Criminal Procedure (Scotland) Act 1995

Criminal Procedure (Scotland) Act 1995

TWENTIETH EDITION

Annotated by
IAIN BRADLEY, Solicitor Advocate
DR ROBERT S. SHIELS, Solicitor Advocate
SHERIFF ALASTAIR N. BROWN, PhD
Act of Adjournal (Criminal Procedure Rules) 1996 annotated by
PETER W. FERGUSON QC

W. GREEN

THOMSON REUTERS

Published in 2021 by Thomson Reuters, trading as W. Green. Thomson Reuters is registered in England & Wales, Company No.1679046. Registered Office and address for service: 5 Canada Square, Canary Wharf, London, E14 5AQ.

For further information on our products and services, visit *http://www.sweetandmaxwell.co.uk*.

Printed and bound in Great Britain by Hobbs the Printers Ltd, Totton, Hampshire

For orders, go to *http://www.tr.com/uki-legal-contact*; Tel: 0345 600 9355.

ISBN (print): 978-0-414-09753-7

ISBN (eBook): 978-0-414-09992-0

ISBN (print and eBook): 978-0-414-09754-4

Please note: the Criminal Procedure (Scotland) Act 1995 will no longer include a CD of forms. Instead, this information can be accessed and downloaded from: *https://www.scotcourts.gov.uk/rules-and-practice/forms/criminal-procedure-forms*.

The content of this book is up-to-date to June 2021.

MAIN TABLE OF CONTENTS

CRIMINAL PROCEDURE (SCOTLAND) ACT 1995

Parts I–VI A4-01
Parts VII–VIII A4-145
Parts IX–I0ZA A4-284
Part XI A4-410.65
Part XII A4-494
Schedules 1–13 A4-596

CRIMINAL JUSTICE (SCOTLAND) ACT 2016

Criminal Justice (Scotland) Act 2016 A170-001

ACT OF ADJOURNAL (CRIMINAL PROCEDURE RULES) 1996

Act of Adjournal (Criminal Procedure Rules) 1996 B1-01
Schedule 1 Powers Under and by Virtue of Which this Act of Adjournal is Made B1-03
Schedule 2 Criminal Procedure Rules 1996 B1-04
Schedule 3 Acts of Adjournal Revoked B1-500

CRIMINAL PROCEDURE (SCOTLAND) ACT 1995

(1995 c. 46) A4-01

An Act to consolidate certain enactments relating to criminal procedure in Scotland.

[8th November 1995]

ARRANGEMENT OF SECTIONS

PART I CRIMINAL COURTS JURISDICTION AND POWERS

The High Court

Sect.

1. Judges in the High Court
2. Fixing of High Court sittings

Solemn courts: general

3. Jurisdiction and powers of solemn courts

The sheriff

4. Territorial jurisdiction of sheriff
5. The sheriff: summary jurisdiction and powers

JP courts

6. JP courts: constitution and prosecutor
7. JP courts: jurisdiction and powers

Sittings of sheriff and JP courts

8. Sittings of sheriff and JP courts

Territorial jurisdiction: general

9. Boundaries of jurisdiction
9A. Competence of justice's actings outwith jurisdiction
10. Crimes committed in different districts
10A. Jurisdiction for transferred cases
11. Certain offences committed outside Scotland
11A. Conspiracy to commit offences outwith Scotland

PART II POLICE FUNCTIONS

Lord Advocate's instructions

12. Instructions by Lord Advocate as to reporting of offences

Detention and questioning

13. Powers relating to suspects and potential witnesses
14. Detention and questioning at police station
14A. Extension of period of detention under section 14
14B. Extension under section 14A: procedure
15. Right of persons arrested or detained to have intimation sent to another person
15A. Right of suspects to have access to a solicitor
16. Drunken persons: power to take to designated place

Arrest: access to solicitor

17. Right of accused to have access to solicitor
17A. Right of person accused of sexual offence to be told about restriction on conduct of defence: arrest

Prints and samples

18. Prints, samples etc. in criminal investigations
18A. Retention of samples etc.: prosecutions for sexual and violent offences
18B. Retention of samples etc. where offer under sections 302 to 303ZA accepted

18C. Section 18B: extension of retention period where relevant offer relates to certain sexual or violent offences
18D. Retention of samples etc. taken or provided in connection with certain fixed penalty offences
18E. Retention of samples etc.: children referred to children's hearings
18F. Retention of samples etc. relating to children: appeals
18G. Retention of samples etc: national security
19. Prints, samples etc. in criminal investigations: supplementary provisions
19A. Samples etc. from persons convicted of sexual and violent offences.
19AA. Samples etc. from sex offenders
19AB. Section 19AA: supplementary provision in risk of sexual harm order cases
19B. Power of constable in obtaining relevant physical data etc.
19C. Sections 18 and 19 to 19AA: use of samples etc.
20. Use of prints, samples etc.

Testing for Class A drugs

20A. Arrested persons: testing for certain Class A drugs
20B. Section 20A: supplementary

Schedule 1 offences

21. Schedule 1 offences: power of constable to take offender into custody

Police liberation

22. Liberation by police
22ZA. Offences where undertaking breached
22ZB. Evidential and procedural provision

PART III BAIL

22A. Consideration of bail on first appearance
23. Bail applications
23A. Bail and liberation where person already in custody
23B. Determination of questions of bail
23C. Grounds relevant as to question of bail
23D. Restriction on bail in certain solemn cases
24. Bail and bail conditions
24A. Bail conditions: remote monitoring of restrictions on movements
24B. Regulations as to power to impose remote monitoring requirements under section 24A
24C. Monitoring of compliance in pursuance of requirements imposed under section 24A
24D. Remote monitoring
24E. Documentary evidence in proceedings for breach of bail conditions being remotely monitored
24F. Bail: extradition proceedings
25. Bail conditions: supplementary
25A. Failure to accept conditions of bail under section 65(8C): continued detention of accused
26. Bail: circumstances where not available
27. Breach of bail conditions: offences
28. Breach of bail conditions: arrest of offender, etc.
29. Bail: monetary conditions
30. Bail review
31. Bail review on prosecutor's application
32. Bail appeal
32A. Bail after conviction: prosecutor's attitude
33. Bail: no fees exigible

PART IV PETITION PROCEDURE

Warrants

34. Petition for warrant
34A. Petition proceedings outwith sheriffdom

Judicial examination

35. Judicial examination
36. Judicial examination: questioning by prosecutor
37. Judicial examination: record of proceedings
38. Judicial examination: rectification of record of proceedings
39. Judicial examination: charges arising in different districts

Committal

40. Committal until liberated in due course of law

PART V CHILDREN AND YOUNG PERSONS

41. Age of criminal responsibility
41A. Prosecution of children under 12
42. Prosecution of children
43. Arrangements where children arrested
44. Detention of children
44A. Appeal against detention in secure accommodation
45. Security for child's good behaviour
46. Presumption and determination of age of child
47. Restriction on report of proceedings involving children
48. Power to refer certain children to reporter
49. Reference or remit to children's hearing
50. Children and certain proceedings
51. Remand and committal of children and young persons

PART VI MENTAL DISORDER

Criminal responsibility of mentally disordered persons

51A. Criminal responsibility of persons with mental disorder

Diminished responsibility

51B. Diminished responsibility

Committal of mentally disordered persons

52. Power of court to commit to hospital an accused suffering from mental disorder

Remit of mentally disordered persons from JP court

52A. Remit of certain mentally disordered persons from JP court to sheriff court

Assessment orders

52B. Prosecutor's power to apply for assessment order
52C. Scottish Ministers' power to apply for assessment order
52D. Assessment order
52E. Assessment order made ex proprio motu: application of section 52D
52F. Assessment order: supplementary
52G. Review of assessment order
52H. Early termination of assessment order
52J. Power of court on assessment order ceasing to have effect

Treatment orders

52K. Prosecutor's power to apply for treatment order
52L. Scottish Ministers' power to apply for treatment order
52M. Treatment order
52N. Treatment order made ex proprio motu: application of section 52M

52P. Treatment order: supplementary
52Q. Review of treatment order
52R. Termination of treatment order
52S. Power of court on treatment order ceasing to have effect

Prevention of delay in trials

52T. Prevention of delay in trials: assessment orders and treatment orders

Effect of assessment and treatment orders on pre-existing mental health orders

52U. Effect of assessment order and treatment order on pre-existing mental health order

Interim compulsion orders

53. Interim compulsion order
53A. Interim compulsion order: supplementary
53B. Review and extension of interim compulsion order
53C. Early termination of interim compulsion order
53D. Power of court on interim compulsion order ceasing to have effect

Acquittal involving mental disorder

53E. Acquittal involving mental disorder

Unfitness for trial

53F. Unfitness for trial
54. Unfitness for trial: further provision

Examination of facts

55. Examination of facts
56. Examination of facts: supplementary provisions

Disposal where accused found not criminally responsible

57. Disposal of case where accused found not criminally responsible or unfit for trial

Compulsion orders

57A. Compulsion order
57B. Compulsion order authorising detention in hospital or requiring residence at place: ancillary provision
57C. Mental health officer's report
57D. Compulsion order: supplementary

Hospital orders and guardianship

58. Order for hospital admission or guardianship
58A. Application of Adults with Incapacity (Scotland) Act 2000
59. Hospital orders: restrictions on discharge

Hospital directions

59A. Hospital direction
59B. Hospital direction: mental health officer's report
59C. Hospital direction: supplementary
60. Appeals against compulsion orders
60A. Appeal by prosecutor against hospital orders etc.
60B. Intervention orders
60C. Acquitted persons: detention for medical examination
60D. Notification of detention under section 60C

Medical evidence

61. Requirements as to medical evidence
61A. Transfer of person to suitable hospital
61B. Specification of hospital unit

Appeals under Part VI

62. Appeal by accused not criminally responsible or unfit for trial

63. Appeal by prosecutor where accused found not criminally responsible or unfit for trial

PART VII SOLEMN PROCEEDINGS

The indictment

64. Prosecution on indictment
65. Prevention of delay in trials
66. Service and lodging of indictment, etc.
67. Witnesses
67A. Failure of witness to attend for, or give evidence on, precognition
68. Productions
69. Notice of previous convictions
70. Proceedings against organisations
70A. Defence statements

Pre-trial proceedings

71. First diet
71A. Further pre-trial diet: dismissal or withdrawal of solicitor representing accused in case of sexual offence
71B. First diet: appointment of trial diet
71C. Written record of state of preparation: sheriff court
72. Preliminary hearing: procedure up to appointment of trial diet
72A. Preliminary hearing: appointment of trial diet
72B. Power to dispense with preliminary hearing
72C. Procedure where preliminary hearing does not proceed
72D. Preliminary hearing: further provision
72E. Written record of state of preparation in certain cases
72F. Engagement, dismissal and withdrawal of solicitor representing accused
72G. Service etc. on accused through a solicitor
73. Preliminary diet: procedure
73A. Consideration of matters relating to vulnerable witnesses where no preliminary diet is ordered
74. Appeals in connection with preliminary diets
75. Computation of certain periods

Adjournment and alteration of diets

75A. Adjournment and alteration of diets
75B. Refixing diets: non-sitting days
75C. Refixing diets: non-suitable days

Plea of guilty

76. Procedure where accused desires to plead guilty
77. Plea of guilty

Notice by accused

78. Special defences, incrimination and notice of witnesses, etc.
79. Preliminary pleas and preliminary issues
79A. Objections to admissibility of evidence raised after first diet or preliminary hearing

Alteration, etc, of diet

80. Alteration and postponement of trial diet
81. Procedure where trial does not proceed
82. Desertion or postponement where accused in custody
83. Transfer of sheriff court solemn proceedings
83ZA. Transfer of sheriff court solemn proceedings within sheriffdom: power of sheriff principal

Continuation of trial diet in the High Court

83A. Continuation of trial diet in the High Court

Jurors for sittings

84. Juries: returns of jurors and preparation of lists
85. Juries: citation and attendance of jurors
86. Jurors: excusal and objections

Non-availability of judge

87. Non-availability of judge
87A. Disposal of preliminary matters at trial diet

Jury for trial

88. Plea of not guilty, balloting and swearing of jury, etc.
89. Jury to be informed of special defence
90. Death or illness of jurors

Obstructive witnesses

90A. Apprehension of witnesses in proceedings on indictment
90B. Orders in respect of witnesses apprehended under section 90A
90C. Breach of bail under section 90B(1)(b)
90D. Review of orders under section 90B(1)(a) or (b)
90E. Appeals in respect of orders under section 90B(1)

Trial

91. Trial to be continuous
92. Trial in presence of accused
93. Record of trial
94. Transcripts of record and documentary productions
95. Verdict by judge alone
96. Amendment of indictment
97. No case to answer
97A. Submissions as to sufficiency of evidence
97B. Acquittals etc. on section 97A(2)(a) submissions
97C. Directions etc. on section 97A(2)(b) submissions
97D. No acquittal on "no reasonable jury" grounds
98. Defence to speak last
99. Seclusion of jury to consider verdict

Verdict and conviction

100. Verdict of jury
101. Previous convictions: solemn proceedings
101A. Post-offence convictions etc.
102. Interruption of trial for other proceedings
102A. Failure of accused to appear

PART VIII APPEALS FROM SOLEMN PROCEEDINGS

103. Appeal sittings
104. Power of High Court in appeals
105. Appeal against refusal of application
105A. Appeal against granting of application
106. Right of appeal
106A. Appeal against automatic sentences where earlier conviction quashed
107. Leave to appeal
107A. Prosecutor's right of appeal: decisions on section 97 and 97A submissions
107B. Prosecutor's right of appeal: decisions on admissibility of evidence

107C.	Appeals under section 107A and 107B: general provisions
107D.	Expedited appeals
107E.	Other appeals under section 107A: appeal against acquittal
107F.	Other appeals under section 107A or 107B: appeal against directions etc.
108.	Lord Advocate's right of appeal against disposal
108A.	Lord Advocate's appeal against decision not to impose automatic sentence in certain cases
109.	Intimation of intention to appeal
110.	Note of appeal
111.	Provisions supplementary to sections 109 and 110
112.	Admission of appellant to bail
113.	Judge's report
113A.	Judge's observations in expedited appeal
114.	Applications made orally or in writing
115.	Presentation of appeal in writing
116.	Abandonment of appeal
117.	Presence of appellant or applicant at hearing
118.	Disposal of appeals
119.	Provision where High Court authorises new prosecution
120.	Appeals: supplementary provisions
121.	Suspension of disqualification, forfeiture, etc.
121A.	Suspension of certain sentences pending determination of appeal
122.	Fines and caution
123.	Lord Advocate's reference
124.	Finality of proceedings and Secretary of State's reference
125.	Reckoning of time spent pending appeal
126.	Extract convictions
127.	Forms in relation to appeals
128.	Fees and expenses
129.	Non-compliance with certain provisions may be waived
130.	Bill of suspension not competent
130A.	Bill of advocation not competent in respect of certain decisions
131.	Prosecution appeal by bill of advocation
132.	Interpretation of Part VIII

PART IX SUMMARY PROCEEDINGS

General

133.	Application of Part IX of Act
134.	Incidental applications
135.	Warrants of apprehension and search
136.	Time limit for certain offences
136A.	Time limits for transferred and related cases
136B.	Time limits where fixed penalty offer etc. made
137.	Alteration of diets
137ZA.	Refixing diets: non-sitting days
137ZB.	Refixing diets: non-suitable days
137A.	Transfer of sheriff court summary proceedings within sheriffdom
137AA.	Transfer of sheriff court summary proceedings within sheriffdom: power of sheriff principal
137B.	Transfer of sheriff court summary proceedings outwith sheriffdom
137C.	Custody cases: initiating proceedings outwith sheriffdom

137CA. Transfer of JP court proceedings within sheriffdom
137CB. Transfer of JP court proceedings outwith sheriffdom
137CC. Custody cases: initiating JP court proceedings outwith sheriffdom
137D. Transfer of JP court proceedings to the sheriff court

Complaints

138. Complaints
139. Complaints: orders and warrants

Citation

140. Citation
141. Manner of citation

Children

142. Summary proceedings against children

Companies

143. Prosecution of companies, etc.

First diet

144. Procedure at first diet
145. Adjournment for inquiry at first calling
145ZA. Adjournment where assessment order made at first calling
145A. Adjournment at first calling to allow accused to appear etc.
146. Plea of not guilty

Pre-trial procedure

147. Prevention of delay in trials
148. Intermediate diet
148A. Interim diet: sexual offence to which section 288C of this Act applies
148B. Pre-trial procedure in sheriff court where no intermediate diet is fixed
148C. Engagement, dismissal and withdrawl of solicitor representing accused
148D. Service etc. on accused through a solicitor
149. Alibi
149A. Notice of defence plea of consent
149B. Notice of defences

Failure of accused to appear

150. Failure of accused to appear
150A. Proceedings in absence of accused

Non-availability of judge

151. Death, illness or absence of judge

Trial diet

152. Desertion of diet
152A. Complaints triable together
153. Trial in presence of accused
154. Proof of official documents
155. Punishment of witness for contempt
156. Apprehension of witness
156A. Orders in respect of witnesses apprehended under section 156
156B. Breach of bail under section 156A(1)(b)
156C. Review of orders under section 156A(1)(a) or (b)
156D. Appeals in respect of orders under section 156A(1)
157. Record of proceedings
158. Interruption of summary proceedings for verdict in earlier trial
159. Amendment of complaint

160. No case to answer
161. Defence to speak last

Verdict and conviction

162. Judges equally divided
163. Conviction: miscellaneous provisions
164. Conviction of part of charge
165. "Conviction" and "sentence" not to be used for children
166. Previous convictions: summary proceedings
166A. Post-offence convictions etc.
166B. Charges which disclose convictions
167. Forms of finding and sentence
168. Caution
169. Detention in precincts of court

Miscellaneous

170. Damages in respect of summary proceedings
171. Recovery of penalties
172. Forms of procedure

PART X APPEALS FROM SUMMARY PROCEEDINGS

General

173. Quorum of Sheriff Appeal Court in relation to appeals
174. Appeals relating to preliminary pleas
175. Right of appeal
175A. Power to refer points of law for the opinion of the High Court

Stated case

176. Stated case: manner and time of appeal
176A. Application of section 176 in relation to certain appeals
177. Procedure where appellant in custody
178. Stated case: preparation of draft
179. Stated case: adjustment and signature
180. Leave to appeal against conviction etc.
181. Stated case: directions by Sheriff Appeal Court
182. Stated case: hearing of appeal
183. Stated case: disposal of appeal
184. Abandonment of appeal

New prosecution

185. Authorisation of new prosecution

Appeals against sentence

186. Appeals against sentence only
187. Leave to appeal against sentence

Disposal of appeals

188. Setting aside conviction or sentence: prosecutor's consent or application
189. Disposal of appeal against sentence
190. Disposal of appeal where appellant not criminally responsible

Miscellaneous

191. Appeal by suspension or advocation on ground of miscarriage of justice
191A. Time limit for lodging bills of advocation and bills of suspension
191B. Bill of advocation not competent in respect of certain decisions
192. Appeals: miscellaneous provisions
193. Suspension of disqualification, forfeiture etc.

193A. Suspension of certain sentences pending determination of appeal
194. Computation of time

PART XA SCOTTISH CRIMINAL CASES REVIEW COMMISSION

The Scottish Criminal Cases Review Commission

194A. Scottish Criminal Cases Review Commission

References to High Court

194B. References by the Commission
194C. Grounds for reference
194D. Further provision as to references
194DA. High Court's power to reject a reference made by the Commission
194E. Extension of Commission's remit to summary cases
194F. Further powers
194G. Supplementary provision

Powers of investigation of Commission

194H. Power to request precognition on oath
194I. Power to obtain documents etc.
194IA. Power to request assistance in obtaining information abroad

Disclosure of information

194J. Offence of disclosure
194K. Exceptions from obligations of non-disclosure
194L. Consent of disclosure

Special circumstances for disclosure

194M. Further exception to section 194J
194N. Effect of the exception
194O. Notification and representations etc.
194P. Consent if UK interest
194Q. Consent if foreign interest
194R. Designated foreign authority
194S. Disapplication of sections 194O to 194R
194T. Final disclosure-related matters

PART 10ZA APPEALS FROM SHERIFF APPEAL COURT

194ZB. Appeal from the Sheriff Appeal Court
194ZC. Appeals: applications and procedure
194ZD. Application for permission for appeal: determination by single judge
194ZE. Further application for permission where single judge refuses permission
194ZF. Applications for permission: further provision
194ZG. Restriction of grounds of appeal
194ZH. Disposal of appeals
194ZI. Procedure where appellant in custody
194ZJ. Abandonment of appeal
194ZK. Finality of proceedings
194ZL. Computation of time

PART XI SENTENCING

General

195. Remit to High Court for sentence
196. Sentence following guilty plea
197. Sentencing guidelines
198. Form of sentence
199. Power to mitigate penalties

Pre-sentencing procedure

200. Remand for inquiry into physical or mental condition
201. Power of court to adjourn case before sentence
202. Deferred sentence
203. Reports
203A. Reports about organisations

Imprisonment, etc.

204. Restrictions on passing sentence of imprisonment or detention
204A. Restriction on consecutive sentences for released prisoners
204B. Consecutive sentences: life prisoners etc.
205. Punishment for murder
205B. Minimum sentence for third conviction of certain offences relating to drug trafficking
205C. Meaning of "conviction" for purposes of sections 205A and 205B
205D. Only one sentence of imprisonment for life to be imposed in any proceedings
206. Minimum periods of imprisonment
207. Detention of young offenders
208. Detention of children convicted on indictment
209. Supervised release orders
210. Consideration of time spent in custody

Sexual or violent offenders

210A. Extended sentences for sex and violent offenders
210AA. Extended sentences for certain other offenders

Approach in domestic abuse cases

210AB. Particular factor as to victim safety

Risk assessment

210B. Risk assessment order
210C. Risk assessment report
210D. Interim hospital order and assessment of risk
210E. The risk criteria
210EA. Application of certain sections of this Act to proceedings under section 210C(7)

Order for lifelong restriction, etc.

210F. Order for lifelong restriction or compulsion order
210G. Disposal of case where certain orders not made

Report of judge

210H. Report of judge

Fines

211. Fines
212. Fines in summary proceedings
213. Remission of fines
214. Fines: time for payment and payment by instalments
215. Application for further time to pay fine
216. Fines: restriction on imprisonment for default
217. Fines: supervision pending payment
218. Fines: supplementary provisions as to payment
219. Fines: periods of imprisonment for non-payment
220. Fines: part payment by prisoners
221. Fines: recovery by civil diligence
222. Transfer of fine orders
223. Transfer of fines: procedure for clerk of court

The mutual recognition of criminal financial penalties

223A. Recognition of financial penalties: requests to other member States
223B. Requests to other member States: procedure on issue of certificate
223C. Requests to other member States: application of provisions relating to fines
223D. Requests to other member States: application of provisions relating to compensation orders
223E. Requests to other member States: application of provisions relating to fixed penalties
223F. Recognition of financial penalties: requests from other member States
223FA. Requests from other member States: procedure where no certificate
223G. Requests from other member States: return of certificate
223H. Requests from other member States: procedure on receipt of certificate
223I. Requests from other member States: action undertaken under certificate
223J. Requests from other member States: application of provisions in relation to fines
223K. Requests from other member States: supplementary provisions in relation to fines
223L. Requests from other member States: action for enforcement where financial penalty not recovered
223M. Requests from other member States: application of provisions relating to orders for compensation
223N. Requests from other member States: supplementary provisions in relation to orders for compensation
223O. Requests from other member States: application of provisions relating to fixed penalties
223P. Transfer of certificates to central authority for England and Wales, or to central authority for Northern Ireland
223Q. The competent authority for Scotland
223R. Accrual of monies obtained from the enforcement of financial penalties
223S. Treatment of compensation monies
223T. Interpretation of sections 223A to 223S

Fines: discharge from imprisonment and penalties

224. Discharge from imprisonment to be specified
225. Penalties: standard scale, prescribed sum and uprating
226. Penalties: exceptionally high maximum fines

Enforcement of fines etc.: fines enforcement officers

226A. Fines enforcement officers
226B. Enforcement orders
226C. Variation for further time to pay
226D. Seizure of vehicles
226E. Deduction from benefits
226F. Powers of diligence
226G. Reference of case to court
226H. Review of actions of FEO
226HA. Judicial co-operation in criminal matters: mutual recognition of financial penalties: requests to other member States
226I. Enforcement of fines, etc.: interpretation

Caution

227. Caution

Community payback orders

227A. Community payback orders
227B. Community payback order: procedure prior to imposition
227C. Community payback order: responsible officer
227D. Community payback order: further provision

227E. Requirement to avoid conflict with religious beliefs, work etc.
227F. Payment of offenders' travelling and other expenses

Offender supervision requirement

227G. Offender supervision requirement

Compensation requirement

227H. Compensation requirement

Unpaid work or other activity requirement

227I. Unpaid work or other activity requirement
227J. Unpaid work or other activity requirement: further provision
227K. Allocation of hours between unpaid work and other activity
227L. Time limit for completion of unpaid work or other activity
227M. Fine defaulters
227N. Offenders subject to more than one unpaid work or other activity requirement
227O. Rules about unpaid work and other activity

Programme requirement

227P. Programme requirement

Residence requirement

227Q. Residence requirement

Mental health treatment requirement

227R. Mental health treatment requirement
227S. Mental health treatment requirements: medical evidence
227T. Power to change treatment

Drug treatment requirement

227U. Drug treatment requirement

Alcohol treatment requirement

227V. Alcohol treatment requirement

Conduct requirement

227W. Conduct requirement

Community payback orders: review, variation etc.

227X. Periodic review of community payback orders
227Y. Applications to vary, revoke and discharge community payback orders
227Z. Variation, revocation and discharge: court's powers
227ZA. Variation of community payback orders: further provision
227ZB. Change of offender's residence to new local authority area

Breach of community payback order

227ZC. Breach of community payback order
227ZD. Breach of community payback order: further provision

Restricted movement requirement

227ZE. Restricted movement requirement
227ZF. Restricted movement requirement: effect
227ZG. Restricted movement requirements: further provision
227ZH. Variation of restricted movement requirement
227ZI. Remote monitoring
227ZJ. Restricted movement requirements: Scottish Ministers' functions
227ZK. Documentary evidence in proceedings for breach of restricted movement requirement

Local authorities: annual consultation about unpaid work

227ZL. Local authorities: annual consultations about unpaid work

Annual reports on community payback orders

227ZM. Annual reports on community payback orders

Community payback order: meaning of "the appropriate court"

227ZN. Meaning of "the appropriate court"

227ZO. Community payback orders: persons residing in England and Wales or Northern Ireland

Probation

228. Probation orders

229. Probation orders: additional requirements

229A. Probation progress review

230. Probation orders: requirement of treatment for mental condition

230A. Requirement for remote monitoring in probation order

231. Probation orders: amendment and discharge

232. Probation orders: failure to comply with requirement

233. Probation orders: commission of further offence

234. Probation orders: persons residing in England and Wales

234A. Non-harassment orders

234AZA. Non-harassment orders: domestic abuse cases

234AA. Antisocial behaviour orders

234AB. Antisocial behaviour orders: notification

234B. Drug treatment and testing order

234C. Requirements and provisions of drug treatment and testing orders

234CA. Requirement for remote monitoring in drug treatment and testing order

234D. Procedural matters relating to drug treatment and testing orders

234E. Amendment of drug treatment and testing order

234F. Periodic review of drug treatment and testing order

234G. Breach of drug treatment testing order

234H. Disposal on revocation of drug treatment and testing order

234J. Concurrent drug treatment and testing and probation orders

234K. Drug treatment and testing orders: interpretation

Supervised attendance

235. Supervised attendance orders

236. Supervised attendance orders in place of fines for 16 and 17 year olds

237. Supervised attendance orders where court allows further time to pay fine

Community service by offenders

238. Community service orders

239. Community service orders: requirements

240. Community service orders: amendment and revocation etc.

241. Community service order: commission of offence while order in force

242. Community service orders: persons residing in England and Wales

243. Community service orders: persons residing in Northern Ireland

244. Community service orders: general provisions relating to persons living in England and Wales or Northern Ireland

245. Community service orders: rules, annual report and interpretation

Restriction of liberty orders

245A. Restriction of liberty orders

245B. Monitoring of restriction of liberty orders

245C. Remote monitoring

245D. Combination of restriction of liberty order with other orders

245DA. Further provision about multiple orders

245E. Variation of restriction of liberty order
245F. Breach of restriction of liberty order
245G. Disposal on revocation of restriction of liberty order
245H. Documentary evidence in proceedings under section 245F
245I. Procedure on variation or revocation of restriction of liberty order
245J. Breach of certain orders: adjourning hearing and remanding in custody etc.

Community reparation orders

245K. Community reparation orders
245L. Community reparation order: notification
245M. Failure to comply with community reparation order: extension of 12 month period
245N. Failure to comply with community reparation order: powers of court
245P. Extension, variation and revocation of order
245Q. Sections 245L, 245N and 245P: meaning of "appropriate court"

Admonition and absolute discharge

246. Admonition and absolute discharge
247. Effect of probation and absolute discharge

Disqualification

248. Disqualification where vehicle used to commit offence
248A. General power to disqualify offenders
248B. Power to disqualify fine defaulters
248C. Application of sections 248A and 248B
248D. Extension of disqualification where sentence of imprisonment also imposed
248E. Effect of sentence of imprisonment in other cases

Compensation

249. Compensation order against convicted person
250. Compensation orders: supplementary provisions
251. Review of compensation order
252. Enforcement of compensation orders: application of provisions relating to fines
253. Effect of compensation order on subsequent award of damages in civil proceedings

Victim surcharge

253F. Victim surcharge
253G. The Victim Surcharge Fund

Forfeiture

254. Search warrant for forfeited articles

European Protection Orders

254A. European Protection Orders: interpretation
254B. Issuing of a European Protection Order
254C. Recognition of a European Protection Order
254D. Implementation of a recognised European Protection Order
254E. Modification and revocation of non-harassment orders made under section 254D

Part XII Evidence

Special capacity

255. Special capacity
255A. Proof of age

Agreed evidence

256. Agreements and admissions as to evidence
257. Duty to seek agreement of evidence
258. Uncontroversial evidence

Hearsay

259. Exceptions to the rule that hearsay evidence is inadmissible
260. Admissibility of prior statements of witnesses
261. Statements by accused

Witness statements

261A. Witness statements: use during trial
262. Construction of sections 259 to 261A

Witnesses

263. Examination of witnesses
264. Spouse or civil partner of accused a compellable witness
265. Witnesses not excluded for conviction, interest, relationship, etc.
266. Accused as witness
267. Witnesses in court during trial
267A. Citation of witnesses for precognition
267B. Order requiring accused to participate in identification procedure

Additional evidence, etc.

268. Additional evidence
269. Evidence in replication
270. Evidence of criminal record and character of accused

Special measures for child witnesses and other vulnerable witnesses

271. Vulnerable witnesses: main definitions
271A. Child and deemed vulnerable witnesses
271B. Further special provision for child witnesses under the age of 12
271BZA. Child witnesses in certain solemn cases: special measures
271BZB. Child witnesses in certain solemn cases: modifications of section 271A
271BZC. Child witnesses in certain solemn cases: modifications of section 271D
271BA. Assessment of witnesses
271C. Vulnerable witness application
271D. Review of arrangements for vulnerable witnesses
271E. Vulnerable witnesses: supplementary provision
271F. The accused
271G. Saving provision
271H. The special measures
271HA. Temporary additional special measures
271HB. Excluding the public while taking evidence
271I. Taking of evidence by a commissioner
271J. Live television link
271K. Screens
271L. Supporters
271M. Giving evidence in chief in the form of a prior statement

Witness anonymity orders

271N. Witness anonymity orders
271P. Applications
271Q. Making and determination of applications
271R. Conditions for making orders
271S. Relevant considerations
271T. Direction to jury
271U. Discharge and variation of order
271V. Appeals
271W. Appeal against the making of a witness anonymity order

271X. Appeal against the refusal to make a witness anonymity order
271Y. Appeal against a variation of a witness anonymity order
271Z. Appeal against a refusal to vary or discharge a witness anonymity order

Evidence on commission and from abroad

272. Evidence by letter of request or on commission
273. Television link evidence from abroad

Evidence from other parts of the United Kingdom

273A. Television link evidence from other parts of the United Kingdom

Evidence relating to sexual offences

274. Restrictions on evidence relating to sexual offences
275. Exceptions to restrictions under section 274
275A. Disclosure of accused's previous convictions where court allows questioning or evidence under section 275
275B. Provisions supplementary to sections 275 and 275A

Expert evidence as to subsequent behaviour of complainer

275C. Expert evidence as to subsequent behaviour of complainer in certain cases

Biological material

276. Evidence of biological material

Transcripts and records

277. Transcript of police interview sufficient evidence
278. Record of proceedings at examination as evidence

Documentary evidence

279. Evidence from documents
279A. Evidence from certain official documents

Routine evidence

280. Routine evidence
281. Routine evidence: autopsy and forensic science reports
281A. Routine evidence: reports of identification prior to trial

Sufficient evidence

282. Evidence as to controlled drugs and medicinal products
283. Evidence as to time and place of video surveillance recordings
284. Evidence in relation to fingerprints

Proof of previous convictions

285. Previous convictions: proof, general
286. Previous convictions: proof in support of substantive charge
286A. Proof of previous conviction by court in other member State

PART XIII MISCELLANEOUS

Lord Advocate

287. Demission from office of Lord Advocate and Solicitor General for Scotland
288. Intimation of proceedings in High Court to Lord Advocate

Convention rights and EU law compatibility issues, and devolution issues

288ZA. Right of Advocate General to take part in proceedings
288ZB. References of compatibility issues to the High Court or Supreme Court
288A. Rights of appeal for Advocate General: compatibility issues and devolution issues
288AA. Appeals to the Supreme Court: compatibility issues
288B. Appeals to the Supreme Court: general

Dockets and charges in sex cases

288BA. Dockets for charges of sexual offences

288BB. Mixed charges for sexual offences
288BC. Aggravation by intent to rape

Trials for sexual offences

288C. Prohibition of personal conduct of defence in cases of certain sexual offences
288D. Appointment of solicitor by court in such cases

Jury directions relating to sexual offences

288DA. Jury direction relating to lack of communication about offence
288DB. Jury direction relating to absence of physical resistance or physical force
288DC. Prohibition of personal conduct of defence in domestic abuse cases

Trials involving vulnerable witnesses

288E. Prohibition of personal conduct of defence in certain cases involving child witnesses under the age of 12
288F. Power to prohibit personal conduct of defence in other cases involving vulnerable witnesses

Application of vulnerable witnesses provisions to proceedings in the district court

288G. Application of vulnerable witnesses provisions to proceedings in the district court

Treason trials

289. Procedure and evidence in trials for treason

Certain rights of accused

290. Accused's right to request identification parade
291. Precognition on oath of defence witnesses

Mode of trial

292. Mode of trial of certain offences

Art and part and attempt

293. Statutory offences: art and part and aiding and abetting
294. Attempt at crime

Legal custody

295. Legal custody

Warrants

296. Warrants for search and apprehension to be signed by judge
297. Execution of warrants and service of complaints, etc.
297A. Re-execution of apprehension warrants

Trial judge's report

298. Trial judge's report

Intimation of certain applications to the High Court

298A. Intimation of bills and of petitions to the nobile officium

Correction of entries

299. Correction of entries
300. Amendment of records of conviction and sentence in summary proceedings

Excusal of irregularities

300A. Power of court to excuse procedural irregularities

Rights of audience

301. Rights of audience

Recovery of documents

301A. Recovery of documents

Fixed penalties

302. Fixed penalty: conditional offer by procurator fiscal
302A. Compensation offer by procurator fiscal

302B. Combined fixed penalty and compensation offer
302C. Recall of fixed penalty or compensation offer
303. Fixed penalty: enforcement
303ZA. Work orders
303ZB. Setting aside of offers and orders

Transfer of rights of appeal of deceased person

303A. Transfer of rights of appeal of deceased person

Electronic proceedings

303B. Electronic summary proceedings

PART XIV GENERAL

304. Criminal Courts Rules Council
305. Acts of Adjournal
306. Information for financial and other purposes
307. Interpretation
308. Construction of enactments referring to detention etc.
308A. Expressions relating to electronic proceedings
309. Short title, commencement and extent

Schedules

Schedule 1—Offences Against Children Under the Age of 17 Years to which Special Provisions Apply
Schedule 2—Examples of Indictments
Schedule 3—Indictments and Complaints
Schedule 4—Supervision and Treatment Orders
Part I—Preliminary
Part II—Making and Effect of Orders
Part III—Revocation and Amendment of Orders
Schedule 5—Forms of Complaint and Charges
Schedule 6—Discharge of and Amendment to Probation Orders
Schedule 7—Supervised Attendance Orders: Further Provisions
Schedule 8—Documentary Evidence in Criminal Proceedings
Schedule 9—Certificates as to Proof of Certain Routine Matters
Schedule 9A—The Commission: Further Provisions
Schedule 10—Certain Offences Triable only Summarily
Schedule 11—Financial Penalties Suitable for Enforcement in Scotland
Schedule 12—Grounds for Refusal to Enforce Financial Penalties
Part 1—The Grounds for Refusal
Part 2—European Framework List (Financial Penalties)
Part 3—Interpretation
Schedule 13—Transfer of Community Payback Orders to England and Wales or Northern Ireland
Part 1—England and Wales
Part 2—Northern Ireland

ABBREVIATIONS

[1] The 1975 Act : Criminal Procedure (Scotland) Act 1975 (c.21). A4-02
The 1980 Act : Bail (Scotland) Act 1980 (c.4).
The 1984 Act : Mental Health (Scotland) Act 1984 (c.36).
The 1993 Act : Prisoners and Criminal Proceedings (Scotland) Act 1993 (c.9).
The 1995 Act : Criminal Procedure (Scotland) Act 1995 (c. 46).

---

[1] Annotations by Iain Bradley, solicitor in Scotland and Robert S. Shiels, solicitor in Scotland. Appeal and sentencing provisions annotated by Sheriff Alastair N. Brown, PhD. Mental health provisions (ss.52A–52U, ss.53–53D and ss.57A–57D) annotated by Ronald Franks, solicitor, and David Cobb, advocate.

The 1996 Act of Adjournal : Act of Adjournal (Criminal Procedure Rules) 1996 (S.I. 1996 No. 513).

Parliamentary Debates

Hansard, H.L. Vol. 565, col. 14; Vol. 566, cols. 384, 581, 894. H.C. Vol. 265, col. 181.

Part I – Criminal Courts Jurisdiction and Powers

The High Court

Judges in the High Court

A4-03 **1.**—(1) The Lord President of the Court of Session shall be the Lord Justice General and shall perform his duties as the presiding judge of the High Court.

(2) Every person who is appointed to the office of one of the Senators of the College of Justice in Scotland shall, by virtue of such appointment, be a Lord Commissioner of Justiciary in Scotland.

(3) If any difference arises as to the rotation of judges in the High Court, it shall be determined by the Lord Justice General, whom failing by the Lord Justice Clerk.

(4) Any Lord Commissioner of Justiciary may preside alone at the trial of an accused before the High Court.

(5) Without prejudice to subsection (4) above, in any trial of difficulty or importance it shall be competent for two or more judges in the High Court to preside for the whole or any part of the trial.

Definitions

A4-03.1 "High Court": s.307(1).
"Lord Commissioner of Justiciary": s.307(1).

[THE NEXT PARAGRAPH IS A4-04]

General Note

A4-04 With one exception, the origins of this section are probably more a matter of legal history than a concern for practitioners. Section 1(5), reflecting the collegiate nature of Scottish judges, permits in any trial of difficulty or importance that it shall be competent for two or more judges in the High Court of Justiciary to provide for the whole or any part of the trial. Such problems tend to arise at short notice and while judges are on circuit but there are still a number of instances of this happening: see *HM Advocate v Cairns*, 1967 J.C. 37; *HM Advocate v MacKenzie*, 1970 S.L.T. 81; *MacNeil v HM Advocate*, 1986 S.C.C.R. 288 and *Copeland v HM Advocate*, 1987 S.C.C.R. 232. The benefit of constituting, in effect, a full bench mid-trial to resolve a critical procedural or evidential issue can be appreciated from *HM Advocate v Malloy (Anthony Francis)* [2012] HCJ 124; 2012 S.C.C.R. 710.

Subs.(3)

This subsection must now probably be read in the context of ss.1 and 2 of the Senior Judiciary (Vacancies and Incapacity) (Scotland) Act 2006 (asp 9).

Subs.(5)

In *Stevens v HM Advocate*, 2002 S.L.T. 1249 an accused sought a declaration that a specific statutory provision was incompatible with a provision of law of human rights. A minute to that effect was dismissed. In the course of the Opinion of the Court it was observed that the power to convene additional judges under s.1(5) of the 1995 Act was not available in the present case as that power related to the High Court of Justiciary sitting as a trial court. That capacity was not one that could hear or determine disputes relating to the compatibility of legislation with human rights under the European Convention of Human Rights.

Fixing of High Court sittings

A4-05 **2.**—(1) The High Court shall sit at such times and places as the Lord Justice General, whom failing the Lord Justice Clerk, may, after consultation with the Lord Advocate, determine.

(2) Without prejudice to subsection (1) above, the High Court shall hold such additional sittings as the Lord Advocate may require.

(3) Where an accused has been cited to, or otherwise required to attend, a diet to be held at any sitting of the High Court, the prosecutor may, at any time before the commencement of the diet or, in the case of a trial diet, the trial, apply to the Court to transfer the case to a diet to be held at a sitting of the Court in another place; and a single judge of the High Court may—

(a) after giving the accused or his counsel an opportunity to be heard; or

(b) on the joint application of all parties,

make an order for the transfer of the case.

(3C) The judge may proceed under subsection (3) above on a joint application of the parties without hearing the parties and, accordingly, he may dispense with any hearing previously appointed for the purpose of considering the application.

(4) Where no diets have been appointed to be held at a sitting of the High Court or if it is no longer expedient that a sitting should take place, it shall not be necessary for the sitting to take place.

(5) If in any case a diet remains appointed to be held at a sitting which does not take place in pursuance of subsection (4) above, subsection (3) above shall apply in relation to the transfer of any other such case to another sitting.

(6) For the purposes of subsection (3) above—

(a) a diet shall be taken to commence when it is called; and

(b) a trial shall be taken to commence when the oath is administered to the jury.

AMENDMENTS

Subss.(3), (4) and (5) as amended, and subss.(3C) and (6) inserted, by Criminal Procedure (Amendment) (Scotland) Act 2004 (asp 5) s.25 and Sch.1 para.2. Brought into force on 1 February 2005 by SSI 2004/405 (C.28) art.2.

DEFINITIONS

"diet": s.307(1). A4-05.1
"High Court": s.307(1).
"judge": s.307(1).
"order": s.307(1).
"prosecutor": s.307(1).

GENERAL NOTE

The general power to settle sittings of the High Court for the disposal of business in the ordinary way is now supplemented with more detailed powers as a result of the amendments to the section. These more detailed powers allow for the transfer of a particular case (a diet or a trial) from one place to another: s.2(3). There need not be a hearing where there is a joint application for such a transfer: s.2(3C). The transfer of such business may be for administrative reasons (existing cases over-running) or there may be other compelling needs (the movement of contentious cases from one location to another). The equivalent in relation to solemn business in sheriff courts is to be found in s.83 of the 1995 Act. A4-05.2

[THE NEXT PARAGRAPH IS A4-06]

Solemn courts: general

Jurisdiction and powers of solemn courts

3.—(1) The jurisdiction and powers of all courts of solemn jurisdiction, except so far as altered or modified by any enactment passed after the commencement of this Act, shall remain as at the commencement of this Act. A4-06

(2) Any crime or offence which is triable on indictment may be tried by the High Court sitting at any place in Scotland.

(3) The sheriff shall, without prejudice to any other or wider power conferred by statute, not be entitled, on the conviction on indictment of an accused, to pass a sentence of imprisonment for a term exceeding five years.

(4) Subject to subsection (5) below, where under any enactment passed or made before 1st January 1988 (the date of commencement of section 58 of the Criminal Justice (Scotland) Act 1987) an offence is punishable on conviction on indictment by imprisonment for a term exceeding two years but the enactment either expressly or impliedly restricts the power of the sheriff to impose a sentence of imprisonment for a term exceeding two years, it shall be competent for the sheriff to impose a sentence of imprisonment for a term exceeding two but not exceeding five years.

(4A) Subject to subsection (5) below, where under any enactment passed or made after 1st January 1988 but before the commencement of section 13 of the Crime and Punishment (Scotland) Act 1997 (increase in sentencing powers of sheriff courts) an offence is punishable on conviction on indictment for a term exceeding three years but the enactment either expressly or impliedly restricts the power of the sheriff to impose a sentence of imprisonment for a term exceeding three years, it shall be competent for the sheriff to impose a sentence of imprisonment for a term exceeding three but not exceeding five years.

(5) Nothing in subsections (4) and (4A) above shall authorise the imposition by the sheriff of a sentence in excess of the sentence specified by the enactment as the maximum sentence which may be imposed on conviction of the offence.

(6) Subject to any express exclusion contained in any enactment, it shall be lawful to indict in the sheriff court all crimes except murder, treason, rape (whether at common law or under section 1(1) of the Sexual Offences (Scotland) Act 2009 (asp 9)), rape of a young child (under section 18 of that Act) and breach of duty by magistrates.

Amendments

Section 3 as amended by Crime and Punishment (Scotland) Act 1997 (c.48) s.13(1). Brought into force on 1 May 2004 by SSI 2004/176 (C.12) art.2.

Subs.(6) as amended by Sexual Offences (Scotland) Act 2009 (asp 9) Sch.5 para.2. Brought into force on 1 December 2010 by SSI 2010/357 (C.21) art.2.

Definitions

A4-06.1 "crime": s.307(1).
"offence": s.307(1).
"sentence": s.307(1).

General Note

A4-07 After conviction on indictment the maximum sentence that a sheriff may competently impose is five years' imprisonment: s.3(3). There is a power to remit a case to the High Court of Justiciary where a sheriff holds that any competent sentence that can be imposed is inadequate: s.195(1). Further, there is a power to remit where a period of imprisonment in default of payment is in contemplation and that period exceeds five years: s.219(8).

Du Plooy v HM Advocate, 2005 J.C. 1 established guidelines with specific regard to discounting sentences for early guilty pleas. In *McGhee v HM Advocate*, 2006 S.C.C.R. 712 a sheriff indicated that he considered the crime admitted by the appellant merited a sentence of six years' imprisonment and discounted it to five years because of the guilty plea. On appeal against the competency of the sentence held that the restriction imposed by s.3(3) falls to be applied to the sentence ultimately fixed by the sheriff, that the question of whether sentence is appropriate for the High Court is a matter for the sheriff, just as is the decision as to whether any competent sentence is inadequate, that when the sheriff holds that the sentence he or she can impose is inadequate it necessarily follows that he is holding that the question of sentence is not appropriate for the High Court, that in these circumstances there is no question of a remit, and it is not for the High Court to consider whether the question of sentence was appropriate for it, that the route by which the sentence reaches the ultimate sentence is not restricted by s.195(1), and that the sentence was competent.

McGhee v HM Advocate, above, was distinguished in *Jordan v HM Advocate*, 2008 S.C.C.R. 618 where it was pointed out that the sentence of the sheriff in *McGhee v HM Advocate*, above, could competently have been imposed under a remit to the High Court of Justiciary. See *Jordan v HM Advocate*, 2008 S.C.C.R. 618 at 625F where it was held that a sentence cannot be more than the statutory maximum.

The High Court of Justiciary (when acting as a court of appeal in a devolution or compatibility issue) is not bound by "retained EU case law". Retained EU case law consists of any principles laid down by, and any decisions of, the Court of Justice of the European Union, as they have effect in EU law im- mediately before the IP ("implementation period") completion day: the European Union (Withdrawal) Act 2018 (Relevant Court) (Retained EU Case Law) Regulations (SI 2020/1525) reg.3(d). The "IP completion day" means 31 December 2020 at 11:00: European Union (Withdrawal) Act 2020 (c.1) s.39(1) to (5).

The sheriff

Territorial jurisdiction of sheriff

4.—(1) Subject to the provisions of this section, the jurisdiction of the sheriffs, within their respective sheriffdoms shall extend to and include all navigable rivers, ports, harbours, creeks, shores and anchoring grounds in or adjoining such sheriffdoms and includes all criminal maritime causes and proceedings (including those applying to persons furth of Scotland) provided that the accused is, by virtue of any enactment or rule of law, subject to the jurisdiction of the sheriff before whom the case or proceeding is raised. **A4-08**

(2) Where an offence is alleged to have been committed in one district in a sheriffdom, it shall be competent to try that offence in a sheriff court in any other district in that sheriffdom.

(3) It shall not be competent for the sheriff to try any crime committed on the seas which it would not be competent for him to try if the crime had been committed on land.

(4) The sheriff shall have a concurrent jurisdiction with every other court of summary jurisdiction in relation to all offences competent for trial in such courts.

DEFINITIONS

"court of summary jurisdiction": s.307(1). **A4-08.1**
"crime": s.307(1).
"offence": s.307(1).

GENERAL NOTE

The ancient lineage of this provision has not been tested much in court: however, in *Lewis v Blair* (1858) 3 Irv. 16 the sheriff had jurisdiction to try a foreign sailor for an offence committed by him aboard a foreign vessel lying within the sheriff's territory, upon a seaman engaged on that vessel. *Shields v Donnelly*, 2000 S.L.T. 147; 1999 S.C.C.R. 890 indicates that while papers may be signed outwith his jurisdiction, a sheriff can only deal with any procedural aspects while within the jurisdiction, and not elsewhere. **A4-09**

A more contemporary example is to be found in *Friel v McKendrick*, 1996 G.W.D. 1–8 in which a passenger appeared at Paisley Sheriff Court on a complaint charged with breach of the peace following his misconduct on an aircraft flying between New York and Glasgow. No objection was taken to the competency of the charge.

It was noted previously that the introduction of the provisions contained in the Sexual Offences (Conspiracy and Incitement) Act 1996 (c.29) raised wide jurisdictional issues. If anything this was a sanguine assessment—see *McCarron v HM Advocate*, 2001 S.L.T. 866; 2001 S.C.C.R. 419 which emphasises the strictly territorial nature of the sheriff's jurisdiction. Curiously, s.11 below would permit a trial, on indictment and in limited circumstances, in the sheriff court of (to repeat the marginal note) "Certain offences committed outside Scotland". Perhaps the addition of listed sexual offences to s.11 might provide an answer to the problems raised in *McCarron*.

The power (or rather lack of it) of Ministers to direct matters to specific sheriffs for judicial consideration is discussed in *Wright, Petitioner*, 2004 S.L.T. 491; 2004 S.C.C.R. 324 (extradition committal proceedings addressed by Scottish Ministers to the sheriff principal being heard by another sheriff).

The sheriff: summary jurisdiction and powers

5.—(1) The sheriff, sitting as a court of summary jurisdiction, shall continue to have all the jurisdiction and powers exercisable by him at the commencement of this Act. **A4-10**

(2) The sheriff shall, without prejudice to any other or wider powers conferred by statute, have power on convicting any person of a common law offence—

(a) to impose a fine not exceeding the prescribed sum;

(b) to ordain the accused to find caution for good behaviour for any period not exceeding 12 months to an amount not exceeding the prescribed sum either in lieu of or in addition to a fine or in addition to imprisonment;

(c) failing payment of such fine, or on failure to find such caution, to award imprisonment in accordance with section 219 of this Act;

(d) to impose imprisonment, for any period not exceeding 12 months.

(3) […]

(4) It shall be competent to prosecute summarily in the sheriff court the following offences—

(a) uttering a forged document;

(b) wilful fire-raising;

(c) robbery; and

(d) assault with intent to rob.

Amendments

Subs.(2)(d) amended and subs.(3) repealed by Criminal Proceedings etc. (Reform) (Scotland) Act 2007 (asp 6) s.43. Brought into force on 10 December 2007 by SSI 2007/479 (C.40) art.3 and Sch.

Definitions

A4-10.1 "caution": s.307(1).
"court of summary jurisdiction": s.307(1).
"fine": s.307(1).
"offence": s.307(1).
"prescribed sum, the": s.225(8).

[THE NEXT PARAGRAPH IS A4-11]

General Note

A4-11 The Criminal Proceedings etc. (Reform) (Scotland) Act 2007 (asp 6) increased the sheriff's sentencing powers in relation to common law offences. This increased range of sentences only applies to proceedings commenced or warranted after 10 December 2007 but note that the date of commission of the offence is irrelevant for these sentencing purposes (*Wilson v Harvie*, 2010 J.C. 105).

The complex interaction of common law and statutory offence penalties was examined in *Minto v Harrower*, 2010 S.L.T. 440, a five judge decision. Thus the inclusion of an offence attracting a higher statutory penalty in a complaint with common law offences only permits the imposition of that statutory maximum penalty for that offence; it cannot be used as a means to enhance or increase the penalties for the common law offences beyond common law levels. With the increased penalties available after 10 December 2007, the arithmetical aspects of *Minto* are now largely academic, but the general sentencing principles discussed remain significant.

Section 178 of the Road Traffic Act 1988 (c.52) makes it an offence to take and drive away a motor vehicle without the consent of the owner or other lawful authority. A contravention of s.178 of the 1988 Act was an offence inferring dishonest appropriation for the purpose of the enhanced penalty following a second or subsequent offence inferring dishonest appropriation of property in terms of s.5(3) of the 1995 Act (*O'Hara v Murray*, 2007 S.C.C.R. 322).

Starrs and Chalmers v Ruxton, 2000 J.C. 208 settled the fate of temporary sheriffs whose mode of appointment was such that their independence was *in law* in doubt and they were replaced by part-time sheriffs (see also *Gibbs v Ruxton*, 2000 J.C. 258).

Stott v Minogue, 2001 S.L.T. (Sh.Ct) 25 provides a rare example of a preliminary challenge by an accused for the trial judge to demonstrate her ability to adjudge issues to his satisfaction. M claimed that it was necessary for him to know whether the judge was impartial and had no affiliations to freemasonry. The sheriff repelled the challenge, citing her judicial oath of impartiality as a sufficient guarantee. See too *Kenny v Howdle*, 2002 S.C.C.R. 814 concerning the powers of an honorary sheriff to deal with procedural appearances, in this case an application for bail after failure to appear for a deferred sentence.

In *Stubbs v The Queen; Davis v The Queen and Evans v The Queen* [2018] UKPC 30; *The Times*, 19 December 2018 there was extensive discussion of the general principles and relevant authorities in regard to circumstances in which a judge should recuse his or herself, in particular in regard to an appeal hearing for a case in which an appellate judge had presided at an earlier aborted jury trial. There seemed to have been no earlier reported decisions relevant to that particular procedural event that was the basis of the objection: at [14]. The general principle from *Stubbs'* case, at [15]–[17], was that the appearance of bias as a result of a pre-determined or pre-judgment was a recognised ground of recusal. It included a clear indication of a prematurely closed mind and extended to any real possibility that a judge would approach a case with anything other than an objective view.

Subs.(1)

The extension, in practice, of the jurisdiction in law of the sheriff sitting as a court of summary jurisdiction to authorise the service of process of English courts in Scotland, and et seperatim to grant process for subsequent service in England is well-established: see the Summary Jurisdiction (Process) Act 1881 (c.24) s.4, and related Schedule for form. That specific function of a court of summary jurisdiction in Scotland is "purely ministerial", and no concern need be shown judicially for any questions regarding the jurisdiction of the English courts in issuing such process or the relevancy of the statements contained therein: *Murphy v Brooks*, 1935 J.C. 11 at 15 per the Lord Justice Clerk (Aitchison). However, the 1881 Act is now excluded by SI 2003/425 art.12C as inserted by SI 2017/1280 Sch. para.3 (both relating to United Kingdom cross-border proceeds of crime authorisations).

Subs.(2)(a)

For a rare example of a fine of, but not exceeding, the prescribed sum in terms of s.5(2)(a) see *Higson v El-Hadji Diouf*, 2003 G.W.D. 29–810 (£5,000 fine). For a discussion of the enhanced and combined effect of ss.5 and 27(3) and (5) see *Penman v Bott*, 2006 S.L.T. 495.

Subs.(2)(d)

In *Nicholson v Lees*, 1996 S.C.C.R. 551 LJC (Ross) said at 558: "where two or more charges are contained in a single complaint, the court cannot competently impose a total period of imprisonment which exceeds in aggregate the upper limit permitted for that court in the particular case by common law or statute". In *Jordan v HM Advocate*, 2008 S.C.C.R. 618 it was held at 625F that the starting point for sentencing cannot competently be more than the statutory maximum when dealing with a contravention of a statutory provision prescribing a maximum sentence. That approach has been maintained in *Jones v Nisbet*, 2013 S.C.C.R. 282 where certain sentences were held to be incompetent.

The maximum competent sentence remains at 12 months in s.5(2)(d), unamended by any recent legislation. However, that period of 12 months has to be understood to be necessarily limited by s.204(3A) of the 1995 Act. That provision asserts that a court must not pass a sentence of imprisonment of 12 months or less on a person unless the court considers that no other method of dealing with the person is appropriate: see the Presumption Against Short Periods of Imprisonment (Scotland) Order 2019 (SSI 2019/236) w.e.f. from 4 July 2019. The Order also modifies the 1995 Act by inserting s.204(3E) which limits the presumption to offences committed on or after the date on which the modification came into effect.

JP courts

JP courts: constitution and prosecutor

6.—(1) […] A4-12

(2) The jurisdiction and powers of the JP court shall be exercisable by a summary sheriff or by one or more justices, and no decision of the court shall be questioned on the ground that it was not constituted as required by this subsection unless objection was taken on that ground by or on behalf of a party to the proceedings not later than the time when the proceedings or the alleged irregularity began.

(3) All prosecutions in a JP court shall proceed at the instance of the procurator fiscal.

(4) […]

(5) The authority of the procurator fiscal to prosecute in JP courts is without prejudice to the authority of any other person to take proceedings there in pursuance of section 43 (prosecutions and penalties) of the Education (Scotland) Act 1980 (c. 44).

(6) In this section, "justice" means a justice of the peace.

AMENDMENTS

Cross-heading and section title substituted, subss.(1), (4) repealed, subss.(5), (6) as substituted and subss.(2), (3) as amended by Criminal Proceedings etc. (Reform) (Scotland) Act 2007 (asp 6) s.80, Sch. para.9(1), (4), (5). Brought into force for the Sheriffdom of Lothian and Borders on 10 March 2008 by SSI 2008/42 (C.4) art.3 and Sch. Brought into force for the Sheriffdom of Grampian, Highland and Islands on 10 June 2008 by SSI 2008/192 (C.19) art.3 and Sch. Brought into force for the Sheriffdom of Glasgow and Strathkelvin on 8 December 2008 by SSI 2008/329 (C.29) art.3 and Sch. Brought into force for the Sheriffdom of Tayside, Central and Fife on 23 February 2009 by SSI 2008/362 (C.30) art.3 and Sch. Brought into force for the Sheriffdom of North Strathclyde on 14 December 2009 by SSI 2009/432 (C.32) art.3 and Sch.1. Remainder in force on 22 February 2010 by SSI 2009/432 (C.32) art. 3 and Sch.2.

Subs.(2) as amended by Courts Reform (Scotland) Act 2014 (asp 8) s.132 and Sch.5 para.39(2). Brought into force on 1 April 2016 (subject to transitional provisions) by SSI 2016/13 art.2 and Sch.1 para.1.

Definitions

A4-12.1 "complaint": s.307(1).
"justice": s.6(6).
"procurator fiscal": s.307(1).

[THE NEXT PARAGRAPH IS A4-13]

General Note

A4-13 The office of stipendiary magistrate was abolished on 1 April 2016 by the 2014 Act s.128.

JP courts: jurisdiction and powers

A4-14 **7.**—(1) [...]

(2) [...]

(3) Except in so far as any enactment (including this Act or an enactment passed after this Act) otherwise provides, it shall be competent for a JP court to—

(a) any common law or statutory offence which is triable summarily;
(b) make such orders and grant such warrants as are appropriate to a court of summary jurisdiction;
(c) anything else (by way of procedure or otherwise) as is appropriate to such a court]

(4) It shall be competent, whether or not the accused has been previously convicted of an offence inferring dishonest appropriation of property, for any of the following offences to be tried in the JP court—

(a) theft or reset of theft;
(b) falsehood, fraud or wilful imposition;
(c) breach of trust or embezzlement,

where (in any such case) the amount concerned does not exceed level 4 on the standard scale.

(5) [...]

(6) The JP court shall, without prejudice to any other or wider powers conferred by statute, be entitled on convicting of a common law offence—

(a) to impose imprisonment for any period not exceeding 60 days;
(b) to impose a fine not exceeding level 4 on the standard scale;
(c) to ordain the accused (in lieu of or in addition to such imprisonment or fine) to find caution for good behaviour for any period not exceeding six months and to an amount not exceeding level 4 on the standard scale;
(d) failing payment of such fine or on failure to find such caution, to award imprisonment in accordance with section 219 of this Act,

but in no case shall the total period of imprisonment imposed in pursuance of this subsection exceed 60 days.

(7) Without prejudice to any other or wider power conferred by any enactment, it shall not be competent for a JP court, as respects any statutory offence—

(a) to impose a sentence of imprisonment for a period exceeding 60 days;
(b) to impose a fine of an amount exceeding level 4 on the standard scale; or
(c) to ordain an accused person to find caution for any period exceeding six months or to an amount exceeding level 4 on the standard scale.

(8) The JP court shall not have jurisdiction to try or to pronounce sentence in the case of any person—

(a) [...]
(b) brought before it accused or suspected of having committed within its jurisdiction any of the following offences—
(i) murder, culpable homicide, robbery, rape (whether at common law or under section 1(1) of the Sexual Offences (Scotland) Act 2009

(asp 9)), rape of a young child (under section 18 of that Act), wilful fire-raising, or attempted wilful fire-raising;
(ii) theft by housebreaking, or housebreaking with intent to steal;
(iii) theft or reset, falsehood fraud or wilful imposition, breach of trust or embezzlement, where the value of the property is an amount exceeding level 4 on the standard scale;
(iv) assault causing the fracture of a limb, assault with intent to ravish, assault to the danger of life, or assault by stabbing;
(v) uttering forged documents or uttering forged bank or banker's notes, or offences under the Acts relating to coinage.

(9) Without prejudice to subsection (8) above, where either in the preliminary investigation or in the course of the trial of any offence it appears that the offence is one which—
(a) cannot competently be tried in the court before which an accused is brought; or
(b) in the opinion of the court in view of the circumstances of the case, should be dealt with by a higher court,

the court may take cognizance of the offence and commit the accused to prison for examination for any period not exceeding four days.

(10) Where an accused is committed as mentioned in subsection (9) above, the prosecutor in the court which commits the accused shall forthwith give notice of the committal to the procurator fiscal of the area within which the offence was committed or to such other official as is entitled to take cognizance of the offence in order that the accused may be dealt with according to law.

AMENDMENTS

Section title substituted, subss.(1), (2) repealed and subss.(3)–(8), (10) as amended by Criminal Proceedings etc. (Reform) (Scotland) Act 2007 (asp 6) s.80, Sch. para.9(2), (4), (5). Brought into force for the Sheriffdom of Lothian and Borders on 10 March 2008 by SSI 2008/42 (C.4) art.3 and Sch. Brought into force for the Sheriffdom of Grampian, Highland and Islands on 10 June 2008 by SSI 2008/192 (C.19) art.3 and Sch. Brought into force for the Sheriffdom of Glasgow and Strathkelvin on 8 December 2008 by SSI 2008/329 (C.29) art.3 and Sch. Brought into force for the Sheriffdom of Tayside, Central and Fife on 23 February 2009 by SSI 2008/362 (C.30) art.3 and Sch. Brought into force for the Sheriffdom of North Strathclyde on 14 December 2009 by SSI 2009/432 (C.32) art.3 and Sch.1. Remainder in force on 22 February 2010 by SSI 2009/432 (C.32) art.3 and Sch.2.

Subs.(8) as amended by Sexual Offences (Scotland) Act 2009 (asp 9) Sch.5 para.2. Brought into force on 1 December 2010 by SSI 2010/357 (C.21) art.2.

Subsection (5) repealed by Courts Reform (Scotland) Act 2014 (asp 18) Sch.5 para.39. Brought into force on 1 April 2016 (subject to transitional provisions) by SSI 2016/13 art.2 and Sch.1 para.1.

DEFINITIONS

"fine": s.307(1). A4-14.1
"level 4": s.225(2) [i.e. £2,500].
"offence": s.307(1).
"procurator fiscal": s.307(1).
"prosecutor": s.307(1).
"sentence": s.307(1).
"standard scale": s.225(1).
"stipendiary magistrate": s.5 of the District Courts (Scotland) Act 1975.

GENERAL NOTE

The office of stipendiary magistrate was abolished on 1 April 2016 by the 2014 Act s.128. A4-15

Sittings of sheriff and JP courts

Sittings of sheriff and JP courts

8.—(1) Notwithstanding any enactment or rule of law, a sheriff court or a JP court— A4-16

(a) shall not be required to sit on any Saturday or Sunday or on a day which by virtue of subsection (2) or (3) below is a court holiday; but

(b) may sit on any day for the disposal of criminal business.

(2) A sheriff principal may in an order made under section 28(1) of the Courts Reform (Scotland) Act 2014 prescribe in respect of criminal business not more than 11 days, other than Saturdays and Sundays, in a calendar year as court holidays in the sheriff courts within his jurisdiction; and may in the like manner prescribe as an additional court holiday any day which has been proclaimed, under section 1(3) of the Banking and Financial Dealings Act 1971, to be a bank holiday either throughout the United Kingdom or in a place or locality in the United Kingdom within his jurisdiction.

(3) A sheriff principal may prescribe not more than 11 days, other than Saturdays and Sundays, in a calendar year as court holidays in the JP courts within his jurisdiction; and he may prescribe as an additional holiday any day which has been proclaimed, under section 1(3) of the said Banking and Financial Dealings Act 1971, to be a bank holiday either throughout the United Kingdom or in a place or locality in the United Kingdom within his jurisdiction.

(4) A sheriff principal may in pursuance of subsection (2) or (3) above prescribe different days as court holidays in relation to different sheriff or JP courts.

AMENDMENTS

Cross-heading and section title and subss.(1), (3), (4) as amended by Criminal Proceedings etc. (Reform) (Scotland) Act 2007 (asp 6) s.80, Sch. para.9(3)–(5). Brought into force for the Sheriffdom of Lothian and Borders on 10 March 2008 by SSI 2008/42 (C.4) art.3 and Sch. Brought into force for the Sheriffdom of Grampian, Highland and Islands on 10 June 2008 by SSI 2008/192 (C.19) art.3 and Sch. Brought into force for the Sheriffdom of Glasgow and Strathkelvin on 8 December 2008 by SSI 2008/329 (C.29) art.3 and Sch. Brought into force for the Sheriffdom of Tayside, Central and Fife on 23 February 2009 by SSI 2008/362 (C.30) art.3 and Sch. Brought into force for the Sheriffdom of North Strathclyde on 14 December 2009 by SSI 2009/432 (C.32) art.3 and Sch.1. Remainder in force on 22 February 2010 by SSI 2009/432 (C.32) art.3 and Sch.2.

Subsections (2) and (3) as amended by Judiciary and Court (Scotland) Act 2008 (asp 6) s.59(2). Brought into force on 16 March 2009 by SSI 2009/83 art.2.

Subsection (2) as amended by Courts Reform (Scotland) Act 2014 (Consequential Provisions) Order 2015 (SSI 2015/150) art.2 and Sch. para.5 (effective 1 April 2015).

GENERAL NOTE

A4-16.1 It is to be noted that, while Parliament in s.8 of the 1995 Act specified what days certain courts might or might not sit on, no *times in terms of hours of the clock* of these permissible days were identified specifically or characterised generally as unlawful or otherwise unacceptable as being unfair. The habit of years of practice settled when courts tend to sit (e.g. from 09.30 or perhaps more commonly 10.00 until the conclusion of business that day) but the patent threats to civil and industrial society during the Second War meant that alternative approaches had to be adopted to enable business and industry to continue.

The severe threat to modern business models following long settled practice from the new coronavirus has added real relevance to past practices and the need for change. The National Records of Scotland include (see ref. HH60/21) a file under the title of "Pleas in absence or staggering of attendance to reduce loss of working time", and reference there to SHHD Circular No.3458 which encouraged the idea of courts in wartime changing practice within the then statutory perimeters to avoid the loss of valuable working time elsewhere. Notably, a letter dated 15 April 1942 in that file mentions the fact of there having been *evening* courts in Kirkintilloch for the prior 30 years.

Territorial jurisdiction: general

Boundaries of jurisdiction

A4-17 **9.**—(1) Where an offence is committed in any harbour, river, arm of the sea or other water (tidal or otherwise) which runs between or forms the boundary of the jurisdiction of two or more courts, the offence may be tried by any one of such courts.

(2) Where an offence is committed on the boundary of the jurisdiction of two or more courts, or within the distance of 500 metres of any such boundary, or partly

within the jurisdiction of one court and partly within the jurisdiction of another court or courts, the offence may be tried by any one of such courts.

(3) Where an offence is committed against any person or in respect of any property in or on any carriage, cart or vehicle employed in a journey by road or railway, or on board any vessel employed in a river, loch, canal or inland navigation, the offence may be tried by any court through whose jurisdiction the carriage, cart, vehicle or vessel passed in the course of the journey or voyage during which the offence was committed.

(4) Where several offences, which if committed in one sheriff court district could be tried together, are alleged to have been committed by any person in different sheriff court districts, the accused may be tried for all or any of those offences—

(a) under one indictment or complaint before the sheriff of any one of the districts; or

(b) under one complaint in the JP court for any one of the districts.

(5) Where an offence is authorised by this section to be tried by any court, it may be dealt with, heard, tried, determined, adjudged and punished as if the offence had been committed wholly within the jurisdiction of such court.

AMENDMENTS

Subs.(4) as amended by Criminal Proceedings etc. (Reform) (Scotland) Act 2007 (asp 6) s.80, Sch. para.9(6). Brought into force for the Sheriffdom of Lothian and Borders on 10 March 2008 by SSI 2008/42 (C.4) art.3 and Sch. Brought into force for the Sheriffdom of Grampian, Highland and Islands on 10 June 2008 by SSI 2008/192 (C.19) art.3 and Sch. Brought into force for the Sheriffdom of Glasgow and Strathkelvin on 8 December 2008 by SSI 2008/329 (C.29) art.3 and Sch. Brought into force for the Sheriffdom of Tayside, Central and Fife on 23 February 2009 by SSI 2008/362 (C.30) art.3 and Sch. Brought into force for the Sheriffdom of North Strathclyde on 14 December 2009 by SSI 2009/432 (C.32) art.3 and Sch.1. Remainder in force on 22 February 2010 by SSI 2009/432 (C.32) art.3 and Sch.2.

DEFINITIONS

"complaints": s.307(1). **A4-17.1**
"indictment": s.307(1).
"offence": s.307(1).
"sheriff court districts": s.307(1).

[THE NEXT PARAGRAPH IS A4-18]

GENERAL NOTE

There seem to have been few modern authorities on the issue of jurisdiction, although the older cases may still provide assistance should doubts arise: see *Lewis v Blair*(1858) 3 Irv. 16; *Witherington* (1881) 4 Couper 475; *Mortensen v Peters* (1906) 5 Adam 121 and *Lipsey v Mackintosh* (1913) 7 Adam 182. **A4-18**

Competence of justice's actings outwith jurisdiction

9A. It is competent for a justice, even if not present within his jurisdiction, to sign any warrant, judgment, interlocutor or other document relating to proceedings within that jurisdiction provided that when he does so he is present within Scotland. **A4-18.1**

AMENDMENTS

Section 9A inserted by Criminal Justice (Scotland) Act 2003 (asp 7) Pt 8 s.59. Brought into force on 27 June 2003 by SSI 2003/288 (C.14).

Section 9A repealed by Criminal Proceedings etc. (Reform) (Scotland) Act 2007 (asp 6) s.80, Sch. para.9(7). Partially brought into force on 10 December 2007 insofar as it relates to justices of the peace as specified in SSI 2007/479 Sch.1 as amended by SSI 2007/527 art.2(5)(b). Brought into force on 8 December 2008 in relation to stipendiary magistrates and the Sheriffdoms of Glasgow and Strathkelvin, Grampian, Highland and Islands and Lothian and Borders (SSI 2008/329 art.2 and Sch.1). Brought into force on 23 February 2009 in relation to stipendiary magistrates for the Sheriffdom of Tayside, Central and Fife as specified in SSI 2008/362 art.3 and Sch.1. Brought into force in relation to stipendiary magistrates for the Sheriffdom of North Strathclyde on 14 December 2009 by SSI 2009/432 (C.32) art.3 and Sch.1. Brought into force in relation to stipendiary magistrates on 22 February 2010 by SSI 2009/432 (C.32) art.3 and Sch.2. Not yet in force otherwise.

GENERAL NOTE

A4-18.2 The case of *Shields v Donnelly*, 2000 S.L.T. 147; 1999 S.C.C.R. 890 emphasised the distinction between the procedural powers exercisable by a judge by virtue of his office and those powers which could only be executed within a territorial jurisdiction. The practical impact of this distinction was that warrants could only competently be granted by a judge while he was within his territorial jurisdiction. This new provision irons out this anomaly which impacted particularly upon sheriffs, many of whom might not reside within their sheriffdom.

[THE NEXT PARAGRAPH IS A4-19]

Crimes committed in different districts

A4-19 **10.**—(1) Where a person is alleged to have committed in more than one sheriff court district a crime or crimes to which subsection (2) below applies, he may be prosecuted in the sheriff court or JP court of such one of those districts as the Lord Advocate determines.

(2) This subsection applies to—

(a) a crime committed partly in one sheriff court district and partly in another;

(b) crimes connected with each other but committed in different sheriff court districts;

(c) crimes committed in different sheriff court districts in succession which, if they had been committed in one such district, could have been tried under one indictment together.

(3) Where, in pursuance of subsection (1) above, a case is tried in the sheriff court or JP court of any sheriff court district, the procurator fiscal of that district shall have power to prosecute in that case even if the crime was in whole or in part committed in a different district, and the procurator fiscal shall have the like powers in relation to such case, whether before, during or after the trial, as he has in relation to a case arising out of a crime or crimes committed wholly within his own district.

AMENDMENTS

Subss.(1)–(3) as amended by Criminal Proceedings etc (Reform) (Scotland) Act 2007 (asp 6) s.80, Sch. para.10. Brought into force on 10 March 2008 by SSI 2008/42 (C.4) art.3 and Sch.

DEFINITIONS

A4-19.1 "crime": s.307(1).
"procurator fiscal": s.307(1).
"sheriff court district": s.307(1).

Jurisdiction for transferred cases

A4-19.2 **10A.**—(1) A sheriff has jurisdiction for any cases which come before the sheriff by virtue of—

(a) section 34A or 83 of this Act; or

(b) section 137A, 137B, 137C or 137D of this Act.

(1A) The jurisdiction of a JP court includes jurisdiction for any cases which come before it by virtue of section 137CA, 137CB or 137CC of this Act.

(2) A procurator fiscal for a sheriff court district shall have—

(a) power to prosecute in any cases which come before a sheriff of that district by virtue of a provision mentioned in subsection (1) above;

(aa) power to prosecute in any cases which come before a JP court of that district by virtue of a provision mentioned in subsection (1A) above;

(b) the like powers in relation to such cases as he has for the purposes of the other cases which come before that sheriff when exercising criminal jurisdiction or (as the case may be) before that JP court.

(3) This section is without prejudice to sections 4 to 10 of this Act.

AMENDMENTS

Section 10A inserted by Criminal Proceedings etc (Reform) (Scotland) Act 2007 (asp 6) s.80, Sch. para.11. Brought into force on 10 March 2008 by SSI 2008/42 (C.4) art.3 and Sch.

Subs.(1A) inserted, subss.(2) and (3) as amended, by Criminal Justice and Licensing (Scotland) Act 2010 (asp 13) Sch.7 para.27. Brought into force on 28 March 2011 by SSI 2011/178 (C.15) art.2, Sch.1 para.1.

[THE NEXT PARAGRAPH IS A4-20]

Certain offences committed outside Scotland

11.—(1) Any British citizen or British subject who in a country outside the United Kingdom does any act or makes any omission which if done or made in Scotland would constitute the crime of murder or of culpable homicide shall be guilty of the same crime and subject to the same punishment as if the act or omission had been done or made in Scotland. **A4-20**

(2) Any British citizen or British subject employed in the service of the Crown who, in a foreign country, when acting or purporting to act in the course of his employment, does any act or makes any omission which if done or made in Scotland would constitute an offence punishable on indictment shall be guilty of the same offence and subject to the same punishment, as if the act or omission had been done or made in Scotland.

(3) A person may be prosecuted, tried and punished for an offence to which this section applies—

(a) in any sheriff court district in Scotland in which he is apprehended or is in custody; or

(b) in such sheriff court district as the Lord Advocate may determine, as if the offence had been committed in that district, and the offence shall, for all purposes incidental to or consequential on the trial or punishment thereof, be deemed to have been committed in that district.

(4) Any person who—

(a) has in his possession in Scotland property which he has stolen in any other part of the United Kingdom; or

(b) in Scotland receives property stolen in any other part of the United Kingdom,

may be prosecuted, tried and punished in Scotland in like manner as if he had stolen it in Scotland.

(5) Where a person in any part of the United Kingdom outside Scotland—

(a) steals or attempts to steal any mail-bag or postal packet in the course of its transmission by post, or any of the contents of such a mail-bag or postal packet; or

(b) in stealing or with intent to steal any such mail-bag or postal packet or any of its contents commits any robbery, attempted robbery or assault with intent to rob,

he is guilty of the offence mentioned in paragraph (a) or (b) as if he had committed it in Scotland and shall be liable to be prosecuted, tried and punished there without proof that the offence was committed there.

(6) Any expression used in subsection (5) and in the Postal Services Act 2000 has the same meaning in that subsection as it has in that Act.

AMENDMENTS

Subss.(5) and (6) inserted by Postal Services Act 2000 (c.26) s.127(4) and Sch.8 para.24. Brought into force by SI 2000/2957 (C.88) art.2(3) and Sch.3 (effective 26 March 2001).

Subss.(3) and (4) as amended by Criminal Justice and Licensing (Scotland) Act 2010 (asp 13) Sch.7 para.28. Brought into force on 28 March 2011 by SSI 2011/178 (C.15) art.2, Sch.1 para.1.

DEFINITIONS

A4-20.1 "crime": s.307(1).
"offence": s.307(1).
"sheriff court district": s.307(1).

GENERAL NOTE

A4-20.2 It should be noted that specific statutory provisions in relation to the commission of "listed sexual offences" abroad by those ordinarily subject to the jurisdiction of the Scottish courts are contained in ss.16A and 16B of the Criminal Law (Consolidation) (Scotland) Act 1995 above.

Conspiracy to commit offences outwith Scotland

A4-20.3 **11A.**—(1) This section applies to any act done by a person in Scotland which would amount to conspiracy to commit an offence but for the fact that the criminal purpose is intended to occur outwith Scotland.

(2) Where a person does an act to which this section applies, the criminal purpose shall be treated as the offence mentioned in subsection (1) above and he shall, accordingly, be guilty of conspiracy to commit the offence.

(3) A person is guilty of an offence by virtue of this section only if the criminal purpose would involve at some stage—

(a) an act by him or another party to the conspiracy; or

(b) the happening of some other event,

constituting an offence under the relevant law; and conduct punishable under that law is an offence under that law for the purposes of this section however it is described in that law.

(3A) In subsection (3) above, "the relevant law" is—

(a) if the act or event was intended to take place in another part of the United Kingdom, the law in force in that part,

(b) if the act or event was intended to take place in a country or territory outwith the United Kingdom, the law in force in that country or territory.

(4) Subject to subsection (6) below, a condition specified in subsection (3) above shall be taken to be satisfied unless, not later than such time as the High Court may, by Act of Adjournal, prescribe, the accused serves on the prosecutor a notice—

(a) stating that, on the facts as alleged with respect to the relevant conduct, the condition is not in his opinion satisfied;

(b) setting out the grounds for his opinion; and

(c) requiring the prosecutor to prove that the condition is satisfied.

(5) In subsection (4) above "the relevant conduct" means the agreement to effect the criminal purpose.

(6) The court may permit the accused to require the prosecutor to prove that the condition mentioned in subsection (4) above is satisfied without the prior service of a notice under that subsection.

(7) In proceedings on indictment, the question whether a condition is satisfied shall be determined by the judge alone.

(8) Nothing in this section—

(a) applies to an act done before the day on which the Criminal Justice (Terrorism and Conspiracy) Act 1998 was passed, or

(b) imposes criminal liability on any person acting on behalf of, or holding office under, the Crown.

AMENDMENTS

Section 11A title and subss.(1) and (3) as amended, subs.(3A) inserted, by Criminal Justice and Licensing (Scotland) Act 2010 (asp 13) s.50. Brought into force on 28 March 2011 by SSI 2011/178 (C.15) art.2, Sch.1 para.1, for all purposes in respect of acts done by a person in Scotland on or after 28 March 2011 which would amount to conspiracy to commit an offence.

GENERAL NOTE

This section was inserted by s.7 of the Criminal Justice (Terrorism and Conspiracy) Act 1998 (c.40). Although it was explained under reference to terrorism during the parliamentary debates, it in fact applies to all offences and all countries the approach originally taken to "sex tourism" cases in s.16A of the Criminal Law (Consolidation) (Scotland) Act 1995 (c.39), which section is now amended so as to restrict its ambit to incitement. Conspiracy in Scotland to commit an offence in a country or territory outside the UK is now dealt with under the present section. **A4-20.4**

Subs. (1)

Any act. Subsection (8) excludes any act done before the Criminal Justice (Terrorism and Conspiracy) Act 1998 (c.40) was passed.

Which would amount to conspiracy to commit an offence but for the fact that the criminal purpose is intended to occur ... outside the United Kingdom. This subsection states the preconditions for the section as a whole to have effect. The case must be one in which there is conduct which, in Scots law would amount to a conspiracy except for the fact that the agreement is to do or achieve something outside the UK.

The section was not discussed in Parliament in its own right. Rather, it was taken along with ss.5 and 6, which make equivalent provision for England and Wales and Northern Ireland. Lord Williams of Mostyn, speaking for the Government, explained the policy intention as follows: "Conspiracy is dealt with in Clause 5 and subsequent clauses. These provisions are designed to close off a gap which has been recognised for some time in our response to international terrorism and other international crime. In our country it is not always an offence to conspire to commit criminal acts outside this country. This section of the Bill deals with those people who try to use our country as a safe place to plot the commission of terrorist offences or other crimes abroad. Terrorism and other forms of organised crime cannot be contained by a line on a map. Crime in one country is often instigated and planned in another. We think that there should not be a hiding place in our jurisdiction for terrorists, those who traffic in arms, drug smugglers, money launderers or counterfeiters ... Some powers already exist in this field. Extra-territorial jurisdiction is available for some offences such as computer misuse and sexual offences against children. Other offences are covered, but only in relation to certain countries, under the Suppression of Terrorism Act ... Your Lordships will find no prohibition of incitement in this Bill. That is deliberate as we did not wish to interfere with a tradition which remains valid, noble and distinctive to our country; that is, that political dissent is important and should be allowed, even when it is disagreeable; in fact, particularly when it is disagreeable...We have included safeguards in Clause 5 and subsequent clauses. The principle of dual criminality—in other words, the conspiracy to commit the unlawful act—depends on the act being unlawful in the foreign country and also in our own domestic jurisdiction" (*Hansard*, H.L. Debs, 3 September 1998, Col. 14).

Lord Williams' remark that "In our country it is not always an offence to conspire to commit criminal acts outside this country" was made against the background of the English case of *Board of Trade v. Owen* [1957] A.C. 602, in which Lord Tucker held that, since the purpose of the criminal law is to protect the Queen's peace and maintain order within the realm, conspiracy to do something in another country is not criminal in English law. This was an essentially nineteenth-century view, reflecting the isolationist approach taken by English courts to jurisdiction over crimes with cross-frontier aspects. That approach has been much criticised in the literature (see, for example, Geoff Gilbert, "Crimes Sans Frontièrs: Jurisdictional Problems in English Law" (1992) 63 *British Yearbook of International Law* 415 and Matthew Goode, "Two New Decisions on Criminal 'Jurisdiction': The Appalling Durability of Common Law", 20 *Criminal Law Journal* 267 (1996) (Australia); but for a contrary view, see Peter Alldridge, " Sex Offenders Act 1997—Territoriality Provisions" [1997] Crim.L.R. 655).

The question whether conspiracy in Scotland to commit crime in a foreign jurisdiction is criminal at common law in Scotland seems never to have been judicially considered. The legislation seems simply to assume that the law of Scotland was as isolationist as that of England and Wales. Since the legislation has now been enacted, the accuracy of that assumption is unlikely ever to be determined. It may, however, be commented that there is no particular reason to suppose that the High Court of Justiciary would have been quite so parochial as its counterparts south of the border, especially since there are in any event material differences between the approaches which the two systems take to jurisdiction in general (see P.W. Ferguson, "Jurisdiction and Criminal Law in Scotland and England", in Robert F. Hunter (ed.), *Justice and Crime*, 1993, 96).

Under the Suppression of Terrorism Act 1978 (c.26), jurisdiction already exists in relation to conspiring within the UK to commit crimes in other Council of Europe countries, India and the United States. This reflects the UK's particular treaty relationships.

Subs.(2)

An act to which this section applies. See subs.(1).

Subs.(3)

This subsection applies a "double" or "dual" criminality test. The acts or events to be carried out in the foreign jurisdiction in pursuance of the criminal purpose which, by subs.(1) must be of a sort which would be criminal in Scotland if carried out here, must also be such as to be criminal by the law of the place where they are intended to take place. There would, for obvious reasons, be difficulties about criminalising in the UK an agreement to do something in a foreign country if that act would be perfectly lawful in the country where it was to be carried out.

The concept of the double criminality test has been developed most fully in relation to extradition law, where in general the conduct for which it is intended to prosecute the fugitive must be criminal in both the state in which he is to be prosecuted and that in which he is found before extradition can take place. The emphasis is always placed on the acts complained of and precise equivalence in the offence creating provisions is not necessary. Nothing in this subsection suggests that a different approach is intended here.

Subs.(4)

A condition specified in subs.(3) above. That is, the double criminality requirement.

Shall be taken to be satisfied. There is a rebuttable presumption that the double criminality requirement is satisfied.

Notwithstanding this, subs.(6) gives the court a discretion to permit the accused to require the prosecutor to prove that the double criminality requirement is satisfied without service of a notice.

A notice. By contrast with notices under, for example, s.280(6)(b) of the present Act, the notice contemplated here cannot simply put the Crown to the proof. The notice must not only state that in the opinion of the accused the double criminality requirement is not satisfied and require the prosecutor to prove it; to be effective it must also state the *grounds* for the accused's opinion. This is likely to involve investigation of foreign law.

Subs.(6)

Since the exercise of the discretion given to the court by this subsection will almost certainly involve the leading of evidence as to the content of foreign law, it seems likely that an adjournment will be required. It might therefore be that the court, in deciding whether to exercise that discretion, will have in mind the three interests which, in terms of *Skeen v McLaren*, 1976 S.L.T. (Notes) 14, it should consider in relation to motions to adjourn (namely that of the accused, that of the prosecutor and the possibility of prejudice to the public interest).

Subs.(8)

Speaking for the Government, Lord Dubs explained that the purpose of this subsection is "not to give minor civil servants carte blanche to pursue criminal careers. It applies to actions which might have to be taken in the course of official duty where there is no exemption. There is a range of circumstances in which technical breaches of the new provisions might otherwise arise. For example, if the police or Customs were planning an undercover operation involving infiltration of an organised crime group, a consignment of drugs or weapons might be tracked to a number of different transit countries, each with a different legal system. There would obviously be no question of prosecution here in those circumstances" (*Hansard*, H.L. Debs, September 3, 1998, Col. 91).

[THE NEXT PARAGRAPH IS A4-21]

PART II – POLICE FUNCTIONS

Lord Advocate's instructions

Instructions by Lord Advocate as to reporting of offences

A4-21 **12.** The Lord Advocate may, from time to time, issue instructions to the chief constable with regard to the reporting, for consideration of the question of prosecution, of offences alleged to have been committed.

AMENDMENTS

Section 12 as amended by Police and Fire Reform (Scotland) Act 2012 (asp 8) Sch.7 para.12(2). Brought into force on April 1, 2013 by SSI 2013/51 art.2.

DEFINITION
"offence": s.307(1). A4-21.1

[THE NEXT PARAGRAPH IS A4-22]

GENERAL NOTE

This section repeats the terms of s.9 of the 1975 Act which, in turn, derived from the Criminal Justice (Scotland) Act 1949 (c.94), s.33. The Lord Advocate's authority to appoint or remove procurators fiscal and delineate their territorial jurisdictions, is found in the Sheriff Courts and Legal Officers (Scotland) Act 1927 (c.35), s.1(2). By s.12 of that Act the Lord Advocate may also after consultation with the Treasury, by Order direct, notwithstanding the terms of any Act of Parliament, that any sheriff court proceedings for contraventions thereof shall proceed at the instance of the procurator fiscal. The Sheriff Courts (Prosecutions for Poaching) Order 1938 is the only instance in which this power has been exercised. A4-22

The Lord Advocate's power to amend or rescind policy, or change the instructions or guidance issued by his predecessors in that office is unfettered; see *MacDonald v HM Advocate*, 1997 S.C.C.R. 408 for its discussion of the constitutional standing of that office.

This generality must now be more narrowly read in light of ECHR considerations introduced by the Scotland Act 1998 (c.46) and the Scotland Act 2012 (c.11).

In the exercise of his role in extradition proceedings (see the Extradition Act 2003 (c.41) s.191) the Lord Advocate fulfils an administrative function as a member of the Scottish Executive not a function in the prosecution of crime.

Thus (unlike criminal proceedings which might give rise to compatibility issues as provided by s.36 of the Scotland Act 2012 (c.11)) his actings in extradition proceedings would still be subject to review as devolution issues. See *Kapri v Lord Advocate* [2013] UKSC 48; 2013 S.C.C.R. 430.

Detention and questioning

Powers relating to suspects and potential witnesses

13.—(1) Where a constable has reasonable grounds for suspecting that a person has committed or is committing an offence at any place, he may require— A4-23

(a) that person, if the constable finds him at that place or at any place where the constable is entitled to be, to give the information mentioned in subsection (1A) below and may ask him for an explanation of the circumstances which have given rise to the constable's suspicion;

(b) any other person whom the constable finds at that place or at any place where the constable is entitled to be and who the constable believes has information relating to the offence, to give the information mentioned in subsection (1A) below.

(1A) That information is—

(a) the person's name;

(b) the person's address;

(c) the person's date of birth;

(d) the person's place of birth (in such detail as the constable considers necessary or expedient for the purpose of establishing the person's identity); and

(e) the person's nationality.

(2) The constable may require the person mentioned in paragraph (a) of subsection (1) above to remain with him while he (either or both)—

(a) subject to subsection (3) below, verifies any information mentioned in subsection (1A) above given by the person;

(b) notes any explanation proffered by the person.

(3) The constable shall exercise his power under paragraph (a) of subsection (2) above only where it appears to him that such verification can be obtained quickly.

(4) A constable may use reasonable force to ensure that the person mentioned in paragraph (a) of subsection (1) above remains with him.

(5) A constable shall inform a person, when making a requirement of that person under—

(a) paragraph (a) of subsection (1) above, of his suspicion and of the general nature of the offence which he suspects that the person has committed or is committing;

(b) paragraph (b) of subsection (1) above, of his suspicion, of the general nature of the offence which he suspects has been or is being committed and that the reason for the requirement is that he believes the person has information relating to the offence;

(c) subsection (2) above, why the person is being required to remain with him;

(d) either of the said subsections, that failure to comply with the requirement may constitute an offence.

(6) A person mentioned in—

(a) paragraph (a) of subsection (1) above who having been required—

(i) under that subsection to give the information mentioned in subsection (1A) above; or

(ii) under subsection (2) above to remain with a constable,

fails, without reasonable excuse, to do so, shall be guilty of an offence and liable on summary conviction to a fine not exceeding level 3 on the standard scale;

(b) paragraph (b) of the said subsection (1) who having been required under that subsection to give the information mentioned in subsection (1A) above fails, without reasonable excuse, to do so shall be guilty of an offence and liable on summary conviction to a fine not exceeding level 2 on the standard scale.

(7) [...]

AMENDMENTS

Subss.(1)(a)(b), (2)(a) and (6)(a)(i)(b) as amended, and subs.(1A) inserted, by Police, Public Order and Criminal Justice (Scotland) Act 2006 (asp 10) s.81(1)–(5). Brought into force on 1 September 2006 by SSI 2006/432 (C.34) art.2.

Subs.(7) repealed by Criminal Justice (Scotland) Act 2016 (asp 1) Sch.2 para.2(a). Brought into force on 25 January 2018 by SSI 2017/345 art.3 and Sch.1 para.1.

Subss.(1B), (1C), (2)(aa), (3A), (5)(ba), (6)(a)(iii) and (8) prospectively inserted, and subss.(2), (5)(d), (6)(a)(i) prospectively amended by Police, Public Order and Criminal Justice (Scotland) Act 2006 (asp 10) s.82.

DEFINITIONS

A4-23.1 "constable": s.307(1) and s.51(1) of the Police (Scotland) Act 1967 (c.77).
"offence": s.307(1).

[THE NEXT PARAGRAPH IS A4-24]

GENERAL NOTE

A4-24 The provisions of s.1 of the 1980 Act, after minor re-numbering of subsections, are re-enacted to form s.13. This section deals with the preliminary stages of police enquiries many of which will never develop into criminal proceedings. It gives a general power to police officers, when they have reasonable cause to suspect that an offence either has occurred or is in the course of commission, to demand information from certain members of the public. Two distinct categories of person are affected by these provisions, those who may have committed an offence, and those who are potential witnesses to an offence.

Powers In Relation To Suspects

A4-25 Subsection (1)(a) relates to any person whom the officer suspects is guilty of such an offence (whether it is an arrestable offence or not), and empowers the constable to demand that person's particulars and an explanation for the conduct which has given rise to suspicion. Note that at this early stage no caution of any sort need be administered and it seems likely that any reply would be admissible subject to the ordinary rules of evidence.

The criteria governing a citizen's right to arrest and search a suspect were discussed by the Appeal Court in *Wightman v McFadyen*, 1999 S.C.C.R. 664 and in the context of drunk driving see the opinion in *Goodson v Higson*, 2002 S.L.T. 202.

If, however, suspicions were sufficiently tangible for the constable to feel a caution to be appropriate, then the s.13 procedure would not be appropriate; the proper approach would be to caution with a view to charging (in the case of non-arrestable offences) or, where the offence could attract a sentence of imprisonment, to consider whether the circumstances would justify the use of the power of arrest. The police may question and charge a suspect in relation to minor offences, without being obliged to arrest him, provided that a caution is administered. Note that s.55 of the Criminal Justice (Scotland) Act 2016 (asp 1) expressly removes any obligation for the police to charge in relation to any offence. The corollary is that in such a situation there would be no obligation to ensure the suspect be offered access to legal advice, this only becoming necessary once taken into custody and arrest procedures are commenced. See *Barrie v Nisbet* [2012] HCJAC 160; 2013 S.C.C.R. 16, an offence of public indecency involving masturbation at 09.00 on Ne'erday.

In the exercise of his power under subs.(1)(a), an officer must first explain the nature of his suspicion and may then require the potential suspect to remain while the veracity of his particulars is established (provided this can be done quickly) and any explanation given may be noted. It will be observed that in terms of subs.(6) failure to provide particulars or to remain while the explanation given is noted by the officer constitutes an offence which attracts arrest without warrant; nonetheless, a suspect is under no more of an obligation to give an explanation than an officer is to note it.

Doubtless a suspect's failure to offer an account may well serve to heighten the constable's existing suspicions. On an equally pragmatic level, an officer's failure to note an explanation given in response to a s.13 requirement would no doubt attract adverse comment in any subsequent proceedings.

No time limit is stipulated in s.13 for the completion of these initial enquiries, except that the procedure for verifying personal particulars must be capable of rapid completion (subs.(3)). While a suspect can be caused to remain for that verification to be made rapidly, it must be emphasised that he cannot be restrained under s.13 while his explanation is examined—that is the role of arrest. Reasonable force can be used to ensure that a suspect remains at the scene for the limited purposes of subs.(2); see *Hume v HM Advocate*, 2005 G.W.D. 22–411.

What then is the status of the suspect who is required to remain in terms of s.13(2) or, worse, restrained at the scene by a constable using his powers under s.13(4)? It might reasonably be felt, not least by the hapless suspect, that he is not at liberty to go and is in the officer's custody. However, reference to s.295 of the Act suggests that legal custody or detention only occurs when a person is required to be taken, or is held for the purpose of being taken, to a place for the purposes of the Act. It is notable that s.13(2) studiously avoids use of the word "detain" and the meaning of being required "to remain" for the limited purposes of the section must surely be something more dilute than detention. It is submitted that the precise status of the suspect is by no means clearly established.

If the view is reached that an accused person has effectively been restrained, or coerced to the point that he has no option but to remain with the police and thus is not at liberty to go about his own business, then de facto he has to be regarded as being detained. In that event, he is then entitled to access to legal advice if any responses or replies are to be admissible in evidence unless, in the whole circumstances, such access at that point would have been impracticable: a general fairness test, as set out in *Miln v Cullen*, 1967 J.C. 21 would have to be applied. See *Ambrose v HM Advocate* [2011] UKSC 43 at [68]–[70]; 2011 S.L.T. 1005 . The admissibility of evidence gleaned as a result of replies made by an accused which themselves fall to be treated as inadmissible raises further complexities; as a general rule the court will then have to consider the overall fairness of the procedure and whether the line of enquiry opened by the admissions would have otherwise been uncovered by the police during further enquiries (*HM Advocate v P* [2011] UKSC 44; 2011 S.L.T. 1097).

Powers In Relation To Potential Witnesses

Subsection (1)(b) applies to persons whom the officer has reason to believe may, wittingly or unwittingly, have information to offer about the offence. It seems that this could extend to the circumstances in which the officer exercised his powers in relation to the suspect under subs.(1)(a): for example, the witness could be a bystander at the time when the suspect gave an explanation to the constable, given if he had not witnessed the offence giving rise to the enquiry. A4-26

First, however, a general explanation of the nature of the alleged offence being investigated must be given by the officer to the potential witness. The officer is also obliged to inform the other party of the belief that he or she possesses information relevant to that investigation and that failure to provide personal particulars in those circumstances is an offence.

Police powers in pursuit of requirements under subs.(1)(b) are more limited than those applicable to suspects, for subs.(4) allows the use of reasonable force to ensure that a suspect remains until the enquiries specified in subs.(2) are quickly completed or noted as the case may be. No force may be employed to cause a witness to remain at the scene. All that can lawfully be demanded of a witness is that he provides his name and address, albeit failure to give these particulars will render him liable to immediate arrest (subs.(7)).

Reasonable grounds for suspicion

The Act does not attempt to define what would constitute "reasonable cause" and nor need it do so. A4-27
The phrase has been minutely examined by the courts, albeit usually in the context of the Road Traffic Acts. Suffice to say that the suspicions formed by the officer need not rest upon personal ocular observa-

tion; they can stem from the observations of other persons, from "information received" or from prior knowledge of the suspect's habits and background, as well as general knowledge of the area being policed.

It will be appreciated that some of the factors giving rise to cause to suspect, may well be inadmissible as evidence, but that would not disentitle the officer from forming his suspicion. The general considerations are discussed in *McNicol v Peters*, 1969 S.L.T. (J.) 261, notably in Lord Wheatley's judgment at pp.265 and 266, from which it can also be seen that even an ill-founded suspicion can still constitute reasonable cause to suspect. Lord Wheatley returned to this topic in *Dryburgh v Galt*, 1981 S.C.C.R. 26 at 29 noting:

> "... the fact that the information on which the police officer formed his suspicion turns out to be ill-founded does not in itself necessarily establish that the police officer's suspicion was unfounded. The circumstances known to the police officer at the time he formed his suspicion constitute the criterion, not the facts as subsequently ascertained."

See too *McKenzie v Murphy*, 2015 S.C.L. 194.

The subtlety of distinctions at this early stage of enquiry are amply illustrated by *Wilson v Procurator Fiscal, Dumfries* [2021] SAC (Crim) 4.

Nonetheless, the Crown will have to establish objectively that the factors which exercised the constable's suspicions would reasonably create a cause to suspect an offence without, at that stage, amounting to sufficient grounds for arrest, or perhaps, charge.

A bald instruction to an officer to apprehend a suspect, without any knowledge, or explanation of the grounds giving rise to suspicion, it is submitted will not suffice; see *HM Advocate v B* [2013] HCJ 71, a case centring upon the exercise of statutory detention powers under the Misuse of Drugs Act 1971 (c.38).

The section is equally silent on the question of defining "any place" or "a place where the constable is entitled to be". The phrases serve to differentiate between the locus of the offence (where the officer can proceed on his enquiries armed with his suspicions) at the time of the offence or later, and elsewhere, in which latter case a right to information may depend upon the legitimacy of the officer's presence there. For example, the constable may be in a public place, or in a private place where access has been gained by warrant, by invitation or for an unrelated legitimate purpose: each of these different situations may subtly impinge upon the ability of the constable to exercise his powers under s.13. It will also be borne in mind that the degree of restraint used to ensure that the suspect remains, must be reasonable.

If it is established that the force employed was unreasonable, i.e. excessive or inappropriate, or both, then that might well nullify any subsequent evidence and constitute a criminal assault upon the suspect. Efforts to enter premises without warrant or the occupier's consent will only be upheld if the urgency of the situation, or gravity of the suspected offence, be substantial (*Gillies v Ralph*, 2008 S.L.T. 978; 2008 S.C.C.R. 887 distinguishing *Turnbull v Scott*, 1990 S.C.C.R. 614). The section itself contains no explicit right of entry or search in pursuance of a detention.

There is a dearth of case authorities dealing with this section, a fact which serves to underline its preliminary nature in the scale of proceedings.

Detention and questioning at police station

A4-28 **14.—** [...]

AMENDMENTS

Subs.(9) as amended, and subs.(10) inserted, by Police, Public Order and Criminal Justice (Scotland) Act 2006 (asp 10) s.81(6). Brought into force on 1 September 2006 by SSI 2006/432 (C.34) art.2.

Subs.(6) as amended by Criminal Procedure (Legal Assistance, Detention and Appeals) (Scotland) Act 2010 (asp 15) s.1. Subss.(2), (4) and (5) as amended by s.3. Brought into force on 30 October 2010.

Section 14 repealed by Criminal Justice (Scotland) Act 2016 (asp 1) Sch.2 para.27(a). Brought into force on 25 January 2018 by SSI 2017/345 art.3 (subject to transitional and savings provisions in arts 4 and 7).

DEFINITIONS

A4-28.1 "constable": s.307 and s.51(1) of the Police (Scotland) Act 1967.
"offence": s.307(1).
"offence punishable by imprisonment": s.307(6).
"prison": s.307(1).

GENERAL NOTE

A4-29 This section was repealed with effect from 25 January 2018 and the active provisions in force from that date are found in the Criminal Justice (Scotland) Act 2016 (asp 1). The General Note has been retained to assist practitioners.

The Criminal Justice (Scotland) Act 2016 (asp 1) abolished the concept of detention introduced in the 1980 Act of the same name (c.62). That concept had been given statutory effect in Scots criminal law on the recommendation of the Thomson Committee which had highlighted both the need for the individual, whose liberty was being interfered with, and the police, to have clarity as to the person's status and to facilitate the investigation of crimes attracting imprisonment. The impact of the Supreme Court decision in *Cadder v HM Advocate* [2012] UKSC 43; 2010 S.L.T. 1125, which held that Convention-compliance required that a detainee must be offered access to legal advice prior to the conduct of police enquiries and was entitled to seek further legal advice during the detention period, was significant as it, in turn, brought about a doubling or even quadrupling of the detention timeframe. (See the Criminal Procedure (Legal Assistance, Detention and Appeals) (Scotland) Act 2010). The 2016 Act reforms drew heavily upon the pattern and provisions of PACE (Police and Criminal Evidence Act 1984 (c.60)) which applied to England and Wales. Unhelpfully for practitioners, some important provisions are to be found as amendments to the 1995 Act; still more are stand-alone provisions in the 2016 Act. It would be optimistic in the extreme to anticipate a consolidating statute in the foreseeable future.

While a citizen may be arrested on warrant granted by a court, it is far more common for apprehension to be initiated by the police. It remains competent for a suspect to attend a police office voluntarily for interview but, standing the impact of *Cadder*, the likelihood is that such an individual (who might once have been detained) will now be arrested, though not officially accused, while police investigations proceed. The telling distinction at the conclusion of the statutory time frame, normally 12 hours, is whether he is charged with an offence and becomes "officially accused", or not. At that stage a range of options arise—release, investigative liberation, liberation on police bail (familiar as the superseded s.22 of the 1995 Act) or continued police custody pending a custodial report to the procurator fiscal.

The development of statutory detention provisions

The concept of detention was introduced into Scots criminal law on the recommendation of the Thomson Committee as a means of providing clarity and flexibility in the previous grey area between voluntary attendance, where (in theory at least) a citizen being so interviewed was free to terminate the interview and leave the police station at any time, and arrest. Thus s.2 of the Criminal Justice (Scotland) Act 1980 (c.62) introduced a six hour maximum period of detention, a formal procedure for timing, documenting or recording the detention period and a new form of statutory caution distinct from the traditional common law caution. These powers can only be exercised by "a constable"; other law enforcement agencies must found upon the statutory powers, if any, vested in their agencies. It follows that questioning during a s.14 detention can only be undertaken by a constable; see *Stone v HM Advocate*, 2009 S.C.C.R. 71. Note too that subs.(9) stipulates that the detainee must be advised of his right to decline to answer any question except for the personal particulars including (where necessary) his nationality. This is the basis for the previously mentioned statutory form of the caution which has to be administered.

The object of detention was to allow time for further enquiry by the police where reasonable cause to suspect the commission of a criminal offence existed but insufficient evidence was immediately available to arrest and charge the detained person. Detention was not, and should not, be regarded as a stratagem for delaying arrest and charge; as soon as it is clear that a sufficiency of evidence exists, detention should cease, and the suspect should be arrested and charged; *Toal v HM Advocate* [2012] HCJAC 123; 2012 S.C.C.R. 735. Equally, if no such further evidence can be found then the suspect has to be released as soon as possible and certainly at the conclusion of the appropriate detention period. Subs.(3) guards against repeated use of the same detention grounds. In this limited timeframe it will occasion no surprise that the focus of enquiry would generally be that of an interview under caution of the accused. The Thomson Committee expended substantial effort in identifying a statutory detention period felt to strike an appropriate balance between the rights of a citizen temporarily deprived of his liberty and the broader public interest in ensuring the effective investigation of crime. As an example of the law of unintended consequences, the outcome of the Supreme Court's decision in *Cadder v HM Advocate* [2010] UKSC 4; 2010 S.L.T. 1125; 2010 S.C.L. 1265 and Convention compliance is peerless: the requirement of access to legal advice before, and during, any detention interview wrought the legislative (and Convention-compliant) response of the Criminal Procedure (Legal Assistance, Detention and Appeals) (Scotland) Act 2010 with a doubling or even quadrupling of the detention timeframe.

Lawful Detention

The elements needed to constitute a lawful detention are not presented chronologically in s.14 but for convenience this course has been followed in the discussion below. **A4-30**

Grounds for Detention

Subsection (1) requires that the constable detaining a suspect must have reasonable grounds for suspecting that he has committed, or is in the course of committing, an imprisonable offence (for discussion of the factors underpinning "reasonable cause to suspect" see note to s.13 above), see *Wilson and Nolan v Robertson*, 1986 S.C.C.R. 700. *Houston v Carnegie*, 2000 S.L.T. 333 is an example of a situation in which the detaining officer had neither sufficient direct knowledge nor information upon which to form reasonable grounds for suspicion. Compare *Stark v Brown*, 1997 S.C.C.R 382. In contrast to s.13 powers (the right to require personal particulars from suspects and potential witnesses, and an explanation of circumstances from suspects) which can be exercised in relation to any offence, s.14 detention is only permissible when the offence under investigation can attract a term of imprisonment on conviction. **A4-31**

It will be seen that the section is not a preventative one, i.e. detention cannot be used to inquire into an offence which has yet to occur. In reality this distinction may be more apparent than real; often matters may have advanced sufficiently to consider that contemplation has blossomed into preparation and, accordingly, an attempt at the suspected offence can be established.

Secondly, the only valid purpose of the detention is to assist in the investigation of the matter at hand. If those inquiries can be shown objectively to have been capable of completion without the necessity of detaining the suspect, then logically, procedures should be regarded as vitiated—that is a determination which commonsense suggests it would be difficult for a court to reach.

Information To Be Given To A Detainee

A4-32 Subsection (6) requires the constable to outline to the suspect the grounds for detention, namely the nature of his suspicions and general details of the offence suspected. It is certain that these steps must be taken at the time when the suspect is detained though, in practice, the grounds will undoubtedly be repeated when the place of detention is reached.

Subsection (9) obliges the officer, before undertaking any questioning of the detainee, to administer the statutory form of caution both when initially detaining the suspect and when presenting him at the place of detention. The statutory caution requires a detainee to furnish his name and address; otherwise he is under no obligation to answer any further questions. Note that in *Tonge v HM Advocate*, 1982 S.C.C.R. 313 the Appeal Court stressed the desirability of administering a common law caution prior to interviews conducted during the detention period.

Best practice also dictates that the statutory caution described above should be administered at the earliest opportunity although failure to do so will not inevitably damage a Crown case fatally. In *Scott v Howie*, 1993 S.C.C.R. 81 the appellant was detained under s.2 of the 1980 Act on suspicion of housebreaking and conveyed to a police office. No statutory caution in terms of s.2(7) (the statutory precursor of s.14(9)), was administered but such a caution was given at the office, as was a common law caution, following which the appellant made a statement whose contents the Crown founded upon. The admitted absence of a statutory caution at the time of detention in the street was not fatal in this instance. However, there can be no doubt that any effort to lead evidence of statements made by the detainee between being stopped by the officers and his arrival at the police office would have foundered on the grounds of inadmissibility.

Reasonable force may be used to effect detention and at that time, or later, to search the suspect's person (see subss.(1), (7) and (8)).

From the moment of detention a suspect is to be regarded as being in legal custody (see s.295 below).

Reference should be made to *Ucak v HM Advocate*, 1999 S.L.T. 392, in which the detention of the accused, a Turk who spoke no English, was held to be lawful although an interpreter was not available during the six hour statutory period; the police had done all that they could to comply.

That judgment has to be regarded as superseded by the Right to Interpretation and Translation in Criminal Proceedings (Scotland) Regulations 2014 (SSI 2014/95), which applies to those who do not speak or understand English, or suffer hearing or speech impairment. Part 2 of the Regulations applies to detention and arrest procedures; Part 3 refers to subsequent court proceedings. The Regulations came into force on May 14, 2014.

Removal To A Police Office Or Other Premises

A4-33 Once detained, the objective has to be to ensure the swift removal of the suspect to a police station or other premises (usually detention will be continued at a police station but that is not demanded by s.14(1)). One of the operational limitations of s.2 of the 1980 Act was that the detainee could only be taken to either a police station or other premises and, once there, could not be removed elsewhere. This could create practical difficulties, for example, in organising a swift identification parade or in detaining individuals for an offence which had been investigated by another officer or had occurred in another police division or area.

European Convention on Human Rights

The Appeal Court was sceptical that detention could properly be regarded as being "charged with an offence", the starting point for application of art.6 (*HM Advocate v Robb*, 2000 J.C. 127) but this aspect has been bypassed in the broader discussion of the right of a suspect or accused to access to legal advice found in *Cadder v HM Advocate*. It now follows that an accused must be informed of his right to legal advice, and offered access to such advice, prior to any interview being undertaken. During interview or other procedures the detainee has a right to access legal advice. Failure to afford such access will certainly render any subsequent admissions made by him inadmissible. *Cadder* may be the first word in this area—it will assuredly not be the last. Thorny issues, such as how early in a police investigation it is necessary to give access to legal advice, whether an accused can exercise a waiver of his rights to such advice, (as *Cadder* in fact did, and as *Jude, Hodgson and Birnie v HM Advocate* [2011] HCJAC 46 suggests one can) or as seems likely, withdraw that waiver subsequently, the extent to which the detainee can require fresh access to advice as further evidence emerges, and whether a co-accused can found upon exculpatory elements of an accused's otherwise inadmissible police interview, all demand early clarification. Application of the general fairness test set out in *Miln v Cullen*, 1967 J.C. 21 necessarily means that any waiver of legal advice exercised by an accused has to stem from informed consent. Thus, the courts would be slow to accept a waiver given by an accused who was, at the time of interview, demonstrably vulnerable. See A4-37 below. For example, see *McCann v HM Advocate* [2013] HCJAC 29; 2013 S.C.C.R. 254, a case involving a waiver of access to legal advice by a child aged 16 years 41 days old which, with little difficulty, was held to be informed and unequivocal, and *Application by Children's Reporter, Alloa in respect of JM* (Case B304/11, Alloa June 6, 2012) in relation to a 12-year-old boy detained for serious sexual offences where age, maturity, lack of understanding of the nature of the charges, and the role of the child and the appropriate adult in the waiver decision were all scrutinized, following *McGowan v B* [2011] UKSC 54.

Although the accused must be given some indication of the broad nature and gravity of the charge under investigation, *GFR v HM Advocate*, 2013 S.C.C.R. 164 holds that he need not be given detailed specification of the allegations to inform his decision whether or not to take legal advice. (See, however, *GM v HM Advocate*, 2013 S.C.C.R. 176 discussed in Notes to s.18). Status as a suspect must be clear to activate any issue of waiver. Administration of a caution in itself is not conclusive of that status; see *Miller v Smith* [2012] HCJAC 166; 2013 S.C.C.R. 169.

Section 14(1) incorporates amendments which were made to s.2 of the 1980 Act by the Criminal Justice and Public Order Act 1994 (c.33) s.129(1). These go some way to answering the logistical difficulties mentioned above. It is now permissible to remove a suspect from the establishment where he has originally been detained to another police office, or other place, for the purpose of facilitating the investigation. So a suspect could be moved between police offices or, say, from a local trading standards office once detained, to a police office for photographing and fingerprinting. A valuable degree of flexibility has been created, but it will be borne in mind that a record of the detention procedures and times, sufficient to comply with the provisions of s.15 has to be maintained (see the notes to s.15 below) and all such inquiries are subject to the time limit stipulated in s.14(2).

Different considerations apply to removal of detainees between jurisdictions in Great Britain and these are examined below.

The requirement to take the accused "as quickly as is reasonably practicable" does not mean that an accused must be conveyed to the closest police station. Operational factors may make detention at a more distant station appropriate. See *Menzies v HM Advocate*, 1995 S.C.C.R. 550 (suspect detained near Airdrie conveyed to Dunfermline).

The Time Factors

Generally, the period of detention will end with the suspect being arrested and charged or, alternatively, released without charge at that time if the grounds of suspicion have not been made out. In the latter case, the police or the Crown would not be barred subsequently from preferring charges arising from the grounds of detention: they would in terms of s.14(3) be unable to detain again using the statutory detention to be found in s.14. In *HM Advocate v Mowat*, 2001 S.L.T. 738; 2001 S.C.C.R. 242 the meaning of subs.(3)'s reference to a further period of detention "on the same grounds or on any grounds arising out of the same circumstances" was reviewed in the absence of any direct authority during M's trial for the murder of C who had been found dead on November 4, 1999. A repetition of detention to enable interview in relation to telephony information gleaned from mobile phones, which had been seized at the time of the earlier detention, was held not to breach s.14(3)'s general prohibition of re-detention arising from the same grounds in *Dunsire v HM Advocate* [2017] HCJAC 30. This decision focused upon the fact that the contents and significance of the phones' contents were both unknown at the time of initial interview; nonetheless, unease has to be voiced that *Dunsire* may permit repeated detention interviews as the Crown case ingathers materials. A4-34

It soon became clear that M had been one of the last people to see C alive. On November 7, 1999 M was detained in relation to an assault upon another man, R, "and other crimes". While so detained he was questioned about the murder, and it was suggested by the defence that the assault upon R itself was attributed to the fact that R had implicated the accused in the murder. Certainly, police enquiries at that stage involved seizure of clothing, fingerprinting and a house search. At the conclusion of his detention M was charged with assaulting R and more than a month later was detained again, but this time for C's murder. It may be that while the offences investigated (and giving rise to detentions) are different, they could properly derive from the same grounds of suspicion. It has to be said that these may be fine distinctions in reality and serve to emphasise the importance of clarity (both in detention records and in the minds of the officers concerned) in the grounds for detention.

It is possible, of course, if unlikely, that at the end of a period of detention the suspect might opt to remain voluntarily to assist enquiries. Procedural laxity similar to that in *HM Advocate v Cowie*, 2012 S.L.T. 709 (discussed in the note to s.18(6) below) arose in *Young v McLintock* [2012] HCJAC 104; Y having been detained in a street, and removed to a police office for search in terms of s.23 of the Misuse of Drugs Act 1971 (c.38), was held in custody while the police sought an intimate body search warrant. This warrant was granted by the sheriff and the search carried out but nothing was done to regularise the accused's status—arrest or formal detention—thus rendering evidence from that search inadmissible.

The end of the detention clearly represents a procedural watershed, for at that point (subject to subs.(b) discussed later) the suspect's status must change to that of a prisoner or a citizen free to return to his own affairs. If procedures laid out in s.14 are complied with, then it would seem that evidence collected during that time will be admissible, despite any subsequent want of procedure; see *Grant v HM Advocate*, 1989 S.C.C.R. 618 where arrest did not occur till some 20 minutes after the end of detention and replies made within the six hours were objected to. The Appeal Court held that subsequent laxity in compliance with formal requirements would not in themselves vitiate what had gone before.

It should not be forgotten that the cross-border enforcement provisions contained in Pt X of the Criminal Justice and Public Order Act 1994 introduce in s.138(6)(a) an allowable period of four hours detention calculated from the time of arrival at a police station outside Scotland, in circumstances described in s.137 of that Act, i.e. where a person is detained in England or Wales for an offence previously committed (or attempted) in Scotland.

So far as Northern Ireland is concerned, quite different provisions, found in s.137(7)(d) apply. A suspect found there and detained in connection with an offence in Scotland can either be taken to the nearest convenient police station in Scotland, or to the nearest designated police station in Northern Ireland, as soon as reasonably practicable (on arrest elsewhere in Great Britain in relation to a Scottish crime, the arresting officer's duty is to take the arrested person either to the nearest convenient police station in Scotland or to a police station within the sheriffdom where the offence is being investigated).

When recourse is had to these cross-border provisions, it should be stressed that it is only competent to convey the detainee to a police office, or to police offices; the references in s.14 of the 1995 Act to "other premises" must then be disregarded.

Lastly, it is worthy of note that the powers of cross-border enforcement bear a surprising, and doubtless unintended, resemblance to the doctrine of hot pursuit which operated in the Scottish and English Borders during the times of the reivers.

Section 14 Detention And Other Statutory Powers

A4-35 As has been mentioned, the inclusion of subs.(b) has substantially affected the previously clear cut operation of s.14. Now detention under the Act may be only a prelude to further statutory periods of detention. The provisions of anti-terrorism legislation and the Customs and Excise Management Act 1979 (c.2) as augmented by the Criminal Justice (Scotland) Act 1987 (c.41) ss.48 to 50 spring to mind. Indeed, it will be noted that the Customs legislation cited is a refinement of the 1980 Act's detention provisions and is generally directed against drug smuggling offences.

Subsection (4) requires that a period of detention under any other enactment upon the same grounds, shall be deducted from the 12-hour period ordinarily available under s.14. A like provision is made specifically in regard to the Prisons (Scotland) Act 1989 (c.45). Section 41(3) of that Act permits temporary detention within a prison for the purpose of investigating the introduction (i.e. smuggling) of forbidden materials by persons into prisons.

Details To Be Recorded

A4-36 In addition to the obligation upon the detaining officer to disclose the nature of his suspicions and the reason for detention, subs.(6) stipulates other requirements which must be complied with by the officer and other police officers who become involved in the detention process later. It is an absolute requirement that (i) the time and place at which detention began, (ii) the general nature of the suspected offence, (iii) the time of arrival at the police office or other premises used for detention, (iv) the time, or times, at which the detainee was informed of his right to refuse to answer questions except those requiring his personal particulars (pursuant to subs.(9)) and his right to request that his solicitor and another person be advised of the fact of his detention as provided by s.15 of the Act, and the particulars of the officer who intimates this information, (v) the times when the above requests were made by the detainee and fulfilled by the police, and (vi) the time when detention terminated and/or the time of arrest should be recorded. All of these requirements simply echo the provisions contained in s.2(4) of the 1980 Act; it should be noted, however, that the corollary of the power in subs.(1) of this Act to remove the detainee from the police office to "any other place", is that subs.(6)(b) demands that the "other place" should be specified in the record if such a power is exercised (although not statutorily required, it would be prudent to record fully the times of removal to that "other place" and return to the police office).

The practice adopted by Scottish police forces is for the detention forms which constitute the record of detention (stipulated now in subs.(6)), to be raised and maintained at police offices from the moment a detainee arrives there. It follows of course that initially the forms raised will necessarily have a retrospective effect since the detention process will have been initiated elsewhere: consequently it is sound practice for the detaining officer to note the time of initiating detention in his notebook.

In *Cummings v HM Advocate*, 1982 S.C.C.R. 108 the only record produced to show that a statutory caution had been administered was contained in the officer's notebook. This was held to constitute a record sufficient for the purposes of s.2(4) of the 1980 Act. Nevertheless, it is sound practice to ensure that the terms of the statutory caution in subs.(9) are repeated at the police office when documentation is raised.

Purpose Of Detention

A4-37 While s.2(5) of the 1980 Act did broadly specify the avenues of inquiry which could be followed during detention, reference now has to be made to ss.18 and 19 of the 1995 Act to appreciate the wide-ranging powers which can be exercised (see notes to ss.18 and 19 below). Subsection (7) preserves the right to question and search the detainee. The power of search was held in *Skirving v Russell*, 1999 G.W.D. 15-701 to include a search of a woman's handbag as well as any pockets in her clothing. In *McIntyre v HM Advocate*, 2005 S.L.T. 757 it was held on appeal that the use, for forensic comparison of his voice against earlier taped malicious phone calls, of a tape recording of the accused's interview under caution while detained was fairly obtained and admissible as evidence. This was despite the fact that neither the accused nor the interviewing officers were aware of this possibility during the interview itself.

Questioning

The physical or psychological fitness of the accused to be questioned fairly often arises as an art.6 Convention issue in the course of trial. This may well lead to a trial within a trial (where evidence is heard by the judge alone outwith the presence of the jury). *Platt v HM Advocate*, 2004 S.L.T. 333; 2004 S.C.C.R. 209 clarifies that the judge applies a proof on the balance of probabilities, but must still give appropriate directions to the jury to emphasise the higher standard of proof which must be applied in their own deliberations. No adverse inference can be drawn from a failure to answer questions put or, as in *Larkin v HM Advocate*, 2005 S.L.T. 1087, to respond "No comment" to such questions.

Following *Platt*, in *Allan v HM Advocate* [2014] HCJAC 60; 2014 S.C.C.R. 540, where a preliminary plea (averring undue police pressure prompting a false confession) had been refused, and the interview thereafter being held admissible, the Appeal Court criticised a jury direction that there had been no challenge to the fairness of the interview, and a further direction that the appellant's evidence as to how he felt during it be disregarded.

In *Stone v HM Advocate*, 2009 S.C.C.R. 71, the Appeal Court held that a strict interpretation of these provisions precluded questioning by anyone other than a police officer. Here in a joint interview conducted by the detaining officer and an HMRC investigator, questioning was largely conducted by the investigator. It is notable that the Court indicated that there would have been nothing improper had the questions been prompted by the investigator and put directly to the detainee by the constable and that the Court reviewed the tenor, fairness and good faith of the interviewing officers (reflecting the excusable irregularity test of *Lawrie v Muir*, 1950 S.L.T. 37). Oddly, the irregular conduct of the interview was prompted by Crown Office guidance.

The tactical use in cross-examination of answers from a police interview, previously deemed inadmissible on *Cadder* grounds, to contradict an accused's evidence is certainly perilous though it does not inevitably result in a miscarriage of justice (see *RMM v HM Advocate*, 2013 S.C.C.R. 79, following *McInnes v HM Advocate* [2010] UKSC 7; 2010 S.C.C.R. 286); the totality of evidence also has to be considered.

Access to solicitor and access to documentation

The Right to Information (Suspects and Accused Persons) (Scotland) Regulations 2014 (SSI 2014/159), framed for compliance with Directive 2012/13/EU of the European Parliament, requires that an affected person be given a written or verbal explanation of his rights, intimation of his status to a solicitor and the opportunity of a legal consultation. Regulation 2(7), echoing s.15(8) of the Act, provides that, exceptionally, questioning may begin or persist without the benefit of such a consultation. Perhaps surprisingly, such a fundamental decision can be exercised by a constable and does not require screening by a more senior officer (see, by contrast, s.14(7)(a) of the Act). The Regulations also provide for a suspect or arrested person to have access to his detention/arrest documentation held by the police, for the express purpose of challenging the lawfulness of those procedures as applied to him. Regulation 4 does not indicate a time frame for exercise of this right or for police compliance with such a request.

Extension of period of detention under section 14

14A.— [...] **A4-37.1**

AMENDMENTS

Section 14A inserted by Criminal Procedure (Legal Assistance, Detention and Appeals) (Scotland) Act 2010 (asp 15) s.3. Brought into force on 30 October 2010.

Section 14A repealed by Criminal Justice (Scotland) Act 2016 (asp 1) Sch.2 para.27(a). Brought into force on 25 January 2018 by SSI 2017/345 art.3 (subject to transitional and savings provisions in arts 4 and 7).

[THE NEXT PARAGRAPH IS A4-37.3]

GENERAL NOTE

This section was repealed with effect from 25 January 2018 and the active provisions in force from that date are found in the Criminal Justice (Scotland) Act 2016 (asp 1). The General Note has been retained to assist practitioners. **A4-37.3**

This section empowers a custody review officer (see subs.(7)) to extend the detention period in serious cases where enquiries are ongoing, from 12 to 24 hours. This power may ordinarily only be exercised once the detainee or his law agent have been given the opportunity to make representations. Given the delicacy of such situations it follows, and subs.(8) demands, that a full record of the procedure and discussions must be maintained by that officer.

Circumstances may arise in such serious cases as s.15(1) recognises when intimation to a named person may be delayed in the interests of the investigation or to facilitate the arrest of other offenders. Section 15A(7) applies the same strictures to intimation to a solicitor. The most extreme position, i.e. no access to legal advice at all prior to, or during, questioning, is permissible in terms of s.15A(8). Standing the *Cadder* judgment it is submitted, however, that such an extreme could probably only find favour with the courts in circumstances where the Crown could justify a derogation from the normal standards set out in the Convention Rights and Freedoms, for which see A130-48 below.

Extension under section 14A: procedure

A4-37.4 **14B.—** [...]

AMENDMENTS

Section 14B inserted by Criminal Procedure (Legal Assistance, Detention and Appeals) (Scotland) Act 2010 (asp 15) s.3. Brought into force on 30 October 2010.

Section 14B repealed by Criminal Justice (Scotland) Act 2016 (asp 1) Sch.2 para.27(a). Brought into force on 25 January 2018 by SSI 2017/345 art.3 (subject to transitional and savings provisions in arts 4 and 7).

[THE NEXT PARAGRAPH IS A4-38]

GENERAL NOTE

This section was repealed with effect from 25 January 2018 and the active provisions in force from that date are found in the Criminal Justice (Scotland) Act 2016 (asp 1).

Right of persons arrested or detained to have intimation sent to another person

A4-38 **15.—** [...]

AMENDMENTS

Subs.(6)(b) substituted by Crime and Punishment (Scotland) Act 1997 (c.48) s.62(1) and Sch.1 para.21 with effect from 1 August 1997 by SI 1997/1712 art.3.

Subss.(1), (4) and title as amended by Criminal Procedure (Legal Assistance, Detention and Appeals) (Scotland) Act 2010 (asp 15) s. 1. Brought into force on 30 October 2010.

Section 15 repealed by Criminal Justice (Scotland) Act 2016 (asp 1) Sch.2 para.27(a). Brought into force on 25 January 2018 by SSI 2017/345 art.3 (subject to transitional and savings provisions in arts 4 and 7).

DEFINITIONS

A4-38.1 "child": s.307(1) as restricted by subs. (6).
"constable": s.307(1) and Police (Scotland) Act 1967 (c.77) s.51(1).
"parent": subs.(6).

[THE NEXT PARAGRAPH IS A4-39]

GENERAL NOTE

A4-39 This section was repealed with effect from 25 January 2018 and the active provisions in force from that date are found in the Criminal Justice (Scotland) Act 2016 (asp 1). The General Note has been retained to assist practitioners.

This section specifies the extent to which arrested or detained persons are entitled to have other persons informed of their circumstances and whereabouts. This must be intimated to the subject as soon as he is presented at the station charge bar or at whatever other place he is being lawfully held in custody. Note that the entitlement does not extend to those attending voluntarily. Section 14(6) requires that the procedure be properly documented at the time of arrival at the police station or "other place", not before.

There are some important differences in the obligations the police are placed under by this section when dealing with arrested, as distinct from detained, persons.

Arrested Persons

A4-40 In the case of arrested persons, subs.(1)(a) only deals with the right to have friends or relatives told this information and, while the arrested person has to be advised of his right to have a named person told of his circumstances, the police can, when there are legitimate grounds for doing so, delay such a notification. Section 17 makes it mandatory for the arrested person to be advised immediately of his right to have a legal representative (whether personally nominated by the person or acting as the duty solicitor under the Legal Aid Scheme) informed of his status and whereabouts. While that section stipulates that the arrested person must be informed of this right immediately on arrest, it does not demand immediate intimation to the solicitor who is named. Nevertheless an unexplained delay in notification would risk an unfavourable interpretation in subsequent proceedings. There is no obligation upon the solicitor to attend the police station (or other named premises) when notification is received from the police.

It should be noted that separate, more extensive, provisions are made in regard to children, and these are discussed below.

Detained Persons

A4-41 Subsection (1)(b) relates to suspects detained in terms of s.14. Their rights to intimation differ from those applicable to arrested persons. At the time of detention at a police office or other place, the detainee must be informed of his entitlement to have his circumstances made known to a reasonably named person and to a solicitor. This right applies equally to situations where the subject is held at a police office or elsewhere but greater latitude is permitted in delaying the implementation of the detainee's demands. Informing either the detainee's reasonably named person or his solicitor, or both, can be delayed. Normally notifications requested by the suspect must be acted upon swiftly, in order to comply with the spirit of the Act unless, as subs.(1) stipulates, there are plausible grounds relative to the matter under investigation or affecting the prospects of apprehending others or relating to the prevention of crime (this last being an undefined catch-all) which justify a temporary withholding of notification.

There is no automatic right of access to a solicitor either prior to, or during a detention interview, but the admissibility of evidence obtained from the accused during the interview must still meet a general test of fairness. See *Paton v Ritchie*, 2000 S.L.T. 239; 2000 S.C.C.R. 151 (following *HM Advocate v Fox*, 1947 J.C. 30) where the accused's appeal was based upon a purported breach of his art.6 rights: the Appeal Court accepted that art.6 could apply even at this early investigative stage in proceedings. Reference should also be made to *R. v Fox; Fox v Chief Constable of Gwent* [1985] 1 W.L.R. 1126; [1985] 3 All E.R. 392, a House of Lords judgement which held that an unlawful arrest did not of itself vitiate subsequent breath test procedures: this case was discussed in *Goodson v Higson*, 2002 S.L.T. 202 where the Appeal Court ruled, on the facts, that there had been no arrest.

Section 15 As Applied To Children

These provisions apply to children aged between eight and 16 years since s.41 statutorily repeats the common law concept of nonage: see also *Merrin v S*, 1987 S.L.T. 193 and the general discussion there of the absence of dole in children under eight years. **A4-42**

In the context of s.15 it will be observed that the definition of "child" found in subs.(6) is narrower than that contained in the Interpretation section (s.308), which in turn refers back to the provisions of the Children (Scotland) Act 1995 (c.36). The narrower definition in subs.(6) has the effect of ensuring that identical provisions apply to all those aged 16 years or more. That section apart, the 1995 Act and Pt II of the Children (Scotland) Act 1995, s.93(2)(b) adhere to the definition of a "child" as either a person less than 16 years old, or a person over the age of 16 years and less than 18 years old who is subject to a supervision requirement.

Subsection (4) places a positive onus upon the police when they think that the person in custody is a child, to take active steps to contact the child's parent or guardian and allow access to the child. This is the case even when it is suspected that the parent or guardian was involved in the offence which gave rise to the child's detention in the first place: subs.(5) allows access to the child to be limited (and, arguably, even refused) where this is essential to the further investigation of the offence under scrutiny or for the safety of the parent or guardian, or both. It is submitted that the grounds for any restriction upon, or refusal of, access in these circumstances should be fully noted by the officers involved. Failure to adhere to these requirements arose in the case of *HM Advocate v GB and DJM*, 1991 S.C.C.R. 533 and a confession obtained by the police was withheld from the jury.

Generally the Act proceeds on the basis that children arrested for offences shall be liberated to appear at court rather than being detained in custody. See s.43 below which sets out the procedures following the arrest of a child.

Observations

Curiously while s.15 demands that the suspect be informed of these rights and (together with s.14(6)(e) and (f)) that a record of the person and solicitor named be kept along with the times of notification, it is not necessary to record when notification is wilfully delayed or the reasons for so doing. It is submitted that where a departure from the usual practice of notification occurs, this should only be done when the following factors are *all* present; (a) the suspect has been informed of his rights of intimation, and (b) has elected names which are deemed unreasonable or as inexpedient (broadly not in the interests of justice for the reasons expressed in subs.(1)) at that time, and (c) has been informed that such intimation will not be made and advised of the grounds for that decision. The suspect cannot simply be left in the dark if the spirit of s.15 is to have any meaning. As was remarked earlier, it would be expedient, with an eye to later proceedings, that the grounds for delaying notification to the suspect's solicitor or friend be recorded along with the other details stipulated in s.14(6)and subs.(3). Failure to comply with the terms of this section would taint any admissions, prints or samples subsequently obtained from the accused. Adapting the *ratio* in *Grant v HM Advocate*, 1989 S.C.C.R. 618 (see notes to s.14 above) suggests that evidence obtained from the accused beforehand would still be admissible. **A4-43**

Right of suspects to have access to a solicitor

15A.— [...] **A4-43.1**

AMENDMENTS

Section 15A inserted by Criminal Procedure (Legal Assistance, Detention and Appeals) (Scotland) Act 2010 (asp 15) s.1. Brought into force on 30 October 2010.

Section 15A repealed by Criminal Justice (Scotland) Act 2016 (asp 1) Sch.2 para.27(a). Brought into force on 25 January 2018 by SSI 2017/345 art.3 (subject to transitional and savings provisions in arts 4 and 7).

[THE NEXT PARAGRAPH IS A4-43.3]

General Note

A4-43.3 This section was repealed with effect from 25 January 2018 and the active provisions in force from that date are found in the Criminal Justice (Scotland) Act 2016 (asp 1). The General Note has been retained to assist practitioners.

This section sets out the right of a detained suspect, an arrested person or one who has attended a police office voluntarily for interview, to have a solicitor informed without delay of each of these developments. More significantly, following *Cadder v HM Advocate* [2010] UKSC 43; 2010 S.L.T. 1125; 2010 S.C.L. 1265, the party involved also has to be advised of his right to a legal consultation (see subs.(5)) and save in exceptional circumstances no questioning can begin until that consultation has occurred. It is clear too from subs.(3)(a) that the individual can also opt to consult as questioning progresses.

Both intimation and consultation may be delayed on the grounds set out in subss.(7) and (8) and, necessarily, the individual involved is obliged to answer questioning directed to obtaining his particulars and cannot withhold these pending such a consultation. *Jude, Hodgson and Birnie v HM Advocate* [2011] HCJAC 46 supports the view that an accused can waive access to his right to a consultation but can only do so having first been informed of that right. Subs.(3)(b) infers that such a waiver need not be irrevocable.

Persistent questioning amounting to interrogation, or refusal of access to a solicitor, can render elements of an interview inadmissible. See *Paul v HM Advocate* [2013] HCJAC 13, an appeal under s.74 of the Act following on a preliminary hearing.

Subs.(8) has been repeated verbatim in the Right to Information (Suspects and Accused Persons) (Scotland) Regulations 2014 (SSI 2014/159). See the discussion at A4-37 above. What might constitute exceptional circumstances remains undecided.

[THE NEXT PARAGRAPH IS A4-44]

Drunken persons: power to take to designated place

A4-44 **16.—** [...]

Amendments

Section 16 repealed by Criminal Justice (Scotland) Act 2016 (asp 1) Sch.2 para.27(a). Brought into force on 25 January 2018 by SSI 2017/345 art.3 (subject to transitional and savings provisions in arts 4 and 7).

Definitions

A4-44.1 "constable": s.307(1) and s.51(1) of the Police (Scotland) Act 1967.
"offence": s.307(1).

[THE NEXT PARAGRAPH IS A4-45]

General Note

A4-45 More in hope than expectation this section repeats the provisions, word for word, of s.5 of the 1980 Act. The original intention of the section was to enable drunken persons to be dealt with other than by criminal prosecution and it gave the police the option of conveying the offender to a designated place for detoxification. The section can only be applied where such designated places exist and to date only pilot schemes have operated.

While a constable may choose to exercise his powers to deliver a drunkard to a designated place, neither he nor the staff there have any power to compel the subject to remain there. It will also be noted that conveyance to a place is entirely without prejudice to any further proceedings arising from the arrest. It is of interest that this section does not require the offence giving rise to arrest to be one specifically of drunkenness, or to have been committed in a public place, only that the offender offended while apparently drunk. That said, the scope of the powers of arrest for common law offences committed by a drunken offender remains hazy: plainly a common law offence witnessed by a constable would qualify, but what is the position when the suspicion of an offence stems from ex parte statements?

Certain statutory powers of arrest of drunken persons do exist. For example, the Civic Government (Scotland) Act 1982 (c.45) s.50(1) created an offence of being drunk and incapable, suggesting a more advanced state of intoxication and incapacity than mere drunkenness, while s.50(5) relates to possession of a firearm or crossbow in a public place while drunk.

The Criminal Justice (Scotland) Act 1980 confined itself to dealing with drunkenness: s.69(c) related to drunken persons on public passenger vehicles en route to designated sporting events; s.74 to drunkenness at a designated sports ground during the currency of a designated sporting event. These provisions are now to be found in Pt 2 of the Criminal Law (Consolidation) (Scotland) Act 1995 (c.39). In the absence of local or centrally funded provision of designated places s.16 is destined to be moribund.

Arrest: access to solicitor

Right of accused to have access to solicitor

17.— [...] A4-46

AMENDMENTS

Section 17 repealed by Criminal Justice (Scotland) Act 2016 (asp 1) Sch.2 para.27(a). Brought into force on 25 January 2018 by SSI 2017/345 art.3 (subject to transitional and savings provisions in arts 4 and 7).

GENERAL NOTE

It is mandatory that an accused person, following arrest, must be informed (i) of his right to have a solicitor informed of this development and that the solicitor's services are required (ii) of his right to a private interview with his solicitor which is to be accorded to him prior to the first court appearance on the charges and (iii) where applicable, of his right to have a solicitor of his choosing present at judicial examination and, if need be, for that examination to be delayed up to 48 hours to permit the attendance of that solicitor. A4-47

There is no obligation upon the solicitor to attend immediately or, indeed, at all but legal advice must be available before the accused's court appearance.

It will be noted that while a request by the accused to have a solicitor informed of his arrest must be acted upon by the police, there is no similar entitlement to have friends or relatives told of his circumstances though this should ordinarily be permitted; see the discussion in Notes to s.15 above regarding "Arrested Persons".

Grounds sufficient to merit arrest can be less than would be needed to prefer charge (*Hay v HM Advocate*, 1998 G.W.D. 35-1780). There is no prohibition on interview by the police after arrest (*Johnston v HM Advocate*, 1994 S.L.T. 300). Following *Cadder v HM Advocate* [2010] UKSC 43; 2010 S.L.T. 1125; 2010 S.C.L. 1265 an accused person subject to such an interview would be required to be informed of his right to further legal consultation in all but the most exceptional circumstances.

See also *Van Lierop v McLeod*, 2000 S.L.T. 291 in relation to the extent of admissibility of answers to questions after arrest.

Right of person accused of sexual offence to be told about restriction on conduct of defence: arrest

17A.— [...] A4-47.1

AMENDMENTS

Section 17A is inserted by Sexual Offences (Procedure and Evidence) (Scotland) Act 2002 (asp 9) Sch.1 para.2. Brought into force by SSI 2002/443 (C.24) art.4 (effective from 1 November 2002).

Subs.(1)(a) as amended by Criminal Justice (Scotland) Act 2003 (asp 7) Sch.4 para.3. Brought into force on 25 November 2003 by SSI 2003/475 (C.26) art.2.

Subs.(1) as amended by Criminal Procedure (Amendment) (Scotland) Act 2004 (asp 5) s.25 and Sch.1 para.3. Brought into force on 4 December 2004 by SSI 2004/405 (C.28) art.2(1).

Subs.(1) as amended by Criminal Justice and Licensing (Scotland) Act 2010 (asp 13) Sch.7 para.29. Brought into force on 28 March 2011 by SSI 2011/178 (C.15) art.2, Sch.1 para.1.

Section 17A repealed by Criminal Justice (Scotland) Act 2016 (asp 1) Sch.2 para.27(a). Brought into force on 25 January 2018 by SSI 2017/345 art.3 (subject to transitional and savings provisions in arts 4 and 7).

DEFINITIONS

"High Court": s.307(1). A4-47.2
"preliminary hearing": s.307(1).

GENERAL NOTE

This section was repealed with effect from 25 January 2018 and the active provisions in force from that date are found in the Criminal Justice (Scotland) Act 2016 (asp 1). The General Note has been retained to assist practitioners. A4-47.3

This section provides that a person charged with any of the sexual offences listed in s.288C of the Act should be advised at the time of arrest of the restrictions upon his conduct of his defence; broadly, he is barred from representing himself and, thus, prevented from precognoscing or cross-examining victims or witnesses in those proceedings. Subs.(2) makes it clear that failure to advise the accused of these restrictions at the time of arrest would not nullify subsequent proceedings. The section is advisory, not mandatory, and it will be remembered that there is an obligation upon the Crown to give note to the accused of these restrictions when serving a complaint or indictment which contains a listed sexual offence. Following the development of victim statements and amendments to s.288C (introduced by ss.14 and 15 of the Criminal Justice (Scotland) Act 2003 (asp 7)), the same restrictions apply to preparation or conduct of any proof of victim statements following conviction of a listed sexual offence.

No person charged with "a listed sexual offence" (see s.288C below) can be personally responsible for the preparation, or conduct of a preliminary hearing, and must engage a lawyer for that purpose. If a lawyer is not instructed then subs.(1)(c) requires the court to appoint a solicitor if the accused has failed to do so, or more likely, has dismissed his solicitor, or the law agent has withdrawn from acting. Note that subs.(1)(a) refers to a "lawyer" while subs.(1)(c) applies more narrowly to "a solicitor".

[THE NEXT PARAGRAPH IS A4-48]

Prints and samples

Prints, samples etc. in criminal investigations

A4-48 **18.**—(1) This section applies where a person has been arrested and is in custody.

(2) A constable may take from the person, or require the person to provide him with, such relevant physical data as the constable may, having regard to the circumstances of the suspected offence or the relevant offence (within the meaning of section 164(3) of the Extradition Act 2003) in respect of which the person has been arrested, reasonably consider it appropriate to take from him or require him to provide, and the person so required shall comply with that requirement.

(3) Subject to subsections (3A) and (4) below and sections 18A to 18G of this Act, all record of any relevant physical data taken from or provided by a person under subsection (2) above, all samples taken under subsection (6) or (6A) below and all information derived from such samples shall be destroyed as soon as possible following a decision not to institute criminal proceedings against the person or on the conclusion of such proceedings otherwise than with a conviction or an order under section 246(3) of this Act.

(3A) Subsection (3) does not apply to—

(a) relevant physical data taken under subsection (2) from, or provided under that subsection by, a person arrested under an extradition arrest power (within the meaning of section 174(2) of the Extradition Act 2003), and

(b) any sample, or any information derived from a sample, taken under subsection (6) or (6A) from a person arrested under such a power (but see section 18H).

(4) The duty under subsection (3) above to destroy samples taken under subsection (6) or (6A) below and information derived from such samples shall not apply—

(a) where the destruction of the sample or the information could have the effect of destroying any sample, or any information derived therefrom, lawfully held in relation to a person other than the person from whom the sample was taken; or

(b) where the record, sample or information in question is of the same kind as a record, a sample or, as the case may be, information lawfully held by or on behalf of the Police Service of Scotland in relation to the person.

(5) No sample, or information derived from a sample, retained by virtue of subsection (4) above shall be used—

(a) in evidence against the person from whom the sample was taken; or

(b) for the purposes of the investigation of any offence.

(6) A constable may, with the authority of an officer of a rank no lower than inspector, take from the person—

(a) from the hair of an external part of the body other than pubic hair, by means of cutting, combing or plucking, a sample of hair or other material;

(b) from a fingernail or toenail or from under any such nail, a sample of nail or other material;

(c) from an external part of the body, by means of swabbing or rubbing, a sample of blood or other body fluid, of body tissue or of other material;

(d) [...]

(6A) A constable, or at a constable's direction a police custody and security officer, may take from the inside of the person's mouth, by means of swabbing, a sample of saliva or other material.

(7) [...]

(7A) For the purposes of this section and, subject to the modification in subsection (7AA), sections 18A to 19C of this Act "relevant physical data" means any—

(a) fingerprint;
(b) palm print;
(c) print or impression other than those mentioned in paragraph (a) and (b) above, of an external part of the body;
(d) record of a person's skin on an external part of the body created by a device approved by the Secretary of State.

(7AA) The modification is that for the purposes of section 19C as it applies in relation to relevant physical data taken from or provided by a person outwith Scotland, subsection (7A) is to be read as if in paragraph (d) the words from "created" to the end were omitted.

(7B) The Secretary of State by order made by statutory instrument may approve a device for the purpose of creating such records as are mentioned in paragraph (d) of subsection (7A) above.

(8) Nothing in this section shall prejudice—

(a) any power of search;
(b) any power to take possession of evidence where there is imminent danger of its being lost or destroyed; or
(c) any power to take relevant physical data or samples under the authority of a warrant.

AMENDMENTS

Subs.(2) as amended by Crime and Punishment (Scotland) Act 1997 (c.48) s.47(1)(a) and (b) with effect from 1 August 1997 in terms of SI 1997/1712 art.3.

Subs.(3) substituted by Crime and Disorder Act 1998 (c.37) Sch.8 para.117(1) and (2) (effective 1 August 1997: SI 1998/2327).

Subss.(7A) and (7B) inserted by s.47(1)(d) of the 1997 Act with effect from 1 August 1997 in terms of SI 1997/1712.

Subs.(7) repealed by Crime and Punishment (Scotland) Act 1997 s.47(1)(c). Brought into force on 17 November 1997 by SI 1997/2694 (C.101) (S.170).

For the purposes of the Terrorism Act 2000 (c.11) s.41 and Sch.7 (where person detained at a police station in Scotland under those provisions), s.18(2) is substituted by Sch.8 para.20 of the 2000 Act.

Subs.(6)(d) repealed, and subs.(6A) inserted, by Criminal Justice (Scotland) Act 2003 (asp 7) Pt 8 s.55. Brought into force on 27 June 2003 by SSI 2003/288 (C.14).

Subss.(3) and (4) as amended by Police, Public Order and Criminal Justice (Scotland) Act 2006 (asp 10) s.101 and Sch.6 para.4(2). Brought into force on1 September 2006 by SSI 2006/432 (C.34) art.2.

Subs.(3) as amended by Police, Public Order and Criminal Justice (Scotland) Act 2006 (asp 10) s.83(1). Brought in to force on 1 January 2007 by SSI 2006/607 (C.46) art.3.

Subss.(3) and (8)(c) as amended by Criminal Justice and Licensing (Scotland) Act 2010 (asp 13) s.77(2)(a) and Sch.7 para.30. Brought into force on 28 March 2011 by SSI 2011/178 (C.15) art.2, Sch.1 para.1.

Subs.(7A) as amended, subs.(7AA) inserted, by Criminal Justice and Licensing (Scotland) Act 2010 (asp 13) s.77(2)(b), (c). Brought into force on 1 August 2011 by SSI 2011/178 (C.15) art.2, Sch.1 para.1.

Subs.(4)(b) as amended by Police and Fire Reform (Scotland) Act 2012 (asp 8) Sch.7 para.12(3). Brought into force on 1 April 2013 by SSI 2013/51 art.2.

Subs.(3) as amended by Protection of Freedoms Act 2012 (c.9) Sch.1 para.6. Brought into force on 31 October 2013 by SI 2013/1814 art.2(k) (subject to transitional provisions specified in SI 2013/1813 art.8).

Subss.(1) and (2) as amended by Criminal Justice (Scotland) Act 2016 (asp 1) Sch.2 para.28(1). Brought into force on 25 January 2018 by SSI 2017/345 art.3 (subject to transitional and savings provisions in art.4).

Subss.(2), (3) as amended, subs.(3A) inserted, by Criminal Justice (Scotland) Act 2016 (Consequential Provisions) Order 2018 (SSI 2018/46) Sch.5 para.1 (effective 25 January 2018).

DEFINITIONS

A4-48.1 "constable": s.307(1) and Police (Scotland) Act 1967 (c.77) s.51(1).
"in custody": s.295.
"relevant physical data": s.18(7A) of the 1995 Act.

[THE NEXT PARAGRAPH IS A4-49]

GENERAL NOTE

A4-49 This section is derived from the Prisoners and Criminal Proceedings (Scotland) Act 1993 (c.9) s.28, which gave effect to the recommendations of the Scottish Law Commission's *Report on Evidence: Blood Group Tests, DNA Tests and Related Matters*, Paper No.120, 1989. The current provisions were intended to give clearer expression to the extent of police powers (those contained in s.2(5)(c) of the 1980 Act being somewhat indeterminate) and to apply equally to arrested suspects and to those detained under s.14 of the 1995 Act. Section 18 does give more extensive sampling powers to the police in subs.(6) than were previously available under the 1980 Act, but note that these can only be exercised after authorisation by a senior police officer, i.e. an officer of inspector rank or higher. The tenor of the Act might suggest that the authorising officer should not be involved in the investigation but this is not expressly stated.

The section stops short of permitting the procuring of evidence by methods which case law has defined as invasive, for example, internal physical examinations, endoscopic or colonoscopic examinations. It remains the case that such extreme invasions of bodily privacy, which involve entering the suspect's body, still require the authority of a sheriff's warrant which has to be obtained by the procurator fiscal. An application for a warrant of this kind can be made at any time, but the court will take account of the nature of the examination or sampling proposed, the degree of physical invasion involved (when set against the public interest in the detection of crime), the stage which proceedings have reached and whether, at that time, there is a prima facie justification for the application. (See *Hay v HM Advocate*, 1968 S.L.T. 334; *HM Advocate v Milford*, 1973 S.L.T. 12; *McGlennan v Kelly*, 1989 S.L.T. 832; *Smith v Cardle*, 1993 S.C.C.R. 609; *Hughes v Normand*, 1993 S.L.T. 113). The extension of this section to entitle the police to recover "relevant physical data" (as defined in subs.(7A)) primarily reflects the technological advances in the field of fingerprinting brought about by electronic "livescan" fingerprinting. "Livescan" is expected to produce higher-definition print quality (improving detection rates) and to deliver an instantaneous comparison of data on file to enable immediate confirmation of an offender's identity on completion of scanning.

Approval for the use of the Digital Biometrics Incorporation (DBI) Tenprinter 1133S, with palm-print option, was given by the Secretary of State with effect from August 8, 1997 by the Electronic Fingerprinting etc. Device Approval Order 1997 (SI 1997/1939 (S.140)).

In the absence of dock identification of the accused as the source of a Livescan fingerprint form used subsequently for comparison purposes, the Appeal Court held the circumstantial web of surrounding evidence—arrest, interview, charge and timings—to provide a sufficiency: *Ross v HM Advocate* [2016] HCJAC 54.

Incidentally note that the phrase "dock identification" was judicially defined in *McMultan v HM Advocate* [2016] HCJAC 89; 2016 S.C.C.R. 496.

Subs.(1)

This stipulates that the section applies to all persons arrested or detained by the police.

Subs.(2)

The reference to an "external part of the body" suggests that physical measurement of a suspect (as in *Smith v Cardle*), would be permissible using s.18 powers but the obtaining of dental impressions (as in *Hay v HM Advocate*) would not and would normally demand a sheriff's warrant. However subs.(8)(b) by implication permits urgent steps to be taken in situations where delay would create a real risk of evidence being irretrievably lost; the legitimacy, or otherwise, of such steps would fall to be considered in any subsequent proceedings.

Subss.(3) and (4)

Superficially, subs.(3) re-enacts the terms of s.2(1)(c) of the 1980 Act which provided for the destruction of fingerprint forms in the event either of their being no proceedings against the accused, or his acquittal following such proceedings. It will be noted that a decision not to proceed against an accused person will not always be because there is an insufficiency of evidence: the Crown may in broad terms decide that prosecution would not be in the public interest for a variety of reasons, or might opt to deal with the matter by way of a warning. It is in these situations, especially where proceedings are maintained against other accused, that intractable problems arise now because of the interaction of subss.(3) and (4).

Subsection (3) refers to "all information derived from such samples" and would seem to be more rigorous than the earlier provisions of s.2(1)(c) of the 1980 Act. The later provision suggests that data obtained as a result of such samples, which could arguably have been retained even after the destruction of the sample material under the 1980 Act, must also be destroyed. Yet while subs.(3) might momentarily be viewed as clarifying the law in this grey area, the terms of subs.(4) serve to qualify and obscure the position.

Subsection (4)(a) permits the retention of the samples, or the information derived from them, where to destroy such would itself "destroy" similar information obtained in relation to a person still accused. Presumably then, sample evidence gathered at an early stage in proceedings from suspect A against whom charges are later dropped, could still be preserved for use as evidence against suspect B now to be prosecuted. In such a situation there would be no obligation upon the police to destroy A's samples at all: they would only be precluded from using them as evidence in any other proceedings against A (see subs.(5) below).

Subsection 4(b) also militates against the general requirement to destroy samples when no proceedings are to follow. In this case both samples and the data derived from them could be preserved to update existing data held by the police about the person concerned, albeit these could not be deployed *directly* in evidence or in the investigation of crime. Since the technology now exists to extract DNA from body samples of the sort specified in subs.(6), this is an issue of no small importance.

There has of course been no judicial interpretation as yet of these subsections.

Subs.(5)

The implications of this provision are discussed above in the Notes to subss.(3) and (4). This appears to open the way to the preservation of databanks derived from samples of previously convicted persons.

Subs.(6)

Samples which can be taken by a police officer are set out in subs.(6) and are those deemed to be of a non-invasive nature. Following *HM Advocate v Cowie* [2011] HCJAC 111; 2012 S.C.L. 219 this statutory power would not extend to buccal swabs (internal swabs from a suspect's cheek), nor would there be a general common law power to recover such swabs in view of their perceived invasive nature. So unless the party gave informed consent, i.e. being aware that he was not obliged to provide such swabs, or compelling issues arose concerning immediate preservation of evidence to prevent its loss or destruction (see, for example *Bell v Hogg*, 1967 J.C. 49) cheek swabs could not be taken from him save by means of a sheriff's warrant. It would, of course, be open to the police to take any other form of sample set out in subs.(6) during the detention period. In practice these samples would normally be obtained by a police casualty surgeon.

The factual circumstances in *Cowie* above were unusual and drawing more general guidance from its facts requires some care (see the cautionary tone in *MacLean v Dunn* [2012] HCJAC 34 para.20). It will be noted, first, that *Cowie* was required to provide samples after her detention period de facto had concluded, when instead of being arrested she was released after charge. Secondly, the form of sample taken was a buccal swab. In either situation, in the absence of informed consent or urgent need to preserve evidence which would otherwise be lost, subsequent evidential use of the samples as source material for forensic comparison undoubtedly would be unlawful: however, the *Cowie* judgment ranges more widely and seeks to address the broader question of whether, after arrest, *any* further samples can be taken from an accused in custody on the grounds that the accused now is ostensibly under the protection of the court. The extent of police powers after arrest remain as set out in *Adair v McGarry*, 1933 J.C. 72 and in *McGovern v HM Advocate*, 1950 J.C. 33; the non-invasive regime of sampling described in subs.(6), as well as fingerprints and photographs, lies within the scope of these common law powers. A substantial distinction applies to invasive samples, such as buccal DNA, pubic hairs or (as in *Hay v HM Advocate*, 1968 S.L.T. 334) dental impressions; should the Crown seek such invasive samples from an accused it becomes necessary, in the absence of informed consent of the accused, to petition the sheriff by incidental application specifying the nature of evidential material sought.

Applications to obtain invasive samples as evidence

Despite the decision in *HM Advocate v Edwards* [2012] HCJAC 9, some unease has to be voiced over the competency of applying to the High Court at first instance. It will be noted that, spurred by whatever expedient, the Crown asserted the competency of such an application which was refused on its merits. The judge had applied a two stage test, seeking special circumstances and an intelligible explanation for the application being necessary. That staged approach was rejected in *MacLean v Dunn* above as being too narrow in its scope; the Court must also heed the gravity of the offence and public interest in successful detection of it, as well as the degree of intrusion involved. Subject to the broad test of fairness set out in *Lawrie v Muir*, 1950 J.C. 19; 1950 S.L.T. 37 and *Stone v HM Advocate*, 2009 S.C.C.R. 71, such applications will generally succeed. (The peculiar difficulties raised by a need for handwriting samples would certainly demand a specific application to the sheriff; see *Davidson v HM Advocate*, 1951 J.C. 33.)

Consent to provision of samples has to be informed; the suspect or accused has to be aware of the nature of the allegations, and of his rights to legal advice and refusal of samples. In *GM v HM Advocate*, 2013 S.C.C.R. 176, in the course of investigation of an allegation of sexual assault, following detention, the accused was questioned at length by a police surgeon conducting a medical examination in the presence of a police officer, without any form of caution, about his conduct earlier that day and made incriminating responses which the Appeal Court ruled inadmissible.

Suspension of invasive sample applications

Notwithstanding the advent of the Sheriff Appeal Court, any Bill of Suspension seeking to stay or prevent procedures covered by a warrant falls to be determined by the High Court of Justiciary, exercising its supervisory jurisdiction over administrative procedures (see *McWilliams v PF, Dumfries* [2016] HCJAC 29, following *Brown v Donaldson*, 2008 J.C. 83).

Subs.(6A)

This new provision enables a constable, or civilian auxiliary acting under his direction, to obtain mouth swab samples from an arrested person. The consent of a senior police officer is now only required by a constable when it is considered that a degree of force will be necessary to obtain relevant samples.

Retention of samples etc.: prosecutions for sexual and violent offences

A4-49.1 **18A.**—(1) This section applies to—

(a) relevant physical data taken or provided under section 18(2), and

(b) any sample, or any information derived from a sample, taken under section 18(6) or (6A),

where the condition in subsection (2) is satisfied.

(2) That condition is that criminal proceedings in respect of a relevant sexual offence or a relevant violent offence were instituted against the person from whom the relevant physical data was taken or by whom it was provided or, as the case may be, from whom the sample was taken but those proceedings concluded otherwise than with a conviction or an order under section 246(3) of this Act.

(3) Subject to subsections (9) and (10) below, the relevant physical data, sample or information derived from a sample shall be destroyed no later than the destruction date.

(4) The destruction date is—

(a) the date of expiry of the period of 3 years following the conclusion of the proceedings; or

(b) such later date as an order under subsection (5) below may specify.

(5) On a summary application made by the chief constable of the Police Service of Scotland within the period of 3 months before the destruction date the sheriff may, if satisfied that there are reasonable grounds for doing so, make an order amending, or further amending, the destruction date.

(6) An application under subsection (5) above may be made to any sheriff—

(a) in whose sheriffdom the person referred to in subsection (2) above resides;

(b) in whose sheriffdom that person is believed by the applicant to be; or

(c) to whose sheriffdom the person is believed by the applicant to be intending to come.

(7) An order under subsection (5) above shall not specify a destruction date more than 2 years later than the previous destruction date.

(8) The decision of the sheriff on an application under subsection (5) above may be appealed to the sheriff principal within 21 days of the decision; and the sheriff principal's decision on any such appeal is final.

(8A) If the sheriff principal allows an appeal against the refusal of an application under subsection (5), the sheriff principal may make an order amending, or further amending, the destruction date.

(8B) An order under subsection (8A) must not specify a destruction date more than 2 years later than the previous destruction date.

(9) Subsection (3) above does not apply where—

(a) an application under subsection (5) above has been made but has not been determined;

(b) the period within which an appeal may be brought under subsection (8) above against a decision to refuse an application has not elapsed; or

(c) such an appeal has been brought but has not been withdrawn or finally determined.

(10) Where—

(a) the period within which an appeal referred to in subsection (9)(b) above may be brought has elapsed without such an appeal being brought;

(b) such an appeal is brought and is withdrawn or finally determined against the appellant; or

(c) an appeal brought under subsection (8) above against a decision to grant an application is determined in favour of the appellant,

the relevant physical data, sample or information derived from a sample shall be destroyed as soon as possible thereafter.

(11) In this section—

"relevant sexual offence" and "relevant violent offence" have", subject to the modification in subsection (12), the same meanings as in section 19A(6) of this Act and include any attempt, conspiracy or incitement to commit such an offence.

(12) The modification is that the definition of "relevant sexual offence" in section 19A(6) is to be read as if for paragraph (g) there were substituted—

"(g) public indecency if it is apparent from the offence as charged in the indictment or complaint that there was a sexual aspect to the behaviour of the person charged;"

AMENDMENTS

Section 18A inserted by Police, Public Order and Criminal Justice (Scotland) Act 2006 (asp 10) s.83(2). Brought in to force on 1 January 2007 by SSI 2006/607 (C.46) art.3.

Subss.(1), (2), (3), (10), (11) as amended, subss.(8A)–(8B) and (12) inserted, by Criminal Justice and Licensing (Scotland) Act 2010 (asp 13) s.77(3). Brought into force on 28 March 2011 by SSI 2011/178 (C.15) art.2, Sch.1 para.1, subject to SSI 2011/178 art.4.

Subss.(5) and (11) as amended by Police and Fire Reform (Scotland) Act 2012 (asp 8) Sch.7 para.12(4). Brought into force on 1 April 2013 by SSI 2013/51 art.2.

GENERAL NOTE

While the police are entitled in terms of s.18 above to take relevant physical data from an individual who has been detained or arrested, the general rule found in s.18(3) is that once a decision has been made not to prosecute or once an acquittal has been achieved or the proceedings discontinued, any sample, and the information derived from it, should be destroyed as soon as possible. Section 18(8) admits of the possibility that action could be taken, generally by the procurator fiscal, to preserve such a sample or the data derived from it but this is exceptional. A4-49.2

Section 18A makes quite different provisions in respect of samples (and the data thus derived) from persons charged but not later convicted of relevant sexual or violent offences as defined in s.19A(6). Essentially, such samples or data can be retained by the criminal authorities for up to three years and that period can be extended by summary application by the chief constable to a relevant sheriff within the final three months. The three-year period can be extended (see subs.(7)) by a further two years; appeal against the sheriff's decision lies to the sheriff principal. Note that the initial three-year time scale is deferred pending any such appeal and that quite separate provisions governing the preservation (and even replacement) of samples and resultant data from convicted persons are to be found in s.19 below in relation to mainstream offenders and s.19A in respect of those convicted of sexual or violent offences.

Retention of samples etc. where offer under sections 302 to 303ZA accepted

18B.—(1) This section applies to— A4-49.3

(a) relevant physical data taken from or provided by a person under section 18(2), and

(b) any sample, or any information derived from a sample, taken from a person under section 18(6) or (6A),

where the conditions in subsection (2) are satisfied.

(2) The conditions are—

(a) the relevant physical data or sample was taken from or provided by the person while the person was in custody in connection with the offence or offences in relation to which a relevant offer is issued to the person, and

(b) the person—

(i) accepts a relevant offer, or

(ii) in the case of a relevant offer other than one of the type mentioned in paragraph (d) of subsection (3), is deemed to accept a relevant offer.

(3) In this section "relevant offer" means—

(a) a conditional offer under section 302,

(b) a compensation offer under section 302A,

(c) a combined offer under section 302B, or

(d) a work offer under section 303ZA.

(4) Subject to subsections (6) and (7) and section 18C(9) and (10), the relevant physical data, sample or information derived from a sample must be destroyed no later than the destruction date.

(5) In subsection (4), "destruction date" means—

(a) in relation to a relevant offer that relates only to—

(i) a relevant sexual offence,

(ii) a relevant violent offence, or

(iii) both a relevant sexual offence and a relevant violent offence,the date of expiry of the period of 3 years beginning with the date on which the relevant offer is issued or such later date as an order under section 18C(2) or (6) may specify,

(b) in relation to a relevant offer that relates to—

(i) an offence or offences falling within paragraph (a), and

(ii) any other offence,the date of expiry of the period of 3 years beginning with the date on which the relevant offer is issued or such later date as an order under section 18C(2) or (6) may specify,

(c) in relation to a relevant offer that does not relate to an offence falling within paragraph (a), the date of expiry of the period of 2 years beginning with the date on which the relevant offer is issued.

(6) If a relevant offer is recalled by virtue of section 302C(5) or a decision to uphold it is quashed under section 302C(7)(a), all record of the relevant physical data, sample and information derived from a sample must be destroyed as soon as possible after—

(a) the prosecutor decides not to issue a further relevant offer to the person,

(b) the prosecutor decides not to institute criminal proceedings against the person, or

(c) the prosecutor institutes criminal proceedings against the person and those proceedings conclude otherwise than with a conviction or an order under section 246(3).

(7) If a relevant offer is set aside by virtue of section 303ZB, all record of the relevant physical data, sample and information derived from a sample must be destroyed as soon as possible after the setting aside.

(8) In this section, "relevant sexual offence" and "relevant violent offence-"have, subject to the modification in subsection (9), the same meanings as in section 19A(6) and include any attempt, conspiracy or incitement to commit such an offence.

(9) The modification is that the definition of "relevant sexual offence" in section 19A(6) is to be read as if for paragraph (g) there were substituted—

"(g) public indecency if it is apparent from the relevant offer (as defined in section 18B(3)) relating to the offence that there was a sexual aspect to the behaviour of the person to whom the relevant offer is issued;"

AMENDMENTS

Section 18B inserted by Criminal Justice and Licensing (Scotland) Act 2010 (asp 13) s.78. Brought into force on 28 March 2011 by SSI 2011/178 (C.15) art.2, Sch.1 para.1, subject to SSI 2011/178 art.5.

Subs.(2)(a) as amended by Criminal Justice (Scotland) Act 2016 (asp 1) Sch.2 para.28(2). Brought into force on 25 January 2018 by SSI 2017/345 art.3 (subject to transitional and savings provisions in art.4).

[THE NEXT PARAGRAPH IS A4-49.5]

Section 18B: extension of retention period where relevant offer relates to certain sexual or violent offences

18C.—(1) This section applies where the destruction date for relevant physical data, a sample or information derived from a sample falls within section 18B(5)(a) or (b). A4-49.5

(2) On a summary application made by the chief constable of the Police Service of Scotland within the period of 3 months before the destruction date, the sheriff may, if satisfied that there are reasonable grounds for doing so, make an order amending, or further amending, the destruction date.

(3) An application under subsection (2) may be made to any sheriff—

(a) in whose sheriffdom the appropriate person resides,

(b) in whose sheriffdom that person is believed by the applicant to be, or

(c) to whose sheriffdom the person is believed by the applicant to be intending to come.

(4) An order under subsection (2) must not specify a destruction date more than 2 years later than the previous destruction date.

(5) The decision of the sheriff on an application under subsection (2) may be appealed to the sheriff principal within 21 days of the decision.

(6) If the sheriff principal allows an appeal against the refusal of an application under subsection (2), the sheriff principal may make an order amending, or further amending, the destruction date.

(7) An order under subsection (6) must not specify a destruction date more than 2 years later than the previous destruction date.

(8) The sheriff principal's decision on an appeal under subsection (5) is final.

(9) Section 18B(4) does not apply where—

(a) an application under subsection (2) has been made but has not been determined,

(b) the period within which an appeal may be brought under subsection (5) against a decision to refuse an application has not elapsed, or

(c) such an appeal has been brought but has not been withdrawn or finally determined.

(10) Where—

(a) the period within which an appeal referred to in subsection (9)(b) may be brought has elapsed without such an appeal being brought,

(b) such an appeal is brought and is withdrawn or finally determined against the appellant, or

(c) an appeal brought under subsection (5) against a decision to grant an application is determined in favour of the appellant,

the relevant physical data, sample or information derived from a sample must be destroyed as soon as possible after the period has elapsed, or, as the case may be, the appeal is withdrawn or determined.

(11) In this section—

"appropriate person" means the person from whom the relevant physical data was taken or by whom it was provided or from whom the sample was taken,

"destruction date" has the meaning given by section 18B(5).

AMENDMENTS

Section 18C inserted by Criminal Justice and Licensing (Scotland) Act 2010 (asp 13) s.78. Brought into force on 28 March 2011 by SSI 2011/178 (C.15) art.2, Sch.1 para.1, subject to SSI 2011/178 art.5.

Subss.(2) and (11) as amended by Police and Fire Reform (Scotland) Act 2012 (asp 8) Sch.7 para.12(5). Brought into force on 1 April 2013 by SSI 2013/51 art.2.

[THE NEXT PARAGRAPH IS A4-49.7]

Retention of samples etc. taken or provided in connection with certain fixed penalty offences

A4-49.7 **18D.**—(1) This section applies to—

(a) relevant physical data taken from or provided by a person under section 18(2), and

(b) any sample, or any information derived from a sample, taken from a person under section 18(6) or (6A),

where the conditions in subsection (2) are satisfied.

(2) The conditions are—

(a) the person was arrested in connection with a fixed penalty offence,

(b) the relevant physical data or sample was taken from or provided by the person while the person was in custody in connection with that offence,

(c) after the relevant physical data or sample was taken from or provided by the person, a constable gave the person under section 129(1) of the 2004 Act—

(i) a fixed penalty notice in respect of that offence (the "main FPN"), or

(ii) the main FPN and one or more other fixed penalty notices in respect of fixed penalty offences arising out of the same circumstances as the offence to which the main FPN relates, and

(d) the person, in relation to the main FPN and any other fixed penalty notice of the type mentioned in paragraph (c)(ii)—

(i) pays the fixed penalty, or

(ii) pays any sum that the person is liable to pay by virtue of section 131(5) of the 2004 Act.

(3) Subject to subsections (4) and (5), the relevant physical data, sample or information derived from a sample must be destroyed before the end of the period of 2 years beginning with—

(a) where subsection (2)(c)(i) applies, the day on which the main FPN is given to the person,

(b) where subsection (2)(c)(ii) applies and—

(i) the main FPN and any other fixed penalty notice are given to the person on the same day, that day,

(ii) the main FPN and any other fixed penalty notice are given to the person on different days, the later day.

(4) Where—

(a) subsection (2)(c)(i) applies, and

(b) the main FPN is revoked under section 133(1) of the 2004 Act,

the relevant physical data, sample or information derived from a sample must be destroyed as soon as possible after the revocation.

(5) Where—

(a) subsection (2)(c)(ii) applies, and

(b) the main FPN and any other fixed penalty notices are revoked under section 133(1) of the 2004 Act, the relevant physical data, sample or information derived from a sample must be destroyed as soon as possible after the revocations.

(6) In this section—

"the 2004 Act" means the Antisocial Behaviour etc. (Scotland) Act 2004 (asp 8),

"fixed penalty notice" has the meaning given by section 129(2) of the 2004 Act,

"fixed penalty offence" has the meaning given by section 128(1) of the 2004 Act.

Amendments

Section 18D inserted by Criminal Justice and Licensing (Scotland) Act 2010 (asp 13) s.79. Brought into force on 28 March 2011 by SSI 2011/178 (C.15) art.2, Sch.1 para.1, subject to SSI 2011/178 art.6.

Subs.(2) as amended by Criminal Justice (Scotland) Act 2016 (asp 1) Sch.2 para.28(3). Brought into force on 25 January 2018 by SSI 2017/345 art.3 (subject to transitional and savings provisions in art.4).

[THE NEXT PARAGRAPH IS A4-49.9]

Retention of samples etc.: children referred to children's hearings

18E.—(1) This section applies to— A4-49.9

(a) relevant physical data taken from or provided by a child under section 18(2); and

(b) any sample, or any information derived from a sample, taken from a child under section 18(6) or (6A),

where subsection (3), (4) or (5) applies.

(2) […]

(3) This subsection applies where—

(a) in relation to a children's hearing arranged in relation to the child under section 69(2) of the 2011 Act, a section 67 ground is that the child has committed an offence mentioned in subsection (6) (a "relevant offence"),

(b) the ground is accepted by the child and each relevant person in relation to the child under section 91(1) or 105(1) of that Act, and

(c) no application to the sheriff under section 93(2)(a) or 94(2)(a) of that Act is made in relation to that ground.

(4) This subsection applies where—

(a) in relation to a children's hearing arranged in relation to the child under section 69(2) of the 2011 Act, a section 67 ground is that the child has committed a relevant offence,

(b) the sheriff, on an application under section 93(2)(a) or 94(2)(a) of that Act, determines under section 108 of that Act that the ground is established, and

(c) no application to the sheriff under section 110(2) of that Act is made in relation to the ground.

(5) This subsection applies where, on an application under section 110(2) of the 2011 Act in relation to the child—

(a) the sheriff is satisfied under section 114(2) or 115(1)(b) of that Act that a section 67 ground which constitutes a relevant offence is established or accepted by the child and each relevant person in relation to the child, or

(b) the sheriff determines under section 117(2)(a) of that Act that—

(i) a section 67 ground which was not stated in the statement of grounds which gave rise to the grounds determination is established, and

(ii) the ground constitutes a relevant offence.

(6) A relevant offence is such relevant sexual offence or relevant violent offence as the Scottish Ministers may by order made by statutory instrument prescribe.

(7) An order under subsection (6) may prescribe a relevant violent offence by reference to a particular degree of seriousness.

(8) Subject to section 18F(8) and (9), the relevant physical data, sample or information derived from a sample must be destroyed no later than the destruction date.

(9) The destruction date is—

(a) the date of expiry of the period of 3 years following—

(i) where subsection (3) applies, the date on which the section 67 ground was accepted as mentioned in that subsection,

(ii) where subsection (4) applies, the date on which the section 67 ground was established as mentioned in that subsection,

(iii) where the section 67 ground is established as mentioned in paragraph (a) of subsection (5), the date on which that ground was established under section 108 of the 2011 Act or, as the case may be, accepted under section 91(1) or 105(1) of that Act, or

(iv) where the section 67 ground is established as mentioned in paragraph (b) of subsection (5), the date on which that ground was established as mentioned in that paragraph,

(b) such later date as an order under section 18F(1) may specify.

(10) No statutory instrument containing an order under subsection (6) may be made unless a draft of the instrument has been laid before, and approved by resolution of, the Scottish Parliament.

(11) In this section—

"the 2011 Act" means the Children's Hearings (Scotland) Act 2011 (asp 1);

"grounds determination" has the meaning given by section 110(1) of the 2011 Act;

"relevant person" has the same meaning as in section 200(1) of the 2011 Act except that it includes a person deemed to be a relevant person by virtue of section 81(3), 160(4)(b) or 164(6) of that Act;

"relevant sexual offence" and "relevant violent offence" have, subject to the modification in subsection (12), the same meanings as in section 19A(6) and include any attempt, conspiracy or incitement to commit such an offence.

"section 67 ground" has the meaning given by section 67(1) of the 2011 Act;

"statement of grounds" has the meaning given by section 89(3) of the 2011 Act.

(12) The modification is that the definition of "relevant sexual offence" in section 19A(6) is to be read as if for paragraph (g) there were substituted—

"(g) public indecency if it is apparent from the section 67 ground relating to the offence that there was a sexual aspect to the behaviour of the child;"

AMENDMENTS

Section 18E inserted by Criminal Justice and Licensing (Scotland) Act 2010 (asp 13) s.80. Brought into force on December 13, 2010 by SSI 2010/413 (C.28) art.2, Sch.1 para.1 (for purposes specified in SSI 2010/413 Sch.1); otherwise brought into force on April 15, 2011 by SSI 2011/178 (C.15) art.2, Sch.1 para.1, subject to SSI 2011/178 art.7.

Subss.(1), (3)-(5), (9)(a), (11) and (12) as amended, subs.(2) repealed, by Children's Hearings (Scotland) Act 2011 (Modification of Primary Legislation) Order 2013 (SSI 2013/211) Sch.1 para.10(2) (effective June 24, 2013).

[THE NEXT PARAGRAPH IS A4-49.11]

Retention of samples etc. relating to children: appeals

18F.—(1) On a summary application made by the chief constable of the Police Service of Scotland within the period of 3 months before the destruction date the sheriff may, if satisfied that there are reasonable grounds for doing so, make an order amending, or further amending, the destruction date. A4-49.11

(2) An application under subsection (1) may be made to any sheriff—

(a) in whose sheriffdom the child mentioned in section 18E(1) resides;

(b) in whose sheriffdom that child is believed by the applicant to be; or

(c) to whose sheriffdom that child is believed by the applicant to be intending to come.

(3) An order under subsection (1) must not specify a destruction date more than 2 years later than the previous destruction date.

(4) The decision of the sheriff on an application under subsection (1) may be appealed to the sheriff principal within 21 days of the decision.

(5) If the sheriff principal allows an appeal against the refusal of an application under subsection (1), the sheriff principal may make an order amending, or further amending, the destruction date.

(6) An order under subsection (5) must not specify a destruction date more than 2 years later than the previous destruction date.

(7) The sheriff principal's decision on an appeal under subsection (4) is final.

(8) Section 18E(8) does not apply where—

(a) an application under subsection (1) has been made but has not been determined;

(b) the period within which an appeal may be brought under subsection (4) against a decision to refuse an application has not elapsed; or

(c) such an appeal has been brought but has not been withdrawn or finally determined.

(9) Where—

(a) the period within which an appeal referred to in subsection (8)(b) may be brought has elapsed without such an appeal being brought;

(b) such an appeal is brought and is withdrawn or finally determined against the appellant; or

(c) an appeal brought under subsection (4) against a decision to grant an application is determined in favour of the appellant,

the relevant physical data, sample or information derived from a sample must be destroyed as soon as possible after the period has elapsed or, as the case may be, the appeal is withdrawn or determined.

(10) In this section—

"destruction date" has the meaning given by section 18E(9).

AMENDMENTS

Section 18F inserted by Criminal Justice and Licensing (Scotland) Act 2010 (asp 13) s.80. Brought into force on April 15, 2011 by SSI 2011/178 (C.15) art.2, Sch.1 para.1.

Subss.(1) and (10) as amended by Police and Fire Reform (Scotland) Act 2012 (asp 8) Sch.7 para.12(6). Brought into force on April 1, 2013 by SSI 2013/51 art.2.

[THE NEXT PARAGRAPH IS A4-49.13]

Retention of samples etc: national security

18G.—(1) This section applies to— A4-49.13

(a) relevant physical data taken from or provided by a person under section 18(2) (including any taken or provided by virtue of paragraph 20 of Schedule 8 to the Terrorism Act 2000),

(b) any sample, or any information derived from a sample, taken from a person under section 18(6) or (6A) (including any taken by virtue of paragraph 20 of Schedule 8 to the Terrorism Act 2000),

(c) any relevant physical data, sample or information derived from a sample taken from, or provided by, a person under section 19AA(3),

(d) any relevant physical data, sample or information derived from a sample which is held by virtue of section 56 of the Criminal Justice (Scotland) Act 2003,and

(e) any relevant physical data, sample or information derived from a sample taken from a person—

(i) by virtue of any power of search

(ii) by virtue of any power to take possession of evidence where there is immediate danger of its being lost or destroyed, or

(iii) under the authority of a warrant.

(2) The relevant physical data, sample or information derived from a sample may be retained for so long as a national security determination made by the relevant chief constable has effect in relation to it.

(3) A national security determination is made if the relevant chief constable determines that is necessary for the relevant physical data, sample or information derived from a sample to be retained for the purposes of national security.

(4) A national security determination—

(a) must be made in writing,

(b) has effect for a maximum of 2 years beginning with the date on which the determination is made, and

(c) may be renewed.

(5) Any relevant physical data, sample or information derived from a sample which is retained in pursuance of a national security determination must be destroyed as soon as possible after the determination ceases to have effect (except where its retention is permitted by any other enactment).

(6) In this section, "the relevant chief constable" means the chief constable of the police force of which the constable who took the relevant physical data, or to whom it was provided, or who took or directed the taking of the sample, was a member.

Amendments

Section 18G inserted by Protection of Freedoms Act 2012 (c.9) Sch.1 para.6. Brought into force on 31 October 2013 by SI 2013/1814 art.2(k) (subject to transitional provisions specified in SI 2013/1813 art.8).

Retention of samples etc.: extradition

18H.—(1) This section applies to-

(a) relevant physical data taken under section 18(2) from, or provided under that subsection by, a person arrested under an extradition arrest power (within the meaning of section 174(2) of the Extradition Act 2003), and

(b) any sample, or any information derived from a sample, taken under section 18(6) or (6A) from a person arrested under an extradition arrest power (within the meaning of section 174(2) of the Extradition Act 2003).

(2) All record of any relevant physical data, all samples and all information derived from such samples must be destroyed as soon as possible following the final determination of the extradition proceedings.

(3) The duty under subsection (2) to destroy samples taken under section 18(6) or (6A) and information derived from such samples does not apply where the circumstances in paragraph (a) or (b) of section 18(4) apply to the sample or

information (and where such circumstances apply, the restrictions in section 18(5) apply to the sample or information retained).

(4) For the purposes of this section, extradition proceedings are finally determined-

(a) if the person is extradited, on the day of the extradition,

(b) if the person is discharged and there is no right of appeal under the Extradition Act 2003 against the decision which resulted in the order for the person's discharge, when the person is discharged, on the day of the discharge,

(c) where the person is discharged at an extradition hearing or by the Scottish Ministers under section 93 of the Extradition Act 2003-

(i) if no application is made to the High Court for leave to appeal against the decision within the period during which such an application may be made, at the end of that period,

(ii) if such an application is made and is refused, on the day of the refusal,

(d) where the High Court orders the person's discharge or dismisses an appeal against a decision to discharge the person-

(i) if no application is made to the High Court for permission to appeal to the Supreme Court within the 28 day period starting with the day of the High Court's decision, at the end of that period,

(ii) if such an application is made to the High Court and is refused, and no application is made to the Supreme Court for permission to appeal to the Supreme Court within the period of 28 days starting with the day of the refusal, at the end of that period,

(iii) if such an application is made to the Supreme Court and is refused, on the day of the refusal,

(iv) if permission to appeal to the Supreme Court is granted, but no appeal is made within the period of 28 days starting with the day on which permission is granted, at the end of that period,

(v) if there is an appeal to the Supreme Court against the High Court's decision, on the day on which the appeal is refused, is abandoned or is upheld with the effect that the person is discharged,

(e) if an appeal to the Supreme Court is upheld with the effect that the person is discharged, on the day of the decision to uphold the appeal.

(5) In subsection (4)-

"extradition hearing" has the meaning given by section 68 or as the case may be section 140 of the Extradition Act 2003,

"extradition proceedings" means proceedings under the Extradition Act 2003.

AMENDMENTS

Section 18H inserted by Criminal Justice (Scotland) Act 2016 (Consequential Provisions) Order 2018 (SSI 2018/46) Sch.5 para.1 (effective 25 January 2018).

[THE NEXT PARAGRAPH IS A4-50]

Prints, samples etc. in criminal investigations: supplementary provisions

19.—(1) Without prejudice to any power exercisable under section 19A of this Act, his section applies where a person convicted of an offence— A4-50

(a) has not, since the conviction, had taken from him, or been required to provide, any relevant physical data or had any impression or sample taken from him; or

(b) has at any time had—

(i) taken from him or been required (whether under paragraph (a) above or under section 18, 19A or 19AA of this Act or otherwise) to provide any physical data; or

(ii) any sample taken from him,

which was not suitable for the means of analysis for which the data were taken or required or the sample was taken or, though suitable, was insufficient (either in quantity or in quality) to enable information to be obtained by that means of analysis.

(2) Where this section applies, a constable may, within the permitted period—

(a) take from or require the convicted person to provide him with such relevant physical data as he reasonably considers it appropriate to take or, as the case may be, require the provision of;

(b) with the authority of an officer of a rank no lower than inspector, take from the person any sample mentioned in any of paragraphs (a) to (c) of subsection (6) of section 18 of this Act by the means specified in that paragraph in relation to that sample; and

(c) take, or direct a police custody and security officer to take, from the person any sample mentioned in subsection (6A) of that section by the means specified in that subsection.

(3) A constable—

(a) may require the convicted person to attend a police station for the purposes of subsection (2) above;

(b) may, where the convicted person is in legal custody by virtue of section 295 of this Act, exercise the powers conferred by subsection (2) above in relation to the person in the place where he is for the time being.

(4) In subsection (2) above, "the permitted period" means—

(a) in a case to which paragraph (a) of subsection (1) above applies, the period of one month beginning with the date of the conviction;

(b) in a case to which paragraph (b) of that subsection applies, the period of one month beginning with the date on which a constable of the Police Service of Scotland receives written intimation that the relevant physical data were or the sample was unsuitable or, as the case may be, insufficient as mentioned in that paragraph.

(5) A requirement under subsection (3)(a) above—

(a) shall give the person at least seven days' notice of the date on which he is required to attend;

(b) may direct him to attend at a specified time of day or between specified times of day.

(6) Any constable may arrest without warrant a person who fails to comply with a requirement under subsection (3)(a) above.

AMENDMENTS

Subss.(1)(a) and (b) as substituted by Crime and Punishment (Scotland) Act 1997 (c.48) s.47(2)(a) with effect from 1 August 1997 in terms of SI 1997/1712 art.3.

Subs.(2)(a) as substituted by the above Act s.47(2)(b) with effect from 1 August 1997 as provided by the Order above.

Subs.(4)(b) as amended by the above Act s.47(2)(c) with effect from 1 August 1997 as provided by the Order above.

Subs.(1) as amended by s.48 of the above Act with effect from 17 November 1997 in terms of SI 1997/2694 (C.101) (S.170).

Subs.(2) as amended by Criminal Justice (Scotland) Act 2003 (asp 7) Pt 8 s.55. Brought into force on June 27, 2003 by SSI 2003/288 (C.14).

Subs.(1)(b)(i) as amended by Police, Public Order and Criminal Justice (Scotland) Act 2006 (asp 10) s.77(3). Brought into force on 1 September 2006 by SSI 2006/432 (C.34) art.2.

Subs.(1)(b) as amended by Criminal Justice and Licensing (Scotland) Act 2010 (asp 13) Sch.7 para.31. Brought into force on 28 March 2011 by SSI 2011/178 (C.15) art.2, Sch.1 para.1.

Subs.(4)(b) as amended by Police and Fire Reform (Scotland) Act 2012 (asp 8) Sch.7 para.12(7). Brought into force on 1 April 2013 by SSI 2013/51 art.2.

DEFINITIONS

"constable": s.307(1) and s.51(1) of the Police (Scotland) Act 1967. A4-50.1
"relevant physical data": s.18(7A) of the 1995 Act.

[THE NEXT PARAGRAPH IS A4-51]

GENERAL NOTE

This section gives the police a general power in the course of investigations or after the conviction of an accused, within the permitted period of one month specified in subs.(4), to obtain relevant physical data as defined in s.18A. (See the General Note at A4-49 above.) The power can be utilised within that time in two distinct situations; (i) when no such samples have been taken since conviction (subs.(1)(a)) and (ii) when the materials obtained in the course of detention or arrest of the person have been either insufficient or deficient for the purposes of analysis (subs.(1)(b)). This section operates without prejudice to the Crown's own rights to petition the court for relevant physical data by way of Incidental Application or petition warrant. A4-51

The previous requirement that police officers had to obtain the consent of a senior police officer before taking mouth swabs from detained or arrested persons has been rescinded. Furthermore the power to take non-invasive samples from such persons has been extended to civilian custody officers. Consent of a senior officer (an inspector or more senior officer) is now only required when it is felt necessary that a degree of force will be needed to procure samples from a suspect or accused person.

The Permitted Period (subs.(4))

The timescale in the event of conviction is unambiguous—one month from the date of that conviction. This would apply equally in the cases of the imposition of a money fine or caution, probation as defined in s.228 below or a deferment of sentence. Subsection (4)(a) provides for an opportunity to correct acts of omission. A4-52

Subsection (4)(b), which applies to suspects under investigation and to those convicted of offences, is by its nature much less precise; the one month timescale is effective from the date upon which the police force instructing a forensic or fingerprint examination of samples previously obtained from the suspect, receives written intimation of their unsuitability. Note that a verbal report to the same effect would not start the clock ticking. It should also be appreciated that subs.(4)(b) does not provide a remedy for situations where no samples had been taken from the suspect; the subsection only operates when samples taken are later found to be defective.

Police Powers Under s.19

The police are entitled, within the permitted period, to require that the accused makes himself available for sampling purposes if he is at liberty or to have access to him for those purposes if he is in custody. No notice need be given to a remand or serving prisoner of the police intention to exercise such powers, but subs.(3)(b) curiously makes it clear that the sampling procedures must be executed, "in the place where he is for the time being": this suggests that the sampling must be carried out in the penal establishment in which the accused is serving his sentence. A4-53

A person at large is entitled to no less than seven days notice of the requirement that he attend at a specified place and may also be directed to attend on a particular day and time (or days and times).

Failure to attend the nominated police station as demanded under s.19(3) renders the subject liable to arrest without warrant, but the Act does not treat such a failure as an offence. A further issue which is unresolved in the Act is the position when a suspect does attend as required, but samples are not sufficient for analysis or indeed no samples are taken at all. It is submitted that in the former case the whole procedure in subs.(4)(b) could be invoked anew, but in the latter, the suspect would have fulfilled his obligation and could not be subjected to the procedure again. Note also that subs.(5) is peremptory and is not qualified by any reasonableness test.

It will be necessary if the power of arrest in subs.(6) is to be invoked, that the police can demonstrate that notice of the requirement has been lawfully served upon the subject.

Samples etc. from persons convicted of sexual and violent offences.

19A.—(1) This section applies where a person— A4-53.1

(a) is convicted on or after the relevant date of a relevant offence and is sentenced to imprisonment;

(b) was convicted before the relevant date of a relevant offence, was sentenced to imprisonment and is serving that sentence on or after the relevant date;

(c) was convicted before the relevant date of a specified relevant offence, was sentenced to imprisonment, is not serving that sentence on that date or at any time after that date but was serving it at any time during the period of five years ending with the day before that date.

(2) Subject to subsections (3) and (4) below, where this section applies a constable may—

(a) take from the person or require the person to provide him with such relevant physical data as the constable reasonably considers appropriate;

(b) with the authority of an officer of a rank no lower than inspector, take from the person any sample mentioned in any of paragraphs (a) to (c) of subsection (6) of section 18 of this Act by the means specified in that paragraph in relation to that sample; and

(c) take, or direct a police custody and security officer to take, from the person any sample mentioned in subsection (6A) of that section by the means specified in that subsection.

(3) The power conferred by subsection (2) above shall not be exercised where the person has previously had taken from him or been required to provide relevant physical data or any sample under subsection (2) of section 19 of this Act in a case where the power conferred by that subsection was exercised by virtue of subsection (1)(a) of that section, under this section or under section 19AA(3) of this Act unless the data so taken or required have been or, as the case may be, the sample so taken or required has been lost or destroyed.

(4) Where this section applies by virtue of—

(a) paragraph (a) or (b) of subsection (1) above, the powers conferred by subsection (2) above may be exercised at any time when the person is serving his sentence; and

(b) paragraph (c) of the said subsection (1), those powers may only be exercised within a period of three months beginning on the relevant date.

(5) Where a person in respect of whom the power conferred by subsection (2) above may be exercised—

(a) is no longer serving his sentence of imprisonment, subsections (3)(a), (5) and (6);

(b) is serving his sentence of imprisonment, subsection (3)(b),

of section 19 of this Act shall apply for the purposes of subsection (2) above as they apply for the purposes of subsection (2) of that section.

(6) In this section—

"conviction" includes—

(a) an acquittal, by reason of the special defence set out in section 51A of this Act;

(b) a finding under section 55(2) of this Act, and "convicted" shall be construed accordingly;

"relevant date" means the date on which section 48 of the Crime and Punishment (Scotland) Act 1997 is commenced;

"relevant offence" means any relevant sexual offence or any relevant violent offence;

"relevant sexual offence" means any of the following offences—

(a) rape at common law;

(b) clandestine injury to women;

(c) abduction of a woman with intent to rape;

(ca) abduction with intent to commit the statutory offence of rape;

(d) assault with intent to rape or ravish;

(da) assault with intent to commit the statutory offence of rape;

(e) indecent assault;
(f) lewd, indecent or libidinous behaviour or practices;
(g) public indecency if the court, in imposing sentence or otherwise disposing of the case, determined for the purposes of paragraph 60 of Schedule 3 to the Sexual Offences Act 2003 (c.42) that there was a significant sexual aspect to the offender's behaviour in committing the offence;
(h) sodomy;
(i) any offence which consists of a contravention of any of the following statutory provisions—
  (i) section 52 of the Civic Government (Scotland) Act 1982 (taking and distribution of indecent images of children);
  (ii) section 52A of that Act (possession of indecent images of children);
  (iii) section 311 of the Mental Health (Care and Treatment) (Scotland) Act 2003 (non consensual sexual acts);
  (iv) section 313 of that Act (persons providing care services: sexual offences);
  (v) section 1 of the Criminal Law (Consolidation)(Scotland) Act 1995 (incest);
  (vi) section 2 of that Act (intercourse with step-child);
  (vii) section 3 of that Act (intercourse with child under 16 years by person in position of trust);
  (viii) section 5(1) or (2) of that Act (unlawful intercourse with girl under 13 years);
  (ix) section 5(3) of that Act (unlawful intercourse with girl aged between 13 and 16 years);
  (x) section 6 of that Act (indecent behaviour towards girl between 12 and 16 years);
  (xi) section 7 of that Act (procuring);
  (xii) section 8 of that Act (abduction and unlawful detention of women and girls);
  (xiii) section 9 of that Act (permitting use of premises for unlawful sexual intercourse);
  (xiv) section 10 of that Act (liability of parents etc in respect of offences against girls under 16 years);
  (xv) section 11(1)(b) of that Act (soliciting for immoral purpose);
  (xvi) section 13(5)(b) and (c) of that Act (homosexual offences); and
(j) any offence which consists of a contravention of any of the following provisions of the Sexual Offences (Scotland) Act 2009 (asp 9)—
  (i) section 1 (rape),
  (ii) section 2 (sexual assault by penetration),
  (iii) section 3 (sexual assault),
  (iv) section 4 (sexual coercion),
  (v) section 5 (coercing a person into being present during a sexual activity),
  (vi) section 6 (coercing a person into looking at a sexual image),
  (vii) section 7(1) (communicating indecently),

(viii) section 7(2) (causing a person to see or hear an indecent communication),
(ix) section 8 (sexual exposure),
(x) section 9 (voyeurism),
(xi) section 18 (rape of a young child),
(xii) section 19 (sexual assault on a young child by penetration),
(xiii) section 20 (sexual assault on a young child),
(xiv) section 21 (causing a young child to participate in a sexual activity),
(xv) section 22 (causing a young child to be present during a sexual activity),
(xvi) section 23 (causing a young child to look at a sexual image),
(xvii) section 24(1) (communicating indecently with a young child),
(xviii) section 24(2) (causing a young child to see or hear an indecent communication),
(xix) section 25 (sexual exposure to a young child),
(xx) section 26 (voyeurism towards a young child),
(xxi) section 28 (having intercourse with an older child),
(xxii) section 29 (engaging in penetrative sexual activity with or towards an older child),
(xxiii) section 30 (engaging in sexual activity with or towards an older child),
(xxiv) section 31 (causing an older child to participate in a sexual activity),
(xxv) section 32 (causing an older child to be present during a sexual activity),
(xxvi) section 33 (causing an older child to look at a sexual image),
(xxvii) section 34(1) (communicating indecently with an older child),
(xxviii) section 34(2) (causing an older child to see or hear an indecent communication),
(xxix) section 35 (sexual exposure to an older child),
(xxx) section 36 (voyeurism towards an older child),
(xxxi) section 37(1) (engaging while an older child in sexual conduct with or towards another older child),
(xxxii) section 37(4) (engaging while an older child in consensual sexual conduct with another older child),
(xxxiii) section 42 (sexual abuse of trust) but only if the condition set out in section 43(6) of that Act is fulfilled,
(xxxiv) section 46 (sexual abuse of trust of a mentally disordered person);

"relevant violent offence" means any of the following offences—

(a) murder or culpable homicide;
(b) uttering a threat to the life of another person;
(c) perverting the course of justice in connection with an offence of murder;
(d) fire raising;
(e) assault;

(f) reckless conduct causing actual injury;
(g) abduction; and
(h) any offence which consists of a contravention of any of the following statutory provisions—
  (i) sections 2 (causing explosion likely to endanger life) or 3 (attempting to cause such an explosion) of the Explosive Substances Act 1883;
  (ii) section 12 of the Children and Young Persons (Scotland) Act 1937 (cruelty to children);
  (iii) sections 16 (possession of firearm with intent to endanger life or cause serious injury), 17 (use of firearm to resist arrest) or 18 (having a firearm for purpose of committing an offence listed in Schedule 2) of the Firearms Act 1968;
  (iv) section 6 of the Child Abduction Act 1984 (taking or sending child out of the United Kingdom); and
  (v) section 47(1) (possession of offensive weapon in public place), 49(1) (possession of article with blade or point in public place), 49A(1) or (2) (possession of article with blade or point or offensive weapon on school premises) or 49C(1) (possession of offensive weapon or article with blade or point in prison) of the Criminal Law (Consolidation) (Scotland) Act 1995 (c.39);

"sentence of imprisonment" means the sentence imposed in respect of the relevant offence and includes—
(a) a compulsion order, a restriction order, a hospital direction and any order under section 57(2)(a) or (b) of this Act; and
(b) a sentence of detention imposed under section 207 or 208 of this Act, and "sentenced to imprisonment" shall be construed accordingly; and any reference to a person serving his sentence shall be construed as a reference to the person being detained in a prison, hospital or other place in pursuance of a sentence of imprisonment; and

"specified relevant offence" means—
(a) any relevant sexual offence mentioned in paragraphs (a), (b), (f) and (i)(viii) of the definition of that expression and any such offence as is mentioned in paragraph (h) of that definition where the person against whom the offence was committed did not consent; and
(b) any relevant violent offence mentioned in paragraph (a) or (g) of the definition of that expression and any such offence as is mentioned in paragraph (e) of that definition where the assault is to the victim's severe injury, but, notwithstanding subsection (7) below, does not include— (i) conspiracy or incitement to commit; and (ii) aiding and abetting, counselling or procuring the commission of, any of those offences.

(6A) In subsection (6)—
(a) the references to "rape" in paragraphs (c) and (d) of the definition of "relevant sexual offence" are to the offence of rape at common law; and
(b) the references in paragraphs (ca) and (da) of that subsection to "the statutory offence of rape" are (as the case may be) to—

(i) the offence of rape under section 1 of the Sexual Offences (Scotland) Act 2009, or

(ii) the offence of rape of a young child under section 18 of that Act.

(7) In this section—

(a) any reference to a relevant offence includes a reference to any attempt, conspiracy or incitement to commit such an offence; and

(b) any reference to—

(i) a relevant sexual offence mentioned in paragraph (i) or (j); or

(ii) a relevant violent offence mentioned in paragraph (h);

of the definition of those expressions in subsection (6) above includes a reference to aiding and abetting, counselling or procuring the commission of such an offence.

AMENDMENTS

Section 19A inserted by Crime and Punishment (Scotland) Act 1997 (c.48) s.48.

Subs.(2) as amended by Criminal Justice (Scotland) Act 2003 (asp 7) Pt 8 s.55. Brought into force on 27 June 2003 by SSI 2003/288 (C.14).

Subs.(6) as amended by Mental Health (Care and Treatment) (Scotland) Act 2003 (Modification of Enactments) Order 2005 (SSI 2005/465) art.2 and Sch.1 para.27(2) (effective 27 September 2005).

Subs.(3) as amended by Police, Public Order and Criminal Justice (Scotland) Act 2006 (asp 10) s.77(4). Brought into force on 1 September 2006 by SSI 2006/432 (C.34) art.2.

Subs.(3) as amended by Police, Public Order and Criminal Justice (Scotland) Act 2006 (asp 10) s.101 and Sch.6, para.4(3). Brought into force on 1 September 2006 by SSI 2006/432 (C.34) art.2.

Subss.(6) and (7) as amended by Sexual Offences (Scotland) Act 2009 (asp 9) Sch.5 para.2. Brought into force on 1 December 2010 by SSI 2010/357 (C.21) art.2.

Subs.(6) as amended, subs.(6A) inserted, by Sexual Offences (Scotland) Act 2009 (Supplemental and Consequential Provisions) Order 2010 (SSI 2010/421) art.2 and Sch. para.1 (effective 1 December 2010).

Subs.(6) as amended by Criminal Justice and Licensing (Scotland) Act 2010 (asp 13) s.81. Brought into force on 28 March 2011 by SSI 2011/178 (C.15) art.2, Sch.1 para.1, subject to SSI 2011/178 art.8.

Subs.(6) (definition of "conviction") as amended by Criminal Justice and Licensing (Scotland) Act 2010 (asp 13) Sch.7 para.32. Brought into force on 25 June 2012 by SSI 2012/160 (C.15) art.3.

GENERAL NOTE

A4-53.1.1 This section identifies the wide range of relevant offences (sexual offences or offences involving violence) in relation to which, post-conviction of an accused or his acquittal on grounds of insanity, the police are empowered to obtain fresh samples after the originals (or the resultant data) have been lost or destroyed. Those powers can be exercised on due notice while the offender is imprisoned or even after release.

[THE NEXT PARAGRAPH IS A4-53.2]

Samples etc. from sex offenders

A4-53.2 **19AA.**—(1) This section applies where a person is subject to—

(a) the notification requirements of Part 2 of the 2003 Act;

(b) an order under section 2 of the Protection of Children and Prevention of Sexual Offences (Scotland) Act 2005 (asp 9) (a risk of sexual harm order); or

(c) an order under section 122A or 123 of the 2003 Act (which makes provision for England and Wales and Northern Ireland corresponding to section 2 of that Act of 2005).

(2) This section applies regardless of whether the person became subject to those requirements or that order before or after the commencement of this section.

(3) Subject to subsections (4) to (8) below, where this section applies a constable may—

(a) take from the person or require the person to provide him with such relevant physical data as the constable considers reasonably appropriate;

(b) with the authority of an officer of a rank no lower than inspector, take from the person any sample mentioned in any of paragraphs (a) to (c) of subsection (6) of section 18 of this Act by the means specified in that paragraph in relation to that sample;

(c) take, or direct a police custody and security officer to take, from the person any sample mentioned in subsection (6A) of that section by the means specified in that subsection.

(4) Where this section applies by virtue of subsection (1)(c) above, the power conferred by subsection (3) shall not be exercised unless the constable reasonably believes that the person's sole or main residence is in Scotland.

(5) The power conferred by subsection (3) above shall not be exercised where the person has previously had taken from him or been required to provide relevant physical data or any sample under section 19(2) or 19A(2) of this Act unless the data so taken or required have been or, as the case may be, the sample so taken has been, lost or destroyed.

(6) The power conferred by subsection (3) above shall not be exercised where the person has previously had taken from him or been required to provide relevant physical data or any sample under that subsection unless the data so taken or required or, as the case may be, the sample so taken—

(a) have or has been lost or destroyed; or

(b) were or was not suitable for the particular means of analysis or, though suitable, were or was insufficient (either in quantity or quality) to enable information to be obtained by that means of analysis.

(7) The power conferred by subsection (3) above may be exercised only—

(a) in a police station; or

(b) where the person is in legal custody by virtue of section 295 of this Act, in the place where the person is for the time being.

(8) The power conferred by subsection (3) above may be exercised in a police station only—

(a) where the person is present in the police station in pursuance of a requirement made by a constable to attend for the purpose of the exercise of the power; or

(b) while the person is in custody in the police station following his arrest in connection with any offence.

(9) A requirement under subsection (8)(a) above—

(a) shall give the person at least seven days' notice of the date on which he is required to attend;

(b) may direct him to attend at a specified time of day or between specified times of day; and

(c) where this section applies by virtue of subsection (1)(b) or (c) above, shall warn the person that failure, without reasonable excuse, to comply with the requirement or, as the case may be, to allow the taking of or to provide any relevant physical data, or to provide any sample, under the power, constitutes an offence.

(10) A requirement under subsection (8)(a) above in a case where the person has previously had taken from him or been required to provide relevant physical data or any sample under subsection (3) above shall contain intimation that the relevant physical data were or the sample was unsuitable or, as the case may be, insufficient, as mentioned in subsection (6)(b) above.

(11) Before exercising the power conferred by subsection (3) above in a case to which subsection (8)(b) above applies, a constable shall inform the person of that fact.

(12) Any constable may arrest without warrant a person who fails to comply with a requirement under subsection (8)(a) above.

(13) This section does not prejudice the generality of section 18 of this Act.

(14) In this section, "the 2003 Act" means the Sexual Offences Act 2003 (c.42).

AMENDMENTS

Section 19AA inserted by Police, Public Order and Criminal Justice (Scotland) Act 2006 (asp 10) s.77(2). Brought into force on 1 September 2006 by SSI 2006/432 (C.34) art.2.

Subs.(1)(c) as amended by Anti-social Behaviour, Crime and Policing Act 2014 (c.12) Sch.11 para.51. Brought into force on 8 March 2015 by SI 2015/373 art.2.

Subs.(8)(b) as amended by Criminal Justice (Scotland) Act 2016 (asp 1) Sch.2 para.28(4). Brought into force on 25 January 2018 by SSI 2017/345 art.3 (subject to transitional and savings provisions in art.4).

Section 19AA: supplementary provision in risk of sexual harm order cases

A4-53.3 **19AB.**—(1) This section applies where section 19AA of this Act applies by virtue of subsection (1)(b) or (c) of that section.

(2) A person who fails without reasonable excuse—

(a) to comply with a requirement made of him under section 19AA(8)(a) of this Act; or

(b) to allow relevant physical data to be taken from him, to provide relevant physical data, or to allow a sample to be taken from him, under section 19AA(3) of this Act,

shall be guilty of an offence.

(3) A person guilty of an offence under subsection (2) above shall be liable on summary conviction to the following penalties—

(a) a fine not exceeding level 4 on the standard scale;

(b) imprisonment for a period—

(i) where the conviction is in the district court, not exceeding 60 days; or

(ii) where the conviction is in the sheriff court, not exceeding 3 months; or

(c) both such fine and such imprisonment.

(4) Subject to subsection (6) below, all record of any relevant physical data taken from or provided by a person under section 19AA(3) of this Act, all samples taken from a person under that subsection and all information derived from such samples shall be destroyed as soon as possible following the person ceasing to be a person subject to any risk of sexual harm orders.

(5) For the purpose of subsection (4) above, a person does not cease to be subject to a risk of sexual harm order where the person would be subject to such an order but for an order under section 6(2) of the 2005 Act or any corresponding power of a court in England and Wales or in Northern Ireland.

(6) Subsection (4) above does not apply if before the duty to destroy imposed by that subsection would apply, the person—

(a) is convicted of an offence; or

(b) becomes subject to the notification requirements of Part 2 of the 2003 Act.

(7) In this section—

"risk of sexual harm order" means an order under—

(a) section 2 of the 2005 Act; or

(b) section 123 of the 2003 Act; and also includes an order under section 122A of the 2003 Act (sexual risk orders);

"the 2005 Act" means the Protection of Children and Prevention of Sexual Offences (Scotland) Act 2005 (asp 9);

"the 2003 Act" has the meaning given by section 19AA(14) of this Act; and
"convicted" shall be construed in accordance with section 19A(6) of this Act.

AMENDMENTS

Section 19AB inserted by Police, Public Order and Criminal Justice (Scotland) Act 2006 (asp 10) s.77(2). Brought into force on 1 September 2006 by SSI 2006/432 (C.34) art.2.

Subs.(7) as amended by Anti-social Behaviour, Crime and Policing Act 2014 (c.12) Sch.11 para.52. Brought into force on 8 March 2015 by SI 2015/373 art.2.

Power of constable in obtaining relevant physical data etc.

19B.—(1) A constable may use reasonable force in— A4-53.4

(a) taking any relevant physical data from a person or securing a person's compliance with a requirement made under section 18(2), 19(2)(a) or 19A(2)(a) of this Act, or under subsection (3)(a) of section 19AA of this Act where that section applies by virtue of subsection (1)(a) of that section;

(b) exercising any power conferred by section 18(6), 19(2)(b) or 19A(2)(b) of this Act, or under subsection (3)(b) of section 19AA of this Act where that section applies by virtue of subsection (1)(a) of that section.

(2) A constable may, with the authority of an officer of a rank no lower than inspector, use reasonable force in (himself) exercising any power conferred by section 18(6A), 19(2)(c) or 19A(2)(c) of this Act, or under subsection (3)(c) of section 19AA of this Act where that section applies by virtue of subsection (1)(a) of that section.

AMENDMENTS

Section 19B inserted by Crime and Punishment (Scotland) Act (c.48) s.48(2).

Section 19B as amended by Criminal Justice (Scotland) Act 2003 (asp 7) Pt 8 s.55. Brought into force on 27 June 2003 by SSI 2003/288 (C.14).

Subss.(1) and (2) as amended by Police, Public Order and Criminal Justice (Scotland) Act 2006 (asp 10) s.77(5). Brought into force on 1 September 2006 by SSI 2006/432 (C.34) art.2.

Sections 18 and 19 to 19AA: use of samples etc.

19C.—(1) Subsection (2) applies to— A4-53.5

(a) relevant physical data taken or provided under section 18(2), 19(2)(a), 19A(2)(a) or 19AA(3)(a) (including any taken or provided by virtue of paragraph 20 of Schedule 8 to the Terrorism Act 2000),

(b) a sample, or any information derived from a sample, taken under section 18(6) or (6A), 19(2)(b) or (c), 19A(2)(b) or (c) or 19AA(3)(b) or (c) (including any taken or provided by virtue of paragraph 20 of Schedule 8 to the Terrorism Act 2000),

(c) relevant physical data or a sample taken from a person—

(i) by virtue of any power of search,

(ii) by virtue of any power to take possession of evidence where there is immediate danger of its being lost or destroyed, or

(iii) under the authority of a warrant,

(d) information derived from a sample falling within paragraph (c), and

(e) relevant physical data, a sample or information derived from a sample taken from, or provided by, a person outwith Scotland which is given by any person to—

(i) the Police Service of Scotland ("the Police Service"),

(ii) the Scottish Police Authority ("the Authority"), or

(iii) a person acting on behalf of the Police Service or the Authority.

(2) The relevant physical data, sample or information derived from a sample may be used—

(a) for the prevention or detection of crime, the investigation of an offence or the conduct of a prosecution,
(b) for the identification of a deceased person or a person from whom the relevant physical data or sample came,
(c) in the interests of national security, or
(d) for the purposes of a terrorist investigation.

(3) Subsections (4) and (5) apply to relevant physical data, a sample or information derived from a sample falling within any of paragraphs (a) to (d) of subsection (1) ("relevant material").

(4) If the relevant material is held by the Police Service, the Authority or a person acting on behalf of the Police Service or the Authority, the Police Service or, as the case may be, the Authority or person may give the relevant material to another person for use by that person in accordance with subsection (2).

(5) The Police Service, the Authority or a person acting on behalf of the Police Service or the Authority may, in using the relevant material in accordance with subsection (2), check it against other relevant physical data, samples and information derived from samples received from another person.

(6) In subsection (2)—
(a) the reference to crime includes a reference to—
(i) conduct which constitutes a criminal offence or two or more criminal offences (whether under the law of a part of the United Kingdom or a country or territory outside the United Kingdom), or
(ii) conduct which is, or corresponds to, conduct which, if it all took place in any one part of the United Kingdom would constitute a criminal offence or two or more criminal offences,
(b) the reference to an investigation includes a reference to an investigation outside Scotland of a crime or suspected crime,
(c) the reference to a prosecution includes a reference to a prosecution brought in respect of a crime in a country or territory outside Scotland, and
(d) "terrorist investigation" has the meaning given by section 32 of the Terrorism Act 2000.

(7) This section is without prejudice to any other power relating to the use of relevant physical data, samples or information derived from a sample.

AMENDMENTS

Section 19C inserted by Criminal Justice and Licensing (Scotland) Act 2010 (asp 13) s.82. Brought into force on August 1, 2011 by SSI 2011/178 (C.15) art.2, Sch.1 para.1, subject to SSI 2011/178 art.9.

Subss.(1)(a), (b), (2) and (6) as amended by Criminal Justice and Licensing (Scotland) Act 2010 (Consequential Provisions and Modifications) Order 2011 (SI 2011/2298) art.3 and Sch.1 (effective September 16, 2011, subject to transitional provisions specified in SI 2011/2298 art.4(1) and (4)).

Subss.(1), (4) and (5) as amended by Police and Fire Reform (Scotland) Act 2012 (asp 8) Sch.7 para.12(8). Brought into force on April 1, 2013 by SSI 2013/51 art.2.

[THE NEXT PARAGRAPH IS A4-54]

Use of prints, samples etc.

A4-54 **20.** [...]

AMENDMENTS

Section 20 repealed by Criminal Justice and Licensing (Scotland) Act 2010 (asp 13) Sch.7 para.33. Brought into force on August 1, 2011 by SSI 2011/178 (C.15) art.2, Sch.1 para.1.

[THE NEXT PARAGRAPH IS A4-55.1]

Testing for Class A drugs

Arrested persons: testing for certain Class A drugs

20A.—(1) Subject to subsection (2) below, where subsection (3) below applies an appropriate officer may— A4-55.1

(a) require a person who has been arrested and is in custody in a police station to provide him with a sample of urine; or

(b) take from the inside of the mouth of such a person, by means of swabbing, a sample of saliva or other material,

which the officer may subject to analysis intended to reveal whether there is any relevant Class A drug in the person's body.

(2) The power conferred by subsection (1) above shall not be exercised where the person has previously been required to provide or had taken from him a sample under that subsection in the same period in custody.

(3) This subsection applies where—

(a) the person is of 16 years of age or more;

(b) the period in custody in the police station has not exceeded 6 hours;

(c) the police station is situated in an area prescribed by order made by statutory instrument by the Scottish Ministers; and

(d) either—

(i) the person's arrest was on suspicion of committing or having committed a relevant offence; or

(ii) a senior police officer who has appropriate grounds has authorised the making of the requirement to provide or the taking of the sample.

(4) Before exercising the power conferred by subsection (1) above, an appropriate officer shall—

(a) warn the person in respect of whom it is to be exercised that failure, without reasonable excuse, to comply with the requirement or, as the case may be, allow the sample to be taken constitutes an offence; and

(b) in a case within subsection (3)(d)(ii) above, inform the person of the giving of the authorisation and the grounds for the suspicion.

(5) Where—

(a) a person has been required to provide or has had taken a sample under subsection (1) above;

(b) any of the following is the case—

(i) the sample was not suitable for the means of analysis to be used to reveal whether there was any relevant Class A drug in the person's body;

(ii) though suitable, the sample was insufficient (either in quantity or quality) to enable information to be obtained by that means of analysis; or

(iii) the sample was destroyed during analysis and the means of analysis failed to produce reliable information; and

(c) the person remains in custody in the police station (whether or not the period of custody has exceeded 6 hours),

an appropriate officer may require the person to provide or as the case may be take another sample of the same kind by the same method.

(6) Before exercising the power conferred by subsection (5) above, an appropriate officer shall warn the person in respect of whom it is to be exercised that failure,

without reasonable excuse, to comply with the requirement or, as the case may be, allow the sample to be taken constitutes an offence.

(7) A person who fails without reasonable excuse—

(a) to comply with a requirement made of him under subsection (1)(a) or (5) above; or

(b) to allow a sample to be taken from him under subsection (1)(b) or (5) above,

shall be guilty of an offence.

(8) In this section—

"appropriate grounds" means reasonable grounds for suspecting that the misuse by the person of any relevant Class A drug caused or contributed to the offence on suspicion of which the person was arrested;

"appropriate officer" means—

(a) a constable; or

(b) a police custody and security officer acting on the direction of a constable;

"misuse" has the same meaning as in the Misuse of Drugs Act 1971 (c.38);

"relevant Class A drug" means any of the following substances, preparations and products—

(a) cocaine or its salts;

(b) any preparation or other product containing cocaine or its salts;

(c) diamorphine or its salts;

(d) any preparation or other product containing diamorphine or its salts;

"relevant offence" means any of the following offences—

(a) theft;

(b) assault;

(c) robbery;

(d) fraud;

(e) reset;

(f) uttering a forged document;

(g) embezzlement;

(h) an attempt, conspiracy or incitement to commit an offence mentioned in paragraphs (a) to (g);

(i) an offence under section 4 of the Misuse of Drugs Act 1971 (c.38) (restriction on production and supply of controlled drugs) committed in respect of a relevant Class A drug;

(j) an offence under section 5(2) of that Act of 1971 (possession of controlled drug) committed in respect of a relevant Class A drug;

(k) an offence under section 5(3) of that Act of 1971 (possession of controlled drug with intent to supply) committed in respect of a relevant Class A drug;

"senior police officer" means a police officer of a rank no lower than inspector.

AMENDMENTS

Section 20A inserted by Police, Public Order and Criminal Justice (Scotland) Act 2006 (asp 10) s.84. Brought into force on January 1, 2007 by SSI 2006/607 (C.46) art.3 and Sch. for the purpose of enabling an order under s.20A(3)(c) of the 1995 Act to be made.

Further brought into force on February 25, 2007 for the purpose specified in SSI 2007/84 (C.12) art.3(1)(a) and on June 12, 2007 so far as not already in force.

DEFINITIONS

A4-55.2 "appropriate grounds": s.20A(8).
"appropriate officer": s.20A(8).
"misuse": s.20A(8).

"relevant Class A drug": s.20A(8).
"relevant offence": s.20A(8).
"senior police officer": s.20A(8).

GENERAL NOTE

The City of Aberdeen, City of Edinburgh and the City of Glasgow have been prescribed for the purposes of s.20A(3)(c) of the 1995 Act. A person who is arrested under suspicion of committing, or having committed a relevant offence specified in s.20A(8) can be tested for the presence of the relevant Class A controlled drug: see the Testing of Arrested Persons for Class A Drugs (Prescribed Area) (Scotland) Order 2007 (SSI 2007/131). **A4-55.3**

Section 20A provides that the police may test a person for a relevant Class A drug if he or she has been arrested under suspicion of committing a relevant offence. The relevant offences are listed in s.20A(8). A person who has been arrested under suspicion of committing any other offence, which is not a relevant offence, can also be tested at the discretion of a senior police officer if he or she believes that misuse of a Class A drug caused or contributed to the offence. Section 20A(8) provides that the Class A drugs that will be tested for are cocaine and diamorphine (heroin). Section 20A(2) provides that the police cannot test a person for a relevant Class A drug if that person has already given a sample for testing after they have been brought to a police station. Section 20A(5) sets out that a further sample can be taken if the original is not suitable for analysis, was insufficient or was destroyed during the testing process.

Subs.(3)

Section 20A(3) sets out the conditions, which must be met before a person is tested for a relevant Class A drug. A sample must also be taken or provided within six hours of that person being brought to a police station. To allow for the policy to be rolled out to particular parts of Scotland and in stages, a sample can only be taken if the Scottish Ministers have made an order by statutory instrument which states that mandatory drugs tests can be carried out in the area in which the police station is located. Such an order will be subject to negative procedure of the Parliament.

Subs.(7)

Section 20A(7) makes it an offence for an arrestee to refuse to comply with a drug test under these powers if required to do so. The maximum penalties for committing this offence are set out in s.20B(6). A constable is required to warn a person of this fact under s.20(4). When a person has been arrested for an offence (other than a relevant offence), a constable must also inform that person that a senior police officer has authorised him or her to take a sample, or require that person to provide a sample. A person must also be told of the reasons why a senior police officer suspects that a Class A drug has been taken.

Assessment following positive test

Section 85 of the Police, Public Order and Criminal Justice (Scotland) Act 2006 provides that an individual who has tested positive for a relevant Class A drug in terms of s.20A of the 1995 Act will be required to attend a drugs assessment with a suitably qualified drugs assessor. A person will be required to remain at that assessment for its duration. Section 86 also sets down that the purpose of the drugs assessment is to establish whether or not the person is dependent on or has a propensity to misuse Class A drugs and whether or not they may benefit from assistance or treatment. There are supplementary provisions in ss.86 to 90 of the Police, Public Order and Criminal Justice (Scotland) Act 2006.

Section 20A: supplementary

20B.—(1) Section 20A of this Act does not prejudice the generality of section 18 of this Act. **A4-55.4**

(2) Each person carrying out a function under section 20A of this Act must have regard to any guidance issued by the Scottish Ministers—

(a) about the carrying out of the function; or
(b) about matters connected to the carrying out of the function.

(3) An order under section 20A(3)(c) shall be subject to annulment in pursuance of a resolution of the Scottish Parliament.

(4) An authorisation for the purposes of section 20A of this Act may be given orally or in writing but, if given orally, the person giving it shall confirm it in writing as soon as is reasonably practicable.

(5) If a sample is provided or taken under section 20A of this Act by virtue of an authorisation, the authorisation and the grounds for the suspicion are to be recorded in writing as soon as is reasonably practicable after the sample is provided or taken.

(6) A person guilty of an offence under section 20A of this Act shall be liable on summary conviction to the following penalties—

(a) a fine not exceeding level 4 on the standard scale;

(b) imprisonment for a period—

(i) where conviction is in the district court, not exceeding 60 days; or

(ii) where conviction is in the sheriff court, not exceeding 3 months; or

(c) both such fine and imprisonment.

(7) Subject to subsection (8) below, a sample provided or taken under section 20A of this Act shall be destroyed as soon as possible following its analysis for the purpose for which it was taken.

(8) Where an analysis of the sample reveals that a relevant Class A drug is present in the person's body, the sample may be retained so that it can be used, and supplied to others, for the purpose of any proceedings against the person for an offence under section 88 of the Police, Public Order and Criminal Justice (Scotland) Act 2006 (asp 10); but—

(a) the sample may not be used, or supplied, for any other purpose; and

(b) the sample shall be destroyed as soon as possible once it is no longer capable of being used for that purpose.

(9) Information derived from a sample provided by or taken from a person under section 20A of this Act may be used and disclosed only for the following purposes—

(a) for the purpose of proceedings against the person for an offence under section 88 of the Police, Public Order and Criminal Justice (Scotland) Act 2006 (asp 10);

(b) for the purpose of informing any decision about granting bail in any criminal proceedings to the person;

(c) for the purpose of informing any decision of a children's hearing arranged to consider the person's case;

(d) where the person is convicted of an offence, for the purpose of informing any decision about the appropriate sentence to be passed by a court and any decision about the person's supervision or release;

(e) for the purpose of ensuring that appropriate advice and treatment is made available to the person.

(10) Subject to subsection (11) below, the Scottish Ministers may by order made by statutory instrument modify section 20A(8) of this Act for either of the following purposes—

(a) for the purpose of adding an offence to or removing an offence from those for the time being listed in the definition of "relevant offence";

(b) for the purpose of adding a substance, preparation or product to or removing a substance, preparation or product from those for the time being listed in the definition of "relevant Class A drug".

(11) An order under subsection (10)(b) may add a substance, preparation or product only if it is a Class A drug (that expression having the same meaning as in the Misuse of Drugs Act 1971 (c.38)).

(12) An order under subsection (10) above shall not be made unless a draft of the statutory instrument containing it has been laid before and approved by resolution of the Scottish Parliament.

AMENDMENTS

Section 20B inserted by Police, Public Order and Criminal Justice (Scotland) Act 2006 (asp 10) s.84. Brought into force on January 1, 2007 by SSI 2006/607 (C.46) art.3 and Sch. for the purpose of enabling an order under s.20A(3)(c) of the 1995 Act to be made.

Further brought into force on February 25, 2007 for the purpose specified in SSI 2007/84 (C.12) art.3(1)(a) and on June 12, 2007 so far as not already in force.

DEFINITIONS

"appropriate grounds": s.20A(8). A4-55.5
"appropriate officer": s.20A(8).
"misuse": s.20A(8).
"relevant Class A drug": s.20A(8).
"relevant offence": s.20A(8).
"senior police officer": s.20A(8).

GENERAL NOTE

Section 20B supplements s.20A of the 1995 Act. Subsections (4) and (5) set out procedures which must be followed if a senior police officer decides that a person should be tested for a Class A drug. Subsection (7) imposes a requirement to destroy a sample, which has been taken under s.20A. Subsection (8) also sets down what the information gathered through a mandatory drugs test can be used for. Section 20B(9) provides that the Scottish Ministers can add to or vary the list of trigger offences and or relevant Class A drugs. Such an order will be made by statutory instrument and will be subject to affirmative procedure. There are supplementary provisions in ss.86 to 90 of the Police, Public Order and Criminal Justice (Scotland) Act 2006. A4-55.6

[THE NEXT PARAGRAPH IS A4-56]

Schedule 1 offences

Schedule 1 offences: power of constable to take offender into custody

21.— [...] A4-56

AMENDMENTS

Subss.(2)–(5) repealed by Criminal Proceedings etc. (Reform) (Scotland) Act 2007 (asp 6) s.7. Brought into force on 10 March 2008 by SSI 2008/42 (C.4) art.3 and Sch.

Section 21 repealed by Criminal Justice (Scotland) Act 2016 (asp 1) Sch.2 para.2(b). Brought into force on 25 January 2018 by SSI 2017/345 art.3 and Sch.1 para.1.

DEFINITION

"constable": s.307(1) and s.51(1) of the Police (Scotland) Act 1967. A4-56.1

[THE NEXT PARAGRAPH IS A4-57]

GENERAL NOTE

Section 136(2) preserves the six month timebar provision in relation to statutory proceedings which are prosecuted summarily. Powers to liberate persons charged with a Sch.1 offence are vested in the officer in charge of the police station to which the accused has been brought. The powers, and penalties for failure to comply with the terms of any undertaking imposed, are identical to those contained in s.22 below, but note that liberation can be utilised for potentially more serious charges under s.21: liberation under s.22 is only competent if the charges preferred could be tried summarily. A4-57

Refer to the discussion in s.22 below.

Evidential Provisions

In proceedings for breach of the terms of a written undertaking made under s.21(2)(a) or the more commonplace provision under s.22(1)(a) below, the Act provides that a copy thereof certified and signed by the liberating officer, shall suffice as proof of the facts contained in it. In entering into such an undertaking an accused person is, in effect, placing himself in a special capacity. Once the court is satisfied as to the terms of the undertaking and that the accused failed to obtemper them, the onus of proof then falls upon an accused to make out reasonable grounds on the balance of probabilities for his failure to attend. A4-58

Penalties

Ordinarily, the statutory maximum penalties of imprisonment or fine are laid down in s.3 (sheriff solemn), s.5(2) (sheriff summary) and s.7(7) (JP courts) and cannot be exceeded *in cumulo*. Exceptions to this generality are provided in ss.21(4) and 22(4) in relation to breach of written undertakings and s.27(5) in regard to breach of bail conditions. In either case the sentence imposed can be added to that imposed for the substantive matter, even if this results in a cumulative sentence or fine higher than that which the Court could normally impose. See *Kelso v Crowe*, 1992 S.C.C.R. 415—sentencing principles where contravention of bail conditions occur. A4-59

Police liberation

Liberation by police

A4-60 **22.—** [...]

AMENDMENTS

A4-60.1 Section 22 amended by Criminal Proceedings etc. (Reform) (Scotland) Act 2007 (asp 6) s.7(2). Brought into force in part (s.7(2)(c)) on 10 December 2007 by SSI 2007/479.

Remaining provisions brought into force on 10 March 2008 by SSI 2008/42 (C.4) art.3 and Sch.

Subs.(2)(b)(i) as amended by Criminal Proceedings etc (Reform) (Scotland) Act 2007 (asp 6) s.80, Sch. para.26. Brought into force for the Sheriffdom of Lothian and Borders on 10 March 2008 by SSI 2008/42 (C.4) art.3 and Sch. Further brought into force for the Sheriffdom of Grampian, Highland and Islands on 2 June 2008 by SSI 2008/192 (C.19) art.3 and Sch. Brought into force for the Sheriffdom of Glasgow and Strathkelvin on 8 December 2008 by SSI 2008/329 (C.29) art.3 and Sch. Brought into force for the Sheriffdom of Tayside, Central and Fife on 23 February 2009 by SSI 2008/362 (C.30) art.3 and Sch. Brought into force for the Sheriffdom of North Strathclyde on 14 December 2009 by SSI 2009/432 (C.32) art.3 and Sch.1. Remainder in force on 22 February 2010 by SSI 2009/432 (C.32) art.3 and Sch.2.

Subs.(1D)(a) as amended by Criminal Proceedings etc. (Reform) (Scotland) Act 2007 (Supplemental Provisions) Order 2008 (SSI 2008/109), with effect from 10 March 2008.

Subss.(1H), (2), (4), (4A), (5) repealed by Criminal Justice and Licensing (Scotland) Act 2010 (asp 13) Sch.7 para.34. Brought into force on 28 March 2011 by SSI 2011/178 (C.15) art.2, Sch.1 para.1.

Section 22 repealed by Criminal Justice (Scotland) Act 2016 (asp 1) Sch.2 para.27(b). Brought into force on 25 January 2018 by SSI 2017/345 art.3 (subject to transitional and savings provisions in arts 4 and 5).

DEFINITIONS

A4-60.2 "Scottish ministers": s.44(2) of the Scotland Act 1998 (c.46).

"procurator fiscal": s.307(1) of the Criminal Procedure (Scotland) Act 1995 (c.46).

[THE NEXT PARAGRAPH IS A4-61]

GENERAL NOTE

A4-61 This section was repealed with effect from 25 January 2018 and the active provisions in force from that date are found in the Criminal Justice (Scotland) Act 2016 (asp 1). The General Note has been retained to assist practitioners.

This section permits the officer in charge of a police station, at his discretion, to liberate an accused person pending the submission of a report to the procurator fiscal, or to liberate him to appear at a named court on a specified future occasion, or to hold the person in custody for appearance at court on the next lawful day. These powers only apply when the charges preferred are capable of being prosecuted summarily, but the fact that a written undertaking has been entered into in no way commits the Crown to proceed summarily. Since a suspect has to consent to abide by the specified terms of an undertaking, it is equally open to him to refuse them and in that event it would be incompetent to proceed in terms of subs.(1)(a). The accused would either have to be detained in custody or be liberated for report.

Evidential Provisions

These are identical to those contained in s.21. See the notes on "Evidential Provisions" in that section.

Penalties (subs.(4))

The implications of this provision mirror those in s.21. Refer to the notes on "Penalties" in that section.

These provisions address the system of discretionary release of accused persons from police custody pending a future court appearance and aim to introduce greater flexibility into these procedures. Prior to December 2007 it was necessary for an individual to have been arrested and charged with an offence by the police before an undertaking form specifying a date, time and court for a court appearance could be issued to the accused by the senior officer (usually a sergeant or inspector) controlling prisoners in a police station. The system had major benefits for police and accused alike: control of the numbers of prisoners in police custody could be regulated to a degree, especially when cell space or police resources were at a premium, while some arrested individuals could be spared the indignities (not to mention the public expense) of being kept in custody pending a court appearance.

Section 22 provides that an individual can be arrested for an offence before being released on an undertaking to appear. He can be charged and released from custody on the authority of the officer charging, or the officer in charge of the station's custody prisoners, and, in addition to the requirement to appear at a specified court at a set time, can now be made subject to interim bail conditions which will apply until such appearance, hence the reference to s.24(5)'s provisions.

Equally welcome from a police perspective, persons who have been apprehended on a summary apprehension warrant (see s.135 of the Act) can be liberated to appear at court using the same procedures instead of being kept in custody—the introduction of s.135(3A) into the 1995 Act puts it beyond doubt that the apprehension of an accused on warrant, and subsequent release on a police undertaking at a later date, is to be regarded as the same as that person being placed before the court in answer to the warrant; this can assume significance when issues of delay in execution of a warrant have to be scrutinised by the court.

It may seem axiomatic, but it remains the case, that the decision to liberate or not rests with the police (who may consult with the fiscal) and is not subject to review. Equally important the forum, and charges, specified by the police when issuing a liberation on undertaking to an accused are not binding upon the procurator fiscal. Thus s.22(1F)(a) empowers the fiscal to rescind the undertaking arrangement (for example to mark a case for no further proceedings or, indeed , to proceed by an initiating warrant) while subs.(1F)(b) enables him to alter any of the essentials of the police undertaking or, prior to any court appearance by the accused, to amend the initial bail conditions set by the police. Notice of any of these changes to the undertaking arrangement is effected by way of citation in accordance with the familiar terms of s.141 of the 1995 Act but, for practical purposes, it is likely that notices would be served by means of personal service in view of the limited timeframes within which undertakings customarily operate. Subss.(1G) and (1H) introduce explanatory provisions. All in all, these reforms have developed the police undertaking into a much more flexible tool for the police and have given the public prosecutor some control over the flow of that work.

Offences and Penalties

In line with the increased penalties for breaches of bail conditions, it will be noted that s.22(2)(b)(ii) quadruples the maximum penalties in the sheriff court for breaches of undertakings. Penalties in the district court remain unchanged. Subsection (4A) as now introduced creates a rebuttable presumption that a person charged with a breach of the section's provisions is guilty of that offence unless a preliminary objection is intimated to the court before any initial plea is tendered. The wording of the subsection reminds that undertakings apply to summary proceedings only.

When libelling bail offences care has to be taken to specify the date when, and the police office where, the undertaking was created as well as the precise terms of the bail condition alleged to have been breached. Despite the evidential presumptions made in subs.(1H), issues of the accused's state of knowledge needed to prove an offence may arise sharply on those rare occasions where, subsequent to liberation of an accused on undertaking, the prosecutor opts to vary the bail conditions imposed (subs.(1F)).

Offences where undertaking breached

22ZA.— [...] **A4-61.0.1**

AMENDMENTS

Section 22ZA inserted by Criminal Justice and Licensing (Scotland) Act 2010 (asp 13) s.55. Brought into force on 28 March 2011 (for all purposes in respect of any breach of undertaking committed on or after 28 March 2011) by SSI 2011/178 (C.15) art.2, Sch.1 para.1.

Section 22ZA repealed by Criminal Justice (Scotland) Act 2016 (asp 1) Sch.2 para.27(b). Brought into force on 25 January 2018 by SSI 2017/345 art.3 (subject to transitional and savings provisions in arts 4 and 5).

DEFINITIONS

"offence": s.307(1) of the Criminal Procedure (Scotland) Act 1995 (c.46). **A4-61.0.2**
"fine": s.307(1) of 1995 Act.
"standard scale": s.225(1) of 1995 Act.
"imprisonment": s.307(1) of 1995 Act.
"JP court": s.7 of the 1995 Act.
"sheriff court": ss.3 to 5 of the 1995 Act.
"subsequent offence": s.22ZA(9) of the 1995 Act.

GENERAL NOTE

This section was repealed with effect from 25 January 2018 and the active provisions in force from that date are found in the Criminal Justice (Scotland) Act 2016 (asp 1). The General Note has been retained to assist practitioners. **A4-61.0.3**

Section 22 above empowers the police to release on bail an arrested person charged with a summary offence; the bail order will ordinarily incorporate the standard bail conditions (see s.24(5) below) and must include an undertaking to appear at a designated court on a set date. It is possible, but rare, for further conditions to be imposed to secure attendance on the specified date and time at court. The express purpose of s.22ZA is to respond to situations where the accused either fails to comply with bail undertaking provisions (subs.(1)) or in terms of subs.(3) prior to the specified date of attendance, commits a further offence. The respective penalties for the two distinct forms of offence are found in subs.(2) which provides for the same summary penalties as the previous section and in s.22ZB(3).

Sentencing

The commission of a subsequent offence while subject to an undertaking is an aggravation (subs.(4)) which may be added to any summary complaint by amendment (s.22ZB(10)) or may be libelled in an indictment. In determining sentence for this aggravated offence the court is obliged to pay heed to the factors set out in subs.(4) but can do so only if the Crown has libelled the aggravation in the complaint or indictment. It will be appreciated that as well as looking to any cognate convictions in Scotland, the court will consider any such equivalent convictions imposed by a court elsewhere in the United Kingdom or in a Member State of the European Union. Perhaps of more general significance, the court in sentencing for an offence committed while the accused was subject of an undertaking, must apportion the total sentence imposed between that offence, and the additional portion attributable to the fact that that offence occurred while the accused was subject of a release on undertaking. No less important, it is competent for the aggravated penalty to be imposed with consecutive effect even if this produces a sentence which exceeds the maximum penalty the court can ordinarily impose (subs.(4)).

For completeness, the court oddly also has the option of remitting the aggravated element of the conviction alone back to the summary court which had been specified in the police undertaking (see s.22ZB(10)) below. (This is discussed further below). That same court may also consider the s.22ZA(1) breach in conjunction with the original undertaking offence if the complaint is amended before trial (see s.22ZB(10)).

Evidential provisions

Section 22ZB provides that the libelling of a s.22ZA(1) aggravation in any complaint will be held as admitted unless challenged by way of a preliminary plea (subs.(3)). Similarly the existence of an undertaking, and its terms, at the time of commission of a subsequent offence has to be challenged at the first calling of a summary complaint, or at a first, or preliminary diet in solemn proceedings.

Proof of the undertaking's terms for the purposes of s.22ZA, or a variation of those terms by the procurator fiscal, can be by means of a certified undertaking form.

As noted earlier, s.22ZB(10) enables the court to which the accused had been given an undertaking (that dealing with "the original offence") to permit amendment of the complaint to include a s.22ZA(1) offence. (Since the Crown are entitled to add this aggravation to a summary complaint at any time before trial, it follows that if this is not done before a plea is first recorded, then the Crown has to forego the benefit of the evidential presumptions in s.22ZB(1)).

It is competent for the court dealing with the subsequent offence (aggravated by its commission while the accused was on a bail undertaking) to remit the s.22ZA(1) element to the court dealing with the original sentence.

Evidential and procedural provision

A4-61.0.4 **22ZB.—** [...]

Amendments

Section 22ZB inserted by Criminal Justice and Licensing (Scotland) Act 2010 (asp 13) s.55. Brought into force on 28 March 2011 (for all purposes in respect of any breach of undertaking committed on or after 28 March 2011) by SSI 2011/178 (C.15) art.2, Sch.1 para.1.

Section 22ZB repealed by Criminal Justice (Scotland) Act 2016 (asp 1) Sch.2 para.27(b). Brought into force on 25 January 2018 by SSI 2017/345 art.3 (subject to transitional and savings provisions in arts 4 and 5).

Definitions

A4-61.0.5 "offence": s.307(1) of the Criminal Procedure (Scotland)Act 1995 (c.46).
"subsequent offence": s.22ZA(9) of the 1995 Act.
"indictment": s.307(1) of the 1995 Act.

General Note

A4-61.0.6 This section was repealed with effect from 25 January 2018 and the active provisions in force from that date are found in the Criminal Justice (Scotland) Act 2016 (asp 1). The General Note has been retained to assist practitioners.

See discussion in General Note to s.22ZA above.

[THE NEXT PARAGRAPH IS A4-61.1]

Part III – Bail

Consideration of bail on first appearance

A4-61.1 **22A.—**(1) On the first occasion on which—

(a) a person accused on petition is brought before the sheriff prior to committal until liberated in due course of law; or

(b) a person charged on complaint with an offence is brought before a judge having jurisdiction to try the offence,

the sheriff or, as the case may be, the judge shall, after giving that person and the prosecutor an opportunity to be heard either admit or refuse to admit that person to bail.

(2) Admittance to or refusal of bail shall be determined before the end of the day (not being a Saturday or Sunday, or a court holiday prescribed for the court which is to determine the question of bail, unless that court is sitting on that day for the disposal of criminal business) after the day on which the person accused or charged is brought before the sheriff or judge.

(3) If, by that time, the sheriff or judge has not admitted or refused to admit the person accused or charged to bail, then that person shall be forthwith liberated.

(4) This section applies whether or not the person accused or charged is in custody when that person is brought before the sheriff or judge.

AMENDMENTS

Section 22A inserted by Bail, Judicial Appointments etc. (Scotland) Act 2000 (asp 9) s.1.

Subss.(1) and (3) amended and subs.(2) substituted by Criminal Proceedings etc. (Reform) (Scotland) Act 2007 (asp 6) s.6. Brought into force on 10 December 2007 by SSI 2007/479.

DEFINITIONS A4-61.2

"complaint": s.307(1).
"offence": s.307(1).
"prosecutor": s.307(1).
"bail": s.307(1).
"sheriff": ss.4 and 5.
"judge": s.307(1).

GENERAL NOTE

The Bail, Judicial Appointments etc. (Scotland) Act 2000 (asp 9) was a legislative response to problems which arose following the advent of the European Convention on Human Rights into Scots law in the Scotland Act 1998 (c.46). A4-61.3

On the first appearance of a person from custody, whether on complaint or on petition, the court is automatically obliged to consider his admission to bail. Thus it would not be necessary at that stage in proceedings to make a formal application on behalf of the accused until the court had first deliberated on the question. Subsection (2) permits the court to continue its consideration of bail for up to 24 hours but subs.(3) provides that if the question is not settled within that time then the accused must be liberated. That does not, of course, bar a prosecution but there would be no bail domicile for the accused. Subsection (4) applies these provisions whether or not the accused is in custody in respect of a separate matter.

The purpose of the amendments to s.22A of the 1995 Act is to ensure that bail applications for those in custody must be decided no later than the end of the day following the court appearance at which bail was sought. This provision replaces the long-standing requirement that any application for bail had to be settled by the court within a 24 hour timescale from the time of application. A sensible degree of flexibility has been introduced: the same timescale also applies to any application for bail made later than a first court appearance (see s.23 of the 1995 Act) or for applications for interim liberation when an appeal against a summary conviction is marked by way of stated case (see s.177 of the 1995 Act).

For a detailed statement of the four key principles for the Crown to oppose bail and to assist the court with bail decisions, see 2012 S.L.T. (News) 150-151. Briefly stated, the four principles are: (i) public protection and personal safety; (ii) public protection; (iii) propensity to reoffend; and (iv) propensity to breach court orders or the risk of absconding.

The ultimate decision on bail is for the court, neither the attitude of the Crown nor the views of a complainer would be determinative, and bail conditions are imposed not due to any Crown policy but because the court considered them to be necessary and appropriate: *HM Advocate v Porch* [2015] HCJAC 111; 2016 S.L.T. 149; (sub nom) *Dunn v Porch*, 2016 S.C.C.R. 55 at [28].

The Community Justice (Scotland) Act 2016 (asp 10) establishes the body corporate known as Community Justice Scotland which has been given certain statutory functions to oversee community justice. By s.1(1)(a) "community justice" means giving effect, inter alia, to "bail conditions". By s.2(1) "bail condition" means (a) conditions imposed by courts to grants of bail; and (b) recognised European Union measures. Also by s.2(1) "recognised European Union measures" means a measure imposed in another member State of the European Union which is recognised in Scotland (with or without adaption) under Sch.2 to the Mutual Recognition of Supervision Measures in the European Union (Scotland) Regulations 2014 (SSI 2014/337).

The 2014 Regulations referred to make provision for a purpose connected with a specified European Council Framework Decision on supervision measures as an alternative to provisional detention. There is extensive authority by reg.3 and Sch.1 for the monitoring of Scottish bail conditions in another State. Further, by reg.4 and Sch.2 there is extensive authority for the monitoring of another State's supervision measures in Scotland.

Academic comment

In the absence of any modern analysis of bail in the Scottish context an American study may assist in laying bare the elements in the judicial decision to grant bail: Laurin P. Gouldin, "Defining Flight Risk" (2018) 85 *University of Chicago Law Review* 677-742 [available freely online]. Much of the commendable paper is concerned with American issues in the context of the law applicable there: American judges have "traditionally relied on a series of statutorily prescribed factors to predict pretrial risks" (p.702). Nevertheless, the elements reviewed as bearing on a decision whether to grant or refuse bail have a certain universal application that might reasonably be considered here as an assistance to comparable decisions by the appropriate judiciary in Scotland.

The factors identified and discussed (pp.703-712) are:

(1) factors that suggest incentives to flee the jurisdiction or to avoid court deliberately: these are (i) the seriousness of the offence; (ii) the weight of evidence;
(2) those factors that suggest an ability to flee the jurisdiction: these are (i) ties outside the jurisdiction; (ii) resources;
(3) those factors that show the connections of anchors of an accused to the jurisdiction and thus by implication discount the flight risk;
(4) those factors that, without suggesting flight from the jurisdiction, nevertheless raise concerns about the reliability or trustworthiness of the accused to return to court. These are: (i) prior record (defaults, non-appearances or lack of co-operation); (ii) substance abuse.

The author of the paper argues for further work on these factors to confirm their "predictive utility" for bail purposes (p.712). The aim is for "risk-assessment tools" that promise a move away from "unbridled judicial discretion and from problematic judicial reliance" on what is said to be intuition: (p.712). The paper is concerned principally with the increasing prison population in America and yet the analysis of failures to appear remains helpful in other jurisdictions.

[THE NEXT PARAGRAPH IS A4-62]

Bail applications

A4-62 **23.**—(1) Any person accused on petition of a crime shall be entitled immediately, on any (other than the first) occasion on which he is brought before the sheriff prior to his committal until liberated in due course of law, to apply to the sheriff for bail, and the prosecutor shall be entitled to be heard against any such application.

(2) The sheriff shall be entitled in his discretion to refuse such application before the person accused is committed until liberated in due course of law.

(3) Where an accused is admitted to bail without being committed until liberated in due course of law, it shall not be necessary so to commit him, and it shall be lawful to serve him with an indictment or complaint without his having been previously so committed.

(4) Where bail is refused before committal until liberation in due course of law on an application under subsection (1) above, the application for bail may be renewed after such committal.

(5) Any sheriff having jurisdiction to try the offence or to commit the accused until liberated in due course of law may, at his discretion, on the application of any person who has been committed until liberation in due course of law for any crime or offence, and having given the prosecutor an opportunity to be heard, admit or refuse to admit the person to bail.

(6) Any person charged on complaint with an offence shall, on any (other than the first) occasion on which he is brought before a judge having jurisdiction to try the offence, be entitled to apply to the judge for bail and the prosecutor shall be entitled to be heard against any such application.

(7) An application under subsection (5) or (6) above shall be disposed of before the end of the day (not being a Saturday or Sunday, or a court holiday prescribed for the court which is to determine the question of bail, unless that court is sitting on that day for the disposal of criminal business) after the day of its presentation to the judge, failing which the accused shall be forthwith liberated.

(8) This section applies whether or not the accused is in custody at the time he appears for disposal of his application.

AMENDMENTS

Subss.(1) and (5) as amended by Bail, Judicial Appointments etc. (Scotland) Act (asp 9) s.12 and Sch. para.7(1).

Subs.(6) substituted by Bail, Judicial Appointments etc. (Scotland) Act (asp 9) s.12 and Sch. para.7(1)(c).

Subs.(7) substituted by Criminal Proceedings etc. (Reform) (Scotland) Act 2007 (asp 6) s.6(2). Brought into force on 10 December 2007 by SSI 2007/479.

DEFINITIONS

"bail": s.307(1). **A4-62.1**
"complaint": s.307(1).
"judge": s.307(1).
"offence": s.307(1).
"prosecutor": s.307(1).

[THE NEXT PARAGRAPH IS A4-63]

GENERAL NOTE

In *AA v HM Advocate* [2016] HCJAC 17 (February 12, 2016) the High Court of Justiciary referred to s.24 and noted that the latter refers to the right of the High Court of Justiciary to admit persons to bail. It remains clear that, where the High Court of Justiciary is seized of a case, such as where an indictment calls at a preliminary hearing, it has the power to hear and determine applications for bail: [2016] HCJAC 17 at [3]. **A4-63**

Subs.(1)

"On petition": This makes it clear that s.23(1) to (5) applies only to those accused at the outset of solemn procedure.

"A crime which is by law bailable": By s.24(1) all crimes are bailable except murder, treason and any others for which the Lord Advocate or the High Court admit the accused to bail. In *Boyle, Petr*, 1993 S.C.C.R. 251 an accused on a murder charge was admitted to bail.

"On any occasion on which he is brought before the sheriff": This makes it certain that the accused must be present at the time of the application to the sheriff.

"Prior to his committal until liberated in due course of law": An application for bail cannot be made after such committal on this wording.

"The prosecutor shall be entitled to be heard": The Crown attitude is crucial but not conclusive, having regard to s.23(2). For examples, see *HM Advocate v Saunders* (1913) 7 Adam 76 and *Mackintosh v McGlinchey*, 1921 J.C. 75.

Subs.(2)

"His discretion": The decision is one for the sheriff although the Crown attitude is crucial. There is no presumption in favour of the Crown on this question. The decision is based on attitude and is not amenable to proof. *Burn, Petr*, 2000 S.L.T. 538 requires the Crown to furnish some information to justify refusal of bail even at the first calling of the petition when moving for commital for further examination. Further, the court indicated that as soon as practicable on the completion of the Crown's further enquiries an accused ought to be brought back before the sheriff.

There are important aspects to which, broadly, the court will have regard when exercising this discretion: (1) the more serious the crime the less willing the court is to allow bail, unless the Crown offers no objection: *Rennie v Dickson* (1907) 5 Adam 372; (2) the previous record of the accused is an important factor: *MacLeod v Wright*, 1959 J.C. 12; (3) the attitude of the Crown; (4) no fixed abode weighs heavily but is not in itself sufficient to determine the question: *HM Advocate v Docherty*, 1958 S.L.T. (Notes) 50; (5) breach of earlier bail, which tends to suggest a contempt for earlier judicial fairness; (6) evidence that the accused will intimidate or threaten witnesses if released.

Subs.(3)

Ordinarily, committal for further examination is followed thereafter by committal until liberated in due course of law. This provision makes it clear that the latter need not necessarily follow the former.

Subs.(4)

A single application for bail is not provided for by this section: an application may be made at the stage of committal for further examination and may be renewed later when the accused next appears. Such an appearance may be for committal until liberated in due course of law or it may be for the purpose of such an application by arrangement.

Subs.(5)

"Jurisdiction": This may be territorial or in terms of statutory powers: see ss.4 and 5.

In *Love, Petr*, 1998 S.L.T. 461, L failed to appear for trial while on bail following committal until liberated in due course of law, and was refused bail on arrest. His application for bail had been made by petition to the nobile officium and L appealed the refusal to the High Court. His appeal by that route was held to be incompetent, the Court noting that s.32(1) was the appropriate avenue for such appeals.

Subs.(6)

"On complaint": This extends shrieval discretion referred to in earlier subsections to "any judge having jurisdiction for the offence". For a definition of "judge", see s.308(1).

Subs.(8)

This subsection rehearses the provision in s.28(3) of the 1975 Act.

The extensive modifications to s.65 of the Act which introduce an entitlement to bail (rather than being liberated) if an accused person has not been indicted within 80 days, and grant bail if a person held in custody, on petition, is not brought before a preliminary hearing within 110 days, or to trial within 140 days of full committal (rather than being declared forever free), are reflected in the amendment to this section.

Note should also be taken of the addition as a condition of bail (where bail would otherwise have been refused) of remote, i.e. electronic, monitoring in pilot schemes in Glasgow, Kilmarnock and Stirling sheriff courts with effect from 18 April 2005. See the Remote Monitoring Requirements (Prescribed Courts) (Scotland) Regulations 2005 (SSI 2007/508). See generally s.24AZ below.

Bail and liberation where person already in custody

A4-63.1 **23A.**—(1) A person may be admitted to bail under section 22A, 23, 65(8C) or 107A(7)(b) of this Act although in custody—

(a) having been refused bail in respect of another crime or offence; or
(b) serving a sentence of imprisonment.

(2) A decision to admit a person to bail by virtue of subsection (1) above does not liberate the person from the custody mentioned in that subsection.

(3) The liberation under section 22A(3), 23(7) or 107A(7)(b) of this Act of a person who may be admitted to bail by virtue of subsection (1) above does not liberate that person from the custody mentioned in that subsection.

(4) In subsection (1) above, "another crime or offence" means a crime or offence other than that giving rise to the consideration of bail under section 22A, 23, 65(8C) or 107A(7)(b) of this Act

AMENDMENTS

Section 23A inserted by Bail, Judicial Appointments etc. (Scotland) Act 2000 (asp 9) s.2.

Subss.(1) and (4) as amended by Criminal Procedure (Amendment) (Scotland) Act 2004 (asp 5) s.25 and Sch.1 para.4. Brought into force on 1 February 2005 by SSI 2004/405 (C.28) art.2.

Subss.(1), (3), (4) as amended by Criminal Justice and Licensing (Scotland) Act 2010 (asp 13) Sch.7 para.35. Brought into force on 28 March 2011 by SSI 2011/178 (C.15) art.2, Sch.1 para.1.

DEFINITIONS

A4-63.2 "bail": s.307(1).
"crime": s.307(1).
"offence": s.307(1).
"imprisonment": s.307(1).

GENERAL NOTE

The 2004 Act reformed a long-standing practice which prevented an accused person from seeking bail until he was in an immediate position to be liberated on bail. Now accused persons serving terms of imprisonment, or on remand in relation to other matters, can competently apply for bail even when the granting of it cannot be given immediate effect. A4-63.3

In *Monterroso v HM Advocate*, 2000 S.C.C.R. 974, the Appeal Court applied a purposive interpretation to subs.(1) and rejected the Crown's efforts to read the provision literally. M had been arrested on arrival in the UK and was remanded in custody on petition charges following a successful Crown bail appeal. Simultaneously the Home Secretary had refused M entry to the country as a result of these criminal allegations, a decision which led to a concurrent remand under the Immigration Act 1971 (c.7). M sought judicial review of this remand, and bail in relation to the criminal charges. The Crown contended that subs.(1) did not competently apply to M's peculiar circumstances. The Appeal Court held it competent to apply for bail but refused bail on the merits. (The civil proceedings are reported as *Monterroso v Secretary of the Home Department*, 2000 G.W.D. 33-1295).

Determination of questions of bail

23B.—(1) Bail is to be granted to an accused person— A4-63.4

(a) except where—

(i) by reference to section 23C of this Act; and

(ii) having regard to the public interest,

there is good reason for refusing bail;

(b) subject to section 23D of this Act.

(2) In determining a question of bail in accordance with subsection (1) above, the court is to consider the extent to which the public interest could, if bail were granted, be safeguarded by the imposition of bail conditions.

(3) Reference in subsections (1)(a)(ii) and (2) above to the public interest includes (without prejudice to the generality of the public interest) reference to the interests of public safety.

(4) The court must (without prejudice to any other right of the parties to be heard) give the prosecutor and the accused person an opportunity to make submissions in relation to a question of bail.

(5) The attitude of the prosecutor towards a question of bail (including as to bail conditions) does not restrict the court's exercise of its discretion in determining the question in accordance with subsection (1) above.

(6) For the purpose of so determining a question of bail (including as to bail conditions), the court may request the prosecutor or the accused person's solicitor or counsel to provide it with information relevant to the question.

(7) However, whether that party gives the court opinion as to any risk of something occurring (or any likelihood of something not occurring) is a matter for that party to decide.

AMENDMENTS

Section 23B inserted by Criminal Proceedings etc. (Reform) (Scotland) Act 2007 (asp 6) s.1. Brought into force on 10 December 2007 by SSI 2007/479 (C.40) art.3 and Schedule.

DEFINITIONS

"bail": s.307(1)
"prosecutor": s.307(1)

GENERAL NOTE

The 2007 Act enacted several statutory provisions in relation to bail. The purpose is to replace long-standing common law principles as developed from case law (see for example *Mackintosh v McGlinchy*, 1921 J.C. 75, *Smith v McC*, 1982 J.C. 67, *Spiers v Maxwell*, 1989 S.L.T. 282 and *M v Watson*, 2009 S.L.T. 1030) with statutory codified procedures. A general entitlement to bail remains, but it should now be noted that s.23B provides that the court is no longer bound to grant bail if it is not opposed by the Crown (contrast this approach with that found in *Speirs v Maxwell* above and, more recently, *M.A.R. v Dyer*, 2005 S.C.C.R. 818). The court is now entitled to apply its own discretion in assessing whether the refusal of bail would be in the public interest, including the interests of justice. A4-63.5

The broad grounds governing refusal of bail are set out in s.23C below but it will be noted that s.23D serves to limit the court's general discretion to grant bail in solemn proceedings when those proceedings involve violent or sexual offences or repeat drug trafficking offences (subss.(2) and (3)). As noted s.23B lays down a general presumption in favour of the grant of bail and entitles the court to decide bail issues irrespective of the Crown's stance (subs.(3)). The broad test to be applied by the court, as subs.(2) provides, is protection of the public interest, and the bail conditions imposed are to be framed with that test in mind.

It will be observed that subs.(4) entitles the court to request (but, apparently, not require) further information from parties to assist it in resolving bail issues. Subs.(5) envisages that the court may solicit opinions from the parties as to the risks associated with a grant of bail but does not oblige those parties to profer such opinions. Nonetheless, a party's failure to comply with a court request either for information or opinion can scarcely strengthen his own submissions.

In *JD and BK v HM Advocate* [2020] HCJAC 15 (3 April 2020) the importance of public safety was considered in the context of the substantial records of the appellants. The appeals by the appellants, against the refusal at first instance of bail, were themselves refused. Reference was made by the court, Lord Justice General (Carloway) at [14], to the "practical terms" in which bail ought not to be granted. These were that

> "bail ought not to be granted where: (1) the accused is charged with a serious offence which, if he were to be convicted, is likely to attract a substantial custodial term (e.g. one in excess of two years); and (2) the nature of his record, or other circumstances, indicate that, were he to be at liberty, he is likely to commit further violent (including sexual and domestic abuse) offences and/or likely to attempt to obstruct justice (including approaching witnesses). These are matters primarily for the judge at first instance to assess. His or her decision should not lightly be interfered with by the appellate courts."

Interestingly, and persuasively, on the question of public safety, it was held in the appeal court in the not dissimilar law of bail in Ireland that the fact that alleged offences were committed in the furtherance of the objectives of an organised crime group was a relevant consideration: *DPP v Curtis and Curtis* [2020] IEAC 85, Birmingham P. at [19] (3 April 2020).

Grounds relevant as to question of bail

A4-63.6 **23C.**—(1) In any proceedings in which a person is accused of an offence, the following are grounds on which it may be determined that there is good reason for refusing bail—

- (a) any substantial risk that the person might if granted bail—
  - (i) abscond; or
  - (ii) fail to appear at a diet of the court as required;
- (b) any substantial risk of the person committing further offences if granted bail;
- (c) any substantial risk that the person might if granted bail—
  - (i) interfere with witnesses; or
  - (ii) otherwise obstruct the course of justice,

  in relation to himself or any other person;
- (d) any other substantial factor which appears to the court to justify keeping the person in custody.

(2) In assessing the grounds specified in subsection (1) above, the court must have regard to all material considerations including (in so far as relevant in the circumstances of the case) the following examples—

- (a) the—
  - (i) nature (including level of seriousness) of the offences before the court;
  - (ii) probable disposal of the case if the person were convicted of the offences;
- (b) whether the person was subject to a bail order when the offences are alleged to have been committed;
- (c) whether the offences before the court are alleged to have been committed—
  - (i) while the person was subject to another court order;
  - (ii) while the person was on release on licence or parole;
  - (iii) during a period for which sentence of the person was deferred;

(d) the character and antecedents of the person, in particular—

(i) the nature of any previous convictions of the person (including convictions [by courts outside [Scotland]]);

(ii) whether the person has previously contravened a bail order or other court order (by committing an offence or otherwise);

(iii) whether the person has previously breached the terms of any release on licence or parole (by committing an offence or otherwise);

(iv) whether the person is serving or recently has served a sentence of imprisonment in connection with a matter referred to in sub-paragraphs (i) to (iii) above;

(e) the associations and community ties of the person.

AMENDMENTS

Section 23C inserted by Criminal Proceedings etc. (Reform) (Scotland) Act 2007(asp 6) s.1. Brought into force on 10 December 2007 by SSI 2007/479 (C.40) art.3 and Sch.

Subsection (2)(d) as amended by Criminal Justice and Licensing (Scotland) Act 2010 (asp 13) Sch.4 para.2. Brought into force on 13 December 2010 by SSI 2010/413 (C.28) art.2 Sch.1 para.1.

Words in subs.(2)(d)(i) were substituted by the Criminal Justice (EU Exit) (Scotland) (Amendment etc.) Regulations 2020 (SSI 2020/339) reg.13(2) (effective December 31, 2020 subject to transitional and saving provision specified in reg.16 of those Regulations.

DEFINITIONS

"offence": s.307(1). A4-63.7
"bail": s.307(1).
"previous convictions": s.307(1).
"imprisonment": s.307(1).

GENERAL NOTE

The grounds for refusal of bail are laid out in this section and the court has to consider whether there is "substantial risk" of an adverse outcome in the event of bail being allowed. The grounds, reflecting long-established case law, are familiar to practitioners: risk of absconding, interference with witnesses or the course of justice (i.e. obstructing the criminal investigation or failing to abide by proposed special bail conditions such as attendance at identification parades or for medical assessment), failure to appear at future diets, or further offending. A4-63.8

Subsection (1)(d) contains a catch-all provision and underlines that the risks defined in the earlier subsections are not exhaustive statements; so, for example, concerns of the accused's safety if at liberty might well be considered as a valid ground for refusal of bail.

In *M v Watson*, 2009 S.L.T. 1030 it was held that (i) the Scottish common law position that bail was to be allowed in every case unless good reason was shown as to why it should not was entirely compliant with art.5 of ECHR; and (ii) s.23D imposed an evidential burden on an accused to rebut the presumption that bail would be refused if the circumstances contained within it are applicable. The court was required to assess all of the information before it with a view to determining whether there was good reason for refusing bail having regard to the relevant risks identified by s.23C, and should not approach by considering whether a persuasive burden or onus had been satisfied.

The effects of the pandemic on questions of bail have been recognised judicially. In *D(J) v HM Advocate* [2020] HCJAC 15; 2020 G.W.D. 14-206 (3 April 2020) three main points arose from an opinion of the court given by the Lord Justice General (Lord Carloway). First, as to the effect of the COVID-19 virus, "in the present crisis, it is not known when accused persons are likely to be tried. In solemn cases, it may be several months before jury trials can be resumed. Meantime there may be an increasing number of those remanded in custody. The length of time during which a person is likely to remain on remand is a factor in deciding whether to grant bail. This factor must be given greater weight than hitherto": at [11]. "The statutory provisions (1995 Act, s.23B) continue to apply to the refusal of bail. In the ordinary case, bail must be granted except where, having regard to the public interest, notably public safety, there is a good reason to refuse bail. The court must consider the extent to which the public interest could be protected by the use of bail conditions. A good reason may arise if there is a substantial risk of the accused: absconding or failing to appear for trial; committing further offences; and interfering with witnesses or otherwise interfering with the course of justice (1995 Act s.23C). Where an accused is charged with a violent offence and has a previous conviction for violence on indictment, he is only to be granted bail in exceptional circumstances (1995 Act s.23D). The provision also applies to sexual and domestic abuse offences along with drug trafficking": at [12].

"As always, each case has to be judged on its own merits by the judge at first instance. In the current crisis, the emphasis must be, albeit not exclusively, on whether bail should be refused on the grounds of public safety. The primary question is whether the accused, if at liberty, will pose a substantial risk of committing further offences; particularly violent (including sexual and domestic abuse) offences. If there is no such risk, the accused ought to be granted bail in the ordinary case. In a s.23D case, exceptional circumstances will exist if there is no such risk. In assessing risk, the court must have regard to the feasibility of imposing conditions, including a curfew": at [13].

Secondly, "[i]n practical terms, bail ought not to be granted where: (1) the accused is charged with a serious offence which, if he were to be convicted, is likely to attract a substantial custodial terms (eg one in excess of two years); and (2) the nature of his record, or other circumstances, indicate that, were he to be at liberty, he is likely to commit further violent (including sexual and domestic abuse) offences and/or is likely to attempt to obstruct justice (including approaching witnesses). These are matters primarily for the judge at first instance to assess. His or her decision should not lightly be interfered with by the appellate courts": at [14]. Finally, "[s]hould the crisis continue beyond the currently predicted period [not specified by the Court in the Opinion], the question of bail may, of course, require to be revisited": at [15].

In *Herbasz v The Regional Court in Gdansk, Poland* [2020] EWHC 2643 (Admin) (7 October 2020) Fordham J was required to consider an application against an earlier refusal of bail in extradition proceedings. The Court noted: "since this is a case of a conviction EAW [European Arrest Warrant after trial], there is no presumption in favour of the grant of bail": at [5]. There were several key factors that were mentioned by the court as to why the applicant was refused bail: at [6]. These included: "a fear of Covid-19". However, it was noted that the applicant had not attended an earlier hearing and he did not say that he was "suffering from Covid-19". It was considered that there was no reason to challenge the earlier view that the applicant was: "attempting to frustrate the proceedings": at [6]. Bail was refused.

Restriction on bail in certain solemn cases

A4-63.9 **23D.**—(1) Where subsection (2) or (3) below applies, a person is to be granted bail in solemn proceedings only if there are exceptional circumstances justifying bail.

(2) This subsection applies where the person—

(a) is accused in the proceedings of an offence falling within subsection (3A); and

(b) has a previous conviction on indictment for an offence falling within subsection (3A).

(3) This subsection applies where the person—

(a) is accused in the proceedings of a drug trafficking offence; and

(b) has a previous conviction on indictment for a drug trafficking offence.

(3A) An offence falls within this subsection if it is—

(a) a violent offence,

(b) a sexual offence, or

(c) a domestic abuse offence.

(4) For the purposes of this section—

"drug trafficking offence" has the meaning given by section 49(5) of the Proceeds of Crime (Scotland) Act 1995 (c. 43);

"domestic abuse offence" means—

(a) an offence under section 1(1) of the Domestic Abuse (Scotland) Act 2018, or

(b) an offence that is aggravated as described in section 1(1)(a) of the Abusive Behaviour and Sexual Harm (Scotland) Act 2016;

"sexual offence" has the meaning given by section 210A(10) and (11) of this Act;

"violent offence" means any offence (other than a sexual offence) inferring personal violence.

(5) Any reference in this section to a conviction on indictment for a type of offence includes—

(a) a conviction on indictment in England and Wales or Northern Ireland for an equivalent offence;

(b) [if the court considers appropriate] a conviction in a member State of the European Union […] which is equivalent to conviction on indictment for an equivalent offence.

(6) Any issue of equivalence arising in pursuance of subsection (5) above is for the court to determine.

(7) This section is without prejudice to section 23C of this Act.

AMENDMENTS

Section 23D inserted by Criminal Proceedings etc. (Reform) (Scotland) Act 2007 (asp 6) s.1. Brought into force on 10 December 2007 by SSI 2007/479 (C.40) art.3 and Sch.

Subsection (2), subs.(5) as amended, subs.(3A) inserted, by Domestic Abuse (Scotland) Act 2018 (asp 5) Sch.1(1)(1) para.1(2) (effective 1 April 2019 in relation to proceedings in respect of acts done or omissions made on or after 1 April 2019).

Definition of "domestic abuse offence" in subs.(4) inserted by Domestic Abuse (Scotland) Act 2018 (asp 5) Sch.1(1)(1) para.1(2)(c) (effective 1 April 2019 in relation to proceedings in respect of acts done or omissions made on or after 1 April 2019).

Words in subs.(5)(b) were inserted by the Criminal Justice (EU Exit) (Scotland) (Amendment etc.) Regulations 2020 (SSI 2020/339) reg.13(3)(a) (effective December 31, 2020 subject to transitional and saving provision specified in reg.16 of those Regulations.

Words omitted from subs.(5)(b) were repealed by the Criminal Justice (EU Exit) (Scotland) (Amendment etc.) Regulations 2020 (SSI 2020/339) reg.13(3)(b) (effective December 31, 2020 subject to transitional and saving provision specified in reg.16 of those Regulations.

DEFINITIONS

"bail": s.307(1). A4-63.10

GENERAL NOTE

While s.23B(3) of the Act now generally entitles the court to consider bail or its refusal irrespective of the attitude of the prosecutor, this section is broadly prescriptive in form and limits the availability of bail in solemn proceedings involving violent offences, sexual offences (see s.210A of the Act), or repeat drug trafficking offences (see both the very broad definition thereof in s.49(2) of the Proceeds of Crime (Scotland) Act 1995 (c.43) and, generally, s.205B of the 1995 Act). Subsection (5) entitles the court to refer to serious convictions recorded against the accused elsewhere in the UK, or within the EU. (It is submitted that this definition would be broad enough to extend to convictions before courts martial). A4-63.11

Subs.(6) neatly entitles the court to determine the applicability of any non-Scottish conviction founded upon by the Crown for itself but, it is argued, that the court's decision on the issue and its impact upon the question of bail, could properly be the subject of appeal as surely as any other grounds.

Despite the prescriptive terms of the section it will be noted that subs.(7) operates without prejudice to the court's general grounds for grant or refusal of bail as set out in s.23C. Still the terms of s.23D would undoubtedly add weight to Crown opposition to bail in cases involving violent or sexual or drug trafficking offences.

In *M v Watson*, 2009 S.L.T. 1030 it was held that (i) that the Scottish common law position that bail was to be allowed in every case unless good reason was shown as to why it should not was entirely compliant with art.5 of ECHR; and (ii) s.23D imposed an evidential burden on an accused to rebut the presumption that bail would be refused if the circumstances contained within it are applicable. The court was required to assess all of the information before it with a view to determining whether there was good reason for refusing bail having regard to the relevant risks identified by s.23C, and should not approach by considering whether a persuasive burden or onus had been satisfied.

"Exceptional circumstances"

The term "exceptional circumstances" in s.23(D)(1) was considered in *HM Advocate v CK*, 2011 S.C.L. 721; 2011 S.C.C.R. 381 on 6 May 2011. The sheriff presiding at an application for bail was persuaded that new legal aid regulations were so disadvantageous to solicitors instructed in solemn cases that the accused ought to be at liberty in order to ensure that her solicitors could prepare the case to ensure that she would get a fair trial. The Crown appealed that decision by the sheriff. After hearing counsel for both sides the appeal court noted (at [11]) that the sheriff, in effect, proceeded to determine the issue of a fair trial at the earliest stage in the proceedings and not at "a hearing designed specifically to discuss that question". The question of bail was considered notwithstanding the provisions of s.23D. Further, at [12], the judicial assessment of whether or not an accused person can obtain, or has obtained, a fair trial for the purposes of art.6 of the ECHR is normally a decision which can only be reached by having regard to all the relevant factors which fall to be taken into account. It must be a rare case where a judge is able to reach a conclusion at a hearing regarding bail that he has before him all the information necessary to reach a properly considered judgement that, unless the accused person who for good reason should otherwise remain in custody is liberated, he or she will inevitably fail to have a fair trial. The Crown appeal was allowed.

Bail and bail conditions

24.—(1) All crimes and offences are bailable. A4-64

(2) Nothing in this Act shall affect the right of the Lord Advocate or the High Court to admit to bail any person charged with any crime or offence.

(2A) Whenever the court grants or refuses bail, it shall state its reasons.

(2B) Where the court—

(a) grants bail to a person accused of a sexual offence (having the meaning given by section 210A(10) and (11) of this Act); and

(b) does so without imposing on the accused further conditions under subsection (4)(b)(i) below,

the court shall also state why it considers in the circumstances of the case that such conditions are unnecessary.

(3) It shall not be lawful to grant bail or release for a pledge or deposit of money, and—

(a) release on bail may be granted only on conditions which subject to subsection (6) below, shall not include a pledge or deposit of money;

(b) liberation may be granted by the police under section 25 of the Criminal Justice (Scotland) Act 2016.

(4) In granting bail the court or, as the case may be, the Lord Advocate shall impose on the accused—

(a) the standard conditions; and

(b) such further conditions as the court or, as the case may be, the Lord Advocate considers necessary to secure—

(i) that the standard conditions are observed;

(ii) […]

(5) The standard conditions referred to in subsection (4) above are conditions that the accused—

(a) appears at the appointed time at every diet relating to the offence with which he is charged of which he is given due notice or at which he is required by this Act to appear;

(b) does not commit an offence while on bail;

(c) does not interfere with witnesses or otherwise obstruct the course of justice whether in relation to himself or any other person;

(ca) does not behave in a manner which causes, or is likely to cause, alarm or distress to witnesses;

(cb) whenever reasonably instructed by a constable to do so—

(i) participates in an identification parade or other identification procedure; and

(ii) allows any print, impression or sample to be taken from the accused;

(d) makes himself available for the purpose of enabling enquiries or a report to be made to assist the court in dealing with him for the offence with which he is charged; and.

(e) where the (or an) offence in respect of which he is admitted to bail is one listed in subsection (7A)(b), does not seek to obtain, otherwise than by way of a solicitor, any precognition of or statement by the complainer in relation to the subject matter of the offence.

(6) The court or, as the case may be, the Lord Advocate may impose as one of the conditions of release on bail a requirement that the accused or a cautioner on his behalf deposits a sum of money in court, but only where the court or, as the case may be, the Lord Advocate is satisfied that the imposition of such condition is appropriate to the special circumstances of the case.

(6A) Subsection (6) above does not apply in relation to an accused admitted to bail under section 65(8C) of this Act.

(7) In any enactment, including this Act and any enactment passed after this Act—

(a) any reference to bail shall be construed as a reference to release on conditions in accordance with this Act or to conditions imposed on bail, as the context requires;

(b) any reference to an amount of bail fixed shall be construed as a reference to conditions, including a sum required to be deposited under subsection (6) above;

(c) any reference to finding bail or finding sufficient bail shall be construed as a reference to acceptance of conditions imposed or the finding of a sum required to be deposited under subsection (6) above.

(7A) For the purpose of subsection (5)(e)—

(a) "complainer" means the person against whom the offence is alleged to have been committed,

(b) the list is—

(i) an offence to which section 288C applies (certain sexual offending),

(ii) an offence to which section 288DC applies (domestic abuse cases).

(8) In this section and sections 25 and 27 to 29 of this Act, references to an accused and to appearance at a diet shall include references respectively to an appellant and to appearance at the court on the day fixed for the hearing of an appeal.

AMENDMENTS

Subs.(1) as amended by Bail, Judicial Appointments etc. (Scotland) Act 2000 (asp 9) s.3(1).

Subs.(5) as amended, and subs.(7A) inserted, by Sexual Offences (Procedure and Evidence) (Scotland) Act 2002 (asp 9) s.5. Brought into force by SSI 2002/443 (C.24) art.4 (effective from 1 November 2002).

Subs.(5)(a) as amended, and subs.(6A) inserted, by Criminal Procedure (Amendment) (Scotland) Act 2004 (asp 5) s.25 and Sch.1 para.5. Brought into force on 1 February 2005 by SSI 2004/405 (C.28) art.2.

Subss.(2A) and (2B) inserted and subs(4)(b)(i) and (5) as amended by Criminal Proceedings etc. (Reform) (Scotland) Act 2007. Brought into force on 10 December 2007 by SSI 2007/479.

Subs.(4)(b)(ii) repealed, subs.(5)(cb) inserted, by Criminal Justice and Licensing (Scotland) Act 2010 (asp 13) s.58. Brought into force on 28 March 2011 (for all purposes where the court grants bail to a person on or after 28 March 2011) by SSI 2011/178 (C.15) art.2, Sch.1 para.1.

Subs.(3)(b) as amended by Criminal Justice (Scotland) Act 2016 (Consequential and Supplementary Modifications) Regulations 2017 (SSI 2017/452) Sch.1 para.12 (effective 25 January 2018).

Subs.(5)(e) amended, subs.(7A) substituted, by Domestic Abuse (Scotland) Act 2018 (asp 5) Sch.1(1)(2) para.2(2) (effective 1 April 2019 in relation to proceedings in respect of acts done or omissions made on or after 1 April 2019).

DEFINITIONS A4-64.1

"bail": s.307(1).
"crime": s.307(1).
"diet": s.307(1).
"High Court": s.307(1).
"offences": s.307(1).
"standard conditions, the": s.24(5).
"witness": s.307(1).
"fine": s.307(1).
"standard scale": s.225(1).
"imprisonment": s.307(1).

[THE NEXT PARAGRAPH IS A4-65]

GENERAL NOTE

An application for bail is largely founded on the presumption of innocence: Scott, Appellant (1890) S. L. Rep. 307 per Lord Stormont Darling and Lord McLaren.

Ordinarily, a bail order granted by the court will echo the terms of subs.(5) but additional conditions can be imposed, including, where circumstances warrant, the imposition of money bail as caution albeit this is unusual (see for example, *Adam v Kirichenko*, 1995 G.W.D. 26-1373). Note, however, that money bail cannot be imposed as a bail condition where an accused, previously in custody, is granted bail pursuant to s.65(8C) below, i.e. where he has not been indicted for trial within 80 days or his custody A4-65 preliminary diet or trial have not commenced within the 110 and 140 day limits. The standard bail conditions now require an accused to attend at any diet or hearing of which he has been given due notice. Attention is drawn to s.24A of the Act which allows the court to impose a remote monitoring restriction on an accused's movements as a further condition of bail.

European authorities were discussed in *Roque v HM Advocate* (Crown Office circular A2/2001) in which the accused, a Portuguese national charged on petition with contravening s.1 of the Road Traffic Act 1988 and refused bail, contended that the risk of absconding was not itself sufficient reason for refusing bail. The court accepted that any distinction between the accused and a United Kingdom national for bail purposes had to have an objective and reasonable justification and would not, of course, be based simply on grounds of nationality but on the interaction of a number of related factors. In the event the bail conditions imposed were stringent requiring deposit of a substantial money sum, residence in Scotland, surrender of passport and regular attendance at a police office. The issues which may arise when an accused's passport is to be surrendered as a special bail condition are discussed at A4-67 below.

Note that additional conditions apply when an accused has been charged on a complaint or (more likely) a petition, with a sexual offence listed in s.288C of the Act. In that event the accused accepts that he must not seek to precognosce the complainer in respect of that offence. It is submitted that in circumstances where the fiscal's subsequent enquiries disclose that the offence charged involves a substantial sexual element (s.288C(4)), or where listed sexual offences are revealed, there are two options; either issue a superseding complaint or petition or seek a review of the earlier bail conditions as permitted by s.31 of the Act.

In *AA v HM Advocate* [2016] HCJAC 17 (12 February 2016) the High Court of Justiciary referred to s.24 and noted that the latter refers to the right of the High Court of Justiciary to admit persons to bail. It remains clear that, where the High Court of Justiciary is seized of a case, such as where an indictment calls at a preliminary hearing, it has the power to hear and determine applications for bail: [2016] HCJAC 17 at [3].

> "Where an indictment has been served, citing an accused to a Preliminary Hearing in the High Court, once that diet has called, the appropriate court to decide any applications for bail is that court. That is because it is inevitable that that court will be apprised of all the relevant information relative to the progress of the case. It is therefore not appropriate to revert to the sheriff once the case has called in the High Court. It follows that the procedure to appeal the original sheriff's decision on bail, after the calling of the Preliminary Hearing, was inappropriate, as was also the procedure which has followed thereon. If an accused person wishes to seek bail upon a trial diet being fixed at a Preliminary Hearing, he should seek that from the Preliminary Hearing judge" at [7].

Bail conditions are imposed not due to any Crown policy but because the court considers them to be necessary and appropriate: *HM Advocate v Porch* [2015] HCJAC 111; 2016 S.L.T. 149; 2016 S.C.L. 128.

s.24(4)(b)

A4-64.1 There seems to be no limit (other than those of reason and common sense) to the "further conditions" that may be imposed in terms of s.24(4)(b) of the 1995 Act: for example, see *Stott v Hussain*, 2004 G.W.D. 10–227 and *Nisbet v McKinlay*, 2009 G.W.D. 18–284.

There requires, however, to be a degree of precision in any condition imposed given the presumption of innocence and the sometimes contradictory restrictions on personal liberty: in *Cameron v Cameron*, 2011 G.W.D. 30-648 a suggested condition not to attend "football matches" was more specifically recorded as not to attend "organised professional football matches". In this respect it may be of interest to note the use of knowledge of the locality in *Burgh of Dunblane, Petitioners*, 1947 S.L.T. (Sh. Ct.) 27. That authority was concerned with a civil matter but it is of relevance as the issue there was also one of the liberty of the subject.

In the interests of the comity of neighbouring jurisdictions, a persuasive authority regarding expedient conditions imposed judicially, and certainly analogous to bail conditions, is that of *Purdue v DPP* [2016] IEHC 619 (8 November 2016). The question for the High Court of Ireland was whether a district judge was correct in law to suspend part of the applicant's sentence of detention on condition that: (1) the applicant did not partake of any alcohol; (2) did not leave a named county of Ireland without the consent of the Probation Service with whom the applicant was then liaising.

In the judgement of Barrett J, relying on various earlier Irish authorities, it was held that the first condition amounted to an ancillary punishment as it did not correspond to the particular circumstances of the offence or indeed the applicant (at [9]). As regards the second condition, there was no evidence before the court to suggest that the restrictions on the liberty of movement could reasonably be considered appropriate to the offences to which the applicant had pleaded guilty, or proportionate or necessary in reducing the likelihood of re-offending. The restriction on movement represented "an unnecessary, unwarranted, and unlawful restriction on, and interference with, [the applicant's] constitutional right to liberty" (at [14]).

Finally, at [15]–[17], it could not be said that the applicant had acquiesced in these conditions merely because he had signed a suspended sentence bond. The alternative to not signing was a custodial sentence to be imposed immediately, and it was noted that the applicant was then still a minor. The decision of the court was that the two conditions complained of were to be removed (at [19]).

For a special bail condition to be imposed in terms of s.24(4)(b) there requires to be a rational connection between the condition and the need to prevent further offending. The condition should not be disproportionate and should be necessary to prevent an accused from committing further offences: *Pollock-Smith v Corrins* [2019] HCJAC 67 at [5].

s.24(5)(cb)

The inclusion as a standard bail condition of a requirement that an accused participate, when required, in an identification parade is not free of difficulty. To begin with it has to be assumed that the parade or procedure would relate only to the matters libelled in the proceedings from which the bail order arose. More fundamental still is the Convention compatibility of an all-encompassing condition at the pre-trial stage. While such a condition can be justifiable and be imposed on a case by case basis, in *Cameron v Cottam* [2012] HCJAC 19; 2012 S.C.C.R. 271, the Appeal Court held that its inclusion as a standard bail condition was not Convention-compliant, observing that Crown opposition to bail might remain necessary until the requisite identification parade had been conducted. Even this option is not devoid of procedural complications, especially in summary proceedings. It may be preferable to place incidental applications for parades before the court.

s.24(6)

The deposit of a sum of money in court as a condition of bail is now probably rare. However, such a deposit is competent and may occur: see *Urquhart, Petitioner*, 2003 G.W.D. 26–735 (French citizen required to lodge money in euros).

Until the advent of the Bail, Judicial Appointments etc. (Scotland) Act 2000 (asp 9), bail in murder cases could only be obtained at the behest of the Lord Advocate (whose refusal to admit to bail could not be challenged) or by petition to the nobile officium: otherwise murder was a non-bailable offence (see, for example, *HM Advocate v Renwicks*, 1998 S.C.C.R. 417; 1999 S.L.T. 407). Now all crimes are potentially bailable albeit s.23D of the Act seeks to restrict its availability for repeat drug trafficking, violent, or sexual offenders. The broad grounds for opposition to, or refusal of, bail are now statutorily set out in s.23C of the Act. It is worth noting that the right of the Lord Advocate to admit persons to bail even after it has been refused, or not sought, at earlier points in the proceedings is preserved.

Subs.(2A)

This provision applied to all bail orders decided upon by the court after 10 December 2007 (orders granted before that date, and continued or varied thereafter are not affected by this subsection) now requires the judge to state the reasons for grant or refusal of a bail application. It has been a common, but by no means universal, practice of judges to make such a pronouncement already; the mandatory provision may improve the processing of any resulting bail appeals. (Even where no application has been made, the court, with a view to being Convention-compliant, already as a matter of course ex proprio motu considers the question of bail).

Subs.(5)

Subs.(5)(ca) adds to the existing standard conditions of bail but as with subs.(2A) above applies only to bail orders granted from 10 December 2007. This new condition is intended to combat conduct which, while falling short of being overtly intimidatory, nonetheless alarms or distresses witnesses or is so intended.

Sensibly subs.(5)(cb) introduced by the Criminal Justice and Licensing (Scotland) Act 2010 (asp 13) adds participation in an identification parade to the standard conditions of bail; the reasonableness test in this measure seems unlikely to evoke much difficulty but it is curious that no express provision setting out the timescale for notice of, or participation in, an identification parade or parades has been included.

European Protection Orders

Following the European Protection Order (Scotland) Regulations 2015 (SSI 2015/107), which enabled Scottish courts to make European Protection Orders and to enforce such orders intimated by member states of the EU, it is conceivable that the terms of a bail order could, on the application of the "protected person", be extended furth of Scotland. See generally s.254A below and note the all-embracing definition there of a "protection measure". Whether an unintended consequence or not, the possibility is postulated in the Scottish Courts Service guidance on these orders.

[THE NEXT PARAGRAPH IS A4-65.4]

Bail conditions: remote monitoring of restrictions on movements

24A. […]

AMENDMENTS

Section 24A inserted by Criminal Procedure (Amendment) (Scotland) Act 2004 (asp 5) s.17. Brought into force on 4 October 2004 by SSI 2004/405 (C.28) art.2(1). **A4-65.4**

Section 24A repealed by Criminal Justice and Licensing (Scotland) Act 2010 (asp 13) s.59. Brought into force on 13 December 2010 by SSI 2010/413 (C.28) art.2, Sch.1 para.1.

Regulations as to power to impose remote monitoring requirements under section 24A

A4-65.5 **24B.** [...]

AMENDMENTS

Section 24B inserted by Criminal Procedure (Amendment) (Scotland) Act 2004 (asp 5) s.17. Brought into force on 4 October 2004 by SSI 2004/405 (C.28) art.2(1).

Section 24B repealed by Criminal Justice and Licensing (Scotland) Act 2010 (asp 13) s.59. Brought into force on 13 December 2010 by SSI 2010/413 (C.28) art.2, Sch.1 para.1.

Monitoring of compliance in pursuance of requirements imposed under section 24A

A4-65.6 **24C.** [...]

AMENDMENTS

Section 24C inserted by Criminal Procedure (Amendment) (Scotland) Act 2004 (asp 5) s.17. Brought into force on 4 October 2004 by SSI 2004/405 (C.28) art.2(1).

Section 24C repealed by Criminal Justice and Licensing (Scotland) Act 2010 (asp 13) s.59. Brought into force on 13 December 2010 by SSI 2010/413 (C.28) art.2, Sch.1 para.1.

Remote monitoring

A4-65.7 **24D.** [...]

AMENDMENTS

Section 24D inserted by Criminal Procedure (Amendment) (Scotland) Act 2004 (asp 5) s.17. Brought into force on 4 October 2004 by SSI 2004/405 (C.28) art.2(1).

Section 24D repealed by Criminal Justice and Licensing (Scotland) Act 2010 (asp 13) s.59. Brought into force on 13 December 2010 by SSI 2010/413 (C.28) art.2, Sch.1 para.1.

Documentary evidence in proceedings for breach of bail conditions being remotely monitored

A4-65.8 **24E.** [...]

AMENDMENTS

Section 24E inserted by Criminal Procedure (Amendment) (Scotland) Act 2004 (asp 5) s.17. Brought into force on 4 October 2004 by SSI 2004/405 (C.28) art.2(1).

Section 24E repealed by Criminal Justice and Licensing (Scotland) Act 2010 (asp 13) s.59. Brought into force on 13 December 2010 by SSI 2010/413 (C.28) art.2, Sch.1 para.1.

Bail: extradition proceedings

A4-65.9 **24F.**—(1) In the application of the provisions of this Part by virtue of section 9(2) or 77(2) of the Extradition Act 2003 (judge's powers at extradition hearing), those provisions apply with the modifications that—

- (a) references to the prosecutor are to be read as references to a person acting on behalf of the territory to which extradition is sought;
- (b) the right of the Lord Advocate mentioned in section 24(2) of this Act applies to a person subject to extradition proceedings as it applies to a person charged with any crime or offence;
- (c) the following do not apply—
  - (i) paragraph (b) of section 24(3); and
  - (ii) subsection (3) of section 30; and
- (d) sections 28(1) and 33 apply to a person subject to extradition proceedings as they apply to an accused.

(2) Section 32 of this Act applies in relation to a refusal of bail, the amount of bail or a decision to allow bail or ordain appearance in proceedings under this Part as the Part applies by virtue of the sections of that Act of 2003 mentioned in subsection (1) above.

(3) The Scottish Ministers may, by order, for the purposes of section 9(2) or 77(2) of the Extradition Act 2003 make such amendments to this Part as they consider necessary or expedient.

(4) The order making power in subsection (3) above shall be exercisable by statutory instrument subject to annulment in pursuance of a resolution of the Scottish Parliament.

AMENDMENTS

Section 24F inserted as s.24A by Extradition Act 2003 (c.41) s.199. Brought into force on 1 January 2004 by SI 2003/3103 (C.122) art.2.

Renumbered to s.24F by Criminal Procedure (Amendment) (Scotland) Act 2004 (Incidental, Supplemental and Consequential Provisions) Order 2005 (SSI 2005/40) art.4(2) (effective 31 January 2005).

DEFINITION

"prosecutor": s.307(1). A4-65.10

GENERAL NOTE

Imprisonment pending the determination of extradition proceedings can be forestalled in appropriate cases by the grant of bail. References to the prosecutor are to be read as referring to the person acting on behalf of the country applying to the Scottish court for an extradition order (subs.(1)(a)); in practice these proceedings are heard by designated Edinburgh sheriffs, once the Crown has initiated the application. A4-65.11

Subs.(1)(b) retains the right of the Lord Advocate to exercise discretion to admit a person, subject to extradition proceedings, to Lord Advocate's bail. The effect of subs.(1)(c) is twofold; it permits pledges or a deposit of money as an element of an extradition bail order and provides that extradition bail reviews will not be subject to any restriction of time as generally apply to criminal proceedings (see s.30(3) below). Although extradition proceedings are civil proceedings it will be noted that any appeal is dealt with by the High Court in terms of s.32 of the present Act.

A police constable has power to arrest any party he suspects to be, or about to be, in breach of an extradition bail order (subs.(1)(d) and s.28(1)). It follows that the arrestee has thereafter to be placed before the court which first considered bail and not the sheriff court within whose territorial jurisdiction he is found (see s.28(2) below).

[THE NEXT PARAGRAPH IS A4-66]

Bail conditions: supplementary

25.—(A1) When granting bail, the court shall (if the accused is present) explain to the accused in ordinary language— A4-66

(a) the effect of the conditions imposed;
(b) the effect of the requirement under subsection (2B) below; and
(c) the consequences which may follow a breach of any of those conditions or that requirement.

(B1) The accused shall (whether or not the accused is present when bail is granted) be given a written explanation in ordinary language of the matters mentioned in paragraphs (a) to (c) of subsection (A1) above.

(C1) Such a written explanation may be contained in the copy of the bail order given to the accused or in another document.

(1) The court shall specify in the order granting bail, a copy of which shall be given to the accused—

(a) the conditions imposed; and
(aa) that breach of a condition imposed is an offence and renders the accused liable to arrest, prosecution and punishment under this Act;
(b) an address, within the United Kingdom (being the accused's normal place

of residence or such other place as the court may, on cause shown, direct) which, subject to subsection (2) below, shall be his proper domicile of citation.

(2) The court may on application in writing by the accused while he is on bail alter the address specified in the order granting bail, and this new address shall, as from such date as the court may direct, become his proper domicile of citation; and the court shall notify the accused of its decision on any application under this subsection.

(2A) Where an application is made under subsection (2) above—

(a) the application shall be intimated by the accused immediately and in writing to the Crown Agent and for that purpose the application shall be taken to be intimated to the Crown Agent if intimation of it is sent to the procurator fiscal for the sheriff court district in which bail was granted; and

(b) the court shall, before determining the application, give the prosecutor an opportunity to be heard.

(2B) Where the domicile of citation specified in an order granting bail ceases to be the accused's normal place of residence, the accused must make an application under subsection (2) above within 7 days of that happening.

(2C) A person who without reasonable excuse contravenes subsection (2B) above is guilty of an offence and is liable—

(a) on conviction in the JP court, to a fine not exceeding level 3 on the standard scale or to imprisonment for a period not exceeding 60 days or to both;

(b) in any other case, to a fine not exceeding level 3 on the standard scale or to imprisonment for a period not exceeding 12 months or to both.

(3) In this section "proper domicile of citation" means the address at which the accused may be cited to appear at any diet relating to the offence with which he is charged or an offence charged in the same proceedings as that offence or to which any other intimation or document may be sent; and any citation at or the sending of an intimation or document to the proper domicile of citation shall be presumed to have been duly carried out.

(4) In this section, references to the court (other than in subsection (2A)) shall, in relation to a person who has been admitted to bail by the Lord Advocate, be read as if they were references to the Lord Advocate.

AMENDMENTS

Subs.(4) inserted by Criminal Procedure (Amendment) (Scotland) Act 2004 (asp 5) s.25 and Sch.1, para.6. Brought into force on October 4, 2004 by SSI 2004/405 (C.28).

Subs.(2A) inserted by Criminal Procedure (Amendment) (Scotland) Act 2004 (asp 5) s.18(2). Brought into force on February 1, 2005 by SSI 2004/405 (C.28) art.2.

Subs.(2A)(a) as amended by Criminal Procedure (Amendment) (Scotland) Act 2004 (Incidental, Supplemental and Consequential Provisions) Order 2005 (SSI 2005/40) art.3.

Subs.(1) as amended and subs.(A1), (B1), (C1), (2B) and (2C) inserted by Criminal Proceedings etc. (Reform) (Scotland) Act 2007 (asp 6) s.2(2). Brought into force on December 10, 2007 by SSI 2007/479.

DEFINITIONS

A4-66.1 "bail": s.307(1).
"order": s.307(1).
"proper domicile of citation": s.25(3).

[THE NEXT PARAGRAPH IS A4-67]

GENERAL NOTE

A4-67 The importance for the Crown of this provision lies in the terms of s.25(2) which allows service of the citation to appear at any diet on the accused at the "proper domicile of citation". The importance for the accused lies in his release but there is a balancing factor of providing such a domicile of citation: change is possible on application but failure to observe the requirements has serious consequences, or may have:

McMahon v MacPhail, 1991 S.C.C.R. 470. Further, the evidence of the points in this section is routine evidence under s.280(1) of and Sch.9 to this Act and may thus be embodied in a certificate for service on the accused.

In *HM Advocate v W.* (High Court of Justiciary, February 2001, unreported) the Crown petitioned the *nobile officium* to rescind a purported order by the sheriff which had altered the accused's bail domicile from an address in Northern Ireland, to an address in Eire. The bail application had not been opposed by the procurator fiscal but the Crown stance, following subs.(1)(b), was that such a variation was ultra vires and thus incapable of consent. The Appeal Court struck out the alteration, and thus reinstated the earlier bail domicile.

A specific condition requiring the accused to surrender his passport should also stipulate that no application should be made either for the issue of a new passport or the issue of a replacement.

Subs.(2A) provides simplified means for an accused to intimate proposed changes to his bail domicile to the Crown Agent rather than to the relevant sheriff clerk or Clerk of Justiciary. It is now permissible to intimate such changes to the local procurator fiscal; see SSI 2005/40, art.3(4).

In the case of an accused admitted to Lord Advocate's bail (see s.24(2) and (6) above) such intimation is to be made to the Lord Advocate.

Subs.(A1)

Utilising well-tried phraseology which features in Part IX of the 1995 Act (see, for example s.234AA(6)) the court is now obliged to explain the standard bail conditions to the accused in everyday language. The accused's (oft-neglected) obligation is to inform the court of any change in address, and he is warned of the penal consequences for any failure on his part to so inform the court.

Subs.(1)

This subsection sets out the information to be contained in all bail orders. Perhaps stating the obvious, particularly when the court is already obliged, in accordance with s.25(A1) now introduced, to explain to an accused in ordinary language the consequences flowing from failure to adhere to the standard bail conditions, this provision added as subs.(1)(aa) now demands that the copy bail order served upon the accused must direct his attention to these consequences.

Subss.(2A) and (2B)

The procedures to be followed when seeking to alter the accused's nominated domicile are found here. Once admitted to bail in criminal proceedings an accused is now placed under an obligation to advise the court of any change to his bail address. This need not necessarily be (but often is) his "domicile of citation" —the address to which any case-related documentation can be served. Application must be made in writing and served upon the Crown within seven days of the change taking effect. Perhaps the significance of this addition to the Criminal Procedure (Scotland) Act 1995 is diminished to an extent by the provisions of s.72G which, in solemn proceedings, permit service of any lawful document in those proceedings on the solicitor nominated by the accused (see s.72F of that Act), an altogether simpler process.

The penalties for an accused's failure to keep the court informed timeously (or even at all) of his removal to another address are set out in subs.(2C)(a) for JP courts (the statutory successor to district courts in Scotland, introduced by s.46 of the 2007 Act), and in subs.(2C)(b) for sheriff summary and all solemn courts.

The latter penalties in part reflect the increased sentencing powers available to sheriff summary courts by means of s.35(1) of the 2006 Act. Curiously, the monetary penalty which can be imposed for such an offence in any proceedings is set at a modest Level 3 fine.Note, however, that these enhanced penalties apply only to contraventions of bail orders granted on or after December 10, 2007; see the Criminal Proceedings etc. (Reform) (Scotland) Act 2007 (Commencement No.2 and Transitional Provisions and Savings) Order 2007 (SSI 2007/479) art. 4.

Failure to accept conditions of bail under section 65(8C): continued detention of accused

25A. An accused who— A4-67.1

(a) is, by virtue of subsection (4) of section 65 of this Act, entitled to be admitted to bail; but

(b) fails to accept any of the conditions imposed by the court on bail under subsection (8C) of that section,

shall continue to be detained under the committal warrant for so long as he fails to accept any of those conditions.

AMENDMENTS

Section 25A inserted by Criminal Procedure (Amendment) (Scotland) Act 2004 (asp 5) s.25 and Sch.1 para.7. Brought into force on February 1, 2005 by SSI 2004/405 (C.28) art.2.

DEFINITIONS

A4-67.2 "bail": s.307(1).

GENERAL NOTE

A4-67.3 Before describing the operation of this section, some explanation of its context is appropriate.

One of the innovations introduced by the 2004 Act has been the restriction upon the operation of s.65(4) where an accused in custody is not indicted or brought to trial within the requisite 80 and 110 days; hitherto the consequence of a failure on the part of the Crown to meet these timescales was that the accused would have to be liberated from custody in the first case, and be forever free of all other process in the second. In neither case would the accused be required to provide a bail address of any kind even though the Crown would almost inevitably seek extensions of the timebars to keep proceedings alive.

Section 65(8C) of the Act as now amended is less final in its terms; henceforth the consequences of (a) failure to serve an indictment within 80 days of full committal, (b) failure to hold a preliminary diet within 110 days, and (c) failure to commence the trial within 140 days, in High Court cases only, entitles the accused to be admitted to bail.

(Note that the more familiar 80 and 110 day time limits for service of an indictment and bringing it to trial still apply to sheriff solemn proceedings). Thus s.25A provides that once an accused remanded on petition has to be granted bail, it falls to the court to set bail conditions. If the accused declines to accept the conditions, he stays in custody—the existing petition committal warrant remaining in force.

Section 25A operates without prejudice to the rights of the prosecutor to seek an extension of any (or all) of the periods mentioned above, or to the power of a single judge or appellate court to refuse bail to the accused on the merits, subject always to the necessary timebar extensions being granted to the Crown.

Bail: circumstances where not available

A4-68 **26.** […]

AMENDMENTS

Deleted by s.4 of the Bail, Judicial Appointments etc. (Scotland) Act 2000 (asp 9).

GENERAL NOTE

A4-69 This section previously contained an absolute prohibition upon the grant of bail where an accused charged with attempted murder, culpable homicide, rape or attempted rape had a previous conviction for such an offence, or murder or manslaughter. The imperative nature of the section is plainly at odds with an accused's art.6 rights under the European Convention. Grounds for opposition to bail are discussed at para.A4-65 above.

Breach of bail conditions: offences

A4-70 **27.**—(1) Subject to subsection (7) below, an accused who having been granted bail fails without reasonable excuse—

(a) to appear at the time and place appointed for any diet of which he has been given due notice or at which he is required by this Act to appear; or

(b) to comply with any other condition imposed on bail,

shall, subject to subsection (3) below, be guilty of an offence and liable on conviction to the penalties specified in subsection (2) below.

(2) The penalties mentioned in subsection (1) above are—

(a) a fine not exceeding level 3 on the standard scale; and

(b) imprisonment for a period—

(i) where conviction is in the JP court, not exceeding 60 days; or

(ii) in any other case, not exceeding 12 months.

(3) Where, and to the extent that, the failure referred to in subsection (1)(b) above consists in the accused having committed an offence while on bail (in this section referred to as "the subsequent offence"), he shall not be guilty of an offence under that subsection but, subject to subsection (4) below, the court which sentences him for the subsequent offence shall, in determining the appropriate sentence or disposal for that offence, have regard to—

(a) the fact that the offence was committed by him while on bail and the number of bail orders to which he was subject when the offence was committed;

(b) any previous conviction of the accused of an offence under subsection (1)(b) above; and

(c) the extent to which the sentence or disposal in respect of any previous conviction of the accused differed, by virtue of this subsection, from that which the court would have imposed but for this subsection.

[(3A) The reference in subsection (3)(b) to any previous conviction of an offence under subsection (1)(b) includes—

(a) any previous conviction by a court in England and Wales or Northern Ireland, and

(b) if the court considers appropriate, any previous conviction by a court in a member State of the European Union,

of an offence that is equivalent to an offence under subsection (1)(b).]

(3B) The references in subsection (3)(c) to subsection (3) are to be read, in relation to a previous conviction by a court referred to in subsection (3A), as references to any provision that is equivalent to subsection (3).

(3C) Any issue of equivalence arising in pursuance of subsection (3A) or (3B) is for the court to determine.

(4) The court shall not, under subsection (3) above, have regard to the fact that the subsequent offence was committed while the accused was on bail unless that fact is libelled in the indictment or, as the case may be, specified in the complaint.

(4A) The fact that the subsequent offence was committed while the accused was on bail shall, unless challenged—

(a) in the case of proceedings on indictment, by giving notice of a preliminary objection in accordance with section 71(2) or 72(6)(b)(i) of this Act; or

(b) in summary proceedings, by preliminary objection before his plea is recorded,

be held as admitted.

(4B) In any proceedings in relation to an offence under subsection (1) above or subsection (7) below, the fact that (as the case may be) an accused—

(a) was on bail;

(b) was subject to any particular condition of bail;

(c) failed to appear at a diet; or

(d) was given due notice of a diet,

shall, unless challenged in the manner described in paragraph (a) or (b) of subsection (4A) above, be held as admitted.

(5) Where the maximum penalty in respect of the subsequent offence is specified by or by virtue of any enactment, that maximum penalty shall, for the purposes of the court's determination, by virtue of subsection (3) above, of the appropriate sentence or disposal in respect of that offence, be increased—

(a) where it is a fine, by the amount for the time being equivalent to level 3 on the standard scale; and

(b) where it is a period of imprisonment—

(i) as respects a conviction in the High Court or the sheriff court, by 6 months; and

(ii) as respects a conviction in the JP court, by 60 days,

notwithstanding that the maximum penalty as so increased exceeds the penalty which it would otherwise be competent for the court to impose.

(6) Where the sentence or disposal in respect of the subsequent offence is, by virtue of subsection (3) above, different from that which the court would have imposed but for that subsection, the court shall state the extent of and the reasons for that difference.

(6A) Where, despite the requirement to have regard to the matters specified in paragraphs (a) to (c) of subsection (3) above, the sentence or disposal in respect of the subsequent offence is not different from that which the court would have imposed but for that subsection, the court shall state (as appropriate, by reference to those matters) the reasons for there being no difference.

(7) An accused who having been granted bail in relation to solemn proceedings fails without reasonable excuse to appear at the time and place appointed for any diet of which he has been given due notice (where such diet is in respect of solemn proceedings) shall be guilty of an offence and liable on conviction on indictment to the following penalties—

(a) a fine; and

(b) imprisonment for a period not exceeding five years.

(8) At any time before the trial of an accused under solemn procedure for the original offence, it shall be competent—

(a) to amend the indictment to include an additional charge of an offence under this section;

(b) to include in the list of witnesses or productions relating to the original offence, witnesses or productions relating to the offence under this section.

(8A) At any time before the trial of an accused in summary proceedings for the original offence, it is competent to amend the complaint to include an additional charge of an offence under this section.

(9) A penalty under subsection (2) or (7) above shall be imposed in addition to any other penalty which it is competent for the court to impose, notwithstanding that the total of penalties imposed may exceed the maximum penalty which it is competent to impose in respect of the original offence.

(9A) The reference in subsection (9) above to a penalty being imposed in addition to another penalty means, in the case of sentences of imprisonment or detention—

(a) where the sentences are imposed at the same time (whether or not in relation to the same complaint or indictment), framing the sentences so that they have effect consecutively;

(b) where the sentences are imposed at different times, framing the sentence imposed later so that (if the earlier sentence has not been served) the later sentence has effect consecutive to the earlier sentence.

(9B) Subsection (9A)(b) above is subject to s.204A of this Act.

(10) A court which finds an accused guilty of an offence under this section may remit the accused for sentence in respect of that offence to any court which is considering the original offence.

(11) In this section "the original offence" means the offence with which the accused was charged when he was granted bail or an offence charged in the same proceedings as that offence.

AMENDMENTS

Subs.(4A) inserted by Criminal Procedure and Investigations Act 1996 (c.25) s.73(2).

Subss.(1)(a) and (4A)(a) as amended by Criminal Procedure (Amendment) (Scotland) Act 2004 (asp 5) s.25 and Sch.1 para.8. Brought into force on February 1, 2005 by SSI 2004/405 (C.28) art.2.

Subss.(2)(b)(ii), (7)(b) and (9) as amended and subss.(4B), (6A), (9A) and (9B) inserted by Criminal Proceedings etc. (Reform) (Scotland) Act 2007 (asp 6) s.3(1), as amended by SSI 2007/540 art.3. Brought into force on December 10, 2007 by SSI 2007/479.

Subss.(2)(b)(i) and (5)(b)(ii) as amended by Criminal Proceedings etc. (Reform) (Scotland) Act 2007 (asp 6) s.80, Sch. para.26. Brought into force for the Sheriffdom of Lothian and Borders on March 10, 2008 by SSI 2008/42 (C.4) art.3 and Sch. Further brought into force for the Sheriffdom of Grampian, Highland and Islands on June 2, 2008 by SSI 2008/192 (C.19) art.3 and Sch. Brought into force for the Sheriffdom of Glasgow and Strathkelvin on December 8, 2008 by SSI 2008/329 (C.29) art.3 and Sch. Brought into force for the Sheriffdom of Tayside, Central and Fife on February 23, 2009 by SSI 2008/362

(C.30) art.3 and Sch. Brought into force for the Sheriffdom of North Strathclyde on December 14, 2009 by SSI 2009/432 (C.32) art.3 and Sch.1. Remainder in force on February 22, 2010 by SSI 2009/432 (C.32) art.3 and Sch.2.

Subss.(3A)–(3C) inserted by Criminal Justice and Licensing (Scotland) Act 2010 (asp 13) Sch.4 para.3. Brought into force on December 13, 2010 by SSI 2010/413 (C.28) art.2, Sch.1 para.1.

Subs.(8A) added by Criminal Justice and Licensing (Scotland) Act 2010 (asp 13) s.62. Brought into force on March 28, 2011 (for all purposes in respect of any breach of bail committed on or after March 28, 2011) by SSI 2011/178 (C.15) art.2, Sch.1 para.1.

Subs.(3A) was substituted by the Criminal Justice (EU Exit) (Scotland) (Amendment etc.) Regulations 2020 (SSI 2020/339) reg.13(4) (effective December 31, 2020 subject to transitional and saving provision specified in reg.16 of those Regulations.

DEFINITIONS A4-70.1

"bail": s.307(1).
"indictment": s.307(1).
"level 3": s.225(2) [i.e. £1,000].
"offence": s.307(1).
"original offence, the": s.27(11).
"sentence": s.307(1).
"standard scale": s.225(1).
"subsequent offence, the": s.27(3).
"complaint": s.307(1).
"diet": s.307(1).
"constable": s.307(1) and Police (Scotland) Act 1967 (c.77) s.51(1).

[THE NEXT PARAGRAPH IS A4-71]

GENERAL NOTE

Subss.(1) and (2)

These subsections create the main bail offences and largely repeat the terms of s.3(1) and (2) of the Bail etc. (Scotland) Act 1980 (c.4). These provisions apply to failures to appear at a diet of summary proceedings and to failures to comply with bail conditions generally in any proceedings. Subs.(7) below lays out the much more substantial penalties arising from a failure to appear at a diet in solemn proceedings. Despite the terms of subs.(1)(b) it may be considered that the circumstances giving rise to a breach of one or other of the standard conditions in relation to solemn proceedings might well give rise to yet more serious common law charges. A4-71

Penalties for offences, as set out in subs.(2), remain surprisingly low given the potential for disruption to court business and inconvenience to witnesses. Subs.(5) does enact slightly more severe penalties where an accused further offends while on bail.

Subs.(1)(a) closes a potential procedural loophole by emphasising that an accused on bail is obliged to attend any mandatory or peremptory diet fixed in the proceedings.

Unsurprisingly, the section's provisions have generated a substantial volume of case law.

For an example of a common bail condition such as "not to approach, contact or attempt to approach or contact" another person see *Cottam v McCloy*, 2009 G.W.D. 32–534 where the breah by attempting to contact was effected by sending text messages to a third party to relay on to the protected person.

Subs.(4)

In *Boyd v HM Advocate*, 2001 J.C. 53 the libelling, as an aggravation of the substantive offence, the fact that it was committed while the accused was already on bail, was submitted to infringe art.6(1) of the European Convention. *Boyd* contended that this would unfairly colour the jury's consideration of the merits: the court rejected this argument and held that a properly directed jury's impartiality would not be tainted by inclusion of a bail aggravation.

Subs.(5)

The maximum penalty which may be imposed upon a summary complaint which incorporates a bail aggravation will ordinarily be one of nine months in the sheriff court and eight months in the district court. The maximum penalty can increase in the sheriff court when the accused has cognate prior convictions as provided in subs.5(3) of the Act. See *Hamilton v Heywood*, 1998 S.L.T. 133.

For a discussion of the effect of s.27(3) and (5) see *Penman v Bott*, 2006 S.L.T. 495. In particular it was held (at 499F–H) that the increased powers conferred by s.27(5) were for the specific purpose identified, thus they could only be used to reflect the bail aggravation: if less than six months was attributed to the bail aggravation, the balance could not be used to increase the period available to be attributed to the substantive offence; conversely, if the period attributable to the substantive offence was less than the maximum which that offence could attract if there were no bail aggravation, the surplus could not be used to augment the extra six months provided for by s.27(5).

Subs.(6)

The court's minute of the sentence imposed state the total sentence and then specify the period of the sentence attributed to the bail offence (*Cochrane v Heywood*, 1998 G.W.D. 13–662).

Subs.(7)

It is commonplace to libel a contravention of s.27(7) as an additional charge in the indictment, indeed subs.(8) permits such a charge to be added by amendment up until the trial starts. In *Slater v HM Advocate* (High Court of Justiciary, November 22, 2000, unreported) this factor, and the *ratio* in *Boyd* (discussed in the Notes to subs.(4) above), caused the Appeal Court to refuse a motion for separation of the s.27(7) charge from others on the indictment. It remains the case that in order to advance a reasonable excuse for failing to appear, an accused may have to give evidence to explain his earlier absence and thus render himself liable to cross-examination on the substantive charges.

In *Creevy v HM Advocate*, 2005 S.C.C.R. 272 where the accused in the course of his trial plead guilty, in the presence of the jury, to an earlier failure to appear and did not give evidence himself, the Appeal Court declined to rule the terms of the prosecutor's speech to the jury, which suggested that this admitted failure was scarcely the act of an innocent man, to be improper. Nevertheless, it remains debatable whether acceptance by an accused that he had no reasonable excuse for failing to appear at a diet necessarily infers that his absence was spurred by his conciousness of his guilt of all, or any, of the charges libelled against him. Compare the earlier approach in *Smith (CC) v HM Advocate*, 2004 S.C.C.R. 521.

Subs.(8)

It has to be observed, however, that the terms of subs.(4A), as applied to solemn proceedings, obviously cannot operate in circumstances where the Crown makes use of the concession contained in subs.(8) and adds a bail offence to the original libel prior to the jury being sworn unless the amendment is made at least two days prior to the first (or the preliminary) diet. Such timeous amendment will preserve the Crown's right to treat the extant bail order as a fact of special capacity and, equally, afford the defence an opportunity to challenge that capacity by preliminary plea. Later amendment would deny the defence that preliminary plea and compel the Crown to prove the existence of the bail order alleged to have been contravened. (At the risk of complicating matters yet further, for the sake of completeness it has to be stressed that subs.(4A) is of no application to s.27 bail offences committed before July 4, 1996; in such cases the applicability of a bail order will always have to be proved.)

The court minutes must refer to grants of bail; see *MacNeill v Smith*, 1984 S.L.T. (Sh. Ct) 63. Any special conditions imposed by the court must be stipulated expressly on the face of the copy bail order served upon the accused (*HM Advocate v Crawford*, 1985 S.L.T. 242). It is clear that the currency of a bail order is not affected by whether any subsequent proceedings are solemn or summary (*McGinn v HM Advocate*, 1991 S.L.T. 266) while in *Mayo v Neizer*, 1994 S.L.T. 931 it was held that bail orders continue for so long as the accused is at liberty even if, as an appellant, he abandons an appeal against sentence and awaits arrest on a consequent warrant. In *Fitzpatrick v Normand*, 1994 S.L.T. 1263 it was held that recall or modification of a bail order must be the subject of an express decision by the court.

It will be observed that s.31 infra entitles the prosecutor to apply for a review of bail or the conditions of bail.

Subs.(8A)

As with the preceding subsection, subs.(8A) entitles the Crown to add a charge alleging a bail condition contravention in summary proceedings; this can be done by amending the complaint at any point up until the summary trial commences, i.e. before the leading of evidence (almost invariably signified by the administration of the oath to the first witness). Note, however, that such late libelling of the bail charge means that the Crown cannot derive comfort from the evidential concessions contained in subss.(4A)(b) and (4B).

Subs. (9)

It is a general rule where one substantive offence involves contravention of a number of separate bail orders, that sentences for the bail offences should be consecutive to any sentence imposed for the substantive offence but concurrent with each other: *Milligan v Normand*, 1996 G.W.D. 24–1367, *Appleton v Vannet*, 1996 G.W.D. 12–698 and *Stuart v Heywood*, 1997 G.W.D. 31–1563. It is not incompetent to impose consecutive sentences for each bail offence (*Whyte v Normand*, 1988 S.C.C.R. 465) and the onus for proving that such an exercise of judicial discretion was inappropriate seems to rest with the appellant rather than requiring justification by the sentencing judge. See *Nicholson v Lees*, 1996 S.C.C.R. 551 (at 561B) which summarises the general principles governing the imposition of concurrent and consecutive sentences and note also *Connal v Carmichael*, 1996 G.W.D. 30–1807. Generally, backdating of a sentence to take account of time on remand awaiting trial is usual, and the reasons for refusal of backdating should be specified in the minutes. However, in the case of a failure to appear for trial, particularly on indictment, it cannot be presumed that backdating will occur even where an acquittal is obtained on the original substantive charges (*Bowers v HM Advocate*, 1997 G.W.D. 31–1562).

Penalties

A substantial increase has been made to the penalty prescribed for breach of bail conditions in s.27 of the 1995 Act on sheriff summary complaint; the previous maximum penalty such bail breaches attracted was a sentence of imprisonment of three months, now raised to twelve months. Such a sentence can be imposed concurrently with, or consecutively to, any other term of imprisonment imposed on conviction and, of course, may be imposed even in the absence of conviction of any substantive charge. Money penalties remain unaltered and note that the existing maximum penalty (level 3 fine and up to 60 days imprisonment or detention) remains unchanged in cases before the district court. Separately by subs.(1)(d) below the Act increases the maximum penalties in solemn procedure from two to five years. These enhanced penalties apply only in relation to contraventions of bail orders granted on or after 10 December 2007; older bail orders attract a maximum penalty in sheriff or solemn proceedings of three months' imprisonment. In keeping with the prescriptive tone of much recent legislation the court must, should it refrain from imposing an additional penalty for a proved breach of a bail condition, expressly minute the reasons for so doing.

Subs.(9A) is a saving provision which empowers the court to exceed its maximum sentencing powers to impose a consecutive sentence once a bail breach has been admitted or proved. Note that such a penalty can be imposed whether the contravention has been libelled in the same proceedings, in separate complaints or indictments calling on the same date, or even when these are called on different dates. All of these measures underscore the intention that bail breaches are ordinarily to merit the imposition of a consecutive sentence. While all parties in *Kyle v HM Advocate*, 2010 S.L.T. 936 agreed that the draftsmanship of this provision could be improved, it is competent to impose a consecutive element in each charge, admitted or proved, to reflect the commission of the offence while on bail. In *Kyle* the issue of the total sentence imposed was not visited since the total sentence imposed by the sheriff did not exceed five years (see s.3(3) above) but refer to subs.(9) above. The only exception to this generality is found in subs.(9B) which covers situations arising from the recall provisions of the Prisoners and Criminal Proceedings (Scotland) Act 1993 (c.9); in those instances an immediate sentence of imprisonment is mandatory.

Evidential provisions

Offending on bail is an aggravation of the substantive offence provided that this capacity is alluded to in the body of any charge which, it is alleged, was committed while the accused was on bail. It is not legitimate when libelling a charge involving breach of a bail condition to add as an aggravation the existence of the bail order which created that condition (*Robertson v Donaldson*, 2007 S.C.C.R. 146). Where a contravention of s.27(1)(b) alleges a breach of a specific bail condition (generally known as a "special bail condition") care has to be taken that the charge accurately echoes the express term, or terms, of the bail order failing which the charge may well be deemed irrelevant (*Dolan v Thomson* Unreported Court of Appeal 3 October 2008).

Subs.(4A) indicates that being subject to bail conditions is a special capacity (on which, see the discussion at s.255 below) and that any objection to that capacity must be intimated in solemn proceedings at the first, or preliminary diet, or prior to tendering a plea to a summary complaint.

The discussion below sets out the convoluted history of this provision (itself an object of wonder) only because it could still be relevant for long-outstanding proceedings.

Prior to the coming into force of the Criminal Procedure (Scotland) Act 1995 it had been judicially determined that bail was a special capacity and, that in the absence of a timeous challenge to that capacity, the Crown did not require to prove that a bail order was in force (*Aitchison v Tudhope*, 1981 J.C. 65; 1981 S.C.C.R. 1). However, the cumulative effect of subss.(3) and (4) is that offending while subject of an earlier bail order now falls to be disposed of as an aggravation of the substantive offence; an enhanced sentence may only be imposed where the prosecutor has specifically libelled the existence of the bail order in the body of the substantive charge itself. When sentencing upon the substantive offence aggravated by being committed while on bail, the court shall impose one allembracing sentence and minute (but apparently not pronounce) the element of sentence attributable to the aggravation (*Hill v HM Advocate*, 1997 S.C.C.R. 376). Where separate offences are prosecuted on distinct complaints, and each offence has been aggravated by being committed while on bail, it is perfectly competent to impose consecutive sentences in relation to both the substantive offences and the aggravations (*Connal v Carmichael*, 1996 G.W.D. 30–1807).

An unintended defect in draftsmanship of the 1995 Act brought about the removal of bail as a special capacity, as it had been since the passing of the Bail etc. (Scotland) Act 1980 (c.4). (See too *Aitchison v Tudhope*, above). This defect was remedied by the amendments to the 1995 Act introduced by the Criminal Procedure and Investigations 1996 (c.25) with effect from 4 July 1996. In those rare cases still extant where the accused was granted bail between 31 March 1996 and 4 July 1996 inclusive, the commission of further offences in breach of such a bail order will be an aggravating feature but the currency of the order itself will have to be proved, and will not be a special capacity.

Being subject of a bail order granted prior to 31 March 1996 (the date upon which the Criminal Justice (Scotland) Act 1995 s.2, the statutory precursor of the 1995 Procedure Act, came into force) falls to be regarded as a special capacity in accordance with case law (*Aitchison v Tudhope*, above) and contraventions of that bail order should be libelled under s.3(1)(b) of the Bail etc. (Scotland) Act 1980 since it was under that legislation that bail was granted.

Different considerations apply where an accused person has been admitted to bail in terms of ss.24 and 25 of the Criminal Procedure (Scotland) Act 1995 after 1 April 1996 (or more rarely, on 31 March

1996 in terms of s.1 of the Criminal Justice (Scotland) Act 1995). In some situations (i.e. where such a bail order is contravened between 31 March 1996 and 4 July 1996) this will be an aggravating feature of the later offence, if the Crown elects to specify the existence of the earlier s.24 bail order in the libel, but will not be a special capacity; however, where there are contraventions of any s.24 bail order libelled as having occurred after 4 July 1996 (the date when the provisions which now appear as s.27(4A) of the 1995 Procedure Act took effect) the existence of that bail order will be both a special capacity and an aggravating factor in sentencing any subsequent substantive offence.

Subs.(4B)

The insertion of subs.(4B) into the 1995 Act both clarifies and extends the scope of the special capacites applying to individuals who are on bail. Hitherto s.27(4A) of the 1995 Act has held the currency of a bail order at the time of committing further offences to be a form of special capacity (for which see generally s.255 below) which had to be challenged once libelled in any charge, failing which the status would not require to be proved. These fresh measures now encompass the fact of bail status, the terms (including any special conditions of bail) contained in the bail order, the failure of the accused to appear at any appointed diet, and proof of awareness of such a diet. The effect of the new measure is to reduce markedly the burden upon the Crown of proving bail contraventions. Any dispute an accused may have with the applicability of any of these bail elements has to be challenged, as s.27(4A) provides, by giving notice at the preliminary, or first, diet in solemn proceedings or by preliminary objection when a summary complaint is first called.

Breach of bail conditions: arrest of offender, etc.

A4-72 **28.**—(1) A constable may arrest without warrant an accused who has been released on bail where the constable has reasonable grounds for suspecting that the accused has broken, is breaking, or is likely to break any condition imposed on his bail.

(1ZA) Where—

(a) a constable who is not in uniform arrests a person under subsection (1), and

(b) the person asks to see the constable's identification,

the constable must show identification to the person as soon as reasonably practicable.

(1A) Where an accused who has been released on bail is arrested by a constable (otherwise than under subsection (1) above), the accused may be detained in custody under this subsection if the constable has reasonable grounds for suspecting that the accused has breached, or is likely to breach, any condition imposed on his bail.

(1B) Subsection (1A) above—

(a) is without prejudice to any other power to detain the accused;

(b) applies even if release of the accused would be required but for that subsection.

(2) An accused who is arrested under subsection (1) above, or is detained under subsection (1A) above, shall wherever practicable be brought before the court to which his application for bail was first made not later than in the course of the first day after his arrest, such day not being, subject to subsection (3) below, a Saturday, a Sunday or a court holiday prescribed for that court under section 8 of this Act.

(3) Nothing in subsection (2) above shall prevent an accused being brought before a court on a Saturday, a Sunday or such a court holiday where the court is, in pursuance of the said section 8, sitting on such day for the disposal of criminal business.

(3A) If—

(a) a person is in custody only by virtue of subsection (1) or (1A), and

(b) in the opinion of a constable there are no reasonable grounds for suspecting that the person has broken, or is likely to break, a condition imposed on the person's bail,

the person must be released from custody immediately.

(3B) An accused is deemed to be brought before a court under subsection (2) or (3) if the accused appears before it by means of a live television link (by virtue of a determination by the court that the person is to do so by such means).

(4) Where an accused is brought before a court under subsection (2) or (3) above, the court, after hearing the parties, may—

(a) recall the order granting bail;
(b) release the accused under the original order granting bail; or
(c) vary the order granting bail so as to contain such conditions as the court thinks it necessary to impose to secure that the accused complies with the requirements of paragraphs (a) to (d) of section 24(5) of this Act.

(4A) In the case of an accused released on bail by virtue of section 65(8C) of this Act—

(a) subsection (2) above shall have effect as if the reference to the court to which his application for bail was first made were a reference to the court or judge which admitted him to bail under that section; and
(b) subsection (4) above shall not apply and subsection (4B) below shall apply instead.

(4B) Where an accused referred to in subsection (4A) above is, under subsection (2) or (3) above, brought before the court or judge which admitted him to bail under section 65(8C)—

(a) the court or judge shall give the prosecutor an opportunity to make an application under section 65(5) of this Act; and
(b) if the prosecutor does not make such an application, or if such an application is made but is refused, the court or judge may—
   (i) release the accused under the original order granting bail; or
   (ii) vary the order granting bail so as to contain such conditions as the court or judge thinks necessary to impose to secure that the accused complies with the requirements of paragraphs (a) to (d) of section 24(5) of this Act.

(5) The same rights of appeal shall be available against any decision of the court under subsection (4) above as were available against the original order of the court relating to bail.

(6) For the purposes of this section and section 27 of this Act, an extract from the minute of proceedings, containing the order granting bail and bearing to be signed by the clerk of court, shall be sufficient evidence of the making of that order and of its terms and of the acceptance by the accused of the conditions imposed under section 24 of this Act.

AMENDMENTS

Subs.(4A) and (4B) inserted by Criminal Procedure (Amendment) (Scotland) Act 2004 (asp 5) s.25 and Sch.1 para.9. Brought into force on 1 February 2005 by SSI 2004/405 (C.28) art.2(1).

Subs.(2) as amended and subss.(1A) and (1B) inserted by Criminal Proceedings etc. (Reform) (Scotland) Act 2007 (asp 6) s.3(2). Brought into force on 10 December 2007 by SSI 2007/479.

Subss.(1ZA), (3A)–(3B) inserted by Criminal Justice (Scotland) Act 2016 (asp 1) Sch.2 para.29(a). Brought into force on 25 January 2018 by SSI 2017/345 art.3 and Sch.1 para.1.

DEFINITION

"bail": s.307(1). A4-72.1

GENERAL NOTE

Additional police powers

With the exception of subss.(1A), (1B) and (4A) these provisions are readily understood. A4-72.2

Subss.(1A) and (1B)

Existing police powers of arrest for breach, or anticipated breach, of bail conditions contained in s.28(1) of the 1995 Act were felt to be limited in scope and could only operate in isolation; so if, for example, an accused had been arrested on an apprehension warrant, or for unpaid fines, and it was thereafter considered that he had also breached bail conditions, no further power of arrest flowed from the bail breach—the power of arrest had already flown off. While the Crown might be able to apply for a review of the bail conditions (see s.31 below) which itself contains a power of arrest, this would have to be effected swiftly since there would be no hold over the accused meantime. The introduction of s.28(1A) addresses this anomaly and entitles the police, where reasonable grounds exist for suspicion that an accused is breaching bail conditions, as well as being liable to arrest on other grounds, to substitute arrest for bail breach if, or when, those other grounds of arrest are ended.

Subs. (4A)

Subs.(4A) deals with a narrow range of offenders—those remand prisoners admitted to bail in solemn proceedings following (a) failure of the Crown to indict within 80 days, (b) failure to hold a preliminary diet in High Court proceedings, or a trial diet in sheriff solemn proceedings within 110 days, or (c) failure to proceed to trial in the High Court within 140 days, each of which failures would entitle the accused to apply for bail. Should such an accused be admitted to bail in terms of s.65(8C) and then breach his bail conditions, subs.(4A) would come into operation.

The subsection requires the accused to be brought back, as soon as practicable, before the court or judge which admitted him to bail, permits the Crown to apply to extend these custody timescales of new, and entitles the court or judge to remand in custody, or to continue or vary the bail order as considered appropriate. Note that the court or judge cannot *ex proprio motu* remand; a motion for a custodial remand must first be made by the Crown or, less likely, the accused must have refused to agree to the bail conditions imposed (see s.25A above).

It is submitted that subs.(4A) would not preclude the Crown from initiating fresh proceedings in the accustomed manner libelling an established (but not an anticipated) breach of bail conditions.

Application of the Criminal Justice (Scotland) Act 2016 to persons arrested and detained under section 28

A4-72.3 **28A.—**(1) Section 7(2) of the Criminal Justice (Scotland) Act 2016 ("the 2016 Act") does not apply to an accused who has been arrested under section 28(1) of this Act.

(2) The following provisions of the 2016 Act apply in relation to a person who is to be brought before a court under section 28(2) or (3) of this Act as they apply in relation to a person who is to be brought before a court in accordance with section 21(2) of the 2016 Act—

(a) section 22,

(b) section 23,

(c) section 24.

(3) In relation to a person who is to be brought before a court under section 28(2) or (3) of this Act, the 2016 Act applies as though—

(a) in section 23(2)—

(i) for paragraph (c) there were substituted—

"(c) that the person is to be brought before the court under section 28 of the 1995 Act in order for the person's bail to be considered.", and

(ii) paragraph (d) were omitted,

(b) in section 24—

(i) in subsection (3)(c), for the words "after being officially accused" there were substituted "after being informed that the person is to be brought before a court under section 28(2) or (3) of the 1995 Act", and

(ii) in subsection (4) , for paragraph (c) there were substituted—

"(c) that the person is to be brought before the court under section 28 of the 1995 Act in order for the person's bail to be considered.",

(c) in section 43(1), for paragraph (d) there were substituted—

"(d) the court before which the person is to be brought under section 28(2) or (3) of the 1995 Act and the date on which the person is to be brought before that court.

AMENDMENTS

Section 28A inserted by Criminal Justice (Scotland) Act 2016 (asp 1) Sch.2 para.30. Brought into force on 25 January 2018 by SSI 2017/345 art.3 and Sch.1 para.1.

GENERAL NOTE

Subs.(1)

Section 28 of the 1995 Act makes provision for the arrest of offenders for breaches of bail conditions. Subs.(1) allows a constable to arrest without warrant an accused who has been released on bail where the constable has reasonable grounds for suspecting that the accused has broken, is breaking, or is likely to break any condition imposed on his bail. A4-72.4

Section 7(2) of the 2016 Act requires that authorisation to keep a person in custody must be sought as soon as reasonably practicable after a person is arrested at a police station, or arrives at a police station, having been taken there in accordance with s.4 of the 2016 Act.

Section 28A provides that s.7(2) of the 2016 Act does not apply to arrests under s.28(1). The reason for that is, presumably, the requirement that, by s.28(2) and (3) of the 1995 Act, such arrested person is brought before a court on the day after arrest. The nature of the alleged breach and that requirement provides the authorisation to keep a person in custody.

Subs.(2)

Specific provision is made by this subsection for the application of s.22 (under 18s to be kept in a place of safety), s.23 (notice to parent that under 18 to be brought before court) and s.24 (notice to local authority that under 18 to be brought before court) to someone brought before court under s.28(2) and (3) of the 1995 Act.

[THE NEXT PARAGRAPH IS A4-73]

Bail: monetary conditions

29.—(1) Without prejudice to section 27 of this Act, where the accused or a cautioner on his behalf has deposited a sum of money in court under section 24(6) of this Act, then— A4-73

(a) if the accused fails to appear at the time and place appointed for any diet of which he has been given due notice, the court may, on the motion of the prosecutor, immediately order forfeiture of the sum deposited;

(b) if the accused fails to comply with any other condition imposed on bail, the court may, on conviction of an offence under section 27(1)(b) of this Act and on the motion of the prosecutor, order forfeiture of the sum deposited.

(2) If the court is satisfied that it is reasonable in all the circumstances to do so, it may recall an order made under subsection (1)(a) above and direct that the money forfeited shall be refunded, and any decision of the court under this subsection shall be final and not subject to review.

(3) A cautioner, who has deposited a sum of money in court under section 24(6) of this Act, shall be entitled, subject to subsection (4) below, to recover the sum deposited at any diet of the court at which the accused appears personally.

(4) Where the accused has been charged with an offence under section 27(1)(b) of this Act, nothing in subsection (3) above shall entitle a cautioner to recover the sum deposited unless and until—

(a) the charge is not proceeded with; or
(b) the accused is acquitted of the charge; or
(c) on the accused's conviction of the offence, the court has determined not to order forfeiture of the sum deposited.

(5) The references in subsections (1)(b) and (4)(c) above to conviction of an offence shall include references to the making of an order in respect of the offence under section 246(3) of this Act.

DEFINITIONS

A4-73.1 "diet": s.307(1).

GENERAL NOTE

A4-73.2 The requirement of bail that a sum of money be deposited in court prior to about 1980 was common enough; although it would seem doubtful now if this section is implemented much, if at all.

Bail review

A4-74 **30.**—(1) This section applies where a court has refused to admit a person to bail or, where a court has so admitted a person, the person has failed to accept the conditions imposed or that a sum required to be deposited under section 24(6) of this Act has not been so deposited.

(1A) This section also applies where a person who has accepted the conditions imposed on his bail wants to have any of them removed or varied.

(2) A court shall, on the application of any person mentioned in subsection (1) or (1A) above, have power to review (in favour of the person) its decision as to bail, or its decision as to the conditions imposed, if—

(a) the circumstances of the person have changed materially; or

(b) the person puts before the court material information which was not available to it when its decision was made.

(2A) On receipt of an application under subsection (2), the court must—

(a) intimate the application to the prosecutor, and

(b) before determining the application, give the prosecutor an opportunity to be heard.

(2AA) Despite subsection (2A)(b), the court may grant the application without having heard the prosecutor if the prosecutor consents.

(2B) Subsection (2C) below applies where an application is made under subsection (2) above by a person convicted on indictment pending the determination of—

(a) his appeal;

(b) any relevant appeal by the Lord Advocate under section 108 or 108A of this Act; or

(c) the sentence to be imposed on, or other method of dealing with, him.

(2C) Where this subsection applies the application shall be—

(a) intimated by the person making it immediately and in writing to the Crown Agent; and

(b) determined not less than 7 days after the date of that intimation.

(3) An application under this section, where it relates to the original decision of the court, shall not be made before the fifth day after that decision and, where it relates to a subsequent decision, before the fifteenth day thereafter.

(4) Nothing in this section shall affect any right of a person to appeal against the decision of a court in relation to admitting to bail or to the conditions imposed.

AMENDMENTS

Subss.(2A)–(2C) inserted by Criminal Procedure (Amendment) (Scotland) Act 2004 (asp 4) s.18(3). Brought into force on 1 February 2005 by SSI 2004/405 (C.28) art.2.

Subs.(1A) inserted and subs.(2) amended by Criminal Proceedings etc. (Reform) (Scotland) Act 2007 (asp 6) s.4(1). Brought into force on 10 December 2007 by SSI 2007/479.

Subss.(2A), (2C) as amended, subs.(2AA) inserted, by Criminal Justice and Licensing (Scotland) Act 2010 (asp 13) s.57. Brought into force on 28 March 2011 (for all purposes in respect of any applications under 1995 c.46 s.30(2) received on or after 28 March 2011) by SSI 2011/178 (C.15) art.2, Sch.1 para.1.

DEFINITIONS A4-74.1

"bail": s.307(1).
"judge": s.307(1).
"Clerk of Justiciary": s.307(1).
"High Court": s.307(1).
"Act of Adjournal": s.305.

[THE NEXT PARAGRAPH IS A4-76]

GENERAL NOTE

This section applies in a number of separate circumstances: e.g. the court may have refused to admit a person to bail. For the general guidelines as to the allowance or refusal of bail, see *Smith v M.*, 1982 S.L.T. 421. Alternatively, a court may have so admitted a person but the person has failed to accept the conditions imposed: for a special condition that was challenged see *Brawls v Walkingshaw*, 1994 S.C.C.R. 7 discussed further in *McDonald v Dickson* 2003 S.C.C.R. 315 (both cases concerning conditions to remain at home). Also, a court may have required the deposit of a sum of money but that has not been done. In any or all of these circumstances, a person may seek to have the original decision reviewed within modest statutory time-limits and yet otherwise appeal the original decision.

A number of amendments have been introduced to ss.30 to 32 of the 1995 Act, dealing with review of bail and bail appeals. The purpose of the amendments in subs.(2) is to put it beyond doubt that a bail review can, in future, only be sought where there has been a material change in the accused's circumstances or there is information now available which was not available to the court at the time of its original decision as to bail, or refusal of bail. The small amendment to subs.(1) enables both the accused and the Crown to seek a review.

The complainer or witness referred to in the grant of bail conditions has no *locus* to appear at, or be independently represented in, the review proceedings. The absence of such an opportunity does not contravene his or her art.8 ECHR rights; see *Dunn v Porch*, 2016 S.C.C.R. 55 discussed in the notes to s.288ZB below.

Note that, once an indictment for High Court proceedings has called at a preliminary hearing, any application for bail, or review of bail, must be considered in that court and not by the sheriff court which received any initiating petition. See *Bail Appeal in A.A. v HM Advocate* [2016] HCJAC 17.

Subss.(2A) and (2AA) as introduced by the Criminal Justice and Licensing (Scotland) Act 2010 (asp 13) requires the court to notify the prosecutor of any application for bail review and to afford him an opportunity to be heard on the merits. Subs.(2AA) enables the court, if it so wishes, to dispense with a review where the Crown has agreed to the application.

Subs.(2A) explicitly provides that the prosecutor now has a right to be heard in *any* application by an accused for review of bail either prior to trial or pending any appeal following conviction on indictment. The same entitlement applies where the Crown appeals claiming undue leniency in sentencing or on a point of law. Intimation of an application for bail review has to be made upon the Crown Agent, and the date of that intimation determines the seven day period within which a hearing must occur.

In *Russell v HM Advocate* [2021] HCJAC 24 the issue was whether the determination of a bail appeal by the Sheriff Appeal Court has the effect that any future applications for review of bail can only competently be entertained by that court rather than by the sheriff at first instance. It was held, at para.[27], that reading s.30(1) and (2) together it is clear that "a court" has power to review "its decision" inter alia to refuse bail if the accused's circumstances have changed or the person puts before the court material information which was not available "to it" when "its decision" was made. A lower court has and continues to have the power to review its original refusal of bail, even though there has been an unsuccessful appeal brought against the refusal of bail by the accused person.

It was also *held*, at para.[29], that where, on the other hand, the appellate court has sustained a defence appeal it had thereby substituted for the first instance decision its own allowance of bail. In such circumstances the appellate court considered that there has been a decision by the appellate court of the type covered by s.30(1) and (2) with the consequence that subsequent applications for review of the appellate decision to allow bail, for example by varying the conditions of bail set by the appellate court, would fall to be considered by the appellate court rather than by the court of first instance. In such circumstances there has been a substantive new decision by the appellate court rather than a mere affirmation of the original decision made by the lower court.

Specific guidance in relation to intimation of appeals to both the respondent and the presiding judge are found in s.32 below.

Bail review on prosecutor's application

31.—(1) On an application by the prosecutor at any time after a court has granted bail to a person the court may, where the prosecutor puts before the court material information which was not available to it when it granted bail to that person, review its decision. A4-76

(2) On receipt of an application under subsection (1) above the court shall—

(a) intimate the application to the person granted bail;

(b) fix a diet for hearing the application and cite that person to attend the diet; and

(c) where it considers that the interests of justice so require, grant warrant to arrest that person.

(2ZA) Despite subsection (2)(b), the court may grant the application without fixing a hearing if the person granted bail consents.

(2A) Subsection (2B) below applies to an application under subsection (1) above where the person granted bail—

(a) was convicted on indictment; and

(b) was granted bail pending the determination of—

(i) his appeal;

(ii) any relevant appeal by the Lord Advocate under section 108 or 108A of this Act; or

(iii) the sentence to be imposed on, or other method of dealing with, him.

(2B) Where this subsection applies, the application shall be heard not more than 7 days after the day on which it is made.

(3) On an application under subsection (1) above the court may—

(a) withdraw the grant of bail and remand the person in question in custody; or

(b) grant bail, or continue the grant of bail, either on the same or on different conditions.

(3A) In relation to an accused admitted to bail under section 65(8C) of this Act—

(a) an application may be made under subsection (1) above only in relation to the conditions imposed on bail; and

(b) paragraph (a) of subsection (3) above shall not apply in relation to any such application.

(4) Nothing in the foregoing provisions of this section shall affect any right of appeal against the decision of a court in relation to bail.

AMENDMENTS

Subss.(2A)–(2B) inserted by Criminal Procedure (Amendment) (Scotland) Act 2004 (asp 5) s.18(4), and subs.(3A) inserted by s.25 and Sch.1 para.10 of the 2004 Act. Brought into force on 1 February 2005 by SSI 2004/405 (C.28) art.2.

Subs.(2ZA) inserted, and subs.(3) as amended, by Criminal Justice and Licensing (Scotland) Act 2010 (asp 13) s.57. Brought into force on 28 March 2011 (for all purposes in respect of any applications under 1995 c.46 s.30(2) received on or after 28 March 2011) by SSI 2011/178 (C.15) art.2, Sch.1 para.1.

DEFINITIONS

A4-76.1 "bail": s.307(1).
"diet": s.307(1).
"prosecutor": s.307(1).

GENERAL NOTE

A4-77 This section enables the prosecutor to apply to the court to reconsider a decision to grant bail. Application must be made on the basis of information relevant to the decision to grant bail which was not available to the court when the decision was taken. Subsection (2) describes the procedure to be followed on receipt of an application by a prosecutor. Subsection (3) specifies the options available to the court on hearing the prosecutor's application. In the absence of this provision under the 1980 Act one reported solution was to petition the court for warrant to apprehend the accused; see *Lockhart v Stokes*, 1981 S.L.T. (Sh. Ct) 71 where efforts to serve an indictment foundered because the domicile given had ceased to be a proper domicile of citation.

The prosecutor's right to bail review is now extended to Crown appeals claiming undue leniency in sentencing or on a point of law.

Subs.(2ZA) provides a mechanism for the Crown's application to be determined without the need for a hearing when the accused intimates consent.

Subs.(3A) deals with situations where the Crown fail to indict an accused, or progress to trial in solemn proceedings within the statutory timescales set out in s.65 of the Act and the accused is then admitted to bail. While the Crown can seek a review of bail in such circumstances this cannot be used as a means to seek withdrawal of that bail, but only to vary or amend the bail conditions previously imposed by the court.

Bail appeal

32.—(1) Where, in any case, bail is refused or where the accused is dissatisfied with the amount of bail fixed, he may appeal to the appropriate Appeal Court which may, in its discretion order intimation to the Lord Advocate or, as the case may be, the prosecutor. **A4-78**

(2) Where, in any case, bail is granted, or, in summary proceedings an accused is ordained to appear, the public prosecutor, if dissatisfied—

(a) with the decision allowing bail;

(b) with the amount of bail fixed; or

(c) in summary proceedings, that the accused has been ordained to appear,

may appeal to the appropriate Appeal Court, and the accused shall not be liberated, subject to subsection (7) below, until the appeal by the prosecutor is disposed of.

(2A) The public prosecutor may, in relation to an accused admitted to bail under section 65(8C) of this Act, appeal under subsection (2) above only in relation to the conditions imposed on bail.

(3) Written notice of appeal shall be immediately given to the opposite party by a party appealing under this section.

(3A) A notice of appeal under this section is to be lodged with the clerk of the court from which the appeal is to be taken.

(3B) When an appeal is made under this section, that clerk shall without delay—

(a) send a copy of the notice of appeal to the judge whose decision is the subject of the appeal; and

(b) request the judge to provide a report of the reasons for that decision.

(3C) The judge shall, as soon as is reasonably practicable, provide that clerk with the judge's report of those reasons.

(3CA) The clerk of the court from which the appeal is to be taken (unless that clerk is the Clerk of Justiciary) must—

(a) send the notice of appeal without delay to the clerk of the appropriate Appeal Court, and

(b) before the end of the day after the day of receipt of the notice of appeal, send the judge's report (if provided by then) to the clerk of the appropriate Appeal Court.

(3D) […]

(3E) […]

(3F) The clerk of the appropriate Appeal Court shall, upon receipt of the notice of appeal, without delay fix a diet for the hearing of the appeal.

(3G) The clerk of the appropriate Appeal Court shall send a copy of the judge's report to—

(a) the accused or his solicitor; and

(b) the Crown Agent.

(3H) In a case where the Sheriff Appeal Court is the appropriate Appeal Court, if the judge's report is not sent as mentioned in subsection (3CA) above—

(a) the appropriate Appeal Court may call for the report to be submitted to it within such period as it may specify; or

(b) if it thinks fit, hear and determine the appeal without the report.

(3I) Subject to subsection (3G) above, the judge's report shall be available only to the appropriate Appeal Court, the parties and, on such conditions as may be prescribed by Act of Adjournal, such other persons or classes of person as may be so prescribed.

(4) An appeal under this section shall be disposed of by the appropriate Appeal Court or any judge of the appropriate Appeal Court in court or in chambers after such inquiry and hearing of parties as shall seem just.

(5) Where an accused in an appeal under this section is under 21 years of age, section 51 of this Act shall apply to the appropriate Appeal Court or, as the case may be, the judge of the appropriate Appeal Court when disposing of the appeal as it applies to a court when remanding or committing a person of the accused's age for trial or sentence.

(6) In the event of the appeal of the public prosecutor under this section being refused, the court may award expenses against him.

(7) When an appeal is taken by the public prosecutor either against the grant of bail or against the amount fixed, the accused to whom bail has been granted (other than an accused to whom subsection (7B) below applies) shall, if the bail fixed has been found by him, be liberated after 72 hours from the granting of the bail, whether the appeal has been disposed of or not, unless the appropriate Appeal Court grants an order for his further detention in custody.

(7B) Where, in relation to an accused admitted to bail under section 65(8C) of this Act, the public prosecutor appeals against the conditions imposed on bail, the accused—

(a) may continue to be detained under the committal warrant for no more than 72 hours from the granting of bail or for such longer period as the appropriate Appeal Court may allow; and

(b) on expiry of that period, shall, whether the appeal has been disposed of or not, be released on bail subject to the conditions imposed.

(8) In computing the period mentioned in subsection (7) above, Sundays and public holidays, whether general or court holidays, shall be excluded.

(9) When an appeal is taken under this section by the prosecutor in summary proceedings against the fact that the accused has been ordained to appear, subsections (7) and (8) above shall apply as they apply in the case of an appeal against the granting of bail or the amount fixed.

(10) Notice to the governor of the prison of the issue of an order such as is mentioned in subsection (7) above within the time mentioned in that subsection bearing to be sent by the clerk of the appropriate Appeal Court or the Crown Agent shall be sufficient warrant for the detention of the accused pending arrival of the order in due course of post.

(11) In this section—

"appropriate Appeal Court" means—

(a) in the case of an appeal under this section against a bail decision of the High Court or a judge of the High Court, that Court,

(b) in the case of an appeal under this section against a bail decision of the Sheriff Appeal Court, the High Court,

(c) in the case of an appeal under this section against a bail decision of a sheriff (whether in solemn or summary proceedings) or a JP court, the Sheriff Appeal Court,

"judge of the appropriate Appeal Court" means—

(a) in a case where the High Court is the appropriate Appeal Court, judge of that Court,

(b) in a case where the Sheriff Appeal Court is the appropriate Appeal Court, Appeal Sheriff,

"the clerk of the appropriate Appeal Court" means—

(a) in a case where the High Court is the appropriate Appeal Court, the Clerk of Justiciary,

(b) in a case where the Sheriff Appeal Court is the appropriate Appeal Court, the Clerk of that Court.

(12) In a case where the Sheriff Appeal Court is the appropriate Appeal Court, the references in subsections (3G)(b) and (10) to the Crown Agent are to be read as references to the prosecutor.

Amendments

Subs.(1) as amended by Bail, Judicial Appointments etc. (Scotland) Act 2000 (asp 9) s.4.

Subss.(2), (5), (7) and (10) as amended by Bail, Judicial Appointments etc. (Scotland) Act 2000 (asp 9) s.12 and Sch. para.7(2).

Subss.(2A) and (7B) inserted, and (7) as amended, by Criminal Procedure (Amendment) (Scotland) Act 2004 (asp 5) s.25 and Sch.1 para.11. Brought into force on 1 February 2005 by SSI 2004/405 (C.28) art.2.

Subss.(3A)-(3I) inserted and subs.(2) amended by Criminal Proceedings etc. (Reform) (Scotland) Act 2007 (asp 6) s.4(2). Brought into force on 10 December 2007 by SSI 2007/479.

Section 32 as amended, subss.(3D) and (3E) substituted by subs.(3CA), and subss.(11), (12) inserted by Courts Reform (Scotland) Act 2014 (asp 18) s.122. Brought into force on 22 September 2015 by SSI 2015/247 (C.35) art.2 and Sch, subject to transitional provisions in art.7.

Definitions

"appropriate Appeal Court": s.32(11) A4-78.1
"bail": s.307(1).
"Clerk of Justiciary": s.307(1).
"complaint": s.307(1).
"governor": s.307(1).
"High Court": s.307(1).
"judge in the appropriate Appeal Court": s.32(11)
"Lords Commissioner of Justiciary": s.307(1).
"order": s.307(1).
"prison": s.307(1).
"prosecutor": s.307(1).
" the clerk of the appropriate Appeal Court": s.32(11)

[THE NEXT PARAGRAPH IS A4-79]

General Note

In its essentials this section provides by subs.(1) that an accused may appeal a refusal of bail, while subs.(2) entitles the Crown to appeal both a grant of bail or, more unusually, in summary proceedings an order ordaining an accused to appear at future diets, i.e. without the imposition of bail conditions. Subs.(3) sets out a requirement for written notice to be provided to the other party, and any resultant appeal can be considered by a single judge in chambers, or during the course of a court hearing of the case. Intimation provisions are found in subs.(12). A4-79

Subs.(7B) addresses the specific procedures set out in s.65(4) and (8D) where a custody case has been indicted into the High Court but no preliminary hearing or trial has occurred timeously; the prosecutor's right of appeal is then restricted to the specific bail conditions imposed, not to the merits of bail itself.

Before the advent of the Sheriff Appeal Court all bail appeals, whether arising from summary or solemn proceedings, were dealt with by the High Court. Now that the Sheriff Appeal Court is fully operational, identifying the *forum* of such appeal requires care in solemn cases (see generally the guidance in *Bail Appeal in A.A. v HM Advocate* [2016] HCJAC 17; 2016 S.C.C.R. 224), the forum of any appeal being determined by the nature, and time line, of the proceedings, bearing in mind too the general principle that an inferior court cannot review a decision of its superior. See subs.(11) above. Thus, the High Court deals with cases in which bail has previously been refused by a judge of that court, while the Sheriff Appeal Court has jurisdiction where refusal has been by a sheriff or JP.

All bail appeals are still heard in Edinburgh; the Sheriff Appeal Court for this purpose consisting of a single judge in chambers at Lawnmarket, Edinburgh.

Appeals or bail reviews following petition proceedings are generally the province of the Sheriff Appeal Court but, once a case is indicted to the High Court and the case has called at a preliminary hearing, management of the case (including bail applications and reviews) rests with a High Court judge. Perversely perhaps, one paradoxical exception springs to mind; should the Crown insist, in circumstances when the accused is on bail, upon not calling a High Court indictment when assigned for its trial, it is suggested that the bail forum would revert to that established, if any, by the original petition.

Section 32(1) affords the means for an appeal against refusal of bail: see *Love, Petr*, 1998 G.W.D. 11-528, discussed at A4-63 above.

The 2004 Act inserted subss.(2A) and (7B) to deal with the particular circumstances arising from the introduction of s.65(8C). Once the Crown has failed to meet the statutory timescales for solemn proceedings applying to remand prisoners, the court may opt to grant bail to the accused while keeping proceedings alive. Any Crown appeal relating to that bail grant must arise from the conditions imposed—the decision upon the merits of bail cannot be challenged.

(The Act does provide remedies in the event of an accused's failure to adhere to the conditions imposed; see the note to s.28(4A) above).

Subs.(7B) requires that any such Crown appeal must be heard within 72 hours unless the High Court has granted a longer period.

It would seem necessary to intimate at the time of marking any appeal that additional time is required since, ordinarily, the committal warrant only extends for 72 hours after which time the bail order, as granted, comes into force.

This section provides the mechanism for appealing bail decisions, an accused appealing in terms of subs.(1), the Crown utilising subs.(2). Each party must give written notice of appeal to the other side and, following on from s.4(2) of the 2007 Act, also to the presiding judge. Subs.(3C) now entitles the judge to furnish a report to the appropriate Appeal Court setting out the reasons for the bail decision now under appeal, and a copy of such report has to be made available to the parties to the appeal (see subs (3G)).

Two points are of note in regard to judge's reports: first, the High Court or single judge has a discretion to deal with a bail appeal even when no judge's report has been furnished or can opt to continue the appeal and order the production of a judge's report (subs.(3H)); secondly, provisions exist to enable other parties, as prescribed by Act of Adjournal, to obtain a copy of a bail appeal report prepared by the judge at first instance.

Jie Lin v HM Advocate [2012] HCJAC 151 is authority for the proposition that it is competent, by way of appeal by bill of suspension, to challenge a decision of a sheriff to grant a warrant for full committal, either because it was defective in form or because its granting would be oppressive, but there was no suggestion therein that a warrant could be suspended in the cause of a bail appeal; that was a statutory appeal under s.32 of the 1995 Act and was not a competent procedure by which to challenge a committal warrant. *Jie Lin v HM Advocate* was explained in *M v HM Advocate* [2013] HCJAC 46; 2013 G.W.D. 13-278.

Subs.(4)

In *DL v HM Advocate* [2007] HCJAC 08; 2007 S.C.C.R. 472; 2008 S.C.R. 25 an accused wished to be present at a bail hearing and it was held that (i) a bail appeal was not part of the determination of a criminal charge and so was not within the scope of art.6 of ECHR (right to a fair trial); (ii) the requirement of art.5(4) (proceedings by which the lawfulness of his detention shall be decided) were met in that the accused was able to be afforded a proper adversarial procedure legal representation; and (iii) justice did not require an accused to be present in these circumstances.

General Note: on and after 22 September 2015

The amendments made to the 1995 Act by s.122 of the Reform Act 2014 (bail appeals) do not apply to bail appeals made to the High Court of Justiciary before 22 September 2015. The effect of these amendments in regard to appeals is to take cognisance of the replacement of the appellate functions in the High Court of Justiciary by the Sheriff Appeals Court, the latter being established by the Reform Act 2014.

The time allotted to bail appeals cannot usually accommodate a debate of any length or complexity but if such a need arose it might be preferable to continue the case to a further hearing for a full debate and to determine it within the first instance process: *O'Leary v HM Advocate* [2014] HCJAC 45; 2014 S.L.T. 711; 2014 S.C.L. 515, at [26]; *HM Advocate v Porch* [2015] HCJAC 111; 2016 S.L.T. 149; 2016 S.C.L. 128, at [46].

Bail after conviction: prosecutor's attitude

A4-79.1 **32A.**—(1) Where—

(a) a person has been convicted in any proceedings of an offence; and
(b) a question of bail (including as to bail conditions) subsequently arises in the proceedings (whether before sentencing or pending appeal or otherwise),

the prosecutor and the convicted person must be given an opportunity to make submissions in relation to the question.

(2) But the attitude of the prosecutor towards the question does not restrict the court's exercise of its discretion in determining the question in accordance with the rules applying in the case.

(3) Despite subsection (1) above, the prosecutor need not be given an opportunity to make submissions in relation to a question of bail arising under section 245J of this Act.

(4) This section is without prejudice to any other right of the parties to be heard.

AMENDMENTS

Section 32A inserted by Criminal Proceedings etc. (Reform) (Scotland) Act 2007 (asp 6) s.5. Brought into force on 10 December 2007 by SSI 2007/479.

DEFINITIONS

A4-79.2

"offence": s.307(1)
"bail": s.307(1)
"prosecutor": s.307(1)

GENERAL NOTE

This 2007 addition to the 1995 Act entitles a prosecutor to be heard in relation to the question of whether a convicted accused should be admitted to bail, or have his bail continued, pending either sentence or an appeal. A4-79.3

Hitherto prosecutors had no locus in such matters once a conviction had been secured. One aspect which has become increasingly important in recent times is the development of proceeds of crime proceedings and civil recovery of funds alleged to have been gained from criminal activity; the Crown might well argue that the continued liberty of the accused post-conviction, when confiscation procedures were active, could prejudice recovery of the funds or assets identified.

It is important to note the caveat in subs.(3). This specifies the situations where the prosecutor has no automatic entitlement to be heard in relation to bail. Following s.245J of the Act, these are breaches or defaults of probation, drug testing and treatment, supervised attendance, community service and restriction of liberty orders. The court may solicit the Crown's stance on bail in these cases but is not statutorily obliged to do so, but in all cases must give the accused an opportunity to be heard in regard to bail until a determinate sentence is imposed. Attendance order (s.236(3) of the Act).

[THE NEXT PARAGRAPH IS A4-80]

Bail: no fees exigible

33. No clerks fees, court fees or other fees or expenses shall be exigible from or awarded against an accused in respect of a decision on bail under section 22A above, an application for bail or of the appeal of such a decision or application to the High Court. A4-80

AMENDMENTS

Section 33 as amended by Bail, Judicial Appointments etc. (Scotland) Act 2000 (asp 9) s.12 and Sch. para.7(3)(a) and (b). Brought into force on 9 August 2000.

DEFINITIONS

A4-80.1

"bail": s.307(1).
"High Court": s.307(1).

[THE NEXT PARAGRAPH IS A4-81]

PART IV – PETITION PROCEDURE

Warrants

Petition for warrant

34.—(1) A petition for warrant to arrest and commit a person suspected of or charged with crime may be in the forms— A4-81

(a) set out in Schedule 2 to this Act; or

(b) prescribed by Act of Adjournal,

or as nearly as may be in such form; and Schedule 3 to this Act shall apply to any such petition as it applies to the indictment.

(2) If on the application of the procurator fiscal, a sheriff is satisfied that there is reasonable ground for suspecting that an offence has been or is being committed by a body corporate, the sheriff shall have the like power to grant warrant for the cita-

tion of witnesses and the production of documents and articles as he would have if a petition charging an individual with the commission of the offence were presented to him.

GENERAL NOTE

A4-82 Solemn proceedings are generally initiated by the presentation of a petition to a sheriff in chambers. The petition may be put before the court along with the person accused of the crime, or the Crown may petition for a warrant to arrest the accused: on occasion where several accused are involved the petition may take both forms. In *Hamilton v HM Advocate*, 1997 S.L.T. 31, a prosecution under the Trades Description Act 1968, it was held that in contrast to England where proceedings were deemed to commence with service of an indictment (an event which would affect calculation of the time-bar on proceedings), in Scotland proceedings commenced with the obtaining of a petition warrant by the prosecutor or by service of an indictment when no initiating petition had been obtained. offences committed by corporate bodies can in terms of subs.(2) also be initiated by way of the same petition procedure and, when granted by the court, give the same powers to the Crown as would a petition against an individual accused. Prior to the enactment of s.74(7) of the 1975 Act the form of petition used for offences committed by such bodies was derived from the Criminal Justice (Scotland) Act 1949 s.40(7); indeed until the Second World War solemn proceedings against companies or other corporate bodies were unknown. Dissolved partnerships cease to be legal entities and cannot then competently be prosecuted. Proceedings would still be competent against individual partners whose personal involvement or responsibility can be established; see *Balmer v HM Advocate*, 2008 S.L.T. 799.

The crimes narrated are charged in the third person and s.40 of the Act requires that the principal petition must be signed by the prosecutor (normally the fiscal or a depute) and by a sheriff both of whom must have a jurisdiction derived from at least one of the charges libelled. A rare exception to these general rules is found in s.34A below. Subsection (1) refers to the forms of indictments set out in Sch.2 to the Act. It will be noted that these charges originated in the Criminal Procedure (Scotland) Act 1887 (c.35) and many are arcane, obsolescent or obsolete.

As a matter of course the warrant granted by the court will authorise (i) the arrest of the accused and require that he be brought before the court for examination, (ii) the search of his abode or other premises for the purpose of such arrest and to gather evidence, (iii) the citation of witnesses and the production to the Crown of documentary and label productions, and (iv) after examination, his committal for further examination or until liberated in due course of law (technically the first-mentioned step is unnecessary in situations where the petition is of even date with the first appearance of the accused or where the accused is a body corporate). In order to fulfil the Crown's obligations under the European Convention on Human Rights arts 5 and 6, a fuller narration of the circumstances which the prosecutor alleges justify the charges libelled in the petition is now routinely served on the accused when the Crown moves for committal for further examination. A fuller outline of the Crown case is likely to follow at full committal. It is usual for this additional information to be put in a paper apart, rather than within the body of the petition itself. Either approach would be acceptable (*Brown v Selfridge*, 2000 S.L.T. 437). See also *Hamilton v Vannet*, 1999 G.W.D. 8-406. It is necessary for the sheriff to consider whether the information provided in a statement provides a sufficiency for committal but no more than a broad outline of the available evidence is required; see *Hynd v Ritchie*, 2002 S.L.T. 984; 2002 S.C.C.R. 755. H's bill of suspension was refused.

Solemn proceedings without a petition warrant

Proceedings generally begin with a petition, or petition warrant, and an appearance by the accused, but it is competent (if increasingly rare) for proceedings to start with service of an indictment upon an accused. This device has the effect of sidestepping the time bar provisions contained in s.65, which are calculated by reference to the date of petition appearance. On the other hand, service of the indictment will have to be made upon the accused (for without the advantage of a domicile of citation there will be no bail conditions in force) and disclosure of the Crown case is unlikely to have been made since no defence solicitor will have been formally engaged; understandably this is a recipe itself for further delay. Additionally, s.288C specifically prohibits an accused from personally conducting his own defence in relation to listed sexual offences and, for practical purposes, makes a petition appearance essential where such charges are to be libelled.

While this device bypasses the statutory protections against delay in proceedings, such as they now are, in s.65 of the Act, delay in proceedings or repeated service of libels without the matters being ventilated in court, could give rise to a compatibility minute alleging oppression and abuse of process. See the discussion of *HM Advocate v Mathieson* unreported 18 January 2016, Kilmarnock Sheriff Court, discussed in *The Journal*, June 2016 p.28, where an abuse of process was held to have occurred and was not appealed by the Crown, and the discussion in *Potts v Procurator Fiscal Hamilton* [2016] SAC (Crim) 25, a summary prosecution initiated after an appeal under s.65 (reported as *Potts v HM Advocate* [2015] HCJAC 124) against any further extension of time bar succeeded.

Warrants for bodily samples or other data from accused

In the absence of voluntary provision by the accused, or the securing by the police of bodily samples by way of the powers contained in s.18 of the Act, a separate warrant would have to be craved by the prosecutor to obtain blood or other body fluid samples where invasive means were to be used. See *Mellors v Normand*, 1996 G.W.D. 14-817 and the authorities cited in the Notes to s.18 above.

Petition proceedings outwith sheriffdom

34A.—(1) Where the prosecutor believes— **A4-82.1**

(a) that, because of exceptional circumstances (and without an order under subsection (3) below), it is likely that there would be an unusually high number of accused persons appearing from custody for the first calling of cases on petition in the sheriff courts in the sheriffdom; and

(b) that it would not be practicable for those courts to deal with all the cases involved, the prosecutor may apply to the sheriff principal for the order referred to in subsection (2) below.

(2) For the purposes of subsection (1) above, the order is for authority for petition proceedings against some or all of the accused persons to be—

(a) taken at a sheriff court in another sheriffdom; and

(b) maintained—

(i) there; or

(ii) at any of the sheriff courts referred to in subsection (1) above as may at the first calling of the case be appointed for further proceedings.

(3) On an application under subsection (1) above, the sheriff principal may make the order sought with the consent of the sheriff principal of the other sheriffdom.

(4) An order under subsection (3) above may be made by reference to a particular period or particular circumstances.

(5) This section does not confer jurisdiction for any subsequent proceedings on indictment.

AMENDMENTS

Section 34A inserted by Criminal Proceedings etc. (Reform) (Scotland) Act 2007 (asp 6) s.31. Brought into force on 10 March 2008 by SSI 2008/42 (C.4) art.3 and Sch.

[THE NEXT PARAGRAPH IS A4-82.3]

DEFINITIONS

"prosecutor": s.307(1). **A4-82.3**
"indictment": s.307(1).

GENERAL NOTE

This section introduces a measure of flexibility at the initial stage of solemn proceedings and enables a prosecutor, faced with an excessive burden of custody business which merits petition proceedings, to move part or all of that court business, from his jurisdiction into any other sheriffdom. Such a step can only be taken with the consent of the sheriff principals of the originating and receiving courts. The section does not require any consideration of the geographical proximity of the affected courts, but in practical terms, that would undoubtedly be a factor which would have to be considered when moving prisoners from one court to another. An order may have regard to a specific event (for example substantial sporting events or political protests of the kind seen during the G8 summit at Gleneagles in 2006) and can be for a specified period of time. **A4-82.4**

The provision appears to be deceptively simple but some procedural matters merit attention: it is submitted that while the petition would ordinarily run in the name of the prosecutor within whose jurisdiction the alleged offences occurred, there would appear to be no obstacle to the petition running instead in the name of the receiving prosecutor. Nonetheless, in order to found jurisdiction in what, ex facie, would appear to be an incompetent petition, devoid of jurisdiction, it is suggested that it would be prudent within the body of the petition to refer to the currency of the s.34A order petition itself; secondly, the committal order ought to be extended to identify the court in which the case would call for full committal at a later date, not least because the papers would have to be retained in the interim lest any application be made for review or appeal of bail, or any other order pronounced by the court, become subject of appeal.

The section is explicit on one matter at least; subs.(5) provides that the fact of transfer at the petition stage does not, of itself, confer jurisdiction upon the receiving sheriffdom in any subsequent indictment proceedings .While it is not explicitly stated, the provisions of subs.(5) only apply to sheriff solemn proceedings; the High Court of Justiciary has an overarching jurisdiction and can sit in any court in Scotland as the Lord Justice General directs.

[THE NEXT PARAGRAPH IS A4-83]

Judicial examination

Judicial examination

A4-83 **35.**—(1) The accused's solicitor shall be entitled to be present at the examination.

(2) The sheriff may delay the examination for a period not exceeding 48 hours from and after the time of the accused's arrest, in order to allow time for the attendance of the solicitor.

(3) [...]

(4) [...]

(4A) An accused charged with an offence listed in subsection (4AA)(b) shall, as soon as he is brought before the sheriff for examination on the charge, be told—

(a) that his case at, or for the purposes of, any relevant hearing in the course of the proceedings may be conducted only by a lawyer;

(b) that it is, therefore, in his interests, if he has not already done so, to get the professional assistance of a solicitor; and

(c) that, if he does not engage a solicitor for the purposes of the conduct of his case at or for the purposes of the hearing, the court will do so.

(4AA) For the purposes of subsection (4A)—

(a) "relevant hearing" is to be construed in accordance with section 288C(1A) or (as the case may be) 288DC(4),

(b) the list is—

(i) an offence to which section 288C applies (certain sexual offending),

(ii) an offence to which section 288DC applies (domestic abuse cases).

(4B) A failure to comply with subsection (4A) above does not affect the validity or lawfulness of the examination or of any other element of the proceedings against the accused.

(5) [...]

(6) Where the accused is brought before the sheriff for further examination the sheriff may delay that examination for a period not exceeding 24 hours in order to allow time for the attendance of the accused's solicitor.

(6A) In proceedings before the sheriff in examination or further examination, the accused is not to be given an opportunity to make a declaration in respect of any charge.

(7) Any proceedings before the sheriff in examination or further examination shall be conducted in chambers and outwith the presence of any co-accused.

(8) This section applies to procedure on petition, without prejudice to the accused being tried summarily by the sheriff for any offence in respect of which he has been committed until liberated in due course of law.

AMENDMENTS

Subss.(4A) and (4B) inserted by Sexual Offences (Procedure and Evidence) (Scotland) Act 2002 (asp 9) Sch.1 para.3.

Subs.(4A) as amended by Criminal Justice (Scotland) Act 2003 (asp 7) Sch.4 para.3. Brought into force on 25 November 2003 by SSI 2003/475 (C.26) art.2.

Subs.(4A) as amended by Criminal Procedure (Amendment) (Scotland) Act 2004 (asp 5) s.25, Sch.1 para.12. Brought into force on 4 December 2004 by SSI 2004/405 (C.28).

Subs.(4A) as amended by Criminal Justice and Licensing (Scotland) Act 2010 (asp 13) Sch.7 para.36. Brought into force on 28 March 2011 by SSI 2011/178 (C.15) art.2, Sch.1 para.1.

Subss.(3), (4), (5) repealed, subs.(6A) inserted, by Criminal Justice (Scotland) Act 2016 (asp 1) s.78. Brought into force on 17 January 2017 by SSI 2016/426 art.2, Sch.1.

Subs.(4A) as amended, subs.(4AA) inserted, by Domestic Abuse (Scotland) Act 2018 (asp 5) Sch.1(1)(2) para.4(2) (effective 1 April 2019 in respect of proceedings commenced on or after 1 April 2019 subject to transitional provision specified in SSI 2018/387 reg.7(2))).

DEFINITIONS

"constable": s.307(1) and s.51(1) of the Police (Scotland) Act 1967. **A4-83.1**
"procurator": s.307(1).
"sheriff": s.4(1) and (4).

[THE NEXT PARAGRAPH IS A4-84]

GENERAL NOTE

Following commencement of s.78 of the Criminal Justice (Scotland) Act 2016 on 17 January 2017 (for which see the Criminal Justice (Scotland) Act 2016 (Commencement No.3 and Saving Provision) Order 2016 (SSI 2016/426)) the procedures of judicial examination, and judicial declaration described in s.35(4), are repealed. By the same token ss.36–39 of the 1995 Act are subject to the same repeal provision. **A4-84**

The Order makes a saving provision which retains ss.35–39 for any judicial examination or declaration conducted before 17 January 2017. Art.3(a) of the Order retains the terms of s.36(10) and (11) of the 1995 Act thus obliging the Crown to investigate, so far as practicable, the terms of any ostensible defence stated in the course of such examination or declaration. It will be appreciated that the Crown was never obliged to examine an accused judicially and that since the inception of the procedure in the 1980 Act have opted increasingly not to do so, leaving the procedure to become moribund; judicial declarations were relatively rare events in modern times.

On a cautionary note (particularly since solemn retrials following conviction and appeal are not unknown, and solemn apprehension warrants for failure to appear at trial or earlier procedural diets generally remain extant for years) care may be needed to retain and lodge transcripts of judicial declarations and examinations conducted before 17 January 2017 at a retrial, or trial after execution of an apprehension warrant, if only to avoid compatibility issues. See, however, *Robertson v HM Advocate,* 1995 S.C.C.R. 152.

The notes which follow relate solely to proceedings prior to 17 January 2017. As with all petition procedure, judicial examination was held in private, outwith the presence of any co-accused or their agents.

The right of an accused person to emit a judicial declaration is preserved by s.35(4) of the 1995 Act and this can be made at any time before service of the indictment. The terms of a previously prepared statement can be declared by an accused provided that the words used are truly his own; it is not permissible for another person, even his solicitor, to edit or style the declaration since this may alter its sense or character (see *Carmichael v Armitage*, 1982 S.C.C.R. 475).

A rare modern example of a declaration being made and not properly recorded either to meet the statutory requirements of s.20B of the 1975 Act or even the common law standards which prevailed prior to the 1980 Act is found in *Robertson v HM Advocate*, 1995 S.C.C.R. 152, discussed in the notes to s.37 below.

Subsection (5) affords the prosecutor an opportunity then, or at a later time, to question the accused either about the contents of such a declaration or about any new admission made to, or heard by, a police officer which is deemed relevant to the charge libelled on the petition.

The prosecutor's right to examine upon any new material certainly can be exercised at any time before service of the indictment and arguably, by inference from *Frame v Houston*, 1991 J.C. 115, up until the trial commences.

Section 17(2) of the 1995 Act stipulates that the accused shall be entitled to a private interview with his solicitor prior to judicial examination or court appearance and s.35(2), in effect, places the court under an obligation to ensure that access to legal advice has been offered. There is no requirement that an accused person must have had such a private interview or be legally represented at his judicial examination, but the court has to draw the accused's attention to his right to such services. Failure to do so may vitiate any admissions made in the course of the declaration by an accused without benefit of legal representation: see *HM Advocate v Goodall* (1888) 2 White 1.

Subsection (6) gives the sheriff a discretion to delay the first examination for a further 24 hours to allow for the attendance of the agent nominated by the accused. Until the first examination has been concluded it is not competent for the accused to apply for bail.

There is no obligation upon the Crown to seek to judicially examine an accused in any petition case; the procedure for conduct of judicial examinations is laid out in s.36 of the Act and ss.37 and 38 specify the form of the record of proceedings. Subs.(4A), most recently amended by the 2004 Act, now directs the sheriff presiding over petition proceedings to inform an accused, who has been charged with a listed sexual offence (this includes offences which appear to contain a substantial sexual element), that he cannot prepare or conduct his defence personally but must be legally represented. See the General Note to s.17A above and note that s.17A(2) makes it plain that a failure to inform the accused of this restriction is not fatal to subsequent proceedings. Additional provisions are found in the Act of Adjournal (Criminal Procedure Rules 1996) Chs 5 and 25.

Subs.(6A)

Subs.(6A), inserted by s.78 of the 2016 Act, removes the common law right of an accused to be given the opportunity to make a declaration at the commencement of a case being prosecuted. The removal of an opportunity for an accused to state in a judicial context an explanation, defence or admission of guilt at the earliest procedural point seems unfair. The power may not have been used much in the modern era, but it may have been forensically significant when it was done.

Judicial examination: questioning by prosecutor

A4-85 **36.** [...]

AMENDMENTS

Section 36 repealed by Criminal Justice (Scotland) Act 2016 (asp 1) s.78. Brought into force on 17 January 2017 by SSI 2016/426 art.2, Sch.1.

DEFINITIONS

A4-85.1 "constable": s.307(1) and s.51(1) of the Police (Scotland) Act 1967.
"prosecutor": s.307(1).

[THE NEXT PARAGRAPH IS A4-86]

GENERAL NOTE

A4-86 Following commencement of s.78 of the Criminal Justice (Scotland) Act 2016 on 17 January 2017 (for which see the Criminal Justice (Scotland) Act 2016 (Commencement No.3 and Saving Provision) Order 2016 (SSI 2016/426)) the procedures of judicial examination, and judicial declaration described in s.35(4), are repealed. By the same token ss.36–39 of the 1995 Act are subject to the same repeal provision. See the fuller discussion at General Note to s.35 above.

Act of Adjournal

Additional provisions are found in the Act of Adjournal (Criminal Procedure Rules) 1996, Chs 5 and 25. See particularly r.5.5.

Judicial examination: record of proceedings

A4-87 **37.** [...]

AMENDMENTS

Subs.(9) as amended by Act of Adjournal (Extension of Time Limit for Service of Transcript of Examination) 1998 (SI 1998/2635: effective December 1, 1998).

Section 37 repealed by Criminal Justice (Scotland) Act 2016 (asp 1) s.78. Brought into force on 17 January 2017 by SSI 2016/426 art.2, Sch.1.

DEFINITION

A4-87.1 "prosecutor": s.307(1).

[THE NEXT PARAGRAPH IS A4-88]

GENERAL NOTE

A4-88 Following commencement of s.78 of the Criminal Justice (Scotland) Act 2016 on 17 January 2017 (for which see the Criminal Justice (Scotland) Act 2016 (Commencement No. 3 and Saving Provision) Order 2016 (SSI 2016/426)) the procedures of judicial examination, and judicial declaration described in s.35(4), are repealed. By the same token ss.36–39 of the 1995 Act are subject to the same repeal provision.

Act of Adjournal

See the Act of Adjournal (Criminal Procedure Rules) 1996 r.5.2 and Form 5.2 which deal with the record of proceedings. The form to be used for intimation where a trial diet has been postponed for the purposs of s.37(7) is found at Form 5.8.

Judicial examination: rectification of record of proceedings

A4-89 **38.** [...]

AMENDMENTS

Section 38 repealed by Criminal Justice (Scotland) Act 2016 (asp 1) s.78. Brought into force on 17 January 2017 by SSI 2016/426 art.2, Sch.1.

DEFINITION

"prosecutor": s.307(1). A4-89.1

[THE NEXT PARAGRAPH IS A4-90]

GENERAL NOTE

Following commencement of s.78 of the Criminal Justice (Scotland) Act 2016 on 17 January 2017 (for which see the Criminal Justice (Scotland) Act 2016 (Commencement No. 3 and Saving Provision) Order 2016 (SSI 2016/426)) the procedures of judicial examination, and judicial declaration described in s.35(4), are repealed. By the same token ss.36–39 of the 1995 Act are subject of the same repeal provision. A4-90

Act of Adjournal

See the Act of Adjournal (Criminal Procedure Rules) 1996 particularly r.5.6 and Forms 5.6-A to 5.6-C.

Judicial examination: charges arising in different districts

39.—(1) An accused against whom there are charges in more than one sheriff court district may be brought before the sheriff of any one such district at the instance of the procurator fiscal of such district for examination on all or any of the charges. A4-91

(2) Where an accused is brought for examination as mentioned in subsection (1) above, he may be dealt with in every respect as if all of the charges had arisen in the district where he is examined.

(3) This section is without prejudice to the power of the Lord Advocate under section 10 of this Act to determine the court before which the accused shall be tried on such charges.

DEFINITIONS

"procurator fiscal": s.307(1). A4-91.1

"sheriff court district": s.307(1).

[THE NEXT PARAGRAPH IS A4-92]

GENERAL NOTE

Following commencement of s.78 of the Criminal Justice (Scotland) Act 2016 on 17 January 2017 (for which see the Criminal Justice (Scotland) Act 2016 (Commencement No. 3 and Saving Provision) Order 2016 (SSI 2016/426)) the procedures of judicial examination, and judicial declaration described in s.35(4), are repealed. By the same token ss.36–39 of the 1995 Act are subject of the same repeal provision. See the fuller discussion at General Note to s.35 above. A4-92

The Lord Advocate's discretion to select which sheriff court shall exercise jurisdiction over offences arising from more than one jurisdiction is preserved by this section.

Committal

Committal until liberated in due course of law

40.—(1) Every petition shall be signed and no accused shall be committed until liberated in due course of law for any crime or offence without a warrant in writing expressing the particular charge in respect of which he is committed. A4-93

(2) Any such warrant for imprisonment which either proceeds on an unsigned petition or does not express the particular charge shall be null and void.

(3) The accused shall immediately be given a true copy of the warrant for imprisonment signed by the constable or person executing the warrant before imprisonment or by the prison officer receiving the warrant.

GENERAL NOTE

The petition should correspond with the forms prescribed in Schs 2 and 3 of the Act or as near as may be; see s.34 above and the general note thereto. A4-94

In *Mellors v Normand*, 1996 J.C. 148 a bill of suspension was taken against full committal on a petition which had charged M with attempting to defeat the ends of justice by his failure to provide blood and saliva samples and dental impressions in compliance with an earlier warrant; while the bill was refused on its merits as being premature, it is noted that the Crown did not challenge its competency. There is no doubt that if an essential feature of a petition charge (designation of accused, a charge and sufficient information in support of the petition) is absent then a bill to suspend a committal warrant would be competent. No such deficiencies were evident in M's case.

Note *McCaffer v Lord Advocate*, 2015 S.L.T. 44, a competent civil action for damages (breach of art.5 of ECHR alleged) where it was argued that the Crown had delayed full disclosure of exculpatory CCTV materials, having secured full committal of the accused. He had subsequently been liberated without further proceedings after the materials were secured and examined and sued the Lord Advocate and the Chief Constable. The action failed on its merits.

PART V – CHILDREN AND YOUNG PERSONS

Age of criminal responsibility

A4-95 **41.** It shall be conclusively presumed that no child under the age of eight years can be guilty of any offence.

DEFINITIONS

A4-95.1 "child": s.307(1) and s.93(2)(b) of the Children (Scotland) Act 1995.

[THE NEXT PARAGRAPH IS A4-96]

GENERAL NOTE

A4-96 This provision repeats the presumption of nonage found in the Children and Young Persons (Scotland) Act 1937 (c.37) s.55. See also Macdonald (5th edn, Edinburgh 1948), p.271.

Consequently proceedings against a child aged less than eight years are incompetent and should be disposed of by means of a plea in bar of trial at a first diet in sheriff and jury proceedings or a preliminary diet in the High Court (refer to ss.71 to 73 below).

Prosecution of children under 12

A4-96.1 **41A.—**(1) A child under the age of 12 years may not be prosecuted for an offence.

(2) A person aged 12 years or more may not be prosecuted for an offence which was committed at a time when the person was under the age of 12 years.

AMENDMENTS

Section 41A inserted by Criminal Justice and Licensing (Scotland) Act 2010 (asp 13) s.52(2). Brought into force on 28 March 2011 by SSI 2011/178 (C.15) art.2, Sch.1 para.1.

DEFINITIONS

A4-96.2 "child": s.307(1) of the 1995 Act and s.93(2)(b) of the Children (Scotland) Act 1995.
"offence": s.307(1) of the 1995 Act.

GENERAL NOTE

A4-96.3 This section reflects the recommendations of the Scottish Law Commission's *Report on Age of Criminal Responsibility* (2002) and, henceforth, both bars prosecution of any offence committed while a child was aged under 12 years and any historical offences committed while an accused was aged below 12 years. This provision renders the preceding section obsolete.

[THE NEXT PARAGRAPH IS A4-97]

Prosecution of children

A4-97 **42.—**(1) A child aged 12 years or more but under 16 years may not be prosecuted for any offence except on the instructions of the Lord Advocate, or at the instance of the Lord Advocate; and no court other than the High Court and the sheriff court shall have jurisdiction over such a child for an offence.

(2) Where a child is charged with any offence, his parent or guardian may in any case, and shall, if he can be found and resides within a reasonable distance, be required to attend at the court before which the case is heard or determined during all the stages of the proceedings, unless the court is satisfied that it would be unreasonable to require his attendance.

(3) […]

(4) For the purpose of enforcing the attendance of a parent or guardian and enabling him to take part in the proceedings and enabling orders to be made against him, rules may be made under section 305 of this Act, for applying, with the necessary adaptations and modifications, such of the provisions of this Act relating to summary proceedings as appear appropriate for the purpose.

(5) The parent or guardian whose attendance is required under this section is—

(a) the parent who has parental responsibilities or parental rights (within the meaning of sections 1(3) and 2(4) respectively of the Children (Scotland) Act 1995) in relation to the child; or

(b) the guardian having actual possession and control of him.

(6) The attendance of the parent of a child shall not be required under this section in any case where the child was before the institution of the proceedings removed from the care or charge of his parent by an order of a court.

(7) […]

(8) Where a local authority receive notification under section 24 of the Criminal Justice (Scotland) Act 2016 they shall make such investigations and submit to the court a report which shall contain such information as to the home surroundings of the child as appear to them will assist the court in the disposal of his case, and the report shall contain information, which the appropriate education authority shall have a duty to supply, as to the school record, health and character of the child.

(9) Any child being conveyed to or from any criminal court, or waiting before or after attendance in such court, shall be prevented from associating with an adult (not being a relative) who is charged with any offence other than an offence with which the child is jointly charged.

(10) […]

AMENDMENTS

Subs.(1) as amended by Criminal Justice and Licensing (Scotland) Act 2010 (asp 13) s.52(3). Brought into force on 28 March 2011 by SSI 2011/178 (C.15) art.2, Sch.1 para.1.

Subss.(3), (7), (10) repealed, subs.(8), (9) as amended by Criminal Justice (Scotland) Act 2016 (asp 1) Sch.2 para.31. Brought into force on 25 January 2018 by SSI 2017/345 art.3 (subject to transitional and savings provisions in art.4).

DEFINITIONS

"child": s.307(1) and s.93(2)(b) of the Children (Scotland) Act 1995. **A4-97.1**
"constable": s.307(1) and s.51(1) of the Police (Scotland) Act 1967.
"High Court": s.307(1).
"local authority": s.307(1).
"parent or guardian": s.42(5) below and in relation to "guardian" only, note also s.307(1).

[THE NEXT PARAGRAPH IS A4-98]

GENERAL NOTE

While it is theoretically the case that reports of criminal offences committed by children will be submitted to the procurator fiscal in the first instance, administrative directions from the Lord Advocate instruct that such reports involving child offenders aged under 16 years will, ordinarily, be referred to the principal reporter for his consideration. Even where there are factors which merit the submission of a report to the procurator fiscal, the police are still required in terms of the Children (Scotland) Act 1995 (c.36) to furnish a copy of the report to the appropriate reporter. Thereafter it is a matter for discussion between the procurator fiscal and the reporter whether the case should be retained for criminal prosecution or dealt with under the previously-mentioned Act. **A4-98**

When the case is retained by the procurator fiscal to initiate a prosecution, it is mandatory in terms of subs.(1) that any proceedings must occur in the sheriff court or a higher court. Rule 6.3 of the 1996 Act of Adjournal enacts that criminal proceedings can only be raised by the procurator fiscal who is, of course, required to comply with the Lord Advocate's directions. The spirit of s.15 of the 1995 Act (which enacts special provisions in regard to the detention of a child, and parental access to a child held in custody) is echoed in s.54: subss.(9) and (10) contain provisions to segregate children from adult offenders while remanded in custody or awaiting trial at court. Oddly, it is not deemed necessary to separate the child entirely from adult accused. Subsection (9) stops short of this and permits detention in custody, or in the court precincts, and transportation to or from court appearances, in the company of adult co-accused or relatives (whether the relatives are, or are not, accused persons).

In a similar spirit, s.142 of the Act stipulates that summary proceedings against a child must be held in private and in different rooms, or on different days, from the criminal courts in which adults appear. The sole exception to this rule is when the child appears on the same complaint or petition as an adult accused; in that event the case has to proceed in the usual "adult" court. The corollary of these provisions so far as an adult co-accused is concerned, is that when charged along with a child on a summary complaint he will necessarily appear in the sheriff, not the district, court.

The scope of s.142 (which replaces s.366(1) of the 1975 Act) extends to appearances from custody, cited diets and trials but it has been held to be directory rather than mandatory in character: failure by the court to obtemper its provisions would not nullify any subsequent conviction; see *Heywood v B*, 1993 S.C.C.R. 554. It is likely that the provisions of s.42 would equally be construed as being directory in nature. Similarly, the 1996 Act of Adjournal r.6.6 indicates that steps should be taken by the court to avoid children attending hearings from mixing with each other by appropriate scheduling of cases and providing suitable supervision of waiting facilities.

Subs.(1)

Amendment to subs.(1) takes account of the reforms introduced by s.41A above; it remains the case that the authority of the Lord Advocate is required before prosecution of a child can be initiated. Any such proceedings must be conducted in the sheriff court or the High Court.

Subss.(3), (7) and (8)

Subsection (3) instructs the police to notify the parent or guardian of the child of the impending court appearance and, wherever practicable, to require parental attendance at the court on the appropriate date. Unreasonable failure to attend the court by a parent or guardian after receipt of such notice can attract criminal penalties and, accordingly, the police should warn of this fact when giving notice of the court date.

Where the child is already in the care of the local authority or has a guardian as a result of a court order, the police are under no duty to advise the parent (defined in subs.(5)(a)) of the proceedings. The date and time of the child's court appearance, and the nature of charges must also be communicated by the police to the local authority within whose boundaries the court is situated. In the event of a finding of guilt, that authority will be responsible for preparing background reports about the child's circumstances for the court.

Act of Adjournal

Refer to Ch.6 of the Act of Adjournal (Criminal Procedure Rules) 1996 for procedural guidance.

Arrangements where children arrested

A4-99 **43.—** [...]

AMENDMENTS

Subss.(1) and (6) substituted by Crime and Punishment (Scotland) Act 1997 (c.48) s.55 with effect from 1 August 1997 in terms of SI 1997/1712 para.3.

Section 43 repealed by Criminal Justice (Scotland) Act 2016 (asp 1) Sch.2 para.27(c). Brought into force on 25 January 2018 by SSI 2017/345 art.3 (subject to transitional and savings provisions in arts 4 and 5).

DEFINITIONS

A4-99.1 "child": s.307(1) and s.93(2)(b) of the Children (Scotland) Act 1995.
"parent or guardian": s.42(5) and in relation to "guardian" only also refer to s.307(1).
"place of safety" : s.307(1) and s.93(1) of the Children (Scotland) Act 1995.
"Principal Reporter": s.93(1) of the Children (Scotland) Act 1995.

[THE NEXT PARAGRAPH IS A4-100]

GENERAL NOTE

A4-100 This section repeats the provisions previously contained in ss.295 and 296 of the 1975 Act with account being taken of the introduction of the Children (Scotland) Act 1995 and small, but significant, changes wrought by the Crime and Punishment (Scotland) Act 1997. It is still to be assumed generally that a child arrested for a criminal offence will be brought before a court without delay, or be liberated on his undertaking, or that of his parent or guardian, to appear at court on a specified date. Subs.(1) as now enacted gives greater discretion to the police to withhold an undertaking. Once an undertaking is entered into, failure to appear at the designated time and place becomes an offence but only in the event of conviction of the original charge which gave rise to the undertaking. The terms of the undertaking can be proved in any proceedings by production of a certified copy of the original form and, it is submitted, that the signatory is in a position of special capacity. While the Act does not specify the form the undertaking should take, subs.(7) clearly envisages that it should be in writing.

In more serious cases as defined in subs.(3), the first effort should be to bring the child before a sheriff forthwith. If that is not practicable, then the senior police officer involved must first endeavour to obtain accommodation for the child in a place of safety, namely a local authority residential establishment, a community home, a hospital, surgery or "other suitable place" whose occupier is willing to take in the child.

Note that while the statutory definition of "a place of safety" in the Children (Scotland) Act s.93(1) includes a police station, this does not hold good for the purposes of s.43(4) of the 1995 Act—police stations are expressly excluded as acceptable accommodation for this purpose. The reason for this apparent anomaly is found later in subs.(4) which stipulates the conditions which must prevail before a child can be held in police custody pending his appearance before the court: broadly, if it is not practical to convey the child to a suitable place of safety or such a place is not available, or the child's character is unruly and militates against his safe detention in an available place of safety, or there are medical grounds which raise concern for his well-being, then continued detention in a police station will be justified. The senior police officer must then certify the reasons for resorting to detention of the child in police custody rather than the preferred option of a place of safety and that certificate must be produced to the court when the child first appears. It will be noted that during such a period of detention, the police are still obliged to keep the child segregated from adult prisoners (see the notes to s.42(9) above).

If the procurator fiscal decides not to proceed with charges against the child, subss.(6) and (7) contain saving provisions to enable the child to be detained pending initial investigation by the principal reporter (see s.56(1) and (6) of the Children (Scotland) Act 1995) and consideration if necessary by a children's hearing within seven days.

Detention of children

44.—(1) Where a child appears before the sheriff in summary proceedings and pleads guilty to, or is found guilty of, an offence to which this section applies, the sheriff may order that he be detained in residential accommodation provided under Part II of the Children (Scotland) Act 1995 by the appropriate local authority for such period not exceeding one year as may be specified in the order in such place (in any part of the United Kingdom) as the local authority may, from time to time, consider appropriate. **A4-101**

(2) This section applies to any offence (other than, if the child is under the age of 16 years, an offence under section 9(1) of the Antisocial Behaviour etc. (Scotland) Act 2004 (asp 8) or that section as applied by section 234AA(11) of this Act) in respect of which it is competent to impose imprisonment on a person of the age of 21 years or more.

(3) Where a child in respect of whom an order is made under this section is detained by the appropriate local authority, that authority shall have the same powers and duties in respect of the child as they would have if he were subject to a compulsory supervision order.

(4) Where a child in respect of whom an order is made under this section is also subject to a compulsory supervision order or interim compulsory supervision order, subject to subsection (6) below, the compulsory supervision order or interim compulsory supervision order shall be of no effect during any period for which he is required to be detained under the order.

(5) The Secretary of State may, by regulations made by statutory instrument subject to annulment in pursuance of a resolution of either House of Parliament, make such provision as he considers necessary as regards the detention in secure accommodation of children in respect of whom orders have been made under this section.

(6) Where a child is detained in residential accommodation in pursuance of an order under—

(a) subsection (1) above, he shall be released from such detention not later than the date by which half the period specified in the order has (following commencement of the detention) elapsed but, without prejudice to subsection (7) below, until the entire such period has so elapsed may be required by the local authority to submit to supervision in accordance with such conditions as they consider appropriate;

(b) subsection (1) above or (8) below, the local authority may at any time review his case and may, in consequence of such review and after having regard to the best interests of the child and the need to protect members of the public, release the child—

(i) for such period and on such conditions as the local authority consider appropriate; or

(ii) unconditionally.

(7) Where a child released under paragraph (a) or (b)(ii) of subsection (6) above is subject to a compulsory supervision order or interim compulsory supervision order, the effect of that order shall commence or, as the case may be, resume upon such release.

(8) If, while released under paragraph (a) or (b) of subsection (6) above (and before the date on which the entire period mentioned in the said paragraph (a) has, following the commencement of the detention, elapsed), a child commits an offence to which this section applies and (whether before or after that date) pleads guilty to or is found guilty of it a court may, instead of or in addition to making any other order in respect of that plea or finding, order that he be returned to the residential accommodation provided by the authority which released him and that his detention in that accommodation or any other such accommodation provided by that authority shall continue for the whole or any part of the period which—

(a) begins with the date of the order for his return; and

(b) is equal in length to the period between the date on which the new offence was committed and the date on which that entire period elapses.

(9) An order under subsection (8) above for return to residential accommodation provided by the appropriate local authority—

(a) shall be taken to be an order for detention in residential accommodation for the purpose of this Act and any appeal; and

(b) shall, as the court making that order may direct, either be for a period of detention in residential accommodation before and to be followed by, or to be concurrent with, any period of such detention to be imposed in respect of the new offence (being in either case disregarded in determining the appropriate length of the period so imposed).

(10) Where a local authority consider it appropriate that a child in respect of whom an order has been made under subsection (1) or (8) above should be detained in a place in any part of the United Kingdom outside Scotland, the order shall be a like authority as in Scotland to the person in charge of the place to restrict the child's liberty to such an extent as that person may consider appropriate having regard to the terms of the order.

(11) In this section—

"the appropriate local authority" means—

(a) where the child usually resides in Scotland, the local authority for the area in which he usually resides;

(b) in any other case, the local authority for the area in which the offence was committed; and

"secure accommodation" means accommodation provided for the purpose of restricting the liberty of children which—

(a) in Scotland, is provided in a residential establishment approved in accordance with regulations made under section 78(2) of the Public Service Reform (Scotland) Act 2010;

(b) in England, is provided in a children's home within the meaning of the Care Standards Act 2000 in respect of which a person is registered under Part 2 of that Act, except that before the coming into force of section 107(2) of the Health and Social Care (Community Health Standards) Act 2003, "secure accommodation" means accommodation in relation to England which—

(i) is provided in a children's home, within the meaning of the Care Standards Act 2000, in respect of which a person is registered under Part 2 of that Act; and

(ii) is approved by the Secretary of State for the purpose of restricting the liberty of children; and

(c) in Wales, is provided in a children's home within the meaning of the Care Standards Act 2000 in respect of which a person is registered under Part 2 of that Act.

AMENDMENTS

Subss.(6), (7), (8), (9) prospectively repealed, and subss.(4) and (10) prospectively amended, by Crime and Punishment (Scotland) Act 1997 (c.48) s.62(1) and Sch.1 para.21(3) but never in force due to repeal of Sch.1 para.21(3) by Crime and Disorder Act 1998 (c.37) Sch.10 para.1 (effective 30 September 1998; SI 1998/2327)

Subs.(2) as amended by Antisocial Behaviour etc. (Scotland) Act 2004 s.10. Brought into force on 28 October 2004 by SSI 2004/420 (C.31).

Subss.(3), (4), (7) and (11) as amended by Children's Hearings (Scotland) Act 2011 (Modification of Primary Legislation) Order 2013 (SSI 2013/1465) Sch.3 para.2 (effective 24 June 2013).

Subs.(11) as amended by Children and Young People (Scotland) Act 2014 (asp 8) Sch.5 para.5(2). Brought into force on 30 September 2015 by SSI 2015/317 art.2 Sch.1 para.1.

Subs.(11) as amended by Children and Young People (Scotland) Act 2014 (Consequential and Saving Provisions) Order 2015 (SSI 2015/907) art.3 (effective 30 September 2015).

DEFINITIONS

"appropriate local authority" : s.44(11). A4-101.1
"child": s.307(1) and s.93(2)(b) of the Children (Scotland) Act 1995.
"offence": s.307(1).
"residential accommodation" : s.307(1).
"secure accommodation": s.44(11) and s.93(1) of the Children (Scotland) Act 1995.
"supervision requirement": s.307(1) and s.70(1) of the Children (Scotland) Act 1995.

[THE NEXT PARAGRAPH IS A4-102]

GENERAL NOTE

This section enables a sheriff sitting summarily to impose a term of detention in residential accommodation of up to one year when an offence, for which imprisonment could competently be imposed upon an adult, is held or admitted to have been committed by a child. The sheriff may then consider immediate use of his powers under s.44 or, in the first instance (and more usually), refer the case under s.49 of the Act to the Principal Reporter for the advice of a children's hearing: when the child is already under a supervision requirement, s.49(3)(b) stipulates that the advice of a children's hearing must be obtained. A4-102

Only a minority of cases will be likely to merit a disposal in terms of s.44 without first obtaining the advice of a children's hearing. The use of s.44 powers is perhaps an indication that the paramount consideration in sentencing has been public safety and the preservation of good order rather than the well-being of the child. Most cases involving juveniles found guilty of offences will continue to require the advice of a children's hearing.

Statutory duties of local authority

When the sheriff either with, or less usually without, advice of a children's hearing imposes detention under s.44, it is then the duty of the Scottish local authority within whose area the child lives, to provide such accommodation at a place within the United Kingdom selected by the authority. However if the child is not ordinarily resident in Scotland then this responsibility falls upon the local authority within whose area the offence was committed. It is not explicitly stated in the Act, but it seems reasonable to assume that, in the event of offences being committed in a number of jurisdictions, responsibility for providing suitable accommodation would rest with the local authority within whose area the sheriff court making the order was situated. A4-103

Subsection (3) provides that the powers and responsibilities of a local authority given charge of such a child will be the same as those regulating supervision requirements and reference to s.70(4) of the Children (Scotland) Act shows that this includes such restrictions on the child's liberty as are deemed appropriate.

Where supervision requirements are imposed by a children's hearing, the hearing can direct that the child resides in residential accommodation or (in more extreme cases) in such accommodation but under secure conditions (see s.70(3) and (8) of the Children (Scotland) Act 1995). Subsection (1) of the 1995 Act states that the court can order that the child "be detained" in residential accommodation, while subs.(5) deals with the regulation of secure accommodation. It is unfortunate that the same phraseology has not been employed consistently in both pieces of legislation, but the provisions of subs.(6) suggest that what is envisaged is placement of the child in secure accommodation and not simply local authority residential care.

Subsection (10) permits the Scottish local authority exercising jurisdiction to remit the child into the custody of persons elsewhere in the United Kingdom when this is felt appropriate. The persons then assuming responsibility for the charge of the child have the same duties and powers as would be vested in an individual under s.44 in Scotland.

Early release provisions and effect of further offences

A4-104 In a manner similar to s.16 of the Prisoners and Criminal Proceedings (Scotland) Act 1993 (c.9) (which deals with the commission of offences by released prisoners during remission), subs.(6) affords a child an opportunity of remission of at least half of the period of detention. This concession can be rescinded if it is established that a further offence has been committed during the remission period and the timescale of the original detention order has not expired (in practice it may be difficult to re-apply the unexpired portion of the detention period since the sentence imposed under s.44 by the sheriff may have been relatively short).

In the event of re-offending being established the court can apply a full range of disposals but subs.(8) makes it competent to return the child to the residential accommodation from which he was earlier released there to serve the unexpired portion of that earlier detention, calculated according to subs.(8). This re-imposition of the order can be instead of, or in addition to, any disposal resulting from the later offence which had been committed during the early release period. Subsection (9) adds that the remaining portion of the original detention order may be served prior to, or concurrent with, the period of detention imposed for the later offence.

Section 44 and existing supervision requirements

A4-105 Where the child appearing before the court is already the subject of a supervision requirement made by a children's hearing, subs.(4) provides for the suspension of that requirement until the appropriate period of detention has been served by the child.

On release from detention (either at the expiry of the full term of detention imposed by the court, or earlier in accordance with subs.(6)(a)), the pre-existing supervision requirement can be resumed. However, even when detention has been imposed by the court, the local authority still has a statutory duty to review the case of any child subject to a supervision requirement (see s.72(6) of the Children (Scotland) Act 1995) and has a discretionary power under the 1995 Act to conduct such a review for children detained by way of a s.44 order—see subs.(6)(b). Indeed, theoretically, such a s.44 review could constitute the first contact between the hearing and the child offender since, as was noted earlier, the statutory obligation upon the sentencing sheriff to seek the advice of a children's hearing before imposing a period of detention upon the child only applies to children who were already subject to a current supervision requirement.

When reviewing the case of a child detained under a s.44 order, the hearing may, following subs.(6) discharge it altogether or vary its terms once due regard has been paid to both the interests of the child and the protection of the public.

Appeal against detention in secure accommodation

A4-105.1 **44A.**—(1) A child, or a relevant person in relation to the child, may appeal to the sheriff against a decision by a local authority to detain the child in secure accommodation in pursuance of an order made under section 44 of this Act.

(2) An appeal under subsection (1) may be made jointly by—

(a) the child and one or more relevant persons in relation to the child; or

(b) two or more relevant persons in relation to the child.

(3) An appeal must not be held in open court.

(4) The sheriff may determine an appeal by—

(a) confirming the decision to detain the child in secure accommodation; or

(b) quashing that decision and directing the local authority to move the child to be detained in residential accommodation which is not secure accommodation.

(5) The Scottish Ministers may by regulations make further provision about appeals under subsection (1).

(6) Regulations under subsection (5) may in particular—

(a) specify the period within which an appeal may be made;

(b) make provision about the hearing of evidence during an appeal;
(c) provide for appeals to the Sheriff Appeal Court and Court of Session against the determination of an appeal.

(7) Regulations under subsection (5) are subject to the affirmative procedure.

(8) In this section—

"relevant person", in relation to a child, means any person who is a relevant person in relation to the child for the purposes of the Children's Hearings (Scotland) Act 2011 (including anyone deemed to be a relevant person in relation to the child by virtue of section 81(3), 160(4)(b) or 164(6) of that Act);

"secure accommodation" has the same meaning as in section 44 of this Act.

AMENDMENTS

Section 44A inserted by Children and Young People (Scotland) Act 2014 (asp 8) s.91. Brought into force on 1 August 2014 by SSI 2014/131 art.2 and Sch.1 para.1 (to enable Scottish Ministers to make regulations under s.44A(5) and (6); not yet in force otherwise).

Subs.(6)(c) as amended by Courts Reform (Scotland) Act 2014 (Consequential and Supplemental Provisions) Order 2015 (SSI 2015/402) Sch.1 para.3 (effective 1 January 2016).

[THE NEXT PARAGRAPH IS A4-106]

Security for child's good behaviour

45.—(1) Where a child has been charged with an offence the court may order his parent or guardian to give security for his co-operation in securing the child's good behaviour. **A4-106**

(2) Subject to subsection (3) below, an order under this section shall not be made unless the parent or guardian has been given the opportunity of being heard.

(3) Where a parent or guardian has been required to attend and fails to do so, the court may make an order under this section.

(4) Any sum ordered to be paid by a parent or guardian on the forfeiture of any security given under this section may be recovered from him by civil diligence or imprisonment in like manner as if the order had been made on the conviction of the parent or guardian of the offence with which the child was charged.

(5) In this section "parent" means either of the child's parents, if that parent has parental responsibilities or parental rights (within the meaning of sections 1(3) and 2(4) respectively of the Children (Scotland) Act 1995) in relation to him.

DEFINITIONS

"child": s.307(1) and s.93(2)(b) of the Children (Scotland) Act 1995. **A4-106.1**
"offence": s.307(1).
"parent": s.45(5) and ss.1(3), 2(4) and 3(5) of the Children (Scotland) Act 1995.
"guardian": s.307(1).

[THE NEXT PARAGRAPH IS A4-107]

GENERAL NOTE

This section permits the court to require caution to be found by the parent or de facto guardian of the child as a surety for parental co-operation in assuring the future good conduct of the child. Such a condition can only be imposed after the parent or guardian has been given an opportunity to be heard by the court, but it has been ruled unnecessary for a formal citation to attend there to have been served upon him; notification made by a police officer would probably suffice. See *White v Jeans* (1911) 6 Adam 489 and *Montgomery v Grey* (1915) 7 Adam 681. Note that subs.(2) does not stipulate that the parent must have been heard, only that the opportunity to be heard has been given. The court under subs.(3) can order attendance by the parent or guardian and require a finding of security, even in the absence of the person concerned. Failure by the parent or guardian to ensure the orderly conduct of the child can result in forfeiture of the amount of security. This can be recovered by civil diligence or by the imprisonment of the guarantor. **A4-107**

Presumption and determination of age of child

A4-108 **46.**—(1) Where a person charged with an offence whose age is not specified in the indictment or complaint in relation to that offence is brought before a court other than for the purpose of giving evidence, and it appears to the court that he is a child, the court shall make due enquiry as to the age of that person, and for that purpose shall take such evidence as may be forthcoming at the hearing of the case, and the age presumed or declared by the court to be the age of that person shall, for the purposes of this Act or the Children and Young Persons (Scotland) Act 1937, be deemed to be the true age of that person.

(2) The court in making any inquiry in pursuance of subsection (1) above shall have regard to the definition of child for the purposes of this Act.

(3) Without prejudice to section 255A of this Act, where in an indictment or complaint for—

(a) an offence under the Children and Young Persons (Scotland) Act 1937;
(b) any of the offences mentioned in paragraphs 3 and 4 of Schedule 1 to this Act; or
(c) an offence under section 1, 10(1) to (3) or 12 of the Criminal Law (Consolidation) (Scotland) Act 1995,

it is alleged that the person by or in respect of whom the offence was committed was a child or was under or had attained any specified age, and he appears to the court to have been at the date of the commission of the alleged offence a child, or to have been under or to have attained the specified age, as the case may be, he shall for the purposes of this Act or the Children and Young Persons (Scotland) Act 1937 or Part I of the Criminal Law (Consolidation) (Scotland) Act 1995 be presumed at that date to have been a child or to have been under or to have attained that age, as the case may be, unless the contrary is proved.

(4) Where, in an indictment or complaint for an offence under the Children and Young Persons (Scotland) Act 1937 or any of the offences mentioned in Schedule 1 to this Act, it is alleged that the person in respect of whom the offence was committed was a child or was a young person, it shall not be a defence to prove that the person alleged to have been a child was a young person or the person alleged to have been a young person was a child in any case where the acts constituting the alleged offence would equally have been an offence if committed in respect of a young person or child respectively.

(5) An order or judgement of the court shall not be invalidated by any subsequent proof that—

(a) the age of a person mentioned in subsection (1) above has not been correctly stated to the court; or
(b) the court was not informed that at the material time the person was subject to a compulsory supervision order or interim compulsory supervision order or that his case had been referred to a children's hearing by virtue of regulations made under section 190 of the Children's Hearings (Scotland) Act 2011 (asp 1).

(6) Where it appears to the court that a person mentioned in subsection (1) above has attained the age of 17 years, he shall for the purposes of this Act or the Children and Young Persons (Scotland) Act 1937 be deemed not to be a child.

(7) In subsection (3) above, references to a child (other than a child charged with an offence) shall be construed as references to a child under the age of 17 years; but except as aforesaid references in this section to a child shall be construed as references to a child within the meaning of section 307 of this Act.

AMENDMENTS

Subss.(1) and (3) inserted by Crime and Punishment (Scotland) Act 1997 (c.48) s.62(1) and Sch.1 para.21(4) with effect from August 1, 1997 by SI 1997/1712 para.3.

Subs.(5)(b) as amended by Children's Hearings (Scotland) Act 2011 (Modification of Primary Legislation) Order 2013 (SSI 2013/211) Sch.1 para.10 (effective June 24, 2013).

DEFINITIONS

"child": s.307(1) and s.93(2)(b) of the Children (Scotland) Act 1995. Note that a more restricted definition is employed in relation to subs.(3) only by virtue of subs.(7). A4-108.1

"offence": s.307(1).

[THE NEXT PARAGRAPH IS A4-109]

GENERAL NOTE

This section repeats the provisions found in the 1975 Act as amended and, in effect, contains saving provisions to prevent proceedings in which children are involved either as witnesses or as accused, being invalidated on account of error as to a child's age. The savings only operate to cure a want of procedure and cannot cure a nullity (note that in addition to the provisions of s.46 which relate specifically to children, the 1995 Act s.307(7) contains a general saving presumption covering adult persons whose age becomes a material factor during criminal proceedings). A4-109

Subss.(1), (5) and (6)

The subsections relate to the age of child offenders appearing before the court and extend to children aged under 16 years, and to any youth up to 18 years of age who at the time of appearing before the court was already the subject of a supervision requirement.

The court should if possible question the child as a means of establishing his age and assess the age by reference to his appearance. Additionally if evidence is led, that too can be scrutinised for indications of the offender's age. The court can then legitimately hold the offender's age to be established and consider the options for disposal of the case if the offence is admitted or proved. Note that if it is concluded on the basis of all the available material that the offender is 17 years old and it is not disclosed that he is subject to local authority supervision, the court can lawfully treat him as a young offender. Subsection (5) enacts that findings or orders pronounced by the court in circumstances where the court has had to deduce the child's age will not be voided if it is subsequently discovered that the court was misled.

Subss.(3) and (7)

These subsections apply when a child is either accused of an offence or is the victim of an offence. The effect of subs.(7) is to distinguish between those who meet the statutory definition of a "child" as promulgated by the 1995 Act and those who fulfil the narrower statutory definition of a "child" found in the Children and Young Persons (Scotland) Act 1937. In relation to the offences specified in Sch.1 to the 1995 Act: in the first case an offender can be aged 17 years or more and continue to be treated as a "child" within the meaning of the 1995 Act provided he is still the subject of a supervision order. However, as a victim the complainer is to be regarded as a child only until his seventeenth birthday is attained. A rebuttable presumption exists that the complainer in the statutory offences specified in subs.(3) was a child at the time of the incident libelled. Similarly where it is averred in a libel that the accused was a "child" in terms of the 1995 Act's statutory definition at the time of committing an offence, and this allegation appears to be confirmed by his bearing and physical appearance, it will be presumed that the offender's age has been established.

Subs.(4)

This subsection prevents the introduction of purely technical defences in cases involving victims who are either children or young persons.

When charged with contravening either of the statutory provisions specified in relation to a child or a young person, an accused cannot base a defence upon a discrepancy between the age of the victim, as stated in the libel, and the actuality when, in either case, an offence would have been committed.

The amendment introduced to subs.(1) by the Crime and Punishment (Scotland) Act 1997 has the effect of removing the court's duty to enquire into the age of a child when his age has been specified in the complaint or indictment. A further presumption as to proof of age, of broader application to witnesses, has been introduced into the 1995 Act as s.255A.

Restriction on report of proceedings involving children

47.—(1) Subject to subsection (3) below, no newspaper report of any proceedings in a court shall reveal the name, address or school, or include any particulars calculated to lead to the identification, of any person under the age of 18 years concerned in the proceedings, either— A4-110

(a) as being a person against or in respect of whom the proceedings are taken; or

(b) as being a witness in the proceedings.

(2) Subject to subsection (3) below, no picture which is, or includes, a picture of a person under the age of 18 years concerned in proceedings as mentioned in subsection (1) above shall be published in any newspaper in a context relevant to the proceedings.

(3) The requirements of subsections (1) and (2) above shall be applied in any case mentioned in any of the following paragraphs to the extent specified in that paragraph—

(a) where a person under the age of 16 years is concerned in the proceedings as a witness only and no one against whom the proceedings are taken is under the age of 18 years, the requirements shall not apply unless the court so directs;

(b) where, at any stage of the proceedings, the court, if it is satisfied that it is in the public interest so to do, directs that the requirements (including the requirements as applied by a direction under paragraph (a) above) shall be dispensed with to such extent as the court may specify; and

(c) where the Secretary of State, after completion of the proceedings, if satisfied as mentioned in paragraph (b) above, by order dispenses with the requirements to such extent as may be specified in the order.

(4) This section shall, with the necessary modifications, apply in relation to sound and television programmes included in a programme service (within the meaning of the Broadcasting Act 1990) as it applies in relation to newspapers.

(5) A person who publishes matter in contravention of this section shall be guilty of an offence and liable on summary conviction to a fine not exceeding level 4 of the standard scale.

(6) In this section, references to a court shall not include a court in England, Wales or Northern Ireland.

Amendments

Subss.(1), (2) and (3)(a) as amended by Victims and Witnesses (Scotland) Act 2014 (asp 1) s.15. Brought into force on 1 September 2015 by SSI 2015/200 art.2 and Sch.

Definition

A4-110.1 "witness": s.307(1).

[THE NEXT PARAGRAPH IS A4-111]

General Note

A4-111 There is a general prohibition upon identifying anyone involved in criminal proceedings as a victim, a witness or an accused when that person is aged less than 18 years of age. The prohibition is intended to prevent the publication or broadcasting of the person's particulars, home address or educational background as well as any details of the circumstances of the case which would be sufficient to establish this information. It extends to photographs of the child, but not of other persons however closely related to the child. Such prohibitions remain in force until the child reaches 18 years of age. See *Caledonian Newspapers, Petrs*, 1995 S.C.C.R. 576 and the general discussion there of the scope of s.169 of the 1975 Act, whose terms are echoed by s.47 of the 1995 Act. Section 47's provisions are mandatory and should not be confused with the general discretionary restrictions on reporting of proceedings set out in High Court Practice Note No.1 of 2015.

In interpreting the phrase "proceedings in a court" as used in this section and which arose in reporting of the Jodi Jones murder case, the court applied a literal, and strict, construction which was held not to apply to the reporting of the arrest by means of a petition warrant of a murder suspect then aged under 16 years of age. The court declined to provide any wider guidance as to the meaning of the phrase (*Frame v Aberdeen Journals Ltd*, 2005 S.L.T. 949; 2005 S.C.C.R. 579).

Subsection (3) permits a relaxation of this prohibition where; (i) the accused is older than 18 years and the child appears as a witness only, not as a victim, though even here it must be noted that the court can direct that the provisions of subs.(1) are to apply; (ii) the court decides during the proceedings that it is in the public interest to identify the person concerned and stipulates the extent of material which may be published or broadcast; (iii) the Secretary of State decides after proceedings are concluded that it is in the public interest for such information, as specified, to be disseminated.

Note that the Act of Adjournal (Criminal Procedure Rules), r.6.9 requires the court to specify the persons whose identities are to be protected or, alternatively may be revealed, along with suitable directions in that regard.

For an example of the application of a s.47 order see *Urquhart v Mackenzie*, 2004 G.W.D. 21—454.

Extent

These provisions do not extend to reports of proceedings arising outwith Scotland. The section does apply to any report of such Scottish proceedings published or broadcast in Scotland or elsewhere in Great Britain. The penalties for contravening s.47 are found in subs.(5).

Act of Adjournal

See the Act of Adjournal (Criminal Procedure Rules) 1996, r.6.7 for procedural directions.

Power to refer certain children to reporter

48.—(1) A court by or before which a person is convicted of having committed an offence to which this section applies may refer— A4-112

(a) a child in respect of whom an offence mentioned in paragraph (a) or (b) of subsection (2) below has been committed; or

(b) any child who is, or who is likely to become, a member of the same household as the person who has committed an offence mentioned in paragraph (b) or (c) of that subsection or the person in respect of whom the offence so mentioned was committed,

to the Principal Reporter, and certify that the offence shall be a ground established for the purposes of the Children's Hearings (Scotland) Act 2011 (asp 1).

(2) This section applies to an offence—

(a) under section 21 of the Children and Young Persons (Scotland) Act 1937;

(b) mentioned in Schedule 1 to this Act; or

(c) in respect of a person aged 17 years or over which constitutes the crime of incest.

AMENDMENTS

Subs.(1) as amended by Children's Hearings (Scotland) Act 2011 (Modification of Primary Legislation) Order 2013 (SSI 2013/211) Sch.1 para.10 (effective 24 June 2013).

DEFINITIONS

"offence": s.307(1). A4-112.1

"Principal Reporter": s.93(1) of the Children (Scotland) Act 1995.

[THE NEXT PARAGRAPH IS A4-113]

GENERAL NOTE

Section 48 entitles the court before which a person is convicted of an offence specified in subs.(2) to take immediate account of the harm done to the child victim, or the risk, or potential risk, of harm to any child who stays or may stay in the same household as the offender. This power also extends to the households of persons convicted of incest. A4-113

With a view to preserving the moral and physical well-being of such children, the court is empowered to certify the grounds for a supervision order to be established, without there being any need for a children's hearing to be constituted to consider the matter. The task of the hearing is confined to consideration in terms of ss.69 and 70 of the Children (Scotland) Act 1995, of the measures necessary to safeguard the welfare of the child or children.

Reference or remit to children's hearing

49.—(1) Where a child who is not subject to a compulsory supervision order or interim compulsory supervision order pleads guilty to, or is found guilty of, an offence the court— A4-114

(a) instead of making an order on that plea or finding, may remit the case to the Principal Reporter to arrange for the disposal of the case by a children's hearing; or

(b) on that plea or finding may request the Principal Reporter to arrange a children's hearing for the purposes of obtaining their advice as to the treatment of the child.

(2) Where a court has acted in pursuance of paragraph (b) of subsection (1) above, the court, after consideration of the advice received from the children's hearing may, as it thinks proper, itself dispose of the case or remit the case as mentioned in paragraph (a) of that subsection.

(3) Where a child who is subject to a compulsory supervision order or interim compulsory supervision order pleads guilty to, or is found guilty of, an offence the court dealing with the case if it is—

(a) the High Court, may; and

(b) the sheriff or JP court, shall,

request the Principal Reporter to arrange a children's hearing for the purpose of obtaining their advice as to the treatment of the child, and on consideration of that advice may, as it thinks proper, itself dispose of the case or remit the case as mentioned in subsection (1)(a) above except that where section 51A of the Firearms Act 1968 or section 29 of the Violent Crime Reduction Act 2006 applies it shall itself dispose of the case.

(4) Subject to any appeal against any decision to remit made under subsection (1)(a) or (7)(b) below, where a court has remitted a case to the Principal Reporter under this section, the jurisdiction of the court in respect of the child shall cease, and his case shall stand referred to a children's hearing.

(5) Nothing in this section shall apply to a case in respect of an offence the sentence for which is fixed by law.

(6) Where a person who is—

(a) not subject to a compulsory supervision order or interim compulsory supervision order;

(b) over the age of 16; and

(c) not within six months of attaining the age of 18,

is charged summarily with an offence and pleads guilty to, or has been found guilty of, the offence the court may request the Principal Reporter to arrange a children's hearing for the purpose of obtaining their advice as to the treatment of the person.

(7) On consideration of any advice obtained under subsection (6) above, the court may, as it thinks proper—

(a) itself dispose of the case; or

(b) where the hearing have so advised, remit the case to the Principal Reporter for the disposal of the case by a children's hearing.

AMENDMENTS

Subs.(4) inserted by Crime and Punishment (Scotland) Act 1997 s.23(a) with effect from August 1, 1997 in terms of SI 1997/1712 art.3.

Subs.(3)(b) inserted by Crime and Disorder Act 1998 (c.37) Sch.8 para.118 (effective September 30, 1998: SI 1998/2327).

Subs.(3) as amended by Criminal Justice Act 2003 (c.44) s.290(2). Brought into force on January 22, 2004 by SI 2004/81 (C.2) .

Section 49 amended by Violent Crime Reduction Act 2006 (c.38) s.49 and Sch.1 para.4(2).

Subs.(3) as amended by Criminal Proceedings etc (Reform) (Scotland) Act 2007 (asp 6) s.80 and Sch. para.26. Brought into force for the Sheriffdom of Lothian and Borders on March 10, 2008 by SSI 2008/42 (C.4) art.3 and Sch. Further brought into force for the Sheriffdom of Grampian, Highland and Islands on June 2, 2008 by SSI 2008/192 (C.19) art.3 and Sch. Brought into force for the Sheriffdom of Glasgow and Strathkelvin on December 8, 2008 by SSI 2008/329 (C.29) art.3 and Sch. Brought into force for the Sheriffdom of Tayside, Central and Fife on February 23, 2009 by SSI 2008/362 (C.30) art.3 and Sch. Brought into force for the Sheriffdom of North Strathclyde on December 14, 2009 by SSI 2009/432 (C.32) art.3 and Sch.1. Remainder in force on February 22, 2010 by SSI 2009/432 (C.32) art.3 and Sch.2.

Subss.(1), (3) and (6)(a) as amended by Children's Hearings (Scotland) Act 2011 (Modification of Primary Legislation) Order 2013 (SSI 2013/211) Sch.1 para.10 (effective June 24, 2013).

DEFINITIONS

"child": s.307(1) and s.93(2)(b) of the Children (Scotland) Act 1995. A4-114.1
"children's hearing": s.93(1) of the Children (Scotland) Act 1995.
"High Court": s.307(1).
"offence": s.307(1).
"Principal Reporter": s.93(1) of the Children (Scotland) Act 1995.
"supervision requirement": s.307(1) and ss.70(1) and 93(1) of the Children (Scotland) Act 1995.

[THE NEXT PARAGRAPH IS A4-115]

GENERAL NOTE

When a child not currently the subject of a supervision requirement admits, or is held to have committed an offence, the court effectively has three options; proceeding to an immediate disposal of the case, or remitting the case to a children's hearing either for their advice or for their consideration and disposal. Subss.(6) and (7) extend these provisions to youths aged up to 17 1/2 years who are convicted on summary complaint. Once the case is remitted to a hearing for disposal, the court's involvement ceases. *S v Miller*, 2001 S.L.T. 531 confirms that since children's hearings are not empowered to impose punishment, their proceedings did not involve the determination of a criminal charge, and as a result are not fully within the ambit of art.6 of the European Convention. Nonetheless, it is acknowledged that the general right to fairly-conducted proceedings would demand compliance with art.6(1). This decision follows *Engel v The Netherlands* (1976) 1 E.H.R.R. 647 which set out the criteria determining whether proceedings are deemed to be criminal proceedings or not, for the purposes of art.6. A4-115

In cases where the child is the subject of a supervision requirement, and thus can be aged up to 17 1/2 years old, admits or is found guilty of an offence in the sheriff or (following the amendment introduced by the 1998 Act in relation only to children already the subject of supervision) the district court, the court must obtain the advice of a children's hearing. On receipt of the hearing's advice the court can dispose of the case or remit the child to the hearing for their decision and disposal. Note that as subs.(3)(b) reads, this procedure would apply equally to summary or solemn cases but that the provisions of s.44 of the Act (which empower a sheriff sitting summarily to order detention of up to one year's duration in residential accommodation) derogate from this general requirement.

Section 208 of the Act empowers solemn courts to impose periods of detention following conviction on indictment.

When the child is convicted before the High Court it is in the discretion of the court to obtain the advice of a children's hearing except where the conviction is for murder since, in that event, the sentence provided by s.205 is a mandatory one of life imprisonment.

Children and certain proceedings

50.—(1) No child under 14 years of age (other than an infant in arms) shall be permitted to be present in court during any proceedings against any other person charged with an offence unless his presence is required as a witness or otherwise for the purposes of justice or the Court consents to his presence. A4-116

(2) Any child present in court when, under subsection (1) above, he is not to be permitted to be so shall be ordered to be removed.

(3) Where, in any proceedings in relation to an offence against, or any conduct contrary to, decency or morality, a person who, in the opinion of the court, is a child is called as a witness, the court may direct that all or any persons, not being—

(a) members or officers of the court;
(b) parties to the case before the court, their counsel or solicitors or persons otherwise directly concerned in the case;
(c) bona fide representatives of news gathering or reporting organisations present for the purpose of the preparation of contemporaneous reports of the proceedings; or
(d) such other persons as the court may specially authorise to be present,

shall be excluded from the court during the taking of the evidence of that witness.

(4) The powers conferred on a court by subsection (3) above shall be in addition and without prejudice to any other powers of the court to hear proceedings *in camera*.

(5) Where in any proceedings relating to any of the offences mentioned in Schedule 1 to this Act, the court is satisfied that the attendance before the court of any person under the age of 17 years in respect of whom the offence is alleged to

have been committed is not essential to the just hearing of the case, the case may be proceeded with and determined in the absence of that person.

(6) Every court in dealing with a child who is brought before it as an offender shall have regard to the welfare of the child and shall in a proper case take steps for removing him from undesirable surroundings.

AMENDMENTS

Subs.(1) as amended by Access to Justice Act 1999 (c.22) s.73(2) (effective September 27, 1999).

DEFINITIONS

A4-116.1 "child": as defined in subs.(1).
"witness": s.307(1).

[THE NEXT PARAGRAPH IS A4-117]

GENERAL NOTE

A4-117 The provisions of this section are of a directory character and non-compliance would not render the proceedings null.

It will be noted that ss.271 and 272 of the 1995 Act allow for applications to be made for a child's evidence to be taken by a commissioner, relayed to the court by means of a remote closed-circuit television link, or to be taken in court while the child is screened from sight of the accused.

Remand and committal of children and young persons

A4-118 **51.**—(1) Where a court remands or commits for trial or for sentence a person under 21 years of age who is charged with or convicted of an offence and is not released on bail or ordained to appear, then, except as otherwise expressly provided by this section, the following provisions shall have effect—

(a) if he is under 16 years of age the court shall commit him to the local authority which it considers appropriate to be detained—

(i) where the court so requires, in secure accommodation (as defined in section 202(1) of the Children's Hearings (Scotland) Act 2011 (asp 1)); and

(ii) in any other case, in a suitable place of safety chosen by the authority;

(aa) if the person has attained the age of 16 years and is subject to a compulsory supervision order or interim compulsory supervision order, the court may commit him to the local authority which it considers appropriate to be detained as mentioned in sub-paragraphs (i) or (ii) of paragraph (a) above or may commit him either to prison or to a young offenders institution;

(b) if he is a person who has attained the age of 16 years and to whom paragraph (aa) above does not apply, then where—

(i) the court has been notified by the Scottish Ministers that a remand centre is available for the reception from that court of persons of his class or description, it shall commit him to a remand centre; or

(ii) the court has not been so notified, it may commit him either to prison or to a young offenders institution;

(bb) […]

(2) Where any person is committed to a local authority under any provision of this Act, that authority shall be specified in the warrant, and he shall be detained by the authority for the period for which he is committed or until he is liberated in due course of law.

(2A) Where any person is committed to a remand centre under any provision of this Act, he shall be detained in a remand centre for the period for which he is committed or until he is liberated in due course of law.

(3) […]

(4) […]

(4A) The local authority which may be appropriate in relation to a power to commit a person under paragraphs (a) or (aa) of subsection (1) may, without prejudice to the generality of those powers, be—

(a) the local authority for the area in which the court is situated;
(b) if the person is usually resident in Scotland, the local authority for the area in which he is usually resident;
(c) if the person is subject to a compulsory supervision order or interim compulsory supervision order, the implementation authority (as defined in section 202(1) of the Children's Hearings (Scotland) Act 2011 (asp 1).

(5) Where by virtue of subsection (1)(aa) or (b)(ii) of this section a person is committed either to prison or to a young offenders institution, the warrant issued by the court is warrant also, without further application to the court in that regard, for committal to whichever of the two the court does not specify.

AMENDMENTS

Subss.(1)(a) and (4) substituted by Crime and Punishment (Scotland) Act 1997 (c.48) s.56 with effect from August 1, 1997 in terms of SI 1997/1712 art.3.

Subss.(1)(aa) inserted by s.56(2) of the above Act with effect from August 1, 1997 in terms of the above Order.

Subs.(4A) inserted by s.56(4) of the above Act and in terms of the above Order.

Section 51 as amended by Criminal Justice (Scotland) Act 2003 (asp 7) Pt 4 s.23. Brought into force on June 27, 2003 by SSI 2003/288 (C.14).

Subss.(1), (2A), (4A), (5) as amended, subss.(3), (4) repealed by Criminal Justice and Licensing (Scotland) Act 2010 (asp 13) s.64. Brought into force on December 13, 2010 by SSI 2010/413 (C.28) art.2, Sch.1 para.1.

Subss.(1), (4A) as amended by Children's Hearings (Scotland) Act 2011 (Modification of Primary Legislation) Order 2013 (SSI 2013/211) Sch.1 para.10 (effective June 24, 2013).

DEFINITIONS

"commits for trial": s.307(1). A4-118.1
"local authority": s.307(1).
"place of safety": s.307(1) of the 1995 Act and, in relation to children see s.93(1) of the Children (Scotland) Act 1995.
"prison": s.307(1).
"remand": s.307(1).
"remand centre": s.307(1).
"secure accommodation": s.93(1) of the Children (Scotland) Act 1995.
"supervision requirement": s.307(1) of the 1995 Act and the Children (Scotland) Act 1995 ss.70(1) and 93(1).

[THE NEXT PARAGRAPH IS A4-119]

GENERAL NOTE

Section 51 applies equally to summary or solemn proceedings and specifies the forms of remand facilities which are to be utilised when persons under 21 years of age are held in custody awaiting trial or remanded for sentence by the court. The aim, so far as practicable, is not to resort to use of remand facilities either before or after any trial unless the circumstances of the case, or the offender, make this unavoidable. The provisions introduced by the 1997 Act reflect the changes brought about by local government reorganisation and give the courts a degree of flexibility when nominating the local authority to provide suitable remand facilities for children and young offenders. It no longer follows that this function must necessarily be met by the local authority within whose boundaries the court is situated; it is now being left to the court to decide the most appropriate authority in the case of each offender. A4-119

In discussing s.43 of the Act it was noted that when it was felt that ordaining or liberating a child to appear at the first diet of the case was considered inappropriate, the options available to the police thereafter would be to remand a child to a place of safety, unless his conduct or circumstances militated against that form of detention. The more stringent restrictions upon the child's liberty, produced by detaining him in police cells pending his appearance before the court from custody could only be justified by the production to the court, on first appearance, of an unruly certificate. A similar philosophy is applied by the courts when it is felt that a child or young person must be remanded in custody for trial or sentence; the broad objective is then to remand the offender to an establishment most suited to the offender's circumstances and so far as possible, to minimise the rigour of the remand regime.

Children Under 16 Years

Prior to the child's appearance from custody before the sheriff, the procurator fiscal and the principal reporter (or their deputes) should already have considered whether such an appearance is necessary or A4-120 whether the child can instead be referred to the reporter in custody or liberated for the reporter to arrange a later children's hearing. Such a consultation process also applies when the offender is aged between 16 and 17 years and six months old and is the subject of a supervision requirement, but failure on the part of the procurator fiscal to consult with the reporter in these circumstances would not vitiate proceedings: see s.46(5) above.

Section 51 only takes effect when the procurator fiscal, having weighed the interests of the child and the broad public interest, elects to retain the case. If the child has been detained in police cells, the procurator fiscal will receive the unruly certificate from the police and has to produce it to the sheriff when the child appears from custody (following s.142 of the 1995 Act it will be observed that in summary proceedings such an appearance should not occur in an adult court (unless there is an adult co-accused) and must be held in private).

Should the procurator fiscal decide that bail will be opposed because of the nature of the offence or the unruliness of the child, he should have established with the local authority before the case is called, whether suitable remand facilities are available. This information should be put before the court in conjunction with a motion to remand the child in custody. In the absence of suitable accommodation, the court, if it refuses bail, will have no option but to consider whether the child is unruly, and if so, certify the child unruly and remand him to a remand institution or an adult prison albeit subs.(4) does permit later variation of the order. It is submitted that while the nature of the offence may well point to the child being unruly or depraved that is not the test; it is the nature of the child himself which should be assessed by the court. See, however, *R.M., Petr*, 1996 S.C.C.R. 92 and the editor's commentary thereon in regard to the implications of a lack of suitable secure accommodation. Note, however, that the reforms introduced by s.64 of the Criminal Justice and Licensing (Scotland) Act 2010 (asp 13) require that any offender under 16 years of age, remanded for trial, must be placed in accommodation selected by the local authority specified by the court.

It ought to be clearly established whether the child is or is not in custody pending trial, since the warrant issued by the court will specify either the centre to which the child is remanded or identify the local authority into whose charge he is placed and (following subs.(1)(a)) the nature of the accommodation to be provided—a place of safety, residential or secure accommodation. The important factor is whether the child is granted bail, and is at liberty, or remanded in custody, since this has an obvious bearing upon the timescale and competency of later proceedings; see ss.65 and 147 of the 1995 Act which re-enact the familiar provisions of ss.101 and 331A of the 1975 Act regarding prevention of delay in proceedings, i.e the 110 day and 40 day rules respectively. The warrant issued by the court will not conclusively determine whether a child is in custody or not, that is ultimately an issue of fact in each case, but the warrant will assuredly be a highly persuasive determining factor. The court must be furnished with comprehensive and accurate information about the precise circumstances of the child and the basis upon which he is held. In *X, Petr*, 1996 S.C.C.R. 436 the Crown was criticised for making representations which were based upon inaccurate information provided by the local authority. The court observed that the Crown had a duty to verify the accuracy of such information for itself and should seek an adjournment for that purpose if necessary.

These comments apply with even greater force when the child appearing before the court is already the subject of a residential supervision order: it is then vital that it is determined whether the child is bailed, and returns to the care of the local authority to continue the current supervision order, or is remanded to secure accommodation provided by the local authority as a preferred alternative to a remand or prison place. It is also essential that the local authority seek a review of the case in terms of subs.(4), should the circumstances of the offender change.

The complications which can arise are amply illustrated in *K v HM Advocate*, 1991 S.C.C.R. 343, where the child was "bailed" to reside at a List D school which in fact contained both secure and residential accommodation. K was bailed to reside in the school's secure unit, instead of being either remanded into the care of the local authority or certified unruly and remanded. The court's well-meant intention was to substitute an earlier warrant which had remanded K to an adult prison with a more suitable regime but, on any view, K was not at liberty and the provisions (then) of s.110 applied, since the bail order had had no practical effect (the solution would have been for the local authority, if it was in agreement, to seek review of the warrant as subs.(4) provides in the 1995 Act).

See also *X, Petr*, 1996 S.C.C.R. 436; following a petition appearance upon a rape charge and refusal of bail, C was held in custody in a remand institution. A review hearing later allowed bail subject to residence in a List D school; although the bail order did not stipulate it, C was kept in secure accommodation by staff solely in execution of the order, and only the issue of instructions by the procurator fiscal for the child's liberation (which were acted upon on the 109th day) stopped the 110 days running. A petition to the *nobile officium* was refused since de facto liberty had been obtained before the expiry of the 110 days.

Note that once a child has been certified unruly by the sheriff it is doubtful whether it can be revoked by anyone, even the certifying sheriff, or formally appealed. In *X, Petr*, supra, the child was certified unruly and remanded in a remand institution after absconding from the local authority home to which he had earlier been bailed. A petition to the *nobile officium* for revocation of the certification was lodged, but the High Court doubted that such an order would be competent; in the absence of Crown opposition the court used its inherent equitable powers to grant a bail order specifying residence in a secure unit. The principles which prompted this decision appear in conflict with the ratio in *K v HM Advocate* above.

A similar situation arose in *Y, Petr*, 1995 S.C.C.R. 457, with the court ruling that a petition to the *nobile officium* was not a competent means for review of an unruly certificate.

Nevertheless, the court substituted a bail order requiring Y to reside in the secure unit of a List D school.

PART VI – MENTAL DISORDER

Criminal responsibility of mentally disordered persons

Criminal responsibility of persons with mental disorder

51A.—(1) A person is not criminally responsible for conduct constituting an offence, and is to be acquitted of the offence, if the person was at the time of the conduct unable by reason of mental disorder to appreciate the nature or wrongfulness of the conduct. **A4-120.1**

(2) But a person does not lack criminal responsibility for such conduct if the mental disorder in question consists only of a personality disorder which is characterised solely or principally by abnormally aggressive or seriously irresponsible conduct.

(3) The defence set out in subsection (1) is a special defence.

(4) The special defence may be stated only by the person charged with the offence and it is for that person to establish it on the balance of probabilities.

(5) In this section, " conduct " includes acts and omissions.

AMENDMENTS

Section 51A inserted by Criminal Justice and Licensing (Scotland) Act 2010 (asp 13) s.168. Brought into force on 25 June 2012 by SSI 2012/160 (C.15) art.3, subject to savings provisions in art.4(2).

DEFINITIONS

"conduct": s.51A(5). **A4-120.2**

"mental disorder": s.328(1) of the Mental Health (Care and Treatment) (Scotland) Act 2003 (asp 13). Brought into force on 5 October 2005 by SSI 2005/161 (C.6).

GENERAL NOTE

This section introduces a new statutory defence to replace the common law defence of insanity. The section provides for a special defence in respect of those who lack criminal responsibility by reason of their mental disorder at the time of the offence with which they are charged. **A4-120.3**

There is scope for anonymity orders in the legislation for the Mental Health Tribunals for Scotland although no comparable authority to make such an order exists in this Part of the 1995 Act. For discussion of the wider issues of open justice even in the context of mental disorder see *MH v HM Advocate* [2019] CSIH 14; 2019 S.L.T. 411, discussed in David Cobb, "Disclosure of mental disorder in court", 2019 S.L.T. (News) 70. For a related case dealing with the fairness of hearings (the convenor of a tribunal participating by phone conference facilities), which may impact on the way evidence in support of orders under this Part of the 1995 Act is obtained, see *MH v Mental Health Tribunal for Scotland* [2019] CSIH 28; 2019 S.L.T. 615.

In *Dunn v W*, 2012 G.W.D. 38-754 (2 November 2012) Sheriff J.A. Baird at Glasgow Sheriff Court made certain observations on s.51A. In particular that (a) it was unclear whether Parliament's intention in s.51A was to introduce a standard less than that which had been required under the prior provision to satisfy the test of "insanity", or merely a change in terminology but not in the relevant test; and (b) it was curious that Parliament had chosen to categorise a s.51A defence as a special defence as, unlike other special defences, if it was upheld the proceedings would not necessarily be ended as the accused was entitled to acquittal but was not free from the potential making of a consequential order by the court in the same proceedings involving a psychiatrically based disposal under s.57 of the 1995 Act. The decision does not seem to have been appealed nor these obiter remarks challenged.

In *Duzgun v HM Advocate* [2020] HCJAC 13; 2020 S.C.C.R. 194 the appellant complained four years after conviction of defective representation by a former solicitor by not having obtained a report from a psychiatrist. The appellant may have been suffering from a mental disorder at the time of the offence but he chose not to plead a defence under s.51A. However, the appellant had not been unwell when that solicitor had taken clear instructions from him and the appellant had given clear instructions not to pursue then the issue of mental responsibility. It would have been a breach of the obligations on the solicitor to the appellant if the solicitor had decided to pursue a line which he had been instructed specifically not to pursue: at [21]. There was no material before the appeal court contradicting the version of events presented by the solicitor: at [22].

Statutory conundrum

There is a complex trail of authorities leading to what might, for the unwary, be an unexpected outcome under s.51A of the 1995 Act, although that result seems to be what Parliament intended. Section 51A provides a statutory defence which is made out when a mental disorder is established on the balance of probabilities and that mental disorder has negated the necessary criminal responsibility for a crime. Such a defence may be proved to the satisfaction of a court or be accepted as such by the Crown.

There are, however, consequences flowing from an acquittal that are not immediately obvious from a reading of s.51A of the 1995 Act alone. The Sexual Offences Act 2003 (c.42) provides by s.135 for the interpretation of the phrase "mentally disordered offenders" and s.135(2A) reflects changes introduced by the Criminal Justice and Licensing (Scotland) Act 2010 (asp 13) Sch.7 para.73. Thus, a person found not guilty of an offence because of insanity, under reference to s.51A of the 1995 Act, will then be subject to the notification requirements in s.80 of the 2003 Act. Notwithstanding an acquittal, or rather perhaps because of the grounds of acquittal, that person will be subject to the intentionally restrictive terms of Pt 2 of the 2003 Act.

Subs.(1)

In *Mackay v HM Advocate* [2017] HCJAC 44 the essence of s.51A was considered. The full report might yet be considered again in appeals given the observation by a defence psychiatrist, at [9], that "psychiatrists were struggling with the new phrase [in s.51A], viz: 'wrongfulness of the conduct'". It is arguable that that encapsulates the long-established problems related to insanity, diminished responsibility, and other mental states of relevance at the time of the commission of crime. The reconciliation of the relevant core issues of medical personnel and lawyers, however either is designated, remains at the centre of continuing discussion.

In *Mackay's* case, above, in deference to the discussion of the issues advocated in the appeal, the court considered some of the history of insanity as a defence at common law and now by statute (see [23]). Further, regarding the precise statutory terms of s.51A, it was asserted that the words of the section were specifically selected. These words "express the defence in quite different language from the common law concept of insanity. They make no mention of alienation of reason, whether substantial, total or absolute [as the older reported cases had done]. They refer to the person being 'unable by reason of mental disorder to appreciate the nature or wrongfulness of the conduct'. This is entirely new phraseology." (at [24])

The court opined that that the "words … 'appreciate' and 'wrongfulness' do not pose any difficulty in interpretation. They are words in common usage. They mean what they mean in ordinary English. It is important, therefore, for the court not to put a spin or gloss on such words by using different words to explain, and thus potentially distort, their plain meaning. This is especially so when directing a jury. Where Parliament has defined the defence in specific, but ordinary, language, the directions must take care to reflect that definition" (at [26]).

The facts of *Mackay's* case are highly contemporaneous in that they concern a soldier (presumably employed by the British Army, although that is not specified) who had served in Afghanistan and who had formed thoughts of directing aggressive acts towards staff at a local tandoori restaurant in Scotland (at [3]). With the passage of time no doubt, there will be other contemporary events that play on the minds of the lieges to a greater or lesser extent although the issues may remain the same.

The court in *Mackay's* case thought it helpful to provide further guidance for similar sorts of cases, subject to the eternal proviso for judicial colleagues that "any charge should always be tailored to the particular circumstances of the case" (at [30]). To that end an "acceptable, although not the only acceptable, form of charge" is provided in the Opinion of the Court and to which reference might be made for consideration in suitable cases in the future (at [30]).

Subs.(2)

The special defence does not apply to a person who at the time of the conduct constituting the offence had a mental disorder which consisted of a psychopathic personality disorder alone.

Further discussion of the medical concepts in s.51A(2) may be found in S.D. Barnes, "Re-evaluating the exclusion of psychopathy from the mental disorder defence in Scots law", 2018 Juridical Review 1–21.

Subs.(4)

This special defence can be raised only by the person charged with the offence. The standard of proof on an accused who states the defence is the balance of probabilities, which corresponds with the common law: see *HM Advocate v Mitchell*, 1951 J.C. 53.

Diminished responsibility

Diminished responsibility

A4-120.4 **51B.**—(1) A person who would otherwise be convicted of murder is instead to be convicted of culpable homicide on grounds of diminished responsibility if the person's ability to determine or control conduct for which the person would otherwise be convicted of murder was, at the time of the conduct, substantially impaired by reason of abnormality of mind.

(2) For the avoidance of doubt, the reference in subsection (1) to abnormality of mind includes mental disorder.

(3) The fact that a person was under the influence of alcohol, drugs or any other substance at the time of the conduct in question does not of itself—

(a) constitute abnormality of mind for the purposes of subsection (1), or

(b) prevent such abnormality from being established for those purposes.

(4) It is for the person charged with murder to establish, on the balance of probabilities, that the condition set out in subsection (1) is satisfied.

(5) In this section, "conduct" includes acts and omissions.

AMENDMENTS

Section 51B inserted by Criminal Justice and Licensing (Scotland) Act 2010 (asp 13) s.168. Brought into force on 25 June 2012 by SSI 2012/160 (C.15) art.3, subject to savings provisions in art.4(2).

DEFINITIONS

"conduct": s.51A(5). A4-120.5

"mental disorder": s.328(1) of the Mental Health (Care and Treatment) (Scotland) Act 2003 (asp 13). Brought into force on 5 October 2005 by SSI 2005/161 (C.6).

GENERAL NOTE

This section sets down a statutory version of the plea of diminished responsibility and the test follows generally the rule from *Galbraith v HM Advocate*, 2002 J.C. 1. By s.51B(1), this special defence is one that applies only in cases of murder. The test from Galbraith's case is whether at the time of the killing the accused was suffering from an abnormality of mind which substantially impaired his or her ability to determine or control his or her conduct. A4-120.6

By s.51B(2), where the accused's condition at the time of an unlawful killing falls within the definitions of both the defence based on mental disorder and diminished responsibility, then an accused has an option of advancing either the defence or the plea. Moreover, the new provision allows for diminished responsibility to be based on the condition of psychopathic personality disorder unlike the common law position: see *Carraher v HM Advocate*, 1946 J.C. 108.

In *Graham v HM Advocate* [2018] HCJAC 57, a reference to the High Court of Justiciary was made by the SCCRC, and consideration was given to a trial in 2008 at which the appellant was convicted of murder. A plea of diminished responsibility was advanced by the defence but it was withdrawn by the trial judge. Provocation remained an issue but that had been rejected by the jury given their verdict.

The reference raised a subsidiary question, stemming from dicta in *Galbraith v HM Advocate*, supra, of whether the evidence of a psychologist is capable of demonstrating, contrary to psychiatric opinion, that an accused suffered from a "mental abnormality" which impaired his or her ability to determine or control their acts at the material time.

At present, provided the test in *Kennedy v Cordia (Services)*, 2016 S.C. (U.K.S.C.) 59 is met, there is no prohibition on people, who are not psychiatrists (i.e. not having a formal medical degree) expressing an opinion on whether a person suffers from an abnormality of mind and whether this was present at the time of a relevant incident: *Graham v HM Advocate* at [123].

In *R. v Dietschmann* [2003] 1 A.C. 1209 the House of Lords approved (at [41]) a direction that: "Drink cannot be taken into account as something which contributed to his mental abnormality and to any impairment of mental responsibility arising from that abnormality." If a jury took the view that the accused's responsibility had been impaired by both mental abnormality and drink, and that he might not have killed if he had not taken drink, then: "the question … is this: has the defendant satisfied you that, despite the drink, his mental abnormality substantially impaired his mental responsibility for his fatal acts, or has he failed to satisfy you of that?"

In *Graham v HM Advocate* [2018] HCJAC 57; 2018 S.C.C.R. 347 the court adopted (at [105]), for common law purposes, the model direction in *R. v Dietschmann* [2003] 1 A.C. 1209, regarding it as consistent with *Brennan v HM Advocate*, 1977 J.C. 38. In *Rodgers v HM Advocate* [2019] HCJAC 27; 2019 G.W.D. 18-284 (at [33]) the court referred to these authorities and noted that: "Abnormality of mind had to be a substantial cause of the impairment for the plea to be open. It need not be the only cause and the impairment 'must not be brought on by the voluntary ingestion of drink or drugs'. If, nevertheless the jury considered that a personality disorder was an operative (i.e. substantial) cause of the accused's action, the plea remained available. It does not seem to be disputed that the common law principles are still apt when considering the statutory provision. If an accused's action at the material time have been substantially impaired by reason of abnormality of mind, then the jury may find diminished responsibility established even if the intoxication also played a part." See also at [35] for approval of *R. v Dietschmann*, ibid., and further discussion.

In *Rodgers v HM Advocate* [2019] HCJAC 27 a second ground of appeal against conviction related to the manner in which a jury should be directed when there is a burden of proof on the defence using the standard of balance of probabilities: at [2] and [25]. It was held at [37] that there had been no material misdirection on the concept of balance of probabilities. It can be dangerous to attempt to reduce the determination to one of combined arithmetical possibilities: following *Milton Keynes BC v Nulty* [2013] 1 W.L.R. 1183 at [34] et seq, and *Re A (Children) (Care Proceedings: Burden of Proof)* [2018] 4 W.L.R. 117 at [56]. The description used by the trial judge was not a substantially erroneous description: *Davies v Taylor* [1974] A.C. 207 at 219–220.

An accused was found guilty of the culpable homicide of his brother on the ground of diminished responsibility. In all the circumstances, an order of lifelong restriction was imposed (in terms of s.210F of the 1995 Act) with a punishment part of the order of 3 years and 7 months. The court commented at sentencing that the order imposed "shares some characteristics with a life sentence": *HM Advocate v Loughton* unreported 24 April 2020 High Court at Edinburgh, Lord Beckett.

"Substantially impaired": English law

It has been asserted authoritatively in the Court of Appeal (Criminal Division) that it is important to emphasise that the judge must carefully consider all the evidence in each case and not feel circumscribed by the psychiatric opinion: *R. v Vowles* [2015] EWCA Crim 45 at [51]; [2015] 2 Cr App R (S) 6; [2015] 1 WLR 5131; [2015] Crim LR 542; [2015] WLR(D) 52.

The English law of diminished responsibility is based on its own statute: s.2 of the Homicide Act 1957. That provision was revised by the Coroners and Justice Act 2009, in s.52 (England and Wales) and s.53 (Northern Ireland). The context is, however, that the defence of diminished responsibility is to be found in cases from both England and Wales, and also Scotland (from whose common law the English defence was derived). The key phrase "substantially impaired" was considered in *R. v Golds* [2016] UKSC 61; [2016] 1 W.L.R. 5231; [2017] 1 Cr. App. R 18. The decision is assessed in M. Gibson, "Diminished Responsibility in Golds and Beyond: Insights and Implications" [2017] Crim.L.R. 543–553; and Elizabeth Stuart-Cole, "Substantially confused? The Paradox of Golds" (2017) 81(2) J.C.L. 99–102.

Following that decision other relevant cases comprise *R. v Squelch* [2017] EWCA Crim 204 (trial judge followed properly the requirements of Golds and left "substantially impaired" to the jury) and *R. v Conroy* [2017] EWCA Crim 81; [2017] 2 Cr. App. R. 26 (autistic spectrum disorder and decision-making process in assessing impairment), from Court of Appeal (Criminal Division). There was also *R. v Blackman* [2017] EWCA Crim 190; [2017] Crim.L.R. 557 (adjustment disorder "substantially impaired" ability at relevant time), from the Court Martial Appeal Court. An attempt to appeal out of time following and relying on the decision in Golds was refused in *R. v Hussain (Imran)* [2019] EWCA Crim 666; [2019] 4 WLUK 299 (CA (Crim Div)).

Fresh psychiatric evidence—English law

The question of fresh evidence arose in *R. v Foy* [2020] EWCA Crim 270 (27 February 2020). After trial, the appellant had been convicted of murder by stabbing a stranger, the attack occurring after substantial ingestion of alcohol and a controlled drug. Psychiatric evidence obtained by the defence before the trial did not support a plea of diminished responsibility. The sole defence at trial was the lack of the necessary intent for murder. Subsequent psychiatric evidence suggested that there was evidence to support a plea of diminished responsibility. The appeal court reviewed recent authorities on the same point: *R. v Foy* [2020] EWCA Crim 270 at [52]–[58]. The court applied the requirements of s.2 of the Homicide Act 1957 and concluded that the fresh evidence in the circumstances could not be adduced and the appeal against conviction was dismissed.

Sentencing principles: diminished responsibility—English law

The Sentencing Council for England and Wales *Guidelines for Manslaughter by Reason of Diminished Responsibility* came into force on 1 November 2018. These were applied, with reference to a number of similar sentencing cases, in *R. v Rodi* [2020] EWCA (Crim) 330 (26 February 2020). The five normative steps are considered there to settling on a fair and just sentence: at [21]–[32]. The ratio of *Rodi's* case is that where there is a conviction for manslaughter by reason of diminished responsibility, the legal responsibility is diminished but not exhausted or extinguished: at [25].

In R. v Westwood [2020] EWCA Crim 598 principles were stated for the sentencing of an offender who suffers from a mental disorder: at [16]–[24]. That was done with reference to the relevant statutory provisions, several recent decisions and the *Guidelines for Manslaughter by Reason of Diminished Responsibility* from the Sentencing Council for England and Wales which took effect on 1 November 2018: at [25]–[26].

Mr. Lall was convicted of manslaughter by reason of diminished responsibility: *R v Lall*[2021] EWCA Crim 404. The trial judge imposed a hospital order and a restriction, without limit of time, on certain statutory authority. The Crown sought leave to appeal on the argument that the sentence was unduly lenient. The psychiatrist who examined Lall were in broad agreement that he suffered from paranoid schizophrenia. The psychosis was of an enduring nature. The doctors were of one view as to the appropriate mental health disposal; viz, that imposed by the trial judge. The appeal court judges thought that Lall's complete lack of insight into his condition was an important feature of the case: at [44]. Every case turns on its own facts, including which regime offers greatest protection to the public: at [47]. As the

Sentencing *Guidelines for Manslaughter by Reason of Diminished Responsibility* states, para.15, the duty of the sentencer is to make their own decision, and the court is not bound to follow expert opinion if there are compelling reasons to set it aside. The Crown in Lall's case had not identified any compelling reasons why the trial judge should have set aside the consensus among three psychiatrists: at [48]. Leave to appeal was refused.

Northern Ireland

In *R. v Dolan* [2020] NICC 7 (28 February 2020) the charge was that of the murder of a woman who lived alone in a remote area. The defendant pled guilty. Colton J referred to the medical evidence in which the defendant was assessed as having an emotionally unstable personality disorder. The characteristics of the disorder impaired substantially the ability of the defendant to form rational judgments and to exert self-control. That was described by the court as the "partial defence" of diminished responsibility, at [35]. It was also observed, at [68], that as a general proposition the court should be careful of comparing sentences imposed in other cases which are inevitably fact sensitive.

[THE NEXT PARAGRAPH IS A4-121]

Committal of mentally disordered persons

Power of court to commit to hospital an accused suffering from mental disorder

52.—(1) Where it appears to the prosecutor in any court before which a person is charged with an offence that the person may be suffering from mental disorder, it shall be the duty of the prosecutor to bring before the court such evidence as may be available of the mental condition of that person. **A4-121**

(2)–(7) [...]

Amendments

Subsections (2)–(7) repealed by Mental Health (Care and Treatment) (Scotland) Act 2003 (asp 13) Sch.5 Pt I. Brought into force on 5 October 2005 by SSI 2005/161 (C.6).

Definitions

"mental disorder": s.328(1) of the Mental Health (Care and Treatment) (Scotland) Act 2003. **A4-121.1**
"offence": s.307(1).
"prosecutor": s.307(1).

General Note

This section amends and consolidates the existing provisions of the court to commit to a specified hospital at the pre-trial stage an accused who appears to be suffering from a mental disorder. The section makes express provision for review of that committal. The committal to hospital is an alternative to remanding such an accused in custody pending trial. Thus the committal to hospital is subject to the maximum remand time limits of 40 days in summary proceedings and 110 days or 140 days as the case may be in solemn proceedings. Before the court can make the hospital committal order three criteria must be met. First, the court must be satisfied on the written or oral evidence of a registered medical practitioner that the accused appears to be suffering from mental disorder, although at this stage it is not necessary for the nature or degree of mental disorder to be established. Secondly, the court must be satisfied that a hospital is *available* for the accused's admission, and thirdly the court must be satisfied that the hospital is *suitable* for the accused's detention pending trial. Accordingly, the registered medical practitioner should confirm to the court that a suitable hospital is prepared to admit the accused. **A4-122**

It should be noted that it is open to anyone with an interest in the case to raise the possibility of an accused's mental disorder with the court. Such interested parties would include the prosecutor, the police, the defence agent and the judge.

Subs.(1)

The breadth of the definition of the word "prosecutor" should be noted for in solemn proceedings it includes Crown counsel. The flexibility implied by this is such that relevant evidence may be brought at what would otherwise be the trial diet in the High Court of Justiciary. The procedure is not contingent on a conviction because of the phrase "is charged with": see *Herron v McCrimmon*, 1969 S.L.T. (Sh. Ct) 37 for circumstances in which a summary complaint was deserted *pro loco et tempore* to place the accused on petition and yet the phrase was still satisfied.

The provision of a psychiatric report by the Crown in compliance with this section's provisions is to be regarded as the fulfilment of a statutory duty which has been placed on the prosecutor for the protection of the accused, and not as an element of the Crown's investigation in furtherance of its case against the accused. Thus in *Sloan v Crowe*, 1996 S.C.C.R. 200 an objection to the competency of proceedings was repelled, and refused on appeal, the defence having asserted that information provided to the Crown in a psychiatric report on the accused unfairly made reference to the offence itself. In *MacDonald v*

Munro, 1996 S.C.C.R. 595 where the psychiatrist had interviewed both the accused and his mother (the complainer) about the circumstances of the offence in compiling his report, it was observed that any prejudicial material would fall to be ignored by the judge and that any attempt by the Crown to found on such material would likely be objectionable. While it was observed in *Tole v HM Advocate*, 2013 S.L.T. 1227 that there was no known bar in terms of art.6 of the ECHR upon the evidential use of such material, provided the accused had had legal advice and had been made aware of his right to silence, the common law position rendered information expressly obtained in pursuance of this section on behalf of the prosecutor, inadmissible.

Whether a person may be suffering from "mental disorder" is a medical question for those qualified to answer the question but that is frequently the most difficult point: in *Allan v HM Advocate*, 1983 S.C.C.R. 183 four psychiatrists divided on precisely that aspect and, if the accused was so suffering, what the best method of disposal would be.

A similar division is apparent in *Jessop v Robertson*, 1989 S.C.C.R. 600 (Sh. Ct) where it was held by a sheriff that: (1) a written report that had been produced by the prosecutor but was not spoken to by a witness at the proof was not admissible; (2) there was an onus on any person alleging unfitness by reason of insanity to satisfy the court of that allegation by corroborated evidence on a balance of probabilities; and (3) in the circumstances of medical division the unfitness had not been proved; and the accused was called upon to plead.

Remit of mentally disordered persons from JP court

Remit of certain mentally disordered persons from JP court to sheriff court

A4-122.1 **52A.** Where—

(a) a person has been charged in a JP court with an offence punishable by imprisonment; and

(b) it appears to the court that the person has a mental disorder,

the JP court shall remit the person to the sheriff in the manner provided by section 7(9) and (10) of this Act.

AMENDMENTS

Section 52A inserted by Mental Health (Care and Treatment) (Scotland) Act 2003 (asp 13) s.130. Brought into force on 5 October 2005 by SSI 2005/161 (C.6).

Section 52A as amended by Criminal Proceedings etc. (Reform) (Scotland) Act 2007 (asp 6) s.80, Sch. para.26. Brought into force for the Sheriffdom of Lothian and Borders on 10 March 2008 by SSI 2008/42 (C.4) art.3 and Sch. Brought into force for the Sheriffdom of Grampian, Highland and Islands on 2 June 2008 by SSI 2008/192 (C.19) art.3 and Sch. Brought into force for the Sheriffdom of Glasgow and Strathkelvin on 8 December 2008 by SSI 2008/329 (C.29) art.3 and Sch. Brought into force for the Sheriffdom of Tayside, Central and Fife on 23 February 2009 by SSI 2008/362 (C.30) art.3 and Sch. Brought into force for the Sheriffdom of North Strathclyde on 14 December 2009 by SSI 2009/432 (C.32) art.3 and Sch.1. Remainder in force on 22 February 2010 by SSI 2009/432 (C.32) art.3 and Sch.2.

DEFINITIONS

A4-122.2 "mental disorder": s.328(1) of the Mental Health (Care and Treatment) (Scotland) Act 2003.
"offence": s.307(1).

GENERAL NOTE

A4-122.3 This section clarifies that where a person charged with an offence punishable by imprisonment and appeari ng to have a mental disorder comes before the JP court, the matter will be remitted to the sheriff court for disposal.

Assessment orders

Prosecutor's power to apply for assessment order

A4-122.4 **52B.—**(1) Where—

(a) a person has been charged with an offence;

(b) a relevant disposal has not been made in the proceedings in respect of the offence; and

(c) it appears to the prosecutor that the person has a mental disorder,

the prosecutor may apply to the court for an order under section 52D(2) of this Act (in this Act referred to as an "assessment order") in respect of that person.

(2) Where the prosecutor applies for an assessment order under subsection (1) above, the prosecutor shall, as soon as reasonably practicable after making the application, inform the persons mentioned in subsection (3) below of the making of the application.

(3) Those persons are—

(a) the person in respect of whom the application is made;

(b) any solicitor acting for the person; and

(c) in a case where the person is remanded in custody, the Scottish Ministers.

(4) In this section—

"court" means any court, other than a JP court, competent to deal with the case; and

"relevant disposal" means—

(a) the liberation in due course of law of the person charged;

(b) the desertion of summary proceedings *pro loco et tempore* or simpliciter;

(c) the desertion of solemn proceedings simpliciter;

(d) the acquittal of the person charged; or

(e) the conviction of the person charged.

AMENDMENTS

Section 52B inserted by Mental Health (Care and Treatment) (Scotland) Act 2003 (asp 13) s.130. Brought into force on 5 October 2005 by SSI 2005/161 (C.6).

Subs.(4) as amended by Criminal Proceedings etc. (Reform) (Scotland) Act 2007 (asp 6) s.80, Sch. para.26. Brought into force for the Sheriffdom of Lothian and Borders on 10 March 2008 by SSI 2008/42 (C.4) art.3 and Sch. Brought into force for the Sheriffdom of Grampian, Highland and Islands on 2 June 2008 by SSI 2008/192 (C.19) art.3 and Sch. Brought into force for the Sheriffdom of Glasgow and Strathkelvin on 8 December 2008 by SSI 2008/329 (C.29) art.3 and Sch. Brought into force for the Sheriffdom of Tayside, Central and Fife on 23 February 2009 by SSI 2008/362 (C.30) art.3 and Sch. Brought into force for the Sheriffdom of North Strathclyde on 14 December 2009 by SSI 2009/432 (C.32) art.3 and Sch.1. Remainder in force on 22 February 2010 by SSI 2009/432 (C.32) art.3 and Sch.2.

Subs.(3)(c) as amended by Mental Health (Scotland) Act 2015 (asp 9) Pt 2 s.38(2)(a). Brought into force on 30 June 2017 by SSI 2017/197 art.2 and Sch.

DEFINITIONS A4-122.5

"assessment order": s.52B(1)(c).
"court": s.52B(4).
"mental disorder": s.328(1) of the Mental Health (Care and Treatment) (Scotland) Act 2003.
"offence": s.307(1).
"prosecutor": s.307(1).
"relevant disposal": s.52B(4).

GENERAL NOTE

This section allows the prosecutor in any criminal proceedings to apply for an assessment order ("AO") to be made relative to an accused who appears to have a mental disorder, at any stage prior to a "relevant disposal" (see subs.(4)) of the case being made (subs.(1)). (It should be noted that desertion of a solemn matter *pro loco et tempore* does not constitute a "relevant disposal" of a matter, nor presumably, does adjournment to a different sitting). The prosecutor must inform the accused and the accused's solicitor about the application for an AO. Where the court has remanded the accused in custody, the Scottish Ministers must also be informed (subss.(2) and (3)). The prosecutor can also apply for a treatment order to be made under s.52K. A4-122.6

The "prosecutor" within the meaning of the 1995 Act is the person prosecuting under solemn procedure or summary procedure in any criminal court: see s.307(1). However, an application cannot be made to a JP court for an AO (subs.(4)). Furthermore, in the conditions specified in s.52B(1) an AO may be sought. Reference needs to be made to s.52D(2) and (5) for the nature and effect of such an AO.

Scottish Ministers' power to apply for assessment order

52C.—(1) Where— A4-122.7

(a) a person has been charged with an offence;

(b) the person has not been sentenced;

(c) the person is remanded in custody; and

(d) it appears to the Scottish Ministers that the person has a mental disorder, the Scottish Ministers may apply to the court for an assessment order in respect of that person.

(2) Where the Scottish Ministers apply for an order under subsection (1) above, they shall, as soon as reasonably practicable after making the application, inform the persons mentioned in subsection (3) below of the making of the application.

(3) Those persons are—

(a) the person in respect of whom the application is made;

(b) any solicitor acting for the person; and

(c) in a case where a relevant disposal has not been made in the proceedings in respect of the offence with which the person is charged, the prosecutor.

(4) In this section, " court " and " relevant disposal " have the same meanings as in section 52B of this Act.

AMENDMENTS

Section 52C inserted by Mental Health (Care and Treatment) (Scotland) Act 2003 (asp 13) s.130. Brought into force on 5 October 2005 by SSI 2005/161 (C.6).

Subs.(1)(c) as amended by Mental Health (Scotland) Act 2015 (asp 9) Pt 2 s.38(2)(b). Brought into force on 30 June 2017 by SSI 2017/197 art.2 and Sch.

DEFINITIONS

A4-122.8 "assessment order": s.52B(1)(c).
"court": s.52B(4).
"offence": s.307(1).
"relevant disposal": s.52B(4).

GENERAL NOTE

A4-122.9 In terms of this section, the Scottish Ministers are entitled to intervene in any criminal proceedings where an accused has been remanded in custody, to apply for an assessment order. This power can be exercised where the accused is remanded in custody but has not been sentenced by the court—cf. s.52B(1)—and appears to the Scottish Ministers to have a mental disorder (subs.(1)). Where the Scottish Ministers intervene under this section, they must notify the accused and the accused's solicitor. The prosecutor must also be advised where a "relevant disposal" (see General Note to s.52B) of the case has not yet been made (subss.(2) and (3)).

Assessment order

A4-122.10 **52D.**—(1) This section applies where an application for an assessment order is made under section 52B(1) or 52C(1) of this Act.

(2) If the court is satisfied—

(a) on the written or oral evidence of a medical practitioner, as to the matters mentioned in subsection (3) below; and

(b) that, having regard to the matters mentioned in subsection (4) below, it is appropriate,

it may, subject to subsection (5) below, make an assessment order authorising the measures mentioned in subsection (6) below and specifying any matters to be included in the report under section 52G(1) of this Act.

(3) The matters referred to in subsection (2)(a) above are—

(a) that there are reasonable grounds for believing—

(i) that the person in respect of whom the application is made has a mental disorder;

(ii) that it is necessary to detain the person in hospital to assess whether the conditions mentioned in subsection (7) below are met in respect of the person; and

(iii) that if the assessment order were not made there would be a significant risk to the health, safety or welfare of the person or a significant risk to the safety of any other person;

(b) that the hospital proposed by the medical practitioner is suitable for the purpose of assessing whether the conditions mentioned in subsection (7) below are met in respect of the person;

(c) that, if an assessment order were made, the person could be admitted to such hospital before the expiry of the period of 7 days beginning with the day on which the order is made; and

(d) that it would not be reasonably practicable to carry out the assessment mentioned in paragraph (b) above unless an order were made.

(4) The matters referred to in subsection (2)(b) above are—

(a) all the circumstances (including the nature of the offence with which the person in respect of whom the application is made is charged or, as the case may be, of which the person was convicted); and

(b) any alternative means of dealing with the person.

(5) The court may make an assessment order only if the person in respect of whom the application is made has not been sentenced.

(6) The measures are—

(a) in the case of a person who, when the assessment order is made, has not been admitted to the specified hospital, the removal, before the end of the day following the 7 days beginning with the day on which the order is made, of the person to the specified hospital by—

(i) a constable;

(ii) a person employed in, or contracted to provide services in or to, the specified hospital who is authorised by the managers of that hospital to remove persons to hospital for the purposes of this section; or

(iii) a specified person;

(b) the detention, for the relevant period given by subsection (6A) below, of the person in the specified hospital; and

(c) during the relevant period given by subsection (6A) below, the giving to the person, in accordance with Part 16 of the Mental Health (Care and Treatment) (Scotland) Act 2003 (asp 13), of medical treatment.

(6A) For the purpose of subsection (6)(b) and (c) above, the relevant period is the period—

(a) beginning with the day on which the order is made,

(b) expiring at the end of the 28 days following that day.

(7) The conditions referred to in paragraphs (a)(ii) and (b) of subsection (3) above are—

(a) that the person in respect of whom the application is made has a mental disorder;

(b) that medical treatment which would be likely to—

(i) prevent the mental disorder worsening; or

(ii) alleviate any of the symptoms, or effects, of the disorder,

is available for the person; and

(c) that if the person were not provided with such medical treatment there would be a significant risk—

(i) to the health, safety or welfare of the person; or

(ii) to the safety of any other person.

(8) The court may make an assessment order in the absence of the person in respect of whom the application is made only if—

(a) the person is represented by counsel or a solicitor;

(b) that counsel or solicitor is given an opportunity of being heard; and

(c) the court is satisfied that it is—

(i) impracticable; or

(ii) inappropriate,

for the person to be brought before it.

(9) An assessment order may include such directions as the court thinks fit for the removal of the person subject to the order to, and detention of the person in, a place of safety pending the person's admission to the specified hospital.

(10) The court shall, as soon as reasonably practicable after making an assessment order, give notice of the making of the order to—

(a) the person subject to the order;

(b) any solicitor acting for the person;

(c) in a case where—

(i) the person has been charged with an offence; and

(ii) a relevant disposal has not been made in the proceedings in respect of the offence,

the prosecutor;

(d) in a case where the person, immediately before the order was made, was remanded in custody, the Scottish Ministers; and

(e) the Mental Welfare Commission.

(11) In this section—

"court" has the same meaning as in section 52B of this Act;

"medical treatment" has the meaning given by section 329(1) of the Mental Health (Care and Treatment) (Scotland) Act 2003 (asp 13);

"relevant disposal" has the same meaning as in section 52B of this Act; and

"specified" means specified in the assessment order.

AMENDMENTS

Section 52D inserted by Mental Health (Care and Treatment) (Scotland) Act 2003 (asp 13) s.130. Brought into force on 5 October 2005 by SSI 2005/161 (C.6).

Subs.(10)(d) as amended by Mental Health (Scotland) Act 2015 (asp 9) Pt 2 s.38(2)(c). Brought into force on 30 June 2017 by SSI 2017/197 art.2 and Sch.

Subs.(6)(a), (b), (c) as amended, subs.(6A) inserted, by Mental Health (Scotland) Act 2015 (asp 9) s.40(2). Brought into force on 30 September 2017 by SSI 2017/197 art.2 and Sch.

DEFINITIONS

A4-122.11 "assessment order": s.52B(1)(c).

"court": s.52B(4).

"medical treatment": s.329(1) of the Mental Health (Care and Treatment) (Scotland) Act 2003.

"mental disorder": s.328(1) of the Mental Health (Care and Treatment) (Scotland) Act 2003.

"offence": s.307(1).

"prosecutor": s.307(1).

"relevant disposal": s.52B(4).

"specified": s.52D(11).

GENERAL NOTE

A4-122.12 Where an application for an assessment order (AO) is made under ss.52B or 52C, or the court decides to make an AO *ex proprio motu* (s.52E), the procedure specified in the new s.52D operates. The court first requires to be satisfied on the evidence of a medical practitioner, that the matters specified in subs.(3) have been established (subs.(2)(a)). These relate essentially to the need to detain the accused for the purposes of conducting an assessment of his or her medical condition and the availability of a suitable hospital for that purpose.

However, the court must be satisfied that the step is justified in all the circumstances, and that no other alternative means of dealing with the accused can be used (subs.(4)). If this test is also satisfied, the court can make an AO, but can only do so in the accused's absence, if the accused is represented (subs.(8)).

An AO is authority for the accused to be taken to the hospital designated in the AO, if necessary preceded by a period of time in a place of safety (subs.(9)), and detained at the hospital for a period of 28 days from the date on which the AO is made (subs.(6)(a) and (b)). The giving of medical treatment in terms of Pt 16 of the Mental Health (Care and Treatment) (Scotland) Act 2003 is also authorised during this period (subs.(6)(c)). During this period, the hospital will assess the matters specified in subs.(7).

Where the court makes an AO, it must notify the persons specified in subs.(10), who are those entitled to be notified of an application for an AO under ss.52B or 52C, with the addition of the Commission. An AO's authority to detain the accused can be suspended by an accused's responsible medical officer (see 2003 Act s.230) in terms of s.221 of the 2003 Act.

Where a person has been detained in hospital and is allowed leave of absence to go on a day trip in the custody of hospital staff that person cannot be said to have "left the hospital" within the meaning of the Mental Health Act 1983 (c.20): *R (CXF) v Central Bedfordshire Council* [2018] EWCA Civ 2852; *The Times* Law Reports, 23 January 2019. The 1983 Act does apply in small part to Scotland: see s.147 of that Act. However, this authority may be persuasive if the question of cessation of detention arises in Scotland.

Subs. (2)

Written or oral evidence of a medical practitioner is required to make an assessment order, although the nature of any specified medical qualification is not referred to in the section. Such evidence may include words spoken by an accused. It is in the public interest for a psychiatrist to explore the detail of the inner workings of the mind of an accused in a hospital rather than a prison. If an accused states something in the course of such examination, which is relevant to the issue of his mental state, such a statement will normally be admissible as part of the proof of that state. If it is not relevant to that state but bears upon the merits of the charge, different considerations will arise: *Tole v HM Advocate* [2013] HCJAC 109; 2013 S.L.T. 1227; 2015 S.C.C.R. 5 at [13].

Assessment order made ex proprio motu: application of section 52D

52E.—(1) Where— A4-122.13

(a) a person has been charged with an offence;

(b) the person has not been sentenced; and

(c) it appears to the court that the person has a mental disorder,

the court may, subject to subsections (2) and (3) below, make an assessment order in respect of that person.

(2) The court may make an assessment order under subsection (1) above only if it would make one under subsections (2) to (11) of section 52D of this Act; and those subsections shall apply for the purposes of subsection (1) above as they apply for the purposes of subsection (1) of that section, references in those subsections to the person in respect of whom the application is made being construed as references to the person in respect of whom it is proposed to make an assessment order.

(3) An assessment order made under subsection (1) above shall, for the purposes of this Act and the Mental Health (Care and Treatment) (Scotland) Act 2003 (asp 13), be treated as if made under section 52D(2) of this Act.

(4) In this section, "court" has the same meaning as in section 52B of this Act.

AMENDMENTS

Section 52E inserted by Mental Health (Care and Treatment) (Scotland) Act 2003 (asp 13) s.130. Brought into force on 5 October 2005 by SSI 2005/161 (C.6).

DEFINITIONS A4-122.14

"assessment order": s.52B(1)(c).
"court": s.52B(4).
"mental disorder": s.328(1) of the Mental Health (Care and Treatment) (Scotland) Act 2003.
"offence": s.307(1).
"relevant disposal": s.52B(4).

GENERAL NOTE

This section is authority for the court to make an assessment order *ex proprio motu* where the grounds set out in s.52D are satisfied. A4-122.15

Assessment order: supplementary

52F.—(1) If, before the end of the day following the 7 days beginning with the day on which an assessment order is made— A4-122.16

(a) in the case of a person who, immediately before the order was made, was in remanded custody, it appears to the Scottish Ministers; or

(b) in any other case, it appears to the court,

that, by reason of emergency or other special circumstances, it is not reasonably practicable for the person to be admitted to the hospital specified in the order, the Scottish Ministers, or, as the case may be, the court, may direct that the person be admitted to the hospital specified in the direction.

(2) Where the court makes a direction under subsection (1) above, it shall, as soon as reasonably practicable after making the direction, inform the person having custody of the person subject to the assessment order of the making of the direction.

(3) Where the Scottish Ministers make a direction under subsection (1) above, they shall, as soon as reasonably practicable after making the direction, inform—

(a) the court;

(b) the person having custody of the person subject to the assessment order; and

(c) in a case where—

(i) the person has been charged with an offence; and

(ii) a relevant disposal has not been made in the proceedings in respect of the offence,

the prosecutor,

of the making of the direction.

(4) Where a direction is made under subsection (1) above, the assessment order shall have effect as if the hospital specified in the direction were the hospital specified in the order.

(5) In this section—

"court" means the court which made the assessment order; and

"relevant disposal" has the same meaning as in section 52B of this Act.

Amendments

Section 52F inserted by Mental Health (Care and Treatment) (Scotland) Act 2003 (asp 13) s.130. Brought into force on 5 October 2005 by SSI 2005/161 (C.6).

Subs.(1)(a) as amended, by Mental Health (Scotland) Act 2015 (asp 9) Pt 2 s.38(2). Brought into force on 30 June 2017 by SSI 2017/197 art.2 and Sch.

Subs.(1) as amended by Mental Health (Scotland) Act 2015 (asp 9) Pt 2 s.40(3). Brought into force on 30 September 2017 by SSI 2017/197 art.2 and Sch, subject to transitional provisions.

Definitions

A4-122.17 "assessment order": s.52B(1)(c).

"court": s.52B(4).

"mental disorder": s.328(1) of the Mental Health (Care and Treatment) (Scotland) Act 2003.

"offence": s.307(1).

"relevant disposal": s.52B(4).

General Note

A4-122.17.1 This section allows the court or the Scottish Ministers—only where an accused is in custody—to change the designation of the hospital required to admit an accused in terms of an assessment order ("AO"), if "by reason of emergency or other special circumstances" (subs.(1)) it is not practicable to admit the accused to the hospital specified in the original order within the seven day period specified in s.52D(6) (see above). The change of designation is effected by direction of the court or the Scottish Ministers as appropriate, and it will be noted that the test is of a stringent nature.

Where a direction is made under this section by a court, it must inform whoever has custody of the accused (see *Renton and Brown's Criminal Procedure*, 6th edn, para.6-03) that the direction has been made (subs.(2)). Where the Scottish Ministers make such a direction, they must also inform the person having custody of the accused, the court and the prosecutor (subs.(3)). A s.52F direction substitutes the hospital specified in the direction for that specified in the original AO, and the rights and obligations under the AO (see General Note to s.52D) pass to the substituted hospital (subs.(4)).

[THE NEXT PARAGRAPH IS A4-122.18]

Review of assessment order

52G.—(1) The responsible medical officer shall, before the end of the day following the 28 days beginning with the day on which the assessment order is made, submit a report in writing to the court— **A4-122.18**

(a) as to whether the conditions mentioned in section 52D(7) of this Act are met in respect of the person subject to the order; and

(b) as to any matters specified by the court under section 52D(2) of this Act.

(2) The responsible medical officer shall, at the same time as such officer submits the report to the court, send a copy of such report—

(a) to the person in respect of whom the report is made;

(b) to any solicitor acting for the person;

(c) in a case where—

(i) the person has been charged with an offence; and

(ii) a relevant disposal has not been made in the proceedings in respect of the offence,

to the prosecutor; and

(d) to the Scottish Ministers.

(3) Subject to subsection (4) below, the court shall, on receiving a report submitted under subsection (1) above, revoke the assessment order and—

(a) subject to subsections (7) and (8) below, make a treatment order; or

(b) commit the person to prison or such other institution to which the person might have been committed had the assessment order not been made or otherwise deal with the person as the court considers appropriate.

(4) If, on receiving a report submitted under subsection (1) above, the court is satisfied that further time is necessary to assess whether the conditions mentioned in section 52D(7) of this Act are met in respect of the person subject to the assessment order, it may, on one occasion only, make an order extending the assessment order for a period not exceeding the relevant period given by subsection (4A) below.

(4A) For the purpose of subsection (4) above, the relevant period is the period—

(a) beginning with the day on which the order would otherwise cease to authorise the detention of the person in hospital,

(b) expiring at the end of the 14 days following that day.

(5) The court may, under subsection (4) above, extend an assessment order in the absence of the person subject to the order only if—

(a) the person is represented by counsel or a solicitor;

(b) that counsel or solicitor is given an opportunity of being heard; and

(c) the court is satisfied that it is—

(i) impracticable; or

(ii) inappropriate,

for the person to be brought before it.

(6) Where the court makes an order under subsection (4) above, it shall, as soon as reasonably practicable after making the order, give notice of the making of the order to—

(a) the persons mentioned in paragraphs (a) and (b) of subsection (2) above;

(b) in a case where—

(i) the person has been charged with an offence; and

(ii) a relevant disposal has not been made in the proceedings in respect of the offence,

the prosecutor;

(c) the Scottish Ministers; and

(d) the person's responsible medical officer.

(7) The court shall make a treatment order under subsection (3)(a) above only if it would make one under subsections (2) to (10) of section 52M of this Act; and those subsections shall apply for the purposes of subsection (3)(a) above as they apply for the purposes of that section, references in those subsections to the person in respect of whom the application is made being construed as references to the person in respect of whom it is proposed to make a treatment order.

(8) A treatment order made under subsection (3)(a) above shall, for the purposes of this Act and the Mental Health (Care and Treatment) (Scotland) Act 2003 (asp 13), be treated as if made under section 52M(2) of this Act.

(9) The responsible medical officer shall, where that officer is satisfied that there has been a change of circumstances since the assessment order was made which justifies the variation of the order, submit a report to the court in writing.

(10) Where a report is submitted under subsection (9) above, the court shall—

(a) if satisfied that the person need not be subject to an assessment order, revoke the order and take any action mentioned in subsection (3)(b) above; or

(b) if not so satisfied—

(i) confirm the order;

(ii) vary the order; or

(iii) revoke the order and take any action mentioned in subsection (3)(b) above.

(11) Sections 52D, 52F, 52H and 52J of this Act and subsections (1) to (3) above apply to the variation of an order under subsection (10)(b)(ii) above as they apply to an assessment order.

(12) In this section—

"court" means the court which made the assessment order;

"relevant disposal" has the same meaning as in section 52B of this Act; and

"responsible medical officer" means the person's responsible medical officer appointed under section 230 of the Mental Health (Care and Treatment) (Scotland) Act 2003 (asp 13).

AMENDMENTS

Section 52G inserted by Mental Health (Care and Treatment) (Scotland) Act 2003 (asp 13) s.130. Brought into force on 5 October 2005 by SSI 2005/161 (C.6).

Subs.(1), (4) as amended, subs.(4A) inserted, by Mental Health (Scotland) Act 2015 (asp 9) Pt 2 s.40(4). Brought into force on 30 September 2017 by SSI 2017/197 art.2 and Sch, subject to transitional provisions.

DEFINITIONS

A4-122.19 "assessment order": s.52B(1)(c).
"court": s.52B(4).
"mental disorder": s.328(1) of the Mental Health (Care and Treatment) (Scotland) Act 2003.
"offence": s.307(1).
"relevant disposal": s.52B(4).
"responsible medical officer": s.230 of the Mental Health (Care and Treatment) (Scotland) Act 2003.
"treatment order": s.52M.

GENERAL NOTE

A4-122.20 Where an assessment order ("AO") has been made by the court, the responsible medical officer ("RMO") (see Mental Health (Care and Treatment) (Scotland) Act 2003 s.230) appointed to the accused must report to the court within 28 days of the AO being made (subs.(1)).

The first duty of the RMO is to advise the court whether the grounds for making the AO have been established, as well as to report on any matters required by the court (see General Note to s.52D). A copy of the report requires to be sent to the accused, the accused's solicitor and to the Scottish Ministers, as well as to the prosecutor where a "relevant disposal" has not been made (subs.(2)).

Once it has the RMO's report, the court can effect a number of disposals, and is empowered to:

(a) revoke the AO and make a treatment order ("TO") relative to the accused (subs.(3)(a)). Before the court makes a TO, the grounds for making a TO would require to be established (subs.(7). See also General Note to s.52M.);

(b) impose a sentence of imprisonment or make any other disposal the court is entitled to make (subs.(3)(b));

(c) extend the AO, on one occasion only, for a period not exceeding seven days for further assessment to take place, but only (where the accused is absent) after hearing representations from counsel or a solicitor acting on the accused's behalf. In this instance, the same people who require to be notified under subs.(2), as well as the accused's RMO, must be notified by the court of the order extending the AO (subs.(5)).

The RMO must also report any change in circumstances which has occurred since the AO was made and which would justify variation of the order (subs.(9)). The court can respond to such information by revoking the AO and proceeding to dispose of the matter, where it is not satisfied that the accused should be subject to the AO (subs.(10)(a)), or it can confirm or vary the AO, or revoke the AO and proceed to dispose of the matter (subss.(10)(b)(i), (ii) and (iii)).

Early termination of assessment order

52H.—(1) This section applies where— A4-122.21

(a) in the case of a person who, when the assessment order is made, has not been removed to the hospital specified in the order, the relevant period given by subsection (1A) below has not expired;

(b) in the case of a person—

(i) who, when the assessment order is made, has been admitted to the hospital specified in the order; or

(ii) who has been removed under paragraph (a) of subsection (6) of section 52D of this Act to the hospital so specified,

the relevant period given by subsection (1A) below has not expired; or

(c) in the case of a person in respect of whom the court has made an order under section 52G(4) of this Act extending the assessment order for a period, the period for which the order was extended has not expired.

(1A) For the purpose of subsection (1)(a) and (b) above, the relevant period is the period—

(a) beginning with the day on which the order is made,

(b) expiring—

(i) as regards subsection (1)(a) above, at the end of the 7 days following the day mentioned in paragraph (a) of this subsection,

(ii) as regards subsection (1)(b) above, at the end of the 28 days following the day mentioned in paragraph (a) of this subsection.

(2) An assessment order shall cease to have effect on the occurrence of any of the following events—

(a) the making of a treatment order in respect of the person subject to the assessment order;

(b) in a case where—

(i) the person subject to the assessment order has been charged with an offence; and

(ii) a relevant disposal had not been made in the proceedings in respect of that offence when the order was made,

the making of a relevant disposal in such proceedings;

(c) in a case where the person subject to the assessment order has been convicted of an offence but has not been sentenced—

(i) the deferral of sentence by the court under section 202(1) of this Act;

(ii) the making of one of the orders mentioned in subsection (3) below or

(iii) the imposition of any sentence.

(3) The orders are—

(a) an interim compulsion order;
(b) a compulsion order;
(c) a guardianship order;
(d) a hospital direction;
(e) any order under section 57 of this Act;
(f) […]

(4) In this section, "relevant disposal" has the same meaning as in section 52B of this Act.

AMENDMENTS

Section 52H inserted by Mental Health (Care and Treatment) (Scotland) Act 2003 (asp 13) s.130. Brought into force on 5 October 2005 by SSI 2005/161 (C.6).

Subsection (3)(e) as amended and subs.(3)(f) repealed by Criminal Justice and Licensing (Scotland) Act 2010 (asp 13) Sch.2 para.2. Brought into force on 13 December 2010 (subject to savings provisions in art.3) by SSI 2010/413 (C.28) art.2, Sch.1 para.1.

Subsection (1) as amended, subs.(1A) inserted, by Mental Health (Scotland) Act 2015 (asp 9) Pt 2 s.40(5). Brought into force on 30 September 2017 by SSI 2017/197 art.2 and Sch, subject to transitional provisions.

DEFINITIONS

A4-122.22 "assessment order": s.52B(1)(c).
"court": s.52B(4).
"relevant disposal": s.52B(4).
"treatment order": s.52M.

GENERAL NOTE

A4-122.23 This section makes a number of provisions for an assessment order ("AO") coming to an end.

Where an accused is subject to an extant AO in terms of subs.(1), the AO will cease where the court makes a treatment order in terms of s.52M, or makes a "relevant disposal" (see General Note to s.52B). Where the accused has been convicted and sentenced or has had sentence deferred by the court, the AO again will cease (subs.(2)(c)(i) and (iii)). Finally, the AO will also cease where the accused is convicted and the court makes a compulsion order (s.57A, as amended), an interim compulsion order (s.53, as amended), a guardianship order (see s.58A), a hospital direction (see s.59A, as amended), or any order the court can make under s.57 of the 1995 Act (disposal where accused found to be insane) in relation to an accused.

Power of court on assessment order ceasing to have effect

A4-122.24 **52J.**—(1) Where, otherwise than by virtue of section 52G(3) or (10) or 52H(2) of this Act, an assessment order ceases to have effect the court shall commit the person who was subject to the order to prison or such other institution to which the person might have been committed had the order not been made or otherwise deal with the person as the court considers appropriate.

(2) In this section, "court" has the same meaning as in section 52B of this Act.

AMENDMENTS

Section 52J inserted by Mental Health (Care and Treatment) (Scotland) Act 2003 (asp 13) s.130. Brought into force on 5 October 2005 by SSI 2005/161 (C.6).

DEFINITIONS

A4-122.25 "assessment order": s.52B(1)(c).
"court": s.52B(4).

GENERAL NOTE

A4-122.25.1 This section makes it clear that where an assessment order ("AO") has been made in relation to an accused, unless the AO comes to an end by virtue of the provisions contained in s.52G(3) or (10) or s.52H(2), the court retains its normal power to sentence an offender (whether or not by imprisonment) where the AO comes to an end.

[THE NEXT PARAGRAPH IS A4-122.26]

Treatment orders

Prosecutor's power to apply for treatment order

52K.—(1) Where— A4-122.26

(a) a person has been charged with an offence;

(b) a relevant disposal has not been made in the proceedings in respect of the offence; and

(c) it appears to the prosecutor that the person has a mental disorder,

the prosecutor may apply to the court for an order under section 52M of this Act (in this Act referred to as a "treatment order") in respect of that person.

(2) Where the prosecutor applies for a treatment order under subsection (1) above, the prosecutor shall, as soon as reasonably practicable after making the application, inform the persons mentioned in subsection (3) below of the making of the application.

(3) Those persons are—

(a) the person in respect of whom the application is made;

(b) any solicitor acting for the person; and

(c) in a case where the person is remanded in custody, the Scottish Ministers.

(4) In this section, "court" and "relevant disposal" have the same meanings as in section 52B of this Act.

AMENDMENTS

Section 52K inserted by Mental Health (Care and Treatment) (Scotland) Act 2003 (asp 13) s.130. Brought into force on 5 October 2005 by SSI 2005/161 (C.6).

Subs.(3)(c) as amended by Mental Health (Scotland) Act 2015 (asp 9) Pt 2 s.38(2)(e). Brought into force on 30 June 2017 by SSI 2017/197 art.2 and Sch.

DEFINITIONS A4-122.27

"assessment order": s.52B(1)(c).
"court": s.52B(4).
"relevant disposal": s.52B(4).
"treatment order": s.52M.

GENERAL NOTE

By virtue of s.52M, a court is entitled to impose a treatment order ("TO") on an accused person who appears to have a mental disorder (see General Note to s.52M). A4-122.28

This section allows the prosecution in any criminal proceedings to apply for a TO to be made relative to an accused who appears to have a mental disorder, at any stage prior to a "relevant disposal" (subs.(1)).

The procedure is similar to, and is available as an alternative to, the prosecutor applying for an assessment order under s.52B. Reference is made to the General Note to s.52B.

The "prosecutor" within the meaning of the 1995 Act is the person prosecuting under solemn procedure or summary procedure in any criminal court: see s.307(1). However, an application cannot be made to a JP court for a TO (s.52M(10)). The provision on this wide definition allows all prosecutors the power to apply for a TO.

Scottish Ministers' power to apply for treatment order

52L.—(1) Where— A4-122.29

(a) a person has been charged with an offence;

(b) the person has not been sentenced;

(c) the person is remanded in custody; and

(d) it appears to the Scottish Ministers that the person has a mental disorder,

the Scottish Ministers may apply to the court for a treatment order in respect of that person.

(2) Where the Scottish Ministers apply for an order under subsection (1) above, they shall, as soon as reasonably practicable after making the application, inform the persons mentioned in subsection (3) below of the making of the application.

(3) Those persons are—

(a) the person in respect of whom the application is made;

(b) any solicitor acting for the person; and

(c) in a case where a relevant disposal has not been made in the proceedings in respect of the offence with which the person is charged, the prosecutor.

(4) In this section, "court" and "relevant disposal" have the same meanings as in section 52B of this Act.

AMENDMENTS

Section 52L inserted by Mental Health (Care and Treatment) (Scotland) Act 2003 (asp 13) s.130. Brought into force on 5 October 2005 by SSI 2005/161 (C.6).

Subs.(1)(c) as amended by Mental Health (Scotland) Act 2015 (asp 9) Pt 2 s.38(2)(f). Brought into force on 30 June 2017 by SSI 2017/197 art.2 and Sch.

DEFINITIONS

A4-122.30 "assessment order": s.52B(1)(c).
"court": s.52B(4).
"mental disorder": s.328(1) of the Mental Health (Care and Treatment) (Scotland) Act 2003.
"offence": s.307(1).
"prosecutor": s.307(1).
"relevant disposal": s.52B(4).
"sentence": s.307(1).
"treatment order": s.52M.

GENERAL NOTE

A4-122.31 This section allows the Scottish Ministers under the conditions set out in s.52L(1)(a) to (c) to apply for a treatment order to be made in respect of an accused person who is in custody, and who appears to have a mental disorder. Intimation to various parties of the making of the application is necessary: s.52L(3).

Again, this procedure is a direct alternative to Scottish Ministers applying for an assessment order under s.52C. See General Note to s.52C.

Treatment order

A4-122.32 **52M.**—(1) This section applies where an application for a treatment order is made under section 52K(1) or 52L(1) of this Act.

(2) If the court is satisfied—

(a) on the written or oral evidence of two medical practitioners, as to the matters mentioned in subsection (3) below; and

(b) that, having regard to the matters mentioned in subsection (4) below, it is appropriate,

it may, subject to subsection (5) below, make a treatment order authorising the measures mentioned in subsection (6) below.

(3) The matters referred to in subsection (2)(a) above are—

(a) that the conditions mentioned in subsection (7) of section 52D of this Act are met in relation to the person in respect of whom the application is made;

(b) that the hospital proposed by the approved medical practitioner and the medical practitioner is suitable for the purpose of giving medical treatment to the person; and

(c) that, if a treatment order were made, such person could be admitted to such hospital before the end of the day following the 7 days beginning with the day on which the order is made.

(4) The matters referred to in subsection (2)(b) above are—

(a) all the circumstances (including the nature of the offence with which the person in respect of whom the application is made is charged or, as the case may be, of which the person was convicted); and

(b) any alternative means of dealing with the person.

(5) The court may make a treatment order only if the person in respect of whom the application is made has not been sentenced.

(6) The measures are—

(a) in the case of a person who, when the treatment order is made, has not been admitted to the specified hospital, the removal, before the end of the day following the 7 days beginning with the day on which the order is made, of the person to the specified hospital by—
   (i) a constable;
   (ii) a person employed in, or contracted to provide services in or to, the specified hospital who is authorised by the managers of that hospital to remove persons to hospital for the purposes of this section; or
   (iii) a specified person;
(b) the detention of the person in the specified hospital; and
(c) the giving to the person, in accordance with Part 16 of the Mental Health (Care and Treatment) (Scotland) Act 2003 (asp 13), of medical treatment.

(7) The court may make a treatment order in the absence of the person in respect of whom the application is made only if—
(a) the person is represented by counsel or solicitor;
(b) that counsel or solicitor is given an opportunity of being heard; and
(c) the court is satisfied that it is—
   (i) impracticable; or
   (ii) inappropriate,

for the person to be brought before it.

(8) A treatment order may include such directions as the court thinks fit for the removal of the person subject to the order to, and detention of the person in, a place of safety pending the person's admission to the specified hospital.

(9) The court shall, as soon as reasonably practicable after making a treatment order, give notice of the making of the order to—
(a) the person subject to the order;
(b) any solicitor acting for the person;
(c) in a case where—
   (i) the person has been charged with an offence; and
   (ii) a relevant disposal has not been made in the proceedings in respect of the offence,

the prosecutor;
(d) in a case where the person, immediately before the order was made—
   (i) was remanded in custody; or
   (ii) was subject to an assessment order and, immediately before that order was made, was in custody,

the Scottish Ministers; and
(e) the Mental Welfare Commission.

(10) In this section—

"court" has the same meaning as in section 52B of this Act;
"medical treatment" has the same meaning as in section 52D of this Act; and
"specified" means specified in the treatment order.

AMENDMENTS

Section 52M inserted by Mental Health (Care and Treatment) (Scotland) Act 2003 (asp 13) s.130. Brought into force on 5 October 2005 by SSI 2005/161 (C.6).

Subs.(9)(d) as amended by Mental Health (Scotland) Act 2015 (asp 9) Pt 2 s.38(2). Brought into force on 30 June 2017 by SSI 2017/197 art.2 and Sch.

Subs.(3)(c), (6)(a) as amended by Mental Health (Scotland) Act 2015 (asp 9) Pt 2 s.41(2). Brought into force on 30 September 2017 by SSI 2017/197 art.2 and Sch.

DEFINITIONS

A4-122.33 "assessment order": s.52B(1)(c).
"court": s.52B(4).
"medical treatment": s.52D.
"mental disorder": s.328(1) of the Mental Health (Care and Treatment) (Scotland) Act 2003.
"offence": s.307(1).
"prosecutor": s.307(1).
"relevant disposal": s.52B(4).
"sentence": s.307(1).
"specified": s.52M(10).
"treatment order": s.52M.

GENERAL NOTE

A4-122.34 Where an application for an treatment order ("TO") is made under ss.52K or 52L, or the court decides to make an TO *ex proprio motu* (s.52N), the procedure specified in the new s.52M operates. The court can only make a TO if it has not already sentenced the accused (subs.(5)).

The court first requires to be satisfied on the evidence of two medical practitioners (cf. s.52D(2)) that the matters specified in subs.(3) have been established (subs.(2)(a)). These relate essentially to the need to detain the accused for the purposes of giving medical treatment (see Pt 16 of the Mental Health (Care and Treatment) (Scotland) Act 2003) and the availability of a suitable hospital for that purpose.

However, the court must be satisfied that the step is justified in all the circumstances, and that no other alternative means of dealing with the accused can be used (subs.(4)). If this test is also satisfied, the court can make a TO, but can only do so in the accused's absence if the accused is represented and it is impracticable or inappropriate for the accused to be brought before the court (subs.(7)).

A TO is authority for the accused to be taken to the hospital designated in the TO, if necessary preceded by a period of time in a place of safety where the court so directs (subs.(8)), and detained at the hospital for an indefinite period (subs.(6)), pending one of the grounds for discharge of the TO arising (see General Notes to ss.52Q and 52R). The giving of medical treatment in terms of Pt 16 of the 2003 Act is also authorised during this period (subs.(6)(c)).

Where the court makes a TO, it must notify the persons specified in subs.(9), who are those entitled to be notified of an application for an assessment order under ss.52B or 52C, with the addition of the Commission. A TO's authority to detain an accused can be suspended by an accused's responsible medical officer (see 2003 Act s.230) in terms of s.224 of the 2003 Act.

Treatment order made ex proprio motu: application of section 52M

A4-122.35 **52N.**—(1) Where—

(a) a person has been charged with an offence;
(b) the person has not been sentenced; and
(c) it appears to the court that the person has a mental disorder,

the court may, subject to subsections (2) and (3) below, make a treatment order in respect of that person.

(2) The court may make a treatment order under subsection (1) above only if it would make one under subsections (2) to (10) of section 52M of this Act; and those subsections shall apply for the purposes of subsection (1) above as they apply for the purposes of subsection (1) of that section, references in those subsections to the person in respect of whom the application is made being construed as references to the person in respect of whom it is proposed to make a treatment order.

(3) A treatment order made under subsection (1) above shall, for the purposes of this Act and the Mental Health (Care and Treatment) (Scotland) Act 2003 (asp 13), be treated as if made under section 52M(2) of this Act.

(4) In this section, "court" has the same meaning as in section 52B of this Act.

AMENDMENTS

Section 52N inserted by Mental Health (Care and Treatment) (Scotland) Act 2003 (asp 13) s.130. Brought into force on 5 October 2005 by SSI 2005/161 (C.6).

DEFINITIONS

A4-122.36 "court": s.52B(4).
"mental disorder": s.328(1) of the Mental Health (Care and Treatment) (Scotland) Act 2003.
"offence": s.307(1).
"sentence": s.307(1).
"treatment order": s.52M.

GENERAL NOTE

This section is authority for the court to make a treatment order *ex proprio motu*, where the grounds set out in s.52M are satisfied. A4-122.37

Treatment order: supplementary

52P.—(1) If, before the end of the day following the 7 days beginning with the day on which the treatment order is made— A4-122.38

(a) in the case of a person to whom subsection (2) below applies, it appears to the Scottish Ministers; or

(b) in any other case, it appears to the court,

that, by reason of emergency or other special circumstances, it is not reasonably practicable for the person to be admitted to the hospital specified in the order, the Scottish Ministers, or, as the case may be, the court, may direct that the person be admitted to the hospital specified in the direction.

(2) This subsection applies to—

(a) a person who is remanded in custody immediately before the treatment order is made; or

(b) a person—

(i) who was subject to an assessment order immediately before the treatment order is made; and

(ii) who was remanded in custody immediately before that assessment order was made.

(3) Where the court makes a direction under subsection (1) above, it shall, as soon as reasonably practicable after making the direction, inform the person having custody of the person subject to the treatment order of the making of the direction.

(4) Where the Scottish Ministers make a direction under subsection (1) above, they shall, as soon as reasonably practicable after making the direction, inform—

(a) the court;

(b) the person having custody of the person subject to the treatment order; and

(c) in a case where—

(i) the person has been charged with an offence; and

(ii) a relevant disposal has not been made in the proceedings in respect of the offence,

the prosecutor,

of the making of the direction.

(5) Where a direction is made under subsection (1) above, the treatment order shall have effect as if the hospital specified in the direction were the hospital specified in the order.

(6) In this section—

"court" means the court which made the treatment order; and

"relevant disposal" has the same meaning as in section 52B of this Act.

AMENDMENTS

Section 52P inserted by Mental Health (Care and Treatment) (Scotland) Act 2003 (asp 13) s.130. Brought into force on 5 October 2005 by SSI 2005/161 (C.6).

Subs.(2) as amended by Mental Health (Scotland) Act 2015 (asp 9) Pt 2 s.38(2). Brought into force on 30 June 2017 by SSI 2017/197 art.2 and Sch.

Subs.(1) as amended by Mental Health (Scotland) Act 2015 (asp 9) Pt 2 s.41(3). Brought into force on 30 September 2017 by SSI 2017/197 art.2 and Sch, subject to transitional provisions.

DEFINITIONS

"assessment order": s.52B(1)(c). A4-122.39

"court": s.52B(4).

"mental disorder": s.328(1) of the Mental Health (Care and Treatment) (Scotland) Act 2003.

"offence": s.307(1).
"relevant disposal": s.52B(4).
"sentence": s.307(1).
"treatment order": s.52M.

GENERAL NOTE

A4-122.39.1 The section allows the court or the Scottish Ministers—only where an accused is in custody or where a treatment order ("TO") immediately follows an assessment order ("AO") and the accused was in custody when the AO was made (subs.(2))—to change the designation of the hospital required to admit an accused in terms of a TO, if "by reason of emergency or other special circumstances" (subs.(1)) it is not practicable to admit the accused there to the hospital specified in the original order within the seven day period specified in s.52M(6) (see above). The change of designation is effected by direction of the court or the Scottish Ministers as appropriate, and it will be noted that the test is of a stringent nature.

Where a direction is made under this section by a court, it must inform whoever has custody of the accused (see General Note to s.52F) that the direction has been made (subs.(3)). Where the Scottish Ministers make such a direction, they must also inform the person having custody of the accused, the court and the prosecutor (subs.(4)). A s.52P direction substitutes the hospital specified in the direction for that specified in the original TO, and the rights and obligations under the TO (see General Note to s.52M) pass to the substituted hospital (subs.(4)).

[THE NEXT PARAGRAPH IS A4-122.40]

Review of treatment order

A4-122.40 **52Q.**—(1) The responsible medical officer shall, where that officer is satisfied—

(a) that any of the conditions mentioned in section 52D(7) of this Act are no longer met in respect of the person subject to the treatment order; or

(b) that there has otherwise been a change of circumstances since the order was made which makes the continued detention of the person in hospital by virtue of the order no longer appropriate,

submit a report in writing to the court.

(2) Where a report is submitted under subsection (1) above, the court shall—

(a) if satisfied that the person need not be subject to the treatment order—

(i) revoke the order; and

(ii) commit the person to prison or such other institution to which the person might have been committed had the order not been made or otherwise deal with the person as the court considers appropriate; or

(b) if not so satisfied—

(i) confirm the order;

(ii) vary the order; or

(iii) revoke the order and take any action mentioned in paragraph (a)(ii) above.

(3) Sections 52M, 52P, this section and sections 52R and 52S of this Act apply to the variation of a treatment order under subsection (2)(b)(ii) above as they apply to a treatment order.

(4) In this section—

"court" means the court which made the treatment order; and

"responsible medical officer" means the person's responsible medical officer appointed under section 230 of the Mental Health (Care and Treatment) (Scotland) Act 2003 (asp 13).

AMENDMENTS

Section 52Q inserted by Mental Health (Care and Treatment) (Scotland) Act 2003 (asp 13) s.130. Brought into force on 5 October 2005 by SSI 2005/161 (C.6).

DEFINITIONS

"assessment order": s.52B(1)(c). A4-122.41
"court": s.52Q(4).
"offence": s.307(1).
"responsible medical officer": s.230 of the Mental Health (Care and Treatment) (Scotland) Act 2003.
"treatment order": s.52M.

GENERAL NOTE

Where a treatment order ("TO") has been made by the court, the responsible medical officer ("RMO") (see 2003 Act s.230) appointed to the accused must report to the court in the event of the TO ceasing to be appropriate (subs.(1)). A4-122.41.1

The RMO must advise the court whether any of the conditions specified in s.52D(7) for making the TO are no longer met (subs.(1)(a); and see General Note to s.52D). If the RMO concluded, for example, that the patient no longer had a mental disorder, this fact would require to be reported to the court.

The RMO must also report on any other change in circumstances of the accused which makes the TO no longer appropriate (subs.(1)(b)). Unlike s.52G, the report only requires to be sent to the court, and there is no provision for a copy to be sent to the accused, the accused's solicitor, the Scottish Ministers or the prosecutor. However, this is likely to be done as a matter of practice.

Once it has the RMO's report, the court can effect a number of disposals, and is empowered to:

(a) revoke the TO, and deal with the accused as it could have done under normal powers, if satisfied that the TO is no longer appropriate (subs.(2)(a)(i)); or

(b) confirm, or vary the TO, or revoke the TO and deal with the accused as it could have done under normal powers (subs.(2)(b)).

[THE NEXT PARAGRAPH IS A4-122.42]

Termination of treatment order

52R.—(1) This section applies— A4-122.42

(a) where, in the case of a person who, when the treatment order is made, has not been removed to the hospital specified in the order, the relevant period given by subsection (1A) below has not expired; or

(b) in the case of a person—

(i) who, when the treatment order is made, has been admitted to the hospital specified in the order; or

(ii) who has been removed under paragraph (a) of subsection (6) of section 52M of this Act to the hospital so specified.

(1A) For the purpose of subsection (1)(a) above, the relevant period is the period—

(a) beginning with the day on which the order is made,

(b) expiring at the end of the 7 days following that day.

(2) A treatment order shall cease to have effect on the occurrence of any of the following events—

(a) in a case where—

(i) the person subject to the treatment order has been charged with an offence; and

(ii) a relevant disposal had not been made in the proceedings in respect of such offence when the order was made,

the making of a relevant disposal in such proceedings;

(b) in a case where the person subject to the treatment order has been convicted of an offence but has not been sentenced—

(i) the deferral of sentence by the court under section 202(1) of this Act;

(ii) the making of one of the orders mentioned in subsection (3) below; or

(iii) the imposition of any sentence.

(3) The orders are—

(a) an interim compulsion order;
(b) a compulsion order;
(c) a guardianship order;
(d) a hospital direction;
(e) any order under section 57 of this Act;
(f) […]

(4) In this section, "relevant disposal" has the same meaning as in section 52B of this Act.

AMENDMENTS

Section 52R inserted by Mental Health (Care and Treatment) (Scotland) Act 2003 (asp 13) s.130. Brought into force on 5 October 2005 by SSI 2005/161 (C.6).

Subsection (3)(e) as amended and subs.(3)(f) repealed by Criminal Justice and Licensing (Scotland) Act 2010 (asp 13) Sch.2 para.3. Brought into force on 13 December 2010 (subject to savings provisions in art.3) by SSI 2010/413 (C.28) art.2, Sch.1 para.1.

Subsection (1)(a) as amended, subs.(1A) inserted, by Mental Health (Scotland) Act 2015 (asp 9) Pt 2 s.41(4). Brought into force on 30 September 2017 by SSI 2017/197 art.2 and Sch, subject to transitional provisions

DEFINITIONS

A4-122.43 "assessment order": s.52B(1)(c).
"court": s.52Q(4).
"offence": s.307(1).
"relevant disposal": s.52B(4).
"responsible medical officer": s.230 of the Mental Health (Care and Treatment) (Scotland) Act 2003.
"treatment order": s.52M.

GENERAL NOTE

A4-122.44 This section makes a number of provisions for a treatment order ("TO") coming to an end. Where an accused is subject to an extant TO in terms of subs.(1), the TO will cease where the court makes a "relevant disposal" (see General Note to s.52A). Where the accused has been convicted and sentenced or has had sentence deferred by the court, the TO again will cease (subs.(2)(a) and (b)).

Finally, the TO will also cease where the accused is convicted and the court makes a compulsion order (s.57A) an interim compulsion order (s.53), a guardianship order (s.58A), a hospital direction (s.59A), or any order the court can make under s.57 (disposal where accused found to be insane), in relation to the accused (subs.(3)).

Power of court on treatment order ceasing to have effect

A4-122.45 **52S.**—(1) Where, otherwise than by virtue of section 52Q(2) or 52R(2) of this Act, a treatment order ceases to have effect the court shall commit the person who was subject to the order to prison or such other institution to which the person might have been committed had the order not been made or otherwise deal with the person as the court considers appropriate.

(2) In this section, "court" has the same meaning as in section 52B of this Act.

AMENDMENTS

Section 52S inserted by Mental Health (Care and Treatment) (Scotland) Act 2003 (asp 13) s.130. Brought into force on 5 October 2005 by SSI 2005/161 (C.6).

DEFINITIONS

A4-122.46 "court": s.52Q(4).
"treatment order": s.52M.

GENERAL NOTE

A4-122.46.1 This section makes it clear that where a treatment order ("TO") has been made in relation to an accused, unless the TO comes to an end by virtue of the provisions contained in ss.52Q(2) or 52R(2), the court retains its normal power to sentence an offender (whether or not by imprisonment) when the TO comes to an end.

[THE NEXT PARAGRAPH IS A4-122.47]

Prevention of delay in trials

Prevention of delay in trials: assessment orders and treatment orders

52T.—(1) Subsections (4) to (9) of section 65 of this Act shall apply in the case of a person committed for an offence until liberated in due course of law who is detained in hospital by virtue of an assessment order or a treatment order as those subsections apply in the case of an accused who is— **A4-122.47**

(a) committed for an offence until liberated in due course of law; and

(b) detained by virtue of that committal.

(2) Section 147 of this Act shall apply in the case of a person charged with an offence in summary proceedings who is detained in hospital by virtue of an assessment order or a treatment order as it applies in the case of an accused who is detained in respect of that offence.

(3) Any period during which, under—

(a) section 221 (as read with sections 222 and 223) of the Mental Health (Care and Treatment) (Scotland) Act 2003 (asp 13); or

(b) section 224 (as read with sections 225 and 226) of that Act,

a patient's detention is not authorised shall be taken into account for the purposes of the calculation of any of the periods mentioned in subsection (4) below.

(4) Those periods are—

(a) the total periods of 80 days, 110 days and 140 days referred to in subsection (4) of section 65 of this Act as applied by subsection (1) above;

(b) those total periods as extended under subsection (5) or, on appeal, under subsection (8) of that section as so applied;

(c) the total of 40 days referred to in section 147 of this Act (prevention of delay in trials in summary proceedings) as applied by subsection (2) above; and

(d) that period as extended under subsection (2) of that section or, on appeal, under subsection (3) of that section as so applied.

AMENDMENTS

Section 52T inserted by Mental Health (Care and Treatment) (Scotland) Act 2003 (asp 13) s.130. Brought into force on 5 October 2005 by SSI 2005/161 (C.6).

Subsections (1) and (4) as amended by Mental Health (Care and Treatment) (Scotland) Act 2003 (Modification of Enactments) Order 2005 (SSI 2005/465) Sch.1 para 32(13) and Sch.2 para.1 (effective 5 October 2005).

Prevention of delay in trials: assessment orders and treatment orders

***52T.**—(1) Subsections (4) to (9), (11), (12)(b) and (13) of section 65 of this Act shall apply in the case of a person committed for an offence until liberated in due course of law who is detained in hospital by virtue of an assessment order or a treatment order as those subsections apply in the case of an accused who is–*

(a) committed for an offence until liberated in due course of law; and

(b) detained by virtue of that committal.

(2) Section 147 of this Act shall apply in the case of a person charged with an offence in summary proceedings who is detained in hospital by virtue of an assessment order or a treatment order as it applies in the case of an accused who is detained in respect of that offence.

(3) Any period during which, under–

(a) section 221 (as read with sections 222 and 223) of the Mental Health (Care and Treatment) (Scotland) Act 2003 (asp 13); or

(b) section 224 (as read with sections 225 and 226) of that Act,

a patient's detention is not authorised shall be taken into account for the purposes of the calculation of any of the periods mentioned in subsection (4) below.

(4) Those periods are–

(a) the total periods of 80 days, 110 days and 140 days referred to in subsection (4) of section 65 of this Act as applied by subsection (1) above;

(b) those total periods as extended under subsection (5) or, on appeal, under subsection (8) of that section as so applied;

(c) the total of 40 days referred to in subsection (1) of section 147 of this Act (prevention of delay in trials in summary proceedings) as applied by subsection (2) above; and

(d) that period as extended under subsection (2) of that section or, on appeal, under subsection (3) of that section as so applied.

(5) In subsection (4)—

(a) the provisions of section 65 referred to in paragraphs (a) and (b) are to be read with subsections (11), (12)(b) and (13) of that section,

(b) the provisions of section 147 referred to in paragraphs (c) and (d) are to be read with subsections (5) and (6) of that section.

AMENDMENTS

In relation to COVID-19, s.52T as amended by Coronavirus (Scotland) Act 2020 (asp 7) Sch.4(4) para.10(2)(a)–(c) (effective 7 April 2020).

[THE NEXT PARAGRAPH IS A4-122.48]

DEFINITIONS

A4-122.48 "assessment order": s.52B(1)(c).
"court": s.52Q(4).
"indictment": s.307(1).
"offence": s.307(1).
"treatment order": s.52M.

GENERAL NOTE

A4-122.48.1 Various statutory time-bars apply to criminal proceedings under ss.65 and 147 of the 1995 Act. This section makes it clear that these time-bars are not affected where an accused is detained in hospital on an assessment order ("AO") or treatment order ("TO"). Similarly, these are not affected by the suspension of an AO by virtue of s.221 of the Mental Health (Care and Treatment) (Scotland) Act 2003 or the suspension of a TO by virtue of s.224 of the 2003 Act (subs.(3)). Any periods of suspension will be taken into account for the purpose of these time-bars.

As previously noted, an accused may be detained under an AO for a period of 28 days, which can be extended for a further seven days (see General Note to ss.52D and 52F). In the case of a TO, the termination of the order may depend on a change in the accused's condition or the making of some other order (see General Note to ss.52Q and 52R), and no specific point at which the termination will occur can be stated in advance. This period will be taken into account for the purpose of these time bars.

[THE NEXT PARAGRAPH IS A4-122.49]

Effect of assessment and treatment orders on pre-existing mental health orders

Effect of assessment order and treatment order on pre-existing mental health order

A4-122.49 **52U.**—(1) This section applies where—

(a) a patient is subject to a relevant order; and

(b) an assessment order or a treatment order is made in respect of the patient.

(2) The relevant order shall cease to authorise the measures specified in it for the period during which the patient is subject to the assessment order or, as the case may be, treatment order.

(3) […]

(4) In this section, a "relevant order" means—

(a) an interim compulsory treatment order made under section 65(2) of the 2003 Act; and

(b) a compulsory treatment order made under section 64(4)(a) of that Act.

AMENDMENTS

Section 52U inserted by Mental Health (Care and Treatment) (Scotland) Act 2003 (asp 13) s.130. Brought into force on 5 October 2005 by SSI 2005/161 (C.6).

Subs.(2) as amended, and subs.(3) repealed, by Mental Health (Care and Treatment) (Scotland) Act 2003 (Modification of Enactments) Order 2005 (SSI 2005/465) Sch.2 para.1 (effective 5 October 2005).

DEFINITIONS

"assessment order": s.52B(1)(c). **A4-122.50**
"court": s.52Q(4).
"relevant order": s.52U(4).
"treatment order": s.52M.

GENERAL NOTE

This section makes it clear that where a patient is subject to a compulsory treatment order ("CTO") or interim compulsory treatment order ("ICTO"), the order will cease to authorise the compulsory measures specified during the period of an assessment order ("AO") or treatment order ("TO") granted in respect of the patient (subs.(1), (2) and (4)). **A4-122.51**

The authority to give medical treatment under Pt 16 of the Mental Health (Care and Treatment) (Scotland) Act 2003 will flow from the AO or TO whilst these orders are in effect (subs.(3)).

It would appear that the CTO or ICTO would revive when the AO or TO comes to an end, although the period of an ICTO may well have come to an end in the meantime. Arrangements may have to be made to extend a CTO which would otherwise come to an end during the period an AO or TO is in effect, to ensure authority to impose compulsory measures remains in place when the AO or TO comes to an end.

The enforcement provisions for non compliance with a community based CTO or ICTO, contained in ss.112 to 120 of the 2003 Act, will not apply during the period of an AO or TO (subs.(3)).

[THE NEXT PARAGRAPH IS A4-123]

Interim compulsion orders

Interim compulsion order

53.—(1) This section applies where a person (referred to in this section and in sections 53A to 53D of this Act as an "offender")— **A4-123**

(a) is convicted in the High Court or the sheriff court of an offence punishable by imprisonment (other than an offence the sentence for which is fixed by law); or

(b) is remitted to the High Court by the sheriff under any enactment for sentence for such an offence.

(2) If the court is satisfied—

(a) on the written or oral evidence of two medical practitioners—

(i) that the offender has a mental disorder; and

(ii) as to the matters mentioned in subsection (3) below; and

(b) that, having regard to the matters mentioned in subsection (4) below, it is appropriate,

it may, subject to subsection (7) below, make an order (in this Act referred to as an "interim compulsion order") authorising the measures mentioned in subsection (8) below and specifying any matters to be included in the report under section 53B(1) of this Act.

(3) The matters referred to in subsection (2)(a)(ii) above are—

(a) that there are reasonable grounds for believing—

(i) that the conditions mentioned in subsection (5) below are likely to be met in respect of the offender; and

(ii) that the offender's mental disorder is such that it would be appropriate to make one of the disposals mentioned in subsection (6) below in relation to the offender;

(b) that the hospital to be specified in the order is suitable for the purpose of assessing whether the conditions mentioned in subsection (5) below are met in respect of the offender;

(c) that, were an interim compulsion order made, the offender could be admitted to such hospital before the end of the day following the 7 days beginning with the day on which the order is made; and

(d) that it would not be reasonably practicable for the assessment mentioned in paragraph (b) above to be made unless an order were made.

(4) The matters referred to in subsection (2)(b) above are—

(a) all the circumstances (including the nature of the offence of which the offender is convicted); and

(b) any alternative means of dealing with the offender.

(5) The conditions referred to in paragraphs (a)(i) and (b) of subsection (3) above are—

(a) that medical treatment which would be likely to—

(i) prevent the mental disorder worsening; or

(ii) alleviate any of the symptoms, or effects, of the disorder,

is available for the offender;

(b) that if the offender were not provided with such medical treatment there would be a significant risk—

(i) to the health, safety or welfare of the offender; or

(ii) to the safety of any other person; and

(c) that the making of an interim compulsion order in respect of the offender is necessary.

(6) The disposals are—

(a) both a compulsion order that authorises detention in hospital by virtue of section 57A(8)(a) of this Act and a restriction order; or

(b) a hospital direction.

(7) An interim compulsion order may authorise detention in a state hospital only if, on the written or oral evidence of the two medical practitioners mentioned in subsection (2)(a) above, it appears to the court—

(a) that the offender requires to be detained in hospital under conditions of special security; and

(b) that such conditions of special security can be provided only in a state hospital.

(8) The measures are—

(a) in the case of an offender who, when the interim compulsion order is made, has not been admitted to the specified hospital, the removal, before the end of the day following the 7 days beginning with the day on which the order is made, of the offender to the specified hospital by—

(i) a constable;

(ii) a person employed in, or contracted to provide services in or to, the specified hospital who is authorised by the managers of that hospital to remove persons to hospital for the purposes of this section; or

(iii) a specified person;

(b) the detention, for a period not exceeding the relevant period given by subsection (8A) below, of the offender in the specified hospital; and

(c) during the relevant period given by subsection (8A) below, the giving to the offender, in accordance with Part 16 of the Mental Health (Care and Treatment) (Scotland) Act 2003 (asp 13), of medical treatment.

(8A) For the purpose of subsection (8)(b) and (c) above, the relevant period is the period—

(a) beginning with the day on which the order is made,
(b) expiring at the end of the 12 weeks following that day.

(9) An interim compulsion order may include such directions as the court thinks fit for the removal of the offender to, and the detention of the offender in, a place of safety pending the offender's admission to the specified hospital.

(10) The court may make an interim compulsion order in the absence of the offender only if—

(a) the offender is represented by counsel or solicitor;
(b) that counsel or solicitor is given an opportunity of being heard; and
(c) the court is satisfied that it is—
  (i) impracticable; or
  (ii) inappropriate,

for the offender to be brought before it.

(11) The court shall, as soon as reasonably practicable after making an interim compulsion order, give notice of the making of the order to—

(a) the person subject to the order;
(b) any solicitor acting for that person;
(c) the Scottish Ministers; and
(d) the Mental Welfare Commission.

(12) Where a court makes an interim compulsion order in relation to an offender, the court—

(a) shall not, at the same time
  (i) make an order under section 200 of this Act;
  (ii) impose a fine;
  (iii) pass sentence of imprisonment;
  (iv) make a compulsion order;
  (v) make a guardianship order;
  (vi) impose a community payback order;
  (vii) make a drug treatment and testing order; or
  (viii) make a restriction of liberty order,

in relation of the offender;

(b) may make any other order which it has power to make apart from this section.

(13) In this section—

"medical treatment" has the same meaning as in section 52D of this Act;
"sentence of imprisonment" includes any sentence or order for detention; and
"specified" means specified in the interim compulsion order.

AMENDMENTS

Section 53 substituted by Mental Health (Care and Treatment) (Scotland) Act 2003 (asp 13) s.131. Brought into force on 5 October 2005 by SSI 2005/161 (C.6).

Subs.(12)(a)(vi)-(vii) substituted with subs.(12)(a)(vi)-(viii) by Criminal Justice and Licensing (Scotland) Act 2010 (asp 13) Sch.2 para.4. Brought into force on 13 December 2010 (subject to savings provisions in art.3) by SSI 2010/413 (C.28).

Subss.(3), (8) as amended, subs.(8A) inserted, by Mental Health (Scotland) Act 2015 (asp 9) Pt 2 s.42(2). Brought into force on 30 September 2017 by SSI 2017/197 art.2 and Sch.

DEFINITIONS

A4-123.1 "court": s.53A(4).
"interim compulsion order": s.53(2).
"medical treatment": s.329(1) of the Mental Health (Care and Treatment) (Scotland) Act 2003.
"sentence of imprisonment": s.53(13).
"specified": s.53(13).

GENERAL NOTE

A4-123.2 Under the original s.53 of the 1995 Act, a court was entitled to make an interim hospital order in relation to an offender, that is a person who has been convicted of an offence (cf. ss.52A-52U which deals with issues which arise prior to conviction). As with other orders made under Pt V of the Mental Health (Scotland) Act 1984, this regime required to be modernised in the light of the Millan Committee's report, *New Directions—Report on the Review of the Mental Health (Scotland) Act 1984* (January 2001).

Accordingly, where a person is convicted of an offence in the High Court or sheriff court which is punishable by imprisonment, the sentencing court will be entitled to make an interim compulsion order ("ICO") under the new ss.53-53E of the 1995 Act.

The court first requires to be satisfied on the evidence of two medical practitioners (cf. s.52D(2)), that the offender has a mental disorder (subs.(2)(a)(i)) and that the matters specified in subss.(3) and (5) have been established (subs.(2)(a)(ii)). This means that the court must be satisfied there are reasonable grounds for believing that medical treatment which would prevent the mental disorder worsening or alleviate its symptoms or effects is available for the offender, (see *R. v Secretary of State for Scotland* [1999] 2 A.C. 512) if the treatment was not provided there would be a significant risk to the offender's health, safety or welfare or the safety of another person, and an ICO is necessary (subs.(3)(a)(i) and (5)). The court must also be satisfied that it would be appropriate to make a compulsion order and restriction order or to make a hospital direction (s.59) in relation to the offender (subs.(3)(a)(ii) and (6)).

The court must further be satisfied that a place is available in a hospital which could assess the offender's condition, could not reasonably be expected to do so in the absence of the ICO, and could admit the offender within seven days of an ICO being made (subs.(3)(b), (c) and (d)).

However, the court must also be satisfied that making an ICO is justified in all the circumstances, and that no other alternative means of dealing with the accused can be used (subs.(4)). If this test is also satisfied, the court can make an ICO, but can only do so in the accused's absence if the accused is represented, and it is impracticable or inappropriate for the accused to be brought before the court (subs.(10)).

An ICO is authority for the accused to be taken to the hospital designated in the ICO, and may include provision for the offender to be taken to a place of safety (see s.307) prior to admission to hospital (subs.(9)) within seven days of the ICO being made (subs.(8)(a)). The detention of the patient at the hospital for a period of up to 12 weeks and the giving of medical treatment under Pt 16 of the Mental Health (Care and Treatment) (Scotland) Act 2003 is also authorised (subs.(8)(b) and (c)).

Where the court makes an ICO, it cannot remand an offender for inquiry under s.200 of the 1995 Act (subs.12(a)(i)), nor can it make any of the other orders specified in subs.(12)(a)(ii)-(viii). Where the court makes a ICO, it must as soon as reasonably practicable notify the persons specified in subs.(11).

An ICO's authority to detain an accused can be suspended by an accused's responsible medical officer (see s.230 of the 2003 Act) in terms of s.224 of the 2003 Act.

[THE NEXT PARAGRAPH IS A4-124]

Interim compulsion order: supplementary

A4-124 **53A.**—(1) If, before the end of the day following the 7 days beginning with the day on which the interim compulsion order is made, it appears to the court, or, as the case may be, the Scottish Ministers, that, by reason of emergency or other special circumstances, it is not reasonably practicable for the offender to be admitted to the hospital specified in the order, the court, or, as the case may be, the Scottish Ministers, may direct that the offender be admitted to the hospital specified in the direction.

(2) Where—

(a) the court makes a direction under subsection (1) above, it shall, as soon as reasonably practicable after making the direction, inform the person having custody of the offender; and

(b) the Scottish Ministers make such a direction, they shall, as soon as reasonably practicable after making the direction, inform—

(i) the court; and

(ii) the person having custody of the offender.

(3) Where a direction is made under subsection (1) above, the interim compulsion order shall have effect as if the hospital specified in the direction were the hospital specified in the order.

(4) In this section, "court" means the court which made the interim compulsion order.

AMENDMENTS

Section 53A inserted by Mental Health (Care and Treatment) (Scotland) Act 2003 (asp 13) s.131. Brought into force on 5 October 2005 by SSI 2005/161 (C.6).

Subs.(1) as amended by Mental Health (Scotland) Act 2015 (asp 9) Pt 2 s.42(3). Brought into force on 30 September 2017 by SSI 2017/197 art.2 and Sch, subject to transitional provisions.

DEFINITIONS

court": s.53A(4). A4-124.1
"interim compulsion order": s.53(2).
"medical treatment": s.329(1) of the Mental Health (Care and Treatment) (Scotland) Act 2003.

GENERAL NOTE

This section allows the court or the Scottish Ministers to change the designation of the hospital required to admit an offender in terms of an interim compulsory order ("ICO"), if "by reason of emergency or other special circumstances" (subs.(1)) it is not practicable to admit the offender to the hospital specified in the original order within the seven day period specified in s.53(8) (see General Note to s.53). A4-124.1.1

The change of designation is effected by direction of the court or the Scottish Ministers as appropriate, and it will be noted that the test is of a stringent nature. Where a direction is made under this section by a court, it must inform whoever has custody of the offender (see *Renton and Brown's Criminal Procedure*, 6th edn, para.6-03) that the direction has been made (subs.(2)(a)). Where the Scottish Ministers make such a direction, they must also inform the persons having custody of the offender and the court (subs.(2)(a) and (b)).

A s.53A direction substitutes the hospital specified in the direction for that specified in the original ICO, and the rights and obligations under the ICO (see General Note to s.53) pass to the substituted hospital (subs.(3)).

[THE NEXT PARAGRAPH IS A4-124.2]

Review and extension of interim compulsion order

53B.—(1) The responsible medical officer shall, before the expiry of the period specified by the court under section 53(8)(b) of this Act, submit a report in writing to the court— A4-124.2

(a) as to the matters mentioned in subsection (2) below; and
(b) as to any matters specified by the court under section 53(2) of this Act.

(2) The matters are—

(a) whether the conditions mentioned in section 53(5) of this Act are met in respect of the offender;
(b) the type (or types) of mental disorder that the offender has; and
(c) whether it is necessary to extend the interim compulsion order to allow further time for the assessment mentioned in section 53(3)(b) of this Act.

(3) The responsible medical officer shall, at the same time as such officer submits the report to the court, send a copy of such report to—

(a) the offender; and
(b) any solicitor acting for the offender.

(4) The court may, on receiving the report submitted under subsection (1) above—

(a) if satisfied that the extension of the order is necessary, extend the order for such period not exceeding the relevant period given by subsection (4A) below as the court may specify, and
(b) if it seems appropriate to do so, direct that the offender be admitted to the hospital specified in the direction.

(4A) For the purpose of subsection (4) above, the relevant period is the period—

(a) beginning with the day on which the order would cease to have effect if it were not extended,

(b) expiring at the end of the 12 weeks following that day.

(5) The court may extend an interim compulsion order under subsection (4) above for a period only if, by doing so, the total period for which the offender will be subject to the order does not exceed the period—

(a) beginning with the day on which the order was first made,

(b) expiring at the end of the 12 months following that day.

(6) The court may, under subsection (4) above, extend an interim compulsion order or make a direction specifying a hospital in the absence of the offender only if—

(a) the offender is represented by counsel or a solicitor;

(b) that counsel or solicitor is given an opportunity of being heard; and

(c) the court is satisfied that it is—

(i) impracticable; or

(ii) inappropriate,

for the offender to be brought before it.

(7) Subsections (1) to (9) of this section shall apply for the purposes of an interim compulsion order extended under subsection (4) above as they apply for the purposes of an interim compulsion order, references in those subsections to the period specified by the court under section 53(8)(b) of this Act being construed as references to the period specified by the court under subsection (4) above.

(7A) Where a direction is made under subsection (4) above, the interim compulsion order has effect as if the hospital specified in the direction were the hospital specified in the order.

(8) Where a report is submitted under subsection (1) above, the court may, before the expiry of the period specified by the court under section 53(8)(b) of this Act—

(a) revoke the interim compulsion order and make one of the disposals mentioned in section 53(6) of this Act; or

(b) revoke the interim compulsion order and deal with the offender in any way (other than by making an interim compulsion order) in which the court could have dealt with the offender if no such order had been made.

(9) In this section—

"court" means the court which made the interim compulsion order; and

"responsible medical officer" means the responsible medical officer appointed in respect of the offender under section 230 of the Mental Health (Care and Treatment) (Scotland) Act 2003 (asp 13).

AMENDMENTS

Section 53B inserted by Mental Health (Care and Treatment) (Scotland) Act 2003 (asp 13) s.131. Brought into force on 5 October 2005 by SSI 2005/161 (C.6).

Subss.(4), (5), (6) as amended, subs.(4A), (7A) inserted, by Mental Health (Scotland) Act 2015 (asp 9) Pt 2 ss.42(4), 45(2). Brought into force on 30 September 2017 by SSI 2017/197 art.2 and Sch.

DEFINITIONS

A4-124.3 "court": s.53B(9).
"interim compulsion order": s.53(2).
"mental disorder": s.328(1) of the Mental Health (Care and Treatment) (Scotland) Act 2003.
"offence": s.307(1).
"offender": s.53(1).
"relevant disposal": s.52B(4).
"responsible medical officer": s.230 of the Mental Health (Care and Treatment) (Scotland) Act 2003.
"treatment order": s.52M.

GENERAL NOTE

Where an interim compulsion order ("ICO") has been made by a court, the responsible medical officer ("RMO") (see s.230 of the Mental Health (Care and Treatment) (Scotland) Act 2003) appointed to the offender must report to the court within the period of the ICO (subs.(1)). A4-124.3.1

The RMO must advise the court whether the conditions specified in s.53(2) for making the ICO are met (subs.(1)(a); see General Note to s.53). If the RMO concluded, for example, that the patient no longer had a mental disorder, this fact would require to be reported to the court. The RMO must also report on any matters specifically identified by the court when making the ICO (subs.(1)(b)).

The RMO must also report specifically on the type of mental disorder (by reference to s.328 of the 2003 Act) which the offender has, and whether the period for assessment allowed under the ICO requires to be extended (subs.(2)(b) and (c)). The report is then sent to the court and a copy sent to the offender and the offender's solicitor (subs.(3)).

Where the court is satisfied that further time to assess the offender's condition is required, it can extend the ICO for a period of up to 12 weeks, provided the cumulative extension does not exceed 12 months from when the ICO was first made (subs.(4) and (5)). The court can only extend an ICO in the accused's absence if the accused is represented and it is impracticable or inappropriate for the accused to be brought before the court (subs.(6)).

Once the assessment is complete, the court can effect a number of disposals and is empowered to:

(a) revoke the ICO, and make an compulsion order with an restriction order or a hospital direction (subs.(8)(a) and s.53(6));

(b) revoke the ICO and deal with the offender as though the order had not been made (subs.(8)(b)).

[THE NEXT PARAGRAPH IS A4-124.4]

Early termination of interim compulsion order

53C.—(1) An interim compulsion order shall cease to have effect if the court— A4-124.4

(a) makes a compulsion order in relation to the offender;

(b) makes a hospital direction in relation to the offender; or

(c) deals with the offender in some other way, including the imposing of a sentence of imprisonment on the offender.

(2) In this section, "court" means the court which made the interim compulsion order.

AMENDMENTS

Section 53C inserted by Mental Health (Care and Treatment) (Scotland) Act 2003 (asp 13) s.131. Brought into force on 5 October 2005 by SSI 2005/161 (C.6).

DEFINITIONS

"compulsion order": s.57A. A4-124.5
"court": s.53C(2).
"hospital direction": s.59A(1).
"offender": s.53(1).

GENERAL NOTE

This section makes it clear that an interim compulsory order will come to an end where the court makes a compulsory order or hospital direction under ss.57A or 59A respectively of the 1995 Act, or else disposes of the matter in some other way including sentencing the offender to imprisonment. A4-124.5.1

[THE NEXT PARAGRAPH IS A4-124.6]

Power of court on interim compulsion order ceasing to have effect

53D.—(1) Where, otherwise than by virtue of section 53B(8) or 53C of this Act, an interim compulsion order ceases to have effect the court may deal with the offender who was subject to the order in any way (other than the making of a new interim compulsion order) in which it could have dealt with the offender if no such order had been made. A4-124.6

(2) In this section, "court" means the court which made the interim compulsion order.

AMENDMENTS

Section 53D inserted by Mental Health (Care and Treatment) (Scotland) Act 2003 (asp 13) s.131. Brought into force on 5 October 2005 by SSI 2005/161 (C.6).

DEFINITIONS

A4-124.7 "court": s.53D(2).
"interim compulsion order": s.53(2).
"offender": s.53(1).

GENERAL NOTE

A4-124.8 This section makes it clear that where an interim compulsory order ("ICO") has been made in relation to an offender, unless the ICO comes to an end by virtue of the provisions contained in ss.53B(8) or 53C, the court retains its normal powers to sentence an offender (whether or not by imprisonment) when the ICO comes to an end.

Acquittal involving mental disorder

Acquittal involving mental disorder

A4-124.9 **53E.**—(1) Where the prosecutor accepts a plea (by the person charged with the commission of an offence) of the special defence set out in section 51A of this Act, the court must declare that the person is acquitted by reason of the special defence.

(2) Subsection (3) below applies where—

(a) the prosecutor does not accept such a plea, and

(b) evidence tending to establish the special defence set out in section 51A of this Act is brought before the court.

(3) Where this subsection applies the court is to—

(a) in proceedings on indictment, direct the jury to find whether the special defence has been established and, if they find that it has, to declare whether the person is acquitted on that ground,

(b) in summary proceedings, state whether the special defence has been established and, if it states that it has, declare whether the person is acquitted on that ground.

AMENDMENTS

Section 53E inserted by Criminal Justice and Licensing (Scotland) Act 2010 (asp 13) s.169. Brought into force on 25 June 2012 by SSI 2012/160 (C.15) art.3.

DEFINITIONS

A4-124.10 "indictment": s.307(1).
"offence": s.307(1).
"prosecutor": s.307(1).

GENERAL NOTE

A4-124.11 This section requires that a court acquitting a person because of a special defence of mental disorder must declare that to be the reason.

Unfitness for trial

Unfitness for trial

A4-124.12 **53F.**—(1) A person is unfit for trial if it is established on the balance of probabilities that the person is incapable, by reason of a mental or physical condition, of participating effectively in a trial.

(2) In determining whether a person is unfit for trial the court is to have regard to—

(a) the ability of the person to—

(i) understand the nature of the charge,

(ii) understand the requirement to tender a plea to the charge and the effect of such a plea,

(iii) understand the purpose of, and follow the course of, the trial,
(iv) understand the evidence that may be given against the person,
(v) instruct and otherwise communicate with the person's legal representative, and

(b) any other factor which the court considers relevant.

(3) The court is not to find that a person is unfit for trial by reason only of the person being unable to recall whether the event which forms the basis of the charge occurred in the manner described in the charge.

(4) In this section "the court" means—

(a) as regards a person charged on indictment, the High Court or the sheriff court,

(b) as regards a person charged summarily, the sheriff court.

AMENDMENTS

Section 53F inserted by Criminal Justice and Licensing (Scotland) Act 2010 (asp 13) s.170. Brought into force on 25 June 2012 by SSI 2012/160 (C.15) art.3.

DEFINITIONS

A4-124.13

"court": s.53F(4).
"indictment": s.307(1).

GENERAL NOTE

A4-124.14

This section represents the modernisation of the law on unfitness for trial following the recommendations by the Scottish Law Commission in the "*Report on Insanity and Diminished Responsibility*" (2004).

In *Murphy v HM Advocate* [2016] HCJAC 118; 2016 G.W.D. 39-691 it was noted, at [61], that there is, in reference to "unfitness for trial", "no stipulation as to the nature of the evidence upon which the court may be satisfied as to unfitness. It is difficult, however, to conceive of circumstances in which the court would make a decision of a mental unfitness said to arise from a medical condition without the evidence of a psychiatrist, psychologist or other appropriate medical professional". Further it was said, at [65]: "The issue of fitness for trial goes to the heart of a person's capacity, and their ability to participate in an effective way in their trial".

In *R. v Roberts* [2019] EWCA Crim 1270; [2020] Crim. L.R. 344 an accused was assessed by three psychiatrists who all agreed that he was not fit to plead or be tried. He later attempted, acting in person, to appeal. The application for leave to appeal was refused as there were no arguable grounds. In any event, it was not competent for him to appeal in person. It can "make no difference that … the accused ostensibly has a keen intelligence and an awareness of the details of his case and of the procedural requirements … the accused's approach is distorted by his mental incapacity such as to render him unfit to participate in the trial process (which is to be taken as extending to an appeal)" at [34].

[THE NEXT PARAGRAPH IS A4-125]

Unfitness for trial: further provision

54.—(1) Where the court is satisfied that a person charged with the commission of an offence is unfit for trial so that his trial cannot proceed or, if it has commenced, cannot continue, the court shall, subject to subsection (2) below— A4-125

(a) make a finding to that effect and state the reasons for that finding;

(b) discharge the trial diet or, in proceedings on indictment where the finding is made at or before the first diet (in the case of proceedings in the sheriff court) or the preliminary hearing (in the case of proceedings in the High Court), that diet or, as the case may be, hearing and order that a diet (in this Act referred to as an "an examination of facts") be held under section 55 of this Act; and

(c) remand the person in custody or on bail or, where the court is satisfied—

(i) on the written or oral evidence of two medical practitioners, that the conditions mentioned in subsection (2A) below are met in respect of the person; and
(ii) that a hospital is available for his admission and suitable for his

detention,

make an order (in this section referred to as a "temporary compulsion order") authorising the measures mentioned in subsection (2B) below in respect of the person until the conclusion of the examination of facts.

(2) Subsection (1) above is without prejudice to the power of the court, on an application by the prosecutor, to desert the diet *pro loco et tempore*.

(2A) The conditions referred to in subsection (1)(c)(i) above are—

(a) that the person has a mental disorder;

(b) that medical treatment which would be likely to—

(i) prevent the mental disorder worsening; or

(ii) alleviate any of the symptoms, or effects, of the disorder,

is available for the person; and

(c) that if the person were not provided with such medical treatment there would be a significant risk—

(a) to the health, safety or welfare of the person; or

(b) to the safety of any other person.

(2B) The measures referred to in subsection (1)(c)(i) above are—

(a) in the case of a person who, when the temporary compulsion order is made, has not been admitted to the specified hospital, the removal, before the end of the day following the 7 days beginning with the day on which the order is made of the person to the specified hospital by—

(i) […]

(ii) person employed in, or contracted to provide services in or to, the specified hospital who is authorised by the managers of that hospital to remove persons to hospital for the purposes of this section; or

(iii) a specified person;

(b) the detention of the person in the specified hospital; and

(c) the giving to the person, in accordance with Part 16 of the Mental Health (Care and Treatment) (Scotland) Act 2003 (asp 13), of medical treatment.

(3) The court may, before making a finding under subsection (1) above as to whether a person is unfit for trial, adjourn the case in order that investigation of his mental or physical condition may be carried out.

(4) The court which made a temporary compulsion order may, at any time while the order is in force, review the order on the ground that there has been a change of circumstances since the order was made and, on such review—

(a) where the court considers that such an order is no longer required in relation to a person, it shall revoke the order and may remand him in custody or on bail;

(b) in any other case, the court may—

(i) confirm or vary the order; or

(ii) revoke the order and make such other order, under subsection (1)(c) above or any other provision of this Act, as the court considers appropriate.

(5) Where it appears to a court that it is not practicable or appropriate for the accused to be brought before it for the purpose of determining whether he is unfit for trial so that his trial cannot proceed, then, if no objection to such a course is taken by or on behalf of the accused, the court may order that the case be proceeded with in his absence.

(6) […]

(7) […]

(8) In this section,

"medical treatment" has the same meaning as in section 52D of this Act;
"specified" means specified in the temporary compulsion order; and
"the court" means—

(a) as regards a person charged on indictment, the High Court or the sheriff court;
(b) as regards a person charged summarily, the sheriff court.

AMENDMENTS

Subs.(1)(b) as amended by Criminal Procedure (Amendment) (Scotland) Act 2004 (asp 5) s.25 and Sch.1 para.13. Brought into force on 1 February 2005 by SSI 2004/405 (C.28) art.2.

Subss.(1)(c), (4), (8) as amended, and subss.(2A), (2B) inserted, by Mental Health (Care and Treatment) (Scotland) Act 2003 (asp 13) Sch.4 para.8(2). Brought into force on 5 October 2005 by SSI 2005/161 (C.6).

Subs.(2B)(a) as amended by Mental Health (Care and Treatment) (Scotland) Act 2003 (Modification of Enactments) Order 2005 (SSI 2005/465) Sch.2 para.1 (effective 5 October 2005: repeal came into force on 27 September 2005 but could not take effect until the commencement of Mental Health (Care and Treatment) (Scotland) Act 2003 (asp 13) Sch.4 para.8(2)(b) on 5 October 2005).

Heading and subss.(1), (3) and (5) as amended, and subss.(6) and (7) repealed, by Criminal Justice and Licensing (Scotland) Act 2010 (asp 13) s.170. Brought into force on 25 June 2012 by SSI 2012/160 (C.15) art.3.

Subs.(2B)(a) as amended by Mental Health (Scotland) Act 2015 (asp 9) Pt 2 s.42(5). Brought into force on 30 September 2017 by SSI 2017/197 art.2 and Sch, subject to transitional provisions.

DEFINITIONS **A4-125.1**

"bail": s.307(1).
"court": s.54(8).
"examination of facts": s.307(1).
"medical practitioner": s.61(1).
"temporary hospital order": s.54(1)(c).

[THE NEXT PARAGRAPH IS A4-126]

GENERAL NOTE

It is interesting to note, by way of a preliminary, that s.52 is concerned with "mental disorder", s.53 is concerned with "mental disorder within the meaning of s.1(2) of the Mental Health (Scotland) Act 1984" and s.54 is concerned with "insanity". **A4-126**

The broad question in a plea-in-bar on grounds of insanity is whether the accused has the capacity to instruct his legal representatives as to his defence and to follow proceedings at his trial. The case of *Stewart v HM Advocate (No.1)*, 1997 S.C.C.R. 330, where such a plea was taken at a preliminary diet in relation to a mentally handicapped accused, emphasises that it is for the judge to decide on assessing the medical evidence whether the plea is made out. See also the case of *McLachlan v Brown*, 1997 S.C.C.R. 457, which confirms that s.54(1) applies not only to cases where the accused is unfit to plead due to mental illness, but also to cases where the accused is unfit to plead due to some mental impairment or handicap. It is conceivable that such a plea-in-bar could also extend to extreme physical defects (see *HM Advocate v Wilson*, 1942 J.C. 75; 1942 S.L.T. 194 approved in *Stewart (No. 1)* above). Also worthy of note is *Stewart v HM Advocate (No. 2)*, 1997 S.C.C.R. 430 where it was held, inter alia, that there is nothing in the legislation to exclude the right of an accused to renew a plea of insanity in bar of trial at a preliminary diet following service of a fresh indictment, despite the fact that such a plea was unsuccessful in respect of the original indictment. The decision recognises the fact that an accused's mental condition may fluctuate, and that accordingly insanity for the purposes of s.54 includes not only insanity by reason of some permanent condition but also insanity by reason of a condition which may alter from time to time. These authorities were also cited in *Hughes v HM Advocate*, 2001 G.W.D. 15-572 when H unsuccessfully contended that his post-accident amnesia should be treated as a plea in bar of trial on the grounds that he would not be able to instruct his defence about the circumstances. The court noted that H had been found to be sane and fit to plead and fully capable of following proceedings, instructing his defence and testing the Crown case, hence the rejection of H's plea.

Subsection (6) of s.54 deals with the special defence of insanity at the time of the offence, as distinct from insanity in bar of trial. Insanity as a defence rests upon alienation of reason at the time of the wrongful act, such that there can have been no mens rea for its commission. Acquittal as a result of a finding of insanity at the time of the offence may arise after trial (s.54(6)) or as a conclusion of an EOF (discussed below and see s.55(4)). In either case the court moves to disposal under s.57 of the Act.

Section 54 requires a court in both solemn and summary proceedings, following a finding that a person is insane so that a trial cannot proceed or continue, to hold an examination of the facts ("EOF") relating to the charges. The section further provides for the court to remand in custody or on bail, or to commit such a person to hospital under a temporary hospital order, until the conclusion of the EOF.

The new procedure very much contrasts with the previous law under which, when a person was found insane in bar of trial, no attempt was made by the court to examine the evidence as to whether the accused did the act with which he is charged. The new procedure requires that there be an examination of the relevant facts. It gives effect to certain recommendations contained in the *Second Thomson Report on Criminal Procedure* (Cmnd. 6218 (1975)). The only circumstances in which an EOF cannot be held are when the Crown applies for and the court agrees to the diet being deserted *pro loco et tempore*.

The novelty of these proceedings is accentuated by the possibility that the hearing to determine insanity may in some circumstances proceed in the absence of the accused: see s.54(5); but it should be borne in mind that the hearing is to be conducted along the lines of a trial in so far as possible, and accordingly proof of the material fact of identification requires to be considered and addressed.

In relation to solemn proceedings, s.54 should be read together with s.67. The latter section sets out the statutory requirements on the Crown for the witnesses and for intimation in writing of the details of the witnesses and where they can be contacted for the purposes of precognition. For that reason the accused or those advising him should have clear intimation of the availability of the two medical practitioners who may give evidence for the Crown of insanity. If the illness has developed immediately prior to the trial then such medical practitioners may be called with leave of the court: see s.67(5). If the defence seek to raise the issue then they must intimate the details of the two medical practitioners: see s.78(4).

In relation to summary proceedings, the approach to the issue is necessarily different. There appears to be no duty on the Crown to intimate the issue in advance of the trial although one would hope that such an important matter would be intimated in the interests of justice. In any event, an adjournment for inquiry at the first calling in terms of s.145(1) would undoubtedly follow where there had been no intimation. The accused or those advising him are under a clear duty to give notice: see s.54(7).

For the purposes of s.54(1) a written report bearing to be signed by a medical practitioner may, subject to the provisions of s.61 being met, be received in evidence without proof of the signature or qualifications of the practitioner: note that s.61(3) entitles the court, in any case, to call the report's author to give oral evidence. Section 54(1)(b) has been amended to take account of the mandatory preliminary diet proceedings in the High Court. At any point in the proceedings, summary or solemn, trial can be discharged if evidence satisfying the requirements of s.54 is produced; the court has then to fix an examination of facts conform to ss.55 and 56.

See s.53F and *Murphy v HM Advocate* [2016] HCJAC 118; 2016 G.W.D. 39-691 for discussion of "unfitness for trial".

Examination of facts

Examination of facts

A4-127 **55.**—(1) At an examination of facts ordered under section 54(1)(b) of this Act the court shall, on the basis of the evidence (if any) already given in the trial and such evidence, or further evidence, as may be led by either party, determine whether it is satisfied—

(a) beyond reasonable doubt, as respects any charge on the indictment or, as the case may be, the complaint in respect of which the accused was being or was to be tried, that he did the act or made the omission constituting the offence; and

(b) on the balance of probabilities, that there are no grounds for acquitting him.

(2) Where the court is satisfied as mentioned in subsection (1) above, it shall make a finding to that effect.

(3) Where the court is not so satisfied it shall, subject to subsection (4) below, acquit the person of the charge.

(4) Where, as respects a person acquitted under subsection (3) above, the court is satisfied as to the matter mentioned in subsection (1)(a) above but it appears to the court that the person was not, because of section 51A of this Act, criminally responsible for the conduct constituting the offence, the court shall state whether the acquittal is by reason of the special defence set out in that section.

(5) Where it appears to the court that it is not practical or appropriate for the accused to attend an examination of facts the court may, if no objection is taken by or on behalf of the accused, order that the examination of facts shall proceed in his absence.

(6) Subject to the provisions of this section, section 56 of this Act and any Act of Adjournal the rules of evidence and procedure and the powers of the court shall, in respect of an examination of facts, be as nearly as possible those applicable in respect of a trial.

(7) For the purposes of the application to an examination of facts of the rules and powers mentioned in subsection (6) above, an examination of facts—

(a) commences when the indictment or, as the case may be, complaint is called; and

(b) concludes when the court—

(i) acquits the person under subsection (3) above;

(ii) makes an order under subsection (2) of section 57 of this Act; or

(iii) decides, under paragraph (e) of that subsection, not to make an order.

AMENDMENTS

Subsection (4) as amended by Criminal Justice and Licensing (Scotland) Act 2010 (asp 13) Sch.7 para.37. Brought into force on 25 June 2012 by SSI 2012/160 (C.15) art.3.

DEFINITIONS

"examination of facts": s.54(1)(b). **A4-127.1**
"offence": s.307(1).

[THE NEXT PARAGRAPH IS A4-128]

GENERAL NOTE

Section 54 establishes the competency of an examination of facts ("EOF") and s.55 specifies the procedure and powers of the court, its findings, and a number of detailed ancillary matters. An EOF is to be held along the lines of a trial as far as possible and, again emphasising the novelty, it may proceed in certain circumstances in the absence of the accused. **A4-128**

It seems important to stress that an EOF need not necessarily be a matter wholly separate from a trial in the conventional sense. Section 54(1) refers to "a person charged with the commission of an offence" being insane "so that his trial cannot proceed or, if it has commenced, cannot continue". On that approach it is easy to imagine under solemn procedure a trial commencing in the ordinary way and after the jury has heard some evidence the defence lawyers (or others) intimating that there is concern about the accused's health. Thereafter, a medical examination might produce the necessary evidence leading the court to make the essential finding (s.54(1)(a)) and the trial diet being discharged and an EOF then being held (s.54(1)(b)). Indeed, the citation of the accused and any witnesses to the trial diet is valid citation to the EOF: see s.56(1) and (2). It follows from the discharge of the trial diet and the terms of s.55 that the jury is released.

Thereafter, at the EOF the court must consider both any evidence already given in the trial and the evidence led at the EOF itself, by either party. The court must then determine whether it is satisfied that the accused did the act or made the omission constituting the offence and that there are no grounds for his acquittal. The standard for the first determination is beyond reasonable doubt and for the second it is on a balance of probabilities (s.55(1)(a) and (b)).

If the court is not satisfied that these standards have been made out the accused is acquitted (s.55(3)). However, if the court is satisfied that the accused did the act or made the omission constituting the offence, but on a balance of probabilities it appears to the court that the accused was insane at the time, acquittal on that ground may competently be determined and stated by the court (s.55(4)).

SUBS.(3)

A determination was provided after the examination of facts in *HM Advocate v Paul Francis Ward* unreported 27 February 2015, High Court of Justiciary at Glasgow, Lord Matthews. The accused was unfit for trial because of his undoubted mental illness. First, on the facts as proved at the hearing the court concluded that the case was a circumstantial one. That did not mean necessarily that the evidence was "sub-standard" (the police were commended for their efforts by the court) but in such a case it is very important that all of the evidence is assessed. Secondly, the result was "a weak Crown case. None of the individual strands on which the Crown rely is compelling". There was evidence of motive, opportunity and suspicious circumstances and the accused "might have" committed the acts that constituted the charge of murder. The test of proof beyond reasonable doubt had not been met. The accused was acquitted in terms of s.55(3). Finally, the court commented that the matter could be "revisited if compelling evidence emerges".

Further, in *HM Advocate v George Watson* unreported 8 July 2016, High Court of Justiciary at Edinburgh, Lord Pentland, the aged accused was unfit for trial because of his undoubted mental illness, assessed as dementia. Evidence was called by the Crown from witnesses and from police officers. The court concluded that there were problems of credibility and reliability with the evidence of the complainers who could attend the examination of facts. Another complainer, who had died, had given statements to the police and the officers who had taken the statements gave evidence. The evidence of the deceased witness was decisive for proof of the charges.

The court had to consider whether there were sufficient "counterbalancing factors" in place to permit a fair and proper assessment of the reliability of the hearsay evidence of the deceased witness to take place: *Al-Khawaja and Tahery v UK*, Grand Chamber, ECHR, 15 December 2011: (2012) 54 E.H.R.R. 23. It was recognised by the Grand Chamber that "there are obvious difficulties in evaluating the credibility and reliability of a witness whose evidence is available only in the form of hearsay statements". Such evidence cannot be tested by cross-examination and, at the examination of facts, the court had no opportunity to see and hear the witness personally.

The court held there to be insufficient counterbalancing factors:

> "[F]irst, there is a complete absence of credible and reliable independent evidence against which the allegations contained in the witness statements could be objectively tested ... secondly, there is a significant body of evidence showing that the three complainers discussed the allegations with one another over a period of some years before they provided statements to the police; thirdly, the evidence of the first two complainers ... is not credible or reliable; and finally, the accused is not capable of providing any evidence in response to the allegations made against him."

Consequently, a fair and proper evaluation of the hearsay evidence could not be made. The accused was acquitted in terms of s.55(3).

Examination of facts: supplementary provisions

A4-129 **56.—**(1) An examination of facts ordered under section 54(1)(b) of this Act may, where the order is made at the trial diet or, in proceedings on indictment, at the first diet (in the case of proceedings in the sheriff court) or the preliminary hearing (in the case of proceedings in the High Court), be held immediately following the making of the order and, where it is so held, the citation of the accused and any witness to the trial diet, first diet or, as the case may be, preliminary hearing shall be a valid citation to the examination of facts.

(2) *[Repealed by Criminal Procedure (Amendment) (Scotland) Act 2004 (asp 5) s.25 and Sch.1 para.14(b). Brought into force on February 1, 2005 by SSI 2004/405 (C.28) art.2.]*

(3) Where an accused person is not legally represented at an examination of facts the court shall appoint counsel or a solicitor to represent his interests.

(4) The court may, on the motion of the prosecutor and after hearing the accused, order that the examination of facts shall proceed in relation to a particular charge, or particular charges, in the indictment or, as the case may be, complaint in priority to other such charges.

(5) The court may, on the motion of the prosecutor and after hearing the accused, at any time desert the examination of facts *pro loco et tempore* as respects either the whole indictment or, as the case may be, complaint or any charge therein.

(6) Where, and to the extent that, an examination of facts has, under subsection (5) above, been deserted *pro loco et tempore*—

(a) in the case of proceedings on indictment, the Lord Advocate may, at any time, raise and insist in a new indictment; or

(b) in the case of summary proceedings, the prosecutor may at any time raise a fresh libel,

notwithstanding any time limit which would otherwise apply in respect of prosecution of the alleged offence.

(7) If, in a case where a court has made a finding under subsection (2) of section 55 of this Act, a person is subsequently charged, whether on indictment or on a complaint, with an offence arising out of the same act or omission as is referred to in subsection (1) of that section, any order made, under section 57(2) of this Act shall, with effect from the commencement of the later proceedings, cease to have effect.

(8) For the purposes of subsection (7) above, the later proceedings are commenced when the indictment or, as the case may be, the complaint is served.

Amendments

Subsection (1) as amended by Criminal Procedure (Amendment) (Scotland) Act 2004 (asp 5) s.25 and Sch.1 para.14(a). Brought into force on 1 February 2005 by SSI 2004/405 (C.28) art.2.

Definitions A4-129.1

"complaint": s.307(1).
"diet": s.307(1).
"examination of facts": s.54(1)(b).
"indictment": s.307(1).
"order": s.307(1).
"prosecutor": s.307(1).

[THE NEXT PARAGRAPH IS A4-130]

General Note

The section makes supplementary provisions for the conduct of examinations of facts ("EOF") in summary and solemn cases. The existing powers of citation to the trial diet in summary cases, or to the first or preliminary or trial diets in solemn proceedings, hold good for any EOF (s.56(1)). Any time limits which might constrain the Crown following an EOF being deserted *pro loco et tempore* are removed (s.56(6)), and the Crown's rights to serve a new complaint or to re-indict are preserved. A4-130

If at the EOF a finding is delivered to the effect that the accused did the act charged as the main offence, thus paving the way for the EOF to move to disposal under s.57, the prosecutor may not wish to prolong the EOF and move to desert the remaining charges under s.56(5). The effect of such desertion *pro loco et tempore* is to terminate the present proceedings, but reserve the Crown's right to reraise proceedings should the accused recover his sanity sufficiently to stand trial. Any disposal order made under s.57 in relation to the previous finding of insanity ceases to have effect from the commencement of the new proceedings, namely when the new indictment or complaint is served (see s.56(7) and (8)). Thus on an accused person sufficiently recovering his sanity, he may be prosecuted in exactly the same terms as those contained in the original indictment or complaint against him, except of course for those charges where he has been acquitted by the court at the EOF. In other words, insanity is no longer a bar to trial. This is in line with case law to the effect that a person found to be insane in bar of trial has not tholed his assize and may be tried upon recovering his sanity or upon it being discovered that he was not insane: see *HM Advocate v Bickerstaff*, 1926 J.C. 5 followed in *HM Advocate v Graham* (High Court of Justiciary, February 16, 1996, unreported).

Disposal where accused found not criminally responsible

Disposal of case where accused found not criminally responsible or unfit for trial

57.—(1) This section applies where— A4-131

(a) a person is acquitted by reason of the special defence set out in section 51A of this Act; or

(b) following an examination of facts under section 55, a court makes a finding under subsection (2) of that section.

(2) Subject to subsection (3) below, where this section applies the court may, as it thinks fit—

(a) subject to subsection (4) below, make a compulsion order (whether or not authorising the detention of the person in a hospital);

(b) subject to subsection (4A) below, make a restriction order in respect of the person (that is, in addition to a compulsion order authorising the detention of the person in a hospital);

(bb) subject to subsections (3A) and (4B) below, make an interim compulsion order in respect of the person;

(c) subject to subsections (4C) and (6) below, make a guardianship order in respect of the person;

(d) subject to subsection (5) below, make a supervision and treatment order (within the meaning of paragraph 1(1) of Schedule 4 to this Act) in respect of the person; or

(e) make no order.

(3) Where the court is satisfied, having regard to a report submitted in respect of the person following an interim compulsion order, that, on a balance of probabilities, the risk his being at liberty presents to the safety of the public at large is high, it shall make orders under both paragraphs (a) and (b) of subsection (2) above in respect of that person.

(3A) The court may make an interim compulsion order under paragraph (bb) of subsection (2) above in respect of a person only where it has not previously made such an order in respect of the person under that paragraph.

(4) For the purposes of subsection (2)(a) above—

(a) subsections (2) to (16) of section 57A of this Act shall apply as they apply for the purposes of subsection (1) of that section, subject to the following modifications—

(i) references to the offender shall be construed as references to the person to whom this section applies; and

(ii) in subsection (4)(b)(i), the reference to the offence of which the offender was convicted shall be construed as a reference to the offence with which the person to whom this section applies was charged;

(b) section 57B of this Act shall have effect subject to the modification that references to the offender shall be construed as references to the person to whom this section applies;

(c) section 57C of this Act shall have effect subject to the following modifications—

(i) references to the offender shall be construed as references to the person to whom this section applies; and

(ii) references to section 57A of this Act shall be construed as references to subsection (2)(a) above; and

(d) section 57D of this Act shall have effect subject to the modification that references to the offender shall be construed as references to the person to whom this section applies.

(4A) For the purposes of subsection (2)(b) above, section 59 of this Act shall have effect.

(4B) For the purposes of subsection (2)(bb) above—

(a) subsections (2) to (13) of section 53 of this Act shall apply as they apply for the purposes of subsection (1) of that section, subject to the following modifications—

(i) references to the offender shall be construed as references to the person to whom this section applies;

(ii) in subsection (3)(a)(ii), the reference to one of the disposals mentioned in subsection (6) of that section shall be construed as a reference to the disposal mentioned in subsection (6)(a) of that section;

(iii) in subsection (4)(a), the reference to the offence of which the offender is convicted shall be construed as a reference to the offence with which the person to whom this section applies is charged; and

(iv) subsection (6)(b) shall not apply;

(b) section 53A of this Act shall have effect subject to the modification that references to the offender shall be construed as references to the person to whom this section applies;

(c) section 53B of this Act shall have effect subject to the following modifications—

(i) references to the offender shall be construed as references to the person to whom this section applies; and

(ii) for paragraphs (a) and (b) of subsection (8) there shall be substituted

", revoke the interim compulsion order and

(a) make an order in respect of the person under paragraph (a), (b), (c) or (d) of subsection (2) of section 57 of this Act; or

(b) decide, under paragraph (e) of that subsection, to make no order in respect of the person."

(d) section 53C of this Act shall have effect subject to the following modifications—

(i) references to the offender shall be construed as references to the person to whom this section applies; and

(ii) for paragraphs (a) to (c) of subsection (1) there shall be substituted—

"(a) makes an order in respect of the person under paragraph (a), (b), (c) or (d) of subsection (2) of section 57 of this Act; or

(b) decides, under paragraph (e) of that subsection, to make no order in respect of the person."

(e) section 53D of this Act shall have effect subject to the modification that the reference to the offender shall be construed as a reference to the person to whom this section applies.

(4C) For the purposes of subsection (2)(c) above, subsections (1A), (6) to (8) and (11) of section 58 of this Act shall apply, subject to the modifications that the reference to a person convicted and any references to the offender shall be construed as references to the person to whom this section applies.

(5) Schedule 4 to this Act shall have effect as regards supervision and treatment orders.

(6) Section 58A of this Act shall have effect as regards guardianship orders made under subsection (2)(c) of this section.

Amendments

Section 57 as amended by Adults with Incapacity (Scotland) Act 2000 (asp 4) s.88 and Sch.5 para.26. Brought into force on 1 April 2002 by SSI 2001/81 (C.2).

Subs.(3) substituted by Criminal Justice (Scotland) Act 2003 (asp 7) Pt 1 s.2(b). Brought into force on 27 June 2003 by SSI 2003/288 (C.14).

Subss.(2), (3) and (4) as amended, and subss.(3A), (4A)–(4C) inserted, by Mental Health (Care and Treatment) (Scotland) Act 2003 (asp 13) Sch.4 para.8(3). Brought into force on 5 October 2005 by SSI 2005/161 (C.6).

Heading and subs.(1)(a) as amended by Criminal Justice and Licensing (Scotland) Act 2010 (asp 13) Sch.7 paras 38 and 39. Brought into force on 25 June 2012 by SSI 2012/160 (C.15) art.3.

Subs.(2) as amended by Mental Health (Scotland) Act 2015 (asp 9) Pt 2 s.39(2). Brought into force on 30 June 2017 by SSI 2017/197 art.2 and Sch.

Definitions

"examination of facts": s.54(1)(b). A4-131.1
"medical practitioner": s.61(1).
"new supervising officer": Sch.4, para.7(1)(b).
"order": s.307(1).
"relevant sheriff court": Sch.4, para.3(2)(b).
"supervised person": Sch.4, para.1(1).
"supervising officer": Sch.4, para.1(1).
"supervision and treatment order": Sch.4, para.1(1).

[THE NEXT PARAGRAPH IS A4-132]

General Note

This section specifies the disposals available to a court at an examination of facts ("EOF") in both solemn and summary proceedings, and to a court acquitting a person on the grounds of insanity at the time of the commission of the offence charged. It provides for the making of a hospital order, with or without a restriction order, a guardianship order, a new disposal (the Supervision and Treatment Order) in A4-132 which the recipient resides in the community under the supervision of a social worker and for the purposes of treatment under a medical practitioner, and, finally, the making of no order at all. The power to specify a hospital contained in subs.(2)(a) includes a power to specify a hospital unit, but only where the court also makes an order in terms of subs.(2)(b), subjecting the person to the special restrictions set out in s.62(1) of the Mental Health (Scotland) Act 1984. The power to specify a hospital unit was introduced by s.9 of the Crime and Punishment (Scotland) Act 1997 with effect from January 1, 1998, and thus allows a measure of flexibility in placing patients at distinct, possibly specialist, mental health units.

Section 57 thus provides a court with a wider range of disposals than was available under the previous law when dealing with an accused who is unfit to plead. Only two observations need to be made in regard to these disposals. First, the new disposal of a Supervision and Treatment Order is only new to Scotland as it has been provided for in the Criminal Procedure (Insanity and Unfitness to Plead) Act 1991 (c.25) for England and Wales. The extensive arrangements for the new disposal are set out in Sch.4 to this Act. Secondly, in only one disposal is the discretion of the court restricted.

Subs.(3), effective from 27 June 2003, was substituted by s.2(b) of the Criminal Justice (Scotland) Act 2003. In fact, in practical terms subs.(3) cannot be followed by the court until s.2(a) of the 2003 Act is commenced. Section 2(A) adds the making of an interim hospital order to the list of disposals already available to the court in s.57(2). For an example of an examination of facts concluding in terms of s.57(2)(d) in the making of a supervision and treatment order, see *Speirs v HM Advocate* [2013] HCJAC 151; 2014 S.C.C.R. 101 (Sy).

Compulsion orders

Compulsion order

A4-132.1 **57A.**—(1) This section applies where a person (in this section and in sections 57C and 57D of this Act, referred to as the "offender")—

(a) is convicted in the High Court or the sheriff court of an offence punishable by imprisonment (other than an offence the sentence for which is fixed by law); or

(b) is remitted to the High Court by the sheriff under any enactment for sentence for such an offence.

(2) If the court is satisfied—

(a) on the written or oral evidence of two medical practitioners, that the conditions mentioned in subsection (3) below are met in respect of the offender; and

(b) that, having regard to the matters mentioned in subsection (4) below, it is appropriate,

it may, subject to subsection (5) below, make an order (in this Act referred to as a "compulsion order") authorising, subject to subsection (7) below, for the relevant period given by subsection (2A) below such of the measures mentioned in subsection (8) below as may be specified in the order.

(2A) For the purpose of subsection (2) above, the relevant period is the period—

(a) beginning with the day on which the order is made,

(b) expiring at the end of the 6 months following that day.

(3) The conditions referred to in subsection (2)(a) above are—

(a) that the offender has a mental disorder;

(b) that medical treatment which would be likely to—

(i) prevent the mental disorder worsening; or

(ii) alleviate any of the symptoms, or effects, of the disorder,

is available for the offender;

(c) that if the offender were not provided with such medical treatment there would be a significant risk—

(i) to the health, safety or welfare of the offender; or

(ii) to the safety of any other person; and

(d) that the making of a compulsion order in respect of the offender is necessary.

(4) The matters referred to in subsection (2)(b) above are—

(a) the mental health officer's report, prepared in accordance with section 57C of this Act, in respect of the offender;
(b) all the circumstances, including—
(i) the nature of the offence of which the offender was convicted; and
(ii) the antecedents of the offender; and
(c) any alternative means of dealing with the offender.

(5) The court may, subject to subsection (6) below, make a compulsion order authorising the detention of the offender in a hospital by virtue of subsection (8)(a) below only if satisfied, on the written or oral evidence of the two medical practitioners mentioned in subsection (2)(a) above, that—
(a) the medical treatment mentioned in subsection (3)(b) above can be provided only if the offender is detained in hospital;
(b) the offender could be admitted to the hospital to be specified in the order before the end of the day following the 7 days beginning with the day on which the order is made; and
(c) the hospital to be so specified is suitable for the purpose of giving the medical treatment to the offender.

(6) A compulsion order may authorise detention in a state hospital only if, on the written or oral evidence of the two medical practitioners mentioned in subsection (2)(a) above, it appears to the court—
(a) that the offender requires to be detained in hospital under conditions of special security; and
(b) that such conditions of special security can be provided only in a state hospital.

(7) Where the court—
(a) makes a compulsion order in respect of an offender; and
(b) also makes a restriction order in respect of the offender,

the compulsion order shall authorise the measures specified in it without limitation of time.

(8) The measures mentioned in subsection (2) above are—
(a) the detention of the offender in the specified hospital;
(b) the giving to the offender, in accordance with Part 16 of the Mental Health (Care and Treatment) (Scotland) Act 2003 (asp 13), of medical treatment;
(c) the imposition of a requirement on the offender to attend—
(i) on specified or directed dates; or
(ii) at specified or directed intervals,

specified or directed places with a view to receiving medical treatment;
(d) the imposition of a requirement on the offender to attend—
(i) on specified or directed dates; or
(ii) at specified or directed intervals,

specified or directed places with a view to receiving community care services, relevant services or any treatment, care or service;
(e) subject to subsection (9) below, the imposition of a requirement on the offender to reside at a specified place;
(f) the imposition of a requirement on the offender to allow—
(i) the mental health officer;
(ii) the offender's responsible medical officer; or
(iii) any person responsible for providing medical treatment, community care services, relevant services or any treatment, care or service to the offender who is authorised for the purposes of this

paragraph by the offender's responsible medical officer,
to visit the offender in the place where the offender resides;

(g) the imposition of a requirement on the offender to obtain the approval of the mental health officer to any change of address; and

(h) the imposition of a requirement on the offender to inform the mental health officer of any change of address before the change takes effect.

(9) The court may make a compulsion order imposing, by virtue of subsection (8)(e) above, a requirement on an offender to reside at a specified place which is a place used for the purpose of providing a care home service only if the court is satisfied that the person providing the care home service is willing to receive the offender.

(10) The Scottish Ministers may, by regulations made by statutory instrument, make provision for measures prescribed by the regulations to be treated as included among the measures mentioned in subsection (8) above.

(11) The power conferred by subsection (10) above may be exercised so as to make different provision for different cases or descriptions of case or for different purposes.

(12) No regulations shall be made under subsection (10) above unless a draft of the statutory instrument containing them has been laid before, and approved by a resolution of, the Scottish Parliament.

(13) The court shall be satisfied as to the condition mentioned in subsection (3)(a) above only if the description of the offender's mental disorder by each of the medical practitioners mentioned in subsection (2)(a) above specifies, by reference to the appropriate paragraph (or paragraphs) of the definition of "mental disorder" in section 328(1) of the Mental Health (Care and Treatment) (Scotland) Act 2003 (asp 13), at least one type of mental disorder that the offender has that is also specified by the other.

(14) A compulsion order—

(a) shall specify—

(i) by reference to the appropriate paragraph (or paragraphs) of the definition of "mental disorder" in section 328(1) of the Mental Health (Care and Treatment) (Scotland) Act 2003 (asp 13), the type (or types) of mental disorder that each of the medical practitioners mentioned in subsection (2)(a) above specifies that the offender has that is also specified by the other; and

(ii) if the order does not, by virtue of subsection (8)(a) above, authorise the detention of the offender in hospital, the name of the hospital the managers of which are to have responsibility for appointing the offender's responsible medical officer; and

(b) may include—

(i) in a case where a compulsion order authorises the detention of the offender in a specified hospital by virtue of subsection (8)(a) above; or

(ii) in a case where a compulsion order imposes a requirement on the offender to reside at a specified place by virtue of subsection (8)(e) above,

such directions as the court thinks fit for the removal of the offender to, and the detention of the offender in, a place of safety pending the offender's admission to the specified hospital or, as the case may be, place.

(15) Where the court makes a compulsion order in relation to an offender, the court—

(a) shall not—

(i) make an order under section 200 of this Act;
(ii) make an interim compulsion order;
(iii) make a guardianship order;
(iv) pass a sentence of imprisonment;
(v) impose a fine;
(vi) impose a community payback order;
(vii) make a drug treatment and testing order; or
(viii) make a restriction of liberty order,

in relation to the offender;

(b) may make any other order that the court has power to make apart from this section.

(16) In this section—

"care home service" has the meaning given by paragraph 2 of schedule 12 to the Public Services Reform (Scotland) Act 2010;

"community care services" has the meaning given by section 12A(8) of the Social Work (Scotland) Act 1968 (c.49);

"medical treatment" has the same meaning as in section 52D of this Act;

"relevant services" has the meaning given by section 20(2) of the Children (Scotland) Act 1995 (c.36);

"responsible medical officer", in relation to an offender, means the responsible medical officer appointed in respect of the offender under section 230 of the Mental Health (Care and Treatment) (Scotland) Act 2003 (asp 13);

"restriction order" means an order under section 59 of this Act;

"sentence of imprisonment" includes any sentence or order for detention; and

"specified" means specified in the compulsion order.

AMENDMENTS

Section 57A inserted by Mental Health (Care and Treatment) (Scotland) Act 2003 (asp 13) s.133. Brought into force on 21 March 2005, only for the purpose of enabling regulations to be made, by SSI 2005/161 (C.6). Coming into force for all other purposes on 5 October 2005.

Subs.(15)(a)(vi)–(vii) substituted with subs.(15)(a)(vi)-(viii) by Criminal Justice and Licensing (Scotland) Act 2010 (asp 13) Sch.2 para.5. Brought into force on 13 December 2010 (subject to savings provisions in art.3) by SSI 2010/413 (C.28) art.2, Sch.1 para.1.

Subs.(16) as amended by Public Services Reform (Scotland) Act 2010 (Consequential Modifications) Order 2011 (SSI 2011/211) Sch.1 para.7 (effective 1 April 2011).

Subs.(16) as amended by Public Bodies (Joint Working) (Scotland) Act 2014 (Consequential Modifications and Saving) Order 2015 (SSI 2015/157) Sch.1 para.3 (effective 1 April 2015).

Subs.(16) as amended by Children and Young People (Scotland) Act 2014 (asp 8) Sch.5 para.5(3). Brought into force on 1 April 2017 by SSI 2016/254 art.3.

Subss.(2), (5)(b) as amended, subs.(2A) inserted, by Mental Health (Scotland) Act 2015 (asp 9) Pt 2 s.43(2). Brought into force on 30 September 2017 by SSI 2017/197 art.2 and Sch.

DEFINITIONS

"care home service": s.2(3) of the Regulation of Care (Scotland) Act 2001. A4-132.2
"community care services": s.5A(4) of the Social Work (Scotland) Act 1968.
"compulsion order": s.57A(1).
"court": s.52B(4).
"medical treatment": s.329(1) of the Mental Health (Care and Treatment) (Scotland) Act 2003.
"mental disorder": s.328(1) of the Mental Health (Care and Treatment) (Scotland) Act 2003.
"offence": s.307(1).
"prosecutor": s.307(1).
"relevant services": s.19(2) of the Children (Scotland) Act 1995.
"restriction order": s.59.
"sentence of imprisonment": s.57A(16).
"specified": s.57A(16).

GENERAL NOTE

This section introduces a new form of mental health disposal for offenders in the form of a compulsion order ("CO"). Before an offender can become subject to a CO, the offender must first have been convicted in the sheriff court or High Court of a sentence punishable by imprisonment (subs.(1)). A4-132.3

The grounds for making a CO are broadly similar to those for making an interim compulsion order ("ICO") (subss.(2)(a) and (3)). However, the medical practitioners reporting on the offender must concur regarding the type of mental disorder (by reference to s.328 of the Mental Health (Care and Treatment) (Scotland) Act 2003) which the offender has (subs.(13)). The court must also have regard in so doing to the terms of a report submitted by a mental health officer ("MHO") under s.57C and also to the circumstances of the case including the nature and antecedents of the offence (subs.(4)) (see also General Note to s.57C).

The purpose of the CO is to ensure that the offender receives medical treatment by compulsory measures, either in the community or by means of detention in hospital, for the offender's mental disorder. The compulsory measures which can be authorised by a CO are essentially those which can be authorised by a compulsory treatment order ("CTO") (subs.(8)). It should be noted, however, that where a CO is made, the court has no power to specify any treatment, care or service as a "recorded matter", this is unlike the position when the CTO is made by the Mental Health Tribunal for Scotland (cf. s.64(4)(a)(ii) of the 2003 Act). The CO may authorise detention and medical treatment in hospital or community based compulsory measures. The making of a CO is a matter for the criminal courts as a mental health disposal for an offender under the 1995 Act. Detention in hospital cannot be authorised by a CO unless the medical practitioners reporting to the court satisfy the court that the medical treatment can be provided only if the patient is detained in hospital, and that a place in a suitable hospital will be available within seven days of the CO being made (subs.(5)). Further specification is required from the medical practitioners if detention in a state hospital is proposed (subs.(6)).

The matters which require to be specified in a CO are set out in subs.(14). When a CO is granted it will authorise the measures specified for a period of six months (subs.(2)). Where a CO authorising detention in hospital is made in conjunction with a restriction order ("RO") (see 1995 Act s.59), it will authorise the measures specified without limit of time (subs.(8)). Part 10 of the Mental Health (Care and Treatment) (Scotland) Act 2003 contains extensive provisions for review of COs and ROs by the Mental Health Tribunal.

Once a court has made a CO, it cannot make any of the orders specified in subs.(15)(a), which include other mental health disposals, and also disposals which the court could make in the ordinary manner. Final disposal of an offender where the making of a CO is being considered in some cases may take a considerable period of time where a lengthy assessment is needed in complex cases. This may be of concern to the victim, and relatives of the victim, of a crime committed by the offender.

The exercise of the authority under s.57A is a matter that is not often, if ever, reported formally as the outcome is the beneficial medical treatment that the subject requires. Examples of the use of the authority do exist: in *HM Advocate v Kerr* unreported 31 January 2017, High Court of Justiciary sitting at Glasgow, the accused pled guilty to culpable homicide on the ground of diminished responsibility. The accused had killed his wife by repeatedly stabbing her. He phoned the police to tell them what he had done. Lord Boyd made a compulsion order in terms of s.57A. The medical inquiries showed the accused to be suffering from a medical disorder, namely a delusional disorder characterised by delusions about his wife's fidelity and police surveillance, both of which were untrue. Other contributing factors included heavy dependence on alcohol and drugs. The court also ordered in terms of s.59 of the 1995 Act that such detention was without limit of time.

Construction of s.57A

It has been observed that the correct construction of s.57A of the 1995 Act is far from straightforward: *FD v Gibson* [2018] SAC (Crim) 2 at [12] (9 January 2018). That was said because of the apparent tension between the necessity test in s.57A(3)(d) and the appropriateness test in s.57A(2)(b) and (4): ibid at [14]. The crucial point in that authority was that the element of necessity was held to be essentially a medical question, meaning that "medical practitioners are entitled to disregard the existence of a compulsory treatment order": ibid at [15]. Reference might also be made to the judicial advice that "[m]edical reports need not be construed as if they were conveyancing documents or commercial contracts": ibid at [18].

Subs.(8)(a)

In recent years there have been several cases that constitute various attempts on appeal to vary an original sentence or disposal on account of some perceived "fresh evidence" relating to the psychiatric assessment of the appellant. Thus in *Jackson v HM Advocate*, 1998 S.C.C.R. 539 the appellant had in 1984 been sentenced to life imprisonment on charges of attempted murder and assault with intent to rape. The original mental illness had abated but the appellant was assessed as having a continuing underlying personality disorder. On that basis the sentence of imprisonment was quashed and in its place a hospital order was imposed with an unlimited restriction on discharge.

In *Baikie v HM Advocate*, 2000 S.C.C.R. 119 the accused was sentenced to 10 years' imprisonment on a charge of attempted murder. Later, while in prison, he was assessed as suffering from schizophrenia and he was so at the time of the crime. He thus had an undiagnosed mental condition at the time of sentencing. In the circumstances, the sentence of imprisonment was quashed and in its place a hospital order was imposed with certain restrictions on discharge. In *Graham v HM Advocate*, 2005 S.C.C.R. 544; [2005] HCJAC 75 the appellant had pled guilty to culpable homicide on the basis of diminished responsibility. He had been sentenced to life imprisonment as his mental condition was stable at the time due to the medication he was taking. There came a time when he stopped taking his medicine and his illness returned. The variation in mental condition was held to meet the test in s.106(3)(a) in that it constituted evidence that had not been heard at the original proceedings. The sentence of imprisonment was quashed and in its place a hospital order was imposed as a more appropriate disposal.

The appellant in *Reid v HM Advocate*, 2008 S.L.T. 293; 2008 S.C.L. 455 had pled guilty to culpable homicide in 1967 and he had been made the subject of a hospital order. That was appealed but refused. The matter was referred back to the High Court of Justiciary by the SCCRC and was heard by three judges: *Reid v HM Advocate*, 2012 S.C.L. 475. On reconsideration it was held that it was arguable that, on the facts, the basis of an assessment made 45 years earlier was not relevant now and an injustice might have been perpetuated. The psychometric tests used showed results that were inconsistent with the diagnosis of a mental disorder. The appeal was remitted to a full bench. Thereafter, in *Reid v HM Advocate* [2012] HCJAC 150; 2013 S.L.T. 65; 2012 S.C.L. 143, the whole matter was considered and the fresh evidence was held to have shown that there had never been a mental disorder as such but an untreatable dissocial personality disorder. Accordingly, the only appropriate sentence was that of life imprisonment. The existing hospital order was quashed and, in its place, a life sentence was imposed with a punishment part of 12 years.

In *Johnstone v HM Advocate* [2013] HCJAC 92; 2012 S.L.T. 1115; 2013 S.C.L. 868 the appellant had pled guilty in 1997 to a charge of culpable homicide and at sentencing he was said, by those medically qualified to assess him, to have a mental disorder in the form of a mental handicap comprising of a mental impairment. A hospital order was made in terms of s.59 as he was said to have posed a danger to the public.

On appeal the "fresh evidence" was said, at [57], to be that other psychiatrists now said that the appellant was either not mentally impaired at the time of sentencing and/or he did not meet the treatability test. The evidence was held not to be "fresh" on the existing authorities when it had been deliberately and reasonably not tendered in the first place. In the circumstances of the appellant it was noted, at [60]:

> "The Court cannot alter Hospital Orders retrospectively merely on the basis of changes in the practice of psychiatric assessment. The issue was whether the Hospital and Restriction Orders were appropriate at the time when they were made, according to the practices then current, albeit perhaps analysed in the light of circumstances which have occurred since sentencing."

The appeal was refused, at [70], as the original disposal was entirely appropriate for the time at which it was made. The court noted that there was no mechanism for achieving a transfer to prison within the current hospital and restriction order system, as there is for a transfer of a prisoner to hospital.

Compulsion order authorising detention in hospital or requiring residence at place: ancillary provision

57B.—(1) Where a compulsion order— A4-132.4

(a) authorises the detention of an offender in a specified hospital; or

(b) imposes a requirement on an offender to reside at a specified place,

this section authorises the removal, before the end of the day following the 7 days beginning with the day on which the order is made, of the offender to the specified hospital or place, by any of the persons mentioned in subsection (2) below.

(2) Those persons are—

(a) a constable;

(b) a person employed in, or contracted to provide services in or to, the specified hospital who is authorised by the managers of that hospital to remove persons to hospital for the purposes of this section; and

(c) a specified person.

(3) In this section, "specified" means specified in the compulsion order.

AMENDMENTS

Section 57B inserted by Mental Health (Care and Treatment) (Scotland) Act 2003 (asp 13) s.133. Brought into force on 21 March 2005, only for the purpose of enabling regulations to be made, by SSI 2005/161 (C.6). Coming into force for all other purposes on 5 October 2005.

Subs.(1) as amended by Mental Health (Scotland) Act 2015 (asp 9) Pt 2 s.43(3). Brought into force on 30 September 2017 by SSI 2017/197 art.2 and Sch.

DEFINITIONS

"compulsion order": s.57A(1). A4-132.5

"specified": s.57B(3).

GENERAL NOTE

Where a compulsion order ("CO") authorises detention in hospital or requires the offender to reside at a specified place (see General Note to s.57A), the persons listed in subs.(2) are authorised to remove the A4-132.5.1

offender there within seven days of the CO being made.

[THE NEXT PARAGRAPH IS A4-132.6]

Mental health officer's report

A4-132.6 **57C.—**(1) This section applies where the court is considering making a compulsion order in relation to an offender under section 57A of this Act.

(2) If directed to do so by the court, the mental health officer shall—

(a) subject to subsection (3) below, interview the offender; and

(b) prepare a report in relation to the offender in accordance with subsection (4) below.

(3) If it is impracticable for the mental health officer to comply with the requirement in subsection (2)(a) above, the mental health officer need not do so.

(4) The report shall state—

(a) the name and address of the offender;

(b) if known by the mental health officer, the name and address of the offender's primary carer;

(c) in so far as relevant for the purposes of section 57A of this Act, details of the personal circumstances of the offender; and

(d) any other information that the mental health officer considers relevant for the purposes of that section.

(5) In this section—

"carer", and "primary", in relation to a carer, have the meanings given by section 329(1) of the Mental Health (Care and Treatment) (Scotland) Act 2003 (asp 13);

"mental health officer" means a person appointed (or deemed to be appointed) under section 32(1) of that Act; and

"named person" has the meaning given by section 329(1) of that Act.

AMENDMENTS

Section 57C inserted by Mental Health (Care and Treatment) (Scotland) Act 2003 (asp 13) s.133. Brought into force on 21 March 2005, only for the purpose of enabling regulations to be made, by SSI 2005/161 (C.6). Coming into force for all other purposes on 5 October 2005.

DEFINITIONS

A4-132.7 "carer": s.329(1) of the Mental Health (Care and Treatment) (Scotland) Act 2003.
"compulsion order": s.57A(1).
"mental health officer": s.32(1) of the Mental Health (Care and Treatment) (Scotland) Act 2003.
"named person": s.32(1) of the Mental Health (Care and Treatment) (Scotland) Act 2003.
"offender": s.53(1).
"primary carer": s.329(1) of the Mental Health (Care and Treatment) (Scotland) Act 2003.

GENERAL NOTE

A4-132.7.1 Before a court can make a compulsion order, it must consider a report on the offender made by a mental health officer ("MHO") (see General Note to s.57A). The MHO's report will contain details of the offender and the offender's primary carer, the personal circumstances of the offender, together with any other relevant information (subs.(4)). The MHO must interview the offender in the course of compiling the report (subs.(2)(a)), but does not have to do so where this is impracticable (subs.(3)). Subs.(5) contains a definition of "named person" although there is no other reference to named person in this section. This would appear to be an omission.

[THE NEXT PARAGRAPH IS A4-132.8]

Compulsion order: supplementary

A4-132.8 **57D.—**(1) If, before the end of the day following the 7 days beginning with the day on which a compulsion order authorising detention of the offender in a hospital is made, it appears to the court, or, as the case may be, the Scottish Ministers, that, by reason of emergency or other special circumstances, it is not reasonably practicable for the offender to be admitted to the hospital specified in the order, the court, or, as the case may be, the Scottish Ministers, may direct that the offender be admitted to the hospital specified in the direction.

(2) Where—

(a) the court makes a direction under subsection (1) above, it shall inform the person having custody of the offender; and

(b) the Scottish Ministers make such a direction, they shall inform—

(i) the court; and

(ii) the person having custody of the offender.

(3) Where a direction is made under subsection (1) above, the compulsion order shall have effect as if the hospital specified in the direction were the hospital specified in the order.

(4) In this section, "court" means the court which made the compulsion order.

AMENDMENTS

Section 57D inserted by Mental Health (Care and Treatment) (Scotland) Act 2003 (asp 13) s.133. Brought into force on 21 March 2005, only for the purpose of enabling regulations to be made, by SSI 2005/161 (C.6). Coming into force for all other purposes on 5 October 2005.

Subs.(1) as amended by Mental Health (Scotland) Act 2015 (asp 9) Pt 2 s.43(4). Brought into force on 30 September 2017 by SSI 2017/197 art.2 and Sch.

DEFINITIONS

"compulsion order": s.57A. A4-132.9

"court": s.57D(4).

"offender": s.53(1).

GENERAL NOTE

This section allows the court or the Scottish Ministers to change the designation of the hospital specified in a compulsion order, if "by reason of emergency or other special circumstances" (subs.(1)) it is not practicable to admit the offender there within the seven day period specified in s.57B(1). This is similar to the provision which applies to interim compulsion orders (see s.53). A4-132.10

[THE NEXT PARAGRAPH IS A4-133]

Hospital orders and guardianship

Order for hospital admission or guardianship

58.—(1) [...] A4-133

(1A) Where a person is convicted in the High Court or the sheriff court of an offence, other than an offence the sentence for which is fixed by law, punishable by that court with imprisonment, and the court is satisfied—

(a) on the evidence of two medical practitioners (complying with section 61 of this Act and with any requirements imposed under section 57(3) of the Adults with Incapacity (Scotland) Act 2000 (asp 4)) that the grounds set out in section 58(1)(a) of that Act apply in relation to the offender;

(b) that no other means provided by or under this Act would be sufficient to enable the offender's interests in his personal welfare to be safeguarded or promoted,

the court may, subject to subsection (2) below, by order place the offender's personal welfare under the guardianship of such local authority or of such other person approved by a local authority as may be specified in the order.

(2) Where the case is remitted by the sheriff to the High Court for sentence under any enactment, the power to make an order under subsection (1A) above shall be exercisable by that court.

(3) Where in the case of a person charged summarily in the sheriff court with an act or omission constituting an offence the court would have power, on convicting

him, to make an order under subsection (1A) above, then, if it is satisfied that the person did the act or made the omission charged, the court may, if it thinks fit, make such an order without convicting him.

(4) [...]

(5) [...]

(6) An order placing a person under the guardianship of a local authority or of any other person (in this Act referred to as a "guardianship order") shall not be made under this section unless the court is satisfied—

(a) on the report of a mental health officer (complying with any requirements imposed by section 57(3) of the Adults with Incapacity (Scotland) Act 2000 (asp 4)) giving his opinion as to the general appropriateness of the order sought, based on an interview and assessment of the person carried out not more than 30 days before it makes the order, that it is necessary in the interests of the personal welfare of the person that he should be placed under guardianship;

(b) that any person nominated to be appointed a guardian is suitable to be so appointed;

(c) that the authority or person is willing to receive that person into guardianship; And

(d) that there is no other guardianship order, under this Act or the Adults with Incapacity (Scotland) Act 2000 (asp 4), in force relating to the person's personal welfare which makes the same provision as the guardianship order which the court proposes to make under this section.

(7) A guardianship order made under this section shall specify (by reference to the appropriate paragraph (or paragraphs) of the definition of "mental disorder" in section 328(1) of the Mental Health (Care and Treatment) (Scotland) Act 2003 (asp 13)) the type (or types) of mental disorder that the person has; and no such order shall be made unless the descriptions of the person's mental disorder by each of the medical practitioners, whose evidence is taken into account under subsection (1A)(a) above, specifies at least one type of mental disorder that is also specified by the other.

(8) Where an order is made under this section, the court shall not pass sentence of imprisonment or impose a fine or impose a community payback order or make a drug treatment and testing order in respect of the offence, but may make any other order which the court has power to make apart from this section; and for the purposes of this subsection "sentence of imprisonment" includes any sentence or order for detention.

(9) [...]

(10) [...]

(11) Section 58A of this Act shall have effect as regards guardianship orders made under this section.

AMENDMENTS

Subss.(4) and (9) amended by Crime and Punishment (Scotland) Act 1997 (c.48) s.62(1) and Sch.1 para.21(6), with effect from1 January 1998 in terms of SI 1997/2323 art.4 and Sch.2.

Subs.(7) as amended by Mental Health (Public Safety and Appeals) (Scotland) Act 1999 (asp 1) s.3(b) (effective 13 September 1999).

Section 58(1), (2), (3), (5)-(7) and (10) as amended by Adults with Incapacity (Scotland) Act 2000 (asp 4) s.88 and Sch.5 para.26. Brought into force on 1 April 2002 by SSI 2001/81 (C.2).

Subs.(11) inserted by Adults with Incapacity (Scotland) Act 2000 (asp 4) s.88 and Sch.5 para.26. Brought into force as above.

Subss.(1A) and (7) as amended by Mental Health (Care and Treatment) (Scotland) Act 2003 (asp 13) Sch.4 para.8(4). Brought into force on 5 October 2005 by SSI 2005/161 (C.6).

Subss.(1), (4), (5), (9) and (10) repealed, and subss.(2), (3), (7) and (11) as amended, by Mental Health (Care and Treatment) (Scotland) Act 2003 (asp 13) Sch.5 Pt I. Brought into force on 5 October 2005 as above.

Subss.(6) and (7) as amended by Adult Support and Protection (Scotland) Act 2007 (asp 10) Sch.1 para.4(a). Brought into force on 5 October 2007 by SSI 2007/334 (C.28) art.2 and Sch.2.

Subs.(8) as amended by Criminal Justice and Licensing (Scotland) Act 2010 (asp 13) Sch.2 para.6. Brought into force on 13 December 2010 (subject to savings provisions in art.3) by SSI 2010/413 (C.28) art.2, Sch.1 para.1.

GENERAL NOTE

See above for the annotation to s.57A(8)(a) and the various authorities on appeal in regard to the making of hospital orders in place of imprisonment and vice versa. A4-134

Application of Adults with Incapacity (Scotland) Act 2000

58A.—(1) Subject to the provisions of this section, the provisions of Parts 1, 5, 6 and 7 of the Adults with Incapacity (Scotland) Act 2000 (asp 4) ("the 2000 Act") apply— A4-134.1

(a) to a guardian appointed by an order of the court under section 57(2)(c), 58(1) or 58(1A) of this Act (in this section referred to as a "guardianship order") whether appointed before or after the coming into force of these provisions, as they apply to a guardian with powers relating to the personal welfare of an adult appointed under section 58 of that Act;

(b) to a person authorised under an intervention order under section 60B of this Act as they apply to a person so authorised under section 53 of that Act.

(2) In making a guardianship order the court shall have regard to any regulations made by the Scottish Ministers under section 64(11) of the 2000 Act and—

(a) shall confer powers, which it shall specify in the order, relating only to the personal welfare of the person;

(b) may appoint a joint guardian;

(c) may appoint a substitute guardian;

(d) may make such consequential or ancillary order, provision or direction as it considers appropriate.

(3) Without prejudice to the generality of subsection (2), or to any other powers conferred by this Act, the court may—

(a) make any order granted by it subject to such conditions and restrictions as appear to it to be appropriate;

(b) order that any reports relating to the person who will be the subject of the order be lodged with the court or that the person be assessed or interviewed and that a report of such assessment or interview be lodged;

(c) make such further inquiry or call for such further information as appears to it to be appropriate;

(d) make such interim order as appears to it to be appropriate pending the disposal of the proceedings.

(4) Where the court makes a guardianship order it shall forthwith send a copy of the interlocutor containing the order to the Public Guardian who shall—

(a) enter prescribed particulars of the appointment in the register maintained by him under section 6(2)(b)(iv) of the 2000 Act;

(b) unless he considers that the notification would be likely to pose a serious risk to the person's health notify the person of the appointment of the guardian; and

(c) notify the local authority and the Mental Welfare Commission of the terms of the interlocutor.

(5) A guardianship order shall continue in force for a period of 3 years or such other period (including an indefinite period) as, on cause shown, the court may determine.

(6) Where any proceedings for the appointment of a guardian under section 57(2)(c) or 58(1) of this Act have been commenced and not determined before the date of coming into force of section 84 of, and paragraph 26 of schedule 5 to, the Adults with Incapacity (Scotland) Act 2000 (asp 4) they shall be determined in accordance with this Act as it was immediately in force before that date.

AMENDMENTS

Section 58A inserted by Adults with Incapacity (Scotland) Act 2000 (asp 4) s.84. Brought into force on 1 April 2002 by SSI 2001/81 (C.2).

Subsection (1)(b) as amended by Adults with Incapacity (Scotland) Act 2000 (asp 4) s.84 (as amended by Regulation of Care (Scotland) Act 2001 (asp 8) Sch.3 para.23(5)) (effective 1 April 2002).

Application of Adults with Incapacity (Scotland) Act 2000

58A.—*(1) Subject to the provisions of this section, the provisions of Parts 1, 5, 6 and 7 of the Adults with Incapacity (Scotland) Act 2000 (asp 4) ("the 2000 Act") apply—*

(a) to a guardian appointed by an order of the court under section 57(2)(c), 58(1) or 58(1A) of this Act (in this section referred to as a "guardianship order") whether appointed before or after the coming into force of these provisions, as they apply to a guardian with powers relating to the personal welfare of an adult appointed under section 58 of that Act;

(b) to a person authorised under an intervention order under section 60B of this Act as they apply to a person so authorised under section 53 of that Act.

(2) In making a guardianship order the court shall have regard to any regulations made by the Scottish Ministers under section 64(11) of the 2000 Act and—

(a) shall confer powers, which it shall specify in the order, relating only to the personal welfare of the person;

(b) may appoint a joint guardian;

(c) may appoint a substitute guardian;

(d) may make such consequential or ancillary order, provision or direction as it considers appropriate.

(3) Without prejudice to the generality of subsection (2), or to any other powers conferred by this Act, the court may—

(a) make any order granted by it subject to such conditions and restrictions as appear to it to be appropriate;

(b) order that any reports relating to the person who will be the subject of the order be lodged with the court or that the person be assessed or interviewed and that a report of such assessment or interview be lodged;

(c) make such further inquiry or call for such further information as appears to it to be appropriate;

(d) make such interim order as appears to it to be appropriate pending the disposal of the proceedings.

(4) Where the court makes a guardianship order it shall forthwith send a copy of the interlocutor containing the order to the Public Guardian who shall—

(a) enter prescribed particulars of the appointment in the register maintained by him under section 6(2)(b)(iv) of the 2000 Act;

(b) unless he considers that the notification would be likely to pose a serious risk to the person's health notify the person of the appointment of the guardian; and

(c) notify the local authority and the Mental Welfare Commission of the terms of the interlocutor.

(5) A guardianship order shall continue in force for a period of 3 years or such other period (including an indefinite period) as, on cause shown, the court may determine.

(5A) The period mentioned in subsection (5) does not, unless it is an indefinite period, run during any period for which this subsection has effect.

(5B) The guardianship order continues to have effect during any period for which subsection (5A) has effect.

(5C) Nothing in subsection (5B) affects any other ground on which the order may cease to have effect.

(6) Where any proceedings for the appointment of a guardian under section 57(2)(c) or 58(1) of this Act have been commenced and not determined before the date of coming into force of section 84 of, and paragraph 26 of schedule 5 to, the Adults with Incapacity (Scotland) Act 2000 (asp 4) they shall be determined in accordance with this Act as it was immediately in force before that date.

AMENDMENTS

In relation to COVID-19, s.58A as amended by Coronavirus (Scotland) Act 2020 (asp 7) Sch.3(2) para.11(2) (effective 7 April 2020).

[THE NEXT PARAGRAPH IS A4-135]

Hospital orders: restrictions on discharge

59.—(1) Where a compulsion order authorising the detention of a person in a hospital by virtue of paragraph (a) of section 57A(8) of this Act is made in respect of a person, and it appears to the court— **A4-135**

(a) having regard to the nature of the offence with which he is charged;

(b) the antecedents of the person; and

(c) the risk that as a result of his mental disorder he would commit offences if set at large,

that it is necessary for the protection of the public from serious harm so to do, the court may, subject to the provisions of this section, further order that the person shall be subject to the special restrictions set out in Part 10 of the Mental Health (Care and Treatment) (Scotland) Act 2003 (asp 13), without limit of time.

(2) An order under this section (in this Act referred to as "a restriction order") shall not be made in the case of any person unless the approved medical practitioner, whose evidence is taken into account by the court under section 57A(2)(a) of this Act, has given evidence orally before the court.

(2A) The court may, in the case of a person in respect of whom it did not, before making the compulsion order, make an interim compulsion order, make a restriction order in respect of the person only if satisfied that, in all the circumstances, it was not appropriate to make an interim compulsion order in respect of the person.

(3) [...]

AMENDMENTS

Subsection (2) as amended by Adults with Incapacity (Scotland) Act 2000 (asp 4) s.88 and Sch.6. Brought into force on 1 April 2002 by SSI 2001/81 (C.2).

Subsections (1) and (2) as amended, and subs.(2A) inserted, by Mental Health (Care and Treatment) (Scotland) Act 2003 (asp 13) Sch.4 para.8(5). Brought into force on 5 October 2005 by SSI 2005/161 (C.6).

Subsection (3) repealed by Mental Health (Care and Treatment) (Scotland) Act 2003 (asp 13) Sch.5 Pt I. Brought into force on 5 October 2005 as above.

DEFINITIONS **A4-135.1**

"offence": s.307(1).

"restriction order": s.59(2).

[THE NEXT PARAGRAPH IS A4-136]

GENERAL NOTE

A4-136 Section 59 makes provision to restrict the discharge of hospital orders made under s.58. As a court may make a further hospital order that amounts to a person being subject to statutory special restrictions without limit of time, the tests to be met are suitably high. Indeed, the aspects of risk and protection in s.59(1) are redolent of the concerns latent in the terms of s.58(5).

In *M v HM Advocate*, 1998 G.W.D. 24-1231, an appeal against the making of a restriction order founding upon a change of opinion by one of the examining psychiatrists subsequent to the sheriff's determination, the Appeal Court held that the only relevant material for the purposes of appeal was that which had been laid before the sheriff; M's case might be considered administratively by the Secretary of State.

The making of a restriction order is ultimately a matter for the Court in the circumstances of each particular case—see *Thomson v HM Advocate*, 1999 S.C.C.R. 640 where the necessary criteria under s.59(1) was held made out and a restriction order made, despite psychiatric evidence that a restriction order was not necessary.

Reference is made in passing to the Mental Health (Public Safety and Appeals) (Scotland) Act 1999 which received Royal Assent on 13 September 1999 and is effective from 1 September 1999. This Act, inter alia, adds public safety to the criteria to be taken into account on an appeal under s.64 of the Mental Health (Scotland) Act 1984 by a person subject to a restriction order. Accordingly, it is provided that the sheriff shall refuse such an appeal if satisfied that the patient is suffering from a mental disorder the effect of which is such that it is necessary, in order to protect the public from serious harm, that the patient continue to be detained in a hospital, "whether for medical treatment or not". The definition of "mental disorder" in s.1(2) of the 1984 Act has been extended to include "personality disorder" (see s.3 of the Mental Health (Public Safety and Appeals) (Scotland) Act 1999, effective from 1 September 1999). This radical provision is subject to a right of appeal to the Court of Session. It is expected that in future greater use will be made of the hospital direction under s.59A of the 1995 Act which allies a period of remedial hospitalisation to a custodial sentence, but of course this hybrid disposal has only been available to the solemn court since 1 January 1998.

Hospital directions

Hospital direction

A4-136.1 **59A.**—(1) This section applies where a person, not being a child, (in this section and in sections 59B and 59C of this Act referred to as the "offender") is convicted on indictment in—

(a) the High Court; or
(b) the sheriff court,

of an offence punishable by imprisonment.

(2) If the court is satisfied—

(a) on the written or oral evidence of two medical practitioners—
   (i) that the conditions mentioned in subsection (3) below are met in respect of the offender; and
   (ii) as to the matters mentioned in subsection (4) below; and
(b) that, having regard to the matters mentioned in subsection (5) below, it is appropriate,

the court may, in addition to any sentence of imprisonment which it has the power or the duty to impose, make, subject to subsection (6) below, a direction (in this Act referred to as a "hospital direction") authorising the measures mentioned in subsection (7) below.

(3) The conditions referred to in subsection (2)(a)(i) above are—

(a) that the offender has a mental disorder;
(b) that medical treatment which would be likely to—
   (i) prevent the mental disorder worsening; or
   (ii) alleviate any of the symptoms, or effects, of the disorder,

   is available for the offender;
(c) that if the offender were not provided with such medical treatment there would be a significant risk—
   (i) to the health, safety or welfare of the offender; or
   (ii) to the safety of any other person; and

(d) that the making of a hospital direction in respect of the offender is necessary.

(4) The matters referred to in subsection (2)(a)(ii) above are—

(a) that the hospital proposed by the two medical practitioners mentioned in subsection (2)(a) above is suitable for the purpose of giving the medical treatment mentioned in paragraph (b) of subsection (3) above to the offender; and

(b) that, were a hospital direction made, the offender could be admitted to such hospital before the end of the day following the 7 days beginning with the day on which the direction is made.

(5) The matters referred to in subsection (2)(b) above are—

(a) the mental health officer's report, prepared in accordance with section 59B of this Act, in respect of the offender;

(b) all the circumstances, including—

(i) the nature of the offence of which the offender was convicted; and

(ii) the antecedents of the offender; and

(c) any alternative means of dealing with the offender.

(6) A hospital direction may authorise detention in a state hospital only if, on the written or oral evidence of the two medical practitioners mentioned in subsection (2)(a) above, it appears to the court—

(a) that the offender requires to be detained in a state hospital under conditions of special security; and

(b) that such conditions of special security can be provided only in a state hospital.

(7) The measures mentioned in subsection (2) above are—

(a) in the case of an offender who, when the hospital direction is made, has not been admitted to the specified hospital, the removal, before the end of the day following the 7 days beginning with the day on which the direction is made, of the offender to the specified hospital by—

(i) a constable;

(ii) a person employed in, or contracted to provide services in or to, the specified hospital who is authorised by the managers of that hospital to remove persons to hospital for the purposes of this section; or

(iii) a specified person;

(b) the detention of the offender in the specified hospital; and

(c) the giving to the offender, in accordance with Part 16 of the Mental Health (Care and Treatment) (Scotland) Act 2003 (asp 13), of medical treatment.

(8) The court shall be satisfied as to the condition mentioned in subsection (3)(a) above only if the description of the offender's mental disorder by each of the medical practitioners mentioned in subsection (2)(a) above specifies, by reference to the appropriate paragraph (or paragraphs) of the definition of "mental disorder" in section 328(1) of the Mental Health (Care and Treatment) (Scotland) Act 2003 (asp 13), at least one type of mental disorder that the offender has that is also specified by the other.

(9) A hospital direction—

(a) shall specify, by reference to the appropriate paragraph (or paragraphs) of the definition of "mental disorder" in section 328(1) of the Mental Health (Care and Treatment) (Scotland) Act 2003 (asp 13), the type (or types) of mental disorder that each of the medical practitioners mentioned in subsection (2)(a) above specifies that is also specified by the other; and

(b) may include such directions as the court thinks fit for the removal of the offender to, and the detention of the offender in, a place of safety pending the offender's admission to the specified hospital.

(10) In this section—

"medical treatment" has the same meaning as in section 52D of this Act; and "specified" means specified in the hospital direction.

AMENDMENTS

Section 59A substituted by Mental Health (Care and Treatment) (Scotland) Act 2003 (asp 13) Sch.4 para.8(6). Brought into force on 5 October 2005 by SSI 2005/161 (C.6).

Subs.(4)(b), (7)(a) as amended by Mental Health (Scotland) Act 2015 (asp 9) Pt 2 s.44(2). Brought into force on 30 September 2017 by SSI 2017/197 art.2 and Sch.

DEFINITIONS

A4-136.2 "hospital direction": s.59A(2).
"indictment": s.307(1).
"medical treatment": s.329(1) of the Mental Health (Care and Treatment) (Scotland) Act 2003.
"mental disorder": s.328(1) of the Mental Health (Care and Treatment) (Scotland) Act 2003.
"sentence": s.307(1).
"specified": s.59A(10).

GENERAL NOTE

A4-136.3 Hospital directions may be made competently after conviction if a court is satisfied on the written or oral evidence of two medical practitioners that the offender has a mental disorder: s.59A(2). There are other conditions to be met: see s.59A(2)(b), (4) and (5). Hospital directions authorise the detention of an offender in a state hospital under conditions of special security where it appears to the court that such conditions of special security can be provided only in a state hospital: s.59A(6). A hospital direction shall specify the type (or types) of mental disorder that each of the medical practitioners specifies and is specified by the other practitioner: s.59A(9).

Hospital direction: mental health officer's report

A4-136.4 **59B.—**(1) This section applies where the court is considering making a hospital direction in relation to an offender under section 59 A of this Act.

(2) If directed to do so by the court, the mental health officer shall—

(a) subject to subsection (3) below, interview the offender; and

(b) prepare a report in relation to the offender in accordance with subsection (4) below.

(3) If it is impracticable for the mental health officer to comply with the requirement in subsection (2)(a) above, the mental health officer need not do so.

(4) The report shall state—

(a) the name and address of the offender;

(b) if known by the mental health officer, the name and address of the offender's primary carer;

(c) in so far as relevant for the purposes of section 59A of this Act, details of the personal circumstances of the offender; and

(d) any other information that the mental health officer considers relevant for the purposes of that section.

(5) In this section, "carer", "primary", in relation to a carer, and "mental health officer" have the same meanings as in section 57C of this Act.

AMENDMENTS

Section 59B inserted by Mental Health (Care and Treatment) (Scotland) Act 2003 (asp 13) Sch.4 para.8(6). Brought into force on 5 October 2005 by SSI 2005/161 (C.6).

DEFINITIONS

A4-136.5 "carer": s.329(1) of Mental Health (Care and Treatment) (Scotland) Act 2003.
"hospital direction": s.59A(2).
"indictment": s.307(1).
"medical treatment": s.329(1) of the Mental Health (Care and Treatment) (Scotland) Act 2003.
"mental disorder": s.328(1) of the Mental Health (Care and Treatment) (Scotland) Act 2003.
"mental health officer": s.32(1) of the Mental Health (Care and Treatment) (Scotland) Act 2003.

"offender": s.53(1).
"primary carer": s.329(1) of the Mental Health (Care and Treatment) (Scotland) Act 2003.
"sentence": s.307(1).

Hospital direction: supplementary

59C.—(1) If, before the end of the day following the 7 days beginning with the day on which a hospital direction is made, it appears to the court, or, as the case may be, the Scottish Ministers, that, by reason of emergency or other special circumstances, it is not reasonably practicable for the offender to be admitted to the hospital specified in the hospital direction, the court, or, as the case may be, the Scottish Ministers, may direct that the offender be admitted to such other hospital as is specified. A4-136.6

(2) Where—

(a) the court makes a direction under subsection (1) above, it shall inform the person having custody of the offender; and

(b) the Scottish Ministers make such a direction, they shall inform—

(i) the court; and

(ii) the person having custody of the offender.

(3) Where a direction is made under subsection (1) above, the hospital direction shall have effect as if the hospital specified in the hospital direction were the hospital specified by the court, or, as the case may be, the Scottish Ministers, under subsection (1) above.

(4) In this section, "court" means the court which made the hospital direction.

Amendments

Section 59C inserted by Mental Health (Care and Treatment) (Scotland) Act 2003 (asp 13) Sch.4 para.8(6). Brought into force on 5 October 2005 by SSI 2005/161 (C.6).

Subs.(1) as amended by Mental Health (Scotland) Act 2015 (asp 9) Pt 2 s.44(3). Brought into force on 30 September 2017 by SSI 2017/197 art.2 and Sch, subject to transitional provisions.

Definitions

"court": s.59C(4). A4-136.7
"hospital direction": s.59A(2).
"offender": s.53(1).

[THE NEXT PARAGRAPH IS A4-137]

Appeals against compulsion orders

60. Where a compulsion order, interim compulsion order (but not an extension thereof), guardianship order, a restriction order or a hospital direction has been made by a court in respect of a person charged or brought before it, he may without prejudice to any other form of appeal under any rule of law (or, where an interim compulsion order has been made, to any right of appeal against any other order or sentence which may be imposed), appeal against that order or, as the case may be, direction in the same manner as against sentence. A4-137

Amendments

Section 60 as amended by Crime and Punishment (Scotland) Act 1997 (c.48) s.6(2) with effect from 1 January 1998 by SI 1997/2323 art.4 and Sch.2.

Section 60 as amended by Mental Health (Care and Treatment) (Scotland) Act 2003 (asp 13) Sch.4 para.8(7). Brought into force on 5 October 2005 by SSI 2005/161 (C.6).

Definitions

"guardianship order": s.58(6). A4-137.1
"hospital direction": s.59A(1).
"restriction order": s.59(2).
"sentence": s.307(1).

[THE NEXT PARAGRAPH IS A4-138]

GENERAL NOTE

A4-138 This section conjoins the right of appeal formerly to be found in ss.280 and 443 of the 1975 Act. The right of appeal against these orders is treated as an appeal against sentence so that, for example, an appeal against a finding on fact under s.55(2) by the court cannot be appealed under s.60. Appeals against findings and orders are dealt with by ss.62 and 63. The right of appeal against the making of a hospital direction was inserted into s.60 by virtue of s.6(2) of the Crime and Punishment (Scotland) Act 1997, with effect from 1 January 1998.

In *Reid v HM Advocate*, 2013 S.L.T. 65; 2013 S.C.L. 143; 2013 S.C.C.R. 70 the appellant had pled guilty to a charge of culpable homicide on the basis of a diagnosis of mental disorder and he was then made subject to a hospital order. There was fresh evidence of a subsequent diagnosis that the appellant was not suffering from a mental disorder but that he did have a personality disorder. The original sentence was quashed and a sentence of imprisonment imposed in its place.

The decision in *Reid v HM Advocate*, above, was distinguished in *Johnstone v HM Advocate*, 2013 S.L.T. 1115; 2013 S.C.L. 868; 2013 S.C.C.R. 487 : whereas in *Reid's* case there had been a misdiagnosis, in *Johnstone's* case the appellant had, after discussing with his counsel the conflicting medical opinion as to his medical condition, accepted a medical order rather than imprisonment. The approach by Johnstone meant that the later allegations did not meet the test for fresh evidence. For further discussion of both these cases see the commentary to s.57A, above.

Appeal by prosecutor against hospital orders etc.

A4-138.1 **60A.**—(1) This section applies where the court, in respect of a person charged or brought before it, has made—

(a) a compulsion order;
(b) a restriction order;
(c) guardianship order;
(d) a decision under section 57(2)(e) of this Act to make no order; or
(e) a hospital direction.

(2) Where this section applies, the prosecutor may appeal against any such order, decision or direction as is mentioned in subsection (1) above—

(a) if it appears to him that the order, decision or direction was inappropriate; or
(b) on a point of law,

and an appeal under this section shall be treated in the same manner as an appeal against sentence under section 108 of this Act.

AMENDMENTS

Section 60A inserted by Crime and Punishment (Scotland) Act 1997 (c.48) s.22 with effect from 1 January 1998 by SI 1997/2323 art.4 and Sch.2.

Subs.(1)(a) and (b) substituted, and subs.(1)(c), (d) and (e) inserted, by Mental Health (Care and Treatment) (Scotland) Act 2003 (asp 13) Sch.4 para.8(8). Brought into force on 5 October 2005 by SSI 2005/161 (C.6).

DEFINITIONS

A4-138.1.1 "court": s.59C(4).
"hospital direction": s.59A(2).
"prosecutor": s.307(1).

[THE NEXT PARAGRAPH IS A4-138.2]

GENERAL NOTE

A4-138.2 This section was inserted by s.22 of the Crime and Punishment (Scotland) Act 1997, with effect from January 1, 1998. It extends the right of appeal of the prosecutor found in s.63 of this Act, to include a right to appeal against hospital orders, etc. made where an accused is found to be insane.

Intervention orders

A4-138.3 **60B.** The court may instead of making a compulsion order or a guardianship order under section 57(2)(c) or 58(1A) of this Act, make an intervention order where it considers that it would be appropriate to do so.

AMENDMENTS

Section 60B inserted by Adults with Incapacity (Scotland) Act 2000 (asp 4) s.88 and Sch.5 para.26. Brought into force on April 1, 2002 by SSI 2001/81 (C.2).

Section 60B as amended by Mental Health (Care and Treatment) (Scotland) Act 2003 (asp 13) Sch.4 para.8(9). Brought into force on October 5, 2005 by SSI 2005/161 (C.6).

Section 60B as amended by Adult Support and Protection (Scotland) Act 2007 (asp 10) Sch.1 para.4(a). Brought into force on October 5, 2007 by SSI 2007/334 (C.28) art.2 and Sch.2.

Acquitted persons: detention for medical examination

60C.—(1) Subject to subsection (7) below, this section applies where a person charged with an offence is acquitted. A4-138.4

(2) If the court by or before which the person is acquitted is satisfied—

(a) on the written or oral evidence of two medical practitioners that the conditions mentioned in subsection (3) below are met in respect of the person; and

(b) that it is not practicable to secure the immediate examination of the person by a medical practitioner,

the court may, immediately after the person is acquitted, make an order authorising the measures mentioned in subsection (4) below for the purpose of enabling arrangements to be made for a medical practitioner to carry out a medical examination of the person.

(3) The conditions referred to in subsection (2)(a) above are—

(a) that the person has a mental disorder;

(b) that medical treatment which would be likely to—

(i) prevent the mental disorder worsening; or

(ii) alleviate any of the symptoms, or effects, of the disorder,

is available for the person; and

(c) that if the person were not provided with such medical treatment there would be a significant risk—

(i) to the health, safety or welfare of the person; or

(ii) to the safety of any other person.

(4) The measures referred to in subsection (2) above are—

(a) the removal of the person to a place of safety by—

(i) a constable; or

(ii) a person specified by the court; and

(b) the detention, subject to subsection (6) below, of the person in that place of safety for a period of 6 hours beginning with the time at which the order under subsection (2) above is made.

(5) If the person absconds—

(a) while being removed to a place of safety under subsection (4) above; or

(b) from the place of safety,

a constable or the person specified by the court under paragraph (a) of that subsection may, at any time during the period mentioned in paragraph (b) of that subsection, take the person into custody and remove the person to a place of safety.

(6) An order under this section ceases to authorise detention of a person if, following the medical examination of the person, a medical practitioner grants—

(a) an emergency detention certificate under section 36 of the Mental Health (Care and Treatment) (Scotland) Act 2003 (asp 13); or

(b) a short-term detention certificate under section 44 of that Act.

(7) This section does not apply in a case where the person is acquitted by reason of the special defence set out in section 51A of this Act.

(8) In this section, "medical treatment" has the same meaning as in section 52D of this Act.

Amendments

Section 60C inserted by Mental Health (Care and Treatment) (Scotland) Act 2003 (asp 13) s.134. Brought into force on March 21, 2005, only for the purpose of enabling regulations to be made, by SSI 2005/161 (C.6). Coming into force for all other purposes on October 5, 2005.

Subs.(7) as amended by Criminal Justice and Licensing (Scotland) Act 2010 (asp 13) Sch.7 para.40. Brought into force on June 25, 2012 by SSI 2012/160 (C.15) art.3.

Definitions

A4-138.5 "mental disorder": s.328(1) of the Mental Health (Care and Treatment) (Scotland) Act 2003.
"medical treatment": s.329(1) of the Mental Health (Care and Treatment) (Scotland) Act 2003.
"offender": s.53(1).

General Note

A4-138.6 After a person charged with an offence is acquitted the court may make an order competently to detain that person in a place of safety for a period of six hours if a court is satisfied on the written or oral evidence of two medical practitioners that the offender has a mental disorder: s.60C(2). There are other conditions to be met: see s.60C(2)(b) and (4). This order seems not to have a specific name but it is, rather, a pragmatic power to have the person acquitted seen for consideration for treatment because it is not practicable to secure the immediate examination of that person by a medical practitioner. Section 60D requires the making of such a place of safety order to be intimated to others.

Notification of detention under section 60C

A4-138.7 **60D.**—(1) This section applies where a person has been removed to a place of safety under section 60C of this Act.

(2) The court shall, before the expiry of the period of 14 days beginning with the day on which the order under section 60C(2) of this Act is made, ensure that the Mental Welfare Commission is given notice of the matters mentioned in subsection (3) below.

(3) Those matters are—

(a) the name and address of the person removed to the place of safety;
(b) the date on and time at which the person was so removed;
(c) the address of the place of safety;
(d) if the person is removed to a police station, the reason why the person was removed there; and
(e) any other matter that the Scottish Ministers may, by regulations made by statutory instrument, prescribe.

(4) The power conferred by subsection (3)(e) above may be exercised so as to make different provision for different cases or descriptions of case or for different purposes.

(5) A statutory instrument containing regulations under subsection (3)(e) above shall be subject to annulment in pursuance of a resolution of the Scottish Parliament.

Amendments

Section 60D inserted by Mental Health (Care and Treatment) (Scotland) Act 2003 (asp 13) s.134. Brought into force on March 21, 2005, only for the purpose of enabling regulations to be made, by SSI 2005/161 (C.6). Coming into force for all other purposes on October 5, 2005.

[THE NEXT PARAGRAPH IS A4-139]

Medical evidence

Requirements as to medical evidence

A4-139 **61.**—(1) Of the medical practitioners whose evidence is taken into account in making a finding under any of the relevant provisions, at least one shall be an approved medical practitioner.

(1A) Of the medical practitioners whose evidence is taken into account under section 52M(2)(a), 53(2)(a), 54(1)(c), 57A(2)(a) or 59A(3)(a) and (b) of this Act, at least one shall be employed at the hospital which is to be specified in the order or, as the case may be, direction.

(2) Written or oral evidence given for the purposes of section 52D(2)(a) or any of the relevant provisions shall include a statement as to whether the person giving the evidence is related to the accused and of any pecuniary interest which that person may have in the admission of the accused to hospital or his reception into guardianship.

(3) For the purposes of making a finding under section 52D(2)(a) of this Act or of any of the relevant provisions a report in writing purporting to be signed by a medical practitioner may, subject to the provisions of this section, be received in evidence without proof of the signature or qualifications of the practitioner; but the court may, in any case, require that the practitioner by whom such a report was signed be called to give oral evidence.

(4) Where any such report as aforesaid is tendered in evidence, otherwise than by or on behalf of the accused, then—

(a) if the accused is represented by counsel or solicitor, a copy of the report shall be given to his counsel or solicitor;

(b) if the accused is not so represented, the substance of the report shall be disclosed to the accused or, where he is a child under 16 years of age, to his parent or guardian if present in court;

(c) in any case, the accused may require that the practitioner by whom the report was signed be called to give oral evidence, and evidence to rebut the evidence contained in the report may be called by or on behalf of the accused,

and where the court is of the opinion that further time is necessary in the interests of the accused for consideration of that report, or the substance of any such report, it shall adjourn the case.

(5) For the purpose of calling evidence to rebut the evidence contained in any such report as aforesaid, arrangements may be made by or on behalf of an accused person detained in a hospital or, as respects a report for the purposes of section 54(1)(c) of this Act, remanded in custody for his examination by any medical practitioner, and any such examination may he made in private.

(6) In this section the "relevant provisions" means sections 52M(2)(a), 53(2)(a), 54(1)(c), 57A(2)(a), 58(1A)(a), 59A(2)(a) and 60C(2)(a).

(7) In this section, "approved medical practitioner" has the meaning given by section 22 of the Mental Health (Care and Treatment) (Scotland) Act 2003 (asp 13).

Amendments

Subss.(1), (2) and (3) as amended by Crime and Punishment (Scotland) Act 1997 (c.48) s.10(2) with effect from January 1, 1998 by SI 1997/2323 art.4, Sch.2.

Subss.(1A) and (6) as inserted by the above Act.

Section 61 as amended by Adults with Incapacity (Scotland) Act 2000 (asp 4) s.88 and Sch.5 para.26. Brought into force on April 1, 2002 by SSI 2001/81 (C.2). See Ward, *Adult Incapacity* (2003), para.11-87.

Subss.(1), (1A), (2), (3) and (6) as amended, and subs.(7) inserted, by Mental Health (Care and Treatment) (Scotland) Act 2003 (asp 13) Sch.4 para.8(10). Brought into force on October 5, 2005 by SSI 2005/161 (C.6).

Subss.(1), (3) and (5) as amended by Criminal Justice and Licensing (Scotland) Act 2010 (asp 13) Sch.7 para.41. Brought into force on June 25, 2012 by SSI 2012/160 (C.15) art.3.

Definitions

"hospital": s.307(1). A4-139.1
"medical practitioner": s.61(1).
"mental disorder": s.58(7).

[THE NEXT PARAGRAPH IS A4-140]

General Note

Section 61 specifies requirements as to medical evidence in respect of (i) a finding of insanity in bar of trial (s.54(1)(a)), (ii) the making of an interim hospital order (s.53(1)), (iii) the making of a temporary A4-140 hospital order (s.54(1)(c)), (iv) the making of a hospital or guardianship order (s.58(1)(a)), and (v) the newly introduced hospital direction (s.59A(3)(a) and (b) as inserted by s.6 of the Crime and Punishment (Scotland) Act 1997 as from January 1, 1998).

One of the purposes of this section is to ensure that medical practitioners who give evidence on the mental health of the person in question do so in the capacity of skilled witnesses, or at least one of them must to meet the terms of s.61(1). In addition, by virtue of subs.1(A) at least one of the medical practitioners involved must be employed in the proposed receiving hospital. This requirement is presumably intended to ensure that facilities will be available at that hospital and that at an early stage a practitioner experienced in the treatment of mental illness has had an input to the case.

Transfer of person to suitable hospital

A4-140.1 **61A.**—(1) Subsection (2) below applies in relation to a person who is subject to—

(a) an assessment order,
(b) a treatment order,
(c) an interim compulsion order, or
(d) a temporary compulsion order (see section 54(1)(c) of this Act).

(2) The person's responsible medical officer may transfer the person from the specified hospital to another hospital.

(3) The responsible medical officer may transfer the person only if satisfied that, for the purpose for which the order in question is made—

(a) the specified hospital is not suitable, and
(b) the other hospital is suitable.

(4) In considering the suitability of each hospital, the responsible medical officer is to have particular regard to the specific requirements and needs in the person's case.

(5) As far before the transfer as practicable, the responsible medical officer must—

(a) inform the person of the reason for the transfer,
(b) notify the managers of the specified hospital, and
(c) obtain the consent of—
  (i) the managers of the other hospital, and
  (ii) the Scottish Ministers.

(6) As soon after the transfer as practicable, the responsible medical officer must notify—

(a) any solicitor known by the officer to be acting for the person, and
(b) the court which made the order in question.

(7) A person may be transferred under subsection (2) above only once with respect to the order in question.

(8) Where a person is transferred under subsection (2) above, the order in question has effect as if the other hospital were the specified hospital.

(9) In this section—

"managers" has the meaning given by section 329(1) of the Mental Health (Treatment and Care) Scotland) Act 2003,

"responsible medical officer" has the meaning given by section 329(4) of that Act,

"specified hospital" means hospital to which the person is admitted by virtue of the order in question.

AMENDMENTS

Section 61A inserted by Mental Health (Scotland) Act 2015 (asp 9) s.46(3). Brought into force on 30 June 2017 by SSI 2017/197 art.2 and Sch.

DEFINITIONS

A4-140.2 "assessment order": s.52D(2).
"interim compulsion order": s.53.

"managers": s.61A(9).
"responsible medical officer": s.61A(9).
"specified hospital": s.61A(9).
"temporary compulsion order": s.54(1)(c).
"treatment order": s.52M

General Note

This provision allows a responsible medical officer to move a patient from one hospital specified in an order of the type mentioned to another hospital. This allows flexibility in the exercise of discretion and removes any uncertainty as to the detention. Notification to interested parties is required as soon as practical. A4-140.3

Specification of hospital unit

61B.—(1) A reference in this Part to a hospital may be read as a reference to a hospital unit. A4-140.4

(2) In the operation of section 61A of this Act in relation to a transfer from one hospital unit to another within the same hospital—

(a) subsection (2) of that section applies by virtue of subsection (1) of that section where the order in question specifies the hospital unit in which the person is to be detained,

(b) in subsection (5) of that section—

(i) paragraph (b) is to be ignored,

(ii) in paragraph (c)(i), the reference to the managers of the other hospital is to be read as a reference to the managers of the hospital in which the person is detained.

(3) For the purposes of this section, "hospital unit" means any part of a hospital which is treated as a separate unit.

Amendments

Section 61B inserted by Mental Health (Scotland) Act 2015 (asp 9) s.47(2). Brought into force on 30 June 2017 by SSI 2017/197 art.2 and Sch.

Definitions

"hospital unit": s.61B(3). A4-140.5

General Note

The discretion allowed to a responsible medical officer by s.61A above is amended to a degree where such transfer is between units of the same hospital. Notification to interested parties is still nevertheless required as soon as practical. A4-140.6

[THE NEXT PARAGRAPH IS A4-141]

Appeals under Part VI

Appeal by accused not criminally responsible or unfit for trial

62.—(1) A person may appeal to the appropriate Appeal Court against— A4-141

(a) a finding made under section 54(1) of this Act that he is unfit for trial so that his trial cannot proceed or continue, or the refusal of the court to make such a finding;

(b) a finding under section 55(2) of this Act; or

(c) an order made under section 57(2) of this Act.

(2) An appeal under subsection (1) above shall be—

(a) in writing; and

(b) lodged—

(i) in the case of an appeal under paragraph (a) of that subsection, not later than seven days after the date of the finding or refusal which is the subject of the appeal;

(ii) in the case of an appeal under paragraph (b), or both paragraphs (b) and (c) of that subsection, not later than 28 days after the conclusion of the examination of facts;

(iii) in the case of an appeal under paragraph (c) of that subsection against an order made on an acquittal, by reason of the special defence set out in section 51A of this Act, not later than 14 days after the date of the acquittal;

(iv) in the case of an appeal under that paragraph against an order made on a finding under section 55(2), not later than 14 days after the conclusion of the examination of facts,

or within such longer period as the appropriate Appeal Court may, on cause shown, allow.

(3) Where the examination of facts was held in connection with proceedings on indictment, subsections (1)(a) and (2)(b)(i) above are without prejudice to section 74(1) of this Act.

(4) Where an appeal is taken under subsection (1) above, the period from the date on which the appeal was lodged until it is withdrawn or disposed of shall not count towards any time limit applying in respect of the case.

(5) An appellant in an appeal under this section shall be entitled to be present at the hearing of the appeal unless the appropriate Appeal Court determines that his presence is not practicable or appropriate.

(6) In disposing of an appeal under subsection (1) above the appropriate Appeal Court may—

(a) affirm the decision of the court of first instance;

(b) make any other finding, order or other disposal which that court could have made at the time when it made the finding or order which is the subject of the appeal; or

(c) remit the case to that court with such directions in the matter as the High Court thinks fit.

(7) Section 60 of this Act shall not apply in relation to any order as respects which a person has a right of appeal under subsection (1)(c) above.

(8) In this section, "appropriate Appeal Court" means—

(a) in the case of an appeal under subsection (1) against a finding or refusal, or an order made, in proceedings on indictment, the High Court;

(b) in the case of an appeal under subsection (1) against a finding or refusal, or an order made, in summary proceedings, the Sheriff Appeal Court.

AMENDMENTS

Subs.(6)(b) as amended by Crime and Punishment (Scotland) Act 1997 (c.48) Sch.1 para.21(7) with effect from 1 January 1998 by SI 1997/2323 art.4, Sch.2.

Heading and subss.(1)(a) and (2)(b) as amended by Criminal Justice and Licensing (Scotland) Act 2010 (asp 13) Sch.7 para.42. Brought into force on 25 June 2012 by SSI 2012/160 (C.15) art.3.

Subss.(1), (2), (5) and (6) as amended, subs.(8) inserted, by Courts Reform (Scotland) Act 2014 (Consequential Provisions No.2) Order 2015 (SSI 2015/338) Sch.2 para.5 (effective 22 September 2015).

DEFINITIONS

A4-141.1 "examination of facts": s.54(1)(b).
"High Court": s.307(1).
"order": s.307(1).

[THE NEXT PARAGRAPH IS A4-142]

GENERAL NOTE

Subs.(1)

A4-142 Under the previous law, ss.174(1) and 375(2) of the 1975 Act enabled a court to find a person insane in bar of trial. An accused person had no right of appeal either against such a finding or against the refusal of any plea or motion that such a finding should be made. The only exception was where the finding was made at a preliminary diet in solemn proceedings in which event the accused had a right of appeal by s.76A(1) of the 1975 Act.

The new section provides the accused under solemn or summary procedure with rights of appeal in relation to any findings, or the refusal to make a finding, that the accused is insane in bar of trial and against findings made by, and orders made at, examinations of fact. Although such appeals must be made in comparatively short periods of time, longer periods may be allowed by the High Court of Justiciary on cause shown. The appellate judges have a broad range of powers to affirm or vary decisions and orders appealed against and to remit cases with directions.

In *ASG v HM Advocate* [2019] HCJAC 91 (a case of causing death by dangerous driving in which an accused was unfit on medical evidence to stand trial because of vascular dementia) the appellate judges of the High Court of Justiciary took the opportunity, at [18], to make some observations about the powers of the court in an appeal under s.62(1) of the 1995 Act against a finding made under s.55(2) of the same Act. It was noted that reference in the statute to "appeal" is quite unqualified. There is no restriction, for example, limiting an appeal to certain grounds. That suggested that in an appeal of this sort the appeal court is in a similar position to the Inner House of the Court of Session when reviewing a decision by a Lord Ordinary. Accordingly, the principles governing the exercise by an appellate court of its powers to interfere with a decision at first instance, which are discussed in *McGraddie v McGraddie*, 2014 S.C. (UKSC) 12; *Henderson v Foxworth Investments Ltd*, 2014 S.C. (UKSC) 203 at [66]–[67]; *Royal Bank of Scotland Plc v Carlyle*, 2015 S.C. (UKSC) 93; and *AW v Greater Glasgow Health Board* [2017] CSIH 58 at [38]–[52], will apply. Also, in *ASG v HM Advocate*, criticism was not made by the appellant of the determination of the primary facts at the examination earlier but criticism was directed on his behalf at the inferences drawn from those facts. The appellate judges also asserted that these matters, the drawing of an inference and the application of the law to the facts, are the sorts of decisions which appellate courts are generally well equipped to reconsider for themselves.

Appeal by prosecutor where accused found not criminally responsible or unfit for trial

63.—(1) The prosecutor may appeal to the appropriate Appeal Court on a point of law against— A4-143

(a) a finding under subsection (1) of section 54 of this Act that an accused is unfit for trial so that his trial cannot proceed or continue;

(b) an acquittal by reason of the special defence set out in section 51A of this Act;

(c) an acquittal under section 55(3) of this Act (whether or not by reason of the special defence set out in section 51A of this Act); or

(d) [...]

(2) An appeal under subsection (1) above shall be—

(a) in writing; and

(b) lodged—

(i) in the case of an appeal under paragraph (a) or (b) of that subsection, not later than seven days after the finding or, as the case may be, the acquittal which is the subject of the appeal;

(ii) in the case of an appeal under paragraph (c) of that subsection, not later than seven days after the conclusion of the examination of facts,

or within such longer period as the appropriate Appeal Court may, on cause shown, allow.

(3) Where the examination of facts was held in connection with proceedings on indictment, subsections (1)(a) and (2)(b)(i) above are without prejudice to section 74(1) of this Act.

(4) A respondent in an appeal under this subsection shall be entitled to be present at the hearing of the appeal unless the appropriate Appeal Court determines that his presence is not practicable or appropriate.

(5) In disposing of an appeal under subsection (1) above the appropriate Appeal Court may—

(a) affirm the decision of the court of first instance;

(b) make any other finding, order or disposal which that court could have made at the time when it made the finding or acquittal which is the subject of the appeal; or

(c) remit the case to that court with such directions in the matter as the appropriate Appeal Court thinks fit.

(6) In this section, "the prosecutor" means, in relation to proceedings on indictment, the Lord Advocate.

(7) In this section, "appropriate Appeal Court" means—

(a) in the case of an appeal under subsection (1) against a finding or an acquittal made in proceedings on indictment, the High Court;

(b) in the case of an appeal under subsection (1) against a finding or an acquittal made in summary proceedings, the Sheriff Appeal Court.

AMENDMENTS

Subs.(5)(b) as amended by Crime and Punishment (Scotland) Act 1997 (c.48) Sch.1 para.21(8) with effect from 1 January 1998 by SI 1997/2323 art.4, Sch.2.

Subs.(1)(d) as repealed by the above Act.

Heading and subs.(1) as amended by Criminal Justice and Licensing (Scotland) Act 2010 (asp 13) Sch.7 para.43. Brought into force on 25 June 2012 by SSI 2012/160 (C.15) art.3.

Subss.(1), (2), (4) and (5) as amended, subs.(7) inserted, by Courts Reform (Scotland) Act 2014 (Consequential Provisions No.2) Order 2015 (SSI 2015/338) Sch.2 para.5 (effective 22 September 2015).

DEFINITIONS

A4-143.1 "examination of facts": s.54(1)(b).
"High Court": s.307(1).
"order": s.307(1).
"prosecutor": s.63(6).

[THE NEXT PARAGRAPH IS A4-144]

GENERAL NOTE

A4-144 Under the previous law, ss.174(1) and 375(2) of the 1975 Act enabled a court to find a person insane in bar of trial. The Crown had no right of appeal against such a finding unless it had been made at a preliminary diet in solemn proceedings, in which event the Crown had a right of appeal by s.76A(1) of the 1975 Act.

This section now provides the Crown with a right of appeal similar to those given to the accused under s.62. The Crown may appeal against a finding of insanity in bar of trial, against a trial verdict of acquittal on the ground of insanity, and against any acquittal at an examination of facts. In each of these the appeal may be only on a point of law. Note also s.60A which allows the prosecutor a right of appeal against hospital orders, etc. made where an accused is found to be insane.

PART VII – SOLEMN PROCEEDINGS

The indictment

Prosecution on indictment

A4-145 **64.**—(1) All prosecutions for the public interest before the High Court or before the sheriff sitting with a jury shall proceed on indictment at the instance of Her Majesty's Advocate.

(2) The indictment may be in the forms—

(a) set out in Schedule 2 to this Act; or

(b) prescribed by Act of Adjournal,

or as nearly as may be in such form.

(3) Indictments in proceedings before the High Court shall be signed by the Lord Advocate or one of his deputes.

(4) Indictments in proceedings before the sheriff sitting with a jury shall be signed by the procurator fiscal, and the words "By Authority of Her Majesty's Advocate" shall be prefixed to the signature of the procurator fiscal.

(5) The principal record and service copies of indictments and all notices of citation, lists of witnesses, productions and jurors, and all other official documents required in a prosecution on indictment may be either written or printed or partly written and partly printed.

(6) Schedule 3 to this Act shall have effect as regards indictments under this Act.

AMENDMENTS

Subs.(1) as amended by Criminal Justice and Licensing (Scotland) Act 2010 (asp 13) s.60(2). Brought into force on 13 December 2010 (subject to savings provisions in art.5) by SSI 2010/413 (C.28) art.2, Sch.1 para.1.

DEFINITIONS

"High Court": s.307(1). A4-145.1
"indictment": s.307(1).
"procurator fiscal": s.307(1).

[THE NEXT PARAGRAPH IS A4-146]

GENERAL NOTE

The provisions dealing with the latitudes as to time, place, capacity and implied terms previously contained in ss.43 to 67 of the 1975 Act, in relation to solemn proceedings, and s.311 relative to summary proceedings, are now incorporated in Sch.3 to the 1995 Act. It remains a moot point what practical benefit is derived from preserving the indictment styles of the 1887 Act as Sch.2 does. The subject of implied charges, or alternative verdicts, was discussed in *McMaster v HM Advocate*, 2001 S.C.C.R. 517 with particular reference to Convention principles. Schedule 3 of the Act was amended by the Criminal Justice and Licensing (Scotland) Act 2010 (asp 13) to enable a charge of uttering to lead, where appropriate, to conviction alternatively of fraud. Section 49 of the 2010 Act created a statutory offence of possession or control of articles for use in the commission of fraud. A4-146

Section 287 of the 1995 Act makes provision for the maintenance of proceedings in the event of the death of, or demission of office by, the Lord Advocate. Even where the Solicitor General exercised his powers in terms of s.287(2) following the resignation of the Lord Advocate in February 2000, it is of note that conform to subs.(4), sheriff and jury indictments continued to have the words "By Authority of Her Majesty's Advocate" upon them. While the terms of subs.(4) appear mandatory (and reflect the fact that a procurator fiscal's commission was protected under the Sheriff Courts and Legal Officers (Scotland) Act 1927 (c.35)) regard has to be paid to *Christie v HM Advocate*, 2004 J.C. 13 where only the words "By Authority" preceded the fiscal's signature. Having regard to the full narrative of the libel, the Appeal Court held there to be neither a nullity nor material prejudice to the appellants. See the broad discussion in *Hester v MacDonald*, 1961 S.C. 370; 1961 S.L.T. 414. A similarly broad approach was evident in the summary case of *Gates v Donnelly*, 2004 S.L.T. 33, discussed at A4-311 below, but the latitude given to the Crown is not unlimited. The decision in *Christie* above has to be read in conjunction with *HM Advocate v Crawford*, 2006 J.C. 57, a case where the indictment served upon the accused was missing the words "By Authority of Her Majesty's Advocate" entirely and was signed by the "Acting Procurator Fiscal". The omission entirely of the first phrase was fatal to proceedings on that indictment; the court did not regard the second phrase (instead of "Procurator Fiscal") as of any moment and was prepared to regard that error as being excusable in character.

Latitude as to dates in charges is granted to the Crown by Sch.3 to the Act at para.4 but subject to the general tests of fairness—set out in *HM Advocate v Hastings*, 1985 S.L.T. 446—and irreversible prejudice, in *McFadyen v Annan*, 1992 S.L.T. 163. See also the discussion of Convention issues in *Stewart v HM Advocate*, 2005 G.W.D. 27-523. Law in this area is not well settled but it is clear that care has to be taken by the Crown when selecting the date or period to be libelled in any charge. Where dates (as distinct from a single date) are libelled, this may well have the effect of removing any latitude in altering either of them, particularly where a time span in excess of one month has been selected. Where the precise date of the offence is not an essential element, and in the absence of any prejudice to the accused, the Crown can move to amend the libel. Practice ordinarily permits a month on either side—what is unresolved is what powers of amendment are open to the Crown where the libel charges the commission of an offence over a longer period. This problem often assumes significance in historic sexual abuse prosecutions. See *Andrew v HM Advocate*, 1982 S.C.C.R. 539 and *Kearney v Ramage*, 2007 S.C.C.R. 35.

The extent of the Crown's power to amend the libel to correspond to evidence led or agreed is discussed at A4-299 below. The libelling of charges in an indictment does not irrevocably commit the Crown to leading evidence in support of all charges at trial; that remains a matter in the discretion of the prosecutor and a decision not to lead evidence cannot ordinarily be regarded as prejudicial per se. See *Donnell v HM Advocate*, 2010 S.C.L. 265. That said, there must be a proper foundation for inclusion of any charge in a criminal libel either as a probative sufficiency or as a means to enable evidence to be led admissibly. The inclusion of charges, or aggravations, where there has never been supporting evidence is certainly improper and may warrant a finding of Crown oppression: see *HM Advocate v JRD* [2015] HCJ 85; 2015 S.C.C.R. 413 in which, unusually, the court deserted the indictment *simpliciter*.

Section 288 below entitles the Lord Advocate to be advised of, and be heard in relation to, any proposed private prosecution; see *X v Sweeney*, 1983 S.L.T. 48 which proceeded by Bill of Criminal Letters, the Lord Advocate offering no objection, following an earlier formal intimation by the Crown to the accused of no further proceedings.

The complex factors involved in the prosecution of a non-natural person (in this case a public limited company charged with culpable homicide following fatalities in a gas explosion) are discussed at length in *Transco Plc v HM Advocate*, 2004 S.L.T. 41. See the discussion "Corporate Culpable Homicide" by P.W. Ferguson in 2004 S.L.T. 97 noting the particular difficulty in attributing mens rea to corporate entities.

Prevention of delay in trials

A4-147 **65.**—(1) Subject to subsections (2) and (3) below, an accused shall not be tried on indictment for any offence unless—

(a) where an indictment has been served on the accused in respect of the High Court, a preliminary hearing is commenced within the period of 11 months; and

(aa) where an indictment has been served on the accused in respect of the sheriff court, a first diet is commenced within the period of 11 months;

(b) in any case, the trial is commenced within the period of 12 months, of the first appearance of the accused on petition in respect of the offence.

(1A) If the preliminary hearing (where subsection (1)(a) above applies), the first diet (where subsection (1)(aa) above applies) or the trial is not so commenced, the accused—

(a) shall be discharged forthwith from any indictment as respects the offence; and

(b) shall not at any time be proceeded against on indictment as respects the offence.

(2) Nothing in subsection (1) or (1A) above shall bar the trial of an accused for whose apprehension a warrant has been granted for failure to appear at a diet in the case.

(3) On an application made for the purpose—

(a) where an indictment has been served on the accused in respect of the High Court, a single judge of that court may, on cause shown, extend either or both of the periods of 11 and 12 months specified in subsection (1) above; or

(b) in any other case, the sheriff may, on cause shown, extend either or both of the periods of 11 and 12 months specified in that subsection.

(3A) An application under subsection (3) shall not be made at any time when an appeal made with leave under s.74(1) of this Act has not been disposed of by the High Court.

(4) Subject to subsections (5) to (9) below, an accused who is committed for any offence until liberated in due course of law shall not be detained by virtue of that committal for a total period of more than—

(a) 80 days, unless within that period the indictment is served on him, which failing he shall be entitled to be admitted to bail; or

(aa) where an indictment has been served on the accused in respect of the High Court—

(i) 110 days, unless a preliminary hearing in respect of the case is commenced within that period, which failing he shall be entitled to be admitted to bail; or

(ii) 140 days, unless the trial of the case is commenced within that period, which failing he shall be entitled to be admitted to bail;

(b) where an indictment has been served on the accused in respect of the sheriff court,

(i) 110 days, unless a first diet in respect of the case is commenced within that period, which failing he shall be entitled to be admitted to bail; or

(ii) 140 days,

unless the trial of the case is commenced within that period, which failing he shall be entitled to be admitted to bail.

(4A) Where an indictment has been served on the accused in respect of the High Court, subsections (1)(a) and (4)(aa)(i) above shall not apply if the preliminary hearing has been dispensed with under section 72B(1) of this Act.

(5) On an application made for the purpose—

(a) in a case where, at the time the application is made, an indictment has not been served on the accused, a single judge of the High Court; or

(b) in any other case, the court specified in the notice served under section 66(6) of this Act,

may, on cause shown, extend any period mentioned in subsection (4) above.

(5A) Before determining an application under subsection (3) or (5) above, the judge or, as the case may be, the court shall give the parties an opportunity to be heard.

(5B) However, where all the parties join in the application, the judge or, as the case may be, the court may determine the application without hearing the parties and, accordingly, may dispense with any hearing previously appointed for the purpose of considering the application.

(6)–(7) […]

(8) The grant or refusal of any application to extend the periods mentioned in this section may be appealed against by note of appeal presented to the High Court; and that Court may affirm, reverse or amend the determination made on such application.

(8A) Where an accused is, by virtue of subsection (4) above, entitled to be admitted to bail, the accused shall, unless he has been admitted to bail by the Lord Advocate, be brought forthwith before—

(a) in a case where an indictment has not yet been served on the accused, a single judge of the High Court; or

(b) in any other case, the court specified in the notice served under section 66(6) of this Act.

(8B) Where an accused is brought before a judge or court under subsection (8A) above, the judge or, as the case may be, the court shall give the prosecutor an opportunity to make an application under subsection (5) above.

(8C) If the prosecutor does not make such an application or, if such an application is made but is refused, the judge or, as the case may be, the court shall, after giving the prosecutor an opportunity to be heard, admit the accused to bail.

(8D) Where such an application is made but is refused and the prosecutor appeals against the refusal, the accused—

(a) may continue to be detained under the committal warrant for no more than 72 hours from the granting of bail under subsection (8C) above or for such longer period as the High Court may allow; and

(b) on expiry of that period, shall, whether the appeal has been disposed of or not, be released on bail subject to the conditions imposed.

(9) For the purposes of this section,

(a) where the accused is cited in accordance with subsection (4)(b) of section 66 of this Act, the indictment shall be deemed to have been served on the accused;

(b) a preliminary hearing shall be taken to commence when it is called;
(ba) a first diet shall be taken to commence when it is called;
(c) a trial shall be taken to commence when the oath is administered to the jury.

(10) In calculating the periods of 11 and 12 months specified in subsections (1) and (3) above there shall be left out of account any period during which the accused is detained, other than while serving a sentence of imprisonment or detention, in any other part of the United Kingdom or in any of the Channel Islands or the Isle of Man in any prison or other institution or place mentioned in subsection (1) or (1A) of section 29 of the Criminal Justice Act 1961 (transfer of prisoners for certain judicial purposes).

AMENDMENTS

Subsection (3A) inserted by Crime and Punishment (Scotland) Act 1997 Sch.1 para.21(9) with effect from 1 August 1997 in terms of SI 1997/1712 art.21(9).

Subsection (1) as amended by Criminal Procedure and Investigations Act 1996 (c.25) s.73(3).

Subsections (1)(a), (b), (1A), (3)(a), (b), (4)(aa), (4A), (5A), (5B), (8A)–(8D), (9)(a)–(c) inserted, subs.(5) substituted and subss.(1)–(3), (4)(a), (b), (9), (10) as amended by Criminal Procedure (Amendment) (Scotland) Act 2004 (asp 5) s.6(2)–(7), (9)–(11). Brought into force on 1 February 2005 by SSI 2004/405 (C.28) art.2.

Subsections (6) and (7) repealed by Criminal Procedure (Amendment) (Scotland) Act 2004 (asp 5) s.6(8). Brought into force on 1 February 2005 by SSI 2004/405 (C.28) art.2.

Subsections (2), (3)(b) as amended by Criminal Proceedings etc. (Reform) (Scotland) Act 2007 (asp 6) ss.26, 80 and Sch. para.12. Brought into force on 10 December 2007 by SSI 2007/479 art.3 and Sch.

Subsections (1), (1A), (4)(b), (9) as amended by Criminal Justice (Scotland) Act 2016 (asp 1) s.79. Brought into force on 29 May 2017 by SSI 2017/99 art.3, for the purposes of any indictment served on an accused on or after that day; not yet in force otherwise.

Prevention of delay in trials.

A4-147A *65.—(1) Subject to subsections (2) and (3) below, an accused shall not be tried on indictment for any offence unless,*

(a) where an indictment has been served on the accused in respect of the High Court, a preliminary hearing is commenced within the period of 11 months; and
(aa) where an indictment has been served on the accused in respect of the sheriff court, a first diet is commenced within the period of 11 months;
(b) in any case, the trial is commenced within the period of 12 months, of the first appearance of the accused on petition in respect of the offence.

(1A) If the preliminary hearing (where subsection (1)(a) above applies), the first diet (where subsection (1)(aa) above applies) or the trial is not so commenced, the accused

(a) shall be discharged forthwith from any indictment as respects the offence; and
(b) shall not at any time be proceeded against on indictment as respects the offence.

(2) Nothing in subsection (1) or (1A) above shall bar the trial of an accused for whose apprehension a warrant has been granted for failure to appear at a diet in the case.

(3) On an application made for the purpose,

(a) where an indictment has been served on the accused in respect of the High Court, a single judge of that court may, on cause shown, extend either or both of the periods of 11 and 12 months specified in subsection (1) above; or
(b) in any other case, the sheriff may, on cause shown, extend either or both of the periods of 11 and 12 months specified in that subsection.

(3A) An application under subsection (3) shall not be made at any time when an appeal made with leave under section 74(1) of this Act has not been disposed of by the High Court.

(4) Subject to subsections (5) to (9) below, an accused who is committed for any offence until liberated in due course of law shall not be detained by virtue of that committal for a total period of more than—

(a) 80 days, unless within that period the indictment is served on him, which failing he shall be entitled to be admitted to bail;

(aa) where an indictment has been served on the accused in respect of the High Court–

(i) 110 days, unless a preliminary hearing in respect of the case is commenced within that period, which failing he shall be entitled to be admitted to bail; or

(ii) 140 days, unless the trial of the case is commenced within that period, which failing he shall be entitled to be admitted to bail; or

(b) where an indictment has been served on the accused in respect of the sheriff court,

(i) 110 days, unless a first diet in respect of the case is commenced within that period, which failing he shall be entitled to be admitted to bail; or

(ii) 140 days,

unless the trial of the case is commenced within that period, which failing he shall be entitled to be admitted to bail.

(4A) Where an indictment has been served on the accused in respect of the High Court, subsections (1)(a) and (4)(aa)(i) above shall not apply if the preliminary hearing has been dispensed with under section 72B(1) of this Act.

(5) On an application made for the purpose–

(a) in a case where, at the time the application is made, an indictment has not been served on the accused, a single judge of the High Court; or

(b) in any other case, the court specified in the notice served under section 66(6) of this Act,

may, on cause shown, extend any period mentioned in subsection (4) above.

(5A) Before determining an application under subsection (3) or (5) above, the judge or, as the case may be, the court shall give the parties an opportunity to be heard.

(5B) However, where all the parties join in the application, the judge or, as the case may be, the court may determine the application without hearing the parties and, accordingly, may dispense with any hearing previously appointed for the purpose of considering the application.

(8) The grant or refusal of any application to extend the periods mentioned in this section may be appealed against by note of appeal presented to the High Court; and that Court may affirm, reverse or amend the determination made on such application.

(8A) Where an accused is, by virtue of subsection (4) above, entitled to be admitted to bail, the accused shall, unless he has been admitted to bail by the Lord Advocate, be brought forthwith before–

(a) in a case where an indictment has not yet been served on the accused, a single judge of the High Court; or

(b) in any other case, the court specified in the notice served under section 66(6) of this Act.

(8B) Where an accused is brought before a judge or court under subsection (8A) above, the judge or, as the case may be, the court shall give the prosecutor an opportunity to make an application under subsection (5) above.

(8C) If the prosecutor does not make such an application or, if such an application is made but is refused, the judge or, as the case may be, the court shall, after giving the prosecutor an opportunity to be heard, admit the accused to bail.

(8D) Where such an application is made but is refused and the prosecutor appeals against the refusal, the accused–

(a) may continue to be detained under the committal warrant for no more than 72 hours from the granting of bail under subsection (8C) above or for such longer period as the High Court may allow; and

(b) on expiry of that period, shall, whether the appeal has been disposed of or not, be released on bail subject to the conditions imposed.

(9) For the purposes of this section,

(a) where the accused is cited in accordance with subsection (4)(b) of section 66 of this Act, the indictment shall be deemed to have been served on the accused;

(b) a preliminary hearing shall be taken to commence when it is called;

(ba) a first diet shall be taken to commence when it is called; and

(c) a trial shall be taken to commence when the oath is administered to the jury.

(10) In calculating the periods of 11 and 12 months specified in subsections (1) and (3) above there shall be left out of account any period during which the accused is detained, other than while serving a sentence of imprisonment or detention, in any other part of the United Kingdom or in any of the Channel Islands or the Isle of Man in any prison or other institution or place mentioned in subsection (1) or (1A) of section 29 of the Criminal Justice Act 1961 (transfer of prisoners for certain judicial purposes).

(11) In calculating any of the periods specified in subsection (12), no account is to be taken of the suspension period.

(12) Those periods are—

(a) any period mentioned in subsection (1), including any such period as extended—

(i) under subsection (3),

(ii) on appeal under subsection (8), or

(iii) under section 74(4)(c),

(b) any period mentioned in subsection (4), including any such period as extended—

(i) under subsection (5), or

(ii) on appeal under subsection (8).

(13) For the purpose of subsection (11), the suspension period is the period of 6 months beginning with whichever is the later of—

(a) the day on which paragraph 10 of schedule 4 of the Coronavirus (Scotland) Act 2020 comes into force,

(b) the day on which—

(i) in relation to a period specified in subsection (12)(a), the accused first appears on petition in respect of the offence, or

(ii) in relation to a period specified in subsection (12)(b), the accused is committed for the offence until liberated in due course of law.

AMENDMENTS

In relation to COVID-19, s.65 as amended by Coronavirus (Scotland) Act 2020 (asp 7) Sch.4(4) para.10(3) (effective 7 April 2020).

DEFINITIONS

"High Court": s.307(1). **A4-147.1**
"indictment": s.307(1).
"offence": s.307(1).
"prison": s.307(1).

[THE NEXT PARAGRAPH IS A4-148]

GENERAL NOTE

A4-148 While the origins of these provisions can be traced back to the Act Anent Wrongeous Imprisonment of 1701 and provide the mandatory time frames for solemn criminal proceedings in Scotland, they have undergone substantial changes since the Criminal Justice (Scotland) Act 1980. Until the introduction of s.6 of that Act, trial proceedings against anyone accused remanded for solemn trial had to be concluded within 110 days; after 1980 the provision was modified to require trial proceedings to commence within the 110 day period. The 2004 Act further alters the time bars in relation to High Court proceedings and substantial procedural changes.

The comprehensive review into High Court procedures conducted by Lord Bonomy ("*Improving Practice: 2002 Review of the Practices and Procedure of the High Court of Justiciary*") focused upon the substantial growth in High Court business in recent years and the six-fold rise in motions for adjournment (many in custody cases) since 1995.

The findings of the Bonomy Report led to a Scottish Executive White Paper "*Modernising Justice in Scotland: The Reform of the High Court of Justiciary*" (2003) and in turn to the Criminal Procedure (Amendment) (Scotland) Act 2004 (asp 5) whose most substantial provisions are to introduce pre-trial preliminary diets in the High Court (drawing heavily upon the first diets long familiar in sheriff solemn cases), a vigorous regime of pre-trial enquiry to ensure that indicted cases are fully prepared for trial, and the reform of the time bar provisions, at least so far as they relate to High Court proceedings. Equally significantly, the outcome for a remanded accused whose case is not commenced within the statutory time scale is that the court may well admit him to bail rather than, as previously, he being forever free of all legal process in relation to the matter.

Since the passing of the 2004 Act the procedural distinctions between sheriff court solemn and High Court proceedings have all but disappeared. The main difference now is found in subs.(4); custody trials in the sheriff court ordinarily must commence within 110 days of full committal, rather than the 140 day time frame applying to High Court custody cases.

It is axiomatic that the statutory provisions found in s.65, whether an accused person is remanded for trial or is at liberty, are triggered by an appearance on petition (see s.34 above) and do not take effect in situations where an accused has been indicted without first having appeared on petition. (See the fuller discussion in the Note to s.34). Less appreciated is the impact upon remanded accused whose remand period, after petition appearance, is interrupted by a sentence of imprisonment or, indeed, a further petition appearance; in such circumstances only the period of remand solely referable to each petition is calculated towards the 110 or 140 day time limits.

Specific provisions in relation to accused remanded for the purposes of assessment of mental health and fitness in both summary and solemn proceedings, are found in s.52T above, but the same statutory time frames (found in ss.65 and 147 of the Act) still apply.

Subss.(1), (1A) and (2)

Subs.(1) now requires that an accused on bail and indicted for trial in the High Court has to be served with an indictment no later than 10 months after the date of his first petition appearance.

Instead of being indicted to a trial diet in the High Court, the accused is now required to appear at a preliminary diet within 11 months of that first appearance: the purposes of the preliminary diet are set out in s.72 below. (These timescales would not apply to an accused who was indicted without a first petition appearance and, as subs.(2) provides, fly off in any solemn proceedings following a failure to appear at any diet—see *Kelly v HM Advocate*, 2002 S.L.T. 43 and *HM Advocate v Taylor*, 1996 S.L.T. 836).

Section 66(6)(b) stipulates that a period of not less than 29 clear days must separate the preliminary and trial diets.

More familiar rules apply to sheriff solemn proceedings; subs.(1)(b) restates the requirement that such bail proceedings must be commenced by indictment within one year of petition appearance. Reference then has to be made to s.66(6)(a) of the Act which provides for a first diet not less than 15 clear days after service of the indictment and a trial diet not less than 29 clear days after that service. A degree of flexibility exists in fixing the first diet since it must also occur not less than 10 clear days before the trial.

In all solemn proceedings it remains possible to tender an accelerated plea on an agreed libel in terms of s.76 of the Act.

Subs.(1A) of the Act provides a new constraint upon solemn bail proceedings by stipulating that they must be commenced by way of a preliminary diet in the High Court, or a trial diet in the sheriff court, within the 11 and 12 month times respectively, or else the accused is forever free of further proceedings in respect of the offence. As mentioned earlier, subs.(2) qualifies this provision as does subs.(3) which preserves the right of parties to apply to the court for an extension of time.

Subss.(3) and (3A)

The periods set out in subs.(1) commence with the date of the accused's first appearance on petition, whether he is committed for further examination as is usual, or fully committed, and halt in the High Court with the commencement of the preliminary hearing within 11 months and in all solemn proceedings, with the commencement of trial within the year. (Calculation of these dates is *de die in diem* not *de momento in momentum*; see *McCulloch v HM Advocate*, 1995 S.L.T. 918 and the discussion on the general topic at A4-292 below).

Prior to service of an indictment upon an accused on bail, *any* application for an extension falls to be considered by the sheriff having jurisdiction over the petition and he retains that power in relation to sheriff solemn proceedings once they are indicted for trial. (See *HM Advocate v Caulfield*, 1999 S.L.T. 1003). Matters are now more problematic in relation to High Court proceedings; once an accused on bail has been indicted, application has to be made to a High Court judge to extend timebars as necessary. More difficult is the position prior to indictment of a bail case self-evidently destined for the High Court, for example a murder or rape, since subs.(3)(b) only empowers a sheriff to extend the 12 (and not the 11) month period.

Application for a prospective or retrospective extension of these timebars would be competent (*Ashcroft v HM Advocate*, 1996 S.C.C.R. 608) but can only be considered afresh where the facts and circumstances are materially different from those argued originally (*Goldie v HM Advocate*, 2003 S.L.T. 1078). Subs.(3A) ensures that no application can be made while an appeal springing from a preliminary or first diet is ongoing.

Extension of 11-month time-bar in High Court proceedings (subs.(3))

A4-148.1 The same broad considerations, and case law, governing extensions of the year time bar upon proceedings apply equally to the statutory 11-month time-bar which has been introduced in High Court proceedings only. Within that 11 month period the court must hold a preliminary hearing diet (see s.72 below). In *HM Advocate v Freeman*, 2006 S.L.T. 35, the Crown in error fixed the preliminary hearing for a Sunday, a *dies non*. Rapidly appreciating the error, a one day extension was sought, and refused, at first instance. The Appeal Court allowed the extension, being critical of the initial lack of clarity of the Crown explanations given to the judge considering the application and doubtful of the defence's stated readiness for trial in a complex case where the libel had been substantially overhauled from the charges in the original petition. No prejudice had been demonstrated by the respondent.

[THE NEXT PARAGRAPH IS A4-149]

Extension of the one year time bar (subs.(3))

A4-149 Any such motion will be considered by a single judge and can be granted on cause shown. The judge does not have an absolute discretion when considering a motion to extend the 12-month (or now, by inference, the 11-month) period. Compare *Langan v HM Advocate*, 1997 S.C.C.R. 306, where the Appeal Court could divine no basis for the sheriff's grant of a retrospective extension and reduced the matter to a summary complaint, and *HM Advocate v Brown*, 1984 S.C.C.R. 347 in which it was held that the sheriff acted unreasonably in granting a defence adjournment while refusing an unopposed Crown motion for an extension. *McCulloch v HM Advocate*, 2001 S.L.T. 113 (discussed at A4-153 below) in which an extension of the year was allowed to enable re-indictment of the case, perhaps surprisingly since the Crown had commented upon the failure of a spouse to give evidence, illustrates the competing interests which must be must be weighed in the balance when considering applications for extension.

It would be a masterpiece of understatement to suggest that not all judicial interpretations of s.65 are easily reconciled; see *Ellis v HM Advocate*, 2001 S.C.C.R. 36 and the unease expressed (at [16]) over the discretionary powers vested by s.65(3), part of a provision ostensibly framed to prevent delay in solemn proceedings. *DMcL v HM Advocate*, 2015 S.C.C.R. 391, may perhaps mark an extreme—a seven year extension to time bar allowed—to enable mutually corroborative charges to be tried. The Appeal Court gave "particularly anxious scrutiny" before upholding such an extension. Significantly no ground of oppression had been led and no intimation of discontinuation of earlier proceedings had been given to the accused or his agent by the Crown.

In considering applications to extend time bar periods, the court will apply the two stage test from *HM Advocate v Swift*, 1984 J.C. 83; 1984 S.C.C.R. 216 at 226, as refined by *Early v HM Advocate*, 2006 S.L.T. 856, a full Bench decision.

Rather than, as hitherto, considering whether the situation has been produced by Crown failure and assessing the seriousness of that, the court must, first, establish whether a sufficient reason has been shown to justify grant of an extension having regard to *all* the circumstances, and, secondly, take account of those circumstances to consider whether its discretion to grant an extension should be exercised. Thus the court should assess any part the accused may have played in the delay by, for example, earlier defence motions to adjourn or discharge diets (see *Mitchell v HM Advocate* [2013] HCJAC 30), and the interests of parties other than the Crown and accused, as well as whether the circumstances were avoidable or not. Refer also to *HM Advocate v Crawford*, 2006 S.L.T. 456. In *Cowan v HM Advocate* [2017] HCJAC 73, notable as a successful defence appeal, the Appeal Court held that the court itself had to apply the first stage test, a matter which, given the nature of such appeals, was not to be considered as capable of concession or agreement by the parties; here the Crown had persistently indicted the accused on what was accepted to be a defective libel.

The scope of the first stage test can be seen in *HM Advocate v Clarke* [2016] HCJAC 2; 2017 S.C.C.R. 301 where the Appeal Court upheld refusal of further Crown application for extensions to time bars to enable investigation and possible incorporation of further petition charges against one of the accused. The court looked to the history of the proceedings and to the impact upon co-accused, not implicated in these fresh charges and who would face further delay to trial.

Significantly in *Clarke* the Appeal Court attached particular weight to the fact that the judge's refusal of extension simply pressed the Crown to begin the trial, and would not result in the proceedings falling. Note too that one of several solutions posited by his counsel in *Clarke*'s case (in an endeavour to expedite the trial) was the addition of an evidential docket to the libel against him alone.

In *Early* (at [8] and [9]) significant distinctions were drawn between errors pointing to positive culpability in the Crown performance on one hand and administrative mishaps on the other, and, indeed, a combination of both.

Systemic failures in the programming of sheriff solemn business, particularly the creation of what are self-evidently oversubscribed sittings demanding the churning of cases, are increasingly argued against the Crown: to date the Appeal Court has shown a marked disinclination to confirm such conclusions. It is evident that the sheriff would have to confirm there to have been such systemic failure: *Uruk v HM Advocate* [2014] HCJAC 46. Equally, however, it is clear, whatever view the Bench at first instance may form, that the presiding sheriff has no power *ex proprio motu* to adjourn a trial, having reached such a view, in the absence of a motion to adjourn. See *Akhtar v Murphy* [2014] HCJAC 80; 2014 S.C.C.R. 475, bills of advocation upheld after the presiding sheriff took such action despite opposition from all parties.

A degree of fault on the part of the Crown would not be fatal to an application for extension of the year period (*Mallison v HM Advocate*, 1987 S.C.C.R. 320 and *McGill v HM Advocate*, 1997 S.C.C.R. 230), but certainly failure to serve an indictment at a domicile of citation would attract particularly rigorous scrutiny (*HM Advocate v Swift*, 1984 S.C.C.R. 216; 1985 S.L.T. 26) while a libel which constituted a nullity would not generally warrant an extension; *Stenton v HM Advocate*, 1999 S.L.T. 255. Similarly, adjournment of a trial to a non-existent sitting, and efforts to constitute a sitting to overcome the error, led to refusal of a last-minute motion for extension of the year (see *Willoughby v HM Advocate*, 2000 S.C.C.R. 73). (Acknowledging that sittings have been abolished in the solemn courts, and that responsibility for the allocation of trial business, and presumably any fault, first rests with the court clerk, judgments more directly in point are awaited). *Rennie v HM Advocate*, 1998 S.C.C.R. 191 is probably an extreme example of the excusal of Crown fault, and may have been not unrelated to the fact that the complainer, in what had begun life as an allegation of rape and had been indicted as shameless indecency, was mentally backward; objection to the libel, which the Crown did not defend, was taken just four days prior to trial—the lateness of this challenge being a factor which the Appeal Court felt had wrongly been taken into consideration by the sheriff. Accordingly, the Appeal Court reviewed the decision to extend the time bar, held the fault on the part of the Crown in serving an indictment which they later conceded to be irrelevant was not entirely inexcusable and paid due regard to the seriousness of the allegations. The extension was upheld on appeal but, whether it accurately reflected the anticipated evidence or not, it could be said that the Crown had been too hasty in conceding that the libel was irrelevant. Remarkably, extensions following desertion of a sexual offences sheriff and jury trial, after the complainer's evidence, with a view to re-indictment as a rape in the High Court was supported by the Appeal Court, no fault being attributed to the Crown (see *TD v HM Advocate* [2013] HCJAC 130; 2013 S.C.C.R. 696). By contrast Crown failure to indict the accused on sexual charges (previously subject of petition appearances and a deserted trial diet at which the complainer had failed to appear), when the accused appeared in later proceedings involving the same complainer, led to refusal of applications to extend time bars substantially and retrospectively. The court found no evidence that the Crown had actively sought to enforce the witness apprehension warrant at all, while the accused had been entitled to regard the earlier conduct of the Crown as a signal of its intentions (*HM Advocate v Collins* [2013] HCJAC 167; 2014 S.C.C.R. 466).

A Crown error in serving an indictment upon the accused to call in Glasgow High Court, but with a Notice of Compearance (see Form 8.2-B at para.B1-96.1) calling him to appear at Paisley, late into the year was held on appeal not to be a major and fundamental error. The Appeal Court seemed to hint that an appearance by the accused at the Glasgow sitting would have sufficed to cure this defect, but taking account of the lack of prejudice to him and the gravity of the offence, allied to the rapidity of the Crown application for extension, felt able to grant an extension of the 12 month period (*HM Advocate v Fitzpatrick*, 2002 S.C.C.R. 758). Lack of urgency on the part of the Crown can be a factor; see *Palmer v HM Advocate*, 2002 S.C.C.R. 908. By way of contrast, Crown dilatoriness in securing a new trial diet following a successful appeal against dismissal of an indictment as irrelevant, inclined neither the sheriff (nor the Appeal Court) to grant the further extensions necessary to re-indict the proceedings; see *HM Advocate v Caldwell* [2010] HCJAC 12.

However, failure on the part of the police to execute service of an indictment timeously or to comply with express instructions are not faults of the prosecutor; see *Welsh v HM Advocate*, 1985 S.C.C.R. 404; *HM Advocate v Davies*, 1993 S.C.C.R. 645; *Coutts v HM Advocate*, 1992 S.C.C.R. 87. Even where the Crown instructed service of an indictment on the last available day with unclear instructions and in the knowledge that the accused had no proper domicile of citation, the Appeal Court felt able to uphold the grant of an extension; it was observed that the terms of the indictment were known to him some days before service and that no claim of prejudice had been advanced (*Finlay v HM Advocate*, 1998 S.L.T. 1235). It is clear that failure to intimate a change of domicile which results in service being unsuccessful at the accused's former address will not count against the Crown (*Black v HM Advocate*, 1990 S.C.C.R. 609); similarly the provision of an incomplete or imprecise address as domicile when seeking bail will not benefit an accused when service at that address proves to be defective (*Brown v HM Advocate*, 1998 S.L.T. 971).

In *Forrester v HM Advocate*, 1997 S.C.C.R. 9 the year had been extended twice already, on Crown motion, due to the prolonged illness of an essential witness. Before applying for a third extension the prosecutor had intimated to the defence, that if a further extension was opposed the Crown intended to lead the evidence of that witness, through use of the hearsay provisions of s.259 of the 1995 Act. The Crown then sought a last extension arguing that the illness of a vital witness was not its fault. A defence appeal against the grant of that third extension, founding inter alia upon the unwillingness of the Crown to lead evidence by means of s.259 for tactical reasons, was refused by the Appeal Court, which distinguished between the technical sufficiency of evidence available using the provisions in s.259 and the desirability of the jury hearing the testimony of such a vital witness and any cross-examination. Recourse to s.259 was not available to the Crown in *HM Advocate v Lewis* (High Court of Justiciary, May 29, 2002, unreported) where a principal witness, whose evidence was essential to proof of sexual offences using *Moorov*, was persistently unfit psychiatrically to give evidence. It was suggested that this condition was a consequence of those offences against her. Trial was postponed six times with appropriate extensions of the year time bar due to the gravity of the offences. Absence of an essential Crown witness, allied to the four day delay in extracting his warrant through "technical problems" was upheld as a legitimate ground for extension of the 12 month time bar in *Neil v HM Advocate*, 2009 G.W.D. 2-32. See too *Early v HM Advocate*, 2006 S.L.T. 856 and also see *HM Advocate v Paterson*, 2013 S.C.C.R. 20. More unusually, the sheriff's decision to desert proceedings *pro loco et tempore* and to extend the year time bar were upheld on appeal in a case where both he, and the prosecutor, had gone too far in comforting a child witness who had broken down in the course of her evidence (see *McKie v HM Advocate*, 1997 S.L.T. 1018, discussed more fully at A4-527 below).

An extension of time has been permitted to enable the Crown to indict an offence committed by the accused late during the year after his petition appearance. In *Campbell v Ritchie*, 1999 S.C.C.R. 914 it was of particular significance that *Moorov* could be applied to both groups of offences. An extension of the year time bar was confirmed on appeal where the Crown, having put three persons on petition, had decided for evidential reasons to split trial proceedings only to find that the initial trial diet against the two other accused (who would be necessary witnesses against H) was delayed for reasons outwith the Crown's control. It was held in *Hogg v HM Advocate*, 2002 S.L.T. 639 that the Crown need not be confronted with losing the right to proceed against H when it was obviously necessary and diligent to precognosce the co-accused before indicting H; and also see *HM Advocate v Paterson*, 2013 S.C.C.R. 20. Similarly, the Crown was not faulted in *Smith v HM Advocate*, 2002 G.W.D. 17-559 in seeking a retrospective extension where a principal witness had changed his evidence against S, and faced prosecution for perjury. The witness reverted to his original account just before his own trial but almost three months elapsed before he was precognosced anew. The court held there to be no prejudice to S and granted the extension. The interplay between ss.65 and 136, and the compatibility of the Crown raising summary proceedings once the year time bar period had expired, was reviewed in *Potts v PF Paisley* [2017] HCJAC 8, discussed in the General Note to s.136 below.

In *HM Advocate v McPhee*, 2007 S.C.C.R. 91, a Crown motion to extend the 11 and 12 month periods was granted to enable a conjoining of trials of the three accused, one of whom had made his petition appearance eight months after the co-accused—this despite evident Crown indecision on how to proceed in the two cases. Several factors were significant: there was sufficient reason, adopting the two stage test set out in *HM Advocate v Swift*, 1985 S.L.T. 26; 1984 S.C.C.R. 216, approved in *Early v HM Advocate*, 2006 S.L.T. 856, to warrant the extension sought; the retrospective extensions sought were short, and while the Crown, only late in the day, had perceived the developing problem well after the last accused made his petition appearance, an application for extension to the 11 month date could only be made before the High Court once the case had been indicted. (Note the absence of discussion of the option in terms of s.65(3)(b) to seek necessary extensions from the sheriff prior to indicting the case.)

Difficulties arising from Crown failure to meet disclosure obligations would be unlikely to attract much sympathy from the Bench. However, in *Paterson v HM Advocate*, 2008 S.L.T. 452; 2008 S.C.C.R. 588 where the self-evidently redacted statement of an important witness had not subsequently been disclosed in full (the Crown first wishing to put witness protection measures in place), and there was no suggestion of wilful concealment by the Crown and confusion over what had, or had not been disclosed, the Appeal Court upheld extensions of the 110 and 140 day, and 11 and 12 month periods.

(Broader questions of disclosure and the fairness of proceedings are discussed in *McInnes v HM Advocate*, 2008 S.L.T. 941; 2008 S.C.C.R. 869 and *McDonald v HM Advocate*, 2008 S.L.T. 993; 2008 S.C.C.R. 954).

A breach of art.6 was held in *Rimmer v HM Advocate*, 2001 G.W.D. 33-1306 where the presiding judge, before whom pleas were tendered and accepted by the Crown, noted that a restraint order laid before the court ran in his name as a former Lord Advocate. He declined to act further and all subsequent procedure was conducted by a fellow judge who permitted the withdrawal of R's pleas and desertion of the diet. The Crown was compelled to seek a retrospective extension to re-indict, the grant of which was appealed unsuccessfully by R. The Appeal Court intriguingly and rather tenuously held there to be fault on the part of the Crown in placing the indictment before the first judge but granted the extension sought. At no point was it alleged that there had been any partiality or impropriety on the part of the judge.

Pressure of business alone will not justify an extension and even when administrative difficulties are founded upon, the court is under an obligation to make enquiry into their nature (see *Dobbie v HM*

Advocate, 1986 S.L.T. 648; *Fleming v HM Advocate*, 1992 S.C.C.R. 575 and *Neil v HM Advocate*, 2010 S.C.C.R. 7). Note that in *Rudge v HM Advocate*, 1989 S.C.C.R. 105 a Crown motion in such circumstances was granted and one persuasive factor was the lack of real prejudice being demonstrated. In *Beattie v HM Advocate*, 1995 S.C.C.R. 606 where a Crown motion to extend the 110 day period was granted, the Court of Appeal disfavoured the view that the non-availability of the trial judge was itself sufficient cause for extending the statutory time-limits. The court was critical of the lack of enquiry made by the trial judge as to possible alternatives and emphasised that the tests involved in extending the 110 day period are more exacting than those applicable to extending the one year period. An extension was granted to the Crown in *HM Advocate v McNally*, 1999 S.L.T 1377 where insufficient jurors were available to deal with the remaining cases in the sitting but the Appeal Court (at 1381F) was at pains not to give the Crown *carte blanche* in the event of a repetition. In *Warnes v HM Advocate*, 2001 S.L.T. 34 a Crown motion for extension of the year time-bar was refused following an appeal by the accused. The Crown, which had given precedence to cases which did not timebar in the sitting over *Warnes* whose case did, had cited pressure of business in a sitting already shortened by Easter holidays. The court was critical of the resources made available by the Scottish Executive and noted that the pressure in the sitting was entirely predictable but had been ignored by the Crown. Efforts to distinguish *Warnes*, by referring to the prior history of adjournments in the case and the pressure of business in its final sitting, failed in *Riaviz v HM Advocate*, 2003 S.L.T. 1110; 2003 S.C.C.R. 444. The complexity of the case allied to Crown efforts both to secure a plea (and broker restitution) in a large fraud case were held to justify extensions of the time bar in *Voudouri v HM Advocate*, 2003 S.C.C.R. 448.

In *CS v HM Advocate* [2021] HCJAC 6 a trial, previously adjourned on defence motion the accused appealed unsuccessfully against a further extension (the case having fallen foul of the interruption to business wrought by the Coronavirus pandemic) founding upon failure by the court authorities to facilitate proceedings within the 6 month suspended period provided by subs.(13).

However, in *Potts v HM Advocate* [2015] HCJAC 124; 2016 S.C.L. 173, a successful appeal against a s.65(3)(b) extension, initially granted to enable the Crown to obtain critical evidence, the Appeal Court noted that the information provided by the Crown to the sheriff in support of their application had been wanting: a series of adjournments of trial minuted as defence adjournments, when scrutinized closely, were necessitated by repeatedly late disclosures of essential evidence. The Crown had repeatedly professed readiness for trial and had signally failed, till the very last moment, to perceive the importance of this last missing chapter of evidence, or taken active steps to obtain it. A timeline of the case's progress (or lack of it) was drawn up and presented to the Appeal Court, an approach which brought clarity to a confused, and sorry, history. Note that the Crown response was to initiate a summary prosecution which was not affected by the earlier solemn appeal, or by s.65's time bar provisions (see *Potts v Procurator Fiscal Hamilton* [2016] SAC (Crim) 25). In *McClymont v HM Advocate* [2020] HCJAC 1 an opposed Crown extension application was granted on grounds that defence failure to lodge a statutory defence statement (see s.70A below) timeously, or indeed at all, had meant that the Crown had consequently been unable to fulfil its statutory disclosure obligations.

Miscalculation of the time bar period on the Crown's part was rejected by the Appeal Court as a valid ground for extension in *Lyle v HM Advocate*, 1992 S.L.T. 467 and *Bennett v HM Advocate*, 1998 S.C.C.R. 23 (but see *Millar v HM Advocate*, 1994 S.L.T. 461 and *Duke v Lees*, 1997 G.W.D. 15-659 discussed below), as has a realisation too late that essential corroborative evidence had not been secured; see *Stewart v HM Advocate*, 1994 S.L.T. 518 where a successful Crown application for extension was overturned on appeal when it was conceded that such additional evidence could have been obtained within the statutory year. Correction of a misnumbered production on the indictment by the Crown without this being made known to the defence or the court was held in *Brown v HM Advocate*, 1999 S.L.T. 1369 to justify refusal of an extension. Detention in England and consequent absence which necessitated an extension was, on the facts, regarded as attributable to the accused, not the Crown (*Duffy v HM Advocate*, 1991 S.C.C.R. 685). Subsection (10) provides some statutory clarification in this area, by enacting that periods of remand served elsewhere in the United Kingdom shall interrupt the advance of the year time bar, an issue which had surfaced (and caused judicial calls for just such a reform) in *HM Advocate v Rowan*, 1994 S.C.C.R. 801. In *Rowan* the Court of Appeal considered a Crown appeal against a refusal of extension of the year period where R was in custody in England on other matters, and the English authorities lacked any powers to transfer him to Scotland; the appeal was allowed and this anomalous situation resulted in the amendment of the Criminal Justice (Scotland) Act 1995, s.15 at the Report Stage (*Hansard*, H.L. Vol. 561, col.39). However, detention as a serving prisoner in Scotland on other charges is not a factor, which can properly be taken into account by the court, when considering an application for extension (*McGill v HM Advocate*, 1997 S.C.C.R. 230).

While an application for extension may be presented orally to the court, the defence are entitled to be heard (*Sandford v HM Advocate*, 1986 S.C.C.R. 573) and to have warning of the motion to be made, albeit no formal notice is necessary (*Ferguson v HM Advocate*, 1992 S.C.C.R. 480; *Cation v HM Advocate*, 1992 S.C.C.R. 480). These last two cases also serve as warnings to the Crown of the risks associated with excusing witnesses without first securing the agreement of the defence: in both cases appeals against extensions of the year period were successful. By contrast see *Berry v HM Advocate*, 1989 S.L.T. 71 where delays in notifying the Crown that a witness on the indictment could not be excused, or his evidence be agreed, resulted in an extension of time which was upheld on appeal. Equally, where adjournment of the trial was on defence motion and, in an oversight, the Crown failed to seek the necessary time-bar extension to preserve the proceedings, the Appeal Court was unimpressed by defence opposition to extension (*McGinlay v HM Advocate*, 1999 S.C.C.R. 779).

Persistent illness or absence of co-accused may not justify extensions if the Crown have not considered proceeding against the accused who is present on his own (*Mejka v HM Advocate*, 1993 S.L.T. 1321; 1993 S.C.C.R. 978).

Where an accused has appeared on successive petitions, the court has to look to each petition individually in order to determine the effective date of the year time bar (*Ross v HM Advocate*, 1990 S.C.C.R. 182). Thus in *HM Advocate v Muir*, 1998 J.C. 20 where M had been remanded on petition and was later released at the trial diet following the failure to appear of a co-accused, only to fail to appear himself at a later trial resulting in a further period of remand after arrest, it was held on appeal that s.65(4) required that both periods of imprisonment had to be added together in calculating the 80 and 110 day periods; appropriate extensions had to be obtained.

It is possible for the time-bar to be extended retrospectively (*HM Advocate v M*, 1987 J.C. 1) and as subs.(2) provides the accused's failure to appear at a first or preliminary diet, or a trial diet, immediately stops the operation of the time-bar. Prospective extension of the time-bar is competent even where no indictment has yet been served is competent (*HM Advocate v Caulfield*, 1999 S.L.T. 1003).

While the provisions of s.65 do not apply directly to private prosecutions by way of a Bill of Criminal Letters, in *G.M.C. v Forsyth*, 1995 S.L.T. 905 the court had regard to the spirit of the statutory provisions in refusing a Bill presented 14 months after proceedings were deserted by the Crown.

In computing the time-scale of any extension, the natural interpretation of such a motion is that the extended period runs from the expiry of the original 12 month period, not from the date upon which the motion for extension is made. This applies equally to applications made under subs.(3) and to cases begun on petition and later reduced to summary complaint (see *Millar v HM Advocate*, 1994 S.L.T. 461 and *Duke v Lees*, 1997 G.W.D. 15-659).

The Note of Appeal in relation to an application for extension of the 12 month period should be on Form 8.1-A of the Act of Adjournal (Criminal Procedure Rules).

Subss.(4) to (7)

A4-149.1 Unlike the 11 and 12 month time bars in solemn bail cases which run from the date of first appearance on petition, calculation of the 80, 110 (and now 140) day time limits which apply to solemn custody trials run from the date of full committal. Prior to the 2004 Act, Crown applications to extend custody time limits could only be granted if the court was satisfied that there had been no fault on the part of the Crown; and all applications had to be made to the High Court, the sheriff dealing with the petition committal warrant or a subsequent solemn trial having no power to extend these remand time limits.

At the heart of s.65 (and no doubt the reason so much case law has been generated) were the peremptory consequences if a necessary extension of the time limits was not obtained either prospectively or retrospectively—an accused would be forever free from all further proceedings arising from the petition warrant.

Several significant changes have followed the 2004 Act. Most notably in relation to High Court proceedings is the introduction of the 80, 110 and 140 day periods to permit the regime of preliminary diets formulated in the *Bonomy Report*, and the additional time for focused preparation of trial business. Prior to service of an indictment, subs.(5) requires applications for extension of any of the custodial periods in solemn proceedings to be made to a single judge in the High Court; however, once the indictment has been served application for extension now falls to be considered by a judge of the court where the case is to be tried—a reform which avoids the need for adjourned or postponed cases to be referred to the High Court simply to obtain a time bar extension.

Subs.(5) preserves the power of the court to extend all, or any, of these periods as appropriate and subs.(8) implies that the court retains the power to refuse an application for extension, a decision which can be appealed.

Ordinarily, the terms of subs.(4)(aa) appear to require the immediate admission of an accused to bail if the Crown fails to adhere to the prescribed time scales, but closer examination of subs.(8A) shows that while providing a mechanism to admit remanded accused to bail, it also preserves the right of the court to refuse bail on a Crown motion. (Subs.(8A) also restates the right of the Lord Advocate to admit the accused to bail administratively). Subs.(8D) enables the Crown to appeal a decision to grant bail but any such appeal must be heard within 72 hours unless *that* period is itself extended by the High Court. (It may be that the court of first instance will have to deal with this further extension since the committal warrant for the accused will otherwise expire after 72 hours and he will then be admitted to bail as of right).

It is important to appreciate that the previous stringent test applied to any application for extension of the solemn remand period has been relaxed—the test now applied to extensions in all solemn proceedings is on cause shown—whereas the 1995 Act required there be no fault on the part of the Crown. Nonetheless the large volume of case law flowing from interpretation of s.65 has not lost its value.

Failure to serve an indictment timeously is not fatal to the proceedings but might give rise to a civil claim and now, would entitle the accused to bail, subject to the provisions in subs.(8A); see also *Farrell v HM Advocate*, 1985 S.L.T. 58; *McCluskey v HM Advocate*, 1993 S.L.T. 897; *HM Advocate v McCann*, 1977 S.L.T. (Notes) 19 and *X, Petitioner*, 1995 S.C.C.R. 407.

It remains the case that the statutory remand periods can be interrupted by liberation of the accused or the imposition of a custodial sentence. The period spent in custody has to be referable solely to the committal order giving rise to the indictment charges to count in the calculation (*HM Advocate v Boyle*, 1972 S.L.T. (Notes) 16; *Harley v HM Advocate*, 1970 S.L.T. (Notes) 6).

Where two or more petitions are conjoined on an indictment the dates of each committal have to be weighed separately in any calculation (*Ross v HM Advocate*, 1990 S.C.C.R. 182).

Similarly, where the 110 days are interrupted by a term of imprisonment, they recommence at the prisoner's earliest release date and not by reference to the working practices of the prison authorities which, in the past, released prisoners whose liberation date fell during a weekend on the Friday before (*Brown v HM Advocate*, 1988 S.C.C.R. 577). The effect of the interaction of subss.(4) to (7) and the revocation of licence provisions contained in s. 17 of the Prisoners and Criminal Proceedings (Scotland) Act 1993 was considered in *Follen v HM Advocate*, 2001 S.C.C.R. 255. F had been released on licence following conviction of contravening s.4(3)(b) of the Misuse of Drugs Act 1971. Within a year of this release he was caught in possession of a substantial quantity of cannabis resin and remanded in custody and, within a week of committal until liberation in due course of law, his licence was recalled and revoked. When indicted he raised devolution issues and pled in bar of trial that he had been detained for more than 110 days. It was held that the period was attributable to the s. 17 order and detention in relation to the original sentence.

[THE NEXT PARAGRAPH IS A4-150]

Case authorities

In *HM Advocate v McTavish*, 1974 S.L.T. 246 a Crown motion for extension, to enable the completion of further forensic tests and to allow further treatment of the accused's mental illness, in circumstances where the Crown was admittedly able to proceed to trial upon the matters libelled in the petition was rejected. In *HM Advocate v Bickerstaff*, 1926 J.C. 65 where trial had been unable to proceed due to the accused's supervening insanity, a Full Bench held the delay as being attributable to the accused, not the Crown. Illness of the judge and of co-accused permitted three extensions (upheld on appeal) in *Young v HM Advocate*, 1990 S.C.C.R. 315, the High Court itself admitting the accused to bail on a murder charge. Two extensions of time, once on the motion of a co-accused and once on Crown motion because of illness of a witness, were allowed in *Johnston (R.) v HM Advocate*, 1993 S.C.C.R. 295. Perhaps the most contentious use of these provisions in which no fault was felt to lie with the Crown is found in *Gildea v HM Advocate*, 1983 S.C.C.R. 144 where an extension was granted on account of a case scheduled earlier in the assize having taken longer than could reasonably be foreseen. Fault on the part of the Crown was argued, but rejected by the Appeal Court, in *Cunningham v HM Advocate*, 2002 S.C.C.R. 499. Prison authorities had failed to serve an indictment upon C timeously. The Crown lodged application to extend the time bar but delayed service of a fresh indictment; defence objections centred upon the failure to re-indict without delay. The Appeal Court noted that the practical outcome of granting the application was not materially different from the outcome had a fresh indictment been served timeously—either way such an extension would have been unavoidable. The application had been made before the expiry of the time bar though there had been delay (compare the approach in *Farrell v HM Advocate*, 2001 S.C.C.R. 720 discussed below). A4-150

Particular difficulty can arise in cases involving children who are remanded into the custody of the local authority pending trial or who are already subject of supervision requirements. It is essential to establish whether bail has been refused, if the child has been bailed into the care of local authority accommodation be that in secure or open accommodation, and whether the residential regime has been altered as a result of the petition appearance or at the initiative of the local authority exercising separate powers under the Children (Scotland) Act 1995. Refer to the Notes "Children Under 16 Years" at A4-120 and the cases of *X, Petr*, 1996 S.C.C.R. 436 and *M, Petr*, 1996 S.C.C.R. 92.

Subs.(8)

It may seem tautological but an appeal against the grant or refusal of an extension of the periods of 80 or 110 days, or 12 months, can only be competently taken where there has de facto been such a grant or refusal. See *McKnight v HM Advocate*, 1996 S.L.T. 834 where an appeal to the nobile officium was ruled incompetent, the sheriff having refused to consider an application for extension at an earlier diet (the case being adjourned through lack of time) and there being no decision to appeal statutorily and no judicial acting to justify recourse to the nobile officium.

"Retrospective Extensions Generally"

Delay in making such an application may itself tell against the Crown. See, for example, *HM Advocate v Caldwell*, 2010 S.L.T. 1023 and *Farrell v HM Advocate*, 2001 S.C.C.R. 720 where, after failures to appear the Crown did not appreciate following re-arrest of the accused that little of the 110 day period remained.

A failure on the part of others to execute explicit instructions issued by the Crown would not be regarded as a fault attributable to the Crown (*Coutts v HM Advocate*, 1992 S.C.C.R. 87) but see also *HM Advocate v Sands (Andrew)*, 2001 S.C.C.R. 786 where an appeal against refusal of an extension failed, the Crown having relied upon inaccurate information supplied by prison authorities as to the length of a prison sentence but, crucially, were dilatory in acting when alerted to the true position by the defence agent.

It will be recalled that, prior to the 2004 Act, in the former two situations no degree of fault on the part of the prosecutor was acceptable—see *HM Advocate v Bickerstaff*, 1926 S.L.T. 121, *Farrell v HM Advocate*, 1985 S.L.T. 58 and *McDowall v Lees*, 1996 S.C. 214. So far as the year time bar was concerned a degree of fault might be excused—*HM Advocate v Davies (Alexander)*, 1993 S.C.C.R. 645; 1994

S.L.T. 296 and *Finlay (Barry Thomas) v HM Advocate*, 1998 S.L.T. 1235. Now, however, the fact that the Crown has been at fault does not, of itself, determine whether any sort of application to extend a time bar should be refused.

Refusal of a retrospective extension may not be the end of the matter. In *HM Advocate v AD* [2018] HCJAC 2 the judge at first instance ruled that charges which had fallen after expiry of the one year time bar, some 18 years earlier, had to be dismissed on the grounds that the "two stage test" set out in *Early v HM Advocate*, 2006 S.L.T. 856 had not been met. Notwithstanding that decision, the Crown repeatedly re-indicted with the same charges (on the argument that they were evidential only and no conviction would be sought in relation to them), or sought to incorporate them by means of amending a charge docket (see s.288BA below). These efforts failed at first instance; the Appeal Court ruled however that such a docket was competent given the breadth of s.288BA(4) unless an unfair trial would result

"Loss of principal petition or indictment"

While s.157 of the Act makes statutory provisions to deal with the loss of the principal complaint in summary proceedings, no similar provision exists in solemn procedure. The most obvious solution would be to petition the court for an extension of the time bar under subss.(3) and (5) and note that it may be necessary in cases involving a remand period to extend each of the 80, 110 and 140 day periods. See, however, *HM Advocate v Fox; HM Advocate v Wilson* (High Court of Justiciary, 5 December 2001, unreported) in both of which the Crown resorted to a petition to the nobile officium. Both cases had been indicted for trial in the same Kilmarnock sitting and had thereafter been adjourned on several occasions until, during a sitting in November 2001, the Clerk could not find the principal indictments and interlocutors. The Crown stance was that no application could be made to the sheriff in accordance with subs.(3) since an indictment had been served on each accused but nor could an application for extension be made to a single High Court judge since there was no principal indictment to lay before the court. The indictments libelled respectively charges of murder and indecent assault and in both cases the Crown was anxious to preserve the trial diet to which witnesses had been cited. Instead, a petition to the nobile officium was lodged along with a copy of each indictment certified as true by the advocate depute who had signed the missing principal indictment craving substitution of the copy and an extension of the time bars. The applications were not contested.

In *Bryceland v HM Advocate*, 2002 S.C.C.R. 995 the Crown used the same approach, petitioning the nobile officium, when the principal indictment had been destroyed after being returned, in error, to the Crown after service of the indictment. In this instance a certified copy of the original indictment was signed by an advocate depute other than the original signatory and was tendered to the court in substitution for the destroyed copy. It is of passing interest that the single judge held it to be competent to place the nobile officium application before a single judge (as had occurred in *BBC, Petitioners (No.3)*, 2002 J.C. 27) rather than before a bench of three judges. In *Bryceland* it was of some moment that the 110 days were running and that the only other course open to the Crown would have been to liberate the accused.

The case is further reported as *Bryceland, Petitioner*, 2003 S.L.T. 54 but that deals with a later application to the nobile officium (as distinct from an appeal) lodged by the accused against the decision at first instance. The competency, or otherwise, of the Crown's petition to the single judge disappointingly was not argued.

New Prosecutions and Time Bar Provisions

Quite distinct time bar provisions govern retrials authorised in terms of s.119 of the Act. See A4-264 below. Curiously, given the spirit of the 2004 Act, no explicit provision has been made to incorporate a preliminary or first diet in the retrial proceedings.

Provisions Relating to Engagement, Dismissal and Withdrawal of Solicitor

Section 72F makes distinct provisions for such situations in solemn proceedings, an issue of particular significance, as subs.(6) recognises, in the context of trials involving listed sexual offences (see s.288C), young children and cases where the court has accorded vulnerable witness status to a witness (s.288F(2)). Section 72(7) applies similar provisions to situations where an accused at a late stage in solemn proceedings—effectively at or after the first or preliminary diet—loses or dispenses with the services of his solicitor.

In either of these distinct situations the court is obliged to fix a further diet not less than 10 clear days before a trial diet (s.72(9)) to confirm fresh legal representation and, implicitly, readiness for trial, and has a discretion to extend any time limit applying to the case. This would doubtless include any necessary extension to a time bar under s.65 but could arguably extend to the timescales for lodging defences and notices.

Service and lodging of indictment, etc.

A4-151 **66.—**(1) This Act shall be sufficient warrant for—

(a) the citation of the accused and witnesses to—

(i) any diet of the High Court to be held on any day, and at any place, the Court is sitting;

(ii) any diet of the sheriff court to be held on any day the court is sitting; or
(iii) any adjournment of a diet specified in sub-paragraph (i) or (ii) above; and
(b) the citation of jurors for any trial to be held—
(i) in the High Court; or
(ii) under solemn procedure in the sheriff court.

(2) The execution of the citation against an accused, witness or juror shall be in such form as may be prescribed by Act of Adjournal, or as nearly as may be in such form.

(3) A witness may be cited by sending the citation to the witness by ordinary or registered post or by the recorded delivery service and a written execution in the form prescribed by Act of Adjournal or as nearly as may be in such form, purporting to be signed by the person who served such citation together with, where appropriate, the relevant post office receipt shall be sufficient evidence of such citation.

(4) The accused may be cited either—
(a) by being served with a copy of the indictment and of the list of the names and addresses of the witnesses to be adduced by the prosecution and of the list of productions (if any) to be put in evidence by the prosecution; or
(b) if the accused, at the time of citation, is not in custody, by a constable affixing to the door of the relevant premises a notice in such form as may be prescribed by Act of Adjournal, or as nearly as may be in such form—
(i) specifying the date on which it was so affixed;
(ii) informing the accused that he may collect a copy of the indictment and of such lists as are mentioned in paragraph (a) above from a police station specified in the notice; and
(iii) calling upon him to appear and answer to the indictment at such diet as shall be so specified.

(4ZA) In subsection (4)(b) above, "the relevant premises" means—
(a) where the accused, at the time of citation, has been admitted to bail, his proper domicile of citation as specified for the purposes of section 25 of this Act; or
(b) in any other case, any premises which the constable reasonably believes to be the accused's dwelling-house or place of business.

(4A) Where a date is specified by virtue of sub-paragraph (i) of subsection (4)(b) above, that date shall be deemed the date on which the indictment is served; and the copy of the indictment referred to in sub-paragraph (ii) of that subsection shall, for the purposes of subsections (12) and (13) below be deemed the service copy.

(4B) Paragraphs (a) and (b) of subsection (6) below shall apply for the purpose of specifying a diet by virtue of subsection (4)(b)(iii) above as they apply for the purpose of specifying a diet in any notice under subsection (6).

(4C) Where—
(a) the accused is cited in accordance with subsection (4)(b) above; and
(b) the charge in the indictment is of committing an offence listed in subsection (14A)(b),

the accused shall, on collecting the indictment, be given a notice containing intimation of the matters specified in subsection (6A)(a) below.

(5) Except in a case to which section 76 of this Act applies, the prosecutor shall on or before the date of service of the indictment lodge the record copy of the indict-

ment with the clerk of court before which the trial is to take place, together with a copy of the list of witnesses and a copy of the list of productions.

(6) If the accused is cited by being served with a copy of the indictment, then except where such service is under section 76(1) of this Act, a notice shall be served on the accused with the indictment calling upon him to appear and answer to the indictment—

(a) where the case is to be tried in the sheriff court, at a first diet not less than 29 clear days after the service of the indictment,

(b) where the indictment is in respect of the High Court, at a diet not less than 29 clear days after the service of the indictment (such a diet being referred to in this Act as a "preliminary hearing").

(6A) Where the charge in the indictment is of committing an offence listed in subsection (14A)(b), the notice served under subsection (6) above shall—

(a) contain intimation to the accused—

(i) that his case at, or for the purposes of, any relevant hearing in the course of the proceedings (including at any commissioner proceedings) may be conducted only by a lawyer;

(ii) that it is, therefore, in his interests, if he has not already done so, to get the professional assistance of a solicitor; and

(iii) that if he does not engage a solicitor for the purposes of the conduct of his case at or for the purposes of the hearing (or at any related commissioner proceedings), the court will do so;

(b) *[Repealed by Criminal Procedure (Amendment) (Scotland) Act 2004 (asp 5) s.1(2). Brought into force on 1 February 2005 by SSI 2004/405 (C.28) art.2.]*

(6AA) A notice affixed under subsection (4)(b) above or served under subsection (6) above shall, where the accused is a body corporate, also contain intimation to the accused—

(a) where the indictment is in respect of the High Court, that, if it does not appear as mentioned in section 70(4) of this Act or by counsel or a solicitor at the preliminary hearing—

(i) the hearing may proceed; and

(ii) a trial diet may be appointed,

in its absence; and

(b) in any case (whether the indictment is in respect of the High Court or the sheriff court), that if it does not appear as mentioned in paragraph (a) above at the trial diet, the trial may proceed in its absence.

(6AB) A notice affixed under subsection (4)(b) or served under subsection (6), where the indictment is in respect of the sheriff court, must contain intimation to the accused that the first diet may proceed and a trial diet may be appointed in the accused's absence.

(6B) A failure to comply with subsection (4C), (6A), (6AA) or (6AB) above does not affect the validity or lawfulness of any notice affixed under subsection (4)(b) above or served under subsection (6) above or any other element of the proceedings against the accused.

(6C) An accused shall be taken to be served with—

(a) the indictment and lists of witnesses and productions; and

(b) the notice referred to in subsection (6) above,

if they are served on the solicitor specified in subsection (6D) below at that solicitor's place of business.

(6D) The solicitor referred to in subsection (6C) above is any solicitor who—

(a) has notified in writing the procurator fiscal for the district in which the charge against the accused was being investigated that he is engaged by the accused for the purposes of his defence; and

(b) has not informed that procurator fiscal that he has been dismissed by, or has withdrawn from acting for, the accused.

(6E) It is the duty of a solicitor who has, before service of an indictment, notified a procurator fiscal that he is engaged by the accused for the purposes of his defence to inform that procurator fiscal in writing forthwith if he is dismissed by, or withdraws from acting for, the accused.

(7) Subject to subsection (4)(b) above, service of the indictment, lists of witnesses and productions, and any notice or intimation to the accused, and the citation of witnesses, whether for precognition or trial, may be effected by any officer of law.

(8) *[Repealed by Criminal Procedure (Amendment) (Scotland) Act 2004 (asp 5) s.7(6). Brought into force on 1 February 2005 by SSI 2004/405 (C.28) art.2.]*

(9) The citation of witnesses may be effected by any officer of law duly authorised; and in any proceedings, the evidence on oath of the officer shall, subject to subsection (10) below, be sufficient evidence of the execution of the citation.

(10) *[Repealed by Criminal Procedure (Amendment) (Scotland) Act 2004 (asp 5) s.25 and Sch.1 para.15(e). Brought into force on 1 February 2005 by SSI 2004/405 (C.28) art.2.]*

(11) No objection to the competency of the officer who served the indictment, or who executed a citation under subsection (4)(b) above, to give evidence in respect of such service or execution shall be upheld on the ground that his name is not included in the list of witnesses served on the accused.

(12) Any deletion or correction made before service on the record or service copy of an indictment shall be sufficiently authenticated by the initials of the person who has signed, or could by law have signed, the indictment.

(13) Any deletion or correction made on a service copy of an indictment, or on any notice of citation, postponement, adjournment or other notice served on an accused shall be sufficiently authenticated by the initials of any procurator fiscal or of the person serving the same.

(14) Any deletion or correction made on any execution of citation or notice or other document so served shall be sufficiently authenticated by the initials of the person serving the same.

(14A) For the purposes of subsections (4C) and (6A)—

(a) "relevant hearing" is to be construed in accordance with section 288C(1A) or (as the case may be) 288DC(4),

(b) the list is—

(i) an offence to which section 288C applies (certain sexual offending),

(ii) an offence to which section 288DC applies (domestic abuse cases).

(15) In subsection (6A) above, "commissioner proceedings" means proceedings before a commissioner appointed under section 271I(1) or by virtue of section 272(1)(b) of this Act.

AMENDMENTS

Subsections (6A) and (6B) inserted by Sexual Offences (Procedure and Evidence) (Scotland) Act 2002 (asp 9) Sch.1 para.4. Brought into force by SSI 2002/443 (C.24) art.4 (effective 1 November 2002).

Section 66 as amended by Criminal Justice (Scotland) Act 2003 (asp 7) Pt 8 s.61. Brought into force on 27 June 2003 by SSI 2003/288 (C.14).

Subsection (6A) as amended by Criminal Justice (Scotland) Act 2003 (asp 7) Sch.4 para.3. Brought into force on 25 November 2003 by SSI 2003/475 (C.26) art.2.

Subs.(1) substituted, subs.(4)(b) as amended and subss.(4ZA), (6C), (6D) and (6E) inserted by Criminal Procedure (Amendment) (Scotland) Act 2004 (asp 5) s.7. Brought into force on 1 February 2005 by SSI 2004/405 (C.28) art.2.

Subs.(6)(a) as amended, and subs.(6)(b) substituted, by Criminal Procedure (Amendment) (Scotland) Act 2004 (asp 5) s.1(1). Brought into force on 1 February 2005 as above.

Subs.(6AA) inserted by Criminal Procedure (Amendment) (Scotland) Act 2004 (asp 5) s.10(5). Brought into force on 1 February 2005 as above.

Subss.(4), (6A)(a)(iii) and (6B) as amended, and subss.(4C), (6A)(a)(zi) inserted, by Criminal Procedure (Amendment) (Scotland) Act 2004 (asp 5) s.25 and Sch.1 para.15(a)-(d). Brought into force on 1 February 2005 as above.

Subs.(6A) amended and subs.(15) inserted by Criminal Proceedings etc. (Reform) (Scotland) Act 2007 (asp 6) s.35. Brought into force on 23 April 2007 by SSI 2007/250 (C.23) art.3.

Subs.(6A)(a) as amended by Criminal Justice and Licensing (Scotland) Act 2010 (asp 13) Sch.7 para.44. Brought into force on 28 March 2011 by SSI 2011/178 (C.15) art.2, Sch.1 para.1.

Subss.(6)(a), (6B) as amended, subs.(6AB) inserted, by Criminal Justice (Scotland) Act 2016 (asp 1) ss.79(3) and 81(2). Brought into force on 29 May 2017 by SSI 2017/99 art.3, for the purposes of any indictment served on an accused on or after that day; not yet in force otherwise.

Subs.(4C)(b), (6A) as amended, subs.(14A) inserted, by Domestic Abuse (Scotland) Act 2018 (asp 5) Sch.1(1) (2) para.4(3) (effective 1 April 2019 in respect of proceedings commenced on or after 1 April 2019 subject to transitional provision specified in SSI 2018/387 reg.7(2)).

DEFINITIONS

A4-151.1 "Clerk of Justiciary" : s.307(1).
"diet": s.307(1).
"High Court": s.307(1).
"indictment": s.307(1).
"officer of law": s.307(1).
"prosecutor": s.307(1).
"sheriff clerk": s.307(1).
"witness": s.307(1).

[THE NEXT PARAGRAPH IS A4-152]

GENERAL NOTE

A4-152 Provisions relating to service of indictments, citations, any notices and proof of service are found in ss.66 and 72G, the latter providing for lawful service of these to be made at the office of the solicitor engaged by the accused (or more rarely, appointed by the court in accordance with ss.288D and 288E). It will be appreciated that s.72F of the Act requires that the appointed solicitor complete and lodge a letter of engagement with both the court and the Crown confirming appointment and requires any subsequent dismissal or withdrawal from acting on behalf of the accused to be intimated formally. (The provisions are discussed in greater detail below).

Service of the indictment as provided in s.66(6) dictates the timetable for the case to call at a preliminary hearing in the High Court, or at a first diet in the sheriff solemn court, not less than 29 days after service. The sole exception to this generality arises in the case of s.76 indictments which involve expedited procedures. The diet fixed dictates the timescales within which a defence statement (s.70A) must be lodged, a written record (s.71C) submitted by all parties, and preliminary pleas and issues, special defences and defence witness lists (ss.78 and 79) be lodged. Only once the court is satisfied that the case is ready to proceed to trial will that diet be assigned. Note that, in sheriff solemn cases, s.71(5) permits the holding of a first diet, and appointment of a trial diet, in the absence of the accused, or continuation for enquiry (s.71(5A)).

Provisions enabling dispensing with a preliminary hearing in the High Court on joint application are found in s.72B but, strictly, do not circumvent the statutory requirement to lodge the formal notices demanded by the Act. In practical terms, however, it has to be recognised that if parties concur that additional preparation time is necessary it is likely that it will be premature to expect compliance with these timescales. It should also be noted that once a trial diet is assigned the defence has fresh obligations to review and update the defence statement in sheriff solemn cases (s.70(4)).

Service of an indictment for High Court proceedings is a procedural watershed. Care must be taken to ensure that matters which hitherto fell within the ambit of the sheriff (as a consequence of the initiating petition warrant) are still competent in that forum. For example, civil restraint proceedings, or review thereof, have been held to be matters for the Court of Session and not the sheriff once a High Court indictment has been served (see *Dunn v PY* [2015] SCEDIN 35), whereas warrants for "relevant physical data" arguably ought still to be considered by the sheriff, notwithstanding the decision in *HM Advocate v Edwards* [2012] HCJAC 9 discussed below.

Various technical matters are dealt with by the section: subs.(1) provides an automatic warrant to cite witnesses to any diet (preliminary, first or trial) in the proceedings and for jurors to be cited for any trial; subs.(4) enables service of an indictment to be made upon an accused by affixing a notice at his bail domicile or wheresoever he is believed to reside or work; see subs.(4ZA). This enables an indictment, which may well contain sensitive material, to be collected from a nominated police office rather than having to be left in public view at a domicile. This may be particularly understandable in indictments detailing allegations of a sexual nature. (See the note "*Listed sexual offences*" which follows). The form of notice to be used for this purpose is found as Form 8.2-A in the Act of Adjournal (Criminal Procedure Rules Amendment) (Criminal Procedure (Amendment) (Scotland) Act 2004) 2005 (SSI 2005/44) while the standard intimation to appear is now Form 8.2-B therein. The execution of service now appears as Form 2.6-G.

Substantial new administrative provisions are to be found in subss.(6C) and (6D). The solicitor engaged by the accused is now obliged to notify the procurator fiscal within whose jurisdiction appearance was made on petition that he is so engaged, and to notify if he ceases to act. (More difficulty will inevitably arise where an accused is indicted without first having appeared on petition). The significance of these measures is seen in subs.(6C) which now enables service of an indictment to be effected in the hands of the nominated solicitor at his place of business. This simple measure removed the absolute need to effect service of the indictment upon the accused but it is suggested that the Crown will ordinarily still seek to do so—in Convention terms the accused must be aware of the allegations he faces; all that appears to be intended is to avoid proceedings falling for a purely technical want of form where no prejudice has been caused to an accused. Attention is directed to *HM Advocate v Holbein*, 2005 S.L.T. 242 which addressed the dilemma facing the Crown when the accused's bail domicile has been demolished. It remains the case that service is validly effected nonetheless by depositing the indictment (or notice to collect it) there; the court confined consideration to this narrow issue and did not explore the possible bail contravention committed by the accused's failure to apply to the court for a change of domicile. The provisions are intended to simplify service of indictments and documents but arguably have still to be shown to fulfil art.6 Convention requirements.

Subs.(5) repeats a time-honoured duty upon the Crown to lodge a record copy of the indictment with the sheriff clerk or Clerk of Justiciary, but where this could once have been regarded as a directory rather than mandatory provision (see, for example, *HM Advocate v Graham*, 1985 S.L.T. 498) lodging now has to be seen as an essential precursor to any solemn diet.

It is competent, though unusual, to run two identical indictments simultaneously against an accused. So in *HM Advocate v Dow*, 1992 S.L.T. 577 where a minute of postponement had been lodged by the defence, and granted by the court, and the Crown was given authority under s.77A(2) of the 1975 Act to serve notice of a new trial diet (the equivalent procedure is now contained in s.80(3) of the 1995 Act) but did not do so, service of a fresh indictment in identical terms was held to be neither oppressive nor incompetent. (See also the notes to s.80 infra.)

In *Smith v HM Advocate*, 1996 S.L.T. 1384 it was discovered, before a preliminary diet, that an error in the minute of notice meant that an incorrect address had been given for the High Court sitting, and a second identical indictment was served. The High Court on appeal held that as the master of the instance it was a matter within the discretion of the Crown which indictment would be called. This suggests that the terms of the indictments themselves (be they identical or not) are not of moment since the Court also indicated that the service of a second indictment implied that the Crown were deserting the first and proceeding on the later indictment.

Provisions relating to service of indictments

New service provisions are found in subs.(4) onwards. Service of an indictment is normally effected upon an accused personally, or by leaving it at his domicile of citation or customary abode, or even *in extremis* by pinning it to a house door. Now it is possible instead to forward a notice to the accused instead of the full indictment (or complaint in summary cases); the notice is dated and informs the accused of the diet (or diets) at which he must appear, and directs him to a specific police office to collect his indictment. As mentioned earlier subs.(6D) allows for an indictment to be taken to be validly served if left at the office of the nominated solicitor. **A4-153**

Either the execution of service of the indictment, or notice, will be sufficient evidence of lawful citation but failure to serve remains fatal to the proceedings on that indictment and cannot be cured by appearance (*McAllister v HM Advocate*, 1985 S.L.T. 399; 1985 S.C.C.R. 36, and *Hester v MacDonald*, 1961 S.C. 370). The aim of the extended service provisions is to avoid the need to leave court documents, which by their nature can contain sensitive material, in places where they may fall into the wrong hands or become common currency in the neighbourhood—this protects the Convention rights of the accused and witnesses alike.

A failure to effect service timeously does not cause the committal warrant granted at the time of appearance on petition to fall, but the Crown will still be obliged to obtemper the timebar requirements set out in s.65 of the Act; see *Jamieson v HM Advocate*, 1990 S.L.T. 845; 1990 S.C.C.R. 137 and the Notes to s.65 above. Service without giving the requisite 29 clear days notice demanded in subs.(6) would not create a nullity and in the absence of an objection to service, which would be taken at a preliminary diet (or first diet in sheriff solemn proceedings), trial could proceed. That 29-day *induciae* can be waived and can be asserted to have been so in the absence of a preliminary challenge (see *HM Advocate v McDonald*, 1984 S.L.T. 426).

Section 66(4A) establishes that the date upon which the notice of an indictment is served upon the accused is to be taken to be the date of service, just as service of the indictment itself would denote.

In *Bryson v HM Advocate*, 1961 S.L.T. 289, an accused bailed to a domicile was subsequently remanded in custody for further charges, but the indictment was served at his original domicile not at the prison, a procedure which was upheld. Service of an indictment without giving the requisite 29 clear days notice stipulated in subs.(6) would not create a nullity and in the absence of an objection to service, which should be taken at a preliminary diet (or at the first diet in sheriff and jury cases), trial could proceed: furthermore the *induciae* can be waived and it can be argued that this has occurred in the absence of a preliminary challenge (see *HM Advocate v McDonald*, 1984 S.L.T. 426).

Listed sexual offences (s.288C of the Act)

A4-153.1 Where the libel contains a sexual offence listed in s.288C of the Act it is provided by s.66(6A) that the accused is to be given an additional notice setting out the special provisions relating to legal representation which apply to such offences, and is to be notified that he has to attend at a mandatory first diet. The form of notice to be used in such cases is now Form 8.2-C in the Act of Adjournal (Criminal Procedure Rules Amendment) (Criminal Procedure (Amendment) (Scotland) Act 2004) 2005 (SSI 2005/44).

Section 66(6B) serves to indicate that the provisions are directory upon the Crown and that a Crown failure to observe them is not fatal to the proceedings themselves (the court having a continuing duty in such cases to ensure that the accused is legally represented throughout the proceedings).

[THE NEXT PARAGRAPH IS A4-154]

Proof of service

A4-154 The form of the Notice of Compearance to be served upon the accused with any indictment has been amended by para.2(12) of the Act of Adjournal (Criminal Procedure Rules Amendment No.3) (Sexual Offences (Procedure and Evidence) (Scotland) Act 2002) 2002 (SSI 2002/454). Consequently, the Notice of Compearance accompanying the indictment is signed by the prosecutor when the indictment itself is signed, rather than completed by the police officer serving the documents. See Form 8.2-B at B1-97 below.

An indictment must be served by an officer of law in the presence of a witness in one of the manners specified in r.2.2 of the 1996 Act of Adjournal, namely (i) by personal service; (ii) by leaving it in the hands of a member of the accused's family, an inmate or employee at the domicile of citation; or (iii) by delivery through, or affixing to the door of the domicile. Similar provisions apply in situations where the accused has no domicile of citation in which event service can be effected at the address which the officer has reasonable cause to believe is occupied by the accused or by personal service.

The execution of service completed by the officer should comply with Form 2.6-AA shown in the Appendix to the 1996 Act of Adjournal and be returned to the prosecutor: the execution will in all likelihood require to be produced to the court if the accused fails to appear at any diet before an arrest warrant will be granted. In *Welsh v HM Advocate*, 1986 S.L.T. 664 a dispute arose as to whether the police could have served the indictment as claimed, since (it was alleged) the building had been demolished. The claim was refuted by the officers but the court noted that even if the accused's assertion had been correct, there would have been a failure to inform the court of a change of domicile.

It is competent in terms of subss.(8) and (11) for the officers effecting service of the indictment to be heard in evidence without their particulars being added to the indictment, a useful provision in the event of later additional charges for failure to appear at a lawful diet.

Witnesses for precognition or trial can be cited in conformity with subs.(3) but in the event of a failure to appear at trial, it may be difficult to persuade the court to grant an arrest warrant, as subs.(10) allows, unless an execution of personal service conforming to Form 2.6-E of the 1996 Act of Adjournal can be exhibited. However, the same Act of Adjournal has introduced a new Form 8.2-D, a reply form to be returned by witnesses cited in indictment cases acknowledging citation and this should be a factor to be taken into account in the event of non-appearance and, incidentally, may alert the Crown at an early stage to any potential shortcomings in citation (it must be doubted that precognition mentioned in subs.(7) can be regarded as "a diet" for the purposes of subs.(10); it is submitted that a warrant for arrest could not properly be sought following failure to appear for precognition, except precognition on oath. The relevant forms of petition for authority to precognosce on oath, are Forms 29.1-A and 29.1-B in the above Act of Adjournal).

For purposes of computation of time, note that in the case of the time limits specified in subs.(6), s.75 enacts that where the final day falls on a *dies non*, the effective date for calculation is the next working day.

Provisions for planning and disposal of sittings

Guidance in relation to the organisation of business intended to supplement existing statutory provisions for High Court sittings is to be found in Memorandum dated 9 January 2002, issued by the Lord Justice General. These provisions which set out responsibilities before, and during, sittings for defence agents and counsel and the Crown, and for the trial judge at the start of sittings, are intended to improve the flow of business in all High Court sittings and can be found in 2002 S.L.T. (News) 28.

Witnesses

A4-155 **67.**—(1) The list of witnesses shall consist of the names of the witnesses together with an address at which they can be contacted for the purposes of precognition.

(2) It shall not be necessary to include in the list of witnesses the names of any witnesses to the declaration of the accused or the names of any witnesses to prove that an extract conviction applies to the accused, but witnesses may be examined in regard to these matters without previous notice.

(3) Any objection in respect of misnomer or misdescription of—

(a) any person named in the indictment; or

(b) any witness in the list of witnesses,

shall be intimated in writing to the court before which the trial is to take place, to the prosecutor and to any other accused, where the case is to be tried in the sheriff court, at or before the first diet and, where the case is to be tried in the High Court, not less than seven clear days before the preliminary hearing; and, except on cause shown, no such objection shall be admitted unless so intimated.

(4) Where such intimation has been given or cause is shown and the court is satisfied that the accused making the objection has not been supplied with sufficient information to enable him to identify the person named in the indictment or to find such witness in sufficient time to precognosce him before the trial, the court may grant such remedy by postponement, adjournment or otherwise as appears to it to be appropriate.

(4A) The prosecutor shall have a duty to cite a witness included in the list only if—

(a) it has been ascertained under—

(i) in the case of proceedings in the High Court, section 72(6)(d); or

(ii) in the case of proceedings in the sheriff court, section 71(1C)(a),

of this Act that the witness is required by the prosecutor or the accused to attend the trial; or

(b) where, in the case of proceedings in the High Court, the preliminary hearing has been dispensed with under subsection (1) of section 72B of this Act, the witness was identified in the application under that subsection as being required by the prosecutor or the accused to attend the trial.

(5) Without prejudice to—

(a) any enactment or rule of law permitting the prosecutor to examine any witness not included in the list of witnesses; or

(b) subsection (6) below,

in any trial it shall be competent with the leave of the court for the prosecutor to examine any witness or to put in evidence any production not included in the listslodged by him, provided that written notice, containing in the case of a witness his name and address as mentioned in subsection (1) above, has been given to the accused by the relevant time.

(5A) In subsection (5) above, "the relevant time" means—

(a) where the case is to be tried in the High Court—

(i) not less then seven clear days before the preliminary hearing; or

(ii) such later time, before the jury is sworn to try the case, as the court may, on cause shown, allow;

(b) where the case is to be tried in the sheriff court, not less than two clear days before the day on which the jury is sworn to try the case.

(6) It shall be competent for the prosecutor to examine any witness or put in evidence any production included in any list or notice lodged by the accused, and it shall be competent for an accused to examine any witness or put in evidence any production included in any list or notice lodged by the prosecutor or by a co-accused.

AMENDMENTS

Subss.(3), (5) as amended, and (4A), (5A) inserted, by Criminal Procedure (Amendment) (Scotland) Act 2004 (asp 5) s.25 and Sch.1 para.16. Brought into force on 1 February 2005 by SSI 2004/405 (C.28) art.2.

DEFINITIONS

A4-155.1 "diet": s.307(1).
"High Court": s.307(1).
"indictment": s.307(1).
"prosecutor": s.307(1).
"witness": s.307(1).

[THE NEXT PARAGRAPH IS A4-156]

GENERAL NOTE

A4-156 Section 67 anticipates that the identity and particulars of most witnesses will be known to the Crown sufficiently early for inclusion in the indictment served upon the accused. Experience suggests otherwise; in custody cases particularly, increasing reliance has been placed upon the use of the provisions in s.67(5) of the Act both for adding witnesses and productions to the indictment.

Objection to any deficiency in the specification of a witness must be intimated in writing to the court and to all parties to the proceedings prior to the first diet in sheriff solemn proceedings and not less than seven days prior to a preliminary hearing in the High Court. Later objection can be made on cause shown (subs.(3)) and distinct time limits apply to both sheriff and jury and High Court proceedings— at or prior to the first diet in the former, seven clear days before the High Court preliminary diet).

Subs.(4A) contains an important reform; whereas previously the inclusion of a witness on an indictment implicitly obliged the Crown to produce that person at the trial diet (even if the witness was hostile, reluctant or had proved uncooperative) or imperil the proceedings, that duty is now a more restricted one; henceforth the obligation is only to cite a witness named on the indictment the need for whose attendance at the trial has been confirmed at the first or preliminary diet. In High Court cases where a preliminary diet has been waived (see s.72B below), the application to dispense with that diet still has to identify the witnesses whose evidence is required at the trial.

Although witnesses are expected to be named in the indictment, later witnesses can be added subject to the provisions in subs.(5A). Note that in sheriff solemn business Criminal Courts Practice Note No.3 of 2015, dated 26 August 2015, whose non-statutory provisions take effect from 1 December 2015, the Crown will be required to explain why witnesses are being added by s.67 notice. (No similar stricture applies to additional productions or label productions added by such notice.) It is conceivable that the late addition of witnesses proposed by the Crown could be refused by the court if no satisfactory explanation for the delay is established.

Again distinct provisions distinguish High Court and sheriff solemn proceedings: later additions can be made up to seven days prior to the preliminary hearing, or right up until the commencement of the trial with leave of the court in High Court cases, but no later than two clear days before the trial in sheriff and jury cases. It may be the height of cynicism to conjecture that the generation of s.67 material, when trial is imminent, might serve the Crown as a means of forcing a late defence motion to adjourn; whatever the cause of such late notices, the High Court obiter in *Holman Fenwick Willan v HM Advocate* [2017] HCJAC 38 at [25], not for the first time, warned that late s.67 notices (and the evidence specified therein) might be refused by the court at the post-indictment stage (sic). Irrespective of the attitude of the defence, it will be noted that acceptance of any s.67 notice is at the court's discretion. Late evidence may still be admitted by agreement of parties in a joint minute of agreement, a procedure in which the court has no part.

Subs.(6) preserves the right of parties to call as witnesses those listed by either the Crown, the accused or any co-accused.

Subs. (5)

As was noted above, the provisions of s.81 in regard to late intimation of witnesses and productions have been preserved in s.67(5) of the 1995 Act: provided due notice has been given to the accused, such evidence can be added to the indictment with leave of the court. However, while an error in describing a witness in a s.67 notice is probably capable of being remedied by amendment in the course of proceedings, given the grounds of amendment in s.96 of the Act, a misdescription of a production either in the list of productions or, later, in a s.67 notice, cannot be so remedied. In *HM Advocate v Swift* 1983 S.C.C.R. 204 an error in the original list of productions was corrected in a s.81 notice which itself misdescribed the production. The sheriff held the terms of s.81 to be peremptory and held evidence arising from the production, a tape, to be inadmissible. It is observed that it would still be open to parties to have such evidence admitted by way of a Minute of Agreement in the course of the trial if they were so minded.

Subsection (5)(a) entitles the prosecutor to examine certain witnesses without having given intimation to the accused. The most obvious categories of witnesses covered by this concession are co-accused whose pleas have been accepted prior to, or during trial, or even by way of an accelerated plea following service of a common indictment (see *Monaghan v HM Advocate*, 1984 S.L.T. 262), witnesses cited by any of the accused, witnesses led in replication in accordance with s.269 of the 1995 Act, police officers proving service of an indictment (s.66(11)), and the officials specified in subs.(2) above.

Failure of witness to attend for, or give evidence on, precognition

67A. [...] A4-156.1

AMENDMENTS

Section 67A inserted by Crime and Punishment (Scotland) Act 1997 (c.48) s.57(1) with effect from 1 August 1997 in terms of SI 1997/1712 art.5.

Section 67A repealed by Criminal Procedure (Amendment) (Scotland) Act 2004 (asp 5) s.25 Sch.1 para.17. Brought into force on 4 October 2004 by SSI 2004/405 (C.28).

[THE NEXT PARAGRAPH IS A4-157]

Productions

68.—(1) [...] A4-157

(2) The accused shall be entitled to see the productions according to the existing law and practice in the office of the sheriff clerk of the district in which the court of the trial diet is situated or, where the trial diet is to be in the High Court in Edinburgh, in the Justiciary Office.

(3) Where a person who has examined a production is adduced to give evidence with regard to it and the production has been lodged, where the case is to be tried in the sheriff court, at least eight days before the trial diet or, where the case is to be tried in the High Court, at least 14 days before the preliminary hearing, it shall not be necessary to prove—

(a) that the production was received by him in the condition in which it was taken possession of by the procurator fiscal or the police and returned by him after his examination of it to the procurator fiscal or the police; or

(b) that the production examined by him is that taken possession of by the procurator fiscal or the police,

unless the accused where the case is to be tried in the sheriff court, at least four days before the trial diet or, where the case is to be tried in the High Court, at least seven days before the preliminary hearing, gives in accordance with subsection (4) below written notice that he does not admit that the production was received or returned as aforesaid or, as the case may be, that it is that taken possession of as aforesaid.

(4) The notice mentioned in subsection (3) above shall be given—

(a) where the case is to be tried in the High Court, to the Crown Agent; and

(b) where the case is to be tried in the sheriff court, to the procurator fiscal.

AMENDMENTS

Subss.(3), (4)(a), (b) as amended by Criminal Procedure (Amendment) (Scotland) Act 2004 (asp 5) s.25 and Sch.1 para.18. Brought into force on 1 February 2005 by SSI 2004/405 (C.28) art.2.

Subs.(1) repealed by Criminal Justice (Scotland) Act 2016 (asp 1) s.78. Brought into force on 17 January 2017 by SSI 2016/426 art.2 and Sch.1 para.1.

DEFINITIONS A4-157.1

"diet": s.307(1).
"High Court": s.307(1).
"procurator fiscal": s.307(1).
"sheriff clerk": s.307(1).

[THE NEXT PARAGRAPH IS A4-158]

GENERAL NOTE

Subsection (3) contains presumptions that (i) productions examined after their recovery by the police or lodging with the procurator fiscal were produced to the witness in the same condition as when recovered or lodged and (ii) that the articles produced to the witness were those seized by the police or procurator fiscal. The presumption only applies to productions lodged not less than eight days before trial in sheriff solemn proceedings, and 14 days prior to the preliminary hearing in High Court cases. A4-158

Any challenge to these presumptions must be made at least four days before a trial in the sheriff court, and no less than seven days prior to the preliminary hearing in the High Court, by notice in accordance with subs.(4).

The interplay of the Crown's statutory duty of disclosure of evidence to the defence, special arrangements for accessing sensitive materials (found in the Criminal Justice and Licensing (Scotland) Act 2010 (asp 13) ss.121 and 160(3)) and the general right of an indicted accused, applying to the court, to inspect productions and label productions set out in s.68(2) of the 1995 Act was examined in *HM Advocate v AM* [2016] HCJAC 34; 2016 S.C.C.R. 227, a case where the defence, following *Davies, Petitioner* cited below, successfully sought fuller access to, and examination of, Joint Investigative Interview (JII) material—video discs of child interviews—than the Crown (operating a blanket policy of restricted disclosure even after productions were listed on the indictment) would allow. The compatibility minute was granted at the preliminary hearing and unsuccessfully appealed by the Crown.

Note that in *Livingston v HM Advocate*, 1991 S.C.C.R. 350 examination of productions and their comparison against the accused's fingerprint forms, which necessitated a motion for the removal of articles from the court during the course of a trial for that purpose, was upheld on appeal. This was viewed as a matter within the discretion of the trial judge, albeit an exceptional procedure. In that case the Lord Justice General (at 356C) echoed the view expressed in *William Turner Davies, Petr*, 1973 S.L.T. (Notes) 36 by the Lord Justice Clerk at 37, that after service of an indictment;

> "the productions ... are lodged with the sheriff clerk who has a duty to retain them in his custody and make them available at the trial. At that stage, the only body with the authority to allow the productions to be inspected and examined is the court, and the proper procedure is to make application to the court thereanent. It is then for the court to decide whether the application should be granted or refused."

Davies had petitioned the *nobile officium* for authority for a defence expert to examine gloves lodged by the Crown as productions before the trial began, but the same principles apply both prior to, and during, trial. The court has to weigh the potential prejudice to the accused in the preparation and presentation of his case against the public interest in the effective prosecution of crime. See also *MacNeil v HM Advocate*, 1986 S.C.C.R. 288, where productions listed in the indictment had not been lodged it was held that objection should have been taken before the jury was sworn and the appropriate remedy in the event of prejudice was an adjournment. It is notable that in *HM Advocate v Sorrie*, (discussed at Notes to s.65(1), (2) and (3) above), the Court of Appeal held that there had been no want of compliance with s.68(2) on the basis that the productions had been lost or destroyed. The absence of an opportunity to examine the missing banknotes was a matter for comment and appropriate direction (the Crown having already undertaken a fingerprint examination of the bank bags which contained the notes initially and averring no likelihood of prejudice in the whole circumstances). This is surely an extreme interpretation and one wonders what approach could have been taken had a written challenge (subs.(3)(b)) been taken.

The procedures regulating the access of jurors to productions are discussed in the notes to s.99 below.

Lodging of productions and their introduction as evidence is only necessary where they are best evidence bearing distinguishing or peculiar features; otherwise there will be no demonstrable prejudice to the accused and no requirement for the items to be produced to the court. See *Maciver v Mackenzie*, 1942 S.L.T. 144, followed most recently in *Friel v Leonard*, 1997 G.W.D. 12–494. Such prejudice to the accused must be of a substantial degree (see *Anderson v Laverock*, 1976 S.L.T. 62 followed in *Allan v Napier*, 1999 G.W.D. 29–1364); mere speculation of possible prejudice to the defence case is not sufficient (*Duke v HM Advocate*, 2001 G.W.D. 21–795). See also *McQuade v Vannet*, 2000 S.C.C.R. 18 where a plea in bar of trial based upon the unavailability of a CCTV video tape which had been viewed by a police officer, found to contain nothing significant, returned to its owner and reused, was repelled. The video tape had never been considered as a production in the summary trial. The Appeal Court noted that if it transpired in the course of the trial the missing production became significant, and its absence then became gravely prejudicial, it would then be appropriate for the court to desert the diet: see *McFadyen v Annan*, 1992 S.L.T. 163; 1992 S.C.C.R. 186. The developing approach to lost CCTV evidence may be seen in *HM Advocate v Haggerty* Unreported High Court of Justiciary 22 January 2003 and *Lennox v HM Advocate* [2008] HCJAC 22; in the former case CCTV material recovered by the police had subsequently been lost or destroyed before the defence had had an opportunity to view it, and it was proposed to lead parole evidence of identification of the accused from police officers who had viewed the tape—this was ruled as inadmissible evidence on grounds of incurable prejudice to the accused; in the latter, the Appeal Court, following an appeal from a preliminary diet, adopted the same approach notwithstanding that the Crown's expressed intention was to have police officers describe an assault without seeking to elicit any identification of the accused. In *Lennox* it will be noted special defences of self defence had been lodged.

HM Advocate v Stuurman, 2003 S.L.T. 1050 establishes that the test to be applied where productions are not produced to the court is whether their absence means that the accused could not receive a fair trial, not simply that there would be a material risk of an unfair trial. See too *Rose v HM Advocate*, 2003 S.L.T. 1050. Requests from the jury to see productions must always be approached with care; again the test to be applied is whether there would be any potential for prejudice to any of the parties; *Barnetson v HM Advocate*, 2003 G.W.D. 30-838.

CB v Brown [2020] SAC (Crim) 3 supports the propriety of a judge examining case productions outwith the presence of parties while considering verdicts, but cautions that no conclusions should be reached without hearing the parties' submissions thereafter.

Section 78 of the Criminal Justice (Scotland) Act 2016 (asp 1) abolished both judicial examinations and judicial declarations. Consequently, subs.(2)(c) removed the requirement to lodge transcripts of these judicial proceedings; while the logic of this provision is unimpeachable it is submitted that some care may be necessary where the original petition appearance occurred before 17 January 2017, and an examination or declaration took place. In such (now rare) circumstances any approved transcript of examination or declaration ought properly to be included in any subsequent indictment. See the discussion at s.35 above.

Notice of previous convictions

69.—(1) No mention shall be made in the indictment of previous convictions; nor shall extracts of previous convictions be included in the list of productions annexed to the indictment. **A4-159**

(2) If the prosecutor intends to place before the court any previous conviction, he shall cause to be served on the accused along with the indictment a notice in the form set out in an Act of Adjournal or as nearly as may be in such form, and any conviction specified in the notice shall be held to apply to the accused unless he gives, in accordance with subsection (3) below, written intimation objecting to such conviction on the ground that it does not apply to him or is otherwise inadmissible.

(3) Intimation objecting to a conviction under subsection (2) above shall be given—

- (a) where the accused is indicted to the High Court, to the Crown Agent not less than seven clear days before the preliminary hearing;
- (b) where the accused is indicted to the sheriff court, to the procurator fiscal at least five clear days before the first day of the sitting in which the trial diet is to be held.

(4) Where notice is given by the accused under section 76 of this Act of his intention to plead guilty and the prosecutor intends to place before the court any previous conviction, he shall cause to be served on the accused along with the indictment a notice in the form set out in an Act of Adjournal or as nearly as may be in such form.

(4A) A notice served under subsection (2) or (4) above shall include any details which the prosecutor proposes to provide under section 101(3A) of this Act; and subsection (3) above shall apply in relation to intimation objecting to the provision of such details, on the grounds that they do not apply to the accused or are otherwise inadmissible, as it applies in relation to intimation objecting to a conviction.

(5) Where the accused pleads guilty at any diet, no objection to any conviction of which notice has been served on him under this section, or to the provision of such details as are, by virtue of subsection (4A) above, included in a notice so served, shall be entertained unless he has, at least two clear days before the diet, given intimation to the procurator fiscal of the district to the court of which the accused is cited for the diet.

(6) This section applies in relation to the alternative disposals mentioned in subsection (7) below as it applies in relation to previous convictions.

(7) Those alternative disposals are—

- (a) a—
  - (i) fixed penalty under section 302(1) of this Act;
  - (ii) compensation offer under section 302A(1) of this Act,

  that has been accepted (or deemed to have been accepted) by the accused in the two years preceding the date of an offence charged;
- (b) a work order under section 303ZA(6) of this Act that has been completed in the two years preceding the date of an offence charged;
- (c) a restoration notice given under subsection (4) of section 20A of the Nature Conservation (Scotland) Act 2004 (asp 6) in respect of which the accused has given notice of intention to comply under subsection (5) of that section in the two years preceding the date of an offence charged.

[(8) Any reference in this section to a previous conviction includes, where relevant, a conviction by a court in any part of the United Kingdom or in any member State of the European Union.]

Amendments

Subsections (3)(a) as amended, and subs.(3)(b) substituted, by Criminal Procedure (Amendment) (Scotland) Act 2004 (asp 5) s.25 and Sch.1 para.19. Brought into force on 1 February 2005 by SSI 2004/405 (C.28) art.2.

Subsection (4A) inserted, and subs.(5) as amended, by Criminal Justice (Scotland) Act 2003 (asp 7) Sch.1 para.2(2). Brought into force on 19 June 2006 by SSI 2006/332 (C.30) art.2(1), subject to art.2(2).

Subsections (6), (7) inserted by Criminal Proceedings etc (Reform) (Scotland) Act 2007 (asp 6) s.53. Brought into force on 10 March 2008 by SSI 2008/42 (C.4) art.3 and Sch.

Subsection (7)(c) inserted by Wildlife and Natural Environment (Scotland) Act 2011 (asp 6) Pt 6 s.40(3)(a). Brought into force on 29 June 2011 by SSI 2011/279 art.2.

Subs.(8) was inserted by the Criminal Justice (EU Exit) (Scotland) (Amendment etc.) Regulations 2020 (SSI 2020/339) reg.13(5) (effective 31 December 2020 subject to transitional and saving provision specified in reg.16 of those Regulations.

Definitions

A4-159.1 "extract of previous conviction": s.307(1).
"indictment": s.307(1).
"prosecutor": s.307(1).

[THE NEXT PARAGRAPH IS A4-160]

General Note

A4-160 The Notice of Previous Convictions which the Crown may place before the court in the event of conviction of the accused should conform to Form 8.3 in the 1996 Act of Adjournal.

Broadly, these provisions echo the terms of s.68 of the 1975 Act but are now specified more clearly. Objection to the accuracy of any previous conviction libelled in an indictment which proceeds to trial now has to be made to the Crown Agent not less than seven days prior to the preliminary hearing in High Court cases, and to the procurator fiscal at least five days before a sheriff and jury trial. In the case of cases which plead, rather than proceeding to trial, any objection to a conviction libelled has to be made to the procurator fiscal not less than two days prior to the diet at which the plea is tendered.

Previous convictions which are under appeal should not be libelled (*McCall v Mitchell* (1911) 6 Adam 303) and no previous conviction omitted from the Notice should be taken into account by the court considering sentence, unless it is disclosed in a social enquiry or other report before the court (*Sharp v Stevenson*, 1948 S.L.T. (Notes) 79).

Although the provisions of subs.(1) appear to be absolute, they must be read in conjunction with s.101(2) of the 1995 Act which permits the leading of evidence of an accused's previous convictions where it is a necessary element of proof of the substantive charge.

The anomalous position of previous convictions libelled against bodies corporate and any named officer in the indictment against that body is discussed in the notes to s.70 below.

Proceedings against organisations

A4-161 **70.**—(1) This section applies to proceedings on indictment against an organisation.

(2) The indictment may be served by delivery of a copy of the indictment together with notice to appear at—

(a) in the case of a body of trustees—
   (i) the dwelling-house or place of business of any of the trustees, or
   (ii) if the solicitor of the body of trustees is known, the place of business of the solicitor,

(aa) in the case of a partnership prosecuted by virtue of section 1 of the Partnerships (Prosecution) (Scotland) Act 2013, the dwelling-house or place of business of any of the partners,

(b) in the case of any other organisation, the registered office or, if there is no registered office or the registered office is not in the United Kingdom, at the principal place of business in the United Kingdom of the organisation.

(3) Where a letter containing a copy of the indictment has been sent by registered post or by the recorded delivery service to any place, an acknowledge-

ment or certificate of the delivery of the letter issued by the postal operator shall be sufficient evidence of the delivery of the letter at that place on the day specified in such acknowledgement or certificate.

(4) An organisation may, for the purpose of—

(a) stating objections to the competency or relevancy of the indictment or proceedings; or

(b) tendering a plea of guilty or not guilty; or

(c) making a statement in mitigation of sentence,

appear by a representative.

(5) Where at the trial diet the organisation does not appear as mentioned in subsection (4) above, or by counsel or a solicitor, the court may—

(a) on the motion of the prosecutor; and

(b) if satisfied as to the matters specified in subsection (5A) below,

proceed with the trial and dispose of the case in the absence of the organisation.

(5A) The matters referred to in subsection (5)(b) above are—

(a) that the organisation was cited in accordance with section 66 of this Act as read with subsection (2) above; and

(b) that it is in the interests of justice to proceed as mentioned in subsection (5) above.

(6) Where an organisation is sentenced to a fine, the fine may be recovered in like manner in all respects as if a copy of the sentence certified by the clerk of the court were an extract decree of the Court of Session for the payment of the amount of the fine by the organisation to the Queen's and Lord Treasurer's Remembrancer.

(7) [...]

(8) In subsection (4) above, "representative" means—

(a) in the case of a body corporate (other than a limited liability partnership), the managing director, secretary or other person in charge, or locally in charge, of its affairs;

(b) in the case of a limited liability partnership, a member of the partnership;

(ba) in the case of a partnership (other than a limited liability partnership), a partner or other person in charge, or locally in charge, of the partnership's affairs;

(bb) in the case of an unincorporated association, the secretary or other person in charge, or locally in charge, of the association's affairs;

(c) in the case of any other organisation, an employee, officer or official of the organisation duly appointed by it for the purposes of the proceedings.

(9) For the purposes of subsection (8)(c) above, a statement—

(a) in the case of a body corporate (other than a limited liability partnership), purporting to be signed by an officer of the body;

(b) in the case of a limited liability partnership, purporting to be signed by a member of the partnership,

(c) in the case of a partnership (other than a limited liability partnership), purporting to be signed by a partner;

(d) in the case of an unincorporated association, purporting to be signed by an officer of the association;

(e) in the case of a government department or a part of the Scottish Administration, purporting to be signed by a senior officer in the department or part,

to the effect that the person named in the statement has been appointed as the representative for the purposes of any proceedings to which this section applies is sufficient evidence of such appointment.

AMENDMENTS

Subs.(3) as amended by Postal Services Act 2000 (Consequential Modifications No. 1) Order 2001 (SI 2001/1149) art.3 and Sch.1 para.104.

Subs.(8) as amended by Limited Liability Partnerships (Scotland) Regulations 2001 (SSI 2001/128) reg.5 and Sch.4.

Subs.(5) as amended, and subss.(5)(a), (b), (5A) inserted, by Criminal Procedure (Amendment) (Scotland) Act 2004 (asp 5) s.10(6). Brought into force on 1 February 2005 by SSI 2004/405 (C.28) art.2.

Subss.(8), (9) substituted for original subs.(8) by Criminal Proceedings etc (Reform) (Scotland) Act 2007 (asp 6) s.28. Brought into force on 10 March 2008 by SSI 2008/42 (C.4) art.3 and Sch.

Section 70 as amended by Criminal Justice and Licensing (Scotland) Act 2010 (asp 13) s.66. Brought into force on 28 March 2011 (for specified purposes) by SSI 2011/178 (C.15) art.2, Sch.1 para.1.

Subs.(2)(aa) inserted by Partnerships (Prosecution) (Scotland) Act 2013 (c.21) s.6(4). Brought into force on 26 April 2013 by s.8 of 2013 Act.

Subs.(7) repealed by Criminal Justice (Scotland) Act 2016 (asp 1) s.83. Brought into force on 17 January 2017 by SSI 2016/426 art.2 and Sch.1 para.1.

DEFINITIONS

A4-161.1 "diet": s.307(1).
"fine": s.307(1).
"indictment": s.307(1).
"prosecutor": s.307(1).
"representative": s.70(8).

[THE NEXT PARAGRAPH IS A4-162]

GENERAL NOTE

A4-162 These provisions apply to solemn proceedings, while s.143 below deals with summary prosecutions, in relation to partnerships, trustees in their corporate capacity and companies and the manner in which such bodies may be legally represented. See the fuller discussion in General Note to s.143. In the absence of contrary provisions, s.70 of the 1995 Act is similarly extended. Note that s.28(7) of the Companies Act 1985 (c.6) provides for the preservation and continuity of legal liabilities when a body corporate changes its name or transfers control; a move from registered to unregistered company status does not affect the validity of existing proceedings or preclude the commencement of proceedings (ss.49 and 50 of that Act). Similar provisions govern the move from unlimited to limited status (ss.51 and 52).

Provisions for service are contained in r.8.2 of the Act of Adjournal (Criminal Procedure Rules Amendment) (Criminal Procedure (Amendment) (Scotland) Act 2004) 2005 (SSI 2005/44) and in Form 8.2-H.

Once the court is satisfied that an indictment has been lawfully served upon a limited company or incorporation, it is entitled, on the motion of the prosecutor, to proceed to consider the evidence at a trial diet and dispose of the case at that time even if the body is unrepresented (it seems implicit from the reference to "the trial diet" in subs.(5) that a failure to appear at any earlier diet has to be treated as a plea of not guilty). If the body prosecuted does elect to make an appearance at any diet, this can be made on its behalf by an authorised representative and need not be by a solicitor or counsel.

The prosecutor may opt to prosecute the corporate body alone, proceed against a responsible officer of the company, or both. In the absence of specific statutory provision in regard to the previous convictions of bodies corporate, the general rules expressed in ss.69 and 101(7) would appear to apply. However, if proceedings are taken solely against an officer of the company as its responsible representative, it would surely be inequitable to libel against him previous convictions incurred by the company.

Subsection (6) enacts that fines imposed upon bodies corporate are recoverable by civil diligence.

The Criminal Justice (Scotland) Act 2016 (Commencement No. 3 and Saving Provision) Order 2016 (SSI 2016/426) repealed s.70(7) of the 1995 Act which itself had already removed any requirement for bodies corporate to have pleas signed on their behalf.

The growing importance of criminal sanctions in cases of environmental pollution and health and safety offences has made prosecutions on indictment of limited companies more commonplace. See, for example, *HM Advocate v Kettle Produce Ltd*, 1996 G.W.D. 3-159 (unauthorised connection between sewage outflow pipe and the public water supply causing widescale illness in the vicinity; fine £60,000) and *Balmoral Group Ltd v HM Advocate*, 1996 S.L.T. 1230 (death of employee struck by crane chain and death of a second employee in a second, unrelated incident; fines of £35,000 and £10,000 respectively).

In *HM Advocate v Transco Plc* (High Court of Justiciary, 25 August 2005, unreported) after a lengthy trial on health and safety charges following the death in a gas explosion of all four members of a family in Larkhall, the accused company was fined £15 million, the equivalent of 4 per cent of the last declared annual profits of the company.

The provisions of s.196 of the Act, which entitle the sentencing judge to reduce the level of penalty imposed following a timeous plea of guilt, apply as much to "organisations" as to individual accused; see, for example, *SD Cameron Ltd v PF Inverness* [2011] HCJAC 128.

The Criminal Justice and Licensing (Scotland) Act 2010 (asp 13) ss.65 and 66 introduce what is intended to be an all-encompassing definition of non-natural personae. See the discussions in the notes to ss.143 and 203A below and the definition "organisation" being imported into s.307(1) of the 1995 Act by s.65 of the 2010 Act. Further provisions in the 2010 Act aim to clarify methods of service of indictments upon such bodies and set out the means by which an appearance can be entered by their representatives. Similar measures in respect of summary proceedings are found in s.143 below.

Defence statements

70A.—(1) This section applies where an indictment is served on an accused. A4-162.1

(2) The accused must lodge a defence statement at least 14 days before the first diet.

(3) The accused must lodge a defence statement at least 14 days before the preliminary hearing.

(4) At least 7 days before the trial diet the accused must—

(a) where there has been no material change in circumstances in relation to the accused's defence since the last defence statement was lodged, lodge a statement stating that fact,

(b) where there has been a material change in circumstances in relation to the accused's defence since the last defence statement was lodged, lodge a defence statement.

(5) If after lodging a statement under subsection (2), (3) or (4) there is a material change in circumstances in relation to the accused's defence, the accused must lodge a defence statement.

(6) Where subsection (5) requires a defence statement to be lodged, it must be lodged before the trial diet begins unless on cause shown the court allows it to be lodged during the trial diet.

(7) The accused may lodge a defence statement—

(a) at any time before the trial diet, or

(b) during the trial diet if the court on cause shown allows it.

(8) As soon as practicable after lodging a defence statement or a statement under subsection (4)(a), the accused must send a copy of the statement to the prosecutor and any co-accused.

(9) In this section, "defence statement" means a statement setting out—

(a) the nature of the accused's defence, including any particular defences on which the accused intends to rely,

(b) any matters of fact on which the accused takes issue with the prosecution and the reason for doing so,

(c) particulars of the matters of fact on which the accused intends to rely for the purposes of the accused's defence,

(d) any point of law which the accused wishes to take and any authority on which the accused intends to rely for that purpose,

(e) by reference to the accused's defence, the nature of any information that the accused requires the prosecutor to disclose, and

(f) the reasons why the accused considers that disclosure by the prosecutor of any such information is necessary.

AMENDMENTS

Section 70A inserted by Criminal Justice and Licensing (Scotland) Act 2010 (asp 13) s.124(3). Brought into force on 6 June 2011 for all purposes in respect of criminal proceedings in which the first appearance of the accused is on or after 6 June 2011 by SSI 2011/178 (C.15) art.2, Sch.1 para.1.

GENERAL NOTE

Fourteen days prior to the first diet or preliminary hearing in solemn proceedings the accused is obliged to lodge a defence statement conform to Form 7A.2-A in the Act of Adjournal (Criminal Procedure Rules Amendment No.4) (Disclosure) 2011 (SSI 2011/242). Given the latitude which the Crown generally has to add late additional witnesses and productions to the indictment in terms of s.67(5) of the Act, as well as its duty to make timeous and full disclosure to the defence, it will be appreciated that the need may well arise for an amended defence statement to be received prior to trial (subs.(5)). The importance of preparation and timely lodging of the defence statement was tellingly highlighted in *McClymont v HM Advocate* [2020] HCJAC 1 in which the defence lodged no defence A4-162.2

statement as a consequence of which the Crown submitted it had been unable to initiate the regime of statutory disclosure (see generally the Criminal Justice and Licensing (Scotland) Act 2010 (asp 13) Part 6). A Crown application to extend the year time bar (s.65(1)(b)) was upheld despite a tortuous procedural history.

Formal notice of special defences or defences of consent, diminished responsibility, automatism or coercion, and notices of incrimination have to be lodged at or prior to the first diet (see s.78 below) but the tenor (if any) of the defence case, including such special defences, has to be outlined earlier in the defence statement and updated if the defence case alters. In *McClymont v HM Advocate* [2020] HCJAC 1 the Appeal Court commented pointedly that the lodging of a defence statement and vigorous judicial scrutiny of its terms were core features at any first diet; particularly any want of disclosure should be stated and examined with the parties (see Criminal Courts Practice Note (No.3 of 2015)).

This provision draws heavily upon the disclosure framework for England and Wales set out in the Criminal Procedure and Investigations Act 1996 (c.25) and specifically upon s.11 therein, but its utility is questionable since the instant provision differs from its progenitor in one critical respect; failure to advance or adhere to the terms of the defence statement in Scotland assumes no evidential significance and cannot be founded upon by parties in the proceedings. What use, if any, can be made of the statutory statement by parties or the court itself as a factor to be considered in sentencing after conviction is no clearer.

What will doubtless be only a preliminary discussion of this provision is found in *Barclay v HM Advocate* [2012] HCJAC 47; 2012 S.C.C.R. 428, holding that the requirement to furnish a defence statement is mandatory and is Convention-compliant and does not demand any self-incrimination on the part of an accused. Indeed, the statutory duty can be fulfilled by a bald denial or a call upon the Crown to prove its case, there being no onus upon an accused to advance a positive defence. A challenge to the alleged incompatibility of the court both framing the Act of Adjournal and deliberating upon the vires thereof was rejected. It remains incumbent upon the trial judge as a general duty to ensure that the accused is not prejudiced in the submission of a defence statement (or an amended statement) by want of disclosure or late service of s.67 notices by the Crown.

[THE NEXT PARAGRAPH IS A4-163]

Pre-trial proceedings

First diet

A4-163 **71.**—(A1) At a first diet in proceedings to which subsection (B1) below applies, the court shall, ascertain whether the accused has engaged a solicitor for the purposes of the conduct of his case at any relevant hearing in the course of the proceedings.

(B1) This subsection applies to proceedings—

(a) in which the accused is charged with a sexual offence to which section 288C of this Act applies,

(aa) in respect of an offence to which section 288DC of this Act applies (domestic abuse cases),

(b) to which section 288E of this Act applies, or

(c) in which an order under section 288F(2) of this Act has been made in relation to any hearing in the course of the proceedings.

(1) At a first diet the court shall, so far as is reasonably practicable, ascertain—

(a) the state of preparation of the prosecutor and of the accused with respect to their cases; and

(b) the extent to which the prosecutor and the accused have complied with the duty under section 257(1) of this Act.

(1ZA) If a written record has been lodged in accordance with section 71C, the court must have regard to the written record when ascertaining the state of preparation of the parties.

(1A) At a first diet, the court shall also—

(a) ascertain whether subsection (1B) below applies to any person who is to give evidence at or for the purposes of any hearing in the course of the proceedings or to the accused, and

(b) if so, consider whether it should make an order under section 271A(7) or 271D(2) of this Act in relation to the person or, as the case may be, the accused.

(1B) This subsection applies—

(a) to a person who is to give evidence at or for the purposes of any hearing in the course of the proceedings if that person is, or is likely to be, a vulnerable witness,

(b) to the accused if, were he to give evidence at or for the purposes of the trial, he would be, or would be likely to be, a vulnerable witness.

(1C) At a first diet, the court—

(a) shall ascertain which of the witnesses included in the list of witnesses are required by the prosecutor or the accused to attend the trial; and

(b) shall, where the accused has been admitted to bail, review the conditions imposed on his bail and may—

(i) after giving the parties an opportunity to be heard; and

(ii) if it considers it appropriate to do so,

fix bail on different conditions.

(2) In addition to the matters mentioned in subsection (1), (1A) and (1C) above the court shall, at a first diet, consider any preliminary plea or preliminary issue (within the meanings given to those terms in section 79(2) of this Act) of which a party has, not less than two clear days before the first diet, given notice to the court and to the other parties.

(2XA) At a first diet the court shall also dispose of any vulnerable witness notice under section 271A(2) or vulnerable witness application under section 271C(2) appointed to be disposed of at that diet.

(2YA) At a first diet, the court shall also ascertain whether there is any objection to the admissibility of any evidence which any party wishes to raise despite not having given the notice referred to in subsection (2) above, and—

(a) if so, decide whether to grant leave under section 79(1) of this Act for the objection to be raised; and

(b) if leave is granted, dispose of the objection unless it considers it inappropriate to do so at the first diet.

(2ZA) Where the court, having granted leave for the objection to be raised, decides not to dispose of it at the first diet, the court may—

(a) appoint a further diet to be held before the trial diet for the purpose of disposing of the objection; or

(b) appoint the objection to be disposed of at the trial diet.

(2A) At a first diet the court may consider an application for the purposes of subsection (1) of section 275 of this Act.

(3) At a first diet the court may ask the prosecutor and the accused any question in connection with any matter which it is required to ascertain or consider under subsection (1), (1A), (2) or (2YA) above or which is relevant to an application for the purposes of subsection (1), (1C) of the said section 275.

(4) The accused shall attend a first diet of which he has been given notice.

(5) A first diet may proceed, and a trial diet may be appointed, notwithstanding the absence of the accused.

(5A) Where, however—

(a) the proceedings in which the first diet is being held are proceedings to which subsection (B1) above applies;

(b) the court has not ascertained (whether at that diet or earlier) that he has engaged a solicitor for the purposes of the conduct of his case at any relevant hearing in the course of the proceedings,

a first diet may not proceed in his absence; and, in such a case, the court shall adjourn the diet and ordain the accused then to attend.

(6) Where the accused appears at the first diet, the accused is to be required at that diet to state how he pleads to the indictment, and section 77 of this Act shall apply where he tenders a plea of guilty.

(7) ...

(7A) In subsections (A1) and (5A)(b), "relevant hearing" means—

(a) in relation to proceedings mentioned in paragraph (a) of subsection (B1), any hearing at, or for the purposes of, which a witness is to give evidence,

(b) in relation to proceedings mentioned in paragraph (b) of that subsection, a hearing referred to in section 288E(2A),

(c) in relation to proceedings mentioned in paragraph (c) of that subsection, a hearing in respect of which an order is made under section 288F.

(8)–(8A) […]

(9) In this section "the court" means the sheriff court.

Amendments

Subss.(A1), (5A) and (8A) inserted by Sexual Offences (Procedure and Evidence) (Scotland) Act 2002 (asp 9) Sch.1 para.5.

Subs.(2A) inserted by Sexual Offences (Procedure and Evidence) (Scotland) Act 2002 (asp 9) s.8(2)(a).

Subs.(3) as amended by Sexual Offences (Procedure and Evidence) (Scotland) Act 2002 (asp 9) s.8(2)(b).

All these changes are brought into force by SSI 2002/443 (C.24) art.4 (effective 1 November 2002).

Subss.(2YA) and (2ZA) inserted, and subs.(3) as amended, by Criminal Procedure (Amendment) (Scotland) Act 2004 (asp 5) s.14(1). Brought into force on 1 February 2005 by SSI 2004/405 (C.28) art.2.

Subs.(1C) inserted, and subss.(2) and (3) as amended, by Criminal Procedure (Amendment) (Scotland) Act 2004 (asp 5) s.19. Brought into force on 1 February 2005 as above.

Subs.(2) as amended by Criminal Procedure (Amendment) (Scotland) Act 2004 (asp 5) s.25, Sch.1 para.20(a). Brought into force on 1 February 2005 as above.

Subss.(8) and (8A) repealed by Criminal Procedure (Amendment) (Scotland) Act 2004 (asp 5) s.25, Sch.1 para.20(b). Brought into force on 1 February 2005 as above.

Subss.(1A) and (1B) inserted, and subss.(2) and (3) as amended, by Vulnerable Witnesses (Scotland) Act 2004 (asp 3) s.2. Brought into force on 1 April 2005 by SSI 2005/168 (C.7) art.2 and Sch. Further brought into force on 1 April 2006 by SSI 2006/59 (C.8). Remainder brought into force on 1 April 2008 by SSI 2008/57 (C.7) art.2.

Subs.(B1) inserted, subs.(5A)(a) as substituted and subs.(A1) as amended by Vulnerable Witnesses (Scotland) Act 2004 (asp 3) s.7(1). Brought into force on 1 April 2005 by SSI 2005/168 (C.7) art.2 and Sch. Further brought into force on 1 April 2006 by the SSI 2006/59 (C.8).

Subs.(2XA) inserted by Criminal Procedure (Amendment) (Scotland) Act 2004 (Incidental, Supplemental and Consequential Provisions) Order 2005 (SSI 2005/40) art.4(3). Brought into force on 31 January 2005 in accordance with art.1.

Subs.(4) as amended by Criminal Proceedings etc (Reform) (Scotland) Act 2007 (asp 6) s.80, Sch. para.12. Brought into force on 10 December 2007 by SSI 2007/479 (C.40) art.3 and Sch.

Subss.(A1), (B1), (1A), (1B) and (5A) as amended, and subs.(7A) inserted, by Criminal Justice and Licensing (Scotland) Act 2010 (asp 13) Sch.7 para.45. Brought into force on 28 March 2011 by SSI 2011/178 (C.15) art.2, Sch.1 para.1.

Subs.(2XA) as amended by Victims and Witnesses (Scotland) Act 2014 (asp 1) s.11(1). Brought into force on 1 September 2015 by SSI 2015/200 art.2 and Sch. subject to transitional provisions in art.4.

Subss.(1), (5), (6), (9) as amended, subs.(1ZA) inserted, subs.(7) repealed, by Criminal Justice (Scotland) Act 2016 (asp 1) ss.80 and 81. Brought into force on 29 May 2017 and 31 July 2017 by SSI 2017/99 art.3, for the purposes of any indictment served on an accused on or after that day; not yet in force otherwise.

Subsection (B1)(aa) inserted by Domestic Abuse (Scotland) Act 2018 (asp 5) Sch.1(1) (2) para.4(4) (effective 1 April 2019 in respect of proceedings commenced on or after 1 April 2019 subject to transitional provision specified in SSI 2018/387 reg.7(2)).

Definitions

A4-163.1 "court": subs.(9).
"diet": s.307(1).
"prosecutor": s.307(1).

[THE NEXT PARAGRAPH IS A4-164]

GENERAL NOTE

"Origins"

Mandatory first diets in sheriff solemn proceedings were introduced by s.13 of the Criminal Justice (Scotland) Act 1995 (c.20). At that time preliminary hearings were optional (and little-used) in High Court cases. Section 71's provisions apply to the first diets while s.72 refers to High Court cases. Exceptionally these procedural hearings may be dispensed with (see s.75A of the Act) on joint application; it is anticipated that such administrative adjournments will actively be encouraged where parties concur that the case is not yet ready for trial. On the other hand continuations of the first diet are expected to be actively discouraged by the Bench (refer to the Criminal Courts Practice Note (No.3 of 2015)). In the absence of concurrence in terms of s.75A, the indictment will have to call on the appointed date for a hearing. **A4-164**

The Act of Adjournal (Criminal Procedure Rules) 1996 governs the conduct of these proceedings and reference should also be made to the Practice Note (No.3 of 2015) which lays out the approach now being applied to solemn court business. For completeness, on a cautionary note, the extent to which an unrepresented accused can properly be required to fulfil the obligations laid out in ss.71 and 71C is questionable.

Accused are now cited only to a first diet, or preliminary hearing, no trial diet being assigned by the Crown, when the indictment is served. Failure of an accused to appear will not necessarily halt either the hearing, or assignment of a trial (s.71(4)) but an accused whose libel falls within the ambit of ss.288C, 288E or 288F(2) must make a personal appearance at the diet or a continuation thereof (see s.71(5A)). Formal notice of special defences or defences of consent, diminished responsibility, automatism or coercion, and notices of incrimination have to be lodged at or prior to the first diet (see s.78 below) but the shape of the defence case has to be outlined earlier—14 days after service of the indictment—in the defence statement (s.70A) and updated if the stated position alters.

See the fuller discussion below at "General Discussion".

Duties of parties prior to first diet court

The first diet is regarded as the "end-point of preparation" rather than the prelude to it and continuation is competent to enable pre-trial disposal of preliminary pleas and issues (s.71(2ZA)). Ordinarily, such pleas or issues should have been raised by notice at least two days prior to the hearing (s.71(2)) but may be moved without such notice with leave of the court (s.71(2YA)).

Responsibility for the management of trial business, previously a Crown task, now rests with the Sheriff Clerk (or Clerk of Justiciary in High Court cases) based upon the information gleaned from the written record (s.71C) and the parties' submissions at the first diet or procedural hearing. Optimal loading of the volume of cases to call in such courts will be agreed between the Crown and the Clerk. In sheriff solemn cases it is the task of the Crown and defence to make known any case listed which they identify as requiring more than 20 minutes consideration by the sheriff.

Duties of the first diet court

Section 71(A1) obliges the court to ensure that an accused charged with committing a listed sexual offence (as set out in s.288C), or charged with any other of the offences specified in s.288E(3) in which a witness is under 12 years of age, is legally represented for both the preparation and conduct of the proceedings.

More generally the first diet court now has a range of tasks to fulfill in addition to ascertaining whether witnesses are covered by these specific statutory provisions: there is an obligation to consider whether any listed witness may be regarded as vulnerable (refer to s.271 of the Act) or equally whether the accused himself is considered vulnerable and in need of special measures to enable him to follow the proceedings or to give evidence (subs.1B); it must ascertain the preparedness of all parties for trial (subs.1(a)); enquire whether evidence capable of agreement has been identified (subs.1(b)) and identify the witnesses whose parole evidence will be required for any trial or hearing (subs.(1C)(a)); consider whether any variation of existing bail conditions is needed (subs.(1C)(b)) and deal with any preliminary pleas or objections to admissibility of evidence (subss.(2) and (2YA)) and, finally, having recorded the accused's pleas, assign a trial diet or invite the Crown to apply for any extension to the relevant time bars affecting the accused.

Procedural matters

First diets can proceed in the absence of an accused and, in the event of a failure to appear and on being satisfied of notice of the diet having been served on the accused, the court has a discretion to grant an apprehension warrant (subss.(4) and (5)). A warrant at this stage has the effect of ending the proceedings upon that indictment against the absent accused, as well as halting any statutory timebar affecting his proceedings. In many cases it may be preferable to maintain the existing indictment especially where there are co-accused.

Attention is directed to the provisions in s.70 governing the citation and trial of bodies corporate; it would for example, be perfectly competent for an officer of the company or other representative to appear instead of a legal representative at the diet. Note too the specific requirements in regard to those charged with listed sexual offences, or who are deemed to be vulnerable, or whose proceedings will involve vulnerable witnesses or witnesses aged less than 12 years; in each of these circumstances the court has to ensure that the accused has been informed of the necessity for legal representation and cannot proceed in his absence until it is satisfied that this has been made known to him.

At the conclusion of the first diet the accused has to be called upon to tender pleas to the charges libelled.

Section 66(6) provides that the first diet must occur not less than 29 clear days after service of the indictment unless the accused has opted for the accelerated procedure for guilty pleas contained in s.76 of the Act.

General Discussion

While preliminary pleas or issues may be resolved at the first diet, s.71(2ZA) anticipates a hearing at a diet continued for the purpose, or at the trial diet itself once it is assigned.

Stewart v HM Advocate, 1997 G.W.D. 23-1145 suggests that, where a case is re-indicted for trial, earlier unsuccessful pleas in bar of trial (in *Stewart* a plea in bar of insanity which had been repelled at first instance and on appeal and is reported as *Stewart v HM Advocate (No.1)*, 1997 S.C.C.R. 330) may competently be restated, the court having the option in terms of s.73(5) and s.80 of the Act to postpone trial to enable further inquiry. It is of course the case that an accused's fitnes for trial can alter between indictments and could thus require to be reconsidered; issues of competency or relevancy, it is submitted, could not be resurrected in the same way.

It will be observed that, adopting the provisions of s.79(1), means that notices specifying any one of the preliminary objections (i.e. competency or relevancy of the libel, objections to the validity of any citation, any plea in bar of trial, motions for separation or conjunction of charges or trials, challenges to any special capacity libelled, including the currency of bail orders, and any objection to the admission of the judicial examination transcript or transcript of an accused's declaration) must be notified not less than two days before the first diet or its continuation.

After consideration of any preliminary pleas or other matters raised before the court it is essential that pleas be tendered and recorded to any charges left on the libel.

Notwithstanding this proposition it is of note that in *Roselli v Vannet*, 1997 S.C.C.R. 655, a summary complaint, advocation of proceedings was held to be competent to review events at an intermediate diet.

Act of Adjournal

A4-164.1 Chapter 9 of the Act of Adjournal (Criminal Procedure Rules) 1996 regulates procedures for first diets and provides appropriate styles. Chapter 9A refers to preliminary hearings in High Court proceedings. Form 9.1 provides the style for raising preliminary pleas or issues.

[THE NEXT PARAGRAPH IS A4-165]

Appeal procedures

A4-165 Appeals arising from decisions of the court at first diets or preliminary diets are considered by the High Court under s.74 of the Act; in the event of an appeal, part, or all of the postponement period can be discounted by the High Court from any time bar calculation and, by implication, this can be done with retrospective effect. Appeals must be raised within two days upon Form 9.12 given in the Act of Adjournal and, if need be, abandoned by Form 9.17. Note that decisions to adjourn the first, or preliminary, diet or to postpone the trial diet cannot be appealed under s.74 (see subs.(2)(a)) but that such decisions can be challenged by an accused in an appeal against conviction or sentence (s.106) and by the Lord Advocate in an appeal against an unduly lenient sentence (s.108).

Further pre-trial diet: dismissal or withdrawal of solicitor representing accused in case of sexual offence

A4-165.1 **71A.** [...]

AMENDMENTS

Section 71A inserted by Sexual Offences (Procedure and Evidence) (Scotland) Act 2002 (asp 9) Sch.1 para.6. Brought into force by SSI 2002/443 (C.24) art.4 (effective 1 November 2002).

Section 71A repealed by Criminal Procedure (Amendment) (Scotland) Act 2004 (asp 5) s.25, Sch.1 para.21. Brought into force on 4 December 2004 by SSI 2004/405 (C.28).

First diet: appointment of trial diet

A4-165.2 **71B.**—(1) At a first diet, unless a plea of guilty is tendered and accepted, the court must—

(a) after complying with section 71, and
(b) subject to subsections (3) to (7),

appoint a trial diet.

(2) Where a trial diet is appointed at a first diet, the accused must appear at the trial diet and answer the indictment.

(3) In appointing a trial diet under subsection (1), in any case in which the 12 month period applies (whether or not the 140 day period also applies in the case)—

(a) if the court considers that the case would be likely to be ready to proceed to trial within that period, it must, subject to subsections (5) to (7), appoint a trial diet for a date within that period, or

(b) if the court considers that the case would not be likely to be so ready, it must give the prosecutor an opportunity to make an application to the court under section 65(3) for an extension of the 12 month period.

(4) Where paragraph (b) of subsection (3) applies—

(a) if such an application as is mentioned in that paragraph is made and granted, the court must, subject to subsections (5) to (7), appoint a trial diet for a date within the 12 month period as extended, or

(b) if no such application is made or if one is made but is refused by the court—

(i) the court may desert the first diet simpliciter or pro loco et tempore, and

(ii) where the accused is committed until liberated in due course of law, the accused must be liberated forthwith.

(5) Subsection (6) applies in any case in which—

(a) the 140 day period as well as the 12 month period applies, and

(b) the court is required, by virtue of subsection (3)(a) or (4)(a) to appoint a trial diet within the 12 month period.

(6) In such a case—

(a) if the court considers that the case would be likely to be ready to proceed to trial within the 140 day period, it must appoint a trial diet for a date within that period as well as within the 12 month period, or

(b) if the court considers that the case would not be likely to be so ready, it must give the prosecutor an opportunity to make an application under section 65(5) for an extension of the 140 day period.

(7) Where paragraph (b) of subsection (6) applies—

(a) if such an application as is mentioned in that paragraph is made and granted, the court must appoint a trial diet for a date within the 140 day period as extended as well as within the 12 month period,

(b) if no such application is made or if one is made but is refused by the court—

(i) the court must proceed under subsection (3)(a) or (as the case may be) (4)(a) to appoint a trial diet for a date within the 12 month period, and

(ii) the accused is then entitled to be admitted to bail.

(8) Where an accused is, by virtue of subsection (7)(b)(ii), entitled to be admitted to bail, the court must, before admitting the accused to bail, give the prosecutor an opportunity to be heard.

(9) On appointing a trial diet under this section in a case where the accused has been admitted to bail (otherwise than by virtue of subsection (7)(b)(ii)), the court, after giving the parties an opportunity to be heard—

(a) must review the conditions imposed on the accused's bail, and

(b) having done so, may, if it considers it appropriate to do so, fix bail on different conditions.

(10) In this section—

"the 12 month period" means the period specified in subsection (1)(b) of section 65 and, in any case in which that period has been extended under subsection (3) of that section, includes that period as so extended,

"the 140 day period" means the period specified in subsection (4)(b)(ii) of section 65 and, in any case in which that period has been extended under subsection (5) of that section, includes that period as so extended.

AMENDMENTS

Section 71B inserted by Criminal Justice (Scotland) Act 2016 (asp 1) s.81(4). Brought into force on 31 July 2017 by SSI 2017/99 art.4.

[THE NEXT PARAGRAPH IS A4-165.5]

Written record of state of preparation: sheriff court

A4-165.5 **71C.**—(1) Subsection (2) applies where—

(a) the accused is indicted to the sheriff court, and

(b) a solicitor—

(i) has notified the court under section 72F(1) that the solicitor has been engaged by the accused for the purposes of conducting the accused's defence, and

(ii) has not subsequently been dismissed by the accused or withdrawn.

(2) The prosecutor and the accused's legal representative must, within the period described in subsection (3), communicate with each other and jointly prepare a written record of their state of preparation with respect to their cases (referred to in this section as "the written record").

(3) The period referred to in subsection (2) begins on the day the accused is served with an indictment and expires at the end of the day falling 14 days later.

(4) The written record must—

(a) be in such form, or as nearly as may be in such form,

(b) contain such information, and

(c) be lodged in such manner,

as may be prescribed by act of adjournal.

(5) The written record must state the manner in which the communication required by subsection (2) was conducted (for example, by telephone, email or a meeting in person).

(6) In subsection (2), "the accused's legal representative" means—

(a) the solicitor referred to in subsection (1), or

(b) where the solicitor has instructed counsel for the purposes of the conduct of the accused's case, either the solicitor or that counsel, or both of them.

(7) In subsection (6)(b), "counsel" includes a solicitor who has a right of audience in the High Court of Justiciary under section 25A of the Solicitors (Scotland) Act 1980.

AMENDMENTS

Section 71C inserted by Criminal Justice (Scotland) Act 2016 (asp 1) s.80(3). Brought into force on 29 May 2017 by SSI 2017/99 art.3, for the purposes of any indictment served on an accused on or after that day; not yet in force otherwise.

GENERAL NOTE

A4-165.6 Within 14 days of service of the indictment all parties are obliged to lodge a written record (WR) jointly setting out the state of preparation for trial in a format which draws heavily upon the experience of preliminary hearings in the High Court. The style is to be found in Criminal Courts Practice Note (No.3 of 2015) and as Form 9.3A in the Scottish Courts site at criminal forms; this can be downloaded for electronic transmission to the Sheriff Clerk. This document should not be confused with the defence statement described in s.70A of the Act which must also be lodged by each defence solicitor.

The WR is central to the scheme of management of court business and details the extent of communication between parties, effectively focusing the issues in the case. While no sanctions are provided for non-compliance, it can be asserted confidently that such a failure is unlikely to be greeted sympathetically by the Bench.

[THE NEXT PARAGRAPH IS A4-166]

Preliminary hearing: procedure up to appointment of trial diet

72.—(1) A preliminary hearing shall be conducted in accordance with this section and section 72A. **A4-166**

(2) The court shall—

(a) where the accused is charged with an offence to which section 288C or 288DC of this Act applies; or

(b) in any case—

(i) in respect of which section 288E of this Act applies; or

(ii) in which an order has been made under section 288F(2) of this Act,

before taking any further step under this section, ascertain whether the accused has engaged a solicitor for the purposes of the conduct of his case at or for the purposes of the preliminary hearing.

(3) After complying with subsection (2) above, the court shall dispose of any preliminary pleas (within the meaning of section 79(2)(a) of this Act) of which a party has given notice not less than 7 clear days before the preliminary hearing to the court and to the other parties.

(4) After disposing of any preliminary pleas under subsection (3) above, the court shall require the accused to state how he pleads to the indictment.

(5) If the accused tenders a plea of guilty, section 77 of this Act shall apply.

(6) After the accused has stated how he pleads to the indictment, the court shall, unless a plea of guilty is tendered and accepted—

(a) in any case—

(i) where the accused is charged with an offence to which section 288C or 288DC of this Act of this Act applies;

(ii) in respect of which section 288E of this Act applies; or

(iii) in which an order has been made under section 288F(2) of this Act,

ascertain whether the accused has engaged a solicitor for the purposes of his defence at the trial;

(b) unless it considers it inappropriate to do so at the preliminary hearing, dispose of—

(i) any preliminary issues (within the meaning of section 79(2)(b) of this Act) of which a party has given notice not less than 7 clear days before the preliminary hearing to the court and to the other parties;

(ii) any vulnerable witness notice under section 271A(2) or vulnerable witness application under section 271C(2) appointed to be disposed of at the preliminary hearing;

(iii) subject to subsection (8) below, any application under section 275(1) or 288F(2) of this Act made before the preliminary hearing (to the extent that the application has not already been disposed of); and

(iv) any other matter which, in the opinion of the court, could be disposed of with advantage before the trial;

(c) ascertain whether there is any objection to the admissibility of any evidence which any party wishes to raise despite not having given the notice referred to in paragraph (b)(i) above, and—

(i) if so, decide whether to grant leave under section 79(1) of this Act for the objection to be raised; and

(ii) if leave is granted, dispose of the objection unless it considers it inappropriate to do so at the preliminary hearing;

(d) ascertain which of the witnesses included in the list of witnesses are required by the prosecutor or the accused to attend the trial;

(e) ascertain whether subsection (7) below applies to any person who is to give evidence at or for the purposes of the trial or to the accused and, if so, consider whether it should make an order under section 271A(7) or 271D(2) of this Act in relation to the person or, as the case may be, the accused; and

(f) ascertain, so far as is reasonably practicable—

(i) the state of preparation of the prosecutor and the accused with respect to their cases; and

(ii) the extent to which the prosecutor and the accused have complied with the duty under section 257(1) of this Act.

(7) This subsection applies—

(a) to a person who is to give evidence at or for the purposes of the trial if that person is, or is likely to be, a vulnerable witness;

(b) to the accused if, were he to give evidence at or for the purposes of the trial, he would be, or would be likely to be, a vulnerable witness.

(8) Where any application or notice such as is mentioned in subsection (6)(b)(iii) above is required by the provision under which it is made or lodged, or by any other provision of this Act, to be made or lodged by a certain time, the court—

(a) shall not be required under that subsection to dispose of it unless it has been made or lodged by that time; but

(b) shall have power to dispose of it to the extent that the provision under which it was made, or any other provision of this Act, allows it to be disposed of notwithstanding that it was not made or lodged in time.

(9) Where the court decides not to dispose of any preliminary issue, application, notice, objection or other matter referred to in subsection (6)(b) or (c) above at the preliminary hearing, it may—

(a) appoint a further diet, to be held before the trial diet appointed under section 72A of this Act, for the purpose of disposing of the issue, application, notice, objection or matter; or

(b) appoint the issue, application, notice, objection or other matter to be disposed of at the trial diet.

AMENDMENT

Section 72 as substituted by Criminal Procedure (Amendment) (Scotland) Act 2004 (asp 5) s.1(3). Brought into force, with exceptions, on 1 February 2005 by SSI 2004/405 (C.28) art.2. Otherwise brought into force on 1 April 2005 by SSI 2004/405 and SSI 2005/168.

Subs.(6)(b)(ii) as amended by Victims and Witnesses (Scotland) Act 2014 (asp 1) s.11(2). Brought into force on 1 September 2015 by SSI 2015/200 art.2 and Sch. subject to transitional provisions in art.4.

Subs.(2)(a), (6)(a)(i) as amended by Domestic Abuse (Scotland) Act 2018 (asp 5) Sch.1(1)(2) para.4(5) (effective 1 April 2019 in respect of proceedings commenced on or after 1 April 2019 subject to transitional provision specified in SSI 2018/387 reg.7(2)).

Subs.(6)(b)(iii) as amended by Vulnerable Witnesses (Criminal Evidence) (Scotland) Act 2019 (asp 8) s.5(7) (effective 20 January 2020).

DEFINITIONS

A4-166.1 "High Court": s.307(1).
"indictment": s.307(1).
"preliminary hearing": s.66(6)(b).

"preliminary issues": s.79(2)(b).
"preliminary pleas": s.79(2)(a).
"prosecutor": s.307(1).
"the court": s.72D(9).
"vulnerable witness": s.307(1).

[THE NEXT PARAGRAPH IS A4-167]

GENERAL NOTE

Background

The Criminal Justice (Scotland) Act 1995 (c.20) introduced mandatory first diets into sheriff and jury proceedings but made the High Court equivalent (the "preliminary diet") optional. This distinction may have stemmed, at least in part, from the logistical difficulties in ensuring the attendance of accused at the High Court in Edinburgh, but two factors conspired to ensure that the once-rare preliminary diet became commonplace; the advent of the European Convention into domestic law following the Scotland Act 1998 (c.46) and the consequent diets to determine devolution issues, and the provisions enacted in relation to listed sexual offences (see ss.274–275B) which demanded advance determination of the scope of questioning at trial. As can be seen, following upon the recommendations of the Bonomy Committee, ss.72 to 72G specify a mandatory (and rigorous) pre-trial regime of judicial scrutiny which is intended to resolve the perceived defects and delays in existing procedures. It is important to recall that with the extended timebars in High Court proceedings introduced by s.67(4)(aa) of the Act, a preliminary diet must be held within 110 days of full committal, and trial within 140 days. Furthermore, earlier notice of preliminary pleas or issues (seven days as against two days) is demanded in High Court proceedings than in sheriff solemn cases. **A4-167**

The Preliminary Hearings Bench Book

Valuable guidance for solemn practitioners, and students alike, is found in the *Preliminary Hearings Bench Book*, available in text or as a download with hyperlinks on the Judiciary of Scotland website as a Judicial Institute publication (see *https://www.judiciary.scot/home/media-information/publications/judicial-institute-publications* [Accessed 7 October 2020]).

Duties of the preliminary diet court

The duties of the court broadly mirror those described in the notes to s.71 above but it must be appreciated that the scope of enquiry by the court in High Court cases is even more extensive.

First, the court has to consider whether any charge libelled falls within the scope of s.288C of the Act as a listed sexual offence, or failing this, whether any offence falls within the scope of s.288E(3) and involves adducing the evidence of a child aged under 12 years at the time of the trial, or will require the evidence of a vulnerable witness (s.288F). In each of these situations the court has to ensure that the accused is alert to the fact that he cannot either prepare the case personally or represent himself in the *preliminary* diet proceedings, and, if need be, arrange for legal representation: while s.288F(3) of the Act appears to permit departure from the need for legal representation in these cases this is only in relation to the conduct of *trial* proceedings, and then strictly on cause shown.

Next, if the accused does not then plead guilty to the charges, the court has to consider any preliminary pleas of which due notice has been given (s.79(2)(a)) before calling upon the accused to plead to any charges remaining. (Refer to Form 9A.1 in SSI 2005/44 for the style of notice).

With a view specifically to the *trial* proceedings now identified, subs.(6)(a) then revisits witness issues as set out in ss.288C, 288E(3) and 288F to ensure that legal representation is available for the conduct of any trial before moving on to consideration of any of the preliminary issues specified in s.79(2)(b) and a more detailed scrutiny of the manner in which evidence will be led by the parties (subs.(6)(b)). This scrutiny will determine the merits of any screen or CCTV applications lodged in relation to child witnesses or vulnerable witnesses, the scope of any application to depart from the general restrictions set down in s.274 of the Act in regard to the questioning of complainers in sexual crimes, and any other matters which could be considered advantageously at that time.

The hearing is also an opportunity for seeking the court's leave to introduce preliminary pleas or preliminary issues (see s.79 below) of which timeous notice has not been given; for the court to resolve with parties which witnesses are required to give parole evidence at the trial (and by implication to identify evidence not in dispute) and to assess what special measures, if any, are necessary for the taking of the evidence of any child or vulnerable witness or, indeed, the accused. It should be noted that s.271A(2)(b) expressly requires the party seeking to lead the child's evidence to state explicitly when *no* special measures are deemed necessary. All questions of admissibility of evidence, as matters of law, are for the judge not the jury, and fall to be considered at this diet once properly brought to the attention of the court. See *Britz v HM Advocate*, 2007 S.L.T. 78, following *Thompson v Crowe*, 1999 S.L.T. 1434; 1999 S.C.C.R. 1003, a five bench decision. Only rarely would it be appropriate to carry the issues, unresolved forward to the trial diet—*Wright v HM Advocate*, 2006 S.C.C.R. 455 has to be viewed as something of an exception to the general rule—and it is almost inconceivable in a solemn trial that predictable issues of admissibility should be deferred until evidence be led before the jury, then heard under reservation (*Atkinson v HM Advocate* [2010] HCJAC 77; 2010 G.W.D. 28-579). See too *HM Advocate v G*, 2010 S.L.T. 239 where defence minutes seeking to found upon psychologists' assessments of the reliability (or otherwise) of child witnesses' testimony as a preliminary issue were deferred till trial, the judge considering that evaluation of the reliability of evidence rested principally with the jury.

Subs.(6)(f) re-enacts the duty of the court to ascertain the readiness of parties for trial (s.72E demands that the parties lodge a written record (following Form 9A.4 in SSI 2005/44) of their efforts to discuss issues) and to investigate the degree to which parties have identified evidence capable of agreement (see s.257 below). Subs.(8) underlines the importance of lodging any notices under ss.275 and 288F timeously but leaves the court a residual discretion to consider such waiver applications, or applications for witnesses to be treated as vulnerable, to the court.

As subs.(9) makes patent it is competent for the court either to appoint a later diet to consider any notices or preliminary pleas or issues, or to continue the matter for consideration at the trial diet itself. (It follows that the trial diet is preserved in either event).

Once all these issues have been resolved the court can proceed to assign the trial diet in accordance with s.72A of the Act.

Dispensing with the preliminary diet

Given the exhaustive range of enquiries the court is now obliged to undertake it may be thought difficult to envisage situations in which no preliminary diet would be needed. Nonetheless, s.72B addresses such rare situations, leaving the parties to lodge written application to the court to waive the diet. It should not be imagined that dispensing with the diet can be deployed as a means of escaping scrutiny by the court; the court has to be satisfied that the case is ready for trial, that there are no preliminary pleas or issues to be settled and no vulnerable witnesses or accused in the case, and that the parties have identified the witnesses whose attendance at trial is not deemed necessary, and should be able to refer to the written record which still must be available for examination by the court (s.72E below).

Note that the time limits for lodging notices or intimations of challenges still apply in the absence of a preliminary diet.

Preliminary hearing: appointment of trial diet

A4-167.1 **72A.**—(1) In any case in which subsection (6) of section 72 applies, the court shall, at the preliminary hearing—

(a) after complying with that subsection;

(b) having regard to earlier proceedings at the preliminary hearing; and

(c) subject to subsections (3) to (7) below,

appoint a trial diet.

(1A) […]

(2) In appointing a trial diet under subsection (1) above, the court may, if satisfied that it is appropriate to do so, indicate that the diet is to be a floating diet for the purposes of section 83A of this Act.

(3) In any case in which the 12 month period applies (whether or not the 140 day period also applies in the case)—

(a) if the court considers that the case would be likely to be ready to proceed to trial within that period, it shall, subject to subsections (5) to (7) below, appoint a trial diet for a date within that period; or

(b) if the court considers that the case would not be likely to be so ready, it shall give the prosecutor an opportunity to make an application to the court under section 65(3) of this Act for an extension of the 12 month period.

(4) Where paragraph (b) of subsection (3) above applies—

(a) if such an application as is mentioned in that paragraph is made and granted, the court shall, subject to subsections (5) to (7) below, appoint a trial diet for a date within the 12 month period as extended; or

(b) if no such application is made or if one is made but is refused by the court—

(i) the court may desert the preliminary hearing simpliciter or *pro loco et tempore*; and

(ii) where the accused is committed until liberated in due course of law, he shall be liberated forthwith.

(5) Subsection (6) below applies in any case in which—

(a) the 140 day period as well as the 12 month period applies; and

(b) the court is required, by virtue of subsection (3)(a) or (4)(a) above, to appoint a trial diet within the 12 month period.

(6) In such a case—

(a) if the court considers that the case would be likely to be ready to proceed to trial within the 140 day period, it shall appoint a trial diet for a date within that period as well as within the 12 month period; or

(b) if the court considers that the case would not be likely to be so ready, it shall give the prosecutor an opportunity to make an application under section 65(5) of this Act for an extension of the 140 day period.

(7) Where paragraph (b) of subsection (6) above applies—

(a) if such an application as is mentioned in that paragraph is made and granted, the court shall appoint a trial diet for a date within the 140 day period as extended as well as within the 12 month period;

(b) if no such application is made or if one is made but is refused by the court

(i) the court shall proceed under subsection (3)(a) or, as the case may be, (4)(a) above to appoint a trial diet for a date within the 12 month period; and

(ii) the accused shall then be entitled to be admitted to bail.

(8) Where an accused is, by virtue of subsection (7)(b)(ii) above, entitled to be admitted to bail, the court shall, before admitting him to bail, give the prosecutor an opportunity to be heard.

(9) On appointing a trial diet under this section in a case where the accused has been admitted to bail (otherwise than by virtue of subsection (7)(b)(ii) above), the court, after giving the parties an opportunity to be heard—

(a) shall review the conditions imposed on his bail; and

(b) having done so, may, if it considers it appropriate to do so, fix bail on different conditions.

(10) In this section—

"the 12 month period" means the period specified in subsection (1)(b) of section 65 of this Act and, in any case in which that period has been extended under subsection (3) of that section, includes that period as so extended; and

"the 140 day period" means the period specified in subsection (4)(aa)(ii) of that section and, in any case in which that period has been extended under subsection (5) of that section, includes that period as so extended.

AMENDMENTS

Section 72A inserted by Sexual Offences (Procedure and Evidence) (Scotland) Act 2002 (asp 9) Sch.1 para.7. Brought into force by SSI 2002/443 (C.24) art.4 (effective 1 November 2002).

Section 72A substituted by Criminal Procedure (Amendment) (Scotland) Act 2004 (asp 5) s.1(3). Brought into force on February 1, 2005 by SSI 2004/405 (C.28) art.2.

Subs.(1) as amended, and subs.(1A) inserted, by Vulnerable Witnesses (Scotland) Act 2004 (asp 3) s.7(3). Brought into force on 1 April 2005 by SSI 2005/168 (C.7) art.2 and Sch. Further brought into force on 1 April 2006 by SSI 2006/59 (C.8) art.2 and Sch.

Subs.(1) as amended, subs.(1A) repealed, by Criminal Justice (Scotland) Act 2016 (asp 1) s.82. Brought into force on 17 January 2017 by SSI 2016/426 art.2 and Sch.1 para.1.

DEFINITIONS A4-167.1.1

"bail": s.307(1).
"diet": s.307(1).
"preliminary hearing": s.66(6)(b).
"the court": s.72D(8).
"the 140 day period": s.72A(10).
"the 12 month period": s.72A(10).

GENERAL NOTE

A4-167.1.2 This section applies only to High Court proceedings (see s.72D(10) below).

Once all preliminary pleas and preliminary issues specified in s.72 have been resolved the accused has to be called upon to tender pleas and, if need be, a trial diet is ordinarily assigned. Subss.(3) to (7) address circumstances where it is considered at the preliminary diet that the case cannot yet proceed to trial and provides mechanisms for extensions of either the 140 day time custody time limit or the year time limit applying to High Court proceedings to be extended. It falls to the prosecutor to make any application necessary to extend the time bar to comply with the terms of s.65(3) or (4) of the Act, failing which the court may opt to desert the indictment *pro loco et tempore* or simpliciter (s.72A(4)) and liberate the accused if he is remanded in relation to the charges.

Assuming that the prosecution so moves, the court in granting such a motion (and extending the requisite time bar) has to fix a fresh trial diet falling within the new time frame for proceedings. If the accused was already bailed, subs.(9) enables the court to review and vary the existing bail terms; in situations where the accused's custody trial cannot occur within 140 days the implicit presumption is that the court following subs.(7)(b)(ii) will admit him to bail but must first hear submissions from the prosecutor on the matter (subs.(8)).

It is submitted that any such submissions merely relate to the conditions to attach to the bail order; separate provision is made in subs.6(b) for the prosecutor to seek an extension of the 140 day period itself—so it should not be thought that the Crown now has no *locus* to seek extension of the period of a custodial remand. Indeed, reference to s.65(4) and (5) of the Act makes it clear that an application for extension can be granted on cause shown—the previous stricter test (which permitted *no* fault on the part of the Crown) has now been superseded.

The definitions in subs.(10) of "the twelve month period" and "the 140 day period" clarify that each period is taken to include any extension of that time limit previously permitted by the court.

Finally, it will be noted that in assigning a trial diet at the preliminary hearing the court has two options; either to appoint a fixed trial diet upon which trial is to commence or, in terms of s.83A(2), to identify the case as a floating trial diet to commence within the days stipulated.

[THE NEXT PARAGRAPH IS A4-167.2]

Power to dispense with preliminary hearing

A4-167.2 **72B.**—(1) The court may, on an application made to it jointly by the parties, dispense with a preliminary hearing and appoint a trial diet if the court is satisfied on the basis of the application that—

(a) the state of preparation of the prosecutor and the accused with respect to their cases is such that the case is likely to be ready to proceed to trial on the date to be appointed for the trial diet;

(b) there are no preliminary pleas, preliminary issues or other matters which require to be, or could with advantage be, disposed of before the trial; and

(c) there are no persons to whom section 72(7) of this Act applies.

(2) An application under subsection (1) above shall identify which (if any) of the witnesses included in the list of witnesses are required by the prosecutor or the accused to attend the trial.

(3) Where a trial diet is to be appointed under subsection (1) above, it shall be appointed in accordance with such procedure as may be prescribed by Act of Adjournal.

(4) Where a trial diet is appointed under subsection (1) above, the accused shall appear at the diet and answer the indictment.

(5) The fact that a preliminary hearing in any case has been dispensed with under subsection (1) above shall not affect the calculation in that case of any time limit for the giving of any notice or the doing of any other thing under this Act, being a time limit fixed by reference to the preliminary hearing.

(6) Accordingly, any such time limit shall have effect in any such case as if it were fixed by reference to the date on which the preliminary hearing would have been held if it had not been dispensed with.

AMENDMENTS

Section 72B inserted by Criminal Procedure (Amendment) (Scotland) Act 2004 (asp 5) s.1(3). Brought into force, with exceptions, on 1 February 2005 by SSI 2004/405 (C.28) art.2. Otherwise brought into force on 1 April 2005 by SSI 2004/405 and SSI 2005/168.

DEFINITIONS A4-167.2.1

"Clerk of Justiciary": s.307(1).
"diet": s.307(1).
"High Court": s.307(1).
"indictment": s.307(1).
"preliminary hearing": s.66(6)(b).
"preliminary issues": s.79(2)(b).
"preliminary pleas": s.79(2)(a).
"the court": s.72D(8).

GENERAL NOTE

This section enables parties on joint application to dispense with the preliminary diet in High Court proceedings. This should not be thought to be a means of avoiding scrutiny of the case by the court which it is normally obliged to undertake at any preliminary hearing (see s.72 above). Applications to dispense must use Form 9A.2 in the Act of Adjournal (Criminal Procedure Rules Amendment) (Criminal Procedure (Amendment) (Scotland) Act 2004) 2005 (SSI 2005/44) and confirm the absence of any preliminary pleas or preliminary issues, identify witnesses whose evidence is not in dispute, and confirm that neither the accused or any witnesses are considered to be vulnerable witnesses (s.271 of the Act sets out exhaustive definitions). A4-167.2.2

For the purposes of timebar calculations, subs.(5) makes it clear that the diet originally fixed for the preliminary hearing now dispensed with still obtains for such purposes and remains the operative date also for calculating the dates for lodging notices, defences, challenges and pleas. Note too that since the normal practice at a preliminary hearing is to record the accused's pleas, the absence of that diet when s.72C is applied means that the accused has to be called upon to plead at the commencement of the trial diet. It might he argued that the giving of joint written notice to the court itself implies that the case is intended to proceed to trial.

[THE NEXT PARAGRAPH IS A4-167.3]

Procedure where preliminary hearing does not proceed

72C.—(1) The prosecutor shall not raise a fresh libel in any case in which the court has deserted a preliminary hearing *simpliciter* unless the court's decision has been reversed on appeal. A4-167.3

(2) Where a preliminary hearing is deserted *pro loco et tempore*, the court may appoint a further preliminary hearing for a later date and the accused shall appear and answer the indictment at that hearing.

(3) Subsection (4) below applies where, at a preliminary hearing—

(a) the hearing has been deserted *pro loco et tempore* for any reason and no further preliminary hearing has been appointed under subsection (2) above; or

(b) the indictment is for any reason not proceeded with and the hearing has not been adjourned or postponed.

(4) Where this subsection applies, the prosecutor may, at any time within the period of two months after the relevant date, give notice to the accused on another copy of the indictment to appear and answer the indictment—

(a) at a further preliminary hearing in the High Court not less than seven clear days after the date of service of the notice; or

(b) where the charge is one that can lawfully be tried in the sheriff court, at a first diet in that court not less than 29 clear days after the service of the notice.

(5) Where notice is given to the accused under subsection (4)(b) above, then for the purposes of section 65(4) of this Act—

(a) the giving of the notice shall be taken to be service of an indictment in respect of the sheriff court; and

(b) the previous service of the indictment in respect of the High Court shall be disregarded.

(6) In subsection (4) above, "the relevant date" means—

(a) where paragraph (a) of subsection (3) above applies, the date on which the diet was deserted as mentioned in that paragraph; or
(b) where paragraph (b) of that subsection applies, the date of the preliminary hearing referred to in that paragraph.

(7) A notice referred to in subsection (4) above shall be in such form as may be prescribed by Act of Adjournal, or as nearly as may be in such form.

AMENDMENTS

Section 72C inserted by Criminal Procedure (Amendment) (Scotland) Act 2004 (asp 5) s.1(3). Brought into force on 1 February 2005 by SSI 2004/405 (C.28) art.2.

Subs.(4)(b) as amended by Criminal Justice (Scotland) Act 2016 (asp 1) s.79(4). Brought into force on 29 May 2017 by SSI 2017/99 art.3, for the purposes of any indictment served on an accused on or after that day; not yet in force otherwise.

DEFINITIONS

A4-167.3.1 "diet" : s.307(1).
"High Court" : s.307(1).
"indictment" : s.307(1).
"preliminary hearing" : s.66(6)(b).
"the court" : s.72D(8).
"the relevant date" : s.72C(4).

GENERAL NOTE

A4-167.3.2 Section 72C applies to proceedings in the High Court (see s.72D(10) below).

The marginal note is perhaps slightly confusing since this section has no application to the most obvious situation where a preliminary hearing does not occur—when the parties jointly dispense with it in proceedings before the High Court in terms of s.72B. Closer scrutiny reveals that s.72C, though primarily relevant (as the reference to a "preliminary hearing" suggests) to the High Court, also applies to sheriff solemn proceedings presumably on the grounds that after preliminary pleas and preliminary issues have been aired the libel remaining might more appropriately proceed in that lower court.

At the preliminary hearing if the case is not ready for trial, the court has several options; an extension of the custody timebars or the year period can be granted to enable the trial then to proceed, the preliminary diet can be continued (and the anticipated trial diet preserved) or the case can be deserted either *pro loco et tempore* or simpliciter causing the existing indictment to fall. Of course none of these provisions affects the other option open to the Crown—not to call the indictment at all.

Subs.(4) provides an abbreviated procedure to re-indict to a fresh preliminary diet, echoing the existing procedures found in s.81 which only apply at an abortive *trial* diet. The same cautionary note has to be sounded; any indictment re-served under either s.72C or 81 will not automatically include any s.67 notices previously served upon the accused. Consequently, care has to be taken to ensure that any such notices are timeously served afresh and, in the case of proceedings still remaining in the High Court, that at least seven clear days are allowed before a new preliminary diet to enable compliance with the "relevant time" provisions set out in s.67(5A) of the Act.

Subs.(5) indicates that any timebar calculation required under s.65 of the Act is unaffected by service of an earlier indictment—calculation begins either with the date upon which the proceedings were deserted *pro loco et tempore* or no trial diet has been fixed at the conclusion of the preliminary diet.

[THE NEXT PARAGRAPH IS A4-167.4]

Preliminary hearing: further provision

A4-167.4 **72D.**—(1) The court may, on cause shown, allow a preliminary hearing to proceed notwithstanding the absence of the accused.

(2) Where—
(a) the accused is a body corporate;
(b) it fails to appear at a preliminary hearing;
(c) the court allows the hearing to proceed in its absence under subsection (1) above; and
(d) no plea is entered on its behalf at the hearing,

it shall be treated for the purposes of proceedings at the preliminary hearing as having pled not guilty.

(3) Where, at a preliminary hearing, a trial diet is appointed, the accused shall appear at the trial diet and answer the indictment.

(4) At a preliminary hearing, the court—

(a) shall take into account any written record lodged under section 72E of this Act; and

(b) may ask the prosecutor and the accused any question in connection with any matter which it is required to dispose of or ascertain under section 72 of this Act.

(5) The proceedings at a preliminary hearing shall be recorded by means of shorthand notes or by mechanical means.

(6) Subsections (2) to (4) of section 93 of this Act shall apply for the purposes of the recording of proceedings at a preliminary hearing in accordance with subsection (5) above as they apply for the purposes of the recording of proceedings at the trial in accordance with subsection (1) of that section.

(7) The Clerk of Justiciary shall prepare, in such form and manner as may be prescribed by Act of Adjournal, a minute of proceedings at a preliminary hearing, which shall record, in particular, whether any preliminary pleas or issues were disposed of and, if so, how they were disposed of.

(8) In this section, references to a preliminary hearing include an adjourned preliminary hearing.

(9) In this section and sections 72 to 72C, "the court" means the High Court.

AMENDMENTS

Section 72D inserted by the Criminal Procedure (Amendment) (Scotland) Act 2004 (asp 5) s.1(3). Brought into force on 1 February 2005 by SSI 2004/405 (C.28) art.2.

DEFINITIONS

"Clerk of Justiciary": s.307(1). A4-167.4.1
"diet": s.307(1).
"High Court": s.307(1).
"indictment": s.307(1).
"preliminary hearing": s.66(6)(b).
"prosecutor": s.307(1).
"the court": s.72D(8).

GENERAL NOTE

This section, as subs.(9) states, deals with procedural aspects arising from preliminary hearings in the High Court. Reference should be made to the General Note to s.72 above. Essentially, the absence of an accused at the preliminary hearing does not prevent the court from considering preliminary pleas and preliminary issues provided that a motion to proceed in absence is made to the court and allowed. In the case of a body corporate (s.70 above) in particular, a failure to appear, or be represented, at the preliminary diet would not vitiate further proceedings; instead the court will record a not guilty plea and move to assigning a trial diet or to proceed as accords. A4-167.4.2

As subs.(4) indicates the court has a duty to investigate the state of readiness of the parties by reference to the written record to be lodged jointly by parties (s.72E and High Court of Justiciary Practice Note No.1 of 2005), and by questioning parties as necessary. The Practice Note envisages that each case hearing will last no more than one hour (para. 11), a clear indication that preparation of the written record is intended to concentrate minds on the live issues in the case. The Practice Note (para.30) also addresses the approach to be adopted if parties consider that the diet cannot be concluded within the one hour timespan.

Once preliminary pleas have been resolved, the accused is to be called upon to tender pleas, and in the event of a trial being required, the High Court then has to proceed to deal with the preliminary issues (reference to the general discussions in ss.71 and 72 above may assist—*Duties of the first diet court; Duties of the preliminary diet court*).

[THE NEXT PARAGRAPH IS A4-167.5]

Written record of state of preparation in certain cases

72E.—(1) This section applies where, in any proceedings in the High Court, a solicitor has notified the Court under section 72F(1) of this Act that he has been engaged by the accused for the purposes of the conduct of his case at the preliminary hearing. A4-167.5

(2) The prosecutor and the accused's legal representative shall, not less than two days before the preliminary hearing—

(a) communicate with each other with a view to jointly preparing a written record of their state of preparation with respect to their cases (referred to in this section as " the written record"); and

(b) lodge the written record with the Clerk of Justiciary.

(3) The High Court may, on cause shown, allow the written record to be lodged after the time referred to in subsection (2) above.

(4) The written record shall—

(a) be in such form, or as nearly as may be in such form;

(b) contain such information; and

(c) be lodged in such manner,

as may be prescribed by Act of Adjournal.

(5) The written record may contain, in addition to the information required by virtue of subsection (4)(b) above, such other information as the prosecutor and the accused's legal representative consider appropriate.

(6) In this section—

"the accused's legal representative" means —

(a) the solicitor referred to in subsection (1) above; or

(b) where the solicitor has instructed counsel for the purposes of the conduct of the accused's case at the preliminary hearing, either the solicitor or that counsel, or both of them; and

"counsel" includes a solicitor who has a right of audience in the High Court of Justiciary under section 25A (rights of audience in various courts including the High Court of Justiciary) of the Solicitors (Scotland) Act 1980 (c.46).

AMENDMENTS

Section 72E inserted by the Criminal Procedure (Amendment) (Scotland) Act 2004 (asp 5), s.2. Brought into force on February 1, 2005 by the Criminal Procedure (Amendment) (Scotland) Act 2004 (Commencement, Transitional Provisions and Savings) Order 2004 (SSI 2004/405 (C.28)), art.2.

DEFINITIONS

A4-167.5.1 "a written report": s.72E(2).
"Clerk of Justiciary": s.307(1).
"counsel": s.72E(6).
"High Court": s.307(1).
"preliminary hearing": s.66(6)(b).
"the accused's legal representative": s.72E(6).
"the written record": s.72E(2)(a).

GENERAL NOTE

A4-167.5.2 This section applies to High Court proceedings and should be read in conjunction with the Act of Adjournal (Criminal Procedure Rules Amendment) (Criminal Procedure (Amendment) (Scotland) Act 2004) 2005 (SSI 2005/44), particularly r.9A.4 and Form 9A.4 which sets out the purpose and format of the written record. Note that the form can now be lodged physically or by means of facsimile or e-mail transmission.

Recent practice has been to hold all preliminary hearings in court 7 at the Court in Glasgow.

Not less than two days before the preliminary diet, it is expected that the parties will have met, discussed preparation of the case and produced a written record conform to Form 9A.4 and lodge this with the Clerk of Justiciary by 2pm two days prior to the hearing. (Later lodging, with leave of the court, is permitted by subs.(3)). High Court of Justiciary Practice Note No. 1 of 2005 states that lodging should be with the Clerk of Justiciary in Glasgow for diets scheduled for there; otherwise records are to be lodged with the Clerk of Justiciary in Edinburgh.

The form of the written record is not intended to be exhaustive. If parties consider that other matters could be considered by the court (for example, the transcription of evidence and its availability for ongoing court use rather than purely for appeal purposes, as arose in *Transco Pic v H.M. Advocate*, 2005 S.L.T. 211) this is permissible.

[THE NEXT PARAGRAPH IS A4-167.6]

Engagement, dismissal and withdrawal of solicitor representing accused

72F.—(1) In any solemn proceedings, it is the duty of a solicitor who is engaged by the accused for the purposes of his defence at any part of the proceedings to notify the court and the prosecutor of that fact forthwith in writing. **A4-167.6**

(2) A solicitor is to be taken to have complied with the duty under subsection (1) to notify the prosecutor of his engagement if, before service of the indictment, he—

(a) notified in writing the procurator fiscal for the district in which the charge against the accused was then being investigated that he was then engaged by the accused for the purposes of his defence; and

(b) had not notified that procurator fiscal in writing that he had been dismissed by the accused or had withdrawn from acting.

(3) Where any such solicitor as is referred to in subsection (1) above—

(a) is dismissed by the accused; or

(b) withdraws,

it is the duty of the solicitor to inform the court and the prosecutor of those facts forthwith in writing.

(4) The prosecutor shall, for the purposes of subsections (1) and (3), be taken to be notified or informed of any fact in accordance with those subsections if—

(a) in proceedings in the High Court, the Crown Agent; or

(b) in solemn proceedings in the sheriff court, the procurator fiscal for the district in which the trial diet is to be held,

is so notified or, as the case may be, informed of the fact.

(5) On being informed in accordance with subsection (3) above of the dismissal or withdrawal of the accused's solicitor in any case to which subsections (6) and (7) below apply, the court shall order that, before the trial diet, there shall be a further pre-trial diet under this section.

(6) This subsection applies to any case—

(a) where the accused is charged with an offence to which section 288C or 288DC of this Act applies;

(b) in respect of which section 288E of this Act applies; or

(c) in which an order has been made under section 288F(2) of this Act.

(7) This subsection applies to any case in which-

(a) the solicitor was engaged for the purposes of the defence of the accused—

(i) in the case of proceedings in the High Court, at the time of a preliminary hearing or, if a preliminary hearing was dispensed with under section 72B(1) of this Act, at the time it was so dispensed with;

(ii) in the case of solemn proceedings in the sheriff court, at the time of a first diet;

(iii) at the time of a diet under this section; or

(iv) in the case of a diet which, under subsection (11) below, is dispensed with, at the time when it was so dispensed with; and

(b) the court is informed as mentioned in subsection (3) above after that time but before the trial diet.

(8) At a diet under this section, the court shall ascertain whether or not the accused has engaged another solicitor for the purposes of his defence at the trial.

(9) A diet under this section shall be not less than 10 clear days before the trial diet.

(10) A court may, at a diet under this section, postpone the trial diet for such period as appears to it to be appropriate and may, if it thinks fit, direct that such period (or some part of it) shall not count towards any time limit applying in respect of the case.

(11) The court may dispense with a diet under this section previously ordered, but only if a solicitor engaged by the accused for the purposes of the defence of the accused at the trial has, in writing—

(a) confirmed his engagement for that purpose; and

(b) requested that the diet be dispensed with.

AMENDMENTS

Section 72F inserted by Criminal Procedure (Amendment) (Scotland) Act 2004 (asp 5) s.8. Brought into force on 1 February 2005 by SSI 2004/405 (C.28) art.2.

Subss.(1), (4) as amended by Criminal Proceedings etc (Reform) (Scotland) Act 2007 (asp 6) s.80, Sch. para.13. Brought into force on 10 December 2007 by SSI 2007/479 (C.40) art.3 and Sch.

Subs.(6)(a) as amended by Domestic Abuse (Scotland) Act 2018 (asp 5) Sch.1(1)(2) para.4(6) (effective 1 April 2019 in respect of proceedings commenced on or after 1 April 2019 subject to transitional provision specified in SSI 2018/387 reg.7(2)).

DEFINITIONS

A4-167.6.1 "diet": s.307(1).
"High Court": s.307(1).
"order": s.307(1).
"preliminary hearing": s.66(6)(b).
"procurator fiscal": s.307(1).

GENERAL NOTE

A4-167.6.2 This section applies to all solemn proceedings and requires the solicitor engaged by the accused to inform both the court and the prosecutor of his identity and contact details. Although subs.(4) stipulates that once a case has been indicted in the High Court intimation should be made to the Crown Agent, prudence would suggest that it would be appropriate to notify the procurator fiscal of first instance of this information. The section also obliges the agent to advise in the event of withdrawal from acting or when dismissed by the accused.

These requirements serve several purposes: identification of the solicitor acting will obviously facilitate communications (particularly important now that High Court proceedings demand the lodging of a written record of discussions between the parties), will immediately alert the court to cases where the accused has not engaged an agent at all (especially vital in cases libelling listed sexual offences under s.288C of the Act where the accused *must* be legally represented) and, as was noted in s.66, service of the indictment may now validly be made in the hands of the defence agent.

Subss.(5) and (9) enable the court to respond to withdrawal or dismissal by fixing a pre-trial hearing for not less than 10 days before the trial diet itself to resolve the issue of legal representation and, as would seem likely, to postpone the trial. Significantly, subs.(10) empowers the court when postponing a trial diet on these grounds to discount any part of the postponement period for calculation of timebars. In keeping with the spirit of this section, it is submitted that the same period could also to be subtracted from any subsequent discount on sentence (see s.196 of the Act), or from any backdate of sentence taking account of the period on remand (s.210 below) but there is no direct authority on the point.

Subs.(11) is a saving provision to permit the cancellation of a diet fixed in terms of subs.(5) once it has been established that an agent has now been engaged for the trial.

Refer also to the fuller discussion of the time bar provisions in the General Note to s.65 above.

[THE NEXT PARAGRAPH IS A4-167.7]

Service etc. on accused through a solicitor

A4-167.7 **72G.**—(1) In any solemn proceedings, anything which is to be served on or given, notified or otherwise intimated to, the accused shall be taken to be so served, given, notified or intimated if it is, in such form and manner as may be prescribed by Act of Adjournal, served on or given, notified or intimated to (as the case may be) the solicitor described in subsection (2) below at that solicitor's place of business.

(2) That solicitor is any solicitor—

(a) who—

(i) has notified the prosecutor under subsection (1) of section 72F of this Act that he is engaged by the accused for the purposes of his defence; and

(ii) has not informed the prosecutor under subsection (3) of that section that he has been dismissed by, or has withdrawn from acting for, the accused; or

(b) who—

(i) has been appointed to act for the purposes of the accused's defence at the trial under section 92 or 288D of this Act; and

(ii) has not been relieved of the appointment by the court.

AMENDMENTS

Section 72G inserted by Criminal Procedure (Amendment) (Scotland) Act 2004 (asp 5) s.12. Brought into force on 4 December 2004 by SSI 2004/405 (C.28).

Subs.(1) as amended by Criminal Proceedings etc (Reform) (Scotland) Act 2007 (asp 6) s.80, Sch. para.13. Brought into force on 10 December 2007 by SSI 2007/479 (C.40) art.3 and Sch.

DEFINITIONS

"prosecutor": s.307(1). A4-167.8

GENERAL NOTE

This section applies in any solemn proceedings and entitles parties, once the case has been indicted, to effect lawful service of any notice upon other parties to the proceedings by lodging it in the hands of an accused's solicitor. Reference should be made to s.72F above. A4-167.9

A separate provision—s.66(6C) of the Act—explicitly enables service of the indictment itself upon the solicitor intimated as acting for the accused.

[THE NEXT PARAGRAPH IS A4-168]

Preliminary diet: procedure

73. […] A4-168

AMENDMENTS

Section 73 repealed by Criminal Procedure (Amendment) (Scotland) Act 2004 (asp 5) s.1(3). Brought into force on 1 February 2005 by SSI 2004/405 (C.28) art.2.

[THE NEXT PARAGRAPH IS A4-169.1]

Consideration of matters relating to vulnerable witnesses where no preliminary diet is ordered

73A. […] A4-169.1

AMENDMENTS

Section 73A, as prospectively inserted by Vulnerable Witnesses (Scotland) Act 2004 (asp 3) s.2(3), repealed by Criminal Procedure (Amendment) (Scotland) Act 2004 (asp 5) s.1(3). Brought into force on 1 February 2005 by SSI 2004/405 (C.28) art.2.

[THE NEXT PARAGRAPH IS A4-170]

Appeals in connection with preliminary diets

74.—(1) Without prejudice to any right of appeal under section 106 or 108 a party may, in accordance with such procedure as may be prescribed by Act of Adjournal, appeal to the High Court against a decision at a first diet or a preliminary hearing. A4-170

(2) An appeal under subsection (1) above—

(a) may not be taken against a decision to adjourn the first diet or, as the case may be, preliminary hearing or to accelerate or postpone the trial diet;

(aza) may not be taken against a decision taken by virtue of section 35 of the Criminal Justice (Scotland) Act 2016;

(aa) may not be taken against a decision taken by virtue of—

(i) in the case of a first diet, section 71(1A),

(ii) in the case of a preliminary hearing, section 72(6)(e),

of this Act;

(ab) may not be taken against a decision at a preliminary hearing, in appointing a trial diet, to appoint or not to appoint it as a floating diet for the purposes of section 83A(2) of this Act;

(b) must be taken not later than seven days after the decision.

(2A) An appeal under subsection (1) may be taken—

(a) in the case of a decision to dismiss the indictment or any part of it, by the prosecutor without the leave of the court,

(b) in any other case, only with the leave of the court of first instance (granted on the motion of a party or *ex proprio motu*).

(3) Where an appeal is taken under subsection (1) above, the High Court may postpone any trial diet that has been appointed for such period as appears to it to be appropriate and may, if it thinks fit, direct that such period (or some part of it) shall not count towards any time limit applying in respect of the case.

(3A) Where an appeal is taken under subsection (1) above against a decision at a preliminary hearing, the High Court may adjourn, or further adjourn, the preliminary hearing for such period as appears to it to be appropriate and may, if it thinks fit, direct that such period (or some part of it) shall not count towards any time limit applying in respect of the case.

(4) In disposing of an appeal under subsection (1) above the High Court—

(a) may affirm the decision of the court of first instance or may remit the case to it with such directions in the matter as it thinks fit;

(b) where the court of first instance has dismissed the indictment or any part of it, may reverse that decision and direct that the court of first instance fix

(i) where the indictment is in respect of the High Court, a further preliminary hearing; or

(ii) where the indictment is in respect of the sheriff court, a trial diet, if it has not already fixed one as regards so much of the indictment as it has not dismissed; and

(c) may on cause shown extend the period mentioned in section 65(1) of this Act.

Amendments

Subs.(4)(a) words deleted by Crime and Punishment (Scotland) Act 1997 (c.48) s.62(1) and Sch.1 para.21(10)(a) with effect from 1 August 1997 as provided by SI 1997/1712 art.3 and Sch.1.

Subs.(4)(c) inserted by Sch.1 para.21(10)(b) of the above-mentioned Act with effect from 1 August 1997 in terms of the above Order.

Subss.(1), (2)(a) and (3) as amended, and subss.(2)(ab), (3A) and (4)(b)(i), (ii) inserted, by Criminal Procedure (Amendment) (Scotland) Act 2004 (asp 5) s.3. Subs.(2)(a) also as amended by 2004 Act s.25 and Sch.1 para.22. Brought into force on 1 February 2005 by SSI 2004/405 (C.28) art.2.

Subs.(2)(aa) inserted by Vulnerable Witnesses (Scotland) Act 2004 (asp 3) s.2(4). Brought into force on 1 April 2005, for certain purposes, by SSI 2005/168 (C.7) art.2. Further brought into force by SSI 2006/59 (C.8). Remainder brought into force on 1 April 2008 by SSI 2008/57 (C.7) art.2.

Subs.(2)(aa)(ii) as amended by Criminal Procedure (Amendment) (Scotland) Act 2004 (asp 5) s.3(b). Brought into force on 1 February 2005 by SSI 2004/405 (C.28) art.2. However, effective 1 April 2005 subject to the commencement of 2004 asp 3 s.2(4).

Subs.(2)(b) as amended by Criminal Justice and Licensing (Scotland) Act 2010 (asp 13) s.72(2). Brought into force on 28 March 2011 by SSI 2011/178 (C.15) art.2, Sch.1 para.1.

Subs.(1) as amended, subs.(2A) inserted, by Criminal Justice (Scotland) Act 2016 (asp 1) s.88. Brought into force on 17 January 2017 by SSI 2016/426 art.2 and Sch.1 para.1.

Subs.(2)(aza) inserted, by Criminal Justice (Scotland) Act 2016 (asp 1) s.81 and Sch.2 para.32. Brought into force on 25 January 2018 by SSI 2017/345 art.3 and Sch.1 para.1.

DEFINITIONS A4-170.1

"first diet": s.71(1).
"High Court": s.307(1).
"preliminary diet": s.72(1).

[THE NEXT PARAGRAPH IS A4-171]

GENERAL NOTE

This section applies to all solemn proceedings and permits limited rights of appeal from decisions arising in the preliminary, or first, diet court. Appeals cannot be taken against scheduling decisions (decisions to adjourn the diet, accelerate or postpone the trial) or against the court's determination as to the vulnerability of an accused or a witness, or in High Court cases against a decision to assign either a fixed or floating trial diet. A4-171

Appeals in regard to preliminary issues or pleas must be taken within seven days of the court's decision (see subs.(2)(b)). While the Crown are entitled to appeal a decision to dismiss an indictment in whole, or part, without leave of the court a defence appeal can only be made with leave of the court of first instance (subs.(2A)). Subs.(2) defines the court's decisions at a first, or preliminary, diet which cannot competently be appealed. While the court of first instance should deal with any necessary extension to the statutory time bar on proceedings when granting leave to appeal (see s.65 above), subs.(4)(c) contains a broader provision to enable the High Court on cause shown to extend any time bars relevant to the proceedings.

Prior to the commencement of the Criminal Justice (Scotland) Act 2016 (asp 1) failure to adhere to the seven day time limit would not necessarily have precluded a late appeal by other avenues. (See, for example, *HM Advocate v Sorrie*, 1997 S.L.T. 250 where the Crown, having failed to appeal a decision upholding S's plea in bar timeously, proceeded by Bill of Advocation, and also secured the necessary extension to the statutory time bar on proceedings. The same route was upheld as competent in Bill of Advocation *Donnelly v AK and AR* [2012] HCJAC 44, the Crown having delayed any form of appeal and possibly never having sought leave to appeal (as was then, but not now, required of all parties).) In contrast to the equivalent summary provision (s.191A), there is no prescriptive time bar upon advocation of a solemn decision. Section 191B of the 1995 Act, inserted by s.92 of the 2016 Act and commenced on 17 January 2017, now explicitly bars use of advocation procedure to review decisions taken at first or preliminary diets.

The relevant procedural forms are 9.6 and 9.11 for raising and abandoning sheriff solemn appeals from first diets, and Forms 9A.7 and 9A.8 in High Court preliminary diets.

Subs.(3) entitles, but does not oblige, the court to deduct the period (or any part of it) taken for such appeals from calculation of timebars applying to the accused, or to any co-accused.

The powers available to the Appeal Court are set out in subs.(4).

Note that even if leave to appeal is granted at the preliminary or first diet, the accused should nonetheless be called upon to plead.

Computation of certain periods

75. Where the last day of any period mentioned in section 66(6), 67(3), 71C(3) or 74 of this Act falls on a Saturday, Sunday or court holiday, such period shall extend to and include the next day which is not a Saturday, Sunday or court holiday. A4-172

AMENDMENTS

Section 75 as amended by Criminal Procedure (Amendment) (Scotland) Act 2004 (asp 5) s.25 and Sch.1 para.23. Brought into force on 1 February 2005 by SSI 2004/405 (C.28) art.2.

Section 75 as amended by Criminal Justice (Scotland) Act 2016 (asp 1) s.80(4). Brought into force on 29 May 2017 by SSI 2017/99 art.3, for the purposes of any indictment served on an accused on or after that day; not yet in force otherwise.

GENERAL NOTE

The timescales specified in s.66(6) refer both to the dates within which a first diet must occur in the sheriff court and the timelapse from service of an indictment until trial; in either event the due date is extended to the next working day. A similar provision covers the time-limit for service of a notice objecting to the description of witnesses in that indictment. The section's reference to s.72 is understandable in that subs.(6) defines "the appropriate period" for notice of the matters to be raised at a preliminary diet. It will be appreciated that s.75's terms do not interfere in any way with the provisions in s.65 against delay. A4-172.1

Adjournment and alteration of diets

Adjournment and alteration of diets

75A.—(1) This section applies where any diet has been fixed in any proceedings on indictment. A4-172.2

(2) The court may, if it considers it appropriate to do so, adjourn the diet.

(3) However—

(a) in the case of a trial diet, the court may adjourn the diet under subsection (2) above only if the indictment is not brought to trial at the diet;

(b) if the court adjourns any diet under that subsection by reason only that, following enquiries for the purpose of ascertaining whether the accused has engaged a solicitor for the purposes of the conduct of his defence at or for the purposes of a preliminary hearing or at a trial, it appears to the court that he has not done so, the adjournment shall be for a period of not more than 48 hours.

(4) A trial diet in the High Court may be adjourned under subsection (2) above to a diet to be held at a sitting of the Court in another place.

(5) The court may, on the application of any party to the proceedings made at any time before commencement of any diet—

(a) discharge the diet; and

(b) fix a new diet for a date earlier or later than that for which the discharged diet was fixed.

(6) Before determining an application under subsection (5) above, the court shall give the parties an opportunity to be heard.

(7) However, where all the parties join in an application under that subsection, the court may determine the application without hearing the parties and, accordingly, may dispense with any hearing previously appointed for the purpose of subsection (6) above.

(8) Where there is a hearing for the purpose of subsection (6) above, the accused shall attend it unless the court permits the hearing to proceed notwithstanding the absence of the accused.

(9) In appointing a new trial diet under subsection (5)(b) above, the court—

(a) shall have regard to the state of preparation of the prosecutor and the accused with respect to their cases and, in particular, to the likelihood of the case being ready to proceed to trial on the date to be appointed for the trial diet; and

(b) may, if it appears to the court that there are any preliminary pleas, preliminary issues or other matters which require to be, or could with advantage be, disposed of or ascertained before the trial, appoint a diet to be held before the trial diet for the purpose of disposing of or, as the case may be, ascertaining them.

(10) A date for a new diet may be fixed under subsection (5)(b) above notwithstanding that the holding of the diet on that date would result in any provision of this Act as to the minimum or maximum period within which the diet is to be held or to commence not being complied with.

(11) In subsections (5) to (9) above, "the court" means—

(a) in the case of proceedings in the High Court, a single judge of that Court; and

(b) in the case of proceedings in the sheriff court, that court.

(12) For the purposes of subsection (5) above—

(a) a diet other than a trial diet shall be taken to commence when it is called; and

(b) a trial diet shall be taken to commence when the jury is sworn.

AMENDMENTS

Section 75A inserted by Criminal Procedure (Amendment) (Scotland) Act 2004 (asp 5) s.15. Brought into force on 1 February 2005 by SSI 2004/405 (C.28) art.2(1).

DEFINITIONS A4-172.3

"diet": s.307(1).
"High Court": s.307(1).
"prosecutor": s.307(1).
"the court": s.75A(11).

GENERAL NOTE

This section applies to all solemn proceedings and introduces the flexibility necessary to accommodate the system of fixed and floating trial diets by pinpointing, at an early stage, cases which clearly are not ready for trial or cannot be scheduled in the assigned trial date or dates. Not only can public expense and inconvenience to witnesses and jury assize members be reduced by altering diets (including trial diets) but suitably flexible business management, combined with the provisions of the section, could result in more effective use of freed court time. A4-172.4

The section enables diets to be altered by application to the court prior to the trial date. A minute can be initiated by a party (see Form 12.2-A) or jointly (Form 12.2-B) as now inserted in the 1996 Act of Adjournal which is discussed at "*Act of Adjournal*" below.

Subs.(3) limits the time allowed for an unrepresented accused to secure legal representation to 48 hours; thereafter, he is to be represented at the preliminary, or first, diet. Subs.(4) usefully provides for adjournment of High Court trials to sittings elsewhere.

Subss.(5) and (7) make it clear that applications to the court for these purposes can be administrative in nature, and do not necessarily require a formal calling of the case provided it is evident that all preliminaries (pleas and issues) identified by then have been canvassed and resolved between the parties in advance of any hearing. (Situations may, of course, arise—such as the grave illness of an accused—which would preclude a trial or restrict the taking of proper instructions, where parties would necessarily have to reserve their positions, but the underlying ethos is that parties should be proactive in identifying areas of agreement and dispute much earlier than on the date of trial). Use of administrative adjournment has been strongly encouraged by the Bench on utility grounds but it has to be stressed that, even where parties are agreed, the grant of the application remains at the discretion of the court which may still require to hear parties.

Note that a diet can be discharged, and an earlier trial diet fixed, as well as the more familiar later adjourned diet but the court is still directed (subs.(9)) to ascertain the parties' state of readiness for trial at the proposed date and can fix a further preliminary, or first, diet for the purpose and to deal with preliminaries.

While a paper procedure (akin to the summary minute of acceleration) can be used by parties individually or jointly, subs.(5) entitles the court to fix a hearing on the application and allows the option of dispensing with the attendance of the accused. At this hearing the full range of enquiries set out in subs.(9) can be undertaken if it is decided to fix a new diet; that diet can be fixed for either earlier or later than the one discharged by the court.

Act of Adjournal

Refer to the Act of Adjournal (Criminal Procedure Rules Amendment) (Criminal Procedure (Amendment) (Scotland) Act 2004) 2005 (SSI 2005/44) which amends, particularly, Ch.12 of the 1996 Act of Adjournal (SI 1996/513).

Refixing diets: non-sitting days

75B.—(1) This section applies where in any proceedings on indictment any diet has been fixed for a non-sitting day. A4-172.5

(2) The court may at any time before the non-sitting day—

(a) discharge the diet; and
(b) fix a new diet for a date earlier or later than that for which the discharged diet was fixed.

(3) That is, by acting—

(a) of the court's own accord; and
(b) without the need for a hearing for the purpose.

(4) In the case of a trial diet—

(a) the prosecutor;
(b) the accused,

shall be entitled to an adjournment of the new diet fixed if the court is satisfied that it is not practicable for that party to proceed with the case on that date.

(5) The power of the court under subsection (1) above is not exercisable for the sole purpose of ensuring compliance with a time limit applying in the proceedings.

(6) In subsections (1) and (2) above, a "non-sitting day" is a day on which the court is under this Act not required to sit.

(7) In subsections (2) to (5) above, "the court" means

(a) in the case of proceedings in the High Court, a single judge of that Court;

(b) in the case of proceedings in the sheriff court, that court.

AMENDMENTS

Section 75B inserted by Criminal Proceedings etc (Reform) (Scotland) Act 2007 (asp 6) s.39. Brought into force on 10 December 2007 by SSI 2007/479 (C.40) art.3 and Sch.

Title as amended by Act of Adjournal (Amendment of the Criminal Procedure (Scotland) Act 1995) (Refixing diets) 2011 (SSI 2011/430) art.2(3) (effective 30 January 2012).

Refixing diets: non-suitable days

A4-172.6 **75C.**—(1) Where in any proceedings on indictment any diet has been fixed for a day which is no longer suitable to the court, it may, of its own accord, at any time before that diet—

(a) discharge the diet; and

(b) fix a new diet for a date earlier or later than that for which the discharged diet was fixed.

(2) [...]

(3) In subsection (1), "the court" means—

(a) in the case of proceedings in the High Court, a single judge of that Court;

(b) in the case of proceedings in the sheriff court, that court.

AMENDMENTS

Section 75C inserted by Act of Adjournal (Amendment of the Criminal Procedure (Scotland) Act 1995) (Refixing diets) 2011 (SSI 2011/430) art.2(2) (effective 30 January 2012).

Subss.(2) and (3) as amended by Act of Adjournal (Criminal Procedure (Scotland) Act 1995 Amendment) (Miscellaneous) 2020 (SSI 2020/93) para.2 (effective 25 March 2020).

DEFINITIONS

A4-172.7 "High Court": s.307(1).
"the court": s.75C(3).

GENERAL NOTE

A4-172.8 Section 75C gives the court the power, in solemn proceedings, to refix diets in respect of days which are no longer suitable to the court. No particular reasons are advanced by the statute for the test of unsuitability. The initiative under this authority lies with the court as it may act of its own accord, which is to say without a motion from the Crown or any accused.

With effect from 25 March 2020, the Act of Adjournal (Criminal Procedure (Scotland) Act 1995 Amendment) (Miscellaneous) 2020 (SSI 2020/93) repealed subs.(2)'s requirement for the views of parties to be considered when re-assigning diets in criminal business. Thus, diets can now competently be fixed of new administratively; sense would suggest that those views would be canvassed where practicable.

The statutory instrument was the first legislative response to counter the anticipated dislocation of criminal court business arising from the coronavirus pandemic.

[THE NEXT PARAGRAPH IS A4-173]

Plea of guilty

Procedure where accused desires to plead guilty

A4-173 **76.**—(1) Where an accused intimates in writing to the Crown Agent that he intends to plead guilty and desires to have his case disposed of at once, the accused may be served with an indictment (unless one has already been served) and a notice to appear at a diet of the appropriate court not less than four clear days after the date of the notice; and it shall not be necessary to lodge or give notice of any list of witnesses or productions.

(2) In subsection (1) above, "appropriate court" means—

(a) in a case where at the time of the intimation mentioned in that subsection an indictment had not been served, either the High Court or the sheriff court; and

(b) in any other case, the court specified in the notice served under section 66(6) of this Act on the accused.

(3) If at any such diet the accused pleads not guilty to the charge or pleads guilty only to a part of the charge, and the prosecutor declines to accept such restricted plea, the diet shall be deserted *pro loco et tempore* and thereafter the cause may proceed in accordance with the other provisions of this Part of this Act; except that in a case mentioned in paragraph (b) of subsection (2) above the court may postpone the trial diet, the first diet or (as the case may be) the preliminary hearing and the period of such postponement shall not count towards any time limit applying in respect of the case.

AMENDMENTS

Subs.(3) as amended by Criminal Procedure (Amendment) (Scotland) Act 2004 (asp 5) s.25 and Sch.1 para.24. Brought into force on 1 February 2005 by SSI 2004/405 (C.28) art.2.

Subs.(3) as amended by Criminal Justice (Scotland) Act 2016 (asp 1) s.81(5). Brought into force on 29 May 2017 by SSI 2017/99 art.3, for the purposes of any indictment served on an accused on or after that day; not yet in force otherwise.

DEFINITIONS

"High Court": s.307(1). **A4-173.1**
"indictment": s.307(1).
"witnesses": s.307(1).

[THE NEXT PARAGRAPH IS A4-174]

GENERAL NOTE

Section 76 re-enacts the familiar accelerated plea provisions of s.102 of the 1975 Act. Although the statute requires written intimation of a proposed plea by the accused to the Crown Agent, it is customary for the letter intimating the terms of the plea to be sent to the procurator fiscal at whose instance the petition charges were raised. It is, of course, competent to serve an indictment without any prior petition but in that event it will be difficult to negotiate a satisfactory plea practically. **A4-174**

On receipt of a letter, the procurator fiscal is under a duty to comply with the Procurator Fiscal Service's Book of Regulations and deliver the letter along with a report outlining his or her views on its merits, or otherwise, to the Crown Agent. While the section stipulates that the letter be sent to the Crown Agent, the Crown as a matter of course indicate the date of its receipt by the procurator fiscal to the court when the plea of guilt is recorded, since this may have a bearing upon any sentence; this is particularly pertinent now given the terms of s.196 of the Act which allows courts discretion to consider as a sentencing parameter, the point in proceedings at which a plea was tendered.

It will be observed that a plea tendered prior to service of any indictment leaves the issue open as to whether the plea should be heard before a sheriff or in the High Court (subs.(2)(a)) and the choice of forum may be a material factor in the plea tendered; by contrast, once an indictment has been served, subs.(2)(b) enacts that a s.76 letter will only have the effect of accelerating the hearing before that court. Rule 10.1-(2) of the 1996 Act of Adjournal provides that cases set down for trial in the High Court, and by necessary inference, charges in which the High Court has exclusive jurisdiction—treason, murder and rape, can be called for disposal in the High Court sitting in Edinburgh instead of at the sitting originally scheduled elsewhere in Scotland. Any charge may be dealt with on a s.76 indictment. It is rare for a murder to be put before the court in this way but it is not unknown: see *HM Advocate v Todd*, 2003 G.W.D. 11-310.

If the plea offered by the accused is acceptable to the Crown, a notice conforming to the style of Form 10.1-A where no indictment has yet been served, or Form 10.1-B, when an indictment has still to be served, will accompany the indictment now served upon the accused. Cases in which a s.76 plea is offered prior to service of an indictment (see subs.(2)(a)) will ordinarily proceed upon an edited indictment which does not include lists of productions and witnesses; this is not an absolute requirement, but obviously economises on Crown resources. Cases which have simply been brought forward after service of the indictment competently proceed on the full indictment previously served on the accused.

The practice of obtaining the accused's written instructions detailing the precise terms of the plea to be tendered is expedient. Refer to A4-179.1 below for a general discussion of the issue.

Subsection (3) works to the benefit of the Crown; if at the accelerated diet the accused reneges on his plea, the court can postpone the trial diet or the preliminary diet (in the High Court) and discount the period of the postponement in any calculation of statutory time-bars. This concession only applies to cases proceeding under subs.(2)(b), i.e. where an accelerated plea has been offered after service of the indictment. Note, however, that Rule 10.1-(3) of the 1996 Act of Adjournal only permits such a postponement when all of the accused have tendered s.76 notices and all are present at the accelerated diet and the court grants the postponement in response to a motion made at that time. It is difficult to envisage practical instances in which these circumstances would apply: it may arise where one (or more) accused recants on a "package" deal involving a number of the accused, thus rendering the totality unacceptable to the Crown. Ordinarily, the Crown would probably accept pleas from other accused and elect to proceed to trial later against the recalcitrant accused and a subs.(3) motion for postponement could then be made quite properly.

The Inducíae

A4-175 This section proceeds upon an *induciae* between service of the edited form of indictment, and its calling, of four clear days. The *induciae* can be waived by the accused but in *McKnight v HM Advocate*, 1991 S.C.C.R. 751 where the accused pleaded to an indictment served upon him 10 minutes beforehand, the Court of Appeal doubted the wisdom of proceeding in such a summary fashion and indicated that the Crown should be hesitant to accept pleas tendered in such circumstances. It may be said too that with the current re-evaluation by the Appeal Court of the relationship between criminal practitioners and clients (after *Anderson v HM Advocate*, 1996 S.L.T. 155), it could be regarded as imprudent to advise clients to waive the four day *induciae*.

Withdrawal of the Plea

A4-176 A plea tendered at the accelerated diet can be withdrawn competently at a later diet, but the court would have to be satisfied that the accused had substantially misunderstood his position and had been prejudiced by that misunderstanding. See *Healy v HM Advocate*, 1990 S.C.C.R. 110, where the indictment had been read over to the accused by the sheriff at the first diet and accepted by the accused who sought to withdraw her plea before a different sheriff at the diet of deferred sentence; and *Paul v HM Advocate* (1914) 7 Adam 343 where the accused sought to change his plea following upon a remit to the High Court for sentence. In *Pickett v HM Advocate*, 2007 S.C.C.R. 389, an appeal against conviction following a guilty plea, the court looked to the absence of any dissent by the accused during narration and mitigation, despite claims of material misapprehension of the pleas tendered and claims of alleged defective representation. Even had this appeal succeeded (the court having ruled *Anderson* grounds to be irrelevant in the context of a plea), counsel properly conceded that a fresh prosecution could follow. Refer also to *Duncan v HM Advocate*, 2009 S.C.C.R. 293; 2009 S.C.L. 571 and *Whillans v Harvie* [2010] HCJAC 91.

Once a plea of guilt is recorded, it cannot be revisited in light of the outcome of any subsequent trial of a co-accused on those charges (*Reedie v HM Advocate*, 2005 S.L.T. 742 and *Duncan v HM Advocate*, 2009 S.C.C.R. 293; 2009 S.C.L. 571). Crown consent to amendment of the pleas is irrelevant; by then the Crown has no locus in the matter. Exceptionally in *Reference by SCCRC re Stewart* [2017] HCJAC 90; 2019 S.C.C.R. 4 a plea to causing death by careless driving, based not upon fault but rather upon a breach of associated statutory driver licensing and insurance provisions, was quashed on appeal as a miscarriage of justice, it being agreed that all parties to the accelerated hearing had proceeded mistakenly on the view that the offence was one of strict liability, the law then being in a state of flux.

So far as the Crown is concerned, any mitigation tendered which is felt to be inconsistent with a guilty plea, or, it is suggested, any defence explanation of the factual circumstances which is disputed, must be made known to the court of first instance. Otherwise, the Crown will likely be held to have acquiesced and will be barred from raising the matter in any appeal (*Bennett v HM Advocate*, 1996 S.C.C.R. 331 and see also s.118(8) below). In the event of such an unsatisfactory plea the court is obliged to invoke the provisions of subs.(3) (refer to A4-174 above). Guidance on the procedures open to the court where disagreement on the terms of the plea surfaces is given in *McCartney v HM Advocate*, 1997 S.C.C.R. 644.

McCartney was followed in *Ross v HM Advocate* [2015] HCJAC 38, a case which summarises current case law and in which it is noted that the sheriff (who had heard some pertinent evidence in the course of a trial) rather than offering the defence the opportunity to lead evidence in mitigation, "ordered" a proof. Note that the court was not bound to accept the defence's factual narrative merely because it had not been challenged or contradicted by the Crown. Divergences of the sort highlighted in *Ross* ought to be relatively rare in solemn proceedings given the prevalence of agreed, written, narratives; the same cannot be said in summary proceedings.

Sentencing Issues

A4-176.1 It has long been tacitly accepted by the courts that the tendering of an acceptable plea utilising this section's provisions can attract a discount on sentence. This reflects a recognition that prosecution resources, court time and witnesses, have all been spared. Nonetheless, there is no automatic entitlement under s.76 to a sentence lower than that which the offence, and offender, would normally merit simply by reason of an early (or accelerated) plea of guilt (see *Tennie v Munro*, 1999 S.C.C.R. 70 and *Murray v HM Advocate*, 2013 S.C.C.R. 88). Reference to the terms of s.196 below makes it clear that the court has a discretion in *all* cases to have regard to the timing, circumstances and purpose of a guilty plea when imposing sentence (*Du Plooy v HM Advocate*, 2003 S.L.T. 1237 and *Gemmell v HM Advocate* [2011] HCJAC 129; 2012 S.C.C.R. 176) but that the scale of discount normally should not exceed one-third of the sentence otherwise in prospect. In *HM Advocate v McKeever* [2016] HCJAC 43, a prosecution for contravention of the Road Traffic Act 1988 s.1, the Crown contended that the one-third discount from a headline six-year imprisonment was unduly lenient since the s.76 letter in acceptable terms was intimated almost nine months after the initial petition appearance. The Appeal Court upheld the discounted sentence, noting that an initial plea in terms of that petition had been submitted within six months but had been rejected since the Crown needed further information and had later added aggravations to the original petition charge.

However, it is observed that in *McKenna v HM Advocate*, 2005 G.W.D. 27-527, where the appellant's s.76 plea had attracted a discount on sentence of only 15 per cent, it was held that use of the accelerated plea procedures ordinarily ought to have merited a discount in the region of 30 per cent, the maximum permissible.

[THE NEXT PARAGRAPH IS A4-177]

Plea of guilty

77.—(1) Where at any diet the accused tenders a plea of guilty to the indictment or any part thereof he shall do so in open court. **A4-177**

(2) Where the plea is to part only of the charge and the prosecutor does not accept the plea, such non-acceptance shall be recorded.

(3) Where an accused charged on indictment with any offence tenders a plea of guilty to any other offence of which he could competently be found guilty on the trial of the indictment, and that plea is accepted by the prosecutor, it shall be competent to convict the accused of the offence to which he has so pled guilty and to sentence him accordingly.

AMENDMENTS

Subs.(1) as amended by Criminal Justice (Scotland) Act 2016 (asp 1) s.83. Brought into force on 17 January 2017 by SSI 2016/426 art.2 and Sch.1 para.1.

DEFINITIONS

"diet": s.307(1). **A4-177.1**
"indictment": s.307(1).
"prosecutor": s.307(1).

[THE NEXT PARAGRAPH IS A4-178]

GENERAL NOTE

With effect from 17 January 2017 the long-standing requirement that an accused had to sign his plea, and that to be countersigned by the presiding judge, was repealed. See s.83 of the Criminal Justice (Scotland) Act 2016 (asp 1) and the Criminal Justice (Scotland) Act 2016 (Commencement No. 3 and Saving Provision) Order 2016 (SSI 2016/426). A similar provision in relation to bodies corporate was introduced, somewhat unnecessarily, to repeal s.70(7) of the 1995 Act which itself had already removed any requirement for bodies corporate to have pleas signed on their behalf. The prosecutor must ensure that any mitigation offered by the accused whose terms are not accepted by the Crown is objected to at the first diet, failing which the Crown will be taken as having acquiesced in the matter (see A4-176 above). **A4-178**

Prosecutor's refusal of pleas

There is no obligation upon the prosecutor to accept a plea of guilt to the libel (indeed, historically, in capital crimes the Crown always elected to prove its case when a guilty plea was offered). **A4-179**

The rules for such eventualities were stated in *Strathern v Sloan*, 1937 J.C. 76 at 80 but had little practical impact once the 1980 Act abolished mandatory pleading diets. The re-introduction of mandatory first diets, and preliminary diets, in ss.71 and 72 of the 1995 Act may render that judgment more topical. If a guilty plea is tendered at the earlier diet but refused by the Crown, the minute should record that the plea was tendered and rejected; it should not record the plea as one of not guilty. At the trial diet the accused should not be called upon to plead *de novo*, in the interim, unless the prosecutor has decided to accept the plea previously tendered (it will be appreciated that the terms of s.196, which have already been discussed in the notes to s.76 above, may well make it advantageous to tender partial pleas at a first diet even if, at that juncture, they are not acceptable to the Crown). If the trial proceeds, and the plea previously tendered becomes acceptable to the Crown, the accused should then be called upon to state his plea publicly. No reference in the course of a trial should be made by the Crown to the fact that such a plea has been proffered. So in *McLean v HM Advocate*, 2007 S.C.C.R. 363 it was also inept for the presiding sheriff to found upon pleas tendered by the accused (and refused by the Crown) as grounds warranting a jury direction that the onus, burden or standard of proof, need no longer be met by the Crown.

Prosecutor's acceptance of pleas

A4-179.1 Following upon *Anderson v HM Advocate*, 1996 S.C.C.R. 487 it is submitted to be a prudent practice to secure a client's written instructions before tendering a guilty plea to the court; this view accords with the Faculty of Advocates' Code of Professional Conduct. In *Crossan v HM Advocate*, 1996 S.C.C.R. 279, C appealed his conviction following a guilty plea to a murder charge (his co-accused having pled guilty to assault), and sought to withdraw his plea the following day, a procedure which was not competent to the court. In terms of s.252(d) of the 1975 Act (now s.104 of the 1995 Act) the Court of Appeal remitted the matter to a single judge for a report on the circumstances surrounding the appeal. It will be noted that the evidence to that judge was not given on oath and was heard in chambers outwith the presence of the accused, it being a matter within the sole discretion of the appointed judge to determine procedures necessary for the preparation of his report.

Recording of pleas

In *Fraser v HM Advocate*, 2004 S.L.T. 592 the Appeal Court was critical of the long-established practice of partial pleas of guilt being tendered in the presence of an assize before jurors were selected to hear the trial. Although at that stage no narration would be given to the court as to the nature of the charges admitted by the accused, and the jury would receive jury copies of the indictment which would include only the charges proceeding to trial, nonetheless the potential for prejudice remained: the Court considered that any partial pleas tendered (and by implication, any pleas formally tendered but rejected) should be tendered and recorded outwith the presence of the unempanelled jurors.

Act of Adjournal

Refer to Ch.10 of the 1996 Act of Adjournal.

Sentencing guidance

A4-179.2 See generally *Du Plooy v HM Advocate*, 2003 S.L.T. 1237 and *Gemmell v HM Advocate* [2011] HCJAC 129; 2012 S.C.C.R. 176. There guidance was given as to the basis of, and scope for, an allowance in the sentencing of an accused in respect of a guilty plea, and the form that such an allowance might take. Further consideration is given to this matter under ss.196 and 197 of this Act, infra.

[THE NEXT PARAGRAPH IS A4-180]

Notice by accused

Special defences, incrimination and notice of witnesses, etc.

A4-180 **78.**—(1) It shall not be competent for an accused to state a special defence or to lead evidence calculated to exculpate the accused by incriminating a co-accused unless—

(a) a plea of special defence or, as the case may be, notice of intention to lead such evidence has been lodged and intimated in writing in accordance with subsection (3) below—

(b) the court, on cause shown, otherwise directs.

(1A) Subsection (1) does not apply where—

(a) the accused lodges a defence statement under section 70A, and

(b) the accused's defence consists of or includes a special defence.

(2) Subsection (1) above shall apply to a plea of diminished responsibility or to a defence of automatism, coercion or, in a prosecution for an offence to which section 288C of this Act applies, consent as if it were a special defence.

(2A) In subsection (2) above, the reference to a defence of consent is a reference to the defence which is stated by reference to the complainer's consent to the act which is the subject matter of the charge or the accused's belief as to that consent.

(2B) In subsection (2A) above, "complainer" has the same meaning as in section 274 of this Act.

(3) A plea or notice is lodged and intimated in accordance with this subsection—

(a) where the case is to be tried in the High Court, by lodging the plea or notice with the Clerk of Justiciary and by intimating the plea or notice to the Crown Agent and to any co-accused not less than seven clear days before the preliminary hearing;

(b) where the case is to be tried in the sheriff court, by lodging the plea or notice with the sheriff clerk and by intimating it to the procurator fiscal and to any co-accused at or before the first diet.

(4) It shall not be competent for the accused to examine any witnesses or to put in evidence any productions not included in the lists lodged by the prosecutor unless—

(a) written notice of the names and addresses of such witnesses and of such productions has been given—

(i) where the case is to be tried in the sheriff court, to the procurator fiscal of the district of the trial diet at or before the first diet; and

(ii) where the case is to be tried in the High Court, to the Crown Agent at least seven clear days before the preliminary hearing; or

(b) the court, on cause shown, otherwise directs.

(5) A copy of every written notice required by subsection (4) above shall be lodged by the accused with the sheriff clerk of the district in which the trial diet is to be held, or in any case the trial diet of which is to be held in the High Court in Edinburgh with the Clerk of Justiciary, at or before

(a) where the case is to be tried in the High Court, the preliminary hearing;

(b) where the case is to be tried in the sheriff court, the trial diet,

for the use of the court.

AMENDMENTS

Subs.(2) as amended by Sexual Offences (Procedure and Evidence) (Scotland) Act 2002 (asp 9) s.6(1)(a).

Subs.(2A) and (2B) inserted by Sexual Offences (Procedure and Evidence) (Scotland) Act 2002 (asp 9) s.6(1)(b).

Brought into force by SSI 2002/443 (C.24) art.4 (effective 1 November 2002).

Subss.(1)(a), (3)(a), (b), (4)(a)(ii) and (5) as amended by Criminal Procedure (Amendment) (Scotland) Act 2004 (asp 5) s.25 and Sch.1 para.25. Brought into force on 1 February 2005 by SSI 2004/405 (C.28) art.2.

Subs.(1A) inserted by Criminal Justice and Licensing (Scotland) Act 2010 (asp 13) s.124. Brought into force on 6 June 2011 (for all purposes in respect of criminal proceedings in which the first appearance of the accused is on or after 6 June 2011) by SSI 2011/178 art.2 and Sch.1 para.1.

Subs.(2) as amended by Criminal Justice and Licensing (Scotland) Act 2010 (asp 13) Sch.7 para.46. Brought into force on 25 June 2012 by SSI 2012/160 (C.15) art.3.

DEFINITIONS

"Clerk of Justiciary": s.307(1). A4-180.1
"High Court": s.307(1).
"procurator fiscal": s.307(1).

[THE NEXT PARAGRAPH IS A4-181]

GENERAL NOTE

Section 78 stipulates the periods of notice to be given by the accused to the prosecutor and any co-accused of any defence, special defence, list of witnesses or productions. On the first calling of the indictment the court is obliged to make enquiry as to the state of readiness of parties for trial (see s.71(1)(a) and s.72(6)(f)). Thus subs.(3)(a) stipulates that such notices in High Court cases must be lodged, and served on all other parties, not less than seven days before the preliminary hearing; subs.(3)(b) governing sheriff solemn cases, requires lodging at, or before, the first diet. Later lodging of special defences, or defences, strictly is not competent but has often been permitted where the Crown consents to late tendering. By contrast, late lodging by the defence of witness lists or productions (which should be lodged to the same timescale) can be permitted on cause shown (subs.(4)(b)). A4-181

The insertion of subss.(2) and (3) adds the defence of consent to the special defences, and notices, which must be intimated in advance of trial to the prosecutor and to co-accused. A defence of consent applies to the category of sexual offences set out in s.288C. Note should also be taken of the procedures in respect of sexual offences now introduced by s.275A of the Act. The equivalent summary provision is found in s.149A of the Act. In this context attention is drawn to the clarification provided by subs.(2A); a defence of consent to a sexual offence specified in s.288C of the Act must relate to the subject matter of the charge and to the accused's belief of consent to that act.

While s.78(1A) allows any defences set out in the "defence statement" (s.70A above) to be taken as lodged, in procedural terms some caution is necessary: the terms of the defence would need to be fully extended in the s.70A document and the terms of any such defence (except notice of incrimination) would require to be available in a format suitable for distribution to the jury. Preparation of more familiar notices of defence has distinct advantages.

Service of Lists and Notices

A4-182 Section 66(6) of the Act stipulates that a first diet, or preliminary hearing, must occur not less than 29 clear days after service of an indictment. Following from this, lists of productions and witnesses should be lodged and intimated not less than seven days before the preliminary hearing in the High Court, and at or prior to the first diet in sheriff solemn proceedings (subs.(4)) unless the court permits late lodging. Section 78(4) enacts that any lists of witnesses or productions (other than those included in the indictment by the prosecutor) must be served upon the Crown, and a copy lodged with the court, no later than at the first diet. Note that there is no obligation to serve these lists upon any co-accused. Failure to lodge the lists timeously renders the examination of either productions or witnesses incompetent unless, in terms of subs.(4)(b), the accused can show cause for this failure. This timescale demands earlier action on the part of the accused than heretofore; s.82(2) of the 1975 Act only stipulated three clear days' notice of witnesses and productions to the prosecutor in any solemn case, calculated by reference to the date on which the jury was sworn.

It will be recalled that at the first diet the sheriff is obliged to enquire as to the state of preparation of the parties for trial (s.71(1)(a)). Accordingly, it may be expected that later lodging of lists will entail a considerable burden in persuading the court that these should still be received. The same can be said for notices of special defences (extended to include defences of coercion and automatism): these have to be served upon the prosecutor and any co-accused at or before the first diet or hearing though, again, a discretion is open to the court to permit late lodging on cause shown.

A special defence is a fact which if established must lead to the acquittal of the accused upon the libel (*Adam v McNeill*, 1971 S.L.T. (Notes) 80). The effect of such a defence, if successful, is to divorce the accused from all blame or culpability in the charge libelled and secure his acquittal. Thus in *McQuade v HM Advocate*, 1996 S.C.C.R. 347 where only one of three accused gave evidence, admitted shooting the deceased during a robbery and implicated his co-accused, it was held on appeal that a notice of incrimination had not been necessary since that evidence could not have secured his acquittal. See also *McShane v HM Advocate*, 1989 S.C.C.R. 687 and *Collins v HM Advocate*, 1991 S.C.C.R. 898: unlike other special defences a notice of incrimination does not require to be read to the jury or be referred to in the course of the judge's charge.

A notice of alibi is not required when it is to be asserted that the accused was at the locus for an innocent purpose (*Balsillie v HM Advocate*, 1993 S.C.C.R. 760). In relation to special defences of self defence, *O'Connell v HM Advocate*, 1997 S.L.T. 564 is authority for the proposition that the particulars of the defence must be properly specified to be received by the court; at an adjourned first diet the special defence had been inspecifically stated causing the sheriff to adjourn the matter further. Where it is averred that the accused was acting in self defence, not of himself but in defence of a third party, it would be prudent to state so explicitly since the trial judge will be obliged to provide specific directions, rather than simply rehearse the standard directions, to meet the novelty of the situation (*Dewar v HM Advocate*, 2009 S.L.T. 670). The defence of coercion or necessity was recognised in *Moss v Howdle*, 1997 S.L.T. 782 following *Thomson v HM Advocate*, 1983 S.L.T. 682; 1983 S.C.C.R. 368. See also the discussion in "Necessity and Coercion in Criminal Law" by P.W. Ferguson, 1997 S.L.T. 127. (The issue of withdrawal of a special defence from a jury where only the thinnest evidence is available is ruled on in *Whyte v HM Advocate*, 1996 J.C. 187.) See also *Carr v HM Advocate*, 2013 S.C.C.R 471 and *Lawson v HM Advocate* [2018] HCJAC 9. Once self-defence has been withdrawn from the jury's consideration, the judge still has a responsibility to consider the need for directions about provocation (*Graham v HM Advocate* [2018] HCJAC 4). Note that in *Telford v HM Advocate* [2018] HCJAC 73 the judge's decision, given the absence of supporting evidence, to withdraw self-defence and provocation pleas, was upheld on appeal.

It is doubtful that a notice of defence, not in proper form, can be treated as complying with the time-limit for notice imposed in subs.(1)(a), but it might serve to indicate a lack of readiness for trial (see s.71(1)(a)) if produced at a first, or preliminary, diet as occurred in *O'Connell*.

Once a special defence has not been insisted upon by counsel then only in the most exceptional circumstances will it still be incumbent upon the trial judge to give jury directions on that defence (*Morrison v HM Advocate* [2021] HCJAC 29).

Note that in terms of Ch.11 of the 1996 Act of Adjournal notices under s.78(1) and lists of witnesses and productions under s.78(4) can be served on the solicitor acting for a co-accused rather than upon the co-accused personally. Despite their effect upon any trial, pleas of diminished responsibility or provocation, which may focus strongly upon technical or medical evidence and necessitate further investigation by the Crown, need not be intimated before trial. See the critical discussion of recent developments in the law of provocation in "Collapsing the Structure of Criminal Law" by James Chalmers in 2001 S.L.T. 241 following *Drury v HM Advocate*, 2001 S.L.T. 1013 which centred upon the nature of provocation wrought by alleged infidelity.

In relation to offences of a sexual nature where the defence is one of consent, subs.(2) requires that to be specified as a special defence. *GW v HM Advocate* [2019] HCJAC 23, approving *KT v Harrower*

[2018] SAC (Crim) 15; 2019 S.C.C.R. 11, stipulates that to provide a basis for that defence the consent being founded upon needs to be proximate in time to the actus and consequently any consent by the complainer to such conduct on previous occasions will rarely be relevant to the instant circumstance. Note too that any consent defence should be expressed briefly and circumspectly; it is not an opportunity to plead the case in the absence of supporting evidence (*GW* at [34]). In the absence of evidence supporting a defence of consent, that defence should be withdrawn from the jury and should not be pursued further in speeches or left as an issue for the jury to consider. See *MacDonald v HM Advocate* [2020] HCJAC 21 at [41] and [42].

It remains open to the prosecutor to waive timeous notice, and to the court to consider the broad interests of justice when assessing whether due cause has been shown for notices to be received late, but such an assessment must surely now take account of any potential prejudice to co-accused since they too are entitled to timeous notification. In *Lowson v HM Advocate*, 1943 J.C. 141, where a list of defence witnesses had not been lodged due to a change of trial venue, the trial judge disallowed the evidence on the view (shared by the procurator fiscal who had objected), that there was no discretion to permit examination of unintimated witnesses; the Lord Justice General (at 145) while noting that the provisions existed to prevent the introduction of evidence which the prosecutor has no means of meeting, stated:

> "But I am clear that rules, being conceived in the interests of the prosecution, may competently, and should, be waived where the interests of justice are better served by waiving them than by insisting on them."

Despite the apparent mandatory nature of many of the 1995 Act's provisions this broad principle should still hold good.

Service of Lists and Notices in the High Court

The advent of preliminary hearings in High Court proceedings has led to the modification of subs.(3)(a); any notices or defences and lists of witnesses and productions need to be lodged, and served upon the prosecutor, at least seven clear days before the preliminary hearing. Notices or defences must also be served on co-accused in the same timescale but there is no obligation to intimate either lists of witnesses or productions to co-accused. Subsection (4)(b) allows these lists to be received late on cause shown, but no such discretion is given to the court to permit late lodging of notices or defences. A4-183

Act of Adjournal

Refer to Ch.11 of the 1996 Act of Adjournal and especially note the alteration to r.11.2 effected by the Act of Adjournal (Criminal Procedure Rules Amendment) (Miscellaneous) 1996; this requires service of notices under s.78(4) on the accused's solicitor.

Preliminary pleas and preliminary issues

79.—(1) Except by leave of the court on cause shown, no preliminary plea or preliminary issue shall be made, raised or submitted in any proceedings on indictment by any party unless his intention to do so has been stated in a notice under section 71(2) or, as the case may be, 72(3) or (6)(b)(i) of this Act. A4-184

(1A) Subsection (1) is subject to section 271Q(8).

(2) For the purposes of this section and those sections—

(a) the following are preliminary pleas, namely—

(i) a matter relating to the competency or relevancy of the indictment;

(ii) an objection to the validity of the citation against a party, on the ground of any discrepancy between the record copy of the indictment and the copy served on him, or on account of any error or deficiency in such service copy or in the notice of citation; and

(iii) a plea in bar of trial; and

(b) the following are preliminary issues, namely—

(i) an application for separation or conjunction of charges or trials;

(ii) a preliminary objection under any of the provisions listed in subsection (3A);

(iia) an application for a witness anonymity order under section 271P of this Act;

(iii) [...]

(iv) an objection by a party to the admissibility of any evidence;

(v) an assertion by a party that there are documents the truth of the contents of which ought to be admitted, or that there is any other matter which in his view ought to be agreed; and

(vi) any other point raised by a party, as regards any matter not mentioned in sub-paragraphs (i) to (v) above, which could in his opinion be resolved with advantage before the trial.

(3) No discrepancy, error or deficiency such as is mentioned in subsection (2)(a)(ii) above shall entitle an accused to object to plead to the indictment unless the court is satisfied that the discrepancy, error or deficiency tended substantially to mislead and prejudice the accused.

(3A) For the purpose of subsection (2)(b)(ii), the provisions are—

(a) section 27(4A)(a) or (4B), 90C(2A), 255 or 255A of this Act,

(b) section 9(6) of the Antisocial Behaviour etc. (Scotland) Act 2004 or that section as applied by section 234AA(11) of this Act,

(c) paragraph 6(5)(b) of schedule 1 to the Criminal Justice (Scotland) Act 2016.

(d) section 1A(2)(b) of the Abusive Behaviour and Sexual Harm (Scotland) Act 2016 or section 7(2)(b) of the Domestic Abuse (Scotland) Act 2018.

(4) Where the court, under subsection (1) above, grants leave for a party to make, raise or submit a preliminary plea or preliminary issue (other than an objection to the admissibility of any evidence) without his intention to do so having been stated in a notice as required by that subsection, the court may—

(a) if it considers it appropriate to do so, appoint a diet to be held before the trial diet for the purpose of disposing of the plea or issue; or

(b) appoint the plea or issue to be disposed of at the trial diet.

AMENDMENTS

Section 79 substituted by Criminal Procedure (Amendment) (Scotland) Act 2004 (asp 5) s.13(1). Brought into force on 1 February 2005 by SSI 2004/405 (C.28) art.2.

Subs.(2)(b)(ii) amended by Antisocial Behaviour etc. (Scotland) Act 2004 (asp 8) s.144 and Sch.4 para.5(2). Brought into force on 28 October 2004 by SSI 2004/420 (C.31) art.3.

Subs.(2)(b)(ii) as amended by Criminal Proceedings etc (Reform) (Scotland) Act 2007 (asp 6) s.80, Sch. para.14. Brought into force on 10 December 2007 by SSI 2007/479 (C.40) art.3 and Sch.

Subs.(1A) inserted and subs.(2) as amended by Criminal Justice and Licensing (Scotland) Act 2010 (asp 13) s.90(2) and Sch.7 para.47. Brought into force on 28 March 2011 by SSI 2011/178 (C.15) art.2, Sch.1 para.1.

Subs.(2)(b)(iii) repealed by Criminal Justice (Scotland) Act 2016 (asp 1) s.78. Brought into force on 17 January 2017 by SSI 2016/426 art.2 and Sch.1 para.1.

Subs.(2) as amended, subs.(3A) inserted, by Criminal Justice (Scotland) Act 2016 (asp 1) Sch.2 para.33. Brought into force on 25 January 2018 by SSI 2017/345 art.3 and Sch.1 para.1.

Subs.(3A)(d) as inserted by Domestic Abuse (Scotland) Act 2018 (asp 5) Sch.1(2) para.10(2) (effective 1 April 2019 in respect of proceedings commenced on or after 1 April 2019 subject to transitional provision specified in SSI 2018/387 reg.7(2)).

DEFINITIONS

A4-184.1 "diet": s.307(1).
"High Court": s.307(1).
"indictment": s.307(1).
"preliminary hearing": s.66(6)(b).
"preliminary issues": s.79(2)(b).
"preliminary pleas": s.79(2)(a).
"the court": s.72D(8).

[THE NEXT PARAGRAPH IS A4-185]

GENERAL NOTE

A4-185 This section applies to all solemn proceedings and has been substantially expanded by the 2004 Act, a reflection of the enhanced role of first diets in sheriff solemn cases and the introduction of mandatory preliminary diets in the High Court.

All preliminary pleas (detailed in subs.(2)(a)) and, thereafter, any preliminary issues (as found in subs.(2)(b)) must be intimated in advance of the appropriate diet; not less than two days before a first diet, and at least seven days before any preliminary diet. Subs.(1) does permit later lodging of notices on cause shown but this has to be viewed as an exceptional measure, and will bring the provisions of subs.(4) into play; the court may then fix a further first or preliminary diet or continue the issues for a hearing at the trial diet, before a jury is selected.

Subs.(3) serves notice that any argument of want of citation has to be directed towards showing the prejudice or confusion caused to the accused—minor errors or discrepancies will not be regarded as fatal to the proceedings.

Attention is drawn to the observations of the Appeal Court in *HM Advocate v Crawford* unreported 22 November 2005, High Court of Justiciary, a case discussed in the Notes to ss.64 and 65 above. "There have to be very compelling reasons before technicalities in procedure, even of a fundamental nature, can be used to avoid a prosecution. It is a fundamental part of our criminal justice system that if technicalities are available to be taken by the defence, they must have a positive result in a sense of prejudice to the accused".

Objections to admissibility of evidence raised after first diet or preliminary Hearing

79A.—(1) This section applies where a party seeks to raise an objection to the admissibility of any evidence after— A4-185.1

(a) in proceedings in the High Court, the preliminary hearing; or

(b) in proceedings on indictment in the sheriff court, the first diet.

(2) The court shall not, under section 79(1) of this Act, grant leave for the objection to be raised if the party seeking to raise it has not given written notice of his intention to do so to the other parties.

(3) However, the court may, where the party seeks to raise the objection after the commencement of the trial, dispense with the requirement under subsection (2) above for written notice to be given.

(4) Where the party seeks to raise the objection after the commencement of the trial, the court shall not, under section 79(1) of this Act, grant leave for the objection to be raised unless it considers that it could not reasonably have been raised before that time.

(5) Where the party seeks to raise the objection before the commencement of the trial and the court, under section 79(1), grants leave for it to be raised, the court shall—

(a) if it considers it appropriate to do so, appoint a diet to be held before the commencement of the trial for the purpose of disposing of the objection; or

(b) dispose of the objection at the trial diet.

(6) In appointing a diet under subsection (5)(a) above, the court may postpone the trial diet for such period as appears to it to be appropriate and may, if it thinks fit, direct that such period (or some part of it) shall not count towards any time limit applying in respect of the case.

(7) The accused shall appear at any diet appointed under subsection (5)(a) above.

(8) For the purposes of this section, the trial shall be taken to commence when the jury is sworn.

AMENDMENTS

Section 79A inserted by Criminal Procedure (Amendment) (Scotland) Act 2004 (asp 5) s.14(2). Brought into force on 1 February 2005 by SSI 2004/405 (C.28) art.2(1).

DEFINITIONS

"diet": s.307(1). A4-185.2
"indictment": s.307(1).
"preliminary issues": s.79(2)(b).
"preliminary pleas": s.79(2)(a).
"prosecutor": s.307(1).

General Note

A4-185.3 The Act stipulates in s.79(2)(b)(iv) that an objection to the admissibility of evidence is now a preliminary issue and, as such, ordinarily should be taken by written notice, timeously served on other parties, at a first or preliminary diet. Such an objection can be raised at these diets even without the requisite period of notice but with leave of the court (see ss.71(2)(YA) and 72(6)(c)).

The present section deals with circumstances where objection to admissibility has not been taken by the time of the first, or preliminary, diet. Even in this situation it is envisaged that objection will first be made known by written notice (subs. (2)), but subs.(3) tacitly acknowledges this to be a counsel of perfection in trial situations and permits the court to dispense with written notice.

Bhowmick V HM Advocate [2018] HCJAC 6 stresses that, standing the evidence previously disclosed by the Crown, the right of the defence to seek further relevant disclosure, and the attendant statutory right to raise a preliminary objection at the first diet or preliminary hearing (s.72(6)(c)), later objection alleging unfairness to an accused has to be rigorously assessed with regard to the totality of these procedures and not solely to the evidence unfolding during the trial.

Objections intimated late

Such objections should be intimated in writing, albeit late, by using Form 9B.1 in the Act of Adjournal (Criminal Procedure Rules Amendment) (Criminal Procedure (Amendment) (Scotland) Act 2004) 2005 (SSI 2005/44).

Subss.(5) and (6) addresses late objections to admissibility intimated before the trial diet: in these circumstances if the court permits late intimation it may fix a fresh first, or preliminary, diet to consider the merits, order the appearance of the accused and postpone the trial diet and discount any part of the intervening period from any time bar calculation; alternatively, defer the issue to be resolved during the trial.

Objections intimated in the course of trial

Subs.(3) preserves the court's long-established power to consider objections to admissibility of evidence in the course of the trial without the prior written notice now demanded in s.79. However, it is important to note that, since it is now expected that such an objection will be taken in advance of the trial, it can only be taken in the course of the trial once the court has been satisfied that it could not reasonably have been raised earlier. Only once this test has been met can the court move on to consider the merits of the objection.

[THE NEXT PARAGRAPH IS A4-186]

Alteration, etc, of diet

Alteration and postponement of trial diet

A4-186 **80.** [...]

Amendments

Section 80 repealed by Criminal Procedure (Amendment) (Scotland) Act 2004 (asp 4) s.25 and Sch.1 para.26. Brought into force on 1 February 2005 by SSI 2004/405 (C.28) art.2.

[THE NEXT PARAGRAPH IS A4-188]

Procedure where trial does not proceed

A4-188 **81.**—(1) The prosecutor shall not raise a fresh libel in a case in which the court has deserted the trial simpliciter unless the court's decision has been reversed on appeal.

(2) Where a trial diet in any proceedings on indictment is deserted pro loco et tempore the court may appoint a further trial diet for a later date and the accused shall appear and answer the indictment at that diet.

(3) In appointing a further trial diet under subsection (2) above, the court—

(a) shall have regard to the state of preparation of the prosecutor and the accused with respect to their cases and, in particular, to the likelihood of the case being ready to proceed to trial on the date to be appointed for the trial diet; and

(b) may, if it appears to the court that there are any preliminary pleas, preliminary issues or other matters which require to be, or could with advantage be, disposed of or ascertained before the trial diet, appoint a diet to be held before the trial diet for the purpose of disposing of or, as the case may be, ascertaining them.

(4) Subsection (5) below applies where, in any proceedings on indictment in which a trial diet has been appointed—

(a) the diet has been deserted pro loco et tempore for any reason and no further trial diet has been appointed under subsection (2) above; or

(b) the indictment falls or is for any other reason not brought to trial and the diet has not been continued, adjourned or postponed.

(5) Where this subsection applies, the prosecutor may, at any time within the period of two months after the relevant date, give notice to the accused on another copy of the indictment to appear and answer the indictment—

(a) where the trial diet referred to in subsection (4) above was in the High Court—

(i) at a further preliminary hearing in that Court not less than seven clear days after service of the notice; or

(ii) where the charge is one that can lawfully be tried in the sheriff court, at a first diet in that court not less than 21 clear days after service of the notice; or

(b) where the trial diet referred to in subsection (4) was in the sheriff court—

(i) at a first diet in that court not less than seven clear days after service of the notice; or

(ii) at a preliminary hearing in the High Court not less than 21 clear days after service of the notice.

(6) Where notice is given to the accused under paragraph (a)(ii) or (b)(ii) of subsection (5) above, then for the purposes of section 65(4) of this Act—

(a) the giving of the notice shall be taken to be service of an indictment in respect of—

(i) in the case of a notice under paragraph (a)(ii) of subsection (5) above, the sheriff court; or

(ii) in the case of a notice under paragraph (b)(ii) of that subsection, the High Court; and

(b) the previous service of the indictment in respect of—

(i) in the case of a notice under paragraph (a)(ii) of subsection (5), the High Court; or

(ii) in the case of a notice under paragraph (b)(ii) of that subsection, the sheriff court,

shall be disregarded.

(7) A notice under subsection (5) above shall be in such form as may be prescribed by Act of Adjournal, or as nearly as may be in such form.

(8) In subsection (5) above, "the relevant date" means—

(a) where paragraph (a) of subsection (4) applies, the date on which the trial diet was deserted as mentioned in that paragraph; or

(b) where paragraph (b) of that subsection applies, the date of the trial diet referred to in that subsection.

AMENDMENTS

Section 81 substituted by Criminal Procedure (Amendment) (Scotland) Act 2004 (asp 5) s.9. Brought into force on 1 February 2005 by SSI 2004/405 (C.28) art.2.

Subs.(4) as amended by Criminal Procedure (Amendment) (Scotland) Act 2004 (Incidental, Supplemental and Consequential Provisions) Order 2005 (SSI 2005/40) art.3.

Subss.(4), (5) as amended by Criminal Justice (Scotland) Act 2016 (Consequential and Transitional Provisions) Regulations 2017 (SSI 2017/221) reg.2 (effective 31 July 2017; subject to transitional provisions).

DEFINITIONS

A4-188.1 "diet": s.307(1).
"High Court": s.307(1).
"indictment": s.307(1).
"preliminary hearing": s.66(6)(b).
"preliminary issues": s.79(2)(b).
"preliminary pleas": s.79(2)(a).
"prosecutor": s.307(1).
"the relevant date": s.81(8).
"witness": s.307(1).

[THE NEXT PARAGRAPH IS A4-189]

GENERAL NOTE

A4-189 These provisions apply to all solemn proceedings and set out the options available at the trial diet should trial not proceed.

Subs.(1)

Subs.(1) simply restates the existing law.

Subs.(2)

Now when the Crown opts to desert *pro loco et tempore* it is open to the court to fix a new trial diet there and then with the existing indictment. Whereas service of a fresh indictment would enable any perceived defects in the indictment, and any s.67 material, to be incorporated into the libel, or the *forum* of proceedings to be changed, preservation of the existing indictment using s.81(2) is unlikely to be a particularly flexible procedural instrument; its primary effect would be to avoid the need for service of a new indictment, or it would seem associated s.67 notices, but that is not the benefit it once was now that service can be effected lawfully in the hands of the accused's solicitor (see s.66(6C) above). Note, however, that subs.(3) also enables the court to appoint a fresh preliminary, or first, diet.

Subs.(2) can be used to re-indict for trial (in sheriff solemn cases at least) in the same *sitting* if that becomes necessary. The same indictment, notices and any defences would remain valid and the case could be empanelled using a fresh jury assize. See *HM Advocate v Johnstone and Kennedy* unreported 25 March 2002, Forfar High Court.

Subss.(3) and (4)

Familiar (but until now little-used) provisions which apply only at the time of the trial diet are repeated, and can be applied when the court either has made no order under subs.(2) or has made no order at all. The Crown is authorised to serve a copy of the indictment on the accused with a reduced *inducíae*. A cautionary note is necessary—using these provisions it is submitted that it becomes necessary to re-serve any s.67 notices.

Identical timescales affect High Court and sheriff solemn proceedings but note that use of the abbreviated procedures can only occur within two months of the "relevant date" (see subs.(8)). It also becomes possible to switch the case from the higher to the lower court or vice versa for trial (see subs.(5)(a)(ii) and (b)(ii)) in either case extending the *induciae*, presumably to effect the transfer of papers. Generally, however, a case can be re-indicted on an *induciae* of as little as seven days—in the High Court to a new preliminary diet—and to a fresh trial diet in the sheriff court; this permits a high degree of flexibility in the allocation of trial business. Support for that view can be found in the Crown discussion in *HM Advocate v Pyne* [2014] HCJAC 129; 2015 S.C.L. 226.

Subs.(5)

Calvey v HM Advocate, 2010 S.C.C.R. 1 centred around the precise terms of the notice used by the Crown to accompany the new copy indictment which had followed the wording of Form 8.2-B too literally and omitted a direct reference to s.81(5). A further cautionary note is necessary when utilising the provisions in subs.(5) particularly having regard to the confetti of s.67 notices which customarily attach to most indictments; the subsection only entitles the Crown to serve a copy of the indictment on a shortened inducíae, it does not incorporate the contents of any s.67 notices, which will likely also need to be served to enable the Crown to proceed to trial.

The Crown may opt for the section's "abbreviated procedure" (see *Ryan v HM Advocate*, 1999 S.C.C.R. 792) but, subject to the expiry of any relevant time bar (see s.65 of the Act), is not irrevocably tied to that indictment alone as the means of continuing the proceedings. Indeed, it is not incompetent to have duplicate indictments existing simultaneously (see *HM Advocate v Dow*, 1992 S.L.T. 577).

Failure to call a s.81 indictment is not fatal—normally it will only mean that the instance of that indictment falls. See *HM Advocate v Pyne* [2014] HCJAC 129; 2015 S.C.L. 226, where the accused had previously failed to appear at a diet resulting in a warrant, and the cessation of the s.65 time bar affecting the original petition proceedings. It does remain open to the accused to argue delay or oppression as preliminary issues in order to place the Crown's conduct of the proceedings under judicial scrutiny.

Subs.(8)

This sets out the two-month timescale which governs use of the section's provisions.

Act of Adjournal

The notice specified in subs.(5) follows the style of Form 8.2–B set out in the 1996 Act of Adjournal except in cases involving "listed sexual offences" conform to s.288C of the 1995 Act, in which event Form 8.2–C is used. Note that both forms presuppose the holding of a preliminary hearing or first diet, and a diet of trial; some adaptation of the wording of the forms may be necessary to reflect the diet (or diets) assigned by the court.

Desertion or postponement where accused in custody

82. Where— A4-190

(a) a diet is deserted *pro loco et tempore*;

(b) a diet is continued, accelerated, postponed or adjourned; or

(c) an order is issued changing the place at which the trial is to take place,

the warrant of committal on which the accused is at the time in custody till liberated in due course of law shall continue in force.

Amendments

Subss.(b) and (c) as amended by Criminal Procedure (Amendment) (Scotland) Act 2004 (asp 5) s.25 and Sch.1 para.27. Brought into force on 1 February 2005 by SSI 2004/405 (C.28) art.2.

Subs.(c) as amended by Criminal Justice (Scotland) Act 2016 (Consequential and Transitional Provisions) Regulations 2017 (SSI 2017/221) reg.2 (effective 31 July 2017; subject to transitional provisions).

General Note

This section keeps the original committal warrant extant in circumstances where the indictment served has not proceeded to trial or a plea. A4-191

Circumstances giving rise to the need to keep the original warrant alive occur in cases of postponement under ss.71(7) and 72(4), s.74(3), adjournment of atrial diet by s.80(1) and desertion *pro loco et tempore* in terms of s.81(1)(a); s.82(c) relates both to situations in which the prosecutor alters the forum of trial (s.81(1)), or the court, before trial, in accordance with s.83 below, grants the prosecutor's motion to transfer the trial to another sheriff court in the sheriffdom.

Transfer of sheriff court solemn proceedings

83.—(1) Where an accused person has been cited to attend a diet of the sheriff court the prosecutor may apply to the sheriff for an order for the transfer of the proceedings to a sheriff court in another district in that sheriffdom and for adjournment to a diet of that court. A4-192

(1A) Where—

(a) an accused person has been cited to attend a diet of the sheriff court; or

(b) paragraph (a) above does not apply but it is competent so to cite an accused person,

and the prosecutor is informed by the sheriff clerk that, because of exceptional circumstances which could not reasonably have been foreseen, it is not practicable for that court (in subsection (2A)(b)(i) below referred to as the "relevant court") or any other sheriff court in that sheriffdom to proceed with the case, the prosecutor—

(i) may, where paragraph (b) above applies, so cite the accused; and

(ii) shall, where paragraph (a) above applies or the accused is so cited by virtue of paragraph (i) above, as soon as practicable apply to the sheriff principal for an order for the transfer of the proceedings to a sheriff court in another sheriffdom and for adjournment to a diet of that court.

(2) On an application under subsection (1) above the sheriff may—

(a) after giving the accused or his counsel or solicitor an opportunity to be heard; or

(b) on the joint application of the parties,

make such order as is mentioned in that subsection.

(2A) On an application under subsection (1A) above the sheriff principal may make the order sought—

(a) provided that the sheriff principal of the other sheriffdom consents; but

(b) in a case where the trial (or part of the trial) would be transferred, shall do so only—

(i) if the sheriff of the relevant court, after giving the accused or his counsel an opportunity to be heard, consents to the transfer; or

(ii) on the joint application of the parties.

(2B) On the application of the prosecutor, a sheriff principal who has made an order under subsection (2A) above may, if the sheriff principal of the other sheriffdom mentioned in that subsection consents—

(a) revoke; or

(ii) vary so as to restrict the effect of,

that order.

(2C) The sheriff may proceed under subsection (2) above on a joint application of the parties without hearing the parties and, accordingly, he may dispense with any hearing previously appointed for the purposes of considering the application.

(3) […]

AMENDMENTS

Subs.(1) substituted by Crime and Punishment (Scotland) Act 1997 (c.48) s.62(1) and Sch.1 para.21(12)(a) with effect from 1 August 1997 in terms of SI 1997/1712 art.3.

Subss.(2) and (3) inserted by s.62(1) and Sch.1 para.21(12) of the above Act with effect from 1 August 1997 by means of the above Order.

Subss.(1), (2) and (3) as amended, and subss.(1A), (2A) and (2B) inserted, by Criminal Justice (Scotland) Act 2003 (asp 7) Pt 8 s.58. Brought into force on 27 June 2003 by SSI 2003/288 (C.14).

Section 83 as amended by Criminal Procedure (Amendment) (Scotland) Act 2004 (asp 5) s.25 and Sch.1 para.28. Brought into force on 1 February 2005 by SSI 2004/405 (C.28) art.2.

DEFINITION

A4-192.1 "prosecutor": s.307(1).

[THE NEXT PARAGRAPH IS A4-193]

GENERAL NOTE

A4-193 This provision was introduced into the 1975 Act by Sch.6, para.41 of the Criminal Justice (Scotland) Act 1995 and is untested. The only changes of note introduced by the 2004 Act are the ability to use these provisions at any point once a case has been indicted; previously, the section only applied to cases due in a trial sitting; and by subs.(2C) to enable the transfer to be effected administratively if parties are agreed. The most obvious use of this section is to permit the transfer of a case to a court equipped to take the evidence of a child via a live television link (see s.271(9) and (10) below), but the section is widely drafted and could, for example, be used to enable the transfer of a sitting to another sheriff court in the sheriffdom if a previous sitting had badly overrun. The amendments introduced by the 1997 Act are of a technical nature, but serve to ensure that the original warrant to cite the accused and witnesses holds good despite any change of venue. Note, however, that s.83 makes no provision for extension of any time bar; reference still has to be had to the general provisions of s.65 above.

The amendments introduced by the Criminal Justice (Scotland) Act 2003 (asp 7) improve mechanisms for the transfer of solemn business to another part of the sheriffdom or, as subs.(1A) now provides, to transfer that business to another sheriffdom in exceptional circumstances. In part this has been a response to the potential for disruption which movement restrictions in areas recently affected by foot and mouth disease had to face. The measures in subs.(1) can be used to deal with pressure of business, or the need for special court facilities available elsewhere in the sheriffdom or perhaps to move proceedings out of the immediate vicinity to preserve public order; by contrast, the provisions in subs.(1A) deal with much less routine situations, are initiated by the sheriff clerk (though it falls to the prosecutor to intimate the application to the accused) and can only be begun with the mutual consent of the affected sheriff principals (subs. (2A)). It falls to the sheriff principal of the original jurisdiction to vary or rescind a transfer order.

(The equivalent summary provisions are set out in ss.137, 137A and 137B of the Act as now amended).

Transfer of sheriff court solemn proceedings within sheriffdom: power of sheriff principal.

83ZA. Where, because of exceptional circumstances which could not reasonably have been foreseen, it is not practicable for a sheriff court in a sheriffdom to proceed with some or all of the proceedings on indictment due to call at a diet, the sheriff principal may, of the sheriff principal's own accord, make an order for— A4-193A

(a) the transfer of the proceedings to a sheriff court in any other district in that sheriffdom; and

(b) adjournment to a diet of that court.

AMENDMENT

Section 83ZA inserted by Act of Adjournal (Criminal Procedure (Scotland) Act 1995 Amendment) (Miscellaneous) 2020 (SSI 2020/93) para.2 (effective 25 March 2020).

GENERAL NOTE

Similar provisions for the transfer of sheriff solemn proceedings could already be found in s.83 of the Act above; the instant provision was introduced by the Act of Adjournal (Criminal Procedure (Scotland) Act 1995 Amendment) (Miscellaneous) 2020 (SSI 2020/93) in the wake of the coronavirus pandemic. The critical features of s.83ZA are that the transfer procedure can be initiated by the Sheriff Principal (rather than the procurator fiscal) and need not involve the parties to the proceedings at all. Paragraph 2(4) enacts an identical provision for sheriff court summary proceedings. A4-193B

[THE NEXT PARAGRAPH IS A4-193.1]

Continuation of trial diet

Continuation of trial diet in the High Court

83A.—(1) Where, in any case which is to be tried in the High Court, the trial diet does not commence on the day appointed for the holding of the diet, the indictment shall fall. A4-193.1

(2) However, where, in appointing a day for the holding of the trial diet, the Court has indicated that the diet is to be a floating diet, the diet and, if it is adjourned, the adjourned diet may, without having been commenced, be continued from sitting day to sitting day—

(a) by minute, in such form as may be prescribed by Act of Adjournal, signed by the Clerk of Justiciary; and

(b) up to such maximum number of sitting days after the day originally appointed for the trial diet as may be so prescribed.

(3) If such a trial diet or adjourned diet is not commenced by the end of the last sitting day to which it may be continued by virtue of subsection (2)(b) above, the indictment shall fall.

(4) For the purposes of this section, a trial diet or adjourned trial diet shall be taken to commence when it is called.

(5) In this section, "sitting day" means any day on which the court is sitting, but does not include any Saturday or Sunday or any day which is a court holiday.

AMENDMENTS

Section 83A inserted by Criminal Procedure (Amendment) (Scotland) Act 2004 (asp 5) s.5. Brought into force on 1 February 2005 by SSI 2004/405 (C.28) art.2.

DEFINITIONS

"Clerk of Justiciary" : s.307(1). A4-193.2
"diet": s.307(1).
"indictment" : s.307(1).
"sitting day" : s.83A(5).

GENERAL NOTE

A4-193.3 The section applies only to High Court proceedings and contains the mechanisms for the fixed and floating trial diets now in place. Following resolution of preliminary pleas and preliminary issues at the preliminary diet, and the recording of pleas, the court will then have assigned any necessary trial to either a fixed diet or a floating trial diet.

Subss.(1) and (4)

An indictment assigned to a fixed trial diet must call on that day. The intention is that the trial should then commence but subs.(4) requires only that the diet be called, not that either a jury be empanelled or evidence led.

Subss.(2) and (3)

Much like a trial assigned to a traditional sitting, a floating trial diet can call for trial within the window of dates previously determined by the court, without having to call day on day. If the case does not proceed to trial, the Crown will require to consider whether to commence the trial diet, i.e. call the case, to seek an adjournment and thus preserve the existing indictment, or simply not call the case at all, bearing in mind the need to comply with the (now) revised timebar provisions in s.65 of the Act.

Continuation of trial diet in the sheriff court

A4-193.4 **83B.**—(1) In the sheriff court a trial diet and, if it is adjourned, the adjourned diet, may, without having been commenced, be continued from sitting day to sitting day—

(a) by minute, in such form as may be prescribed by act of adjournal, signed by the sheriff clerk,

(b) up to such maximum number of sitting days after the day originally appointed for the trial diet as may be so prescribed.

(2) The indictment falls if a trial diet, or adjourned diet, is not commenced by the end of the last sitting day to which it may be continued by virtue of subsection (1).

(3) For the purposes of this section, a trial diet or adjourned trial diet is to be taken to commence when it is called.

(4) In this section, "sitting day" means any day on which the court is sitting but does not include any Saturday or Sunday or any day which is a court holiday.

AMENDMENTS

Section 83B inserted by Criminal Justice (Scotland) Act 2016 (asp 1) s.81(6). Brought into force on 28 August 2017 by SSI 2017/99 art.5.

GENERAL NOTE

A4-193.5 This section provides the procedural mechanisms necessary to operate the regime of fixed and floating trial diets introduced into sheriff solemn procedures; its terms echo those found in s.83A which applied to High Court trial diets. Refer to the General Note there.

[THE NEXT PARAGRAPH IS A4-194]

Jurors for sittings

Juries: returns of jurors and preparation of lists

A4-194 **84.**—(1) For the purposes of a trial, the sheriff principal shall return such number of jurors as he thinks fit or, in relation to a trial in the High Court, such other number as the Lord Justice Clerk or any Lord Commissioner of Justiciary may direct.

(2) The Lord Justice General, whom failing the Lord Justice Clerk, may give directions as to the areas from which and the proportions in which jurors are to be summoned for trials to be held in the High Court, and for any such trial the sheriff principal of the sheriffdom in which the trial is to take place shall requisition the required number of jurors from the areas and in the proportions so specified.

(3) Where a sitting of the High Court is to be held at a town in which the High Court does not usually sit, the jury summoned to try any case in such a sitting shall be summoned from the lists of potential jurors of the sheriff court district in which the town is situated.

(4) For the purpose of a trial in the sheriff court, the sheriff principal must furnish the clerk of court with a list of names, containing the number of persons required, from lists of potential jurors of—

(a) the sheriff court district in which the trial is to be held (the "local district"), and

(b) if the sheriff principal considers it appropriate, any other sheriff court district or districts in the sheriffdom in which the trial is to be held ("other districts").

(4A) Where the sheriff principal furnishes a list containing names of potential jurors of other districts, the sheriff principal may determine the proportion as between the local district and the other districts in which jurors are to be summoned.

(5) The sheriff principal, in any return of jurors made by him to a court, shall take the names in regular order, beginning at the top of the lists of potential jurors in each of the sheriff court districts, as required; and as often as a juror is returned to him, he shall mark or cause to be marked, in the lists of potential jurors of the respective sheriff court districts the date when any such juror was returned to serve; and in any such return he shall commence with the name immediately after the last in the preceding return, without regard to the court to which the return was last made, and taking the subsequent names in the order in which they are entered, as directed by this subsection, and so to the end of the lists respectively.

(6) Where a person whose name has been entered in the lists of potential jurors dies, or ceases to be qualified to serve as a juror, the sheriff principal, in making returns of jurors in accordance with the Jurors (Scotland) Act 1825, shall pass over the name of that person, but the date at which his name has been so passed over, and the reason therefor, shall be entered at the time in the lists of potential jurors.

(7) [...]

(8) The persons to serve as jurors at trials in the High Court sitting at a particular place on a particular day shall be listed and their names and addresses shall be inserted in one roll, and the list made up under this section shall be known as the "list of assize".

(9) When more than one case is set down for trial in the High Court sitting at a particular place on a particular day, it shall not be necessary to prepare more than one list of assize, and such list shall be the list of assize for all trials to be held in the High Court sitting in that particular place on that particular day; and the persons included in such list shall be summoned to serve generally for all such trials, and only one general execution of citation shall be returned against them; and a copy of the list of assize, certified by one of the clerks of court, shall have the like effect, for all purposes for which the list may be required, as the principal list of assize authenticated as aforesaid.

(10) No irregularity in—

(a) making up the lists in accordance with the provisions of this Act;

(b) transmitting the lists;

(c) [...]

(d) summoning jurors; or

(e) in returning any execution of citation,

shall constitute an objection to jurors whose names are included in the jury list, subject to the ruling of the court in relation to the effect of an objection as to any criminal act by which jurors may be returned to serve in any case contrary to this Act or the Jurors (Scotland) Act 1825.

AMENDMENTS

Subs.(8) and (9) as amended, and subs.10(c) repealed, by Criminal Procedure (Amendment) (Scotland) Act 2004 (asp 5) s.25 and Sch.1 para.29. Brought into force on 1 February 2005 by SSI 2004/405 (C.28) art.2.

Subss.(3), (4), (5) as amended, (4A) inserted, (7) repealed by Criminal Justice and Licensing (Scotland) Act 2010 (asp 13) s.93(2). Brought into force on 13 December 2010 by SSI 2010/413 (C .28) art.2, Sch.1 para.1.

DEFINITIONS

A4-194.1 "High Court": s.307(1).
"Lord Commissioner of Justiciary" : s.307(1).
"Lord Justice Clerk": s.307(1).
"Lord Justice General": s.1(1).

[THE NEXT PARAGRAPH IS A4-195]

GENERAL NOTE

A4-195 This section lays out the administrative procedures to be followed in drawing up and maintaining a list of assize. Particularly note that subs.(9) makes it competent for those who have served on a jury during the sitting to be balloted for later trials in the sitting.

Rule 13.1 of the 1996 Act of Adjournal requires the clerk of court to pay heed to the postponement or adjournment of trials under s.74(5), the postponement of trial following upon the withdrawal of an accelerated plea of guilty (s.76(3)) and the alteration and postponement of a trial during a sitting, when drawing up lists of jurors.

Act of Adjournal

Refer to Ch.13 of the 1996 Act of Adjournal.

Juries: citation and attendance of jurors

A4-196 **85.**—(1) It shall not be necessary to serve any list of jurors upon the accused …

(2) A list of jurors shall—

(a) be prepared and kept in such form and manner; and
(b) contain such minimum number of names, as may be prescribed by Act of Adjournal.

(2A) The clerk of the court before which the trial is to take place shall, on an application made to him by or on behalf of an accused, supply the accused, free of charge on the day on which the trial diet is called, and before the oath has been administered to the jurors for the trial of the accused, with a copy of a list of jurors prepared under subsection (2) above.

(2B) Where an accused has been supplied under subsection (2A) above with a list of jurors—

(a) neither he nor any person acting on his behalf shall make a copy of that list, or any part thereof; and
(b) he or his representatives shall return the list to the clerk of the court after the oath has been administered to the jurors for his trial.

(2C) A person who fails to comply with subsection (2B) above shall be guilty of an offence and shall be liable on summary conviction to a fine not exceeding level 1 on the standard scale.

(3) It shall not be necessary to summon all the jurors contained in any list of jurors under this Act, but it shall be competent to summon such jurors only, commencing from the top of the list, as may be necessary to ensure a sufficient number for the trial of the cases which remain for trial at the date of the citation of the jurors, and such number shall be fixed by the clerk of the court in which the trial diet is to

be called, or in any case in the High Court by the Clerk of Justiciary, and the jurors who are not so summoned shall be placed upon the next list issued, until they have attended to serve.

(4) The sheriff clerk of—

(a) the sheriffdom in which the High Court is to sit, or

(b) the sheriff court district in which a trial in the sheriff court is to be held,

shall fill up and sign a proper citation addressed to each juror, and shall cause the same to be transmitted to him by letter, sent to him at his place of residence as stated in the lists of potential jurors or to be served on him by an officer of law; and a certificate under the hand of such sheriff clerk of the citation of any jurors or juror in the manner provided in this subsection shall be a legal citation.

(4A) Citation of a juror may also be effected by an electronic citation which is sent—

(a) by or on behalf of the sheriff clerk; and

(b) by means of electronic communication,

to the home or business email address of the juror.

(4B) Citation under subsection (4A) above is a legal citation if the sheriff clerk possesses a legible version of an electronic communication which—

(a) is signed by electronic signature by the person who signed the citation;

(b) includes the citation; and

(c) bears to have been sent to the home or business email address of the juror being cited.

(4C) In subsection (4A) above, an "electronic citation" is a citation in electronic form which—

(a) is capable of being kept in legible form; and

(b) is signed by electronic signature by or on behalf of the sheriff clerk.

(5) The sheriff clerk of the sheriffdom in which the High Court is to sit on any particular day shall issue citations to the whole jurors required for trials to be held in the High Court sitting in the sheriffdom on that day, whether the jurors reside in that or in any other sheriffdom.

(6) Persons cited to attend as jurors may, unless they have been excused in respect thereof under section 1 or 1A of the Law Reform (Miscellaneous Provisions) (Scotland) Act 1980, be fined up to level 3 on the standard scale if they fail to attend in compliance with the citation.

(7) A fine imposed under subsection (6) above may, on application, be remitted—

(a) by a Lord Commissioner of Justiciary where imposed in the High Court;

(b) by the sheriff court where imposed in the sheriff court, and no court fees or expenses shall be exigible in respect of any such application.

(8) A person shall not be exempted by sex or marriage from the liability to serve as a juror.

AMENDMENTS

Subss.(1) and (2) as amended by Crime and Punishment (Scotland) Act 1997 (c.48) s.58 with effect from 1 August 1997 (SI 1997/1712 art.3).

Subs.(2), (4) and (5) as amended by Criminal Procedure (Amendment) (Scotland) Act 2004 (asp 5) s.25 and Sch.1 para.30. Brought into force on 1 February 2005 by SSI 2004/405 (C.28) art.2.

Subss.(4) and (6) as amended by Criminal Justice and Licensing (Scotland) Act 2010 (asp 13) s.93(3) and Sch.7 para.48. Brought into force on 13 December 2010 by SSI 2010/413 (C.28) art.2, Sch.1 para.1.

Subss.(4A)–(4C) inserted by Criminal Proceedings etc. (Reform) (Scotland) Act 2007 (asp 6) s.29. Brought into force on 1 November 2012 by SSI 2012/274 (C.28) art.2 and Sch.

Subs.(4) as amended by Courts Reform (Scotland) Act 2014 (asp 18) Sch.5 para.44. Brought into force on 1 April 2015 by SSI 2015/77 art.2, Sch.1 para.1.

DEFINITIONS

A4-196.1 "Clerk of Justiciary" : s.307(1).
"High Court": s.307(1).
"indictment" : s.307(1).
"Lord Commissioner of Justiciary" : s.307(1).
"sheriff clerk": s.307(1).
"electronic citation": s.85

[THE NEXT PARAGRAPH IS A4-197]

GENERAL NOTE

A4-197 This section, amended by the 1997 Act, removes the accused's right to receive a copy of the List of Assize once his indictment has been served upon him; from August 1, 1997 the right is limited to sight of the Assize List on the day the case is called for trial.

The modified provision is directed against intimidation of jurors and was introduced into the 1997 Act at a late stage (January 20, 1997) without opposition. "Jury nobbling" has become a recognised phenomenon in other jurisdictions and the potential for abuse which advance access to jurors' particulars could present is obvious. Concern was heightened by the discovery of a current High Court Assize List circulating amongst prisoners.

Both the accused and his agent are only entitled to sight of the Assize List on the day the indictment calls for trial and may neither retain, nor copy, the List which must be returned to the Clerk once the jury is empanelled. It will be noted that subs.(2B) creates a criminal offence for any breach of that provision.

Persons made subject to probation, drug testing and treatment, community service, restriction of liberty and community orders either before or after the coming into force of s.78 of the Criminal Justice (Scotland) Act 2003 (asp 7) on 27 June 2003 are disqualified from jury service. A saving provision in subs.(3) requires the individual cited for service to attend the assize nonetheless.

Court clerks are empowered to cite jurors by electronic means.

Jurors: excusal and objections

A4-198 **86.**—(1) Where, before a juror is sworn to serve, the parties jointly apply for him to be excused the court shall, notwithstanding that no reason is given in the application, excuse that juror from service.

(2) Nothing in subsection (1) above shall affect the right of the accused or the prosecutor to object to any juror on cause shown.

(3) If any objection is taken to a juror on cause shown and such objection is founded on the want of sufficient qualification as provided by section 1(1) of the Law Reform (Miscellaneous Provisions) (Scotland) Act 1980, such objection shall be proved only by the oath of the juror objected to.

(4) No objection to a juror shall be competent after he has been sworn to serve.

DEFINITION

A4-198.1 "prosecutor": s.307(1).

[THE NEXT PARAGRAPH IS A4-199]

GENERAL NOTE

A4-199 Reference should be made to Chapter 14 of the Act of Adjournal (Criminal Procedure Rules) 1996 which lays out the procedures for selection of the jury from the assize (which must number at least 30 persons (r.14.1A)).

The right of peremptory challenge to a number of jurors without showing cause was abolished by s.8 of the Criminal Justice (Scotland) Act 1995 and subs.(1) was substituted; where parties concur, jurors can still be excused without cause being shown, a measure largely intended to enable patently unsuitable or unfit jurors to be relieved of possible selection without open challenge. Although the obvious time for such an agreement to be reached is when the assize presents itself for ballot, the section does not rule out an earlier agreement between parties after the list of assize has been inspected. The court has no power to intervene in the matter.

Subsection (2) preserves the traditional right of challenge on cause shown to a juror selected in the ballot. "Cause shown" has to relate to the juror personally and to his inability to try the case impartially or without importing personal knowledge of the circumstances of the alleged offence or of the parties listed in the indictment. So in *HM Advocate v Devine* (1962) 78 S.C. Rep. 173, objection on the basis that a juror had already served on a jury in the same assize dealing with a similar incident to that now libelled at the same *locus*, and might thus be against the accused, was repelled.

In *McCadden v HM Advocate*, 1985 S.C.C.R. 282 the court disfavoured any suggestion that vetting of a jury was permissible. Objections to jurors must be stated as subs.(4) provides, before the jury is sworn; thereafter they cannot be entertained (also see *McArthur v HM Advocate* , 1902 S.L.T. 310). Once balloted, any concern over irregular conduct, or incapacity, is a matter for the judge—parties remain entitled to make concerns known to the judge (generally through the clerk)—and fall within the ambit of s.90 of the Act.

The Law Reform (Miscellaneous Provisions) (Scotland) Act 1980 (c.55) provides that persons aged between 18 and 71 years, ordinarily resident in the United Kingdom and registered as an elector, are qualified for jury service. Older persons have the right to seek exemption as of right. Schedule 1 to that Act lists those individuals exempted, barred or disqualified from jury service.

Non-availability of judge

Non-availability of judge

87.—(1) Where the court is unable to proceed owing to the death, illness or absence of the presiding judge, the clerk of court may convene the court (if necessary) and— **A4-200**

(a) in a case where no evidence has been led, adjourn the diet and any other diet appointed for the same day to—

(i) a time later the same day, or a date not more than seven days later, when he believes a judge will be available; or

(ii) a later date not more than two months after the date of the adjournment; or

(b) in a case where evidence has been led—

(i) adjourn the diet and any other diet appointed for the same day to a time later the same day, or a date not more than seven days later, when he believes a judge will be available; or

(ii) with the consent of the parties, desert the diet *pro loco et tempore*.

(2) Where a diet has been adjourned under sub-paragraph (i) of either paragraph (a) or paragraph (b) of subsection (1) above the clerk of court may, where the conditions of that subsection continue to be satisfied, further adjourn the diet under that sub-paragraph; but the total period of such adjournments shall not exceed seven days.

(3) Where a diet has been adjourned under subsection (1)(b)(i) above the court may, at the adjourned diet—

(a) further adjourn the diet; or

(b) desert the diet *pro loco et tempore*.

(4) Where a diet is deserted in pursuance of subsection (1)(b)(ii) or (3)(b) above, the Lord Advocate may raise and insist in a new indictment, and—

(a) where the accused is in custody it shall not be necessary to grant a new warrant for his incarceration, and the warrant or commitment on which he is at the time in custody till liberation in due course of law shall continue in force; and

(b) where the accused is at liberty on bail, his bail shall continue in force.

AMENDMENTS

Subs.(1) as amended by Criminal Procedure (Amendment) (Scotland) Act 2004 (asp 5) s.25 and Sch.1 para.31. Brought into force on 1 February 2005 by SSI 2004/405 (C.28) art.2.

DEFINITIONS **A4-200.1**

"bail": s.307(1).
"indictment" : s.307(1).

[THE NEXT PARAGRAPH IS A4-201]

GENERAL NOTE

This section provides powers to the clerk of court in the event of illness or death of the presiding judge to convene the court and defer the day's business to a later date or dates. **A4-201**

Two different situations are envisaged: first, where no evidence has been led (subs.(1)(a)), the clerk may, in the absence of an available judge, adjourn any such case for a maximum of seven days to enable a judge to attend, or alternatively, *ex proprio motu* adjourn the case for up to two months. Subs.(2) limits the cumulative total of these adjournments to seven days.

On the other hand where evidence has already been led (subs.(1)(b)) the options are to adjourn the-case for up to seven days, or with the consent of parties, desert the diet *pro loco et tempore*. In the absence of this consent, resort then has to be had to an adjournment of the trial for up to seven days; in terms of subs.(3) it only becomes competent (in the absence of the parties' concurrence) for the clerk to desert the diet after a first adjournment under subs.(1)(b)(i) has elapsed.

Subs.(4) maintains the right of the Lord Advocate, where a trial has been interrupted through the unavailability of the judge and has been deserted *pro loco et tempore*, to re-indict the case. While the original warrant for committal remains in force, and the Lord Advocate can "insist" upon the proceedings, which surely suggests that there would be no need to extend timebars, prudence would suggest it would be expedient to seek extensions of any timebars for the avoidance of any doubt.

Disposal of preliminary matters at trial diet

A4-201.1 **87A.** Where—

(a) any preliminary plea or issue; or

(b) in a case to be tried in the High Court, any application, notice or other matter referred to in section 72(6)(b)(iii) or (iv) of this Act,

is to be disposed of at the trial diet, it shall be so disposed of before the jury is sworn, unless, where it is a preliminary issue consisting of an objection to the admissibility of any evidence, the court at the trial diet considers it is not capable of being disposed of before then.

AMENDMENTS

Section 87A inserted by Criminal Procedure (Amendment) (Scotland) Act 2004 (asp 5) s.13(2). Brought into force on 1 February 2005 by SSI 2004/405 (C.28) art.2.

DEFINITIONS

A4-201.2 "High Court": s.307(1).
"preliminary issues": s.79(2)(b).
"preliminary pleas": s.79(2)(a).

GENERAL NOTE

A4-201.3 Preliminary pleas or issues of related matters are now required to be disposed of at preliminary hearings but if they are to be disposed of at the trial diet then this section requires that they are disposed of before the jury is sworn. The section allows for the proviso (in effect a proof before answer) that where a preliminary issue consists of an objection to the admissibility of any evidence then it may be disposed of in the course of the trial diet.

[THE NEXT PARAGRAPH IS A4-202]

Jury for trial

Plea of not guilty, balloting and swearing of jury, etc.

A4-202 **88.—**(1) Where the accused pleads not guilty, the clerk of court shall record that fact and proceed to ballot the jury.

(2) The jurors for the trial shall be chosen in open court by ballot from the list of persons summoned in such manner as shall be prescribed by Act of Adjournal, and the persons so chosen shall be the jury to try the accused, and their names shall be recorded in the minutes of the proceedings.

(3) It shall not be competent for the accused or the prosecutor to object to a juror on the ground that the juror has not been duly cited to attend.

(4) Notwithstanding subsecction (1) above, the jurors chosen for any particular trial may, when that trial is disposed of, without a new ballot serve on the trials of other accused, provided that—

(a) the accused and the prosecutor consent;

(b) the names of the jurors are contained in the list of jurors; and

(c) the jurors are duly sworn to serve on each successive trial.

(5) When the jury has been balloted, the clerk of court shall inform the jury of the charge against the accused—

(a) by reading the words of the indictment (with the substitution of the third person for the second); or

(b) if the presiding judge, because of the length or complexity of the indictment, so directs, by reading to the jury a summary of the charge approved by the judge,

and copies of the indictment shall be provided for each member of the jury without lists of witnesses or productions.

(6) After reading the charge as mentioned in subsection (5) above and any special defence as mentioned in section 89(1) of this Act, the clerk of court shall administer the oath in common form.

(7) The court may excuse a juror from serving on a trial where the juror has stated the ground for being excused in open court.

(8) Where a trial which is proceeding is adjourned from one day to another, the jury shall not be secluded during the adjournment, unless, on the motion of the prosecutor or the accused or *ex proprio motu* the court sees fit to order that the jury be kept secluded.

Definition

"prosecutor" : s.307(1). A4-202.1

[THE NEXT PARAGRAPH IS A4-203]

General Note

This section deals with the selection of a trial jury from the list of assize prepared beforehand. Ch. 14 of the Act of Adjournal 1996 regulates the mechanics of the ballot and Forms 14.3.-A and 14.3.-B respectively stipulate the oath or affirmation to be administered to all jurors. While parties can concur to excuse jurors without showing cause (see the notes to s.86 above), in any other case objection to a juror serving on the jury must be on cause shown: the right to peremptory challenge of jurors has been abolished. It remains the case that a juror who is not exempted or disqualified from service by the provisions of the Law Reform (Miscellaneous Provisions) (Scotland) Act 1980, s.1 must serve on the jury unless he can give reason in terms of subs.(7) why he should be excused. Ordinarily, personal knowledge of the circumstances of the case, or of the accused or witnesses, would be telling factors but ultimately the determining factor has to be whether the court can be assured that the juror can try the accused according to the evidence, without importing outside knowledge or prejudice; if there is any doubt, fairness dictates that the juror should not be called upon to serve. In *Hay v HM Advocate*, 1995 S.C.C.R. 639 an appeal was taken founding on the fact that two of the jurors had knowledge of the accused (a fact made known to the clerk and the sheriff by five of the assize) while a third juror had had dealings with an associate of the accused; no challenge had been given to the selection of the jury. The Appeal Court noted that the sheriff followed the guidance given in *Pullar v HM Advocate*, 1993 S.C.C.R. 514 and emphasised (at 643C) that the issues raised in the appeal should properly have been aired prior to the trial; the appeal against conviction was dismissed. A4-203

Before the jury is empanelled, the clerk of court is required to have made the assembled assize aware of the particulars of the accused and of any witness named in the charges on the indictment and to have advised them to inform him of any prior knowledge of these parties which they have (*Pullar v HM Advocate*).

The presiding judge should also make enquiry of the jurors once the indictment has been read to them and before evidence is led, if they know of any reason why they should not serve (*Spink v HM Advocate*, 1989 S.C.C.R. 413 and also *Russell v HM Advocate*, 1992 S.L.T. 25). The ineligibility of a juror for jury service will not of itself nullify a conviction; in the face of the terms of the juror's oath to try the accused solely on the evidence led, an appeal on these grounds would only succeed if it could be demonstrated to an objective standard that there was a lack of impartiality. See *R v HM Advocate*, 2005 G.W.D. 28-521, where a former police officer who had served in another police area, who had served on R's jury was disqualified from jury service, as ineligible, in a later trial in the same sitting.

Following *B v HM Advocate*, 2006 S.L.T. 143, it would seem that the presiding sheriff, even before ordering the ballot of jurors, has to be content that there is an adequate number comprising the panel from which a ballot is to be made. The appellant principally objected to the sex mix of the selected jury (7 males and 15 females which, in the event, produced a jury of 3 men and 12 women) and did so when the case was called for trial. This submission was rejected by the sheriff who ordered the jury to be balloted. On appeal the court's approach was that the pool of available jurors for the assize on that day (only 22 from 60, and equal numbers of men and women, the missing 38 having been excused or failing to attend) was far too small; the sheriff ought to have considered an adjournment of the diet until the following day when a much larger pool was due to attend. Authority was granted to the Crown for a retrial. The Act of

Adjournal (Criminal Procedure Rules) 1996 lays out the procedures for selection of the jury from the assize which must number at least 30 persons (r.14.1A).

Subsection (4) re-enacts the rarely-used provision of s.132 of the 1975 Act: a jury which has just concluded a trial can be selected to sit in the following case in the sitting without the necessity of a ballot. However, this abbreviated procedure can only be used where; (i) the accused and the Crown consent and thus have no challenge on cause shown and; (ii) the jurors themselves pronounce no personal knowledge of the case, the accused or witnesses. Furthermore, it is implicit that the whole of that prior jury must serve in the new case and subs.(4)(c) stipulates that the jury must be put on oath anew. A consent to the use of this shortened procedure can be withdrawn by an objection from the accused which is stated before the jury has been sworn (Daniel or Donald Stuart, Re (1829) Bell's Notes 237). Chapter 14 of the Act of Adjournal provides a short form of minute, recording the particulars of the jury by reference to the record of proceedings of the previous trial.

While subs.(5)(b) allows for a summary form of the indictment charges approved by the judge to be read to the jury, it is interesting to note that this is not a matter which has to be addressed expressly at either a first or preliminary diet (the same observation could equally be made in relation to the provision in s.89(2) which allows for a condensed version of any special defence to be read to the jury instead of the notice intimated to the court).

Unempanelled jurors are not released until evidence is begun and the trial is lawfully under way.

Subsection (8) is broadly drafted. The statutory authority for the overnight accommodation of jurors who are deliberating upon their verdict is contained in s.99(4) below. Hence, subs.(8) would appear to be intended for use at earlier points in the trial, while evidence is still being led.

Jury to be informed of special defence

A4-204 **89.**—(1) Subject to subsection (2) below, where the accused has lodged a plea of special defence, the clerk of court shall, after informing the jury, in accordance with section 88(5) of this Act, of the charge against the accused, and before administering the oath, read to the jury the plea of special defence.

(2) Where the presiding judge on cause shown so directs, the plea of special defence shall not be read over to the jury in accordance with subsection (1) above; and in any such case the judge shall inform the jury of the lodging of the plea and of the general nature of the special defence.

(3) Copies of a plea of special defences shall be provided for each member of the jury.

DEFINITION

A4-204.1 "judge": s.307(1).

[THE NEXT PARAGRAPH IS A4-205]

GENERAL NOTE

A4-205 Section 78 of the Act requires that any special defence must be intimated to the court, and all other parties, at or before the first diet in sheriff solemn cases, and not less than seven clear days before the preliminary diet in High Court proceedings. Although it is possible to dispense with the preliminary diet in the High Court (s.72B) except, it is submitted, in cases involving listed sexual offences (see s.288C below), it remains the case in terms of s.72B(5) that the date of that diet still determines when notices have to be lodged and intimated. It will be noted that in addition to the well-understood categories of special defence, s.78(2) adds defences of coercion and automatism (see for the latter *Sorley v HM Advocate*, 1992 S.LT. 867 and *Ross v HM Advocate*, 1991 S.LT. 564) and, in s.288C cases, the defence of consent.

Once the indictment is read to the jury by the clerk of court, the next procedure is to read the terms of any special defence over to the jury. Failure to read over the special defence will not necessarily amount to a miscarriage of justice; see *Moar v HM Advocate*, 1949 J.C. 31. Indeed, it is often asserted that the only purpose of a notice of special defence is to give notice to the Crown of a possible line of defence evidence and, accordingly, the reading over of the terms of a notice which may not ultimately form a part of the defence case is both unnecessary and likely to confuse. Refer to *Mullen v HM Advocate*, 1978 S.L.T. (Notes) 33. Nonetheless, the provisions of s.89 are unequivocal: the terms of the notice must be made known to the jury before the trial begins. Subsection (2) allows the judge following a motion by one or other of the parties to withhold the full terms of the notice from the jury and to substitute a condensed account of the notice's meaning. In this context it has to be assumed that the terms of subs.(3), which instructs the distribution of copies of the notice of special defence, would not be adhered to, since that would appear to defeat the purpose of editing the original notice as lodged.

A plea of insanity must always be made known to the jury since the accused's state of mind at the time of the commission of the crime is a fundamental issue. It is not proper to read over a notice of incrimination of a co-accused; see *Collins v HM Advocate*, 1991 S.C.C.R. 898.

Death or illness of jurors

90.—(1) Where in the course of a trial— A4-206

(a) a juror dies; or

(b) the court is satisfied that it is for any reason inappropriate for any juror to continue to serve as a juror,

the court may in its discretion, on an application made by the prosecutor or an accused, direct that the trial shall proceed before the remaining jurors (if they are not less than twelve in number), and where such direction is given the remaining jurors shall be deemed in all respects to be a properly constituted jury for the purpose of the trial and shall have power to return a verdict accordingly whether unanimous or, subject to subsection (2) below, by majority.

(2) The remaining jurors shall not be entitled to return a verdict of guilty by majority unless at least eight of their number are in favour of such verdict and if, in any such case, the remaining jurors inform the court that—

(a) fewer than eight of their number are in favour of a verdict of guilty; and

(b) there is not a majority in favour of any other verdict,

they shall be deemed to have returned a verdict of not guilty.

GENERAL NOTE

This section regulates the composition of the jury which, of course, must comprise of 15 people at the outset of the trial, and stipulates that a majority verdict in any case requires eight of the jury at least to favour a guilty verdict. Once the trial has begun, the size of the jury can be reduced by reason of death, illness or other suitable cause (including misconduct by a juror himself) but in no case can the trial proceed with a jury numbering less than 12 persons. Recent experience in long-running trials might have suggested that the preservation of jurors' numbers is no small feat; see for example the sheriff's note in *MacDonald v HM Advocate*, 1995 S.C.C.R. 663 which lends an insight into the major logistical problems experienced in lengthy trials. A4-207

Informal discussion between parties and the presiding judge as to how to resolve the identified impasse can occur in chambers and outwith the accused's presence, but the interaction of ss.90 and 92 of the Act makes it clear that any formal motion under s.90 must be made in his presence. The sole exception to this would (perhaps) be circumstances where s.92(2) applies. *MacKay v HM Advocate* [2015] HCJAC 55 may assist.

The subsection does not of course require that the trial must proceed with a reduced number of jurors though that is the normal procedure; it would be open to the court to consider motions to desert the trial diet and to exercise such powers as were competent to the court under s.65 of the Act to extend statutory time-bars. However, in *HM Advocate v Khan*, 1997 S.C.C.R. 100 where a juror was certified unfit in the course of a trial, leaving less than 12 jurors to continue, and the sheriff refused a Crown motion to adjourn the trial for a period to permit the juror to return to health, instead deserting the trial *pro loco et tempore*, Crown advocation of that sentence was upheld, the Appeal Court having regard to both the length of proceedings and possible prejudice to the accused in a retrial.

The procedure to be followed when the jury seeks guidance on the calculation of their verdict is described in *Kerr v HM Advocate*, 1992 S.C.C.R. 281; 1992 S.L.T. 1031, where the trial judge was handed a slip of paper from the jury showing a split verdict, eight for acquittal, seven (the arithmetical majority) for guilt and after further direction a conviction resulted; quashed on appeal.

Obstructive witnesses

Apprehension of witnesses in proceedings on indictment

90A.—(1) In any proceedings on indictment, the court may, on the application of any of the parties, issue a warrant for the apprehension of a witness if subsection (2) or (3) below applies in relation to the witness. A4-207.1

(2) This subsection applies if the witness, having been duly cited to any diet in the proceedings, deliberately and obstructively fails to appear at the diet.

(3) This subsection applies if the court is satisfied by evidence on oath that the witness is being deliberately obstructive and is not likely to attend to give evidence at any diet in the proceedings without being compelled to do so.

(4) For the purposes of subsection (2) above, a witness who, having been duly cited to any diet, fails to appear at the diet is to be presumed, in the absence of any evidence to the contrary, to have so failed deliberately and obstructively.

(5) An application under subsection (1) above—

(a) may be made orally or in writing;

(b) if made in writing—

(i) shall be in such form as may be prescribed by Act of Adjournal, or as nearly as may be in such form; and

(ii) may be disposed of in court or in chambers after such inquiry or hearing (if any) as the court considers appropriate.

(6) A warrant issued under this section shall be in such form as may be prescribed by Act of Adjournal or as nearly as may be in such form.

(7) A warrant issued under this section in the form mentioned in subsection (6) above shall imply warrant to officers of law—

(a) to search for and apprehend the witness in respect of whom it is issued;

(b) to bring the witness before the court;

(c) in the meantime, to detain the witness in a police station, police cell or other convenient place; and

(d) so far as is necessary for the execution of the warrant, to break open shut and lockfast places.

(8) It shall not be competent, in any proceedings on indictment, for a court to issue a warrant for the apprehension of a witness otherwise than in accordance with this section.

(9) A person apprehended under a warrant issued under this section shall wherever practicable be brought before the court not later than in the course of the first day on which—

(a) in the case of a warrant issued by a single judge of the High Court, that Court;

(b) in any other case, the court,

is sitting after he is taken into custody.

(10) In this section and section 90B, "the court" means —

(a) where the witness is to give evidence in proceedings in the High Court, a single judge of that Court; or

(b) where the witness is to give evidence in proceedings on indictment in the sheriff court, any sheriff court with jurisdiction in relation to the proceedings.

AMENDMENTS

Section 90A inserted by Criminal Procedure (Amendment) (Scotland) Act 2004 (asp 5) s.11. Brought into force on February 1, 2005 by SSI 2004/405 (C.28) art.2.

Subs.(10) as amended by Criminal Proceedings etc (Reform) (Scotland) Act 2007 (asp 6) s.80, Sch. para.15. Brought into force on December 10, 2007 by SSI 2007/479 (C.40) art.3 and Sch.

DEFINITIONS

A4-207.1.1 "diet": s.307(1).
"indictment": s.307(1).
"the Court": s.90A(10).
"witness": s.307(1).

GENERAL NOTE

A4-207.1.2 This section applies only to solemn proceedings and is in response to the conclusions of the Bonomy Report, "*Modernising Justice in Scotland: The Reform of the High Court of Justiciary*" (Scottish Executive, 2003) that witness problems were the cause of the bulk of Crown motions for adjournments of trial.

Thus, a substantial portion of the Criminal Procedure (Amendment) (Scotland) Act 2004 was devoted to policing errant or reluctant witnesses as can be seen from the following sections. It will be noted that the 1995 Act already contains provisions to permit the admission of the evidence of missing witnesses (s.259(2)(c)) and of prior statements by uncooperative witnesses at trial (s.259(2)(e)).

The present section enables any party to apply to the court by means of Form 13A.2-A in the Act of Adjournal (Criminal Procedure Rules Amendment) (Criminal Procedure (Amendment) (Scotland) Act

2004) 2005 (SSI 2005/44), or verbally at a diet, for a witness apprehension warrant. The section applies at any point in the proceedings and the application can be considered, as appropriate, in court or in chambers.

The court has to be satisfied that the witness has misconducted himself as specified in either subss.(2) or (3) and this is without prejudice to any right to reach a subsequent determination of contempt.

In the case of subs.(2) it is noted that a failure to appear at a cited diet will prima facie be construed as deliberate or wilful. Subs.(3) depends upon evidence on oath and suggests that conduct both before and after any successful service of a witness citation can be taken into account by the court.

The warrant is granted for execution by officers of law whose powers under warrant are set out in subs.(7); these echo the terms of ordinary search warrants but require the apprehended witness to be produced before a judge of the court which issued the warrant as soon as practicable. Generally, it has to be assumed that warrants will be sought by the Crown but application can competently be made by the defence. Section 90B deals with the options which the court can exercise in relation to the witness.

[THE NEXT PARAGRAPH IS A4-207.2]

Orders in respect of witnesses apprehended under section 90A

90B.—(1) Where a witness is brought before the court in pursuance of a warrant issued under section 90A of this Act, the court shall, after giving the parties and the witness an opportunity to be heard, make an order— A4-207.2

(a) detaining the witness until the conclusion of the diet at which the witness is to give evidence;

(b) releasing the witness on bail; or

(c) liberating the witness.

(2) The court may make an order under subsection (1)(a) or (b) above only if it is satisfied that—

(a) the order is necessary with a view to securing that the witness appears at the diet at which the witness is to give evidence; and

(b) it is appropriate in all the circumstances to make the order.

(2A) Whenever the court makes an order under subsection (1) above, it shall state the reasons for the terms of the order.

(3) Subsection (1) above is without prejudice to any power of the court to—

(a) make a finding of contempt of court in respect of any failure of a witness to appear at a diet to which he has been duly cited; and

(b) dispose of the case accordingly.

(4) Where—

(a) an order under subsection (1)(a) above has been made in respect of a witness; and

(b) at, but before the conclusion of, the diet at which the witness is to give evidence, the court in which the diet is being held excuses the witness,

that court, on excusing the witness, may recall the order under subsection (1)(a) above and liberate the witness.

(5) On making an order under subsection (1)(b) above in respect of a witness, the court shall impose such conditions as it considers necessary with a view to securing that the witness appears at the diet at which he is to give evidence.

(6) However, the court may not impose as such a condition a requirement that the witness or a cautioner on his behalf deposit a sum of money in court.

(7) Where the court makes an order under subsection (1)(a) above in respect of a witness, the court shall, on the application of the witness—

(a) consider whether the imposition of a remote monitoring requirement would enable it to make an order under subsection (1)(b) above releasing the witness on bail subject to a movement restriction condition; and

(b) if so—

(i) make an order under subsection (1)(b) above releasing the witness on bail subject to such a condition (as well as such other conditions required to be imposed under subsection (5) above); and

(ii) in the order, impose, as a further condition under subsection (5) above, a remote monitoring requirement.

(8) Subsections (7) to (19) of section 24A of this Act apply in relation to remote monitoring requirements imposed under subsection (7)(b)(ii) above and to the imposing of such requirements as they apply to remote monitoring requirements imposed under section 24A(1) or (2) of this Act and the imposing of such requirements, but with the following modifications—

(a) references to a remote monitoring requirement imposed under section 24A(1) or (2) of this Act shall be read as if they included references to a remote monitoring requirement imposed under subsection (7)(b)(ii) above;

(b) references to the accused shall be read as if they were references to the witness in respect of whom the order under subsection (1)(b) above is made.

(9) The powers conferred and duties imposed by sections 24B to 24D of this Act are exercisable in relation to remote monitoring requirements imposed under subsection (7)(b)(ii) above as they are exercisable in relation to remote monitoring requirements imposed under subsection (1) or (2) of section 24A of this Act; and—

(a) references in those sections to remote monitoring requirements shall be read accordingly; and

(b) references to the imposition of any requirement as a further condition of bail shall be read as if they were references to the imposition of the requirement as a further condition under subsection (5) above.

(10) Section 25 of this Act (which makes provision for an order granting bail to specify the conditions imposed on bail and the accused's proper domicile of citation) shall apply in relation to an order under subsection (1)(b) above as it applies to an order granting bail, but with the following modifications—

(a) references to the accused shall be read as if they were references to the witness in respect of whom the order under subsection (1)(b) above is made;

(b) references to the order granting bail shall be read as if they were references to the order under subsection (1)(b) above;

(c) subsection (3) shall be read as if for the words from "relating" to "offence" in the third place where it occurs there were substituted "at which the witness is to give evidence".

(11) In this section—

(a) "a movement restriction condition" means, in relation to a witness released on bail under subsection (1)(b) above, a condition imposed under subsection (5) above restricting the witness's movements, including such a condition requiring the witness to be, or not to be, in any place or description of place for, or during, any period or periods or at any time.

(b) "a remote monitoring requirement" means, in relation to a movement restriction condition, a requirement that compliance with the condition be remotely monitored.

AMENDMENTS

Section 90B inserted by Criminal Procedure (Amendment) (Scotland) Act 2004 (asp 5) s.11. Brought into force (with the exception of subss.(7)–(9) and (11)(b)) on 1 February 2005 by SSI 2004/405 (C.28) art.2 for the purposes specified in Sch.1.

Subs.(2A) inserted by Criminal Proceedings etc. (Reform) (Scotland) Act 2007 (asp 6) s.27. Brought into force on 10 December 2007 by SSI 2007/479.

DEFINITIONS A4-207.2.1

"a movement restriction condition": s.90B(11)(a).
"a remote monitoring requirement": s.90B(11)(b).
"bail": s.307(1).
"indictment": s.307(1).
"the Court": s.90A(10).
"witness": s.307(1).
"offence": s.307(1)

GENERAL NOTE

Applying only to solemn proceedings, this section lays out the procedures for the court in dealing with a witness apprehended under a s.90A warrant. Previously a witness apprehended on warrant was either held in custody pending the trial proceedings and the hearing of his evidence or had to petition the nobile officium for bail—a time-consuming, costly and not necessarily swift resolution. Section 90B provides a statutory framework for bail appplications in such circumstances and study of ss.90A to 90E of the Act underlines the efforts already devoted to the problem of reluctant or errant witnesses. Yet within two years of these legislative provisions being commenced the topic has been revisited and reworked, this time to ensure that the same statutory regime is applied to both solemn and summary proceedings—the latter provisions, now found in ss.156A to 156D, perhaps making up in comprehensivness what they palpably lack in elegance. A4-207.2.2

The alternatives open to the court on the appearance from custody of the witness are described in subs.(1) but release on bail or a remand in custody pending the trial proceedings can only be deployed if the court is satisfied that the measure is appropriate to ensure appearance at the diet and no determination can be reached until both the parties and the witness himself have been heard.

Bail conditions much like those which apply to accused persons can be imposed and might, for example, require surrender of passport or signing at given times at a police station, but, following subs.(6), cannot include the finding of money bail or caution by the witness or a guarantor. Review of the conditions is competent; see s.90D of the Act. No less important, s.90E provides mechanisms for appealing decisions of the court, appeals being open to the witness, the Crown and the accused.

Section 90B(2A) requires the court dealing with suitably obstructive witnesses in solemn proceedings to state its reasons when bail is refused and a witness is remanded in custody pending trial, when bail is granted pending the trial, or when a witness brought before it on warrant is simply ordained to attend; this last option seems the least likely to be used given the circumstances.

[THE NEXT PARAGRAPH IS A4-207.3]

Breach of bail under section 90B(1)(b)

90C.—(1) A witness who, having been released on bail by virtue of an order under subsection (1)(b) of section 90B of this Act, fails without reasonable excuse— A4-207.3

(a) to appear at any diet to which he has been cited; or
(b) to comply with any condition imposed under subsection (5) of that section,

shall be guilty of an offence and liable on conviction on indictment to the penalties specified in subsection (2) below.

(2) Those penalties are—

(a) a fine; and
(b) imprisonment for a period not exceeding two years.

(2A) In any proceedings in relation to an offence under subsection (1) above, the fact that (as the case may be) a person—

(a) was on bail;
(b) was subject to any particular condition of bail;
(c) failed to appear at a diet;
(d) was cited to a diet,

shall, unless challenged by giving notice of a preliminary objection in accordance with section 71(2) or 72(6)(b)(i) of this Act, be held as admitted.

(3) Subsection (4) below applies in proceedings against a witness for an offence under paragraph (b) of subsection (1) above where the condition referred to in that paragraph is—

(a) a movement restriction condition (within the meaning of section 90B(11) of this Act) in respect of which a remote monitoring requirement has been imposed under section 90B(7)(b)(ii) of this Act; or

(b) a requirement imposed under section 24D(3)(b) (as extended by section 90B(9)) of this Act.

(4) In proceedings in which this subsection applies, evidence of—

(a) in the case referred to in subsection (3)(a) above, the presence or absence of the witness at a particular place at a particular time; or

(b) in the case referred to in subsection (3)(b) above, any tampering with or damage to a device worn or carried by the witness for the purpose of remotely monitoring his whereabouts,

may, subject to subsections (7) and (8) below, be given by the production of the document or documents referred to in subsection (5) below.

(5) That document or those documents is or are a document or documents bearing to be—

(a) a statement automatically produced by a device specified in regulations made under section 24D(4) (as extended by section 90B(9)) of this Act by which the witness's whereabouts were remotely monitored; and

(b) a certificate signed by a person nominated for the purpose of this paragraph by the Scottish Ministers that the statement relates to—

(i) in the case referred to in subsection (3)(a) above, the whereabouts of the witness at the dates and times shown in the statement; or

(ii) in the case referred to in subsection (3)(b) above, any tampering with or damage to the device.

(6) The statement and certificate mentioned in subsection (5) above shall, when produced in the proceedings, be sufficient evidence of the facts set out in them.

(7) Neither the statement nor the certificate mentioned in subsection (5) above shall be admissible in evidence unless a copy of both has been served on the witness prior to the trial.

(8) Without prejudice to subsection (7) above, where it appears to the court that the witness has had insufficient notice of the statement or certificate, it may adjourn the trial or make an order which it thinks appropriate in the circumstances.

(9) In subsections (7) and (8), "the trial" means the trial in the proceedings against the witness referred to in subsection (3) above.

(10) Section 28 of this Act shall apply in respect of a witness who has been released on bail by virtue of an order under section 90B(1)(b) of this Act as it applies to an accused released on bail, but with the following modifications—

(a) references to an accused shall be read as if they were references to the witness;

(b) in subsection (2), the reference to the court to which the accused's application for bail was first made shall be read as if it were a reference to the court which made the order under section 90B(1)(b) of this Act in respect of the witness; and

(c) in subsection (4)—

(i) references to the order granting bail and original order granting bail shall be read as if they were references to the order under section 90B(1)(b) and the original such order respectively;

(ii) paragraph (a) shall be read as if at the end there were inserted "and make an order under section 90B(1)(a) or (c) of this Act in respect of the witness"; and

(iii) paragraph (c) shall be read as if for the words from "complies" to the end there were substituted "appears at the diet at which the witness is to give evidence".

Amendments

Section 90C inserted by Criminal Procedure (Amendment) (Scotland) Act 2004 (asp 5) s. 11. Brought into force (with the exception of subss.(3)-(9)) on February 1, 2005 by SSI 2004/405 (C.28) art.2 for the purposes specified in Sch. 1.

Subs.(2A) inserted by Criminal Proceedings etc. (Reform) (Scotland) Act 2007 (asp 6) s.27. Brought into force on December 10, 2007 by SSI 2007/479.

Definitions

"bail": s.307(1). A4-207.3.1
"diet": s.307(1).
"trial": s.90C(9).
"witness": s.307(1).

General Note

This section creates offences for any breach of bail conditions by a witness and extends to matters of evidential proof where a remote monitoring requirement has been imposed. Powers of arrest without warrant, mirroring those applied to bailed accused by s.28 of the Act, are applied to witnesses by s.90C(10). Significantly, arrest can be used against a witness who, it is anticipated, is *likely* to breach his bail conditions. A4-207.3.2

Section 90C(2A) imports several presumptions in the proof of any criminal proceedings alleging a breach of a witness bail order. Any challenge to these four presumptions has to be made known at the first diet in sheriff solemn proceedings and by notice in advance of the preliminary hearing in any High Court proceedings. It may be observed however that the penalty for breach of a witness bail order is restricted to a fine, or two years imprisonment, or both. This tariff still may not adequately reflect the gravity of the witness' offence and may impel the Crown instead to libel a common law offence of attempting to defeat the ends of justice which could attract unlimited fines or imprisonment. It will be recognised however that the presumptions only apply to proof of statutory offences under s.90C of the 1995 Act, not to any associated common law offences. Evidentially these provisions are far-reaching and need to be considered well before any preliminary, or first, diet. Particular care would be required in High Court proceedings before anyone charged in solemn proceedings with contravening s.90C should opt to waive the preliminary hearing as s.72B of the 1995 Act permits.

[THE NEXT PARAGRAPH IS A4-207.4]

Review of orders under section 90B(1)(a) or (b)

90D.—(1) Where a court has made an order under subsection (1)(a) of section 90B of this Act, the court may, on the application of the witness in respect of whom the order was made, and after giving the parties and the witness an opportunity to be heard— A4-207.4

(a) recall the order; and
(b) make an order under subsection (1)(b) or (c) of that section in respect of the witness.

(2) Where a court has made an order under subsection (1)(b) of section 90B of this Act, the court may, after giving the parties and the witness an opportunity to be heard—

(a) on the application of the witness in respect of whom the order was made—
  (i) review the conditions imposed under subsection (5) of that section at the time the order was made; and
  (ii) make a new order under subsection (1)(b) of that section and impose different conditions under subsection (5) of that section;
(b) on the application of the party who made the application under section 90A(1) of this Act in respect of the witness, review the order and the conditions imposed under subsection (5) of section 90B at the time the order was made, and
  (i) recall the order and make an order under subsection (1)(a) of that section in respect of the witness; or

(ii) make a new order under subsection (1)(b) of that section and impose different conditions under subsection (5) of that section.

(3) The court may not review an order by virtue of subsection (1) or (2) above unless—

(a) in the case of an application by the witness, the circumstances of the witness have changed materially; or

(b) in that or any other case, the witness or

party making the application puts before the court material information which was not available to it when it made the order which is the subject of the application.

(4) An application under this section by a witness—

(a) where it relates to the first order made under section 90B(1)(a) or (b) of this Act in respect of the witness, shall not be made before the fifth day after that order is made;

(b) where it relates to any subsequent such order, shall not be made before the fifteenth day after the order is made.

(5) On receipt of an application under subsection (2)(b) above the court shall—

(a) intimate the application to the witness in respect of whom the order which is the subject of the application was made;

(b) fix a diet for hearing the application and cite the witness to attend the diet; and

(c) where it considers that the interests of justice so require, grant warrant to arrest the witness.

(6) Nothing in this section shall affect any right of a person to appeal against an order under section 90B(1).

Amendments

Section 90D inserted by Criminal Procedure (Amendment) (Scotland) Act 2004 (asp 5) s.11. Brought into force on February 1, 2005 by SSI 2004/405 (C.28) art.2.

Subss.(1), (2) and (3) amended by Criminal Proceedings etc. (Reform) (Scotland) Act 2007 (asp 6) ss.27, 80 and Sch. para. 15. Brought into force on December 10, 2007 by SSI 2007/479 art.3 and Sch.

Subs.(3) as amended by Criminal Justice and Licensing (Scotland) Act 2010 (asp 13) Sch.7 para.49. Brought into force on December 13, 2010 by SSI 2010/413 (C.28) art.2, Sch.1 para.1.

Definitions

A4-207.4.1 "bail": s.307(1).
"diet": s.307(1).
"trial": s.90C(9).
"witness": s.307(1).

General Note

A4-207.4.2 This section applies to witnesses in solemn proceedings and allows for review of the terms of a bail order, the making of a bail order where bail has previously been refused by the court and a material change in circumstances has occurred or fresh information is now available, or the outright removal of a bail order. All parties are entitled to be heard; note too that subs.(1) relates to any such application by the witness himself, while subs.(2)(b) is initiated by the party who originally craved the warrant for the witness' apprehension and has to be read in conjunction with subs.(5). Written application for a warrant in these circumstances should follow the style of Form 13A.2-A in the Act of Adjournal (Criminal Procedure Rules Amendment) (Criminal Procedure (Amendment) (Scotland) Act 2004) 2005 (SSI 2005/44).

By way of clarification, subs.(4) sets out the timescales for applications for review or further review of the court's decision; these apply only to applications by the affected witness.

[THE NEXT PARAGRAPH IS A4-207.5]

Appeals in respect of orders under section 90B(1)

A4-207.5 **90E.**—(1) Any of the parties specified in subsection (2) below may appeal to the High Court against—

(a) any order made under subsection (1)(a) or (c) of section 90B of this Act; or

(b) where an order is made under subsection (1)(b) of that section—
(i) the order;
(ii) any of the conditions imposed under subsection (5) of that section on the making of the order; or
(iii) both the order and any such conditions.

(2) The parties referred to in subsection (1) above are—
(a) the witness in respect of whom the order which is the subject of the appeal was made;
(b) the prosecutor; and
(c) the accused.

(3) A party making an appeal under subsection (1) above shall intimate it to the other parties specified in subsection (2) above and, for that purpose, intimation to the Crown Agent shall be sufficient intimation to the prosecutor.

(4) An appeal under this section shall be disposed of by the High Court or any Lord Commissioner of Justiciary in court or in chambers after such inquiry and hearing of the parties as shall seem just.

(5) Where the witness in respect of whom the order which is the subject of an appeal under this section was made is under 21 years of age, section 51 of this Act shall apply to the High Court or, as the case may be, the Lord Commissioner of Justiciary when disposing of the appeal as it applies to a court when remanding or committing a person of the witness's age for trial or sentence.

AMENDMENTS

Section 90E inserted by Criminal Procedure (Amendment) (Scotland) Act 2004 (asp 5) s.11. Brought into force on February 1, 2005 by SSI 2004/405 (C.28) art.2.

Subs.(3) as amended by Criminal Proceedings etc (Reform) (Scotland) Act 2007 (asp 6) s.80, Sch. para. 15. Brought into force on December 10, 2007 by SSI 2007/479 (C.40) art.3 and Sch.

DEFINITIONS

"High Court": s.307(1). A4-207.6
"prosecutor": s.307(1).
"witness": s.307(1).

GENERAL NOTE

Applying to solemn proceedings, this section enables appeals to the High Court by any witness refused witness bail or made subject to bail conditions which he considers to be unduly onerous. As with other bail orders in the Act, the prosecutor has a right of appeal but so too does an accused, or any co-accused. Subs.(5) specifies the form of remand facilities to be used for the detention of witnesses under 21 years of age by drawing upon the provisions of s. 51 of the Act which ordinarily apply to accused persons. A4-207.7

[THE NEXT PARAGRAPH IS A4-208]

Trial

Trial to be continuous

91. Every trial shall proceed from day to day until it is concluded unless the court sees cause to adjourn over a day or days. A4-208

GENERAL NOTE

Although it is generally the case that trials will continue from day to day until concluded, this section affords the presiding judge an element of discretion in allowing for variations from that norm when appropriate. See *MacDonald v HM Advocate*, 1995 S.C.C.R. 663 for an insight into the conduct of longer trials. A4-209

Section 102 below permits the interruption of proceedings to receive the verdict in another case. See also rr.14.8 and 14.9 of the 1996 Act of Adjournal.

Trial in presence of accused

A4-210 **92.**—(1) Without prejudice to section 54 of this Act, and subject to subsections (2) and (2A) below, no part of a trial shall take place outwith the presence of the accused.

(2) If during the course of his trial an accused so misconducts himself that in the view of the court a proper trial cannot take place unless he is removed, the court may order—

(a) that he is removed from the court for so long as his conduct makes it necessary; and

(b) that the trial proceeds in his absence,

but if he is not legally represented the court shall appoint a solicitor to represent his interests during such absence.

(2A) If—

(a) after evidence has been led which substantially implicates the accused in respect of the offence charged in the indictment or, where two or more offences are charged in the indictment, any of them, the accused fails to appear at the trial diet; and

(b) the failure to appear occurred at a point in proceedings where the court is satisfied that it is in the interests of justice to do so,

then the court may, on the motion of the prosecutor and after hearing the parties on the motion, proceed with the trial and dispose of the case in the absence of the accused.

(2B) Where a motion is made under subsection (2A) above, the court shall—

(a) if satisfied that there is a solicitor with authority to act for the purposes of—

(i) representing the accused's interests at the hearing on the motion; and

(ii) if the motion is granted, the accused's defence at the trial allow that solicitor to act for those purposes; or

(b) if there is no such solicitor, at its own hand appoint a solicitor to act for those purposes.

(2C) It is the duty of a solicitor appointed under subsection (2) or (2B)(b) above to act in the best interests of the accused.

(2D) In all other respects, a solicitor so appointed has, and may be made subject to, the same obligations and has, and may be given, the same authority as if engaged by the accused; and any employment of and instructions given to counsel by the solicitor shall proceed and be treated accordingly.

(2E) Where the court is satisfied that—

(a) a solicitor allowed to act under subsection (2B)(a) above no longer has authority to act; or

(b) a solicitor appointed under subsection (2) or (2B)(b) above is no longer able to act in the best interests of the accused,

the court may relieve that solicitor and appoint another solicitor for the purposes referred to in subsection (2) or, as the case may be, (2B) above.

(2F) Subsections (2B)(b) and (2E) above shall not apply in the case of proceedings

(a) in respect of a sexual offence to which section 288C of this Act applies; or

(aa) in respect of an offence to which section 288DC of this Act applies;

(b) in respect of which section 288E of this Act applies; or

(c) in which an order has been made under section 288F(2) of this Act.

(3) From the commencement of the leading of evidence in a trial for rape or the like the judge may, if he thinks fit, cause all persons other than the accused and counsel and solicitors to be removed from the court-room.

(4) In this section—

(a) references to a solicitor appointed under subsection (2) or (2B)(b) above include references to a solicitor appointed under subsection (2E) above;

(b) "counsel" includes, in relation to the High Court of Justiciary, a solicitor who has a right of audience in that Court under section 25A of the Solicitors (Scotland) Act 1980 (c.46).

AMENDMENTS

Subss.(1) and (2) as amended, and subs.(2A)–(2F), (4) inserted, by Criminal Procedure (Amendment) (Scotland) Act 2004 (asp 5) s.10. Brought into force on 1 February 2005 by SSI 2004/405 (C.28) art.2.

Subs.(2F)(b) as amended, and subs.(2F)(c) inserted, by Criminal Procedure (Amendment) (Scotland) Act 2004 (Incidental, Supplemental and Consequential Provisions) Order 2005 (SSI 2005/40) art.3.

Subs.(2F)(aa) as inserted by Domestic Abuse (Scotland) Act 2018 (asp 5) Sch.1(1) (2) para.4(7) (effective 1 April 2019 in respect of proceedings commenced on or after 1 April 2019 subject to transitional provision specified in SSI 2018/387 reg.7(2)).

DEFINITIONS

"counsel": s.92(4)(b). A4-210.1
"judge": s.307(1).

[THE NEXT PARAGRAPH IS A4-211]

GENERAL NOTE

The hearing of evidence in all cases should occur in the presence of the accused unless he so misconducts himself as to necessitate his removal from the court. In *Aitken v Wood*, 1921 J.C. 84 magistrates examined alleged injuries on the complainer's arm in private. Breach of this provision, which arose from removal of the accused from court in the course of his evidence due to a legal debate, was held to be fundamental even without any evidence of prejudice in *Drummond v HM Advocate*, 2003 S.L.T. 295; oddly, the Crown was held to be responsible to a significant extent in not reminding the court that such a procedure would be inept and application for a retrial was refused. The conviction was quashed. See also *Livingston v HM Advocate*, 1991 S.C.C.R. 350; 1992 S.L.T. 481, where the removal of productions from the court for expert examination during the trial was held not to breach the general prohibition then contained in s.145 of the 1975 Act. In *McColl v HM Advocate*, 1989 S.C.C.R. 229; 1989 S.L.T. 691 the clerk of court was called to the jury room and was asked for guidance upon the judge's directions which he gave; the conviction was quashed. See also *Kerr v HM Advocate*, 1992 S.C.C.R. 281; 1992 S.L.T. 1031 discussed in the notes to s.90 above. A4-211

The need for the accused to follow the evidence, and to be capable of giving informed instruction to counsel during trial is well-recognised as essential for a fair trial; see *Erkurt v Higson*, 2004 J.C. 23; 2004 S.L.T. 21; 2004 S.C.C.R. 87; *Hassan v HM Advocate*, 2013 S.L.T. 217 and *Lee v HM Advocate* [2016] HCJAC 39; 2016 S.C.C.R. 247. In the first instance it is for the defence to satisfy themselves that the accused's interpretation arrangements are effective and to draw any difficulty with these to the court's attention immediately.

While the courts are generally public courts, subs.(3) permits the presiding judge in cases involving a charge of rape or other charges of a sexual nature to close the court to the public from the outset of proceedings. Further provisions in regard to the line of questioning permissible in sexual offences are to be found at s.274 below. Specifically in relation to the evidence of children, it will also be recalled that s.50(3) enables the court to be cleared of all but the immediately interested parties during the hearing of that evidence. The general principle need not extend to any proceedings deemed necessary in connection with an appeal: see *Crossan v HM Advocate*, 1996 S.C.C.R. 279 discussed at A4-178 above.

The distinction between matters of an administrative character (which can be dealt with outwith the presence of the accused) and matters intrinsic to the trial itself (where the accused's presence is a prerequisite except in the circumstances set out in s.54 or in s.92(2) above) was discussed in *Thomson v HM Advocate*, 1998 S.L.T. 364. See more recently *Lindsay v HM Advocate*, 2005 S.C.C.R. 515 and *MacKay v HM Advocate* [2015] HCJAC 55, a case involving enquiries into the extent of a declared familiarity between a juror and the accused. *MacKay* underlines the importance of maintaining an accurate record of proceedings whether they properly occur in, or outwith, the presence of the accused.

Subs.(2A) introduces a contentious measure to deal with an accused who absents himself during the course of his trial on indictment: on the motion of the prosecutor, and after hearing submissions, the court can order that the trial continue in absence. Despite the novelty of the provision, one has to question how readily it can be used to any sustainable effect.

Leaving aside the practicality of such a provision where identification of the accused may still be in issue, subs.(2A) lays out the tests to be applied by the court in considering such a motion—once an accused has been substantially implicated upon a charge (or one of the charges) on the indictment and the court is satisfied that it is in the interests of justice to do so, there is a discretion to proceed with the trial, and if need be to appoint a solicitor to continue with the defence of the case. It is submitted that the court might consider the effects of an aborted trial upon the witnesses who have given, or are still waiting to give, evidence under these circumstances, but would also have to take account of the significance or gravity of the charge in which the accused has been substantially implicated in the context of the entire libel, and the form and content of the defence case up to that point in the proceedings. Bluntly, it is difficult to see how this provision could be applied in solemn proceedings except where the bulk of evidence, including, arguably, defence evidence, had been led before the accused absented himself; further, in the event of a conviction it cannot be assumed that the court would already be in possession of the necessary social enquiry reports to pass sentence competently, a problem which need not arise where an accused had been removed from the court on account of misconduct.

It might be felt better in the circumstances set out in subs.(2A), for the Crown to adopt a robust stance—in seeking withdrawal of bail—where the evidence led has substantially implicated the accused upon grave charges, rather than courting the risk of using a procedure so fraught with jurisprudential difficulty.

The scope of the provisions in subs.(3) is shown by *HM Advocate v Mola*, 2007 S.L.T. 462; in the course of trial of an accused charged with culpably and recklessly infecting the complainer with HIV, the court not only used its powers to exclude the public from hearing the complainer's evidence but issued a s.11 order in terms of the Contempt of Court Act 1981 (c.49) prohibiting identification of the complainer during the proceedings and in all time coming. No objection had been taken and the court clearly proceeded on the basis that the offence charged was in the nature of a sexual offence.

Act of Adjournal

See Form 14.7 in the 1996 Act of Adjournal.

Record of trial

A4-212 **93.**—(1) The proceedings at the trial of any person who, if convicted, is entitled to appeal under Part VIII of this Act, shall be recorded by means of shorthand notes or by mechanical means.

(2) A shorthand writer shall—

(a) sign the shorthand notes taken by him of such proceedings and certify them as being complete and correct; and

(b) retain the notes.

(3) A person recording such proceedings by mechanical means shall—

(a) certify that the record is true and complete;

(b) specify in the certificate the proceedings or, as the case may be, the part of the proceedings to which the record relates; and

(c) retain the record.

(4) The cost of making a record under subsection (1) above shall be defrayed, in accordance with scales of payment fixed for the time being by Treasury, out of money provided by Parliament.

(5) In subsection (1) above "proceedings at the trial" means the whole proceedings including, without prejudice to that generality—

(a) discussions—

(i) on any objection to the relevancy of the indictment;

(ii) with respect to any challenge of jurors; and

(iii) on all questions arising in the course of the trial;

(b) the decision of the court on any matter referred to in paragraph (a) above;

(c) the evidence led at the trial;

(d) any statement made by or on behalf of the accused whether before or after the verdict;

(e) the judge's charge to the jury;

(f) the speeches of counsel or agent;

(g) the verdict of the jury;

(h) the sentence by the judge.

DEFINITION
"judge": s.307(1). A4-212.1

[THE NEXT PARAGRAPH IS A4-213]

GENERAL NOTE

A shorthand or recorded record of the entire proceedings in all solemn cases must be maintained and preserved lest a call is made (in terms of s.94) for them to be produced. Additionally Chap.14 of the Act of Adjournal 1996 enacts that the trial judge is obliged to preserve and authenticate his own notes of evidence and produce them (or a certified copy) to the High Court when requested. The same rules stipulate that where reliance is placed on a recording of the proceedings instead of shorthand notes, the clerk of court must record the fact in his minutes of proceedings. A4-213

On appeal in *Kyle v HM Advocate*, 1987 S.C.C.R. 116, weight was placed by the appellant upon the apparent inconsistency of a part of the judge's charge, the shorthand notes having been certified as accurate. In fact the terms of the notes suggested that the shorthand writer had some doubts about the accuracy of that section of the transcription; the High Court held that while the notes had to be so certified, the court was not bound to accept them as such and that, in any event, no miscarriage of justice had occurred.

However the absence of a shorthand record altogether has been held to have left the Appeal Court in doubt as to additional directions given to the jury, the sheriff having re-convened the court in the absence of the shorthand writer in breach of the provisions of s.274(1) of the 1975 Act. The aggravated element of the conviction which had been the reason for further directions was quashed and a lesser conviction substituted (see *McLaughlan v HM Advocate*, 1995 G.W.D. 38–1935).

Comparison of this decision with that in *Carroll v HM Advocate*, 1999 S.L.T. 1185; 1999 S.C.C.R. 617 is instructive; on one reading the sheriff had wilfully proceeded with his directions to the jury in the knowledge that no record of the proceedings was being made in McLaughlan whereas in Carroll none of the parties was aware of a defect in the recording equipment, and this only became an issue when an appeal on entirely unrelated grounds was taken and the defect discovered. The Appeal Court declined to quash the conviction simply on account of the absence of a record of trial, looked to the judge's report and ruled that the appellant would have to point to an irregularity or misdirection to maintain an appeal. The Court declined to regard the absence of a record as fatal to any conviction.

Transcripts of record and documentary productions

94.—(1) The Clerk of Justiciary may direct that a transcript of a record made under section 93(1) of this Act, or any part thereof, be made and delivered to him for the use of any judge. A4-214

(2) Subject to subsection (3) below, the Clerk of Justiciary shall, if requested to do so by—

(a) the Secretary of State or, subject to subsection (2B) below, the prosecutor; or

(b) any other person, not being a person convicted at the trial, on payment of such charges as may be fixed for the time being by Treasury,

direct that such a transcript be made and sent to the person who requested it.

(2A) If—

(a) on the written application of a person convicted at the trial and granted leave to appeal; and

(b) either of the conditions in subsection (2AZA) is met or it is otherwise in the interests of justice to do so,

a judge of the High Court may order, and in that event, the Clerk of Justiciary shall direct, on payment of such charges as are mentioned in paragraph (b) of subsection (2) above, that such a transcript be made and sent to that person.

(2AZA) The conditions mentioned in subsection (2A)(b) are that—

(a) a ground of appeal, for which leave to appeal has been granted, reveals a significant dispute between that ground and the report of the trial judge on the nature and extent of the evidence, speech or other part of the record to which the application relates; or

(b) the trial judge's report does not, in relation to a ground of appeal for which leave to appeal has been granted, provide a sufficient narrative of the nature and extent of the evidence, speech or other part of the record to which the application relates.

(2AA) Subsection (2A) applies to a person mentioned in subsection (2AB) as it applies to a person convicted at the trial, with the modification that the reference to the transcript in subsection (2A) is to be construed as a reference to the transcript of the record made of proceedings at the trial resulting in the acquittal mentioned in subsection (2AB)(b).

(2AB) The person mentioned in subsection (2AA) is a person who—

(a) is convicted of the offence mentioned in subsection (1) of section 11 of the Double Jeopardy (Scotland) Act 2011 (asp 16);

(b) is subsequently acquitted of an offence mentioned in subsection (2) of that section; and

(c) desires to appeal, under subsection (7) of that section, against the conviction of the offence mentioned in paragraph (a).

(2B) Where, as respects any person convicted at the trial, the Crown Agent has received intimation under section 107(10) of this Act, the prosecutor shall not be entitled to make a request under subsection (2)(a) above; but if, on the written application of the prosecutor and on cause shown, a judge of the High Court so orders, the Clerk of Justiciary shall direct that such a transcript be made and sent to the prosecutor.

(2C) Any application under subsection (2A) above shall—

(a) be made within 14 days after the date on which leave to appeal was granted or within such longer period after that date as a judge of the High Court may, on written application and on cause shown, allow; and

(aa) set out, for each ground of appeal to which the application relates, the particular evidence, speech or other part of the record required; and

(b) be intimated forthwith by the applicant to the prosecutor.

(2D) The prosecutor may, within 7 days after receiving intimation under subsection (2C)(b) above, make written representations to the court as respects the application under subsection (2A) above (the application being determined without a hearing).

(2E) Any application under subsection (2B) above shall—

(a) be made within 14 days after the receipt of intimation mentioned in that subsection or within such longer period after that receipt as a judge of the High Court may, on written application and on cause shown, allow; and

(b) be intimated forthwith by the prosecutor to the person granted leave to appeal.

(2F) The person granted leave to appeal may, within 7 days after receiving intimation under subsection (2E)(b) above, make written representations to the court as respects the application under subsection (2B) above (the application being determined without a hearing).

(3) The Secretary of State may, after consultation with the Lord Justice General, by order made by statutory instrument provide that in any class of proceedings specified in the order the Clerk of Justiciary shall only make a direction under subsection (2)(b) above if satisfied that the person requesting the transcript is of a class of person so specified and, if purposes for which the transcript may be used are so specified, intends to use it only for such a purpose; and different purposes may be so specified for different classes of proceedings or classes of person.

(4) Where subsection (3) above applies as respects a direction, the person to whom the transcript is sent shall, if purposes for which that transcript may be used are specified by virtue of that subsection, use it only for such a purpose.

(5) A statutory instrument containing an order under subsection (3) above shall be subject to annulment in pursuance of a resolution of either House of Parliament.

(6) A direction under subsection (1) or (2) above may require that the transcript be made by the person who made the record or by such competent person as may be specified in the direction; and that person shall comply with the direction.

(7) A transcript made in compliance with a direction under subsection (1) or (2) above—

(a) shall be in legible form; and

(b) shall be certified by the person making it as being a correct and complete transcript of the whole or, as the case may be, the part of the record purporting to have been made and certified, and in the case of shorthand notes signed, by the person who made the record.

(8) The cost of making a transcript in compliance with a direction under subsection (1) or (2)(a) above shall be defrayed, in accordance with scales of payment fixed for the time being by the Treasury, out of money provided by Parliament.

(9) The Clerk of Justiciary shall, on payment of such charges as may be fixed for the time being by the Treasury, provide a copy of any documentary production lodged in connection with an appeal under this Part of this Act to such of the following persons as may request it—

(a) the prosecutor;

(b) any person convicted in the proceedings;

(c) any other person named in, or immediately affected by, any order made in the proceedings; and

(d) any person authorised to act on behalf of any of the persons mentioned in paragraphs (a) to (c) above.

AMENDMENTS

Subs.(2) as amended and subss.(2A)–(2F) inserted by Criminal Justice (Scotland) Act 2003 (asp 7) Pt 8 s.65. Brought into force on June 27, 2003 by SSI 2003/288 (C.14).

Subss.(2AA), (2AB) inserted by Double Jeopardy (Scotland) Act 2011 (asp 16) Sch.1 para.7. Brought into force on November 28, 2011 by SSI 2011/365 (C.34) art.3.

Subss.(2A), (2C) as amended, and subs.(2AZA) inserted, by Act of Adjournal (Amendment of the Criminal Procedure (Scotland) Act 1995) (Transcripts) 2012 (SSI 2012/272) art.2 (effective November 12, 2012), subject to transitional provisions specified in art.3.

DEFINITIONS

"Clerk of Justiciary": s.307(1). A4-214.1
"judge": s.307(1).
"Lord Justice General": s.307(1).

[THE NEXT PARAGRAPH IS A4-215]

GENERAL NOTE

The effect of certification of a transcript of evidence as correct was raised in *Kyle v HM Advocate*, 1987 S.C.C.R. 116. See the discussion in the notes to s.93 above. A4-215

In *HM Advocate v Nulty*, 2000 S.L.T. 528: 2000 S.C.C.R. 431, a retrial in which the Crown gave notice of its intention to utilise the hearsay provisions found in s.259 of the Act, to lodge the testimony of a principal witness from the abortive trial, she now being unfit to testify, it is of note that use was made of the original tapes of evidence rather than a transcript of evidence. (It could be argued that the tape was now the best evidence.) The admissibility of this evidence was upheld on appeal in *N v HM Advocate*, 2003 S.L.T. 761.

Provisions introduced by s.65 of the Criminal Justice (Scotland) Act 2003 (asp 7) would entitle persons other than a convicted accused (or of course the Crown) to apply to the court for a transcript of proceedings, on cause shown. The Crown would be entitled to be heard in response to such an application.

The primary purpose of the transcript of evidence is to provide an official record of the proceedings should an appeal occur: see *Transco Plc v HM Advocate*, 2005 S.L.T. 211. The appellant company appealed against the decision of the judge hearing the preliminary diet who refused a motion for simultaneous transcription (LiveNote) of the trial proceedings expected to last at least six months. It was implicit that such a transcription (extended daily) would constitute the official record of the trial proceedings as, indeed, occurred during the Lockerbie trial. *Transco Plc* does not entirely exclude the possibility (all parties and the court agreeing) of such a record being kept of the proceedings but does emphasise the extra-statutory nature of such an arrangement.

See generally the Transcript of Criminal Proceedings (Scotland) Order 1993 (SI 1993/2226 (S.236)) and the Transcripts of Criminal Proceedings (Scotland) Amendment Order 1995 (SI 1995/1751(S.121)).

Verdict by judge alone

A4-216 **95.**—(1) Where, at any time after the jury has been sworn to serve in a trial, the prosecutor intimates to the court that he does not intend to proceed in respect of an offence charged in the indictment, the judge shall acquit the accused of that offence and the trial shall proceed only in respect of any other offence charged in the indictment.

(2) Where, at any time after the jury has been sworn to serve in a trial, the accused intimates to the court that he is prepared to tender a plea of guilty as libelled, or such other plea as the Crown is prepared to accept, in respect of any offence charged in the indictment, the judge shall accept the plea tendered and shall convict the accused accordingly.

(3) Where an accused is convicted under subsection (2) above of an offence—

(a) the trial shall proceed only in respect of any other offence charged in the indictment; and

(b) without prejudice to any other power of the court to adjourn the case or to defer sentence, the judge shall not sentence him or make any other order competent following conviction until a verdict has been returned in respect of every other offence mentioned in paragraph (a) above.

DEFINITIONS

A4-216.1 "indictment": s.307(1).
"judge": s.307(1).
"offence": s.307(1).
"prosecutor": s.307(1).

[THE NEXT PARAGRAPH IS A4-217]

GENERAL NOTE

A4-217 Section 95 deals with situations in the course of a trial in which the jury is not called upon to reach a verdict upon the evidence, either because the Crown has withdrawn a charge (subs.(1)) or acceptable pleas have been tendered (subs.(2)). In the latter case, it is implicit that acceptance of pleas tendered is signified by the prosecutor subscribing his minute of acceptance following the signatures of the accused and the presiding judge. Subsection (2) also deals with the tendering of a partial plea in circumstances where other charges remain outstanding against the accused. In that situation, where the prosecutor is maintaining the other charges on the libel, care must be taken to ensure that the prosecutor's endorsement is restricted solely to the charges in relation to which the plea was tendered.

It will be noted that the onus of assenting to the pleas tendered strictly lies with the trial judge, not with the jury. No sentence can competently be pronounced until a verdict is reached on all the charges on the indictment.

In determining sentence, the court may take account of the point in the proceedings at which a plea or pleas were tendered (see s.196 below).

Particularly in solemn proceedings the court will not readily consent to the withdrawal of a guilty plea; see *Weightman v HM Advocate*, 1997 G.W.D. 3–85 and the discussion at A4-174 and A4-178 above.

Amendment of indictment

A4-218 **96.**—(1) No trial shall fail or the ends of justice be allowed to be defeated by reason of any discrepancy or variance between the indictment and the evidence.

(2) It shall be competent at any time prior to the determination of the case, unless the court see just cause to the contrary, to amend the indictment by deletion, alteration or addition, so as to—

(a) cure any error or defect in it;

(b) meet any objection to it; or

(c) cure any discrepancy or variance between the indictment and the evidence.

(3) Nothing in this section shall authorise an amendment which changes the character of the offence charged, and, if it appears to the court that the accused may in any way be prejudiced in his defence on the merits of the case by any amendment made under this section, the court shall grant such remedy to the accused by adjournment or otherwise as appears to the court to be just.

(4) An amendment made under this section shall be sufficiently authenticated by the initials of the clerk of the court.

DEFINITION

"indictment": s.307(1). A4-218.1

[THE NEXT PARAGRAPH IS A4-219]

GENERAL NOTE

Schedule 3 of the Act states the general rules concerning latitudes in time and place, implied terms and implied alternatives. Section 96 re-enacts the provisions contained in s.123 of the 1975 Act relating to the power of amendment of an indictment in the course of a trial. The Crown may seek leave to amend the terms of the libel at a first, or preliminary, diet to meet any preliminary objection, but s.96 deals with such motions in the course of trial. While wide powers of amendment are available to the Crown this is qualified by the provisos that; (i) they cannot be used to introduce an essential requisite into a criminal charge—a fundamentally defective libel cannot be cured (*Stevenson v McLevy* (1879) 4 Couper 196 and *Thomson, Petr*, 1997 S.L.T. 322 where the libel lacked a *locus delicti*) and (ii) they must not change the character of the charge to such a degree as to prejudice the accused's defence on the merits (see subs.(3)). Any amendment has to be justified to the court, and while amendment of either the libel or the description of a witness can be craved, amendment of the description of a production in the indictment is not competent (see *HM Advocate v Swift*, 1983 S.C.C.R. 204 discussed in the notes to s.67(5)). *Thomson, Petr*, cited above also indicates that there can be no question of a tholed assize where the libel itself was a fundamental nullity. The point in proceedings when amendment is moved is a significant factor; see *Phillips v Houston*, 2003 G.W.D. 29–805, a summary case, where objection had been taken promptly to evidence not covered by the libel and amendment was not then sought till the close of the Crown case. See generally *Paterson v HM Advocate*, 2008 S.C.C.R. 605 (statutory charges amended to common law libel) and *Iqbal v HM Advocate* [2015] HCJAC 71 (more extensive dates added to a fraud libel). A4-219

Amendment of an indictment which omitted the accused's name in one of the three charges (the murder charge), when he had been correctly described in the instance, has been allowed (*Keane v HM Advocate*, 1986 S.C.C.R. 491); the decision might have been quite different if there had been other accused on the indictment.

In the event that amendment is allowed by the court, the remedy for the accused is ordinarily adjournment. The presiding judge's decision on the issue will only be overturned on appeal if the Appeal Court is satisfied that the public interest or the interest of the accused has been adversely affected (see *Cumming v Frame* (1909) 6 Adam 57).

Customarily, deletions from the libel are made to bring it into line with the extent of corroborated evidence heard by the jury. See however *Clarke v Ruxton*, 1997 G.W.D. 10–408 in relation, at least, to sexual offences discussed at para.A4-406.1 below. Amendment of the libel can only be initiated by the prosecutor; in *TG v HM Advocate* [2018] HCJAC 58 convictions of charges in which the jury had sought, and been permitted by the trial judge, to amend the libel by adding a *locus delictus* were quashed on appeal.

See *TD v HM Advocate* [2013] HCJAC 130; 2013 S.C.C.R. 696 where, once the evidence of the complainer had been led and discrepancies in her parole evidence and previously disclosed (and undisclosed) material made it clear that she was alleging rape, and not the penetrative sexual assault libelled, the sheriff permitted desertion of the trial and granted an extension to the time bars.

No case to answer

97.—(1) Immediately after the close of the evidence for the prosecution, the accused may intimate to the court his desire to make a submission that he has no case to answer both— A4-220

(a) on an offence charged in the indictment; and

(b) on any other offence of which he could be convicted under the indictment.

(2) If, after hearing both parties, the judge is satisfied that the evidence led by the prosecution is insufficient in law to justify the accused being convicted of the offence charged in respect of which the submission has been made or of such other offence as is mentioned, in relation to that offence, in paragraph (b) of subsection (1)

above, he shall acquit him of the offence charged in respect of which the submission has been made and the trial shall proceed only in respect of any other offence charged in the indictment.

(3) If, after hearing both parties, the judge is not satisfied as is mentioned in subsection (2) above, he shall reject the submission and the trial shall proceed, with the accused entitled to give evidence and call witnesses, as if such submission had not been made.

(4) A submission under subsection (1) above shall be heard by the judge in the absence of the jury.

DEFINITIONS

A4-220.1 "indictment": s.307(1).
"judge": s.307(1).
"offence": s.307(1).

GENERAL NOTE

A4-221 The no case to answer submission was introduced into Scots criminal law by the Criminal Justice (Scotland) Act 1980 s.19 and the terms of that section are repeated in s.97 above. A common law submission could always be made at the conclusion of evidence, before the judge's charge but a s.97 submission, unlike the common law type, is concerned only with the sufficiency of evidence, not its quality. A helpful discussion of the approach to be followed in assessing circumstantial evidence and its evidential significance is found in *MacPherson v HM Advocate* [2019] HCJAC 21; 2019 S.C.C.R. 129, while *Duthie v HM Advocate* [2021] HCJAC 23, a Full Bench decision, authoritatively addresses the particular problems of assessing sufficiency and mutual corroboration in the context of sexual offences. Qualitative assessments are matters solely for the jury; see, for example, *HM Advocate v Mason* [2015] HCJAC 1; 2015 S.C.L. 277 (following *HM Advocate v Fox*, 1998 S.L.T. 348; 1998 S.C.C.R. 115 at 138F) a successful Crown appeal under ss.107A and 110 below. The judge's task at this stage is summarized in *Fox v HM Advocate*, 1998 S.C.C.R. 115 at 138G onwards. The submission is made outwith the presence of the jury and can relate to any, or all, of the charges on the indictment. Note that s.97 refers to "an offence" not "a charge" on the indictment; so where a number of offences are libelled as part of one charge a submission can competently be made upon each offence: the Crown cannot, by creative draftsmanship, withhold the right of an accused to make a s.97 motion (see *Cordiner v HM Advocate*, 1991 S.C.C.R. 652).

It will be observed that a submission can be made in regard to the charge libelled or any other offence which is implied by the libel but, in practical terms, the starting point will be the sufficiency, or otherwise, of the charge libelled before proceeding to a consideration of any alternative charge. Any challenge to the competency or admissibility of evidence must be raised at, or prior to, the point in proceedings at which that evidence is being received by the court; it is too late to air such issues at the point of a no case to answer submission when no prior objection has been taken (*McGee v McNaughtan*, 1996 G.W.D. 17–977).

If in terms of subs.(3) the accused's submissions are rejected, he has to decide whether or not to lead evidence, a dilemma heightened by the introduction of the prosecutor's right to comment upon the failure of the accused to lead evidence (see s.32 of the Criminal Justice (Scotland) Act 1995). It remains to be seen what use will be made of this provision and to what effect. What is the position if the judge incorrectly rejects a submission of no case to answer and the accused then leads evidence which confirms the Crown case? The problem was recognised but not addressed in *Little v HM Advocate*, 1983 S.C.C.R. 56. The same problems occurred in *Mackie v HM Advocate*, 1994 S.C.C.R. 277 and there the judge read the elements of the charge as a unity in what was, by any standard, a complex libel.

It is permissible for the Crown to submit to the jury at the conclusion of evidence that the withdrawal of charges at the submission stage does not necessarily reflect adversely upon prosecution witnesses; it is however one step too far to suggest that the accused might still have committed the offences of which he had been acquitted earlier (see *Dudgeon v HM Advocate*, 1988 S.C.C.R. 147). In that case the improper remarks of the prosecutor were held to have been cured by the directions of the trial judge and no miscarriage to have resulted.

Attention is directed to the terms of ss.97A and 107A, inserted by s.74 of the Criminal Justice and Licensing (Scotland) Act 2010 (asp 13) which, in solemn cases, provides the Crown with a broad right of appeal against a successful common law submission by the defence. The 2010 Act has introduced several new forms of Crown appeals during the course of trial proceedings; appeals can be initiated against the upholding of a statutory submission (s.107A), a finding during the leading of Crown evidence that an element of it is inadmissible (s.107B), and a common law submission in relation to the whole or a part of the libel (ss.97A and 107A). Each of these forms of appeal, in the course of the trial itself, proceeds as an expedited appeal (s.107D).

Submissions as to sufficiency of evidence

97A.—(1) Immediately after one or other (but not both) of the appropriate events, the accused may make either or both of the submissions mentioned in subsection (2) in relation to an offence libelled in an indictment (the "indicted offence"). A4-221.1

(2) The submissions are—

(a) that the evidence is insufficient in law to justify the accused's being convicted of the indicted offence or any other offence of which the accused could be convicted under the indictment (a "related offence"),

(b) that there is no evidence to support some part of the circumstances set out in the indictment.

(3) For the purposes of subsection (1), "the appropriate events" are—

(a) the close of the whole of the evidence,

(b) the conclusion of the prosecutor's address to the jury on the evidence.

(4) A submission made under this section must be heard by the judge in the absence of the jury.

AMENDMENTS

Section 97A inserted by Criminal Justice and Licensing (Scotland) Act 2010 (asp 13) s.73. Brought into force on March 28, 2011 (for all purposes in respect of any trial which commences on or after March 28, 2011, with a trial taken to have commenced in solemn proceedings when the oath is administered to the jury and in summary proceedings when the first witness is sworn) by SSI 2011/178 (C.15) art.2, Sch.1 para.1.

GENERAL NOTE

This section introduces a statutory replacement for the common law submission in solemn proceedings but makes some telling amendments to the existing law, notably a Crown right of appeal found in s.107A of the Act. To appreciate the significance of this statutory provision some comment is necessary upon procedures prior to the advent of s.97A. A4-221.2

Until the passage of the Criminal Justice (Scotland) Act 1980 which introduced the concept of a no case to answer submission at the close of the Crown evidence, the only form of legal submission upon the evidence open to the defence was a common law submission. This was made at the close of all evidence in the proceedings and addressed either, or both, the sufficiency and quality of the evidence. This form of submission, necessarily made outwith the presence of the jury, remains competent in solemn proceedings (albeit modified by the statutory provisions in s.97A). Strictly it should be made only after the close of the prosecutor's speech by which time he is *functus* and thus cannot reply; due to that stricture the Crown often consents to the common law submission being made before speeches to the jury, a timing which can shorten the proceedings or, at least, gives the opportunity to identify the likely focus of the defence speech if one has to be made to the jury. It has to be stressed that a common law submission can result in the trial judge making his own assessment of the sufficiency of the evidence and the quality of that evidence, the Crown having no right of reply or appeal against what may result in an acquittal—the jury being directed to confirm the verdict. The reforms introduced in the 2010 Act make several radical changes to these long-standing procedures.

Section 97A(3) enables the accused to make a statutory submission on the whole, or part of the libel, once—either at the close of all evidence or after the prosecutor's speech to the jury. The Crown must be given an opportunity to respond to such a submission. The submission can be directed against an indicted offence or any of its implied alternatives (s.97A(2)(a)) or against elements of the libel for which there is no supporting evidence (s.97A(2)(b)). The court's powers in considering these submissions, particularly to direct amendment of the libel to reflect any insufficiency or deficiency, are found in ss.97B and 97C respectively. As noted earlier, both parties must be given the opportunity to be heard and the judge is expressly barred from applying his own assessment of the quality of the evidence (s.97D); that evaluation is the exclusive province of the jury.

Prosecution appeals

One of the radical reforms brought by the 2010 Act is the prosecutor's right of appeal against the court's decision—the court generally being obliged to adjourn the trial proceedings for up to two days if the Crown so moves to enable consideration of an appeal. To initiate such an appeal notice has to be given to the court immediately after acquittal and, if necessary, the prosecutor may then seek an adjournment of proceedings for up to two days to consider the issue. On resumption of proceedings the prosecutor must then advise the court if an appeal is to proceed, pending the outcome of which the trial stands adjourned. The court has only a limited discretion (see subss.(2) and (3)) to refuse these Crown motions. The court can refuse such a motion but only when it considers that it would not be in the interests of justice as defined in s.107A(4). This will require heed to be paid inter alia to the immediate impact upon the instant proceedings and the impact upon any subsequent prosecution should the proposed Crown appeal succeed. See s.107A below. It is also of immediate importance for parties to consider whether ad interim an order under s.4(2) of the Contempt of Court Act 1981 (c.41) should be sought to restrict or postpone any media report of the proceedings—see s.107A(7) below.

No less important, parties will have to consider whether the accused affected by the decision should now be admitted to, or refused, bail; the court, in terms of s.107A(8), can only order detention in custody if the trial judge considers that there is an arguable appeal.

Similar mechanisms found in s.107B, as inserted by the 2010 Act, are introduced in relation to prosecution appeals against adverse decisions on the admissibility of Crown evidence. It will be noted that this form of appeal can arise only before the conclusion of Crown evidence, that the trial judge can permit such an appeal on the prosecutor's motion or *ex proprio motu*, and that s.107B(4) sets a different, less stringent, test for this type of appeal—whether there are arguable grounds and, perhaps more difficult to gauge until much of the Crown evidence has been led, what effect that adverse finding will have on the strength of the prosecution case.

HM Advocate v Hutchison [2013] HCJAC 91 is an example of a successful Crown appeal at this stage of trial proceedings. Note that the Appeal Court decision was issued five days after the acquittal complained of, and that the jury verdict in turn was one of acquittal.

Acquittals etc. on section 97A(2)(a) submissions

A4-221.3 **97B.**—(1) This section applies where the accused makes a submission of the kind mentioned in section 97A(2)(a).

(2) If the judge is satisfied that the evidence is insufficient in law to justify the accused's being convicted of the indicted offence, then—

(a) where the judge is satisfied that the evidence is also insufficient in law to justify the accused's being convicted of a related offence—

(i) the judge must acquit the accused of the indicted offence, and

(ii) the trial is to proceed only in respect of any other offence libelled in the indictment,

(b) where the judge is satisfied that the evidence is sufficient in law to justify the accused's being convicted of a related offence, the judge must direct that the indictment be amended accordingly.

(3) If the judge is not satisfied as is mentioned in subsection (2)—

(a) the judge must reject the submission, and

(b) the trial is to proceed as if the submission had not been made.

(4) The judge may make a decision under this section only after hearing both (or all) parties.

(5) An amendment made by virtue of this section must be sufficiently authenticated by the initials of the judge or the clerk of court.

(6) In this section, "indicted offence" and "related offence" have the same meanings as in section 97A.

Amendments

Section 97B inserted by Criminal Justice and Licensing (Scotland) Act 2010 (asp 13) s.73. Brought into force on March 28, 2011 (for all purposes in respect of any trial which commences on or after March 28, 2011, with a trial taken to have commenced in solemn proceedings when the oath is administered to the jury and in summary proceedings when the first witness is sworn) by SSI 2011/178 (C.15) art.2, Sch.1 para.1.

General Note

A4-221.4 Refer to the discussion in General Note to s.97A above.

Directions etc. on section 97A(2)(b) submissions

A4-221.5 **97C.**—(1) This section applies where the accused makes a submission of the kind mentioned in section 97A(2)(b).

(2) If the judge is satisfied that there is no evidence to support some part of the circumstances set out in the indictment, the judge must direct that the indictment be amended accordingly.

(3) If the judge is not satisfied as is mentioned in subsection (2)—

(a) the judge must reject the submission, and

(b) the trial is to proceed as if the submission had not been made.

(4) The judge may make a decision under this section only after hearing both (or all) parties.

(5) An amendment made by virtue of this section must be sufficiently authenticated by the initials of the judge or the clerk of court.

AMENDMENTS

Section 97C inserted by Criminal Justice and Licensing (Scotland) Act 2010 (asp 13) s.73. Brought into force on March 28, 2011 (for all purposes in respect of any trial which commences on or after March 28, 2011, with a trial taken to have commenced in solemn proceedings when the oath is administered to the jury and in summary proceedings when the first witness is sworn) by SSI 2011/178 (C.15) art.2, Sch.1 para.1.

GENERAL NOTE

Refer to the discussion in General Note to s.97A above. A4-221.6

No acquittal on "no reasonable jury" grounds

97D.—(1) A judge has no power to direct the jury to return a not guilty verdict on any charge on the ground that no reasonable jury, properly directed on the evidence, could convict on the charge. A4-221.7

(2) Accordingly, no submission based on that ground or any ground of like effect is to be allowed.

AMENDMENTS

Section 97D inserted by Criminal Justice and Licensing (Scotland) Act 2010 (asp 13) s.73. Brought into force on March 28, 2011 (for all purposes in respect of any trial which commences on or after March 28, 2011, with a trial taken to have commenced in solemn proceedings when the oath is administered to the jury and in summary proceedings when the first witness is sworn) by SSI 2011/178 (C.15) art.2, Sch.1 para.1.

GENERAL NOTE

Refer to the discussion in General Note to s.97A above. A4-221.8

[THE NEXT PARAGRAPH IS A4-222]

Defence to speak last

98. In any trial the accused or, where he is legally represented, his counsel or solicitor shall have the right to speak last. A4-222

GENERAL NOTE

There has been, in practice, a development of discussion between Crown and defence representation in order to settle how best to present in all the surrounding facts and circumstances both the explanation of how the crime in issue was committed and any explanation falling short of full exculpation that the defence wish to put before the court: see R. McPherson "The Rise of the Agreed Narrative in Scottish Criminal Procedure" (2013) *Juridical Review* 141–156. However that might be, in everyday practice it seems clear that the defence retain a right to speak last. A4-222.1

[THE NEXT PARAGRAPH IS A4-223]

Seclusion of jury to consider verdict

99.—(1) When the jury retire to consider their verdict, the clerk of court shall enclose the jury in a room by themselves and, except in so far as provided for, or is made necessary, by an instruction under subsection (4) below, neither he nor any other person shall be present with the jury while they are enclosed. A4-223

(2) Except in so far as is provided for, or is made necessary, by an instruction under subsection (4) below, while the jury are enclosed and until they intimate that they are ready to return their verdict—

(a) subject to subsection (3) below, no person shall visit the jury or communicate with them; and

(b) no juror shall come out of the jury room other than to receive or seek a direction from the judge or to make a request—
   (i) for an instruction under subsection (4)(a), (c) or (d) below; or
   (ii) regarding any matter in the cause.

(3) Nothing in paragraph (a) of subsection (2) above shall prohibit the judge, or any person authorised by him for the purpose, communicating with the jury for the purposes—

(a) of giving a direction, whether or not sought under paragraph (b) of that subsection; or
(b) responding to a request made under that paragraph.

(4) The judge may give such instructions as he considers appropriate as regards—

(a) the provision of meals and refreshments for the jury;
(b) the making of arrangements for overnight accommodation for the jury and, unless under subsection (7) below the court permits them to separate, for their continued seclusion if such accommodation is provided;
(c) the communication of a personal or business message, unconnected with any matter in the cause, from a juror to another person (or vice versa); or
(d) the provision of medical treatment, or other assistance, immediately required by a juror.

(5) If the prosecutor or any other person contravenes the provisions of this section, the accused shall be acquitted of the crime with which he is charged.

(6) During the period in which the jury are retired to consider their verdict, the judge may sit in any other proceedings; and the trial shall not fail by reason only of his so doing.

(7) The court may, if it thinks fit, permit the jury to separate even after they have retired to consider their verdict.

AMENDMENTS

Subss.(1), (2) and (4)(b) as amended, and subs.(7) inserted, by Criminal Justice (Scotland) Act 2003 (asp 7) Pt 12 s.79. Brought into force on June 27, 2003 by SSI 2003/288 (C.14).

DEFINITIONS

A4-223.1 "judge": s.307(1).
"prosecutor": s.307(1).

[THE NEXT PARAGRAPH IS A4-224]

GENERAL NOTE

A4-224 Until the point at which the jury is directed to retire to consider its verdict, all proceedings in a trial must take place in the presence of the accused (see s.92). Once the jury withdraws to the jury room, s.99 stipulates that no contact should be made with its members unless the jury requests directions or has need to seek assistance from the court. The provisions of s.99 are mandatory and conduct constituting a breach (subs.(5)) is fatal to any conviction. The reforms introduced into s.99 by the Criminal Justice (Scotland) Act 2003 (asp 7) substantially relax the provisions which required the seclusion, or supervised corralling, of the jury once it had retired to consider its verdict. Until the passage of the Criminal Justice (Scotland) Act 1980 (c.62) once a jury retired to consider its verdict, no interruptions were permitted until the jury returned. The 1980 Act enabled the jury to break from protracted deliberations and to retire to supervised accommodation until the following day: the latest reforms introduce a judicial discretion to permit jurors to break from deliberations and to "separate", or more prosaically—go home, until directed to return to court to continue consideration of their verdict.

One might be forgiven for sensing the dead hands of misplaced economy and bureaucratic convenience; we may perhaps lament a further dilution of a distinct Scottish legal tradition which underpinned the unique importance, even mystique, of jury service; what cannot be gainsaid is that the new provisions do not explicitly address the sort of problems which no doubt will occur in practice.

First, although it is not evident from the textual changes now introduced into s.99 itself (by dint of some ungainly draftsmanship), the Criminal Justice (Scotland) Act 2003 s.79 stipulates that seclusion of the jury, until a verdict is reached, is no longer mandatory. Thus in each case the matter lies in the discretion of the trial judge.

Secondly, s.88(8) of the 1995 Act contains a power (scarcely used) for the jury to be secluded throughout the proceedings; thus a motion for seclusion could be made at any point during the trial where deemed appropriate, but it is submitted that this should certainly be made outwith the presence of either jurors or the potential jurors of an assize—indeed there would be obvious merit in applying to the court by means of a preliminary diet (s.72(d) of the Act) where possible.

Yet the most likely scenario, which can be expected to cast up unprecedented difficulties, is that of the errant juror who fails to return to court after "separation". It is submitted that the priority at this stage is to avoid delay to the jury's deliberations and that the appropriate course, rather than any form of delay or desertion, ought to be for the court to review the position in accordance with s.90 of the Act, and to proceed with a reduced number of jurors so far as this is possible and appropriate.

Points of appeal have arisen from allegations of inappropriate communication between the jury and court officials; the Appeal Court may remit the case for enquiry and report under s.104(d) below (see for example *Squire v HM Advocate*, 1998 G.W.D. 28–1410) but has emphasised that such enquiry should confine itself to establishing the factual background and must not concern itself with the jury's deliberations. In *Simpson v HM Advocate*, 2001 G.W.D. 16–603 an appeal founded on the fact that the sheriff had declined to desert proceedings after a letter discussing the trial evidence and passing comment was found on a stairwell only 10m from the jury room. The sheriff in open court asked all jury members if they knew of the letter and in the absence of a positive response allowed trial to continue. The Appeal Court upheld the sheriff's approach, noting that the extent of investigation was one within his discretion and had to be directed to preserving the integrity of the proceedings.

In *Swankie v HM Advocate*, 1999 S.C.C.R. 1, an appeal against conviction rested on the alleged conduct during jury deliberations of a juror in making known a previous conviction of the accused, an incident which was stated to have been disclosed by another juror to an acquaintance of S. (Such a disclosure would have been in breach of s.8 of the Contempt of Court Act 1981). The appeal proceeded by way of an affidavit from the acquaintance. Leaving aside the hearsay nature of the affidavit, the Appeal Court itself examined the quality of the evidence before the jury and the apparent extent of its deliberations, cast doubt on the veracity of the affidavit and declined to initiate a s.104 enquiry.

By contrast in *McLean v HM Advocate*, 2001 S.L.T. 1096, where the sheriff's enquiry confirmed that after the jury had deliberated, but before a verdict was pronounced, a jury member had disclosed knowledge of a previous conviction of the accused, the Appeal Court was not satisfied that an unimpeachable verdict had been achieved. Although the sheriff had directly interrogated the juror as to whether this knowledge had influenced her verdict, and noted that the revealed conviction (of shoplifting) was minor when set against the charges being tried, this could not suffice to remove taint from the proceedings. Authority was granted for a retrial.

A growing problem, despite explicit judicial directions to jurors on the topic, has been of jurors accessing information about the case or its participants from the internet, and subsequent dissemination of that information to other jurors. In *Attorney General v Dallas* [2012] 1 W.L.R. 991; [2012] Cr.App.R. 32, a juror's misconduct resulted in abandonment of the trial and, following prosecution under the Contempt of Court Act 1981 (c.49) s.8(1), a sentence of six months' imprisonment. The Lord Justice General commented that:

> "misuse of the internet by a juror is always a most serious irregularity and an effective custodial sentence is inevitable."

By contrast in *Goddard v HM Advocate* [2019] HCJAC 48 the Appeal Court declined to quash a conviction following disclosure by one member of the assize to another (who subsequently was empanelled) of a Google enquiry showing the accused to have a conviction for violence. Significantly this speculative exercise had been undertaken prior to jury selection, could not be shown to have prejudiced the juror or to have been further communicated. (The circumstances had come to light in a juror's feedback form). Some discussion of whether the juror selected ought to have disclosed these prior events to the court when selected, might have been helpful; doubtless the riposte would be that, notwithstanding, the juror would still have been bound by the oath or affirmation taken when balloted.

In *Howden, Petitioner* [2015] HCJAC 91; 2015 S.C.C.R. 418 a juror's £500 fine for contempt was upheld on appeal, after she accessed Facebook, in defiance of express judicial directions, to ascertain whether a witness who had given evidence was a friend's brother. The sheriff's preliminary allencompassing admonition against use of social media was approved (at [16]).

More serious still, in *Attorney General v Fraill* [2011] EWHC 1629 Admin; [2012] Crim. L.R. 286 a juror made Facebook contact with an acquitted accused as the trial continued, the two discussing elements of the case, actings which attracted eight months' imprisonment.

The limits for investigation of a jury's deliberations were considered in *Scottish Criminal Cases Review Commission, Petitioners*, 2001 S.L.T. 1198 where the Commission sought to make enquiry of jurors in a murder trial as to events prior to their retiral to consider verdicts. The court confirmed the legitimacy of such enquiries, the Commission being anxious not to fall foul of the contempt of court provisions contained in s.8 of the Contempt of Court Act 1981 (c.49) which bar investigations into any jury's deliberations once it has retired to consider verdicts. It was also made clear that the Commission could not petition the court to carry out investigations on its behalf; the court's own powers of investigation under s.104 of the 1995 Act exist for the limited purpose of dealing with appeals under ss.106 and 108 of that Act. See also *Carberry v HM Advocate* [2013] HCJAC 101; 2013 S.C.C.R. 587.

An important distinction has emerged, following *R. v Pan* [2001] 2 SCR 344, a Canadian Supreme Court decision, and *Clow v HM Advocate*, 2007 S.L.T. 517; 2007 S.C.C.R. 201, between factors intrinsic and those extrinsic to the deliberations of the jury. The former, concerned as they are with the confidential deliberations of the jury once secluded, remain confidential and will not be explored by the court; the latter, involving conduct or events during the currency otherwise of the trial might be scrutinised by the court and might properly be a subject of enquiry for the Scottish Criminal Cases Review Commission; see *Scottish Criminal Cases Review Commission, Petitioners*, 2010 S.L.T. 976, and *Casey v HM Advocate*, 2010 S.L.T. 1020.

Subss. (2) and (3)

A4-224.1 Unfortunately the cases arising from s.153 (the statutory predecessor to s.99) tend to suggest that in their zeal to provide for the seclusion of the jury, officers of the court have on occasion overlooked the obligations (now) created by s.92 and trespassed into matters which should have been dealt with in open court.

It is the jury's right to examine productions referred to in the evidence but subject to any directions given by the court. The procedure to be followed is laid out in *Hamilton v HM Advocate*, 1980 J.C. 66; the Clerk LJ (at 69) stated:

> "If the jury make a request to see a production, this request should be communicated to the clerk of court who should inform counsel on both sides and then refer the matter to the trial judge for his decision."

A practice has developed, in part to delay the jury's deliberations as little as possible and to avoid the need to reconvene the court repeatedly, of trial judges clarifying with the parties which productions can, and which cannot, be given to the jury on request. This is done in open court immediately after the jury retires and has the merit of focusing this issue even before the need arises and commits parties' views to the record. There is no statutory authority for this procedure but, it is submitted, it complies with the directions in *Hamilton*. Support for this reading can be found in *Bertram v HM Advocate*, 1990 S.C.C.R. 394, where the judge in his charge permitted access to all productions admitted in evidence during the trial. See also *Martin v HM Advocate*, 1989 S.C.C.R. 546 where the sheriff gave directions which were inspecific and were acted upon by the clerk of court without reference to the parties and *Boyle v HM Advocate*, 1990 S.C.C.R. 480 where productions not spoken of in evidence were given to the jurors in error. Once the error was appreciated, the sheriff gave further directions to the jury to ignore the content of these productions; the conviction was upheld in the circumstances.

It is clear that the question of access to productions is one upon which parties should be heard; it is not an administrative matter to be resolved between the clerk of court and the presiding judge. The complex issues which can surface are amply illustrated by *Collins v HM Advocate*, 1991 S.C.C.R. 898 where the trial judge withheld statements by various of the accused on the grounds that they could be misapplied and wrongly used as evidence against other accused. Similar problems arose, but were dealt with quite differently (the judge allowing transcripts of police interviews given by all accused to be made available following a request by the jury, but giving additional directions on the inadmissibility against others of statements made outwith their presence) in *Munro v HM Advocate*, 2000 S.L.T. 950. It is of note that the Appeal Court considered it might well be preferable in such circumstances to lead evidence by means of edited transcripts.

In the past, difficulty has also been caused by the interpretation of the provisions against contact being made with the jury room (subs.(2)). In *Brownlie v HM Advocate* (1966) S.C.C.R. Supp. 14, the clerk of court on the judge's instructions went to the jury room door and asked if the jury had understood the judge's direction. This had followed earlier difficulty and further directions. The appeal, which had founded upon both the recall of the jury for further directions and the judge's actions in causing the clerk to communicate with the jury was refused. The right of the judge to recall the jury for further directions was upheld in *McBeth v HM Advocate* (1976) S.C.C.R. Supp. 123.

In *Cunningham v HM Advocate*, 1984 J.C. 37 written requests for directions were delivered to the judge in chambers in the presence of both counsel and dealt with by further written directions; these events occurred outwith the presence of the accused and were not recorded in the shorthand notes. While the conviction was quashed, the court held that the Crown was not at fault and gave authority for fresh proceedings, surely the only just solution in the circumstances. An appeal against conviction on grounds of miscarriage was refused where a jury's request for further directions could not be dealt with by the judge for over an hour, since another jury was being empanelled. In the interval the jury reached a verdict and it is of note that the Appeal Court took note of the discriminating nature of that verdict as evidence of a considered, and not a capricious, jury (*Brown v HM Advocate*, 1997 S.L.T. 611). *McColl v HM Advocate*, 1989 S.L.T. 691 is a rare example of communication of an order so extreme as to constitute a miscarriage, a decision the Court of Appeal reached after granting authority to parties to precognosce the clerk of court. The clerk had given formal directions to the jurors on the instructions of the presiding judge and the court did not reconvene; no record existed of the communings between the clerk and the jurors, all of which had occurred outwith the presence of the accused. It was by no means clear whether the circumstances had been brought to the attention of both counsel but the lack of a record of proceedings was critical and the verdict was overturned.

Difficulties have arisen when the court has been faced with a verdict at odds with the judge's directions: in *Whyte v HM Advocate*, 2000 S.L.T. 544 the Crown case rested entirely on application of the *Moorov* doctrine, and the court was advised by the foreman that guidance was needed because the jury was coming to two dissimilar verdicts. Additional directions were given but, on appeal, *Whyte* contended that once such an impasse had been reached in a *Moorov* case he should have been acquitted. The Appeal Court noted that no settled verdict had been reached and, following *Took v HM Advocate*, 1989 S.L.T.

425, indicated that where different verdicts would be mutually inconsistent, further directions would be appropriate. Broadly, where the jury seeks to return a verdict patently at odds with the judge's directions, or returns a verdict which simply is not lawful, it is no part of the court's function to let a verdict based on confusion, error or inconsistency pass unchecked. The judge in such circumstances must consider issuing further directions to assist the jury to reach a clear and sustainable verdict (see *Cameron (J.P.) v HM Advocate*, 1999 S.C.C.R. 476). In *TG v H.M. Advocate* [2018] HCJAC 58 the jury was permitted to amend the libel by altering the locus delictus, despite there having been no motion to do so by the prosecutor [see s.96 above]: conviction upon these charges was quashed.

In *McGill v HM Advocate*, 2001 S.C.C.R. 28 an unsuccessful appeal founded upon the form of deletions made by the jury to a libel of attempted rape.

A novel problem (but one likely to concern courts in the future) arose in *Matthewson v HM Advocate*, 1989 S.C.C.R. 101 when the jury asked to be shown parts of a video tape produced in evidence. The only operator available was the procurator fiscal depute who, in the presence of counsel for one of the accused and the clerk, showed a juror how to operate the video recorder, the jury having had to return to the court in order to view the tape. In *Gray v HM Advocate*, 1999 S.L.T. 533; 1999 S.C.C.R. 24, an assault and robbery in which video evidence was central to identification of the accused by witnesses who had seen him earlier that day, the trial judge refused a jury request to view the video again. On appeal against conviction the Appeal Court distinguished between the jurors viewing the tape again for the purpose of testing the accuracy and reliability of the witnesses' evidence (which could be permitted in open court) and undertaking an investigation or assessment of the contents of the tape for themselves (which would be unacceptable). *Gray* holds that it is competent to grant such jury requests; however, it has to be doubted that such subtle distinctions will be clear to the jury even after additional directions. (The propriety of introducing interpretative evidence, most pertinently of identification solely based upon reviewing CCTV evidence, is discussed in *Henry v HM Advocate* [2012] HCJAC 128). The jury also sought assistance from the court in *Moir v HM Advocate*, 1993 S.L.T. 1191 to "hear if possible ... all or part of the evidence given by [J]". Plainly at that stage in proceedings the witness could not be recalled and, in the absence of a transcript, the judge had declined to read over his own notes of evidence lest this influence the jury's own recall. The Appeal Court (at 1197) followed *Hamilton v HM Advocate*, 1938 S.L.T. 333 at 337 and held that the notes could have been read if the judge so chose, but that the issue was one which fell to the judge's discretion in determining the best way to conduct the case and not subject to review by the Appeal Court. The considerations governing the extent of a jury's access to productions are discussed in *Barnetson v HM Advocate*, 2003 G.W.D. 30–838.

Subs.(4)

At earlier stages in the proceedings, arrangements for accommodating jurors overnight during adjournments of trial can be made (s.88(8)) and it is presumed that the requirements of subs.(4) would then be applied to those situations. Once the jury has been charged there is no doubt that its deliberations should be interrupted only for the purposes of subs.(4). It is implicit that the jury should be unhindered in its deliberations and should in no way be pressured directly or indirectly to hasten to a verdict. See *McKenzie v HM Advocate*, 1986 S.C.C.R. 94 and *Love v HM Advocate*, 1995 S.C.C.R. 501. The distinction between eliciting a report on the jury's progress (necessary for the planning of accommodation) and pressing for a conclusion, can be a fine, but telling, one. Contrast *Robertson v HM Advocate*, 1996 S.C.C.R. 243 and *Sinclair v HM Advocate*, 1996 S.C.C.R. 221. An entirely illegitimate approach, suggesting that the issues before the jury were in short compass, and could be resolved quickly by a simple vote (the trial judge having already commented adversely in the jury's presence upon the length of counsel's speech) rather than discussion of the evidence, was identified by the Appeal Court in *Dyer v HM Advocate*, 2009 S.C.C.R. 194. It was noted that any discussion of the rate of progress in a trial should be conducted outwith the presence of the jury. It would seem to be good practice to remind jurors that they should reach a verdict in their own good time and should feel under no pressure to reach a verdict. An alternative, and perhaps less satisfactory, approach was used by the sheriff in *Eraker v HM Advocate*, 1997 G.W.D. 5–183 when the jury was asked if they were happy to consider "at least in the first instance trying to make a decision this evening"; presumably, since this left the jury to resolve whether to try to reach a verdict later that day (as they did) rather than directing them to do so, no element of pressure was evident. A4-224.2

Subsection (7), which was introduced by the 2003 Act, permits the trial judge, where appropriate, to interrupt the jury's deliberations after they have been charged and allow its members to break off and to return home rather than being in continued seclusion (subs.4(b)) and accommodated overnight. The greater element of discretion now found in subs.(7) greatly eases the burden on jurors, and on the court, of having to arrange suitable secluded accommodation at very short notice. The task of securing suitable accommodation (say) in Edinburgh during Festival time is not one for either the fainthearted or the parsimonious.

It is submitted, though the section is silent on the matter, that it would be prudent when utilising subs.(7)'s powers for the trial judge to make further explicit directions to the jurors not to discuss, or deliberate upon, the evidence until the court has reconvened.

Subs.(5)

In *Carswell v HM Advocate*, 2009 J.C. 59 a juror slipped out of the jury room to have a cigarette but was stopped on his way out of the court by the clerk and complied with a direction to return to the jury room. The juror had had no opportunity to communicate with any other person. Applying *Thomson v HM Advocate*, 1998 S.L.T. 364; 1997 S.C.C.R. 121, the court held this to be an irregularity, breaching subs.(2) A4-224.3

but not a breach of the more fundamental provisions of subs.(5) which had been directed against the prosecutor, or anyone at his instigation, seeking to influence jurors.

A further counterblast against tobacco was delivered in *HM Advocate v Paterson* [2012] HCJAC 105; 2012 S.C.C.R. 621 where the court officer permitted three jurors to part from the jury immediately after it had been directed to retire to consider verdicts; predictably, this course had been to enable the trio to enjoy a last cigarette before being sequestered. More surprisingly, when the incident was made known to parties, it was approached as a breach of subs.(5), causing them to concur in the acquittal of the accused by the court. The proper course would have been a desertion *pro loco et tempore*, a step which despite the Crown's contribution to the inept disposal, the Appeal Court, in dealing with a Crown Bill of Advocation, imposed.

No less surprisingly, the trial judge held a breach of both subss.(2) and (5) to have occurred in *Bill of Advocation re HM Advocate v MacDonald* [2016] HCJAC 121 when a juror absented herself from the jury's deliberations to make an urgent personal phone call. Following enquiry, the judge thereafter formally acquitted the accused in the absence of any material pointing to improper influence or pressure on the juror or jurors; see *Thomson* above. Again, the Appeal Court substituted desertion *pro loco et tempore* and quashed the acquittal.

Subs.(6)

This provision was introduced by the Prisoners and Criminal Proceedings (Scotland) Act 1993 (c.9) s.40(1) into the 1975 Act as s.155A. Section 91 enacts that trials shall proceed from day to day until concluded, while the marginal note stipulates "Trial to be continuous". Technical objections as to want of procedure of the sort raised in *Boyle v HM Advocate* above should not occur. The logical corollary of subs.(6) is s.102 below which permits other proceedings to be interrupted for the taking of a verdict, deal with the requests of, or issue further directions to, the jury in a prior trial. Section 158 of the Act allows summary proceedings to be interrupted for the same purposes.

[THE NEXT PARAGRAPH IS A4-225]

Verdict and conviction

Verdict of jury

A4-225 **100.—**(1) The verdict of the jury, whether the jury are unanimous or not, shall be returned orally by the foreman of the jury unless the court directs a written verdict to be returned.

(2) Where the jury are not unanimous in their verdict, the foreman shall announce that fact so that the relative entry may be made in the record.

(3) The verdict of the jury may be given orally through the foreman of the jury after consultation in the jury box without the necessity for the jury to retire.

GENERAL NOTE

A4-226 The jury's verdict can be returned competently in court immediately on conclusion of the judge's charge; it is not essential that they retire to the jury room (subs.(3)) or deliberate for any length of time (*Crowe v HM Advocate*, 1990 J.C. 112).

The verdict should be delivered orally to the court, a written verdict being competent only when the court has previously directed that the verdict be given to the court in that form. In part this ensures that all proceedings occur within the view and hearing of the accused; see *Kerr v HM Advocate*, 1992 S.L.T. 1031; 1992 S.C.C.R. 281 discussed in the notes to s.90. It has been held in *MacDermid (John Anderson) v HM Advocate*, 1948 J.C. 12 that the judge is not obliged to explain the meaning of the not proven verdict on the grounds that it is well-understood in Scotland. That assessment is questionable but the High Court has repeatedly warned judges against attempting to differentiate between the not proven and not guilty verdicts in jury charges; see most recently *Cussick (Barry) v HM Advocate*, 2001 S.L.T. 1316; 2001 S.C.C.R. 683 and *Sweeney v HM Advocate*, 2002 S.C.C.R. 131.

It is improper during trial proceedings to voice criticism of the not proven verdict, since it is a legitimate verdict in all but the most exceptional circumstances (see *Morrison v HM Advocate* [2013] HCJAC 108; 2013 S.C.C.R. 626 where the Appeal Court criticized the Crown for airing such views and the sheriff for not providing contrary corrective directions). *Reid v HM Advocate*, 1947 S.L.T. 150 then is a rare instance of the not proven verdict being withdrawn standing the nature of the evidence. The presiding judge is obliged to explain the meaning of a majority verdict to the jury and it must be made clear that at least eight of the jury are minded to convict: the jury will only be asked whether the verdict is unanimous or by a majority and no further enquiry should be made into the arithmetic involved (*Pullar v HM Advocate*, 1993 J.C. 126). The manner of calculating a majority has to be well understood by jurors particularly because of the availability (usually) of three verdicts and because the size of the jury can be reduced in certain circumstances to consist of as few as 12 jurors (s.90(1)). Refer to *Affleck v HM Advocate*, 1987 S.C.C.R. 150. In *Docherty v HM Advocate*, 1997 J.C. 196 confusion arose in a murder trial where the jury had voted by a majority for a guilty verdict, but were divided as to whether to convict for murder or culpable homicide. The Appeal Court held that those who had voted for an acquittal should not thereafter vote upon which of the alternative verdicts of guilt should be pronounced. Of consent, a conviction of culpable homicide was substituted by the Appeal Court. In the light of *Docherty* it would seem that modification of the standard directions given to juries would be appropriate in cases where alternative charges are libelled.

Once the verdict has been recorded by the clerk of court, read back to them and assented as correct, it cannot be subject to further consideration by the trial court, the verdict being finally pronounced (see *McGarry v HM Advocate*, 1959 J.C. 30). It has been held, however, that failure to read back a verdict to the jury is not itself fatal to the conviction (*Torri v HM Advocate*, 1923 J.C. 52).

Jury deletions of words or phrases from the libel are permissible but must leave sufficient specification to constitute a crime in Scots law: no *nomen juris* is necessary but the criminal conduct must be narrated. If all specification has been removed from the libel, the judge should refuse to accept the verdict and direct the jury to reconsider further. See *Took v HM Advocate*, 1988 S.C.C.R. 495; *Whyte v HM Advocate*, 1989 S.C.C.R. 553; *Marcus v HM Advocate* [2013] HCJAC 58 and *Goldie v HM Advocate* [2020] HCJAC 9. Contrast *Dennie v HM Advocate* [2018] HCJAC 67 where deletions to the libel specified by the jury's verdict while retaining its aggravating features were upheld as neither perverse nor unreasonable.

How far even an appellate court can venture in exploring the nature of a jury's deliberations is discussed in "Jury Secrecy and Criminal Appeals" by P. W. Ferguson in 2004 S.L.T. 43.

Previous convictions: solemn proceedings

101.—(1) Previous convictions against the accused shall not, subject to subsection (2) below and section 275A(2) of this Act, be laid before the jury, nor shall reference be made to them in presence of the jury before the verdict is returned. **A4-227**

(2) Nothing in subsection (1) above shall prevent the prosecutor—

(a) asking the accused questions tending to show that he has been convicted of an offence other than that with which he is charged, where he is entitled to do so under section 266 of this Act; or

(b) leading evidence of previous convictions where it is competent to do so under section 270 of this Act, and nothing in this section or in section 69 of this Act shall prevent evidence of previous convictions being led in any case where such evidence is competent in support of a substantive charge.

(3) Previous convictions shall not, subject to section 275A(1) of this Act, be laid before the presiding judge until the prosecutor moves—

(a) for sentence; or

(b) for a risk assessment order (or the court at its own instance proposes to make such an order).

and in that event the prosecutor shall lay before the judge a copy of the notice referred to in subsection (2) or (4) of section 69 of this Act

(3A) Where, under paragraph (b) of subsection (3) above, the prosecutor lays previous convictions before the judge, he shall also provide the judge with such details regarding the offences in question as are available to him.

(4) On the conviction of the accused it shall be competent for the court, subject to subsection (5) below, to amend a notice of previous convictions so laid by deletion or alteration for the purpose of curing any error or defect.

(5) […]

(6) Any conviction which is admitted in evidence by the court shall be entered in the record of the trial.

(7) Where a person is convicted of an offence, the court may have regard to any previous conviction in respect of that person in deciding on the disposal of the case.

(8) Where any such intimation as is mentioned in section 69 of this Act is given by the accused, it shall be competent to prove any previous conviction included in a notice under that section in the manner specified in section 285, or as the case may be 286A, of this Act, and the provisions of the section in question shall apply accordingly.

(9) This section, except subsection (2) above, applies in relation to the alternative disposals mentioned in subsection (10) below as it applies in relation to previous convictions.

(10) Those alternative disposals are—

(a) a—

(i) fixed penalty under section 302(1) of this Act;

(ii) compensation offer under section 302A(1) of this Act, that has been accepted (or deemed to have been accepted) by the accused in the two years preceding the date of an offence charged;

(b) a work order under section 303ZA(6) of this Act that has been completed in the two years preceding the date of an offence charged;

(c) a restoration notice given under subsection (4) of section 20A of the Nature Conservation (Scotland) Act 2004 (asp 6) in respect of which the accused has given notice of intention to comply under subsection (5) of that section in the two years preceding the date of an offence charged.

(11) Nothing in this section or in section 69 of this Act shall prevent the prosecutor, following conviction of an accused of an offence—

(a) to which a fixed penalty offer made under section 302(1) of this Act related;

(b) to which a compensation offer made under section 302A(1) of this Act related;

(c) to which a work offer made under section 303ZA(1) of this Act related; or

(d) to which a restoration notice given under section 20A(4) of the Nature Conservation (Scotland) Act 2004 (asp 6) related, providing the judge with information about the making of the offer (including the terms of the offer) or, as the case may be, about the giving of the notice (including the terms of the notice).

[(12) Any reference in this section to a previous conviction includes, where relevant, a conviction by a court in any part of the United Kingdom or in any member State of the European Union.]

AMENDMENTS

Subs.(5) repealed by Crime and Punishment (Scotland) Act 1997 (c.48) s.31 with effect from 1 August 1997 (SI 1997/1712 art.3).

Subss.(1) and (3) as amended by Sexual Offences (Procedure and Evidence) (Scotland) Act 2002 (asp 9) s.10(1). Brought into force by SSI 2002/443 (C.24) art.4 (effective 1 November 2002).

Subs.(8) as amended by Criminal Justice (Scotland) Act 2003 s.57(2). Brought into force on 27 June 2003 by SSI 2003/288 (C.14).

Subs.(3) as amended, and subs.(3A) inserted, by Criminal Justice (Scotland) Act 2003 (asp 7) Sch.1 para.2(3). Brought into force on 19 June 2006 by SSI 2006/332 (C.30) art.2(1), subject to art.2(2).

Subss.(9)–(11) inserted by Criminal Proceedings etc. (Reform) (Scotland) Act 2007 (asp 6) s.53. Brought into force on 10 March 2008 by SSI 2008/42 (C.4) art.3 and Sch subject to savings in art.6.

Subs.(10)(c) and (11)(d) inserted and subs.(11) as amended by Wildlife and Natural Environment (Scotland) Act 2011 (asp 6) Pt 6 s.40(3)(b). Brought into force on 29 June 2011 by SSI 2011/279 art.2.

Subs.(12) was inserted by the Criminal Justice (EU Exit) (Scotland) (Amendment etc.) Regulations 2020 (SSI 2020/339) reg.13(6) (effective 31 December 2020 subject to transitional and saving provision specified in reg.16 of those Regulations.

DEFINITIONS

A4-227.1 "judge": s.307(1).
"previous conviction": s.307(5).
"prosecutor": s.307(1).

[THE NEXT PARAGRAPH IS A4-228]

GENERAL NOTE

A4-228 In Scots criminal proceedings the previous convictions of an accused will not normally be made known to the court until a conviction is recorded and the prosecutor moves for sentence. There are now three exceptions to the general rule; first, where the existence of a conviction, and proof of it, is essential to the proof of the substantive charge; secondly, where the accused or his witnesses represent that he is of good character, or impugn the character or motives of the prosecution witnesses or prosecutor; and finally where invasive questioning in respect of a complainer has been admitted in terms of s.275 of the Act and the court, thereafter has granted the prosecutor the right to refer to relevant convictions of the accused pursuant to s.275A of the Act. This last only applies where the charge is one involving an offence specified in s.288C and unusually, arguably, has the joint purpose of showing the proclivity of the accused to commit the listed sexual offence libelled as well as undermining credibility and reliability by reference to his relevant conviction: by contrast use of record under the second exception is only intended to go to credibility and reliability. These fine distinctions may be more apparent than real.

Previous convictions specified in the body of the libel

Previous convictions may only be mentioned in the body of a charge where the fact of conviction places the accused in a specific category essential for commission of the offence, for example, a driving disqualification, or being a registered sex offender. Even then care has to be exercised to libel only what is strictly necessary to establish the offending capacity. See *MacDonald v HM Advocate*, 2008 S.C.C.R. 181 where the libel was held to stray into collateral areas, notably the *modus* used previously by the accused in the offence which had led to the imposition of a custodial sentence.

So far as sexual offence libels are concerned, inclusion of a s.288BA docket has been held not to breach the provisions of subs.(1) above, but considerable care would be needed to avoid that provision being breached in the course of evidence. See *HM Advocate v Moynihan* [2018] HCJAC 43; 2019 S.C.C.R. 61.

Previous convictions in the course of trial

The discussion above referred to the three exceptions to the general rule barring reference to an accused's previous convictions in the course of trial. In the following discussion only the first two situations are discussed, trials involving listed sexual offences involve more complex procedures; see ss.274 – 275A below. There are two accepted exceptions to this general rule: first, where proof of the conviction is an essential to proof of the substantive charge (for example, driving while disqualified, or contravening the provisions of the Firearms Act 1968 (c.27) s.21, or prison-breaking—see *Russell v HM Advocate*, 1993 S.L.T. 358; *Varey v HM Advocate*, 1986 S.L.T. 321 and *Harkin v HM Advocate*, 1996 S.L.T. 1004); secondly, when the accused has represented himself to be of good character or impugned the character of prosecution witnesses, the complainer or the prosecutor (see ss.266(4) and 270(1)). The prosecutor is also under a duty not to question the accused in a fashion calculated to show that he has been involved in other criminal charges which are not before the court. The general principles are discussed in *Deighan v MacLeod*, 1959 J.C. 25 at [29], approved in *Sivero v HM Advocate* [2013] HCJAC 1.

The consequences of revealing previous convictions, even when this is done by the prosecutor, are not necessarily fatal; much depends on the circumstances in which the section's provisions were breached, whether the information was wilfully elicited or was imparted unexpectedly, what objection, if any, was offered to the evidence and who sought the evidence in the first place. The Appeal Court will generally defer to the judgment of the trial judge since it is considered that he is best equipped to place the remarks, and their impact on the fairness of the trial, in context; see *Fraser v HM Advocate*, 2014 J.C. 115; 2013 S.C.C.R. 674 and *Crombie v HM Advocate* [2014] HCJAC 118. *Sivero v HM Advocate* cited above is an example of an unconsidered, and superfluous, question by the prosecutor eliciting a prejudicial response from an experienced police witness; while not held to be a breach of the section, since there was no deliberate intent on the prosecutor's part, the Appeal Court quashed conviction only of the second of the two charges libelled holding there to have been a miscarriage of justice; this outcome may seem perverse but is explained by the fact that the accused had pled guilty to the first charge, only, at the outset which had been refused by the Crown. The approach adopted by the Court of Appeal is to consider whether a miscarriage of justice has occurred (having regard, inter alia, to any steps taken by the trial judge to address the issue, or consciously avoid it, in his charge) and then to consider whether the breach constituted a sufficiently substantial miscarriage to merit the quashing of the conviction or amendment of the verdict. So in *McCuaig v HM Advocate*, 1982 J.C. 59 where a police officer in response to a question from the trial judge read over the full terms of a charge preferred to him, making reference to the accused's previous convictions, it was held that no substantial miscarriage had occurred. Similarly in *Binks v HM Advocate*, 1984 S.C.C.R. 335; 1985 S.L.T. 59 where in reading a statement given by the accused, a Customs officer during his examination-in-chief read the phrase "I don't want to go back to jail again", the court took the view that the mere disclosure of a previous conviction might be of little or no significance in the circumstances of the case. In *Lewry v HM Advocate* [2013] HCJAC 62; 2013 S.C.C.R. 396, repeated, and deliberate, comment upon an accused's demeanour during interview by a police officer, contrasting it (unfavourably) with the officer's general dealings with him was severely criticised on appeal. While acknowledging the dilemma which the sheriff faced in directing the jury about the improper remarks (in this case making no comment at all having refused motions to desert proceedings) the Appeal Court opined that the sheriff in assessing whether the comments made were "certain" or "likely" to influence the jury as a whole set the test too high, the remarks then being sufficient to justify desertion of the trial *pro loco et tempore*. See generally *Kepple v HM Advocate*, 1936 J.C. 76, *HM Advocate v McIlwain*, 1965 S.L.T. 311 and *Penman v Stott*, 2001 S.C.C.R. 911.

By contrast a very similar reply to caution and charge to that in *Binks* elicited by the prosecutor in *Graham v HM Advocate*, 1984 S.L.T. 67 was held to be deliberate and fatal to conviction. Compare *McAvoy v HM Advocate*, 1991 S.C.C.R. 123 in which the prosecutor asked a police officer about "known associates" of the accused a question, which though criticised by the Appeal Court, was held not to have breached the provisions. The central issue in studying the conduct of the prosecutor is whether the disclosure came about as a result of calculation or unacceptable want of care on his part, or whether it occurred unexpectedly or as part of a wilful ploy by a witness or co-accused. See *Deeney v HM Advocate*, 1986 S.C.C.R. 393 where a witness mentioned that the accused was on licence at the time of offences, an answer not anticipated from the Crown's question and which was held not to have breached the section's provisions. More recently in *Robertson v HM Advocate*, 1995 S.C.C.R. 497 where a Crown witness repeatedly referred to the accused being provided accommodation by SACRO (Scottish Association for Care and Resettlement of Offenders), using only the acronym and without divulging the objects of the organisation, the disclosure was held to be accidental and to have been dealt with sensitively in the judge's charge to the jury. In *Campbell v HM Advocate*, 1999 S.L.T. 399 (driving while disqualified) the prosecutor's brief questioning of C about his previous conviction notwithstanding that C had stated no preliminary objection to the special capacity, was upheld. The court took the view that the Crown could still elect to prove the terms of the qualifying conviction; see the discussion at A4-495 below. Revelations under cross-examination of a Crown witness, whose convictions were being rehearsed, of a common conviction with the accused did not dispose the court to grant a desertion of trial, the jury being directed to treat the information (15 years old) as irrelevant. See *Donnell v HM Advocate*, 2009 S.C.C.R. 918.

It will be noted that the section bars any reference to an accused's previous convictions (unless the provisions of subs.(2) apply) but this cannot guard against wilful conduct on the part of co-accused or defence witnesses; in such circumstances this is almost certain to be prejudicial but the court will not rush to hold that a miscarriage has occurred. See *Slane v HM Advocate*, 1984 S.L.T. 293 and *Griffith v HM Advocate* [2013] HCJAC 84; 2013 S.C.C.R. 448 and the Notes to s.266 below. In the first instance the judge presiding at the trial has to decide whether to mention such inadmissible evidence in order to direct that it be disregarded or whether, in the whole circumstances, it is more discreet, and effective, to say nothing at all and in so doing avoid resurrecting the objectionable evidence (see *Fyfe v HM Advocate*, 1989 S.C.C.R. 429; 1990 S.L.T. 50 and *Gallagher v HM Advocate*, 1992 G.W.D. 6-355).

The deletion of subs.(5) introduced by the 1997 Act means that it is now competent to amend the schedule of previous convictions to correct errors. This concession would have had a considerable impact if the Government had commenced the scheme of automatic sentences set out in Pt I of the 1997 Act; in that scheme the precise terms of a prior conviction would have dictated whether a re-offending accused was subject to an automatic sentence on indictment.

Previous convictions and the sentencing process

A4-228.1 When moving for sentence the Crown is entitled to place a schedule detailing previous convictions before the court as material relevant to sentence. The question now is what in the way of more detailed information about the nature and circumstances of prior background, including convictions, should be disclosed to the court, and considered by it. Until now the directions laid down in *Connell v Mitchell*, 1909 S.C. (J.) 13 (broadly that the court could not look behind previous convictions) had been applied, albeit previous convictions not libelled by the Crown but revealed in social enquiry reports could be taken into account once the accused had been given the opportunity to challenge them or comment (*Sillars v Copeland*, 1966 J.C. 8). Otherwise the court would seek no more information as to the factual circumstances of previous offences.

In *Riley v HM Advocate*, 1999 J.C. 308; 1999 S.L.T. 1076; 1999 S.C.C.R. 644, the Appeal Court has signalled a broader approach and has approved a practice of the Crown serving extracts of convictions whose factual detail is being founded upon in any narration. Nonetheless it was emphasised that a sentencing court would not wish to become embroiled in disputes over the fine detail of convictions, and would limit scrutiny to the terms of charges, and only then in exceptional cases.

The purpose of schedules of previous convictions and social enquiry reports is to enable the sentencing judge to pass an appropriate disposal having regard to all the known circumstances: thus in *Penman v HM Advocate*, 1999 S.C.C.R. 740 where no previous convictions were put before the court but a report referred to convictions for offences committed subsequent to the sexual misconduct libelled, the Appeal Court approved the use of this information provided that the record was not treated as an aggravating feature. Penman's recent pattern of offending justified the view that he was a danger to the public.

Following *Penman*, if a schedule of convictions applying to the accused placed before the court is materially deficient, for example, omitting significant convictions, subs.(4) would, subject to a general test of fairness and any necessary adjournment for instructions, entitle the Crown to move to amend the schedule prior to the completion of sentencing; see *HM Advocate v Hollywood*, 2010 G.W.D. 12-213. Section 300A below may also support this approach.

Moving for sentence

A4-228.2 Ordinarily following the pronouncement of the jury's verdict, the prosecutor is invited to proceed and will lay any convictions before the court. *Noon v HM Advocate*, 1960 J.C. 52 is authority for the proposition that no particular form of words is required of the prosecutor; his actions in placing any schedule of convictions signals his intention. However, in *Arthur, Petitioner*, 2003 S.L.T. 90 a murder trial in which the judge proceeded straight to imposition of the mandatory sentence of life imprisonment on pronouncement of the verdict, without inviting the Crown to address the court, the sentence but, significantly not the conviction, was quashed and the case was remitted to the trial judge to sentence according to law.

Road Traffic Offenders Act 1988 (c.53).

See the notes at A4-359 below.

European Convention on Human Rights

In *Andrew v HM Advocate*, 2000 S.L.T. 402 the Appeal Court rejected the contention that disclosure of an accused's previous conviction in the course of trial necessarily amounted to a breach of art.6(1) or (2). It is of note that the disclosure arose through no fault of the Crown. **A4-228.3**

Inclusion of convictions imposed by courts in the European Union

The effect of s.57 of the Criminal Justice (Scotland) Act 2003 (asp 7) is to permit the inclusion of an accused's convictions from these courts in any schedule of convictions served upon an accused in Scottish criminal proceedings. Such convictions can be proved by certification of known fingerprints in much the same manner as was applied to UK convictions by s.285 of the 1995 Act.

Post-offence convictions etc.

101A.—(1) This section applies where an accused person is convicted of an offence ("offence O") on indictment. **A4-228.4**

(2) The court may, in deciding on the disposal of the case, have regard to—

(a) any conviction in respect of the accused which occurred on or after the date of offence O but before the date of conviction in respect of that offence,

(b) any of the alternative disposals in respect of the accused that are mentioned in subsection (3).

(3) Those alternative disposals are—

(a) a—

(i) fixed penalty under section 302(1) of this Act, or

(ii) compensation offer under section 302A(1) of this Act,

that has been accepted (or deemed to have been accepted) on or after the date of offence O but before the date of conviction in respect of that offence,

(b) a work order under section 303ZA(6) of this Act that has been completed on or after the date of offence O but before the date of conviction in respect of that offence.

(4) The court may have regard to any such conviction or alternative disposal only if it is—

(a) specified in a notice laid before the court by the prosecutor, and

(b) admitted by the accused or proved by the prosecutor (on evidence adduced then or at another diet).

(5) A reference in this section to a conviction which occurred on or after the date of offence O is a reference to such a conviction by a court in any part of the United Kingdom or [, where the court considers appropriate, in any] member State of the European Union.

AMENDMENTS

Section 101A inserted by Criminal Justice and Licensing (Scotland) Act 2010 (asp 13) s.70. Brought into force on 28 March 2011 (for all purposes in respect of offences committed on or after 28 March 2011) SSI 2011/178 (C.15) art.2, Sch.1 para.1.

Words in subs.(5) were substituted by the Criminal Justice (EU Exit) (Scotland) (Amendment etc.) Regulations 2020 (SSI 2020/339) reg.13(7) (effective 31 December 2020 subject to transitional and saving provision specified in reg.16 of those Regulations.

DEFINITIONS

"conviction": s.307(1) of the Criminal Procedure (Scotland) Act 1995 as amended by s.71(1) of and Sch.4 to the Criminal Justice and Licensing (Scotland) Act 2010 (asp 13). **A4-228.5**

"offence": s.307(1) of the Criminal Procedure (Scotland) Act 1995.

"indictment": s.307(1) of the above Act.

GENERAL NOTE

A4-228.6 This section applies to any solemn proceedings; the equivalent in summary proceedings is found in s.166A below. The sentencing court is entitled (but not obliged) to heed any conviction or disposal of an offence committed since the date of commission of an offence in the libel before the court. However, this provision only becomes operative after the Crown has served a notice (additional to any schedule of convictions initially served on the accused) or, perhaps, has amended the schedule of convictions in terms of s.101(5) above to reflect the new conviction. Note that a qualifying conviction or disposal could arise from any court within a Member State of the EU; see generally s.71 of the Criminal Justice and Licensing (Scotland) Act 2010 (asp 13) and Sch.4 of that Act.

While the section refers both to post-offence convictions and to non-court disposals (subs.(3)), it is difficult to envisage a situation in solemn proceedings where the accused's fate would be much affected, if at all, by the acceptance, or deemed acceptance, of a qualifying fixed penalty or compensation offer. It is submitted that the court might properly have regard to post-offence convictions disclosed in a social enquiry report or quite properly adverted to in a plea in mitigation.

It would be sound Crown practice, once alerted to the fact that a previously bailed or ordained accused was now in custody, to make some diligent enquiry into the circumstances leading to that custody, and especially the date of each offence to assess whether a qualifying conviction has occurred.

[THE NEXT PARAGRAPH IS A4-229]

Interruption of trial for other proceedings

A4-229 **102.**—(1) When the jury have retired to consider their verdict, and the diet in another criminal cause has been called, then, subject to subsection (3) below, if it appears to the judge presiding at the trial to be appropriate, he may interrupt the proceedings in such other cause—

(a) in order to receive the verdict of the jury in the preceding trial, and thereafter to dispose of the case;

(b) to give a direction to the jury in the preceding trial upon any matter upon which the jury may wish a direction from the judge or to hear any request from the jury regarding any matter in the cause.

(2) Where in any case the diet of which has not been called, the accused intimates to the clerk of court that he is prepared to tender a plea of guilty as libelled or such qualified plea as the Crown is prepared to accept, or where a case is remitted to the High Court for sentence, then, subject to subsection (3) below, any trial then proceeding may be interrupted for the purpose of receiving such plea or dealing with the remitted case and pronouncing sentence or otherwise disposing of any such case.

(3) In no case shall any proceedings in the preceding trial take place in the presence of the jury in the interrupted trial, but in every case that jury shall be directed to retire by the presiding judge.

(4) On the interrupted trial being resumed the diet shall be called de novo.

(5) In any case an interruption under this section shall not be deemed an irregularity, nor entitle the accused to take any objection to the proceedings.

DEFINITIONS

A4-229.1 "High Court": s.307(1).
"judge": s.307(1).

[THE NEXT PARAGRAPH IS A4-230]

GENERAL NOTE

A4-230 This section and, in some circumstances, s.99(6) fall to be read in conjunction. While s.91 of the Act requires that the trial shall proceed from day to day, procedural difficulties can develop when it is necessary to interpose other solemn business. See for example *Boyle v HM Advocate*, 1990 S.C.C.R. 480. These problems became yet more acute when a jury trial had spilled over from a previous sitting; then the disposal of business called to the later (delayed) sitting often demanded dexterity of a high order. Section 102 admits a degree of flexibility into the administration of court business but it will be noted that when a jury trial is interrupted to deal with other business before the court, that jury is to be excluded until the fresh business is concluded.

The section also enables a jury in a later trial to be empanelled while an earlier jury deliberates, a provision which may assist on occasion to utilise court time more effectively.

Rule 14.8. of the 1996 Act of Adjournal enacts that a minute of continuation shall be entered in the minutes of the interrupted trial; Rule 14.9.-(1) permits other matters, which have been deferred for sentence to await the outcome of the jury trial, to be called once a verdict has been reached in that trial without the need to adjourn.

It will be observed that it is still necessary to call the diet anew after any such interruption (subs.(4)).

Failure of accused to appear

102A.—(1) In proceedings on indictment, an accused person who without reasonable excuse fails to appear at a diet of which the accused has been given due notice (apart from a diet which the accused is not required to attend) is— A4-230.1

(a) guilty of an offence; and
(b) liable on conviction on indictment to a fine or to imprisonment for a period not exceeding 5 years or to both.

(2) In proceedings on indictment, where an accused person fails to appear at a diet of which the accused has been given due notice (apart from a diet which the accused is not required to attend), the court may grant a warrant to apprehend the accused.

(3) It is not, otherwise than under subsection (2) above, competent in any proceedings on indictment for a court to grant a warrant for the apprehension of an accused person for failure to appear at a diet.

(4) However, it remains competent for a court to grant a warrant on petition (as referred to in section 34 of this Act) in respect of an offence under—

(a) subsection (1) above;
(b) section 27(7) of this Act,

whether or not a warrant has been granted under subsection (2) above in respect of the same failure to appear to which that offence relates.

(5) Where a warrant to apprehend an accused person is granted under subsection (2) above at any stage prior to conviction, the indictment falls as respects that accused.

(6) Subsection (5) above is subject to any order to different effect made by the court when granting the warrant.

(7) An order under subsection (6) above—

(a) for the purpose of proceeding with the trial in the absence of the accused under section 92(2A) (where the warrant is granted at a trial diet), may be made on the motion of the prosecutor;
(b) for any other purpose, may be made on the motion of the prosecutor or of the court's own accord.

(8) A warrant granted under subsection (2) above shall be in such form as may be prescribed by Act of Adjournal or as nearly as may be in such form.

(9) A warrant granted under subsection (2) above (in the form mentioned in subsection (8) above) shall imply warrant to officers of law—

(a) to search for and apprehend the accused;
(b) to bring the accused before the court;
(c) in the meantime, to detain the accused in a police station, police cell or other convenient place; and
(d) so far as is necessary for the execution of the warrant, to break open shut and lockfast places.

(10) An accused apprehended under a warrant granted under subsection (2) above shall wherever practicable be brought before the court not later than in the course of the first day on which the court is sitting after the accused is taken into custody.

(11) Where the accused is brought before the court in pursuance of a warrant granted under subsection (2) above, the court shall make an order—

(a) detaining the accused until liberated in due course of law; or

(b) releasing the accused on bail.

(12) For the purposes of subsection (11) above, the court is to have regard to the terms of the indictment in relation to which the warrant was granted even if that indictment has fallen.

(13) In a case where a warrant is granted under subsection (2) above, any period of time during which the accused was detained in custody—

(a) as regards that case; and

(b) prior to the making of an order under subsection (11) above,

does not count towards any time limit applying in that case by virtue of section 65(4) of this Act.

(14) For the purposes of subsection (13) above—

(a) detention as regards a case includes, in addition to detention as regards the indictment in relation to which the warrant was granted (whether or not that indictment has fallen), detention as regards any preceding petition;

(b) it is immaterial whether or not further proceedings are on a fresh indictment.

(15) At any time before the trial of an accused person on indictment, it is competent—

(a) to amend the indictment so as to include an additional charge of an offence under subsection (1) above;

(b) to include, in the list of witnesses or productions associated with the indictment, witnesses or productions relating to that offence.

(16) In this section, "the court" means—

(a) where the accused failed to appear at the High Court—

(i) for the purposes of subsections (10) to (12) above, that Court (whether or not constituted by a single judge);

(ii) otherwise, a single judge of that Court;

(b) where the accused failed to appear at a sheriff court, any sheriff court with jurisdiction in relation to the proceedings.

AMENDMENTS

Section 102A inserted by Criminal Proceedings etc (Reform) (Scotland) Act 2007 (asp 6) s.32. Brought into force on December 12, 2007 by SSI 2007/479 (C.40) art.3 and Sch.

Subss.(4)(b), (5) as amended by Criminal Proceedings etc. (Reform) (Scotland) Act 2007 (Supplemental Provisions) Order 2008 (SSI 2008/109), with effect from March 10, 2008.

Subs.(4)(b) as amended by Criminal Justice and Licensing (Scotland) Act 2010 (asp 13) Sch.7 para.50. Brought into force on March 28, 2011 by SSI 2011/178 (C.15) art.2, Sch.1 para.1.

GENERAL NOTE

A4-230.2 The complex provisions in this section which apply only to solemn proceedings are relevant to failures of an accused to appear at any point, up to and including any appeal proceedings. The penalties for failure to appear are significantly increased to a fine, or detention or imprisonment for up to five years, or both such fine and period of detention or imprisonment.

Several procedural changes, whose significance should not be underestimated, have been introduced by s.102A. At the time when an accused fails to appear, the court and the Crown seeks a warrant for arrest; the only warrant which the court may now grant is a statutory warrant in terms of s.102A(2) (it is no longer competent to grant a due course of law warrant at this point in proceedings). In contrast to previous practice, once a s.102A warrant has been granted and executed, the accused must, so far as practicable, be brought before the sheriff custody court on the next lawful day (s.102A(10)) in sheriff solemn cases, or before a single High Court judge in proceedings which had been indicted in that court. On that appearance the question of bail will doubtless be considered and the court will then be entitled to consider both the terms of the fallen indictment as well as the circumstances of the failure to appear. Subs.(11) empowers the court either to remand in custody or to grant bail; there seems to be no provision to permit the court to ordain an accused in these circumstances.

Ordinarily, the effect of granting a s.102A warrant, as in previous practice, is that the proceedings fall in relation to that accused alone (subs.(5)) unless the court in terms of subs.(6) orders otherwise. The stated purpose of this latter subsection is to permit the court to fix a trial in absence of the acccused, for which see generally s.92(2A) and the General Notes to that section and to s.150 below. Less clear is the impact of a failure of an accused to appear at the sentencing stage of proceedings: on one reading of subs.(5) once a warrant is granted the proceedings are brought to an end because the indictment then falls; it is submitted that that was scarcely the intention of the Scottish Parliament but the problem might be side-stepped if the court, when granting warrant, minuted in terms of subs.(6) that the proceedings be maintained pending apprehension of the accused.

It may be argued from both a Crown perspective, and that of the accused, that the most significant change wrought by s.102A is to be found in subs.(11) which has a considerable impact upon the time bar provisions of s.65 of the 1995 Act. Henceforth, an accused who obtains bail at the petition stage, or after an indictment has been served, and subsequently fails to appear at a diet, stands to have any earlier period spent in custody discounted from calculation of the period he can, competently, be remanded de novo in custody awaiting trial. Subs.(11) does not indicate how any backdating of a sentence ultimately imposed is to be approached (see generally s.210 of the 1995 Act) but in the case of an accused enjoying interim liberation pending appeal who subsequently failed to appear before the Appeal Court, a case could be argued for loss of backdating on any sentence ultimately imposed.

In rare circumstances it is conceivable that an accused may have been indicted without having made an appearance on petition leaving the only avenues open to the Crown to seek a s.102A warrant from the trial court or on an initiating petition in terms of s.102A(1), or more speculatively, to raise a petition libelling an attempt to defeat the ends of justice. Normally, however, it is important to observe that the availability of a s.102A warrant seems to be entirely without prejudice to the Crown's right to seek a petition warrant libelling a contravention of s.27 of the Act, founding upon the failure to appear as a breach of any bail order then in force: expedient use of an initiating warrant can enable the Crown to preserve the existing indictment (rather than risk its loss) by calling the indictment and taking a s.102A warrant. (Situations can often arise where such a cessation is not felt to be in the public interest, for example in cases involving a number of accused or vulnerable witnesses, or in trials where a substantial volume of evidence has already been led or complex logistics are involved).

Note that it is competent to amend any live indictment peremptorily to incorporate an additional failure to appear charge and any necessary witnesses or productions.

[THE NEXT PARAGRAPH IS A4-231]

Part VIII – Appeals from Solemn Proceedings

Appeal sittings

103.—(1) The High Court shall hold both during session and during vacation such sittings as are necessary for the disposal of appeals and other proceedings under this Part of this Act. **A4-231**

(2) Subject to subsection (3) below, for the purpose of hearing and determining any appeal or other proceeding under this Part of this Act three of the Lords Commissioners of Justiciary shall be a quorum of the High Court, and the determination of any question under this Part of this Act by the court shall be according to the votes of the majority of the members of the court sitting, including the presiding judge, and each judge so sitting shall be entitled to pronounce a separate opinion.

(3) For the purpose of hearing and determining any appeal under section 106(1)(b) to (e) of this Act, or any proceeding connected therewith, two of the Lords Commissioners of Justiciary shall be a quorum of the High Court, and each judge shall be entitled to pronounce a separate opinion; but where the two Lords Commissioners of Justiciary are unable to reach agreement on the disposal of the appeal, or where they consider it appropriate, the appeal shall be heard and determined in accordance with subsection (2) above.

(4) Subsections (1) to (3) above shall apply to cases certified to the High Court by a single judge of the said court and to appeals by way of advocation in like manner as they apply to appeals under this Part of this Act.

(5) The powers of the High Court under this Part of this Act—

(a) to extend the time within which intimation of intention to appeal and note of appeal may be given;

(b) to allow the appellant to be present at any proceedings in cases where he is not entitled to be present without leave; and

(c) to admit an appellant to bail,

may be exercised by any judge of the High Court, sitting and acting wherever convenient, in the same manner as they may be exercised by the High Court, and subject to the same provisions.

(6) Where a judge acting under subsection (5) above refuses an application by an appellant to exercise under that subsection any power in his favour, the appellant shall be entitled to have the application determined by the High Court.

(6A) Where a judge acting under subsection (5)(c) above grants an application by an appellant to exercise that power in his favour, the prosecutor shall be entitled to have the application determined by the High Court.

(7) Subject to subsections (5), (6) and (6A) above and without prejudice to it, preliminary and interlocutory proceedings incidental to any appeal or application may be disposed of by a single judge.

(8) In all proceedings before a judge under section (5) above, and in all preliminary and interlocutory proceedings and applications except such as are heard before the full court, the parties may be represented and appear by a solicitor alone.

AMENDMENTS

Subss.(3), (4) and (7) as amended by Crime and Punishment (Scotland) Act 1997 (c.48) s.62(1) and Sch.1 para.21(13) with effect from August 1, 1997 in terms of SI 1997/1712 art.3.

Subs.(6A) inserted, and subs.(7) as amended, by Criminal Justice (Scotland) Act 2003 (asp 7) Pt 8 s.66. Brought into force on June 27, 2003 by SSI 2003/288 (C.14).

DEFINITIONS

A4-232 "appellant": s.132.
"bail": s.307(1).
"High Court" s.307(1).
"judge": s.307(1).
"Lords Commissioners of Justiciary": s.307(1).
"sentence": s. 132.

GENERAL NOTE

A4-232.1 Part VIII of the Act deals with appeals under solemn procedure and it should be read with Ch. 15 of the Criminal Procedure Rules (infra). Note that the 1995 Act introduced what was a new distinction between conviction appeals and sentence appeals so far as the quorum of the court is concerned. Although the general quorum remains three, for sentence appeals the quorum is, in terms of s. 103(3), two judges. It is thought that the situation in which the two judges have been unable to agree, so that three judges are required, has not occurred in practice.

In cases not covered by the 1995 Act it is for the court to determine the appropriate quorum—*Express Newspapers Plc Petr*, 1999 S.C.C.R. 262.

If one of the judges in a court is subsequently held not to be impartial then proceedings are treated as if he had not been present. If there are insufficient judges remaining to form a quorum then there is no validly constituted court and hence no valid interlocutor in terms of s.124—*Hoekstra v HM Advocate (No.2)*, 2000 S.C.C.R. 368.

Subsection (4)—certification is a procedure whereby a judge on circuit can refer a point of law for decision by the High Court: see *HM Advocate v Cunningham*, 1963 J.C. 80 and *HM Advocate v Burns*, 1967 J.C. 15.

Subsection (5)—The quorum is one judge in relation to the matters of extending the time within which intimation of intention to appeal and note of appeal may be given, of allowing the appellant to be present at any proceedings in cases where leave is necessary and to admit the appellant to bail.

[THE NEXT PARAGRAPH IS A4-233]

Power of High Court in appeals

A4-233 **104.**—(1) Without prejudice to any existing power of the High Court, it may for the purposes of an appeal under section 106(1), 107A, 107B or 108 of this Act—

(a) order the production of any document or other thing connected with the proceedings;

(b) hear any evidence relevant to any alleged miscarriage of justice or order such evidence to be heard by a judge of the High Court or by such other person as it may appoint for that purpose;

(c) take account of any circumstances relevant to the case which were not before the trial judge;

(d) remit to any fit person to enquire and report in regard to any matter or circumstance affecting the appeal;

(e) appoint a person with expert knowledge to act as assessor to the High Court in any case where it appears to the court that such expert knowledge is required for the proper determination of the case.

(2) The evidence of any witnesses ordered to be examined before the High Court or before any judge of the High Court or other person appointed by the High Court shall be taken in accordance with the existing law and practice as to the taking of evidence in criminal trials in Scotland.

(3) The appellant or applicant and the respondent or counsel on their behalf shall be entitled to be present at and take part in any examination of any witness to which this section relates.

Amendments

Subs.(1)(b) as amended by Crime and Punishment (Scotland) Act 1997 Sch.1 para.21.

Subs.(1) as amended by Criminal Justice and Licensing (Scotland) Act 2010 (asp 13) s.75. Brought into force on March 28, 2011 by SSI 2011/178 (C.15) art.2, Sch.1 para.1.

Definitions

"appellant": s.132. **A4-233.1**

"High Court": s.307(1).

"judge": s.307(1).

[THE NEXT PARAGRAPH IS A4-234]

General Note

The central question in appeals against conviction is whether there has been a miscarriage of justice: s.106(3). The essence of s.104 is to allow the High Court of Justiciary, in addition to any existing powers, statutory powers relating to the investigation of an allegation of a miscarriage of justice. **A4-234**

Subsection (1)(a): In *Hoekstra v HM Advocate (No.1)*, 2000 S.C.C.R. 263 "disclosure minutes" were prepared by the appellants seeking recovery of new material not available at the trial. It was held that "in general terms the court should not order the Crown to disclose new material in the course of an appeal unless the court was satisfied that the material was likely to be of value for the purpose of evaluating the grounds of appeal and determining whether or not there had been a miscarriage of justice, but the court might be prepared to consider ordering the production of new material which was shown to be of potential importance even if it was not material which was, on a strict reading, relevant to an existing ground of appeal, provided that the material sought could provide the basis for a new or amended ground of appeal which the appellant should, at a late stage be allowed to advance". The court declined in that case to order disclosure. A further petition for recovery was presented in respect of the fresh appeal proceedings. It was argued that the general disclosure of documents was appropriate so that the appellants could investigate the whole background of the prosecution and trial. The Appeal Court disagreed holding that the production of material must relate to the grounds of appeal and the statutory requirements of the 1995 Act—*Hoekstra v HM Advocate (No.5)*, 2001 S.C.C.R. 121. In *Porter & Smith Petrs*, 2000 G.W.D. 2-46 a petition for commission and diligence was sought and granted in respect of material evidence not heard at the trial, the existence of which did not become known until later confiscation proceedings.

Subsection (1)(b) has been amended by the Crime and Punishment (Scotland) Act 1997 Sch.1 para.21(14). The word "additional" has been removed in light of the new ground of appeal in s.106(3). For cases where evidence was heard by the Appeal Court see *Morland v HM Advocate*, 1985 S.C.C.R. 316; *Kinnon v HM Advocate*, 1997 S.C.C.R. 552; *O'Neill v HM Advocate*, 1996 G.W.D. 29-1728 and *Daly v HM Advocate*, 1997 G.W.D. 22-1067; *Jackson v HM Advocate*, 1998 S.C.C.R. 539; subs.(1)(c), see *Rubin v HM Advocate*, 1984 S.C.C.R. 96; *Carrington v HM Advocate*, 1994 S.C.C.R. 567 and *Tarbett v HM Advocate*, 1994 S.C.C.R. 867; subs.(1)(d), see *McCadden v HM Advocate*, 1985 S.C.C.R. 282; *Robertson v HM Advocate*, 1996 S.C.C.R. 243; *Crossan v HM Advocate*, 1996 S.C.C.R. 279; *Squire v HM Advocate*, 1998 G.W.D. 28-1410; *Feely v HM Advocate*, 2000 G.W.D. 12-422 and *Kerr v HM Advocate*, 1999 S.C.C.R. 763. As Sheriff Gordon points out in his commentary the remit to a single judge required to be specific in its terms so as not to conflict with s.8 of the Contempt of Court Act 1981.

The form an investigation should take is set out in *Squire v HM Advocate*, 1998 G.W.D. 28-1410, a case concerning alleged communications between the jury and the clerk of court. In considering the question of an alleged miscarriage of justice, in *Clark v HM Advocate*, 2000 S.C.C.R. 767 the tape of part of the judge's charge was played to the Appeal Court.

Appeal against refusal of application

A4-235 **105.**—(1) When an application or applications have been dealt with by a judge of the High Court, under section 103(5) of this Act, the Clerk of Justiciary shall—

(a) notify to the applicant the decision in the form prescribed by Act of Adjournal or as nearly as may be in such form; and

(b) where all or any of such applications have been refused, forward to the applicant the prescribed form for completion and return forthwith if he desires to have the application or applications determined by the High Court as fully constituted for the hearing of appeals under this Part of this Act.

(2) Where the applicant does not desire a determination as mentioned in subsection (1)(b) above, or does not return within five days to the Clerk the form duly completed by him, the refusal of his application or applications by the judge shall be final.

(3) Where an applicant who desires a determination by the High Court as mentioned in subsection (1)(b) above—

(a) is not legally represented, he may be present at the hearing and determination by the High Court of the application;

(b) is legally represented, he shall not be entitled to be present without leave of the court.

(3A) Subsection (3) does not entitle an applicant to be present at the hearing and determination of an application under section 111(2) unless the High Court has made a direction under section 111(4)(b).

(4) When an applicant duly completes and returns to the Clerk of Justiciary within the prescribed time the form expressing a desire to be present at the hearing and determination by the court of the applications mentioned in this section, the form shall be deemed to be an application by the applicant for leave to be so present, and the Clerk of Justiciary, on receiving the form, shall take the necessary steps for placing the application before the court.

(4A) An application by a convicted person for a determination by the High Court of a decision of a judge acting under section 103(5)(c) of this Act to refuse to admit him to bail shall be intimated by him immediately and in writing to the Crown Agent.

(5) If the application to be present is refused by the court, the Clerk of Justiciary shall notify the applicant; and if the application is granted, he shall notify the applicant and the Governor of the prison where the applicant is in custody and the Secretary of State.

(6) For the purpose of constituting a Court of Appeal, the judge who has refused any application may sit as a member of the court, and take part in determining the application.

AMENDMENTS

Subs.(4A) inserted by Criminal Justice (Scotland) Act 2003 (asp 7) Pt 8 s.66. Brought into force on 27 June 2003 by SSI 2003/288 (C.14).

Subs.(3A) inserted by Criminal Justice (Scotland) Act 2016 (asp 1) s.90(1). Brought into force on 17 January 2017 by SSI 2016/426 art.2 and Sch.1 para.1.

DEFINITIONS

A4-235.1 "clerk of justiciary": s.307(1).
"High Court": s.307(1).
"judge": s.307(1).

[THE NEXT PARAGRAPH IS A4-236]

GENERAL NOTE

Under s.103(5) the quorum is one judge in relation to the matters of extending the time within which intimation of intention to appeal and note of appeal may be given, of allowing the appellant to be present at any proceedings in cases where leave is necessary and to admit the appellant to bail. A4-236

Section 105 prescribes the procedure to appeal against a refusal of an application under s.103(5). Such an appeal (not being an appeal against sentence) requires to be heard by three judges. It is strange to see that for the purposes of constituting a Court of Appeal, the judge who has refused any application may sit as a member of the court, and take part in determining the application: s. 105(6).

Appeal against granting of application

105A.—(1) Where the prosecutor desires a determination by the High Court as mentioned in subsection (6A) of section 103 of this Act, he shall apply to the judge immediately after the power in subsection (5)(c) of that section is exercised in favour of the appellant. A4-236.1

(2) Where a judge acting under section 103(5)(c) of this Act has exercised that power in favour of the appellant but the prosecutor has made an application under subsection (1) above—

(a) the appellant shall not be liberated until the determination by the High Court; and

(b) that application by the prosecutor shall be heard not more than seven days after the making of the application,

and the Clerk of the Justiciary shall forward to the appellant the prescribed form for completion and return forthwith if he desires to be present at the hearing.

(3) At a hearing and determination as mentioned in subsection (2) above, if the appellant—

(a) is not legally represented, he may be present;

(b) is legally represented, he shall not be entitled to be present without leave of the court.

(4) If the appellant completes and returns the form mentioned in subsection (2) above indicating a desire to be present at the hearing, the form shall be deemed to be an application by the appellant for leave to be so present, and the Clerk of Justiciary, on receiving the form, shall take the necessary steps for placing the application before the court.

(5) If the application to be present is refused by the court, the Clerk of Justiciary shall notify the appellant; and if the application is granted, he shall notify the appellant and the Governor of the prison where the applicant is in custody and the Scottish Ministers.

(6) For the purposes of constituting a Court of Appeal, the judge who exercised the power in section 103(5)(c) of this Act in favour of the appellant may sit as a member of the court, and take part in determining the application of the prosecutor.

AMENDMENTS

Section 105A inserted by Criminal Justice (Scotland) Act 2003 (asp 7) Pt 8 s.66. Brought into force on 27 June 2003 by SSI 2003/288 (C.14).

[THE NEXT PARAGRAPH IS A4-237]

Right of appeal

106.—(1) Any person convicted on indictment may, with leave granted in accordance with section 107 of this Act, appeal in accordance with this Part of this Act, to the High Court— A4-237

(a) against such conviction;

(b) subject to subsection (2) below, against the sentence passed on such conviction;

(ba) against the making of an order for lifelong restriction;

(bb) against any decision not to exercise the power conferred by section 205A(3) or 205B(3) of this Act;
(c) against his absolute discharge or admonition;
(d) against any drug treatment and testing order;
(dza) against any disposal under section 227ZC(7)(a) to (c) or (e) or (8)(a) of this Act;
(da) against any decision to remit made under section 49(1)(a) of this Act;
(db) [...]
(dc) [...]
(e) against any order deferring sentence; or
(f) against
  (i) both such conviction and, subject to subsection (2) below, such sentence or disposal or order;
  (ii) [...]
  (iii) [...]

(2) There shall be no appeal against any sentence fixed by law.

(3) By an appeal under subsection (1) above a person may bring under review of the High Court any alleged miscarriage of justice, which may include such a miscarriage based on—
(a) subject to subsections (3A) to (3D) below, the existence and significance of evidence which was not heard at the original proceedings; and
(b) the jury's having returned a verdict which no reasonable jury, properly directed, could have returned.

(3A) Evidence such as is mentioned in subsection (3)(a) above may found an appeal only where there is a reasonable explanation of why it was not so heard.

(3B) Where the explanation referred to in subsection (3A) above or, as the case may be, (3C) below is that the evidence was not admissible at the time of the original proceedings, but is admissible at the time of the appeal, the court may admit that evidence if it appears to the court that it would be in the interests of justice to do so.

(3C) Without prejudice to subsection (3A) above, where evidence such as is mentioned in paragraph (a) of subsection (3) above is evidence—
(a) which is—
  (i) from a person; or
  (ii) of a statement (within the meaning of section 259(1) of this Act) by a person,

who gave evidence at the original proceedings; and
(b) which is different from, or additional to, the evidence so given,

it may not found an appeal unless there is a reasonable explanation as to why the evidence now sought to be adduced was not given by that person at those proceedings, which explanation is itself supported by independent evidence.

(3D) For the purposes of subsection (3C) above, "independent evidence" means evidence which—
(a) was not heard at the original proceedings;
(b) is from a source independent of the person referred to in subsection (3C) above; and
(c) is accepted by the court as being credible and reliable.

(4) Any document, production or other thing lodged in connection with the proceedings on the trial of any person who, if convicted, is entitled or may be authorised to appeal under this Part of this Act, shall, in accordance with subsections (5) to (9) below, be kept in the custody of the court in which the conviction took place.

(5) All documents and other productions produced at the trial of a convicted person shall be kept in the custody of the court of trial in such manner as it may direct until any period allowed under or by virtue of this Part of this Act for lodging intimation of intention to appeal has elapsed.

(6) Where no direction is given as mentioned in subsection (5) above, such custody shall be in the hands of the sheriff clerk of the district of the court of the second diet to whom the clerk of court shall hand them over at the close of the trial, unless otherwise ordered by the High Court on an intimation of intention to appeal being lodged, and if within such period there has been such lodgement under this Part of this Act, they shall be so kept until the appeal, if it is proceeded with, is determined.

(7) Notwithstanding subsections (5) and (6) above, the judge of the court in which the conviction took place may, on cause shown, grant an order authorising any of such documents or productions to be released on such conditions as to custody and return as he may deem it proper to prescribe.

(8) All such documents or other productions so retained in custody or released and returned shall, under supervision of the custodian thereof, be made available for inspection and for the purpose of making copies of documents or productions to a person who has lodged an intimation of intention to appeal or as the case may be, to the convicted person's counsel or agent, and to the Crown Agent and the procurator fiscal or his deputes.

(9) Where no intimation of intention to appeal is lodged within the period mentioned in subsection (6) above, all such documents and productions shall be dealt with as they are dealt with according to the existing law and practice at the conclusion of a trial; and they shall be so dealt with if, there having been such intimation, the appeal is not proceeded with.

AMENDMENTS

Subs.(3) as amended by Crime and Punishment (Scotland) Act 1997 (c.48) s.17 with effect from August 1, 1997 in terms of SI 1997/1712 art.3.

Subs.(1)(bb) inserted by Crime and Punishment (Scotland) Act 1997 (c.48) s.18 with effect from October 20, 1997 in terms of SI 1997/2323 art.3, Sch.1; amended by Crime and Disorder Act 1998 (c.37) Sch.8 para.119 (effective September 30, 1998: SI 1998/2327).

Subs.(1)(da) inserted by Crime and Punishment (Scotland) Act 1997 (c.48) s.23 with effect from August 1, 1997 in terms of SI 1997/1712 art.3.

Subs.(1)(d) as amended by Crime and Disorder Act 1998 (c.37) s.94 and Sch.6 para.5. Brought into force on September 30, 1998 by SI 1998/2327 (C.53).

Subs.(1)(db)(dc) and (f)(ii)(iii) inserted, and subs.(1)(f) as amended, by Protection of Children (Scotland) Act 2003 (asp 5) s.16(2). Brought into force on January 10, 2005 by SSI 2004/522 (C.38) art.2.

Subs.(1)(ba) inserted by Criminal Justice (Scotland) Act 2003 Sch.1 para.2(4). Brought into force on June 19, 2006 by SSI 2006/332 (C.30) art.2(1), subject to art.2(2).

Subs.(1)(d) as amended, and subs.(dza) inserted, by Criminal Justice and Licensing (Scotland) Act 2010 (asp 13) Sch.2 para.7. Brought into force on December 13, 2010 (subject to savings provisions in art.3) by SSI 2010/413 (C.28) art.2, Sch.1 para.1.

Subss.(1)(db), (1)(dc), and (1)(f)(ii), (iii) repealed by Protection of Vulnerable Groups (Scotland) Act 2007 (asp 14) Sch.4 para.14. Brought into force on February 28, 2011 by SSI 2011/157 (C.13) art.2, subject to savings specified in art.5(1).

DEFINITIONS

"community service order": s.238. A4-237.1
"High Court": s.307(1).
"indictment": s.307(1).
"judge": s.307(1).
"probation order": s.228.
"procurator fiscal": s.307(1).
"sentence": s.307(1).
"sheriff court": s.307(1).

[THE NEXT PARAGRAPH IS A4-238]

GENERAL NOTE

A4-238 An appeal under s.106 must be "with leave granted in accordance with s.107 of this Act". Reference may be made to that section and the General Note to it for a full understanding of this hurdle to be cleared.

Assuming that leave has been granted, an appeal against conviction alone is possible under s.106(1)(a) and against both conviction and sentence disposal or other order under s.106(1)(f). The hearing of these appeals will be by three judges: s.103(2). Further assuming that leave has been granted, an appeal against sentence and other similar disposals is possible under s.106(1)(b) to (e) inclusive. The hearing of these appeals will be by two judges: s.103(2).

Subs.(1)

From October 20, 1997, a convicted person can also appeal against a decision to impose a minimum sentence for drug trafficking. From August 1, 1997 a convicted person can appeal against any decision by the court to remit to the Principal Reporter in terms of s.49(1)(a) to arrange for disposal by a Children's Hearing.

In *George v HM Advocate*, 2012 S.C.L. 54, the appeal court faced the potentially embarrassing argument that the convicted offender was entitled to a reduction in sentence because of an unreasonable delay at avizandum following the hearing of his appeal against conviction. The appellant had been convicted in April 2006 of 18 charges relating to the abuse of children at a residential school where he was a teacher and he was sentenced to 10 years' imprisonment. In March 2007 he lodged a note of appeal against conviction and was granted interim liberation. The appeal procedure was protracted, with numerous procedural hearings, and the appeal was not heard until July 2010. The hearing, which involved the giving of evidence, took two weeks and the judgment ran to 100 pages. The appeal against conviction was refused and the appellant then appealed against the sentence on the ground that the nine months it took for the appeal court to deliver its decision was excessive. It was suggested that three months would have been enough. The court did not agree that three months would have been sufficient, especially because the appeal hearing finished on the last day of term and members of the court were then immediately on vacation. The court did agree that nine months exceeded what would have been reasonable and held, accordingly, that there had been an infringement of art.6 ECHR. However, the court considered that the mere acknowledgement of that infringement constituted sufficient just satisfaction. It had taken more than four years for the appellant to prepare his appeal and during that whole period he had been at liberty. The sentence reflected the gravity of the offence and the need to protect the public and deter others. The appeal was refused.

Subs.(2)

There is no appeal against any sentence fixed by law. The clearest example of this is the sentence of imprisonment for life for murder: s.205(1). A minimum recommendation can be appealed: see s.205(6).

Subs.(3)

A4-238.1 In *Harper v HM Advocate*, 2005 S.C.C.R. 245 Lord Osborne, giving the decision of the court, stressed that before the Appeal Court can disturb a conviction, a miscarriage of justice must be identified and that "it has never been recognised by the court that some general concern, or unease, could be a basis upon which a conviction could be disturbed". In context, what this means is that it must be possible to identify and articulate some particular miscarriage of justice. The point was reiterated by the Lord Justice General (Hamilton) in *Mitchell v HM Advocate*, 2008 S.C.C.R. 469 at 548 (para.185). This is not to say, however, that the concept is a narrow one. In *Drummond v HM Advocate*, 2003 S.L.T. 295 the court held that the phrase "miscarriage of justice" must on occasion be given a somewhat extended meaning, and must cover all the various situations which, in the past, under summary procedure were viewed in terms of incompetency and/or oppression, including excess of jurisdiction, where the diet is not properly constituted and where the verdict is one which is not open on the indictment.

In *McInnes v HM Advocate*, 2010 S.C.C.R. 286, Lord Hope of Craighead (in the Supreme Court) distinguished the so-called threshold and consequences tests. He said (paras 19 and 20):

> "Two questions arise in a case of this kind to which a test must be applied. The tests in each case are different, and they must be considered and applied separately. The first question is whether the material which has been withheld from the defence was material which ought to have been disclosed. The test here is whether the material might have materially weakened the Crown case or materially strengthened the case for the defence … The Lord Advocate's failure to disclose material that satisfies this test is incompatible with the accused's article 6 Convention rights. In the case of police statements, the position is clear. Applying the materiality test, all police statements of any witnesses on the Crown list must be disclosed to the defence before the trial …
>
> "The second question is directed to the consequences of the violation. This is the question that arises at the stage of an appeal when consideration is given to the appropriate remedy: see *Spiers v Ruddy*. In that case it was the reasonable time guarantee that was in issue, but I think that the ratio of that case applies generally. As Lord Bingham of Cornhill put it in paragraph 17, the Lord Advocate does not act incompatibly with a person's Convention right by continuing to prosecute after the breach has occurred. A trial is not to be taken to have been unfair just because of the non-disclosure. The significance and consequences of the non-disclosure must be assessed. The ques-

tion at the stage of an appeal is whether, given that there was a failure to disclose and having regard to what actually happened at the trial, the trial was nevertheless fair and, as Lady Cosgrove said in *Kelly v HM Advocate*, paragraph 35, as a consequence there was no miscarriage of justice ... The test that should be applied is whether, taking all the circumstances of the trial into account, there is a real possibility that the jury would have arrived at a different verdict."

The test which the court should apply in determining whether to quash a conviction or to substitute an amended verdict was considered in *Smith v HM Advocate*, 2001 S.L.T. 438. The court held where the Crown accept that a jury's verdict must be set aside but contend that, on the correct factual basis, the court should substitute a different verdict of guilty, the onus of satisfying the court that it should do so must rest on the Crown. When deciding whether to substitute an amended verdict of guilty the Appeal Court should consider what a reasonable jury, properly instructed, would have done. See also *Murray v HM Advocate*, 2001 S.L.T. 435.

For an example of a misdirection which did not constitute a miscarriage of justice, see *Blyth v HM Advocate*, 2006 J.C. 64. In *Gonshaw v Bamber*, 2004 S.L.T. 1270, there was a miscarriage of justice where a no case to answer submission was wrongly repelled and the accused, in giving evidence after he should have been acquitted, supplied the deficiency in the Crown case.

Where a question of miscarriage of justice is raised in connection with a very old case—as may happen on a review from the Scottish Criminal Cases Review Commission—*Coughbrough's Executrix v HM Advocate*, 2010 S.C.C.R. 473 may be helpful. In that case, the court followed the approach of Lord Woolf CJ in *R. v Hanratty* [2002] 2 Cr. App. R. 30, where it was held that current standards are to be applied in judging the fairness of a trial, whenever that trial took place, but that non compliance with rules which were not current at the time of the trial may need to be treated differently from non compliance with rules which were in force at that time.

In *Gordon v HM Advocate*, 2010 S.C.C.R. 589 the appeal court observed that the fact that the appellant did not give evidence at the trial may be a factor to be borne in mind at the appellate stage in determining whether a miscarriage of justice has occurred. The court also observed that if a party who is aware of facts, such as deficiencies in the police investigation, which he regards as oppressive or unfair under art.6 of the European Convention on Human Rights, elects not to tender a plea in bar of trial or does not move the court to desert the diet if it appears during a trial that the deficiencies have deprived him of a fair trial, it ought to be regarded as at least difficult for him to maintain later that a miscarriage of justice has occurred because of circumstances which could have been focused on at first instance.

Since the test is miscarriage of justice, it follows that defective representation can be a ground of appeal—see *Anderson v HM Advocate*, 1996 J.C. 29. In *Woodside v HM Advocate* [2009] HCJAC 19, the Lord Justice Clerk restated the test. It is, he said, "not a performance appraisal in which the court decides whether this question or that should or should not have been put; or whether this line of defence or that should or should not have been pursued. The appellant must demonstrate that there was a complete failure to present his defence either because his counsel or solicitor advocate disregarded his instructions or because he conducted the defence as no competent practitioner could reasonably have conducted it". That, the Lord Justice Clerk said, "is a narrow question of precise and limited scope". The court in *Woodside* also stressed the necessity for practitioners to co-operate promptly and properly when the High Court asks for information in connection with an *Anderson* appeal arising out of a defence which they conducted. In *JB v HM Advocate* 2009 S.L.T. 284, the court recalled that passages in *Anderson* stress the importance of the client's instructions and noted similar passages in other cases. In that case, counsel had formed the view that insisting, in his speech to the jury, upon the accused's position that the complainers were lying was likely to do more harm than good and so he suggested to the jury that the complainers might be honest but mistaken. The court recalled that, in *Anderson*, the Lord Justice General said that counsel must not conduct a defence "in a way which is contrary to the instructions he has received as to the basic nature of it" and took the view that departing from the instructions given by the appellant in *JB* had deprived him of a fair trial. The conviction was quashed.

Subs. 3(a)

In *Al Megrahi v HM Advocate*, 2002 J.C. 99, the Lord Justice General (Cullen) delivered what was to be described in *Coughbrough v HM Advocate*, 2008 S.C.C.R. 317 as "the most authoritative and recent elaboration of the approach to be followed in cases involving fresh evidence", as follows (at para.219):

"1. The court may allow an appeal against conviction on any ground only if it is satisfied that there has been a miscarriage of justice.
2. In an appeal based on the existence and significance of additional evidence not heard at the trial, the court will quash the conviction if it is satisfied that the original jury, if it had heard the new evidence, would have been bound to acquit.
3. Where the court cannot be satisfied that the jury would have been bound to acquit, it may nevertheless be satisfied that a miscarriage of justice has occurred.
4. Since setting aside the verdict of a jury is no light matter, before the court can hold that there has been a miscarriage of justice it will require to be satisfied that the additional evidence is not merely relevant but also of such significance that it will be reasonable to conclude that the verdict of the jury, reached in ignorance of its existence, must be regarded as a miscarriage of justice.
5. The decision on the issue of the significance of the additional evidence is for the appeal court, which will require to be satisfied that it is important and of such a kind and quality

> that it was likely that a reasonable jury properly directed would have found it of material assistance in its consideration of a critical issue at the trial.
>
> 6. The appeal court will therefore require to be persuaded that the additional evidence is (a) capable of being regarded as credible and reliable by a reasonable jury, and (b) likely to have had a material bearing on, or a material part to play in, the determination by such a jury of a critical issue at the trial."

Further explanation, consistent with this, was given by the Lord Justice Clerk (Gill) in delivering the opinion of the Appeal Court in *Fraser v HM Advocate*, 2008 S.C.C.R. 407 at 437–438 (paras 131–133):

> "Sections 106(3) and 106(3A) of the 1995 Act regulate fresh evidence appeals in the context of the single ground of appeal that the 1995 Act allows, namely miscarriage of justice. Before new evidence can be considered by the court, the appellant must furnish a reasonable explanation why it was not heard at the trial. Unless there is a reasonable explanation, the appeal cannot succeed, no matter how significant the proposed new evidence may be.
>
> If the appellant provides such an explanation, the onus being on him, the court must consider whether the new evidence would have been capable of being regarded by a reasonable jury as credible and reliable. If the court is so satisfied, it must next consider the cogency of the new evidence. The new evidence must be important evidence of such a kind and quality that it was likely to have been found by a reasonable jury, under proper directions, to have been of material assistance in their consideration of a critical issue that emerged at the trial.
>
> At that stage the appeal can succeed only if the court is satisfied that if the jury had heard the new evidence, they would have been bound to acquit; or that the new evidence is of such significance that it is reasonable to conclude that the verdict of the jury, reached in ignorance of its existence, must be regarded as a miscarriage of justice. Since there is a danger that fresh evidence may assume greater strength than it would have had if it had been led at the trial, it is essential that this court should assess it in the context of the whole evidence led at the trial." (Citations of authority omitted from the quotation).

Subs. 3(b)

A4-238.2 Section 2(1) of the Criminal Appeal (Scotland) Act 1926 (c.15) provided inter alia that a verdict of a jury could be set aside on the grounds that it was unreasonable or could not be supported by the evidence, but the proviso to the section required a "substantial miscarriage of justice" before an appeal would be allowed (see *Webb v HM Advocate*, 1927 J.C. 92). The test of unreasonableness was as set out in the current provision namely a verdict which no reasonable jury properly directed could have returned (see *Slater v HM Advocate*, 1928 J.C. 94). In *Macmillan v HM Advocate*, 1927 J.C. 62 and *Webb*, above, the court stated that the Appeal Court was not a court of review and it could not upset a verdict because it disagreed with a jury's view of evidence or credibility of witnesses. There had to be circumstances of a special character before the court would set aside a jury's verdict.

Post 1980 legislation did not contain provision for review of unreasonable verdicts provoking concern about verdicts considered to be unsafe.

The Sutherland Committee recognised that the test to be applied in the current legislation is very similar to the test applied by the Appeal Court under the 1926 legislation. They envisaged that an appeal based on this subsection would succeed only in exceptional cases. They expected however "a broader recognition of the potential for such cases" than with the 1926 Act. Subs.3(b) was considered by the Appeal Court in *King v HM Advocate*, 1999 S.C.C.R. 330. It was held that the Appeal Court could quash the verdict of a jury only if satisfied that, on the evidence led at the trial, no reasonable jury could have been satisfied beyond a reasonable doubt that the accused was guilty. (The court observed that this formulation was not dissimilar to that in *Webb* but gave no indication whether in future cases it would be as strictly interpreted.) At p.333E to F the Lord Justice General stated "the test is objective; the court must be able to say that no reasonable jury *could* have returned a guilty verdict on the evidence before them. Since in any case where the provision is invoked the jury will ex hypothesi have returned a guilty verdict, their verdict will have implied they were satisfied beyond a reasonable doubt that the Appellant was guilty. What the appellant must establish therefore is that, on the evidence led at the trial, no reasonable jury could have been satisfied beyond a reasonable doubt that the appellant was guilty." The Appeal Court will not simply substitute their view of the evidence for the jury's view. There will not be a miscarriage of justice simply because the Appeal Court might have entertained a reasonable doubt on the evidence. In determining such cases the Appeal Court will have regard to the fact that the jury had the advantage of seeing and hearing the evidence. In *King* four witnesses led by the Crown contradicted the Crown case in that they claimed to have seen the deceased alive and well some three hours after the murder allegedly occurred. The Appeal Court held that the jury would have been entitled to accept or reject the evidence of the four witnesses and it could not be said that no reasonable jury could have been satisfied beyond a reasonable doubt that the appellant was guilty and appeal refused; see also *McAllan v HM Advocate*, 1999 G.W.D. 18-826 and *Donnelly v HM Advocate*, 2000 S.C.C.R. 861.

A verdict cannot be attacked under this provision on the basis of "fresh evidence" as the attack must be based on evidence actually before the jury: see *Campbell and Steele v HM Advocate*, above. Otherwise an appellant would be able to circumvent subss.(3A) to (3D).

Subs. (3)(b)

The test for an appeal on this ground was explained in the Opinion of the Appeal Court, delivered by the Lord Justice General, in *Mitchell v HM Advocate*, 2008 S.C.C.R. 469 at 521 (para.111): "Although in consideration of such a ground of appeal it may be necessary to consider individual items of evidence, it is important to notice that it is the verdict, that is, the conclusion on the whole evidence, which must be considered. Moreover the ground is only made out if no reasonable jury, properly directed, *could* have returned the verdict in question … The test is objective … This court is not entitled to quash the verdict of the jury merely because, on the basis of the record of the evidence, it would have reached a different view from that which the jury plainly reached …" (emphasis in original).

Subs. (3A)

Additional evidence required to be evidence which was not available and could not have reasonably been made available at the trial. The test was an exacting one and had to be fully satisfied see *Carr v Lees*, 1993 S.C.C.R. 316 and *Tolmie v HM Advocate*, 1997 G.W.D. 26-1312. The reasonable availability test has now gone and all that is required is that a "reasonable explanation" be provided as to why the evidence was not heard at the original proceedings see subs.(3 A). **A4-238.3**

"Reasonable explanation". The Sutherland Committee recommended no attempt be made to qualify or interpret the term and that it be a matter for the court to decide. They did consider that the comments of Lord Justice-Clerk Thomson in *Gallacher v HM Advocate*, 1951 J.C. 38 regarding an adequate explanation for a failure to produce fresh evidence at a trial were relevant. His Lordship stated:

> "No general rule can possibly be laid down and the explanation in any particular case must be viewed, not in the light of any technicality or rule of practice or procedure but solely in the light of the dominating consideration that we may order new evidence if we think it necessary or expedient in the interests of justice."

The Appeal Court in *Campbell and Steele v HM Advocate*, above, considered that although the words "necessary or expedient in the interests of justice", which were used by the Lord Justice-Clerk in reference to s.6 of the 1926 Act, were not included in subs.(3A) in determining whether the terms of that subsection were satisfied the court should have regard to the interests of justice according to the circumstances of the particular case. As the Lord Justice-Clerk states "the underlying intention of the new legislation is that the court should take a broad and flexible approach in taking account of the circumstances of the particular case".

A "reasonable explanation" Lord Sutherland defined as an "explanation which, in the circumstances of the particular case is one which the court is persuaded to regard as some justification for the failure to lead the evidence bearing in mind the context that what is being enquired into is an alleged miscarriage of justice which in turn involves the concept of the interests of justice as a whole".

Lord McCluskey considered that "where an appellant is able to tender an explanation which cannot be shown without enquiry to be untrue and which is one that the court can objectively regard as plausible, sufficient and not unreasonable" the Appeal Court would then ask if it was necessary or expedient in the interests of justice to hear the evidence. The L.J.C. stated that the explanation must be adequate to account for the fact that a witness evidence was not heard.

It is for the appellant to satisfy the test of reasonable explanation in subs.(3A) and reasonable explanation will be interpreted in an objective way. The Court must be persuaded to treat the explanation as genuine rather than as true as the latter would require what Lord McCluskey describes as "preliminary proof as to the truth or otherwise of the explanation" and hence "depart dramatically from the relatively simple approach which the Sutherland Committee recommended, the Government expressly accepted and which Parliament approved and enacted".

The L.J.C. and Lord Sutherland agreed with the English Court of Appeal in *R. v Shields and Patrick* [1977] Crim.L.R. 281 that a decision not to call a witness whose evidence was viewed as dangerous would seldom be a reasonable explanation. Their Lordships considered that a tactical decision not to call a witness could not provide a reasonable explanation nor could an appellant being unaware of the existence of a witness or if aware, not aware he was able or willing to give evidence of any significance. The Lord Justice-Clerk did however go on to state that if the appellant could show that at the time of the trial he had no good reason for thinking that the witness existed or as the case might be that he would give the evidence in question then this might amount to a reasonable explanation. It "might depend on the steps which the appellant could reasonably be expected to have taken in the light of what was known at the time". Failure by defence solicitors to precognosce a witness on the Crown list could not, according to Lord Sutherland, amount to a reasonable explanation.

In the English case of *R. v Beresford* (1971) 56 Cr.App.R. 143 the court confirmed that in order to satisfy the reasonable explanation requirement "the court has in general to be satisfied that the evidence could not with reasonable diligence have been obtained for use at the trial".

In *Hall v HM Advocate*, 1998 S.C.C.R. 525 the Appeal Court accepted that a reasonable explanation existed in respect of a witness who had not been on the Crown list of witnesses, who had given two statements to the police making no mention of the evidence he was now giving and who at the time he was interviewed by the police was anxious to conceal his presence near to the locus. The appellant argued that given the witness' position at the time of the trial the defence could not, in the exercise of reasonable diligence, have been aware of the significance of the witness. The Appeal Court also agreed to hear the evidence of a witness who was on the list of Crown witnesses but who was not called at the trial diet. Her evidence had become significant in the light of the first witness whose evidence was to be heard. Her significance, it was argued, could not have been discovered by the defence at the time. The Appeal Court stressed that even if there is a reasonable explanation provided the evidence will only be heard if it is "significant evidence" in the light of the test set out in *Cameron v HM Advocate*, 1987 S.C.C.R. 608 at 619.

The Appeal Court in *Hall v HM Advocate*, above observed that adequate specification should be given in the grounds of appeal of what is proposed to be adduced as additional evidence and what is merely a change in the evidence.

In *Hall v HM Advocate (No. 2)*, 1999 S.C.C.R. 130, in quashing the conviction, it was held that the terms of subs.(3A) suggest that the reasonable explanation question should be looked at from the point of view of those who represented the appellant at the time of the trial, which includes the period when the defence was being prepared and that if it was shown that despite reasonable steps having been taken to investigate the case, it did not appear that a person would provide information which would be of assistance, whether by way of challenging the Crown case or advancing the case for the defence, there could be a reasonable explanation of why the witness was not adduced at the trial. In attempting to satisfy the subs.(3A) requirements it is important that the appellant should be able to point to information as to what was known to those who represented the appellant at the time and what steps they took to investigate the defence. Information should also be provided regarding any reason or reasons for thinking no further enquiries were necessary, if appropriate—*Barr v HM Advocate*, 1999 S.C.C.R. 13.

In *Mills v HM Advocate*, 1999 S.C.C.R. 202 it was held that the decision not to call an incriminee as a witness at a trial precluded his evidence and evidence of alleged confessions made by him being led in terms of s. 106(3) at the stage of an appeal as the test in subs.(3A) had not been satisfied. The Crown conceded in that case that the fact that a co-accused did not give evidence and could not be compelled to give evidence amounted to a reasonable explanation. The court, however reserved their opinion regarding this concession. They did suggest that in such circumstances a motion for separation of trials would have been appropriate. As Sheriff Gordon notes in his commentary on this case if such a motion was refused it could be argued that the test in subs.(3A) had been satisfied.

In *Karling v HM Advocate*, 1999 S.C.C.R. 359 the Appeal Court observed that a reasonable explanation why evidence was not led from one witness does not necessarily apply to another witness. If a reasonable explanation is advanced regarding part of a witness' evidence it does not necessarily apply to the whole of their evidence. In that case a reasonable explanation for not seeking further expert opinion was held to have been made out where a defence expert provided advice to the appellant's solicitors confirming the Crown evidence as to one possible cause of death. The Court rejected this explanation regarding another possible cause of death which had been raised at the trial. If the existence of a witness is not known this may amount to a reasonable explanation *Fraser v HM Advocate*, 2000 S.C.C.R. 755. However, a deliberate decision by the appellant to advance a completely false defence at trial did not do so in *Lyon v HM Advocate*, 2003 S.C.C.R. 692. In *McIntyre v HM Advocate*, 2005 S.C.C.R. 380, it was held that a tactical decision made at trial not to lead certain evidence could not afford a reasonable explanation such as to allow fresh evidence to be considered on appeal.

Subs. (3B)

In *Conway v HM Advocate*, 1996 S.C.C.R. 570 the accused was unable to benefit from a change in the hearsay provisions where his trial had been concluded prior to a change in the rules, the court holding that the evidence must have been admissible at the original trial. Under the new provision the law current at the date of the hearing of the appeal would apply.

Subs. (3C)

Mitchell v HM Advocate, 1989 S.C.C.R. 502 and *Brodie v HM Advocate*, 1993 S.C.C.R. 371 established that the Appeal Court will not entertain an appeal on the basis that a witness who has given evidence at the trial wishes to change his story. The Sutherland Committee recommended that this be changed but added the proviso that the reason for the change of testimony be supported by additional credible and reliable evidence. The Government originally rejected this proposal but at the committee stage in the House of Lords introduced the present provision. The section relates not only to oral evidence from a person but also a statement under the exceptions to the hearsay provisions in terms of s.259. The evidence sought to be adduced can be different or additional. A reasonable explanation must be provided as to why the evidence sought to be led was not given by that person at the trial. The section also provides for a check in the form of "independent evidence" which is defined in subs.(3D) to support the reasonable explanation.

The main ground of appeal in *Campbell and Steele v HM Advocate*, above, was the changing of the evidence of a material witness. The Lord Justice Clerk and Lord Sutherland considered that in such appeals the words "without prejudice to subs.(3A)" meant that the first hurdle to be overcome was that a reasonable explanation had to be provided by the appellant as to why the evidence was not heard and thereafter a reasonable explanation would be required from the witness as to why the evidence was not given.

Lord McCluskey in his opinion however dissented from the two reasonable explanations requirement. As His Lordship points out there are cases where a witness cannot or will not provide an explanation hence the reference to the hearsay provisions in s.259. Parliament's intention was not to so prejudice an appellant.

Reasonable explanation in this subsection is as defined for subs.(3A).

In *Hall v HM Advocate*, above, the appellant sought to argue that a transcript of a police interview (post conviction) with a witness who gave evidence at the trial was a statement that fell within s.106(3C)(a)(ii), namely evidence different or additional to that given at the trial. As the requirements of s.259(2) had not been satisfied the attempt to rely on subs.(3C)(a)(ii) foundered. The appellant then sought to rely on subs.(3C)(a)(i) namely that it was evidence from a person different or additional to the evidence given at the trial. The reasonable explanation for not giving this evidence at the trial was said to be that the witness was a fantasist or untruthful. Independent evidence was said to come from other false allegations made. The Appeal Court held that the reasonable explanation test was not satisfied. No explanation had been provided by the witness. The Appeal Court considered it unnecessary to express a concluded view on whether the reasonable explanation should come from the witness himself. The Court also held that there was no independent evidence to support the explanation. See also *McLay v HM Advocate*, 2000 S.C.C.R. 579.

Subs. (3D)

The independent evidence must satisfy three requirements. In respect of part (a) it is the evidence which requires not to have been heard, not the witness and therefore if a witness is called to give evidence at a trial diet but not asked about a particular matter then the provision would be satisfied—or as in the case of *Cameron v HM Advocate*, 1994 S.C.C.R. 502 a witness could state that they were not prepared to give evidence to that effect at the trial. The Sutherland Committee considered that the additional supporting evidence could be evidence which was heard at the trial but clearly given the terms of part (a) this could not be the case. **A4-238.4**

Part (b) provides that the evidence must be independent of the person who is changing his story. This was discussed in some detail at the committee stage in the House of Lords (see *Hansard*, H.L. 10 March 1997 cols 37–39). The Lord Advocate explained that independent evidence could derive from a relative or colleague, more importantly however, the independent evidence should relate to the reason why the new evidence was not given at the earlier trial and should not relate to the particulars of the new account. This would cover the situation in *McCormack* above where an accused was suffering from amnesia (see the comments of Hope LJ and the Lord Advocate in *Hansard*, H.L. 10 March 1997 col.39) and the independent evidence could be from a doctor that the accused was suffering from this condition. If however the reasonable explanation is that the witness had been pressurised into withholding evidence it may be difficult to find independent evidence to support this.

In *Campbell and Steele v HM Advocate*, supra, the appellants sought to employ, as independent evidence inter alia the evidence of police officers of what Love said during interview post conviction of the two accused. The Appeal Court held that this could not be independent evidence as the evidence was of statements from the same source, i.e. Love.

Part (c) provides that the evidence must be credible and reliable.

It is for the Appeal Court to decide whether or not the evidence is credible and reliable.

Subss. (4)–(9)

The remaining subsections of s.106 are concerned with the custody of trial documents, productions and related matters. The emphasis in Scotland on real evidence means that there are or can be a substantial quantity of material to be kept safe for the possible consideration of the appellate judges or until such time as it seems reasonable to consider that there is not to be an appeal. In *Strock, Petr*, 1996 S.C.C.R. 432 the court indicated that the proviso in s.270(2) of the 1975 Act now s.106(7) can operate even though an appeal against conviction was pending. If the outstanding appeal relates to the person seeking release of productions conditions might have to be imposed as to custody and return of productions.

[THE NEXT PARAGRAPH IS A4-239]

Sentence

The foregoing note is directed principally to any alleged miscarriage of justice in relation to conviction but it is competent to bring under review of the High Court of Justiciary any alleged miscarriage of justice, including one which arises in relation to sentence on the basis of evidence not *heard at the original proceedings*: see *Renton and Brown* (5th edn) para.11–47, at p.208. At any rate in appeals against sentence the test is no longer (as before 1980) whether the sentence was harsh and oppressive but whether it was excessive: *Addison v Mackinnon*, 1983 S.C.C.R. 52; *Donaldson v HM Advocate*, 1983 S.C.C.R. 216. A bold statement that a sentence is excessive might reasonably be said to be lacking in specification. There must be an indication of the circumstances to be relied on. One important reason for that is to allow the trial judge or the sheriff to report fully upon them for the appellate judges, see Practice Note "*Appeals in Solemn Procedure and Appeals against Sentence in Summary Procedure*", 29 March 1985. For an example of an appeal against sentence on the basis of fresh evidence see *Baikie v HM Advocate*, 2000 S.C.C.R. 119. Medical reports obtained post sentence disclosed the appellant was suffering from an undiagnosed mental condition at the time of sentence. A hospital order was substituted. In *Gemmell v HM Advocate* [2011] HCJAC 129 at para.[81], the Lord Justice Clerk (Gill) said that "[w]here the sentencer has given cogent reasons either for allowing the discount in question [under s.196] or for declining to apply a discount at all, I consider that it is only in exceptional circumstances that this court should interfere". **A4-239**

Appeal against automatic sentences where earlier conviction quashed

A4-239.1 **[106A.**—(1) This subsection applies where—

(a) a person has been sentenced under section 205A(2) of this Act;

(b) he had, at the time at which the offence for which he was so sentenced was committed, only one previous conviction for a qualifying offence or a relevant offence within the meaning of that section; and

(c) after he has been so sentenced, the conviction mentioned in paragraph (b) above has been quashed.]

(2) This subsection applies where—

(a) a person has been sentenced under section 205B(2) of this Act;

(b) he had, at the time at which the offence for which he was so sentenced was committed, only two previous convictions for class A drug trafficking offences within the meaning of that section; and

(c) after he has been so sentenced, one of the convictions mentioned in paragraph (b) above has been quashed.

(3) Where subsection (1) or (2) above applies, the person may appeal under section 106(1)(b) of this Act against the sentence imposed on him under [section 205A(2) or, as the case may be], 205B(2) of this Act.

(4) An appeal under section 106(1)(b) of this Act by virtue of subsection (3) above—

(a) may be made notwithstanding that the person has previously appealed under that section; and

(b) shall be lodged within two weeks of the quashing of the conviction as mentioned in subsection (1)(c) or, as the case may be, (2)(c) above.

(5) Where an appeal is made under section 106(1)(b) by virtue of this section, the following provisions of this Act shall not apply in relation to such an appeal, namely—

(a) section 121; and

(b) section 126.

AMENDMENTS

Section 106A inserted by Crime and Punishment (Scotland) Act 1997 (c.48) s.19 with effect from October 20, 1997 in terms of SI 1997/2323 art.3, Sch.1.

Subs.(1) prospectively inserted by the above.

Subs.(3) inserted by the above and effective except in so far as it refers to s.205(A)(2) of the 1995 Act.

[THE NEXT PARAGRAPH IS A4-239.3]

GENERAL NOTE

A4-239.3 Where an earlier conviction which qualified an accused of a minimum sentence for drug trafficking is quashed by the Appeal Court, an accused who has received the minimum sentence may appeal. The appeal is in terms of s.106(1)(b) and must be made within two weeks of the conviction being quashed. A previous appeal against sentence does not preclude an appeal under this section.

Subs.(5) provides that suspension of disqualification etc. and the provisions relating to extract convictions shall not apply where there is an appeal under this section.

[THE NEXT PARAGRAPH IS A4-240]

Leave to appeal

A4-240 **107.**—(1) The decision whether to grant leave to appeal for the purposes of section 106(1) of this Act shall be made by a judge of the High Court who shall—

(a) if he considers that the documents mentioned in subsection (2) below disclose arguable grounds of appeal, grant leave to appeal and make such comments in writing as he considers appropriate; and

(b) in any other case—

(i) refuse leave to appeal and give reasons in writing for the refusal; and

(ii) where the appellant is on bail and the sentence imposed on his conviction is one of imprisonment, grant a warrant to apprehend and imprison him.

(2) The documents referred to in subsection (1) above are—

(a) the note of appeal lodged under section 110(1)(a) of this Act;

(b) in the case of an appeal against conviction or sentence in a sheriff court, the certified copy or, as the case may be, the record of the proceedings at the trial;

(c) where the judge who presided at the trial furnishes a report under section 113 of this Act, that report; and

(d) where, by virtue of section 94(1) of this Act, a transcript of the charge to the jury of the judge who presided at the trial is delivered to the Clerk of Justiciary, that transcript.

(2A) In respect of an appeal by virtue of section 11(7) of the Double Jeopardy (Scotland) Act 2011 (asp 16), the "report under section 113" in subsection (2)(c) means—

(a) the report of the judge who presided at the trial resulting in the appellant's acquittal for an offence mentioned in section 11(2) of that Act;

(b) where an appeal against conviction was taken before that acquittal, the report of the judge who presided at the trial resulting in the conviction in respect of which leave to appeal is sought prepared at that time; and

(c) any other report of that judge furnished under section 113.

(3) A warrant granted under subsection (1)(b)(ii) above shall not take effect until the expiry of the period of 14 days mentioned in subsection (4) below (and if that period is extended under subsection (4A) below before the period being extended expires, until the expiry of the period as so extended) without an application to the High Court for leave to appeal having been lodged by the appellant under that subsection.

(4) Where leave to appeal is refused under subsection (1) above the appellant may, within 14 days of intimation under subsection (10) below, apply to the High Court for leave to appeal.

(4A) The High Court may, on cause shown, extend the period of 14 days mentioned in subsection (4) above, or that period as extended under this subsection, whether or not the period to be extended has expired (and if that period of 14 days has expired, whether or not it expired before section 62 of the Criminal Justice (Scotland) Act 2003 (asp 7) came into force).

(5) In deciding an application under subsection (4) above the High Court shall—

(a) if, after considering the documents mentioned in subsection (2) above and the reasons for the refusal, the court is of the opinion that there are arguable grounds of appeal, grant leave to appeal and make such comments in writing as the court considers appropriate; and

(b) in any other case—

(i) refuse leave to appeal and give reasons in writing for the refusal; and

(ii) where the appellant is on bail and the sentence imposed on his conviction is one of imprisonment, grant a warrant to apprehend and imprison him.

(6) Consideration whether to grant leave to appeal under subsection (1) or (5) above shall take place in chambers without the parties being present.

(7) Comments in writing made under subsection (1)(a) or (5)(a) above may, without prejudice to the generality of that provision, specify the arguable grounds of appeal (whether or not they are contained in the note of appeal) on the basis of which leave to appeal is granted.

(8) Where the arguable grounds of appeal are specified by virtue of subsection (7) above it shall not, except by leave of the High Court on cause shown, be competent for the appellant to found any aspect of his appeal on any ground of appeal contained in the note of appeal but not so specified.

(9) Any application by the appellant for the leave of the High Court under subsection (8) above—

(a) shall be made within 14 days of the date of intimation under subsection (10) below; and

(b) shall, within 14 days of that date, be intimated by the appellant to the Crown Agent.

(9A) The High Court may, on cause shown, extend the periods of 14 days mentioned in subsection (9) above.

(10) The Clerk of Justiciary shall forthwith intimate—

(a) a decision under subsection (1) or (5) above; and

(b) in the case of a refusal of leave to appeal, the reasons for the decision,

to the appellant or his solicitor and to the Crown Agent.

AMENDMENTS

Subs.(4) inserted by Crime and Punishment (Scotland) Act 1997 (c.48) Sch.1 para.21(15) with effect from August 1, 1997 in terms of SI 1997/1712 art.3.

Subs.(3) as amended, and subs.(4A) inserted, by Criminal Justice (Scotland) Act 2003 (asp 7) Pt 8 s.62. Brought into force on June 27, 2003 by SSI 2003/288 (C.14).

Subs.(9) as amended and subs.(9A) inserted by Criminal Proceedings etc (Reform) (Scotland) Act 2007 (asp 6) s.80, Sch. para.16(1). Brought into force on April 23, 2007 by SSI 2007/250 (C.23) art.3.

Subs.(2A) inserted by Double Jeopardy (Scotland) Act 2011 (asp 16) Sch.1 para.8. Brought into force on November 28, 2011 by SSI 2011/365 (C.34) art.3.

DEFINITIONS

A4-240.1 "bail": s.307(1).
"High Court": s.307(1).
"judge": s.307(1).

[THE NEXT PARAGRAPH IS A4-241]

GENERAL NOTE

A4-241 It is probably more convenient in seeking to understand the full import of this section to consider the law under the headings of, on the one hand, leave to appeal and, on the other, application for leave to appeal. Separate consideration of the hearing must be made.

Leave to appeal

A4-242 Section 106 allows a right of appeal to any person convicted on indictment and such appeal may be against conviction or sentence or both. The right of appeal is conditional on a ground of leave to appeal by a judge of the High Court of Justiciary in terms of s.107. Before the judge can decide the grant he must have documents before him and these are specified as the note of appeal, the certified copy or actual record of proceedings for a sheriff court trial, a judge's report and a transcript of the charge to the jury by the judge, as necessary: subs.(2). Having considered these documents the judge must decide whether they disclose arguable grounds of appeal: subs.(1)(a). The action that follows such a decision depends on which way the decision goes. Before considering the alternatives the turning point requires analysis: what are "arguable grounds of appeal"?

To answer that question one might start with "High Court of Justiciary Practice Note" dated March 29, 1985 (*Renton and Brown* (6th edn) Appendix E, at p.729). There, judicial criticism is directed predominantly at grounds of appeal which are found in notes of appeal to be "wholly unspecific". The examples given in the Note are, first, an allegation of "misdirection" without any specification whatever. Secondly, "insufficient evidence" without any specification of the particular point, if any, which is to be taken. Examples are also given in relation to appeals against sentence where the ground of appeal is "more often than not equally uninformative" with a bare allegation of a sentence being excessive or severe.

The Practice Note indicated in terms that it was intended to remind practitioners that grounds of appeal must be stated with sufficient specification to identify the particular criticism of the conviction or sentence which the appellant hopes to present at the hearing.

It can readily be seen that appellate judges require detail in the grounds of appeal such as allows some insight as to the appellant's complaint. Detail alone may not take matters far: although the allegation of a miscarriage of justice is the only ground of appeal, there are various particular grounds of appeal, which are commonly advanced as a basis for the conclusion that there has been a miscarriage of justice.

Lord McCluskey in *Criminal Appeals* (1992) at pp.177–189 discusses some of the possible types or categories of appeal: it may be that there is alleged to have been a misdirection by the presiding judge (by omission, with an error of law, or regarding corroboration), that the conduct of the trial judge, the prosecutor or the defence advocate was improper, that the proceedings were incompetent or that there were some other irregularities. There are ample precedents for all these allegations. In short, "arguable grounds of appeal" are such to indicate, in Lord McCluskey's words, ibid. at p.177, "clarity, accuracy, brevity and comprehensiveness" and which invite a conclusion that there has been in law a miscarriage of justice.

The judge of the High Court of Justiciary who will consider the documents to decide whether they disclose arguable grounds of appeal does so in chambers without the parties being present: s.107(6). If the judge considers that the documents do disclose arguable grounds of appeal he then grants leave to appeal and he makes such comments in writing as he considers appropriate: s.107(1)(a). If the judge considers that the documents do not disclose arguable grounds of appeal he then refuses leave to appeal and he gives reasons in writing for the refusal: subs.(1)(b)(i).

The appellant, who is at this stage on bail and who had a sentence of imprisonment imposed on conviction, will then be the subject of a warrant to apprehend granted by the judge and on implementation the appellant will be imprisoned: subs.(1)(b)(ii).

The warrant to apprehend and imprison under subs.(1)(b)(ii) shall not take effect until the expiry of the period of 14 days during which period the appellant may, in effect, appeal by making an application to the High Court of Justiciary: subs.(4). If no such application is to be made then the appellant's solicitor has the time available to arrange for the client to surrender to the warrant.

Application for leave to appeal

There are no statutory grounds for the reason for, in effect, appealing the decision of the single judge in chambers. The provision merely states that if leave to appeal is refused under subs.(1) then the appellant may within 14 days of intimation apply to the High Court of Justiciary for leave to appeal against the original conviction or sentence or both: subs.(4). **A4-243**

Who decides the application in terms of subs.(4) depends on what is at issue, namely, on appeal against conviction, sentence or conviction and sentence. By s.103(2) "for the purpose of hearing and determining any appeal or other proceeding under this Part of this Act" the quorum is three judges, except that by s.103(3) for appeals against sentence alone the quorum is two judges.

The various judges of the High Court of Justiciary who must consider the documents to decide whether they disclose arguable grounds of appeal do so in chambers without the parties being present: subs.(6).

In deciding the application the judges must consider the documents that had been before the single judge in chambers and also consider the reasons for the earlier refusal but thereafter, if the court is of the opinion that there are arguable grounds of appeal, then the court should grant leave to appeal and make such comments in writing as the court considers appropriate: subs.(5)(a). In any other case, leave to appeal will be refused with reasons in writing and a warrant to apprehend and imprison is to be granted if appropriate: subs.(5)(b). In *McCluskey v HM Advocate* [2012] HCJAC 125, the Appeal Court commented that, where a sifting judge identifies arguable grounds of appeal not specified in the note of appeal, it would generally be appropriate to request a supplementary report from the trial or sentencing judge.

In *Connolly Petr*, 1997 S.L.T. 689 it was held that it was incompetent to invoke the *nobile officium* where an application in terms of s.107(4) was not lodged timeously.

Hearing of appeal

Regard must be paid to the comments in writing made either by the single judge in chambers by subs.(1)(a) or by a greater number of judges in chambers by subs.(5)(a). The importance of the comments in writing lies in the possibility that they "may specify the arguable grounds of appeal (whether or not they are contained in the note of appeal) on the basis of which leave to appeal is granted": subs.(7). **A4-244**

It is very easy to imagine on the wording of subs.(1)(a) a single judge in chambers granting leave to appeal, not on the original grounds in the note of appeal, but on the basis of comments in writing which amend, alter or distil the original grounds in the note of appeal. The new grounds of appeal, having been specified, in effect dictate the ground of appeal to be argued at the hearing: subs.(8).

The appellant who wishes to found any aspect of his appeal on any ground of appeal contained in the note of appeal but not so specified in the comments in writing provided under subs.(1)(a) or subs.(5)(a) may seek leave of the High Court of Justiciary to do so: subs.(8). Application for such leave under subs.(8) must be made not less than seven days before the date fixed for the hearing of the appeal: subs.(9). It is not immediately clear from a reading of the statute as to whom an application under subs.(8) will be directed. As it is not so much an appeal as a request to broaden an approach to an appeal it may simply be returned to those who made the comments in writing under subss.(1)(a) or (5)(a).

In *Milne v HM Advocate*, 1998 G.W.D. 17–848, the Appeal Court held that in determining the appeal it was irrelevant that the sifting judge considered the matter arguable.

Subs. (1)

A4-244.1 Where the sifting judge deems some, but not all, of the grounds of appeal to be arguable, that does not constitute a refusal of the other grounds, such as to entitle the accused to pursue an appeal to second sift in terms of subsection (4). Rather, his remedy his to seek the leave specified in subsection (8) (*Beggs, Petitioner*, 2005 1 J.C. 174).

Subs. (4)

Once application has been made for leave to appeal, the second sift can take place at any time and does not have to wait for the expiry of the 14 days (*Gary Strang, Petitioner*, 2006 J.C. 100). Accordingly, if the practice described in *Ryan, Petitioner*, 2002 S.L.T. 275, of applying for leave and having counsel submit further representations, is to be used, it needs to be made clear to the Justiciary Office that such representations are to follow.

Subs. (5)

Second sift judges are entitled to adopt the reasoning of the first sift judge without further elaboration (*Timothy McSorley, Petitioner, 2005 S.C.C.R. 508*).

Subs. (8)

The obtaining of leave under subs (8) involves satisfying the arguability test (*Donnell v HM Advocate*, 2005 S.C.C.R. 728). It also involves cause shown and in *Beggs v HM Advocate*, 2006 S.C.C.R. 25 the Lord Justice General explained that this means satisfying the court that there is a good reason why the appellant should be able to rely on a ground which has not been specified under subs.(7). What will be a good reason will depend on the circumstances of the case and examples of things which might suffice are given in the Lord Justice General's opinion.

Leave is not available in a case where appeal is taken against both conviction and sentence and the appeal against sentence fails both stages of the sift (*McLeod v HM Advocate*, 2006 J.C. 147).

In *Birnie v HM Advocate* [2015] HCJAC 54, counsel for the appellant wished to argue a ground of appeal which had been refused at both first and second sifts. It was contended that the decision at sift had been wrong. The court refused to allow that to be done. The Lord Justice Clerk (Carloway) said:

> "An application under section 107(8) of the 1995 Act to argue a ground, for which not only has leave not been granted but has actually been refused at sift, is not to be seen as a form of appeal against the decision taken at sift. The sift decision is final at that stage of the proceedings. It is not simply a matter of asking the court to reconsider the question of the arguability of the ground of appeal. The appellant must show that there is 'good reason' for reinstating the ground, such as some change in circumstances, or a patent error or misunderstanding of the grounds of appeal by the sifting judge or court, or, indeed, that the point is of such significance that it would not be in the interests of justice to exclude it."

Prosecutor's right of appeal: decisions on section 97 and 97A submissions

A4-244.2 **107A.**—(1) The prosecutor may appeal to the High Court against—

(a) an acquittal under section 97 or 97B(2)(a), or

(b) a direction under section 97B(2)(b) or 97C(2).

(2) If, immediately after an acquittal under section 97 or 97B(2)(a), the prosecutor moves for the trial diet to be adjourned for no more than 2 days in order to consider whether to appeal against the acquittal under subsection (1), the court of first instance must grant the motion unless the court considers that there are no arguable grounds of appeal.

(3) If, immediately after the giving of a direction under section 97B(2)(b) or 97C(2), the prosecutor moves for the trial diet to be adjourned for no more than 2 days in order to consider whether to appeal against the direction under subsection (1), the court of first instance must grant the motion unless the court considers that it would not be in the interests of justice to do so.

(4) In considering whether it would be in the interests of justice to grant a motion for adjournment under subsection (3), the court must have regard, amongst other things, to—

(a) whether, if an appeal were to be made and to be successful, continuing with the diet would have any impact on any subsequent or continued prosecution,

(b) whether there are any arguable grounds of appeal.

(5) An appeal may not be brought under subsection (1) unless the prosecutor intimates intention to appeal—

(a) immediately after the acquittal or, as the case may be, the giving of the direction,

(b) if a motion to adjourn the trial diet under subsection (2) or (3) is granted, immediately upon resumption of the diet, or

(c) if such a motion is refused, immediately after the refusal.

(6) Subsection (7) applies if—

(a) the prosecutor intimates an intention to appeal under subsection (1)(a), or

(b) the trial diet is adjourned under subsection (2).

(7) Where this subsection applies, the court of first instance must suspend the effect of the acquittal and may—

(a) make an order under section 4(2) of the Contempt of Court Act 1981 (c.49) (which gives a court power, in some circumstances, to order that publication of certain reports be postponed) as if proceedings for the offence of which the person was acquitted were pending or imminent,

(b) after giving the parties an opportunity of being heard, order the detention of the person in custody or admit him to bail.

(8) The court may, under subsection (7)(b), order the detention of the person in custody only if the court considers that there are arguable grounds of appeal.

AMENDMENTS

Section 107A inserted by Criminal Justice and Licensing (Scotland) Act 2010 (asp 13) s.74. Brought into force on March 28, 2011 (for all purposes in respect of any trial which commences on or after March 28, 2011, with a trial taken to have commenced in solemn proceedings when the oath is administered to the jury and in summary proceedings when the first witness is sworn) by SSI 2011/178 (C.15) art.2, Sch.1 para.1.

GENERAL NOTE

Refer to the general discussion in General Notes to ss.97 and 97A above. It will be noted that the instant section provides a route for an expedited form of Crown appeal during the currency of a trial, and that the Crown is entitled to move for an adjournment as of right for up to two days to permit consideration of whether or not to proceed with such an appeal. An appeal can be taken against the upholding of either a no case to answer or a common law submission and, although subs.(2) does not state it explicitly, its interaction with subss.(1)(a) and (7) has the effect of suspending an acquittal during the two day adjournment; presumably, on the resumption of the proceedings, the court has to affirm its decision if the Crown has not insisted upon its right of appeal. A Crown appeal may also be initiated against a decision to restrict the Crown's libel to a related offence and the necessary amendment of the libel by the court. Again, while it is perhaps a technical issue primarily and the section is silent on the subject, it is submitted that any amendment ordered by the court in light of opposed defence submissions must be suspended to await the outcome of the adjournment for consideration. **A4-244.3**

Grounds for refusal of Crown adjournment

Subs.(3) requires the court to grant a Crown motion to adjourn for consideration unless it is considered not to be in the interest of justice; as well as weighing the merits of the appeal itself, the court has the yet more problematic task of assessing the impact of a successful appeal on the immediate, or any subsequent, prosecution—a task made more complex still if there are other accused to be considered. Furthermore, while subs.(4) highlights two important factors the court must assess before refusing a Crown motion for adjournment, that is not exhaustive of the factors which might be taken into account by the court.

Other considerations

It has to be emphasised that the provisions of the section only take effect once the Crown makes a motion to adjourn for consideration. That motion has to be made immediately after court's decision under ss.97 or 97A and has the effect of suspending the accused's acquittal. At the same time, subs.(7) necessarily empowers the court to make an order under s.4(2) of the Contempt of Court Act 1981 (c.49) to order postponement of any media report. (No such order is necessary where the decision has been a direction to restrict the libel since, by definition, the proceedings remain active).

The final matter to be resolved by the court when acquitting the accused of the libel in accordance with subs.(1)(a) is whether the accused should be admitted to bail or be detained in custody. The test to be applied is whether the Crown has a stateable appeal (subss.(7) and (8)).

The section is silent upon how this appeal procedure will impact upon the trial of co-accused against whom a sufficiency of evidence has been established. It is submitted to be good practice, when the Crown returns to court resolved to maintain a s.107A appeal, that it be in a position to furnish all parties with the precise terms of the appeal grounds it seeks to place before the Appeal Court, and be able to provide the trial court with the date identified for the appeal to be heard by the Appeal Court. Lack of this information will assuredly disrupt parties' preparations and impact adversely upon the flow of business in both the trial and appellate court.

HM Advocate v Mason [2015] HCJAC 1; 2015 S.L.T. 41 is an instance of the speed of expedited procedure, following a successful no case to answer submission and criticism of the trial judge transgressing into the province of the jury by applying a qualitative, rather than a quantitative, test to the evidence.

Prosecutor's right of appeal: decisions on admissibility of evidence

A4-244.4 **107B.**—(1) The prosecutor may appeal to the High Court against a finding, made after the jury is empanelled and before the close of the evidence for the prosecution, that evidence that the prosecution seeks to lead is inadmissible.

(2) The appeal may be made only with the leave of the court of first instance, granted—

(a) on the motion of the prosecutor, or

(b) on that court's initiative.

(3) Any motion for leave to appeal must be made before the close of the case for the prosecution.

(4) In determining whether to grant leave to appeal the court must consider—

(a) whether there are arguable grounds of appeal, and

(b) what effect the finding has on the strength of the prosecutor's case.

AMENDMENTS

Section 107B inserted by Criminal Justice and Licensing (Scotland) Act 2010 (asp 13) s.74. Brought into force on March 28, 2011 (for all purposes in respect of any trial which commences on or after March 28, 2011, with a trial taken to have commenced in solemn proceedings when the oath is administered to the jury and in summary proceedings when the first witness is sworn) by SSI 2011/178 (C.15) art.2, Sch.1 para.1.

Appeals under section 107A and 107B: general provisions

A4-244.5 **107C.**—(1) In an appeal brought under section 107A or 107B the High Court may review not only the acquittal, direction or finding appealed against but also any direction, finding, decision, determination or ruling in the proceedings at first instance if it has a bearing on the acquittal, direction or finding appealed against.

(2) The test to be applied by the High Court in reviewing the acquittal, direction or finding appealed against is whether it was wrong in law.

AMENDMENTS

Section 107C inserted by Criminal Justice and Licensing (Scotland) Act 2010 (asp 13) s.74. Brought into force on March 28, 2011 (for all purposes in respect of any trial which commences on or after March 28, 2011, with a trial taken to have commenced in solemn proceedings when the oath is administered to the jury and in summary proceedings when the first witness is sworn) by SSI 2011/178 (C.15) art.2, Sch.1 para.1.

Expedited appeals

A4-244.6 **107D.**—(1) Subsection (2) applies where—

(a) the prosecutor intimates intention to appeal under section 107A or leave to appeal is granted by the court under section 107B, and

(b) the court is able to obtain confirmation from the Keeper of the Rolls that it would be practicable for the appeal to be heard and determined during an adjournment of the trial diet.

(2) The court must inform both parties of that fact and, after hearing them, must decide whether or not the appeal is to be heard and determined during such an adjournment.

(3) An appeal brought under section 107A or 107B which is heard and determined during such an adjournment is referred to in this Act as an "expedited appeal".

(4) If the court decides that the appeal is to be an expedited appeal the court must, pending the outcome of the appeal—

(a) adjourn the trial diet, and

(b) where the appeal is against an acquittal, suspend the effect of the acquittal.

(5) Where the court cannot obtain from the Keeper of the Rolls confirmation of the kind mentioned in subsection (1)(b), the court must inform the parties of that fact.

(6) Where the High Court in an expedited appeal determines that an acquittal of an offence libelled in the indictment was wrong in law it must quash the acquittal and direct that the trial is to proceed in respect of the offence.

AMENDMENTS

Section 107D inserted by Criminal Justice and Licensing (Scotland) Act 2010 (asp 13) s.74. Brought into force on March 28, 2011 (for all purposes in respect of any trial which commences on or after March 28, 2011, with a trial taken to have commenced in solemn proceedings when the oath is administered to the jury and in summary proceedings when the first witness is sworn) by SSI 2011/178 (C.15) art.2, Sch.1 para.1.

Other appeals under section 107A: appeal against acquittal

107E.—(1) This section applies where— A4-244.7

(a) an appeal brought under section 107A is not an expedited appeal,

(b) the appeal is against an acquittal, and

(c) the High Court determines that the acquittal was wrong in law.

(2) The court must quash the acquittal.

(3) If the prosecutor seeks leave to bring a new prosecution charging the accused with the same offence as that libelled in the indictment, or a similar offence arising out of the same facts as the offence libelled in the indictment, the High Court must grant the prosecutor authority to do so in accordance with section 119, unless the court considers that it would be contrary to the interests of justice to do so.

(4) If—

(a) no motion is made under subsection (3), or

(b) the High Court does not grant a motion made under that subsection,

the High Court must in disposing of the appeal acquit the accused of the offence libelled in the indictment.

AMENDMENTS

Section 107E inserted by Criminal Justice and Licensing (Scotland) Act 2010 (asp 13) s.74. Brought into force on 28 March 2011 (for all purposes in respect of any trial which commences on or after 28 March 2011, with a trial taken to have commenced in solemn proceedings when the oath is administered to the jury and in summary proceedings when the first witness is sworn) by SSI 2011/178 (C.15) art.2, Sch.1 para.1.

Other appeals under section 107A or 107B: appeal against directions etc.

107F.—(1) This section applies where— A4-244.8

(a) an appeal brought under section 107A or 107B is not an expedited appeal, and

(b) the appeal is not against an acquittal.

(2) The court of first instance must desert the diet *pro loco et tempore* in relation to any offence to which the appeal relates.

(3) The trial is to proceed only if another offence of which the accused has not been acquitted and to which the appeal does not relate is libelled in the indictment.

(4) However, if the prosecutor moves for the diet to be deserted *pro loco et tempore* in relation to such other offence, the court must grant the motion.

(5) If the prosecutor seeks leave to bring a new prosecution charging the accused with the same offence as that libelled in the indictment, or a similar offence arising out of the same facts as the offence libelled in the indictment, the High Court must grant the prosecutor authority to do so in accordance with section 119, unless the court considers that it would be contrary to the interests of justice to do so.

AMENDMENTS

Section 107F inserted by Criminal Justice and Licensing (Scotland) Act 2010 (asp 13) s.74. Brought into force on 28 March 2011 (for all purposes in respect of any trial which commences on or after 28 March 2011, with a trial taken to have commenced in solemn proceedings when the oath is administered to the jury and in summary proceedings when the first witness is sworn) by SSI 2011/178 (C.15) art.2, Sch.1 para.1.

[THE NEXT PARAGRAPH IS A4-245]

Lord Advocate's right of appeal against disposal

A4-245 **108.**—(1) Where a person has been convicted on indictment, the Lord Advocate may, in accordance with subsection (2) below, appeal against any of the following disposals, namely—

(a) a sentence passed on conviction;
(b) a decision under section 209(1)(b) of this Act not to make a supervised release order;
(c) a decision under section 234A(2) of this Act not to make a non-harassment order;
(ca) a decision under section 92 of the Proceeds of Crime Act 2002 not to make a confiscation order;
(cb) a decision under section 22A of the Serious Crime Act 2007 not to make a serious crime prevention order;
(cb) a decision under section 36(2) of the Regulatory Reform (Scotland) Act 2014 not to make a publicity order;
(cc) a decision under section 41(2) of that Act not to make a remediation order;
(cd) a decision under section 97B(2) of the Proceeds of Crime Act 2002 to make or not to make a compliance order;
(cd) a decision under section 30(2) of the Health (Tobacco, Nicotine etc. and Care) (Scotland) Act 2016 not to make a remedial order,
(ce) a decision under section 30(2) of that Act not to make a publicity order,
(d) […]
(dd) a drug treatment and testing order;
(e) […]
(f) a decision to remit to the Principal Reporter made under section 49(1)(a) of this Act;
(g) an order deferring sentence;
(h) an admonition; or
(i) an absolute discharge.

(2) An appeal under subsection (1) above may be made—

(a) on a point of law;
(b) where it appears to the Lord Advocate, in relation to an appeal under—
    (i) paragraph (a), (h) or (i) of that subsection, that the disposal was unduly lenient;

(ii) paragraph (b), (c), (ca), (cb), (cc), (cd) or (ce) of that subsection, that the decision not to make the order in question was inappropriate;

(iii) paragraph (cd) or (dd) of that subsection, that the making of the order concerned was unduly lenient or was on unduly lenient terms;

(iv) under paragraph (f) of that subsection, that the decision to remit was inappropriate;

(v) under paragraph (g) of that subsection, that the deferment of sentence was inappropriate or was on unduly lenient conditions.

(2A) In deciding whether to appeal under subsection (1) in any case, the Lord Advocate must have regard to any sentencing guidelines which are applicable in relation to the case.

(3) For the purposes of subsection (2)(b)(i) above in its application to a confiscation order by virtue of section 92(11) of the Proceeds of Crime Act 2002, the reference to the disposal being unduly lenient is a reference to the amount required to be paid by the order being unduly low.

AMENDMENTS

Section 108 substituted by Crime and Punishment (Scotland) Act 1997 (c.48) s.21 with effect from 1 August 1997 in terms of SI 1997/1712 art.3.

Subss.(1) and (2) as amended by Crime and Disorder Act 1998 (c.37) s.94 and Sch.6 para.6. Brought into force on 30 September 1998 by SI 1998/2327 (C.53).

Subss.(1) and (2) as amended, and subs.(3) inserted, by Proceeds of Crime Act 2002 (c.29) Pt 3 s.115. Brought into force on 24 March 2003 by SSI 2003/210 (C.44).

Subss.(1)(d) and (e) repealed, and subs.(2)(b) as amended, by Criminal Justice and Licensing (Scotland) Act 2010 (asp 13) Sch.2 para.8. Brought into force on 13 December 2010 (subject to savings provisions in art.3) by SSI 2010/413 (C.28) art.2, Sch.1 para.1.

Subss.(1) and (2) as amended by Regulatory Reform (Scotland) Act 2014 (asp 3) s.44(2). Brought into force on 30 June 2014 by SSI 2014/160 art.2 and Sch.1 para.1.

Subs.(2A) inserted by Criminal Justice and Licensing (Scotland) Act 2010 (asp 13) s.6(7). Brought into force on 19 October 2015 by SSI 2015/336 art.2.

Subs.(1)(cd) inserted, and subs.(2)(b) as amended, by Serious Crime Act 2015 (c.9) s.17(2). Brought into force on 1 March 2016 by SSI 2016/11 reg.2(b).

Subs.(1)(cb) inserted by Serious Crime Act 2015 (c.9) Sch.4 para.14. Brought into force on 1 March 2016 by SI 2016/148 reg.3(h).

Subs.(1)(cd), (ce) inserted, subs.(2)(b) as amended, by Health (Tobacco, Nicotine etc. and Care) (Scotland) Act 2016 (asp 14) s.31(2). Brought into force on 1 October 2017 by SSI 2017/294 reg.2 and Sch.1 para.1. Note: possible drafting error so second subs.(1)(cd) inserted.

DEFINITIONS

"community service order": s.238. A4-245.1
"indictment": s.307(1).
"probation order": s.228.

[THE NEXT PARAGRAPH IS A4-246]

GENERAL NOTE

As there was no tariff for sentences in the criminal courts of Scotland the selection of the appropriate sentence was clearly a matter for the individual discretion of the sentencer: *Strawhorn v Mcleod*, 1987 S.C.C.R. 413. The present Act invites the High Court of Justiciary, in appropriate circumstances, to pronounce an opinion on the sentence or other disposal or order which is appropriate in any similar case: ss.118(7) and 189(7). The Crown can appeal on a point of law (e.g. *HM Advocate v Foley*, 1999 G.W.D. 17–788) or on the ground that the sentence or other disposal is either unduly lenient or inappropriate as provided in subs.(2). A4-246

The Crown right of appeal against an unduly lenient sentence can only proceed in circumstances where "it appears" that a sentence is unduly lenient: s.228A of the 1975 Act as amended, and now s.108 of the present Act. A new reorganised s.108 was introduced by s.21(1) of the Crime and Punishment (Scotland) Act 1997 with effect from August 1, 1997. It introduces a right of appeal by the Lord Advocate against decisions by a court not to make a supervised release order; non harassment order and decision to remit to the principal Reporter. The right to bring an appeal under this section entitles the Crown to take an interest in sentencing which they did not have before—*HM Advocate v McKinlay*, 1998 S.C.C.R. 201.

The first appeal taken by the Crown was successful: see *HM Advocate v McPhee*, 1994 S.C.C.R. 830. There have been a number of appeals since then and the Appeal Court has indicated that a high standard of care and accuracy is expected of the Crown who do not require leave to appeal: see *HM Advocate v Mackay*, 1996 S.C.C.R. 410; *HM Advocate v Ross*, 1996 S.C.C.R. 107 and *HM Advocate v Wallace*, 1999 S.L.T. 1134. The grounds of appeal must be specific although the Appeal Court have allowed amendments to same: see *HM Advocate v Lee*, 1996 S.C.C.R. 205. In *Mackay*, supra, the court deplored the Crown's seeking to abandon the appeal at the hearing.

Furthermore the Crown must ensure that if they challenge a sentence as being unduly lenient the basis for the challenge has properly been laid in the trial court: see *HM Advocate v Bennett*, 1996 S.C.C.R. 331. If the Crown seek to maintain a sentence was unduly lenient because due consideration had not been given to a particular factor by a trial judge then the Crown have to show that the factor was fully drawn to the trial judge's attention: see *HM Advocate v Donaldson*, 1997 S.C.C.R. 738. Relevant factors to be taken into account in the determination of such appeals are the forum in which the Crown choose to proceed—see *HM Advocate v Robertson*, 1997 G.W.D. 5–187; the nature of any pleas accepted by the Crown: see *HM Advocate v Campbell*, 1997 S.L.T. 354 and if a non custodial option was imposed whether or not it was complied with—*HM Advocate v Jamieson*, 1996 S.C.C.R. 836; *HM Advocate v Carnall*, 1999 G.W.D. 31–1485; *HM Advocate v Paterson*, 2000 S.C.C.R. 309; *HM Advocate v Drain*, 2000 S.C.C.R. 256 but cf. *HM Advocate v McKinlay*, 1998 S.C.C.R. 201. The Crown are not specifically entitled to ask for a deterrent sentence—*HM Advocate v McKinlay*, 1998 S.C.C.R. 201.

The court will not grant an appeal by the Crown against sentence lightly and it is not enough that the Appeal Court judges would have passed a different sentence (*HM Advocate v McCourt* [2013] HCJAC 114 at [36]). Before the Appeal Court will interfere with a sentence it must be unduly lenient or inappropriate as provided by the section. Unduly lenient was defined in *HM Advocate v Bell*, 1995 S.L.T. 350 and *HM Advocate v O'Donnell*, 1995 S.C.C.R. 745 namely "The sentence must be seen to be unduly lenient. That means that it must fall outside the range of sentences which the judge at first instance, applying his mind to all the relevant factors, could reasonably have considered appropriate". It was held in *HM Advocate v Carnall*, 1999 G.W.D. 31–1485 even if the Appeal Court considered that an order was unduly lenient the court still has a discretion in terms of s.118(4) as to the course to adopt in determining disposal of the appeal. Due weight will be given by the Appeal Court to the views of the trial judge especially where he has had the advantage of seeing and hearing all the evidence— *HM Advocate v Wheldon*, 1998 S.C.C.R. 710. Lord Johnstone in that case described the task facing the Crown in such appeals as "formidable".

In *HM Advocate v Lee*, supra the court observed that although it was not the practice of the Appeal Court to lay down sentencing guidelines decisions of the Appeal Court in appeals against sentence especially unduly lenient sentence appeals do from time to time provide guidelines as to what is or is not appropriate and that a judge who fails to take account of that guidance cannot be said to have acted within the proper limits of his discretion as a sentencer: see *HM Advocate v Lee*, supra. Section 197 of this Act now provides that a court in passing sentence shall have regard to any relevant opinion pronounced in terms of ss.118(7) or 189(7). The question of setting down minimum sentences was rejected in *HM Advocate v Mackay*, supra.

Guidelines can be found in *HM Advocate v Brough*, 1996 S.C.C.R. 377 (lewd and libidinous practices; teacher; custodial sentence well nigh inevitable); *HM Advocate v McPhee*, 1994 S.C.C.R. 830 (supply of Class A drug to teenage girls; custodial sentences must be imposed): *HM Advocate v Fallan*, 1996 S.L.T. 314 (unprovoked sexual attack on stranger in street at night; custodial sentence should normally be imposed); contrast *HM Advocate v Currie*, 2008 S.L.T. 1055 (17-year-old convicted of unlawful intercourse with a 13-year-old girl, who had met him for that specific purpose, and the attempted rape of another; *held* that the sentencing judge was entitled, in the particular circumstances of the case, to take the view that a custodial sentence was not likely to achieve the necessary change in the attitude, maturity and behaviour of the respondent and to select, instead, Community Service); *HM Advocate v Lee*, 1996 S.C.C.R. 205 (being concerned in the supply of a Class A drug; substantial custodial sentence will be inevitable) and *HM Advocate v Carnall*, supra; *HM Advocate v Jamieson*, 1996 S.C.C.R. 836 (assault to severe injury and danger of life; only in an unusual case should the court refrain from imposing custodial sentence) see also *HM Advocate v Smith*, 1998 S.C.C.R. 637; *HM Advocate v Spiers*, 1997 S.L.T. 1401 (a custodial sentence was the only appropriate disposal where an assault occurred by stabbing with a broken bottle). The Appeal Court declined to set down a minimum sentence for culpable homicide where death was caused by kicking—*HM Advocate v Wheldon*, supra. The Appeal Court has also provided guidelines in appeals under this section as to factors that a judge is entitled to take into account in determining sentence. The fact that an accused pled guilty to a reduced charge is a mitigatory factor which a judge can take into account—*HM Advocate v Brand*, 1998 S.C.C.R. 71. A judge is not obliged to take account of an early plea of guilty but is entitled to give it the weight appropriate in the circumstances—*HM Advocate v Forrest*, 1998 S.C.C.R. 153. In cases involving kicking and punching it is appropriate for a sentencing judge to have regard to the nature of the conduct in determining whether an attack is violent and savage rather than the resulting injuries—*HM Advocate v Allan*, 2000 S.C.C.R. 219. For other Crown appeals see *HM Advocate v Gordon and Foy*, 1996 S.C.C.R. 274; *HM Advocate v McColl*, 1996 S.C.C.R. 523; *HM Advocate v Callaghan*, 1996 S.C.C.R. 709; *HM Advocate v McPherson*, 1996 S.C.C.R. 802; *HM Advocate v Campbell*, 1997 S.L.T. 354; *HM Advocate v McC.*, 1996 S.C.C.R. 842; *HM Advocate v McK.*, 1996 S.C.C.R. 866; *HM Advocate v M.*, 1997 S.L.T. 359; *HM Advocate v Scottish Hydro Electric plc*, 1997 S.L.T. 359 and *HM Advocate v Speirs*, 1997 S.C.C.R. 479; *HM Advocate v Hodgson*, 1998 S.C.C.R. 320; *HM Advocate v Heron*, 1998 S.C.C.R. 449 and *HM Advocate v Carpenter*, 1998 S.C.C.R. 706; *HM Advocate v Duff*, 1999 S.C.C.R. 193; *HM Advocate v Davidson*, 1999 S.C.C.R. 729; *HM Advocate v Millard*, 2000 G.W.D. 25–939 and *HM Advocate v Briody*, 2000 G.W.D. 29–1138.

The Crown has a right under s.121A to seek suspension of a probation order, community service order, supervised attendance order and restriction of liberty order pending determination of the appeal.

Failure to exercise this right is a factor which the Appeal Court will take into account in determining appeals against sentence by the Crown—*HM Advocate v Carnall*, above.

In *Urqhart v Campbell* [2006] HCJAC 76; 2006 S.C.C.R. 656 the court said that, in principle, proceedings in such an appeal where the consequence, if the appeal is allowed, is likely to be the imposition of a more severe sentence, ought not to take place outwith the presence of the respondent and that it would not be satisfactory to hear the appeal in the respondent's absence and, then, if it was successful, continue it to enable the respondent to be present when the new sentence was imposed. Although the context of this was summary proceedings, the court said in terms that the same principle applies in a solemn appeal where the accused is not in custody.

Subs.(1)(a)

In *HM Advocate v CH* [2017] HCJAC 82, the Appeal Court confirmed that the Lord Advocate's right of appeal under this section extends to a decision not to impose an extended sentence.

Lord Advocate's appeal against decision not to impose automatic sentence in certain cases

108A. Where the court has exercised the power conferred by section 205A(3) or 205B(3) of this Act, the Lord Advocate may appeal against that decision. A4-246.1

AMENDMENTS

Section 108A inserted by Crime and Punishment (Scotland) Act 1997 (c.48) s.18(2) with effect from 20 October 1997 in terms of SI 1997/2323 art.3 and Sch.1; as amended by Crime and Disorder Act 1998 (c.37) Sch.8 para.120 (effective 30 September 1998: SI 1998/2327).

Section 108A as amended by Crime and Disorder Act 1998 Sch.8 para.120.

[THE NEXT PARAGRAPH IS A4-246.3]

GENERAL NOTE

Some account of the origins of this involved section has to be attempted; it involves a provision on the statute book not brought into force, a provision now live and a third which has been repealed without ever coming into force. A4-246.3

Section 108A was introduced into the 1995 Act by the Crime and Punishment (Scotland) Act 1997 (c.48) s.18(2) to afford the Lord Advocate a specific right of appeal against the court's decision not to impose: (i) an automatic life sentence on conviction of a qualifying offence (s.205A of the 1995 Act as prospectively inserted by the 1997 Act s.1); (ii) an automatic minimum sentence on a third solemn conviction for drug trafficking (s.205B of the 1995 Act as now in force); or (iii) a supervised release order on conviction of a qualifying offence (s.209 of the 1995 Act as prospectively substituted by s.4 of the 1997 Act).

To date only the second provision, s.205B has been brought into force but it remains open for the regime of automatic life sentences to be activated should this be desired. The 1998 amendment to s.108A takes account of the fact that s.4 of the 1997 Act has been repealed; see Sch.10 of the 1998 Act.

[THE NEXT PARAGRAPH IS A4-247]

Intimation of intention to appeal

109.—(1) Subject to section 111(2) of this Act and to section 99 of the Proceeds of Crime Act 2002 (postponement), where a person desires to appeal under section 106(1)(a) or (f) of this Act, he shall within two weeks of the final determination of the proceedings, lodge with the Clerk of Justiciary written intimation of intention to appeal which shall identify the proceedings and be in as nearly as may be the form prescribed by Act of Adjournal. A4-247

(1A) Where a person desires to appeal under section 106(1)(a) of this Act by virtue of section 11(7) of the Double Jeopardy (Scotland) Act 2011 (asp 16), subsection (1) applies with the following modifications—

(a) for the words "two weeks of the final determination of the proceedings" substitute "two weeks of the date on which the person is acquitted of an offence mentioned in section 11(2) of the Double Jeopardy (Scotland) Act 2011 (asp 16)"; and

(b) the reference to identifying the proceedings is to be construed as a reference to identifying—

(i) the proceedings which resulted in the conviction desired to be appealed; and

(ii) the proceedings which resulted in the person's acquittal as mentioned in section 11(7) of the Double Jeopardy (Scotland) Act 2011 (asp 16).

(1B) Subsections (5) to (9) of section 106 of this Act do not apply where the modifications specified in subsection (1A) apply.

(2) A copy of intimation given under subsection (1) above shall be sent to the Crown Agent.

(3) On intimation under subsection (1) above being lodged by a person in custody, the Clerk of Justiciary shall give notice of the intimation to the Secretary of State.

(4) Subject to subsection (5) below, for the purposes of subsection (1) above and section 106(5) to (7) of this Act, proceedings shall be deemed finally determined on the day on which sentence is passed in open court.

(5) Where in relation to an appeal under section 106(1)(a) of this Act sentence is deferred under section 202 of this Act, the proceedings shall be deemed finally determined on the day on which sentence is first so deferred in open court.

(6) Without prejudice to section 10 of the said Act of 1995, the reference in subsection (4) above to "the day on which sentence is passed in open court" shall, in relation to any case in which, under subsection (1) of that section, a decision has been postponed for a period, be construed as a reference to the day on which that decision is made, whether or not a confiscation order is then made or any other sentence is then passed.

AMENDMENTS

Subs.(1) as amended by Proceeds of Crime Act 2002 (c.29) Sch.11 para.29(2). Brought into force on March 24, 2003 by SSI 2003/210 (C.44).

Subss.(1A), (1B) inserted by Double Jeopardy (Scotland) Act 2011 (asp 16) Sch.1 para.9. Brought into force on November 28, 2011 by SSI 2011/365 (C.34) art.3.

DEFINITIONS

A4-247.1 "Clerk of Justiciary": s.307(1).
"sentence": s.307(1).

[THE NEXT PARAGRAPH IS A4-248]

GENERAL NOTE

A4-248 It is crucial to recall that the right of appeal under s.106(1) relates to all convictions on indictment. It is as important to know that all appeals following conviction on indictment are initiated in the justiciary office and not in the sheriff court. The intimation of an intention to appeal required under this section is important for it gives an office in Edinburgh notice of an appeal from a trial that may have occurred in any one of the sheriff courts of Scotland or one of the towns where the High Court has been on circuit. Those who may be required to produce notes or reports can thus be put on notice. Where there are several accused on one indictment the trial of all of them must be brought to a finality before any one of them can exercise the right of appeal: see *Evans, Petr*, 1991 S.C.C.R. 160.

Once an intimation of intention to appeal against conviction is lodged a transcript of the charge to the jury will be ordered to enable the grounds of appeal to be prepared. The unavailability of the transcript will not necessarily result in the appeal being allowed. Prejudice must be shown—*Carroll v HM Advocate*, 1999 J.C. 302.

Subs.(1)

In *Graham v HM Advocate* [2013] HCJAC 149, the Appeal Court said that, although the notice is only a formal document, it is far from being without importance. It alerts the trial judge to the prospect of an appeal, triggers extension of the charge to the jury and preserves evidence in the form of documents and labelled productions. In dealing with an application to lodge a notice late, the question for the court is where the balance of justice comes to rest. The applicant needs to persuade the court that there is a reasonable explanation for the delay and that the grounds of appeal are likely to succeed. The greater the delay, the stronger the grounds require to be.

Note of appeal

110.—(1) Subject to section 111(2) of this Act— A4-249

(a) within eight weeks of lodging intimation of intention to appeal or, in the case of an appeal under section 106(1)(b) to (e) of this Act, within two weeks of the appropriate date (being, as the case may be, the date on which sentence was passed, the order disposing of the case was made, sentence was deferred or the previous conviction was quashed as mentioned in section 106A(1)(c) or (2)(c) of this Act) (or, as the case may be, of the making of the order disposing of the case or deferring sentence) in open court, the convicted person may lodge a written note of appeal with the Clerk of Justiciary who shall send a copy to the judge who presided at the trial and to the Crown Agent; or, as the case may be,

(b) within four weeks of the passing of the sentence in open court, the Lord Advocate may lodge such a note with the Clerk of Justiciary, who shall send a copy to the said judge and to the convicted person or that person's solicitor.

(c) where the prosecutor intimates intention to appeal under section 107A(1), Criminal Procedure (Scotland) Act 1995 within 7 days after the acquittal or direction appealed against, the prosecutor may, except in the case of an expedited appeal, lodge such a note with the Clerk of Justiciary, who must send a copy to the judge and to the accused or to the accused's solicitor,

(d) within 7 days after leave to appeal under section 107B(1) is granted, the prosecutor may, except in the case of an expedited appeal, lodge such a note with the Clerk of Justiciary, who must send a copy to the judge and to the accused or to the accused's solicitor,

(e) in the case of an expedited appeal, as soon as practicable after the decision as to hearing and determining the case is made under section 107D(2), the prosecutor may—

(i) lodge such a note with the Clerk of Justiciary, and

(ii) provide a copy to the judge and to the accused or to the accused's solicitor.

(2) The period of eight weeks mentioned in paragraph (a) of subsection (1) above may be extended, before it expires, by the Clerk of Justiciary.

(3) A note of appeal shall—

(a) identify the proceedings;

(b) contain a full statement of all the grounds of appeal; and

(c) be in as nearly as may be the form prescribed by Act of Adjournal.

(3A) In respect of a written note of appeal relating to an appeal by virtue of section 11(7) of the Double Jeopardy (Scotland) Act 2011 (asp 16)—

(a) subsection (1) applies as if the reference to the judge who presided at the trial were a reference to—

(i) the judge who presided at the trial resulting in the conviction to which the written note of appeal relates; and

(ii) the judge who presided at the trial for an offence mentioned in section 11(2) of that Act resulting in the convicted person's acquittal; and

(b) subsection (3)(a) applies as if the reference to the proceedings were a reference to—

(i) the proceedings which resulted in the conviction to which the written note of appeal relates; and

(ii) the proceedings which resulted in the convicted person's acquittal.

(4) Except by leave of the High Court on cause shown, it shall not be competent for an appellant to found any aspect of his appeal on a ground not contained in the note of appeal.

(5) Subsection (4) above shall not apply as respects any ground of appeal specified as an arguable ground of appeal by virtue of subsection (7) of section 107 of this Act.

(6) On a note of appeal under section 106(1)(b) to (e) of this Act being lodged by an appellant in custody the Clerk of Justiciary shall give notice of that fact to the Secretary of State.

AMENDMENTS

Subs.(1)(a) as amended by Crime and Punishment (Scotland) Act 1997 (c.48) s.19(2) with effect from October 20, 1997 in terms of SI 1997/2323 art.3 and Sch.1.

Subss.(1)(a) and (2) as amended by Act of Adjournal (Criminal Appeals) 2002 (SSI 2002/387) art.2 with effect from August 26, 2002 in accordance with art.1(2).

Subs.(1) as amended by Criminal Procedure (Amendment) (Scotland) Act 2004 (asp 5) s.24(2). Brought into force on October 4, 2004 by SSI 2004/405 (C.28).

Subs.(1)(a) as amended by Criminal Proceedings etc (Reform) (Scotland) Act 2007 (asp 6) s.80, Sch. para.16(2). Brought into force on December 10, 2007 by SSI 2007/479 (C.40) art.3 and Sch.

Subs.(1)(a) as amended by Protection of Vulnerable Groups (Scotland) Act 2007 (asp 14) Sch.4 para.15. Brought into force on 28 February 2011 by SSI 2011/157 (C.13) art.2, subject to savings specified in art.5(1).

Subs.(1)(c), (d) and (e) inserted by Criminal Justice and Licensing (Scotland) Act 2010 (asp 13) s.76. Brought into force on 28 March 2011 (for all purposes in respect of any trial which commences on or after 28 March 2011, with a trial taken to have commenced in solemn proceedings when the oath is administered to the jury and in summary proceedings when the first witness is sworn) by SSI 2011/178 (C.15) art.2, Sch.1 para.1.

Subs.(3A) inserted by Double Jeopardy (Scotland) Act 2011 (asp 16) Sch.1 para.10. Brought into force on 28 November 2011 by SSI 2011/365 (C.34) art.3.

DEFINITIONS

A4-249.1 "Clerk of Justiciary": s.307(1).
"judge": s.307(1).

[THE NEXT PARAGRAPH IS A4-250]

GENERAL NOTE

A4-250 Three periods of time are envisaged by this section. First, for all solemn appeals against conviction or conviction and sentence written intimation of intention to appeal should be lodged within two weeks of the final determination with the Clerk of Justiciary by s.109(1). Thereafter a convicted person has six weeks to lodge a written note of appeal. Alternatively, and secondly, if the appeal is only against sentence then the period is two weeks from the date sentence was passed, or order disposing of the case was made, or sentence deferred etc.: subs.(1)(a). It is clear that if conviction is accepted fewer papers are required and less preparatory work is necessary. Thirdly, if the Crown wishes to appeal (against, for example, what appears to be an unduly lenient sentence) a note of appeal must be lodged within four weeks: subs.(1)(b).

Those lodging notes of appeal must have regard to two important points. The note of appeal must contain a full statement of all the grounds of appeal: subs.(3)(b). There are a number of reported cases that emphasise the importance of specification; see, for example, *Mitchell v HM Advocate*, 1991 S.C.C.R. 216. *Smith v HM Advocate*, 1983 S.C.C.R. 30: *Lindsay v HM Advocate*, 1993 S.C.C.R. 868, and *McGregor v HM Advocate*, 1996 G.W.D. 9–471. If the grounds of appeal are deficient the presiding judge may be unable to fully comment on the appeal—*MacLeay v HM Advocate*, 2000 G.W.D. 8–278. In *HM Advocate v Bagan*, 1996 G.W.D. 29–1734 the court observed that there was a professional responsibility to ensure that grounds of appeal were formulated which had a sound basis in fact. The importance is accentuated by the new requirement to disclose arguable grounds of appeal in the note of appeal for the consideration of a single judge in chambers to obtain leave to appeal: s.107(1)(a) and (2)(a).

Further, it is not competent, except by leave of the High Court of Justiciary on cause shown. for an appellant to found any aspect of his appeal on a ground not contained in the note of appeal: subs.(4). The narrow approach is also emphasised earlier in the Act: s.107(8). If a ground of appeal is abandoned it cannot be resurrected at a later stage—*McGinty v HM Advocate*, 2000 J.C. 277. That said, it is in practice possible to amend grounds of appeal and to add additional grounds, even at a late stage, because the court is chiefly concerned with whether or not there has been a miscarriage of justice and tends to be flexible.

In *Strachan v HM Advocate* [2011] HCJAC 28 Lord Carloway explained (at [13]–[17]) that:

> "The 1995 Act is generous in the time that it affords appellants to consider and formulate grounds of appeal… The statutory scheme envisages that, by the end of the period, a convicted person will have lodged a Note containing 'a *full* statement of *all* the grounds of appeal' (s.110(3)(b)) (emphasis

added). The idea is that an appellant, having had adequate time for preparation, will not be allowed to argue any other grounds without leave of the court (s.110(4)). That leave ought to be the exception rather than the rule… In determining whether to allow an amendment to a Note of Appeal, the court must, of course, have firmly in mind the need to ensure that a convicted person's right to a fair trial (including, where permitted, an appeal) in terms of Article 6 of the European Convention is adequately protected. Within that context, however, the court must have procedural rules, which all appellants can take advantage of but with which they must also be expected to comply, to ensure that all appeals are dealt with efficiently and fairly. Reasonably enforced procedural rules and practices are essential components of a fair and expeditious appellate process. Such a process is, in turn, a core element of a criminal justice system that works effectively to ensure the protection of those who are subject to its procedures and to promote the interests of justice… Given the time afforded to an appellant to consider and formulate his grounds of appeal, it should only be in exceptional cases that leave to amend ought to arise as an issue at all and thereafter be permitted… There are many considerations which may be taken into account in determining whether to grant leave to amend. One is the apparent strength of the proposed amended ground. The stronger it is, the more probable it will be that the court will exercise its discretion to allow amendment. But the background to the late presentation of the ground is also a consideration. If the point sought to be raised is one which was not focussed, as it might have been, at first instance, it is less likely that the court will be sympathetic to its introduction outwith the statutory time limits. The cogency of the reason for the point not having been included in the original Note of Appeal is also a factor. But change of counsel should not normally be regarded as affording an advantage to an appellant seeking to expand the scope of his appeal … The timing of the application for amendment is a factor. In the context of the relatively new procedure for the written presentation of appeals, the making of an application after the time for lodging the written case and argument has expired is unlikely to be regarded as satisfactory in all but the most exceptional of circumstances."

See also *McCarthy v HM Advocate*, 2008 S.C.C.R. 902 and *DS v HM Advocate*, 2008 S.C.C.R. 929.

Provisions supplementary to sections 109 and 110

111.—(1) Where the last day of any period mentioned in sections 109(1) and 110(1) of this Act falls on a day on which the office of the Clerk of Justiciary is closed, such period shall extend to and include the next day on which such office is open. **A4-251**

(2) Any period mentioned in section 109(1) or 110(1)(a) of this Act may be extended at any time by the High Court in respect of any convicted person; and an application for such extension may be made under this subsection and shall be in as nearly as may be the form prescribed by Act of Adjournal.

(2ZA) Where an application under subsection (2) is received after the period to which it relates has expired, the High Court may extend the period only if it is satisfied that doing so is justified by exceptional circumstances.

(2ZB) In considering whether there are exceptional circumstances for the purpose of subsection (2ZA), the High Court must have regard to—

(a) the length of time that has elapsed between the expiry of the period and the making of the application,

(b) the reasons stated in accordance with subsection (2A)(a)(i),

(c) the proposed grounds of appeal.

(2A) An application under subsection (2) must—

(a) state—

(i) the reasons why the applicant failed, or expects to fail, to comply with the time limit, and

(ii) the proposed grounds of appeal, and

(b) be intimated in writing by the applicant to the Crown Agent.

(2B) If the prosecutor so requests within 7 days of receipt of intimation of the application under subsection (2A)(b), the prosecutor must be given an opportunity to make representations before the application is determined.

(2C) […]

(3) […]

(4) An application under subsection (2) is to be dealt with by the High Court—
(a) in chambers, and
(b) unless the Court directs otherwise, without the parties being present.
(5) If the High Court extends a period under subsection (2), it must—
(a) give reasons for the decision in writing, and
(b) give the reasons in ordinary language.

AMENDMENTS

Subs.(3) inserted by Criminal Procedure (Amendment) (Scotland) Act 2004 (asp 5) s.24(3). Brought into force on 4 October 2004 by SSI 2004/405 (C.28).

Subss.(2A), (2B), (2C) inserted by Criminal Procedure (Legal Assistance, Detention and Appeals) (Scotland) Act 2010 (asp 15) s.5. Brought into force on 30 October 2010.

Subs.(3) repealed by Protection of Vulnerable Groups (Scotland) Act 2007 (asp 14) Sch.4 para.16. Brought into force on 28 February 2011 by SSI 2011/157 (C.13) art.2, subject to savings specified in art.5(1).

Subss.(2ZA), (2ZB), (4), (5) inserted, subs.(2A) as amended, subs.(2C) repealed by Criminal Justice (Scotland) Act 2016 (asp 1) s.90. Brought into force on 17 January 2017 by SSI 2016/426 art.2 and Sch.1 para.1.

DEFINITIONS

A4-251.1 "Clerk of Justiciary": s.307(1).
"High Court": s.307(1).

GENERAL NOTE

A4-251.2 For examples of extensions considered, see *Spence v HM Advocate*, 1945 J.C. 59 and *Birrell v HM Advocate*, 1993 S.C.C.R. 812. See *Grant v HM Advocate*, 1996 G.W.D. 19–1077—an appeal against refusal to extend the time.

[THE NEXT PARAGRAPH IS A4-252]

Admission of appellant to bail

A4-252 **112.**—(1) Subject to subsections (2), (2A) and (9) below, the High Court may, if it thinks fit, on the application of a convicted person, admit him to bail pending the determination of—
(a) his appeal; or
(b) any relevant appeal by the Lord Advocate under section 108 or 108A of this Act.

(2) The High Court shall not admit a convicted person to bail under subsection (1) above unless—
(a) the application for bail—
(i) states reasons why it should be granted; and
(ii) where he is the appellant and has not lodged a note of appeal in accordance with section 110(1)(a) of this Act, sets out the proposed grounds of appeal.
(b) […]

(2A) Where—
(a) the convicted person is the appellant and has not lodged a note of appeal in accordance with section 110(1)(a) of this Act; or
(b) the Lord Advocate is the appellant,

the High Court shall not admit the convicted person to bail under subsection (1) above unless it considers there to be exceptional circumstances justifying admitting him to bail.

(3) A person who is admitted to bail under subsection (1) above shall, unless the High Court otherwise directs, appear personally in court on the day or days fixed for the hearing of the appeal.

(4) Where an appellant fails to appear personally in court as mentioned in subsection (3) above, the court may—

(a) if he is the appellant—
  (i) decline to consider the appeal; and
  (ii) dismiss it summarily; or
(b) whether or not he is the appellant—
  (i) consider and determine the appeal; or
  (ii) without prejudice to section 27 of this Act, make such other order as the court thinks fit.

(5) For the purposes of subsections (1), (3) and (4) above, "appellant" includes not only a person who has lodged a note of appeal but also one who has lodged an intimation of intention to appeal.

(6) Subject to subsections (7) and (9) below, the High Court may, if it thinks fit, on the application of a convicted person, admit him to bail pending the determination of any appeal under section 288AA of this Act or paragraph 13(a) of Schedule 6 to the Scotland Act 1998 and the disposal of the proceedings by the High Court thereafter.

(7) The High Court shall not admit a convicted person to bail under subsection (6) above unless
(a) the application for bail states reasons why it should be granted and the High Court considers there to be exceptional circumstances justifying admitting the convicted person to bail, and
(b) where the appeal relates to conviction on indictment, the prosecutor has had an opportunity to be heard on the application.

(8) A person who is admitted to bail under subsection (6) above shall, unless the High Court otherwise directs, appear personally in the High Court at any subsequent hearing in the High Court in relation to the proceedings; and if he fails to do so the court may, without prejudice to section 27 of this Act, make such order as it thinks fit.

(9) An application for the purposes of subsection (1) or (6) above by a person convicted on indictment shall be—
(a) intimated by him immediately and in writing to the Crown Agent; and
(b) heard not less than seven days after the date of that intimation.

AMENDMENTS

Subs.(1)(b) as amended by Crime and Punishment (Scotland) Act 1997 (c.48) s.18(3) with effect from October 20, 1997 in terms of SI 1997/2323 art.3, Sch.1.

Subss.(6), (7) and (8) inserted by Scotland Act 1998 (Consequential Modifications) (No.1) Order 1999 (SI 1999/1042) art.3, Sch. para.13 (effective 6 May 1999).

Subss.(1), (2), (6) and (7) as amended, and subss.(2A) and (9) inserted, by Criminal Justice (Scotland) Act 2003 (asp 7) Pt 8 s.66. Brought into force on 27 June 2003 by SSI 2003/288 (C.14).

Subs.(2) as amended by Criminal Proceedings etc (Reform) (Scotland) Act 2007 (asp 6) s.80, Sch. para.16(3). Brought into force on 10 December 2007 by SSI 2007/479 (C.40) art.3 and Sch.

Subs.(6) as amended by Scotland Act 2012 (c.11) s.36(10). Brought into force on 22 April 2013 by SI 2013/6 art.2(c).

DEFINITIONS

"appellant": s.112(5). A4-252.1
"bail": s.307(1).
"High Court": s.307(1).

[THE NEXT PARAGRAPH IS A4-253]

GENERAL NOTE

This section regulates the power which the High Court has long possessed to admit an appellant to bail. It should be read in the light of High Court of Justiciary Practice Note No.1 of 2012 (Interim liberation), which is important and succinct enough to reproduce in full (see also Division C, para.C1-52): A4-253

"1. The purpose of this practice note is to inform practitioners of the court's understanding of, and approach to, the granting of interim liberation.

2. Section 112(2)(a)(ii) of the Act of 1995 provides that where the appellant has not lodged a note of appeal the application for bail must set out the proposed grounds of appeal. The purpose of this provision is to allow the court to make an assessment as to whether the grounds are arguable. However, even if that is done, section 112(2A) provides that it is only in 'exceptional circumstances' that interim liberation should be granted in advance of the note of appeal. The court will, ordinarily, be justified in refusing an application in hoc statu pending the result of the sift; this will be especially so where there is no report from the judge dealing with the grounds of appeal.
3. The issues mentioned in paragraph 2 do not apply where leave to appeal has been granted. That being said, the grant of leave to appeal does not provide an 'automatic passport' to liberation. The onus is on the appellant to demonstrate circumstances justifying the grant of liberation pending a hearing on the appeal and the court will take into account the strength of the grounds of appeal before determining whether it is in the interests of justice to grant the application.
4. It is not a good reason for granting an application for interim liberation only to state that, if it were not granted, any sentence may have been served by the time of any appeal hearing, albeit that that is a factor in deciding whether to grant liberation in short sentence appeals.
5. The court will bear in mind that the presumption of innocence ceases to apply after conviction. Although in summary cases the grant of leave to appeal is likely to be a strong indicator that liberation ought to follow, the same consideration does not apply with equivalent force in solemn cases, where the appellant stands convicted of what is likely to be a serious offence. Indeed, interim liberation should not be granted where (i) the appellant poses a danger to the public; or (ii) the appellant is likely to abscond or otherwise interfere with the course of justice.
6. Where a person has been in custody pending trial, it will not normally be appropriate to grant that person interim liberation following upon their conviction. In this situation, the appellant will already have been deemed unsuitable for bail and, unless circumstances have changed since the refusal of bail, the same considerations which justified refusal of bail ought to apply with greater force, in the absence of the presumption of innocence, at the stage of interim liberation."

Judge's report

A4-254 **113.**—(1) Subject to subsections (1A) to (1D), as soon as is reasonably practicable after receiving the copy note of appeal sent to him under any of paragraphs (a) to (d) of section 110(1) of this Act, the judge who presided at the trial shall furnish the Clerk of Justiciary with a written report giving the judge's opinion on the case generally and on the grounds contained in the note of appeal.

(1A) Subsections (1B) to (1D) apply where the copy note of appeal mentioned in subsection (1) relates to an appeal by virtue of section 11(7) of the Double Jeopardy (Scotland) Act 2011 (asp 16).

(1B) The reference in subsection (1) to the judge who presided at the trial is to be construed as a reference to—

(a) the judge who presided at the trial for an offence mentioned in section 11(2) of that Act resulting in the appellant's acquittal; and

(b) where subsection (1C) applies, the judge who presided at the trial resulting in the conviction to which the copy note of appeal relates.

(1C) This subsection applies—

(a) where, in connection with the appeal, the High Court calls for the report to be furnished by the judge mentioned in subsection (1B)(b); and

(b) it is reasonably practicable for the judge to furnish the report.

(1D) For the purposes of subsections (1) to (1C), it is irrelevant whether or not the judge mentioned in subsection (1B)(b) had previously furnished a report under subsection (1).

(2) The Clerk of Justiciary shall send a copy of the judge's report—

(a) to the convicted person or his solicitor;

(b) to the Crown Agent; and

(c) in a case referred under Part XA of this Act, to the Commission.

(3) Where the judge's report is not furnished as mentioned in subsections (1)–(5) above, the High Court may call for the report to be furnished within such period as it may specify or, if it thinks fit, hear and determine the appeal without the report.

(4) Subject to subsection (2) above, the report of the judge shall be available only to the High Court, the parties and, on such conditions as may be prescribed by Act of Adjournal, such other persons or classes of persons as may be so prescribed.

AMENDMENTS

Subs.(2)(c) as amended by Crime and Punishment (Scotland) Act 1997 Sch.1 para.21(16) (effective April 1, 1999: SI 1999/652).

Subs.(1) as amended by Criminal Justice and Licensing (Scotland) Act 2010 (asp 13) s.76. Brought into force on March 28, 2011 (for all purposes in respect of any trial which commences on or after March 28, 2011, with a trial taken to have commenced in solemn proceedings when the oath is administered to the jury and in summary proceedings when the first witness is sworn) by SSI 2011/178 (C.15) art.2, Sch.1 para.1.

Subss.(1) and (3) as amended, subss.(1A)–(1D) inserted, by Double Jeopardy (Scotland) Act 2011 (asp 16) Sch.1 para.11. Brought into force on November 28, 2011 by SSI 2011/365 (C.34) art.3.

DEFINITIONS

"Clerk of Justiciary": s.307(1). A4-254.1
"High Court": s.307(1).
"judge": s.307(1).

GENERAL NOTE

In *McLaren v HM Advocate*, 1994 S.C.C.R. 855 the Appeal Court observed that where more than one accused has appealed against conviction or sentence the trial judge should prepare separate reports and it is desirable these be self-contained and set out points the judge considers appropriate in response to the grounds of appeal. A4-254.2

Where the ground of appeal is based on the wrongful rejection of a no case to answer submission the form of the judge's report should be as set out in *Horne v HM Advocate*, 1991 S.C.C.R. 248 and *Vetters v HM Advocate*, 1994 S.C.C.R. 305. It was observed in *McPhelim v HM Advocate*, 1996 S.C.C.R. 647 that judges should comment on all grounds of appeal and not just those raising questions of fact. Delay by a trial judge in producing a report for the Appeal Court was only one factor to be considered in assessing the issue of reasonable time in terms of art.6—*HM Advocate v McGlinchey*, 2000 S.C.C.R. 593.

The duties of a trial judge, in furnishing a report in terms of this section were emphasised in *McCutcheon v HM Advocate*, 2001 G.W.D. 18–694. In *Ogilvie v Heywood*, 2001 G.W.D. 18–695 the Appeal Court disapproved of comments by a trial judge regarding the bringing of the appeal. In *Megrahi v HM Advocate*, 2001 G.W.D. 26–1014 it was held that the requirement upon the judge to produce a report was mandatory.

Judge's observations in expedited appeal

113A.—(1) On receiving a note of appeal given under section 110(1)(e), the judge who presided at the trial may give the Clerk of Justiciary any written observations that the judge thinks fit on— A4-254.3

(a) the case generally,
(b) the grounds contained in the note of appeal.

(2) The High Court may hear and determine the appeal without any such written observations.

(3) If written observations are given under subsection (1), the Clerk of Justiciary must give a copy of them to—

(a) the accused or the accused's solicitor, and
(b) the prosecutor.

(4) The written observations of the judge are available only to—

(a) the High Court,
(b) the parties, and
(c) any other person or classes of person prescribed by Act of Adjournal, in accordance with any conditions prescribed by Act of Adjournal.

AMENDMENTS

Section 113A inserted by Criminal Justice and Licensing (Scotland) Act 2010 (asp 13) s.76. Brought into force on March 28, 2011 (for all purposes in respect of any trial which commences on or after March 28, 2011, with a trial taken to have commenced in solemn proceedings when the oath is administered to the jury and in summary proceedings when the first witness is sworn) by SSI 2011/178 (C.15) art.2, Sch.1 para.1.

[THE NEXT PARAGRAPH IS A4-255]

Applications made orally or in writing

A4-255 **114.** Subject to any provision of this Part of this Act or to rules made under section 305 of this Act to the contrary, any application to the High Court may be made by the appellant or respondent as the case may be or by counsel on his behalf, orally or in writing.

AMENDMENTS

Section 114 as amended by Act of Adjournal (Criminal Appeals) 2003 (SSI 2003/387) art.2. Brought into force on September 1, 2003 in accordance with art.1.

DEFINITIONS

A4-255.1 "appellant": s.132.
"High Court": s.307(1).

[THE NEXT PARAGRAPH IS A4-256]

Presentation of appeal in writing

A4-256 **115.**—(1) Subject to rules made under section 305 of this Act, if an appellant desires to present his case and his argument in writing instead of orally he shall, at least four days before the diet fixed for the hearing of the appeal—

(a) intimate this desire to the Clerk of Justiciary;
(b) lodge with the Clerk of Justiciary three copies of his case and argument; and
(c) send a copy of the intimation, case and argument to the Crown Agent.

(2) Any case or argument presented as mentioned in subsection (1) above shall be considered by the High Court.

(3) Unless the High Court otherwise directs, the respondent shall not make a written reply to a case and argument presented as mentioned in subsection (1) above, but shall reply orally at the diet fixed for the hearing of the appeal.

(4) Unless the High Court otherwise allows, an appellant who has presented his case and argument in writing shall not be entitled to submit in addition an oral argument to the court in support of the appeal.

AMENDMENTS

Section 115 as amended by Act of Adjournal (Criminal Appeals) 2003 (SSI 2003/387) art.2. Brought into force on September 1, 2003 in accordance with art.1.

DEFINITIONS

A4-256.1 "appellant": s.132.
"Clerk of Justiciary": s.307(1).
"High Court": s.307(1).

GENERAL NOTE

A4-256.2 It is interesting to note the willingness of the Appeal Court in certain cases to entertain written submissions both from appellants and the Lord Advocate: see *Anderson v HM Advocate*, 1996 S.C.C.R. 114. In *Campbell v HM Advocate*, 1998 S.C.C.R. 214, the court ordered the Crown to lodge a written history of the case.

[THE NEXT PARAGRAPH IS A4-257]

Abandonment of appeal

116.—(1) An appellant may abandon his appeal by lodging with the Clerk of Justiciary a notice of abandonment in as nearly as may be the form prescribed by Act of Adjournal; and on such notice being lodged the appeal shall be deemed to have been dismissed by the court. **A4-257**

(2) A person who has appealed against both conviction and sentence (or, as the case may be, against both conviction and a decision mentioned in section 106(1)(bb) or both conviction and disposal and order) may abandon the appeal in so far as it is against conviction and may proceed with it against sentence (or, as the case may be, decision, disposal or order) alone.

AMENDMENTS

Subs.(2) as amended by Crime and Punishment (Scotland) Act 1997 (c.48) s.18(4) with effect from October 20, 1997 in terms of SI 1997/2323 art.3 and Sch.1.

Subs.(2) substituted by Protection of Children (Scotland) Act 2003 (asp 5) s.16(3). Brought into force on January 10, 2005 by SSI 2004/522 (C.38) art.2.

Subs.(2) as amended by Criminal Proceedings etc (Reform) (Scotland) Act 2007 (asp 6) s.80, Sch. para.16(4). Brought into force on December 10, 2007 by SSI 2007/479 (C.40) art.3 and Sch.

Subs.(2) as substituted by Protection of Vulnerable Groups (Scotland) Act 2007 (asp 14) Sch.4 para.17. Brought into force on February 28, 2011 by SSI 2011/157 (C.13) art.2, subject to savings specified in art.5(1).

DEFINITIONS

"appellant": s.132. **A4-257.1**
"Clerk of Justiciary": s.307(1).
"sentence": s.132.

GENERAL NOTE

In *Hendry and Beaton v HM Advocate*, 2006 S.C.C.R. 178 a bench of 5 judges considered the question of abandonment of a sentence appeal in light of the existence of conflicting authorities. The Court approved of the principle articulated in *West v HM Advocate*, 1955 S.L.T. 425, in which it was said that the appellant has the right to abandon only up to the point at which the hearing begins and counsel addresses the court. Thereafter, dismissal of the appeal is in the discretion of the court. This is because it would be a denial of justice to allow an appellant to argue his appeal and then, when he realises he will probably fail, to permit him to abandon and take refuge in what the court may consider to be an inappropriate sentence. The Lord Justice General in West said that "accused person who choose to exercise their rights to appeal … must realise that though they may succeed in securing a reduction of sentence, they also run the risk of a long sentence being imposed". **A4-257.2**

Where a Notice of Abandonment has been lodged the competent mode of reinstating the appeal is by petition to the nobile officium: see *Young, Petr*, 1994 S.L.T. 269 and *McIntosh, Petr*, 1995 S.C.C.R. 327.

The Crown seeking to abandon an appeal against an unduly lenient sentence at the hearing was deplored in the case of *HM Advocate v Mackay*: see s.108, above.

An appellant who has appealed against conviction and the imposition of a minimum sentence may abandon the appeal against conviction and proceed only with the appeal against sentence—s.18(4) of the Crime and Punishment (Scotland) Act 1997.

[THE NEXT PARAGRAPH IS A4-258]

Presence of appellant or applicant at hearing

117.—(1) Where an appellant or applicant is in custody the Clerk of Justiciary shall notify— **A4-258**

(a) the appellant or applicant;
(b) the Governor of the prison in which the appellant or applicant then is; and
(c) the Secretary of State,

of the probable day on which the appeal or application will be heard.

(2) The Secretary of State shall take steps to transfer the appellant or applicant to a prison convenient for his appearance before the High Court at such reasonable time before the hearing as shall enable him to consult his legal adviser, if any.

(3) A convicted appellant, notwithstanding that he is in custody, shall be entitled to be present if he desires it, at the hearing of his appeal.

(4) When an appellant or applicant is to be present at any diet—

(a) before the High Court or any judge of that court; or
(b) for the taking of additional evidence before a person appointed for that purpose under section 104(1)(b) of this Act, or
(c) for an examination or investigation by a special commissioner in terms of section 104(1)(d) of this Act,

the Clerk of Justiciary shall give timeous notice to the Secretary of State, in the form prescribed by Act of Adjournal or as nearly as may be in such form.

(5) A notice under subsection (4) above shall be sufficient warrant to the Secretary of State for transmitting the appellant or applicant in custody from prison to the place where the diet mentioned in that subsection or any subsequent diet is to be held and for reconveying him to prison at the conclusion of such diet.

(6) […]

(7) Where the Lord Advocate is the appellant, subsections (1) to (5) above shall apply in respect of the convicted person, if in custody, as they apply to an appellant or applicant in custody.

(8) The Secretary of State shall, on notice under subsection (4) above from the Clerk of Justiciary, ensure that sufficient male and female prison officers attend each sitting of the court, having regard to the list of appeals for the sitting.

(9) When the High Court fixes the date for the hearing of an appeal or of an application under section 111(2) of this Act, the Clerk of Justiciary shall give notice to the Crown Agent and to the solicitor of the convicted person, or to the convicted person himself if he has no known solicitor.

AMENDMENTS

Subs.(6) repealed, subs.(7) as amended, by Criminal Justice (Scotland) Act 2016 (asp 1) s.110(2). Brought into force on 17 January 2017 by SSI 2016/426 art.2 and Sch.1 para.1.

DEFINITIONS

A4-258.1 "appellant": s.132.
"Clerk of Justiciary": s.307(1).
"diet": s.307(1).
"governor": s.307(1).
"High Court": s.307(1).
"judge": s.307(1).

GENERAL NOTE

A4-258.2 An appellant who is in custody need not be present at his appeal hearing: see *Manuel v HM Advocate*, 1958 J.C. 41 where the accused accepted counsel's advice that it was not in his best interest to be there. However if an appellant does wish to be present subs.(3) entitles him to be there.

[THE NEXT PARAGRAPH IS A4-259]

Disposal of appeals

A4-259 **118.—**(1) The High Court may, subject to subsection (4) below, dispose of an appeal against conviction by—

(a) affirming the verdict of the trial court;
(b) setting aside the verdict of the trial court and either quashing the conviction or, subject to subsection (2) below, substituting therefor an amended verdict of guilty; or
(c) setting aside the verdict of the trial court and quashing the conviction and granting authority to bring a new prosecution in accordance with section 119 of this Act.

(1A) Where an appeal against conviction is by virtue of section 11(7) of the Double Jeopardy (Scotland) Act 2011 (asp 16), paragraph (c) of subsection (1) does not apply.

(2) An amended verdict of guilty substituted under subsection (1) above must be one which could have been returned on the indictment before the trial court.

(3) In setting aside, under subsection (1) above, a verdict the High Court may quash any sentence imposed on the appellant (or, as the case may be, any disposal or order made) as respects the indictment, and—

(a) in a case where it substitutes an amended verdict of guilty, whether or not the sentence (or disposal or order) related to the verdict set aside; or

(b) in any other case, where the sentence (or disposal or order) did not so relate,

may pass another (but not more severe) sentence or make another (but not more severe) disposal or order in substitution for the sentence, disposal or order so quashed.

(4) The High Court may, subject to subsection (5) below, dispose of an appeal against sentence by—

(a) affirming such sentence; or

(b) if the Court thinks that, having regard to all the circumstances, including any evidence such as is mentioned in section 106(3) of this Act, a different sentence should have been passed, quashing the sentence and passing another sentence whether more or less severe in substitution therefor,

and, in this subsection, "appeal against sentence" shall, without prejudice to the generality of the expression, be construed as including an appeal under 106(1)(ba), (bb), (c), (d), (da), (e) or (f), and any appeal under section 108, of this Act; and other references to sentence shall be construed accordingly.

(4AA) [...]

(4A) On an appeal under section 108A of this Act, the High Court may dispose of the appeal—

(a) by affirming the decision and any sentence or order passed;

(b) where it is of the opinion mentioned in section 205A(3) or, as the case may be, 205B(3) of this Act but it considers that a different sentence or order should have been passed, by affirming the decision but quashing any sentence or order passed and passing another sentence or order whether more or less severe in substitution therefor; or

(c) in any other case, by setting aside the decision appealed against and any sentence or order passed by the trial court and where the decision appealed against was taken under—

(i) subsection (3) of section 205A of this Act, by passing the sentence mentioned in subsection (2) of that section;

(ii) subsection (3) of section 205B of this Act, by passing a sentence of imprisonment of at least the length mentioned in subsection (2) of that section; or

(iii) [...]

(5) In relation to any appeal under section 106(1) of this Act, the High Court shall, where it appears to it that the appellant committed the act charged against him but that he was not, because of section 51A of this Act, criminally responsible for it, dispose of the appeal by—

(a) setting aside the verdict of the trial court and substituting therefor a verdict of acquittal by reason of the special defence set out in section 51A of this Act; and

(b) quashing any sentence imposed on the appellant (or disposal or order made) as respects the indictment and—

(i) making, in respect of the appellant, any order mentioned in section 57(2)(a) to (d) of this Act; or

(ii) making no order.

(6) Subsections (3) to (6) of section 57 of this Act shall apply to an order made under subsection (5)(b)(i) above as they apply to an order made under subsection (2) of that section.

(7) In disposing of an appeal under section 106(1)(b) to (f) or 108 of this Act the High Court may, without prejudice to any other power in that regard, pronounce an opinion on

(a) the sentence or other disposal or order which is appropriate in any similar case;

(b) […]

(8) No conviction, sentence, judgment, order of court or other proceeding whatsoever in or for the purposes of solemn proceedings under this Act—

(a) shall be quashed for want of form; or

(b) where the accused had legal assistance in his defence, shall be suspended or set aside in respect of any objections to—

(i) the relevancy of the indictment, or the want of specification therein; or

(ii) the competency or admission or rejection of evidence at the trial in the inferior court,

unless such objections were timeously stated.

(9) The High Court may give its reasons for the disposal of any appeal in writing without giving those reasons orally.

AMENDMENTS

Subs.(4)(b) as amended by Crime and Punishment (Scotland) Act 1997 (c.48) Sch.1 para.21(17) with effect from 1 August 1997 in terms of SI 1997/1712 art.3. As amended by Crime and Punishment (Scotland) Act 1997 (c.48) s.18(5) with effect from 20 October 1997 in terms of SI 1997/2323 art.3, Sch.1.

Subs.(4A) inserted by Crime and Punishment (Scotland) Act 1997 (c.48) s.18(5) with effect from 20 October 1997 in terms of SI 1997/2323 art.3, Sch.1.

Subs.(9) inserted by Crime and Punishment (Scotland) Act 1997 (c.48) Sch.1 para.21(17) with effect from 1 August 1997 in terms of SI 1997/1712 art.3.

Subs.(4A)(c)(iii) repealed by the 1998 Act Sch.8 para.121.

Subss.(4AA) and (7)(b) inserted, and subs.(7) as amended, by Protection of Children (Scotland) Act 2003 (asp 5) s.16(4). Brought into force on 10 January 2005 by SSI 2004/522 (C.38) art.2.

Subs.(6) as amended by Mental Health (Care and Treatment) (Scotland) Act 2003 (asp 13) Sch.4 para.8(11). Brought into force on 5 October 2005 by SSI 2005/161 (C.6).

Subs.(4) as amended by Criminal Proceedings etc (Reform) (Scotland) Act 2007 (asp 6) s.80, Sch. para.16(5). Brought into force on 10 December 2007 by SSI 2007/479 (C.40) art.3 and Sch.

Subs.(4) as amended by Criminal Justice and Licensing (Scotland) Act 2010 (asp 13) Sch.2 para.9. Brought into force on 13 December 2010 (subject to savings provisions in art.3) by SSI 2010/413 (C.28) art.2, Sch.1 para.1.

Subss.(4) and (7) as amended, subs.(4AA) repealed, by Protection of Vulnerable Groups (Scotland) Act 2007 (asp 14) Sch.4 para.18. Brought into force on 28 February 2011 by SSI 2011/157 (C.13) art.2, subject to savings specified in art.5(1).

Subs.(1A) inserted by Double Jeopardy (Scotland) Act 2011 (asp 16) Sch.1 para.12. Brought into force on 28 November 2011 by SSI 2011/365 (C.34) art.3.

Subs.(5) as amended by Criminal Justice and Licensing (Scotland) Act 2010 (asp 13) Sch.7 para.51. Brought into force on 25 June 2012 by SSI 2012/160 (C.15) art.3.

DEFINITIONS

A4-259.1 "appeal against sentence": s.118(4).
"High Court": s.307(1).
"sentence": s.307(1).

[THE NEXT PARAGRAPH IS A4-260]

GENERAL NOTE

Appeal against conviction

Subsection (1) is concerned with appeals against conviction following solemn proceedings. The High Court of Justiciary may dispose of an appeal by affirming the verdict of the trial court: subs.(1)(a). Alternatively, the High Court of Justiciary may dispose of an appeal by setting aside the verdict of the trial court: subs.(1)(b) and (c). The Appeal Court cannot, under s.118, authorise the withdrawal of a plea of guilty (*Pickett v HM Advocate*, 2007 S.C.C.R. 389). What follows after setting aside the verdict depends on what has gone wrong and how that is to be corrected. The Appeal Court is not obliged to give effect to a concession by the Crown at the appeal. It is for the court to determine if there has been a miscarriage of justice—*Duffy v HM Advocate*, 1999 G.W.D. 37–1791. In *Santini v HM Advocate*, 2000 S.C.C.R. 726 the Appeal Court declined to accept a Crown concession to restrict the libel to 2 days on the basis that there was no justification in law for this. **A4-260**

The High Court of Justiciary may set aside the verdict and quash the conviction and that may be done where the irregularity was substantial: e.g. *Gardiner v HM Advocate*, 1978 S.L.T. 118. Alternatively, the High Court of Justiciary may set aside the verdict and substitute therefor an amended verdict of guilty: e.g. *Salmond v HM Advocate*, 1991 S.C.C.R. 43 in which it was clear that the jury held some criminal behaviour proved but returned an incorrect verdict owing to a misunderstanding of the law. See *White v HM Advocate*, 1989 S.C.C.R. 553 and *Ainsworth v. HM Advocate*, 1996 S.C.C.R. 631.

The Appeal Court has a discretionary power to quash a conviction where a miscarriage of justice has occurred. Prior to the Criminal Justice (Scotland) Act 1980 the court was under a duty to do so providing that the miscarriage was a substantial one. The duty and proviso were removed by the 1980 Act. In *McCuaig* the amendments introduced by the 1980 Act were interpreted as giving a wider power to the Appeal Court than the previous legislation. See Sir Gerald Gordon's full commentary thereon at pp.128–129 and *McAvoy v HM Advocate*, 1982 S.C.C.R. 263. The test which the court should apply in determining whether to quash a conviction or to substitute an amended verdict was considered in *Smith v HM Advocate*, 2001 S.C.C.R. 143.

The High Court of Justiciary may set aside the verdict of the trial court and quash the conviction and grant, on statutory grounds, authority to bring a new prosecution: e.g. *Mackenzie v HM Advocate*, 1982 S.C.C.R. 499 through many cases to *McDade v HM Advocate*, 1994 S.C.C.R. 627. See *Sinclair v HM Advocate*, 1996 S.C.C.R. 221; *O'Neill v HM Advocate*, 1996 G.W.D. 4–183; *Hutton v HM Advocate*, 1996 G.W.D. 31–1907; *Hobbins v HM Advocate*, 1996 S.C.C.R. 637, *McPhelim v HM Advocate*, 1996 S.C.C.R. 647; *Hoy v HM Advocate*, 1997 S.L.T. 26; *Hemphill v HM Advocate*, 2001 S.C.C.R. 361 and *McLean v HM Advocate*, 2001 G.W.D. 7-24.

The setting aside of the verdict of the trial court and the quashing of the conviction in the context of a misdirection to the jury does not necessarily lead to the grant of authority to bring a new prosecution. In *Farooq v HM Advocate*, 1993 S.L.T. 1271 the ages of child witnesses and the generally unsatisfactory nature of the evidence resulted in such authority being refused. In *Jones v HM Advocate*, 1991 S.C.C.R. 290 the appellants were convicted of murder. They then gave evidence for the Crown at the trial of another on the same charge having been called as socii. The appellants' convictions were set aside on appeal. Authority to bring prosecution was refused as the setting aside of the conviction operated retroactively and as the appellants had given evidence for the Crown as socii they were immune from prosecution. See also *Kerr v HM Advocate*, 1992 S.C.C.R. 281. In *Hoy v HM Advocate*, 1998 S.C.C.R. 8, authority for a second retrial was refused on the basis that there had been insufficient evidence before the jury to convict of murder. Repeated indictments do not necessarily preclude authority being granted for a new prosecution—*Callan v HM Advocate*, 1999 S.C.C.R. 57 (murder charge and no fault on the part of the Crown) but see *Cameron v HM Advocate*, 1999 S.C.C.R. 11 (appellant previously undergone two trials and long delay in proceedings—authority refused). See also *Muirhead v HM Advocate*, 1999 G.W.D. 4-176 and *Cathcart v HM Advocate*, 1999 G.W.D. 5-241. In *Glancy v HM Advocate*, 2001 S.C.C.R. 385 authority for a fresh prosecution was refused due to the age of the offence and the fact the accused had been in custody for four months, the equivalent of a nine month sentence. The power in subs.(1) to set aside the verdict of the court necessarily requires a comparable power to deal with the question of sentence. Subsection (3) allows variation of sentence but whenever a sentence is varied a substituted sentence may only be the same or less than the original sentence. An appeal against conviction alone does not allow a variation of sentence for the imposition of a more severe sentence: cf. the earlier position, e.g. in *O 'Neil v HM Advocate*, 1976 S.L.T. (Notes) 7.

Appeals against sentence

Subsection (4) is concerned with appeals against sentence following solemn proceedings. The High Court of Justiciary may dispose of an appeal by affirming the sentence complained of: subs.(4)(a). Alternatively, the High Court of Justiciary may dispose of an appeal by quashing the sentence complained of and passing another sentence "whether more or less severe" in substitution. In doing the latter, the High Court of Justiciary may have regard to additional evidence such as that mentioned in s.106(3) of this Act. **A4-261**

An example of a more severe sentence being substituted is to be found in *Donnelly v HM Advocate*, 1988 S.C.C.R. 386 where 18 months' detention was quashed and two years' detention substituted for a youth who had a CS gas canister at a football match. In *Stewart v HM Advocate (No.2)*, 2006 S.L.T. 560, the Appeal Court observed that, far from it being an affront to justice for it to increase the sentence where the case has been referred to it by the Scottish Criminal Cases Review Commission (as senior counsel for the appellant contended), it has the power to do exactly that. In contrast, a less serious sentence was substituted in *McIntyre v HM Advocate*, 1994 G.W.D. 28-1687 where 20 years' imprisonment was quashed and was substituted with 14 years' imprisonment for culpable homicide for throwing or pouring acid on another. See also *Donnell v HM Advocate*, 1997 G.W.D. 17-762 where the Appeal Court declined to exercise their power under subs.(4). The new subs.(4A) was added by s.18(5) of the Crime and Punishment Act 1997 with effect from October 20, 1997. This provides that on appeal by the prosecutor in terms of s.108A the court can (1) affirm the original decision; or (2) whilst agreeing that the minimum sentence should not be imposed for the reasons set out in s.205B(3) alter the sentence or (3) impose the appropriate sentence prescribed by the Act.

Sentencing guidance

A4-262 A most notable use of the authority in s.118(7), above, is the appeal of *Du Plooy v HM Advocate*, 2003 S.L.T. 1237. There guidance was given as to the basis of, and scope for, an allowance in the sentencing of an accused in respect of a guilty plea, and the form that such an allowance might take. For another example, see *Gill v HM Advocate*, 2010 S.C.C.R. 922. Further consideration is given to this matter under ss.196 and 197 of this Act, below.

Section 8 of the Criminal Justice and Licensing (Scotland) Act 2010 provides that, where the High Court of Justiciary pronounces an opinion under s.118(7), the Court may require the Scottish Sentencing Council to prepare, for the Court's approval, sentencing guidelines on any matter, or review any sentencing guidelines published by the Council on any matter. The Council must comply with such a requirement and, in doing so, must have regard to the High Court's reasons for making the requirement.

Supplementary provisions

A4-262.1 In relation to any appeal under s.106(1) of this Act, the High Court of Justiciary is required to set aside the verdict of the trial court and quash the sentence and make an order where it appears that the appellant committed the act charged against him but that he was insane when he did so: subss. (5) and (6).

When disposing of appeals against sentence generally, the High Court of Justiciary may pronounce an opinion on the sentence or other disposal or order which is appropriate in any similar case: subs.(7). In *O 'Neill v HM Advocate*, 1998 S.C.C.R. 644 the Appeal Court set out guidelines for dealing with confidential material in mitigation. In *HM Advocate v Carnall*, 1999 G.W.D. 31-1485 the Appeal Court observed that although reference in the course of an appeal hearing to disposals in previous, similar appeals against sentence may indicate to some extent the appropriate level of sentence for an offence they could not provide guidance to the whole range of sentences appropriate. See also *HM Advocate v Wheldon*, 1999 J.C. 5.

Two other matters may have important consequences for appeals. First, no conviction, sentence, judgment, order of court or other proceedings whatsoever in or for the purposes of solemn proceedings shall be quashed for want of form: subs.(8)(A).

Secondly, and similarly, no conviction, sentence, judgment, order of court or other proceeding whatsoever in or for the purposes of solemn proceedings, where the accused had legal assistance in his defence, shall be suspended or set aside in respect of any objection to, either, the relevancy of the indictment, or the want of specification, or, the competency or admission or rejection of evidence at trial in the lower court, unless such objections were timeously stated: subs.(8)(b)(i) and (ii).

The concept of timeous objection was to be found in s.454 of the 1975 Act in relation to summary trials and it was said to be "special to summary trials": *Renton and Brown* (5th edn) para.14-61 at p.300. For a recent case of how the section worked, see *McPherson v McNaughton*, 1992 S.L.T. 600. See notes at s.192.

Subsection (9) was introduced by para.21(17) of Sch.1 to the Crime and Punishment Act with effect from August 1, 1997. This provides that the High Court may give written reasons without giving these reasons orally. This does away with the necessity of having advisings. The deletion of s.118(4A)(c)(iii) occurs as a consequence of the repeal of s.4 of the 1997 Act wrought by the 1998 Act Sch.10.

Subs.(8)

The Appeal Court said in *McFadden and Spark v HM Advocate*, 2009 S.C.C.R. 902 that it will only sustain arguments relating to the admissibility of evidence where no objection was taken at or before the trial in very exceptional circumstances, amounting to an Anderson appeal based on defective representation.

[THE NEXT PARAGRAPH IS A4-263]

Provision where High Court authorises new prosecution

A4-263 **119.**—(1) Subject to subsection (2) below, where authority is granted under section 118(1)(c) or 107E(3) or 107F(5) of this Act, a new prosecution may be brought charging the accused with the same or any similar offence arising out of the same facts; and the proceedings out of which the appeal arose shall not be a bar to such new prosecution.

(2) In a new prosecution under this section—

(a) where authority for the prosecution is granted under section 118(1)(c), the accused must not be charged with an offence more serious than that of which the accused was convicted in the earlier proceedings,

(b) where authority for the prosecution is granted under section 107E(3), the accused must not be charged with an offence more serious than that of which the accused was acquitted in the earlier proceedings,

(c) where authority for the prosecution is granted under section 107F(5), the accused must not be charged with an offence more serious than that originally libelled in the indictment in the earlier proceedings.

(2A) In a new prosecution under this section brought by virtue of section 107F(5), the circumstances set out in the indictment are not to be inconsistent with any direction given under section 97B(2)(b) or 97C(2) in the proceedings which gave rise to the appeal in question unless the High Court, in disposing of that appeal, determined that the direction was wrong in law.

(3) No sentence may be passed on conviction under the new prosecution which could not have been passed on conviction under the earlier proceedings.

(4) A new prosecution may be brought under this section, notwithstanding that any time limit, other than the time limit mentioned in subsection (5) below, for the commencement of such proceedings has elapsed.

(5) Proceedings in a prosecution under this section shall be commenced within two months of the date on which authority to bring the prosecution was granted.

(6) In proceedings in a new prosecution under this section it shall, subject to subsection (7) below, be competent for either party to lead any evidence which it was competent for him to lead in the earlier proceedings.

(7) The indictment in a new prosecution under this section shall identify any matters as respects which the prosecutor intends to lead evidence by virtue of subsection (6) above which would not have been competent but for that subsection.

(8) For the purposes of subsection (5) above, proceedings shall be deemed to be commenced—

(a) in a case where a warrant to apprehend the accused is granted—

(i) on the date on which the warrant is executed; or

(ii) if it is executed without unreasonable delay, on the date on which it is granted;

(b) in any other case, on the date on which the accused is cited.

(9) Where the two months mentioned in subsection (5) above elapse and no new prosecution has been brought under this section, the order under section 118(1)(c) of this Act setting aside the verdict or under section 107E(3) or 107F(5) granting authority to bring a new prosecution shall have the effect, for all purposes, of an acquittal.

(10) On granting authority under section 118(1)(c) or 107E(3) or 107F(5) of this Act to bring a new prosecution, the High Court shall, after giving the parties an opportunity of being heard, order the detention of the accused person in custody or admit him to bail.

(11) Section 65(4)(aa) and (b) and (4A) to (9) of this Act (prevention of delay in trials) shall apply to an accused person who is detained under subsection (10) above as they apply to an accused person detained by virtue of being committed until liberated in due course of law.

Amendments

Subs.(8)(a), (b) as amended by Criminal Procedure (Amendment) (Scotland) Act 2004 (asp 5) s.25 and Sch.1 para.32. Brought into force on February 1, 2005 by SSI 2004/405 (C.28) art.2.

Subs.(11) as amended by Criminal Proceedings etc (Reform) (Scotland) Act 2007 (asp 6) s.80, Sch. para.16(6). Brought into force on December 10, 2007 by SSI 2007/479 (c .40) art.3 and Sch.

Subss.(1), (2), (9) and (10) as amended, and subs.(2A) inserted, by Criminal Justice and Licensing (Scotland) Act 2010 (asp 13) s.76. Brought into force on March 28, 2011 (for all purposes in respect of any trial which commences on or after March 28, 2011, with a trial taken to have commenced in solemn proceedings when the oath is administered to the jury and in summary proceedings when the first witness is sworn) by SSI 2011/178 (C.15) art.2, Sch.1 para.1.

DEFINITIONS

A4-263.1 "High Court": s.307(1).
"offence": s.307(1).
"prosecutor": s.307(1).
"sentence": s.307(1).

[THE NEXT PARAGRAPH IS A4-264]

GENERAL NOTE

A4-264 Section 119 sets out the procedures for retrial following the quashing of a conviction on appeal but the critical issue is the form of libel which the Crown may use when re-indicting. A number of different situations may arise from the original trial: as well as being convicted of the offence since successfully appealed, the accused may have plead to other charges, have been acquitted, or the Crown may have withdrawn some parts of the libel either due to a perceived insufficiency, or because these had been included for evidential purposes only or to focus issues for the jury.

Subs. (1)

There have been a considerable number of new prosecutions on statutory authority in its earlier form: see, e.g. *Mackenzie v HM Advocate*, 1982 S.C.C.R. 499, *King v HM Advocate*, 1985 S.C.C.R. 322, *McGhee v HM Advocate*, 1991 S.C.C.R. 510, and *Allison v HM Advocate*, 1994 S.C.C.R. 464. The grant of such authority does not mean that the Crown is bound to initiate new proceedings: see e.g. *Sinclair v HM Advocate*, 1990 S.C.C.R. 412.

Subs. (2)

In a new prosecution under s.119 the accused is not to be charged with an offence more serious than that of which he was convicted in the earlier proceedings. The clearest example of this restriction is the case of Daniel Boyle. He had been charged with murder and after trial in the High Court of Justiciary at Glasgow he was convicted of culpable homicide in November 1991.He was sentenced to 10 years' detention. He appealed against conviction and that verdict was set aside in July 1992: *Boyle v HM Advocate*, 1993 S.L.T. 577. The High Court of Justiciary, in setting aside that verdict, granted authority to the Crown to bring a new prosecution in accordance with s.254(1)(c) of the 1975 Act.

A new indictment with a charge of murder was served on Boyle on July 30, 1992 for trial on August 31, 1992 but the trial diet was overtaken by an appeal by the Crown against a decision at a preliminary diet: see s.76A of the 1975 Act. The Crown appeal arose in this way: at the preliminary diet the accused argued that the jury, having returned a verdict of culpable homicide, had barred the Crown from indicting Boyle for the more serious crime of murder. The Crown argued otherwise.

At the preliminary diet the judge held that the action of the Crown was competent in law but unfair in the circumstances and dismissed the indictment. The Crown appeal from the preliminary diet was allowed, it being for the Crown not the court to decide any charges brought, and the indictment for murder was remitted to the trial court to proceed: *HM Advocate v Boyle*, 1992 S.C.C.R. 939.

Thereafter, Boyle petitioned the *nobile officium* of the High Court of Justiciary to complain that that court had exceeded its own authority in the original appeal in setting aside certain charges on the indictment which Boyle had been convicted of but had not appealed. The petition was refused: *Boyle, Petr*, 1993 S.L.T. 1085.

For the sake of completeness it should be added that at the adjourned trial diet in November 1992 the trial was again adjourned to January 1993 because of difficulties that the Crown had with citing witnesses. Boyle had been in custody since August 1991 and he again petitioned the *nobile officium* of the High Court of Justiciary, this time for bail. That was granted (unusually for those on a murder charge) in terms of s.35 of the 1975 Act: *Boyle, Petr*, 1993 S.C.C.R. 251. Daniel Boyle was acquitted at his second murder trial.

Subs. (3)

This provision ensures that at a second trial in the event of conviction a sentence cannot competently be passed if it could not have been passed on conviction under the earlier proceedings.

Subs. (4)

This provision permits a new prosecution notwithstanding any existing time-limits except for that in subs.(5). It is submitted that calculation of the two month time bar specified falls to be calculated *de die in diem*, the normal rule; see *Lees v Lovell*, 1992 S.L.T. 967 discussed at A4-291 below. It will be noted that the summary provision for fresh proceedings following illness of a judge is drafted in almost identical terms.

Subs. (5)

Proceedings in a prosecution under s.119 must be commenced within two months of the date on which authority to bring the prosecution was granted. Authority for a new prosecution was granted in *Maillie v HM Advocate*, 1993 S.C.C.R. 535. Delay in implementing a subsequent petition warrant results in that petition being dismissed: *Friel v Mailley*, 1993 S.C.C.R. 928.

Where an accused has been remanded in custody pending a retrial this provision has the effect of requiring the Crown to re-indict within 60 days of the date upon which the court grants authority for a retrial, rather than the customary 80 day period, following full committal on petition, as set out in s.65 above. It is submitted that, while there would be no time bar upon proceedings in a retrial where the accused is on bail, once an indictment has been served the position in custody cases is quite different; the authority for retrial would become the operative date for calculation of a 110 day period. Thus in *HM Advocate v Donnelly*, (High Court of Justiciary, December 2000, unreported) the Crown obtained a retrospective extension of the 110 days when D's trial was adjourned on defence motion beyond the period without an extension having been granted at the time. The Appeal Court's warrant for a retrial was by that time the only authority the Crown had for keeping D in custody or serving an indictment, the original petition warrant having long since expired.

Subss.(6) to (7)

The requirements of s.119(7) apply to cases where evidence could be led only in terms of s.119(6). If the evidence is admissible in terms of e.g. *Nelson v HM Advocate*, 1994 S.C.C.R. 192 and *Cairns v HM Advocate*, 1967 J.C. 37 then subs.(7) does not apply—*Diamond v HM Advocate*, 1999 S.C.C.R. 411.

Subss. (8) to (11)

In *McPhelim v HM Advocate*, 1997 S.C.C.R. 87 the Crown raised an indictment within the statutory two months but the indictment was thereafter deserted *pro loco et tempore*. A fresh indictment was raised outwith the two month period. This was held to be competent as proceedings had been commenced timeously.

The competency by subs.(10) of bail for the accused reflects the position that Boyle found himself in and that resulted in his petition to the *nobile officium*: see *Boyle, Petr*, 1993, above.

Appeals: supplementary provisions

120.—(1) Where— A4-265

(a) intimation of the diet appointed for the hearing of the appeal has been made to the appellant;

(b) no appearance is made by or on behalf of an appellant at the diet; and

(c) no case or argument in writing has been timeously lodged,

the High Court shall dispose of the appeal as if it had been abandoned.

(2) The power of the High Court to pass any sentence under this Part of this Act may be exercised notwithstanding that the appellant (or, where the Lord Advocate is the appellant, the convicted person) is for any reason not present.

(3) When the High Court has heard and dealt with any application under this Part of this Act, the Clerk of Justiciary shall (unless it appears to him unnecessary so to do) give to the applicant if he is in custody and has not been present at the hearing of such application notice of the decision of the court in relation to the said application.

(4) On the final determination of any appeal under this Part of this Act or of any matter under section 103(5) of this Act, the Clerk of Justiciary shall give notice of such determination—

(a) to the appellant or applicant if he is in custody and has not been present at such final determination;

(b) to the clerk of the court in which the conviction took place; and

(c) to the Secretary of State.

DEFINITIONS

"appellant": s.132. A4-265.1

"diet": s.307(1).

"High Court": s.307(1).

[THE NEXT PARAGRAPH IS A4-266]

GENERAL NOTE

A4-266 These supplementary provisions in practice are important because a not inconsiderable number of appeals are refused for want of insistence. The appellant cannot, however, fail to meet any obligation placed on him and expect to have the court overlook it. In *Manson, Petr*, 1991 S.L.T. 96 the petitioner sought to have heard an appeal against sentence which had been dismissed for want of insistence. Manson claimed not to have been notified of the date of appeal but he had failed to notify the court of a change of address as required by s.2(2) of the 1980 Act and the petition was refused.

In *Boyle, Petr*, 1992 S.C.C.R. 949 the Appeal Court held that intimation under the then s.261 of the Criminal Procedure (Scotland) Act 1975 was not an interlocutor and is open to correction by the court, the opinion of the court being the best evidence of what was decided by the court.

Suspension of disqualification, forfeiture, etc.

A4-267 **121.**—(1) Any disqualification, forfeiture or disability which attaches to a person by reason of a conviction shall not attach—

(a) for the period of four weeks from the date of the verdict against him; or

(b) where an intimation of intention to appeal or, in the case of an appeal under section 106(1)(b) to (e), 108 or 108A of this Act, a note of appeal is lodged, until the appeal, if it is proceeded with, is determined.

(2) The destruction or forfeiture or any order for the destruction or forfeiture of any property, matter or thing which is the subject of or connected with any prosecution following upon a conviction shall be suspended—

(a) for the period of four weeks after the date of the verdict in the trial; or

(b) where an intimation of intention to appeal or, in the case of an appeal under section 106(1)(b) to (e), 108 or 108A of this Act, a note of appeal is lodged, until the appeal, if it is proceeded with, is determined.

(3) This section does not apply in the case of any disqualification, destruction or forfeiture or order for destruction or forfeiture under or by virtue of any enactment which makes express provision for the suspension of the disqualification, destruction or forfeiture or order for destruction or forfeiture pending the determination of an appeal against conviction or sentence.

(4) Where, upon conviction, a fine has been imposed on a person or a compensation order has been made against him under section 249 of this Act, then, for a period of four weeks from the date of the verdict against such person or, in the event of an intimation of intention to appeal (or in the case of an appeal under section 106(1)(b) to (e), 108 or 108A of this Act a note of appeal) being lodged under this Part of this Act, until such appeal, if it is proceeded with, is determined—

(a) the fine or compensation order shall not be enforced against that person and he shall not be liable to make any payment in respect of the fine or compensation order; and

(b) any money paid by that person under the compensation order shall not be paid by the clerk of court to the person entitled to it under subsection (9) of the said section 249.

(5) In this section—

(a) "appeal" includes an appeal under section 288AA of this Act or paragraph 13(a) of Schedule 6 to the Scotland Act 1998; and

(b) in relation to such an appeal, references to an appeal being determined are to be read as references to the disposal of the proceedings by the High Court following determination of the appeal.

AMENDMENTS

Subss.(1)(b), (2)(b) and (4) as amended by Crime and Punishment (Scotland) Act 1997 (c.48) s.18(6) with effect from October 20, 1997 interms of SI 1997/2323 art.3, Sch.1.

Subs.(5) inserted by Scotland Act 1998 (Consequential Modifications) (No.1) Order 1999 (SI 1999/1042) art.3, Sch.1 para.13(3) (effective May 6, 1999).

Subs.(5)(a) as amended by Scotland Act 2012 (c.11) s.36(10). Brought into force on April 22, 2013 by SI 2013/6 art.2(c).

DEFINITION

"fine": s.307(1). A4-267.1

Suspension of certain sentences pending determination of appeal

121A.—(1) Where an intimation of intention to appeal or, in the case of an appeal under section 106(1)(b) to (e), 108 or 108A of this Act, a note of appeal is lodged, the court may on the application of the appellant direct that the whole, or any remaining part, of a relevant sentence shall be suspended until the appeal, if it is proceeded with, is determined. A4-267.2

(2) Where the court has directed the suspension of the whole or any remaining part of a person's relevant sentence, the person shall, unless the High Court otherwise directs, appear personally in court on the day or days fixed for the hearing of the appeal.

(3) Where a person fails to appear personally in court as mentioned in subsection

(2) above, the court may—

(a) if he is the appellant—

(i) decline to consider the appeal; and

(ii) dismiss it summarily; or

(b) whether or not he is the appellant—

(i) consider and determine the appeal; or

(ii) make such other order as the court thinks fit.

(4) In this section "relevant sentence" means any one or more of the following—

(aa) a community payback order;

(d) a restriction of liberty order.

(5) Subsections (1), (2) and (4) above apply to an appeal under section 288AA of this Act or paragraph 13(a) of Schedule 6 to the Scotland Act 1998 and, in relation to such an appeal—

(a) references to an appeal being determined are to be read as references to the disposal of the proceedings by the High Court following determination of the appeal; and

(b) the reference in subsection (2) to the hearing of the appeal is to be read as a reference to any subsequent hearing in the High Court in relation to the proceedings.

(6) Where a person fails to appear personally in court as mentioned in subsection (2) as read with subsection (5) above, the court may make such order as it thinks fit.

AMENDMENTS

Section 121A inserted by Crime and Punishment (Scotland) Act 1997 (c.48) s.24 with effect from August 1, 1997 interms of SI 1997/1712 art.3.

Subs.(4)(d) inserted by Crime and Punishment (Scotland) Act 1997 (c.48) s.24 (effective July 1, 1998: SI 1998/2323).

Subss.(5) and (6) inserted by Scotland Act 1998 (Consequential Modifications) (No.1) Order 1999 (SI 1999/1042) art.3, Sch.1 para.13(4) (effective May 6, 1999).

Subs.(1) as amended by Protection of Children (Scotland) Act 2003 (asp 5) s.16(5). Brought into force on January 10, 2005 by SSI 2004/522 (C.38) art.2.

Subs.(4) as amended by Criminal Justice and Licensing (Scotland) Act 2010 (asp 13) Sch.2 para.10. Brought into force on December 13, 2010 (subject to savings provisions in art.3) by SSI 2010/413 (C.28) art.2, Sch.1 para.1.

Subs.(1) as amended by Protection of Vulnerable Groups (Scotland) Act 2007 (asp 14) Sch.4 para.19. Brought into force on February 28, 2011 by SSI 2011/157 (C.13) art.2, subject to savings specified in art.5(1).

Subs.(5) as amended by Scotland Act 2012 (c.11) s.36(10). Brought into force on April 22, 2013 by SI 2013/6 art.2(c).

[THE NEXT PARAGRAPH IS A4-267.4]

General Note

A4-267.4 With effect from August 1, 1997 sentences detailed in subs.(4) are to be suspended pending the determination of an appeal. This should prevent the situation as arose in *HM Advocate v Jamieson*, 1996 S.C.C.R. 836 where an accused had completed the majority of a community service order and paid most of a compensation order prior to the hearing of an appeal. The Crown appeal against sentence was refused. In *HM Advocate v McKinlay*, 1998 S.C.C.R. 201, however, the Appeal Court upheld a Crown appeal against sentence despite completion of community service. Partial completion of probation and community service will be taken into account in any subsequent unduly lenient sentence appeal *HM Advocate v Paterson*, 2000 S.C.C.R. 309 and *HM Advocate v Drain*, 2000 S.C.C.R. 256. The fact that the Crown failed to exercise its right under s.121A is a relevant factor in determining unduly lenient sentence appeals—*HM Advocate v Carnall*, 1999 G.W.D. 31-1485.

[THE NEXT PARAGRAPH IS A4-268]

Fines and caution

A4-268 **122.**—(1) Where a person has on conviction been sentenced to payment of a fine and in default of payment to imprisonment, the person lawfully authorised to receive the fine shall, on receiving it, retain it until the determination of any appeal in relation to the conviction or sentence.

(2) If a person sentenced to payment of a fine remains in custody in default of payment of the fine he shall be deemed, for the purposes of this Part of this Act, to be a person sentenced to imprisonment.

(3) An appellant who has been sentenced to the payment of a fine, and has paid it in accordance with the sentence, shall, in the event of his appeal being successful, be entitled, subject to any order of the High Court, to the return of the sum paid or any part of it.

(4) A convicted person who has been sentenced to the payment of a fine and has duly paid it shall, if an appeal against sentence by the Lord Advocate or any appeal by the Lord Advocate or the Advocate General for Scotland under section 288AA of this Act or paragraph 13(a) of Schedule 6 to the Scotland Act 1998 results in the sentence being quashed and no fine, or a lesser fine than that paid, being imposed, be entitled, subject to any order of the High Court, to the return of the sum paid or as the case may be to the return of the amount by which that sum exceeds the amount of the lesser fine.

(5) In subsections (1) and (3) above, "appeal" includes an appeal under section 288AA of this Act or paragraph 13(a) of Schedule 6 to the Scotland Act 1998.

Amendments

Subs.(4) as amended by Scotland Act 1998 (Consequential Modifications) (No.1) Order 1999 (SI 1999/1042) art.3, Sch.1 para.13(5)(a) (effective May 6, 1999).

Subs.(5) inserted by Scotland Act 1998 (Consequential Modifications) (No.1) Order 1999 (SI 1999/1042) art.3, Sch.1 para.13(5)(b) (effective May 6, 1999).

Subs.(4)–(5) as amended by Scotland Act 2012 (c.11) s.36(10). Brought into force on April 22, 2013 by SI 2013/6 art.2(c).

Definitions

A4-268.1 "appellant": s.132.
"fine": s.307(1).
"High Court": s.307(1).

[THE NEXT PARAGRAPH IS A4-269]

Lord Advocate's reference

123.—(1) Where a person tried on indictment is acquitted or convicted of a charge, the Lord Advocate may refer a point of law which has arisen in relation to that charge to the High Court for their opinion; and the Clerk of Justiciary shall send to the person and to any solicitor who acted for the person at the trial, a copy of the reference and intimation of the date fixed by the Court for a hearing. **A4-269**

(2) The person may, not later than seven days before the date so fixed, intimate in writing to the Clerk of Justiciary and to the Lord Advocate either—

(a) that he elects to appear personally at the hearing; or

(b) that he elects to be represented thereat by counsel,

but, except by leave of the Court on cause shown, and without prejudice to his right to attend, he shall not appear or be represented at the hearing other than by and in conformity with an election under this subsection.

(3) Where there is no intimation under subsection (2)(b) above, the High Court shall appoint counsel to act at the hearing as *amicus curiae*.

(4) The costs of representation elected under subsection (2)(b) above or of an appointment under subsection (3) above shall, after being taxed by the Auditor of the Court of Session, be paid by the Lord Advocate.

(5) The opinion on the point referred under subsection (1) above shall not affect the acquittal or, as the case may be, conviction in the trial.

DEFINITIONS

"Clerk of Justiciary" : s.307(1). **A4-269.1**
"High Court": s.307(1).
"indictment" : s.307(1).

[THE NEXT PARAGRAPH IS A4-270]

GENERAL NOTE

There is no appeal against acquittal in solemn proceedings: see the terms of s.106(1) of this Act. It is incompetent in such proceedings to advocate either a verdict of acquittal by a jury, or an acquittal by a judge on a submission of no case to answer. However, should there then be a doubt about the law to be applied then the Lord Advocate may invoke the reference procedure provided by s.123. The expression "a point of law which has arisen in relation to that charge" in subs.(1) relates "not merely to points of law which are in some general way inherent in the charge itself but also to points of law which have actually arisen in the proceedings which led to acquittal or conviction … including points of law which arise from any defence which is advanced against the charge", *Lord Advocate's Reference (No. 1 of 2000)*, 2001 S.C.C.R. 296 at 333. It was open to the court to hear arguments on what were contended by the defence to be the real issues in the case. **A4-270**

A few such references have been taken on a diverse range of points of law: see *Lord Advocate's Reference No. 1 of 1983*, 1984 S.C.C.R. 62 (taped interviews); *Lord Advocate's Reference No. 1 of 1985*, 1987 S.L.T. 187 (perjury); *Lord Advocate's Reference No. 1 of 1992*, 1992 S.L.T. 1010 (building societies); *Lord Advocate's Reference No. 2 of 1992*, 1992 S.C.C.R. 960 (joke as motive); *Lord Advocate's Reference No. 1 of 1994*, 1995 S.L.T. 248 (supply of a controlled drug), *Lord Advocate's Reference No. 1 of 1996*, 1996 S.C.C.R. 516 (bankers' books) and *Lord Advocate's Reference (No.1 of 2000)*, 2001 S.C.C.R.296 (malicious mischief, necessity and international law).

The costs of representation elected under s.123(2)(b) are, after being taxed by the Auditor of the Court of Session, paid by the Lord Advocate: s.123(4).

Finality of proceedings and Secretary of State's reference

124.—(1) Nothing in this Part or Part XA of this Act shall affect the prerogative of mercy. **A4-271**

(2) Subject to Part XA and section 288AA of this Act and paragraph 13(a) of Schedule 6 to the Scotland Act 1998, every interlocutor and sentence pronounced by the High Court under this Part of this Act shall be final and conclusive and not subject to review by any court whatsoever and, except for the purposes of an appeal under section 288AA of this Act or paragraph 13(a) of that Schedule, it shall be incompetent to stay or suspend any execution or diligence issuing from the High Court under this Part of this Act.

(3)–(5) […]

AMENDMENTS

Subss.(1) and (2) as amended by Crime and Punishment (Scotland) Act 1997 Sch.1 para.21(18).

Subs.(2) as amended by Scotland Act 1998 (Consequential Modifications) (No.1) Order 1999 (SI 1999/1042) art.3, Sch.1 para.13(6) (effective 6 May 1999).

Subss.(3)–(5) repealed by Crime and Punishment (Scotland) Act 1997 Sch.1 para.21(18) and Sch.3 (effective 1 April 1999: SI 1999/652).

Subs.(2) as amended by Scotland Act 2012 (c.11) s.36(10). Brought into force on 22 April 2013 by SI 2013/6 art.2(c).

Subs.(2) as amended by Criminal Justice (Scotland) Act 2016 (asp 1) s.94. Brought into force on 17 January 2017 by SSI 2016/426 art.2 and Sch.1 para.1.

DEFINITIONS

A4-271.1 "High Court": s.307(1).
"sentence": s.132.

[THE NEXT PARAGRAPH IS A4-272]

GENERAL NOTE

Subs.(1)

A4-272 The prerogative of mercy remains unaffected by the provisions in Pt VIII of the 1995 Act. Precisely what this subsection means, in the context of subs.(3), is a matter of some interest. Some assistance may be found in *HM Advocate v Waddell*, 1976 S.L.T. (Notes) 61 and C. Gane "The Effect of a Pardon in Scots Law", 1980 J.R. 18.

Subs.(2)

In *McIntyre (Colin McLean) v HM Advocate*, 2009 S.C.C.R. 719 and *Harris (Stuart) v HM Advocate*, 2010 S.C.C.R. 50, the Appeal Court emphasised that the effect of s.124 is that once an appeal against conviction on indictment has been finally determined it is not competent for the Appeal Court to review that decision at the instance of an unsuccessful appellant or the Crown except under the express statutory powers governing references from the Scottish Criminal Cases Review Commission (see Part XA of this Act). In particular, a petition to the *nobile officium* is not competent.

This limitation applies to interlocutors and sentences pronounced by the High Court in appeals from solemn proceedings—*Express Newspapers Plc Petrs*, 1999 S.C.C.R. 262. Subsection (2) has been amended to permit appeals to the Judicial Committee of the Privy Council in terms of the Scotland Act 1998.

The *nobile officium* cannot be invoked to review the merits of decisions of the court exercising its appellate jurisdiction but it can be used to alter or correct an order pronounced by the Appeal Court where the court has exceeded its powers. See *Perrie Petr*, 1991 S.C.C.R. 475; *Beattie Petr*, 1997 S.C.C.R. 949; *Windsor Petr*, 1994 S.C.C.R. 59 and *Granger, Petr*, 2001 S.C.C.R. 337. In that case not even a decision by the ECtHR that failure to provide legal aid for an appeal constituted a breach of G's human rights permitted the appellant to use the nobile officium to review the merits of the Appeal Court's refusal of an appeal against conviction. In *Express Newspapers Plc Petrs*, above, a petition to the *nobile officium* was used to appeal fines imposed for contempt of court.

A valid interlocutor cannot be pronounced if a quorum of the Appeal Court is not constituted—*Hoekstra v HM Advocate (No.2)*, 2000 S.C.C.R. 368. The resulting setting aside of the courts interlocutor was thereafter held not to amount to an attempt by the Appeal Court to amend s.124(2) (finality of interlocutors) and did not give rise to a devolution issue. The Privy Council confirmed "except in regard to devolution issues as defined by para. 1 the position remains that every interlocutor of the High Court of Justiciary is final and conclusive and not subject to review by any court whatsoever", *Hoekstra v HM Advocate (No.4)*, 2000 S.C.C.R. 1121.

Reckoning of time spent pending appeal

A4-273 **125.**—(1) Subject to subsection (2) below, where a convicted person is admitted to bail under section 112 of this Act, the period beginning with the date of his admission to bail and ending on the date of his readmission to prison in consequence of the determination or abandonment of—

(a) his appeal; or, as the case may be,

(b) any relevant appeal by the Lord Advocate under section 108 or 108A of this Act,

shall not be reckoned as part of any term of imprisonment under his sentence.

(2) The time, including any period consequent on the recall of bail during which an appellant is in custody pending the determination of his appeal or, as the case

may be, of any relevant appeal by the Lord Advocate under section 108 or 108A of this Act shall, subject to any direction which the High Court may give to the contrary, be reckoned as part of any term of imprisonment under his sentence.

(3) Subject to any direction which the High Court may give to the contrary, imprisonment of an appellant or, where the appellant is the Lord Advocate, of a convicted person—

(a) who is in custody in consequence of the conviction or sentence appealed against, shall be deemed to run as from the date on which the sentence was passed;

(b) who is in custody other than in consequence of such conviction or sentence, shall be deemed to run or to be resumed as from the date on which his appeal was determined or abandoned;

(c) who is not in custody, shall be deemed to run or to be resumed as from the date on which he is received into prison under the sentence.

(4) In this section references to a prison and imprisonment shall include respectively references to a young offenders institution or place of safety or, as respects a child sentenced to be detained under section 208 of this Act, the place directed by the Secretary of State and to detention in such institution, centre or place of safety, or, as respects such a child, place directed by the Secretary of State and any reference to a sentence shall be construed as a reference to a sentence passed by the court imposing sentence or by the High Court on appeal as the case may require.

AMENDMENT

Subss.(1)(b) and (2) as amended by Crime and Punishment (Scotland) Act 1997 (c.48) s. 18(7) with effect from October 20, 1997 in terms of SI 1997/2323 art.3, Sch.1.

DEFINITIONS

"bail": s.307(1). A4-273.1
"prison": s.307(1).
"sentence": s. 132.
"young offender's institution": s.307(1).

GENERAL NOTE

Subsections 1 and 2 have been amended with effect from October 20, 1997 to provide that where an appellant is released on bail pending an appeal under s. 108A by the Lord Advocate this shall not be reckoned towards the calculation of the period of imprisonment. A4-273.2

Subsection (2)—see *Scott v HM Advocate*, 1946 J.C. 68 where an accused made a frivilous application for extension of time. The court refused to direct that the time he was treated as an appellant should count as part of his sentence.

[THE NEXT PARAGRAPH IS A4-274]

Extract convictions

126. No extract conviction shall be issued— A4-274

(a) during the period of four weeks after the day on which the conviction took place, except in so far as it is required as a warrant for the detention of the person convicted under any sentence which has been pronounced against him; nor

(b) where an intimation of intention to appeal or, in the case of an appeal under section 106(1)(b) to (e), 108 or 108A of this Act, a note of appeal is lodged, until the appeal, if it is proceeded with, is determined.

AMENDMENT

Subs.(b) as amended by Crime and Punishment (Scotland) Act 1997 (c.48) s. 18(8) with effect from October 20, 1997 in terms of SI 1997/2323 art.3, Sch.1.

DEFINITIONS

A4-274.1 "extract conviction": s.307(1).
"sentence": s.132.

GENERAL NOTE

A4-274.2 This has been amended with effect from October 20, 1997 to include appeals under s.108A.

[THE NEXT PARAGRAPH IS A4-275]

Forms in relation to appeals

A4-275 **127.**—(1) The Clerk of Justiciary shall furnish the necessary forms and, instructions in relation to intimations of intention to appeal, notes of appeal or notices of application under this Part of this Act to—

(a) any person who demands them; and
(b) to officers of courts, governors of prisons, and such other officers or persons as he thinks fit.

(2) The governor of a prison shall cause the forms and instructions mentioned in subsection (1) above to be placed at the disposal of prisoners desiring to appeal or to make any application under this Part of this Act.

(3) The governor of a prison shall, if requested to do so by a prisoner, forwarded on the prisoner's behalf to the Clerk of Justiciary any intimation, note or notice mentioned in subsection (1) above given by the prisoner.

DEFINITIONS

A4-275.1 "Clerk of Justiciary": s.307(1).
"governor": s.307(1).
"prison": s.307(1).

[THE NEXT PARAGRAPH IS A4-276]

Fees and expenses

A4-276 **128.** Except as otherwise provided in this Part of this Act, no court fees, or other fees or expenses shall be exigible from or awarded against an appellant or applicant in respect of an appeal or application under this Part of this Act.

Non-compliance with certain provisions may be waived

A4-277 **129.**—(1) Non-compliance with—

(a) the provisions of this Act set out in subsection (3) below; or
(b) any rule of practice for the time being in force under this Part of this Act relating to appeals,

shall not prevent the further prosecution of an appeal if the High Court or a judge thereof considers it just and proper that the non-compliance is waived or, in the manner directed by the High Court or judge, remedied by amendment or otherwise.

(2) Where the High Court or a judge thereof directs that the non-compliance is to be remedied, and the remedy is carried out, the appeal shall proceed.

(3) The provisions of this Act referred to in subsection (1) above are:—

section 94
section 103(1), (4), (6) and (7)
section 104(2) and (3)
section 105
section 106(4)
section 111
section 114
section 115

section 116
section 117
section 120(1), (3) and (4)
section 121
section 122
section 126
section 128.

(4) This section does not apply to any rule of practice relating to appeals under section 60 of this Act.

DEFINITIONS

"High Court": s.307(1). A4-277.1
"judge": s.307(1).

[THE NEXT PARAGRAPH IS A4-278]

GENERAL NOTE

This general saving power permits an appeal against conviction or sentence to proceed notwithstanding non-compliance with the rules specified in s.129(3) if it appears just and proper to proceed or if a consequential problem can be remedied. A4-278

Bill of suspension not competent

130. It shall not be competent to appeal to the High Court by bill of suspension against any conviction, sentence, judgement or order pronounced in any proceedings on indictment in the sheriff court. A4-279

DEFINITIONS

"indictment": s.307(1). A4-279.1
"sentence": s.132.

[THE NEXT PARAGRAPH IS A4-280]

GENERAL NOTE

The origins of this section lie in the Criminal Appeal (Scotland) Act 1926 which, by s.13, abolished appeal by suspension, but appeal by advocation from the sheriff in solemn procedure remained competent. A bill of suspension for an appeal by a witness found in contempt in the course of solemn proceedings in the sheriff court was held competent in *Butterworth v Herron*, 1975 S.L.T. (Notes) 56. This was later over-ruled when five judges held in *George Outram & Co. v Lees*, 1992 S.L.T. 32 that the correct mode of appeal was a petition to the *nobile officium*. In *Mellors v Normand (No.2)*, 1996 J.C. 148 the Appeal Court held it was appropriate to use a bill of suspension to suspend a committal warrant. A4-280

Bill of advocation not competent in respect of certain decisions

130A. It is not competent to bring under review of the High Court by way of bill of advocation a decision taken at a first diet or a preliminary hearing. A4–280.1

AMENDMENTS

Section 130A inserted by Criminal Justice (Scotland) Act 2016 (asp 1) s.92. Brought into force on 17 January 2017 by SSI 2016/426 art.2 and Sch.1 para.1.

[THE NEXT PARAGRAPH IS A4-281]

Prosecution appeal by bill of advocation

131.—(1) Without prejudice to section 74 of this Act, the prosecutor's right to bring a decision under review of the High Court by way of bill of advocation in accordance with existing law and practice shall extend to the review of a decision of any court of solemn jurisdiction. A4-281

(2) Where a decision to which a bill of advocation relates is reversed on the review of the decision the prosecutor may, whether or not there has already been a trial diet at which evidence has been led, proceed against the accused by serving

him with an indictment containing, subject to subsection (3) below, the charge or charges which were affected by the decision.

(3) The wording of the charge or charges referred to in subsection (2) above shall be as it was immediately before the decision appealed against.

DEFINITIONS

A4-281.1 "High Court": s.307(1).
"prosecutor": s.307(1).

[THE NEXT PARAGRAPH IS A4-282]

GENERAL NOTE

A4-282 In *HM Advocate v Sinclair*, 1987 S.L.T. 161 a shrieval decision to desert an indictment *pro loco et tempore* was successfully challenged by the Crown. The competency of the use of advocation by the Crown to review a sheriff's decision during the currency, rather than at the conclusion, of proceedings, and before final judgment was upheld in *HM Advocate v Khan*, 1997 S.C.C.R. 100 and in *HM Advocate v Shepherd*, 1997 S.C.C.R. 246 (see *A4–207* above). In *HM Advocate v Sorrie*, 1996 S.C.C.R. 778 the Appeal Court indicated that if the Crown seek to use a bill of advocation rather than an appeal in terms of s.74 of the Act the accused should be alerted to the fact. In *HM Advocate v Khan*, 1997 S.C.C.R. 100 the Crown successfully brought a Bill of Advocation against a sheriff's refusal to adjourn a diet and to grant a defence motion to discharge a juror while in *HM Advocate v Fleming*, 2005 S.C.C.R. 324, a decision by the trial judge in High Court proceedings, unusually, to desert simpliciter rather than *pro loco et tempore* was advocated.

Notwithstanding the marginal heading to the section, *Donnelly v AK and AR* [2012] HCJAC 44 affirms that advocation is a remedy available to both Crown and defence (see the discussion at A4-171 above). While no time bar applies to solemn advocation, it is important to note that as well as any implied or direct waiver of appeal, undue delay may be construed as acquiescence and close this appeal route.

As *HM Advocate v Paterson* [2012] HCJAC 105 illustrates, even substantial fault or procedural error on the Crown's part (here conceding acquittal instead of desertion *pro loco*) will not bar Advocation as a remedy.

Interpretation of Part VIII

A4-283 **132.** In this Part of this Act, unless the context otherwise requires—

"appellant" includes a person who has been convicted and desires to appeal under this Part of the Act;

"sentence" includes any order of the High Court made on conviction with reference to the person convicted or his wife or children, and any recommendation of the High Court as to the making of a deportation order in the case of a person convicted and the power of the High Court to pass a sentence includes a power to make any such order of the court or recommendation, and a recommendation so made by the High Court shall have the same effect for the purposes of Articles 20 and 21 of the Aliens Order 1953 as the certificate and recommendation of the convicting court.

PART IX – SUMMARY PROCEEDINGS

General

Application of Part IX of Act

A4-284 **133.**—(1) This Part of this Act applies to summary proceedings in respect of any offence which might prior to the passing of this Act, or which may under the provisions of this or any Act, whether passed before or after the passing of this Act, be tried summarily.

(2) Without prejudice to subsection (1) above, this Part of this Act also applies to procedure in all courts of summary jurisdiction in so far as they have jurisdiction in respect of—

(a) any offence or the recovery of a penalty under any enactment or rule of law which does not exclude summary procedure as well as, in accordance with section 211(3) and (4) of this Act, to the enforcement of a fine imposed in solemn proceedings; and

(b) any order *ad factum praestandum*, or other order of court or warrant competent to a court of summary jurisdiction.

(3) Where any statute provides for summary proceedings to be taken under any public general or local enactment, such proceedings shall be taken under this Part of this Act.

(4) Nothing in this Part of this Act shall—

(a) extend to any complaint or other proceeding under or by virtue of any statutory provision for the recovery of any rate, tax, or impost whatsoever; or

(b) affect any right to raise any civil proceedings.

(5) Except where any enactment otherwise expressly provides, all prosecutions under this Part of this Act shall be brought at the instance of the procurator fiscal.

DEFINITIONS

"court of summary jurisdiction": s.5(1) and (2) and s.307(1). **A4-284.1**
"offence": s.307(1).
"statute": s.307(1).
"summarily": s.5(1) and (2) and s.7(5) and (6).

[THE NEXT PARAGRAPH IS A4-285]

GENERAL NOTE

Part IX of the Act regulates the procedure in all summary cases including proceedings raised under local enactments as well as statutory provisions which apply generally. Revenue offences involving the Inland Revenue and HM Customs and Excise only adopt the procedures in Pt IX of the Act insofar as expressly stipulated within their relevant statutes. **A4-285**

It will be seen that subs.(2)(a) provides that summary provisions also apply to the enforcement of monetary fines imposed following solemn convictions and to the enforcement of fines imposed by other courts in Scotland, England and Wales unless such a jurisdiction is specifically excluded.

Incidental applications

134.—(1) This section applies to any application to a court for any warrant or order of court— **A4-286**

(a) as incidental to proceedings by complaint; or

(b) where a court has power to grant any warrant or order of court, although no subsequent proceedings by complaint may follow thereon.

(2) An application to which this section applies may be made by petition at the instance of the prosecutor in the form prescribed by Act of Adjournal.

(3) Where it is necessary for the execution of a warrant or order granted under this section, warrant to break open shut and lockfast places shall be implied.

DEFINITION

"complaint": s.307(1). **A4-286.1**

[THE NEXT PARAGRAPH IS A4-287]

GENERAL NOTE

This section determines that the form specified in the 1996 Act of Adjournal (Form 16.4.-A) shall be used for applications to the court by the prosecutor or the accused when summary proceedings have begun (subs.(1)(a)) or when the prosecutor, in carrying out his investigative role, seeks a search warrant, or other warrant, from a sheriff or magistrate even before any person has been charged with an offence (subs.(1)(b)); this latter provision will doubtless remain the most common use of this section. Examples of the range of warrants sought, can be found in *Carmichael, Complainer*, 1993 S.L.T. 305 (to precognosce a complainer on oath); *Frame v Houston*, 1992 S.L.T. 205 (warrant for hair samples of accused sought after indictment served); *Normand, Complainer*, 1992 S.L.T. 478 (warrant at common law to inspect bankers' books before proceedings have begun). **A4-287**

Summary warrants to apprehend which are used to commence proceedings and empower the arrest of a known accused are granted under s.139(1)(c) below.

In addition to the statutory power of apprehension and search enacted in s.135 below, a multiplicity of statutes contain their own express powers of search, detention and arrest, notably the Misuse of Drugs Act 1971, the Road Traffic Act 1988 and the Firearms Act 1968: these express provisions override the general powers contained in s.134.

In *Douglas v Crowe*, 1991 G.W.D. 40-2457 the procurator fiscal resorted to incidental application procedure to have citations as defence witnesses for himself and the Law Officers rescinded on the grounds that they had no evidence to offer pertinent to the case; the accused, on appeal, stated that citations had been served because he had a separate grievance against the procurator fiscal. His appeal by advocation was refused.

Note that where one of the parties has declined to make a joint application to the court to alter a diet as enabled by s.137 below, s.137(4) permits the use of an incidental application to put the matter before the court for consideration.

Reduction of incidental applications is by way of a bill of suspension. See, for example, *McIntyre v Munro*, 1999 G.W.D. 9–419 where an inept apprehension warrant was quashed.

Warrants of apprehension and search

A4-288 **135.**—(1) A warrant of apprehension or search may be in the form prescribed by Act of Adjournal or as nearly as may be in such form, and any warrant of apprehension or search shall, where it is necessary for its execution, imply warrant to officers of law to break open shut and lockfast places.

(2) A warrant of apprehension of an accused in the form mentioned in subsection (1) above shall imply warrant to officers of law to search for and to apprehend the accused, and to bring him before the court issuing the warrant, or before any other court competent to deal with the case, to answer to the charge on which such warrant is granted, and, in the meantime, until he can be so brought, to detain him in a police station, police cell, or other convenient place.

(3) […]

(4) […]

(5) A warrant of apprehension or other warrant shall not be required for the purpose of bringing before the court an accused who has been apprehended without a written warrant or who attends without apprehension in answer to any charge made against him.

Amendments

Subs.(3) as amended and subs.(4) repealed by Criminal Proceedings etc (Reform) (Scotland) Act 2007 (asp 6) ss.7(3), 80, Sch. para.17. Brought into force on 10 March 2008 by SSI 2008/42 (C.4) art.3 and Sch.

Subs.(3) repealed by Criminal Justice (Scotland) Act 2016 (asp 1) Sch.2 para.27(d). Brought into force on 25 January 2018 by SSI 2017/345 art.3 (subject to transitional and savings provisions in art.4).

Definition

A4-288.1 "officers of law": s.307(1).

[THE NEXT PARAGRAPH IS A4-289]

General Note

A4-289 As subs.(5) makes clear, the provisions of this section are intended to initiate proceedings against an accused whose identity is known to the prosecutor but who, for one reason or another, has not been apprehended and brought before the court to answer the charge against him. Rule 16.5-(1) of the 1996 Act of Adjournal stipulates that such warrants are to follow the styles shown as Forms 16.5-A and B (Warrants to apprehend following a failure to appear at a diet are granted under s.150 of the Act).

While the power granted by warrant under subs.(2) is to arrest the accused, it is competent for the prosecutor instead to exercise a discretion to invite the accused to appear at a specified court or police station on a given date and thus avoid the pains of arrest; see *Spowart v Burr* (1895) 1 Adam 539. It was held in *Young v Smith*, 1981 S.L.T. (Notes) 101; 1981 S.C.C.R. 85 that where an accused attended voluntarily in response to such an invitation the warrant had not been executed. Similarly failure to respond to such an invitation with the result that a warrant is executed, cannot work to the benefit of the accused (*Young v McLeod*, 1993 S.C.C.R. 479 where pleas of undue delay were repelled). *CH v Donnelly* [2013] HCJAC 17; 2013 S.C.C.R. 160 is a rare example of an initiating apprehension warrant being suspended by the Appeal Court, the accused's agent having previously been informed, apparently incorrectly by a member of the fiscal's staff, that there were to be no proceedings, and the full background not being made known to the sheriff thereafter when the Crown craved the warrant.

The wording of subss.(3) and (4) paraphrases the terms of s.321(3) of the 1975 Act and, following *Robertson v MacDonald*, 1993 S.L.T. 1337; 1992 S.C.C.R. 916 would appear to be directory rather than mandatory in its effect. In *Robertson*, the accused had been arrested upon a petition warrant, granted at Wick Sheriff Court, in Glasgow. He was conveyed to Wick and made his appearance on summary complaint four days later when he took objection to the competency of proceedings. Albeit a breach of the subsection had occurred, the court upheld Crown submissions that itself did not vitiate proceedings. A challenge to the granting of a summary complaint initiating warrant is found in *McMillan v PF Paisley* [2017] SAC (Crim) 2. There a Bill of Suspension was sought to be argued before the Sheriff Appeal Court which declined jurisdiction since the warrant had been granted by the sheriff in his administrative capacity before summary proceedings had commenced and, as such, remained privative to the High Court. The acid test, applied in this instance, is the point at which the warrant is sought. In *McMillan* the prosecutor had obtained the warrant conform to s.135(1) before any proceedings had been activated and, at that point, no complaint had formally called. By contrast an expediency warrant, craved in terms of s.139(1)(b) once the complaint was called in open court and when an absent accused could be shown to the court's satisfaction to have notice of that diet would seem to be referable to the Sheriff Appeal Court. The judgment itself confusingly describes the warrant as "an expediency or initiating warrant"—the latter form is discussed at s.139 Notes—but correctly distinguishes the marked procedural differences between the two which impelled the SAC's declinature of jurisdiction.

So far as search warrants are concerned it is well-understood that it is incompetent to look behind the grant of a warrant (*Allan v Tant*, 1986 S.C.C.R. 175; *HM Advocate v Rae*, 1992 S.C.C.R. 1) and there is a general presumption of regularity where the warrant appears *ex facie* valid (*MacNeill, Complainer*, 1984 S.LT. 157 and *HM Advocate v Beggs (No.4)*, 2002 S.L.T. 163). A distinction has to be drawn between review of an *ex facie* valid warrant which requires a Bill of Suspension in the High Court to be challenged, and, on the other hand, issues of admissibility of evidence garnered prior to granting of a warrant or beyond the scope of the warrant granted which in solemn procedure can be addressed by means of a s.71 minute in the court of first instance without such suspension; see *Sturrock v HM Advocate* [2016] HCJAC 97; 2017 S.C.C.R. 340, a three judge decision remitted to a court of five judges whose decision is reported as *AS v HM Advocate* [2016] HCJAC 126. Refer also to the Notes to ss.296 and 297 below.

Time limit for certain offences

136.—(1) Proceedings under this Part of this Act in respect of any offence to which this section applies shall be commenced— **A4-290**

(a) within six months after the contravention occurred;

(b) in the case of a continuous contravention, within six months after the last date of such contravention,

and it shall be competent in a prosecution of a contravention mentioned in paragraph (b) above to include the entire period during which the contravention occurred.

(2) This section applies to any offence triable only summarily and consisting of the contravention of any enactment, unless the enactment fixes a different time limit.

(3) For the purposes of this section proceedings shall be deemed to be commenced on the date on which a warrant to apprehend or to cite the accused is granted, if the warrant is executed without undue delay.

Time limit for certain offences.

136.—*(1) Proceedings under this Part of this Act in respect of any offence to which this section applies shall be commenced—* **A4-290A**

(a) within 12 months after the contravention occurred;

(b) in the case of a continuous contravention, within 12 months after the last date of such contravention,

and it shall be competent in a prosecution of a contravention mentioned in paragraph (b) above to include the entire period during which the contravention occurred.

(2) This section applies to any offence triable only summarily and consisting of the contravention of any enactment, unless the enactment fixes a different time limit.

(3) For the purposes of this section proceedings shall be deemed to be commenced on the date on which a warrant to apprehend or to cite the accused is granted, if the warrant is executed without undue delay.

Amendment

In relation to COVID-19, s.136 as amended by Coronavirus (Scotland) Act 2020 (asp 7) Sch.4(4) para.10(4) (effective 7 April 2020).

Definition

A4-290.1 "offence": s.307(1).

[THE NEXT PARAGRAPH IS A4-291]

General Note

A4-291 The peremptory nature of these provisions in the 1975 Act inevitably produced a substantial volume of case law. Section 136 appears to re-enact the terms of s.331 of the 1975 Act which applied a six-month time bar to the raising of summary prosecutions of statutory offences; however subs.(2) now restricts the operation of the provisions to cases which are triable summarily only, and to statutory enactments which contain their own express time bar provisions. See for example *Gilday v Ritchie*, 1999 G.W.D. 32-1528, a prosecution under the Misuse of Drugs Act 1971 on summary complaint, where it was held that the statute's specific time bar was not set aside by the terms of s.136 above.

Note that this time-bar provision, which now applies to a more limited number of statutory offences than were affected by s.331 of the 1975 Act, does not apply to the libelling of common law offences. While pleas to the competency of proceedings on the grounds of time-bar should now be less commonplace, it may be noted that a delay on the part of the Crown in initiating proceedings could well justify a plea of *mora*. (For *mora* see generally *Tudhope v McCarthy*, 1985 J.C. 48; 1985 S.L.T. 392; *McFarlane v Jessop*, 1988 S.L.T. 596; 1988 S.C.C.R. 186; *Connachan v Douglas*, 1990 S.L.T. 563; 1990 S.C.C.R.101).

The issue of *mora* was not argued explicitly in *Higson v Morrison*, 2001 G.W.D. 16-600 where M had taken objection, on Convention grounds, to proceedings against him under the Road Traffic Act 1988. These had been initiated by means of certification by the Lord Advocate specifying the date upon which sufficient information came to his knowledge to justify proceedings. M's challenge to proceedings failed under s.136 since the offence was not triable only summarily but the sheriff expressed some unease about the conclusive nature of such certification—the court having no power to look behind it—and opined that proceedings initiated so long after the event might be capable of reduction on the basis that they offended against Convention rights. The court did not review the public interest considerations which arguably underpin the kinds of offence which can be certified by the Lord Advocate; these tend to be offences, for example driving without insurance, or driving while disqualified, where discovery of the offence might take some time.

Proceedings will normally be commenced by the postal service of a citation and service copy complaint upon the accused, but can also be started by an initiating warrant or by obtaining an assigned diet within the six-month period for a diet outwith that period; the question of whether the prosecutor has complied with the statutory timebar provisions has to be approached differently in each of these situations. Service by post of a complaint timeously to call at a diet within the six-month date offers no difficulty; the proceedings commence on the date of posting of the complaint. The same rule applies to the service of a complaint to call at a diet after the expiry of six-months; in that event the proceedings are still competent, provided that the complaint is sent and received within the six-month date and calls at the cited diet (see *Keily v Tudhope*, 1986 S.C.C.R. 351; 1987 S.L.T. 99; *Orr v Lowdon*, 1987 S.C.C.R. 515 and *Slater v Howdle*, 2002 G.W.D. 31-1063); it is desirable that the prosecutor is able to produce an execution of service of the complaint in that latter situation.

Different considerations apply when the prosecutor elects to proceed instead by way of either an initiating warrant or by a warrant to cite the accused to an assigned diet. The grant of either form of warrant signals the commencement of the proceedings and to preserve those proceedings the warrant must in either case be executed without undue delay. It must be emphasised however that while an initiating warrant may well be a valid basis for proceedings months later (if the prosecutor can show that there was no undue delay on his part, a matter discussed later), in the case of a warrant to cite the complaint will either stand or fall on the date of the assigned diet (*Tudhope v Buckner*, 1985 S.C.C.R. 352).

If service has not been effected upon the accused prior to the diet then the complaint necessarily falls. The only option available to the prosecutor should he learn of difficulty in effecting service of a warrant to cite, is to withdraw the warrant and reraise by means of an initiating warrant if this can be done before the expiry of the timebar.

Once an initiating warrant or a warrant to cite has been obtained, any undue delay in its execution must not be attributable to the actions (or inactions) of the prosecutor. Generally, reported cases have focused upon what constitutes "undue delay" and it has to be stressed that even where a warrant to cite an accused to a diet outwith the six-month period is granted timeously, the prosecutor must still effect service of the complaint swiftly. The onus of proof of "no undue delay" rests with the Crown and if facts are in dispute, the court should hear evidence of the steps taken to execute the warrant (*McCartney v Tudhope*, 1985 S.C.C.R. 373; 1986 S.L.T. 159). An incorrect address in the instance of the complaint and frustrated efforts to serve at the correct address by post and personally were held not to constitute "undue delay"; see *McKay v Normand*, 1995 G.W.D. 39-1995.

Statutory Exceptions

It is well understood that where a statute provides specific time limits for procedures or proceedings, then those time limits apply and are not affected by the generality of s.136; see for example *Gilday v Ritchie*, 2000 S.C.C.R. 53, a Misuse of Drugs Act 1971 prosecution which was time-barred. **A4-291.1**

[THE NEXT PARAGRAPH IS A4-292]

Computation of Time

The six-month period is calculated *de die in diem* and not *de momento in momentum* (see *Tudhope v Lawson*, 1983 S.C.C.R. 435; *Lees v Lovell*, 1992 S.L.T. 967; 1992 S.C.C.R. 557 following *Keenan v Carmichael*, 1991 S.C.C.R. 680), i.e. excluding the date of offence. **A4-292**

In the exceptional circumstances produced by the death, illness or absence of the judge, which has interrupted a part-heard trial, s.151(2) permits a new prosecution of a statutory complaint raised within two months of its desertion, notwithstanding the usual timebar on statutory proceedings.

Undue Delay

Warrants are sought for arrest or for the assignment of a diet for a date usually outwith the normal prescriptive period. Undue delay where established is fatal to proceedings on that complaint and the result of such a finding is to preclude any further proceedings on a statutory (but not a common law) charge. The delay has to be attributable to the prosecutor alone and will be assessed according to the facts of each case. The presiding judge has a broad discretion in deciding the issue. Execution of the warrant extends to any action taken by the prosecutor to effect citation whether by post or other means (*Lockhart v Bradley*, 1977 S.L.T. 5); "undue delay" was defined in *Smith v Peter Walker and Son (Edinburgh)*, 1978 J.C. 44. **A4-293**

Examples of undue delay are found in *Carmichael v Sardar and Sons*, 1983 S.C.C.R. 433 (unexplained period of six days), *Harvey v Lockhart*, 1991 S.C.C.R. 83; 1992 S.L.T. 68 (14 days but the sheriff had erred in reaching a decision without hearing explanations for the delay), *Robertson v Carmichael*, 1993 S.C.C.R. 841 (four days unexplained and not investigated).

Undue delay was not established in *Stagecoach v MacPhail*, 1986 S.C.C.R. 184 (seven days between warrant to cite and service), *Anderson v Lowe*, 1991 S.C.C.R. 712 (warrant mislaid in Sheriff Clerk's office for three days), *Buchan v McNaughtan*, 1990 S.C.C.R. 688; 1991 S.L.T. 410 (delay attributed to conduct of accused), *Young v MacPhail*, 1991 S.C.C.R. 630; 1992 S.L.T. 98 (a warrant granted for accused then serving a prison sentence in England not being executed until his date of release), or in *Melville v Normand*, 1996 S.L.T. 826 (a combination of public holidays, the warrant being sent to the wrong police office and execution being delayed by the police until the conclusion of the accused's High Court trial on other charges, this last practice being viewed as a sound one), *Alexander v Normand*, 1997 S.L.T. 370 (a delay of 13 days before issuing the warrant to the police where the time-bar was still two months away followed by three abortive attempts to execute the warrant), *McGlennan v Singh*, 1993 S.C.C.R. 341 (16 days lapsed from grant of warrant till its execution, but the sheriff had moved too summarily in finding against the Crown).

The period to be taken into account in assessing delay is from the date of granting of the warrant until its execution, not the time from the expiry of the prescriptive period until the execution of the warrant (see *MacNeill v Cowie*, 1984 S.C.C.R. 449; *McNellie v Walkingshaw*, 1990 S.C.C.R. 428; 1991 S.L.T. 892) but it must be emphasised that the issue of delay will only arise where service is effected outwith the six-month time-bar period. Hence in *Chow v Lees*, 1997 S.C.C.R. 253, where the prosecutor was granted an apprehension warrant shortly before expiry of the time-bar and elected to invite the accused to appear voluntarily on a date after that expiry, the Appeal Court directed the sheriff (who had repelled a plea to the competency) to consider the issue of undue delay; it had taken Crown over a week to instruct an invitation to be sent to the accused and a further week to intimate to him a date for his appearance.

Reduction of Proceedings to Summary Complaint

The anticipated impact of the decision in *Gardner v Lees*, 1996 S.C.C.R. 168, which required that any petition proceedings later reduced to a summary complaint had to be concluded within a year of the original appearance on petition, has been blunted by the express provisions of the Criminal Procedure and Investigations Act 1996 (c.25) s.73(3). This statutory provision, which amended s.65(1) of the 1995 Act, has the effect of removing any time-bar on such summary proceedings while restating the time-bar applicable to solemn proceedings (carried over from s.101 of the 1975 Act, i.e. one year from petition appearance to the date of commencement of indictment proceedings). The effects of the interplay between ss.65 and 136 of the Act are amply illustrated by *Potts v PF Paisley* [2017] HCJAC 8. P originally appeared on petition and was subsequently indicted on a charge of domestic housebreaking involving theft of a sum of £50,000. A series of abortive jury trial diets, re-indictments and extensions to the year time bar followed. Ultimately, the sheriff's grant of yet a further Crown motion to adjourn, with attendant s.65 extension to afford the prosecution a further opportunity to obtain necessary evidence, was successfully overturned on appeal to the High Court. Section 65(1A)(b) precluded further solemn proceedings but, in the absence of oppression, could not bar the Crown from initiating (albeit tardily) a summary complaint. **A4-294**

While *Gardner v Lees* may assist in understanding the constitutional origins of the statutory timebar, the jurisprudential justification for applying those principles equally to non-custodial summary proceedings was, to say the least, doubtful; the leap of logic which required summary trial proceedings to be concluded within a year (rather than commenced as s.101 demanded of solemn proceedings) was more questionable still. Effectively the statutory amendment to s.65 brings the law back to that stated in *MacDougall v Russell*, 1985 S.C.C.R. 441 and *Whitelaw v Dickinson*, 1993 S.C.C.R. 164. See A4-149 in relation to the computation of the time of such proceedings and *Duke v Lees*, 1997 G.W.D. 15-659.

Time limits for transferred and related cases

A4-294.1 **136A.—**(1) This section applies where the prosecutor recommences proceedings by complaint containing both—

(a) a charge to which proceedings—

(i) transferred to a court by authority of an order made under section 137A or 137CA of this Act; or

(ii) transferred to, or taken at, a court by authority of an order made under 137B or 137CB of this Act,

relate; and

(b) a charge to which previous proceedings at that court relate.

(2) Where this section applies, proceedings for an offence charged in that complaint are, for the purposes of—

(a) section 136 of this Act (so far as applying to the offence);

(b) any provision of any other enactment for a time limit within which proceedings are to be commenced (so far as applying to the offence); and

(c) any rule of law relating to delay in bringing proceedings (so far as applying to the offence),

to be regarded as having been commenced when any previous proceedings for the offence were first commenced.

AMENDMENTS

Section 136A inserted by Criminal Proceedings etc (Reform) (Scotland) Act 2007 (asp 6) s.23. Brought into force on 10 March 2008 by SSI 2008/42 (C.4) art.3 and Sch.

Subs.(1) as amended by Criminal Justice and Licensing (Scotland) Act 2010 (asp 13) Sch.7 para.52. Brought into force on 28 March 2011 by SSI 2011/178 (C.15) art.2 Sch.1 para.1.

DEFINITIONS

A4-294.2 "prosecutor": s.307(1).
"complaint": s.307(1).
"offence":s.307(1).

GENERAL NOTE

A4-294.3 The new section ensures that any case transferred under the provisions in ss.137A or 137B, and which has necessitated the raising of a fresh complaint does not a result fall foul of the time bar for the initiation of proceedings. Essentially the time bar is to be taken as the date upon which the proceedings were commenced or initiated in the originating court rather than the date when proceedings began in the receiving sheriffdom. While this provision infers that any transfer of case requires the fresh commencement of proceedings, it is debatable whether this is entirely conclusive. It is arguable that existing proceedings on a summary complaint could be maintained after a transfer order if a specific minute so specified.

Time limits where fixed penalty offer etc. made

A4-294.4 **136B.—**(1) For the purposes of section 136 of this Act, and any provision of any other enactment for a time limit within which proceedings are to be commenced, in calculating the period since a contravention occurred—

(a) where a fixed penalty offer is made under section 302(1) of this Act, the period between the date of the offer and—

(i) the receipt by the procurator fiscal of a notice under section 302(4) of this Act;

(ii) a recall of the fixed penalty by virtue of section 302C of this Act,

shall be disregarded;

(b) where a compensation offer is made under section 302A(1) of this Act, the period between the date of the offer and—
    (i) the receipt by the procurator fiscal of a notice under section 302A(4) of this Act;
    (ii) a recall of the offer by virtue of section 302C of this Act,
shall be disregarded;

(c) where a work offer is made under section 303ZA(1) of this Act, the period between the date of the offer and—
    (i) if the alleged offender does not accept the offer in the manner described in section 303ZA(5) of this Act, the last date for notice of acceptance of the offer;
    (ii) if the alleged offender accepts the offer as so described, but fails to complete the subsequent work order, the date specified for completion of the order,
shall be disregarded.

(2) A certificate purporting to be signed by or on behalf of the prosecutor which states a period to be disregarded by virtue of subsection (1) above is sufficient authority for the period to be disregarded.

AMENDMENTS

Section 136B inserted by Criminal Proceedings etc (Reform) (Scotland) Act 2007 (asp 6) s.54. Brought into force on 10 March 2008 by SSI 2008/42 (C.4) art.3 and Sch.

[THE NEXT PARAGRAPH IS A4-295]

Alteration of diets

137.—(1) Where a diet has been fixed in a summary prosecution, it shall be competent for the court, on a joint application in writing by the parties or their solicitors, to discharge the diet and fix an earlier diet in lieu. A4-295

(2) Where the prosecutor and the accused make joint application to the court (orally or in writing) for postponement of a diet which has been fixed, the court shall discharge the diet and fix a later diet in lieu unless the court considers that it should not do so because there has been unnecessary delay on the part of one of more of the parties.

(3) Where all the parties join in an application under subsection (2) above, the court may proceed under that subsection without hearing the parties.

(4) Where the prosecutor has intimated to the accused that he desires to postpone or accelerate a diet which has been fixed, and the accused refuses, or any of the accused refuse, to make a joint application to the court for that purpose, the prosecutor may make an incidental application for that purpose under section 134 of this Act; and after giving the parties an opportunity to be heard, the court may discharge the diet and fix a later diet or, as the case may be, an earlier diet in lieu.

(5) Where an accused had intimated to the prosecutor and to all the other accused that he desires such postponement or acceleration and the prosecutor refuses, or any of the other accused refuse, to make a joint application to the court for that purpose, the accused who has so intimated may apply to the court for that purpose; and, after giving the parties an opportunity to be heard, the court may discharge the diet and fix a later diet or, as the case may be, an earlier diet in lieu.

DEFINITIONS

"diet": s.307(1). A4-295.1
"prosecutor": s.307(1).

General Note

A4-295.2 This section provides procedures for applications to the court for alteration of summary diets on joint motion, and for such applications to be made by a party in the absence of agreement of all parties. While the amendments made to subs.(1) by the 2007 Act might be thought to apply to any summary proceedings, the marginal note or heading above, and the terms of s.137B below, indicate that the intention is to apply these provisions to sheriff summary proceedings Where all parties concur in making a written application timeously, the court can dispose of it administratively. Note however that the court's power to refuse an application for postponement on grounds of unnecessary delay by one of the parties suggests that a hearing would be required before the motion could be decided by the court.

Subss.(4) and (5) respectively provide for the prosecutor and the accused to make application individually to the court for variation of the diet in situations where other parties will not concur. The prosecutor should make application by way of an incidental application (see s.134 above) while the accused, although it is not stipulated in subs.(5), can petition using Form 16.7 provided in the 1996 Act of Adjournal.

In *White v Ruxton*, 1996 S.C.C.R. 427 it was held in the absence of a court minute recording a new diet of trial fixed by Joint Minute of Acceleration that the minute itself, whose terms were not in dispute, was sufficient for the purpose. Objections to the competency of the proceedings were rejected.

Similar provisions in relation to indictments are found in ss.75A and 75B of the 1995 Act as amended.

[THE NEXT PARAGRAPH IS A4-296]

Refixing diets: non-sitting days

A4-296 **137ZA.**—(1) This section applies where in a summary prosecution any diet has been fixed for a non-sitting day.

(2) The court may at any time before the non-sitting day—

(a) discharge the diet; and

(b) fix a new diet for a date earlier or later than that for which the discharged diet was fixed.

(3) That is, by acting—

(a) of the court's own accord; and

(b) without the need for a hearing for the purpose.

(4) In the case of a trial diet—

(a) the prosecutor;

(b) the accused,

shall be entitled to an adjournment of the new diet fixed if the court is satisfied that it is not practicable for that party to proceed with the case on that date.

(5) The power of the court under subsection (1) above is not exercisable for the sole purpose of ensuring compliance with a time limit applying in the proceedings.

(6) In subsections (1) and (2) above, a "non-sitting day" is a day on which the court is under this Act not required to sit.

Amendments

Section 137ZA inserted by Criminal Proceedings etc (Reform) (Scotland) Act 2007 (asp 6) s.39. Brought into force on 10 December 2007 by SSI 2007/479 (C.40) art.3 and Sch.

Title as amended by Act of Adjournal (Amendment of the Criminal Procedure (Scotland) Act 1995) (Refixing diets) 2011 (SSI 2011/430) art.2(5) (effective 30 January 2012).

Refixing diets: non-suitable days

A4-296.0.1 **137ZB.**—(1) Where in a summary prosecution any diet has been fixed for a day which is no longer suitable to the court it may, of its own accord, at any time before that diet—

(a) discharge the diet; and

(b) fix a new diet for a date earlier or later than that for which the discharged diet was fixed.

(2) […]

Amendments

Section 137ZB inserted by Act of Adjournal (Amendment of the Criminal Procedure (Scotland) Act 1995) (Refixing diets) 2011 (SSI 2011/430) art.2(4) (effective 30 January 2012).

Subsection (2) repealed by Act of Adjournal (Criminal Procedure (Scotland) Act 1995 Amendment) (Miscellaneous) 2020 (SSI 2020/93) (effective 25 March 2020).

[THE NEXT PARAGRAPH IS A4-296.1]

Transfer of sheriff court summary proceedings within sheriffdom

137A.—(1) Where this subsection applies, the prosecutor may apply to the sheriff for an order for the transfer of the proceedings to a sheriff court in any other district in that sheriffdom and for adjournment to a diet of that court. **A4-296.1**

(1A) Subsection (1) above applies—

(a) where the accused person has been cited in summary proceedings to attend a diet of the court; or

(b) if the accused person has not been cited to such a diet, where summary proceedings against the accused have been commenced in the court.

(2) On an application under subsection (1) above the sheriff may make such order as is mentioned in that subsection.

AMENDMENTS

Section 137A inserted by Criminal Justice (Scotland) Act 2003 (asp 7) Pt 8 s.58. Brought into force on 27 June 2003 by SSI 2003/288 (C.14).

Subsection (1) as amended and subs.(1A) inserted by Criminal Proceedings etc (Reform) (Scotland) Act 2007 (asp 6) s.22. Brought into force on 10 March 2008 by SSI 2008/42 (C.4) art.3 and Sch.

GENERAL NOTE

This new provision entitles the prosecutor, at any point in the proceedings, to apply to the sheriff for authority to cite accused persons, and transfer the proceedings to elsewhere in the sheriffdom. Section 137B enables the sheriff clerk to inform the prosecutor of exceptional factors which would justify the transfer of existing business, and cited diets, to another sheriffdom. (Some assistance may be found in the General Notes to s.83 above). The transfer arrangements between sheriffdoms are contingent upon there being agreement between the sheriff principals involved *before* any application by the prosecutor is granted. In summary proceedings it is conceivable that joint minute procedures could be utilised to transfer ongoing proceedings under both these sections. **A4-296.1.1**

Transfer of sheriff court summary proceedings within sheriffdom: power of sheriff principal

137AA. Where, because of exceptional circumstances which could not reasonably have been foreseen, it is not practicable for a sheriff court in a sheriffdom to proceed with some or all of the summary cases due to call at a diet, the sheriff principal may, of the sheriff principal's own accord, make an order for— **A4-296.1.2**

(a) the transfer of the proceedings to a sheriff court in any other district in that sheriffdom; and

(b) adjournment to a diet of that court.

AMENDMENT

Section 137AA inserted by Act of Adjournal (Criminal Procedure (Scotland) Act 1995 Amendment) (Miscellaneous) 2020 (SSI 2020/93) para.2 (effective 25 March 2020).

GENERAL NOTE

Similar provisions for the transfer of sheriff court proceedings are to be found in s.137 above; the instant provision was introduced by the Act of Adjournal (Criminal Procedure (Scotland) Act 1995 Amendment) (Miscellaneous) 2020 (SSI 2020/93) in the wake of the coronavirus pandemic. The critical features of s.137AA are that the transfer procedure can be initiated by the Sheriff Principal (rather than the procurator fiscal) and need not involve the parties to the proceedings at all. Paragraph 2(3) of the same statutory instrument enacts an identical provision for sheriff solemn proceedings. **A4-296.1.3**

[THE NEXT PARAGRAPH IS A4-296.2]

Transfer of sheriff court summary proceedings outwith sheriffdom

137B.—(1) Where the sheriff clerk informs the prosecutor that, because of exceptional circumstances which could not reasonably have been foreseen, it is not **A4-296.2**

practicable for the sheriff court or any other sheriff court in the sheriffdom to proceed with some or all of the summary cases due to call at a diet, the prosecutor shall as soon as practicable apply to the sheriff principal for an order for—

(a) the transfer of the proceedings to a sheriff court in another sheriffdom; and

(b) adjournment to a diet of that court.

(1A) Where this subsection applies, the prosecutor may apply to the sheriff for an order for—

(a) the transfer of the proceedings to a sheriff court in another sheriffdom; and

(b) adjournment to a diet of that court,

if there are also summary proceedings against the accused person in that court in the other sheriffdom.

(1B) Subsection (1A) above applies—

(a) where the accused person has been cited in summary proceedings to attend a diet of the court; or

(b) if the accused person has not been cited to such a diet, where summary proceedings against the accused have been commenced in the court.

(1C) Where the prosecutor intends to take summary proceedings against an accused person in the sheriff court, the prosecutor may apply to the sheriff for an order for authority for the proceedings to be taken at a sheriff court in another sheriffdom if there are also summary proceedings against the accused person in that court in the other sheriffdom.

(2) On an application under subsection (1) above the sheriff principal may make the order sought, provided that the sheriff principal of the other sheriffdom consents.

(2A) On an application under subsection (1A) or (1C) above, the sheriff is to make the order sought if—

(a) the sheriff considers that it would be expedient for the different cases involved to be dealt with by the same court; and

(b) a sheriff of the other sheriffdom consents.

(3) On the application of the prosecutor, a sheriff principal who has made an order under subsection (2) above may, if the sheriff principal of the other sheriffdom mentioned in that subsection consents—

(a) revoke; or

(b) vary so as to restrict the effect of,

that order.

(4) On the application of the prosecutor, the sheriff who has made an order under subsection (2A) above (or another sheriff of the same sheriffdom) may, if a sheriff of the other sheriffdom mentioned in paragraph (b) of that subsection consents—

(a) revoke; or

(b) vary so as to restrict the effect of,

that order.

AMENDMENTS

Section 137B inserted by Criminal Justice (Scotland) Act 2003 (asp 7) Pt 8 s.58. Brought into force on 27 June 2003 by SSI 2003/288 (C.14).

Subs.(1) substituted and subss.(1A)-(1C), (2A), (4) inserted by Criminal Proceedings etc (Reform) (Scotland) Act 2007 (asp 6) s.22. Brought into force on 10 March 2008 by SSI 2008/42 (C.4) art.3 and Sch.

Subs.(4) as amended by Criminal Justice and Licensing (Scotland) Act 2010 (asp 13) Sch.7 para.53. Brought into force on 28 March 2011 by SSI 2011/178 art.2 and Sch.1 para.1.

GENERAL NOTE

Section 137A of the 1995 Act already permitted summary cases to be moved for administrative reasons, within a sheriffdom for further procedure. That procedure has been extended slightly now and permits transfer of business to other sheriffdoms. Again this can be triggered either by identifying undue pressure of business or, in relation to individual accused, by associating live cases against an accused in other sheriffdoms. In each case it is the prosecutor who must elect to initiate either a transfer of business, or of an individual case. Note that it is only the prosecutor who is shedding or shifting business who can seek its transfer; the fiscal in the receiving jurisdiction has no such power. In all cases it will be appreciated, as subs.(2A) states, that sheriffs in both (or all) jurisdictions affected by the proposal must consent to tranfers before they can be approved. A4-296.3

Custody cases: initiating proceedings outwith sheriffdom

137C.—(1) Where the prosecutor believes— A4-296.4

(a) that, because of exceptional circumstances (and without an order under subsection (3) below), it is likely that there would be an unusually high number of accused persons appearing from custody for the first calling of cases in summary prosecutions in the sheriff courts in the sheriffdom; and

(b) that it would not be practicable for those courts to deal with all the cases involved, the prosecutor may apply to the sheriff principal for the order referred to in subsection (2) below.

(2) For the purposes of subsection (1) above, the order is for authority for summary proceedings against some or all of the accused persons to be—

(a) taken at a sheriff court in another sheriffdom; and

(b) maintained—

(i) there; or

(ii) at any of the sheriff courts referred to in subsection (1) above as may at the first calling of the case be appointed for further proceedings.

(3) On an application under subsection (1) above, the sheriff principal may make the order sought with the consent of the sheriff principal of the other sheriffdom.

(4) An order under subsection (3) above may be made by reference to a particular period or particular circumstances.

AMENDMENTS

Section 137C inserted by Criminal Proceedings etc (Reform) (Scotland) Act 2007 (asp 6) s.22. Brought into force on March 10, 2008 by SSI 2008/42 (C.4) art.3 and Sch.

GENERAL NOTE

This new section enables the prosecutor to apply to his sheriff principal to transfer some part of the sheriffdom's summary custody business to another sheriffdom when it is considered that there will be exceptional pressure upon his custody court facilities. It seems implicit, from a reading of subs (b), that a transfer out of the jurisdiction should be considered only once it is clear that other courts within the "home" sheriffdom cannot deal with the business. Again the agreement of both (or all) sheriffs principal has to be secured before a transfer can be ordered. A4-296.5

Subs.(4) allows that an order can be in response to a specific situation (for example large scale protests of the sort seen during the G8 conference at Gleneagles in Perthshire) or for a specified time period, but neither is essential for a transfer order to be lawful. Theoretically nothing precludes the transfer of proceedings against only some of the accused, in a multiple accused case, either to elsewhere in the sheriffdom or even to another sheriffdom.

Transfer of JP court proceedings within sheriffdom

137CA.—(1) Subsection (2) applies— A4-296.5.1

(a) where the accused person has been cited in summary proceedings to attend a diet of a JP court, or

(b) if the accused person has not been cited to such a diet, where summary proceedings against the accused have been commenced in a JP court.

(2) The prosecutor may apply to a justice for an order for the transfer of the proceedings to another JP court in the sheriffdom (and for adjournment to a diet of that court).

(3) On an application under subsection (2), the justice may make the order sought.

(4) In this section and sections 137CB and 137CC, "justice" does not include the sheriff.

AMENDMENTS

Section 137CA inserted by Criminal Justice and Licensing (Scotland) Act 2010 (asp 13) s.61. Brought into force on March 28, 2011 by SSI 2011/178 (C.15) art.2, Sch.1 para.1.

DEFINITIONS

A4-296.5.2 "JP court": s.307(1).
"justice": s.137CA(4).
"prosecutor": s.307(1).

GENERAL NOTE

A4-296.5.3 This section allows for the transfer of JP court proceedings within a sheriffdom on the application of the prosecutor. The section does not specify that any particular reason need be given for the application. The application is made to a justice.

Transfer of JP court proceedings outwith sheriffdom

A4-296.5.4 **137CB.**—(1) Subsection (2) applies where the clerk of a JP court informs the prosecutor that, because of exceptional circumstances which could not reasonably have been foreseen, it is not practicable for the JP court or any other JP court in the sheriffdom to proceed with some or all of the summary cases due to call at a diet.

(2) The prosecutor shall as soon as practicable apply to the sheriff principal for an order for the transfer of the proceedings to a JP court in another sheriffdom (and for adjournment to a diet of that court).

(3) Subsection (4) applies where—

(a) either—

(i) the accused person has been cited in summary proceedings to attend a diet of a JP court, or

(ii) if the accused person has not been cited to such a diet, summary proceedings against the accused have been commenced in a JP court, and

(b) there are also summary proceedings against the accused person in a JP court in another sheriffdom.

(4) The prosecutor may apply to a justice for an order for the transfer of the proceedings to a JP court in the other sheriffdom (and for adjournment to a diet of that court).

(5) Subsection (6) applies where—

(a) the prosecutor intends to take summary proceedings against an accused person in a JP court, and

(b) there are also summary proceedings against the accused person in a JP court in another sheriffdom.

(6) The prosecutor may apply to a justice for an order for authority for the proceedings to be taken at a JP court in the other sheriffdom.

(7) On an application under subsection (2), the sheriff principal may make the order sought with the consent of the sheriff principal of the other sheriffdom.

(8) On an application under subsection (4) or (6), the justice is to make the order sought if—

(a) the justice considers that it would be expedient for the different cases involved to be dealt with by the same court, and

(b) a justice of the other sheriffdom consents.

(9) On the application of the prosecutor, the sheriff principal who has made an order under subsection (7) may, with the consent of the sheriff principal of the other sheriffdom—

(a) revoke the order, or

(b) vary it so as to restrict its effect.

(10) On the application of the prosecutor, the justice who has made an order under subsection (8) (or another justice of the same sheriffdom) may, with the consent of a justice of the other sheriffdom—

(a) revoke the order, or

(b) vary it so as to restrict its effect.

AMENDMENTS

Section 137CB inserted by Criminal Justice and Licensing (Scotland) Act 2010 (asp 13) s.61. Brought into force on March 28, 2011 by SSI 2011/178 (C.15) art.2, Sch.1 para.1.

DEFINITIONS

"JP court": s.307(1). A4-296.5.5
"justice": s.137CA(4).
"prosecutor": s.307(1).

GENERAL NOTE

This section allows for the transfer of JP court proceedings from one sheriffdom to another where exceptional circumstances exist, which could not reasonably have been foreseen, preventing cases calling at that JP court or any other JP court within the sheriffdom. The application may be made to the sheriff principal or to a justice. A4-296.5.6

Custody cases: initiating JP court proceedings outwith sheriffdom

137CC.—(1) Subsection (2) applies where the prosecutor believes— A4-296.5.7

(a) that, because of exceptional circumstances (and without an order under subsection (3)), it is likely that there would be an unusually high number of accused persons appearing from custody for the first calling of cases in summary prosecutions in the JP courts in the sheriffdom, and

(b) that it would not be practicable for those courts to deal with all the cases involved.

(2) The prosecutor may apply to the sheriff principal for an order authorising summary proceedings against some or all of the accused persons to be—

(a) taken at a JP court in another sheriffdom, and

(b) maintained—

(i) at that JP court, or

(ii) at any of the JP courts referred to in subsection (1) as may at the first calling of the case be appointed for further proceedings.

(3) On an application under subsection (2), the sheriff principal may make the order sought with the consent of the sheriff principal of the other sheriffdom.

(4) An order under subsection (3) may be made by reference to a particular period or particular circumstances.

AMENDMENTS

Section 137CC inserted by Criminal Justice and Licensing (Scotland) Act 2010 (asp 13) s.61. Brought into force on March 28, 2011 by SSI 2011/178 (C.15) art.2, Sch.1 para.1.

DEFINITIONS

"JP court": s.307(1). A4-296.5.8
"justice": s.137CA(4).
"prosecutor": s.307(1).

GENERAL NOTE

A4-296.5.9 This section applies to custody courts and allows for the transfer of JP court proceedings from one sheriffdom to another where because of exceptional circumstances it is likely that there would be an unusually high number of accused appearing from custody at the first calling of cases in summary prosecutions. The section presumes that there is no existing order that authorises such a transfer. The application may be made to the sheriff principal.

[THE NEXT PARAGRAPH IS A4-296.6]

Transfer of JP court proceedings to the sheriff court

A4-296.6 **137D.**—(1) Where an accused person is due to be sentenced at a sheriff court for an offence, the prosecutor may apply to the sheriff for an order for—

(a) the transfer to the sheriff court of any case against the accused in respect of which sentencing is pending at any JP court in the sheriffdom; and

(b) the case to call at a diet of the sheriff court.

(2) On an application under subsection (1) above, the sheriff is to make the order sought if the sheriff considers that it would be expedient for the different cases to be disposed of at the same court at the same time.

(3) If, in a case transferred under subsection (1) above, the finding of guilt was before a justice of the peace, the sentencing powers of the sheriff in the case are restricted to those of the justice.

AMENDMENTS

Section 137D inserted by Criminal Proceedings etc (Reform) (Scotland) Act 2007 (asp 6) s.22. Brought into force on March 10, 2008 by SSI 2008/42 (C.4) art.3 and Sch.

GENERAL NOTE

A4-296.7 Section 137D enables a sheriff, considering sentencing an accused in the sheriff court, to order the transfer of any JP court case, upon which the accused is awaiting sentence, to the sheriff court. As was noted in the last three sections, the initiative for conjoining these cases rests with the prosecutor but what, in theory looks to be a sensible and efficient means of disposal may not always be open to the court, for example, where there are co-accused and issues of comparative sentencing arise. Section 137D(2) restricts the sentence which can be imposed upon the transferred charges to the statutory maxima which the accused would have been liable to on conviction in the court of first instance. Again it is the prosecutor in the sheriff court who has the option of initiating a transfer request; the initiative cannot be taken by the JP court (or particularly in Glasgow, the Stipendiary) in terms of the section but a discretion, in restricted circumstances, to effect transfers from the JP to sheriff court is still found in s.7(9) of the 1995 Act.

A saving provision dealing with the time bar implications of cases being transferred (with the exception of s.7(9) cases just mentioned) is contained in s.136A of the 1995 Act.

[THE NEXT PARAGRAPH IS A4-297]

Complaints

Complaints

A4-297 **138.**—(1) All proceedings under this Part of this Act for the trial of offences or recovery of penalties shall be instituted by complaint signed by the prosecutor or by a solicitor on behalf of a prosecutor other than the procurator fiscal.

(2) The complaint shall be in the form—

(a) set out in Schedule 5 to this Act; or

(b) prescribed by Act of Adjournal,

or as nearly as may be in such form.

(3) A solicitor may appear for and conduct any prosecution on behalf of a prosecutor other than the procurator fiscal.

(4) Schedule 3 to this Act shall have effect as regards complaints under this Act.

DEFINITIONS

"complaint": s.307(1). A4-297.1
"judge": s.307(1).
"procurator fiscal": s.307(1).
"prosecutor": s.307(1).

[THE NEXT PARAGRAPH IS A4-298]

GENERAL NOTE

The complaint will ordinarily proceed at the instance of the procurator fiscal having jurisdiction over a locus where it is alleged an offence was committed. Section 138 also permits other authorised prosecutors (for example the local education authority) to initiate proceedings by a complaint and to prosecute such cases. A4-298

The form of complaint should correspond to Form 16.1.-A in the 1996 Act of Adjournal, a style identical to the format used under the 1975 Act. The citation form now shown in Form 16.1.-B is similarly familiar. Examples of statutory charges are given in Sch.5 to the Act which in turn adopts the somewhat esoteric charges listed as indictment styles in Sch.2; Sch.5 may lack some of the colour of the earlier schedule but at least has the merit of being of some practical (if limited) use. More importantly, the provisions of Sch.3 in relation to implied terms and alternative verdicts, which were previously contained in s.312 of the 1975 Act are applied to all summary complaints. See for example *MacQueen v Hingston*, 1997 S.C.C.R. 561, a Skye Bridge case in which, on appeal, it was held that the Crown was not obliged to lead proof of the currency of an Order where no preliminary plea to relevancy had been taken. The subject of implied charges, and alternative verdicts, was fully discussed in *McMaster v HM Advocate*, 2001 S.C.C.R. 517. No *nomen juris* need be stipulated in a complaint (see *Lippe v Wilson*, 1997 G.W.D. 17-766 and A4-146 above).

The scope of the Crown's extensive powers of amendment were illustrated in *Robertson v Klos*, 2006 S.C.C.R. 52, dated 1 December 2005, a case notable not least for the video recorded speed of the vehicle driven on public roads—156 miles per hour—while its driver used a mobile phone. The sheriff had held during trial that no Notice of Intended Prosecution had been served timeously on the accused, as registered owner of the vehicle, the Crown being unable to rebut the claim. The Appeal Court held that the sheriff had erred in refusing a Crown motion to amend the charge to one at common law of culpable and reckless conduct on the facts proved, in place of the original charge of dangerous driving. (*Wimpey Homes Holdings Ltd v Lees*, 1993 S.L.T. 564; 1991 S.C.C.R. 447 discussed at A4-313 and A4-495, distinguished).

Note that the court has no power *ex proprio motu* to amend the libel and has to be moved to do so by the Crown, and consider defence submissions, before an amendment is permissible; see *Anderson v Griffiths*, 2005 S.L.T. 86; 2005 S.C.C.R. 41 discussed at A1-102.3 above.

Essential Elements of a Complaint

The principal complaint has to be signed by the prosecutor but only the citation form to the accused need be signed (1996 Act of Adjournal, Rule 16.2.-(1)). Rule 16.2.-(2) suggests that signature of any part of the papers sent to an accused as a service copy complaint would be sufficient to render proceedings competent. Failure by the prosecutor to sign the principal complaint creates a nullity (*Lowe v Bee*, 1989 S.C.C.R. 476) which cannot be treated as a procedural irregularity (*Shahid v Brown* [2010] HCJAC 100): loss of the principal complaint has till now been held to be fatal to proceedings and could not be remedied by seeking to substitute a certified copy (*McSeveney v Annan*, 1990 S.C.C.R. 573; *Wilson v Carmichael*, 1992 S.L.T. 54; 1991 S.C.C.R. 587; *Scott v MacKay*, 1983 S.C.C.R. 210). However, s.157 of the Act now permits the substitution of a certified copy of the complaint in the event of such loss. A4-299

A discrepancy between the libel in the principal complaint and the service copy is no more than a technical defect unless it can be shown that the variation has caused substantial prejudice (*Fletcher v Webster*, 1991 S.L.T. 256; 1991 S.C.C.R. 379 following *Dunsmore v Threshie* (1896)2 Adam 202).

Rule 16.1 above directs that the copy complaint should include a reply form and a means form, which again are familiar in appearance; failure to include these two forms will not vitiate proceedings on that complaint (r.16.3.).

It will be noted that this section does not require a complaint to include notices of penalty; such notices were previously essential to any sentence upon conviction of a statutory offence on summary complaint. The complaint should include any previous convictions to be founded upon by the prosecutor in the event of a conviction of the accused; previous convictions are discussed in notes to s.166 below.

Although it is statutorily enacted that any proceedings must be initiated by the procurator fiscal or an authorised prosecutor, the cases of *Thomson v Scott; Walker v Emslie* (1899) 3 Adam 102 and *Hill v Finlayson* (1883) 5 Couper 284 support the view that the court itself has an inherent power to appoint a prosecutor *pro hac vice* to conduct those proceedings in the event of the death, illness or unavoidable absence of the prosecutor.

Schedule 3 to the Act

This schedule sets out well-established parameters for amending libels and applies equally to solemn and summary procedure. See the discussion at A4-146 above.

Complaints: orders and warrants

A4-300 **139.**—(1) On any complaint under this Part of this Act being laid before a judge of the court in which the complaint is brought, he shall have power on the motion of the prosecutor—

(a) to pronounce an order assigning a diet for the disposal of the case to which the accused may be cited as mentioned in section 141 of this Act;

(b) to grant warrant to apprehend the accused where this appears to the judge expedient;

(c) to grant warrant to search the person, dwelling-house and repositories of the accused and any place where he may be found for any documents, articles, or property likely to afford evidence of his guilt of, or guilty participation in, any offence charged in the complaint, and to take possession of such documents, articles or property;

(d) to grant any other order or warrant of court or warrant which may be competent in the circumstances.

(2) The power of a judge under subsection (1) above—

(a) to pronounce an order assigning a diet for the disposal of the case may be exercised on his behalf by the clerk of court;

(b) to grant a warrant to apprehend the accused shall be exercisable notwithstanding that there is power whether at common law or under any Act to apprehend him without a warrant.

DEFINITIONS

A4-300.1 "complaint": s.307(1).
"judge": s.307(1).
"prosecutor": s.307(1).

[THE NEXT PARAGRAPH IS A4-301]

GENERAL NOTE

A4-301 As subs.(2)(a) provides, cited diets are normally assigned administratively by the clerk of court, the judge initially needing only to be involved in considering the grant of an expediency or initiating warrant (subs.(1)(b)) or search warrants (subs.(1)(c)). It is the responsibility of the prosecutor to indicate to the clerk whether a specific date for the complaint to be called is needed; the complaint itself will show whether an assigned diet is craved and it then falls to the prosecutor to ensure that service is effected timeously (see notes to s.136 above).

When the prosecutor decides to begin proceedings by means of an initiating warrant the practice is for the complaint to be considered by the judge in chambers without hearing the prosecutor; it is unusual, but perfectly competent for the judge to require the prosecutor to specify the grounds which lie behind the application for a warrant. Commonly an initiating warrant will be necessary in order to obtain the accused's fingerprints or other samples in an admissible fashion or to place him before an identification parade.

As its name suggests, an expediency warrant is granted at the discretion of the court where a complaint is already current before the court and serves to keep the proceedings on it alive, provided that there are then reasonable grounds for believing that the complaint has been validly served: such a warrant cannot be used to validate a defect in the service of a complaint or as a means of overcoming a statutory timebar which would otherwise nullify the proceedings. In *Heywood v McLennan*, 1994 S.C.C.R. 1 where a complaint had been continued without plea, and later was established not to have been served, the depute moved to desert the case *pro loco et tempore* and sought an initiating warrant on that complaint. In such circumstances the proper course should have been to raise a fresh complaint craving an initiating warrant, the first complaint having fallen. See also *Lees v Malcolm*, 1992 S.C.C.R. 589. The distinction between an initiating warrant and an expediency warrant may seem of little moment since each provides a mechanism for bringing an accused person before a summary court; it can be telling, however, should the accused seek to have the warrant suspended. See *McMillan v PF Paisley* [2017] SAC (Crim) 2 discussed in Notes to s.135 above.

The extent of the procurator fiscal's common law power to apply for a search warrant as part of his investigative role, before proceedings are initiated, was discussed in *MacNeill, Complainer*, 1983 S.C.C.R. 450.

Citation

Citation

140.—(1) This Act shall be a sufficient warrant for **A4-302**

(a) [...]

(b) the citation of the accused and witnesses in a summary prosecution to any ordinary sitting of the court or to any special diet fixed by the court or any adjournment thereof.

(2) Without prejudice to section 141(2A) of this Act, such citation shall be in the form prescribed by Act of Adjournal or as nearly as may be in such form and shall, in the case of the accused, proceed on an induciae of at least 48 hours unless in the special circumstances of the case the court fixes a shorter induciae.

(2A) Where the charge in the complaint in respect of which an accused is cited is of committing an offence listed in subsection (2C)(c), the citation shall include or be accompanied by notice to the accused—

(a) that his case at, or for the purposes of, any relevant hearing in the course of the proceedings (including at any commissioner proceedings) may be conducted only by a lawyer,

(b) that it is, therefore, in his interests, if he has not already done so, to get the professional assistance of a solicitor; and

(c) that, if he does not engage a solicitor for the purposes of the conduct of his case at, or for the purposes of, the hearing (or at any related commissioner proceedings), the court will do so.

(2B) A failure to comply with subsection (2A) above does not affect the validity or lawfulness of any such citation or any other element of the proceedings against the accused.

(2C) For the purposes of subsection (2A)—

(a) "commissioner proceedings" means proceedings before a commissioner appointed under section 271I(1) or by virtue of section 272(1)(b),

(b) "relevant hearing" is to be construed in accordance with section 288C(1A) or (as the case may be) 288DC(4),

(c) the list is—

(i) an offence to which section 288C applies (certain sexual offending),

(ii) an offence to which section 288DC applies (domestic abuse cases).

(3) [...]

AMENDMENTS

Subss.(1) and (1)(a) inserted by Crime and Punishment (Scotland) Act 1997 (c.48) s.57(2) with effect from 1 August 1997 in terms of SI 1997/1712 art.3.

Subs.(3) deleted by s.57(2)(b) of the Act above in terms of the above Order.

Subss.(2A) and (2B) inserted by Sexual Offences (Procedure and Evidence) (Scotland) Act 2002 (asp 9) Sch.1 para.8. Brought into force by SSI 2002/443 (C.24) art.4 (effective 1 November 2002).

Subs.(2) as amended by Criminal Justice (Scotland) Act 2003 (asp 7) Pt 8 s.61. Brought into force on 27 June 2003 by SSI 2003/288 (C.14).

Subs.(2A) as amended by Criminal Justice (Scotland) Act 2003 (asp 7) Sch.4 para.3. Brought into force on 25 November 2003 by SSI 2003/475 (C.26) art.2.

Subs.(1)(a) repealed by Criminal Procedure (Amendment) (Scotland) Act 2004 (asp 5) s.25, Sch.1 para.33. Brought into force on 4 October 2004 by SSI 2004/405 (C.28).

Subs.(2A) as amended and subs.(2C) inserted by Criminal Proceedings etc. (Reform) (Scotland) Act 2007 (asp 6) s.35. Brought into force on 23 April 2007 by SSI 2007/250 (C.23) art.3.

Subs.(2A) as amended by Criminal Justice and Licensing (Scotland) Act 2010 (asp 13) Sch.7 para.54. Brought into force on 28 March 2011 by SSI 2011/178 (C.15) art.2, Sch.1 para.1.

Subs.(2A) as amended, subs.(2C) substituted, by Domestic Abuse (Scotland) Act 2018 (asp 5) Sch.1(1)(2) para.4(8) (effective 1 April 2019 in respect of proceedings commenced on or after 1 April 2019 subject to transitional provision specified in SSI 2018/387 reg.7(2)).

DEFINITIONS

A4-302.1 "diet": s.307(1).
"judge": s.307(1).
"prosecutor": s.307(1).

[THE NEXT PARAGRAPH IS A4-303]

GENERAL NOTE

A4-303 Chapter 16 of the 1996 Act of Adjournal provides that the citation of an accused shall be by Form 16.1-B while witnesses should be cited by post using Form 16.6-A and, personally, by Form 16.6-C. Omission of the date of the diet from the accused's citation creates a nullity (*Beattie v MacKinnon*, 1977 J.C. 64).

As with solemn witness citations, the Act of Adjournal envisages that any witness cited postally to attend, will acknowledge receipt of the citation by returning a pre-paid envelope with a further form (Form 16.6-B) within 14 days of citation. The objective of this reform, particularly now that intermediate diets are to be mandatory in summary cases (see s.148 below), is to enable parties to be in a position to advise the court confidently about their readiness for trial; however well-intended this provision may be, serious doubts must remain as to its practical worth. No citation of a witness or an accused is valid until the principal complaint has been signed (*Stewart v Lang* (1894) 1 Adam 493).

Subsection (2) prescribes an *induciae* in the case of service of a citation upon an accused of at least 48 hours. This period, in the case of postal citation, is reckoned from 24 hours after the time of posting (see s.141(6) below). The *induciae* can of course be waived by the accused or, exceptionally, be reduced by the court itself on cause shown, but must not be so shortened as to prejudice the accused in the conduct of his defence. No such time scale is applied to the citation of witnesses but Rule 16.6 in the Act of Adjournal plainly envisages a greater period of notice being given to witnesses.

As well as providing for the citation of accused and witnesses in summary prosecutions, subs.(1) as now amended provides a mechanism for the prosecutor to obtain a warrant to cite witnesses for precognition even before any proceedings are active before the court. See also s.67A of Act dealing with the failure of a witness to attend for precognition by the prosecutor. Both petition and summary warrants as a matter of course give power to the prosecutor to cite for precognition but subs.(1) enables the Crown to make preliminary investigations even before proceedings are initiated; it is usual to petition the court by way of an incidental application in circumstances where it is believed that witnesses will not attend for precognition voluntarily. This procedure is rarely used.

Manner of citation

A4-304 **141.**—(1) The citation of the accused or a witness in a summary prosecution to any ordinary sitting of the court or to any special diet fixed by the court or to any adjourned sitting or diet shall be effected by an officer of law or other person—

(a) delivering the citation to him personally; or

(b) leaving it for him—

(i) at his dwelling-house or place of business with a resident or (as the case may be) employee there; or

(ii) where he has no known dwelling-house or place of business, at any other place in which he may be resident at the time.

(2) Notwithstanding subsection (1) above, citation may also be effected—

(a) where the accused or witness is the master of, or a seaman or person employed in a vessel, if the citation is left with a person on board the vessel and connected with it;

(b) where the accused is an organisation other than a body of trustees or a partnership prosecuted by virtue of section 1 of the Partnerships (Prosecution) (Scotland) Act 2013—

(i) if the citation is left at its ordinary place of business with a partner, director, secretary or other official; or

(ii) if it is cited in the same manner as if the proceedings were in a civil court;

(c) where the accused is a body of trustees, if the citation is left with any one of them who is resident in Scotland or with their known solicitor in Scotland; or

(d) where the accused is a partnership prosecuted by virtue of section 1 of the

Partnerships (Prosecution) (Scotland) Act 2013, if the citation is left with any one of the partners who is resident in Scotland;

in sub-paragraph (b)(i) of this subsection references to the director or secretary or other official, in relation to a limited liability partnership, are to any member of the limited liability partnership.

(2A) Notwithstanding subsection (1) above and section 140(2) of this Act, citation of the accused may also be effected by an officer of law affixing to the door of the accused's dwelling-house or place of business a notice in such form as may be prescribed by Act of Adjournal, or as nearly as may be in such form—

(a) specifying the date on which it was so affixed;

(b) informing the accused that he may collect a copy of the complaint from a police station specified in the notice; and

(c) calling upon him to appear and answer the complaint at such diet as shall be so specified.

(2B) Where the citation of the accused is effected by notice under subsection (2A) above, the inducíae shall be reckoned from the date specified by virtue of paragraph (a) of that subsection.

(3) Subject to subsection (4) below and without prejudice to the effect of any other manner of citation, the citation of the accused or a witness to a sitting or diet or adjourned sitting or diet as mentioned in subsection (1) above shall be effective if it is—

(a) in the case of the accused signed by the prosecutor and sent by post in a registered envelope or through the recorded delivery service or by ordinary post; and

(b) in the case of a witness, sent by or on behalf of the prosecutor by ordinary post,

to the dwelling-house or place of business of the accused or witness or, if he has no known dwelling-house or place of business, to any other place in which he may be resident at the time.

(3A) Subject to subsection (4) below and without prejudice to the effect of any other manner of citation, the citation of the accused or a witness to a sitting or diet or adjourned sitting or diet as mentioned in subsection (1) above shall also be effective if an electronic citation is sent—

(a) by or on behalf of the prosecutor; and

(b) by means of electronic communication,

to the home or business email address of the person.

(4) Where the accused fails to appear at a diet or sitting or adjourned diet or sitting to which he has been cited in the manner provided by this section, sections 143(7), 150(3) and 150A(1) of this Act shall not apply unless it is proved to the court that he received the citation or that its contents came to his knowledge.

(5) The production in court of any letter or other communication (including a legible version of an electronic communication) purporting to be written by or on behalf of an accused who has been cited as mentioned in subsection (2A) or (3) above in such terms as to infer that the contents of such citation came to his knowledge, shall be admissible as evidence of that fact for the purposes of subsection (4) above.

(5ZA) The production in court of a legible version of an electronic communication which—

(a) bears to have come from an accused's email address; and

(b) is in such terms as to infer that the contents of an electronic citation sent as mentioned in subsection (3A) above came to the accused's knowledge, shall (even if not purporting to be written by or on behalf of the accused) be admissible as evidence of those facts for the purposes of subsection (4) above.

(5A) The citation of a witness to a sitting or diet or adjourned sitting or diet as mentioned in subsection (1) above shall be effective if—

(a) it is sent by or on behalf of the accused's solicitor by ordinary post—

(i) to the dwelling-house or place of business of the witness; or

(ii) if he has no known dwelling-house or place of business, to any other place in which he may be resident at the time; or

(b) an electronic citation is sent by or on behalf of the accused's solicitor by means of electronic communication to the home or business email address of the witness.

(5B) Where a witness fails to appear at a diet or sitting or adjourned diet or sitting to which he has been cited in the manner provided by this section, subsection (2) of section 156 of this Act shall not apply unless it is proved to the court that he received the citation or that its contents came to his knowledge.

(6) When the citation of any person is effected by post in terms of this section or any other provision of this Act to which this section is applied, the induciae shall be reckoned from 24 hours after the time of posting.

(6A) When the citation of any person is effected by electronic citation under subsection (3A) above, the induciae shall be reckoned from the end of the day on which the citation was sent.

(7) It shall be sufficient evidence that—

(a) a citation has been sent by post in terms of this section or any other provision of this Act mentioned in subsection (6) above, if there is produced in court a written execution, signed by the person who signed the citation in the form prescribed by Act of Adjournal, or as nearly as may be in such form, together with the post office receipt for the relative registered or recorded delivery letter; or

(b) citation has been effected by notice under subsection (2A) above, if there is produced in court a written execution, in such form as may be prescribed by Act of Adjournal, or as nearly as may be in such form, signed by the officer of law who affixed the notice.

(7A) It shall be sufficient evidence that citation has been effected electronically under subsection (3A) or (5A)(b) above if there is produced in court a legible version of an electronic communication which—

(a) is signed by electronic signature by the person who signed the citation;

(b) includes the citation; and

(c) bears to have been sent to the home or business email address of the person being cited.

(7B) In this section, an "electronic citation" is a citation in electronic form which—

(a) is capable of being kept in legible form; and

(b) is signed by electronic signature—

(i) in the case of citation of the accused, by the prosecutor;

(ii) in the case of citation of a witness, by or on behalf of the prosecutor or the accused's solicitor.

AMENDMENTS

Subs.(3) as amended by Crime and Punishment (Scotland) Act 1997 (c.48) s.62(1) and Sch.1 para.21(19)(a) with effect from August 1, 1997 in terms of SI 1997/1712 art.3.

Subss.(3)(a), (b) as amended, and (5A) inserted, by the 1997 Act s.62 and Sch.1 para.21(19) with effect from August 1, 1997 in terms of the above Order.

Subs.(2) as amended by Limited Liability Partnerships (Scotland) Regulations 2001 (SSI 2001/128) reg.5 and Sch.4.

Subss.(2A) and (2B) inserted, and subss.(3), (5) and (7) as amended, by Criminal Justice (Scotland) Act 2003 (asp 7) Pt 8 s.61. Brought into force on June 27, 2003 by SSI 2003/288 (C.14).

Subs.(1) substituted, subss.(3), (4), (5), (5A) as amended and subss.(3A), (5ZA), (5B), (6A), (7A), (7B) inserted by Criminal Proceedings etc (Reform) (Scotland) Act 2007 (asp 6) ss.8 and 14(1). Brought into force on December 10, 2007 by SSI 2007/479 (C.40) art.3 and Sch.

Subs.(2)(b) as amended by Criminal Justice and Licensing (Scotland) Act 2010 (asp 13) s.68. Brought into force on March 28, 2011 (for specified purposes) by SSI 2011/178 (C.15) art.2, Sch.1 para.1.

Subs.(2) as amended by Partnerships (Prosecution) (Scotland) Act 2013 (c.21) s.6(5). Brought into force on April 26, 2013 by s.8 of 2013 Act.

DEFINITIONS

"diet": s.307(1). A4-304.1
"prosecutor": s.307(1).
"witness": s.307(1).
"officer of law": s.307(1).
"electronic communication": s.15(1) of the Electronic Communications Act 2000 (c.7) and s.8 of the Criminal Proceedings etc (Reform) (Scotland) Act 2007 (asp 6).

[THE NEXT PARAGRAPH IS A4-305]

GENERAL NOTE

The broad intention of this section is to extend the power of lawful citation of an accused or a witness, in summary prosecutions, to persons other than officers of law and to enable the use of electronic citation to any diet of the court. The provisions apply equally to the prosecutor and the defence solicitor in the proceedings. Section 305A below introduces electronically initiated and maintained summary proceedings and these provisions, two of which are of particular interest, flow from that section: subs.(5ZA) entitles the court to take account of any electronic response received from an accused who has failed to appear at a diet of the court; the amended terms of subs.(5A) permit electronic communications to be used by defence solicitors in proceedings. Subsection (5B) affords some protection for witnesses whose apprehension is sought following a failure to appear at a court diet of which notice was sent by electronic means—the court will still require to be satisfied that the errant witness was aware of the citation or had knowledge of its terms before granting a warrant for apprehension. A4-305

Attention is drawn to the wider range of "organisations" covered by subs.(2)(b) above once the amendments introduced by the Criminal Justice and Licensing (Scotland) Act 2010 (asp 13) take effect. See the discussions in general notes to ss.143 and 203A. For solemn proceedings refer to s.70 above.

Coronavirus (Scotland) Act 2020 (asp 7)

Section 5 of, and Sch.4 to, the above Act of necessity makes substantial changes to the competent means of service of complaints and any relevant notices, including electronic transmission. See Sch.4 paras 1 and 1A.

Children

Summary proceedings against children

142.—(1) Where summary proceedings are brought in respect of an offence alleged to have been committed by a child, the sheriff shall sit either in a different building or room from that in which he usually sits or on different days from those on which other courts in the building are engaged in criminal proceedings: and no person shall be present at any sitting for the purposes of such proceedings except— A4-306

(a) members and officers of the court;
(b) parties to the case before the court, their solicitors and counsel, and witnesses and other persons directly concerned in that case;
(c) bona fide representatives of news gathering or reporting organisations present for the purpose of the preparation of contemporaneous reports of the proceedings;
(d) such other persons as the court may specially authorise to be present.

(2) A sheriff sitting summarily for the purpose of hearing a charge against, or an application relating to, a person who is believed to be a child may, if he thinks fit to do so, proceed with the hearing and determination of the charge or application, notwithstanding that it is discovered that the person in question is not a child.

(3) When a sheriff sitting summarily has remanded a child for information to be obtained with respect to him, any sheriff sitting summarily in the same place—

(a) may in his absence extend the period for which he is remanded provided that he appears before a sheriff or a justice at least once every 21 days;

(b) when the required information has been obtained, may deal with him finally,

and where the sheriff by whom he was originally remanded has recorded a finding that he is guilty of an offence charged against him it shall not be necessary for any court which subsequently deals with him under this subsection to hear evidence as to the commission of that offence, except in so far as it may consider that such evidence will assist the court in determining the manner in which he should be dealt with.

(4) Any direction in any enactment that a charge shall be brought before a juvenile court shall be construed as a direction that he shall be brought before the sheriff sitting as a court of summary jurisdiction, and no such direction shall be construed as restricting the powers of any justice or justices to entertain an application for bail or for a remand, and to hear such evidence as may be necessary for that purpose.

(5) This section does not apply to summary proceedings before the sheriff in respect of an offence where a child has been charged jointly with a person who is not a child.

DEFINITIONS

A4-306.1 "justice": s.307(1).
"offence": s.307(1).
"sheriff" : s.5(1).

[THE NEXT PARAGRAPH IS A4-307]

GENERAL NOTE

A4-307 Section 42 stipulates that where criminal offences alleged to have been committed by children are prosecuted by the criminal courts, rather than being referred to the Principal Reporter, such offences must be prosecuted in the sheriff court or a higher court (see generally the discussion in the notes to s.42 above). This stipulation does not extend to cases in which a co-accused is over 16 years old; in that event the proceedings can be taken in any court if it is felt that referring the child to the children's panel is inappropriate and proceedings must be taken against both parties.

The district court will not have jurisdiction over complaints against juvenile offenders but subs.(4) provides that this is without prejudice to any right of a justice (as defined in s.307(1) this includes sheriffs, stipendiary magistrates and justices of the peace) to determine applications for bail or remand.

The object of subs.(1) is to ensure that the juvenile criminal proceedings brought against children are conducted in court facilities distinct from those used in the course of summary proceedings against young persons and adults. This is intended to prevent the child coming into contact with older offenders and means that a separate juvenile court should convene to hear any custody, diet or trial business whose accused are solely children. The provision is directory in character and nonobservance of it is not fatal to a finding of guilt (*Heywood v B*, 1993 S.C.C.R. 554).

Chapter 6 of the 1996 Act of Adjournal also provides that efforts be made to prevent the mixing of children attending any juvenile court hearing.

In addition to requiring separate courts for juvenile hearings, s.142 enacts that those proceedings will not be held in open court; access is restricted to the parties specified by subs.(1)(a) to (c) and is otherwise at the discretion of the court.

Subsection (2) preserves the validity of any finding made by a court which has proceeded on the mistaken belief that the accused, or one of the accused, is a child.

Subsection (3) provides for an administrative continuation of a juvenile's case by another sheriff in the absence of the sheriff who made the original remand for information and, in situations where the latter sheriff is unavailable at the time of receipt of that information, his colleague may dispose of the case. A period of remand of a juvenile can exceed 21 days provided that the child is brought before a justice at least once every 21 days.

Companies

Prosecution of companies, etc.

143.—(1) Without prejudice to any other or wider powers conferred by statute, this section shall apply in relation to the prosecution by summary procedure of an organisation. **A4-308**

(2) Proceedings may be taken against the organisation in its corporate capacity, and in that event any penalty imposed shall be recovered by civil diligence in accordance with section 221 of this Act.

(3) Proceedings may be taken against an individual representative of a partnership, association or body corporate as follows:—

(a) in the case of a partnership or firm, any one of the partners, or the manager or the person in charge or locally in charge of its affairs;

(b) in the case of an association or body corporate, the managing director or the secretary or other person in charge, or locally in charge, of its affairs,

may be dealt with as if he was the person offending, and the offence shall be deemed to be the offence of the partnership, association or body corporate; and in paragraph 3(b) of this subsection references to the managing director or the secretary, in relation to a limited liability partnership, are to any member of the limited liability partnership.

(4) An organisation may, for the purpose of—

(a) stating objections to the competency or relevancy of the complaint or proceedings;

(b) tendering a plea of guilty or not guilty;

(c) making a statement in mitigation of sentence,

appear by a representative.

(5) In subsection (4) above, "representative" means—

(a) an individual representative as mentioned in subsection (3) above; or

(b) an employee, officer or official of the organisation duly appointed by it for the purpose of the proceedings.

(6) For the purposes of subsection (5)(b) above, a statement—

(a) in the case of a body corporate (other than a limited liability partnership), purporting to be signed by an officer of the body;

(b) in the case of a limited liability partnership, purporting to be signed by a member of the partnership;

(c) in the case of a partnership (other than a limited liability partnership), purporting to be signed by a partner of the partnership;

(d) in the case of an association, purporting to be signed by an officer of the association,

(e) in the case of a government department or part of the Scottish Administration, purporting to be signed by a senior officer in the department or part,

to the effect that the person named in the statement has been appointed as the representative for the purposes of any proceedings to which this section applies is sufficient evidence of such appointment.

(7) Where at a diet (apart from a diet fixed for the first calling of the case) an organisation does not appear as mentioned in subsection (4) above, or by counsel or a solicitor, the court may—

(a) on the motion of the prosecutor or, in relation to sentencing, of its own accord; and

(b) if satisfied as to the matters specified in subsection (8) below,

proceed to hear and dispose of the case in the absence of the organisation.

(8) The matters referred to in subsection (7)(b) above are—

(a) that citation has been effected or other intimation of the diet has been received; and

(b) that it is in the interests of justice to proceed as mentioned in subsection (7) above.

(9) The reference in subsection (7) above to proceeding to hear and dispose of the case includes, in relation to a trial diet, proceeding with the trial.

Amendments

Subs.(3) as amended by Limited Liability Partnerships (Scotland) Regulations 2001 (SSI 2001/128) reg.5 and Sch.4.

Subss.(4)-(9) inserted by Criminal Proceedings etc (Reform) (Scotland) Act 2007 (asp 6) s.17. Brought into force on March 10, 2008 by SSI 2008/42 (C.4) art.3 and Sch.

Subss.(1), (2), (4), (5)(b), (6), (7) as amended by Criminal Justice and Licensing (Scotland) Act 2010 (asp 13) s.67. Brought into force on March 28, 2011 (for specified purposes) by SSI 2011/178 (C.15) art.2, Sch.1 para.1.

Definitions

A4-308.1 "offence": s.307(1).
"complaint": s.307(1).
"sentence": s.307(1).
"diet": s.307(1).
"prosecutor": s.307(1).

[THE NEXT PARAGRAPH IS A4-309]

General Note

A4-309 The leading discussion of the extent of culpability of a limited company, as distinct from its officers, managers or employees, is found in *Transco Plc v HM Advocate*, 2004 S.L.T. 41 and *MacLachlan v Harris*, 2009 S.C.C.R. 783 which emphasises that prosecution of an individual company officer is as a representative of that company or entity, not in a personal capacity. If personal responsibility is sought to be brought home to the individual for his own actings this has to be libelled expressly.

See generally the notes to s.70 above.

An unincorporated company may be charged in the name of the company or the partners' names or both (*City and Suburban Dairies v Mackenna*, 1918 J.C. 105). The same approach can be followed against partnerships.

Proceedings against a registered club can be taken against its office bearers (*Burnette v Mackenna*, 1917 J.C. 20).

It is competent to proceed against directors of a limited company or against a manager or employee locally responsible for its affairs (*Bean v Sinclair*, 1930 J.C. 31) but previous convictions libelled against the company cannot be used against that individual (*Campbell v MacPherson* (1910) 6 Adam 394). A manager can competently represent the company at any diet (*McAlpine v Ronaldson* (1901) 3 Adam 405). Only convictions libelled against the accused company can be founded upon by the Crown, but where such convictions exist and have not been libelled against the company, it is not open to the defence to make claims at odds with the terms of those convictions; *Massily Packaging (U.K.) Ltd v MacDonald*, 1997 G.W.D. 3-87.

Amendment of the complaint where the company is incorrectly named is problematical; see *Hoyers (U.K.) v Houston*, 1991 S.L.T. 934; 1991 S.C.C.R. 919 where the description of the accused was amended at the trial diet, by which time a new complaint would have been timebarred. In *Ralston v Carmichael*, 1995 J.C. 206 a complaint against "Henry Ralston Ltd" was amended to "Henry Ralston" when it was discovered that the limited company did not exist; an appearance and correspondence had already passed before the amendment was sought and it could not be contended that prejudice was caused by the amendment. The issues are whether the error in the name or designation is trivial and if an appearance is made in answer to the complaint (*Poli v Thomson* (1910) 5 Adam 261); in that event amendment is competent.

For service of citations against bodies corporate, see s.141 above.

Subs.(5) extends s.143 of the 1995 Act in relation to the prosecution of companies, trusts, partnerships and limited liability partnerships on summary complaint and, it will be noted, now fully takes account of the development of this last legal persona. The basis upon which each of these bodies can make appearance in the proceedings is now set out in subss.(4) to (6). No less important procedures are now in place to enable the court to proceed to trial, and to sentence, in the absence of representation of the accused entity, provided that the prosecutor can satisfy the court (subs.(8)) that intimation of the diet had been effected and that to so proceed is in the interests of justice. This provision applies to any summary proceedings against the company and should be distinguished from circumstances where an individual officer or manager of the company is also prosecuted on the same complaint; the court may only proceed in the absence of that individual in the more limited circumstances prescribed by s.150(5) of the Act.

Criminal prosecutions of trusts in Scotland are, to say the least, infrequent; for that reason attention is drawn to the full discussion of their criminal liability in *Aitkenhead v Fraser*, 2006 S.L.T. 711.

The extended provisions described above are also applied to solemn proceedings by the 2007 Act (see s.70 above as now amended).

See also the discussions in the notes to ss.70 and 203A.

First diet

Procedure at first diet

144.—(1) Where the accused is present at the first calling of the case in a summary prosecution and— A4-310

(a) the complaint has been served on him, or
(b) the complaint or the substance thereof has been read to him, or
(c) he has legal assistance in his defence,

he shall, unless the court adjourns the case under the section 145 or 145ZA of this Act and subject to subsection (4) below, be asked to plead to the charge.

(2) Where the accused is not present at a calling of the case in a summary prosecution and either—

(a) the prosecutor produces to the court written intimation that the accused pleads not guilty or pleads guilty; or
(b) counsel or a solicitor, or a person not being counsel or a solicitor who satisfies the court that he is authorised by the accused, appears on behalf of the accused and tenders a plea of not guilty or a plea of guilty,

subsection (3) below shall apply.

(3) Where this subsection applies—

(a) in the case of a plea of not guilty, this Part of this Act except section 146(2) shall apply in like manner as if the accused had appeared and tendered the plea; and
(b) in the case of a plea of guilty, the court may, if the prosecutor accepts the plea, proceed to hear and dispose of the case in the absence of the accused in like manner as if he had appeared and pled guilty, or may, if it thinks fit, continue the case to another diet and require the attendance of the accused with a view to pronouncing sentence in his presence.

(3ZA) Where the prosecutor is not satisfied, in relation to a written intimation of a plea—

(a) that the intimation of the plea has been made or authorised by the accused; or
(b) that the terms of the plea are clear,

the court may continue the case to another diet.

(3ZB) The clerk of court may perform the functions of the court under

(a) subsections (2) and (3) above in relation to a plea of not guilty;
(b) subsection (3ZA) above,

without the court being properly constituted.

(3A) Where an accused charged with an offence listed in subsection (3AA)(b) is present, whether or not with a solicitor, at a calling of the case in a summary prosecution, he shall be told—

(a) that his case at, or for the purposes of, any relevant hearing in the course of the proceedings may be conducted only by a lawyer;
(b) that it is, therefore, in his interests, if he has not already done so, to get the professional assistance of a solicitor; and
(c) that if he does not engage a solicitor for the purposes of the conduct of his case at, or for the purposes of, the hearing, the court will do so.

(3AA) For the purposes of subsection (3A)—

(a) "relevant hearing" is to be construed in accordance with section 288C(1A) or (as the case may be) 288DC(4),

(b) the list is—

(i) an offence to which section 288C applies (certain sexual offending),

(ii) an offence to which section 288DC applies (domestic abuse cases).

(3B) A failure to comply with subsection (3A) above does not affect the validity or lawfulness of anything done at the calling of the case or any other element of the proceedings against the accused.

(4) Any objection to the competency or relevancy of a summary complaint or the proceedings thereon, or any denial that the accused is the person charged by the police with the offence shall be stated before the accused pleads to the charge or any plea is tendered on his behalf.

(5) No objection or denial such as is mentioned in subsection (4) above shall be allowed to be stated or issued at any future diet in the case except with the leave of the court, which may be granted only on cause shown.

(6) Where in pursuance of subsection (3)(b) above the court proceeds to hear and dispose of a case in the absence of the accused, it shall not pronounce a sentence of imprisonment or of detention in a young offenders institution, remand centre or other establishment.

(7) In this section a reference to a plea of guilty shall include a reference to a plea of guilty to only part of the charge, but where a plea of guilty to only part of a charge is not accepted by the prosecutor it shall be deemed to be a plea of not guilty.

(8) It shall not be competent for any person appearing to answer a complaint, or for counsel or a solicitor appearing for the accused in his absence, to plead want of due citation or informality therein or in the execution thereof.

(9) In this section, a reference to the first calling of a case includes a reference to any adjourned diet fixed by virtue of section 145, 145ZA or 145A of this Act.

AMENDMENTS

Subss.(3A) and (3B) inserted by Sexual Offences (Procedure and Evidence) (Scotland) Act 2002 (asp 9) Sch.1 para.9. Brought into force by SSI 2002/443 (C.24) art.4 (effective 1 November 2002).

Subs.(9) as amended by Criminal Justice (Scotland) Act 2003 (asp 7) Pt 8 s.63. Brought into force on 27 June 2003 by SSI 2003/288 (C.14).

Subs.(3A) as amended by Criminal Justice (Scotland) Act 2003 (asp 7) Sch.4 para.3. Brought into force on 25 November 2003 by SSI 2003/475 (C.26) art.2.

Subs.(2) as amended by Criminal Proceedings etc. (Reform) (Scotland) Act 2007 (asp 6) s.9. Brought into force on 10 December 2007 by SSI 2007/479.

Subss.(3ZA)-(3ZB) inserted by Criminal Proceedings etc. (Reform) (Scotland) Act 2007 (asp 6) s.9. Brought into force on 10 December 2007 by SSI 2007/479.

Subss.(1) and (9) as amended by Adult Support and Protection (Scotland) Act 2007 (asp 10) Pt 4 s.75(a). Brought into force on 30 June 2007 by SSI 2007/334 art.2 and Sch.1 para.1.

Subs. (3A) as amended by Criminal Justice and Licensing (Scotland) Act 2010 (asp 13) Sch.7 para.55. Brought into force on 28 March 2011 by SSI 2011/178 (C.15) art.2, Sch.1 para.1.

Subs.(3A) as amended, subs.(3AA) inserted, by Domestic Abuse (Scotland) Act 2018 (asp 5) Sch.1(1)(2) para.4(9) (effective 1 April 2019 in respect of proceedings commenced on or after 1 April 2019 subject to transitional provision specified in SSI 2018/387 reg.7(2)).

DEFINITIONS

A4-310.1 "complaint": s.307(1).
"diet": s.307(1).
"imprisonment": s.308.
"prosecutor": s.307(1).
"sentence": s.307(1).
"young offenders institution": s.307(1).

[THE NEXT PARAGRAPH IS A4-311]

GENERAL NOTE

Appearance at a first diet cures any deficiency in citation (subs.(8)); the accused can make an appearance in person, by way of attendance at court by a solicitor or other authorised representative or by letter. Want of form, which is curable by appearance, should not be confused with a nullity; an unsigned complaint (*Lowe v Bee*, 1989 S.C.C.R. 476; *McLeod v Millar*, 2004 S.C.C.R. 419), a complaint which failed to specify a date or locus or in which the court had no jurisdiction (*McMillan v Grant*, 1924 J.C. 13; *Duffy v Ingram*, 1987 S.C.C.R. 286) or a missing principal complaint (*McSeveney v Annan*, 1990 S.C.C.R. 573) are all fundamental procedural defects which cannot be remedied. Note in the last instance, the terms of s.157 which appear to permit the use of a certified copy complaint to preserve proceedings. See too *Gates v Donnelly*, 2004 S.L.T. 33 where the accused appeared at the pleading diet to voice objection to an unsigned citation; held appearance had cured any want of citation. **A4-311**

While the law does not go so far as to hold that any want or defect in citation is cured by the appearance of the accused or his law agent, when it is asserted that a complaint has not been proceeded with or served timeously (see s.136 above) there is some onus upon him to establish the facts giving rise to the preliminary plea (*Shaw v Dyer*, 2002 S.L.T. 826).

Before any plea is tendered any plea in bar, plea to the competency or relevancy (including any allegation of undue delay in executing any warrant to apprehend or cite), notice that the accused disputes having been cautioned and charged with the offences libelled should be stated (subs.(4)), as should any objection to the libelling of a special capacity (s.255).

Failure to sign the citation of an accused, unlike a failure to sign the principal complaint, does not create a nullity. In *Gates v Donnelly*, 2004 S.L.T. 33 the Appeal Court approved the reasoning of the sheriff in holding that the purpose of the complaint is to inform the accused of the allegations he faces, and that such a defect—an unsigned citation, would be of little moment unless particular prejudice could be shown to have been suffered by the accused.

Subss.(3ZA) and (3ZB)

In keeping with so many of the summary procedure reforms in the 2007 Act, this is an endeavour to streamline the handling of cited summary cases. In essence any such cases can be progressed without the involvement of a judge and, to that end, subs.(3ZA) entitles the prosecutor to decide whether the terms of a letter plea are properly made out, while subs.(3ZB) enables the clerk of court to continue any such cases to a later diet. and to alert the accused that a future non-appearance may entitle the court to proceed to trial in his absence. Thus the administrative functions of the court including the fixing of trial diets can be performed without a judge. For the avoidance of doubt these provisions do not apply to personal appearances at diets by the accused which must still be conducted in the presence of a judge. It remains open to the Crown at an attended diet to advise the court that it may be moved to hear a trial in absence of the accused should he fail to appear for trial (see the amendments to s.146 below).

Mental Disorder

Section 52 expressly, and s.145 impliedly, require both the prosecutor and the court to ensure that the accused is not suffering any mental disorder and the diet should be adjourned without plea for the purpose of investigation (in the former section the prosecutor should place medical evidence before the court; in the latter the court itself may adjourn without plea, to enable the prosecutor to obtain a medical report). Until the issue is resolved, any continuation is to be treated as a first diet (subs.(9)). See generally the notes at A4-122 above, *Sloan v Crowe*, 1996 S.C.C.R. 200 and *MacDonald v Munro*, 1996 S.C.C.R. 595 for discussion of the Crown's obligations under this section. **A4-312**

Pleas to Competency and Relevancy and Special Capacity

Subsection (5) stipulates that any such pleas must normally be stated at the first diet, though subs.(9) has the effect of permitting a continuation without pleaunder s.145, to permit proper formulation of any such objections. After the first diet, any objection can only be heard on cause shown; in *HM Advocate v Bell* (1892) 3 White 313, the court at a second diet was held to be entitled to consider such objections not previously stated where otherwise a gross injustice would result. See also *McLeay v Hingston*, 1994 S.L.T. 720; 1994 S.C.C.R. 116 where objection to a complaint devoid of a locus was stated only part way through a trial, the Appeal Court noting that the case could have been adjourned pending resolution of an appeal, the sheriff having repelled objections and granted leave to appeal. The introduction of mandatory intermediate diets in all summary cases (see s.148 below) may serve to limit the late introduction of any such motion. **A4-313**

The Appeal Court has indicated that it is primarily a matter for the discretion of the trial judge whether or not to entertain late pleas to competency, relevancy or capacity (which of course necessarily involve the withdrawal of any pleas previously tendered in regard to the charges) and that that discretion will only be reviewed in light of fundamental objections (*Henderson v Ingram*, 1982 S.C.C.R. 135). See also *Scott v Annan*, 1981 S.C.C.R. 172; 1982 S.L.T. 90; *Wimpey Homes Holdings v Lees*, 1993 S.L.T. 564.

The principal ground for consideration of a plea to relevancy of a complaint is whether the libel is sufficiently specific to give the defence fair notice of the offences (*Clydesdale Group v Normand*, 1994 S.L.T. 1302). *MK v Procurator Fiscal, Kilmarnock* [2021] SAC (Crim) 3 underlines the distinction between a plea to the competency (which if upheld will result in dismissal of the complaint) and one to the relevancy which is capable of amendment if required. In *MK* the complaint, contained several indecent sexual communications offences allegedly committed "within the jurisdiction of Kilmarnock Sheriff Court", the court took the locus as not being the essence of the offence and the latitude taken being necessary to protect the complainer. Two points are of note; an earlier Crown amendment of the complaint to add a town within the jurisdiction was considered to have been unnecessary on appeal; secondly, the defence conceded that their case was not prejudiced by the lack of greater specification.

If a preliminary plea is wholly sustained, then the complaint falls. In the event that the complaint is upheld in whole or part, ordinarily the accused should then be called upon to plead to the charges (a continuation without plea, for example to obtain further instructions, would be competent in terms of s.145). It is important to note that even if the defence move for, or are granted, leave to appeal against the decision relating to the preliminary plea (by way of s.174 below), a plea of guilty or not guilty should be tendered and recorded and a trial diet assigned as necessary (see *Lafferty v Jessop*, 1989 S.L.T. 846; 1989 S.C.C.R. 451 and *Jessop v First National Securities*, 1988 S.C.C.R. 1). Note that in the latter case having decided the issue of relevancy, the sheriff, no doubt conscious that his decision was likely to be appealed, canvassed the views of parties and decided to issue a written note of his judgment. Procedurally the proper course would have been to give no decision and continue the case to a later diet for the judgment or, alternatively, give his decision and defer any written comment for his Report, should an appeal be taken against the judgment and the call upon the accused to plead.

Although the court may continue a case for the personal appearance of the accused for sentence (subs.(3)(b)), it does not follow that sentence is contingent upon such an appearance (see *Taylor v Lees*, 1993 S.C.C.R. 947). The only stricture upon sentence in absence is stated in subs.(6); a sentence of imprisonment or detention can only be imposed when an accused is personally present.

The prosecutor is never obliged to accept a plea of guilty either to the whole or part of a complaint: (*Kirkwood v Coalburn District Cooperative Society*, 1930 J.C. 38). However where a plea of guilt is tendered, it has been held that appeal by way of bill of suspension will rarely be appropriate; see *Aitken v Reith*, 1996 G.W.D. 2-79 where following a letter plea of guilty and a personal appearance for sentence, the accused subsequently claimed to have been unaware that he had been charged with dangerous, rather than careless, driving and had been too timid to withdraw his plea at the deferred diet. A Bill of Suspension, alleging a material misunderstanding by the accused of the potential penalties following conviction, was considered and refused in *Whillans v Harvie* [2010] HCJAC 91, a case which comprehensively reviews the authorities on withdrawal of pleas.

The court would require to be satisfied that the accused had substantially misunderstood his position and been prejudiced, or had been unreasonably pressured by his solicitor into pleading and had been prejudiced as a result (see *Blockley v Cameron* [2013] HCJAC 2; 2013 S.C.C.R. 181, *McGuire v Normand*, 1997 G.W.D. 3-86; *Simpson v McKay*, 1997 G.W.D. 14-588 where the Crown's narration went unchallenged; *Kerr v Friel*, 1997 S.C.C.R. 317 a "plea of convenience" case; and *Bieniwoski v Ruxton*, 1997 G.W.D. 23-1143 a plea to dangerous driving by speeding, allegedly tendered in ignorance of the penalties, the conviction was not suspended, the Appeal Court noting the service of a penalty notice on the accused).

Crombie v Clark, 2001 S.L.T. 635 is something of a curiosity, being referred to the Appeal Court by the Scottish Criminal Cases Review Commission (see s.194C below) as a possible miscarriage of justice without any further investigation of the factual background. C's objection had been to the quantum in his guilty plea to evasion of betting and gaming duties, rather than to a plea tendered in error; indeed he had failed to consult further with a solicitor despite an adjournment being granted by the sheriff for that express purpose. For its part the court examined the whole history of the case and was not content that the conviction or sentence would have been materially different if C's contentions had been aired at the time.

Where the accused is present in court, the terms of his plea should be confirmed directly from him, even if he is represented; failure to follow the procedure set out in the Act of Adjournal (Criminal Procedure Rules) 1996, r.18.1(1) creates a nullity (*McGowan v Ritchie*, 1997 S.C.C.R. 322 where authority for fresh proceedings on the original charges libelled was granted).

In *Ettinger v McFadyen*, 2000 G.W.D. 22-851 the Appeal Court held it to be a breach of natural justice for the sheriff, having found an unexplained period of delay on the part of the Crown in initiating proceedings, to permit an adjournment for the Crown to produce further evidence after parties had concluded submissions. See also *McAnea v HM Advocate*, 2001 S.L.T. 12; 2000 S.C.C.R. 779 where the trial judge, having ruled upon defence objections to a line of evidence, was held to have wrongly permitted further Crown submissions on the point thereafter.

Coronavirus (Scotland) Act 2020 (asp 7)

Section 5 of, and Sch.4 para.2 to, the above act makes substantial, and expedient, changes to the competent means of appearance at a diet. Ordinarily, appearance can be achieved by personal appearance, appearance by a nominated solicitor, by letter by or on behalf of an accused, or by electronic means. The court has an over-arching power to require personal appearance (subpara (1)) and can specify the form of participation of an accused at any trial diet but may only specify proceedings by electronic means if satisfied that the interest of justice can still be maintained. These general provisions are distinct from the earlier statutory power to conduct trials in absence of an accused (s.150A of the Act).

Adjournment for inquiry at first calling

A4-314 **145.**—(1) Where the accused is present at the first calling of a case in a summary prosecution the court may, in order to allow time for inquiry into the case or for any other cause which it considers reasonable, adjourn the case under this section, for such period as it considers appropriate, without calling on the accused to plead to any charge against him but remanding him in custody or on bail or ordaining him to appear at the diet thus fixed; and, subject to subsections (2) and (3) below, the court may from time to time so adjourn the case.

(2) Where the accused is remanded in custody, the total period for which he is so remanded under this section shall not exceed 21 days and no one period of adjournment shall, except on special cause shown, exceed 7 days.

(3) Where the accused is remanded on bail or ordained to appear, no one period of adjournment shall exceed 28 days.

AMENDMENTS

Subsection (1) as amended by Criminal Justice (Scotland) Act 2003 (asp 7) Pt 8 s.63. Brought into force on 27 June 2003 by SSI 2003/288 (C.14).

DEFINITIONS

"bail": s.307(1). A4-314.1
"diet": s.307(1).
"remand": s.307(1).

GENERAL NOTE

The court's power to continue a case without plea on the motion of a party or *ex proprio motu* is preserved. However where an accused is remanded in custody in relation to the complaint before the court, no continuation should exceed seven days save on cause shown, and the total period of continuations cannot exceed 21 days (subs.(2)). It will be remembered that the period involved in any such continuation has to be included in the calculation of time spent in custody awaiting summary trial since the bringing of the complaint (see s.147 below). A4-314.2

The maximum period of adjournment allowed at any one time in cases where the accused is bailed or ordained to appear is 28 days (subs.(3)). A continuation without plea for debate would appear not to be subject to the time limit imposed by subs.(3) following the *ratio* in *Pearson v Crowe*, 1994 S.L.T. 378, but is obviously affected by the strictures imposed in custody cases by subs.(2).

Adjournment where assessment order made at first calling

145ZA. Where the accused is present at the first calling of a case in a summary prosecution the court may, where it makes an assessment order in respect of the accused, adjourn the case under this section for a period not exceeding 28 days without calling on the accused to plead to any charge against him; and the court may so adjourn the case for a further period not exceeding 7 days. A4-315

AMENDMENTS

Section 145ZA inserted by Adult Support and Protection (Scotland) Act 2007 (asp 10) Pt 4 s.75(b). Brought into force on 30 June 2007 by SSI 2007/334 art.2 and Sch.1 para.1.

Adjournment at first calling to allow accused to appear etc.

145A.—(1) Without prejudice to section 150 of this Act, where the accused is not present at the first calling of the case in a summary prosecution, the court may (whether or not the prosecutor is able to provide evidence that the accused has been duly cited) adjourn the case under this section for such period as it considers appropriate; and subject to subsections (2) and (3) below, the court may from time to time so adjourn the case. A4-315.1

(2) An adjournment under this section shall be—

(a) for the purposes of allowing—

(i) the accused to appear in answer to the complaint; or

(ii) time for inquiry into the case; or

(b) for any other cause the court considers reasonable.

(3) No one period of adjournment under this section shall exceed 28 days.

(4) The clerk of court may perform the functions of the court under subsection (1) above without the court being properly constituted.

Amendments

Section 145A inserted by Criminal Justice (Scotland) Act 2003 (asp 7) Pt 8 s.63. Brought into force on 27 June 2003 by SSI 2003/288 (C.14).

Subsection (4) inserted by Criminal Proceedings etc. (Reform) (Scotland) Act 2007 (asp 6) s.9. Brought into force on 10 December 2007 by SSI 2007/479.

Subsection (1) amended by Criminal Proceedings etc. (Reform) (Scotland) Act 2007 (asp 6) s.14. Brought into force on 10 December 2007 by SSI 2007/479.

Definitions

A4-315.2 "prosecutor": s.307(1) of the 1995 Act.

General Note

A4-315.3 This section enables any summary case in which an accused has been cited to appear at its first calling, or any subsequent calling (as distinct from custody or apprehension warrant cases where by definition an accused will appear before the court), to proceed without the court first having to be satisfied that the diet has been intimated to the accused. Adjournment may simply enable the Crown to produce proof at the later (adjourned) diet that the accused had been lawfully cited in accordance with s.141 of the Act but s.145A also allows the Crown to intimate continuation dates to an accused in an endeavour to secure appearance or a letter plea. See *Chilcott v Richardson* [2012] HCJAC 7; 2012 S.C.C.R. 222.

Some notes of caution must be sounded: at the time of appearance finally being secured, the court will require to ascertain that the accused is fully aware of the terms of the complaint before it; it may often be the case in such cases that no schedule of previous convictions will in fact have been served upon the accused (see s.166(2) below); finally, in the circumstances to which s.145A applies, it must be doubtful the Crown could seek to move on to a trial in absence of the accused—see ss.150A and 155 below.

In *Chilcott* the Crown advanced the questionable assertion (para.22) that the proceedings commenced—a matter of significance where statutory time bars or issues of delay arose—only once an appearance, in terms of the Act, was made. Presumably, it would be argued that commencement could validly be established if the Crown could instead establish awareness or avoidance of the complaint.

[THE NEXT PARAGRAPH IS A4-316]

Plea of not guilty

A4-316 **146.**—(1) This section applies where the accused in a summary prosecution—

(a) pleads not guilty to the charge; or

(b) pleads guilty to only part of the charge and the prosecutor does not accept the partial plea.

(2) The court may proceed to trial at once unless either party moves for an adjournment and the court considers it expedient to grant it.

(3) The court may adjourn the case for trial to as early a diet as is consistent with the just interest of both parties, and the prosecutor shall, if requested by the accused, furnish him with a copy of the complaint if he does not already have one.

(3ZA) Where a case is adjourned under subsection (3) above, the court shall intimate to the accused the trial diet assigned and any intermediate diet fixed.

(3ZB) When intimating a diet under subsection (3ZA) above, the court shall inform the accused that, if he fails to appear at any diet in the proceedings in respect of the case, the court might hear and dispose of the case in his absence.

(3A) Where, under subsection (3) above, the prosecutor furnishes an accused charged with an offence listed in subsection (3AA)(b) with a copy of the complaint, it shall be accompanied by a notice to the accused—

(a) that his case at, or for the purposes of, any relevant hearing in the course of the proceedings may be conducted only by a lawyer,

(b) that it is, therefore, in his interests, if he has not already done so, to get the professional assistance of a solicitor; and

(c) that, if he does not engage a solicitor for the purposes of the conduct of his case at, or for the purposes of, the hearing, the court will do so.

(3AA) For the purposes of subsection (3A)—

(a) "relevant hearing" is to be construed in accordance with section 288C(1A) or (as the case may be) 288DC(4),

(b) the list is—

(i) an offence to which section 288C applies,
(ii) an offence to which section 288DC applies.

(3B) A failure to comply with subsection (3A) above does not affect the validity or lawfulness of any such copy complaint or any other element of the proceedings against the accused.

(4) Where the accused is brought before the court from custody the court shall inform the accused of his right to an adjournment of the case for not less than 48 hours and if he requests such adjournment before the prosecutor has commenced his proof, subject to subsection (5) below, the adjournment shall be granted.

(5) Where the court considers that it is necessary to secure the examination of witnesses who otherwise would not be available, the case may proceed to trial at once or on a shorter adjournment than 48 hours.

(6) Where the accused is in custody, he may be committed to prison or to legalised police cells or to any other place to which he may lawfully be committed pending trial—

(a) if he is neither granted bail nor ordained to appear; or
(b) if he is granted bail on a condition imposed under section 24(6) of this Act that a sum of money is deposited in court, until the accused or a cautioner on his behalf has so deposited that sum.

(7) The court may from time to time at any stage of the case on the motion of either party or *expropprio motu* grant such adjournment as may be necessary for the proper conduct of the case, and where from any cause a diet has to be continued from day to day it shall not be necessary to intimate the continuation to the accused.

(8) It shall not be necessary for the prosecutor to establish a charge or part of a charge to which the accused pleads guilty.

(9) The court may, in any case where it considers it expedient, permit any witness for the defence to be examined prior to evidence for the prosecution having been led or concluded, but in any such case the accused shall be entitled to lead additional evidence after the case for the prosecution is closed.

AMENDMENTS

Subss.(3A) and (3B) inserted by Sexual Offences (Procedure and Evidence) (Scotland) Act 2002 (asp 9) Sch.1 para.10. Brought into force by SSI 2002/443 (C.24) art.4 (effective 1 November 2002).

Subs.(3A) as amended by Criminal Justice (Scotland) Act 2003 (asp 7) Sch.4 para.3. Brought into force on 25 November 2003 by SSI 2003/475 (C.26) art.2.

Subss.(3ZA) and (3ZB) inserted by Criminal Proceedings etc. (Reform) (Scotland) Act 2007 (asp 6) s.10. Brought into force on 10 December 2007 by SSI 2007/479.

Subs.(3A) as amended by Criminal Justice and Licensing (Scotland) Act 2010 (asp 13) Sch.7 para.56. Brought into force on 28 March 2011 by SSI 2011/178 (C.15) art.2, Sch.1 para.1.

Subs.(3A) as amended, subs.(3AA) inserted, by Domestic Abuse (Scotland) Act 2018 (asp 5) Sch.1(1)(2) para.4(10) (effective 1 April 2019 in respect of proceedings commenced on or after 1 April 2019 subject to transitional provision specified in SSI 2018/387 reg.7(2)).

DEFINITIONS A4-316.1

"bail": s.307(1).
"diet": s.307(1).
"legalised police cells": s.307(1).
"prison": s.307(1).
"prosecutor": s.307(1).

[THE NEXT PARAGRAPH IS A4-317]

GENERAL NOTE

Provided that any preliminary pleas have been repelled, the accused should then be called upon to plead to the charges still current on the complaint. A guilty plea may then be recorded. Guidance on the principles applying where an accused, having pled guilty initially, later seeks to alter that plea to one of not guilty, can be found in the Notes to s.76 at A4-176. *Adebayo v PF Paisley* [2015] HCJAC 79 at [11] may also assist. The prosecutor may, but is not obliged to, accept any partial pleas tendered. Subject to the exceptional provisions of subs.(5), in custody cases the accused is entitled to an *induciae* of 48 hours before his trial occurs, an *induciae* which he may waive, but his right to which the court must make A4-317 known to him; failure to do so will almost certainly vitiate any conviction (see *Ferguson v Brown*, 1942 J.C. 113). The refusal of an adjournment which is needed, in order to enable the accused to lead evidence in support of his alibi defence once trial has begun, may constitute oppression: *McKellar v Dickson* (1898) 2 Adam 504.

In accordance with subs.(2), the court can proceed to trial immediately unless any of the parties moves for an adjournment. In practice, such a peremptory diet of trial is rare though subs.(5) allows for such a trial then or within 48 hours, where this is essential to secure witnesses' evidence even in custody cases. It is perfectly competent to adjourn the trial once such evidence has been heard or at any point in any summary trial (subs.(7)).

Unless the court has misdirected itself in law, or wholly disregarded a relevant factor when considering a motion to adjourn, its decision will not be reversed by the Appeal Court (*Berry, Petitioner*, 1985 S.C.C.R. 106). Thus, a JP's decision to refuse a Crown motion to adjourn through lack of time, only to adjourn the trial shortly after it had commenced, was upheld in *Walker v Dunn* [2015] HCJAC 119; 2016 S.C.L. 178, the Appeal Court being content that proper consideration had been given to all relevant factors. Contrast *Shaan v PF Paisley* [2016] SAC (Crim) 12, a successful Crown Bill of Advocation, following a justice's refusal of a Crown motion to adjourn brought about by an essential Crown witness now being in London and unwilling to attend. The Sheriff Appeal Court ruled both that consideration of the potential expense involved in bringing that witness from London to a future trial was not a legitimate factor, and that the court had not properly considered what prejudice (if any) an adjournment would cause the accused.

Subsection (6) permits a remand in custody in cases where bail is either not granted or not sought, or more unusually, where a sum of money bail is required to be deposited with the court as an additional bail condition in terms of s.24(6).

Subsection (7) allows for adjournments. An adjournment occurs when a case calls at a settled diet, being a date fixed earlier, and then is put back: see *Mitchell v Reith*, 2004 S.C.C.R. 433 at 435 (para.6). This is contrasted with a postponement that occurs when the date of the diet is altered in advance of the date set originally: *Mitchell v Reith*, 2004 S.C.C.R. 433. When considering a motion to adjourn, the judge has to balance the competing interests of the accused, the prosecutor and the broader public interest. The Appeal Court has concluded that the local judge, familiar with local circumstances, is best placed to decide the issue and will only interfere where the judge has misdirected himself in law or has come to a decision no reasonable court of first instance could have achieved (see *Patterson v PF, Airdrie* [2012] HCJAC 61 and *Bowden v Harvie* [2015] HCJAC 11; 2015 S.C.L. 32).

Guidance on the courses which the court may follow where there is disagreement between the parties in the factual narration is given in *McCartney v HM Advocate*, 1997 S.C.C.R. 644.

Subsection (9) echoes the little-used terms of s.337(h) of the 1975 Act and permits the calling of defence evidence prior to, or during, Crown evidence. It is suggested that this provision envisages the leading of defence evidence, a preferable alternative to the Crown, as an expedient means of assisting the defence—calling defence witnesses during the Crown case formally, then leaving the defence to lead the witness' evidence in cross-examination.

Subsections (3ZA) and (3ZB) enable the court, on receipt of a plea of not guilty, to fix trial and intermediate diets and to advise the accused that a trial may proceed in his absence. See generally the note to s.144 above. This provision came into effect on 10 December 2007.

Coronavirus (Scotland) Act 2020 (asp 7)

Attention is directed to Guidance in respect of Facilitating Pleas of Guilty issued on 11 May 2020 setting out the special procedural arrangements needed in an era of social distancing and virtual courts. Practice Note No.2 of 2020 para.8 provides a hyperlink.

Pre-trial procedure

Prevention of delay in trials

A4-318 **147.**—(1) Subject to subsections (2) and (3) below, a person charged with an offence in summary proceedings shall not be detained in that respect for a total of more than 40 days after the bringing of the complaint in court unless his trial is commenced within that period, failing which he shall be liberated forthwith and thereafter he shall be for ever free from all question or process for that offence.

(2) On an application made for the purpose, the sheriff may, on cause shown—

(a) extend the period mentioned in subsection (1) above; and

(b) order the accused to be detained awaiting trial,

for such period as the sheriff thinks fit.

(2A) Before determining an application under subsection (2) above, the sheriff shall give the parties an opportunity to be heard

(2B) However, where all the parties join in the application, the sheriff may determine the application without hearing the parties and, accordingly, may dispense with any hearing previously appointed for the purpose of considering the application.

(3) The grant or refusal of any application to extend the period mentioned in subsection (1) above may be appealed against by note of appeal presented to the Sheriff Appeal Court; and that Court may affirm, reverse or amend the determination made on such application.

(4) For the purposes of this section, a trial shall be taken to commence when the first witness is sworn.

AMENDMENTS

Subsections (2), (2A), (2B) substituted for original subs.(2) by Criminal Proceedings etc (Reform) (Scotland) Act 2007 (asp 6) s.11. Brought into force on 10 March 2008 by SSI 2008/42 (C.4) art.3 and Schedule.

Subsection (3) as amended by Courts Reform (Scotland) Act 2014 (Consequential Provisions No.2) Order 2015 (SSI 2015/338) Sch.2 para.5 (effective 22 September 2015).

Prevention of delay in trials

147.—(1) Subject to subsections (2) and (3) below, a person charged with an offence in summary proceedings shall not be detained in that respect for a total of more than 40 days after the bringing of the complaint in court unless his trial is commenced within that period, failing which he shall be liberated forthwith and thereafter he shall be for ever free from all question or process for that offence. **A4-318A**

(2) On an application made for the purpose, the sheriff may, on cause shown—

(a) extend the period mentioned in subsection (1) above; and

(b) order the accused to be detained awaiting trial,

for such period as the sheriff thinks fit.

(2A) Before determining an application under subsection (2) above, the sheriff shall give the parties an opportunity to be heard.

(2B) However, where all the parties join in the application, the sheriff may determine the application without hearing the parties and, accordingly, may dispense with any hearing previously appointed for the purpose of considering the application.

(3) The grant or refusal of any application to extend the period mentioned in subsection (1) above may be appealed against by note of appeal presented to the Sheriff Appeal Court; and that Court may affirm, reverse or amend the determination made on such application.

(4) For the purposes of this section, a trial shall be taken to commence when the first witness is sworn.

(5) In calculating the period mentioned in subsection (1), including any such period as extended either under subsection (2) or on appeal under subsection (3), no account is to be taken of the suspension period.

(6) For the purpose of subsection (5), the suspension period is the period of 3 months beginning with whichever is the later of—

(a) the day on which paragraph 10 of schedule 4 of the Coronavirus (Scotland) Act 2020 comes into force,

(b) the day on which the complaint is brought in court.

AMENDMENTS

In relation to COVID-19, s.147 as amended by Coronavirus (Scotland) Act 2020 (asp 7) Sch.4(4) para.10(5) (effective 7 April 2020).

DEFINITIONS **A4-318.1**

"complaint": s.307(1).
"High Court": s.307(1).
"judge": s.307(1).

"offence": s.307(1).
"prosecutor": s.307(1).
"sheriff": s.5(1).
"witness": s.307(1).

[THE NEXT PARAGRAPH IS A4-319]

GENERAL NOTE

A4-319 This section preserves the provisions introduced into the 1975 Act by s.14(2) of the Criminal Justice (Scotland) Act 1980 to limit the period of remand affecting persons awaiting summary trial. A person remanded in custody in terms of s.146(6) may only be held in custody pending trial for 40 days in relation to that complaint. Specific provisions in relation to accused remanded for the purposes of assessment of mental health and fitness in both summary and solemn proceedings are found in s.52T above, but the same statutory time frames to prevent delay in proceedings (see ss.65 and 147) apply.

Note that the period only begins from "the bringing of the complaint" so a period on remand following an appearance on petition would not, it is submitted, be included in calculation of the 40 days, notwithstanding the recent decision in *Gardner v Lees*, 1996 S.C.C.R. 186 (itself since superseded by the terms of s.65(1) as now amended) which dealt with a non-custodial reduction of petition proceedings to summary proceedings.

Similarly, the period spent in custody must be attributable wholly to matters awaiting trial; a person serving a sentence, or a person remanded for trial but who then becomes a serving prisoner thus effectively interrupting the remand period, cannot benefit from the protection of the provisions against delay in trial. However in *Lockhart v Robb*, 1988 S.C.C.R. 381 it was held by the sheriff that a remand for pre-sentencing reports on another complaint did not interrupt the running of 40 days in a custody complaint.

Two extensions were permitted where the accused's plea in bar on grounds of insanity had to be investigated by the Crown, and through no fault on the Crown's part one of the reports was not available to the court; the accused was remanded awaiting trial for 70 days (*Sweeney v Douglas*, 1997 G.W.D. 28-1408).

In calculating the 40 day period, the whole of the day on which the remand order is made is discounted, while the whole of the final day is included: see *Hazlett v McGlennan*, 1992 S.C.C.R. 799; 1993 S.L.T. 74 and the discussion "Computation of Time" in notes to s.136 above. As subs.(4) enacts, the period expires when the trial begins. In *Grugen v Jessop*, 1988 S.C.C.R. 182 the accused took a Bill of Advocation founding upon the actions of the prosecutor who commenced his trial on the fortieth day, in the knowledge that the trial would have to be adjourned only part-heard due to the known unavailability of Crown witnesses. The Appeal Court refused the Bill and declined to hold these procedures to be an abuse of process.

The court on application can extend the 40 day period on the grounds specified in subs.(2); considerations similar to those applying to s.65(4) in solemn procedure are relevant. Appeal to the High Court against such extension proceeds on Form 17.1 while Rule 17.1.-(2) of the 1996 Act of Adjournal stipulates service of copies of the Form upon the prosecutor and the clerk of court. Appeals against extensions of the 40 day period are marked using Form 17.1 in the Act of Adjournal.

Subs.(2) preserves the power of a sheriff, in summary proceedings, to extend the total custody remand period awaiting trial beyond the 40 day limit which ordinarily applies. Hitherto, s.147(2) required particularly that there be no fault on the part of the prosecutor (a similar requirement in solemn proceedings had already been relaxed in solemn proceedings by the Criminal Procedure (Amendment) (Scotland) Act 2004 (asp 5)) but a broader test "on cause shown" has now been introduced. Although parties are entitled to be heard (and will be should an extension be opposed) subs.(2B) allows the sheriff to determine the application administratively if there is a joint application for extension of the remand period. Note, however, that the sheriff is not obliged to grant a joint application for extension but would, at least, be obliged to fix a hearing if minded to refuse the application. Appeal to the High Court in relation to such extension (or refusal thereof) is by means of Form 17.1 and is regulated by Rule 17.1 in the 1996 Act of Adjournal.

Although extradition applications to the Scottish courts are dealt with as summary applications, and generally follow summary procedural rules, (see the Extradition Act 2003 (c.41) s.9(2)), the person subject to the application is not an accused as such, and the proceedings are not governed by s.147's provisions against delay in trials (see above). See *HM Advocate (sic) v Havrilova*, 2012 S.C.C.R. 361.

Intermediate diet

A4-320 **148.**—(1) The court may, when adjourning a case for trial in terms of section 146(3) of this Act, and may also, at any time thereafter, whether before, on or after any date assigned as a trial diet, fix a diet (to be known as an intermediate diet) for the purpose of ascertaining, so far as is reasonably practicable, whether the case is likely to proceed to trial on any date assigned as a trial diet and, in particular—

(a) the state of preparation of the prosecutor and of the accused with respect to their cases;

(b) whether the accused intends to adhere to the plea of not guilty; and

(ba) how many witnesses are required by—

(i) the prosecutor;

(ii) the accused,

to attend the trial; and

(c) the extent to which the prosecutor and the accused have complied with the duty under section 257(1) of this Act.

(1A) At an intermediate diet in summary proceedings in the sheriff court, the court shall also:

(a) ascertain whether subsection (1B) below applies to any person who is to give evidence at or for the purposes of the trial or to the accused, and

(b) if so, consider whether it should make an order undersection 271A(7) or 271D(2) of this Act in relation to person or, as the case may be, the accused.

(1B) This subsection applies:

(a) to a person who is to give evidence at or for the purposes of the trial if that person is, or is likely to be, a vulnerable witness,

(b) to the accused if, were he to give evidence at or for the purposes of the trial, he would be, or would be likely to be, a vulnerable witness.

(2) Where at an intermediate diet the court concludes that the case is unlikely to proceed to trial on the date assigned for the trial diet, the court—

(a) may postpone the trial diet; and

(b) may fix a further intermediate diet.

(3) The court may, if it considers it appropriate to do so, adjourn an intermediate diet.

(3AA) At an intermediate diet, the court shall also dispose of any application for a witness anonymity order under section 271P of this Act of which notice has been given in accordance with section 271Q(2)(a) of this Act.

(3A) At an intermediate diet, the court may consider an application for the purposes of subsection (1) of section 275 of this Act; and, notwithstanding subsection (1) above, the court may fix a diet under that subsection for the purpose only of considering such an application.

(3B) Subsection (3A) above shall not operate so as to relieve any court prescribed by order under subsection (7) below of its duty, which arises by virtue of the operation of that subsection, to fix an intermediate diet for the purpose mentioned in subsection (1) above.

(4) At an intermediate diet, the court shall make such enquiry of the parties as is reasonably required for the purposes of subsections (1) and (3A) above.

(5) The accused shall attend an intermediate diet of which he has received intimation or to which he has been cited unless—

(a) he is legally represented; and

(b) the court considers that, on cause shown, he need not attend.

(6) A plea of guilty may be tendered at the intermediate diet.

(7) The foregoing provisions of this section shall have effect as respects any court prescribed by the Secretary of State by order, in relation to proceedings commenced after such date as may be so prescribed, with the following modifications—

(a) in subsection (1), for the word "may" where it first appears there shall be substituted "shall, subject to subsection (1A) below,"; and

(b) after subsection (1) there shall be inserted the following subsections—

"(1A) If, on a joint application by the prosecutor and the accused made at any time before the commencement of the intermediate diet, the court considers it inappropriate to have such a diet, the duty under subsection (1) above shall not apply and the court shall discharge any such diet already fixed.

(1B) The court may consider an application under subsection (1A) above without hearing the parties.".

(8) An order under subsection (7) above shall be made by statutory instrument, which shall be subject to annulment in pursuance of a resolution of either House of Parliament.

AMENDMENTS

Subss.(1) and (7)(a) as amended by Criminal Procedure (Intermediate Diets) (Scotland) Act 1998 (c.10) s.1 (effective 8 April 1998).

Subss.(3A) and (3B) inserted by Sexual Offences (Procedure and Evidence) (Scotland) Act 2002 (asp 9) s.8(5)(a). Brought into force by SSI 2002/443 (C.24) art.4 (effective 1 November 2002).

Subs.(4) as amended by Sexual Offences (Procedure and Evidence) (Scotland) Act 2002 (asp 9) s.8(5)(b). Brought into force as above.

Subs.(4) as amended, and subss.(1A) and (1B) inserted by Vulnerable Witnesses (Scotland) Act 2004 (asp 3) s.2(5). Brought into force on 1 April 2007 (only in respect of child witness and referred to in s.27(1)(a) of the 1995 Act) by SSI 2007/101 (C.13) art.2. Remainder brought into force on 1 April 2008 by SSI 2008/57 (C.7) art.2.

Subss.(1), (2) and (3) as amended and subs.(4) substituted by Criminal Proceedings etc. (Reform) (Scotland) Act 2007 (asp 6) s.18. Brought into force on 10 December 2007 by SSI 2007/479.

Subs.(3AA) inserted by Criminal Justice and Licensing (Scotland) Act 2010 (asp 13) s.90. Brought into force on 28 March 2011 by SSI 2011/178 (C.15) art.2, Sch.1 para.1.

Subs.(5)(b) as amended by Act of Adjournal (Amendment of the Criminal Procedure (Scotland) Act 1995 and Criminal Procedure Rules 1996) (Miscellaneous) 2014 (SSI 2014/242) para.2(2) (effective 10 October 2014).

DEFINITIONS

A4-320.1 "diet": s.307(1).
"prosecutor": s.307(1).

[THE NEXT PARAGRAPH IS A4-321.1]

GENERAL NOTE

Intermediate diets were introduced in 1980 to address the perceived waste of resources, and the inconvenience to witnesses resulting from the large numbers of summary cases which did not, for one reason or another, proceed at trial diets. Until the passage of the Criminal Justice (Scotland) Act 1995 (c.20) the role of the Bench at intermediate diets was largely formal–the court doing little more than noting (and accepting, with varying scepticism) parties' assurances as to readiness; the 1995 legislation introduced a more pro–active role, tasking the Bench with ascertaining the state of preparation of parties for the impending trial, and dealing with preliminary issues in an endeavour to utilise court time more effectively. It remains the case that parties can utilise subs.(7)'s chamber procedure (by way of joint written application) to discharge the scheduled intermediate diet but the court is not obliged to accede to the request and can fix a hearing of parties to enable fuller discussion.

It will be readily apparent that s.148 has been extensively augmented since its introduction. Significant procedural and practical reforms have developed in response (in large part) to the Coronavirus crisis; attention must be directed to Practice Notes Nos.3 and 4 of 2020. No.3 initiated remote appearances by witnesses and accused, electronic communication of applications to the court and a substantially augmented Written Record. Practice Note No.4 introduced yet another procedural layer into summary proceedings in the shape of a Pre Intermediate Diet Meeting (PIDM) in an effort to compel dialogue between parties in advance of the intermediate diet itself. After the PIDM any substantial change to parties' positions should, so far as possible, be dealt with by way of s.137 either by Joint Minute or by party application. Receipt of PIDM reports will assist the Sheriff Clerk to draw up a working schedule of intermediate diet hearings (and i identified trials); separate procedures for unrepresented accused are set out in paras. [13] to [15], but it will be borne in mind that s.288C of the principal 1995 Act is peremptory that for certain sexual charges an accused must be legally represented, while s.288E applies a more general requirement of legal representation in relation to child witnesses under 12 years of age, and s.288F enables similar strictures to apply (on application) to non–sexual offences involving vulnerable witnesses.

At the intermediate diet as well as continuing the case to its assigned trial diet, or disposing of any pleas, subs.(2) vests the court with a discretion to postpone the scheduled trial or to enable an intermediate diet itself to be adjourned still preserving the trial diet. Subsequent legislation requires the court to consider vulnerable witness applications and the scope of permitted questioning of the complainer where listed sexual offences are libelled issues, though it should be emphasised that such matters can, if necessary, still be aired, or re-visited, prior to commencement of the subsequent trial.

Section 257 of the Act places parties under a duty to identify the extent of evidence capable of agreement and to be mindful that the court should ascertain the extent of evidence agreed, as well as reviewing any Statements of Uncontroversial Evidence served in accordance with s.258 of the Act at the time of the intermediate diet.

The court in considering an adjournment motion at any point must reflect on the prejudice to an accused, to the prosecutor and to the public interest (*McCowan v Dunn*[2013] HCJAC 119). Bill of Advocation of *Archer v Dunn* [2016] SAC (Crim) 23 is unusual in that the Sheriff's report gave no indication of any such consideration prior to granting an adjournment. An appellate court will only interfere with such a decision when it can be established that the judge misdirected himself in law or reached a decision no reasonable judge, possessed of the facts, could have reached (see *Paterson v McPherson* [2012] HCJAC 61). *Archer v Dunn* sits in contrast to *Kane v Procurator Fiscal, Hamilton* [2018] SAC (Crim) 337 and note particularly the judicial dicta at [8] critical of use of Advocation procedures .

Coronavirus (Scotland) Act 2020 (asp 7)

The advent of the COVID-19 virus early in 2020 resulted in the rapid enactment of the above Act and led to the issue of two Practice Notes. The first enables the conduct of virtual summary trials in the Highlands and Islands centred on Aberdeen and Inverness Sheriff Courts; the second, dated 1 June 2020, establishes procedures for the phased re-introduction of summary criminal business, bringing a requirement for significant documentation to be completed by all parties. While numerous elements echo those found in written records in solemn cases (see s.71C above), the paperwork is more comprehensive still to address the distinct issues arising from virtual trials. Born of necessity, and in haste, in response to the coronavirus pandemic, it will be intriguing to see how that unhappy event may leave its mark on the future shape of summary criminal procedure.

Interim diet required in certain sexual or domestic abuse cases

148A.—(1) Where, in a case which is adjourned for trial, the charge is of committing an offence listed in subsection (10), the court shall order that, before the trial diet, there shall be a diet under this section and ordain the accused then to attend. **A4-321.1**

(2) At a diet under this section, the court shall ascertain whether or not the accused has engaged a solicitor for the purposes of his defence at the trial.

(3) Where, following inquiries for the purposes of subsection (2) above, it appears to the court that the accused has not engaged a solicitor for the purposes of his defence at his trial, it may adjourn the diet under this section for a period of not more than 48 hours and ordain the accused then to attend.

(4) A diet under this section may be conjoined with an intermediate diet.

(5) A court may, at a diet under this section, postpone the trial diet.

(6) The court may dispense with a diet under this section previously ordered, but only if a solicitor engaged by the accused for the purposes of the defence of the accused at the trial has, in writing—

(a) confirmed his engagement for that purpose; and

(b) requested that the diet be dispensed with.

(7) Where—

(a) a solicitor has requested, under subsection (6) above, that a diet under this section be dispensed with; and

(b) before that diet has been held or dispensed with, the solicitor—

(i) is dismissed by the accused; or

(ii) withdraws,

the solicitor shall forthwith inform the court in writing of those facts.

(8) It is the duty of a solicitor who—

(a) was engaged for the purposes of the defence of the accused at the trial—

(i) at the time of a diet under this section; or

(ii) in the case of a diet which, under subsection (6) above, is dispensed with, at the time when it was so dispensed with; and

(b) after that time but before the trial diet—

(i) is dismissed by the accused; or

(ii) withdraws,

forthwith to inform the court in writing of those facts.

(9) On being so informed, the court shall order a further diet under this section.

(10) For the purposes of this section, the list is—

(a) an offence to which section 288C applies,

(b) an offence to which section 288DC applies.

AMENDMENTS

Section 148A inserted by Sexual Offences (Procedure and Evidence) (Scotland) Act 2002 (asp 9) Sch.1 para.11. Brought into force by SSI 2002/443 (C.24) art.4 (effective 1 November 2002).

Subsection (1), (10) as amended, title of s.148A substituted, by Domestic Abuse (Scotland) Act 2018 (asp 5) Sch.1(1)(2) para.4(11) and (12) (effective 1 April 2019 in respect of proceedings commenced on or after 1 April 2019 subject to transitional provision specified in SSI 2018/387 reg.7(2)).

GENERAL NOTE

A4-321.2 Refer to discussion at A4-321 above.

Pre-trial procedure in sheriff court where no intermediate diet is fixed

A4-321.3 **148B.**—(1) Where, in any summary proceedings in the sheriff court, no intermediate diet is fixed, the court shall, at the trial diet before the first witness is sworn—

(a) ascertain whether subsection (2) below applies to any person who is to give evidence at or for the purposes of the trial or to the accused and, if so, consider whether it should make an order under section 271A(7) or 271D(2) of this Act in relation to the person or, as the case may be, the accused, and

(b) if—

(i) section 288E of this Act applies to the proceedings, or

(ii) an order under section 288F(2) has been made in the proceedings,

ascertain whether or not the accused has engaged a solicitor for the purposes of his defence at the trial.

(2) This subsection applies—

(a) to a person who is to give evidence at or for the purposes of the trial if that person is, or is likely to be, a vulnerable witness,

(b) to the accused if, were he to give evidence at or for the purposes of the trial, he would be, or be likely to be, a vulnerable witness.

(3) Where, following inquiries for the purposes of subsection (1)(b) above, it appears to the court that the accused has not engaged a solicitor for the purposes of his defence at the trial, the court may adjourn the trial diet for a period of not more than 48 hours and ordain the accused then to attend.

(4) At the trial diet, the court may ask the prosecutor and the accused any question in connection with any matter which it is required to ascertain or consider under subsection (1) above.

AMENDMENTS

Section 148B inserted by Vulnerable Witnesses (Scotland) Act 2004 (asp 3) s.9. Brought into force on 1 April 2007 (only in respect of child witness and referred to in s.27(1)(a) of the 1995 Act) by SSI 2007/101 (C.13) art.2. Remainder brought into force on 1 April 2008 by SSI 2008/57 (C.7) art.2.

DEFINITIONS

A4-321.4 "diet": s.307(1).
"prosecutor": s.307(1).
"vulnerable witness": s.271.

GENERAL NOTE

A4-321.5 This section covers the procedural possible event of a trial in a summary case that has not been preceded by an intermediate diet. Section 148B applies to a vulnerable witness or to an accused who (if giving evidence) would be a vulnerable witness: see s.148B(2). In these circumstances the court must, at the trial diet before the first witness is sworn, see if s.148B(2) does apply and whether there may be a prohibition on an accused personally cross-examining a complainer and ascertain whether or not the accused has engaged a solicitor for the purposes of his defence at the trial. If it appears that there is no solicitor so engaged then the court may adjourn the trial diet for a period of not more than 48 hours: s.148B(3).

See the fuller discussion at s.148C below.

Engagement, dismissal and withdrawl of solicitor representing accused

148C.—(1) In summary proceedings, it is the duty of a solicitor who is engaged by the accused for the purposes of his defence at trial to notify the court and the prosecutor of that fact forthwith in writing. **A4-321.6**

(2) The duty under subsection (1) above shall be regarded as having been complied with if the solicitor has represented the accused at the first calling of the case—

(a) by submitting a written intimation of the accused's plea as described in subsection (2)(a) of section 144 of this Act; or

(b) by appearing on behalf of the accused—

(i) as described in subsection (2)(b) of that section; or

(ii) with the accused present,

and has, when acting as described in paragraph (a) or (b) above, notified the court and the prosecutor orally or in writing that the solicitor is also engaged by the accused for the purposes of his defence at trial.

(3) Where a solicitor referred to in subsection (1) above—

(a) is dismissed by the accused; or

(b) withdraws,

it is the duty of the solicitor to notify the court and the prosecutor of that fact forthwith in writing.

AMENDMENTS

Section 148C inserted by Criminal Proceedings etc (Reform) (Scotland) Act 2007 (asp 6) s.21. Brought into force on December 10, 2007 by SSI 2007/479 (C.40) art.3 and Sch.

DEFINITIONS

"prosecutor": s.307(1). **A4-321.7**
"Act of Adjournal": s.305.

GENERAL NOTE

The introduction into the 1995 Act first, of s.148B, and now s.148C, which relate only to summary proceedings, mirrors earlier procedures introduced for solemn proceedings by the Criminal Procedure (Amendment) (Scotland) Act 2004 (asp 5). **A4-321.8**

Once service of the complaint (or, arguably, notice of its content) has been effected upon the accused, any other document which has to be served upon the accused can, instead, be served upon the nominated solicitor. This all-embracing provision is intended to override express evidential concessions found elsewhere in the 1995 Act; for example, the routine evidence provisions of ss.280 to 282. It is submitted that it does not apply, however, in instances where the charges are "listed sexual offences" or where witnesses are children under 12 years of age: both these situations demand that specific information is made known to the accused by notice since he is statutorily barred from acting on his own behalf (see generally ss.288C and 288E of the 1995 Act).

Section 148B obliges the solicitor acting for the accused to make his appointment known to the court and to the prosecutor (but not to co-accused) either by an express written notice, by a letter plea or by personal appearance at the first, or pleading diet, or any continuation thereof. The nominated solicitor is also obliged (subs.(3)) to inform the court if, for any reason, he ceases to act for the accused. It follows that any solicitor appointed at a later stage in the proceedings is under a duty to advise the prosecutor and the court of this development.

Service etc. on accused through a solicitor

148D.—(1) In summary proceedings, anything which is to be served on or given, notified or otherwise intimated to, the accused (except service of a complaint) shall be taken to be so served, given, notified or intimated if it is, in such form and manner as may be prescribed by Act of Adjournal, served on or given, notified or intimated to (as the case may be) the solicitor described in subsection (2) below at that solicitor's place of business. **A4-321.9**

(2) That solicitor is any solicitor—

(a) who

(i) has given notice under subsection (1) of section 148C of this Act that that solicitor is engaged by the accused for the purposes of the accused's defence at the trial; and

(ii) has not given notice under subsection (3) of that section;

(b) who has represented the accused as mentioned in subsection (2) of that section; and—

(i) has given notice as mentioned in that subsection; and

(ii) has not given notice under subsection (3) of that section; or

(c) who—

(i) has been appointed to act for the purposes of the accused's defence at the trial under section 150A(4)(b) or (7) or 288D of this Act; and

(ii) has not been relieved of the appointment by the court.

Amendments

Section 148D inserted by Criminal Proceedings etc (Reform) (Scotland) Act 2007 (asp 6) s.21. Brought into force on December 10, 2007 by SSI 2007/479 (C.40) art.3 and Sch.

[THE NEXT PARAGRAPH IS A4-322]

Alibi

A4-322 **149.** [...]

Amendments

This section and s.149A repealed and replaced by s.149B below by Criminal Proceedings etc. (Reform) (Scotland) Act 2007 (asp 6) s.19. Brought into force on December 10, 2007 by SSI 2007/479.

Notice of defence plea of consent

A4-323 **149A.** [...]

Amendments

This section and s.149 repealed and replaced by s.149B below by Criminal Proceedings etc. (Reform) (Scotland) Act 2007 (asp 6) s.19. Brought into force on December 10, 2007 by SSI 2007/479.

Notice of defences

A4-323.1 **149B.**—(1) It is not competent for an accused in a summary prosecution to found on a defence to which this subsection applies unless—

(a) notice of the defence has been given to the prosecutor in accordance with subsection (5) below; or

(b) the court, on cause shown, allows the accused to found on the defence despite the failure so to give notice of it.

(2) Subsection (1) above applies—

(a) to a special defence;

(b) to a defence which may be made out by leading evidence calculated to exculpate the accused by incriminating a co-accused;

(c) to a defence of automatism or coercion;

(d) in a prosecution for an offence to which section 288C of this Act applies, to a defence of consent.

(2A) Subsection (1) does not apply where—

(a) the accused lodges a defence statement under section 125 of the Criminal Justice and Licensing (Scotland) Act 2010 (asp 13),

(b) the statement is lodged—

(i) where an intermediate diet is to be held, at or before the diet, or

(ii) where such a diet is not to be held, no later than 10 clear days before the trial diet, and

(c) the accused's defence consists of or includes a defence to which that subsection applies.

(3) In subsection (2)(d) above, the reference to a defence of consent is a reference to the defence which is stated by reference to the complainer's consent to the act which is the subject matter of the charge or the accused's belief as to that consent.

(4) In subsection (3) above, "complainer" has the same meaning as in section 274 of this Act.

(5) Notice of a defence is given in accordance with this subsection if it is given—

(a) where an intermediate diet is to be held, at or before that diet; or
(b) where such a diet is not to be held, no later than 10 clear days before the trial diet,

together with the particulars mentioned in subsection (6) below.

(6) The particulars are—

(a) in relation to a defence of alibi, particulars as to time and place; and
(b) in relation to that or any other defence, particulars of the witnesses who may be called to give evidence in support of the defence.

(7) Where notice of a defence to which subsection (1) above applies is given to the prosecutor, the prosecutor is entitled to an adjournment of the case.

(8) The entitlement to an adjournment under subsection (7) above may be exercised whether or not—

(a) the notice was given in accordance with subsection (5) above;
(b) the entitlement could have been exercised at an earlier diet.

AMENDMENTS

This section substituted for ss.149 and 149A by Criminal Proceedings etc. (Reform) (Scotland) Act 2007 (asp 6) s.19. Brought into force on December 10, 2007 by SSI 2007/479.

Subs.(2A) inserted by Criminal Justice and Licensing (Scotland) Act 2010 (asp 13) s.125(7). Brought into force on June 6, 2011 (for all purposes in respect of criminal proceedings in which the recording of a plea of not guilty against an accused charged on summary complaint is on or after June 6, 2011) by SSI 2011/178 (C.15) art.2, Sch.1 para.1.

DEFINITIONS

A4-323.2

"prosecutor": s.307(1).
"complainer": s.274(2).
"intermediate diet": s.148(1).

GENERAL NOTE

A4-323.3

This section's provisions substitute both s.149 of the 1995 Act dealing with intimation of alibi defences in summary trials, and the more recent provision found in s.149A which required intimation in advance of a consent defence when the charge was a "listed sexual offence" (see s.288C below). Echoing the approach adopted in solemn proceedings, it is now mandatory for the defence to give advance notice of intention to lead any special defence, including automatism or coercion, and to do so much earlier than hitherto. The familiar, and till now legitimate, practice of tendering such a plea at the beginning of a summary trial diet, leaving the Crown with the dilemma of either proceeding to trial immediately with minimal further preparation or seeking an adjournment at the very last moment (with attendant inconvenience to witnesses and loss of court time) is at an end for most cases. The timescale for lodging defences is set out in subs.(5) while subs.(6) specifies the detail to be included in defences. Later notice of a special defence can be permitted on cause shown but it should be noted that once notice of such a defence is given to the Crown at any point in the proceedings, the Crown will still be entitled to an adjournment of the proceedings.

It is worthy of note that this amended provision now specifies all the categories of special defence whereas s.149 of the 1995 Act only referred to that of alibi. For avoidance of doubt, entrapment has to be regarded as a plea in bar of any trial rather than a special defence (see the discussion in *HM Advocate v Brown*, 2002 S.L.T. 809).

[THE NEXT PARAGRAPH IS A4-324]

Failure of accused to appear

A4-324 **150.**—(1) This section applies where the accused in a summary prosecution fails to appear at any diet of which he has received intimation, or to which he has been cited other than a diet which, by virtue of section 148(5) of this Act, he is not required to attend.

(2) The court may adjourn the proceedings to another diet, and order the accused to attend at such diet, and appoint intimation of the diet to be made to him.

(3) The court may grant warrant to apprehend the accused.

(3A) The grant, under subsection (3) above, at an intermediate diet, or a diet under section 148A of this Act, of a warrant to apprehend the accused has the effect of discharging the trial diet as respects that accused.

(3B) Subsection (3A) above is subject to any order to different effect made by the court when granting the warrant.

(3C) An order under subsection (3B) above—

(a) for the purpose of having a trial in absence of the accused under section 150A of this Act, may be made on the motion of the prosecutor;

(b) for any other purpose, may be made on the motion of the prosecutor or of the court's own accord.

(4) Intimation under subsection (2) above shall be sufficiently given by an officer of law, or by letter signed by the clerk of court or prosecutor and sent to the accused at his last known address by registered post or by the recorded delivery service, and the production in court of the written execution of such officer or of an acknowledgement or certificate of the delivery of the letter issued by the postal operator shall be sufficient evidence of such intimation having been duly given.

(5) [...]

(6) [...]

(7) [...]

(8) An accused who without reasonable excuse fails to attend any diet of which he has been given due notice, shall be guilty of an offence and liable on summary conviction—

(a) to a fine not exceeding level 3 on the standard scale; and

(b) to a period of imprisonment not exceeding—

(i) in the JP court, 60 days; or

(ii) in the sheriff court, 12 months.

(9) A penalty under subsection (8) above shall be imposed in addition to any other penalty which it is competent for the court to impose, notwithstanding that the total of penalties imposed may exceed the maximum penalty which it is competent to impose in respect of the original offence.

(9A) The reference in subsection (9) above to a penalty being imposed in addition to another penalty means, in the case of sentences of imprisonment or detention—

(a) where the sentences are imposed at the same time (whether or not in relation to the same complaint), framing the sentences so that they have effect consecutively;

(b) where the sentences are imposed at different times, framing the sentence imposed later so that (if the earlier sentence has not been served) the later sentence has effect consecutive to the earlier sentence.

(9B) Subsection (9A)(b) above is subject to section 204A of this Act.

(9C) In any proceedings in relation to an offence under subsection (8) above, the fact that (as the case may be) an accused—

(a) failed to appear at a diet; or
(b) was given due notice of a diet,

shall, unless challenged by preliminary objection before his plea is recorded, be held as admitted.

(10) At any time before the trial in the prosecution in which the failure to appear occurred, it is competent to amend the complaint to include an additional charge of an offence under subsection (8).

AMENDMENTS

Subs.(4) as amended by Postal Services Act 2000 (Consequential Modifications No.1) Order 2001 (SI 2001/1149) art.3 and Sch.1 para.104.

Subss.(3A) and (3B) inserted by Criminal Procedure (Amendment) (Scotland) Act 2002 (asp 4) s.1 (effective 9 March 2002).

Subs.(3A) as amended by Sexual Offences (Procedure and Evidence) (Scotland) Act 2002 (asp 9) Sch.1 para.12. Brought into force by SSI 2002/443 (C.24) art.4 (effective 1 November 2002).

Subs.(3C) inserted and subss.(5)-(7) repealed by Criminal Proceedings etc. (Reform) (Scotland) Act 2007 (asp 6) s.14; subss.(8) and (9) as amended and subs.(9A)-(9C) inserted by s.15 of the 2007 Act. All brought into force on 10 December 2007 by SSI 2007/479.

Subs.(8) as ameneded by Criminal Proceedings etc. (Reform) (Scotland) Act 2007 (asp 6) s.80, Sch. para.26. Brought into force for the Sheriffdom of Lothian and Borders on 10 March 2008 by SSI 2008/42 (C.4) art.3 and Sch. Brought into force for the Sheriffdom of Grampian, Highland and Islands on 2 June 2008 by SSI 2008/192 (C.19) art.3 and Sch. Brought into force for the Sheriffdom of Glasgow and Strathkelvin on 8 December 2008 by SSI 2008/329 (C.29) art.3 and Sch. Brought into force for the Sheriffdom of Tayside, Central and Fife on 23 February 2009 by SSI 2008/362 (C.30) art.3 and Sch. Brought into force for the Sheriffdom of North Strathclyde on 14 December 2009 by SSI 2009/432 (C.32) art.3 and Sch.1. Remainder in force on 22 February 2010 by SSI 2009/432 (C.32) art.3 and Sch.2.

Subs.(10) substituted by Criminal Justice and Licensing (Scotland) Act 2010 (asp 13) s.62(2). Brought into force on 28 March 2011 (for all purposes in respect of any breach of bail committed on or after 28 March 2011)by SSI 2011/178 (C.15) art.2, Sch.1 para.1.

DEFINITIONS

"complaint": s.307(1). **A4-324.1**
"diet": s.307(1).
"imprisonment": s.307(6).
"offence": s.307(1).
"officer of law": s.307(1).
"prosecutor": s.307(1).

GENERAL NOTE

Section 141, which specifies the methods of citation of accused, and this section which deals with the consequences of a failure by an accused to appear at a summary diet need to be considered together. Intimation of any diet can be made by notice sent by registered or recorded post, by personal service of such a notice by an officer of law, or by the fixing of the diet in the accused's presence. While s.141 relates to the way in which proceedings are launched, s.150 has general application once a complaint has been placed before the court until the proceedings are concluded. **A4-325**

The failure by an accused to attend a diet of which he has been given notice lawfully, entitles the prosecutor to seek an apprehension warrant in terms of s.150 and to libel a further complaint founding upon failure to appear. The penalties disclosed in subs.(8) are in addition to any penalty the court may impose on the original complaint and, cumulatively, the penalties exacted on the original and second complaint can competently exceed the statutory ceilings fixed in summary proceedings; these are defined in s.5(2) and (3) for the sheriff court, and in s.7(6) and (7) in relation to the district court.

On proof of citation or notice of a diet being produced to the court, the prosecutor may seek a warrant to apprehend the accused. The court may grant a warrant or continue the diet to a later diet and order intimation of the diet on the accused as provided by subs.(2). This underlines the importance of the Crown being able to exhibit evidence of service of the complaint or of intimation of the diet when required by the court. See *Beattie v Mackinnon*, 1977 J.C. 64 where no date of citation had been placed on the accused's citation and service copy complaint, a fact unknown to the court when a warrant to apprehend was granted following an apparent failure to appear.

The court is not obliged to issue a warrant following failure to appear by the accused (subs.(2) permits adjournment of proceedings) but must pronounce some order and cannot simply refrain from action; see *Skeen v Sullivan*, 1980 S.L.T. (Notes) 11. Equally, the prosecutor can only proceed under this section to take a warrant, when he is satisfied that service of the complaint has been effected and, hence, that it is validly before the court for further procedure; see *Lees v Malcolm*, 1992 S.L.T. 1137; 1992 S.C.C.R. 589 where a fresh complaint was raised to maintain proceedings, and *Heywood v McLennan*, 1994 S.C.C.R. 1 where efforts were made to "convert" an unserved complaint into an initiating warrant, despite the complaint having fallen.

Subsections (5), (6) and (7) provide for trial proceedings in the absence of the accused only once the court is satisfied that the accused has either been cited or received an intimation of the diet deemed necessary by the court.

Subss.(3A) and (3B)

In *Reynolds v Dyer*, 2002 S.L.T. 331 it was held that the discharge of a trial diet, which was a peremptory diet, should not be left to implication and that the granting of a warrant at an intermediate diet did not per se discharge a trial diet. The statutory changes in the Criminal Procedure (Amendment) (Scotland) Act 2002 reversed that decision and thereby reinstated the usual practice in the summary courts.

The amended penalties found in s.150(8) of the Act have the effect of increasing the penalties upon an accused following his failure to appear at a summary diet in the sheriff court. The maximum penalty for such an offence is quadrupled from a term of 3, to 12, months imprisonment or detention; the penalty in the JP court (see s.59 of the 2007 Act) remains unchanged at 60 days. Still more to the point the amendments made to s.150(9) now require that any such sentence, whether it is imposed in either the JP or sheriff court, shall be imposed consecutively to any other term of detention or imprisonment pronounced by the court on the substantive offence or offences and this, whether the principal charge and failure to appear charge are dealt with at the same or separate diets. This may of course result in the court passing custodial sentences whose total substantially exceeds the powers normally available to the court (see ss.5(2) and (3) and 7(6) of the 1995 Act).

The only exception to this generality occurs when the person so convicted has been released on licence and is thus liable to recall—see s.204A of the 1995 Act. Subsection (9C) as now introduced into the 1995 Act repeats a now familiar drafting formula and holds the s.150 charge to be admitted unless objection is taken at the pleading diet (or its continuation) before any plea is tendered.

Subs.(10)

Subs.(10), as introduced by the 2010 Act cited above, entitles the Crown to add a charge alleging a failure to appear at a diet by the accused to an existing summary complaint; this can be done by amending the complaint at any point up until the summary trial commences, i.e. before the leading of evidence (almost invariably signified by the administration of the oath to the first witness). The disadvantage for the Crown in leaving amendment of the complaint until such a late point in the proceedings is that the major evidential concession in subs.(9C) is lost; plainly there is benefit in libelling the additional charge at the earliest opportunity to utilise the concession.

Where the accused person is on bail, and fails to appear at a diet, refer instead to s.27 of the 1995 Act above.

Proceedings in absence of accused

A4-325.1 **150A.**—(1) Where the accused does not appear at a diet (apart from a diet fixed for the first calling of the case), the court—

(a) on the motion of the prosecutor or, in relation to sentencing, of its own accord; and

(b) if satisfied as to the matters specified in subsection (2) below,

may proceed to hear and dispose of the case in the absence of the accused in like manner as if the accused were present.

(2) The matters referred in subsection (1)(b) above are—

(a) that citation of the accused has been effected or the accused has received other intimation of the diet; and

(b) that it is in the interests of justice to proceed as mentioned in subsection (1) above.

(3) In subsection (1) above, the reference to proceeding to hear and dispose of the case includes, in relation to a trial diet, proceeding with the trial.

(4) Where the court is considering whether to proceed in pursuance of subsection (1) above, it shall—

(a) if satisfied that there is a solicitor with authority to act—

(i) for the purposes of representing the accused's interests at the hearing on whether to proceed that way; and

(ii) if it proceeds that way, for the purposes of representing the accused's further interests at the diet (including, in relation to a trial diet, presenting a defence at the trial),

allow that solicitor to act for those purposes; or

(b) if there is no such solicitor, at its own hand appoint a solicitor to act for those purposes if it considers that it is in the interests of justice to do so.

(5) It is the duty of a solicitor appointed under subsection (4)(b) above to act in the best interests of the accused.

(6) In all other respects, a solicitor so appointed has, and may be made subject to, the same obligations and has, and may be given, the same authority as if engaged by the accused; and any employment of and instructions given to counsel by the solicitor shall proceed and be treated accordingly.

(7) Where the court is satisfied that—

(a) a solicitor allowed to act under subsection (4)(a) above no longer has authority to act; or

(b) a solicitor appointed under subsection (4)(b) above is no longer able to act in the best interests of the accused,

the court may relieve that solicitor and appoint another solicitor for the purposes referred to in subsection (4) above.

(8) Subsections (4)(b) and (7) above do not apply in the case of proceedings—

(a) in respect of a sexual offence to which section 288C of this Act applies;

(aa) in respect of an offence to which section 288DC of this Act applies;

(b) in respect of which section 288E of this Act applies; or

(c) in which an order has been made under section 288F(2) of this Act.

(9) Reference in this section to a solicitor appointed under subsection (4)(b) above includes reference to a solicitor appointed under subsection (7) above.

(10) Where the court proceeds in pursuance of subsection (1) above, it shall not in the absence of the accused pronounce a sentence of imprisonment or detention.

(11) Nothing in this section prevents—

(a) a warrant being granted at any stage of proceedings for the apprehension of the accused;

(b) a case subsequently being adjourned (in particular, with a view to having the accused present at any proceedings).

Amendments

Section 150A inserted by the Criminal Proceedings etc. (Reform) (Scotland) Act 2007 (asp 6), s.14. Brought into force on 10 December 2007, by the Criminal Proceedings etc. (Reform) (Scotland) Act 2007 (Commencement No. 2 and Transitional Provisions and Savings) Order 2007 (SSI 2007/479).

Subs.(8)(aa) as inserted by Domestic Abuse (Scotland) Act 2018 (asp 5) Sch.1(1)(2) para.4(13) (effective 1 April 2019 in respect of proceedings commenced on or after 1 April 2019 subject to transitional provision specified in SSI 2018/387 reg.7(2)).

Definitions

"prosecutor": s.307(1). A4-325.2
"diet": s.307(1).
"imprisonment": s.307(1).
"young offenders institution": s.307(1) of the 1995 Act and the Prisons (Scotland) Act 1989.

General Note

Section 150 of the 1995 Act originally made limited (and little-used) provisions for summary proceedings in the absence of an accused. Generally the offences involved could not attract imprisonment following conviction and a trial in absence could only occur when the court could be satisfied that the accused had had advance notice of such a possibility. A4-325.3

The insertion into the Act of ss.150(3C) and 150A has brought about some subtle (but telling) refinements of procedure; now it is open to the court to order to a trial absence of the accused on either the prosecutor's motion or that of the court *ex proprio motu* and thereafter to proceed to impose a non-custodial, and final, sentence once satisfied that an accused has received notification of the diet and that it is in the interests of justice to proceed. While s.150A(10) does not allow the court to impose a sentence of imprisonment or detention in the absence of an accused, that does not, of itself, prevent the court from hearing evidence and reaching a determination on the evidence, thereafter granting a warrant for apprehension enabling the accused to be brought before the court for sentence. The critical issues then, are whether the court considers at the outset (and, obviously, in ignorance of the accused's criminal history) that a trial in absence is appropriate and that the evidence offered to the court is adequately tested. Some further comments may be pertinent: first, it remains the case that the court cannot impose any sentence which depends upon the accused's consent—notably probation or community service; secondly, that the provision may well be better suited to situations where there is only a single accused (thorny issues of comparative justice between co-accused are then avoided); thirdly, that an appointed solicitor can continue to act on behalf of the accused if content that he is adequately instructed, failing which the court can appoint a solicitor to conduct the defence if it considers it in the interests of justice so to do. Whether a solicitor would be content to act in such circumstances is more debatable. It is submitted, with caution, that there would be merit in receiving an express mandate from clients in advance of a summary trial defining the extent (if any) of the instructions especially where a custodial sentence could be in prospect; this would surely provide the court with the information needed to satisfy the requirements of s.150A(7). Finally, it is observed that use of trial in absence can only be of value where issues of identification of the accused have already been resolved or the Crown can invoke the little-known (and even less-used) presumption respecting identification found in s.280(9) of the Act or other statutory presumptions.

Section 150A(8) makes numerous saving provisions to allow the provisions of ss. 288C to 288F—cases involving listed sexual offences, and child and vulnerable witnesses—to stand.

Finally, attention is directed to the increased penalties, and evidential presumptions, governing failures of accused to appear at appointed summary diets; these are discussed in the Notes to s.150 above.

[THE NEXT PARAGRAPH IS A4-326]

Non-availability of judge

Death, illness or absence of judge

A4-326 **151.**—(1) Where the court is unable to proceed owing to the death, illness or absence of the presiding judge, it shall be lawful for the clerk of court—

(a) where the diet has not been called, to convene the court and adjourn the diet;

(b) where the diet has been called but no evidence has been led, to adjourn the diet; and

(c) where the diet has been called and evidence has been led—

(i) with the agreement of the parties, to desert the diet *pro loco et tempore*; or

(ii) to adjourn the diet.

(2) Where, under subsection (1)(c)(i) above, a diet has been deserted *pro loco et tempore*, any new prosecution charging the accused with the same or any similar offence arising out of the same facts shall be brought within two months of the date on which the diet was deserted notwithstanding that any other time limit for the commencement of such prosecution has elapsed.

(3) For the purposes of subsection (2) above, a new prosecution shall be deemed to commence on the date on which a warrant to apprehend or to cite the accused is granted, if such warrant is executed without undue delay.

Definitions

A4-326.1 "judge": s.307(1).
"offence": s.307(1).

[THE NEXT PARAGRAPH IS A4-327]

General Note

A4-327 The purpose of this section is to provide for the adjournment, or desertion *pro loco et tempore*, of summary proceedings where the court cannot proceed due to the death, illness or absence of the "presiding judge", a phrase equally applicable to sheriff or district court proceedings. Similar provisions, taking due account of differences in procedure, apply to solemn proceedings by s.87 above.

In summary proceedings the court has a common law authority to fix a new diet when a judge is taken ill during a trial and therefore the possibility of postponement of a trial, for that same reason, was acknowledged in s.331A(2)(a) of the 1975 Act. However until the passage of s.30 of the Criminal Justice (Scotland) Act 1995, no statutory provision existed in summary cases to regulate proceedings in the event of the death of a judge. In *Clarke v Fraser*, 2002 S.L.T. 745, the Appeal Court refused to uphold a purported adjournment of a District Court proof where the court could not convene due to severe weather and the clerk and the judge having spoken over the phone, the clerk opted to adjourn in the absence of the judge at a place other than the court itself. The Appeal Court noted that since the court could not convene the remedy would have been for the Crown to petition the *nobile officium* as a means of preserving the complaint.

Desertion of the diet necessarily means that the instance in the complaint falls. To preserve the public interest, particularly in cases which would otherwise be time-barred in accordance with s.136 above, subs.(2) permits the re-raising of any proceedings deserted in terms of s.151. In that event proceedings can be initiated anew, but must be effected upon the accused without undue delay (for "undue delay" see generally the notes to s.136 above).

A separate provision dealing with the illness or death of a judge in the course of preparation of an appeal by stated case is found at s.176(4).

Trial diet

Desertion of diet

152.—(1) It shall be competent at the diet of trial, at any time before the first witness is sworn, for the court, on the application of the prosecutor, to desert the diet *pro loco et tempore*. A4-328

(2) If, at a diet of trial, the court refuses an application by the prosecutor to adjourn the trial or to desert the diet *pro loco et tempore*, and the prosecutor is unable or unwilling to proceed with the trial, the court shall desert the diet simpliciter.

(3) Where the court has deserted a diet simpliciter under subsection (2) above (and the court's decision in that regard has not been reversed on appeal), it shall not be competent for the prosecutor to raise a fresh libel.

DEFINITIONS A4-328.1

"diet": s.307(1).
"prosecutor": s.307(1).
"trial": s.307(1).
"witness": s.307(1).

[THE NEXT PARAGRAPH IS A4-329]

GENERAL NOTE

The terms of s.338A of the 1975 Act are preserved. Section 147(4) of this Act enacts that a trial begins when the first witness is sworn; until that time it is open to the prosecutor to move the court to desert the diet *pro loco et tempore*, or to move to adjourn the trial. Once either of these motions has been made however, the court can refuse the motion and, instead, desert the trial simpliciter, a step which brings proceedings to an end. In some instances the Crown might better achieve its purpose simply by not calling the case for trial at all, since, although the instance in the current complaint would fall, the right to proceed might still be retained. It remains the case, as subs.(3) states, that the unreasonable refusal by the judge of a Crown motion to adjourn or desert *pro loco et tempore* can still be appealed. A4-329

In *Tudhope v Gough*, 1982 S.C.C.R. 157 it was held competent for the Crown to move to desert *pro loco* even after the refusal of a motion to adjourn and see *Fay v Vannet*, 1998 S.L.T. 1099, where desertion of a complaint of police assault by the prosecutor following the sheriff's refusal of adjournment was competently followed by a fresh complaint of common law assault, a step which was held not to be oppressive. In *Fay v Vannet*, 1998 S.L.T. 1099 it was affirmed that desertion simpliciter could only be exercised by the court in terms of s.152(2) after refusal of both of the prosecutor's motions to adjourn and to desert *pro loco et tempore*. A more novel, but inappropriate, use of desertion simpliciter is found in *MacLeod v Williamson*, 1993 S.L.T. 144 where the sheriff did so *ex proprio motu* having overheard witnesses during an adjournment and having drawn the nature of the eavesdropping to the attention of the prosecutor.

The Appeal Court indicated that if the sheriff had come to the view that he could no longer preside over the trial, he should have discharged the trial diet and fixed a new diet to go before another sheriff; desertion simpliciter was invalid. In a similar vein, see *Carmichael v Monaghan* 1986 S.C.C.R. 598.

In *McMahon v Hamilton*, 1992 S.C.C.R. 351, the prosecutor deserted one of two charges on a complaint simpliciter, a plea of not guilty being recorded for the second charge. Issue was thereafter taken with the competency of proceeding on the latter charge. The plea to competency was repelled but the Appeal Court, rather than express any view on the competency of deserting a charge (as distinct from a complaint) simpliciter elected to treat both charges as live and to treat the minuting of the pleas as *pro non scripto*: it remains unresolved whether such a motion is competent or not, though the simplest solution is surely to accept a plea of not guilty to the charge in normal circumstances. In *Mitchell v HM Advocate*, 2004 S.L.T. 151 the Crown's decision to desert not one, but two, prior complaints to enable substitution of a complaint containing still more serious charges was upheld; only if the accused can demonstrate oppression, i.e. that he cannot now receive a fair trial due to the gravity of the prejudice resulting from the proceedings, could a motion to desert *pro loco et tempore* be refused.

See *Normand v West*, 1992 S.C.C.R. 76 as an example of an unreasonable refusal by the court to permit an adjournment in the absence of essential witnesses. Desertion simpliciter by the court and the premature ending of a prosecution is a step which, in *Tudhope v Laurie*, 1979 S.L.T. (Notes) 13 at 14, "must be exercised only after the most careful consideration on weighty grounds and with due and accurate regard to the interests which will be affected or prejudiced by that exercise".

See also *Normand v Milne*, 1996 G.W.D. 19-1078, where the Crown succeeded on appeal by advocation against the sheriff's refusal to permit a desertion *pro loco*. The Appeal Court may have signalled a more rigorous (and less tolerant) approach to repeated Crown motions to adjourn caused by failure to trace or cite witnesses; see *Donaldson v Kelly*, 2004 S.C.C.R. 153.

Ruxton v Borland, 2000 S.L.T. 612; 2000 S.C.C.R. 484 re-introduces a measure of familiarity, and clarity, to summary proceedings after the uncertainties produced by the Appeal Court in *Mitchell v Vannet*, 1999 S.L.T 934, which bore to follow *Handley v Pirie*, 1977 S.L.T. 30, both of which *Ruxton v Borland*, a five judge decision, has overruled. Following this decision and its three judge precursor (found at 2000 G.W.D. 9-326) it can be said that after the tendering of a plea of not guilty on a summary complaint, it is only necessary thereafter to ascertain whether the plea previously tendered is adhered to, and that unless there is evident prejudice to the accused, there is no necessity for the same judge to deal with the case at all times once it has been put down for trial.

Complaints triable together

A4-329.1 **152A.—**(1) Where—

(a) two or more complaints against an accused call for trial in the same court on the same day; and

(b) they each contain one or more charges to which the accused pleads not guilty,

the prosecutor may apply to the court for those charges to be tried together at that diet despite the fact that they are not all contained in the one complaint.

(2) On an application under subsection (1) above, the court is to try those charges together if it appears to the court that it is expedient to do so.

(3) For the purposes of subsections (1) and (2) above, any other charges contained in the complaints are (without prejudice to further proceedings as respects those other charges) to be disregarded.

(4) Where charges are tried together under this section, they are to be treated (including, in particular, for the purposes of and in connection with the leading of evidence, proof and verdict) as if they were contained in one complaint.

(5) But the complaints mentioned in subsection (1)(a) above are, for the purposes of further proceedings (including as to sentence), to be treated as separate complaints.

AMENDMENTS

Section 152A inserted by Criminal Proceedings etc. (Reform) (Scotland) Act 2007 (asp 6) s.13. Brought into force on 10 December 2007 by SSI 2007/479.

DEFINITIONS

A4-329.2 "complaint": s.307(1).
"prosecutor": s.307(1).

GENERAL NOTE

A4-329.3 In keeping with the broad theme of the summary criminal reforms in the 2007 Act, economising on court resources and time, this section makes a statutory provision enabling the prosecutor in summary proceedings to seek to conjoin complaints against the accused when two or more are due to call for trial on the same date. There may be procedural savings in such a move, but it could carry the prospect of a conjunction being sought to enable the *Moorov* doctrine to be applied where available evidence on an existing complaint suddenly proved to be deficient. It will be noted that the section does not explore the issues which might arise should either of the complaints involve co-accused. Nonetheless, as subs.(2) makes clear the court retains a discretion to grant or refuse a motion of this sort and must treat the complaints as separate at the time of imposing any sentence.

[THE NEXT PARAGRAPH IS A4-330]

Trial in presence of accused

A4-330 **153.—**(1) Subject to section 150A of this Act and subsection (2) below, no part of a trial shall take place outwith the presence of the accused.

(2) If during the course of his trial an accused so misconducts himself that in the view of the court a proper trial cannot take place unless he is removed, the court may order—

(a) that he is removed from the court for so long as his conduct makes it necessary; and

(b) that the trial proceeds in his absence,

but if he is not legally represented the court shall appoint counsel or a solicitor to represent his interests during such absence.

Amendments

Subs.(1) as amended by Criminal Proceedings etc. (Reform) (Scotland) Act 2007 (asp 6) s.14. Brought into force on 10 December 2007 by SSI 2007/479.

Definition

"trial": s.307(1). A4-330.1

[THE NEXT PARAGRAPH IS A4-331]

General Note

Subject to the statutory enactments which permit trial in the absence of the accused (see s.150(5)), it is generally the case that any trial can only competently proceed in the accused's presence (see *Aitken v Wood*, 1921 J.C. 84) for justice to be seen to be done. Section 153 introduces a further exception to the generality in circumstances where the accused so misconducts himself as to preclude proper conduct of the case. In that event the accused can be removed from the court and trial continue with the accused represented by his solicitor or counsel, or if he has not been legally represented, by an agent appointed by the court to act on his behalf, during the period of absence. This provision does not, of course, resolve what action the court may take at the conclusion of the trial to deal with any contempt. A4-331

The general principle that justice must not only be done, but be seen to be done, underpins this provision. Unreasonable fetters upon an accused's ability to cross-examine, as in *McGeechan v Higson*, 2000 G.W.D. 39-1445 where the magistrate had restricted the accused, who was defending himself, to cross-examining witnesses only on their answers to Crown questions, offend against that principle. See the general guidance provided for these situations in *Beckley v Ramage*, 2009 S.C.C.R. 93. Similarly in *McKee v Brown*, 2001 S.C.C.R. 6, where the trial judge accidentally saw the schedule of convictions which had been left with the complaint after withdrawal of an earlier guilty plea, and expressed misgivings but still felt bound by the decision in *Tudhope v O'Neill*, 1984 S.L.T. 424; 1984 S.C.C.R. 276 (discussed at A4-359 below), conviction was quashed. The obligation to ensure the fairness of proceedings persists even after a verdict has been reached on the evidence. In *Doherty v Mc-Glennan*, 1997 S.L.T. 444 a conviction was quashed where the sheriff, having convicted the accused, then deferred sentence and invited the complainer (a local Member of Parliament) to meet in chambers. *Harper v Heywood*, 1998 S.L.T. 644, is perhaps an extreme example of unjudicial conduct which resulted in the quashing of the conviction and authority being granted for a new prosecution. However expressions of sympathy towards a victim during sentence of an accused, which caused an accused to aver that his conviction had resulted from the sheriff's sympathy, were held not to be improper, the court having moved from weighing the evidence to sentence (*Bagan v Normand*, 1997 G.W.D. 14-596). Compare *Ogilvie v Heywood*, 2001 G.W.D. 18-695 where the judge expressed regret to a witness at the conclusion of her evidence that she had had to travel from England by saying "In fact, I am sorry that this happened at all". The Appeal Court accepted that an impartial observer would have felt that the sheriff had already reached a concluded view on the evidence. In *Lowe v Brown*, 1997 S.C.C.R. 341, the Appeal Court observed that judges should question witnesses with restraint and avoid any indication of disbelieving a witness' account during examination. In *Clark v HM Advocate*, 2000 S.L.T. 1107; 2000 S.C.C.R. 767 the Appeal Court listened to the tape of the sheriff's charge to the jury and quashed the accused's conviction on the ground that the tone used in posing a series of rhetorical questions was such as to intrude into the jury's role as masters of fact. Injudicious comment by the sheriff in the course of trial, hastening defence cross-examination, and giving a clear impression that his mind was made up resulted in the quashing of conviction in *Murray v Watt*, 2002 G.W.D. 2-64. The conduct of the presiding judge in response to what was described as the agent's intemperate and repeated cross-examination of witnesses did not breach the broad principles discussed: see *Mullen v Procurator Fiscal, Inverness* [2018] SAC (Crim) 8. By contrast inappropriate, unfounded and, at points, inadmissible, questioning, and summary dismissal of properly taken defence objections, by the presiding sheriff attracted withering comment from the Appeal Court; perhaps fortuitously the subsequent appeal was decided on other grounds. See *Ahmed v HM Advocate* [2020] HCJAC 37.

The court has a duty to ensure that where the accused or any witness in the proceedings requires the services of an interpreter, suitable steps are taken to ensure that such evidence is properly presented to it as a matter of fairness. (Generally, the court is obliged to provide interpretation services for an accused and the prosecutor and defence are to make arrangements for their own witnesses, but that is not the end of the matter.) See *Kroupa v Donnelly* [2013] HCJAC 113; 2013 S.C.C.R. 662, K being unrepresented and calling a defence witness with limited command of English. Further, with effect from 19 May 2014, note the extensive right of access to interpretation and translation facilities provided to suspects and accused persons by the Right to Interpretation and Translation in Criminal Proceedings (Scotland) Regulations (SSI 2014/95). Care has to be taken to ensure that the interpreter assisting witnesses, or the accused, can objectively be regarded as independent and particularly has had no involvement during the investigation of the proceedings; see *McDougall v HM Advocate* [2015] HCJAC 88; 2015 S.C.C.R 407. The respective roles of the accused's legal representative and the court itself are set out in *Lee v HM Advocate* [2016] HCJAC 39; 2016 S.C.C.R. 247 following *Hassan v HM Advocate*, 2013 S.L.T. 217. The same general principle applies when the judge examines productions, label productions and (by logical extension) any CCTV or audio evidence outwith the presence of parties; *CB v Brown* [2020] SAC (Crim) 3 confirms the regularity of such enquiries but cautions that no findings should be reached without then hearing the parties' submissions.

Section 153(1)'s principles need not apply however in relation to enquiries conducted in connection with appeals where further evidence is heard; see *Crossan v HM Advocate*, 1996 S.C.C.R. 279 and the discussion at A4-179 above. It is noted that the accused's counsel and solicitor were present in chambers during the appointed judge's examination of evidence.

The equivalent provision in solemn proceedings is found at s.92(2) above.

Proof of official documents

A4-332 **154.** […]

AMENDMENTS

Section 154 repealed by Crime and Punishment (Scotland) Act 1997 (c.48) s.28.

GENERAL NOTE

A4-333 This section was deleted by s.28(1) of the Crime and Punishment (Scotland) Act 1997 and its provisions are now to be found in s.279A of the Act which extends the provisions in relation to official documents to all criminal proceedings. Section 154, which only applied to summary proceedings, ceased to have effect from 1 August 1997 in terms of SI 1997/1712.

Punishment of witness for contempt

A4-334 **155.—**(1) If a witness in a summary prosecution—

(a) wilfully fails to attend after being duly cited; or

(b) unlawfully refuses to be sworn; or

(c) after the oath has been administered to him refuses to answer any question which the court may allow; or

(d) prevaricates in his evidence,

he shall be deemed guilty of contempt of court and be liable to be summarily punished forthwith for such contempt by a fine not exceeding level 3 on the standard scale or by imprisonment for any period not exceeding 21 days.

(2) Where punishment is summarily imposed as mentioned in subsection (1) above, the clerk of court shall enter in the record of the proceedings the acts constituting the contempt or the statements forming the prevarication.

(3) Subsections (1) and (2) above are without prejudice to the right of the prosecutor to proceed by way of formal complaint for any such contempt where a summary punishment, as mentioned in the said subsection (1), is not imposed.

(4) Any witness who, having been duly cited in accordance with section 140 of this Act—

(a) fails without reasonable excuse, after receiving at least 48 hours' notice, to attend for precognition by a prosecutor at the time and place mentioned in the citation served on him; or

(b) refuses when so cited to give information within his knowledge regarding any matter relative to the commission of the offence in relation to which such precognition is taken,

shall be liable to the like punishment as is provided in subsection (1) above.

DEFINITIONS

A4-334.1 "prosecutor": s.307(1).

"witness": s.307(1).

[THE NEXT PARAGRAPH IS A4-335]

GENERAL NOTE

Note that this section of the Act deals with strictly defined forms of contemptuous conduct by a witness in summary proceedings. This is distinct from the court's general inherent powers to maintain orderly conduct of proceedings and from the statutory provisions which permit the Crown itself to initiate proceedings for contempt (see the Contempt of Court Act 1981 (c.49)).

Nevertheless, the same general themes, and procedural guidance, apply to all of these circumstances, and are discussed below.

Factors constituting contempt of court were reviewed generally, by a bench of five judges, in *Robertson v HM Advocate; HM Advocate v Gough*, 2007 S.L.T. 1153; 2008 S.C.C.R. 20 the first dealing with prevarication and contempt by a witness in solemn proceedings, the second involving the insistence of the accused on appearing naked before the court. The complex jurisprudential factors involved in a solicitor's duties to his client and to the court, and the broader considerations of art.10 rights were examined in *Anwar, Respondent*, 2008 S.L.T. 710; 2008 S.C.C.R. 709 which concerned a solicitor's comments upon trial proceedings, some of which were held to be inaccurate or misleading, albeit no contempt was established. **A4-335**

Contempt can be constituted by overt misconduct in proceedings before the court or, more rarely, outwith the court when clearly allied to those proceedings. In the latter situation a complaint of contempt is generally initiated by a written complaint or by a party's verbal motion to the court drawing the alleged contempt to its notice (*HM Advocate v Airs*, 1975 J.C. 64; 1975 S.L.T. 177); since the alleged misconduct occurred outwith the presence of the court, the judge must invoke a thoroughgoing investigation (especially if the complaint is directed against professional witnesses or court officials) and provide an adequate opportunity for notice of the allegation and a considered response to it. Care should be taken to ascertain that the Crown is not intending to initiate criminal proceedings. Failure to obey an order of the court does not necessarily constitute a contempt: see *AB and CD, Petitioners*, 2015 S.C.L.R. 664, a case involving social workers in a children's hearing.

The law of contempt as applied to media reporting of proceedings, is comprehensively discussed in *Scottish Daily Record and Sunday Mail v HM Advocate*, 2009 S.L.T. 363. Notwithstanding the powers of civil imprisonment provided by the Civil Imprisonment (Scotland) Act 1882 (c.42), non-payment of aliment ordered by the court in ongoing divorce proceedings is not a criminal contempt of court: see *Petition to the Nobile Officium by ADM* [2013] CSIH 69.

A finding of contempt will only be justified where there has been wilful or deliberate conduct or an affront or challenge to the court's authority (*Johnston v Normand*, 1997 G.W.D. 3-81, *McTavish v Hamilton*, 1997 G.W.D. 11-451 and, generally, *McMillan v Carmichael*, 1993 S.C.C.R. 943; 1994 S.L.T. 510). A measure of magnanimity was shown to the accused in *Williams v Clark*, 2001 G.W.D. 20-758, W having been held in contempt for having a mobile phone ringing while in the dock despite clear warning notices in the court building. One might be moved to sympathy for the judge but the Appeal Court felt that he might well have concluded disrespect on W's part also from earlier conduct in the court and upon which submissions had not then been sought. It bears repeating that the test for contempt is high one; the conduct must be wilful or signal deliberate disrespect for the court. See *Cameron v Orr* 1995 S.L.T. 589; 1995 S.C.C.R. 365 followed in *Strathern v Harvie* [2015] HCJAC 107; 2016 S.C.C.R. 22. A solicitor can be held in contempt, in the course of proceedings applying the same test, should he refuse to comply with the clear ruling of the court (*Blair-Wilson, Petr*, 1997 S.L.T. 621). It is competent to found upon factors preceding the immediate misconduct complained of in reaching a finding of contempt; see *Hainey v HM Advocate* [2012] HCJAC 144 in which the Appeal Court upheld a finding based upon the appellant's failure to obtemper citation without satisfactory explanation, and as well as her subsequent demeanour in the witness box. While that view was reached with some hesitation, the court did observe that it was not in the advantageous position of the trial judge witnessing the conduct, and a mitigatory factor was identified in the heated exchanges between counsel and the appellant. Note that a wilful failure to appear on the part of a witness is a contempt of court. The nature of that act means that, unlike prevarication, it is not capable of purgation; see *Lyons v Fraser* [2016] HCJAC 92; 2016 S.C.C.R. 584.

The court must indicate that consideration is being given to making a finding of contempt and afford the party an opportunity to explain the circumstances and submit why such a finding should not be made (*Johnston v Normand* above, *Harkness v Westwater*, 1997 G.W.D. 15-650 and *Dickson v Reith*, 1997 G.W.D. 23-1139). The broad lesson from all these cases is that the court has to proceed with cool deliberation, specify the nature of the misconduct, give the offending party ample opportunity to explain himself and, possibly, purge any contempt, rather than leaping too swiftly to an untenable conclusion which will not be supported. Even before embarking upon such a procedure the judge ought first to ascertain whether the Crown is intending to raise its own proceedings in response to the alleged willful misconduct. If the Crown proposes to instruct its own enquiries then the court should not proceed with its own investigation. See *Scott v Procurator Fiscal, Falkirk* [2014] HCJAC 134.

In minuting the act which constituted the contempt, care must be taken to specify in detail the nature of the misconduct; see *Strang v Annan*, 1991 S.L.T. 676; *Sze v Wilson*, 1992 S.L.T. 569; 1992 S.C.C.R. 54. In *Riaviz v Howdle*, 1996 S.L.T. 747 the Appeal Court proceeded to deal with a bill of suspension (following a finding of prevarication) despite the absence of minutes recording the witness' misconduct; the court founded upon the contents of the sheriff's report and applied a purposive, rather than literal, reading of this section. Since s.155(1) refers to punishment "forthwith", there is no necessity to obtain social enquiry reports and the punishment imposed is not a "any disposal" (see *Forrest v Wilson*, 1994 S.L.T. 490; 1993 S.C.C.R. 631 and the statutory definition of "any disposal" at s.307(1)). Although subs.(4) refers back to the provisions of subs.(1), it would appear that the same comments would apply. As subs.(1) states the maximum penalty following a finding of contempt or prevarication is a sentence of 21 days' imprisonment; see *Logan v McGlennan*, 1999 J.C. 285.

It follows that the range of options available for summary disposal under s.155 is limited to those set out in subs.(1); it is not competent to consider the range of sentencing options generally available in Part XI of the Act when a court is imposing a sentence; see *Robertson and Gough v HM Advocate* [2007] HCJAC 63; 2008 S.C.C.R. 20 followed in *Meade v Corrins* [2020] SAC (Crim) 4. Note that where contempt proceedings are initiated by the Crown (as distinct from the court as s.155 provides) these proceed in terms of the Contempt of Court Act 1981 (c.49).

It is appropriate when sentencing individuals guilty of prevarication to consider both punishment and deterrence as elements of sentence. See *Cowan v HM Advocate*, 2009 S.L.T. 434.

The factors justifying precognition on oath are set out in *Carmichael, Complainer*, 1992 S.C.C.R. 553, where a Bill of Advocation followed refusal of an application to precognosce on oath. Precognition on oath applications by the defence proceed by way of s.291 below.

European Convention on Human Rights

In *Mair (Bryan), Petitioner*, 2002 S.L.T. (Sh.Ct) 2 it was submitted that this section's provisions contravened art.6 of the European Convention since the presiding judge was simultaneously accuser, prosecutor and judge, roles incompatible with Convention rights. The court acknowledged the apparent contradictions inherent in s.155 but recognised that the competing public interest in preserving the authority of the court had to prevail. In any event even had it been decided that the section was incompatible with art.6 this could have been justified in terms of s.6(2)(b) of the Human Rights Act 1998 (c.42). See too *Little (Cheryl)*, 2002 S.L.T. (Sh. Ct) 12. In summary it is submitted that provided the well-established procedures set out in case law are adhered to, then the requirements of art.6 will be satisfied.

Memorandum by the Lord Justice-General on Contempt of Court

Attention is drawn to the memorandum, dated 1 April 2003 which provides general directions in relation to potential contempts by individuals and by news media. See para.C1-26 in Division C, Practice Notes, below and also in Renton and Brown's Criminal Procedure, 6th Edition, at App.C.

High Court Practice Note No.1 of 2015

This Practice Note, "Reporting Restrictions", superseded Practice Note No.1 of 2007 with effect from 1 April 2015. Procedures for the imposition and review of reporting restrictions upon proceedings are now found in SSI 2015/84 discussed below.

Act of Adjournal (Criminal Procedure Rules Amendment) (Reporting Restrictions) 2015 (SSI 2015/84)

The court has a power to restrict the reporting of proceedings on cause shown. This proceeds by way of an interim order initially which falls to be intimated to "interested persons" as defined in the Act of Adjournal. Interested persons may apply to be heard and applications for revocation or variation of the order proceed by means of Form 56.3.

Note that the mandatory provision in s.47 of the Act on reporting of proceedings in which a child is an accused or witness remains in force.

Apprehension of witness

A4-336 **156.—**(1) In any summary proceedings, the court may, on the application of any of the parties, issue a warrant for the apprehension of a witness if subsection (2) or (3) below applies in relation to the witness.

(2) This subsection applies if the witness, having been duly cited to any diet in the proceedings, deliberately and obstructively fails to appear at the diet.

(3) This subsection applies if the court is satisfied by evidence on oath that the witness is being deliberately obstructive and is not likely to attend to give evidence at any diet in the proceedings without being compelled to do so.

(4) For the purposes of subsection (2) above, a witness who, having been duly cited to any diet, fails to appear at the diet is to be presumed, in the absence of any evidence to the contrary, to have so failed deliberately and obstructively.

(5) An application under subsection (1) above—

(a) may be made orally or in writing;

(b) if made in writing—

(i) shall be in such form as may be prescribed by Act of Adjournal, or as nearly as may be in such form; and
(ii) may be disposed of in court or in chambers after such enquiry or hearing (if any) as the court considers appropriate.

(6) A warrant issued under this section shall be in such form as may be prescribed by Act of Adjournal or as nearly as may be in such form.

(7) A warrant issued under this section in the form mentioned in subsection (6) above shall imply warrant to officers of law—
(a) to search for and apprehend the witness in respect of whom it is issued;
(b) to bring the witness before the court;
(c) in the meantime, to detain the witness in a police station, police cell or other convenient place; and
(d) so far as necessary for the execution of the warrant, to break open shut and lockfast places.

(8) It shall not be competent in summary proceedings for a court to issue a warrant for the apprehension of a witness otherwise than in accordance with this section.

(9) Section 135(3) of this Act makes provision as to bringing before the court a person apprehended under a warrant issued under this section.

(10) In this section and section 156A, "the court" means the court in which the witness is to give evidence.

AMENDMENTS

Section 156 substituted, together with ss.156A-156D, for original s.156 by Criminal Proceedings etc (Reform) (Scotland) Act 2007 (asp 6) s.16. Brought into force on 10 March 2008 by SSI 2008/42 (C.4) art.3 and Sch.

DEFINITIONS
"diet": s.307(1). A4-336.1
"witness": s.307(1).
"warrant": s.307(1).

GENERAL NOTE

Powers matching those dealing with obstructive witnesses in solemn procedure (s.90A of the 1995 Act) are now introduced into all summary criminal procedures. A warrant for the apprehension of a witness duly cited to a diet subject, presumably, to it being established first that the witness is a competent individual. As with s.90A the court has to be satisfied by evidence on oath that the witness has been properly cited to attend at a diet, that there has been a failure to appear at that properly constituted diet of the court and that such failure has been both deliberate and obstructive as the section presumes. Warrant applications, written or oral, can be heard in open court within the presence of the accused or, as is more commonplace, in chambers outwith his presence. The powers granted to the police in terms of a witness apprehension warrant are broadly similar to those contained in initiating warrants granted against accused persons. A4-336.2

It will be noted that it is open to any party to the proceedings to seek a witness apprehension warrant.

Orders in respect of witnesses apprehended under section 156

156A.—(1) Where a witness is brought before the court in pursuance of a warrant issued under section 156 of this Act, the court shall, after giving the parties and the witness an opportunity to be heard, make an order— A4-336.3
(a) detaining the witness until the conclusion of the diet at which the witness is to give evidence;
(b) releasing the witness on bail; or
(c) liberating the witness.

(2) The court may make an order under subsection (1)(a) or (b) above only if it is satisfied that—
(a) the order is necessary with a view to securing that the witness appears at the diet at which the witness is to give evidence; and
(b) it is appropriate in all the circumstances to make the order.

(3) Whenever the court makes an order under subsection (1) above, it shall state the reasons for the terms of the order.

(4) Subsection (1) above is without prejudice to any power of the court to—

(a) make a finding of contempt of court in respect of any failure of a witness to appear at a diet to which he has been duly cited; and

(b) dispose of the case accordingly.

(5) Where—

(a) an order under subsection (1)(a) above has been made in respect of a witness; and

(b) at, but before the conclusion of, the diet at which the witness is to give evidence, the court in which the diet is being held excuses the witness,

that court, on excusing the witness, may recall the order under subsection (1)(a) above and liberate the witness.

(6) On making an order under subsection (1)(b) above in respect of a witness, the court shall impose such conditions as it considers necessary with a view to securing that the witness appears at the diet at which he is to give evidence.

(7) However, the court may not impose as such a condition a requirement that the witness or a cautioner on his behalf deposit a sum of money in court.

(8) Section 25 of this Act shall apply in relation to an order under subsection (1)(b) above as it applies to an order granting bail, but with the following modifications—

(a) references to the accused shall be read as if they were references to the witness in respect of whom the order under subsection (1)(b) above is made;

(b) references to the order granting bail shall be read as if they were references to the order under subsection (1)(b) above;

(c) subsection (3) shall be read as if for the words from "relating" to "offence" in the third place where it occurs there were substituted "at which the witness is to give evidence".

AMENDMENTS

Section 156A substituted, together with ss.156, 156B–156D, for original s.156 by Criminal Proceedings etc (Reform) (Scotland) Act 2007 (asp 6) s.16. Brought into force on March 10, 2008 by SSI 2008/42 (C.4) art.3 and Sch.

GENERAL NOTE

A4-336.4 Section 156A now introduced for summary proceedings in the 1995 Act draws heavily upon the provisions governing solemn proceedings which came from the Criminal Procedure (Amendment) (Scotland) Act 2004 (asp 5); each provides mechanisms for dealing with errant witnesses brought before the court after arrest on warrant. Such a witness can be detained until the conclusion of the trial diet and not simply until he has given his evidence, or released on bail (but following subs.(7) below not money bail or caution), or liberated to appear at the trial diet.

Subsection (2), in effect, creates a presumption that the witness should ordinarily be admonished to appear at the future proceedings unless the court is satisfied and states that more stern measures—bail conditions or a custodial remand—are needed to ensure the witness' appearance at the diet of trial. The bail order granted by the court not only requires the witness to appear at the future diet but obliges him, as s.25 of the 1995 Act states, to apply to the court if he wishes to alter his domicile. Curiously, while subs. (4), for ease of reference, endeavours to place the status of accused and witness on an equal footing by substitution of "witness" for "accused" in the bail provisions of the 1995 Act, the powers of arrest without warrant set out in s.28 of that Act in relation to accused do not seem to extend to witnesses admitted to bail. It may be of course that a common law crime might be libelled against a witness in such circumstances and thus justify arrest of a witness. Section 156B below also introduces offences and penalties for breach of witness bail orders.

The court retains its power to make a finding of contempt against a witness who has failed to appear in defiance of a lawful citation. or otherwise has misconducted himself during the summary proceedings: see generally s.155 of the Criminal Procedure (Scotland) Act 1995.

Breach of bail under section 156A(1)(b)

156B.—(1) A witness who, having been released on bail by virtue of an order under subsection (1)(b) of section 156A of this Act, fails without reasonable excuse— A4-336.5

(a) to appear at any diet to which he has been cited; or

(b) to comply with any condition imposed under subsection (6) of that section, shall be guilty of an offence and liable on summary conviction to the penalties specified in subsection (2) below.

(2) Those penalties are—

(a) a fine not exceeding level 3 on the standard scale; and

(b) imprisonment for a period—

(i) where conviction is in the JP court, not exceeding 60 days;

(ii) where conviction is in the sheriff court, not exceeding 12 months.

(3) In any proceedings in relation to an offence under subsection (1) above, the fact that (as the case may be) a person—

(a) was on bail;

(b) was subject to any particular condition of bail;

(c) failed to appear at a diet;

(d) was cited to a diet,

shall, unless challenged by preliminary objection before his plea is recorded, be held as admitted.

(4) Section 28 of this Act shall apply in respect of a witness who has been released on bail by virtue of an order under section 156A(1)(b) of this Act as it applies to an accused released on bail, but with the following modifications

(a) references to an accused shall be read as if they were references to the witness;

(b) in subsection (2), the reference to the court to which the accused's application for bail was first made shall be read as if it were a reference to the court which made the order under section 156A(1)(b) of this Act in respect of the witness;

(c) in subsection (4)—

(i) references to the order granting bail and original order granting bail shall be read as if they were references to the order under section 156A(1)(b) of this Act and the original such order respectively;

(ii) paragraph (a) shall be read as if at the end there were inserted "and make an order under section 156A(1)(a) or (c) of this Act in respect of the witness";

(iii) paragraph (c) shall be read as if for the words from "complies" to the end there were substituted "appears at the diet at which the witness is to give evidence".

AMENDMENTS

Section 156B substituted, together with ss.156, 156A, 156C–156D, for original s.156 by Criminal Proceedings etc (Reform) (Scotland) Act 2007 (asp 6) s.16. Brought into force on March 10, 2008 by SSI 2008/42 (C.4) art.3 and Sch.

GENERAL NOTE

Once the court has made a witness bail order, and the witness subsequently fails to comply with any of the bail conditions, he is liable to prosecution and to the penalties on conviction set out in s.156B. Again a special capacity is created and there are broad presumptions holding that the accused was on bail, the tems of such bail, that he had been cited to appear at the appointed diet and failed to do so. Each of these presumptions prevails unless challenged by way of preliminary objection. A4-336.6

Review of orders under section 156A(1)(a) or (b)

A4-336.7 **156C.**—(1) Where a court has made an order under subsection (1)(a) of section 156A of this Act, the court may, on the application of the witness in respect of whom the order was made and after giving the parties and the witness an opportunity to be heard—

(a) recall the order; and

(b) make an order under subsection (1)(b) or (c) of that section in respect of the witness.

(2) Where a court has made an order under subsection (1)(b) of section 156A of this Act, the court may, after giving the parties and the witness an opportunity to be hear—

(a) on the application of the witness in respect of whom the order was made—

(i) review the conditions imposed under subsection (6) of that section at the time the order was made; and

(ii) make a new order under subsection (1)(b) of that section and impose different conditions under subsection (6) of that section;

(b) on the application of the party who made the application under section 156(1) of this Act in respect of the witness, review the order and the conditions imposed under subsection (6) of section 156A of this Act at the time the order was made, and—

(i) recall the order and make an order under subsection (1)(a) of that section in respect of the witness; or

(ii) make a new order under subsection (1)(b) of that section and impose different conditions under subsection (6) of that section.

(3) The court may not review an order by virtue of subsection (1) or (2) above unless—

(a) in the case of an application by the witness, the circumstances of the witness have changed materially; or

(b) in that or any other case, the witness or party making the application puts before the court material information which was not available to it when it made the order which is the subject of the application.

(4) An application under this section by a witness—

(a) where it relates to the first order made under section 156A(1)(a) or (b) of this Act in respect of the witness, shall not be made before the fifth day after that order is made;

(b) where it relates to any subsequent such order, shall not be made before the fifteenth day after the order is made.

(5) On receipt of an application under subsection (2)(b) above the court shall—

(a) intimate the application to the witness in respect of whom the order which is the subject of the application was made;

(b) fix a diet for hearing the application and cite the witness to attend the diet; and

(c) where it considers that the interests of justice so require, grant warrant to arrest the witness.

(6) Nothing in this section shall affect any right of a person to appeal against an order under section 156A(1).

AMENDMENTS

Section 156C substituted, together with ss.156, 156A, 156B, 156D, for original s.156 by Criminal Proceedings etc (Reform) (Scotland) Act 2007 (asp 6) s.16. Brought into force on March 10, 2008 by SSI 2008/42 (C.4) art.3 and Sch.

General Note

This section provides a review procedure for any witness either remanded in custody pending the trial diet (subs.(1)) or whose attendance has been enforced by imposition of a bail order and bail conditions (subs.(2)). Note that subs.(2)(b) enables the party (usually the Crown) who sought the witness' initial apprehension to apply to the court for review; such a variation could be aimed at altering the terms of a bail order or to have the bail order rescinded and the witness remanded in custody. The court can then be craved to grant a fresh witness arrest warrant to enable that person to be brought before court for review of a subs.(2)(b) application—see generally subs.(5) below. A4-336.8

Each procedure is by means of an application to the originating court, following which a hearing must be fixed to afford other parties (quaere including co-accused) the opportunity to be heard. In the case of a witness remanded in custody, the court may exercise a discretion to recall the remand and can then either admit him to bail or liberate him. In the case of a witness allowed bail, the court has an option to vary the bail conditions but cannot simply liberate. In all cases the test which any application for review must meet is a familiar one and is found in subs.(3). Since the rationale of a witness apprehension warrant is to compel attendance at any relevant hearing, it might be thought that a change in a witness' circumstances since the court made its order would be of little persuasive weight; far more reliance is likely to be placed upon the discovery of factors not known at the time when the order was made.

The time scales for review are set out in subs.(4), while subs.(6) enables a witness to appeal against the terms of any court order, remanding him or placing him upon bail conditions as a means of ensuring future attendance. See generally s.156D below.

[THE NEXT PARAGRAPH IS A4-337]

Appeals in respect of orders under section 156A(1)

156D.—(1) Any of the parties specified in subsection (2) below may appeal to the Sheriff Appeal Court against— A4-337

(a) any order made under subsection (1)(a) or (c) of section 156A of this Act;
(b) where an order is made under subsection (1)(b) of that section—
  (i) the order;
  (ii) any of the conditions imposed under subsection (6) of that section on the making of the order; or
  (iii) both the order and any such conditions.

(2) The parties referred to in subsection (1) above are—
(a) the witness in respect of whom the order which is the subject of the appeal was made;
(b) the prosecutor; and
(c) the accused.

(3) A party making an appeal under subsection (1) above shall intimate it to the other parties specified in subsection (2) above; and, for that purpose, intimation to the Crown Agent shall be sufficient intimation to the prosecutor.

(4) An appeal under this section shall be disposed of by the Sheriff Appeal Court or any Appeal Sheriff in court or in chambers after such enquiry and hearing of the parties as shall seem just.

(5) Where the witness in respect of whom the order which is the subject of an appeal under this section was made is under 21 years of age, section 51 of this Act shall apply to the Sheriff Appeal Court or, as the case may be, Appeal Sheriff when disposing of the appeal as it applies to a court when remanding or committing a person of the witness's age for trial and sentence.

Amendments

Section 156D substituted, together with ss.156, 156A–156C, for original s.156 by Criminal Proceedings etc (Reform) (Scotland) Act 2007 (asp 6) s.16. Brought into force on March 10, 2008 by SSI 2008/42 (C.4) art.3 and Sch.

Subss.(1), (4) and (5) as amended by Courts Reform (Scotland) Act 2014 (Consequential Provisions No.2) Order 2015 (SSI 2015/338) Sch.2 para.5 (effective September 22, 2015).

General Note

This section entitles a witness, any accused or the prosecutor to appeal the terms of any order made by the court under s.156A(1) including any particular bail conditions imposed. Appeal is to a single High A4-337.1

Court judge in chambers and any appeal has to be intimated to other parties. In the case of a witness aged under 21 years at the time of the order being made, the provisions of s.51 of the 1995 Act (which enable the court to remand children and certain young persons into the care of a local authority) are to be followed by the appellate judge.

Record of proceedings

A4-338 **157.**—(1) Proceedings in a summary prosecution shall be conducted summarily *viva voce* and, except where otherwise provided and subject to subsection (2) below, no record need be kept of the proceedings other than the complaint, or a copy of the complaint certified as a true copy by the procurator fiscal, the plea, a note of any documentary evidence produced, and the conviction and sentence or other finding of the court.

(2) Any objection taken to the competency or relevancy of the complaint or proceedings, or to the competency or (subject to subsection (3) below) admissibility of evidence, shall, if either party desires it, be entered in the record of the proceedings.

(3) An application for the purposes of subsection (1) of section 275 of this Act, together with the court's decision on it, the reasons stated therefor and any conditions imposed and directions issued under subsection (7) of that section shall be entered in the record of the proceedings.

Amendments

Subs.(2) as amended by Sexual Offences (Procedure and Evidence) (Scotland) Act 2002 (asp 9) s.8(6)(a).

Subs.(3) inserted by Sexual Offences (Procedure and Evidence) (Scotland) Act 2002 (asp 9) s.8(6)(b). Brought into force by SSI 2002/443 (C.24) art.4 (effective 1 November 2002).

Definitions

A4-338.1 "complaint": s.307(1).
"procurator fiscal": s.307(1).

General Note

s.157(1)

A4-339 *"except where otherwise provided, no record need be kept of [summary] proceedings other than"* In *Barr v Ingram*, 1977 S.L.T. 173 an appeal was taken after summary trial on the ground that the proceedings prior to conviction were irregular and vitiated by fundamental nullity. The accused had attended for trial at the time and date appointed by the court. After the calling of the case, it was adjourned three times in the course of the day and these adjournments were not minuted.

The accused argued on appeal that such adjournments must be minuted otherwise the proceedings fell. It was held that adjournments within the date of citation (as opposed to adjournments to a later date) did not require to be minuted. The appeal was refused.

It is a procedural irregularity if the court minutes are not signed off on the date of proceedings by the clerk, but this may be capable of correction under s.300A of the Act. See the discussion to s.300A below.

In *Higson v Clark*, 2003 S.L.T. 253; 2004 S.C.C.R. 161 the respondent was charged on summary complaint and pleaded not guilty. A trial diet and an intermediate diet were fixed, but the minutes made no reference to the intermediate diet, and the case did not appear on the court roll for the date of the intermediate diet. The case did not call on the date of the intermediate diet.

When the case called at the trial diet the sheriff amended the minutes to include the fixing of the intermediate diet, and then dismissed the complaint as incompetent in the light of the failure of the Crown to call the case at the intermediate diet. The Crown appealed to the High Court, and submitted that the purported amendment came too late. Parties accepted that an intermediate diet was a peremptory diet.

It was held, applying *Barr v Ingram*, supra, that on the hypothesis that an intermediate diet was peremptory there was no reason not to apply to it the same stringency as applied to adjourned diets, including the formal requirement that it be constituted in writing, and that there had been no effectual fixing of the intermediate diet and the sheriff had erred in upholding the plea to the competency. The appeal was allowed and the case remitted to the sheriff to proceeds as accords.

"or a copy of the complaint certified as a true copy by the Procurator Fiscal" These words were inserted into s.359 of the 1995 Act by the Criminal Justice (Scotland) Act 2003 Sch.6 para.128. The current s.157 is derived from s.359. The loss of the principal or court copy of a summary complaint would have previously vitiated proceedings may now be cured. Although no similar statutory provision exists for the loss of an indictment there have been authorities on the problem: see the note "Loss of indictment" at A4-150 above.

Interruption of summary proceedings for verdict in earlier trial

158. Where the sheriff is sitting in summary proceedings during the period in which the jury in a criminal trial in which he has presided are retired to consider their verdict, it shall be lawful, if he considers it appropriate to do so, to interrupt those proceedings— A4-340

(a) in order to receive the verdict of the jury and dispose of the cause to which it relates;

(b) to give a direction to the jury on any matter on which they may wish one from him, or to hear a request from them regarding any matter,

and the interruption shall not affect the validity of the proceedings nor cause the instance to fall in respect of any person accused in the proceedings.

DEFINITION

"sheriff" : s.307(1). A4-340.1

GENERAL NOTE

This section was introduced by the Prisoners and Criminal Proceedings (Scotland) Act 1993 (c.9) s.40.It provides for more efficient use of court time by enabling the sheriff to deal with summary business while a jury charged by him earlier is considering its verdict. Chapter 18 of the 1996 Act of Adjournal makes provision for the interruption of summary proceedings on conviction of the accused, to enable the court to consider conviction or sentence in other cases proceeding before the court (see r.18.5). A4-341

Section 102 of this Act enacts equivalent provisions relative to the interruption of sheriff and jury trials.

Amendment of complaint

159.—(1) It shall be competent at any time prior to the determination of the case, unless the court see just cause to the contrary, to amend the complaint or any notice of previous conviction relative thereto by deletion, alteration or addition, so as to— A4-342

(a) cure any error or defect in it;

(b) meet any objection to it; or

(c) cure any discrepancy or variance between the complaint or notice and the evidence.

(2) Nothing in this section shall authorise an amendment which changes the character of the offence charged, and, if it appears to the court that the accused may in any way be prejudiced in his defence on the merits of the case by any amendment made under this section, the court shall grant such remedy to the accused by adjournment or otherwise as appears to the court to be just.

(3) An amendment made under this section shall be sufficiently authenticated by the initials of the clerk of the court.

DEFINITIONS

"complaint": s.138 and Sch.5. A4-342.1

"offence": s.307(1).

"previous conviction": s.307(5).

GENERAL NOTE

The Act permits wide powers of amendment to a summary complaint but subject to the proviso that the amendment proposed must not alter the character of the offence charged, and cannot be used to validate a complaint which is radically defective in its essentials (*Stevenson v McLevy* (1879) 4 Couper 196; *Lowe v Bee*, 1989 S.C.C.R. 476). Note that no one can be competently convicted upon a complaint which is a fundamental nullity and, accordingly, there has been no tholed assize (*Thomson, Petr*, 1997 S.L.T.322). A4-343

The court cannot amend the complaint *ex proprio motu* in the absence of such a motion from the prosecutor (*Grant v Lockhart*, Crown Office Circular A3/91). The refusal or grant of a proposed amendment rests in the discretion of the trial judge and will not readily be interfered with by the Appeal Court (*Cumming v Frame* (1909) 6 Adam 57). Such a motion can be made at any point in the case prior to the determination of proceedings (see *Cochrane v The West Calder Cooperative Society*, 1978 S.L.T. (Notes) 22 and *Matheson v Ross* (1885) 5 Couper 582, where the date libelled was found to be incorrect after the close of the Crown case, the accused not being prejudiced and declining an adjournment). The point in the proceedings at which amendment is moved can itself be significant; in *MacArthur v MacNeill*, 1986 S.C.C.R. 552; 1987 S.L.T. 299 the Crown sought to amend a road traffic complaint, substituting failure to supply a blood specimen in a libel which originally averred failure to provide breath specimens at the close of evidence, a manoeuvre which the Appeal Court held to have changed the character of the offence (compare with *Fenwick v Valentine*, 1994 S.L.T. 485; 1993 S.C.C.R. 892).

See also *Phillips v Houston*, 2003 S.C.C.R. 653 where a Crown motion to amend the libel to add previously unspecified sexual misconduct at the close of the Crown evidence was rejected on appeal. The Appeal Court observed that amendment might properly have been allowed if it had been moved when the evidence first came out and objection to it had been taken.

Amendment of the Preamble and Instance

A4-344 Adding a heading to the complaint to read "Under the Summary Jurisdiction (Scotland) Acts 1864 and 1881, and the Criminal Procedure (Scotland) Act 1887" by amendment, was allowed in *Finlayson v Bunbury* (1898) 2 Adam 478; correction of the heading on a complaint which referred to a District Court jurisdiction when the accused had been cited to, and the case called in, the relevant sheriff court was upheld on appeal (*Doonin Plant v Lees*, 1994 S.L.T. 313; 1993 S.C.C.R. 511).

Altering the name of the accused even after the statutory time bar has expired was allowed in *Hoyers (UK) v Houston*, 1991 S.L.T. 934; 1991 S.C.C.R. 919 and see also *Ralston v Carmichael*, 1995 G.W.D. 38-1933 discussed in Notes to s.143 above. More curiously in *Montgomery Transport v Walkingshaw*, 1992 S.C.C.R. 17 the complainers brought a Bill of Suspension following a guilty plea to a complaint which, it was later discovered, had libelled the wrong section of the statute albeit the narrative accurately set out the offence: they argued the complaint to be a nullity, but the High Court treated it as merely irrelevant and capable of amendment noting that the complainers had not taken objection before the sheriff.

However in *Lockhart v British School of Motoring*, 1982 S.C.C.R. 188, amendment to the libel was refused on the grounds that, if allowed, it would deprive co-accused of a statutory defence. Amendment to change the identity of the accused was refused in *Valentine v Thistle Leisure*, 1983 S.C.C.R. 515; by contrast, amendment of a nature which altered the capacity of the accused was allowed on appeal in *Tudhope v Chung*, 1985 S.C.C.R. 139.

Amendment of Offence Dates

A4-345 See *Matheson v Ross* cited above. In *Duffy v Ingram* (also cited above), where the offence date was omitted in the first charge and adopted in the second charge and detailed as "said 30 November 1985" in the last charge on the complaint, an objection to relevancy was repelled by the sheriff who allowed amendments to cure the defects in the libel. In *McFadyen v Kerr*, 2002 G.W.D. 9-281, following dismissal of a complaint as a nullity which did not contain the year in an offence date, a Crown Bill of Advocation succeeded. In fact the complaint contained a bail aggravation dated 5 October 2000 and the trial occurred on 20 November of that year; on that basis *Duffy v Ingram* was binding, and the bill was passed and case remitted to the sheriff to proceed.

Amendment of Locus

A4-346 It is generally competent to amend the locus stated in a summary charge so as to bring the libel into accord with the evidence, and amendment should be permitted unless it alters the nature of the charge. Amendment is permissible even if it involves including a locus outwith the court's jurisdiction (see *Craig v Keane*, 1982 S.L.T. 198; 1981 S.C.C.R. 166 and, more generally, *Belcher v MacKinnon*, 1987 S.L.T. 298).

In *Herron v Gemmell*, 1975 S.L.T. (Notes) 93 the sheriff refused an amendment to add "Glasgow" to the specification "on the road on the Glasgow Inner Ring Road, at a part thereof near Charing Cross underpass" a decision which was overturned on appeal. This approach was followed in *Strawbridge v Murphy* [2014] HCJAC 32, which has a broader discussion on specification of the locus.

A more radical amendment in *Brown v McLeod*, 1986 S.C.C.R. 615 had the effect of extending the locus to include driving between two towns. In response, the sheriff offered the defence the opportunity of an adjournment to lead additional evidence in light of the amendment but this was declined. His decision was upheld on appeal. Similarly in *Tudhope v Fulton*, 1986 S.C.C.R. 567 amendment of the *locus delicti*, where the offence was failure to provide breath specimens at an incorrectly specified police office, was allowed on appeal; this follows reasoning similar to that employed in *Belcher v MacKinnon* cited above.

Where the *locus* is inspecific, as above, the acid test is whether the details specified in the libel are sufficient to enable the court to determine that it has jurisdiction; see *Yarrow Shipbuilders v Normand* 1995 S.L.T. 1215; 1995 S.C.C.R. 224, *Caven v Cumming* 1998 S.L.T. 768 and *MK v Procurator Fiscal, Kilmarnock* [2021] SAC (Crim) 3, discussed in detail at s.144 above.

Amendment and Statutory Offences

A4-347 Amendment may be used to alter an incorrectly specified contravention of statute or regulations, but must not change the nature of the offence libelled. In *MacKenzie v Brougham*, 1985 S.L.T. 276; 1984 S.C.C.R. 434, the charge narrated the statute and regulations contravened but omitted reference to the precise regulation which created a criminal offence and was poorly specified; it was held that the complaint was not a nullity and could be cured by amendment. Amendment of a complaint to reflect the terms of the current statutory legislation is competent even where this renders an accused liable, on conviction, to an increased penalty (*Wadbister Offshore Ltd v Adam*, 1998 S.L.T. 1230 following *Cook v Jessop* cited below). The broad test to be applied is whether the charge as specified affords the defence fair notice of what the Crown was seeking to prove; see *Blair v Keane*, 1981 S.L.T. (Notes) 4; *Clydesdale Group v Normand*, 1994 S.L.T. 1302; 1993 S.C.C.R. 958; *Gullett v Hamilton*, 1997 G.W.D. 14-592.

In *Sterling-Winthrop Group v Allan*, 1987 S.C.C.R. 25, a prosecution under the Health and Safety at Work etc. Act 1974 (c.37), objections to the relevancy of charges were repelled by the sheriff. Before the Appeal Court the Crown sought, and were permitted, to amend the charges to meet the objections previously stated. Even where a repealed statute has been libelled, amendment of the charge to make reference to the correct statutory provision is permissible, despite the greater penalties which can be imposed. See *Cook v Jessop*, 1990 J.C. 286, where a charge of harbouring an escaper from an approved school was made, contrary to the Children and Young Persons (Scotland) Act 1937, a statute which had been repealed and replaced by the Social Work (Scotland) Act 1968: it will be noted, however, that the libel gave clear warning of the character of the offence and there could be little cause to argue prejudice or lack of specification of the *species facti* (see also *High-Clad Roofing v Carmichael*, "The Scotsman" Law Reports, February 24, 1989, where the wrong regulation under the Factories Act 1961 (c.34) had been libelled).

Schedule 3 of the Act contains the provisions relating to latitudes in time and place and alternative verdicts which previously appeared in s.312 of the 1975 Act. Particularly, the terms of paras 11 to 14 are of significance in relation to the libelling of statutory offences.

The Nomen Juris

It is well accepted that the charge in an indictment need not specify the *nomen juris* of the alleged crime, it being sufficient that the facts described in the libel are relevant and set forth a crime known to the law of Scotland (*Cameron v HM Advocate*, 1971 S.L.T. 333 (piracy)). By the same token, since it is the *species facti* which indicate the nature of the crime complained of, and not the *nomen juris* attached (*Lippe v Wilson*, 1997 G.W.D. 17-766), it follows that amendment of the *nomen juris* is competent (see *Dyce v Aitchison*, 1985 S.L.T. 512 (contempt of court libelled)). **A4-348**

Authentication of amendments

In *PF, Airdrie v Carmichael* [2015] HCJAC 81 the Appeal Court noted the absence of authenticated amendments to complaint charges. Neither the complaint nor the terms of the sheriff's report clarified the precise terms of the conviction under appeal and nor did the court minutes. The conviction was ultimately quashed for this and other reasons. **A4-348.1**

[THE NEXT PARAGRAPH IS A4-349]

No case to answer

160.—(1) Immediately after the close of the evidence for the prosecution, the accused may intimate to the court his desire to make a submission that he has no case to answer both— **A4-349**

(a) on an offence charged in the complaint; and

(b) on any other offence of which he could be convicted under the complaint were the offence charged the only offence so charged.

(2) If, after hearing both parties, the judge is satisfied that the evidence led by the prosecution is insufficient in law to justify the accused being convicted of the offence charged in respect of which the submission has been made or of such other offence as is mentioned, in relation to that offence, in paragraph (b) of subsection (1) above, he shall acquit him of the offence charged in respect of which the submission has been made and the trial shall proceed only in respect of any other offence charged in the complaint.

(3) If, after hearing both parties, the judge is not satisfied as is mentioned in subsection (2) above, he shall reject the submission and the trial shall proceed, with the accused entitled to give evidence and call witnesses, as if such submission had not been made.

DEFINITIONS

"complaint": s.307(1). **A4-349.1**

"judge": s.307(1).

"offence": s.307(1).

[THE NEXT PARAGRAPH IS A4-350]

GENERAL NOTE

A4-350 A fuller discussion of this provision is found at s.97 above and a helpful summation of the approach to adopt in relation to circumstantial evidence is found in *MacPherson v HM Advocate* [2019] HCJAC 21; 2019 S.C.C.R. 129. The sufficiency in law of evidence presented by the prosecution falls to be considered at the close of the Crown case. The assessment of evidence by the judge at this stage in proceedings is not a qualitative one. The sole issue is whether there is a sufficiency of evidence for the charge; see, for example, *HM Advocate v Mason* [2015] HCJAC 1; 2015 S.C.L. 277 (following *HM Advocate v Fox*, 1998 S.L.T. 335; 1998 S.C.C.R. 115 at 138F). The criteria for acceptance or rejection of a no case to answer submission were set out in *Williamson v Wither*, 1981 S.C.C.R. 214, but the court must also assess the admissibility at that stage of evidence led in support of the prosecution case (see *Jessop v Kerr*, 1989 S.C.C.R. 417) and make known the result of this assessment. See also *Gonshaw v Bamber*, 2004 S.L.T. 1270 where the Appeal Court held that the sheriff had erred in rejecting a submission of no case to answer and the accused simply should not have been placed in a dilemma as to whether or not to lead evidence in his defence. In the absence of a sufficiency of evidence at that point in the proceedings a miscarriage of justice had occurred. Where, however, no submission is made when it should have been, and the accused then gives evidence, that omission cannot properly constitute a miscarriage of justice (*EM v PF, Inverness* [2015] HCJAC 8). The related issue of defective representation was not discussed.

The court must give both parties the opportunity to make submissions before reaching a decision on sufficiency, and cannot consider the issue in the absence of a motion from the accused (*Stewart v Lowe*, 1991 S.C.C.R. 317—a case in which the sheriff had rejected a submission without having heard from the prosecutor, and convicted the accused without first hearing from the defence agent; see also *Taylor v Douglas*, 1984 S.L.T. 69). Where a number of submissions are advanced, the court is obliged to determine upon them all, rather than dismissing the case upon a consideration of only one. Consideration of all submissions avoids needless duplication of appeal procedures in the event of the Crown successfully appealing the court's original decision on sufficiency (*Lockhart v Milne*, 1992 S.C.C.R. 864). In *Duffin v Normand*, 1993 S.C.C.R. 864 (followed in *Duke v Griffiths*, 2010 S.C.C.R. 44 which disapproved *Johnston v Dyer*, 2007 S.C.C.R. 494), the court having rejected a submission under the section, and there being no defence evidence, proceeded to convict without hearing further from the parties: the court is obliged to hear submissions at the close of evidence upon the quality of evidence, an issue which cannot be considered at the time of a s.160 submission. The conviction was quashed.

The form of questions to be posed in stated cases challenging decisions on submissions of no case to answer are discussed in the commentary to *Cassidy v Normand*, 1994 S.C.C.R. 325, while guidance on the form of the stated case itself is given in *Keane v Bathgate*, 1983 S.L.T. 651, since at that stage in the case the court cannot state findings-in-fact.

It will be noted that in *Tudhope v Stewart*, 1986 S.L.T. 659; 1986 S.C.C.R. 384 it was held that use of a no case to answer submission, founding upon the inadmissibility of evidence which had earlier been led without objection, was inappropriate (see also *Skeen v Murphy*, 1978 S.L.T. (Notes) 2 and *McGee v McNaughton*, 1996 G.W.D. 17-977, discussed at A4-221 above; as a general rule objections to the admissibility of evidence should be taken at the time when that evidence is tendered).

In *Walls v Heywood*, 2000 S.L.T. 841; 2000 S.C.C.R. 21 where the lay magistrate returned a guilty verdict at the s.160 stage, and had to be corrected by the assessor, it was held on appeal, following *Lorimar v Normand*, 1997 S.L.T.1277; 1997 S.C.C.R. 582 that the necessity for an intervention by the assessor might lead an impartial observer to conclude that the judge had reached a verdict prematurely.

Defence to speak last

A4-351 **161.** In any trial the accused or, where he is legally represented, his counsel or solicitor shall have the right to speak last.

GENERAL NOTE

A4-352 "There is no doubt that the panel is entitled to the last word in criminal trials": *Watson v Stuart* (1878) 4 Couper 67. See also *Duffin v Normand* discussed in the notes to s.160 above. Similarly, following conviction the defence must be offered the opportunity to plead in mitigation, before sentence is considered (*Meikle v Lees*, 1997 G.W.D. 3-88).

In *Watson v Griffiths*, 2004 G.W.D 34-694 it was held that even if there had been a breach of s.161 any such breach did not automatically lead to the proceedings being regarded as null. It was seriously doubted in the circumstances of this case whether there had been a breach and it was held that there had been no oppression

Verdict and conviction

Judges equally divided

162. In a summary prosecution in a court consisting of more than one judge, if the judges are equally divided in opinion as to the guilt of the accused, the accused shall be found not guilty of the charge or part thereof on which such division of opinion exists. A4-353

DEFINITION
"judge": s.307(1). A4-353.1

[THE NEXT PARAGRAPH IS A4-354]

GENERAL NOTE

Where two judges sit and reach different verdicts, no conviction can follow (*Dorward v Mackay* (1870) 1 Couper 392). A4-354

Conviction: miscellaneous provisions

163.—(1) Where imprisonment is authorised by the sentence of a court of summary jurisdiction, an extract of the finding and sentence in the form prescribed by Act of Adjournal shall be a sufficient warrant for the apprehension and commitment of the accused, and no such extract shall be void or liable to be set aside on account of any error or defect in point of form. A4-355

(2) In any proceedings in a court of summary jurisdiction consisting of more than one judge, the signature of one judge shall be sufficient in all warrants or other proceedings prior or subsequent to conviction, and it shall not be necessary that the judge so signing shall be one of the judges trying or dealing with the case otherwise.

DEFINITIONS
"court of summary jurisdiction": s.307(1). A4-355.1
"imprisonment": s.307(1).
"judge": s.307(1).

[THE NEXT PARAGRAPH IS A4-356]

Conviction of part of charge

164. A conviction of a part or parts only of the charge or charges libelled in a complaint shall imply dismissal of the rest of the complaint. A4-356

DEFINITIONS
"complaint": s.307(1). A4-356.1

[THE NEXT PARAGRAPH IS A4-357]

"Conviction" and "sentence" not to be used for children

165. The words "conviction" and "sentence" shall not be used in relation to children dealt with summarily and any reference in any enactment, whether passed before or after the commencement of this Act, to a person convicted, a conviction or a sentence shall in the case of a child be construed as including a reference to a person found guilty of an offence, a finding of guilt or an order made upon such a finding as the case may be. A4-357

DEFINITIONS
"child": s.307(1) and the Children (Scotland) Act 1995 s.93(2)(b). A4-357.1
"enactment": s.307(1).
"finding of guilt": s.307(8).
"sentence": s.307(1).

Previous convictions: summary proceedings

A4-358 **166.—**(1) This section shall apply where the accused in a summary prosecution has been previously convicted of any offence and the prosecutor has decided to lay a previous conviction before the court.

(2) A notice in the form prescribed by Act of Adjournal or as nearly as may be in such form specifying the previous conviction shall be served on the accused with the complaint where he is cited to a diet, and where he is in custody the complaint and such a notice shall be served on him before he is asked to plead.

(3) The previous conviction shall not, subject to section 275A(1) of this Act, be laid before the judge until he is satisfied that the charge is proved.

(4) If a plea of guilty is tendered or if, after a plea of not guilty, the accused is convicted the prosecutor shall lay the notice referred to in subsection (2) above before the judge, and—

(a) in a case where the plea of guilty is tendered in writing the accused shall be deemed to admit any previous conviction set forth in the notice, unless he expressly denies it in the writing by which the plea is tendered;

(b) in any other case the judge or the clerk of court shall ask the accused whether he admits the previous conviction,

and if such admission is made or deemed to be made it shall be entered in the record of the proceedings; and it shall not be necessary for the prosecutor to produce extracts of any previous convictions so admitted.

(5) Where the accused does not admit any previous conviction, the prosecutor unless he withdraws the conviction shall adduce evidence in proof thereof either then or at any other diet.

(6) A copy of any notice served on the accused under this section shall be entered in the record of the proceedings.

(7) Where a person is convicted of an offence, the court may have regard to any previous conviction in respect of that person in deciding on the disposal of the case.

(8) Nothing in this section shall prevent the prosecutor—

(a) asking the accused questions tending to show that the accused has been convicted of an offence other than that with which he is charged, where he is entitled to do so under section 266 of this Act; or

(b) leading evidence of previous convictions where it is competent to do so—

(i) […]

(ii) under section 270 of this Act.

(9) This section, except subsection (8) above, applies in relation to the alternative disposals mentioned in subsection (10) below as it applies in relation to previous convictions.

(10) Those alternative disposals are—

(a) a—

(i) fixed penalty under section 302(1) of this Act;

(ii) compensation offer under section 302A(1) of this Act,

that has been accepted (or deemed to have been accepted) by the accused in the two years preceding the date of an offence charged;

(b) a work order under section 303ZA(6) of this Act that has been completed in the two years preceding the date of an offence charged;

(c) a restoration notice given under subsection (4) of section 20A of the Nature Conservation (Scotland) Act 2004 (asp 6) in respect of which the accused has given notice of intention to comply under subsection (5) of that section in the two years preceding the date of an offence charged.

(11) Nothing in this section shall prevent the prosecutor, following conviction of an accused of an offence—

(a) to which a fixed penalty offer made under section 302(1) of this Act related;

(b) to which a compensation offer made under section 302A(1) of this Act related;

(c) to which a work offer made under section 303ZA(1) of this Act related; or

(d) to which a restoration notice given under section 20A(4) of the Nature Conservation (Scotland) Act 2004 (asp 6) related,

providing the judge with information about the making of the offer (including the terms of the offer) or, as the case may be, about the giving of the notice (including the terms of the notice).

[(12) Any reference in this section to a previous conviction includes, where relevant, a conviction by a court in any part of the United Kingdom or in any member State of the European Union.]

AMENDMENTS

Subs.(3) as amended by Sexual Offences (Procedure and Evidence) (Scotland) (Act) 2002 (asp 9) s.10(2). Brought into force by SSI 2002/443 (C.24) art.4 (effective November 1, 2002).

Subs.(8)(b) as amended by Criminal Proceedings etc. (Reform) (Scotland) Act 2007 (asp 6) s.12. Brought into force on 10 December 2007 by SSI 2007/479.

Subss.(9)–(11) inserted by Criminal Proceedings etc (Reform) (Scotland) Act 2007 (asp 6) s.53. Brought into force on 10 March 2008 by SSI 2008/42 (C.4) art.3 and Sch.

Subss.(10)(c) and (11)(d) inserted and subs.(11) as amended by Wildlife and Natural Environment (Scotland) Act 2011 (asp 6) Pt 6 s.40(3)(b). Brought into force on 29 June 2011 by SSI 2011/279 art.2.

Words in subs.(12) was inserted by the Criminal Justice (EU Exit) (Scotland) (Amendment etc.) Regulations 2020 (SSI 2020/339) reg.13(8) (effective 31 December 2020 subject to transitional and saving provision specified in reg.16 of those Regulations.

DEFINITIONS

"complaint": s.307(1). A4-358.1
"diet": s.307(1).
"judge": s.307(1).
"offence": s.307(1).
"previous conviction": s.307(1).
"prosecutor": s.307(1).

GENERAL NOTE

The general principles of placing previous convictions before the court are discussed in the notes to s.101 above. Unless adducing a previous conviction is necessary to prove the substantive charge, or the accused has either attacked the character of Crown witnesses or misrepresented his own character, no reference can be made to the accused's criminal record until he has been convicted. A4-359

Any previous convictions to be founded upon by the Crown for the purposes of sentence must accompany the citation and service copy complaint (see Rule 16.1.—(4) and Form 16.1-E in the 1996 Act of Adjournal) and have to be laid before the court by the prosecutor; see *Clark v Connell*, 1952 J.C. 119; 1952 S.L.T. 421; convictions which have not been libelled cannot be considered by the court (*Adair v Hill*, 1943 J.C. 9 and *Massily Packaging (UK) Ltd v MacDonald*, 1997 G.W.D. 3-87 discussed at A4-309 above) except where they are referred to in a social enquiry report prepared for the purpose of sentence (*Sharp v Stevenson*, 1948 S.L.T. (Notes) 79; *Sillars v Copeland*, 1966 C.L.R. 686); in such circumstances the accused should be afforded the opportunity of admitting or denying such additional convictions. The growth of European Union legislation raises previously unconsidered issues. In *Redman v Sehmel*, 1997 G.W.D. 9-370, the accused plead guilty to contravening Articles of the Sea Fishing (Enforcement of Community Control Measures) Order 1994, by failing to record his vessel's true catch and admitted a prior conviction for the same offence only weeks earlier imposed by an Irish court. While not a conviction imposed by a UK court, it is submitted that the earlier conviction was competently libelled in the circumstances; attention is drawn to the terms of s.57(5) of the Criminal Justice (Scotland) Act 2003 (asp 7) which has extended the definition of "previous conviction" to include previous convictions imposed upon an accused by courts in member states of the European Union. European convictions can competently be libelled in a schedule of previous convictions, and can be proved by certification of fingerprints as set out in s.286A of the Act in any criminal proceedings with effect from 27 June 2003.

It will be noted that subs.(4)(a) continues the presumption that any convictions not expressly disputed by the accused when tendering a letter plea are held to be admitted. Difficulty can arise where the plea contained in a letter is rejected by the prosecutor; care then has to be taken to ensure that any schedule of convictions is not retained with the complaint at any subsequent diet, though this has been held not to amount to laying of convictions before the court by the prosecutor (see *O'Neill v Tudhope*, 1984 S.L.T.

424; 1984 S.C.C.R. 276). See also *McKee v Brown*, 2000 G.W.D. 34-1302 where, after a change of plea, the accused's schedule of convictions remained with the complaint and was seen and troubled the trial judge, the conviction was quashed. It would have been preferable for the proceedings to be deserted but parties may have felt compelled to proceed with the trial because the case (which centred on Road Traffic Act offences) would otherwise be timebarred.

The use of extract convictions as evidence in support of a substantive charge, for example the Road Traffic Act 1988 (c.52) s.103 (driving while disqualified) has generated a considerable volume of case law. The cardinal rule is that so far as practicable, the extract used must disclose only the minimum necessary to prove the currency of a disqualification and nothing more (see *Mitchell v Dean*, 1979 S.L.T. (Notes) 12; *Boustead v McLeod*, 1979 S.L.T. (Notes) 48) but note also *Moffat v Robertson* 1983 S.C.C.R. 392 in which a defence appeal against conviction, founding upon the use of an extract conviction which libelled both driving without a licence and without insurance, was held *not* to be prejudicial.

The general principles applicable to the disclosure either wilfully or inadvertently by the prosecutor are discussed in the notes to s.101; see also *Kerr v Jessop*, 1991 S.C.C.R. 27, an instance of questioning too far and thus breaching the provision and *Carmichael v Monaghan*, 1987 S.L.T. 338; 1986 S.C.C.R. 598, where the sheriff's decision that there had been a breach by the unanticipated revelation that the accused had been apprehended in relation to a means warrant, was overruled. *Kerr v Jessop* was followed in *MacLean v Buchanan*, 1997 S.L.T. 91, the sheriff holding that the adducing of a reply in breach of this provision (but which had been led without objection) was the result of inexperience or lack of preparation, a careless incident which had not been pressed further.

Section 32 of the Road Traffic Offenders Act 1988 (c.53) permits a court, when considering discretionary or obligatory disqualification from driving, to refer to a DVLA printout where the accused does not produce his driving licence. *Hamilton v Ruxton*, 2001 S.L.T. 351; 2001 S.C.C.R. 1 clarifies that such a printout can be founded upon whether the accused fails to produce his licence, has already been disqualified or has never held a licence at all. Similarly in *Clampett v Stott*, 2001 S.C.C.R. 860; 2001 G.W.D. 33-1307 no breach of the section occurred where the Crown had lodged copy papers in support of an allegation that the accused had been subject of a (disputed) bail order which disclosed previous convictions. The Appeal Court ruled that the convictions had not been produced in pursuance of s.166 and, in any event, the convictions had been unknown to the sheriff until the accused directed attention to them in support of a motion for acquittal. The Crown's actions were considered to be careless, not deliberate.

Refer to s.285 in relation to proof of previous convictions by means of a certificate completed on behalf of the Chief Constable and s.286, which provides means by which the service of extract convictions upon the accused can be treated as sufficient evidence.

Post-offence convictions etc.

A4-359.1 **166A.**—(1) This section applies where an accused person is convicted of an offence ("offence O") on summary complaint.

(2) The court may, in deciding on the disposal of the case, have regard to—

(a) any conviction in respect of the accused which occurred on or after the date of offence O but before the date of conviction in respect of that offence,

(b) any of the alternative disposals in respect of the accused that are mentioned in subsection (3).

(3) Those alternative disposals are—

(a) a—

(i) fixed penalty under section 302(1) of this Act, or

(ii) compensation offer under section 302A(1) of this Act,

that has been accepted (or deemed to have been accepted) on or after the date of offence O but before the date of conviction in respect of that offence,

(b) a work order under section 303ZA(6) of this Act that has been completed on or after the date of offence O but before the date of conviction in respect of that offence.

(4) The court may have regard to any such conviction or alternative disposal only if it is—

(a) specified in a notice laid before the court by the prosecutor, and

(b) admitted by the accused or proved by the prosecutor (on evidence adduced then or at another diet).

(5) A reference in this section to a conviction which occurred on or after the date of offence O is a reference to such a conviction by a court in any part of the United Kingdom or [, where the court considers appropriate, in any] member State of the European Union.

AMENDMENTS

Section 166A inserted by Criminal Proceedings etc (Reform) (Scotland) Act 2007 (asp 6) s.12. Brought into force on 10 March 2008 by SSI 2008/42 (C.4) art.3 and Sch.

Section 166A substituted by Criminal Justice and Licensing (Scotland) Act 2010 (asp 13) s.70(2). Brought into force on 28 March 2011 (for all purposes in respect of offences committed on or after 28 March 2011) by SSI 2011/178 (C.15) art.2 Sch.1 para.1.

Words in subs.(5) were substituted by the Criminal Justice (EU Exit) (Scotland) (Amendment etc.) Regulations 2020 (SSI 2020/339) reg.13(9) (effective 31 December 2020 subject to transitional and saving provision specified in reg.16 of those Regulations.

DEFINITIONS

"conviction": s.307(1) of the Criminal Procedure (Scotland) Act 1995 as amended by s.71(1) of and Sch.4 to the Criminal Justice and Licensing (Scotland) Act 2010 (asp 13). A4-359.2
"offence": s.307(1) of the Criminal Procedure (Scotland) Act 1995.
"complaint": s.307(1) of the above Act.

GENERAL NOTE

This section applies to any summary proceedings and overhauls the existing provision; the equivalent in solemn proceedings is found in s.101A above. The sentencing court is entitled (but not obliged) to heed any conviction or disposal of an offence committed since the date of commission of an offence in the libel before the court. However, this provision only becomes operative after the Crown has served a notice (additional to any schedule of convictions initially served on the accused) or, perhaps, has amended the schedule of convictions in terms of s.101(5) above to reflect the new conviction. Note that a qualifying conviction or disposal could arise from any court within a Member State of the EU—see the fuller note at s.101A above. A4-359.3

It will be observed that the section refers both to post-offence convictions and to non-court disposals (subs.(3)) accepted, or deemed to have been accepted, by the accused. It is submitted that the court validly may still have regard to post-offence convictions disclosed in a social enquiry report or quite properly mentioned in a plea in mitigation. Still it would be sound Crown practice, once alerted to the fact that a previously bailed or ordained accused was now in custody, to make some diligent enquiry into the circumstances leading to that custody, particularly the date of each offence to assess whether a qualifying conviction has occurred.

Charges which disclose convictions

166B.—(1) Nothing in section 166 of this Act prevents— A4-359.4

(a) the prosecutor leading evidence of previous convictions where it is competent to do so as evidence in support of a substantive charge;

(b) the prosecutor proceeding with a charge—

(i) which discloses a previous conviction; or

(ii) in support of which evidence of a previous conviction may competently be led, on a complaint which includes a charge in relation to which the conviction is irrelevant; or

(c) the court trying a charge—

(i) which discloses a previous conviction; or

(ii) in support of which evidence of a previous conviction may competently be led, together with a charge on another complaint in relation to which the conviction is irrelevant.

(2) But subsections (1)(b) and (c) above apply only if the charges are of offences which—

(a) relate to the same occasion; or

(b) are of a similar character and amount to (or form part of) a course of conduct.

(3) The reference in subsection (1)(c) above to trying a charge together with a charge on another complaint means doing so under section 152A of this Act.

AMENDMENTS

Section 166B inserted by the Criminal Proceedings etc (Reform) (Scotland) Act 2007 (asp 6), s.12. Brought into force on December 10, 2007 by the Criminal Proceedings etc. (Reform) (Scotland) Act 2007 (Commencement No. 2 and Transitional Provisions and Savings) Order 2007 (SSI 2007/479 (C.40)), art.3 and Sch.

DEFINITIONS

A4-359.5 "prosecutor": s.307(1).
"complaint": s.307(1).

GENERAL NOTE

A4-359.6 This new measure which applies only to summary proceedings is of both evidential and procedural significance. From a prosecutor's stance it may also serve to halt the proliferation of complaints which can arise out of a single incident or course of conduct: while there are valid reasons for withholding charges which would infer the existence of previous convictions from a jury, it is difficult to discern the same rationale in the context of a summary trial.

It will be borne in mind that Scottish criminal procedure ordinarily did not permit the prosecutor to disclose the existence of an accused's previous convictions to the court until a conviction had been secured. For this reason separate complaints had to be raised to avoid inadvertent, or premature, disclosure of an accused's criminal history, notably in cases involving disqualified driving or being a known thief (see Civic Government (Scotland) Act 1982 (c.45)). The only exceptions to this broad rule had been where the existence of the conviction was a necessary precursor to the commission of an offence (again, most obviously disqualification from driving) or where, during a trial, the court ruled that the conduct of the defence had fallen foul of the provisions of either ss.266 or 270 of the 1995 Act. In reality most experienced judges would be able to surmise the existence of previous convictions; while such insight in the past cannot be shown to have influenced courts' deliberations on the merits, it is beyond dispute that the need for separate complaints added to the numbers of summary trials to be factored into court business schedules.

The new provision will permit all charges from an incident or course of criminal conduct to be libelled in the same complaint with consequent savings in court time. This would not preclude the possibility of a motion being made, on cause shown, for a separation of charges. Some further economy in court time is brought by s.152A of the 1995 Act, which permits the prosecutor to seek the conjoining of separate complaints against an accused when they are due to call for trial on the same day. This reform is made yet more flexible by the advent of s.166B's provisions.

[THE NEXT PARAGRAPH IS A4-360]

Forms of finding and sentence

A4-360 **167.**—(1) Every sentence imposed by a court of summary jurisdiction shall unless otherwise provided be pronounced in open court in the presence of the accused, but need not be written out or signed in his presence.

(2) The finding and sentence and any order of a court of summary jurisdiction, as regards both offences at common law and offences under any enactment, shall be entered in the record of the proceedings in the form, as nearly as may be, prescribed by Act of Adjournal.

(3) The record of the proceedings shall be sufficient warrant for all execution on a finding, sentence or order and for the clerk of court to issue extracts containing such executive clauses as may be necessary for implement thereof.

(4) When imprisonment forms part of any sentence or other judgement, warrant for the apprehension and interim detention of the accused pending his being committed to prison shall, where necessary, be implied.

(5) Where a fine imposed by a court of summary jurisdiction is paid at the bar it shall not be necessary for the court to refer to the period of imprisonment applicable to the non-payment thereof.

(6) Where several charges at common law or under any enactment are embraced in one complaint, a cumulo penalty may be imposed in respect of all or any of such charges of which the accused is convicted.

(7) Subject to section 204A of this Act, a court of summary jurisdiction may frame—

(a) a sentence following on conviction; or

(b) an order for committal in default of payment of any sum of money or for contempt of court,

so as to take effect on the expiry of any previous sentence for a term or order which, at the date of the later conviction or order, the accused is undergoing.

(7A) Where the court imposes a sentence as mentioned in paragraph (a) of subsection (7) above for an offence committed after the coming into force of this subsection, the court may—

(a) if the person is serving or is liable to serve the punishment part of a previous sentence, frame the sentence to take effect on the day after that part of that sentence is or would be due to expire; or

(b) if the person is serving or is liable to serve the punishment parts of two or more previous sentences, frame the sentence to take effect on the day after the later or (as the case may be) latest expiring of those parts is or would be due to expire.

(7B) Where it falls to the court to sentence a person who is subject to a previous sentence in respect of which a punishment part requires to be (but has not been) specified, the court shall not sentence the person until such time as the part is either specified or no longer requires to be specified.

(7C) In subsections (7A) and (7B) above, any reference to a punishment part of a sentence shall be construed by reference to—

(a) the punishment part of the sentence as is specified in an order mentioned in section 2(2) of the 1993 Act; or

(b) any part of the sentence which has effect, by virtue of section 10 of the 1993 Act or the schedule to the Convention Rights (Compliance) (Scotland) Act 2001 (asp 7), as if it were the punishment part so specified,

and "the 1993 Act" means the Prisoners and Criminal Proceedings (Scotland) Act 1993 (c.9).

(8) It shall be competent at any time before imprisonment has followed on a sentence for the court to alter or modify it; but no higher sentence than that originally pronounced shall be competent, and—

(a) the signature of the judge or clerk of court to any sentence shall be sufficient also to authenticate the findings on which such sentence proceeds; and

(b) the power conferred by this subsection to alter or modify a sentence may be exercised without requiring the attendance of the accused.

AMENDMENTS

Subs.(7) inserted by Crime and Disorder Act 1998 (c.37) Sch.8 para.122 (effective September 30, 1998: SI 1998/2327).

Subs.(7) as amended, and subss.(7A)-(7C) inserted, by Criminal Justice (Scotland) Act 2003 (asp 7) Pt 4 s.26. Brought into force on December 1, 2003 by SSI 2003/475 (C.26) art.2.

DEFINITIONS A4-360.1

"complaint": s.307(1).
"court of summary jurisdiction": s.307(1).
"enactment": s.307(1).
"fine": s.307(1).
"imprisonment": s.307(6).
"judge": s.307(1).
"offences": s.307(1).
"prison": s.307(1).
"sentence": s.307(1).

[THE NEXT PARAGRAPH IS A4-361]

GENERAL NOTE

A4-361 While sentence is normally pronounced in the accused's presence this does not apply to the circumstances covered by s.150(5) or, arguably, where the accused misconducts himself in the course of his trial (s.153(2)) provided he is legally represented. Section 144(6) of the Act provides that sentences of imprisonment or detention cannot be imposed in the absence of the accused. Confusion over findings or correction of findings, following the justice's evident confusion over the role played by each of the accused, resulted in the quashing of convictions in *Taylor v Craigen*, 2002 G.W.D. 38-1251.

Subsection (6) enacts that *cumulo* sentences can be imposed in relation to all the charges libelled on a complaint; conversely if the Crown elects to place on separate complaints, matters which could properly have been incorporated in one complaint, then consecutive sentences should not be imposed; *Kesson v Heatly*, 1964 J.C. 40. See also *Noble v Guild*, 1987 S.C.C.R. 518 where a delay in imposing a sentence of imprisonment rendered it incompetent to apply imprisonment consecutive to a term which by then was already being served. However, where an accused was sentenced on indictment to 18-months' detention and had outstanding fines, the Appeal Court upheld the imposition of the alternative periods of detention in lieu of the fines, these being effective consecutive to each other, and to the 18-months' sentence (*Cartledge v McLeod*, 1988 S.L.T. 389; 1988 S.C.C.R. 129). The fact that an earlier sentence is the subject of appeal, and thus is not being "undergone", does not debar a court sentencing in respect of other matters from imposing a consecutive sentence to begin at such time as the matter under appeal is resolved (*Thorne v Stott*, 1999 G.W.D. 28-1332).

The appropriateness and effect upon eligibility for licence of consecutive terms of detention were discussed in *Clayton, Petr*, 1992 S.L.T. 404.

Section 218(2) sets out the table of fines and alternative periods of imprisonment applicable to proceedings under the Act. The minimum period of imprisonment which can be imposed summarily is five days (see s.205).

Caution

A4-362 **168.**—(1) This section applies with regard to the finding, forfeiture, and recovery of caution in any proceedings under this Part of this Act.

(2) Caution may be found by consignation of the amount with the clerk of court, or by bond of caution signed by the cautioner.

(3) Where caution becomes liable to forfeiture, forfeiture may be granted by the court on the motion of the prosecutor, and, where necessary, warrant granted for the recovery of the caution.

(4) Where a cautioner fails to pay the amount due under his bond within six days after he has received a charge to that effect, the court may—

(a) order him to be imprisoned for the maximum period applicable in pursuance of section 219 of this Act to that amount or until payment is made; or
(b) if it considers it expedient, on the application of the cautioner grant time for payment; or
(c) instead of ordering imprisonment, order recovery by civil diligence in accordance with section 221 of this Act.

DEFINITIONS

A4-362.1 "imprisonment": s.306(7).
"prosecutor": s.307(1).

[THE NEXT PARAGRAPH IS A4-363]

Detention in precincts of court

A4-363 **169.** [...]

AMENDMENTS

Section 169 repealed by Criminal Justice and Licensing (Scotland) Act 2010 (asp 13) s.16(2). Brought into force on December 13, 2010 by SSI 2010/413 (C.28) art.2, Sch.1 para.1.

[THE NEXT PARAGRAPH IS A4-365]

Miscellaneous

Damages in respect of summary proceedings

170.—(1) No judge, clerk of court or prosecutor in the public interest shall be found liable by any court in damages for or in respect of any proceedings taken, act done, or judgment, decree or sentence pronounced in any summary proceedings under this Act, unless— A4-365

(a) the person suing has suffered imprisonment in consequence thereof; and

(b) such proceedings, act, judgment, decree or sentence has been quashed; and

(c) the person suing specifically avers and proves that such proceeding, act, judgment, decree or sentence was taken, done or pronounced maliciously and without probable cause.

(2) No such liability as aforesaid shall be incurred or found where such judge, clerk of court or prosecutor establishes that the person suing was guilty of the offence in respect whereof he had been convicted, or on account of which he had been apprehended or had otherwise suffered, and that he had undergone no greater punishment than was assigned by law to such offence.

(3) No action to enforce such liability as aforesaid shall lie unless it is commenced within two months after the proceeding, act, judgment decree or sentence founded on, or in the case where the Act under which the action is brought fixes a shorter period, within that shorter period.

(4) In this section "judge" shall not include "sheriff", and the provisions of this section shall be without prejudice to the privileges and immunities possessed by sheriffs.

Definitions A4-365.1

"imprisonment": s.307(6).
"judge": ss.170(6) and 307(1).
"prosecutor": s.307(1).
"sentence": s.307(1).

[THE NEXT PARAGRAPH IS A4–366]

General Note

In the conduct of proceedings on indictment the Lord Advocate, and subordinates appointed by him to prepare and conduct such proceedings, enjoy absolute privilege and thus immunity from actions for damages (see *Hester v MacDonald*, 1961 S.C. 370; 1961 S.L.T. 414). This immunity extends to procurators fiscal in solemn proceedings but is restricted in summary proceedings by the operation of s.170: the right to seek damages from the criminal authorities in relation to any summary proceedings is available to an accused person who can satisfy all the requirements of subs.(1); see *Graham v Strathern*, 1924 S.C. 699. Any proceedings must be commenced within two months of the conduct complained of or any shorter period specifically stated. Subsection (2) provides immunity from civil liability for court officials only while they are proceeding under the Act (*Graham v Strathern* at 724; *Ferguson v MacDonald* (1885) 12 Rettie 1083). The practical effect of subs.(4) is to afford a sheriff sitting in summary proceedings a greater degree of immunity at common law, than was conferred on other judges in summary proceedings. See the extensive discussion of the issue in *Russell v Dickson*, 1997 G.W.D. 22-1058. A4-366

See *Bell v McGlennan*, 1992 S.L.T. 237, where proceedings were held to have been competently raised against the prosecutor as vicariously liable over the retention of property as evidence in a case which did not proceed, due to the intervention of the statutory time bar.

Maliciously and without probable cause

The most difficult legal obstacle for a pursuer seeking damages in respect of summary proceedings is the requirement to aver and prove that the action complained of had been taken or done *maliciously and without probable cause*: see s.170(1)(c) above. The difficulty lies in the requirement that the standard of averment and proof is high, requiring the basis of any claim of malice to be described with particular clarity in the pleadings: *McKie v Strathclyde Joint Police Board*, 2004 S.L.T. 982

In *Findlay v McGowan*, 2010 G.W.D. 12-225 photographs that had been productions were destroyed on the instruction of a procurator fiscal depute as part of the discontinuance of a summary prosecution. Such an act attracted the protection of s.170. In taking that decision an erroneous instruction led to certain items being destroyed needlessly. In the absence of averments of malice and want of probable cause, the claim by the pursuer for reparation for the loss failed. The sheriff observed that it had long been recognised that the protection afforded to public officials is not for their personal benefit, but for the benefit and in the interests of the general public. In the case of prosecutors the public interest lies in having crime properly investigated and prosecuted without having constantly to look over their shoulders for fear of causing some harm along the way, whether to an accused person, a witness or a member of the public.

The section's terms demanding malice on the part of the prosecutor to trigger any liability in damages sit uneasily with art.5 of the European Convention on Human Rights; see generally *McCaffer v Lord Advocate*, 2015 S.L.T. (Sh Ct) 44, a civil action arising from petition proceedings, following *Keegan v United Kingdom* (2007) E.H.R.R. 33.

Rule of immunity abolished

The whole of s.170 and the associated case law requires now to be reconsidered in the context of *Whitehouse and Clark v Lord Advocate* [2019] CSIH 52 (30 October 2019) because in that five judge decision *Hester v MacDonald,* 1961 S.C. 370 was overruled, at [124], in regard to the common law absolute privilege in the context of solemn procedure. Specific reference was made by the Lord President (Carloway) to s.170 of the 1995 Act, at [91]:

> "The existence of this regime is of no material relevance to the question of immunity in solemn cases. It exists as a matter of policy applicable only in the prosecution of what will inevitably be relatively minor offences. Whether parts of it might be challenged on Convention grounds may be for another day."

Recovery of penalties

A4-367 **171.—**(1) All penalties, for the recovery of which no special provision has been made by any enactment may be recovered by the public prosecutor in any court having jurisdiction.

(2) Where a court has power to take cognisance of an offence the penalty attached to which is not defined, the punishment therefore shall be regulated by that applicable to common law offences in that court.

DEFINITIONS

A4-367.1 "offence": s.307(1).
"prosecutor": s.307(1).

[THE NEXT PARAGRAPH IS A4-368]

GENERAL NOTE

A4-368 Unless it is expressly stipulated to the contrary by statute, the public prosecutor holds a general title to prosecute for the recovery of penalties (subs.(1)). In the absence of any express provision, the competent punishment in summary proceedings shall be dictated by reference to the penalties applicable to common law offences (see s.21).

Forms of procedure

A4-369 **172.—**(1) The forms of procedure for the purposes of summary proceedings under this Act and appeals therefrom shall be in such forms as are prescribed by Act of Adjournal or as nearly as may be in such forms.

(2) All warrants (other than warrants of apprehension or search), orders of court, and sentences may be signed either by the judge or by the clerk of court, and execution upon any warrant, order of court, or sentence may proceed either upon such warrant, order of court, or sentence itself or upon an extract thereof issued and signed by the clerk of court.

(3) Where, preliminary to any procedure, a statement on oath is required, the statement may be given before any judge, whether the subsequent procedure is in his court or another court.

DEFINITIONS

A4-369.1 "judge": s.307(1).
"sentence": s.307(1).

[THE NEXT PARAGRAPH IS A4-370]

GENERAL NOTE

The 1996 Act of Adjournal substantially revises the format of many forms to be utilised in criminal proceedings. **A4-370**

Although subs.(2) provides that all warrants (except those for apprehension or search) may be subscribed by the judge or the clerk of court, and that extracts thereof shall be equally valid, this presupposes that the order or warrant must first have been granted by a judge (see *Skeen v Ives Cladding*, 1976 S.L.T. (Notes) 31). Failure to complete proper minutes of proceedings and thus maintain a proper record of the proceedings is a fundamental defect (*Heywood v Stewart* C.O. Circ. A54/91).

PART X – APPEALS FROM SUMMARY PROCEEDINGS

General

Quorum of Sheriff Appeal Court in relation to appeals

173.—(1) For the purpose of hearing and determining any appeal under this Part of this Act, or any proceeding connected therewith, three of the Appeal Sheriffs shall be a quorum of the Sheriff Appeal Court, and the determination of any question under this Part of this Act by the court shall be according to the votes of the majority of the members of the court sitting, including the presiding Appeal Sheriff, and each Appeal Sheriff so sitting shall be entitled to pronounce a separate opinion. **A4-371**

(2) For the purpose of hearing and determining appeals under section 175(2)(b), (c) or (cza) of this Act, or any proceeding connected therewith, two of the Appeal Sheriffs shall be a quorum of the Sheriff Appeal Court, and each Appeal Sheriff shall be entitled to pronounce a separate opinion; but where the two Appeal Sheriffs are unable to reach agreement on the disposal of the appeal, or where they consider it appropriate, the appeal shall be heard and determined in accordance with subsection (1) above.

AMENDMENTS

Subs.(2) as amended by Protection of Children (Scotland) Act 2003 (asp 5) s.16(6). Brought into force on 10 January 2005 by SSI 2004/522 (C.38) art.2.

Subs.(2) as amended by Criminal Justice and Licensing (Scotland) Act 2010 (asp 13) Sch.2 para.11. Brought into force on 13 December 2010 (subject to savings provisions in art.3) by SSI 2010/413 (C.28) art.2, Sch.1 para.1.

Subs.(2) as amended by Protection of Vulnerable Groups (Scotland) Act 2007 (asp 14) Sch.4 para.20. Brought into force on 28 February 2011 by SSI 2011/157 (C.13) art.2, subject to savings specified in art.5(1).

Subss.(1), (2) as amended by Courts Reform (Scotland) Act 2014 (asp 8) Sch.3 para.2. Brought into force on 22 September 2015 by SSI 2015/247 (C.35) art.2 and Sch, subject to transitional provisions in art.6.

GENERAL NOTE

Appeals in terms of s.175 and appeals in relation to preliminary pleas under s.174 lie to the Sheriff Appeal Court, established by the Courts Reform (Scotland) Act 2014. Reference should be made to Ch.19 of the Act of Adjournal (Criminal Procedure Rules) 1996 and to the Sheriff Appeal Court Criminal Practice Note (No.1 of 2015) of 28 September 2015 (see para.C3-01 below) as well as to Part X of the present Act. It should be noted that, in terms of s.194ZB, there is a further appeal, on a point of law, to the High Court but only with the permission of that court. **A4-372**

Subs.(1)

Any appeal under this Part of this Act. This is subject to an exception in subs.(2) for appeals under the provisions there specified (broadly speaking, appeals against sentence).

Three of the Appeal Sheriffs. In terms of s.49 of the Courts Reform (Scotland) Act 2014, all Sheriffs Principal are Appeal Sheriffs. To their number are added sheriffs of at least five years' standing appointed as Appeal Sheriffs in terms of s.50 of that Act. Those sheriffs continue to serve in their ordinary shrieval capacity as well as sitting as Appeal Sheriffs. In terms of s.48 of the 2014 Act, a decision of the Sheriff Appeal Court on the interpretation or application of the law is binding in proceedings (including solemn proceedings before a sheriff and jury) before a sheriff anywhere in Scotland, in proceedings before a justice of the peace court anywhere in Scotland, and in proceedings before the Sheriff Appeal Court, except in a case where the court hearing the proceedings is constituted by a greater number of Appeal Sheriffs than those constituting the court which made the decision.

Shall be a quorum. This subsection prescribes the quorum but does not preclude the convening of a larger court as provided for by s.58 of the 2014 Act.

Subs.(2)

The quorum for sentence appeals is two but, in the event of disagreement, this subsection provides for the hearing of the appeal by a Bench of at least three. This follows the practice when summary appeals were heard by the High Court.

Appeals relating to preliminary pleas

A4-373 **174.**—(1) Without prejudice to any right of appeal under section 175(1) to (6) or 191 of this Act, a party may, in accordance with such procedure as may be prescribed by Act of Adjournal, appeal to the Sheriff Appeal Court against a decision of the court of first instance (other than a decision not to grant leave under subsection (1A)(b)) which relates to such objection or denial as is mentioned in section 144(4) of this Act; but such appeal must be taken not later than seven days after such decision.

(1A) An appeal under subsection (1) may be taken—

(a) in the case of a decision to dismiss the complaint or any part of it, by the prosecutor without the leave of the court,

(b) in any other case, only with the leave of the court of first instance (granted on the motion of a party or ex proprio motu).

(2) Where an appeal is taken under subsection (1) above, the Sheriff Appeal Court may postpone the trial diet (if one has been fixed) for such period as appears to it to be appropriate and may, if it thinks fit, direct that such period (or some part of it) shall not count towards any time limit applying in respect of the case.

(2A) Subsection (3) applies where—

(a) the court grants leave to appeal under subsection (1), or

(b) the prosecutor—

(i) indicates an intention to appeal under subsection (1), and

(ii) by virtue of subsection (1A)(a), does not require the leave of the court.

(3) Where this subsection applies, the court of first instance shall not proceed to trial at once under subsection (2) of section 146 of this Act; and subsection (3) of that section shall be construed as requiring sufficient time to be allowed for the appeal to be taken.

(4) In disposing of an appeal under subsection (1) above the Sheriff Appeal Court may affirm the decision of the court of first instance or may remit the case to it with such directions in the matter as it thinks fit; and where the court of first instance had dismissed the complaint, or any part of it, may reverse that decision and direct that the court of first instance fix a trial diet (if it has not already fixed one as regards so much of the complaint as it has not dismissed.)

AMENDMENTS

Subs.(1) as amended by Criminal Justice and Licensing (Scotland) Act 2010 (asp 13) s.72(3). Brought into force on 28 March 2011 by SSI 2011/178 (C.15) art.2, Sch.1 para.1.

Subss.(1), (2) and (4) as amended by Courts Reform (Scotland) Act 2014 (asp 8) Sch.3 para.3. Brought into force on 22 September 2015 by SSI 2015/247 (C.35) art.2 and Sch, subject to transitional provisions in art.6.

Subss.(1), (3) as amended, subss.(1A), (2A) inserted, by Criminal Justice (Scotland) Act 2016 (asp 1) s.87. Brought into force on 17 January 2017 by SSI 2016/426 art.2 and Sch.1 para.1.

DEFINITIONS

A4-373.1 "diet": s.307(1).

[THE NEXT PARAGRAPH IS A4-374]

GENERAL NOTE

By contrast with what is possible under solemn procedure, the scope for the raising of preliminary issues under summary procedure is distinctly limited. Section 144, which deals with procedure at the first diet under summary procedure, contemplates only objections to competency or relevancy and denials that the accused is the person charged by the police. The present section follows that by providing for an appeal relating to preliminary pleas only in relation to matters mentioned in s.144(4). Accordingly, it does not provide an avenue of appeal in relation to other decisions which a sheriff or JP might take at the pre-trial stage. Such decisions would include matters such as the making or refusal of witness anonymity orders and the making of orders under the Criminal Justice and Licensing (Scotland) Act 2010 in relation to disclosure. Matters not mentioned in s.144(4) often have their own, discrete, appeal procedures. It will be important, in any case in which such a question arises, to identify the correct mode of appeal. The powers of the Sheriff Appeal Court in dealing with appeals relating to preliminary pleas are set out in subs.(4). **A4-374**

Subs.(1)

Right of appeal under s.175. That is, an appeal against conviction and/or sentence.

Or s.191. That is, appeal by suspension or advocation on the ground of miscarriage of justice.

With the leave of the court … and in accordance with such procedure as may be prescribed. The detailed procedure for appeals relating to preliminary pleas is prescribed by r.19.1. By r.19.1(1), the accused may apply for leave only after stating how he pleads. By r.19.1(2), he must do so (and the court must decide whether to grant leave) immediately following the decision in question.

Such appeal must be taken not later than seven days after such decision. What this means is that the note of appeal in Form 19.1-A must be lodged with the clerk of court within seven days (see r.19.1(4) and (5)).

Subss.(2) and (3)

These subsections should be read carefully. The underlying theory of the Act is that the court may proceed to summary trial summarily—that is, at once after the plea is tendered (s.146(2)). In practice, however, that only happens in cases involving foreign witnesses who wish to return home or in fisheries cases in which a foreign registered vessel has been detained. At the time of writing (December 2015), sheriff courts are usually fixing trials at least 12 weeks after the pleading diet (and custody trials close to the 40 day time limit prescribed by s.147(1)). Timescales of that sort will usually allow time for the appeal to be dealt with but subs.(2) and (3) aim to ensure that the appeal can be dealt with before the trial diet. The starting point is subs.(3), which disapplies s.146(2) when leave to appeal is granted and which (assuming that the whole complaint has not been dismissed) requires the first instance court, in selecting a date for trial, to allow time for an appeal to be taken (that is, for the note of appeal to be lodged). Thereafter, subs.(2) empowers the Sheriff Appeal Court, in a case in which an appeal actually is taken, to postpone the trial. The obvious, though unstated, purpose is to allow time for the appeal to be decided. At the time of writing, it is not known how long that is likely to be. Note that subs.(2) empowers the Sheriff Appeal Court to direct that any postponement is not to count towards any time limit. It is thought that the only relevant time limit which exists in summary criminal procedure is the 40 day custody time limit prescribed by s.147(1). It is assumed that, in practice, first instance courts will fix trials far enough ahead to allow the appeal to be dealt with without the need for the Sheriff Appeal Court to exercise the power conferred by subs.(2), though it remains to be seen whether that will be possible in custody trials.

Right of appeal

175.—(1) This section is without prejudice to any right of appeal under section 191 of this Act. **A4-375**

(2) Any person convicted, or found to have committed an offence, in summary proceedings may, with leave granted in accordance with section 180 or, as the case may be, 187 of this Act, appeal under this section to the Sheriff Appeal Court—

(a) against such conviction, or finding;

(b) against the sentence passed on such conviction;

(c) against his absolute discharge or admonition or any drug treatment and testing order or any order deferring sentence;

(cza) against any disposal under section 227ZC(7)(a) to (c) or (e) or (8)(a) of this Act;

(ca) against any decision to remit made under section 49(1)(a) or (7)(b) of this Act;

(cb) […]; or

(d) against
  (i) both such conviction and such sentence or disposal or order;
  (ii) […]
  (iii) […]

(3) The prosecutor in summary proceedings may appeal under this section to the Sheriff Appeal Court on a point of law—
(a) against an acquittal in such proceedings; or
(b) against a sentence passed on conviction in such proceedings.

(4) The prosecutor in summary proceedings, in any class of case specified by order made by the Secretary of State, may, in accordance with subsection (4A) below, appeal to the Sheriff Appeal Court against any of the following disposals, namely—
(a) a sentence passed on conviction;
(b) a decision under section 209(1)(b) of this Act not to make a supervised release order;
(c) a decision under section 234A(2) of this Act not to make a non-harassment order;
(ca) a decision under section 92 of the Proceeds of Crime Act 2002 not to make a confiscation order;
(cb) a decision under section 22A of the Serious Crime Act 2007 not to make a serious crime prevention order;
(cb) a decision under section 36(2) of the Regulatory Reform (Scotland) Act 2014 not to make a publicity order;
(cc) a decision under section 41(2) of that Act not to make a remediation order;
(cd) a decision under section 97B(2) of the Proceeds of Crime Act 2002 to make or not to make a compliance order;
(cd) a decision under section 30(2) of the Health (Tobacco, Nicotine etc. and Care) (Scotland) Act 2016 not to make a remedial order;
(ce) a decision under section 30(2) of that Act not to make a publicity order
(d) […]
(dd) a drug treatment and testing order;
(e) […]
(f) a decision to remit to the Principal Reporter made under section 49(1)(a) or (7)(b) of this Act;
(g) an order deferring sentence;
(h) an admonition; or
(i) an absolute discharge.

(4A) An appeal under subsection (4) above may be made—
(a) on a point of law;
(b) where it appears to the Lord Advocate, in relation to an appeal under—
  (i) paragraph (a), (h) or (i) of that subsection, that the disposal was unduly lenient;
  (ii) paragraph (b), (c), (ca), (cb), (cc), (cd) or (ce) of that subsection, that the decision not to make the order in question was inappropriate:
  (iii) paragraph (cd) or (dd) of that subsection, that the making of the order concerned was unduly lenient or was on unduly lenient terms;
  (iv) under paragraph (f) of that subsection, that the decision to remit was inappropriate;

(v) under paragraph (g) of that subsection, that the deferment of sentence was inappropriate or was on unduly lenient conditions.

(4B) For the purposes of subsection (4A)(b)(i) above in its application to a confiscation order by virtue of section 92(11) of the Proceeds of Crime Act 2002, the reference to the disposal being unduly lenient is a reference to the amount required to be paid by the order being unduly low.

(4C) In deciding whether to appeal under subsection (4) in any case, the prosecutor must have regard to any sentencing guidelines which are applicable in relation to the case.

(5) By an appeal under subsection (2) above, an appellant may bring under review of the Sheriff Appeal Court any alleged miscarriage of justice which may include such a miscarriage based, subject to subsections (5A) to (5D) below, on the existence and significance of evidence which was not heard at the original proceedings.

(5A) Evidence which was not heard at the original proceedings may found an appeal only where there is a reasonable explanation of why it was not so heard.

(5B) Where the explanation referred to in subsection (5A) above or, as the case may be, (5C) below is that the evidence was not admissible at the time of the original proceedings, but is admissible at the time of the appeal, the court may admit that evidence if it appears to the court that it would be in the interests of justice to do so.

(5C) Without prejudice to subsection (5A) above, where evidence such as is mentioned subsection (5) above is evidence—

(a) which is—

(i) from a person; or

(ii) of a statement (within the meaning of section 259(1) of this Act) by a person,

who gave evidence at the original proceedings; and

(b) which is different from, or additional to, the evidence so given,

it may not found an appeal unless there is a reasonable explanation as to why the evidence now sought to be adduced was not given by that person at those proceedings, which explanation is itself supported by independent evidence.

(5D) For the purposes of subsection (5C) above, "independent evidence" means evidence which—

(a) was not heard at the original proceedings;

(b) is from a source independent of the person referred to in subsection (5C) above; and

(c) is accepted by the court as being credible and reliable.

(5E) By an appeal against acquittal under subsection (3) above a prosecutor may bring under review of the Sheriff Appeal Court any alleged miscarriage of justice.

(6) The power of the Secretary of State to make an order under subsection (4) above shall be exercisable by statutory instrument; and any order so made shall be subject to annulment in pursuance of a resolution of either House of Parliament.

(7) Where a person desires to appeal under subsection (2)(a) or (d) or (3) above, he shall pursue such appeal in accordance with sections 176 to 179, 181 to 185, 188, 190 and 192(1) and (2) of this Act.

(8) A person who has appealed against both conviction and sentence may abandon the appeal in so far as it is against conviction and may proceed with it against sentence alone, subject to such procedure as may be prescribed by Act of Adjournal.

(9) Where a convicted person or as the case may be a person found to have committed an offence desires to appeal under subsection (2)(b) or (c) above, or the

prosecutor desires so to appeal by virtue of subsection (4) above, he shall pursue such appeal in accordance with sections 186, 189(1) to (6), 190 and 192(1) and (2) of this Act; but nothing in this section shall prejudice any right to proceed by bill of suspension, or as the case may be advocation, against an alleged fundamental irregularity relating to the imposition of sentence.

(10) Where any statute provides for an appeal from summary proceedings to be taken under any public general or local enactment, such appeal shall be taken under this Part of this Act.

AMENDMENTS

Subs.(2)(a) inserted by Crime and Punishment (Scotland)Act 1997 (c.48) s.23 with effect from 1 August 1997 in terms of SI 1997/1712 art.3.

Subs.(4) inserted by Crime and Punishment (Scotland) Act 1997 (c.48) s.21 with effect from 1 August 1997 in terms of SI 1997/1712 art.3.

Subs.(5) inserted by Crime and Punishment (Scotland)Act 1997 (c.48) s.17(2) with effect from 1 August 1997 in terms of SI 1997/1712 art.3.

Subs.(5C) as amended by Crime and Disorder Act 1998 (c.37) Sch.8 para.123 (effective 30 September 1998: SI 1998/2327).

Subss.(2)(c), (4) and (4A) as amended by Crime and Disorder Act 1998 (c.37) s.94 and Sch.6 para.7. Brought into force on 30 September 1998 by SI 1998/2327 (C.53).

Subss.(4) and (4A) as amended, and subs.(4B) inserted, by Proceeds of Crime Act 2002 (c.29) Pt 3 s.115. Brought into force on 24 March 2003 by SSI 2003/210 (C.44).

Subs.(2)(cb), (d)(ii)(iii) inserted, and subss.(2)(c), (d), (8), (9) as amended, by Protection of Children (Scotland) Act 2003 (asp 5) s.16(7). Brought into force on 10 January 2005 by SSI 2004/522 (C.38) art.2.

Subss.(2)(c), (4A) as amended, subs.(cza) inserted, and subs.(4)(d) and (e) repealed, by Criminal Justice and Licensing (Scotland) Act 2010 (asp 13) Sch.2 para.12. Brought into force on 13 December 2010 (subject to savings provisions in art.3) by SSI 2010/413 (C.28) art.2, Sch.1 para.1.

Subss.(2), (8) and (9) as amended by Protection of Vulnerable Groups (Scotland) Act 2007 (asp 14) Sch.4 para.21. Brought into force on 28 February 2011 by SSI 2011/157 (C.13) art.2, subject to savings specified in art.5(1).

Subss.(4) and (4A) as amended by Regulatory Reform (Scotland)Act 2014 (asp 3) s.44(3). Brought into force on 30 June 2014 by SSI 2014/160 art.2 and Sch.1 para.1.

Subss.(2), (3), (4), (5), (5E) as amended by Courts Reform (Scotland) Act 2014 (asp 8) Sch.3 para.4. Brought into force on 22 September 2015 by SSI 2015/247 (C.35) art.2 and Sch, subject to transitional provisions in art.6.

Subs.(4C) inserted by Criminal Justice and Licensing (Scotland) Act 2010 (asp 13) s.6(8). Brought into force on 19 October 2015 by SSI 2015/336 art.2.

Subs.(4)(cd) inserted, subs.(4A) as amended, by Serious Crime Act 2015 (c.9) s.17(3). Brought into force on 1 March 2016 by SSI 2016/11 reg.2.

Subs.(4) and (4A) as amended by Serious Crime Act 2015 (c.9) Sch.4 para.15. Brought into force on 1 March 2016 by SI 2016/148 reg.3.

Subss.(4) and (4A)(b) as amended by Health (Tobacco, Nicotine etc. and Care) (Scotland) Act 2016 (asp 14) s.31(3). Brought into force on 1 October 2017 by SSI 2017/294 reg.2 and Sch.1 para.1. Note: possible drafting error so a second subs.(4)(cd) has been inserted.

DEFINITIONS

A4-375.1 "community service order": s.238.
"offence": s.307(1).
"probation order": s.228.
"prosecutor": s.307(1).
"sentence": s.307(1).

[THE NEXT PARAGRAPH IS A4-376]

GENERAL NOTE

A4-376 Except for Bills of Advocation and Suspension (as to which, see s.191), s.175 is the core provision in relation to appeals against conviction and/or disposal (a wider category than "sentence") under summary procedure. Subs.(2) provides for appeals by the accused. Leave is required and an appeal is available only in relation to the matters specified in the subsection. The ground is miscarriage of justice (subs.(5)), a phrase with an extended meaning which covers all the various situations which, in times past, under summary procedure were viewed in terms of incompetency and/or oppression, including excess of jurisdiction, where the diet is not properly constituted, and where the verdict is one which is not open on the indictment (*Drummond v HM Advocate*, 2003 S.C.C.R. 108, at [14]). Subs.(3) provides for appeals by the prosecutor on a point of law in relation to acquittal or sentence. Subs.(4) provides for appeals by the prosecutor in relation to disposal in specified classes of case, on a point of law or, according to the particular kind of decision which it is sought to criticise, undue leniency or inappropriateness. Prosecutors' appeals do not require leave but appeals under subs.(4) on the ground of undue leniency or inappropriateness do depend on the Lord Advocate taking the view specified in subs.(4A)(b). It is not enough for an individual procurator fiscal to form the view that a disposal is unduly lenient or inappropriate. The note of appeal by a prosecutor must be lodged within four weeks of the passing of the sentence (s.186(2)(b)).

Subs.(2)

Against such conviction. The appeal is by application for a stated case, in terms of s.176.

Against the sentence passed… Appeals under s.175(2)(b), (c) or (cza) which do not seek to bring the conviction itself under review are by note of appeal in terms of s.186.

Disposal under section 227ZC(7)(a) to (c)… The provision referred to deals with breaches of Community Payback Orders.

Remit made under section 49(1)… That is, a remit to the children's hearing for disposal.

Subs.(4)

Any class of case specified by order. The Prosecutor's Right of Appeal in Summary Proceedings (Scotland) Order 1996 (SI 1996/2548) specifies any case in which, on or after 1 November 1996, (a) sentence is passed, or (b) an order deferring sentence is made, or (c) the person is admonished or discharged absolutely.

Subs.(5)

Subss.(5) to (5D) are the direct equivalent of s.106(3) to (3D) and the commentary to those provisions should be consulted.

Power to refer points of law for the opinion of the High Court

175A.—(1) In an appeal under this Part, the Sheriff Appeal Court may refer a point of law to the High Court for its opinion if it considers that the point is a complex or novel one. A4-376.1

(2) The Sheriff Appeal Court may make a reference under subsection (1)—

(a) on the application of a party to the appeal proceedings, or

(b) on its own initiative.

(3) On giving its opinion on a reference under subsection (1), the High Court may also give a direction as to further procedure in, or disposal of, the appeal.

AMENDMENTS

Section 175A inserted by Courts Reform (Scotland) Act 2014 (asp 8) s.120. Brought into force on 22 September 2015 by SSI 2015/247 (C.35) art.2 and Sch.

GENERAL NOTE

It is primarily for the Sheriff Appeal Court to decide whether a case is complex or novel and the Sheriff Appeal Court's view is determinative. The High Court cannot normally refuse to entertain a reference (*Wilson v Shanks*, 2018 S.C.C.R. 302). A4-376.2

The procedure applicable to a reference to the High Court is prescribed in Ch.19D of the Criminal Procedure Rules. Whether the reference is contemplated as a result of an application by a party or because the Sheriff Appeal Court proposes to make a reference on its own initiative, a diet must be fixed at which parties may be heard on the question of whether a reference should be made. If the Sheriff Appeal Court decides to make the reference, the reasons for that decision must be given and recorded. The reference itself is then drafted (using the prescribed form) by whichever of the parties the court directs to do that. No doubt the reasons recorded by the court will inform that part of the draft which sets out the reasons why the Sheriff Appeal Court considers the point to be novel or complex. There is provision in r.19D.4 for adjustment of the draft and, in r.19D.4(3) for further adjustment as required by the court. In due course, the High Court is empowered (by r.19D.5) to make such order as it thinks fit to determine the reference and a certified copy of the opinion of the High Court must be sent to the Sheriff Appeal Court along with any direction as to further procedure given in terms of subs.(3). Rule 19D.6 provides that, on receipt, the Sheriff Appeal Court is to give its own directions as to further procedure and these, together with the opinion of the High Court, are to be given to the parties.

[THE NEXT PARAGRAPH IS A4-377]

Stated case

Stated case: manner and time of appeal

A4-377 **176.**—(1) An appeal under section 175(2)(a) or (d) or (3) of this Act shall be by application for a stated case, which application shall—

(a) be made within one week of the final determination of the proceedings;

(b) contain a full statement of all the matters which the appellant desires to bring under review and, where the appeal is also against sentence or disposal or order, the ground of appeal against that sentence or disposal or order; and

(c) be signed by the appellant or his solicitor and lodged with the clerk of court,

and a copy of the application shall, within the period mentioned in paragraph (a) above, be sent by the appellant to the respondent or the respondent's solicitor.

(2) The clerk of court shall enter in the record of the proceedings the date when an application under subsection (1) above was lodged.

(3) The appellant may, at any time within the period of three weeks mentioned in subsection (1) of section 179 of this Act, or within any further period afforded him by virtue of section 181 (1) of this Act, amend any matter stated in his application or add a new matter; and he shall intimate any such amendment, or addition, to the respondent or the respondent's solicitor.

(4) Where such an application has been made by the person convicted, and the judge by whom he was convicted dies before signing the case or is precluded by illness or other cause from doing so, it shall be competent for the convicted person to present a bill of suspension to the Sheriff Appeal Court and to bring under the review of that court any matter which might have been brought under review by stated case.

(5) The record of the procedure in the inferior court in an appeal mentioned in subsection (1) above shall be as nearly as may be in the form prescribed by Act of Adjournal.

AMENDMENTS

Subs.(4) as amended by Courts Reform (Scotland) Act 2014 (asp 8) Sch.3 para.5. Brought into force on 22 September 2015 by SSI 2015/247 (C.35) art.2 and Sch, subject to transitional provisions in art.6.

GENERAL NOTE

Subs. (1)

A4-378 An application for stated case is not competent until the cause has been finally determined and sentence pronounced: see *Lee v Lasswade Local Authority* (1893) 5 Couper 329 and *Torrance v Miller* (1892) 3 White 254.

A case is finally determined when particulars of conviction and sentence are entered in the record of proceedings: see *Tudhope v Colbert*, 1978 S.L.T. (Notes) 57 and *Tudhope v Campbell*, 1979 J.C. 24. Where sentence is deferred in terms of s.202 then the final determination for summary proceedings is the date on which sentence is first deferred.

An application for a stated case is an application for a document that sets forth "the particulars of any matters competent for review which the appellant desires to bring under the review of the High Court, and of the facts, if any, proved in the case, and any point of law decided, and the grounds of the decision": subs.(2).

The nature and content of a stated case is emphasised because of the requirement in subs.(1)(b) that the application for a stated case contain "a full statement of all the matters which the appellant desires to bring under review". If the application does not have a comprehensive and accurate description of the point at issue the stated case will in the fullness of time reflect that.

It is not easy for a trial judge to prepare a stated case when the application is inadequate but the weight of High Court authority is in favour of the attempt being made. Although it was held in *Durant v Lockhart*, 1986 S.C.C.R. 23 (and reiterated in *Dickson v Valentine*, 1988 S.C.C.R. 325) that a sheriff was justified in refusing to state a case where the application did not contain the full statement required and it was recognised in *Leonard, Petitioner*, 1995 S.C.C.R. 39 that there may be cases in which the ground of appeal is so deficient that the Sheriff or JP cannot properly state a case at all. In *McTaggart, Petitioner*, 1987 S.C.C.R. 638 , the High Court (in directing a Sheriff to state a case) made it clear that it is not for a

Sheriff to determine the relevancy of the ground of appeal and, by refusing to state a case, to apply a sift to determine which cases are heard by the appeal court. In *Crowe, Petitioner*, 1994 S.C.C.R. 784 it was held that an application which contained a series of questions could constitute the necessary "full statement". Giving the opinion of the court, the Lord Justice General (Hope) said:

> "What is required is that the matter to be brought under review should be identified with sufficient specification to enable a case to be stated".

A further concern arising from applications for stated cases that do not contain full statements relates to the hearing of the appeal. An application for a stated case, and in turn the stated case itself, that does not properly focus the real issue can unduly hamper those presenting the appeal: *Cameron v Normand*, 1997 G.W.D. 9–367. In *Walton v Crowe*, 1993 S.C.C.R. 885 an attempt by the appellant to raise an issue which had not been mentioned in the application was refused. That restriction can also apply to the Crown: *Normand v Walker*, 1994 S.C.C.R. 875.

The main practical problem is the failure to meet the requirements of subs.(1)(b) about a full statement. Making an application within one week of the final determination is less of a general problem: see subs.(1)(a) which must be read with s.194(3) for the meaning of "final determination".

Subs. (3)

The draft stated case that follows from a proper application may on authority be amended or added to and if that is done there must be intimation to the other side.

Subs. (4)

An appeal cannot proceed on the basis of a draft stated case. Either there is a signed stated case to found the appeal or there is not. If there is no stated case in the terms set out in this subsection then the correct mode is a bill of suspension: see *Brady v Barbour*, 1994 S.C.C.R. 890 and *Clark v Ruxton*, 1997 G.W.D. 10–408.

Application of section 176 in relation to certain appeals

176A.—(1) Section 176 applies in relation to an appeal under section 175(2)(a) by virtue of section 11(7) of the Double Jeopardy (Scotland) Act 2011 (asp 16) with the following modifications. **A4-378.1**

(2) In subsection (1)(a), for the words "one week of the final determination of the proceedings" substitute "one week of the date on which the appellant is acquitted of an offence mentioned in section 11(2) of the Double Jeopardy (Scotland) Act 2011 (asp 16)".

(3) In subsection (2), the reference to the proceedings is to be construed as a reference to the proceedings resulting in the appellant's acquittal as mentioned in section 11(7) of the Double Jeopardy (Scotland) Act 2011 (asp 16).

(4) In subsection (5), the reference to the inferior court is to be construed as a reference to the court which acquitted the appellant of an offence under section 11(2) of the Double Jeopardy (Scotland) Act 2011 (asp 16).

AMENDMENTS

Section 176A inserted by Double Jeopardy (Scotland) Act 2011 (asp 16) Sch.1 para.13. Brought into force on 28 November 2011 by SSI 2011/365 (C.34) art.3.

[THE NEXT PARAGRAPH IS A4-379]

Procedure where appellant in custody

177.—(1) If an appellant making an application under section 176 of this Act is in custody, the court of first instance may— **A4-379**

(a) grant bail;

(b) grant a sist of execution;

(c) make any other interim order.

(2) An application for bail shall be disposed of by the court before the end of the day (not being a Saturday or Sunday, or a court holiday prescribed for the court which is to determine the question of bail, unless that court is sitting on that day for the disposal of criminal business) after the day on which the application is made.

(3) If bail is refused or the appellant is dissatisfied with the conditions imposed, he may, within 24 hours after the judgment of the court, appeal against it by a note of appeal written on the complaint and signed by himself or his solicitor, and the complaint and proceedings shall thereupon be transmitted to the Clerk of the Sheriff Appeal Court, and the Sheriff Appeal Court or any Appeal Sheriff thereof, either in court or in chambers, shall have power to review the decision of the inferior court and to grant bail on such conditions as the Court or Appeal Sheriff may think fit, or to refuse bail.

(4) No clerks' fees, court fees or other fees or expenses shall be exigible from or awarded against an appellant in custody in respect of an appeal to the Sheriff Appeal Court against the conditions imposed or on account of refusal of bail by a court of summary jurisdiction.

(5) If an appellant who has been granted bail does not thereafter proceed with his appeal, the inferior court shall have power to grant warrant to apprehend and imprison him for such period of his sentence as at the date of his bail remained unexpired and, subject to subsection (6) below, such period shall run from the date of his imprisonment under the warrant or, on the application of the appellant, such earlier date as the court thinks fit, not being a date later than the date of expiry of any term or terms of imprisonment imposed subsequently to the conviction appealed against.

(6) Where an appellant who has been granted bail does not thereafter proceed with his appeal, the court from which the appeal was taken shall have power, where at the time of the abandonment of the appeal the person is in custody or serving a term or terms of imprisonment imposed subsequently to the conviction appealed against, to order that the sentence or, as the case may be, the unexpired portion of that sentence relating to that conviction should run from such date as the court may think fit, not being a date later than the date on which any term or terms of imprisonment subsequently imposed expired.

(7) The court shall not make an order under subsection (6) above to the effect that the sentence or, as the case may be, unexpired portion of the sentence shall run other than concurrently with the subsequently imposed term of imprisonment without first notifying the appellant of its intention to do so and considering any representations made by him or on his behalf.

(8) Subsections (6) and (7) of section 112 of this Act (bail pending determination of appeals under section 288AA of this Act or paragraph 13(a) of Schedule 6 to the Scotland Act 1998) shall apply to appeals arising in summary proceedings as they do to appeals arising in solemn proceedings.

AMENDMENTS

Subs.(8) inserted by Scotland Act 1998 (Consequential Modifications) (No.1) Order 1999 (SI 1999/1042) art.3, Sch.1 para.13(7) (effective May 6, 1999).

Subss.(2) and (3) as amended by Criminal Proceedings etc. (Reform) (Scotland) Act 2007 (asp 6) s.6, 80 and Sch. para.18(1). Brought into force on December 10, 2007 by SSI 2007/479 art.3 and Sch.

Subs.(8) as amended by Scotland Act 2012 (c.11) s.36(10). Brought into force on April 22, 2013 by SI 2013/6 art.2(c).

Subss.(3), (4) as amended by Courts Reform (Scotland) Act 2014 (asp 8) Sch.3 para.6. Brought into force on September 22, 2015 by SSI 2015/247 (C.35) art.2 and Sch, subject to transitional provisions in art.6.

DEFINITIONS

A4-379.1 "bail": s.307(1).
"order": s.307(1).

[THE NEXT PARAGRAPH IS A4-380]

GENERAL NOTE

This section sets out the immediate procedure if the appellant makes an application for a stated case and is in custody. If bail is sought an application would be disposed of within 24 hours of such an application or, if refused, a note of appeal may be lodged to review the decision to refuse: subss.(2) and (3). High Court of Justiciary Practice Note No.1 of 2012 (Interim liberation), which is reproduced in the annotations to s.112 above (and also in Division C, para.C1-52), states that in summary cases the grant of leave to appeal is likely to be a strong indicator that liberation ought to follow A4-380

Appeals are frequently not pursued despite the initial enthusiasm. Where the appellant is at liberty when he abandons his appeal the warrant to imprison him in accordance with his sentence shall run from the date of his imprisonment under the warrant or, on application, such earlier date as the court thinks fit, not being a date later than the date of expiry of any term of imprisonment imposed subsequently to the conviction appealed against: subs.(5).

This may be contrasted with the circumstances where the appellant is in custody when he abandons his appeal, then the unexpired portion of that sentence should run from such date as the court thinks fit, not being a date later than the date on which any term of imprisonment subsequently imposed expired: subs.(6).

Subsection (7) gives statutory effect to *Proudfoot v Wither*, 1990 S.L.T. 742 and requires sentences under subs.(6) to be served concurrently but if the court is minded to do otherwise then the appellant must be notified and the court must consider any representations he wishes to make.

Stated case: preparation of draft

178.—(1) Within three weeks of the final determination of proceedings in respect of which an application for a stated case is made under section 176 of this Act— A4-381

(a) where the appeal is taken from the JP court and the trial was presided over by a justice of the peace or justices of the peace, the Clerk of Court; or

(b) in any other case the judge who presided at the trial,

shall prepare a draft stated case, and the clerk of the court concerned shall forthwith issue the draft to the appellant or his solicitor and a duplicate thereof to the respondent or his solicitor.

(1A) Where an application for a stated case under section 176 of this Act relates to an appeal by virtue of section 11(7) of the Double Jeopardy (Scotland) Act 2011 (asp 16)—

(a) the reference in subsection (1) to the final determination of proceedings is to be construed as a reference to the date on which the appellant is acquitted of an offence mentioned in section 11(2) of that Act; and

(b) the reference in subsection (1)(b) to the judge who presided at the trial is to be construed as a reference to the judge who presided at the trial resulting in the conviction in respect of which the application for a stated case is made.

(2) A stated case shall be, as nearly as may be, in the form prescribed by Act of Adjournal, and shall set forth the particulars of any matters competent for review which the appellant desires to bring under the review of the Sheriff Appeal Court, and of the facts, if any, proved in the case, and any point of law decided, and the grounds of the decision.

AMENDMENTS

Subs.(1)(a) as amended by Criminal Proceedings etc. (Reform) (Scotland) Act 2007 (asp 6) s.80 and Sch. para.26. Brought into force for the Sheriffdom of Lothian and Borders on March 10, 2008 by SSI 2008/42 (C.4) art.3 and Sch. Brought into force for the Sheriffdom of Grampian, Highland and Islands on June 2, 2008 by SSI 2008/192 (C.19) art.3 and Sch. Brought into force for the Sheriffdom of Glasgow and Strathkelvin on December 8, 2008 by SSI 2008/329 (C.29) art.3 and Sch. Brought into force for the Sheriffdom of Tayside, Central and Fife on February 23, 2009 by SSI 2008/362 (C.30) art.3 and Sch. Brought into force for the Sheriffdom of North Strathclyde on December 14, 2009 by SSI 2009/432 (C.32) art.3 and Sch.1. Remainder in force on February 22, 2010 by SSI 2009/432 (C.32) art.3 and Sch.2.

Subs.(1A) inserted by Double Jeopardy (Scotland) Act 2011 (asp 16) Sch.1 para.14. Brought into force on November 28, 2011 by SSI 2011/365 (C.34) art.3.

Subs.(2) as amended by Courts Reform (Scotland) Act 2014 (asp 8) Sch.3 para.7. Brought into force on 22 September 2015 by SSI 2015/247 (C.35) art.2 and Sch, subject to transitional provisions in art.6.

Definition

A4-381.1 "judge": s.307(1).

General Note

A4-381.2 In the JP court the draft stated case is prepared by the clerk of court: see *Mackinnon v McGarry*, 1988 S.L.T. (Sh. Ct.) 15. In *Clarke v Ruxton*, 1997 G.W.D. 10–408 the accused had to proceed by way of a bill of suspension following the death of the sheriff before a stated case could be prepared.

Subs.(2)

The form of the draft stated case has been considered a number of times and the following guidelines have been given: (1) it is not necessary to narrate the charges, though appeal courts do find it helpful; (2) the facts proved should be fully set out: see *Gordon v Hansen* (1914) 7 Adam 441; *Waddell v Kinnaird*, 1922 J.C. 40; *Gordon v Allan*, 1987 S.L.T. 400; *Duncan v MacLeod*, 1997 G.W.D. 13–550; (3) it should set out objections taken to admissibility or rejection of evidence and the reasons for upholding or repelling same should be explained: see *Falconer v Brown* (1893) 1 Adam 96; (4) any findings in fact made should be based on the whole evidence: see *Jordan v Allan*, 1989 S.C.C.R. 202 and *Bowman v Jessop*, 1989 S.C.C.R. 597; (5) where a no case to answer submission is made then the form of the stated case should be as set out in *Wingate v MacGlennan*, 1991 S.C.C.R. 133. See also *MacDonald v Normand*, 1994 S.C.C.R. 121; *Cassidy v Normand*, 1994 S.C.C.R. 325, and *Thomson v Barber*, 1994 S.C.C.R. 485; (6) the reasons for the final decision should be set out: see *Lyon v Don Brothers, Buist & Co*, 1944 J.C. 1 including the reasons the evidence was believed or disbelieved. See *Petrovich v Jessop*, 1990 S.C.C.R. 1; *Roberton v McGlennan*, 1994 S.C.C.R. 394, and *Leask v Vannet*, 1996 G.W.D. 36–1960; (7) questions should be stated for the opinion of the court: see *Needes v MacLeod*, 7 November 1984, unreported. Notwithstanding that questions are not properly framed the court may proceed: see *Robertson v Aitchison*, 1981 S.C.C.R. 149; *Marshall v Smith* 1983 S.C.C.R. 156, and *Waddell v MacPhail*, 1986 S.C.C.R. 593. In *Jackson v Vannet*, 1997 G.W.D. 23–1146 the stated case was sent back for restatement where the justice did not summarise the entire evidence of a number of essential witnesses.

[THE NEXT PARAGRAPH IS A4-382]

Stated case: adjustment and signature

A4-382 **179.—**(1) Subject to section 181(1) of this Act, within three weeks of the issue of the draft stated case under section 178 of this Act, each party shall cause to be transmitted to the court and to the other parties or their solicitors a note of any adjustments he proposes be made to the draft case or shall intimate that he has no such proposal.

(2) The adjustments mentioned in subsection (1) above shall relate to evidence heard or purported to have been heard at the trial and not to such evidence as is mentioned in section 175(5) of this Act.

(3) Subject to section 181(1) of this Act, if the period mentioned in subsection (1) above has expired and the appellant has not lodged adjustments and has failed to intimate that he has no adjustments to propose, he shall be deemed to have abandoned his appeal; and subsection (5) of section 177 of this Act shall apply accordingly.

(4) If adjustments are proposed under subsection (1) above or if the judge desires to make any alterations to the draft case there shall, within one week of the expiry of the period mentioned in that subsection or as the case may be of any further period afforded under section 181(1) of this Act, be a hearing (unless the appellant has, or has been deemed to have, abandoned his appeal) for the purpose of considering such adjustments or alterations.

(5) Where a party neither attends nor secures that he is represented at a hearing under subsection (4) above, the hearing shall nevertheless proceed.

(6) Where at a hearing under subsection (4) above—

(a) any adjustment proposed under subsection (1) above by a party (and not withdrawn) is rejected by the judge; or

(b) any alteration proposed by the judge is not accepted by all the parties,

that fact shall be recorded in the minute of the proceedings of the hearing.

(7) Within two weeks of the date of the hearing under subsection (4) above or, where there is no hearing, within two weeks of the expiry of the period mentioned in subsection (1) above, the judge shall (unless the appellant has been deemed to have abandoned the appeal) state and sign the case and shall append to the case—

(a) any adjustment, proposed under subsection (1) above, which is rejected by him, a note of any evidence rejected by him which is alleged to support that adjustment and the reasons for his rejection of that adjustment and evidence; and

(b) a note of the evidence upon which he bases any finding of fact challenged, on the basis that it is unsupported by the evidence, by a party at the hearing under subsection (4) above.

(8) As soon as the case is signed under subsection (7) above the clerk of court—

(a) shall send the case to the appellant or his solicitor and a duplicate thereof to the respondent or his solicitor; and

(b) shall transmit a certified copy of the complaint, the minute of proceedings and any other relevant documents to the Clerk of the Sheriff Appeal Court.

(9) Subject to section 181(1) of this Act, within one week of receiving the case the appellant or his solicitor, as the case may be, shall cause it to be lodged with the Clerk of the Sheriff Appeal Court.

(10) Subject to section 181(1) of this Act, if the appellant or his solicitor fails to comply with subsection (9) above the appellant shall be deemed to have abandoned the appeal; and subsection (5) of section 177 of this Act shall apply accordingly.

(11) In relation to a draft stated case under section 178 of this Act relating to an appeal by virtue of section 11(7) of the Double Jeopardy (Scotland) Act 2011 (asp 16)—

(a) the reference in subsection (1) to the court is to be construed as a reference to the court by which the appellant was convicted; and

(b) the references in this section to the judge are to be construed as references to the judge who presided at the trial resulting in that conviction.

AMENDMENTS

Subs.(2) as amended by Crime and Punishment (Scotland) Act 1997 (c.48) Sch.1 para.21(20) with effect from 1 August 1997 in terms of SI 1997/1712 art.3.

Subs.(8)(b) as amended by Act of Adjournal (Amendment of the Criminal Procedure (Scotland) Act 1995) (Appeal by Stated Case) 2009 (SSI 2009/108) art.2 (effective 8 April 2009).

Subs.(11) inserted by Double Jeopardy (Scotland) Act 2011 (asp 16) Sch.1 para.15. Brought into force on 28 November 2011 by SSI 2011/365 (C.34) art.3.

Subss.(8)(b), (9) as amended by Courts Reform (Scotland) Act 2014 (asp 8) Sch.3 para.8. Brought into force on 22 September 2015 by SSI 2015/247 (C.35) art.2 and Sch, subject to transitional provisions in art.6.

DEFINITIONS

"judge": s.307(1). **A4-382.1**

[THE NEXT PARAGRAPH IS A4-383]

GENERAL NOTE

There are only two practical points which need to be emphasised. First, many appeals are deemed to be abandoned because adjustments are not lodged or because the appellant does not intimate that he has no adjustments to propose. This requirement still exists in subs.(3). Similarly, within one week of receiving the stated case itself it should be lodged with the Clerk of the Sheriff Appeal Court: subs.(9). Failure to comply with that requirement also results in an appeal being deemed to be abandoned: subs.(10). **A4-383**

Secondly, adjustments must relate to the evidence heard or purported to have been heard at trial not to any fresh evidence: subs.(2). Adjustments can be proposed to: (1) findings in fact: see *Wilson v Carmichael*, 1982 S.C.C.R. 528; (2) the trial judge's note: see *Ballantyne v MacKinnon*, 1983 S.C.C.R. 97, and *MacDonald v Scott*, 1993 S.C.C.R. 78; and (3) questions of law: see *O'Hara v Tudhope*, 1984 S.C.C.R. 283. However, if any adjustments are rejected by the judge then reasons for that rejection must be given: subs.(7)(a). The court can take account of material rejected by the sheriff: see *Wilson v Carmichael* above, and s.182 below.

In *Amoco (UK) Exploration Company v Frame* [2008] HCJAC 49 (16 September 2008) the sheriff rejected proposed adjustments (relating to evidence about a statutory defence) and gave as his reason that they did not accord with his recollection or the inferences he had drawn. The Advocate depute was able to confirm to the Appeal Court that evidence to support the matters dealt with in the proposed adjustments in question had indeed been led in the course of the trial and that no contrary evidence had been led on behalf of the Crown. The Court considered that the sheriff's approach was unsatisfactory and that he had not given any good reason for rejecting the adjustments in question. In the circumstances, the Court considered that it was open to them to have regard to the various matters of fact which were set out in the adjustments.

Where reasons are not given the case may be remitted for the purpose of having reasons given. That was done in *Owens v Crowe*, 1994 S.C.C.R. 310 and on reporting the sheriff gave sound reasons.

Leave to appeal against conviction etc.

A4-384 **180.—**(1) The decision whether to grant leave to appeal for the purposes of section 175(2)(a) or (d) of this Act shall be made by an Appeal Sheriff of the Sheriff Appeal Court who shall—

(a) if he considers that the documents mentioned in subsection (2) below disclose arguable grounds of appeal, grant leave to appeal and make such comments in writing as he considers appropriate; and

(b) in any other case—

(i) refuse leave to appeal and give reasons in writing for the refusal; and

(ii) where the appellant is on bail and the sentence imposed on his conviction is one of imprisonment, grant a warrant to apprehend and imprison him.

(2) The documents referred to in subsection (1) above are—

(a) the stated case lodged under subsection (9) of section 179 of this Act; and

(b) the documents transmitted to the Clerk of the Sheriff Appeal Court under subsection (8)(b) of that section.

(3) A warrant granted under subsection (1)(b)(ii) above shall not take effect until the expiry of the period of 14 days mentioned in subsection (4) below (and if that period is extended under subsection (4A) below before the period being extended expires, until the expiry of the period as so extended) without an application to the Sheriff Appeal Court for leave to appeal having been lodged by the appellant under subsection (4) below.

(4) Where leave to appeal is refused under subsection (1) above the appellant may, within 14 days of intimation under subsection (10) below, apply to the Sheriff Appeal Court for leave to appeal.

(4A) The Sheriff Appeal Court may, on cause shown, extend the period of 14 days mentioned in subsection (4) above, or that period as extended under this subsection, whether or not the period to be extended has expired (and if that period of 14 days has expired, whether or not it expired before section 25(1) of the Criminal Proceedings etc. (Reform) (Scotland) Act 2007 (asp 6) came into force).

(5) In deciding an application under subsection (4) above the Sheriff Appeal Court shall—

(a) if, after considering the documents mentioned in subsection (2) above and the reasons for the refusal, the court is of the opinion that there are arguable grounds of appeal, grant leave to appeal and make such comments in writing as the court considers appropriate; and

(b) in any other case—

(i) refuse leave to appeal and give reasons in writing for the refusal; and

(ii) where the appellant is on bail and the sentence imposed on his conviction is one of imprisonment, grant a warrant to apprehend and imprison him.

(6) The question whether to grant leave to appeal under subsection (1) or (5) above shall be considered and determined in chambers without the parties being present.

(7) Comments in writing made under subsection (1)(a) or (5)(a) above may, without prejudice to the generality of that provision, specify the arguable grounds of appeal (whether or not they are contained in the stated case) on the basis of which leave to appeal is granted.

(8) Where the arguable grounds of appeal are specified by virtue of subsection (7) above it shall not, except by leave of the Sheriff Appeal Court on cause shown, be competent for the appellant to found any aspect of his appeal on any ground of appeal contained in the stated case but not so specified.

(9) Any application by the appellant for the leave of the Sheriff Appeal Court under subsection (8) above—

(a) shall be made within 14 days of the date of intimation under subsection (10) below; and

(b) shall, within 14 days of that date, be intimated by the appellant to the prosecutor.

(9A) The Sheriff Appeal Court may, on cause shown, extend the periods of 14 days mentioned in subsection (9) above.

(10) The Clerk of the Sheriff Appeal Court shall forthwith intimate—

(a) a decision under subsection (1) or (5) above; and

(b) in the case of a refusal of leave to appeal, the reasons for the decision,

to the appellant or his solicitor and to the prosecutor.

AMENDMENTS

Subs.(3) as amended and subs.(4A) inserted by Criminal Proceedings etc. (Reform) (Scotland) Act 2007 (asp 6) s.25. Brought into force on 10 December 2007 by SSI 2007/479.

Subs.(9) as amended and subs.(9A) inserted by Criminal Proceedings etc (Reform) (Scotland) Act 2007 (asp 6) s.80 and Sch. para.18(2). Brought into force on 23 April 2007 by SSI 2007/250 (C.23) art.3.

Section 180 as amended by Courts Reform (Scotland) Act 2014 (asp 8) Sch.3 para.9. Brought into force on 22 September 2015 by SSI 2015/247 (C.35) art.2 and Sch, subject to transitional provisions in art.6.

DEFINITIONS

"bail": s.307(1). A4-384.1

"judge": s.307(1).

[THE NEXT PARAGRAPH IS A4-385]

GENERAL NOTE

This section mirrors so far as possible the provisions for solemn appeals which are to be found in s.107. Reference therefore might conveniently be made to the general note to that section. A4-385

In *Akram v HM Advocate*, 2010 S.C.C.R. 30 a person convicted under summary procedure petitioned the *nobile officium* successfully to set aside the decision of the second sift and consider the question of leave to appeal *de novo*. The majority held the petition to be competent but it should be noted that Lord Emslie dissented in some detail and that a differently constituted court, in *Harris (Stuart) v HM Advocate*, 2010 S.C.C.R. 50, agreed with Lord Emslie that the case might require to be revisited.

In *FB v Murphy*, 2015 S.C.C.R. 175 it was emphasised that the decisions at sift are to be taken under reference to the questions posed in the stated case, not to the content of the original application for a stated case.

[THE NEXT PARAGRAPH IS A4-389]

Stated case: directions by Sheriff Appeal Court

A4-389 **181.**—(1) Without prejudice to any other power of relief which the Sheriff Appeal Court may have, where it appears to that court on application made in accordance with subsection (2) below, that the applicant has failed to comply with any of the requirements of—

(a) subsection (1) of section 176 of this Act; or

(b) subsection (1) or (9) of section 179 of this Act,

the Sheriff Appeal Court may direct that such further period of time as it may think proper be afforded to the applicant to comply with any requirement of the aforesaid provisions.

(1A) Where an application for a direction under subsection (1)—

(a) is made by the person convicted, and

(b) relates to the requirements of section 176(1),

the Sheriff Appeal Court may make a direction only if it is satisfied that doing so is justified by exceptional circumstances.

(1B) In considering whether there are exceptional circumstances for the purpose of subsection (1A), the Sheriff Appeal Court must have regard to—

(a) the length of time that has elapsed between the expiry of the period mentioned in section 176(1)(a) and the making of the application,

(b) the reasons stated in accordance with subsection (2A)(a)(i),

(c) the proposed grounds of appeal.

(2) Any application for a direction under subsection (1) above shall be made in writing to the Clerk of the Sheriff Appeal Court and shall state the ground for the application, and, in the case of an application for the purposes of paragraph (a) of subsection (1) above, notification of the application shall be made by the appellant or his solicitor to the clerk of the court from which the appeal is to be taken, and the clerk shall thereupon transmit the complaint, documentary productions and any other proceedings in the cause to the Clerk of the Sheriff Appeal Court.

(2A) An application for a direction under subsection (1) in relation to the requirements of section 176(1) of this Act must—

(a) state—

(i) the reasons why the applicant failed to comply with the requirements of section 176(1), and

(ii) the proposed grounds of appeal, and

(b) be intimated in writing by the applicant to the respondent or the respondent's solicitor.

(2B) If the respondent so requests within 7 days of receipt of intimation of the application under subsection (2A)(b), the respondent must be given an opportunity to make representations before the application is determined.

(2C) […]

(3) The Sheriff Appeal Court shall dispose of any application under subsection (1) above in like manner as an application to review the decision of an inferior court on a grant of bail, but shall have power—

(a) to dispense with a hearing; and

(b) to make such enquiry in relation to the application as the court may think fit,

and when the Sheriff Appeal Court has disposed of the application the Clerk of the Sheriff Appeal Court shall inform the clerk of the inferior court of the result.

(4) […]

(5) If the Sheriff Appeal Court makes a direction under subsection (1), it must—

(a) give reasons for the decision in writing, and

(b) give the reasons in ordinary language.

Amendments

Subs.(4) inserted by Criminal Procedure (Amendment) (Scotland) Act 2004 (asp 5) s.24(4). Brought into force on 4 October 2004 by SSI 2004/405 (C.28).

Subss.(2A), (2B) and (2C) inserted, and subs.(3) as amended by Criminal Procedure (Legal Assistance, Detention and Appeals) (Scotland) Act 2010 (asp 15) s.5. Brought into force on 30 October 2010.

Subs.(4) repealed by Protection of Vulnerable Groups (Scotland) Act 2007 (asp 14) Sch.4 para.22. Brought into force on 28 February 2011 by SSI 2011/157 (C.13) art.2, subject to savings specified in art.5(1).

Subss.(1), (2), (3) and heading, as amended by Courts Reform (Scotland) Act 2014 (asp 8) Sch.3 para.10. Brought into force on 22 September 2015 by SSI 2015/247 (C.35) art.2 and Sch, subject to transitional provisions in art.6.

Subss.(1A), (1B), (5) inserted, subs.(2C) repealed, subs.(3)(a) as amended, by Criminal Justice (Scotland) Act 2016 (asp 1) s.89. Brought into force on 17 January 2017 by SSI 2016/426 art.2 and Sch.1 para.1.

General Note

The complex arrangements for applying for a stated case and thereafter attending to adjustments and hearings will all be done within a short time frame: see s.176(1) and s.179(1) to (9). A pragmatic power is granted to the Sheriff Appeal Court to afford an appropriate further time to comply with these arrangements: s.181(1). An application for a grant is made in writing: s.181(2). A hearing is not necessary and the High Court may make enquiry: subs.(5). **A4-390**

Stated case: hearing of appeal

182.—(1) A stated case under this Part of this Act shall be heard by the Sheriff Appeal Court on such date as it may fix. **A4-391**

(2) For the avoidance of doubt, where an appellant, in his application under section 176(1) of this Act (or in a duly made amendment or addition to that application), refers to an alleged miscarriage of justice, but in stating a case under section 179(7) of this Act the inferior court is unable to take the allegation into account, the Sheriff Appeal Court may nevertheless have regard to the allegation at a hearing under subsection (1) above.

(3) Except by leave of the Sheriff Appeal Court on cause shown, it shall not be competent for an appellant to found any aspect of his appeal on a matter not contained in his application under section 176(1) of this Act (or in a duly made amendment or addition to that application).

(4) Subsection (3) above shall not apply as respects any ground of appeal specified as an arguable ground of appeal by virtue of subsection (7) of section 180 of this Act.

(5) Without prejudice to any existing power of the Sheriff Appeal Court, that court may in hearing a stated case—

(a) order the production of any document or other thing connected with the proceedings;

(b) hear any evidence relevant to any alleged miscarriage of justice or order such evidence to be heard by an Appeal Sheriff at the Sheriff Appeal Court or by such other person as it may appoint for that purpose;

(c) take account of any circumstances relevant to the case which were not before the trial judge;

(d) remit to any fit person to enquire and report in regard to any matter or circumstance affecting the appeal;

(e) appoint a person with expert knowledge to act as assessor to the Sheriff Appeal Court in any case where it appears to the court that such expert knowledge is required for the proper determination of the case;

(f) take account of any matter proposed in any adjustment rejected by the trial judge and of the reasons for such rejection;

(g) take account of any evidence contained in a note of evidence such as is mentioned in section 179(7) of this Act.

(6) The Sheriff Appeal Court may at the hearing remit the stated case back to the inferior court to be amended and returned.

AMENDMENTS

Subs.(5)(b) as amended by Crime and Punishment (Scotland) Act 1997 (c.48) Sch.1 para.21(21) with effect from 1 August 1997 in terms of SI 1997/1712 art.3.

Subss.(1), (2), (3), (5) and (6) as amended by Courts Reform (Scotland) Act 2014 (asp 8) Sch.3 para.11. Brought into force on 22 September 2015 by SSI 2015/247 (C.35) art.2 and Sch, subject to transitional provisions in art.6.

DEFINITIONS

A4-391.1 "single court": s.307(1).

[THE NEXT PARAGRAPH IS A4-392]

GENERAL NOTE

A4-392 The court in *Egan v Normand*, 1997 S.C.C.R. 211 observed that it was unacceptable for an appellant at the hearing of an appeal to seek a postponement to allow enquiries to be made into a possible ground of appeal based on *Anderson v HM Advocate*. It remains the position (notwithstanding earlier strictures) that if in an application for a stated case a miscarriage of justice is alleged but for some reason has not been dealt with in the stated case itself, the Sheriff Appeal Court at a hearing of the appeal may still have regard to the earlier allegation: subs.(2). An appellant cannot himself found on a matter not contained in the application for a stated case without the leave of the court: subs.(3). See *West v McNaughtan*, 1990 S.C.C.R. 439; *Stein v Lowe*, 1991 S.C.C.R. 692; *Fulton v Lees*, 1992 S.C.C.R. 923; *Normand v Walker*, 1994 S.C.C.R. 875, and *Campbell v McClory*, 1996 G.W.D. 28–1659. However, if the appellant wishes to extend his position beyond any ground of appeal specified as an arguable ground of appeal then he may not do so: subs.(4).

Prior to disposing of the appeal the Sheriff Appeal Court has a wide range of powers to assist in attaining justice: subs.(5). Re para.(b) see *MacLeod v Lowe*, 1993 S.L.T. 475 and *Marshall v MacDougall*, 1987 S.L.T. 123. Re para.(c) see *Hogg v Heattle*, 1961 S.L.T. 38. Re para.(d) *Marshall v MacDougall*, above, but see also *Faroux v Brown*, 1996 S.C.C.R. 891. Paragraph (f) see *Wilson v Carmichael*, 1982 S.C.C.R. 528; *Paterson v Lees*, 1992 S.C.C.R. 300; *Ballantyne v MacKinnon*, 1983 S.C.C.R. 97 and *MacDonald v Scott*, 1993 S.C.C.R. 78. Subsection 6—see *Jackson v Vannet*, 1997 G.W.D. 23–1146.

Subs.(3)

In *Watt v Ralph*, 2007 S.C.C.R. 70, the Appeal Court said that, where a case has been stated and there subsequently arise other matters on which an appellant wishes to rely, he should make an application for leave under s.182(3), in writing, promptly, in a document headed "Application under s.182(3) of the Criminal Procedure (Scotland) Act 1995", setting out clearly and succinctly the basis upon which the application is made. That document should be lodged in court and intimated to the Crown sufficiently far in advance of the day on which leave is to be sought to allow the Court and the Crown time to give it mature consideration. Although the Court did not say so, it seems reasonable to assume that one element in that consideration is likely to be the obtaining of a report from the sheriff dealing with the proposed additional matters.

Stated case: disposal of appeal

A4-393 **183.**—(1) The Sheriff Appeal Court may, subject to subsection (3) below and to section 190(1) of this Act, dispose of a stated case by—

(a) remitting the cause to the inferior court with its opinion and any direction thereon;

(b) affirming the verdict of the inferior court;

(c) setting aside the verdict of the inferior court and either quashing the conviction or, subject to subsection (2) below, substituting therefor an amended verdict of guilty; or

(d) setting aside the verdict of the inferior court and granting authority to bring a new prosecution in accordance with section 185 of this Act.

(1A) Where an appeal against conviction is by virtue of section 11(7) of the Double Jeopardy (Scotland) Act 2011 (asp 16), paragraphs (a) and (d) of subsection (1) do not apply.

(2) An amended verdict of guilty substituted under subsection (1)(c) above must be one which could have been returned on the complaint before the inferior court.

(3) The Sheriff Appeal Court shall, in an appeal—

(a) against both conviction and sentence, subject to section 190(1) of this Act, dispose of the appeal against sentence; or

(b) by the prosecutor, against sentence, dispose of the appeal,

by exercise of the power mentioned in section 189(1) of this Act.

(4) In setting aside, under subsection (1) above, a verdict the Sheriff Appeal Court may quash any sentence imposed on the appellant as respects the complaint, and—

(a) in a case where it substitutes an amended verdict of guilty, whether or not the sentence related to the verdict set aside; or

(b) in any other case, where the sentence did not so relate,

may pass another (but not more severe) sentence in substitution for the sentence so quashed.

(5) For the purposes of subsections (3) and (4) above, "sentence" shall be construed as including disposal or order.

(6) Where an appeal against acquittal is sustained, the Sheriff Appeal Court may—

(a) convict and, subject to subsection (7) below, sentence the respondent;

(b) remit the case to the inferior court with instructions to convict and sentence the respondent, who shall be bound to attend any diet fixed by the court for such purpose; or

(c) remit the case to the inferior court with their opinion thereon.

(7) Where the Sheriff Appeal Court sentences the respondent under subsection (6)(a) above it shall not in any case impose a sentence beyond the maximum sentence which could have been passed by the inferior court.

(8) Any reference in subsection (6) above to convicting and sentencing shall be construed as including a reference to—

(a) convicting and making some other disposal; or

(b) convicting and deferring sentence.

(9) The Sheriff Appeal Court shall have power in an appeal under this Part of this Act to award such expenses both in the High Court and in the inferior court as it may think fit.

(10) Where, following an appeal, other than an appeal under section 175(2)(b) or (3) of this Act, the appellant remains liable to imprisonment or detention under the sentence of the inferior court, or is so liable under a sentence passed in the appeal proceedings the Sheriff Appeal Court shall have the power where at the time of disposal of the appeal the appellant—

(a) was at liberty on bail, to grant warrant to apprehend and imprison or detain the appellant for a term, to run from the date of such apprehension, not longer than that part of the term or terms of imprisonment or detention specified in the sentence brought under review which remained unexpired at the date of liberation;

(b) is serving a term or terms of imprisonment or detention imposed in relation to a conviction subsequent to the conviction appealed against, to exercise the like powers in regard to him as may be exercised, in relation to an appeal which has been abandoned, by a court of summary jurisdiction in pursuance of section 177(6) of this Act.

Amendments

Subs.(1A) inserted by Double Jeopardy (Scotland) Act 2011 (asp 16) Sch.1 para.16. Brought into force on 28 November 2011 by SSI 2011/365 (C.34) art.3.

Section 183 as amended by Courts Reform (Scotland) Act 2014 (asp 8) Sch.3 para.12. Brought into force on 22 September 2015 by SSI 2015/247 (C.35) art.2 and Sch, subject to transitional provisions in art.6.

Definitions

A4-393.1 "sentence": s.183(5).

[THE NEXT PARAGRAPH IS A4-394]

General Note

A4-394 The general approach to disposing of appeals by way of stated case in s.183 is very similar to the general approach to disposing of solemn appeals in s.118. Reference may be made to the General Note to that section.

Abandonment of appeal

A4-395 **184.**—(1) An appellant in an appeal such as is mentioned in section 176(1) of this Act may at any time prior to lodging the case with the Clerk of the Sheriff Appeal Court abandon his appeal by minute signed by himself or his solicitor, written on the complaint or lodged with the clerk of the inferior court, and intimated to the respondent or the respondent's solicitor, but such abandonment shall be without prejudice to any other competent mode of appeal, review, advocation or suspension.

(2) Subject to section 191 of this Act, on the case being lodged with the Clerk of the Sheriff Appeal Court, the appellant shall be held to have abandoned any other mode of appeal which might otherwise have been open to him.

Amendments

Subss.(1), (2) as amended by Courts Reform (Scotland) Act 2014 (asp 8) Sch.3 para.13. Brought into force on 22 September 2015 by SSI 2015/247 (C.35) art.2 and Sch, subject to transitional provisions in art.6.

New prosecution

Authorisation of new prosecution

A4-396 **185.**—(1) Subject to subsection (2) below, where authority is granted under section 183(1)(d) of this Act, a new prosecution may be brought charging the accused with the same or any similar offence arising out of the same facts; and the proceedings out of which the stated case arose shall not be a bar to such prosecution.

(2) In a new prosecution under this section the accused shall not be charged with an offence more serious than that of which he was convicted in the earlier proceedings.

(3) No sentence may be passed on conviction under the new prosecution which could not have been passed on conviction under the earlier proceedings.

(4) A new prosecution may be brought under this section, notwithstanding that any time limit (other than the time limit mentioned in subsection (5) below) for the commencement of such proceedings has elapsed.

(5) Proceedings in a prosecution under this section shall be commenced within two months of the date on which authority to bring the prosecution was granted.

(6) In proceedings in a new prosecution under this section it shall, subject to subsection (7) below, be competent for either party to lead any evidence which it was competent for him to lead in the earlier proceedings.

(7) The complaint in a new prosecution under this section shall identify any matters as respects which the prosecutor intends to lead evidence by virtue of subsection (6) above which would not have been competent but for that subsection.

(8) For the purposes of subsection (5) above, proceedings shall be deemed to be commenced—

(a) in a case where such warrant is executed without unreasonable delay, on the date on which a warrant to apprehend or to cite the accused is granted; and

(b) in any other case, on the date on which the warrant is executed.

(9) Where the two months mentioned in subsection (5) above elapse and no new prosecution has been brought under this section, the order under section 183(1)(d) of this Act setting aside the verdict shall have the effect, for all purposes, of an acquittal.

(10) On granting authority under section 183(1)(d) of this Act to bring a new prosecution, the Sheriff Appeal Court may, after giving the parties an opportunity of being heard, order the detention of the accused person in custody; but an accused person may not be detained by virtue of this subsection for a period of more than 40 days.

AMENDMENTS

Subs.(10) as amended by Courts Reform (Scotland) Act 2014 (asp 8) Sch.3 para.14. Brought into force on September 22, 2015 by SSI 2015/247 (C.35) art.2 and Sch, subject to transitional provisions in art.6.

GENERAL NOTE

See notes to s.183, para.(d) above, for examples. In *Heywood, Petr*, 1998 S.C.C.R. 335, the Crown brought a petition to the nobile officium to amend the record of the interlocutor pronounced by the court which did not reflect the fact that the Crown had been granted leave to raise a fresh prosecution in respect of all charges. In granting the petition the court held that as the order granting authority had been pronounced in open court the Crown needed no further authority to bring a fresh prosecution. **A4-396.1**

[THE NEXT PARAGRAPH IS A4-397]

Appeals against sentence

Appeals against sentence only

186.—(1) An appeal under 175(2)(b), (c) or (cza), or by virtue of section 175(4), of this Act shall be by note of appeal, which shall state the ground of appeal. **A4-397**

(2) The note of appeal shall, where the appeal is—

(a) under 175(2)(b), (c) or (cza) be lodged, within one week of—

(i) the passing of the sentence; or

(ii) the making of the order disposing of the case or deferring sentence,

(iii) […]

with the clerk of the court from which the appeal is to be taken; or

(b) by virtue of section 175(4) be so lodged within four weeks of such passing or making.

(3) The clerk of court on receipt of the note of appeal shall—

(a) send a copy of the note to the respondent or his solicitor; and

(b) obtain a report from the judge who sentenced the convicted person or, as the case may be, who disposed of the case or deferred sentence.

(4) Subject to subsection (5) below, the clerk of court shall within two weeks of the passing of the sentence or within two weeks of the disposal or order against which the appeal is taken—

(a) send to the Clerk of the Sheriff Appeal Court the note of appeal, together with the report mentioned in subsection (3)(b) above, a certified copy of the complaint, the minute of proceedings and any other relevant documents; and

(b) send copies of that report to the appellant and respondent or their solicitors.

(5) The sheriff principal of the sheriffdom in which the judgment was pronounced may, on cause shown, extend the period of two weeks specified in subsection (4) above for such period as he considers reasonable.

(6) Subject to subsection (4) above, the report mentioned in subsection (3)(b) above shall be available only to the Sheriff Appeal Court, the parties and, on such conditions as may be prescribed by Act of Adjournal, such other persons or classes of persons as may be so prescribed.

(7) Where the judge's report is not furnished within the period mentioned in subsection (4) above or such period as extended under subsection (5) above, the Sheriff Appeal Court may extend such period, or, if it thinks fit, hear and determine the appeal without the report.

(8) Section 181 of this Act shall apply where an appellant fails to comply with the requirement of subsection (2)(a) above as they apply where an applicant fails to comply with any of the requirements of section 176(1) of this Act.

(9) An appellant under 175(2)(b), (c) or (cza), or by virtue of section 175(4), of this Act may at any time prior to the hearing of the appeal abandon his appeal by minute, signed by himself or his solicitor, lodged—

(a) in a case where the note of appeal has not yet been sent under subsection (4)(a) above to the Clerk of the Sheriff Appeal Court, with the clerk of court;

(b) in any other case, with the Clerk of the Sheriff Appeal Court,

and intimated to the respondent.

(10) Sections 176(5), 177 and 182(5)(a) to (e) of this Act shall apply to appeals under 175(2)(b), (c) or (cza), or by virtue of section 175(4), of this Act as they apply to appeals under section 175(2)(a) or (d) of this Act, except that, for the purposes of such application to any appeal by virtue of section 175(4), references in subsections (1) to (4) of section 177 to the appellant shall be construed as references to the convicted person and subsections (6) and (7) of that section shall be disregarded.

AMENDMENTS

Subs.(5) as amended by Bail, Judicial Appointments etc. (Scotland) Act 2000 (asp 9) s.12 and Sch. para.7(4).

Subs.(2) as amended by Criminal Procedure (Amendment) (Scotland) Act 2004 (asp 5) s.24(5). Brought into force on 4 October 2004 by SSI 2004/405 (C.28).

Subss.(1), (2), (9), (10) as amended by Protection of Children (Scotland) Act 2003 (asp 5) s.16(8). Brought into force on 10 January 2005 by SSI 2004/522 (C.38) art.2.

Subs.(5) as amended by Criminal Proceedings etc. (Reform) (Scotland) Act 2007 (asp 6) s.25. Brought into force on 10 December 2007 by SSI 2007/479.

Subss.(1), (2)(a), (9), (10) as amended by Criminal Justice and Licensing (Scotland) Act 2010 (asp 13) Sch.2 para.13. Brought into force on 13 December 2010 (subject to savings provisions in art.3) by SSI 2010/413 (C.28) art.2 Sch.1 para.1.

Subss.(1), (2), (9) and (10) as amended by Protection of Vulnerable Groups (Scotland) Act 2007 (asp 14) Sch.4 para.23. Brought into force on 28 February 2011 by SSI 2011/157 (C.13) art.2, subject to savings specified in art.5(1).

Subss.(4), (6), (7), (9) as amended by Courts Reform (Scotland) Act 2014 (asp 8) Sch.3 para.15. Brought into force on 22 September 2015 by SSI 2015/247 (C.35) art.2 and Sch, subject to transitional provisions in art.6.

DEFINITIONS

A4-397.1 "judge": s.307(1).
"sentence": s.307(1).

[THE NEXT PARAGRAPH IS A4-398]

GENERAL NOTE

A4-398 An appeal against sentence is taken by note of appeal, lodged within one week of the sentence appealed against (or within four weeks in the case of a prosecutor's appeal). The note of appeal is required to state the ground of appeal (subs.(1)) and this has sometimes been construed quite strictly. In *Campbell v McDougall*, 1991 S.C.C.R. 218, the note of appeal simply asserted "The sentence is excessive. No previous convictions libelled". The High Court refused the appeal because of "the complete and total lack of any ground of appeal being stated in the grounds of appeal which are stated to the sheriff". It is, however, arguable that the same principles should be applied as are applied to applications for stated cases (see the annotations to s.176). In particular, following *Crowe, Petitioner*, 1994 S.C.C.R. 784, it might well be that the appeal can proceed if the matter to be brought under review is identified with sufficient specification to enable a report to be written.

Leave to appeal against sentence

187.—(1) The decision whether to grant leave to appeal for the purposes of 175(2)(b), (c) or (cza) of this Act shall be made by an Appeal Sheriff of the Sheriff Appeal Court who shall— **A4-399**

(a) if he considers that the note of appeal and other documents sent to the Clerk of the Sheriff Appeal Court under section 186(4)(a) of this Act disclose arguable grounds of appeal, grant leave to appeal and make such comments in writing as he considers appropriate; and

(b) in any other case—

(i) refuse leave to appeal and give reasons in writing for the refusal; and

(ii) where the appellant is on bail and the sentence imposed on his conviction is one of imprisonment, grant a warrant to apprehend and imprison him.

(2) A warrant granted under subsection (1)(b)(ii) above shall not take effect until the expiry of the period of 14 days mentioned in subsection (3) below (and if that period is extended under subsection (3A) below before the period being extended expires, until the expiry of the period as so extended) without an application to the Sheriff Appeal Court for leave to appeal having been lodged by the appellant under subsection (3) below.

(3) Where leave to appeal is refused under subsection (1) above the appellant may, within 14 days of intimation under subsection (9) below, apply to the Sheriff Appeal Court for leave to appeal.

(3A) The Sheriff Appeal Court may, on cause shown, extend the period of 14 days mentioned in subsection (3) above, or that period as extended under this subsection, whether or not the period to be extended has expired (and if theat period of 14 days has expired, whether or not it expired before section 25(3) of the Criminal Proceedings etc. (Reform) (Scotland) Act (asp 6) came into force).

(4) In deciding an application under subsection (3) above the Sheriff Appeal Court shall—

(a) if, after considering the note of appeal and other documents mentioned in subsection (1) above and the reasons for the refusal, it is of the opinion that there are arguable grounds of appeal, grant leave to appeal and make such comments in writing as he considers appropriate; and

(b) in any other case—

(i) refuse leave to appeal and give reasons in writing for the refusal; and

(ii) where the appellant is on bail and the sentence imposed on his conviction is one of imprisonment, grant a warrant to apprehend and imprison him.

(5) The question whether to grant leave to appeal under subsection (1) or (4) above shall be considered and determined in chambers without the parties being present.

(6) Comments in writing made under subsection (1)(a) or (4)(a) above may, without prejudice to the generality of that provision, specify the arguable grounds of appeal (whether or not they are contained in the note of appeal) on the basis of which leave to appeal is granted.

(7) Where the arguable grounds of appeal are specified by virtue of subsection (6) above it shall not, except by leave of the Sheriff Appeal Court on cause shown, be competent for the appellant to found any aspect of his appeal on any ground of appeal contained in the note of appeal but not so specified.

(8) Any application by the appellant for the leave of the Sheriff Appeal Court under subsection (7) above—

(a) shall be made within 14 days of the date of intimation under subsection (9) below; and

(b) shall, within 14 days of that date, be intimated by the appellant to the prosecutor.

(8A) The Sheriff Appeal Court may, on cause shown, extend the periods of 14 days mentioned in subsection (8) above.

(9) The Clerk of the Sheriff Appeal Court shall forthwith intimate—

(a) a decision under subsection (1) or (4) above; and

(b) in the case of a refusal of leave to appeal, the reasons for the decision,

to the appellant or his solicitor and to the prosecutor.

AMENDMENTS

Subs.(1) as amended by Protection of Children (Scotland) Act 2003 (asp 5) s.16(9). Brought into force on 10 January 2005 by SSI 2004/522 (C.38) art.2.

Subs.(2) as amended and subs.(3A) inserted by Criminal Proceedings etc. (Reform) (Scotland) Act 2007 (asp 6) s.25. Brought into force on 10 December 2007 by SSI 2007/479.

Subs.(8) as amended and subs.(8A) inserted by Criminal Proceedings etc (Reform) (Scotland) Act 2007 (asp 6) s.80 and Sch. para.18(3). Brought into force on 23 April 2007 by SSI 2007/250 (C.23) art.3.

Subs.(1) as amended by Criminal Justice and Licensing (Scotland) Act 2010 (asp 13) Sch.2 para.14. Brought into force on 13 December 2010 (subject to savings provisions in art.3) by SSI 2010/413 (C.28) art.2, Sch.1 para.1.

Subs.(1) as amended by Protection of Vulnerable Groups (Scotland) Act 2007 (asp 14) Sch.4 para.24. Brought into force on 28 February 2011 by SSI 2011/157 (C.13) art.2, subject to savings specified in art.5(1).

Section 187 as amended by Courts Reform (Scotland) Act 2014 (asp 8) Sch.3 para.16. Brought into force on September 22, 2015 by SSI 2015/247 (C.35) art.2 and Sch, subject to transitional provisions in art.6.

DEFINITIONS

A4-399.1 "bail": s.307(1).
"judge": s.307(1).
"sentence": s.307(1).

[THE NEXT PARAGRAPH IS A4-400]

GENERAL NOTE

A4-400 The procedure to be followed in regard to appeals against summary sentences necessarily requires leave to appeal. The note of appeal containing the ground of appeal is placed before a single judge in chambers along with, principally, the trial judge's report: subs.(1)(a). There is consideration and determination without the parties being present: subs.(5). As there is no longer the opportunity to explain or expand upon the grounds of appeal by advocacy the written note of appeal assumes far greater significance: such a note no longer merely initiates an appeal, it is now the substance of the leave to appeal. When leave to appeal is refused further application can be made: subs.(3) which follows identical procedure under, e.g. s.180(3).

Disposal of appeals

Setting aside conviction or sentence: prosecutor's consent or application

A4-401 **188.—**(1) Without prejudice to section 175(3) or (4) of this Act, where—

(a) an appeal has been taken under section 175(2) of this Act or by suspension or otherwise and the prosecutor is not prepared to maintain the judgment appealed against he may, by a relevant minute, consent to the conviction or sentence or, as the case may be, conviction and sentence ("sentence" being construed in this section as including disposal or order) being set aside either in whole or in part; or

(b) no such appeal has been taken but the prosecutor is, at any time, not prepared to maintain the judgment on which a conviction is founded or the sentence imposed following such conviction he may, by a relevant minute, apply for the conviction or sentence or, as the case may be, conviction and sentence to be set aside.

(2) For the purposes of subsection (1) above, a "relevant minute" is a minute, signed by the prosecutor—

(a) setting forth the grounds on which he is of the opinion that the judgment cannot be maintained; and

(b) written on the complaint or lodged with the clerk of court.

(3) A copy of any minute under subsection (1) above shall be sent by the prosecutor to the convicted person or his solicitor and the clerk of court shall—

(a) thereupon ascertain and note on the record, whether that person or solicitor desires to be heard by the Sheriff Appeal Court before the appeal, or as the case may be application, is disposed of; and

(b) thereafter transmit the complaint and relative proceedings to the Clerk of the Sheriff Appeal Court.

(4) The Clerk of the Sheriff Appeal Court, on receipt of a complaint and relative proceedings transmitted under subsection (3) above, shall lay them before any Appeal Sheriff of the Sheriff Appeal Court either in court or in chambers who, after hearing parties if they desire to be heard, may—

(a) set aside the conviction or the sentence, or both, either in whole or in part and—

(i) award such expenses to the convicted person, both in the Sheriff Appeal Court and in the inferior court, as the Appeal Sheriff may think fit;

(ii) where the conviction is set aside in part, pass another (but not more severe) sentence in substitution for the sentence imposed in respect of that conviction; and

(iii) where the sentence is set aside, pass another (but not more severe) sentence; or

(b) refuse to set aside the conviction or sentence or, as the case may be, conviction and sentence, in which case the complaint and proceedings shall be returned to the clerk of the inferior court.

(5) Where an appeal has been taken and the complaint and proceedings in respect of that appeal returned under subsection (4)(b) above, the appellant shall be entitled to proceed with the appeal as if it had been marked on the date of their being received by the clerk of the inferior court on such return.

(6) Where an appeal has been taken and a copy minute in respect of that appeal sent under subsection (3) above, the preparation of the draft stated case shall be delayed pending the decision of the Sheriff Appeal Court.

(7) The period from an application being made under subsection (1)(b) above until its disposal under subsection (4) above (including the day of application and the day of disposal) shall, in relation to the conviction to which the application relates, be disregarded in any computation of time specified in any provision of this Part of this Act.

Amendments

Subss.(3), (4), (6) as amended by Courts Reform (Scotland) Act 2014 (asp 8) Sch.3 para.17. Brought into force on September 22, 2015 by SSI 2015/247 (C.35) art.2 and Sch, subject to transitional provisions in art.6.

Definitions

A4-401.1 "complaint": s.307(1).
"prosecutor": s.307(1).
"relevant minute": s.188(2).
"sentence": s.188(1)(a).

[THE NEXT PARAGRAPH IS A4-402]

General Note

A4-402 A set of procedural or other circumstances may have arisen resulting in a clear and unequivocal miscarriage of justice having occurred so that the Crown would not wish to maintain a judgment. This section provides for a conviction being set aside with the prosecutor's consent or on the prosecutor's application depending on the circumstances.

Subsection (2)(a)—in *MacRae v Hingston*, 1992 S.L.T. 1197 the Appeal Court made it clear that where the procedure under this section is to be used any minute should be accompanied by sufficient material to satisfy the single judge that grounds of law exist to set aside the conviction.

Subs.(4)(b)— see *O'Brien v Adair*, 1947 J.C. 180 where the court refused to set aside a conviction. On the general question of expenses see *Lawrie & Symington Ltd v Donaldson*, 2009 S.L.T. 723; 2009 S.C.C.R. 640.

Disposal of appeal against sentence

A4-403 **189.**—(1) An appeal against sentence by note of appeal shall be heard by the Sheriff Appeal Court on such date as it may fix, and the Sheriff Appeal Court may, subject to section 190(1) of this Act, dispose of such appeal by—

(a) affirming the sentence; or

(b) if the Court thinks that, having regard to all the circumstances, including any evidence such as is mentioned in section 175(5) of this Act, a different sentence should have been passed, quashing the sentence and, subject to subsection (2) below, passing another sentence, whether more or less severe, in substitution therefor.

(2) In passing another sentence under subsection (1)(b) above, the Court shall not in any case increase the sentence beyond the maximum sentence which could have been passed by the inferior court.

(2A) […]

(3) The Sheriff Appeal Court shall have power in an appeal by note of appeal to award such expenses both in the Sheriff Appeal Court and in the inferior court as it may think fit.

(4) Where, following an appeal under section 175(2)(b) or (c), or by virtue of section 175(4), of this Act, the convicted person remains liable to imprisonment or detention under the sentence of the inferior court or is so liable under a sentence passed in the appeal proceedings, the Sheriff Appeal Court shall have power where at the time of disposal of the appeal the convicted person—

(a) was at liberty on bail, to grant warrant to apprehend and imprison or detain the appellant for a term, to run from the date of such apprehension, not longer than that part of the term or terms of imprisonment or detention specified in the sentence brought under review which remained unexpired at the date of liberation; or

(b) is serving a term or terms of imprisonment or detention imposed in relation to a conviction subsequent to the conviction in respect of which the sentence appealed against was imposed, to exercise the like powers in regard to him as may be exercised, in relation to an appeal which has been abandoned, by a court of summary jurisdiction in pursuance of section 177(6) of this Act.

(5) In subsection (1) above, "appeal against sentence" shall, without prejudice to the generality of the expression, be construed as including an appeal under section 175(2)(c) or (cza), and any appeal by virtue of section 175(4), of this Act; and without prejudice to subsection (6) below, other references to sentence in that subsection and in subsection (4) above shall be construed accordingly.

(6) In disposing of any appeal in a case where the accused has not been convicted, the Sheriff Appeal Court may proceed to convict him; and where it does, the reference in subsection (4) above to the conviction in respect of which the sentence appealed against was imposed shall be construed as a reference to the disposal or order appealed against.

(7) In disposing of an appeal under section 175(2)(b) to (d), (3)(b) or (4) of this Act the Sheriff Appeal Court may, without prejudice to any other power in that regard, pronounce an opinion on—

(a) the sentence or other disposal or order which is appropriate in any similar case;

(b) [...]

AMENDMENTS

Subs.(1)(b) as amended by Crime and Punishment (Scotland) Act 1997 (c.48) Sch.1 para.21(22) with effect from 1 August 1997 in terms of SI 1997/1712 art.3.

Subss.(2A), (7)(b) inserted, and (7) as amended, by Protection of Children (Scotland) Act 2003 (asp 5) s.16(10). Brought into force on 10 January 2005 by SSI 2004/522 (C.38) art.2.

Subs.(5) as amended by Criminal Justice and Licensing (Scotland) Act 2010 (asp 13) Sch.2 para.15. Brought into force on 13 December 2010 (subject to savings provisions in art.3) by SSI 2010/413 (C.28) art.2, Sch.1 para.1.

Subs.(2A) repealed and subs.(7) as amended by Protection of Vulnerable Groups (Scotland) Act 2007 (asp 14) Sch.4 para.25. Brought into force on 28 February 2011 by SSI 2011/157 (C.13) art.2, subject to savings specified in art.5(1).

Subss.(1), (3), (4), (6), (7) as amended by Courts Reform (Scotland) Act 2014 (asp 8) Sch.3 para.18. Brought into force on 22 September 2015 by SSI 2015/247 (C.35) art.2 and Sch, subject to transitional provisions in art.6.

DEFINITIONS

"appeal against sentence": s.189(5). A4-403.1
"sentence": s.307(1).

[THE NEXT PARAGRAPH IS A4-404]

GENERAL NOTE

Subs. (1)

The sole test for appeals is whetherthere has been a miscarriage ofjustice and the question in relation to sentence is whether the sentence complained of is excessive: *Addison v Mackinnon* 1983 S.C.C.R. 52: *Donaldson v HM Advocate*, 1983 S.C.C.R. 216. The Sheriff Appeal Court may affirm the sentence or quash it and impose another of greater or lesser severity. The latter option is not often used to increase a summary sentence although it has been done: *Briggs v Guild*, 1987 S.C.C.R. 141. The appellate court is not authorised to alter a sentence on a charge which has not been appealed: see *Allan, Petr*, 1993 S.C.C.R. 686. In *Kelly v Vannet*, 2000 S.L.T. 75 in an appeal against sentence itwas held that the appellant had pled to a non offence and an absolute discharge was substituted. A4-404

Disposal of appeal where appellant not criminally responsible

190.—(1) In relation to any appeal under section 175(2) of this Act, the Sheriff Appeal Court shall, where it appears to it that the appellant committed the act charged against him but that he was not, because of section 51A of this Act, criminally responsible for it, dispose of the appeal by— A4-405

(a) setting aside the verdict of the inferior court and substituting therefor a verdict of acquittal by reason of the special defence set out in section 51A of this Act; and

(b) quashing any sentence imposed on the appellant as respects the complaint and—

(i) making, in respect of the appellant, any order mentioned in section 57(2)(a) to (d) of this Act; or

(ii) making no order.

(2) Subsections (3) to (6) of section 57 of this Act shall apply to an order made under subsection (1)(b)(i) above as it applies to an order made under subsection (2) of that section.

AMENDMENTS

Subs.(2) as amended by Mental Health (Care and Treatment) (Scotland) Act 2003 (asp 13) Sch.4 para.8(12). Brought into force on 5 October 2005 by SSI 2005/161 (C.6).

Heading and subs.(1) as amended by Criminal Justice and Licensing (Scotland) Act 2010 (asp 13) Sch.7 paras 57 and 58. Brought into force on 25 June 2012 by SSI 2012/160 (C.15) art.3.

Subs.(1) as amended by Courts Reform (Scotland) Act 2014 (asp 8) Sch.3 para.19. Brought into force on 22 September 2015 by SSI 2015/247 (C.35) art.2 and Sch, subject to transitional provisions in art.6.

Miscellaneous

Appeal by suspension or advocation on ground of miscarriage of justice

A4-406 **191.**—(1) Notwithstanding section 184(2) of this Act, a party to a summary prosecution may, where an appeal under section 175 of this Act would be incompetent or would in the circumstances be inappropriate, appeal to the Sheriff Appeal Court, by bill of suspension against a conviction or, as the case may be, by advocation against an acquittal on the ground of an alleged miscarriage of justice in the proceedings.

(2) Where the alleged miscarriage of justice is referred to in an application under section 176(1) of this Act, for a stated case as regards the proceedings (or in a duly made amendment or addition to that application), an appeal under subsection (1) above shall not proceed without the leave of the Sheriff Appeal Court until the appeal to which the application relates has been finally disposed of or abandoned.

(3) Sections 182(5)(a) to (e), 183(1)(d) and (4) and 185 of this Act shall apply to appeals under this section as they apply to appeals such as are mentioned in section 176(1) of this Act.

(4) This section is without prejudice to any rule of law relating to bills of suspension or advocation in so far as such rule of law is not inconsistent with this section.

AMENDMENTS

Subss.(1)-(3) as amended by Courts Reform (Scotland) Act 2014 (asp 8) Sch.3 para.20. Brought into force on 22 September 2015 by SSI 2015/247 (C.35) art.2 and Sch, subject to transitional provisions in art.6.

GENERAL NOTE

A4-406.1 The classic definition of a Bill of Suspension is Lord Wheatley's in *McGregor v MacNeil*, 1975 J.C. 57:

> "Suspension is a competent method of review, available in summary proceedings only when some step in the procedure has gone wrong or some factor has emerged which satisfies the court that a miscarriage of justice has taken place resulting in a failure to do justice to the accused."

Suspension, then, is available only to the accused and, in terms of s.130 of this Act, only in summary cases. It is a process whereby a warrant, conviction or judgment issued by an inferior judge may be reviewed. The present section is concerned with appeals against conviction. The Bill of Advocation is available to both prosecution and defence (see *Durant v Lockhart*, 1985 S.C.C.R. 72) and in both solemn and summary proceedings. It is also available at any stage of proceedings. Here, we are concerned with its use in summary proceedings as a mode of appeal against acquittal. So far as possible, procedure is (by subs.(3) equiparated to that in appeals by stated case.

Time limit for lodging bills of advocation and bills of suspension

191A.—(1) This section applies where a party wishes— A4-406.2

(a) to appeal to the Sheriff Appeal Court under section 191(1) of this Act by bill of suspension against a conviction or by advocation against an acquittal, or

(b) to appeal to the Sheriff Appeal Court against, or to bring under review of the Sheriff Appeal Court, any other decision in a summary prosecution by bill of suspension or by advocation.

(2) The party must lodge the bill of suspension or bill of advocation within 3 weeks of the date of the conviction, acquittal or, as the case may be, other decision to which the bill relates.

(3) The Sheriff Appeal Court may, on the application of the party, extend the time limit in subsection (2).

(4) An application under subsection (3) must—

(a) state—

(i) the reasons why the applicant failed to comply with the time limit in subsection (2), and

(ii) the proposed grounds of appeal or review, and

(b) be intimated in writing by the applicant to the other party to the prosecution.

(5) If the other party so requests within 7 days of receipt of intimation of the application under subsection (4)(b), the other party must be given an opportunity to make representations before the application is determined.

(6) Any representations may be made in writing or, if the other party so requests, orally at a hearing; and if a hearing is fixed, the applicant must also be given an opportunity to be heard.

AMENDMENTS

Section 191A inserted by Criminal Procedure (Legal Assistance, Detention and Appeals) (Scotland) Act 2010 (asp 15) s.6. Brought into force on 30 October 2010, subject to s.6(2) of the 2010 Act.

Subs.(1) as amended by Courts Reform (Scotland) Act 2014 (asp 8) Sch.3 para.21. Brought into force on 22 September 2015 by SSI 2015/247 (C.35) art.2 and Sch, subject to transitional provisions in art.6.

GENERAL NOTE

Such bills are intended to provide a swift remedy for readily discernible errors or irregularities especially of a procedural kind. Thus it is important that this avenue of review is taken up quickly after the occurrence giving rise to complaint; to benefit from the concession in subs.(3) extending the timescale for lodging, the affected party must first be able to account satisfactorily for the delay. In considering any Bill the court tests whether the stated point of appeal has substantial merit giving sufficient cause to suspend the interlocutor (or conviction). See *MacDonald v Procurator Fiscal, Dornoch* [2013] HCJAC 48 and *AMI v Dunn* [2014] HCJAC 9, both late bills refused. See *CH v Donnelly* [2013] HCJAC 17; 2013 S.C.C.R. 160, successful suspension of an initiating apprehension warrant, and *Blockley v Cameron* [2013] HCJAC 2; 2013 S.C.C.R. 181, the quashing of a sentence after the sheriff refused a motion to withdraw a guilty plea previously tendered. A4-406.3

Bill of advocation not competent in respect of certain decisions

191B. It is not competent to bring under review of the Sheriff Appeal Court by way of bill of advocation a decision of the court of first instance that relates to such objection or denial as is mentioned in section 144(4). A4-406.4

AMENDMENTS

Section 191B inserted by Criminal Justice (Scotland) Act 2016 (asp 1) s.93. Brought into force on 17 January 2017 by SSI 2016/426 art.2 and Sch.1 para.1.

[THE NEXT PARAGRAPH IS A4-407]

Appeals: miscellaneous provisions

A4-407 **192.**—(1) Where an appellant has been granted bail, whether his appeal is under this Part of this Act or otherwise, he shall appear personally in court at the diet appointed for the hearing of the appeal.

(2) Where an appellant who has been granted bail does not appear at such a diet, the Sheriff Appeal Court shall either—

(a) dispose of the appeal as if it had been abandoned (in which case subsection (5) of section 177 of this Act shall apply accordingly); or

(b) on cause shown permit the appeal to be heard in his absence.

(3) No conviction, sentence, judgement, order of court or other proceeding whatsoever in or for the purposes of summary proceedings under this Act—

(a) shall be quashed for want of form; or

(b) where the accused had legal assistance in his defence, shall be suspended or set aside in respect of any objections to—

(i) the relevancy of the complaint, or to the want of specification therein; or

(ii) the competency or admission or rejection of evidence at the trial in the inferior court,

unless such objections were timeously stated.

(4) The provisions regulating appeals shall, subject to the provisions of this Part of this Act, be without prejudice to any other mode of appeal competent.

(5) Any officer of law may serve any bill of suspension or other writ relating to an appeal.

AMENDMENTS

Subs.(2) as amended by Courts Reform (Scotland) Act 2014 (asp 8) Sch.3 para.23. Brought into force on 22 September 2015 by SSI 2015/247 (C.35) art.2 and Sch, subject to transitional provisions in art.6.

DEFINITIONS

A4-407.1 "bail": s.307(1).
"officer of law": s.307(1).
"sentence": s.307(1).

[THE NEXT PARAGRAPH IS A4-408]

GENERAL NOTE

A4-408 Subsection (3)(a)—see *Paterson v MacLennan* (1914) 7 Adam 128 where the accused was found guilty but not as libelled. The appeal was refused. See also *Ogilvie v Mitchell* (1903) 4 Adam 273; *Miller v Brown*, 1941 J.C. 2, and *Gilmour v Gray*, 1951 J.C. 70.

Subsection (2)—in *Gemmell v MacDougall*, 1993 S.C.C.R. 238 the appeal by stated case was continued on a number of occasions because the appellant was medically unfit to attend. On the motion of the Crown and in the presence of counsel for the appellant the appeal was heard in the absence of the appellant, the view being taken that as the appeal was on a question of law the appellant would not be prejudiced by his absence.

In *Pratt v Normand*, 1995 S.C.C.R. 881 the appellant failed to appear at the hearing of his appeal. The case was continued to give him an opportunity to appear. At the continued hearing he appeared and gave an explanation with which the Appeal Court were not satisfied. They refused the appeal for want of insistence: see also *Flynn v Vannet*, 1997 G.W.D. 31-1555.

First, highly pedantic points cannot be taken on procedural or other matters as no conviction, sentence, judgment, order of court or other proceedings in or for the purposes of summary proceedings can be quashed for want of form: subs.(3)(a).

Secondly, the failure to object timeously to the relevancy of the complaint or to the want of specification or to the competency or admission or rejection of evidence prevents later suspension of a conviction or sentence if the accused had legal assistance: subs.(3)(b). See e.g. *Jardine v Howdle*, 1997 S.C.C.R. 294 where an appeal against conviction, founding on the sheriff's placing a 13-yearold child on oath without ascertaining the age of a child witness or satisfying himself that the child understood the nature of the oath, was refused, no objection having been taken at the time.

If, however, the objection amounts to a fundamental nullity then this can be challenged at any time: see *Czajkowski v Lewis*, 1956 J.C. 8; *Coventry v Douglas*, 1944 J.C. 13; *Rendle v Muir*, 1952 J.C. 115; *Aitkenhead v Cuthbert*, 1962 J.C. 12, and *Shaw v Smith*, Crown Office circular A43/78.

Suspension of disqualification, forfeiture etc.

193.—(1) Where upon conviction of any person— A4-409

(a) any disqualification, forfeiture or disability attaches to him by reason of such conviction; or

(b) any property, matters or things which are the subject of the prosecution or connected therewith are to be or may be ordered to be destroyed or forfeited,

if the court before which he was convicted thinks fit, the disqualification, forfeiture or disability or, as the case may be, destruction or forfeiture or order for destruction or forfeiture shall be suspended pending the determination of any appeal against conviction or sentence (or disposal or order).

(2) Subsection (1) above does not apply in respect of any disqualification, forfeiture or, as the case may be, destruction or forfeiture or order for destruction or forfeiture under or by virtue of any enactment which contains express provision for the suspension of such disqualification, forfeiture or, as the case may be, destruction or forfeiture or order for destruction or forfeiture pending the determination of any appeal against conviction or sentence (or disposal or order).

(3) Where, upon conviction, a fine has been imposed upon a person or a compensation order has been made against him under section 249 of this Act—

(a) the fine or compensation order shall not be enforced against him and he shall not be liable to make any payment in respect of the fine or compensation order; and

(b) any money paid under the compensation order shall not be paid by the clerk of court to the entitled person under subsection (9) of that section,

pending the determination of any appeal against conviction or sentence (or disposal or order).

Suspension of certain sentences pending determination of appeal

193A.—(1) Where a convicted person or the prosecutor appeals to the Sheriff Appeal Court under section 175 of this Act, the court may on the application of the appellant direct that the whole, or any remaining part, of a relevant sentence shall be suspended until the appeal, if it is proceeded with, is determined. A4-409.1

(2) Where the court has directed the suspension of the whole or any remaining part of a person's relevant sentence, the person shall, unless the Sheriff Appeal Court otherwise directs, appear personally in court on the day or days fixed for the hearing of the appeal.

(3) Where a person fails to appear personally in court as mentioned in subsection (2) above, the court may—

(a) if he is the appellant—

(i) decline to consider the appeal; and

(ii) dismiss it summarily; or

(b) whether or not he is the appellant—

(i) consider and determine the appeal; or

(ii) make such other order as the court thinks fit.

(4) In this section "relevant sentence" means any one or more of the following—

(aa) a community payback order;

(d) a restriction of liberty order;

(e) […].

Amendments

Section 193A inserted by Crime and Punishment (Scotland) Act 1997 (c.48) s.24(2) with effect from 1 August 1997 in terms of SI 1997/1712 art.3.

Subs.(4)(d) inserted by Crime and Punishment (Scotland) Act 1997 (c.48) s.24(2) (effective 1 July 1998: SI 1998/2323).

Subs.(4)(e) inserted by Antisocial Behaviour etc. (Scotland) Act 2004 (asp 8) s.144(1), Sch.4 para.5(3). Brought into force on 28 October 2004 by SSI 2004/420 (C.31).

Subs.(1) as amended by Protection of Children (Scotland) Act 2003 (asp 5) s.16(11). Brought into force on 10 January 2005 by SSI 2004/522 (C.38) art.2.

Subs.(4) as amended by Criminal Justice and Licensing (Scotland) Act 2010 (asp 13) Sch.2 para.16. Brought into force on 13 December 2010 (subject to savings provisions in art.3) by SSI 2010/413 (C.28) art.2, Sch.1 para.1.

Subs.(1) as amended by Protection of Vulnerable Groups (Scotland) Act 2007 (asp 14) Sch.4 para.26. Brought into force on 28 February 2011 by SSI 2011/157 (C.13) art.2, subject to savings specified in art.5(1).

Subss.(1), (2) as amended by Courts Reform (Scotland) Act 2014 (asp 8) Sch.3 para.24. Brought into force on 22 September 2015 by SSI 2015/247 (C.35) art.2 and Sch, subject to transitional provisions in art.6.

[THE NEXT PARAGRAPH IS A4-409.3]

GENERAL NOTE

A4-409.3 With effect from August 1, 1997 certain sentences as detailed in subs.(4) can be suspended pending the determination of an appeal. Prevents a situation as arose in *HM Advocate v Jamieson*, 1996 S.C.C.R. 836.

[THE NEXT PARAGRAPH IS A4-410]

Computation of time

A4-410 **194.**—(1) If any period of time specified in any provision of this Part of this Act relating to appeals expires on a Saturday, Sunday or court holiday prescribed for the relevant court, the period shall be extended to expire on the next day which is not a Saturday, Sunday or such court holiday.

(2) The sheriff principal of the sheriffdom in which the judgement was pronounced may, on cause shown, extend any period specified in sections 178(1) and 179(4) and (7) of this Act for such period as he considers reasonable.

(3) For the purposes of sections 176(1)(a) and 178(1) of this Act, summary proceedings shall be deemed to be finally determined on the day on which sentence is passed in open court; except that, where in relation to an appeal—

(a) under section 175(2)(a) or (3)(a); or

(b) in so far as it is against conviction, under section 175(2)(d),

of this Act sentence is deferred under section 202 of this Act, they shall be deemed finally determined on the day on which sentence is first so deferred in open court.

AMENDMENTS

Subs.(2) as amended by Bail, Judicial Appointments etc. (Scotland) Act 2000 (asp 9) s.12 and Sch. para.7(5).

Subs.(2) as amended by Criminal Proceedings etc. (Reform) (Scotland) Act 2007 (asp 6) s.25. Brought into force on 10 December 2007 by SSI 2007/479.

PART XA – SCOTTISH CRIMINAL CASES REVIEW COMMISSION

The Scottish Criminal Cases Review Commission

Scottish Criminal Cases Review Commission

A4-410.1 **194A.**—(1) There shall be established a body corporate to be known as the Scottish Criminal Cases Review Commission (in this Act referred to as "the Commission").

(2) The Commission shall not be regarded as the servant or agent of the Crown or as enjoying any status, immunity or privilege of the Crown; and the Commission's property shall not be regarded as property of, or held on behalf of, the Crown.

(3) The Commission shall consist of not fewer than three members.

(4) The members of the Commission shall be appointed by Her Majesty on the recommendation of the Secretary of State.

(5) At least one third of the members of the Commission shall be persons who are legally qualified; and for this purpose a person is legally qualified if he is an advocate or solicitor of at least ten years' standing.

(6) At least two thirds of the members of the Commission shall be persons who appear to the Secretary of State to have knowledge or experience of any aspect of the criminal justice system; and for the purposes of this subsection the criminal justice system includes, in particular, the investigation of offences and the treatment of offenders.

(7) Schedule 9A to this Act, which makes further provision as to the Commission, shall have effect.

AMENDMENTS

Section 194A inserted by s.25 of Crime and Punishment (Scotland) Act 1997 with effect from 1 January 1998 as provided by SI 1997/3004 (C.110) (S.190).

GENERAL NOTE

This part of the Act provides for a Scottish Criminal Cases Review Commission. The Sutherland Commission recommended the setting up of a new body to consider alleged miscarriages of justice and to refer deserving cases to the Court of Appeal. The Secretary of State would be removed from this process. The Committee was of the view that the Secretary of State's role was incompatible with the constitutional separation of powers between the executive and the courts. An independent body would be seen to be impartial. The Committee recognised that the Secretary of State was however accountable to Parliament whilst the Commission would be subject to judicial review. A4-410.1.1

The Sutherland Committee reported there was a strong body of opinion that there was no need for change, and defects in the system would be remedied by the amended ground of appeal. The Government latched onto this and made no provision for the Commission in the Bill. Despite the best efforts of Lord McCluskey at the committee stage in the House of Lords, the Government resisted amendments to remedy the omission (see *Hansard*, HL, March 10, 1997, cols 56 to 62). The legislative timetable however resulted in a Government concession (see *Hansard*, HL, March 10, 1997, cols 945 to 952). The provisions on the whole follow the Sutherland Committee's recommendations.

Further provisions for the workings of the Commission can be found in Sch.9A.

s.194A

Provision is made for at least three members of the Commission and the Sutherland Committee envisaged that these will be part-time appointments. At least one-third of the members requires to be legally qualified and at least two-thirds need knowledge or experience of the investigation of offences and treatment of offenders. There are currently seven commissioners.

[THE NEXT PARAGRAPH IS A4-410.2]

References to High Court

References by the Commission

194B.—(1) The Commission on the consideration of any conviction of a person or of the sentence (other than sentence of death) passed on a person who has been convicted on indictment or complaint may, if they think fit, at any time, and whether or not an appeal against such conviction or sentence has previously been heard and determined by the High Court or the Sheriff Appeal Court, refer the whole case to the High Court and the case shall be heard and determined, subject to any directions the High Court may make, as if it were an appeal under Part VIII or, as the case may be, Part X of this Act. A4-410.2

(2) The power of the Commission under this section to refer to the High Court the case of a person convicted shall be exercisable whether or not that person has petitioned for the exercise of Her Majesty's prerogative of mercy.

(3) This section shall apply in relation to a finding under section 55(2) and an order under section 57(2) of this Act as it applies, respectively, in relation to a conviction and a sentence.

(3A) For the purposes of an appeal under Part X of this Act in a case referred to the High Court under subsection (1)—

(a) the High Court may exercise in the case all the powers and jurisdiction that the Sheriff Appeal Court would, had the case been an appeal to that Court, have had in relation to the case by virtue of section 118 of the Courts Reform (Scotland) Act 2014, and

(b) accordingly, Part X of this Act has effect in relation to the case subject to the following modifications—

(i) references to the Sheriff Appeal Court are to be read as references to the High Court,

(ii) references to an Appeal Sheriff are to be read as references to a judge of the High Court,

(iii) references to the Clerk of the Sheriff Appeal Court are to be read as reference to the Clerk of Justiciary.

(4) For the purposes of this section "person" includes a person who is deceased.

AMENDMENTS

Section 194B inserted by s.25 of Crime and Punishment (Scotland) Act 1997 with effect from 1 April 1999 as provided by SI 1999/652.

Subs.(1) as amended by SI 1999/1181, para.3 (effective 1 April 1999).

Subs.(1) as amended by Criminal Procedure (Legal Assistance, Detention and Appeals) (Scotland) Act 2010 (asp 15) s.7. Brought into force on 30 October 2010.

Subs.(1) as amended, (3A) inserted, by Courts Reform (Scotland) Act 2014 (asp 8) s.121. Brought into force on 22 September 2015 by SSI 2015/247 (C.35) art.2 and Sch.

Section 194B heading and subs.(1) as amended by Criminal Justice (Scotland) Act 2016 (asp 1) s.96(2), (3). Brought into force on 17 January 2017 by SSI 2016/426 art.2 and Sch.1 para.1.

GENERAL NOTE

s.194B

A4-410.2.1 *Subs.(1)* A reference can be made at any time (in *Preece v HM Advocate* [1981] Crim.L.R. 783, the reference by the Secretary of State was made seven years after conviction) *post conviction*, whether or not the case has been previously heard by the Appeal Court. The appeal is then treated as an ordinary appeal. The Commission may, as could the Secretary of State, refer the whole case or part thereof to the Appeal Court (see e.g. *Slater v HM Advocate*, 1928 J.C. 94; *Gallacher v HM Advocate*, 1951 J.C. 38 and *Beattie v HM Advocate*, 1995 J.C. 33). The first reference by the SCCRC was *Bonca-Tomaszewski v HM Advocate*, 2000 J.C. 586. It was held that the Appeal Court in considering the reference would proceed on the basis of current understanding of common law and present day standards although that could result in the court criticising their predecessors by reference to different criteria than applied then.

Once a reference is made the provisions relating to either solemn or summary appeals apply as applicable. In e.g. *Bonca Tomaszewski v HM Advocate* following the Commission's reference the applicant proceeded by lodging grounds of appeal. In *Crombie v Clark*, 2001 S.L.T. 635 the applicant lodged a Bill of Suspension following the reference.

Subs.(2) The prerogative of mercy is still exercisable by the Secretary of State but the Commission may refer a case even if a petition for the Royal Prerogative has previously been made.

Subs.(3) A reference can be made in respect of a finding that an accused committed an act where he is insane in bar of trial and also in respect of disposals where an accused is insane at the time of the offence.

Subs.(4) A reference can be made in respect of a deceased.

[THE NEXT PARAGRAPH IS A4-410.3]

Grounds for reference

A4-410.3 **194C.**—(1) The grounds upon which the Commission may refer a case to the High Court are that they believe—

(a) that a miscarriage of justice may have occurred; and

(b) that it is in the interests of justice that a reference should be made.

(2) […]

AMENDMENTS

Section 194C inserted by s.25 of Crime and Punishment (Scotland) Act 1997 with effect from 1 April 1999 as provided by SI 1999/652.

Section 194C as amended by Criminal Procedure (Legal Assistance, Detention and Appeals) (Scotland) Act 2010 (asp 15) s.7. Brought into force on 30 October 2010.

Subs.(2) repealed by Criminal Justice (Scotland) Act 2016 (asp 1) s.96(4). Brought into force on 17 January 2017 by SSI 2016/426 art.2 and Sch.1 para.1.

GENERAL NOTE

s.194C

The administrative criteria by which the Secretary of State assessed cases involving a miscarriage of justice was considered by the Sutherland Committee. The criteria were whether there was relevant material to suggest a miscarriage of justice and further, would the Appeal Court as a matter of law entertain the case on a reference. **A4-410.3.1**

The Committee considered that the criteria for references by the commission should reflect the "broad and flexible miscarriage of justice" ground of appeal. It appears that part (a) incorporates the previous criteria used by the Secretary of State, there being no point in referring an alleged miscarriage of justice which the appeal court as a matter of law would not entertain.

The Committee also recommended that the normal appeal procedures should have been exhausted but this has not been incorporated in the current provisions.

In *Crombie v Clark*, 2001 S.L.T. 635 the Appeal Court held that the question of whether or not it was in the interests of justice for a reference to be made was a matter for the Commission and not the Appeal court. As Sir Gerald Gordon comments at pages 240–241 the Commission only requires "to believe there may have been" a miscarriage of justice. The Appeal Court require to be satisfied that there has. The reasons for the Commission's belief or material on which it is based are not considered by the Court. The Appeal Court in *Crombie* expressed surprise that the merits of the applicant's defence were not considered when the Commission determined whether they believed there had been a miscarriage of justice.

[THE NEXT PARAGRAPH IS A4-410.4]

Further provision as to references

194D.—(1) A reference of a conviction, sentence or finding may be made under section 194B of this Act whether or not an application has been made by or on behalf of the person to whom it relates. **A4-410.4**

(2) In considering whether to make a reference the Commission shall have regard to—

(a) any application or representations made to the Commission by or on behalf of the person to whom it relates;

(b) any other representations made to the Commission in relation to it; and

(c) any other matters which appear to the Commission to be relevant.

(3) In considering whether to make a reference the Commission may at any time refer to the High Court for the Court's opinion any point on which they desire the Court's assistance; and on a reference under this subsection the High Court shall consider the point referred and furnish the Commission with their opinion on the point.

(4) Where the Commission make a reference to the High Court under section 194B of this Act they shall—

(a) give to the Court a statement of their reasons for making the reference; and

(b) send a copy of the statement to every person who appears to them to be likely to be a party to any proceedings on the appeal arising from the reference.

(4A) The grounds for an appeal arising from a reference to the High Court under section 194B of this Act must relate to one or more of the reasons for making the reference contained in the Commission's statement of reasons.

(4B) Despite subsection (4A), the High Court may, if it considers it is in the interests of justice to do so, grant leave for the appellant to found the appeal on additional grounds.

(4C) An application by the appellant for leave under subsection (4B) must be made and intimated to the Crown Agent within 21 days after the date on which a copy of the Commission's statement of reasons is sent under subsection (4)(b).

(4D) The High Court may, on cause shown, extend the period of 21 days mentioned in subsection (4C).

(4E) The Clerk of Justiciary must intimate to the persons mentioned in subsection (4F)—

(a) a decision under subsection (4B), and

(b) in the case of a refusal to grant leave for the appeal to be founded on additional grounds, the reasons for the decision.

(4F) Those persons are—

(a) the appellant or the appellant's solicitor, and

(b) the Crown Agent.

(5) In every case in which—

(a) an application has been made to the Commission by or on behalf of any person for the reference by them of any conviction, sentence or finding; but

(b) the Commission decide not to make a reference of the conviction, sentence or finding,

they shall give a statement of the reasons for their decision to the person who made the application.

AMENDMENTS

Section 194D inserted by s.25 of Crime and Punishment (Scotland) Act 1997 with effect from 1 April 1999 as provided by SI 1999/652.

Subss.(4A)–(4F) inserted by Criminal Justice and Licensing (Scotland) Act 2010 (asp 13) s.83. Brought into force on 5 November 2010 (subject to savings provisions in arts 3 and 4) by SSI 2010/385 art.2.

GENERAL NOTE

s.194D

A4-410.4.1 *Subs.(1)* This allows an application to be made to the Commission on someone's behalf, e.g. someone who is mentally ill or deceased. Although the Sutherland Committee recommended that this should be allowed only if there was a good reason, this requirement has not been incorporated.

Subs.(2) In *R. v Secretary of State for Home Department, ex p. Hickey (No.2)* [1995] 1 All E.R. 490, it was held that prior to the Secretary of State's decision regarding a referral, a petitioner should be given the opportunity to make representations upon whatever material had been revealed by the Secretary of State's enquiries and that sufficient disclosure should be given to enable the petitioner to present his case.

It may well be that the Commission will have to disclose relevant material to enable the applicant to make full representations.

Subs.(3) This is not limited to a point of law. Hopefully this may be used to clarify points such as mentioned above.

Subs.(4) A statement of reasons for making the reference must be sent to every person the Commission considers likely to be a party to any proceedings. In most cases this will just be the Crown and the accused but there is also the possibility of a co-accused. The principal statement of reasons is given to the court.

In *Bonca-Tomaszewski v HM Advocate*, 2000 J.C. 586 after the reference was lodged by the SCCRC the appellant lodged fresh grounds of appeal. Following a procedural hearing the court suggested that the grounds of appeal be amended to include the original grounds of appeal and ordered written submissions. In *Crombie v Clark*, 2001 S.L.T. 635 once the reference was made by the Commission, the complainer lodged a Bill of Suspension. The Appeal Court held that the court must proceed on the material in the Bill and not in the letter of referral.

Subs.(5) If a decision is taken not to make a reference, a statement of reasons must be given to the applicant. The decision will no doubt be subject to judicial review.

High Court's power to reject a reference made by the Commission

194DA.— […] A4-410.4.2

Amendments

Section 194DA inserted by Criminal Procedure (Legal Assistance, Detention and Appeals) (Scotland) Act 2010 (asp 15) s.7. Brought into force on 30 October 2010.

Section 194DA repealed by Criminal Justice (Scotland) Act 2016 (asp 1) s.96(5). Brought into force on 17 January 2017 by SSI 2016/426 art.2 and Sch.1 para.1.

[THE NEXT PARAGRAPH IS A4-410.5]

Extension of Commission's remit to summary cases

194E.—(1) The Secretary of State may by order provide for this Part of this Act to apply in relation to convictions, sentences and findings made in summary proceedings as they apply in relation to convictions, sentences and findings made in solemn proceedings, and may for that purpose make in such an order such amendments to the provisions of this Part as appear to him to be necessary or expedient. A4-410.5

(2) An order under this section shall be made by statutory instrument, and shall not have effect unless a draft of it has been laid before and approved by a resolution of each House of Parliament.

Amendments

Section 194E inserted by s.25 of Crime and Punishment (Scotland) Act 1997 with effect from 1 January 1998 as provided by SI 1997/3004 (C.110) (S.190).

General Note

s.194E

The Sutherland Committee considered that the Commission should also be able to consider summary cases but that to ensure that priority was given to solemn cases and to ensure that the Commission was not overwhelmed, then the Secretary of State could extend the Commission's remit at a later stage to summary cases. The Committee envisaged that the Commission would rarely have to consider summary cases as the existing appeal procedures for summary cases were well established. The Commission remit was extended to summary cases by means of the Scottish Criminal Cases Review Commission (Application to Summary Proceedings) Order 1999 (SI 1999/1181). A4-410.5.1

In *Crombie v Clark*, 2001 S.L.T. 635 proceedings commenced by a reference by the Commission in a summary case. C subsequently appealed by Bill of Suspension.

[THE NEXT PARAGRAPH IS A4-410.6]

Further powers

194F. The Commission may take any steps which they consider appropriate for assisting them in the exercise of any of their functions and may, in particular— A4-410.6

(a) themselves undertake inquiries and obtain statements, opinions or reports; or

(b) request the Lord Advocate or any other person to undertake such inquiries or obtain such statements, opinions and reports.

Amendments

Section 194F inserted by s.25 of the Crime and Punishment (Scotland) Act 1997 with effect from April 1, 1999 as provided by the Crime and Punishment (Scotland) Act 1997 (Commencement No. 5 and Transitional Provisions and Savings) Order 1999 (SI 1999/652).

General Note

s.194F

The Commission has power to undertake enquiries, obtain statements, opinions or reports or request the Lord Advocate or others to do so. As the emphasis is on independence and justice being seen to be done the Commission undertakes the majority of enquiries themselves employing a number of case workers. Previously, investigations were dealt with through Crown Office, the Procurator Fiscal or the police—including the precognition of witnesses, obtaining forensic reports, etc. One of the major criti- A4-410.6.1

cisms of the old procedure was that those bodies responsible for prosecuting a person thereafter were involved in investigating any alleged miscarriage of justice.

[THE NEXT PARAGRAPH IS A4-410.7]

Supplementary provision

A4-410.7 **194G.**—(1) The Secretary of State may by order make such incidental, consequential, transitional or supplementary provisions as may appear to him to be necessary or expedient for the purpose of bringing this Part of this Act into operation, and, without prejudice to the generality of the foregoing, of dealing with any cases being considered by him under section 124 of this Act at the time when this Part comes into force, and an order under this section may make different provision in relation to different cases or classes of case.

(2) An order under this section shall be made by statutory instrument subject to annulment in pursuance of a resolution of either House of Parliament.

AMENDMENTS

Section 194G inserted by s.25 of the Crime and Punishment (Scotland) Act 1997 with effect from January 1, 1998 as provided by the Crime and Punishment (Scotland) Act 1997 (Commencement No. 4) Order 1997 (SI 1997/3004 (C.110) (S.190)).

Powers of investigation of Commission

Power to request precognition on oath

A4-410.8 **194H.**—(1) Where it appears to the Commission that a person may have information which they require for the purposes of carrying out their functions, and the person refuses to make any statement to them, they may apply to the sheriff under this section.

(2) On an application made by the Commission under this section, the sheriff may, if he is satisfied that it is reasonable in the circumstances, grant warrant to cite the person concerned to appear before the sheriff in chambers at such time or place as shall be specified in the citation, for precognition on oath by a member of the Commission or a person appointed by them to act in that regard.

(3) Any person who, having been duly cited to attend for precognition under subsection (2) above and having been given at least 48 hours notice, fails without reasonable excuse to attend shall be guilty of an offence and liable on summary conviction to a fine not exceeding level 3 on the standard scale or to imprisonment for a period not exceeding 21 days; and the court may issue a warrant for the apprehension of the person concerned ordering him to be brought before a sheriff for precognition on oath.

(4) Any person who, having been duly cited to attend for precognition under subsection (2) above, attends but—

(a) refuses to give information within his knowledge or to produce evidence in his possession; or

(b) prevaricates in his evidence,

shall be guilty of an offence and shall be liable to be summarily subjected to a fine not exceeding level 3 on the standard scale or to imprisonment for a period not exceeding 21 days.

AMENDMENTS

Section 194H inserted by s.25 of the Crime and Punishment (Scotland) Act 1997 with effect from April 1, 1999 as provided by the Crime and Punishment (Scotland) Act 1997 (Commencement No. 5 and Transitional Provisions and Savings) Order 1999 (SI 1999/652).

GENERAL NOTE

New s.194H

This allows for precognition on oath. Other parties would not be entitled to be present (see Hume Vol. ii. 82). For a discussion of the general nature of precognitions see *HM Advocate v McSween* 2007 SCCR 310. **A4-410.8.1**

[THE NEXT PARAGRAPH IS A4-410.9]

Power to obtain documents etc.

194I.—(1) Where the Commission believe that a person or a public body has possession or control of a document or other material which may assist them in the exercise of any of their functions, they may apply to the High Court for an order requiring that person or body— **A4-410.9**

(a) to produce the document or other material to the Commission or to give the Commission access to it; and

(b) to allow the Commission to take away the document or other material or to make and take away a copy of it in such form as they think appropriate,

and such an order may direct that the document or other material must not be destroyed, damaged or altered before the direction is withdrawn by the Court.

(2) The duty to comply with an order under this section is not affected by any obligation of secrecy or other limitation on disclosure (including any such obligation or limitation imposed by or by virtue of any enactment) which would otherwise prevent the production of the document or other material to the Commission or the giving of access to it to the Commission.

(3) The documents and other material covered by this section include, in particular, any document or other material obtained or created during any investigation or proceedings relating to—

(a) the case in relation to which the Commission's function is being or may be exercised; or

(b) any other case which may be in any way connected with that case (whether or not any function of the Commission could be exercised in relation to that other case).

(4) In this section—

"Minister" means a Minister of the Crown as defined by section 8 of the Ministers of the Crown Act 1975;

"public body" means

(a) the Police Service of Scotland;

(b) any government department, local authority or other body constituted for the purposes of the public service, local government or the administration of justice; or

(c) any other body whose members are appointed by Her Majesty, any Minister, the Scottish Minister or any government department or whose revenues consist wholly or mainly of money provided by Parliament.

AMENDMENTS

Section 194I inserted by s.25 of the Crime and Punishment (Scotland) Act 1997 with effect from April 1, 1999 as provided by SI 1999/652.

Subs.(4)(c) as amended by Scotland Act 1998 (Consequential Modifications) (No.2) Order 1999 (SI 1999/1820) art.4 and Sch.2 para.122(2) (effective July 1, 1999).

Subs.(4) as amended by Police and Fire Reform (Scotland) Act 2012 (asp 8) Sch.7 para.12(9) and Sch.8 para.1. Brought into force on April 1, 2013 by SSI 2013/51 art.2.

[THE NEXT PARAGRAPH IS A4-410.9.2]

General Note

A4-410.9.2 The Commission's broad rights to recover and examine documents were upheld in *Scottish Criminal Cases Review Commission v HM Advocate*, 2001 S.L.T. 905; 2000 S.C.C.R. 842, where the Crown had opposed access to its papers. The Appeal Court held that SCCRC were not precluded from recovering e.g. departmental documents, the nature and circumstance of the creation of the document not being sufficient objection to recovery. While the court accepted that there might be certain classes of documents which would warrant denial of access to the Commission, the Crown still had to justify refusal of a request for materials by the Commission. On the other hand it would be difficult for the Commission to make out a case for access to documents whose contents were entirely unknown to it. The court held that averments setting out the history of the case satisfied the requirements of s.194I. It was recognised that it was only when the SCCRC saw the documents they would be able to ascertain if they were material.

Power to request assistance in obtaining information abroad

A4-410.9.3 **194IA.**—(1) Where it appears to the Commission that there may be information which they require for the purposes of carrying out their functions, and the information is outside the United Kingdom, they may apply to the High Court to request assistance.

(2) On an application made by the Commission under subsection (1), the High Court may request assistance if satisfied that it is reasonable in the circumstances.

(3) In this section, "request assistance" means request assistance in obtaining outside the United Kingdom any information specified in the request for use by the Commission for the purposes of carrying out their functions.

(4) Section 8 of the Crime (International Co-operation) Act 2003 (c.32) (sending requests for assistance) applies to requests for assistance under this section as it applies to requests for assistance under section 7 of that Act.

(5) Subsections (2), (3) and (6) of section 9 of that Act (use of evidence obtained) apply to information obtained pursuant to a request for assistance under this section as they apply under subsection (1) of that section to evidence obtained pursuant to a request for assistance under section 7 of that Act.

Amendments

Section 194IA inserted by Criminal Justice and Licensing (Scotland) Act 2010 (asp 13) s.105. Brought into force on December 13, 2010 by SSI 2010/413 (C.28).

[THE NEXT PARAGRAPH IS A4-410.10]

Disclosure of information

Offence of disclosure

A4-410.10 **194J.**—(1) A person who is or has been a member or employee of the Commission shall not disclose any information obtained by the Commission in the exercise of any of their functions unless the disclosure of the information is excepted from this section by section 194K or 194M of this Act.

(2) A member of the Commission shall not authorise the disclosure by an employee of the Commission of any information obtained by the Commission in the exercise of any of their functions unless the authorisation of the disclosure of the information is excepted from this section by section 194K or 194M of this Act.

(3) A person who contravenes this section is guilty of an offence and liable on summary conviction to a fine of an amount not exceeding level 5 on the standard scale.

Amendments

Section 194J inserted by s.25 of the Crime and Punishment (Scotland) Act 1997 with effect from April 1, 1999 as provided by SI 1999/652.

Subss.(1) and (2) as amended by Criminal Cases (Punishment and Review) (Scotland) Act 2012 (asp 7) s.3(2). Brought into force on September 24, 2012 by SSI 2012/249 art.3.

[THE NEXT PARAGRAPH IS A4-410.12]

Exceptions from obligations of non-disclosure

194K.—(1) The disclosure of information, or the authorisation of the disclosure of information, is excepted from section 194J of this Act by this section if the information is disclosed, or is authorised to be disclosed— A4-410.12

(a) for the purposes of any criminal, disciplinary or civil proceedings;
(b) in order to assist in dealing with an application made to the Secretary of State for compensation for a miscarriage of justice;
(c) by a person who is a member or an employee of the Commission to another person who is a member or an employee of the Commission;
(d) in any statement or report required by this Act;
(e) in or in connection with the exercise of any function under this Act; or
(f) in any circumstances in which the disclosure of information is permitted by an order made by the Secretary of State.

(2) The disclosure of information is also excepted from section 194J of this Act by this section if the information is disclosed by an employee of the Commission who is authorised to disclose the information by a member of the Commission.

(3) The disclosure of information, or the authorisation of the disclosure of information, is also excepted from section 194J of this Act by this section if the information is disclosed, or is authorised to be disclosed, for the purposes of—

(a) the investigation of an offence; or
(b) deciding whether to prosecute a person for an offence,

unless the disclosure is or would be prevented by an obligation or other limitation on disclosure (including any such obligation or limitation imposed by, under or by virtue of any enactment) arising otherwise than under that section.

(4) Where the disclosure of information is excepted from section 194J of this Act by subsection (1) or (2) above, the disclosure of the information is not prevented by any obligation of secrecy or other limitation on disclosure (including any such obligation or limitation imposed by, under or by virtue of any enactment) arising otherwise than under that section.

(5) The power to make an order under subsection (1)(f) above is exercisable by statutory instrument which shall be subject to annulment in pursuance of a resolution of either House of Parliament.

AMENDMENTS

Section 194K inserted by s.25 of the Crime and Punishment (Scotland) Act 1997 with effect from April 1, 1999 as provided by SI 1999/652).

[THE NEXT PARAGRAPH IS A4-410.14]

Consent of disclosure

194L.—(1) Where a person or body is required by an order under section 194I of this Act to produce or allow access to a document or other material to the Commission and notifies them that any information contained in the document or other material to which the order relates is not to be disclosed by the Commission without his or its prior consent, the Commission shall not disclose the information without such consent. A4-410.14

(2) Such consent may not be withheld unless—

(a) (apart from section 194I of this Act) the person would have been prevented by any obligation of secrecy or other limitation on disclosure from disclosing the information without such consent; and
(b) it is reasonable for the person to withhold his consent to disclosure of the information by the Commission.

(3) An obligation of secrecy or other limitation on disclosure which applies to a person only where disclosure is not authorised by another person shall not be taken for the purposes of subsection (2)(a) above to prevent the disclosure by the person of information to the Commission unless—

(a) reasonable steps have been taken to obtain the authorisation of the other person; or

(b) such authorisation could not reasonably be expected to be obtained.".

AMENDMENTS

Section 194L inserted by s.25 of the Crime and Punishment (Scotland) Act 1997 with effect from April 1, 1999 as provided by SI 1999/652.

[THE NEXT PARAGRAPH IS A4-410.16]

Special circumstances for disclosure

Further exception to section 194J

A4-410.16 **194M.**—(1) The disclosure of information, or the authorisation of disclosure of information, is excepted from section 194J by this section if—

(a) the conditions specified in subsection (2) are met, and

(b) the Commission have determined that it is appropriate in the whole circumstances for the information to be disclosed.

(2) The conditions are that—

(a) the information relates to a case that has been referred to the High Court under section 194B(1),

(b) the reference concerns—

(i) a conviction, or

(ii) a finding under section 55(2), and

(c) the case has fallen, or has been abandoned, under the provisions or other rules applying by virtue of section 194B(1).

AMENDMENTS

Section 194M inserted by Criminal Cases (Punishment and Review) (Scotland) Act 2012 (asp 7) s.3(3). Brought into force on September 24, 2012 by SSI 2012/249 art.3.

[THE NEXT PARAGRAPH IS A4-410.18]

Effect of the exception

A4-410.18 **194N.**—(1) Where the disclosure of information is excepted from section 194J by section 194M, the disclosure of the information is not prevented by any obligation of confidentiality or other limitation on disclosure arising otherwise than under section 194J.

(2) For the purpose of subsection (1), such an obligation or limitation does not include one imposed–

(a) by, under or by virtue of any enactment, or

(a) by any interdict or other court order applying in connection with this section.

AMENDMENTS

Section 194N inserted by Criminal Cases (Punishment and Review) (Scotland) Act 2012 (asp 7) s.3(3). Brought into force on September 24, 2012 by SSI 2012/249 art.3.

[THE NEXT PARAGRAPH IS A4-410.20]

Notification and representations etc.

194O.—(1) When considering for the purpose of section 194M(1) the question of whether it is appropriate for the information to be disclosed, the Commission have the following duties. A4-410.20

(2) The Commission must—

(a) so far as practicable, take reasonable measures to—

(i) notify each of the affected persons of the possibility that the information may be disclosed, and

(ii) seek the views of each of them on the question, and

(b) to such extent (and in such manner) as they think fit, consult the other interested persons.

(3) The Commission must—

(a) allow the prescribed period for each of the affected and other interested persons involved to take steps (including legal action) in their own favour in relation to the question, and

(b) have regard to any material representations made to them on the question by any of those affected and other interested persons within the prescribed period.

(4) The Commission must have regard to any other factors that they believe to be significant in relation to the question.

(5) In subsections (2) and (3)—

(a) the references to the affected persons are to the persons—

(i) to whom the information directly relates, or

(ii) from whom the information was obtained, whether directly or indirectly,

(b) the references to the other interested persons are to (so far as not among the affected persons)—

(i) the Lord Advocate, and

(ii) such additional persons (if any) as appear to the Commission to have a substantial interest in the question.

(6) In subsection (3), the references to the prescribed period in relation to a particular person are to—

(a) the period of 6 weeks, or

(b) such longer period as the Commission may set,

starting with the date on which the notification was sent to, or (as the case may be) consultation was initiated with respect to, the person.

(7) Subsections (3) and (6) are inapplicable in relation to a particular person if the Commission cannot reasonably ascertain the person's whereabouts.

Amendments

Section 194O inserted by Criminal Cases (Punishment and Review) (Scotland) Act 2012 (asp 7) s.3(3). Brought into force on September 24, 2012 by SSI 2012/249 art.3.

[THE NEXT PARAGRAPH IS A4-410.22]

Consent if UK interest

194P.—(1) Unless subsection (3) is complied with, section 194M(1) is of no effect in relation to any information falling within subsection (2). A4-410.22

(2) Information falls within this subsection if it—

(a) is held by the Commission, and

(b) at any time, has been supplied by the UK Government under arrangements of any kind.

(3) This subsection is complied with if, at any time, the UK Government has in connection with section 194M(1) given its consent to disclosure of the information.

(4) In this section, "the UK Government" means a Minister of the Crown or a department of the Government of the United Kingdom.

AMENDMENTS

Section 194P inserted by Criminal Cases (Punishment and Review) (Scotland) Act 2012 (asp 7) s.3(3). Brought into force on September 24, 2012 by SSI 2012/249 art.3.

[THE NEXT PARAGRAPH IS A4-410.24]

Consent if foreign interest

A4-410.24 **194Q.**—(1) Unless subsection (3) is complied with, section 194M(1) is of no effect in relation to any information falling within subsection (2).

(2) Information falls within this subsection if it—

(a) is held by the Commission, and

(b) at any time, has been supplied by a designated foreign authority under arrangements of any kind.

(3) This subsection is complied with if the designated foreign authority has in connection with section 194M(1) given its consent to disclosure of the information, by virtue of—

(a) the arrangements concerned, or

(b) subsection (4).

(4) Where not previously given by virtue of those arrangements, it is for the Commission to seek the designated foreign authority's consent to disclosure of the information.

(5) Subsection (1) does not apply if the information also falls within section 194P(2).

AMENDMENTS

Section 194Q inserted by Criminal Cases (Punishment and Review) (Scotland) Act 2012 (asp 7) s.3(3). Brought into force on September 24, 2012 by SSI 2012/249 art.3.

[THE NEXT PARAGRAPH IS A4-410.26]

Designated foreign authority

A4-410.26 **194R.**—(1) The references in section 194Q to a designated foreign authority are to a current or previous authority of a prosecutorial, judicial or other character which is or was located within a country or territory outwith the United Kingdom.

(2) But, if in connection with subsection (4) of that section—

(a) the Commission cannot reasonably identify or find the particular authority in question, or

(b) they are unsuccessful in their reasonable attempts to communicate with it,

the references in subsections (3) and (4) of that section to the designated foreign authority are to be read as if they were to the relevant foreign government.

(3) In the application of subsection (2), paragraph (a) of subsection (3) of that section is to be ignored.

(4) In subsection (2)—

(a) the references to the Commission include their acting with the Lord Advocate's help,

(b) the reference to the relevant foreign government—

(i) is to the government of the other country or territory,

(ii) in the event of doubt as to the status or operation of a governmental system in the other country or territory, is to be regarded as being to the body described in subsection (5).

(5) That is, the principal body in it (for the time being (if any)) that is recognised by the Government of the United Kingdom as having responsibility for exercising governmental control centrally.

AMENDMENTS

Section 194R inserted by Criminal Cases (Punishment and Review) (Scotland) Act 2012 (asp 7) s.3(3). Brought into force on 24 September 2012 by SSI 2012/249 art.3.

[THE NEXT PARAGRAPH IS A4-410.28]

Disapplication of sections 194O to 194R

194S.—(1) Sections 194O to 194R cease to have effect if subsection (2) prevails. **A4-410.28**

(2) This subsection prevails where, on their preliminary examination of the question to which section 194O(1) relates, the Commission determine for the purpose of section 194M(1) that it is manifestly inappropriate for the information to be disclosed.

(3) But—

(a) if there is a material change in any significant factor on which the determination depended, it is open to the Commission to re-examine the question (and this is to be regarded as another preliminary examination of the question),

(b) where they choose to re-examine the question, the effect of sections 194O to 194R is restored unless subsection (2) again prevails.

AMENDMENTS

Section 194S inserted by Criminal Cases (Punishment and Review) (Scotland) Act 2012 (asp 7) s.3(3). Brought into force on 24 September 2012 by SSI 2012/249 art.3.

[THE NEXT PARAGRAPH IS A4-410.30]

Final disclosure-related matters

194T.—(1) If the Commission decide in pursuance of section 194M(1) to disclose the information— **A4-410.30**

(a) subsection (2) applies initially, and

(b) subsection (3) applies subsequently.

(2) Before disclosing the information, the Commission must—

(a) so far as practicable, take reasonable measures to notify of the decision—

(i) each of the affected persons, and

(ii) to the same extent as they were consulted under section 194O(2)(b), the other interested persons, and

(b) allow the prescribed period for each of the affected and other interested persons involved to take steps (including legal action) in their own favour in relation to the decision.

(3) In disclosing the information, the Commission must—

(a) explain the context in which the information is being disclosed by them (including by describing the background to the case), and

(b) where (for any reason) other information relating to the case remains undisclosed by them, explicitly state that fact,

and do so along with the material by which the disclosure is made.

(4) In subsection (2), the references to the affected and other interested persons are to be construed in accordance with section 194O(5).

(5) In subsection (2)(b), the reference to the prescribed period in relation to a particular person is to—

(a) the period of 6 weeks, or

(b) such longer period as the Commission may set,

starting with the date on which the notification was sent to the person.

(6) Subsections (2)(b) and (5) are inapplicable in relation to a particular person if the Commission cannot reasonably ascertain the person's whereabouts.

(7) In subsection (3)(b), the reference to other information is to any other information obtained by the Commission in the exercise of their functions.

AMENDMENTS

Section 194T inserted by Criminal Cases (Punishment and Review) (Scotland) Act 2012 (asp 7) s.3(3). Brought into force on 24 September 2012 by SSI 2012/249 art.3.

[THE NEXT PARAGRAPH IS A4-410.32]

PART 10ZA – APPEALS FROM SHERIFF APPEAL COURT

Appeal from the Sheriff Appeal Court

A4-410.32 **194ZB.**—(1) An appeal on a point of law may be taken to the High Court against any decision of the Sheriff Appeal Court in criminal proceedings, but only with the permission of the High Court.

(2) An appeal under subsection (1) may be taken by any party to the appeal in the Sheriff Appeal Court.

(3) The High Court may give permission for an appeal under subsection (1) only if the Court considers that—

(a) the appeal would raise an important point of principle or practice, or

(b) there is some other compelling reason for the Court to hear the appeal.

(4) An application for permission for an appeal under subsection (1) must be made before the end of the period of 14 days beginning with the day on which the decision of the Sheriff Appeal Court that would be the subject of the appeal was made.

(5) The High Court may extend the period of 14 days mentioned in subsection (4) if satisfied that doing so is justified by exceptional circumstances.

AMENDMENTS

Section 194ZB inserted by Courts Reform (Scotland) Act 2014 (asp 8) s.119. Brought into force on 22 September 2015 by SSI 2015/247 (C.35) art.2 and Sch.

[THE NEXT PARAGRAPH IS A4-410.34]

GENERAL NOTE

A4-410.34 If an appeal requires leave, there is no appeal before the court unless and until leave is granted and a note of appeal which is refused leave is of no effect and is incompetent and the decision of the Sheriff Appeal Court to grant or refuse leave cannot be appealed: *Mackay v Murphy* [2015] SAC (Crim) 2; 2016 S.C.C.R. 83.

Where an appeal under this section proceeds, there is no authority for the Sheriff Appeal Court to provide a report to the High Court (*Stolarczyk v Harrower*, 2017 S.C.C.R. 229, at [17]).

Appeals: applications and procedure

A4-410.35 **194ZC.**—(1) An appeal under section 194ZB(1) is to be made by way of note of appeal.

(2) A note of appeal must specify the point of law on which the appeal is being made.

(3) For the purposes of considering and deciding an appeal under section 194ZB(1)—

(a) three of the judges of the High Court are to constitute a quorum of the Court,

(b) decisions are to be taken by a majority vote of the members of the Court sitting (including the presiding judge),

(c) each judge sitting may pronounce a separate opinion.

AMENDMENTS

Section 194ZC inserted by Courts Reform (Scotland) Act 2014 (asp 8) s.119. Brought into force on September 22, 2015 by SSI 2015/247 (C.35) art.2 and Sch.

[THE NEXT PARAGRAPH IS A4-410.38]

Application for permission for appeal: determination by single judge

194ZD.—(1) An application to the High Court for permission for an appeal under section 194ZB(1) is to be determined by a single judge of the High Court. **A4-410.38**

(2) If the judge gives permission for the appeal, the judge may make comments in writing in relation to the appeal.

(3) If the judge refuses permission for the appeal—

(a) the judge must give reasons in writing for the refusal, and
(b) where the appellant is on bail and the sentence imposed on the appellant on conviction is one of imprisonment, the judge must grant a warrant to apprehend and imprison the appellant.

(4) A warrant under subsection (3)(b) does not take effect until the expiry of the period of 14 days mentioned in section 194ZE(1) (or, where that period is extended under section 194ZE(2) before the period being extended expires, until the expiry of the period as so extended) without an application for permission having been lodged by the appellant under section 194ZE(1).

AMENDMENTS

Section 194ZD inserted by Courts Reform (Scotland) Act 2014 (asp 8) s.119. Brought into force on September 22, 2015 by SSI 2015/247 (C.35) art.2 and Sch.

[THE NEXT PARAGRAPH IS A4-410.41]

Further application for permission where single judge refuses permission

194ZE.—(1) Where the judge refuses permission for the appeal under section 194ZD, the appellant may, within the period of 14 days beginning with the day on which intimation of the decision is given under section 194ZF(2), apply again to the High Court for permission for the appeal. **A4-410.41**

(2) The High Court may extend the period of 14 days mentioned in subsection (1), or that period as extended under this subsection, whether or not the period to be extended has expired.

(3) The High Court may extend a period under subsection (2) only if satisfied that doing so is justified by exceptional circumstances.

(4) Three of the judges of the High Court are to constitute a quorum for the purposes of considering an application under subsection (1).

(5) If the High Court gives permission for the appeal, the Court may make comments in writing in relation to the appeal.

(6) If the High Court refuses permission for the appeal—

(a) the Court must give reasons in writing for the refusal, and
(b) where the appellant is on bail and the sentence imposed on the appellant on conviction is one of imprisonment, the Court must grant a warrant to apprehend and imprison the appellant.

AMENDMENTS

Section 194ZE inserted by Courts Reform (Scotland) Act 2014 (asp 8) s.119. Brought into force on September 22, 2015 by SSI 2015/247 (C.35) art.2 and Sch.

[THE NEXT PARAGRAPH IS A4-410.44]

Applications for permission: further provision

A4-410.44 **194ZF.**—(1) An application for permission for an appeal under section 194ZB(1) is to be considered and determined (whether under section 194ZD or 194ZE)—

(a) in chambers without the parties being present,

(b) by reference to section 194ZB(3), and

(c) on the basis of consideration of—

(i) the note of appeal under section 194ZC(1), and

(ii) such other document or information (if any) as may be specified by act of adjournal.

(2) The Clerk of Justiciary must, as soonas possible, intimate to the appellant or the appellant's solicitor and to the Crown Agent—

(a) a decision under section 194ZD or 194ZE determining the application for permission for an appeal, and

(b) in the case of a refusal of permission for the appeal, the reasons for the decision.

Amendments

Section 194ZF inserted by Courts Reform (Scotland) Act 2014 (asp 8) s.119. Brought into force on April 1, 2015 by SSI 2015/77 art.2 only for the purpose specified in SSI 2015/77 Sch.1; not yet in force otherwise.

[THE NEXT PARAGRAPH IS A4-410.47]

Restriction of grounds of appeal

A4-410.47 **194ZG.**—(1) Comments in writing made under section 194ZD(2) or 194ZE(5) may specify the arguable grounds of appeal (whether or not they were stated in the note of appeal) on the basis of which permission for the appeal was given.

(2) Where the arguable grounds of appeal are specified under subsection (1), the appellant may not, except with the permission of the High Court on cause shown, found any aspect of the appeal on a ground of appeal stated in the application for permission but not specified under subsection (1).

(3) An application by the appellant for permission under subsection (2) must—

(a) be made before the end of the period of 14 days beginning with the date of intimation under section 194ZF(2), and

(b) be intimated by the appellant to the Crown Agent before the end of that period.

(4) The High Court may extend the period of 14 days mentioned in subsection (3) if satisfied that doing so is justified by exceptional circumstances.

(5) The appellant may not, except with the permission of the High Court on cause shown, found any aspect of the appeal on a matter not stated in the note of appeal (or in a duly made amendment or addition to the note of appeal).

(6) Subsection (5) does not apply in relation to a matter specified as an arguable ground of appeal under subsection (1).

Amendments

Section 194ZG inserted by Courts Reform (Scotland) Act 2014 (asp 8) s.119. Brought into force on September 22, 2015 by SSI 2015/247 (C.35) art.2 and Sch.

[THE NEXT PARAGRAPH IS A4-410.50]

Disposal of appeals

A4-410.50 **194ZH.**—(1) In disposing of an appeal under section 194ZB(1), the High Court may—

(a) remit the case back to the Sheriff Appeal Court with its opinion and any direction as to further procedure in, or disposal of, the case, or
(b) exercise any power that the Sheriff Appeal Court could have exercised in relation to disposal of the appeal proceedings before that Court.

(2) So far as necessary for the purposes or in consequence of the exercise of a power by the High Court by virtue of subsection (1)(b)—
(a) references in Part X to the Sheriff Appeal Court are to be read as including references to the High Court, and
(b) references in Part X to a verdict of or sentence passed by the inferior court are to be read as incuding references to a verdict of or sentence passed by the Sheriff Appeal Court in disposing of the appeal before it.

(3) Subsections (1)(b) and (2) do not affect any power in relation to the consideration or disposal of appeals that the High Court has apart from those subsections.

Amendments

Section 194ZH inserted by Courts Reform (Scotland) Act 2014 (asp 8) s.119. Brought into force on September 22, 2015 by SSI 2015/247 (C.35) art.2 and Sch.

[THE NEXT PARAGRAPH IS A4-410.53]

Procedure where appellant in custody

194ZI.—(1) Section 177 (procedure where appellant in custody) applies in the case where a party making an appeal (other than an excepted appeal) under section 194ZB(1) is in custody as it applies in the case where an appellant making an application under section 176 is in custody. **A4-410.53**

(2) In subsection (1), "excepted appeal" means an appeal against a decision of the Sheriff Appeal Court in—
(a) an appeal under section 32, or
(b) an appeal under section 177(3).

Amendments

Section 194ZI inserted by Courts Reform (Scotland) Act 2014 (asp 8) s.119. Brought into force on September 22, 2015 by SSI 2015/247 (C.35) art.2 and Sch.

[THE NEXT PARAGRAPH IS A4-410.56]

Abandonment of appeal

194ZJ. An appellant in an appeal under section 194ZB(1) may at any time abandon the appeal by minute to that effect— **A4-410.56**
(a) signed by the appellant or the appellant's solicitor,
(b) lodged with the Clerk of Justiciary, and
(c) intimated to the respondent or the respondent's solicitor.

Amendments

Section 194ZJ inserted by Courts Reform (Scotland) Act 2014 (asp 8) s.119. Brought into force on September 22, 2015 by SSI 2015/247 (C.35) art.2 and Sch.

[THE NEXT PARAGRAPH IS A4-410.59]

Finality of proceedings

194ZK.—(1) Every interlocutor and sentence (including disposal or order) pronounced by the High Court in disposing of an appeal relating to summary proceedings is final and conclusive and not subject to review by any court whatsoever. **A4-410.59**

(2) Subsection (1) is subject to—

(a) Part XA and section 288AA, and
(b) paragraph 13(a) of Schedule 6 to the Scotland Act 1998.

(3) It is incompetent to stay or suspend any execution or diligence issuing from the High Court under this Part, except for the purposes of an appeal under—
(a) section 288AA, or
(b) paragraph 13(a) of Schedule 6 to the Scotland Act 1998.

Amendments

Section 194ZK inserted by Courts Reform (Scotland) Act 2014 (asp 8) s.119. Brought into force on September 22, 2015 by SSI 2015/247 (C.35) art.2 and Sch.

[THE NEXT PARAGRAPH IS A4-410.62]

Computation of time

A4-410.62 **194ZL.** If any period of time specified in this Part expires on a Saturday, Sunday or court holiday prescribed for the relevant court, the period is extended to expire on the next day which is not a Saturday, Sunday or such a court holiday.

Amendments

Section 194ZL inserted by Courts Reform (Scotland) Act 2014 (asp 8) s.119. Brought into force on September 22, 2015 by SSI 2015/247 (C.35) art.2 and Sch.

[THE NEXT PARAGRAPH IS A4-410.65]

Part XI – Sentencing

General Note

Sentencing Part

A4-410.65 Thomson has expressed the view that "as every practitioner knows, sentencing, and in particular custodial sentencing, has become significantly more complex in recent years. Sentencing is now, in all its particulars, a creature of statute alone". He goes on to explain that Parliament has, of late, tended to insert express statements as to the purpose of sentencing into the legislation itself, rather than leaving this to the good sense and discretion of the sentencer and he observes that:

> "While this no doubt fulfils two functions in that it makes sentencing more transparent and allows the public a greater understanding of the considerations behind certain sentences as selected, it cannot be regarded as making the task of the sentencer any easier" (Douglas J.C. Thomson, "The punishment part of a discretionary life sentence-a difficulty remains" 2011 S.L.T. 105).

Sir Gerald Gordon is less polite. Introducing Ch.23 of *Renton and Brown's Criminal Procedure*, 6th Edition, he writes:

> "What follows is an attempt, which may not be entirely successful, to state in intelligible English the current effect of the dog's breakfast which has resulted from both the United Kingdom and Scottish Parliaments' restless desire to tamper with the law ... dealing with the disposal of offenders".

[THE NEXT PARAGRAPH IS A4-411]

General

Remit to High Court for sentence

A4-411 **195.**—(1) Where at any diet in proceedings on indictment in the sheriff court, sentence falls to be imposed but the sheriff holds that any competent sentence which he can impose is inadequate or it appears to him that the criteria mentioned in section 210E of this Act (that is to say, the risk criteria) may be met so that, in either case, the question of sentence is appropriate for the High Court, he shall—
(a) endorse upon the record copy of the indictment a certificate of the plea or the verdict, as the case may be;

(b) by interlocutor written on the record copy remit the convicted person to the High Court for sentence; and

(c) append to the interlocutor a note of his reasons for the remit,

and a remit under this section shall be sufficient warrant to bring the accused before the High Court for sentence and shall remain in force until the person is sentenced.

(2) Where under any enactment an offence is punishable on conviction on indictment by imprisonment for a term exceeding five years but the enactment either expressly or impliedly restricts the power of the sheriff to impose a sentence of imprisonment for a term exceeding five years, it shall be competent for the sheriff to remit the accused to the High Court for sentence under subsection (1) above; and it shall be competent for the High Court to pass any sentence which it could have passed if the person had been convicted before it.

(3) When the Clerk of Justiciary receives the record copy of the indictment he shall send a copy of the note of reasons to the convicted person or his solicitor and to the Crown Agent.

(4) Subject to subsection (3) above, the note of reasons shall be available only to the High Court and the parties.

AMENDMENTS

Subs.(2) as amended by Crime and Punishment (Scotland) Act 1997 (c.48) s.13(3). Brought into force on May 1, 2004 by SSI 2004/176 (C.12).

Subs.(1) as amended by Criminal Justice (Scotland) Act 2003 (asp 7) Sch.1 para.2(5). Brought into force on June 19, 2006 by SSI 2006/332 (C.30) art.2(1), subject to art.2(2).

DEFINITIONS

"Clerk of Justiciary": s.307(1). A4-411.1
"diet": s.307(1).
"enactment": s.307(1).
"High Court": s.307(1).
"indictment": s.307(1).
"sentence": s.307(1).

[THE NEXT PARAGRAPH IS A4-412]

GENERAL NOTE

Subs.(1)

This subsection reproduces the terms of s.104(1) of the 1975 Act in requiring a remit where "the sheriff holds that any competent sentence which he can impose is inadequate so that the question of sentence is appropriate for the High Court". This contrasts with the original position in s.31 of the Criminal Procedure (Scotland) Act 1887 (c.35) which required a remit if the sheriff held that if the case was "of so grave a nature" that the question of punishment should be disposed of by the High Court of Justiciary. Care must be taken that the plea and remit are properly authenticated: *HM Advocate v Galloway* (1894) 1 Adam 375 and *HM Advocate v McDonald* (1896) 3 S.L.T. 317. The sheriff who remits the accused merely means the sheriff who has the duty to sentence: *Borland v HM Advocate*, 1976 S.L.T. (Notes) 12. A4-412

Subs.(2)

This subsection reproduces the terms of s.104(1A) of the 1975 Act as amended. The maximum competent sentence must be considered by the sheriff before remit, and where there are two or more indictments, each indictment must be considered separately. Where the maximum sentence which could be imposed on an indictment was within the competence of the sheriff then he must deal with that indictment: *HM Advocate v Anderson*, 1946 J.C. 81. Each of several indictments must be considered separately: *HM Advocate v Stern*, 1974 S.L.T. 2.

Sentence following guilty plea

196.—(1) In determining what sentence to pass on, or what other disposal or order to make in relation to, an offender who has pled guilty to an offence, a court shall take into account— A4-413

(a) the stage in the proceedings for the offence at which the offender indicated his intention to plead guilty, and

(b) the circumstances in which that indication was given.

(1A) In passing sentence on an offender referred to in subsection (1) above, the court shall—

(a) state whether, having taken account of the matters mentioned in paragraphs (a) and (b) of that subsection, the sentence imposed in respect of the offence is different from that which the court would otherwise have imposed; and

(b) if it is not, state reasons why it is not.

(2) Where the court is passing sentence on an offender under section 205B(2) of this Act and that offender has pled guilty to the offence for which he is being so sentenced, the court may, after taking into account the matters mentioned in paragraphs (a) and (b) of subsection (1) above, pass a sentence of less than seven years imprisonment or, as the case may be, detention but any such sentence shall not be of a term of imprisonment or period of detention of less than five years, two hundred and nineteen days.

AMENDMENTS

Subs.(2) inserted by Crime and Punishment (Scotland) Act 1997 (c.48) s.2(2) with effect from 20 October 1997 in terms of SI 1997/2323 art.3 and Sch.1.

Subs.(1) as amended, and subs.(1A) inserted, by Criminal Procedure (Amendment) (Scotland) Act 2004 (asp 5) s.20. Brought into force on 4 October 2004 by SSI 2004/405 (C.28).

DEFINITION

A4-413.1 "sentence": s.307(1).

[THE NEXT PARAGRAPH IS A4-414]

GENERAL NOTE

A4-414 The rationale of this provision, requiring a sentencing court to take account of the utilitarian value to the justice system of early pleas of guilt, and discount the sentence which a conviction would otherwise attract, was set out in *Du Plooy v HM Advocate*, 2003 S.L.T. 1237; 2003 S.C.C.R. 640 and refined further in *HM Advocate v Booth*, 2005 S.L.T. 337. Unsurprisingly, given its nature, this section has attracted a substantial volume of case law all of which must now be read under reference to *Gemmell v HM Advocate* 2012 S.C.C.R. 176 (reaffirmed in *Wilson v Shanks*, 2018 S.C.C.R. 302) discussed below. This case signalled the abandonment of any rigid or formalised scale of sentencing reduction; indeed, as both *Booth* and *Gemmell* decisions say, while a reduction in sentence may ordinarily follow upon a timely plea of guilt, there is in fact no automatic right to a reduction at all. Moreover, *Gemmell* indicates that the protection of the public, as well as any mitigatory material, must be factored into the sentence at the outset and confirms that (s.196(2) apart) the section does not empower the sentencing court to reduce a statutory minimum sentence.

Sentencers have first to consider the appropriate sentence having regard to the factual circumstances, public protection, the accused's record and any mitigatory plea, then factor in the timing of the plea to consider whether a discount from the appropriate sentence ought to be granted, and finally the scale of such discount. Only once this process is completed should the court then move on to consider backdating of sentence in respect of time spent on remand prior to sentence (see generally s.210 below).

In *MacLeod (Carol Anne) v HM Advocate*, unreported but digested by Graeme Brown in [2017] Crim. L.B. 149–7, the sentencing judge would have taken a starting point of five years but, because the appellant had spent five months on remand, took a starting point of four years. (She was bailed to await the outcome against a co-accused so the sentence could not just be backdated). He then discounted that for the plea to three years. It was argued on appeal that the correct approach was to select a starting point, apply the discount and then take into account the period on remand. Lords Carloway and Turnbull endorsed the approach of the sentencing judge. Lord Carloway said

> "the appropriate course is to select a starting point which will have taken into account all relevant matters, including any period spent on remand. Only once that starting point has been selected should the discount be applied".

It is axiomatic that parties should be in a position to inform the court of the stage in proceedings when the plea, in the form tendered to it, was proposed and accepted. As well as a time line, the terms of the plea (whether accepted or rejected at that point) ought to be properly documented, or formally minuted, at any preliminary hearing or first diet. See *Spence v HM Advocate*, 2007 S.C.C.R. 592 and the general warning to practitioners from the Appeal Court in *HM Advocate v Simpson* [2009] HCJAC 41; 2009 S.C.C.R. 554.

Note that while s.131 of the Criminal Justice and Licensing (Scotland) Act 2010 (asp 13) provides that the duties of disclosure incumbent on the prosecutor cease from the time of a guilty plea being recorded, the Convention compatibility of that section must be open to question. (See General Note to said section at para.A160-133). The sentencing phase of proceedings is still subject to the requirements of art.6 ECHR and, in any case, the prosecutor would still have an overriding obligation to ensure that material favourable to the accused's case be communicated to his agent and the court once known.

In cases involving road traffic offences, the scale of penalty points can be susceptible to discount as a part of the sentencing process (*Watt v PF Dunfermline* [2016] SAC (Crim) 2).

Practice Notes

Practice Note (No.1 of 2008) Recording of Sentencing Discount requires all sentencing courts openly to record the sentence imposed upon an accused and to specify any discount applied, and the base sentence which would otherwise have applied in the absence of a guilty plea. These calculations, and the justification for the discount, or absence thereof, should be set out in any appeal report.

In the interests of sentencing transparency the Appeal Court has reiterated that the sentencing judge should first calculate and state the determinate sentence which would have been imposed in the event of trial then apply any discount considered appropriate to reflect the whole circumstances and timing of the guilty plea (*Raffan v HM Advocate*, 2009 J.C. 133). Scots criminal procedure deprecates any effort to solicit an indication in advance of the plea of the likely sentence from the trial judge (*Allan v HM Advocate*, 2009 S.C.C.R. 331).

Subs.(1)

Sentence: In *Gemmell v HM Advocate* [2011] HCJAC 129, it was held that, subject to subs.(2), where that applies, the requirements of the section apply to the whole sentence, including any disqualification from driving or endorsement of penalty points on a licence, though a sentence must not be discounted below the statutory minimum. The only exception is the extension period contemplated in s.210A. See also *MacLean v Procurator Fiscal Stornoway* [2015] HCJAC 77, a case where the judge had reflected an early guilty plea to Road Traffic Act offences by including reductions to penalty points which fell below the statutory tariffs.

A court shall take into account: In *Gemmell* the Lord Justice Clerk (Lord Gill) said that the wording of s.196 "indicates that the decisions whether to allow a discount and, if so, what discount to allow, remain a matter for the discretion of the sentencer" (at [29]). The discounting process was analysed in three stages, namely (1) to decide what the sentence would be if no question of a discount arose (which the appeal court referred to as the "headline" sentence); (2) to decide whether there should be a discount; and (3) if so, to decide what the amount of it should be (at [27]). In *Gemmell*, the Lord Justice Clerk (Gill) described the assessment of the headline sentence and the assessment of any discount as "separate processes governed by separate criteria" (at [37]).

The assessment of the headline sentence is not discussed here. As to whether there should be a discount at all, although it is clear from *Gemmell* and also from *Du Plooy v HM Advocate*, 2005 1 J.C. 1 that there is no absolute entitlement to a discount, the Lord Justice Clerk, in *Gemmell*, observed that "[s]ince there will always be some benefit in an early plea, if only in the administrative benefits that flow from it, I find it difficult to imagine circumstances in which an early plea would not entitle the accused to at least a token discount".

See *Murray v HM Advocate*, 2013 S.C.C.R. 88, an appeal against sentence following a s.76 plea centred on the limited discount on sentence, in which unusually the headline sentence was increased. The court noted that the appellant had admitted guilt to the police at the outset, but that a period of two months followed his petition appearance before s.76 procedures began. In any event, there were no positive utilitarian factors since there had never been any question of the vulnerable elderly complainers ever being called to give evidence.

The level of discount requires much more attention. Prior to *Gemmell*, there was a tendency to think in terms of a sliding scale but the court in that case disapproved of that approach. The Lord Justice Clerk said that the only relevant consideration in relation to the matter of a discount is how far the so-called utilitarian benefits of the early plea have been achieved (at [38]) and that when the court comes to the second and third stages of its consideration, "the two questions to be answered are how early the plea was tendered and the extent to which the tendering of it furthered the objective justification set out in *Du Plooy*". It will be recalled that that objective justification is that the tendering of a plea of guilty is likely to save public money and court time, and in general avoid inconvenience to witnesses or, in certain types of cases, avoid additional distress being caused by their being required to give evidence or be precognosced for that purpose (*Du Plooy*, per Lord Justice General (Cullen) at [16]). In *Gemmell*, Lord Eassie said that utilitarian benefit should be assessed on a broad brush basis and that the principle criterion should be the timing of the plea (at [146]). It is incorrect to limit the discount so as to avoid what the sentencer regards as disproportionate dilution of the headline sentence (*Kindness v HM Advocate* [2014] HCJAC 5). It is also incorrect to increase the discount on account of the backlog in the courts, or on account of difficulties in prisons, brought about by COVID-19 (*HM Advocate v Lindsay*, 2020 S.C.C.R. 324).

In *Gemmell* the court held that the following matters relate to headline sentence but have no relevance to discounting: previous convictions and protection of the public; assistance to the authorities; remorse; unco-operative behaviour. The strength of the Crown case does not operate to reduce the discount, contrary to what was said in a number of cases decided before *Gemmell*.

The following observations in *Spence v HM Advocate*, 2007 S.C.C.R. 592 at [14] should be read in light of the foregoing general principles:

> "The extent of the discount will be on a sliding scale ranging at its greatest from one-third, or in exceptional circumstances possibly more, to nil. The utilitarian value of an early plea will be influenced by, among other things, the extent of the public resources which will be expended in preparing a case for trial and presenting it at trial. After an accused has appeared on petition, investigation and preparation will to an increasing extent be undertaken by the Crown prior to the service of an indictment. Among other courses open to an accused person during that period is the giving of written intimation to the Crown under section 76 of the 1995 Act of his intention to plead guilty and his desire to have his case disposed of at once. If a clear indication of an intention to plead guilty is given during that period (and is adhered to), we would expect that a discount in the order of one-third might be afforded. Such an indication at the first calling of a case at a preliminary hearing (or in the sheriff court at a first diet) might attract a discount in the order of one-quarter. Thereafter, any discount can be expected to reduce further. A plea at the trial diet should not ordinarily exceed one-tenth and in some circumstances may be less than that or nil"."

In *McInally v Procurator Fiscal, Edinburgh* [2016] SAC (Crim) 5, the sentencing sheriff, in dealing with a particularly bad contravention of s.3 of the Road Traffic Act 1988, did not discount the penalty points. He imposed eight points (the maximum provided for being nine). In the Opinion of the Court, delivered by Sheriff Principal MM Stephen QC, the Sheriff Appeal Court said that discount is not an automatic entitlement and that the issue for that court is whether the sheriff has given cogent reasons for not discounting penalty points. She said that it is only in exceptional cases that there will be interference with a discretionary decision on discount. She also said that the sheriff had "afforded the appellant a generously discounted penalty by … declining to disqualify".

The stage in the proceedings … at which the offender indicated his intention to plead guilty: It is an intention to plead guilty which matters, not an enquiry about whether the Crown would accept a particular plea; and the clearest manifestation of that intention is a formal plea duly tendered and recorded. The benefit will be lost, however, if the accused takes advantage of the rejection of the plea by the Crown to run a substantive defence, even if the eventual conviction is for no more than was offered (for all of this, see Lord Marnoch in *Balgowan v HM Advocate*, 2011 S.C.C.R. 143 at [5]). See, however, *Rippon v HM Advocate*, 2012 S.C.C.R. 699, a murder libel in which a discount of one sixth was applied, on appeal, following the guidelines in *Boyle v HM Advocate*, 2010 J.C. 66 to sentence imposed at a continued preliminary diet, the continuation being needed to enable clarification of the accused's fitness to plead to the libel before a guilty plea was tendered.

The circumstances in which that indication was given: In *HM Advocate v Thomson*, 2006 S.C.C.R. 265 and again in *Gemmell v HM Advocate* [2011] HCJAC 129 the Lord Justice Clerk (Lord Gill) emphasised that it is specious to argue that an accused is justified in withholding an early plea yet invoking s.196 where there has been a delay in obtaining disclosure from the Crown. In *Thomson*, he said "[i]f an accused person has committed the crime charged he can plead guilty to it at the outset and benefit from his plea by way of discount when the sentence is assessed; or he can defer pleading until he is sure that the Crown have a corroborated case, in the knowledge that a sentence discount may be reduced or refused altogether. That is the choice that he must make. He cannot have it both ways" (at [27]).

See also Graeme Brown's article entitled "Discounts and discretion—Gemmell v HM Advocate", 2012 Crim. L.B. 115–1 (February 2012).

The section's provisions do not empower the sentencing court to apply any form of discount to the unexpired portion of any sentence still live in terms of s.16 of the Prisoners and Criminal Proceedings (Scotland) Act 1993 (c.9); see *Ottaway v HM Advocate* [2012] HCJAC 36; 2012 S.L.T. 662. The sentencing judge, where it is competent to do so, may elect to modify that unexpired portion but not by means of s.196.

The period of time an accused has spent on bail curfew conditions awaiting trial does not constitute part of a sentence and thus cannot merit a sentencing discount save in the most exceptional circumstances, for example, the trial having been extremely delayed and the accused having no role in that delay (see *McGill v HM Advocate* [2013] HCJAC 150).

Sentencing guidelines

A4-415 **197.** Without prejudice to any rule of law, a court in passing sentence shall have regard to any relevant opinion pronounced under section 118(7) or section 189(7) of this Act.

General Note

A4-416 For guidance on sentencing in relation to the production of cannabis, see *Zhi Pen Lin v HM Advocate* [2007] HCJAC 62.

For guidance on sentencing in relation to indecent images of children, see *HM Advocate v Graham*, 2011 J.C. 1 and *Moore v HM Advocate* [2018] HCJAC 40.

For guidance on sentencing in relation to benefit fraud, see *Gill v Thomson*, 2012 J.C. 137 read in the light of *Bradley v Procurator Fiscal, Falkirk* [2010] HCJAC 136 and *Ryan v Procurator Fiscal, Aberdeen* [2014] HCJAC 106.

For guidance on sentencing young offenders, see *Murray v HM Advocate* [2018] HCJAC 27 (and *HM v HM Advocate* [2018] HCJAC 26 for guidance on sentencing adults who committed serious sexual offences when they were children).

Form of sentence

198.—(1) In any case the sentence to be pronounced shall be announced by the judge in open court and shall be entered in the record in the form prescribed by Act of Adjournal. A4-417

(2) In recording a sentence of imprisonment, it shall be sufficient to minute the term of imprisonment to which the court sentenced the accused, without specifying the prison in which the sentence is to be carried out; and an entry of sentence, signed by the clerk of court, shall be full warrant and authority for any subsequent execution of the sentence and for the clerk to issue extracts for the purposes of execution or otherwise.

(3) In extracting a sentence of imprisonment, the extract may be in the form set out in an Act of Adjournal or as nearly as may be in such form.

Definitions

"sentence": s.307(1). A4-417.1

General Note

O'Neill v HM Advocate, 1999 S.L.T. 364 establishes that all information which an accused seeks to place before a sentencing court as mitigation must be produced in open court. (In *O'Neill's* case information showing his previous co-operation with the police was produced to the trial judge who declined to consider the papers on the basis that the contents could not be discussed publicly.) A4-417.2

In *Steele v HM Advocate*, 2002 S.L.T. 868 the court was reconvened after sentence had been imposed upon the accused when it was realised that no disqualification from driving had been pronounced. On appeal the accused's contention was that no such disqualification could be imposed upon him by the judge; it was argued that the judge was by that stage functus officio and enjoyed no *locus* to sentence. The Appeal Court was satisfied that a valid sentence had been passed in open court.

[THE NEXT PARAGRAPH IS A4-418]

Power to mitigate penalties

199.—(1) Subject to subsection (3) below, where a person is convicted of the contravention of an enactment and the penalty which may be imposed involves— A4-418

(a) imprisonment;

(b) the imposition of a fine;

(c) the finding of caution for good behaviour or otherwise whether or not imposed in addition to imprisonment or a fine,

subsection (2) below shall apply.

(2) Where this subsection applies, the court, in addition to any other power conferred by statute, shall have power—

(a) to reduce the period of imprisonment;

(b) to substitute for imprisonment a fine (either with or without the finding of caution for good behaviour);

(c) to substitute for imprisonment or a fine the finding of caution;

(d) to reduce the amount of the fine;

(e) to dispense with the finding of caution.

(3) Subsection (2) above shall not apply—

(a) in relation to an enactment which carries into effect a treaty, convention, or agreement with a foreign state which stipulates for a fine of a minimum amount;

(b) to proceedings taken under any Act relating to any of Her Majesty's regular or auxiliary forces; or

(c) to any proceedings in which the court on conviction is under a duty to impose a sentence under section 205A(2) or 205B(2) of this Act.

(4) Where, in summary proceedings, a fine is imposed in substitution for imprisonment, the fine—

(a) in the case of an offence which is triable either summarily or on indictment, shall not exceed the prescribed sum; and
(b) in the case of an offence triable only summarily, shall not exceed level 4 on the standard scale.

(5) Where the finding of caution is imposed under this section—
(a) in respect of an offence which is triable only summarily, the amount shall not exceed level 4 on the standard scale and the period shall not exceed that which the court may impose under this Act; and
(b) in any other case, the amount shall not exceed the prescribed sum and the period shall not exceed 12 months.

AMENDMENTS

Subs.(3)(c) inserted by Crime and Punishment (Scotland) Act 1997 Sch.1, para.21 with effect from October 20, 1997 as provided by SI 1997/2323.

DEFINITIONS

A4-418.1 "fine": s.307(1).
"indictment": s.307(1).
"level 4": s.225(2) [i.e. £2,500].
"prescribed sum": s.225(8).
"standard scale": s.225(1).

GENERAL NOTE

A4-418.2 This section applies to all proceedings, subject to the express restrictions set out in subs.(3), and empowers the court to modify or amend sentences previously imposed. As the section description makes clear, the provisions can only be used to mitigate (reduce) sentence. Subs.(3) specifies the circumstances in which no exercise of this general post-sentencing discretion is permissible.

[THE NEXT PARAGRAPH IS A4-419]

Pre-sentencing procedure

Remand for inquiry into physical or mental condition

A4-419 **200.**—(1) Without prejudice to any powers exercisable by a court under section 201 of this Act, where—
(a) the court finds that an accused has committed an offence punishable with imprisonment; and
(b) it appears to the court that before the method of dealing with him is determined an inquiry ought to be made into his physical or mental condition,

subsection (2) below shall apply.

(2) Where this subsection applies the court shall—
(a) for the purpose of inquiry solely into his physical condition, remand him in custody or on bail;
(b) for the purpose of inquiry into his mental condition (whether or not in addition to his physical condition), remand him in custody or on bail or, where the court is satisfied—
(i) on the written or oral evidence of a medical practitioner, that the person appears to be suffering from a mental disorder; and
(ii) that the accused could be admitted to a hospital that is suitable for his detention,

make an order committing him to that hospital,

for such period or periods, no single period exceeding three weeks, as the court thinks necessary to enable a medical examination and report to be made.

(3) Where the court is of the opinion that a person ought to continue to be committed to hospital for the purpose of inquiry into his mental condition following the

expiry of the period specified in an order for committal to hospital under paragraph (b) of subsection (2) above, the court may—

(a) if the condition in sub-paragraph (i) of that paragraph continues to be satisfied and he could be admitted to a hospital that is suitable for his continued detention, renew the order for such further period not exceeding three weeks as the court thinks necessary to enable a medical examination and report to be made; and

(b) in any other case, remand the person in custody or on bail in accordance with subsection (2) above.

(4) An order under subsection (3)(a) above may, unless objection is made by or on behalf of the person to whom it relates, be made in his absence.

(5) Where, before the expiry of the period specified in an order for committal to hospital under subsection (2)(b) above, the court considers, on an application made to it, that committal to hospital is no longer required in relation to the person, the court shall revoke the order and may make such other order, under subsection (2)(a) above or any other provision of this Part of this Act, as the court considers appropriate.

(6) Where an accused is remanded on bail under this section, it shall be a condition of the order granting bail that he shall—

(a) undergo a medical examination by a duly qualified registered medical practitioner or, where the inquiry is into his mental condition, and the order granting bail so specifies, two such practitioners; and

(b) for the purpose of such examination, attend at an institution or place, or on any such practitioner specified in the order granting bail and, where the inquiry is into his mental condition, comply with any directions which may be given to him for the said purpose by any person so specified or by a person of any class so specified,

and, if arrangements have been made for his reception, it may be a condition of the order granting bail that the person shall, for the purpose of the examination, reside in an institution or place specified as aforesaid, not being an institution or place to which he could have been remanded in custody, until the expiry of such period as may be so specified or until he is discharged therefrom, whichever first occurs.

(7) On exercising the powers conferred by this section to remand in custody or on bail the court shall—

(a) where the person is remanded in custody, send to the institution or place in which he is detained; and

(b) where the person is released on bail, send to the institution or place at which or the person by whom he is to be examined,

a statement of the reasons for which it appears to the court that an inquiry ought to be made into his physical or mental condition, and of any information before the court about his physical or mental condition.

(8) On making an order of committal to hospital under subsection (2)(b) above the court shall send to the hospital specified in the order a statement of the reasons for which the court is of the opinion that an inquiry ought to be made into the mental condition of the person to whom it relates, and of any information before the court about his mental condition.

(9) A person remanded under this section may, before the expiry of the period of 24 hours beginning with his remand, appeal to the appropriate Appeal Court by note of appeal against the refusal of bail or against the conditions imposed and a person committed to hospital under this section may, at any time during the period when the order for his committal, or, as the case may be, renewal of such order, is in force, appeal to the appropriate Appeal Court by note of appeal against the order of

committal, and the appropriate Appeal Court, either in court or in chambers, may after hearing parties—

(a) review the order and grant bail on such conditions as it thinks fit; or
(b) confirm the order; or
(c) in the case of an appeal against an order of committal to hospital, revoke the order and remand the person in custody.

(9A) A note of appeal under subsection (9) above is to be—

(a) lodged with the clerk of the court from which the appeal is to be taken; and
(b) sent without delay by that clerk (where not the clerk of the appropriate Appeal Court) to the clerk of the appropriate Appeal Court.

(10) The court may, on cause shown, vary an order for committal to hospital under subsection (2)(b) above by substituting another hospital for the hospital specified in the order.

(11) Subsection (2)(b) above shall apply to the variation of an order under subsection (10) above as it applies to the making of an order for committal to hospital.

(12) In this section—

"appropriate Appeal Court" means—

(a) in the case of an appeal under subsection (9) against a decision of the High Court, that Court;
(b) in the case of an appeal under subsection (9) against a decision of a sheriff (whether in solemn or summary proceedings) or a JP court, the Sheriff Appeal Court; and

"the clerk of the appropriate Appeal Court" means—

(a) in a case where the High Court is the appropriate Appeal Court, the Clerk of Justiciary;
(b) in a case where the Sheriff Appeal Court is the appropriate Appeal Court, the Clerk of that Court.

AMENDMENTS

Subss.(2)(b) and (3)(a) as amended by Mental Health (Care and Treatment) (Scotland) Act 2003 (asp 13) Sch.4, para.8(13). Brought into force on October 5, 2005 by SSI 2005/161 (C.6).

Subs.(9) as amended by Mental Health (Care and Treatment) (Scotland) Act 2003 (asp 13) s.132 and Sch.5. Brought into force on October 5, 2005 as above.

Subs.(9) as amended and subs.(9A) inserted by Criminal Proceedings etc. (Reform) (Scotland) Act 2007 (asp 6) s.6. Brought into force on December 10, 2007 by SSI 2007/479.

Subss.(9) and (9A) as amended, subs.(12) inserted, by Courts Reform (Scotland) Act 2014 (Consequential Provisions No.2) Order 2015 (SSI 2015/338) Sch.2 para.5 (effective September 22, 2015).

DEFINITIONS

A4-419.1 "bail": s.307(1).
"hospital": s.307(1).
"registered medical practitioner": s.2 of the Medical Act 1983 (c.54).

[THE NEXT PARAGRAPH IS A4-420]

Power of court to adjourn case before sentence

A4-420 **201.**—(1) Where an accused has been convicted or the court has found that he committed the offence and before he has been sentenced or otherwise dealt with, subject to subsection (3) below, the court may adjourn the case for the purpose of enabling inquiries to be made or of determining the most suitable method of dealing with his case.

(2) Where the court adjourns a case solely for the purpose mentioned in subsection (1) above, it shall remand the accused in custody or on bail or ordain him to appear at the adjourned diet.

(3) Subject to section 21(9) of the Criminal Justice (Scotland) Act 2003 (asp 7), a court shall not adjourn the hearing of a case as mentioned in subsection (1) above for any single period exceeding four weeks or, on cause shown, eight weeks.

(4) An accused who is remanded under this section may appeal to the appropriate Appeal Court against the refusal of bail or against the conditions imposed within 24 hours of his remand, by note of appeal, and the appropriate Appeal Court, either in court or in chambers, may—

(a) review the order appealed against and either grant bail on such conditions as it thinks fit or ordain the accused to appear at the adjourned diet; or

(b) confirm the order.

(5) A note of appeal under subsection (4) above is to be—

(a) lodged with the clerk of the court from which the appeal is to be taken; and

(b) sent without delay by that clerk (where not the clerk of the appropriate Appeal Court) to the clerk of the appropriate Appeal Court.

(6) In this section—

"appropriate Appeal Court" means—

(a) in the case of an appeal under subsection (4) against a decision of the High Court, that Court;

(b) in the case of an appeal under subsection (4) against a decision of a sheriff (whether in solemn or summary proceedings) or a JP court, the Sheriff Appeal Court; and

"the clerk of the appropriate Appeal Court" means—

(a) in a case where the High Court is the appropriate Appeal Court, the Clerk of Justiciary;

(b) in a case where the Sheriff Appeal Court is the appropriate Appeal Court, the Clerk of that Court.

AMENDMENTS

Subsection (3) as amended by Criminal Justice (Scotland) Act 2003 (asp 7) Pt 8 s.67. Brought into force on 27 June 2003 by SSI 2003/288 (C.14).

Subsection (3) as amended by Criminal Justice (Scotland) Act 2003 (asp 7) Pt 3 s.21(10). Brought into force on 10 June 2004 by SSI 2004/240 (C.16).

Subsection (4) as amended and subs.(5) inserted by Criminal Proceedings etc. (Reform) (Scotland) Act 2007 (asp 6) ss.6, 80 and Sch. para18(4). Brought into force on 10 December 2007 by SSI 2007/479 art.3 and Sch.

Subsections (4) and (5) as amended, subs.(6) inserted, by Courts Reform (Scotland) Act 2014 (Consequential Provisions No.2) Order 2015 (SSI 2015/338) Sch.2 para.5 (effective 22 September 2015).

Power of court to adjourn case before sentence

201.—*(1) Where an accused has been convicted or the court has found that he committed the offence and before he has been sentenced or otherwise dealt with, subject to subsection (3) below, the court may adjourn the case for the purpose of enabling inquiries to be made or of determining the most suitable method of dealing with his case.* A4-420A

(2) Where the court adjourns a case solely for the purpose mentioned in subsection (1) above, it shall remand the accused in custody or on bail or ordain him to appear at the adjourned diet.

(3) The court may adjourn the hearing of a case as mentioned in subsection (1) for such period as it considers appropriate.

(4) An accused who is remanded under this section may appeal to the appropriate Appeal Court against the refusal of bail or against the conditions imposed within 24 hours of his remand, by note of appeal, and the appropriate Appeal Court, either in court or in chambers, may—

(a) review the order appealed against and either grant bail on such conditions as it thinks fit or ordain the accused to appear at the adjourned diet; or

(b) confirm the order.

(5) A note of appeal under subsection (4) above is to be—

(a) lodged with the clerk of the court from which the appeal is to be taken; and

(b) sent without delay by that clerk (where not the clerk of the appropriate Appeal Court) to the clerk of the appropriate Appeal Court.

(6) In this section—

"appropriate Appeal Court" means—

(a) in the case of an appeal under subsection (4) against a decision of the High Court, that Court;

(b) in the case of an appeal under subsection (4) against a decision of a sheriff (whether in solemn or summary proceedings) or a JP court, the Sheriff Appeal Court; and

"the clerk of the appropriate Appeal Court" means—

(a) in a case where the High Court is the appropriate Appeal Court, the Clerk of Justiciary;

(b) in a case where the Sheriff Appeal Court is the appropriate Appeal Court, the Clerk of that Court.

AMENDMENTS

In relation to COVID-19, s.201 as amended by Coronavirus (Scotland) Act 2020 (asp 7) Sch.4(4) para.10(6) (effective 7 April 2020).

DEFINITIONS

A4-420.1 "bail": s.307(1).
"diet": s.307(1).
"remand": s.307(1).

GENERAL NOTE

A4-421 The antecedent provisions conjoined for this section have produced a considerable number of authorities, those provisions being ss.179 and 380 of the 1975 Act as amended. The principal point to note is that it is of paramount importance for courts at first instance to have in mind the clear statutory distinction between adjourning a case before sentence and deferring sentence. In *HM Advocate v Clegg*, 1991 S.L.T. 192 it was held that to obtain various reports for sentencing the correct approach is to adjourn the case and not to defer sentence, a distinction that was emphasised in *McRobbie v HM Advocate*, 1990 S.C.C.R 767. Refer also to *Airlie v Heywood*, 1996 S.C.C.R. 562 where sentence had been deferred for good behaviour, social inquiry reports and to ascertain the effect of conviction upon the accused's taxi licence; it was held that the adjournment had been at common law and was not a statutory one limited to eight weeks.

Subs.(3)

At the very least when adjourning a case for sentence in excess of four weeks, it must be recorded in the minutes that the adjournment was on cause shown otherwise the Appeal Court can have no inkling of its purpose (*Dingwall v Vannet*, 1997 S.C.C.R. 515). Although there is no requirement that the reason for such a length of adjournment be stated either in court or in the minutes themselves, it would seem sensible (if only as a means of answering any points taken on appeal) that such steps be taken. See too *Napier v Dyer*, 2001 S.L.T. 1298 in which following a guilty plea and deferment of sentence, the accused was permitted to tender a late plea to the competency of proceedings founding upon the role of a temporary sheriff at an earlier point in the case (see *Starrs v Ruxton*, 2000 S.L.T. 42; 1999 S.C.C.R. 1052). Rather than the court permitting withdrawal of earlier pleas, the diet was adjourned; the accused later asserted that further proceedings were now incompetent in his bill of advocation. The Appeal Court agreed that procedure had gone awry but held that no particular form of wording was necessary in minuting such an adjournment where the court's intention was clear.

The necessity of abiding by the statutory time-limits was shown in *Wilson v Donald*, 1993 S.L.T. 31 because, while the continuation was recorded as a deferred sentence, the obtaining of a DVLA printout during a period greater than three weeks was an adjournment to which the time-limits applied. This point was applied in *Holburn v Lees*, 1993 S.C.C.R. 426 and *Burns v Wilson*, 1993 S.C.C.R. 418 although it was held that convictions were unaffected by these appeals on procedural points although the sentences were suspended: see also *McCulloch v Scott*, 1993 S.L.T. 901.

A further distinction became apparent in *Douglas v Jamieson*, 1993 S.L.T. 816 and *Douglas v Peddie*, 1993 S.C.C.R. 717 where it was held that with a combination of guilty and not guilty pleas leading to an adjourned trial diet the court was exercising its power at common law to adjourn at any stage when it seemed appropriate to do so. See also *Mcleod v Hutton (Sh.Ct)*, 1993 S.C.C.R. 747.

The statutory distinction was also held not to apply in *Johnstone v Lees*, 1994 S.L.T. 551 where an adjournment of eight weeks to await the outcome of other cases was deemed competent at common law. In *Gifford v HM Advocate*, 2011 S.C.C.R. 751 adjournment beyond eight weeks for a proof in mitigation was held not to be adjournment in terms of s.201 but rather an adjournment for evidence before proceeding to sentence. A continuation for a proof of a previous conviction is a matter at common law: *Burns v Lees*, 1994 S.C.C.R. 780. "Cause shown" (subs.(3)(9b)) was held to extend to an extension of the four week period of deferment at Christmas where a social worker had requested additional time to obtain additional material for the accused's report (*Porteous v Hamilton*, 1996 G.W.D. 21–1199).

In the authorities cited, objection to the competency of the various proceedings was taken timeously and to delay without explanation a complaint about competency may amount to acquiescence especially with a long passage of time and a payment of fines as ordered: *Storie v Friel*, 1993 S.C.C.R. 955.

In *Long v HM Advocate*, 1984 S.C.C.R. 161 it was held that review of the court's decision on bail (s.30 of the 1975 Act and this Act) had no application to bail in relation to the power of the court to adjourn a case before sentence.

An adjournment for a proof in mitigation is an adjournment at common law and does not engage s.201(3): *McSporran v HM Advocate* [2011] HCJAC 56.

Deferred sentence

202.—(1) It shall be competent for a court to defer sentence after conviction for a period and on such conditions as the court may determine. A4-422

(2) If it appears to the court which deferred sentence on an accused under subsection (1) above that he has been convicted during the period of deferment, by a court in any part of the United Kingdom or [, where the court which deferred sentence considers appropriate, by a court in any] member State of the European Union of an offence committed during that period and has been dealt with for that offence, the court which deferred sentence may—

(a) issue a warrant for the arrest of the accused; or

(b) instead of issuing such a warrant in the first instance, issue a citation requiring him to appear before it at such time as may be specified in the citation,

and on his appearance or on his being brought before the court it may deal with him in any manner in which it would be competent for it to deal with him on the expiry of the period of deferment.

(3) Where a court which has deferred sentence on an accused under subsection (1) above convicts him of another offence during the period of deferment, it may deal with him for the original offence in any manner in which it would be competent for it to deal with him on the expiry of the period of deferment, as well as for the offence committed during the said period.

Amendments

Subsection (2) as amended by Criminal Justice and Licensing (Scotland) Act 2010 (asp 13) Sch.4 para.4. Brought into force on 13 December 2010 by SSI 2010/413 art.2 and Sch.1 para.1.

Words in subs.(2) were substituted by the Criminal Justice (EU Exit) (Scotland) (Amendment etc.) Regulations 2020 (SSI 2020/339) reg.13(10) (effective December 31, 2020 subject to transitional and saving provision specified in reg.16 of those Regulations.

Definition

"sentence": s.307(1). A4-422.1

[THE NEXT PARAGRAPH IS A4-423]

GENERAL NOTE

A4-423 It is of paramount importance for courts at first instance to have in mind the clear statutory distinction between adjourning a case before sentence and deferring sentence. Regard might be had to the cases in the General Note to s.201 of this Act for the authorities arising from this distinction. The note by A.D. Smith on Deferred Sentences in Scotland, 1968 S.L.T. (Notes) 153 is still of interest.

In *Valentine v Parker*, 1992 S.C.C.R. 695 an appeal was taken during a deferred sentence but in the absence of the court papers the sheriff held the calling of the case on the appropriate date for consideration was incompetent. A Crown Bill of Advocation was passed and it was held by the High Court of Justiciary that the deferred sentence had been superceded by the appeal proceedings and the case was remitted to the sheriff for sentence.

In *Maitland v McNaughtan*, 1996 G.W.D. 22–1261 sentence had been deferred for good behaviour. The Appeal Court held that the sheriff erred in holding M to be in breach, when a conviction, for an offence which predated the deferment, and a pending trial, for an offence alleged to have occurred during the period of deferment, were disclosed: the correct approach would have been to defer to await the outcome of the trial.

In *Hart v Hingston*, 2001 G.W.D. 16–620 where following upon a deferment of sentence for good behaviour, and H having failed to maintain payments of other fines, this was held not to be sufficient to entitle the sheriff to conclude that there had been a breach of good behaviour.

In *Fletcher v Walkingshaw*, 1997 G.W.D. 8–327 where sentences of imprisonment were imposed upon the accused, after an initial deferment for restitution had not been complied with, the Appeal Court took account of a non-analogous record and the social enquiry report obtained before deferral, which had concluded that a custodial sentence was inappropriate; a probation order allied to community service (as proposed in the report) was substituted.

When deferring sentence it is probably unwise for the judge either to predict or promise a particular disposal. Any such statement would not be binding on the judge himself or any other judge called upon to dispose of the case (*Laing v Heywood*, 1998 S.C.C.R. 458). When deferring sentence for good behaviour the conditions imposed should not be unduly restrictive—the aim is to confirm that the accused is capable of behaving "in ordinary life in an acceptable way"; see *Islam v Heywood*, 1999 S.C.C.R. 68.

Reports

A4-424 **203.**—(1) Where a person specified in section 27(1)(b)(i) to (vi) of the Social Work (Scotland) Act 1968 commits an offence, the court shall not dispose of the case without obtaining from the local authority in whose area the person resides a report as to—

(a) the circumstances of the offence; and
(b) the character of the offender, including his behaviour while under the supervision, or as the case may be subject to the order, so specified in relation to him.

(1A) However, if there is available to the court a report from a local authority—

(a) of the kind described in subsection (1)(b) above; and
(b) which was prepared in relation to the person not more than 3 months before the person was convicted of the offence,

the court need not obtain another report of that kind before disposing of the case unless it considers, following representations made by or on behalf of the person as to the person's circumstances, that it is appropriate to obtain another report.

(1B) Nothing in subsection (1) or (1A) above requires the court to obtain a report if the court is satisfied, having regard to its likely method of dealing with the case before it for disposal, that the report would not be of any material assistance.

(2) In subsection (1) above, "the court" does not include a JP court.

(3) Where, in any case, a report by an officer of a local authority is made to the court with a view to assisting the court in determining the most suitable method of dealing with any person in respect of an offence, a copy of the report shall be given by the clerk of the court to—

(a) the offender,
(b) the offender's solicitor (if any), and
(c) the prosecutor.

AMENDMENTS

Subsections (1A) and (1B) inserted by Criminal Proceedings etc. (Reform) (Scotland) Act 2007 (asp 6) s.24. Brought into force on 10 December 2007 by SSI 2007/479.

Subsection (2) as amended by Criminal Proceedings etc (Reform) (Scotland) Act 2007 (asp 6) s.80 and Sch. para.26. Brought into force for the Sheriffdom of Lothian and Borders on 10 March 2008 by SSI 2008/42 (C.4) art.3 and Sch. Brought into force for the Sheriffdom of Grampian, Highland and Islands on 2 June 2008 by SSI 2008/192 (C.19) art.3 and Sch. Brought into force for the Sheriffdom of Glasgow and Strathkelvin on 8 December 2008 by SSI 2008/329 (C.29) art.3 and Sch. Brought into force for the Sheriffdom of Tayside, Central and Fife on 23 February 2009 by SSI 2008/362 (C.30) art.3 and Sch. Brought into force for the Sheriffdom of North Strathclyde on 14 December 2009 by SSI 2009/432 (C.32) art.3 and Sch.1. Remainder in force on 22 February 2010 by SSI 2009/432 (C.32) art.3 and Sch.2.

Subsection (3) as amended by Criminal Justice and Licensing (Scotland) Act 2010 (asp 13) s.20(2). Brought into force on 1 February 2011 (subject to savings provisions in art.3) by SSI 2010/413 (C.28) art.2 Sch.1 para.1.

DEFINITIONS

"local authority": s.307(1). A4-424.1
"offence": s.307(1).
"prosecutor": s.307(1).

GENERAL NOTE

This section requires the court to obtain a report targeted on new offences by an offender who is subject to statutory supervision. So in *Hendry v HM Advocate*, 1999 G.W.D. 21–1004, a sentence of imprisonment was suspended on appeal where the sheriff had failed to obtain a local authority report on H who was on probation at the time of the offence. The obligation to obtain such a report exists even where the accused lives outwith Scotland, as in *Williams v Kennedy*, 2002 G.W.D. 15–496, where the accused who resided in Wales and was there subject of a probation order had been convicted of a further offence in Scotland. The provisions of the section only apply when the person committing the offences libelled is already subject to the provisions of s.27(1)(b) of the Social Work (Scotland) Act 1968 (see *Townsley v McGlennan*, 1998 S.L.T. 104). The circumstances of the new offences are an aspect distinct from the offender's behaviour on supervision. A4-425

This addition to s.203 of the 1995 Act effects a sensible, and overdue, alteration to a long-standing sentencing requirement concerning offenders subject of statutory supervision who had therafter been convicted of a further offence; whereas formerly the court could not competently pass sentence without first obtaining an individual report in each case from the local authority's supervising (probation) officer—often an exercise which served only to delay sentence and added little of significance in such situations—the new measure now enables the court to take account of any such report prepared within 3 months before the date of conviction. More signicant still subs.(1B) removes the mandatory requirement upon the court to order a probation report at all if the judge feels it will not assist in determining sentence.

Section 20 of the 2010 Act amended subs.(3) above to provide that the prosecutor must also be provided with a copy of any report upon the offender.

Reports about organisations

203A.—(1) This section applies where an organisation is convicted of an offence. A4-425.1

(2) Before dealing with the organisation in respect of the offence, the court may obtain a report into the organisation's financial affairs and structural arrangements.

(3) The report is to be prepared by a person appointed by the court.

(4) The person appointed to prepare the report is referred to in this section as the "reporter".

(5) The court may issue directions to the reporter about—

(a) the information to be contained in the report,

(b) the particular matters to be covered by the report,

(c) the time by which the report is to be submitted to the court.

(6) The court may order the organisation to give the reporter and any person acting on the reporter's behalf—

(a) access at all reasonable times to the organisation's books, documents and other records,

(b) such information or explanation as the reporter thinks necessary.

(7) The reporter's costs in preparing the report are to be paid by the clerk of court, but the court may order the organisation to reimburse to the clerk all or a part of those costs.

(8) An order under subsection (7) may be enforced by civil diligence as if it were a fine.

(9) On submission of the report to the court, the clerk of court must provide a copy of the report to—

(a) the organisation,

(b) the organisation's solicitor (if any), and

(c) the prosecutor.

(10) The court must have regard to the report in deciding how to deal with the organisation in respect of the offence.

(11) If the court decides to impose a fine, the court must, in determining the amount of the fine, have regard to—

(a) the report, and

(b) if the court makes an order under subsection (7), the amount of costs that the organisation is required to reimburse under the order.

(12) Where the court—

(a) makes an order under subsection (7), and

(b) imposes a fine on the organisation,

any payment by the organisation is first to be applied in satisfaction of the order under subsection (7).

(13) Where the court also makes a compensation order in respect of the offence, any payment by the organisation is first to be applied in satisfaction of the compensation order before being applied in accordance with subsection (12).

Amendments

Section 203A inserted by Criminal Justice and Licensing (Scotland) Act 2010 (asp 13) s.22. Brought into force on 28 March 2011 (for all purposes in respect of offences committed on or after 28 March 2011) by SSI 2011/178 (C.15) art.2, Sch.1 para.1.

Definitions

A4-425.2 "organisation": s.48 of the Act.

General Note

A4-425.3 As the General Note to s.143 above suggests, prosecution of bodies corporate are not without difficulty; see for example *Aitkenhead v Fraser*, 2006 S.L.T. 711, the application of summary proceedings to trusts and trusts, or *Balmer v HM Advocate* [2008] HCJAC 44, a solemn prosecution of a dissolved partnership. The 2010 Act introduced several related provisions, notably the all-encompassing concept of an "organisation" in s.65 of that Act (added to s.307(1) of the 1995 Act) and the refinement in regard to partnerships in a stand-alone provision of s.53 of that Act. Broadly, the objective has been to place partners in partnerships on the same plane as directors of bodies corporate in relation to statutory criminal offences, much as partners of limited liability partnerships are already—see the Limited Liability Partnerships (Scotland) Regulations 2001 (SSI 2001/128).

Sentencing such bodies has caused difficulty. Witness the £15 million fine imposed in *HM Advocate v Transco Plc* (Unreported 25 August 2005 High Court of Justiciary) following a multiple fatal gas explosion and, more tellingly, the accountancy exercise undertaken by the Crown in its successful appeal against an unduly lenient sentence in *HM Advocate v Doonin Plant Ltd* [2010] HCJAC 80. Gauging a meaningful financial penalty is now tackled statutorily by the option of assessment of the organisation's worth or means. The court has a discretion to appoint a reporter to evaluate the financial standing of the organisation. The costs (or a stipulated proportion of the cost) of preparation of his report, ordered by the court, will ordinarily have first call on any fine exigible (subs.(11)) except where the court imposes either a compensation order or a fine combined with a compensation order; then satisfaction of that order has first call.

[THE NEXT PARAGRAPH IS A4-426]

Imprisonment, etc.

Restrictions on passing sentence of imprisonment or detention

A4-426 **204.**—(1) A court shall not pass a sentence of imprisonment or of detention in respect of any offence, nor impose imprisonment, or detention, under section 214(2) of this Act in respect of failure to pay a fine, on an accused who is not legally represented in that court and has not been previously sentenced to imprisonment or detention by a court in any part of the United Kingdom [or, where the court passing sentence considers appropriate, by a court in any] member State of the European Union, unless the accused either—

(a) applied for legal aid and the application was refused on the ground that he was not financially eligible; or

(b) having been informed of his right to apply for legal aid, and having had the opportunity, failed to do so.

(2) A court shall not pass a sentence of imprisonment on a person of or over twenty-one years of age who has not been previously sentenced to imprisonment or detention by a court in any part of the United Kingdom [or, where the court passing sentence considers appropriate, by a court in any] member State of the European Union unless the court considers that no other method of dealing with him is appropriate.

(2A) For the purpose of determining under subsection (2) above whether any other method of dealing with such a person is appropriate, the court, unless it has made a risk assessment order in respect of the person, shall take into account—

(a) such information as it has been able to obtain from an officer of a local authority or otherwise about his circumstances;

(b) any information before it concerning his character and mental and physical condition;

(c) its power to make a hospital direction in addition to imposing a sentence of imprisonment.

(3) Where a court of summary jurisdiction passes a sentence of imprisonment on any such person as is mentioned in subsection (2) above, the court shall state the reason for its opinion that no other method of dealing with him is appropriate, and shall have that reason entered in the record of the proceedings.

(3A) A court must not pass a sentence of imprisonment for a term of 12 months or less on a person unless the court considers that no other method of dealing with the person is appropriate.

(3B) Where a court passes such a sentence, the court must—

(a) state its reasons for the opinion that no other method of dealing with the person is appropriate, and

(b) have those reasons entered in the record of the proceedings.

(3C) The Scottish Ministers may by order made by statutory instrument substitute for the number of months for the time being specified in subsection (3A) another number of months.

(3D) An order under subsection (3C) is not to be made unless a draft of the statutory instrument containing the order has been laid before and approved by resolution of the Scottish Parliament.

(3E) A modification of the number of months specified in subsection (3A), by an order made under subsection (3C), applies only to offences committed on or after the date on which the modification comes into force.

(4) The court shall, for the purpose of determining whether a person has been previously sentenced to imprisonment or detention by a court in any part of the United Kingdom—

(a) disregard a previous sentence of imprisonment which, having been suspended, has not taken effect under section 23 of the Powers of Criminal Courts Act 1973 or under section 19 of the Treatment of Offenders Act (Northern Ireland) 1968;

(b) construe detention as meaning—

(i) in relation to Scotland, detention in a young offenders institution or detention centre;

(ii) in relation to England and Wales a sentence of youth custody, borstal training or detention in a young offender institution or detention centre; and

(iii) in relation to Northern Ireland, detention in a young offenders centre.

(4A) The court shall, for the purpose of determining whether a person has been previously sentenced to imprisonment or detention by a court in a member State of the European Union […]—

(a) disregard any previous sentence of imprisonment which, being the equivalent of a suspended sentence, has not taken effect;

(b) construe detention as meaning an equivalent sentence to any of those mentioned in subsection (4)(b).

(4B) Any issue of equivalence arising in pursuance of subsection (4A) is for the court to determine.

(5) This section does not affect the power of a court to pass sentence on any person for an offence the sentence for which is fixed by law.

(6) In this section—

"legal aid" means legal aid for the purposes of any part of the proceedings before the court;

"legally represented" means represented by counsel or a solicitor at some stage after the accused is found guilty and before he is dealt with as referred to in subsection (1) above.

Amendments

Subsection (2): words deleted by s.6(3) of the Crime and Punishment (Scotland) Act 1997 with effect from 1 January 1998 as provided by SI 1997/2323 art.4 and Sch.2.

Subsection (2A) inserted by s.6(3) of the above Act and commenced on 1 January 1998 in terms of the above Order.

Subsection (2A) as amended by Criminal Justice (Scotland) Act 2003 (asp 7) Sch.1 para.2(6). Brought into force on 19 June 2006 by SSI 2006/332 (C.30) art.2(1), subject to art.2(2).

Subsections (1), (2) as amended, subs.(4A)–(4B) inserted, by Criminal Justice and Licensing (Scotland) Act 2010 (asp 13) Sch.4 para.5. Brought into force on 13 December 2010 by SSI 2010/413 (C.28) art.2 Sch.1 para.1.

Subsections (3A)–(3D) inserted by Criminal Justice and Licensing (Scotland) Act 2010 (asp 13) s.17. Brought into force on 1 February 2011 by SSI 2010/413 (C.28) art.2 Sch.1 para.1.

Subsection (3A) as amended by Presumption Against Short Periods of Imprisonment (Scotland) Order (SSI 2019/236) art.2 (effective 4 July 2019).

Subsection (3E) inserted by Presumption Against Short Periods of Imprisonment (Scotland) Order (SSI 2019/236) art.3 (effective 3 July 2019).

Words in subs.(1) were substituted by the Criminal Justice (EU Exit) (Scotland) (Amendment etc.) Regulations 2020 (SSI 2020/339) reg.13(11)(a) (effective 31 December 2020 subject to transitional and saving provision specified in reg.16 of those Regulations.

Words omitted from subs.(4A) were repealed by the Criminal Justice (EU Exit) (Scotland) (Amendment etc.) Regulations 2020 (SSI 2020/339) reg.13(11)(b) (effective 31 December 2020 subject to transitional and saving provision specified in reg.16 of those Regulations.

Definitions

A4-426.1 "court of summary jurisdiction": s.307(1).
"fine": s.307(1).
"impose imprisonment": s.307(1).
"legal aid": s.204(6).
"legally represented": s.204(6).
"offence": s.307(1).
"sentence": s.307(1).

[THE NEXT PARAGRAPH IS A4-427]

GENERAL NOTE

This section conjoins the provisions in ss.41 and 42 of the 1980 Act. Imprisonment as a sentence or as a penalty for fine default can only be imposed once the accused has been legally represented in the proceedings (subs.(1)). In addition the court can now impose a hospital direction (discussed at ss.59 and 60 above) as part of such sentence or penalty. In all cases there is a general obligation to have regard to any information about the accused's character, physical and mental condition. A4-427

Subs.(3A) enables the Scottish Ministers by order to vary the minimum term of imprisonment or detention which can be imposed by Scottish criminal courts. Hitherto a court was only obliged to minute the reasons for imposition of such a term on the first occasion of imposing it on those offenders aged over 21 years. It will be noted that the court is now obliged to minute such reasons in all cases where imprisonment or detention is imposed. Note too that s.206 of the Act now prohibits the imposition of such a sentence unless it is of at least 15 days' duration.

Two authorities are worth considering here. First, the duty (in subs.(2)) to obtain information from a local authority "or otherwise" is not fulfilled by obtaining information from the prosecution or the defence: *Auld v Herron*, 1969 J.C. 4. It should be noted that the duty is qualified by the phrase "such information as it can" although that is not defined. Secondly, the imprisonment or detention relates only to the UK and that necessarily excludes the Republic of Ireland: *Mawhinney v HM Advocate*, 1950 S.L.T. 135. It is difficult to see why imprisonment or detention elsewhere is excluded in this way but it may be information bearing on the accused's character. While it is not necessary for the sentencing judge to enumerate the other disposals considered before arriving at a custodial sentence, for the purposes of compliance with the requirements of subs.(2), and particularly in preparing a report for any appeal, a judge should indicate that the sentencing options have been fully considered (*Keogh v Watt*, 2000 S.C.C.R. 443).

Should the report contain material which is disputed, care has to be taken to assess whether this can be dealt with by means of a proof in mitigation or whether the material really contains fresh allegations of criminality which must be considered separately; see *Ross v HM Advocate*, 2002 S.L.T. 925.

Subs.(2)

In *RC v HM Advocate*, 2020 SCCR 20, it was held, under reference to art.3 ECHR, that, where a court has decided to impose a sentence of imprisonment on a person with a severe medical condition, it should defer sentence for a period to ensure that the prison authorities are put on notice to expect him and to make suitable arrangements for his care.

Restriction on consecutive sentences for released prisoners

204A. A court sentencing a person to imprisonment or other detention shall not order or direct that the term of imprisonment or detention shall commence on the expiration of any other such sentence from which he has been released at any time under the existing or new provisions within the meaning of Schedule 6 to the Prisoners and Criminal Proceedings (Scotland) Act 1993. A4-427.1

AMENDMENTS

Section 204A inserted by Crime and Disorder Act 1998 (c.37) s.112 (effective 30 September 1998: SI 1998/2327).

DEFINITIONS

"imprisonment": s.307(1) of the 1995 Act. A4-427.2
"detention": s.307(1) of the 1995 Act.
"sentence": s.307(1) of the 1995 Act.

GENERAL NOTE

In keeping with the provisions in s.111(1) of the 1998 Act, which added s.1A to the Prisoners and Criminal Proceedings (Scotland) Act 1993 (c.9), this section stipulates that prisoners released on licence who are sentenced, in relation to other offences, to another term of imprisonment should not receive a sentence running consecutive to the expiry of that imprisonment term. only by imposing an immediate and concurrent sentence of further imprisonment (which may of course result in incarceration beyond the end of the earlier sentence) can the release provisions set down in the 1993 Act, as amended, function effectively. A4-427.3

This provision came into force on September 30, 1998 in terms of SI 1998/2327.

See for example, *HM Advocate v Graham*, 1999 G.W.D. 26-1235 and *Thomson, Petr*, 2000 G.W.D. 8-289.

In *McIntosh v HM Advocate*, 2003 G.W.D. 31-868 the Appeal Court approved the practice of the Crown drawing the attention of the court imposing sentence to a pre-existing sentence, the balance of which had been re-imposed upon the accused.

The Appeal Court repeated the requirement that the Crown be in a position to furnish full information to sentencing courts as to whether the accused has been subject of recall to prison (s.17 of the 1993 Act) or had been at liberty thanks to early release at the time of committing a further offence (s.16). See *Stuart v HM Advocate*, 2010 S.L.T. 981.

Consecutive sentences: life prisoners etc.

A4-427.4 **204B.**—(1) This section applies in respect of sentencing for offences committed after the coming into force of this section.

(2) Where, in solemn proceedings, the court sentences a person to imprisonment or other detention, the court may—

(a) if the person is serving or is liable to serve the punishment part of a previous sentence, frame the sentence to take effect on the day after that part of that sentence is or would be due to expire; or

(b) if the person is serving or is liable to serve the punishment parts of two or more previous sentences, frame the sentence to take effect on the day after the later or (as the case may be) latest expiring of those parts is or would be due to expire.

(3) Where, in such proceedings, it falls to the court to sentence a person who is subject to a previous sentence in respect of which a punishment part requires to be (but has not been) specified, the court shall not sentence the person until such time as the part is either specified or no longer requires to be specified.

(4) Where the court sentences a person to a sentence of imprisonment or other detention for life, for an indeterminate period or without limit of time, the court may, if the person is serving or is liable to serve for any offence—

(a) a previous sentence of imprisonment or other detention the term of which is not treated as part of a single term under section 27(5) of the 1993 Act; or

(b) two or more previous sentences of imprisonment or other detention the terms of which are treated as a single term under that section of that Act,

frame the sentence to take effect on the day after the person would (but for the sentence so framed and disregarding any subsequent sentence) be entitled to be released under the provisions referred to in section 204A of this Act as respects the sentence or sentences.

Amendments

Section 204B inserted by Criminal Justice (Scotland) Act 2003 (asp 7) Pt 4 s.26. Brought into force on 1 December 2003 by SSI 2003/475 (C.26) art.2.

Definitions

A4-427.5 "detention": s.307(1) of the 1995 Act.
"imprisonment": s.307(1) of the 1995 Act.
"sentence": s.307(1) of the 1995 Act.

General Note

A4-427.6 This new section provides a court, when sentencing a person for an offence committed after the section comes into force and where that person is already serving a sentence of imprisonment, to order that: (a) a life sentence may commence, in the existing life prisoner, on the expiry of the punishment part of the existing life sentence or, if the prisoner is already serving a determinate sentence, at the point at which the scottish Ministers would otherwise be required to release the prisoner; and (b) a determinate sentence may commence, in the case of an existing life prisoner, on the expiry of the punishment of the existing life sentence. This provision applies only to solemn proceedings as summary proceedings are dealt with in terms of s.167 of the 1995 Act as amended.

[THE NEXT PARAGRAPH IS A4-428]

Punishment for murder

A4-428 **205.**—(1) Subject to subsections (2) and (3) and section 205D below, a person convicted of murder shall be sentenced to imprisonment for life.

(2) Where a person convicted of murder is under the age of 18 years he shall not be sentenced to imprisonment for life but to be detained without limit of time and shall be liable to be detained in such place, and under such conditions, as the Secretary of State may direct.

(3) Where a person convicted of murder has attained the age of 18 years but is under the age of 21 years he shall not be sentenced to imprisonment for life but to be detained in a young offenders institution and shall be liable to be detained for life.

(4)-(6) […]

Amendments

Section 205 as amended by Convention Rights (Compliance) (Scotland) Act 2001 (asp 7) s.2. Brought into force on 8 October 2001 by SSI 2001/274 (C.12).

Definitions

"judge": s.307(1). A4-428.1
"sentence": s.307(1).

[THE NEXT PARAGRAPH IS A4-429]

General Note

Chalmers v HM Advocate [2014] HCJAC 247; 2014 S.C.C.R. 291, a full Bench decision, confirms that following conviction of murder in conjunction with other offences, only one sentence—detention for life or life imprisonment—can be imposed. The punishment part of that sentence can properly be adjusted to reflect the gravity of all the offences before the court following a motion for sentence. (C had been convicted of murder and of a protracted course of conduct thereafter aimed at concealing the murder.) The judgment overturns *Cameron v HM Advocate* [2011] HCJAC 29; 2011 G.W.D. 14-328. A4-429

In assessing the punishment part of sentence the court is required to reflect current sentencing mores, not the sentencing practices prevailing at the time of the offence—see *Docherty v HM Advocate* [2016] HCJAC 49; 2016 S.C.L. 627, a murder committed almost 30 years earlier, since which time the accused had had an exemplary career in the armed forces and a settled domestic relationship.

Minimum sentence for third conviction of certain offences relating to drug trafficking

205B.—(1) This section applies where— A4-429.1

(a) a person is convicted on indictment in the High Court of a class A drug trafficking offence committed after the commencement of section 2 of the Crime and Punishment (Scotland) Act 1997;

(b) at the time when that offence was committed, he had attained the age of at least 18 years and had two previous convictions for relevant offences, irrespective of—

(i) whether either of those offences was committed before or after the commencement of section 2 of the Crime and Punishment (Scotland) Act 1997;

(ii) the court in which any such conviction was obtained; and

(iii) his age at the time of the commission of either of those offences; and

(c) one of the offences mentioned in paragraph (b) above was committed after he had been convicted of the other.

(1A) In subsection (1), "relevant offence" means—

(a) in relation to a conviction by a court in any part of the United Kingdom, a class A drug trafficking offence;

(b) in relation to a conviction by a court in a member State of the European Union [which the court passing sentence considers appropriate to take into account], an offence that is equivalent to a class A drug trafficking offence.

(1B) Any issue of equivalence arising in pursuance of subsection (1A)(b) is for the court to determine.

(2) Subject to subsection (3) below, where this section applies the court shall sentence the person—

(a) where he has attained the age of 21 years, to a term of imprisonment of at least seven years; and

(b) where he has attained the age of 18 years but is under the age of 21 years, to detention in a young offenders institution for a period of at least seven years.

(3) The court shall not impose the sentence otherwise required by subsection (2) above where it is of the opinion that there are specific circumstances which—

(a) relate to any of the offences or to the offender; and

(b) would make that sentence unjust.

(4) For the purposes of section 106(2) of this Act a sentence passed under subsection (2) above in respect of a conviction for a class A drug trafficking offence shall not be regarded as a sentence fixed by law for that offence.

(5) In this section "class A drug trafficking offence" means a drug trafficking offence committed in respect of a class A drug; and for this purpose—

"class A drug" has the same meaning as in the Misuse of Drugs Act 1971;

"drug trafficking offence" means an offence specified in paragraph 2 or (so far as it relates to that paragraph) paragraph 10 of Schedule 4 to the Proceeds of Crime Act 2002.

[(6) Any reference in this section to a previous conviction includes, where relevant, a conviction by a court in any part of the United Kingdom or in any member State of the European Union.]

Amendments

Section 205B inserted by Crime and Punishment (Scotland) Act 1997 (c.48) s.2 with effect from 20 January 1998 as provided by SI 1997/2323 art.3, Sch.1.

Subs.(5) as amended by Proceeds of Crime Act 2002 (c.29) Sch.11 para.29(3). Brought into force on 24 March 2003 by SSI 2003/210 (C.44).

Subs.(1) as amended, subs.(1A)-(1B) inserted, by Criminal Justice and Licensing (Scotland) Act 2010 (asp 13) Sch.4 para.6. Brought into force on 13 December 2010 by SSI 2010/413 (C.28) art.2, Sch.1 para.1.

Words in subs.(6) was inserted by the Criminal Justice (EU Exit) (Scotland) (Amendment etc.) Regulations 2020 (SSI 2020/339) reg.13(12)(a) (effective December 31, 2020 subject to transitional and saving provision specified in reg.16 of those Regulations.

Subs.(1A)(b) were substituted by the Criminal Justice (EU Exit) (Scotland) (Amendment etc.) Regulations 2020 (SSI 2020/339) reg.13(12)(b) (effective 31 December 2020 subject to transitional and saving provision specified in reg.16 of those Regulations.

Definitions

A4-429.2 "indictment": s.307(1) of the 1995 Act.

"High Court": s.307(1) of the Act.

"class A drug": s.2(1) and Sch.2 Pt I of the Misuse of Drugs Act 1971 (c.38).

"drug trafficking offence": s.49(5) of the Proceeds of Crime (Scotland) Act 1995 (c.43); s. 1(3) of the Drug Trafficking Act 1994 (c.37); Proceeds of Crime (Northern Ireland) Order 1996.

"offence": s.307(1) of the 1995 Act.

"United Kingdom": Sch.1 of the Interpretation Act 1978 (c.30).

"conviction": s.3 of the 1997 Act.

"young offenders institutution": s.307(1) of the 1995 Act.

"sentence": s.307(1) of the 1995 Act.

General Note

A4-429.3 This section was introduced into the 1995 Act by s.2 of the Crime and Punishment (Scotland) Act with effect from 20 October 1997 as provided by the Crime and Punishment (Scotland) Act 1997 (Commencement No. 2 and Transitional and Consequential Provisions) 1997 (SI 1997/2323).

Section 205B provides that, where a person convicted of a drug trafficking offence before the High Court in relation to a class A drug, has two distinct prior convictions for trafficking in class A drugs (a number of incidents conjoined in one conviction would not suffice), he shall be sentenced to a minimum period of imprisonment or detention of seven years. Reference to the legislation mentioned in subs.(5) shows that "drug trafficking offence" has a much wider meaning than merely dealing in, or being concerned in, the supply of controlled drugs. It is important to note that the two prior convictions can have been imposed by any United Kingdom court at any time—these provisions can operate retrospectively. Subsection (1)(b) stipulates that such a minimum sentence can only be imposed upon an offender who had reached 18 years of age at the time of committing the third offence.

Reservations have to be expressed, however, as to whether information currently available in previous convictions will highlight that the prior convictions related specificaly to class A drugs. This problem may lead the Crown to lodge certified copies of the complaints or indictments, and related Minutes of Procedure, and perhaps a s.285 certificate (now a Secretary of State's rather than a Chief Constable's certificate, following s.59 of the 1997 Act) to lay out the provenance of previous convictions.

It will be appreciated that the broad intention of s.205B is to limit the sentencing discretion available to judges when dealing with recidivist drug trafficking offenders but the wording of s.205B(3) is not free of difficulty, particularly when read along with s. 196(2) of the 1995 Act. While the Government adhered to the familiar notion that a sentencing court would have to look to the circumstances of the current offence before it, and to any previous convictions, the Lord Advocate did concede that "the procedure for laying details of the circumstances of the first qualifying offence before the court will have to be addressed" (*Hansard*, 4 March 1997, col. 1821). It is submitted that it would be quite proper for the court to have regard to the sentences imposed in relation to the earlier convictions, and that in something of a departure from current sentencing practices, subs.(3) suggests that some investigation of the factual background to those convictions could be undertaken by the court. This is a marked departure from the principles set out in *Connell v Mitchell* (1908) 5 A. 641 and *Baker v McFadyean*, 1952 S.L.T. (Notes) 69 which disapproved of "looking behind convictions". See, however, the discussion at A4-228 above.

Interestingly, it was only after the Committee stage of the Crime and Punishment (Scotland) Bill that the Government moved an amendment to s. 196 of the 1995 Act to permit the sentencing court to pass a lower sentence where a guilty plea had been tendered. (This it will be noted pre-dated *Du Plooy v HM Advocate*, 2003 S.L.T 1237; 2003 S.C.C.R. 640 which formulated general rules on the discounting of sentences following a guilty plea as permitted by s. 196 of the Act). The prescriptive tone of S.205B, with its limited admission of judicial sentencing discretion, and the broader, permissive approach in s. 196 do not sit together comfortably. Section 196(2) of the Act makes express provision for a statutory reduction in sentence to one of 5 years, 219 days, a figure which, not by chance, reflects a 20 per cent discount against the mandatory minimum which a third Class A drug dealing offence would ordinarily attract. The issue is whether the sentencing court can exercise its discretionary powers (in s.205B(3)) irrespective of whether an accused pleads guilty or is convicted after trial and, in the former case, also permit a broad s. 196 discount for the guilty plea.

In *HM Advocate v McGale* (High Court of Justiciary, 7 April 2005, unreported) the court held that it could exercise that discretion and apply a s.196 discount on that sentence and take account of time spent on remand awaiting trial (s.210). It has to be doubted that this was the form of sentencing regime envisaged when s.205B was introduced by Parliament (the court was not referred to *Hansard* and, almost uniquely, s. 199 of the Act, which generally permits the court to mitigate a sentence previously passed, is expressly disapplied to s.205B(2) by s. 199(3)). Arguably, a preferable approach would be to disregard s. 196 entirely in imposing sentence and proceed simply by exercising the discretion vested in the court by s.205B(3). In doing so, the factors giving rise to the reduction to the otherwise mandatory sentence would have to be stated and could properly include the timing of the plea if that was appropriate.

Section 205B(4) preserves the right of appeal against sentence since s.205B provides for an automatic, not a mandatory sentence; by definition the latter form of sentence cannot be appealed.

Meaning of "conviction"

Reference to s.205C below reveals that the automatic sentence for a third relevant drug trafficking offence will apply even if one, or both, of the earlier convictions was disposed of by way of admonition or a probation order. Such a disposal would, in the event of conviction after trial for a third drug trafficking offence, still fall to be considered under subs.(3) above as a ground for refraining from imposing the seven year minimum sentence.

Meaning of "conviction" for purposes of sections 205A and 205B

205C.—(1) For the purposes of paragraph (b) of subsection (1) of each sections 205A and 205B of this Act "conviction" includes— **A4-429.4**

(a) a finding of guilt in respect of which the offender was admonished under section 181 of the Criminal Procedure (Scotland) Act 1975 (admonition); and

(b) a conviction for which an order is made placing the offender on probation,

and related expressions shall be construed accordingly.

AMENDMENTS

Section 205C inserted by Crime and Punishment (Scotland) Act 1997 (c.48) s.3 (in part) with effect from 20 October 1997 as provided by SI 1997/2323 art.3, Sch.1.

DEFINITIONS

"admonished": s.246 of the Criminal Procedure (Scotland) Act 1995. **A4-429.5**
"probation": s.247 of said Act.

"offence": s.307(1) of said Act.
"Class A drug": s.2(1) and Sch.2, Part I of the Misuse of Drugs Act 1971.
"drug trafficking offence": s.49(5) of the Proceeds of Crime (Scotland) Act 1995, s.1(3) of the Drug Trafficking Act 1994 and s.1(3) of the Proceeds of Crime (Northern Ireland) Order 1996.

GENERAL NOTE

A4-429.6 This section defines the meaning of "conviction", a concept central to the operation of Part I of the 1997 Act. It will be recalled that the 1997 Act introduced two "automatic" sentences, requiring the High Court to impose life sentences in a range of serious offences and minimum sentences for class A drug trafficking offences. The incoming Government has not commenced the regime of automatic life sentences specified in s.1 of the 1997 Act, and has commenced onlypart of s.205B (the full text of the section appears as s.3 of the 1997 Act) with effect from 20 October 1997.

The ethos of the 1997 Act, which sought to impose more severe penalties upon offenders by removing large elements of sentencing discretion fromjudges, is still to be found in s.205B: it will be noted that the imposition of a probation order, an order which as s.247(1) of the 1995 Act provides, is not deemed to be a conviction, is nonetheless a disposal for the purposes of s.205B, counting as a conviction. (As originally drafted even absolute and conditional discharges were included also as "convictions" but this was withdrawn late in the life of the Bill).

Although the mechanism is in place to permit drug trafficking convictions imposed by military courts martial to count as prior convictions forthe purposes of s.205B (see subs.(2) of s.205B as it appears in the 1997 Act) no steps have been taken to activate that provision as yet.

Only one sentence of imprisonment for life to be imposed in any proceedings

A4-429.7 **205D.** Where a person is convicted on the same indictment of more than one offence for which the court must impose or would, apart from this section, have imposed a sentence of imprisonment for life, only one such sentence shall be imposed in respect of those offences.

AMENDMENTS

Section 205D inserted by Convention Rights (Compliance) (Scotland) Act 2001 (asp 7) s.2. Brought into force on October 8, 2001 by SSI 2001/274 (C.12).

GENERAL NOTE

A4-429.8 This section applies to those convicted of murder which, as s.205 of the Act provides, attracts a mandatory life sentence on conviction, and to accused whose conduct is deemed sufficiently grave as to warrant a discretionary life sentence. In either situation only one life sentence should be imposed by the court, the punishment part being varied if other offences still before the sentencing court are considered grave in their own right. If the Crown moves for sentence on all remaining charges then it is submitted to be good practice that sentence be imposed in relation to "lesser" charges concurrently: this can assume significance in the event of subsequent appeal procedures. See *Chalmers v HM Advocate* [2014] HCJAC 247; 2014 S.C.C.R. 291.

Minimum periods of imprisonment

A4-430 **206.**—(1) No person shall be sentenced to imprisonment by a court of summary jurisdiction for a period of less than 15 days.

(2)-(6) [...]

AMENDMENTS

Subs.(1) as amended, subss.(2)-(6) repealed by Criminal Justice and Licensing (Scotland) Act 2010 (asp 13) s.16(3). Brought into force on 13 December 2010 by SSI 2010/413 (C.28) art.2, Sch.1 para.1.

DEFINITIONS

A4-430.1 "imprisonment": s.307(1).
"court of summary jurisdiction": s.307(1).

GENERAL NOTE

A4-430.2 The minimum period of imprisonment has been raised from 5 to 15 days in accord with the general presumption in the 2010 Act against short terms of detention or imprisonment.

Detention of young offenders

A4-431 **207.**—(1) It shall not be competent to impose imprisonment on a person under 21 years of age.

(2) Subject to section 205(2) and (3), 205A(2)(b) and 205B(2)(b) of this Act and to subsections (3) and (4) below, a court may impose detention (whether by way of sentence or otherwise) on a person, who is not less than 16 but under 21 years of age, where but for subsection (1) above the court would have power to impose a period of imprisonment; and a period of detention imposed under this section on any person shall not exceed the maximum period of imprisonment which might otherwise have been imposed.

(3) The court shall not under subsection (2) above impose detention on an offender unless it is of the opinion that no other method of dealing with him is appropriate; and the court shall state its reasons for that opinion, and, except in the case of the High Court, those reasons shall be entered in the record of proceedings.

(3A) Subsections (2) and (3) above are subject to—

(a) Section 51A(2) of the Firearms Act 1968 (minimum sentences for certain firearms offences); and

(b) Section 29(8) of the Violent Crime Reduction Act 2006 (minimum sentence of detention for certain offences relating to dangerous weapons).

(4) To enable the court to form an opinion under subsection (3) above, it shall obtain from an officer of a local authority or otherwise such information as it can about the offender's circumstances; and it shall also take into account any information before it concerning the offender's character and physical and mental condition.

(4A) In forming an opinion under subsection (3) above the court shall take into account its power to make a hospital direction in addition to imposing a period of detention.

(4B) Subsections (4) and (4A) above apply to the forming of an opinion under the enactments mentioned in subsection Criminal Procedure (Scotland) Act above as they apply to the forming of an opinion under subsection (3) above.]

(5) A sentence of detention imposed under this section shall be a sentence of detention in a young offenders institution.

Amendments

Subs.(2) as amended by Crime and Punishment (Scotland) Act 1997 (c.48) Sch.1 para.21 with effect from October 20, 1997 in terms of SI 1997/2323) art.3 and Sch.1.

Subs.(4A) inserted by Crime and Punishment (Scotland) Act 1997 s.6(4) with effect from 1 January 1998 in terms of SI 1997/2323 art.4 and Sch.2.

Subss.(3A) and (4B) inserted by Violent Crime Reduction Act (c.38) s.49 and Sch.1 para.4(3) (effective 6 April 2007).

Definitions

A4-431.1

"imprisonment": s.307(1).
"hospital direction": s.9A of the 1997 Act.
"local authority": s.307(1).
"young offender's institution": s.307(1).

[THE NEXT PARAGRAPH IS A4-432]

General Note

The correct approach for the court in deciding the issue of detention for a young offender is to ask, in terms of subs.(3), what methods of dealing with the accused are appropriate. If the court is of the opinion that no method other than detention is appropriate then detention should be imposed: see *Milligan v Jessop*, 1988 S.C.C.R. 137; *Dunsmore v Allan*, 1991 S.C.C.R. 946 and *Divers v Friel*, 1994 S.L.T. 247 in which the approaches were flawed. Having formed the opinion that no other method of dealing with the accused is appropriate, the court is required to state its reasons for that opinion and those reasons shall be entered in the record of proceedings. For the effect of failure to obtemper an earlier version of this subsection, see *Binnie v Farrell*, 1972 S.L.T. 212. The common reasons so stated are "character, gravity or nature of the offence" and "previous record of the accused", variations of which were used in *Dunsmore v Allan*, above. Some support for these are to be found in s.214(4) of this Act. A4-432

It is acknowledged that the sentences imposed upon those committing offences as young offenders necessarily reflect a more complex range of considerations than generally arise with adults convicted of similar indictable offences. In addition to considerations of deterrence and punishment, and protection of the public, the court has to pay regard to the welfare of the child and his eventual reintegration into society. While the sentencing judge may refer to the range of sentences imposed upon adult offenders for like offences as a starting point, the expectation when these factors have been fully weighed is that the sentence imposed for offences committed by a child or young person will be significantly lower: see the guidance in *McCormick v HM Advocate* [2016] HCJAC 50; 2016 S.C.L. 651, which also observed that when dealing with an adult offender, convicted of historic offences committed in youth, the issue of reintegration into society need not feature.

It is not sufficient for the purposes of subs.(3) for the sentencing judge to recall the terms of earlier reports upon the accused. The Appeal Court did approve the use of an up-to-date report prepared in regard to other proceedings provided that a copy of that report is placed before the court; see *Bain v McNaughtan*, 1999 S.L.T. 410. Some care has to be taken when considering previously undisclosed material in such a report; thus in *Ross v HM Advocate*, 2002 S.L.T. 925 where the report discussed allegations about the accused's conduct while on remand awaiting sentence, the sheriff wrongly proceeded to hold a proof upon matters which were plainly fresh criminal allegations. This procedure was held to be flawed by the Appeal Court which emphasised that at that stage there could only be a proof in mitigation upon factors relevant to sentence. The reasons for imposition of such a custodial sentence must be expressly minuted; see *Finnigan v HM Advocate* [2016] HCJAC 88.

The court may now incorporate a hospital direction into any sentence of detention imposed upon a young offender. See generally s.59A above.

Detention of children convicted on indictment

A4-433 **208.**—(1) Subject to section 205 of this Act and subsection (3) below, where a child is convicted on indictment and the court is of the opinion that no other method of dealing with him is appropriate, it may sentence him to be detained for a period which it shall specify in the sentence; and the child shall during that period be liable to be detained in such place and on such conditions as the Secretary of State may direct.

(1A) Where the court imposes a sentence of detention on a child, the court must—

(a) state its reasons for the opinion that no other method of dealing with the child is appropriate, and

(b) have those reasons entered in the record of the proceedings.

(2) Subsections (1) and (1A) above are subject to—

(a) section 51A(2) of the Firearms Act 1968 (minimum sentences for certain firearms offences); and

(b) section 29(9) of the Violent Crime Reduction Act 2006 (minimum sentence of detention for certain offences relating to dangerous weapons).

(3) If the child is under the age of 16 years, the power conferred by subsection (1) above shall not be exercisable in respect of a conviction for an offence under section 9(1) of the Antisocial Behaviour etc. (Scotland) Act 2004 (asp 8) or that section as applied by section 234AA(11) of this Act.

AMENDMENTS

Section 208 as amended by Criminal Justice Act 2003 (c.44) s.290(3). Brought into force on 22 January 2004 by SI 2004/81 (C.2) art.3.

Section 208 as amended by Antisocial Behaviour etc. (Scotland) Act 2004 (asp 8) s.10(3) and (4). Brought into force on 28 October 2004 by SSI 2004/420 (C.31).

Subs.(2) as substituted by Violent Crime Reduction Act 2006 (c.38) s.49 and Sch.1 para.4(4) (effective 6 April 2007).

Subs.(1A) inserted, subs.(2) as amended, by Criminal Justice and Licensing (Scotland) Act 2010 (asp 13) s.21. Brought into force on 1 February 2011 by SSI 2010/413 (C.28) art.2, Sch.1 para.1.

DEFINITIONS

A4-433.1 "child": s.307(1).
"indictment": s.307(1).
"sentence": s.307(1).

[THE NEXT PARAGRAPH IS A4-434]

GENERAL NOTE

A4-434 The correct approach for the court in deciding the issue of detention for a child convicted on indictment is the same as that for young offenders, namely to ask what methods of dealing with the child are appropriate. If the court is of the opinion that no method other than detention is appropriate then the child shall be detained for a specified period. See for example *Sneddon v HM Advocate*, 1998 G.W.D. 22-1131. Subs.(1A) requires any solemn court sentencing a child to a period of detention to minute the reasons for concluding that no other form of sentence was appropriate. This amendment gives statutory effect to what was already common practice in Scottish courts. (The equivalent provision in relation to summary proceedings is found at s.207(3) above)

In *R.J.K. v HM Advocate*, 1993 S.L.T. 237 it was held that (in relation to s.206 of the 1975 Act from which this section is derived) the sentence of detention "without limit of time" is a specified sentence and the absence of those words from the section did not impose any restriction on a courtto pass such a sentence. Such a sentence, however, is in effect a life sentence: *R.F. v HM Advocate*, 1994 S.C.C.R. 71.

Supervised release orders

209.—(1) Where a person is convicted on indictment of an offence other than a sexual offence within the meaning of section 210A of this Act and is sentenced to imprisonment for a term of less than four years, the court on passing sentence may, if it considers that it is necessary to do so to protect the public from serious harm from the offender on his release, make such order as is mentioned in subsection (3) below. A4-435

(2) A court shall, before making an order under subsection (1) above, consider a report by a relevant officer of a local authority about the offender and his circumstances and, if the court thinks it necessary, hear that officer.

(3) The order referred to in subsection (1) above (to be known as a "supervised release order") is that the person, during a relevant period—

(a) be under the supervision of a relevant officer of a local authority or of an officer of a local probation board appointed for or assigned to a petty sessions area or (as the case may be) an officer of a provider of probation services acting in a local justice area (such local authority or the justices for such area to be designated under section 14(4) or 15(1) of the Prisoners and Criminal Proceedings (Scotland) Act 1993);

(b) comply with;

(i) such requirements as may be imposed by the court in the order; and

(ii) such requirements as that officer may reasonably specify,

for the purpose of securing the good conduct of the person or preventing, or lessening the possibility of, his committing a further offence (whether or not an offence of the kind for which he was sentenced); and

(c) comply with the standard requirements imposed by virtue of subsection (4)(a)(i) below.

(4) A supervised release order—

(a) shall—

(i) without prejudice to subsection (3)(b) above, contain such requirements (in this section referred to as the "standard requirements"); and

(ii) be as nearly as possible in such form,

as may be prescribed by Act of Adjournal;

(b) for the purposes of any appeal or review constitutes part of the sentence of the person in respect of whom the order is made; and

(c) shall have no effect during any period in which the person is subject to a licence under Part I of the said Act of 1993.

(5) Before making a supervised release order as respects a person the court shall explain to him, in as straightforward a way as is practicable, the effect of the order and the possible consequences for him of any breach of it.

(6) The clerk of the court by which a supervised release order is made in respect of a person shall—

(a) forthwith send a copy of the order to the person and to the Secretary of State; and

(b) within seven days after the date on which the order is made, send to the Secretary of State such documents and information relating to the case and to the person as are likely to be of assistance to a supervising officer.

(7) In this section—

"relevant officer" has the same meaning as in Part I of the Prisoners and Criminal Proceedings (Scotland) Act 1993;

"relevant period" means such period as may be specified in the supervised release order, being a period—

(a) not exceeding twelve months after the date of the person's release; and

(b) no part of which is later than the date by which the entire term of imprisonment specified in his sentence has elapsed; and

"supervising officer" means, where an authority has or justices have been designated as is mentioned in subsection (3)(a) above for the purposes of the order, any relevant officer or, as the case may be, officer of a local probation board or officer of a provider of probation services who is for the time being supervising for those purposes the person released.

(7A) Where a person—

(a) is serving a sentence of imprisonment and on his release from that sentence will be subject to a supervised release order; and

(b) is sentenced to a further term of imprisonment, whether that term is to run consecutively or concurrently with the sentence mentioned in paragraph (a) above,

the relevant period for any supervised release order made in relation to him shall begin on the date when he is released from those terms of imprisonment; and where there is more than one such order he shall on his release be subject to whichever of them is for the longer or, as the case may be, the longest period.

(8) This section applies to a person sentenced under section 207 of this Act as it applies to a person sentenced to a period of imprisonment.

AMENDMENTS

Subsection (1) as amended by Crime and Disorder Act 1998 (c.37) s.86(2) (effective 30 September 1998: SI 1998/2327).

Subsection (7A) inserted by Crime and Punishment (Scotland) Act 1997 Sch.1 para.21(26) (effective 1 April 1999: SI 1999/652).

Subsection (3)(a) as amended by Criminal Justice and Court Services Act 2000 (c.43) s.74 and Sch.7 para.4. Brought into force by SI 2001/919 (C.33) art.2(f)(ii) (effective 1 April 2001).

Subsection (7) as amended by Criminal Justice and Court Services Act 2000 (c.43) s.74 and Sch.7 para.121. Brought into force as above.

Subsections (3)(a) and (7) as amended by Offender Management Act 2007 (ConsequentialAmendments) Order 2008 (SI 2008/912) Sch.1(1) para.11(2) (effective 1 April 2008).

DEFINITIONS

A4-435.1 "local authority": s.307(1).
"relevant officer": s.209(7).
"relevant period": s.209(7).
"supervised release order": s.209(3).
"supervising officer": s.209(7).

GENERAL NOTE

A4-435.2 Supervised release orders are not available to solemn courts when sentencing offenders for any sexual offence now specified in s.210A(8) of the 1995 Act (see the General Notes to s.210); in *Craig v HM Advocate*, 2000 G.W.D. 34-1313 the Appeal Court accepted Crown submissions that, having been convicted of sexual offences, the accused should have been made subject of an extended sentence order in terms of s.210A of the Act, not a supervised release order (see also *O'Hare v HM Advocate*, 2002 S.L.T. 925 (Note)). Note however that the court declined to impose an extended sentence on appeal on the grounds that the social enquiry report prepared originally had not addressed the risk to the public posed by the accused. It is s.209 that empowers solemn courts to make such orders in relation to offenders sentenced to imprisonment for a period of less than four years. Separate provisions, introducing extended sentences for sexual offenders, and for violent offenders sentenced to more than four years imprisonment, are to be found in s.210A. These provisions came into force on September 30, 1998 in terms of the Crime and DisorderAct 1998 (Commencement No.2 and Transitional Provisions) Order 1998 (SI 1998/2327); the provisions do not apply to sex offences committed before 30 September 1998—supervised release orders could still be imposed in such circumstances.

Since the purpose of such an order is public protection it follows that the provisions of s.196 of the Act, which provide for possible reductions on sentence for timeous guilty pleas, do not extend to SROs. It should also be noted that the SRO takes effect from the date of any early release from the term of imprisonment imposed but cannot run beyond the date when that term expires. See *O'Neil v HM Advocate* [2016] HCJAC 565; 2016 S.C.L. 657, explaining *Robertson v HM Advocate*, an ongoing appeal considered in the course of *Gemmell v HM Advocate* [2011] HCJAC 129; 2012 S.L.T. 484; 2012 S.C.C.R. 176.

Act of Adjournal

The style of supervised release order is set out in Form 20.3 in the 1996 Act of Adjournal as amended by the Act of Adjournal (Criminal Procedure Rules Amendment) (Miscellaneous) 2000 (SSI 2000/65) which came into force on 7 April 2000; whose text is found in 2000 S.L.T. 121. **A4-435.3**

Subs.(5)

The possible consequences of a breach of a supervised release order are dealt with in s.18 of the Prisoners and Criminal Proceedings (Scotland) Act 1993. The court may order the person to be returned to prison for the whole or any part of the period which begins with the date of the order for his return and is equal to the period between the date of the first proven failure and the date on which supervision under the supervised release order would have ceased. Alternatively, the court may vary the order as it could on an application for variation under s.15(4) of the 1993 Act.

[THE NEXT PARAGRAPH IS A4-436]

Consideration of time spent in custody

210.—(1) A court, in passing a sentence of imprisonment or detention on a person for an offence, shall— **A4-436**

(a) in determining the period of imprisonment or detention, have regard to any period of time spent in custody by the person on remand awaiting trial or sentence, or spent in custody awaiting extradition to the United Kingdom otherwise than from a category 1 territory, or spent in hospital awaiting trial or sentence by virtue of an assessment order, a treatment order or an interim compulsion order or by virtue of an order made under section 200 of this Act;

(b) specify the date of commencement of the sentence; and

(c) if the person—

(i) has spent a period of time in custody on remand awaiting trial or sentence; or

(ii) is an extradited prisoner who was extradited to the United Kingdom otherwise than from a category 1 territory, or

(iii) has spent a period of time in hospital awaiting trial or sentence by virtue of an assessment order, a treatment order or an interim compulsion order or by virtue of an order under section 200 of this Act,

and the date specified under paragraph (b) above is not earlier than the date on which sentence was passed, state its reasons for not specifying an earlier date so however that a period of time spent both in custody on remand and, by virtue of section 47(1) of the Crime (international Cooperation) Act 2003 or regulation 20 or 54 of the Criminal Justice (European Investigation Order) Regulations 2017, abroad is not for any reason to be discounted in a determination under paragraph (a) above or specification under paragraph (b) above.

(1A) Subsection (1B) applies where—

(a) a court is passing a sentence of imprisonment or detention on a person for an offence, and

(b) the person is an extradited prisoner who was extradited to the United Kingdom from a category 1 territory.

(1B) The court shall specify—

(a) the period of time spent in custody awaiting extradition, and

(b) the date of commencement of the sentence in accordance with subsection (1C).

(1C) The date of commencement of the sentence is to be a date the relevant number of days earlier than the date the sentence would have commenced had the person not spent time in custody awaiting extradition.

(1D) In subsection (1C), "the relevant number of days" means the number of days in the period specified under subsection (1B)(a).

(2) A prisoner is an extradited prisoner for the purposes of this section if—

(a) he was tried for the offence in respect of which his sentence of imprisonment was imposed—

(i) after having been extradited to the United Kingdom; and

(ii) without having first been restored to the state from which he was extradited or having had an opportunity of leaving the United Kingdom; and

(b) he was for any period in custody while awaiting such extradition.

(2A) In this section, "category 1 territory" means a territory designated under the Extradition Act 2003 for the purposes of Part 1 of that Act.

(3) [...]

AMENDMENTS

Subss.(1)(a) and (1)(c)(iii) inserted by Crime and Punishment (Scotland)Act 1997 (c.48) s.12 and commenced on 1 August 1997 by SI 1997/1712 art.3.

Subs.(1)(c) as amended by Crime (International Co-operation) Act 2003 (c.32) Sch.5 para.65. Brought into force on 26 April 2004 by SI 2004/786 (C.32).

Subs.(1)(a) and (c) as amended by Mental Health (Care and Treatment) (Scotland)Act 2003 (asp 13) Sch.4 para.8(13) and Sch.5. Brought into force on 5 October 2005 by SSI 2005/161 (C.6).

Subs.(1) as amended, subs.(3) repealed and subs.(1A)-(1D), (2A) inserted, by Anti-social Behaviour, Crime and Policing Act 2014 (c.12) s.172. Brought into force on21 July 2014 by SI 2014/1916 art.2(q).

Subs(1)(c) as amended by Criminal Justice (European Investigation Order) Regulations 2017 (SI 2017/730) Sch.3 para.3 (effective 31 July 2017).

DEFINITION

A4-436.1 "sentence": s.307(1).

[THE NEXT PARAGRAPH IS A4-437]

GENERAL NOTE

A4-437 The obligation placed on a court by this section is to "have regard to any period of time spent in custody by the person awaiting trial or sentence, or spent in custody awaiting extradition to the United Kingdom". The 1997 Act extended this obligation to any prisoner spending time on remand in hospital prior to plea or trial to ascertain his mental state (s.52 of the 1995 Act), prior to sentence when an interim hospital order had been made (s.53 of that Act as amended) or when remanded to hospital during a deferment of sentence (s.200 of the 1995 Act). This obligation normally exists even when the conviction is one of murder which, of course, carries a mandatory life sentence; while subs.(1)(a) has no application in such a case the remaining provisions do, and can affect the date upon which a prisoner might first be eligible for parole (*Elliott v HM Advocate*, 1997 G.W.D. 1-15).

In effect, it is submitted, the court should have such a period in mind when selecting a sentence: it does not follow that such a period should be deducted automatically or that the sentence passed should be backdated to a commencement date that in effect deducts the period in mind. In practice, however, many sentences are backdated to a suitable commencement date: for a survey of the very considerable number of authorities on this point see *Backdating Sentences of Imprisonment* (1995) 40 J.L.S. 383. The considerations behind the sentence being imposed should be explicable and explicitly stated and the whole period spent on remand (or, if preferred, since arrest) should customarily be taken into account provided it is solely referable to those proceedings; *Simpson v HM Advocate*, 2008 S.L.T. 271;2008 S.C.C.R. 126.

While the extent and seriousness of the accused's previous convictions and the gravity of the offences before the court are factors which would justify not backdating a term of imprisonment (see for example *Robertson v HM Advocate*, 1996 G.W.D. 14-836; *Wilson v Lees*, 1996 G.W.D. 8-441, and *Grant v HM Advocate*, 1996 G.W.D. 25-1421), due attention has to be paid to the extent of the charges where the accused has been convicted when set against those libelled originally: see *Johnston v Wilson*, 1996 G.W.D. 17-986; *Craig v HM Advocate*, 1997 G.W.D. 8-306 and *Blacklock v HM Advocate*, 1998 G.W.D. 7-328 and *Pugh v Hingston*, 1999 G.W.D. 13-605.

Time spent on remand resulting from an accused's own failure to appear for trial is unlikely to merit backdating (*Galbraith v Vannet*, 1998 G.W.D. 5-215 following *Wojciechowski v McLeod*, 1992 S.C.C.R. 563) but backdating only to the date of intimation of an acceptable plea, rather than to the date of being taken into custody, will only be upheld if reasons for so doing are stated (*Taylor v HM Advocate*, 1998 G.W.D. 28-1415). However contrast *McAuley v McLeod*, 1998 G.W.D. 37-1918 where a breach of bail and an appalling record of shoplifting offences was held to justify a refusal to backdate sentence.

Even following a conviction for murder, the mandatory sentence of life imprisonment should be backdated unless there are sound reasons stated to the contrary (*Elliott v HM Advocate (No.2)*, 1997 S.L.T. 1229).

Ordinarily the reasons for refraining from backdating have to be noted when sentence is imposed (subs.(1)(c)) as in *Young v HM Advocate*, 1996 G.W.D. 15-667 and *McGhee v HM Advocate*, 1997 G.W.D. 17-772, cases in which regard was had to offending while on bail or very soon after the commission of other offences; failure to state them generally results in sentence being backdated on appeal (*Egan v McGlennan*, 1996 G.W.D. 17-985 and *Dailly v HM Advocate*, 1996 S.C.C.R. 580). In the latter case matters were further complicated by the need to take account of s.16 of the Prisoners and Criminal Proceedings (Scotland) 1993 which makes no provision for backdating; such sentences either must be served before any additional sentence imposed by the court or concurrently with such additional sentence. See also *McLaughlin v HM Advocate*, 1996 G.W.D. 23-1315 in which the sheriff refrained from backdating on the basis that, had he done so, he would have remitted the accused to the High Court for sentence. The Court of Appeal paid the same regard to the accused's record, albeit that had not been expressly referred to in the sentencing minutes.

In *Hutcheson v HM Advocate*, 2001 S.C.C.R. 43, which might seem to follow upon *Douglas v HM Advocate*, 1997 S.C.C.R. 671 (where the sentencing judge had refrained from backdating as an alternative to remitting to the High Court for sentence), the sentencing High Court judge adopted an idiosyncratic approach, and one which the Appeal Court seemed reluctant to commend; H's sentence for assault to severe injury and danger of life committed while on bail, was not backdated on the basis that such a brutal attack truly merited a more severe punishment, the time spent in custody being used to offset the sentence which would otherwise have been imposed. It would surely have been more satisfactory to have imposed an appropriate sentence first, then consider whether or not to backdate. It should be noted that these provisions have no application to "curfew" bail conditions (*McGill v HM Advocate*; *Harrison v PF Perth* [2013] HCJAC 150).

Sexual or violent offenders

Extended sentences for sex, violent and terrorist offenders

210A.—(1) Where a person is convicted on indictment of a sexual, violent or terrorism offence, the court may, if it— **A4-437.1**

(a) intends, in relation to—

(i) a sexual offence, to pass a determinate sentence of imprisonment; or

(ii) a violent or terrorism offence, to pass such a sentence for a term of four years or more; and

(b) considers that the period (if any) for which the offender would, apart from this section, be subject to a licence would not be adequate for the purpose of protecting the public from serious harm from the offender,

pass an extended sentence on the offender.

(2) An extended sentence is a sentence of imprisonment which is the aggregate of—

(a) the term of imprisonment ("the custodial term") which the court would have passed on the offender otherwise than by virtue of this section; and

(b) a further period ("the extension period") for which the offender is to be subject to a licence and which is, subject to the provisions of this section, of such length as the court considers necessary for the purpose mentioned in subsection (1)(b) above.

(3) The extension period shall not exceed, in the case of—

(a) a sexual offence, ten years;

(b) a violent offence, ten years; and

(c) a terrorism offence, ten years.

(4) A court shall, before passing an extended sentence, consider a report by a relevant officer of a local authority about the offender and his circumstances and, if the court thinks it necessary, hear that officer.

(5) The term of an extended sentence passed for a statutory offence shall not exceed the maximum term of imprisonment provided for in the statute in respect of that offence.

(6) Subject to subsection (5) above, a sheriff may pass an extended sentence which is the aggregate of a custodial term not exceeding the maximum term of imprisonment which he may impose and an extension period not exceeding five years.

(7) The Secretary of State may by order—

(a) amend paragraph (b) of subsection (3) above by substituting a different period, not exceeding ten years, for the period for the time being specified in that paragraph; and

(b) make such transitional provision as appears to him to be necessary or expedient in connection with the amendment.

(8) The power to make an order under subsection (7) above shall be exercisable by statutory instrument; but no such order shall be made unless a draft of the order has been laid before, and approved by a resolution of, each House of Parliament.

(9) An extended sentence shall not be imposed where the sexual or violent offence was committed before the commencement of section 86 of the Crime and Disorder Act 1998.

(10) For the purposes of this section—

"licence" and "relevant officer" have the same meaning as in Part I of the Prisoners and Criminal Proceedings (Scotland) Act 1993;

"sexual offence" means—

(i) rape at common law;

(ii) clandestine injury to women;

(iii) abduction of a woman or girl with intent to rape or ravish;

(iiia) abduction with intent to commit the statutory offence of rape;

(iv) assault with intent to rape or ravish;

(iva) assault with intent to commit the statutory offence of rape;

(v) indecent assault;

(vi) lewd, indecent or libidinous behaviour or practices;

(vii) shameless indecency;

(viii) sodomy;

(ix) an offence under section 170 of the Customs and Excise Management Act 1979 in relation to goods prohibited to be imported under section 42 of the Customs Consolidation Act 1876, but only where the prohibited goods include indecent photographs of persons;

(x) an offence under section 52 of the Civic Government (Scotland) Act 1982 (taking and distribution of indecent images of children);

(xi) an offence under section 52A of that Act (possession of indecent images of children);

(xii) an offence under section 1 of the Criminal Law (Consolidation) (Scotland) Act 1995 (incest);

(xiii) an offence under section 2 of that Act (intercourse with a stepchild);

(xiv) an offence under section 3 of that Act (intercourse with child under 16 by person in position of trust);

(xv) an offence under section 5 of that Act (unlawful intercourse with girl under 16);

(xvi) an offence under section 6 of that Act (indecent behaviour towards girl between 12 and 16);

(xvii) an offence under section 8 of that Act (abduction of girl under 18 for purposes of unlawful intercourse);

(xviii) an offence under section 10 of that Act (person having parental responsibilities causing or encouraging sexual activity in relation to a girl under 16);

(xix) an offence under subsection (5) of section 13 of that Act (homosexual offences);

(xx) an offence under section 3 of the Sexual Offences (Amendment) Act 2000 (abuse of position of trust);

(xxi) an offence under section 311(1) of the Mental Health (Care and Treatment) (Scotland) Act 2003 (asp 13) (non-consensual sexual acts);

(xxii) an offence under section 1 of the Protection of Children and Prevention of Sexual Offences (Scotland) Act 2005 (asp 9) (meeting a child following certain preliminary conduct);

(xxiii) an offence under section 9 of that Act (paying for sexual services of a child);

(xxiv) an offence under section 10 of that Act (causing or inciting provision by child of sexual services or child pornography);

(xxv) an offence under section 11 of that Act (controlling a child providing sexual services or involved in pornography);

(xxvi) an offence under section 12 of that Act (arranging or facilitating provision by child of sexual services or child pornography),

(xxvii) an offence which consists of a contravention of any of the following provisions of the Sexual Offences (Scotland) Act 2009 (asp 9)—

- (A) section 1 (rape),
- (B) section 2 (sexual assault by penetration),
- (C) section 3 (sexual assault),
- (D) section 4 (sexual coercion),
- (E) section 5 (coercing a person into being present during a sexual activity),

(F) section 6 (coercing a person into looking at a sexual image),
(G) section 7(1) (communicating indecently),
(H) section 7(2) (causing a person to see or hear an indecent communication),
(I) section 8 (sexual exposure),
(J) section 9 (voyeurism),
(K) section 11 (administering a substance for sexual purposes),
(L) section 18 (rape of a young child),
(M) section 19 (sexual assault on a young child by penetration),
(N) section 20 (sexual assault on a young child),
(O) section 21 (causing a young child to participate in a sexual activity),
(P) section 22 (causing a young child to be present during a sexual activity)
(Q) section 23 (causing a young child to look at a sexual image),
(R) section 24(1) (communicating indecently with a young child),
(S) section 24(2) (causing a young child to see or hear an indecent communication),
(T) section 25 (sexual exposure to a young child),
(U) section 26 (voyeurism towards a young child),
(V) section 28 (having intercourse with an older child),
(W) section 29 (engaging in penetrative sexual activity with or towards an older child),
(X) section 30 (engaging in sexual activity with or towards an older child),
(Y) section 31 (causing an older child to participate in a sexual activity),
(Z) section 32 (causing an older child to be present during a sexual activity),
(ZA) section 33 (causing an older child to look at a sexual image),
(ZB) section 34(1) (communicating indecently with an older child),
(ZC) section 34(2) (causing an older child to see or hear an indecent communication),
(ZD) section 35 (sexual exposure to an older child),
(ZE) section 36 (voyeurism towards an older child),
(ZF) section 37(1) (engaging while an older child in sexual conduct with or towards another older child),
(ZG) section 37(4) (engaging while an older child in consensual sexual conduct with another older child),
(ZH) section 42 (sexual abuse of trust),
(ZI) section 46 (sexual abuse of trust of a mentally disordered person);

(xxviii) an offence (other than one mentioned in the preceding paragraphs) where the court determines for the purposes of this paragraph that there was a significant sexual aspect to the offender's behaviour in committing the offence;

"imprisonment" includes—

(i) detention under section 207 of this Act; and

(ii) detention under section 208 of this Act;

"terrorism offence" means—

(a) an offence under any of the following provisions of the Terrorism Act 2000—

(i) section 11 (membership of a proscribed organisation),

(ii) section 12 (inviting support for a proscribed organisation),

(iii) section 54 (weapons training),

(iv) section 56 (directing a terrorist organisation),

(v) section 57 (possession of article for terrorist purposes),

(vi) section 58 (collection of information likely to be of use to a terrorist),

(vii) section 58A (publishing information about members of the armed forces etc),

(viii) section 58B (entering or remaining in a designated area), or

(ix) section 59 (inciting terrorism overseas),

(b) an offence under any of the following provisions of the Anti-terrorism, Crime and Security Act 2001—

(i) section 47 (use etc of nuclear weapons),

(ii) section 50 (assisting or inducing certain weapons-related acts overseas), or

(iii) section 113 (use of noxious substance or thing to cause harm or intimidate),

(c) an offence under any of the following provisions of the Terrorism Act 2006—

(i) section 1 (encouragement of terrorism),

(ii) section 2 (dissemination of terrorist publications),

(iii) section 5 (preparation of terrorist acts),

(iv) section 6 (training for terrorism),

(v) section 8 (attendance at a place used for terrorist training),

(vi) section 9 (making or possession of radioactive device or material),

(vii) section 10 (misuse of radioactive device or material for terrorist purposes etc), or

(viii) section 11 (terrorist threats relating to radioactive devices etc),

(d) an offence of aiding, abetting, counselling, procuring or inciting the commission of an offence specified in paragraphs (a) to (c),

(e) an offence of attempting to commit such an offence,

(f) an offence of conspiring to commit such an offence; and.

"violent offence" means any offence (other than an offence which is a sexual offence within the meaning of this section) inferring personal violence.

(11) In subsection (10)—

(a) any reference to a "sexual offence" includes—

(i) a reference to any attempt, conspiracy or incitement to commit that offence; and

(ii) except in the case of an offence under paragraphs (i) to (viii) of the definition of "sexual offence" in that subsection, a reference to aiding and abetting, counselling or procuring the commission of that offence;

(b) the references to "rape" in paragraphs (iii) and (iv) of the definition of "sexual offence" are to the offence of rape at common law; and

(c) the references to "the statutory offence of rape" in paragraphs (iiia) and (iva) of that definition are (as the case may be) to—

(i) the offence of rape under section 1 of the Sexual Offences (Scotland) Act 2009, or

(ii) the offence of rape of a young child under section 18 of that Act.

(12) An extended sentence may be passed by reference to paragraph (xxviii) only if the offender is or is to become, by virtue of Schedule 3 to the Sexual Offences Act 2003 (c.42), subject to the notification requirements of Part 2 of that Act.

AMENDMENTS

Section 210A inserted by Crime and Disorder Act 1998 (c.37) s.86 (effective 30 September 1998: SI 1998/2327).

Subs.(10)(xx) inserted by Sexual Offences (Amendment) Act 2000 (c.44) s.6(2).

Subs.(3)(b) as amended by Extended Sentences for Violent Offenders (Scotland) Order 2003 (SSI 2003/48) art.2 (effective 28 January 2003).

Subs.(6) as amended by Criminal Procedure (Amendment) (Scotland) Act 2004 (asp 5) s.21. Brought into force on 4 October 2004 by SSI 2004/405 (C.28).

Subs.(10) as amended by Mental Health (Care and Treatment) (Scotland) Act 2003 (asp 13) s.312. Brought into force on 5 October 2005 by SSI 2005/161 (C.6).

Subs.(10) as amended by Criminal Proceedings etc (Reform) (Scotland) Act 2007 (asp 6) s.80 and Sch. para.(19). Brought into force on 23 April 2007 by SSI 2007/250 (C.23) art.3.

Subs.(10) as amended by Sexual Offences (Scotland) Act 2009 (asp 9) Sch.5 para.2. Brought into force on 1 December 2010 by SSI 2010/357 (C.21) art.2.

Subss.(10), (11) as amended by Sexual Offences (Scotland) Act 2009 (Supplemental and Consequential Provisions) Order 2010 (SSI 2010/421) Sch.1 para.1(3) (effective 1 December 2010).

Subs.(10) as amended, subs.(12) inserted, by Criminal Justice and Licensing (Scotland) Act 2010 (asp 13) s.23. Brought into force on 13 December 2010 by SSI 2010/413 (C.28) art.2, Sch.1 para.1.

Subss.(1), (3), (10) (insertion of definition of "terrorism offence") and heading as amended by Counter-Terrorism and Border Security Act 2019 c.3, Pt 1 c.2 s.10. Brought into force on 12 April 2019 by 2019 c.3 s.27(3) subject to transitional provisions specified in 2019 c.3 s.25(3).

DEFINITIONS

A4-437.2 "indictment": s.307(1) of the 1995 Act.

"sexual offence": s.210A(8) of the 1995 Act as inserted by s.86(1) of the 1998 Act.

"violent offence": as last above.

"imprisonment": s.307(1) of the 1995 Act and s.210A(8) of that Act as inserted by s.86(1) of the 1998 Act.

GENERAL NOTE

A4-437.3 This section inserted into the 1995 Act as s.210A has to be read in conjunction with s.26A of the Prisoners and Criminal Proceedings (Scotland) Act 1993 (c.9) which, confusingly, inserts "extended sentence" provisions into that latter Act.

Solemn courts imposing imprisonment for serious sexual offences or violent crimes attracting a term of imprisonment of four years or more now have a discretion to place the offender on licence, and thus subject to recall, when it is considered that the offender may pose a serious threat to public safety after his release.

(Section 87 of the 1998 Act is inserted into Pt I of the Prisoners and Criminal Proceedings (Scotland) Act 1993 and ss.12 and 17 of the 1993 Act set out the meaning of "licence"; however, Schs 1 and 3 of the Crime and Punishment (Scotland) Act 1997 (c.48) contain prospective changes to these sections.)

Henceforth, courts opting to place an offender on licence for a qualifying offence will impose an extended sentence comprising the period of imprisonment or detention (dubbed "the custodial term") and a period of licence ("the extension term"). Subsection (10)by defining "imprisonment" under reference to ss.207 and 208 of the 1995 Act stipulates that these discretionary sentencing powers can be applied to children and young offenders as well as to adult offenders. The provisions can only apply to determinate sentences—those serving indeterminate sentences, i.e. life imprisonment, are dealt with separately. While subs.(4) requires the court to obtain and consider both a social enquiry report and an offender risk assessment before imposing an extended sentence (*Robertson v HM Advocate*, 2004 S.L.T. 888 and *Crawford v HM Advocate* [2015] HCJAC 70), no such stricture applies to offenders sentenced to life imprisonment for violent, as opposed to sexual, offences—see *Hamilton v HM Advocate*, 2005 S.C.C.R. 316. A conviction now of public indecency (rather than the obsolescent shameless indecency specified in subs.(10)(vii)) can attract an extended sentence. See *Clark v HM Advocate*, 2008 S.L.T. 787. While the custodial element of sentence may be discounted in terms of s.196 of the Act to reflect the utility value of a guilty plea, given the broader public protection aim of an extended sentence, no such discount could properly be applied to that second element of sentence. Similar reasoning applies to supervised release orders, discussed at s.208 above. See the Note to subs.(2) below.

It has to be emphasised that extended sentences are discretionary and, necessarily, only operate in circumstances where a term of imprisonment has been imposed on indictment and it is felt that the offender will constitute a threat to public safety on release and, then, subject to several qualifications. While it is proper to impose an extended sentence, when it is felt that the period of licence after early release is insufficient to protect the public from serious harm, consideration has still to be given to the extension period necessary for that purpose (*Fleming v HM Advocate*, 2002 G.W.D. 2-69). A common law "sexual offence" as defined by s.210A(10) can involve a period of licence of up to 10 years, while the extended sentence for a statutory "sexual offence" is to be not more than the maximum period of imprisonment statutorily provided for that offence, or the 10 year ceiling already mentioned, whichever is lower. It will be recalled that some statutory sexual offences, notably contraventions of ss.1 to 4 and 18 to 21 of the Sexual Offences (Scotland) Act 2009 (asp 9) can attract life imprisonment. It is submitted that s.210A(3) and (4) have to be read in conjunction.

The new provisions in s.210A in regard to violent offences only apply to sentences of over four years' imprisonment, the point at which prisoners are regarded as long-term prisoners (see s.27 of the 1993 Act) and in such cases the "extension period" cannot exceed five years. If the violent offence has been a statutory crime then, again, the extension period will be the lower of either the maximum period of imprisonment available under statute, or five years, due to the interaction of s.210A(3) and (4). It is worth noting that subs.(7) empowers the Secretary of State to increase "the extension period" in relation to violent offences (but not sexual offences) from the five years set out in subs.(3)(b) up to 10 years, by order. Subs.(10)(xxviii) adds a catch all, empowering the court in its discretion to hold that the offence of which the accused has been convicted involved a significant sexual element and thus to impose an extended sentence. Note, however, that in such circumstances subs.(12) then stipulates that an extended sentence may only be applied if the convicted offender is already subject of the notification requirements in the Sexual Offences Act 2003 (c.46) or if the court has now resolved to impose such requirements as part of its sentence.

For those convicted of a violent offence and sentenced to less than four years' imprisonment the option open to the court is to impose a supervised release order; see s.209 above.

Thus, where a number of offences, including a violent offence, together attract imposition of a cumulo sentence exceeding four years, it is only competent to incorporate an extended sentence when the qualifying violent offence itself leads to imposition of a sentence of four years or more; see *Crawford v HM Advocate* [2015] HCJAC 70.

See the discussion of *Craig v HM Advocate*, 2000 G.W.D. 34—1313 and *O'Hare v HM Advocate*, 2002 S.L.T. 925 (Note) at A4-435.2 above.

Subs.(1)(a)(ii)

A sentence for a term of four years or more. Charges cannot be taken together to cross this threshold. In *Crawford v HM Advocate*, 2015 S.C.C.R. 345 the appellant pled guilty to a series of offences and the sheriff imposed consecutive sentences in excess of four years. One of the charges was assault and robbery, in respect of which he was sentenced to three years' imprisonment. On a related charge of dangerous driving, he was sentenced to nine months' imprisonment, consecutively. The total, including the sentences for other, unrelated offences, was four years eight months. The sheriff imposed an extended sentence. The appeal court held that the only violent offence was the assault and robbery and that the threshold for an extended sentence was, therefore, not crossed.

Subs.(1)(b)

For the purpose of protecting the public from serious harm. It is not legitimate to impose an extended sentence on the basis that the custodial part is not long enough to allow the offender to complete a course designed to reduce the risk of re-offending. Nor can it be maintained that the risk that an offender, who has been convicted of accessing pornographic images of children, will repeat the offence involves serious harm to the public. The argument that, by providing an audience, that offender creates a risk that similar images will be created in the future, so that the offender poses a risk to those who might be subjected to such photography, is excessively "convoluted" (*Wood v HM Advocate*, 2017 S.C.C.R. 100 at [27]).

Subs.(2)

In terms of *Gemmell v HM Advocate* [2011] HCJAC 129, discounting in terms of s.196 does not apply to the extension period, because it is the period assessed as necessary for the protection of the public from serious harm. The correct approach is to consider first the ordinary determinate custodial sentence which the crime would attract, discount that according to the timing of the plea, consider the adequacy of the licence period and then, if an extension is necessary, decide the length of that extension on a basis independent of the timing of the guilty plea (see especially the Opinion of Lord Eassie at [142]).

Subs.(9)

For an example of a case in which this was overlooked, see *PM v HM Advocate*, 2011 S.L.T. 1047.

Extended sentences for certain other offenders

A4-437.4 **210AA.** Where a person is convicted on indictment of abduction but the offence is other than is mentioned in paragraph (iii) of the definition of "sexual offence" in subsection (10) of section 210A of this Act, that section shall apply in relation to the person as it applies in relation to a person so convicted of a violent offence.

AMENDMENTS

Section 210AA inserted by Criminal Justice (Scotland) Act 2003 (asp 7) Pt 3 s.20. Brought into force on 27 June 2003 by SSI 2003/288 (C.14).

Approach in domestic abuse cases

Particular factor as to victim safety

A4-437.4.1 **210AB.—**(1) When sentencing a person convicted of an offence listed in subsection (2)(b), the court must have particular regard to the aim of ensuring that the victim is not the subject of a further such offence committed by the convicted person.

(2) For the purpose of subsection (1)—

(a) "victim" means the person against whom the offence was committed,

(b) the list is—

(i) an offence under section 1(1) of the Domestic Abuse (Scotland) Act 2018,

(ii) an offence that is aggravated as described in section 1(1)(a) of the Abusive Behaviour and Sexual Harm (Scotland) Act 2016.

AMENDMENT

S.210AB inserted by Domestic Abuse (Scotland) Act 2018 (asp 5) Sch.1(1)(4) para.8(2) (effective 1 April 2019 in respect of proceedings commenced on or after 1 April 2019 subject to transitional provision specified in SSI 2018/387 reg.7(2)).

[THE NEXT PARAGRAPH IS A4-437.5]

Risk assessment

Risk assessment order

A4-437.5 **210B.—**(1) This subsection applies where it falls to the High Court to impose sentence on a person convicted of an offence other than murder and that offence—

(a) is (any or all)—

(i) a sexual offence (as defined in section 210A(10) of this Act);

(ii) a violent offence (as so defined);

(iii) an offence which endangers life; or

(b) is an offence the nature of which, or circumstances of the commission of which, are such that it appears to the court that the person has a propensity to commit any such offence as is mentioned in sub-paragraphs (i) to (iii) of paragraph (a) above.

(2) Where subsection (1) above applies, the court, at its own instance or (provided that the prosecutor has given the person notice of his intention in that regard) on the motion of the prosecutor, if it considers that the risk criteria may be met, shall make an order under this subsection (a "risk assessment order") unless—

(a) the court makes an interim compulsion order by virtue of section 210D(1) of this Act in respect of the person; or

(b) the person is subject to an order for lifelong restriction previously imposed.

(3) A risk assessment order is an order—

(a) for the convicted person to be taken to a place specified in the order, so that there may be prepared there—

(i) by a person accredited for the purposes of this section by the Risk Management Authority; and

(ii) in such manner as may be so accredited,

a risk assessment report (that is to say, a report as to what risk his being at liberty presents to the safety of the public at large); and

(b) providing for him to be remanded in custody there for so long as is necessary for those purposes and thereafter there or elsewhere until such diet as is fixed for sentence.

(4) On making a risk assessment order, the court shall adjourn the case for a period not exceeding ninety days.

(5) The court may on one occasion, on cause shown, extend the period mentioned in subsection (4) above by not more than ninety days; and it may exceptionally, where by reason of circumstances outwith the control of the person to whom it falls to prepare the risk assessment report (the "assessor"), or as the case may be of any person instructed under section 210C(5) of this Act to prepare such a report, the report in question has not been completed, grant such further extension as appears to it to be appropriate.

(6) There shall be no appeal against a risk assessment order or against any refusal to make such an order.

Amendments

Section 210B inserted by Criminal Justice (Scotland) Act 2003 (asp 7) s.1(1). Brought into force on 19 June 2006 by SSI 2006/332 (C.30) art.2(1), subject to art.2(2).

Subs.(2)(a) as amended by Mental Health (Care and Treatment) (Scotland) Act 2003 (Modification of Enactments) Order 2005 (SSI 2005/465) Sch.1 para.34(2) (effective 19 June 2006).

General Note

Sections 210B-210H set out the mechanisms for imposition of an Order for Lifelong Restriction (an "OLR"), a sentencing option only in High Court convictions for the range of serious offences as specified in s.210B(1). It will be noted that separate procedures apply to murder convictions (see s.205). The Crown will generally seek such an addition to sentence when moving for sentence and must advise the accused of that intention before so doing; the court *ex proprio motu* also has a discretion to initiate investigation of the risk criteria. **A4-437.5.1**

In either situation sentence will require to be further deferred for up to 90 days to enable preparation of a risk assessment report (see s.210C). Pending that report, a risk assessment order must be made unless a previous OLR exists for the accused, or his mental health requires instead an interim compulsion order, for which see, generally, s.57 above. Section 210E specifies the risk criteria which will justify an OLR, and which have to be assessed in the report.

There is no appeal for, or against, the making of a risk assessment order or interim compulsion order (s.210B(6) above).

Ferguson v HM Advocate [2014] HCJAC 19; 2014 S.L.T. 431; 2014 S.C.C.R. 244 is a helpful decision, examining the range of sentencing options available once a risk assessment report has been prepared. It is stressed that, even if the court is not satisfied that an OLR is a necessary element of sentence, the court could still (and assuredly will) competently impose an extended sentence (see ss.210A and 210AA).

Equally importantly, if it is concluded that the risk criteria are not established, and hence an OLR is not appropriate, then an indeterminate sentence of life imprisonment or detention for life cannot be imposed (s.210G (2)).

Risk assessment report

A4-437.6 **210C.**—(1) The assessor may, in preparing the risk assessment report, take into account not only any previous conviction of the convicted person but[, including a conviction by a court in any part of the United Kingdom or in any member State of the European Union,] also any allegation that the person has engaged in criminal behaviour (whether or not that behaviour resulted in prosecution and acquittal).

(2) Where the assessor, in preparing the risk assessment report, takes into account any allegation that the person has engaged in criminal behaviour, the report is to—

(a) list each such allegation;
(b) set out any additional evidence which supports the allegation; and
(c) explain the extent to which the allegation and evidence has influenced the opinion included in the report under subsection (3) below.

(3) The assessor shall include in the risk assessment report his opinion as to whether the risk mentioned in section 210B(3)(a) of this Act is, having regard to such standards and guidelines as are issued by the Risk Management Authority in that regard, high, medium or low.

(4) The assessor shall submit the risk assessment report to the High Court by sending it, together with such documents as are available to the assessor and are referred to in the report, to the Principal Clerk of Justiciary, who shall then send a copy of the report and of those documents to the prosecutor and to the convicted person.

(5) The convicted person may, during the period of his detention at the place specified in the risk assessment order, himself instruct the preparation (by a person other than the assessor) of a risk assessment report; and if such a report is so prepared then the person who prepares it shall submit it to the court by sending it, together with such documents as are available to him (after any requirement under subsection (4) above is met) and are referred to in the report, to the Principal Clerk of Justiciary, who shall then send a copy of it and of those documents to the prosecutor.

(6) When the court receives the risk assessment report submitted by the assessor a diet shall be fixed for the convicted person to be brought before it for sentence.

(7) If, within such period after receiving a copy of that report as may be prescribed by Act of Adjournal, the convicted person intimates, in such form, or as nearly as may be in such form, as may be so prescribed—

(a) that he objects to the content or findings of that report; and
(b) what the grounds of his objection are,

the prosecutor and he shall be entitled to produce and examine witnesses with regard to—

(i) that content or those findings; and
(ii) the content or findings of any risk assessment report instructed by the person and duly submitted under subsection (5) above.

AMENDMENTS

Section 210C inserted by Criminal Justice (Scotland) Act 2003 (asp 7) s.1(1). Brought into force on 19 June 2006 by SSI 2006/332 (C.30) art.2(1), subject to art.2(2).

Words in subs.(1) was inserted by the Criminal Justice (EU Exit) (Scotland) (Amendment etc.) Regulations 2020 (SSI 2020/339) reg.13(13) (effective 31 December 2020 subject to transitional and saving provision specified in reg.16 of those Regulations.

Interim hospital order and assessment of risk

210D.—(1) Where subsection (1) of section 210B of this Act applies, the High Court, if— A4-437.7

(a) it may make an interim compulsion order in respect of the person under section 53 of this Act; and

(b) it considers that the risk criteria may be met,

shall make such an order unless the person is subject to an order for lifelong restriction previously imposed.

(2) Where an interim hospital order is made by virtue of subsection (1) above, a report as to the risk the convicted person's being at liberty presents to the safety of the public at large shall be prepared by a person accredited for the purposes of this section by the Risk Management Authority and in such manner as may be so accredited.

(3) Section 210C(1) to (4) and (7) (except paragraph (ii)) of this Act shall apply in respect of any such report as it does in respect of a risk assessment report.

AMENDMENTS

Section 210D inserted by Criminal Justice (Scotland) Act 2003 (asp 7) s.1(1). Brought into force on 19 June 2006 by SSI 2006/332 (C.30) art.2(1), subject to art.2(2).

Subs.(1)(a) as amended by Mental Health (Care and Treatment) (Scotland) Act 2003 (Modification of Enactments) Order 2005 (SSI 2005/465) Sch.1 para.34(2) (effective 19 June 2006).

The risk criteria

210E. For the purposes of sections 195(1), 210B(2), 210D(1) and 210F(1) and (3) of this Act, the risk criteria are that the nature of, or the circumstances of the commission of, the offence of which the convicted person has been found guilty either in themselves or as part of a pattern of behaviour are such as to demonstrate that there is a likelihood that he, if at liberty, will seriously endanger the lives, or physical or psychological well-being, of members of the public at large. A4-437.8

AMENDMENTS

Section 210E inserted by Criminal Justice (Scotland) Act 2003 (asp 7) s.1(1). Brought into force on 19 June 2006 by SSI 2006/332 (C.30) art.2(1), subject to art.2(2).

Application of certain sections of this Act to proceedings under section 210C(7)

210EA.—(1) Sections 271 to 271M, 274 to 275C and 288C to 288F of this Act (in this section referred to as the "applied sections") apply in relation to proceedings under section 210C(7) of this Act as they apply in relation to proceedings in or for the purposes of a trial, references in the applied sections to the "trial" and to the "trial diet" being construed accordingly. A4-437.9

(2) But for the purposes of this section the references—

(a) in sections 271(1)(a) and 271B(1)(b) to the date of commencement of the proceedings in which the trial is being held or is to be held; and

(b) in section 288E(2)(b) to the date of commencement of the proceedings,

are to be construed as references to the date of commencement of the proceedings in which the person was convicted of the offence in respect of which sentence falls to be imposed (such proceedings being in this section referred to as the "original proceedings").

(3) And for the purposes of this section any reference in the applied sections to—

(a) an "accused" (or to a person charged with an offence) is to be construed as a reference to the convicted person except that the reference in section 271(2)(e)(iii) to an accused is to be disregarded;

(b) an "alleged" offence is to be construed as a reference to any or all of the following—
(i) the offence in respect of which sentence falls to be imposed;
(ii) any other offence of which the convicted person has been convicted;
(iii) any alleged criminal behaviour of the convicted person; and
(c) a "complainer" is to be construed as a reference to any or all of the following—
(i) the person who was the complainer in the original proceedings;
(ii) in the case of any such offence as is mentioned in paragraph (b)(ii) above, the person who was the complainer in the proceedings relating to that offence;
(iii) in the case of alleged criminal behaviour if it was alleged behaviour directed against a person, the person in question.

(4) Where—
(a) any person who is giving or is to give evidence at an examination under section 210C(7) of this Act gave evidence at the trial in the original proceedings; and
(b) a special measure or combination of special measures was used by virtue of section 271A, 271C or 271D of this Act for the purpose of taking the person's evidence at that trial,

that special measure or, as the case may be, combination of special measures is to be treated as having been authorised, by virtue of the same section, to be used for the purpose of taking the person's evidence at or for the purposes of the examination.

(5) Subsection (4) above does not affect the operation, by virtue of subsection (1) above, of section 271D of this Act.

AMENDMENTS

Section 210EA inserted by Management of Offenders etc. (Scotland) Act 2005 (asp 14) s.19. Brought into force on 20 June 2006 by SSI 2006/331 (C.29) art.3(1), subject to art.3(2).

Order for lifelong restriction, etc.

Order for lifelong restriction or compulsion order

A4-437.10 **210F.**—(1) The High Court, at its own instance or on the motion of the prosecutor, if it is satisfied, having regard to—
(a) any risk assessment report submitted under section 210C(4) or (5) of this Act;
(b) any report submitted by virtue of section 210D of this Act;
(c) any evidence given under section 210C(7) of this Act; and
(d) any other information before it,

that, on a balance of probabilities, the risk criteria are met, in a case where it may make a compulsion order in respect of the convicted person under section 57A of this Act, either make such an order or make an order for lifelong restriction in respect of that person and in any other case make an order for lifelong restriction in respect of that person.

(2) An order for lifelong restriction constitutes a sentence of imprisonment, or as the case may be detention, for an indeterminate period.

(3) The prosecutor may, on the grounds that on a balance of probabilities the risk criteria are met, appeal against any refusal of the court to make an order for lifelong restriction.

AMENDMENTS

Section 210F inserted by Criminal Justice (Scotland) Act 2003 (asp 7) s.1(1). Brought into force on 19 June 2006 by SSI 2006/332 (C.30) art.2(1), subject to art.2(2).

Subs.(1) as amended by Management of Offenders etc. (Scotland) Act 2005 (asp 14) s.14(2) and (3). Brought into force on 20 June 2006 by SSI 2006/331 (C.29) art.3(1), subject to art.3(2).

GENERAL NOTE

An Order for Lifelong Restriction (an "OLR") is only competent in proceedings where sentence is being imposed in the High Court. In *Kinloch and Quinn v HM Advocate*, 2016 S.C.C.R. 25 it was emphasised that the language of the legislation is clear in requiring not only that there be a serious risk posed by the offender but also a link between the offence and that risk. Note that distinct procedures govern murder convictions, for which see ss.205 and 205D above. **A4-437.10.1**

The assessment procedures occur post-conviction, apply the risk criteria set out in s.210E, and can be initiated by the court *ex proprio motu* or in response to an express motion from the prosecutor following a qualifying conviction (see s.210B(1)). No OLR can be imposed without the preparation first and consideration of a risk assessment report, unless the accused has previously been the subject of an OLR or is subject to an interim compulsion order (s.210D). The court may adjourn proceedings for up to 90 days to enable preparation of the risk assessment report.

Perplexingly, in *Henderson v HM Advocate*, 2009 S.C.C.R. 30 it was held that these procedures did not constitute a punishment, a view since reversed by the Appeal Court in *McCluskey v HM Advocate* [2012] HCJAC 125. It will be appreciated that the OLR procedures are separate from the requirements governing life sentences and should not influence the calculation of "the punishment part" of the sentence as described in s.2 of the Prisoners and Criminal Proceedings (Scotland) Act 1993 (c.9) for which see *Petch v HM Advocate*, 2011 S.C.C.R. 199 and *McCluskey*, above.

Cases involving a combination of common law and statutory offences have given some difficulty: there is clear authority that a cumulative sentence can properly be imposed with such a combination of offences (*Gemmell v HM Advocate*, 2012 S.C.C.R. 176) or for a series of statutory offences (*McDade v HM Advocate*, 1997 S.C.C.R. 52) but clarification has been necessary on the competence of imposing a cumulo OLR particularly where the duration of that order would necessarily exceed the maximum sentence competent for the statutory offences. In *Henderson*, a firearms case, the Crown had conceded that an OLR could not be imposed since this would exceed the statutory maximum penalty (five years) but a more sophisticated analysis has since been applied in *McCluskey*, above, following *HM Advocate v Austin* Unreported 21 March 2011 High Court; essentially the existence of a statutory maximum sentence for a qualifying offence does not prevent the sentencing judge from imposing an OLR but only one such order should be imposed, whether it be for one offence in the libel or a combination thereof in the indictment before the court. *McCluskey* provides a working example of the complexities of High Court sentencing and underlines that calculation of the punishment part must only occur after tallying all the separate offences.

The trial judge is obliged to consider the terms of the Risk Assessment Report (see s.210C above) which assesses the offender against the public risk criteria (s.210E) but is not bound by the conclusions reached by the report's author. See *Ferguson v HM Advocate* [2014] HCJAC 19; 2014 S.L.T. 431; 2014 S.C.C.R. 244 and *Laird v HM Advocate* 2015 HCJAC 90; 2015 S.C.C.R. 434.

Subs.(1)

As originally enacted, the words following para.(d) were "that, on a balance of probabilities, the risk criteria are met, shall make an order for lifelong restriction in respect of the convicted person". In the longer formula which was substituted in 2005, the word "shall" has been omitted. In *Johnstone v HM Advocate*, 2011 S.C.C.R.470, the appeal court held that Parliament had not intended to delete the word "shall" and refused an appeal based on the argument that the provision had become meaningless. In the same case, the court held that orders for lifelong restriction are ECHR compatible.

[THE NEXT PARAGRAPH IS A4-437.11]

Disposal of case where certain orders not made

210G.—(1) Where, in respect of a convicted person— **A4-437.11**

(a) a risk assessment order is not made under section 210B(2) of this Act, or (as the case may be) an interim compulsion order is not made by virtue of section 210D(1) of this Act, because the court does not consider that the risk criteria may be met; or

(b) the court considers that the risk criteria may be met but a risk assessment order, or (as the case may be) an interim hospital order, is not so made because the person is subject to an order for lifelong restriction previously imposed,

the court shall dispose of the case as it considers appropriate.

(2) Where, in respect of a convicted person, an order for lifelong restriction is not made under section 210F of this Act because the court is not satisfied (in accordance with subsection (1) of that section) that the risk criteria are met, the court, in disposing of the case, shall not impose on the person a sentence of imprisonment for life, detention for life or detention without limit of time.

AMENDMENTS

Section 210G inserted by Criminal Justice (Scotland) Act 2003 (asp 7) s.1(1). Brought into force on 19 June 2006 by SSI 2006/332 (C.30) art.2(1), subject to art.2(2).

Subs.(1)(a) as amended by Mental Health (Care and Treatment) (Scotland) Act 2003 (Modification of Enactments) Order 2005 (SSI 2005/465) Sch.1 para.34(2) (effective 19 June 2006).

Report of judge

Report of judge

A4-437.12 **210H.**—(1) This subsection applies where a person falls to be sentenced—

(a) in the High Court for an offence (other than murder) mentioned in section 210B(1) of this Act; or

(b) in the sheriff court for such an offence prosecuted on indictment.

(2) Where subsection (1) above applies, the court shall, as soon as reasonably practicable, prepare a report in writing, in such form as may be prescribed by Act of Adjournal—

(a) as to the circumstances of the case; and

(b) containing such other information as it considers appropriate,

but no such report shall be prepared if a report is required to be prepared under section 21(4) of the Criminal Justice (Scotland) Act 2003 (asp 7).

AMENDMENTS

Section 210H inserted by Criminal Justice (Scotland) Act 2003 (asp 7) s.1(1). Brought into force on 19 June 2006 by SSI 2006/332 (C.30) art.2(1), subject to art.2(2).

[THE NEXT PARAGRAPH IS A4-438]

Fines

Fines

A4-438 **211.**—(1) Where an accused who is convicted on indictment of any offence (whether triable only on indictment or triable either on indictment or summarily other than by virtue of section 292(6) of this Act) would apart from this subsection be liable to a fine of or not exceeding a specified amount, he shall by virtue of this subsection be liable to a fine of any amount.

(2) Where any Act confers a power by subordinate instrument to make a person liable on conviction on indictment of any offence mentioned in subsection (1) above to a fine or a maximum fine of a specified amount, or which shall not exceed a specified amount, the fine which may be imposed in the exercise of that power shall by virtue of this subsection be a fine of an unlimited amount.

(3) Any sentence or decree for any fine or expenses pronounced by a sheriff court or JP court may be enforced against the person or effects of any party against whom the sentence or decree was awarded—

(a) in the district where the sentence or decree was pronounced; or

(b) in any other such district.

(4) A fine imposed by the High Court shall be remitted for enforcement to, and shall be enforceable as if it had been imposed by—

(a) where the person upon whom the fine was imposed resides in Scotland, the sheriff for the district where that person resides; and

(b) where that person resides outwith Scotland, the sheriff before whom he was brought for examination in relation to the offence for which the fine was imposed.

(5) [...]

(6) [All] fines and expenses imposed in proceedings under this Act shall be paid to the [clerk of any court, or to any other person (or class of person) authorised by the Scottish Ministers for the purpose], to be accounted for to the person entitled to such fines and expenses, and it shall not be necessary to specify in any sentence the person entitled to payment of such fines or expenses unless it is necessary to provide for the division of the penalty.

(7) A court in determining the amount of any fine to be imposed on an offender shall take into consideration, amongst other things, the means of the offender so far as known to the court.

AMENDMENTS

Subs.(5) repealed and subs.(6) as amended by Criminal Proceedings etc. (Reform) (Scotland) Act 2007 (asp 6) s.80 and Sch. para.20(1). Brought into force (words in square brackets in para.(6) brought into force except for the purposes of any fines or expenses which require to be paid to the clerk of any district court) on 10 March 2008 by SSI 2008/42 (C.4) art.3 and Sch.

Subs.(3) as amended by Criminal Proceedings etc. (Reform) (Scotland) Act 2007 (asp 6) s.80 and Sch. para.26. Brought into force for the Sheriffdom of Lothian and Borders on 10 March 2008 by SSI 2008/42 (C.4) art.3 and Sch. Further brought into force for the Sheriffdom of Grampian, Highland and Islands on 2 June 2008 by SSI 2008/192 (C.19) art.3 and Sch. Brought into force for the Sheriffdom of Glasgow and Strathkelvin on 8 December 2008 by SSI 2008/329 (C.29) art.3 and Sch. Brought into force for the Sheriffdom of Tayside, Central and Fife on 23 February 2009 by SSI 2008/362 (C.30) art.3 and Sch. Brought into force for the Sheriffdom of North Strathclyde on 14 December 2009 by SSI 2009/432 (C.32) art.3 and Sch.1. Remainder in force on 22 February 2010 by SSI 2009/432 (C.32) art.3 and Sch.2.

Subs.(6) as amended by Mutual Recognition of Criminal Financial Penalties in the European Union (Scotland) Order 2009 (SSI 2009/342) art.7 (effective 12 October 2009).

Words in subs.(6) were substituted by the Criminal Justice (EU Exit) (Scotland) (Amendment etc.) Regulations 2020 (SSI 2020/339) reg.3(2) (effective 31 December 2020 subject to transitional and saving provision specified in reg.6 of those Regulations.

DEFINITIONS

"fine": s.307(1). **A4-438.1**
"High Court": s.307(1).
"indictment": s.307(1).
"sentence": s.307(1).
"witness": s.307(1).

GENERAL NOTE

The fine (which is defined in s.307(1) in terms which include an excise penalty: *Melville v Thomson*, 2006 S.L.T. 1017) is the most commonly imposed sentence. A court sentencing a person convicted on indictment may impose a fine of any amount (see s.3(1) of this Act). As a result of subs.(1) of the present section, that is true even where the offence is a statutory one which carries a specified maximum penalty and even if the offence in question can ordinarily be prosecuted only summarily. Moreover, in terms of s.199, even where an Act, in creating a statutory offence, provides only for imprisonment (rare, or possibly unknown, in modern legislative practice), the court may substitute a fine. It follows from subs.(1) of the present section that, on indictment, that substituted fine may be unlimited. **A4-439**

The power of the sheriff to impose a fine on summary conviction of a common law offence is limited by s.5(2)(a) to the prescribed sum—an expression defined by s.225(8) as £10,000 or such sum as is substituted by Order. At the time of writing (March 2013) no such Order has been made and the prescribed sum is, accordingly, £10,000. The power of a JP court to impose a fine on summary conviction of a common law offence is limited by s.7(6)(b) to level 4 on the Standard Scale. The Standard Scale is set out in s.225(2) and level 4 is £2,500. The general rule is that any fine imposed should be capable of being paid within one year, based upon the information made known to the court of current circumstances, not upon a speculative assessment of potential future earnings. See *Jackson v PF, Perth* [2016] SAC (Crim) 1.

The levels of fine which may be imposed on summary conviction of a statutory offence are prescribed in the statute which creates the offence (sometimes by reference to another statute—see for example the Road Traffic (Offenders) Act 1988 Sch.2, which prescribes the penalties applicable to offences under the Road Traffic Act 1988, the Road Traffic (Consequential Provisions) Act 1988 and the Road Traffic Regulation Act 1984). Two things must be noted. First, irrespective of the maximum fine provided for by statute, the JP court is still limited to level 4 on the Standard Scale unless there is specific provision for a that court to impose a higher fine (see s.7(7)(b)). It is believed that no such provision exists. Secondly, some statutes make provision for exceptionally high fines on summary conviction and those fines are available in the sheriff court. For an example, see the Environmental Protection Act 1990 s.33(8).

Provision about time to pay is made by s.214. In most cases, the court must allow at least seven days to pay the fine or the first instalment. In some cases, time to pay may be refused and in those cases the court may exercise its power to impose imprisonment (unless the fine is paid forthwith). That power is governed principally by s.219 but is constrained by s.227M which provides that, where the fine or instalment which is unpaid does not exceed level 2 on the Standard Scale (£500) a level 1 unpaid work requirement must be imposed rather than imprisonment. Where time to pay is granted (as it usually is), the court must normally make an enforcement order under s.226B. That order is administered by a fines enforcement officer whose functions are set out in s.226A. It is also open to the sentencing court, in terms of s.217, to make an order placing the offender under supervision for the purposes of assisting and advising him in relation to a fine. There is provision in s.221 for the recovery of fines by civil diligence but that is not usually ordered except in the case of corporate bodies.

Fines imposed in the High Court are remitted to the sheriff court for enforcement in terms of subs.(4) of the present section.

Subs.(7)

Take into consideration. This is not the same as being limited by the means of the offender. There is some basis in *Buchan v McNaughtan*, 1990 S.C.C.R. 13 for thinking that impecuniosity is not a bar to the imposition of a significant fine. Dealing with a careless driving and drink driving case, Lord Brand said

> "[i]t cannot be allowed to be thought by any motorist that he can, with impunity, contravene these sections of the Road Traffic Act. If, in light of the appellant's impecuniosity and his state of health, it appears to be impossible for him to pay the pecuniary penalties that have been imposed upon him, then he must have recourse to the means court to have the matter determined there. So far as the present appeal is concerned, it must be refused."

As Sir Gerald Gordon observed in his commentary on the case, however, it is not clear what the means enquiry court is supposed to do.

In *Foster v Buchan*, 2020 S.C.C.R. 184, the Sheriff Appeal Court rejected the proposition that there is a general rule that fines should be set at such a level that the offender can pay them within one year, though sentencers might find considering whether payment can be made within 12–18 months to be a useful and realistic check of the level of fine to be imposed.

Amongst other things. Comparative justice might be an issue. In *Scott v Lowe*, 1990 S.C.C.R. 15, the sheriff was faced with four offenders who had engaged in fraud together. They were equal in their culpability but had very different incomes. The sheriff fined each of them five weeks' income and the appeal court held that to be an appropriate way to select sentence.

The means of the offender. In *St Clare v Wilson*, 1994 S.L.T. 564 this expression was held to include an offer by a third party to pay the fine. In that case, the appellant was the master of a fishing vessel who pled guilty to various sea fishing offences. The sheriff was told that the company which owned the vessel would pay the fine and imposed a very substantial fine on that basis. The appeal against sentence was not successful and Lord Cowie, delivering the Opinion of the Court said (under reference to the identically worded statutory predecessor of subs.(7)), "[t]he words of the section do not restrict the consideration of the amount of the fine to the "personal" means of the appellant … the words are capable of a much wider interpretation … The benefit which an offender is expected to gain from an offer by a third party to pay his fine is in our opinion as much part of his means as his personal income" (at 565J-L).

So far as known to the court. The information available to the court tends to be quite limited. Although a company convicted of an offence, in respect of which its financial position would be relevant to determining the level of a fine, must place before the court sufficiently detailed information about its financial position to enable the court to see the complete picture without having to resort to speculation (*HM Advocate v Munro and Sons (Highland) Ltd*, 2009 S.L.T. 233 at 238, [30] per Lord Nimmo Smith; *HM Advocate v Doonin Plant Ltd*, 2011 S.L.T. 25 at 30B-C, [21] per Lord Clarke), no similar requirement appears to have been articulated in relation to individuals (but see s.212 which allows the court to order that individuals should be searched for money which might be applied to payment of the fine).

Fines in summary proceedings

A4-440 **212.**—(1) Where a court of summary jurisdiction imposes a fine on an offender, the court may order him to be searched, and any money found on him on apprehension or when so searched or when taken to prison or to a young offenders institution in default of payment of the fine, may, unless the court otherwise directs and subject to subsection (2) below, be applied towards payment of the fine, and the surplus if any shall be returned to him.

(2) Money shall not be applied as mentioned in subsection (1) above if the court is satisfied that it does not belong to the person on whom it was found or that the loss of the money will be more injurious to his family than his imprisonment or detention.

(3) When a court of summary jurisdiction, which has adjudged that a sum of money shall be paid by an offender, considers that any money found on the offender on apprehension, or after he has been searched by order of the court, should not be applied towards payment of such sum, the court, shall make a direction in writing to that effect which shall be written on the extract of the sentence which imposes the fine before it is issued by the clerk of the court.

(4) An accused may make an application to such a court either orally or in writing, through the governor of the prison in whose custody he may be at that time, that any sum of money which has been found on his person should not be applied in payment of the fine adjudged to be paid by him.

(5) A person who alleges that any money found on the person of an offender is not the property of the offender, but belongs to that person, may apply to such court either orally or in writing for a direction that the money should not be applied in payment of the fine adjudged to be paid, and the court after enquiry may so direct.

(6) A court of summary jurisdiction, which has adjudged that a sum of money shall be paid by an offender, may order the attendance in court of the offender, if he is in prison, for the purpose of ascertaining the ownership of money which has been found on his person.

(7) A notice in the form prescribed by Act of Adjournal, or as nearly as may be in such form, addressed to the governor of the prison in whose custody an offender may be at the time, signed by the judge of a court of summary jurisdiction shall be a sufficient warrant to the governor of such prison for conveying the offender to the court.

DEFINITIONS

"court of summary jurisdiction": s.307(1). A4-440.1
"fine": s.307(1).

Act of Adjournal

The procedure set out in subs.(1) uses Form 20.4-A in the 1996 Act of Adjournal. The notice described in subs.(7) follows the style of Form 20.4-B in that Act of Adjournal.

[THE NEXT PARAGRAPH IS A4-441]

Remission of fines

213.—(1) A fine may at any time be remitted in whole or in part by— A4-441

(a) in a case where a transfer of fine order under section 222 of this Act is effective and the court by which payment is enforceable is, in terms of the order, a court of summary jurisdiction in Scotland, that court; or

(b) in any other case, the court which imposed the fine or, where that court was the High Court, by which payment was first enforceable.

(2) Where the court remits the whole or part of a fine after imprisonment has been imposed under section 214(2) or (4) of this Act, it shall also remit the whole period of imprisonment or, as the case may be, reduce the period by an amount which bears the same proportion to the whole period as the amount remitted bears to the whole fine.

(3) The power conferred by subsection (1) above shall be exercisable without requiring the attendance of the accused.

DEFINITIONS

"court of summary jurisdiction": s.307(1). A4-441.1
"fine": s.307(1).
"High Court": s.307(1).

[THE NEXT PARAGRAPH IS A4-442]

GENERAL NOTE

A4-442 In *Tudhope v Furphy*, 1982 S.C.C.R. 575 a sheriff held inter alia that he has power to reduce or extinguish a compensation order in circumstances where it had subsequently been discovered that the payee had died before the order was made.

Fines: time for payment and payment by instalments

A4-443 **214.**—(1) Where a court has imposed a fine on an offender or ordered him to find caution the court shall, subject to subsection (2) below, allow him at least seven days to pay the fine or the first instalment thereof or, as the case may be, to find caution; and any reference in this section and section 216 of this Act to a failure to pay a fine or other like expression shall include a reference to a failure to find caution.

(2) If on the occasion of the imposition of a fine—

(a) the offender appears to the court to possess sufficient means to enable him to pay the fine forthwith; or

(b) on being asked by the court whether he wishes to have time for payment, he does not ask for time; or

(c) he fails to satisfy the court that he has a fixed abode; or

(d) the court is satisfied for any other special reason that no time should be allowed for payment,

the court may refuse him time to pay the fine and, if the offender fails to pay, may exercise its power to impose imprisonment and, if it does so, shall state the special reason for its decision.

(3) In all cases where time is not allowed by a court for payment of a fine, the reasons of the court for not so allowing time shall be stated in the extract of the finding and sentence as well as in the finding and sentence itself.

(4) Where time is allowed for payment of a fine or payment by instalments is ordered, the court shall not, on the occasion of the imposition of a fine, impose imprisonment in the event of a future default in paying the fine or an instalment thereof unless the offender is before it and the court determines that, having regard to the gravity of the offence or to the character of the offender, or to other special reason, it is expedient that he should be imprisoned without further inquiry in default of payment; and where a court so determines, it shall state the special reason for its decision.

(5) Where a court has imposed imprisonment in accordance with subsection (4) above, then, if at any time the offender asks the court to commit him to prison, the court may do so notwithstanding subsection (1) of this section.

(6) Nothing in the foregoing provisions of this section shall affect any power of the court to order a fine to be recovered by civil diligence.

(7) Where time has been allowed for payment of a fine imposed by the court, it may, on an application by or on behalf of the offender, and after giving the prosecutor an opportunity of being heard, allow further time for payment.

(8) Without prejudice to subsection (2) above, where a court has imposed a fine on an offender, the court may, of its own accord or on the application of the offender, order payment of that fine by instalments of such amounts and at such time as it may think fit.

(9) Where the court has ordered payment of a fine by instalments it may—

(a) allow further time for payment of any instalment thereof;

(b) order payment thereof by instalments of lesser amounts, or at longer intervals, than those originally fixed,

and the powers conferred by this subsection shall be exercisable without requiring the attendance of the accused.

DEFINITIONS
"caution": s.227. A4-443.1
"fine": s.307(1).

[THE NEXT PARAGRAPH IS A4-444]

GENERAL NOTE

This section states the general rule that, subject to the exceptions specified in subs.(2), courts must allow time to pay fines (or, in the rare cases in which it is imposed, to find caution for good behaviour). It is open to the court to allow time to pay even where that has not been requested by the accused (*Fraser v Herron*, 1968 J.C. 1). Subs.(8) authorises courts to allow payment by instalments. The time to be allowed is seven days (subs.(1)) and it applies to payment of the fine as a whole or payment of the first instalment (the more usual situation). Subss.(7) and (9) confer on the court a wide power to allow further time for payment or to reduce the instalments ordered. Note that s.215 makes provision for applications for further time to pay a fine. A4-444

Where time is allowed, subs.(4) precludes the court from, at the same time as it imposes the fine, imposing the alternative of imprisonment in the event of future default unless (a) the offender is before it (so the option is simply not available if the court proceeds to sentence on the basis of a letter pleading guilty); and (b) it is expedient, on one of three grounds, to order that he should be imprisoned without further enquiry in default of payment. Those grounds are (i) the gravity of the offence; (ii) the character of the offender; or (iii) "other special reason". The reason must be stated. It is important to recognise that these rules apply to the fixing of the alternative for a future default in payment, which may never happen. The gravity of the offence is regarded by the legislation as relevant to that situation. It is not, however, a basis for refusing time to pay at all, as the Appeal Court made clear in *Barbour v Robertson, Ram v Robertson*, 1943 J.C. 46. The Lord Justice Clerk (Cooper) said that

> "where the offence is of such a grave character as to warrant the imposition of a term of imprisonment, the proper course is definitely to impose such a sentence, either without the option of a fine or with a fine in addition; and not to purport to impose a merely pecuniary penalty, but, by making that penalty of large amount and by refusing to allow time for payment, as in effect to convert the imposition of the fine into the imposition of a sentence of imprisonment without the option of a fine."

Subs.(2)

This subsection specifies the exceptions to the general rule that time must be allowed for payment of fines. Note that s.204(1) precludes the imposition of a sentence under this subsection on any person who is not legally represented unless he has been refused legal aid on financial grounds or has failed to apply for legal aid.

The offender appears ... to possess sufficient means It seems likely that an offender could only appear to have sufficient means to pay the fine forthwith if he has with him sufficient cash to enable him to do so. In terms of s.212, the court has the power to order that offenders are to be searched and (with some qualifications) any money found applied to payment of a fine.

He does not ask for time. This is not the same as stating that he will not pay. In such a case, the court, having determined that a fine is appropriate, should impose that fine (*Sheridan v MacDonald*, 1996 G.W.D. 9-481). Presumably the offender will then not ask for time to pay and subs.(2)(b) will come into play at that point.

He fails to satisfy the court that he has a fixed abode. The fines enforcement mechanism in s.226A et seq. is predicated upon the offender having a "residence" (see e.g. s.226A(4) and (6)).

Subs.(4)

Unless the offender is before it. Without this, the ability of the accused to make representations is limited. In *Campbell v Jessop*, 1988 S.L.T. 160 the imposition of the alternative other than in open court and in the absence of both the accused and his agent was held to be oppressive.

The gravity of the offence. Buchanan v Hamilton, 1988 S.C.C.R. 379 makes the point that it is the *gravity* of the offence, not its nature, which is in issue. *Dunlop v Allan*, 1984 S.C.C.R. 329 decides that an offence which is not punishable by imprisonment cannot be regarded as an offence of gravity so as to enable the offence itself to provide a special reason for imposing the alternative of imprisonment. See, however, *Finnie v Mcleod*, 1983 S.C.C.R. 387, in which the sheriff imposed a fine and "in view of the nature of the offence" imposed the alternative of thirty days' imprisonment. He reported that "The case was one of bare faced shoplifting ... security personnel in the shop had watched the appellant and the co-accused go to a part of the store where children's boots were on display. The co-accused took a pair of boots and gave them to the appellant. A shopping bag was then emptied of its contents, the boots put in the bottom, and the contents on top of them. They then went to another display section where they took another pair of boots, for which they paid at the checkout ... On the day in question she had gone to kit out her son. She could not also afford boots for her daughter and she had succumbed to temptation ... I was of the view that although the appellant was a first offender such a barefaced theft merited a significant fine. It was not committed on the spur of the moment because it involved co-operation between the two accused". This was attacked as, in effect, a sentence of imprisonment with the first option of a fine. The Lord Justice General (Emslie) said "we do not follow fully the reasoning which underlies that proposition, and having regard to what the sheriff says in his note we think that [this] was the very case in which it was appropriate for the sheriff to take the course he did".

Character of the offender. In *Paterson v McGlennan*, 1991 J.C. 141, the Lord Justice General (Hope) drew a distinction between the gravity of the offence and the character of the offender and said that the only point which was being made in *Dunlop v Allan* was that an offence which is not punishable by imprisonment cannot be regarded as an offence of gravity so as to enable the offence itself to provide a special reason for imposing the alternative of imprisonment. But, he said, the character of the offender may be such as to indicate, irrespective of the nature of his offence, that he is unlikely to pay the fine, or may delay in doing so, unless pressure is put on him at the outset to ensure payment. Where previous convictions are the basis of the adverse assessment of the accused's character, it will be significant if the number or nature of the previous convictions is such as to show that he is unlikely to pay a fine unless forced to do so.

Special reason. In *Paterson v McGlennan*, 1991 J.C. 141, the Lord Justice General (Hope) said that the reason why a special reason is needed is that it deprives the offender of the chance to come before a means enquiry court and ask for further time to pay.

Subs.(7)

This subsection provides that the court "may", on the application of the offender allow further time for payment. Such applications are regulated by s.215, subs.(3) of which provides that the court "shall" allow further time for payment unless either the failure has been wilful or the offender has no reasonable prospect of being able to pay if further time is allowed.

Application for further time to pay fine

A4-445 **215.**—(1) An application by an offender for further time in which to pay a fine imposed on him by a court, or of instalments thereof, shall be made, subject to subsection (2) below, to that court.

(2) Where a transfer of fine order has been made under section 222 of this Act, section 90 of the Magistrates' Courts Act 1980 or Article 95 of the Magistrates' Courts (Northern Ireland) Order 1981, an application under subsection (1) above shall be made to the court specified in the transfer order, or to the court specified in the last transfer order where there is more than one transfer.

(3) A court to which an application is made under this section shall allow further time for payment of the fine or of instalments thereof, unless it is satisfied that the failure of the offender to make payment has been wilful or that the offender has no reasonable prospect of being able to pay if further time is allowed.

(4) An application made under this section may be made orally or in writing.

DEFINITION

A4-445.1 "fine": s.307(1).

Act of Adjournal

Orders under subs. (3) follow the style set out in Form 20.5 to the 1996 Act of Adjournal. See r. 20.5.

GENERAL NOTE

A4-445.2 Subss.(1) and (2) of this section identify the court to which applications for further time to pay should be made as the court which imposed the fine or, where a transfer of fine order has been made, the court to which the fine has been transferred. Subs.(4) permits applications to be made orally or in writing and underlies procedure where a person is brought before a means enquiry court and offers payment by instalments. The section is not, however, purely formal. Subs.(3) gives the court no discretion. Further time to pay *must* be allowed unless either the failure has been wilful or the offender has no reasonable prospect of being able to pay if further time is allowed.

In *HM Advocate v Cheung*, 2013 S.L.T. (Sh Ct) 131, it is pointed out that this section has no application to the enforcement of confiscation orders under the Proceeds of Crime Act 2002.

[THE NEXT PARAGRAPH IS A4-446]

Fines: restriction on imprisonment for default

A4-446 **216.**—(1) Where a court has imposed a fine or ordered the finding of caution without imposing imprisonment in default of payment, subject to subsection (2) below, it shall not impose imprisonment on an offender for failing to make payment of the fine or, as the case may be, to find caution, unless on an occasion subsequent to that sentence the court has enquired into in his presence the reason why the fine has not been paid or, as the case may be, caution has not been found.

(2) Subsection (1) above shall not apply where the offender is in prison.

(3) A court may, for the purpose of enabling enquiry to be made under this section—

(a) issue a citation requiring the offender to appear before the court at a time and place appointed in the citation; or

(b) issue a warrant of apprehension.

(4) On the failure of the offender to appear before the court in response to a citation under this section, the court may issue a warrant of apprehension.

(5) The citation of an offender to appear before a court in terms of subsection (3)(a) above shall be effected in like manner, mutatis mutandis, as the citation of an accused to a sitting or diet of the court under section 141 of this Act, and—

(a) the citation shall be signed by the clerk of the court before which the offender is required to appear, instead of by the prosecutor; and

(b) the forms relating to the citation of an accused shall not apply to such citation.

(6) The following matters shall be, or as nearly as may be, in such form as is prescribed by Act of Adjournal—

(a) the citation of an offender under this section;

(b) if the citation of the offender is effected by an officer of law, the written execution, if any, of that officer of law;

(c) a warrant of apprehension issued by a court under subsection (4) above; and

(d) the minute of procedure in relation to an enquiry into the means of an offender under this section.

(7) Where a child would, if he were an adult, be liable to be imprisoned in default of payment of any fine the court may, if it considers that none of the other methods by which the case may legally be dealt with is suitable, order that the child be detained for such period, not exceeding one month, as may be specified in the order in a place chosen by the local authority in whose area the court is situated.

DEFINITIONS

"caution": s.227. **A4-446.1**
"fine": s.307(1).
"officer of law": s.307(1).
"prosecutor": s.307(1).

[THE NEXT PARAGRAPH IS A4-447]

GENERAL NOTE

Imprisonment in terms of s.219 is the ultimate answer to default. Section 214(2) provides for imprisonment where the court refuses time to pay, while s.214(4) provides for imprisonment in respect of future default. The present section deals with the situation in which neither of those subsections of s.214 has been employed, where time for payment has been allowed and where the offender defaults. It places a restriction on the power to imprison for failure to pay. Unless the offender is in prison (see subs.(2)), the court may not proceed in that way unless it has enquired, in the presence of the offender, into the reason why the fine has not been paid (subs.(1)). Subs.(3) gives the court power to cite the offender to court or to grant warrant to apprehend for that enquiry. The options available to the court in addition to imprisonment are to allow further time to pay, either on the application of the offender (ss.214(7) and 215) or *ex proprio motu* (s.214(9)); to remit the fine (s.213); to place the offender under supervision (s.217) or to make a Community Payback Order with a requirement of unpaid work (s.227M). The imposition of consecutive custodial sentences in default of payment has been doubted: *Stevenson v McGlennan*, 1990 S.L.T. 842 and *Robertson v Jessop*, 1989 S.L.T. 843. Imprisonment under this authority must be immediate imprisonment: *Craig v Smith*, 1990 S.C.C.R. 328. **A4-447**

This section does not provide an avenue for resolution of unmet confiscation orders imposed under the Proceeds of Crime Act 2002 (c .29). That Act contains its own express provisions (ss.116 and 117) in the event of non-payment and for interest to be added to the outstanding principal sum; see *HM Advocate v Cheung*, 2013 S.L.T. (Sh Ct) 131 (judgment of Sheriff A.N. Brown).

Act of Adjournal

Refer to r.20.6 and to Forms 20.6–A to 20.6–C.

Fines: supervision pending payment

A4-448 **217.**—(1) Where an offender has been allowed time for payment of a fine, the court may, either on the occasion of the imposition of the fine or on a subsequent occasion, order that he be placed under the supervision of such person, in this section referred to as the "supervising officer", as the court may from time to time appoint for the purpose of assisting and advising the offender in regard to payment of the fine.

(2) An order made in pursuance of subsection (1) above shall remain in force so long as the offender to whom it relates remains liable to pay the fine or any part of it unless the order ceases to have effect or is discharged under subsection (3) below.

(3) An order under this section shall cease to have effect on the making of a transfer of fine order under section 222 of this Act in respect of the fine or may be discharged by the court that made it without prejudice, in either case, to the making of a new order.

(4) Where an offender under 21 years of age has been allowed time for payment of a fine, the court shall not order the form of detention appropriate to him in default of payment of the fine unless—

(a) he has been placed under supervision in respect of the fine; or
(b) the court is satisfied that it is impracticable to place him under supervision.

(5) Where a court, on being satisfied as mentioned in subsection (4)(b) above, orders the detention of a person under 21 years of age without an order under this section having been made, the court shall state the grounds on which it is so satisfied.

(6) Where an order under this section is in force in respect of an offender, the court shall not impose imprisonment in default of the payment of the fine unless before doing so it has—

(a) taken such steps as may be reasonably practicable to obtain from the supervising officer a report, which may be oral, on the offender's conduct and means, and has considered any such report; and
(b) in a case where an enquiry is required by section 216 of this Act, considered such enquiry.

(7) When a court appoints a different supervising officer under subsection (1) above, a notice shall be sent by the clerk of the court to the offender in such form, as nearly as may be, as is prescribed by Act of Adjournal.

(8) The supervising officer shall communicate with the offender with a view to assisting and advising him in regard to payment of the fine, and unless the fine or any instalment thereof is paid to the clerk of the court within the time allowed by the court for payment, the supervising officer shall report to the court without delay after the expiry of such time, as to the conduct and means of the offender.

(9) Where an enforcement order has been made under section 226B of this Act in relation to payment of the fine, the supervising officer shall, instead of reporting under subsection (8) above to the court, report under that subsection to the fines enforcement officer dealing with the order.

AMENDMENTS

Subs.(9) inserted by Criminal Proceedings etc (Reform) (Scotland) Act 2007 (asp 6) s.80, Sch. para.20(2). Brought into force on March 10, 2008 by SSI 2008/42 (C.4) art.3 and Sch.

DEFINITION
"fine": s.307(1). A4-448.1

Act of Adjournal

The notice specified in subs.(7), in accordance with r.20.7 in the 1996 Act of Adjournal, is in the style set out in Form 20.7.

GENERAL NOTE

Although the power to order supervision is used most often in relation to young offenders, it may also be appropriate where the offender is subject to a hospital order: *Muirhead v Normand*, 1995 S.C.C.R. 632. A4-448.2

[THE NEXT PARAGRAPH IS A4-449]

Fines: supplementary provisions as to payment

218.—(1) Where under the provisions of section 214 or 217 of this Act a court is required to state a special reason for its decision or the grounds on which it is satisfied that it is undesirable or impracticable to place an offender under supervision, the reason or, as the case may be, the grounds shall be entered in the record of the proceedings along with the finding and sentence. A4-449

(2) Any reference in the said sections 214 and 217 to imprisonment shall be construed, in the case of an offender on whom by reason of his age imprisonment may not lawfully be imposed, as a reference to the lawful form of detention in default of payment of a fine appropriate to that person, and any reference to prison shall be construed accordingly.

(3) Where a warrant has been issued for the apprehension of an offender for non-payment of a fine, the offender may, notwithstanding section 211(6) of this Act, pay such fine in full to a constable; and the warrant shall not then be enforced and the constable shall remit the fine to the clerk of court.

DEFINITIONS
"fine": s.307(1). A4-449.1
"impose imprisonment": s.307(1).

[THE NEXT PARAGRAPH IS A4-450]

Fines: periods of imprisonment for non-payment

219.—(1) Subject to sections 214 to 218 of this Act and subsection (1A) below— A4-450

(a) a court may, when imposing a fine, impose a period of imprisonment in default of payment; or
(b) where no order has been made under paragraph (a) above and a person fails to pay a fine, or any part or instalment of a fine, by the time ordered by the court (or, where section 214(2) of this Act applies, immediately) the court may, subject to section 235(1) of this Act, impose a period of imprisonment for such failure either with immediate effect or to take effect in the event of the person failing to pay the fine or any part or instalment of it by such further time as the court may order,

whether or not the fine is imposed under an enactment which makes provision for its enforcement or recovery.

(1A) Subsection (1) shall not apply to a fine imposed for an offence under section 107 of the Antisocial Behaviour etc. (Scotland) Act 2004 (asp 8).

(2) Subject to the following subsections of this section, the maximum period of imprisonment which may be imposed under subsection (1) above or for failure to find caution, shall be as follows—

Amount of Fine or Caution	Maximum Period of Imprisonment
Not exceeding £200	7 days
Exceeding £200 but not exceeding £500	14 days
Exceeding £500 but not exceeding £1,000	28 days
Exceeding £1,000 but not exceeding £2,500	45 days
Exceeding £2,500 but not exceeding £5,000	3 months
Exceeding £5,000 but not exceeding £10,000	6 months
Exceeding £10,000 but not exceeding £20,000	12 months
Exceeding £20,000 but not exceeding £50,000	18 months
Exceeding £50,000 but not exceeding £100,000	2 years
Exceeding £100,000 but not exceeding £250,000	3 years
Exceeding £250,000 but not exceeding £1 Million	5 years
Exceeding £1 Million	10 years

(3) Where an offender is fined on the same day before the same court for offences charged in the same indictment or complaint or in separate indictments or complaints, the amount of the fine shall, for the purposes of this section, be taken to be the total of the fines imposed.

(4) Where a court has imposed a period of imprisonment in default of payment of a fine, and—

(a) an instalment of the fine is not paid at the time ordered; or

(b) part only of the fine has been paid within the time allowed for payment,

the offender shall be liable to imprisonment for a period which bears to the period so imposed the same proportion, as nearly as may be, as the amount outstanding at the time when warrant is issued for imprisonment of the offender in default bears to the original fine.

(5) Where no period of imprisonment in default of payment of a fine has been imposed and—

(a) an instalment of the fine is not paid at the time ordered; or

(b) part only of the fine has been paid within the time allowed for payment,

the offender shall be liable to imprisonment for a maximum period which bears, as nearly as may be, the same proportion to the maximum period of imprisonment which could have been imposed by virtue of the Table in subsection (2) above in default of payment of the original fine as the amount outstanding at the time when he appears before the court bears to the original fine.

(6) If in any sentence or extract sentence the period of imprisonment inserted in default of payment of a fine or on failure to find caution is in excess of that competent under this Part of this Act, such period of imprisonment shall be reduced to the

maximum period under this Part of this Act applicable to such default or failure, and the judge who pronounced the sentence shall have power to order the sentence or extract to be corrected accordingly.

(7) The provisions of this section shall be without prejudice to the operation of section 220 of this Act.

(8) Where in any case—

(a) the sheriff considers that the imposition of imprisonment for the number of years for the time being specified in section 3(3) of this Act would be inadequate; and

(b) the maximum period of imprisonment which may be imposed under subsection (1) above (or under that subsection as read with either or both of sections 252(2) of this Act and section 118(2), (2A) and (2B) of the Proceeds of Crime Act 2002) exceeds that number of years,

he shall remit the case to the High Court for sentence.

AMENDMENTS

Subs.(8)(b) as amended by Proceeds of Crime Act 2002 (c.29) Sch.11 para.29(4). Brought into force by SSI 2003/210 (C.44).

Subs.(1) as amended, and (1A) inserted, by Antisocial Behaviour etc. (Scotland) Act 2004 (asp 8) s.144(1) and Sch.4 para.5(4). Brought into force on 4 April 2005 by SSI 2004/420 (C.31).

Subs.(8)(b) as amended by Serious Crime Act 2015 (c.9) s.19(3). Brought into force, subject to savings provisions, on 1 March 2016 by SSI 2016/11 reg.2.

DEFINITIONS A4-450.1

"caution": s.227.
"fine": s.307(1).
"impose imprisonment": s.307(1).
"order": s.307(1).

[THE NEXT PARAGRAPH IS A4-451]

GENERAL NOTE

Imprisonment under s.219(1) is the ultimate remedy for failure to pay a fine but its availability is limited by s.214(2) (which limits the power to impose immediate imprisonment as an alternative to paying a fine), s.214(4) (which limits the power to impose imprisonment for a future default) and s.216 (which limits the power to impose imprisonment in respect of established default.) It should be noted that, in terms of s.248B, the court has the option, where it could impose imprisonment for fine default, of imposing disqualification from driving. A4-451

Subs.(1)(a) empowers the court, when imposing a fine, to impose a period of imprisonment in default of payment. It is not necessary to obtain a social work report before making such an order (*Sullivan v McLeod*, 1980 S.L.T. (Notes) 99). The power is limited by s.214(4) which requires that the offender should be present in court and that the court must be satisfied, by reference to the gravity of the offence, the character of the offender or other special reason, that the making of such an order is expedient. Subs.(1)(b) empowers the court to impose imprisonment in default where the offender fails to pay the fine or (more usually) an instalment within the time allowed by the court. Both parts of subs.(1) require to be read in light of s.227M. In terms of that section, where the fine or the instalment does not exceed level 2 on the standard scale (£500), the court must impose a level 1 community payback order instead of imprisonment under subs.(1). For higher fines or instalment, the court may impose such an order. Where the fine or instalment does not exceed level 1 (£200) the hours imposed must not exceed 50.

Fines: part payment by prisoners

220.—(1) Where a person committed to prison or otherwise detained for failure to pay a fine imposed by a court pays to the governor of the prison, under conditions prescribed by rules made under the Prisons (Scotland) Act 1989, any sum in part satisfaction of the fine, the term of imprisonment imposed under section 219 of this Act in respect of the fine shall be reduced (or as the case may be further reduced) by a number of days bearing as nearly as possible the same proportion to such term as the sum so paid bears to the amount of the fine outstanding at the commencement of the imprisonment. A4-452

(2) The day on which any sum is paid as mentioned in subsection (1) above shall not be regarded as a day served by the prisoner as part of the said term of imprisonment.

(3) All sums paid under this section shall be handed over on receipt by the governor of the prison to the clerk of the court in which the conviction was obtained, and thereafter paid and applied *pro tanto* in the same manner and for the same purposes as sums adjudged to be paid by the conviction and sentence of the court, and paid and recovered in terms thereof, are lawfully paid and applied.

(4) In this section references to a prison and to the governor thereof shall include respectively references to any other place in which a person may be lawfully detained in default of payment of a fine, and to an officer in charge thereof.

AMENDMENTS

Subs.(1) as amended by Criminal Justice (Scotland) Act 2003 (asp 7) Sch.4 para.3. Brought into force on 27 June 2003 by SSI 2003/288 (C.14).

DEFINITIONS

A4-452.1 "fine": s.307(1).
"governor": s.307(1).
"prison": s.307(1).

[THE NEXT PARAGRAPH IS A4-453]

Fines: recovery by civil diligence

A4-453 **221.**—(1) Where any fine falls to be recovered by civil diligence in pursuance of this Act or in any case in which a court may think it expedient to order a fine to be recovered by civil diligence, there shall be added to the finding of the court imposing the fine a warrant for civil diligence in a form prescribed by Act of Adjournal which shall have the effect of authorising—

(a) the charging of the person who has been fined to pay the fine within the period specified in the charge and, in the event of failure to make such payment within that period—
  (i) the execution of an arrestment;
  (ii) the attachment of articles belonging to him; and
  (iii) the execution of a money attachment,

  and, if necessary for the purpose of executing the attachment, or the money attachment, the opening of shut and lockfast places;

(b) an arrestment other than an arrestment of earnings in the hands of his employer,

and such diligence, whatever the amount of the fine imposed, may be executed in the same manner as if the proceedings were on an extract decree of the sheriff in a summary cause.

(2) Subject to subsection (3) below, proceedings by civil diligence under this section may be taken at any time after the imposition of the fine to which they relate.

(3) No such proceedings shall be authorised after the offender has been imprisoned in consequence of his having defaulted in payment of the fine.

(4) Where proceedings by civil diligence for the recovery of a fine or caution are taken, imprisonment for non-payment of the fine or for failure to find such caution shall remain competent and such proceedings may be authorised after the court has imposed imprisonment for, or in the event of, the non-payment or the failure but before imprisonment has followed such imposition.

AMENDMENTS

Subs.(1)(a) as amended by Debt Arrangement and Attachment (Scotland) Act 2002 (asp 17) Sch.3 para.25. Brought into force on 30 December 2002 by Royal Assent.

Subs.(1)(a) as amended by Bankruptcy and Diligence etc. (Scotland) Act 2007 (asp 3) Sch.5 para.23. Brought into force on 23 November 2009 by SSI 2009/369 art.3 and Sch.1.

DEFINITION

"fine": s.307(1). A4-453.1

GENERAL NOTE

Prior to the 1995 Act the primary use of civil diligence as a criminal sanction was against bodies corporate. Note however that s.303(2)(a)(i) below now provides that in the event of default in payment of a fiscal fine, recovery of sums outstanding is enforced by civil diligence rather than by means courts. A4-453.2

Act of Adjournal

Form 20.8 in the 1996 Act of Adjournal appears to be the style approved for the purposes of subs.(1) above.

[THE NEXT PARAGRAPH IS A4-454]

Transfer of fine orders

222.—(1) Where a court has imposed a fine on a person convicted of an offence and it appears to the clerk of the court that he is residing— A4-454

(a) within the jurisdiction of another court in Scotland; or

(b) in any petty sessions area in England and Wales; or

(c) in any petty sessions district in Northern Ireland,

that clerk may order that payment of the fine shall be enforceable by that other court or in that petty sessions area or petty sessions district as the case may be.

(1A) Where a court has imposed a fine on a person convicted of an offence, and it appears to the clerk of court that there is a fine imposed by another court (of whatever kind) in the same sheriffdom, that clerk may order that payment of the fine is to be enforceable by that other court.

(2) An order under this section (in this section referred to as a "transfer of fine order") shall specify the court by which or the petty sessions area or petty sessions district in which payment is to be enforceable and, where the court to be specified in a transfer of fine order is a court of summary jurisdiction, it shall, in any case where the order is made by the sheriff clerk, be a sheriff court.

(3) Subject to subsections (4) and (5) below, where a transfer of fine order is made with respect to any fine under this section, any functions under any enactment relating to that sum which, if no such order had been made, would have been exercisable by the court which made the order or by the clerk of that court shall cease to be so exercisable.

(4) Where, in relation to a transfer of fine order made under subsection (1)(a) above—

(a) the clerk of the court specified in the order is satisfied, after inquiry, that the offender is not residing within the jurisdiction of that court; and

(b) the clerk of that court, within 14 days of receiving the notice required by section 223(1) of this Act, sends to the clerk of the court which made the order notice to that effect,

the order shall cease to have effect.

(5) Where a transfer of fine order ceases to have effect by virtue of subsection (4) above, the functions referred to in subsection (3) above shall again be exercisable by the court which made the order or, as the case may be, by the clerk of that court.

(6) Where a transfer of fine order under this section, section 90 of the Magistrates' Courts Act 1980 or Article 95 of the Magistrates' Courts (Northern Ireland) Order 1981 specifies a court of summary jurisdiction in Scotland, that court

and the clerk of that court shall have all the like functions under this Part of this Act in respect of the fine or the sum in respect of which that order was made (including the power to make any further order under this section) as if the fine or the sum were a fine imposed by that court and as if any order made under this section, the said Act of 1980 or the said Order of 1981 in respect of the fine or the sum before the making of the transfer of fine order had been made by that court.

(7) The functions of the court to which subsection (6) above relates shall be deemed to include the court's power to apply to the Secretary of State under any regulations made by him under section 24(1)(a) of the Criminal Justice Act 1991 (power to deduct fines etc. from income support).

(8) Where a transfer of fine order under section 90 of the Magistrates' Courts Act 1980, Article 95 of the Magistrates' Courts (Northern Ireland) Order 1981, or this section provides for the enforcement by a sheriff court in Scotland of a fine imposed by the Crown Court, the term of imprisonment which may be imposedunder this Part of this Act shall be the term fixed in pursuance of section 139 of the Powers of Criminal Courts (Sentencing) Act 2000 by the Crown Court or a term which bears the same proportion to the term so fixed as the amount of the fine remaining due bears to the amount of the fine imposed by that court, notwithstanding that the term exceeds the period applicable to the case under section 219 of this Act.

AMENDMENTS

Subs.(1), (2) as amended and subs.(1A) inserted by Criminal Proceedings etc. (Reform) (Scotland) Act 2007 (asp 6) s.80, Sch. para.20(3). Brought into force (subs.(1A) brought into force only for the Sheriffdom of Lothian and Borders) on 10 March 2008 by SSI 2008/42 (C.4) art.3 and Sch. Subs.(1A) further brought into force for the Sheriffdom of Grampian, Highland and Islands on 2 June 2008 by SSI 2008/192 (C.19) art.3 and Sch; brought into force for the Sheriffdom of Glasgow and Strathkelvin on 8 December 2008 by SSI 2008/329 (C.29) art.3 and Sch; and brought into force for the Sheriffdom of Tayside, Central and Fife on 23 February 2009 by SSI 2008/362 (C.30) art.3 and Sch. Brought into force for the Sheriffdom of North Strathclyde on 14 December 2009 by SSI 2009/432 (C.32) art.3 and Sch.1. Remainder in force on 22 February 2010 by SSI 2009/432 (C.32) art.3 and Sch.2.

Subs.(8) as amended by Serious Crime Act 2015 (c.9) Sch.4 para.16. Brought into force on 1 March 2016 by SSI 2016/11 reg.2.

DEFINITIONS

A4-454.1 "fine": s.307(1).
"order": s.222(2).
"transfer of fine order": s.307(1).

Act of Adjournal

See r.20.9 and Forms 20.9–A to 20.9–C in the 1996 Act of Adjournal.

GENERAL NOTE

A4-454.2 Where a transfer of fine order has been made, applications for further time to pay must be made to the court to which the fine has been transferred (s.215(2)). That court also has power to remit the fine (s.213(1)(a)).

[THE NEXT PARAGRAPH IS A4-455]

Transfer of fines: procedure for clerk of court

A4-455 **223.**—(1) Where the clerk of a court makes a transfer of fine order under section 222 of this Act, that clerk shall send to the clerk of the court specified in the order—

(a) a notice in the form prescribed by Act of Adjournal, or as nearly as may be in such form;

(b) a statement of the offence of which the offender was convicted; and

(c) a statement of the steps, if any, taken to recover the fine,

and shall give him such further information, if any, as, in his opinion, is likely to assist the court specified in the order in recovering the fine.

(2) In the case of a further transfer of fine order, the clerk of court who made the order shall send to the clerk of the court by which the fine was imposed a copy of the notice sent to the clerk of the court specified in the order.

(3) The clerk of the court specified in a transfer of fine order shall, as soon as may be after he has received the notice mentioned in subsection (1)(a) above, send an intimation to the offender in the form prescribed by Act of Adjournal or as nearly as may be in such form.

(4) The clerk of court speciffed in a transfer of fine order shall remit or otherwise account for any payment received in respect of a fine imposed by a court outwith Scotland to the clerk of the court by which the fine was imposed, and if the sentence has been enforced otherwise than by payment of the fine, he shall inform the clerk of court how the sentence was enforced.

AMENDMENTS

Subss.(1), (2), (4) as amended by Criminal Proceedings etc (Reform) (Scotland) Act 2007 (asp 6) s.80, Sch. para.20(4). Brought into force on 10 March 2008 by SSI 2008/42 (C.4) art.3 and Sch.

DEFINITIONS A4-455.1

"fine": s.307(1).
"order": s.307(1).
"transfer of fine order": s.222(2).

Act of Adjournal

See r.20.9 and Forms 20.9–A for subs.(1) and Form 20.9–B for subs.(2).

The mutual recognition of criminal financial penalties

Recognition of financial penalties: requests to other member States

223A.— *(Repealed by the Criminal Justice (EU Exit) (Scotland) (Amendment etc.) Regulations 2020 (SSI 2020/339) reg.3(3) (effective December 31, 2020 subject to transitional and saving provision specified in reg.6 of those Regulations).*

Requests to other member States: procedure on issue of certificate

223B.— *(Repealed by the Criminal Justice (EU Exit) (Scotland) (Amendment etc.) Regulations 2020 (SSI 2020/339) reg.3(3) (effective December 31, 2020 subject to transitional and saving provision specified in reg.6 of those Regulations).* A4-455.5

Requests to other member States: application of provisions relating to fines

223C. *(Repealed by the Criminal Justice (EU Exit) (Scotland) (Amendment etc.) Regulations 2020 (SSI 2020/339) reg.3(3) (effective December 31, 2020 subject to transitional and saving provision specified in reg.6 of those Regulations).* A4-455.8

Requests to other member States: application of provisions relating to compensation orders

223D.— *(Repealed by the Criminal Justice (EU Exit) (Scotland) (Amendment etc.) Regulations 2020 (SSI 2020/339) reg.3(3) (effective December 31, 2020 subject to transitional and saving provision specified in reg.6 of those Regulations).* A4-455.11

Requests to other member States: application of provisions relating to fixed penalties

223E.— *(Repealed by the Criminal Justice (EU Exit) (Scotland) (Amendment etc.) Regulations 2020 (SSI 2020/339) reg.3(3) (effective December 31, 2020 subject to transitional and saving provision specified in reg.6 of those Regulations).* A4-455.14

Recognition of financial penalties: requests from other member States

A4-455.17 **223F.—** *(Repealed by the Criminal Justice (EU Exit) (Scotland) (Amendment etc.) Regulations 2020 (SSI 2020/339) reg.3(3) (effective December 31, 2020 subject to transitional and saving provision specified in reg.6 of those Regulations).*

Requests from other member States: procedure where no certificate

A4-455.19.1 **223FA.—** *(Repealed by the Criminal Justice (EU Exit) (Scotland) (Amendment etc.) Regulations 2020 (SSI 2020/339) reg.3(3) (effective December 31, 2020 subject to transitional and saving provision specified in reg.6 of those Regulations).*

Requests from other member States: return of certificate

A4-455.20 **223G.** [...]

AMENDMENTS

Section 223G inserted by Mutual Recognition of Criminal Financial Penalties in the European Union (Scotland) Order 2009 (SSI 2009/342) art.3 (effective 12 October 2009).

Section 223G repealed by Mutual Recognition of Criminal Financial Penalties in the European Union (Scotland) (No.1) Order 2014 (SSI 2014/322) art.5 (effective 1 December 2014).

GENERAL NOTE

A4-455.22 Section 223G made provision for the return of requests for enforcement to the other Member State in certain specified circumstances. In such cases no enforcement action was to be carried out in Scotland following the return of the enforcement request.

Requests from other member States: procedure on receipt of certificate

A4-455.23 **223H.—** *(Repealed by the Criminal Justice (EU Exit) (Scotland) (Amendment etc.) Regulations 2020 (SSI 2020/339) reg.3(3) (effective December 31, 2020 subject to transitional and saving provision specified in reg.6 of those Regulations).*

Requests from other member States: action undertaken under certificate

A4-455.26 **223I.—** *(Repealed by the Criminal Justice (EU Exit) (Scotland) (Amendment etc.) Regulations 2020 (SSI 2020/339) reg.3(3) (effective December 31, 2020 subject to transitional and saving provision specified in reg.6 of those Regulations).*

Requests from other member States: application of provisions in relation to fines

A4-455.29 **223J.** *(Repealed by the Criminal Justice (EU Exit) (Scotland) (Amendment etc.) Regulations 2020 (SSI 2020/339) reg.3(3) (effective December 31, 2020 subject to transitional and saving provision specified in reg.6 of those Regulations).*

Requests from other member States: supplementary provisions in relation to fines

A4-455.32 **223K.—** *(Repealed by the Criminal Justice (EU Exit) (Scotland) (Amendment etc.) Regulations 2020 (SSI 2020/339) reg.3(3) (effective December 31, 2020 subject to transitional and saving provision specified in reg.6 of those Regulations).*

Requests from other member States: action for enforcement where financial penalty not recovered

A4-455.34 **223L.** (Repealed by the Criminal Justice (EU Exit) (Scotland) (Amendment etc.) Regulations 2020 (SSI 2020/339) reg.3(3) (effective December 31, 2020 subject to transitional and saving provision specified in reg.6 of those Regulations).

Requests from other member States: application of provisions relating to orders for compensation

223M. (Repealed by the Criminal Justice (EU Exit) (Scotland) (Amendment etc.) Regulations 2020 (SSI 2020/339) reg.3(3) (effective December 31, 2020 subject to transitional and saving provision specified in reg.6 of those Regulations). **A4-455.37**

Requests from other member States: supplementary provisions in relation to orders for compensation

223N. (Repealed by the Criminal Justice (EU Exit) (Scotland) (Amendment etc.) Regulations 2020 (SSI 2020/339) reg.3(3) (effective December 31, 2020 subject to transitional and saving provision specified in reg.6 of those Regulations). **A4-455.40**

Requests from other member States: application of provisions relating to fixed penalties

223O.— (Repealed by the Criminal Justice (EU Exit) (Scotland) (Amendment etc.) Regulations 2020 (SSI 2020/339) reg.3(3) (effective December 31, 2020 subject to transitional and saving provision specified in reg.6 of those Regulations). **A4-455.43**

Transfer of certificates to central authority for England and Wales, or to central authority for Northern Ireland

223P.— [Repealed by the Criminal Justice (EU Exit) (Scotland) (Amendment etc.) Regulations 2020 (SSI 2020/339) reg.3(3) (effective December 31, 2020 subject to transitional and saving provision specified in reg.6 of those Regulations]. **A4-455.46**

The competent authority for Scotland

223Q.— [Repealed by the Criminal Justice (EU Exit) (Scotland) (Amendment etc.) Regulations 2020 (SSI 2020/339) reg.3(3) (effective December 31, 2020 subject to transitional and saving provision specified in reg.6 of those Regulations]. **A4-455.49**

Accrual of monies obtained from the enforcement of financial penalties

223R.— [Repealed by the Criminal Justice (EU Exit) (Scotland) (Amendment etc.) Regulations 2020 (SSI 2020/339) reg.3(3) (effective December 31, 2020 subject to transitional and saving provision specified in reg.6 of those Regulations]. **A4-455.52**

Treatment of compensation monies

223S.— (Repealed by the Criminal Justice (EU Exit) (Scotland) (Amendment etc.) Regulations 2020 (SSI 2020/339) reg.3(3) (effective December 31, 2020 subject to transitional and saving provision specified in reg.6 of those Regulations). **A4-455.55**

Interpretation of sections 223A to 223S

223T.— (Repealed by the Criminal Justice (EU Exit) (Scotland) (Amendment etc.) Regulations 2020 (SSI 2020/339) reg.3(3) (effective December 31, 2020 subject to transitional and saving provision specified in reg.6 of those Regulations). **A4-455.58**

Fines: discharge from imprisonment and penalties

Discharge from imprisonment to be specified

224. All warrants of imprisonment in default of payment of a fine, or on failure to find caution, shall specify a period at the expiry of which the person sentenced **A4-456**

shall be discharged, notwithstanding the fine has not been paid, or caution found.

DEFINITIONS

A4-456.1 "caution": s.307(1).
"fine": s.307(1).

[THE NEXT PARAGRAPH IS A4-457]

Penalties: standard scale, prescribed sum and uprating

A4-457 **225.**—(1) There shall be a standard scale of fines for offences triable only summarily, which shall be known as "the standard scale".

(2) The standard scale is shown below—

Level on the scale	Amount of Fine
1	£ 200
2	£ 500
3	£1,000
4	£2,500
5	£5,000

(3) Any reference in any enactment, whenever passed or made, to a specified level on the standard scale shall be construed as referring to the amount which corresponds to that level on the standard scale referred to in subsection (2) above.

(4) If it appears to the Secretary of State that there has been a change in the value of money since the relevant date, he may by order substitute for the sum or sums for the time being specified in the provisions mentioned in subsection (5) below such other sum or sums as appear to him justified by the change.

(5) The provisions referred to in subsection (4) above are—

(a) subsection (2) above;

(b) subsection (8) below;

(c) section 219(2) of this Act;

(d) column 5 or 6 of Schedule 4 to the Misuse of Drugs Act 1971 so far as the column in question relates to the offences under provisions of that Act specified in column 1 of that Schedule in respect of which the maximum fines were increased by Part II of Schedule 8 to the Criminal Justice and Public Order Act 1994.

(6) In subsection (4) above "the relevant date" means—

(a) in relation to the first order made under that subsection, the date the last order was made under section 289D(1) of the Criminal Procedure (Scotland) Act 1975; and

(b) in relation to each subsequent order, the date of the previous order.

(7) An order under subsection (4) above—

(a) shall be made by statutory instrument subject to annulment in pursuance of a resolution of either House of Parliament and may be revoked by a subsequent order thereunder; and

(b) without prejudice to Schedule 14 to the Criminal Law Act 1977, shall not affect the punishment for an offence committed before that order comes into force.

(8) In this Act "the prescribed sum" means £10,000 or such sum as is for the time being substituted in this definition by an order in force under subsection (4) above.

AMENDMENTS

Subs.(8) as amended by the Criminal Proceedings etc (Reform) (Scotland) Act 2007 (asp 6) s.48. Brought into force on December 10, 2007 by the Criminal Proceedings etc. (Reform) (Scotland) Act 2007 (Commencement No. 2 and Transitional Provisions and Savings) Order 2007 (SSI 2007/479 (C.40)) art.3 and Sch.

DEFINITIONS A4-457.1

"fine": s.307(1).
"prescribed sum": s.225(8).
"relevant date": s.225(4).
"standard scale": s.225(1).

[THE NEXT PARAGRAPH IS A4-458]

Penalties: exceptionally high maximum fines

226.—(1) The Secretary of State may by order amend an enactment specifying a sum to which this subsection applies so as to substitute for that sum such other sum as appears to him— A4-458

(a) to be justified by a change in the value of money appearing to him to have taken place since the last occasion on which the sum in question was fixed; or
(b) to be appropriate to take account of an order altering the standard scale which has been made or is proposed to be made.

(2) Subsection (1) above applies to any sum which—

(a) is higher than level 5 on the standard scale; and
(b) is specified as the fine or the maximum fine which may be imposed on conviction of an offence which is triable only summarily.

(3) The Secretary of State may by order amend an enactment specifying a sum to which this subsection applies so as to substitute for that sum such other sum as appears to him—

(a) to be justified by a change in the value of money appearing to him to have taken place since the last occasion on which the sum in question was fixed; or
(b) to be appropriate to take account of an order made or proposed to be made altering the statutory maximum.

(4) Subsection (3) above applies to any sum which—

(a) is higher than the statutory maximum; and
(b) is specified as the maximum fine which may be imposed on summary conviction of an offence triable either on indictment or summarily.

(5) An order under this section—

(a) shall be made by statutory instrument subject to annulment in pursuance of a resolution of either House of Parliament; and
(b) shall not affect the punishment for an offence committed before that order comes into force.

(6) In this section "enactment" includes an enactment contained in an Act or subordinate instrument passed or made after the commencement of this Act.

DEFINITIONS A4-458.1

"enactment": s.226(6) and s.307(1).
"fine": s.307(1).
"standard scale": s.225(1).

Enforcement of fines etc.: fines enforcement officers

Fines enforcement officers

A4-458.2 **226A.**—(1) The Scottish Ministers may authorise persons (including classes of person) to act as fines enforcement officers for any or all of the purposes of this section and sections 226B to 226H of this Act.

(2) A FEO has the general functions of—

(a) providing information and advice to offenders as regards payment of relevant penalties;

(b) securing compliance of offenders with enforcement orders (including as varied under section 226C(1) of this Act).

(3) Where an offender is subject to two or more relevant penalties, a FEO—

(a) in exercising the function conferred by subsection (2)(b) above;

(b) in considering whether or not to vary an enforcement order under section 226C(1) of this Act,

shall have regard to that fact and to the total amount which the offender is liable to pay in respect of them.

(4) Where an enforcement order as respects an offender has been made in a sheriff court district other than that in which the offender resides, a FEO for the district in which the offender resides may (whether or not those districts are in the same sheriffdom) take responsibility for exercising functions in relation to the order.

(5) A FEO taking responsibility for exercising functions by virtue of subsection (4) above is to notify that fact to—

(a) the offender; and

(b) any FEO for the district in which the enforcement order was made.

(6) Notification under subsection (5)(b) above has the effect of transferring functions in relation to the enforcement order—

(a) from any FEO for the district in which the order was made; and

(b) to a FEO for the district in which the offender resides.

(7) The Scottish Ministers may by regulations make further provision as to FEOs and their functions.

(8) Regulations under subsection (7) above are not made unless a draft of the statutory instrument containing the regulations has been laid before, and approved by a resolution of, the Scottish Parliament.

AMENDMENTS

Section 226A inserted by the Criminal Proceedings etc (Reform) (Scotland) Act 2007 (asp 6) s.55. Brought into force, except for the purposes of any relevant penalty which requires to be paid in any district court, on 10 March 2008 by the Criminal Proceedings etc. (Reform) (Scotland) Act 2007 (Commencement No.3 and Savings) Order 2008 (SSI 2008/42 (C.4)) art.3 and Sch.

Enforcement orders

A4-458.3 **226B.**—(1) When a court grants time to pay (or further time to pay) a relevant penalty (or an instalment of it) under section 214 or 215 of this Act, the court shall make an enforcement order under this subsection in relation to payment of the penalty.

(2) Despite subsection (1) above, a court need not make an enforcement order where it considers that it would not be appropriate to do so in the circumstances of the case.

(3) Where, by virtue of subsection (2) above, a court does not make an enforcement order under subsection (1) above, it may subsequently make an enforcement order under that subsection in relation to payment of the penalty.

(4) Where—

(a) a person has accepted (or is deemed to have accepted)—
(i) a fixed penalty offer under section 302(1) of this Act; or
(ii) a compensation offer under section 302A(1) of this Act; and
(b) payment (or payment of an instalment) has not been made as required by the offer,

the relevant court may make an enforcement order under this subsection in relation to the payment due.

(5) Where—
(a) a person is liable to pay—
(i) a fixed penalty notice given under section 54 (giving notices for fixed penalty offences), or section 62 (fixing notices to vehicles) of the Road Traffic Offenders Act 1988 (c.53), which has been registered under section 71 of that Act; or
(ii) by virtue of section 131(5) of the Antisocial Behaviour etc. (Scotland) Act 2004 (asp 8), a fixed penalty notice given under section 129 (fixed penalty notices) of that Act; and
(b) payment (or payment of an instalment) has not been made as required by the penalty,

the relevant court may make an enforcement order under this subsection in relation to the payment due.

(6) Where there is transferred to a court in Scotland a fine—
(a) imposed by a court in England and Wales; and
(b) in relation to which a collection order (within the meaning of Part 4 of Schedule 5 to the Courts Act 2003 (c.39)) has been made,

the relevant court may make an enforcement order under this subsection in relation to payment of the fine.

(6A) Where—
(a) a certificate requesting enforcement under the Framework Decision on financial penalties and a decision, or a certified copy of the decision, requiring payment of the financial penalty to which the certificate relates has been referred to the competent authority for Scotland by virtue of section 223H(2) of this Act; and
(b) by virtue of section 223I(1) the competent authority for Scotland is satisfied that none of the grounds for refusal to enforce the financial penalty as specified in Schedule 12 to this Act apply,

the relevant court may make an enforcement order under this subsection in relation to payment of the financial penalty (which, for the purposes of this subsection, is deemed to be a relevant penalty).

(7) An enforcement order under subsection (4), (5), (6) or (6A) above may be made—
(a) on the oral or written application of the clerk of court; and
(b) without the offender being present.

(8) An enforcement order shall—
(a) state the amount of the relevant penalty;
(b) require payment of the relevant penalty in accordance with—
(i) such arrangements as to the amount of the instalments by which the relevant penalty should be paid and as to the intervals at which such instalments should be paid;
(ii) such other arrangements,

as the order may specify;
(c) provide contact details for the FEO dealing with the enforcement order;

(d) explain the effect of the enforcement order.

(9) Where a court makes (or is to make) an enforcement order in relation to a fine—

(a) a court may not impose imprisonment—

(i) under section 214(4) of this Act; or

(ii) under section 219(1) of this Act,

in respect of the fine;

(b) a court may not—

(i) allow further time for payment under subsection (9)(a) of section 214 of this Act; or

(ii) make an order under subsection (9)(b) of that section,

in respect of the fine;

(c) the offender may not make an application under section 215(1) of this Act in respect of the fine.

(10) Paragraphs (a) to (c) of subsection (9) above apply for so long as the enforcement order continues to have effect.

(11) An enforcement order ceases to have effect if—

(a) the relevant penalty is paid (including by application of any proceeds of enforcement action); or

(b) it is revoked under section 226G(9)(a) of this Act.

Amendments

Section 226B inserted by Criminal Proceedings etc. (Reform) (Scotland) Act 2007 (asp 6) s.55. Brought into force, except for the purposes of any relevant penalty which requires to be paid in any district court, on 10 March 2008 by SSI 2008/42 (C.4) art.3 and Sch.

Subs.(6A) inserted and subs.(7) as amended by Mutual Recognition of Criminal Financial Penalties in the European Union (Scotland) Order 2009 (SSI 2009/342) art.5 (effective 12 October 2009).

Variation for further time to pay

A4-458.4 **226C.**—(1) A FEO dealing with an enforcement order may—

(a) on the application of the offender; and

(b) having regard to the circumstances of the offender,

vary the arrangements specified in the order for payment of the relevant penalty.

(2) That is, by—

(a) allowing the offender further time to pay the penalty (or any instalment of it);

(b) allowing the offender to pay the penalty by instalments of such lesser amounts, or at such longer intervals, as those specified in the enforcement order.

(3) An application by an offender for the purpose of subsection (1) above may be made orally or in writing.

(4) A FEO shall notify the offender concerned of any—

(a) variation under subsection (1) above;

(b) refusal of an application for variation under that subsection.

Amendments

Section 226C inserted by Criminal Proceedings etc. (Reform) (Scotland) Act 2007 (asp 6) s.55. Brought into force, except for the purposes of any relevant penalty which requires to be paid in any district court, on 10 March 2008 by SSI 2008/42 (C.4) art.3 and Sch.

Seizure of vehicles

A4-458.5 **226D.**—(1) A FEO may, for the purpose mentioned in subsection (2) below, direct that a motor vehicle belonging to the offender be—

(a) immobilised;

(b) impounded.

(2) The purpose is of obtaining the amount of a relevant penalty which has not been paid in accordance with an enforcement order.

(3) For the purposes of this section—

(a) a vehicle belongs to an offender if it is registered under the Vehicle Excise and Registration Act 1994 (c.22) in the offender's name;

(b) a reference—

(i) to a vehicle being immobilised is to its being fitted with an immobilisation device in accordance with regulations made under subsection (12) below;

(ii) to a vehicle being impounded is to its being taken to a place of custody in accordance with regulations made under that subsection;

(c) a direction under subsection (1) above is referred to as a "seizure order".

(4) A FEO shall notify the offender concerned that a seizure order has been carried out.

(5) Where—

(a) a seizure order has been carried out; and

(b) at the end of such period as may be specified in regulations made under subsection (12) below, any part of the relevant penalty remains unpaid,

a FEO may apply to the relevant court for an order under subsection (6) below.

(6) The court may make an order under this subsection—

(a) for the sale or other disposal of the vehicle in accordance with regulations made under subsection (12) below;

(b) for any proceeds of the disposal to be applied in accordance with regulations made under that subsection in payment of or towards the unpaid amount of the relevant penalty;

(c) for any remainder of those proceeds to be applied in accordance with regulations made under that subsection in payment of or towards any reasonable expenses incurred by the FEO in relation to the seizure order;

(d) subject to paragraphs (b) and (c) above, for any balance to be given to the offender.

(7) Where, before a vehicle which is the subject of a seizure order is disposed of—

(a) a third party claims to own the vehicle; and

(b) either—

(i) a FEO is satisfied that the claim is valid (and that there are no reasonable grounds for believing that the claim is disputed by the offender or any other person from whose possession the vehicle was taken); or

(ii) the sheriff, on an application by the third party, makes an order that the sheriff is so satisfied,

the seizure order ceases to have effect.

(8) An application for the purposes of subsection (7)(b)(ii) above does not preclude any other proceedings for recovery of the vehicle.

(9) A person commits an offence if, without lawful authority or reasonable excuse, the person removes or attempts to remove—

(a) an immobilisation device fitted;

(b) a notice fixed,

to a motor vehicle in pursuance of a seizure order.

(10) A person guilty of an offence under subsection (9) above is liable on summary conviction to a fine not exceeding level 3 on the standard scale.

(11) A seizure order must not be made in respect of a vehicle—

(a) which displays a valid disabled person's badge; or
(b) in relation to which there are reasonable grounds for believing that it is used primarily for the carriage of a disabled person.

(12) The Scottish Ministers may make regulations for the purposes of and in connection with this section.

(13) Regulations under subsection (12) above may, in particular, include provision—

(a) as to circumstances in which a seizure order may (or may not) be made;
(b) as regards the value of a vehicle seizable compared to the amount of a relevant penalty which is unpaid;
(c) by reference to subsection (3)(a) and (7) above or otherwise, for protecting the interests of owners of vehicles apart from offenders;
(d) relating to subsections (3)(b), (5)(b) and (6) above;
(e) as to the fixing of notices to vehicles to which an immobilisation device has been fitted;
(f) as to the keeping and release of vehicles immobilised or impounded (including as to conditions of release);
(g) as to the payment of reasonable fees, charges or other costs in relation to—
  (i) the immobilisation or impounding of vehicles;
  (ii) the keeping, release or disposal of vehicles immobilised or impounded.

(14) Regulations under subsection (12) above shall be made by statutory instrument subject to annulment in pursuance of a resolution of the Scottish Parliament.

(15) In this section—

"disabled person's" badge means a badge issued, or having effect as if issued, under regulations made under section 21 of the Chronically Sick and Disabled Persons Act 1970 (c.44);

"immobilisation device" has the same meaning as in section 104(9) of the Road Traffic Regulation Act 1984 (c.27);

"motor vehicle" means a mechanically propelled vehicle intended or adapted for use on roads (except that section 189 of the Road Traffic Act 1988 (c.52) applies for the purposes of this section as it applies for the purposes of that Act).

AMENDMENTS

Section 226D inserted by the Criminal Proceedings etc (Reform) (Scotland) Act 2007 (asp 6) s.55. Brought into force, except for the purposes of any relevant penalty which requires to be paid in any district court, on 10 March 2008 by the Criminal Proceedings etc. (Reform) (Scotland) Act 2007 (Commencement No.3 and Savings) Order 2008 (SSI 2008/42 (C.4)) art.3 and Sch.

GENERAL NOTE

A4-458.5.1 The powers conferred by s.226D(12) of the 1995 Act as amended have allowed the Scottish Ministers to make the Enforcement of Fines (Seizure and Dispoal of Vehicles) (Scotland) Regulations 2008 (SSI 2008/103). These Regulations, in short, allow fines enforcement officers to seize a vehicle belonging to an offender who has failed to pay a relevant penalty under an enforcement order, and make provision for an associated scheme.

Deduction from benefits

226E.—(1) A FEO may, for the purpose mentioned in subsection (2) below, request the relevant court to make an application under regulations made under section 24(1)(a) of the Criminal Justice Act 1991 (c.53) for deductions as described in that section. **A4-458.6**

(2) The purpose is of obtaining the amount of a relevant penalty which has not been paid in accordance with an enforcement order.

AMENDMENTS

Section 226E inserted by the Criminal Proceedings etc (Reform) (Scotland) Act 2007 (asp 6) s.55. Brought into force, except for the purposes of any relevant penalty which requires to be paid in any district court, on 10 March 2008 by the Criminal Proceedings etc. (Reform) (Scotland) Act 2007 (Commencement No.3 and Savings) Order 2008 (SSI 2008/42 (C.4)) art.3 and Sch.

Powers of diligence

226F.—(1) When a court makes an enforcement order, it shall grant a warrant for civil diligence in the form prescribed by Act of Adjournal. **A4-458.7**

(2) A warrant granted under subsection (1) above authorises a FEO to execute the types of diligence mentioned in subsection (3) below for the purpose mentioned in subsection (4) below.

(3) The types of diligence are—

(a) arrestment of earnings; and

(b) arrestment of funds standing in accounts held at any bank or other financial institution.

(4) The purpose is of obtaining the amount of a relevant penalty which has not been paid in accordance with an enforcement order.

(5) The types of diligence mentioned in subsection (3) above may (whatever the amount of the relevant penalty concerned) be executed by an FEO in the same manner as if authorised by a warrant granted by the sheriff in a summary cause.

(6) However, the power of FEOs to execute the types of diligence mentioned in subsection (3) above is subject to such provision as the Scottish Ministers may by regulations make.

(7) Provision in regulations under subsection (6) above may, in particular—

(a) specify circumstances in which the types of diligence mentioned in subsection (3) above are (or are not) to be executed by a FEO;

(b) modify the application of any enactment (including subsection (5) above) or rule of law applying in relation to those types of diligence in so far as they may be executed by a FEO.

(8) Regulations under subsection (6) above shall be made by statutory instrument subject to annulment in pursuance of a resolution of the Scottish Parliament.

AMENDMENTS

Section 226F inserted by the Criminal Proceedings etc (Reform) (Scotland) Act 2007 (asp 6) s.55. Brought into force, except for the purposes of any relevant penalty which requires to be paid in any district court, on 10 March 2008 by the Criminal Proceedings etc. (Reform) (Scotland) Act 2007 (Commencement No. 3 and Savings) Order 2008 (SSI 2008/42 (C.4)) art.3 and Sch.

Reference of case to court

226G.—(1) A FEO may refer an enforcement order to the relevant court where— **A4-458.8**

(a) the FEO believes that payment of a relevant penalty, or any remaining part of a relevant penalty, to which an enforcement order relates is unlikely to be obtained;

(b) for any other reason (including failure of the offender to co-operate with the FEO) the FEO considers it expedient to do so.

(2) A FEO may make a reference under subsection (1) above at any time from the day after the enforcement order is made.

(3) When making a reference under subsection (1) above, the FEO shall provide the court with a report on the circumstances of the case.

(4) A report under subsection (3) above shall include, in particular—

(a) a copy of any report from a supervising officer received by the FEO under section 217(9) of this Act; and

(b) information about—

(i) the steps taken by the enforcement officer to obtain payment of or towards the relevant penalty; and

(ii) any effort (or lack of effort) made by the offender to make payment of or towards the penalty.

(5) Where a reference is made under subsection (1) above, the relevant court shall enquire of the offender as to the reason why the relevant penalty (or an instalment of it) has not been paid.

(6) Subsection (5) above does not apply where the offender is in prison.

(7) Subsections (3) to (7) of section 216 of this Act apply in relation to subsection (5) above as they apply in relation to subsection (1) of that section.

(8) After the court has considered—

(a) the report provided by the FEO under subsection (3) above; and

(b) any information obtained by enquiry under subsection (5) above,

the court may dispose of the case as mentioned in subsection (9) below.

(9) That is, the court may—

(a) revoke the enforcement order and deal with the offender as if the enforcement order had never been made;

(b) vary the enforcement order;

(c) confirm the enforcement order as previously made;

(d) direct the FEO to take specified steps to secure payment of or towards the relevant penalty in accordance with the enforcement order (including as varied under paragraph (b) above);

(e) make such other order as it thinks fit.

AMENDMENTS

Section 226G inserted by Criminal Proceedings etc. (Reform) (Scotland) Act 2007 (asp 6) s.55. Brought into force, except for the purposes of any relevant penalty which requires to be paid in any district court, on 10 March 2008 by SSI 2008/42 (C.4) art.3 and Sch.

Review of actions of FEO

A4-458.9 **226H.**—(1) The offender may apply to the relevant court for review—

(a) in relation to an enforcement order—

(i) of any variation under section 226C(1) of this Act;

(ii) of any refusal of an application for variation under that section;

(b) of the making of a seizure order under section 226D(1) of this Act.

(2) An application under subsection (1) above requires to be made within 7 days of notification under section 226C(4) of this Act or (as the case may be) section 226D(4) of this Act.

(3) On an application under subsection (1) above, the relevant court may—

(a) confirm, vary or quash the decision of the FEO;

(b) make such other order as it thinks fit.

AMENDMENTS

Section 226H inserted by Criminal Proceedings etc. (Reform) (Scotland) Act 2007 (asp 6) s.55. Brought into force, except for the purposes of any relevant penalty which requires to be paid in any district court, on 10 March 2008 by SSI 2008/42 (C.4) art.3 and Sch.

Judicial co-operation in criminal matters: mutual recognition of financial penalties: requests to other member States

226HA.— [Repealed by the Criminal Justice (EU Exit) (Scotland) (Amendment etc.) Regulations 2020 (SSI 2020/339) reg.3(5) (effective December 31, 2020 subject to transitional and saving provision specified in reg.6 of those Regulations]. A4-458.10

Enforcement of fines, etc.: interpretation

226I.—(1) [In] this section and [sections 226A to 226H] of this Act— A4-458.13

[…]

"enforcement order" is to be construed in accordance with [section 226B(1) and (4) to (6)] of this Act;

"FEO" means a fines enforcement officer;

[…]

"offender" means the person who is liable to pay a relevant penalty;

"relevant court"—

(a) in the case of a fine or compensation order, means—

(i) the court which imposed the penalty; or

(ii) where the penalty is transferred to another court, that other court;

(b) in the case of another relevant penalty (apart from a penalty specified by order for the purposes of this section), means—

(i) the court whose clerk is specified in the notice to the offender; or

(ii) where the penalty is transferred to another court, that other court;

(c) in the case of a penalty specified by order for the purposes of this section, means—

(i) the court whose clerk is specified in the notice to the offender;

(ii) where the penalty is transferred to another court, that other court; or

(iii) such other court as the order may specify for those purposes;

(d) *(Repealed by the Criminal Justice (EU Exit) (Scotland) (Amendment etc.) Regulations 2020 (SSI 2020/339) reg.3(6)(a)(v) (effective December 31, 2020 subject to transitional and saving provision specified in reg.6 of those Regulations).*

"relevant penalty" means —

(a) a fine;

(b) a compensation order imposed under section 249 of this Act;

(c) a fixed penalty offer made under section 302(1) of this Act;

(d) a compensation offer made under section 302A(1) of this Act;

(e) a fixed penalty notice given under section 54 (giving notices for fixed penalty offences) or section 62 (fixing notices to vehicles) of the Road Traffic Offenders Act 1988 (c.53);

(f) a fixed penalty notice given under section 129 (fixed penalty notices) of the Antisocial Behaviour etc. (Scotland) Act 2004 (asp 8);

(g) such other penalty as the Scottish Ministers may by order specify for the purposes of this section.

(1A) *(Repealed by the Criminal Justice (EU Exit) (Scotland) (Amendment etc.) Regulations 2020 (SSI 2020/339) reg.3(6)(b) (effective December 31, 2020 subject to transitional and saving provision specified in reg.6 of those Regulations).*

(2) An order specifying a penalty or a court for the purpose of this section shall be made by statutory instrument which shall be subject to annulment in pursuance of a resolution of the Scottish Parliament.

AMENDMENTS

Section 226I inserted by Criminal Proceedings etc. (Reform) (Scotland) Act 2007 (asp 6) s.55. Brought into force, except for the purposes of any relevant penalty which requires to be paid in any district court, on March 10, 2008 by SSI 2008/42 (C.4) art.3 and Sch.

Section 226I as amended by Mutual Recognition of Criminal Financial Penalties in the European Union (Scotland) Order 2009 (SSI 2009/342) art.6 (effective 12 October 2009).

Words in subs.(1) were substituted by the Criminal Justice (EU Exit) (Scotland) (Amendment etc.) Regulations 2020 (SSI 2020/339) reg.3(6)(a)(i) and (ii) (effective 31 December 2020 subject to transitional and saving provision specified in reg.6 of those Regulations.

Definitions omitted from subs.(1) were repealed by the Criminal Justice (EU Exit) (Scotland) (Amendment etc.) Regulations 2020 (SSI 2020/339) reg.3(6)(a)(iii) (effective 31 December 2020 subject to transitional and saving provision specified in reg.6 of those Regulations.

Words in the definition of "enforcement order" were substituted by the Criminal Justice (EU Exit) (Scotland) (Amendment etc.) Regulations 2020 (SSI 2020/339) reg.3(6)(a)(iv) (effective 31 December 2020 subject to transitional and saving provision specified in reg.6 of those Regulations.

Caution

Caution

A4-459 **227.** Where a person is convicted on indictment of an offence (other than an offence the sentence for which is fixed by law) the court may, instead of or in addition to imposing a fine or a period of imprisonment, ordain the accused to find caution for good behaviour for a period not exceeding 12 months and to such amount as the court considers appropriate.

DEFINITIONS

A4-459.1 "fine": s.307(1).
"impose imprisonment": s.307(1).
"indictment": s.307(1).
"offence": s.307(1).

Community payback orders

Community payback orders

A4-459.2 **227A.—**(1) Where a person (the "offender") is convicted of an offence punishable by imprisonment, the court may, instead of imposing a sentence of imprisonment, impose a community payback order on the offender.

(2) A community payback order is an order imposing one or more of the following requirements—

(a) an offender supervision requirement,
(b) a compensation requirement,
(c) an unpaid work or other activity requirement,
(d) a programme requirement,
(e) a residence requirement,
(f) a mental health treatment requirement,
(g) a drug treatment requirement,
(h) an alcohol treatment requirement,
(i) a conduct requirement.

(3) Subsection (4) applies where—

(a) a person (the "offender") is convicted of an offence punishable by a fine (whether or not it is also punishable by imprisonment), and
(b) where the offence is also punishable by imprisonment, the court decides not to impose—
(i) a sentence of imprisonment, or
(ii) a community payback order under subsection (1) instead of a sentence of imprisonment.

(4) The court may, instead of or as well as imposing a fine, impose a community payback order on the offender imposing one or more of the following requirements—
(a) an offender supervision requirement,
(b) a level 1 unpaid work or other activity requirement,
(c) a conduct requirement.

(5) A justice of the peace court may only impose a community payback order imposing one or more of the following requirements—
(a) an offender supervision requirement,
(b) a compensation requirement,
(c) an unpaid work or other activity requirement,
(d) a residence requirement,
(e) a conduct requirement.

(6) Subsection (5)(c) is subject to section 227J(4).

(7) The Scottish Ministers may by order made by statutory instrument amend subsection (5) so as to add to or omit requirements that may be imposed by a community payback order imposed by a justice of the peace court.

(8) An order is not to be made under subsection (7) unless a draft of the statutory instrument containing the order has been laid before and approved by resolution of the Scottish Parliament.

(9) In this section and sections 227B to 227ZK, except where the context requires otherwise—

"court" means the High Court, the sheriff or a justice of the peace court,
"imprisonment" includes detention.

AMENDMENTS

Section 227A inserted by Criminal Justice and Licensing (Scotland) Act 2010 (asp 13) s. 14(1). Brought into force on 1 February 2011 (subject to savings provisions in art.3(1)) by SSI 2010/413 art.2 and Sch. 1 para. 1.

DEFINITIONS

"community payback order": s.227A(2). A4-459.3
"court": s.227A(10).
"imprisonment": s.227A(10).
"level 1 unpaid work or other activity requirement": s.227A(10).
"offender": s.227A(1).

GENERAL NOTE

This section introduces community payback orders, which replace probation, community service orders and supervised attendance orders, whilst seeking to reproduce some of the previously existing community sentencing options in a package tailored for the particular offender. A restricted version of the community payback order (limited to offender supervision, a "level 1" unpaid work or other activity requirement and a conduct requirement) may be imposed alongside a fine. JP courts may only impose community payback orders in that same restricted form, with the addition of residence and conduct requirements. A4-459.4

Subs.(1)

The community payback order is available only (i) in relation to offences punishable by imprisonment and (ii) in a limited form, to offences punishable by fines. It is defined by subs.(2). The order cannot be imposed without the willingness of the offender to comply with the requirements (s.227B(9)(b)). On imposing a community payback order on an offender, the court may include provision for the order to be reviewed periodically (s.227X). In terms of s.227ZC(7), breach of a community payback order exposes the offender to the risk of a fine not exceeding level 3 on the standard scale, of revocation of the order with the court then dealing with the offender for the original offence, or of imprisonment.

Subs. (2)

It is important to note that this subsection should be read in the light of subs.(5) which restricts the power of a JP court to make community payback orders to orders consisting of offender supervision requirements, compensation requirements, unpaid work or other sentencing requirements and residence requirements. An "offender supervision requirement" is a requirement that, during the specified period (at least 6 months and not more than three years), the offender must attend appointments with the responsible officer (an officer of the local authority who will supervise the person) at such time and place as may be determined by the responsible officer, for the purpose of promoting the offender's rehabilitation (s.227G). Such a requirement must be imposed in the circumstances specified in s.227G(2). A compensation requirement is a requirement that the offender must pay compensation for any personal injury, loss or damage (s.227H). An unpaid work or other activity requirement is a requirement that the offender must, during the period specified by the court, for the specified number of hours (at least 20 and not more than 300), undertake unpaid work, or unpaid work and another activity (s.227I). A programme requirement is a requirement that the offender must participate in a specified course or other planned set of activities, taking place over a period of time, and provided to individuals or groups of individuals for the purpose of addressing "offending behavioural needs" (s.227P). A residence requirement is a requirement that, during the specified period, the offender must reside at a specified place. The length of the period cannot be more than that of the offender supervision requirement which must be imposed at the same time (s.227Q). A mental health treatment requirement is a requirement that the offender must submit, during the specified period, to treatment by or under the direction of a registered medical practitioner or a registered psychologist (or both) with a view to improving the offender's mental condition (s.227R). There are complex rules in ss.227R, 227S and 227T about the conditions which must be satisfied before such a requirement can be imposed, the means by which those conditions can be satisfied and how changes may be made in the treatment. A drug treatment requirement is a requirement that the offender must submit, during the specified period, to treatment by or under the direction of a specified person with a view to reducing or eliminating the offender's dependency on, or propensity to misuse, drugs (s.227U); and an alcohol treatment requirement is a similar order with a view to the reduction or elimination of the offender's dependency on alcohol (s.227V). Finally, a conduct requirement is a requirement that the offender must, during the specified period (not more than three years), do or refrain from doing specified things (S.227W).

Subs. (3)

This subsection and subs.(4) (which is the operative subsection) should be read together. They deal with offences punishable by fines. They empower the court to impose a community payback order as well as, or instead of, a fine; but in that case the order is restricted to an offender supervision requirement, a level 1 unpaid work or other activity requirement (as to which, see s.227I(5)) or a conduct requirement. The power arises in relation to every offence punishable by a fine. It is not restricted to those offences for which imprisonment is a possibility (subs.(3)(a)). It also arises where the court could have imposed imprisonment or a community payback order as an alternative in terms of subs.(1) but decides not to do so (subs.(3)(b)).

Subs. (6)

The section referred to limits the power of the JP court to impose a level 2 unpaid work or other activity requirement (as to which, see s.227I(5)).

Community payback order: procedure prior to imposition

A4-459.5 **227B.**—(1) This section applies where a court is considering imposing a community payback order on an offender.

(2) The court must not impose the order unless it is of the opinion that the offence, or the combination of the offence and one or more offences associated with it, was serious enough to warrant the imposition of such an order.

(3) Before imposing a community payback order imposing two or more requirements, the court must consider whether, in the circumstances of the case, the requirements are compatible with each other.

(4) The court must not impose the order unless it has obtained, and taken account of, a report from an officer of a local authority containing information about the offender and the offender's circumstances.

(5) An Act of Adjournal may prescribe—

(a) the form of a report under subsection (4), and
(b) the particular information to be contained in it.

(6) Subsection (4) does not apply where the court is considering imposing a community payback order—
(a) imposing only a level 1 unpaid work or other activity requirement, or
(b) under section 227M(2).

(7) The clerk of the court must give a copy of any report obtained under subsection (4) to—
(a) the offender,
(b) the offender's solicitor (if any), and
(c) the prosecutor.

(8) Before imposing the order, the court must explain to the offender in ordinary language—
(a) the purpose and effect of each of the requirements to be imposed by the order,
(b) the consequences which may follow if the offender fails to comply with any of the requirements imposed by the order, and
(c) where the court proposes to include in the order provision under section 227X for it to be reviewed, the arrangements for such a review.

(9) The court must not impose the order unless the offender has, after the court has explained those matters, confirmed that the offender—
(a) understands those matters, and
(b) is willing to comply with each of the requirements to be imposed by the order.

(10) Subsection (9)(b) does not apply where the court is considering imposing a community payback order under section 227M(2).

AMENDMENTS

Section 227B inserted by Criminal Justice and Licensing (Scotland) Act 2010 (asp 13) s.14(1). Brought into force on 1 February 2011 (subject to savings provisions in art.3(1)) by SSI 2010/413 art.2 and Sch.1 para.1.

DEFINITIONS

"community payback order": s.227A(2). A4-459.6
"prosecutor": s.307(1).

GENERAL NOTE

Two parts of this section are of practical importance. The first is the requirement, in subs.(4) for a social enquiry report before a community payback order is imposed (except where the requirement is for a level 1 unpaid work or other activity requirement or is imposed in relation to fine default). The second, is the requirement, in subs.(8) for the order to be explained to the offender). A4-459.7

Community payback order: responsible officer

227C.—(1) This section applies where a court imposes a community payback order on an offender. A4-459.8

(2) The court must, in imposing the order—
(a) specify the locality in which the offender resides or will reside for the duration of the order,
(b) require the local authority within whose area that locality is situated to nominate, within two days of its receiving a copy of the order, an officer of the authority as the responsible officer for the purposes of the order,
(c) require the offender to comply with any instructions given by the responsible officer—
(i) about keeping in touch with the responsible officer, or
(ii) for the purposes of subsection (3),

(d) require the offender to report to the responsible officer in accordance with instructions given by that officer,

(e) require the offender to notify the responsible officer without delay of—

(i) any change of the offender's address, and

(ii) the times, if any, at which the offender usually works (or carries out voluntary work) or attends school or any other educational establishment, and

(f) where the order imposes an unpaid work or other activity requirement, require the offender to undertake for the number of hours specified in the requirement such work or activity as the responsible officer may instruct, and at such times as may be so instructed.

(3) The responsible officer is responsible for—

(a) making any arrangements necessary to enable the offender to comply with each of the requirements imposed by the order,

(b) promoting compliance with those requirements by the offender,

(c) taking such steps as may be necessary to enforce compliance with the requirements of the order or to vary, revoke or discharge the order.

(4) References in this Act to the responsible officer are, in relation to an offender on whom a community payback order has been imposed, the officer for the time being nominated in pursuance of subsection (2)(b).

(5) In reckoning the period of two days for the purposes of subsection (2)(b), no account is to be taken of a Saturday or Sunday or any day which is a local or public holiday in the area of the local authority concerned.

Amendments

Section 227C inserted by Criminal Justice and Licensing (Scotland) Act 2010 (asp 13) s.14(1). Brought into force on 1 February 2011 (subject to savings provisions in art.3(1)) by SSI 2010/413 art.2 and Sch.1 para.1.

Definitions

A4-459.9 "community payback order": s.227A(2).
"responsible officer": s.227C(4).

General Note

A4-459.10 The "responsible officer" is the key figure in the implementation of the community payback order and this section provides for his or her appointment and specifies his or her particular responsibilities (in subs.(3)). Subs.(2)(c) provides that the court must, in imposing the order, require the offender to comply with instructions given by the responsible officer, inter alia in connection with compliance with the order. A failure to comply with those instructions would, accordingly, constitute a breach of the order and expose the offender to the risk of proceedings in terms of s.227ZC.

Community payback order: further provision

A4-459.11 **227D.**—(1) Where a community payback order is imposed on an offender, the order is to be taken for all purposes to be a sentence imposed on the offender.

(2) On imposing a community payback order, the court must state in open court the reasons for imposing the order.

(3) The imposition by a court of a community payback order on an offender does not prevent the court imposing a fine or any other sentence (other than imprisonment), or making any other order, that it would be entitled to impose or make in respect of the offence.

(4) Where a court imposes a community payback order on an offender, the clerk of the court must ensure that—

(a) a copy of the order is given to—

(i) the offender, and

(ii) the local authority within whose area the offender resides or will reside, and

(b) a copy of the order and such other documents and information relating to the case as may be useful are given to the clerk of the appropriate court (unless the court imposing the order is that court).

(5) A copy of the order may be given to the offender—

(a) by being delivered personally to the offender, or

(b) by being sent—

(i) by a registered post service (as defined in section 125(1) of the Postal Services Act 2000 (c.26)), or

(ii) by a postal service which provides for the delivery of the document to be recorded.

(6) A community payback order is to be in such form, or as nearly as may be in such form, as may be prescribed by Act of Adjournal.

AMENDMENTS

Section 227D inserted by Criminal Justice and Licensing (Scotland) Act 2010 (asp 13) s. 14(1). Brought into force on February 1, 2011 (subject to savings provisions in art.3(1)) by SSI 2010/413 art.2 and Sch. 1 para. 1.

DEFINITIONS

"appropriate court": s.227ZN. A4-459.12
"community payback order": s.227A(2).
"responsible officer": s.227C(4).

GENERAL NOTE

This section makes it clear that the court may combine a community payback order with any other disposal (other than imprisonment). It also requires the court to state the reason for the order when it is made and it requires the clerk of court to ensure that a copy of the order is given to the offender. It is thought that failure to comply with these particular requirements would not, of themselves, invalidate the order. A4-459.13

Requirement to avoid conflict with religious beliefs, work etc.

227E.—(1) In imposing a community payback order on an offender, the court must ensure, so far as practicable, that any requirement imposed by the order avoids— A4-459.14

(a) a conflict with the offender's religious beliefs,

(b) interference with the times, if any, at which the offender normally works (or carries out voluntary work) or attends school or any other educational establishment.

(2) The responsible officer must ensure, so far as practicable, that any instruction given to the offender avoids such a conflict or interference.

AMENDMENTS

Section 227E inserted by Criminal Justice and Licensing (Scotland) Act 2010 (asp 13) s. 14(1). Brought into force on February 1, 2011 (subject to savings provisions in art.3(1)) by SSI 2010/413 art.2 and Sch. 1 para. 1.

DEFINITIONS

"community payback order": s.227A(2). A4-459.15

GENERAL NOTE

The obligation is to avoid conflicts "so far as practicable". In most cases, it will be subs.(2) which will be relevant because the detail of the arrangements for compliance with the order are for the responsible officer (s.227(C)(3)). A4-459.16

Payment of offenders' travelling and other expenses

227F.—(1) The Scottish Ministers may by order made by statutory instrument provide for the payment to offenders of travelling or other expenses in connection with their compliance with requirements imposed on them by community payback orders. A4-459.17

(2) An order under subsection (1) may—

(a) specify expenses or provide for them to be determined under the order,

(b) provide for the payments to be made by or on behalf of local authorities,

(c) make different provision for different purposes.

(3) An order under subsection (1) is subject to annulment in pursuance of a resolution of the Scottish Parliament.

AMENDMENTS

Section 227F inserted by Criminal Justice and Licensing (Scotland) Act 2010 (asp 13) s. 14(1). Brought into force on February 1, 2011 (subject to savings provisions in art.3(1)) by SSI 2010/413 art.2 and Sch. 1 para. 1.

DEFINITIONS

A4-459.18 "community payback order": s.227A(2).

GENERAL NOTE

A4-459.19 A statutory instrument made under this section may make provision for the payment of travelling and other expenses.

Offender supervision requirement

Offender supervision requirement

A4-459.20 **227G.**—(1) In this Act, an "offender supervision requirement" is, in relation to an offender, a requirement that, during the specified period, the offender must attend appointments with the responsible officer or another person determined by the responsible officer, at such time and place as may be determined by the responsible officer, for the purpose of promoting the offender's rehabilitation.

(2) On imposing a community payback order, the court must impose an offender supervision requirement if—

(a) the offender is under 18 years of age at the time the order is imposed, or

(b) the court, in the order, imposes—

(i) a compensation requirement,

(ii) a programme requirement,

(iii) a residence requirement,

(iv) a mental health requirement,

(v) a drug treatment requirement,

(vi) an alcohol treatment requirement, or

(vii) a conduct requirement.

(3) The specified period must be at least 6 months and not more than 3 years.

(4) Subsection (3) is subject to subsection (5) and section 227ZE(4).

(5) In the case of an offender supervision requirement imposed on a person aged 16 or 17 along with only a level 1 unpaid work or other activity requirement, the specified period must be no more than whichever is the greater of—

(a) the specified period under section 227L in relation to the level 1 unpaid work or other activity requirement, and

(b) 3 months.

(6) In this section, "specified", in relation to an offender supervision requirement, means specified in the requirement.

AMENDMENTS

Section 227G inserted by Criminal Justice and Licensing (Scotland) Act 2010 (asp 13) s.14(1). Brought into force on 1 February 2011 (subject to savings provisions in art.3(1)) by SSI 2010/413 art.2 and Sch.1 para.1.

DEFINITIONS

A4-459.21 "community payback order": s.227A(2).
"responsible officer": s.227C(4).

"specified period": s.227G(4).

GENERAL NOTE

In terms of s.227C the responsible officer is responsible for promoting compliance with the order. The present section adds a rehabilitative purpose to the relationship between the responsible officer and the offender. An offender supervision requirement must be imposed in the circumstances set out in subs.(2) but the imposition of such a requirement is not excluded in other circumstances. Except in the circumstances referred to in subs.(5) and s.227ZE(4) (a restricted movement requirement) the period must be between 6 months and 3 years. A4-459.22

Compensation requirement

Compensation requirement

227H.—(1) In this Act, a "compensation requirement" is, in relation to an offender, a requirement that the offender must pay compensation for any relevant matter in favour of a relevant person. A4-459.23

(2) In subsection (1)—

"relevant matter" means any personal injury, loss, damage or other matter in respect of which a compensation order could be made against the offender under section 249 of this Act, and

"relevant person" means a person in whose favour the compensation could be awarded by such a compensation order.

(3) A compensation requirement may require the compensation to be paid in a lump sum or in instalments.

(4) The offender must complete payment of the compensation before the earlier of the following—

(a) the end of the period of 18 months beginning with the day on which the compensation requirement is imposed,

(b) the beginning of the period of 2 months ending with the day on which the offender supervision requirement imposed under section 227G(2) ends.

(5) The following provisions of this Act apply in relation to a compensation requirement as they apply in relation to a compensation order, and as if the references in them to a compensation order included a compensation requirement—

(a) section 249(3), (4), (5) and (8) to (10),

(b) section 250(2),

(c) section 251(1), (1A) and (2)(b),

(d) section 253,

[(e) section 253C,

(f) section 253D, and

(g) section 253H.]

AMENDMENTS

Section 227H inserted by Criminal Justice and Licensing (Scotland) Act 2010 (asp 13) s. 14(1). Brought into force on 1 February 2011 (subject to savings provisions in art.3(1)) by SSI 2010/413 art.2 and Sch. 1 para. 1.

Section 227H(5)(e)-(g) inserted and the word "and" immediately following paragraph (c) is repealed by the Victims and Witnesses (Scotland) Act 2014 (Supplementary Provisions) Order 2021 (SSI 2021/57) art.2(2)(a) and (b) effective (3 February 2021).

DEFINITIONS

"community payback order": s.227A(2). A4-459.24

"compensation requirement": s.227H(1).

"offender supervision requirement": s.227G(1).

GENERAL NOTE

A4-459.25 This section makes it possible for a court to impose a requirement to pay compensation as part of a community payback order. It does not replace the existing compensation order mechanism, set out in s.249. Indeed, subs.(5) applies provisions relevant to ordinary compensation orders to compensation requirements.

Unpaid work or other activity requirement

Unpaid work or other activity requirement

A4-459.26 **227I.**—(1) In this Act, an "unpaid work or other activity requirement" is, in relation to an offender, a requirement that the offender must, for the specified number of hours, undertake—

(a) unpaid work, or
(b) unpaid work and other activity.

(2) Whether the offender must undertake other activity as well as unpaid work is for the responsible officer to determine.

(3) The nature of the unpaid work and any other activity to be undertaken by the offender is to be determined by the responsible officer.

(4) The number of hours that may be specified in the requirement must be (in total)—

(a) at least 20 hours, and
(b) not more than 300 hours.

(5) An unpaid work or other activity requirement which requires the work or activity to be undertaken for a number of hours totalling no more than 100 is referred to in this Act as a "level 1 unpaid work or other activity requirement".

(6) An unpaid work or other activity requirement which requires the work or activity to be undertaken for a number of hours totalling more than 100 is referred to in this Act as a "level 2 unpaid work or other activity requirement".

(7) The Scottish Ministers may by order made by statutory instrument substitute another number of hours for any of the numbers of hours for the time being specified in subsections (4) to (6).

(8) An order under subsection (7) may only substitute for the number of hours for the time being specified in a provision mentioned in the first column of the following table a number of hours falling within the range set out in the corresponding entry in the second column.

Provision	*Range*	
	No fewer than	*No more than*
Subsection (4)(a)	10 hours	40 hours
Subsection (4)(b)	250 hours	350 hours
Subsections (5) and (6)	70 hours	150 hours

(9) An order under subsection (7) is subject to annulment in pursuance of a resolution of the Scottish Parliament.

(10) In this section, "specified", in relation to an unpaid work or other activity requirement, means specified in the requirement.

AMENDMENTS

Section 227I inserted by Criminal Justice and Licensing (Scotland) Act 2010 (asp 13) s. 14(1). Brought into force on February 1, 2011 (subject to savings provisions in art.3(1)) by SSI 2010/413 art.2 and Sch. 1 para. 1.

DEFINITIONS

A4-459.27 "level 1 unpaid work or other activity requirement": s.227I(5).
"level 2 unpaid work or other activity requirement": s.227I(6).

"specified": s.227I(10).
"unpaid work or other activity requirement": s.227I(1).

GENERAL NOTE

This section, together with ss.227J-227O provides for an unpaid work or other activity requirement. An unpaid work or other activity requirement is a requirement that the offender must undertake either unpaid work or unpaid work plus another activity for a specified number of hours within the period specified in the requirement. It may be concurrent with any existing unpaid work requirement. It may be used in place of a prison sentence where an offender fails to pay a fine. It is for the court to specify the number of hours (at least 20 but not more than 300) but for the responsible officer to determine the nature of the work and decide whether the offender must undertake another activity as well as unpaid work and, if so, how the time is to be allocated (subject to the parameters in s.227K). The Act makes a distinction between a level 1 requirement (which is for no more than 100 hours) and a level 2 requirement (which is for more than 100 hours). Section 227J(4) precludes a JP court from imposing a level 2 requirement. An unpaid work or other activity requirement can only be imposed where the offender is at least 16 years old and, in the case of a level 2 requirement, only if the court is satisfied, having obtained a social enquiry report, that the offender is a suitable person for the requirement. A4-459.28

Unpaid work or other activity requirement: further provision

227J.—(1) A court may not impose an unpaid work or other activity requirement on an offender who is under 16 years of age. A4-459.29

(2) A court may impose such a requirement on an offender only if the court is satisfied, after considering the report mentioned in section 227B(4), that the offender is a suitable person to undertake unpaid work in pursuance of the requirement.

(3) Subsection (2) does not apply where the court is considering imposing a community payback order—

(a) imposing only a level 1 unpaid work or other activity requirement, or
(b) under section 227M(2).

(4) A justice of the peace court may impose a level 2 unpaid work or other activity requirement only if—

(a) the Scottish Ministers by regulations made by statutory instrument so provide, and
(b) the requirement is imposed in such circumstances and subject to such conditions as may be specified in the regulations.

(5) Regulations are not to be made under subsection (4) unless a draft of the statutory instrument containing them has been laid before and approved by resolution of the Scottish Parliament.

AMENDMENTS

Section 227J inserted by Criminal Justice and Licensing (Scotland) Act 2010 (asp 13) s.14(1). Brought into force on February 1, 2011 (subject to savings provisions in art.3(1)) by SSI 2010/413 art.2 and Sch. 1 para. 1.

DEFINITIONS

"level 2 unpaid work or other activity requirement": s.227I(6). A4-459.30
"unpaid work or other activity requirement": s.227I(1).

GENERAL NOTE

This section sets out the restrictions on the making of an unpaid work or other activity requirement. This section includes a power for the Scottish Ministers to make regulations to allow Justice of the Peace courts to impose level 2 unpaid work and activity requirements. A4-459.31

See the General Note to s.227I.

Allocation of hours between unpaid work and other activity

227K.—(1) Subject to subsection (2), it is for the responsible officer to determine how many out of the number of hours specified in an unpaid work or other activity requirement are to be allocated to undertaking, respectively— A4-459.32

(a) unpaid work, and
(b) any other activity to be undertaken.

(2) The number of hours allocated to undertaking an activity other than unpaid work must not exceed whichever is the lower of—

(a) 30% of the number of hours specified in the requirement, and

(b) 30 hours.

(3) The Scottish Ministers may by order made by statutory instrument—

(a) substitute another percentage for the percentage for the time being specified in subsection (2)(a),

(b) substitute another number of hours for the number of hours for the time being specified in subsection (2)(b).

(4) An order is not to be made under subsection (3) unless a draft of the statutory instrument containing the order has been laid before and approved by resolution of the Scottish Parliament.

Amendments

Section 227K inserted by Criminal Justice and Licensing (Scotland) Act 2010 (asp 13) s. 14(1). Brought into force on February 1, 2011 (subject to savings provisions in art.3(1)) by SSI 2010/413 art.2 and Sch.1 para.1.

General Note

A4-459.33 See the General Note to s.227I.

A split between unpaid work and other activity may competently be determined by the responsible officer subject to the maximum number of hours of other activity that may be counted towards the requirement.

Time limit for completion of unpaid work or other activity

227L.—(1) The number of hours of unpaid work and any other activity that the offender is required to undertake in pursuance of an unpaid work or other activity requirement must be completed by the offender before the end of the specified period beginning with the imposition of the requirement.

(2) The "specified period" is—

(a) in relation to a level 1 unpaid work or other activity requirement, 3 months or such longer period as the court may specify in the requirement,

(b) in relation to a level 2 unpaid work or other activity requirement, 6 months or such longer period as the court may specify in the requirement.

Amendments

Section 227L inserted by Criminal Justice and Licensing (Scotland) Act 2010 (asp 13) s.14(1). Brought into force on 1 February 2011 (subject to savings provisions in art.3(1)) by SSI 2010/413 art.2 and Sch. 1 para. 1.

Time limit for completion of unpaid work or other activity

A4-459.34 ***227L.—(1)*** *The number of hours of unpaid work and any other activity that the offender is required to undertake in pursuance of an unpaid work or other activity requirement must be completed by the offender before the end of the specified period beginning with the imposition of the requirement.*

(2) The "specified period" is—

(a) in relation to a level 1 unpaid work or other activity requirement, 3 months or such longer period as the court may specify in the requirement,

(b) in relation to a level 2 unpaid work or other activity requirement, 6 months or such longer period as the court may specify in the requirement.

Amendments

In relation to COVID-19, s.227L as amended by Coronavirus (Scotland) Act 2020 (asp 7) Sch.4(6) para.13(2) and (3) (effective 7 April 2020).

Definitions

A4-459.35 "level 1 unpaid work or other activity requirement": s.227I(5).

"level 2 unpaid work or other activity requirement": s.227I(6).

"specified period": s.227L(2).
"unpaid work and other activity requirement": s.227I(1).

GENERAL NOTE

See the General Note to s.227I. A4-459.36

The number of hours of unpaid work must be completed by the end of the specified period and this section makes the appropriate provisions in that regard.

Fine defaulters

227M.—(1) This section applies where— A4-459.37

(a) a fine has been imposed on an offender in respect of an offence,

(b) the offender fails to pay the fine or an instalment of the fine,

(c) the offender is not serving a sentence of imprisonment, and

(d) apart from this section, the court would have imposed a period of imprisonment on the offender under section 219(1) of this Act in respect of the failure to pay the fine or instalment.

(2) Instead of imposing a period of imprisonment under section 219(1) of this Act, the court—

(a) where the amount of the fine or the instalment does not exceed level 2 on the standard scale, must impose a community payback order on the offender imposing a level 1 unpaid work or other activity requirement,

(b) where the amount of the fine or the instalment exceeds that level, may impose such a community payback order.

(3) The court, in imposing a community payback order under subsection (2) on a person aged 16 or 17, must also impose an offender supervision requirement.

(4) Where the amount of the fine or the instalment does not exceed level 1 on the standard scale, the number of hours specified in the requirement must not exceed 50.

(5) On completion of the hours of unpaid work and any other activity specified in an unpaid work or other activity requirement imposed under this section, the fine in respect of which the requirement was imposed is discharged (or, as the case may be, the outstanding instalments of the fine are discharged).

(6) If, after a community payback order is imposed on an offender under this section, the offender pays the fine or the full amount of any outstanding instalments, the appropriate court must discharge the order.

(7) Subsection (2) is subject to sections 227J(1) and 227N(2), (3) and (7).

(8) In this section, "court" does not include the High Court.

AMENDMENTS

Section 227M inserted by Criminal Justice and Licensing (Scotland) Act 2010 (asp 13) s.14(1). Brought into force on 1 February 2011 (subject to savings provisions in art.3(1)) by SSI 2010/413 art.2 and Sch.1 para.1.

DEFINITIONS

"appropriate court": s.227ZN. A4-459.38
"community payback order": s.227A(2).
"court": s.227M(10).
"level 1 unpaid work or other activity requirement": s.227I(5).
"level 2 on the standard scale": s.225(1) and (2) [£500].
"level 2 unpaid work or other activity requirement": s.227I(6).

GENERAL NOTE

See the General Note to s.227I. A4-459.39

This section provides, inter alia, that where the offender has defaulted on a fine not exceeding £500, and where the court in disposing of the matter would otherwise have imposed a custodial sentence, then the court must impose a community payback order with level 1 unpaid work and other activity requirements. The number of hours is limited to 50 for the requirement where the fine that has been imposed does not exceed £200.

Offenders subject to more than one unpaid work or other activity requirement

A4-459.40 **227N.**—(1) This section applies where—

(a) a court is considering imposing an unpaid work or other activity requirement on an offender (referred to as the "new requirement"), and

(b) at the time the court is considering imposing the requirement, there is already in effect one or more of the following orders—

(i) a community payback order imposing such a requirement on the same offender;

(ii) a community service order under this Act in relation to the same offender;

(iii) a probation order under this Act imposing an unpaid work requirement on the same offender;

(iv) a supervised attendance order under this Act in relation to the same offender.

(1A) In this section references to an "existing requirement" are—

(a) in relation to a community payback order, to the unpaid work or other activity requirement imposed on the offender by the order;

(b) in relation to a community service order or a probation order, to the unpaid work requirement imposed on the offender by the order;

(c) in relation to a supervised attendance order, to the requirement imposed on the offender by the order by virtue of section 235(2) of this Act.

(2) The court may, in imposing the new requirement, direct that it is to be concurrent with any existing requirement.

(3) Where the court makes a direction under subsection (2), hours of unpaid work or other activity undertaken after the new requirement is imposed count for the purposes of compliance with that requirement and the existing requirement.

(4) Subsection (5) applies where the court does not make a direction under subsection (2).

(5) The maximum number of hours which may be specified in the new requirement is the number of hours specified in section 227I(4)(b) less the aggregate of the number of hours still to be completed under each existing requirement at the time the new requirement is imposed.

(6) In calculating that aggregate, if any existing requirement is concurrent with another (by virtue of a direction under subsection (2)), hours that count for the purposes of compliance with both (or, as the case may be, all) are to be counted only once.

(7) Where that maximum number is less than the minimum number of hours that can be specified by virtue of section 227I(4)(a), the court must not impose the new requirement.

AMENDMENTS

Section 227N inserted by Criminal Justice and Licensing (Scotland) Act 2010 (asp 13) s. 14(1). Brought into force on February 1, 2011 (subject to savings provisions in art.3(1)) by SSI 2010/413 art.2 and Sch. 1 para. 1.

Subss.(1)(b) and (5) as amended, subs.(1 A) inserted, by Criminal Justice and Licensing (Scotland) Act 2010 (Consequential and Supplementary Provisions) Order 2011 (SSI 2011/25) Sch.1 para.1 (effective February 1, 2011).

DEFINITIONS

A4-459.41 "existing requirement": s.227N(1)(b).
"new requirement": s.227N(1)(a).
"unpaid work or other activity requirement": s.227I(1).

GENERAL NOTE

A4-459.42 See the General Note to s.227I.

An offender may competently be made the subject of an unpaid work or other activity requirement even although he is already subject to such a requirement. The inhibition placed on such an option is that, by s.227N(4) and (5), the total number of hours must not exceed 300.

Rules about unpaid work and other activity

227O.—(1) The Scottish Ministers may make rules by statutory instrument for or in connection with the undertaking of unpaid work and other activities in pursuance of unpaid work or other activity requirements. A4-459.43

(2) Rules under subsection (1) may in particular make provision for—

(a) limiting the number of hours of work or other activity that an offender may be required to undertake in any one day,

(b) reckoning the time spent undertaking unpaid work or other activity,

(c) the keeping of records of unpaid work and any other activity undertaken.

(3) Rules under subsection (1) may—

(a) confer functions on responsible officers,

(b) contain rules about the way responsible officers are to exercise functions under this Act.

(4) Rules under subsection (1) are subject to annulment in pursuance of a resolution of the Scottish Parliament.

AMENDMENTS

Section 227O inserted by Criminal Justice and Licensing (Scotland) Act 2010 (asp 13) s. 14(1). Brought into force on February 1, 2011 (subject to savings provisions in art.3(1)) by SSI 2010/413 art.2 and Sch. 1 para. 1.

DEFINITIONS

"unpaid work or other activity requirement": s.227I(1). A4-459.44

GENERAL NOTE

See the General Note to s.227I. A4-459.45

This section gives the Scottish Ministers the power to make rules for regulating performance of unpaid work and other activity requirements including in relation to a daily maximum number of hours, calculations of time undertaken, provision for travel expenses and record keeping.

Programme requirement

Programme requirement

227P.—(1) In this Act, a "programme requirement" is, in relation to an offender, a requirement that the offender must participate in a specified programme, at the specified place and on the specified number of days. A4-459.46

(2) In this section, "programme" means a course or other planned set of activities, taking place over a period of time, and provided to individuals or groups of individuals for the purpose of addressing offending behavioural needs.

(3) A court may impose a programme requirement on an offender only if the specified programme is one which has been recommended by an officer of a local authority as being suitable for the offender to participate in.

(4) If an offender's compliance with a proposed programme requirement would involve the co-operation of a person other than the offender, the court may impose the requirement only if the other person consents.

(5) A court may not impose a programme requirement that would require an offender to participate in a specified programme after the expiry of the period specified in the offender supervision requirement to be imposed at the same time as the programme requirement (by virtue of section 227G(2)(b)).

(6) Where the court imposes a programme requirement on an offender, the requirement is to be taken to include a requirement that the offender, while attend-

ing the specified programme, complies with any instructions given by or on behalf of the person in charge of the programme.

(7) In this section, "specified", in relation to a programme requirement, means specified in the requirement.

AMENDMENTS

Section 227P inserted by Criminal Justice and Licensing (Scotland) Act 2010 (asp 13) s. 14(1). Brought into force on February 1, 2011 (subject to savings provisions in art.3(1)) by SSI 2010/413 art.2 and Sch. 1 para. 1.

DEFINITIONS

A4-459.47 "programme": s.227P(2).
"programme requirement": s.227P(1).
"specified": s.227P(7).

GENERAL NOTE

A4-459.48 A programme requirement is a requirement that the offender must, at a specified place and for a specified number of days, participate in a specified course or other planned set of activities, taking place over a period of time, and provided to individuals or groups of individuals for the purpose of addressing "offending behavioural needs". It is only available to the court as a disposal if the social enquiry report recommends it as one suitable for the offender. The effect of subs.(4) is that the making of such an order is also dependent on the consent of those running the programme.

Residence requirement

Residence requirement

A4-459.49 **227Q.**—(1) In this Act, a "residence requirement" is, in relation to an offender, a requirement that, during the specified period, the offender must reside at a specified place.

(2) The court may, in a residence requirement, require an offender to reside at a hostel or other institution only if the hostel or institution has been recommended as a suitable place for the offender to reside in by an officer of a local authority.

(3) The specified period must not be longer than the period specified in the offender supervision requirement to be imposed at the same time as the residence requirement (by virtue of section 227G(2)(b)).

(4) In this section, "specified", in relation to a residence requirement, means specified in the requirement.

AMENDMENTS

Section 227Q inserted by Criminal Justice and Licensing (Scotland) Act 2010 (asp 13) s. 14(1). Brought into force on February 1, 2011 (subject to savings provisions in art.3(1)) by SSI 2010/413 art.2 and Sch. 1 para. 1.

DEFINITIONS

A4-459.50 "residence requirement": s.227Q(1).
"specified": s.227Q(4).

GENERAL NOTE

A4-459.51 A residence requirement can only be imposed in association with an offender supervision requirement and can only be made in relation to a hostel or other institution if the hostel or other institution has been recommended as a suitable place in terms of subs.(2).

Mental health treatment requirement

Mental health treatment requirement

A4-459.52 **227R.**—(1) In this Act, a "mental health treatment requirement" is, in relation to an offender, a requirement that the offender must submit, during the specified period, to treatment by or under the direction of a registered medical practitioner or a registered psychologist (or both) with a view to improving the offender's mental condition.

(2) The treatment to which an offender may be required to submit under a mental health treatment requirement is such of the kinds of treatment described in subsection (3) as is specified; but otherwise the nature of the treatment is not to be specified.

(3) Those kinds of treatment are—

(a) treatment as a resident patient in a hospital (other than a State hospital) within the meaning of the Mental Health (Care and Treatment) (Scotland) Act 2003 (asp 13) ("the 2003 Act"),

(b) treatment as a non-resident patient at such institution or other place as may be specified, or

(c) treatment by or under the direction of such registered medical practitioner or registered psychologist as may be specified.

(4) A court may impose a mental health treatment requirement on an offender only if the court is satisfied—

(a) on the written or oral evidence of an approved medical practitioner (within the meaning of the 2003 Act), that Condition A is met,

(b) on the written or oral evidence of the registered medical practitioner or registered psychologist by whom or under whose direction the treatment is to be provided, that Condition B is met, and

(c) that Condition C is met.

(5) Condition A is that—

(a) the offender suffers from a mental condition,

(b) the condition requires, and may be susceptible to, treatment, and

(c) the condition is not such as to warrant the offender's being subject to—

(i) a compulsory treatment order under section 64 of the 2003 Act, or

(ii) a compulsion order under section 57A of this Act.

(6) Condition B is that the treatment proposed to be specified is appropriate for the offender.

(7) Condition C is that arrangements have been made for the proposed treatment including, where the treatment is to be of the kind mentioned in subsection (3)(a), arrangements for the offender's reception in the hospital proposed to be specified in the requirement.

(8) The specified period must not be longer than the period specified in the offender supervision requirement to be imposed at the same time as the mental health treatment requirement (by virtue of section 227G(2)(b)).

(9) In this section, "specified", in relation to a mental health treatment requirement, means specified in the requirement.

AMENDMENTS

Section 227R inserted by Criminal Justice and Licensing (Scotland) Act 2010 (asp 13) s. 14(1). Brought into force on February 1, 2011 (subject to savings provisions in art.3(1)) by SSI 2010/413 art.2 and Sch. 1 para. 1.

DEFINITIONS

"mental health treatment requirement": s.227R(1). A4-459.53
"specified": s.227R(9).
"the 2003 Act": s.227R(3)(a).

GENERAL NOTE

Sections 227R to 227T provide for mental health treatment requirements. The regime is well described in the Revised Explanatory Notes, published for Stage 2 of the Bill: A4-459.54

"Section 227R(1) provides a definition, including purpose, of a mental health treatment requirement. Subsection (2) indicates that subject to certain specified types of treatment listed in subsection (3) the nature of the treatment is not to be specified. Before imposing a mental health requirement subsection (4) requires the court to be satisfied on the basis of evidence submitted by appropriately qualified individuals that three conditions (A-C) have been met. Subsection (5) sets out the considerations in relation to Condition A in that the offender must be suffering from a mental condition, which requires and may be susceptible to treatment and that other specified orders are not appropriate. Condition B is set out in subsection (6) and requires the proposed treatment to be appropriate for the offender. Condition C is set out in subsection (7) and requires that arrangements must have been made for the proposed treatment. Subsection (8) requires that the period for which the offender must submit to the treatment should be no longer than the specified period in the offender supervision requirement to be imposed at the same time as the mental health treatment requirement. Subsection (9) defines the specified treatment or specified period as being the treatment or period specified by the court in the requirement.

"Section 227S(1) provides that proof of signature or qualifications on a report from an approved medical practitioner is not necessary when the report is submitted in evidence for imposition of a mental health treatment requirement. Subsections (2) and (3) state that the offender and his/her solicitor must receive a copy of the report of the medical evidence and the case may be adjourned to give the offender further time to consider the report. Where the offender is being detained in hospital or remanded to custody, subsections (4) and (5) make provision for an examination of the offender by an approved medical practitioner for the purposes of challenging the evidence to be presented in court. Subsection (6) provides for any such examination to be undertaken in private.

"Section 227T(1) to (3) enable the practitioner under whose direction the treatment is being carried out to make arrangements where appropriate for the offender to receive a different kind of treatment or to receive it at a different place. Subsection (4) states that the treatment to be provided must be of a kind which could have been specified in the original requirement. An exception is set out in subsection (5) which allows for the offender to receive treatment as a residential patient in an institution or place which it might not have been possible to specify for that purpose in the original requirement. Subsection (6) requires the agreement of the offender and the responsible officer to the proposed changes, for the agreement of a registered medical practitioner to accept the offender as a patient and where the offender is to be a resident patient for him/her to be received as such. Subsection (7) requires the court to be informed of changes under this section and for the newly arranged treatment to be regarded as required under the CPO."

Mental health treatment requirements: medical evidence

A4-459.55 **227S.**—(1) For the purposes of section 227R(4)(a) or (b), a written report purporting to be signed by an approved medical practitioner (within the meaning of the Mental Health (Care and Treatment) (Scotland) Act 2003 (asp 13)) may be received in evidence without the need for proof of the signature or qualifications of the practitioner.

(2) Where such a report is lodged in evidence otherwise than by or on behalf of the offender, a copy of the report must be given to—

(a) the offender, and
(b) the offender's solicitor (if any).

(3) The court may adjourn the case if it considers it necessary to do so to give the offender further time to consider the report.

(4) Subsection (5) applies where the offender is—

(a) detained in a hospital under this Act, or
(b) remanded in custody.

(5) For the purpose of calling evidence to rebut any evidence contained in a report lodged as mentioned in subsection (2), arrangements may be made by or on behalf of the offender for an examination of the offender by a registered medical practitioner.

(6) Such an examination is to be carried out in private.

AMENDMENTS

Section 227S inserted by Criminal Justice and Licensing (Scotland) Act 2010 (asp 13) s. 14(1). Brought into force on February 1, 2011 (subject to savings provisions in art.3(1)) by SSI 2010/413 art.2 and Sch. 1 para. 1.

GENERAL NOTE

See the General Note to s.227R above. A4-459.56

General questions of an evidential nature are settled by the provisions of this section.

Power to change treatment

227T.—(1) This section applies where— A4-459.57

(a) a mental health treatment requirement has been imposed on an offender, and

(b) the registered medical practitioner or registered psychologist by whom or under whose direction the offender is receiving the treatment to which the offender is required to submit in pursuance of the requirement is of the opinion mentioned in subsection (2).

(2) That opinion is—

(a) that the offender requires, or that it would be appropriate for the offender to receive, a different kind of treatment (whether in whole or in part) from that which the offender has been receiving, or

(b) that the treatment (whether in whole or in part) can be more appropriately given in or at a different hospital or other institution or place from that where the offender has been receiving treatment.

(3) The practitioner or, as the case may be, psychologist may make arrangements for the offender to be treated accordingly.

(4) Subject to subsection (5), the treatment provided under the arrangements must be of a kind which could have been specified in the mental health treatment requirement.

(5) The arrangements may provide for the offender to receive treatment (in whole or in part) as a resident patient in an institution or place even though it is one that could not have been specified for that purpose in the mental health treatment requirement.

(6) Arrangements may be made under subsection (3) only if—

(a) the offender and the responsible officer agree to the arrangements,

(b) the treatment will be given by or under the direction of a registered medical practitioner or registered psychologist who has agreed to accept the offender as a patient, and

(c) where the treatment requires the offender to be a resident patient, the offender will be received as such.

(7) Where arrangements are made under subsection (3)—

(a) the responsible officer must notify the court of the arrangements, and

(b) the treatment provided under the arrangements is to be taken to be treatment to which the offender is required to submit under the mental health treatment requirement.

AMENDMENTS

Section 227T inserted by Criminal Justice and Licensing (Scotland) Act 2010 (asp 13) s. 14(1). Brought into force on February 1, 2011 (subject to savings provisions in art.3(1)) by SSI 2010/413 art.2 and Sch. 1 para. 1.

GENERAL NOTE

See the General Note to S.227R above. A4-459.58

The directing nature of the mental health treatment requirement is allowed to be changed by s.227T so that the practitioner under whose direction the treatment is being carried out may make arrangements where appropriate for the offender to receive a different kind of treatment or to receive it at a different place. The court must be informed of the changes to the requirement thus preserving a general and independent superintendence of the treatment.

Drug treatment requirement

Drug treatment requirement

A4-459.59 **227U.**—(1) In this Act, a "drug treatment requirement" is, in relation to an offender, a requirement that the offender must submit, during the specified period, to treatment by or under the direction of a specified person with a view to reducing or eliminating the offender's dependency on, or propensity to misuse, drugs.

(2) The treatment to which an offender may be required to submit under a drug treatment requirement is such of the kinds of treatment described in subsection (3) as is specified (but otherwise the nature of the treatment is not to be specified).

(3) Those kinds of treatment are—

(a) treatment as a resident in such institution or other place as is specified,

(b) treatment as a non-resident at such institution or other place, and at such intervals, as is specified.

(4) The specified person must be a person who has the necessary qualifications or experience in relation to the treatment to be provided.

(5) The specified period must not be longer than the period specified in the offender supervision requirement to be imposed at the same time as the drug treatment requirement (by virtue of section 227G(2)(b)).

(6) A court may impose a drug treatment requirement on an offender only if the court is satisfied that—

(a) the offender is dependent on, or has a propensity to misuse, any controlled drug (as defined in section 2(1)(a) of the Misuse of Drugs Act 1971 (c.38)),

(b) the dependency or propensity requires, and may be susceptible to, treatment, and

(c) arrangements have been, or can be, made for the proposed treatment including, where the treatment is to be of the kind mentioned in subsection (3)(a), arrangements for the offender's reception in the institution or other place to be specified.

(7) In this section, "specified", in relation to a drug treatment requirement, means specified in the requirement.

Amendments

Section 227U inserted by Criminal Justice and Licensing (Scotland) Act 2010 (asp 13) s.14(1). Brought into force on February 1, 2011 (subject to savings provisions in art.3(1)) by SSI 2010/413 art.2 and Sch.1 para.1.

Definitions

A4-459.60 "drug treatment requirement": s.227U(1).
"specified": s.227U(7).

General Note

A4-459.61 The purpose of a drug treatment requirement is to reduce or eliminate the offender's dependency on, or propensity to misuse, drugs. It can only be imposed in association with an offender supervision requirement.

Alcohol treatment requirement

Alcohol treatment requirement

A4-459.62 **227V.**—(1) In this Act, an "alcohol treatment requirement" is, in relation to an offender, a requirement that the offender must submit, during the specified period, to treatment by or under the direction of a specified person with a view to the reduction or elimination of the offender's dependency on alcohol.

(2) The treatment to which an offender may be required to submit under an alcohol treatment requirement is such of the kinds of treatment described in subsection (3) as is specified (but otherwise the nature of the treatment is not to be specified).

(3) Those kinds of treatment are—

(a) treatment as a resident in such institution or other place as is specified,
(b) treatment as a non-resident at such institution or other place, and at such intervals, as is specified,
(c) treatment by or under the direction of such person as is specified.

(4) The person specified under subsection (1) or (3)(c) must be a person who has the necessary qualifications or experience in relation to the treatment to be provided.

(5) The specified period must not be longer than the period specified in the offender supervision requirement to be imposed at the same time as the alcohol treatment requirement (by virtue of section 227G(2)(b)).

(6) A court may impose an alcohol treatment requirement on an offender only if the court is satisfied that—

(a) the offender is dependent on alcohol,
(b) the dependency requires, and may be susceptible to, treatment, and
(c) arrangements have been, or can be, made for the proposed treatment, including, where the treatment is to be of the kind mentioned in subsection (3)(a), arrangements for the offender's reception in the institution or other place to be specified.

(7) In this section, "specified", in relation to an alcohol treatment requirement, means specified in the requirement.

AMENDMENTS

Section 227V inserted by Criminal Justice and Licensing (Scotland) Act 2010 (asp 13) s.14(1). Brought into force on February 1, 2011 (subject to savings provisions in art.3(1)) by SSI 2010/413 art.2 and Sch.1 para.1.

DEFINITIONS

"alcohol treatment requirement": s.227V(1). **A4-459.63**
"specified": s.227V(7).

GENERAL NOTE

The purpose of an alcohol treatment requirement is to reduce or eliminate the offender's dependency on, or propensity to misuse, alcohol. It can only be imposed in association with an offender supervision requirement. **A4-459.64**

Conduct requirement

Conduct requirement

227W.—(1) In this Act, a "conduct requirement" is, in relation to an offender, a requirement that the offender must, during the specified period, do or refrain from doing specified things. **A4-459.65**

(2) A court may impose a conduct requirement on an offender only if the court is satisfied that the requirement is necessary with a view to—

(a) securing or promoting good behaviour by the offender, or
(b) preventing further offending by the offender.

(3) The specified period must be not more than 3 years.

(4) The specified things must not include anything that—

(a) could be required by imposing one of the other requirements listed in section 227A(2), or

(b) would be inconsistent with the provisions of this Act relating to such other requirements.

(5) In this section, "specified", in relation to a conduct requirement, means specified in the requirement.

AMENDMENTS

Section 227W inserted by Criminal Justice and Licensing (Scotland) Act 2010 (asp 13) s.14(1). Brought into force on February 1, 2011 (subject to savings provisions in art.3(1)) by SSI 2010/413 art.2 and Sch.1 para.1.

DEFINITIONS

A4-459.66 "conduct requirement": s.227W(1).
"specified": s.227W(5).

GENERAL NOTE

A4-459.67 This section was added during the Parliamentary progress of the Bill and it represents a kind of fall back. It empowers a court to require an offender to do or refrain from doing specified things where that objective cannot be achieved by one of the other components of a community payback order. The court can only impose such a requirement if satisfied that the requirement is necessary with a view to securing or promoting good behaviour by the offender or preventing further offending and it cannot be for more than three years.

In *Kirk and Hunter v Brown*, 2012 S.C.C.R. 558 the Appeal Court suspended *simpliciter* a requirement in community payback orders made against the complainers requiring them, for a period of 12 months, to refrain from committing any criminal offence. In explaining the Court's reasoning, Lord Clarke said: "It appeared to us that, having regard to the statutory language employed, the Scottish Parliament had, in providing for conduct requirements, as specified in section 227W(2), done so expressly for the purpose of seeking or promoting the good behaviour of the offender or preventing further offending by him. In other words any such requirement is to be seen as providing *a means* which the court considers necessary to achieve *the end* of good behaviour on the part of the offender. To impose a requirement to be of good behaviour or to refrain generally from committing criminal offences would be to impose the end as a requirement, not to impose a requirement to seek or promote that end." The Court considered that s.227G(1) and (2) emphasise the rehabilitative nature of the requirement imposed.

Community payback orders: review, variation etc.

Periodic review of community payback orders

A4-459.68 **227X.**—(1) On imposing a community payback order on an offender, the court may include in the order provision for the order to be reviewed at such time or times as may be specified in the order.

(2) A review carried out in pursuance of such provision is referred to in this section as a "progress review".

(3) A progress review may be carried out by the court which imposed the community payback order or (if different) the appropriate court, and, where those courts are different, the court must specify in the order which of those courts is to carry out the reviews.

(4) A progress review is to be carried out in such manner as the court carrying out the review may determine.

(5) Before each progress review, the responsible officer must give the court a written report on the offender's compliance with the requirements imposed by the community payback order in the period to which the review relates.

(6) The offender must attend each progress review.

(7) If the offender fails to attend a progress review, the court may—

(a) issue a citation requiring the offender's attendance, or

(b) issue a warrant for the offender's arrest.

(8) The unified citation provisions apply in relation to a citation under subsection (7)(a) as they apply in relation to a citation under section 216(3)(a) of this Act.

(9) Subsections (10) and (11) apply where, in the course of carrying out a progress review in respect of a community payback order, it appears to the court that the offender has failed to comply with a requirement imposed by the order.

(10) The court must—

(a) provide the offender with written details of the alleged failure,

(b) inform the offender that the offender is entitled to be legally represented, and

(c) inform the offender that no answer need be given to the allegation before the offender—

(i) has been given an opportunity to take legal advice, or

(ii) has indicated that the offender does not wish to take legal advice.

(11) The court must then—

(a) if it is the appropriate court, appoint another hearing for consideration of the alleged failure in accordance with section 227ZC, or

(b) if it is not the appropriate court, refer the alleged failure to that court for consideration in accordance with that section.

(12) On conclusion of a progress review in respect of a community payback order, the court may vary, revoke or discharge the order in accordance with section 227Z.

AMENDMENTS

Section 227X inserted by Criminal Justice and Licensing (Scotland) Act 2010 (asp 13) s.14(1). Brought into force on February 1, 2011 (subject to savings provisions in art.3(1)) by SSI 2010/413 art.2 and Sch.1 para.1.

DEFINITIONS

"community payback order": s.227A(2). A4-459.69
"progress review": s.227X(2).
"the appropriate court": s.227ZN.

GENERAL NOTE

Sections 227X to 227ZA make provision for periodic review of community payback orders and for their variation, revocation or discharge. It is a matter for the discretion of the court whether a progress review is included in the original order. The key to variation, revocation or discharge is whether the step contemplated is in the interests of justice having regard to circumstances which have arisen since the order was imposed (s.227Z(2)). A4-459.70

Applications to vary, revoke and discharge community payback orders

227Y.—(1) The appropriate court may, on the application of either of the persons mentioned in subsection (2), vary, revoke or discharge a community payback order in accordance with section 227Z. A4-459.71

(2) Those persons are—

(a) the offender on whom the order was imposed,

(b) the responsible officer in relation to the offender.

AMENDMENTS

Section 227Y inserted by Criminal Justice and Licensing (Scotland) Act 2010 (asp 13) s.14(1). Brought into force on February 1, 2011 (subject to savings provisions in art.3(1)) by SSI 2010/413 art.2 and Sch.1 para.1.

DEFINITIONS

"community payback order": s.227A(2). A4-459.72
"the appropriate court": s.227ZN.

GENERAL NOTE

See the General Note to s.227X. A4-459.73

Variation, revocation and discharge: court's powers

227Z.—(1) This section applies where a court is considering varying, revoking or discharging a community payback order imposed on an offender. A4-459.74

(2) The court may vary, revoke or discharge the order only if satisfied that it is in the interests of justice to do so having regard to circumstances which have arisen since the order was imposed.

(3) Subsection (2) does not apply where the court is considering varying the order under section 227ZC(7)(d).

(4) In varying an order, the court may, in particular—

(a) add to the requirements imposed by the order,
(b) revoke or discharge any requirement imposed by the order,
(c) vary any requirement imposed by the order,
(d) include provision for progress reviews under section 227X,
(e) where the order already includes such provision, vary that provision.

(5) In varying a requirement imposed by the order, the court may, in particular—

(a) extend or shorten any period or other time limit specified in the requirement,
(b) in the case of an unpaid work or other activity requirement, increase or decrease the number of hours specified in the requirement,
(c) in the case of a compensation requirement, vary the amount of compensation or any instalment.

(6) The court may not, under subsection (5)(b), increase the number of hours beyond the appropriate maximum.

(7) The appropriate maximum is the number of hours specified in section 227I(4)(b) at the time the unpaid work or other activity requirement being varied was imposed less the aggregate of the number of hours of unpaid work or other activity still to be completed under each other unpaid work or other activity requirement (if any) in effect in respect of the offender at the time of the variation (a "current requirement").

(8) In calculating that aggregate, if any current requirement is concurrent with another (by virtue of a direction under section 227N(2)), hours that count for the purposes of compliance with both (or, as the case may be, all) are to be counted only once.

(9) The court may not, under subsection (5)(c), increase the amount of compensation beyond the maximum that could have been awarded at the time the requirement was imposed.

(10) Where the court varies a restricted movement requirement imposed by a community payback order, the court must give a copy of the order making the variation to the person responsible for monitoring the offender's compliance with the requirement.

(11) Where the court revokes a community payback order, the court may deal with the offender in respect of the offence in relation to which the order was imposed as it could have dealt with the offender had the order not been imposed.

(12) Subsection (11) applies in relation to a community payback order imposed under section 227M(2) as if the reference to the offence in relation to which the order was imposed were a reference to the failure to pay in respect of which the order was imposed.

(13) Where the court is considering varying, revoking or discharging the order otherwise than on the application of the offender, the court must issue a citation to the offender requiring the offender to appear before the court (except where the offender is required to appear by section 227X(6)) or 227ZC(2)(b).

(14) If the offender fails to appear as required by the citation, the court may issue a warrant for the arrest of the offender.

(15) The unified citation provisions apply in relation to a citation under subsection (13) as they apply in relation to a citation under section 216(3)(a) of this Act.

AMENDMENTS

Section 227Z inserted by Criminal Justice and Licensing (Scotland) Act 2010 (asp 13) s.14(1). Brought into force on 1 February 2011 (subject to savings provisions in art.3(1)) by SSI 2010/413 art.2 and Sch.1 para.1.

DEFINITIONS

"a current requirement": s.227Z(7). A4-459.75
"community payback order": s.227A(2).
"unpaid work or other activity requirement": s.227I(1).

GENERAL NOTE

See the General Note to s.227X. A4-459.76

If it is in the interests of justice to revoke, vary or discharge a community payback order a court may do so competently. The options available to the court are set out in this section.

The imposition of a period of imprisonment or detention for other matters after the imposition of a payback order will not necessarily justify its revocation; the court should first consider the feasibility of continuing the order before imposing an alternative form of disposal. See *Robertson v HM Advocate*, 2013 S.C.C.R. 270 (Sy).

The power in subs.(5) of variation of an order can be exercised prospectively or retrospectively: see *Stewart v Dunn* [2015] HCJAC 93; 2015 S.C.C.R 443. *Stewart* underlines that when the court decides to vary an order by adding to its existing requirements it does so by means of s.227ZA below.

Variation of community payback orders: further provision

227ZA.—(1) This section applies where a court is considering varying a community payback order imposed on an offender. A4-459.77

(2) The court must not make the variation unless it has obtained, and taken account of, a report from the responsible officer containing information about the offender and the offender's circumstances.

(3) An Act of Adjournal may prescribe—

(a) the form of a report under subsection (2), and
(b) the particular information to be contained in it.

(4) Subsection (2) does not apply where the court is considering varying a community payback order—

(a) so that it imposes only a level 1 unpaid work or other activity requirement, or
(b) imposed under section 227M(2).

(5) The clerk of the court must give a copy of any report obtained under subsection (2) to—

(a) the offender,
(b) the offender's solicitor (if any).

(6) Before making the variation, the court must explain to the offender in ordinary language—

(a) the purpose and effect of each of the requirements to be imposed by the order as proposed to be varied,
(b) the consequences which may follow if the offender fails to comply with any of the requirements imposed by the order as proposed to be varied, and
(c) where the court proposes to include in the order as proposed to be varied provision for a progress review under section 227X, or to vary any such provision already included in the order, the arrangements for such a review.

(7) The court must not make the variation unless the offender has, after the court has explained those matters, confirmed that the offender—

(a) understands those matters, and
(b) is willing to comply with each of the requirements to be imposed by the order as proposed to be amended.

(8) Where the variation would impose a new requirement—

(a) the court must not make the variation if the new requirement is not a requirement that could have been imposed by the order when it was imposed,

(b) if the new requirement is one which could have been so imposed, the court must, before making the variation take whatever steps the court would have been required to take before imposing the requirement had it been imposed by the order when it was imposed.

(9) Subsection (8)(a) does not prevent the imposition of a restricted movement requirement under section 227ZC(7)(d).

(10) In determining for the purpose of subsection (8)(a) whether an unpaid work or other activity requirement is a requirement that could have been imposed by the order when the order was imposed, the effect of section 227N(7) is to be ignored.

(11) Where the variation would vary any requirement imposed by the order, the court must not make the variation if the requirement as proposed to be varied could not have been imposed, or imposed in that way, by the order when it was imposed.

(12) Subsections (4) and (5) of section 227D apply, with the necessary modifications, where a community payback order is varied as they apply where such an order is imposed.

AMENDMENTS

Section 227ZA inserted by Criminal Justice and Licensing (Scotland) Act 2010 (asp 13) s.14(1). Brought into force on 1 February 2011 (subject to savings provisions in art.3(1)) by SSI 2010/413 art.2 and Sch.1 para.1.

DEFINITIONS

A4-459.78 "community payback order": s.227A(2).

GENERAL NOTE

A4-459.79 See the General Note to s.227X.

A report is required to be obtained by a court from the responsible officer before a community payback order is made: s.227ZA(2) makes several requirements before a variation is made, including the court explaining in ordinary language to the offender the purpose and effect of each of the proposed varied requirements, the consequences of non-compliance and also any variations to progress review arrangements.

Where the court decides to vary an order by adding to its existing requirements it does so in terms of this section; s.227Z(5) above applies to variations of existing requirements.

Change of offender's residence to new local authority area

A4-459.80 **227ZB.**—(1) The section applies where—

(a) the offender on whom a community payback order has been imposed proposes to change, or has changed, residence to a locality ("the new locality") situated in the area of a different local authority from that in which the locality currently specified in the order is situated, and

(b) the court is considering varying the order so as to specify the new local authority area in which the offender resides or will reside.

(2) The court may vary the order only if satisfied that arrangements have been, or can be, made in the local authority area in which the new locality is situated for the offender to comply with the requirements imposed by the order.

(3) If the court considers that a requirement ("the requirement concerned") imposed by the order cannot be complied with if the offender resides in the new locality, the court must not vary the order so as to specify the new local authority area unless it also varies the order so as to—

(a) revoke or discharge the requirement concerned, or

(b) substitute for the requirement concerned another requirement that can be so complied with.

(4) Where the court varies the order, the court must also vary the order so as to require the local authority for the area in which the new locality is situated to nominate an officer of the authority to be the responsible officer for the purposes of the order.

AMENDMENTS

Section 227ZB inserted by Criminal Justice and Licensing (Scotland) Act 2010 (asp 13) s.14(1). Brought into force on 1 February 2011 (subject to savings provisions in art.3(1)) by SSI 2010/413 art.2 and Sch.1 para.1.

DEFINITIONS

"community payback order": s.227A(2). A4-459.81
"the new locality": s.227ZB(1)(a).

GENERAL NOTE

See the General Note to s.227X. A4-459.82

Breach of community payback order

Breach of community payback order

227ZC.—(1) This section applies where it appears to the appropriate court that an offender on whom a community payback order has been imposed has failed to comply with a requirement imposed by the order. A4-459.83

(2) The court may—

(a) issue a warrant for the offender's arrest, or

(b) issue a citation to the offender requiring the offender to appear before the court.

(3) If the offender fails to appear as required by a citation issued under subsection (2)(b), the court may issue a warrant for the arrest of the offender.

(4) The unified citation provisions apply in relation to a citation under subsection (2)(b) as they apply in relation to a citation under section 216(3)(a) of this Act.

(5) The court must, before considering the alleged failure—

(a) provide the offender with written details of the alleged failure,

(b) inform the offender that the offender is entitled to be legally represented, and

(c) inform the offender that no answer need be given to the allegation before the offender—

(i) has been given an opportunity to take legal advice, or

(ii) has indicated that the offender does not wish to take legal advice.

(6) Subsection (5) does not apply if the offender has previously been provided with those details and informed about those matters under section 227X(10) of this Act.

(7) Where the order was imposed under section 227A, if the court is satisfied that the offender has failed without reasonable excuse to comply with a requirement imposed by the order, the court may—

(a) impose on the offender a fine not exceeding level 3 on the standard scale,

(b) where the order was imposed under section 227A(1), revoke the order and deal with the offender in respect of the offence in relation to which the order was imposed as it could have dealt with the offender had the order not been imposed,

(c) where the order was imposed under section 227A(4), revoke the order and impose on the offender a sentence of imprisonment for a term not exceeding—

(i) where the court is a justice of the peace court, 60 days,
(ii) in any other case, 3 months,

(d) vary the order so as to impose a new requirement, vary any requirement imposed by the order or revoke or discharge any requirement imposed by the order, or

(e) both impose a fine under paragraph (a) and vary the order under paragraph (d).

(8) Where the order was imposed under section 227M(2), if the court is satisfied that the offender has failed without reasonable excuse to comply with a requirement imposed by the order, the court may—

(a) revoke the order and impose on the offender a period of imprisonment for a term not exceeding—
(i) where the court is a justice of the peace court, 60 days,
(ii) in any other case, 3 months, or

(b) vary—
(i) the number of hours specified in the level 1 unpaid work or other activity requirement imposed by the order, and
(ii) where the order also imposes an offender supervision requirement, the specified period under section 227G in relation to the requirement.

(9) Where the court revokes a community payback order under subsection (7)(b) or (c) and the offender is, in respect of the same offence, also subject to—

(a) a drug treatment and testing order, by virtue of section 234J, or
(b) a restriction of liberty order, by virtue of section 245D(3),

the court must, before dealing with the offender under subsection (7)(b) or (c), revoke the drug treatment and testing order or, as the case may be, restriction of liberty order.

(9A) Where under subsection (8)(a) the court revokes the order and imposes on the offender a period of imprisonment, liability to pay the fine in respect of which the order was imposed (or, as the case may be, any instalments of the fine that are unpaid on the date that the period of imprisonment is imposed) is discharged.

(10) If the court is satisfied that the offender has failed to comply with a requirement imposed by the order but had a reasonable excuse for the failure, the court may, subject to section 227Z(2), vary the order so as to impose a new requirement, vary any requirement imposed by the order or revoke or discharge any requirement imposed by the order.

(11) Subsections (7)(b) and (c) and (9) are subject to section 42(9) of the Criminal Justice (Scotland) Act 2003 (asp 7) (powers of drugs courts to deal with breach of community payback orders).

Amendments

Section 227ZC inserted by Criminal Justice and Licensing (Scotland) Act 2010 (asp 13) s.14(1). Brought into force on 1 February 2011 (subject to savings provisions in art.3(1)) by SSI 2010/413 art.2 and Sch.1 para.1.

Subs.(9A) inserted by Criminal Justice and Licensing (Scotland) Act 2010 (Consequential and Supplementary Provisions) Order 2011 (SSI 2011/25) Sch.1 para.1 (effective 1 February 2011).

Definitions

A4-459.84 "community payback order": s.227A(2).
"level 3 on the standard scale": s.225(1) and (2) [£1000].
"responsible officer": s.227C(4).
"restricted movement requirement": s.227ZD(1).
"the appropriate court": s.227ZN.

GENERAL NOTE

Sections 227ZC to 227ZD provide a mechanism for dealing with breach of community payback orders. Where it appears to the court (presumably on the basis of a report by the responsible officer) that there has been a failure of compliance, the court may issue a warrant for the arrest of the offender or cite him or her to appear before the court. Thereafter, if the court is "satisfied" that the offender has failed without reasonable cause to comply with a requirement imposed by the order the court may proceed in terms of subs.(7) or (8) of this section as appropriate. The Act does not make provision for the means by which the court may be so satisfied except that s.227ZD makes it possible for failure without reasonable excuse to be established on the evidence of one witness (presumably the responsible officer in most cases) and for failure to pay compensation to be established by a certificate from the clerk of court. In both these cases, the evidence specified will be sufficient in law but it is not said to be conclusive. Once a breach is established, the court may proceed in a number of ways. One of those ways is by varying the order to impose a restricted movement requirement in terms of s.227ZE, qv. **A4-459.85**

The distinction between circumstances justifying breach proceedings, rather than review, should be discerned. A conviction for an offence committed after the raising of a CPO certainly risks breach but if the offence pre-dated the order then a review would be appropriate; see *Laing v Procurator Fiscal Kirkcaldy* 2016 SAC (Crim) 22.

In the event of a breach of a community payback order imposed in terms of s.227A(1) or such an order allied to a fine (s.227A(4)) the offender should be sentenced of new for committing the offence which gave rise to the order. No separate sentence should be imposed in respect of the order itself [see *Russell v Harrower* [2018] SAC (Crim) 7; 2018 S.L.T. (Sh Ct) 176; 2018 S.C.C.R. 114].

Breach of community payback order: further provision

227ZD.—(1) Evidence of one witness is sufficient for the purpose of establishing that an offender has failed without reasonable excuse to comply with a requirement imposed by a community payback order. **A4-459.86**

(2) Subsection (3) applies in relation to a community payback order imposing a compensation requirement.

(3) A document bearing to be a certificate signed by the clerk of the appropriate court and stating that the compensation, or an instalment of the compensation, has not been paid as required by the requirement is sufficient evidence that the offender has failed to comply with the requirement.

(4) The appropriate court may, for the purpose of considering whether an offender has failed to comply with a requirement imposed by a community payback order, require the responsible officer to provide a report on the offender's compliance with the requirement.

AMENDMENTS

Section 227ZD inserted by Criminal Justice and Licensing (Scotland) Act 2010 (asp 13) s.14(1). Brought into force on 1 February 2011 (subject to savings provisions in art.3(1)) by SSI 2010/413 art.2 and Sch.1 para.1.

DEFINITIONS

"community payback order": s.227A(2). **A4-459.87**
"level 1 unpaid work or other activity requirement": s.227A(10).
"the appropriate court": s.227ZN.

GENERAL NOTE

See the General Note to s.227ZC above. **A4-459.88**

Restricted movement requirement

Restricted movement requirement

227ZE.—(1) The requirements which the court may impose under section 227ZC(7)(d) include a restricted movement requirement. **A4-459.89**

(2) If the court varies a community payback order under section 227ZC(7)(d) so as to impose a restricted movement requirement, the court must also vary the order so as to impose an offender supervision requirement, unless an offender supervision requirement is already imposed by the order.

(3) The court must ensure that the specified period under section 227G in relation to the offender supervision requirement is at least as long as the period for which the restricted movement requirement has effect and, where the community payback order already imposes an offender supervision requirement, must vary it accordingly, if necessary.

(4) The minimum period of 6 months in section 227G(3) does not apply in relation to an offender supervision requirement imposed under subsection (2).

(5) Where the court varies the order so as to impose a restricted movement requirement, the court must give a copy of the order making the variation to the person responsible for monitoring the offender's compliance with the requirement.

(6) If during the period for which the restricted movement requirement is in effect it appears to the person responsible for monitoring the offender's compliance with the requirement that the offender has failed to comply with the requirement, the person must report the matter to the offender's responsible officer.

(7) on receiving a report under subsection (6), the responsible officer must report the matter to the court.

AMENDMENTS

Section 227ZE inserted by Criminal Justice and Licensing (Scotland) Act 2010 (asp 13) s. 14(1). Brought into force on 1 February 2011 (subject to savings provisions in art.3(1)) by SSI 2010/413 art.2 and Sch.1 para.1.

DEFINITIONS

A4-459.90 "other relevant restricted movement order": s.227ZF(4).
"responsible officer": s.227C(4).
"restricted movement requirement": s.227ZF(1).
"specified": s.227ZF(12).

GENERAL NOTE

A4-459.91 A "restricted movement requirement" is a requirement that restricts the movement by an offender to such an extent as is specified in the terms of the requirement: s.227ZF(1) and (8). In particular, the offender may be required *to be* in a specified place at a specified time or during specified periods or *not to be* in a specified place or a specified class of place at a specified time or during specified periods: s.227ZF(2). To a large degree s.227ZF replicates some of the provisions of s.245A of the 1995 Act (restriction of liberty orders).

Restricted movement requirement: effect

A4-459.92 **227ZF.**—(1) In this Act, a "restricted movement requirement" is, in relation to an offender, a requirement restricting the offender's movements to such extent as is specified.

(2) A restricted movement requirement may in particular require the offender—

(a) to be in a specified place at a specified time or during specified periods, or

(b) not to be in a specified place, or a specified class of place, at a specified time or during specified periods.

(3) In imposing a restricted movement requirement containing provision under subsection (2)(a), the court must ensure that the offender is not required, either by the requirement alone or the requirement taken together with any other relevant requirement or order, to be at any place for periods totalling more than 12 hours in any one day.

(4) in subsection (3), "other relevant requirement or order" means—

(a) any other restricted movement requirement in effect in respect of the offender at the time the court is imposing the requirement referred to in subsection (3), and

(b) any restriction of liberty order under section 245A in effect in respect of the offender at that time.

(5) A restricted movement requirement—

(a) takes effect from the specified day, and
(b) has effect for such period as is specified.

(6) The period specified under subsection (5)(b) must be—
(a) not less than 14 days, and
(b) subject to subsections (7) and (8), not more than 12 months.

(7) Subsection (8) applies in the case of a restricted movement requirement imposed for failure to comply with a requirement of a community payback order—
(a) where the offender was under 18 years of age at the time the order was imposed, or
(b) where the only requirement imposed by the order is a level 1 unpaid work or other activity requirement.

(8) The period specified under subsection (5)(b) must be not more than—
(a) where the order was imposed by a justice of the peace court, 60 days, or
(b) in any other case, 3 months.

(9) A court imposing a restricted movement requirement must specify in it—
(a) the method by which the offender's compliance with the requirement is to be monitored, and
(b) the person who is to be responsible for monitoring that compliance.

(10) The Scottish Ministers may by regulations made by statutory instrument substitute—
(a) for the number of hours for the time being specified in subsection (3) another number of hours,
(b) for the number of months for the time being specified in subsection (6)(b) another number of months.

(11) Regulations are not to be made under subsection (10) unless a draft of the statutory instrument containing the regulations has been laid before and approved by resolution of the Scottish Parliament.

(12) In this section, "specified", in relation to a restricted movement requirement, means specified in the requirement.

AMENDMENTS

Section 227ZF inserted by Criminal Justice and Licensing (Scotland) Act 2010 (asp 13) s.14(1). Brought into force on 1 February 2011 (subject to savings provisions in art.3(1)) by SSI 2010/413 art.2and Sch.1 para.1.

DEFINITIONS

"other relevant requirement or order": s.227ZF(4). A4-459.93
"restricted movement order": s.227ZF(1).
"specified": s.227ZD(12).

GENERAL NOTE

A restricted movement requirement is a requirement restricting the offender's movements as specified. That is the generality. Subs.(2) provides that it *may* in particular require the offender to be or not to be in a specified place at a specified time or during specified periods. This implies that it may also specify other restrictions, though it is not easy to imagine what those might be. Any restriction cannot, by subs.(3), be imposed for more than 12 hours per day. Nor can it subsist for more than 12 months (subs.(7)) (or for less than 14 days, though that seems less likely to be an issue). Provision must be made for monitoring (s.227ZG) and that may include remote monitoring (s.227ZI). Breach of a restricted movement requirement may be proved in the manner specified in s.227ZK. A4-459.94

Restricted movement requirements: further provision

227ZG.—(1) A court may not impose a restricted movement requirement requiring the offender to be, or not to be, in a specified place unless it is satisfied that the offender's compliance with the requirement can be monitored by the method specified in the requirement. A4-459.95

(2) Before imposing a restricted movement requirement requiring the offender to be in a specified place, the appropriate court must obtain and consider a written

report by an officer of the local authority in whose area the place is situated on—

(a) the place, and

(aa) the suitability of the place (particularly with a view to maximising the prospect of the offender's compliance with the requirement and minimising the risk of reoffending by the offender),

(b) the attitude of any person (other than the offender) likely to be affected by the enforced presence of the offender at the place.

(3) The court may, before imposing the requirement, hear the officer who prepared the report.

Amendments

Section 227ZG inserted by Criminal Justice and Licensing (Scotland) Act 2010 (asp 13) s.14(1). Brought into force on 1 February 2011 (subject to savings provisions in art.3(1)) by SSI 2010/413 art.2and Sch.1 para.1.

Subs.(2) as amended, subs.(2)(aa) inserted, by Management of Offenders (Scotland) Act 2019 (asp 14) Sch.1(1) para.5(2) (effective 11 October 2019).

Definitions

A4-459.96 "restricted movement requirement": s.227ZF(1).
"the appropriate court": s.227ZN.

General Note

A4-459.97 See the General Note to s.227ZF above.

Section 227ZG further replicates some of the provisions of s.245A of the 1995 Act (restriction of liberty orders).

Variation of restricted movement requirement

A4-459.98 **227ZH.**—(1) This section applies where—

(a) a community payback order which is in force in respect of an offender imposes a restricted movement requirement requiring the offender to be at a particular place specified in the requirement for any period, and

(b) the court is considering varying the requirement so as to require the offender to be at a different place ("the new place").

(2) Before making the variation, the appropriate court must obtain and consider a written report by an officer of the local authority in whose area the new place is situated on—

(a) the new place, and

(aa) the suitability of the new place (particularly with a view to maximising the prospect of the offender's compliance with the requirement and minimising the risk of reoffending by the offender),

(b) the attitude of any person (other than the offender) likely to be affected by the enforced presence of the offender at the new place.

(3) The court may, before making the variation, hear the officer who prepared the report.

Amendments

Section 227ZH inserted by Criminal Justice and Licensing (Scotland) Act 2010 (asp 13) s.14(1). Brought into force on 1 February 2011 (subject to savings provisions in art.3(1)) by SSI 2010/413 art.2 and Sch.1 para.1.

Subs.(2) as amended, subs.(2)(aa) inserted, by Management of Offenders (Scotland) Act 2019 (asp 14) Sch.1(1) para.5(3) (effective 11 October 2019).

Definitions

A4-459.99 "community payback order": s.227A(2).
"restricted movement requirement": s.227ZD(1).
"the appropriate court": s.227ZN.
"the new place": s.227ZH(1)(b).

[THE NEXT PARAGRAPH IS A4-460]

GENERAL NOTE

See the General Note to s.227ZF above. A4-460

The section makes it competent for a court to consider an application from the offender to vary the terms of a restricted movement requirement to change the specified address. Before agreeing to the variation the court must consider a report as required by s.227ZH(2) of the 1995 Act.

Remote monitoring

227ZI. Section 245C of this Act, and regulations made under that section, apply in relation to the imposition of, and compliance with, restricted movement requirements as they apply in relation to the imposition of, and compliance with, restriction of liberty orders. A4-460.1

AMENDMENTS

Section 227ZI inserted by Criminal Justice and Licensing (Scotland) Act 2010 (asp 13) s. 14(1). Brought into force on 1 February 2011 (subject to savings provisions in art.3(1)) by SSI 2010/413 art.2 and Sch.1 para.1.

GENERAL NOTE

Section 227ZI applies s.245C of the 1995 Act (remote monitoring of compliance with restriction of liberty orders) to remote monitoring requirements. A4-460.2

See the General Note to s.227ZF above.

Restricted movement requirements: Scottish Ministers' functions

227ZJ.—(1) The Scottish Ministers may by regulations made by statutory instrument prescribe— A4-460.3

(a) which courts, or class or classes of courts, may impose restricted movement requirements,

(b) the method or methods of monitoring compliance with a restricted movement requirement which may be specified in such a requirement,

(c) the class or classes of offender on whom such a requirement may be imposed.

(2) Regulations under subsection (1) may make different provision about the matters mentioned in paragraphs (b) and (c) of that subsection in relation to different courts or classes of court.

(3) Regulations under subsection (1) are subject to annulment in pursuance of a resolution of the Scottish Parliament.

(4) The Scottish Ministers must determine the person, or class or description of person, who may be specified in a restricted movement requirement as the person to be responsible for monitoring the offender's compliance with the requirement (referred to in this section as the "monitor").

(5) The Scottish Ministers may determine different persons, or different classes or descriptions of person, in relation to different methods of monitoring.

(6) The Scottish Ministers must notify each court having power to impose a restricted movement requirement of their determination.

(7) Subsection (8) applies where—

(a) the Scottish Ministers make a determination under subsection (4) changing a previous determination made by them, and

(b) a person specified in a restricted movement requirement in effect at the date the determination takes effect as the monitor is not a person, or is not of a class or description of person, mentioned in the determination as changed.

(8) The appropriate court must—

(a) vary the restricted movement requirement so as to specify a different person as the monitor,

(b) send a copy of the requirement as varied to that person and to the responsible officer, and

(c) notify the offender of the variation.

AMENDMENTS

Section 227ZJ inserted by Criminal Justice and Licensing (Scotland) Act 2010 (asp 13) s. 14(1). Brought into force on 1 February 2011 (subject to savings provisions in art.3(1)) by SSI 2010/413 art.2 and Sch.1 para.1.

DEFINITIONS

A4-460.4 "monitor": s.227ZJ(4).
"restricted movement requirement": s.227ZF(1).
"the appropriate court": s.227ZN.

GENERAL NOTE

A4-460.5 See the General Note to s.227ZF above.

This section makes various provisions with respect to the functions of the Scottish Ministers, replicating some provisions from ss.245A and 245B of the 1995 Act.

Subss.(1) to (3)

These subsections provide for the Scottish Ministers to prescribe by regulation the court or classes of courts which may impose restricted movement requirements, the method of monitoring which may be used to monitor compliance with the restricted movement requirement and the class of offender who may be made subject to a restricted movement requirement.

Subss.(4) and (5)

These subsections require the Scottish Ministers to determine the person or persons responsible for monitoring compliance with the restricted movement requirement and provides for different persons to be determined for different methods of monitoring.

Subss.(6) to (8)

These subsections require the Scottish Ministers to advise the court of who is responsible for monitoring compliance with the restricted movement requirement, enabling the court to specify the relevant details on the order. The Scottish Ministers must also advise the courts if there is any change in the persons responsible for monitoring compliance, and for those courts to vary the restricted movement requirement to specify the new responsible persons, to send a copy of the varied order to the new responsible person and to notify the offender of the variation.

Documentary evidence in proceedings for breach of restricted movement requirement

A4-460.6 **227ZK.**—(1) This section applies for the purposes of establishing in any proceedings whether an offender on whom a restricted movement requirement has been imposed has complied with the requirement.

(2) Evidence of the presence or absence of the offender at a particular place at a particular time may be given by the production of a document or documents bearing to be—

(a) a statement automatically produced by a device specified in regulations made under section 245C of this Act, by which the offender's whereabouts were remotely monitored, and

(b) a certificate signed by a person nominated for the purposes of this paragraph by the Scottish Ministers that the statement relates to the whereabouts of the offender at the dates and times shown in the statement.

(3) The statement and certificate are, when produced in evidence, sufficient evidence of the facts stated in them.

(4) The statement and certificate are not admissible in evidence at any hearing unless a copy of them has been served on the offender before the hearing.

(5) Where it appears to any court before which the hearing is taking place that the offender has not had sufficient notice of the statement or certificate, the court may adjourn the hearing or make any order that it considers appropriate.

AMENDMENTS

Section 227ZK inserted by Criminal Justice and Licensing (Scotland) Act 2010 (asp 13) s.14(1). Brought into force on 1 February 2011 (subject to savings provisions in art.3(1)) by SSI 2010/413 art.2 and Sch.1 para.1.

DEFINITIONS

"restricted movement requirement": s.227ZF(1). A4-460.7

GENERAL NOTE

This section specifies the documentary evidence (in the form of statements and certificates) for proof that an offender has complied with a restricted movement requirement. Details of the presence or otherwise of an offender at the specified address at the date and time shown on the document is sufficient evidence of the facts. A4-460.8

See also the General Note to s.227ZF above.

Local authorities: annual consultation about unpaid work

Local authorities: annual consultations about unpaid work

227ZL.—(1) Each local authority must, for each year, consult prescribed persons about the nature of unpaid work and other activities to be undertaken by offenders residing in the local authority's area on whom community payback orders are imposed. A4-460.9

(2) In subsection (1), "prescribed persons" means such persons, or class or classes of person, as may be prescribed by the Scottish Ministers by regulations made by statutory instrument.

(3) A statutory instrument containing regulations under subsection (2) is to be subject to annulment in pursuance of a resolution of the Scottish Parliament.

AMENDMENTS

Section 227ZL inserted by Criminal Justice and Licensing (Scotland) Act 2010 (asp 13) s. 14(1). Brought into force on 1 February 2011 (subject to savings provisions in art.3(1)) by SSI 2010/413 art.2 and Sch.1 para.1.

DEFINITIONS

"community payback order": s.227A(2). A4-460.10
"prescribed persons": s.227ZL(2).

Annual reports on community payback orders

Annual reports on community payback orders

227ZM.—(1) Each local authority must, as soon as practicable after the end of each reporting year, prepare a report on the operation of community payback orders within their area during that reporting year, and send a copy of the report to Community Justice Scotland. A4-460.11

(2) The Scottish Ministers may issue directions to local authorities about the content of their reports under subsection (1); and local authorities must comply with any such directions.

(3) Community Justice Scotland must, in relation to each reporting year, lay before the Scottish Parliament and publish a report that collates and summarises the data included in the various reports under subsection (1).

(3A) A report under subsection (3) must be laid before the Parliament, and published, together with, or as part of, the corresponding report under section 27 of the Community Justice (Scotland) Act 2016.

(3B) The reference in subsection (3A) to the corresponding report under section 27 of the Community Justice (Scotland) Act 2016 is, in relation to a report under subsection (3) for a particular reporting year, a reference to the report under that section which requires to be published as soon as reasonably practicable after that 31 March.

(4) In this section, "reporting year" means a year ending with 31 March.

Amendments

Section 227ZM inserted by Criminal Justice and Licensing (Scotland) Act 2010 (asp 13) s.14(1). Brought into force on 1 April 2011 (subject to savings provisions in art.3(1)) by SSI 2010/413 art.2 and Sch.1 para.1.

Subss.(1), (3), (4) as amended, subs.(3A), (3B) inserted, by Community Justice (Scotland) Act 2016 (asp 10) Sch.2 para.2. Brought into force on 1 April 2017 by SSI 2017/33 reg.2(3).

Definitions

A4-460.12 "community payback order": s.227A(2).
"reporting year": s.227ZM(4).

Community payback order: meaning of "the appropriate court"

Meaning of "the appropriate court"

A4-460.13 **227ZN.**—(1) In sections 227A to 227ZK, "the appropriate court" means, in relation to a community payback order—

(a) where the order was imposed by the High Court of Justiciary, that Court,
(b) where the order was imposed by a sheriff, a sheriff having jurisdiction in the locality mentioned in subsection (2),
(c) where the order was imposed by a justice of the peace court—
(i) the justice of the peace court having jurisdiction in that locality, or
(ii) if there is no justice of the peace court having jurisdiction in that locality, a sheriff having such jurisdiction.

(2) The locality referred to in subsection (1) is the locality for the time being specified in the community payback order under section 227C(2)(a).

Amendments

Section 227ZN inserted by Criminal Justice and Licensing (Scotland) Act 2010 (asp 13) s.14(1). Brought into force on 1 February 2011 (subject to savings provisions in art.3(1)) by SSI 2010/413 art.2 and Sch.1 para.1.

Definitions

A4-460.14 "community payback order": s.227A(2).
"the appropriate court": s.227ZN(1).

Community payback orders: persons residing in England and Wales or Northern Ireland

A4-460.15 **227ZO.** Schedule 13 to this Act, which makes provision for the transfer of community payback orders to England and Wales or Northern Ireland, has effect.

Amendments

Section 227ZO inserted by Criminal Justice and Licensing (Scotland) Act 2010 (Consequential Provisions and Modifications) Order 2011 (SI 2011/2298) art.3 and Sch.1 (effective 16 September 2011, subject to transitional provisions specified in s i 2011/2298 art.4(4)).

[THE NEXT PARAGRAPH IS A4-461]

Probation

Probation orders

A4-461 **228.** [...]

AMENDMENTS

Section 228 repealed by Criminal Justice and Licensing (Scotland) Act 2010 (asp 13) Sch.2 para.17. Brought into force on 13 December 2010 (subject to savings provisions in art.3) by SSI 2010/413 (C.28) art.2, Sch.1 para.1.

Probation orders: additional requirements

229. [...] A4-462

AMENDMENTS

Section 229 repealed by Criminal Justice and Licensing (Scotland) Act 2010 (asp 13) Sch.2 para.17. Brought into force on 13 December 2010 (subject to savings provisions in art.3) by SSI 2010/413 (C.28) art.2, Sch.1 para.1.

[THE NEXT PARAGRAPH IS A4-462.3]

Probation progress review

229A. [...] A4-462.3

AMENDMENTS

Section 229A repealed by Criminal Justice and Licensing (Scotland) Act 2010 (asp 13) Sch.2 para.17. Brought into force on 13 December 2010 (subject to savings provisions in art.3) by SSI 2010/413 (C.28) art.2, Sch.1 para.1.

[THE NEXT PARAGRAPH IS A4-463]

Probation orders: requirement of treatment for mental condition

230. [...] A4-463

AMENDMENTS

Section 230 repealed by Criminal Justice and Licensing (Scotland) Act 2010 (asp 13) Sch.2 para.17. Brought into force on 13 December 2010 (subject to savings provisions in art.3) by SSI 2010/413 (C.28) art.2, Sch.1 para.1.

[THE NEXT PARAGRAPH IS A4-463.2]

Requirement for remote monitoring in probation order

230A. [...] A4-463.2

AMENDMENTS

Section 230A inserted by Criminal Justice (Scotland) Act 2003 (asp 7) Pt 6 s.46. Brought into force on 27 June 2003 by SSI 2003/288 (C.14).

Section 230A repealed by Criminal Justice and Licensing (Scotland) Act 2010 (asp 13) Sch.2 para.17. Brought into force on 13 December 2010 (subject to savings provisions in art.3) by SSI 2010/413 (C.28) art.2, Sch.1 para.1.

[THE NEXT PARAGRAPH IS A4-464]

Probation orders: amendment and discharge

231. [...] A4-464

AMENDMENTS

Section 231 repealed by Criminal Justice and Licensing (Scotland) Act 2010 (asp 13) Sch.2 para.17. Brought into force on 13 December 2010 (subject to savings provisions in art.3) by SSI 2010/413 (C.28) art.2, Sch.1 para.1.

Probation orders: failure to comply with requirement

232. [...] A4-465

AMENDMENTS

Section 232 repealed by Criminal Justice and Licensing (Scotland) Act 2010 (asp 13) Sch.2 para.17. Brought into force on 13 December 2010 (subject to savings provisions in art.3) by SSI 2010/413 (C.28) art.2, Sch.1 para.1.

Probation orders: commission of further offence

A4-466 **233.** [...]

AMENDMENTS

Section 233 repealed by Criminal Justice and Licensing (Scotland) Act 2010 (asp 13) Sch.2 para.17. Brought into force on 13 December 2010 (subject to savings provisions in art.3) by SSI 2010/413 (C.28) art.2, Sch.1 para.1.

Probation orders: persons residing in England and Wales

A4-467 **234.** [...]

AMENDMENTS

Section 234 repealed by Criminal Justice and Licensing (Scotland) Act 2010 (asp 13) Sch.2 para.17. Brought into force on 13 December 2010 (subject to savings provisions in art.3) by SSI 2010/413 (C.28) art.2, Sch.1 para.1.

[THE NEXT PARAGRAPH IS A4-467.1.1]

Non-harassment orders

A4-467.1.1 **234A.**—(1) This section applies where a person is—

(a) convicted of an offence involving misconduct towards another person ("the victim"),

(b) acquitted of such an offence by reason of the special defence set out in section 51A, or

(c) found by a court to be unfit for trial under section 53F in respect of such an offence and the court determines that the person has done the act or made the omission constituting the offence.

(1A) The prosecutor may apply to the court to make (instead of or in addition to dealing with the person in any other way) a non-harassment order against the person.

(1B) A non-harassment order is an order requiring the person to refrain, for such period (including an indeterminate period) as may be specified in the order, from such conduct in relation to the victim as may be specified in the order.

(2) On an application under subsection (1A) above the court may, if it is satisfied on a balance of probabilities that it is appropriate to do so in order to protect the victim from harassment (or further harassment), make a non-harassment order.

(2A) The court may, for the purpose of subsection (2) above, have regard to any information given to it for that purpose by the prosecutor—

(a) about any other offence involving misconduct towards the victim—

(i) of which the person against whom the order is sought has been convicted, or

(ii) as regards which the person against whom the order is sought has accepted (or has been deemed to have accepted) a fixed penalty or compensation offer under section 302(1) or 302A(1) or as regards which a work order has been made under section 303ZA(6),

(b) in particular, by way of—

(i) an extract of the conviction along with a copy of the complaint or indictment containing the charge to which the conviction relates, or

(ii) a note of the terms of the charge to which the fixed penalty offer, compensation offer or work order relates.

(2B) But the court may do so only if the court may, under section 101 or 101A (in a solemn case) or section 166 or 166A (in a summary case), have regard to the conviction or the offer or order.

(2BA) The court may, for the purpose of subsection (2) above, have regard to any information given to it for that purpose by the prosecutor about any other offence involving misconduct towards the victim—

(a) in respect of which the person against whom the order is sought was acquitted by reason of the special defence set out in section 51A, or

(b) in respect of which the person against whom the order is sought was found by a court to be unfit for trial under section 53F and the court determined that the person had done the act or made the omission constituting the offence.

(2C) The court must give the person against whom the order is sought an opportunity to make representations in response to the application.

(3) A non-harassment order made by a criminal court may be appealed against—

(a) if the order was made in a case falling within subsection (1)(a) above, as if the order were a sentence,

(b) if the order was made in a case falling within subsection (1)(b) or (c) above, as if the person had been convicted of the offence concerned and the order were a sentence passed on the person for the offence.

(3A) A variation or revocation of a non-harassment order made under subsection (6) below may be appealed against—

(a) if the order was made in a case falling within subsection (1)(a) above, as if the variation or revocation were a sentence,

(b) if the order was made in a case falling within subsection (1)(b) or (c) above, as if the person had been convicted of the offence concerned and the variation or revocation were a sentence passed on the person for the offence.

(4) Any person who is in breach of a non-harassment order shall be guilty of an offence and liable—

(a) on conviction on indictment, to imprisonment for a term not exceeding 5 years or to a fine, or to both such imprisonment and such fine; and

(b) on summary conviction, to imprisonment for a period not exceeding 6 months or to a fine not exceeding the statutory maximum, or to both such imprisonment and such fine.

(4A) [...]

(4B) [...]

(5) [...]

(6) The person against whom a non-harassment order is made, or the prosecutor at whose instance the order is made, may apply to the court which made the order for its revocation or variation and, in relation to any such application the court concerned may, if it is satisfied on a balance of probabilities that it is appropriate to do so, revoke the order or vary it in such manner as it thinks fit, but not so as to increase the period for which the order is to run.

(7) For the purposes of this section—

"harassment" and "conduct" are to be construed in accordance with section 8 of the Protection from Harassment Act 1997 (c.40),

"misconduct" includes conduct that causes alarm or distress.

AMENDMENTS

Section 234A inserted by Protection from Harassment Act 1997 (c.40) s.11.

Subs.(5) repealed by Crime and Punishment (Scotland) Act 1997 (c.48) s.62(1) and Sch.1 para.21(30) with effect from 1 August 1997 in terms of SI 1997/1712 art.3.

Subs.(4) as amended, and subss.(4A) and (4B) inserted, by Criminal Justice (Scotland) Act 2003 (asp 7) Pt 6 s.49. Brought into force on 27 June 2003 by SSI 2003/288 (C.14).

Subss.(1), (2), (7) as amended, subss.(2A)–(2C) inserted, by Criminal Justice and Licensing (Scotland) Act 2010 (asp 13) s.15. Brought into force on 28 March 2011 (for all purposes where the misconduct complained of occurred on or after 28 March 2011) by SSI 2011/178 (C.15) art.2, Sch.1 para.1.

Subss.(1), (2), (2A), (2C), (3) as amended, subss.(1A), (1B), (2BA), (3A) inserted, by Abusive Behaviour and Sexual Harm (Scotland) Act 2016 (asp 22) s.5. Brought into force on 24 April 2017 by SSI 2017/93 reg.2(1), subject to transitional provisions in reg.4.

Subss.(4A), (4B) repealed by Criminal Justice (Scotland) Act 2016 (asp 1) Sch.2 para.3(1). Brought into force on 25 January 2018 by SSI 2017/345 art.3 and Sch.1 para.1.

[THE NEXT PARAGRAPH IS A4-467.2]

DEFINITIONS

A4-467.2 "compensation offer": s.302A(1) of the 1995 Act.
"conduct": s.8 of Protection from Harassment Act 1997 (c.40).
"fixed penalty": s.302(1) of the 1995 Act.
"harassment": s.8 of Protection from Harassment Act 1997 (c.40).
"misconduct": s.234A(7).
"offence": s.307(1) of the 1995 Act.
"prosecutor": s.307(1) of the Criminal Procedure (Scotland) Act 1995 (c.46).
"work order": s.303ZA(1) of the 1995 Act.

GENERAL NOTE

Subs.(1)

A4-467.3 *Misconduct.* In terms of subs.(7), this includes conduct that causes alarm or distress.

Towards a person. In *Robertson v Vannet*, 1999 S.L.T. 1081 this expression was held to include the father of the appellant's former girlfriend when the appellant made telephone calls to her in which he threatened violence to her and her father (it being established that the father knew of the threats). In *Kergan v Dunn*, 2013 S.C.C.R. 237, it was held to include three breaches of a bail condition designed to protect the appellant's ex partner by prohibiting him from entering the block of flats where she lived. Contrast *SJS v HM Advocate*, 2016 S.C.C.R. 12, in which the appellant was convicted of threatening and abusive conduct towards his estranged wife (in contravention of s.38(1) of the Criminal Justice and Licensing (Scotland) Act 2010) in the presence of their children, who were distressed by the conduct. It was held that there is a "threshold requirement" for misconduct towards the victim and that the mere fact that the children were witnesses to the conduct did not qualify it as misconduct "towards" them.

Subs.(2)

In *S v HM Advocate* [2015] HCJAC 64; 2015 S.C.L. 840; 2015 G.W.D. 24-432 it was held: first, that s.234A(2) has a "threshold" requirement of misconduct towards the victim (at [7]); secondly, while some individuals may be affected adversely by the actions of a person who may be subject to an order, such misconduct could be regarded as harassment. However, charges against that person had to specify an offence involving misconduct towards those individuals (at [8]).

Subs.(7)

Section 8 of the Protection from Harassment Act 1997 provides that "conduct" includes speech and that "harassment" of a person includes causing the person alarm or distress. That section is invoked only for these definitions and s.8(5), which makes it incompetent for a civil court to make a non-harassment order under that Act while the defender is subject to an interdict. It does not prevent a criminal court from making an order under the present section (*Robertson v Vannet*). In the allegation of "approaching" someone named in a charge that may be taken as "nearing" that other person, and the question is the proximity of the parties at the material time: see *Harvie v Murphy*, 2015 S.C.C.R. 363 at [30], in which there had been a chance meeting between parties.

Alternative orders

Reference might be made to the Abusive Behaviour and Sexual Harm (Scotland) Act 2016 (asp 22) by which it is now competent to make sexual harm prevention orders and sexual risk orders which have, in practice, a policy intention of protecting individuals as might a non-harassment order.

Non-harassment orders: domestic abuse cases

A4-467.3.1 **234AZA.**—(1) Section 234A applies subject to this section if an offence referred to in subsection (1) of that section is one listed in subsection (2)(c).

(2) For the purposes of this section—
(a) "victim" has the same meaning as it has in section 234A,
(b) "child" has the same meaning as given by section 5(11) of the Domestic Abuse (Scotland) Act 2018,
(c) the list is—
(i) an offence under section 1(1) of the Domestic Abuse (Scotland) Act 2018,
(ii) an offence that is aggravated as described in section 1(1)(a) of the Abusive Behaviour and Sexual Harm (Scotland) Act 2016.

(3) A non-harassment order in the person's case may include provision for the order to apply in favour of any of the following, in addition to the victim—
(a) in any circumstances, a child usually residing with the person or a child usually residing with the victim (or a child usually residing with both the person and the victim),
(b) where the offence is one under section 1(1) of the Domestic Abuse (Scotland) Act 2018, and is aggravated as described in section 5(1)(a) of that Act, a child to whom the aggravation relates,

if the court is satisfied that it is appropriate for the child to be protected by the order.

(4) The court must—
(a) without an application by the prosecutor, consider the question of whether to make a non-harassment order in the person's case,
(b) after hearing the prosecutor as well as the person, make such an order unless of a negative conclusion on the question,
(c) if of a negative conclusion on the question, explain the basis for this.

(5) Here, a negative conclusion on the question is the conclusion by the court that there is no need for—
(a) the victim, or
(b) the children (if any) in mind by virtue of subsection (3),

to be protected by such an order.

(6) In the operation of section 234A along with subsection (4)—
(a) subsection (1A) of that section is of no effect (and the reference in subsection (2) of that section to an application under subsection (1A) of that section is to be ignored),
(b) further—
(i) the references in subsections (2A), (2BA) and (2C) of that section to the person against whom the order is sought are to be read as being to the person in whose case the making of a non-harassment order is being considered,
(ii) the reference in subsection (2C) of that section to representations in response to the application is to be read as being to representations on the question of whether to make a nonharassment order,
(iii) the reference in subsection (6) of that section to the prosecutor at whose instance the order is made is to be read as being to the prosecutor in the case in which the non-harassment order is made.

(7) For the avoidance of doubt, nothing in this section affects the ability to make a non-harassment order in the case instead of or in addition to dealing with the person in any other way.

AMENDMENT

Section 234AZA inserted by Domestic Abuse (Scotland) Act 2018 (asp 5) Sch.1(1)(4) para.9(2) (effective 1 April 2019 in respect of proceedings commenced on or after 1 April 2019 subject to transitional provision specified in SSI 2018/387 reg.7(2)).

Subsection (4)(a) as amended by Management of Offenders (Scotland) Act 2019 (asp 14) Sch.1(1) para.3(2) (effective 11 October 2019).

GENERAL NOTE

A4-467.3.1A It is clear from the statutory language that the test in s.234AZA is entirely different from that in s.234A (and see *Finlay v Corrins* [2020] SAC (Crim) 1). Under s.234A(2), the making of the order is discretionary, triggered by a Crown motion and involves the court being satisfied on a balance of probabilities that the order is "appropriate". By contrast, s.234AZA requires the court to make an order in any case in which there is a conviction under s.1 of the Domestic Abuse (Scotland) Act 2018 or in which the aggravation under s.1 of the Abusive Behaviour and Sexual Harm (Scotland) Act 2016 forms part of the conviction unless the court is satisfied that there is no need for the victim to be protected from the offender. Section 234AZA(4)(c) requires a judge who reaches such a "negative conclusion" to explain the basis for that conclusion. That basis requires to be rational. It is not enough that the facts do not satisfy the court that an order is necessary. Rather, there must be a basis for deciding that an order is not necessary. It is suggested that the court must be satisfied that there is some factor in play which will operate to reduce the risk of further abuse to such a level that, having regard to the provisions of s.210AB (which requires a sentencing court in a domestic abuse case to have particular regard to the aim of ensuring that the victim is not the subject of a further offence committed by the convicted person), it can be said that the order is not needed.

It is worth bearing in mind that a plea of guilty to a charge with the 2016 Act aggravation means that the appellant admits that he intended to cause the complainer either physical or psychological harm (as defined in s.1(7) of the 2016 Act) or was reckless about doing so. A conviction at trial with the aggravation involves a finding to that effect. That is made explicitly clear by s.1(2) of the 2016 Act. The aggravation is not merely a tautologous restatement of the proposition that the complainer was the appellant's partner or ex-partner. Rather, it establishes that at the time of the crime the appellant either intended to do harm or was reckless about doing harm. Many solicitors overlook that. That intention or recklessness is relevant to the consideration of a non-harassment order.

Antisocial behaviour orders

A4-467.3.2 **234AA.**—(1) Where subsection (2) below applies, the court may, instead of or in addition to imposing any sentence which it could impose, make an antisocial behaviour order in respect of a person (the "offender").

(2) This subsection applies where—

(a) the offender is convicted of an offence;

(b) […]

(c) in committing the offence, he engaged in antisocial behaviour; and

(d) the court is satisfied, on a balance of probabilities, that the making of an antisocial behaviour order is necessary for the purpose of protecting other persons from further antisocial behaviour by the offender.

(3) For the purposes of subsection (2)(c) above, a person engages in antisocial behaviour if he—

(a) acts in a manner that causes or is likely to cause alarm or distress; or

(b) pursues a course of conduct that causes or is likely to cause alarm or distress,

to at least one person who is not of the same household as him.

(4) Subject to subsection (5) below, an antisocial behaviour order is an order which prohibits, indefinitely or for such period as may be specified in the order, the offender from doing anything described in the order.

(5) The prohibitions that may be imposed by an antisocial behaviour order are those necessary for the purpose of protecting other persons from further antisocial behaviour by the offender.

(6) Before making an antisocial behaviour order, the court shall explain to the offender in ordinary language—

(a) the effect of the order and the prohibitions proposed to be included in it;

(b) the consequences of failing to comply with the order;

(c) the powers the court has under subsection (8) below; and

(d) the entitlement of the offender to appeal against the making of the order.

(7) Failure to comply with subsection (6) shall not affect the validity of the order.

(8) On the application of the offender in respect of whom an antisocial behaviour order is made under this section, the court which made the order may, if satisfied on a balance of probabilities that it is appropriate to do so—

(a) revoke the order; or

(b) subject to subsection (9) below, vary it in such manner as it thinks fit.

(9) Where an antisocial behaviour order specifies a period, the court may not, under subsection (8)(b) above, vary the order by extending the period.

(10) An antisocial behaviour order made under this section, and any revocation or variation of such an order under subsection (8) above, shall be taken to be a sentence for the purposes of an appeal.

(11) Section 9 (breach of orders) of the Antisocial Behaviour etc. (Scotland) Act 2004 applies in relation to antisocial behaviour orders made under this section as that section applies in relation to antisocial behaviour orders made under section 4 of that Act.

(12) In this section, "conduct" includes speech; and a course of conduct must involve conduct on at least two occasions.

AMENDMENTS

Section 234AA inserted by Antisocial Behaviour etc. (Scotland) Act 2004 (asp 8) s.118. Brought into force on 28 October 2004 by SSI 2004/420 (C.31).

Subs.(2)(b) repealed by Criminal Justice and Licensing (Scotland) Act 2010 (asp 13) s.52(4). Brought into force on 28 March 2011 by SSI 2011/178 (C.15) art.2, Sch.1 para.1.

Subs.(11) as amended by Criminal Justice (Scotland) Act 2016 (asp 1) Sch.2 para.3(2). Brought into force on 25 January 2018 by SSI 2017/345 art.3 and Sch.1 para.1.

DEFINITIONS

"antisocial behaviour": s.234AA(3) of the 1995 Act and s.143(1) of the 2004 Act. A4-467.3.3
"conduct": s.234AA(12) of the 1995 Act and see also s.143(2) of the 2004 Act.
"offender": s.234AA(1) of the 1995 Act.

GENERAL NOTE

Antisocial behaviour orders

Amongst the various options now available to the court at the sentencing stage is that of an antisocial behaviour order: s.234AA(1). That provision provides that the court "may, instead of or in addition to imposing any sentence which it could impose" make such an order. There are conditions to satisfy but as the offender must be at least 10 years of age when the offence was committed and the test is one of a balance of probabilities that is necessary to prevent further such behaviour then the court is left with a wide discretion: s.234AA(2). A4-467.3.4

"Conduct"

The phrase "antisocial behaviour" includes a course of conduct that causes or is likely to cause alarm or distress: s.234AA(3)(b). "Conduct" includes speech and a course of conduct must involve conduct on at least two occasion: s.234AA(12).

Antisocial behaviour orders: notification

234AB.—(1) Upon making an antisocial behaviour order under section 234AA of this Act, the court shall— A4-467.3.5

(a) serve a copy of the order on the offender; and

(b) give a copy of the order to the local authority it considers most appropriate.

(2) Upon revoking an antisocial behaviour order under subsection (8)(a) of that section, the court shall notify the local authority to whom a copy of the order was given under subsection (1)(b) above.

(3) Upon varying an antisocial behaviour order under subsection (8)(b) of that section, the court shall—

(a) serve a copy of the order as varied on the offender; and

(b) give a copy of the order as varied to the local authority to whom a copy of the order was given under subsection (1)(b) above.

(4) For the purposes of this section, a copy is served on an offender if—

(a) given to him; or

(b) sent to him by registered post or the recorded delivery service.

(5) A certificate of posting of a letter sent under subsection (4)(b) issued by the postal operator shall be sufficient evidence of the sending of the letter on the day specified in such certificate.

(6) In this section, "offender" means the person in respect of whom the antisocial behaviour order was made.

AMENDMENTS

Section 234AB inserted by Antisocial Behaviour etc. (Scotland) Act 2004 (asp 8) s.118. Brought into force on 28 October 2004 by SSI 2004/420 (C.31).

DEFINITIONS

A4-467.3.6 "conduct": s.234AA(12) of the 1995 Act and see also s.143(2) of the 2004 Act.
"local authority": s.143(1) of the 2004 Act.
"offender": s.234AB(6) of the 1995 Act.

GENERAL NOTE

A4-467.3.7 This section provides for the procedure to be adopted when making an antisocial behaviour order.

[THE NEXT PARAGRAPH IS A4-467.4]

Drug treatment and testing order

A4-467.4 **234B.—**(1) This section applies where a person of 16 years of age or more is convicted of an offence, other than one for which the sentence is fixed by law, committed on or after the date on which section 89 of the Crime and Disorder Act 1998 comes into force.

(2) Subject to the provisions of this section, the court by or before which the offender is convicted may, if it is of the opinion that it is expedient to do so instead of sentencing him, make an order (a "drug treatment and testing order") which shall—

(a) have effect for a period specified in the order of not less than six months nor more than three years ("the treatment and testing period"); and

(b) include the requirements and provisions mentioned in section 234C of this Act.

(3) A court shall not make a drug treatment and testing order unless it—

(a) has been notified by the Secretary of State that arrangements for implementing such orders are available in the area of the local authority proposed to be specified in the order under section 234C(6) of this Act and the notice has not been withdrawn;

(b) has obtained a report by, and if necessary heard evidence from, an officer of the local authority in whose area the offender is resident about the offender and his circumstances; and

(c) is satisfied that—

(i) the offender is dependent on, or has a propensity to misuse, drugs;

(ii) his dependency or propensity is such as requires and is susceptible to treatment; and

(iii) he is a suitable person to be subject to such an order.

(4) For the purpose of determining for the purposes of subsection (3)(c) above whether the offender has any drug in his body, the court may by order require him to provide samples of such description as it may specify.

(5) A drug treatment and testing order or an order under subsection (4) above shall not be made unless the offender expresses his willingness to comply with its requirements.

(6) The Secretary of State may by order—

(a) amend paragraph (a) of subsection (2) above by substituting a different period for the minimum or the maximum period for the time being specified in that paragraph; and

(b) make such transitional provisions as appear to him necessary or expedient in connection with any such amendment.

(7) The power to make an order under subsection (6) above shall be exercisable by statutory instrument; but no such order shall be made unless a draft of the order has been laid before and approved by resolution of each House of Parliament.

(8) A drug treatment and testing order shall be as nearly as may be in the form prescribed by Act of Adjournal.

AMENDMENT

Section 234B inserted by the Crime and Disorder Act 1998 (c.37), s.89 (effective September 30, 1998: SI 1998/2327).

DEFINITIONS

"offence": s.307(1) of the 1995 Act. A4-467.5
" sentence": s.307(1) of the 1995 Act.
"drug treatment and testing order": ss.234B(2) and 234C(1) of the 1995 Act as inserted by ss.89 and 90 of the 1998 Act.

GENERAL NOTE

The provisions contained in ss.89 to 95 of the 1998 Act introduced a new form of court disposal for Scottish courts, the drug treatment and testing order (referred to henceforth as a DTTO), and echo the measures applied to England and Wales by ss.58 to 60 of that Act. The Scottish measures are all inserted in the 1995 Procedure Act as ss.234B to 234J and came into force on September 30, 1998 in terms of the Crime and Disorder Act 1998 (Commencement No.2 and Transitional Provisions) Order 1998 (SI 1998/2327.) A4-467.6

It will be observed that the provisions owe much to existing procedures used in relation to probation orders, a clear signal that the object of a DTTO is rehabilitation, rather than punishment, of the offender. A DTTO is an alternative to a criminal sentence, cannot be imposed following conviction of murder, and can be for a specified period of between six months and three years duration (subs.(2)) subject to several criteria being met. A DTTO can be imposed on its own or combined concurrently with either a probation order (see s.234J(1)) or a restriction of liberty order, or combined with both such orders (implied by s.234H(3)). The court must first receive a report indicating that the offender, who has to be aged 16 years or older, abuses drugs and that his condition is amenable to treatment (subs.(3)) aimed at reducing or ending his susceptibility to misuse drugs (s.234C(1)).

Secondly, the offender must express willingness to comply with the order which will be supervised by an officer nominated by the local authority and, particularly, must consent to attend an establishment for appropriate medical treatment (as an in-patient or out-patient or both), make himself available to the supervising officer as necessary and provide appropriate samples to enable his compliance with the order, and his progress, to be monitored (s.234C(2) and (3)).

The court can only impose a DTTO once the Secretary of State has given notice that suitable arrangements have been put in place in the locale (s.234B(3)) and once satisfied that appropriate medical care facilities are available there to provide the treatment proposed (s.234B(3)). In addition to the background report which must be furnished to it, the court is empowered to require the offender to provide samples for the purpose of confirming the presence of drugs in his body (s.234B(4)). This power is intended only for use at the investigative stage; once a DTTO has been imposed, samples for monitoring compliance are got using s.234C(2) and (3) of the Act.

Subsection (6) entitles the Secretary of State to alter the length of DTTOs, which can be imposed, by Statutory Instrument and gives a broad discretion to enact transitional arrangements.

Two points are worthy of note: it is not necessary that the offence giving rise to the DTTO was itself drug-related (though that will often be so)—what matters are the offender's circumstances; secondly, subs.(3)(b) stipulates that the duty of providing a report to the court rests with the local authority within whose area the offender resides—it does not follow that any element of the DTTO has to be provided in that area. However for practical purposes, like probation, a DTTO depends upon the offender having a regular abode, a qualification which may exclude rootless offenders with drug problems unless suitable in-patient or residential facilities are available.

Section 234G provides penalties for failure to comply with the requirements of a DTTO and entitles the court to issue either a citation or an apprehension warrant to bring an offender before it.

Reference should also be made to Sch.6 to the 1998 Act which imports a number of amendments to enable DTTOs to be combined with both probation and restriction of liberty orders. Part II of the same Schedule contains provisions to deal with appeals arising from a sentence which includes a DTTO.

Requirements and provisions of drug treatment and testing orders

A4-467.7 **234C.** —(1) A drug treatment and testing order shall include a requirement ("the treatment requirement") that the offender shall submit, during the whole of the treatment and testing period, to treatment by or under the direction of a specified person having the necessary qualifications or experience ("the treatment provider") with a view to the reduction or elimination of the offender's dependency on or propensity to misuse drugs.

(2) The required treatment for any particular period shall be

(a) treatment as a resident in such institution or place as may be specified in the order; or

(b) treatment as a non-resident in or at such institution or place, and at such intervals, as may be so specified;

but the nature of the treatment shall not be specified in the order except as mentioned in paragraph (a) or (b) above.

(3) A court shall not make a drug treatment and testing order unless it is satisfied that arrangements have been made for the treatment intended to be specified in the order (including arrangements for the reception of the offender where he is required to submit to treatment as a resident).

(4) A drug treatment and testing order shall include a requirement ("the testing requirement") that, for the purpose of ascertaining whether he has any drug in his body during the treatment and testing period, the offender shall provide during that period, at such times and in such circumstances as may (subject to the provisions of the order) be determined by the treatment provider, samples of such description as may be so determined.

(5) The testing requirement shall specify for each month the minimum number of occasions on which samples are to be provided.

(6) A drug treatment and testing order shall specify the local authority in whose area the offender will reside when the order is in force and require that authority to appoint or assign an officer (a "supervising officer") for the purposes of subsections (7) and (8) below.

(7) A drug treatment and testing order shall—

(a) provide that, for the treatment and testing period, the offender shall be under the supervision of a supervising officer;

(b) require the offender to keep in touch with the supervising officer in accordance with such instructions as he may from time to time be given by that officer, and to notify him of any change of address; and

(c) provide that the results of the tests carried out on the samples provided by the offender in pursuance of the testing requirement shall be communicated to the supervising officer.

(8) Supervision by the supervising officer shall be carried out to such extent only as may be necessary for the purpose of enabling him—

(a) to report on the offender's progress to the appropriate court;

(b) to report to that court any failure by the offender to comply with the requirements of the order; and

(c) to determine whether the circumstances are such that he should apply to that court for the variation or revocation of the order.

AMENDMENTS

Section 234C inserted by Crime and Disorder Act 1998 (c.37) s.90 (effective September 30, 1998: SI 1998/2327).

DEFINITIONS

"drug treatment and testing order": ss.234B(2) and 234C(1) of the 1995 Act as inserted by ss.89 and 90 of the 1998 Act. **A4-467.8**

"offender": s.5 of the Crime and Punishment (Scotland) Act 1997 (c.48).

"local authority": s.234K of the 1995 Act as inserted by s.95(1) of the 1998 Act.

GENERAL NOTE

This section indicates that the purpose of a drug treatment and testing order (hereafter referred to as a "DTTO") is to provide the offender with a programme to curb, or end, his propensity to misuse drugs. It came into force on September 30, 1998; see generally the Note to s.234B above. **A4-467.9**

Section 234C(2) enacts that appropriate treatment may be delivered by in-patient or out-patient treatment as directed, or varied, by the treatment provider specified in the order. The treatment provider is responsible for monitoring the medical aspects, including the regime of periodic sampling for drug testing purposes—a compulsory element in all DTTOs (subs.(4)), while a nominated member of the social work department is given the general duty to oversee the offender's conduct and to provide compulsory reports on the progress of the offender to the court (s.234F(1)).

In addition to the general requirements set out in s.234B(3) above, the court has to satisfy itself that satisfactory arrangements for the form of treatment identified as necessary in the report to combat the offender's misuse of drugs are in place (s.234C(3)); to stipulate the minimum number of testing samples to be provided monthly by the offender; to set the timescale (at least initially) for reviews of the order and require the supervising officer to provide a written progress report for consideration at each review (s.234F(1)). Each report must incorporate the results of drug tests and an assessment of the offender's progress by the treatment provider.

It may be appreciated that DTTOs will draw heavily upon medical and social work resources and demand similar commitment from the offenders involved. Failure to comply with the terms of a DTTO are to be reported to the court by the supervising officer who is also empowered to seek variation or revocation of the order (s.234C(8)). The offender himself can also apply to the court for variation or revocation of the order—see s.234E as inserted by s.92 of the 1998 Act.

Requirement for remote monitoring in drug treatment and testing order

234CA.—(1) A drug treatment and testing order may include a requirement that during such period as may be specified in the requirement, being a period not exceeding twelve months, the offender comply with such restrictions as to his movements as the court thinks fit; and paragraphs (a) and (b) of subsection (2) of section 245A of this Act (with the qualification of paragraph (a) which that subsection contains) shall apply in relation to any such requirement as they apply in relation to a restriction of liberty order. **A4-467.9.1**

(2) The clerk of the court shall cause a copy of a drug treatment and testing order which includes such a requirement to be sent to the person who is to be responsible for monitoring the offender's compliance with the requirement.

(3) If, within the period last specified by virtue of subsection (1) above or (6)(d) below, it appears to the person so responsible that the offender has failed to comply with the requirement the person shall so inform the supervising officer appointed by virtue of section 234C(6) of this Act, who shall report the matter to the court.

(4) Section 245H shall apply in relation to proceedings under section 234G of this Act as respects a drug treatment and testing order which includes such a requirement as it applies in relation to proceedings under section 245F of this Act.

(5) Sections 245A(6) and (8) to (11), 245B and 245C of this Act shall apply in relation to the imposition of, or as the case may be compliance with, requirements included by virtue of subsection (1) above in a drug treatment and testing order as those sections apply in relation to the making of, or as the case may be compliance with, a restriction of liberty order.

(6) In relation to a drug testing order which includes such a requirement, section 234E of this Act shall apply with the following modifications—

(a) the persons who may make an application under subsection (1) of that section shall include the person responsible for monitoring the offender's compliance with the requirement, but only in so far as the application relates to the requirement;

(b) the reference in subsection (2) of that section to the supervising officer shall be construed as a reference to either that officer or the person so responsible;

(c) where an application is made under subsection (1) of that section and relates to the requirement, the persons to be heard under subsection (3) of that section shall include the person so responsible;

(d) the ways of varying the order which are mentioned in subsection (3)(a) of that section shall include increasing or decreasing the period specified by virtue of subsection (1) above (or last specified by virtue of this paragraph) but not so as to increase that period above the maximum mentioned in subsection (1) above; and

(e) the reference in subsection (5) of that section—

(i) to the supervising officer shall be construed as a reference to either that officer or the person so responsible; and

(ii) to sections 234B(5) and 234D(1) shall be construed as including a reference to section 245A(6) and (11).

(7) Where under section 234E or 234G(2)(b) of this Act the court varies such a requirement, the clerk of court shall cause a copy of the amended drug treatment and testing order to be sent—

(a) to the person responsible for monitoring the offender's compliance with the requirement; and

(b) where the variation comprises a change in who is designated for the purposes of such monitoring, to the person who, immediately before the order was varied, was so responsible.

AMENDMENTS

Section 234CA inserted by Criminal Justice (Scotland) Act 2003 (asp 7) Pt 6 s.47(2). Brought into force on June 27, 2003 by SSI 2003/288 (C.14).

GENERAL NOTE

A4-467.9.2 Drug treatment and testing orders may be made in terms of s.234B of the Criminal Procedure (Scotland) Act 1995 and require the offender to submit to treatment designed to reduce or eliminate drug dependency. The present section makes it possible to add a requirement for remote monitoring, much as in relation to probation orders.

[THE NEXT PARAGRAPH IS A4-467.10]

Procedural matters relating to drug treatment and testing orders

A4-467.10 **234D.**—(1) Before making a drug treatment and testing order, a court shall explain to the offender in ordinary language—

(a) the effect of the order and of the requirements proposed to be included in it;

(b) the consequences which may follow under section 234G of this Act or 42(4) of the Criminal Justice (Scotland) Act 2003 (asp 7) (powers of drugs court) if he fails to comply with any of those requirements;

(c) that the court has power under section 234E of this Act to vary or revoke the order on the application of either the offender or the supervising officer; and

(d) that the order will be periodically reviewed at intervals provided for in the order.

(2) Upon making a drug treatment and testing order the court shall—

(a) give, or send by registered post or the recorded delivery service, a copy of the order to the offender;

(b) send a copy of the order to the treatment provider;

(c) send a copy of the order to the chief social work officer of the local authority specified in the order in accordance with section 234C(6) of this Act; and

(d) where it is not the appropriate court, send a copy of the order (together with such documents and information relating to the case as are considered useful) to the clerk of the appropriate court.

(3) Where a copy of a drug treatment and testing order has under subsection (2)(a) been sent by registered post or by the recorded delivery service, an acknowledgement or certificate of delivery of a letter containing a copy order issued by the postal operator shall be sufficient evidence of the delivery of the letter on the day specified in such acknowledgement or certificate.

Amendments

Section 234D inserted by Crime and Disorder Act 1998 (c.37) s.91 (effective September 30, 1998: SI 1998/2327).

Subs.(3) as amended by Postal Services Act 2000 (Consequential Modifications No. 1) Order 2001 (SI 2001/1149) art.3 and Sch.1 para.104.

Subs.(1)(b) as amended by Criminal Justice (Scotland) Act 2003 (asp 7) Pt 5 s.42(11). Brought into force on June 27, 2003 by SSI 2003/288 (C.14).

Definitions

"drug treatment and testing order": ss.234B(2) and 234C(1) as inserted by ss.89 and 90 of the 1998 Act. **A4-467.11**

"offender": s.5 of the Crime and Punishment (Scotland) Act 1997 (c.48).

"supervising officer": s.234C(6) of the 1995 Act as inserted by s.90 of the 1998 Act.

General Note

In addition to the provisions of s.234B(2) and s.234C which specify the nature of a drug treatment and testing order and the court's powers, this section sets out the obligation of the court to explain (as it would when imposing a probation order) the effects of the order and his obligations. Subs.(2) permits personal or postal intimation of the order upon the offender, and stipulates that notification has also to be given to the treatment provider (see s.234C(1)), to the local authority and, where necessary, to the sheriff clerk or clerk of court of the court within whose jurisdiction the offender will reside while subject to the drug treatment and testing order—a situation which will arise where the order has to be transferred from the court which dealt with the original offences. **A4-467.12**

This section came into force on September 30, 1998 in terms of SI 1998/2327; see the Notes to s.234B above.

Amendment of drug treatment and testing order

234E.—(1) Where a drug treatment and testing order is in force either the offender or the supervising officer may apply to the appropriate court for variation or revocation of the order. **A4-467.13**

(2) Where an application is made under subsection (1) above by the supervising officer, the court shall issue a citation requiring the offender to appear before the court.

(2A) The unified citation provisions apply in relation to a citation under this section as they apply in relation to a citation under section 216(3)(a) of this Act.

(3) On an application made under subsection (1) above and after hearing both the offender and the supervising officer, the court may by order, if it appears to it in the interests of justice to do so—

(a) vary the order by—

(i) amending or deleting any of its requirements or provisions;

(ii) inserting further requirements or provisions; or

(iii) subject to subsection (4) below, increasing or decreasing the treatment and testing period; or

(b) revoke the order.

(4) The power conferred by subsection (3)(a)(iii) above shall not be exercised so as to increase the treatment and testing period above the maximum for the time being specified in section 234B(2)(a) of this Act, or to decrease it below the minimum so specified.

(5) Where the court, on the application of the supervising officer, proposes to vary (otherwise than by deleting a requirement or provision) a drug treatment and testing order, sections 234B(5) and 234D(1) of this Act shall apply to the variation of such an order as they apply to the making of such an order.

(6) If an offender fails to appear before the court after having been cited in accordance with subsection (2) above, the court may issue a warrant for his arrest.

(7) This section is subject to section 234CA(6) of this Act.

AMENDMENTS

Section 234E inserted by Crime and Disorder Act 1998 (c.37) s.92 (effective September 30, 1998: SI 1998/2327).

Subs.(7) inserted by Criminal Justice (Scotland) Act 2003 (asp 7) Pt 6 s.47(3). Brought into force on June 27, 2003 by SSI 2003/288 (C.14).

Subs.(2A) inserted by Criminal Justice (Scotland) Act 2003 (asp 7) Pt 8 s.60(1). Brought into force on October 27, 2003 by SSI 2003/475 (C.26) art.2.

DEFINITIONS

A4-467.14 "drug treatment and testing order": ss.234B(2) and 234C(1) of the 1995 Act as inserted by ss.89 and 90 of the 1998 Act.

"offender": s.5 of the Crime and Punishment (Scotland) Act 1997 (c.48).

"supervising officer": s.234C(6) of the 1995 Act as inserted by s.90 of the 1998 Act.

"citation": s.141 of the 1995 Act.

"appropriate court": s.234K of the 1995 Act as inserted by s.95 of the 1998 Act.

GENERAL NOTE

A4-467.15 On the application of either the offender, or his supervising officer, the court can be requested to vary the terms of a drug treatment and testing order (hereafter referred to as a "DTTO") or to revoke the order entirely. Note that while the court may continue, vary or revoke the order (or indeed specify additional requirements) after hearing parties, it must adhere to the terms of s.234B(2), i.e. it cannot alter the period of a DTTO which must be of not less than six months and not more than three years' duration.

On receipt of an application from the supervising officer for amendment or revocation of the DTTO, the court, if it considers there to be merit in the application, shall cite the offender to attend a hearing (subs.(4)). Note however that it is not mandatory to cite the offender to appear if the court intends only to delete a requirement or vary a provision of the order.

These procedures are in addition to, and distinct from, the mandatory programme of periodic reviews of all DTTOs set out in s.234F below; and came into force on September 30, 1998 in terms of SI 1998/2327; see generally the Notes to s.234B above.

Periodic review of drug treatment and testing order

A4-467.16 **234F.**—(1) A drug treatment and testing order shall—

(a) provide for the order to be reviewed periodically at intervals of not less than one month;

(b) provide for each review of the order to be made, subject to subsection (5) below, at a hearing held for the purpose by the appropriate court (a "review hearing");

(c) require the offender to attend each review hearing;

(d) provide for the supervising officer to make to the court, before each review, a report in writing on the offender's progress under the order; and

(e) provide for each such report to include the test results communicated to the supervising officer under section 234C(7)(c) of this Act and the views of the treatment provider as to the treatment and testing of the offender.

(1A) A review hearing may be held whether or not the prosecutor elects to appear.

(2) At a review hearing the court, after considering the supervising officer's report, may amend any requirement or provision of the order.

(3) The court—

(a) shall not amend the treatment or testing requirement unless the offender expresses his willingness to comply with the requirement as amended;

(b) shall not amend any provision of the order so as reduce the treatment and testing period below the minimum specified in section 234B(2)(a) of this Act or to increase it above the maximum so specified; and

(c) except with the consent of the offender, shall not amend any requirement or provision of the order while an appeal against the order is pending.

(4) If the offender fails to express his willingness to comply with the treatment or testing requirement as proposed to be amended by the court, the court may revoke the order.

(5) If at a review hearing the court, after considering the supervising officer's report, is of the opinion that the offender's progress under the order is sastisfactory, the court may so amend the order as to provide for each subsequent review to be made without a hearing.

(6) A review without a hearing shall take place in chambers without the parties being present.

(7) If at a review without a hearing the court, after considering the supervising officer's report, is of the opinion that the offender's progress is no longer satisfactory, the court may issue a warrant for the arrest of the offender or may, if it thinks fit, instead of issuing a warrant in the first instance, issue a citation requiring the offender to appear before that court as such time as may be specified in the citation.

(8) Where an offender fails to attend—

(a) a review hearing in accordance with a requirement contained in a drug treatment and testing order; or

(b) a court at the time specified in a citation under subsection (7) above, the court may issue a warrant for his arrest.

(9) Where an offender attends the court at a time specified by a citation issued under subsection (7) above—

(a) the court may exercise the powers conferred by this section as if the court were conducting a review hearing; and

(b) so amend the order as to provide for each subsequent review to be made at a review hearing.

AMENDMENTS

Section 234F inserted by Crime and Disorder Act 1998 (c.37) s.92 (effective September 30, 1998: SI 1998/2327).

Subs.(1A) inserted by Criminal Justice (Scotland) Act 2003 (asp 7) Pt 8 s.64. Brought into force on June 27, 2003 by SSI 2003/288 (C.14).

DEFINITIONS

"drug treatment and testing order": ss.234B(2) and 234C(1) of the 1998 Act as inserted by ss.89 and 90 of the 1998 Act. **A4-467.17**

"review hearing": s.234F(1)(b) of the 1998 Act.

"offender": s.5 of the Crime and Punishment (Scotland) Act 1997 (c.48).

"the appropriate court": s.234K of the 1995 Act as inserted by s.95(1) of the 1998 Act.

GENERAL NOTE

This section sets out the mandatory procedures for review of an offender's performance of a drug treatment and testing order at a hearing. Each such order must specify the timescale for hearings, a process which operates separately from the right of either the offender, or the supervising officer, to apply to the court for variation or revocation of an order (see s.234E as inserted by s.92(1) of the 1998 Act). **A4-467.18**

Prior to the due review date the supervising officer is required to furnish a written report on the offender's progress to the court. Subsection (3) stipulates that the results of all "testing requirements" made by the "treatment officer" and any observations should be incorporated in each review report. Although the offender is required to attend all review hearings until that requirement is waived by the court in terms of subs.(5), nothing expressly stipulates that he be provided with a copy of the supervising officer's report.

The court is empowered to review, and amend, the terms of the existing order's treatment or testing requirements only with the offender's consent (subs.(3)(a)). Failing consent at this stage, the DTTO must proceed unaltered or be revoked but it should be noted that different considerations apply once the offender is held to have been in breach of his order; see s.234G(2) below.

As has been mentioned the offender's attendance at review hearings is mandatory until such time as the court itself resolves that his progress is sufficiently satisfactory to vary the DTTO, and dispense with such attendance. Future reviews would then be held in chambers and based solely on consideration of the supervising officer's report.

In the event of an adverse report being placed before the court in chambers, subs.(7) entitles the court either to cite the offender to appear at a specified time or, alternatively, to issue an arrest warrant. Failure to appear at a review as specified in the DTTO (subs.(1)(c)) or in answer to a citation issued by the court following receipt of an unsatisfactory report (subs.(7)) will entitle the court to issue an arrest warrant. A failure to appear on being given due notice can be treated as a breach of the order and attract the penalties set out in s.234G(2) of the 1995 Act (inserted by s.93 of the 1998 Act). Once a DTTO has been established to have been breached the court may elect to continue the order but strictly, in those circumstances, no longer needs the consent of the offender, albeit it would seem fairly fruitless to persist with treatment in the absence of consent.

These provisions came into force on September 30, 1998; see SI 1998/2327.

Breach of drug treatment testing order

A4-467.19 **234G.**—(1) If at any time when a drug treatment and testing order is in force it appears to the appropriate court that the offender has failed to comply with any requirement of the order, the court may issue a citation requiring the offender to appear before the court at such time as may be specified in the citation or, if it appears to the court to be appropriate, it may issue a warrant for the arrest of the offender.

(1A) The unified citation provisions apply in relation to a citation under this section as they apply in relation to a citation under section 216(3)(a) of this Act.

(2) If it is proved to the satisfaction of the appropriate court that the offender has failed without reasonable excuse to comply with any requirement of the order, the court may by order—

(a) without prejudice to the continuation in force of the order, impose a fine not exceeding level 3 on the standard scale;
(b) vary the order so however that any extension of the period of a requirement imposed by virtue of section 234CA of this Act shall not increase that period above the maximum mentioned in subsection (1) of that section; or
(c) revoke the order.

(2A) Subsections (6) and (11) of section 245A of this Act apply to the variation, under paragraph (b) of subsection (2) above, of a requirement imposed as is mentioned in that paragraph as they apply to the making of a restriction of liberty order.

(3) For the purposes of subsection (2) above, the evidence of one witness shall be sufficient evidence.

(4) A fine imposed under this section in respect of a failure to comply with the requirements of a drug treatment and testing order shall be deemed for the purposes of any enactment to be a sum adjudged to be paid by or in respect of a conviction or a penalty imposed on a person summarily convicted.

AMENDMENTS

Section 234G inserted by Crime and Disorder Act 1998 (c.37), s.93 (effective September 30, 1998: SI 1998/2327).

Subs.(2)(b) as amended, and subs.(2A) inserted, by Criminal Justice (Scotland) Act 2003 (asp 7) Pt 6 s.47. Brought into force on June 27, 2003 by SSI 2003/288 (C.14).

Subs.(1A) inserted by Criminal Justice (Scotland) Act 2003 (asp 7) Pt 8 s.60. Brought into force on October 27, 2003 by SSI 2003/475 (C.26) art.2.

DEFINITIONS

A4-467.20 "drug treatment and testing order": ss.234B(2) and 234C(1) of the 1995 Act as inserted by ss.89 and 90 of the 1998 Act.

"the appropriate court": s.234K of the 1998 Act as inserted by s.95(1) of the 1998 Act.

"offender": s.5 of the Crime and Punishment (Scotland) Act 1997 (c.48).
"citation": s.141 of the 1995 Act.
"fine": s.307(1) of the 1995 Act.
"standard scale": s.225(1) of the 1995 Act.
"witness": s.307(1) of the 1995 Act.

GENERAL NOTE

Failure to comply with the requirements of a drug treatment and testing order (hereafter referred to as a "DTTO") which, it is submitted, can include a failure to appear at a review hearing as well as refusal to provide test samples or to co-operate with either the supervising or treatment officers, is an offence which can be proved on the evidence of one witness, i.e. without the necessity of corroborated evidence. Conviction attracts a monetary penalty up to Level 3 on the standard scale, and also entitles the court, as subs.(3) provides, to vary or revoke the order. In the latter case reference then has to be made to s.234H below which entitles the court to impose any other disposal competent at the time of the making of the DTTO. **A4-467.21**

Once the court has received information pointing to a breach of a DTTO it can either cite the offender to appear at a designated time or issue an arrest warrant. Plainly, when the offender subsequently appears before the court, he will be called upon to admit or deny breaching the order (a procedure already familiar in relation to alleged breaches of probation or community service orders) and, in the case of a denial, a proof will require to be fixed. The procedures for dealing with a reported breach were considered in *Tweedie v Higson*, 2002 S.L.T. 443 a case in which the purported order did not specify the particulars of those to be responsible for providing treatment.

Subsection (4) provides that any fine imposed after a breach has been established shall fall subject to the fine provisions of the 1995 Act (see ss.211 to 223), and the offence itself may be libelled as a conviction.

It is submitted, with hesitation, that once a DTTO has been breached and the court decides to vary the terms of the order (rather than revoking it), and proceeds "by order" as subs.(2) allows, it is no longer necessary to secure the offender's willingness to comply with the revised terms of the order. Nonetheless, having regard to the resource implications of DTTOs, it would seem sensible to obtain an undertaking from the offender as to his future conduct, failing which to consider the range of alternative sentencing disposals.

These provisions came into force on September 30, 1998; see SI 1998/2327.

Disposal on revocation of drug treatment and testing order

234H.—(1) Where the court revokes a drug treatment and testing order under section 234E(3)(b), 234F(4) or 234G(2)(c) of this Act, it may dispose of the offender in any way which would have been competent at the time when the order was made. **A4-467.22**

(2) In disposing of an offender under subsection (1) above, the court shall have regard to the time for which the order has been in operation.

(3) Where the court revokes a drug treatment and testing order as mentioned in subsection (1) above and the offender is, in respect of the same offence, also subject to a community payback order, by virtue of section 234J, or a restriction of liberty order, by virtue of section 245D, the court shall, before disposing of the offender under subsection (1) above, revoke the community payback order or restriction of liberty order (as the case may be).

(4) This section is subject to section 42(8) of the Criminal Justice (Scotland) Act 2003 (asp 7) (powers of drugs court).

AMENDMENTS

Section 234H inserted by Crime and Disorder Act 1998 (c.37) s.93 (effective September 30, 1998: SI 1998/2327).

Subs.(4) inserted by Criminal Justice (Scotland) Act 2003 (asp 7) Pt 5 s.42(11). Brought into force on June 27, 2003 by SSI 2003/288 (C.14).

Subss.(1) and (3) as amended by Criminal Justice and Licensing (Scotland) Act 2010 (asp 13) Sch.2 para. 18. Brought into force on December 13, 2010 (subject to savings provisions in art.3) by SSI 2010/413 (C.28) art.2, Sch.1 para.1.

[THE NEXT PARAGRAPH IS A4-467.24]

Concurrent drug treatment and testing and probation orders

A4-467.24 **234J.**—(1) Notwithstanding section 234B(2) of this Act, where the court considers it expedient that the offender should be subject to a drug treatment and testing order and to a community payback order, it may make both such orders in respect of the offender.

(2) In deciding whether it is expedient for it to exercise the power conferred by subsection (1) above, the court shall have regard to the circumstances, including the nature of the offence and the character of the offender and to the report submitted to it under section 234B(3)(b) of this Act.

(3) Where the court makes both a drug treatment and testing order and a community payback order by virtue of subsection (1) above, the clerk of the court shall send a copy of each of the orders to the following—

(a) the treatment provider within the meaning of section 234C(1);

(ba) the local authority within whose area the offender will reside for the duration of each order.

(4) Where the offender by an act or omission fails to comply with a requirement of an order made by virtue of subsection (1) above—

(a) if the failure relates to a requirement contained in a community payback order and is dealt with under section 227ZC(7)(d) of this Act, the court may, in addition, exercise the power conferred by section 234G(2)(b) of this Act in relation to the drug treatment and testing order; and

(b) if the failure relates to a requirement contained in a drug treatment and testing order and is dealt with under section 234G(2)(b) of this Act, the court may, in addition, exercise the power conferred by section 227ZC(7)(d) of this Act in relation to the community payback order.

(5) Where an offender by an act or omission fails to comply with both a requirement contained in a drug treatment and testing order and in a community payback order to which he is subject by virtue of subsection (1) above, he may, without prejudice to subsection (4) above, be dealt with as respects that act or omission either under section 227ZC(7) of this Act or under section 234G(2) of this Act but he shall not be liable to be otherwise dealt with in respect of that act or omission.

(6) Schedule 6 to this Act (Part I of which makes further provision in relation to the combination of drug treatment and testing orders with other orders and Part II of which makes provision in relation to appeals) shall have effect.

AMENDMENTS

Section 234J inserted by Crime and Disorder Act 1998 (c.37) s.94 (effective September 30, 1998: SI 1998/2327).

Subss.(1), (3), (3)(b)-(c), (4)(a), (b), (5) as amended by Criminal Justice and Licensing (Scotland) Act 2010 (asp 13) Sch.2 para.19. Brought into force on December 13, 2010 (subject to savings provisions in art.3) by SSI 2010/413 (C.28) art.2, Sch.1 para.1.

[THE NEXT PARAGRAPH IS A4-467.26]

Drug treatment and testing orders: interpretation

A4-467.26 **234K.** In sections 234B to 234J of this Act—

"the appropriate court" means—

(a) where the drug treatment and testing order has been made by the High Court, that court;

(b) in any other case, the court having jurisdiction in the area of the local authority for the time being specified in the order under section 234C(6) of this Act, being a sheriff or JP court according to whether the order had been made by a sheriff or district court, but in a case where an order has been made by a district court and there is no district court in that area, the sheriff court; and

"local authority" means a council constituted under section 2 of the Local Government etc. (Scotland) Act 1994 and any reference to the area of such an authority is a reference to the local government area within the meaning of that Act for which it is so constituted.

AMENDMENTS

Section 234K inserted by Crime and Disorder Act 1998 (c.37) s.95(1) (effective September 30, 1998: SI 1998/2327).

Subs.(b) as amended by Criminal Proceedings etc. (Reform) (Scotland) Act 2007 (asp 6) s.80, Sch. para.26. Brought into force for the Sheriffdom of Lothian and Borders on March 10, 2008 by SSI 2008/42 (C.4) art.3 and Sch. Brought into force for the Sheriffdom of Grampian, Highland and Islands on June 2, 2008 by SSI 2008/192 (C.19) art.3 and Sch. Brought into force for the Sheriffdom of Glasgow and Strathkelvin on December 8, 2008 by SSI 2008/329 (C.29) art.3 and Sch. Brought into force for the Sheriffdom of Tayside, Central and Fife on February 23, 2009 by SSI 2008/362 (C.30) art.3 and Sch. Brought into force for the Sheriffdom of North Strathclyde on December 14, 2009 by SSI 2009/432 (C.32) art.3 and Sch.1. Remainder in force on February 22, 2010 by SSI 2009/432 (C.32) art.3 and Sch.2.

[THE NEXT PARAGRAPH IS A4-467.28]

GENERAL NOTE

It is evident that drug treatment and testing orders can be imposed by any Scottish criminal court, and that for the purposes of delivering the appropriate measures of treatment and supervision, it is competent for the offender to be supervised by a local authority other than that within whose area he offended. It should not be assumed that the local authority within whose area the offender resides (and which must furnish a background report—see s.234B(3) of the 1995 Act as inserted by s.89 of the 1998 Act) will necessarily be the authority named in the DTTO; much will depend upon the availability of suitable treatment facilities, residential or otherwise. **A4-467.28**

[THE NEXT PARAGRAPH IS A4-468]

Supervised attendance

Supervised attendance orders

235. [...] **A4-468**

AMENDMENTS

Subss.(3)(a) and (4)(b) as amended by Criminal Justice (Scotland) Act 2003 (asp 7) Pt 6 s.50. Brought into force on June 27, 2003 by SSI 2003/288 (C.14).

Subss.(1) and (6) as amended, and subss.(2A) and (4A) inserted by Antisocial Behaviour etc. (Scotland) Act 2004 (asp 8) s. 144(1) and Sch.4 para.5. Brought into force on April 4, 2005 by SSI 2004/420 (C.31).

Section 235 repealed by Criminal Justice and Licensing (Scotland) Act 2010 (asp 13) Sch.2 para.20. Brought into force on December 13, 2010 (subject to savings provisions in art.3) by SSI 2010/413 (C.28) art.2, Sch.1 para.1.

[THE NEXT PARAGRAPH IS A4-470]

Supervised attendance orders in place of fines for 16 and 17 year olds

236. [...] **A4-470**

AMENDMENTS

Subss.(1) and (6) as amended by Criminal Justice (Scotland) Act 2003 (asp 7) Pt 6 s.50. Brought into force on June 27, 2003 by SSI 2003/288 (C.14).

Section 236 repealed by Criminal Justice and Licensing (Scotland) Act 2010 (asp 13) Sch.2 para.20. Brought into force on December 13, 2010 (subject to savings provisions in art.3) by SSI 2010/413 (C.28) art.2, Sch.1 para.1.

[THE NEXT PARAGRAPH IS A4-472]

Supervised attendance orders where court allows further time to pay fine

A4-472 **237.** [...]

AMENDMENTS

Section 237 repealed by Criminal Justice and Licensing (Scotland) Act 2010 (asp 13) Sch.2 para.20. Brought into force on December 13, 2010 (subject to savings provisions in art.3) by SSI 2010/413 (C.28) art.2, Sch.1 para.1.

Community service by offenders

Community service orders

A4-473 **238.** [...]

AMENDMENTS

Subs.(1) substituted by Community Service by Offenders (Hours of Work) (Scotland) Order 1996 (SI 1996/1938) art.3.

Subs.(11) as amended by Postal Services Act 2000 (Consequential Modifications No. 1) Order 2001 (SI 2001/1149) art.3 and Sch.1 para. 104.

Section 238 repealed by Criminal Justice and Licensing (Scotland) Act 2010 (asp 13) Sch.2 para.20. Brought into force on December 13, 2010 (subject to savings provisions in art.3) by SSI 2010/413 (C.28) art.2, Sch.1 para.1.

Community service orders: requirements

A4-474 **239.** [...]

AMENDMENT

Subs.(4A) inserted by Criminal Justice (Scotland) Act 2003 (asp 7) Pt 8 s.60. Brought into force on October 27, 2003 by SSI 2003/475 (C.26) art.2.

Subs.(3) as amended by Antisocial Behaviour etc. (Scotland) Act 2004 (asp 8) s. 144(1) and Sch.4 para.5(6). Brought into force on October 28, 2004 by SSI 2004/420 (C.31).

Subs.(4) as amended and subs.(4ZA) inserted by Criminal Proceedings etc (Reform) (Scotland) Act 2007 (asp 6) s.57. Brought into force on December 10, 2007 by SSI 2007/479 (C.40) art.3 and Sch.

Section 239 repealed by Criminal Justice and Licensing (Scotland) Act 2010 (asp 13) Sch.2 para.20. Brought into force on December 13, 2010 (subject to savings provisions in art.3) by SSI 2010/413 (C.28) art.2, Sch.1 para.1.

Community service orders: amendment and revocation etc.

A4-475 **240.** [...]

AMENDMENTS

Subs.(4) inserted by Criminal Justice (Scotland) Act 2003 (asp 7) Pt 8 s.60. Brought into force on October 27, 2003 by SSI 2003/475 (C.26) art.2.

Section 240 repealed by Criminal Justice and Licensing (Scotland) Act 2010 (asp 13) Sch.2 para.20. Brought into force on December 13, 2010 (subject to savings provisions in art.3) by SSI 2010/413 (C.28) art.2, Sch.1 para.1.

Community service order: commission of offence while order in force

A4-476 **241.** [...]

AMENDMENTS

Subs.(4) inserted by Crime and Punishment (Scotland) Act 1997 (c.48) s.26(2) with effect from August 1, 1997 in terms of SI 1997/1712 art.3.

Section 241 repealed by Criminal Justice and Licensing (Scotland) Act 2010 (asp 13) Sch.2 para.20. Brought into force on December 13, 2010 (subject to savings provisions in art.3) by SSI 2010/413 (C.28) art.2, Sch.1 para.1.

[THE NEXT PARAGRAPH IS A4-478]

Community service orders: persons residing in England and Wales

A4-478 **242.** [...]

Amendments

Subss.(1)(a), (2)(b) and (3)(b) as amended by Powers of Criminal Courts (Sentencing) Act 2000 (c.6) s. 165 and Sch.9 para. 177.

Subs.(1)(a), (2)(b) and (3)(b) as amended by Criminal Justice and Court Services Act 2000 (c.43) s.74 and Sch.7 para.124. Brought into force by SI 2001/919 (C.33) art.2(f)(ii) (effective April 1, 2001).

Subss.(1)(a)(ii), (iii), (2)(b), (3)(b) as amended by Criminal Justice Act 2003 (c.44) s.304 and Sch.32 para.71. Brought into force on April 4, 2005 by SI 2005/950 (C.42) art.2 and Sch.1.

Subs.(3)(b) as amended by Offender Management Act 2007 (Consequential Amendments) Order 2008 (SI 2008/912) Sch.1(1) para.11(5) (effective April 1, 2008).

Subss.(1)(a), (2)(b) and (3)(b) as amended by Criminal Justice and Immigration Act 2008 (c.4) Sch.4 para.45. Brought into force on November 30, 2009 by SI 2009/3074 subject to transitory, transitional and savings provisions as specified in 2008 c.4 Sch.27 paras 1(1) and 5.

Section 242 repealed by Criminal Justice and Licensing (Scotland) Act 2010 (asp 13) Sch.2 para.20. Brought into force on December 13, 2010 (subject to savings provisions in art.3) by SSI 2010/413 (C.28) art.2, Sch.1 para.1.

Community service orders: persons residing in Northern Ireland

243. […] A4-479

Amendments

Section 243 repealed by Criminal Justice and Licensing (Scotland) Act 2010 (asp 13) Sch.2 para.20. Brought into force on December 13, 2010 (subject to savings provisions in art.3) by SSI 2010/413 (C.28) art.2, Sch.1 para.1.

Community service orders: general provisions relating to persons living in England and Wales or Northern Ireland

244. […] A4-480

Amendments

Subs.(6)(b) as amended by Powers of Criminal Courts (Sentencing) Act 2000 (c.6) s. 165 and Sch.9 para. 178.

Subss.(4), (5) and (6) as amended by Criminal Justice and Court Services Act 2000 (c.43) s.74 and Sch.7 para.125. Brought into force by SI 2001/919 (C.33) art2(f)(ii) (effective April 1, 2001).

Subs.(3) substituted by Criminal Justice and Court Services Act 2000 (c.43) s.74 and Sch.7 para.125. Brought into force as above.

Section 244 is prospectively amended by Justice (Northern Ireland) Act 2002 (c.26) Sch.4 para.37.

Subss.(3)(a), (4)(a), (5), (6), (b)(ii) as amended by Criminal Justice Act 2003 (c.44) s.304 and Sch.32 para.72. Brought into force on April 4, 2005 by SI 2005/950 (C.42) art.2 and Sch.1.

Subss.(3)(a), (4)(a), (5) and (6) as amended by Criminal Justice and Immigration Act 2008 (c.4) Sch.4 para.46. Brought into force on November 30, 2009 by SI 2009/3074 subject to transitory, transitional and savings provisions as specified in 2008 c.4 Sch.27 paras 1(1) and 5.

Section 244 repealed by Criminal Justice and Licensing (Scotland) Act 2010 (asp 13) Sch.2 para.20. Brought into force on December 13, 2010 (subject to savings provisions in art.3) by SSI 2010/413 (C.28) art.2, Sch.1 para.1.

Community service orders: rules, annual report and interpretation

245. […] A4-481

Amendments

Subs.(5)(b) as amended by Criminal Proceedings etc. (Reform) (Scotland) Act 2007 (asp 6) s.80, Sch. para.26. Brought into force for the Sheriffdom of Lothian and Borders on 10 March 2008 by SSI 2008/42 (C.4) art.3 and Sch. Brought into force for the Sheriffdom of Grampian, Highland and Islands on 2 June 2008 by SSI 2008/192 (C.19) art.3 and Sch. Brought into force for the Sheriffdom of Glasgow and Strathkelvin on 8 December 2008 by SSI 2008/329 (C.29) art.3 and Sch. Brought into force for the Sheriffdom of Tayside, Central and Fife on 23 February 2009 by SSI 2008/362 (C.30) art.3 and Sch. Brought into force for the Sheriffdom of North Strathclyde on 14 December 2009 by SSI 2009/432 (C.32) art.3 and Sch.1. Remainder in force on 22 February 2010 by SSI 2009/432 (C.32) art.3 and Sch.2.

Section 245 repealed by Criminal Justice and Licensing (Scotland) Act 2010 (asp 13) Sch.2 para.20. Brought into force on 13 December 2010 (subject to savings provisions in art.3) by SSI 2010/413 (C.28) art.2, Sch.1 para.1.

[THE NEXT PARAGRAPH IS A4-481.2]

Restriction of liberty orders

Restriction of liberty orders

A4-481.2 **245A.**—(1) Without prejudice to section 245D of this Act, where a person is convicted of an offence punishable by imprisonment (other than an offence the sentence for which is fixed by law) the court may, instead of imposing on him a sentence of, or including, imprisonment or any other form of detention, make an order under this section (in this Act referred to as a "restriction of liberty order") in respect of him.

(2) A restriction of liberty order may restrict the offender's movements to such extent as the court thinks fit and, without prejudice to the generality of the foregoing, may include provision—

(a) requiring the offender to be in such place as may be specified for such period or periods in each day or week as may be specified;

(b) requiring the offender not to be in such place or places, or such class or classes of place or places, at such time or during such periods, as may be specified.

(2A) In making a restriction of liberty order containing provision under subsection (2)(a), the court must ensure that the offender is not required, either by the order alone or the order taken together with any other relevant order or requirement, to be in any place or places for a period or periods totalling more than 12 hours in any one day.

(2B) In subsection (2A), "other relevant order or requirement" means—

(a) any other restriction of liberty order in effect in respect of the offender at the time the court is making the order referred to in subsection (2A), and

(b) any restricted movement requirement under section 227ZF in effect in respect of the offender at that time.

(3) A restriction of liberty order may be made for any period up to 12 months.

(4) Before making a restriction of liberty order, the court shall explain to the offender in ordinary language—

(a) the effect of the order;

(b) the consequences which may follow any failure by the offender to comply with the requirements of any order; and

(c) that the court has power under section 245E of this Act to review the order on the application either of the offender or of any person responsible for monitoring the order,

and the court shall not make the order unless the offender agrees to comply with its requirements.

(5) The clerk of the court by which a restriction of liberty order is made shall—

(a) cause a copy of the order to be sent—

(i) to any person who is to be responsible for monitoring the offender's compliance with the order; and

(ii) if the offender resides (or is to reside) in a place outwith the jurisdiction of the court making the order, to the clerk of a court within whose jurisdiction that place is; and

(b) cause a copy of the order to be given to the offender or sent to him by registered post or by the recorded delivery service; and an acknowledgment or certificate of delivery of a letter containing such copy order issued by the Post Office shall be sufficient evidence of the delivery of the letter on the day specified in such acknowledgment or certificate.

(6) Before making a restriction of liberty order which will require the offender to remain in a specified place or places the court shall—

(a) obtain and consider a written report by an officer of a local authority about—

(i) the place or places proposed to be specified; and

(ia) the suitability of what is proposed (particularly with a view to maximising the prospect of the offender's compliance with the order and minimising the risk of reoffending by the offender);

(ii) be affected by the enforced presence there of the offender; and

(b) if it considers it necessary, hear the officer who prepared the report.

(7) A restriction of liberty order shall be taken to be a sentence for the purposes of this Act and of any appeal.

(8) The Secretary of State may by regulations prescribe—

(a) which courts, or class or classes of courts, may make restriction of liberty orders;

(b) what method or methods of monitoring compliance with such orders may be specified in any such order by any such court; and

(c) the class or classes of offenders in respect of which restriction of liberty orders may be made,

and different provision may be made in relation to the matters mentioned in paragraphs (b) and (c) above in relation to different courts or classes of court.

(9) [...]

(10) Regulations under subsection (8) above may make such transitional and consequential provisions, including provision in relation to the continuing effect of any restriction of liberty order in force when new regulations are made, as the Secretary of State considers appropriate.

(11) A court shall not make a restriction of liberty order which requires an offender to be in or, as the case may be, not to be in, a particular place or places unless it is satisfied that his compliance with that requirement can be monitored by the means of monitoring which it intends to specify in the order.

(11A) A court shall not make a restriction of liberty order in respect of an offender who is under 16 years of age unless, having obtained a report on the offender from the local authority in whose area he resides, it is satisfied as to the services which the authority will provide for his support and rehabilitation during the period when he is subject to the order.

(12) The Secretary of State may by regulations substitute for the period of—

(a) hours for the time being mentioned in subsection (2A) above; or

(b) months for the time being mentioned in subsection (3) above, such period of hours or, as the case may be, months as may be prescribed in the regulations.

(13) Regulations under this section shall be made by statutory instrument.

(14) A statutory instrument containing regulations made under subsection (8) above shall be subject to annulment in pursuance of a resolution of either House of Parliament.

(15) No regulations shall be made under subsection (12) above unless a draft of the regulations has been laid before, and approved by a resolution of, each House of Parliament.

AMENDMENTS

Section 245A inserted by Crime and Punishment (Scotland) Act 1997 (c.48) s.5 (in part) with (effective 1 July 1998: SI 1997/2323).

Subss.(8)-(15) inserted by Crime and Punishment (Scotland) Act 1997 (c.48) s.5 (in part) with effect from 20 October 1997 in terms of SI 1997/2323 (S.155) art.3 and Sch.1.

Subs.(1) as amended by Criminal Justice (Scotland) Act 2003 (asp 7) Pt 6 s.50. Brought into force on 27 June 2003 by SSI 2003/288 (C.14).

Subs.(5) as amended by Criminal Justice (Scotland) Act 2003 (asp 7) Pt 6 s.43. Brought into force on 27 June 2003 by SSI 2003/288 (C.14).

Subs.(6) as amended by Criminal Procedure (Amendment) (Scotland) Act 2004 (asp 5) s.25 and Sch.1 para.35. Brought into force on 4 October 2004 by SSI 2004/405 (C.28).

Subs.(11A) inserted by Antisocial Behaviour etc. (Scotland) Act 2004 (asp 8) s.121(3). Brought into force on 4 April 2005 by SSI 2004/420 (C.31).

Subs.(1) as amended by Antisocial Behaviour etc. (Scotland) Act 2004 (asp 8) ss.121(2), 144(2) and Sch.5. Brought into force on 4 April 2005 as above.

Subs.(9) as amended by Criminal Proceedings etc (Reform) (Scotland) Act 2007 (asp 6) s.80, Sch. para.26. Brought into force for the Sheriffdom of Lothian and Borders on 10 March 2008 by SSI 2008/42 (C.4) art.3 and Sch. Brought into force for the Sheriffdom of Grampian, Highland and Islands on 2 June 2008 by SSI 2008/192 (C.19) art.3 and Sch. Brought into force for the Sheriffdom of Glasgow and Strathkelvin on 8 December 2008 by SSI 2008/329 (C.29) art.3 and Sch. Brought into force for the Sheriffdom of Tayside, Central and Fife on 23 February 2009 by SSI 2008/362 (C.30) art.3 and Sch. Brought into force for the Sheriffdom of North Strathclyde on 14 December 2009 by SSI 2009/432 (C.32) art.3 and Sch.1. Remainder in force on 22 February 2010 by SSI 2009/432 (C.32) art.3 and Sch.2.

Subss.(2), (12)(a) as amended, subss.(2A)-(2B) inserted, by Criminal Justice and Licensing (Scotland) Act 2010 (asp 13) Sch.2 para.21. Brought into force on 13 December 2010 (subject to savings provisions in art.3) by SSI 2010/413 (C.28) art.2, Sch.1 para.1.

Subs.(9) repealed by Courts Reform (Scotland) Act 2014 (asp 18) Sch.5 para.39. Brought into force on 1 April 2016 by SSI 2016/13 art.2, Sch.1 para.1.

Subs.(4)(a) as amended by Management of Offenders (Scotland) Act 2019 (asp 14) Sch.1(1) para.7(3)(d) (effective 11 October 2019).

Subs.(6)(a) as amended, subs.(6)(a)(ia) as inserted, by Management of Offenders (Scotland) Act 2019 (asp 14) Sch.1(1) para.5(4) (effective 11 October 2019).

DEFINITIONS

A4-481.3 "restriction of liberty order": s.5 of the 1997 Act.
"offender": s.5 of the 1997 Act.
"stipendiary magistrate": s.5 of the District Courts (Scotland) Act 1975 and s.7(5) of the 1995 Act.
"justice": ss.6 and 307(1) of the 1995 Act.
"probation order": s.228 of the 1995 Act.
"fine": s.307(1) of the 1995 Act.
"standard scale": s.225(1) of the 1995 Act.

GENERAL NOTE

A4-481.4 This section was brought into the 1995 Act by the Crime and Punishment (Scotland) Act 1997 (c.48) s.5 and introduced the concept of curfew into Scottish criminal procedure and, more controversially, aimed to monitor compliance by means of electronic tagging. The provisions apply to adults and young offenders but not to child offenders.

Orders can stand alone or operate in conjunction with community service or probation orders or the newer drug testing and treatment orders found in s.234B of the Act but (as with these other alternatives to custodial sentences) can only be imposed with the consent of the accused. The duration of the order can be for up to 12 months and for up to 12 hours in a day, can restrict the accused's movements so as to prohibit his attendance, or require his attendance, at specified premises. Thus a restriction of liberty order (henceforth "RLO") can be used to bar an individual from licensed premises or football grounds, or to require attendance elsewhere. Monitoring of compliance is by way of electronic tagging and the broad aim has been to use the disposal as an alternative to custody in fairly minor cases with attendant cost savings; it is estimated that the costs of such schemes run at about half the level of custodial alternatives. Equally it is not competent to impose a RLO in disposing of a summary contempt of court; see *Meade v Corrins* [2020] SAC (Crim) 4 and s.155(1) above. The section does not permit one condition, at least, in combination with any RLO; it is not competent to link a community service order with any RLO, the two being distinct forms of penalty (*Macauley v Houston*, 2005 S.L.T. 834).

Note that RLOs cannot be imposed in murder cases where the sentence is fixed by law and, as with other non-custodial alternatives, must be assented to by the accused once its workings have been explained to him in plain language. Unusually, subs.(6) also requires the court to take soundings from, and consider the impact upon, persons likely to be affected by the nomination of a place where the RLO is to be served. It seems probable that this would involve consultation with social work services.

Delegated legislation

The means of enforcing the restriction of liberty orders is brought into effect by the Restriction of Liberty Order (Scotland) Regulations 2006 (SSI 2006/8) which by reg.2 came into force on 16 April 2006.

Monitoring of restriction of liberty orders

245B.—(1) Where the Secretary of State, in regulations made under section 245A(8) of this Act, empowers a court or a class of court to make restriction of liberty orders he shall notify the court or each of the courts concerned of the person or class or description of persons who may be designated by that court for the purpose of monitoring an offender's compliance with any such order. A4-481.5

(2) A court which makes a restriction of liberty order in respect of an offender shall include provision in the order for making a person notified by the Secretary of State under subsection (1) above, or a class or description of persons so notified, responsible for the monitoring of the offender's compliance with it.

(3) Where the Secretary of State changes the person or class or description of persons notified by him under subsection (1) above, any court which has made a restriction of liberty order shall, if necessary, vary the order accordingly and shall notify the variation to the offender.

AMENDMENTS

Section 245B inserted by Crime and Punishment (Scotland) Act 1997 (c.48) s.5 (effective 1 July 1998: SI 1997/2323).

GENERAL NOTE

s.245B

In addition to his general regulatory duties set out in s.245A(10), the Secretary of State is required to intimate to any court empowered to make restriction of liberty orders the particulars of the individual person or category of persons who shall monitor offenders' compliance with orders. This provision would permit the nomination of a named individual or a generic description, say, employees of an authorised monitoring organisation. A4-481.5.1

In the event of a change of monitor it is the court's responsibility to notify the offender of this alteration. Observe that s.254B is not explicit as to how such notification is to be effected but, it is suggested, that guidance may be had from s.254A(6) above. It is submitted that although subs.(3) refers to "variation" of the order this is a quite distinct procedure from variation of an order as set out in s.245E: in the former case the court simply intimates a change of monitor to an offender without any court hearing.

[THE NEXT PARAGRAPH IS A4-481.6]

Remote monitoring

245C.—(1) The Secretary of State may make such arrangements, including contractual arrangements, as he considers appropriate with such persons, whether legal or natural, as he thinks fit for the remote monitoring of the compliance of offenders with restriction of liberty orders, and different arrangements may be made in relation to different areas or different forms of remote monitoring. A4-481.6

(2) A court making a restriction of liberty order which is to be monitored remotely may include in the order a requirement that the offender—

(a) shall, either continuously or for such periods as may be specified, wear or carry a device for the purpose of enabling the remote monitoring of his compliance with the order to be carried out, and

(b) shall not tamper with or intentionally damage the device or knowingly allow it to be tampered with or intentionally damaged.

(3) The Secretary of State shall by regulations specify devices which may be used for the purpose of remotely monitoring the compliance of an offender with the requirements of a restriction of liberty order.

(4) Regulations under this section shall be made by statutory instrument subject to annulment in pursuance of a resolution of either House of Parliament.

AMENDMENTS

Section 245C inserted by Crime and Punishment (Scotland) Act 1997 (c.48) s.5 (effective July 1, 1998: SI 1997/2323).

Subs.(2) as amended by Criminal Procedure (Amendment) (Scotland) Act 2004 (asp 5) s.25 and Sch.1 para.36. Brought into force on October 4, 2004 by SSI 2004/405 (C.28).

GENERAL NOTE

s.245C

A4-481.7 This section empowers the Secretary of State to select contractors to carry out electronic tagging of offenders and remote monitoring, and to designate the types of electronic devices which may be placed on the person of offenders.

Delegated legislation

The means of enforcing the restriction of liberty orders is brought into effect by the Restriction of Liberty Order (Scotland) Regulations 2006 (SSI 2006/8) which by reg.2 came into force on April 16, 2006.

Combination of restriction of liberty order with other orders

A4-481.8 **245D.**—(1) Subsection (3) applies where the court—

(a) intends to make a restriction of liberty order under section 245A(1) of this Act; and

(b) considers it expedient that the offender should also be subject to

(i) in the case of an offender who is under 16 years of age, a community payback order imposed under section 227A(1) of this Act

(ii) in the case of an offender who is 16 years of age or more, a community payback order imposed under section 227A(1) of this Act or a drug treatment and testing order made under section 234B(2) of this Act.

(2) In deciding whether it is expedient to make a community payback order or drug treatment and testing order by virtue of paragraph (b) of subsection (1) above, the court shall—

(a) have regard to the circumstances, including the nature of the offence and the character of the offender; and

(b) obtain a report as to the circumstances and character of the offender.

(3) Where this subsection applies, the court, notwithstanding sections 234(2) and 245A(1) of this Act, may make a restriction of liberty order and

(a) in the case of an offender who is under 16 years of age, a community payback order;

(b) in the case of an offender who is 16 years of age or more, either a community payback order or a drug treatment and testing order.

(4) Where the court makes a restriction of liberty order and a community payback order by virtue of subsection (3) above, the clerk of court shall send a copy of each order to—

(a) any person responsible for monitoring the offender's compliance with the restriction of liberty order; and

(b) the local authority within whose area the offender will reside for the duration of each order.

(5) Where the court makes a restriction of liberty order and a drug treatment and testing order by virtue of subsection (3) above, the clerk of court shall send a copy of each order to—

(a) any person responsible for monitoring the offender's compliance with the restriction of liberty order;

(b) the treatment provider, within the meaning of section 234C(1) of this Act; and

(c) the officer of the local authority who is appointed or assigned to be the supervising officer under section 234C(6) of this Act.

(6) […]

(7) Where the offender by an act or omission fails to comply with a requirement of an order made by virtue of subsection (3) above—

(a) if the failure relates to a requirement imposed by a community payback order and is dealt with under section 227ZC(7)(d) of this Act, the court may, in addition, exercise the powers conferred by section 245F(2) of this Act in relation to the restriction of liberty order;

(b) if the failure relates to a requirement contained in a drug treatment and testing order and is dealt with under section 234G(2)(b) of this Act, the court may, in addition, exercise the powers conferred by section 245F(2)(b) of this Act in relation to the restriction of liberty order; and

(c) if the failure relates to a requirement contained in a restriction of liberty order and is dealt with under section 245F(2)(b) of this Act, the court may, in addition, exercise the powers conferred by section 227ZC(7)(d) of this Act in relation to a community payback order and by section 234G(2)(b) of this Act in relation to a drug treatment and testing order to which, in either case, the offender is subject by virtue of subsection (3) above.

(8) In any case to which this subsection applies, the offender may, without prejudice to subsection (7) above, be dealt with as respects that case under section 227ZC or, as the case may be, section 234G or section 245F(2) of this Act but he shall not be liable to be otherwise dealt with as respects that case.

(9) Subsection (8) applies in a case where—

(a) the offender by an act or omission fails to comply with both a requirement contained in a restriction of liberty order and in a community payback order to which he is subject by virtue of subsection (3) above;

(b) the offender by an act or omission fails to comply with both a requirement contained in a restriction of liberty order and in a drug treatment and testing order to which he is subject by virtue of subsection (3) above;

(c) […]

AMENDMENTS

Section 245D inserted by Crime and Punishment (Scotland) Act 1997 (c.48) s.5 (effective July 1, 1998: SI 1997/2323).

Section 245D as substituted by Crime and Disorder Act 1998 (c.37) s.94 and Sch.6 para.3. Brought into force on 30 September 1998 by SI 1998/2327 (C.53).

Subsection (1)(b) as amended, and subss.(1)(b)(i), (3)(a), (b) inserted, by Antisocial Behaviour etc. (Scotland) Act 2004 (asp 8) s.144(1), Sch.4 para.5(7). Brought into force on 4 April 2005 by SSI 2004/420 (C.31).

Subsections (1)(b), (2), (3), (3)(a), (3)(b), (4), (4)(b), (7)(a), (b), (c), (8), (9)(a) as amended, subss.(6), (9)(c) repealed, by Criminal Justice and Licensing (Scotland) Act 2010 (asp 13) Sch.2 para.22. Brought into force on 13 December 2010 (subject to savings provisions in art.3) by SSI 2010/413 (C.28) art.2 Sch.1 para.1.

GENERAL NOTE

s.245D

The well-established principle that a probation order is an alternative to sentence is adhered to in s.228(1) of the 1995 Act but, practically, is considerably eroded in the current Act. For the purposes of an automatic sentence under ss.1 and 2 of the Act, probation, following conviction of a qualifying offence, is viewed no differently from any other sentencing disposal. A restriction of liberty order can be imposed in conjunction with other non-custodial disposals, including probation, and is held to be a sentence (s.245A(10)). It has already been noted that the procedures which a court must follow before imposing a restriction of liberty order (s.245A(4)) draw heavily upon the existing practices in relation to probation orders, albeit additional conditions have to be met before a tagging order can be initiated. Where a court opts to impose a probation order along with a restriction of liberty order it imposes two separate orders and thus, must specify both the person to be responsible for operating remote monitoring of the offender and the local authority responsible for supervising probation. It will be recalled that a restriction of liberty order can only subsist for a year (s.245A(3)) whereas a probation order can exceptionally last up to three years from the date of the order. A4-481.9

These dual orders inevitably create difficulty when one or other order, or both, needs to be breached or varied. Subsection (3) enacts that where a "linked" probation order is held not to have been complied with, the court may also vary the RLO but, it is postulated that it will then be necessary to ensure that the RLO complies with the time limits laid out in s.245A(3). Similarly where a "linked" RLO is varied following non-compliance, the court is also empowered to call up and vary the terms of the concurrent probation order. The provisions of subs.(3) do not apply to breaches of unassociated probation and restriction of liberty orders which contain the same requirements; these are dealt with once only in accordance with subs.(4), thus avoiding double jeopardy.

Further provision about multiple orders

245DA.—(1) Subsection (2) applies where the court—

(a) makes any of the listed orders in relation to an offender, and
(b) knows that the offender is already subject to another of the listed orders.

The clerk of court must send a copy of whichever of the listed orders is then made to—

(a) any person responsible for monitoring the offender's compliance with whichever of the other listed orders the offender is already subject to (so far as the person's identity can reasonably be ascertained), and
(b) the local authority within whose area the offender resides.

The listed orders are—

(a) a restriction of liberty order
(b) a community payback order,
(c) a drug treatment and testing order.

(4)

In the listed orders, the reference to a community payback order does not include such an order if imposed under section 227M(2).

AMENDMENTS

Section 245DA inserted by Management of Offenders (Scotland) Act 2019 (asp 14) Sch.1(1) para.4(2) (effective 11 October 2019).

Variation of restriction of liberty order

A4-481.10 **245E.**—(1) Where a restriction of liberty order is in force either the offender or any person responsible for monitoring his compliance with the order may—

(a) except in a case to which paragraph (b) below applies, apply to the court which made the order, or
(b) where a copy of the order was, under section 245A(5)(a)(ii) of this Act or subsection (7)(a) below, sent to the clerk of a different court, apply to that different court (or, if there has been more than one such sending, the different court to which such a copy has most recently been so sent),

for a review of it.

(2) On an application made under subsection (1) above, and after hearing both the offender and any person responsible for monitoring his compliance with the order, the court may by order, if it appears to it to be in the interests of justice to do so—

(a) vary the order by—
   (i) amending or deleting any of its requirements;
   (ii) inserting further requirements; or
   (iii) subject to subsection (3) of section 245A of this Act, increasing the period for which the order has to run; or
(b) revoke the order.

(3) Where the court, on the application of a person other than the offender, proposes to—

(a) exercise the power conferred by paragraph (a) of subsection (2) above to vary (otherwise than by deleting a requirement) a restriction of liberty order, it shall issue a citation requiring the offender to appear before the court and section 245A(4) shall apply to the variation of such an order as it applies to the making of an order; and

(b) exercise the power conferred by subsection (2)(b) above to revoke such an order and deal with the offender under section 245G of this Act, it shall issue a citation requiring him to appear before the court.

(3A) The unified citation provisions apply in relation to a citation under this section as they apply in relation to a citation under section 216(3)(a) of this Act.

(4) If an offender fails to appear before the court after having been cited in accordance with subsection (3) above, the court may issue a warrant for his arrest.

(4A) Before varying a restriction of liberty order so as to require the offender to remain in a specified place or places or so as to specify a different place or different places in which the offender is to remain, the court shall—

(a) obtain and consider a written report by an officer of a local authority about—

(i) the place or places proposed to be specified, and

(ia) the suitability of what is proposed (particularly with a view to maximising the prospect of the offender's compliance with the order and minimising the risk of reoffending by the offender);

(ii) the attitude of persons likely to be affected by any enforced presence there of the offender; and

(b) if it considers it necessary, hear the officer who prepared the report.

(5) Where a reason for an application by the offender under subsection (1) above is that he proposes to reside in a place outwith the jurisdiction of the court to which that application is made, and the court is satisfied that suitable arrangements can be made, in the district where that place is, for monitoring his compliance with the order it may—

(a) vary the order to permit or make practicable such arrangements; and

(b) where the change in residence necessitates or makes desirable a change in who is designated for the purpose of such monitoring, vary the order accordingly.

(6) Before varying a restriction of liberty order for the reason mentioned in subsection (5) above, the court shall—

(a) if the order will require the offender to remain in a specified place or in specified places—

(i) obtain and consider a report by an officer of a local authority about the same matters as are to be included in a report under subsection (4A)(a);

(ii) if it considers it necessary, hear the officer who prepared the report; and

(b) satisfy itself that his compliance with that requirement can be monitored by the means of monitoring specified, or which it intends to specify, in the order.

(7) Where a restriction of liberty order is varied as is mentioned in subsection (5) above, the clerk of the court shall send a copy of the order as so varied to—

(a) the clerk of a court within whose jurisdiction the place of proposed residence is;

(b) the person who, immediately before the order was varied, was responsible for monitoring the person's compliance with it; and

(c) the person who, in consequence of the variation, is to have that responsibility.

(8) If, in relation to an application made for such reason as is mentioned in subsection (5) above, the court is not satisfied as is mentioned in that subsection, it may—

(a) refuse the application; or
(b) revoke the order.

AMENDMENTS

Section 245E inserted by Crime and Punishment (Scotland) Act 1997 (c.48) s.5 (effective July 1, 1998: SI 1997/2323).

Subs.(1) as amended, and subss.(5)-(8) inserted, by Criminal Justice (Scotland) Act 2003 (asp 7) Pt 6 s.43. Brought into force on June 27, 2003 by SSI 2003/288 (C.14).

Subs.(3A) inserted by Criminal Justice (Scotland) Act 2003 (asp 7) Pt 8 s.60. Brought into force on October 27, 2003 by SSI 2003/475 (C.26) art.2.

Subs.(4A) inserted, and subs.(6) as amended, by Criminal Procedure (Amendment) (Scotland) Act 2004 (asp 5) s.25 and Sch.1 para.37. Brought into force on October 4, 2004 by SSI 2004/405 (C.28).

Subs.(1)(b) as amended by Antisocial Behaviour etc. (Scotland) Act 2004 (asp 8) s.144(1), Sch.4 para.5(8). Brought into force on April 4, 2005 by SSI 2004/420 (C.31).

Subs.(4A)(a) and (6)(a)(i) as amended, subs.(4A)(a)(ia) inserted, by Management of Offenders (Scotland) Act 2019 (asp 14) Sch.1(1) para.5(5) (effective 11 October 2019).

GENERAL NOTE

s.245E

A4-481.11 During the currency of a restriction of liberty order it is open to both the offender and his monitoring supervisor to apply to the court for its review. As was noted at s.245B(3) it is not necessary to make an application for review when all that is sought is variation of the particulars of the monitoring supervisor. (The court has its own intrinsic power to deal with alleged failures to comply with the terms of an RLO in s.245F below).

Where application is made by the supervisor for a purpose other than revocation of the order or deletion of a requirement, subs.(3)(a) makes it clear that it is necessary to specify what variation is proposed. Thereafter the court, if it considers that alteration of the order could be in the interests of justice, shall cite the offender to appear before it; on varying the order the court is obliged to comply with s.245A(5) and explain the effects plainly to the offender.

If the supervisor seeks revocation of the RLO, the court if satisfied that this in the interests of justice, shall issue a citation ordering the offender to appear. Failure to appear after being duly cited will entitle the court to issue an apprehension warrant (s.245E(4)).

At the review hearing the court requires to hear both parties and is only obliged to vary the order if it is felt to be in the interests of justice. In that event the RLO can be revoked or altered by adding to, amending or deleting requirements but subject to the requirements set out in s.245A(3) that it must be completed in a 12 month period—six months in the case of a child offender.

On revocation of the RLO the court can pronounce any other disposal competent at the time the order was made but is obliged to take account of the length of time for which the RLO operated. Where dual tagging and probation orders had been imposed on the offender, the court when revoking the RLO has also to discharge the probation order (s.245G below).

Breach of restriction of liberty order

A4-481.12 **245F.**—(1) If at any time when a restriction of liberty order is in force it appears—

(a) except in a case to which paragraph (b) below applies, to the court which made the order, or
(b) where a copy of the order was, under section 245A(5)(a)(ii) or 245E(7)(a) of this Act, sent to the clerk of a different court, to that different court (or, if there has been more than one such sending, the different court to which such a copy has most recently been so sent),

that the offender has failed to comply with any of the requirements of the order the court in question may issue a citation requiring the offender to appear before the it at such time as may be specified in the citation or, if it appears to that court to be appropriate, it may issue a warrant for the arrest of the offender.

(1A) The unified citation provisions apply in relation to a citation under this section as they apply in relation to a citation under section 216(3)(a) of this Act.

(2) If it is proved to the satisfaction of that court that the offender has failed without reasonable excuse to comply with any of the requirements of the order it may by order—

(a) without prejudice to the continuance in force of the order, impose a fine not exceeding level 3 on the standard scale;

(b) vary the restriction of liberty order; or

(c) revoke that order.

(2A) For the purposes of subsection (2) above, evidence of one witness shall be sufficient evidence.

(3) A fine imposed under this section in respect of a failure to comply with the requirements of a restriction of liberty order shall be deemed for the purposes of any enactment to be a sum adjudged to be paid by or in respect of a conviction or a penalty imposed on a person summarily convicted.

(4) Where a court varies a restriction of liberty order under subsection (2) above it may do so in any of the ways mentioned in paragraph (a) of section 245E(2) of this Act.

AMENDMENTS

Section 245F inserted by Crime and Punishment (Scotland) Act 1997 (c.48) s.5 (effective July 1, 1998: SI 1997/2323).

Subss.(1), (2) and (4) as amended by Criminal Justice (Scotland) Act 2003 (asp 7) Pt 6 s.43. Brought into force on June 27, 2003 by SSI 2003/288 (C.14).

Subs.(1A) inserted by Criminal Justice (Scotland) Act 2003 (asp 7) Pt 8 s.60. Brought into force on October 27, 2003 by SSI 2003/475 (C.26) art.2.

Subs.(2A) inserted by Criminal Proceedings etc (Reform) (Scotland) Act 2007 (asp 6) s.58. Brought into force on December 10, 2007 by SSI 2007/479 (C.40) art.3 and Sch.

GENERAL NOTE

s.245F

The court's own powers to initiate breach proceedings are contained in this section. It will be noted that s.245E deals with the rights of both the offender and the monitoring supervisor to seek review of the terms of an order. Where the court has reason to believe that the offender has failed to comply with the terms of the order, it may cite him or issue an arrest warrant. A4-481.13

Once it is proved or admitted that a breach of a requirement has occurred, the court may impose a fine up to level 3, before resolving whether to continue or revoke the order or vary it in any of the ways specified in s.245E(2)(a) to (c). Any fine is governed by the provisions of Pt XI of the 1995 Act.

Subs.(2)

In *Whitham v HM Advocate*, 2013 S.C.C.R. 612, it was held that a person who is arrested and kept in custody has a reasonable excuse for not being within his domicile address during the specified periods.

Disposal on revocation of restriction of liberty order

245G.—(1) Where the court revokes a restriction of liberty order under section 245E(2)(b) or 245F(2) of this Act, it may dispose of the offender in any way which would have been competent at the time when the order was made, but in so doing the court shall have regard to the time for which the order has been in operation. A4-481.14

(2) Where the court revokes a restriction of liberty order as mentioned in subsection (1) above, and the offender is, in respect of the same offence, also subject to a community payback order or a drug treatment and testing order, by virtue of section 245D(3), it shall before disposing of the offender under subsection (1) above, revoke the community payback order or drug treatment and testing order.

(3) Where the court orders a community payback order or a drug treatment and testing order revoked the clerk of the court shall forthwith give copies of that order to the persons mentioned in subsection (4) or, as the case may be, (5) of section 245D of this Act.

(4) […]

Amendments

Section 245G inserted by Crime and Punishment (Scotland) Act 1997 (c.48) s.5 (effective July 1, 1998: SI 1997/2323).

Section 245G as amended by Crime and Disorder Act 1998 (c.37) s.94 and Sch.6 para.3. Brought into force on September30, 1998 by SI 1998/2327 (C.53).

Subs.(2) as amended by Antisocial Behaviour etc. (Scotland) Act 2004 (asp 8) s.144(1), Sch.4 para.5(9). Brought into force on April 4, 2005 by SSI 2004/420 (C.31).

Subss.(2), (3) as amended, and subs.(4) repealed, by Criminal Justice and Licensing (Scotland) Act 2010 (asp 13) Sch.2 para.23. Brought into force on December 13, 2010 (subject to savings provisions in art.3) by SSI 2010/413 (C.28) art.2, Sch.1 para.1.

General Note

s.245G

A4-481.15 On revocation of an RLO the court can dispose of the offender's case in any way competent at the time of the imposition of the order. In cases where an RLO has been initiated in association with a probation order, the court when revoking the RLO must also discharge the probation order.

When revoking an order and taking account of the period during which it operated, the court need not limit itself to an arithmetical calculation of the order's duration before it was breached; a qualitative assessment of the accused's compliance and performance can also be appropriate [*Flannigan v Orr* [2018] SAC (Crim) 17 at para.11].

Documentary evidence in proceedings under section 245F

A4-481.16 **245H.**—(1) Evidence of the presence or absence of the offender at a particular place at a particular time may, subject to the provisions of this section, be given by the production of a document or documents bearing to be—

(a) a statement automatically produced by a device specified in regulations made under section 245C of this Act, by which the offender's whereabouts were remotely monitored; and

(b) a certificate signed by a person nominated for the purpose of this paragraph by the Secretary of State that the statement relates to the whereabouts of the offender at the dates and times shown in the statement.

(2) The statement and certificate mentioned in subsection (1) above shall, when produced at a hearing, be sufficient evidence of the facts set out in them.

(3) Neither the statement nor the certificate mentioned in subsection (1) above shall be admissible in evidence unless a copy of both has been served on the offender prior to the hearing and, without prejudice to the foregoing, where it appears to the court that the offender has had insufficient notice of the statement or certificate, it may adjourn a hearing or make any order which it thinks appropriate in the circumstances.

Amendments

Section 245H inserted by Crime and Punishment (Scotland) Act 1997 (c.48) s.5 (effective 1 July 1998: SI 1997/2323).

Subs.(1)(b) as amended by Antisocial Behaviour etc. (Scotland) Act 2004 (asp 8) s.144(1), Sch.4 para.5(10). Brought into force on 4 April 2005 by SSI 2004/420 (C.31).

General Note

s.245H

A4-481.17 This section provides for a certificated statement showing the presence or absence of the offender at a specified place on a specific occasion to be used as evidence in proceedings.

The statement, automatically generated by an approved monitoring device and certified by an authorised official, will be sufficient evidence if it has been served along with the certificate upon the offender prior to the court hearing. The court may adjourn the hearing to allow sufficient time for the offender to consider the material laid before him.

Procedure on variation or revocation of restriction of liberty order

A4-481.18 **245I.** Where a court exercises any power conferred by sections 232(3A), 245E(2) or 245F(2)(b) or (c) of this Act, the clerk of the court shall forthwith give copies of the order varying or revoking the restriction of liberty order to any person responsible for monitoring the offender's compliance with that order and that person shall give a copy of the order to the offender.".

AMENDMENTS

Section 245I inserted by Crime and Punishment (Scotland) Act 1997 (c.48) s.5 (effective 1 July 1998: SI 1997/2323).

[THE NEXT PARAGRAPH IS A4-481.20]

GENERAL NOTE

s.245I

At any time when the court varies or revokes an RLO or an RLO linked to a probation order, it is obliged to issue a copy of its interlocutor to the monitoring supervisor who, in turn, is responsible for ensuring that notification is served upon the offender. **A4-481.20**

Breach of certain orders: adjourning hearing and remanding in custody etc.

245J.—(1) Where an offender appears before the court in respect of his apparent failure to comply with a requirement of, as the case may be, a community payback order, drug treatment and testing order, or restriction of liberty order the court may, for the purpose of enabling inquiries to be made or of determining the most suitable method of dealing with him, adjourn the hearing. **A4-481.21**

(2) Where, under subsection (1) above, the court adjourns a hearing it shall remand the offender in custody or on bail or ordain him to appear at the adjourned hearing.

(3) A court shall not so adjourn a hearing for any single period exceeding four weeks or, on cause shown, eight weeks.

(4) An offender remanded under this section may appeal against the refusal of bail, or against the conditions imposed, within 24 hours of his remand.

(5) Any such appeal shall be to the appropriate Appeal Court by note of appeal, and the appropriate Appeal Court either in court or in chambers, may after hearing the appellant—

- (a) review the order appealed against and either grant bail on such conditions as it thinks fit or ordain the appellant to appear at the adjourned hearing; or
- (b) confirm the order.

(6) A note of appeal under subsection (5) above is to be—

- (a) lodged with the clerk of the court from which the appeal is to be taken; and
- (b) sent without delay by that clerk (where not the clerk of the appropriate Appeal Court) to the clerk of the appropriate Appeal Court.

(7) In this section—

"appropriate Appeal Court" means—

- (a) in the case of an appeal under subsection (4) against a decision of the High Court, that Court;
- (b) in the case of an appeal under subsection (4) against a decision of a sheriff (whether in solemn or summary proceedings) or a JP court, the Sheriff Appeal Court; and

"the clerk of the appropriate Appeal Court" means—

- (a) in a case where the High Court is the appropriate Appeal Court, the Clerk of Justiciary;
- (b) in a case where the Sheriff Appeal Court is the appropriate Appeal Court, the Clerk of that Court.

AMENDMENTS

Section 245J inserted by Criminal Justice (Scotland) Act 2003 (asp 7) Pt 6 s.48. Brought into force on June 27, 2003 by SSI 2003/288 (C.14).

Subs.(5) amended and subs.(6) inserted by Criminal Proceedings etc. (Reform) (Scotland) Act 2007 (asp 6) ss.6, 80 and Sch. para.21. Brought into force on December 10, 2007 by SSI 2007/479 art.3 and Sch.

Subss.(1), (2), (4) as amended by Criminal Justice and Licensing (Scotland) Act 2010 (asp 13) Sch.2 para.24. Brought into force on December 13, 2010 (subject to savings provisions in art.3) by SSI 2010/413 (C.28) art.2, Sch.1 para.1.

Subss.(5), (6) as amended, subs.(7) inserted, by Courts Reform (Scotland) Act 2014 (Consequential Provisions No.2) Order 2015 (SSI 2015/338) Sch.2 para.5 (effective September 22, 2015).

GENERAL NOTE

A4-481.22 Proceedings for breach of various sentencing orders has always been rather ad hoc. The present section makes it possible for courts to do what they have tended to do anyway—that is, to adjourn the hearing for up to four weeks (eight on cause shown) for inquiries to be made (a euphemism for a proof) or to determine the most suitable way to deal with the offender. The offender may be remanded in custody, "remanded" on bail (the creeping anglicisation of the language of the statute is to be regretted—elsewhere in the Act, a person is "admitted to" bail) or ordained to appear. A bail appeal is available (but not, it seems, a bail review).

Community reparation orders

Community reparation orders

A4-481.23 **245K.** [...]

AMENDMENTS

Section 245K inserted by Antisocial Behaviour etc. (Scotland) Act 2004 (asp 8) s.120. Brought into force on October 28, 2004 by SSI 2004/420 (C.31).

Section 245K repealed by Criminal Justice and Licensing (Scotland) Act 2010 (asp 13) Sch.2 para.25. Brought into force on December 13, 2010 (subject to savings provisions in art.3) by SSI 2010/413 (C.28) art.2, Sch.1 para.1.

Community reparation order: notification

A4-481.24 **245L.** [...]

AMENDMENTS

Section 245L inserted by Antisocial Behaviour etc. (Scotland) Act 2004 (asp 8) s.120. Brought into force on October 28, 2004 by SSI 2004/420 (C.31).

Section 245L repealed by Criminal Justice and Licensing (Scotland) Act 2010 (asp 13) Sch.2 para.25. Brought into force on December 13, 2010 (subject to savings provisions in art.3) by SSI 2010/413 (C.28) art.2, Sch.1 para.1.

Failure to comply with community reparation order: extension of 12 month period

A4-481.25 **245M.** [...]

AMENDMENTS

Section 245M inserted by Antisocial Behaviour etc. (Scotland) Act 2004 (asp 8) s.120. Brought into force on October 28, 2004 by SSI 2004/420 (C.31).

Section 245M repealed by Criminal Justice and Licensing (Scotland) Act 2010 (asp 13) Sch.2 para.25. Brought into force on December 13, 2010 (subject to savings provisions in art.3) by SSI 2010/413 (C.28) art.2, Sch.1 para.1.

Failure to comply with community reparation order: powers of court

A4-481.26 **245N.** [...]

AMENDMENTS

Section 245N inserted by Antisocial Behaviour etc. (Scotland) Act 2004 (asp 8) s.120. Brought into force on October 28, 2004 by SSI 2004/420 (C.31).

Section 245N repealed by Criminal Justice and Licensing (Scotland) Act 2010 (asp 13) Sch.2 para.25. Brought into force on December 13, 2010 (subject to savings provisions in art.3) by SSI 2010/413 (C.28) art.2, Sch.1 para.1.

Extension, variation and revocation of order

245P. […] A4-481.27

Amendments

Section 245P inserted by Antisocial Behaviour etc. (Scotland) Act 2004 (asp 8) s.120. Brought into force on October 28, 2004 by SSI 2004/420 (C.31).

Section 245P repealed by Criminal Justice and Licensing (Scotland) Act 2010 (asp 13) Sch.2 para.25. Brought into force on December 13, 2010 (subject to savings provisions in art.3) by SSI 2010/413 (C.28) art.2, Sch.1 para.1.

Sections 245L, 245N and 245P: meaning of "appropriate court"

245Q. […] A4-481.28

Amendments

Section 245Q inserted by Antisocial Behaviour etc. (Scotland) Act 2004 (asp 8) s.120. Brought into force on October 28, 2004 by SSI 2004/420 (C.31).

Section 245Q as amended by Criminal Proceedings etc. (Reform) (Scotland) Act 2007 (asp 6) s.80, Sch. para.26. Brought into force for the Sheriffdom of Lothian and Borders on March 10, 2008 by SSI 2008/42 (C.4) art.3 and Sch. Brought into force for the Sheriffdom of Grampian, Highland and Islands on June 2, 2008 by SSI 2008/192 (C.19) art.3 and Sch. Brought into force for the Sheriffdom of Glasgow and Strathkelvin on December 8, 2008 by SSI 2008/329 (C.29) art.3 and Sch. Brought into force for the Sheriffdom of Tayside, Central and Fife on 3 February 2009 by SSI 2008/362 (C.30) art.3 and Sch. Brought into force for the Sheriffdom of North Strathclyde on 14 December 2009 by SSI 2009/432 (C.32) art.3 and Sch.1. Remainder in force on 22 February 2010 by SSI 2009/432 (C.32) art.3 and Sch.2.

Section 245Q repealed by Criminal Justice and Licensing (Scotland) Act 2010 (asp 13) Sch.2 para.25. Brought into force on 13 December 2010 (subject to savings provisions in art.3) by SSI 2010/413 (C.28) art.2, Sch.1 para.1.

[THE NEXT PARAGRAPH IS A4-482]

Admonition and absolute discharge

Admonition and absolute discharge

246.—(1) A court may, if it appears to meet the justice of the case, dismiss with an admonition any person convicted by the court of any offence. A4-482

(2) Where a person is convicted on indictment of an offence (other than an offence the sentence for which is fixed by law), if it appears to the court, having regard to the circumstances including the nature of the offence and the character of the offender, that it is inexpedient to inflict punishment it may instead of sentencing him make an order discharging him absolutely.

(3) Where a person is charged before a court of summary jurisdiction with an offence (other than an offence the sentence for which is fixed by law) and the court is satisfied that he committed the offence, the court, if it is of the opinion, having regard to the circumstances including the nature of the offence and the character of the offender, that it is inexpedient to inflict punishment may without proceeding to conviction make an order discharging him absolutely.

Amendments

Subss.(2), (3) as amended by Criminal Justice and Licensing (Scotland) Act 2010 (asp 13) Sch.2 para.26. Brought into force on 13 December 2010 (subject to savings provisions in art.3) by SSI 2010/413 (C.28) art.2, Sch.1 para.1.

Definitions

A4-482.1

"court of summary jurisdiction": s.307(1).
"indictment": s.307(1).
"offence": s.307(1).
"probation order": s.307(1).

GENERAL NOTE

A4-482.2 The legal effect of an absolute discharge is stipulated in s.247, below. In *McLay v Ruxton*, 1996 G.W.D. 23-1311 the Appeal Court granted an absolute discharge after allowing a motion to appeal against conviction to be made at the bar.

It is legitimate to take into account the effect of a conviction on an offender's employment when deciding whether to discharge him absolutely. In *Galloway v Mackenzie*, 1991 S.C.C.R. 548, a person who was employed as a careers officer was provoked to lash out when youths threw fireworks at him and his children. A conviction was likely to have a serious effect on his employment. The Appeal Court granted an absolute discharge. In *Kheda v Lees*, 1995 S.C.C.R. 63 the appellant was a nurse. He too had been provoked (in his case, by youths constantly kicking a football against his door and tramping though his garden). He had threatened to puncture their football and he brandished a knife. The Appeal Court held that the sheriff ought to have made absolute discharge. Contrast *Gibson v McTaggart* [2019] SAC (Crim) 3, a successful Crown appeal against that disposal which, the Sheriff Appeal Court held, had given undue weight to the reduction in quantum when compared with the intrinsic gravity of the crime of embezzlement charged.

As subs.(3) makes clear the court does not move to conviction; see *Murphy v SB*, 2014 S.C.C.R. 501, where the High Court, drawing on s.299 below, corrected a recording of conviction to uphold a subsequent absolute discharge. Despite the general aim expressed in subs.(1), refraining from conviction does not avoid the offender notification requirements set out in the Sexual Offences (Scotland) Act 2009; as the court noted in *HM Advocate v KH*, 2014 S.C.C.R. 485, where an absolute discharge had originally been imposed upon a 15-year-old boy charged with a sexual assault, this paradox arises from interplay with the Powers of Criminal Courts (Sentencing) Act 2000 (c.6) ss.14 and 167(2).

It is submitted that if parties and the court are satisfied, despite the libel, that no substantial sexual conduct was involved in an offence and that such notification requirements are inappropriate, then the only option would be for the Crown not to seek conviction at all; a tall order. *KH* was a successful Crown appeal against an unduly lenient sentence so the above dilemma did not arise.

[THE NEXT PARAGRAPH IS A4-483]

Effect of probation and absolute discharge

A4-483 **247.**—(1) Subject to the following provisions of this section, a conviction of an offence for which an order is made discharging the offender absolutely shall be deemed not to be a conviction for any purpose other than the purposes of the proceedings in which the order is made and of laying it before a court as a previous conviction in subsequent proceedings for another offence.

(2) Without prejudice to subsection (1) above, the conviction of an offender who is discharged absolutely as aforesaid shall in any event be disregarded for the purposes of any enactment which imposes any disqualification or disability upon convicted persons, or authorises or requires the imposition of any such disqualification or disability.

(3) Subsections (1) and (2) above shall not affect any right to appeal.

(4) Where a person charged with an offence has at any time previously been discharged absolutely in respect of the commission by him of an offence it shall be competent, in the proceedings for that offence, to lay before the court the order of absolute discharge in like manner as if the order were a conviction.

(5) Where an offender is discharged absolutely by a court of summary jurisdiction, he shall have the like right of appeal against the finding that he committed the offence as if that finding were a conviction.

(6) [...]

AMENDMENTS

Subss.(1), (2) as amended, subs.(6) repealed, by Criminal Justice and Licensing (Scotland) Act 2010 (asp 13) Sch.7 para.59. Brought into force on 28 March 2011 by SSI 2011/178 (C.15) art.2, Sch.1 para.1.

DEFINITIONS

A4-483.1 "court of summary jurisdiction": s.307(1).
"offence": s.307(1).
"probation": s.307(1).

[THE NEXT PARAGRAPH IS A4-484]

Disqualification

Disqualification where vehicle used to commit offence

248.—(1) Where a person is convicted of an offence (other than one triable only summarily) and the court which passes sentence is satisfied that a motor vehicle was used for the purposes of committing or facilitating the commission of that offence, the court may order him to be disqualified for such a period as the court thinks fit from holding or obtaining a licence to drive a motor vehicle granted under Part III of the Road Traffic Act 1988. **A4-484**

(2) A court which makes an order under subsection (1) above disqualifying a person from holding or obtaining a licence under Part III of the Road Traffic Act 1988 shall require him to produce—

(a) any such licence;
(b) any Community licence (within the meaning of that Part); and
(c) any counterpart of a licence mentioned in paragraph (a) or (b) above,

held by him.

(3) Any reference in this section to facilitating the commission of an offence shall include a reference to the taking of any steps after it has been committed for the purpose of disposing of any property to which it relates or of avoiding apprehension or detection.

(4) In relation to licences, other than Community licences which came into force before 1st June 1990, the reference in subsection (2) above to the counterpart of a licence shall be disregarded.

AMENDMENTS

Subs.(2) substituted, and subs.(4) as amended, by Driving Licences (Community Driving Licences) Regulations 1996 (SI 1996/1974) (effective 1 January 1997).

DEFINITIONS

"offence": s.307(1). **A4-484.1**
"order": s.307(1).

GENERAL NOTE

Separate statutory powers to enable forfeiture of motor vehicles used during the commission of Road Traffic Act offences are found in the Road Traffic Offenders Act 1988 (c.53) s.33A and are unique to Scotland; see, for example, *Li v Dunn* [2016] SAC (Crim)7; 2016 S.C.C.R. 272 and *Duncan v Procurator Fiscal, Lerwick* [2016] SAC (Crim) 9. **A4-484.1.1**

General power to disqualify offenders

248A.—(1) Subject to subsection (2) below, the court by or before which a person is convicted of an offence may, in addition to or instead of dealing with him in any other way, order him to be disqualified from holding or obtaining a licence to drive a motor vehicle granted under Part III of the Road Traffic Act 1988 for such period as it thinks fit. **A4-484.1.2**

(2) Where the person is convicted of an offence for which the sentence is fixed by law, subsection (1) above shall have effect as if the words "or instead of" were omitted.

(3) Subsections (2) and (4) of section 248 of this Act shall apply for the purposes of this section as they apply for the purposes of that section.

AMENDMENTS

Section 248A inserted by Crime and Punishment (Scotland) Act 1997 (c.48) s.15 with effect from 1 January 1998 in terms of SI 1997/2323 art.3 and Sch.1.

[THE NEXT PARAGRAPH IS A4-484.2]

DEFINITIONS

A4-484.2 "offence": s.307(1) of the 1995 Act.
"disqualified": s.98(1) of the Road Traffic Offenders Act 1988.
"motor vehicle": s.185(1) of the Road Traffic Act 1988.

GENERAL NOTE

A4-484.3 This section, introduced at a late stage in the life of the Crime and Punishment (Scotland) Bill, gives courts or categories of courts selected by the Secretary of State, a general power of disqualification from driving as an element of sentence on conviction of any offence. This power is quite distinct from the specific provisions found in s.248 and may be used even where the offence leading to conviction was neither a road traffic contravention nor a crime involving the use of a motor vehicle in its commission. The section took effect on January 1, 1998 but only for offences committed after that date.

Section 248B of the Act, which took effect on the same date, provides for disqualification as a sentencing alternative to imprisonment in cases of fine default. It has to be said that these two provisions passed into law with little or no Parliamentary discussion.

A s.248A disqualification can be imposed as an element of any sentence including a sentence fixed by law (subs.(2)), and applies to an offender irrespective of whether or not he possesses a driving licence; subs.(3) serves to make it clear that any driving licence held by an accused will require to be produced to the court and it may now be necessary for agents to advise clients to ensure that driving licences are available at any court diet, and for agents to be ready to address the court on this aspect of sentence.

It is important to observe that this general power of disqualification may be imposed even where the original offence did not involve the use of a motor vehicle in the commission of the offence.

It remains to be seen how far, if at all, the sentencing principles, already established in relation to disqualification for Road Traffic offences, can properly apply to s.248A or s.248B disqualifications: notably where a conviction or sentence is under appeal, what mechanism, if any, exists for suspension of disqualification? It does not appear that the general provisions of ss.39 to 41 of the Road Traffic Offenders Act 1988 (c.53) can be read into ss.248A and 248B. A fuller discussion is found in the annotations to s.15 of the Crime and Punishment (Scotland)Act 1997 at para.A5-038.

Power to disqualify fine defaulters

A4-484.4 **248B.**—(1) This section applies where the court has power to impose a period of imprisonment in default of payment of a fine, or any part or instalment of a fine.

(2) Where this section applies, the court may, instead of imposing such a period of imprisonment as is mentioned in subsection (1) above, order that where the offender is in default he shall be disqualfied from holding a licence to drive a motor vehicle granted under Part III of the Road Traffic Act 1988 for such period not exceeding twelve months as the court thinks fit.

(3) Where an order has been made under subsection (2) above in default of payment of any fine, or any part or instalment of a fine—

(a) on payment of the fine to any person authorised to receive it, the order shall cease to have effect; and

(b) on payment of any part of that fine to any such person, the period of disqualification to which the order relates shall be reduced (or, as the case may be, further reduced) by a number of days bearing as nearly as possible the same proportion to such period as the sum so paid bears to the amount of the fine outstanding at the commencement of that period.

(4) Subsections (2) and (4) of section 248 of this Act shall apply for the purposes of this section as they apply for the purposes of that section.

(5) Section 19 of the Road Traffic Offenders Act 1988 (proof of disqualification in Scottish proceedings) shall apply to an order under subsection (2) above as it applies to a conviction or extract conviction.

(6) The Secretary of State may by order made by statutory instrument vary the period specified in subsection (2) above; but not such order shall be made unless a draft of the order has been laid before, and approved by a resolution of, each House of Parliament.

AMENDMENTS

Section 248B inserted by Crime and Punishment (Scotland) Act 1997 (c.48) s.15 with effect from 1 January 1998 in terms of SI 1997/2323 art.3 and Sch.1.

DEFINITIONS

"imprisonment": s.307(1) of the 1995 Act. A4-484.5

"fine": s.307(1).

"extract conviction": s.307(1) above.

GENERAL NOTE

It is important to recognise that the power to disqualify only arises where the court has power to imprison in default of payment. That power to imprison is constrained in various ways, but one which might be important if the court is considering disqualification is s.227M which prevents a court from imposing imprisonment in default of payment where the fine does not exceed level 2 and obliges a court, instead, to impose a level 1 community payback order. Where the power to disqualify does arise, the Act does not provide guidance about how the duration of that disqualification is to be calculated (within the maximum of 12 months set by subs.(2)). A4-484.5.1

[THE NEXT PARAGRAPH IS A4-484.6]

Application of sections 248A and 248B

248C.—(1) The Secretary of State may by order prescribe which courts, or class or classes of courts, may make orders under section 248A or 248B of this Act. A4-484.6

(2) An order made under subsection (1) above shall be made by statutory instrument and any such instrument shall be subject to annulment in pursuance of a resolution of either House of Parliament.

(3) Where an order has been made under subsection (1) above, section 248(1) of this Act shall not apply as respects any court, or class or classes of court prescribed by the order.

AMENDMENTS

Section 248C inserted by Crime and Punishment (Scotland) Act 1997 (c.48) s.15 with effect from 20 October 1997 in terms of SI 1997/2323 art.3 and Sch.1.

Subs.(1) as amended by Criminal Proceedings etc. (Reform) (Scotland) Act 2007 (asp 6) s.80, Sch. paras 22, 26. Brought into force for the Sheriffdom of Lothian and Borders on 10 March 2008 by SSI 2008/42 (C.4) art.3 and Sch. Brought into force for the Sheriffdom of Grampian, Highland and Islands on 2 June 2008 by SSI 2008/192 (C.19) art.3 and Sch. Brought into force for the Sheriffdom of Glasgow and Strathkelvin on 8 December 2008 by SSI 2008/329 (C.29) art.3 and Sch. Brought into force for the Sheriffdom of Tayside, Central and Fife on 23 February 2009 by SSI 2008/362 (C.30) art.3 and Sch. Brought into force for the Sheriffdom of North Strathclyde on 14 December 2009 by SSI 2009/432 (C.32) art.3 and Sch.1. Remainder in force on 22 February 2010 by SSI 2009/432 (C.32) art.3 and Sch.2.

Subs.(1) as amended by Courts Reform (Scotland) Act 2014 (asp 18) Sch.5 para.39. Brought into force on 1 April 2016 by SSI 2016/13 art.2, Sch.1 para.1.

[THE NEXT PARAGRAPH IS A4-484.8]

GENERAL NOTE

Section 248C was brought into force on 20 October 1997 and empowers the Secretary of State to make orders to prescribe the particular courts, or categories of courts, which will ultimately have power to impose driving disqualification as a penalty on conviction of any offence (s.248A) or as an alternative to imprisonment following fine default (s.248B). The main provisions came into effect on January 1, 1998. A4-484.8

The purpose of this section, introduced at a late stage to the Bill, is to make disqualification from driving available as a punishment for a broad range of offences, including fine default. The majority of s.15 is inserted into the 1995 Procedure Act as ss.248A, 248B and 248C and to s.252, with only a small addition (subs.(3)) to the Proceeds of Crime (Scotland) Act 1995. Despite, or perhaps because of, the brevity of the draftsmanship, the mechanics of this new legislation are by no means clear and much depends upon the extent to which the provisions of the Road Traffic Offenders Act 1988 are held to apply to it.

Some concern was expressed during debate of this provision that the court should not impose a s.248 disqualification until suitability reports had first been considered; while social enquiry reports would usually have been sought before the court could consider imprisonment, such reports are not generally obtained in respect of fine defaulters who can now be disqualified under s.248B, as an alternative to imprisonment, for fine default. The Lord Advocate indicated that the new disqualification provisions would be tested by a number of pilot schemes in both urban and rural areas before consideration is given to their more widespread introduction. (*Hansard*, H.L., 19 March 1997, col. 942).

Extension of disqualification where sentence of imprisonment also imposed

A4-484.9 **248D.**—(1) This section applies where a person is convicted of an offence for which the court—

(a) imposes a sentence of imprisonment, and

(b) orders the person to be disqualified under section 248 or 248A of this Act from holding or obtaining a driving licence.

(2) The order under section 248 or 248A of this Act must provide for the person to be disqualified for the appropriate extension period, in addition to the discretionary disqualification period.

(3) The discretionary disqualification period is the period for which, in the absence of this section, the court would have disqualified the person under section 248 or 248A of this Act.

(4) The appropriate extension period is—

(a) in the case of a life prisoner, a period equal to the punishment part of the life sentence;

(b) in the case of a custody and community prisoner, a period equal to half the custody part of the sentence of imprisonment;

(c) in the case of a person serving an extended sentence, a period equal to half the confinement term;

(d) in any other case, a period equal to half the sentence of imprisonment imposed.

(5) If a period determined under subsection (4) includes a fraction of a day, that period is to be rounded up to the nearest number of whole days.

(6) For the purposes of subsection (4), a sentence is to be taken to start on the date of commencement of the sentence.

(7) Subsection (8) applies where an amending order provides for a different proportion ("the new proportion") to be substituted for the proportion of a prisoner's sentence referred to in section 6(4)(a) of the Custodial Sentences and Weapons (Scotland) Act 2007 (asp 17) ("the 2007 Act").

(8) The Secretary of State may by order provide that the proportion specified in subsection (4)(b) and (c) of this section is to be read, in the case of a sentence of imprisonment to which the amending order relates, as a reference to the new proportion.

(9) An order under subsection (8) is to be made by statutory instrument and a draft of the statutory instrument containing the order must be laid before, and approved by a resolution of, each House of Parliament.

(10) In this section—

"amending order" means an order made by the Scottish Ministers under section 7 of the 2007 Act;

"confinement term" has the meaning given by section 210A(2)(a) of this Act;

"custody and community prisoner" has the meaning given by section 4 of the 2007 Act;

"custody part" has the meaning given by section 6(3) of the 2007 Act;

"extended sentence" has the meaning given by section 210A of this Act;

"life prisoner" has the meaning given by section 4 of the 2007 Act;

"punishment part" has the meaning given by section 4 of the 2007 Act;

"sentence of imprisonment" includes—

(a) an order for detention in residential accommodation under section 44 of this Act, and

(b) a sentence of detention under section 205, 207 or 208 of this Act.

AMENDMENTS

S.248D inserted by Coroners and Justice Act 2009 (c. 25) Sch.16 para.3 (effective 16 July 2018: insertion has effect on 16 July 2018 as specified in SI 2018/733 art.2(b) subject to transitional provisions specified in 2009 (c.25) Sch.22 paras 29, 35(2) and 36).

Effect of sentence of imprisonment in other cases

248E.—(1) This section applies where a person is convicted of an offence for which a court proposes to order the person to be disqualified under section 248 or 248A from holding or obtaining a driving licence and— **A4-484.10**

(a) the court proposes to impose on the person a sentence of imprisonment for another offence, or

(b) at the time of sentencing for the offence, a sentence of imprisonment imposed on the person on an earlier occasion has not expired.

(2) In determining the period for which the person is to be disqualified under section 248 or 248A, the court must have regard to the consideration in subsection (3) if and to the extent that it is appropriate to do so.

(3) The consideration is the diminished effect of disqualification as a distinct punishment if the person who is disqualified is also detained in pursuance of a sentence of imprisonment.

(4) If the court proposes to order the person to be disqualified under section 248 or 248A and to impose a sentence of imprisonment for the same offence, the court may not in relation to that disqualification take that sentence of imprisonment into account for the purposes of subsection (2).

(5) In this section "sentence of imprisonment" has the same meaning as in section 248D.

AMENDMENTS

S.248E inserted by Coroners and Justice Act 2009 (c. 25) Sch.16 para.3 (effective 16 July 2018: insertion has effect on 16 July 2018 as specified in SI 2018/733 art.2(b) subject to transitional provisions specified in 2009 (c.25) Sch.22 paras 29, 35(2) and 36).

[THE NEXT PARAGRAPH IS A4-485]

Compensation

Compensation order against convicted person

249.—(1) Where a person is convicted of an offence the court, instead of or in addition to dealing with him in any other way, may make an order (in this Part of this Act referred to as "a compensation order") requiring him to pay compensation in favour of the victim for any— **A4-485**

(a) personal injury, loss or damage caused directly or indirectly; or

(b) alarm or distress caused directly,

to the victim.

(1A) For the purposes of subsection (1) above, "victim" means—

(a) a person against whom; or

(b) a person against whose property,

the acts which constituted the offence were directed.

(1B) Where a person is convicted of an offence, the court may (instead of or in addition to dealing with the person in any other way), in accordance with subsections (3A) to (3C), make a compensation order requiring the convicted person to pay compensation in favour of—

(a) the victim, or

(b) a person who is liable for funeral expenses in respect of which subsection (3C)(b) allows a compensation order to be made.

(1C) For the purposes of subsection (1B)(a), "victim" means—

(a) a person who has suffered personal injury, loss or damage in respect of which a compensation order may be made by virtue of subsection (3A), or

(b) a relative (as defined in Schedule 1 to the Damages (Scotland) Act 1976 (c.13)) who has suffered bereavement in respect of which subsection (3C)(a) allows a compensation order to be made.

(2) It shall not be competent for a court to make a compensation order—

(a) where, under section 246(2) of this Act, it makes an order discharging him absolutely;

(ab) where, under section 227A of this Act, it imposes a community payback order;

(c) at the same time as, under section 202 of this Act, it defers sentence.

(3) Where, in the case of an offence involving dishonest appropriation, or the unlawful taking and using of property or a contravention of section 178(1) of the Road Traffic Act 1988 (taking motor vehicle without authority etc.) the property is recovered, but has been damaged while out of the owner's possession, that damage, however and by whomsoever it was in fact caused, shall be treated for the purposes of subsection (1) above as having been caused by the acts which constituted the offence.

(3A) A compensation order may be made in respect of personal injury, loss or damage (apart from loss suffered by a person's dependents in consequence of a person's death) that was caused directly or indirectly by an accident arising out of the presence of a motor vehicle on a road if—

(a) it was being used in contravention of section 143(1) of the Road Traffic Act 1988 (c.52), and

(b) no compensation is payable under arrangements to which the Secretary of State is a party.

(3B) Where a compensation order is made by virtue of subsection (3) or (3A), the order may include an amount representing the whole or part of any loss of (including reduction in) preferential rates of insurance if the loss is attributable to the accident.

(3C) A compensation order may be made—

(a) for bereavement in connection with a person's death resulting from the acts which constituted the offence,

(b) for funeral expenses in connection with such a death,

except where the death was due to an accident arising out of the presence of a motor vehicle on a road.

(4) Unless (and to the extent that) subsections (3) to (3C) allow a compensation order to be made, no compensation order shall be made in respect of—

(a) loss suffered in consequence of the death of any person; or

(b) injury, loss or damage due to an accident arising out of the presence of a motor vehicle on a road.

(5) In determining whether to make a compensation order against any person, and in determining the amount to be paid by any person under such order, the court shall take into consideration his means so far as known to the court.

(6) […]

(7) In solemn proceedings there shall be no limit on the amount which may be awarded under a compensation order.

(8) In summary proceedings—

(a) a sheriff shall have power to make a compensation order awarding in respect of each offence an amount not exceeding the prescribed sum;

(b) a judge of a JP court shall have power to make a compensation order awarding in respect of each offence an amount not exceeding level 4 on the standard scale.

(8A) In summary proceedings before the sheriff, where the fine or maximum fine to which a person is liable on summary conviction of an offence exceeds the prescribed sum, the sheriff may make a compensation order awarding in respect of the offence an amount not exceeding the amount of the fine to which the person is so liable.

(9) Payment of any amount under a compensation order shall be made to the clerk of the court who shall account for the amount to the person entitled thereto.

(10) Only the court shall have power to enforce a compensation order.

(11) This section is subject to section 34 of the Regulatory Reform (Scotland) Act 2014.

AMENDMENTS

Subs.(1) as amended and subs.(1A) inserted by Criminal Proceedings etc. (Reform) (Scotland) Act 2007 (asp 6) s.49. Brought into force on 10 March 2008 by SSI 2008/42 (C.4) art.3 and Sch.

Subs.(8) as amended by Criminal Proceedings etc. (Reform) (Scotland) Act 2007 (asp 6) s.80, Sch. paras 22, 26. Brought into force for the Sheriffdom of Lothian and Borders on 10 March 2008 by SSI 2008/42 (C.4) art.3 and Sch. Brought into force for the Sheriffdom of Grampian, Highland and Islands on 2 June 2008 by SI 2008/192 (C.19) art.3 and Sch. Brought into force for the Sheriffdom of Glasgow and Strathkelvin on 8 December 2008 by SSI 2008/329 (C.29) art.3 and Sch. Brought into force for the Sheriffdom of Tayside, Central and Fife on 23 February 2009 by SSI 2008/362 (C.30) art.3 and Sch. Brought into force for the Sheriffdom of North Strathclyde on 14 December 2009 by SSI 2009/432 (C.32) art.3 and Sch.1. Remainder in force on 22 February 2010 by SSI 2009/432 (C.32) art.3 and Sch.2.

Subs.(2)(b) as amended by Criminal Justice and Licensing (Scotland) Act 2010 (asp 13) Sch.2 para.27. Brought into force on 13 December 2010 (subject to savings provisions in art.3) by SSI 2010/413 (C.28) art.2, Sch.1 para.1.

Subss.(1), (4), (4)(b) as amended, subss.(1B), (1C), (3A)-(3C), (8A) inserted, and subs.(6) repealed, by Criminal Justice and Licensing (Scotland) Act 2010 (asp 13) s.115(1). Brought into force on 28 March 2011 (for all purposes in respect of offences committed on or after 28 March 2011) by SSI 2011/178 (C.15) art.2, Sch.1 para.1.

Subs.(11) inserted by Regulatory Reform (Scotland) Act 2014 (asp 3) Sch.3 para.12. Brought into force on 30 June 2014 by SSI 2014/160 art.2 and Sch.1 para.1.

Subs.(8) as amended by Courts Reform (Scotland) Act 2014 (asp 18) Sch.5 para.39. Brought into force on 1 April 2016 by SSI 2016/13 art.2, Sch.1 para.1.

DEFINITIONS

"compensation order": s.249(1). A4-485.1
"offence": s.307(1).
"probation order": s.307(1).
"prescribed sum": s.225(8)
"standard scale": s.225(1).

[THE NEXT PARAGRAPH IS A4-486]

GENERAL NOTE

Compensation orders have probably not been sought for as many offences as they might have but that may merely reflect the impecunious state of most convicted people in Scotland. Nevertheless the law to date has been clarified by several decisions: in *Stewart v HM Advocate*, 1982 S.C.C.R. 203 it was held on appeal that an order made in respect of "inconvenience suffered" was not open to criticism. A4-486

In *Carmichael v Siddique*, 1985 S.C.C.R. 145 a sheriff rejected an argument that a compensation order was competent and appropriate only where the legal position was clear and bereft of complexities and the damage was capable of precise valuation and was not great. Such an argument has not, apparently, been put forward again. In *Collins v Lowe*, 1990 S.C.C.R. 605 it was held on appeal that it was competent to make a compensation order in addition to custodial sentences, an approach followed in *Moses v MacDonald*, 1996 G.W.D. 1-62 where compensation was fixed to cover a vehicle insurance excess and other costs in addition to a maximum custodial sentence. In *Robertson v Lees*, 1992 S.C.C.R. 545 the Appeal Court observed that the fact that the accused was a first offender was not a relevant factor when setting the amount of compensation: equally it has been held to be irrelevant that the complainer was insured (see *Ely v Donnelly*, 1996 S.C.C.R. 537 which also holds that the guidelines relating to the period of time allowable for repayment of fines, have no bearing upon repayment of compensation orders). See also *Galbraith v Gilchrist*, 2001 G.W.D. 31-1231 where a £250 fine and £500 compensation order was imposed payable at the rate of £5 weekly; the fine was reduced to £150 with an order for £350 solely having regard to the excessive time needed for repayment.

In *Sullivan v McLeod*, 1998 S.L.T. 552, the construction of "at the same time" in subs.(2)(c) was raised: S had been convicted on a summary complaint containing two charges and a deferred sentence was imposed on one charge, a compensation order on the other. While observing that such a disposal would only rarely be appropriate, the Appeal Court held that all that subs.(2)(c) sought to prevent was the imposition of both a deferment of sentence and a compensation order for the same offence. Where a number of offences appeared on the same complaint, separate disposals could be considered in relation to each charge but *no cumulo* sentence could incorporate both a deferred sentence and a compensation order.

For a discussion of s.249(3) see *O'Hara v Murray*, 2007 S.C.C.R. 322 where observations were made on the three categories of dishonest appropriation and separately the unlawful taking and using of property again a contravention of s.178 of the Road Traffic Act 1988 (c.52).

With the commencement of s.49 of the Criminal Proceedings etc. (Reform) (Scotland) Act 2007 (asp 6) on March 10, 2008, compensation orders were extended to apply to offences causing alarm or distress caused directly to the victim, in addition to the earlier provisions involving personal injury, loss or damage. It is not necessary for the libel to include an allegation of this sort before a compensation order can be imposed; it is sufficient that the facts disclosed to the accused or his agent and narrated (if not challenged in any plea) or held as proved after trial, indicate such an effect upon the victim. See generally *Campbell v Stott*, 2001 S.L.T. 112; 2001 S.C.C.R. 10. Nonetheless, compensation cannot be awarded to a group or individual unconnected with the events prompting a compensation order. In *HM Advocate v Nelson* 1996 S.L.T. 1073 the Crown successfully appealed against a purported compensation award to Victim Support where that organisation had had no involvement in the incidents libelled, the award being quashed as incompetent. Imposition of a compensation order by the court may present practical difficulties should the Crown elect to appeal a sentence as unduly lenient; see *HM Advocate v Jamieson*, 1997 S.L.T. 955, discussed at A4-462.2 above.

In *Heafey v Craigen*, 2001 G.W.D. 16-615 a compensation order of £200 had been imposed. An appeal against sentence was allowed on the basis that the appellant had not been given the opportunity to dispute the valuation or been informed that the compensation might be ordered. It was observed, while not wishing to lay down a general rule, that it appeared that at least in many cases where there was a plea of guilty by letter or the accused was not present, it might be right to continue the matter if compensation was contemplated given potential disputes about the valuation of damages and circumstances where it might be proper to ask whether a complainer should receive compensation. See *also Shaw v Donnelly*, 2003 S.L.T. 255 where a compensation order was imposed without sufficient enquiry into the accuracy of a repair estimate, or any opportunity to challenge same. Similar issues of assessing compensation for damage to a car arose in *Grant v Griffiths*, 2004 S.C.C.R. 136, where the court also paid heed to the extent to which the complainer had provoked the criminal conduct.

Questions of causation must be examined closely, especially from the accused's point of view, for in *Nazir v Normand*, 1994 S.C.C.R. 265 the appellant caused and permitted another to drive an uninsured car and the appellant's appeal against a consequential compensation order was refused.

Finally, Parliament has not given the court power to make a compensation order where the impact of an offender's behaviour falls short of the infliction of personal injury: *Brown v Laing*, 2004 S.L.T. 646.

Compensation orders: supplementary provisions

A4-487 **250.**—(1) Where a court considers that in respect of an offence it would be appropriate to impose a fine and to make a compensation order but the convicted person has insufficient means to pay both an appropriate fine and an appropriate amount in compensation the court should prefer a compensation order.

(2) Where a convicted person has both been fined and had a compensation order made against him in respect of the same offence or different offences in the same proceedings, a payment by the convicted person shall first be applied in satisfaction of the compensation order.

(3) For the purposes of any appeal or review, a compensation order is a sentence.

(4) Where a compensation order has been made against a person, a payment made to the court in respect of the order shall be retained until the determination of any appeal in relation to the order.

DEFINITIONS

A4-487.1 "compensation order": s.249(1).
"offence": s.307(1).

[THE NEXT PARAGRAPH IS A4-488]

GENERAL NOTE

A4-488 There are, having regard to subs.(3), several reported cases in which a compensation order has been appealed. For example, in *Brown v Normand*, 1988 S.C.C.R. 229 a sentence of a fine and a compensation order was appealed on the ground that the sentence was excessive and it was allowed. Appeals were similarly allowed in *Smillie v Wilson*, 1990 S.L.T. 582, *Hughes v Brown*, 1990 G.W.D. 13-670, *Crawford v McGlennan*, 1990 G.W.D 21-1170, *McMahon v Hamilton*, 1990 G.W.D. 372124, *Wilson v Brown*, 1992 G.W.D. 6-288, *Currie v Webster*, 1992 G.W.D. 13-722 and *Clark v O'Brien*, 1995 G.W.D. 20-1130. Such appeals were refused in *McPhail v Hamilton*, 1991 G.W.D. 24-1375 and *Barclay v Douglas*, 1994 G.W.D. 1-37.

Review of compensation order

251.—(1) Without prejudice to the power contained in section 213 of this Act, (as applied by section 252 of this Act), at any time before a compensation order has been complied with or fully complied with, the court, on the application of the person against whom the compensation order was made, may discharge the compensation order or reduce the amount that remains to be paid if it appears to the court that— **A4-489**

(a) [...]

(b) that property the loss of which is reflected in the compensation order has been recovered.

(1A) On the application of the prosecutor at any time before a compensation order has been complied with (or fully complied with), the court may increase the amount payable under the compensation order if it is satisfied that the person against whom it was made—

(a) because of the availability of materially different information about financial circumstances, has more means than were made known to the court when the order was made, or

(b) because of a material change of financial circumstances, has more means than the person had then.

(2) In subsection (1) above "the court" means—

(a) in a case where, as respects the compensation order, a transfer of fine order under section 222 of this Act (as applied by the said section 252) is effective and the court by which the compensation order is enforceable is in terms of the transfer of fine order a court of summary jurisdiction in Scotland, that court; or

(b) in any other case, the court which made the compensation order or, where that court was the High Court, by which the order was first enforceable.

AMENDMENTS

Subs.(1) as amended by Criminal Proceedings etc (Reform) (Scotland) Act 2007 (asp 6) s.49. Brought into force on 10 March 2008 by SSI 2008/42 (C.4) art.3 and Sch.

Subs.(1)(a) repealed, subs.(1A) added, by Criminal Justice and Licensing (Scotland)Act 2010 (asp 13) s.115(2). Brought into force on 28 March 2011 (for all purposes in respect of offences committed on or after 28 March 2011) by SSI 2011/178 (C.15) art.2, Sch.1 para.1.

DEFINITIONS

"compensation order": s.249(1). **A4-489.1**

"court": s.251(2).

[THE NEXT PARAGRAPH IS A4-490]

Enforcement of compensation orders: application of provisions relating to fines

252.—(1) The provisions of this Act specified in subsection (2) below shall, subject to any necessary modifications and to the qualifications mentioned in that subsection, apply in relation to compensation orders as they apply in relation to fines; and section 91 of the Magistrates' Courts Act 1980 and article 96 of the Magistrates' Courts (Northern Ireland) Order 1981 shall be construed accordingly. **A4-490**

(2) The provisions mentioned in subsection (1) above are—

section 211(3), (4) and (7) to (9) (enforcement of fines);

section 212 (fines in summary proceedings);

section 213 (power to remit fines), with the omission of the words "or (4)" in subsection (2) of that section;
section 214 (time for payment) with the omission of—

(a) the words from "unless" to "its decision" in subsection (4); and
(b) subsection (5);

section 215 (further time for payment);
section 216 (reasons for default);
section 217 (supervision pending payment of fine);
section 218 (supplementary provisions), except that subsection (1) of that section shall not apply in relation to compensation orders made in solemn proceedings;
subject to subsection (3) below, section 219(1)(b), (2), (3), (5), (6) and (8) (maximum period of imprisonment for non-payment of fine);
section 220 (payment of fine in part by prisoner);
section 221 (recovery by civil diligence);
section 222 (transfer of fine orders);
section 223 (action of clerk of court on transfer of fine order);
section 224 (discharge from imprisonment to be specified); and
section 248B (driving disqualification for fine defaulters) so far as it relates to the power conferred by section 219(1)(b).

(3) In the application of the provisions of section 219 of this Act mentioned in subsection (2) above for the purposes of subsection (1) above—

(a) a court may impose imprisonment in respect of a fine and decline to impose imprisonment in respect of a compensation order but not vice versa; and
(b) where a court imposes imprisonment both in respect of a fine and of a compensation order the amounts in respect of which imprisonment is imposed shall, for the purposes of subsection (2) of the said section 219, be aggregated.

AMENDMENTS

Subs.(2) as amended by Crime and Punishment (Scotland) Act 1997 (c.48) s.15(2) with effect from January 1, 1998 in terms of SI 1997/2323 art.4 and Sch.2.

Subs.(2) inserted by the above provisions.

DEFINITION

A4-490.1 "fines": s.307(1).

[THE NEXT PARAGRAPH IS A4-491]

Effect of compensation order on subsequent award of damages in civil proceedings

A4-491 **253.**—(1) This section shall have effect where a compensation order or a service compensation order or award has been made in favour of any person in respect of any injury, loss, damage, alarm or distress and a claim by him in civil proceedings for damages in respect thereof subsequently falls to be determined.

(2) The damages in the civil proceedings shall be assessed without regard to the order or award; but where the whole or part of the amount awarded by the order or award has been paid, the damages awarded in the civil proceedings shall be restricted to the amount (if any) by which, as so assessed, they exceed the amount paid under the order or award.

(3) Where the whole or part of the amount awarded by the order or award remains unpaid and damages are awarded in a judgment in the civil proceedings, then, unless the person against whom the order or award was made has ceased to be

liable to pay the amount unpaid (whether in consequence of an appeal, or of his imprisonment for default or otherwise), the court shall direct that the judgment—

(a) if it is for an amount not exceeding the amount unpaid under the order or award, shall not be enforced; or

(b) if it is for an amount exceeding the amount unpaid under the order or award, shall not be enforced except to the extent that it exceeds the amount unpaid,

without the leave of the court.

(4) In this section a "service compensation order or award" means—

(a) an order requiring the payment of compensation under paragraph 11 of—

(i) Schedule 5A to the Army Act 1955;

(ii) Schedule 5A to the Air Force Act 1955; or

(iii) Schedule 4A to the Naval Discipline Act 1957; or

(b) an award of stoppages payable by way of compensation under any of those Acts.

AMENDMENTS

Subs.(1) as amended by Criminal Proceedings etc (Reform) (Scotland) Act 2007 (asp 6) s.49. Brought into force on March 10, 2008 by SSI 2008/42 (C.4) art.3 and Sch.

DEFINITIONS

"compensation orders": s.249(1). A4-491.1

"order": s.307(1).

"service compensation order": s.253(4).

[THE NEXT PARAGRAPH IS A4-492.16]

GENERAL NOTE

Following *Goodhall v Carmichael*, 1984 S.C.C.R. 247 it is clear that credible though uncorroborated evidence is sufficient to settle the value of the loss to be compensated, a practice that is now consistent with the civil law of evidence. The appeal by Goodhall was dismissed without Opinions being delivered. However, in an article following that appeal it was said that Lord Wheatley had commented during the appeal that "the whole point of compensation orders was to save victims the need to go to the civil courts": C.J. Docherty and G. Maher, "Corroboration and Compensation Orders", 1984 S.L.T. (News) 125 at 126.

Restitution order

[Restitution order where conviction of police assault etc.

253A.—(1) This section applies where a person ("P") is convicted of an offence under section 90(1) of the Police and Fire Reform (Scotland) Act 2012 (police assault etc.).

(2) The court, instead of or in addition to dealing with P in any other way, may make an order to be known as a restitution order requiring P to pay an amount not exceeding the prescribed sum (as defined in section 225(8)).

(3) The Scottish Ministers may by regulations amend subsection (2) so as to substitute for the amount for the time being specified such other amount as may be prescribed by, or determined in accordance with, the regulations.

(4) Any amount paid in respect of a restitution order is to be paid to the clerk of any court or any other person (or class of person) authorised by the Scottish Ministers for the purpose.

(5) Regulations under subsection (3) are subject to the negative procedure.

[(6) A restitution order is to be treated as a sentence for the purposes of any appeal under this Act.]

Amendments

Section 253A inserted by the Victims and Witnesses (Scotland) Act 2014 (asp 1) s.25 (effective 10 February 2021: insertion has effect as SSI 2020/405 art.2(b) subject to transitional provisions specified in SSI 2020/405 art.3).

Section 253A(6) inserted by the Victims and Witnesses (Scotland) Act 2014 (Supplementary Provisions) Order 2021 (SSI 2021/57) art.2(3) (effective 10 February 2021: insertion came into force on February 3, 2021 but could not take effect until the commencement of s.253A on 10 February 2021).

[The Restitution Fund

253B.—(1) A person to whom any amount is paid under section 253A in respect of a restitution order must pay the amount to the Scottish Ministers.

(2) The Scottish Ministers must pay any amount received by virtue of subsection (1) into a fund to be known as the Restitution Fund.

(3) The Scottish Ministers must establish, maintain and administer the Restitution Fund for the purpose of securing the provision of support services for persons who have been assaulted as mentioned in section 90(1) of the Police and Fire Reform (Scotland) Act 2012 ("victims").

(4) Any payment out of the fund may be made only to—

(a) a person who provides or secures the provision of support services for victims, or

(b) the Scottish Ministers or, with the consent of the Scottish Ministers, a person specified by order by virtue of subsection (5) in respect of outlays incurred in administering the fund.

(5) The Scottish Ministers may delegate to such person as they may specify by order the duties imposed on them by subsection (3) of establishing, maintaining and administering the Restitution Fund.

(6) The Scottish Ministers may by order make further provision about the administration of the Restitution Fund including provision for or in connection with—

(a) specifying persons or classes of person to or in respect of whom payments may be made out of the fund (but subject to subsection (4)),

(b) the making of payments out of the fund,

(c) requiring financial or other records to be kept,

(d) the making of reports to the Scottish Government containing such information and in respect of such periods as may be specified.

(7) An order under subsection (5) or (6) is subject to the affirmative procedure.

(8) In this section, "support services" , in relation to a victim, means any type of service or treatment which is intended to benefit the physical or mental health or wellbeing of the victim.]

Amendments

Section 253B inserted by the Victims and Witnesses (Scotland) Act 2014 (asp 1) s.25 (effective 25 August 2020: as SSI 2020/237 reg.2(2) subject to transitional provisions specified in SSI 2020/405 art.3).

[Restitution order, fine and compensation order: order of preference

253C.—(1) Subsection (2) applies where a court considers in relation to an offence that it would be appropriate—

(a) to make a restitution order,

(b) to impose a fine, and

(c) to make a compensation order.

(2) If the person convicted of the offence ("P") has insufficient means to pay an appropriate amount under a restitution order, to pay an appropriate fine and to pay an appropriate amount in compensation, the court should prefer a compensation order and then a restitution order over a fine.

(3) Subsection (4) applies where a court considers in relation to an offence that it would be appropriate—

(a) to make a restitution order, and

(b) to impose a fine or make a compensation order.

(4) If P has insufficient means to pay an appropriate amount under a restitution order and to pay an appropriate fine or, as the case may be, an appropriate amount in compensation, the court should prefer a compensation order and then a restitution order over a fine.]

AMENDMENTS

S.253C inserted by the Victims and Witnesses (Scotland) Act 2014 (asp 1) s.25 (effective 10 February 2021: insertion has effect as SSI 2020/405 art.2(b) subject to transitional provisions specified in SSI 2020/405 art.3).

[Application of receipts

253D.—(1) This section applies where the court makes a restitution order in relation to a person ("P") convicted of an offence and also in respect of the same offence or different offences in the same proceedings—

(a) imposes a fine and makes a compensation order, or

(b) imposes a fine or makes a compensation order.

(2) A payment by P must be applied in the following order—

(a) the payment must first be applied in satisfaction of the compensation order,

(b) the payment must next be applied in satisfaction of the restitution order,

(c) the payment must then be applied in satisfaction of the fine.]

AMENDMENTS

Section 253D inserted by the Victims and Witnesses (Scotland) Act 2014 (asp 1) s.25 (effective 10 February 2021: insertion has effect as SSI 2020/405 art.2(b) subject to transitional provisions specified in SSI 2020/405 art.3).

[Enforcement: application of certain provisions relating to fines

253E.—(1) The provisions of this Act specified in subsection (2) apply in relation to restitution orders as they apply in relation to fines but subject to the modifications mentioned in subsection (2) and to any other necessary modifications.

(2) The provisions are—

[(za) section 121(4),

(zb) section 193(3),]

(a) section 211(3) and (7),

(b) section 212,

(c) section 213 (with the modification that subsection (2) is to be read as if the words "or (4)" were omitted),

(d) section 214(1) to (4) and (6) to (9) (with the modification that subsection (4) is to be read as if the words from "unless" to "decision" were omitted),

(e) sections 215 to 217,

(f) subject to subsection (3) below, section 219(1)(b), (2), (3), (5), (6) and (8),

(g) sections 220 to 224,

(h) section 248B.

(3) In the application of the provisions of section 219 mentioned in subsection (2)(f) for the purposes of subsection (1)—

(a) a court may impose imprisonment in respect of a fine and decline to impose imprisonment in respect of a restitution order but not vice versa,

(b) where a court imposes imprisonment both in respect of a fine and a restitution order, the amounts in respect of which imprisonment is imposed are to be aggregated for the purposes of section 219(2).]

AMENDMENTS

Section 253E inserted by the Victims and Witnesses (Scotland) Act 2014 (asp 1) s.25 (effective 10 February 2021: insertion has effect as SSI 2020/405 art.2(b) subject to transitional provisions specified in SSI 2020/405 art.3).

Section 253E(2)(za) and (zb) inserted by the Victims and Witnesses (Scotland) Act 2014 (Supplementary Provisions) Order 2012 (SSI 2021/57) art.2(4) (effective February 10, 2021: insertion came into force on February 3, 2021 but could not take effect until the commencement of s.253E on February 10, 2021).

[THE NEXT PARAGRAPH IS A4-492.16]

Victim surcharge

Victim surcharge

A4-492.16 **253F.**—(1) This section applies where—

(a) a person ("P") is convicted of an offence other than an offence, or offence of a class, that is prescribed by regulations by the Scottish Ministers,
(b) the court does not make a restitution order, and
(c) the court imposes a sentence, or sentence of a class, that is so prescribed.

(2) Except in such circumstances as may be prescribed by regulations by the Scottish Ministers, the court, in addition to dealing with P in any other way, must order P to pay a victim surcharge of such amount as may be so prescribed.

(3) Despite subsection (2), if P is convicted of two or more offences in the same proceedings, the court must order P to pay only one victim surcharge in respect of both or, as the case may be, all the offences.

(4) Any sum paid in respect of a victim surcharge is to be paid to the clerk of any court or any other person (or class of person) authorised by the Scottish Ministers for the purpose.

(5) Regulations under this section may make different provision for different cases and in particular may include provision—

(a) prescribing different amounts for different descriptions of offender,
(b) prescribing different amounts for different circumstances.

(6) Where provision is made by virtue of subsection (5), the Scottish Ministers may by regulations make provision for determining which victim surcharge is payable in the circumstances mentioned in subsection (3).

(7) Regulations under this section are subject to the affirmative procedure.

AMENDMENTS

Section 253F inserted by Victims and Witnesses (Scotland) Act 2014 (asp 1) s.26. Brought into force on 13 August 2014 by SSI 2014/210 (C.17) art.2 (only for the purpose of making regulations under s.253F; 25 November 2019 otherwise).

[THE NEXT PARAGRAPH IS A4-492.19]

The Victim Surcharge Fund

A4-492.19 **253G.**—(1) A person to whom any sum is paid under section 253F(4) in respect of a victim surcharge must pay the sum to the Scottish Ministers.

(2) The Scottish Ministers must pay any sum received by virtue of subsection (1) into a fund to be known as the Victim Surcharge Fund.

(3) The Scottish Ministers must establish, maintain and administer the Victim Surcharge Fund for the purpose of securing the provision of support services for persons who are or appear to be the victims of crime and prescribed relatives of such persons.

(4) Any payment out of the fund may be made only to—

(a) a person who is or appears to be the victim of crime,

(b) a prescribed relative of a person who is or appears to be the victim of crime,
(c) a person who provides or secures the provision of support services for persons who are or appear to be victims of crime, or
(d) the Scottish Ministers or, with the consent of the Scottish Ministers, a person specified by order by virtue of subsection (5) in respect of outlays incurred in administering the fund.

(5) The Scottish Ministers may delegate to such person as they may specify by order the duties imposed on them by subsection (3) of establishing, maintaining and administering the Victim Surcharge Fund.

(6) The Scottish Ministers may by regulations make further provision about the administration of the Victim Surcharge Fund including provision for or in connection with—

(a) the making of payments out of the fund,
(b) the keeping of financial and other records,
(c) the making of reports to the Scottish Government containing such information and in respect of such periods as may be specified.

(7) An order under subsection (5) and regulations under subsection (6) are subject to the affirmative procedure.

(8) In this section—

"prescribed" means prescribed by the Scottish Ministers by regulations,
"support services", in relation to a person who is or appears to be the victim of crime, means any type of service or treatment which is intended to benefit the physical or mental health or wellbeing of the person or a prescribed relative of the person

(9) Regulations under subsections (3), (4) and (8) are subject to the negative procedure.

AMENDMENTS

Section 253G inserted by Victims and Witnesses (Scotland) Act 2014 (asp 1) s.26. Brought into force on 13 August 2014 by SSI 2014/210 (C.17) art.2 (only for the purpose of making an order and regulations under s.253G; 25 November 2019 except for the purposes specified in SSI 2019/283 art.2(b); not yet in force otherwise).

Application of receipts

253H.—(1) This section applies where the court orders the payment of a victim surcharge in relation to a person ("P") convicted of an offence and also in respect of the same offence or different offences in the same proceedings— A4-492.20

(a) imposes a fine and makes a compensation order, or
(b) imposes a fine or makes a compensation order.

(2) A payment by P must be applied in the following order—

(a) the payment must first be applied in satisfaction of the compensation order,
(b) the payment must next be applied in satisfaction of the victim surcharge,
(c) the payment must then be applied in satisfaction of the fine.

AMENDMENTS

Section 253H inserted by Victims and Witnesses (Scotland) Act 2014 (asp 1) s.26. Brought into force on 25 November 2019 by SSI 2019/283 art.2(c) and (d)).

Enforcement: application of certain provisions relating to fines

253J.—(1) The provisions of this Act specified in subsection (2) apply in relation to victim surcharges as they apply in relation to fines but subject to the modifications mentioned in subsection (2) and to any other necessary modifications. A4-492.21

(2) The provisions are—

[(za) section 121(4),
(zb) section 193(3),]
(a) section 211(3) and (4),
(b) section 212,
(c) section 213 (with the modification that subsection (2) is to be read as if the words "or (4)" were omitted),
(d) section 214(1) to (4) and (6) to (9) (with the modification that subsection (4) is to be read as if the words from "unless" to "decision" were omitted),
(e) sections 215 to 218,
(f) subject to subsection (3) below, section 219(1)(b) , (2), (3) , (5), (6) and (8),
(g) sections 220 to 224,
(h) section 248B.

(3) In the application of the provisions of section 219 mentioned in subsection (2)(f) for the purposes of subsection (1)—
(a) a court may impose imprisonment in respect of a fine and decline to impose imprisonment in respect of a victim surcharge but not vice versa,
(b) where a court imposes imprisonment both in respect of a fine and a victim surcharge, the amounts in respect of which imprisonment is imposed are to be aggregated for the purposes of section 219(2).

AMENDMENTS

Section 253J inserted by Victims and Witnesses (Scotland) Act 2014 (asp 1) s.26. Brought into force on 25 November 2019 by SSI 2019/283 art.2(c) and (d)).

Section 253J(2)(za) and (zb) inserted by the Victims and Witnesses (Scotland) Act 2014 (Supplementary Provisions) Order 2021 (SSI 2021/57) art.2(6) (effective 3 February 2021).

Forfeiture

Search warrant for forfeited articles

A4-493 **254.**—(1) Where a court has made an order for the forfeiture of an article, the court or any justice may, if satisfied on information on oath—
(a) that there is reasonable cause to believe that the article is to be found in any place or premises; and
(b) that admission to the place or premises has been refused or that a refusal of such admission is apprehended,
issue a warrant of search which may be executed according to law.

(2) In subsection (1), "article" includes animal.

AMENDMENTS

Section 254 renumbered to s.254(1) and subs.(2) inserted by Criminal Justice and Licensing (Scotland) Act 2010 (asp 13) Sch.7 para.60. Brought into force on 28 March 2011 by SSI 2011/178 (c.15) art.2, Sch.1 para.1.

[THE NEXT PARAGRAPH IS A4-493.2]

European Protection Orders

European Protection Orders: interpretation

A4-493.2 **254A.** In this section and in sections 254B, 254C, 254D and 254E, except where the context otherwise requires—

"competent authority" means the judicial or equivalent authority in a member state of the European Union which has power to issue and recognise a European Protection Order;

"European Protection Order" means a decision—
(a) taken in relation to a protection measure by a competent authority in a member state of the European Union; and
(b) on the basis of which the competent authority of another member state of the European Union may take any appropriate measure or measures under its own national law with a view to continuing the protection of the protected person,

"issuing state" in relation to a European Protection Order, means the member state of the European Union, other than the United Kingdom, whose competent authority has issued the Order;

"offender" in relation to a protection measure or, as the case may be, a non-harassment order made under section 254D(1), means the individual whose conduct is the subject of the measure or order;

"protected person" in relation to a protection measure or, as the case may be, a non-harassment order made under section 254D(1), means the individual who is the object of the protection given by the measure or order;

"protection measure" means a decision taken in criminal matters which is intended to protect a protected person from the criminal conduct of the offender by imposing one or more of the following prohibitions or restrictions—
(a) prohibiting the offender from entering certain localities, places or defined areas where the protected person resides or visits;
(b) prohibiting the offender from contacting, or regulating the offender's contact with, the protected person in any form (for example by telephone, electronic or ordinary mail or fax); or
(c) prohibiting the offender from coming closer than a prescribed distance to the protected person or regulating the approach of the offender to the protected person within such a distance.

AMENDMENTS

Section 254A inserted by European Protection Order (Scotland) Regulations 2015 (SSI 2015/107) reg.2 (effective 11 March 2015).

GENERAL NOTE

A4-493.4 This section and the four following were inserted by the European Protection Order (Scotland) Regulations 2015 (SSI 2015/107) and came into force on 11 March 2015. By way of background s.234A of the Act makes provision for the imposition of a non-harassment order (an NHO) both in civil proceedings and as a sentencing option, or as an element of any sentence, upon an accused in criminal proceedings. Once an NHO is imposed, breach of its terms is a criminal offence.

Sections 254A to 254E empower Scottish criminal courts, when fixing "protection measures" for the purpose of protecting an affected person from future harassment by that accused, on application, to extend their scope to the jurisdictions of member states of the European Union. The protected person should be notified of this sentencing option and can, where appropriate, make application (once a s.234A order has been imposed) for issue of a European Protection Order (EPO) for enforcement in an executing state where the accused stays or intends to stay.

The provisions, executed by a sheriff, cover the issuing and format of such an order and also set out procedures for mutual recognition and enforcement of orders by member states. Unless one of the exceptions set out in s.254C(2) exists, the sheriff must recognize and enforce a member state EPO issued by a competent authority, by imposing a non-harassment order. Refusal of an EPO, or the need for additional information to allow fuller consideration, must be notified to the issuing state and the protected person. Note that the sheriff is expected, so far as possible, to reflect the EPO's restrictions and conditions but it is a fine point how much latitude is available to the courts to reflect local circumstances.

The offender, protected person and issuing state all must be notified of the sheriff's imposition of a non-harassment order and its operative conditions (s.254D(6) and (7)). Section 254E provides for modification or revocation of EPOs; the section make no provisions for appeal. It has to be assumed that appeal procedures to the High Court would be by way of Bill of Suspension.

Issuing of a European Protection Order

A4-493.5 **254B.**—(1) A protected person, or an authorised representative of such a person, may apply to a court for a European Protection Order.

(2) A court may issue a European Protection Order in respect of a protected person if the court is satisfied that—

(a) a protection measure which has been taken in Scotland is in force; and
(b) the protected person—
(i) resides or stays in the executing state, or
(ii) has decided to reside or stay in the executing state.

(3) In deciding whether to issue a European Protection Order, the court must take into account—

(a) the period or periods of time during which the protected person intends to reside or stay in the executing state; and
(b) the seriousness of the need for protection of the protected person.

(4) Where the court decides not to issue a European Protection Order, the court must inform the protected person of that decision.

(5) Where a court issues a European Protection Order under subsection (2) the court must, as soon as reasonably practicable, transmit the European Protection Order to the competent authority of the executing state.

(6) Where a European Protection Order has been issued by a court under subsection (2) and the court subsequently modifies or revokes the protection measure on which it is based, the court must, as soon as reasonably practicable—

(a) modify or revoke the European Protection Order accordingly; and
(b) inform the competent authority of the executing state of that decision.

(7) For the purposes of this section—

"court" means the High Court, the Sheriff Appeal Court, a sheriff or a justice of the peace court; and

"executing state" means a member state of the European Union, other than the United Kingdom in which the protected person resides, stays, or intends to reside or stay.

AMENDMENTS

Section 254B inserted by European Protection Order (Scotland) Regulations 2015 (SSI 2015/107) reg.2 (effective March 11, 2015).

Subs.(7) as amended by Courts Reform (Scotland) Act 2014 (Consequential Provisions No.2) Order 2015 (SSI 2015/338) Sch.2 para.5 (effective September 22, 2015).

[THE NEXT PARAGRAPH IS A4-493.8]

Recognition of a European Protection Order

A4-493.8 **254C.**—(1) This section applies where a sheriff receives a European Protection Order from a competent authority of an issuing state.

(2) Except where one or more grounds specified in subsection (3) applies, the sheriff must recognise the European Protection Order.

(3) The grounds are—

(a) the sheriff, after complying with subsection (4), decides that the European Protection Order is incomplete;
(b) the European Protection Order does not relate to a protection measure;
(c) the prohibitions or restrictions contained in the European Protection Order have been adopted in relation to conduct that does not constitute a criminal offence in Scotland;
(d) the protection created by the prohibitions or restrictions contained in the

European Protection Order derives from the execution of a penalty or measure that is covered by an amnesty under the law of Scotland;

(e) there is immunity conferred on the offender in Scotland, which would make it impossible to adopt a protection measure following recognition of the European Protection Order;

(f) criminal proceedings against the offender for the conduct in relation to which the prohibitions or restrictions contained in the European Protection Order have been adopted would be prohibited in Scotland under any enactment had the conduct occurred in Scotland;

(g) recognition of the European Protection Order would be inconsistent with the rule against double jeopardy provided for in section 1(1) of the Double Jeopardy (Scotland) Act 2011;

(h) the offender, by reason of the offender's age, could not have been held criminally responsible for the conduct in relation to which the prohibitions or restrictions contained in the European Protection Order have been adopted had the conduct occurred in Scotland;

(i) the prohibitions or restrictions contained in the European Protection Order relate to a criminal offence which, under the law of Scotland, is regarded as having been committed, wholly or for a major or essential part, within Scotland.

(4) Where the sheriff considers that the European Protection Order is incomplete, the sheriff must—

(a) inform the competent authority of the issuing state in writing;

(b) request that the competent authority of the issuing state provide the missing information; and

(c) allow the competent authority of the issuing state such reasonable period of time as the sheriff may specify in order to comply with that request.

(5) Where the sheriff refuses to recognise a European Protection Order on any of the grounds specified in subsection (3), the sheriff must inform the competent authority of the issuing state and the protected person of the refusal and the grounds of refusal.

AMENDMENTS

Section 254C inserted by European Protection Order (Scotland) Regulations 2015 (SSI 2015/107) reg.2 (effective March 11, 2015).

[THE NEXT PARAGRAPH IS A4-493.11]

Implementation of a recognised European Protection Order

254D.—(1) Where a sheriff recognises a European Protection Order under section 254C(2), the sheriff must make a non-harassment order in relation to the offender requiring the offender to refrain from such conduct in relation to the protected person as may be specified in the order for such period (which includes an indeterminate period) as may be so specified. **A4-493.11**

(2) Subsection (4) of section 234A applies to a non-harassment order made under subsection (1) of this section as it applies to a non-harassment order made under section 234A subject to the restrictions in paragraph 1(1)(d) of Schedule 2 to the European Communities Act 1972.

(3) Subsections (4A) and (4B) of section 234A apply to a non-harassment order made under subsection (1) of this section as they apply to a non-harassment order made under section 234A.

(4) A non-harassment order made under subsection (1) may impose on the offender only such requirements as to the offender's conduct—

(a) as may constitute a protection measure; and
(b) which correspond, to the highest degree possible, to the prohibitions or restrictions contained in the European Protection Order.

(5) In considering which requirements to specify in a non-harassment order made under subsection (1), the sheriff must consider—
(a) the nature of the prohibitions or restrictions contained in the European Protection Order; and
(b) the duration of the prohibitions or restrictions contained in the European Protection Order.

(6) Where a sheriff makes a non-harassment order under subsection (1), the sheriff must provide the information in subsection (7) to—
(a) the offender;
(b) the competent authority of the issuing state; and
(c) the protected person.

(7) The information is—
(a) that the non-harassment order has been made;
(b) that a breach of the non-harassment order is an offence under section 234A(4);
(c) information about the punishments to which the offender may be liable following conviction for an offence under section 234A(4); and
(d) information about the powers of arrest available to a constable under section 234A(4A) and (4B).

(8) Where the offender is convicted of an offence consisting of, or involving, a breach of a non-harassment order made under subsection (1), the convicting court must notify the competent authority of the issuing state.

AMENDMENTS

Section 254D inserted by European Protection Order (Scotland) Regulations 2015 (SSI 2015/107) reg.2 (effective March 11, 2015).

[THE NEXT PARAGRAPH IS A4-493.14]

Modification and revocation of non-harassment orders made under section 254D

A4-493.14 **254E.**—(1) This section applies to non-harassment orders made under section 254D(1).

(2) Where a sheriff is informed by a competent authority of an issuing state that the European Protection Order to which a non-harassment order relates has been modified, the sheriff must—
(a) modify the non-harassment order so that the requirements as to the offender's conduct contained in the modified non-harassment order correspond, to the highest degree possible, to the prohibitions or restrictions contained in the modified European Protection Order;
(b) where the information submitted by the competent authority of the issuing state in relation to the modification of the European Protection Order is incomplete, refuse to modify the non-harassment order until the missing information is provided by the competent authority of the issuing state; or
(c) where the prohibitions or restrictions contained in the modified European Protection Order no longer constitute a protection measure, revoke the non-harassment order.

(3) A sheriff may, on the application of an offender to whom a non-harassment order relates, modify the order on either or both of the following grounds—
(a) that the requirements as to the offender's conduct contained in the non-

harassment order do not correspond, or do not correspond sufficiently, to the prohibitions or restrictions contained in the European Protection Order to which the non-harassment order relates;

(b) the European Protection Order to which the non-harassment order relates has been modified by the competent authority of the issuing state and the non-harassment order should be modified in a similar manner.

(4) Where a sheriff is informed by a competent authority of an issuing state that the European Protection Order to which a non-harassment order relates has been revoked or withdrawn, the sheriff must revoke the non-harassment order.

(5) A sheriff may, on the application of an offender to whom a non-harassment order relates, revoke the order on any of the following grounds—

(a) the recognition of the European Protection Order to which the non-harassment order relates should have been refused on one of the grounds specified in section 254C(3);

(b) the protected person no longer resides or stays in Scotland;

(c) where the prohibitions or restrictions contained in the European Protection Order have been modified and no longer constitute a protection measure;

(d) the European Protection Order has been revoked or withdrawn by the competent authority of the issuing state; or

(e) a decision on supervision measures, within the meaning of Article 4 of Framework Decision 2009/829/JHA, which includes the prohibitions or restrictions contained in the European Protection Order, is transferred to Scotland after the recognition of the European Protection Order.

(6) Where a sheriff modifies or revokes a non-harassment order under this section, the sheriff must inform—

(a) the competent authority of the issuing state; and

(b) where possible—

(i) the protected person, and

(ii) the offender.

Amendments

Section 254E inserted by European Protection Order (Scotland) Regulations 2015 (SSI 2015/107) reg.2 (effective March 11, 2015).

[THE NEXT PARAGRAPH IS A4-494]

Part XII – Evidence

Special capacity

Special capacity

255. Where an offence is alleged to be committed in any special capacity, as by the holder of a licence, master of a vessel, occupier of a house, or the like, the fact that the accused possesses the qualification necessary to the commission of the offence shall, unless challenged— **A4-494**

(a) in the case of proceedings on indictment, by giving notice of a preliminary objection in accordance with section 71(2) or 72(6)(b)(i) of this Act; or

(b) in summary proceedings, by preliminary objection before his plea is recorded,

be held as admitted.

AMENDMENTS

Subs.(a) as amended by Criminal Procedure (Amendment) (Scotland) Act 2004 (asp 5) s.25 and Sch.1 para.38. Brought into force on 1 February 2005 by SSI 2004/405 (C.28) art.2.

DEFINITIONS

A4-494.1 "indictment": s.307(1).
"offence": s.307(1).

[THE NEXT PARAGRAPH IS A4-495]

GENERAL NOTE

A4-495 This section relates both to solemn and summary procedure. A special capacity is a capacity which is special to the accused and is necessary to the commission of the offence.

In order to take advantage of this evidential concession, a prosecutor has to give notice in the libel of the capacity upon which he intends to found. Failure to do so will compel the prosecution to lead sufficient evidence to establish that the accused did possess the capacity essential to the commission of the offence. Furthermore, if the Crown libels a special capacity and then proceeds to conduct its case by leading evidence of the fact, it risks being held to have waived the benefit of the presumption (*Wimpey Homes Holdings v Lees*, 1993 S.L.T. 564; 1991 S.C.C.R. 447; *Smith v Ross*, 1937 J.C. 65). Note that production of an extract conviction in support of a charge of driving while disqualified does not constitute a waiver of the presumption by the Crown (*Paton v Lees*, 1992 S.C.C.R. 212).

A special capacity is not implied in any charge so while no express formula of words is required, it must be patent that the accused was acting in that capacity at the time of the offence (*Ross v Simpson*, 1994 S.C.C.R. 847).

Any denial of special capacity must be stated before any plea is tendered at the first calling of a summary complaint (s.144(4)) unless the court, being satisfied on cause shown (s.144(5)), permits objection or denial at a later diet.

In relation to solemn proceedings objection has to be stated, before the recording of any plea, and timeously in advance of either the first diet (s.71(2)) or preliminary hearing (s.72(3)). It should also be noted for both summary and solemn proceedings that express formal objection to the terms of any s.258 statement of uncontroversial evidence alleging such special capacity must also be lodged (see application by *Travers v HM Advocate* [2018] HCJAC 8).

Examples of special capacity are: being subject to bail conditions in terms of the Bail etc. (Scotland) Act 1980 and, now, in terms of s.27(4) of the 1995 Act as amended, being subject of bail conditions imposed after July 4, 1996; being a common prostitute (*Allan v McGraw*, 1986 S.C.C.R. 257); being a known thief as defined in s.58 of the Civic Government (Scotland) Act 1982 (c.45) (*Newlands v MacPhail*, 1991 S.C.C.R. 88); being a disqualified driver (*Paton v Lees*, cited above); ownership of a vessel (*Thomas W. Ward Ltd v Waugh*, 1934 J.C. 13); and in certain circumstances, being the parent of a child (*Ross v Simpson*, 1994 S.C.C.R. 847). It is submitted that ss.233 and 241 above which relate to offences committed at placements by those subject to probation or community service orders equally create categories of special capacity as well as being aggravated offences. See *McClory v MacKinnon*, 1996 S.C.C.R. 367 in relation to the construction of "occupier".

Proof of age

A4-495.1 **255A.** Where the age of any person is specified in an indictment or complaint, it shall, unless challenged—

(a) in the case of proceedings on indictment by giving notice of a preliminary objection in accordance with section 71(2) or 72(6)(b)(i) of this Act; or

(b) in summary proceedings—

  (i) by preliminary objection before the plea of the accused is recorded; or

  (ii) by objection at such later time as the court may in special circumstances allow,

be held as admitted.

AMENDMENTS

Section 255A inserted by Crime and Punishment (Scotland) Act 1997 (c.48) s.27 with effect from 1 August 1997 by SI 1997/1712 art.3.

Subs.(a) as amended by Criminal Procedure (Amendment) (Scotland) Act 2004 (asp 5) s.25 and Sch.1 para.39. Brought into force on 1 February 2005 by SSI 2004/405 (C.28) art.2.

DEFINITIONS

A4-495.2 "complaint": s.307(1) of the 1995 Act.
"indictment": s.307(1) of the 1995 Act.

GENERAL NOTE

This provision was introduced into the 1997 Act at a relatively late stage and would apply to witness particulars in cases where the age of a witness is a necessary element of the offence, notably the broad range of sexual offences now contained in Part I of the Criminal Law (Consolidation) (Scotland) Act 1995, and in the Licensing (Scotland) Act 1976. This provision is sufficiently broadly drafted to apply to circumstances where the libel indicates the age of the victim as an aggravating factor, for example in assaults or housebreakings, as well as where the age of the accused is a necessary element of the offence, as in the Firearms Act 1968 s.22 (acquisition and possession of firearms by minors). **A4-495.3**

It may be that specification of a witness's age in the list of witnesses on an indictment could create a rebuttable presumption. Any objection to specification of the age of a victim, witness or accused must be specified at a preliminary (or first) diet in solemn proceedings, or, in summary proceedings, by preliminary objection prior to tendering any plea (s.144(4) of the 1995 Act).

[THE NEXT PARAGRAPH IS A4-496]

Agreed evidence

Agreements and admissions as to evidence

256.—(1) In any trial it shall not be necessary for the accused or for the prosecutor— **A4-496**

(a) to prove any fact which is admitted by the other; or

(b) to prove any document, the terms and application of which are not in dispute between them,

and, without prejudice to paragraph 1 of Schedule 8 to this Act, copies of any documents may, by agreement of the parties, be accepted as equivalent to the originals.

(2) For the purposes of subsection (1) above, any admission or agreement shall be made by lodging with the clerk of court a minute in that behalf signed—

(a) in the case of an admission, by the party making the admission or, if that party is the accused and he is legally represented, by his counsel or solicitor; and

(b) in the case of an agreement, by the prosecutor and the accused or, if he is legally represented, his counsel or solicitor.

(3) Where a minute has been signed and lodged as aforesaid, any facts and documents admitted or agreed thereby shall be deemed to have been duly proved.

DEFINITIONS

"prosecutor": s.307(1). **A4-496.1**
"trial": s.307(1).

[THE NEXT PARAGRAPH IS A4-497]

GENERAL NOTE

This section applies to both solemn and summary procedure and provides for the lodging of Minutes of Agreement or Minutes of Admissions describing facts accepted as established in the proceedings. Documentary evidence or copies thereof can be admitted in this way; where such evidence is not formally agreed, or is not agreed with sufficient celerity, then recourse can be had to the provisions of s.258 which permits service of a statement of what is felt to be uncontroversial evidence upon other parties or, alternatively, the use of the procedures for setting up documentary evidence contained in Sch.8 (this preserves the terms of Sch.3 of the Prisoners and Criminal Proceedings (Scotland) Act 1993 (c.9)). **A4-497**

It will be recalled that there is no timescale stipulated for agreement of evidence by Minutes of Agreement or Admission and, indeed, these can be prepared and lodged at any point in proceedings before evidence is closed; by contrast s.258 demands a response from the other party in seven days to any statement of facts served validly and is only available prior for use more than 14 days before trial. *McClymont v HM Advocate* [2020] HCJAC 1 emphasises that where parties at a first diet (in that case) or, by extension, at a preliminary hearing, indicate in the written record that evidence has been agreed, it is incumbent upon the parties to produce and lodge it at that time. This will enable judicial consideration of the terms and save valuable court time at any trial.

Guidance upon the importance of accurate draftsmanship, and particularly highlighting the facts upon which parties are agreed, rather than expressing unanimity that the contents of reports or documents are accepted, is found in *Liddle v HM Advocate* [2012] HCJAC 68; 2012 S.C.C.R. 478.

Duty to seek agreement of evidence

A4-498 **257.**—(1) Subject to subsection (2) below, the prosecutor and the accused (or each of the accused if more than one) shall each identify any facts which are facts—

(a) which he would, apart from this section, be seeking to prove;

(b) which he considers unlikely to be disputed by the other party (or by any of the other parties); and

(c) in proof of which he does not wish to lead oral evidence,

and shall, without prejudice to section 258 of this Act, take all reasonable steps to secure the agreement of the other party (or each of the other parties) to them; and the other party (or each of the other parties) shall take all reasonable steps to reach such agreement.

(2) Subsection (1) above shall not apply in relation to proceedings as respects which the accused (or any of the accused if more than one) is not legally represented.

(3) The duty under subsection (1) above applies—

(a) in relation to proceedings on indictment, from the date of service of the indictment until the swearing of the jury or, where intimation is given under section 76 of this Act, the date of that intimation; and

(b) in relation to summary proceedings, from the date on which the accused pleads not guilty until the swearing of the first witness or, where the accused tenders a plea of guilty at any time before the first witness is sworn, the date when he does so.

(4) Without prejudice to subsection (3) above, in relation to proceedings on indictment, the parties to the proceedings shall, in complying with the duty under subsection (1) above, seek to ensure that the facts to be identified, and the steps to be taken in relation to those facts, are identified and taken—

(a) in the case of the High Court, before the preliminary hearing;

(b) in the case of the sheriff court, before the first diet.

(5) Without prejudice to subsection (3) above, in relation to summary proceedings, the parties to the proceedings shall, in complying with the duty under subsection (1) above, seek to ensure that the facts to be identified, and the steps to be taken in relation to those facts, are identified and taken before any intermediate diet that is to be held.

AMENDMENTS

Subs.(4) inserted by Criminal Procedure (Amendment) (Scotland) Act 2004 (asp 5) s.25 and Sch.1 para.40. Brought into force on 1 February 2005 by SSI 2004/405 (C.28) art.2.

Subs.(5) inserted by Criminal Proceedings etc. (Reform) (Scotland) Act 2007 (asp 6) s.20. Brought into force on 10 December 2007 by SSI 2007/479.

Subs.(4) as amended by Criminal Proceedings etc. (Reform) (Scotland) Act 2007 (asp 6) s.30. Brought into force on 10 December 2007 by SSI 2007/479.

DEFINITIONS

A4-498.1 "indictment": s.307(1).
"prosecutor": s.307(1).

[THE NEXT PARAGRAPH IS A4-499]

GENERAL NOTE

A4-499 The general duty of pleaders before all Scottish criminal courts to seek to identify evidence which could be agreed formally, without the necessity of leading it ad longem, was given a statutory footing by this section . More recent legislation which applied only to proceedings in the High Court required parties to to make an active endeavour to identify such evidence and to report upon it at the preliminary diet. The same formalised duty is extended to solemn proceedings in the sheriff court, and has to be executed in time for the first diet (refer generally to s.71 of the 1995 Act).

The purpose of this, and the following section, is to identify evidence which is capable of being received without the need for its introduction by parole evidence and the need for witnesses to attend court. Prior to the introduction of these provisions there was no onus upon any party to identify, or agree, formal or uncontroversial evidence and while a duty is now placed on parties to consider such material, there is no sanction for failure to do so. The prosecutor and, only where he is legally represented the accused, are each required to identify factual evidence felt to be capable of agreement and to take all reasonable steps to agree these matters before trial. The purpose of this provision and s.258 below were considered at length in *HM Advocate v Ashif* [2015] HCJAC 100, a seven Bench decision.

Section 256 provides a mechanism for agreement of evidence, or for the admission of facts by one party; s.258 enacts a procedure for service of statements of fact upon other parties. Subsection (3) provides two different timescales during which the duties imposed on parties persist: in solemn proceedings this is the period from service of the indictment until the commencement of trial (see s.64(9)) or, in the case of accelerated pleas, until the accused gives notice in writing of a plea which is accepted by the Crown (see s.76(1)); in summary proceedings, the period from the date of the plea being recorded (s.146(1)) until trial begins (s.147(4)) or a plea of guilty is intimated.

Attention is also directed to High Court of Justiciary Practice Note No.1 of 2018 (see C1-78) regulating the management of lengthy or complex trials. Paragraph 4 directs all parties to consider use of s.258 procedures during the preparation for trial, and to utilise the provisions of s.256 Minutes during the trial itself to agree uncontentious evidence.

Uncontroversial evidence

258.—(1) This section applies where, in any criminal proceedings, a party (in this section referred to as "the first party") considers that facts which that party would otherwise be seeking to prove are unlikely to be disputed by the other parties to the proceedings. **A4-500**

(2) Where this section applies, the first party may prepare and sign a statement—

(a) specifying the facts concerned; or

(b) referring to such facts as set out in a document annexed to the statement,

and shall, not less than the relevant period before the relevant diet, serve a copy of the statement and any such document on every other party.

(2ZA) In subsection (2) above, the "relevant period" means—

(a) where the relevant diet for the purpose of that subsection is an intermediate diet in summary proceedings, 7 days;

(b) in any other case, 14 days.

(2A) In subsection (2) above, "the relevant diet" means—

(a) in the case of proceedings in the High Court, the preliminary hearing;

(aa) in summary proceedings in which an intermediate diet is to be held, that diet;

(b) in any other case, the trial diet.

(3) Unless any other party serves on the first party, not more than seven days after the date of service of the copy on him under subsection (2) above or by such later time as the court may in special circumstances allow, a notice that he challenges any fact specified or referred to in the statement, the facts so specified or referred to shall be deemed to have been conclusively proved.

(4) Where a notice is served under subsection (3) above, the facts specified or referred to in the statement shall be deemed to have been conclusively proved only in so far as unchallenged in the notice.

(4AA) Where in summary proceedings the relevant diet for the purposes of subsection (4A) above is an intermediate diet, an application under that subsection may be made at (or at any time before) that diet.

(4A) Where a notice is served under subsection (3) above, the court may, on the application of any party to the proceedings made not less than 48 hours before the relevant diet, direct that any challenge in the notice to any fact is to be disregarded for the purposes of subsection (4) above if the court considers the challenge to be unjustified.

(4B) In subsection (4A) above, "the relevant diet" means—

(a) in proceedings in the High Court, the preliminary hearing;

(b) in solemn proceedings in the sheriff court, the first diet.

(c) in summary proceedings—
  (i) in which an intermediate diet is to be held, that diet;
  (ii) in which such a diet is not to be held, the trial diet.

(4C) In proceedings in the High Court, the Court may, on cause shown, allow an application under subsection (4A) above to be made after the time limit specified in that subsection.

(4D) In summary proceedings, the court may allow an application under subsection (4A) above to be made late if the court is satisfied that a timeous application would not have been practicable.

(5) Subsections (3) and (4) above shall not preclude a party from leading evidence of circumstances relevant to, or other evidence in explanation of, any fact specified or referred to in the statement.

(6) Notwithstanding subsections (3) and (4) above, the court—
(a) may, on the application of any party, where it is satisfied that there are special circumstances; and
(b) shall, on the joint application of all the parties,

direct that the presumptions in those subsections shall not apply in relation to such fact specified or referred to in the statement as is specified in the direction.

(7) An application under subsection (6) above may be made at any time after the commencement of the trial and before the commencement of the prosecutor's address to the court on the evidence.

(8) Where the court makes a direction under subsection (6) above it shall, unless all the parties otherwise agree, adjourn the trial and may, without prejudice to section 268 of this Act, permit any party to lead evidence as to any such fact as is specified in the direction, notwithstanding that a witness or production concerned is not included in any list lodged by the parties and that the notice required by sections 67(5) and 78(4) of this Act has not been given.

(9) A copy of a statement or a notice required, under this section, to be served on any party shall be served in such manner as may be prescribed by Act of Adjournal; and a written execution purporting to be signed by the person who served such copy or notice together with, where appropriate, the relevant post office receipt shall be sufficient evidence of such service.

AMENDMENTS

Subss.(4A)–(4C) inserted, by Criminal Procedure (Amendment) (Scotland) Act 2004 (asp 5) s.16. Subs.(2) as amended and subs.(2A) inserted by s.25 and Sch.1 para.41 of the 2004 Act. Brought into force on 1 February 2005 by SSI 2004/405 (C.28) art.2.

Subs.(2), (2A), (4A) and (4B) as amended and subs.(2ZA), inserted by Criminal Proceedings etc. (Reform) (Scotland) Act 2007 (asp 6) s.20. Brought into force on 10 December 2007 by SSI 2007/479.

Subs.(4D) inserted by Criminal Proceedings etc. (Reform) (Scotland) Act 2007 (asp 6) s.20, as amended by SSI 2007/540 art.4 (effective 10 December 2007).

Subs.(4AA) inserted by Criminal Justice and Licensing (Scotland) Act 2010 (asp 13) Sch.7 para.61. Brought into force on 28 March 2011 by SSI 2011/178 (C.15) art.2, Sch.1 para.1.

DEFINITIONS

A4-500.1 "diet": s.307(1).
"prosecutor": s.307(1).
"the relevant diet": s.258(2A) and (4B).

[THE NEXT PARAGRAPH IS A4-501]

GENERAL NOTE

A4-501 This section now applies equally to summary and solemn proceedings and the amendments reflect an effort to rationalise the provisions covering uncontroversial evidence. Thus a statement identifying evidence which any party believes to be uncontentious now has to be served upon other parties to summary proceedings not less than 7 days before an intermediate diet . In circumstances where no intermediate diet has been fixed in summary proceedings, subs.(2ZA) also indicates that any such statement has to be served not less than 14 days before the trial diet. In this latter situation it is submitted that the court could justifiably exercise its discretion to permit any challenge, or counterchallenge, to the notice. In solemn proceedings a statement must be served not less than 14 days before the preliminary diet in High Court proceedings, and 14 days before any sheriff and jury trial (subs.(2ZA)).

This provision was considered in a seven Bench decision, *HM Advocate v Ashif* [2015] HCJAC 100, when it was noted that the requirement upon parties to identify uncontentious evidence was proportionate and did not infringe an accused's art.6 Convention rights, and that subs.(4A), enacted by the Holyrood Parliament, which empowers the court to discard challenges to a notice which are considered unjustified, was neither ultra vires nor did it infringe an accused's right to silence. In all discussion of s.258 it should be borne in mind that each party to proceedings is entitled to lodge a s.258 notice, albeit the procedure is generally utilised by the Crown. Note too that the procedure can only be used to identify formal or uncontroversial material not (as was held to have occurred in the notice in the *Ashif* case) to advance as facts the contested issues, identified from the libel which are at the heart of the proceedings themselves.

Spurred in part by the lessons from *Ashif*, High Court of Justiciary Practice Note No.1 of 2018 (see C1-78) obliges parties in any lengthy or complex trial, expected to exceed eight weeks in duration, to identify facts they consider to be undisputed and to formulate appropriate s.258 notices. It can be expected that some judicial rigour will be brought to bear on parties; while the Practice Note is framed by reference to High Court proceedings its spirit seems certain to be applied in similar sheriff court proceedings.

Challenges to s.258 notice

Challenges to such notices have to be intimated to other parties within 7 days from service of the notice (or at such later time as the court in its discretion permits) failing which the contents of the notice will be deemed to be proved conclusively (s.258(3) being unaltered by the 2007 Act) unless the court is persuaded, or the parties jointly concur, that this presumptiion should be waived (see s.258(6) and (7)).

The Act remains silent as to how statements of fact, modified or unmodified by challenge, are to be introduced into the record of proceedings; they may be treated in the same way as a Minute of Agreement, being read to a jury by the clerk of court or simply be tendered to the judge in a summary trial but this is not settled. Parties serving statements of fact will need to preserve, and be able to exhibit to the court, a copy notice and completed execution of service. Given the complexities of s.258 the attractions of using a Minute of Agreement to identify and introduce undisputed evidence become obvious.

It is no part of counsel's (or by inference a law agent's) duty to accede to an accused's blanket instruction not to agree evidence—counsel owes a professional responsibility to the court in the administration of justice (see *Ashif* above at [69]–[71]). That said this element of the judgment may yet face further appeals. It is worth noting that where a special capacity (see s.255 above) is averred in the statement it is necessary to challenge that capacity both by (s.258(3)) and by a preliminary objection (see application by *Travers v HM Advocate* [2018] HCJAC 8).

Hearsay

Exceptions to the rule that hearsay evidence is inadmissible

259.—(1) Subject to the following provisions of this section, evidence of a statement made by a person otherwise than while giving oral evidence in court in criminal proceedings shall be admissible in those proceedings as evidence of any matter contained in the statement where the judge is satisfied— A4-502

(a) that the person who made the statement will not give evidence in the proceedings of such matter for any of the reasons mentioned in subsection (2) below;

(b) that evidence of the matter would be admissible in the proceedings if that person gave direct oral evidence of it;

(c) that the person who made the statement would have been, at the time the statement was made, a competent witness in such proceedings; and

(d) that there is evidence which would entitle a jury properly directed, or in summary proceedings would entitle the judge, to find that the statement was made and that either—

(i) it is contained in a document; or

(ii) a person who gave oral evidence in the proceedings as to the statement has direct personal knowledge of the making of the statement.

(2) The reasons referred to in paragraph (a) of subsection (1) above are that the person who made the statement—

(a) is dead or is, by reason of his bodily or mental condition, unfit or unable to give evidence in any competent manner;

(b) is named and otherwise sufficiently identified, but is outwith the United

Kingdom and it is not reasonably practicable to secure his attendance at the trial or to obtain his evidence in any other competent manner;

(c) is named and otherwise sufficiently identified, but cannot be found and all reasonable steps which, in the circumstances, could have been taken to find him have been so taken;

(d) having been authorised to do so by virtue of a ruling of the court in the proceedings that he is entitled to refuse to give evidence in connection with the subject matter of the statement on the grounds that such evidence might incriminate him, refuses to give such evidence; or

(e) is called as a witness and either—

(i) refuses to take the oath or affirmation; or

(ii) having been sworn as a witness and directed by the judge to give evidence in connection with the subject matter of the statement refuses to do so,

and in the application of this paragraph to a child, the reference to a witness refusing to take the oath or affirmation or, as the case may be, to having been sworn shall be construed as a reference to a child who has refused to accept an admonition to tell the truth or, having been so admonished, refuses to give evidence as mentioned above.

(3) Evidence of a statement shall not be admissible by virtue of subsection (1) above where the judge is satisfied that the occurrence of any of the circumstances mentioned in paragraphs (a) to (e) of subsection (2) above, by virtue of which the statement would otherwise be admissible, is caused by—

(a) the person in support of whose case the evidence would be given; or

(b) any other person acting on his behalf,

for the purpose of securing that the person who made the statement does not give evidence for the purposes of the proceedings either at all or in connection with the subject matter of the statement.

(4) Where in any proceedings evidence of a statement made by any person is admitted by reference to any of the reasons mentioned in paragraphs (a) to (c) and (e)(i) of subsection (2) above—

(a) any evidence which, if that person had given evidence in connection with the subject matter of the statement, would have been admissible as relevant to his credibility as a witness shall be admissible for that purpose in those proceedings;

(b) evidence may be given of any matter which, if that person had given evidence in connection with the subject matter of the statement, could have been put to him in cross-examination as relevant to his credibility as a witness but of which evidence could not have been adduced by the cross-examining party; and

(c) evidence tending to prove that that person, whether before or after making the statement, made in whatever manner some other statement which is inconsistent with it shall be admissible for the purpose of showing that he has contradicted himself.

(5) Subject to subsection (6) below, where a party intends to apply to have evidence of a statement admitted by virtue of subsection (1) above he shall, by the relevant time, give notice in writing of—

(a) that fact;

(b) the witnesses and productions to be adduced in connection with such evidence; and

(c) such other matters as may be prescribed by Act of Adjournal, to every other party to the proceedings and, for the purposes of this subsection, such evidence may be led notwithstanding that a witness or production concerned is not included in any list lodged by the parties and that the notice required by sections 67(5) and 78(4) of this Act has not been given.

(5A) In subsection (5) above, "the relevant time" means—

(a) in the case of proceedings in the High Court—

(i) not less than 7 days before the preliminary hearing; or

(ii) such later time, before the trial diet, as the judge may on cause shown allow;

(b) in any other case, before the trial diet.

(6) A party shall not be required to give notice as mentioned in subsection (5) above where—

(a) the grounds for seeking to have evidence of a statement admitted are as mentioned in paragraph (d) or (e) of subsection (2) above; or

(b) he satisfies the judge that there was good reason for not giving such notice.

(7) If no other party to the proceedings objects to the admission of evidence of a statement by virtue of subsection (1) above, the evidence shall be admitted without the judge requiring to be satisfied as mentioned in that subsection.

(8) For the purposes of the determination of any matter upon which the judge is required to be satisfied under subsection (1) above—

(a) except to the extent that any other party to the proceedings challenges them and insists in such challenge, it shall be presumed that the circumstances are as stated by the party seeking to introduce evidence of the statement; and

(b) where such a challenge is insisted in, the judge shall determine the matter on the balance of probabilities, and he may draw any reasonable inference—

(i) from the circumstances in which the statement was made or otherwise came into being; or

(ii) from any other circumstances, including, where the statement is contained in a document, the form and contents of the document.

(9) Where evidence of a statement has been admitted by virtue of subsection (1) above on the application of one party to the proceedings, without prejudice to anything in any enactment or rule of law, the judge may permit any party to lead additional evidence of such description as the judge may specify, notwithstanding that a witness or production concerned is not included in any list lodged by the parties and that the notice required by sections 67(5) and 78(4) of this Act has not been given.

(10) Any reference in subsections (5), (6) and (9) above to evidence shall include a reference to evidence led in connection with any determination required to be made for the purposes of subsection (1) above.

AMENDMENTS

Subsection (5) as amended, and subs.(5A) inserted, by the Criminal Procedure (Amendment) (Scotland) Act 2004 (asp 5) s.25 and Sch.1 para.42. Brought into force on 1 February 2005 by the Criminal Procedure (Amendment) (Scotland) Act 2004 (Commencement, Transitional Provisions and Savings) Order 2004 (SSI 2004/405 (C.28)) art.2.

Exceptions to the rule that hearsay evidence is inadmissible

***259.**—(1) Subject to the following provisions of this section, evidence of a statement made by a person otherwise than while giving oral evidence in court in criminal proceedings shall be admissible in those proceedings as evidence of any matter contained in the statement where the judge is satisfied—* A4-502A

(a) that the person who made the statement will not give evidence in the proceedings of such matter for any of the reasons mentioned in subsection (2) or (2A) below;

(b) that evidence of the matter would be admissible in the proceedings if that person gave direct oral evidence of it;

(c) that the person who made the statement would have been, at the time the statement was made, a competent witness in such proceedings; and

(d) that there is evidence which would entitle a jury properly directed, or in summary proceedings would entitle the judge, to find that the statement was made and that either—

(i) it is contained in a document; or

(ii) a person who gave oral evidence in the proceedings as to the statement has direct personal knowledge of the making of the statement.

(2) The reasons referred to in paragraph (a) of subsection (1) above are that the person who made the statement—

(a) is dead or is, by reason of his bodily or mental condition, unfit or unable to give evidence in any competent manner;

(b) is named and otherwise sufficiently identified, but is outwith the United Kingdom and it is not reasonably practicable to secure his attendance at the trial or to obtain his evidence in any other competent manner;

(c) is named and otherwise sufficiently identified, but cannot be found and all reasonable steps which, in the circumstances, could have been taken to find him have been so taken;

(d) having been authorised to do so by virtue of a ruling of the court in the proceedings that he is entitled to refuse to give evidence in connection with the subject matter of the statement on the grounds that such evidence might incriminate him, refuses to give such evidence; or

(e) is called as a witness and either—

(i) refuses to take the oath or affirmation; or

(ii) having been sworn as a witness and directed by the judge to give evidence in connection with the subject matter of the statement refuses to do so,

and in the application of this paragraph to a child, the reference to a witness refusing to take the oath or affirmation or, as the case may be, to having been sworn shall be construed as a reference to a child who has refused to accept an admonition to tell the truth or, having been so admonished, refuses to give evidence as mentioned above.

(2A) The reasons referred to in paragraph (a) of subsection (1) also include that—

(a) to have the person who made the statement physically attend the trial would give rise to a particular risk—

(i) to the person's wellbeing attributable to coronavirus, or

(ii) of transmitting coronavirus to others, and

(b) it is not reasonably practicable for the person to give the evidence in any other competent manner.

(3) Evidence of a statement shall not be admissible by virtue of subsection (1) above where the judge is satisfied that the occurrence of any of the circumstances mentioned in paragraphs (a) to (e) of subsection (2) or in subsection (2A) above, by virtue of which the statement would otherwise be admissible, is caused by—

(a) the person in support of whose case the evidence would be given; or

(b) any other person acting on his behalf,

for the purpose of securing that the person who made the statement does not give evidence for the purposes of the proceedings either at all or in connection with the subject matter of the statement.

(4) Where in any proceedings evidence of a statement made by any person is admitted by reference to any of the reasons mentioned in paragraphs (a) to (c) and (e)(i) of subsection (2) or in subsection (2A) above—

(a) any evidence which, if that person had given evidence in connection with the subject matter of the statement, would have been admissible as relevant to his credibility as a witness shall be admissible for that purpose in those proceedings;

(b) evidence may be given of any matter which, if that person had given evidence in connection with the subject matter of the statement, could have been put to him in cross-examination as relevant to his credibility as a witness but of which evidence could not have been adduced by the cross-examining party; and

(c) evidence tending to prove that that person, whether before or after making the statement, made in whatever manner some other statement which is inconsistent with it shall be admissible for the purpose of showing that he has contradicted himself.

(5) Subject to subsection (6) below, where a party intends to apply to have evidence of a statement admitted by virtue of subsection (1) above he shall, by the relevant time, give notice in writing of—

(a) that fact;

(b) the witnesses and productions to be adduced in connection with such evidence; and

(c) such other matters as may be prescribed by Act of Adjournal,

to every other party to the proceedings and, for the purposes of this subsection, such evidence may be led notwithstanding that a witness or production concerned is not included in any list lodged by the parties and that the notice required by sections 67(5) and 78(4) of this Act has not been given.

(5A) In subsection (5) above, "the relevant time" means–

(a) in the case of proceedings in the High Court–

(i) not less than 7 days before the preliminary hearing; or

(ii) such later time, before the trial diet, as the judge may on cause shown allow;

(b) in any other case, before the trial diet.

(6) A party shall not be required to give notice as mentioned in subsection (5) above where—

(a) the grounds for seeking to have evidence of a statement admitted are as mentioned in paragraph (d) or (e) of subsection (2) above; or

(b) he satisfies the judge that there was good reason for not giving such notice.

(7) If no other party to the proceedings objects to the admission of evidence of a statement by virtue of subsection (1) above, the evidence shall be admitted without the judge requiring to be satisfied as mentioned in that subsection.

(8) For the purposes of the determination of any matter upon which the judge is required to be satisfied under subsection (1) above—

(a) except to the extent that any other party to the proceedings challenges them and insists in such challenge, it shall be presumed that the circumstances are as stated by the party seeking to introduce evidence of the statement; and

(b) where such a challenge is insisted in; the judge shall determine the matter on the balance of probabilities, and he may draw any reasonable inference—

(i) from the circumstances in which the statement was made or otherwise came into being; or

(ii) from any other circumstances, including, where the statement is contained in a document, the form and contents of the document.

(9) Where evidence of a statement has been admitted by virtue of subsection (1) above on the application of one party to the proceedings, without prejudice to anything in any enactment or rule of law, the judge may permit any party to lead additional evidence of such description as the judge may specify, notwithstanding that a witness or production concerned is not included in any list lodged by the parties and that the notice required by sections 67(5) and 78(4) of this Act has not been given.

(10) Any reference in subsections (5), (6) and (9) above to evidence shall include a reference to evidence led in connection with any determination required to be made for the purposes of subsection (1) above.

(11) In subsection (2A), "coronavirus" has the meaning given by section 1 of the Coronavirus (Scotland) Act 2020.

Amendments

In relation to COVID-19, s.259 as amended by Coronavirus (Scotland) Act 2020 (asp 7) Sch.4(5) para.11(2)(a)–(e) (effective 7 April 2020).

Definitions

A4-502.1 "child": s.307(1).
"criminal proceedings": s.262(3).
"document": s.262(3).
"judge": s.307(1).
"statement": s.262(1).
"witness": s.307(1).

[THE NEXT PARAGRAPH IS A4-503]

General Note

A4-503 This section statutorily extends the grounds for the admission of hearsay evidence in criminal proceedings and, in subs.(5) onwards, sets out the procedures necessary in most circumstances for such evidence to be received. It is important to note that while a "statement" is very widely defined in s.262(1), anything by nature of a precognition, save for a precognition on oath, is excluded from the ambit of s.259. The distinction between a statement and a precognition was revisited in *HM Advocate v Beggs (No.3)*, 2002 S.L.T. 153; 2001 S.C.C.R. 891 in which a police statement taken in the course of enquiries was held not to be a precognition; the statement had been taken from the witness on the initiative of the police (not on the instructions of the fiscal) and the witness had been given the opportunity to read it over and correct it. In *HM Advocate v Khder*, 2009 S.C.C.R. 187 Crown efforts to found upon an edited version of a statement of the complainer (the victim of a sexual crime who had since died in an accident) to omit reference to a crime not charged, surprisingly failed on the grounds that the act of editing had produced a precognition which would not be admissible in terms of this section. *Khder*'s strictures must now be approached with caution; the time-honoured distinction between precognitions and witness statements (the former being viewed as inadmissible on account of the witness's account being filtered through another's mind, and being prepared from a partial stance (rather than objectively) in support of one party), classically expounded in *Kerr v HM Advocate*, 1958 J.C. 14, has been diluted. (Note also the statutory exclusion of precognitions, but not precognitions on oath, in s.262(1)(b) below). This flows from *Beurskens v HM Advocate* [2014] HCJAC 99; 2014 S.C.C.R. 447 where not only its timing in the detection/investigative process, but the fact of the account being signed by the witness, was held to be significant. Standing a strong dissenting judgment in Beurskens, a three judge decision, the law in this area is not yet settled. It is stressed that the section's provisions operate in addition to, and do not replace, the categories of hearsay evidence which can be accepted by the courts at common law (see s.262(4), below); for that reason some mention is necessary of the pre-existing categories of hearsay evidence which were recognised as exceptions to the general bar on hearsay evidence.

Following *HM Advocate v Bain*, 2002 S.L.T. 340 it would appear that although a judge is bound to permit the admission of hearsay evidence if it complies with the requirements of subs.(7) that does not debar the judge from considering whether the statement, or statements, can be fairly put before the jury. In *Bain* the Crown had given due notice of the leading of evidence from a deceased witness at the outset of the trial and no objection had been taken by the defence. Nonetheless, the Crown accepted that elements of at least one of the statements were contradicted by other evidence the Crown founded upon; on that basis the trial judge had to consider how the Crown interpreted this evidence for the jury and, indeed, assess afresh whether it could fairly be considered as sufficiently reliable for the jury to found upon. See too *McKenna v HM Advocate*, 2003 S.L.T. 769, the appeal arising from *HM Advocate v McKenna*, 2000 S.L.T. 508; 2000 S.C.C.R. 159 discussed below.

The trial judge has a continuing duty, as any trial in which hearsay evidence has been led continues, to assess whether the admission of that evidence should be permitted in the light of the evidence as it unfolds. If it becomes clear that the evidence is unfair to the party (or parties) against whom it is admitted, the trial judge may have to direct, at the very least, that the jury disregard the evidence.

In the case of evidence led by the Crown it might also be necessary to uphold a submission of no case to answer, or to desert the trial *ex proprio motu*, or direct the jury to acquit; see *N v HM Advocate*, 2003 S.L.T. 761. This function can only properly be exercised by the trial judge in the light of the evidence. Once it is established that the qualifications set out in subss.(1) and (2) have been met, the court has no power to refuse to allow the evidence to be led, but can withdraw it from consideration as evidence (once led) if its admission would result in unfairness.

(The self-evident fact that other parties cannot cross-examine this chapter of evidence does not, of itself, constitute unfairness since Scottish courts will still require corroboration of essential facts before any conviction is possible).

Efforts to utilise the section's provisions to introduce admissions made by a co-accused, notably when police interviews were deemed not to be admissible as evidence, as direct evidence have understandably enjoyed little success; see *Brand v HM Advocate*, 2012 S.C.C.R. 451 and *Murphy v HM Advocate*, 2012 S.C.C.R. 542.

Categories of hearsay admissible at common law

First, it is well-established that statements made by a deceased witness, while hearsay in character, are admissible; see *HM Advocate v Irving*, 1978 J.C. 28, but it is unsettled whether this exception extends either as far as writings of a deceased, particularly if authorship is in dispute (the *Lauderdale Peerage* case (1885) 10 App. Cas. 692), or to a dying deposition. More tentatively, a statement made by a witness deemed permanently insane since its making could perhaps be adduced as evidence provided that it could be established that he had been lucid at the time when it was made (*HM Advocate v Monson* (1893) 1 Adam 114). It is thought that a statement by a prisoner of war might be received as evidence.

It is well-established that statements forming part of the res gestae are admissible as are incriminating or mixed statements made by an accused, and that hearsay evidence can be admitted where it would be impossible to lead primary evidence, this on the basis that such hearsay now qualifies as best evidence. The making of prior inconsistent statements can be used as a means of discrediting a witness, but previous consistent statements cannot be used to bolster credibility; in neither case, however, is the prior statement admissible as evidence of its contents. In addition to statutory exceptions such as the Bankers' Book Evidence Act 1879 and the provisions now contained in Sch.8 to the 1996 Act concerning categories of business documents, case law has also allowed evidence at second hand—of identification or description of an accused (*Muldoon v Herron*, 1970 J.C. 30), of a vehicle (*Frew v Jessop*, 1990 J.C. 15), and more recently, of a statement whose detail had been forgotten by a witness but assented to in evidence (*Jamieson v HM Advocate (No.2)*, 1994 S.C.C.R. 610).

While it might seem that the list of expected categories of hearsay evidence which can be adduced as evidence is endless, the fact remains that Scottish courts have exercised extreme caution before admitting such evidence largely on the grounds that it cannot be subjected to cross-examination and must be inherently less reliable than parole evidence. Yet the bar on admissible hearsay may cause unnecessary expense, probably smacks of pettifoggery and contrivance to lay witnesses whose flow of testimony is artificially constrained, and certainly can militate against the broader interests of justice: see especially the cases of *Perrie v HM Advocate*, 1991 S.C.C.R. 255 and *McLay v HM Advocate*, 1994 S.C.C.R. 397 in both of which it had been held inadmissible to lead evidence made to third parties by an incriminee.

The Scottish Law Commission's Report, "*Hearsay Evidence in Criminal Proceedings*" (No. 149) and, to an extent, the experience of English courts in applying Pt 2 of the Criminal Justice Act 1988 (c.33) (which drew heavily upon the Roskill Report, "*Report of the Departmental Inquiry on Fraud Trials*", Lord Chancellor's Department 1986), as well as the *Perrie* and *McLay* cases, have all influenced the shape of Pt 12 of the 1995 Act. Section 259 broadens the categories of hearsay evidence which can be introduced into proceedings but provides a right to other parties to challenge such evidence—in which event the court will require to adjudicate prior to the commencement of a trial, and to lead counter-evidence in rebuttal.

Subs. (1)

Subsection (1) sets out several tests which any hearsay material has to meet before it can be founded upon, namely, the unavailability of the maker of the statement (for one of the reasons specified in subs.(2) below); the admissibility of the evidence had it been given in parole form (a ground which demands both that the evidence adduced is competent and does not contain hearsay, and that the maker of the statement would have qualified as a witness); and finally that the making of the statement can itself be proved by direct evidence. The witness' statement need not be in written form provided that other witnesses can speak to its contents but nor can it be by nature a precognition (a distinction itself often more apparent than real nowadays).

In *HM Advocate v Beggs (No.3)*, 2002 S.L.T. 153 the Crown moved to lead evidence, of the accused's general interest in picking up young men, in the form of a statement from a witness since deceased. Following a trial within a trial (on which now see *Crooks v Russell*, 2002 S.L.T. 221; 2002 S.C.C.R. 216), the Crown's contention that the statement was not a precognition since it had been taken by a police officer in the course of enquiries into the movements of the accused after an apprehension warrant had been granted (and then was incorporated into extradition proceedings against the accused), was accepted. The defence had founded upon *Kerr v HM Advocate*, 1958 J.C. 14 both as setting out the general test of a precognition and as authority for the view that it was for the Crown to satisfy the court that the account being tendered was not by way of being a precognition. In the interest of clarity it may be noted that the issue of lifting the veil of confidentiality on the precognition process was discussed in *Kerr v HM Advocate*, 2002 S.L.T. 582; 2002 S.C.C.R. 275.

Subs. (2)

Subss.(1)(a) and (2) define the categories of witness whose testimony can be introduced admissibly as evidence in their absence. Section 259 is the sole means of introducing such evidence and it is generally crucial that due notice of an intention to introduce it is given timeously and in proper form (see subss. (5) and (5A)). The only exceptions to the requirement for notice in advance of trial are seen in subs.(6) and are only triggered by reluctance or recalcitrance on the part of an otherwise competent witness during the trial itself. Subs.(6)(b) enables the court to exercise a discretion to waive the period of notice for evidence which could competently be placed before the court but it is not available as a means of introducing further categories of witness, and evidence, to those specified in subs. (2). See *HM Advocate v Malloy* [2012] HCJ 124; 2012 S.C.C.R. 710, a three judge decision in the course of an ongoing murder trial, which followed two unreported cases *HM Advocate v Parracho*, IN764 / 08 and *HM Advocate v Clancy*, Glasgow High Court, 10 February 1997. (In *Clancy*, which arose in the infancy of this provision, an unsuccessful attempt had been made during a murder trial to introduce a statement of the victim, without notice, on a common law basis).

Malloy confirms that (standing the saving provision of s.264(2) discussed at para.22 in that judgment) s.259 sets out the only method for introducing admissible hearsay evidence; it is exhaustive of the categories of such evidence and, at para.21, confirms that the prior notice provisions exist to enable other parties the opportunity to investigate the proposed evidence in advance of the trial. It is submitted that dying depositions are to be considered competent for the purposes of s.259 applications. In *HM Advocate v Johnston*, 2004 S.L.T. 1055, a murder trial, where the Crown sought to lead the police statement of the now-deceased boyfriend of the victim which had become significant in conjunction with DNA evidence, the trial judge repelled objections of an inherent unfairness, in art.6 Convention terms, in using that statement in evidence. In *Lees v HM Advocate* [2016] HCJAC 16 the Crown use was upheld of a 999 recording of the complainer (who had since died in unrelated circumstances) alleging an assault by the accused, and her later signed police statement, to afford mutual corroboration of a second complainer who gave parole evidence of similar conduct. The deceased's witness statement was spoken to by the police officers who responded to her call; they also observed her distress and damage at the locus consistent with her account, but this last material, while arguably lending support to her credibility, was not necessary for admissibility purposes.

More problematic, as *Glass v HM Advocate* [2018] HCJAC 70; 2018 S.C.C.R. 379 illustrates, is ascertaining that a witness whose "bodily or mental function" is asserted to preclude parole evidence, can be shown conclusively to be unable to give evidence by any other competent means as subs.(2)(a) requires; in *Glass* the position was that while physically able to attend court, the witness had suffered permanent memory loss resulting from a subsequent head injury, but the extent of that loss upon ability to testify had not been fully explored. While hearsay evidence in the form of his earlier statement was allowed at trial, the Crown on appeal, conceded that the necessary foundations had not been laid. The solution offered by the Appeal Court, in the absence of such conclusive medical information, was to point to s.260's provisions to ascertain whether first, the witness would acknowledge his signature on the statement, then assert its truthfulness, as a prelude to adopting it as evidence. Presumably, though the judgment did not venture further, if the s.260 avenue proved fruitless, then the witness' statement might yet be capable of being introduced in terms of s.259 under the exemption from notice procedure of s.259(6)(b) and from the evidence of incapacity now evident in court; how far a jury could follow the ratio for such jurisprudential fine-tuning is a moot point.

Section 259(2)(b) enables the statement of a witness abroad to be received in evidence, but only once it can be shown, if required, that it is not reasonable to use other competent evidential devices, such as live television link, or letters of request or commission.

Paragraph (c), in a fashion similar to the last paragraph, enables statements of identifiable witnesses who have disappeared to be admitted as evidence but only if it can be shown, if required, that all reasonable steps have been taken to trace the witness beforehand. Paragraph (d) deals with admissions of incriminees; it will now be possible to tender evidence of statements allegedly made by an incriminee who has been brought before the court but refuses to testify on grounds of self-incrimination.

Subtle differences exist between the last provision and the next, contained in para.(e)(i), which deals with a witness who simply misconducts himself and refuses to testify, or prevaricates. In *Cowie v HM Advocate*, 2009 S.C.C.R. 838 the court was satisfied that a witness was refusing to testify on the basis of reports received from the macer and clerk of court that the witness was refusing to re-enter the court, and received her evidence by means of an earlier statement. The Appeal Court rejected submissions that the witness ought to have been produced before the court, if need be forcibly, a conclusion doubtless strengthened by the reported mien of the witness earlier in her evidence. Paragraph (e) can apply to the evidence of a child "who has refused an admonition to tell the truth or, having been so admonished, refuses to give evidence"; this phrase would obviously apply to a recalcitrant child witness but would not apply to situations in which the child proved to be unable to give evidence or was tongue-tied. *MacDonald v HM Advocate*, 1999 S.L.T. 533; 1999 S.C.C.R. 146 indicates that the judge must have seen the child witness and actively admonished the child to answer and been met with a refusal, but see *SRS v PF Tain* [2016] SAC (Crim) 3 where, from information provided by court staff and the Crown, the trial judge concluded that a distressed child witness, aged 10 years, would not even enter the remotely-sited CCTV room to give evidence, and instead permitted use of the child's prior statement in terms of subs.(2)(e)(ii). A further category of child witness has to be recognised—the child who does not understand the nature of the admonition; in such a case it is doubtful that an earlier statement could be taken in evidence at all, since the child was not a "competent witness" when the statement was made (subs.(1)(c)).

Several caveats have to be entered: first, subs.(3) precludes the application of s.259's provisions where the judge is satisfied the party tendering the evidence, or his followers, have colluded in bringing about the unavailability or recalcitrance of the witness identified. This provision would readily apply to assisting in, or engineering the disappearance of a witness (arguably an attempt to pervert the course of justice in many circumstances) but more complex issues might arise for example in child abuse cases where emotional pressures may be brought to bear on the child.

Secondly, subs.(5) stipulates that for hearsay evidence to be admitted in most circumstances notice of the intention to do so must be served on all other parties before the trial. (The form of notice is found in Form 21.3 in the 1996 Act of Adjournal.) The notice has to be in the proper form and relate to the correct statement: in *McPhee (William McAllister) v HM Advocate*, 2002 S.L.T. 90; 2001 S.C.C.R. 674 the Crown had attached the wrong statement to the s.259 notice served upon the accused but was permitted to lead the evidence in question on the basis that the accused had suffered no prejudice. The Appeal Court quashed the conviction upon that charge on the grounds that no "good reason" had been shown for the omission as subs.(6)(b) demanded and prejudice (or its lack) was not a relevant factor. Broadly, notice has to be served where it is anticipable that a witness will be unavailable; subs.(6) exempts situations described in para.(2)(d) and (e) namely, failures to testify by incriminees or by witnesses who misconduct themselves, from the normal requirement of advance notice. Thirdly, a failure to challenge appropriate notice under subs.(5) means that the statement's contents can be lead in evidence without further ado (subs.(7)). Nonetheless, it is submitted that some circumspection is necessary here: it cannot be right that the terms of subs.(7) would preclude a common law challenge during the proceedings if it is demonstrable that the evidence being adduced would ordinarily be incompetent or otherwise inadmissible.

Only in the event of a challenge does the presiding judge have to decide the issue before the trial commences (subs.(8)) and it will be noted that it is presumed that the terms of the Form 21.3 are correct, a presumption which is capable of rebuttal, and that the issue is determined on the balance of probabilities. The main benefit of subs.(8) is that a "trial within a trial" to resolve the admissibility of the statement can be avoided, thus saving time and inconvenience to all involved since the issue will be aired, possibly by leading evidence, before trial. Subsection (4) permits parties to lead evidence to support the credibility of the absent witness, challenge his credibility, or demonstrate prior inconsistent statements. (The only exceptions to this generality occur in the circumstances outlined in subs.(2)(d) and (e)(i) where, by definition, no evidence has been heard from the witness.) Reference to "any proceedings" suggests that such evidence could well be adduced before the judge determining the admissibility of a challenged notice. However a decision to refuse to allow a s.259 application, either on its merits or on grounds of unjustified late lodging, by a judge at a preliminary hearing, should not readily be reviewed at trial (see *Murphy v HM Advocate* [2012] HCJAC 74).

Subs. (5A)(a)

Murphy v HM Advocate [2012] HCJAC 74 (following *HM Advocate v Forrester* 2007 S.C.C.R. 216) emphasises that the correct time for lodging of s.259 applications in High Court proceedings is seven days prior to the preliminary hearing, not at any later continuation of that hearing. Later lodging is at the discretion of the hearing judge, or trial judge, as the case may be, once cause has been shown for the later application. It is possible only in the most extreme cases that a later application could be moved as a cure for a procedural irregularity on the part of the accused (see s.300A(5)(b)(ii) below) but only once the hurdle presented by s.300A(7) has been overcome.

Although it may be self-evident, the above hearsay provisions do not extend to statements made by an accused in his favour (see s.261(1) below). Less obviously, given the terms of s.261(2) of the Act, a statement by a co-accused B can be adduced as evidence by an accused A where B declines to give evidence: the statement can be used as evidence by A but not by B. Section 261(4) provides that this can only occur where A has given notice in terms of s.259(5) and, it is submitted, where it can be shown that no pressure was exerted by A to prevent B testifying, and the Crown itself has not lead B's statement. To say the least the interplay of ss.259 and 261 is likely to create situations of byzantine complexity, particularly in cases involving several accused; will all accused founding upon B's statement require to serve a s.259 notice as prudence might suggest?

Finally, it will be noted that both s.259(5) and (9) permit the leading of witnesses or productions, not formally intimated, either for the purpose of setting up a hearsay statement or, with leave of the court, as additional evidence.

European Convention on Human Rights

The introduction of the Convention into Scots criminal law has undoubtedly led to a re-appraisal of many well-accepted practices. For that reason the discussion which follows is necessarily of some length, albeit the basic issue—the need to achieve a proper balance between a fair trial for the accused and the need to detect and suppress serious crime (*Irving v HM Advocate*, 1978 J.C. 28)—remains unchanged.

HM Advocate v McKenna, 2000 S.L.T. 508; 2000 S.C.C.R. 159 was an early challenge under the Convention to the Crown's stated intention to lead hearsay evidence and was notable also because objection was permitted to be taken prior to trial in its exceptional circumstances. Ordinarily it is expected that the leading of s.259 evidence will be considered by the court at the outset of the trial proceedings after service of the appropriate notices. Following upon *HM Advocate v Bain*, 2002 S.L.T. 340 it is submitted that it is essential (particularly where no objection has been taken in terms of subs.(7)) to determine from the outset whether the court has, or has not, accepted that the hearsay evidence identified can be led. In *Bain* the Crown laid an application under subs.(2)(a) before the court without objection from the defence before the jury was sworn only to be met with an objection at the point in evidence when the statement was about to be lead. The trial judge doubted, despite the lack of objection at the outset, that he had granted the application and, in any event, the grant of an application as admissible in the proceedings would not itself settle issues of evidential admissibility. Rejecting defence submissions that Convention rights were being breached because the deceased's accounts were at odds with each other and that this evidence could not be cross-examined (much as had occurred in *McKenna*), Lord Reed noted that the question of fairness could be revisited as the evidence emerged.

In *McKenna* the Crown advanced seven broad principles to be applied to the leading of hearsay evidence in a manner compatible with Convention rights. Particularly, it was significant that leading such evidence was not per se in conflict with such rights provided that the accused had the opportunity to challenge the statement and, more important, following *Kostovski v The Netherlands* (1989) 12 E.H.R.R. 434 and *Asch v Austria* (1992) 15 E.H.R.R.597 that this is not either the sole or main evidence. In his judgment Lord Caplan noted that the European Court has not laid down prescriptive rules (a difficult, if not impossible, task given the variety of criminal law systems) but proceeds by an overall assessment of the whole proceedings, not individual elements.

The defence minutes were repelled in *McKenna*; the accused raised objection by preliminary diet to the Crown leading evidence of a statement from the third person present at the scene of a murder, and since identified as a suspect but who had since died, on grounds that not only could this evidence not be subject to cross-examination but that there was evidence that the witness would likely have given a partial and self-serving account. Particular emphasis was placed upon alleged oppression on the part of the Crown (in contravention of the European Convention) in seeking to lead evidence of this sort; the Crown responded by outlining seven general principles (which the Court approved) in relation to the leading of hearsay evidence from a deceased person foremost of which was the fact that this was neither the sole or principal evidence against the accused. On appeal, the Appeal Court indicated that only on rare occasions could the issue of the potential for prejudice to the achievement of a fair trial be determined in advance of the trial itself (compare the approach in *Brown v Stott*, 2000 S.C.C.R. 314 where the fundamental issue, as a matter of law, of a suspect's right not to be called upon to incriminate himself, notwithstanding the terms of the Road Traffic Act 1988 (c.52) s.172, was so resolved). A contemporary demonstration of the *McKenna* approach can be seen in *Graham v HM Advocate* [2018] HCJAC 69; 2019 S.C.CR. 19 dealing with no fewer than seven mixed statements made by the complainer, a distressed and disturbed young woman, since deceased.

The view of the European Court of Human Rights, expressed in *R. v Khawaja and Tahery* (2009) 49 E.H.R.R. 1, was that the use of hearsay evidence as the sole or decisive evidence in criminal trial proceedings necessarily offends against art.6(3)(d) Convention rights "to examine or have examined witnesses against [an accused]", with a view to enabling adversarial argument, except where the accused had connived at the absence or fearfulness of the witness. That approach was firmly negatived by the Supreme Court in *R. v Horncastle* [2009] UKSC 14 and by the European Court itself in *Case of Horncastle and Others v United Kingdom* (Application 4184/10), by judgment of 16 December 16 2014. Sole or decisive evidence might be counterbalanced by other procedural safeguards; the acid test in all cases is the overall fairness of the proceedings themselves. See *Schatschaschwili v Germany* (2016) 63 EHRR 14 followed in *AS v HM Advocate* [2020] HCJAC 42.

Note that in *Horncastle*, the European Court adjudged that the evidence complained of was not sole or, indeed, decisive at all in the trial.

In *Patterson v HM Advocate*, 2000 S.L.T. 302 the Appeal Court ruled as competent evidence for the purposes of the section, the statement of a deceased witness who had intimated to the defence that she was an alcoholic and had given her police statement while under the influence of drink. It was held that the reliability of the witness was not a determining factor in assessing the competency of her statement. Note that the Court also held that it was not necessary for the Crown to meet an inspecific challenge to the witness' mental capacity by proving her sanity; the general evidential presumption (that witnesses are deemed to have the ordinary physical and mental faculties) applied.

In *HM Advocate v Nulty*, 2000 S.L.T. 528 the Crown sought to lead evidence of a complainer in a rape trial by reference to her taped evidence from an earlier trial diet which had, unfortunately, been deserted for procedural reasons. Since giving her evidence and being cross-examined at the first trial, the complainer had become mentally unwell and was unfit to give evidence, causing the Crown to use the best evidence available, her prior testimony. Two points are of note; first, the court apparently had no difficulty in reconciling this approach with the terms of subs.(1) which excludes from the ambit of s.259 oral evidence given in the course of criminal proceedings, no doubt on the basis that the evidence to be received had not been given in the instant proceedings; second, the trial judge was unwilling to hold that unfairness necessarily arose because the accused could not cross-examine the complainer. Following *Doorson v Netherlands* (1996) 22 E.H.R.R. 330 fairness had to be assessed overall and had to take account of the balance between the defence's interests and those of the victims.

It will only rarely be proper for the judge at a preliminary diet to determine conclusively whether hearsay evidence should be allowed in terms of s.259. Such a decision can only be reached where the court can, at that stage, pre-emptively determine that the admission of that evidence would inevitably result in the entire proceedings being rendered unfair; *HM Advocate v M*, 2003 S.L.T. 1151.

Convention arguments were aired in *Campbell v HM Advocate*, 2004 S.L.T. 135; 2003 S.C.C.R. 779 with little success, but this appeal succeeded on grounds of the inadequate directions given to the jury as to how to approach hearsay evidence which was of an essential corroborative character.

Admissibility of prior statements of witnesses

260.—(1) Subject to the following provisions of this section, where a witness gives evidence in criminal proceedings, any prior statement made by the witness shall be admissible as evidence of any matter stated in it of which direct oral evidence by him would be admissible if given in the course of those proceedings. A4-504

(2) A prior statement shall not be admissible under this section unless—

(a) the statement is contained in a document;

(b) the witness, in the course of giving evidence, indicates that the statement was made by him and that he adopts it as his evidence; and

(c) at the time the statement was made, the person who made it would have been a competent witness in the proceedings.

(3) For the purposes of this section, any reference to a prior statement is a reference to a prior statement which, but for the provisions of this section, would not be admissible as evidence of any matter stated in it.

(4) Subsections (2) and (3) above do not apply to a prior statement—

(a) contained in a precognition on oath; or

(b) made in other proceedings, whether criminal or civil and whether taking place in the United Kingdom or elsewhere,

and, for the purposes of this section, any such statement shall not be admissible unless it is sufficiently authenticated.

(5) A prior statement made by a witness shall not, in any proceedings on indictment, be inadmissible by reason only that it is not included in any list of productions lodged by the parties.

AMENDMENTS

Subs.(5) inserted by Criminal Procedure (Amendment) (Scotland) Act 2004 (asp 5) s.23. Brought into force on 4 October 2004 by SSI 2004/405 (C.28).

DEFINITIONS

"criminal proceedings": s.262(3). A4-504.1
"statement": s.262(1).
"witness": s.307(1).

[THE NEXT PARAGRAPH IS A4-505]

GENERAL NOTE

This section applies to solemn and summary proceedings and permits the introduction of prior statements, as specified by subs.(2), by a witness in criminal proceedings as evidence of any matter therein of which direct oral evidence from him would have been admissible in the course of those proceedings. In essence the section permits the adoption of earlier statements, suitably authenticated, and is perceptibly influenced by the decision of the High Court in *Jamieson v HM Advocate (No. 2)*, 1995 S.L.T. 666. Nevertheless, this statutory provision rests upon its own terms and is not simply a repetition of *Jamieson*; in that case there was a claimed loss of memory, a factor which would not satisfy the test in subs.(3) above. See *Hughes v HM Advocate*, 2009 S.L.T. 325. It is submitted that where the witness could now no longer testify on medical grounds, recourse to the admissible hearsay provisions in s.259 might be fruitful. A4-505

Note that the witness has both to acknowledge being the originator of the statement and adopt it as his evidence (subs.(2)(b)), circumstances which did not prevail in either *Muldoon v Herron*, 1970 J.C. 30; 1970 S.L.T. 228 (a judgment which the court founded upon in *Jamieson*) or in *Smith v HM Advocate*,

1986 S.C.C.R. 135. In both those cases police witnesses' accounts of the witness' evidence replaced the testimony of the witnesses themselves. If a witness can adopt a prior statement as this section provides, *McNee v Ruxton*, 1997 G.W.D. 13–545 is authority perhaps for the proposition that witness B can adopt the statement of another witness, witness A, as his own. The corollary however surely must be that either witness can have a prior inconsistent statement made by either witness put to him.

Reference should be made to the stand alone provision in s.54 of the Criminal Justice and Licensing (Scotland) Act 2010 (asp 3) entitling the prosecutor to provide a copy of a witness's statement to that witness before the witness is called to give evidence.

The distinction between this section, which in effect enables witnesses to rely upon accurate statements made earlier (but whose details are now forgotten) such that these can form part of the evidence, and section 263 which enables a prior statement to be put as a means, at least initially, only of challenging the credibility or reliability of a witness, can quickly become blurred; see *Ogilvie v HM Advocate*, 1999 S.L.T. 1068. In this case the Crown plainly utilised the (rarely used) power in s.263(2) of the Act to interpose another witness during the witness' evidence, albeit prematurely. See also *Pupkis v Thomson*, 2002 G.W.D. 17–554 and *A v HM Advocate* [2012] HCJAC 29; mixed testimony of a witness, adopting only parts of a statement whose provenance and verity has been accepted by him while denying other elements within it, is problematic. The adopted parts can be used as evidence; the parts denied can only be utilized for the purpose of assessing the witness' reliability and credibility. This is so even if the accuracy of the entire statement is confirmed in evidence by the officer who noted its terms. The distinctly different uses the jury can make of elements within a witness' mixed statement must be made subject of express direction to the jury. See *Morrison v HM Advocate*, 2013 S.C.C.R. 626 and *Moynihan v HM Advocate* [2016] HCJAC 85; 2016 S.C.C.R. 548: failure to direct upon the evidential import of an adopted (or partially adopted) prior statement may well constitute a material misdirection. The vital factor, if the statement has not been adopted by the witness, is to direct the jury that the statement put cannot be used to prove fact but solely for the purpose of assessing both the witness's credibility and reliability.

Where the witness has adopted the statement, rather than disavowing it, there is no need for the police officer who noted it to be led in evidence to establish its provenance. See *Matulewicz v PF Alloa* [2014] HCJAC 7.

The effect of subs. (4) is to remove the need for a witness to adopt the terms of his precognition on oath (which of course had to be signed as an acknowledgment of its accuracy by the witness at the conclusion of the precognition proceedings) or for him to confirm the accuracy of testimony given in earlier judicial proceedings.

Reference to r.21.4 and Form 21.4 in the 1996 Act of Adjournal indicates that only statements of the type specified in subs. (4) require to be certified with such an authentication docquet; authentication need not be docquetted by the originator of the statement, the certificate of a party present at the making of the statement would suffice. Note that any prior statement by a witness would be admissible if given as a precognition on oath or in the course of any court proceedings once properly authenticated.

The above certification procedures are not required for any other sort of statement; in such cases it would be sufficient for the witness to assent to the truth of an earlier account which is produced to the court in document form. See s.262(2) and (3) for definitions. It will be noted that nothing in either ss.260 or 262 would permit the use of a precognition.

The different evidential significance of a s.260 and s.263 statement is discussed at A4–511 below.

Practice Notes

Practice Note No.1 of 2014 requires that, where it is intended to put a prior statement to a witness either to contradict the evidence given, or to "extend" such evidence and that statement has not been formally lodged as a production, then a copy should be immediately available for the trial judge. Part of the purpose of the Note is to avoid delaying proceedings so it is submitted that best practice would be to ensure that a copy is to hand for each of the parties to the proceedings.

Statements by co-accused

A4-506 **261.**—(1) Subject to the following provisions of this section, nothing in sections 259 and 260 of this Act shall apply to a statement made by the accused.

(2) Evidence of a statement made by an accused shall be admissible by virtue of the said section 259 at the instance of another accused in the same proceedings as evidence in relation to that other accused.

(3) For the purposes of subsection (2) above, the first mentioned accused shall be deemed—

(a) where he does not give evidence in the proceedings, to be a witness refusing to give evidence in connection with the subject matter of the statement as mentioned in paragraph (e) of subsection (2) of the said section 259; and

(b) to have been, at the time the statement was made, a competent witness in the proceedings.

(4) Evidence of a statement shall not be admissible as mentioned in subsection (2) above unless the accused at whose instance it is sought to be admitted has given notice of his intention to do so as mentioned in subsection (5) of the said section 259; but subsection (6) of that section shall not apply in the case of notice required to be given by virtue of this subsection.

AMENDMENTS

Heading substituted by Criminal Justice (Scotland) Act 2016 (asp 1) s.109(2). Brought into force on 25 January 2018 by SSI 2017/345 art.3 subject to transitional provisions.

DEFINITIONS

"made": s.262(3). A4-506.1
"statement": s.262(1).
"witness": s.307(1).

GENERAL NOTE

This section applies to solemn and summary proceedings. Its effect is to exclude a statement made by the accused from the provisions of ss.259 and 260. However, statements made by an accused, which are hearsay, may become admissible against that accused when introduced by another accused in the same proceedings. Use of this procedure will normally require a Notice in terms of s.259(5) prior to trial (see notes to s.259 above at para.A4-503). The general rule against statements by an accused implicating a co–accused made outwith that person's presence, or hearing, is set out in *CS v HM Advocate* [2021] HCJAC 6; the limitations on the use of such statements must be explained to the jury and specific direction provided A4-506.2

Statements by accused

261ZA.—(1) Evidence of a statement to which this subsection applies is not inadmissible as evidence of any fact contained in the statement on account of the evidence's being hearsay. A4-506.3

(2) Subsection (1) applies to a statement made by the accused in the course of the accused's being questioned (whether as a suspect or not) by a constable, or another official, investigating an offence.

(3) Subsection (1) does not affect the issue of whether evidence of a statement made by one accused is admissible as evidence in relation to another accused.

AMENDMENTS

Section 261ZA inserted by Criminal Justice (Scotland) Act 2016 (asp 1) s.109. Brought into force on 25 January 2018 by SSI 2017/345 art.3 subject to transitional provisions.

[THE NEXT PARAGRAPH IS A4-506.5]

GENERAL NOTE

Subject to the general rules of admissibility, this section provides that any response made by an accused during questioning by an investigating officer, whether an admission of guilt, exculpatory, setting out a statutory defence or mixed in nature (on the last see, notably, *McCutcheon v HM Advocate*, 2002 S.L.T. 27; 2002 S.C.C.R. 101), shall be available as evidence in relation to that accused. See also s.261ZB below which renders as admissible, any responses made after judicially-authorised questioning of an accused, after charge. Section 261 still governs the more complex situations involving statements by an accused which implicate, or are preyed in aid, by a co-accused. A4-506.5

Statements made after charge

Exception to rule on inadmissiblity

261ZB. Evidence of a statement made by a person in response to questioning carried out in accordance with authorisation granted under section 35 of the Criminal Justice (Scotland) Act 2016 is not inadmissible on account of the statement's being made after the person has been charged with an offence. A4-506.6

AMENDMENTS

Section 261ZB inserted by Criminal Justice (Scotland) Act 2016 (asp 1) Sch.2 para.34. Brought into force on 25 January 2018 by SSI 2017/345 art.3 and Sch.1 para.1.

GENERAL NOTE

A4-507 This section renders admissible any responses made by an accused to judicially-authorised questioning as provided by s.35 of the 2016 Act. Both sections are as yet untested.

Witness statements

Witness statements: use during trial

A4-507.1 **261A.**—(1) Subsection (2) applies where—

(a) a witness is giving evidence in criminal proceedings,
(b) the witness has made a prior statement,
(c) the prosecutor has seen or has been given an opportunity to see the statement, and
(d) the accused (or a solicitor or advocate acting on behalf of the accused in the proceedings) has seen or has been given an opportunity to see the statement.

(2) The court may allow the witness to refer to the statement while the witness is giving evidence.

AMENDMENTS

Section 261A inserted by Criminal Justice and Licensing (Scotland) Act 2010 (asp 13) s.85(2). Brought into force on 28 March 2011 (for all purposes in respect of criminal proceedings in which the first appearance of the accused, or the recording of a plea of not guilty against an accused charged on summary complaint, is on or after 28 March 2011) by SSI 2011/178 (C.15) art.2, Sch.1 para.1.

DEFINITIONS

A4-507.2 "witness": s.307(1).
"statement": s.262(1).
"prosecutor": s.307(1).

GENERAL NOTE

A4-507.3 This provision clarifies the procedures which can, with the consent of the court, enable a witness in criminal proceedings to refer to (and presumably adopt or challenge) his prior statements in the course of giving evidence. While primarily applicable to Crown witnesses whose statements must have been disclosed to the defence, the provision can apply equally to a defence witness but then can only take effect once the prosecutor has been offered prior sight of the statement in question. Note that neither party can bar a witness access to a qualifying statement by declining to accept a copy of it. It remains in the court's general discretion however to refuse any witness the use of such a statement.

[THE NEXT PARAGRAPH IS A4-508]

Construction of sections 259 to 261A

A4-508 **262.**—(1) For the purposes of sections 259 to 261A of this Act, a "statement" includes—

(a) any representation, however made or expressed, of fact or opinion; and
(b) any part of a statement, but does not include a statement in a precognition other than a precognition on oath.

(2) For the purposes of the said sections 259 to 261A a statement is contained in a document where the person who makes it—

(a) makes the statement in the document personally;
(b) makes a statement which is, with or without his knowledge, embodied in a document by whatever means or by any person who has direct personal knowledge of the making of the statement; or
(c) approves a document as embodying the statement.

(3) In the said sections 259 to 261A—

"criminal proceedings" include (other than in section 261A) any hearing by the sheriff of an application made by virtue of section 93(2)(a) or 94(2)(a) of the Children's Hearings (Scotland) Act 2011 (asp 1) to determine whether a ground is established, in so far as the application relates to the commission of an offence by the child, or for a review of such a determination;;

"document" includes, in addition to a document in writing—

(a) any map, plan, graph or drawing;

(b) any photograph;

(c) any disc, tape, sound track or other device in which sounds or other data (not being visual images) are recorded so as to be capable (with or without the aid of some other equipment) of being reproduced therefrom; and

(d) any film, negative, tape, disc or other device in which one or more visual images are recorded so as to be capable (as aforesaid) of being reproduced therefrom;

"film" includes a microfilm;

"made" includes (other than in section 261A) allegedly made.

(4) Nothing in the said sections 259 to 261A shall prejudice the admissibility of a statement made by a person other than in the course of giving oral evidence in court which is admissible otherwise than by virtue of those sections.

AMENDMENTS

Section 262 as amended by Criminal Justice and Licensing (Scotland) Act 2010 (asp 13) s.85(3). Brought into force on 28 March 2011 (for all purposes in respect of criminal proceedings in which the first appearance of the accused, or the recording of a plea of not guilty against an accused charged on summary complaint, is on or after 28 March 2011) by SSI 2011/178 (C.15) art.2, Sch.1 para.1.

Subs.(3) as amended by Children's Hearings (Scotland) Act 2011 (Modification of Primary Legislation) Order 2013 (SSI 2013/211) Sch.1 para.10 (effective 24 June 2013).

DEFINITIONS

"child": s.307(1). A4-508.1

"indictment": s.307(1).

"sheriff": ss.4(4) and 5(1).

[THE NEXT PARAGRAPH IS A4-509]

GENERAL NOTE

These provisions apply both to solemn and summary proceedings and generally exclude a statement made by an accused from the provisions of ss.259 and 260. Subs.(2) does permit a limited right to a co-accused to found upon, as evidence, statements made by an accused. This right, as subs.(3) makes clear, only begins when that accused has not given evidence himself and can only be exercised after the co-accused has given requisite notice of the terms of the statement to be founded upon (in terms of s.259) and already lodged a notice of incrimination; *McIntyre v HM Advocate*, 2009 S.L.T. 716, It should be noted, first, that it is implicit that the admissions to be founded upon must constitute a statement as defined in s.262(1); secondly, quite different considerations apply when the accused's utterances are led in evidence by the Crown for, in that situation, there would be a right to cross-examine without notice but only to the extent of the material elicited in evidence in chief. A4-509

See the discussion in *Beurskens v HM Advocate*, 2014 S.C.C.R. 447.

Though a precognition is regarded as a confidential document and, as such, not itself disclosable, the gist of it would still constitute part of the material which the Crown would ordinarily be obliged to disclose to the defence. See generally ss.121-123 of the Criminal Justice and Licensing (Scotland) Act 2010 (asp 13).

Witnesses

Examination of witnesses

263.—(1) In any trial, it shall be competent for the party against whom a witness is produced and sworn in causa to examine such witness both in cross and in causa. A4-510

(2) The judge may, on the motion of either party, on cause shown order that the examination of a witness for that party ("the first witness") shall be interrupted to permit the examination of another witness for that party.

(3) Where the judge makes an order under subsection (2) above he shall, after the examination of the other witness, permit the recall of the first witness.

(4) In a trial, a witness may be examined as to whether he has on any specified occasion made a statement on any matter pertinent to the issue at the trial different from the evidence given by him in the trial; and evidence may be led in the trial to prove that the witness made the different statement on the occasion specified.

(5) In any trial, on the motion of either party, the presiding judge may permit a witness who has been examined to be recalled.

Definitions

A4-510.1 "judge": s.307(1).
"trial": s.307(1).
"witness": s.307(1).

[THE NEXT PARAGRAPH IS A4-511]

General Note

A4-511 This section applies to solemn and summary proceedings. Subsections (2) and (3) which permit the interruption of a witness' testimony to allow evidence to be taken from another of the party's witnesses was introduced by the Criminal Justice (Scotland) Act 1980 (c.62) Sch.6 para.54. By implication such a motion could only be made during the examination or re-examination of the first witness, not during cross-examination.

Subsection (4) repeats the familiar terms of ss.147 and 349 of the 1975 Act in relation to prior inconsistent statements by witnesses. This rule does not apply to precognitions which cannot, of course, be put to witnesses unless they are precognitions on oath (see *Kerr v HM Advocate*, 1958 J.C. 14; *K.J.C. v HM Advocate*, 1994 S.C.C.R. 560). See also *Coll, Petr*, 1977 S.L.T. 58, a petition to the nobile officium by a witness to order destruction of his precognition on oath before giving evidence at the trial proceedings.

The second part of subs.(4) does not become operative until the witness has been specifically asked whether he made the statement (*McTaggart v HM Advocate*, 1934 J.C. 33 and *Leverage v HM Advocate*, 2009 S.C.C.R. 371) and that it was made on a specified occasion (*Paterson v HM Advocate*, 1998 S.L.T. 117). Subsection (4) has to be read in conjunction with s.269(1) and (2); with leave of the court it is competent to lead additional evidence (to prove the making of the prior statement) by way of productions and witnesses' evidence even if no notice has been given of them in the trial indictment. Following *Leckie v HM Advocate*, 2002 S.L.T. 595 it is not necessary that the entire terms of the prior statement be lead in evidence; what matters is that the gist of the earlier account be put in unequivocal terms for the witness to admit or dispute. In *Leckie* the Crown had objected to defence efforts to put anything other than a full statement, line by line. It is competent to examine a witness upon the terms of another witness' statement where the former witness has previously adopted that statement, or its terms, as his own; see *McNee v Ruxton* 1998 S.L.T. 140. In *HM Advocate v Hislop*, 1994 S.L.T. 333 a Crown witness, who claimed to be unable to recall events, stated that she had told the police what had happened. The prosecutor put her account to her by means of her earlier tape-recorded interview and a transcript of it, both of which were listed as productions. Objections to this use of the section's provisions were repelled. See also the notes to s.260 at A4-505 above. The distinction between the admission of a prior statement by means of s.263 and s.260 is vital: a s.263 statement used in the course of proceedings does not itself constitute evidence against the accused but serves only as a test of the credibility and reliability of the maker of the statement once its provenance has been proved; by contrast a s.260 statement (or indeed a *Jamieson* statement) will be primary evidence but only once it has been adopted by the witness as his evidence (see *Ogilvie*, 1999 G.W.D. 14-632). In any proceedings in which a party utilises s.263's provisions it is incumbent upon the trial judge to direct the jury as to the limited purpose and effect of such prior inconsistent statement (*HM Advocate v Haggerty* [2009] HCJAC 31 and *Clark v HM Advocate* [2016] HCJAC 11; 2016 S.C.C.R. 203); it tests the credibility of the witness, and remains hearsay admissible only for that limited purpose, cannot be deployed by the party leading the witness to bolster the witness's credibility, and can become primary evidence capable of replacing the witness's parole evidence only if, or when, "adopted", i.e. assented to as accurate by the witness. (*De recenti* statements by a complainer to the first natural confidant or utterances lying within the res gestae remain as special exceptions to the foregoing generality).

In *Hemming v HM Advocate*, 1998 S.L.T. 213, H was charged with attempted murder and petitioned the High Court for a commission and diligence to recover witness statements. The object was to attack the credibility of Crown witnesses by demonstrating variations in their accounts as the police investigation proceeded. In the instant case the Court held there to be compelling grounds for overriding the public interest objections raised by the Crown. Compare the approach taken by a court of five judges in *McLeod, Petr*, 1998 S.L.T. 233 (at 244J-L) in which the parameters to be met by an accused seeking a diligence to recover documents are formulated.

Refer also to the discussion of *Ogilvie v HM Advocate*, 1999 S.L.T. 1068 in the Notes to s.260 above.

It is well understood that a *socius criminis* once called to give evidence for the Crown, enjoys immunity from prosecution in relation to the matter. The defence are entitled to criticise the witness' testimony on the grounds of that immunity and, if they do so, it is generally proper for the trial judge to direct attention to this immunity; see generally *Docherty v HM Advocate*, 1987 S.L.T. 784. In *Mason v HM Advocate*, 2000 S.L.T. 1004 no such criticism of a witness' evidence had been voiced by the defence and it was held that there was no automatic duty incumbent upon the trial judge to give such directions; indeed it might be risky to do so without an appreciation of the considerations giving rise to the defence approach.

In *HM Advocate v Megrahi (No.2)*, 2000 S.L.T. 1399 a transcript of evidence given by a witness before a magistrate in a foreign jurisdiction (in this instance, Malta) was admitted as evidence, the Scottish Court in the Netherlands rejecting defence objections that the statement being put to the witness was akin to a precognition.

In *Trotter v HM Advocate*, 2001 S.L.T. 296 the accused, who had been charged with possessing controlled drugs with intent to supply during a visit to prison, had called his father, a serving prisoner, as a witness. The witness gave evidence in court in handcuffs; while the Appeal Court rejected claims that T had been deprived of a fair trial, since the jury could not fail to be aware of his father's status, an opinion was delivered that handcuffs should only be used where security was a real concern and then only after the issues had been considered between the Crown and the judge.

In *Jeffrey v HM Advocate*, 2002 S.L.T. 1407; 2002 S.C.C.R 822, which centred upon the adequacy of defence representation (following *Anderson v HM Advocate*, 1996 J.C. 29; 1999 S.L.T. 155; 1999 S.C.C.R. 114), a secondary point of appeal was the decision of the sheriff not to exercise his discretion to recall the complainer, a seven year old child, to enable an (apparently) inconsistent earlier statement to be put to her. The statement, of which the defence had a copy at the time, had not been put to the child in cross-examination. The Appeal Court upheld the sheriff's approach to the issue. There is, however, no statutory obligation upon the party founding upon a prior inconsistent statement to lead evidence of its contents at all, if a witness denies them (see *Leverage* above). The issue is primarily an ethical one; as that case indicates there has to be some basis for such questioning and not simply a speculative shot in the dark.

Spouse or civil partner of accused a compellable witness

264.—(1) The spouse or civil partner of an accused is a competent and compellable witness for the prosecution, the accused or any co-accused in the proceedings against the accused. **A4-512**

(2) Subsection (1) is, if the spouse or civil partner is a co-accused in the proceedings, subject to any enactment or rule of law by virtue of which an accused need not (by reason of being an accused) give evidence in the proceedings

(3) Subsection (1) displaces any other rule of law that would (but for that subsection) prevent or restrict, by reference to the relationship, the giving of evidence by the spouse or civil partner of an accused.

AMENDMENTS

Section 264 substituted by Criminal Justice and Licensing (Scotland) Act 2010 (asp 13) s.86(1). Brought into force on March 28, 2011 (for specified purposes) by SSI 2011/178 (C.15) art.2, Sch.1 para.1.

DEFINITIONS

"witness": s.307(1). **A4-512.1**

[THE NEXT PARAGRAPH IS A4-513]

GENERAL NOTE

The term "spouse" still applies only to persons married to each other, not to those who co-habit (*Casey v HM Advocate*, 1993 S.L.T. 33). The effect of this provision which applies to all prosecutions raised after March 28, 2011 is to abolish the long-standing right of a spouse, when called as a witness in criminal proceedings involving that spouse, by any party other than the spouse, to elect whether or not to give evidence. (Civil partnerships while explicitly recognised in the legislation are now also in an identical position). The only exception to this broad rule against compellability arose when the witness, estranged or not, was the victim or complainer in proceedings; in such circumstances the witness became compellable (*Hay v McClory*, 1993 S.C.C.R. 1115) and could no longer choose whether to give evidence. **A4-513**

It will be noted that the reforms introduced by s.63 of the Criminal Justice and Licensing (Scotland) Act 2010 also remove the long-standing prohibition upon the prosecutor passing comment upon the failure of a spouse to give evidence on behalf of a partner.

The workings, and it might be said the iniquities especially where co-accused were involved, of the long-standing right of a spouse to withhold evidence in proceedings involving a marital partner can be seen in *Hunter v HM Advocate*, 1984 S.L.T. 434 and in *Bates v HM Advocate*, 1989 S.L.T. 701; 1989 S.C.C.R. 338. These authorities will remain relevant for proceedings raised before the March 28, 2011.

Witnesses not excluded for conviction, interest, relationship, etc.

A4-514 **265.**—(1) Every person adduced as a witness who is not otherwise by law disqualified from giving evidence, shall be admissible as a witness, and no objection to the admissibility of a witness shall be competent on the ground of—

(a) conviction of or punishment for an offence;
(b) interest;
(c) agency or partial counsel;
(d) the absence of due citation to attend; or
(e) his having been precognosced subsequently to the date of citation.

(2) Where any person who is or has been an agent of the accused is adduced and examined as a witness for the accused, it shall not be competent for the accused to object, on the ground of confidentiality, to any question proposed to be put to such witness on matter pertinent to the issue of the guilt of the accused.

(3) No objection to the admissibility of a witness shall be competent on the ground that he or she is the father, mother, son, daughter, brother or sister, by consanguinity or affinity, or uncle, aunt, nephew or niece, by consanguinity of any party adducing the witness in any trial.

(4) It shall not be competent for any witness to decline to be examined and give evidence on the ground of any relationship mentioned in subsection (3) above.

Definitions

A4-514.1 "conviction": s.307(5).
"witness": s.307(1).

[THE NEXT PARAGRAPH IS A4-515]

General Note

A4-515 This section permits parties' evidence to be heard irrespective of their character or interest or relationship. See generally *Dow v McKnight*, 1949 J.C. 38. Subsection (2) provides that the accused's solicitor, or former solicitor, can be adduced as a witness by the accused; the agent cannot be objected to on the grounds that he has been present in court (*Campbell v Cochrane*, 1928 J.C. 25).

Accused as witness

A4-516 **266.**—(1) Subject to subsections (2) to (8) below, the accused shall be a competent witness for the defence at every stage of the case, whether the accused is on trial alone or along with a co-accused.

(2) The accused shall not be called as a witness in pursuance of this section except upon his own application or in accordance with subsection (9) or (10) below.

(3) An accused who gives evidence on his own behalf in pursuance of this section may be asked any question in cross-examination notwithstanding that it would tend to incriminate him as to the offence charged.

(4) An accused who gives evidence on his own behalf in pursuance of this section shall not be asked, and if asked shall not be required to answer, any question tending to show that he has committed, or been convicted of, or been charged with, any offence other than that with which he is then charged, or is of bad character, unless—

(a) the proof that he has committed or been convicted of such other offence is admissible evidence to show that he is guilty of the offence with which he is then charged; or
(b) the accused or his counsel or solicitor has asked questions of the witnesses for the prosecution with a view to establishing the accused's good character or impugning the character of the complainer, or the accused has given evidence of his own good character, or the nature or conduct of the defence is such as to involve imputations on the character of the prosecutor or of the witnesses for the prosecution or of the complainer; or

(c) the accused has given evidence against any other person charged in the same proceedings.

(5) In a case to which paragraph (b) of subsection (4) above applies, the prosecutor shall be entitled to ask the accused a question of a kind specified in that subsection only if the court, on the application of the prosecutor, permits him to do so.

(5A) Nothing in subsections (4) and (5) above shall prevent the accused from being asked, or from being required to answer, any question tending to show that he has been convicted of an offence other than that with which he is charged if his conviction for that other offence has been disclosed to the jury, or is to be taken into consideration by the judge, under section 275A(2) of this Act.

(6) An application under subsection (5) above in proceedings on indictment shall be made in the course of the trial but in the absence of the jury.

(7) In subsection (4) above, references to the complainer include references to a victim who is deceased.

(8) Every person called as a witness in pursuance of this section shall, unless otherwise ordered by the court, give his evidence from the witness box or other place from which the other witnesses give their evidence.

(9) The accused may—

(a) with the consent of a co-accused, call that other accused as a witness on the accused's behalf; or

(b) ask a co-accused any question in cross-examination if that co-accused gives evidence,

but he may not do both in relation to the same co-accused.

(10) The prosecutor or the accused may call as a witness a co-accused who has pleaded guilty to or been acquitted of all charges against him which remain before the court (whether or not, in a case where the co-accused has pleaded guilty to any charge, he has been sentenced) or in respect of whom the diet has been deserted; and the party calling such co-accused as a witness shall not require to give notice thereof, but the court may grant any other party such adjournment or postponement of the trial as may seem just.

(11) Where, in any trial, the accused is to be called as a witness he shall be so called as the first witness for the defence unless the court, on cause shown, otherwise directs.

AMENDMENTS

Subs.(5A) inserted by Sexual Offences (Procedure and Evidence) (Scotland) Act 2002 (asp 9) s.10(3). Brought into force by SSI 2002/443 (C.24) art.4 (effective 1 November 2002).

DEFINITIONS

"diet": s.307(1). A4-516.1
"offence": s.307(1).
"prosecutor": s.307(1).
"trial": s.307(1).
"witness": s.307(1).

[THE NEXT PARAGRAPH IS A4-517]

GENERAL NOTE

The accused cannot be compelled to give evidence on his own behalf in his own trial, but his failure to do so can be the subject of comment, with restraint, by the trial judge when charging a jury (see *Scott (A.T.) v HM Advocate*, 1946 J.C. 90; *Brown v MacPherson*, 1918 J.C. 3 and *McIntosh v HM Advocate*, 1946 J.C. 90). The Criminal Justice (Scotland) Act 1995 (c.20) s.32 removed a long-standing prohibition upon such comment by the prosecutor. *Dempsey v HM Advocate*, 1995 S.C.C.R. 431, a case arising from comments by both prosecutor and judge while the prohibition was current, is of note, as is *Morrison v HM Advocate*, 2013 S.C.C.R. 626. The latter case highlights the responsibility of all parties in the proceedings to intervene; in *Morrison* it is pertinent to note that the accused had entered into a joint minute of agreement with the Crown and so had led evidence, and that the prosecutor, in his jury speech, chose to introduce material which had not been led in evidence. A4-517

There was previous authority that in some cases, the proved facts may raise a presumption that the accused committed the crime libelled, and failure by the accused to put forward an explanation sufficient to raise a reasonable doubt in the minds of the jury could occasion comment legitimately (see *HM Advocate v Hardy*, 1938 J.C. 144; *McIlhargey v Herron*, 1972 J.C. 38).

Barnes v HM Advocate, 2000 G.W.D. 35-1330 demonstrates the sort of complex issues which can arise when an accused is exposed to cross-examination by others' counsel. It is one thing for a prior record to be revealed inadvertently in the course of questioning but in *Barnes*, the Appeal Court held that his counsel had expressly questioned a co-accused about *Barnes*' involvement in the assault libelled (a fact clearly evident from earlier evidence) solely as a means of drawing out the co-accused's criminal history. Such a tactic flew in the face of the section's purpose, and during the trial, *Barnes*' counsel had been refused the right to cross-examine on record; (*Murdoch v HM Advocate*, 1978 S.L.T. 10 distinguished). *Hanlin v McFadyen*, 2000 S.C.C.R. 428 confirms that no witness citation is necessary when it is intended to call a co-accused upon whom the court has already deferred sentence. In *Hanlin* the sheriff had declined an accused's motion to adjourn trial founded upon the failure of the co-accused to appear for sentence, no witness citation having been served.

While the prosecutor can only question an accused on his record with leave of the court once the character of the accused or Crown witnesses has been put in issue by that accused (s.266(4)(b)), *Griffith v HM Advocate* [2013] HCJAC 84 supports the view voiced in *Barnes* and in *McCourtney* (1978 S.L.T. 10) that once an accused expressly or implicitly incriminates, or attacks the character of, his co accused, he risks his own relevant convictions record being explored by that accused to undermine credit and character and, more significantly, that there is no discretion, subject to the ordinary rules of evidence applying to all witnesses, on the part of the trial judge to disallow such questioning, notwithstanding the general duty of the judge to preserve the fairness of the proceedings (see *N v HM Advocate*, 2003 S.L.T. 761; 2003 S.C.C.R. 378). It may be of some significance that G had only lodged a special defence of alibi, and extended his testimony to implicate his co accused. It is nonetheless difficult to resist a sense that the potential for injustice is conspicuous and to doubt how much of it can be forestalled by judicial directions to jurors.

With regard to the reform which became s.32 of the Criminal Justice (Scotland) Act 1995, during the Committee Stage of the Bill (*Hansard*, H.L. Vol. 560, col. 416), the Lord Advocate observed: "Where the law itself only allows comment with restraint, and only for inferences to be drawn in narrow circumstances, it would be a foolish prosecutor indeed who went further than that."

Subss.(2) and (3)

No other party can compel an accused person to give evidence in any trial unless he has already been convicted or acquitted of all charges libelled. The accused may give evidence on his own behalf but ordinarily should do so before leading any other evidence (s.263(2) permits application to be made only for the interruption of evidence to enable the examination of another witness). Once he elects to give evidence the accused can be cross-examined on any issue subject only to the limitations imposed upon the prosecutor by subs.(4); these restrictions do not apply to co-accused who are entitled to cross-examine an accused as to his criminal record if the accused, directly or impliedly, gives evidence against them (*McCourtney v HM Advocate*, 1978 S.L.T. 10; *Burton v HM Advocate*, 1979 S.L.T. (Notes) 59). Much of the case law originates from the problems created by cross-incrimination of accused (see *Sandlan v HM Advocate*, 1983 S.L.T. 519 which involved prejudicial evidence against first accused elicited in cross-examination of Crown witnesses by second accused without adequate opportunity for first accused to examine anew; in *HM Advocate v Ferrie*, 1983 S.C.C.R. 1 the use, by the Crown, as a witness of an accused who tendered partial pleas during trial was upheld; *Dodds v HM Advocate*, 1987 S.C.C.R. 678; 1988 S.L.T. 194; an accused who had had his partial pleas accepted, then gave evidence in relation to the outstanding charge and was cross-examined by the co-accused in relation to all charges libelled, unsuccessfully appealed.

If in the conduct of his defence, either in cross-examination of prosecution witnesses or in his own evidence, the accused attacks the character of the complainer, impugns the conduct of the prosecutor or represents himself falsely to be of good character, the accused is liable to lose the customary protection of subs.(4). See, for example, *Penman v HM Advocate* [2018] HCJAC 71; 2019 S.C.C.R. 41. As subs.(5) makes clear, that protection can only properly be withdrawn by the court after the prosecutor has made that motion outwith the presence of any jury: see *Khan v HM Advocate*, 2010 S.L.T. 1004. The court must consider the motion (see *Leggate v HM Advocate*, 1988 S.L.T. 665; 1988 S.C.C.R. 391). In relation to witnesses the general rule is that it is incompetent to found upon extract convictions of a witness, rather than the witness's own testimony, as evidence of the facts behind those convictions, particularly if such a conviction is subject to appeal; see *HM Advocate v Duffy*, 2009 S.C.C.R. 20, following *Howitt v HM Advocate*, 2000 SL.T. 449; 2000 S.C.C.R. 195. The obligation upon the Crown to disclose witnesses' previous convictions is not absolute. Only convictions, pending cases or administrative fines which are material, that is bear upon the credibility or character of the witness and, as such, materially weaken the Crown case or enhance that of the defence need be disclosed. On balance there is a general presumption in favour of disclosure (see *HM Advocate v Murtagh*, 2009 S.C.C.R. 790, following *McDonald v HM Advocate*, 2008 S.L.T. 993; 2009 S.C.C.R. 954) which may be over-ridden in extreme situations by the privacy rights of a witness. So, in *Cairney v HM Advocate* [2019] HCJAC 87 a conviction was quashed where the Crown had failed to pursue and disclose any English convictions recorded against a complainer which were subsequently considered relevant to his credibility.

The prosecutor has to exercise care to avoid breaching the statutory provisions, particularly in the heat of cross-examination: in *Cordiner v HM Advocate*, 1993 S.L.T. 2; 1991 S.C.C.R. 652 the prosecutor challenged the accused that he had sought to instigate another witness to pervert the course of justice by false testimony, a crime not charged. No objection had been taken at the time and the Court of Appeal held that while the section had been breached technically, the appellant had waived compliance. The difficulties involved for prosecutor and defence alike in the face of fingerprint evidence are apparent in *Robertson v HM Advocate*, 2003 S.L.T. 127. The Appeal Court, following *Jones v DPP* [1962] A.C. 635, considered that the words "tending to show" in subs.(4) meant "to suggest to the jury".

A third situation (robust cross-examination of witnesses which elicits prejudicial material) will not inevitably result in desertion of the proceedings. The test to be applied in all three situations is a high one (the court tending to distinguish breaches by the prosecutor or police and professional witnesses from those by lay witnesses), namely whether the remarks or evidence so compromised the fairness of the trial that desertion becomes imperative to avoid a miscarriage of justice. See *Fraser v HM Advocate*, 2014 J.C. 115 followed in *Jackson v HM Advocate* [2017] HCJAC 72 and *Cameron v HM Advocate* [2017] HCJAC 74. In *Cameron* factually inaccurate, and prejudicial, details of the accused's criminal history were given gratuitously by a witness during tense cross-examination. Having heard submissions from parties in relation to a defence motion to desert proceedings, the sheriff was upheld in applying the *Fraser* test and exercising discretion to make only indirect reference to the evidence.

Note that subs.(7) has the effect of extending the protection given to the character of the complainer by subs.(4)(b) to deceased victims; it is not necessary that the deceased died as a result of being the victim of the crime charged. A curious variation upon subs.(4)(c) is found in *Marshall v HM Advocate*, 1996 G.W.D. 27-1577 where the jury was provided a copy of a co-accused's 22 page police interview transcript which made reference to M having previously being released from jail. M's appeal against conviction was refused, it being noted that the relevant passage had not been referred to in evidence and the sheriff had consciously decided not to draw attention to it or issue directions. See also *Sinclair v MacDonald*, 1996 J.C. 145; 1996 S.C.C.R. 466 where defence cross-examination had gone too far and amounted to attacks on character.

Witnesses in court during trial

267.—(1) The court may, on an application by any party to the proceedings, permit a witness to be in court during the proceedings or any part of the proceedings before he has given evidence if it appears to the court that the presence of the witness would not be contrary to the interests of justice. A4-518

(2) Without prejudice to subsection (1) above, where a witness has, without the permission of the court and without the consent of the parties to the proceedings, been present in court during the proceedings, the court may, in its discretion, admit the witness, where it appears to the court that the presence of the witness was not the result of culpable negligence or criminal intent, and that the witness has not been unduly instructed or influenced by what took place during his presence, or that injustice will not be done by his examination.

DEFINITIONS

"witness": s.307(1). A4-518.1

[THE NEXT PARAGRAPH IS A4-519]

GENERAL NOTE

It is a matter for the court whether the evidence of a witness present in court during the trial should be taken into account. The court should consider whether there has been any criminative intent or wilful neglect on the part of the witness, the likely effect upon his testimony of his earlier presence in court and the likelihood of injustice being done by the exclusion of that evidence in the case. A4-519

See *MacDonald v Mackenzie*, 1947 J.C. 169; it is the task of the party tendering the witness' evidence to satisfy the court that the evidence should be admitted notwithstanding the improper presence in court. The evidence of a solicitor engaged in the case cannot be objected to on the ground of his earlier presence in court (*Campbell v Cochrane*, 1928 J.C. 25).

Citation of witnesses for precognition

267A.—(1) This Act shall be sufficient warrant for the citation of witnesses for precognition by the prosecutor, whether or not any person has been charged with the offence in relation to which the precognition is taken. A4-519.1

(1A) Subsection (1) extends to citation for precognition by the prosecutor where a European investigation order having effect by virtue of Part 3 of the Criminal Justice (European Investigation Order) Regulations 2017 contains a request for a person in Scotland to be heard under regulations 35 to 37 of those Regulations.

(2) Such citation shall be in the form prescribed by Act of Adjournal or as nearly as may be in such form.

(3) A witness who, having been duly cited—

(a) fails without reasonable excuse, after receiving at least 48 hours notice, to attend for precognition by a prosecutor at the time and place mentioned in the citation served on him; or

(b) refuses when so cited to give information within his knowledge regarding any matter relative to the commission of the offence in relation to which the precognition is taken,

shall be guilty of an offence and shall be liable on summary conviction to a fine not exceeding level 3 on the standard scale or to a term of imprisonment not exceeding 21 days.

AMENDMENTS

Section 267A inserted by Criminal Procedure (Amendment) (Scotland) Act 2004 (asp 5) s.22. Brought into force on 4 October 2004 by SSI 2004/405 (C.28).

Subs.(1A) inserted by Criminal Justice (European Investigation Order) Regulations 2017 (SI 2017/730) Sch.3 para.3 (effective 31 July 2017).

DEFINITIONS

A4-519.2 "fine": s.307(1).
"level 3": s.225(2).
"offence": s.307(1).
"prosecutor": s.307(1).
"standard scale": s.225(1).

GENERAL NOTE

A4-519.3 New s.267A re-enacts in an updated form what was s.67A of the 1995 Act. In particular, s.267A provides that the 1995 Act is itself sufficient warrant to cite a witness for precognition and that citation shall be in the form prescribed by Act of Adjournal or as nearly as possible in such form. It is an offence for a witness fail to attend or to give information within his knowledge: s.267A(3).

Order requiring accused to participate in identification procedure

A4-519.4 **267B.—**(1) The court may, on an application by the prosecutor in any proceedings, make an order requiring the accused person to participate in an identification parade or other identification procedure.

(2) The application may be made at any time after the proceedings have been commenced.

(3) The court—

(a) shall (if the accused is present) allow the accused to make representations in relation to the application;

(b) may, if it considers it appropriate to do so (where the accused is not present), fix a hearing for the purpose of allowing the accused to make such representations.

(4) Where an order is made under subsection (1) above, the clerk of court shall (if the accused is not present) have notice of the order effected as respects the accused without delay.

(5) Notice under subsection (4) above shall (in relation to any proceedings) be effected in the same manner as citation under section 141 of this Act.

(6) It is sufficient evidence that notice has been effected under subsection (5) above if there is produced a written execution—

(a) in the form prescribed by Act of Adjournal or as nearly as may be in such form; and

(b) signed by the person who effected notice.

(7) In relation to notice effected by means of registered post or the recorded delivery service, the relevant post office receipt requires to be produced along with the execution mentioned in subsection (6) above.

(8) A person who, having been given due notice of an order made under subsection (1) above, without reasonable excuse fails to comply with the order is—

(a) guilty of an offence; and
(b) liable on summary conviction to a fine not exceeding level 3 on the standard scale or to imprisonment for a period not exceeding 12 months or to both.

(9) For the purpose of subsection (5) above, section 141 of this Act is to be read with such modifications as are necessary for its application in the circumstances.

(10) In this section, "the court" means

(a) in the case of proceedings in the High Court, a single judge of that Court;
(b) in any other case, any court with jurisdiction in relation to the proceedings.

AMENDMENTS

Section 267B inserted by Criminal Proceedings etc (Reform) (Scotland) Act 2007 (asp 6) s.34. Brought into force on 10 December 2007 by SSI 2007/479 (C.40) art.3 and Sch.

DEFINITIONS

"prosecutor": s.307(1). **A4-519.5**
"offence": s.307(1).
"fine": s.307(1).
"standard": s.225(1).
"imprisonment": s.307(1).

GENERAL NOTE

This section is a further measure designed to add flexibility into Scottish criminal procedure. It empowers the prosecutor to apply to the court in any proceedings to order the accused to participate in an identification parade or in identification procedures—a recognition of the increasing use of Viper image capture procedures and, indeed, the increasing demands for pre-court identification of accused brought about by the extension of vulnerable witness provisions—see generally s.271 below. It is also noted that the Act has enhanced the use of trials in absence of accused and that, in some cases identification may well have to be resolved as an issue before such a trial is viable. The application can be made verbally to the court in the presence of the accused, or by written application to fix a hearing for parties to be heard. Intimation is by standard postal methods. **A4-519.6**

Until this reform the Crown could seek attendance at an identification parade as a condition of bail (a step which was only feasible on petition), or place the accused on petition and seek a remand in order that a parade could be held in the period between committal for further examination and full committal. Now it has to be stressed that an order for an identification parade can be sought in any criminal proceedings.

Subs.(8) makes it an offence to fail to adhere to the court's order under the section and the penalties range from a Level 3 fine up to a period of imprisonment (or, presumably, detention) of one year, a scale which reflects the application of the provision to both summary and solemn criminal proceedings.

On a cautionary note attention is directed to subs.(10) which sets out the forum for applications. While it is clear that applications have to be directed to a High Court judge once proceedings have been indicted in that court, the position is arguably less clear in relation to other solemn or summary proceedings; while it is the case that applications generally fall to be considered by the court before which the proceedings are being heard, the subsection permits applications to be made to any court with jurisdiction in relation to the proceedings which might not be quite the same thing.

[THE NEXT PARAGRAPH IS A4-520]

Additional evidence, etc.

Additional evidence

268.—(1) Subject to subsection (2) below, the judge may, on a motion of the prosecutor or the accused made— **A4-520**

(a) in proceedings on indictment, at any time before the commencement of the speeches to the jury;
(b) in summary proceedings, at any time before the prosecutor proceeds to address the judge on the evidence,

permit him to lead additional evidence.

(2) Permission shall only be granted under subsection (1) above where the judge—

(a) considers that the additional evidence is prima facie material; and

(b) accepts that at the commencement of the trial either—

(i) the additional evidence was not available and could not reasonably have been made available; or

(ii) the materiality of such additional evidence could not reasonably have been foreseen by the party.

(3) The judge may permit the additional evidence to be led notwithstanding that—

(a) in proceedings on indictment, a witness or production concerned is not included in any list lodged by the parties and that the notice required by sections 67(5) and 78(4) of this Act has not been given; or

(b) in any case, a witness must be recalled.

(4) The judge may, when granting a motion in terms of this section, adjourn or postpone the trial before permitting the additional evidence to be led.

(5) In this section "the commencement of the trial" means—

(a) in proceedings on indictment, the time when the jury is sworn; and

(b) in summary proceedings, the time when the first witness for the prosecution is sworn.

DEFINITIONS

A4-520.1 "commencement of proceedings": s.268(5).
"indictment": s.307(1).
"judge": s.307(1).
"prosecutor": s.307(1).

[THE NEXT PARAGRAPH IS A4-521]

GENERAL NOTE

A4-521 Additional evidence can be led in both solemn or summary proceedings provided that the criteria in subs.(2) are satisfied. In solemn proceedings such evidence can be received notwithstanding that the relevant productions or witnesses have not been specified in the indictment (subs.(3)(a)); in either solemn or summary trials the additional evidence can be taken from witnesses whose evidence has already been heard. In making a motion for additional evidence to be heard, the party has to demonstrate some knowledge of the likely content of that evidence and its potential materiality, as well as persuade the court that the conditions set out in subs.(2) can be satisfied. Even then the judge retains an overall discretion not to admit the additional evidence (*Kerr v HM Advocate*, 2002 G.W.D. 5-157).

In *Cushion v HM Advocate*, 1994 S.L.T. 410; 1993 S.C.C.R. 356 a review of the trial judge's refusal to admit additional evidence was appealed under the explanation that the court had not been given a full background, and that the judge's decision might have been more favourable to the application; the Appeal Court declined to review the application under s.149(1) of the 1975 Act.

In *Hyslop v HM Advocate* [2018] HCJAC 75; 2019 S.C.C.R. 49, CCTV evidence, which had never been lodged with the Crown or deemed significant enough to obtain and disclose to parties [despite its existence being mentioned in the police summary and referred to in an admission by the accused upon which the Crown founded] was admitted as additional evidence. Two further features, possibly not entirely unconnected, are noteworthy; the Appeal Court excused the sheriff's admitted failure to elicit the views of the (by then) unrepresented accused on the Crown motion; the trial scheduled for four to six days lasted an extraordinary 38 days by which time one might feel parties' positions had crystallised.

Evidence in replication

A4-522 **269.**—(1) The judge may, on a motion of the prosecutor made at the relevant time, permit the prosecutor to lead additional evidence for the purpose of—

(a) contradicting evidence given by any defence witness which could not reasonably have been anticipated by the prosecutor; or

(b) providing such proof as is mentioned in section 263(4) of this Act.

(2) The judge may permit the additional evidence to be led notwithstanding that—

(a) in proceedings on indictment, a witness or production concerned is not included in any list lodged by the parties and that the notice required by sections 67(5) and 78(4) of this Act has not been given; or

(b) in any case, a witness must be recalled.

(3) The judge may when granting a motion in terms of this section, adjourn or postpone the trial before permitting the additional evidence to be led.

(4) In subsection (1) above, "the relevant time" means—

(a) in proceedings on indictment, after the close of the defence evidence and before the commencement of the speeches to the jury; and

(b) in summary proceedings, after the close of the defence evidence and before the prosecutor proceeds to address the judge on the evidence.

DEFINITIONS

"indictment": s.307(1). A4-522.1
"judge": s.307(1).
"prosecutor": s.307(1).
"relevant time, the": s.269(4).

[THE NEXT PARAGRAPH IS A4-523]

GENERAL NOTE

Evidence in replication may be led with leave of the court to contradict defence evidence which could not be anticipated by the prosecutor, or for the purpose of proving a prior statement of a witness whose evidence is now at variance (s.263(4)). A4-523

In assessing whether the prosecutor could have expected the testimony led by the defence, the court may well enquire about the preparations for trial; in both *MacGillivray v Johnston (No. 2)*, 1994 S.L.T. 1012 and *Neizer v Johnston*, 1993 S.C.C.R. 772 a decisive factor in refusing such a motion in each case was the Crown's awareness of the existence of witnesses who had been precognosced but had not been led in evidence.

Note that replication can only be used to counter defence evidence and cannot be used by the Crown to contradict earlier prosecution evidence (see *Campbell v Allan*, 1988 S.C.C.R. 47).

Evidence of criminal record and character of accused

270.—(1) This section applies where— A4-524

(a) evidence is led by the defence, or the defence asks questions of a witness for the prosecution, with a view to establishing the accused's good character or impugning the character of the prosecutor, of any witness for the prosecution or of the complainer; or

(b) the nature or conduct of the defence is such as to tend to establish the accused's good character or to involve imputations on the character of the prosecutor, of any witness for the prosecution or of the complainer.

(2) Where this section applies the court may, without prejudice to section 268 of this Act, on the application of the prosecutor, permit the prosecutor to lead evidence that the accused has committed, or has been convicted of, or has been charged with, offences other than that for which he is being tried, or is of bad character, notwithstanding that, in proceedings on indictment, a witness or production concerned is not included in any list lodged by the prosecutor and that the notice required by sections 67(5) and 78(4) of this Act has not been given.

(3) In proceedings on indictment, an application under subsection (2) above shall be made in the course of the trial but in the absence of the jury.

(4) In subsection (1) above, references to the complainer include references to a victim who is deceased.

DEFINITIONS

"prosecutor": s.307(1). A4-524.1
"witness": s.307(1).

[THE NEXT PARAGRAPH IS A4-525]

GENERAL NOTE

A4-525 The purpose of this section is to provide a balanced picture where the defence, as a matter of tactics, elects to present the accused as being of good character or brings out the faults of witnesses or a deceased person. A cursory examination might suggest that subs.(2) is very similar to the more familiar terms of s.266(4)(b) and (c). Section 266 only enables the prosecutor or other accused to question the accused as to his history and character where such defence tactics have been pursued by the accused and the prosecutor, at least, may only do so with leave of the court (s.266(5)). It is important to note that s.266(4) is limited in scope: it is only activated when the accused gives evidence on his own behalf.

By contrast, subs.(2) is much more radical and enables the prosecution to lead evidence (without prior notice but with leave of the court) in rebuttal to demonstrate the history and character of the accused, if the defence has led evidence of his good character, or attacked the character of Crown witnesses or the prosecutor. The introduction of this provision in the Criminal Justice (Scotland) Act 1995 s.24 was not without controversy, given its nature, but it is clear that the conduct of the defence case in the future may require a good deal more circumspection than was necessary hitherto, even where the accused does not give evidence. It may also be said that subs.(1)(b) by its reference to "the nature or conduct of the defence" lacks both the familiarity and clarity of subs.(1)(a).

While the accused may found upon the previous convictions of Crown witnesses, it is clear that only in exceptional circumstances will the court permit scrutiny of, or questioning about, the factual circumstances giving rise to a previous conviction (see *Brady v HM Advocate*, 1986 S.C.C.R. 191): only when the previous conviction relates directly to the circumstances of the current trial can questioning be extended.

Special measures for child witnesses and other vulnerable witnesses

Vulnerable witnesses: main definitions

A4-526 **271.**—(1) For the purposes of this Act, a person who is giving or is to give evidence at, or for the purposes of, a hearing in relevant criminal proceedings is a vulnerable witness if—

(a) the person is under the age of 18 on the date of commencement of the proceedings in which the hearing is being or is to be held,

(b) there is a significant risk that the quality of the evidence to be given by the person will be diminished by reason of—

(i) mental disorder (within the meaning of section 328 of the Mental Health (Care and Treatment) (Scotland) Act 2003), or

(ii) fear or distress in connection with giving evidence at the trial.

(c) the offence is alleged to have been committed against the person in proceedings for—

(i) an offence listed in any of paragraphs 36 to 59ZL of Schedule 3 to the Sexual Offences Act 2003,

(ii) an offence under section 22 of the Criminal Justice (Scotland) Act 2003 (traffic in prostitution etc.),

(iii) an offence under section 4 of the Asylum and Immigration (Treatment of Claimants, etc.) Act 2004 (trafficking people for exploitation),

(iiia) an offence of human trafficking (see section 1 of the Human Trafficking and Exploitation (Scotland) Act 2015),

(iv) an offence the commission of which involves domestic abuse, or

(v) an offence of stalking, or

(d) there is considered to be a significant risk of harm to the person by reason only of the fact that the person is giving or is to give evidence in the proceedings.

(1AA) The Scottish Ministers may by order subject to the affirmative procedure modify subsection (1)(c).

(1A) […]

(2) In determining whether a person is a vulnerable witness by virtue of subsection (1)(b) or (d) above, the court shall take into account—

(a) the nature and circumstances of the alleged offence to which the proceedings relate,
(b) the nature of the evidence which the person is likely to give,
(c) the relationship (if any) between the person and the accused,
(d) the person's age and maturity,
(e) any behaviour towards the person on the part of—
(i) the accused,
(ii) members of the family or associates of the accused,
(iii) any other person who is likely to be an accused or a witness in the proceedings, and
(f) such other matters, including—
(i) the social and cultural background and ethnic origins of the person,
(ii) the person's sexual orientation,
(iii) the domestic and employment circumstances of the person,
(iv) any religious beliefs or political opinions of the person, and
(v) any physical disability or other physical impairment which the person has,

as appear to the court to be relevant.

(3) For the purposes of subsection (1)(a), section 271B(1)(b) and sections 271BZA to 271BZC, proceedings shall be taken to have commenced—
(a) where it is relevant to a court's consideration of whether to authorise the use of the special measure of taking evidence by commissioner (on its own or in combination with any other special measure) and the accused has appeared on petition, on the date when the accused appeared on petition, or
(b) in any other case, on the date when the indictment or, as the case may be, complaint is served on the accused.

(4) In subsection (1)(b) above, the reference to the quality of evidence is to its quality in terms of completeness, coherence and accuracy.

(4A) In determining whether a person is a vulnerable witness under subsection (1)(b) or (d), the court must—
(a) have regard to the best interests of the witness, and
(b) take account of any views expressed by the witness.

(5) In this section and sections 271A to 271M of this Act—

"child witness" means a vulnerable witness referred to in subsection (1)(a),
"court" means the High Court or the sheriff court,
"deemed vulnerable witness" means a vulnerable witness referred to in subsection (1)(c),
"hearing in relevant criminal proceedings" means any hearing in the course of any criminal proceedings in the High Court or the sheriff court..

(6) In sections 271A to 271M of this Act, "special measure" means any of the special measures set out in, or prescribed under, section 271H below.

AMENDMENTS

Section 271 substituted by Vulnerable Witnesses (Scotland) Act 2004 (asp 3) s.1(1). Brought into force (except for the reference to s.271I in subss.(5) and (6)), for specified purposes, on 1 April 2005 by SSI 2005/168 (C.7) art.2 and Sch.

Further brought into force for specified purposes on 30 November 2005 by SSI 2005/590 art.2 and Sch.1.

Further brought into force for specified purposes on 1 April 2006 by SSI 2006/59 (C.8).

Further brought into force for specified purposes on 1 April 2007 by SSI 2007/101 (C.13) art.2.

Remainder brought into force on 1 April 2008 by SSI 2008/57 (C.7) art.2.

Subss.(1), (5) as amended by Criminal Justice and Licensing (Scotland) Act 2010 (asp 13) s.87(2). Brought into force on 28 March 2011 (for all purposes in respect of criminal proceedings commenced on or after 28 March 2011, with proceedings taken to have commenced when a report of the case has been received by the procurator fiscal) by SSI 2011/178 (C.15) art.2, Sch.1 para.1.

Subs.(1A) inserted by Criminal Justice and Licensing (Scotland) Act 2010 (asp 13) s.88(b). Brought into force on 28 March 2011 (for all purposes in respect of criminal proceedings commenced on or after 28 March 2011, with proceedings taken to have commenced when a report of the case has been received by the procurator fiscal) by SSI 2011/178 art.2 and Sch.1 para.1.

Subss.(1) and (2) as amended, subs.(1AA) and (4A) inserted, subs.(1A) repealed by Victims and Witnesses (Scotland) Act 2014 (asp 1) s.10. Subs.(5) as amended by 2014 asp 1 s.11. Brought into force on 1 September 2015 by SSI 2015/200 art.2 and Sch. subject to transitional provisions in art.4.

Subs.(1)(c)(iiia) inserted by Human Trafficking and Exploitation (Scotland) Act 2015 (asp 12) Sch.1 para.1. Brought into force on 31 May 2016 by SSI 2016/128 (C.12) art.2 and Sch.

Subs.(3) as amended by Vulnerable Witnesses (Criminal Evidence) (Scotland) Act 2019 (asp 8) s.5(6)(a). Brought into force on 20 January 2020 by SSI 2019/392 Sch.1, subject to transitional provisions in reg.4.

Subs.(3) as amended by Vulnerable Witnesses (Criminal Evidence) (Scotland) Act 2019 (asp 8) s.5(6)(b). Brought into force on 20 January 2020 by SSI 2019/392 Sch.1, subject to transitional provisions in reg.3; not yet in force otherwise.

DEFINITIONS

A4-526.1 "court": s.271(5).
"proceedings": s.271(3).
"quality of evidence": s.271(4).
"special measures": s.271H.
"trial": s.271(5).
"vulnerable witness": s.271(1).

[THE NEXT PARAGRAPH IS A4-527]

GENERAL NOTE

A4-527 A brief discussion of the development of these provisions may assist: ss.271 to 271M introduced the regime of special measures available to "vulnerable witnesses" (see s.271 above) when called to give evidence in Scottish courts, setting out the procedures for placing vulnerable witness applications before the courts.

Previously there had been no automatic entitlement to any special treatment for children or other vulnerable witnesses—the need for departure from the time-honoured tradition of parole evidence being determined on a case by case basis. The statutory framework laid down in s.271A applied initially in High Court and sheriff court trials but has since been extended to preliminary hearings and debates, to district court trials and to fatal accident and sudden death enquiries. It comprises automatic entitlement to special measures for children under 18 years old and discretionary entitlement on cause shown for other vulnerable witnesses.

Children under 12 years of age benefited from enhanced procedures—essentially a presumption against the child witness giving evidence in court or within the court precincts, while children aged between 12 and 18 years were placed within a more flexible regime as were witnesses whose deemed vulnerability arose from mental disorder (s.271(1)(b)(i)) or fear and distress caused by the court proceedings (s.271(1)(b)(ii)). In the case of non-child witnesses it falls to the party intending to call that witness to prepare a vulnerability assessment in support of any vulnerable witness application and to identify the special measure or measures considered to best assist the witness to give evidence in the proceedings (s.271BA).

The Vulnerable Witnesses (Criminal Evidence) (Scotland) Act 2019 (asp 8) aims to enhance the existing provisions governing the testimony of child witnesses (as defined in s.271(1)(a) of the 1995 Act), apart from the accused, in most solemn proceedings. The charge, or charges, libelled in these proceedings will determine whether or not the child witness qualifies for modified standard special measures, specifically evidence on commission, or utilising testimony in the form of a prior statement (s.271M(1)). Otherwise standard special measures as described previously will obtain if application is granted by the court. The earlier legislation generally sought to take the witness's evidence contemporaneously but the 2019 Act goes a step further; henceforth the aim of this legislation as now found in s.271BZA, in all but the most exceptional circumstances, is to ensure that the child's entire evidence is recorded in advance of the trial proceedings. The Act stipulates procedures considered necessary to bring this about including, in s.271I(1ZA) the statutory introduction of a preparatory hearing (a "ground rules hearing") in cases involving a commissioner, tasked with detailed consideration of the length and form of questioning, the appropriate special measures, and any outstanding issues relating to the witness in terms of ss.275 and 288F. The Scottish Legal Aid Board considers that the existing criminal legal aid rules will be sufficient to categorise and fee the additional appearances for solicitors and counsel. It is important to appreciate that with the advent of the 2019 Act in solemn proceedings there are two possible routes, ss.271B and 271BZA, to secure the evidence of child witnesses, and that the latter provision is considerably more prescriptive in tone. On a cautionary note, all parties will have to be alert to the need for the earliest possible identification of affected witnesses and, if the ground rules and witness examination hearings are to operate effectively, issues of admissibility and disclosure will require similarly prompt consideration. See too Practice Note No.1 of 2017 and Practice Note No.1 of 2019.

Section 9 of the 2019 Act stipulates that the operation of the Act will have to be reported upon by the Scottish Ministers to evaluate whether the reform measures have assisted affected witnesses' participation in the criminal justice system. The opportunity has not been taken to study whether witnesses' testimony delivered at a remove from the jury is perceived differently from traditional parole evidence.

It has to be emphasised that before the discretionary entitlement is excused by the court there requires to be a significant risk that the quality of the evidence to be given will be diminished by reason of that mental disorder or fear or distress: s.271(1).

In determining whether a person is a vulnerable witness with discretionary entitlement there is a wide range of various circumstances that the court may weigh in the balance: see s.271(2)(a) to (f) for the full range. These wider circumstances mean that assistance may now be extended to, amongst others, victims of sexual offences, domestic abuse or witnesses who have been intimidated.

These provisions have been operative only in proceedings before the High Court and in the sheriff court. The effect of the amendments introduced by s.64 of the Criminal Justice and Licensing (Scotland) Act 2010 has been to extend vulnerable witness provisions as set out in ss.271–271M of the 1995 Act to any preliminary diets or debate hearings where evidence requires to be lead, and arguably to examination of facts procedures (s.54(1)(b) of the 1995 Act) since the last-mentioned are not trials as such. It should also be noted that the relevant (qualifying) age for vulnerable child witnesses—witnesses automatically entitled to standard special measures—is extended to 18 years of age for the range of serious people trafficking offences specified in subs.(1A).

These provisions were extended to fatal accident and sudden death inquiries by the Fatal Accident and Sudden Deaths Inquiry Procedure (Scotland) Rules 2007 (SSI 2007/478) which provide specific forms for vulnerable witness issues.

Reference should also be made to witness anonymity orders now found in ss.271N–271Y which give a statutory basis for yet further forms of protection for certain vulnerable witnesses.

Justice of the Peace Court

The special measures provided for in this section have been extended to the JP court by the Justice of the Peace Courts (Special Measures) (Scotland) Order 2015 (SSI 2015/447) art.3(1).

Child and deemed vulnerable witnesses

271A.—(1) Where a child witness or a deemed vulnerable witness is to give evidence at or for the purposes of a hearing in relevant criminal proceedings, the witness is entitled, subject to— **A4-527.1**

(a) subsections (2) to (13) below, and

(b) section 271D of this Act,

to the benefit of one or more of the special measures for the purpose of giving evidence.

(2) A party citing or intending to cite a child witness or a deemed vulnerable witness shall, by the required time, lodge with the court a notice (referred to in this Act as a "vulnerable witness notice")—

(a) specifying the special measure or measures which the party considers to be the most appropriate for the purpose of taking the witness's evidence, or

(b) if the party considers that the witness should give evidence without the benefit of any special measure, stating that fact.

(3) A vulnerable witness notice shall contain or be accompanied by—

(a) a summary of any views expressed for the purposes of section 271E(2)(b) of this Act, and

(b) such other information as may be prescribed by Act of Adjournal.

(3A) In the case where a vulnerable witness notice under subsection (2)(a) specifies only a standard special measure—

(a) subsection (3)(a) does not apply, and

(b) subsection (5) has effect as if the words "not earlier than 7 days and" were omitted.

(4) The court may, on cause shown, allow a vulnerable witness notice to be lodged after the required time.

(4A) Any party to the proceedings may, not later than 7 days after a vulnerable witness notice has been lodged, lodge with the court a notice (referred to in this section as an "objection notice") stating—

(a) an objection to any special measure (other than a standard special measure) specified in the vulnerable witness notice that the party considers to be inappropriate, and

(b) the reasons for that objection.

(4B) The court may, on cause shown, allow an objection notice to be lodged after the period referred to in subsection (4A).

(4C) If an objection notice is lodged in accordance with subsection (4A) or (4B)—

(a) subsection (5)(a)(ii) does not apply to the vulnerable witness notice, and

(b) the court must make an order under subsection (5A).

(5) The court shall, not earlier than 7 days and not later than 14 days after a vulnerable witness notice has been lodged, consider the notice in the absence of the parties and, subject to sections 271B to 271BZB of this Act—

(a) in the case of a notice under subsection (2)(a) above—

(i) if a standard special measure is specified in the notice, make an order authorising the use of that measure for the purpose of taking the witness's evidence, and

(ii) if any other special measure is specified in the notice and the court is satisfied on the basis of the notice that it is appropriate to do so, make an order authorising the use of the special measure (in addition to any authorised by virtue of an order under sub-paragraph (i) above) for the purpose of taking the witness's evidence,

(b) in the case of a notice under subsection (2)(b) above, if—

(i) the summary of views accompanying the notice under subsection (3)(a) above indicates that the witness has expressed a wish to give evidence without the benefit of any special measure, and

(ii) the court is satisfied on the basis of the notice that it is appropriate to do so,

make an order authorising the giving of evidence by the witness without the benefit of any special measure, or

(c) if—

(i) paragraph (a)(ii) or (b) above would apply but for the fact that the court is not satisfied as mentioned in that paragraph, or

(ii) in the case of a notice under subsection (2)(b), the summary of views accompanying the notice under subsection (3)(a) above indicates that the witness has not expressed a wish to give evidence without the benefit of any special measure,

make an order under subsection (5A) below.

(5A) That order is an order—

(a) in the case of proceedings in the High Court where the preliminary hearing is yet to be held, appointing the vulnerable witness notice to be disposed of at that hearing;

(b) in the case of proceedings on indictment in the sheriff court where the first diet is yet to be held, appointing the vulnerable witness notice to be disposed of at that diet; or

(c) in any other case, appointing a diet to be held before the hearing at which the evidence is to be given and requiring the parties to attend the diet.

(6) Subsection (7) below applies where—

(a) it appears to the court that a party intends to call a child witness or a deemed vulnerable witness to give evidence at or for the purposes of a hearing in relevant criminal proceedings,

(b) the party has not lodged a vulnerable witness notice in respect of the witness by the time specified in subsection (2) above, and

(c) the court has not allowed a vulnerable witness notice in respect of the witness to be lodged after that time under subsection (4) above.

(7) Where this subsection applies, the court shall—

(a) order the party to lodge a vulnerable witness notice in respect of the witness by such time as the court may specify, or

(b) where the court does not so order—

(i) in the case of proceedings on indictment where this subsection applies at or before the preliminary hearing or, as the case may be, the first diet, at that hearing or diet make an order under subsection (9) below; or

(ii) in any other case, make an order appointing a diet to be held before the hearing at which the evidence is to be given and requiring the parties to attend the diet.

(8) On making an order under subsection (5A)(c) or (7)(b)(ii) above, the court may postpone the hearing at which the evidence is to be given.

(8A) Subsection (9) below applies to—

(a) a preliminary hearing or first diet, so far as the court is—

(i) by virtue of an order under subsection (5A)(a) or (b) above, disposing of a vulnerable witness notice at the hearing or diet; or

(ii) by virtue of subsection (7)(b)(i) above, to make an order under subsection (9) at the hearing or diet; and

(b) a diet appointed under subsection (5A)(c) or (7)(b)(ii) above.

(9) Subject to section 271B, at a hearing or diet to which this subsection applies, the court, after giving the parties an opportunity to be heard—

(a) in a case where any of the standard special measures has been authorised by an order under subsection (5)(a)(i) above, may make an order authorising the use of such further special measure or measures as it considers appropriate for the purpose of taking the witness's evidence, and

(b) in any other case, shall make an order—

(i) authorising the use of such special measure or measures as the court considers to be the most appropriate for the purpose of taking the witness's evidence, or

(ii) that the witness is to give evidence without the benefit of any special measure.

(10) Subject to section 271B, the court may make an order under subsection (9)(b)(ii) above only if satisfied—

(a) where the witness has expressed a wish to give evidence without the benefit of any special measure, that it is appropriate for the witness so to give evidence, or

(b) in any other case, that—

(i) the use of any special measure for the purpose of taking the evidence of the witness would give rise to a significant risk of prejudice to the fairness of the hearing at which the evidence is to be given or otherwise to the interests of justice, and

(ii) that risk significantly outweighs any risk of prejudice to the interests of the witness if the order is made.

(11) A hearing or diet to which subsection (9) above applies may—

(a) on the application of the party citing or intending to cite the witness in respect of whom the diet is to be held, or

(b) of the court's own motion,

be held in chambers.

(12) A diet appointed under subsection (5A)(c) or (7)(b)(ii) above in any case may be conjoined with any other diet to be held before the hearing at which the evidence is to be given.

(13) A party lodging a vulnerable witness notice or an objection notice shall, at the same time, intimate the notice to the other parties to the proceedings.

(13A) In subsections (2) and (4) above, "the required time" means—

(a) any time before a date has been fixed for one of the following—

(i) a preliminary hearing in the High Court;

(ii) a first diet in the sheriff court, or

(iii) a hearing at which the evidence is to be given, or

(b) if a date has been fixed—

(i) for a preliminary hearing in the High Court, no later than 14 clear days before the preliminary hearing,

(ii) for a first diet in the sheriff court in the case of proceedings on indictment, no later than 7 clear days before the first diet, or

(iii) in a case in which the proceedings are not to take place in the High Court or on indictment in the sheriff court, for a hearing at which the evidence is to be given, no later than 14 clear days before that hearing.

(14) In this section, references to a standard special measure are to any of the following special measures—

(a) the use of a live television link in accordance with section 271J of this Act,

(b) the use of a screen in accordance with section 271K of this Act, and

(c) the use of a supporter in accordance with section 271L of this Act.

(15) The Scottish Ministers may, by order subject to the affirmative procedure—

(a) modify subsection (14),

(b) in consequence of any modification made under paragraph (a)—

(i) prescribe the procedure to be followed when standard special measures are used, and

(ii) so far as is necessary, modify sections 271A to 271M of this Act.

AMENDMENTS

Sections 271A inserted by Vulnerable Witnesses (Scotland) Act 2004 (asp 3) s.1(1). Brought into force, for specified purposes, on 1 April 2005 by SSI 2005/168 (C.7) art.2 and Sch.

Subss.(2), (4), (5), (8), (9), (11) and (12) as amended, subs.(7)(b) substituted and subss.(5A), (8A), (13A) inserted by Criminal Procedure (Amendment) (Scotland) Act 2004 (asp 5) s.25, Sch.1 para.43. Brought into force on 1 April 2005 by SSI 2004/405 (C.28) art.2 and Sch.2.

Further brought into force for specified purposes on 1 April 2007 by SSI 2007/101 (C.13) art.2

Remainder brought into force on 1 April 2008 by SSI 2008/57 (C.7) art.2.

Subss.(1), (5A)(c), (6)(a), (7)(b), (8), (10)(b), (12), (13A)(c) as amended by Criminal Justice and Licensing (Scotland) Act 2010 (asp 13) s.87(3). Brought into force on 28 March 2011 (for all purposes in respect of criminal proceedings commenced on or after 28 March 2011, with proceedings taken to have commenced when a report of the case has been received by the procurator fiscal) by SSI 2011/178 (C.15) art.2, Sch.1 para.1.

Section 271A as amended by Victims and Witnesses (Scotland) Act 2014 (asp 1) ss.11, 12, 13 and 14. Brought into force on 1 September 2015 by SSI 2015/200 art.2 and Sch. subject to transitional provisions in art.4.

Subsection (3A) as amended by Vulnerable Witnesses (Criminal Evidence) (Scotland) Act 2019 (asp 8) s.7(2) effective 20 January 2020.

Subsection (5) as amended by Vulnerable Witnesses (Criminal Evidence) (Scotland) Act 2019 (asp 8) s.10(2) effective 20 January 2020.

Subsection (9) as amended by Vulnerable Witnesses (Criminal Evidence) (Scotland) Act 2019 (asp 8) s.2(3)(a) effective 20 January 2020.

Subsection (10) as amended by Vulnerable Witnesses (Criminal Evidence) (Scotland) Act 2019 (asp 8) s.2(3)(b) effective 20 January 2020.

Subsection (13A) substituted by Vulnerable Witnesses (Criminal Evidence) (Scotland) Act 2019 (asp 8) s.8(2) effective 20 January 2020.

Definitions

A4-527.2
"child witness notice": s.271A(2).
"court": s.271(5).
"proceedings": s.271(3).
"special measures": s.271H.
"trial": s.271(5).

General Note

A4-527.3
This section sets out the various powers in regard to the method by which a child witness may competently give evidence.

Refer to the discussion at A4-527 above.

Subs.(1)

This entitles all child witnesses to give their evidence with the help of at least one of the special measures.

Subss.(2) and (13)

This requires the party calling the child witness to submit a notice to the court and at the same time intimate it to all other parties at least 14 clear days before the trial. That notice must set out the special measures that the party calling the witness considers to be the most appropriate.

Subs.(3)

Where a child has expressed a view then details of that view must be included in the notice.

Subs.(3A)

This subsection enables the court to give immediate consideration to any vulnerable witness notice seeking only standard special measures, abandoning a previous requirement that any such notice had to lie for seven days before its terms could be considered. In the event that a notice under s.271A seeks measures additional to standard special measures then it will be appreciated that the seven day lying time remains in place to give time for parties to make objection to the proposed variations.

Section 6 of the Vulnerable Witnesses (Criminal Evidence) (Scotland) Act 2019 (asp 8) envisages that in cases now falling within the scope of s.271BZA, as now enacted, a simplified form of procedure will dispense with very many vulnerable witness notices provided that statutory timelines are met. The provision remains prospective, not being commenced in the transitional regulations SSI 2019/392 which generally took effect on 20 January 2020.

Subs.(4)

The time limit specified in s.271A(2) may on cause shown be disregarded.

Subss.(5) and (6)

This provides that a court must consider a child witness notice within seven days of that notice being lodged. If the court is satisfied that there are necessary special measures or that the child has expressed a wish not to have special measures then the appropriate authority for either option may be given: s.271A(5)(a) and (6). If the court is not satisfied that there are necessary special measures or that the child has not expressed a wish to give evidence without special measures then a diet may be set down under s.271A(10) and parties maybe ordained to attend: s.271A(5)(b) and (6).

Subss.(7) and (8)

If a child witness order is not lodged in time a court has power to order that such a notice is lodged or to arrange for a diet to be held before the trial.

Subs.(9)

The making of an order to hold a diet to consider a child witness order may also be accompanied by an order to postpone the trial diet.

Subs.(10)

The court must give parties the opportunity to be heard on the question of a child witness order. Thereafter, special measures may be authorised or the evidence of a child may be authorised to be given without special measures. The conditions for making such an order are set out in s.271A(11).

Subs.(11)

The effect of this provision is that an order can only be made in one of the two sets of circumstances. First, if a child wishes to give evidence without the benefit of special measures then that may be authorised if it is appropriate to do so: s.271A(11)(a). Secondly, in any other case, a child may be required to give evidence without the benefit of special measures where there is the risk of prejudicing the fairness of the trial significantly outweighs any risk of prejudice to the child: s.271A(11)(b).

Subs.(12)

It is competent to have child witness notice hearings concurrent with other hearings prior to the trial.

Subs.(13A)

The purpose of the amendments introduced in this subsection are to inject an element of flexibility by permitting early preparation of vulnerable witness notices. Timeframes need no longer have to be set by reference to the service of an indictment or complaint, and its associated procedural diets. Instead once the anticipated forum of proceedings is known, then at any point after first appearance of an accused. once a diet or hearing has been fixed then familiar time scales—14 days before a preliminary hearing, or evidential hearing, or seven days before a sheriff solemn first diet.

Justice of the Peace Court

The special measures provided for in this section have been extended to the JP court by the Justice of the Peace Courts (Special Measures) (Scotland) Order 2015 (SSI 2015/447) art.3(1).

Further special provision for child witnesses under the age of 12

A4-527.4 **271B.**—(1) This section applies where a child witness—

(a) is to give evidence at, or for the purposes of, a hearing in relevant criminal proceedings in respect of any offence specified in subsection (2) below, and

(b) is under the age of 12 on the date of commencement of the proceedings in which the hearing is being or to be held.

(2) The offences referred to in subsection (1)(a) above are—

(a) murder,

(b) culpable homicide,

(c) [...]

(d) any offence which involves an assault on, or injury or a threat of injury to, any person (including any offence involving neglect or ill-treatment of, or other cruelty to, a child),

(e) abduction, and

(f) plagium.

(g) an offence to which section 288C applies (certain sexual offending),

(h) an offence under section 1(1) of the Domestic Abuse (Scotland) Act 2018,

(i) an offence that is aggravated as described in section 1(1)(a) of the Abusive Behaviour and Sexual Harm (Scotland) Act 2016.

(3) Subsection (4) applies if the child witness expresses a wish to be present in the court-room for the purpose of giving evidence.

(4) The court must make an order under section 271A or, as the case may be, 271D which has the effect of requiring the child witness to be present in the courtroom for the purpose of giving evidence unless the court considers that it would not be appropriate for the child witness to be present there for that purpose.

(4A) Where the court is required to make an order having the effect mentioned in subsection (4), an order made by the court under section 271A(5)(a) may authorise the use of a special measure or measures other than those specified in the vulnerable witness notice if that would result in the order having the effect mentioned in subsection (4).

(5) Subsection (6) applies if the child witness—

(a) does not express a wish to be present in the court-room for the purpose of giving evidence, or

(b) expresses a wish to give evidence in some other way.

(6) The court may not make an order under section 271A or 271D having the effect mentioned in subsection (4) unless the court considers that—

(a) the giving of evidence by the child witness in some way other than by being present in the court-room for that purpose would give rise to a significant risk of prejudice to the fairness of the trial or otherwise to the interests of justice, and

(b) that risk significantly outweighs any risk of prejudice to the interests of the child witness if the order were to be made.

(7) This section does not apply in a case to which section 271BZA applies.

AMENDMENTS

Section 271B inserted by Vulnerable Witnesses (Scotland) Act 2004 (asp 3) s.1(1). Brought into force, for specified purposes, on 1 April 2005 by SSI 2005/168 (C.7) art.2 and Sch.

Further brought into force for specified purposes on 1 April 2007 by SSI 2007/101 (C.13) art.2

Remainder brought into force on 1 April 2008 by SSI 2008/57 (C.7) art.2.

Subss.(1)(a)(b), (3)(b) as amended by Criminal Justice and Licensing (Scotland) Act 2010 (asp 13) s.87(4). Brought into force on 28 March 2011 (for all purposes in respect of criminal proceedings commenced on or after 28 March 2011, with proceedings taken to have commenced when a report of the case has been received by the procurator fiscal) by SSI 2011/178 (C.15) art.2, Sch.1 para.1.

Subs.(3) as substituted, and subss.(4)–(6) inserted, by Victims and Witnesses (Scotland) Act 2014 (asp 1) s.14(1). Brought into force on 1 September 2015 by SSI 2015/200 art.2 and Sch. subject to transitional provisions in art.4.

Subs.(2)(c) repealed, subs.(2)(g)–(i) added, by Domestic Abuse (Scotland) Act 2018 (asp 5) Sch.1(1)(3) para.6(2) (effective 1 April 2019 in respect of proceedings commenced on or after 1 April 2019 subject to transitional provision specified in SSI 2018/387 reg.7(2)).

Subs.(4A) inserted by Vulnerable Witnesses (Criminal Evidence) (Scotland) Act 2019 (asp 8) s.2(2)(a) effective 20 January 2020.

Subs.(7) inserted by Vulnerable Witnesses (Criminal Evidence) (Scotland) Act 2019 (asp 8) s.2(2)(b) effective 20 January 2020.

DEFINITION

"trial": s.271(5). A4-527.5

GENERAL NOTE

When introduced the section's provisions applied only in the High and Sheriff Courts as might be expected given the gravity of offences specified in subs.(2). They were extended to the JP court by the Justice of the Peace Courts (Special Measures) (Scotland) Order 2015 (SSI 2015/447), reflecting the incorporation of the previous district court structure into the Scottish Courts Service and the increased sentencing powers which the JP court were accorded. The Fatal Accident and Sudden Deaths Inquiry (Procedure) (Scotland) Rules 2007 (SSI 2007/478) extended the provisions to vulnerable witnesses in general. For adult vulnerable witnesses in qualifying cases refer to s.271 above. A4-527.6

The broad approach of s.271B is that the court may not make an order that has the effect of requiring a child witness giving evidence in relation to a subs.(2) offence to be present in the court; such evidence would be received by remote link to the court. Two exceptions to the generality were acknowledged; first, where it was considered that the absence of the child from the court would be prejudicial to a fair trial; secondly, where the child expressed a personal preference to be present. As subs.(6)(b) stipulates the court has to balance the competing factors and the barriers to dispensing with the special provisions are set high. The application of the provisions to a child accused is covered by s.271F(2).

Justice of the Peace Court

The special measures provided for in this section have been extended to the JP court by the Justice of the Peace Courts (Special Measures) (Scotland) Order 2015 (SSI 2015/447) art.3(1).

Child witnesses in certain solemn cases: special measures

A4-527.6A **271BZA.**—(1) This section applies where a child witness, other than the accused, is to give evidence at, or for the purposes of, a hearing in relevant criminal proceedings which are—

(a) solemn proceedings, and
(b) in respect of an offence listed in subsection (2).

(2) The offences are—

(a) murder,
(b) culpable homicide,
(c) assault to the danger of life,
(d) abduction,
(e) plagium,
(f) a sexual offence to which section 288C applies,
(g) an offence under section 1(1) of the Domestic Abuse (Scotland) Act 2018,
(h) an offence that is aggravated as described in section 1(1)(a) of the Abusive Behaviour and Sexual Harm (Scotland) Act 2016,
(i) an offence that would have fallen within paragraph (fb) if section 1 of the Abusive Behaviour and Sexual Harm (Scotland) Act 2016 had been in force when the offence was allegedly committed,
(j) an offence of human trafficking (see section 1 of the Human Trafficking and Exploitation (Scotland) Act 2015),
(k) an offence under section 4 of the Human Trafficking and Exploitation (Scotland) Act 2015 (slavery, servitude and forced or compulsory labour),
(l) an offence under section 1 of the Prohibition of Female Genital Mutilation (Scotland) Act 2005 (offence of female genital mutilation),
(m) an offence under section 3 of the Prohibition of Female Genital Mutilation (Scotland) Act 2005 (aiding and abetting female genital mutilation),
(n) an attempt to commit an offence mentioned in any of paragraphs (a) to (m).

(3) The court must enable all of the child witness's evidence to be given in advance of the hearing unless the court is satisfied that an exception is justified under subsection (7) or (8).

(4) For the purposes of this section, the court enables all of the child witness's evidence to be given in advance of the hearing if—

(a) the court makes an order under section 271A which satisfies the following requirements—
  (i) it authorises the use of one or both of the special measures listed in subsection (5) for the purpose of taking all of the child witness's evidence,
  (ii) it does not authorise the use of an incompatible special measure for the purpose of taking any of the child witness's evidence, and
  (iii) it does not authorise the giving of any of the child witness's evidence without the benefit of any special measure, and
(b) the court, if it commences a review under section 271D before the hearing has commenced, does not make an order under that section which—
  (i) revokes the order made under section 271A, or
  (ii) varies it in such a way that it no longer satisfies the requirements set out in paragraph (a)(i), (ii) and (iii).

(5) The special measures mentioned in subsection (4)(a)(i) are—

(a) taking of evidence by a commissioner in accordance with section 271I,

(b) giving evidence in chief in the form of a prior statement in accordance with section 271M.

(6) In this section, "incompatible special measure" means a special measure which is capable of being used only if the child witness gives evidence at the hearing (whether or not its use would require the child witness to be present in the courtroom).

(7) An exception is justified if—

(a) the giving of all of the child witness's evidence in advance of the hearing would give rise to a significant risk of prejudice to the fairness of the hearing or otherwise to the interests of justice, and

(b) that risk significantly outweighs any risk of prejudice to the interests of the child witness if the child witness were to give evidence at the hearing.

(8) An exception is justified if—

(a) the child witness is aged 12 or over on the date of commencement of the proceedings in which the hearing is being or is to be held,

(b) the child witness expresses a wish to give evidence at the hearing, and

(c) it would be in the child witness's best interests to give evidence at the hearing.

(9) The Scottish Ministers may by regulations—

(a) modify subsection (2),

(b) remove the condition set out in subsection (1)(b) and the list of offences in subsection (2).

(10) Regulations under subsection (9) are subject to the affirmative procedure.

AMENDMENT

Section 271BZA inserted by Vulnerable Witnesses (Criminal Evidence) (Scotland) Act 2019 (asp 8) s.1(2) effective 20 January 2020: insertion has effect on 20 January 2020 as SSI 2019/392 Sch.1 subject to transitional provisions specified in SSI 2019/392 reg.3; not yet in force otherwise.

GENERAL NOTE

For brevity in this discussion references henceforth will be to the "1995 Act" (the Criminal Procedure (Scotland) Act 1995 (c.46)) and to the "2019 Act" (the Vulnerable Witnesses (Criminal Evidence) (Scotland) Act 2019 (asp 8)). **A4-527.6B**

The 2019 Act aims to enhance the existing provisions governing the testimony of child witnesses (as defined in s.271(1)(a) of the 1995 Act), apart from the accused, in most solemn proceedings. The charge, or charges, libelled in these proceedings in turn determine whether or not the child witness qualifies for modified standard special measures, specifically evidence on commission, or utilising testimony in the form of a prior statement (s.271M(1)). Otherwise standard special measures, as described in the last paragraph, would have to be considered by the court hearing applications.

The range of qualifying offences now set out in subs.(2) of the 2019 Act above closely resembles the offences specified in the 1995 Act s.271B which had required additional arrangements for child witnesses aged under 12 years. These latter measures were introduced by the Vulnerable Witnesses (Scotland) Act 2004 (asp 3) and established as the norm the practice of beaming the child's parole evidence contemporaneously from an adjacent or remote site into the court during the court proceedings. As subs.(3) of the new section makes clear, the 2019 Act takes matters further; henceforth the aim of the legislation, in all but the most exceptional circumstances, is to ensure that the child's entire evidence is recorded in advance of the trial proceedings, and the Act lays down procedures considered necessary to bring this about. A general balancing provision remains in subss.(7) and (8) where, exceptionally, the court considers evidence in this form would risk significant prejudice to fairness at the trial so far outweighing the child's own welfare, that these special measures would have to be set aside. Even at that point the court cannot immediately require the child's evidence to be delivered in open court (see s.271A(10D) as now introduced. Note too that the court may (but is not obliged) to take heed of preferences expressed by older child witnesses, i.e. aged 12 years or more. As might be expected in all situations where the evidence of a child is indicated, it falls to the party identifying any such witness to apply to the court by a vulnerable witness notice conform to ss.271A(2) or 271A(2)(a) and for the court to fix a hearing on the notice's merits.

(Note that in cases now covered by the 2019 Act the range of standard special measures available (see s.271A(14) of the 1995 Act) is further extended).

Importantly, service of an indictment is not a necessary precursor to initiate these enhanced procedures; indeed, particularly with younger children there may be merit in securing the child's parole evidence at a very early juncture after the relevant petition appearance of the accused. (See s.271I(4A) as now inserted in the 1995 Act).

The section preserves the option for children aged 12 years or over to seek to give evidence in open court but subject to the court's over-riding discretion to apply a broader assessment of the child's best interests (subs.(8)). Though it must be approached as an exceptional circumstance, subs.(7) retains the court's power to require contemporaneous testimony (subject to any relevant special measures) of a child witness in limited circumstances.

Relevant cases—those whose petition charges meet the test of subs.(2) and look likely to be indicted in the High Court—in which a petition appearance was made on or after 20 January 2020, or qualifying High Court cases indicted for dates from 20 October 2020 onwards, will be subject to these provisions.

In anticipation of the enhanced witness arrangements on 18 November 2019 a dedicated evidence and hearings suite, under the aegis of the Scottish Courts and Tribunals Service (SCTS), was opened in Glasgow; other centres are to follow.

Child witnesses in certain solemn cases: modifications of section 271A

A4-527.6C **271BZB.**—(1) In a case to which section 271BZA applies, section 271A applies with the following modifications.

(2) References to a standard special measure are to be read as references to any of the following special measures (and subsection (14) is to be read accordingly)—

(a) taking of evidence by a commissioner in accordance with section 271I,

(b) use of a supporter in accordance with section 271L,

(c) giving evidence in chief in the form of a prior statement in accordance with section 271M.

(3) Section 271A(2) has effect as if—

(a) the words "Subject to section 271AA," were omitted,

(b) the words "or a deemed vulnerable witness" were omitted.

(4) Section 271A has effect as if the following subsection were inserted after subsection (2)—

"(2A) A vulnerable witness notice must—

(a) state that section 271BZA applies, and

(b) explain why the party considers that an exception is justified under section 271BZA(7) or (8) if the notice—

(i) does not specify one or both of the special measures listed in section 271BZA(5) for the purpose of taking all of the child witness's evidence,

(ii) specifies an incompatible special measure (as defined in section 271BZA(6)) for the purpose of taking any of the child witness's evidence, or

(iii) states that the party considers that the child witness should give any of the child witness's evidence without the benefit of any special measure.".

(5) Section 271A has effect as if the following subsections were inserted after subsection (10)—

"(10A) Subsections (5), (9) and (10) are subject to subsections (10B) to (10F).

(10B) Where the court is considering a notice in accordance with subsection (5) and the notice does not specify one or both of the special measures mentioned in section 271BZA(5) for the purpose of taking all of the child witness's evidence, the court may nonetheless make an order which has the effect of authorising the use of one or both of those special measures for that purpose.

(10C) Unless the court is satisfied that an exception is justified under section 271BZA(7) or (8), an order made by the court under this section—

(a) must authorise the use of one or more of the special measures mentioned in section 271BZA(5) for the purpose of taking all of the child witness's evidence,

(b) must not authorise the use of an incompatible special measure (as defined in section 271BZA(6)) for the purpose of taking any of the child witness's evidence, and

(c) must not authorise the giving of any of the child witness's evidence without the benefit of any special measure.

(10D) Even if the court is satisfied that an exception is justified under section 271BZA(7) or (8), an order made by the court under this section must not have the effect of requiring the child witness to be present in the courtroom to give evidence unless the court is satisfied that subsection (10E) or (10F) applies.

(10E) This subsection applies if—

(a) the giving of evidence by the child witness in some way other than by being present in the courtroom for that purpose would give rise to a significant risk of prejudice to the fairness of the hearing or otherwise to the interests of justice, and

(b) that risk significantly outweighs any risk of prejudice to the interests of the child witness if the child witness were to be present in the courtroom to give evidence.

(10F) This subsection applies if—

(a) the child witness is aged 12 or over on the date of commencement of the proceedings in which the hearing is being held or is to be held,

(b) the child witness expresses a wish to be present in the courtroom to give evidence, and

(c) it would be in the child witness's best interests to be present in the courtroom to give evidence."

AMENDMENT

Section 271BZB inserted by Vulnerable Witnesses (Criminal Evidence) (Scotland) Act 2019 (asp 8) s.1(2) effective 20 January 2020 as SSI 2019/392 Sch.1, subject to transitional provisions in reg.3; not yet in force otherwise.

GENERAL NOTE

This section introduces the modifications necessary to differentiate between a vulnerable witness application proceeding under s.271 and the enhanced provisions introduced for qualifying solemn cases by s.271BZA. In particular, subs.(2) describes the enhanced measures (confusingly perhaps described as a "standard special measure") available to the court, beyond those set out in s.271H of the 1995 Act, when considering a vulnerable witness application. Parties are required to indicate if it is known or anticipated that s.271A or s.271BZA applies—dictating both future procedures and the powers which the court then can call upon under the legislation. **A4-527.6D**

Child witnesses in certain solemn cases: modifications of section 271D

271BZC.—(1) In a case to which section 271BZA applies, section 271D applies with the following modifications. **A4-527.6E**

(2) Section 271D has effect as if—

(a) subsections (3A) to (3C) were omitted,

(b) subsection (4A) were omitted, and

(c) the following subsections were inserted after subsection (4A)—

(4B) Subsections (2) to (4) are subject to subsections (4C) to (4H).

(4C) Unless the hearing has already commenced when the court commences its review or the court is satisfied that an exception is justified under section 271BZA(7) or (8), an order made by the court under this section must not—

(a) revoke the earlier order, or

(b) vary it in such a way that it no longer satisfies the requirements set out in section 271BZA(4)(a)(i), (ii) and (iii).

(4D) An order made by the court under this section must have the effect of authorising the use of the special measure of taking of evidence by a commissioner in accordance with section 271I if—

(a) that is requested by any party to the proceedings, and

(b) the earlier order authorises only the special measure of giving evidence in chief in the form of a prior statement in accordance with section 271M.

(4E) However, an order made by the court under this section need not have the effect described in subsection (4D) if—

(a) the hearing has already commenced when the court commences its review, or

(b) the court is satisfied that an exception is justified under section 271BZA(7) or (8).

(4F) Even if the hearing has already commenced when the court commences its review or the court is satisfied that an exception is justified under section 271BZA(7) or (8), an order made under this section must not have the effect of requiring the child witness to be present in the courtroom to give evidence unless the court is satisfied that subsection (4G) or (4H) applies.

(4G) This subsection applies if—

(a) the giving of evidence by the child witness in some way other than by being present in the courtroom for that purpose would give rise to a significant risk of prejudice to the fairness of the hearing or otherwise to the interests of justice, and

(b) that risk significantly outweighs any risk of prejudice to the interests of the child witness if the child witness were to be present in the courtroom to give evidence.

(4H) This subsection applies if—

(a) the child witness is aged 12 or over on the date of commencement of the proceedings in which the hearing is being held or is to be held,

(b) the child witness expresses a wish to be present in the courtroom to give evidence, and

(c) it would be in the child witness's best interests to be present in the courtroom to give evidence.]

Amendment

Section 271BZC inserted by Vulnerable Witnesses (Criminal Evidence) (Scotland) Act 2019 (asp 8) s.1(2) effective 20 January 2020 as SSI 2019/392 Sch.1, subject to transitional provisions in reg.3; not yet in force otherwise.

[THE NEXT PARAGRAPH IS A4-527.6.1]

Assessment of witnesses

A4-527.6.1 **271BA.**—(1) This section applies where a party intends to cite a witness other than a child witness or a deemed vulnerable witness to give evidence at, or for the purposes of, a hearing in relevant criminal proceedings.

(2) The party intending to cite the witness must take reasonable steps to carry out an assessment under subsection (3).

(3) An assessment must determine whether the person—

(a) is likely to be a vulnerable witness, and

(b) if so, what special measure or combination of special measures ought to be used for the purpose of taking the person's evidence.

(4) In determining under subsection (3)(a) whether a person is likely to be a vulnerable witness the party must—

(a) take into account the matters mentioned in section 271(2),

(b) have regard to the best interests of the person, and

(c) take account of any views expressed by the person.

Amendments

Section 271BA inserted by Victims and Witnesses (Scotland) Act 2014 (asp 1) s.16. Brought into force on 1 September 2015 by SSI 2015/200 art.2 and Sch, subject to transitional provisions in art.4.

[THE NEXT PARAGRAPH IS A4-527.7]

Vulnerable witness application

A4-527.7 **271C.**—(1) This section applies where a party citing or intending to cite a person (other than a child witness or a deemed vulnerable witness) to give evidence at, or for the purposes of, a hearing in relevant criminal proceedings (such a person being referred to in this section as "the witness") and, having carried out an assessment under section 271BA, considers—

(a) that the witness is likely to be a vulnerable witness, and

(b) that a special measure or combination of special measures ought to be used for the purpose of taking the witness's evidence.

(2) Where this section applies, the party citing or intending to cite the witness shall, by the required time, make an application (referred to as a "vulnerable witness application") to the court for an order authorising the use of one or more of the special measures for the purpose of taking the witness's evidence.

(3) A vulnerable witness application shall—

(a) specify the special measure or measures which the party making the application considers to be the most appropriate for the purpose of taking the evidence of the witness to whom the application relates, and

(b) contain or be accompanied by—

(i) a summary of any views expressed for the purposes of section 271E(2)(b) of this Act, and

(ii) such other information as may be prescribed by Act of Adjournal.

(4) The court may, on cause shown, allow a vulnerable witness application to be made after the required time.

(4A) Any party to the proceedings may, not later than 7 days after a vulnerable witness application has been lodged, lodge with the court a notice (referred to in this section as "an objection notice") stating—

(a) an objection to any special measure specified in the vulnerable witness application that the party considers to be inappropriate, and

(b) the reasons for that objection.

(4B) The court may, on cause shown, allow an objection notice to be lodged after the period referred to in subsection (4A).

(4C) If an objection notice is lodged in accordance with subsection (4A) or (4B)—

(a) subsection (5) does not apply to the vulnerable witness application, and

(b) the court must make an order under subsection (5A).

(5) The court shall, not earlier than 7 days and not later than 14 days after a vulnerable witness application is made to it, consider the application in the absence of the parties and—

(a) make an order authorising the use of the special measure or measures specified in the application if satisfied on the basis of the application that—

(i) the witness in respect of whom the application is made is a vulnerable witness,

(ii) the special measures or measures specified in the application are the most appropriate for the purpose of taking the witness's evidence, and

(iii) it is appropriate to do so after having complied with the duty in subsection (8) below, or

(b) if not satisfied as mentioned in paragraph (a) above, make an order under subsection (5A) below.

(5A) That order is an order—

(a) in the case of proceedings in the High Court where the preliminary hearing is yet to be held, appointing the vulnerable witness application to be disposed of at that hearing,

(b) in the case of proceedings on indictment in the sheriff court where the first diet is yet to be held, appointing the vulnerable witness application to be disposed of at that diet, or

(c) in any other case, appointing a diet to be held before the hearing at which the evidence is to be given and requiring the parties to attend the diet.

(6) On making an order under subsection (5A)(c) above, the court may postpone the hearing at which the evidence is to be given.

(6A) Subsection (7) below applies to—

(a) a preliminary hearing or first diet so far as the court is, by virtue of an order under subsection (5A)(a) or (b) above disposing of a vulnerable witness application at the hearing or diet, and

(b) a diet appointed under subsection (5A)(c) above.

(7) At a hearing or diet to which this subsection applies, the court may—

(a) after giving the parties an opportunity to be heard, and

(b) if satisfied that the witness in respect of whom the application is made is a vulnerable witness,

make an order authorising the use of such special measure or measures as the court considers to be the most appropriate for the purpose of taking the witness's evidence.

(8) In deciding whether to make an order under subsection (5)(a) or (7) above, the court shall—

(a) have regard to—

(i) the possible effect on the witness if required to give evidence without the benefit of any special measure, and

(ii) whether it is likely that the witness would be better able to give evidence with the benefit of a special measure, and

(b) take into account the matters specified in subsection (2)(a) to (f) of section 271 of this Act.

(9) A hearing or diet to which subsection (7) above applies may—

(a) on the application of the party citing or intending to cite the witness in respect of whom the diet is to be held, or

(b) of the court's own motion,

be held in chambers.

(10) A diet appointed under subsection (5A)(c) above in any case may be conjoined with any other diet to be held before the hearing at which the evidence is to be given.

(11) A party making a vulnerable witness application or an objection notice shall, at the same time, intimate the application or, as the case may be, the notice to the other parties to the proceedings.

(12) In subsections (2) and (4) above, "the required time" means—

(a) in the case of proceedings in the High Court, no later than 14 clear days before the preliminary hearing,

(b) in the case of proceedings on indictment in the sheriff court, no later than 7 clear days before the first diet,

(c) in any other case, no later than 14 clear days before the hearing at which the evidence is to be given.

Amendments

Section 271C inserted by Vulnerable Witnesses (Scotland) Act 2004 (asp 3) s.1(1). Brought into force, for specified purposes, on 1 April 2006 by SSI 2006/59 (C.8).

Remainder brought into force on 1 April 2008 by SSI 2008/57 (C.7) art.2.

Subss.(2), (4), (5)(b), (6), (7), (9), (10) as amended, and subss.(5A), (6A), (12) inserted, by Criminal Procedure (Amendment) (Scotland) Act 2004 (asp 5) s.25, Sch.1 para.44. Brought into force on 1 April 2006 by SSI 2004/405 (C.28) art.2(2) and Sch.2.

Subss.(1), (5A)(c), (6), (10), (12)(c) as amended by Criminal Justice and Licensing (Scotland) Act 2010 (asp 13) s.87(5). Brought into force on 28 March 2011 (for all purposes in respect of criminal proceedings commenced on or after 28 March 2011, with proceedings taken to have commenced when a report of the case has been received by the procurator fiscal) by SSI 2011/178 (C.15) art.2, Sch.1 para.1.

Section 271C as amended by Victims and Witnesses (Scotland) Act 2014 (asp 1) ss.11, 16, 17. Brought into force on 1 September 2015 by SSI 2015/200 art.2 and Sch, subject to transitional provisions in art.4.

Definitions

A4-527.8 "special measures": s.271H.
"vulnerable witness": s.271(1).
"vulnerable witness application": s.271C(2).

General Note

A4-527.9 This section sets out the various powers in regard to the method by which a vulnerable witness may competently give evidence.

Subs.(1)

This entitles a witness likely to be a vulnerable witness to give evidence with a special measure or a combination of special measures.

Subs.(2)

Where it is proposed to take evidence from a vulnerable witness by means of a special measure then not less than 14 clear days before the trial diet a vulnerable witness application should be made to obtain the necessary authority of the court.

Subs.(3)

A vulnerable witness application is required to specify the special measure sought and should be accompanied by relevant papers.

Subs.(4)

Notwithstanding the time limit set for a vulnerable witness application a court may allow such an application to be heard on other days.

Subs.(5)

Not later than seven days after a vulnerable witness application is made the court must consider the application in the absence of parties. If the court is satisfied with the application then an order is to be made authorising the use of special measures. If the court is not satisfied in regard to any of the specified aspects then the parties should be ordained to attend at a diet.

Subs.(6)

The court at a diet must give parties an opportunity to be heard and then, if satisfied that the relevant witness is a vulnerable witness, make an order authorising the use of a special measure.

Subs.(7)

The court in deciding whether to make an order must have regard to the possible effect on a witness if required to give evidence without the benefit of any special measure and whether it is likely that the witness would be better able to give evidence with the benefit of a special measure. Various circumstances are to be taken into consideration: see s.271(2)(a) to (f) inclusive.

Subs.(8)

It is competent to hear a vulnerable witness application concurrent with other hearings prior to the trial.

Subs.(9)

A party making a vulnerable witness application must intimate that to the other parties to the proceedings.

Justice of the Peace Court

The special measures provided for in this section have been extended to the JP court by the Justice of the Peace Courts (Special Measures) (Scotland) Order 2015 (SSI 2015/447) art.3(1).

Review of arrangements for vulnerable witnesses

271D.—(1) In any case in which a person who is giving or is to give evidence at or for the purposes of a hearing in relevant criminal proceedings (referred to in this section as the "witness") is or appears to the court to be a vulnerable witness, the court may at any stage in the proceedings (whether before or after the commencement of the hearing or before or after the witness has begun to give evidence)— **A4-527.10**

(a) on the application of any party to the proceedings, or

(b) of its own motion,

review the current arrangements for taking the witness's evidence and, after giving the parties an opportunity to be heard, make an order under subsection (2) below.

(2) The order which may be made under this subsection is—

(a) where the current arrangements for taking the witness's evidence include the use of a special measure or combination of special measures authorised by an order under section 271A or 271C of this Act or under this subsection (referred to as the "earlier order"), an order varying or revoking the earlier order, or

(b) where the current arrangements for taking the witness's evidence do not include any special measure, an order authorising the use of such special measure or measures as the court considers most appropriate for the purpose of taking the witness's evidence.

(3) An order under subsection (2)(a) above varying an earlier order may—

(a) add to or substitute for any special measure authorised by the earlier order such other special measure as the court considers most appropriate for the purpose of taking the witness's evidence, or

(b) where the earlier order authorises the use of a combination of special measures for that purpose, delete any of the special measures so authorised.

(3A) If an earlier order has the effect of enabling all of the witness's evidence to be given in advance of the hearing, the court may not make an order under subsection (2)(a) varying the earlier order in such a way that it no longer has that effect.

(3B) However, the court may vary the earlier order in the way mentioned in subsection (3A) if the hearing has already commenced when the court commences its review or if the court is satisfied—

(a) where the witness has expressed a wish to give evidence at the hearing, that it is appropriate for the witness to do so, or

(b) in any other case, that—

(i) if the court does not vary the earlier order in that way, there would be a significant risk of prejudice to the fairness of the hearing or otherwise to the interests of justice, and

(ii) that risk significantly outweighs any risk of prejudice to the interests of the witness if the court were not to vary the earlier order in that way.

(3C) For the purposes of this section, an order has the effect of enabling all of the witness's evidence to be given in advance of the hearing if—

(a) it authorises the use of one or both of these special measures for the purpose of taking all of the witness's evidence—

(i) taking of evidence by a commissioner in accordance with section 271I,

(ii) giving evidence in chief in the form of a prior statement in accordance with section 271M,

(b) it does not authorise the use of a special measure which is capable of being used only if the witness gives evidence at the hearing (whether or not its use would require the witness to be present in the courtroom), and

(c) it does not authorise the giving of any of the witness's evidence without the benefit of any special measure.

(4) Subject to section 271B, the court may make an order under subsection (2)(a) above revoking an earlier order only if satisfied—

(a) where the witness has expressed a wish to give or, as the case may be, continue to give evidence without the benefit of any special measure, that it is appropriate for the witness so to give evidence, or

(b) in any other case, that—

(i) the use, or continued use, of the special measure or measures authorised by the earlier order for the purpose of taking the witness's evidence would give rise to a significant risk of prejudice to the fairness of the hearing or otherwise to the interests of justice, and

(ii) that risk significantly outweighs any risk of prejudice to the interests of the witness if the order is made.

(5) Subsection (8) of section 271C of this Act applies to the making of an order under subsection (2)(b) of this section as it applies to the making of an order under subsection (5)(a) or (7) of that section but as if the references to the witness were to the witness within the meaning of this section.

(6) In this section, "current arrangements" means the arrangements in place at the time the review under this section is begun.

(6A) In this section, "court" includes a commissioner appointed under section 271I(1).

(7) This section is subject to sections 271B to 271BZC.

AMENDMENTS

Section 271D inserted by Vulnerable Witnesses (Scotland) Act 2004 (asp 3) s.1(1). Brought into force (except for subs.(5) and the reference to s.271C in subs.(2)(a)), for specified purposes, on 1 April 2005 by SSI 2005/168 (C.7) art.2 and Sch.

Subss.(3A)–(3C) inserted by Vulnerable Witnesses (Criminal Evidence) (Scotland) Act 2019 (asp 8) s.4(2) effective 20 January 2020 as SSI 2019/392 Sch.1; not yet in force otherwise.

Subs.(6A) inserted by Vulnerable Witnesses (Criminal Evidence) (Scotland) Act 2019 (asp 8) s.5(8) effective 20 January 2020.

Subs.(7) as amended by Vulnerable Witnesses (Criminal Evidence) (Scotland) Act 2019 (asp 8) s.10(3) effective 20 January 2020.

Further brought into force for specified purposes on 1 April 2006 by SSI 2006/59 (C.8).

Further brought into force (except for subs.(5) and the reference to s.271C in subs.(2)(a)) for specified purposes on 1 April 2007 by SSI 2007/101 (C.13) art.2.

Remainder brought into force on 1 April 2008 by SSI 2008/57 (C.7) art.2.

Subss.(1), (4)(b) as amended by Criminal Justice and Licensing (Scotland) Act 2010 (asp 13) s.87(6). Brought into force on 28 March 2011 (for all purposes in respect of criminal proceedings commenced on or after 28 March 2011, with proceedings taken to have commenced when a report of the case has been received by the procurator fiscal) by SSI 2011/178 (C.15) art.2, Sch.1 para.1.

Subs.(1)(a) as amended and subs.(7) inserted by Victims and Witnesses (Scotland) Act 2014 (asp 1) ss.14(3) and 18. Brought into force on 1 September 2015 by SSI 2015/200 art.2 and Sch, subject to transitional provisions in art.4.

DEFINITIONS

"court": s.271(5). **A4-527.11**
"current arrangements": s.271D(6).
"earlier order": s.271D(2)(a).
"special measures": s.271H.
"vulnerable witness": s.271(1).
"witness": s.271D(2).

GENERAL NOTE

This section enables the court at any time, up to and including when a vulnerable witness is giving evidence in a trial, to review the arrangements for the taking of their evidence. The court may make an order regarding the arrangements at the request of the party who is calling the witness or of its own accord: s.271D(1). The court may make an order for a special measure to be used by a vulnerable witness in circumstances where an order has not previously been made: s.271D(2)(b). Such an order may add a special measure, or substitute a special measure in the previous order for another special measure that is considered more appropriate: s.271D(3)(a). Where a previous order contains a combination of special measures, the number of measures to be used can be reduced: s.271D(3)(b). **A4-527.12**

An order that special measures may no longer be used can only be made in two instances: first, where the court is satisfied that it is appropriate to revoke the use of special measures as the witness does not wish to use them: s.271D(4)(a). Secondly, where the court is satisfied that there is a risk of prejudice to the fairness of the trial that significantly outweighs the risk of prejudice to the witness: s.271D(4)(b). In making an order the court must take into account the circumstances in s.271(2)(a) to (f) inclusive.

It is perhaps curious that in proceedings in which "special measures" as defined in s.271H are deemed necessary, there is no statutory provision for the party against whom an adult vulnerable witness' evidence is intended to be led, to be heard on the merits of the application prior to it being considered by the court.

The Act has introduced special measures as of right for witnesses aged under 16 years (s.271A) with still more extensive requirements for children aged under 12 years (s.271B) and in such circumstances all that is normally required is intimation of the application's terms to that party: it is only when the application is not lodged timeously that the court may appoint a hearing (s.271A(7)) to enable parties to be heard at the outset. Specific special measures for adult vulnerable witnesses (ss.271 and 271C) are considered by the court on a case by case basis.

Once special measures have been specified by the court, it can, on its own initiative, or at the behest only of the mover of the application, review the measures prescribed earlier, or vary those measures at any time up to, and including, the time when the witness' evidence is being led. Subs.(2)(a) seems to have excluded applications granted in terms of s.271B from such review.

As a matter of statutory interpretation it is only once a review has been initiated that the affected party has a right to make representations—he normally would have no right to oppose the grant of the application ab initio. However, as *I v Dunn*, 2012 S.L.T. 983; 2012 S.C.C.R. 673 highlights, this sits uneasily with the general duty of the court to guard against significant prejudice to the fairness of the proceedings, and the preservation of an accused's art.6 rights and, indeed, opens the way to review by means of preliminary plea or a devolution minute (see s.98 of, and Sch.6 to, the Scotland Act 1998 (c.46)). In the absence of these mechanisms it would have to be doubted that the terms of s.271D could be viewed as Convention-compliant and notwithstanding *I v Dunn* above, grave reservations remain about the Convention-compliance of a review occurring after a witness has begun to give evidence. In such circumstances it is submitted, albeit on no authority, that desertion *pro loco* might seem to be a more prudent option.

It should be appreciated from what follows that it is important that parties at the earliest time can predict both the probable forum for proceedings and the nature of the charges to be libelled.

Following the insertion of subss.(3A) to (3C) by the Vulnerable Witnesses (Criminal Evidence) (Scotland) Act 2019 (asp 8) a measure of caution now has to be applied to the generality of s.271 which allowed courts a discretion to vary vulnerable witness arrangements by the court. with effect from 20 January 2020, when s.4 of that Act commenced in relation to qualifying High Court proceedings, the broad intention is that the court (subject to the caveat provided by subs.(3B)) shall not vary an order previously granted. It will be borne in mind that the enhanced provisions apply to the range of solemn offences specified in s.271BZA; otherwise the proceedings are still governed by the earlier provision described below.

Justice of the Peace Court

The special measures provided for in this section have been extended to the JP court by the Justice of the Peace Courts (Special Measures) (Scotland) Order 2015 (SSI 2015/447) art.3(1).

Vulnerable witnesses: supplementary provision

A4-527.13 **271E.**—(1) Subsection (2) below applies where—

(a) a party is considering for the purposes of a vulnerable witness notice or a vulnerable witness application which of the special measures is or are the most appropriate for the purpose of taking the evidence of the person to whom the notice or application relates, or

(b) the court is making an order under section 271A(5)(a)(ii) or (b) or (9), 271C or 271D of this Act.

(2) The party or, as the case may be, the court shall—

(a) have regard to the best interests of the witness, and

(b) take account of any views expressed by—

(i) the witness (having regard, where the witness is a child witness, to the witness's age and maturity), and

(ii) where the witness is a child witness, the witness's parent (except where the parent is the accused).

(3) For the purposes of subsection (2)(b) above, where the witness is a child witness—

(a) the witness shall be presumed to be of sufficient age and maturity to form a view if aged 12 or older, and

(b) in the event that any views expressed by the witness are inconsistent with any views expressed by the witness's parent, the views of the witness shall be given greater weight.

(4) In this section—

"parent", in relation to a child witness, means any person having parental responsibilities within the meaning of section 1(3) of the Children (Scotland) Act 1995 (c.36) in relation to the child witness,

"the witness" means—
(a) in the case referred to in subsection (1)(a) above, the person to whom the notice or application relates,
(b) in the case referred to in subsection (1)(b) above, the person to whom the order would relate.

AMENDMENTS

Section 271E inserted by Vulnerable Witnesses (Scotland) Act 2004 (asp 3) s.1(1). Brought into force (except for the reference to s.271C in subs.(1)(b)), for specified purposes, on 1 April 2005 by SSI 2005/168 (C.7) art.2 and Sch.

Further brought into force for specified purposes on 1 April 2006 by SSI 2006/59 (C.8).

Further brought into force (except for the reference to s.271C in subs.(1)(b)) for specified purposes on 1 April 2007 by SSI 2007/101 (C.13) art.2.

Remainder brought into force on 1 April 2008 by SSI 2008/57 (C.7) art.2.

Subs.(1)(a) as amended by Victims and Witnesses (Scotland) Act 2014 (asp 1) s.11(7). Brought into force on 1 September 2015 by SSI 2015/200 art.2 and Sch, subject to transitional provisions in art.4.

DEFINITIONS

"child witness notice": s.271A(2). **A4-527.14**
"court": s.271(5).
"parent": s.271E(4).
"special measures": s.271H.
"the witness": s.271E(4).
"vulnerable witness": s.271(1).
"vulnerable witness application": s.271C(2).

GENERAL NOTE

Section 271E(1) to (3) require the party calling the witness and the court in determining a special measures order to consider the best interests and views of the witness when deciding the special measures most appropriate for the purpose of taking the evidence. With regard to child witnesses the views of the parents of the child are also to be considered unless that person is the accused. **A4-527.15**

The section ensures that children over 12 years are presumed to be able to give a view, and in the case of children under 12 years, the age and maturity of the child are to be considered in determining whether they can express a view on the special measures to be used. In the event that the views of the child and the parent differ then the views of the child are to be given greater weight.

Justice of the Peace Court

The special measures provided for in this section have been extended to the JP court by the Justice of the Peace Courts (Special Measures) (Scotland) Order 2015 (SSI 2015/447) art.3(1).

The accused

271F.—(1) For the purposes of the application of subsection (1) of section 271 of this Act to the accused (where the accused is giving or is to give evidence at or for the purposes of a hearing in relevant criminal proceedings), subsection (2) of that section shall have effect as if— **A4-527.16**
(a) for paragraph (c) there were substituted—
"(c) whether the accused is to be legally represented at the hearing and, if not, the accused's entitlement to be so legally represented,", and
(b) for paragraph (e) there were substituted—
"(e) any behaviour towards the accused on the part of—
(i) any co-accused or any person who is likely to be a co-accused in the proceedings,
(ii) any witness or any person who is likely to be a witness in the proceedings, or
(iii) members of the family or associates of any of the persons mentioned in sub-paragraphs (i) and (ii) above.".

(2) Where, if the accused were to give evidence at or for the purposes of the hearing, he would be a child witness—
(a) section 271A of this Act shall apply in relation to the accused subject to the following modifications—

(i) references to a witness shall be read as if they were references to the accused,

(ii) references to the party citing or intending to cite a witness shall be read as if they were references to the accused, and

(iii) subsection (6) shall have effect as if for paragraph (a) there were substituted—

"(a) it appears to the court that the accused, if he were to give evidence at or for the purposes of a hearing in relevant criminal proceedings, would be a child witness," and,

(b) section 271B of this Act shall apply in relation to the accused as if—

(i) for subsection (1) there were substituted—

"(1) This section applies where the accused—

(a) if he were to give evidence at or for the purposes of a hearing in relevant criminal proceedings would be a child witness, and

(b) is under the age of 12 on the date of commencement of the proceedings.", and

(ii) in subsection (3), references to the child witness were references to the accused.

(3) Subsection (4) below applies where the accused—

(a) considers that, if he were to give evidence at or for the purposes of a hearing in relevant criminal proceedings, he would be a vulnerable witness other than a child witness, and

(b) has not decided to give evidence without the benefit of any special measures.

(4) Where this subsection applies, subsections (2) to (11) of section 271C of this Act shall apply in relation to the accused subject to the following modifications—

(a) references to the witness shall be read as if they were references to the accused,

(b) references to the party citing or intending the cite the witness shall be read as if they were references to the accused, and

(c) in subsection (8)(b), the reference to subsection (2)(a) to (f) of section 271 of this Act shall be read as if it were a reference to that subsection as modified by subsection (1) above.

(5) Section 271D of this Act shall apply in any case where it appears to the court that the accused, if he were to give evidence at or for the purposes of the hearing, would be a vulnerable witness as it applies in the case referred to in subsection (1) of that section but subject to the following modifications—

(a) references to the witness shall be read as if they were references to the accused,

(b) references to the party citing or intending to cite the witness shall be read as if they were references to the accused.

(6) Where the witness within the meaning of section 271E of this Act is the accused, that section shall have effect in relation to the witness as if—

(a) in subsection (1), paragraph (a) were omitted, and

(b) in subsection (2), the words "The party or, as the case may be," were omitted.

(7) Section 271M of this Act shall have effect, where the vulnerable witness is the accused, as if the reference in subsection (2) to the party citing the vulnerable witness were a reference to the accused.

(8) The following provisions of this Act shall not apply in relation to a vulnerable witness who is the accused—

(a) section 271H(1)(c) and (ea),
(b) section 271I(3).

AMENDMENTS

Section 271F inserted by Vulnerable Witnesses (Scotland) Act 2004 (asp 3) s.1(1). Brought into force (except for subss.(3), (4), (8)(b)), for specified purposes, on 1 April 2005 by SSI 2005/168 (C.7) art.2 and Sch.

Subs.(8)(b) brought into force for specified purposes on 30 November 2005 by SSI 2005/590 art.2 and Sch.1.
Further brought into force for specified purposes on 1 April 2006 by SSI 2006/59 (C.8).
Further brought into force for specified purposes on 1 April 2007 by SSI 2007/101 (C.13) art.2.
Remainder brought into force on 1 April 2008 by SSI 2008/57 (C.7) art.2.

Subss.(1), (2), (3), (5) as amended by Criminal Justice and Licensing (Scotland) Act 2010 (asp 13) s.87(7). Brought into force on 28 March 2011 (for all purposes in respect of criminal proceedings commenced on or after 28 March 2011, with proceedings taken to have commenced when a report of the case has been received by the procurator fiscal) by SSI 2011/178 (C.15) art.2, Sch.1 para.1.

Subs.(2) as amended by Victims and Witnesses (Scotland) Act 2014 (asp 1) s.11(7). Subs.(8)(a) as amended by s.20(3). Brought into force on 1 September 2015 by SSI 2015/200 art.2 and Sch subject to transitional provisions in art.4.

DEFINITIONS

"child witness notice": s.271A(2). A4-527.17
"court": s.271(5).
"vulnerable witness": s.271(1).

GENERAL NOTE

This section sets out the provisions for allowing an accused, if considered to be vulnerable, to give his or her evidence with the use of a special measure. The provisions of ss.271 to 271M will apply to the accused as a vulnerable witness but with certain modifications. Section 271 is modified for the accused by amending the factors to be taken into account under s.271(2) in determining vulnerability, including the fact that the accused is entitled to or will have legal representation. The accused is also not entitled to use screens as a special measure for the giving of his or her evidence. A4-527.18

Justice of the Peace Court

The special measures provided for in this section have been extended to the JP court by the Justice of the Peace Courts (Special Measures) (Scotland) Order 2015 (SSI 2015/447) art.3(1).

Saving provision

271G. Nothing in sections 271A to 271F of this Act affects any power or duty which a court has otherwise than by virtue of those sections to make or authorise any special arrangements for taking the evidence of any person. A4-527.19

AMENDMENTS

Section 271G inserted by Vulnerable Witnesses (Scotland) Act 2004 (asp 3) s.1(1). Brought into force (except in respect of s.271C), for specified purposes, on 1 April 2005 by SSI 2005/168 (C.7) art.2 and Sch.
Further brought into force for specified purposes on 1 April 2006 by SSI 2006/59 (C.8).
Further brought into force for specified purposes on 1 April 2007 by SSI 2007/101 (C.13) art.2.

DEFINITIONS

"court": s.271(5). A4-527.20

GENERAL NOTE

This section ensures that the existing common law powers to make or authorise special arrangements for vulnerable witnesses' evidence are not removed by the new ss.271A to 271F. In *Hampson v HM Advocate*, 2003 S.L.T. 94 the court established common law power to regulate proceedings and permitted the complainer, who did not fall within the statutory provisions set out in s.271, to give evidence from behind screens but visible to the accused. The test in an application made prior to the commencement of a trial was whether if the application was granted the proposed arrangement would affect the right of the accused to such an extent that the trial would inevitably be unfair: *HM Advocate v Smith*, 2000 S.C.C.R. 910. A4-527.21

Justice of the Peace Court

The special measures provided for in this section have been extended to the JP court by the Justice of the Peace Courts (Special Measures) (Scotland) Order 2015 (SSI 2015/447) art.3(1).

The special measures

A4-527.22 **271H.**—(1) The special measures which may be authorised to be used under section 271A, 271C or 271D of this Act for the purpose of taking the evidence of a vulnerable witness are—

(a) taking of evidence by a commissioner in accordance with section 271I of this Act,

(b) use of a live television link in accordance with section 271J of this Act,

(c) use of a screen in accordance with section 271K of this Act,

(d) use of a supporter in accordance with section 271L of this Act,

(e) giving evidence in chief in the form of a prior statement in accordance with section 271M of this Act, and

(ea) excluding the public during the taking of the evidence in accordance with section 271HB of this Act,

(f) [...]

(1A) The Scottish Ministers may, by order subject to the affirmative procedure—

(a) modify subsection (1),

(b) in consequence of any modification made under paragraph (a)—

(i) prescribe the procedure to be followed when special measures are used, and

(ii) so far as is necessary, modify sections 271A to 271M of this Act.

(2) [...]

(3) Provision may be made by Act of Adjournal regulating, so far as not regulated by sections 271I to 271M of this Act, the use in any proceedings of any special measure authorised to be used by virtue of section 271A, 271C or 271D of this Act.

AMENDMENTS

Section 271H inserted by Vulnerable Witnesses (Scotland) Act 2004 (asp 3) s.1(1). Brought into force (except for subs.(1)(a) and the references in subss.(1) and (3) to s.271C), for specified purposes, on 1 April 2005 by SSI 2005/168 (C.7) art.2 and Sch.

Subs.(1)(a) brought into force for specified purposes on 30 November 2005 by SSI 2005/590 art.2 and Sch.1.

Further brought into force for specified purposes on 1 April 2006 by SSI 2006/59 (C.8).

Further brought into force for specified purposes on 1 April 2007 by SSI 2007/101 (C.13) art.2.

Remainder brought into force on 1 April 2008 by SSI 2008/57 (C.7) art.2.

Subss.(1)(ea) and (1A) inserted, subss.(1)(f) and (2) repealed by Victims and Witnesses (Scotland) Act 2014 (asp 1) ss.20 and 21. Brought into force on 1 September 2015 by SSI 2015/200 art.2 and Sch, subject to transitional provisions in art.4.

DEFINITIONS

A4-527.23 "court": s.271(5).
"vulnerable witness": s.271(1).

GENERAL NOTE

A4-527.24 The special measures that may be made available to vulnerable witnesses in order that they may give their evidence are listed in this section. The various competent measures in s.271H(1)(a) to (e) inclusive probably represent the best available measures but there may yet be others. Section 271H(1)(f) allows the Scottish Ministers a power to make provision for other special measures by way of statutory instrument.

Justice of the Peace Court

The special measures provided for in this section have been extended to the JP court by the Justice of the Peace Courts (Special Measures) (Scotland) Order 2015 (SSI 2015/447) art.3(1).

Temporary additional special measures

A4-527.24.1 **271HA.**—(1) The Scottish Ministers may, by order subject to the affirmative procedure, specify additional measures which for the time being are to be treated as special measures listed in section 271H(1).

(2) An order under subsection (1) may make different provision for different courts or descriptions of court or different proceedings or types of proceedings.

(3) An order under subsection (1) must specify—

(a) the area in which the additional measures may be used,

(b) the period during which the additional measures may be used, and

(c) the procedure to be followed when the additional measures are used.

AMENDMENTS

Section 271HA inserted by Victims and Witnesses (Scotland) Act 2014 (asp 1) s.19. Brought into force on 1 September 2015 by SSI 2015/200 art.2 and Sch, subject to transitional provisions in art.4

[THE NEXT PARAGRAPH IS A4-527.24.4]

Excluding the public while taking evidence

271HB.—(1) This section applies where the special measure to be used in respect of a vulnerable witness is excluding the public during the taking of the evidence of the vulnerable witness. **A4-527.24.4**

(2) The court may direct that all or any persons other than those mentioned in subsection (3) are excluded from the court during the taking of the evidence.

(3) The persons are—

(a) members or officers of the court,

(b) parties to the case before the court, their counsel or solicitors or persons otherwise directly concerned in the case,

(c) bona fide representatives of news gathering or reporting organisations present for the purpose of the preparation of contemporaneous reports of the proceedings,

(d) such other persons as the court may specially authorise to be present.

AMENDMENTS

Section 271HB inserted by Victims and Witnesses (Scotland) Act 2014 (asp 1) s.20. Brought into force on 1 September 2015 by SSI 2015/200 art.2 and Sch, subject to transitional provisions in art.4.

[THE NEXT PARAGRAPH IS A4-527.25]

Taking of evidence by a commissioner

271I.—(1) Where the special measure to be used is taking of evidence by a commissioner, the court shall appoint a commissioner to take the evidence of the vulnerable witness in respect of whom the special measure is to be used. **A4-527.25**

(1ZA) A court which appoints a commissioner under subsection (1) must—

(a) fix a date for the proceedings before the commissioner, and

(b) fix a date for a hearing (to be known as a "ground rules hearing") for the purpose of preparing for the proceedings.

(1ZB) The ground rules hearing is to be presided over by—

(a) a judge of the court which appointed the commissioner if—

(i) the court directs that the ground rules hearing be conjoined with another hearing or diet that is to be held before the date of the proceedings to which the ground rules hearing relates and that hearing or diet is presided over by a judge, or

(ii) it is not reasonably practicable for the ground rules hearing to be presided over by the commissioner appointed to preside over the proceedings to which the ground rules hearing relates, or

(b) in any other case, the commissioner appointed to preside over the proceedings to which the ground rules hearing relates.

(1ZC) In cases where a judge presides over a ground rules hearing in accordance with subsection (1ZB)(a), references to the commissioner in subsection (1ZD) are to be read as references to the judge.

(1ZD) The commissioner presiding over a ground rules hearing must—

(a) ascertain the length of time the parties expect to take for examination-in-chief and cross-examination, including any breaks that may be required,

(b) to the extent that the commissioner considers it appropriate to do so, decide on the form and wording of the questions that are to be asked of the vulnerable witness,

(c) if the commissioner considers it appropriate to do so, authorise the use of a supporter at the proceedings, in accordance with section 271L,

(d) if the commissioner considers that there are steps that could reasonably be taken to enable the vulnerable witness to participate more effectively in the proceedings, direct that those steps be taken,

(e) subject to section 72(8) which applies in relation to the commissioner as it applies in relation to the court, dispose of any application that—

(i) has been made under section 275(1) or 288F(2), and

(ii) has not yet been disposed of by the court,

(f) consider whether the proceedings should take place on the date fixed by the court and postpone the proceedings if the commissioner considers that it is in the interests of justice to do so having regard to all the circumstances, including—

(i) whether the parties are likely to be ready for the proceedings to take place on the date fixed by the court and if not, the reasons for that,

(ii) any views expressed by the parties on whether the proceedings should be postponed, and

(iii) whether postponement is in the interests of the vulnerable witness, and

(g) consider and, if appropriate, make a decision on, any other matter that the commissioner considers could be usefully dealt with before the proceedings take place.

(1A) Proceedings before a commissioner appointed under subsection (1) above shall, if the court so directed when authorising such proceedings or it was so directed at the ground rules hearing, take place by means of a live television link between the place where the commissioner is taking, and the place from which the witness is giving, evidence.

(2) Proceedings before a commissioner appointed under subsection (1) above shall be recorded by video recorder.

(3) An accused—

(a) shall not, except by leave of the court on special cause shown, be present—

(i) in the room where such proceedings are taking place; or

(ii) if such proceedings are taking placeby means of a live television link, in the same room as the witness

(b) is entitled by such means as seem suitable to the court to watch and hear the proceedings.

(4) The recording of the proceedings made in pursuance of subsection (2) above shall be received in evidence without being sworn to by witnesses.

(4A) It is not necessary (in solemn cases) for an indictment to have been served before—

(a) a party may lodge a vulnerable witness notice which specifies the special measure of taking evidence by commissioner as the special measure or one of the special measures which the party considers to be the most appropriate for the purpose of taking the witness's evidence,

(b) a court may make an order authorising the use of the special measure of taking evidence by commissioner, whether on its own or in combination with any other special measure specified in the same vulnerable witness notice,

(c) a court may appoint a commissioner under subsection (1), or

(d) proceedings may take place before a commissioner appointed under subsection (1).

(5) Sections

(a) 274;

(b) 275;

(c) 275B except subsection (2)(b);

(d) 275C;

(e) 288C;

(f) 288E; and

(g) 288F,

of this Act apply in relation to proceedings before a commissioner appointed under subsection (1)(b) above as they apply in relation to a trial.

(6) In the application of those sections in relation to such proceedings-

(a) the commissioner acting in the proceedings is to perform the functions of the court as provided for in thoses sections;

(b) references-

(i) in thoses sections, except sections 275(3)(c) and (7)(c), to a trial or a trial diet;

(ii) in those sections, except sections 275(3)(e) and 288F(2), (3) and (4), to the court, shall be read accordingly; (c) the reference in section 275B(1) to 14 days shall be read as reference to 7 days.

(7) In a case where it falls to the court to appoint a commissioner under subsection (1) above, the commissioner shall be a person described in subsection (8) below.

(8) The persons are-

(a) where the proceedings before the commissioner are for the purposes of a trial which the court (when it appoints the commissioner) expects will be in the High Court, a judge of the Hight Court; or

(b) in any other case, a sheriff.

AMENDMENTS

Section 271I inserted by Vulnerable Witnesses (Scotland) Act 2004 (asp 3) s.1(1). Brought into force, for specified purposes, on 30 November 2005 by SSI 2005/590 art.2 and Sch.1.

Further brought into force for specified purposes on 1 April 2007 by SSI 2007/101 (C.13) art.2.

Remainder brought into force on 1 April 2008 by SSI 2008/57 (C.7) art.2.

Subs.(3) as amended and subss.(1A) and (5)–(8) inserted by Criminal Proceedings etc. (Reform) (Scotland) Act 2007 (asp 6) s.35. Brought into force on 23 April 2007 by SSI 2007/250 (C.23) art.3.

Subss (1ZA)–(1ZD) inserted by Vulnerable Witnesses (Criminal Evidence) (Scotland) Act 2019 (asp 8) s.5(2) effective 20 January 2020 as SSI 2019/392 Sch.1, subject to transitional provisions in reg.4.

Subs.(1A) as amended by Vulnerable Witnesses (Criminal Evidence) (Scotland) Act 2019 (asp 8) s.5(3) effective 20 January 2020 as SSI 2019/392 Sch.1, subject to transitional provisions in reg.4.

Subs.(4A) inserted by Vulnerable Witnesses (Criminal Evidence) (Scotland) Act 2019 (asp 8) s.5(4) effective 20 January 2020.

Subs.(8)(a) as amended by Vulnerable Witnesses (Criminal Evidence) (Scotland) Act 2019 (asp 8) s.5(5) effective 20 January 2020.

DEFINITIONS

"court": s.271(5). A4-527.26

"special measures": s.271H.

"vulnerable witness": s.271(1).

GENERAL NOTE

A4-527.27 Two distinct routes to obtaining the evidence of vulnerable child witnesses on commission now co-exist in the Criminal Procedure (Scotland) Act 1995, in the form of s.271B and s.271BZA. The former more generally-applied provision sets out the discretionary powers vested in all Scottish courts to appoint a commissioner for that purpose and is only activated once an indictment or complaint has been served. The latter, introduced by the Vulnerable Witnesses (Criminal Evidence) (Scotland) Act 2019 (asp 8), provides a much more prescriptive route, and several innovative procedures, to securing such evidence. The General Note below comments upon the s.271I insofar as it deals with applications flowing from s.271B. A separate Note is annexed and refers specifically to the latter statutory mechanisms set out in s.271(1ZA) which currently apply to High Court proceedings, or anticipated High Court proceedings, involving the offences listed in s.271BZA.

This section allows evidence on commission to be used as a special measure for vulnerable witnesses. The court may appoint a commissioner to take the evidence of a vulnerable witness in advance of the trial. An accused may be present with the agreement of the commissioner but at least must be able to watch and listen by some means while the evidence of that witness is taken. Proceedings heard before a commissioner must be recorded by video. That recording of proceedings must be received in evidence at a trial without necessarily being sworn to by a witness.

In *MacLennan v HM Advocate* [2015] HCJAC 128, following grant of a Crown application to have the Joint Investigative Interviews (JII) of two infant child complainers received as their evidence in chief, the commission in relation to the children was held over a year after their original complaints. It is notable that no timeous objection to the admissibility of either JII had been lodged (see s.271C(4A)), the appeal founding on art.6 Convention issues said to arise from the procedural delays prior to the commissions. The court acknowledged the importance of early scrutiny of such testimony but observed with concern that the trigger for any of the vulnerable witness procedures was service of an indictment or complaint. Note that s.271C(4B) does permit late objection, on cause shown, but that that procedure in no way expedites consideration of the original vulnerable witness application.

In solemn proceedings the time scale for initiating vulnerable witness procedures (see s.271A(13A)) is dictated by the date of the preliminary, or first, diet and the citing of, or decision to cite, such a witness. This may result in a substantial delay before the evidence of the complainer can be obtained by commission. In *MacLennan v HM Advocate* [2015] HCJAC 128; 2016 S.C.L. 202 the Crown, unopposed, as a special measure, used the contents of JIIs (joint investigative interviews) as evidence-in-chief for two child witnesses, whose cross-examination and re-examination was to be conducted before the commissioner; the Appeal Court voiced concern at the substantial delay between the JIIs and subsequent commission which application of s.271A(13A) involved. Note that there had been no defence challenge to the special measure itself (see s.271C(4A)).

Subss.(1ZA) to (1ZD) and (4A)

Section 271BZB(2) above extended the range of measures available to the court in qualifying cases. Most notable amongst these is the statutory inclusion of procedures for evidence to be taken by a commissioner rather than this being at the discretion of the court. Such evidence would, of course, be taken prior to the trial hearing. but in contrast to the position hitherto, as subs.(4A) states, the commissioner's involvement can be sought much earlier—even before service of any indictment—and before such evidential hearing the court will have to conduct a ground rules hearing (a GRH) to facilitate the subsequent evidential diet.; it is incumbent upon the parties to predict the probable forum for proceedings and the nature of the charges to be libelled. (As an aside it is essential that disclosure issues and identification of any significant labels and productions required for the evidential hearing are resolved at the ground rules hearing if not sooner).

The GRH may stand alone and be conducted, if possible, by the appointed commissioner or may form part of a procedural hearing and be conducted by the presiding judge. Either way subs.(1ZD) lays out the purpose of the hearing, which can include consideration of any outstanding s.275 application or s.288C issue over representation, both issues which have to be resolved prior to any examination of the witness (It is implicit that the GRH would deal with s.275 applications relating to the witness rather than more widely). Notably the commissioner or judge conducting the GRH has a discretion at the GRH to order further resources they identify as assisting the witness better to give evidence (The Explanatory notes to the Act posit that a live TV link might be incorporated if it was felt that the witness' wellbeing would be better met by being out with the examination suite).

Attention is directed to subs.(1ZD)(f) which enables either the judge dealing with the GRH or the appointed commissioner to issue a postponement of the proceedings.

Justice of the Peace Court

The special measures provided for in this section have been extended to the JP court by the Justice of the Peace Courts (Special Measures) (Scotland) Order 2015 (SSI 2015/447) art.3(1).

Live television link

271J.—(1) Where the special measure to be used is a live television link, the court shall make such arrangements as seem to it appropriate for the vulnerable witness in respect of whom the special measure is to be used to give evidence from a place outside the court-room where the hearing is to take place by means of a live television link between that place and the court-room. A4-527.28

(2) The place from which the vulnerable witness gives evidence by means of the link—

(a) may be another part of the court building in which the court-room is located or any other suitable place outwith that building, and

(b) shall be treated, for the purposes of the proceedings at the hearing, as part of the court-room whilst the witness is giving evidence.

(3) Any proceedings conducted by means of a live television link by virtue of this section shall be treated as taking place in the presence of the accused.

(4) Where—

(a) the live television link is to be used in proceedings in a sheriff court, but

(b) that court lacks accommodation or equipment necessary for the purpose of receiving such a link,

the sheriff may by order transfer the proceedings to any other sheriff court in the same sheriffdom which has such accommodation or equipment available.

(5) An order may be made under subsection (4) above—

(a) at any stage in the proceedings (whether before or after the commencement of the hearing), or

(b) in relation to any part of the proceedings.

AMENDMENTS

Section 271J inserted by Vulnerable Witnesses (Scotland) Act 2004 (asp 3) s.1(1). Brought into force, for specified purposes, on 1 April 2005 by SSI 2005/168 (C.7) art.2 and Sch.

Further brought into force for specified purposes on 1 April 2006 by SSI 2006/59 (C.8).

Further brought into force for specified purposes on 1 April 2007 by SSI 2007/101 (C.13) art.2.

Remainder brought into force on 1 April 2008 by SSI 2008/57 (C.7) art.2.

Subss.(1), (2)(b), (5)(a) as amended by Criminal Justice and Licensing (Scotland) Act 2010 (asp 13) s.87(8). Brought into force on 28 March 2011 (for all purposes in respect of criminal proceedings commenced on or after 28 March 2011, with proceedings taken to have commenced when a report of the case has been received by the procurator fiscal) by SSI 2011/178 (C.15) art.2, Sch.1 para.1.

DEFINITIONS

"court": s.271(5). A4-527.29
"special measures": s.271H.
"trial": s.271(5).
"vulnerable witness": s.271(1).

GENERAL NOTE

The giving of evidence by means of a live television link is known already: see *HM Advocate v Cinci*, 2002 G.W.D. 27-934. This new provision refers to the use of a live television link as a special measure for vulnerable witnesses. Section 271J(1) imposes a duty on the court to make suitable arrangements for the evidence of a vulnerable witness to be given from outside the courtroom by a live television link. Section 271J(2) allows for this to happen from either another part of the courtroom building or any suitable place that can be identified away from the court building. A4-527.30

Section 271J(3) provides that when a live link is used in these proceedings it will be treated as taking place in the presence of the accused. Section 271J(4) makes it competent for the court to transfer a case, or part of a case, in which it is intended that a live television link be used from a court lacking suitable accommodation or equipment to another court within the same sheriffdom.

Justice of the Peace Court

The special measures provided for in this section have been extended to the JP court by the Justice of the Peace Courts (Special Measures) (Scotland) Order 2015 (SSI 2015/447) art.3(1).

Screens

A4-527.31 **271K.—**(1) Where the special measure to be used is a screen, the screen shall be used to conceal the accused from the sight of the vulnerable witness in respect of whom the special measure is to be used.

(2) However, the court shall make arrangements to ensure that the accused is able to watch and hear the vulnerable witness giving evidence.

(3) Subsections (4) and (5) of section 271J of this Act apply for the purpose of the use of a screen under this section as they apply for the purpose of the use of a live television link under that section but as if—

(a) references to the live television link were references to the screen, and
(b) the reference to receiving such a link were a reference to the use of a screen.

AMENDMENTS

Section 271K inserted by Vulnerable Witnesses (Scotland) Act 2004 (asp 3) s.1(1). Brought into force, for specified purposes, on 1 April 2005 by SSI 2005/168 (C.7) art.2 and Sch.

Further brought into force for specified purposes on 1 April 2006 by SSI 2006/59 (C.8).

Further brought into force for specified purposes on 1 April 2007 by SSI 2007/101 (C.13) art.2.

Remainder brought into force on 1 April 2008 by SSI 2008/57 (C.7) art.2.

DEFINITIONS

A4-527.32 "court": s.271(5).
"vulnerable witness": s.271(1).

GENERAL NOTE

A4-527.33 This section provides for the use of screens where a vulnerable witness is giving evidence in a criminal trial. The purpose of the screen is to conceal the accused from the sight of the vulnerable person while the latter is giving evidence. There is a duty on the court to ensure that the accused is able to see and hear the witness giving evidence.

Justice of the Peace Court

The special measures provided for in this section have been extended to the JP court by the Justice of the Peace Courts (Special Measures) (Scotland) Order 2015 (SSI 2015/447) art.3(1).

Supporters

A4-527.34 **271L.—**(1) Where the special measure to be used is a supporter, another person ("the supporter") nominated by or on behalf of the vulnerable witness in respect of whom the special measure is to be used may be present alongside the witness to support the witness while the witness is giving evidence.

(2) Where the person nominated as the supporter is to give evidence at that or any other hearing in the proceedings, that person may not act as the supporter at any time before giving evidence.

(3) The supporter shall not prompt or otherwise seek to influence the witness in the course of giving evidence.

AMENDMENTS

Section 271L inserted by Vulnerable Witnesses (Scotland) Act 2004 (asp 3) s.1(1). Brought into force, for specified purposes, on 1 April 2005 by SSI 2005/168 (C.7) art.2 and Sch.

Further brought into force for specified purposes on 1 April 2006 by SSI 2006/59 (C.8).

Further brought into force for specified purposes on 1 April 2007 by SSI 2007/101 (C.13) art.2.

Remainder brought into force on 1 April 2008 by SSI 2008/57 (C.7) art.2.

Subs.(2) as amended by Criminal Justice and Licensing (Scotland) Act 2010 (asp 13) s.87(9). Brought into force on 28 March 2011 (for all purposes in respect of criminal proceedings commenced on or after 28 March 2011, with proceedings taken to have commenced when a report of the case has been received by the procurator fiscal) by SSI 2011/178 (C.15) art.2, Sch.1 para.1.

DEFINITIONS

A4-527.35 "supporter": s.271L.
"vulnerable witness": s.271(1).

GENERAL NOTE

This section allows for a person to be nominated by a vulnerable witness to accompany the witness into the courtroom or the room where the witness is to give evidence by live television link. The nominated person is known as the supporter. The person nominated as a supporter may not act as such at any time prior to giving evidence. The supporter cannot be allowed to prompt the vulnerable witness when the latter is giving evidence. A4-527.36

Justice of the Peace Court

The special measures provided for in this section have been extended to the JP court by the Justice of the Peace Courts (Special Measures) (Scotland) Order 2015 (SSI 2015/447) art.3(1).

Giving evidence in chief in the form of a prior statement

271M.—(1) This section applies where the special measure to be used in respect of a vulnerable witness is giving evidence in chief in the form of a prior statement. A4-527.37

(2) A statement made by the vulnerable witness which is lodged in evidence for the purposes of this section by or on behalf of the party citing the vulnerable witness shall, subject to subsection (3) below, be admissible as the witness's evidence in chief, or as part of the witness's evidence in chief, without the witness being required to adopt or otherwise speak to the statement in giving evidence in court.

(3) Section 260 of this Act shall apply to a statement lodged for the purposes of this section as it applies to a prior statement referred to in that section but as if—

(a) references to a prior statement were references to the statement lodged for the purposes of this section,

(b) in subsection (1), the words "where a witness gives evidence in criminal proceedings" were omitted, and

(c) in subsection (2), paragraph (b) were omitted.

(4) This section does not affect the admissibility of any statement made by any person which is admissible otherwise than by virtue of this section.

(5) In this section, "statement" has the meaning given in section 262(1) of this Act.

AMENDMENTS

Section 271M inserted by Vulnerable Witnesses (Scotland) Act 2004 (asp 3) s.1(1). Brought into force, for specified purposes, on 1 April 2005 by SSI 2005/168 (C.7) art.2 and Sch.

Further brought into force for specified purposes on 1 April 2006 by SSI 2006/59 (C.8).

Further brought into force for specified purposes on 1 April 2007 by SSI 2007/101 (C.13) art.2.

Remainder brought into force on 1 April 2008 by SSI 2008/57 (C.7) art.2.

DEFINITIONS

"special measures": s.271H. A4-527.38

"statement": ss.271M(5) and 262(1).

"vulnerable witness": s.271(1).

GENERAL NOTE

Section 271M(1) and (2) allow for a previous statement made by a vulnerable witness and which has been reliably recorded on video or in some other way to be used as their main evidence without the need for the witness having to adopt the statement: cf. *Jamieson v HM Advocate*, 1994 S.L.T. 537 and also s.260(2)(b) of the 1995 Act. A4-527.39

Justice of the Peace Court

The special measures provided for in this section have been extended to the JP court by the Justice of the Peace Courts (Special Measures) (Scotland) Order 2015 (SSI 2015/447) art.3(1).

Witness anonymity orders

Witness anonymity orders

A4-527.40 **271N.**—(1) A court may make an order requiring such specified measures to be taken in relation to a witness in criminal proceedings as the court considers appropriate to ensure that the identity of the witness is not disclosed in or in connection with the proceedings.

(2) The court may make such an order only on an application made in accordance with sections 271P and 271Q, if satisfied of the conditions set out in section 271R having considered the matters set out in section 271S.

(3) The kinds of measures that may be required to be taken in relation to a witness include in particular measures for securing one or more of the matters mentioned in subsection (4).

(4) Those matters are—

(a) that the witness's name and other identifying details may be—

(i) withheld,

(ii) removed from materials disclosed to any party to the proceedings,

(b) that the witness may use a pseudonym,

(c) that the witness is not asked questions of any specified description that might lead to the identification of the witness,

(d) that the witness is screened to any specified extent,

(e) that the witness's voice is subjected to modulation to any specified extent.

(5) Nothing in this section authorises the court to require—

(a) the witness to be screened to such an extent that the witness cannot be seen by the judge or the jury,

(b) the witness's voice to be modulated to such an extent that the witness's natural voice cannot be heard by the judge or the jury.

(6) An order made under this section is referred to in this Act as a "witness anonymity order".

(7) In this section "specified" means specified in the order concerned.

Amendments

Section 271N inserted by Criminal Justice and Licensing (Scotland) Act 2010 (asp 13) s.90. Brought into force on 28 March 2011 by SSI 2011/178 (C.15) art.2, Sch.1 para.1.

[THE NEXT PARAGRAPH IS A4-527.42]

General Note

A4-527.42 These substantial provisions relating to witness anonymity orders were introduced at a late stage in the passage of the Criminal Justice and Licensing (Scotland) Act 2010 and provide a statutory footing for such measures. On receipt of an application conforming to the requirements of ss.271P and s.271Q below, which can come from either the accused, or more usually the Crown, the court must be satisfied that the conditions in s.271Q and the statutory considerations set out in s.271R have been met. Particularly notable is s.271S(2)(f) which requires the court to weigh whether other less comprehensive means could be deployed to protect the witness rather than recourse to an order.

A Witness Anonymity Order, as s.271N(4) makes clear, can contain a wide range of witness protection measures—anonymity when giving evidence, use of a pseudonym, the redaction of disclosable materials to prevent identification, use of "screening" and, it seems, disguise of the witness's voice. (It may be of some moment that in specifying the special measures relevant to vulnerable witnesses, s.271H of the Act refers to use of a screen, and not "screening" as here.)

The application must be determined by the court before the commencement of the trial itself (s.271Q(11))—arguably this is sufficiently broadly defined to permit use in most cases of the anonymity measures even at a preliminary debate or evidential hearing—and any application has to be lodged with the court in time for the preliminary or first diet in solemn proceedings, or before any intermediate diet in summary cases. A measure of latitude for later applications is available in summary cases, see s.271Q(2)(b) and (4). It is open to the court to postpone or further adjourn a trial once an application has been received (s.271Q(10)) but all parties must be afforded the opportunity of being heard before any determination (s.271P(6)).

Some comments are necessary: first, appeals against the refusal or making of an order, or its individual elements, are available with leave of the court of first instance (s.271V) and these will not impact upon any operative time bar in the case; secondly, less obviously, given the strictures governing applications in s.271P, the earliest possible steps must be taken to identify a witness's need for an Order and to tailor disclosure of evidence and the framing of libels, notices and disclosure schedules accordingly (s.271P(5)–(6)). The court retains a residual common law power to deal with the circumstances of witnesses who do not fulfil the vulnerability criteria in s.271C or the personal risk criteria set out in s.271R; see *Petition to Nobile Officium by Mr A* [2017] HCJAC 91 in which the alleged victim of an extortion, prosecuted summarily, belatedly had to seek the upholding of a s.11 contempt of court order to prevent further public disclosure of his identity in news media. Albeit the Crown might seek to advance a very broad interpretation of "the public interest", s.271R(3)(b) is narrowly drafted.

Applications

271P.—(1) An application for a witness anonymity order to be made in relation to a witness in criminal proceedings may be made to the court by the prosecutor or the accused. **A4-527.43**

(2) Where an application is made by the prosecutor, the prosecutor—

(a) must (unless the court directs otherwise) inform the court of the identity of the witness, but

(b) is not required to disclose in connection with the application—

(i) the identity of the witness, or

(ii) any information that might enable the witness to be identified,

to any other party to the proceedings (or to the legal representatives of any other party to the proceedings).

(3) Where an application is made by the accused, the accused—

(a) must inform the court and the prosecutor of the identity of the witness, but

(b) if there is more than one accused, is not required to disclose in connection with the application—

(i) the identity of the witness, or

(ii) any information that might enable the witness to be identified,

to any other accused (or to the legal representatives of any other accused).

(4) Subsections (5) and (6) apply where the prosecutor or the accused proposes to make an application under this section in respect of a witness.

(5) Any relevant information which is disclosed by or on behalf of that party before the determination of the application must be disclosed in such a way as to prevent—

(a) the identity of the witness, or

(b) any information that might enable the witness to be identified,

from being disclosed except as required by subsection (2)(a) or (3)(a).

(6) Despite any provision in this Act to the contrary, any relevant list, application or notice lodged, made or given by that party before the determination of the application must not—

(a) disclose the identity of the witness, or

(b) contain any other information that might enable the witness to be identified,

but the list, application or notice must, instead, refer to the witness by a pseudonym.

(7) "Relevant information" means any document or other material which falls to be disclosed, or is sought to be relied on, by or on behalf of the party concerned in connection with the proceedings or proceedings preliminary to them.

(8) "Relevant list, application or notice" means—

(a) a list of witnesses,

(b) a list of productions,

(c) a notice under section 67(5) or 78(4) relating to the witness,

(d) a motion or application under section 268, 269 or 270 relating to the witness,

(e) any other motion, application or notice relating to the witness.

(9) The court must give every party to the proceedings the opportunity to be heard on an application under this section.

(10) Subsection (9) does not prevent the court from hearing one or more of the parties to the proceedings in the absence of an accused and the accused's legal representatives, if it appears to the court to be appropriate to do so in the circumstances of the case.

(11) Nothing in this section is to be taken as restricting any power to make rules of court.

AMENDMENTS

Section 271P inserted by Criminal Justice and Licensing (Scotland) Act 2010 (asp 13) s.90. Brought into force on 28 March 2011 by SSI 2011/178 (C.15) art.2, Sch.1 para.1.

[THE NEXT PARAGRAPH IS A4-527.45]

GENERAL NOTE

A4-527.45 Refer to the discussion in the General Note to s.271N above.

Making and determination of applications

A4-527.46 **271Q.—**(1) In proceedings on indictment, an application under section 271P is a preliminary issue (and sections 79 and 87A and other provisions relating to preliminary issues apply accordingly).

(2) No application under section 271P may be made in summary proceedings by any party unless notice of the party's intention to do so has been given—

(a) if an intermediate diet has been fixed, before that diet,

(b) if no intermediate diet has been fixed, before the commencement of the trial.

(3) Subsection (2) is subject to subsections (4) and (8).

(4) In summary proceedings in which an intermediate diet has been fixed, the court may, on cause shown, grant leave for an application under section 271P to be made without notice having been given in accordance with subsection (2)(a).

(5) Subsection (6) applies where—

(a) the court grants leave for a party to make an application under section 271P without notice having been given in accordance with subsection (2)(a), or

(b) notice of a party's intention to make such an application is given in accordance with subsection (2)(b).

(6) The application must be disposed of before the commencement of the trial.

(7) Subsection (8) applies where a motion or application is made under section 268, 269 or 270 to lead the evidence of a witness.

(8) Despite section 79(1) and subsection (2) above, an application under section 271P may be made in respect of the witness at the same time as the motion or application under section 268, 269 or 270 is made.

(9) The application must be determined by the court before continuing with the trial.

(10) Where an application is made under section 271P, the court may postpone or adjourn (or further adjourn) the trial diet.

(11) In this section, "commencement of the trial" means the time when the first witness for the prosecution is sworn.

Amendments

Section 271Q inserted by Criminal Justice and Licensing (Scotland) Act 2010 (asp 13) s.90. Brought into force on 28 March 2011 by SSI 2011/178 (C.15) art.2, Sch.1 para.1.

[THE NEXT PARAGRAPH IS A4-527.48]

General Note

Refer to the discussion in the General Note to s.271N above. **A4-527.48**

Conditions for making orders

271R.—(1) This section applies where an application is made for a witness anonymity order to be made in relation to a witness in criminal proceedings. **A4-527.49**

(2) The court may make the order only if it is satisfied that Conditions A to D below are met.

(3) Condition A is that the proposed order is necessary—

(a) in order to protect the safety of the witness or another person or to prevent any serious damage to property, or

(b) in order to prevent real harm to the public interest (whether affecting the carrying on of any activities in the public interest or the safety of a person involved in carrying on such activities or otherwise).

(4) Condition B is that, having regard to all the circumstances, the effect of the proposed order would be consistent with the accused's receiving a fair trial.

(5) Condition C is that the importance of the witness's testimony is such that in the interests of justice the witness ought to testify.

(6) Condition D is that—

(a) the witness would not testify if the proposed order were not made, or

(b) there would be real harm to the public interest if the witness were to testify without the proposed order being made.

(7) In determining whether the measures to be specified in the order are necessary for the purpose mentioned in subsection (3)(a), the court must have regard in particular to any reasonable fear on the part of the witness—

(a) that the witness or another person would suffer death or injury, or

(b) that there would be serious damage to property,

if the witness were to be identified.

Amendments

Section 271R inserted by Criminal Justice and Licensing (Scotland) Act 2010 (asp 13) s.90. Brought into force on 28 March 2011 by SSI 2011/178 (C.15) art.2, Sch.1 para.1.

[THE NEXT PARAGRAPH IS A4-527.51]

General Note

Refer to the discussion in the General Note to s.271N above. **A4-527.51**
See *Griffiths v R*, 2014 S.C.L. 61, a sheriff court judgment of 2013.

Relevant considerations

271S.—(1) When deciding whether Conditions A to D in section 271R are met in the case of an application for a witness anonymity order, the court must have regard to— **A4-527.52**

(a) the considerations mentioned in subsection (2), and

(b) such other matters as the court considers relevant.

(2) The considerations are—

(a) the general right of an accused in criminal proceedings to know the identity of a witness in the proceedings,

(b) the extent to which the credibility of the witness concerned would be a relevant factor when the witness's evidence comes to be assessed,
(c) whether evidence given by the witness might be material in implicating the accused,
(d) whether the witness's evidence could be properly tested (whether on grounds of credibility or otherwise) without the witness's identity being disclosed,
(e) whether there is any reason to believe that the witness—
(i) has a tendency to be dishonest, or
(ii) has any motive to be dishonest in the circumstances of the case,
having regard in particular to any previous convictions of the witness[, including any convictions by a court in any part of the United Kingdom or in any member State of the European Union,] and to any relationship between the witness and the accused or any associates of the accused,
(f) whether it would be reasonably practicable to protect the witness's identity by any means other than by making a witness anonymity order specifying the measures that are under consideration by the court.

Amendments

Section 271S inserted by Criminal Justice and Licensing (Scotland) Act 2010 (asp 13) s.90. Brought into force on 28 March 2011 by SSI 2011/178 (C.15) art.2, Sch.1 para.1.

Words in subs.(2)(e)(ii) were inserted by the Criminal Justice (EU Exit) (Scotland) (Amendment etc.) Regulations 2020 (SSI 2020/339) reg.13(14) (effective 31 December 2020 subject to transitional and saving provision specified in reg.16 of those Regulations.

General Note

A4-527.54 Refer to the discussion in the General Note to s.271N above.

Direction to jury

A4-527.55 **271T.—**(1) Subsection (2) applies where, in a trial on indictment, any evidence has been given by a witness at a time when a witness anonymity order applied to the witness.

(2) The judge must give the jury such direction as the judge considers appropriate to ensure that the fact that the order was made in relation to the witness does not prejudice the accused.

Amendments

Section 271T inserted by Criminal Justice and Licensing (Scotland) Act 2010 (asp 13) s.90. Brought into force on 28 March 2011 by SSI 2011/178 (C.15) art.2, Sch.1 para.1.

[THE NEXT PARAGRAPH IS A4-527.58]

Discharge and variation of order

A4-527.58 **271U.—**(1) This section applies where a court has made a witness anonymity order in relation to any criminal proceedings.

(2) The court may discharge or vary (or further vary) the order if it appears to the court to be appropriate to do so in view of the provisions of sections 271R and 271S that applied to the making of the order.

(3) The court may do so—
(a) on an application made by a party to the proceedings if there has been a material change of circumstances since the relevant time, or
(b) on its own initiative.

(4) The court must give every party to the proceedings the opportunity to be heard—
(a) before determining an application made to it under subsection (3)(a), and
(b) before discharging or varying the order on its own initiative.

(5) Subsection (4) does not prevent the court from hearing one or more of the parties to the proceedings in the absence of an accused and the accused's legal representatives, if it appears to the court to be appropriate to do so in the circumstances of the case.

(6) In subsection (3)(a) "the relevant time" means—

(a) the time when the order was made, or

(b) if a previous application has been made under that subsection, the time when the application (or the last application) was made.

AMENDMENTS

Section 271U inserted by Criminal Justice and Licensing (Scotland) Act 2010 (asp 13) s.90. Brought into force on 28 March 2011 by SSI 2011/178 (C.15) art.2, Sch.1 para.1.

[THE NEXT PARAGRAPH IS A4-527.61]

Appeals

271V.—(1) The prosecutor or the accused may appeal to the appropriate Appeal Court against— **A4-527.61**

(a) the making of a witness anonymity order under section 271N,

(b) the kinds of measures that are required to be taken in relation to a witness under a witness anonymity order made under that section,

(c) the refusal to make a witness anonymity order under that section,

(d) the discharge of a witness anonymity order under section 271U,

(e) the variation of a witness anonymity order under that section, or

(f) the refusal to discharge or vary a witness anonymity order under that section.

(2) The appeal may be brought only with the leave of the court of first instance, granted—

(a) on the motion of the party making the appeal, or

(b) on its own initiative.

(3) The procedure in relation to the appeal is to be prescribed by Act of Adjournal.

(4) If an appeal is brought under this section—

(a) the period between the lodging of the appeal and its determination does not count towards any time limit applying in respect of the case,

(b) the court of first instance or the appropriate Appeal Court may do either or both of the following—

(i) postpone or adjourn (or further adjourn) the trial diet,

(ii) extend any time limit applying in respect of the case.

(5) An appeal under this section does not affect any right of appeal in relation to any other decision of any court in the criminal proceedings.

(6) In this section, "appropriate Appeal Court" means—

(a) in the case of an appeal under this section against a decision made in proceedings on indictment, the High Court;

(b) in the case of an appeal under this section against a decision made in summary proceedings, the Sheriff Appeal Court.

AMENDMENTS

Section 271V inserted by Criminal Justice and Licensing (Scotland) Act 2010 (asp 13) s.90. Brought into force on 28 March 2011 by SSI 2011/178 (C.15) art.2, Sch.1 para.1.

Subss.(1) and (4) as amended, subs.(6) inserted, by Courts Reform (Scotland) Act 2014 (Consequential Provisions No.2) Order 2015 (SSI 2015/338) Sch.2 para.5 (effective 22 September 2015).

[THE NEXT PARAGRAPH IS A4-527.64]

Appeal against the making of a witness anonymity order

A4-527.64 **271W.**—(1) This section applies where—

(a) an appeal is brought under section 271V(1)(a) against the making of a witness anonymity order, and

(b) the court hearing the appeal determines that the decision of the judge at first instance was wrong in law.

(2) The court hearing the appeal must discharge the order and the trial is to proceed as if the order had not been made.

Amendments

Section 271W inserted by Criminal Justice and Licensing (Scotland) Act 2010 (asp 13) s.90. Brought into force on 28 March 2011 by SSI 2011/178 (C.15) art.2, Sch.1 para.1.

Subss.(1) and (2) as amended by Courts Reform (Scotland) Act 2014 (Consequential Provisions No.2) Order 2015 (SSI 2015/338) Sch.2 para.5 (effective 22 September 2015).

General Note

A4-527.65 The express aim of a conduct requirement is to secure the rehabilitation of the offender to prevent future offending so the imposition of a requirement of good behaviour was held not to be competent (*Kirk v Brown* [2012] HCJAC 96).

[THE NEXT PARAGRAPH IS A4-527.67]

Appeal against the refusal to make a witness anonymity order

A4-527.67 **271X.**—(1) This section applies where—

(a) an appeal is brought under section 271V(1)(c) against the refusal to make a witness anonymity order in relation to a witness in criminal proceedings, and

(b) the court hearing the appeal determines that the decision of the judge at first instance was wrong in law.

(2) The court hearing the appeal must make an order requiring such specified measures to be taken in relation to the witness in the proceedings as the court considers appropriate to ensure that the identity of the witness is not disclosed in or in connection with the proceedings.

Amendments

Section 271X inserted by Criminal Justice and Licensing (Scotland) Act 2010 (asp 13) s.90. Brought into force on 28 March 2011 by SSI 2011/178 (C.15) art.2, Sch.1 para.1.

Subs.(1) and (2) as amended by Courts Reform (Scotland) Act 2014 (Consequential Provisions No.2) Order 2015 (SSI 2015/338) Sch.2 para.5 (effective 22 September 2015).

[THE NEXT PARAGRAPH IS A4-527.70]

Appeal against a variation of a witness anonymity order

A4-527.70 **271Y.**—(1) This section applies where—

(a) an appeal is brought under section 271V(1)(e) against a variation of a witness anonymity order, and

(b) the court hearing the appeal determines that the decision of the judge at first instance was wrong in law.

(2) The court hearing the appeal must discharge the variation.

(3) If the court hearing the appeal determines that it is appropriate to make an additional variation in view of the provisions of sections 271R and 271S, the court may do so.

Amendments

Section 271Y inserted by Criminal Justice and Licensing (Scotland) Act 2010 (asp 13) s.90. Brought into force on 28 March 2011 by SSI 2011/178 (C.15) art.2, Sch.1 para.1.

Subs.(1), (2) and (3) as amended by Courts Reform (Scotland) Act 2014 (Consequential Provisions No.2) Order 2015 (SSI 2015/338) Sch.2 para.5 (effective 22 September 2015).

[THE NEXT PARAGRAPH IS A4-527.73]

Appeal against a refusal to vary or discharge a witness anonymity order

271Z.—(1) This section applies where— A4-527.73

(a) an appeal is brought under section 271V(1)(f) against a refusal to discharge or vary a witness anonymity order, and

(b) the court hearing the appeal determines that the decision of the judge at first instance was wrong in law.

(2) The court hearing the appeal must discharge the order, or make the variation, as the case requires.

(3) If, in the case of a variation, the court hearing the appeal determines that it is appropriate to make an additional variation in view of the provisions of sections 271R and 271S, the court may do so.

AMENDMENTS

Section 271Z inserted by Criminal Justice and Licensing (Scotland) Act 2010 (asp 13) s.90. Brought into force on 28 March 2011 by SSI 2011/178 (C.15) art.2, Sch.1 para.1.

Subs.(1), (2) and (3) as amended by Courts Reform (Scotland) Act 2014 (Consequential Provisions No.2) Order 2015 (SSI 2015/338) Sch.2 para.5 (effective 22 September 2015).

[THE NEXT PARAGRAPH IS A4-528]

Evidence on commission and from abroad

Evidence by letter of request or on commission

272.—(1) In any criminal proceedings in the High Court or the sheriff court the prosecutor or the defence may, at an appropriate time, apply to a judge of the court in which the trial is to take place (or, if that is not yet known, to a judge of the High Court) for— A4-528

(a) the issue of a letter of request to a court, or tribunal, exercising jurisdiction in a country or territory outside the United Kingdom, Channel Islands and Isle of Man for the examination of a witness resident in that country or territory; or

(b) the appointment of a commissioner to examine, at any place in the United Kingdom, Channel Islands, or Isle of Man, a witness who—

(i) by reason of being ill or infirm is unable to attend the trial diet; or

(ii) is not ordinarily resident in, and is, at the time of the trial diet, unlikely to be present in, the United Kingdom, Channel Islands or the Isle of Man.

(2) A hearing, as regards any application under subsection (1) above by a party, shall be conducted in chambers but may be dispensed with if the application is not opposed.

(3) An application under subsection (1) above may be granted only if the judge is satisfied that—

(a) the evidence which it is averred the witness is able to give is necessary for the proper adjudication of the trial; and

(b) there would be no unfairness to the other party were such evidence to be received in the form of the record of an examination conducted by virtue of that subsection.

(4) Any such record as is mentioned in paragraph (b) of subsection (3) above shall, without being sworn to by witnesses, be received in evidence in so far as it either accords with the averment mentioned in paragraph (a) of that subsection or

can be so received without unfairness to either party.

(5) Where any such record as is mentioned in paragraph (b) of subsection (3) above, or any part of such record, is not a document in writing, that record or part shall not be received in evidence under subsection (4) above unless it is accompanied by a transcript of its contents.

(6) The procedure as regards the foregoing provisions of this section shall be prescribed by Act of Adjournal; and without prejudice to the generality of the power to make it, such an Act of Adjournal may provide for the appointment of a person before whom evidence may be taken for the purposes of this section.

(7) In subsection (1) above, "appropriate time" means as regards—

(a) solemn proceedings, any time before the oath is administered to the jury;

(b) summary proceedings, any time before the first witness is sworn,

or (but only in relation to an application under paragraph (b) of that subsection) any time during the course of the trial if the circumstances on which the application is based had not arisen, or would not have merited such application, within the period mentioned in paragraph (a) or, as the case may be, (b) of this subsection.

(8) In subsection (3) and (4) above, "record" includes, in addition to a document in writing—

(a) any disc, tape, soundtrack or other device in which sounds or other data (not being visual images) are recorded so as to be capable (with or without the aid of some other equipment) of being reproduced therefrom; and

(b) any film (including microfilm), negative, tape, disc or other device in which one or more visual images are recorded so as to be capable (as aforesaid) of being reproduced therefrom.

(9) This section is without prejudice to any existing power at common law to adjourn a trial diet to the place where a witness is.

(10) Sections—

(a) 274;

(b) 275;

(c) 275B except subsection (2)(b);

(d) 275C;

(e) 288C;

of this Act apply in relation to proceedings in which a commissioner examines a witness under subsection (1)(b) above as they apply in relation to a trial.

(11) In the application of those sections in relation to such proceedings—

(a) the commissioner acting in the proceedings is to perform the functions of the court as provided for in thoses sections;

(b) references—

(i) in thoses sections, except sections 275(3)(c) and (7)(c), to a trial or a trial diet;

(ii) in those sections, except sections 275(3)(e), to the court, shall be read accordingly;

(c) the reference in section 275B(1) to 14 days shall be read as reference to 7 days.

(12) In a case where it falls to the court to appoint a commissioner under subsection (1)(b) above, the commissioner shall be a person described in subsection (13) below.

(13) The persons are—

(a) where the proceedings before the commissioner are for the purposes of a trial in the High Court, a judge of the Hight Court; or

(b) in any other case, a sheriff.

(14) This section does not apply to a witness who or evidence that is the subject of a European investigation order made under Part 2 of the Criminal Justice (European Investigation Order) Regulations 2017.

AMENDMENTS

Subss.(10)–(13) inserted by Criminal Proceedings etc. (Reform) (Scotland) Act 2007 (asp 6) s.35. Brought into force on 23 April 2007 by SSI 2007/250 (C.23) art.3.

Subs.(14) inserted by Criminal Justice (European Investigation Order) Regulations 2017 (SI 2017/730) Sch.3 para.3 (effective 31 July 2017).

[THE NEXT PARAGRAPH IS A4-528.2]

DEFINITIONS

"appropriate time": s.272(7). A4-528.2
"High Court": s.307(1).
"judge": s.307(1).
"prosecutor": s.307(1).
"record": s.272(8).
"trial": s.307(1).
"witness": s.307(1).

[THE NEXT PARAGRAPH IS A4-529]

GENERAL NOTE

This section applies to solemn and summary proceedings and can apply in circumstances in which the court might otherwise have to convene elsewhere in order to hear a witness' testimony. Chapters 23 and 24 of the 1996 Act of Adjournal regulates the form in which applications for Letters of Request of the taking of evidence on Commission are to be made. The procedures only operate in the Sheriff and High Courts. A4-529

Subsection (7) stipulates that such applications can normally only be made before trial proceedings have begun (although see the exceptional provisions available for applications which of necessity need to be made in the course of the trial). As subs.(1) states, any application should be made to a judge within whose jurisdiction the trial is due to take place, or, if no trial diet has been assigned, to a High Court judge. This requirement will be of limited applicability to summary cases since it would only rarely be necessary to seek Letters or a Commission once a trial had been fixed. The application in terms of Rule 23.1.–(4) has to be intimated to other parties and any hearing will occur in chambers if the application is opposed.

This statutory provision is the sole basis for such applications, there being no common law alternative; see *HM Advocate v M*, 2010 S.L.T. 5 where defence submissions that other means of delivering such evidence—notably a live television link broadcast from witnesses' homes—ought to be preferred and could be ordered at common law, were rejected by the court. The classes of witness in relation to whom applications can be made are set out in subs.(1) but the judge has to be satisfied that the factors stipulated in subs.(3) are met before the application is allowed. Furthermore the granting of the application does not of itself mean that the testimony obtained has to be admitted as evidence: the court on receipt of the record (which must be accompanied by a written transcript) still has to consider whether its contents can be fairly admitted in accordance with the rules of evidence.

In considering the grant of an application, the court has to consider the test set out in subs.(3). It is essential that due weight is given to the potential unfairness to those in the trial who are deprived of the opportunity of oral cross-examination should Letters or a Commission be permitted (see *Muirhead v HM Advocate*, 1983 S.C.C.R. 133). In *Land, Petr*, 1991 S.L.T. 931; 1991 S.C.C.R. 138 while an application by the Crown to take the evidence on commission of a 91-year-old witness was granted, and it was conceded that the sheriff's discretion was not subject to review, it was held that the issue of fairness to the accused still fell to be considered at the trial and, if necessary, on appeal.

Subss.(1) and (3) were used to obtain the evidence of several housebound elderly witnesses, all alleged victims of fraud or theft, by means of examination on an open commission (i.e. with full examination and cross-examination) with the trial judge as commissioner, outwith the accused's presence. A transcript of the commission could then be read over to the jury. Defence objections that such arrangements were inferior to a televised link to the court which could, and should, be provided by the court, were rejected. Note that the court paid heed to the practicability (cost implications) of the various methods of securing the evidence and considered no art.6 Convention point arose; *HM Advocate v M*, 2010 S.L.T. 5; 2010 S.C.C.R. 79.

See also *HM Advocate v Lesacher*, 1982 S.C.C.R. 418 where the trial had to be delayed to allow for the presentation of Letters of Request to West Germany through diplomatic channels.

Refer to Ch.23 of the 1996 Act of Adjournal for provisions as to expenses, transmission of Letters and custody of documents. Note in particular that Rule 23.6. specifies that such evidence cannot be led or referred to in trial proceedings until a motion to that effect has been made and granted.

It will be observed that requests for live television links for evidence to be taken contemporaneously from abroad during proceedings (s.273 below) are initiated by way of the Letter of Request procedures described above.

Attention is directed to Practice Note No.3 of 2005 which provides comprehensive guidance as to the preparatory steps required of practitioners before the court can consider an application, and details the powers of the appointed commissioner. It is likely that the Practice Note will be revised during 2017 as further provisions of the Criminal Justice (Scotland) Act 2016 in relation to vulnerable witnesses are commenced.

Television link evidence from abroad

A4-530 **273.**—(1) In any criminal proceedings in the High Court or the sheriff court a person other than the accused may give evidence through a live television link if—

(a) the witness is outside the United Kingdom;
(b) an application under subsection (2) below for the issue of a letter of request has been granted; and
(c) the court is satisfied as to the arrangements for the giving of evidence in that manner by that witness.

(2) The prosecutor or the defence in any proceedings referred to in subsection (1) above may apply to a judge of the court in which the trial is to take place (or, if that court is not yet known, to a judge of the High Court) for the issue of a letter of request to—

(a) a court or tribunal exercising jurisdiction in a country or territory outside the United Kingdom where a witness is ordinarily resident; or
(b) any authority which the judge is satisfied is recognised by the government of that country or territory as the appropriate authority for receiving requests for assistance in facilitating the giving of evidence through a live television link,

requesting assistance in facilitating the giving of evidence by that witness through a live television link.

(3) An application under subsection (2) above shall be granted only if the judge is satisfied that—

(a) the evidence which it is averred the witness is able to give is necessary for the proper adjudication of the trial; and
(b) the granting of the application—
  (i) is in the interests of justice; and
  (ii) in the case of an application by the prosecutor, is not unfair to the accused.

(5) This section does not apply to a witness who or evidence that is the subject of a European investigation order made under Part 2 of the Criminal Justice (European Investigation Order) Regulations 2017.

AMENDMENTS

Subs.(1) as amended by Criminal Justice and Licensing (Scotland) Act 2010 (asp 13) s.91(2). Brought into force on 28 March 2011 (for all purposes in respect of criminal proceedings commenced on or after 28 March 2011, with proceedings taken to have commenced when a report of the case has been received by the procurator fiscal) by SSI 2011/178 (C.15) art.2, Sch.1 para.1.

Subs.(5) inserted by Criminal Justice (European Investigation Order) Regulations 2017 (SI 2017/730) Sch.3 para.3 (effective 31 July 2017).

DEFINITIONS

A4-530.1 "High Court": s.307(1).
"judge": s.307(1).
"prosecutor": s.307(1).
"sheriff": s.307(1).
"trial": s.307(1).
"witness": s.307(1).

[THE NEXT PARAGRAPH IS A4-531]

GENERAL NOTE

In criminal proceedings, in the High Court or sheriff courts, application by way of the Letter of Request procedure outlined in s.272 above can be made for a live television link to take the evidence of witnesses who are outwith the United Kingdom. The factors determining whether such an application should be allowed by the court are laid out in subs.(2). For an example of the application of this section see *HM Advocate v Cinci*, 2002 G.W.D. 27-934. A4-531

Standing the need for a letter of request to initiate such a television link, use of this provision will generally be confined to solemn proceedings. Note that s.273A has introduced similar provisions to permit television links to courts elsewhere in the United Kingdom.

Evidence from other parts of the United Kingdom

Television link evidence from other parts of the United Kingdom

273A.—(1) In any criminal proceedings in the High Court or the sheriff court a person other than the accused may give evidence through a live television link if— A4-531.1

(a) the witness is within the United Kingdom but outside Scotland,

(b) an application under this section for the issue of a letter of request has been granted, and

(c) the court is satisfied as to the arrangements for the giving of evidence in that manner by that witness.

(2) The prosecutor or the defence in any proceedings referred to in subsection (1) may apply for the issue of a letter of request.

(3) The application must be made to a judge of the court in which the trial is to take place or, if that court is not yet known, to a judge of the High Court.

(4) The judge may, on an application under this section, issue a letter to a court or tribunal exercising jurisdiction in the place where the witness is ordinarily resident requesting assistance in facilitating the giving of evidence by that witness through a live television link, if the judge is satisfied of the matters set out in subsection (5).

(5) Those matters are—

(a) that the evidence which it is averred the witness is able to give is necessary for the proper adjudication of the trial,

(b) that the granting of the application—

(i) is in the interests of justice, and

(ii) in the case of an application by the prosecutor, is not unfair to the accused.

AMENDMENTS

Section 273A inserted by Criminal Justice and Licensing (Scotland) Act 2010 (asp 13) s.91(3). Brought into force on 28 March 2011 (for all purposes in respect of criminal proceedings commenced on or after 28 March 2011, with proceedings taken to have commenced when a report of the case has been received by the procurator fiscal) by SSI 2011/178 (C.15) art.2, Sch.1 para.1.

[THE NEXT PARAGRAPH IS A4-532]

Evidence relating to sexual offences

Restrictions on evidence relating to sexual offences

274.—(1) In the trial of a person charged with an offence to which section 288C of this Act applies, the court shall not admit, or allow questioning designed to elicit evidence which shows or tends to show that the complainer— A4-532

(a) is not of good character (whether in relation to sexual matters or otherwise);

(b) has, at any time, engaged in sexual behaviour not forming part of the subject matter of the charge;

(c) has, at any time (other than shortly before, at the same time as or shortly after the acts which form part of the subject matter of the charge), engaged in such behaviour, not being sexual behaviour, as might found the inference that the complainer—

(i) is likely to have consented to those acts; or

(ii) is not a credible or reliable witness; or

(d) has, at any time, been subject to any such condition or predisposition as might found the inference referred to in sub-paragraph (c) above.

(2) In subsection (1) above, "complainer" means the person against whom the offence referred to in that subsection is alleged to have been committed; and the reference to engaging in sexual behaviour includes a reference to undergoing or being made subject to any experience of a sexual nature.

AMENDMENTS

Section 274 substituted by Sexual Offences (Procedure and Evidence) (Scotland) Act 2002 (asp 9) s.7. Brought into force by SSI 2002/443 (C.24) art.4 (effective 1 November 2002).

GENERAL NOTE

A4-533 This section applies equally to summary and solemn proceedings and introduces entirely new procedures to limit the scope of questioning relating to a complainer's character, sexual behaviour or history. Offences covered by these provisions are set out in s.288C(2) of the Act and, it should be noted, in subs.(4) of that section which adds offences held to contain a substantial sexual element in the offence. Significantly too the general definition here applies equally to the Crown and the defence and extends to the complainer's history as a victim of sexual conduct just as much as a willing participant in sexual conduct.

In order to lift the prohibition, a party has to make application in writing in accordance with s.275, setting out the grounds which are argued to justify an exception being made to the general bar on such questioning, unless special cause can be shown, not less than 14 clear days before trial. So far as an accused is concerned, as s.275A makes clear, the corollary is that the Crown will be obliged to place any relevant previous conviction, served on the accused, before the court on conclusion of its consideration of the application. The intention is that any such conviction, unless its accuracy is challenged, will be admitted in evidence during the trial proceedings. Procedures are established for proof of previous convictions or for showing that a conviction has a substantial sexual element. Issues may become more complex in cases involving co-accused.

The High Court has emphasised repeatedly that the starting point in any consideration is to ascertain that the material whose admission is sought is admissible at common law; only if that test is satisfied can the court then look to the merits of the application; see *RG v HM Advocate* [2019] HCJAC 18; 2019 S.C.C.R. 172 (Sy) following *LL v HM Advocate* [2018] HCJAC 35 and *M v HM Advocate (No.2)*, 2013 SLT 380; 2013 S.C.C.R. 215. The primary issue tends to be whether the material is of direct relevance or is simply collateral in nature and thus falling foul of the prohibitions in subs.(1). It should be stressed that the validity of an application is not settled by Crown acquiescence; in *RN v HM Advocate* [2020] HCJAC 3 the Appeal Court emphasised that the court itself must be satisfied that the matters specified are admissible as evidence. Thereafter the court has to be satisfied that the requirements of s.275(3) are fully met.

There may well be force to the argument that these provisions do not extend to former complainers whose evidence is introduced by means of a s.288BA docket in support of a subsequent sexual offence libel (see *HM Advocate v Moynihan* [2018] HCJAC 43; 2019 S.C.C.R. 61).

Act of Adjournal

The Act of Adjournal (Criminal Procedure Rules Amendment No.3) (Sexual Offences (Procedure and Evidence) (Scotland) Act 2002) 2002 (SSI 2002/454) adds procedural rules and new forms of intimation covering solemn and summary cases involving sexual offences.

Exceptions to restrictions under section 274

A4-534 **275.**—(1) The court may, on application made to it, admit such evidence or allow such questioning as is referred to in subsection (1) of section 274 of this Act if satisfied that—

(a) the evidence or questioning will relate only to a specific occurrence or occurrences of sexual or other behaviour or to specific facts demonstrating—

(i) the complainer's character; or

(ii) any condition or predisposition to which the complainer is or has been subject;

(b) that occurrence or those occurrences of behaviour or facts are relevant to establishing whether the accused is guilty of the offence with which he is charged; and

(c) the probative value of the evidence sought to be admitted or elicited is significant and is likely to outweigh any risk of prejudice to the proper administration of justice arising from its being admitted or elicited.

(2) In subsection (1) above—

(a) the reference to an occurrence or occurrences of sexual behaviour includes a reference to undergoing or being made subject to any experience of a sexual nature;

(b) "the proper administration of justice" includes—

(i) appropriate protection of a complainer's dignity and privacy; and

(ii) ensuring that the facts and circumstances of which a jury is made aware are, in cases of offences to which section 288C of this Act applies, relevant to an issue which is to be put before the jury and commensurate to the importance of that issue to the jury's verdict,

and, in that subsection and in sub-paragraph (i) of paragraph (b) above, "complainer" has the same meaning as in section 274 of this Act.

(3) An application for the purposes of subsection (1) above shall be in writing and shall set out—

(a) the evidence sought to be admitted or elicited;

(b) the nature of any questioning proposed;

(c) the issues at the trial to which that evidence is considered to be relevant;

(d) the reasons why that evidence is considered relevant to those issues;

(e) the inferences which the applicant proposes to submit to the court that it should draw from that evidence; and

(f) such other information as is of a kind specified for the purposes of this paragraph in Act of Adjournal.

(4) The party making such an application shall, when making it, send a copy of it—

(a) when that party is the prosecutor, to the accused; and

(b) when that party is the accused, to the prosecutor and any co-accused.

(5) The court may reach a decision under subsection (1) above without considering any evidence; but, where it takes evidence for the purposes of reaching that decision, it shall do so as if determining the admissibility of evidence.

(6) The court shall state its reasons for its decision under subsection (1) above, and may make that decision subject to conditions which may include compliance with directions issued by it.

(7) Where a court admits evidence or allows questioning under subsection (1) above, its decision to do so shall include a statement—

(a) of what items of evidence it is admitting or lines of questioning it is allowing;

(b) of the reasons for its conclusion that the evidence to be admitted or to be elicited by the questioning is admissible;

(c) of the issues at the trial to which it considers that that evidence is relevant.

(8) A condition under subsection (6) above may consist of a limitation on the extent to which evidence—

(a) to be admitted; or

(b) to be elicited by questioning to be allowed,

may be argued to support a particular inference specified in the condition.

(9) Where evidence is admitted or questioning allowed under this section, the court at any time may—

(a) as it thinks fit; and

(b) notwithstanding the terms of its decision under subsection (1) above or any condition under subsection (6) above,

limit the extent of evidence to be admitted or questioning to be allowed.

AMENDMENTS

Section 275 substituted by Sexual Offences (Procedure and Evidence) (Scotland) Act 2002 (asp 9) s.8(1). Brought into force by SSI 2002/443 (C.24) art.4 (effective 1 November 2002).

DEFINITION

A4-535 "trial": s.307(1).

GENERAL NOTE

Refer to the discussion at A4-533. Where a party seeks to lead evidence about the complainer's sexual history or behaviour in face of the general prohibition laid down in s.274 of the Act, notice must be given in writing, ordinarily, not less than 14 clear days before trial. The section applies equally to the Crown and the defence and the object of the section is to ensure that the thrust of questioning is relevant to the issues of fact before the court rather than merely calculated to belittle or humiliate the complainer by raising tangential issues. Several factors are noteworthy: the purpose of the 14 day *induciae* specified in s.275B below is to ensure that the application is raised as far as possible, before the trial rather than at the point when evidence, especially that of the complainer, is being lead so applications should be considered at first or preliminary diets in solemn proceedings (see ss.71 and 72 of the Act as now amended) or at intermediate diets in summary trials; secondly, the court has to consider a broad test—the proper administration of justice—and, to do so, must weigh the comparative benefit to the accused in having such evidence against the impact it might have upon the privacy and dignity of the complainer; third, in considering the application the court may hear evidence and, fourth, while imposing any conditions or limits upon questioning the court nonetheless has to maintain a watching brief (subs.(9)) to limit the evidence admitted under s.275 in the course of the trial. From all of this it follows that in dealing with s.275 applications the court may well seek evidence from parties who were not originally listed as witnesses at all, for example medical practitioners, psychologists or social workers, the aim being to minimise the procedural interruptions which might otherwise occur during the trial itself.

In response to a successful application the Crown is directed to lay before the court any relevant previous convictions. See the fuller discussion on this aspect in the General Note to s.275A below.

The terms of the court's decision upon the application must be properly preserved to enable the trial judge to fulfil the Bench's responsibilities under s.275—to monitor adherence to the line, and scope, of questioning permitted under the application and to control its tone and content. See *MacDonald v HM Advocate* [2020] HCJAC 21 at [33] and [34], an instance of wholesale failure by all parties to adhere to the section's requirements.

The court was critical of the unresponsive stance adopted by the Crown in dealing with the original application and during the trial proceedings themselves.

Notwithstanding *MacDonald* above it is clear from Petition to Nobile Officium by *RR v HM Advocate and LV* [2021] HCJAC 21, a Full Bench decision, that neither the complainer or her legal representatives have a locus to be heard on the merits of a s.275 application. Still it will be observed that the application itself was held to be competent and, perhaps more importantly, the court emphasised the responsibility upon the Crown firstly, to keep the complainer informed of the progress of the case (including the anticipated s.275 hearing) and secondly, to ascertain the complainer's stance upon the averments in the s.275 application before it has been considered by the court. One might reflect whether, in our accusatorial system, fairness might be better served by effective precognition where possible.

Case law

While much depends upon the facts in individual cases, some propositions can now be tentatively advanced: the earlier permissive approach adopted by the courts, where applications were rarely challenged or argued, is now much less evident. A general discussion of the development of these procedures is found in *Moir v HM Advocate (No.1)*, 2005 1 J.C. 102; *MM v HM Advocate*, 2004 S.C.C.R. 658 which also held the provisions to be ECHR compliant.

See the discussion of *RN v HM Advocate* [2020] HCJAC 3 in the General Note to the preceding section.

Broadly, any application has to found upon specific and directly relevant allegations, from identifiable sources, which are demonstrated to be necessary to challenge the reliability or credibility of the complainer's testimony (*Cumming v HM Advocate*, 2003 S.C.C.R. 261). Thus, evidence of an earlier predispositon of the complainer to lie or fabricate demonstrably fantastical stories can be brought out (*Mackay v HM Advocate*, 2005 J.C. 24). If the defence elects to produce expert evidence of "false memory syndrome" as a means of challenging the veracity of the complainer, the Crown is entitled to lead evidence in rebuttal. (The diagnosis is one which is still controversial in psychiatric opinion.) A thorough analysis of the range of case law in this field was provided in Lord MacPhail's judgment in *HM Advocate v A*, 2005 S.L.T. 975.

Expert evidence as to the psychiatric condition of the witness, insofar as it would impinge on truthfulness, or explain the response to questioning, or accurate recall was discussed in *Green v HM Advocate*, 1983 S.C.C.R. 42 and in *McBrearty v HM Advocate*, 2004 S.L.T. 917; 2004 S.C.C.R. 337. Where it can be shown to be material to an accused's defence, questions about earlier consensual intercourse between the parties may be permitted (*Tant v HM Advocate*, 2003 S.C.C.R. 506) but such earlier consent will not itself be sufficient to make out a defence of consent (see *GW v HM Advocate* [2019] HCJAC 23); earlier false allegations of rape may be permitted but only where it is intended to do more than proceed by bald assertions—colourable evidence has to be identified in support of an application (*Thomson v HM Advocate*, 2001 S.C.C.R. 162 revisited and approved in *Thomson v HM Advocate*, 2010 S.L.T. 678). *Thomson* underlines the fundamental distinction between admissible, material evidence and collateral issues which are not germane to the libel and thus not admissible. Here though the trial judge dealt with the matter on its merits under ss.274 and 275, it could more properly have been decided at common law, the provisions of the sections not overriding existing common law. See *Moir v HM Advocate*, 2007 S.L.T. 452; 2007 S.C.C.R. 159, the post-trial appeal arising from *MM v HM Advocate* cited above, and *Ronald v HM Advocate*, 2007 S.L.T. 1170; 2007 S.C.C.R. 451.

In *CJM v HM Advocate* [2013] HCJAC 22; 2013 S.C.C.R. 215, a Full Bench decision, the Appeal Court reviewed whether the issue aired in the s.275 application (a prior allegation by one of the four complainers of sexual assault which had resulted in her being cautioned but not prosecuted for wasting police time) was admissible at common law and hence could form the basis of an application. The material was held to be collateral—removed in time and character from the charges now libeled—and thus inadmissible. Note too that, as the Crown argued, even once this hurdle was negotiated, an application had to go on to fulfill all the requirements of subs.(1)(a) to (c).

In any application it has to be emphasised that there has to be a soundly-argued basis for the line of evidence being sought and that speculative "fishing", or evidence solely directed towards demeaning or distressing the complainer will not be permitted. Since s.275, applications have to be lodged for consideration at the first diet, or preliminary hearing, the applicant may well have to be ready at that stage in the proceedings to lead evidence in support of the application. Refusal of an application at that point does not necessarily prevent the trial court reconsidering issues as evidence emerges, and the relevance of the questioning proposed earlier in the s.275 application emerges: the court's broader duty to ensure the fairness of the proceedings as the trial develops, remains.

Disclosure of accused's previous convictions where court allows questioning or evidence under section 275

275A.—(1) Where, under section 275 of this Act, a court (or, in proceedings before a commissioner appointed under section 271I(1) or by virtue of section 272(1)(b) of this Act, a commissioner) on the application of the accused allows such questioning or admits such evidence as is referred to in section 274(1) of this Act, the prosecutor shall forthwith place before the presiding judge any previous relevant conviction of the accused. **A4-535.1**

(2) [Subject to subsection (2A) any] conviction placed before the judge under subsection (1) above shall, unless the accused objects, be—

(a) in proceedings on indictment, laid before the jury;

(b) in summary proceedings, taken into consideration by the judge.

[(2A) Where the conviction is a relevant conviction by virtue of subsection (10)(aa)(ii), subsection (2) applies only if the judge considers it appropriate.]

(3) An extract of [a conviction referred to in subsection (2)] may not be laid before the jury or taken into consideration by the judge unless such an extract was appended to the notice, served on the accused under section 69(2) or, as the case may be, 166(2) of this Act, which specified that conviction.

(4) An objection under subsection (2) above may be made only on one or more of the following grounds—

(a) where the conviction bears to be a relevant conviction by virtue only of paragraph (b) of subsection (10) below, that there was not a substantial sexual element present in the commission of the offence for which the accused has been convicted;

(b) that the disclosure or, as the case may be, the taking into consideration of the conviction would be contrary to the interests of justice;

(c) in proceedings on indictment, that the conviction does not apply to the accused or is otherwise inadmissible;

(d) in summary proceedings, that the accused does not admit the conviction.

(5) Where—

(a) an objection is made on one or more of the grounds mentioned in paragraphs (b) to (d) of subsection (4) above; and

(b) an extract of the conviction in respect of which the objection is made was not appended to the notice, served on the accused under section 69(2) or, as the case may be, 166(2) above, which specified that conviction,

the prosecutor may, notwithstanding subsection (3) above, place such an extract conviction before the judge.

(6) In summary proceedings, the judge may, notwithstanding subsection (2)(b) above, take into consideration any extract placed before him under subsection (5) above for the purposes only of considering the objection in respect of which the extract is disclosed.

(7) In entertaining an objection on the ground mentioned in paragraph (b) of subsection (4) above, the court shall, unless the contrary is shown, presume that the disclosure, or, as the case may be, the taking into consideration, of a conviction is in the interests of justice.

(8) An objection on the ground mentioned in paragraph (c) of subsection (4) above shall not be entertained unless the accused has, under subsection (2) of section 69 of this Act, given intimation of the objection in accordance with subsection (3) of that section.

(9) In entertaining an objection on the ground mentioned in paragraph (d) of subsection (4) above, the court shall require the prosecutor to withdraw the conviction or adduce evidence in proof thereof.

(10) For the purposes of this section a "relevant conviction" is, subject to subsection (11) below–

(a) a conviction for an offence to which section 288C of this Act applies by virtue of subsection (2) thereof;

[(aa) a conviction by a court in—

(i) England and Wales or Northern Ireland, or

(ii) a member State of the European Union,

of an offence that is equivalent to one to which section 288C of this Act applies by virtue of subsection (2) thereof; or]

(b) where a substantial sexual element was present in the commission of any other offence in respect of which the accused has previously been convicted, a conviction for that offence,

which is specified in a notice served on the accused under section 69(2) or, as the case may be, 166(2) of this Act.

(10A) Any issue of equivalence arising in pursuance of subsection (10)(aa) is for the court to determine.

(11) A conviction for an offence other than an offence to which section 288C of this Act applies by virtue of subsection (2) thereof is not a relevant conviction for the purposes of this section unless an extract of that conviction containing information which indicates that a sexual element was present in the commission of the offence was appended to the notice, served on the accused under section 69(2) or, as the case may be, 166(2) of this Act, which specified that conviction.

AMENDMENTS

Section 275A inserted by Sexual Offences (Procedure and Evidence) (Scotland) Act 2002 (asp 9) s.10(4). Brought into force by SSI 2002/443 (C.24) art.4 (effective 1 November 2002).

Subs.(1) as amended by Criminal Proceedings etc. (Reform) (Scotland) Act 2007 (asp 6) s.35. Brought into force on 23 April 2007 by SSI 2007/250 (C.23) art.3

Subss.(10A), (10)(aa) inserted, subs.(10)(a) as amended, by Criminal Justice and Licensing (Scotland) Act 2010 (asp 13) Sch.4 para.7. Brought into force on 13 December 2010 by SSI 2010/413 (C.28) art.2 and Sch.1 para.1.

Words in subs.(2) were substituted by the Criminal Justice (EU Exit) (Scotland) (Amendment etc.) Regulations 2020 (SSI 2020/339) reg.13(15)(a) (effective December 31, 2020 subject to transitional and saving provision specified in reg.16 of those Regulations.

Subs.(2A) was inserted by the Criminal Justice (EU Exit) (Scotland) (Amendment etc.) Regulations 2020 (SSI 2020/339) reg.13(15)(b) (effective December 31, 2020 subject to transitional and saving provision specified in reg.16 of those Regulations.

Words in subs.(3) were substituted by the Criminal Justice (EU Exit) (Scotland) (Amendment etc.) Regulations 2020 (SSI 2020/339) reg.13(15)(c) (effective December 31, 2020 subject to transitional and saving provision specified in reg.16 of those Regulations.

GENERAL NOTE

Refer to the General Notes to ss.274 and 275 above. It is noted that the corollary of success for an accused with a s.275 application is that the Crown is obliged to place any relevant convictions and supporting extract convictions if the sexual context is not self-evident. All such convictions must first have been served upon the accused by the customary notice, and will then be placed before the trial court in the course of evidence unless the accused at the s.275 hearing can successfully challenge their validity or show that he had not been served with them. The only other ground for ignoring a relevant conviction would be that its disclosure in trial proceedings would be contrary to the interests of justice (subs.(4)(b)). In *HM Advocate v S*, 2005 G.W.D. 26–504 it was held that this section's provisions did not offend against art.6 of ECHR. An accused whose application under s.275 has been granted by the court can still argue that disclosure of his relevant previous convictions should not follow automatically. Essentially the argument is that disclosure would be disproportionately harmful to his fair trial when set against the (limited) purpose of his application (*HM Advocate v S*, 2005 G.W.D. 26–504). See, generally, *Leggate v HM Advocate*, 1988 S.L.T. 665; 1988 S.C.C.R. 391. **A4-535.1.1**

Section 275A is densely drafted and looks likely to attract more than its fair share of procedural appeals and case decisions as well as proofs of previous convictions. This assessment does not even begin to take account of the labyrinthine complexities which will develop in cases involving more than a single accused. For these reasons attention is directed to the discussion of *Riley v HM Advocate*, 1999 J.C. 308; 1999 S.L.T. 1076; 1999 S.C.C.R. 644 at A4–228.1 above, in relation to the uses of relevant extract convictions, and to the provisions for proof of previous convictions found at ss.285 and 286 below.

One important qualification to this discussion must be noted in solemn proceedings—the accused can only dispute a conviction for the purpose of s.275A if he has already challenged the accuracy of the notice of previous convictions served upon him with his indictment. See s.69(3) of the Act. Failure to comply with this provision would not, it is submitted, nullify any subsequent conviction.

Provisions supplementary to sections 275 and 275A

275B.—(1) An application for the purposes of subsection (1) of section 275 of this Act shall not, unless on special cause shown, be considered by the court unless made **A4-535.2**

(a) in the case of proceedings in the High Court, not less than 7 clear days before the preliminary hearing; or

(b) in any other case, not less than 14 clear days before the trial diet.

(2) Where—

(a) such an application is considered; or

(b) any objection under subsection (2) of section 275A of this Act is entertained,

during the course of the trial, the court shall consider that application or, as the case may be, entertain that objection in the absence of the jury, the complainer, any person cited as a witness and the public.

AMENDMENTS

Section 275B inserted by Sexual Offences (Procedure and Evidence) (Scotland) Act 2002 (asp 9) s.10(4). Brought into force by SSI 2002/443 (C.24) art.4 (effective 1 November 2002).

Subs.(1)(a) and (b) inserted by Criminal Procedure (Amendment) (Scotland) Act 2004 (asp 5) s.25 and Sch.1 para.45. Brought into force on 1 February 2005 by SSI 2004/405 (C.28) art.2.

GENERAL NOTE

Ordinarily any application to the court to waive the restrictions upon evidence relating to the sexual history or background of the complainer must be intimated at least 14 clear days before trial. This timing **A4-535.3** enables such applications to be considered at first or preliminary diets in solemn proceedings, or at the intermediate diet in summary proceedings. Although later notice may be permitted, this will only be on special cause shown, an indication that this has to be seen as available only in exceptional circumstances. Subs.(2) stipulates that if notice is first given at the trial diet then any consideration of an application, or any resultant s.275A hearing in relation to relevant convictions, must be considered by the court *in camera*.

Expert evidence as to subsequent behaviour of complainer

Expert evidence as to subsequent behaviour of complainer in certain cases

A4-535.4 **275C.**—(1) This section applies in the case of proceedings in respect of

(a) any offence to which section 288C of this Act applies.

(b) an offence under section 1(1) of the Domestic Abuse (Scotland) Act 2018,

(c) an offence that is aggravated as described in section 1(1)(a) of the Abusive Behaviour and Sexual Harm (Scotland) Act 2016.

(2) Expert psychological or psychiatric evidence relating to any subsequent behaviour or statement of the complainer is admissible for the purpose of rebutting any inference adverse to the complainer's credibility or reliability as a witness which might otherwise be drawn from the behaviour or statement.

(3) In subsection (2) above—

"complainer" means the person against whom the offence to which the proceedings relate is alleged to have been committed,

"subsequent behaviour or statement" means any behaviour or statement subsequent to, and not forming part of the acts constituting, the offence to which the proceedings relate and which is not otherwise relevant to any fact in issue at the trial.

(3A) Where the offence is as referred to in subsection (1)(b) above, the reference in the last definition in subsection (3) above to any behaviour or statement subsequent to the offence includes any behaviour or statement subsequent to a particular part of the course of behaviour of which the offence consists.

(4) This section does not affect the admissibility of any evidence which is admissible otherwise than by virtue of this section.

Amendments

Section 275C inserted by Vulnerable Witnesses (Scotland) Act 2004 (asp 3) s.5. Brought into force, for all purposes, on 1 April 2005 by SSI 2005/168 (C.7) art.2 and Sch.

Subs.(1) as amended, subs.(3A) inserted, by Domestic Abuse (Scotland) Act 2018 (asp 5) Sch.1(1)(3) para.7(2) (1 April 2019 in respect of proceedings commenced on or after 1 April 2019 subject to transitional provision specified in SSI 2018/387 reg.7(2)).

Definitions

A4-535.5 "complainer": s.275C(3).
"statement": ss.271M(5) and 262(1).
"subsequent behaviour or statement": s.275C(3).

General Note

A4-535.6 Section 288C of the 1995 Act introduced a prohibition on the personal conduct by the accused of the defence case in certain specified sexual offences. This new s.275C allows for certain expert witness evidence to be admitted in cases involving relevant sexual offences. That evidence may only be admitted for the purpose of explaining the behaviour of the complainer in order to rebut any inference adverse to the credibility and reliability of the complainer that might otherwise be drawn from that behaviour. The new provision does not restrict the use of expert evidence that is admissible by existing law.

[THE NEXT PARAGRAPH IS A4-536]

Biological material

Evidence of biological material

276.—(1) Evidence as to the characteristics and composition of any biological material deriving from human beings or animals shall, in any criminal proceedings, be admissible notwithstanding that neither the material nor a sample of it is lodged as a production. A4-536

(2) A party wishing to lead such evidence as is referred to in subsection (1) above shall, where neither the material nor a sample of it is lodged as a production, make the material or a sample of it available for inspection by the other party unless the material constitutes a hazard to health or has been destroyed in the process of analysis.

GENERAL NOTE

This section dispenses with the need to produce in court certain biological materials in relation to which evidence is to be led in proceedings. Ordinarily in solemn proceedings the accused is entitled to inspect any productions (see s.68(2)); no such provision is found in summary proceedings given their character. Section 276 arises from considerations of public health and constitutes an exception to the authority that allows an accused to see productions. A4-537

Transcripts and records

Transcript of police interview sufficient evidence

277.—(1) Subject to subsection (2) below, for the purposes of any criminal proceedings, a document certified by the person who made it as an accurate transcript made for the prosecutor of the contents of a tape (identified by means of a label) purporting to be a recording of an interview between— A4-538

(a) a police officer and an accused person;

(b) a person commissioned, appointed or authorised under section 6(3) of the Customs and Excise Management Act 1979 and an accused person; or

(c) a person authorised by the Scottish Environment Protection Agency under section 108 of the Environment Act 1995 and an accused person.

shall be received in evidence and be sufficient evidence of the making of the transcript and of its accuracy.

(2) Subsection (1) above shall not apply to a transcript—

(a) unless a copy of it has been served on the accused not less than 14 days before

(i) in the case of proceedings in the High Court, the preliminary hearing;

(ii) in any other case, his trial; or

(b) if the accused, not less than

(i) in the case of proceedings in the High Court, seven days before the preliminary hearing;

(ii) in any other case, six days before his trial;

or (in either case) by such later time before his trial as the court may in special circumstances allow, has served notice on the prosecutor that the accused challenges the making of the transcript or its accuracy.

(3) A copy of the transcript or a notice under subsection (2) above shall be served in such manner as may be prescribed by Act of Adjournal; and a written execution purporting to be signed by the person who served the transcript or notice, together with, where appropriate, the relevant post office receipt shall be sufficient evidence of such service.

(4) Where subsection (1) above does not apply to a transcript, if the person who made the transcript is called as a witness his evidence shall be sufficient evidence of the making of the transcript and of its accuracy.

(5) Subsection (1) is without prejudice to section 108(12) of the Environment Act 1995.

Amendments

Subss.(2)(a)(i), (ii) and (b)(i), (ii) inserted, and subs.(2)(b) as amended, by Criminal Procedure (Amendment) (Scotland) Act 2004 (asp 5) s.25 and Sch.1 para.46. Brought into force on 1 February 2005 by SSI 2004/405 (C.28) art.2.

Subs.(1) as amended, and subs.(5) inserted, by Regulatory Reform (Scotland) Act 2014 (asp 3) Sch.3 para.31. Brought into force on 30 June 2014 by SSI 2014/160 art.2 and Sch.1 para.1.

Definition

A4-538.1 "prosecutor": s.307(1).

[THE NEXT PARAGRAPH IS A4-539]

General Note

A4-539 This section permits the admission as evidence of a transcript of any interview conducted by the police or Customs officers with the accused on tape. The transcript, prepared by a person appointed by the procurator fiscal, has to be certified by that person and a copy of it has to be served (subs.(3)) on the accused not less than 14 days before trial (subs.(2)(a)). Any challenge to the accuracy of the transcript has to be intimated to the prosecutor not less than six days before trial normally, or later on cause shown. It appears that a challenge to the accuracy of the transcript can be met conclusively by calling the person who prepared it but this would not preclude the alternative of playing the tape, provided its contents did not breach ss.101(1) and 166(3) and disclose previous convictions or contain other inadmissible material. These factors explain why the prosecution will often prepare and lodge an edited transcript deleting any such untoward references: in that event the jury, or the judge in summary proceedings, should only be referred to the edited transcript in the course of evidence.

Note that, unlike the transcript of any judicial examination, which must be lodged in solemn proceedings (see the notes to ss.36 and 37), this section does not oblige the prosecutor to lodge a transcript of taped interview.

Record of proceedings at examination as evidence

A4-540 **278.**(1) [...]

Amendments

Subs.(2)(a) as amended by Criminal Procedure (Amendment) (Scotland) Act 2004 (asp 5) s.25 and Sch.1 para.47. Brought into force on 1 February 2005 by SSI 2004/405 (C.28) art.2.

Section 278 repealed by Criminal Justice (Scotland) Act 2016 (asp 1) s.78(2)(e). Brought into force on 17 January 2017 by SSI 2016/426 art.2 and Sch.1 para.1, subject to savings.

General Note

A4-541 Following commencement of s.78 of the Criminal Justice (Scotland) Act 2016 on 17 January 2017 (for which see the Criminal Justice (Scotland) Act 2016 (Commencement No. 3 and Saving Provision) Order 2016 (SSI 2016/426)) the procedures of judicial examination, and judicial declaration described in s.35(4), are repealed. By the same token, s.278 was also repealed though it is submitted that this repealed provision might better be regarded meantime as obsolescent . Refer to the discussion at s.35 of the instant Act.

Documentary evidence

Evidence from documents

A4-542 **279.** Schedule 8 to this Act, which makes provision regarding the admissibility in criminal proceedings of copy documents and of evidence contained in business documents, shall have effect.

General Note

A4-543 Schedule 8 to the Act restates the terms of Sch.3 to the Prisoners and Criminal Proceedings (Scotland) Act 1993 which provides for the certification of documentary evidence, particularly business documents, and validates the use of certified copies of documents (as defined in Sch.(8)), which may in some instances contain hearsay material, as best evidence in criminal proceedings. It will be noted that the provisions of this section would not preclude use of the Bankers' Books Evidence Act 1879 (c.11) in suitable circumstances; there are two means of proving entries in bankers' books though it has to be said that generally the Sch.8 provisions are more widely drafted (see *Lord Advocate's Reference No. 1 of 1996*, 1996 G.W.D. 21–1189).

HM Advocate v AB [2012] HCJAC 13; 2012 S.C.C.R. 336 offers a vigorous examination of the purposes of certification and the extent to which defective docquets can be corrected prior to trial. Broadly, such certificates do not constitute a part of any production to which they relate or are annexed; thus alteration or amendment of certificates even at that late stage is permissible. See also General Note to s.68 above.

Act of Adjournal

Forms 26.1–A to 26.1–C are provided in the 1996 Act of Adjournal for authentication of documents, and setting up business documents, and providing a means for certification of evidence which is not to be found in business documents. This last class of certificate can be tendered in proceedings without the need for the person certifying to attend court as a witness.

Evidence from certain official documents

279A.—(1) Any letter, minute or other official document issuing from the office of or in custody of any of the departments of state or government in the United Kingdom or any part of the Scottish Administration which— A4-543.1

(a) is required to be produced in evidence in any prosecution; and
(b) according to the rules and regulations applicable to such departments may competently be so produced,

shall when so produced be prima facie evidence of the matters contained in it without being produced or sworn to by any witness.

(2) A copy of any such document as is mentioned in subsection (1) above bearing to be certified by any person having authority to certify it shall be treated as equivalent to the original of that document and no proof of the signature of the person certifying the copy or of his authority to certify it shall be necessary.

(3) Any order made by any of the departments of state or government or the Scottish Parliament or any local authority or public body made under powers conferred by any statute or a print or a copy of such order, shall when produced in a prosecution be received as evidence of the due making, confirmation, and existence of the order without being sworn to by any witness and without any further or other proof.

(4) Subsection (3) above is without prejudice to any right competent to the accused to challenge any order such as is mentioned in that subsection as being ultra vires of the authority making it or any other competent ground.

(5) Where an order such as is mentioned in subsection (3) above is referred to in the indictment or, as the case may be, the complaint, it shall not be necessary to enter it in the record of the proceedings as a documentary production.

(6) The provisions of this section are in addition to, and not in derogation of, any powers of proving documents conferred by statute or existing at common law.

AMENDMENTS

Section 279A inserted by Crime and Punishment (Scotland) Act 1997 (c.48) s.28(2); commenced with effect from August 1, 1997 in terms of SI 1997/1712 art.3.

Subss.(1) and (3) as amended by Scotland Act 1998 (Consequential Modifications) (No.2) Order 1999 (SI 1999/1820) art.4 and Sch.2 para.122(4) (effective July 1, 1999).

DEFINITIONS

"document": s.279 and Sch.8, para.8 to the 1995 Act. A4-543.2
"order": s.307(1) of the 1995 Act.
"United Kingdom": s.5 of and Sch.1 to the Interpretation Act 1978 (c.30).

GENERAL NOTE

This section supercedes s.154 of the 1995 Act and makes provisions for the admissibility of official documents as evidence in any criminal proceedings. Apart from minor rewording, and associated renumbering of subsections, the new provision is all but identical to the old but, importantly, extends to solemn proceedings. A4-543.3

Either the original document or a certified copy of it can be used in proceedings without the need for it to be listed as a production or set up by parole evidence: the only proviso is that there must be valid certification of the document or a copy of it. These specific evidential concessions go beyond the provisions found in Sch.8 to the 1995 Act; particularly note that there is no requirement to lodge the relevant Order, Local Government Order or Statutory Instrument as a production in proceedings. Reference should also be made to the statutory presumptions found in Sch.3 para.12 of the 1995 Act.

The procedure to be followed when a challenge is made to the validity of an Order was discussed in *Johnston v McGillivray*, 1993 S.L.T. 120 and in *Neizer v Johnston*, 1993 S.C.C.R. 772.

[THE NEXT PARAGRAPH IS A4-544]

Routine evidence

Routine evidence

A4-544 **280.**—(1) For the purposes of any proceedings for an offence under any of the enactments specified in column 1 of Schedule 9 to this Act, a certificate purporting to be signed by a person or persons specified in column 2 thereof, and certifying the matter specified in column 3 thereof shall, subject to subsection (6) below, be sufficient evidence of that matter and of the qualification or authority of that person or those persons.

(2) The Secretary of State may by order—

(a) amend or repeal the entry in Schedule 9 to this Act in respect of any enactment; or

(b) insert in that Schedule an entry in respect of a further enactment.

(3) An order under subsection (2) above may make such transitional, incidental or supplementary provision as the Secretary of State considers necessary or expedient in connection with the coming into force of the order.

(3A) For the purposes of any criminal proceedings, a report purporting to be signed by a person authorised by the Scottish Environment Protection Agency for the purpose of this subsection is sufficient evidence of any fact or conclusion as to fact contained in the report and of the authority of the signatory.

(4) For the purposes of any criminal proceedings, a report purporting to be signed by two authorised forensic scientists shall, subject to subsection (5) below, be sufficient evidence of any fact or conclusion as to fact contained in the report and of the authority of the signatories.

(5) A forensic scientist is authorised for the purposes of subsection (4) above if—

(a) he is authorised for those purposes by the Secretary of State; or

(b) he—

(i) [...]

(ii) [...]

(iii) is authorised for those purposes by the chief constable of the police force maintained for the police area of that authority.

(6) Subsections (1), (3A) and (4) above shall not apply to a certificate or, as the case may be, report tendered on behalf of the prosecutor or the accused—

(a) unless a copy has been served on the other party not less than fourteen days before

(i) in the case of proceedings in the High Court, the preliminary hearing;

(ii) in any other case, the trial; or

(b) where the other party, not more than seven days after the date of service of the copy on him under paragraph (a) above or by such later time as the court may in special circumstances allow, has served notice on the first party that he challenges the matter, qualification or authority mentioned in subsection (1) above or as the case may be the fact, conclusion or authority mentioned in subsection (3A) or (4) above.

(7) A copy of a certificate or, as the case may be, report required by subsection (6) above, to be served on the accused or the prosecutor or of a notice required by that subsection or by subsection (1) or (2) of section 281 of this Act to be served on the prosecutor shall be served in such manner as may be prescribed by Act of Adjournal; and a written execution purporting to be signed by the person who served such certificate or notice, together with, where appropriate, the relevant post office receipt shall be sufficient evidence of service of such a copy.

(8) Where, following service of a notice under subsection (6)(b) above, evidence is given in relation to a report referred to in subsection (4) above by both of the forensic scientists purporting to have signed the report, the evidence of those forensic scientists shall be sufficient evidence of any fact (or conclusion as to fact) contained in the report.

(9) At any trial of an offence it shall be presumed that the person who appears in answer to the complaint is the person charged by the police with the offence unless the contrary is alleged.

(10) An order made under subsection (2) or (5)(b)(ii) above shall be made by statutory instrument.

(11) No order shall be made under subsection (2) above unless a draft of the order has been laid before, and approved by a resolution of, each House of Parliament.

(12) A statutory instrument containing an order under subsection (5)(b)(ii) above shall be subject to annulment pursuant to a resolution of either House of Parliament.

AMENDMENTS

Subs.(6)(b) amended by Crime and Punishment (Scotland) Act 1997 (c.48) s.62(1) and Sch.1 para.21(32) with effect from August 1, 1997 in terms of SI 1997/1712 art.3.

Subs.6(a) as amended by Criminal Procedure (Amendment) (Scotland) Act 2004 (asp 5) s.25 and Sch.1 para.48. Brought into force on February 1, 2005 by SSI 2004/405 (C.28) art.2.

Subs.(5)(b)(i) and (ii) repealed by Police and Fire Reform (Scotland) Act 2012 (asp 8) Sch.8 para.1. Brought into force on April 1, 2013 by SSI 2013/51 art.2.

Subs.(6) as amended, and subs.(3A) inserted, by Regulatory Reform (Scotland) Act 2014 (asp 3) Sch.3 para.31. Brought into force on June 30, 2014 by SSI 2014/160 art.2 and Sch.1 para.1.

DEFINITIONS

"complaint": s.307(1). **A4-544.1**
"constable": s.307(1) and s.51(1) of the Police (Scotland) Act 1967 (c. 77).
"offence": s.307(1).
"prosecutor": s.307(1).
"trial": s.307(1).

[THE NEXT PARAGRAPH IS A4-545]

GENERAL NOTE

Unlike s.26(2) of the Criminal Justice (Scotland) Act 1980 which applied only to summary proceedings, the effect of subs.(4) is to apply these provisions relating to routine evidence prepared by authorised forensic scientists to both summary and solemn proceedings. The provisions of s.281 are equally available to prosecution and defence alike provided the authors of the report are authorised scientists. **A4-545**

It will be noted that subs.(5) broadens the definition of "forensic scientist" to include police constables or police employees appointed by their Chief Constable. The provisions in regard to service of forensic reports are repeated in subs.(6) and the form of certificate, as provided by Ch.27 of the 1996 Act of Adjournal, may broadly follow the style of Form 27.2.

Challenges to the contents of a report must be by notice served on the other party not more than seven days after service of the report (note that by contrast, s.26(3) of the 1980 Act allowed challenge up to six days before the trial). Failing such challenge, the contents of the report shall be received as sufficient evidence. Much of the case law generated by s.26 of the 1980 Act related to attacking certificated evidence, which had not been formally challenged, on the basis that the facts contained in the reports did not themselves satisfy the statutory requirements. See *Normand v Wotherspoon*, 1994 S.L.T. 487; 1993 S.C.C.R. 912; *Straker v Orr*, 1994 S.C.C.R. 251; *McCrindle v Walkingshaw*, 1994 S.C.C.R. 299; *O'Brien v McCreadie*, 1994 S.C.C.R. 516. For more recent discussion of the presumptions as to service of such reports see *Lawrence v Vannet*, 1998 G.W.D. 40–2041. Objection to the contents of a forensic report served under s.280 (on the basis that the authors had not stated that they had analysed the drugs identified) without having intimated a challenge under subs.(6)(b) was repelled on appeal in *Meek v HM Advocate*, 2000 G.W.D. 9–323.

The section makes various other provisions intended to reduce the unnecessary attendance of witnesses at court. The Secretary of State may add to the list of matters which may be introduced into evidence by certificate, by way of subordinate legislation. This will enable suitable matters to be added to the list as they are identified without the need to wait for a suitable opportunity to incorporate them in primary legislation (subss.(2) and (3)).

This section puts it beyond doubt that the facts and conclusions as to facts spoken to either in the report or in subsequent oral evidence based on the report, are sufficient for the purpose of proving those facts. Such evidence can still be attacked on the grounds of credibility or unreliability.

Subsection (9) repeats the terms of s.26(5) and enacts a presumption that the party answering the complaint is the person charged by the police. Unless a challenge is intimated on behalf of the accused before a plea has been tendered, the presumption will hold good and it then becomes unnecessary to identify the accused in the course of the trial, always provided that it has been established that the person responsible for the offence had been charged. See *Rollo v Wilson*, 1988 S.C.C.R. 312 where the sheriff recalled a police witness to confirm evidence of identification; on appeal it was held that the s.26(5) presumption had in any event rendered the recall unnecessary: in *Hamilton v Ross*, 1992 S.L.T. 384; 1991 S.C.C.R. 165 the Appeal Court raised the issue of the presumption in response to a Crown appeal against a no case to answer motion; the issue had not been aired before that time but the Crown was still entitled to benefit from the provision.

Routine evidence: autopsy and forensic science reports

A4-546 **281.**—(1) Where in a trial an autopsy report is lodged as a production by the prosecutor it shall be presumed that the body of the person identified in that report is the body of the deceased identified in the indictment or complaint, unless the accused not less than

(i) in the case of proceedings in the High Court, seven days before the preliminary hearing;

(ii) in any other case, six days before the trial;

or (in either case) by such later time before the trial as the court may in special circumstances allow, gives notice that the contrary is alleged.

(2) At the time of lodging an autopsy or forensic science report as a production the prosecutor may intimate to the accused that it is intended that only one of the pathologists or forensic scientists purporting to have signed the report shall be called to give evidence in respect thereof; and, where such intimation is given, the evidence of one of those pathologists or forensic scientists shall be sufficient evidence of any fact or conclusion as to fact contained in the report and of the qualifications of the signatories, unless the accused, not less than

(i) in the case of proceedings in the High Court, seven days before the preliminary hearing;

(ii) in any other case, six days before the trial;

or (in either case) by such later time before the trial as the court may in special circumstances allow, serves notice on the prosecutor that he requires the attendance at the trial of the other pathologist or forensic scientist also.

(3) Where, following service of a notice by the accused under subsection (2) above, evidence is given in relation to an autopsy or forensic science report by both of the pathologists or forensic scientists purporting to have signed the report, the evidence of those pathologists or forensic scientists shall be sufficient evidence of any fact (or conclusion as to fact) contained in the report.

AMENDMENTS

Subss.(1), (2) as amended, and subss.(1)(i), (ii), (2)(i), (ii) inserted, by Criminal Procedure (Amendment) (Scotland) Act 2004 (asp 5) s.25 and Sch.1 para.49. Brought into force on February 1, 2005 by SSI 2004/405 (C.28) art.2.

DEFINITIONS

"indictment": s.307(1). A4-546.1
"complaint": s.307(1).
"prosecutor": s.307(1).
"trial": s.307(1).

[THE NEXT PARAGRAPH IS A4-547]

GENERAL NOTE

It is presumed, unless a challenge is notified to the prosecutor not less than six days before any trial (or later on cause shown), that the person referred to in any autopsy report founded upon in the proceedings is the same person as specified in the libel. Subsection (2) entitles the prosecutor to serve notice that he will call only one of the joint authors of a forensic of autopsy report, a concession designed to minimise inconvenience to such witnesses if their evidence is not in dispute. Again, a challenge to such a notice has to be intimated not less than six days before trial (or later on cause shown). Rule 27.1 in the 1996 Act of Adjournal requires that such notice will be in writing. A4-547

The practice has developed in solemn cases of incorporating the subs.(2) notice to the accused in the List of Productions incorporated in the indictment.

The evidential impact of the presumption in subs.(2) was discussed in *Bermingham v HM Advocate*, 2004 S.L.T. 692; 2004 S.C.C.R. 354 which recognises that it is competent for forensic scientists to incorporate elements of hearsay evidence in their reports in relation to work or findings generated by supervised assistants.

Routine evidence: reports of identification prior to trial

281A.—(1) Where in a trial the prosecutor lodges as a production a report naming— A4-547.1

(a) a person identified in an identification parade or other identification procedure by a witness, and
(b) that witness,

it shall be presumed, subject to subsection (2) below, that the person named in the report as having been identified by the witness is the person of the same name who appears in answer to the indictment or complaint.

(2) That presumption shall not apply—

(a) unless the prosecutor has, by the required time, served on the accused a copy of the report and a notice that he intends to rely on the presumption, or
(b) if the accused—
  (i) not more than 7 days after the date of service of the copy of the report, or
  (ii) by such later time as the court may in special circumstances allow,

  has served notice on the prosecutor that he intends to challenge the facts stated in the report.

(3) In subsection (2)(a) above, "the required time" means—

(a) in the case of proceedings in the High Court—
  (i) not less than 14 clear days before the preliminary hearing; or
  (ii) such later time, being not less than 14 clear days before the trial, as the court may, in special circumstances, allow;
(b) in any other case, not less than 14 clear days before the trial.

AMENDMENTS

Section 281A inserted by Vulnerable Witnesses (Scotland) Act 2004 (asp 3) s.4. Brought into force, for all purposes, on April 1, 2005 by SSI 2005/168 (C.7) art.2 and Sch.

Subs.(2)(a) as amended and subs.(3) inserted by Criminal Procedure (Amendment) (Scotland) Act 2004 (asp 5) s.25 and Sch.1 para.50. Brought into force on April 1, 2005 by SSI 2004/405 (C.28) art.2 and Sch.2.

Subs.(3) as amended by Criminal Procedure (Amendment) (Scotland) Act 2004 (Incidental, Supplemental and Consequential Provisions) Order 2005 (SSI 2005/40) art.3.

DEFINITIONS

A4-547.2 "prosecutor": s.307(1).
"trial": s.307(1).
"witness": s.271E(4).

GENERAL NOTE

A4-547.3 First, s.281A(1) provides that if the witness has previously identified the accused in an identification procedure before the start of the trial then that witness need not make a dock identification at the trial. A report is lodged naming the person that the witness has identified in the procedure as the accused. That report becomes a production in the case.

Secondly, the presumption of correct identification does not apply unless the prosecutor has served a copy of the report on the accused with a notice that it is intended to rely upon that statutory presumption. The prosecutor has not less than 14 clear days before the trial to serve the documents. The accused may not more than seven days after the service of the copy report serve a notice on the prosecutor that it is intended to challenge the facts stated in the report. Special circumstances may allow a later service of such a notice by an accused.

[THE NEXT PARAGRAPH IS A4-548]

Sufficient evidence

Evidence as to controlled drugs and medicinal products

A4-548 **282.**—(1) For the purposes of any criminal proceedings, evidence given by an authorised forensic scientist, either orally or in a report purporting to be signed by him, that a substance which satisfies either of the conditions specified in subsection (2) below is—

(a) a particular controlled drug or medicinal product; or
(b) a particular product which is listed in the British Pharmacopoeia as containing a particular controlled drug or medicinal product,

shall, subject to subsection (3) below, be sufficient evidence of that fact notwithstanding that no analysis of the substance has been carried out.

(2) Those conditions are—

(a) that the substance is in a sealed container bearing a label identifying the contents of the container; or
(b) that the substance has a characteristic appearance having regard to its size, shape, colour and manufacturer's mark.

(3) A party proposing to rely on subsection (1) above ("the first party") shall, not less than 14 days before the relevant diet, serve on the other party ("the second party")—

(a) a notice to that effect; and
(b) where the evidence is contained in a report, a copy of the report,

and if the second party serves on the first party, not more than seven days after the date of service of the notice on him, a notice that he does not accept the evidence as to the identity of the substance, subsection (1) above shall not apply in relation to that evidence.

(3A) In subsection (3) above, "the relevant diet" means—

(a) in the case of proceedings in the High Court, the preliminary hearing;
(b) in any other case, the trial diet.

(4) A notice or copy report served in accordance with subsection (3) above shall be served in such manner as may be prescribed by Act of Adjournal; and a written execution purporting to be signed by the person who served the notice or copy together with, where appropriate, the relevant post office receipt shall be sufficient evidence of such service.

(5) In this section—

"controlled drug" has the same meaning as in the Misuse of Drugs Act 1971; and

"medicinal product" has the same meaning as in the Medicines Act 1968.

AMENDMENTS

Subs.(3) as amended, and subs.(3A) inserted, by Criminal Procedure (Amendment) (Scotland) Act 2004 (asp 5) s.25 and Sch.1 para.51. Brought into force on February 1, 2005 by SSI 2004/405 (C.28) art.2.

DEFINITIONS

"controlled drug": s.282(5) and s.2(1)(a) of the Misuse of Drugs Act 1971 (c.38). A4-548.1
"medicinal product": s.282(5) and s.130(1) of the Medicines Act 1968 (c.67).
"trial": s.307(1).

[THE NEXT PARAGRAPH IS A4-549]

GENERAL NOTE

This section, introduced by the Criminal Justice (Scotland) Act 1995, s.25, enables evidence to be given, in certain circumstances, by an authorised forensic scientist in any criminal proceedings to the effect that a substance is listed in British Pharmacopoiea as being, or containing, a controlled drug or medicinal product. Instead of demanding the conduct of a chemical examination to establish identification, s.282 allows forensic identification to be achieved by reference either to the label on a sealed container or, as is more common, to the size, colour, shape and markings on the substance; this latter method is commonplace in medical practice and in the pharmaceutical industry and there seems little virtue in requiring a higher standard than that in criminal proceedings particularly when subs.(3)(b) preserves the rights of the other party to give formal notice of challenge to that evidence. **A4-549**

Any such forensic report can be served in accordance with subs.(3) not less than 14 days prior to trial may broadly follow the style of Form 27, and must be challenged within seven days of the date of service, not receipt. Such a report must be served on all other parties in the proceedings.

Evidence as to time and place of video surveillance recordings

283.—(1) For the purposes of any criminal proceedings, a certificate purporting to be signed by a person responsible for the operation of a video surveillance system and certifying— **A4-550**

(a) the location of the camera;
(b) the nature and extent of the person's responsibility for the system; and
(c) that visual images (and any sounds) recorded on a particular device are images (and sounds), recorded by the system, of (or relating to) events which occurred at a place specified in the certificate at a time and date so specified,

shall, subject to subsection (2) below, be sufficient evidence of the matters contained in the certificate.

(2) A party proposing to rely on subsection (1) above ("the first party") shall, not less than 14 days before the relevant diet, serve on the other party ("the second party") a copy of the certificate and, if the second party serves on the first party, not more than seven days after the date of service of the copy certificate on him, a notice that he does not accept the evidence contained in the certificate, subsection (1) above shall not apply in relation to that evidence.

(2A) In subsection (2) above, "the relevant diet" means—

(a) in the case of proceedings in the High Court, the preliminary hearing;
(b) in any other case, the trial diet.

(3) A copy certificate or notice served in accordance with subsection (2) above shall be served in such manner as may be prescribed by Act of Adjournal; and a written execution purporting to be signed by the person who served the copy or notice together with, where appropriate, the relevant post office receipt shall be sufficient evidence of such service.

(4) In this section, "video surveillance system" means apparatus consisting of a camera mounted in a fixed position and associated equipment for transmitting and

recording visual images of events occurring in any place (and includes associated equipment for transmitting and recording sounds relating to such events).

Amendments

Subs.(2) amended, and subs.(2A) inserted, by Criminal Procedure (Amendment) (Scotland) Act 2004 (asp 5) s.25 and Sch.1 para.52. Brought into force on February 1, 2005 by SSI 2004/405 (C.28) art.2.

Subs.(1) as amended by Criminal Proceedings etc (Reform) (Scotland) Act 2007 (asp 6) s.80, Sch. para.23. Brought into force on December 10, 2007 by SSI 2007/479 (C.40) art.3 and Sch.

Definition

A4-550.1 "video surveillance systems": s.283(4).

[THE NEXT PARAGRAPH IS A4-551]

General Note

A4-551 As originally propounded this evidential concession was intended to provide a convenient means of introducing the evidence garnered from city centre surveillance systems without the necessity of requiring the formality of attendance by the system's operators at court. Evidence from home or private CCTV sources was expected to be introduced using the provisions of s.279 and Sch.8 to the Act. The distinction is now more apparent than real, and often resolved by agreement of evidence during preliminary diets rather than adherence to the formal mechanisms of service and challenge set out in subss.(2) and (3). The section provides an evidential concession but is not, of course, the sole means of introducing such evidence (see *Procurator Paisley v McLean* [2019] SAC (Crim) 2).

Any want of compliance in completion of the provenance certification should ordinarily be challenged timeously as subs.(2) states, not in the course of the trial itself (see *Wishart v Procurator Fiscal, Kirkcaldy* 2021 SAC (Crim) 1 when it should no longer be entertained. No such notice of challenge is necessary where the issue is either the applicability of the CCTV material to the libel, or the factual interpretation of the images shown.

Issues of interpretation of CCTV images, and admissibility, have also developed in case law. Where images demand expert assessment (for example as to the ages of children shown in indecent images or the lighting pattern of vehicles, or case linkage analysis) the witness' expertise, and the soundness of the methodology used, will have to be established—a civil case, *Cordia v Kennedy* [2016] UKSC 6 affords valuable guidance and, as examples, see *HDJS v HM Advocate* [2018] HCJAC 14; *Young v HM Advocate*, 2014 S.C.C.R. 649. Generally, where the imagery is of sound quality, and its provenance is established or agreed, an actus reus captured on CCTV is real evidence in its own right. It then falls to the masters of fact—jury or judge—to assess the criminality in what is shown; it does not require to be filtered through a witness' eyes. See *Gubinas v HM Advocate*, 2017 S.C.C.R. 463; *Gannon v HM Advocate* [2017] HCJAC 58 and *Shuttleton v Orr* [2019] HCJAC 12.

Henderson v Shanks [2019] SAC (Crim) 18 may be seen as something of a watershed; the Sheriff Appeal Court viewed the same CCTV material of alleged dangerous driving as had the summary sheriff and reached entirely opposite conclusions as to fact and law; the conviction was quashed.

Evidence in relation to fingerprints

A4-552 **284.**—(1) For the purposes of any criminal proceedings, a certificate purporting to be signed by a person authorised in that behalf by a chief constable and certifying that relevant physical data (within the meaning of section 18(7A) of this Act) was taken from or provided by thereon were taken from a person designated in the certificate at a time, date and place specified therein shall, subject to subsection (2) below, be sufficient evidence of the facts contained in the certificate.

(2) A party proposing to rely on subsection (1) above ("the first party") shall, not less than 14 days before the relevant diet, serve on any other party to the proceedings a copy of the certificate, and, if that other party serves on the first party, not more than seven days after the date of service of the copy on him, a notice that he does not accept the evidence contained in the certificate, subsection (1) above shall not apply in relation to that evidence.

(2A) Where the first party does not serve a copy of the certificate on any other party as mentioned in subsection (2) above, he shall not be entitled to rely on subsection (1) above as respects that party.

(2B) In subsection (2) above, "the relevant diet" means—

(a) in the case of proceedings in the High Court, the preliminary hearing;

(b) in any other case, the trial diet.

(3) A copy certificate or notice served in accordance with subsection (2) above shall be served in such manner as may be prescribed by Act of Adjournal; and a written execution purporting to be signed by the person who served the copy or notice together with, where appropriate, the relevant post office receipt shall be sufficient evidence of such service.

AMENDMENTS

Subs.(1) substituted by Crime and Punishment (Scotland) Act 1997 s.47(4)(a) with effect from 1 August 1997 in terms of SI 1997/1712 art.3.

Subss.(2) and (2A) substituted by s.47(4)(b) of the 1997 Act and effected by the Order specified above.

Subs.(2) as amended by Criminal Justice (Scotland) Act 2003 (asp 7) Pt 8 s.54. Brought into force on 27 June 2003 by SSI 2003/288 (C.14).

Subs.(2) as amended, and subs.(2B) inserted, by Criminal Procedure (Amendment) (Scotland) Act 2004 (asp 5) s.25 and Sch.1 para.53. Brought into force on 1 February 2005 by SSI 2004/405 (C.28) art.2.

DEFINITIONS

"constable": s.307(1) and s.51(1) of the Police (Scotland) Act 1967. A4-552.1

"relevant physical data": s.18(7A) of the 1995 Act.

[THE NEXT PARAGRAPH IS A4-553]

GENERAL NOTE

The reforms to s.284 introduced by the Crime and Punishment (Scotland) Act 1997 s.47(4) further abbreviates the procedures for presentation of fingerprint evidence in the Scottish criminal courts. Formerly certificates signed by two police constables on any fingerprint report, giving details of the obtaining of the prints from the person named in the certificate, provided a sufficiency of evidence unless challenged timeously: from 1 August 1997 certification of the taking of relevant physical data can be made by one authorised person, a role which can obviously be undertaken by nominated civilian staff. Ultimately the aim seems to be for a member of staff at the database end, rather than the officers present with the person being fingerprinted, to certify the form produced by the Livescan equipment. A4-553

Subsections (2) and (2A) require the party relying upon this provision to serve a copy of the signed certificate on the affected party to the proceedings and, once served, the evidence in the copy shall be sufficient, cannot be challenged and will be conclusive as to its contents. With effect from 27 June 2003, subs.(2) reinstates the right of an accused to challenge the sufficiency of the certificate evidence served upon him; the Crime and Punishment (Scotland) Act 1997 s.47(4) had created a conclusive presumption which it was felt (on an admittedly narrow construction) might not be Convention-compliant.

Any party relying upon these provisions (almost invariably the Crown) will have to be able to produce executions of service of documentation to the court.

Proof of previous convictions

Previous convictions: proof, general

285.—(1) A previous conviction may be proved against any person in any criminal proceedings by the production of such evidence of the conviction as is mentioned in this subsection and subsections (2) to (6) below and by showing that his fingerprints and those of the person convicted are the fingerprints of the same person. A4-554

(2) A certificate purporting to be signed by or on behalf of the chief constable of the Police Service of Scotland or the Commissioner of Police of the Metropolis, containing particulars relating to a conviction extracted from the criminal records kept by the person by whom, or on whose behalf, the certificate is signed, and certifying that the copies of the fingerprints contained in the certificate are copies of the fingerprints appearing from the said records to have been taken in pursuance of rules for the time being in force under sections 12 and 39 of the Prisons (Scotland) Act 1989, or regulations for the time being in force under section 16 of the Prison Act 1952, from the person convicted on the occasion of the conviction or on the occasion of his last conviction, shall be sufficient evidence of the conviction or, as the

case may be, of his last conviction and of all preceding convictions and that the copies of the fingerprints produced on the certificate are copies of the fingerprints of the person convicted.

(3) Where a person has been apprehended and detained in the custody of the police in connection with any criminal proceedings, a certificate purporting to be signed by the chief constable concerned or a person authorised on his behalf, certifying that the fingerprints produced thereon were taken from him while he was so detained, shall be sufficient evidence in those proceedings that the fingerprints produced on the certificate are the fingerprints of that person.

(4) A certificate purporting to be signed by or on behalf of the governor of a prison or of a remand centre in which any person has been detained in connection with any criminal proceedings, certifying that the fingerprints produced thereon were taken from him while he was so detained, shall be sufficient evidence in those proceedings that the fingerprints produced on the certificate are the fingerprints of that person.

(5) A certificate purporting to be signed by or on behalf of the chief constable of the Police Service of Scotland, and certifying that the fingerprints, copies of which are certified as mentioned in subsection (2) above by or on behalf of the chief constable of the Police Service of Scotland or the Commissioner of Police of the Metropolis to be copies of the fingerprints of a person previously convicted and the fingerprints certified by or on behalf of a chief constable or a governor as mentioned in subsection (3) or (4) above, or otherwise shown, to be the fingerprints of the person against whom the previous conviction is sought to be proved, are the fingerprints of the same person, shall be sufficient evidence of the matter so certified.

(6) An extract conviction of any crime committed in any part of the United Kingdom bearing to have been issued by an officer whose duties include the issue of extract convictions shall be received in evidence without being sworn to by witnesses.

(7) It shall be competent to prove a previous conviction or any fact relevant to the admissibility of the conviction by witnesses, although the name of any such witness is not included in the list served on the accused; and the accused shall be entitled to examine witnesses with regard to such conviction or fact.

(8) An official of any prison in which the accused has been detained on such conviction shall be a competent and sufficient witness to prove its application to the accused, although he may not have been present in court at the trial to which such conviction relates.

(9) The method of proving a previous conviction authorised by this section shall be in addition to any other method of proving the conviction.

(10) In this section "fingerprint" includes any record of the skin of a person's finger created by a device approved by the Secretary of State under section 18(7B) of this Act.

Amendments

Subs.(2) substituted by Crime and Punishment (Scotland) Act 1997 (c.48) s.59(2) with effect from 1 August 1997 as enacted by SI 1997/1712 art.3.

Subs.(5) substituted by the 1997 Act s.59(3) and enacted from 1 August 1997 by the above Order.

Subs.(10) inserted by the 1997 Act s.47(5) and enacted from 1 August 1997 by the above Order.

Subs.(2), (5) as amended by Police and Fire Reform (Scotland) Act 2012 (Consequential Modifications and Savings) Order 2013 (SSI 2013/119) Sch.1 para.16(a) and (b) (effective 1 April 2013).

Definitions

A4-554.1 "conviction": s.307(5).

General Note

This section carries over the provisions relating to proof of previous convictions by use of proved fingerprints. This procedure can be deployed to prove previous convictions which have been disputed by the accused or, in limited circumstances, as evidence in support of a substantive charge (see also s.286 below). Use is made of the fingerprint forms completed at the time of the accused's admission to a prison (subs.(4)) or when routinely detained in police custody in relation to the charges libelled (subs.(3)). A4-555

It is not necessary to list as witnesses those prison officials or court officers whose only role is to speak to the fact of a previous conviction or extract conviction.

Certification was previously the responsibility of the Chief Constable of Strathclyde Police but, following amendments to the Police (Scotland) Act 1967 (c.77) made by s.46 of the 1997 Act, responsibility for this core service now lies with the Scottish Secretary.

The development of "livescan" electronic fingerprinting is reflected in subs.(10). See the discussion at A4-49 above. The Electronic Fingerprinting etc. Device Approval (Scotland) Order 1997 (SI 1997/1939) approved the use of the Digital Biometrics Corporation (D.B.I.) Tenprinter 1133S with effect from August 8, 1997.

Previous convictions: proof in support of substantive charge

286.—(1) Without prejudice to section 285(6) to (9) or, as the case may be, section 166 of this Act, where proof of a previous conviction [including a conviction by a court in a member State of the European Union] is competent in support of a substantive charge, any such conviction or an extract of it shall, if— A4-556

(a) it purports to relate to the accused and to be signed by the clerk of court having custody of the record containing the conviction; and

(b) a copy of it has been served on the accused not less than 14 days before the relevant diet,

be sufficient evidence of the application of the conviction to the accused unless, within seven days of the date of service of the copy on him, he serves notice on the prosecutor that he denies that it applies to him.

(1A) In subsection (1)(b) above, "the relevant diet" means—

(a) in the case of proceedings in the High Court, the preliminary hearing;

(b) in any other case, the trial diet.

(2) A copy of a conviction or extract conviction served under subsection (1) above shall be served on the accused in such manner as may be prescribed by Act of Adjournal, and a written execution purporting to be signed by the person who served the copy together with, where appropriate, the relevant post office receipt shall be sufficient evidence of service of the copy.

(3) The reference in subsection (1)(a) above to "the clerk of court having custody of the record containing the conviction" includes, in relation to a previous conviction by a court in [a] member State of the European Union, a reference to any officer of that court or of that State having such custody.

Amendments

Subs.(3) inserted by Criminal Justice (Scotland) Act 2003 (asp 7) Pt 8 s.57(3). Brought into force on 27 June 2003 by SSI 2003/288 (C.14).

Subs.(1)(b) as amended, and subs.(1A) inserted, by Criminal Procedure (Amendment) (Scotland) Act 2004 (asp 5) s.25 and Sch.1 para.54. Brought into force on 1 February 2005 by SSI 2004/405 (C.28) art.2.

Words in subs.(1) were inserted by the Criminal Justice (EU Exit) (Scotland) (Amendment etc.) Regulations 2020 (SSI 2020/339) reg.13(16)(a) (effective 31 December 2020 subject to transitional and saving provision specified in reg.16 of those Regulations.

Word in subs.(3) were inserted by the Criminal Justice (EU Exit) (Scotland) (Amendment etc.) Regulations 2020 (SSI 2020/339) reg.13(16)(b) (effective 31 December 2020 subject to transitional and saving provision specified in reg.16 of those Regulations.

Definitions

"previous conviction": s.307(5). A4-556.1

"trial": s.307(1).

GENERAL NOTE

A4-557 Where it is necessary to lead evidence of a conviction in support of a substantive charge, this section provides for the use in evidence, of a relevant certified extract conviction. A copy of the extract conviction has to be served on the accused not less than 14 days before trial and any challenge to it must be intimated within seven days of service. Use of a s.286 certificate may well serve to pre-empt any such challenge. In solemn proceedings the completed execution of service should be lodged as a production.

See generally the discussion on the admissibility of evidence of previous convictions in the notes to ss.101 and 166 above and, in regard to European Union convictions, the notes to ss.285 and 286A of the Act.

Proof of previous conviction by court in other member State

A4-557.1 **286A.**—(1) A previous conviction by a court in [a] member State of the European Union may be proved against any person in any criminal proceedings by the production of evidence of the conviction and by showing that his fingerprints and those of the person convicted are the fingerprints of the same person.

(2) A certificate—

(a) bearing—

(i) to have been sealed with the official seal of a Minister of the State in question; and

(ii) to contain particulars relating to a conviction extracted from the criminal records of that State; and

(b) including copies of fingerprints and certifying that those copies—

(i) are of fingerprints appearing from those records to have been taken from the person convicted on the occasion of the conviction, or on the occasion of his last conviction; and

(ii) would be admissible in evidence in criminal proceedings in that State as a record of the skin of that person's fingers,

shall be sufficient evidence of the conviction or, as the case may be, of the person's last conviction and of all preceding convictions and that the copies of the fingerprints included in the certificate are copies of the fingerprints of the person convicted.

(3) A conviction bearing to have been—

(a) extracted from the criminal records of the State in question; and

(b) issued by an officer of that State whose duties include the issuing of such extracts,

shall be received in evidence without being sworn to by witnesses.

(4) Subsection (9) of section 285 of this Act applies in relation to this section as it does in relation to that section.

AMENDMENTS

Section 286A inserted by Criminal Justice (Scotland) Act 2003 (asp 7) Pt 8 s.57(4). Brought into force on 27 June 2003 by SSI 2003/288 (C.14).

Words in subs.(1) were substituted by the Criminal Justice (EU Exit) (Scotland) (Amendment etc.) Regulations 2020 (SSI 2020/339) reg.13(17) (effective 31 December 2020 subject to transitional and saving provision specified in reg.16 of those Regulations.

GENERAL NOTE

A4-557.2 This section provides for proof by fingerprint certificate of a previous conviction imposed upon an accused by a member state of the European Union, when included in a schedule of convictions. The provision follows the terms of s.285 of the Act which apply to proof of United Kingdom convictions.

PART XIII – MISCELLANEOUS

Lord Advocate

Demission from office of Lord Advocate and Solicitor General for Scotland

A4-558 **287.**—(1) All indictments which have been raised at the instance of Her Majesty's Advocate shall remain effective notwithstanding the holder of the office of Lord Advocate subsequently having died or demitted office and may be taken up and proceeded with by his successor or the Solicitor General.

(2) During any period when the office of Lord Advocate is vacant it shall be lawful to indict accused persons at the instance of Her Majesty's Advocate or the Solicitor General.

(2A) Any such indictments in proceedings at the instance of the Solicitor General may be signed by the Solicitor General.

(2B) All indictments which have been raised at the instance of the Solicitor General shall remain effective notwithstanding the holder of the office of Solicitor General subsequently having died or demitted office and may be taken up and proceeded with by his successor or the Lord Advocate.

(2C) Subsection (2D) applies during any period when the offices of Lord Advocate and Solicitor General are both vacant.

(2D) It is lawful to indict accused persons at the instance of Her Majesty's Advocate.

(3) The advocates depute shall not demit office when a Lord Advocate dies or demits office but shall continue in office until their successors receive commissions.

(4) The advocates depute and procurators fiscal shall have power, notwithstanding any vacancy in the office of Lord Advocate or Solicitor General, to take up and proceed with any indictment which—

(a) by virtue of subsection (1) or (2B) above, remains effective;
(b) by virtue of subsection (2) above, is raised at the instance of the Solicitor General; or
(c) by virtue of subsection (2D) above, is raised at the instance of Her Majesty's Advocate.

(5) For the purposes of this Act, where, but for this subsection, demission of office by one Law Officer would result in the offices of both being vacant, he or, where both demit office on the same day, the person demitting the office of Lord Advocate shall be deemed to continue in office until the warrant of appointment of the person succeeding to the office of Lord Advocate is granted.

(6) The Lord Advocate shall enter upon the duties of his office immediately upon the grant of his warrant of appointment.

AMENDMENTS

Subs.(6) as amended by Scotland Act 1998 (Consequential Modifications) (No.1) Order 1999 (SI 1999/1042) art.4 and Sch.2 para.11 and Sch.2, Pt III.

Subss.(2A)–(2D), (4)(c) inserted, title substituted, and subss.(1), (2), (4), (4)(a), (b) as amended, by Criminal Justice and Licensing (Scotland) Act 2010 (asp 13) s.60(4). Brought into force on 13 December 2010 (subject to savings provisions in art.5) by SSI 2010/413 (C.28) art.2 and Sch.1 para. 1.

DEFINITIONS

"indictment": s.307(1). A4-558.1
"procurator fiscal": s.307(1).

GENERAL NOTE

The Lord Advocate has the universal and exclusive title to prosecute on indictment. This section is concerned with the consequences of the decession of office by Lord Advocate. This section puts into statutory form a variety of authorities that have evolved or been passed over the years: see Macdonald *Criminal Law of Scotland* (5th edn) (W. Green, Edinburgh) at p.212. The adoption of the grammatical neuter in the 2010 Act recognises that the holder of the office of Lord Advocate might now be a member of either sex. The section also signals a recognition of the range of constitutional possibilities arising from the death or demission of office of either, or both, of the Law Officers and contains transitional provisions intended to preserve proceedings. In short, the section provides for the continuity of Crown business notwithstanding a change of Lord Advocate. A4-559

Two points are worth noting. First, during any period when the office of Lord Advocate is vacant it shall be lawful to indict accused persons in the name of the Solicitor General then in office: subs.(2). It is clear that such indictments may be taken up by the new Lord Advocate on his appointment: *HM-Solicitor General v Lavelle* (1913) 7 Adam 255. Secondly, the Lord Advocate shall enter upon the duties of his office immediately upon the grant of his warrant: subs.(6). Before this provision the Lord Advocate could not act until the Royal Warrant appointing him reached Crown Office, he was not entitled to act merely on notice of his appointment appearing in the Edinburgh Gazette: *Halliday v Wilson* (1891) 3 White 38.

Only in the most exceptional, and unequivocal, of circumstances can an indication as to the form, and forum, of proceedings by the Procurator Fiscal to a defence agent fetter the Lord Advocate's discretion. See *Murphy v HM Advocate*, 2002 S.L.T. 1416; 2002 S.C.C.R. 969 in which a letter was sent by the Fiscal to the defence agent providing an assessment of the evidence and an indication that petition proceedings would be reduced to summary complaint; this pronouncement had been communicated to the accused without the knowledge or authority of Crown counsel. (The separate issue of whether, given the background, it would be oppressive for the Crown to maintain the proceedings in any form was not explored in this appeal). Refer also to *Cook v HM Advocate*, 2003 G.W.D. 3-66.

Section 287 ought to be read with s.48 of the Scotland Act 1998 (c.46) as the latter provision deals specifically with the Scottish Law Officers. In particular, s.48(2) provides that the Lord Advocate and the Solicitor General may at any time resign and shall do so if Parliament resolves that the Scottish Executive no longer enjoys the confidence of the Parliament. For a definition of which office holders constitute the "Scottish Executive" see s.44(1) of the 1998 Act. It is provided also that where the Lord Advocate resigns in consequence of such a resolution of a lack of confidence, the Lord Advocate shall be deemed to continue in office until the warrant of appointment of the person succeeding to the office of Lord Advocate is granted, but only for the purpose of exercising retained functions (see s.48(3)). The provision made by s.48(3) of the 1998 Act is without prejudice to s.287 of the 1995 Act.

Intimation of proceedings in High Court to Lord Advocate

A4-560 **288.**—(1) In any proceeding in the High Court (other than a proceeding to which the Lord Advocate or a procurator fiscal is a party) it shall be competent for the court to order intimation of such proceeding to the Lord Advocate.

(2) On intimation being made to the Lord Advocate under subsection (1) above, the Lord Advocate shall be entitled to appear and be heard in such proceeding.

Definitions

A4-560.1 "High Court": s.307(1).
"procurator fiscal": s.307(1).

General Note

A4-561 This section is probably concerned with Bill of Criminal letters which have not been presented to the Lord Advocate for concurrence or with petitions to the *nobile officium* of the High Court of Justiciary. The ordinary practice would be to intimate to the Lord Advocate but individuals proceeding without legal representation, for example, might not know of that practice.

Convention rights and EU law compatibility issues, and devolution issues

Right of Advocate General to take part in proceedings

A4-561.0.1 **288ZA.**—(1) The Advocate General for Scotland may take part as a party in criminal proceedings so far as they relate to a compatibility issue.

(2) In this section "compatibility issue" means a question, arising in criminal proceedings, as to—

- (a) whether a public authority has acted (or proposes to act)—
  - (i) in a way which is made unlawful by section 6(1) of the Human Rights Act 1998, or
  - (ii) in a way which is incompatible with EU law, or
- (b) whether an Act of the Scottish Parliament or any provision of an Act of the Scottish Parliament is incompatible with any of the Convention rights or with EU law.

(3) In subsection (2)—

- (a) "public authority" has the same meaning as in section 6 of the Human Rights Act 1998;
- (b) references to acting include failing to act;
- (c) "EU law" has the meaning given by section 126(9) of the Scotland Act 1998.

Amendments

Section 288ZA inserted by Scotland Act 2012 (c.11) s.34(3). Brought into force on 22 April 2013 by SI 2013/6 art.2(a).

General Note

In *Carlin v HM Advocate*, 2013 S.C.C.R. 706; 2013 G.W.D. 34-669 the appellant had his application to lodge late an intimation of an intention to appeal refused. It was said to be highly questionable whether the appellant should be allowed to resurrect an appeal four years and nine months after an earlier intimation of such intent had been withdrawn. A4-561.0.2

[THE NEXT PARAGRAPH IS A4-561.0.4]

References of compatibility issues to the High Court or Supreme Court

288ZB.—(1) Where a compatibility issue has arisen in criminal proceedings before a court, other than a court consisting of two or more judges of the High Court, the court may, instead of determining it, refer the issue to the High Court. A4-561.0.4

(2) The Lord Advocate or the Advocate General for Scotland, if a party to criminal proceedings before a court, other than a court consisting of two or more judges of the High Court, may require the court to refer to the High Court any compatibility issue which has arisen in the proceedings.

(3) The High Court may, instead of determining a compatibility issue referred to it under subsection (2), refer it to the Supreme Court.

(4) Where a compatibility issue has arisen in criminal proceedings before a court consisting of two or more judges of the High Court, otherwise than on a reference, the court may, instead of determining it, refer it to the Supreme Court.

(5) The Lord Advocate or the Advocate General for Scotland, if a party to criminal proceedings before a court consisting of two or more judges of the High Court, may require the court to refer to the Supreme Court any compatibility issue which has arisen in the proceedings otherwise than on a reference.

(6) On a reference to the Supreme Court under this section—

(a) the powers of the Supreme Court are exercisable only for the purpose of determining the compatibility issue

(b) for that purpose the Court may make any change in the formulation of that issue that it thinks necessary in the interests of justice.

(7) When it has determined a compatibility issue on a reference under this section, the Supreme Court must remit the proceedings to the High Court.

(8) An issue referred to the High Court or the Supreme Court under this section is referred to it for determination.

(9) In this section "compatibility issue" has the meaning given by section 288ZA.

Amendments

Section 288ZB inserted by Scotland Act 2012 (c.11) s.35. Brought into force on 22 April 2013 by SI 2013/6 art.2(b).

General Note

Dunn v Porch, 2016 S.C.C.R. 55 is a rare, and bemusing, example of a referral by the court at first instance following the raising of a compatibility issue by P, who had been refused variation of his bail conditions (which, despite her views being made known to the Crown, barred him from contact with his partner pending trial). P asserted that Crown opposition to variation was in pursuit of a blanket policy which offended against art.8 of ECHR but was opaque in identifying any incompatible act of the bail judge, who also had to balance the public interest in reaching a bail decision. A4-561.0.5

Three procedural points are of note; first, in a novel twist the complainer was accorded a role as a party to the hearing at first instance and was represented at the appeal hearing, which resolved that she had no locus and that there was no incompatibility issue since her art.8 rights were preserved by other means; secondly, the court, following *O'Leary v HM Advocate* [2014] HCJAC 45 reiterated that before initiating a referral on compatibility grounds, the presiding judge was required to undertake an analysis and posit a solution for consideration by the High Court; thirdly, it has to be doubted that that court could do anything more than adjudge upon the alleged incompatibility, the section providing the Appeal Court with no remedial powers.

Rights of appeal for Advocate General: compatibility issues and devolution issues

A4-561.1 **288A.**—(1) This section applies where—

(a) a person is acquitted or convicted of a charge (whether on indictment or in summary proceedings), and

(b) the Advocate General for Scotland was a party to the proceedings.

(2) Where the Advocate General for Scotland was a party in pursuance of paragraph 6 of Schedule 6 to the Scotland Act 1998 (devolution issues), the Advocate General may refer to the High Court for their opinion any devolution issue which has arisen in the proceedings

(2A) Where the Advocate General for Scotland was a party in pursuance of section 288ZA, the Advocate General may refer to the High Court for their opinion any compatibility issue (within the meaning of that section) which has arisen in the proceedings.

(2B) If a reference is made under subsection (2) or (2A) the Clerk of Justiciary shall send to the person acquitted or convicted and to any solicitor who acted for that person at the trial a copy of the reference and intimation of the date fixed by the Court for a hearing.

(3) The person may, not later than seven days before the date so fixed, intimate in writing to the Clerk of Justiciary and to the Advocate General for Scotland either—

(a) that he elects to appear personally at the hearing, or

(b) that he elects to be represented by counsel at the hearing,

but, except by leave of the Court on cause shown, and without prejudice to his right to attend, he shall not appear or be represented at the hearing other than by and in conformity with an election under this subsection.

(4) Where there is no intimation under subsection (3)(b), the High Court shall appoint counsel to act at the hearing as amicus curiae.

(5) The costs of representation elected under subsection (3)(b) or of an appointment under subsection (4) shall, after being taxed by the Auditor of the Court of Session, be paid by the Advocate General for Scotland out of money provided by Parliament.

(6) The opinion on the point referred under subsection (2) or (2A) shall not affect the acquittal or (as the case may be) conviction in the trial.

Amendments

Section 288A inserted by Scotland Act 1998 (c.46) Sch.8 para.32 and brought into force by SI 1998/3178 art.2, Sch.3 (effective 6 May 1999).

Subss.(1), (2) and (6) as amended by Scotland Act 2012 (c.11) s.34(5)-(8). Brought into force on 22 April 2013 by SI 2013/6 art.2(c).

[THE NEXT PARAGRAPH IS A4-561.3]

General Note

A4-561.3 The Advocate General for Scotland is to be the new law officer with the responsibility for Scottish legal matters in regard to the United Kingdom. Where questions arise as to the competency of legislation, or the actings of some members of the Scottish Executive or related questions, the Advocate General may institute proceedings for the determination of such a devolution issue. It follows then that there requires to be a mode of appeal and that is provided for by s.288A and s.288B of the 1995 Act.

In *O'Neill v HM Advocate*, 2013 S.C.C.R. 401 (SC) a question arose as to whether certain appeals were to be dealt with as devolution issues or compatibility issues. It was held, first, that the delay ground was a convertible devolution issue and so became a compatibility issue; and, secondly, the High Court of Justiciary had statutory power to refer any devolution issue to the Supreme Court, and that that was what seemed to have happened in respect of the apparent bias ground, which also fell to be treated as a compatibility issue.

Appeals to the Supreme Court: compatibility issues

288AA.—(1) For the purpose of determining any compatibility issue an appeal lies to the Supreme Court against a determination in criminal proceedings by a court of two or more judges of the High Court. A4-561.3.1

(2) On an appeal under this section—

(a) the powers of the Supreme Court are exercisable only for the purpose of determining the compatibility issue;

(b) for that purpose the Court may make any change in the formulation of that issue that it thinks necessary in the interests of justice.

(3) When it has determined the compatibility issue the Supreme Court must remit the proceedings to the High Court.

(4) In this section "compatibility issue" has the same meaning as in section 288ZA.

(5) An appeal under this section against a determination lies only with the permission of the High Court or, failing that permission, with the permission of the Supreme Court.

(6) Subsection (5) does not apply if it is an appeal by the Lord Advocate or the Advocate General for Scotland against a determination by the High Court of a compatibility issue referred to it under section 288ZB(2).

(7) An application to the High Court for permission under subsection (5) must be made—

(a) within 28 days of the date of the determination against which the appeal lies, or

(b) within such longer period as the High Court considers equitable having regard to all the circumstances.

(8) An application to the Supreme Court for permission under subsection (5) must be made—

(a) within 28 days of the date on which the High Court refused permission under that subsection, or

(b) within such longer period as the Supreme Court considers equitable having regard to all the circumstances.

AMENDMENTS

Section 288AA inserted by Scotland Act 2012 (c.11) s.36(6). Brought into force on 22 April 2013 by SI 2013/6 art.2(c).

[THE NEXT PARAGRAPH IS A4-561.4]

Appeals to the Supreme Court: general

288B.—(1) This section applies where the Supreme Court determines an appeal under section 288AA of this Act or paragraph 13(a) of Schedule 6 to the Scotland Act 1998 against a determination by the High Court in the ordinary course of proceedings. A4-561.4

(2) The determination of the appeal shall not affect any earlier acquittal or earlier quashing of any conviction in the proceedings.

(3) Subject to subsection (2) above, the High Court shall have the same powers in relation to the proceedings when remitted to it by the Supreme Court as it would have if it were considering the proceedings otherwise than as a trial court.

AMENDMENTS

Section 288B inserted by Scotland Act 1998 (c.46) Sch.8 para.32 and brought into force by SI 1998/3178 art.2, Sch.3 (effective 6 May 1999).

Subss.(1) and (3) as amended by Constitutional Reform Act 2005 (c.4) s.40(9) and Sch.9 para.86. Brought into force on 1 October 2009 by SI 2009/1604 art.2(d).

Subs.(1) as amended by Scotland Act 2012 (c.11) s.36(8)-(9). Brought into force on 22 April 2013 by SI 2013/6 art.2(c).

Dockets and charges in sex cases

Dockets for charges of sexual offences

A4-561.4.1 **288BA.**—(1) An indictment or a complaint may include a docket which specifies any act or omission that is connected with a sexual offence charged in the indictment or complaint.

(2) Here, an act or omission is connected with such an offence charged if it—

(a) is specifiable by way of reference to a sexual offence, and

(b) relates to—

(i) the same event as the offence charged, or

(ii) a series of events of which that offence is also part.

(3) The docket is to be in the form of a note apart from the offence charged.

(4) It does not matter whether the act or omission, if it were instead charged as an offence, could not competently be dealt with by the court (including as particularly constituted) in which the indictment or complaint is proceeding.

(5) Where under subsection (1) a docket is included in an indictment or a complaint, it is to be presumed that—

(a) the accused person has been given fair notice of the prosecutor's intention to lead evidence of the act or omission specified in the docket, and

(b) evidence of the act or omission is admissible as relevant.

(6) The references in this section to a sexual offence are to—

(a) an offence under the Sexual Offences (Scotland) Act 2009,

(b) any other offence involving a significant sexual element.

Amendments

Section 288BA inserted by Criminal Justice and Licensing (Scotland) Act 2010 (asp 13) s.63. Brought into force on 1 December 2010 by SSI 2010/357 (C.21) art.2.

Definitions

A4-561.4.2 "a sexual offence": s.288BA(6).

General Note

A4-561.4.3 This section permits as a matter of relevancy a note apart from the offence charged on an indictment or a summary complaint, which note specifies any act or omission that is connected with the sexual offence charged. The note seems to suggest a possibility of evidence being led in much the same sort of way that similar fact evidence is led in English law.

The origins of s.288BA might be thought to flow from *HM Advocate v Joseph*, 1929 J.C. 55; 1929 S.L.T. 414. Certainly, that is a decision of a single judge on circuit. Yet, having regard to the impressive range of authorities in Scots and English law (some of which are very early but remain authoritative) provided by the Crown, the point in *Joseph's* case may well be accepted by a modern court convened to consider the same point. A charge of uttering a forged document was intended by the Crown to be proved by evidence that included acts in Belgium. It was held that while the relevant incident in Belgium could not be made the subject of a substantive charge, that incident and the crime charged were sufficiently closely connected to admit evidence relating to that foreign incident being used by the prosecution for the purpose of supporting the other domestic charges. The test would appear from the opinion (at 56–7; 416) to be sufficient connection or "nexus" between the relevant incidents.

Whether that earlier decision was relied upon by the Crown over the subsequent years is uncertain but perhaps the point was never put in issue. More recently, in *Climent v HM Advocate* [2015] HCJAC 92; 2015 S.C.L. 965; 2015 S.C.C.R. 423, in the context of the evidence of crimes in Scotland, there was apparently relevant evidence of an event in France. However, the evidence of Parisian episodes had not be presented to the jury as capable of providing corroboration of any charges, and for that reason inter alia a specific conviction was quashed.

A docket might be added to include charges deleted from the indictment where their inclusion would be incompetent for time bar reasons and the court had refused an extension of that time bar. The conduct complained of in the reported case formed part of a sequence of events capable of providing corroboration of other charges on the indictment in terms of the *Moorov* doctrine: *HM Advocate v AD* [2018] HCJAC 2; 2018 J.C. 109; 2018 S.L.T. 101; 2018 S.C.C.R. 42.

The logic of s.288BA(5)(b) [that there is a statutory presumption of relevancy] when taken with *HM Advocate v AD* must mean that at any police interview prior to a suspect being charged the interviewing officers may fairly ask the suspect questions about events elsewhere in the world outside Scotland if these incidents formed part of a sequence of events capable of providing corroboration for an event in Scotland.

At the very least, and this may be a prosecutor's point, such questioning at interview, while bearing on events outside Scotland of relevance to events within the jurisdiction, would provide fair notice of what might be specified in a docket later: see s.288BA(5)(a). Developments of what constitutes a relevant locus include s.3 of the Domestic Abuse (Scotland) Act 2018 which provides explicitly for an extra-territorial jurisdiction.

Of considerable importance is *HM Advocate v Moynihan* [2018] HCJAC 43 (decided on 8 August 2018 and published 5 March 2019). The indictment against Moynihan contained a single charge of attempted rape in May 2008 and in the docket intimation of an attempt to lead evidence of an act amounting to rape in May 2008, a crime of which the accused had been convicted. The appeal court held that there was no logical basis for treating evidence which relates to a matter which could not competently be formulated as a charge, being already the subject of a conviction, differently from circumstances where a charge would be incompetent for other reasons. There is no logical basis for allowing evidence of an act which, by virtue of being time barred, can never amount to more than an allegation, yet refusing to admit evidence of an act which has been established by corroborated evidence: at [14]. Suitable directions were needed to ensure that the jury were not told that the docket matter had already resulted in a conviction against the same accused: at [15]–[16].

In the time between decision and publication of the *HM Advocate v Moynihan* [2018] HCJAC 43; 2019 S.C.C.R. 61. opinion the charge on the indictment was proved to the satisfaction of the jury and the accused sentenced to nine years' imprisonment and his name was ordered to remain on the Sex Offenders Register indefinitely: *HM Advocate v Moynihan*, High Court of Justiciary sitting at Livingston, Lord Woolman, Unreported, 18 February 2019.

Practice Note No.2 of 2016 requires a docket authorised by s.288BA to be read out to the jury for whom copies of the docket ought also to be provided. A trial judge may explain the purpose of the docket in introductory remarks to the jury.

RKS v HM Advocate [2020] HCJAC 19 underlines the importance of any objection to inclusion of a docket in the libel being taken timeously, ordinarily as a preliminary issue. The Appeal Court noted the bar, created by s.118(8) of the Act, on initiating the issue at the appellate stage.

In a first instance case it was held that s.288BA of the 1995 Act, which only applies with sexual offences, has the purpose of establishing a course of conduct: *Corrins v Ogilvie* [2020] SC DUNF 5 (1 August 2019), Sheriff J MacDonald, Dunfermline Sheriff Court, at [29]. Further, "as a general rule the addition of what may be termed a 'docket' is already permissible at common law in summary procedure": [41].

Mixed charges for sexual offences

288BB.—(1) An indictment or a complaint may include a charge that is framed as mentioned in subsection (2) or (3) (or both). **A4-561.4.4**

(2) That is, framed so as to comprise (in a combined form) the specification of more than one sexual offence.

(3) That is, framed so as to—

(a) specify, in addition to a sexual offence, any other act or omission, and

(b) do so in any manner except by way of reference to a statutory offence.

(4) Where a charge in an indictment or a complaint is framed as mentioned in subsection (2) or (3) (or both), the charge is to be regarded as being a single yet cumulative charge.

(5) The references in this section to a sexual offence are to an offence under the Sexual Offences (Scotland) Act 2009.

AMENDMENTS

Section 288BB inserted by Criminal Justice and Licensing (Scotland) Act 2010 (asp 13) s.63. Brought into force on 1 December 2010 by SSI 2010/357 (C.21) art.2.

DEFINITIONS

"a sexual offence": s.288BA(6). **A4-561.4.5**

GENERAL NOTE

A docket in the form of a note apart from a charge on an indictment or on a summary complaint may relevantly be framed so as to cover more than one sexual offence. **A4-561.4.6**

Aggravation by intent to rape

288BC.—(1) Subsection (2) applies as respects a qualifying offence charged in an indictment or a complaint. **A4-561.4.7**

(2) Any specification in the charge that the offence is with intent to rape (however construed) may be given by referring to the statutory offence of rape.

(3) In this section—

(a) the reference to a qualifying offence is to an offence of assault or abduction (and includes attempt, conspiracy or incitement to commit such an offence),

(b) the reference to the statutory offence of rape is (as the case may be) to—

(i) the offence of rape under section 1 of the Sexual Offences (Scotland) Act 2009, or

(ii) the offence of rape of a young child under section 18 of that Act.

AMENDMENTS

Section 288BC inserted by Criminal Justice and Licensing (Scotland) Act 2010 (asp 13) s.63. Brought into force on 1 December 2010 by SSI 2010/357 (C.21) art.2.

DEFINITIONS

A4-561.4.8 "a qualifying offence": s.288BC(3)(a).
"the statutory offence of rape": s.288BC(3)(b).

GENERAL NOTE

A4-561.4.9 Any specification in a charge that the offence is with intent to rape may be given by referring to the statutory offence of rape.

[THE NEXT PARAGRAPH IS A4-561.5]

Trials for sexual offences

Prohibition of personal conduct of defence in cases of certain sexual offences

A4-561.5 **288C.**—(1) An accused charged with a sexual offence to which this section applies is prohibited from conducting his case in person at, or for the purposes of, any relevant hearing in the course of proceedings (other than proceedings in a JP court) in respect of the offence.

(1A) In subsection (1), "relevant hearing" means a hearing at, or for the purposes of, which a witness is to give evidence.

(2) This section applies to the following sexual offences—

(a) rape (whether at common law or under section 1(1) of the Sexual Offences (Scotland) Act 2009 (asp 9));

(b) sodomy;

(c) clandestine injury to women;

(d) abduction of a woman or girl with intent to rape;

(da) abduction with intent to commit the statutory offence of rape;

(e) assault with intent to rape;

(ea) assault with intent to commit the statutory offence of rape;

(f) indecent assault;

(g) indecent behaviour (including any lewd, indecent or libidinous practice or behaviour);

(h) an offence under section 311 (non-consensual sexual acts) or 313 (persons providing care services: sexual offences) of the Mental Health (Care and Treatment) (Scotland) Act 2003;

(i) an offence under any of the following provisions of the Criminal Law (Consolidation) (Scotland) Act 1995 (c.39)—

(i) sections 1 to 3 (incest and related offences);

(ii) section 5 (unlawful sexual intercourse with girl under 13 or 16);

(iii) section 6 (indecent behaviour toward girl between 12 and 16);

(iv) section 7(2) and (3) (procuring by threats etc.);

(v) section 8 (abduction and unlawful detention);
(vi) section 10 (seduction, prostitution, etc. of girl under 16);
(vii) section 13(5)(b) or (c) (homosexual offences);

(j) an offence under any of the following provisions of the Sexual Offences (Scotland) Act 2009 (asp 9)—

(i) section 2 (sexual assault by penetration),
(ii) section 3 (sexual assault),
(iii) section 4 (sexual coercion),
(iv) section 5 (coercing a person into being present during a sexual activity),
(v) section 6 (coercing a person into looking at a sexual image),
(vi) section 7(1) (communicating indecently),
(vii) section 7(2) (causing a person to see or hear an indecent communication),
(viii) section 8 (sexual exposure),
(ix) section 9 (voyeurism),
(x) section 18 (rape of a young child),
(xi) section 19 (sexual assault on a young child by penetration),
(xii) section 20 (sexual assault on a young child),
(xiii) section 21 (causing a young child to participate in a sexual activity),
(xiv) section 22 (causing a young child to be present during a sexual activity),
(xv) section 23 (causing a young child to look at a sexual image),
(xvi) section 24(1) (communicating indecently with a young child),
(xvii) section 24(2) (causing a young child to see or hear an indecent communication),
(xviii) section 25 (sexual exposure to a young child),
(xix) section 26 (voyeurism towards a young child),
(xx) section 28 (having intercourse with an older child),
(xxi) section 29 (engaging in penetrative sexual activity with or towards an older child),
(xxii) section 30 (engaging in sexual activity with or towards an older child),
(xxiii) section 31 (causing an older child to participate in a sexual activity),
(xxiv) section 32 (causing an older child to be present during a sexual activity),
(xxv) section 33 (causing an older child to look at a sexual image),
(xxvi) section 34(1) (communicating indecently with an older child),
(xxvii) section 34(2) (causing an older child to see or hear an indecent communication),
(xxviii) section 35 (sexual exposure to an older child),
(xxix) section 36 (voyeurism towards an older child),
(xxx) section 37(1) (engaging while an older child in sexual conduct with or towards another older child),
(xxxi) section 37(4) (engaging while an older child in consensual sexual conduct with another older child),
(xxxii) section 42 (sexual abuse of trust) but only if the condition set out in section 43(6) of that Act is fulfilled,
(xxxiii) section 46 (sexual abuse of trust of a mentally disordered person); and

(k) attempting to commit any of the offences set out in paragraphs (a) to (j).

(3) This section applies also to an offence in respect of which a court having jurisdiction to try that offence has made an order under subsection (4) below.

(4) Where, in the case of any offence, other than one set out in subsection (2) above, that court is satisfied that there appears to be such a substantial sexual element in the alleged commission of the offence that it ought to be treated, for the purposes of this section, in the same way as an offence set out in that subsection, the court shall, either on the application of the prosecutor or *ex proprio motu*, make an order under this subsection.

(5) The making of such an order does not affect the validity of anything which—

(a) was done in relation to the alleged offence to which the order relates; and

(b) was done before the order was made.

(6) The Scottish Ministers may by order made by statutory instrument vary the sexual offences to which this section applies by virtue of subsection (2) above by modifying that subsection.

(7) No such statutory instrument shall be made, however, unless a draft of it has been laid before and approved by resolution of the Scottish Parliament.

(8) […]

(9) In subsection (2)—

(a) the references to "rape" in paragraphs (d) and (e) are to the offence of rape at common law; and

(b) the references to "the statutory offence of rape" in paragraphs (da) and (ea) are (as the case may be) to—

(i) the offence of rape under section 1 of the Sexual Offences (Scotland) Act 2009, or

(ii) the offence of rape of a young child under section 18 of that Act.

AMENDMENTS

Section 288C inserted by Sexual Offences (Procedure and Evidence) (Scotland) Act 2002 (asp 9) s.1. Brought into force by SSI 2002/443 (C.24) art.4 (effective 1 November 2002).

Subs.(1) as amended by Criminal Justice (Scotland) Act 2003 (asp 7) Pt 2 s.15(2). Brought into force on 25 November 2003 by SSI 2003/475 (C.26) art.2.

Subs.(1)(a), (b) inserted by Criminal Procedure (Amendment) (Scotland) Act 2004 (asp 5) s.4(1). Subs.(1)(b) as amended and subs.(8) inserted by s.25 and Sch.1 para.55 of the 2004 Act. Brought into force on 1 February 2005 by SSI 2004/405 (C.28) art.2.

Subs.(2)(h) as amended by Mental Health (Care and Treatment) (Scotland) Act 2003 (Modification of Enactments) Order 2005 (SSI 2005/465) art.2 and Sch.1 para.27(5) (effective 27 September 2005).

Subs.(2) as amended by Sexual Offences (Scotland) Act 2009 (asp 9) Sch.5 para.2. Brought into force on 1 December 2010 by SSI 2010/357 (C.21) art.2.

Subss.(2)(da), (ea), (9) inserted by Sexual Offences (Scotland) Act 2009 (Supplemental and Consequential Provisions) Order 2010 (SSI 2010/421) Sch.1 para.1 (effective 1 December 2010).

Subs.(8) repealed, subs.(1) amended, by Criminal Justice and Licensing (Scotland) Act 2010 (asp 13) s.69(2). Brought into force on 28 March 2011 (for all purposes in respect of criminal proceedings commenced on or after 28 March 2011, with proceedings taken to have commenced when a report of the case has been received by the procurator fiscal) by SSI 2011/178 (C.15) art.2, Sch.1 para.1.

GENERAL NOTE

A4-561.5.1 Following strongly adverse press comment upon the case of *HM Advocate v Anderson* (Perth High Court, 8 June 2000, unreported), the Scottish Parliament rapidly responded with the Sexual Offences (Procedure and Evidence) (Scotland) Act 2002 (asp 9). Anderson had defended himself and cross-examined the complainers at considerable length. Coming as this did after several highly-publicised trials of a similar nature south of the border, it was felt that reliance upon judicial discretion to marshall cross-examination was not enough. This section sets out procedures to prevent accused representing themselves in trials for a sexual offence or in cases which appear to involve a substantial sexualised element (some species of breach of the peace, for example). It will be noted that these provisions apply to proceedings in any Scottish criminal court and that restrictions are also introduced to debar such an accused from conducting precognition on oath of the complainer (see s.291(4) below).

When a person is taken into police custody following arrest, or exercise of an arrest warrant, in relation to a relevant sexual offence, the police are obliged to advise that he must be represented by a lawyer, selected by him or by the court (see s.20 of the Criminal Justice (Scotland) Act 2016 (asp 1).

The onus is generally upon the Crown to identify the proceedings as fulfilling the demands of s.288C at the time of indicting or serving a complaint by serving notice upon the accused. The only exception to this general rule is found in subs.(4) where the court, *ex proprio motu* or on application of the prosecutor, can initiate an order. Only if the accused asserts that he is not so represented will a s.288C hearing be necessary but in that situation, the court must follow the directions in s.288D and ensure that legal representation, and legal aid, are in place (see the Legal Aid (Scotland) Act 1986, s.22 as now amended).

Due to the differences between summary and solemn procedures, and between procedures in sheriff and jury and High Court trials, different mechanisms exist to meet the demands of s.288C. In summary proceedings the citation is accompanied by a notice from the prosecutor indicating that the accused cannot conduct his own defence, or the accused is advised personally or through his law agent during a personal appearance. Individuals tendering a letter pleading not guilty would have to attend an intermediate diet in due course. Adjournment for the purpose of enquiry as to legal representation is competent for up to 48 hours.

It is submitted that a s.288C hearing has no other purpose and cannot be used as an means to introduce other preliminary issues.

The bar on an accused representing himself in such cases was held not to contravene the right to fair trial enshrined in art.6 of the European Convention on Human Rights. See *McCarthy v HM Advocate*, 2008 S.C.C.R 902. Further, where the indictment libels both sexual offences (which are subject to this section's provisions) and other crimes, the section's provisions apply to all charges in the libel and a motion for separation of charges would only succeed if the accused could demonstrate exposure to material prejudice (*McCarthy* above at [38]).

[THE NEXT PARAGRAPH IS A4-561.6]

Appointment of solicitor by court in such cases

288D.—(1) This section applies in the case of proceedings (other than proceedings in a JP court) in respect of a sexual offence to which section 288C above applies. **A4-561.6**

(2) Where the court ascertains that—

(a) the accused has not engaged a solicitor for the purposes of

(i) the conduct of his case at, or for the purposes of, any relevant hearing (within the meaning of section 288C(1A)) in the proceedings; or

(ii) […]

(iii) the conduct of his case at any commissioner proceedings; or

(b) having engaged a solicitor for those purposes, the accused has dismissed him; or

(c) the accused's solicitor has withdrawn,

then, where the court is not satisfied that the accused intends to engage a solicitor or, as the case may be, another solicitor for those purposes, it shall, at its own hand, appoint a solicitor for those purposes.

(3) A solicitor so appointed is not susceptible to dismissal by the accused or obliged to comply with any instruction by the accused to dismiss counsel.

(4) Subject to subsection (3) above, it is the duty of a solicitor so appointed—

(a) to ascertain and act upon the instructions of the accused; and

(b) where the accused gives no instructions or inadequate or perverse instructions, to act in the best interests of the accused.

(5) In all other respects, a solicitor so appointed has, and may be made subject to, the same obligations and has, and may be given, the same authority as if engaged by the accused; and any employment of and instructions given to counsel by the solicitor shall proceed and be treated accordingly.

(6) Where the court is satisfied that a solicitor so appointed is no longer able to act upon the instructions, or in the best interests, of the accused, the court may relieve that solicitor of his appointment and appoint another solicitor for the purposes referred to in subsection (2)(a) above.

(6A) Where, in realation to commissioner proceedings, the commissioner is satisfied that a solicitor so appointed is no longer able to act upon the instructions, or in the best interests, of the accused, the commissioner is (for the purpose of the application of subsection (6) above) to refer the case to the court.

(7) The references in subsections (3) to (6A) above to "a solicitor so appointed" include references to a solicitor appointed under subsection (6) above.

(8) In this section "counsel" includes a solicitor who has right of audience in the High Court of Justiciary under section 25A (rights of audience in various courts including the High Court of Justiciary) of the Solicitors (Scotland) Act 1980 (c.46).

(9) In this section, "commissioner proceedings" means proceedings before a commissioner appointed under section 271I(1) or by virtue of section 272(1)(b) of this Act.

AMENDMENTS

Section 288D inserted by Sexual Offences (Procedure and Evidence) (Scotland) Act 2002 (asp 9) s.2(1). Brought into force by SSI 2002/443 (C.24) art.4 (effective 1 November 2002).

Subs.(2)(a) as amended by Criminal Justice (Scotland) Act 2003 (asp 7) Pt 2 s.15. Brought into force on 25 November 2003 by SSI 2003/475 (C.26) art.2.

Subs.(2)(a)(i), (ii) inserted by Criminal Procedure (Amendment) (Scotland) Act 2004 (asp 5) s.4(2). Subs.(2)(a)(ii) as amended by s.25 and Sch.1 para.56 of the 2004 Act. Brought into force on 1 February 2005 by SSI 2004/405 (C.28) art.2.

Subss.(2), (6) and (7) as amended, and subss.(6A) and (9) inserted by Criminal Proceedings etc. (Reform) (Scotland) Act 2007 (asp 6) s.35. Brought into force on 23 April 2007 by SSI 2007/250 (C.23) art.3.

Subss.(1) and (6) as amended, subs.(2)(a)(i)(ii) substituted, by Criminal Justice and Licensing (Scotland) Act 2010 (asp 13) s.69(3). Brought into force on 28 March 2011 (for all purposes in respect of criminal proceedings commenced on or after 28 March 2011, with proceedings taken to have commenced when a report of the case has been received by the procurator fiscal) by SSI 2011/178 (C.15) art.2, Sch.1 para.1.

GENERAL NOTE

A4-561.7 The purpose of this provision is discussed at A4-561.5.1 above.

There seems to have been no Scottish appeal about this section since but if there should be then, comparatively speaking, it may be of interest to note that in *R. v Altzenberger* 2018 BCCA 296 (27 July 2018) there was a challenge to a *discretionary* judicial decision to appoint a lawyer for the purpose of cross-examining the appellant's former mother-in-law. The Court of Appeal of British Columbia held, at [47]-[51], that that appeal court "owes deference to the judge's decision to appoint counsel to cross-examine the complainant". Some of the other grounds of appeal alleged ineffective assistance rendered by the court-appointed lawyer: at [51]-[75]. The court did not accede to these grounds of appeal.

Jury directions relating to sexual offences

Jury direction relating to lack of communication about offence

A4-561.7.1 **288DA.**—(1) Subsection (2) applies where, in a trial on indictment for a sexual offence—

(a) evidence is given which suggests that the person against whom the offence is alleged to have been committed—

(i) did not tell, or delayed in telling, anyone, or a particular person, about the offence, or

(ii) did not report, or delayed in reporting, the offence to any investigating agency, or a particular investigating agency, or

(b) a question is asked, or a statement is made, with a view to eliciting, or drawing attention to, evidence of that nature.

(2) In charging the jury, the judge must advise that—

(a) there can be good reasons why a person against whom a sexual offence is committed may not tell others about it or report it to an investigating agency, or may delay in doing either of those things, and

(b) this does not, therefore, necessarily indicate that an allegation is false.

(3) Subsection (2) does not apply if the judge considers that, in the circumstances of the case, no reasonable jury could consider the evidence, question or statement by reason of which subsection (2) would otherwise apply to be material to the question of whether the alleged offence is proved.

(4) For the purposes of this section—

"investigating agency" means—

(a) a police force maintained for the area where the offence is alleged to have been committed,

(b) any other person who has functions (to any extent) of investigating crime in the area where the offence is alleged to have been committed,

"sexual offence" has the same meaning as in section 210A, except that it does not include—

(a) an offence under section 170 of the Customs and Excise Management Act 1979, or

(b) an offence under section 52A of the Civic Government (Scotland) Act 1982.

Amendments

Section 288DA inserted by Abusive Behaviour and Sexual Harm (Scotland) Act 2016 (asp 22) s.6. Brought into force on 24 April 2017 by SSI 2017/93 reg.2(1)(c).

Definitions

"indictment": s.307(1). **A4-561.7.2**
"investigating agency": s.288DA(4).
"judge": s.307(1).
"sexual offence": s.288DA(4).

General Note

Section 288DA makes provision for a jury direction relating to a lack of communication by a complainer about an alleged offence. That judicial direction follows when "evidence is given" of such a delay. No specification is given in s.288DA(1)(a) of how or when that evidence is given or who gives it. It would seem then that the parole evidence of a police officer of noting the first complaint made about a matter, say, 12 years after an incident engages the requirement for such a direction. **A4-561.7.3**

A degree of specification is found in s.288DA(1)(b), namely that a question being asked or a statement being made engages that provision. The requirement to give a judicial direction by s.288DA(2) is ameliorated by s.288DA(3) which allows for a degree of judicial discretion over the point if the judge considers it correct to do so in the circumstances allowed by the statute. It is unnecessary on a plain reading of s.288DA(3) for parties to be heard on the exercise of that judicial discretion. See, for example, *Donegan v HM Advocate* [2019] HCJAC 10; 2019 S.C.C.R. 106.

Jury direction relating to absence of physical resistance or physical force

288DB.—(1) Subsection (2) applies where, in a trial on indictment for a sexual offence— **A4-561.7.4**

(a) evidence is given which suggests that the sexual activity took place without physical resistance on the part of the person against whom the offence is alleged to have been committed, or

(b) a question is asked, or a statement is made, with a view to eliciting, or drawing attention to, evidence of that nature.

(2) In charging the jury, the judge must advise that—

(a) there can be good reasons why a person against whom a sexual offence is committed might not physically resist the sexual activity, and

(b) an absence of physical resistance does not, therefore, necessarily indicate that an allegation is false.

(3) Subsection (2) does not apply if the judge considers that, in the circumstances of the case, no reasonable jury could consider the evidence, question or statement by reason of which subsection (2) would otherwise apply to be material to the question of whether the alleged offence is proved.

(4) Subsection (5) applies where, in a trial on indictment for a sexual offence—

(a) evidence is given which suggests that the sexual activity took place without the accused using physical force to overcome the will of the person against whom the offence is alleged to have been committed, or

(b) a question is asked, or a statement is made, with a view to eliciting, or drawing attention to, evidence of that nature.

(5) In charging the jury, the judge must advise that—

(a) there can be good reasons why a person may, in committing a sexual offence, not need to use physical force to overcome the will of the person against whom the offence is committed, and

(b) an absence of physical force does not, therefore, necessarily indicate that an allegation is false.

(6) Subsection (5) does not apply if the judge considers that, in the circumstances of the case, no reasonable jury could consider the evidence, question or statement by reason of which subsection (5) would otherwise apply to be material to the question of whether the alleged offence is proved.

(7) For the purposes of this section—

"sexual activity" means the sexual activity which is the subject of the alleged sexual offence,

"sexual offence" means—

(a) rape (whether at common law or under section 1(1) of the Sexual Offences (Scotland) Act 2009),

(b) indecent assault,

(c) sodomy,

(d) clandestine injury to women,

(e) an offence under section 2 of the Sexual Offences (Scotland) Act 2009 (sexual assault by penetration),

(f) an offence under section 3 of that Act (sexual assault),

(g) an offence under section 4 of that Act (sexual coercion).

AMENDMENTS

Section 288DB inserted by Abusive Behaviour and Sexual Harm (Scotland) Act 2016 (asp 22) s.6. Brought into force on 24 April 2017 by SSI 2017/93 reg.2(1)(c).

DEFINITIONS

A4-561.7.5 "indictment": s.307(1).
"judge": s.307(1).
"sexual activity": s.288DB(7).
"sexual offence": s.288DB(7).

GENERAL NOTE

A4-561.7.6 Section 288DB(1), (2) and (3) are concerned with the absence of any *physical resistance* made by a complainer. Section 288DB(4), (5) and (6) are concerned with the absence of any *physical force* used by an accused.

In regard to both the elements of physical resistance and physical force the concepts of "sexual activity" and "sexual offence" are defined in the section.

Consideration of the circumstances of the evidence, questions and judicial discretion mentioned above for s.288DA would also seem to be apposite in the context envisaged for s.288DB.

See for example, *MacDonald v HM Advocate* [2020] HCJAC 21 at [46] an instance where a judicial direction under subs.(2) should have been given to the jury.

Prohibition of personal conduct of defence in domestic abuse cases

A4-561.7.7 **288DC.**—(1) This section applies to—

(a) an offence under section 1(1) of the Domestic Abuse (Scotland) Act 2018,

(b) an offence that is aggravated as described in section 1(1)(a) of the Abusive Behaviour and Sexual Harm (Scotland) Act 2016.

(2) An accused in proceedings for an offence to which this section applies is prohibited from conducting the accused's case in person at, or for the purposes of, any relevant hearing in the course of the proceedings.

(3) Section 288D applies in the case of proceedings in respect of an offence to which this section applies as it does in the case of proceedings in respect of an offence to which section 288C applies (and a reference in section 288D to a relevant hearing is to be read accordingly).

(4) In subsection (2), "relevant hearing" means a hearing at, or for the purposes of, which a witness is to give evidence.

Amendment

Section 288DC inserted by Domestic Abuse (Scotland) Act 2018 (asp 5) Sch.1(1)(2) para.4(14) (effective 1 April 2019 in respect of proceedings commenced on or after 1 April 2019 subject to transitional provision specified in SSI 2018/387 reg.7(2)).

Definitions

"relevant hearing": s.288DC(4).

General Note

This provision restricts the extent to which an accused might conduct his own case either during preliminary hearings or at the trial itself.

[THE NEXT PARAGRAPH IS A4-561.8]

Trials involving vulnerable witnesses

Prohibition of personal conduct of defence in certain cases involving child witnesses under the age of 12

288E.—(1) […] A4-561.8

(2) This section applies to any proceedings (other than proceedings in the JP court)—

(a) in respect of any offence specified in subsection (3) below, and
(b) in which a child witness who is under the age of 12 on the date of commencement of the proceedings is to give evidence at or for the purposes of any hearing in the course of the proceedings.

(2A) The accused is prohibited from conducting his case in person at, or for the purposes of, any hearing at, or for the purposes of, which the child witness is to give evidence.

(3) The offences referred to in subsection (2)(a) above are—

(a) murder,
(b) culpable homicide,
(c) any offence which—
    (i) involves an assault on, or injury or threat of injury to, any person (including any offence involving neglect or ill-treatment of, or other cruelty to, a child), but
    (ii) is not an offence to which section 288C or 288DC of this Act applies,
(d) abduction, and
(e) plagium.

(4) Section 288D of this Act applies in the case of proceedings to which this section applies as it applies in the case of proceedings in respect of a sexual offence to which section 288C of this Act applies as if references to a relevant hearing were references to a hearing referred to in subsection (2A) above.

(5) In proceedings to which this section applies, the prosecutor shall, at the same time as intimating to the accused under section 271A(13) of this Act a vulnerable witness notice in respect of a vulnerable witness referred to in subsection (2)(b) above, serve on the accused a notice under subsection (6).

(6) A notice under this subsection shall contain intimation to the accused—

(a) that his case at, or for the purposes of, any hearing in the course of the proceedings at, or for the purposes of, which the child witness is to give evidence may be conducted only by a lawyer,

(b) that it is therefore in his interests, if he has not already done so, to get the professional assistance of a solicitor, and

(c) that if he does not engage a solicitor for the purposes of the conduct of his case at or for the purposes of the hearing, the court will do so.

(7) A failure to comply with subsection (5) or (6) above does not affect the validity or lawfulness of any vulnerable witness notice or any other element of the proceedings against the accused.

(8) […]

(9) For the purposes of subsection (2)(b) above, proceedings shall be taken to have commenced when the indictment or, as the case may be, the complaint is served on the accused.

Amendments

Section 288E inserted by Vulnerable Witnesses (Scotland) Act 2004 (asp 3) s.6. Brought into force, for specified purposes, on 1 April 2005 by SSI 2005/168 (C.7) art.2 and Sch. Further brought into force for specified purposes on 1 April 2006 by SSI 2006/59 (C.8) art.2 and Sch.

Subss.(1) and (6)(c) as amended and subss.(1)(a), (b) and (6)(za) inserted by Criminal Procedure (Amendment) (Scotland) Act 2004 (asp 5) s.4(3). Brought into force on 1 April 2005 by SSI 2004/405 (C.28) art.2 and Sch.2.

Further brought into force for specified purposes on 1 April 2007 by SSI 2007/101 (C.13) art.2.
Remainder brought into force on 1 April 2008 by SSI 2008/57 (C.7) art.2.

Subs.(2) as amended by Criminal Proceedings etc. (Reform) (Scotland) Act 2007 (asp 6) s.80, Sch. para.26. Brought into force for the Sheriffdom of Lothian and Borders on 10 March 2008 by SSI 2008/42 (C.4) art.3 and Sch. Brought into force for the Sheriffdom of Grampian, Highland and Islands on 2 June 2008 by SSI 2008/192 (C.19) art.3 and Sch. Brought into force for the Sheriffdom of Glasgow and Strathkelvin on 8 December 2008 by SSI 2008/329 (C.29) art.3 and Sch. Brought into force for the Sheriffdom of Tayside, Central and Fife on 23 February 2009 by SSI 2008/362 (C.30) art.3 and Sch. Brought into force for the Sheriffdom of North Strathclyde on 14 December 2009 by SSI 2009/432 (C.32) art.3 and Sch.1. Remainder in force on 22 February 2010 by SSI 2009/432 (C.32) art.3 and Sch.2.

Subss.(1), (8) repealed, subs.(2)(b), (4), (5), (6)(za), (a), (c) as amended, and subs.(2A) inserted, by Criminal Justice and Licensing (Scotland) Act 2010 (asp 13) s.69(4). Brought into force on 28 March 2011 (for all purposes in respect of criminal proceedings commenced on or after 28 March 2011, with proceedings taken to have commenced when a report of the case has been received by the procurator fiscal) by SSI 2011/178 (C.15) art.2, Sch.1 para.1.

Subss.(5) and (7) as amended by Victims and Witnesses (Scotland) Act 2014 (asp 1) s.11(9). Brought into force on 1 September 2015 by SSI 2015/200 art.2 and Sch, subject to transitional provisions in art.4.

Subs.(3)(c)(ii) as amended by Domestic Abuse (Scotland) Act 2018 (asp 5) Sch.1(1)(2) para.4(15) (effective 1 April 2019 in respect of proceedings commenced on or after 1 April 2019 subject to transitional provision specified in SSI 2018/387 reg.7(2)).

Definitions

A4-561.9 "court": s.271(5).
"prosecutor": s.307(1).
"trial": s.307(1).
"vulnerable witness": s.271(7).

General Note

A4-561.10 Section 288C of the 1995 Act introduced a prohibition on the personal conduct of the defence case by an accused in the trial of certain specified sexual offences. The new s.288E applies to murder, culpable homicide and other offences that involve generally speaking assaults (excluding matters covered by s.288C). The new s.288E, if such a matter is charged, covers a child witness who is under 12 years on the date of the commencement of proceedings and who is to give evidence. The test is whether the use of this procedure is in the best interests of the child witness. The prosecutor must serve a child witness notice on an accused by s.271A(3) and at the same time serve a notice by s.288E(6). The latter notice advises an accused that for the offence charged the defence may only be conducted by a lawyer.

Justice of the Peace Court

The power to prohibit personal conduct of a defence by an accused provided for in this section has been extended to the JP court by the Justice of the Peace Courts (Special Measures) (Scotland) Order 2015 (SSI 2015/447) art.3(1).

Power to prohibit personal conduct of defence in other cases involving vulnerable witnesses

288F.—(1) This section applies in the case of proceedings in respect of any offence, other than proceedings— A4-561.11

(a) in the JP court,
(b) in respect of a sexual offence to which section 288C of this Act applies, or
(ba) in respect of an offence to which section 288DC of this Act applies,
(c) to which section 288E of this Act applies,

where a vulnerable witness is to give evidence at, or for the purposes of, any hearing in the course of the proceedings.

(2) If satisfied that it is in the interests of the vulnerable witness to do so, the court may—

(a) on the application of the prosecutor, or
(b) of its own motion,

make an order prohibiting the accused from conducting his case in person at any hearing at, or for the purposes of, which the vulnerable witness is to give evidence.

(3) However, the court shall not make an order under subsection (2) above if it considers that—

(a) the order would give rise to a significant risk of prejudice to the fairness of the hearing or otherwise to the interests of justice, and
(b) that risk significantly outweighs any risk of prejudice to the interests of the vulnerable witness if the order is not made.

(4) The court may make an order under subsection (2) above relation to a hearing after, as well as before, the hearing has commenced.

(4A) […]

(5) Section 288D of this Act applies in the case of proceedings in respect of which an order is made under this section as it applies in the case of proceedings in respect of a sexual offence to which section 288C of this Act applies and as if references to a relevant hearing were references to any hearing in respect of which an order is made under this section.

(6) […]

AMENDMENTS

Section 288F inserted by Vulnerable Witnesses (Scotland) Act 2004 (asp 3) s.6. Brought into force, for specified purposes, on 1 April 2005 by SSI 2005/168 (C.7) art.2 and Sch. Further brought into force for specified purposes on 1 April 2006 by SSI 2006/59 (C.8) art.2 and Sch.

Subs.(4A) inserted by Criminal Procedure (Amendment) (Scotland) Act 2004 (asp 5) s.4(4). Brought into force on 1 April 2005 by SSI 2004/405 (C.28) art.2 and Sch.2.

Further brought into force for specified purposes on 1 April 2007 by SSI 2007/101 (C.13) art.2.

Remainder brought into force on 1 April 2008 by SSI 2008/57 (C.7) art.2.

Subs.(1)(a) as amended by Criminal Proceedings etc. (Reform) (Scotland) Act 2007 (asp 6) s.80, Sch. para.26. Brought into force for the Sheriffdom of Lothian and Borders on 10 March 2008 by SSI 2008/42 (C.4) art.3 and Sch. Further brought into force for the Sheriffdom of Grampian, Highland and Islands on 2 June 2008 by SSI 2008/192 (C.19) art.3 and Sch. Brought into force for the Sheriffdom of Glasgow and Strathkelvin on 8 December 2008 by SSI 2008/329 (C.29) art.3 and Sch. Brought into force for the Sheriffdom of Tayside, Central and Fife on 23 February 2009 by SSI 2008/362 (C.30) art.3 and Sch. Brought into force for the Sheriffdom of North Strathclyde on 14 December 2009 by SSI 2009/432 (C.32) art.3 and Sch.1. Remainder in force on 22 February 2010 by SSI 2009/432 (C.32) art.3 and Sch.2.

Subss.(1), (2), (3)(a), (4), (5) as amended, and subss.(4A), (6) repealed, by Criminal Justice and Licensing (Scotland) Act 2010 (asp 13) s.69(5). Brought into force on 28 March 2011 (for all purposes in respect of criminal proceedings commenced on or after 28 March 2011, with proceedings taken to have commenced when a report of the case has been received by the procurator fiscal) by SSI 2011/178 (C.15) art.2, Sch.1 para.1.

Subs.(1)(ba) inserted by Domestic Abuse (Scotland) Act 2018 (asp 5) Sch.1(1)(2) para.4(16) (effective 1 April 2019 in respect of proceedings commenced on or after 1 April 2019 subject to transitional provision specified in SSI 2018/387 reg.7(2)).

DEFINITIONS

"court": s.271(5). A4-561.12
"prosecutor": s.307(1).

"trial": s.307(1).
"vulnerable statement proof": s.288E(5A).
"vulnerable witness": s.271(7).

GENERAL NOTE

A4-561.13 Section 288C of the 1995 Act introduced a prohibition on the personal conduct of the defence case by an accused in the trial of certain specified sexual offences. The new s.288F extends that type of prohibition to cases (other than ones with sexual offences and those specified in s.288F(3)) if a vulnerable witness is giving evidence in the trial. The test is whether the use of this procedure is in the best interests of the vulnerable witness. There seems to be a balance that requires to be found in this as no such order of prohibition can be made if there is a significant risk of prejudice to the fairness of the trial and that risk outweighs any prejudice to the interests of the vulnerable witness. If an order is made the court also appoints a solicitor for the accused.

Justice of the Peace Court

The power to prohibit personal conduct of a defence by an accused provided for in this section has been extended to the JP court by the Justice of the Peace Courts (Special Measures) (Scotland) Order 2015 (SSI 2015/447) art.3(1).

Application of vulnerable witnesses provisions to proceedings in the district court

Application of vulnerable witnesses provisions to proceedings in the district court

A4-561.14 **288G.**—(1) The Scottish Ministers may by order made by statutory instrument provide for any of sections—

(a) 271 to 271M,
(b) 288E, and
(c) 288F,

of this Act to apply, subject to such modifications (if any) as may be specified in the order, to proceedings in the JP court.

(2) An order under subsection (1) may—

(a) make such incidental, supplemental, consequential, transitional, transitory or saving provision as the Scottish Ministers think necessary or expedient,
(b) make different provision for different JP courts or descriptions of JP court or different proceedings or types of proceedings,
(c) modify any enactment.

(3) An order under this section shall not be made unless a draft of the statutory instrument containing the order has been laid before, and approved by resolution of, the Scottish Parliament.

AMENDMENTS

Section 288G inserted by Vulnerable Witnesses (Scotland) Act 2004 (asp 3) s.10. Brought into force on 1 July 2015 by SSI 2015/244 (C.34) art.2.

Subss.(1), (2) as amended by Criminal Proceedings etc. (Reform) (Scotland) Act 2007 (asp 6) s.80, Sch. para.26. Brought into force for the Sheriffdom of Lothian and Borders on 10 March 2008 by SSI 2008/42 (C.4) art.3 and Sch. Brought into force for the Sheriffdom of Grampian, Highland and Islands on 2 June 2008 by SSI 2008/192 (C.19) art.3 and Sch. Brought into force for the Sheriffdom of Glasgow and Strathkelvin on 8 December 2008 by SSI 2008/329 (C.29) art.3 and Sch. Brought into force for the Sheriffdom of Tayside, Central and Fife on 23 February 2009 by SSI 2008/362 (C.30) art.3 and Sch. Brought into force for the Sheriffdom of North Strathclyde on 14 December 2009 by SSI 2009/432 (C.32) art.3 and Sch.1. Remainder in force on 22 February 2010 by SSI 2009/432 (C.32) art.3 and Sch.2.

DEFINITION

A4-561.15 "vulnerable witness": s.271(7).

GENERAL NOTE

A4-561.16 There is no reason in principle as to why cases tried in the district courts should not proceed where there are or may be vulnerable witnesses. This is all the more so given the existence of stipendiary magistrates in the district court with the summary powers of a sheriff: see s.7(5) of the 1995 Act. This new s.288G allows the Scottish Ministers a power to apply the vulnerable witness provisions to the district court.

Use of live television link

Participation through live television link

288H.—(1) Where the court so determines at any time before or at a specified hearing, a detained person is to participate in the hearing by means of a live television link. **A4-561.17**

(2) The court—

(a) must give the parties in the case an opportunity to make representations before making a determination under subsection (1),

(b) may make such a determination only if it considers that to do so is not contrary to the interests of justice.

(3) The court may require a detained person to participate by means of a live television link in any proceedings at a specified hearing or otherwise in the case for the sole purpose of considering whether to make a determination under subsection (1) with respect to a specified hearing.

(4) Where a detained person participates in any specified hearing or other proceedings by means of a live television link—

(a) a place of detention is, for the purposes of the hearing or other proceedings, deemed to be part of the court-room, and

(b) accordingly, the hearing is or other proceedings are deemed to take place in the presence of the detained person.

(5) In this section—

"court-room" includes chambers,

"live television link" means live television link between a place of detention and the court-room in which any specified hearing is or other proceedings are to be held or (as the case may be) any specified hearing is or other proceedings are being held.

Amendments

Section 288H as inserted by Criminal Justice (Scotland) Act 2016 (asp 1) s.110(1). Brought into force on 25 January 2018 by SSI 2017/345 art.3.

Definitions

"court-room": s.288H(5). **A4-561.18**
"detained person": s.288L.
"live television link": s.288H(5).
"place of detention": s.288L.
"specified hearing": s.288L.

General Note

The terms of this section might appear at first reading to be somewhat peremptory: by subs.(1), where a court determines it, a detained person "is to" participate in a hearing. However, a right of making representations is allowed by subs.(2). Also, by subs.(3), a court "may require" a detained person to participate in relevant hearings. Yet, s.288I offers reassurance that the procedure envisaged by these sections is not directed at matters of proof. The routine procedure of committal and other hearings that hitherto have required the movement of large numbers of prisoners between jails and detention facilities to be at courts for the ordinary hours can be avoided by this legislation. Section 288K empowers the Lord Justice General to specify the types of hearing in which these live television links to court may be used. It is not competent for such links be used to conduct trial proceedings (see s.288I(1) below). **A4-561.19**

Evidence and personal appearance

288I.—(1) No evidence as to a charge on any complaint or indictment may be led or presented at a specified hearing in respect of which there is a determination under section 288H(1). **A4-561.20**

(2) The court—

(a) may, at any time before or at a specified hearing, revoke a determination under section 288H(1),

(b) must do so in relation to a detained person if it considers that it is in the interests of justice for the detained person to appear in person.

(3) The court may postpone a specified hearing to a later day if, on the day on which a specified hearing takes place or is due to take place—

(a) the court decides not to make a determination under section 288H(1) with respect to the hearing, or

(b) the court revokes such a determination under subsection (2).

AMENDMENTS

Section 288I as inserted by Criminal Justice (Scotland) Act 2016 (asp 1) s.110(1). Brought into force on 25 January 2018 by SSI 2017/345 art.3.

DEFINITIONS

A4-561.21 "complaint": s.307(1).
"detained person": s.288L.
"indictment": s.307(1).
"place of detention": s.288L.
"postpone": s.288J(3).
"specified hearing": s.288L.

GENERAL NOTE

A4-561.22 By subs.(1) it is certain that the procedure envisaged by these sections is not directed at matters of proof. The phrase "led or presented" in that context means that the agreement of evidence in the form of a minute which is put before the court at a preliminary hearing or diet is permissible.

Effect of postponement

A4-561.23 **288J.**—(1) Except where a postponement under section 288I(3) is while section 21(2) of the Criminal Justice (Scotland) Act 2016 applies to a detained person, the following do not count towards any time limit arising in the person's case if the postponement in the case is to the next day on which the court is sitting—

(a) that next day,

(b) any intervening Saturday, Sunday or court holiday.

(2) Even while section 21(2) of the Criminal Justice (Scotland) Act 2016 applies to a detained person, that section does not prevent a postponement under section 288I(3) in the person's case.

(3) In section 288I and this section, "postpone" includes adjourn.

AMENDMENTS

Section 288J as inserted by Criminal Justice (Scotland) Act 2016 (asp 1) s.110(1). Brought into force on 25 January 2018 by SSI 2017/345 art.3.

DEFINITIONS

A4-561.24 "detained person": s.288L.
"postpone": s.288J(3).

GENERAL NOTE

A4-561.25 Certain adjustments in time are required in the context of the provisions arising out of the use of live television links. While the Scottish Parliament has thought that these adjustments are necessary as a matter of fairness and given the application at the relevant point of the presumption of innocence, the periods of time envisaged by these adjustments barely, which is to say just pass, the hurdle of de minimis.

Specified hearings

A4-561.26 **288K.**—(1) The Lord Justice General may by directions specify types of hearing at the High Court, sheriff court and JP court in which a detained person may participate in accordance with section 288H(1).

(2) Directions under subsection (1) may specify types of hearing by reference to—

(a) the venues at which they take place,

(b) particular places of detention,

(c) categories of cases or proceedings to which they relate.

(3) Directions under subsection (1) may—

(a) vary or revoke earlier such directions,

(b) make different provision for different purposes.

(4) The validity of any proceedings is not affected by the participation of a detained person by means of a live television link in a hearing that is not a specified hearing.

(5) In this section, "hearing" includes any diet or hearing in criminal proceedings which may be held in the presence of an accused, a convicted person or an appellant in the proceedings.

Amendments

Section 288K as inserted by Criminal Justice (Scotland) Act 2016 (asp 1) s.110(1). Brought into force on 25 January 2018 by SSI 2017/345 art.3.

Definitions

"detained person": s.288L. A4-561.27
"hearing": s.288K(5).

General Note

This section is the key authority in this brief tranche of sections: the directions of the Lord Justice General once intimated will of course settle the precise procedural point to be dealt with by live television link. The understanding of how precisely these sections work will, of course, depend on the points they apply to. Some indication has been provided by the legislation, but the definition of "hearing" in s.288K(5) is not absolute and only "includes" the types mentioned. A4-561.28

Defined terms

288L. For the purpose of sections 288H to 288K— A4-561.29

"detained person" means person who is—

(a) an accused, a convicted person or an appellant in the case to which a specified hearing relates, and

(b) imprisoned or otherwise lawfully detained (whether or not in connection with an offence) at any place in Scotland,

"place of detention" means place in which a detained person is imprisoned or detained,

"specified hearing" means hearing of a type specified in directions having effect for the time being under section 288K.

Amendments

Section 288L as inserted by Criminal Justice (Scotland) Act 2016 (asp 1) s.110(1). Brought into force on 25 January 2018 by SSI 2017/345 art.3.

[THE NEXT PARAGRAPH IS A4-562]

Treason trials

Procedure and evidence in trials for treason

289. The procedure and rules of evidence in proceedings for treason and misprision of treason shall be the same as in proceedings according to the law of Scotland for murder. A4-562

General Note

It has been the rule in England since the Treason Act 1800 (see now the Criminal Law Act 1967, s.12(7)) that trials for treason and misprision should be governed by the rules applicable to trials for murder. This section restates the position in Scotland which was clarified in s.39 of the 1980 Act. The substantive law of trespass remains English, but the Treason Acts of 1800 and 1945 were repealed by s.83(3) of and Sch.8 to the 1980 Act, along with what remained of the Treason Act 1708. A4-563

Certain rights of accused

Accused's right to request identification parade

A4-564 **290.—**(1) Subject to subsection (2) below, the sheriff may, on an application by an accused at any time after the accused has been charged with an offence, order that, in relation to the alleged offence, the prosecutor shall hold an identification parade in which the accused shall be one of those constituting the parade.

(2) The sheriff shall make an order in accordance with subsection (1) above only after giving the prosecutor an opportunity to be heard and only if—

(a) an identification parade, such as is mentioned in subsection (1) above, has not been held at the instance of the prosecutor;

(b) after a request by the accused, the prosecutor has refused to hold, or has unreasonably delayed holding, such an identification parade; and

(c) the sheriff considers the application under subsection (1) above to be reasonable.

DEFINITIONS

A4-564.1 "offence": s.307(1).
"prosecutor": s.307(1).
"sheriff": s.4(1) and (4).

[THE NEXT PARAGRAPH IS A4-565]

GENERAL NOTE

A4-565 This section re-enacts the provisions of s.10 of the Criminal Justice (Scotland) Act 1980. It is open to the accused to make an application for an identification parade to be held by the prosecutor; (i) where no such parade has been conducted; (ii) where the prosecutor has refused a request by the accused for such a parade, or else been dilatory in organising the parade; and (iii) where the application appears reasonable to the sheriff. An application under s.290 can only be made after charges have been preferred against the accused and once the sheriff has heard the prosecutor on the merits of the charge.

The style of application is found in the 1996 Act of Adjournal, Ch.28; note that the style applies to circumstances where either an indictment has been served or summary proceedings have begun.

In *Wilson v Tudhope*, 1985 S.C.C.R. 339 two Crown attempts to hold an identification parade failed because witnesses were unwilling to attend. The defence craved, and were granted, an identification parade, the sheriff opining that it would be competent to cite witnesses to attend such a parade.

See *Beattie v Hingston*, 1999 S.L.T. 362, where the Appeal Court suspended the sheriff's refusal of B's petition for a parade, the s.290 hearing having had to be fixed too early (in view of the imminent trial diet) for intimation to be given to B. Consequently B. was not present and, more importantly, the local agent who had been instructed to lodge the application had only slight knowledge of the factual background to the case. Note that the Appeal Court reserved opinion upon defence submissions that the s.290 hearing should have been held in open court; it is submitted that given that identification of an accused is plainly to be an issue at trial, there would be little to be gained (and much to be risked) by arguing the merits of an application in open court.

On a general note attention is directed to *Holland v HM Advocate*, 2005 1 S.C. (P.C.) 3 (Privy Council DRA No.1 of 2004) which discusses the use of dock identification and how far it can be said to intrude upon an accused's art.6 Convention rights to a fair trial.

C v HM Advocate, 2013 S.L.T. 27; 2012 S.C.C.R. 702 supports the view that an application can be refused as unreasonable if made too late. In C after refusal of a defence application for an identification parade, the matter proceeded as a devolution issue. The Appeal Court in upholding the sheriff's reasoning, also founded on the fact that the witnesses' statements obtained by the police (previously disclosed to the defence) indicated that several of the witnesses stated an ability to identify the accused. Broader questions of the propriety of dock identification are discussed in *Toal v HM Advocate* [2012] HCJAC 123; 2012 S.C.C.R. 735 and in *McLean v HM Advocate* [2011] HCJAC 99; 2011 S.C.C.R. 633.

Perhaps surprisingly, given the Parliamentary energy devoted to witness vulnerability issues, this section infers that the parade has to be in the conventional one-way mirror form, rather than the VIPER image selection model generally favoured by the Crown for cases involving vulnerable witnesses.

Precognition on oath of defence witnesses

A4-566 **291.—**(1) The sheriff may, on the application of an accused, grant warrant to cite any person (other than a co-accused), who is alleged to be a witness in relation to any offence of which the accused has been charged, to appear before the sheriff in chambers at such time or place as shall be specified in the citation, for precognition on oath by the accused or his solicitor in relation to that offence, if the court is satisfied that it is reasonable to require such precognition on oath in the circumstances.

(2) Any person who, having been duly cited to attend for precognition under subsection (1) above and having been given at least 48 hours notice, fails without reasonable excuse to attend shall be guilty of an offence and shall be liable on summary conviction to a fine not exceeding level 3 on the standard scale or to imprisonment for a period not exceeding 21 days; and the court may issue a warrant for the apprehension of the person concerned, ordering him to be brought before a sheriff for precognition on oath.

(3) Any person who, having been duly cited to attend for precognition under subsection (1) above, attends but—

(a) refuses to give information within his knowledge or to produce evidence in his possession; or

(b) prevaricates in his evidence,

shall be guilty of an offence and shall be liable to be summarily subjected forthwith to a fine not exceeding level 3 on the standard scale or to imprisonment for a period not exceeding 21 days.

(4) This section does not, however, extend to the citation of the complainer for precognition by the accused in person.

(5) In subsection (4) above, "complainer" has the same meaning as in section 274 of this Act.

(6) A warrant is not to be granted under this section for the citation for precognition by the accused in person of any child under the age of 12 on the relevant date where the offence in relation to which the child is alleged to be a witness is one specified in section 288E(3) of this Act.

(7) In subsection (6) above, "the relevant date" means—

(a) where an indictment or complaint in respect of the offence has been served on the accused at the time of the application, the date on which the indictment or complaint was so served, or

(b) where an indictment or complaint in respect of the offence has not been so served, the date on which the application under subsection (1) above is made.

AMENDMENT

Subss.(4) and (5) inserted by Sexual Offences (Procedure and Evidence) (Scotland) Act 2002 (asp 9) s.4. Brought into force by SSI 2002/443 (C.24) art.4 (effective November 1, 2002).

Subss.(6) and (7) inserted by Vulnerable Witnesses (Scotland) Act 2004 (asp 3) s.8. Brought into force on April 1, 2005 by SSI 2005/168 (C.7) art.2 and Sch. Further brought into force for specified purposes on April 1, 2007 by SSI 2007/101 (C.13) art.2.

DEFINITIONS

"enactment": s.307(1). A4-566.1
"imprisonment": ss.307(6) and 309.
"indictment": s.307(1).
"offence": s.307(1).

[THE NEXT PARAGRAPH IS A4-567]

GENERAL NOTE

A warrant to cite a witness for precognition on oath may be craved by the defence once charges have been preferred and cause can be shown to justify the use of this *compulsitor*; the power should be exercised with caution (*Low v MacNeill*, 1981 S.C.C.R. 243). A4-567

In *Drummond, Petr*, 1998 S.L.T. 757 where an unrepresented accused petitioned the nobile officium for authority to interview police witnesses on tape, the High Court observed, in refusing the application, that the appropriate course would have been to make an application under s.291.

It is not competent to make an application of this sort prior to full committal on petition, since, in the period between committal for further examination and full committal the Crown are still completing enquiries; see *Cirignaco, Petr*, 1985 S.C.C.R. 157 where precognition on oath of the complainer was sought with a view to secure early release on bail. Refusal on the part of potential witnesses to assist defence investigations, even after joint approaches by both the defence and the Crown, resulted in the grant of warrant to cite for precognition (*Brady v Lockhart*, 1985 S.C.C.R. 349). It is likely that an application for precognition on oath without first having sought the assistance of the Crown will be treated as premature.

A warrant for precognition on oath can only be sought prior to the trial (and conviction or acquittal) of the accused (see *Gilmour, Petr*, 1994 S.C.C.R. 872). In *Campbell v HM Advocate*, 1997 S.L.T. 577 the Appeal Court, with some hesitation, refused Crown advocation of a warrant to precognose a police officer who was not a witness in a murder trial, in relation to earlier dealings with a Crown witness; the broad intention was to undermine the credibility of the Crown witness. It is of note that the original warrant was entirely unqualified, and that the warrant for precognition was upheld by the Appeal Court largely on the basis of the case being a murder trial and of undertakings given by counsel to the court.

Failure to attend for precognition after lawful citation, prevarication, or failure to furnish information is an offence liable to peremptory punishment (subs.(3)); in such circumstances the court is not obliged to obtain social enquiry or other reports before sentencing such misconduct.

Pleas of legal privilege will not necessarily be conclusive where application is made to precognosce an accused's solicitor on oath; see *Kelly v Vannet*, 1999 G.W.D. 4-175. Crown applications proceed as incidental applications in terms of s.134 of the 1995 Act. For a discussion of the general nature of precognitions see *HM Advocate v McSween*, 2007 S.C.C.R. 310.

Refer to Ch.29 of the 1996 Act of Adjournal for directions on procedures and styles.

The intention of the Sexual Offences (Procedure and Evidence) (Scotland) Act 2002 (asp 9) was to prevent either cross-examination or precognition of victims of sexual offences by the alleged perpetrator. (See the General Note to s.288C above). The addition of subs.(4) extends these prohibitions to precognition on oath of a victim by the accused. Note too that s.24(5) of the Act introduces a specific bail condition in these circumstances precluding such precognition.

Mode of trial

Mode of trial of certain offences

A4-568 **292.**—(1) Subject to subsection (6) below, the offences mentioned (and broadly described) in Schedule 10 to this Act shall be triable only summarily.

(2) An offence created by statute shall be triable only summarily if—

(a) the enactment creating the offence or any other enactment expressly so provides (in whatever words); or

(b) subject to subsections (4) and (5)(a) below, the offence was created by an Act passed on or before 29 July 1977 (the date of passing of the Criminal Law Act 1977) and the penalty or maximum penalty in force immediately before that date, on any conviction of that offence, did not include any of the following—

(i) a fine exceeding £400;

(ii) imprisonment for a period exceeding 3 months;

(iii) a fine exceeding £50 in respect of a specified quantity or number of things, or in respect of a specified period during which a continuing offence is committed.

(3) […]

(4) An offence created by statute which is triable only on indictment shall continue only to be so triable.

(5) An offence created by statute shall be triable either on indictment or summarily if—

(a) the enactment creating the offence or any other enactment expressly so provides (in whatever words); or

(b) it is an offence to which neither subsection (2) nor subsection (4) above applies.

(6) An offence which may under any enactment (including an enactment in this Act or passed after this Act) be tried only summarily, being an offence which, if it had been triable on indictment, could competently have been libelled as an additional or alternative charge in the indictment, may (the provisions of this or any other enactment notwithstanding) be so libelled, and tried accordingly.

(7) Where an offence is libelled and tried on indictment by virtue of subsection (6) above, the penalty which may be imposed for that offence in that case shall not exceed that which is competent on summary conviction.

AMENDMENTS

Subs.(2) as amended and subs.(3) repealed by Criminal Proceedings etc (Reform) (Scotland) Act 2007 (asp 6) s.80, Sch. para.24. Brought into force on 10 December 2007 by SSI 2007/479 (C.40) art.3 and Sch.

DEFINITIONS A4-568.1

"enactment": s.307(1).
"fine": s.307(1).
"imprisonment": s.307(6).
"indictment": s.307(1).
"offence": s.307(1).

[THE NEXT PARAGRAPH IS A4-569]

GENERAL NOTE

Offences triable summarily only are listed in Sch.10 and in subs.(2) and can extend to offences defined in s.5(3) notwithstanding the fact that these create liability to a sentence of six months' imprisonment on a second or subsequent conviction in the sheriff court. It will be recalled that s.136(2) enacts that the six-month time limit for the commencement of statutory offences applies only to offences triable summarily only. A4-569

Offences which by statute may only be prosecuted summarily can be libelled along with other charges on an indictment but, in that event, any sentence which may be imposed on conviction of that offence shall be restricted to that which could have been passed summarily (subs.(6)).

Art and part and attempt

Statutory offences: art and part and aiding and abetting

293.—(1) A person may be convicted of, and punished for, a contravention of any enactment, notwithstanding that he was guilty of such contravention as art and part only. A4-570

(2) Without prejudice to subsection (1) above or to any express provision in any enactment having the like effect to this subsection, any person who aids, abets, counsels, procures or incites any other person to commit an offence against the provisions of any enactment shall be guilty of an offence and shall be liable on conviction, unless the enactment otherwise requires, to the same punishment as might be imposed on conviction of the first-mentioned offence.

DEFINITIONS

"enactment": s.307(1). A4-570.1
"offence": s.307(1).

[THE NEXT PARAGRAPH IS A4-571]

GENERAL NOTE

Art and part guilt can apply equally to common law and statutory offences. See *Vaughan v HM Advocate*, 1979 S.L.T. 49 where the accused though not himself within the forbidden degrees, was convicted under the Incest Act 1567 as an actor. A4-571

It is considered in light of the Interpretation Act 1978 (c.30) that the word "enactment" extends only to Acts of Parliament and does not apply to Acts of the Scottish Parliament. Nonetheless, Scots common law imports the concept of art and part guilt into statutory offences: the practical impact of this unintended lacuna is slight.

Attempt at crime

294.—(1) Attempt to commit any indictable crime is itself an indictable crime. A4-572

(2) Attempt to commit any offence punishable on complaint shall itself be an offence punishable on complaint.

GENERAL NOTE

A4-572.1 For a brief discussion of s.294 see *RCB v HM Advocate* [2016] HCJAC 63; 2016 S.C.C.R. 374.

[THE NEXT PARAGRAPH IS A4-573]

Legal custody

Legal custody

A4-573 **295.** Without prejudice to section 13 of the Prisons (Scotland) Act 1989 (c.45) (legal custody of prisoners), any person required or authorised by or under this Act or any other enactment to be taken to any place, or to be detained or kept in custody is, while being so taken or detained or kept, in legal custody.

AMENDMENT

Section 295 as amended by Criminal Justice (Scotland) Act 2003 (asp 7) Pt 4 s.24. Brought into force on 27 June 2003 by SSI 2003/288 (C.14).

DEFINITION

A4-573.1 "enactment": s.307(1).

[THE NEXT PARAGRAPH IS A4-574]

GENERAL NOTE

A4-574 The definition of legal custody applies to the status of persons either detained or arrested under the Act or other statutory powers. The anomalous position of a person suspected of committing an offence and required to remain where found by police officers (see s.13(1) and (2) above) has already been discussed; such an individual is not then in legal custody.

This definition is of relevance to the death of any prisoner as there are easily conceivable circumstances in which a death occurs during custody which would of course necessitate a mandatory public inquiry in terms of s.1(1)(a)(ii) of the Fatal Accidents and Sudden Deaths Inquiry (Scotland) Act 1976 (c.14).

Moreover, once a client is in custody certain security consequences apply for a solicitor, and presumably counsel, which have been discussed in *HM Advocate v Collins* [2014] HCJAC 11; 2014 S.L.T. 372; 2014 S.C.L. 225; 2014 S.C.C.R. 105; 2014 G.W.D. 6-120.

Warrants

Warrants for search and apprehension to be signed by judge

A4-575 **296.** Any warrant for search or apprehension granted under this Act shall be signed by the judge granting it, and execution upon any such warrant may proceed either upon the warrant itself or upon an extract of the warrant issued and signed by the clerk of court.

DEFINITION

A4-575.1 "judge": s.307(1).

[THE NEXT PARAGRAPH IS A4-576]

GENERAL NOTE

A4-576 This section applies to the grant of warrants of apprehension or search by a justice of the peace, sheriff or High Court judge. Ordinarily such warrants are craved from judges in the lower courts. See s.135 of the Act and the notes thereto.

The status of the judge granting a warrant was unsuccessfully challenged in *McFarlane v Gilchrist*, 2002 S.L.T. 521. Objection had been taken in the light of *Starrs v Ruxton*, 2000 S.L.T. 42; 1999 S.C.C.R. 1052 which had centred upon the impartiality of temporary judges in the context of trial proceedings. A common law warrant, dated only "November 2000", was upheld as valid. The Crown appealed against the sheriff's decision to uphold preliminary objections to the validity of search. The Appeal Court took account of the fact that, unlike statutory warrants, no time limits applied to the execution of a common law warrant; the warrant under question was *ex facie* valid.

A distinction has to be drawn between statutory warrants, the execution of which must comply with the statutory time limit stated in the relevant legislation, and common law warrants which carry no time limit; in *HM Advocate v Foulis*, 2002 S.L.T. 761 objection was taken to evidence recovered under an undated common law warrant. The Appeal Court ruled this warrant to be *ex facie* valid, there being no prescription applying to common law warrants. (Since by their very nature search warrants are intended to be executed swiftly, Convention issues of delay would be unlikely to be germane).

In *Lord Advocate's Reference (No.1 of 2002)*, 2002 S.L.T. 1017, following *Hepburn v Brown*, 1998 J.C. 63; 1997 S.C.C.R. 698, it was held on appeal that the sheriff erred in disallowing evidence obtained following an examination of computer equipment and images by a police civilian specialist who had not been specified in the body of the search warrant. (Prudence would suggest that the warrant ought to be sufficiently broadly drafted to avoid such objections, since the court stressed that the regularity or otherwise of a warrant depended upon the circumstances in each case). Different considerations had applied in relation to a warrant obtained under statute by Customs and Excise officers since the Customs and Excise Management Act 1979 (c.2) required that the number of officers involved in the search had to be stipulated in the body of the warrant; see *Singh (Manjit) v HM Advocate*, 2001 S.L.T. 812; 2001 S.C.C.R. 348.

In *Graham v Higson*, 2002 S.L.T. 1382 the accused proceeded by means of a Bill of Suspension after having precognosced the justice who had granted a statutory search warrant. The Appeal Court ordered a report from the justice who could not recall the information given to him in support of the warrant. G argued unsuccessfully that the justice had not exercised his judicial duty of scrutiny properly and that the warrant should be quashed. Paradoxically, given the oft-expressed unwillingness of the Court to look behind the circumstances leading to grant of warrants, no comment was made about the propriety of precognition here.

A Bill of Suspension, rather than a preliminary plea, was raised in *Knaup v Hutchison*, 2002 S.C.C.R. 879 following service of an indictment alleging contravention of the Misuse of Drugs Act 1971 s.4(3)(b), and precognition of the Crown witnesses. Precognition disclosed that the officer craving the warrant did so on the basis that the accused was concerned in the supplying of controlled drugs and was suspected to be due to take delivery of drugs imminently; the defence contention was that the sheriff could not recall the circumstances giving rise to grant of the warrant and, in any event, that grant was premature, the accused not then being in possession of such drugs. The court proceeded on the customary basis that the warrant was *ex facie* valid and the sheriff's lack of recall was of no moment almost two years on, but accepted that a warrant could not be granted prospectively. See also *Stewart v Harvie* [2015] HCJAC 13; 2016 S.C.C.R. 1, a Bill of Suspension which failed to suspend a drugs search warrant.

Ex facie valid warrants were attacked, unsuccessfully, by Bill of Suspension in *Crawford v Dyer*, 2003 G.W.D. 1-18, where C, whose rented premises had been searched previously, contended that this information ought to have been disclosed to the sheriff when the warrant was sought and that C should have been given notice of the warrant and the opportunity then to be heard.

Attention is directed to the terms of s.9A of the Act which now enable justices (a definition which applies equally to justices of the peace and to sheriffs) to sign warrants which they could competently grant, but while outwith their territorial jurisdiction. This provision came into force from 27 June 2003; warrants granted before that date would still be subject to the caveats set out in *Shields v Donnelly*, 2000 S.L.T. 147; 1999 S.C.C.R. 890.

Execution of warrants and service of complaints, etc.

297.—(1) Any warrant granted by a justice may, without being backed or endorsed by any other justice, be executed throughout Scotland in the same way as it may be executed within the jurisdiction of the justice who granted it. A4-577

(2) Any complaint, warrant, or other proceeding for the purposes of any summary proceedings under this Act may without endorsation be served or executed at any place within Scotland by any officer of law, and such service or execution may be proved either by the oath in court of the officer or by production of his written execution.

(3) A warrant issued in the Isle of Man for the arrest of a person charged with an offence may, after it has been endorsed by a justice in Scotland, be executed there by the person bringing that warrant, by any person to whom the warrant was originally directed or by any officer of law of the sheriff court district where the warrant has been endorsed in like manner as any such warrant issued in Scotland.

(4) In subsection (3) above, "endorsed" means endorsed in the like manner as a process to which section 4 of the Summary Jurisdiction (Process) Act 1881 applies.

(5) The Indictable Offences Act Amendment Act 1868 shall apply in relation to the execution in Scotland of warrants issued in the Channel Islands.

Definitions

"justice": s.307(1). A4-577.1
"offence": s.307(1).

"officer of law": s.307(1).

[THE NEXT PARAGRAPH IS A4-578]

GENERAL NOTE

A4-578 This section reflects the reform introduced by s.9 of the Criminal Justice (Scotland) Act 1995 and applies to all warrants granted in Scotland. It removes the need for a warrant, granted by a justice for execution outwith his jurisdiction, to be "backed" by another justice. A degree of caution is necessary since this reform does not extend to warrants granted in Scotland for execution in England and Wales.

Historically, a warrant granted for execution within the jurisdiction of a justice could always be executed without further ado, but matters were less straightforward when the warrant was granted for execution elsewhere in Scotland, and thoroughly byzantine when the warrant had to be executed in England and Wales: these are discussed in turn below.

Historically, the sheriff's power to grant warrants to the police extended only to officers of forces responsible for policing within the sheriffdom (see *Dyer, Applicant*, 2008 S.C.C.R. 192) but it is submitted that this would not preclude application to the sheriff specifying the need for those officers to utilise the assistance or expertise of other police forces, officers of SPA, or other enforcement agencies if the circumstances demanded. The critical factor remains (in the absence of rare express statutory exceptions) that the prosecutor can satisfy the sheriff that the offence, or a material element of its furtherance, occurred within the court's jurisdiction. The legislative response to *Dyer* was a stand-alone provision in the Criminal Justice and Licensing (Scotland) Act 2010 (s.56) ostensibly to extend powers of search to officers of the now defunct Scottish Drug Enforcement Agency. Section 297 of the Act applies to "any officer of law" as modified by SI 2018/46 paras 6 and 7, and Schs 2 and 3 confirm that the scope of the Act extends, as before, to officers of British Transport Police, Ministry of Defence Police and Civil Nuclear Constabulary and now also to immigration officers and to authorised HMRC officers, officers of the National Crime Agency and to the various military policing arms, in certain circumstances. Mercifully, such complexities have remained of academic, rather than practical, concern. Much helpful discussion on the question of shrieval jurisdiction is found in *Ashraf v Dunn* [2011] HCJAC 106; 2012 S.C.C.R. 597, a Bill of Suspension initiated at a very late stage in proceedings, well after service of the indictment or disclosure of the Crown case. As well as enabling the sheriff or JP to grant relevant search warrants to be executed by officers of UK national forces whose ambit would include the sheriffdom, such as the British Transport Police or Ministry of Defence Police, this power could be extended to officers of police forces policing areas outwith the jurisdiction and, indeed, outwith Scotland entirely. Much helpful discussion on the question of shrieval jurisdiction can be found in *Ashraf v Dunn* [2011] HCJAC 106; 2012 S.C.C.R. 597, a Bill of Suspension launched at a very late stage in proceedings, well after service of the indictment or disclosure of the Crown case.

Procedurally, such a Bill would remain competent even if no preliminary plea had been intimated in time for the first or preliminary diet (see s.71(2) and (2YA) above) and, critically, does not require the consideration of, or leave to appeal from, the court of first instance. Notwithstanding the advent of the Sheriff Appeal Court, it remains the case that any Bill of Suspension seeking to stay or prevent procedures covered by a warrant falls to be determined by the High Court of Justiciary, exercising its supervisory jurisdiction over administrative procedures (see *McWilliams v PF, Dumfries* [2016] HCJAC 29, following *Brown v Donaldson*, 2008 J.C. 83).

The procedure to be followed in recovering client files from solicitors where legal privilege is asserted is set out in Bill of Suspension, *Clyde and Co (Scotland) LLP v Richardson* [2016] HCJAC 93; 2016 S.C.C.R. 480. Still more care has to be exercised where the ultimate intention is to endorse the warrant for execution outwith Scotland; see *Holman Fenwick Willan LLP v Orr* [2017] HCJAC 38; 2017 S.C.C.R. 309. In *Clyde and Co.* the Crown did not argue against the suspension sought. Several notable issues appear in *Holman*: the warrant conspicuously failed to identify the potential evidential materials as being in any way privileged or to make known that the case had already been indicted in the High Court. The Appeal Court (at [22]) held that privilege is a matter for the client, not the agent, to assert—a counsel of perfection. Unless there is clarity in the warrant, recovered materials will be sealed until client instructions can be sought, either in relation to a bill of suspension or appointment of a commissioner to examine the papers. In this case, the warrant was quashed and the Appeal Court cautioned that, notwithstanding the decision in *Frame v Houston*, 1991 J.C. 115; 1991 S.C.C.R. 436; 1992 S.L.T. 205, evidential materials, after such late applications, risked not being admitted as evidence under s.67 procedure.

It is important to note that suspension procedure is only appropriate where there is consensus as to the factual background giving rise to the Bill. If there is a necessity to determine the factual background (for example by means of a proof hearing, or a judicial inquiry) then this avenue is nugatory. See generally *AS v HM Advocate* [2016] HCJAC 126.

A Bill is not an appropriate instrument to review a conditional fixed penalty issued by the procurator fiscal (s.302) or, indeed, a compensation offer (s.302A). See the General Note to s.302 below.

Warrants craved for execution outwith the jurisdiction of the court, but in Scotland, included a crave requesting the concurrence of judges in that other place in the granting of the warrant. This necessitated application to be made to two courts before the warrant could be executed, an anachronistic, time-consuming, and invariably unnecessary, procedure. Following *Shields v Donnelly*, 2000 S.L.T. 147; 2000 S.C.C.R. 890 it was established that a warrant had to be granted within the territorial jurisdiction of the court; but see now s.9A at para. A4-18.2.

Warrants craved in Scotland for execution in England and Wales require to be "backed" and "endorsed" in accordance with the Summary Jurisdiction (Process) Act 1881 (c.24): in those circumstances the warrant obtained from the Scottish court has to be docquetted in compliance with the Act and then presented to the relevant magistrates' court having jurisdiction. However in England and Wales warrant procedures are generally regulated by Pt II of the Police and Criminal Evidence Act 1984 (c.60) and, thus, the court competent to grant warrants under PACE is determined by whether it is "special procedure" material (which requires a Crown Court warrant), or not.

PACE failed to take account of cross-border warrants, or the need to preserve the position of warrants granted, and backed, by Scottish courts, when it repealed the 1881 Act's provisions for England and Wales and introduced the Pt II provisions. These shortcomings have now been remedied for warrants granted by English and Welsh courts in relation to materials lying within Scotland by s.86 of the Criminal Justice and Police Act 2001; for practical purposes a Circuit judge is placed on the same footing as a magistrate and the wording of the 1881 docquet is used.

The position in relation to the cross-border execution of Scottish warrants in England and Wales is set out in *R. v Manchester Stipendiary Magistrate, ex p. Granada Television Ltd* [2000] 2 W.L.R. 1, H.L.(E) by the judgement of Lord Hope of Craighead. This case involved the use of a Scottish common law search warrant, endorsed in accordance with the 1881 Act by the Manchester Stipendiary Magistrate, to search a broadcaster's premises for evidential materials arising from a television programme. The competency of the warrant was upheld on final appeal. Note that following upon the reforms wrought by the Criminal Justice and Police Act 2001, the decision in *HM Advocate (for Duncan Hodge)*, 2000 S.C.C.R. 439 has been superseded. In that decision, which centred upon efforts to execute an English Circuit Court warrant in Scotland, the Appeal Court reserved opinion upon whether a petition to the nobile officium could have been used to meet the shortcomings. It is submitted that matters might still be dealt with satisfactorily in many instances by means of a common law warrant obtained by the Procurator Fiscal for the public interest. More surprisingly perhaps, in *Paterson v Thomson*, 2010 J.C. 44, a Bill of Suspension against a pro forma JP warrant, which had not included a reference to "Glasgow" when defining the premises to be searched there under the Misuse of Drugs Act 1971, failed on the basis of the other information contained in the warrant and the fact that the Crown demonstrated that there was only one street of that name not just within the JP district but within the United Kingdom.

Note should also be taken of the terms of s.81 of the Criminal Justice (Scotland) Act 2003 (asp 7) which enables "backed" search warrants issued in Northern Irish courts, authorising the search of premises in Scotland, to be endorsed by the relevant Scottish court. One could be forgiven for pondering why this straightforward provision could not simply have been incorporated into s.297 rather than standing alone in the 2003 Act.

A full discussion of the factors, such as danger to life or property, or urgency to protect or preserve evidence which might otherwise be imperiled, can be found in *Freeburn v HM Advocate* [2012] HCJAC 135; 2013 S.L.T.70. Note too that the courts distinguish between evidents recovered irregularly in the course of an investigation—which may, or may not, affect their admissibility—if the irregularity is held to be excusable [see *Lawrie v Muir*, 1950 J.C. 19 and *Melville v Procurator Fiscal, Dundee* [2018] SAC (Crim) 14] and items stumbled upon entirely fortuitously, which involve no such irregularity or potential inadmissibility. *Melville v Procurator Fiscal, Dundee* [2018] SAC (Crim) 14 strikes a contemporary note: texts inadvertently uncovered by the complainer's husband who had surreptitiously gained forensic access to her mobile phone, as he sought to confirm his suspicions of an affair between her and the accused, whilst (on Crown concession) irregularly obtained, was admissible evidence.

See also *Meo v Watson* [2013] HCJAC 76, where following a credible report from a Scottish Power electrician of suspected cannabis cultivation there, police officers entered a, by now, empty flat and surveyed the scene but delayed any search till a search warrant had been obtained. *M's* Bill of Suspension was refused. Similar considerations arose in *O'Neill v Procurator Fiscal, Paisley* [2015] HCJAC 136 where ongoing cannabis cultivation was found by firefighters and an extensive search was conducted by police without a search warrant for several hours. Again the appellant's Bill was refused.

Re-execution of apprehension warrants

297A.—(1) This section applies where a person has been apprehended under a warrant (the "original warrant") granted under this Act in relation to any proceedings. A4-578.1

(2) If the person absconds, the person may be re-apprehended under the original warrant (and as if that warrant had not been executed to any extent).

(3) If, for any reason, it is not practicable to bring the person before the court as required under a provision of this Act applying in the case, the person is to be brought before the court as soon as practicable after the relevant reason ceases to prevail.

(4) Despite subsection (3) above, if—

(a) the original warrant was granted in solemn proceedings; and

(b) the impracticability arises because the person needs medical treatment or care,

the person may be released.

(5) A person released under subsection (4) above may be re-apprehended under the original warrant (and as if that warrant had not been executed to any extent).

(6) Subsection (3) above does not affect the operation of section 22(1B) of this Act (which relates to liberation on an undertaking of persons apprehended under warrant granted in summary proceedings).

(7) Nothing in this section prevents a court from granting a fresh warrant for the apprehension of the person.

(8) Subject to this section are—

(a) any rule of law as to bringing a person before a court in pursuance of a warrant granted on petition (as referred to in section 34 of this Act);

(b) section 102A(10) of this Act;

(c) section 135(3) (including as applying in relation to sections 22(1B) and 156) of this Act;

(d) section 90A(9) of this Act.

AMENDMENTS

Section 297A inserted by Criminal Proceedings etc (Reform) (Scotland) Act 2007 (asp 6) s.33. Brought into force on 10 December 2007 by SSI 2007/479 (C.40) art.3 and Sch.

GENERAL NOTE

A4-578.2 This section applies to the broad range of apprehension warrants in both solemn and summary procedure and confronts the problems which can, on occasion, arise after an accused has been arrested on warrant but before he can be placed before the court. Ordinarily Scottish criminal procedure demands that any person arrested on criminal charges should be put before the court on the next lawful day or as soon as reasonably practicable. Considerable logistical and procedural difficulties can develop if, for any reason, an accused arrested on warrant is, or becomes, unfit to appear before the court - the problem being that the apprehension warrant having been executed, is now spent. Until the reform introduced by s.297A the only option for the Crown was to seek a fresh apprehension warrant on the same charges—a duplication which presented challenges for the police and the court alike. Section 297A now gives the police and prosecuting authorities a degree of flexibility in these circumstances by enabling them to release the accused and re-arrest him once they are satisfied that the circumstances, which precluded his scheduled court appearance, have ended: this discretion can be exercised without the need to obtain a fresh warrant but operates without prejudice to the right of the prosecutor to seek a warrant de novo if he so wishes. As can be seen, the scope of the provision extends to petition apprehension warrants, to warrants granted after failure to appear at a subsequent solemn diet (see generally s.102A(10)), summary apprehension warrants and witness apprehension warrants from solemn or summary proceedings. The provision does not however extend to means apprehension warrants granted by the courts for unpaid fines.

[THE NEXT PARAGRAPH IS A4-579]

Trial judge's report

Trial judge's report

A4-579 **298.**—(1) Without prejudice to section 113 of this Act, the High Court may, in relation to—

(a) an appeal under section 106(1), 108 or 108A of this Act;

(b) an appeal by way of bill of suspension or advocation; or

(c) a petition to the nobile officium,

at any time before the appeal is finally determined or, as the case may be, petition finally disposed of, order the judge who presided at the trial, passed sentence or otherwise disposed of the case to provide to the Clerk of Justiciary a report in writing giving the judge's opinion on the case generally or in relation to any particular matter specified in the order.

(2) The Clerk of Justiciary shall send a copy of a report provided under subsection (1) above to the convicted person or his solicitor, the Crown Agent and, in relation to cases referred under Part XA of this Act, the Commission.

(2A) Without prejudice to section 186(3)(b) of this Act, the Sheriff Appeal Court may, in relation to—

(a) an appeal under section 175(2) to (4) of this Act; or

(b) an appeal by way of bill of suspension or advocation,

at any time before the appeal is finally determined order the judge who presided at the trial, passed sentence or otherwise disposed of the case to provide to the Clerk of the Sheriff Appeal Court a report in writing giving the judge's opinion in the case generally or in relation to any particular matter specified in the order.

(2B) The Clerk of the Sheriff Appeal Court must send a copy of the report provided under subsection (2A) above to the convicted person or their solicitor, the prosecutor and, in relation to cases referred under Part XA of this Act, the Commission.

(3) Subject to subsections (2) and (2B) above, the report of the judge shall be available only to the High Court or the Sheriff Appeal Court (as the case may be), the parties and, on such conditions as may be prescribed by Act of Adjournal, such other persons or classes of persons as may be so prescribed.

AMENDMENTS

Subs.(1)(a) inserted by Crime and Punishment (Scotland) Act 1997 (c.48) Sch.1 para. 21(33)(a) with effect from 20 October 1997 in terms of SI 1997/2323 art.3 and Sch.1.

Subs.(2) as amended by Crime and Punishment (Scotland) Act 1997 (c.48) Sch.1 para.21(33)(b) (effective 1 April 1999: SI 1999/652).

Subss.(1) and (3) as amended, subss.(2A), (2B) inserted, by Courts Reform (Scotland) Act 2014 (Consequential Provisions No.2) Order 2015 (SSI 2015/338) Sch.2 para.5 (effective 22 September 2015).

DEFINITIONS

"Clerk of Justiciary": s.307(1). **A4-579.1**
"judge": s.307(1).

[THE NEXT PARAGRAPH IS A4-580]

GENERAL NOTE

This new provision reinforces the statutory duty on judges at first instance to provide a report in the event of an appeal: the section allows the High Court of Justiciary to order further reports of a general or specific nature. This may be necessary because, for example, the note of appeal may not contain, as is required by s.110(3)(b), a full statement of all the grounds of appeal. Alternatively, difficulty or uncertainty in relation to a material point may have arisen at the hearing of the appeal and the trial judge's opinion may be thought necessary in the circumstances. In *Brady v Barbour*, 1994 S.C.C.R. 890 the sheriff, for whatever reason, did not produce a draft stated case and thus placed the High Court of Justiciary in some difficulty. This provision allows further orders to be made for reports. The role of s.298 was commented on in *Megrahi v HM Advocate*, 2001 G.W.D. 26-1014. **A4-580**

Intimation of certain applications to the High Court

Intimation of bills and of petitions to the nobile officium

298A.—(1) This subsection applies where the prosecutor requires to intimate to the respondent— **A4-580.1**

(a) a bill of advocation;

(b) a petition to the nobile officium;

(c) an order of the High Court or the Sheriff Appeal Court relating to such a bill or (as the case may be) petition.

(2) Where subsection (1) above applies, the requirement may be met by serving on the respondent or the respondent's solicitor a copy of the bill, petition or (as the case may be) order.

(3) Service under subsection (2) above may (in relation to any proceedings) be effected—

(a) on the respondent, in the same manner as citation under section 141 of this Act;

(b) on the respondent's solicitor, by post.

(4) This subsection applies where a person requires to intimate to the prosecutor—

(a) a bill of suspension or advocation;
(b) a petition to the nobile officium;
(c) an order of the High Court or the Sheriff Appeal Court relating to such a bill or (as the case may be) petition.

(5) Where subsection (4) above applies, the requirement may be met by serving on the prosecutor a copy of the bill, petition or (as the case may be) order.

(6) Service under subsection (5) above may (in relation to any proceedings) be effected by post.

(7) It is sufficient evidence that service has been effected under subsection (3) or (6) above if there is produced a written execution—

(a) in the form prescribed by Act of Adjournal or as nearly as may be in such form; and
(b) signed by the person who effected service.

(8) In relation to service effected by means of registered post or the recorded delivery service, the relevant post office receipt requires to be produced along with the execution mentioned in subsection (7) above.

(9) A party who has service effected under subsection (3) or (6) above must, as soon as practicable thereafter, lodge with the Clerk of Justiciary or the Clerk of the Sheriff Appeal Court (as the case may be) a copy of the execution mentioned in subsection (7) above.

(10) For the purpose of subsection (3)(a) above, section 141 of this Act is to be read with such modifications as are necessary for its application in the circumstances.

(11) This section is without prejudice to any rule of law or practice by virtue of which things of the kinds mentioned in subsections (1) and (4) above (including copies) may be intimated or served.

AMENDMENTS

Section 298A inserted by Criminal Proceedings etc (Reform) (Scotland) Act 2007 (asp 6) s.38. Brought into force on 10 December 2007 by SSI 2007/479 (C.40) art.3 and Sch.

Subss.(1), (4) and (9) as amended by Courts Reform (Scotland) Act 2014 (Consequential Provisions No.2) Order 2015 (SSI 2015/338) Sch.2 para.5 (effective 22 September 2015).

[THE NEXT PARAGRAPH IS A4-581]

Correction of entries

Correction of entries

A4-581 **299.**—(1) Subject to the provisions of this section, it shall be competent to correct any entry in—

(a) the record of proceedings in a prosecution; or
(b) the extract of a sentence passed or an order of court made in such proceedings,

in so far as that entry constitutes an error of recording or is incomplete.

(2) An entry mentioned in subsection (1) above may be corrected—

(a) by the clerk of the court, at any time before either the sentence or order of the court is executed or, on appeal, the proceedings are transmitted to the Clerk of Justiciary or the Clerk of the Sheriff Appeal Court (as the case may be);
(b) by the clerk of the court, under the authority of the court which passed the

sentence or made the order, at any time after the execution of the sentence or order of the court but before such transmission as is mentioned in paragraph (a) above; or

(c) by the clerk of the court under the authority of the High Court or the Sheriff Appeal Court (as the case may be) in the case of a remit under subsection (4)(b) below.

(3) A correction in accordance with paragraph (b) or (c) of subsection (2) above shall be intimated to the prosecutor and to the former accused or his solicitor.

(4) Where during the course of an appeal, the court hearing the appeal becomes aware of an erroneous or incomplete entry, such as is mentioned in subsection (1) above, the court—

(a) may consider and determine the appeal as if such entry were corrected; and

(b) either before or after the determination of the appeal, may remit the proceedings to the court of first instance for correction in accordance with subsection (2)(c) above.

(5) Any correction under subsections (1) and (2) above by the clerk of the court shall be authenticated by his signature and, if such correction is authorised by a court, shall record the name of the judge or judges authorising such correction and the date of such authorisation.

AMENDMENTS

Subss.(2) and (4) as amended by Courts Reform (Scotland) Act 2014 (Consequential Provisions No.2) Order 2015 (SSI 2015/338) Sch.2 para.5 (effective 22 September 2015).

DEFINITIONS

"clerk of Court": s.114 of the Criminal Justice (Scotland) Act 1995. A4-581.1
"Clerk of Justiciary": s.307(1).
"High Court": s.307(1).
"judge": s.307(1).
"order": s.307(1).
"sentence": s.307(1).

GENERAL NOTE

See *Heywood, Petr*, 1998 G.W.D. 13-639. An unauthenticated correction has no effect (see *Fitzgerald v Vannet*, 2000 S.C.C.R. 422) where corrections made in error, but not initialled, were disregarded. The Appeal Court utilised its power under s.299(4)(a) to remit the complaint back to the court of first instance having directed correction of defective minutes. A4-581.2

Section 299 operates only where it is clear that the record does not reflect the sentence which was in fact passed: *Iqbal v Harvie* [2016] HCJAC 38; 2016 S.C.C.R. 258.

[THE NEXT PARAGRAPH IS A4-582]

Amendment of records of conviction and sentence in summary proceedings

300.—(1) Without prejudice to section 299 of this Act, where, on an application in accordance with subsection (2) below, the Sheriff Appeal Court is satisfied that a record of conviction or sentence in summary proceedings inaccurately records the identity of any person, it may authorise the clerk of the court which convicted or, as the case may be, sentenced the person to correct the record. A4-582

(2) An application under subsection (1) above shall be made after the determination of the summary prosecution and may be made by any party to the summary proceedings or any other person having an interest in the correction of the alleged inaccuracy.

(3) The Sheriff Appeal Court shall order intimation of an application under subsection (1) above to such persons as it considers appropriate and shall not

determine the application without affording to the parties to the summary proceedings and to any other person having an interest in the correction of the alleged inaccuracy an opportunity to be heard.

(4) The power of the High Court under this section may be exercised by a single judge of the High Court in the same manner as it may be exercised by the High Court, and subject to the same provisions.

AMENDMENTS

Subss.(1) and (3) as amended by Courts Reform (Scotland) Act 2014 (Consequential Provisions No.2) Order 2015 (SSI 2015/338) Sch.2 para.5 (effective 22 September 2015).

DEFINITIONS

A4-582.1 "clerk of Court": s.114(1) of the Criminal Justice (Scotland) Act 1995.
"Clerk of Justiciary": s.308(1).

Excusal of irregularities

Power of court to excuse procedural irregularities

A4-582.2 **300A.**—(1) Any court may excuse a procedural irregularity—

(a) of a kind described in subsection (5) below; and
(b) which has occurred in relation to proceedings before that court,

if the conditions mentioned in subsection (4) below are met.

(2) In appeal proceedings, the court hearing the appeal may excuse a procedural irregularity—

(a) of that kind; and
(b) which has occurred in relation to earlier proceedings in the case that is the subject of the appeal,

if those conditions are met.

(3) A court may proceed under subsection (1) or (2) above on the application of the prosecutor or an accused person (having given the other an opportunity to be heard).

(4) The conditions are that—

(a) it appears to the court that the irregularity arose because of—
  (i) mistake or oversight; or
  (ii) other excusable reason; and
(b) the court is satisfied in the circumstances of the case that it would be in the interests of justice to excuse the irregularity.

(5) A procedural irregularity is an irregularity arising at any stage of proceedings—

(a) from—
  (i) failure to call or discharge a diet properly;
  (ii) improper adjournment or continuation of a case;
  (iii) a diet being fixed for a non-sitting day;
(b) from failure of—
  (i) the court; or
  (ii) the prosecutor or the accused,

  to do something within a particular period or otherwise comply with a time limit;
(c) from failure of the prosecutor to serve properly a notice or other thing;
(d) from failure of the accused to—
  (i) intimate properly a preliminary objection;
  (ii) intimate properly a plea or defence;
  (iii) serve properly a notice or other thing;

(e) from failure of—
(i) the court; or
(ii) the prosecutor or the accused,
to fulfil any other procedural requirement.

(6) Subsection (1) above does not authorise a court to excuse an irregularity arising by reason of the detention in custody of an accused person for a period exceeding that fixed by this Act.

(7) Subsection (1) above does not apply in relation to any requirement as to proof including, in particular, any matter relating to—
(a) admissibility of evidence;
(b) sufficiency of evidence; or
(c) any other evidential factor.

(7A) Subsection (1) does not authorise a court to excuse a failure to do any of the following things timeously—
(a) lodge written intimation of intention to appeal in accordance with section 109(1),
(b) lodge a note of appeal in accordance with section 110(1)(a),
(c) make an application for a stated case under section 176(1),
(d) lodge a note of appeal in accordance with section 186(2)(a).

(8) Where a court excuses an irregularity under subsection (1) above, it may make such order as is necessary or expedient for the purpose of—
(a) restoring the proceedings as if the irregularity had never occurred;
(b) facilitating the continuation of the proceedings as if it had never occurred, for example—
(i) altering a diet;
(ii) extending any time limit;
(iii) appointing a diet for further procedure or granting an adjournment or continuation of a diet;
(c) protecting the rights of the parties.

(9) For the purposes of this section—
(a) a reference to an accused person, except the reference in subsection (6) above, includes reference to a person who has been convicted of an offence;
(b) something is done properly if it is done in accordance with a requirement of an enactment or any rule of law.

(10) In subsection (5)(a)(iii) above, a "non-sitting day" is a day on which the court is under this Act not required to sit.

(11) This section is without prejudice to any provision of this Act under which a court may—
(a) alter a diet; or
(b) extend—
(i) a period within which something requires to be done; or
(ii) any other time limit.

(12) This section is without prejudice to any rule of law by virtue of which it may be determined by a court that breach, in relation to criminal proceedings—
(a) of a requirement of an enactment; or
(b) of a rule of law,
does not render the proceedings, or anything done (or purported to have been done) for the purposes of or in connection with proceedings, invalid.

AMENDMENTS

Section 300A inserted by Criminal Proceedings etc (Reform) (Scotland) Act 2007 (asp 6) s.40. Brought into force on 10 December 2007 by SSI 2007/479 (C.40) art.3 and Sch.

Subs.(2) as amended by Courts Reform (Scotland) Act 2014 (Consequential Provisions No.2) Order 2015 (SSI 2015/338) Sch.2 para.5 (effective 22 September 2015).

Subs.(7A) inserted by Criminal Justice (Scotland) Act 2016 (asp 1) s.91. Brought into force on 17 January 2017 by SSI 2016/426 art.2 and Sch.1 para.1.

GENERAL NOTE

A4-582.3 In *Murray v Campbell* (1878) 16 S. L. Rep. 71 there was a complaint on appeal of an unreasonable departure from ordinary summary procedure. The appeal was refused when it was admitted at the bar that the Crown had merely provided too much information, and that the appellant had not suffered any prejudice as a consequence. In *William and Anderson v Linton* (1878) 16 S. L. Rep. 180 an appeal was taken in circumstances where in a court of first instance a guilty plea was recorded during a sitting of the court at a point during the temporary absence of instructed counsel elsewhere in the building to consult law books. That was an irregularity of the nature that would now be excusable competently, especially as the court had not understood fully the extent of their authority

Some of the contentious issues still arising from the excusal of procedural errors can be found in the early case of *Riddell v Stevenson* (1881)8 R. (J.) 17. An appeal had been taken when a sentence of imprisonment was imposed on one specific date and yet the minute recorded the date as that of the day before the true date. The correction was made after the prisoner was removed from the court. The warrant of imprisonment seems to have had the wrong date on it.

Lord Craighill noted (at p.18) that: "The record is the only authentic evidence of what was done, and if it be erroneous, or if it has been altered unauthorisedly after proceedings have terminated, there is nothing trustworthy upon which the warrant can be supported. I think it of the utmost importance that we should discountenance irregularity in the records of a criminal, or indeed any Court."

Lord Young (at p.19) took the opposite view: "The minutes of procedure of Court of criminal justice may be, and frequently are, corrected by striking or words and sentences, and writing in others, and being a record written by a public officer of proceedings in an open Court there is no presumption or room for suspicion of impropriety." See further observations (at p.20) and, in particular, the view that the clerk's certificate is not the conviction or the sentence.

The Lord Justice Clerk was required to decide these conflicting views and he sided with the former colleague (at p.21): "I cannot think that the alteration is a matter of indifference. I think that more injustice would be done by giving encouragement to laxity in criminal proceedings … than by granting this suspension. It may be that … the prisoner in this case suffered no injustice by the error, but we are here dealing with criminal proceedings and a criminal sentence, where accuracy is absolutely essential." Appeal allowed.

It may be that procedural errors in the past were pled on the basis of appeals and refused as insufficiently serious to support an appellate plea of a miscarriage of justice, or even simply that the complaint was *de minimis*. In short, there may be other missed authorities of relevance to a modern statutory power of excusal. In *Gallie v Ferguson* (1883) 21 S. L. Reporter 120 the error of omission was one of trivia. After a minor infraction of the law was held proved the written interlocutor from the court recorded the sentence with the word "shillings" omitted so that the formal record of the sentence did not say what the fine amounted to in sterling money. The appeal was refused. Lord Young commented, p.121, that in the ordinary course of business it was known that the fine was announced by the magistrates, by implication in open court, and that must have been done in the present case, as the 15 shillings had been paid. It was noted also that the appeal had not been brought on the ground of the innocence of the accused, but only because a word was missing from the interlocutor.

Further, there is an essential difference between an error and that which is beyond merely slovenly and is altogether illegal and improper: *Stewart v Lang and Sinclair* (1894) 32 32 S. L. Reporter 67 per Lord Trayner at p.68.

Not every error necessarily requires correction or even prejudices an accused: in *Gea Catalan v Spain* (1995) 20 E.H.H.R. 266 a typing error was reproduced when documents were copied, but, in the procedural circumstances, the appellant could not say that he had not been given full information as to the nature of the charge against him.

The terms of this section appear permissive in scope but it is essential first to distinguish between procedural irregularities, covered by s.300A, and anything which constitutes a fundamental nullity and hence incapable of being corrected using s.300A. The rules of statutory interpretation as applied to the section are strictly construed by the Appeal Court and rendered much earlier case law governing procedural irregularities redundant. The "proceedings" specified in s.300A(1)(b) are those before the court at the time of the irregularity in question. Note too that the Appeal Court will require the fullest explanation (which will generally come from the Crown) of the circumstances giving rise to the error. In *Shahid v Brown* [2010] HCJAC 100: 2011 J.C. 119 where a guilty plea had been tendered on an unsigned (and thus inept) complaint, the section could offer no remedy. Contrast *PF, Aberdeen v RL* [2015] HCJAC 21, where earlier court minutes had not been signed off by the clerk (causing the instance to fall on that date) and steps were taken subsequently before the sheriff to cure the error, the court held that s.300A could be applied. On the merits the application was refused having failed the interests of justice test (subs.(4)(b)).

In solemn proceedings this section does not provide a mechanism for remedying late lodging of notices; see *Murphy v HM Advocate* [2012] HCJAC 74; 2012 S.C.L. 855 and, generally, s.79(1) above. Failure to lodge a s.259 application timeously may in limited circumstances constitute a procedural irregularity; in *Murphy* above the Appeal Court indicated that the judge determining the issue would be entitled to examine the full procedural history of the case.

For other examples of the use of s.300A, see *HM Advocate v Hollywood*, 2010 G.W.D. 12–213 where a schedule of previous convictions had been served on the accused but several pages were missing. The Crown had a corrected version available which was substituted under authority of s.300A. There was no unfairness to the accused. Counsel for the accused conceded the competence of the action of the Crown but declined to agree to the matter having been done. Further, in *Gifford v HM Advocate*, 2011 S.C.C.R. 751 at [23], s.300A did not apply as the particular requirements of the section had not been satisfied.

In *Swan v Logue* 2013 S.C.C.R. 360 there were procedural circumstances which were such as to allow a sheriff to excuse a failure to serve a summary complaint on a regular induciae without hearing parties. An appeal by bill of suspension was refused. In *Newlands v HM Advocate*, 2014 S.C.C.R. 25 it was held that the statutory provision in s.300 preserved the pre-existing power of courts to hold proceedings to be valid notwithstanding a failure to comply with a specific statutory requirement or a rule of law. In the circumstances a petition to the *nobile officium* was refused.

See *Newlands v HM Advocate*, 2014 S.C.C.R. 25 for discussion of the relationship between s.300A(5) and s.300A(12) which also concerned the use of a certified copy indictment in place of the record copy after the latter had been lost.

In *Murphy v L* [2015] HCJAC 21; 2015 G.W.D. 12-201 it was held that s.300A entitled the Crown to make the motion for rectification of an error and the sheriff in the circumstances of this case erred. When s.300A(1)(b) referred to a court excusing a procedural irregularity that had occurred in relation to "proceedings before that court", it meant proceedings that were before that court on the date when the alleged irregularity had occurred, and s.300A(8) entitled the court in such circumstances to restore proceedings as if the irregularity had never occurred: *Shahid v Brown* [2010] HCJAC 100; 2011 J.C. 119 distinguished. Observed: that s.300A(4) entitled the court to grant relief on the ground, inter alia, that it would be in the interests of justice to excuse the irregularity, which might be relevant where a minor error for which there was a reasonable explanation would otherwise result in the failure of a prosecution on a serious charge but also necessitated a consideration of the accused's interests, and in considering whether the Crown had discharged the onus the courts had to give the fullest possible account of the circumstances in which the error occurred.

[THE NEXT PARAGRAPH IS A4-583]

Rights of audience

Rights of audience

301.—(1) Without prejudice to section 103(8) of this Act, any solicitor who has, by virtue of section 25A (rights of audience) of the Solicitors (Scotland) Act 1980, a right of audience in relation to the High Court of Justiciary shall have the same right of audience in that court as is enjoyed by an advocate. **A4-583**

(2) Any person who has complied with the terms of a scheme approved under section 26 of the Law Reform (Miscellaneous Provisions) (Scotland) Act 1990 (consideration of applications made under section 25) shall have such rights of audience before the High Court of Justiciary as may be specified in an Act of Adjournal made under subsection (7)(b) of that section.

GENERAL NOTE

The vital importance of avoiding the potential appearance of conflicts of interest in the choice of representation between the instructed solicitor advocate and the nominated solicitor (or firm) was highlighted in *Woodside v HM Advocate*, 2009 S.C.C.R. 355 and revisited by the Appeal Court in *Yazdanparast v HM Advocate* [2015] HCJAC 82. Neither appeal succeeded on the merits. **A4-583.0.1**

[THE NEXT PARAGRAPH IS A4-583.1]

Recovery of documents

Recovery of documents

301A.—(1) It is competent for the sheriff court to make, in connection with any criminal proceedings mentioned in subsection (2) below, the orders mentioned in subsection (3) below. **A4-583.1**

(2) The proceedings are—

(a) solemn proceedings in that sheriff court;

(b) summary proceedings—

(i) in that sheriff court;

(ii) in any JP court in that sheriff court's district.

(3) The orders are—

(a) an order granting commission and diligence for the recovery of documents;

(b) an order for the production of documents.

(4) An application for the purpose may not be made—

(a) in connection with solemn proceedings, until the indictment has been served on the accused or the accused has been cited under section 66(4)(b) of this Act;

(b) in connection with summary proceedings, until the accused has answered the complaint.

(5) A decision of the sheriff on an application for an order under subsection (1) above may be appealed to the appropriate Appeal Court.

(6) In an appeal under subsection (5) above, the appropriate Appeal Court may uphold, vary or quash the decision of the sheriff.

(7) The prosecutor is entitled to be heard in any—

(a) application for an order under subsection (1) above;

(b) appeal under subsection (5) above, even if the prosecutor is not a party to the application or (as the case may be) appeal.

(8) The competence of the High Court to make, in connection with criminal proceedings, the orders mentioned in subsection (3) above is restricted to making them in connection with proceedings in that court.

(9) In this section, "appropriate Appeal Court" means—

(a) in the case of an appeal under subsection (5) against a decision made in solemn proceedings, the High Court;

(b) in the case of an appeal under subsection (5) against a decision made in summary proceedings, the Sheriff Appeal Court.

AMENDMENTS

Section 301A inserted by Criminal Proceedings etc (Reform) (Scotland) Act 2007 (asp 6) s.37. Brought into force on 10 December 2007 by SSI 2007/479 (C.40) art.3 and Sch.

Subsections (5), (6) as amended, subs.(9) inserted, by Courts Reform (Scotland) Act 2014 (Consequential Provisions No.2) Order 2015 (SSI 2015/338) Sch.2 para.5 (effective 22 September 2015).

DEFINITIONS

A4-583.2 "indictment": s.307(1).
"complaint": s.307(1).
"High Court": s.307(1).
"prosecutor": s.307(1).

GENERAL NOTE

A4-583.3 This new provision as s.301A of the 1995 Act gives the sheriff court jurisdiction to deal with all applications for commission and diligence, or recovery of documents, except for cases indicted in the High Court. Hitherto all such procedures had to be placed before the High Court. It is axiomatic that applications can only be made to the sheriff in relation to cases in which the court enjoys territorial jursdiction and that, in solemn cases, application can only be made once an indictment has been served; in summary proceedings an application is only competent once an accused has appeared before court on his summary complaint (thus it would not be competent for a defence agent to seek materials, for example, in the knowledge that an apprehension warrant was still to be executed against the accused).

The High Court will now be required only to deliberate upon applications arising from proceedings indicted in that court but, as subs.(5) makes clear, appeals from any decision by the sheriff are to be considered by the High Court whose appellate powers are set out in subs.(6). It remains the case that the prosecutor is entitled to be heard in regard to any application for commision and diligence.

[THE NEXT PARAGRAPH IS A4-584]

Fixed penalties

Fixed penalty: conditional offer by procurator fiscal

302.—(1) Where a procurator fiscal receives a report that a relevant offence has been committed he may send to the alleged offender a notice under this section (referred to in this section as a conditional offer); and where he issues a conditional offer the procurator fiscal shall notify the clerk of court specified in it of the issue of the conditional offer and of its terms. **A4-584**

(2) A conditional offer—

(a) shall give such particulars of the circumstances alleged to constitute the offence to which it relates as are necessary for giving reasonable information about the alleged offence;

(b) shall state—

(i) the amount of the appropriate fixed penalty for that offence;

(ii) if the penalty is to be payable by instalments, the amount of the instalments and the intervals at which they should be paid;

(c) shall indicate that if, within 28 days of the date on which the conditional offer was issued, or such longer period as may be specified in the conditional offer, the alleged offender accepts the offer by making payment in respect of the fixed penalty to the clerk of court specified in the conditional offer at the address therein mentioned, any liability to conviction of the offence shall be discharged;

(ca) shall indicate—

(i) that the alleged offender may refuse the conditional offer by giving notice to the clerk of court in the manner specified in the conditional offer before the expiry of 28 days, or such longer period as may be specified in the conditional offer, beginning on the day on which the conditional offer is made;

(ii) that unless the alleged offender gives such notice, the alleged offender will be deemed to have accepted the conditional offer (even where no payment is made in respect of the offer);

(iii) that where the alleged offender is deemed as described in subparagraph (ii) above to have accepted the conditional offer any liability to conviction of the offence shall be discharged except where the offer is recalled under section 302C of this Act;

(d) shall state that proceedings against the alleged offender shall not be commenced in respect of that offence until the end of a period of 28 days from the date on which the conditional offer was issued, or such longer period as may be specified in the conditional offer;

(e) shall state—

(i) that the acceptance of the offer in the manner described in paragraph (c) above, or deemed acceptance of the offer as described in paragraph (ca)(ii) above, shall not be a conviction nor be recorded as such;

(ii) that the fact that the offer has been accepted, or deemed to have been accepted, may be disclosed to the court in any proceedings for an offence committed by the alleged offender within the period of two years beginning on the day of acceptance of the offer;

(iia) that that fact may be disclosed to the court also in any proceedings for an offence to which the alleged offender is, or is liable to become, subject at such time as the offer is accepted;

(iii) that if the offer is not accepted, that fact may be disclosed to the court in any proceedings for the offence to which the conditional offer relates;

(f) shall state that refusal of a conditional offer under paragraph (ca)(i) above will be treated as a request by the alleged offender to be tried for the offence; and

(g) shall explain the right to request a recall of the fixed penalty under section 302C of this Act.

(3) A conditional offer may be made in respect of more than one relevant offence and shall, in such a case, state the amount of the appropriate fixed penalty for all the offences in respect of which it is made.

(4) The clerk of court shall—

(a) without delay, notify the procurator fiscal who issued the conditional offer when a notice as described in subsection (2)(ca)(i) above has been received in respect of the offer; or

(b) following the expiry of the period of 28 days referred to in subsection (2)(c) above or such longer period as may be specified in the offer, notify the procurator fiscal if no such notice has been received.

(4A) A conditional offer is accepted by the alleged offender making any payment in respect of the appropriate fixed penalty.

(4B) Where an alleged offender to whom a conditional offer of a fixed penalty is made does not give notice as described in subsection (2)(ca)(i) above, the alleged offender is deemed to have accepted the conditional offer.

(4C) Where—

(a) an alleged offender accepts a conditional offer as described in subsection (4A) above; or

(b) an alleged offender is deemed to have accepted a conditional offer under subsection (4B) above and the fixed penalty is not recalled,

no proceedings shall be brought against the alleged offender for the offence.

(5) […]

(6) […]

(7) The Secretary of State shall, by order, prescribe a scale of fixed penalties for the purpose of this section.

(7A) The amount of the maximum penalty on the scale prescribed under subsection (7) above may not exceed £300 or such higher sum as the Scottish Ministers may by order specify.

(8) An order under subsection (7) or (7A) above—

(a) may contain provision as to the payment of fixed penalties by instalments; and

(b) shall be made by statutory instrument, which shall not be made unless a draft of the instrument has been laid before, and approved by resolution of, the Scottish Parliament.

(8A) The alleged offender shall be presumed to have received a conditional offer under subsection (1) above if the offer is sent to—

(a) the address given by the alleged offender in a request for recall under section 302C(1) of this Act of an earlier offer in the same matter; or

(b) any address given by the alleged offender to the clerk of court specified in the offer, or to the procurator fiscal, in connection with the offer.

(8B) For the purposes of section 141(4) of this Act, the accused shall be presumed to have received any citation effected at—

(a) the address to which a conditional offer under subsection (1) above was sent provided it is proved that the accused received the offer; or

(b) any address given by the accused to the clerk of court specified in the offer, or to the procurator fiscal, in connection with the offer.

(9) In this section—

(a) "a relevant offence" means any offence in respect of which an alleged offender could competently be tried before a district court, but shall not include a fixed penalty offence within the meaning of section 51 of the Road Traffic Offenders Act 1988 nor any other offence in respect of which a conditional offer within the meaning of sections 75 to 77 of that Act may be sent; and

(b) "the appropriate fixed penalty" means such fixed penalty on the scale prescribed under subsection (7) above as the procurator fiscal thinks fit having regard to the circumstances of the case.

AMENDMENTS

Subsection (9) as amended by Wireless Telegraphy Act 2006(c.36) s.123 and Sch.7 para.16 (effective 8 February 2007).

Subsections (2), (7), (8), (9) as amended, subss.(5), (6) repealed, and subss.(4A), (4B), (4C), (7A), (8A), (8B) inserted by Criminal Proceedings etc (Reform) (Scotland) Act 2007 (asp 6) s.50. Brought into force on 10 March 2008 by SSI 2008/42 (C.4) art.3 and Sch.

Subsection (2)(e)(iia) inserted by Criminal Justice and Licensing (Scotland) Act 2010 (asp 13) s.70(3). Brought into force on 28 March 2011 (for all purposes in respect of offences committed on or after 28 March 2011) by SSI 2011/178 (C.15) art.2, Sch.1 para.1.

Fixed penalty: conditional offer by procurator fiscal

302.—*(1) Where a procurator fiscal receives a report that a relevant offence has been committed he may send to the alleged offender a notice under this section (referred to in this section as a conditional offer); and where he issues a conditional offer the procurator fiscal shall notify the clerk of court specified in it of the issue of the conditional offer and of its terms.* **A4-584A**

(2) A conditional offer—

(a) shall give such particulars of the circumstances alleged to constitute the offence to which it relates as are necessary for giving reasonable information about the alleged offence;

(b) shall state—

(i) the amount of the appropriate fixed penalty for that offence;

(ii) if the penalty is to be payable by instalments, the amount of the instalments and the intervals at which they should be paid;

(c) shall indicate that if, within 28 days of the date on which the conditional offer was issued, or such longer period as may be specified in the conditional offer, the alleged offender accepts the offer by making payment in respect of the fixed penalty to the clerk of court specified in the conditional offer at the address therein mentioned, any liability to conviction of the offence shall be discharged;

(ca) shall indicate—

(i) that the alleged offender may refuse the conditional offer by giving notice to the clerk of court in the manner specified in the conditional offer before the expiry of 28 days, or such longer period as may be specified in the conditional offer, beginning on the day on which the conditional offer is made;

(ii) that unless the alleged offender gives such notice, the alleged of-

fender will be deemed to have accepted the conditional offer (even where no payment is made in respect of the offer);

(iii) that where the alleged offender is deemed as described in sub-paragraph (ii) above to have accepted the conditional offer any liability to conviction of the offence shall be discharged except where the offer is recalled under section 302C of this Act;

(d) shall state that proceedings against the alleged offender shall not be commenced in respect of that offence until the end of a period of 28 days from the date on which the conditional offer was issued, or such longer period as may be specified in the conditional offer;

(e) shall state—

(i) that the acceptance of the offer in the manner described in paragraph (c) above, or deemed acceptance of the offer as described in paragraph (ca)(ii) above, shall not be a conviction nor be recorded as such;

(ii) that the fact that the offer has been accepted, or deemed to have been accepted, may be disclosed to the court in any proceedings for an offence committed by the alleged offender within the period of two years beginning on the day of acceptance of the offer;

(iia) that that fact may be disclosed to the court also in any proceedings for an offence to which the alleged offender is, or is liable to become, subject at such time as the offer is accepted;

(iii) that if the offer is not accepted, that fact may be disclosed to the court in any proceedings for the offence to which the conditional offer relates;

(f) shall state that refusal of a conditional offer under paragraph (ca)(i) above will be treated as a request by the alleged offender to be tried for the offence; and

(g) shall explain the right to request a recall of the fixed penalty under section 302C of this Act.

(3) A conditional offer may be made in respect of more than one relevant offence and shall, in such a case, state the amount of the appropriate fixed penalty for all the offences in respect of which it is made.

(4) The clerk of court shall—

(a) without delay, notify the procurator fiscal who issued the conditional offer when a notice as described in subsection (2)(ca)(i) above has been received in respect of the offer; or

(b) following the expiry of the period of 28 days referred to in subsection (2)(c) above or such longer period as may be specified in the offer, notify the procurator fiscal if no such notice has been received.

(4A) A conditional offer is accepted by the alleged offender making any payment in respect of the appropriate fixed penalty.

(4B) Where an alleged offender to whom a conditional offer of a fixed penalty is made does not give notice as described in subsection (2)(ca)(i) above, the alleged offender is deemed to have accepted the conditional offer.

(4C) Where—

(a) an alleged offender accepts a conditional offer as described in subsection (4A) above; or

(b) an alleged offender is deemed to have accepted a conditional offer under subsection (4B) above and the fixed penalty is not recalled,

no proceedings shall be brought against the alleged offender for the offence.

(7) The Secretary of State shall, by order, prescribe a scale of fixed penalties for the purpose of this section.

(7A) The amount of the maximum penalty on the scale prescribed under subsection (7) above may not exceed £500 or such higher sum as the Scottish Ministers may by order specify.

(8) An order under subsection (7) or (7A) above—

(a) may contain provision as to the payment of fixed penalties by instalments; and

(b) shall be made by statutory instrument, which shall not be made unless a draft of the instrument has been laid before, and approved by resolution of, the Scottish Parliament.

(8A) The alleged offender shall be presumed to have received a conditional offer under subsection (1) above if the offer is sent to—

(a) the address given by the alleged offender in a request for recall under section 302C(1) of this Act of an earlier offer in the same matter; or

(b) any address given by the alleged offender to the clerk of court specified in the offer, or to the procurator fiscal, in connection with the offer.

(8B) For the purposes of section 141(4) of this Act, the accused shall be presumed to have received any citation effected at—

(a) the address to which a conditional offer under subsection (1) above was sent provided it is proved that the accused received the offer; or

(b) any address given by the accused to the clerk of court specified in the offer, or to the procurator fiscal, in connection with the offer.

(9) In this section—

(a) "a relevant offence" means any offence in respect of which an alleged offender could be tried summarily, but shall not include a fixed penalty offence within the meaning of section 51 of the Road Traffic Offenders Act 1988 nor any other offence in respect of which a conditional offer within the meaning of sections 75 to 77 of that Act may be sent; and

(b) "the appropriate fixed penalty" means such fixed penalty on the scale prescribed under subsection (7) above as the procurator fiscal thinks fit having regard to the circumstances of the case.

Amendments

In relation to COVID-19, s.302(7A) as amended by Coronavirus (Scotland) Act 2020 (asp 7) Sch.4(2) para.7(2) (effective 7 April 2020).

Definitions

"appropriate fixed penalty": s.302(9). **A4-584.1**
"offence": s.307(1).
"procurator fiscal": s.307(1).
"relevant offence": s.302(9).
"standard scale": s.225(1).

[THE NEXT PARAGRAPH IS A4-585]

General Note

This section extends the range of fixed penalties which the procurator fiscal can offer to persons reported to him for offences other than Road Traffic offences. The "fiscal fine" was introduced by the Criminal Justice (Scotland) Act 1987 and then permitted procurator fiscals to use the offer of a £25 fixed fine to alleged offenders as an alternative to prosecution. Payment or part-payment of such a fine brought an end to the procurator fiscal's involvement and was not recorded as a criminal conviction. In 1987 the £25 fine, fixed by statutory instrument, equalled half the Level 1 fine on the standard scale; Level 1 is now a sum of £200. Section 302 permits the Secretary of State by statutory instrument, to set a range of fixed penalty bands from which the procurator fiscal can choose, according to the circumstances of the case as reported, when offering the option of a fiscal fine. Subsection (7) enacts that the bands must not exceed Level 1 on the standard scale. **A4-585**

One of the difficulties identified in the operation of the earlier fiscal fine system was that where several offences were reported against an accused as a result of an incident, the fiscal, if he chose to offer the option of such a fine, had to select one charge only from those reported. In the event of nonpayment only the single charge selected previously could later be libelled against the accused; subs.(3) statutorily permits the offer of more than one fiscal fine against an accused following an incident and, hence, in the event of refusal of the offer it will be open to the prosecutor to libel several charges, not just one as before.

The administration and collection of fines remains the responsibility of the clerk of court. Whereas the old fiscal fine system required payment of the entire £25 fine within 28 days, and to an extent limited the range of offenders who could be offered that option, subs.(1)(c) enacts that payment of the full amount or a pre-determined instalment is to be made within 28 days, or a specified longer period. Once either sort of payment is received, the prosecutor is barred from prosecuting those offences. It is then the task of the clerk of court to enforce collection of any unpaid balance (see s.303 below).

It will be appreciated that the thrust of s.302 is to extend the use of fiscal fines as an alternative to prosecution. If successful, the broadened fixed penalty conditional offer scheme may reduce the pressure of criminal business in the lower courts. Failure to pay a fixed penalty timeously can be expected to result in a prosecution for the offence highlighted in the notice. The court convicting of that offence should reach its own view upon the appropriate sentence and need not take account of the fine level stipulated in the unpaid fixed penalty; see *Fyfe v Walker*, 1998 G.W.D. 16–828.

Neither a Bill of Suspension nor a petition to the *nobile officium* is an appropriate instrument to review a conditional fixed penalty issued by the procurator fiscal or, following the same reasoning, a compensation offer (s.302A) since at that stage neither is a criminal proceeding. See *JQ v PF Paisley* [2017] HCJAC 9. In any event, s.302C provides mechanisms for recall or review of such offers, which, exceptional circumstances apart, are intended to be conclusive (subs.(8)).

Compensation offer by procurator fiscal

A4-585.1 **302A.**—(1) Where a procurator fiscal receives a report that a relevant offence has been committed he may send to the alleged offender a notice under this section (referred to in this section as a compensation offer); and where he issues a compensation offer the procurator fiscal shall notify the clerk of court specified in it of the issue of the offer and of its terms.

(2) A compensation offer—

(a) shall give such particulars of the circumstances alleged to constitute the offence to which it relates as are necessary for giving reasonable information about the alleged offence;

(b) shall state—

(i) the amount of compensation payable;

(ii) if the compensation is to be payable by instalments, the amount of the instalments and the intervals at which they should be paid;

(c) shall indicate that if, within 28 days of the date on which the offer was issued, or such longer period as may be specified in the offer, the alleged offender accepts the offer by making payment in respect of the offer to the clerk of court specified in the offer at the address therein mentioned, any liability to conviction of the offence shall be discharged;

(d) shall indicate—

(i) that the alleged offender may refuse the offer by giving notice to the clerk of court in the manner specified in the offer before the expiry of 28 days, or such longer period as may be specified in the offer, beginning on the day on which the offer is made;

(ii) that unless the alleged offender gives such notice, the alleged offender will be deemed to have accepted the offer (even where no payment is made in respect of the offer);

(iii) that where the alleged offender is deemed as described in subparagraph (ii) above to have accepted the offer any liability to conviction of the offence shall be discharged except where the offer is recalled under section 302C of this Act;

(e) shall state that proceedings against the alleged offender shall not be commenced in respect of that offence until the end of a period of 28 days from the date on which the offer was made, or such longer period as may be specified in the offer;

(f) shall state—

(i) that the acceptance of the offer in the manner described in paragraph (c) above, or deemed acceptance of the offer as described in paragraph (d)(ii) above, shall not be a conviction nor be recorded as such;

(ii) that the fact that the offer has been accepted, or deemed to have been accepted, may be disclosed to the court in any proceedings for an offence committed by the alleged offender within the period of two years beginning on the day of acceptance of the offer;

(iia) that that fact may be disclosed to the court also in any proceedings for an offence to which the alleged offender is, or is liable to become, subject at such time as the offer is accepted;

(iii) that if the offer is not accepted, that fact may be disclosed to the court in any proceedings for the offence to which the offer relates;

(g) shall state that refusal of an offer under paragraph (d)(i) above will be treated as a request by the alleged offender to be tried for the offence; and

(h) shall explain the right to request a recall of the offer under section 302C of this Act.

(3) A compensation offer may be made in respect of more than one relevant offence and shall, in such a case, state the amount payable in respect of the offer for all the offences in relation to which it is issued.

(4) The clerk of court shall—

(a) without delay, notify the procurator fiscal who issued the compensation offer when a notice as described in subsection (2)(d)(i) above has been received in respect of the offer; or

(b) following the expiry of the period of 28 days referred to in subsection (2)(c) above or such longer period as may be specified in the offer, notify the procurator fiscal if no such notice has been received.

(5) A compensation offer is accepted by the alleged offender making any payment in respect of the offer.

(6) Where an alleged offender to whom a compensation offer is made does not give notice as described in subsection (2)(d)(i) above, the alleged offender is deemed to have accepted the offer.

(7) Where—

(a) an alleged offender accepts a compensation offer as described in subsection (5) above; or

(b) an alleged offender is deemed to have accepted a compensation offer under subsection (6) above and the offer is not recalled, no proceedings shall be brought against the alleged offender for the offence.

(8) The Scottish Ministers shall by order prescribe the maximum amount of a compensation offer; but that amount shall not exceed level 5 on the standard scale.

(9) An order under subsection (8) above shall be made by statutory instrument; and any such instrument shall be subject to annulment in pursuance of a resolution of the Scottish Parliament.

(10) The alleged offender shall be presumed to have received a compensation offer under subsection (1) above if the offer is sent to—

(a) the address given by the alleged offender in a request for recall under section 302C(1) of this Act of an earlier offer in the same matter; or

(b) any address given by the alleged offender to the clerk of court specified in the offer, or to the procurator fiscal, in connection with the offer.

(11) For the purposes of section 141(4) of this Act, the accused shall be presumed to have received any citation effected at—

(a) the address to which a compensation offer under subsection (1) above was sent provided it is proved that the accused received the offer; or

(b) any address given by the accused to the clerk of court specified in the offer, or to the procurator fiscal, in connection with the offer.

(12) The clerk of court shall account for the amount paid under a compensation offer to the person entitled thereto.

(13) In this section, a "relevant offence" means any offence—

(a) in respect of which an alleged offender could be tried summarily; and

(b) on conviction of which it would be competent for the court to make a compensation order under section 249 of this Act.

AMENDMENTS

Section 302A inserted by Criminal Proceedings etc (Reform) (Scotland) Act 2007 (asp 6) s.50. Brought into force on 10 March 2008 by SSI 2008/42 (C.4) art.3 and Sch.

With effect from 10 March 2008 for the purposes of this section, the maximum amount of a compensation offer is £5,000: see the Criminal Procedure (Scotland) Act 1995 Compensation Offer (Maximum Amount) Order 2008 (SSI 2008/7) art.2.

Subs.(2)(f)(iia) inserted by Criminal Justice and Licensing (Scotland) Act 2010 (asp 13) s.70(4). Brought into force on 28 March 2011 (for all purposes in respect of offences committed on or after 28 March 2011) by SSI 2011/178 (C.15) art.2, Sch.1 para.1.

DEFINITIONS

A4-585.1.1 "offence": s.307(1) of the 1995 Act.
"procurator fiscal": s.307(1) of the 1995 Act.
"relevant offence": s.302A(13) of the 1995 Act.

[THE NEXT PARAGRAPH IS A4-585.2]

GENERAL NOTE

A4-585.2 Section 50 of the 2007 Act provides for considerable changes in procedures relating to existing alternatives to prosecution, and introduces by means of s.302A of the 1995 Act, as amended, a new alternative to prosecution, to be known as the compensation offer. Sections 302 and 303 of the 1995 Act deal with conditional offers of a fixed penalty by prosecutors (generally known as "fiscal fines"). This section makes various amendments to these existing sections and also introduces a number of new sections into the 1995 Act.

New s.302A—compensation offer

Section 50(2) introduces three new sections into the 1995 Act, and of these s.302A creates compensation offers by procurators fiscal and provides a mechanism for their operation. In practice, procedures for compensation offers will be similar to those for existing conditional offers.

The 2007 Act introduced a further alternative to prosecution in the shape of the compensation offer, administered in broadly the same fashion as the fiscal fines created in 1987. Section 302B enables the prosecutor to issue a "combined offer" of both. This scheme is administrative, not criminal, and recovery of any unpaid sums is by way of civil diligence. Accordingly, review beyond that statutorily provided for in s.302C of the Act rests in the jurisdiction of the civil courts. See the discussion at s.302 above.

Combined fixed penalty and compensation offer

A4-585.3 **302B.**—(1) The procurator fiscal may send to an alleged offender a notice under sections 302(1) and 302A(1) of this Act in respect of the same relevant offence (referred to in this section as a "combined offer").

(2) A combined offer shall be contained in the one notice.

(3) In addition to the information required to be provided under sections 302(2) and 302A(2) of this Act, the combined offer shall state—

(a) that the combined offer consists of both a fixed penalty offer and a compensation offer;

(b) the whole amount of the combined offer; and

(c) that liability to conviction of the offence shall not be discharged unless the whole of the combined offer is accepted.

(4) Any acceptance or deemed acceptance of part of a combined offer shall be treated as applying to the whole of the offer.

AMENDMENTS

Section 302B inserted by Criminal Proceedings etc (Reform) (Scotland) Act 2007 (asp 6) s.50. Brought into force on 10 March 2008 by SSI 2008/42 (C.4) art.3 and Sch.

[THE NEXT PARAGRAPH IS A4-585.5]

Recall of fixed penalty or compensation offer

302C.—(1) Where an alleged offender is deemed to have accepted— **A4-585.5**

(a) a fixed penalty offer by virtue of section 302(2)(ca)(ii) of this Act; or

(b) a compensation offer by virtue of section 302A(2)(d)(ii) of this Act, the alleged offender may request that it be recalled.

(2) A request for recall under subsection (1) above is valid only if—

(a) the alleged offender claims that he—

(i) did not receive the offer concerned; and

(ii) would (if he had received it) have refused the offer; or

(b) the alleged offender claims that—

(i) although he received the offer concerned, it was not practicable by reason of exceptional circumstances for him to give notice of refusal of the offer; and

(ii) he would (but for those circumstances) have refused the offer.

(3) A request for recall of a fixed penalty offer or a compensation offer requires to be made—

(a) to the clerk of court referred to in the offer; and

(b) no later than 7 days after the expiry of the period specified in the offer for payment of the fixed penalty or compensation offer or, where a notice is sent in pursuance of section 303(1A)(a) of this Act, no later than 7 days after it is sent.

(4) The clerk of court may, on cause shown by reference to subsection (2) above, consider a request for recall of such an offer despite its being made outwith the time limit applying by virtue of subsection (3)(b) above.

(5) The clerk of court may, following receipt of such a request—

(a) uphold the fixed penalty offer or compensation offer; or

(b) recall it.

(6) The alleged offender may, within 7 days of a decision under subsection (5)(a) above, apply to the court specified in the offer for a review of the decision (including as it involves a question which arose by reference to subsections (2) to (4) above).

(7) In a review under subsection (6) above, the court may—

(a) confirm or quash the decision of the clerk;

(b) in either case, give such direction to the clerk as the court considers appropriate.

(8) The decision of the court in a review under subsection (6) above shall be final.

(9) The clerk of court shall, without delay, notify the procurator fiscal of—

(a) a request for recall under subsection (1) above;

(b) an application for review under subsection (6) above;

(c) any decision under subsection (5) or (7) above.

(10) For the purposes of this section, a certificate given by the procurator fiscal as to the date on which a fixed penalty offer or compensation order was sent shall be sufficient evidence of that fact.

Amendments

Section 302C inserted by Criminal Proceedings etc (Reform) (Scotland) Act 2007 (asp 6) s.50. Brought into force on 10 March 2008 by SSI 2008/42 (C.4) art.3 and Sch.

[THE NEXT PARAGRAPH IS A4-586]

Fixed penalty: enforcement

A4-586 **303.—**(1) Subject to subsections (1A) and (2) below, where an alleged offender accepts a fixed penalty offer under section 302 of this Act or a compensation offer under section 302A of this Act, any amount of it which is outstanding at any time shall be treated as if the penalty or offer were a fine imposed by the court (the clerk of which is specified in the notice).

(1A) No action shall be taken to enforce a fixed penalty or compensation offer which an alleged offender is deemed to have accepted by virtue of section 302(2)(ca)(ii) or section 302A(2)(d)(ii) of this Act unless—

(a) the alleged offender is sent a notice—
  (i) of the intention to take enforcement action; and
  (ii) which explains the right to request a recall of the penalty or offer under section 302C of this Act;
(b) any request for recall made under that section has been finally disposed of.

(2) In the enforcement of a fixed penalty or compensation offer which is to be treated as a fine in pursuance of subsection (1) above—

(a) any reference, howsoever expressed, in any enactment whether passed or made before or after the coming into force of this section to—
  (i) the imposition of imprisonment or detention in default of payment of a fine shall be construed as a reference to enforcement by means of civil diligence;
  (ii) the finding or order of the court imposing the fine shall be construed as a reference to a certificate given in pursuance of subsection (3) below;
  (iii) the offender shall be construed as a reference to the alleged offender;
  (iv) the conviction of the offender shall be construed as a reference to the acceptance of the conditional offer by the alleged offender;
(b) the following sections of this Act shall not apply—
  section 211(7);
  section 213(2);
  section 214(1) to (6);
  section 216(7);
  section 219, except subsection (1)(b);
  section 220;
  section 221(2) to (4);
  section 222(8); and
  section 224.

(3) For the purposes of any proceedings in connection with, or steps taken for, the enforcement of any amount of a fixed penalty or compensation offer which is outstanding, a document purporting to be a certificate signed by the clerk of court

for the time being responsible for the collection or enforcement of the penalty or compensation offer as to any matter relating to the penalty shall be conclusive of the matter so certified.

(4) The Secretary of State may, by order made by statutory instrument subject to annulment in pursuance of a resolution of either House of Parliament, make such provision as he considers necessary for the enforcement in England and Wales of any penalty, treated in pursuance of subsection (1) above as a fine, which is transferred as a fine to a court in England and Wales.

(5) The Department of Justice in Northern Ireland may by order make such provision as it considers necessary for the enforcement in Northern Ireland of any penalty, treated in pursuance of subsection (1) above as a fine, which is transferred as a fine to a court in Northern Ireland.

(6) The power of the Department of Justice to make an order under subsection (5) is exercisable by statutory rule for the purposes of the Statutory Rules (Northern Ireland) Order 1979.

(7) An order made by the Department of Justice under subsection (5) is subject to negative resolution (within the meaning of section 41(6) of the Interpretation Act (Northern Ireland) 1954).

AMENDMENTS

Subs.(1) substituted, subs.(1A) inserted and subss.(2), (3) as amended by Criminal Proceedings etc (Reform) (Scotland) Act 2007 (asp 6) s.50. Brought into force on 10 March 2008 by SSI 2008/42 (C.4) art.3 and Sch.

Subs.(4) as amended and subss.(5)–(7) inserted by Northern Ireland Act 1998 (Devolution of Policing and Justice Functions) Order 2010 (SI 2010/976) Sch.14 para.32 (effective 12 April 2010 subject to transitional provisions).

DEFINITIONS

"appropriate fixed penalty": s.302(9)(b). **A4-586.1**
"enactment": s.307(1).
"fine": s.307(1).
"impose detention": s.307(1).
"impose imprisonment": s.307(1).

GENERAL NOTE

The collection of fiscal fines remains the responsibility of the clerk of court. In the event of only partial payment of the instalments due to meet such a fine, subs.(2) allows recovery of the balance due by way of civil diligence. Subsection (3) provides that for the purpose of such enforcement the clerk of court is empowered to certify conclusively the sums due. **A4-586.2**

Subsection (2) has the effect of removing criminal sanctions for the enforcement of unpaid fiscal fines.

Work orders

303ZA.—(1) Where a procurator fiscal receives a report that a relevant offence has been committed he may send the alleged offender a notice under this section (referred to in this section as a work offer) which offers the alleged offender the opportunity of performing unpaid work. **A4-586.3**

(2) The total number of hours of unpaid work shall be not less than 10 nor more than 50.

(3) A work offer—

(a) shall give such particulars of the circumstances alleged to constitute the offence to which it relates as are necessary for giving reasonable information about the alleged offence;

(b) shall state—

(i) the number of hours of unpaid work which the alleged offender is required to perform;

(ii) the date by which that work requires to be completed;

(c) shall indicate that if the alleged offender—

(i) accepts the work offer; and

(ii) completes the work to the satisfaction of the supervising officer,

any liability to conviction of the offence shall be discharged;

(d) shall state that proceedings against the alleged offender shall not be commenced in respect of that offence until the end of a period of 28 days from the date on which the offer was issued, or such longer period as may be specified in the offer;

(e) shall state—

(i) that acceptance of a work offer in the manner described in subsection (5) below shall not be a conviction nor be recorded as such;

(ia) that if a work offer is not accepted, that fact may be disclosed to the court in any proceedings for the offence to which the offer relates;

(ii) that the fact that a resultant work order has been completed may be disclosed to the court in any proceedings for an offence committed by the alleged offender within the period of two years beginning on the day of acceptance of the offer;

(iia) that that fact may be disclosed to the court also in any proceedings for an offence to which the alleged offender is, or is liable to become, subject at such time as the offer is accepted;

(iii) that if a resultant work order is not completed, that fact may be disclosed to the court in any proceedings for the offence to which the order relates.

(4) A work offer may be made in respect of more than one relevant offence and shall, in such a case, state the total amount of work requiring to be performed in respect of the offences in relation to which it is made.

(5) An alleged offender accepts a work offer by giving notice to the procurator fiscal specified in the order before the expiry of 28 days, or such longer period as may be specified in the offer, beginning on the day on which the offer is made.

(6) If (and only if) the alleged offender accepts a work offer, the procurator fiscal may make an order (referred to in this section as a work order) against the alleged offender.

(7) Notice of a work order—

(a) shall be sent to the alleged offender as soon as reasonably practicable after acceptance of the work offer; and

(b) shall contain—

(i) the information mentioned in subsection (3)(b) above; and

(ii) the name and contact details of the person who is to act as supervisor ("the supervising officer") in relation to the alleged offender.

(8) The procurator fiscal shall notify the local authority which will be responsible for supervision of an alleged offender of the terms of any work order sent to the alleged offender.

(9) Where a work order is made, the supervising officer shall—

(a) determine the nature of the work which the alleged offender requires to perform;

(b) determine the times and places at which the alleged offender is to perform that work;

(c) give directions to the alleged offender in relation to that work;

(d) provide the procurator fiscal with such information as the procurator fiscal may require in relation to the alleged offender's conduct in connection with the requirements of the order.

(10) In giving directions under subsection (9)(c) above, a supervising officer shall, so far as practicable, avoid—

(a) any conflict with the alleged offender's religious beliefs;

(b) any interference with the times at which the alleged offender normally—

(i) works (or carries out voluntary work); or

(ii) attends an educational establishment.

(11) The supervising officer shall, on or as soon as practicable after the date referred to in subsection (3)(b)(ii) above, notify the procurator fiscal whether or not the work has been performed to the supervising officer's satisfaction.

(12) Where an alleged offender completes the work specified in the work order to the satisfaction of the supervising officer, no proceedings shall be brought against the alleged offender for the offence.

(13) The Scottish Ministers may, by regulations, make provision for the purposes of subsection (9) above (including, in particular, the kinds of activity of which the work requiring to be performed may (or may not) consist).

(14) Regulations under subsection (13) above shall be made by statutory instrument which shall be subject to annulment in pursuance of a resolution of the Scottish Parliament.

(15) For the purposes of section 141(4) of this Act, the accused shall be presumed to have received any citation effected at—

(a) the address to which a work offer was sent provided it is proved that the accused received the offer; or

(b) any address given, in connection with the offer, by the accused to the procurator fiscal specified in the offer.

(16) In this section, a "relevant offence" means any offence in respect of which an alleged offender could be tried summarily.

AMENDMENTS

Section 303ZA inserted by Criminal Proceedings etc (Reform) (Scotland) Act 2007 (asp 6) s.51. Brought into force for certain purposes on 2 June 2008 by SSI 2008/192 (C.19) art.3 and Sch. The Schedule thereof states that s.303ZA comes into force on that date: "only for the purpose of making a work order where one or more of the alleged offences in relation to which the work order is to be made was committed in any of the local authority areas of Highland, South Lanarkshire, West Dunbartonshire or West Lothian and in respect of which arrangements have been made by a local authority within those areas for the supervision of any such work order".

Subs.(3)(e)(ia), (iia) inserted, and subs.(3)(e)(ii), (iii) as amended, by Criminal Justice and Licensing (Scotland) Act 2010 (asp 13) s.70(5). Brought into force on 28 March 2011 (for all purposes in respect of offences committed on or after 28 March 2011) by SSI 2011/178 (C.15) art.2, Sch.1 para.1.

[THE NEXT PARAGRAPH IS A4-587]

Setting aside of offers and orders

303ZB.—(1) Where this subsection applies, the procurator fiscal may set aside— **A4-587**

(a) a fixed penalty offer made under section 302(1) of this Act;

(b) a compensation offer made under section 302A(1) of this Act;

(c) a work offer made under section 303ZA(1) of this Act;

(d) a work order made under section 303ZA(6) of this Act.

(2) Subsection (1) above applies where, on the basis of information which comes to the procurator fiscal's attention after the offer or (as the case may be) order has been made, the procurator fiscal considers that the offer or (as the case may be) order should not have been made in respect of the alleged offender.

(3) The procurator fiscal may act under subsection (1)(a) to (c) above even where the offer has been accepted (including, in the case of an offer mentioned in subsection (1)(a) or (b) above, deemed to have been accepted).

(4) Where the procurator fiscal acts under subsection (1) above, the procurator fiscal shall give the alleged offender notice—

(a) of the setting aside of the offer or (as the case may be) order; and
(b) indicating that any liability of the alleged offender to conviction of the alleged offence is discharged.

AMENDMENTS

Section 303ZB inserted by Criminal Proceedings etc (Reform) (Scotland) Act 2007 (asp 6) s.52. Brought into force on 10 March 2008 by SSI 2008/42 (C.4) art.3 and Sch.

Transfer of rights of appeal of deceased person

Transfer of rights of appeal of deceased person

A4-587.1 **303A.**—(1) Where a person convicted of an offence has died, any person may, subject to the provisions of this section, apply to the appropriate Appeal Court for an order authorising him to institute or continue any appeal which could have been or has been instituted by the deceased.

(2) An application for an order under this section may be lodged with the clerk of the appropriate Appeal Court within three months of the deceased's death or at such later time as the appropriate Appeal Court may, on cause shown, allow.

(3) Where the Commission makes a reference to the High Court under section 194B of this Act in respect of a person who is deceased, any application under this section must be made within one month of the reference.

(4) Where an application is made for an order under this section and the applicant—

(a) is an executor of the deceased; or
(b) otherwise appears to the appropriate Appeal Court to have a legitimate interest,

the appropriate Appeal Court shall make an order authorising the applicant to institute or continue any appeal which could have been instituted or continued by the deceased; and, subject to the provisions of this section, any such order may include such ancillary or supplementary provision as the appropriate Appeal Court thinks fit.

(5) The person in whose favour an order under this section is made shall from the date of the order be afforded the same rights to carry on the appeal as the deceased enjoyed at the time of his death and, in particular, where any time limit had begun to run against the deceased the person in whose favour an order has been made shall have the benefit of only that portion of the time limit which remained unexpired at the time of the death.

(6) In this section "appeal" includes any sort of application, whether at common law or under statute, for the review of any conviction, penalty or other order made in respect of the deceased in any criminal proceedings whatsoever.

(7) In this section—

"appropriate Appeal Court" means—

(a) in the case of an appeal proposed to be instituted or continued before the High Court, the High Court;
(b) in the case of an appeal proposed to be instituted or continued before the Sheriff Appeal Court, the Sheriff Appeal Court; and

"the clerk of the appropriate Appeal Court" means—

(a) in a case where the High Court is the appropriate Appeal Court, the Clerk of Justiciary;

(b) in a case where the Sheriff Appeal Court is the appropriate Appeal Court, the Clerk of that Court.

AMENDMENTS

Section 303A inserted by Crime and Punishment (Scotland) Act 1997 (c.48) s.20 with effect from 1 August 1997 in terms of SI 1997/1712 art.3; 1 April 2009 otherwise.

Subss.(1), (2), (4) as amended, subs.(7) inserted, by Courts Reform (Scotland) Act 2014 (Consequential Provisions No.2) Order 2015 (SSI 2015/338) Sch.2 para.5 (effective 22 September 2015).

GENERAL NOTE

This introduces provision whereby an executor or a person with a legitimate interest can institute or continue an appeal (of any kind) where an accused person dies. Such a person has three months from the date of death to apply to the High Court. An application can be allowed at a later time on cause shown. It appears that it does not apply where a person is applying to the SCCRC, as an appeal would not be instituted until a reference was made by the Commission. **A4-587.2**

Where the Criminal Review Commission makes a reference in respect of a deceased person then within one month of the reference an application under this section must be made.

Subsection (5) only allows the applicant the remainder of any time limit running against the deceased. This would appear harsh but given that the person is afforded the same rights as a deceased, they too would be entitled to apply for extensions of time under the relevant statutory provisions, e.g. s.11 of the Criminal Procedure (Scotland) Act 1995 (c.46).

The procedure under s.303A was followed in *Cowan v HM Advocate*, 2001 G.W.D. 18–692 and the conviction quashed.

Electronic proceedings

Electronic summary proceedings

303B.—(1) For the purposes of section 138(1) of this Act— **A4-587.3**

(a) institution of proceedings may be effected by electronic complaint;

(b) the requirement for signing is satisfied in relation to an electronic complaint by an electronic signature;

(c) the requirement for signing may be satisfied in relation to any other complaint by an electronic signature.

(2) The references in the other provisions of this Act to a complaint include an electronic complaint unless the context otherwise requires.

(3) Where proceedings are instituted by electronic complaint, in the event of any conflict between—

(a) the principal electronic complaint kept by the clerk of court for the purposes of the proceedings; and

(b) any other document (whether in electronic or other form) purporting to be the complaint,

the principal electronic complaint prevails.

(4) The requirement in section 85(4) of this Act for signing may be satisfied by electronic signature.

(5) The requirement in section 136B(2) of this Act for signing may be satisfied by electronic signature.

(6) The requirement in section 141(3)(a) of this Act for signing may be satisfied by electronic signature.

(7) The requirement in section 159(3) of this Act for authentication by initials is satisfied in relation to an electronic complaint by authentication by electronic signature.

(8) The requirements in section 172(2) of this Act for signing by the clerk of court may be satisfied by electronic signature.

(9) The requirements in section 258(2) and (9) of this Act for signing may be satisfied in relation to summary proceedings by electronic signature.

(10) The requirement in section 299(5) of this Act for authentication by signature is satisfied in relation to—

(a) proceedings which are recorded in electronic form;
(b) any extract of sentence, or order made, which is recorded in electronic form,

by authentication by electronic signature.

AMENDMENTS

Section 303B inserted by Criminal Proceedings etc (Reform) (Scotland) Act 2007 (asp 6) s.41(1). Subs.(6) brought into force on 10 December 2007 by SSI 2007/479 (C.40) art.3 and Sch.

Subss.(1)–(5) and (7)–(10) brought into force on 1 November 2012 by SSI 2012/274 (C.28) art.2 and Sch.

DEFINITIONS

A4-587.4 "complaint: s.307(1).
"Scottish Ministers": s.44(2) of the Scotland Act 1998 (c.48).

GENERAL NOTE

A4-587.5 This is one of a substantial number of measures introduced by the Criminal Proceedings etc. (Reform) (Scotland) Act 2007 (asp 6) to streamline the operation of summary criminal proceedings. As the marginal heading makes clear this reform permits the use of an electronic complaint, validated by an electronically—generated signature of the prosecutor, in any summary proceedings. Subsection (5) similarly allows for amendment of an electronic complaint by electronic signature, while subs.(7) enables corrections to be made to such complaints by electronic means. This provision will enable online transmission of complaints from the procurator fiscal to the clerk of court and for electronic preservation, as principals, of summary complaints and minutes. Subssections (8) to (10) are interpretative and also empower the Scottish Ministers, by statutory instrument, to introduce modifications at least in relation to the form of acceptable electronic signatures. Looking to subs.(2) it will be noted that the Scottish Ministers are given broader powers to regulate the keeping in electronic form of records of summary criminal proceedings. It will be seen that the Act now introduces service of complaints and witness citations by electronic means.

[THE NEXT PARAGRAPH IS A4-588]

PART XIV – GENERAL

Criminal Courts Rules Council

A4-588 **304.**—(1) There shall be established a body, to be known as the Criminal Courts Rules Council (in this section referred to as "the Council") which shall have the functions conferred on it by subsection (9) below.

(2) The Council shall consist of—
(a) the Lord Justice General, the Lord Justice Clerk and the Clerk of Justiciary;
(b) a further Lord Commissioner of Justiciary appointed by the Lord Justice General;
(c) the following persons appointed by the Lord Justice General after such consultation as he considers appropriate—
(zi) one Appeal Sheriff;
(i) two sheriffs;
(ii) two members of the Faculty of Advocates;
(iii) two solicitors;
(iv) one sheriff clerk; and
(v) one person appearing to him to have a knowledge of the procedures and practices of the JP court;
(d) two persons appointed by the Lord Justice General after consultation with the Lord Advocate, at least one of whom must be a procurator fiscal;
(e) two persons appointed by the Lord Justice General after consultation with the Secretary of State, at least one of whom must be a person appearing to the Lord Justice General to have—
(i) a knowledge of the procedures and practices of the courts exercising criminal jurisdiction in Scotland; and

(ii) an awareness of the interests of victims of crime and of witnesses in criminal proceedings; and

(f) any persons appointed under subsection (3) below.

(3) The Lord Justice General may appoint not more than two further persons, and the Secretary of State may appoint one person, to membership of the Council.

(4) The chairman of the Council shall be the Lord Justice General or such other member of the Council, being a Lord Commissioner of Justiciary, as the Lord Justice General may nominate.

(5) The members of the Council appointed under paragraphs (b) to (f) of subsection (2) above shall, so long as they retain the respective qualifications mentioned in those paragraphs, hold office for three years and be eligible for reappointment.

(6) Any vacancy in the membership of the Council by reason of the death or demission of office, prior to the expiry of the period for which he was appointed, of a member appointed under any of paragraphs (b) to (f) of subsection (2) above shall be filled by the appointment by the Lord Justice General or, as the case may be, the Secretary of State, after such consultation as is required by the paragraph in question, of another person having the qualifications required by that paragraph, and a person so appointed shall hold office only until the expiry of that period.

(7) The Council shall meet—

(a) at intervals of not more than 12 months; and

(b) at any time when summoned by the chairman or by three members of the Council,

but shall, subject to the foregoing, have power to regulate the summoning of its meetings and the procedure at such meetings.

(8) At any meeting of the Council six members shall be a quorum.

(9) The functions of the Council shall be—

(a) to keep under general review the procedures and practices of the courts exercising criminal jurisdiction in Scotland (including any matters incidental or relating to those procedures or practices); and

(b) to consider and comment on any draft Act of Adjournal submitted to it by the High Court, which shall, in making the Act of Adjournal, take account to such extent as it considers appropriate of any comments made by the Council under this paragraph.

(10) In the discharge of its functions under subsection (9) above the Council may invite representations on any aspect of the procedures and practices of the courts exercising criminal jurisdiction in Scotland (including any matters incidental or relating to those procedures or practices) and shall consider any such representations received by it, whether or not submitted in response to such an invitation.

AMENDMENTS

Subs.(2)(c)(v) as amended by Criminal Proceedings etc. (Reform) (Scotland) Act 2007 (asp 6) s.80, Sch. para.26. Brought into force for the Sheriffdom of Lothian and Borders on 10 March 2008 by SSI 2008/42 (C.4) art.3 and Sch. Brought into force for the Sheriffdom of Grampian, Highland and Islands on 2 June 2008 by SSI 2008/192 (C.19) art.3 and Sch. Brought into force for the Sheriffdom of Glasgow and Strathkelvin on 8 December 2008 by SSI 2008/329 (C.29) art.3 and Sch. Brought into force for the Sheriffdom of Tayside, Central and Fife on 23 February 2009 by SSI 2008/362 (C.30) art.3 and Sch. Brought into force for the Sheriffdom of North Strathclyde on 14 December 2009 by SSI 2009/432 (C.32) art.3 and Sch.1. Remainder in force on 22 February 2010 by SSI 2009/432 (C.32) art.3 and Sch.2.

Subs.(2)(c)(zi) inserted by Courts Reform (Scotland) Act 2014 (asp 18) Sch.5 para.15. Brought into force on 22 September 2015 by SSI 2015/247 (C.35) art.2 and Sch.

DEFINITIONS

"Lord Commissioner of Justiciary": s.307(1). A4-588.1
"procurator fiscal": s.307(1).

[THE NEXT PARAGRAPH IS A4-589]

General Note

A4-589 This innovation established a Rules Council for criminal court proceedings with functions broadly comparable to the existing Scottish Rules Council for civil court proceedings. The new body will assist the High Court of Justiciary in the discharge of its existing court procedural rule-making functions.

Acts of Adjournal

A4-590 **305.**—(1) The High Court may by Act of Adjournal—

(a) regulate the practice and procedure in relation to criminal procedure;

(b) make such rules and regulations as may be necessary or expedient to carry out the purposes and accomplish the objects of any enactment (including an enactment in this Act) in so far as it relates to criminal procedure;

(c) subject to subsection (5) below, to fix and regulate the fees payable in connection with summary criminal proceedings; and

(d) to make provision for the application of sums paid under section 220 of this Act and for any matter incidental thereto.

(1A) Subsection (1) above extends to making provision by Act of Adjournal for something to be done in electronic form or by electronic means.

(2) The High Court may by Act of Adjournal modify, amend or repeal any enactment (including an enactment in this Act) in so far as that enactment relates to matters with respect to which an Act of Adjournal may be made under subsection (1) above.

(3) No rule, regulation or provision which affects the governor or any other officer of a prison shall be made by Act of Adjournal except with the consent of the Secretary of State.

(4) The Clerk of Justiciary may, with the sanction of the Lord Justice General and the Lord Justice Clerk, vary the forms set out in an Act of Adjournal made under subsection (1) above or any other Act whether passed before or after this Act from time to time as may be found necessary for giving effect to the provisions of this Act relating to solemn procedure.

(5) Nothing in paragraph (c) of subsection (1) above shall empower the High Court to make any provision that the Scottish Ministers are empowered to make under section 107(1) of the Courts Reform (Scotland) Act 2014.

Amendments

Subs.(4) as amended by Courts Reform (Scotland) Act 2014 (Consequential Provisions No.2) Order 2015 (SSI 2015/338) art.2 (effective 22 September 2015).

Subs.(1A) inserted by Criminal Justice (Scotland) Act 2016 (asp 1) s.111. Brought into force on 17 January 2017 by SSI 2016/426 art.2 and Sch.1 para.1.

Definitions

A4-590.1 "governor": s.307(1).
"High Court": s.307(1).
"officer of a prison": s.307(1).

[THE NEXT PARAGRAPH IS A4-591]

General Note

A4-591 The High Court of Justiciary is best placed to know how to regulate its own procedure and it does so by Act of Adjournal on statutory authority. The previous powers of ss.282 and 457 of the 1975 Act have been combined in this single provision which relates to "criminal procedure". Variations in the wording of these sections have been removed. Differences as between other statutory powers to make Acts of Adjournal have been removed with this single provision: see, e.g. s.32A of the 1980 Act which allowed provisions the court thought "necessary and expedient", a wider power than that of necessity under the 1975 Act. A lengthy examination of the nature of the powers vested in the High Court to regulate its proceedings was undertaken in *Dickson v HM Advocate*, 2001 S.L.T. 674; 2001 S.C.C.R. 397, a five judge decision which followed upon a three judge hearing convened in the course of trial. The issues had not been raised earlier by devolution minute. D submitted that the court could not independently and impartially deliberate upon whether the Act of Adjournal (Devolution Rules) 1999 (SI 1999/1346) were Convention compliant, arguing that the matter had to be resolved by the Privy Council, and in any event, D had been prejudiced on the merits by the lack of a full judgment during the trial. The thrust of s.305

was summarised by Lord Hope of Craighead in *Montgomery v HM Advocate*, 2001 S.L.T. 37; 2000 S.C.C.R. 1044.

Information for financial and other purposes

306.—(1) The Secretary of State shall in each year publish such information as he considers expedient for the purpose of— **A4-592**

(a) enabling persons engaged in the administration of criminal justice to become aware of the financial implications of their decisions; or

(b) facilitating the performance by such persons of their duty to avoid discriminating against any persons on the ground of race or sex or any other improper ground.

(2) Publication under subsection (1) above shall be effected in such manner as the Secretary of State considers appropriate for the purpose of bringing the information to the attention of the persons concerned.

Interpretation

307.—(1) In this Act, unless the context otherwise requires— **A4-593**

"alcohol treatment requirement" has the meaning given in section 227V(1);

"assessment order" has the meaning given by section 52D of this Act;

"bail" means release of an accused or an appellant on conditions, or conditions imposed on bail, as the context requires;

"child", except in section 46(3) of and Schedule 1 to this Act, has the meaning assigned to that expression for the purposes of section 199 of the Children's Hearings (Scotland) Act 2011 (asp 1);

"child witness" shall be construed in accordance with section 271(1)(a) of this Act;

"children's hearing" is to be construed in accordance with section 5 of the Children's Hearings (Scotland) Act 2011 (asp 1);

"Clerk of Justiciary" shall include assistant clerk of justiciary and shall extend and apply to any person duly authorised to execute the duties of Clerk of Justiciary or assistant clerk of justiciary;

"Clerk of the Sheriff Appeal Court" includes Deputy Clerk of the Sheriff Appeal Court and any person authorised to carry out the functions of Clerk of the Sheriff Appeal Court;

["the Commission" has the meaning given by section 194A(1) of this Act;]

"commit for trial" means commit until liberation in due course of law;

"community payback order" means a community payback order (within the meaning of section 227A(2)) imposed under section 227A(1) or (4) or 227M(2);

"compensation requirement" has the meaning given in section 227H(1);

"complaint" includes a copy of the complaint laid before the court;

"compulsion order" means an order under section 57(2)(a) or 57A(2) of this Act;

"compulsory supervision order" has the meaning given by section 83 of the Children's Hearings (Scotland) Act 2011 (asp 1);

"conduct requirement" has the meaning given in section 227W(1);

"constable" has the same meaning as in the Police and Fire Reform (Scotland) Act 2012;

"conviction", in relation to a previous conviction by a court outside Scotland, means a final decision of a criminal court establishing guilt of a criminal offence;

"court of summary jurisdiction" means a court of summary criminal jurisdiction;

"court of summary criminal jurisdiction" includes the sheriff court and JP court;

"crime" means any crime or offence at common law or under any Act of Parliament whether passed before or after this Act, and includes an attempt to commit any crime or offence;

"devolution issue" has the same meaning as in Schedule 6 to the Scotland Act 1998;

"diet" includes any continuation of a diet;

"drug treatment and testing order" has the meaning assigned to it in section 234B(2) of this Act;

"drug treatment requirement" has the meaning given in section 227U(1);

"enactment" includes an enactment contained in a local Act and any order, regulation or other instrument having effect by virtue of an Act;

"examination of facts" means an examination of facts held under section 55 of this Act;

"existing" means existing immediately before the commencement of this Act;

"extract conviction" and "extract of previous conviction" include certified copy conviction, certificate of conviction, and any other document lawfully issued from any court of justice of the United Kingdom as evidence of a conviction and also include a conviction extracted and issued as mentioned in section 286A(3)(a) and (b) of this Act;

"fine" includes—

(a) any pecuniary penalty, (but not a pecuniary forfeiture or pecuniary compensation);

(b) an instalment of a fine;

(c) a victim surcharge imposed under section 253F;[or]

[(d) a restitution order;]

"governor" means, in relation to a contracted out prison within the meaning of section 106(4) of the Criminal Justice and Public Order Act 1994, the director of the prison;

"guardian", in relation to a child, includes any person who, in the opinion of the court having cognizance of any case in relation to the child or in which the child is concerned, has for the time being the charge of or control over the child;

"guardianship order" has the meaning assigned to it by section 58 of this Act;

"High Court" and "Court of Justiciary" shall mean "High Court of Justiciary" and shall include any court held by the Lords Commissioners of Justiciary, or any of them;

"hospital" means—

(a) any hospital vested in the Secretary of State under the National Health Service (Scotland) Act 1978;

(aa) any hospital managed by a National Health Service Trust established under section 12A of that Act;

(b) any private hospital as defined in section 12(2) of the Mental Health (Scotland) Act 1984; and

(c) any State hospital;

"hospital direction" has the meaning assigned to it by section 59A(1) of this Act.

"impose detention" or "impose imprisonment" means pass a sentence of detention or imprisonment, as the case may be, or make an order for committal in default of payment of any sum of money or for contempt of court;

"indictment" includes any indictment whether in the sheriff court or the High Court framed in the form set out an Act of Adjournal or as nearly as may be in such form;

"interim compulsion order" has the meaning given by section 53 of this Act;

"interim compulsory supervision order" has the meaning given by section 86 of the Children's Hearings (Scotland) Act 2011 (asp 1);

"JP court" means a justice of the peace court;

"judge", in relation to solemn procedure, means a judge of a court of solemn criminal jurisdiction and, in relation to summary procedure, means any sheriff or any judge of a JP court;

"justice" includes the sheriff and any justice of the peace;

"justice of the peace" means a justice of the peace appointed under section 67 of the Criminal Proceedings etc. (Reform) (Scotland) Act 2007 (asp 6);;

"legalised police cells" has the like meaning as in the Prisons (Scotland) Act 1989;

"local authority" has the meaning assigned to it by section 1(2) of the Social Work (Scotland) Act 1968;

"local probation board" means a local probation board established under section 4 of the Criminal Justice and Court Services Act 2000;

"Lord Commissioner of Justiciary" includes Lord Justice General and Lord Justice Clerk;

"mental disorder" has the meaning given by section 328(1) of the Mental Health (Care and Treatment) (Scotland) Act 2003 (asp 13);

"mental health treatment requirement" has the meaning given in section 227R(1);

"Mental Welfare Commission" means the Mental Welfare Commission for Scotland;

"offence" means any act, attempt or omission punishable by law;

"offender supervision requirement" has the meaning given in section 227G(1);

"officer of law" includes, in relation to the service and execution of any warrant, citation, petition, indictment, complaint, list of witnesses, order, notice, or other proceeding or document—

(a) any macer, messenger-at-arms, sheriff officer or other person having authority to execute a warrant of the court;

(b) any constable;

(ba) an officer of Revenue and Customs acting with the authority (which may be general or specific) of the Commissioners for Her Majesty's Revenue and Customs;

(bb) subject to subsection (1AA) below, an immigration officer acting with the authority (which may be general or specific) of the Secretary of State;

(c) any person who is appointed under section 26 of the Police and Fire Reform (Scotland) Act 2012 who is either authorised by the chief constable of the Police Service of Scotland in relation to such service and execution or is a police custody and security officer;

(d) where the person upon whom service or execution is effected is in prison at the time of service on him, any prison officer; and

(e) any person or class of persons authorised in that regard for the time being by the Lord Advocate or by the Secretary of State;

"order" means any order, byelaw, rule or regulation having statutory authority;

"order for lifelong restriction" means an order under section 210F(1) of this Act;

"organisation" means—

(a) a body corporate;
(b) an unincorporated association;
(c) a partnership;
(d) a body of trustees;
(e) a government department;
(f) a part of the Scottish Administration;
(g) any other entity which is not an individual;

"patient" means a person suffering or appearing to be suffering from mental disorder;

"place of safety", in relation to a person not being a child, means any police station, prison or remand centre, or any hospital the board of management of which are willing temporarily to receive him, and in relation to a child has the meaning given by section 202(1) of the Children's Hearings (Scotland) Act 2011 (asp 1);

"postal operator" has the meaning assigned to it by section 27 of the Postal Services Act 2011;

"preliminary hearing" shall be construed in accordance with section 66(6)(b) of this Act and, where in any case a further preliminary hearing is held or to be held under this Act, includes the diet consisting of that further preliminary hearing;

"preliminary issue" shall be construed in accordance with section 79(2)(b) of this Act;

"preliminary plea" shall be construed in accordance with section 79(2)(a) of this Act;

"the prescribed sum" has the meaning given by section 225(8) of this Act;

"prison" does not include a naval, military or air force prison;

"prison officer" and "officer of a prison" means, in relation to a contracted out prison within the meaning of section 106(4) of the Criminal Justice and Public Order Act 1994, a prisoner custody officer within the meaning of section 114(1) of that Act;

[…];

"procurator fiscal" means the procurator fiscal for a sheriff court district, and includes assistant procurator fiscal and procurator fiscal depute and any person duly authorised to execute the duties of the procurator fiscal;

"programme requirement" has the meaning given in section 227P(1);

"prosecutor"—

(a) for the purposes of proceedings other than summary proceedings, includes Crown Counsel, procurator fiscal, any other person prosecuting in the public interest and any private prosecutor; and
(b) for the purposes of summary proceedings, includes procurator fiscal, and any other person prosecuting in the public interest and complainer and any person duly authorised to represent or act for any public prosecutor;

"registered psychologist" means a person registered in the part of the register maintained under the Health and Social Work Professions Order 2001 which relates to practitioner psychologists;

"remand" means an order adjourning the proceedings or continuing the case and giving direction as to detention in custody or liberation during the period of adjournment or continuation and references to remanding a person or remanding in custody or on bail shall be construed accordingly;

"remand centre" has the like meaning as in the Prisons (Scotland) Act 1989;

"residence requirement" has the meaning given in section 227Q(1);

"responsible officer", in relation to a community payback order, is to be construed in accordance with section 227C;

"restricted movement requirement" has the meaning given in section 227ZF(1);

"restriction order" has the meaning assigned to it by section 59 of this Act;

"risk assessment order" means an order under section 210B(2) of this Act;

"risk assessment report" has the meaning given by section 210B(3)(a) of this Act;

"sentence", whether of detention or of imprisonment, means a sentence passed in respect of a crime or offence and does not include an order for committal in default of payment of any sum of money or for contempt of court;

"sheriff clerk" includes sheriff clerk depute, and extends and applies to any person duly authorised to execute the duties of sheriff clerk;

"sheriff court district" extends to the limits within which the sheriff has jurisdiction in criminal matters whether by statute or at common law;

"State hospital" has the meaning assigned to it in Part VIII of the Mental Health (Scotland) Act 1984;

"statute" means any Act of Parliament, public general, local, or private, and any Provisional Order confirmed by Act of Parliament;

"training school order" has the same meaning as in the Social Work (Scotland) Act 1968;

"treatment order" has the meaning given by section 52M of this Act;

"unfit for trial" has the meaning given by section 53F of this Act;

["the unified citation provisions" means section 216(5) and (6)(a) and (b) of this Act;]

"unpaid work or other activity requirement" has the meaning given in section 227I(1), and "level 1 unpaid work or other activity requirement" and "level 2 unpaid work or other activity requirement" are to be construed in accordance with section 227I(5) and (6) respectively;

"vulnerable witness" shall be construed in accordance with section 271(1) of this Act;

"witness" includes haver;

"young offenders institution" has the like meaning as in the Prisons (Scotland) Act 1989.

(1A) [...]

(1AA) The inclusion of immigration officers as "officers of law" shall have effect only in relation to immigration offences and nationality offences.

(1AB) In subsection (1AA)—

"immigration offence" means—

(a) an offence involving conduct which relates to the entitlement of one or more persons who are not nationals of the United

Kingdom to enter, transit across, or be in, the United Kingdom (including conduct which relates to conditions or other controls on any such entitlement); or

(b) (insofar as it is not an offence within paragraph (a)) an offence under the Immigration Acts or in relation to which a power of arrest is conferred on an immigration officer by the Immigration Acts;

"nationality offence" means an offence involving conduct which is undertaken for the purposes of, or otherwise in relation to, an enactment in—

(a) the British Nationality Act 1981;
(b) the Hong Kong Act 1985;
(c) the Hong Kong (War Wives and Widows) Act 1996;
(d) the British Nationality (Hong Kong) Act 1997;
(e) the British Overseas Territories Act 2002;
(f) an instrument made under any of those Acts.

(1AC) In subsection (1AB), "the Immigration Acts" has the meaning given by section 61 of the UK Borders Act 2007.

(1B) In any proceedings (whether civil or criminal) under or arising from this Act—

(a) a certificate of the Commissioners for Her Majesty's Revenue and Customs that an officer of Revenue of Customs, or

(b) a certificate of the Secretary of State that an immigration officer, had the authority,

to exercise a power or function conferred by a provision of this Act shall be conclusive evidence of that fact.

(2) References in this Act to a court do not include references to a service court; and nothing in this Act shall be construed as affecting the punishment which may be awarded by a service court for an offence under section 42 of the Armed Forces Act 2006.

(2A) In subsection (2), "service court" means—

(a) the Court Martial;
(b) the Summary Appeal Court;
(c) the Court Martial Appeal Court; or
(d) the Supreme Court on an appeal brought from the Court Martial Appeal Court.

(3) […]

(4) Any reference in this Act to a previous sentence of imprisonment shall be construed as including a reference to a previous sentence of penal servitude; any such reference to a previous sentence of Borstal training shall be construed as including a reference to a previous sentence of detention in a Borstal institution.

(5) Except where the context requires otherwise—

(a) any reference in this Act to a previous conviction is to be construed as a reference to a previous conviction by a court in any part of the United Kingdom […]

(b) any reference in this Act to a previous sentence is to be construed as a reference to a previous sentence passed by any such court;

(c) any reference to a previous conviction of a particular offence is to be construed, in relation to a previous conviction by a court outside Scotland, as a reference to a previous conviction of an equivalent offence; and

(d) any reference to a previous sentence of a particular kind is to be construed, in relation to a previous sentence passed by a court outside Scotland, as a reference to a previous sentence of an equivalent kind.

(6) References in this Act to an offence punishable with imprisonment shall be construed, in relation to any offender, without regard to any prohibition or restriction imposed by or under any enactment, including this Act, upon the imprisonment of offenders of his age.

(7) Without prejudice to section 46 of this Act, where the age of any person at any time is material for the purposes of any provision of this Act regulating the powers of a court, his age at the material time shall be deemed to be or to have been that which appears to the court, after considering any available evidence, to be or to have been his age at that time.

(8) References in this Act to findings of guilty and findings that an offence has been committed shall be construed as including references to pleas of guilty and admissions that an offence has been committed.

AMENDMENTS

Subs.(1) as amended by Crime and Punishment (Scotland) Act 1997 (c.48) s.62(1) and Sch.1 para.21(34)(b) with effect from 1 August 1997 in terms of SI 1997/1712 art.3.

Subs.(1) as amended by Crime and Punishment (Scotland) Act 1997 (c.48) s.6(5) with effect from 1 January 1998 in terms of SI 1997/2323 Sch.2.

Section 307 as amended by Crime and Disorder Act 1998 (c.37) Sch.8 para.124 (effective 30 September 1998: SI 1998/2327).

Subs.(1) as amended by Crime and Disorder Act 1998 (c.37) s.95.

Subsection (1) as amended by Scotland Act 1998 (c.46) s.125(1) and Sch.8 para.31(3).

Subsection (1) as amended by Criminal Justice and Court Services Act 2000 (c.43) s.74 and Sch.7 para.126. Brought into force by SI 2001/919 (C.33) art.2(f)(ii) (effective 1 April 2001).

Subsection (1) as amended by Postal Services Act 2000 (Consequential Modifications No.1) Order 2001 (SI 2001/1149) art.3 and Sch.1 para.104.

Section 307 as amended by Regulation of Care (Scotland) Act 2001 (asp 8) s.79 and Sch.3 para.20. Brought into force on 1 October 2001 by SSI 2001/304 (C.13).

Subsections (1) and (5) as amended by Criminal Justice (Scotland) Act 2003 (asp 7) Pt 8 s.57(5). Brought into force on 27 June 2003 by SSI 2003/288 (C.14).

Subsection (1) as amended by Criminal Justice (Scotland) Act 2003 (asp 7) Pt 12 s.76(11). Brought into force on 27 June 2003 by SSI 2003/288 (C.14).

Subsection (1) as amended by Criminal Justice (Scotland) Act 2003 (asp 7) Pt 8 s.60(2). Brought into force on 27 October 2003 by SSI 2003/475 (C.26) art.2.

Subsection (1) as amended by Criminal Justice (Scotland) Act 2003 (asp 7) Sch.1 para.2(7). Brought into force on 19 June 2006 by SSI 2006/332 (C.30) art.2(1), subject to art.2(2).

Subsection (1) as amended by Criminal Procedure (Amendment) (Scotland) Act 2004 (asp 5) s.25 and Sch.1 para.57. Brought into force on 1 February 2005 by SSI 2004/405 (C.28) art.2.

Subsection (1) as amended by Mental Health (Care and Treatment) (Scotland) Act 2003 (asp 13) Sch.4 para.8(16) and Sch.5. Brought into force on 5 October 2005 by SSI 2005/161 (C.6).

Subsection (1) as amended by Vulnerable Witnesses (Scotland) Act 2004 (asp 3) s.1(2). Brought into force, for specified purposes, on 2 July 2007 by SSI 2007/329 (C.26). Remainder brought into force on 1 April 2008 by SSI 2008/57 (C.7) art.2.

In subs.(1) definition “justice of the peace” inserted by Criminal Proceedings etc. (Reform) (Scotland) Act 2007 (asp 6) s.80, Sch. para.25(b). Brought into force on 12 December 2007 by SSI 2007/479 (C.40) art.3 and Sch.

In subs.(1) definition “JP court” inserted by Criminal Proceedings etc (Reform) (Scotland) Act 2007 (asp 6) s.80, Sch. para.25(c). Brought into force on 10 March 2008 by SSI 2008/42 (C.4) art.3 and Sch.

In subs.(1) definitions “court of summary criminal jurisdiction” and “judge” as amended and definition “stipendiary magistrate” inserted by Criminal Proceedings etc. (Reform) (Scotland) Act 2007 (asp 6) s.80, Sch. para.25(a), (d). Brought into force for the Sheriffdom of Lothian and Borders on 10 March 2008 by SSI 2008/42 (C.4) art.3 and Sch. Brought into force for the Sheriffdom of Grampian, Highland and Islands on 2 June 2008 by SSI 2008/192 (C.19) art.3 and Sch. Brought into force for the Sheriffdom of Glasgow and Strathkelvin on 8 December 2008 by SSI 2008/329 art.3 and Sch.1 para.1. Brought into force for the Sheriffdom of Tayside, Central and Fife on 23 February 2009 by SSI 2008/362 (C.30) art.3 and Sch. Brought into force for the Sheriffdom of North Strathclyde on 14 December 2009 by SSI 2009/432 (C.32) art.3 and Sch.1. Remainder in force on 22 February 2010 by SSI 2009/432 (C.32) art.3 and Sch.2.

In subs.(1) definition of “officer of the law” as amended by Finance Act 2007 (c.11) Sch.23 para.9. Subss.(1A) and (1B) inserted by Finance Act 2007 (c.11) Sch.23 para.10. Brought into force on 1 December 2007 by SI 2007/3166 art.3(b).

Subsection (2) as amended and subs.(2A) inserted by Armed Forces Act 2006 (c.52) Sch.16 para.133. Brought into force on 31 October 2009 by SI 2009/1167 art.4.

In subs.(1) definition of “chartered psychologist” deleted and defintion of “registered psychologist” inserted by Health Care and Associated Professions (Miscellaneous Amendments and Practitioner Psychologists) Order 2009 (SI 2009/1182) Sch.5 para.3 (effective 13 May 2009 for the purpose of conferring, amending, or substituting powers enabling rules or orders to be made subject to transitional provisions specified in SI 2009/1182 art.5; 1 July 2009 otherwise).

In subs.(1) definition of "conviction" inserted, and subs.(5) substituted, by Criminal Justice and Licensing (Scotland) Act 2010 (asp 13) Sch.4 para.8. Brought into force on 13 December 2010 by SSI 2010/413 (C.28) art.2 and Sch.1 para.1.

Subsection (1) as amended, and subs.(3) repealed, by Criminal Justice and Licensing (Scotland) Act 2010 (asp 13) Sch.2 para.28. Brought into force on 13 December 2010 (subject to savings provisions in art.3) by SSI 2010/413 (C.28) art.2 and Sch.1 para.1.

In subs.(1) definition of "organisation" inserted by Criminal Justice and Licensing (Scotland) Act 2010 (asp 13) s.65. Brought into force on 28 March 2011 (for specified purposes) by SSI 2011/178 (C.15) art.2, Sch.1 para.1.

In subs.(1) definition of "postal operator" as amended by Postal Services Act 2011 (c.5) Sch.12 para.146. Brought into force on 1 October 2011 by SI 2011/2329 art.3(1).

In subs.(1) definition of "unfit for trial" inserted by Criminal Justice and Licensing (Scotland) Act 2010 (asp 13) Sch.7 para.62. Brought into force on 25 June 2012 by SSI 2012/160 (C.15) art.3. In subs.(1) definition of "registered psychologist" as amended by Health and Social Care Act 2012 (c.7) Pt 7 s.213(8). Brought into force on 1 August 2012 by SI 2012/1319 art.2(4).

In subs.(1) definitions of "constable" and "officer of law" as amended by Police and Fire Reform (Scotland) Act 2012 (asp 8) Sch.7 para.12(10). Brought into force on 1 April 2013 by SSI 2013/51 art.2.

Subs.(1) as amended by Children's Hearings (Scotland) Act 2011 (Modification of Primary Legislation) Order 2013 (SSI 2013/211) Sch.1 para.10 (effective 24 June 2013).

Subsection (1AA) inserted, and subs.(1B) as amended, by Crime and Courts Act 2013 (c.22) s.55(13). Brought into force on 25 June 2013 by SI 2013/1042 art.4(d), subject to savings and transitional provisions.

In subs.(1) definition of "officer of law", subs.(bb) inserted by Crime and Courts Act 2013 (c.22) s.55(13). Brought into force on 25 June 2013 by SI 2013/1042 art.4(d), subject to savings and transitional provisions.

In subs.(1) definition of "justice" as amended, and definition of "stipendiary magistrate" repealed, by Courts Reform (Scotland) Act 2014 (asp 18) Sch.5 para.39. Brought into force on 1 April 2016 by SSI 2016/13 art.2 Sch.1 para.1.

In subs.(1) definition of "Clerk of the Sheriff Appeal Court" inserted by Courts Reform (Scotland) Act 2014 (asp 18) Sch.3 para.26. Brought into force on 22 September 2015 by SSI 2015/247 art.2 Sch.1 para.1.

In subs.(1) definition of "officer of law", para.(ba) repealed by Criminal Finances Act 2017 (c.22) s.18(3). Brought into force on 27 June 2017 by s.58(4)(b).

Subsection (1A) repealed by Criminal Finances Act 2017 (c.22) s.18(3). Brought into force on 27 June 2017 by s.58(4)(b).

In subs.(1), definition of "compulsion order" as amended by Mental Health (Scotland) Act 2015 (asp 9) s.53(2). Brought into force on 30 June 2017 by SSI 2017/197 art.2 and Sch.1 para.1.

Subsection (1A) as amended, subss.(1AB), (1AC) inserted by Criminal Justice (Scotland) Act 2016 (Consequential Provisions) Order 2018 (SI 2018/46) art.15 (effective 25 January 2018), subject to savings.

Words omitted from subs.(5)(a) were repealed by the Criminal Justice (EU Exit) (Scotland) (Amendment etc.) Regulations 2020 (SSI 2020/339) reg.13(18) (effective December 31, 2020 subject to transitional and saving provision specified in reg.16 of those Regulations.

In s.307(1) in the definition of "fine" para.(d) inserted by the Victims and Witnesses (Scotland) Act 2014 (Supplementary Provisions) Order 2021 (SSI 2021/57) art.2(7)(b) (effective February 3, 2021).

General Note

A4-593.1 For specific judicial explanation of the term "conviction" reference might be made to *HM Advocate v Dempster* (1862) 4 Irvine 143 where it was settled that an English conviction of theft was equivalent to a Scottish conviction. In *HM Advocate v Jacques* (1871) 9 S. L. Rep. 69 it was held that it was no objection to an English conviction that it had been under a statute and not at common law. In *HM Advocate v Whyte* (1873) it was held that it was irrelevant that the nature or details of the theft were not specified in a previous conviction.

In the definition of "extract conviction" reference is made to "certificate of conviction". In *Fairfield Sentry Ltd (in liquidation) v Quilvest Finance Ltd* [2014] UKPC 9 it was held (at [5]) that "the word 'certificate' had no standard meaning and the question of what constituted a certificate was dependant on the commercial or legal context in which the term appeared". In the decision of the Board (at [27]) "as a matter of language, a 'certificate' ordinarily meant (i) a statement in writing; (ii) issued by an authoritative source, which (iii) was communicated by whatever method to a recipient or class of recipients intended to rely on it, and (iv) conveyed information, (v) in a form or context which showed that it was intended to be definitive. There was no reason to think that a document had to satisfy any further formal requirements unless its purpose or legal context plainly required them".

The law and circumstances relating to a court passing a sentence on a "child" in the context of s.307 of the 1995 Act as amended resulted in judicial reference to the concept of "a statutory child", which included those individuals between the ages of 16 and 18 years subject to compulsory measures of supervision: *HM Advocate v O'D (G)* [2019] HCJAC 33; 2019 S.L.T. 813; 2019 S.C.C.R. 242; (2019) GWD 18-295 at [8].

For consideration of the meaning of "sentence" in the context of an appeal concerning a finding of contempt of court by failing to attend having been lawfully cited as a witness for a sheriff court case see *Meade v Corrins* [2020] SAC (Crim) 4; 2020 S.C.C.R. 371.

Construction of enactments referring to detention etc.

308. In any enactment— **A4-594**

(a) any reference to a sentence of imprisonment as including a reference to a sentence of any other form of detention shall be construed as including a reference to a sentence of detention under section 207 of this Act; and

(b) any reference to imprisonment as including any other form of detention shall be construed as including a reference to detention under that section.

Expressions relating to electronic proceedings

308A.—(1) In this Act, an "electronic complaint" is a complaint in electronic form which is capable of being— **A4-594.1**

(a) transmitted by means of electronic communication;

(b) kept in legible form.

(2) In this Act, unless the context otherwise requires—

"electronic communication" is to be construed in accordance with section 15(1) of the Electronic Communications Act 2000 (c.7);

"electronic signature" is to be construed in accordance with section 7(2) of the Electronic Communications Act 2000, but includes a version of an electronic signature which is reproduced on a paper document.

(3) The Scottish Ministers may by order modify the meaning of "electronic signature" provided for in subsection (2) above for the purpose of such provisions of this Act as are specified in the order.

(4) An order under subsection (3) above shall be made by statutory instrument subject to annulment in pursuance of a resolution of the Scottish Parliament.

AMENDMENTS

Section 308A inserted by Criminal Proceedings etc. (Reform) (Scotland) Act 2007 (asp 6) s.41(2).
Subss.(2)–(4) brought into force on 10 December 2007 by SSI 2007/479 (C.40) art.3 and Sch.

Subs.(1) brought into force on 1 November 2012 by SSI 2012/274 (C.28) art.2 and Sch.

[THE NEXT PARAGRAPH IS A4-595]

Short title, commencement and extent

309.—(1) This Act may be cited as the Criminal Procedure Act 1995. **A4-595**

(2) This Act shall come into force on 1 April 1996.

(3) Subject to subsections (4) and (5) below, this Act extends to Scotland only.

(4) The following provisions of this Act and this section extend to England and Wales—

section 44;

section 47;

section 209(3) and (7);

section 234(4) to (11);

section 244;

section 252 for the purposes of the construction mentioned in subsection (1) of that subsection;

section 303(4) to (7);

Part 1 of Schedule 13 (and section 227ZO).

(5) The following provisions of this Act and this section extend to Northern Ireland—

section 44;
section 47;
section 244;
section 252 for the purposes of the construction mentioned in subsection (1) of that subsection;
section 303(4) to (7);
Part 2 of Schedule 13 (and section 227ZO).

(6) Section 297(3) and (4) of this Act and this section also extend to the Isle of Man.

Amendments

Subss.(4) and (5) as amended by Northern Ireland Act 1998 (Devolution of Policing and Justice Functions) Order 2010 (SI 2010/976) Sch.14 para.32 (effective 12 April 2010 subject to transitional provisions).

Subss.(4) and (5) as amended by Criminal Justice and Licensing (Scotland) Act 2010 (Consequential Provisions and Modifications) Order 2011 (SI 2011/2298) art.3 and Sch.1 (effective 16 September 2011, subject to transitional provisions specified in SI 2011/2298 art.4(4)).

General Note

Subs.(3)

A4-595.1 The 1995 Act extends, subject to slight exceptions, to Scotland only but it should be noted, for the avoidance of doubt that in ordinary practice dockets added to certain indictments on the authority of s.288BA of the 1995 Act now seem to permit, as a matter of course, relevant evidence to be admitted of events occurring outside the jurisdiction of Scotland. For an indication of the possible limitation of the term "Scots law" to the context in which it is used see *Donaldson v Scottish Legal Aid Board* [2014] CSIH 31; 2014 S.L.T. 459; 2014 G.W.D. 12-218.

[THE NEXT PARAGRAPH IS A4-596]

SCHEDULES

SCHEDULE 1

Offences Against Children Under the Age of 17 Years to which Special Provisions Apply

Section 21

A4-596 **1.** Any offence under Part I of the Criminal Law (Consolidation) (Scotland) Act 1995.

1A. Any offence under section 18 (rape of a young child) or 28 (having intercourse with an older child) of the Sexual Offences (Scotland) Act 2009 (asp 9).

1B. Any offence under section 19 (sexual assault on a young child by penetration) or 29 (engaging in penetrative sexual activity with or towards an older child) of that Act.

1C. Any offence under section 20 (sexual assault on a young child) or 30 (engaging in sexual activity with or towards an older child) of that Act.

1D. Any offence under section 42 of that Act (sexual abuse of trust) towards a child under the age of 17 years but only if the condition set out in section 43(6) of that Act is fulfilled.

2. Any offence under section 12, 15, 22 or 33 of the Children and Young Persons (Scotland) Act 1937.

2A. Any offence under the Prohibition of Female Genital Mutilation (Scotland) Act 2005 where the person mutilated or, as the case may be, proposed to be mutilated, is a child under the age of 17 years.

2B. Any offence under section 52 or 52A of the Civic Government (Scotland) Act 1982 in relation to an indecent photograph or pseudophotograph of a child under the age of 17 years.

2C. Any offence under section 1, 9, 10, 11 or 12 of the Protection of Children and Prevention of Sexual Offences (Scotland) Act 2005 in respect of a child under the age of 17 years.

3. Any other offence involving bodily injury to a child under the age of 17 years.

4. Any offence involving the use of lewd, indecent or libidinous practice or behaviour towards a child under the age of 17 years.

4A. Any offence under section 5 (coercing a person into being present during a sexual activity), 6 (coercing a person into looking at a sexual image), 7 (communicating indecently etc.), 8 (sexual exposure) or 9 (voyeurism) of the Sexual Offences (Scotland) Act 2009 (asp 9) towards a child under the age of 17 years.

4B. Any offence under any of sections 21 to 26 or 31 to 37 of that Act (certain sexual offences relating to children).

AMENDMENTS

Para.2A inserted by Prohibition of Female Genital Mutilation (Scotland) Act 2005 (asp 8) s.7(1). Brought into force on September 1, 2005 in accordance with s.8.

Paras 2B and 2C inserted by Protection of Children and Prevention of Sexual Offences (Scotland) Act 2005 (asp 9) Sch.para.2. Brought into force on October 7, 2005 by SSI 2005/480 (C.24).

Paras 1A, 1B, 1C, 1D, 4A, and 4B inserted by Sexual Offences (Scotland) Act 2009 (asp 9) Sch.5 para.2. Brought into force on December 1, 2010 by SSI 2010/357 (C.21) art.2.

Para.2B as amended by Criminal Justice and Licensing (Scotland) Act 2010 (asp 13) s.41(2). Brought into force on December 13, 2010 by SSI 2010/413 (C.28) art.2 Sch.1 para.1.

SCHEDULE 2

EXAMPLES OF INDICTMENTS

Sections 34 & 64(2)

"A.B. (*name and address, that given in the declaration being sufficient*), you are indicted at the instance of Her Majesty's Advocate, and the charge against you is that on 20th 199, in a shop in George Street, Edinburgh, occupied by John Cruikshank, draper, you did steal a shawl and a boa." **A4-597**

"... You did rob Charles Doyle, a cattle dealer, of Biggar, Lanarkshire, of a watch and chain and £36 of money..."

"... You did break into the house occupied by Andrew Howe, banker's clerk, and did there steal twelve spoons, a ladle, and a candlestick..."

"... You did force open (*or* attempt to force open) a lockfast cupboard and did thus attempt to steal therefrom..."

"... You did place your hand in one of the packets of Thomas Kerr, commercial traveller, 115 Main Street, Perth, and did thus attempt to steal..."

"... You did assault Lewis Mann, station-master of Earlston, and compress his throat and attempt to take from him a watch and chain..."

"... You did, while in the employment of James Pentland, accountant in Frederick Street, Edinburgh, embezzle £4,075 of money..."

"... You did, while acting as commercial traveller to Brown and Company, merchants in Leith, at the times and places specified in the inventory hereto subjoined, receive from the persons therein set forth the respective sums of money therein specified for the said Brown and Company, and did embezzle the same (or did embezzle £470 of money, being part thereof)..."

"... You did pretend to Norah Omond, residing there, that you were a collector of subscriptions for a charitable society, and did thus induce her to deliver to you £15 of money as a subscription thereto, which you appropriated to your own use..."

"... You did reset a watch and chain, pocket book and £15.55 of money, the same having been dishonestly appropriated by theft or robbery..."

"... You did utter as genuine a bill, on which the name of John Jones bore to be signed as acceptor, such signature being forged by (*here describe in general terms how the bill was uttered, and add where the bill is produced*), and said bill of exchange is No. of the productions lodged herewith..."

"... You did utter as genuine a letter bearing to be a certificate of character of you, as a domestic servant, by Mary Watson, of 15 Bon Accord Street, Aberdeen, what was written above the signature of Mary Watson having been written there by some other person without her authority by handing it to Ellen Chisholm of Panmore Street, Forfar, to whom you were applying for a situation (*here add when the letter is produced*), and said letter is No. of the productions lodged herewith..."

"... You did utter a cheque signed by Henry Smith for £8 sterling, which had been altered without his authority by adding the letter Y to eight and the figure 0 to figure 8, so as to make it read as a cheque for XC11,480 sterling, by presenting such altered cheque for payment to Allen Brown, Cashier of the Bank of Scotland at Callander (*here add when the cheque is produced*), and said cheque is No. of the productions lodged herewith..."

"... You did, when examined under section 45 of the Bankruptcy (Scotland) Act 1985 before Hubert Hamilton Esquire, sheriff of the Lothians and Borders, depone (*here state the general nature of the false statement*), in order to defraud your creditors..."

"... You did, sequestration having been awarded on your estate on the 20th March 1991, conceal property consisting of (*here state generally the property concealed*), falling under your sequestration, in order to defraud your creditor, by burying it in the garden of your house in Troon Street, Kilmarnock (or by removing it to the house of James Kidd, your son, No. 17 Greek Street, Port-Glasgow)..."

"... You did set fire to a warehouse occupied by Peter Cranston in Holly Lane, Greenock, and the fire took effect on said warehouse, and this you did wilfully (*or* culpably and recklessly)..."

"... You did set fire to the shop in Brown Street, Blairgowrie, occupied by you, with intent to defraud the Liverpool, London, and Globe Insurance Company, and the fire took effect on said shop..."

"... You did assault Theresa Unwin, your wife, and did beat her and did murder her..."

"... You did stab Thomas Underwood, baker, of Shiels Place, Oban, and did murder him..."

"... You did administer poison to Vincent Wontner, your son, and did murder him..."

"... You did strangle Mary Shaw, mill-worker, daughter of John Shaw, residing at Juniper Green, in the county of Midlothian, and did murder her..."

"... You were delivered of a child now dead or amissing, and you did conceal your pregnancy and did not call for or use assistance at the birth, contrary to the *Concealment of Birth (Scotland) Act 1809*..."

"… You did assault Hector Morrison, carter, of 20 Buccleuch Street, Dalkeith, and did beat him with your fists and with a stick, and did break his arm…"

"… You did ravish Harriet Cowan, mill-worker, of 27 Tweed Row, Peebles…"

"… You did attempt to ravish Jane Peters, servant, at Glen House, near Dunbar…"

"… You did, when acting as railway signalman, cancel a danger signal and allow a train to enter on a part of the line protected by the signals under your charge, and did cause a collision, and did kill William Peters, commercial traveller, of Brook Street, Carlisle, a passenger in said train…"

"… You formed part of a riotous mob, which, acting of common purpose, obstructed A. B., C. D., and E. F., constables of the Northern constabulary on duty, and assaulted them, and forcibly took two persons whom they had arrested from their custody…"

"… You did, being the lawful husband of Helen Hargreaves, of 20 Teviot Row, Edinburgh, and she being still alive, bigamously marry Dorothy Rose, a widow, of 7 Blacks Row, Brechin, and did cohabit with her as her husband…"

"… You being sworn as a witness in a civil cause, then proceeding in the sheriff court, deponed (*here set forth the statements said to be false*) the truth as you knew being that (*here state the true facts*)…"

"… You did suborn James Carruthers, scavenger, 12 Hercles Street, Edinburgh, to depone as a witness in the sheriff court of Edinburgh, that (*here set forth the statements said to be false*), and he did (*time and place*) depone to that effect, the truth as you knew being (*here state the true facts*)…"

"… You did deforce John Macdonald, a sheriff officer of Renfrewshire, and prevent him serving a summons issued by the sheriff of Renfrewshire upon Peter M'Innes, market gardener in Renfrew…"

AMENDMENTS

Sch.2 para.1 as amended by Criminal Justice and Licensing (Scotland) Act 2010 (asp 13) s.60(5). Brought into force on December 13, 2010 (subject to savings provisions in art.5) by SSI 2010/413 (C.28) art.2, Sch.1 para.1.

SCHEDULE 3

INDICTMENTS AND COMPLAINTS

Sections 64(6) and 138(4)

A4-598 **1.** An accused may be named and designed—

(a) according to the existing practice; or

(b) by the name given by him and designed as of the place given by him as his residence when he is examined or further examined; or

(c) by the name under which he is committed until liberated in due course of law.

2. It shall not be necessary to specify by any *nomen juris* the offence which is charged, but it shall be sufficient that the indictment or complaint sets forth facts relevant and sufficient to constitute an indictable offence or, as the case may be, an offence punishable on complaint.

3. It shall not be necessary to allege that any act or commission or omission charged was done or omitted to be done "wilfully" or "maliciously", or "wickedly and feloniously", or "falsely and fraudulently" or "knowingly", or "culpably and recklessly", or "negligently", or in "breach of duty", or to use such words as "knowing the same to be forged", or "having good reason to know", or "well knowing the same to have been stolen", or to use any similar words or expressions qualifying any act charged, but such qualifying allegation shall be implied in every case.

4.—(1) The latitude formerly used in stating time shall be implied in all statements of time where an exact time is not of the essence of the charge.

(2) The latitude formerly used in stating any place by adding to the word "at", or to the word "in", the words "or near", or the words "or in the near neighbourhood thereof" or similar words, shall be implied in all statements of place where the actual place is not of the essence of the charge.

(3) Subject to sub-paragraph (4) below, where the circumstances of the offence charged make it necessary to take an exceptional latitude in regard to time or place it shall not be necessary to set forth the circumstances in the indictment, or to set forth that the particular time or the particular place is to the prosecutor unknown.

(4) Where exceptional latitude is taken as mentioned in sub-paragraph (3) above, the court shall, if satisfied that such exceptional latitude was not reasonable in the circumstances of the case, give such remedy to the accused by adjournment of the trial or otherwise as shall seem just.

(5) Notwithstanding sub-paragraph (4) above, nothing in any rule of law shall prohibit the amendment of an indictment or, as the case may be, a complaint to include a time outwith the exceptional latitude if it appears to the court that the amendment would not prejudice the accused.

(6) The latitude formerly used in describing quantities by the words "or thereby", or the words "or part thereof", or the words "or some other quantity to the prosecutor unknown" or similar words, shall be implied in all statements of quantities.

(7) The latitude formerly used in stating details connected with the perpetration of any act regarding persons, things or modes by inserting general alternative statements followed by the words "to the prosecutor unknown" or similar words, shall be implied in every case.

(8) In this paragraph references to latitude formerly used are references to such use before the commencement of—

(a) in the case of proceedings on indictment, the Criminal Procedure (Scotland) Act 1887; and

(b) in the case of summary proceedings, the Summary Jurisdiction (Scotland) Act 1908.

5. The word "money" shall include cheques, banknotes, postal orders, money orders and foreign currency.

6. Any document referred to shall be referred to by a general description and, where it is to be produced in proceedings on indictment, by the number given to it in the list of productions for the prosecution.

7. In an indictment which charges a crime importing personal injury inflicted by the accused, resulting in death or serious injury to the person, the accused may be lawfully convicted of the aggravation that the assault or other injurious act was committed with intent to commit such crime.

8.—(1) In an indictment or a complaint charging the resetting of property dishonestly appropriated—

(a) having been taken by theft or robbery; or

(b) by breach of trust, embezzlement or falsehood, fraud and wilful imposition,

it shall be sufficient to specify that the accused received the property, it having been dishonestly appropriated by theft or robbery, or by breach of trust and embezzlement, or by falsehood, fraud and wilful imposition, as the case may be.

(2) Under an indictment or a complaint for robbery, theft, breach of trust and embezzlement or falsehood, fraud and wilful imposition, an accused may be convicted ofreset.

(3) Under an indictment or a complaint for robbery, breach of trust and embezzlement, or falsehood, fraud and wilful imposition, an accused may be convicted of theft.

(3A) Under an indictment or a complaint for breach of trust and embezzlement, an accused may be convicted offalsehood, fraud and wilful imposition.

(3B) Under an indictment or a complaint for falsehood, fraud and wilful imposition, an accused may be convicted ofbreach oftrust and embezzlement.

(4) Under an indictment or a complaint for theft, an accused may be convicted of breach of trust and embezzlement, or of falsehood, fraud and wilful imposition, or may be convicted of theft, although the circumstances proved may in law amount to robbery.

(5) The power conferred by sub-paragraphs (2) to (4) above to convict a person of an offence other than that with which he is charged shall be exercisable by the sheriff court before which he is tried notwithstanding that the other offence was committed outside the jurisdiction of that sheriff court.

9.—(1) Where two or more crimes or acts of crime are charged cumulatively, it shall be lawful to convict of any one or more of them.

(2) Any part of the charge in an indictment or complaint which itself constitutes an indictable offence or, as the case may be an offence punishable on complaint, shall be separable and it shall be lawful to convict the accused ofthat offence.

(3) Where any crime is charged as having been committed with a particular intent orwith particular circumstances of aggravation, it shall be lawful to convict of the crime without such intent or aggravation.

10.—(1) Under an indictment or, as the case may be, a complaint which charges a completed offence, the accused may be lawfully convicted of an attempt to commit the offence.

(2) Under an indictment or complaint charging an attempt, the accused may be convicted of such attempt although the evidence is sufficient to prove the completion of the offence said to have been attempted.

(3) Under an indictment or complaint which charges an offence involving personal injury inflicted by the accused, resulting in death or serious injury to the person, the accused may be lawfully convicted of the assault or other injurious act, and may also be lawfully convicted of the aggravation that the assault or other injurious act was committed with intent to commit such offence.

11. In an indictment or complaint charging a contravention of an enactment the description of the offence in the words of the enactment contravened, or in similar words, shall be sufficient.

12. In a complaint charging a contravention of an enactment—

(a) the statement that an act was done contrary to an enactment shall imply a statement—

(i) that the enactment applied to the circumstances existing at the time and place of the offence;

(ii) that the accused was a person bound to observe the enactment;

(iii) that any necessary preliminary procedure had been duly gone through; and

(iv) that all the circumstances necessary to a contravention existed, and, in the case of the contravention of a subordinate instrument, such statement shall imply a statement that the instrument was duly made, confirmed, published and generally made effectual according to the law applicable, and was in force at the time and place in question; and

(b) where the offence is created by more than one section of one or more statutes or subordinate instruments, it shall be necessary to specify only the leading section or one of the leading sections.

13. In the case of an offence punishable under any enactment, it shall be sufficient to allege that the offence was committed contrary to the enactment and to refer to the enactment founded on without setting out the words of the enactment at length.

14. Where—

(a) any act alleged in an indictment or complaint as contrary to any enactment is also criminal at common law; or

(b) where the facts proved under the indictment or complaint do not amount to a contravention of the enactment, but do amount to an offence at common law, it shall be lawful to convict of the common law offence.

15. Where the evidence in a trial is sufficient to prove the identity of any person, corporation or company, or of any place, or of anything, it shall not be a valid objection to the sufficiency of the evidence that any particulars specified in the indictment or complaint relating to such identity have not been proved.

16. Where, in relation to an offence created by or under an enactment any exception, exemption, proviso, excuse, or qualification, is expressed to have effect whether by the same or any other enactment, the exception, exemption, proviso, excuse or qualification need not be specified or negatived in the indictment or complaint, and the prosecution is not required to prove it, but the accused may do so.

17. It shall be competent to include in one indictment or complaint both common law and statutory charges.

18. In any proceedings under the Merchant Shipping Acts it shall not be necessary to produce the official register of the ship referred to in the proceedings in order to prove the nationality of the ship, but the nationality of the ship as stated in the indictment or, as the case may be, complaint shall, in the absence of evidence to the contrary, be presumed.

19. In offences inferring dishonest appropriation of property brought before a court whose power to deal with such offences is limited to cases in which the value of such property does not exceed level 4 on the standard scale it shall be assumed, and it shall not be necessary to state in the charge, that the value of the property does not exceed that sum.

Amendments

Para.8(3A)–(3B) added by Criminal Justice and Licensing (Scotland) Act 2010 (asp 13) s.48. Brought into force on March 28, 2011 (for all purposes in respect of offences committed on or after March 28, 2011) by SSI 2011/178 (C.15) art.2, Sch.1 para.1.

General Note

A4-598.1 In *Momoh v McFadyen*, 2003 S.C.C.R. 679 the opinion of the court was reserved as to the true construction and effect of para.16 of Sch.3.

Sch.3 para.16

In *Cunningham v HM Advocate*, 2012 S.C.C.R. 605 it was observed that Sch.3 para.16 is a statutory reflection of an underlying and perhaps wider principle that a negative averment made by one party which is peculiarly within the knowledge of the other need not be proved. Further, when an accused pleads a particular exemption, or excuse peculiarly within his knowledge, he is required to establish that excuse or exemption

[THE NEXT PARAGRAPH IS A4-599]

SCHEDULE 4

Supervision and Treatment Orders

Section 57(5)

Part I

Preliminary

A4-599 **1.**—(1) In this Schedule "supervision and treatment order" means an order requiring the person in respect of whom it is made ("the supervised person")—

(a) to be under the supervision of a social worker who is an officer of the local authority for the area where the supervised person resides or is to reside (in this Schedule referred to as "the supervising officer") for such period, not being more than three years, as is specified in the order;

(b) to comply during that period with instructions given to him by the supervising officer regarding his supervision; and

(c) to submit during that period to treatment by or under the direction of a medical practitioner with a view to the improvement of his mental condition.

(2) The Secretary of State may by order amend sub-paragraph (1) above by substituting, for the period for the time being specified in that sub-paragraph, such period as may be specified in the order.

(3) An order under sub-paragraph (2) above may make any amendment to paragraph 8(2) below which the Secretary of State considers necessary in consequence of the order.

(4) The power of the Secretary of State to make orders under sub-paragraph (2) above shall be exercisable by statutory instrument subject to annulment in pursuance of a resolution of either House of Parliament.

PART II

MAKING AND EFFECT OF ORDERS

Circumstances in which orders may be made

2.—(1) The court shall not make a supervision and treatment order unless it is satisfied— **A4-599.1**

(a) that, having regard to all the circumstances of the case, the making of such an order is the most suitable means of dealing with the person; and

(b) on the written or oral evidence of two or more approved medical practitioners, that the mental condition of the person—

(i) is such as requires and may be susceptible to treatment; but

(ii) is not such as to warrant the making of an order under paragraph (a) of subsection (2) of section 57 of this Act (whether with or without an order under paragraph (b) of that subsection) or an order under paragraph (c) of that subsection.

(2) The court shall not make a supervision and treatment order unless it is also satisfied—

(a) that the supervising officer intended to be specified in the order is willing to undertake the supervision; and

(b) that arrangements have been made for the treatment intended to be specified in the order.

(3) Subsections (3) to (5) of section 61 of this Act shall have effect with respect to proof of a person's mental condition for the purposes of sub-paragraph (1) above as they have effect with respect to proof of an offender's mental condition for the purposes of section 58(1)(a) of this Act.

(4) In this Schedule "approved medical practitioner" has the meaning given by section 22(4) of the Mental Health (Care and Treatment) (Scotland) Act 2003 (asp 13).

AMENDMENTS

Para.2(1)(b) as amended by Adults with Incapacity (Scotland) Act 2000 (asp 4) Sch.6. Brought into force on April 1, 2002 by SSI 2001/81 (C.2).

Para.2(1)(b) as amended, and para.2(4) inserted, by Mental Health (Care and Treatment) (Scotland) Act 2003 (Modification of Enactments) Order 2005 (SSI 2005/465) art.2 and Sch.1para.27(6) (effective September 27, 2005).

Making of orders and general requirements

3.—(1) A supervision and treatment order shall specify the local authority area in which the supervised person resides or will reside. **A4-599.2**

(2) Before making such an order, the court shall explain to the supervised person in ordinary language—

(a) the effect of the order (including any requirements proposed to be included in the order in accordance with paragraph 5 below); and

(b) that the sheriff court for the area in which the supervised person resides or will reside (in this Schedule referred to as "the relevant sheriff court") has power under paragraphs 6 to 8 below to review the order on the application either of the supervised person or of the supervising officer.

(3) After making such an order, the court shall forthwith give a copy of the order to—

(a) the supervised person;

(b) the supervising officer; and

(bb) the medical practitioner by whom or under whose supervision the supervised person is to be treated under the order;

(c) the person in charge of any institution in which the supervised person is required by the order to reside.

(4) After making such an order, the court shall also send to the relevant sheriff court—

(a) a copy of the order; and

(b) such documents and information relating to the case as it considers likely to be of assistance to that court in the exercise of its functions in relation to the order.

(5) Where such an order is made, the supervised person shall comply with such instructions as he may from time to time be given by the supervising officer regarding his supervision and shall keep in touch with that officer and notify him of any change of address.

Obligatory requirements as to medical treatment

4.—(1) A supervision and treatment order shall include a requirement that the supervised person shall submit, during the period specified in the order, to treatment by or under the direction of a medical practitioner with a view to the improvement of his mental condition. **A4-599.3**

(2) The treatment required by the order shall be such one of the following kinds of treatment as may be specified in the order, that is to say—

(a) treatment as a non-resident patient at such institution or place as may be specified in the order; and

(b) treatment by or under the direction of such medical practitioner as may be so specified; but the nature of the treatment shall not be specified in the order except as mentioned in paragraph (a) or (b) above.

(3) Where the medical practitioner by whom or under whose direction the supervised person is being treated for his mental condition in pursuance of a supervision and treatment order is of the opinion that part of the treatment can be better or more conveniently given at an institution or place which—

(a) is not specified in the order; and

(b) is one at which the treatment of the supervised person will be given by or under the direction of a medical practitioner,

he may, with the consent of the supervised person, make arrangements for him to be treated accordingly.

(4) Where any such arrangements as are mentioned in sub-paragraph (3) above are made for the treatment of a supervised person—

(a) the medical practitioner by whom the arrangements are made shall give notice in writing to the supervising officer, specifying the institution or place at which the treatment is to be carried out; and

(b) the treatment provided for by the arrangements shall be deemed to be treatment to which he is required to submit in pursuance of the supervision and treatment order.

Optional requirements as to residence

A4-599.4 5.—(1) Subject to sub-paragraphs (2) to (4) below, a supervision and treatment order may include requirements as to the residence of the supervised person.

(2) Such an order may not require the supervised person to reside as a resident patient in a hospital.

(3) Before making such an order containing any such requirement, the court shall consider the home surroundings of the supervised person.

(4) Where such an order requires the supervised person to reside in any institution, the period for which he is so required to reside shall be specified in the order.

PART III

REVOCATION AND AMENDMENT OF ORDERS

Revocation of order in interests of health or welfare

A4-599.5 6. Where a supervision and treatment order is in force in respect of any person and, on the application of the supervised person or the supervising officer, it appears to the relevant sheriff court that, having regard to circumstances which have arisen since the order was made, it would be in the interests of the health or welfare of the supervised person that the order should be revoked, the court may revoke the order.

Amendment of order by reason of change of residence

A4-599.6 7.—(1) This paragraph applies where, at any time while a supervision and treatment order is in force in respect of any person, the relevant sheriff court is satisfied that—

(a) the supervised person proposes to change, or has changed, his residence from the area specified in the order to the area of another local authority;

(b) a social worker who is an officer of the other local authority ("the new supervising officer") is willing to undertake the supervision; and

(c) the requirements of the order as respects treatment will continue to be complied with.

(2) Subject to sub-paragraph (3) below the court may, and on the application of the supervising officer shall, amend the supervision and treatment order by substituting the other area for the area specified in the order and the new supervising officer for the supervising officer specified in the order.

(3) Where a supervision and treatment order contains requirements which, in the opinion of the court, can be complied with only if the supervised person continues to reside in the area specified in the order, the court shall not amend the order under this paragraph unless it also, in accordance with paragraph 8 below, either—

(a) cancels those requirements; or

(b) substitutes for those requirements other requirements which can be complied with if the supervised person ceases to reside in that area.

Amendment of requirements of order

A4-599.7 8.—(1) Without prejudice to paragraph 7 above, but subject to sub-paragraph (2) below, the relevant sheriff court may, on the application of the supervised person or the supervising officer, by order amend a supervision and treatment order—

(a) by cancelling any of the requirements of the order; or

(b) by inserting in the order (either in addition to or in substitution for any such requirement) any requirement which the court could include if it were the court by which the order was made and were then making it.

(2) The power of the court under sub-paragraph (1) above shall not include power to amend an order by extending the period specified in it beyond the end of three years from the date of the original order.

Amendment of requirements in pursuance of medical report

9.—(1) Where the medical practitioner by whom or under whose direction the supervised person is being treated for his mental condition in pursuance of any requirement of a supervision and treatment order— **A4-599.8**

(a) is of the opinion mentioned in sub-paragraph (2) below; or
(b) is for any reason unwilling to continue to treat or direct the treatment of the supervised person,

he shall make a report in writing to that effect to the supervising officer and that officer shall apply under paragraph 8 above to the relevant sheriff court for the variation or cancellation of the requirement.

(2) The opinion referred to in sub-paragraph (1) above is—

(a) that the treatment of the supervised person should be continued beyond the period specified in the supervision and treatment order;
(b) that the supervised person needs different treatment, being treatment of a kind to which he could be required to submit in pursuance of such an order;
(c) that the supervised person is not susceptible to treatment; or
(d) that the supervised person does not require further treatment.

Supplemental

10.—(1) On the making under paragraph 6 above of an order revoking a supervision and treatment order, the sheriff clerk shall forthwith give a copy of the revoking order to the supervising officer and to the medical practitioner by whom or under whose supervision the supervised person was treated under the supervision and treatment order. **A4-599.9**

(2) On receipt of a copy of the revoking order the supervising officer shall give a copy to the supervised person and to the person in charge of any institution in which the supervised person was required by the order to reside.

11.—(1) On the making under paragraph 7 or 8 above of an order amending a supervision and treatment order, the sheriff clerk shall forthwith—

(a) if the order amends the supervision and treatment order otherwise than by substituting a new area or a new place for the one specified in that order, give a copy of the amending order to the supervising officer and to the medical practitioner by whom or under whose supervision the supervised person has been treated under the supervision and treatment order;
(b) if the order amends the supervision and treatment order in the manner excepted by paragraph (a) above, send to the new relevant sheriff court—
    (i) a copy of the amending order; and
    (ii) such documents and information relating to the case as he considers likely to be of assistance to that court in exercising its functions in relation to the order;

and in a case falling within paragraph (b) above, the sheriff clerk shall give a copy of the amending order to the supervising officer.

(2) On receipt of a copy of an amending order the supervising officer shall give a copy to the supervised person and to the person in charge of any institution in which the supervised person is or was required by the order to reside.

12. On the making, revocation or amendment of a supervision and treatment order the supervising officer shall give a copy of the order or, as the case may be, of the order revoking or amending it, to the Mental Welfare Commission for Scotland.

AMENDMENTS

Para.3(3)(bb) inserted by the Crime and Punishment (Scotland) Act 1997 (c. 48), Sched. 1, para. 21(35) with effect from January 1, 1998 as provided by the Crime and Punishment (Scotland) Act 1997 (Commencement No. 2 and Transitional and Consequential Provisions) Order 1997 (S.I. 1997 No. 2323) art. 4, Sched. 2.

Paras 10(1) and 11(1)(a) as amended by the above provisions with effect from January 1, 1998.

[THE NEXT PARAGRAPH IS A4-600]

SCHEDULE 5

FORMS OF COMPLAINT AND CHARGES

Section 138(2)

The following Forms are additional to those contained in Schedule 2 to this Act, *all of which, in so far as applicable to charges which may be tried summarily, are deemed to be incorporated in this* Schedule:— **A4-600**

You did assault A.L. and strike him with your fists.

You did conduct yourself in a disorderly manner and commit a breach of the peace.

You did threaten violence to the lieges and commit a breach of the peace.

You did fight and commit a breach of the peace.

You did publicly expose your person in a shameless and indecent manner in presence of the lieges.

You did obtain from A.N. board and lodging to the value of £16 without paying and intending not to pay therefor.

You did maliciously knock down 20 metres of the coping of a wall forming the fence between two fields on the said farm.

You did maliciously place a block of wood on the railway line and attempt to obstruct a train.

You did drive a horse and cart recklessly to the danger of the lieges.

You did break into a poultry house and steal three fowls.

You did steal a coat which you obtained from R.O. on the false representation that you had been sent for it by her husband.

having received from D.G. £6 to hand to E.R., you did on (date) at (place) steal the said sum.

having received from G.R. a watch in loan, you did on at, sell it to E.G., and steal it.

having found a watch, you did, without trying to discover its owner, sell it on at, to O.R., and steal it.

You did acquire from K.O., a private in the Third Battalion a military jacket and waist belt, contrary to section 195 of the Army Act 1955.

You, being a person whose estate has been sequestrated, did obtain credit from W.A. to the extent of £260 without informing him that your estate had been sequestrated and that you had not received your discharge, contrary to section 67(9) of the Bankruptcy (Scotland) Act 1985.

You, being the occupier of the said house, did use the same for the purpose of betting with persons resorting thereto, contrary to section 1 of the Betting, Gaming and Lotteries Act 1963.

You did frequent and loiter in the said street for the purpose of betting and receiving bets, contrary to section 8 of the Betting, Gaming and Lotteries Act 1963.

You did assault L.S., a constable of the Police, while engaged in the execution of his duty, and with a stick strike him on the face to the great effusion of blood contrary to section 41 of the Police (Scotland) Act 1967.

You did wilfully neglect your children K.I., aged seven years; J.I., aged five years; and H.I., aged three years, by failing to provide them with adequate food and clothing, and by keeping them in a filthy and verminous condition, contrary to section 12 of the Children and Young Persons (Scotland) Act 1937.

You are the owner of a dog which is dangerous and not kept under proper control, and which on in did chase a flock of sheep, contrary to section 2 of the Dogs Act 1871, section 2, as amended by section 1 of the Dogs Act 1906, whereby you are liable to be ordered to keep the said dog under proper control or to destroy it.

You, being a parent of D.U., a child of school age, aged, who has attended school, and the said child having failed, between and, without reasonable excuse, to attend regularly at the said school, you are thereby guilty of an offence against section 35 of the Education (Scotland) Act 1980.

You did sell and deliver to N.C. to his prejudice an article of food namely; gallons of sweet milk which was not of the nature, substance and quality of the article demanded by him and was not genuine sweet milk in respect that it was deficient in milk fat to the extent of per cent, or thereby in that it contained only per cent, of milk fat, conform to certificate of analysis granted on (date) by A.N. analytical chemist (address), public analyst for (a copy of which certificate of analysis is annexed hereto) of a sample of the said milk taken (specify time and place) by L.O., duly appointed sampling officer for, acting under the direction of the local authority for the said burgh, while the said milk was in course of delivery to the said N.C. contrary to the Food Act 1984, and the Sale of Milk Regulations 1901.

You did take part in gaming in the street contrary to sections 5 and 8 of the Gaming Act 1968.

…

…

…

You did present or cause to be presented to W.E., Assessors for a return in which you falsely stated that the yearly rent of your House. No. Street, was £20, instead of £30, contrary to section 7 of the Lands Valuation (Scotland) Act 1854.

You did drive a motor car recklessly contrary to section 2 of the Road Traffic Act 1988.

You did act as a pedlar without having obtained a certificate, contrary to section 4 of the Pedlars' Act 1871.

…

You did travel in a railway carriage without having previously paid your fare, and with intent to avoid payment thereof, contrary to section 5(3)(a) of the Regulation of Railways Act 1889.

Having on within the house No. Street, given birth to a female child, you did fail, within twenty-one days thereafter, to attend personally and give information to C.W., registrar of births, deaths, and marriages for (Registration District), of the particulars required to be registered concerning the birth, contrary to sections 14 and 53 of the Registration of Births, Deaths, and Marriages (Scotland) Act 1965.

You did take two salmon during the annual close time by means of cobles and sweep nets, contrary to section 15 of the Salmon Fisheries (Scotland) Act 1868.

You had in your possession for use for trade a counter balance which was false, and two weights, which were unjust, contrary to the Weights and Measures Act 1985, section 17.

Amendments

Sch.5 as amended by Postal Services Act 2000 (Consequential Modifications No. 1) Order 2001 (SI 2001/1149) art. 3 and Sch.2.

Sch.5 as amended by Manufacture and Storage of Explosives Regulations 2005 (SI 2005/1082) reg.28(1), Sch.5 para.21. Brought into force on 26 April 2005 in accordance with reg.1.

Sch.5 as amended by Animal Health and Welfare (Scotland) Act 2006 (Consequential Provisions) Order 2006 (SSI 2006/536) art.2(3) and Sch.3 (effective 3 November 2006).

Sch.5 (entries relating to the Licensing (Scotland) Act 1976) as amended by Licensing (Scotland) Act 2005 (Consequential Provisions) Order 2009 (SSI 2009/248) Sch.2 para.1 (effective 1 September 2009).

Sch.5 (entries relating to the Night Poaching Act 1828, the Game (Scotland) Act 1832 and the Poaching Prevention Act 1862) as amended by Wildlife and Natural Environment (Scotland) Act 2011 (Consequential Modifications) Order 2012 (SSI 2012/215) Sch.1 para.1 (effective 2 July 2012).

General Note

In regard to the second entry to Sch.5 ("You did conduct yourself in a disorderly manner and commit a breach of the peace") it has been observed that it would normally be proper, having regard to E.C.H.R., Art.7, not to rely on the minimal statutory form of the charge but to specify the conduct said to constitute the breach of the peace: *Smith v Donnelly*, 2001 S.L.T. 1007 at 1012J–K. *Butcher v Jessop*, 1989 S.L.T. 593 was not followed in that regard. While it was not commented upon in *Smith v Donnelly*, ibid, there seems no reason in principle to suppose that some of the other statutory forms in the Schedule are necessarily in any different category: some degree of specification is needed in the description of the behaviour said to constitute the charge to allow an accused to understand the case that is to be accepted or refuted. A few of the statutory forms of a charge in Sch.5 do incorporate a degree of specification.

SCHEDULE 6

Discharge of and Amendment to Probation Orders

[…]

Amendments

Sch.6 repealed by Criminal Justice and Licensing (Scotland) Act 2010 (asp 13) Sch.2 para.29. Brought into force on 13 December 2010 (subject to savings provisions in art.3) by SSI 2010/413 (C.28) art.2 Sch.1 para.1. **A4-601**

SCHEDULE 7

Supervised Attendance Orders: Further Provisions

[…]

Amendments

Sch.7 repealed by Criminal Justice and Licensing (Scotland) Act 2010 (asp 13) Sch.2 para.29. Brought into force on 13 December 2010 (subject to savings provisions in art.3) by SSI 2010/413 (C.28) art.2 Sch.1 para.1. **A4-602**

SCHEDULE 8

Documentary Evidence in Criminal Proceedings

Section 279

Production of copy documents

1.—(1) For the purposes of any criminal proceedings a copy of, or of a material part of, a document, purporting to be authenticated in such manner and by such person as may be prescribed, shall unless the court otherwise directs, be— **A4-603**

(a) deemed a true copy; and

(b) treated for evidential purposes as if it were the document, or the material part, itself,

whether or not the document is still in existence.

(2) For the purposes of this paragraph it is immaterial how many removes there are between a copy and the original.

(3) In this paragraph "copy" includes a transcript or reproduction.

Statements in business documents

2.—(1) Except where it is a statement such as is mentioned in paragraph 3(b) and (c) below, a statement in a document shall be admissible in criminal proceedings as evidence of any fact or opinion of which direct oral evidence would be admissible, if the following conditions are satisfied— **A4-603.1**

(a) the document was created or received in the course of, or for the purposes of, a business or undertaking or in pursuance of the functions of the holder of a paid or unpaid office;

(b) the document is, or at any time was, kept by a business or undertaking or by or on behalf of the holder of such an office; and

(c) the statement was made on the basis of information supplied by a person (whether or not the maker of the statement) who had, or may reasonably be supposed to have had, personal knowledge of the matters dealt with in it.

(2) Sub-paragraph (1) above applies whether the information contained in the statement was supplied directly or indirectly unless, in the case of information supplied indirectly, it appears to the court that any person through whom it was so supplied did not both receive and supply it in the course of a business or undertaking or as or on behalf of the holder of a paid or unpaid office.

(3) Where in any proceedings a statement is admitted as evidence by virtue of this paragraph—

(a) any evidence which, if—

(i) the maker of the statement; or

(ii) where the statement was made on the basis of information supplied by another person, such supplier,

had been called as a witness, would have been admissible as relevant to the witness's credibility shall be so admissible in those proceedings;

(b) evidence may be given of any matter which, if the maker or as the case may be the supplier had been called as a witness, could have been put to him in cross-examination as relevant to his credibility but of which evidence could not have been adduced by the cross-examining party; and

(c) evidence tending to prove that the maker or as the case may be the supplier, whether before or after making the statement or supplying the information on the basis of which the statement was made, made (in whatever manner) some other representation which is inconsistent with the statement shall be admissible for the purpose of showing that he has contradicted himself.

(4) In sub-paragraph (3)(c) above, "representation" does not include a representation in a precognition.

3. A statement in a document shall be admissible in criminal proceedings as evidence of the fact that the statement was made if—

(a) the document satisfies the conditions mentioned in sub-paragraph (1)(a) and (b) of paragraph 2 above;

(b) the statement is made, whether directly or indirectly, by a person who in those proceedings is an accused; and

(c) the statement, being exculpatory only, exculpates the accused.

Documents kept by businesses etc.

A4-603.2 **4.** Unless the court otherwise directs, a document may in any criminal proceedings be taken to be a document kept by a business or undertaking or by or on behalf of the holder of a paid or unpaid office if it is certified as such by a docquet in the prescribed form and purporting to be authenticated, in such manner as may be prescribed—

(a) by a person authorised to authenticate such a docquet on behalf of the business or undertaking by which; or

(b) by, or by a person authorised to authenticate such a docquet on behalf of, the office-holder by whom,

the document was kept.

Statements not contained in business documents

A4-603.3 **5.**—(1) In any criminal proceedings, the evidence of an authorised person that—

(a) a document which satisfies the conditions mentioned in paragraph 2(1)(a) and (b) above does not contain a relevant statement as to a particular matter; or

(b) no document, within a category of documents satisfying those conditions, contains such a statement,

shall be admissible evidence whether or not the whole or any part of that document or of the documents within that category and satisfying those conditions has been produced in the proceedings.

(2) For the purposes of sub-paragraph (1) above, a relevant statement is a statement which is of the kind mentioned in paragraph 2(1)(c) above and which, in the ordinary course of events—

(a) the document; or

(b) a document within the category and satisfying the conditions mentioned in that subparagraph,

might reasonably have been expected to contain.

(3) The evidence referred to in sub-paragraph (1) above may, unless the court otherwise directs, be given by means of a certificate by the authorised person in the prescribed form and purporting to be authenticated in such manner as may be prescribed.

(4) In this paragraph, "authorised person" means a person authorised to give evidence—

(a) on behalf of the business or undertaking by which; or

(b) as or on behalf of the office-holder by or on behalf of whom,

the document is or was kept.

Additional evidence where evidence from business documents challenged

A4-603.4 **6.**—(1) This sub-paragraph applies where—

(a) evidence has been admitted by virtue of paragraph 2(3) above: or

(b) the court has made a direction under paragraph 1(1), 4 or 5(3) above.

(2) Where sub-paragraph (1) above applies the judge may. without prejudice to sections 268 and 269 of this Act—

(a) in solemn proceedings, on a motion of the prosecutor or defence at any time before the commencement of the speeches to the jury:

(b) in summary proceedings, on such a motion at any time before the prosecutor proceeds to address the judge on the evidence, permit him to lead additional evidence of such description as the judge may specify.

(3) Subsections (3) and (4) of section 268 of this Act shall apply in relation to sub-paragraph (2) above as they apply in relation to subsection (1) of that section.

General

7.—(1) Nothing in this Schedule— **A4-603.5**

(a) shall prejudice the admissibility of a statement made by a person other than in the course of giving oral evidence in court which is admissible otherwise than by virtue of this Schedule;

(b) shall affect the operation of the Bankers' Books Evidence Act 1879;

(c) shall apply to—

(i) proceedings commenced; or

(ii) where the proceedings consist of an application to the sheriff by virtue of section 42(2)(c) of the Social Work (Scotland) Act 1968, an application made.

before this Schedule comes into force.

For the purposes of sub-paragraph (1)(c)(i) above, solemn proceedings are commenced when the indictment is served.

8. In this Schedule—

"business" includes trade, profession or other occupation:

"criminal proceedings" includes any hearing by the sheriff of an application made by virtue of section 93(2)(a) or 94(2)(a) of the Children's Hearings (Scotland) Act 2011 (asp 1) to determine whether a ground is established, in so far as the application relates to the commission of an offence by the child, or for a review of such a determination;

"document" includes, in addition to a document in writing—

(a) any map, plan, graph or drawing;

(b) any photograph;

(c) any disc, tape, sound track or other device in which sounds or other data (not being visual images) are recorded so as to be capable, with or without the aid of some other equipment, of being reproduced therefrom; and

(d) any film, negative, tape, disc or other device in which one or more visual images are recorded so as to be capable (as aforesaid) of being produced therefrom;;

"film" includes a microfilm;

"made" includes allegedly made;

"prescribed" means prescribed by Act of Adjournal:

"statement" includes any representation (however made or expressed) of fact or opinion, including an instruction, order or request, but, except in paragraph 7(1)(a) above, does not include a statement which falls within one or more of the following descriptions—

(a) a statement in a precognition;

(b) a statement made for the purposes of or in connection with—

(i) pending or contemplated criminal proceedings; or

(ii) a criminal investigation; or

(c) a statement made by an accused person in so far as it incriminates a co-accused; and

"undertaking" includes any public or statutory undertaking, any local authority and any government department.

AMENDMENTS

Para.8 as amended by Children's Hearings (Scotland) Act 2011 (Modification of Primary Legislation) Order 2013 (SSI 2013/211) Sch.1 para.10 (effective June 24, 2013).

GENERAL NOTE

Sch.8 generally

In *HM Advocate v AB*, 2012 J.C. 283; 2012 S.C.L. 351; 2012 S.C.C.R. 336 there is extensive discussion (see especially [32]-[34]) about the nature of this schedule and the docquets attached to productions. There was also reference to a duty on the part of the defence to co-operate with the Crown. **A4-603.6**

[THE NEXT PARAGRAPH IS A4-604]

A4-604

SCHEDULE 9

CERTIFICATES AS TO PROOF OF CERTAIN ROUTINE MATTERS

Enactment	Persons who may purport to sign certificates	Matters which may be certified
The Parks Regulations Acts 1872 to 1974.	An officer authorised to do so by the Secretary of State.	That, on a date specified in the certificate— (a) copies of regulations made under those Acts, prohibiting such activity as may be so specified, were displayed at a location so specified; (b) in so far as those regulations prohibited persons from carrying out a specified activity in the park without written permission, such permission had not been given to a person so specified.
The Firearms Act 1968 (c. 27).	[1], [12]As respects the matters specified in paragraph (a) of column 3, a constable or a person employed by a police authority, if the constable or person is authorised to do so by the chief constable of the Police Service of Scotland; and as respects the matters specified in paragraph (b) of column 3, an officer authorised to do so by the Secretary of State or a member of staff of the Scottish Administration who is authorised to do so by the Scottish Ministers.	In relation to a person identified in the certificate, that on a date specified therein— (a) he held, or as the case may be did not hold, a firearm certificate or shotgun certificate (within the meaning of that Act); (b) [1]he possessed, or as the case may be did not possess, an authority (which as regards as possessed authority, shall be described in the certificate) given under section 5 of that Act by the Secretary of State or, by virtue of provision made under section 63 of the Scotland Act 1998, the Scottish Ministers.
The Misuse of Drugs Act 1971 (c. 38) Sections 4, 5, 6, 8, 9, 12, 13, 19 and 20 (various offences concerning controlled drugs).	Two analysts who have analysed the substance and each of whom is either a person possessing the qualifications (qualifying persons for appointments as public analysts) prescribed by regulations made under section 76 of the Food Act 1984 (c. 30), or section 30 of the Food Safety Act 1990 (c. 16), or a person authorised by the Secretary of State to make analyses for the purposes of the provisions of the Misuse of Drugs Act 1971 mentioned in column 1.	The type, classification, purity, weight and description of any particular substance identified in the certificate by reference to a label or otherwise, which is alleged to be a controlled drug within the meaning of section 2 of the Act referred to in column 1.
The Immigration Act 1971 (c. 77)	An officer authorised to do so by the Secretary of State.	In relation to a person identified in the certificate—

Enactment	Persons who may purport to sign certificates	Matters which may be certified
Section 24(1)(a) in so far as it relates to entry in breach of a deportation order, section 24(1)(b) and section 26(1)(f) in so far as it relates to a requirement of regulations (various offences concerning persons entering, or remaining in, the United Kingdom).		(a) the date, place or means of his arrival in, or any removal of him from, the United Kingdom; (b) any limitation on, or condition attached to, any leave for him to enter or remain in the United Kingdom; (c) the date and method of service of any notice of, or of variations of conditions attached to, such leave.
[…][10] Customs and Excise Management Act 1979 The following provisions in so far as they have effect in relation to the prohibitions contained in sections 20 and 21 of the Forgery and Counterfeiting Act 1981 namely— Sections 50(2) and (3) Section 68; and Section 170 (various offences committed in connection with contraventions of prohibitions on the import and export of counterfeits or currency notes or protected coins).	Two officials authorised to do so by the Secretary of State, being officials of the authority or body which may lawfully issue the currency notes or protected coins referred to in column 3 hereof.	That the coin or note identified in the certificate by reference to a label or otherwise is a counterfeit of a currency note or protected coin; where "currency note" has the meaning assigned to it by section 27(1)(a) of the Forgery and Counterfeiting Act 1981, and "protected coin" means any coin which is customarily use as money in the United Kingdom, any of the Channel Islands, the Isle of Man or the Republic of Ireland.
The Forgery and Counterfeiting Act 1981 Sections 14 to 16 (certain offences relating to counterfeiting).	Two officials authorised to do so by the Secretary of State, being officials of the authority or body which may lawfully issue the currency notes or protected coins referred to in column 3 hereof.	That the coin or note identified in the certificate by reference to a label or otherwise is a counterfeit of a currency note or protected coin; where "currency note" has the meaning assigned to it by section 27(1)(a) of the Forgery and Counterfeiting Act 1981, and "protected coin" means any coin which is customarily used as money in the United Kingdom, any of the Channel Islands, the Isle of Man or the Republic of Ireland.
The Wildlife and Countryside Act 1981 (c. 69) [11]Sections 1, 5, 6(1) to (3), 7, 8, 9(1), (2), (4) and (5), 10A(1), 11(1) and (2), 11G(1), 11I(1), 13(1) and (2), 14, 14ZC and 14A (certain offences relating to protection of wild animals or wild plants).	An officer of the appropriate authority (within the meaning of section 16(9) of that Act) authorised to do so by the authority.	In relation to a person specified in the certificate that, on a date so specified, he held, or as the case may be did not hold, a licence under section 16 of that Act and, where he held such a licence— (a) the purpose for which the licence was granted; and (b) the terms and conditions of the licence.
The Civic Government (Scotland) Act 1982 (c. 45).	A person authorised to do so by the Secretary of State.	In relation to a person identified in the certificate, that on a date specified therein he held, or as the case may be, did

Enactment	Persons who may purport to sign certificates	Matters which may be certified
		not hold, a licence under a provision so specified of that Act.
The Road Traffic Regulation Act 1984 (c. 27).	Two police officers who have tested the apparatus.	The accuracy of any particular— (a) speedometer fitted to a police vehicle; (b) odometer fitted to a police vehicle; (c) radar meter; or (d) apparatus for measuring speed, time or distance, identified in the certificate by reference to its number or otherwise.
The Video Recordings Act 1984 (c. 39)		

Enactment	Persons who may purport to sign certificates	Matters which may be certified
Sections 9 to 14 (offences relating to the supply and possession of video recordings in contravention of that Act).	[1]A person authorised to do so by the Secretary of State, being a person who has examined the record maintained in pursuance of arrangements made by the designated authority and in the case of a certificate in terms of— (a) sub-paragraph (a) in column 3, the video work mentioned in that sub-paragraph; (b) sub-paragraph (b) in that column, both video works mentioned in that sub-paragraph.	[2]That the record shows any of the following— (a) in respect of a video work (or part of a video work) contained in a video recording identified by the certificate, that by a date specified no classification certificate has been issued; (b) in respect of a video work which is the subject of a certificate under sub-paragraph (a) above, that the video work differs in a specified way from another video work contained in a video recording identified in the certificate under this sub-paragraph and that, on a date specified, a classification certificate was issued in respect of that other video work; (c) that, by a date specified, no classification certificate had been issued in respect of a video work having a particular title; (d) that, on a date specified, a classification certificate was issued in respect of a video work having a particular title and that a document which is identified in the certificate under this sub-paragraph is a copy of the classification certificate so issued; expressions used in column 2, or in this column, of this entry being construed in accordance with that Act; and in each of sub-paragraphs (a) to (d) above "specified" means specified in the certificate under that sub-paragraph.
The Road Traffic Act 1988 (c. 52)		
Section 165(3) (offence of failure to give name and address and to produce vehicle documents when required by constable).	A constable.	In relation to a person specified in the certificate, that he failed, by such date as may be so specified, to produce such documents as may be so specified at a police station so specified.
The Control of Pollution (Amendment) Act 1989 (c. 14)		

[1] Substituted by Crime and Punishment (Scotland) Act 1997 (c.48) s.30 with effect from 1 August 1997 in terms of SI 1997/1712 para.3.
[2] Substituted by Crime and Punishment (Scotland) Act 1997 (c.48) s.30 with effect from 1 August 1997 in terms of SI 1997/1712 para.3.

Enactment	Persons who may purport to sign certificates	Matters which may be certified
Section 1 (offence of transporting controlled waste without registering).	An officer of a regulation authority within the meaning of that Act authorised to do so by the authority.	In relation to a person specified in the certificate, that on a date so specified he was not a registered carrier of controlled waste within the meaning of that Act.
The Environmental Protection Act 1990 (c. 43)		
Section 33(1)(a) and (b) (prohibition on harmful depositing, treatment or disposal of waste).	An officer of a waste regulation authority within the meaning of that Act authorised to do so by the authority.	In relation to a person specified in the certificate that, on a date so specified, he held, or as the case may be he did not hold, a waste management licence.
Section 34(1)(c) (duty of care as respects transfer of waste).	An officer of a waste regulation authority within the meaning of that Act authorised to do so by the authority.	In relation to a person specified in the certificate, that on a date so specified he was not an authorised person within the meaining of section 34(3)(b) or (d) of that Act.
[1]The Social Security Administration Act 1992 (c. 5)		
Section 112(1) (false statements etc. to obtain payments).	Any officer authorised to do so by the Secretary of State.	In relation to a person identified in the certificate— (a) the assessment, award, or nature of any benefit applied for by him; (b) the transmission or handing over of any payment to him.
The Criminal Justice and Public Order Act 1994 (c. 33)		
Paragraph 5 of Schedule 6 (offence of making false statements to obtain certification as prisoner custody officer).	An officer authorised to do so by the Secretary of State.	That— (a) on a date specified in the certificate, an application for a certificate under section 114 of that Act was received from a person so specified; (b) the application contained a statement so specified; (c) a person so specified made, on a date so specified, a statement in writing in terms so specified.

[1] Amended by Criminal Procedure and Investigations Act 1996 (c.25) s.73(4).

Enactment	Persons who may purport to sign certificates	Matters which may be certified
This Act		
[1]Sections 24(3) to (8), 25, 27 to 29 and 90C(1)	The Clerk of Justiciary or the clerk of court.	In relation to a person specified in the certificate, that— (a) an order granting bail under that Act was made on a date so specified by a court so specified; (b) the order or a condition of it so specified was in force on a date so specified; (c) notice of the time and place appointed for a diet so specified was given to him in a manner so specified; (d) as respects a diet so specified, he failed to appear.
Section 150(8) (offence of failure of accused to appear at diet after due notice).	The clerk of court.	That, on a date specified in the certificate, he gave a person so specified, in a manner so specified, notice of the time and place appointed for a diet so specified.
[2]The Communications Act 2003		
Section 363(1) and (2) (offence of unauthorised installation or use of a television receiver)	A person authorised to do so by the British Broadcasting Corporation	In relation to premises at an address specified in the certificate, whether on a date so specified any television licence (for the purposes of that section) was, in records maintained on behalf of the Corporation in relation to such licences, recorded as being in force; and, if so, particulars so specified of such record of that licence.
[3]The Building (Scotland) Act 2003 (asp 8).		
Section 8(1) and (2) (prohibition of work for construction or demolition of, or provision of services, fittings or equipment for, building, or conversion of building, without warrant)	An officer of a local authority authorised to do so by the authority.	In relation to a building specified in the certificate, that on a date so specified, the local authority had not— (a) granted a warrant under section 9 for the work or, as the case may be, conversion, or (b) received a copy of such a warrant granted by a verifier other than the authority

[1] Amended by Criminal Procedure (Amendment) (Scotland) Act 2004 (asp 5) s.25 and Sch.1 para.58. Brought into force on 1 February 2005 by SSI 2004/405 (C.28) art.2.
[2] Inserted by Communications Act 2003 (c.21) Sch.17 para.133. Brought into force on 1 April 2004 by SI 2003/3142 (C.125). Entry relating to the Wireless Telegraphy Act 1949 repealed by Communications Act 2003 (c.21) Sch.19. Brought into force as previous.
[3] Inserted by Building (Scotland) Act 2003 (asp 8) Sch.6 para.22. Entry relating to the Building (Scotland) Act 1959 (c.24) repealed. Brought into force on 1 May 2005 by SSI 2004/404 (C.27).

Enactment	Persons who may purport to sign certificates	Matters which may be certified
Section 21(5) (offence of occupying building when no completion certificate has been accepted)	An officer of a local authority authorised to do so by the authority	That, on a date specified in the certificate, the local authority had not— (a) accepted under section 18(1) a completion certificate in respect of construction or conversion in relation to a building so specified, (b) received a copy of such a certificate accepted under section 18(1) by a verifier other than the authority, or (c) received a copy of a permission for temporary occupation or use of the building so specified granted under section 21(3)
Section 43(1) (offence of occupying building, following evacuation, without notice from local authority)	An officer of a local authority authorised to do so by the authority	That, on a date specified in the certificate, the local authority had not given a person notice under section 42(7)
[1]The Antisocial Behaviour etc. (Scotland) Act 2004 (asp 8), section 45(1).	An officer of a local authority within the meaning of that Act authorised to do so by the authority.	That a level of noise specified in the certificate was measured at a time and in a place specified in the certificate using an approved device within the meaning of that Act.
[…][2, 3]		
[4]The Licensing (Scotland) Act 2005 (asp 16)	A person authorised to do so by the Scottish Ministers.	In relation to a person identified in the certificate, that on a date specified in that certificate that person held, or as the case may be did not hold, a licence issued under that Act. In relation to a premises licence or occasional licence issued under that Act and held by a person identified in the certificate, the conditions to which that licence is subject.

[1] Inserted by Antisocial Behaviour etc. (Scotland) Act 2004 (asp 8) s.144(1) and Sch.4 para.5(12). Brought into force on 5 November 2004 by SSI 2004/420 (C.31).

[2] Inserted by Water Environment (Consequential Savings and Provisions) (Scotland) order 2006 (SSI 2006/181) art.2, Sch.1 para.9 (effective 1 April 2006). Entry relating to the Control of Pollution Act 1974 (c.40) repealed by the same provision.

[3] Entry relating to the Water Environment (Controlled Activities) (Scotland) Regulations 2005 repealed and entry relating to the Water Environment (Controlled Activities) (Scotland) Regulations 2011 inserted by Regulatory Reform (Scotland) Act 2014 (asp 3) Sch.3 para.31(4). Brought into force on 30 June 2014 by SSI 2014/160 art.2 and Sch.1 para.1.

[4] Inserted by Licensing (Scotland) Act 2005 (Consequential Provisions) Order 2009 (SSI 2009/248) Sch.1 para.6 (effective 1 September 2009).

Enactment	Persons who may purport to sign certificates	Matters which may be certified
[1]The Water Environment (Controlled Activities) (Scotland) Regulations 2011 (SSI 2011/209)		
Regulation 44	A person authorised to do so by the Scottish Environment Protection Agency	That the person has analysed a sample identified in the certificate (by label or otherwise) and that the sample is of a nature and composition specified in the certificate.
Regulations made by virtue of section 18 of the Regulatory Reform (Scotland) Act 2014 (asp 3)	A person authorised to do so by a regulator (within the meaning of paragraph 3(1) of schedule 2 to that Act)	That the person has analysed a sample identified in the certificate (by label or otherwise) and that the sample is of a nature and composition specified in the certificate. In relation to a person specified in the certificate that, on a date and in relation to an activity so specified, the person held or, as the case may be, did not hold a permit (within the meaning of paragraph 34 of schedule 2 to that Act) granted by such a regulator and, where the person held such a permit, any condition to which the permit is subject. In relation to a person specified in the certificate that, on a date and in relation to an activity so specified, the person held or, as the case may be, did not hold registration (within the meaning of paragraph 34 of schedule 2 to that Act) granted by such a regulator and, where the person held such registration— (a) any condition to which the registration is subject; (b) whether the registration subsisted on the date specified in the certificate. In relation to a person specified in the certificate that, on a date and in relation to an activity so specified, the person had given notification (within the meaning of paragraph 34 of schedule 2 to that Act) to such a regulator and, where the person gave such notification, whether the notification subsisted on the date specified in the certificate.

[1] Entry relating to the Water Environment (Controlled Activities) (Scotland) Regulations 2005 repealed and entry relating to the Water Environment (Controlled Activities) (Scotland) Regulations 2011 inserted by Regulatory Reform (Scotland) Act 2014 (asp 3) Sch.3 para.31(4). Brought into force on 30 June 2014 by SSI 2014/160 art.2 and Sch.1 para.1.

Enactment	Persons who may purport to sign certificates	Matters which may be certified
		In relation to a permit or registration (in each case within the meaning of paragraph 34 of schedule 2 to that Act) a description of any variation, transfer, surrender, suspension or revocation of the permit or registration.
		In relation to a person specified in the certificate that, on a date so specified, such regulator served on the person a notice mentioned in paragraph 18 of schedule 2 to that Act.
		That such a regulator has, in pursuance of paragraph 4(3)(d) of schedule 2 to that Act, made general binding rules as mentioned in that paragraph, or has, in pursuance of paragraph 11 of that schedule, made standard rules as mentioned in that paragraph; and the content of those general binding rules or standard rules.
[1]The Air Weapons and Licensing (Scotland) Act 2015	A constable or a person employed by the Scottish Police Authority, if the constable or person is authorised to do so by the chief constable of the Police Service of Scotland.	In relation to a person identified in the certificate, that on the date specified in the certificate the person held, or as the case may be, did not hold, an air weapon certificate (within the meaning of Part 1 of that Act).

[1] Entry relating to the Air Weapons and Licensing (Scotland) Act 2015 inserted Air Weapons and Licensing (Scotland) Act 2015 (asp 10) Sch.2 para.2. Brought into force on 31 December 2016 by SSI 2016/130 art.3.

AMENDMENTS

[1] As amended by Scotland Act 1998 (Consequential Modifications) (No. 2) Order 1999 (SI 1999/1820) art.4 and Sch.2 para.122(5) (effective 1 July 1999).

[10] Entry relating to the Licensing (Scotland) Act 1976 repealed by Licensing (Scotland) Act 2005 (Consequential Provisions) Order 2009 (SSI 2009/248) Sch.2 para.1 (effective 1 September 2009).

[11] Entry relating to the Wildlife and Countryside Act 1981 as amended by Wildlife and Natural Environment (Scotland) Act 2011 (Consequential Modifications) Order 2012 (SSI 2012/215) Sch.1 para.1 (effective 2 July 2012).

[12] Entry relating to the Firearms Act 1968 (c.27) as amended by Police and Fire Reform (Scotland) Act 2012 (asp 8) Sch.7 para.12(11). Brought into force on 1 April 2013 by SSI 2013/51 art.2.

SCHEDULE 9A

THE COMMISSION: FURTHER PROVISIONS

Membership

1. Her Majesty shall, on the recommendation of the Secretary of State, appoint one of the members of the Commission to be the chairman of the Commission. **A4-604.1**

2.—(1) Subject to the following provisions of this paragraph, a person shall hold and vacate office as a member of the Commission, or as chairman of the Commission, in accordance with the terms of his appointment.

(2) An appointment as a member of the Commission may be full-time or part-time.

(3) The appointment of a person as a member of the Commission, or as chairman of the Commission, shall be for a fixed period of not longer than five years.

(4) Subject to sub-paragraph (5) below, a person whose term of appointment as a member of the Commission, or as chairman of the Commission, expires shall be eligible for re-appointment.

(5) No person may hold office as a member of the Commission for a continuous period which is longer than ten years.

(6) A person may at any time resign his office as a member of the Commission, or as chairman of the Commission, by notice in writing addressed to Her Majesty.

(7) Her Majesty may at any time remove a person from office as a member of the Commission if satisfied—

(a) that he has without reasonable excuse failed to discharge his functions as a member for a continuous period of three months beginning not earlier than six months before that time;

(b) that he has been convicted of a criminal offence;

(c) that a bankruptcy order has been made against him, or his estate has been sequestrated, or he has made a composition or arrangement with, or granted a trust deed for, his creditors; or

(d) that he is unable or unfit to discharge his functions as a member.

(8) If the chairman of the Commission ceases to be a member of the Commission he shall also cease to be chairman.

Members and employees

3.—(1) The Commission shall—

(a) pay to members of the Commission such remuneration;

(b) pay to or in respect of members of the Commission any such allowances, fees, expenses and gratuities; and

(c) pay towards the provisions of pensions to or in respect of members of the Commission any such sums,

as the Commission are required to pay by or in accordance with directions given by the Secretary of State.

(2) Where a member of the Commission was, immediately before becoming a member, a participant in a scheme under section 1 of the Superannuation Act 1972, the Minister for the Civil Service may determine that his term of office as a member shall be treated for the purposes of the scheme as if it were service in the employment or office by reference to which he was a participant in the scheme; and his rights under the scheme shall not be affected by sub-paragraph (1)(c) above.

(3) Where—

(a) a person ceases to hold office as a member of the Commission otherwise than on the expiry of his term of appointment; and

(b) it appears to the Secretary of State that there are special circumstances which make it right for him to receive compensation,

the Secretary of State may direct the Commission to make to him a payment of such amount as the Secretary of State may determine.

4.—(1) The Commission may appoint a chief executive and such other employees as the Commission think fit, subject to the consent of the Secretary of State as to their number and terms and conditions of service.

(2) The Commission shall—

(a) pay to employees of the Commission such remuneration; and

(b) pay to or in respect of employees of the Commission any such allowances, fees, expenses and gratuities,

as the Commission may, with the consent of the Secretary of State, determine.

(3) Employment by the Commission shall be included among the kinds of employment to which a scheme under section 1 of the Superannuation Act 1972 may apply.

5. The Commission shall pay to the Minister for the Civil Service, at such times as he may direct, such sums as he may determine in respect of any increase attributable to paragraph 3(2) or 4(3) above in the sums payable out of money provided by Parliament under the Superannuation Act 1972.

Procedure

6.—(1) The arrangements for the procedure of the Commission including the quorum for meetings) shall be such as the Commission may determine.

(2) The arrangements may provide for the discharge, under the general direction of the Commission, of any function of the Commission—

(a) in the case of the function specified in sub-paragraph (3) below, by a committee consisting of not fewer than three members of the Commission; and

(b) in any other case, by any committee of, or by one or more of the members or employees of, the Commission.

(3) The function referred to in sub-paragraph (2)(a) above is making a reference to the High Court under section 194B of this Act.

(4) The validity of any proceedings of the Commission (or of any committee of the Commission) shall not be affected by—

(a) any vacancy among the members of the Commission or in the office of chairman of the Commission; or

(b) any defect in the appointment of any person as a member of the Commission or as chairman of the Commission.

(5) Where—

(a) a document or other material has been produced to the Commission under section 194I of this Act, or they have been given access to a document or other material under that section, and the Commission have taken away the document or other material (or a copy of it); and

(b) the person who produced the document or other material to the Commission, or gave them access to it, has notified the Commission that he considers that its disclosure to others may be contrary to the interests of national security,

the Commission shall, after consulting that person, deal with the document or material (or copy) in a manner appropriate for safeguarding the interests of national security.

Evidence

7. A document purporting to be—

(a) duly executed under the seal of the Commission; or

(b) signed on behalf of the Commission,

shall be received in evidence and, unless the contrary is proved, taken to be so executed or signed.

Annual reports and accounts

8.—(1) As soon as possible after the end of each financial year of the Commission, the Commission shall send to the Secretary of State a report on the discharge of their functions during that year.

(2) Such a report may include an account of the working of the provisions of Part XA of this Act and recommendations relating to any of those provisions.

(3) The Secretary of State shall lay before each House of Parliament, and cause to be published, a copy of every report sent to him under sub-paragraph (1).

9.—(1) The Commission shall—

(a) keep proper accounts and proper records in relation to the accounts; and

(b) prepare a statement of accounts in respect of each financial year of the Commission.

(2) The statement of accounts shall contain such information and shall be in such form as the Secretary of State may direct.

(3) The Commission shall send the statement of accounts to the Secretary of State within such period after the end of the financial year to which the statement relates as the Secretary of State may direct.

(3A) The Scottish Ministers shall send the statement of accounts to the Auditor General for Scotland for auditing.

(4) [...]

10. For the purposes of this Schedule the Commission's financial year shall be the period of twelve months ending with 31st March; but the first financial year of the Commission shall be the period beginning with the date of establishment of the Commission and ending with the first 31st March which falls at least six months after that date.

Expenses

11. The Secretary of State shall defray the expenses of the Commission up to such amount as may be approved by him.

Amendments

Schedule 9A inserted by s.25 of Crime and Punishment (Scotland) Act 1997 with effect from April 1, 1999 as provided by SI 1999/652.

Para.9(2) as amended by Scotland Act 1998 (Consequential Modifications) (No. 2) Order 1999 (SI 1999/1820) art. 4 and Sch.2 para.122(3) (effective July 1, 1999).

Para.9(3) as amended by Public Finance and Accountability (Scotland) Act 2000 (asp 1) s.26 and Sch.4 para.14(a).

Para.9(3A) as inserted by Public Finance and Accountability (Scotland) Act 2000 (asp 1) s.26 and Sch.4 para.14(b).

Para.9(4) repealed by Public Finance and Accountability (Scotland) Act 2000 (asp 1) s.26 and Sch.4 para.14(c).

[THE NEXT PARAGRAPH IS A4-605]

SCHEDULE 10

Certain Offences Triable only Summarily

Section 292(1)

Night Poaching Act 1828 (c.69)

1. […] **A4-605**

Amendments

Para.1 repealed by Wildlife and Natural Environment (Scotland) Act 2011 (Consequential Modifications) Order 2012 (SSI 2012/215) Sch.1 para.1 (effective July 2, 2012).

Public Meeting Act 1908 (c.66)

2. Offences under section 1(1) of the Public Meeting Act 1908 (endeavour to break up a public meeting). **A4-605.1**

Post Office Act 1953 (c.36)

3. […] **A4-605.2**

Amendments

Para.3 repealed by the Postal Services Act 2000 (Consequential Modifications No. 1) Order 2001 (SI 2001/1149) art.3 and Sch.2.

Betting, Gaming and Lotteries Act 1963 (c.2)

4. Offences under the following provisions of the Betting, Gaming and Lotteries Act 1963— **A4-605.3**

(a) section 7 (restriction of betting on dog racecourses);
(b) section 10(5) (advertising licensed betting offices);
(c) section 11(6) (person holding bookmaker's or betting agency permit employing a person disqualified from holding such a permit);
(d) section 18(2) (making unauthorised charges to bookmakers on licensed track);
(e) section 19 (occupiers of licensed tracks not to have any interest in bookmaker thereon);
(f) section 21 (betting with young persons); and
(g) section 22 (betting circulars not to be sent to young persons).

Theatres Act 1968 (c.54)

5. Offences under section 6 of the Theatres Act 1968 (provocation of breach of the peace by means of public performance of play). **A4-605.4**

Criminal Law (Consolidation) (Scotland) Act 1995 (c.39)

6. Offences under section 12(1) of the Criminal Law (Consolidation) (Scotland) Act 1995 (allowing child under 16 to be in brothel). **A4-605.5**

[THE NEXT PARAGRAPH IS A4-606]

SCHEDULE 11

Financial Penalties Suitable for Enforcement in Scotland

Section 223F(7)

A4-606 *(Sch.11 was repealed by the Criminal Justice (EU Exit) (Scotland) (Amendment etc.) Regulations 2020 (SSI 2020/339) reg.3(7) (effective December 31, 2020 subject to transitional and saving provision specified in reg.6 of those Regulations).*

SCHEDULE 12

Grounds for Refusal to Enforce Financial Penalties

(Sch.11 was repealed by the Criminal Justice (EU Exit) (Scotland) (Amendment etc.) Regulations 2020 (SSI 2020/339) reg.3(7) (effective 31 December 2020 subject to transitional and saving provision specified in reg.6 of those Regulations).

SCHEDULE 13

Transfer of Community Payback Orders to England and Wales or Northern Ireland

Section 227ZO

Part 1

England and Wales

A4-608 **1.**—(1) This paragraph applies where the court is considering imposing a community payback order under section 227A of this Act on an offender who—

(a) resides in England and Wales, or

(b) when the order takes effect, will reside in England and Wales.

(2) The court must not impose the order unless—

(a) the offender has attained the age of 16 years, and

(b) the court is satisfied that arrangements have been, or can be, made in the relevant area—

(i) for the offender to comply with the requirements imposed by the order in accordance with arrangements that exist in the relevant area for offenders to comply with the same or broadly similar requirements imposed by the corresponding order, and

(ii) for the appointment of a responsible officer.

A4-609 **2.**—(1) This paragraph applies where—

(a) an offender on whom a community payback order has been imposed under section 227A of this Act proposes to change, or has changed, residence to a locality in England and Wales ("the new locality"), and

(b) the court is considering varying the order so as to specify the relevant area in which the offender resides or will reside.

(2) The court must not vary the order unless—

(a) the offender has attained the age of 16 years, and

(b) the court is satisfied as mentioned in paragraph 1(2)(b).

(3) If the court considers that a requirement ("the requirement concerned") imposed by the order cannot be complied with if the offender resides in the new locality, the court must not vary the order so as to specify the relevant area unless it also varies the order so as to—

(a) revoke or discharge the requirement concerned, or

(b) substitute for the requirement concerned another requirement that can be so complied with.

(4) The court must not make a variation under sub-paragraph (3) unless it is satisfied as mentioned in paragraph 1(2)(b) (reading the reference there to the order as a reference to the order as proposed to be varied).

A4-610 **3.**—(1) This paragraph applies where the court is considering—

(a) imposing a community payback order by virtue of paragraph 1, or

(b) varying a community payback order by virtue of paragraph 2.

(2) Before imposing or, as the case may be, varying the order, the court must explain to the offender in ordinary language—

(a) the requirements of the legislation relating to the corresponding order,

(b) the powers of the home court under that legislation and this Schedule, and

(c) the court's powers under this Act.

(3) The court must not impose or, as the case may be, vary the order unless the offender has, after the court has explained those matters, confirmed that the offender—

(a) understands those matters, and

(b) is willing to comply with the requirements referred to in sub-paragraph (2)(a).

(4) Sub-paragraphs (2) and (3) do not affect sections 227B(8) and (9) and 227ZA(6) and (7) of this Act.

(5) Sections 227B(4), 227ZA(2), 227ZG(2) and 227ZH(2) of this Act have effect as if the references in them to a report by an officer of a local authority or a report by the responsible officer included references to a report by an officer of a relevant service.

(6) Sections 227R and 227S of this Act have effect as if the references in them to an approved medical practitioner (within the meaning of the Mental Health (Care and Treatment) (Scotland) Act 2003) included references to a registered medical practitioner approved for the purposes of section 12 of the Mental Health Act 1983.

4.—(1) The court may not, in a community payback order imposed by virtue of paragraph 1, impose a compensation requirement. **A4-611**

(2) Where the court would, but for sub-paragraph (1), have imposed a compensation requirement, the court must instead make a compensation order under section 249(1) of this Act.

(3) Sub-paragraph (4) applies where—

(a) the court varies a community payback order by virtue of paragraph 2, and

(b) the order imposes a compensation requirement.

(4) The court must—

(a) also vary the order so as to revoke the compensation requirement, and

(b) make a compensation order under section 249(1) of this Act in respect of the amount remaining to be paid under the compensation requirement.

(5) Sub-paragraphs (2) and (4)(b) are subject to sub-paragraph (8).

(6) Paragraph (ab) of section 249(2) of this Act does not apply to the making of a compensation order by virtue of this paragraph.

(7) Before making a compensation order by virtue of this paragraph, the court must explain to the offender in ordinary language—

(a) the purpose and effect of the compensation order, and

(b) the consequences which may follow if the offender fails to comply with the order in England and Wales.

(8) The court must not make the compensation order unless the offender has, after the court has explained those matters, confirmed that the offender—

(a) understands those matters, and

(b) is willing to comply with the order.

5.—(1) This paragraph applies where the court— **A4-612**

(a) imposes a community payback order by virtue of paragraph 1, or

(b) varies a community payback order by virtue of paragraph 2.

(2) The court must, in the order—

(a) specify the relevant area in which the offender resides or will reside,

(b) specify, in relation to each requirement imposed by the order, the requirement of the corresponding order which the court considers to be the same as or broadly similar to those imposed by the community payback order,

(c) where—

(i) the order imposes a restricted movement requirement, and

(ii) a corresponding order imposing the same or broadly similar requirement would also impose an electronic monitoring requirement,

specify in accordance with sub-paragraph (3) the person responsible for monitoring compliance with the restricted movement requirement.

(3) The person specified under sub-paragraph (2)(c) must be of a description specified in an order made by the Secretary of State by virtue of section 215(3) of the 2003 Act.

(4) The clerk of the court must ensure that a copy of the order, and such other documents and information relating to the case as may be useful, are given to—

(a) the clerk of the home court,

(b) the relevant service in the area in which the offender resides or will reside, and

(c) if a person is specified under sub-paragraph (2)(c), that person.

(5) Sections 227C and 227D(4)(a)(ii) and (b) of this Act do not apply in relation to a community payback order imposed by virtue of paragraph 1.

6.—(1) This paragraph applies where the court has— **A4-613**

(a) imposed a community payback order by virtue of paragraph 1, or

(b) varied a community payback order by virtue of paragraph 2.

(2) The order has effect in England and Wales as if it were a corresponding order made by a court in that jurisdiction.

(3) The home court may exercise in relation to the order any power under the legislation relating to the corresponding order that the home court could exercise, other than—

(a) a power to discharge or revoke the order (other than in circumstances where the offender is convicted of a further offence and the court imposes a custodial sentence),

(b) a power to deal with the offender in respect of the offence in relation to which the order was imposed as the offender could have been dealt with had the order not been imposed,

(c) where the order imposes an unpaid work or other activity requirement, a power to vary the order by substituting for the number of hours of work specified in it a greater number than the court which imposed the order could have specified,

(d) where the order imposed a restricted movement requirement, a power to vary the order by substituting for the period specified in it a longer period than the court which imposed it could have specified.

(4) Sub-paragraph (5) applies where it appears to the home court—

(a) on information from the responsible officer, that the offender has failed to comply with any of the requirements of the order, or

(b) on the application of the offender or the responsible officer, that it would be in the interests of justice to—

(i) discharge the order, or

(ii) revoke the order and deal with the offender as mentioned in sub-paragraph (3)(b).

(5) The home court may—

(a) refer the matter to the appropriate Scottish court, and

(b) require the offender to appear before that court.

(6) Where the matter is referred under sub-paragraph (5) to the appropriate Scottish court, that court may—

(a) if the offender fails to appear as required under sub-paragraph (5)(b), issue a warrant for the offender's arrest, and

(b) deal with the matter—

(i) where it is referred by virtue of sub-paragraph (4)(a), in accordance with section 227ZC of this Act, or

(ii) where it is referred by virtue of sub-paragraph (4)(b), as if it were an application under section 227Y of this Act to vary, revoke or discharge the order.

(7) Where the matter is referred by virtue of sub-paragraph (4)(a), the home court must also send to the appropriate Scottish court—

(a) a certificate signed by the clerk of the home court certifying that the offender has failed to comply with such requirements of the order as are specified in the certificate, and

(b) such other documents and information relating to the case as may be useful.

(8) The certificate mentioned in sub-paragraph (7)(a) is, for the purposes of any proceedings before the appropriate Scottish court, sufficient evidence of the failure mentioned in the certificate.

(9) Where, in dealing with the matter by virtue of sub-paragraph (6)(b), the appropriate Scottish court is considering varying the order (or has varied the order) the provisions of this Part apply in relation to the proposed variation (or the order as varied) as they apply where the court is considering imposing a community payback order (or has imposed a community payback order) by virtue of paragraph 1.

(10) Section 227G(3) of this Act does not apply where the appropriate Scottish court is considering imposing a restricted movement requirement by virtue of sub-paragraph (6)(b)(i).

A4-614 7.—(1) In this Part—

"the 2003 Act" means the Criminal Justice Act 2003;

"the 2008 Act" means the Criminal Justice and Immigration Act 2008;

"the appropriate Scottish court" means, in relation to an order to which paragraph 6 applies—

(a) the court in Scotland which imposed the order by virtue of paragraph 1, or

(b) where the order has been varied by virtue of paragraph 2 or 6(6)(b), the court in Scotland which made the last such variation;

"corresponding order" means —

(a) in relation to an offender who is under the age of 18, a youth rehabilitation order within the meaning of Part 1 of the 2008 Act,

(b) in relation to any other offender, a community order within the meaning of Part 12 of the 2003 Act;

"the home court" means the magistrates' court acting for the local justice area in which the offender resides or will reside;

"relevant area" means —

(a) in relation to an offender who is under the age of 18, the area of the local authority (within the meaning given by section 7(1) of the 2008 Act) where the offender resides or will reside,

(b) in relation to any other offender, the local justice area where the offender resides or will reside;

"relevant service" means —

(a) in relation to an offender who is under the age of 18, a youth offending team within the meaning given by section 7(1) of the 2008 Act,

(b) in relation to any other offender, a provider of a probation service within the meaning of Part 1 of the Offender Management Act 2007;

"responsible officer" —

(a) in relation to an offender who is under the age of 18, has the meaning given in section 4 of the 2008 Act,

(b) in relation to any other offender, has the meaning given in section 197 of the 2003 Act.

(2) Subject to sub-paragraph (1), any word or expression used in this Part which is also used in any of sections 227A to 227ZK of this Act has the same meaning as it has for the purposes of those sections.

Amendments

Sch.13 Pt 1 inserted by Criminal Justice and Licensing (Scotland) Act 2010 (Consequential Provisions and Modifications) Order 2011 (SI 2011/2298) art.3 and Sch.1 (effective September 16, 2011, subject to transitional provisions specified in SI 2011/2298 art.4(4)).

Part 2

Northern Ireland

8.—(1) This paragraph applies where the court is considering imposing a community payback order under section 227A of this Act on an offender who— A4-615

(a) resides in Northern Ireland, or

(b) when the order takes effect, will reside in Northern Ireland.

(2) The court must not impose the order unless—

(a) the offender has attained the age of 16 years, and

(b) the court is satisfied that arrangements have been, or can be, made in the relevant area—

(i) for the offender to comply with the requirements imposed by the order in accordance with arrangements that exist in the relevant area for offenders to comply with the same or broadly similar requirements imposed by the corresponding order, and

(ii) for the supervision of the offender by the relevant service.

9.—(1) This paragraph applies where— A4-616

(a) an offender on whom a community payback order has been imposed under section 227A of this Act proposes to change, or has changed, residence to a locality in Northern Ireland ("the new locality"), and

(b) the court is considering varying the order so as to specify the relevant area in which the offender resides or will reside.

(2) The court must not vary the order unless—

(a) the offender has attained the age of 16 years, and

(b) the court is satisfied as mentioned in paragraph 8(2)(b).

(3) If the court considers that a requirement ("the requirement concerned") imposed by the order cannot be complied with if the offender resides in the new locality, the court must not vary the order so as to specify the relevant area unless it also varies the order so as to—

(a) revoke or discharge the requirement concerned, or

(b) substitute for the requirement concerned another requirement that can be so complied with.

(4) The court must not make a variation under sub-paragraph (3) unless it is satisfied as mentioned in paragraph 8(2)(b) (reading the reference there to the order as a reference to the order as proposed to be varied).

10.—(1) This paragraph applies where the court is considering— A4-617

(a) imposing a community payback order by virtue of paragraph 8, or

(b) varying a community payback order by virtue of paragraph 9.

(2) Before imposing or, as the case may be, varying the order, the court must explain to the offender in ordinary language—

(a) the requirements of the legislation relating to the corresponding order,

(b) the powers of the home court under that legislation and this Schedule, and

(c) the court's powers under this Act.

(3) The court must not impose or, as the case may be, vary the order unless the offender has, after the court has explained those matters, confirmed that the offender—

(a) understands those matters, and

(b) is willing to comply with the requirements referred to in sub-paragraph (2)(a).

(4) Sub-paragraphs (2) and (3) do not affect sections 227B(8) and (9) and 227ZA(6) and (7) of this Act.

(5) Sections 227B(4), 227ZA(2), 227ZG(2) and 227ZH(2) of this Act have effect as if the references in them to a report by an officer of a local authority or a report by the responsible officer included references to a report by a relevant service or an officer of a relevant service.

(6) Sections 227R and 227S of this Act have effect as if the references in them to an approved medical practitioner (within the meaning of the Mental Health (Care and Treatment) (Scotland) Act 2003) included references to a registered medical practitioner approved by the Health and Social Care Regulation and Quality Improvement Authority for the purposes of Part 2 of the Mental Health (Northern Ireland) Order 1986.

11.—(1) The court may not, in a community payback order imposed by virtue of paragraph 8, impose a compensation requirement. A4-618

(2) Where the court would, but for sub-paragraph (1), have imposed a compensation requirement, the court must instead make a compensation order under section 249(1) of this Act.

(3) Sub-paragraph (4) applies where—

(a) the court varies a community payback order by virtue of paragraph 9, and

(b) the order imposes a compensation requirement.

(4) The court must—

(a) also vary the order so as to revoke the compensation requirement, and

(b) make a compensation order under section 249(1) of this Act in respect of the amount remaining to be paid under the compensation requirement.

(5) Sub-paragraphs (2) and (4)(b) are subject to sub-paragraph (8).

(6) Paragraph (ab) of section 249(2) of this Act does not apply to the making of a compensation order by virtue of this paragraph.

(7) Before making a compensation order by virtue of this paragraph, the court must explain to the offender in ordinary language—

(a) the purpose and effect of the compensation order, and

(b) the consequences which may follow if the offender fails to comply with the order in Northern Ireland.

(8) The court must not make the compensation order unless the offender has, after the court has explained those matters, confirmed that the offender—

(a) understands those matters, and

(b) is willing to comply with the order.

A4-619 12.—(1) This paragraph applies where the court—

(a) imposes a community payback order by virtue of paragraph 8, or

(b) varies a community payback order by virtue of paragraph 9.

(2) The court must, in the order—

(a) specify the relevant area in which the offender resides or will reside,

(b) specify, in relation to each requirement imposed by the order, the requirement of the corresponding order which the court considers to be the same as or broadly similar to those imposed by the community payback order,

(c) where—

(i) the order imposes a restricted movement requirement, and

(ii) a corresponding order imposing the same or broadly similar requirement would also impose an electronic monitoring requirement, specify in accordance with sub-paragraph (3) the person responsible for monitoring compliance with the restricted movement requirement.

(3) The person specified under sub-paragraph (2)(c) must be of a description specified in an order made by virtue of article 40(3) of the Criminal Justice (Northern Ireland) Order 2008.

(4) The clerk of the court must ensure that a copy of the order, and such other documents and information relating to the case as may be useful, are given to—

(a) the clerk of the home court,

(b) the relevant service in the area in which the offender resides or will reside, and

(c) if a person is specified under sub-paragraph (2)(c), that person.

(5) Sections 227C and 227D(4)(a)(ii) and (b) of this Act do not apply in relation to a community payback order imposed by virtue of paragraph 8.

A4-620 13.—(1) This paragraph applies where the court has—

(a) imposed a community payback order by virtue of paragraph 8, or

(b) varied a community payback order by virtue of paragraph 9.

(2) The order has effect in Northern Ireland as if it were a corresponding order made by a court in that jurisdiction.

(3) The home court may exercise in relation to the order any power under the legislation relating to the corresponding order that the home court could exercise, other than—

(a) a power to discharge or revoke the order (other than in circumstances where the offender is convicted of a further offence and the court imposes a custodial sentence),

(b) a power to deal with the offender in respect of the offence in relation to which the order was imposed as the offender could have been dealt with had the order not been imposed,

(c) where the order imposes an unpaid work or other activity requirement, a power to vary the order by substituting for the number of hours of work specified in it a greater number than the court which imposed the order could have specified,

(d) where the order imposed a restricted movement requirement, a power to vary the order by substituting for the period specified in it a longer period than the court which imposed it could have specified.

(4) Sub-paragraph (5) applies where it appears to the home court—

(a) on information from the responsible officer, that the offender has failed to comply with any of the requirements of the order, or

(b) on the application of the offender or the responsible officer, that it would be in the interests of justice to—

(i) discharge the order, or

(ii) revoke the order and deal with the offender as mentioned in sub-paragraph (3)(b).

(5) The home court may—

(a) refer the matter to the appropriate Scottish court, and

(b) require the offender to appear before that court.

(6) Where the matter is referred under sub-paragraph (5) to the appropriate Scottish court, that court may—

(a) if the offender fails to appear as required under sub-paragraph (5)(b), issue a warrant for the offender's arrest, and

(b) deal with the matter—

(i) where it is referred by virtue of sub-paragraph (4)(a), in accordance with section 227ZC of this Act, or

(ii) where it is referred by virtue of sub-paragraph (4)(b), as if it were an application under section 227Y of this Act to vary, revoke or discharge the order.

(7) Where the matter is referred by virtue of sub-paragraph (4)(a), the home court must also send to the appropriate Scottish court—

(a) a certificate signed by the clerk of the home court certifying that the offender has failed to comply with such requirements of the order as are specified in the certificate, and

(b) such other documents and information relating to the case as may be useful.

(8) The certificate mentioned in sub-paragraph (7)(a) is, for the purposes of any proceedings before the appropriate Scottish court, sufficient evidence of the failure mentioned in the certificate.

(9) Where, in dealing with the matter by virtue of sub-paragraph (6)(b), the appropriate Scottish court is considering varying the order (or has varied the order) the provisions of this Part apply in relation to the proposed variation (or the order as varied) as they apply where the court is considering imposing a community payback order (or has imposed a community payback order) by virtue of paragraph 1.

(10) Section 227G(3) of this Act does not apply where the appropriate Scottish court is considering imposing a restricted movement requirement by virtue of sub-paragraph (6)(b)(i).

14.—(1) In this Part— **A4-621**

"the 1996 Order" means the Criminal Justice (Northern Ireland) Order 1996;

"the appropriate Scottish court" means, in relation to an order to which paragraph 13 applies—

(a) the court in Scotland which imposed the order by virtue of paragraph 8, or

(b) where the order has been varied by virtue of paragraph 9 or 13(6)(b), the court in Scotland which made the last such variation;

"corresponding order" means a community order, within the meaning of article 2 of the 1996 Order";

"the home court" means a court of summary jurisdiction acting for the petty sessions district in which an offender resides or proposes to reside;

"relevant area" means the petty sessions district in Northern Ireland where the offender resides or will reside;

"relevant service" means the Probation Board for Northern Ireland;

"responsible officer" has the meaning given in article 17(3) of the 1996 Order;

(2) Subject to sub-paragraph (1), any word or expression used in this Part which is also used in any of sections 227A to 227ZK of this Act has the same meaning as it has for the purposes of those sections.

Amendments

Sch.13 Pt 2 inserted by Criminal Justice and Licensing (Scotland) Act 2010 (Consequential Provisions and Modifications) Order 2011 (SI 2011/2298) art.3 and Sch.1 (effective September 16, 2011, subject to transitional provisions specified in SI 2011/2298 art.4(4)).

[THE NEXT PARAGRAPH IS A170-001]

CRIMINAL JUSTICE (SCOTLAND) ACT 2016

(2016 asp 1) **A170-001**

An Act of the Scottish Parliament to make provision about criminal justice including as to police powers and rights of suspects and as to criminal evidence, procedure and sentencing; to establish the Police Negotiating Board for Scotland; and for connected purposes.

The Bill for this Act of the Scottish Parliament was passed by the Parliament on 8th December 2015 and received Royal Assent on 13th January 2016

Arrangement of Sections

Part 1 Arrest and Custody

Chapter 1 Arrest by Police

Arrest without warrant

Sect.

1. Power of a constable
2. Exercise of the power

Procedure following arrest

3. Information to be given on arrest
4. Arrested person to be taken to police station
5. Information to be given at police station
6. Information to be recorded by police

Chapter 2 Custody: Person Not Officially Accused

Keeping person in custody

7. Authorisation for keeping in custody
8. Information to be given on authorisation
9. 12 hour limit: general rule
10. 12 hour limit: previous period
11. Authorisation for keeping in custody beyond 12 hour limit
12. Information to be given on authorisation under section 11
13. Custody review
14. Test for sections 7,11 and 13
15. Medical treatment

Investigative liberation

16. Release on conditions
17. Conditions ceasing to apply
18. Modification or removal of conditions
19. Review of conditions

Chapter 3 Custody: Person Officially Accused

Person to be brought before court

20. Information to be given if sexual offence
21. Person to be brought before court
22. Under 18s to be kept in place of safety prior to court
23. Notice to parent that under 18 to be brought before court
24. Notice to local authority that under 18 to be brought before court

Police liberation

25. Liberation by police
26. Release on undertaking

27. Modification of undertaking
28. Rescission of undertaking
29. Expiry of undertaking
29A. Expiry of undertaking: coronavirus-related reason for non-appearance
30. Review of undertaking

Chapter 4 Police Interview

Rights of suspects

31. Information to be given before interview
32. Right to have solicitor present
33. Consent to interview without solicitor

Person not officially accused

34. Questioning following arrest

Person officially accused

35. Authorisation for questioning
36. Authorisation: further provision
37. Arrest to facilitate questioning

Chapter 5 Rights of Suspects in Police Custody

Intimation and access to another person

38. Right to have intimation sent to other person
39. Right to have intimation sent: under 18s
40. Right of under 18s to have access to other person
41. Social work involvement in relation to under 18s

Vulnerable persons

42. Support for vulnerable persons

Intimation and access to a solicitor

43. Right to have intimation sent to solicitor
44. Right to consultation with solicitor

Chapter 6 Police Powers and Duties

Powers of police

45. Use of reasonable force
46. Common law power of entry
47. Common law power of search etc.
48. Power of search etc. on arrest
49. Taking drunk persons to designated place

Duties of police

50. Duty not to detain unnecessarily
51. Duty to consider child's wellbeing
52. Duties in relation to children in custody
53. Duty to inform Principal Reporter if child not being prosecuted

Chapter 7 General

Common law and enactments

54. Abolition of pre-enactment powers of arrest
55. Abolition of requirement for constable to charge
56. Consequential modification

Code of practice about investigative functions

57. Code of practice about investigative functions

Modifications to Part as it applies in certain cases

57A. Arrest without warrant otherwise than in respect of an offence

57B. Arrest under warrant other than an initiating warrant
57C. Modifications applying by virtue of sections 57A and 57B
57D. Arrest under an extradition arrest power

Disapplication of Part

58. Disapplication in relation to service offences
59. Disapplication in relation to terrorism offences

Powers to modify Part

60. Further provision about application of Part
61. Further provision about vulnerable persons

Interpretation of Part

62. Meaning of constable
63. Meaning of officially accused
64. Meaning of police custody

PART 2 SEARCH BY POLICE

Chapter 1 Search of Person not in Police Custody

Lawfulness of search by constable

65. Limitation on what enables search
66. Cases involving removal of person
67. Public safety at premises or events
68. Duty to consider child's wellbeing

Miscellaneous and definitions

69. Publication of information by police
70. Provisions about possession of alcohol
71. Matters as to effect of sections 65, 66 and 70
72. Meaning of constable etc.

Chapter 2 Code of Practice

Making and status of code

73. Contents of code of practice
74. Review of code of practice
75. Legal status of code of practice

Procedure applying to code

76. Consultation on code of practice
77. Bringing code of practice into effect

PART 3 SOLEMN PROCEDURE

78-83. [Not reproduced]

PART 4 SENTENCING

84. Maximum term for weapons offences

Prisoners on early release

85. Sentencing under the 1995 Act
86. Sentencing under the 1993 Act

PART 5 APPEALS AND SCCRC

87-96. [Not reproduced]

PART 6 MISCELLANEOUS

Chapter 1 Publication of Prosecutorial Test

97. Publication of prosecutorial test

Chapter 2 Support for Vulnerable Persons

98. Meaning of appropriate adult support
99. Responsibility for ensuring availability of appropriate adults

100. Assessment of quality of appropriate adult support
101. Training for appropriate adults
102. Recommendations from quality assessor and training provider
103. Duty to ensure quality assessment takes place
104. Elaboration of regulation-making powers under this Chapter
105. Procedure for making regulations under this Chapter
106. Other powers of Ministers unaffected

Chapter 3 Notification if Parent of under 18 Imprisoned

107. Child's named person to be notified
108. Definition of certain expressions

Chapter 4 Statements and Procedure

Statements by accused

109. Statements by accused

Use of technology

110. Live television links
111. Electronic proceedings

Chapter 5 Authorisation Under Part III of the Police Act 1997

112. Authorisation of persons other than constables

Chapter 6 Police Negotiating Board for Scotland

113. Establishment and functions
114. Consequential and transitional

PART 7 FINAL PROVISIONS

Ancillary and definition

115. Ancillary regulations
116. Meaning of "the 1995 Act"

Commencement and short title

117. Commencement
118. Short title

Schedule 1—Breach of Liberation Condition
Schedule 2—Modifications in Connection with Part 1
Part 1 — Provisions as to Arrest
Part 2—Further Modifications
Schedule 3—Police Negotiating Board for Scotland

PROGRESS OF THE BILL

A170-002 Introduced by Kenny MacAskill MSP on 20 June 2013
Stage 1 debate: 27 February 2014
Stage 1 report by lead committee (Justice Committee) published 6 February 2014
Bill considered by Justice Committee on fifteen occasions (including the taking of evidence on eleven days) between 25 June 2013 and 4 February 2014
Stage 2 debate (day 1) 8 September 2015
Stage 2 debate (day 2) 22 September 2015
Stage 3 debate 8 December 2015
Passed 8 December 2015
Royal Assent 13 January 2016

INTRODUCTION AND GENERAL NOTE

A170-003 [1]The Criminal Justice (Scotland) Act 2016 concerns what were described at the time the Bill was introduced to the Scottish Parliament as: "essential reforms to the Scottish criminal justice system to

---

[1] Annotated by Robert S. Shiels, solicitor advocate in Scotland and Iain Bradley, solicitor advocate in Scotland.

enhance efficiency and bring the appropriate balance to the justice system so that rights are protected whilst ensuring effective access to justice for victims of crime", Policy Memorandum, para.2.

The origins of the 2016 Act are to be found in three sources: first, there are provisions which have been developed from the recommendations of Lord Carloway's Review of Scottish Criminal Law and Practice; secondly, there are provisions which have been developed from the recommendations of the Independent Review of Sheriff and Jury Procedure by Sheriff Principal Edward Bowen QC; and, thirdly, a number of additional provisions which develop key justice priorities of the Scottish Government.

The Criminal Justice (Scotland) Act 2016 is in seven Parts. Part 1 deals with arrest and custody; Part 2 covers search by the police; Part 3 provides for solemn procedure; Part 4 deals with sentencing matters; Part 5 covers appeals and the Scottish Criminal Case Review Commission; Part 6 provides for miscellaneous matters; and Pt 7 covers general and ancillary provisions.

COMMENCEMENT

The Criminal Justice (Scotland) Act 2016 (asp 1) provides by s.117(1)(a) and (b) that on 14 January 2016 the following were brought into force: **A170-004**

- Section 71;
- Sections 73 to 77.
- Part 7 (ss.115–118).

The Criminal Justice (Scotland) Act 2016 (Commencement No.1 and Saving Provision) Order 2016 (SSI 2016/95) brought into force on 10 March 2016:

- Section 84.

The Criminal Justice (Scotland) Act 2016 (Commencement No.2) Order 2016 (SSI 2016/199) brought into force on 1 July 2016:

- Section 112.

The Criminal Justice (Scotland) Act 2016 (Commencement No.3 and Saving Provision) Order 2016 (SSI 2016/426) brought into force on 17 January 2017:

- Sections 60–64 inclusive.
- Section 78.
- Sections 82 and 83.
- Sections 87–101 inclusive.
- Sections 104–106 inclusive.
- Section 110(2)(a).
- Section 111(1).

Note: by art.3 of SSI 2016/426 the effect of s.36(1) of the 1995 Act (otherwise repealed by s.78 of the 2016 Act) is continued in relation to judicial examinations occurring before 17 January 2017. Other interim and conditional provisions are made.

The Criminal Justice (Scotland) Act 2016 (Commencement No.4, Transitional, Transitory, and Savings Provisions) Order (SSI 2017/99 (C.8)) brought into force the following sections on the dates stated:

- Sections 65–69 inclusive (11 May 2017).
- Section 72 (11 May 2017).
- Sections 79–80 inclusive (29 May 2017).
- Section 81(1), (2) and (5) (29 May 2017).
- Section 81(3) and (4) (31 July 2017).
- Section 81(6) and (7) (28 August 2017).

Note: by art.6 of SSI 2017/99 extensive transitory provisions are made about the adjournment and alteration of diets calling before 28 August 2017.

The Criminal Justice (Scotland) Act 2016 (Commencement No.5, Transitional and Saving Provisions) Order 2017 (SSI 2017/345) brought into force on 25 January 2018:

- Sections 1 to 41 inclusive (and, by s.16, Sch.1 to the Act);
- Sections 43 to 59 inclusive (and, by s.56, Sch.2 to the Act);
- Section 97.
- Section 109.
- Section 110(1) and (2)(b).

Note: by arts 4 to 10 inclusive of the SSI referred to above transitional and saving provisions are made for some procedures beginning before and concluding after the appointed day of 25 January 2018.

The Criminal Justice (Scotland) Act 2016 (Commencement No.6 and Transitional Provision) Order 2019 (SSI 2019/363) brought into force the following sections on 10 January 2020:

- Section 42.
- Section 102.

- Section 103.

Note: by art.4 of SSI 2019/363 as a transitional provision, s.42 of the 2016 Act only applies to persons arrested by a constable on or after 10 January 2020.

Particular modifications applicable to the police

In terms of the Police, Public Order and Criminal Justice (Scotland) Act 2006 s.33A(b)(i), the Police Investigation and Review Commissioner (PIRC) has a general function, where directed to do so by the appropriate prosecutor, to investigate any circumstance in which there is an indication that a person serving with the police may have committed an offence. The Police Investigations and Review Commissioner (Application and Modification of the Criminal Justice (Scotland) Act 2016) Order 2017 (SSI 2017/465) makes both general modifications (art.3) and specific modifications (art.4). The effect of these modifications is that when a PIRC investigator exercises the powers of a constable in pursuit of an investigation of a police officer then the ordinary requirements of the procedural rules apply.

Consequential modifications

Regulations were required to amend several other provisions made under the Legal Aid (Scotland) Act 1986 (c.47) following the coming into force of the 2016 Act: see the Criminal Legal Assistance (Miscellaneous Amendments) (Scotland) Regulations 2017 (SSI 2017/466).

Professional qualification of solicitor

In matters relating to the exercise of the professional rights associated with the qualification of solicitor there may be a "need for vigilance": *FF v AFMS Ltd* [2020] SC GLA 31 (9 July 2020) per Sheriff John N McCormick, at [1]. "Solicitors with practicing certificates spend time and expense on continuing professional development and, where events go awry, their regulatory professional body and insurers provide a route for the aggrieved. Standards are thereby maintained": [2020] SC GLA 31 at [28]. While that decision at first instance concerned the competency of a civil petition, the issue of professional qualification raised is nevertheless relevant to the procedural aspects of the 2016 Act.

An arrested person has a right, by s.32, to have a solicitor present when being interviewed. Yet, such an arrested person may consent to be interviewed without a solicitor present: see s.33, both of the 2016 Act. Also, intimation sent to a solicitor under s.43 and access to a solicitor in terms of s.44, both of the 2016 Act. No definition of "solicitor" is given in the 2016 Act.

In Scotland, no person can be said to be qualified to practise as a solicitor unless (a) he or she has been admitted as a solicitor; (b) his or her name is on the roll; and (c) he or she has in force a certificate issued by the Council in accordance with the provisions of this Part authorising him or her to practise as a solicitor (a "practising certificate"): see the Solicitors (Scotland) Act 1980 s.4. That Act also sets out the details of the requirements to fulfil for such admission and to obtain a practising certificate.

The Scottish Legal Aid Board is required to maintain a Criminal Legal Assistance Register of (a) solicitors who are eligible to provide criminal legal assistance; and (b) the firms with which the solicitors so eligible are connected: see the amended Legal Aid (Scotland) Act 1986 (c.47) s.25A(1). Further, only those solicitors whose names appear on that Register may provide criminal legal assistance; and a solicitor may provide criminal legal assistance only when working in the course of a connection with a registered firm: see s.25A(3) of the 1986 Act.

Several points may be inferred from this brief discussion of the law of lawyers: first, solicitors in other jurisdictions need to have met the requirements referred to above to entitle them to either be advised of arrest or give appropriate advice on the law of Scotland. Secondly, those who are not entitled to give advice on the law of Scotland cannot be properly be insured against any professional faults in connection with the law of Scotland. Thirdly, from a reading of the relevant law, as explained in the decision of *FF v AFMS Ltd* [2020] SC GLA 31, the possession of a valid practising certificate is the necessary test for meeting the professional qualification of solicitor in terms of the 2016 Act.

Expectation of privacy

While it is not an invariable rule in English law, a suspect under a police investigation had a legitimate expectation of privacy as against the police force both in relation to the investigation and in relation to a search of his home. If that information got into the hands of a media organisation it retained its private quality, therefore the suspect had an expectation of privacy as against the media organisation too: *Richard v BBC* [2018] EWHC 1837 (Ch); *Times*, 23 July 2018. It has since been announced that the BBC will not appeal the decision against them: *Sunday Times*, 5 August 2018 (pp.1 and 2).

In general, a person has a reasonable expectation of privacy in the fact and the details of a police investigation, or equivalent inquiry by an authorised prosecuting authority into his activities, up until the point when he was charged with an offence: *ZXC v Bloomberg LP* [2020] EWHC Civ 611; *The Times* Law Reports 30 June 2020.

The first civil authority cited is of course from English law and is an apparently unchallenged decision of a single judge. It remains to be seen what, if any, the authority the decision carries in comparable cases in Scotland: most likely it is very persuasive, given the attention given in pleadings and in the judgment.

In so far as the case carries weight in Scots criminal procedure, it might be posited that while police investigations into sexual abuse of children is a matter of legitimate public interest ordinary rules still apply.

Yet, it did not follow that the identity of the subject of the investigation also attracted that characterisation. Accordingly, individuals in Scotland, who attend police stations voluntarily for interview are, at the very least, suspects not officially accused and should be allowed to leave police premises with the forensic presumption of innocence intact.

The civil vindication of personal rights differs markedly from the application of what are, in practice, constitutional rights of the first order arising from criminal procedure, but the decisions emerging out of the pursuit by Sir Cliff Richard of such vindication serve to remind practitioners of all disciplines that the inherent fairness of the essential issues may very well elide easy classification, and may apply in both spheres.

Pragmatic arrangements, such as voluntary attendance, for the police avoid the necessity of obtaining arrest warrants and the necessary use of scarce resources being sent to arrest an individual. That arrangement should not be regarded as an acceptance by a co-operating person of any guilt and therefore a weaker position in law. Such an approach undermines that role and function of the courts. Co-operation may be regarded by some as implied deference to the position of the police but that should not be regarded as an acceptance or admission of responsibility in a generic sense.

The Strasbourg jurisprudence

It is safe to say that modern Scottish criminal procedure is infused with the requirements of the Strasbourg jurisprudence and other European requirements: e.g. s.5(3) of the 2016 Act and the Letter of Rights on Arrest. Time will tell of the relevance to, or effects on, criminal procedure of the European Union (Notification of Withdrawal) Act 2017. In the meantime, notice requires to be taken by practitioners of decisions from the European Court of Human Rights such as that of *Beuze v Belgium* (Application No.71409/10), 9 November 2018 as the decision might reasonably be seen to be highly relevant to several sections of the 2016 Act, and perhaps other legislation elsewhere. The decision of that court was unanimous and yet, of the 17 judges, four of their number issued a separate concurring opinion. The minority agreed with the decision of the court but took issue with the reasoning of the majority view.

Beuze, relying on art.6 ss.1 and 3(c) of ECHR, alleged, first, that he had been deprived of his right of access to a lawyer while in police custody, without being given sufficient information about his right to remain silent and his right not to be compelled to incriminate himself, and secondly, that he had not been assisted by a lawyer during subsequent police interviews, examinations by an investigating judge and other investigative acts in the course of the judicial investigation: see at [2]. Referring to earlier authorities from the court, in particular *Salduz v Turkey* (2008) 49 EHHR 19, Beuze submitted that these laid down an absolute principle not allowing for any case-specific assessment: at [38].

Following *Salduz v Turkey*, in *Beuze v Belgium* the court considered the question of the consequences, in terms of overall fairness, of the admissibility in evidence of statements made by the accused in the absence of access to a lawyer. The stages of analysis were first looking at whether or not there were compelling reasons to justify the restriction on the right to a lawyer, then examining the overall fairness of the proceedings. That test had been followed by other courts: at [138]–[139].

The importance of *Beuze v Belgium* lies in the development there of the concept of compelling reasons with the frequent assertion that the test of compelling reasons is "a stringent one": at [142]. There is discussion of the fairness of the proceedings as a whole and the relationship of the two stages of the test: at [144]–[149]. The court provided a "non-exhaustive" list of relevant factors for the overall assessment of fairness: at [150].

The court reiterated that restrictions on access to a lawyer for compelling reasons, at the pre-trial stage, are permitted only in exceptional circumstance, must be of a temporary nature and must be based on an individual assessment of the particular case: at [161]. Conversely, "very strict scrutiny" is called for where the restriction on the right of access to a lawyer is not based on "any compelling reasons": at [145], [165], [170], [193] and [194].

The court found there to be significant procedural defects in the Belgium criminal procedure in the context of the prosecution at the pre-trial stage of *Beuze*: at [193]. The decision in favour of the accused was of a violation of the law and a decision that the finding constituted in itself sufficient yet just satisfaction for non-pecuniary damage sustained by the accused.

The minority but concurring opinion believed that the reasoning of the majority in *Beuze v Belgium* diminished the significance of the minimum rights or guarantees. Specific reference was made there to member states who had made amendments to domestic law and would become disgruntled with the diminishing effect of the reasoning of the majority. Specific reference was made to the example of Scots law and *Cadder v HM Advocate* [2010] UKSC 43: see Separate Opinion, [26] and fn 33.

Solicitor

There are throughout the 2016 Act references to a "solicitor", a term that is not defined in the Act, nor in s.307(1) of the 1995 Act. Thus, in s.3 of the 2016 Act the arrested person must be told of his or her right to have intimation sent to a solicitor (s.3(e)(i) and s.43) and the right to access to a solicitor (s.3(e)(ii) and s.44). Specifically, there is a right of an accused to have a solicitor present while being interviewed by a constable (s.32(2)).

In practice, the distinction does not matter as local solicitors who practice in the area of criminal law are well-known to the police through their professional business. However, there is nothing in the 2016 Act that requires it to be the same solicitor to receive intimation, and who is also to be given access for consultation, or who is then to attend for interview. The practicalities of place and time, often dictate different solicitors are involved: intimation to one named solicitor might lead to a different solicitor from the same firm attending at the police station for access to a client.

It may be that someone from, say, Liverpool arrested in Dumfries wishes intimation to a solicitor in England and also requires the attendance of a solicitor for a professional presence at interview. Whether intimation to a solicitor in another jurisdiction (a) satisfies the terms of the 2016 Act, and (b) is an obligation on the police in Scotland to carry out remains unsettled. It is certain, however, that the solicitor attending to be present at an interview, being conducted within the requirements of the 2016 Act, requires to be qualified as a solicitor in Scotland, and to have the appropriate professional indemnity insurance.

There have been a few instances of lawyers from another jurisdiction appearing in Scotland to conduct business falling properly to be dealt with under Scots law without having obtained the qualification leading to enrolment in Scotland. One example is that of *Stevenson v Christie*, Kilmarnock Sheriff Court, 17 February 1908, Sheriff A.J. Loutitt Laing, unreported but see (1908) 24 Scottish Law Review 62–65. In a charge of driving a motor car at speed, the accused wished to employ a specialist solicitor in London, although the accused could not point to any authority in support of his application. The request was considered by the court and no precedent could be found. The application to allow an English-qualified solicitor to practice in a Scottish court was refused, counsel at the Scots Bar was subsequently instructed. The same approach might be said to be the position now for police interviews under the 2016 Act.

ABBREVIATIONS

A170-005 "the 1993 Act": Prisoners and Criminal Proceedings (Scotland) Act 1993 (c.9).
"the 1995 Act": Criminal Procedure (Scotland) Act 1995 (c.46).

PART 1 – ARREST AND CUSTODY

Chapter 1 – Arrest by Police

Arrest without warrant

Power of a constable

A170-006 **1.**—(1) A constable may arrest a person without a warrant if the constable has reasonable grounds for suspecting that the person has committed or is committing an offence.

(2) In relation to an offence not punishable by imprisonment, a constable may arrest a person under subsection (1) only if the constable is satisfied that it would not be in the interests of justice to delay the arrest in order to seek a warrant for the person's arrest.

(3) Without prejudice to the generality of subsection (2), it would not be in the interests of justice to delay an arrest in order to seek a warrant if the constable reasonably believes that unless the person is arrested without delay the person will—

(a) continue committing the offence, or

(b) obstruct the course of justice in any way, including by—

(i) seeking to avoid arrest, or

(ii) interfering with witnesses or evidence.

(4) For the avoidance of doubt, an offence is to be regarded as not punishable by imprisonment for the purpose of subsection (2) only if no person convicted of the offence can be sentenced to imprisonment in respect of it.

DEFINITIONS

A170-007 "constable": s.62.

GENERAL NOTE

A170-008 Section 1 sets out the powers of a police constable to arrest, without a warrant, a person suspected of having committed or to be committing an offence in Scotland. The definition in s.62 of the 2016 Act merely refers the reader to s.99(1) of the Police and Fire Reform (Scotland) Act 2012 (asp 8). Section 99(1) defines "constable" as an individual holding the office of constable who is serving as a constable in the Police Service of Scotland, and includes various categories of office-holder specified including, e.g. "special constable". The availability of this power to officers engaged in cross-border policing, non-territorial police forces, immigration officers, officers of HMRC and the National Crime Agency and, in certain circumstances to military police personnel, are found in the Criminal Justice (Scotland) Act 2016 (Consequential Provisions) Order SI 2018/46, particularly in the Schedules thereto, which invite careful reading.

The Code of Practice on the Exercise of Powers Stop and Search of the Person in Scotland, made on 9 March 2017 and in force from 11 May 2017, does not apply where a person has been arrested: see Code, para.3.2. The Code is reproduced below at C2-50.

Subs.(1)

This subsection provides that a constable who has reasonable grounds to suspect that a person has committed or is committing an offence may arrest that person without a warrant.

The issue of arrest where it is thought necessary to prevent the commission of an offence was the issue in *R (on the application of Hicks) v Commissioner of Police for the Metropolis* [2017] UKSC 9; [2017] AC 256; [2017] 2 WLR 824; [2018] 1 All ER 374; [2017] 2 WLUK 377 (where it was held to be ECHR compliant). That decision was then the subject of an application, which was declared inadmissible to the ECHR, which court agreed with the UK Supreme Court: *Eisenman-Renyard v United Kingdom* (application 57884/17: 28 March 2018), with seven other similar cases.

There is judicial discussion of the meaning of "arrest" in the context of the exclusion clauses of a policy of insurance in *Burnett v International Insurance Company of Hanover Ltd* [2019] CSIH 9; 2019 S.L.T. 483 at [45], [46]–[47] and [71]. That context does not necessarily render all the dicta irrelevant: Lord Brodie observed at [46] that: "While "arrest" most immediately suggests the action of a police officer, and therefore by extension that of someone making a 'citizen's arrest', in apprehending a suspected criminal, the expression 'wrongful arrest' is habile to describe any interference with the liberty of another which, if not justified, might render the person who is guilty of such interference liable in damages". Lord Drummond Young observed at [70] that: "In legal usage the word 'arrest', in relation to persons, normally signifies apprehension by legal authority. The expression "wrongful arrest" signifies an attempt to apprehend a person without reasonable justification or displaying malice or using excessive force."

Subs.(2)

Section 1(2) qualifies the power of a constable to arrest a person without warrant for having committed "an offence which is not punishable by imprisonment". The arresting constable must have reasonable grounds for suspecting the person and that constable must also be satisfied that the "interests of justice" would not be met if the person was not immediately arrested for the offence. The phrase "interests of justice" is not specifically defined but relevant factors are set out below in subs.(3) below.

Subs.(3)

The factors referred to in regard to subs.(2) are those that may be relevant in applying the "interests of justice" test.

Subs.(4)

This subsection is said to be included for the avoidance of doubt. The double negative seems imperative to an understanding of it. An offence is to be regarded as *not* punishable by imprisonment for the purpose of subs.(2) only if *no* person convicted of the offence can be sentenced to imprisonment in respect of it.

ADDITIONAL GENERAL NOTE: CROSS BORDER

It is provided generally by the Criminal Justice and Public Order Act 1994 (c.33) s.137(2), that a constable of a police force in Scotland may arrest someone in England and Wales, or Northern Ireland, and exercise the same powers as would be competently exercised if the arrested person had been in Scotland.

Additional provisions have been made by the Policing and Crime Act 2017 (c.3) which sets out rules for the extensions of cross-border powers of arrest in urgent cases. The 2017 Act allows a constable of a police force in Scotland, "if satisfied that it would not be in the interests of justice to delay the arrest to obtain a warrant", to arrest without warrant.

The 2017 Act, by s.116, inserts new ss.137A–D into the Criminal Justice and Public Order Act 1994. The new sections were brought into effect by the Policing and Crime Act 2017 (Commencement No.7) Regulations 2018 (S.I. 2018 No.227 (C.22)) reg.2 (w.e.f. 1 March 2018).

The important point for present purposes is that the provisions of the 2016 Act bearing on the rights of an arrested person are now applicable to such an urgent cross-border arrest: see esp. s.137D(3) of the 1994 Act as amended. There it is specified what precise terms of the 2016 Act must be adhered to when such an arrest is made.

Contempt of Court Act 1981 (c.49)

Once an arrest has been effected this Act provides that proceedings are "live", that media reports or comment are accordingly limited in scope, and strict liability in terms of the legislation applies. By contrast, an exercise of detention powers in terms of s.14 of the 1995 Act did not fall within the scope of the 1981 Act since "detention" was not sufficient to activate those provisions. Further caution is now necessary since the 2016 Act introduced distinctions between persons not officially accused, some of whom may be subject of conditional investigative liberation, others who may be released without charge, and still others who become officially accused.

Citizen's arrest

A170-008.1 The criteria governing a citizen's right to arrest and search a suspect were discussed by the Appeal Court in *Wightman v McFadyen*, 1999 S.C.C.R. 664 and in the context of drunk driving see the opinion in *Goodson v Higson*, 2002 S.L.T. 202.

Present concerns about vigilantes and their increasing involvement with the investigation of crime is well-known: see e.g. Editorial, "Vigilantes and admissibility of evidence" (2018) 155 Crim L.B. 1-3; and F. Stark, "Non-state entrapment", Arch. Rev. 2018, 10, 6-9, and the cases considered there. A number of legal issues arise in regard to such group action and not least surrounding the power of arrest of an alleged suspect. There may well be in the ensuing discussion of these cases some consideration of the power of constables in the context of earlier vigilante groups.

In *Sutherland v HM Advocate* [2020] UKSC 32; 2020 S.C.C.R. 331; *The Times* Law Report, 20 July 2020 it was held that admitting evidence from an online "paedophile hunter" group was not a breach of an accused's right to privacy. However, the facts of the case indicated that the appellant had been lured to a meeting place by members of the paedophile hunter group who "remained with him until the police arrived": at [3]. The question of whether, and when, there was an arrest by the civilians did not arise as an issue in these particular circumstances but it may do in others of a similar nature as the appellant was, as others in a similar position have been, in effect restricted in his movement.

However, that question may not arise, as the state has no supervening positive obligation to protect the appellant's interests that would prevent the Lord Advocate, as the public prosecutor, from making use of the evidence to investigate or prosecute the crime. On the contrary, the relevant positive obligation on the public prosecutor is to ensure that the criminal law could be applied effectively to deter sexual offences against children. Article 8 of ECHR has the effect that the public prosecutor should be entitled to, and might indeed be obliged to, make use of the evidence in bringing a prosecution against him: at [64].

General discussion

If, however, suspicions were sufficiently tangible for the constable to feel a caution to be appropriate the proper approach would be to caution with a view to charging (in the case of non-arrestable offences) or, where the offence could attract a sentence of imprisonment, to consider whether the circumstances would justify the use of the power of arrest. The police may question and charge a suspect in relation to minor offences, without being obliged to arrest him, provided that a caution is administered. Note that s.55 of the Criminal Justice (Scotland) Act 2016 (asp 1) expressly removes any obligation for the police to charge in relation to any offence. The corollary is that in such a situation there would be no obligation to ensure the suspect be offered access to legal advice, this only becoming necessary once taken into custody and arrest procedures are commenced. See *Barrie v Nisbet* [2012] HCJAC 160; 2013 S.C.C.R. 16, an offence of public indecency involving masturbation at 09.00 on Ne'erday.

In the exercise of his power an officer must first explain the nature of his suspicion and may then require the potential suspect to remain while the veracity of his particulars is established (provided this can be done quickly) and any explanation given may be noted.

Powers In Relation To Potential Witnesses

Section 13(1)(b) of the 1995 Act applies to persons whom the officer has reason to believe may, wittingly or unwittingly, have information to offer about the offence. It seems that this could extend to the circumstances in which the officer exercised his powers in relation to the suspect under s.13(1)(a): for example, the witness could be a bystander at the time when the suspect gave an explanation to the constable, given if he had not witnessed the offence giving rise to the enquiry.

First, however, a general explanation of the nature of the alleged offence being investigated must be given by the officer to the potential witness. The officer is also obliged to inform the other party of the belief that he or she possesses information relevant to that investigation and that failure to provide personal particulars in those circumstances is an offence.

Police powers in pursuit of requirements under s.13(1)(b) are more limited than those applicable to suspects, for s.13(4) allows the use of reasonable force to ensure that a suspect remains until the enquiries specified in s.13(2) are quickly completed or noted as the case may be. No force may be employed to cause a witness to remain at the scene. All that can lawfully be demanded of a witness is that he provides his name and address, albeit failure to give these particulars will render him liable to immediate arrest (s.13(7)).

Reasonable grounds for suspicion

The 2016 Act does not attempt to define what would constitute "reasonable cause" and nor need it do so. The phrase has been minutely examined by the courts, albeit usually in the context of the Road Traffic Acts. Suffice to say that the suspicions formed by the officer need not rest upon personal ocular observation; they can stem from the observations of other persons, from "information received" or from prior knowledge of the suspect's habits and background, as well as general knowledge of the area being policed.

It will be appreciated that some of the factors giving rise to cause to suspect, may well be inadmissible as evidence, but that would not disentitle the officer from forming his suspicion. The general considerations are discussed in *McNicol v Peters*, 1969 S.L.T. (J.) 261, notably in Lord Wheatley's judgment at pp.265 and 266, from which it can also be seen that even an ill-founded suspicion can still constitute reasonable cause to suspect. Lord Wheatley returned to this topic in *Dryburgh v Galt*, 1981 S.C.C.R. 26 at 29 noting:

> "... the fact that the information on which the police officer formed his suspicion turns out to be ill-founded does not in itself necessarily establish that the police officer's suspicion was unfounded. The circumstances known to the police officer at the time he formed his suspicion constitute the criterion, not the facts as subsequently ascertained."

See too *McKenzie v Murphy*, 2015 S.C.L. 194.

Nonetheless, the Crown will have to establish objectively that the factors which exercised the constable's suspicions would reasonably create a cause to suspect an offence without, at that stage, amounting to sufficient grounds for arrest, or perhaps, charge.

A bald instruction to an officer to apprehend a suspect, without any knowledge, or explanation of the grounds giving rise to suspicion, it is submitted will not suffice; see *HM Advocate v B* [2013] HCJ 71, a case centring upon the exercise of statutory detention powers under the Misuse of Drugs Act 1971 (c.38).

See too *Wilson and Nolan v Robertson*, 1986 S.C.C.R. 700 and *Houston v Carnegie*, 2000 S.L.T. 333, the latter an example of a situation in which the detaining officer had neither sufficient knowledge nor information upon which to form reasonable grounds for suspicion.

If it is established that the force employed was unreasonable, i.e. excessive or inappropriate, or both, then that might well nullify any subsequent evidence and constitute a criminal assault upon the suspect. Efforts to enter premises without warrant or the occupier's consent will only be upheld if the urgency of the situation, or gravity of the suspected offence, be substantial (*Gillies v Ralph*, 2008 S.L.T. 978; 2008 S.C.C.R. 887 distinguishing *Turnbull v Scott*, 1990 S.C.C.R. 614). The section itself contains no explicit right of entry or search in pursuance of a detention.

There is a dearth of case authorities dealing with this section, a fact which serves to underline its preliminary nature in the scale of proceedings.

[THE NEXT PARAGRAPH IS A170-009]

Exercise of the power

2.—(1) A person may be arrested under section 1 more than once in respect of the same offence. **A170-009**

(2) A person may not be arrested under section 1 in respect of an offence if the person has been officially accused of committing the offence or an offence arising from the same circumstances as the offence.

(3) Where—

(a) a constable who is not in uniform arrests a person under section 1, and

(b) the person asks to see the constable's identification,

the constable must show identification to the person as soon as reasonably practicable.

Definitions

"constable": s.62. **A170-010**

"officially accused": s.63.

General Note

Once an individual has been officially accused (see s.63 below) note that the Act introduced a procedure in ss.35–37 to enable the criminal authorities, criminal proceedings being extant, to crave a warrant for arrest to facilitate further questioning. **A170-011**

Subs.(1)

Section 2(1) provides that an individual may be arrested under s.1 more than once for the same offence. It seems that depending on the circumstances, no doubt, an individual may be arrested, questioned and released and subsequently arrested again if, as an example, further evidence is obtained.

Subs.(2)

Section 2(2) provides that the power to arrest again by s.2(1) does not apply to individuals who have been "officially accused" of having committed the offence or an offence arising from the same circumstances. By s.63 "officially accused" means that a constable has charged the accused or the prosecutor initiates proceedings against that person in respect of the offence.

In *Dunsire v HM Advocate* [2017] HCJAC 30; 2017 S.C.L. 615; 2017 S.C.C.R. 348 the phrase "arising out of the same circumstances" was considered in regard to detention under s.14(3) of the 1995 Act. It was held that those circumstances must be those on the basis of which the constable had formed the view that he had reasonable grounds for suspicion and had initiated the detention and must have been in existence at least immediately before the initiation of the detention: [9]. The learned commentator, at 2017 S.C.C.R. 353, thought that to be "a very wide meaning", allowing for the possibility of repeat detention.

Given the different statutory context of the exercise now of the power of arrest it is difficult be sure if the prohibition on re-arrest including the phrase "arising from of the same circumstances as the offence" in s.2(2) of the 2016 Act would be construed as widely as the phrase in *Dunsire's* case. The loss in law of the intermediate stage of "detention" means that the police simply "arrest" which is a more complete action. Investigations may be assumed to be continuing with detention but are thought to be complete with arrest. It is to be recalled the person may have been charged with an offence, and the liberty of the subject would be in issue. The phrases in the two subsections are slightly different, being "out of" in s.14(3) and "from" in s.2(2), but that hardly seems to matter.

Subs.(3)

Section 2(3) requires a constable who is not in uniform to show his or her identification, as soon as reasonably practicable, when requested to do so by an individual being arrested.

Procedure following arrest

Information to be given on arrest

A170-012 **3.** When a constable arrests a person (or as soon afterwards as is reasonably practicable), a constable must inform the person—

- (a) that the person is under arrest,
- (b) of the general nature of the offence in respect of which the person is arrested (if any),
- (c) of the reason for the arrest,
- (d) that the person is under no obligation to say anything, other than to give the information specified in section 34(4), and
- (e) of the person's right to have—
  - (i) intimation sent to a solicitor under section 43, and
  - (ii) access to a solicitor under section 44.

AMENDMENTS

Subs.(b) as amended by Criminal Justice (Scotland) Act 2016 (Modification of Part 1 and Ancillary Provision) Regulations 2017 (SSI 2017/453) reg.2 (effective 25 January 2018).

DEFINITIONS

A170-013 "constable": s.62.

GENERAL NOTE

A170-014 Section 3 lays out the information which must be provided by a constable to an arrested person at the time of arrest, or as soon thereafter as reasonably practicable. It does not necessarily follow that this information must be given by the constable responsible for effecting the arrest, though that would be the norm.

Note that the caution specified in subs.(d) falls short of the terms of the familiar common law caution. Indeed, failure to administer the statutory caution might not fatally damage the Crown case if the position can be equiperated to that in *Scott v Howie*, 1993 S.C.C.R. 81, a decision centring upon failure to administer a statutory caution when the accused was detained under the 1980 Act's detention provisions

The arrested person has to be advised of his dual right both to have intimation of arrest sent to a solicitor and of the right of "access" to a solicitor; s.44 more accurately stipulates a right to consult with a solicitor. Section 5 below provides that this information must be repeated at the police station.

The consistent judicial policy of general application, amounting in effect to a tolerable silence, gives rise to two legal points after an accused has been told that he or she is under no obligation to say anything, now other than provide certain personal details of identification. These points are that any such silence does not form a part of the case against the accused, and that silence does not provide a link with the suspected crime or offence: *Jameson v Barty* (1893) 1 Adam 91.

Subs.(d)

The statutory concession made for an accused is, in Scotland, that he or she "is under no obligation to say anything" after arrest by a police constable. The same statutory concession is patent in s.34(4) of the 2016 Act (questioning following arrest). That approach is to be assessed as contrasting with the provision in the Social Security Assistance (Investigation of Offences) (Scotland) Regulations 2020 (SSI 2020/11). There authorised officers have the power to require information by the service of a notice: see reg.4. There are restrictions on that power to require information and on requirements to provide it: reg.5. Legal privilege is preserved: reg.5(3). However, no person is required by a notice under reg.4 to provide any information that incriminates, or tends to incriminate, either the person or the person's spouse or civil person: reg.5(4).

On occasions it is a matter of acute professional judgement as to whether answering certain questions incriminate, or tend to incriminate, an interviewee or a client. In any event, it is not certain that authorised officers necessarily must disclose the true nature and full extent of the alleged criminality or other improper conduct tending to be contrary to the relevant social security statutes then under investigation. It is a matter for comment that a police constable is constrained completely in a manner in which an authorised officer authorised by the Scottish Ministers is not. Interviews by question and answer, without any suggestion of improper conduct by those in authority, often serve by concession in answers to narrow the issues for proof and thereby may be said to incriminate.

Arrested person to be taken to police station

4.—(1) Where a person is arrested by a constable outwith a police station, a constable must take the person as quickly as is reasonably practicable to a police station. **A170-015**

(1A) But subsection (1) need not be complied with if—

(a) either the warrant under which the person was arrested or an enactment requires that following the arrest the person be taken to a particular place (other than a police station), and

(b) the taking of the person to that place would be unnecessarily delayed by taking the person to a police station first.

(2) Subsection (1) ceases to apply, and the person must be released from police custody immediately, if—

(a) the person has been arrested in respect of an offence without a warrant,

(b) the person has not yet arrived at a police station in accordance with this section, and

(c) in the opinion of a constable there are no reasonable grounds for suspecting that the person has committed—

(i) the offence in respect of which the person was arrested, or

(ii) an offence arising from the same circumstances as that offence.

(3) For the avoidance of doubt, subsection (1) ceases to apply if, before arriving at a police station in accordance with this section, the person is released from custody under—

(a) section 25(2), or

(b) section 28(3A) of the 1995 Act.

AMENDMENTS

Subsection (1A) inserted, subs.(2)(a) as amended, by Criminal Justice (Scotland) Act 2016 (Modification of Pt 1 and Ancillary Provision) Regulations 2017 (SSI 2017/453) reg.2 (effective 25 January 2018).

DEFINITIONS

"constable": s.62. **A170-016**

GENERAL NOTE

Subs.(1)

This places a duty on a constable to take an arrested person to a police station as quickly as is reasonably practicable after arrest if that person is not arrested at a police station. **A170-017**

Subs.(2)

Section 4(2) provides circumstances as to when the duty under s.4(1) to take the person to the police station can cease to apply prior to arrival at a police station. These are "(a) the person has been arrested without warrant; (b) the person has not yet arrived at a police station in accordance with this section; *and* [emphasis added] (c) in the opinion of a constable there are no reasonable grounds for suspecting that the person has committed (i) the offence in respect of which the person was arrested, *or* [emphasis added] (ii) an offence arising from the same circumstances as that offence".

Subs.(3)

Section 4(3) also clarifies that the requirement to take the person to the police station will also cease to apply if, before arriving at a police station, that person is released under the provisions contained within s.25(2) of the 2016 Act (liberation by police) or s.28(3A) of the 1995 Act.

The 2016 Act elsewhere amends the 1995 Act. By s.56 and Sch.2 of the 2016 Act a new s.28(3A) is inserted into the 1995 Act and that applies if (a) a person is in custody only by virtue of subs.(1) or (1A), and (b) in the opinion of a constable there are no reasonable grounds for suspecting that the person has broken, or is likely to break, a condition imposed on the person's bail, in which case the person must be released from custody immediately.

Information to be given at police station

A170-018 **5.**—(1) Subsections (2) and (3) apply when—

(a) a person is in police custody having been arrested at a police station, or

(b) a person is in police custody and has been taken to a police station in accordance with section 4.

(2) The person must be informed as soon as reasonably practicable—

(a) that the person is under no obligation to say anything, other than to give the information specified in section 34(4),

(b) of any right the person has to have intimation sent and to have access to certain persons under—

(i) section 38,

(ii) section 40,

(iii) section 43,

(iv) section 44.

(3) The person must be provided as soon as reasonably practicable with such information (verbally or in writing) as is necessary to satisfy the requirements of Articles 3 and 4 of Directive 2012/13/EU of the European Parliament and of the Council on the right to information in criminal proceedings.

GENERAL NOTE

A170-019 After arrest and when at a police station, by s.5(2)(a) a person is under no obligation to say anything, other than provide a few details bearing on personal identification. Similarly, but not identically on the words of the statute, on questioning following arrest, by s.34(4) the person arrested is under no obligation to answer any question, other than provide a few details bearing on personal identification. Whether either of these statutorily sanctioned silences in the face of questioning by a representative of authority is *either* a right derived wholly from the principle against self-incrimination *or* an entitlement of citizens to adopt silence in these circumstances as a matter of constitutional principle is a political question that may more appropriately be for legislatures to determine.

The potential differences between the true nature of the right to silence may require depending on circumstances to be clarified in judicial remarks to a jury at the conclusion of the evidence. The point, however, has been considered by judges of the Republic of Ireland: *Sweeney v Ireland* [2017] IEHC 702, per Baker J at [41]–[42]. That was appealed to the Supreme Court of Ireland: *Sweeney v Ireland* [2019] IEHC 39 (28 May 2019). There was concern in the latter court at the procedural manner, agreed facts, in which the issue was considered: "It should be clearly stated that any issue as to whether a charge was capable of being dealt with in a constitutional fashion and as to whether there had in fact been any trammelling on the right to silence or undermining of the privilege against self-incrimination could only be analysed in the context of the nature of the evidence which the State proposed to lead against Michael Sweeney", Charleton J, at [2]. The court held, by reference to foreign cases including two from Scotland, that the relevant statutory provision of Irish law, challenged below, was not incompatible with the Constitution and the order of the High Court was reversed.

Subs.(1)

Section 5(1) sets out the information that must be provided as soon as reasonably practicable to a person arrested while at a police station and also to those taken to a police station under arrest.

Subs.(2)

This subsection sets out the various matters that the arrested person must be informed of, as soon as reasonably practicable. These include that the arrested person has a right not to say anything other than to provide information relating to their identity as specified in s.34(4) of the 2016 Act. Also, the arrested person requires to be told of the right to have intimation sent and to have access to certain persons under ss.38, 40, 43 and 44, the latter two concern access to solicitors.

On being brought to a police custody suite any arrested person, not officially accused, is routinely asked for some personal details for identification as allowed by statute. Additionally, that arrested person is asked what are described as routine questions, and is advised generally to answer accurately and honestly. The purpose of these welfare questions would seem to be to discover if the arrested person believes that medical attention is necessary or desirable for themselves and thus to allow the custody staff some information to enable them to assess the condition, particularly the vulnerability, of the arrested person and whether that person possesses a threat to themselves or others. As that person is, as a matter of fact, in the custody of the police, a degree of responsibility or accountability rests on the Police Service for Scotland: see Inquiries into Fatal Accidents and Sudden Deaths etc. (Scotland) Act 2016 (asp 2) s.2(4)(a) and (5). That responsibility is separate from any civil law duty of care.

In *Mitchell v Harrower* [2017] SAC (Crim) 14; 2017 S.L.T. (Sh. Ct) 207; 2017 S.C.L. 1066; 2017 S.C.C.R. 512 an appeal against conviction for domestic assault was sustained. Replies by an appellant to standard welfare questions had inadvertently related to the offence and the appellant had neither been afforded access to legal representation nor reminded of his right to silence. The answer given provided corroboration of an essential fact. The appellate court accepted that the custody sergeant had acted in good faith throughout and that the questions asked were not intended to elicit any information: at [9]. The enquiries into the appellant's welfare should be inadmissible in relation to matters beyond that: at [12]. The appellate court regarded the fact that the appellant was advised to answer the welfare questions accurately and honestly as "a particularly important feature" because that statement conflicted with the terms of the caution which had earlier been administered to him and may have been considered to have over-ridden the caution: at [15].

Subs.(3)

By this subsection the arrested person "must be provided as soon as reasonably practicable with such information (verbally or in writing) as is necessary to meet the requirements of arts 3 and 4 of Directive 2012/13/EU of the European Parliament and of the Council which concern the right to information in criminal proceedings". As the directive may not be immediately to hand for most practitioners it seems expedient to reproduce that below for ease of reference.

Directive 2012/13/EU of 22 May 2012 on the right to information in criminal proceedings

Article 3

Right to information about rights

1. Member States shall ensure that suspects or accused persons are provided promptly with information concerning at least the following procedural rights, as they apply under national law, in order to allow for those rights to be exercised effectively:

(a) the right of access to a lawyer;
(b) any entitlement to free legal advice and the conditions for obtaining such advice;
(c) the right to be informed of the accusation, in accordance with Article 6;
(d) the right to interpretation and translation;
(e) the right to remain silent.

2. Member States shall ensure that the information provided for under paragraph 1 shall be given orally or in writing, in simple and accessible language, taking into account any particular needs of vulnerable suspects or vulnerable accused persons.

Article 4

Letter of rights on arrest

1. Member States shall ensure that suspects or accused persons who are arrested or detained are provided promptly with a written Letter of Rights. They shall be given an opportunity to read the Letter of Rights and shall be allowed to keep it in their possession throughout the time that they are deprived of liberty.

2. In addition to the information set out in Article 3, the Letter of Rights referred to in paragraph 1 of this Article shall contain information about the following rights as they apply under national law:

(a) the right of access to the materials of the case;
(b) the right to have consular authorities and one person informed;
(c) the right of access to urgent medical assistance; and
(d) the maximum number of hours or days suspects or accused persons may be deprived of liberty before being brought before a judicial authority.

3. The Letter of Rights shall also contain basic information about any possibility, under national law, of challenging the lawfulness of the arrest; obtaining a review of the detention; or making a request for provisional release.

4. The Letter of Rights shall be drafted in simple and accessible language. An indicative model Letter of Rights is set out in [an] Annex [to the Directive].

5. Member States shall ensure that suspects or accused persons receive the Letter of Rights written in a language that they understand. Where a Letter of Rights is not available in the appropriate language, suspects or accused persons shall be informed of their rights orally in a language that they understand. A Letter of Rights in a language that they understand shall then be given to them without undue delay.

Article 6

Right to information about the accusation

1. Member States shall ensure that suspects or accused persons are provided with information about the criminal act they are suspected or accused of having committed. That information shall be provided promptly and, in such detail, as is necessary to safeguard the fairness of proceedings and the effective exercise of the rights of the defence.

2. Member States shall ensure that suspects or accused persons who are arrested or detained are informed of the reasons for their arrest or detention, including the criminal act they are suspected or accused of having committed.

3. Member States shall ensure that, at the latest on submission of the merits of the accusation to a court, detailed information is provided on the accusation, including the nature and legal classification of the criminal offence, as well as the nature of participation by the accused.

4. Member States shall ensure that suspects or accused persons are informed promptly of any changes in the information given in accordance with this Article where this is necessary to safeguard the fairness of the proceedings.

Rights to interpretation and translation

Reference should be made to the Right to Interpretation and Translation in Criminal Proceedings (Scotland) Regulations 2014 (SSI 2014/95) which applies to those who do not speak or understand English or suffer hearing or speech impairment. Part 2 of the Regulations refers to arrest and custody procedures; Part 3 refers to subsequent court proceedings. *Ucak v HM Advocate*, 1999 S.L.T. 392 may offer some general assistance.

Information to be recorded by police

A170-020 **6.**—(1) There must be recorded in relation to any arrest by a constable—

(a) the time and place of arrest,

(b) either—
(i) the general nature of the offence in respect of which the person is arrested, or
(ii) if the person is arrested otherwise than in respect of an offence, the reason for the arrest,
(c) if the person is taken from one place to another while in police custody (including to a police station in accordance with section 4)—
(i) the place from which, and time at which, the person is taken, and
(ii) the place to which the person is taken and the time at which the person arrives there,
(d) the time at which, and the identity of the constable by whom, the person is informed of the matters mentioned in section 3,
(e) the time at which the person ceases to be in police custody.

(2) Where relevant, there must be recorded in relation to an arrest by a constable—
(a) the reason that the constable who released the person from custody under subsection (2) of section 4 formed the opinion mentioned in paragraph (c) of that subsection,
(b) the time at which, and the identity of the person by whom, the person is—
(i) informed of the matters mentioned in subsection (2) of section 5, and
(ii) provided with information in accordance with subsection (3) of that section,
(c) the time at which, and the identity of the person by whom, the person is informed of the matters mentioned in section 20,
(d) the time at which the person requests that intimation be sent under—
(i) section 38,
(ii) section 43,
(e) the time at which intimation is sent under—
(i) section 38,
(ii) section 41,
(iii) section 42,
(iv) section 43.

(3) Where a person is in police custody and not officially accused of committing an offence, there must be recorded the time, place and outcome of any decision under section 7.

(4) Where a person is held in police custody by virtue of authorisation given under section 7 there must be recorded—
(a) the time at which the person is informed of the matters mentioned in section 8,
(b) the time, place and outcome of any custody review under section 13,
(c) the time at which any interview in the circumstances described in section 15(6) begins and the time at which it ends.

(5) If a constable considers whether to give authorisation under section 11 there must be recorded—
(a) whether a reasonable opportunity to make representations has been afforded in accordance with subsection (4)(a) of that section,
(b) if the opportunity referred to in paragraph (a) has not been afforded, the reason for that,
(c) the time, place and outcome of the constable's decision, and
(d) if the constable's decision is to give the authorisation—

(i) the grounds on which it is given,

(ii) the time at which, and the identity of the person by whom, the person is informed and reminded of things in accordance with section 12, and

(iii) the time at which the person requests that intimation be sent under section 12(3)(a) and the time at which it is sent.

(6) Where a person is held in police custody by virtue of authorisation given under section 11 there must be recorded—

(a) the time, place and outcome of any custody review under section 13,

(b) the time at which any interview in the circumstances described in section 15(6) begins and the time at which it ends.

(7) If a person is released from police custody on conditions under section 16, there must be recorded—

(a) details of the conditions imposed, and

(b) the identity of the constable who imposed them.

(8) If a person is charged with an offence by a constable while in police custody, there must be recorded the time at which the person is charged.

AMENDMENTS

Subs.(1)(b) as amended by Criminal Justice (Scotland) Act 2016 (Modification of Part 1 and Ancillary Provision) Regulations 2017 (SSI 2017/453) reg.2 (effective 25 January 2018).

DEFINITIONS

A170-021 "constable": s.62.

GENERAL NOTE

A170-022 The Code of Practice on the Exercise of Powers of Stop and Search of the Person in Scotland, made on 9 March 2017 and in force from 11 May 2017, requires a record to be kept of any search to which the Code of Practice cited applies. An exception may be that in s.67: see Code, para.9.1. The Code is reproduced below at C2-50.

In addition to the obligation upon the arresting officer to specify the nature of his suspicions and the reason for arrest (see s.3 above), further requirements must be complied with by the officer and others who become involved in the arrest process later. Section 6 sets out the regime of information about the alleged offence and offender which must be recorded and maintained by the police, essentially detailing the custody of the individual, and recording the information provided to him during this period. The details specified in s.3 above need to be recorded anew, but more important still, the date, time and place where the arrestee is taken to must be recorded and preserved: it is essential to appreciate that, in contrast to previous detention provisions, the 12-hour custodial period (and any extension or cessation thereof) begins from the time recorded at the police office not at the time of initial arrest. Given the increased centralisation of police custody facilities, this means that significant time may elapse between the time of apprehension and the commencement of s.6 procedures. Broadly, periods when the person is receiving medical treatment at a hospital once in police custody, and before charge, will not count towards the 12-hour computation or any authorised extension of the same (s.15 below); any interview conducted during the time at hospital, or in transit to or from there, will count towards the computation (s.15(6)).

Documentation is required to record compliance with the terms of s.5, providing a record that statutory rights to information, including the administration of the statutory caution (s.5(2)(a)), have been fulfilled. At this time, the force custody officer has to address the statutory test set by s.7; broadly, that it is necessary and proportionate to enable investigation that the party be held in police custody as a preliminary before processing the arrest.

Since the arrested person generally is entitled to have others informed of his current situation (s.38), a record has to be maintained to detail the steps taken to relay this information to the named person; the occurrence of a 6-hour custody review and the measures taken to inform a solicitor and to afford access to legal advice (s.43) similarly must be noted.

Procedurally, should it be decided that the arrest be discontinued, a record of the decision, and its timing is required. Ordinarily, a decision to charge the arrestee requires to be executed within the statutory 12-hour period, but if it is considered that the offence is an indictable matter and decided (after addressing the s.7 test) that the original 12-hour period of arrest requires to be extended, the terms of subs.(5) have to be met. Since the *Cadder* judgment, the practice of Police Scotland has been to detail communications with the suspect's solicitor on a SARF (Solicitor Access Recording Form) separately and this looks likely to continue despite the information which s.6 demands be recorded. In the context of record–keeping, attention is directed to *Cummings v HM Advocate*, 1982 S.C.C.R. 108 where the only record produced to show that a statutory caution had been administered was in the constable's notebook; this was held to be a record sufficient to meet statutory requirements.

Subs.(1)

Section 6(1) provides a list of the information to be recorded in respect of all arrests. The subsection itself does not specify how or where that information is to be recorded. It may be assumed that, in practice, there will be a series of hardcopy police forms or alternatively computer entries that may be downloaded, docketed and signed as evidence of the requirements of all or any one the subsections having been fulfilled. There may be both options, one for proof at court and the other for police records.

Subs.(2)

This subsection requires any decisions, intimations or provision of information under other sections of this Act to be recorded.

Subss.(3) and (4)

Decisions under s.7 (Authorisation for keeping in custody) require to be recorded and so too do those under s.8 (Information to be given on authorisation), s.13 (Custody review) and s.15(6) (Medical treatment).

Subss.(5) and (6)

Decisions under s.11 (Authorisation for keeping in custody beyond 12 hour limit) require to be recorded.

Subs.(7)

Decisions under s.16 (Release from police custody on conditions) require to be recorded.

Subs.(8)

The time of the charging of a person must be recorded.

Chapter 2 – Custody: Person not Officially Accused

Keeping person in custody

Authorisation for keeping in custody

7.—(1) Subsection (2) applies where— A170-023

(a) a person is in police custody having been arrested in respect of an offence without a warrant, and

(b) since being arrested, the person has not been charged with an offence by a constable.

(2) Authorisation to keep the person in custody must be sought as soon as reasonably practicable after the person—

(a) is arrested at a police station, or

(b) arrives at a police station, having been taken there in accordance with section 4.

(3) Authorisation may be given only by a constable who—

(a) is of the rank of sergeant or above, and

(b) has not been involved in the investigation in connection with which the person is in police custody.

(4) Authorisation may be given only if that constable is satisfied that the test in section 14 is met.

(5) If authorisation is refused, the person may continue to be held in police custody only if—

(a) a constable charges the person with an offence, or

(b) the person is detained under section 28(1A) of the 1995 Act (which allows for detention in connection with a breach of bail conditions).

AMENDMENTS

Subs.(1)(a) as amended by Criminal Justice (Scotland) Act 2016 (Modification of Part 1 and Ancillary Provision) Regulations 2017 (SSI 2017/453) reg.2 (effective 25 January 2018).

DEFINITIONS

A170-024 "constable": s.62.

GENERAL NOTE

Subs.(1)

A170-025 Section 7(1) sets out the procedure for keeping a person in custody where the person has been arrested but without there having been a warrant to do so *and* the arrested person has not been charged with an offence by a constable.

Subs.(2)

This subsection provides that authorisation to keep the person in custody must be sought as soon as reasonably practicable after the person is arrested at a police station or arrives at a police station following arrest.

Subss.(3) and (4)

These provide that authorisation to keep a person in custody may only be given by a constable of the rank of sergeant or above who has not been involved in the investigation in connection with which the person is in custody and if the test set out in s.14 has been met.

Subs.(5)

This subsection provides that if authorisation to keep a person in custody is refused then the person can continue to be held in custody only if charged with an offence, or the person is detained for detention in connection with a breach of bail conditions.

Information to be given on authorisation

A170-026 **8.** At the time when authorisation to keep a person in custody is given under section 7, the person must be informed of—

(a) the reason that the person is being kept in custody, and

(b) the 12 hour limit arising by virtue of section 9 and the fact that the person may be kept in custody for a further 12 hours under section 11.

GENERAL NOTE

A170-027 Section 8 provides that, at the time when authorisation is given to keep a person in custody under s.7, the person must be informed of the reason they are being kept in custody and that they may only be kept in custody without charge for a period of 12 hours. That person must also be informed when authorisation is given under s.7 that a further extension of 12 hours may be authorised under s.11.

12 hour limit: general rule

A170-028 **9.—**(1) Subsection (2) applies when—

(a) a person has been held in police custody for a continuous period of 12 hours, beginning with the time at which authorisation was given under section 7, and

(b) during that period the person has not been charged with an offence by a constable.

(2) The person may continue to be held in police custody only if—

(a) a constable charges the person with an offence,

(b) authorisation to keep the person in custody has been given under section 11, or

(c) the person is detained under section 28(1A) of the 1995 Act (which allows for detention in connection with a breach of bail conditions).

DEFINITIONS

A170-029 "constable": s.62.

GENERAL NOTE

Section 9 provides that a person may not continue to be held in custody after a continuous period of 12 hours unless that person is then charged with an offence by a constable or authorisation has been given to extend that arrest for a further 12 hours under s.11. **A170-030**

The period of 12 hours begins at the point when authorisation to keep a person in custody is given by a constable in accordance with s.7. After the expiry of 12 hours if the person is not charged, they must be released, perhaps conditionally, if appropriate (see s.16).

12 hour limit: previous period

10.—(1) Subsection (2) applies where— **A170-031**

(a) a person is being held in police custody by virtue of authorisation given under section 7,

(b) authorisation has been given under that section to hold the person in police custody on a previous occasion, and

(c) the offence in connection with which the authorisation mentioned in paragraph (a) has been given is the same offence or arises from the same circumstances as the offence in connection with which the authorisation mentioned in paragraph (b) was given.

(2) The 12 hour period mentioned in section 9 is reduced by the length of the period during which the person was held in police custody by virtue of the authorisation mentioned in subsection (1)(b).

(3) Subsections (5) and (6) of section 15 apply for the purpose of calculating the length of the period during which the person was held in police custody by virtue of the authorisation mentioned in subsection (1)(b).

GENERAL NOTE

Where a person is held in custody on more than one occasion for the same or a related offence, s.10 provides that the 12 hour maximum period of custody (see s.9 for the general rule) is reduced by any earlier period during which the person was held in custody for that offence. **A170-032**

Authorisation for keeping in custody beyond 12 hour limit

11.—(1) A constable may give authorisation for a person who is in police custody to be kept in custody for a continuous period of 12 hours, beginning when the 12 hour period mentioned in section 9 ends. **A170-033**

(2) Authorisation may be given only by a constable who—

(a) is of, or above, the rank of—

(i) inspector, if a constable believes the person to be 18 years of age or over,

(ii) chief inspector, if a constable believes the person to be under 18 years of age, and

(b) has not been involved in the investigation in connection with which the person is in police custody.

(3) Authorisation may be given only if—

(a) the person has not been held in police custody by virtue of authorisation given under this section in connection with—

(i) the offence in connection with which the person is in police custody, or

(ii) an offence arising from the same circumstances as that offence, and

(b) the constable is satisfied that—

(i) the test in section 14 will be met when the 12 hour period mentioned in section 9 ends,

(ii) the offence in connection with which the person is in police custody is an indictable offence, and

(iii) the investigation is being conducted diligently and expeditiously.

(4) Before deciding whether or not to give authorisation the constable must—

(a) where practicable afford a reasonable opportunity to make verbal or written representations to—

(i) the person, or

(ii) if the person so chooses, the person's solicitor, and

(b) have regard to any representations made.

(5) If authorisation is given, it is deemed to be withdrawn if the person is released from police custody before the 12 hour period mentioned in section 9 ends.

(6) Subsection (7) applies when—

(a) by virtue of authorisation given under this section, a person has been held in police custody for a continuous period of 12 hours (beginning with the time at which the 12 hour period mentioned in section 9 ended), and

(b) during that period the person has not been charged with an offence by a constable.

(7) The person may continue to be held in police custody only if—

(a) a constable charges the person with an offence, or

(b) the person is detained under section 28(1A) of the 1995 Act (which allows for detention in connection with a breach of bail conditions).

DEFINITIONS

A170-034 "constable": s.62.

GENERAL NOTE

A170-035 The section sets out the tests to be applied by the independent custody review officer before authorising an extension of 12 hours to the customary 12-hour limit specified in s.10 above. It will be noted that this can only be granted if the offence, or one of the offences, is indictable, and an assessment of the need to keep the individual in custody to enable full and expeditious investigation has been made. Furthermore, the qualitative test set out in s.14 is expected to be met within that additional 12-hour period. Authorisation can only be given by an officer holding the rank of inspector where the person is believed to be over 18 years old (subs.(2)(a)(i)); in relation to anyone believed to be under 18 years old authority for extension has to be obtained from an officer holding chief inspector rank or above (subs.(2)(a)(ii)). It does not follow that the responsible officer has to be at the police station in which the person is being held.

As part of the assessment process the authorising officer is obliged to take and document reasonable steps to permit the accused or his lawyer to make representations (presumably disputing the need for the extension being sought) all of which must be recorded (s.6(5) above). This consultation process is to precede any determination. Once authorisation is granted s.12 stipulates that as soon as reasonably practicable the person must be so informed, and advised of his right to have his solicitor advised too.

Subs.(5)

This subsection clarifies that any authorisation to extend beyond the initial 12 hours is deemed to have been withdrawn if the person is released prior to those initial 12 hours elapsing.

Subss.(6) and (7)

These subsections provide that after the expiry of the further 12 hours the person can only continue to be held in police custody if charged, or detained under s.28(1A) of 1995 Act (detention in connection with a breach of bail conditions).

Information to be given on authorisation under section 11

A170-036 **12.**—(1) This section applies when authorisation to keep a person in custody is given under section 11.

(2) The person must be informed—

(a) that the authorisation has been given, and

(b) of the grounds on which it has been given.

(3) The person—

(a) has the right to have the information mentioned in subsection (2) intimated to a solicitor, and

(b) must be informed of that right.

(4) The person must be reminded about any right which the person has under Chapter 5.

(5) Subsection (4) does not require that a person be reminded about a right to have intimation sent under either of the following sections if the person has exercised the right already—

(a) section 38,

(b) section 43.

(6) Information to be given under subsections (2), (3)(b) and (4) must be given to the person as soon as reasonably practicable after the authorisation is given.

(7) Where the person requests that intimation be sent under subsection (3)(a), the intimation must be sent as soon as reasonably practicable.

General Note

Section 12 specifies the information which must be provided by a constable to an arrested person when authorisation to extend the arrest under s.11 is granted. This information is to be given as soon as reasonably practicable after authorisation. **A170-037**

Subs.(4) is a saving provision which requires intimation to be sent, if requested by the party in custody, to the person or persons specified in ss.38 to 43, if the party has not already made such a request earlier in the arrest period.

Custody review

13.—(1) A custody review must be carried out— **A170-038**

(a) when a person has been held in police custody for a continuous period of 6 hours by virtue of authorisation given under section 7, and

(b) again, if authorisation to keep the person in police custody is given under section 11, when the person has been held in custody for a continuous period of 6 hours by virtue of that authorisation.

(2) A custody review entails the consideration by a constable of whether the test in section 14 is met.

(3) A custody review must be carried out by a constable who—

(a) is of the rank of inspector or above, and

(b) has not been involved in the investigation in connection with which the person is in police custody.

(4) If the constable is not satisfied that the test in section 14 is met, the person may continue to be held in police custody only if—

(a) a constable charges the person with an offence, or

(b) the person is detained under section 28(1A) of the 1995 Act (which allows for detention in connection with a breach of bail conditions).

Definitions

"constable": s.62. **A170-039**

"custody review": s.13(2).

General Note

Subss.(1) and (2)

Section 13(1) and (2) provide that where a person has been held in police custody for a continuous period of six hours and has not been charged with an offence, a decision must be made on whether to continue to keep that person in custody. That decision is referred to as "a custody review". That decision to continue or discontinue custody must be made as soon as reasonably practicable after the expiry of the period of six hours which started when the authorisation under s.7 was given. In making that decision, the test set out in s.14 is applied. **A170-040**

Subs.(3)

Under s.13(3) the decision in regard to custody must be made by a constable of the rank of inspector or above, who has not been involved in the investigation in connection with which the person is in custody. If the test set out in s.14 is not met, the person may continue to be held in custody only if they are charged with an offence. This section also provides that where an arrest has been extended under s.11, and if the person remains in custody, that there must be a further 6 hour review after this extension period has begun.

Test for sections 7,11 and 13

A170-041 **14.**—(1) For the purposes of sections 7(4), 11(3)(b) and 13(2), the test is that—

(a) there are reasonable grounds for suspecting that the person has committed an offence, and

(b) keeping the person in custody is necessary and proportionate for the purposes of bringing the person before a court or otherwise dealing with the person in accordance with the law.

(2) Without prejudice to the generality of subsection (1)(b), in considering what is necessary and proportionate for the purpose mentioned in that subsection regard may be had to—

(a) whether the person's presence is reasonably required to enable the offence to be investigated fully,

(b) whether the person (if liberated) would be likely to interfere with witnesses or evidence, or otherwise obstruct the course of justice,

(c) the nature and seriousness of the offence.

GENERAL NOTE

Subs.(1)

A170-042 Generally, s.14 sets out the test for keeping a person in custody under ss.7(4), 11(3)(b) and reviewing continuation of that period of custody after six hours under s.13(2). Section 14(1) provides that the test for keeping a person in custody is whether there are reasonable grounds for suspecting that the person has committed an offence *and* keeping the person in custody is *necessary and proportionate* (see subs.(2) below) for the purposes of bringing the person before a court or otherwise dealing with the person by law.

Subs.(2)

In considering what constitutes "necessary and proportionate" regard may be had to the factors detailed in s.14(2). The section refers only to the need to have "regard" for these factors which are not all necessary and simultaneously or so it would seem.

A provision in English law (s.38(1)(b)(ii) of the Police and Criminal Evidence Act 1984) is not incompatible with art.5 of ECHR (right to liberty and security) in so far as it purports to authorise the detention of minors in their own interests. The claimant had been detained for about 13 hours in order to be brought to court. The assessment by the custody sergeant of the risk of violence to the claimant had he been released was based on a consideration of the specific circumstances and the context of the offence (rival gang fights) and not merely on generic considerations: *Archer v Commissioner of Police of the Metropolis* [2020] EWHC 1567 (QB); [2020] WLR(D) 348 at [57]–[59].

Medical treatment

A170-043 **15.**—(1) Subsection (2) applies when—

(a) a person is in police custody having been arrested without a warrant,

(b) since being arrested, the person has not been charged with an offence by a constable, and

(c) the person is at a hospital for the purpose of receiving medical treatment.

(2) If authorisation to keep the person in custody has not been given under section 7, that section has effect as if—

(a) each reference in subsection (2) of that section to a police station were a reference to the hospital, and

(b) the words after the reference to a police station in paragraph (b) of that subsection were omitted.

(3) Where authorisation is given under section 7 when a person is at a hospital, authorisation under that section need not be sought again if, while still in custody, the person is taken to a police station in accordance with section 4.

(4) Subsections (5) and (6) apply for the purpose of calculating the 12 hours mentioned in sections 9 and 11.

(5) Except as provided for in subsection (6), no account is to be taken of any period during which a person is—

(a) at a hospital for the purpose of receiving medical treatment, or
(b) being taken as quickly as is reasonably practicable—
(i) to a hospital for the purpose of receiving medical treatment, or
(ii) to a police station from a hospital to which the person was taken for the purpose of receiving medical treatment.

(6) Account is to be taken of any period during which a person is both—

(a) at a hospital, or being taken to or from one, and
(b) being interviewed by a constable in relation to an offence which the constable has reasonable grounds to suspect the person of committing.

GENERAL NOTE

Subss.(1) and (2)

Subsections (1) and (2) apply to a person who is taken into police custody having been arrested without a warrant, has not been charged with an offence *and* the person is at a hospital for the purpose of receiving medical treatment. These provisions taken together provide that authority to keep a person in custody may be given as though s.7 applies in the hospital as it does in a police station. **A170-044**

Subs.(3)

Where authorisation is given under s.7 when a person is at hospital, authorisation under that section need not be sought again if, while still in custody, the person is taken to a police station in accordance with s.4.

Subss.(4) and (5)

For the purpose of calculating the 12 hour maximum period of custody set out in s.9, *no* account will be taken of any time during which a person is at a hospital for the purpose of receiving medical treatment or being taken as quickly as is reasonably practicable to a hospital for that purpose or to a police station from a hospital to which that person had been taken for the purpose of receiving medical treatment: see s.15(5).

Account is to be taken of any period during which a person is both at a hospital, or being taken to or from one and being interviewed by a constable in relation to an offence which the constable has reasonable grounds to suspect the person of committing: see s.15(6).

It would seem that what is intended by this means of obtaining a division of essentially the same tasks is to allow towards the reckoning of any 12 hour period any interview that a constable might carry out with a person in custody while in transit to and from the hospital or any interview that a constable might carry out with a person in custody while at hospital.

Investigative liberation

Release on conditions

16.—(1) Subsection (2) applies where— **A170-045**

(a) a person is being held in police custody by virtue of authorisation given under section 7,
(b) a constable has reasonable grounds for suspecting that the person has committed a relevant offence, and
(c) either—
(i) the person has not been subject to a condition imposed under subsection (2) in connection with a relevant offence, or
(ii) it has not been more than 28 days since the first occasion on which a condition was imposed on the person under subsection (2) in connection with a relevant offence.

(2) If releasing the person from custody, a constable may impose any condition that an appropriate constable considers necessary and proportionate for the purpose

of ensuring the proper conduct of the investigation into a relevant offence (including, for example, a condition aimed at securing that the person does not interfere with witnesses or evidence).

(3) A condition under subsection (2)—

(a) may not require the person to be in a specified place at a specified time,

(b) may require the person—

(i) not to be in a specified place, or category of place, at a specified time, and

(ii) to remain outwith that place, or any place falling within the specified category (if any), for a specified period.

(4) A condition imposed under subsection (2) is a liberation condition for the purposes of schedule 1.

(5) In subsection (2), "an appropriate constable" means a constable of the rank of sergeant or above.

(6) In this section, "a relevant offence" means—

(a) the offence in connection with which the authorisation under section 7 has been given, or

(b) an offence arising from the same circumstances as that offence.

DEFINITIONS

A170-046 "constable": s.62.
"a relevant offence": s.16(6).
"an appropriate constable": s.16(5).

GENERAL NOTE

A170-047 This provision was introduced by the 2016 Act and applies to persons who have been arrested but not, as yet, officially accused and charged, before being released from custody. It should not be confused with the more familiar concept of release on a police undertaking after charge now found in ss.25 and 26 building upon the foundations laid by s.22 of the Criminal Procedure (Scotland) Act 1995. The mechanism provided by s.16 enables the police to continue with investigation of the circumstances of the relevant offence giving rise to the earlier arrest while imposing conduct conditions upon the released person for up to 28 days. Sense suggests that a person could not be re-arrested for the same relevant offence then made subject of a further investigative liberation after expiry of the 28-day period. It also follows that arrest and charge, or official accusation, during that period would halt the investigative liberation conditions (see s.17(1)(b) below).

Chapter 3 of the Act also lays out procedures to be applied during the period of investigative liberation enabling the police to remove or modify release conditions and to serve notice of such variations on the suspect. Section 19 provides for shrieval review (including removal) of the conditions imposed. Form 66.2-A introduced by the Act of Adjournal (Criminal Procedure Rules 1996 Amendment) (Miscellaneous) 2018 (SSI 2018/12) stipulates that a hearing has to be fixed within seven days, a factor which may render applications made later in the 28 day period futile.

Observe that s.16's provisions may be applied to any offence whether potentially summary or solemn in nature.

Subs.(2)

Subsection (2) provides that a constable of the rank of sergeant or above (see s.16(5)) may authorise the release of a person from custody on any condition which is necessary and proportionate for the purpose of ensuring the proper conduct of the investigation into a relevant offence.

Subs.(4)

Schedule 1 of the 2016 Act specifies offences and penalties for breach of both liberation conditions and undertakings, and evidential presumptions relating to proof of such offences. Note that any challenge to what is, effectively, a special capacity, or to the conditions imposed upon the accused, must be made prior to plea in summary proceedings, and at the first diet or preliminary hearing in solemn proceedings.

Paragraph 2 sets out the sentencing provisions for the offence. Paragraph 3 makes provision for breach by committing an offence. Paragraph 4 concerns matters related to a failure to comply with the terms of an investigative liberation condition. Paragraph 5 concerns matters related to a failure to comply with an undertaking other than the requirement to attend at court. Paragraph 6 sets down evidential presumptions. Paragraph 7 provides guidance on interpretation.

Schedule 1 to this Act is reproduced below at paras A170-262–A170-268.

Conditions ceasing to apply

17.—(1) A condition imposed on a person under section 16(2) ceases to apply— A170-048

(a) at the end of the day falling 28 days after the first occasion on which a condition was imposed on the person under section 16(2) in connection with a relevant offence, or

(b) before then, if—

(i) the condition is removed by a notice under section 18,

(ii) the person is arrested in connection with a relevant offence,

(iii) the person is officially accused of committing a relevant offence, or

(iv) the condition is removed by the sheriff under section 19.

(2) In subsection (1), "a relevant offence" means—

(a) the offence in connection with which the condition was imposed, or

(b) an offence arising from the same circumstances as that offence.

DEFINITIONS

"a relevant offence": s.17(2). A170-049

GENERAL NOTE

Section 17 provides when conditions imposed on a person under s.16(2) cease to apply. These are broadly, after 28 days in force: s.17(1)(a). Alternative ways of conditions ending are by removal under s.18, arrest for a relevant offence, officially accused of committing an offence or removal judicially: s.17(2)(i)–(iv). A170-050

Modification or removal of conditions

18.—(1) A constable may by notice modify or remove a condition imposed under section 16(2). A170-051

(2) A notice under subsection (1)—

(a) is to be given in writing to the person who is subject to the condition,

(b) must specify the time from which the condition is modified or removed.

(3) A constable of the rank of inspector or above must keep under review whether or not—

(a) there are reasonable grounds for suspecting that a person who is subject to a condition imposed under section 16(2) has committed a relevant offence, and

(b) the condition imposed remains necessary and proportionate for the purpose of ensuring the proper conduct of the investigation into a relevant offence.

(4) Where the constable referred to in subsection (3) is no longer satisfied as to the matter mentioned in paragraph (a) of that subsection, a constable must give notice to the person removing any condition imposed in connection with a relevant offence.

(5) Where the constable referred to in subsection (3) is no longer satisfied as to the matter mentioned in paragraph (b) of that subsection, a constable must give notice to the person—

(a) modifying the condition in question, or

(b) removing it.

(6) Where a duty to give notice to a person arises under subsection (4) or (5), the notice—

(a) is to be given in writing to the person as soon as practicable, and

(b) must specify, as the time from which the condition is modified or removed, the time at which the duty to give the notice arose.

(7) The modification or removal of a condition under subsection (1), (4) or (5) requires the authority of a constable of the rank of inspector or above.

(8) In this section, "a relevant offence" means—

(a) the offence in connection with which the condition was imposed, or

(b) an offence arising from the same circumstances as that offence.

DEFINITIONS

A170-052 "constable": s.62.
"a relevant offence": s.18(8).

GENERAL NOTE

Subs.(2)

A170-053 Under s.18(2) a notice about the modification or removal of a condition must be given in writing to the person who is subject to it and must specify the time from which the condition is modified or removed. Any modification or removal of a condition requires to be approved by a constable of the rank of an inspector or above: s.18(3). This power gives the police the flexibility to adjust conditions in light of changed circumstances.

Subs.(3)

Section 18(3) provides that a constable of the rank of inspector or above must keep under review whether or not there are reasonable grounds for suspecting that a person who is subject to a condition imposed under s.16(2) has committed a relevant offence, and whether the condition imposed remains necessary and proportionate for the purpose of ensuring the proper conduct of the investigation into a relevant offence.

Subss.(4) and (5)

If the inspector is no longer satisfied that there are reasonable grounds for suspecting that a person who is subject to a condition has committed a relevant offence, the person must be given notice of the removal of the condition. If no longer satisfied that a condition is necessary and proportionate, again the person must be given notice that the condition is being modified or removed.

Subs.(6)

Section 18(6) provides that any such notice must be given in writing to the person as soon as practicable and it must specify as the time from which the condition is modified or removed, the time at which the duty to give the notice arose, i.e. the time at which the decision is made by an appropriate constable, to remove or modify the condition.

Review of conditions

A170-054 **19.**—(1) A person who is subject to a condition imposed under section 16(2) may apply to the sheriff to have the condition reviewed.

(2) Before disposing of an application under this section, the sheriff must give the procurator fiscal an opportunity to make representations.

(3) If the sheriff is not satisfied that the condition is necessary and proportionate for the purpose for which it was imposed, the sheriff may—

(a) remove the condition, or

(b) impose an alternative condition that the sheriff considers to be necessary and proportionate for that purpose.

(4) For the purposes of sections 17 and 18, a condition imposed by the sheriff under subsection (3)(b) is to be regarded as having been imposed under section 16(2).

GENERAL NOTE

Subs.(2)

A170-055 Section 19(1) provides that a person who is subject to a condition imposed under s.16(2) may make an application for review to a sheriff. Section 19(2) requires the sheriff to give the procurator fiscal an opportunity to make representations before the review is determined.

Subs.(3)

Section 19(3) provides that where the sheriff is not satisfied that the condition imposed is necessary and proportionate, the sheriff may remove it or impose an alternative condition which the sheriff considers to be necessary and proportionate for that purpose.

Subs.(4)

Section 19(4) provides that a condition imposed on review by the sheriff under s.19(3)(b) is to be regarded as having been imposed by a constable under s.16(2). This provides that the conditions set by the sheriff have the same effect and are to be taken as having started when set by the police, i.e. the 28 day period is calculated from the date on which the police conditions were set. Conditions imposed by the sheriff can be modified or removed under s.19(1) in the same manner as police conditions.

Chapter 3 – Custody: Person Officially Accused

Person to be brought before court

Information to be given in particular cases

20.—(1) Subsection (2) applies when— **A170-056**

(a) a person is in police custody having been arrested under a warrant in respect of an offence listed in subsection (3)(b), or

(b) a person—

(i) is in police custody having been arrested without a warrant, and

(ii) since being arrested, the person has been charged by a constable with an offence listed in subsection (3)(b).

(2) The person must be informed as soon as reasonably practicable—

(a) that the person's case at, or for the purposes of, any relevant hearing in the course of the proceedings may be conducted only by a lawyer,

(b) that it is, therefore, in the person's interests to get the professional assistance of a solicitor, and

(c) that if the person does not engage a solicitor for the purposes of the conduct of the person's case at or for the purposes of the hearing, the court will do so.

(3) For the purposes of subsections (1) and (2)—

(a) "relevant hearing" is to be construed in accordance with section 288C(1A) or (as the case may be) 288DC(4) of the 1995 Act,

(b) the list is—

(i) an offence to which section 288C of the 1995 Act applies (certain sexual offending),

(ii) an offence to which section 288DC of the 1995 Act applies (domestic abuse cases).

Subs.(1)(a), (b)(ii), (2)(a) as amended, subs.(3) inserted, title of s.20 substituted, by Domestic Abuse (Scotland) Act 2018 (asp 5) Sch.1(1)(2) para.5 and (effective 1 April 2019 in respect of proceedings commenced on or after 1 April 2019 subject to transitional provision specified in SSI 2018/387 reg.7(2)).

DEFINITIONS

"constable": s.62. **A170-057**

GENERAL NOTE

Subs.(1)

Section 20(1) contains the criteria that are to be applied to establish whether a person falls within this section. The person must have been arrested in respect of a warrant for a sexual offence to which s.288C of the 1995 Act applies or, if arrested without warrant and since being arrested, have been charged by a constable for a sexual offence to which s.288C of the 1995 Act applies. **A170-058**

Subs.(2)

Section 20(2) contains the information that a person, who falls within the criteria contained within subs.(1), must give. The person must be informed that certain hearings in the course of their case may only be conducted by a lawyer. The person must also be given notice that it is in their interests to engage the professional assistance of a solicitor at, or for the purposes of, those hearings and if the person does not engage the assistance of a solicitor then the court will do so.

Person to be brought before court

A170-059 **21.**—(1) Subsection (2) applies to a person when—

(a) the person is in police custody having been arrested under a warrant granted for the purpose of having the person brought before a court in connection with an offence which the person is officially accused of committing), or

(b) the person—

(i) is in police custody having been arrested without a warrant, and

(ii) since being arrested in respect of an offence, the person has been charged with an offence by a constable.

(2) The person must be brought before a court (unless released from custody under section 25)—

(a) if practicable, before the end of the first day on which the court is sitting after the day on which this subsection began to apply to the person, or

(b) as soon as practicable after that.

(3) A person is deemed to be brought before a court in accordance with subsection (2) if the person appears before it by means of a live television link (by virtue of a determination by the court that the person is to do so by such means).

AMENDMENTS

Subs.(1) as amended by Criminal Justice (Scotland) Act 2016 (Modification of Part 1 and Ancillary Provision) Regulations 2017 (SSI 2017/453) reg.2 (effective 25 January 2018).

DEFINITIONS

A170-060 "constable": s.62.

GENERAL NOTE

Subss.(1) and (2)

A170-061 Section 21(1) and (2) provide in effect that, wherever practicable, persons kept in custody after being arrested under a warrant, or arrested without a warrant and subsequently charged with an offence by a constable, must be brought before a court by the end of the next court day or as soon as practicable after that.

Subs.(3)

Section 21(3) provides that individuals are to be considered as having been brought before a court if they appear by live television link.

Under 18s to be kept in place of safety prior to court

A170-062 **22.**—(1) Subsection (2) applies when—

(a) a person is to be brought before a court in accordance with section 21(2), and

(b) either—

(i) a constable believes the person is under 16 years of age, or

(ii) the person is subject to a compulsory supervision order, or an interim compulsory supervision order, made under the Children's Hearings (Scotland) Act 2011.

(2) The person must (unless released from custody under section 25) be kept in a place of safety until the person can be brought before the court.

(3) The place of safety in which the person is kept must not be a police station unless an appropriate constable certifies that keeping the person in a place of safety other than a police station would be—

(a) impracticable,
(b) unsafe, or
(c) inadvisable due to the person's state of health (physical or mental).

(4) A certificate under subsection (3) must be produced to the court when the person is brought before it.

(5) In this section—

"an appropriate constable" means a constable of the rank of inspector or above,
"place of safety" has the meaning given in section 202(1) of the Children's Hearings (Scotland) Act 2011.

DEFINITIONS

"an appropriate constable": s.22(5). **A170-063**
"place of safety": s.22(5).

GENERAL NOTE

Section 22 provides that individuals under 16 years of age and those subject to compulsory supervision orders who are being brought to court are consequently following s.22(2) only to be kept in a place of safety before being brought to court. Subs.(3) follows well-established practice that a police station cannot be regarded as a place of safety unless one of the factors set out is fulfilled. The grounds for departing from that general principle, and specifying a police station as the place of safety, must be certified by a police officer of inspector rank or above, and the completed certificate must be placed before the court when a custodial appearance is made. It is implicit that the police station in question must be identified. **A170-064**

Notice to parent that under 18 to be brought before court

23.—(1) Subsection (2) applies when a person who is 16 years of age or over and subject to a supervision order or under 16 years of age— **A170-065**

(a) is to be brought before a court in accordance with section 21(2), or
(b) is released from police custody on an undertaking given under section 25(2)(a).

(2) A parent of the person mentioned in subsection (1) (if one can be found) must be informed of the following matters—

(a) the court before which the person is to be brought,
(b) the date on which the person is to be brought before the court,
(c) the general nature of the offence which the person has been officially accused of committing, and
(d) that the parent's attendance at the court may be required under section 42 of the 1995 Act.

(3) Subsection (2) does not require any information to be given to a parent if a constable has grounds to believe that giving the parent the information mentioned in that subsection may be detrimental to the wellbeing of the person mentioned in subsection (1).

(4) In this section—

"parent" includes guardian and any person who has the care of the person mentioned in subsection (1),
"supervision order" means compulsory supervision order, or interim compulsory supervision order, made under the Children's Hearings (Scotland) Act 2011.

DEFINITIONS

"parent": s.23(4). **A170-066**
"supervision order": s.23(4).

GENERAL NOTE

A170-067 Section 23 makes provision for circumstances where a person who is under 16 years of age, or is aged 16 or over and subject to a supervision order, is to be brought before a court in accordance with s.23(2) or released from police custody on an undertaking, and, where possible, certain information must be provided to the parent of such a person. The requirement to give such information may be dispensed with if a constable believes that it would be detrimental to the wellbeing of the person being brought before the court or released on undertaking: s.23(3).

Notice to local authority that under 18 to be brought before court

A170-068 **24.**—(1) The appropriate local authority must be informed of the matters mentioned in subsection (4) when—

(a) a person to whom either subsection (2) or (3) applies is to be brought before a court in accordance with section 21(2), or

(b) a person to whom subsection (2) applies is released from police custody on an undertaking given under section 25(2)(a).

(2) This subsection applies to—

(a) a person who is under 16 years of age,

(b) a person who is—

(i) 16 or 17 years of age, and

(ii) subject to a compulsory supervision order, or an interim compulsory supervision order, made under the Children's Hearings (Scotland) Act 2011.

(3) This subsection applies to a person if—

(a) a constable believes the person is 16 or 17 years of age,

(b) since being arrested, the person has not exercised the right to have intimation sent under section 38, and

(c) on being informed or reminded of the right to have intimation sent under that section after being officially accused, the person has declined to exercise the right.

(4) The matters referred to in subsection (1) are—

(a) the court before which the person mentioned in paragraph (a) or (as the case may be) (b) of that subsection is to be brought,

(b) the date on which the person is to be brought before the court, and

(c) the general nature of the offence which the person has been officially accused of committing.

(5) For the purpose of subsection (1), the appropriate local authority is the local authority in whose area the court referred to in subsection (4)(a) sits.

DEFINITIONS

A170-069 "appropriate local authority": s.24(5).

GENERAL NOTE

A170-070 Section 24 sets out the circumstances, in regard to an individual under the age of 18 years who is to be brought to court, in which a local authority requires to be advised of the following information: the court before which the person is to be brought, the date the person is to be brought before the court and the general nature of the offence which the person has been officially accused of committing. The local authority is that in the area where the court sits.

There are two sets of circumstances which require the local authority to be notified. First, where a person who is (i) under 16 years, (ii) 16 or 17 years of age and subject to either a compulsory supervision order or an interim compulsory supervision order, or (iii) believed to be 16 or 17 years of age and has declined the right to have intimation sent under s.38 is brought before a court in accordance with s.24(2). Secondly, where a person is under 16 or 17 years and subject to compulsory supervision is released from police custody on an undertaking given under s.25(2)(a).

Subs.(4) specifies the information to be provided.

Police liberation

Liberation by police

25.—(1) Subsection (2) applies when— **A170-071**

(a) a person is in police custody having been arrested under a warrant (other than a warrant granted under section 37(1)), or

(b) a person—

(i) is in police custody having been arrested without a warrant, and

(ii) since being arrested, the person has been charged with an offence by a constable.

(2) A constable may—

(a) if the person gives an undertaking in accordance with section 26, release the person from custody,

(b) release the person from custody without such an undertaking,

(c) refuse to release the person from custody.

(3) Where a person is in custody as mentioned in subsection (1)(a), the person may not be released from custody under subsection (2)(b).

(4) A constable is not to be subject to any claim whatsoever by reason of having refused to release a person from custody under subsection (2)(c).

DEFINITIONS

"constable": s.62. **A170-072**

GENERAL NOTE

It will be noted that s.50 of the Act requires officers of law to ensure that persons are not held unreasonably or unnecessarily in custody. Accordingly, s.25 applies to those who have been officially accused (i.e. arrested for, and charged with, an offence) and allows the police a general discretion to liberate an accused on undertaking conditions pending court appearance. Note, however, that the procedure cannot be used where arrest was pursuant to the execution of an apprehension warrant (subs.(3)). Section 25 closely resembles its statutory precursor—s.22 of the 1995 Act, in dealing with liberation on undertakings—but unlike the earlier provision which was restricted to offences which might be tried summarily, now in theory at least, a s.25 undertaking can be applied to any offence. Any undertaking must stipulate the date and court an accused must attend and must be assented to by the accused. Once such an appearance is made, the undertaking conditions will cease to have effect, any issue of bail and attendant conditions becoming the responsibility of the court (see s.29 below) **A170-073**

Significantly, in addition to long-familiar conditions as to conduct (see s.26(2) and (3)), further curfew or geographical exclusion conditions can be imposed. In the 1995 Act the imposition of any additional conditions had to be approved by an officer of rank inspector or above: in the 2016 Act subs.(5) divides approval between officers of sergeant rank or above. Practically, much may depend upon general guidance issued by the Lord Advocate, or specific instructions given by the procurator fiscal.

Section 25(4) underlines the discretionary nature of these powers; no action in delict can be founded upon a refusal to release an accused on undertaking conditions. The section makes no similar provision in regard to a decision to release an accused. A limited right to seek a shrieval review only of the terms of a curfew or general exclusion condition (whether imposed by the police or, later, by the procurator fiscal under s.27 of the Act) is found in s.30. (See Form 66.3-A in the Act of Adjournal (Criminal Procedure Rules 1996 Amendment) (Miscellaneous) 2018 (SSI 2018/12)).

Offences and penalties, and evidential provisions are contained in Sch.1 to the Act.

Release on undertaking

26.—(1) A person may be released from police custody on an undertaking given under section 25(2)(a) only if the person signs the undertaking. **A170-074**

(2) The terms of an undertaking are that the person undertakes to—

(a) appear at a specified court at a specified time, and

(b) comply with any conditions imposed under subsection (3) while subject to the undertaking.

(3) The conditions which may be imposed under this subsection are—

(a) that the person does not—

(i) commit an offence,

(ii) interfere with witnesses or evidence, or otherwise obstruct the course of justice,

(iii) behave in a manner which causes, or is likely to cause, alarm or distress to witnesses,

(b) any further condition that a constable considers necessary and proportionate for the purpose of ensuring that any conditions imposed under paragraph (a) are observed.

(4) Conditions which may be imposed under subsection (3)(b) include—

(a) a condition requiring the person—

(i) to be in a specified place at a specified time, and

(ii) to remain there for a specified period,

(b) a condition requiring the person—

(i) not to be in a specified place, or category of place, at a specified time, and

(ii) to remain outwith that place, or any place falling within the specified category (if any), for a specified period.

(5) For the imposition of a condition under subsection (3)(b)—

(a) if it is of the kind described in subsection (4)(a), the authority of a constable of the rank of inspector or above is required,

(b) if it is of any other kind, the authority of a constable of the rank of sergeant or above is required.

(6) The requirements imposed by an undertaking to attend at a court and comply with conditions are liberation conditions for the purposes of schedule 1.

DEFINITIONS

A170-075 "liberation conditions": s.26(6).

GENERAL NOTE

Subs.(1)

A170-076 Where release on an undertaking is being considered by the police such release necessarily requires to be signed by the individual. There is no provision, in the Act in general or s.26 in particular, as to what is to be done if the arrested person declines to sign an undertaking form as envisaged by s.26(1). Of course, the prospect of immediate release from police custody is in itself an inducement for an arrested person to sign the appropriate form. However, there may be reasons that would lead a person to decline to sign the form.

Subss.(2) and (3)

Section 26(2) specifies the terms of an undertaking and s.26(3)(a) provides for the standard conditions (not referred to or defined as such) and any further conditions which may be imposed. The latter conditions in terms of subs.(3)(b) are those that a constable considers necessary and proportionate for the purpose of ensuring that any conditions under subs.(3)(a) are observed.

The conditions can include a timed curfew or a geographical exclusion from a specified area or category of premises in addition to the "standard conditions" set out in subs.(3)(a). The additional conditions can be subject to review on application to the sheriff (refer to s.30 below).

The test in subs.(3) is whether "a" constable (therefore not necessarily one involved in any relevant investigation) believes that "any" further condition is necessary and proportionate to ensure observation of those in subs.(2). There is no provision in the section for what is to be done if the arrested person does not accept the condition as being necessary and proportionate and declines to sign an undertaking. It cannot be said that the constable might always simply detain further the arrested person until a signature is provided. Section 50 (see below) places a duty on a constable not to detain such a person unreasonably or unnecessarily.

Subs.(4)

There are examples of the further conditions, being considered necessary and proportionate, that may be imposed under s.26(3)(b).

Subs.(5)

Further conditions under s.26(3)(b), if it is of the kind described in s.26(4)(b) (conditions requiring a person to be in a specified place at a specified time and to remain there for a specified period), may only be imposed by a constable of the rank of inspector or above: s.26(5)(a).

Other conditions under s.26(3)(b) considered necessary and proportionate may be imposed by a constable of the rank of sergeant or above: s.26(5)(b).

Subs.(6)

The requirements imposed by an undertaking to attend court and comply with conditions are liberation conditions for the purposes of Sch.1.

Modification of undertaking

27.—(1) The procurator fiscal may by notice modify the terms of an undertaking given under section 25(2)(a) by— **A170-077**

(a) changing the court specified as the court at which the person is to appear,

(b) changing the time specified as the time at which the person is to appear at the court,

(c) removing or altering any condition imposed under section 26(3).

(2) A condition may not be altered under subsection (1)(c) so as to forbid or require something not forbidden or required by the terms of the condition when the person gave the undertaking.

(3) Notice under subsection (1) must be effected in a manner by which citation may be effected under section 141 of the 1995 Act.

DEFINITIONS

"procurator fiscal": s.307(1) of the 1995 Act. **A170-078**

GENERAL NOTE

Section 27(1) enables the procurator fiscal by notice (effected as set out in s.27(3)) to modify an undertaking given under s.25(2)(a), either by changing the time or place of the court hearing or removing or altering a condition in the undertaking. The manner of citation may be effected as under s.141 of the 1995 Act (manner of citation). **A170-079**

Shrieval review, limited to the terms of a curfew or general exclusion condition (whether imposed by the police or, as here, by the procurator fiscal), is found in s.30 below. (See Form 66.3-A in the Act of Adjournal (Criminal Procedure Rules 1996 Amendment) (Miscellaneous) 2018 (SSI 2018/12)). Curiously, subs.(1)(c) empowers the procurator fiscal to modify *any* undertaking condition imposed upon an accused. It is no doubt intended that the prosecutor might vary a curfew or general exclusion condition rather than the standard undertaking conditions.

Rescission of undertaking

28.—(1) The procurator fiscal may by notice rescind an undertaking given under section 25(2)(a) (whether or not the person who gave it is to be prosecuted). **A170-080**

(2) The rescission of an undertaking by virtue of subsection (1) takes effect at the end of the day on which the notice is sent.

(3) Notice under subsection (1) must be effected in a manner by which citation may be effected under section 141 of the 1995 Act.

(4) A constable may arrest a person without a warrant if the constable has reasonable grounds for suspecting that the person is likely to fail to comply with the terms of an undertaking given under section 25(2)(a).

(5) Where a person is arrested under subsection (4) or subsection (6) applies—

(a) the undertaking referred to in subsection (4) or (as the case may be) (6) is rescinded, and

(b) this Part applies as if the person, since being most recently arrested, has been charged with the offence in connection with which the person was in police custody when the undertaking was given.

(6) This subsection applies where—

(a) a person who is subject to an undertaking given under section 25(2)(a) is in police custody (otherwise than as a result of having been arrested under subsection (4)), and

(b) a constable has reasonable grounds for suspecting that the person has failed, or (if liberated) is likely to fail, to comply with the terms of the undertaking.

(7) The references in subsections (4) and (6)(b) to the terms of the undertaking are to the terms of the undertaking subject to any modification by—

(a) notice under section 27(1), or

(b) the sheriff under section 30(3)(b).

DEFINITIONS

A170-081 "constable": s.62.

"procurator fiscal": s.307(1) of the 1995 Act.

GENERAL NOTE

Subss.(1) and (2)

A170-082 Section 28(1) enables the procurator fiscal to rescind an undertaking under s.25(2)(a) regardless of whether the person who gave the undertaking is to be prosecuted. The rescission takes effect at the end of the day the notice is sent to the person who gave the undertaking.

Subs.(3)

Section 28(3) provides that notice of rescission "must" be made in a manner by which citation may be effected under s.141 of the 1995 Act.

Subs.(4)

Section 28(4) provides a constable with a power of arrest to if the constable has reasonable grounds for believing that the person is likely to fail to comply with the terms of an undertaking as contained within s.25(2)(a).

Subs.(5)

This subsection provides that, when a person is arrested under subs.(4) or is arrested otherwise than in accordance with the undertaking, as in subs.(6), the undertaking is rescinded and the person is deemed to be in custody, as if charged with the original offence for which an undertaking was given.

Subs.(7)

Section 28(7) provides that reference contained within subss.(4) and (6)(b) to the terms of the undertaking also refer to any undertaking modified by notice made under s.27(1) or by a sheriff under s.30(3)(b).

Expiry of undertaking

A170-083 **29.**—(1) An undertaking given under section 25(2)(a) expires—

(a) at the end of the day on which the person who gave it is required by its terms to appear at a court, or

(b) if subsection (2) applies, at the end of the day on which the person who gave it is brought before a court having been arrested under the warrant mentioned in that subsection.

(2) This subsection applies where—

(a) a person fails to appear at court as required by the terms of an undertaking given under section 25(2)(a), and

(b) on account of that failure, a warrant for the person's arrest is granted.

(3) The references in subsections (1)(a) and (2)(a) to the terms of the undertaking are to the terms of the undertaking subject to any modification by notice under section 27(1).

Expiry of undertaking

***29.—(1)** An undertaking given under section 25(2)(a) expires—* A170-083.1

(a) at the end of the day on which the person who gave it is required by its terms to appear at a court (but see section 29A), or

(b) if subsection (2) applies, at the end of the day on which the person who gave it is brought before a court having been arrested under the warrant mentioned in that subsection.

(2) This subsection applies where—

(a) a person fails to appear at court as required by the terms of an undertaking given under section 25(2)(a), and

(b) on account of that failure, a warrant for the person's arrest is granted.

(3) The references in subsections (1)(a) and (2)(a) to the terms of the undertaking are to the terms of the undertaking subject to any modification by notice under section 27(1).

AMENDMENTS

In relation to COVID-19, subs.(1)(a) as amended by Coronavirus (Scotland) (No.2) Act 2020 (asp 10) Sch.2(1) para.6(2) (effective 27 May 2020).

[THE NEXT PARAGRAPH IS A170-084]

GENERAL NOTE

Section 29(1) provides that an undertaking under s.25(2)(a) expires in two circumstances: these are either (a) at the end of the day when the person was required to have appeared at court, or (b) at the end of the day when a person appears at court having been arrested on a warrant for failing to appear as required by the terms of the undertaking. Section 29(2) applies when a person fails to appear at court as required by an undertaking and, on account of that failure, a warrant to arrest the person is granted. It is not immediately clear what the application of s.29(2) applies to. A170-084

Expiry of undertaking: coronavirus-related reason for non-appearance

29A.—(1) A court may modify the terms of an undertaking given under section 25(2)(a) by changing the time at which the person who gave it is to appear at the court if— A170-084.1

(a) the person has failed to appear at court as required by the terms of the undertaking,

(b) the court considers that the failure to appear is attributable to a reason relating to coronavirus, and

(c) the court does not consider it appropriate to grant a warrant for the person's arrest on account of the failure to appear.

(2) Where a court modifies the terms of an undertaking under subsection (1), the procurator fiscal must give notice of the modification to the person who gave the undertaking as soon as reasonably practicable.

(3) Notice under subsection (2) must be effected in a manner by which citation may be effected under section 141 of the 1995 Act.

(4) The reference in subsection (1) to the terms of an undertaking are to the terms of the undertaking subject to any modification by notice under section 27(1).

(5) A reference in any enactment to the modification of the terms of an undertaking under section 27(1) is to be treated as including modification under subsection (1).

(6) In subsection (1)(b), "coronavirus" has the meaning given by section 1 of the Coronavirus (Scotland) Act 2020.

AMENDMENTS

In relation to COVID-19, s.29A is inserted by Coronavirus (Scotland) (No.2) Act 2020 (asp 10) Sch.2(1) para.6(3) (effective 27 May 2020).

[THE NEXT PARAGRAPH IS A170-085]

Review of undertaking

A170-085 **30.**—(1) A person who is subject to an undertaking containing a condition imposed under section 26(3)(b) may apply to the sheriff to have the condition reviewed.

(2) Before disposing of an application under this section, the sheriff must give the procurator fiscal an opportunity to make representations.

(3) If the sheriff is not satisfied that the condition is necessary and proportionate for the purpose for which it was imposed, the sheriff may modify the terms of the undertaking by—

(a) removing the condition, or

(b) imposing an alternative condition that the sheriff considers to be necessary and proportionate for that purpose.

GENERAL NOTE

A170-086 Section 30(1) enables a person subject to an undertaking to apply to the sheriff for review. Section 30(2) provides that the sheriff must provide the procurator fiscal with an opportunity to make representations with regard to the review.

This section affords an accused a limited right to judicial scrutiny of conditions imposed by the police or the procurator fiscal as part of a release on undertaking (see s.25). Shrieval review is confined to the terms of a curfew or general exclusion condition, whether imposed by the police or by the procurator fiscal. (See Form 66.3-A in the Act of Adjournal (Criminal Procedure Rules 1996 Amendment) (Miscellaneous) 2018 (SSI 2018/12)). There is no power to remove or amend the standard conditions of an undertaking or to overrule the procurator fiscal's exercise of any other powers found in s.27 above.

Chapter 4 – Police Interview

Rights of suspects

Information to be given before interview

A170-087 **31.**—(1) Subsection (2) applies to a person who—

(a) is in police custody, or

(b) is attending at a police station or other place voluntarily for the purpose of being interviewed by a constable.

(2) Not more than one hour before a constable interviews the person about an offence which the constable has reasonable grounds to suspect the person of committing, the person must be informed—

(a) of the general nature of that offence,

(b) that the person is under no obligation to say anything other than to give the information specified in section 34(4),

(c) about the right under section 32 to have a solicitor present during the interview, and

(d) if the person is in police custody, about any right which the person has under Chapter 5.

(3) A person need not be informed under subsection (2)(d) about a right to have intimation sent under either of the following sections if the person has exercised the right already—

(a) section 38,

(b) section 43.

(4) For the purpose of subsection (2), a constable is not to be regarded as interviewing a person about an offence merely by asking the person for the information specified in section 34(4).

(5) Where a person is to be interviewed by virtue of authorisation granted under section 35, before the interview begins the person must be informed of what was specified by the court under subsection (6) of that section.

DEFINITIONS
"police custody": s.64. A170-088

GENERAL NOTE

Subs.(1)

Section 31 applies to a person who is either in police custody, as defined in the 2016 Act, or has voluntarily attended a police station, or other place, for the purpose of being interviewed by the police. A170-089

Subs.(2)

This subsection requires a constable to inform a person suspected of committing an offence of their rights not more than one hour before any interview commences. Broadly, these rights are: (a) the right to be informed of the general nature of that offence; (b) the right not to say anything other than to provide the person's name, address, date of birth, place of birth and nationality as required by s.34(4); (c) the right to have a solicitor present during any interview; and (d) if the person is being held in police custody, any rights which the person has under Ch.5 of this Act (intimation and access to other people and to legal advice).

The authority requiring the constable to provide the information specified, especially that under s.31(2)(a) [the general nature of the offence for which a suspect has been arrested] is the Right to Information (Suspects and Accused Persons) (Scotland) Regulations 2014 (SSI 2014/159). That imports EU Directive 2012/13/EU into criminal proceedings in Scotland. For ease of reference arts 3, 4 and 6 of that Directive have been reproduce earlier in the annotations for the 2016 Act: see s.5 and para.A170-019, infra.

Subs.(3)

This provides that if a person has already exercised their right to have another person or solicitor informed of their custody, then the police are not required to inform the person of these rights a second time.

Subs.(4)

A constable is not to be regarded as interviewing a person about an offence merely by asking for the person's name, address, date of birth, place of birth and nationality.

Subs.(5)

If a person is being interviewed as authorised by s.35 of this Act (which permits the court to authorise a constable to question someone who has been officially accused of an offence), the person must be told before the start of the interview about any conditions attached by the court under s.35(6) when authorising the questioning.

Right to have solicitor present

32.—(1) Subsections (2) and (3) apply to a person who— A170-090

(a) is in police custody, or

(b) is attending at a police station or other place voluntarily for the purpose of being interviewed by a constable.

(2) The person has the right to have a solicitor present while being interviewed by a constable about an offence which the constable has reasonable grounds to suspect the person of committing.

(3) Accordingly—

(a) unless the person consents to being interviewed without having a solicitor present, a constable must not begin to interview the person about the offence until the person's solicitor is present, and

(b) the person's solicitor must not be denied access to the person at any time while a constable is interviewing the person about the offence.

(4) Despite subsection (3)(a) a constable may, in exceptional circumstances, proceed to interview the person without a solicitor being present if it is necessary to interview the person without delay in the interests of—

(a) the investigation or the prevention of crime, or

(b) the apprehension of offenders.

(5) A decision to allow the person to be interviewed without a solicitor present by virtue of subsection (4) may be taken only by a constable who—

(a) is of the rank of sergeant or above, and

(b) has not been involved in investigating the offence about which the person is to be interviewed.

(6) For the purposes of subsections (2) and (3), a constable is not to be regarded as interviewing a person about an offence merely by asking the person for the information specified in section 34(4).

(7) Where a person consents to being interviewed without having a solicitor present, there must be recorded—

(a) the time at which the person consented, and

(b) any reason given by the person at that time for waiving the right to have a solicitor present.

DEFINITIONS

A170-091 "constable": s.62.

"police custody": s.64.

GENERAL NOTE

Cadder v HM Advocate [2010] UKSC 43; 2010 S.C. (U.K.S.C.) 13 required the police to advise an arrested person as a suspect of his or her right to a legal consultation before any interview occurred. Private arrangements in that regard may, of course, be made between an arrested person in these circumstances and a solicitor of their choice. Otherwise, a general duty is placed on the Scottish Legal Aid Board to make arrangements for a solicitor to be available for the purpose of providing advice and assistance: Criminal Legal Assistance (Duty Scheme) (Scotland) Regulations 2011 (SSI 2011/163) reg.3(1).

Subss.(1) and (2)

A170-092 Where a person who is either in police custody or has voluntarily attended a police station, or other place, for the purpose of being interviewed by a constable about an offence, that person has a right to have a solicitor present during the police interview where the constable reasonably suspects that person of committing that offence.

The apparently absolute nature of the terms of s.32(2) of the 2016 Act require to be read in the context of the law as applied to admittedly extreme cases. Thus, it has been held that it is a justified interference with the right to legal assistance guaranteed by art.6(3)(c) of the ECHR for the police to use powers under anti-terrorism legislation to question suspected bomb plotters without granting them access to a lawyer. The subsequent admission at trial of statements obtained during such questioning had not prejudiced their right to a fair trial as guaranteed by art.6(1): *Ibrahim v UK, Application number 50541/08: The Times Law Report* 19 December 2016.

This case arose out of the major incidents on 7 July 2005 when four suicide bombs exploded on three underground trains in central London killing 52 people and injuring countless others. Also, on 21 July 2005 four bombs were detonated on the London transport system but failed to explode. The perpetrators on this occasion fled the scene but were later arrested. The applicants had been arrested and they were temporarily refused legal assistance to enable the police on statutory authority to conduct "safety interviews". These were allowed by statute for the urgent purpose of protecting life and preventing serious damage to property.

There was no such degree of urgency in *R. v McLaughlin* [2018] NICC 10 (19 June 2018) although the facts and circumstances of the case revealed what was a well-organised murder of a prison officer. The locus was Northern Ireland but evidence was sought to be led from police officers from the Republic of Ireland. The court noted that two requests in an interview for access to a solicitor for the purpose of legal consultation outside of that interview were "ignored and glossed over": Colton J. at [184]. Reference was made to the defence argument that: "the interviews were conducted in defiance of generally accepted international norms that prevented him from having practical and effective legal representation during his interviews, protection which is closely linked to the internationally recognised protection of the right of silence". Mention was made then to *Cadder v HM Advocate*, 2011 S.C. (UKSC) 13 at [186]. The court was also of the view that the fact that the interviewee did not have the benefit of a solicitor present in the course of the 12 interviews, despite his request, is a relevant factor in considering the fairness and reliability of the evidence: at [189].

Subs.(3)

This subsection provides that, unless a person has consented to be interviewed without a solicitor present, a constable must not start to interview the person about the alleged offence until a solicitor is present and must not deny the solicitor access to the person at any time during interview.

Subs.(4)

A constable may start to interview the person without a solicitor present if satisfied it is necessary to interview the person without delay in the interests of the investigation or prevention of crime, or the apprehension of offenders. If a solicitor becomes available during such time as the police are interviewing a person, the solicitor must be allowed access to that person.

The *Ibrahim v UK* case cited above under the heading subss.(1) and (2) later came to be considered at Strasbourg, ECHR (Grand Chamber): [2017] Crim. L.R. 877. The relevance of the case in the context of "exceptional circumstances" under s.32(4) of the 2016 Act has been considered in T. Convery, "Delay in access to legal assistance at interview", 2018 Crim. L.B. 152 5–7.

Subs.(5)

There is a high test of "exceptional circumstances" in which a constable may start to interview the person without a solicitor present. The decision to do so may be taken only by a constable who is of the rank of sergeant or above, and who has not been involved in investigating the offence about which the individual is about to be interviewed.

Subs.(6)

A constable is not to be regarded as interviewing a person about an offence merely by asking for the information specified in s.34(4) namely, a person's name, address, date of birth, place of birth and nationality. Thus, a constable does not have to inform the person of their rights, as detailed in s.31(2), before asking the person for these details.

Subs.(7)

Interview without the presence of solicitor on the agreement of the person being interviewed requires the recording of the time at which the person consented and any reason given by the interviewee at that time for waiving that right.

Consent to interview without solicitor

33.—(1) Subsections (2) and (3) apply for the purpose of section 32(3)(a). **A170-093**

(2) A person may not consent to being interviewed without having a solicitor present if—

(a) the person is under 16 years of age

(b) the person is 16 or 17 years of age and subject to a compulsory supervision order, or an interim compulsory supervision order, made under the Children's Hearings (Scotland) Act 2011, or

(c) the person is 16 years of age or over and, owing to mental disorder, appears to a constable to be unable to—

(i) understand sufficiently what is happening, or

(ii) communicate effectively with the police.

(3) A person to whom this subsection applies (referred to in subsection (5) as "person A") may consent to being interviewed without having a solicitor present only with the agreement of a relevant person.

(4) Subsection (3) applies to a person who is—

(a) 16 or 17 years of age, and

(b) not precluded by subsection (2)(b) or (c) from consenting to being interviewed without having a solicitor present.

(5) For the purpose of subsection (3), "a relevant person" means—

(a) if person A is in police custody, any person who is entitled to access to person A by virtue of section 40(2),

(b) if person A is not in police custody, a person who is—

(i) at least 18 years of age, and

(ii) reasonably named by person A.

(6) In subsection (2)(c)—

(a) "mental disorder" has the meaning given by section 328 of the Mental Health (Care and Treatment) (Scotland) Act 2003,

(b) the reference to the police is to any—

(i) constable, or
(ii) person appointed as a member of police staff under section 26(1) of the Police and Fire Reform (Scotland) Act 2012.

DEFINITIONS

A170-094 "a relevant person": s.33(5).
"mental disorder": s.328 of the Mental Health (Care and Treatment) (Scotland) Act 2003.
"person A": s.33(5).
"police": s.33(6)(b).

GENERAL NOTE

A170-095 On the recent authorities, a valid waiver is a voluntary, informed and unequivocal decision not to have a solicitor present at the time of interview: *McGowan v B* [2011] UKSC 54; 2012 UKSC 182; 2012 S.L.T. 37; 2012 S.C.L. 65. It is a matter for the court of first instance as to whether a suspect has understood the implications of a refusal of legal assistance: *Barclay v Harvie* [2015] HCJAC 110; 2016 S.C.L. 101. Section 33 of this Act concerns the group of potential interviewees who may be presumed in law not to have the capacity to waive the right validly.

This section seems to be difficult to apply in practice in what are likely to be quite commonly recurring circumstances. Section 33(2) provides that a person in specified categories may not consent to being interviewed without having a solicitor present. Police officers in practice as potential interviewers, or as custody staff in the cells, are apt to read the terms of the section and conclude, not unreasonably, that a suspect as a person about to be interviewed must have a solicitor present.

What is to be done if such a person as a matter of personal choice *does not wish* to have a solicitor present at interview? The context in which that uncertainty has to be dealt with is that the Law Society of Scotland *Code of Conduct for Criminal Work* (an undated version of which is freely available online at the Society's website) contains the following:

> "Article 1—Seeking Business: (1) A solicitor shall seek or accept only those instructions which emanate from the client properly given and should not accept instructions given as a result of an inducement or subject to any improper constraint or condition."

That Article is followed by extensive guidance which need not reproduced here in its entirety. The relevant part, given the context of the peremptory nature of s.33(2) of the 2016 Act, is as follows:

> "A solicitor should accept instructions only from the client directly and not from a third party on behalf of the client. [...] instructions must come directly from the person detained and not by virtue of the police arranging for a specific solicitor to be contacted who is unknown to and has not been requested by the accused."

Accepting instructions from the client directly "and not from a third party" may be easier said than done in practical terms when the police phone, for example, to advise that a solicitor is required to attend. The term "third party" is not defined in either the Law Society of Scotland Code of Conduct for Criminal Conduct or the Police Service of Scotland Solicitor Access Guidance. However, the true issue is one of a client and solicitor relationship (principal and agent in law) and any person not involved in that legal relationship must be a third party which must include the police in whatever context they work. The term "third party" cannot be restricted by, for example, the police to mean someone other than the police, such as a near relative. An agency cannot be imposed on an unwilling or indifferent principal.

The practical answer as to what should be done by the police when there is a physical absence of a solicitor is to be found in s.32(4)(a) and (b) of the 2016 Act which allows for the *exceptional circumstances* in which a constable may proceed to interview without a solicitor present. That decision is a matter peculiarly within the discretion of the police because at that stage only they know the strength of any potential case against the suspect based on what is or is not a sufficiency of evidence. Nonetheless it would then be prudent, to say the least, to ensure that the circumstances giving rise to an operational departure from the norm are fully explained and documented.

Subs.(1)

By s.32(3)(a) unless a person consents to being interviewed without having a solicitor present, a constable must not begin to interview the person about the offences until the person's solicitor is present. In general terms anyone may decline to have a solicitor present when being interviewed by the police. However, this section provides for specific categories of individuals who may not waive that right and thus require to have a solicitor present. For the purpose of s.32(3)(a), subss.(2) and (3) apply.

Subs.(2)

A person under 16 years of age may not consent to be interviewed without a solicitor present: s.33(2)(a).

A person aged 16 or 17 and subject to a compulsory supervision order or an interim compulsory supervision order made under the Children's Hearings (Scotland) Act may not consent to be interviewed without a solicitor present: s.33(2)(b).

A person aged 16 years and over who, owing to a mental disorder, is considered by a constable to be unable to understand sufficiently what is happening or to communicate effectively with the police may not consent to be interviewed without a solicitor present: s.33(2)(c).

Subs.(3), (4) and (5)

A person who is 16 or 17 years of age and not subject to a compulsory supervision order or interim compulsory supervision order or suffering from a mental disorder may consent to be interviewed without a solicitor present with the agreement of a relevant person: s.33(4)(a).

If the person aged 16 or 17 years is in police custody, a relevant person means any person who could by s.40(2) have access to the person: s.33(5)(a).

If the person aged 16 or 17 is not in police custody, a relevant person means a person who is at least 18 years of age and is reasonably named by the 16 or 17 year old: s.33(5)(b).

Subs.(6)

The term "mental disorder" referred to in s.33(6)(a) is defined as meaning in s.238(1)(c) of the Mental Health (Care and Treatment) (Scotland) Act 2003, inter alia, "any learning disability however caused or manifested". In *R. v Jones* [2018] EWCA Crim 2816 (21 December 2018) an issue there illustrates the inherent difficulties for everyone. Trial and conviction were in 2008 and a decade or so later, the appellant was assessed by several experts as having "a significant learning disability" and that mental disorder "may have been masked at the time of his trial": at [66]–[71]. Trial counsel advised, confidentiality having been waived, that it had been apparent at the time of the trial that the appellant had learning difficulties, but that there were never any signs that he failed to understand the allegations, the legal proceedings or that he was incapable of providing instructions. On the contrary, the appellant had been able to provide clear and consistent instructions on two fundamental issues at the trial: at [72]–[76]. Submissions for the prosecution at the appeal included the point that the father of the appellant and an experienced solicitor were present during his interview, and the appellant was able to answer questions asked of him up until the point when he exercised his right to silence: at [80]. The appeal court held that the new evidence met the appropriate test. Appeal against conviction was allowed.

Person not officially accused

Questioning following arrest

34.—(1) Subsections (2) and (4) apply where— **A170-096**

(a) a person is in police custody in relation to an offence, and

(b) the person has not been officially accused of committing the offence or an offence arising from the same circumstances as the offence.

(2) A constable may put questions to the person in relation to the offence.

(3) For the avoidance of doubt, nothing in this section is to be taken to mean that a constable cannot put questions to the person in relation to any other matter.

(4) The person is under no obligation to answer any question, other than to give the following information—

(a) the person's name,

(b) the person's address,

(c) the person's date of birth,

(d) the person's place of birth (in such detail as a constable considers necessary or expedient for the purpose of establishing the person's identity), and

(e) the person's nationality.

(5) Subsection (2) is without prejudice to any rule of law as regards the admissibility in evidence of any answer given.

Definitions

"constable": s.62. **A170-097**

Foreword

Chapter 4 of the 2016 Act is headed "Police Interview". It would seem that in law an interview is merely a constable asking a person questions about an offence (s.35(1)). A constable may engage with a suspect in a "voluntary interview" that includes an attendance at a police station. The interviewee might be regarded as a suspect by the constable, and the interview is unregulated.

Whatever the earlier practice, the allegedly voluntary nature avoids, intentionally or otherwise, the statutory safeguards provided in the 2016 Act. These include time limits and access to independent legal advice.

An assertion by a constable that a person being asked questions at such a voluntary interview will be arrested if an attempt is made by the interviewee to leave the police station suggests that an unregulated interview is not voluntary.

An interview under the inhibiting but statutory conditions of the 2016 Act is surely always to be preferred. The controlled conditions in the statute provide protection for the constable (against later complaints of unfairness) when asking questions. The restraints also provide protection for the person in custody.

There is a danger in assuming problems that arise elsewhere are necessarily to be found in Scotland especially when the prescriptive rules are so different. Merely replicating the problems of others is to be avoided but for possible issues see Harriet Pierpoint, "The risks of voluntary interviews" [2020] Crim L.R. 818.

General Note

A170-098 Section 34 allows a constable to question a person following arrest provided the person has not been officially accused of the offence. "Officially charged" by s.63 means charged with the offence by the police or where a prosecutor has started proceedings in relation to the offence, or an offence arising from the same circumstances. The person to be interviewed has the right, however, not to answer any questions but must provide the police with specific details of identification (see s.34(4)), i.e. their name, address, date of birth, place of birth and nationality. Under s.34(5), at any subsequent trial of that person, the use in evidence of any answers given by a person during questioning is subject to the laws on admissibility.

It is crucial to locate any police questioning in its correct common law or statutory context because either of these regimes affects powers and therefore outcomes. In *Wilson v Brown* [2021] SAC Crim 4, a single vehicle road traffic accident case, the appellant had not been arrested. After the accident, he was asked to take a seat in a police vehicle: [5]. The police questions that followed commenced with the single statutory requirement as to who was driving the particular vehicle at the relevant time. The Court asserted generally that the "law will protect a suspect from improper or coercive questioning carried out in an intimidating or oppressive manner": [13]. Further, the "question of fairness must be considered in its correct context which involves careful consideration of the facts and circumstances of each case": [14]. The appellant was asked by the policeman what he could tell him about the accident. That was considered on appeal not to be capable of being "categorised as questioning designed to elicit an incriminating response. The fact that an incriminating response emerged does not render a fair question or process unfair": [14]. The locus of the interview, if that is what it was, formed the basis of some concern at the appeal: "[c]onducting the interview in the back of the police vehicle, whilst not ideal, cannot be considered either intimidating or oppressive given the locus of the accident on a major traffic route which at that precise area was classified as a motorway. Practical considerations would suggest that conducting the interview at the roadside might be unsafe and nosy": [14]. The appeal against conviction was refused. *Observed*: arguably, an interview at a police station, even with a solicitor in attendance, is more intimidating for a person than questions asked in the back seat of a police car: [17].

"under no obligation to answer any question"

The literature on the right to silence exercisable by individuals in the face of questioning by representatives of authority is substantial. [For example, see the texts discussed more fully below]. Scots law does not positively assert that right; instead the concept is expressed in the negative. Section 5(2)(a) of the 2016 Act provides that a person having been arrested at a police station, or arrested and taken to a police station, "*must be informed as soon as reasonably practicable that [he] is under no obligation to say anything*" other than to give the particulars specified in s.34(4) above. Different considerations apply where, rather than a response to police questioning, the person makes an unsolicited and spontaneous comment or admission against interest: see *Mullen v HM Advocate* [2011] HCJAC 55; 2011 G.W.D. 19-451.

Not all questioning under s.34 is necessarily used as evidence as there may not be subsequent criminal proceedings, or the contents of interview have no meaningful evidential use for either side. On occasions, these interviews may be referred to, or put in evidence, in, for example, civil care proceedings. Whether, and if so to what extent, adverse findings may be inferred in civil proceedings from silence at a police interview in the context of their investigation is not a question properly for discussion now. However, it would be, in the civil context, a relevant consideration in all the circumstances that a person who was interviewed and did not answer questions from a constable had been advised in that regard by a criminal lawyer: In *T and J (Children), Re* [2020] EWCA Civ 1344; [2021] 4 W.L.R. 25.

The absence of an obligation in Scots law to answer *any* question [s.34(4)'s strictures apart] means that there is no requirement that a suspect must expressly and repeatedly invoke the right to remain silent in answer to questioning as occurs in some adversarial jurisdictions: see the controversial case *Salinas v Texas* 133 U.S.S.Ct. 2174 (2013).

An appeal in the Republic of Ireland turned on their law of evidence and procedure. However, it is notable that the appellant had in answer to specific questions: either (i) made no reply; or (ii) said "no comment" in answer to questions; or (iii) said words to the effect that he had already given his account and he would not be commenting further. The court observed that "those types of answers" will generally be referred to as "no comment" answers: *DPP v SM* [2020] IECA 170 at [8]. Also, it was said that the crucial importance is that "the centrality of the right of silence" is recognised and the risk of improper adverse inferences being drawn should be kept to a minimum: [2020] IECA 170 at [32].

Statutory exceptions

There are notable statutory derogations from the general right to silence, carrying criminal penalties for non-compliance, the most familiar of which are the police powers in the Road Traffic Act 1988 (c.52) ss.172 and 178 to require specified individuals to provide information identifying a vehicle's driver; see too *Brown v Stott*, 2001 S.L.T. 59; 2001 S.C.C.R. 62; [2001] U.K.H.R.R. 333.

The Regulation of Investigatory Powers Act 2000 (c.23) s.49 and s.53(1), (5A), (6) and (7)(c) empower the criminal authorities to require a haver of disclosable information to provide specified information to enable investigative access: thus, in *R. v Nicholson*, Southampton Crown Court, unreported (31 August 2018), the defendant, arrested on suspicion of murder of a teenage girl, declined to provide his Facebook password, information which detectives considered essential to access that account as part of their investigations. He was sentenced to 14 months' imprisonment for that failure. Note too that there are substantial powers available to authorised officers to demand information under penalty within the Terrorism Act 2000 (c.11), s.53 and Sched 7, regs 2 and 18, and s.89.

Texts and articles

It is "undoubtedly the case that saying things which are untrue to the police in the course of an enquiry can constitute the crime of attempting to pervert the course of justice": *HM Advocate v Turner (Graham)* [2020] HCJ 12 per Lord Turnbull at [27] (17 January 2020: Opinion released 9 December 2020). See ibid at [33] for reference to similar earlier cases and academic contributions. Any consideration of the legal advice given by solicitors to their clients around, for example, a formal police interview requires to be considered in the context of these authorities.

Useful general discussions, reviewing the political and legal developments shaping the changes to the right to silence under English law, are found in A Owusu-Bempah, *Defendant Participation in the Criminal Process* (London: Routledge, 2017) and H. Quirk, *The Rise and Fall of the Right of Silence* (London: Routledge, 2017). For discussion of the Salinas case, see Ian C. Kerr, "Beyond Salinas v Texas: Why An Express Invocation Requirement Should Not Apply To Post-Arrest Silence", *Columbia Law Review* 161, 489-532 (2016), and esp. fn.5 on p.490 for various US cases as to the meaning of "silence" [free online].

Section 34(4) does not on a fair reading of its terms prohibit an accused from saying anything other than in response to direct questions from a constable. It is not unknown in practice for an accused, after consultation with a solicitor, to provide (in writing as a possible subsequent production or merely by reading out words into the taped record) a prepared and relevant statement and then declining to answer any subsequent questions from a constable. The approach of providing the police with such a prepared statement, after consultation with a solicitor, is a familiar one in the Crown Court in England: *Farah v Abdullah* [2020] EWHC 825 (QB) per Linden J at [212].

Person officially accused

Authorisation for questioning

35.—(1) The court may authorise a constable to question a person about an offence after the person has been officially accused of committing the offence. **A170-099**

(2) The court may grant authorisation only if it is satisfied that allowing the person to be questioned about the offence is necessary in the interests of justice.

(3) In deciding whether to grant authorisation, the court must take into account—

(a) the seriousness of the offence,

(b) the extent to which the person could have been questioned earlier in relation to the information which the applicant believes may be elicited by the proposed questioning,

(c) where the person could have been questioned earlier in relation to that information, whether it could reasonably have been foreseen at that time that the information might be important to proving or disproving that the person has committed an offence.

(4) Where subsection (5) applies, the court must give the person an opportunity to make representations before deciding whether to grant authorisation.

(5) This subsection applies where—

(a) a warrant has been granted to arrest the person in respect of the offence, or

(b) the person has appeared before a court in relation to the offence.

(6) Where granting authorisation, the court—

(a) must specify the period for which questioning is authorised, and

(b) may specify such other conditions as the court considers necessary to ensure that allowing the proposed questioning is not unfair to the person.

(7) A decision of the court—

(a) to grant or refuse authorisation, or

(b) to specify, or not to specify, conditions under subsection (6)(b), is final.

(8) In this section, "the court" means—

(a) where an indictment has been served on the person in respect of the High Court, a single judge of that court,

(b) in any other case, the sheriff.

DEFINITIONS

A170-100 "constable": s.62.
"the court": s.35(8).

GENERAL NOTE

A170-101 This section introduces a procedure enabling a constable to question an officially accused person after charge. Subsection (3) infers that the provision will only be granted in serious cases. An application can be initiated by the police before the party has appeared before court, or by the prosecutor, once formal court proceedings have been initiated by means of an apprehension warrant, or by an appearance before the court. In all cases the applicant will require to justify the grounds for the request to satisfy the parameters of subss.(2) and(3) and the court's decision is final (subs.(7)). Form 66.4–A in the Act of Adjournal (Criminal Procedure Rules 1996 Amendment) (Miscellaneous) 2018 (SSI 2018/12) refers and can include a crave for an apprehension warrant where necessary. It will be observed that s.36(3) permits both oral and written applications, but in either case the hearing of the applicant is conducted in private. It is posited that oral applications might be made by the police at the pre-court stage, and might equally be made by the prosecutor in the course of summary or solemn proceedings before the trial commences. In all cases the questioning sought must be undertaken by a constable but the identity of the officer authorised to effect it is not specified.

Since the case is still *sub judice*, common sense suggests that any hearing on the merits ought also to be conducted in private. As subs.(7) makes clear there is no appeal from the court's decision.

It is conceivable that the provision might be used to enable questioning about additional evidence uncovered since charge, or the recovery of significant forensic results which might be put to the accused, but it must be stressed that any questioning must relate to the offence previously charged or indicted. The nature of the questioning, explanation of, and justification for, its belated introduction will have to be set before the court; note that in some, but not all, circumstances it is mandatory in terms of subs.(4) that the accused be given the opportunity to respond to the application. This right does not extend to a party still to be brought before court.

Once the accused has been brought before court the shape of the proposed questioning will necessarily have to be divulged at that hearing; thus it may be considered that the provision will be limited in scope, and may have the secondary purpose, intended or not, of spelling out the strength of the prosecution case to an accused and his lawyer.

Form 66.4–B in the above Act of Adjournal details the extent of the powers of questioning permitted, and the duration and location of such questioning. Issues may yet arise over the terms of para.3 of the form which enables questioning about the offence or "an offence arising from the same circumstances as the offence". Section 35(1) seems more restrictive in its terms, but this is as yet untested. It would seem reasonable to assume that any such questioning, conducted by the police or responsible reporting agency, would be conducted on tape or otherwise recorded, but there is no specification of how the proceedings are to be preserved evidentially. Possibly the judge might specify the means of preserving the questioning within the warrant.

Perhaps the most perplexing aspect of this procedure is that, as ss.35(8) and 36(5) provide, it can be initiated at such a late point in the proceedings. It will be seen that there is no express provision for extension of statutory time bars to accommodate the procedure. A power of arrest is available to enable an accused to be brought before the court for authorised questioning (see s.37).

The fruits of the questioning, subject to the general rules of admissibility, will be admissible as evidence against, or perhaps for, that accused; see ss.261ZA and 261ZB of the 1995 Act as now amended by the 2016 Act.

Authorisation: further provision

A170-102 **36.**—(1) An application for authorisation may be made—

(a) where section 35(5) applies, by the prosecutor, or

(b) in any other case, by a constable.

(2) In subsection (1)(a), "the prosecutor" means—

(a) where an indictment has been served on the person in respect of the High Court, Crown Counsel, or
(b) in any other case, the procurator fiscal.

(3) Where an application for authorisation is made in writing (rather than orally) it must—
(a) be made in such form as may be prescribed by act of adjournal (or as nearly as may be in such form), and
(b) state whether another application has been made for authorisation to question the person about the offence or an offence arising from the same circumstances as the offence.

(4) Authorisation ceases to apply as soon as either—
(a) the period specified under section 35(6)(a) expires, or
(b) the person's trial in respect of the offence, or an offence arising from the same circumstances as the offence, begins.

(5) For the purpose of subsection (4)(b), a trial begins—
(a) in proceedings on indictment, when the jury is sworn,
(b) in summary proceedings, when the first witness for the prosecution is sworn.

(6) In this section—

"authorisation" means authorisation under section 35,
"the offence" means the offence referred to in section 35(1).

DEFINITIONS

"authorisation": s.36(6). **A170-103**
"constable": s.62.
"the offence": s.36(6).
"the prosecutor": s.36(2).

GENERAL NOTE

Subs.(1)

This sets out who may make an application for authorisation. Where the case has commenced against the accused person in terms of s.35(5) (warrant granted or actual appearance), then subs.(1)(a) provides that the application must be made by a prosecutor; otherwise by subs.(1)(b) the application should be made by a constable. **A170-104**

Any questioning will fall to be conducted by a constable, normally (but who need not be) an officer serving with Police Service of Scotland. Questioning is not conducted by the prosecutor. (The wide scope of the statutory definition of "constable" is discussed at A4-578 above). Partly this may be explained by a desire to ensure that the provisions of Chapter 4 of the Act govern procedures once the application has been granted; those familiar with the operation of the 1995 Act concerning judicial examinations, which were repealed by the 2016 Act, might well wonder whether a variation on those procedures might have been a more appropriate route at such an advanced stage of the trial proceedings.

Section 37 below enables the court to grant an arrest warrant to facilitate police questioning.

Subss.(2) and (3)

This explicitly provides that an application for further police questioning can be made even after service of an indictment or summary complaint but, as subss.(4) and (5) make clear, is not competent once a trial is held to have commenced.

Subs.(3)(a) gives the High Court of Justiciary the power to prescribe, in an Act of Adjournal, the form in which a written application seeking authorisation must be made and a written application should closely follow that form.

Subs.(3)(b), by requiring an applicant to include details of any previous applications for authorisation to question the accused person, either about the same offence, or about another offence arising out of the same circumstances, will ensure that the court has information about any such previous applications.

Subs.(4)

This subsection sets out when authorisation to question the accused person comes to an end: either when the period stipulated by the court under s.35(6)(a) expires; or, by s.36(4), in practical terms when the trial of the accused person starts.

Subs.(5)

By this subsection and for the purposes of s.36(4)(b), a trial begins in proceedings on indictment when the jury is sworn and in a summary prosecution when the first witness for the prosecution is sworn.

Arrest to facilitate questioning

A170-105 **37.**—(1) On granting authorisation under section 35, the court may also grant a warrant for the person's arrest if it seems to the court expedient to do so.

(2) The court must specify in a warrant granted under subsection (1) the maximum period for which the person may be detained under it.

(3) The person's detention under a warrant granted under subsection (1) must end as soon as—

(a) the period of the person's detention under the warrant becomes equal to the maximum period specified under subsection (2),

(b) the authorisation ceases to apply (see section 36(4)), or

(c) in the opinion of the constable responsible for the investigation into the offence referred to in section 35(1), there are no longer reasonable grounds for suspecting that the person has committed—

(i) that offence, or

(ii) an offence arising from the same circumstances as that offence.

(4) For the purpose of subsection (3)(a), the period of the person's detention under the warrant begins when the person—

(a) is arrested at a police station, or

(b) arrives at a police station, having been taken there in accordance with section 4.

(5) For the avoidance of doubt—

(a) if the person is on bail when a warrant under subsection (1) is granted, the order admitting the person to bail is not impliedly recalled by the granting of the warrant,

(b) if the person is on bail when arrested under a warrant granted under subsection (1)—

(i) despite being in custody by virtue of the warrant the person remains on bail for the purpose of section 24(5)(b) of the 1995 Act,

(ii) when the person's detention under the warrant ends, the bail order continues to apply as it did immediately before the person's arrest,

(c) if the person is subject to an undertaking given under section 25(2)(a), the person remains subject to the undertaking despite—

(i) the granting of a warrant under subsection (1),

(ii) the person's arrest and detention under it.

GENERAL NOTE

Subs.(1)

A170-106 This provides that the court may, as well as granting a warrant for the purposes of questioning by s.35, grant a warrant for the arrest of an accused person if it is expedient to do so.

Subs.(2)

When the court grants an application for a warrant it must put a time limit on the period for which the person can be detained to be questioned.

Subs.(3)

Provision is made as to when the accused person's detention, under a warrant granted in terms of this section, must come to an end.

The investigating officer's power in subs.(3)(c) can be seen to relate only to the duration, and cessation, of the s.35 authorisation of further questioning but a note of scepticism has to be sounded at the notion that that officer would (or indeed, should) assume responsibility for a decision as to sufficiency of evidence after proceedings had been initiated.

Subs.(4)

The detention of an accused person under a warrant granted in terms of s.37(1) is necessarily limited by s.37(2) and that makes it possible to determine when the period specified has expired. By subs.(4) the period of detention under the warrant begins when the person is arrested at a police station or arrives at a police station having been taken there in accordance with s.4 of this Act.

Subs.(5)

Subsections (5)(a) and (b) assert that a warrant under s.37 does not operate to recall or affect the operation of any bail order that the accused person might be on, whether in the same proceedings or not.

While the accused person is in custody, having been detained and arrested on the warrant, s.24(5)(b) of the 1995 Act, which makes it a condition of bail that the accused does not commit an offence while on bail, remains in force.

This means that if the person commits an offence while detained in custody under a warrant granted in terms of this section, it would be a breach of that condition of bail. Once the accused person's detention ends, the bail order applies in full, including any conditions attached to that order.

Subsection (5)(c) provides that, where an accused person has been liberated on an undertaking in terms of s.25 of this Act (liberation by police), the terms and conditions of the undertaking remain in force where a warrant is granted for the accused person, and continue in force after arrest and detention on that warrant.

Chapter 5 – Rights of Suspects in Police Custody

Intimation and access to another person

Right to have intimation sent to other person

38.—(1) A person in police custody has the right to have intimation sent to another person of— A170-107

(a) the fact that the person is in custody,

(b) the place where the person is in custody.

(2) Intimation under subsection (1) must be sent—

(a) where a constable believes that the person in custody is under 16 years of age, regardless of whether the person requests that it be sent,

(b) in any other case, if the person requests that it be sent.

(3) The person to whom intimation is to be sent under subsection (1) is—

(a) where a constable believes that the person in custody is under 16 years of age, a parent of the person,

(b) in any other case, an adult reasonably named by the person in custody.

(4) Intimation under subsection (1) must be sent—

(a) as soon as reasonably practicable, or

(b) if subsection (5) applies, with no more delay than is necessary.

(5) This subsection applies where an appropriate constable considers some delay to be necessary in the interests of—

(a) the investigation or prevention of crime,

(b) the apprehension of offenders, or

(c) safeguarding and promoting the wellbeing of the person in custody, where a constable believes that person to be under 18 years of age.

(6) In subsection (5), "an appropriate constable" means a constable who—

(a) is of the rank of sergeant or above, and

(b) has not been involved in the investigation in connection with which the person is in custody.

(7) The sending of intimation may be delayed by virtue of subsection (5)(c) only for so long as is necessary to ascertain whether a local authority will arrange

for someone to visit the person in custody under section 41(2).

(8) In this section and section 39—

"adult" means person who is at least 18 years of age,

"parent" includes guardian and any person who has the care of the person in custody.

Definitions

A170-108 "adult": s.38(8).
"an appropriate constable": s.38(6).
"parent": s.38(8).
"police custody": s.64.

General Note

A170-109 As a general provision s.38 allows a person in police custody the right to have someone else informed that the he or she is in police custody and where they are being held in custody. This intimation must be sent as soon as reasonably practicable after the person arrives at a police station unless "some delay" is considered necessary in the interests of the investigation or prevention of crime, the apprehension of offenders or safeguarding and promoting the wellbeing of the person where a constable believes that person to be under 18 years of age: s.38(4) and (5). "Some delay" is undefined in this Act.

Where such a delay is required, it should be for no longer than necessary: s.38(4)(b). The sending of intimation may be delayed until it has been ascertained whether a local authority will arrange for someone to visit the person in custody under s.41(2). If a constable believes that the person in police custody is under 16 years of age then, by s.38(2)(a) and (3)(a), a parent must be informed, regardless of whether the person requests that intimation be sent.

Subs.(2) is mandatory in its terms; a parent, guardian or person *in loco parentis* of an arrested person believed to be aged under 16 years and held in police custody, must be advised of both the arrest and whereabouts. The sole ground for delaying such intimation, where subs.(2) otherwise applies, would be that set out in subs.(5)(c) and qualified by subs.(7).

Section 51 below imposes a general duty upon the police in dealing with those 18 years or less to safeguard and promote the wellbeing of that individual. Those held in police custody should, so far as practicable, be segregated from adult offenders there (see s.52).

It seems likely that any interpretation of s.38(1) will require to be a generous or liberal one depending on the circumstances. In *Essex Police v Transport Arendonk BVBA* [2020] EWHC 212 (QB) (23 January 2020) there was a *civil* claim in tort for theft of a valuable load from a parked lorry which followed the lorry driver being arrested for drunk-driving and taken to a police station elsewhere. The accused driver asked for intimation to be sent to his employer to advise him of the whereabouts of the lorry. The phone number was in the unattended lorry and it seems that, notwithstanding a stated intention, the police did not go back to the lorry to retrieve the relevant phone number. The civil claim was said to be hopeless for an employer to rely on a breach of a private right under s.56(1) of the Police and Criminal Evidence Act 1984 (c.60) (the English provision that equates with s.38(1) of the 2016 Act). However, the court held, at [96], that the hopeless nature of that particular claim did not "exclude the existence of a duty on appropriate facts to tell an owner that his driver ha[d] been arrested and that his lorry ha[d] been left in a layby, or alternatively *a duty to permit the driver to tell his employer*". That suggestion of a common law duty in addition to the statutory duty arises in the context of an alleged breach of a duty of care but the existence of a parallel duty for criminal cases is not difficult to argue.

Right to have intimation sent: under 18s

A170-110 **39.**—(1) This section applies where a constable believes that a person in police custody is under 18 years of age.

(2) At the time of sending intimation to a person under section 38(1), that person must be asked to attend at the police station or other place where the person in custody is being held.

(3) Subsection (2) does not apply if—

(a) a constable believes that the person in custody is 16 or 17 years of age, and

(b) the person in custody requests that the person to whom intimation is to be sent under section 38(1) is not asked to attend at the place where the person in custody is being held.

(4) Subsections (5) and (6) apply where—

(a) it is not practicable or possible to contact, within a reasonable time, the person to whom intimation is to be sent by virtue of section 38(3),

(b) the person to whom intimation is sent by virtue of section 38(3), if asked to attend at the place where the person in custody is being held, claims to be unable or unwilling to attend within a reasonable time, or

(c) a local authority, acting under section 41(9)(a), has advised against sending intimation to the person to whom intimation is to be sent by virtue of section 38(3).

(5) Section 38(3) ceases to have effect.

(6) Attempts to send intimation to an appropriate person under section 38(1) must continue to be made until—

(a) an appropriate person is contacted and agrees to attend, within a reasonable time, at the police station or other place where the person in custody is being held, or

(b) if a constable believes that the person in custody is 16 or 17 years of age, the person requests that (for the time being) no further attempt to send intimation is made.

(7) In subsection (6), "an appropriate person" means—

(a) if a constable believes that the person in custody is under 16 years of age, a person the constable considers appropriate having regard to the views of the person in custody,

(b) if a constable believes that the person in custody is 16 or 17 years of age, an adult who is named by the person in custody and to whom a constable is willing to send intimation without a delay by virtue of section 38(5)(a) or (b).

(8) The reference in subsection (4)(a) to its not being possible to contact a person within a reasonable time includes the case where, by virtue of section 38(5)(a) or (b), a constable delays sending intimation to the person.

DEFINITIONS

"an appropriate person": s.39(7). A170-111

"police custody": s.64.

GENERAL NOTE

If a constable believes that a person in police custody is under 18 years of age, the person sent intimation under s.38 must be asked to attend at the police station or other place where the person is being held: s.39(2). A170-112

For those under 16 years the person sent intimation means a parent of the person and for those aged 16 and 17 years, an adult named by them: s.39(7).

The requirement in subs.(2) does not apply if a constable believes that the person in police custody is 16 or 17 years of age and has requested that the person notified under s.38 should not be asked to attend: s.39(3).

Whether "an appropriate person" in terms of s.39(7) is in Scots law is to be regarded as the same as "an appropriate adult" in English law remains to be decided. Assuming the concepts are the same, and they would appear to be given the similar context, then regard may be had to the line of cases from *DPP v Blake* [1989] 1W.L.R. 432 at 437 leading to *McPhee v The Queen* [2016] UKPC 2959 at [11]; The Times Law Reports, December 23, 2016. In the latter, it was reasserted that

> "an appropriate adult had to be informed that he was not expected to act simply as an observer. The purposes of his presence were, first, to advise the person being questioned and to observe whether or not the interview was being conducted properly and fairly; and, secondly, to facilitate communication with the person being interviewed."

It may be then that in Scotland if an appropriate person attends then the individual concerned must engage with the police as they will have assumed by attendance a quasi-advisory role.

Right of under 18s to have access to other person

40.—(1) Access to a person in police custody who a constable believes is under 16 years of age must be permitted to— A170-113

(a) a parent of the person,

(b) where a parent is not available, a person sent intimation under section 38 in respect of the person in custody.

(2) Access to a person in police custody who a constable believes is 16 or 17 years of age must be permitted to a person sent intimation under section 38 in respect of the person in custody where the person in custody wishes to have access to the person sent intimation.

(3) Access to a person in custody under subsection (1) or (2) need not be permitted to more than one person at the same time.

(4) In exceptional circumstances, access under subsection (1) or (2) may be refused or restricted so far as the refusal or restriction is necessary—

(a) in the interests of—

(i) the investigation or prevention of crime, or

(ii) the apprehension of offenders, or

(b) for the wellbeing of the person in custody.

(5) A decision to refuse or restrict access to a person in custody under subsection (1) or (2) may be taken only by a constable who—

(a) is of the rank of sergeant or above, and

(b) has not been involved in the investigation in connection with which the person is in custody.

(6) In this section, "parent" includes guardian and any person who has the care of the person in custody.

DEFINITIONS

A170-114 "parent": s.40(6).
"police custody": s.64.

GENERAL NOTE

A170-115 This section provides for children under 18 years of age in police custody to have access to another person. Under s.40(1) all children under 16 years of age in police custody must have access, in the first instance, to any parent to provide support. Subs.(1)(b) ensures that where a parent is not available, the child has access to another appropriate adult sent intimation under s.38, subject to the caveats in s.38(4). Section 40(2) provides similar rights of access for those aged 16 or 17 years. However, the adult granted access to the 16 or 17 year old does not have to be their parent. Subs.(3) provides that access need not be permitted to more than one person at the same time.

Social work involvement in relation to under 18s

A170-116 **41.**—(1) Intimation of the fact that a person is in police custody and the place where the person is in custody must be sent to a local authority as soon as reasonably practicable if—

(a) a constable believes that the person may be subject to a supervision order, or

(b) by virtue of subsection (5)(c) of section 38, a constable has delayed sending intimation in respect of the person under subsection (1) of that section.

(2) A local authority sent intimation under subsection (1) may arrange for someone to visit the person in custody if—

(a) the person is subject to a supervision order, or

(b) the local authority—

(i) believes the person to be under 16 years of age, and

(ii) has grounds to believe that its arranging someone to visit the person would best safeguard and promote the person's wellbeing (having regard to the effect of subsection (4)(a)).

(3) Before undertaking to arrange someone to visit the person in custody under subsection (2), the local authority must be satisfied that anyone it arranges to visit the person in custody will be able to make the visit within a reasonable time.

(4) Where a local authority arranges for someone to visit the person in custody under subsection (2)—

(a) sections 38 and 40 cease to have effect, and

(b) the person who the local authority has arranged to visit the person in custody must be permitted access to the person in custody.

(5) In exceptional circumstances, access under subsection (4)(b) may be refused or restricted so far as the refusal or restriction is necessary—

(a) in the interests of—

(i) the investigation or prevention of crime, or

(ii) the apprehension of offenders, or

(b) for the wellbeing of the person in custody.

(6) A decision to refuse or restrict access to a person in custody under subsection (4)(b) may be taken only by a constable who—

(a) is of the rank of sergeant or above, and

(b) has not been involved in the investigation in connection with which the person is in custody.

(7) Where a local authority sent intimation under subsection (1) confirms that the person in custody is—

(a) over 16 years of age, and

(b) subject to a supervision order,

sections 38 to 40 are to be applied in respect of the person as if a constable believes the person to be under 16 years of age.

(8) Subsection (9) applies where a local authority might have arranged for someone to visit a person in custody under subsection (2) but—

(a) chose not to do so, or

(b) was precluded from doing so by subsection (3).

(9) The local authority may—

(a) advise a constable that the person to whom intimation is to be sent by virtue of section 38(3) should not be sent intimation if the local authority has grounds to believe that sending intimation to that person may be detrimental to the wellbeing of the person in custody, and

(b) give advice as to who might be an appropriate person to a constable considering that matter under section 39(7) (and the constable must have regard to any such advice).

(10) In this section, "supervision order" means compulsory supervision order, or interim compulsory supervision order, made under the Children's Hearings (Scotland) Act 2011.

DEFINITIONS

"police custody": s.64. A170-117

"supervision order": s.41(10).

GENERAL NOTE

Section 41 makes provision for a local authority to be notified of the fact that a person is in police custody and where the person is being held, where a constable believes that the person may be subject to a supervision order or has delayed intimation by s.38(5). A170-118

Following intimation under subs.(1), a local authority may arrange for someone to visit the person in custody if that person is subject to a supervision order or the local authority believes the person to be under 16 years of age and arranging a visit would best safeguard and promote the person's wellbeing. The local authority must be satisfied the visit will be made within a reasonable time before arranging the visit: s.42(3).

Where a local authority arranges for someone to visit the person in custody, ss.38 and 40 cease to have effect (see s.41(4)(a)) until such time as the local authority confirms that the person in custody is over 16 years and subject to a supervision order. Sections 38 to 40 will then apply as if a constable believes the person to be under 16 years of age: s.41(7). The person who the local authority arranges to visit the person in custody must be permitted access to that person (s.41(4)(b)) unless, in exceptional circumstances, such access would affect the investigation or prevention of crime, the apprehension of offenders or the wellbeing of the person in custody: s.41(5).

Where a local authority chooses not to arrange a visit or could not do so within a reasonable time, the authority may advise a constable that the person to whom intimation is to be sent under s.38(3) should not be sent intimation if the authority has grounds to believe that such intimation may be detrimental to the person in custody and may give advice as to who might be an appropriate person to a constable who is considering the matter under s.39(7).

Vulnerable persons

Support for vulnerable persons

A170-119 **42.**—(1) Subsection (2) applies where—

(a) a person is in police custody,
(b) a constable believes that the person is 16 years of age or over, and
(c) owing to mental disorder, the person appears to the constable to be unable to—
  (i) understand sufficiently what is happening, or
  (ii) communicate effectively with the police.

(2) With a view to facilitating the provision of support of the sort mentioned in subsection (3) to the person as soon as reasonably practicable, the constable must ensure that intimation of the matters mentioned in subsection (4) is sent to a person who the constable considers is suitable to provide the support.

(3) That is, support to—

(a) help the person in custody to understand what is happening, and
(b) facilitate effective communication between the person and the police.

(4) Those matters are—

(a) the place where the person is in custody, and
(b) that support of the sort mentioned in subsection (3) is, in the view of the constable, required by the person.

(5) In this section—

(a) "mental disorder" has the meaning given by section 328 of the Mental Health (Care and Treatment) (Scotland) Act 2003,
(b) the references to the police are to any—
  (i) constable, or
  (ii) person appointed as a member of police staff under section 26(1) of the Police and Fire Reform (Scotland) Act 2012.

DEFINITIONS

A170-120 "mental disorder": s.328 of the Mental Health (Care and Treatment) (Scotland) Act 2003.
"police": s.42(5)(b).
"police custody": s.64.

GENERAL NOTE

A170-121 The Code of Practice on the Exercise of Powers Stop and Search of the Person in Scotland, made on 9 March 2017 and in force from 11 May 2017, makes certain provisions for support to be provided for vulnerable adults: see Code, para.8.1–8.13. The Code is reproduced below at C2-50.

Section 42 makes provision to identify vulnerable adults in police custody. Thereafter, such adults are to be provided with support to assist communication between them and the police. It is thought that in practice, this support is likely to be that provided by an appropriate adult though that term is not used in this Act.

Subss.(1), (2) and (4)

To ensure support is provided as soon as is reasonably practicable, subss.(1), (2) and (4) make certain requirements. They provide when read together that, where a constable considers that a person in police custody is age 16 or over and is unable, because of a mental disorder, to understand what is happening or to communicate effectively, the constable must make sure that a suitable person is told where the person is being held (this is not always at the police station and could be, for example, at a hospital) and that they require the support of an appropriate adult.

Subs.(3)

This subsection provides that the role of the person considered suitable is to assist a vulnerable person to understand what is happening and to facilitate effective communication between the vulnerable person and the police.

Intimation and access to a solicitor

Right to have intimation sent to solicitor

43.—(1) A person who is in police custody has the right to have intimation sent to a solicitor of any or all of the following— A170-122

(a) the fact that the person is in custody,

(b) the place where the person is in custody,

(c) that the solicitor's professional assistance is required by the person,

(d) if the person has been officially accused of an offence—

(i) whether the person is to be released from custody, and

(ii) where the person is not to be released, the court before which the person is to be brought in accordance with section 21(2) and the date on which the person is to be brought before that court.

(2) Where the person requests that intimation be sent under subsection (1), the intimation must be sent as soon as reasonably practicable.

DEFINITIONS

"police custody": s.64. A170-123

GENERAL NOTE

A170-124 Section 43 affords a person in police custody the right to have a solicitor informed, as soon as reasonably practicable after a request is made by the person in police custody, that that person is being held in police custody, where they are being held and that the professional assistance of a solicitor is required. If the person has been officially accused of an offence, the person has the right to have a solicitor informed whether they are to be released from custody or, if not, of the court before which the person is to be brought and the day on which the person will be brought before court.

Right to consultation with solicitor

44.—(1) A person who is in police custody has the right to have a private consultation with a solicitor at any time. A170-125

(2) In exceptional circumstances, the person's exercise of the right under subsection (1) may be delayed so far as that is necessary in the interests of—

(a) the investigation or the prevention of crime, or

(b) the apprehension of offenders.

(3) A decision to delay the person's exercise of the right under subsection (1) may be taken only by a constable who—

(a) is of the rank of sergeant or above, and

(b) has not been involved in the investigation in connection with which the person is in custody.

(4) In subsection (1), "consultation" means consultation by such method as may be appropriate in the circumstances and includes (for example) consultation by telephone.

DEFINITIONS

"consultation": s.44(4). A170-126

"police custody": s.64.

GENERAL NOTE

A170-127 Section 44 provides for the right of a person in police custody to have a private consultation with a solicitor at any time.

The police can delay the exercise of this right only so far as necessary in the interest of the investigation or prevention of crime, or the apprehension of offenders: s.44(2).

The decision to delay the exercise of a right by a person in custody may be taken only by a constable of the rank of sergeant or above, and who has not been involved in the investigation in connection with which the person is in custody: s.44(3).

A consultation is defined as a consultation by such means as considered appropriate, for example, by telephone, an example provided in the subsection: s.44(4).

The breadth of s.44(1) in establishing an absolute right to a private consultation is remarkable. While s.44(2) tends to suggest that the right relates to the subject matter for which a suspect has been arrested, s.44(1) does not in terms specify that. As consultations are private a suspect may (and wide experience anecdotally suggests they do) require a consultation about anything.

Private arrangements may, of course, be made between a person in custody who wishes a private consultation with a solicitor of their choice. Otherwise, a general duty is place on the Scottish Legal Aid Board to make arrangements for a solicitor to be available for the purpose of providing advice and assistance: Criminal Legal Assistance (Duty Scheme) (Scotland) Regulations 2011 (SSI 2011/163) reg.3(1).

Subs.(2)

As the norm is not specified in the section or elsewhere it is virtually impossible to state definitively in advance what might constitute "exceptional circumstances". At best, it might only be suggested that the statutory right is to consult with a solicitor, and not anyone else, and that such right of consultation can only be delayed for the specific reasons identified in s.44(2)(a) or (b). The inhibiting factor on the right of consultation is only one of delay and not denial. The subject matter of the consultation cannot be proscribed as such conversations are privileged professionally. Little in the way of enlightenment may be obtained, it is respectfully suggested, from other case law on the phrase "exceptional circumstances" as those cases are very specific to their statutory contexts: see e.g. W.J. Stewart, *Scottish Contemporary Judicial Dictionary of Words and Phrases* (Edinburgh: W Green, 1995) pp.201–202.

Chapter 6 – Police Powers and Duties

Powers of police

Use of reasonable force

A170-128 **45.** A constable may use reasonable force—

(a) to effect an arrest,

(b) when taking a person who is in police custody to any place.

DEFINITIONS

A170-129 "constable": s.62.

GENERAL NOTE

A170-130 A constable may use reasonable force to effect an arrest and when taking a person in custody to any place. Neither "reasonable force" nor "any place" are defined in this Act.

Common law power of entry

A170-131 **46.** Nothing in this Part affects any rule of law concerning the powers of a constable to enter any premises for any purpose.

DEFINITIONS

A170-132 "constable": s.62.

GENERAL NOTE

A170-133 Any existing powers of a constable to enter any premises for any purposes are not affected by this Act.

Common law power of search etc.

A170-134 **47.—**(1) Nothing in this Part affects any rule of law by virtue of which a constable may exercise a power of the type described in subsection (2).

(2) The type of power is a power that a constable may exercise in relation to a person by reason of the person's having been arrested and charged with an offence by a constable.

(3) Powers of the type described in subsection (2) include the power to—

(a) search the person,

(b) seize any item in the person's possession,

(c) cause the person to participate in an identification procedure.

DEFINITIONS
"constable": s.62. A170-135

GENERAL NOTE

Section 47 preserves any existing powers of a constable in relation to a person arrested and charged, for example, to search them, seize items in their possession and place them in an identification parade. A170-136

Power of search etc. on arrest

48.—(1) A constable may exercise in relation to a person to whom subsection (2) applies any power of the type described in section 47(2) which the constable would be able to exercise by virtue of a rule of law if the person had been charged with the relevant offence by a constable. A170-137

(2) This subsection applies to a person who—

(a) is in police custody having been arrested without a warrant, and

(b) has not, since being arrested, been charged with an offence by a constable.

(3) In subsection (1), "the relevant offence" means the offence in connection with which the person is in police custody.

DEFINITIONS
"constable": s.62. A170-138
"the relevant offence": s.48(3).
"police custody": s.64.

GENERAL NOTE

Section 48 preserves the powers which can be exercised by a constable in relation to a person after arrest and charge can also be exercised between the arrest of a person and that person being charged. A170-139

Taking drunk persons to designated place

49.—(1) Where— A170-140

(a) a person is liable to be arrested in respect of an offence by a constable without a warrant, and

(b) the constable is of the opinion that the person is drunk,

the constable may take the person to a designated place (and do so instead of arresting the person).

(2) Nothing done under subsection (1)—

(a) makes a person liable to be held unwillingly at a designated place, or

(b) prevents a constable from arresting the person in respect of the offence referred to in that subsection.

(3) In this section, "designated place" is any place designated by the Scottish Ministers for the purpose of this section as a place suitable for the care of drunken persons.

DEFINITIONS
"constable": s.62. A170-141
"designated place": s.49(3).

GENERAL NOTE

Section 49(1) of the 2016 Act is very similar as a matter of policy to s.5 of the Criminal Justice (Scotland) Act 1980 (c.62) which was repealed after 15 years. The new section allows the police to take a person who is considered to be drunk to a designated place (as designated by the Scottish Ministers on authority of this section). The purpose of the exercise of power in the section is not specified. It may be intended that this removal is a form of alternative to prosecution although that is not stated to be so. A170-142

The power does not, however, require the person to remain unwillingly at such a place nor does it prevent a constable from subsequently arresting the person. The assessment of the state of being "drunk" is the opinion of the constable. There is no reference to "drugged" or any other condition other than what seems to be intended, viz, alcohol intoxication.

Duties of police

Duty not to detain unnecessarily

A170-143 **50.** A constable must take every precaution to ensure that a person is not unreasonably or unnecessarily held in police custody.

DEFINITIONS

A170-144 "constable": s.62.
"police custody": s.64.

GENERAL NOTE

A170-145 No criminal penalty attaches directly by this section to a failure on the part of a constable to take every precaution to ensure that a person is not unreasonably or unnecessarily held in police custody. The consequence of a failure must be a breach of duty of care in the civil context.

Duty to consider child's wellbeing

A170-146 **51.**—(1) Subsection (2) applies when a constable is deciding whether to—

(a) arrest a child,
(b) hold a child in police custody,
(c) interview a child about an offence which the constable has reasonable grounds to suspect the child of committing, or
(d) charge a child with committing an offence.

(2) In taking the decision, the constable must treat the need to safeguard and promote the wellbeing of the child as a primary consideration.

(3) For the purposes of this section, a child is a person who is under 18 years of age.

DEFINITIONS

A170-147 "child": s.51(3).
"constable": s.62.
"police custody": s.64.

GENERAL NOTE

A170-148 Section 51 requires that in making decisions to arrest a child (being a person under the age of 18 years), hold a child in police custody, interview a child about an offence which the child is suspected of committing, or charge a child with an offence, a constable must treat the need to safeguard and promote the well-being of the child as a primary consideration.

Duties in relation to children in custody

A170-149 **52.**—(1) A child who is in police custody at a police station is, so far as practicable, to be prevented from associating with any adult who is officially accused of committing an offence other than an adult to whom subsection (2) applies.

(2) This subsection applies to an adult if a constable believes that it may be detrimental to the wellbeing of the child mentioned in subsection (1) to prevent the child and adult from associating with one another.

(3) For the purposes of this section—

"child" means person who is under 18 years of age,
"adult" means person who is 18 years of age or over.

DEFINITIONS

A170-150 "adult": s.52(3).
"child": s.52(3).
"police custody": s.64.

GENERAL NOTE

A170-151 A child who is in police custody at a police station should, so far as practicable, be prevented from associating with any adult who is officially accused of committing an offence unless a constable believes it would be detrimental to the child's wellbeing to prevent them from associating with that particular adult.

This is not a theoretical duty nor an impractical one as the duty may extend, paradoxically, to some of the most serious cases. In *HM Advocate v X* Unreported 7 March 2016 High Court of Justiciary sitting at Aberdeen, in the trial before Lady Stacey and a jury, the charge against the 16-year-old accused was that of the murder by stabbing of a fellow student at the same school.

Duty to inform Principal Reporter if child not being prosecuted

53.—(1) Subsections (2) and (3) apply if— **A170-152**

(a) a person is being kept in a place of safety in accordance with section 22(2) when it is decided not to prosecute the person for any relevant offence, and

(b) a constable has reasonable grounds for suspecting that the person has committed a relevant offence.

(2) The Principal Reporter must be informed, as soon as reasonably practicable, that the person is being kept in a place of safety under subsection (3).

(3) The person must be kept in a place of safety under this subsection until the Principal Reporter makes a direction under section 65(2) of the Children's Hearings (Scotland) Act 2011.

(4) An offence is a "relevant offence" for the purpose of subsection (1) if—

(a) it is the offence with which the person was officially accused, leading to the person being kept in the place of safety in accordance with section 22(2), or

(b) it is an offence arising from the same circumstances as the offence mentioned in paragraph (a).

(5) In this section, "place of safety" has the meaning given in section 202(1) of the Children's Hearings (Scotland) Act 2011.

DEFINITIONS

"place of safety": s.53(5). **A170-153**
"relevant offence": s.53(5).

GENERAL NOTE

The Principal Reporter must be informed as soon as reasonably practicable that the person, a child within the meaning of the 2016 Act, is being kept in a place of safety until the Principal Reporter makes a statutory direction. **A170-154**

Chapter 7 – General

Common law and enactments

Abolition of pre-enactment powers of arrest

54. A constable has no power to arrest a person without a warrant in respect of an offence that has been or is being committed other than— **A170-155**

(a) the power of arrest conferred by section 1,

(b) the power of arrest conferred by section 41(1) of the Terrorism Act 2000.

DEFINITIONS

"constable": s.62. **A170-156**

GENERAL NOTE

Section 54 provides that the only power of arrest which the police have to take a person into police custody is that in s.1 of this Act and s.41(1) of the Terrorism Act 2000. **A170-157**

For modification of primary and secondary legislation to remove powers of arrest abolished by s.54 and to remove other obsolete references to detention see SSI 2017/452, which came into force on 25 January 2018. These regulations also contain some transitional provisions for individuals detained or arrested before the appointed day and still in custody after then.

Abolition of requirement for constable to charge

A170-158 **55.** Any rule of law that requires a constable to charge a person with an offence in particular circumstances is abolished.

DEFINITIONS

A170-159 "constable": s.62.

GENERAL NOTE

A170-160 A constable does not have to charge a suspect with a crime at any time and s.55 abolishes any rule of law that requires such a charge to be made.

Consequential modification

A170-161 **56.** Schedule 2 contains repeals and other provisions consequential on this Part.

Code of practice about investigative functions

Code of practice about investigative functions

A170-162 **57.**—(1) The Lord Advocate must issue a code of practice on—

(a) the questioning, and recording of questioning, of persons suspected of committing offences, and

(b) the conduct of identification procedures involving such persons.

(2) The Lord Advocate—

(a) must keep the code of practice issued under subsection (1) under review,

(b) may from time to time revise the code of practice.

(3) The code of practice is to apply to the functions exercisable by or on behalf of—

(a) the Police Service of Scotland,

(b) such other bodies as are specified in the code (being bodies responsible for reporting offences to the procurator fiscal).

(4) Before issuing the code of practice, the Lord Advocate must consult publicly on a draft of the code.

(5) When preparing a draft of the code of practice for public consultation, the Lord Advocate must consult—

(a) the Lord Justice General,

(b) the Faculty of Advocates,

(c) the Law Society of Scotland,

(d) the Scottish Police Authority,

(e) the chief constable of the Police Service of Scotland,

(f) the Scottish Human Rights Commission,

(g) the Commissioner for Children and Young People in Scotland,

(ga) any body which the Lord Advocate intends to specify in the code under subsection (3)(b) and (where relevant) the Secretary of State, and

(h) such other persons as the Lord Advocate considers appropriate.

(6) The Lord Advocate must lay before the Scottish Parliament a copy of the code of practice issued under this section.

(7) A court or tribunal in civil or criminal proceedings must take the code of practice into account when determining any question arising in the proceedings to which the code is relevant.

(8) Breach of the code of practice does not of itself give rise to grounds for any legal claim whatsoever.

(9) Subsections (3) to (8) apply to a revised code of practice under subsection (2)(b) as they apply to the code of practice issued under subsection (1).

AMENDMENTS

Subs.(5)(ga) inserted by Criminal Justice (Scotland) Act 2016 (Consequential Provisions) Order 2018 (SI 2018/46) art.10(4)(b) (effective 25 January 2018).

GENERAL NOTE

The effect of this section is that the Lord Advocate must issue a code of practice on the matters specified in the respective subs.(1)(a) and 1(b) and (2) and to keep such a code of practice under review. The code will apply to the Police Service of Scotland and such other bodies specified in the code who report offences to the procurator fiscal. **A170-163**

It is to be inferred from the obligation (in subs.6)) on the Lord Advocate to lay a copy of the code of practice before the Scottish Parliament that the code will be put into the public domain. The code must be considered to have a status that is in essence instructive, rather than anything else, as breach of the code (by subs.(8)) does not of itself give rise to grounds for "any legal claim whatsoever".

Code of practice about investigative functions

Notwithstanding the apparently limited terms of s.57, the Lord Advocate may competently, in a code of practice, deal with matters that are outside the legislative competence of the Scottish Parliament. Accordingly, the restrictions in s.29(2)(b) and (c) of the Scotland Act 1998 (c.46) do not constrain the contents of the code of practice. The code of practice is to apply to the Police Service of Scotland and it may apply to such other bodies as are named within that code of practice (being bodies responsible for reporting offences to the procurator fiscal). Yet, the Lord Advocate may specify a body in the code of practice to whom that code applies notwithstanding that it is outwith the legislative competence of the Scottish Parliament to make provision about that body of functions which are excisable by it or on its behalf. The code of practice is necessarily restricted, by the terms of the statutory instrument aftermentioned, to the questioning, and recording of questioning, of persons suspected of committing an offence; and to the conduct of identification procedures involving such persons: see SI 2018/46 art.10. Brought into force on 17 January 2018 by SI 2018/46 art.2(1)(b).

Modifications to Part as it applies in certain cases

Arrest without warrant otherwise than in respect of an offence

57A.—(1) In a case where— **A170-163.1**

(a) a constable arrests a person without a warrant, and

(b) the arrest is not in respect of an offence,

this Part applies subject to the modifications set out in section 57C.

(2) For the avoidance of doubt, where it is stated (in whatever terms) that a provision applies in the case of a person arrested without a warrant only if the arrest is in respect of an offence, subsection (1) does not cause that provision to apply in the case of a person who has been arrested otherwise than in respect of an offence.

(3) For the avoidance of doubt, the powers of arrest conferred by the following enactments are (for the purposes of this Part) powers to arrest otherwise than in respect of an offence—

(a) sections 6D and 7(5A) of the Road Traffic Act 1988 1;

(b) section 40 of the Prisons (Scotland) Act 1989 2;

(c) sections 19(6), 19AA(12) and 28(1) of the 1995 Act 3;

(d) section 4(1) of the Protection from Abuse (Scotland) Act 2001;

(e) section 5 of the Extradition Act 2003 4;

(f) section 28 of the Adult Support and Protection (Scotland) Act 2007.

AMENDMENTS

Section 57A inserted by Criminal Justice (Scotland) Act 2016 (Modification of Part 1 and Ancillary Provision) Regulations 2017 (SSI 2017/453) reg.2 (effective 25 January 2018).

DEFINITIONS

"constable": s.62. **A170-163.2**

GENERAL NOTE

This section, taken with ss. 57B and 57C, modify the 2016 Act in relation to its application to people who have been arrested by the police on a legal basis other than s.1 of the 2016 Act. The last authority cited gives a constable the power to arrest someone without a warrant on the strength of a suspicion that the person has committed an offence. These sections modify that position. **A170-163.3**

Arrest under warrant other than an initiating warrant

A170-163.4 **57B.**—(1) In a case where a person is arrested by a constable under a relevant warrant, this Part applies subject to the modifications set out in section 57C.

(2) For the avoidance of doubt, subsection (1) does not cause section 21(2) to apply in the case of a person arrested under a relevant warrant.

(3) In this section, "relevant warrant" means any warrant other than one granted for the purpose of having a person brought before a court in connection with an offence which the person is officially accused of committing.

AMENDMENTS

Section 57B inserted by Criminal Justice (Scotland) Act 2016 (Modification of Part 1 and Ancillary Provision) Regulations 2017 (SSI 2017/453) reg.2 (effective 25 January 2018).

DEFINITIONS

A170-163.5 "constable": s.62.
"relevant warrant": s.57B(3).

GENERAL NOTE

A170-163.6 See the general note for s.57A.

Modifications applying by virtue of sections 57A and 57B

A170-163.7 **57C.**—(1) The modifications referred to in sections 57A(1) and 57B(1) are as follows.

(2) Chapter 3 applies as though for the words "brought before a court in accordance with section 21(2)" (in each place where they occur) there were substituted "brought before a court in accordance with an enactment, rule of law or a term of the warrant under which the person was arrested".

(3) Section 23(2) applies as though—

(a) paragraph (c) read "the reason that the person is to be brought before the court,", and

(b) paragraph (d) were omitted.

(4) Section 24 applies as though-

(a) in subsection (3)(c), for the words "officially accused" there were substituted "informed that the person is to be brought before a court", and

(b) subsection (4)(c) read "the reason that the person is to be brought before the court."

(5) Section 43(1) applies as though for paragraph (d) there were substituted—

"(d) if there is a requirement to bring the person before a court in accordance with an enactment, rule of law or a term of the warrant under which the person was arrested—

(i) whether the person is to be released from custody, and

(ii) where the person is not to be released, the court before which the person is to be brought in accordance with the requirement and the date on which the person is to be brought before that court."

AMENDMENTS

Section 57C inserted by Criminal Justice (Scotland) Act 2016 (Modification of Part 1 and Ancillary Provision) Regulations 2017 (SSI 2017/453) reg.2 (effective 25 January 2018).

DEFINITIONS

A170-163.8 "constable": s.62.

GENERAL NOTE

A170-163.9 The modifications referred to in ss.57A and 57B are set out in s.57C.

Arrest under an extradition arrest power

57D.—(1) In a case where a person is arrested under an extradition arrest power (within the meaning of section 174(2) of the Extradition Act 2003), this Part applies subject to the following further modifications. **A170-163.10**

(2) The following do not apply—

(a) sections 3 and 4,

(b) sections 25 to 30,

(c) section 50.

(3) In section 5—

(a) subsection (1)(b) is to be read as if the words "in accordance with section 4" were omitted,

(b) subsection (2)(a) is to be read as if the words "other than to give the information specified in section 34(4)" were omitted, and

(c) subsection (3) is to be read as if the words "of Articles 3 and 4" were omitted.

(4) Section 6 is to be read as if—

(a) in subsection (1)(c) the words "in accordance with section 4" were omitted,

(b) subsection (1)(d) were omitted,

(c) subsection (2)(a) were omitted,

(d) subsection (2)(c) were omitted, and

(e) subsections (3) to (8) were omitted.

(6) Section 23 is to be read as if—

(a) subsection (1)(b) were omitted,

(b) subsection (2)(d) were omitted.

(7) Section 24 is to be read as if subsection (1)(b) were omitted.

(8) Section 48 is to be read as if—

(a) for subsection (2) there were substituted—

> "(2) This subsection applies to a person who is in police custody having been arrested under an extradition arrest power (within the meaning of section 174(2) of the Extradition Act 2003).", and

(b) for subsection (3) there were substituted—

> "(3) In subsection (1), "the relevant offence" means the offence that would have been committed were the act constituting the relevant offence (within the meaning of section 164(3) of the Extradition Act 2003) done in Scotland."

AMENDMENTS

Section 57D inserted by Criminal Justice (Scotland) Act 2016 (Consequential Provisions) Order 2018 (SI 2018/46) art.9 and Sch.5 para.2 (effective 25 January 2018, being the day on which s.14 of the 1995 Act (c.46) was repealed).

[THE NEXT PARAGRAPH IS A170-164]

Disapplication of Part

Disapplication in relation to service offences

58.—(1) References in this Part to an offence do not include a service offence. **A170-164**

(2) Nothing in this Part applies in relation to a person who is arrested in respect of a service offence.

(2A) This section is subject to Schedule 4 to the Criminal Justice (Scotland) Act 2016 (Consequential Provisions) Order 2018 (SI 2018/46).

(3) In this section, "service offence" has the meaning given by section 50(2) of the Armed Forces Act 2006.

AMENDMENTS

Subs.(2A) inserted by Criminal Justice (Scotland) Act 2016 (Consequential Provisions) Orders 2018 (SSI 2018/46) art.24 (effective 25 January 2018, being the day on which s.14 of the 1995 Act (c.46) was repealed).

DEFINITIONS

A170-165 "service offence": s.50(2) of the Armed Forces Act 2006.

GENERAL NOTE

A170-166 Service offences are not included in this Part of this Act. Service offences are those offences committed by service personnel under the Armed Forces Act 2006.

Disapplication in relation to terrorism offences

A170-167 **59.**—(1) Nothing in this Part applies in relation to a person who is arrested under section 41(1) of the Terrorism Act 2000.

(2) Subsection (1) is subject to paragraph 18 of Schedule 8 to the Terrorism Act 2000.

GENERAL NOTE

A170-168 Part 1 of this Act, dealing with arrest and custody, does not apply to persons arrested under the Terrorism Act 2000.

Powers to modify Part

Further provision about application of Part

A170-169 **60.**—(1) The Scottish Ministers may by regulations modify this Part to provide that some or all of it—

(a) applies in relation to persons to whom it would otherwise not apply because of—

(i) section 58, or

(ii) section 59,

(b) does not apply in relation to persons arrested otherwise than under section 1.

(2) The Scottish Ministers may by regulations make such modifications to this Part as seem to them necessary or expedient in relation to its application to persons mentioned in subsection (1).

(3) Regulations under this section may make different provision for different purposes.

(4) Regulations under this section are subject to the affirmative procedure.

GENERAL NOTE

A170-170 This section allows the Scottish Ministers by regulations to modify Part 1 to either provide that some or all of it applies to persons to whom it otherwise does not apply because of ss.58 and 59, or to dis-apply some or all of it so that it does not operate in relation to people who have been arrested otherwise than in respect of an offence.

Further provision about vulnerable persons

A170-171 **61.**—(1) The Scottish Ministers may by regulations—

(a) amend subsections (2)(c) and (6) of section 33,

(b) amend subsections (1)(c), (3) and (5) of section 42,

(c) specify descriptions of persons who may for the purposes of subsection (2) of section 42 be considered suitable to provide support of the sort mentioned in subsection (3) of that section (including as to training, qualifications and experience).

(2) Regulations under subsection (1) are subject to the affirmative procedure.

GENERAL NOTE

Section 61 allows the Scottish Ministers to modify, by regulations, the provisions which provide that those aged over 16 and who have a mental disorder are unable to consent to being interviewed without a solicitor being present. A170-172

Interpretation of Part

Meaning of constable

62. In this Part, "constable" has the meaning given by section 99(1) of the Police and Fire Reform (Scotland) Act 2012. A170-173

GENERAL NOTE

The definition of "constable" in s.99(1) of the Police and Fire Reform (Scotland) Act 2012 (asp 8) is in the following terms: ""constable" means an individual holding the office of constable who is serving as a constable of the Police Service and includes (a) the chief constable, (b) other senior officers, (c) any special constable, (d) any constable on temporary service outwith the Police Service, and (e) any individual engaged on temporary service as a constable of the Police Service under arrangements made under section 16 [of the 2012 Act] (Temporary service as constable of the Police Service of Scotland)". A170-174

A constable of British Transport Police has all the powers of a constable, including any powers conferred on a constable during the continuance of his or her appointment: *Smith v Dudgeon*, 1982 S.C.C.R. 451.

Meaning of officially accused

63. For the purposes of this Part, a person is officially accused of committing an offence if— A170-175

(a) a constable charges the person with the offence, or
(b) the prosecutor initiates proceedings against the person in respect of the offence.

GENERAL NOTE

This section defines the meaning of "officially accused" for the purposes of this Part. A170-176

Meaning of police custody

64.—(1) For the purposes of this Part, a person is in police custody from the time the person is arrested by a constable until any one of the events mentioned in subsection (2) occurs. A170-177

(2) The events are—

(a) the person is released from custody,
(b) the person is brought before a court in accordance with section 21(2),
(c) the person is brought before a court under section 28(2) or (3) of the 1995 Act,
(ca) the person is brought before a court in accordance with—
  (i) any other enactment or rule of law which requires that a person in custody be brought before a court, or
  (ii) a term of the warrant under which the person was arrested,
(cb) the person is transferred in accordance with the law into the custody of a person who is neither—
  (i) a constable, nor
  (ii) a member of police staff appointed under section 26(1) of the Police and Fire Reform (Scotland) Act 2012,
(d) the Principal Reporter makes a direction under section 65(2)(b) of the Children's Hearings (Scotland) Act 2011 that the person continue to be kept in a place of safety.

AMENDMENTS

Subs.(2) as amended by Criminal Justice (Scotland) Act 2016 (Modification of Part 1 and Ancillary Provision) Regulations 2017 (SSI 2017/453) reg.2 (effective 25 January 2018).

DEFINITIONS

A170-178 "constable": s.62.

GENERAL NOTE

A170-179 This section defines the meaning of "police custody" for the purposes of this Part.

PART 2 – SEARCH BY POLICE

Chapter 1 – Search of Person not in Police Custody

Lawfulness of search by constable

Limitation on what enables search

A170-180 **65.**—(1) This section applies in relation to a person who is not in police custody.

(2) It is unlawful for a constable to search the person otherwise than—

(a) in accordance with a power of search conferred in express terms by an enactment, or

(b) under the authority of a warrant expressly conferring a power of search.

DEFINITIONS

A170-181 "constable": s.62.
"police custody": s.64.

GENERAL NOTE

A170-182 Where a person is not in police custody a constable may only search that person on statutory authority or when in possession of a warrant.

Cases involving removal of person

A170-183 **66.**—(1) A person who is not in police custody may be searched by a constable while the person is to be, or is being, taken to or from any place—

(a) by virtue of any enactment, warrant or court order requiring or permitting the constable to do so, or

(b) in circumstances in which the constable believes that it is necessary to do so with respect to the care or protection of the person.

(2) A search under this section is to be carried out for the purpose of ensuring that the person is not in, or does not remain in, possession of any item or substance that could cause harm to the person or someone else.

(3) Anything seized by a constable in the course of a search carried out under this section may be retained by the constable.

DEFINITIONS

A170-184 "constable": s.62.
"police custody": s.64.

GENERAL NOTE

A170-185 Where a person is not in police custody a constable may search that person while the person is to be, or is being, taken to or from any place on lawful authority or the constable believes such a search is necessary for the care and protection of the person. The question of harm to the person being searched or anyone else is important in regard to such a search. Anything recovered by a constable during such a search may be retained.

The Code of Practice on the Exercise of Powers Stop and Search of the Person in Scotland, made on 9 March 2017 and in force from 11 May 2017, is the document to which regard must be had in exercising the authority under s.66: see Code, Annex A. The Code is reproduced below at C2-50.

Subs.(1)(b)

The belief of the constable of the necessity for a search on a strict reading of the subsection is not required to follow on "reasonable suspicion". The statutory reason for the search is ostensibly the care and protection of the person being searched, and thus probably very little in the way of a belief of necessity is required on the part of a constable. In these circumstances the exercise of the authority is perhaps to be considered as wholly a matter of necessity generally. No reason for such a search would seem to be required to be given to the individual being searched, following the analogy in *Karia v Secretary of State for the Home Department* [2018] EWCA Civ 1673; *Times*, September 5, 2018 (customs officer stopping and searching baggage).

Public safety at premises or events

67.—(1) A person who is not in police custody may be searched by a constable if— **A170-186**

(a) the person—

(i) is seeking to enter, or has entered, relevant premises, or

(ii) is seeking to attend, or is attending, a relevant event, and

(b) the further criteria are met.

(2) Premises are or an event is relevant if—

(a) the premises may be entered, or the event may be attended, by members of the public (including where dependent on possession of a ticket or on payment of a charge), and

(b) the entry or the attendance is controlled, at the time of the entry or the attendance, by or on behalf of the occupier of the premises or the organiser of the event.

(3) The further criteria to be met are that—

(a) the entry or the attendance is subject to a condition, imposed by the occupier of the premises or the organiser of the event, that the person consents to being searched, and

(b) the person informs the constable that the person consents to being searched by the constable.

(4) A search under this section is to be carried out for the purpose of ensuring the health, safety or security of people on the premises or at the event.

(5) Anything seized by a constable in the course of a search carried out under this section may be retained by the constable.

DEFINITIONS

"constable": s.62. **A170-187**
"police custody": s.64.
"relevant event": s.67(2).
"relevant premises": s.67(2).

GENERAL NOTE

The generality of the terms of this section make it desirable to consider the detail as the powers in the section will apply to a very large range of sporting, social and other gatherings. **A170-188**

The Code of Practice on the Exercise of Powers Stop and Search of the Person in Scotland, made on 9 March 2017 and in force from 11 May 2017, is the document to which regard must be had in exercising the authority under s.67: see Code, para.9.1 and Annex A. The Code is reproduced below at C2-50.

Subs.(1)

A person who is not in police custody may be searched when that person is seeking to enter or has entered relevant premises or a relevant event.

Subs.(2)

The relevant premises or the relevant events are those that: (a) may be attended by members of the public, by ticket or payment, and (b) entry or attendance is controlled by or on behalf of the occupier of the premises or the organiser of the event. The link of "and" between the subsections suggests that both must be met for the section to apply. The further criteria to be met are specified in subs.(3).

Subs.(3)

The further criteria is that entry or attendance includes a condition that those there agree to a search and the person then tells a constable that they agree to a search. The link of "and" between the subsections suggests that both must be met for the section to apply.

Subs.(4)

The purpose of a search is to ensure the health and safety or security of "people on the premises or at the event": the breadth of that terms tends to suggest that the people protected includes the security or other employees there and not only other patrons.

Subs.(5)

Anything recovered by a constable during such a search may be retained.

Duty to consider child's wellbeing

A170-189 **68.**—(1) Subsection (2) applies when a constable is deciding whether to search a child who is not in police custody.

(2) In taking the decision, the constable must treat the need to safeguard and promote the wellbeing of the child as a primary consideration.

(3) For the purposes of this section, a child is a person who is under 18 years of age.

DEFINITIONS

A170-190 "constable": s.62.
"police custody": s.64.

GENERAL NOTE

A170-191 A child for this section is a person who is under the age of 18 years. In taking a decision to search a child, a constable must treat the need to safeguard and promote the wellbeing of the child as a primary consideration.

The Code of Practice on the Exercise of Powers Stop and Search of the Person in Scotland, made on 9 March 2017 and in force from 11 May 2017, is the document to which regard must be had in exercising the authority under s.68: see Code, paras 7.1–7.33. The Code is reproduced below at C2-50.

Miscellaneous and definitions

Publication of information by police

A170-192 **69.**—(1) The Police Service of Scotland must ensure that, as soon as practicable after the end of each reporting year, information is published on how many times during the reporting year a search was carried out by a constable—

(a) of a person not in police custody, and
(b) otherwise than under the authority of a warrant expressly conferring a power of search.

(2) So far as practicable, the information is to disclose (in addition)—

(a) how many persons were searched on two or more occasions,
(b) the age and gender, and the ethnic and national origin, of the persons searched,
(c) the proportion of searches that resulted in—
  (i) something being seized by a constable,
  (ii) a case being reported to the procurator fiscal,
(d) the number of complaints made to the Police Service of Scotland about the carrying out of searches (or the manner in which they were carried out).

(3) In this section, "reporting year" means a yearly period ending on 31 March.

DEFINITIONS

A170-193 "police custody": s.64.
"reporting year": s.69(3).

GENERAL NOTE

Concern amongst Parliamentarians and some members of the public about the general practice by the police of stopping and searching specific groups of people led to extensive political discussion about recent police practices. This section calls on the police to record and state statistically what has been done. A170-194

Provisions about possession of alcohol

70.—(1) The Scottish Ministers may by regulations amend section 61 (confiscation of alcohol from persons under 18) of the Crime and Punishment (Scotland) Act 1997 so as to confer on a constable a power, exercisable in addition to the power in subsection (1) or (2) of that section— A170-195

(a) to search a person for alcoholic liquor,
(b) to dispose of anything found in the person's possession that the constable believes to be such liquor.

(2) Prior to laying before the Scottish Parliament a draft of an instrument containing regulations under this section, the Scottish Ministers must—

(a) consult publicly on the regulations that they are proposing to make,
(b) send a copy of the proposed regulations to—
  (i) the chief constable of the Police Service of Scotland,
  (ia) the chief constable of the British Transport Police Force,
  (ib) the chief constable of the Civil Nuclear Constabulary,
  (ic) the chief constable of the Ministry of Defence Police,
  (ii) the Scottish Human Rights Commission,
  (iii) the Commissioner for Children and Young People in Scotland, and
  (iv) such other persons as the Scottish Ministers consider appropriate.

(3) When laying before the Scottish Parliament a draft of an instrument containing regulations under this section, the Scottish Ministers must also so lay a statement—

(a) giving reasons for wishing to make the regulations as currently framed (and confirming whether the regulations will amend the relevant enactment in the same way as shown in the proposed regulations),
(b) summarising—
  (i) the responses received by them to the public consultation on the proposed regulations,
  (ii) the representations made to them by the persons to whom a copy of the proposed regulations was sent.

(4) Regulations under this section are subject to the affirmative procedure.

AMENDMENTS

Subs.(2)(b) as amended by Criminal Justice (Scotland) Act 2016 (Consequential Provisions) Orders 2018 (SSI 2018/46) art.24 (effective 17 January 2018).

Note: section 70 is not yet in force.

GENERAL NOTE

The local and delegated legislation allowed a general practice by the police in some parts of Scotland of stopping and searching people for alcoholic liquor. This section allows the Scottish Ministers by delegated legislation to amend the relevant principal legislation. A170-196

Matters as to effect of sections 65, 66 and 70

71.—(1) The day appointed for the coming into force of sections 65 and 66 is to be the same as the day from which a code of practice required by section 73(1) has effect by virtue of the first regulations made under section 77. A170-197

(2) If no regulations under section 70 are made before the end of the 2 years beginning with the day from which a code of practice required by section 73(1) has

effect by virtue of the first regulations made under section 77, section 70 is to be regarded as repealed at the end of that period.

DEFINITIONS

A170-198 "constable": s.62.

GENERAL NOTE

A170-199 This section prescribes co-ordinated times for the coming into force of s.65 (limitation on what enables search), s.66 (cases involving removal of persons) and s.70 (provisions about possession of alcohol) and time limits for doing so.

Meaning of constable etc.

A170-200 **72.** In this Chapter—

"constable" has the meaning given by section 99(1) of the Police and Fire Reform (Scotland) Act 2012,

"police custody" has the same meaning as given for the purposes of Part 1 (see section 64).

Chapter 2 – Code of Practice

Making and status of code

Contents of code of practice

A170-201 **73.**—(1) The Scottish Ministers must make a code of practice about the carrying out of a search of a person who is not in police custody.

(2) A code of practice must set out (in particular)—

(a) the circumstances in which a search of such a person may be carried out,

(b) the procedure to be followed in carrying out such a search,

(c) in relation to such a search—

(i) the record to be kept,

(ii) the right of someone to receive a copy of the record.

(3) A code of practice is to apply to the functions exercisable by a constable.

(4) In this section—

"constable" has the meaning given by section 99(1) of the Police and Fire Reform (Scotland) Act 2012,

"police custody" has the same meaning as given for the purposes of Part 1 (see section 64).

(5) In this Chapter, a reference to a code of practice means one required by subsection (1) (but see also section 74(5)).

DEFINITIONS

A170-202 "constable": s.62.
"police custody": s.64.

GENERAL NOTE

A170-203 This section follows on from the duty placed on the Police Service of Scotland by s.69 of this Act.

The Code of Practice on the Exercise of Powers Stop and Search of the Person in Scotland, made on 9 March 2017 and in force from 11 May 2017, is the document made in terms of s.73. The Code is reproduced below at C2-50.

Subs.(2)(c)

For details of "the record to be kept" see the Code Practice on the Exercise of Powers Stop and Search of the Person in Scotland at paras 9.1–9.3. The Code is reproduced below at C2-50.

Review of code of practice

74.—(1) The Scottish Ministers may revise a code of practice in light of a review conducted under subsection (2). A170-204

(2) The Scottish Ministers must conduct a review of a code of practice as follows—

(a) a review is to begin no later than 2 years after the code comes into effect,

(b) subsequently, a review is to begin no later than 4 years after—

(i) if the code is revised in light of the previous review under this subsection, the coming into effect of the revised code, or

(ii) otherwise, the completion of the previous review under this subsection.

(3) So far as practicable, a review conducted under subsection (2) must be completed within 6 months of the day on which the review begins.

(4) In deciding when to conduct a review in accordance with subsection (2), the Scottish Ministers must have regard to representations put to them on the matter by—

(a) the Scottish Police Authority,

(b) the chief constable of the Police Service of Scotland,

(c) Her Majesty's Inspectors of Constabulary in Scotland.

(d) the British Transport Police Authority,

(e) the chief constable of the British Transport Police Force,

(f) the Civil Nuclear Police Authority,

(g) the chief constable of the Civil Nuclear Constabulary,

(h) the chief constable of the Ministry of Defence Police, or

(i) the Secretary of State.

(5) For the purposes of—

(a) section 73(3) and this section (except subsection (2)(a)), and

(b) sections 75, 76 (except subsection (3)) and 77 (except subsection (3)),

a reference to a code of practice includes a revised code as allowed by subsection (1).

AMENDMENTS

Subs.(4) as amended by Criminal Justice (Scotland) Act 2016 (Consequential Provisions) Orders 2018 (SSI 2018/46) art.11 (effective 17 January 2018).

DEFINITIONS

"constable": s.62. A170-205

"police custody": s.64.

GENERAL NOTE

This section follows on from the developments in ss.69 and 73 of this Act. A170-206

Legal status of code of practice

75.—(1) A court or tribunal in civil or criminal proceedings must take a code of practice into account when determining any question arising in the proceedings to which the code is relevant. A170-207

(2) Breach of a code of practice does not of itself give rise to grounds for any legal claim whatsoever.

GENERAL NOTE

The enthusiasm of the Scottish Parliament for codes of practice has led to this provision that requires "a court or tribunal in civil or criminal proceedings" to take into account a relevant code when determining any question arising in proceedings to which the code applies. Standing the effective disapplication under subs.(2), it would seem that the potential effect of subs.(1) must be very much constrained. A170-208

The Code of Practice on the Exercise of Powers Stop and Search of the Person in Scotland, made on 9 March 2017 and in force from 11 May 2017, is the document to which regard must be had in terms of s.75: see Code, para.3.5. The Code is reproduced below at C2-50.

Procedure applying to code

Consultation on code of practice

A170-209 **76.**—(1) Prior to making a code of practice, the Scottish Ministers must consult publicly on a draft of the code.

(2) When preparing a draft of a code of practice for public consultation, the Scottish Ministers must consult—

(a) the Lord Justice General,
(b) the Faculty of Advocates,
(c) the Law Society of Scotland,
(d) the Scottish Police Authority,
(e) the chief constable of the Police Service of Scotland,
(ea) the British Transport Police Authority,
(eb) the chief constable of the British Transport Police Force,
(ec) the Civil Nuclear Police Authority,
(ed) the chief constable of the Civil Nuclear Constabulary,
(ee) the chief constable of the Ministry of Defence Police,
(ef) the Commissioners for Her Majesty's Revenue and Customs,
(eg) the Director of Border Revenue,
(eh) the National Crime Agency,
(ei) for each of the persons mentioned in paragraphs (ea) to (eh), the Secretary of State.
(f) the Police Investigations and Review Commissioner,
(g) the Scottish Human Rights Commission,
(h) the Commissioner for Children and Young People in Scotland, and
(i) such other persons as the Scottish Ministers consider appropriate.

(3) Subsection (1) or (2) is complied with in relation to a code of practice having (or to have) effect for the first time even if the consultation has been initiated before the day on which this section comes into force.

AMENDMENTS

Subs.(2) as amended by Criminal Justice (Scotland) Act 2016 (Consequential Provisions) Orders 2018 (SSI 2018/46) art.11 (effective 17 January 2018).

Bringing code of practice into effect

A170-210 **77.**—(1) A code of practice has no effect until the day appointed for the code by regulations made by the Scottish Ministers.

(2) When laying before the Scottish Parliament a draft of an instrument containing regulations bringing a code of practice into effect, the Scottish Ministers must also so lay a copy of the code.

(3) No later than at the end of the 12 months beginning with the day on which this section comes into force, there must be so laid a draft of an instrument containing regulations bringing a code of practice into effect.

(4) Regulations under this section are subject to the affirmative procedure.

PART 3 – SOLEMN PROCEDURE

[Not reproduced]

A170-211 **78–83.** *[These provisions make amendments and add sections to the Criminal Procedure (Scotland) Act 1995]*

PART 4 – SENTENCING

Maximum term for weapons offences

84. *[Amends ss.47, 49, 49A and 49C of the Criminal Law (Consolidation) (Scotland) Act 1995]* A170-212

Prisoners on early release

Sentencing under the 1995 Act

85. *[Inserts s.200A into the 1995 Act]* A170-213

Sentencing under the 1993 Act

86. *[Amends s.16 of the Prisoners and Criminal Proceedings (Scotland) Act 1993]* A170-214

PART 5 – APPEALS AND SCCRC

[Not reproduced]

87–96. *[These provisions make amendments and add sections to the Criminal Procedure (Scotland) Act 1995]* A170-215

PART 6 – MISCELLANEOUS

Chapter 1 – Publication of Prosecutorial Test

Publication of prosecutorial test

97.—(1) The Lord Advocate must make available to the public a statement setting out in general terms the matters about which a prosecutor requires to be satisfied in order to initiate, and continue with, criminal proceedings in respect of any offence. A170-216

(2) The reference in subsection (1) to a prosecutor is to one within the Crown Office and Procurator Fiscal Service.

DEFINITIONS

"prosecutor": s.97(2). A170-217

GENERAL NOTE

It is likely that the statement of the test will embody much of what is known and published already about initiating and continuing criminal proceedings which are, of course, two different matters. A published prosecutorial test would be a notable development. In *Phan v HM Advocate* [2018] HCJAC 7; 2018 S.C.C.R. 133 it was recognised that an option not to prosecute a person for a particular crime has always been available in Scotland; it being a matter for the Lord Advocate to decide whether to do so in the public interest: at [38]. Although the court may give due deference to the Lord Advocate in taking a decision not to prosecute, that decision could be reviewed by the court where an accused advanced a plea in bar of trial on the grounds of oppression, and that such a review might very well succeed if, for example, the decision had been taken without regard to the Lord Advocates instructions or if any prospective trial would inevitably be unfair: at [40]. Quite how the public might come to know of the Lord Advocate's instructions in an individual case remains uncertain given rights around Crown confidentiality. A published prosecutorial test could clarify the Lord Advocate's instructions in general, and thus provide A170-218 another means of assessing whether a prosecutor has reached an appropriate decision. Specific instructions in regard to particular facts and circumstances of individual cases may yet be considered to raise different issues.

Chapter 2 – Support for Vulnerable Persons

Meaning of appropriate adult support

A170-219 **98.**—(1) For the purposes of this Chapter, "appropriate adult support" means—

(a) support of the sort mentioned in subsection (3) of section 42 that is provided to a person about whom intimation has been sent under subsection (2) of that section, and

(b) such other support for vulnerable persons in connection with a criminal investigation or criminal proceedings as the Scottish Ministers specify by regulations.

(2) In regulations under subsection (1)(b), the Scottish Ministers may, in particular, specify support by reference to—

(a) the purpose it is to serve,

(b) the description of vulnerable persons to whom it is to be available, and

(c) the circumstances in which it is to be available.

(3) For the purposes of this section—

"vulnerable person" means a person who, owing to mental disorder, is—

(a) unable to understand sufficiently what is happening, or

(b) communicate effectively, in the context of a criminal investigation or criminal proceedings,

"mental disorder" has the meaning given by section 328 of the Mental Health (Care and Treatment) (Scotland) Act 2003.

(4) The Scottish Ministers may by regulations amend the definitions of "vulnerable person" and "mental disorder" in subsection (3) for the purpose of making them consistent with (respectively) subsections (1)(c) and (5)(a) of section 42.

DEFINITIONS

A170-220 "appropriate adult support": s.98(1).
"mental disorder": s.98(3).
"vulnerable person": s.98(3).

GENERAL NOTE

A170-221 Section 42 of this Act makes provision to identify vulnerable adults in police custody and to provide them with support to assist communication between them and the police. In practice, this support is likely to be that provided by an "appropriate adult" though that term is not used in this Act.

This section specifies the sort of support that may be required to meet the duties imposed by s.42 and allows the Scottish Ministers the authority to make regulations for that support to assist vulnerable adults in connection with a criminal investigation or criminal proceedings.

The Code of Practice on the Exercise of Powers Stop and Search of the Person in Scotland, made on 9 March 2017 and in force from 11 May 2017, is the document to which regard must be had in relation to vulnerable adults in terms of s.98: see Code, paras 8.1–8.13. The Code is reproduced below at C2–50.

For the purposes of Ch.2 of Pt 6 of the 2016 Act the meaning of "appropriate adult support" has been extended. It now includes support at any stage during a police investigation for victims, witnesses and those suspected or accused of committing an offence: see reg.3 of the Criminal Justice (Scotland) Act 2016 (Support for Vulnerable Persons) Regulations 2019 (SSI 2019/437). The remaining regulations confer commensurate duties on others with an interest in these procedures.

Responsibility for ensuring availability of appropriate adults

A170-222 **99.** The Scottish Ministers may by regulations—

(a) confer on a person the function of ensuring that people are available to provide appropriate adult support—

(i) throughout Scotland, or

(ii) in a particular part of Scotland, and

(b) make provision about how that function may or must be discharged.

DEFINITIONS

"appropriate adult support": s.98(1). A170-223

GENERAL NOTE

This section allows the Scottish Ministers to make regulations in accordance with the function of ensuring that people are available to provide appropriate adult support. A170-224

Assessment of quality of appropriate adult support

100. The Scottish Ministers may by regulations— A170-225

(a) confer on a person the functions of—

(i) assessing the quality of whatever arrangements may be in place to ensure that people are available to provide appropriate adult support, and

(ii) assessing the quality of any appropriate adult support that is provided, and

(b) make provision about how those functions may or must be discharged.

DEFINITIONS

"appropriate adult support": s.98(1). A170-226

GENERAL NOTE

This section allows the Scottish Ministers to make regulations in accordance with the function of assessing the quality of any appropriate adult support that is provided. A170-227

Training for appropriate adults

101. The Scottish Ministers may by regulations— A170-228

(a) confer on a person the function of—

(i) giving to people who provide, or wish to provide, appropriate adult support training in how to provide that support,

(ii) giving to other people specified by the Scottish Ministers in the regulations training in how to deal with people who need appropriate adult support, and

(b) make provision about how that function may or must be discharged.

DEFINITIONS

"appropriate adult support": s.98(1). A170-229

GENERAL NOTE

This section allows the Scottish Ministers to make regulations in accordance with the provision of training for appropriate adult support. A170-230

Recommendations from quality assessor and training provider

102.—(1) A person upon whom a function has been conferred by virtue of section 100 or 101 may— A170-231

(a) make to a provider of appropriate adult support recommendations about the way that appropriate adult support is provided,

(b) make to the Scottish Ministers recommendations about the exercise of their powers under section 61 and the provisions of this Chapter.

(2) A provider of appropriate adult support must have regard to any recommendation made to it under subsection (1)(a).

(3) The Scottish Ministers must have regard to any recommendation made under subsection (1)(b).

(4) In this section, "a provider of appropriate adult support" means a person upon whom the function of ensuring that people are available to provide appropriate adult support has been conferred by virtue of section 99.

DEFINITIONS

A170-232 "a provider of appropriate adult support": s.102(4).
"appropriate adult support": s.98(1).

GENERAL NOTE

A170-233 This section places duties on a person on whom a function has been conferred (by ss.100 or 101) to have regard to recommendations made by a quality assessor or a training provider.

Duty to ensure quality assessment takes place

A170-234 **103.** If, by virtue of regulations under section 99, a person has the function of ensuring that people are available to provide appropriate adult support, it is the Scottish Ministers' duty to ensure that there is a person discharging the functions mentioned in section 100(a).

GENERAL NOTE

A170-235 It is the duty of Scottish Ministers to ensure that there is, as a matter of fact, a person discharging the function of assessing the quality of any appropriate adult support that is provided.

Elaboration of regulation-making powers under this Chapter

A170-236 **104.**—(1) A power under this Chapter to confer a function on a person by regulations may be exercised so as to confer the function, or aspects of the function, on more than one person.

(2) A power under this Chapter to make provision by regulations about how a function may or must be discharged may, in particular, be exercised so as to—

(a) require or allow the person discharging the function to enter into a contract with another person,
(b) require the person discharging the function to have regard to any guidance about the discharge of the function issued by the Scottish Ministers.

(3) The powers under this Chapter to make regulations may be exercised so as to—

(a) make such provision as the Scottish Ministers consider necessary or expedient in consequence of, or for the purpose of giving full effect to, any regulations made in exercise of a power under this Chapter,
(b) modify any enactment (including this Act),
(c) make different provision for different purposes.

GENERAL NOTE

A170-237 The powers under this Part of the Act to make regulations are further explained in this section.

Procedure for making regulations under this Chapter

A170-238 **105.**—(1) Regulations under this Chapter are subject to the affirmative procedure.

(2) Prior to laying a draft Scottish statutory instrument containing regulations under this Chapter before the Scottish Parliament for approval by resolution, the Scottish Ministers must consult publicly.

Other powers of Ministers unaffected

106. Nothing in this Chapter is to be taken to imply that the powers it gives to the Scottish Ministers to confer functions are the only powers that they have to confer those (or similar) functions. **A170-239**

Chapter 3 – Notification if Parent of Under 18 Imprisoned

Child's named person to be notified

107.—(1) This section applies where a person is admitted to any penal institution for imprisonment or detention arising from— **A170-240**

(a) anything done by a court of criminal jurisdiction (including the imposition of a sentence, the making of an order or the issuing of a warrant),

(b) anything done under section 17 or 17A of the Prisoners and Criminal Proceedings (Scotland) Act 1993 (as to the recall of a prisoner),

(c) anything done by virtue of the Extradition Act 2003 (particularly section 9(2) or 77(2) of that Act), or

(d) the operation of any other enactment concerning criminal matters (including penal matters).

(2) The Scottish Ministers must ensure that the person is asked—

(a) whether the person is a parent of a child, and

(b) if the person claims to be a parent of a child, to—

(i) state the identity of the child, and

(ii) give information enabling the identity of the service provider in relation to the child to be ascertained.

(3) If the identity of the service provider can be ascertained by or on behalf of the Scottish Ministers without undue difficulty in light of anything disclosed by the person, they must ensure that the service provider is notified of—

(a) the fact of the person's admission to the penal institution,

(b) what has been stated by the person about the identity of the child, and

(c) such other matters disclosed by the person as appear to them to be relevant for the purpose of the exercise of the named person functions with respect to the child.

(4) In addition, the Scottish Ministers must ensure that the service provider is notified of anything disclosed by the person about the identity of any other child—

(a) of whom the person claims to be a parent, and

(b) the service provider in relation to whom is unknown to them.

(5) No requirement is imposed by subsection (2) if the person's admission to the penal institution is on—

(a) returning after—

(i) any unauthorised absence, or

(ii) any temporary release in accordance with prison rules, or

(b) being transferred from—

(i) any other penal institution,

(ii) any secure accommodation in which the person has been kept, or

(iii) any hospital in which the person has been detained, so as to be given medical treatment for a mental disorder, by virtue of Part VI of the 1995 Act or the Mental Health (Care and Treatment) (Scotland) Act 2003.

(6) Each of the requirements imposed by subsections (2) to (4) is to be fulfilled without unnecessary delay.

(7) The references in subsections (2) to (4) to the Scottish Ministers are to them in their exercise of functions in connection with the person's imprisonment or detention in the penal institution.

(8) The references in subsections (3) and (4) to disclosure by the person are to such disclosure in response to something asked under subsection (2).

DEFINITIONS

A170-241 "child": s.108.
"named person functions": s.108.
"parent": s.108.
"penal institution": s.108.
"prison rules": s.108.
"secure accommodation": s.108.
"service provider": s.108.

GENERAL NOTE

A170-242 Section 107 places a duty on the Scottish Ministers to ensure, without unnecessary delay, when a person is admitted to specific penal institutions that the person is asked whether he or she is the parent of a child and, where relevant, the identity of the child and the "service provider". Thereafter, if the child is identified then the service provider is notified. The duty on the Scottish Ministers is restricted to initial admissions and not after a temporary release or transfer within the penal system.

Definition of certain expressions

A170-243 **108.** In this Chapter—

"child" means a person who is under 18 years of age,

"named person functions" has the meaning given by section 32 of the Children and Young People (Scotland) Act 2014,

"parent" includes any person who—

(a) is a guardian of a child,

(b) is liable to maintain, or has care of, a child, or

(c) has parental responsibilities in relation to a child (as construed by reference to section 1(1) to (3) of the Children (Scotland) Act 1995),

"penal institution" means —

(a) any prison, other than—

(i) a naval, military or air force prison, or

(ii) any legalised police cells (within the meaning of section 14(1) of the Prisons (Scotland) Act 1989),

(b) any remand centre (within the meaning of section 19(1)(a) of the Prisons (Scotland) Act 1989), or

(c) any young offenders institution (within the meaning of section 19(1)(b) of the Prisons (Scotland) Act 1989,

"prison rules" means rules made under section 39 of the Prisons (Scotland) Act 1989,

"secure accommodation" means accommodation provided in a residential establishment, approved in accordance with regulations made under section 78(2) of the Public Services Reform (Scotland) Act 2010, for the purpose of restricting the liberty of children,

"service provider" in relation to a child has the meaning given by section 32 of the Children and Young People (Scotland) Act 2014.

Chapter 4 – Statements and Procedure

Statements by accused

A170-244 **109.** *[Not reproduced]*

GENERAL NOTE

New s.261ZA of the 1995 Act (as inserted by s.109) will modify the common law rule on the admissibility of hearsay evidence in criminal proceedings, as it applies to certain types of statement made by an accused. A170-245

Use of technology

Live television links

110. *[Not reproduced]* A170-246

GENERAL NOTE

Each of ss.288H to 288K of the 1995 Act (as inserted by s.110) are not reproduced here. In general terms they make provision for the participation of detained persons in hearings by means of live television link from the place of detention. A170-247

Electronic proceedings

111. *[Not reproduced]* A170-248

GENERAL NOTE

Section 111 inserts s.305(1A) into the 1995 Act and that provides that the power of the High Court of Justiciary to regulate criminal procedure through Acts of Adjournal includes the power to make provision in respect of electronic proceedings. The subsection provides an authority that relates to "something" to be done. A170-249

Chapter 5 – Authorisation under Part III of the Police Act 1997

Authorisation of persons other than constables

112. In section 108 (interpretation of Part III) of the Police Act 1997, after subsection (1) there is inserted— A170-250

"(1A) A reference in this Part to a staff officer of the Police Investigations and Review Commissioner is to any person who—

(a) is a member of the Commissioner's staff appointed under paragraph 7A of schedule 4 to the Police, Public Order and Criminal Justice (Scotland) Act 2006, or

(b) is a member of the Commissioner's staff appointed under paragraph 7 of that schedule to whom paragraph 7B(2) of that schedule applies.".

GENERAL NOTE

Section 112 amends police legislation to allow directly employed members of the staff of the Police Investigations and Review Commissioner, who have been designated by the Commissioner to take charge or assist in investigations, to make certain applications to the Commissioner for authorisation under Part III of the Police Act 1997. It also allows the Commissioner to designate a member of directly employed staff to authorise certain applications in the Commissioner's absence if the matter is urgent. A170-251

Chapter 6 – Police Negotiating Board for Scotland

Establishment and functions

113. *[Not reproduced]* A170-252

GENERAL NOTE

These sections deal with the establishment and functions of a Police Negotiating Board for Scotland. A170-253

Consequential and transitional

114. *[Not reproduced]* A170-254

GENERAL NOTE

The section deals with certain legal matters following the establishment of a Police Negotiating Board for Scotland. A170-255

PART 7 – FINAL PROVISIONS

Ancillary and definition

Ancillary regulations

A170-256 **115.**—(1) The Scottish Ministers may by regulations make such supplemental, incidental, consequential, transitional, transitory or saving provision as they consider necessary or expedient for the purposes of or in connection with this Act.

(2) Regulations under this section—

(a) are subject to the affirmative procedure if they add to, replace or omit any part of the text of an Act (including this Act),

(b) otherwise, are subject to the negative procedure.

GENERAL NOTE

A170-257 This section allows in broad terms for delegated legislation by the Scottish Ministers in relation to any aspect of this Act.

Meaning of "the 1995 Act"

A170-258 **116.** In this Act, "the 1995 Act" means the Criminal Procedure (Scotland) Act 1995.

Commencement and short title

Commencement

A170-259 **117.**—(1) The following provisions come into force on the day after Royal Assent—

(a) sections 71 and 73 to 77,

(b) this Part.

(2) The other provisions of this Act come into force on such day as the Scottish Ministers may by order appoint.

(3) An order under subsection (2) may include transitional, transitory or saving provision.

GENERAL NOTE

A: Date of Royal Assent: 13 January 2016

A170-260 Sections 71 and 73 to77 and Part 7 (ss.115-118) came into force on the day after Royal Assent.

B. Such other date as Scottish Ministers may appoint

The remaining provisions of this Act will be brought into force in due course.

Short title

A170-261 **118.** The short title of this Act is the Criminal Justice (Scotland) Act 2016.

SCHEDULE 1

BREACH OF LIBERATION CONDITION

(introduced by ss.16(4) and 26(6))

Offence of breaching condition

A170-262 **1.**—(1) A person commits an offence if, without reasonable excuse, the person breaches a liberation condition by reason of—

(a) failing to comply with an investigative liberation condition,

(b) failing to appear at court as required by the terms of an undertaking, or

(c) failing to comply with the terms of an undertaking, other than the requirement to appear at court.

(2) Sub-paragraph (1) does not apply where (and to the extent that) a person breaches a liberation condition by reason of committing an offence (in which case see paragraph 3).

(3) It is competent to amend a complaint to include an additional charge of an offence under subparagraph (1) at any time before the trial of a person in summary proceedings for—

(a) the original offence, or

(b) an offence arising from the same circumstances as the original offence.

(4) In sub-paragraph (3), "the original offence" is the offence in connection with which—

(a) an investigative liberation condition was imposed, or

(b) an undertaking was given.

Sentencing for the offence

2.—(1) A person who commits an offence under paragraph 1(1) is liable on summary conviction to— **A170-263**

(a) a fine not exceeding level 3 on the standard scale, or

(b) imprisonment for a period—

(i) where conviction is in the justice of the peace court, not exceeding 60 days,

(ii) where conviction is in the sheriff court, not exceeding 12 months.

(2) A penalty under sub-paragraph (1) may be imposed in addition to any other penalty which it is competent for the court to impose, even if the total of penalties imposed exceeds the maximum penalty which it is competent to impose in respect of the original offence.

(3) The reference in sub-paragraph (2) to a penalty being imposed in addition to another penalty means, in the case of sentences of imprisonment or detention—

(a) where the sentences are imposed at the same time (whether or not in relation to the same complaint), framing the sentences so that they have effect consecutively,

(b) where the sentences are imposed at different times, framing the sentence imposed later so that (if the earlier sentence has not been served) the later sentence has effect consecutive to the earlier sentence.

(4) Sub-paragraph (3)(b) is subject to section 204A (restriction on consecutive sentences for released prisoners) of the 1995 Act.

(5) Where a person is to be sentenced in respect of an offence under paragraph 1(1), the court may remit the person for sentence in respect of it to any court which is considering the original offence.

(6) In sub-paragraphs (2) and (5), "the original offence" is the offence in connection with which—

(a) the investigative liberation condition was imposed, or

(b) the undertaking was given.

Breach by committing offence

3.—(1) This paragraph applies— **A170-264**

(a) where (and to the extent that) a person breaches a liberation condition by reason of committing an offence ("offence O"), but

(b) only if the fact that offence O was committed while the person was subject to the liberation condition is specified in the complaint or indictment.

(2) In determining the penalty for offence O, the court must have regard—

(a) to the fact that offence O was committed in breach of a liberation condition,

(b) if the breach is by reason of the person's failure to comply with the terms of an investigative liberation condition, to the matters mentioned in paragraph 4(1),

(c) if the breach is by reason of the person's failure to comply with the terms of an undertaking other than the requirement to appear at court, to the matters mentioned in paragraph 5(1).

(3) Where the maximum penalty in respect of offence O is specified by (or by virtue of) an enactment, the maximum penalty is increased—

(a) where it is a fine, by the amount equivalent to level 3 on the standard scale,

(b) where it is a period of imprisonment—

(i) as respects conviction in the justice of the peace court, by 60 days,

(ii) as respects conviction in the sheriff court or the High Court, by 6 months.

(4) The maximum penalty is increased by sub-paragraph (3) even if the penalty as so increased exceeds the penalty which it would otherwise be competent for the court to impose.

(5) In imposing a penalty in respect of offence O, the court must state—

(a) where the penalty is different from that which the court would have imposed had sub-paragraph (2) not applied, the extent of and the reasons for that difference,

(b) otherwise, the reasons for there being no such difference.

Matters for paragraph 3(2)(b)

4.—(1) For the purpose of paragraph 3(2)(b), the matters are— **A170-265**

(a) the number of offences in connection with which the person was subject to investigative liberation conditions when offence O was committed,

(b) any previous conviction the person has for an offence under paragraph 1(1)(a),

(c) the extent to which the sentence or disposal in respect of any previous conviction differed, by virtue of paragraph 3(2), from that which the court would have imposed but for that paragraph.

(2) In sub-paragraph (1)—

(a) in paragraph (b), the reference to any previous conviction includes any previous conviction by a court in England and Wales, Northern Ireland or a member State of the European Union (other than the United Kingdom) for an offence that is equivalent to an offence under paragraph 1(1)(a),

(b) in paragraph (c), the references to paragraph 3(2) are to be read, in relation to a previous conviction by a court referred to in paragraph (a) of this sub-paragraph, as references to any provision that is equivalent to paragraph 3(2).

(3) Any issue of equivalence arising under sub-paragraph (2)(a) or (b) is for the court to determine.

Matters for paragraph 3(2)(c)

A170-266 **5.**—(1) For the purpose of paragraph 3(2)(c), the matters are—

(a) the number of undertakings to which the person was subject when offence O was committed,

(b) any previous conviction the person has for an offence under paragraph 1(1)(c),

(c) the extent to which the sentence or disposal in respect of any previous conviction differed, by virtue of paragraph 3(2), from that which the court would have imposed but for that paragraph.

(2) In sub-paragraph (1)—

(a) in paragraph (b), the reference to any previous conviction includes any previous conviction by a court in England and Wales, Northern Ireland or a member State of the European Union (other than the United Kingdom) for an offence that is equivalent to an offence underparagraph 1(1)(c),

(b) in paragraph (c), the references to paragraph 3(2) are to be read, in relation to a previous conviction by a court referred to in paragraph (a) of this sub-paragraph, as references to any provision that is equivalent to paragraph 3(2).

(3) Any issue of equivalence arising under sub-paragraph (2)(a) or (b) is for the court to determine.

Evidential presumptions

A170-267 **6.**—(1) In any proceedings in relation to an offence under paragraph 1(1), the facts mentioned in sub-paragraph (2) are to be held as admitted unless challenged by preliminary objection before the person's plea is recorded.

(2) The facts are—

(a) that the person breached an undertaking by reason of failing to appear at court as required by the terms of the undertaking,

(b) that the person was subject to a particular—

(i) investigative liberation condition, or

(ii) condition under the terms of an undertaking.

(3) In proceedings to which sub-paragraph (4) applies—

(a) something in writing, purporting to impose investigative liberation conditions and bearing to be signed by a constable, is sufficient evidence of the terms of the investigative liberation conditions imposed under section 16(2),

(b) something in writing, purporting to be an undertaking and bearing to be signed by the person said to have given it, is sufficient evidence of the terms of the undertaking at the time that it was given,

(c) a document purporting to be a notice (or a copy of a notice) under section 18, 27 or 28, is sufficient evidence of the terms of the notice.

(4) This sub-paragraph applies to proceedings—

(a) in relation to an offence under paragraph 1(1), or

(b) in which the fact mentioned in paragraph 3(1)(b) is specified in the complaint or indictment.

(5) In proceedings in which the fact mentioned in paragraph 3(1)(b) is specified in the complaint or indictment, that fact is to be held as admitted unless challenged—

(a) in summary proceedings, by preliminary objection before the person's plea is recorded, or

(b) in the case of proceedings on indictment, by giving notice of a preliminary objection in accordance with section 71(2) or 72(6)(b)(i) of the 1995 Act.

Interpretation

A170-268 **7.** In this schedule—

(a) references to an investigative liberation condition are to a condition imposed under section 16(2) or 19(3)(b) subject to any modification by notice under section 18(1) or (5)(a),

(b) references to an undertaking are to an undertaking given under section 25(2)(a),

(c) references to the terms of an undertaking are to the terms of an undertaking subject to any modification by—

(i) notice under section 27(1), or

(ii) the sheriff under section 30(3)(b).

SCHEDULE 2

Modifications In Connection With Part 1

(introduced by section 56)

Part 1

Provisions as to Arrest

Criminal Procedure (Scotland) Act 1995

1. The 1995 Act is amended as follows. **A170-269**

2. These provisions are repealed— **A170-270**

(a) in section 13, subsection (7),

(b) section 21.

3.—(1) In section 234A, subsections (4A) and (4B) are repealed. **A170-271**

(2) In subsection (11) of section 234AA, for the words from the beginning to "those sections apply" there is substituted "Section 9 (breach of orders) of the Antisocial Behaviour etc. (Scotland) Act 2004 applies in relation to antisocial behaviour orders made under this section as that section applies".

Miscellaneous enactments

4. In section 4 of the Trespass (Scotland) Act 1865, for the words from the beginning to "every in the last place where it occurs there is substituted "A". **A170-272**

5. In subsection (3) of section 1 of the Public Meeting Act 1908, the words from ", and if he refuses" to the end are repealed. **A170-273**

6. In the Firearms Act 1968, section 50 is repealed. **A170-274**

7. In the Civic Government (Scotland) Act 1982— **A170-275**

(a) in section 59, subsections (1), (2) and (5) are repealed,

(b) in subsection (3), for the words "he can be delivered into the custody" there is substituted "the arrival",

(c) in section 65, subsections (4) and (5) are repealed,

(d) in subsection (1) of section 80, for the words from "and taken" to the end there is substituted "by a constable".

8. In the Child Abduction Act 1984, section 7 is repealed. **A170-276**

9. In section 11 of the Protection of Badgers Act 1992, paragraph (c) of subsection (1) is repealed. **A170-277**

10. In the Criminal Justice and Public Order Act 1994, section 60B is repealed. **A170-278**

11. In section 8B of the Olympic Symbol etc. (Protection) Act 1995, subsections (2) and (3) are repealed. **A170-279**

12. In the Criminal Law (Consolidation) (Scotland) Act 1995— **A170-280**

(a) in section 7, subsection (4) is repealed,

(b) in section 47, subsection (3) is repealed,

(c) in section 48, subsection (3) is repealed,

(d) in section 50, subsections (3) and (5) are repealed.

13. In the Deer (Scotland) Act 1996, section 28 is repealed. **A170-281**

14. In section 61 of the Crime and Punishment (Scotland) Act 1997, subsection (5) is repealed. **A170-282**

15. In section 7 of the Protection of Wild Mammals (Scotland) Act 2002, paragraph (a) of subsection (1) is repealed. **A170-283**

16. In the Fireworks Act 2003— **A170-284**

(a) in section 11A, subsection (6) is repealed,

(b) section 11Bis repealed.

17. In section 307 of the Criminal Justice Act 2003, subsection (4) is repealed. **A170-285**

18. In theAntisocial Behaviour etc. (Scotland) Act 2004— **A170-286**

(a) section 11 is repealed,

(b) in section 22, subsections (3) and (4) are repealed,

(c) section 38 is repealed.

19. In section 130 of the Serious Organised Crime and Police Act 2005, subsection (3) is repealed. **A170-287**

20. In the Animal Health and Welfare (Scotland) Act 2006, in schedule 1— **A170-288**

(a) paragraph 16 is repealed,

(b) in paragraph 18(b)(i), the words "except paragraph 16" are repealed.

21. In the Prostitution (Public Places) (Scotland) Act 2007, section 2 is repealed. **A170-289**

22. In section 32 of the Glasgow Commonwealth Games Act 2008, subsections (3) and (4) are repealed. **A170-290**

23. In section 7 of the Tobacco and Primary Medical Services (Scotland) Act 2010, subsection (4) is repealed. **A170-291**

24. In each of sections 169(2) and 170(2) of the Children's Hearings (Scotland) Act 2011, the words "arrested without warrant and" are repealed. **A170-292**

A170-293 **25.** In section 9 of the Forced Marriage etc. (Protection and Jurisdiction) (Scotland) Act 2011, subsections (2) and (3) are repealed.

PART 2

FURTHER MODIFICATIONS

The 1995 Act

A170-294 **26-34.** *[These provisions make further modifications to the 1995 Act]*

Other enactments

A170-295 **35.** In subsection (2)(a) of section 8A of the Legal Aid (Scotland) Act 1986, for the words "section 15A of the Criminal Procedure (Scotland) Act 1995 (right of suspects to have access to a solicitor)" there is substituted "section 32 (right to have solicitor present) of the Criminal Justice (Scotland) Act 2016".

A170-296 **36.** In section 6D of the Road Traffic Act 1988, for subsection (2A) there is substituted—

"(2A) Instead of, or before, arresting a person under this section, a constable may detain the person at or near the place where the preliminary test was, or would have been, administered with a view to imposing on the person there a requirement under section 7.".

A170-297 **37.** In Schedule 8 to the Terrorism Act 2000—

(a) in paragraph 18—

(i) in sub-paragraph (2), for the words from "and" at the end of paragraph (a) to the end of the sub-paragraph there is substituted—

"(ab) intimation is to be made under paragraph 16(1) whether the person detained requests that it be made or not, and

(ac) section 40 (right of under 18s to have access to other person) of the Criminal Justice (Scotland) Act 2016 applies as if the detained person were a person in police custody for the purposes of that section.",

(ii) after sub-paragraph (3) there is inserted—

"(4) For the purposes of sub-paragraph (2)—

"child" means a person under 16 years of age,

"parent" includes guardian and any person who has the care of the child mentioned in sub-paragraph (2).",

(b) in paragraph 20(1), the words "or a person detained under section 14 of that Act" are repealed,

(c) in paragraph 27—

(i) in sub-paragraph (4), paragraph (a) is repealed,

(ii) sub-paragraph (5) is repealed.

A170-298 **38.** In the schedule to the Sexual Offences (Procedure and Evidence) (Scotland) Act 2002, paragraph 2 is repealed.

A170-299 **39.** In the Criminal Procedure (Legal Assistance, Detention and Appeals) (Scotland) Act 2010, sections 1, 3 and 4 are repealed.

A170-300 **40.** In the Children's Hearings (Scotland) Act 2011—

(a) in section 65—

(i) for subsection (1) there is substituted—

"(1) Subsection (2) applies where the Principal Reporter is informed under subsection (2) of section 53 of the Criminal Justice (Scotland) Act 2016 that a child is being kept in a place of safety under subsection (3) of that section.",

(ii) in subsection (2), for the words "in the" there is substituted "in a",

(b) in section 66(1), for sub-paragraph (vii) there is substituted—

"(vii) information under section 53 of the Criminal Justice (Scotland) Act 2016, or",

(c) in section 68(4)(e)(vi), for the words "section 43(5) of the Criminal Procedure (Scotland) Act 1995 (c.46)" there is substituted "section 53 of the Criminal Justice (Scotland) Act 2016",

(d) in section 69, for subsection (3) there is substituted—

"(3) If—

(a) the determination under section 66(2) is made following the Principal Reporter receiving information under section 53 of the Criminal Justice (Scotland) Act 2016, and

(b) at the time the determination is made the child is being kept in a place of safety,

the children's hearing must be arranged to take place no later than the third day after the Principal Reporter receives the information mentioned in paragraph (a).",

(e) in section 72(2)(b), for the words "in the" there is substituted "in a".

41. In section 20 of the Police and Fire Reform (Scotland) Act 2012, subsections (2) and (3) are repealed. **A170-301**

SCHEDULE 3

Police Negotiating Board for Scotland

(introduced by section 113)

[Not reproduced] **A170-302**

General Note

This schedule inserts Schedule 2A into the Police and Fire Reform (Scotland) Act 2012. **A170-303**

[THE NEXT PARAGRAPH IS B1-01]

ACT OF ADJOURNAL (CRIMINAL PROCEDURE RULES) 1996

(SI 1996/513) B1-01

Made 29 February 1996.
Coming into force 1 April 1996.

The Lord Justice General, Lord Justice Clerk and Lords Commissioners of Justiciary under and by virtue of the powers conferred on them by section 305 of the Criminal Procedure (Scotland) Act 1995, the provisions specified in Schedule 1 to this Act of Adjournal and of all other powers enabling them in that behalf, do hereby enact and declare:

Citation and commencement

1.—(1) This Act of Adjournal may be cited as the Act of Adjournal (Criminal Procedure Rules) 1996 and shall come into force on 1st April 1996. B1-01.1

(2) This Act of Adjournal shall be inserted in the Books of Adjournal.

Criminal Procedure Rules

2. Schedule 2 to this Act of Adjournal shall have effect for the purpose of providing rules of procedure in the High Court of Justiciary, in the sheriff court in the exercise of its criminal jurisdiction and in a justice of the peace court. B1-01.2

AMENDMENT

Para.2 as substituted by the Act of Adjournal (Criminal Procedure Rules Amendment) (Criminal Proceedings etc. (Reform) (Scotland) Act 2007) 2008 (SSI 2008/61) r.2 (effective 10 March 2008).

Revocations

3. The Acts of Adjournal mentioned in Schedule 3 to this Act of Adjournal are revoked to the extent specified in the third column of that Schedule. B1-01.3

[THE NEXT PARAGRAPH IS B1-02]

INTRODUCTION AND GENERAL NOTE

[1] On the foundation of the High Court of Justiciary in 1672 the High Court was given the power "to regulate the inferior officers thereof, and order every other thing concerning the said Court" (see s.6 of the Act 1672 c.40 (now repealed)). The High Court under this power has passed various Acts of Adjournal relating to the forms of procedure in that Court, the organisation of circuits of the Court and sundry other matters. However, by the Act of Adjournal (Consolidation) 1988 (SI 1988/110) of 21 January 1988, all previous Acts of Adjournal were revoked and since that date subsequent alterations in criminal procedure have been effected by amendment of the consolidating Act of Adjournal which provided a detailed code of rules of criminal procedure (hereinafter referred to as "the 1988 Rules"). B1-02

With the enactment of the Criminal Procedure (Scotland) Act 1995 which repealed the Criminal Procedure (Scotland) Act 1975, itself a consolidation statute, a new Act of Adjournal became necessary. The Act of Adjournal (Criminal Procedure Rules) 1996 provides a new set of rules which are contained in Sch.2 to the Act of Adjournal and are to be known as the Criminal Procedure Rules 1996 (see r.1.1). These rules, as the 1988 Rules did, make provision for criminal procedure both in solemn and summary proceedings. The same policy is adopted with the Criminal Procedure Rules 1996 as was followed with the 1988 Rules and accordingly when the need for change in the rules becomes evident, an Act of Adjournal is passed to amend the consolidating Act of Adjournal of 1996. This process was commenced within just six months of the coming into force of the Criminal Procedure Rules 1996 and has continued on a regular basis. However, as a result of the Criminal Procedure (Amendment) (Scotland) Act 2004 (asp 5) which has effected significant changes to the procedure to be followed in High Court cases, a substantial amendment of the Criminal Procedure Rules 1996 became recently necessary. This was effected by the Act of Adjournal (Criminal Procedure Rules Amendment) (Criminal Procedure (Amend-

---

[1] Annotations by Peter W. Ferguson, Q.C.

ment) (Scotland) Act 2004) 2005 (SSI 2005/44) which came into force on 1 February 2005. Allied with this statutory instrument is the Act of Adjournal (Criminal Procedure Rules Amendment No.3) (Vulnerable Witnesses (Scotland) Act 2004) 2005 (SSI 2005/188) which came into force on 1 April 2005. The principal purpose of the latter Act of Adjournal is to substitute a new Ch.22 for the previous chapter which dealt with the evidence of children. The new chapter is much more extensive because it requires to reflect the considerable extension in the scope of protection afforded to the now enlarged category of "vulnerable witnesses" for whom provision is made in the Vulnerable Witnesses (Scotland) Act 2004 (asp 3).

One provision in the 1995 Act which requires special notice is s.305(2) which provides that the High Court may by Act of Adjournal "modify, amend or repeal any enactment (including an enactment in this Act) in so far as that enactment relates to matters in respect to which an Act of Adjournal may be made under subs.(1) above." For all material purposes the matters with respect to which this Act of Adjournal has been made are given in s.305(1) and are (a) the regulation of the practice and procedure in relation to criminal procedure and (b) the making of such rules and regulations "as may be necessary or expedient to carry out the purposes and accomplish the objects of any enactment (including an enactment in this Act) in so far as it relates to criminal procedure". An example of the exercise of this power to amend primary legislation is to be found in the Act of Adjournal (Extension of Time Limit for Service of Transcript of Examination) 1998 (SI 1998/2635) which came into force on 1 December 1998 and amended s.37(9) of the 1995 Act to allow for the disposal of applications for extension by the High Court or a single judge either in chambers or in public. A very recent example is the Act of Adjournal (Criminal Appeals) 2003 (SSI 2003/387), para.2 which amends ss.114 and 115(1) of the 1995 Act so as to allow for appeals against sentence in both solemn and summary cases (including the Lord Advocate's appeals against unduly lenient disposals) to be presented in writing only.

Section 305(2) is in its terms a "Henry VIII clause" because it gives to the High Court by way of statutory instrument the power to change the law as Parliament has expressed it in statute. This gives rise to difficulty. Virtually the same provision was contained in the 1975 Act (see ss.282(2) and 457(d)) and it has been stated that having regard to the limits placed upon the High Court's powers by these provisions, an Act of Adjournal may be ultra vires (see (Lord) McCluskey, *Criminal Appeals*, para. 1.06). To the extent that an Act of Adjournal sought to make provision for matters which did not relate to criminal procedure, that is no doubt true although Lord McCluskey did also note that Lord Justice Clerk Ross received with little enthusiasm a submission that the 1988 Rules were ultra vires (see *Wither v Cowie*, 1991 S.L.T. 401 at 405K). However, standing the power of the High Court by Act of Adjournal to amend, modify or repeal the 1995 Act, is it permissible to have regard to the terms of the Act of Adjournal when construing the 1995 Act? Usually a statutory instrument is of no assistance since it exists only as a creature of its parent statute. But by virtue of s.305(2) it is arguable that this progeny can refashion its parent. Indeed, the more precise question may be whether, when there is conflict between the Act of Adjournal and the 1995 Act, the 1995 Act is to be treated as impliedly repealed on the principle *leges posteriores priores abrogant*.

This issue has been considered (although perhaps not fully considered) in some recent decisions. In *McLeay v Hingston*, 1994 S.L.T. 720 at 723J-K Lord Justice General Hope said: "the purpose of the rules in the Act of Adjournal is to give effect to the provisions of the [1975] statute, not control their meaning or to provide an aid to their interpretation. The meaning and effect of s.334(2A) is to be found by examining the words used by Parliament, not by construing the terms of the Act of Adjournal." In *Walkingshaw v Robison and Davidson Ltd*, 1989 S.C.C.R. 359 Lord Justice Clerk Ross said at 362B: "Certainly it is not correct to hold that the Act of Adjournal has in some way limited the scope of the subsection of the Act of Parliament." However, one can set against these dicta what Lord Justice Clerk Ross said in *Lafferty v Jessop*, 1989 S.L.T. 846 at 848K that the terms of r.128 in the 1988 Rules "make it perfectly clear that leave to appeal against a decision under s.334(2A) cannot be sought or granted until after the accused has stated how he pleads to the charge or charges set out in the complaint." (See also *Stevenson v MeGlennan*, 1990 S.L.T. 842.)

Human Rights Act 1998, press reporting and contempt of court

Section 4(2) of the Contempt of Court Act 1981 provides the court with a power to order that publication of any report of any proceedings, or part of such proceedings, should be postponed for such period as the court thinks necessary for the purpose of avoiding a substantial risk of prejudice to the administration of justice. As a result of the "cardinal importance" which the courts now attach to freedom of the press and (because of the incorporation of Art. 10 of the European Convention) the need for any restriction on that freedom to be proportionate and no more than is necessary to promote the legitimate object of the restriction (*McCartan Turkington Breen (A Firm) v Times Newspapers Ltd* [2000] 3 W.L.R. 1670 at 1679H-1680,per Lord Bingham of Comhill) s. 12 of the Human Rights Act 1998 was enacted. Section 12(2) requires that before relief which might affect the right to freedom of expression is granted the court should be satisfied that if any affected person is not present or represented, all practicable steps to notify him have been taken or that there are compelling reasons why he should not be notified. Section 12 does not, however, apply to remedies or orders pronounced in criminal proceedings (s. 12(5)).

Notwithstanding that deliberate omission and no doubt in view of the cardinal importance of a free press, which was implicitly recognised prior to the Human Rights Act 1998 by the Appeal Court in *Scottish Daily Record and Sunday Mail Ltd, Petrs*, 1999 S.L.T. 624 at 628C (when the right of the press to be heard in any decision to pronounce an order under s.4(2) or the terms in which it should be couched (whether before or after it was pronounced) was emphasised on an analogy with proceedings for interim interdict pronounced on an ex parte basis: see 628F-G), the Appeal Court recently took an unusual step.

In *Galbraith v HM Advocate*, 2000 S.C.C.R. 935 in the course of an appeal against a murder conviction in which the appellant gave notice of an intention to seek an order under s.4(2) prohibiting reporting of the appeal proceedings until determination of the appeal or of any retrial, the Appeal Court informed the agents for various media interests of the motion. At the resumed hearing the media were represented. The Appeal Court again recognised that "[p]rima facie ... the media have a substantial interest in the making or refusal of such orders and in their scope" (at 941A) but reserved its opinion on whether any order should be made for an initially limited period so as to allow the media to make representations on the order and its terms at a later hearing. The court also observed that the Scottish Courts website was the place for journalists and others to look when concerned to know whether an order had been made (941D-E). In *BBC, Petitioners*, 2002 S.L.T. 2 (para.4), the trial judge (Lord Osborne) made an order under s.4(2) but provided that, while it was to be immediately effective, it should only become "final" at 5 pm on the second working day after it was pronounced, in order to give the media and other interested parties the opportunity to move for recall or variation of the order. A similar practice was adopted by Lord Hodge when he made an order under s.11 of the Contempt of Court Act 1981 in *HM Advocate v M*, 2007 S.L.T. 462; 2007 S.C.C.R. 124 (sub nom *HM Advocate v Mola*).The present practice is for copies of s.4(2) orders to be immediately sent by e-mail to various newspapers and broadcasting organisations and their agents: see para.4.

This area of practice seems, with respect, to be an appropriate matter for which provision should be made in the Criminal Procedure Rules. The Rules could set out a procedure to be followed for motions for s.4(2) orders to be raised and for them to be intimated to the media by various means, the manner of, and time for, representations to be made, the holding of a hearing on the motion, the notification to all interested persons of the terms of the order and the duration of the order.

As Lord McCluskey noticed in *Scottish Daily Record and Sunday Mail Ltd, Petrs*, above (at 627F), s. 159 of the Criminal Justice Act 1988 provides for England and Wales a right of appeal by a "person aggrieved" by the making of an order under s.4(2) but there is no equivalent provision for Scotland. There is at present an application to the European Court of Human Rights in which complaint is made that there were violations of arts 6, 10 and 13 of the Convention in respect of a s.4(2) order made by the Appeal Court in the course of hearing the Crown's bill of advocation in *HM Advocate v Fleming*, 2005 S.C.C.R. 324. The application complains that the media were denied an opportunity to be represented and to make submissions at a hearing where it was anticipated that an order would be sought; and that as there is no equivalent to s. 159 in Scotland, the media were denied an effective remedy (see *Mackay and BBC Scotland v United Kingdom* (Application No. 10734/05) [2008] E.C.H.R. 214).

SCHEDULE 1

POWERS UNDER AND BY VIRTUE OF WHICH THIS ACT OF ADJOURNAL IS MADE

Preamble

B1-03

Column 1	**Column 2**	**Column 3**
Relevant enactment conferring power	**Relevant amending enactment**	**Relevant provision in Schedule 2**
Section 1 of the Public Records (Scotland) Act 1937 (c. 43)		Rule 3.6
Section 2A(3) of the Backing of Warrants (Republic of Ireland) Act 1965 (c. 45)	Inserted by paragraph 5 of Schedule 1 to the Criminal Justice Act 1988 (c. 33) and continued by section 37(5) of the Extradition Act 1989 (c. 33)	Rule 30.3(2) and (6)
Section 8 of the Backing of Warrants (Republic of Ireland) Act 1965 (c.45)	Amended by paragraph 5 of Schedule 4 to the Criminal Procedure (Consequential Provisions) (Scotland) Act 1995 (c. 40)	Chapter 30
Section 38 of the Legal Aid (Scotland) Act 1986 (c. 47)		Chapter 33
Section 90(4) of the Debtors (Scotland) Act 1987 (c. 18)		Rule 20.8(2)
Section 10(3) of the Extradition Act 1989 (c. 33)		Rule 34.2(2) to (8)
Section 14(3) of, and paragraph 9(3) of Schedule 1 to, the Extradition Act 1989 (c. 33)		Rule 34.5
Section 8(5) of the Computer Misuse Act 1990 (c. 18)		Rule 35.1

Column 1 **Relevant enactment conferring power**	Column 2 **Relevant amending enactment**	Column 3 **Relevant provision in Schedule 2**
Section 10 of the Criminal Justice (International Co-operation) Act 1990 (c. 5)		Chapter 36
Section 19(2) of the Prisoners and Criminal Proceedings (Scotland) Act 1993 (c. 9)		Rule 15.2(6)
Section 18(7) of the Proceeds of Crime (Scotland) Act 1995 (c. 43)		Rule 37.2

SCHEDULE 2

Criminal Procedure Rules 1996

Paragraph 2

Arrangement of Rules

Part I Preliminary and administration

Chapter 1 Citation, Interpretation Etc.

Rule	
1.1.	Citation of these Rules
1.2.	Interpretation
1.3.	Forms
1.4.	Direction relating to Advocate General

Chapter 2 Service of Documents

2.1.	Service on Crown
2.2.	Citation in solemn proceedings
2.2A.	Citation in solemn proceedings by service on solicitor
2.3.	General provisions for service
2.3A.	Service etc. on accused through a solicitor
2.4.	Service on witnesses
2.5.	Service by post
2.6.	Forms of execution of service
2.7.	Proof of service furth of Scotland

Chapter 3 Court Records

3.1.	Books of Adjournal
3.2.	Form of minuting in solemn proceedings
3.3.	Interlocutors in High Court to be signed by clerk of court
3.4.	Record copies of indictments etc. to be inserted in record books
3.5.	Form of recording warrants for remission of sentences
3.5A.	Registers kept by High Court
3.6.	Custody and transmission of records

Chapter A4 Excusal of Procedural Irregularities

A4.1.	Application to court to excuse procedural irregularity

Part II General

Chapter 4 Bail

4.1.	Application to alter address in bail order
4.2.	Attendance of accused at Crown bail appeals

Chapter 5 Judicial Examination

5.1.	Procedure in examination

5.2. Record of examination
5.3. Verbatim record
5.4. Use of tape recorders
5.5 Questions by prosecutor
5.6. Rectification of errors in transcript
5.7. Alteration of time limits by sheriff
5.8. Postponement of trial diet by sheriff
5.9. Postponement of trial diet by High Court
5.10. Alteration of time limits by High Court

Chapter 6 Proceedings Involving Children

6.1. Interpretation of this Chapter
6.2. Application of summary procedure
6.3. Assistance for unrepresented child
6.4. Procedure in summary proceedings
6.5. Failure to comply with probation order
6.6. Separation of children at sittings
6.7. Restrictions on reports of proceedings involving children

Chapter 7 Mental Disorder

7.1. Application for assessment orders
7.2. Assessment orders ex proprio motu
7.3. Applications for treatment orders
7.4. Treatment orders ex proprio motu
7.5. Variation of assessment orders or review of treatment orders
7.6. Interim compulsion order
7.7. Assessment, treatment and interim compulsion orders: specified hospital
7.8. Compulsion orders and hospital directions: specified hospital
7.9 Appeals

Chapter 7A Disclosure

7A.1. Interpretation
7A.2. Defence statements
7A.3. Applications for ruling on disclosure
7A.4. Review of ruling on disclosure
7A.5. Appeal against ruling
7A.6. Applications for orders preventing or restricting disclosure: prosecutor
7A.7. Applications for orders preventing or restricting disclosure: Secretary of State
7A.8. Special Counsel
7A.9. Appeals
7A.10. Review of section 145 and 146 orders
7A.11. Review by court of section 145 and 156 orders
7A.12. Applications during trials etc.
7A.13. Storage of sensitive information

Part III Solemn proceedings

Chapter 8 The Indictment

8.1. Appeals in relation to extension of time for trial
8.1A. Further provision as respects extension of twelve months period for commencement of trial on indictment
8.1B. Fresh indictment as alternative to serving notice fixing new trial diet
8.2. Citation of accused and witnesses
8.3. Notice of previous convictions

Chapter 8A Engagement, Dismissal and Withdrawal of Solicitors in Solemn Proceedings

8A.1. Notification

8A.2. Further pre-trial diet

Chapter 8B Failure of Accused to Appear

8B.1. Failure of accused to appear: form of warrant

Chapter 8C Transfer of Proceedings (Sheriff Court)

8C.1. Transfer of solemn proceedings outwith sheriffdom

Chapter 9 First Diets (Sheriff Court)

9.1. Minute giving notice of preliminary pleas or preliminary issues

9.2. Procedure on lodging minute

9.3. Orders for further diets under section 71 of the Act of 1995

9.4. Procedure at first diet

9.5. Applications for leave to appeal

9.6. Note of appeal

9.7. Procedure on lodging note of appeal

9.8. Report of sheriff

9.9. Intimation of order postponing trial diet

9.10. Orders of appeal court

9.11. Abandonment of appeal

Chapter 9A Preliminary Hearings (High Court of Justiciary)

9A.1. Notice of preliminary pleas and preliminary issues

9A.2. Applications to dispense with preliminary hearings

9A.3. Notice to appear where preliminary hearing deserted

9A.3A. Instruction of representation

9A.4. Written record of state of preparation

9A.5. Proceedings at preliminary hearing

9A.6. Applications for leave to appeal

9A.7. Note of appeal

9A.8. Abandonment of appeal

Chapter 9B Objections to the Admissibility of Evidence Raised after First Diet or Preliminary Hearing

9B.1. Notice etc. of objections raised after first diet or preliminary hearing

Chapter 10 Plea of Guilty

10.1. Procedure for plea of guilty

Chapter 11 Notices by Accused in Relation to Defence

11.1. Notices of special defence etc.

11.2. Notices by accused of witnesses and productions

Chapter 12 Adjournment and Alteration of Diets in Solemn Proceedings

12.1. Adjournment

12.2. Applications for alteration of diet

12.3. Orders fixing diet for hearing of application to alter diet

12.4. Calling of diet for hearing application

12.5 Joint applications without hearing

12.6. Form of notice where trial diet does not take place

12.7. Floating diets in the High Court of Justiciary

Chapter 13 Summoning of Jurors

13.1. List of jurors

13.2. Citation of jurors

Chapter 13A Witnesses

13A.1 Citation of witnesses for precognition

13A.2. Warrants for apprehension
13A.3. Review of orders
13A.4. Appeals

Chapter 14 Procedure at Trial in Solemn Proceedings

14.1. Recording of not guilty plea
14.1A. Minimum number of jurors for balloting jury
14.2. Balloting of jurors
14.3. Form of oath or affirmation to jurors
14.4. Jurors chosen for one trial may continue to serve
14.5. Form of oath or affirmation to witnesses
14.6. Sheriff's notes of evidence
14.7. Form of record of proceedings
14.8. Interruption of trial for other proceedings
14.8A. Interruption of proceedings for the tendering of pleas
14.9. Interruption of proceedings for conviction or sentence
14.10. Issue of extract convictions

Chapter 15 Appeals from Solemn Proceedings

15.1. Register and lists of appeals
15.2. Forms of appeal
15.3. Appeals against refusal of applications heard by single judge
15.4. Extension of time by Clerk of Justiciary
15.5. Intimation of appeal against sentence of death
15.5A Procedural hearing
15.6. Abandonment of appeals
15.7. Note of proceedings at trial
15.8. Clerk to give notice of date of hearing
15.9. Continuation of hearings
15.10. Note to be kept of appeal
15.11. Suspension of disqualification from driving pending appeal
15.12. Provisions supplemental to rule 15.11(3)
15.12A. Suspension of sentence under s.121A of the Act of 1995
15.13. Suspension of disqualification etc. under section 121 of the Act of 1995
15.14. Remits in applications for leave to appeal
15.15. Amended grounds of appeal
15.15A. Requirement for case and argument
15.15B. Hearing of appeal
15.16. Presentation of solemn sentence appeal in writing
15.16A. Copying of transcripts to other parties
15.17 Lodging and intimation of transcripts

PART IV SUMMARY PROCEEDINGS

Chapter 16 Complaints

16.1. Form of complaints and related notices and forms
16.2. Signature of prosecutor
16.3. Effect of failure by prosecutor to comply with certain requirements
16.4. Further procedural forms
16.4A Incidental applications out of hours
16.5. Form of certain warrants
16.6. Citation of witnesses
16.7. Applications for alteration of diets

Chapter 16A Engagement, Dismissal and Withdrawal of Solicitors in Summary Proceedings

16A.1. Notification

Chapter 17 Summary Pre-trial Procedure

17.A1. Applications for extension of period of detention
17.1. Appeals against extension of period of detention
17.2. Notice of defences

Chapter 17A Transfer of Summary Proceedings

17A.1. Transfer of summary proceedings

Chapter 18 Procedure at Trial in Summary Proceedings

18.1. Accused to plead personally and to receive intimation of diets
18.2. Form of oath or affirmation to witnesses
18.3. Warrants for apprehension of witnesses
18.3A. Review by witnesses of orders made under section 156A
18.3B. Citation of witnesses under section 156C(5)
18.3C. Appeals in respect of orders made under section 156A(1)
18.4. Record of proceedings to be written or printed
18.5. Interruption of proceedings after conviction
18.6. Detention in precincts of court

Chapter 19 Appeals from Summary Proceedings

19.1. Appeals relating to preliminary pleas
19.2. Forms for appeals by stated case
19.3. Forms for appeals against sentence only
19.4. Extension of time for appeals
19.5. Abandonment of appeals by stated case
19.6. Abandoning appeals against conviction only
19.7. Abandonment of appeals against sentence only
19.8. Intimation of abandonment
19.9. Applications for suspension of disqualification from driving in appeals
19.10. Applications for suspension of disqualification from driving in bills of suspension
19.10A. Suspension of sentence under s.193A of the Act of 1995
19.11. Solicitor entering appearance etc.
19.12. Duty to print stated case etc.
19.13. Duty of solicitor in bill of suspension
19.14. List of appeals
19.15. Diet for interim suspension
19.16. Intimation of determination of appeal
19.17. Suspension of disqualification etc. under section 193 of the Act of 1995
19.18. Remits in applications for leave to appeal
19.18A. Presentation of summary conviction appeals in writing
19.18B. Hearing of appeal presented in writing
19.19 Presentation of summary sentence appeal in writing

Chapter 19A Alteration by Clerk of Justiciary of Place Where Case to be Heard

19A.1. Power of clerk of Justiciary to alter place where case to be heard

Chapter 19B Scottish Criminal Cases Review Commission

19B.1. References
19B.2. Applications for requests for assistance

Chapter 19C Risk Assessment

19C.1. Risk assessment orders
19C.2. Reports

19C.3. Objections to reports

PART IVA APPEALS AND REFERRALS FROM SHERIFF APPEAL COURT

Chapter 19D Referral of Point of Law for Opinion of the High Court of Justiciary

19D.1. Interpretation of this Chapter
19D.2. Notice of intention to seek reference
19D.3. Reference proposed by the Sheriff Appeal Court on its own initiative
19D.4. Preparation of a reference
19D.5. Procedure before the High Court
19D.6. Procedure on receipt of opinion of the High Court

Chapter 19E Appeals to High Court of Justiciary

19E.1. Forms for appeals
19E.2. Lodging of appeal
19E.3. Documents to be considered in determining an application for permission
19E.4. Solicitor entering appearance etc.
19E.5. List of appeals
19E.6. Intimation of determination of appeal
19E.7. Abandonment of appeal

PART V SENTENCING

Chapter 20 Sentencing

20.1. Form of sentence of death
20.2. Detention in police custody instead of imprisonment
20.3. Supervised release orders
20.3A. Sexual offences to which Part 2 of the Sexual Offences Act 2003 applies
20.4. Application of money found on offender towards fine
20.5. Extension of time for payment of fine
20.6. Forms for enquiry for non-payment of fine
20.7. Supervision of payment of fine
20.8. Forms of warrant for execution and charge for payment of fine or other financial penalty
20.9. Transfer of fines
20.9A. Enforcement orders
20.9AA. Application for release of vehicle
20.9B. Application for an order for sale or disposal of a vehicle
20.9C. Application by a third party claiming to own vehicle
20.9D. Review of actions of fines enforcement officer
20.10. Probation orders
20.10A. Form and notification of non-harassment order
20.10B. Variation or revocation of non-harassment order
20.11. Supervised attendance orders
20.12. Community service orders
20.12A. Restriction of liberty orders
20.12B. Drug treatment and testing orders
20.12C. Community reparation orders
20.13. Terms of compensation orders in record of proceedings
20.14. Legal disability of person entitled to compensation
20.15. Variation of compensation orders
20.16. Discharge or reduction of compensation order
20.17. Use of certified copy documents in certain proceedings
20.18. Form of extract of sentence
20.19. Reduction of disqualification period for drink-drive offenders

20.20.	Antisocial behaviour orders
20.21.	Orders for lifelong restriction
20.22	Community payback orders
20.23	Supervision default orders

PART VI EVIDENCE

Chapter 21 Uncontroversial Evidence, Hearsay and Prior Statements

21.1.	Notice of uncontroversial evidence
21.2.	Notice of challenge of evidence as uncontroversial
21.2A.	Application for direction that challenge be disregarded
21.3.	Notice of intention to have hearsay statement admitted
21.4.	Authentication of certain prior statements of witnesses
21.5.	Form of application to introduce evidence relating to sexual offences
21.6	Notice of intention to rely on presumption of identification

Chapter 22 Evidence of Vulnerable Witnesses

22.1.	Vulnerable witness notice: non-standard special measures
22.1ZA.	Vulnerable witness notice: standard special measures
22.1A.	Vulnerable witness application
22.2.	Procedure on lodging vulnerable witness notice or vulnerable witness application
22.2A.	Objections to special measures
22.3.	Intimation of an order under section 271A
22.3A.	Intimation of an order under section 271C
22.4.	Review of arrangements for vulnerable witnesses
22.5.	Procedure for review
22.6.	Intimation of the order
22.7.	Notice of prohibition of personal conduct of defence
22.8.	Application for prohibition of personal conduct of defence
22.9.	Transfer of cases
22.10.	Evidence in chief in form of prior statement
22.11.	Appointment of commissioner
22.12.	The commission
22.13.	Video recording of commission
22.14.	Custody of video recording and documents
22.15.	Applications for leave for accused to be present at commission

Chapter 22A Witness Anonymity Orders

22A.1.	Application for witness anonymity order
22A.2.	Notice of application in summary proceedings
22A.3.	Discharge and variation of witness anonymity order
22A.4.	Appeals

Chapter 23 Letters of Request

23.1.	Applications for letters of request
23.2.	Powers of court in applications
23.3.	Expenses
23.4.	Transmission of letters of request
23.5.	Custody of documents
23.6.	Prohibition of reference to evidence without leave

Chapter 23A Television Link Evidence

23A.1	Application for television link evidence
23A.2	Powers of the court in applications
23A.3	Expenses

23A.4 Transmission of letters of request
23A.5 Procedural diet

Chapter 24 Evidence on Commission

24.1. Applications to take evidence on commission
24.2. Appointment of commissioner
24.3. Expenses
24.4. The commission
24.5. Commissioner's report
24.6. Custody of documents
24.7. Prohibition of reference to evidence without leave

Chapter 25 Record of Judicial Examination as Evidence in Solemn Proceedings

25.1. Use of transcript of judicial examination

Chapter 26 Documentary Evidence

26.1. Authentication of copies of documents

Chapter 27 Routine Evidence, Sufficient Evidence and Proof of Previous Convictions

27.1. Notices in relation to use of autopsy and forensic science reports
27.2. Form of certificates in relation to certain evidence
27.3. Form of notice in relation to certain evidential certificates
27.4. Notices under section 16A(4) of the Criminal Law (Consolidation) (Scotland) Act 1995
27.5. Notice under section 16B(4) of Criminal Law (Consolidation) (Scotland) Act 1995

Chapter 27A Recovery of Documents

27A.1. Appeal against decision of sheriff

PART VII MISCELLANEOUS PROCEDURES

Chapter 28 Identification Procedures

28.1. Applications for identification parade
28.2. Order requiring accused to participate in identification procedure

Chapter 29 Precognition on Oath of Defence Witnesses

29.1. Applications for warrant to cite for precognition
29.2. Orders for taking precognition
29.3. Citation to attend for precognition
29.4. Record of proceedings
29.5. Fees of shorthand writer

Chapter 29A Service of Bills of Advocation and Suspension and Petitions to the Nobile Officium

29A.1. Service of bill or petition

Chapter 29B Contempt of Court

29B.1. Application of this Chapter
29B.2. Withdrawal of jury
29B.3. Criminal prosecution
29B.4. Procedure where the prosecutor does not intend to bring criminal proceedings
29B.5. Statement of facts
29B.6. The contempt hearing
29B.7. Adjournment of the hearing
29B.8. Remand appeal
29B.9. Minute of proceedings

Chapter 30 Proceedings for the Execution of Irish Warrants

Chapter 31 References to the European Court of Justice

31.1. Interpretation of this Chapter

31.2. Notice of references in solemn proceedings
31.3. Notice of references in summary proceedings
31.3A. References in proceedings in the Sheriff Appeal Court
31.4. Proceedings on appeal etc. to the High Court
31.5. Preparation of case for reference
31.6. Procedure on receipt of preliminary ruling
31.7. Appeals against references

Chapter 32 Annoying Creatures

32.1. Interpretation of this Chapter
32.2. Form of application to district court and service

Chapter 33 Legal Aid

33.1. Interpretation of this Chapter
33.2. Legal aid in High Court
33.3. Discontinuance of entitlement to legal aid
33.4. Statements on oath
33.5. Intimation of determination of High Court
33.6. Intimation of appointment of solicitor by court in proceedings in respect of sexual offence

Chapter 34 Extradition

34.1. Interpretation of this Chapter
34.1A. Provisional arrest
34.2. Arrest under provisional warrant
34.2A. Procedural hearing
34.3. Application for leave to appeal
34.3A. Hearing of appeals
34.4. Time limits
34.5 Applications for extension of time
34.6. Consent to extradition
34.7. Post-extradition matters
34.8. Part 3 warrants

Chapter 34A Interpretation and Translation in European Arrest Warrant Proceedings

34A.1. Interpretation and application
34A.2. Right to interpretation assistance
34A.3. Right to translation of Part 1 warrant
34A.4. Application for review of a determination about rights to interpretation or translation
34A.5. Application for a direction relating to interpretation or translation
34A.6. Applications under rule 34A.4 and 34A.5
34A.7. Information to be recorded by the clerk of court
34A.8. Provision of interpretation assistance and translation free of charge

Chapter 35 Computer Misuse Act 1990

35.1. Notices in relation to relevance of external law

Chapter 36 Crime (International Co-operation) Act 2003

36.1. Interpretation of this Chapter
36.2. Effecting citation or service of documents outside the United Kingdom
36.3. Proof of citation or service outside the United Kingdom
36.4. Applications for requests for assistance
36.5. Hearing of applications for requests for assistance
36.6. Register of applications for requests for assistance
36.7. Notification of requests for assistance

36.8. Citation for proceedings before a nominated court
36.9. Proceedings before a nominated court
36.9A. Time period for consideration of overseas freezing order
36.9B. Form of warrant for seizure and retention of evidence
36.9C. Application for release of evidence
36.10. Provision of interpreters
36.11. Court record of proceedings before a nominated court

Chapter 37 Proceedings under the Proceeds of Crime (Scotland) Act 1995

37.1. Orders to make material available
37.2. Discharge and variation of orders
37.3. Warrants to search premises
37.4. Orders under sections 25 and 26
37.5. Appeals under section 27

Chapter 37AA Proceedings under the Proceeds of Crime Act 2002

37AA.1 Interpretation of this Chapter

Confiscation

37AA.2 Confiscation orders
37AA.2A. Confiscation orders: certification
37AA.2B. Compliance orders
37AA.2C. Compliance orders: discharge and variation
37AA.2D. Compliance orders: breach
37AA.3 Disposal of family home
37AA.4 Application for postponement
37AA.5 Statement of information
37AA.5A. Initial period of adjustment
37AA.5B. First procedural hearing
37AA.5C. Second procedural hearing
37AA.5D. Preparation for determination hearing
37AA.5E. Hearing to check preparation
37AA.5F. General provision on adjustment
37AA.5G. Public holidays
37AA.6 Reconsideration of case, benefit or available amount
37AA.7 Variation or discharge of confiscation order
37AA.8 Time for payment
37AA.9 Hearings

Investigations

37AA.10 Application, discharge and variation

Chapter 37A Proceedings under Section 7 of the Knives Act 1997

37A. Proceedings under Section 7 of the Knives Act 1997

Chapter 38 Transfer of Rights of Appeal of Deceased Persons

38. Applications for transfer under section 303A of the Act of 1995

Chapter 39 Proceedings under Criminal Law (Consolidation) (Scotland) Act 1995

39.1. Orders to make material available
39.2. Discharge and variation of orders
39.3. Warrants to search premises

Chapter 40 Compatibility Issues and Devolution Issues

40.1. Interpretation
40.2. Raising compatibility issues and devolution issues: solemn proceedings
40.3. Raising compatibility issues and devolution issues: summary proceedings

40.4. Raising compatibility issues and devolution issues: other proceedings
40.5. Specification of compatibility issue or devolution issue
40.6. Time for raising compatibility issue or devolution issue
40.7. Intimation of compatibility issues and devolution issues to the Advocate General
40.8. Participation of Advocate General in proceedings
40.9. Appeals to the Supreme Court
40.10. Reference of compatibility issues and devolution issues to the High Court
40.11. Reference of compatibility issues and devolution issues to the Supreme Court
40.12. Orders pending determination of compatibility issues or devolution issues
40.13. Procedure on receipt of determination of compatibility issue or devolution issue
40.14. Procedure following determination of an appeal by the Supreme Court
40.15. Orders mitigating the effect of certain decisions

Chapter 41 Human Rights Act 1998

41.1. Application and interpretation
41.2. Evidence of judgments etc
41.3. Declaration of incompatibility

Chapter 42 Convention Rights (Compliance) (Scotland) Act 2001

42.1. Application and interpretation
42.2. Intimation
42.3. Disputed or additional documents
42.4. Procedural hearing

Chapter 43 Terrorism Act 2000 and Anti-terrorism, Crime and Security Act 2001

43.1. Interpretation
43.2. Applications under the Act of 2000 or 2001

Chapter 44 International Criminal Court Act 2001

44.1. Interpretation of this Chapter
44.2. Consent to surrender
44.3. Waiver of right to review

Chapter 45 Fur Farming (Prohibition) (Scotland) Act 2002

45.1. Interpretation of this Chapter
45.2. Representations in forfeiture orders

Chapter 46 Parental Directions under the Sexual Offences Act 2003

46.1. Young offenders: parental directions
46.2. Applications to vary, renew or discharge parental directions

Chapter 47 Protection of Children (Scotland) Act 2003

Chapter 47A Protection of Vulnerable Groups (Scotland) Act 2007

47A.1 References under the Protection of Vulnerable Groups (Scotland) Act 2007

Chapter 48 Protection of Children and Prevention of Sexual Offences (Scotland) Act 2005

48.1. Interpretation
48.2. Sexual offences prevention orders
48.3. Variation, renewal or discharge of sexual offences prevention orders

Chapter 49 Financial Reporting Orders

Chapter 50 Football Banning Orders

50.1. Interpretation
50.2. Football banning orders
50.3. Variation or termination of football banning orders

Chapter 51 Animal Health and Welfare

51.1 Interpretation

51.2	Deprivation Orders
51.3	Representations
51.4	Forms of appeal by person with interest in animal
51.5	Disqualification Orders
51.6	Termination or variation of disqualification orders
	Chapter 52 Investigation of Revenue and Customs Offences
52.1	Interpretation
52.2	Production Orders
52.3	Revenue and Customs warrants
52.4	Applications for variation, discharge or failure to comply with sections 23F or 23G
	Chapter 53 Review of Fixed Penalty or Compensation Conditional Offers by Procurator Fiscal
53.1.	Review by court of fixed penalty or compensation conditional offers by procurator Fiscal
	Chapter 54 Mutual Recognition of Criminal Financial Penalties
54.1.	Form of certificate
	Chapter 55 Recovery Orders under Section 27K(3) of the Civic Government (Scotland) Act 1982
	Chapter 56 Reporting Restrictions
56.1.	Interpretation and application of this Chapter
56.2.	Interim orders: notification to interested persons
56.3.	Interim orders: representations
56.4.	Notification of reporting restrictions
56.5.	Applications for variation or revocation
	Chapter 57 Regulation of Investigatory Powers Act 2000
57.1.	Interpretation
57.2.	Disclosed information: hearing
	Chapter 58 Control of Dogs (Scotland) Act 2010
58.1.	Interpretation
58.2.	Application for discharge of disqualification
58.3.	Appeal to the High Court
58.4.	Hearing and intimation
	Chapter 59 Double Jeopardy (Scotland) Act 2011
59.1.	Interpretation
59.2.	Exceptions to the rule against Double Jeopardy: applications by the Lord Advocate
59.3.	Other subsequent prosecutions: applications by the prosecutor
59.4.	Hearing and determination of applications
59.5	Appeal to the High Court
	Chapter 60 Regulatory Reform (Scotland) Act 2014
60.1.	Interpretation
60.2.	Publicity orders
60.3.	Remediation orders
60.4.	Variation of remediation order
	Chapter 61 European Protection Orders
61.1.	Interpretation
61.2.	Information about European Protection Orders
61.3.	Application for a European Protection Order
61.4.	Issuing of a European Protection Order
61.5.	Recognition of a European Protection Order

61.6. Implementation of a recognised European Protection Order

61.7. Modification and revocation of a non-harassment order

61.8. Translation free of charge

61.9. Where competent authority not known

Chapter 62 Request for Final Decision and Reasons

62.1. Application and interpretation of this Chapter

62.2. Form in which information to be provided

Chapter 63 Serious Crime Prevention Orders

63.1. Interpretation of this Chapter

63.2. Serious crime prevention orders

63.3. Variation or replacement of serious crime prevention orders

63.4. Extension of serious crime prevention orders

63.5. Notification of making or variation of order

Chapter 64 Trafficking and Exploitation Prevention Orders

64.1. Interpretation

64.2. Trafficking and exploitation prevention order

64.3. Variation, renewal or discharge of trafficking and exploitation prevention order

64.4. Representations by a third party claiming an interest in a vehicle, ship or aircraft

Chapter 65 Psychoactive Substances Act 2016

65.1. Interpretation of this Chapter

65.2. Prohibition orders

65.3. Variation or discharge of orders

65.4. Notification of making, variation or discharge of orders

65.5. Forfeiture orders

65.6. Forfeiture orders: representations

Chapter 66 Review of Liberation Conditions and Authorisation for Questioning

66.1. Interpretation of this Chapter

66.2. Review of investigative liberation conditions

66.3. Review of undertaking conditions

66.4. Authorisation for questioning

Chapter 67 European Investigation Orders

67.1. Interpretation of this Chapter

67.2. Application for a European investigation order

67.3. Variation or revocation of a European investigation order

67.4. Citation for proceedings before a nominated court

67.5. Proceedings before a nominated court

67.6. Time periods

67.7. Form of warrnat giving effect to European investigation order

67.8. Application to revoke or vary search warrant or to authorise the release of evidence

67.9. Application to vary or revoke a customer information order or an account monitoring order

67.10. Provision of interpreters

67.11. Court record of proceedings before a nominated court

Chapter 68 Approval of Sentencing Guidelines

68.1. Interpretation of this Chapter

68.2. Application for approval of sentencing guidelines

68.3. Consideration and determination of an application

Chapter 69 Labour Market Enforcement Orders
69.1. Interpretation of this Chapter
69.2. Variation and discharge of a labour market enforcement order
69.3. Appeals
Annex: Notes for Completion of Form 31.5
Schedule 3

[THE NEXT PARAGRAPH IS B1-04]

PART I

PRELIMINARY AND ADMINISTRATION

Chapter 1

Citation, Interpretation Etc.

Citation of these Rules

1.1. These Rules may be cited as the Criminal Procedure Rules 1996. **B1-04**

Interpretation

1.2.—(1) In these Rules, unless the context otherwise requires— **B1-04.1**

"the Act of 1995" means the Criminal Procedure (Scotland) Act 1995;
"counsel" means a practising member of the Faculty of Advocates or a solicitor having a right of audience before the High Court by virtue of section 25A of the Solicitors (Scotland) Act 1980;

(2) Unless the context otherwise requires, a reference to a specified Chapter, Part, rule or form is a reference to the Chapter, Part, rule, or form in the appendix to these Rules, so specified in these Rules; and a reference to a specified paragraph, sub-paragraph or head is a reference to that paragraph of the rule or form, that sub-paragraph of the paragraph or that head of the sub-paragraph, in which the reference occurs.

Forms

1.3. Where there is a reference to the use of a form in these Rules, that form in the appendix to these Rules, or a form substantially to the same effect, shall be used with such variation as circumstances may require. **B1-04.2**

Direction relating to Advocate General

1.4. The Lord Justice General may, by direction, specify such arrangements as he considers necessary for, or in connection with, the appearance in court of the Advocate General for Scotland. **B1-04.3**

AMENDMENTS

Chapter 1 as amended by Act of Adjournal (Criminal Procedure Rules Amendment No. 3) 1999 (SI 1999/1387) para.2(2)(a) (effective 19 May 1999).

Rule 1.4 inserted by Act of Adjournal (Criminal Procedure Rules Amendment No. 3) 1999 (SI 1999/1387) para.2(2)(b) (effective 19 May 1999).

[THE NEXT PARAGRAPH IS B1-05]

GENERAL NOTE

Rule 1.3 gives a degree of latitude to individual courts to adapt the forms set out in the Appendix to the Rules (as r.2(3) of the 1988 Rules did). Moreover, special power is given by s.305(4) of the 1995 Act to the Clerk of Justiciary, with the sanction of the Lord Justice General and the Lord Justice Clerk to vary the forms which are set out in the Appendix to the Rules. This power is, however, confined to variations necessary for giving effect to the provisions of the 1995 Act relating to solemn procedure only. It should also be noted that where the form has not been followed, care should be taken, when effecting variations, to ensure that the substance of the rule is followed: see *Stevenson v McGlennan*, 1990 S.L.T. 842. **B1-05**

Chapter 2

Service of Documents

Service on Crown

2.1. Any document that requires to be sent to or served on the Lord Advocate or the prosecutor under any enactment or rule of law shall be sent to or served on, as the case may be— **B1-06**

(a) if it relates to a case set down for trial in the High Court, the Crown Agent;
(b) if it relates to a case set down for trial in the sheriff court or district court, the appropriate procurator fiscal.

Citation in solemn proceedings

B1-06.1 **2.2.—**(1) Subject to rule 2.4 (service on witnesses), this rule applies to the citation of, and service on, an accused under section 66(4)(a) of the Act of 1995 (service and lodging of indictment, etc.).

(2) Service shall be effected by an officer of law—

(a) delivering the document to the accused personally;

(b) leaving the document in the hands of a member of the family of the accused or other occupier or employee at the proper domicile of citation of the accused;

(c) affixing the document to the door of, or depositing it in, the proper domicile of citation of the accused; or

(d) where the officer of law serving the document has reasonable grounds for believing that the accused, for whom no proper domicile of citation has been specified, is residing at a particular place but is unavailable—

(i) leaving the document in the hands of a member of the family of the accused or other occupier or employee at that place; or

(ii) affixing the document to the door of, or depositing it in, that place.

(3) In this rule, "proper domicile of citation" means the address at which the accused may be cited to appear at any diet relating to the offence with which he is charged or an offence charged in the same proceedings as that offence or to which any other intimation or document may be sent.

AMENDMENTS

Rule 2.2 as amended by Act of Adjournal (Criminal Procedure Rules Amendment No.2) (Miscellaneous) 2003 (SSI 2003/468) para.2. Brought into force on 27 October 2003 in accordance with para.1.

Citation in solemn proceedings by service on solicitor

B1-06.1.1 **2.2A.** Where the documents mentioned in section 66(6C) of the Act of 1995 (citation by service on solicitor) are to be served on a solicitor under that section, they shall be—

(a) delivered to the solicitor personally at the solicitor's place of business;

(b) left for the solicitor with an employee or partner of the solicitor at the solicitor's place of business; or

(c) posted to the solicitor's place of business by the first class recorded delivery service,

with a notice in Form 2.2A.

AMENDMENTS

Rule 2.2A inserted by Act of Adjournal (Criminal Procedure Rules Amendment) (Criminal Procedure (Amendment) (Scotland) Act) 2005 (SSI 2005/44) para.2(5) (subject to para.2(2)-(4)) (effective 1 February 2005).

[THE NEXT PARAGRAPH IS B1-06.2]

General provisions for service

B1-06.2 **2.3.—**(1) Subject to the following paragraphs of this rule and to rule 2.3A, the citation of, or the service of any document on, a person under or by virtue of the Act of 1995, these Rules or any other enactment shall, unless otherwise provided in the relevant enactment, be effected in the same manner, with the necessary modifications, as the citation of an accused in summary proceedings under section 141 of that Act (manner of citation) or under rule 2.2 of these Rules (citation in solemn proceedings).

(1A) The citation of a person to appear before the sheriff under an enactment mentioned in paragraph (1B) is to be effected in the same manner, with the necessary modifications, as the citation of an accused in summary proceedings under section 141 of the Act of 1995 (manner of citation), but—

(a) the citation is to be signed by the sheriff clerk instead of the prosecutor;

(b) the forms relating to the citation of an accused do not apply to such a citation.

(1B) The enactments are—

(a) section 256AC(1)(a) of;

(b) section 256C(1)(a) of; and

(c) paragraph 8(1)(a) of schedule 19A of,

the Criminal Justice Act 2003, as applied by paragraph 8(2) or (4) of schedule 1 of the Crime (Sentences) Act 1997.

(2) […]

(3) The citation in Form 29.3 of a person to attend a diet fixed for taking his precognition on oath under section 291 of the Act of 1995 (precognition on oath of defence witnesses) shall be made by personal service on him by an officer of law acting on the instructions of the accused or his solicitor.

AMENDMENTS

Rule 2.3 as amended by Act of Adjournal (Criminal Procedure Rules Amendment No.2) (Miscellaneous) 2003 (SSI 2003/468) para.2. Brought into force on 27 October 2003 in accordance with para.1.

Rule 2.3(1) as amended by Act of Adjournal (Criminal Procedure Rules Amendment No.4) (Criminal Procedure (Amendment) (Scotland) Act 2004) 2004 (SSI 2004/434) para.2 (effective 4 October 2004).

Rule 2.3(1A) and (1B) inserted by Act of Adjournal (Criminal Procedure Rules 1996 Amendment) (No.3) (Supervision Default Orders) 2016 (SSI 2016/300) para.2(2) (effective 31 October 2016).

Service etc. on accused through a solicitor

2.3A.—(1) Where anything is to be served on, given, notified or intimated to a solicitor under section 72G or section 148D of the Act of 1995 it shall be— B1-06.2.1

(a) delivered to the solicitor personally;

(b) left for the solicitor with an employee or partner of the solicitor at the solicitor's place of business; or

(c) posted to the solicitor's place of business by the first class recorded delivery service, with a notice in Form 2.3A.

(1A) The citation of a person to appear before the sheriff under an enactment mentioned in paragraph (1B) is to be effected in the same manner, with the necessary modifications, as the citation of an accused in summary proceedings under section 141 of the Act of 1995 (manner of citation), but—

(a) the citation is to be signed by the sheriff clerk instead of the prosecutor;

(b) the forms relating to the citation of an accused do not apply to such a citation.

(1B) The enactments are—

(a) section 256AC(1)(a) of;

(b) section 256C(1)(a) of; and

(c) paragraph 8(1)(a) of schedule 19A of,

the Criminal Justice Act 2003, as applied by paragraph 8(2) or (4) of schedule 1 of the Crime (Sentences) Act 1997.

(2) Paragraph (3) applies where a party requires to intimate—

(a) a vulnerable witness notice in accordance with section 271A(13) of the Act of 1995 (child and deemed vulnerable witnesses); or

(b) a vulnerable witness application in accordance with section 271C(11) of the Act of 1995 (vulnerable witness application).

(3) Intimation may be given to a solicitor under section 72G or 148D of the Act of 1995 by—

(a) any of the methods specified in paragraph (1); or

(b) sending it to the solicitor via the CJSM system, if that solicitor is a CJSM user.

(4) In this rule—

"CJSM user" means a solicitor who has an active account on the CJSM system;

"CJSM system" means the Criminal Justice Secure eMail system managed by the Ministry of Justice to facilitate the transmission of encrypted sensitive information between criminal justice organisations and practitioners.

AMENDMENTS

Rule 2.3A inserted by Act of Adjournal (Criminal Procedure Rules Amendment No.4) (Criminal Procedure (Amendment) (Scotland) Act 2004) 2004 (SSI 2004/434) para.2 (effective 4 October 2004).

Rule 2.3A as amended by Act of Adjournal (Criminal Procedure Rules Amendment No.6) (Criminal Proceedings etc. (Reform) (Scotland) Act 2007) 2007 (SSI 2007/511) para.2 (effective 10 December 2007).

Rule 2.3A as amended by Act of Adjournal (Criminal Procedure Rules 1996 and Act of Adjournal (Criminal Procedure Rules 1996 Amendment) (No. 4) (Sheriff Appeal Court) 2015 Amendment) (Miscellaneous) 2015 (SSI 2015/295) para.2 (effective 1 September 2015).

Rule 2.3(1A) and (1B) inserted Act of Adjournal (Criminal Procedure Rules 1996 Amendment) (No.3) (Supervision Default Orders) 2016 (SSI 2016/300) para.2 (effective 31 October 2016).

[THE NEXT PARAGRAPH IS B1-06.3]

Service on witnesses

2.4.—(1) Service of a citation by the prosecution or defence on a witness in any proceedings may, in the first instance, be by post. B1-06.3

(2) Where citation of a witness has been attempted by post but has not been effected, or the witness has not returned Form 8.2-D or Form 16.6-B, as the case may be, within the period prescribed in rule 8.2(3) or 16.6(1), as the case may be, citation of that witness shall be effected by an officer of law delivering the document to the witness personally.

Service by post

2.5.—(1) Subject to any provision in the Act of 1995 or of these Rules, service by post shall be by registered post, ordinary first class post or the first class recorded delivery service. B1-06.4

(2) Where the citation of, or service on, any person is effected by post under these Rules, the date of citation shall be deemed to be the day after the date of posting.

AMENDMENTS

Rule 2.5(1) as amended by Act of Adjournal (Criminal Procedure Rules Amendment No.4) (Criminal Procedure (Amendment) (Scotland) Act 2004) 2004 (SSI 2004/434) para.2 (effective 4 October 2004).

Forms of execution of service

2.6.—(1) The execution of service of a citation and notice to appear of a person accused on indictment referred to in rule 8.2(1) (citation of accused and witnesses) shall be in Form 2.6-A. B1-06.5

(1A) The execution of a citation of a person accused on indictment referred to in rule 8.2(1A) (citation of accused by affixing a notice) shall be in Form 2.6-AA.

(2) The execution of service of a complaint on an accused shall be in Form 2.6-B.

(2A) The execution of a citation of an accused referred to in rule 16.1(2A) (citation of accused by affixing a notice) shall be in Form 2.6-BA.

(3) The execution of personal service of a citation of a witness cited to appear at a trial on indictment shall be in Form 2.6-C.

(4) The execution of personal service of a citation of a witness cited to appear at a trial on summary complaint shall be in Form 2.6-D.

(5) The execution of a citation referred to in—

(a) rule 20.3(2) or (3) (supervised release orders: form of citation of offender) shall be in Form 2.6-EA;

(b)-

(d) […]

(e) rule 20.12A(3) or (4) (restriction of liberty orders: forms of citation of offender) shall be in Form 2.6-EE;

(f) rule 20.12B(2) or (3) (drug treatment and testing orders: forms of citation of offender) shall be in Form 2.6-EF; and

(h) rule 20.22(2) (community payback orders: failure to attend progress review) shall be in Form 2.6-EH;

(i) rule 20.22(4) (community payback orders: breach of community payback order) shall be in Form 2.6-EI; and

(j) rule 20.22(5) (community payback orders: hearing of applications to vary, revoke and discharge community payback orders) shall be in Form 2.6-EJ.

(k) rule 20.23(4) (supervision default orders: failure to comply) shall be in Form 2.6-EK;

(l) rule 20.23(5) (supervision default orders: hearing of application to amend or vary) shall be in Form 2.6-EL.

(6) The execution of a citation or service under rule 2.3(1) (general provisions for service) shall, with the necessary modifications, be in Form 2.6-F.

(7) The execution of service of documents under rule 2.2A (citation in solemn proceedings by service on solicitor) or rule 2.3A (service etc. on accused through a solicitor) shall be in Form 2.6-G.

Amendments

Rule 2.6 as amended by Act of Adjournal (Criminal Procedure Rules Amendment No.2) (Miscellaneous) 2003 (SSI 2003/468) para.2. Brought into force on 27 October 2003 in accordance with para.1.

Rule 2.6(7) inserted by Act of Adjournal (Criminal Procedure Rules Amendment) (Criminal Procedure (Amendment) (Scotland) Act) 2005 (SSI 2005/44) para.2(6) (subject to para.2(2)-(4)) (effective 1 February 2005).

Rule 2.6(5) as amended by Act of Adjournal (Criminal Procedure Rules Amendment No.2) (Miscellaneous) 2005 (SSI 2005/160) para.2 (effective 31 March 2005).

Rule 2.6(5) as amended by Act of Adjournal (Criminal Procedure Rules Amendment No.4) (Miscellaneous) 2010 (SSI 2010/418) para.2 (effective 1 February 2011; subject to savings in para.2(8)).

Rule 2.6(5) as amended by Act of Adjournal (Criminal Procedure Rules 1996 Amendment) (No.3) (Supervision Default Orders) 2016 (SSI 2016/300) para.2 (effective 31 October 2016).

Proof of service furth of Scotland

B1-06.6 **2.7.** Where any citation of an accused is served in England, Wales or Northern Ireland by an officer effecting such service in accordance with section 39(3) of the Criminal Law Act 1977 (citation of person charged with crime or offence to appear before a court in Scotland), the evidence of—

(a) that officer on oath, or

(b) written execution of service by him,

shall be sufficient evidence of that service.

[THE NEXT PARAGRAPH IS B1-07]

General Note

B1-07 Chapter 2 deals with the appropriate modes of service of any document which, under the 1995 Act or the 1996 Rules, requires to be served on accused, witnesses, jurors or other persons to whom notice must be given. Separate rules are provided for service on the Crown as represented by the Lord Advocate in solemn proceedings or the procurator fiscal in sheriff and jury trials and summary proceedings; for service on accused persons charged on indictment; and for service on accused persons in summary proceedings and for all witnesses (who should, in the first instance, be served by post). Special provision is also made in r.2.3(1A) for the unusual case where service is effected by the sheriff clerk when a supervision default order (which relates to an offender whose post-release supervision has been transferred from England or Wales to Scotland) requires to be made, amended or revoked. In such a case the general rule laid down in s.141 of the 1995 Act is applied but the sheriff clerk rather than the prosecutor must sign the citation.

This chapter is concerned with how service is to be effected on accused persons, whether natural or legal, and not with whether certain persons are amenable to criminal prosecution. In summary procedure, s.143 of the 1995 Act makes provision for prosecution of legal persons including legal non-persons. Partnerships (including limited liability partnerships: see s.1(2) of the Limited Liability Partnerships Act 2000), unincorporated associations, companies and bodies of trustees may be prosecuted by way of summary procedure. When this is to be done, these entities are to be cited in "their corporate capacity" (1995 Act, s.143(2); see *Aitkenhead v Fraser* [2006] HCJAC 51; 2006 S.L.T.711; 2006 S.C.C.R. 411) although proceedings may also be taken against specified individuals of the partnership, association or company (but not trustees) and in such a case the offence shall be deemed to be the offence of the partnership, association or company (s.143(3)).

So far as solemn proceedings are concerned, s.70 of the 1995 Act makes special provision for service of indictments on "bodies corporate" and specifies special rules which are adapted to accommodate the non-natural character of the corporate accused (such as appearance, representation and tendering of pleas). The forebear of s.70 has been held to apply to firms (see *Mackay Bros v Gibb*, 1969 J.C.26; *Douglas v Phoenix Motors*, 1970 S.L.T. (Sh. Ct.) 57). The High Court has also expressed the tentative opinion that the rules prescribed by s.143 for bodies of trustees would be likely "to apply equally to cases on indictment against trustees" (*Aitkenhead v Fraser*, 2006 S.L.T. 711 (para.6); see Ferguson, "Trusts and criminal liability", 2006 S.L.T. (News) 175).

When a partnership is dissolved for whatever reason, it can no longer be prosecuted for any offence of which it could be liable because the separate legal personality of the partnership is then and there extinguished (*Balmer v HM Advocate*, 2008 S.L.T. 799; 2008 S.C.L. 1070) and there is thereafter no "person" capable of being made a party to the prosecution for offences committed prior to dissolution.

The Crown

Rule 2.1 repeats the terms of r.166 of the 1988 Rules with the omission, however, of reference to the Act of Adjournal as being itself a rule of law but it is thought that no significance can be attached to that omission. Accordingly, when an application is made, for example, under r.4.1(1) to alter the accused's address specified in his bail order, service of the application should be made in accordance with r.2.1. Failure by a sheriff clerk to give notice to the procurator fiscal under r.4.1(5) of the accused's new bail address would justify an extension of the 12 month period under s.65(3) if the Crown encountered difficulties in effecting service of the indictment (see *Black v HM Advocate*, 1990 S.C.C.R. 609). Unlike r.166 of the 1988 Rules, r.2.1(b) expressly refers to the district court now.

It is specifically provided that the provisions in r.2.1 have no application to service on the "relevant authority" (i.e. the Lord Advocate, where appropriate, and the Advocate General for Scotland) of minutes which seek to raise devolution issues in terms of Part I of Sch.6 to the Scotland Act 1998 (c.46): see r.40.1(3). In such cases the relevant provisions are set out in rr.40.2, 40.3 and 40.4 (which includes proceedings for contempt of court: Practice Note of May 6, 1999 see C1-14, infra).

Service of indictment, Notice of previous convictions, etc.

Section 66(2) provides that the execution of the citation against an accused in solemn proceedings shall be in such form as may be prescribed by Act of Adjournal, or as nearly as may be in such form. The indictment should be served by an officer of law who must be a macer, messenger-at-arms, sheriff officer or other officer having authority to execute a warrant of court; any constable and any other person employed by the appropriate chief constable under s.9 of the Police (Scotland) Act 1967 for the assistance of constables and who has been authorised by the chief constable to effect service and execution of documents; any person or class of persons authorised to effect service and execution by the Lord Advocate or Secretary of State; and any prison officer when the accused is in prison (see s.307(1) of the 1995 Act). Three principal modes of service are provided: (1) personal service on the accused wherever he is found within the jurisdiction; (2) service at his bail address on a family member who must be an occupier of that address, or an occupier such as a tenant of that address, or an employee. It is submitted that reference to employee is reference to the accused's employee or an employee of a member of the accused's family or of an occupier of that address and is not restricted to the accused's domestic servants; (3) leaving the document attached to the door or behind the door at the accused's bail address. This list (which is identical to r.167 of the 1988 Rules) is exhaustive of the manner of citation and (3) is apt when no family member, occupier or appropriate employee is present. A fourth manner of citation is also specified (in r.2.2(2) (3)) but applies only where there is no bail address and the accused is not on remand in respect of the charges in the indictment.

Once an accused has been granted bail on condition inter alia that he reside at a specified address, that address is the accused's "proper domicile of citation" and can only be altered with the leave of the sheriff under s.25(2) of the 1995 Act (see Chapter 4). The Appeal Court has explained that the "whole point" of the bail address being specified by the court in the bail order granted under ss.24 and 25 of the 1995 Act is that it then becomes the address at which the accused may be cited to appear (see *Brown v HM Advocate*, 1998 S.L.T. 971). The Crown is therefore under no obligation to look behind the address and thus, if the accused has given the incorrect address on being admitted to bail, he cannot later found on that fact to complain of defective citation when resisting the Crown's application for an extension of the 12-month period. Service will be validly effected on the accused at that address whether or not it is the accused's correct address (see *Reilly v HM Advocate*, 1995 S.C.C.R. 45). Moreover, r.2.2(b) has been held to give an option to the Crown as to how service might be effected and service of an indictment at the accused's bail address was held to be valid even though by the time of service the accused had been arrested and detained in prison on unrelated charges (see *Jamieson v HM Advocate*, 1990 S.L.T. 845).

However, where the proper domicile of citation has ceased to exist because it has been demolished, unless the accused has been permitted to alter his domicile of citation under s.25(2) of the 1995 Act, the correct course for the Crown to take is to affix the indictment and citation to "the nearest place as could reasonably be regarded as the equivalent" of that address (see *Welsh v HM Advocate*, 1986 S.C.C.R.

233). The Crown is not entitled to rely on r.2.2(2)(d)(ii) and put the service copy through the letterbox of the residence to which the police have subsequently come to understand the accused has removed. That is because that particular rule is intended to cover cases where the sheriff court has not specified a domicile of citation (e.g. where the accused has never appeared on petition). Since the bail address has not been altered, it remains—even though no longer physically in existence—the proper domicile of citation (see *HM Advocate v Holbein* (unreported), December 15, 2004 (para.7)).

Service generally

In practice an accused in summary proceedings, as well as witnesses in both solemn and summary proceedings, will be cited in accordance with the rules relating to citation in summary proceedings under s.141 of the 1995 Act. Effective citation is achieved by (1) delivering the citation to the accused or witness personally wherever he is found within the jurisdiction; or (2) leaving it for that person at his dwelling-house or place of business with a resident or employee at that place; or (3) where that person has no known dwelling-house or place of business, at any other place in which he may be resident at the time (see e.g. *HM Advocate v Finlay*, 1998 S.C.C.R. 103). In *Garrow v HM Advocate*, 1999 S.L.T. 1202 the Appeal Court held that s.66(3) of the 1995 Act did not operate to interfere with the right of the Crown to proceed by the traditional means of personal citation of witnesses in solemn cases. Rule 2.2 provided a variety of methods for service of a citation of a witness and all such methods were usually available subject to the qualification in r.2.4 that citation might, in the first instance, be by post. It is a matter for the Crown but once postal service has failed they are obliged next to attempt personal citation. When an accused person following upon his conviction on indictment is placed on probation and either fails to comply with the requirement of his probation order (see s.232 of the 1995 Act) or commits a further offence during the probation period (see s.233 of the 1995 Act), citation to attend a diet in respect of breach of his probation order should also be as aforesaid. However, when a witness has been cited to a diet under a warrant from the sheriff in order for his precognition to be taken on oath, personal service is required no doubt because an execution of personal service is the best evidence that a witness knew of the diet and his obligation to attend and such knowledge is essential to proof of guilt on a charge of failing to attend under s.291(2) of the 1995 Act.

Postal service

Postal service is a most cost-effective means of service and r.2.5 provides the types of postal service which are valid and makes express the rule that the date of receipt of a citation through the post is not the date of citation (see *Lockhart v Bradley*, 1977 S.L.T. 5). Where postal service has been selected in respect of a witness but has been ineffective, r.2.4(2) requires that personal service be thereafter attempted. Repeated attempts at postal service are irrelevant. Thus where, for example, the defence maintain at a trial diet that an essential witness is absent and has not been successfully served with a citation by post, the court will be entitled to refuse an adjournment if the defence has failed to attempt personal service and has simply attempted postal service again.

[THE NEXT PARAGRAPH IS B1-12]

Chapter 3

Court Records

Books of Adjournal

B1-12 **3.1.**—(1) The Edinburgh Book of Adjournal and the Book of Adjournal for cases heard outwith Edinburgh shall respectively contain—

(a) in the case of a trial in the High Court—

(i) the record copy of the indictment;

(ii) the minute of proceedings prepared by the Clerk of Justiciary;

(iii) the relative printed list of assize;

(b) in the case of a petition to the High Court—

(i) the record copy of the petition;

(ii) the minute of proceedings prepared by the Clerk of Justiciary;

(2) The Edinburgh Book of Adjournal shall contain the Acts of Adjournal.

(3) The minute of proceedings referred to in paragraph (1) shall be signed by the Clerk of Justiciary; and, on being so signed, shall have effect and shall be treated for all purposes, including extracts, as a true and sufficient record of the proceedings to which it relates.

Form of minuting in solemn proceedings

B1-12.1 **3.2.** Subject to the provisions of any other enactment, the forms of minuting in solemn proceedings before the sheriff shall be in accordance with the forms used in the High Court.

Interlocutors in High Court to be signed by clerk of court

B1-12.2 **3.3.** In the High Court, an interlocutor shall be distinctly minuted or entered in the record, and that entry shall be signed by the clerk of court.

Record copies of indictments etc. to be inserted in record books

3.4.—(1) The record copies of indictments brought before the High Court, and the record copies of all printed proceedings in that court, shall be inserted in the books of adjournal, either at their proper place in the body of such books, or at the end of the volume in which the relative procedure is recorded (in which case they shall be distinctly referred to as so appended); and the books of adjournal so made up and completed shall be and be taken to be and be used as the books of adjournal of that court. **B1-12.3**

(2) Where an indictment in solemn proceedings in a sheriff court is either wholly or partly printed, a copy of it, either wholly or partly printed, shall be inserted in the record book of court, either in its proper place in the body of that book or at the end of the volume in which the relative procedure is recorded (in which case it shall be distinctly referred to as so appended).

Form of recording warrants for remission of sentences

3.5. The Clerk of Justiciary shall cause all warrants under the royal sign manual for remission of sentences received by him to be bound in volumes and indexed, and a note of each warrant referring to a High Court sentence shall be entered in the margin of the minute book opposite the case to which it relates. **B1-12.4**

Registers kept by High Court

3.5A. Any register kept by the High Court, whether or not under or by virtue of these Rules, may be kept either— **B1-12.5**

(a) in documentary form; or
(b) in electronic form (that is to say in a form accessible only by electronic means).

Custody and transmission of records

3.6.—(1) Subject to the following provisions of this rule, the records of the High Court shall, after the Keeper of the Records of Scotland and the Clerk of Justiciary have consulted as to what records or parts of them may first be destroyed as not being considered to have a value for legal purposes or for historical or other research, be transmitted to the Keeper of the Records of Scotland under arrangements to be agreed between him and the Clerk of Justiciary. **B1-12.6**

(2) The Clerk of Justiciary and the Keeper of the Records of Scotland shall arrange for such transmissions at intervals of not less than five years nor more than 10 years from the date of the immediately preceding transmission and after similar consultation, for such periods as may be deemed by them to be appropriate.

(3) The Lord Justice General or Lord Justice-Clerk may make a direction from time to time in relation to the retention, disposal, transmission or destruction by the Clerk of Justiciary of any document or category of document in the records of the High Court.

AMENDMENT

Rule 3.5A inserted by the Act of Adjournal (Criminal Procedure Rules Amendment No. 3) 1999 (SI 1999/1387), para.2(3) (effective May 19, 1999).

Rule 3.1 as amended by Act of Adjournal (Criminal Procedure Rules Amendment No.2) (Miscellaneous) 2003 (SSI 2003/468), r.2. Brought into force on October 27, 2003 in accordance with art.1.

[THE NEXT PARAGRAPH IS B1-13]

GENERAL NOTE

Chapter 3 provides mainly for the administration of the court records of the High Court but also assimilates the sheriff court to the High Court in respect of the forms of minuting to be employed in proceedings on indictment. **B1-13**

Rule 3.1

The rule retains the historic distinction between sittings of the High Court at Edinburgh and circuits of the High Court outside the capital. The books of record in the High Court were described (see *Green's Encyclopaedia of the Laws of Scotland*, Vol. 8, s.v. "Justiciary, High Court of", para. 1496) as consisting of the Minute Book written in court by the clerk of court and the Books of Adjournal. A full and correct copy of the minute book at Edinburgh was written out and bound with relative principal indictments and petitions in an appendix. This volume was known as the "Books of Adjournal" (Encyclopaedia, supra, para. 1501). This rule now seems of only historic significance because of the computerisation of High Court records. When an accused now pleads guilty he has to sign a sheet of paper attesting to that fact because there is no physical Minute Book for him to sign.

Rule 3.1(1)(b)

Provides for petitions which can either be heard by a single judge of the High Court as in a petition under r.15.11(1)(b) (application to suspend ad interim a disqualification imposed by the High Court pending determination of an appeal against sentence) or be heard by a quorum of judges of the High Court as in a petition to the nobile officium. Historically the record of proceedings of the High Court in its appellate jurisdiction was kept under the title "Justiciary Appeal Book" and a separate minute book was kept for solemn criminal appeals (which were heard under the Criminal Justice (Scotland) Act 1926) (Encyclopaedia, supra, para. 1504). No provision is made in r.3.1 for court records relating to appeals (e.g. stated cases, bills of suspension or advocation, notes of appeal against decisions on competency or relevancy or in respect of conviction on indictment) which are all heard by the High Court sitting in its appellate capacity. Rule 15.1(1) does however provide that the Clerk of Justiciary shall keep a register of all cases in which he receives intimation of intention to appeal in solemn proceedings or in which notes of appeal are lodged under s. 108 by the Crown against unduly lenient sentences or under s. 106 by the accused who has been granted leave by the High Court to appeal against his conviction and/or sentence in solemn proceedings under s.107.

Rule 3.1(2)

Confirms the historic practice of inserting all Acts of Adjournal in the Books of Adjournal kept for sittings of the High Court at Edinburgh.

Rule 3.1(3)

"[H]ave effect and shall be treated for all purposes ... as a true ... record": it is unclear whether this rule entails, for example, that the summary of proceedings, if it incorrectly recorded a sentence, would take precedence over a judge's report to the High Court setting out the sentence which he actually imposed. Section 299(4)(b) empowers the High Court on appeal, when it becomes aware of an erroneous entry in the record of the proceedings, to remit the proceedings to the court of first instance for correction. It is however suggested that r.3.1(3) is not intended to alter the import of s.299(4)(b) and that the summary of proceedings is true only when the High Court considers that it is accurate.

Rule 3.2

Minuting is the recording of the significant details of the proceedings such as the place, date, judge's name, the Crown and Defence Counsel's name, whether a plea has been taken to the competency or relevancy of the indictment or proceedings, the jury members, the verdict, the sentence, etc. Form 3.1-A is the form of summary of the proceedings prescribed for High Court trials by r.3.1(1)(a)(ii) and should accordingly be employed in sheriff and jury trials also.

Rule 3.3

The term "interlocutor" is not defined in s.307(1) of the 1995 Act notwithstanding the fact that s.124(2) of the 1995 Act reproduces ss.262 and 281 of the 1975 Act and declares that "every interlocutor and sentence pronounced by the High Court ... shall be final and conclusive". The High Court has observed that "it is not the practice of the High Court in appeals under solemn procedure to issue interlocutors signed by the presiding judge" (*Perrie, Petitioner*, 1992 S.L.T. 655 at 657J; 1991 S.C.C.R. 475 at 480L; and *Boyle, Petitioner*, 1993 S.L.T. 1085 at 1088I–J) although in petitions to the nobile officium interlocutors are pronounced, presumably on the view that such petitions are proceedings sui generis and neither solemn nor summary in character (see *Express Newspapers plc, Petitioners*, 1999 S.L.T. 644 (Five Judges)). The reference to "interlocutor" has been described as unfortunate (see *Windsor, Petitioner*, 1994 S.L.T. 604 at 612H; 1994 S.C.C.R. 59 at 69C, per Lord Sutherland) but it was accepted in both *Perrie* and *Windsor* that "interlocutor" in s.262 (1995 Act, s. 124(2)) covers any judgment or order pronounced by the High Court (cf. *Church v HM Advocate*, 1996 S.C.C.R. 29 at 31A-B) but does not include a notice of determination under s. 120(4) of the 1995 Act of an appeal given by the Clerk of Justiciary. Where there is conflict between the notice of determination and the opinion of the court, the opinion is the best evidence of what was decided by the court (see, *Boyle, Petitioner*, above). A minimum recommendation in a mandatory life sentence case is not an "interlocutor" (see *Draper, Petitioner*, 1996 S.C.C.R. 324). In *Heywood, Petitioner*, 1998 G.W.D. 13-639, it was held that the interlocutor pronounced in open court in a summary appeal was the court's order and that the document subsequently issued by the Clerk of Justiciary was merely the record of the interlocutor. Accordingly it is unnecessary to seek rectification of the record when the order pronounced in open court accurately expresses the court's decision in the appeal although for the avoidance of doubt, such rectification can be granted.

Prior to the radical reforms of criminal procedure effected by the Criminal Procedure (Scotland) Act 1887, it was the practice of the High Court sitting as a trial court to issue interlocutors (e.g. sustaining the relevancy of the indictment or repelling the defences, before remitting the libel to "the knowledge of the assize") but now orders pronounced by the High Court as a trial court are not generally termed "interlocutors". Practice does, however, vary on occasion. For example, at present where the trial court appoints a hearing on an accused's minute for postponement of the forthcoming trial diet in terms of s.80 of the 1995 Act, the order assigning the diet is recorded as an interlocutor.

It is unclear what the effect of a total failure to comply with r.3.3 would be in appeal proceedings. So far as minuting of adjournments at first instance from day to day (outwith a sitting of the court) is concerned, the rule is that this must be done in order to preserve the instance (Renton and Brown, *Criminal Procedure* (6th ed.), paras 18-17 and 21-13), either before the expiry of midnight on the day of the adjournment or, perhaps, before the case next calls in court (see *Pettigrew v Ingram*, 1982 S.L.T. 435; *Heywood v Stewart*, 1992 S.L.T. 1106). This rule of the common law requires that the adjournment be to a fixed time and place. If the minute is not signed it is held to be no minute at all (*McLean v Falconer* (1895) 22 R. (J.) 39; 1 Adam 564) and the instance falls at midnight on the day of the purported adjournment. This rule applies only to trial proceedings because diets in appeal proceedings are not peremptory (see Notes to r.15.9) but if the minute in, for example, a Crown bill of advocation, is not signed, is the effect the same? It is suggested that it is not; the rule, though couched in mandatory terms, is directory only and does not entail that the Crown appeal fails.

Rule 3.4(1)

This rule confirms the practice of the High Court as to the inclusion of record copies of indictments in the Books of Adjournal (see, note on r.3.1, above).

Rule 3.4(2)

This rule applies the High Court practice in respect of indictments to the record books of the sheriff court.

Rule 3.5

Where a convicted person has successfully petitioned for the exercise of Her Majesty's Mercy his sentence is remitted (though his conviction stands: *HM Advocate v Waddell*, 1976 S.L.T. (Notes) 61). The more common name now for such remission of sentence is a royal pardon which is only granted where there is no other remedy for rectifying a miscarriage of justice (see *Stair Memorial Encyclopaedia of the Laws of Scotland*, "Criminal Procedure", paras 1.54 and 8.73). The fact that a sentence has been remitted is to be recorded in the appropriate minute book. The rule apparently envisages that only High Court sentences will be remitted as no reference is made to sheriff court sentences.

Rule 3.6

Not all records or proceedings in the High Court are of legal or historical interest and only those which can be considered to be in one or other of these two categories will be preserved by the Keeper of the Records of Scotland.

Chapter A4
Excusal of Procedural Irregularities

Application to court to excuse procedural irregularity

A4.1.—(1) An application made in writing under section 300A of the Act of 1995 (power of court to excuse procedural irregularities) shall be in Form A4.1 and shall be served on the other parties to the proceedings. B1-13.1

(2) On an application referred to in paragraph (1) being made, the court may appoint a diet for a hearing and intimate the diet to the other parties.

AMENDMENTS

Chapter A4 inserted by Act of Adjournal (Criminal Procedure Rules Amendment No.6) (Criminal Proceedings etc. (Reform) (Scotland) Act 2007) 2007 (SSI 2007/511) para.3 (effective 10 December 2007).

GENERAL NOTE

Section 300A of the 1995 Act was inserted by s.40 of the Criminal Proceedings etc (Reform) (Scotland) Act 2007 and brought into force on 10 December 2007. Section 300A(1) gives any court the power to excuse a procedural irregularity of various kinds specified in s.300A(5) occurring in the course of the proceedings before that court if certain conditions are satisfied. In relation to appeal proceedings, if these conditions are met, the High Court is given power to excuse these kinds of procedural irregularity where they have occurred in relation to earlier proceedings in the case which is the subject of appeal before the High Court. Thus procedural irregularities which went unnoticed (or uncorrected) in the lower court can be cured by the High Court when hearing an appeal from the lower court; and, of course, under s.300A(1) the High Court can also cure any such irregularities which occur in the course of proceedings before it. B1-13.2

This new power can be invoked by either the prosecutor or the accused person but no provision is made for third parties who may have brought proceedings before the High Court by petition to the nobile officium (see s.300A(9)(a)). This power of any court (whether exercising solemn or summary jurisdiction) is invoked by the relevant party making application for excusal of the irregularity. Section 300A(3) does not stipulate that the application must be in writing but r.A4.1(1) makes that necessary, presumably on the sound view that the application will then contain a clear statement of the precise irregularity which it is sought to have excused and the reason for the irregularity arising so that, if the court exercises its power, it will be clear from the court record what exactly has been corrected: hence the terms of para.2 of Form A4.1.

Section 300A nowhere provides that there should be intimation of the application to the other parties to the proceedings or that the court should fix a hearing but both these matters are covered by this new rule. The application must be intimated to the other parties; failure to do so will justify immediate dismissal of the application. The court is entitled to order a hearing on the application and for that purpose the court will order intimation of the diet to the parties (r.A4.1(2)).

Kinds of excusable procedural irregularity

The power to excuse irregularities is discretionary. The kinds of irregularities which may be excused are specified in s.300A(5). They arise at any stage of proceedings (a) from failure to call or discharge a diet properly; improper adjournment or continuation of a case; a diet being fixed for a non-sitting day (i.e. a day on which the court is under the 1995 Act not obliged to sit: s.300A(10)); (b) from failure of the court or prosecutor or accused to do something "within a particular period or otherwise comply with a time limit"; (c) from failure of the prosecutor to serve properly a notice or other thing; (d) from failure of the accused "to intimate properly" a preliminary objection, plea or defence (see s.78(1) and (2) in respect of special defences, defences of non-insane automatism and coercion and the claim of consent in answer to a charge of a sexual offence) or his failure to serve properly a notice or other thing; and (e) from failure of the court or prosecutor or accused "to fulfil any other procedural requirement". Something is done "properly" if it is done "in accordance with a requirement of an enactment or any rule of law" (s.300A(9)(b)).

This power does not authorise a court to excuse an irregularity which arises "by reason of the detention in custody of an accused person for a period exceeding that fixed by this Act" (i.e. in breach of ss.65 and 147) (s.300A(6)). Nor is this power applicable in relation to any requirement as to proof including, in particular, any matter relating to the admissibility or sufficiency of evidence or "any other evidential factor" (s.300A(7)).

Conditions for excusing procedural irregularity

The court's discretion to excuse any of the foregoing irregularities must be exercised only where the following conditions are met. These are that the court is satisfied that (a) the irregularity arose because of "mistake or oversight or other excusable reason" and (b) in the circumstances of the case it would be in the interests of justice to excuse the irregularity (s.300A(3)).

The phrase in s.300A(3) is almost identical to that employed in R.C.S. r.2.1 under which the Court of Session may now relieve a party from the consequences of a failure to comply with a provision of the Rules shown to be due to "mistake, oversight or such other excusable cause". That provision replaced the earlier power which was more circumscribed because it included the qualification that the mistake, oversight or other cause should not be "wilful non-observance" of the rule relief from non-compliance with which was sought. A wilful failure to comply with the relevant rules is, however, unlikely to be excused by a criminal court. But, as under R.C.S. r.2.1, it can be expected that the failure of the accused person's solicitor will count for exercise of the dispensing power and that a solicitor's ignorance of the rules of procedure will be a proper ground for the exercise of the power (see the court of five judges' decision in *Grier v Wimpey Plant & Transport Ltd*, 1994 S.L.T. 714 at 719). The power thus could be exercised by the High Court to allow an appeal to be taken against a decision of the sheriff at a first diet or of the High Court at a preliminary hearing outwith the period prescribed by s.74(2)(b) (viz. not later than two days after the decision). But as with civil procedure, failure to obtain leave to appeal under s.74(1) will not be curable, as to excuse that failure would be to frustrate the object of the requirement to obtain leave to appeal (cf. *Robertson v Robertson's Exr*, 1991 S.C. 21 at 24, per Lord President Hope).

Consequences of granting application

Where the court is satisfied that it should excuse the irregularity, it may make such order as is necessary or expedient for the purpose of restoring the proceedings as if the irregularity had not occurred; for facilitating the continuation of the proceedings as if the irregularity had not occurred; and for protecting the rights of the parties (s.300A(8)).

[THE NEXT PARAGRAPH IS B1-14]

PART II

GENERAL

Chapter 4

Bail

Application to alter address in bail order

B1-14 **4.1.**—(1) An application under section 25(2) of the Act of 1995 (alteration of address specified in the order granting bail) shall—

(a) include the following information—

(i) identification of the proceedings in which the order was made;

(ii) details of the new address; and

(iii) reasons for the proposed change of address; and

(b) be served on—

(i) the clerk of the court which made the order; and

(ii) the prosecutor.

(2) The prosecutor shall, within seven days of receipt of the copy of the application, notify the clerk of court in writing whether or not he intends to oppose the application.

(3) Where the prosecutor notifies the clerk of court that he does not intend to oppose the application, the court shall proceed to dispose of the application and may do so in the absence of the applicant.

(4) Where the prosecutor notifies the clerk of court that he intends to oppose the application, the clerk of court shall arrange a hearing before the court in chambers at which the applicant and the prosecutor may appear or be represented.

(5) The clerk of court shall give notice in writing of the decision of the court on an application referred to in paragraph (1) to—

(a) the applicant;
(b) the prosecutor; and
(c) any co-accused.

(6) Where—

(a) the application is made by a witness who has been granted bail under section 90B(1)(b) of the Act of 1995; and
(b) the warrant to apprehend the witness under section 90A(1) of the Act of 1995 was issued on the application of a party other than the prosecutor,

paragraphs (1) to (5) shall also apply to that party as they apply to the prosecutor.

AMENDMENTS

Rule 4.1(6) inserted by Act of Adjournal (Criminal Procedure Rules Amendment) (Criminal Procedure (Amendment) (Scotland) Act) 2005 (SSI 2005/44) para.2(7) (subject to para.2(2)–(4)) (effective 1 February 2005).

Attendance of accused at Crown bail appeals

4.2.—(1) Where an appeal is made under section 32(2) of the Act of 1995 the accused may attend the hearing of the appeal. **B1-14.1**

(2) Where the accused wishes to attend the hearing of the appeal, he shall inform the clerk of the appropriate Appeal Court not later than 24 hours before the hearing is due to take place.

(3) In this rule, "clerk of the appropriate Appeal Court" has the meaning given by section 32(11) of the Act of 1995.

AMENDMENTS

Rule 4.2 inserted by Act of Adjournal (Criminal Procedure Rules Amendment No.4) (Miscellaneous) 2010 (SSI 2010/418) para.3 (effective 13 December 2010).

Rule 4.2 as amended by Act of Adjournal (Criminal Procedure Rules 1996 Amendment) (No. 4) (Sheriff Appeal Court) 2015 (SSI 2015/245) para.4 (effective 22 September 2015 subject to savings provisions in para.6).

Rule 4.2(3) inserted by the Act of Adjournal (Criminal Procedure Rules 1996 Amendment) (No.4) (Sheriff Appeal Court) 2015 (SSI 2015/245) r.4(2)(b) (effective 22 September 2015 subject to savings specified in r.6(2) of that SI).

GENERAL NOTE

Apart from previous convictions, the most important factor in the refusal of bail in most cases is the suitability of the accused's bail address which becomes his "domicile of citation" under s.25(1)(b) of the 1995 Act. For accused persons the bail address is the place at which service of most documents is effected. That has been described as "the whole point" of the bail address being specified in the bail order granted to the accused (see *Brown v HM Advocate*, 1998 S.L.T. 971 at 973, per Lord Justice General Rodger). Accordingly, alteration of the bail address can only be effected with leave of the sheriff. All applications for alteration in the bail address must be served on both the clerk of the court which made the order and the procurator fiscal of the appropriate sheriff court district. The procurator fiscal is entitled to oppose the application and, if he does so, the sheriff will hear the application in chambers. It is imperative that an alteration in the bail address should be intimated to the Crown and any co-accused since they require to be advised of the new bail address at which documents should be served. Failure to give the Crown notice of the alteration of the bail address can have serious consequences under s.65(3) of the 1995 Act for the accused (see, e.g. *Black v HM Advocate*, 1990 S.C.C.R. 609). **B1-15**

Chapter 5

Judicial Examination

Procedure in examination

5.1. Subject to the following provisions of this Chapter, the procedure to be followed in relation to examination of the accused under sections 35 and 39 of the Act of 1995 (which relate to judicial examination) on any charge shall be in accordance with existing law and practice. **B1-16**

AMENDMENTS

Rule 5.1 as amended by Act of Adjournal (Criminal Procedure Rules 1996 Amendment) (Miscellaneous) 2017 (SSI 2017/144) para.2(2) (effective 29 May 2017).

Record of examination

5.2.(1) The record of all proceedings under the sections of the Act of 1995 mentioned in rule 5.1 (procedure in examination) shall be kept by the sheriff clerk in Form 5.2, and shall be kept by him with the petition containing the charge or charges in respect of which the accused is brought before the sheriff for examination. **B1-16.1**

(2) The sheriff clerk shall transmit to the prosecutor a certified copy of the petition under section 34 of the Act of 1995 (petition for warrant) and the record of proceedings—

(a) in relation to proceedings at which the accused is liberated in due course of law, on the conclusion of those proceedings; and

(b) in relation to any further examination, on the conclusion of that examination.

Verbatim record

B1-16.2 **5.3.** [...]

AMENDMENTS

Rule 5.3 repealed by Act of Adjournal (Criminal Procedure Rules 1996 Amendment) (Miscellaneous) 2017 (SSI 2017/144) para.2(2) (effective 29 May 2017).

Use of tape recorders

B1-16.3 **5.4.** [...]

AMENDMENTS

Rule 5.4 repealed by Act of Adjournal (Criminal Procedure Rules 1996 Amendment) (Miscellaneous) 2017 (SSI 2017/144) para.2(2) (effective 29 May 2017).

Questions by prosecutor

B1-16.4 **5.5** [...]

AMENDMENTS

Rule 5.5 repealed by Act of Adjournal (Criminal Procedure Rules 1996 Amendment) (Miscellaneous) 2017 (SSI 2017/144) para.2(2) (effective 29 May 2017).

Rectification of errors in transcript

B1-16.5 **5.6.** [...]

AMENDMENTS

Rule 5.6 repealed by Act of Adjournal (Criminal Procedure Rules 1996 Amendment) (Miscellaneous) 2017 (SSI 2017/144) para.2(2) (effective 29 May 2017).

Alteration of time limits by sheriff

B1-16.6 **5.7.** [...]

AMENDMENTS

Rule 5.7 repealed by Act of Adjournal (Criminal Procedure Rules 1996 Amendment) (Miscellaneous) 2017 (SSI 2017/144) para.2(2) (effective 29 May 2017).

Postponement of trial diet by sheriff

B1-16.7 **5.8.** [...]

AMENDMENTS

Rule 5.8 repealed by Act of Adjournal (Criminal Procedure Rules 1996 Amendment) (Miscellaneous) 2017 (SSI 2017/144) para.2(2) (effective 29 May 2017).

Postponement of trial diet by High Court

B1-16.8 **5.9.** [...]

AMENDMENTS

Rule 5.9 repealed by Act of Adjournal (Criminal Procedure Rules 1996 Amendment) (Miscellaneous) 2017 (SSI 2017/144) para.2(2) (effective 29 May 2017).

Alteration of time limits by High Court

B1-16.9 **5.10.** [...]

AMENDMENTS

Rule 5.10 repealed by Act of Adjournal (Criminal Procedure Rules 1996 Amendment) (Miscellaneous) 2017 (SSI 2017/144) para.2(2) (effective 29 May 2017).

[THE NEXT PARAGRAPH IS B1-17]

GENERAL NOTE

B1-17 Sections 35–39 of the 1995 Act provide at the Crown's discretion for the accused to be judicially examined before the sheriff at his first or subsequent appearance on petition in respect of the charge or charges contained in the petition and in respect of any extra-judicial confession (whether incriminatory in whole or in part) made to or in the hearing of a constable as defined in the Police (Scotland) Act 1967. The accused is also entitled, if he chooses, to emit a declaration made in his own words at such appearance (see *Robertson v HM Advocate*, 1994 S.C.C.R. 152 for an example of a declaration being emitted by an accused). Section 36(9) provides that the procedure in relation to judicial examination by the Crown shall be prescribed by Act of Adjournal.

Rule 5.1

Existing law and practice has been established principally since 1980 when judicial examination was reintroduced by the Criminal Justice (Scotland) Act 1980 but the 1995 Act has widened the prosecutor's right to question the accused so that he may now ask the accused whether he admits any or a part of the charge(s). The prosecutor is not entitled to cross-examine the accused or to reiterate questions which the accused has declined to answer. The sheriffs duty is to ensure fairness to the accused and he must advise the accused that he is not obliged to answer any questions but that his failure to do so may be commented on at his trial by the court, the Crown or any co-accused if he has advanced a defence at his trial which he could appropriately have stated but had not stated at judicial examination. It is suggested here that if the sheriff fails to administer this caution to the accused, the answers which the accused gives to questions at judicial examination will be inadmissible in evidence at his trial on the same principle as governs the admissibility of extra-judicial confessions. The accused should also be told by the sheriff that he is entitled to consult his solicitor before answering any questions (although the solicitor is not entitled to intervene either by way of objection to the prosecutor's questions or to volunteer advice to the accused) and that if his answers disclose an ostensible defence, the Crown is under a duty (under s.36(10)) to investigate the defence so far as is reasonably practicable (see s.36(6)). The duty under s.36(10) is administrative in character and requires the Crown to divulge the results of their investigations but only if requested to do so before trial: see *McDermott v. H.M. Advocate*, 2000 S.L.T. 366. It seems unlikely however that a failure to give such advice under s.36(6) will automatically render inadmissible evidence of what was said at judicial examination. An omission of this nature is in an entirely different position from a failure to administer the caution.

Rule 5.2

A certified copy of the petition is crucial to judicial examination as it is the basis on which the prosecutor may question the accused. In the event of comment at the trial being made about the accused's silence or statements at judicial examination, the trial court will require to examine the petition in order to determine the legitimacy of such comment in the light of the charges which the accused originally faced at judicial examination. The certified copy petition need not however be lodged by the Crown and included with the list of productions annexed to the indictment (see r.5.5(5)).

Rule 5.3

Rule 5.3(1) and (2). There is no obligation to record the judicial examination by means of both a shorthand writer and a tape recorder but when a shorthand writer is employed, the sheriff clerk should also operate a tape recorder.

Rule 5.3(4).

A declaration by the accused should also be recorded in full: see *Robertson v H.M. Advocate*, 1995 S.C.C.R. 153.

Rule 5.3(7).

It is the Crown's duty to serve the transcript of the judicial examination on the accused and a failure to do so precludes use of the transcript as evidence at the trial.

Rule 5.4

When a tape recorder is employed, two tapes should be simultaneously recorded so that Tape A which is retained by the sheriff clerk until the criminal process is concluded, can be used to verify the accuracy of Tape B which is delivered to the Crown.

Rule 5.5

Rule 5.5 (1) and (2). If the sheriff does not receive a copy of the extra-judicial confession, no questioning of the accused about it can be permitted at the judicial examination.

Rule 5.5(3). As the accused is not put on oath any untruths told at judicial examination by an accused will not warrant prosecution for perjury although they could warrant a charge of attempting to pervert the course of justice or of perverting the course of justice.

Rule 5.5(4). Section 36(8) of the 1995 Act permits a prosecutor, judge and any co-accused to comment on the accused's having declined to answer a question put to him at judicial examination, only where and in so far as the accused or any of his witnesses in evidence have averred something which could have been stated appropriately in answer to a question which the accused declined to answer at judicial examination. It is here suggested that the judge should be invited by the Crown or counsel for the co-accused, outwith the presence of the jury, to permit comment to be made before adverse comment is in fact made. The 1995 Act does not expressly give to the trial judge a controlling discretion but the rule clearly envisages that the trial judge's permission should be applied for. The procedure followed should accordingly be the same procedure as is followed when the Crown seeks leave of the court to cross-examine an accused on his criminal record. The trial judge's discretion when it is exercised to allow adverse comment to be made on the accused's silence, will be capable of challenge on appeal as a ground for alleging a miscarriage of justice because it has been held that comment should be made only with restraint and without undue emphasis: see *McEwan v H.M. Advocate*, 1992 S.L.T. 317; 1990 S.C.C.R. 401.

Rule 5.6

Section 38 of the 1995 Act permits the sheriff to order rectification of the transcript of the judicial examination if it contains an error or is incomplete. The Crown or the accused must within 10 days of service of the transcript, serve notice on the other party that the Crown or accused considers that there is an error or that the transcript is incomplete. Within 14 days of service of that notice the party seeking rectification must apply to the sheriff for an order rectifying the transcript and the sheriff must within seven days of that application to him hear parties in chambers although, if there is agreement between the Crown and the accused that the transcript is defective the sheriff may dispense with the hearing. There is no appeal against the sheriff's decision which is declared by s.38(4) to be final but presumably that declaration only applies at the pre-trial stage to avoid delay which could be occasioned by appeal and does not prevent the accused from raising the matter in the Appeal Court in the event that he is convicted. It would be odd indeed if the sheriff's decision could not be challenged on the basis that it had caused a miscarriage of justice.

Rules 5.7 and 5.8

Where the time available before trial does not permit the Crown to comply with the requirement in s.36(6) to serve the transcript of the judicial examination on the accused and his solicitor (where appropriate) within 14 days of the judicial examination, or does not allow compliance with the time-limits under s.38(1) (see r.5.6), the sheriff can direct that those time-limits should be modified. In an extreme case the sheriff can also postpone the trial diet under s.37(7)(b) but r.5.8 prohibits such an order when the case is set down for trial in the High Court. The sheriff in such a case must (under r.5.9) report the case to the Clerk of Justiciary so that the High Court can determine whether or not to postpone the trial diet. The sheriff is directed by s.77(8) of the 1995 Act that postponement of the trial diet is incompetent *unless* he considers that modification of the time-limit would not be practicable. Presumably the same consideration applies when the High Court has to determine whether or not the trial diet should be postponed although s.37(8) refers only to sheriffs.

Rule 5.10

Section 37(9) permits the High Court to extend the time-limits referred to in the preceding note. A single judge of the High Court will hear the application which must be made by way of petition. Although no form of petition is provided for by the Rules, it is suggested here that the petition should set forth (i) the name(s) of the accused; (ii) the date of the judicial examination; (iii) the dates of service of the transcript (where appropriate) or service of the notice under s.38(1); (iv) the error or incompleteness which is complained of in the transcript of the judicial examination (where appropriate); (v) the date of the trial diet; and (vi) the circumstances necessitating alteration of the relevant time-limit.

Chapter 6

Proceedings involving Children

Interpretation of this Chapter

B1-18 **6.1.** In this Chapter—

"the Act of 1937" means the Children and Young Persons (Scotland) Act 1937;
"court" means the sheriff sitting as a court of summary jurisdiction.

Application of summary procedure

B1-18.1 **6.2.** The procedure in summary proceedings shall apply, in relation to proceedings against a child as it applies to proceedings against an adult, subject to the provisions of the Act of 1937, the Act of 1995 and this Chapter.

Assistance for unrepresented child

B1-18.2 **6.3.**—(1) Where a child is unrepresented in any proceedings, the parent or guardian of the child may assist him in conducting his defence.

(2) Where the parent or guardian of the child cannot be found, or cannot in the opinion of the court reasonably be required to attend, the court may allow a relative or other responsible person to assist the child in conducting his defence.

Procedure in summary proceedings

B1-18.3 **6.4.** In a case where a child is brought before a court on a complaint, the sheriff—

(a) shall explain to the child the substance of the charge in simple language suitable to his age and understanding, and shall then ask the child whether he admits the charge;

(b) if satisfied, after trial or otherwise, that the child has committed an offence, shall so inform the child and—
   (i) the child and his parent, guardian, relative or other responsible person assisting the child, or the person representing the child, shall be given an opportunity to make a statement, and
   (ii) shall obtain such information as to the general conduct, home surroundings, school record, health and character of the child as may enable the sheriff to deal with the case in the best interests of the child and may remand the child for such enquiry as may be necessary; and
(c) if the sheriff considers it necessary in the interests of the child while considering disposal after conviction, may require the parent, guardian, relative or other responsible person assisting the child, or the person representing the child, or the child, as the case may be, to withdraw from the court.

Failure to comply with probation order

6.5. […] **B1-18.4**

AMENDMENTS

Rule 6.5 repealed by Act of Adjournal (Criminal Procedure Rules Amendment No.4) (Miscellaneous) 2010 (SSI 2010/418) para.2 (effective February 1, 2011; subject to savings in para.2(8)).

Separation of children at sittings

6.6.—(1) The court shall take steps, so far as possible, to prevent children attending sittings of the court from mixing with one another. **B1-18.5**

(2) If this cannot be achieved by holding separate sittings or fixing different hours for the different cases and types of cases coming before it, the court may order additional waiting rooms to be brought into use or may provide for an attendant in the waiting room.

Restrictions on reports of proceedings involving children

6.7.—(1) Any direction made by a court under subsection (3)(a) (person under 16 is a witness only) of section 47 (restriction on report of proceedings involving children) of the Act of 1995 shall specify the person in respect of whom the direction is made. **B1-18.6**

(2) Any direction made by a court under subsection (3)(b) of section 47 of the Act of 1995 (restrictions dispensed with) shall specify the person in respect of whom the direction is made and the extent to which the provisions of the section are dispensed with in relation to that person.

(3) Any such direction shall be pronounced in open court and its terms shall be recorded in the record of proceedings; and the direction as so recorded shall be authenticated by the signature of the clerk of court.

[THE NEXT PARAGRAPH IS B1-19]

GENERAL NOTE

Sections 41 to 51 of the 1995 Act contain special provisions for cases involving children who are under 16 years of age. Chapter 6 provides rules which relate only to the sheriff court exercising its summary jurisdiction (r. 6.1). Children cannot competently be prosecuted in the district court (see s.42(1)). Section 42(4) provides that for the purpose of enforcing the attendance of a parent or guardian of a child who is being prosecuted, and for enabling the parent or guardian to take part in the conduct of the child's defence and enabling orders to be made against the parent or guardian (see s.45(1)—order that parent or guardian give security for his co-operation in securing his child's good behaviour), rules may be made by Act of Adjournal for applying, with the necessary adaptations and modifications, such of the provisions of the 1995 Act relating to summary procedure as appear appropriate for the purpose. Rule 6.2 provides that the procedures for children are to be the same as the procedures for adults except in so far as the 1995 Act, the Children and Young Persons (Scotland) Act 1937 and Chapter 6 provide different or additional rules. **B1-19**

Rule 6.3

Section 42(2) of the 1995 Act provides that where a child under 16 years is charged, his parent (who is the person having parental responsibilities or parental rights under s.1(3) and s.2(4)respectively of the Children (Scotland) Act 1995) or his guardian having actual possession and control of the child (see s.42(5)) may be required to attend at the court during all stages of the proceedings and, if such parent or guardian can be found and resides within a reasonable distance of the court, he *shall* require to attend. When a child is arrested a warning must be given to the parent or guardian by the police that he should attend at court (see s.42(3)). It is suggested here that the purpose of these provisions is two-fold: (i) to inform the parent or guardian of what is happening to his child, and (ii) to allow him the opportunity to assist his child both in the conduct of his defence in court and in the child being of good behaviour. Rule 6.3(1) obliges the sheriff to allow the parent or guardian to assist in his child's defence but only where his child has no legal representation. Rule 6.3(2) goes further than the 1995 Act because another relative or responsible person can be permitted to assist in the defence even though no requirement to attend court can be made in respect of that relative or responsible person.

Rule 6.4

This rule imposes duties on the sheriff irrespective of whether the child is legally represented or not. It is open to question, however, whether failure to explain the charge, or to afford the parent an opportunity to make a statement, would respectively vitiate conviction or sentence. See *Heywood v. B*, 1993 S.C.C.R. 554. The local authority responsible for the particular sheriff court district will by the stage of conviction have received notification from the chief constable of the area in which the offence was committed, of the day and time when and the nature of the charge on which the child is brought before the court (see s.42(7)). That local authority is placed under a duty (by s.42(8)) to make investigations and to submit a report to the court. The report should deal with the child's home surroundings, school record (which the appropriate education authority is under a duty to supply), health and character.

Rule 6.5

The duties to serve the notice on the child either with the citation or personally and to explain to the child the effect of the notice, are no doubt important but it is open to question whether failure to discharge these duties would necessarily vitiate the proceedings. These duties also apply whether or not the child has legal representation or is accompanied by his parent, guardian, other relative or responsible person.

Rule 6.6

Section 42(9) requires inter alia that while a child accused is waiting at court he should be prevented from associating with an adult (not being a relative) who is charged with any offence other than an offence with which the child is jointly charged. This rule applies to all children whether they are witnesses, accused or complainers. When an attendant is required, at least for a child accused, the attendant must be female if the child is female.

Rule 6.7

No newspaper report of any court proceedings should reveal the name, address or school, or include any particulars which are calculated to lead to the identification of the child who is concerned in the proceedings either as an accused or as a witness (see s.47(1)). Furthermore, no picture which is or includes a picture of such a child should be published in a context relevant to the proceedings (see s.47(2)). These restrictions apply mutatis mutandis to radio and television broadcasts (see s.47(4)). However, where the child is concerned in the proceedings only as a witness, these restrictions do not apply unless the court so directs (see s.47(3)). The court can also dispense with these restrictions when at any stage in the proceedings it is satisfied that it is in the public interest to lift reporting restrictions. In both the imposing of the restrictions in respect of a child who is a witness only, and the lifting of the restrictions in respect of any child concerned in the proceedings, the order is specific to named individuals.

Article 10(1) of the European Convention on Human Rights guarantees the right to freedom of expression but subject to certain limited qualifications (set out in Art. 10(2)) which must be prescribed by law and necessary in a democratic society. Two such justifications are "the protection of health or morals … [or] the reputation or rights of others". The effect of European jurisprudence is that when there is a violation of the right, the burden is cast on the violator to show that the restriction is legitimate and proportionate to one of the objects set out in Art. 10(2) such as the protection of the reputation of others. It is for consideration whether the restrictions on press reporting of summary cases involving children as accused are compatible with Art. 10 since they apply a blanket ban on reporting subject to a discretionary power in the court to disapply them on being asked to do so. The press have an interest in asking for the reporting restrictions to be disapplied. No doubt the press could not be prevented from appearing in the course of the proceedings (or even after the conclusion of them?) to ask for the restrictions to be lifted and it may be that they could also invoke the nobile officium in order to appeal against a refusal by the court to lift reporting restrictions. See Introduction and General Note at B1-02.

Chapter 7

Mental Disorder

Application for assessment orders

B1-20 **7.1.**—(1) A written application under—

(a) section 52B(1) of the Act of 1995 (assessment order: prosecutor); or

(b) section 52C(1)of the Act of 1995 (assessment order: Scottish Ministers),

shall be in Form 7.1.

(2) Where an application is made under paragraph (1)—

(a) the court shall appoint a diet for hearing the application; and

(b) the clerk of court shall intimate the diet to the applicant, the person in respect of whom the application is made or the solicitor for that person, the governor of any institution in which the person in respect of whom the application is made is detained and, where the application is by the Scottish Ministers, the prosecutor.

Assessment orders ex proprio motu

B1-20.1 **7.2.** Where the court considers making an assessment order under section 52E of the Act of 1995 (assessment order: *ex proprio motu*) and considers it appropriate to do so—

(a) the court shall appoint a diet for parties to be heard; and

(b) the clerk of court shall intimate the diet to the prosecutor, the person in respect of whom the order may be made or the solicitor for that person, and the governor of any institution in which the person in respect of whom the application is made is detained.

Applications for treatment orders

7.3.—(1) A written application under— **B1-20.2**

(a) section 52K(1) of the Act of 1995 (treatment order: prosecutor); or
(b) section 52L(1) of the Act of 1995 (treatment order: Scottish Ministers),

shall be in Form 7.3.

(2) Where an application is made under paragraph (1)—

(a) the court shall appoint a diet for hearing the application; and
(b) the clerk of court shall intimate the diet to the applicant, the person in respect of whom the application is made or the solicitor for that person, the governor of any institution in which the person in respect of whom the application is made is detained, and where the application is by the Scottish Ministers, the prosecutor.

Treatment orders ex proprio motu

7.4. Where the court considers making a treatment order under section 52N of the Act of 1995 (treatment order: *ex proprio motu*) and considers it appropriate to do so— **B1-20.3**

(a) the court shall appoint a diet for parties to be heard; and
(b) the clerk of court shall intimate the diet to the prosecutor, the person in respect of whom the order may be made or the solicitor for that person, and the governor of any institution in which the person in respect of whom the application is made is detained.

Variation of assessment orders or review of treatment orders

7.5. Where the court receives a report under section 52G(9) (report for variation of assessment order) or section 52Q(1) (report for review of treatment order) of the Act of 1995— **B1-20.4**

(a) the court shall, by interlocutor in Form 7.5, appoint a hearing for parties to be heard and where appropriate, grant warrant to authorised officers of the hospital or officers of law, to bring the offender from the hospital to the court for that diet; and
(b) the clerk of court shall intimate the diet to the prosecutor, the person in respect of whom the order has been made or the solicitor for that person.

Interim compulsion order

7.6.—(1) Subject to paragraph (2), where the court receives a report under section 53B(1) of the Act of 1995 (interim compulsion order)— **B1-20.5**

(a) the court shall—
 (i) by interlocutor in Form 7.6, appoint a hearing for parties to be heard and where appropriate, grant warrant to authorised officers of the hospital or officers of law, to bring the offender from the hospital to the court for that diet;
 (ii) discharge the diet already fixed; and
(b) the clerk of court shall intimate the diet to the prosecutor, the person in respect of whom the order has been made or the solicitor for that person.

(2) Where the report referred to in paragraph (1) is received within 14 days before the diet already fixed, paragraph (1) shall not apply.

Assessment, treatment and interim compulsion orders: specified hospital

7.7. Where the court makes a direction under section 52F(1)(b) (assessment order: specified hospital), section 52P(1)(b) (treatment order: specified hospital) or section 53A(1) (interim compulsion order: specified hospital) of the Act of 1995 the court shall send a copy of the direction to the person in respect of whom the order has been made, the solicitor for that person, the prosecutor and the Scottish Ministers. **B1-20.6**

Compulsion orders and hospital directions: specified hospital

7.8. Where the court makes a direction under 57D(1) (compulsion order: specified hospital) or specifies another hospital in a direction under section 59C(1) (hospital direction: specified hospital) of the Act of 1995 the court shall send a copy of the direction or specification, as the case may be, to the person in respect of whom the order has been made and the solicitor for that person. **B1-20.7**

Appeals

7.9—(1) An appeal under: **B1-20.8**

(a) section 62 of the Act of 1995 (appeal by accused in case involving insanity); or
(b) section 63 of the Act of 1995 (appeal by prosecutor in case involving insanity),

shall be made by lodging a note of appeal in Form 7.9.

(2) At the same time as lodging a note of appeal under paragraph (1), the applicant shall send a copy to the other parties.

(3) As soon as possible after the lodging of a note of appeal under paragraph (1), the clerk of the appropriate Appeal Court shall request a report from the judge who made the finding, order or acquittal which is the subject of the appeal.

(4) In this rule, "clerk of the appropriate Appeal Court" means—

(a) in a case where the High Court is the appropriate Appeal Court, the Clerk of Justiciary;

(b) in a case where the Sheriff Appeal Court is the appropriate Appeal Court, the Clerk of the Sheriff Appeal Court.

AMENDMENTS

Rule 7.9 inserted by Act of Adjournal (Criminal Procedure Rules Amendment No. 3) (Miscellaneous) 2007 (SSI 2007/276) para.2(2) (effective2 May 2007).

Rule 7.9 as amended by Act of Adjournal (Criminal Procedure Rules 1996 Amendment) (No. 4) (Sheriff Appeal Court) 2015 (SSI 2015/245) para.4 (effective 22 September 2015 subject to savings provisions in para.6).

[THE NEXT PARAGRAPH IS B1-21]

GENERAL NOTE

B1-21 This chapter was substituted for the previous and much briefer Ch.7 by para.2 of the Act of Adjournal (Criminal Procedure Rules Amendment No.4) (Mental Health (Care and Treatment) (Scotland) Act 2003) 2005 (SSI 2005/457) with effect from 5 October 2005. The 2003 Act introduced a new procedure to be followed when persons charged with an offence suffer from a mental disorder. These procedures are to be found in ss.52B–52U of the 1995 Act and introduce two new forms of order. Both orders can only be made in respect of a person charged with an offence but not yet sentenced for it (see ss.52D(5) and 52M(5)).

Assessment orders

An assessment order under s.52D can be made by any court other than the district court (which must remit to the sheriff court any person charged with an offence when it appears to the court that that person has a mental disorder: s.52A) when the court is satisfied on the evidence (written or oral) of one medical practitioner (who need not be a psychiatric specialist) that there are reasonable grounds for believing: (1) that the person charged has a mental disorder; (2) that it is necessary to detain him in hospital to assess him to determine whether he has a mental disorder which is amenable to treatment and would, were he not to receive treatment, pose a significant risk either to his health, safety and welfare or to another person's safety (s.52D(7)); (3) that if the assessment order were not made there would be a significant risk to his health, safety and welfare or such a risk to the safety of another person; (4) that the proposed hospital is suitable for such assessment; (5) that if the order were made, the person could be admitted to the specific hospital before the expiry of seven days beginning with the day on which the order is made; and (6) that it would not be reasonably practicable to carry out the assessment unless the order were made.

An assessment order can be sought by both the prosecutor (s.52B) and the Scottish Ministers (s.52C), although in the latter case the person must be in custody, and it can also be made by the court *ex proprio motu* (s.52E). The order confines the person for a period of 28 days (which can be extended on one occasion only for a further period not exceeding seven days: s.52G(4)) during which time a psychiatric specialist (the "responsible medical officer" appointed under s.230 of the Mental Health (Care and Treatment) (Scotland) Act 2003 to treat the person) will assess the person and prepare a report which is to be submitted to the court making the order *before* the expiry of the 28-day period (s.52G(1)). No provision is made for the effect of a failure to submit the report timeously but in light of the House of Lords' decisions in *R. v Soneji* [2005] 3 W.L.R. 303 and *R. v Knights* [2005] 3 W.L.R. 330 (as to the proper construction of apparently mandatory statutory provisions in penal legislation) it seems likely that the assessment order would not be thereby invalidated and that accordingly the court would be entitled to consider the terms of the report and proceed as allowed by s.52G(3).

Treatment orders

The court can make a treatment order under s.52M. That order is envisaged as one of the outcomes of an assessment order followed by a report to the court on the condition of the person charged with but not yet sentenced for an offence (see s.52G(3)(a)). As with assessment orders, both the prosecutor (s.52K) and the Scottish Ministers (s.52L) may apply for a treatment order (although in the latter case the person must be in custody at the time of application) and the court may make a treatment order *ex proprio motu* (s.52N).

The court can only make a treatment order when it is satisfied on the evidence (whether written or oral) of *two* medical practitioners: (1) that the conditions for making an assessment order set out in s.52D(7) exist (namely, the person has a mental disorder which is amenable to treatment and if treatment were not given there would be a significant risk either to the person's health, safety or welfare or to another person's safety); (2) that the proposed hospital and the proposed medical practitioner are suitable for the purposes of giving the necessary treatment; (3) that if an order were made, the person could be admitted to the specified hospital before the expiry of seven days beginning with the day on which the order is made; and when the court is also satisfied that having regard to the offence and the alternative means of dealing with the person, it is appropriate to make such an order (s.52M(2)). The order authorises the detention of the person in a specified hospital for medical treatment (s.52M(6)).

Interim Compulsion Orders and Compulsion Orders

Sections 131 and 133 of the Mental Health (Care and Treatment) (Scotland) Act 2003 also amended the 1995 Act by substituting a new s.53 and inserting s.57A so as to make provision for respectively interim compulsion orders and compulsion orders. These orders are available to the court only in respect of persons who have been convicted of an offence (referred to as "the offender": s.53(1)). The court requires to be satisfied on the written or oral evidence of *two* medical practitioners that the offender has a mental disorder and that much the same conditions applicable to treatment orders are met before an interim compulsion order can be made (see s.53(2)-(5)). Additionally, the court must be satisfied that there are reasonable grounds for believing that the mental disorder is such that it would be appropriate to make either a compulsion order and a restriction order or a hospital direction (s.53(6)). An interim compulsion order may authorise detention in a state hospital but only if two medical practitioners satisfy the court that the offender requires to be detained under conditions of special security and that such conditions can only be provided in a state hospital (s.53(7)).

An interim compulsion order authorises the offender's confinement in a specified hospital for a period not exceeding 12 weeks beginning with the day on which the order is made for the purposes of giving the offender medical treatment (s.53(8)). Before the expiry of the specified period the offender's responsible medical officer must submit to the court making the order a report under s.53B setting out the medical officer's assessment of the offender's mental state, the type or types of mental disorder from which he is suffering and whether it is necessary to extend the duration of the order to allow further time for the assessment (s.53B(2)). The court may extend the period of the order but only if the total period of confinement does not exceed 12 months (s.53B(5)).

Compulsion orders can be made in respect of offenders under s.57A and may authorise the detention of the offender in a specified hospital (including a state hospital but only where the offender's treatment can only be provided in conditions of special security provided by a state hospital) for a period of six months beginning with the day on which the order is made but can alternatively impose requirements on an offender to attend a specified hospital for treatment as an outpatient on specified or directed dates or at specified or directed intervals, or to attend at a place for community care services, or to reside at a specified place or to do several other specified things (including obtaining approval for a change of address).

Chapter 7A

Disclosure

Interpretation

7A.1. In this Chapter— **B1-21.1**

"the 2010 Act" means the Criminal Justice and Licensing (Scotland) Act 2010;

"classified" means has a status under any scheme operated by the United Kingdom Government for the protection of information which limits those who may see the information to those with a special security clearance;

"appropriate security clearance" means the special security clearance required under the scheme concerned;

"appropriate security conditions" means the security conditions for the storage of the information required under the scheme concerned.

Defence statements

7A.2.—(1) A defence statement lodged under section 70A of the Act of 1995, or section 125 or section 126 of the 2010 Act, shall be in Form 7A.2-A. **B1-21.2**

(2) A statement lodged before the trial diet under section 70A(4)(a) of the Act of 1995, or section 126(2)(a) of the 2010 Act, shall be in Form 7A.2-B.

Applications for ruling on disclosure

7A.3.—(1) An application under section 128(2), section 139(2) or section 140E(2) of the 2010 Act shall be in Form 7A.3. **B1-21.3**

(2) Not less than 48 hours before lodging the application the applicant shall send a copy of the application to the prosecutor.

(3) Where the court appoints a hearing on an application the clerk of court shall intimate the date and time of the hearing to the parties.

Amendments

Rule 7A.3(1) as amended by Act of Adjournal (Criminal Procedure Rules Amendment No.7) (Double Jeopardy (Scotland) Act 2011) 2011 (SSI 2011/387) para.2 (effective November 28, 2011).

Review of ruling on disclosure

7A.4.—(1) An application under section 129(2), section 140(2) or section 140F(2) of the 2010 Act shall be in Form 7A.4. **B1-21.4**

(2) Not less than 48 hours before lodging the application the applicant shall send a copy of the application to the prosecutor.

(3) Where the court appoints a hearing on an application the clerk of court shall intimate the date and time of the hearing to the parties.

AMENDMENTS

Rule 7A.4 as amended by Act of Adjournal (Criminal Procedure Rules Amendment No.7) (Double Jeopardy (Scotland) Act 2011) 2011 (SSI 2011/387) para.2 (effective November 28, 2011).

Appeal against ruling

B1-21.5 **7A.5.**—(1) An appeal under section 130(1) of the 2010 Act shall be made by lodging a note of appeal in Form 7A.5.

(2) At the same time as lodging a note of appeal the appellant shall send a copy of the note of appeal to the other parties.

(3) Where the court appoints a hearing on the appeal the clerk of court shall intimate the date and time of the hearing to the parties.

Applications for orders preventing or restricting disclosure: prosecutor

B1-21.6 **7A.6.**—(1) An application by the prosecutor for a non-notification order and an exclusion order under section 142(2)(a) of the 2010 Act shall be in Form 7A.6-A.

(2) An application by the prosecutor for an exclusion order under section 142(2)(b) or section 142(3) of the 2010 Act shall be in Form 7A.6-B.

(3) An application by the prosecutor for a section 145 order under section 141(5) of the 2010 Act shall be in Form 7A.6-C.

(4) On an application being lodged the clerk of court shall—

(a) appoint a hearing on the application;

(b) intimate the date and time of the hearing to those parties who are entitled to be heard or represented at the hearing.

AMENDMENTS

Rule 7A.6(2) as amended by Act of Adjournal (Criminal Procedure Rules Amendment No.5) (Miscellaneous) 2011 (SSI 2011/290) para.2 (effective July 12, 2011).

Applications for orders preventing or restricting disclosure: Secretary of State

B1-21.7 **7A.7.**—(1) An application by the Secretary of State for a section 146 order under section 146(1) of the 2010 Act shall be in Form 7A.7-A.

(2) An application by the Secretary of State for a restricted notification order and a non-attendance order under section 147(2)(a) of the 2010 Act shall be in Form 7A.7-B.

(3) An application by the Secretary of State for a non-attendance order under section 147(2)(b) or section 147(3) of the 2010 Act shall be in Form 7A.7-C.

(4) On an application being lodged the clerk of court shall—

(a) appoint a hearing on the application;

(b) intimate the date and time of the hearing to those parties who are entitled to be heard or represented at the hearing.

AMENDMENTS

Rule 7A.7(3) as amended by Act of Adjournal (Criminal Procedure Rules Amendment No.5) (Miscellaneous) 2011 (SSI 2011/290) para.2 (effective July 12, 2011).

Special Counsel

B1-21.8 **7A.8.**—(1) This rule applies to the appointment of special counsel under section 150(2) of the 2010 Act.

(2) Special counsel shall be appointed from a list of persons who have been nominated for that purpose by the Lord Justice General.

(3) Where the information which is the subject of the application or appeal concerned is classified, the person appointed must have appropriate security clearance.

Appeals

B1-21.9 **7A.9.**—(1) Any appeal mentioned in section 153 of the 2010 Act shall be made by lodging a note of appeal in Form 7A.9.

(2) At the same time as lodging a note of appeal the appellant shall send a copy of the note of appeal to those parties who are entitled to be heard in the appeal.

(3) On an appeal being lodged the clerk of court shall—

(a) appoint a hearing on the appeal;

(b) intimate the date and time of the hearing to those parties who are entitled to be heard in the appeal.

Review of section 145 and 146 orders

B1-21.10 **7A.10.**—(1) This rule applies to the review of—

(a) a section 145 order under section 155(2) of the 2010 Act;

(b) a section 146 order under section 156(2) of the 2010 Act.

(2) An application shall be in Form 7A.10.

(3) On an application being lodged the clerk of court shall—

(a) appoint a hearing on the application;

(b) intimate the date and time of the hearing to those parties who are entitled to be heard on the application.

Review by court of section 145 and 156 orders

7A.11.—(1) This rule applies where the court appoints a hearing under section 157(3) of the 2010 Act. B1-21.11

(2) The clerk of court shall intimate the date and time of the hearing to those parties who would be entitled to be heard on an application mentioned in Rule 7A.10.

Applications during trials etc.

7A.12.—(1) This rule applies where a case has called for its trial diet, or any other hearing. B1-21.12

(2) During the diet or hearing, an application for—

(a) any of the orders mentioned in Rule 7A.6 or Rule 7A.7;
(b) any of the reviews mentioned in Rule 7A.10,

may be made verbally (that is without the need for a form).

Storage of sensitive information

7A.13.—(1) This rule applies where the court, in considering any application or appeal mentioned in this Chapter, receives or has had disclosed to it information which is classified. B1-21.13

(2) The record of the hearing and any retained documents shall be stored by the court in appropriate security conditions.

AMENDMENTS

Chapter 7A inserted by Act of Adjournal (Criminal Procedure Rules Amendment No.4) (Disclosure) 2011 (SSI 2011/242) para.2 (effective June 6, 2011).

GENERAL NOTE

Chapter 7A came into force on June 6, 2011. Its promulgation was necessary in order to give effect to the detailed statutory provisions of the Criminal Justice and Licensing (Scotland) Act 2010 (asp 13). Part 6 of the 2010 Act deals with disclosure in criminal proceedings, both solemn and summary. The enactment of a statutory code for disclosure was recommended by Lord Coulsfield in his report (*Review of the Law and Practice of Disclosure in Criminal Proceedings in Scotland*, September 2007). In particular, Lord Coulsfield recommended that the formulation given by the full bench in *McLeod v HM Advocate (No.2)*, 1998 J.C. 67 of what requires to be disclosed, should be adopted in statute to clarify the law in Scotland (recommendation 1, para.5.34). Recommendation 5 proposed that that statutory definition should be to disclose to the defence, "all material evidence or information which would tend to exculpate the accused whether by weakening the Crown case or providing a defence to it" (para.5.46.1). B1-21.14

That prosecutor's duty is set down in s.121 of the 2010 Act. Under s.121(2) as soon as practicable after either the accused appears on petition for the first time (or on indictment when no petition procedure has been followed) or a plea of not guilty has been recorded in summary proceedings, the prosecutor must (a) review all the information that may be relevant to the case for or against the accused of which the prosecutor is aware, and (b) disclose to the accused the information to which subs.(3) applies. Subsection (3) applies that duty of disclosure to information if: "(a) the information would materially weaken or undermine the evidence that is likely to be led by the prosecutor in the proceedings against the accused, (b) the information would materially strengthen the accused's case, or (c) the information is likely to form part of the evidence to be led by the prosecutor in the proceedings against the accused".

Section 122 further provides that in solemn cases (but not summary proceedings), where the prosecutor has disclosed information under s.121(2)(b), he must as soon as practicable thereafter disclose to the accused details of any information which the prosecutor is not required to disclose under s.121(2)(b) but which "may be relevant to the case for or against the accused" (s.122(2)). However it is expressly provided that the prosecutor need not disclose details of sensitive information (s.122(3)). Information is "sensitive" where there would be a risk, if it were to be disclosed, of causing serious injury, or death, to any person; or of obstructing or preventing the prevention, detection, investigation or prosecution of crime; or causing serious prejudice to the public interest (s.122(4)).

The common law rules about disclosure are abolished in so far as they are replaced by or are inconsistent with the provisions of Part 6 of the 2010 Act (s.160(2)). Furthermore, the accused (including an appellant) is not entitled to seek the disclosure or recovery of the same information by or from the prosecutor by means of any other procedure at common law "on grounds that are substantially the same as any of those on which the earlier disclosure application [under the 2010 Act] was made" (s.160(5)). Where the prosecutor is required by the various provisions of the 2010 Act to make disclosure, he need not disclose anything that has already been disclosed to the accused in relation to the same matter (whether because the same matter has been the subject of an earlier petition, indictment or complaint or otherwise) (s.127(2)).

The duty of disclosure is a continuing one. During the period beginning with the prosecutor's compliance with the duty under s.121(2)(b) and ending with the conclusion of the proceedings against that accused, the prosecutor must from time to time review all the information that may be relevant to the case for or against the accused of which the prosecutor is aware and disclose to the accused any new information which is revealed by that review (s.123(2)). That duty to review and disclose new information, once complied with, also triggers the duty (akin to s.122(2)) to disclose details of any other information that may be relevant to the case for or against the accused of which the prosecutor is aware (s.123(3)) but subject also to the exception in respect of sensitive information as defined in s.122(4) (s.123(4) and (5)). Proceedings are concluded if (1) a plea of guilty is recorded against the accused; (2) the accused is acquitted; (3) the proceedings against the accused are deserted simpliciter; (4) the accused is convicted and does not appeal against conviction before the expiry of the time allowed for such an appeal; (5) the accused is convicted and appeals against that conviction before the expiry of the time allowed for such an appeal; (6) the proceedings are deserted pro loco et tempore for any reason and no further trial diet is appointed; and (7) the indictment or summary complaint falls or is for any other reason not brought to trial, the diet is not continued, adjourned or postponed and "no further proceedings are in contemplation" (s.123(6)).

Where an accused pleads guilty and that plea is recorded against him, the prosecutor who has not by then complied with his duty of disclosure is released from that duty in so far as it relates to the disclosure of information which but for that plea would have been likely to have formed part of the evidence to be led by the prosecutor in the proceedings against the accused (s.131(2)). However, where that plea is withdrawn, as can easily occur in summary proceedings, the duty is revived (s.131(3)).

The Crown's duty of disclosure continues even after the conclusion of proceedings at first instance. Section 133(2) provides that where appellate proceedings are instituted in relation to an appellant, the Crown must, as soon as practicable after the appeal is initiated by a "relevant act", undertake a review of all information of which the prosecutor is aware that relates to the grounds of appeal and disclose to the appellant any information which falls within s.133(3). The information which falls within s.133(3) is: (a) information which the Crown was required to disclose in the earlier proceedings but did not disclose; (b) information which the prosecutor during the earlier proceedings considered was not covered by paras (a) or (b) of s.121(3) but which he now considers would be covered by one or other of these paragraphs; or (c) information of which the Crown has become aware since the disposal of the trial proceedings where that information would have been subject to the disclosure duty had it been known to the prosecutor during the earlier proceedings. But the prosecutor need not disclose anything which he has already disclosed (s.133(4)).

Appellate proceedings are defined in s.132 as follows: (i) solemn appeals under s.106 of the 1995 Act and summary appeals under s.175 of the 1995 Act; (ii) an appeal to the Supreme Court against a determination of a devolution issue by the High Court of Justiciary; (iii) an appeal against conviction by bill of suspension or advocation; (iv) a petition to the nobile officium "in respect of a matter arising out of criminal proceedings which brings under review an alleged miscarriage of justice which is based on the existence and significance of new evidence"; (v) an appeal by an accused in a case involving insanity against a finding made in respect of him under s.55(2) of the 1995 Act at an examination of facts; and (vi) references by the Scottish Criminal Cases Review Commission of convictions or findings made under s.55(2) of the 1995 Act.

The duty in appellate proceedings is triggered by the "relevant act": in solemn and summary conviction appeals, the grant of leave to appeal; in Supreme Court proceedings, the grant of leave by the High Court or special leave by the Supreme Court; in bills and petitions, by the service of a certified copy of the bill or petition and the interlocutor granting the first order for service of the bill or petition; in insanity appeals, the lodging of the appeal; and in Commission references, the lodging of the grounds of appeal (in summary conviction cases, that is done by bill of suspension) by the person to whom the reference relates (s.133(5)).

There is also a continuing duty on the prosecutor once an appeal has been initiated. The prosecutor must from time to time review all information relating to the grounds of appeal of which he is aware and disclose any information that falls under s.133(3) (s.134(2)). He need not disclose anything already disclosed (s.134(3)). This duty continues until either the accused abandons his appeal or the appeal is finally disposed of by the High Court (s.134(5)).

Rule 7A.2

B1-21.15 The new disclosure procedure imposes a duty on the accused in solemn proceedings to lodge a defence statement. The duty is to lodge the defence statement at least 14 days before the first diet in the sheriff court or the preliminary hearing in the High Court (s.70A(2) and (3) of the 1995 Act respectively). In summary proceedings the accused may lodge a defence statement. In either set of circumstances, the consequence of the lodging of the defence statement is that the prosecutor must, as soon as practicable after receiving the defence statement, review all the information that may be relevant to the case for or against the accused of which the prosecutor is aware and disclose any information to which s.121(3) applies (in solemn proceedings, s.124(2); in summary cases, s.125(4)).

A defence statement must set forth the following details (s.70A(9) for solemn proceedings; s.125(2) for summary cases): (1) the nature of the accused's defence, including any particular defences on which he intends to rely; (2) any matters of fact on which the accused takes issue with the Crown and the reason for doing so; (3) the particulars of the matters of fact on which the accused intends to rely for the purposes of the accused's defence; (4) any point of law which the accused wishes to take and any authority on which the accused intends to rely for that purpose; (5) the nature of any information that the accused requires the Crown to disclose as identified by reference to the accused's defence; and (6) the reasons for the accused's considering that disclosure of that information is necessary.

Items (5) and (6) are crucial to the system of disclosure. They provide the basis for the accused's entitlement to apply to the court for a ruling on whether s.121(3) (the general duty of disclosure) applies to that specific information (see s.128(2)). See Rule 7A.3 below.

Rule 7A.3

Where the accused considers that the prosecutor has failed in responding to the defence statement to disclose to the accused an item of information to which s.121(3) applies, he may apply for a ruling from the court as to whether the duty of disclosure in s.121(3) applies to it. The application must set out the following details: (1) where the accused is charged with more than one offence, the charge or charges to which the application relates; (2) a description of the information in question; and (3) the accused's grounds for considering that the duty of disclosure applies to the information in question (s.128(3)). On receipt of an application the court must appoint a hearing at which the application is to be considered and determined (s.128(4)) but may dispose of the application without a hearing if the court considers that it either fails to set out the three requirements in s.128(3) or otherwise fails to disclose "any reasonable grounds for considering that s.121(3) applies to the information in question" (s.128(5)). At the hearing the court must give the Crown an opportunity to be heard on the application before determining it (s.128(6)). Except where it is impracticable to do so, the application should be determined by the JP, sheriff or judge who is presiding, or is to preside, at the accused's trial (s.128(8)).

Rule 7A. 4

Where the application is refused in whole or in part and subsequently—but prior to the conclusion of the proceedings against the accused (as defined in s.129(11) which sets out the same termini as s.123(6))—the accused becomes aware of information (referred to as "secondary information") which was unavailable to the court when it made its initial ruling under s.128(7), the accused may apply to the court which made the ruling for a review of the ruling (s.129(1) and (2)). The application for review must be made in writing and set forth the following matters: (1) where the accused is charged with more than one offence, the charge or charges to which the application relates; (2) a description of the information in question and the secondary information; and (3) the accused's grounds for considering that the duty of disclosure under s.121(3) applies to the information in question (s.129(3)). **B1-21.16**

As with the initial application for a ruling, the court must appoint a hearing on the application for a review of the original ruling but need not do so if the application fails to set forth the matters set out in s.129(3) or fails otherwise to disclose reasonable grounds for considering that the duty of disclosure applies to the information in question (s.129(5)). The review hearing should also be assigned to the JP, sheriff or judge who dealt with the original application unless it is impracticable to do so (s.129(8)). Nothing in these procedures affects any rights of appeal available under s.130 to the accused in respect of the ruling being reviewed (s.129(9)). See Rule 7A.5 below.

Rule 7A.5

This new procedure provides for an interlocutory appeal in respect of the trial court's ruling on disclosure. The Crown or accused may, within the period of seven days beginning with the day on which the ruling is made under s.128, appeal to the High Court against that ruling (s.130(1)). In disposing of such an appeal (which is without prejudice to any other right of appeal which any party may have in relation to the ruling under s.128: see s.130(4)), the High Court may affirm the original ruling or remit the case to the court of first instance with such directions as the High Court thinks appropriate (s.130(3)).

Rule 7A.6

A "section 145 order" is one which the prosecutor applies for where he has information which he should disclose but he considers that the disclosure of that information would be "likely to cause a real risk of substantial harm or damage to the public interest" (s.141(4)). A section 145 order can only be determined after any application for a non-notification order or an exclusion order has been determined by the court (s.145(1)(b)). A non-notification order is an order under s.143 prohibiting notice being given to the accused of (a) the making of an application for the following orders, namely a section 145 order to which the non-notification order relates, the non-notification order itself and any exclusion order; and (b) the determination of those applications. An exclusion order is an order under s.143 or 144 prohibiting the accused from attending or making representations in proceedings for the determination of the application for a section 145 order to which the exclusion order relates (s.142(5)). **B1-21.17**

Rule 7A.7

Where the prosecutor proposes to disclose to an accused, an appellant or as the case may be a person, information which he is required to disclose, or where he proposes to disclose information which he is not required to disclose by virtue of Pt 6 of the 2010 Act, the Secretary of State may apply to the court for an order referred to as a "section 146 order" in relation to that information (s.146(1)). That order prevents or restricts disclosure of information which would otherwise be disclosed by the prosecutor. Where such an order is sought in solemn proceedings the Secretary of State may also seek a restricted notification order and a non-attendance order (s.147(2)); and in summary proceedings he may also seek a non-attendance order (s.147(3)). A restricted notification order is an order prohibiting notice being given to the accused of (a) the making of the applications for the section 146 order, the restricted notification order and the non-attendance order and (b) the hearing appointed to determine whether a restricted notification order should be made (s.148(3)).

A restricted notification order may be made where the court is satisfied of the following conditions: (a) that disclosure to the accused of the making of the application for a section 146 order would be "likely to cause a real risk of substantial harm or damage to the public interest" and (b) that, having regard to all the circumstances, the making of a restricted notification order would be "consistent with the accused's receiving a fair trial" (s.148(6)). That test is elaborated on: references to an accused's having a fair trial include references to the appellant or other person to whom the prosecutor is required to disclose the item of information having received a fair trial (s.146(14)).

Rule 7A.8

B1-21.18 Where the court is determining applications for non-notification orders, exclusion orders, section 145 orders, restricted notification orders, non-attendance orders and section 146 orders, or applications for review of the grant or refusal of any of the foregoing orders, or appeals relating to any of the foregoing orders (under s.153), the court may appoint a person (to be known as "special counsel") to represent the interests of the accused in relation to the determination of the application, review or appeal (as the case maybe) (s.150(2)). But this appointment can only be made where the court considers that it is necessary to ensure that the accused receives a fair trial (s.150(3)). The prosecutor may appeal to the High Court against a decision of the court not to appoint special counsel in any case (s.150(7)) and the Secretary of State may appeal against the decision not to appoint a special counsel in a restricted notification case (s.150(8)). The accused may appeal against a decision not to appoint a special counsel in any case other than a non-notification case or a restricted notification case (s.150(9)).

Only persons who are solicitors or Members of the Faculty of Advocates may be appointed as special counsel (s.151). The role of special counsel is set out in s.152: it is his duty, in relation to the determination of the relevant application or appeal, "to act in the best interests of the accused with a view only to ensuring that the accused receives a fair trial" (s.152(1)). Special counsel is entitled to see the confidential information but must not disclose any of it to the accused or the accused's representatives (s.152(2)). Special counsel appointed in a non-notification case or a restricted notification case must not disclose to the accused or his representatives the making of the relevant application or appeal, or otherwise communicate with the accused or his representatives about the relevant application or appeal (s.152(3)). In any other case, special counsel must not communicate with the accused or his representatives about the relevant application or appeal except (a) with the court's permission and, (b) where permission is given, in accordance with such conditions as the court may impose (s.152(4)).

Rule 7A.9

The prosecutor is entitled to appeal to the High Court against the making of section 145 and 146 orders, restricted notification orders and non-attendance orders and against the refusal of applications for non-notification orders, exclusion orders and section 145 orders (s.153(1)). The accused may appeal against the making of exclusion orders, section 145 and 146 orders and non-attendance orders (s.153(2)). The Secretary of State may appeal against the making of section 146 orders and against the refusal of applications for restricted notification orders, non-attendance orders and section 146 orders (s.153(3)). Special counsel may appeal against the making of non-notification orders and section 145 orders in relation to the same item of information (s.153(4)). The same is true where special counsel has been appointed in relation to applications for restricted notification orders: he may appeal against the making of that order and the section 146 order in relation to the same item of information (s.153(5)). Any appeal must be lodged with Justiciary Office "not later than 7 days after the decision appealed against" (s.153(6)).

[THE NEXT PARAGRAPH IS B1-22]

PART III

SOLEMN PROCEEDINGS

Chapter 8

The Indictment

Appeals in relation to extension of time for trial

B1-22 **8.1.**—(1) A note of appeal under section 65(8) of the Act of 1995 (appeal to High Court against grant or refusal of extension of time) in respect of an appeal from a decision under section 65(3) of that Act (extension of periods for commencement of preliminary hearing or trial diet) shall be in Form 8.1-A.

(2) A note of appeal under section 65(8) of the Act of 1995 in respect of an appeal from a decision under section 65(5) of that Act (extension of 80, 110 or 140 days period of committal) shall be in Form 8.1-B.

(3) A note of appeal mentioned in paragraph (1) or (2) shall be served by the appellant on—

(a) the respondent;
(b) any co-accused; and
(c) the clerk of the court against the decision of which the appeal is taken.

(4) The appellant shall lodge with the Clerk of Justiciary—

(a) the note of appeal; and
(b) the execution of service in respect of the persons mentioned in paragraph (3).

(5) The clerk of the court against the decision of which the appeal is taken shall, as soon as practicable after being served with the note of appeal, transmit to the Clerk of Justiciary the original application and all the relative documents; and the Clerk of Justiciary shall, on receiving them, assign the appeal to the roll and intimate the date of the diet to the appellant and the respondent.

(6) Where the judge's or sheriff's report is not included in the documents mentioned in paragraph (5) the Clerk of Justiciary shall request the report from the clerk of the court against the decision of which the appeal is taken.

AMENDMENTS

Rule 8.1 as amended by Act of Adjournal (Criminal Procedure Rules Amendment) (Criminal Procedure (Amendment) (Scotland) Act) 2005 (SSI 2005/44) para.2(8) (subject to para.2(2)-(4)) (effective February 1, 2005).

Rule 8.1(6) inserted by Act of Adjournal (Criminal Procedure Rules Amendment) (Miscellaneous) 2012 (SSI 2012/125) para.2 (effective June 4, 2012).

Further provision as respects extension of twelve months period for commencement of trial on indictment

8.1A. […] B1-22.1

AMENDMENTS

Rule 8.1A inserted by Act of Adjournal (Criminal Procedure Rules) (Amendment) 1999 (SI 1999/78: effective March 1, 1999).

Rule 8.1A repealed by Act of Adjournal (Criminal Procedure Rules Amendment) (Criminal Procedure (Amendment) (Scotland) Act) 2005 (SSI 2005/44) para.2(9) (subject to para.2(2)-(4)) (effective February 1, 2005).

[THE NEXT PARAGRAPH IS B1-22.3]

Fresh indictment as alternative to serving notice fixing new trial diet

8.1B. […] B1-22.3

AMENDMENTS

Rule 8.1B inserted by Act of Adjournal (Criminal Procedure Rules) (Amendment) 1999 (SI 1999/78: effective March 1, 1999).

Rule 8.1B repealed by Act of Adjournal (Criminal Procedure Rules Amendment) (Criminal Procedure (Amendment) (Scotland) Act) 2005 (SSI 2005/44) para.2(9) (subject to para.2(2)-(4)) (effective February 1, 2005).

Citation of accused and witnesses

8.2.—(1) Subject to paragraph (5), the notice to be affixed to the door of the relevant premises for the purposes of section 66(4)(b) of the Act of 1995 shall be in Form 8.2-A. B1-22.4

(2) Subject to paragraph (5), the notice for the purposes of section 66(6) of the Act of 1995 to be served on a person accused on indictment shall be in Form 8.2-B or, where the charge is of committing a sexual offence to which section 288C of that Act applies or, where it is known by the prosecutor that the offence is one to which section 288E of that Act (prohibition of personal conduct of defence where a child witness is under the age of 12) applies, Form 8.2-C.

(3) The form of postal citation of a witness under section 66(1) of the Act of 1995 shall be in Form 8.2-D; and the witness shall return Form 8.2-E to the procurator fiscal, or the accused person or his solicitor, as the case may be, in the prepaid envelope provided, within 14 days after the date of citation.

(4) The form of personal citation of a witness under section 66(1) of the Act of 1995 shall be in Form 8.2-F.

(5) Where the accused is an organisation,

(a) the notice to be affixed to the door of the relevant premises for the purposes of section 66(4)(b) of the Act of 1995 shall be in Form 8.2-G;

(b) the notice for the purposes of section 66(6) of the Act of 1995 shall be in Form 8.2-H

AMENDMENTS

Rule 8.2 substituted by Act of Adjournal (Criminal Procedure Rules Amendment) (Criminal Procedure (Amendment) (Scotland) Act) 2005 (SSI 2005/44) para.2(10) (subject to para.2(2)-(4)) (effective February 1, 2005).

Rule 8.2(2) as amended by Act of Adjournal (Criminal Procedure Rules Amendment No.3) (Vulnerable Witnesses (Scotland) Act 2004) 2005 (SSI 2005/188) para.2, subject to the conditions in para.2(2) (effective April 1, 2005).

Rule 8.2(5) as amended by Act of Adjournal (Criminal Procedure Rules Amendment No.3) (Miscellaneous) 2011 (SSI 2011/194) para.2 (effective March 28, 2011).

Notice of previous convictions

8.3. Any notice to be served on an accused under section 69(2) of the Act of 1995 (notice of previous convictions) shall be in Form 8.3. B1-22.5

[THE NEXT PARAGRAPH IS B1-23]

GENERAL NOTE

Rule 8.1

The wording of this rule does not take account of the combined effect of the five judge decision in *Gardner v Lees*, 1996 S.L.T. 342; 1996 S.C.C.R. 168 and *Normand v Walker*, 1996 S.L.T. 418. It is now recognised that it is competent to apply for an extension of the 12 month time-limit in summary B1-23 proceedings. An extension can also be granted retrospectively: see *McGowan v Friel*, High Court of Justiciary, February 1, 1996 (unreported) which was approved by a bench of five judges in *McDowall v Lees*, 1996 S.L.T. 871; 1996 S.C.C.R. 719. However, the change in the law effected by these decisions (and *McDonald v Gordon*, 1996 S.C.C.R. 740) is now superseded by s.73 of the Criminal Procedure and Investigation Act 1996 which amends the 1995 Act to restrict the freedom conferred by s.65 from further process when the 12 month period has expired to proceedings on indictment, thereby reinstating the effect of *MacDougall v Russell*, 1986 S.L.T. 403. So the wording of the rule is now apt.

Where a sheriff refuses to be addressed on an application by the Crown for an extension of the 12 month period, no appeal under s.65 is competent because there is no decision to grant or refuse the application, nor can the unsuccessful applicant competently petition the nobile officium of the High Court. A subsequent application for extension is accordingly competent (*McKnight v HM Advocate*, 1996 S.L.T. 834). It has also been held that since the circumstances of the granting of an arrest warrant are—for policy reasons of securing certainty in criminal proceedings—irrelevant to the application of the proviso to s.101(1) of the 1975 Act (now s.65(2) of the 1995 Act), an accused for whose apprehension a warrant has been mistakenly granted should seek review of the warrant by means of a bill of suspension as soon as he becomes aware that proceedings are being continued against him outwith the 12 month period in reliance on the warrant (*HM Advocate v Taylor*, 1996 S.L.T. 836; 1996 S.C.C.R. 510).

Rule 8.1A

The rule provides for an exception to the general principle that all significant stages in solemn proceedings should be conducted in the presence of the accused. Any extension granted in excess of the period applied for would be incompetent and render subsequent trial proceedings fundamentally null.

Rule 8.1B

If further witnesses are to be examined or further productions put in evidence at the trial beyond those listed in the schedule annexed to the original record copy of the indictment or in any s.67 notice (served before leave was given to serve a notice fixing a new trial diet) then the prosecutor will require to serve a further s.67 notice timeously.

Rule 8.2

The reference in r.8.2(5) to a "body corporate" must be understood in the context of s.70 of the 1995 Act. That provision deals with the prosecution of bodies corporate on indictment and may be distinguished from s.143 which is headed "Prosecution of companies, etc." and specifically identifies its scope as being "a partnership, association, body corporate or body of trustees" (s.143(1)). Section 70 does not define the expression "body corporate". However, the predecessor of s.70 was held to extend beyond limited liability companies and to include firms (*Mackay Bros v Gibb*, 1969 J.C. 26). Furthermore, the High Court has expressed the obiter opinion that the rules laid down in s.143 for bodies of trustees would be likely to apply equally to cases on indictment against trustees (*Aitkenhead v Fraser*, 2006 S.L.T. 711, para.6).

Rule 8.3

The notice of previous convictions should be served on the accused along with his citation and the indictment so that he can timeously object to any previous convictions which do not relate to him or are otherwise incompetently libelled by giving written intimation under s.69(2). Intimation of his objection should be given at least five clear days before the first day of the sitting in which the trial diet is to be held (see s.69(3)).

Chapter 8A

Engagement, Dismissal and Withdrawal of Solicitors in Solemn Proceedings

Notification

B1-23.1 **8A.1.**—(1) The notification to the court in writing under section 72F(1) of the Act of 1995 that a solicitor has been engaged by the accused for the purposes of his defence in any part of proceedings on indictment shall be in Form 8A.1-A.

(2) The notification to the court in writinf under section 72F(2) of the Act of 1995 that a solicitor has been dismissed by the accused or has withdrawn from acting shall be in Form 8A.1-B.

Further pre-trial diet

B1-23.2 **8A.2.**—(1) An order for a further pre-trial diet under section 72F(5) of the Act of 1995 may be signed by the clerk of court.

(2) An order mentioned in paragraph (1) shall be intimated by the clerk of court to all parties and to the governor of any institution in which the accused is detained.

AMENDMENT

Chapter 8A inserted by Act of Adjournal (Criminal Procedure Rules Amendment No.4) (Criminal Procedure (Amendment) (Scotland) Act 2004) 2004 (SSI 2004/434) r.2 (effective 4 October 2004).

Rule 8A.2(1) as amended by Act of Adjournal (Criminal Procedure Rules Amendment No.5) (Miscellaneous) 2004 (SSI 2004/481) r.2 (effective 26 November 2004).

GENERAL NOTE

Section 5 of the Criminal Procedure (Amendment) (Scotland) Act 2004 inserted S.72F into the Act. That provision applies to three types of case (s.72F(4)). First, where the accused is prohibited from conducting his defence personally because it is a sexual offence, he must engage a lawyer or the court will appoint one to act for him (see S.288C of the 1995 Act); secondly, in cases to which S.288E applies (i.e. certain cases involving child witnesses under 12 years of age); and, thirdly, in cases where the court has made an order under s.288F(2) of the 1995 Act (i.e. where there are vulnerable witnesses). Section 72F(1) provides that in any proceedings on indictment "it is the duty of a solicitor who is engaged by the accused for the purposes of his defence at any part of the proceedings to notify the court and the prosecutor of that fact forthwith". However, the solicitor is deemed to have complied with that duty if, before the indictment is served, he has notified the procurator fiscal of the district "in which the charge against the accused was then being investigated" that he has been engaged and has not notified the procurator fiscal that he has been sacked or has withdrawn from acting (s.72F(2)(a)). The notifications must be in writing: a telephone call will not suffice (though presumably an e-mail or a fax will). B1-23.3

Section 72F(2) provides, as a consequence of the foregoing, that where the solicitor withdraws or is sacked, it is his duty to inform the court and the prosecutor of that fact "forthwith in writing". When the court is so informed, the court comes under a duty to order a further pre-trial diet to be held so that legal representation can be inquired into and if necessary ordered (s.72F(3)).

Chapter 8B

Failure of Accused to Appear

Failure of accused to appear: form of warrant

8B.1. A warrant for the apprehension of an accused under section 102A of the Act of 1995 (failure of accused to appear in solemn proceedings) shall be in Form 8B.1. **B1-23.4**

AMENDMENT

Chapter 8B inserted by Act of Adjournal (Criminal Procedure Rules Amendment No.6) (Criminal Proceedings etc. (Reform) (Scotland) Act 2007) 2007 (SSI 2007/511) r.4 (effective 10 December 2007).

GENERAL NOTE

Section 102A was inserted by s.32 of the Criminal Proceedings etc. (Reform) (Scotland) Act 2007 and brought into force on 12 December 2007 (see SSI 2007/479). Section 102A(1) provides that it is an offence, triable only on indictment and punishable by a maximum sentence of five years' imprisonment, for an accused person in solemn proceedings to fail, without reasonable excuse, to appear at any diet of which he has been given notice (except where the accused has been excused attendance). Where an accused fails to appear at such a diet, the court may grant warrant to apprehend him (s.102A(2)). It is incompetent for a court in any proceedings on indictment to grant warrant for the accused's apprehension for failure to appear at such a diet otherwise than under s.102A(2) (s.102A(3)) although it remains competent for the sheriff to grant a warrant on a petition at the procurator fiscal's instance under s.34(1) of the 1995 Act to arrest and commit an accused in respect of an offence under s.102A(1) or s.27(1)(a) or (7) of the 1995 Act (s.102A(4)). **B1-23.5**

The usual effect of the granting of a warrant under s.102A(2) at any stage prior to conviction is that the "indictment falls as respects that accused" (s.102A(5)) but that consequence is qualified. The court when granting the warrant may make an order "to different effect" (s.102A(6)) either for the purpose of proceeding, on the prosecutor's motion, with the trial in that accused's absence under s.92(2A)—when, prior to disposal of the case, the accused absents himself—or "for any other purpose" where either the prosecutor so moves or the court ex proprio motu determines (s.102A(7)). This rule provides the form in which such warrants under s.102A(2) should be granted (s.102A(8)).

It is worthy of note that s.102A applies to all solemn proceedings and not just trial proceedings. Hence the definition which is given for "the court" in s.102A(16)(a). For example, a person who is on bail pending appeal against a decision taken at a preliminary hearing in the High Court and fails to appear at his appeal hearing will be liable to apprehension on a warrant under s.102A(2) granted by the Criminal Appeal Court and may subsequently be prosecuted on indictment for that failure.

Chapter 8C

Transfer of Proceedings (Sheriff Court)

Transfer of solemn proceedings outwith sheriffdom

8C.1. A written application by the prosecutor under section 34A of the Act of 1995 (initiating proceedings outwith sheriffdom: exceptional circumstances) shall be in Form 8C.1. **B1-23.6**

AMENDMENTS

Chapter 8C inserted by Act of Adjournal (Criminal Procedure Rules Amendment) (Miscellaneous) 2009 (SSI 2009/144) r.2 (effective 30 April 2009).

GENERAL NOTE

B1-23.7 Section 34A of the 1995 Act was inserted by s.31 of the Criminal Proceedings etc. (Reform) (Scotland) Act 2007 and brought into force on March 10, 2008 (see SSI 2008/42). The prosecutor may apply to the sheriff principal of the sheriffdom in which the prosecutor's district lies for an order under s.34A(2) where he believes (a) that because of exceptional circumstances (and without such an order being made) it is likely that there will be "an unusually high number of accused persons appearing from custody for the first calling of cases on petition in the sheriff courts in the sheriffdom" and (b) that it will not be practicable for those courts to deal with all of these petition cases (s.34A(1)). The order, which may be made by the sheriff principal only if the sheriff principal of the relevant other sheriffdom consents (s.34A(3)), is for authority for petition proceedings against some or all of the accused (a) to be taken at a sheriff court in that other sheriffdom and (b) for these proceedings to be maintained there or at any of the sheriff courts in the transferring sheriffdom as may, at the first calling of the case, be appointed for further proceedings (s.34A(2)).

Such an order allows the prosecutor to transfer some or all of his petition cases outwith his sheriffdom and for them to be dealt with there or, after the first calling, for them to be returned to his sheriffdom. The order may be limited to a particular period or to particular circumstances (s.34A(4)). The order does not confer jurisdiction on the receiving sheriffdom in respect of any subsequent proceedings on indictment (s.34A(5)).

[THE NEXT PARAGRAPH IS B1-24]

Chapter 9

First Diets (Sheriff Court)

Minute giving notice of preliminary pleas or preliminary issues

B1-24 **9.1.**—(1) Any notice given under section 71(2) of the Act of 1995 (notice of preliminary pleas or preliminary issues before first diet) shall be by minute in Form 9.1.

(2) That minute shall be lodged with the sheriff clerk and served on every other party by the minuter.

Procedure on lodging minute

B1-24.1 **9.2.** On the lodging of a minute under rule 9.1 (minute giving notice of preliminary pleas or preliminary issues) with a certificate of execution of service, the sheriff clerk shall endorse on the minute the time and date on which it was received.

Orders for further diets under section 71 of the Act of 1995

B1-24.2 **9.3.**—(1) An order for a further diet under section 71(2ZA) of the Act of 1995 (further diet to consider objection to the admissibility of evidence) may be signed by the sheriff clerk.

(2) Intimation of the terms of an order—

(a) mentioned in paragraph (1); or

(b) for an adjourned diet under section 71(5A) of the Act of 1995 (adjournment of first diet),

shall be given by the sheriff clerk to the governor of any institution in which the accused is detained.

Written record of state of preparation

B1-24.2.1 **9.3A.**—(1) A written record referred to in section 71C of the Act of 1995 (written record of state of preparation: sheriff court) shall be in Form 9.3A.

(2) A written record under paragraph (1) must be lodged no later than two court days before the first diet and may be lodged by electronic means.

AMENDMENTS

Rule 9.3A inserted by Act of Adjournal (Criminal Procedure Rules 1996 Amendment) (Miscellaneous) 2017 (SSI 2017/144) para.2(3) (effective 29 May 2017).

[THE NEXT PARAGRAPH IS B1-24.3]

Procedure at first diet

B1-24.3 **9.4.**—(1) A first diet shall commence on the diet being called.

(2) A record of the proceedings at the first diet, including—

(a) a note of the decision made by the court in respect of any notice placed before it;

(b) any adjournment

(c) the plea stated under section 71(6) of the Act of 1995 (plea at first diet); and

(d) the date appointed for the trial diet,

shall be kept in accordance with existing law and practice.

AMENDMENTS

Rule 9.4 as amended by Act of Adjournal (Criminal Procedure Rules 1996 Amendment) (Miscellaneous) 2017 (SSI 2017/144) para.2(3) (effective 29 May 2017).

Applications for leave to appeal

9.5.—(1) An application for leave to appeal to the High Court under section 74(1) of the Act of 1995 (appeal against a decision of the sheriff at a first diet) shall be made by motion to the sheriff at that diet immediately following the making of the decision in question, and shall be granted or refused at that time. **B1-24.4**

(2) A decision under this rule shall be recorded in the minute of proceedings.

Note of appeal

9.6.—(1) An appeal under section 74(1) of the Act of 1995 against a decision of the sheriff at a first diet shall be made by lodging a note of appeal in Form 9.6. **B1-24.5**

(2) The note of appeal shall be lodged with the sheriff clerk not later than seven days after the making of the decision in question.

AMENDMENTS

Rule 9.6 as amended by Act of Adjournal (Criminal Procedure Rules Amendment) (Miscellaneous) 2012 (SSI 2012/125) para.3 (effective 4 June 2012).

Procedure on lodging note of appeal

9.7.—(1) On the lodging of a note of appeal with the sheriff clerk, he shall, in those cases where leave to appeal is required, endorse on it a certificate that leave to appeal has been granted and the date and time of lodging. **B1-24.6**

(2) As soon as possible after the lodging of a note of appeal with the sheriff clerk, he shall—

(a) send a copy of the note of appeal to the other parties or their solicitors;

(b) request a report on the circumstances relating to the decision from the sheriff; and

(c) transmit the note of appeal to the Clerk of Justiciary with a certified copy of—

(i) the indictment;

(ii) the record of proceedings; and

(iii) any other relevant document.

AMENDMENTS

Rule 9.7 as amended by Act of Adjournal (Criminal Procedure Rules 1996 Amendment) (Miscellaneous) 2017 (SSI 2017/144) para.2(3) (effective 29 May 2017).

Report of sheriff

9.8.—(1) The sheriff, on receiving a request for a report under rule 9.7(2)(b) (report on circumstances relating to decision) shall, as soon as possible, send his report to the Clerk of Justiciary. **B1-24.7**

(2) The Clerk of Justiciary shall, on receiving the report of the sheriff—

(a) send a copy of the report to the parties or their solicitors;

(b) arrange for a hearing of the appeal as soon as possible; and

(c) cause to be copied any documents necessary for the appeal.

Intimation of order postponing trial diet

9.9.—(1) Where, in relation to an appeal under section 74(1) of the Act of 1995 (appeal in connection with first diet) in a case set down for trial in the sheriff court, the High Court makes an order under section 74(3) of that Act (postponement of trial diet), the Clerk of Justiciary shall send a copy of the order to— **B1-24.8**

(a) the sheriff clerk;

(b) all parties to the proceedings; and

(c) the governor of any institution in which any accused is detained.

(2) If, in relation to any case a trial diet has been postponed by virtue of an order mentioned in paragraph (1), any requirement to call that diet shall have effect only in relation to the date to which the diet has been postponed.

Orders of appeal court

9.10. The Clerk of Justiciary shall intimate to the sheriff clerk the decision of the High Court disposing of an appeal under section 74(1) of the Act of 1995 in relation to a first diet. **B1-24.9**

Abandonment of appeal

9.11.—(1) An appellant who has taken an appeal under section 74(1) of the Act of 1995 (appeal in connections with first diet) may abandon the appeal at any time before the hearing of the appeal. **B1-24.10**

(2) An abandonment of such an appeal shall be made by lodging a minute of abandonment in Form 9.11 with the Clerk of Justiciary.

(3) The Clerk of Justiciary, on receiving such a minute of abandonment, shall inform the sheriff clerk and the other parties or their solicitors.

(4) The sheriff, on the sheriff clerk being so informed, may proceed as accords with the case.

AMENDMENTS

Chapter 9 substituted by Act of Adjournal (Criminal Procedure Rules Amendment) (Criminal Procedure (Amendment) (Scotland) Act) 2005 (SSI 2005/44) para.2(11) (subject to para.2(2)–(4)) (effective 1 February 2005).

[THE NEXT PARAGRAPH IS B1-25]

GENERAL NOTE

B1-25 Paragraph 2(11) of the Act of Adjournal (Criminal Procedure Rules Amendment) (Criminal Procedure (Amendment) (Scotland) Act) 2005 replaced, as from 1 February 2005, the old Ch.9 which had made provision for preliminary diets in the High Court and first diets in the sheriff court (but see the General Note at C1-31 for the applicability of the new procedure). The first diet was mandatory although preliminary diets were held only when a judge of the High Court was obliged, or in the exercise of his discretion considered it appropriate, to order that one be held.

Preliminary pleas and issues

Preliminary pleas are defined in s.79(2)(a) of the 1995 Act (as amended by s.13(1) of the Criminal Procedure (Amendment) (Scotland) Act 2004) as follows: (1) challenges to the competency or relevancy of the indictment; (2) objections to the validity of the accused's citation; and (3) pleas in bar of trial (such as insanity, tholed assize, nonage and oppression (by, for example, prejudicial pre-trial publicity or abuse of process by the prosecutor)).

Preliminary issues are defined in s.79(2)(b) as follows: (1) applications for separation or conjunction of charges or trials; (2) objections under ss.27(4A)(a), 255 or 255A of the 1995 Act (respectively challenges to the deemed admission that the offence was committed while on bail, that it was committed in any special capacity or that the age of any person specified in the indictment is true), or under s.9(6) of the Antisocial Behaviour etc. (Scotland) Act 2004 or under that section as applied by s.234AA(11) of the 1995 Act; (3) applications under s.278(2) of the 1995 Act (to have the court direct that the record of proceedings at judicial examination, or a part of that record, should not be read to the jury); (4) objections by either Crown or defence to the admissibility of any evidence; (5) assertions by either Crown or defence that there are documents the truth of the contents of which ought to be admitted, or that there is any other matter which in the applicant's view should be agreed; and (6) any other point raised by either Crown or defence as regards any matter which (not being mentioned in (1) to (5) above) "could in his opinion be resolved with advantage before the trial".

Section 71(2) of the 1995 Act requires the sheriff at a first diet to "consider" any preliminary plea or issue of which notice has been given in terms of s.79(1). In *Wright v HM Advocate*, 2006 S.C.C.R. 455 (July 4, 2006, unreported) the sheriff had continued consideration of an objection to the admissibility of evidence of an identification parade to the trial diet. The High Court held that the sheriff was not required to determine or dispose of the issue at the first diet and was entitled to continue consideration of the issue to the trial diet to hear evidence before determining the issue.

The importance of these provisions is made clear when regard is had to s.79A. This provision was inserted by the Criminal Procedure (Amendment) (Scotland) Act 2004 and brought into force on February 1, 2005. The section provides that the court, after the commencement of the trial, shall not grant leave for an objection to be raised to the admissibility of any evidence "if the party seeking to raise it has not given written notice of his intention to do so to the other parties" (s.79A(2)) unless "it considers that it could not reasonably have been raised before that time" (s.79A(4)) in which event the court may dispense with the requirement of written notice (s.79A(3)). Thus, all objections to the admissibility of evidence must be taken by way of written notice before the preliminary hearing when they are recognised by the defence: this avoids ambushing the prosecution. Moreover, it will be irrelevant that the basis of the objection was not recognised by the defence if in the court's opinion the basis of the objection should have been recognised at a stage prior to trial. What remains to be determined is the scope of this important provision: what is meant by an objection to the admissibility of any evidence? Real evidence recovered under a search warrant which it is argued is defective in a material respect must be covered by the phrase; so also the admissibility of extra-judicial admissions by an accused. But where an objection is taken to a forensic scientist's report on the basis that the witness cannot speak to its terms because he himself did not conduct the tests, is that objection covered by s.79A? It seems that it is preferable that objections to the foundations of expert reports, from scientists, forensic accountants, pathologists and the like should be subject to s.79A.

Procedure at first diet

In addition to disposing of preliminary pleas and issues, the sheriff has certain other obligations. First, he must, where the accused is charged with a sexual offence listed in s.288C(2) (in respect of which an accused is prohibited from defending himself in person), ascertain whether the accused has engaged a solicitor for his defence at trial (s.71(A1)). Secondly, the sheriff must, so far as is reasonably practicable, ascertain whether the case is likely to proceed to trial on the date assigned as the trial diet and, in particular, ascertain the state of preparation of both Crown and defence with respect to their cases and the extent to which the parties have complied with their duties under s.257(1) of the 1995 Act to identify any facts which seem likely to be capable of agreement (s.71(1)(a) and (b)). Thirdly, the sheriff must ascertain which witnesses the Crown and defence will respectively require to attend at trial and, where the accused is on bail, review the bail conditions (so as, where appropriate, to vary them) (s.71(1C)). Fourthly, the sheriff must ascertain whether there is any objection to the admissibility of evidence which either the Crown or defence wishes to raise despite that party's not having given timeous notice of that preliminary issue and, if there is, the sheriff must decide whether to grant leave (which is granted on cause shown: s.79(1)) for the objection to be raised and, where the sheriff grants leave, dispose of the objection unless he considers it inappropriate to do so as the first diet (s.71(2YA)).

Rule 9.4 provides that a record of the proceedings shall be kept in accordance with "existing law and practice" and must include a record of the sheriff's decision on any notice under s.71(2) which has been placed before him. The effect of a failure to record all decisions on the various notices which might be argued at a first diet is not stated.

The accused must attend the first diet of which he has been given notice and if he fails to do so, the sheriff may grant warrant for his apprehension (s.71(4)). However, a first diet may proceed in the accused's absence (s.71(5)) but that is expressly not so in the case of an accused who is charged with a sexual offence listed in s.288C(2) and in respect of whom the court has not yet ascertained whether he has engaged a solicitor to represent him at trial (s.71(5A)). In such an eventuality, the sheriff must adjourn the diet and ordain the absent accused to appear.

After the business of the first diet is disposed of whether by decision or adjournment, the accused should then be called on to state how he pleads to the indictment (s.71(6)).

Objections to admissibility of evidence

As mentioned above, at the first diet the sheriff is also obliged to ascertain whether the parties have any objection to the admissibility of evidence of which no timeous notice has been given and if there is such an objection, he must decide whether to allow it to be raised late and then either dispose of the objection or, where that is inappropriate (because, for example, evidence requires to be led), appoint a further diet to be held before the trial diet for the purpose of disposing of the objection or direct the objection to be disposed of at the trial diet (s.71(2ZA)). (See *Wright*, above.)

Appeals

Section 74(1) of the 1995 Act provides that, without prejudice to the accused's right of appeal against conviction and sentence and the Lord Advocate's right of appeal against disposal or his right to appeal by bill of advocation (see ss.106, 108 and 131), a party dissatisfied with the sheriff's decision at a first diet may appeal to the High Court by note of appeal in accordance with such procedure as is provided for by Act of Adjournal. Rule 9.6 provides that the note of appeal should be in Form 9.6 and must be lodged with the sheriff clerk not later than two days after the making of the decision (Rule 9.6(2)).

There is no automatic right to appeal. The accused and Crown require leave of the sheriff to appeal by note of appeal under s.74(1) although the Crown has an unfettered right to bring a bill of advocation. Thus, even where leave has been obtained by the Crown but the Crown has failed to exercise that right of appeal within the time limit, the Crown is entitled to present a bill of advocation (see *HM Advocate v Shepherd*, 1997 S.C.C.R. 246 at 249, per Lord Justice Clerk Cullen). Even if it is clear that review by bill of advocation of a decision in the sheriff court is only available to the prosecutor (and not also to the accused), that in itself does not establish a breach of any requirement under art.6 of the European Convention as to equality of arms: see *HM Advocate v K(A)*, 2012 S.C.C.R. 421, para. 11).

Leave to appeal may be granted either on the party's motion or by the sheriff ex proprio motu. However, an appeal may not be taken, and leave should not therefore be given by the sheriff for appeal to be brought, against a decision to adjourn the first diet (for whatever reason) or to accelerate or postpone the trial diet (s.74(2)(a)).

Chapter 9A

Preliminary Hearings (High Court of Justiciary)

Notice of preliminary pleas and preliminary issues

9A.1.—(1) Any notice given under section 72(3) (notice of preliminary pleas) or section 72(6)(b)(i) (notice of preliminary issues) of the Act of 1995 shall be by minute in Form 9A. 1. **B1-25.1**

(2) A minute under paragraph (1) shall be lodged with the Clerk of Justiciary and served on every other party by the minuter.

Applications to dispense with preliminary hearings

9A.2.—(1) An application to dispense with a preliminary hearing shall made in Form 9A.2. **B1-25.2**

(2) Prior to making an application under paragraph (1), the parties shall consult with the Clerk of Justiciary as to a suitable date for a trial diet.

(3) An application under paragraph (1) shall indicate whether or not a date for a trial diet has been agreed by the parties with the Clerk of Justiciary and shall give details of any applicable time limits under section 65 of the Act of 1995.

(4) On the lodging of an application under paragraph (1), the Clerk of Justiciary shall attach it to the record copy of the indictment and place it before a judge in chambers.

(5) The order made by the judge in chambers in respect of the application shall be—

(a) recorded by endorsation on the record copy of the indictment;
(b) signed by the Clerk of Justiciary;
(c) entered in the record of proceedings; and
(d) intimated by the Clerk of Justiciary to the applicants or their solicitors.

(6) The Clerk of Justiciary shall send to the governor of any institution in which any accused is detained a copy of any order of the court dispensing with a preliminary hearing.

Notice to appear where preliminary hearing deserted

B1-25.3 **9A.3.** A notice referred to in section 72C(4) of the Act of 1995 (notice to appear at further preliminary hearing) shall be in Form 8.2-B or, where the charge is of committing a sexual offence to which section 288C of the Act of 1995 (prohibition of personal conduct of defence in cases of certain sexual offences) applies, Form 8.2-C.

Instruction of representation

B1-25.3.1 **9A.3A.**—(1) This rule applies where—

(a) the accused has been cited to answer an indictment at a preliminary hearing in the Fligh Court; and

(b) a solicitor has given notification under section 72F(1) of the Act of 1995 of having been engaged by the accused.

(2) Where the accused is charged with murder, before the preliminary hearing the accused's solicitor must—

(a) take reasonable steps to identify a selection of Queen's Counsel who appear to be available to accept instructions to represent the accused;

(b) inform the accused of the accused's right to be represented by Queen's Counsel;

(c) give the accused a copy of Form 9A.3A-A; and

(d) give the accused a summary of the selection referred to in subparagraph (a).

(3) In any other case, before the preliminary hearing the accused's solicitor must—

(a) take reasonable steps to identify a selection of counsel who appear to be available to accept instructions to represent the accused;

(b) give the accused a copy of Form 9A.3A-B; and

(c) give the accused a summary of the selection referred to in subparagraph (a).

(4) In this rule "Queen's Counsel" means counsel holding the rank of Queen's Counsel or Queen's Counsel, Solicitor Advocate.

AMENDMENTS

Rule 9A.3A inserted by Act of Adjournal (Criminal Procedure Rules 1996 Amendment) (No.3) (Instruction of Representation in the High Court) 2016 (SSI 2016/201) para.2 (effective 3 October 2016).

[THE NEXT PARAGRAPH IS B1-25.4]

Written record of state of preparation

B1-25.4 **9A.4.**—(1) A written record referred to in section 72E of the Act of 1995 (written record of the state of preparation in certain cases) shall be in Form 9A.4 and shall contain the information indicated in that form.

(2) A written record under paragraph (1) may be lodged by sending a copy by facsimile or other electronic means followed by the lodging of the principal and the time and date of lodging shall be the date and time on which the copy was received by the Clerk of Justiciary.

(3) A written record under paragraph (1) which is lodged after 2pm on the last date for lodging under section 72E of that Act shall be deemed to have been lodged on the next day after that date.

Proceedings at preliminary hearing

B1-25.5 **9A.5.**—(1) Any order under section 72(9)(a) (appointment of further diet) of the Act of 1995 shall be intimated by the Clerk of Justiciary to the parties or their solicitors.

(2) On the making of an order mentioned in paragraph (1), the Clerk of Justiciary shall send a copy of the order to the governor of any institution in which the accused is detained.

(3) On the appointment of a trial diet, the Clerk of Justiciary shall intimate the date of that diet to the governor of any institution in which the accused is detained.

Applications for leave to appeal

B1-25.6 **9A.6.**—(1) An application for leave to appeal to the High Court under section 74(1) of the Act of 1995 against a decision of the High Court at a preliminary hearing shall be made by motion to the court at that hearing immediately following the making of the decision in question, and shall be granted or refused at that time.

(2) A decision made under this rule shall be recorded in the record of proceedings.

Note of appeal

B1-25.7 **9A.7.**—(1) An appeal under section 74(1) of the Act of 1995 against a decision of the High Court at a preliminary hearing shall be made by lodging a note of appeal in Form 9A.7 with the Clerk of Justiciary.

(2) The appellant shall send a copy of a note of appeal under paragraph (1) to the other parties.

Abandonment of appeal

B1-25.8 **9A.8.**—(1) An appellant who has taken an appeal under section 74(1) of the Act of 1995 (appeals against decision at a preliminary hearing) may abandon the appeal at any time before the hearing of the appeal.

(2) An abandonment of such appeal shall be made by lodging a minute of abandonment in Form 9A.8.

AMENDMENTS

Chapter 9A inserted by Act of Adjournal (Criminal Procedure Rules Amendment) (Criminal Procedure (Amendment) (Scotland) Act) 2005 (SSI 2005/44) para.2(11) (subject to para.2(2)-(4)) (effective 1 February 2005).

GENERAL NOTE

Lord Bonomy's Review of High Court practice (see *Improving Practice*, November 2002) was principally concerned with solving the problems created by the frequency with which High Court trials were adjourned (see P.W. Ferguson, "High Court Practice and Procedure", 2003 S.L.T. (News) 129-136). The Scottish Executive responded to Lord Bonomy's Report with a White Paper (*Modernising Justice in Scotland: The reform of the High Court of Justiciary*, para.16) by accepting his recommendation that there should be a mandatory pre-trial hearing in all High Court cases. That recommendation was implemented by the Criminal Procedure (Amendment) (Scotland) Act 2004 which amended the 1995 Act to introduce ss.72 and 72A into that statute. **B1-25.9**

A preliminary hearing must be held in all cases unless the High Court dispenses with such a hearing. Section 72B gives to the High Court the power, on an application to it jointly by the Crown and the defence, to dispense with the preliminary hearing and to appoint a trial diet where the court is satisfied of certain matters. These matters are: (1) that the state of the Crown and defence's preparations for trial is such that "the case is likely to be ready to proceed to trial on the date to be appointed for the trial diet" and (2) that there are no preliminary pleas, preliminary issues or other matters which require to be, or could with advantage be, disposed of before the trial diet (s.72B(1)). The joint application must be in Form 9A.2 which requires parties to state the expected length of the trial and specify which witnesses the parties shall require to be in attendance at the trial diet.

For the definition of preliminary pleas and preliminary issues, see the annotations to Ch.9, supra.

Rule 9A.3A

This rule (which came into force on 3 October 2016) follows on from concerns which first surfaced in the Appeal Court in 2009 (in *Woodside v HM Advocate* [2009] HCJAC 19; 2009 S.L.T. 371; 2009 S.C.C.R. 350) and arose again in *Addison v HM Advocate* [2014] HCJAC 110; 2015 J.C. 107; 2014 S.L.T. 995; 2014 S.C.C.R. 608. Most recently, in an appeal from a murder conviction, the Appeal Court again expressed concerns about the nature of informed choice made available to persons and commented that the fact that this issue continued to surface suggested very strongly that the current rules were inadequate to achieve their end and that consideration should be given to their amendment (*Yazdanparast v HM Advocate* [2015] HCJAC 82; 2015 S.C.C.R. 374 (at [30]).

Where a person is charged with murder and has been cited to appear at a preliminary hearing, his solicitor *must* "take reasonable steps to identify a selection of Queen's Counsel who appear to be available to accept instructions to represent the accused" (r.9A.3A(2)(a)). The expression "Queen's Counsel" is defined as counsel holding the rank of QC (viz. senior counsel in the Faculty of Advocate) or "Queen's Counsel, Solicitor Advocate" (r.9A.3A(4)). This is a mandatory professional requirement which closely mirrors what Lord Justice General Gill stated in Addison (at [25]): "To make such a decision [as to professional representation] the client must be advised of his options for representation. A mere recital of those options is no more than a formality if it is not supplemented by advice, a point on which the practice rules are silent. In my view, it is the duty of the accused's solicitor to take all reasonable steps to ascertain which members of the Bar and solicitor advocates experienced in this area are, or may be, available to conduct the defence. Only then can a worthwhile decision on representation be made."

The solicitor must thereafter do three other things: (1) inform his client of "his right to be represented by Queen's Counsel"; (2) give his client a copy of Form 9A.3A-A (Form of information regarding right to be represented by Queen's Counsel) explaining the significance of the QC status and advising that an accused may choose to be represented by a lawyer who is not a QC; and (3) give his client a summary of the selection of Queen's Counsel previously identified by the solicitor (r.9A.3A(2)(b)-(d)).

In all other cases the accused's solicitor must follow much the same procedure as in murder cases except for informing the accused of his right to be represented by a QC (r.9A.3A(3)).

Written Record of State of Preparation

Rule 9A.4 makes provision for an essential part of the new procedure. Both the Crown and the defence must submit to the court a written record of its state of preparation. Schedule 1 is to be completed by the prosecutor and Sch.2 is for the defence to complete. The High Court has issued Practice Note (No.1 of 2005), paras 7-10 of which are intended to guide practitioners as to what is expected of them by the court when complying with the obligation in s.72E to prepare a written record of preparation. It is imperative that the parties communicate with each other in sufficient time before the preliminary hearing with a view to preparing the joint written record. For preliminary hearings to be held in Glasgow, Form 9A.4 should be lodged with the Clerk of Justiciary in Glasgow. In all other cases the form should be lodged with the Justiciary Office in Edinburgh.

Appeals

A party desiring to bring under review a decision at a preliminary hearing must apply by motion to the judge at that hearing immediately following the making of the decision (r.9A.6(1)). In *HM Advocate v*

Fleming [2005] HCJ 02 (October 28, 2005) Lord Brodie held that it was necessary for a party to apply for leave to appeal against his decision on a question relating to the recovery of documents even though his decision was not given at a preliminary hearing. The rationale of that conclusion was that while the diet at which the decision was made was not a preliminary hearing, the question was a preliminary issue (see para.22).

Chapter 9B

Objections to the Admissibility of Evidence Raised after First Diet or Preliminary Hearing

Notice etc. of objections raised after first diet or preliminary hearing

B1-25.10 **9B.1.**—(1) Any notice given under section 79A(2) of the Act of 1995(objections to the admissibility of evidence after first diet or preliminary hearing) shall be by minute in Form 9B.1 and shall be served on the other parties by the minuter.

(2) On the lodging of a minute under paragraph (1), the Clerk of Justiciary or the sheriff clerk, as the case may be, shall place the minute before a judge in chambers.

(3) On considering the minute in the absence of the parties or of any person acting on their behalf, the judge shall appoint—

(a) a further diet to be held before the trial diet for the purpose of hearing the parties on whether leave should be granted for the objection to be raised; or
(b) the question of whether leave should be granted under section 79A(2) of the Act of 1995 for the objection to be disposed of at the trial diet.

(4) The Clerk of Justiciary or the sheriff clerk, as the case may be, shall intimate the order under paragraph (3) to the parties and to the governor of any institution in which the accused is detained.

AMENDMENTS

Chapter 9B inserted by Act of Adjournal (Criminal Procedure Rules Amendment) (Criminal Procedure (Amendment) (Scotland) Act) 2005 (SSI 2005/44) para.2(11) (subject to para.2(2)-(4)) (effective 1 February 2005).

[THE NEXT PARAGRAPH IS B1-26]

Chapter 10

Plea of Guilty

Procedure for plea of guilty

B1-26 **10.1.**—(1) A notice to appear at a diet of the appropriate court served on an accused under section 76(1) of the Act of 1995 (procedure where accused desires to plead guilty) shall—

(a) if an indictment has not already been served, be in Form 10.1-A;
(b) if an indictment has already been served, be in Form 10.1-B.

(2) In any case set down for trial in the High Court, any diet fixed by virtue of section 76(1) of the Act of 1995 may be called before the High Court sitting in Edinburgh whether or not—

(a) the case has already been set down for trial elsewhere, or
(b) any notice has already been served on the accused under section 66(6) of that Act (notice of first diet and trial diet or preliminary hearing).

(3) In the application of subsection (3) of section 76 of the Act of 1995, the court may postpone the trial diet under that section if, but only if—

(a) all the accused have been served with a notice in accordance with subsection (1) of that section;
(b) all the accused are present at the diet called by virtue of subsection (1) of that section; and
(c) a motion to postpone the trial diet is made to the court at that diet.

(4) Where the court grants that motion, the order granting it shall—

(a) be endorsed on the record copy of the indictment;
(b) be signed by the presiding judge;
(c) be entered in the record of proceedings; and
(d) […]

(5) A copy of the order shall be sent by the clerk of court to the governor of any institution in which any accused is detained.

(6) Any requirement to call the diet in any case where such an order has been made shall have effect only in relation to the postponed trial diet.

AMENDMENT

Rule 10.1(2) as amended, and r. 10.1(4)(d) repealed, by the Act of Adjournal (Criminal Procedure Rules Amendment) (Criminal Procedure (Amendment) (Scotland) Act) 2005 (SSI 2005/44), r.2(12) (subject to r.2(2)-(4)) (effective February 1, 2005).

GENERAL NOTE

B1-27 Section 76 of the 1995 Act provides that an accused, who desires to plead guilty and to have his case disposed of "at once", can give written intimation of that desire to the Crown Agent. The written intimation must be given to the Crown Agent irrespective of whether the accused has been already indicted for trial in either the sheriff court or the High Court. An indictment (with a schedule of previous convictions where appropriate: s.69(4)) can then be served (if one has not already been served) without there being appended thereto any list of witnesses or productions, and it shall not be necessary for productions to be lodged in court. The accused will also be served with a notice to appear at a diet at which he can plead guilty, the diet being not less than four clear days after the date of the notice.

On receipt of a "section 76 letter" (such written intimation was known under the 1975 Act as a "section 102 letter"), the Crown can elect, if no indictment has by then been served, to indict in the High Court or the sheriff court. The election of the forum is sometimes influenced by prior negotiations with the Crown when consideration is being given by the accused's agents to submitting an offer to plead. Where, however, the accused thereafter pleads not guilty at a diet which had been fixed by reason of such a s.76 letter, or the accused otherwise reneges on the terms of his written intimation and offers a restricted plea, the diet is to be deserted *pro loco et tempore* and the court may postpone the trial diet. Any period of such postponement of the trial diet is not to count towards the statutory time-limit.

The Justiciary Office has announced (see 2000 S.L.T. (News) 147) that persons wishing to plead guilty in High Court cases may have these cases called and dealt with at the first day of a High Court sitting local to the case and the Crown Office has stated that ideally at least six weeks' notice should be given to the Crown and that the procurator fiscal will advise the accused's representatives whether particular petition cases are regarded as being of High Court potential. When submitting a letter under s.76, the procurator fiscal should be advised of the sitting of the High Court at which the accused wishes his case dealt with.

Rule 10.1(1)

It is essential that a notice is served on the accused as he is being called to a diet and his failure to appear when he is on bail will constitute an offence only if he has been given due notice of the time and place appointed for the diet (see s.27(1)(a) of the 1995 Act).

Rule 10.1(3)

Where an indictment has already been served on the accused and some but not all of the accused submit s.76 letters which lead the Crown to serve a notice upon the accused to appear at an earlier diet for the court to receive their pleas of guilty, the accused who have not submitted s.76 letters will not be present. Plainly they should not be prejudiced so far as the time-limits are concerned and the court is therefore prevented from postponing the trial diet unless all the accused have been served with a notice and are present at the diet called by virtue of that notice.

Chapter 11

Notices by accused in Relation to Defence

Notices of special defence etc.

11.1.—(1) Where a notice under section 78(1) of the Act of 1995 (plea of special defence etc.) is to be served on a co-accused, that notice may be served on his solicitor. **B1-28**

Notices by accused of witnesses and productions

11.2. Any notice given by an accused under section 78(4) of the Act of 1995 (notice of witnesses and productions) shall be served on any co-accused or his solicitor. **B1-28.1**

AMENDMENT

Rule 11.2 as amended by Act of Adjournal (Criminal Procedure Rules Amendment) (Miscellaneous) (SI 1996/2147 (s.171)) (effective September 9, 1996).

[THE NEXT PARAGRAPH IS B1-29]

GENERAL NOTE

Section 78(1) of the 1995 Act provides that in solemn proceedings it shall not be competent for the accused to state a special defence (which is deemed to include a defence of coercion or automatism (s.78(2)) or lead evidence calculated to exculpate himself by incriminating his co-accused, unless he lodges and intimates the plea or notice (under s.78(3)) to the Clerk of Justiciary, the Crown Agent and any co-accused not less than 10 clear days before the trial diet in the High Court and, if the trial is to take place in the sheriff court, to the sheriff clerk and the procurator fiscal at or before the first diet. A special defence can be received at a continued first diet without the necessity of the accused's showing cause under s.78(1)(b) of the 1995 Act because any diet includes a continuation of a diet (s.307(1)): see *O'Connell v H.M. Advocate*, 1996 S.C.C.R. 674. In *Trotter v. H.M. Advocate*, 2000 S.C.C.R. 968 the notice of a defence of coercion was not given in accordance with s.78(1) but was allegedly mentioned in chambers in the presence of the Crown and the sheriff. The sheriff withdrew the defence from the jury's consideration. The Appeal Court did not, however, require to consider the propriety of this decision as they held that the defence was not, in any event, open to the accused on the evidence. **B1-29**

Section 78(4) of the 1995 Act provides that in solemn proceedings it shall not be competent for the accused to examine any witnesses or put in evidence any productions which are not included in the lists lodged by the Crown appended to the indictment unless written notice of the names and addresses of these witnesses and of such productions have been given to the procurator fiscal at or before the first diet where the case is to be tried in the sheriff court or to the Crown Agent at least 10 days before the day on which the jury is sworn if the case is to be tried in the High Court, or unless the court on "cause shown" otherwise directs. A copy of any notice must be lodged with the appropriate court of trial.

Rule 11.2 therefore extends the right to receive notice of witnesses and productions to co-accused (or his solicitor) because a co-accused no doubt may be affected by the evidence which other accused persons propose to lead. Thus for example where an accused has given notice of his intention to incriminate a co-accused not less than 10 clear days before the trial diet in the High Court to the Crown and to the co-accused under s.78(1), or has given notice to the Crown and co-accused of a defence of coercion by a co-accused or automatism caused by a co-accused under s.78(2), there may be witnesses not on the Crown list upon whom the co-accused intends to rely.

Rule 11.2 does not however contain a time-limit. It might have been preferable for the same time-limits which are stipulated for in s.78(4) to be included in the rule. It is therefore open to an accused to withhold giving notice to the co-accused until immediately before the first Crown witness is sworn. Such a tactic may hamper a co-accused in the conduct of his defence in court. For that reason it is at least arguable that the draftsman intended that the time-limit in s.78(4) should be implied into r.11.2. In the event that no notice to a co-accused is given at all under r.11.2 it is open to question what the court will do. If the witness or production is intended to support a notice of incrimination of a co-accused, the co-accused cannot complain of prejudice by failure to serve a notice on him since he will have been made aware of the line of evidence at least 10 clear days before the trial diet (in High Court cases) by service of a notice of incrimination under s.78(1). If the witness or production relates to a special defence (e.g. self-defence or alibi) no prejudice at all could be founded on. However it may not be necessary for prejudice to be demonstrated to the court if r.11.2 is held to be mandatory (see e.g. Lord Justice Clerk's opinion in *Robertson v H.M. Advocate*, 1995 S.C.C.R. 152). It seems likely however that the High Court will require prejudice to be demonstrated before a breach of r.11.2 will be held to constitute a miscarriage of justice. In the course of a trial, a short adjournment might be considered all that is necessary to remedy the effects of failure to obtemper the rule.

Furthermore, it is noteworthy that since a notice of incrimination under s.78(1) requires to be given *only* where the line of evidence will have the *dual* effect of exculpating the accused by showing the co-accused committed the crime (*McQuade v HM Advocate*, 1996 S.C.C.R. 347) r.11.2 gives a co-accused some notice of another accused's intention to incriminate him albeit that the evidence will not wholly exculpate the incriminator, at least where evidence will be led from a witness not on the Crown list.

Chapter 12

Adjournment and Alteration of Diets in Solemn Proceedings

Adjournment

B1-30 **12.1.**—(1) Where circumstances arise in which the court may adjourn a diet under section 75A(2) of the Act of 1995 (adjournment and alteration of diets), and the prosecutor proposes such an adjournment, he may for that purpose require the diet to be called on the date for which it was originally fixed at such time as he thinks appropriate.

(2) The presence of the accused in court when the diet was so called and adjourned shall be sufficient intimation to him of the adjourned diet.

(3) If the diet was so called and adjourned in the absence of the accused, the prosecutor shall forthwith serve on the accused an intimation of adjournment in Form 12.1.

(4) The calling and the adjournment of the diet including a record as to the presence or absence of the accused, as the case may be, shall be endorsed by the clerk of court on the record copy indictment and entered in the record of proceedings in accordance with existing law and practice.

(5) A copy of the order of the court adjourning the diet under section 75A(2) of the Act of 1995 shall be sent by the clerk of court to the governor of any institution in which the accused is detained.

Applications for alteration of diet

B1-30.1 **12.2.**—(1) Subject to paragraph (2), an application under section 75A(5) of the Act of 1995 (application for alteration of diet) shall be made by minute in Form 12.2-A.

(2) Where all parties join in the application, the application shall be made by joint minute in Form 12.2-B.

(3) A minute under this rule shall be lodged—

(a) in the case of proceedings in the High Court, with the Clerk of Justiciary,

(b) in the case of proceedings in the sheriff court, with the sheriff clerk.

Orders fixing diet for hearing of application to alter diet

B1-30.2 **12.3.** Where a minute referred to in rule 12.2 (applications for alteration of diet) has been lodged, the court shall, or, in a case in which all parties join in the application, may, make an order endorsed on the minute—

(a) fixing a diet for a hearing of the application; and

(b) for service of the minute with the date of the diet on all parties.

Calling of diet for hearing application

B1-30.3 **12.4.** A diet fixed under rule 12.3 (orders fixing diet for hearing application to alter diet) shall be held in open court in the presence of all parties unless the court permits the hearing to proceed in the absence of the accused under section 75A(8) of the Act of 1995, and shall be commenced by the calling of the diet.

Joint applications without hearing

12.5—(1) Where, in the case of a joint application under subsection (5) of section 75 A of the Act of 1995 (application for alteration of diet), the court proposes to proceed without hearing the parties by virtue of subsection (7) of that section (joint application for alteration of diet), the clerk of court shall on the lodging of the minute attach it to the record copy of the indictment and place it before a judge in chambers. **B1-30.4**

(2) The order made by the judge in chambers in respect of the joint application shall be—

(a) recorded by endorsation on the record copy of the indictment;
(b) signed by the clerk of court;
(c) entered in the record of proceedings; and
(d) intimated by the clerk of court to the applicants or their solicitors.

(3) The clerk of court shall send to the governor of any institution in which the accused is detained a copy of the following orders of the court—

(a) an order under rule 12.3 (order fixing diet for hearing of application to alter diet);
(b) an order under section 65(3) or (5) of the Act of 1995 (extension of time limits); and
(c) an order under section 75A(5) of the Act of 1995(discharging a diet and fixing a new diet).

Form of notice where trial diet does not take place

12.6. A notice referred to in section 81(5) of the Act of 1995 (notice to appear where trial diet has not taken place) shall be in Form 8.2-B or, where the charge is of committing a sexual offence to which section 288C of that Act (prohibition of personal conduct of defence in cases of certain sexual offences) applies, Form 8.2-C. **B1-30.5**

Floating diets in the High Court of Justiciary and continued diets in the sheriff court

12.7.—(1) A minute referred to in section 83A(2)(a) of the Act of 1995 (minute of continuation of floating trial diet) shall be in Form 12.7. **B1-30.6**

(1A) A minute referred to in section 83B of the Act of 1995 (continuation of trial diet in the sheriff court)(c) shall be in Form 12.7.

(2) The maximum number of days for which a floating diet in the High Court or continued diet in the sheriff court may be continued from sitting day to sitting day shall be four days after the day originally appointed for the trial diet.

AMENDMENT

Chapter 12 substituted by Act of Adjournal (Criminal Procedure Rules Amendment) (Criminal Procedure (Amendment) (Scotland) Act) 2005 (SSI 2005/44) para.2(13) (subject to para.2(2)–(4)) (effective 1 February 2005).

Rule 12.7 as amended by Act of Adjournal (Criminal Procedure Rules 1996 Amendment) (Miscellaneous) 2017 (SSI 2017/144) para.2(4) (effective 28 August 2017).

[THE NEXT PARAGRAPH IS B1-31]

GENERAL NOTE

Chapter 12 in its original form was concerned with s. 80 of the 1995 Act (which made provision for alteration and postponement of a trial diet). That provision was repealed by s.25 of, and para.26 to Sch.1 to the Criminal Procedure (Amendment) (Scotland) Act 2004 with effect from February 1, 2005. From that date S.75A was inserted into the 1995 Act by s. 15 of the 2004 Act. Section 75A now regulates adjournment and alteration of diets. Under the reforms introduced by the 2004 Act, the old system of the Crown's indicting a trial for a sitting of the High Court has been abolished and indictments call the accused to a preliminary hearing on a fixed date. However, the practice of "sittings" in solemn proceedings in the sheriff court has not been abolished by the amendments made to s.66(1) of the 1995 Act by s.7 of the Criminal Procedure (Amendment) (Scotland) Act 2004 (*HM Advocate v Thompson* [2010] HCJAC 6, para.9). Once the case is considered ready for trial, the court fixes a trial diet which is either a fixed diet or a floating diet. In either event, a specific date is identified. Section 75A applies where any diet has been fixed in any proceedings on indictment (subs.(1)) and so applies to sheriff court as well as High Court cases. **B1-31**

Section 75A(2) provides, as the common law always has provided, that the court may, if it considers it appropriate to do so, adjourn the diet. However, adjournment of trial diets has to receive special treatment. First, the court (either a single judge of the High Court or the sheriff, as appropriate: s.75A(11)) may adjourn a trial diet "only if the indictment is not brought to trial at the diet" (s.75A(3)(a)). Trial diets commence when the jury is sworn (s.75A(12)(b)) and not on the calling of the diet (as is the rule for all other diets: s.75A(12)(a)). Secondly, a trial diet cannot be adjourned for more than 48 hours where the *only* reason for the adjournment is the failure of the accused to engage a solicitor for the purposes of conducting his defence at the trial (s.75A(3)(b)). This rule applies also to preliminary hearings.

High Court trial diets (but apparently not preliminary hearings, although s.72(9)(a) contains no restriction on venue for a continued hearing) may be adjourned to a diet to be held at a sitting of the court in another place (s.75A(4)). When determining an application to discharge a fixed diet and appoint another diet (which, except in the special case of trial diets, may be earlier or later than the diet originally fixed (see s.75A(5)(b))), the court must give parties an opportunity to be heard (s.75A(6)) unless parties are ultimately agreed in the application (s.75A(7)). The accused must attend any such hearing unless the court permits him to be absent (s.75A(8)).

Rule 12.1

Section 75A(2) allows adjournment of all fixed diets but note the special provisions in subs.(3) relating to both trial diets and diets (whether trial diets or preliminary hearings) which require to be adjourned only because of the accused's being unrepresented by a solicitor at these diets.

Rule 12.1(3) is on its face mandatory: "the prosecutor shall forthwith serve on an accused an intimation of adjournment". However, the Crown's failure to do so will not necessarily be fatal. In *Carruthers v HM Advocate*, 1994 J.C. 8; 1994 S.L.T. 900; 1993 S.C.C.R. 825 there was a failure to comply with r.41(4) of the 1988 Rules. That rule provided that "the prosecutor shall immediately serve on the accused an intimation of adjournment". Lord Justice General Hope stated (1994 S.L.T. 900 at 902; 1993 S.C.C.R. 825 at 930): "The intention of the rule has to be seen against the background of s.77 of the 1975 Act. If one is concerned to find out whether a provision is directory or mandatory it is relevant to consider the purpose of the rule and its context, and to examine also the consequences if that rule is not observed. The proper view to take of the rule in this case is that its purpose is to provide notice to the accused of a competent adjournment. Failure to give that notice does not affect the competency of the adjournment as such. What it does do, or may do, is result in an absence of notice and possible prejudice to the accused ... [W]here it cannot be suggested that there is any prejudice, the failure to observe the rule can have no adverse consequences, and it certainly cannot lead to the falling of the indictment."

Similarly, a failure to make the necessary endorsement on the record copy of the indictment, or to make the necessary entry in the record of proceedings, will not be fatal because there can never be any prejudice to the accused (cf. *R. v Soneji* [2005] 3 W.L.R. 303 and *R. v Knights* [2005] 3 W.L.R. 330).

Rule 12.4

A hearing on the minute in Form 12.2-A is itself a fixed diet under r. 12.3(a) must be intimated to all parties (r. 12.3(b)). The hearting must be in open court and in the presence of all parties unless the accused is excused attendance. No provision is made in s.75A for the hearing to be in open court (nor was any such requirement made in s.80(5) (now repealed)) but this rule makes that requirement. This contrasts with the chambers hearing which is all that is necessary when the parties are agreed on the adjournment and make a joint application under s.75A(7) and r.12.5.

Rule 12.5

Where the accused is in custody and there is a joint motion to adjourn, the prison governor must receive *copies* of the orders made on the original minute to adjourn (before it is agreed among the parties) and of the orders extending the time limits (where relevant) and fixing a new diet. This requirement is not simply to keep the governor informed of the next diet to which the accused must be brought from custody to appear (or to advise the governor of the continuing lawfulness of the accused's pre-trial incarceration) but presumably so that these copies can be transmitted to the accused for his information.

Rule 12.6

Section 81(2) provides (unlike the old position before amendment by the 2004 Act) that where a solemn trial diet is deserted *pro loco et tempore* the court may appoint a further trial diet for a later date. That will not always happen and in that event, s.81(4)(a) permits the prosecutor in the High Court, at any time within two months after the desertion of the diet, to give notice (under s.81(5)) to the accused on another copy of the (original) indictment to appear and answer the indictment at a further preliminary hearing (or, if the prosecutor so chooses, a first diet for further proceedings on the indictment to be taken in the lower court). Similarly, where the original indictment was due for trial in the sheriff court, the prosecutor can call upon the accused to appear at a further trial diet in that court not less than seven clear days after service of the notice or the prosecutor can elect to proceed against the accused in the High Court and in that event the notice should call the accused to appear at a preliminary hearing.

The prosecutor's power to give notice for the above purposes is not, however, limited to desertion of the trial diet. Under s.81(4)(b), where the indictment falls or is for any other reason not brought to trial and the diet has not been "continued, adjourned or postponed", the Crown may in its discretion proceed under s.81(5). In such a case, the Crown must give notice in the same fashion at any time within the period of two months after the date of the trial diet (see s.81(8)(b)).

Chapter 13

Summoning of Jurors

List of jurors

B1-32 **13.1.**—(1) A list of jurors shall—

(a) contain not less than 40 names;
(b) be prepared under the directions of the clerk of court before which the trial is to take place;
(c) be kept at the office of the sheriff clerk of the district in which the court of the trial diet is situated; and
(d) be headed "List of Assize for the sitting of the High Court of Justiciary (or the sheriff court of.at.) on the.of.".

(2) The clerk of the court before which the trial is to take place, in preparing a list of jurors for the trial diet, shall have regard, in determining the number of jurors to be listed, to the powers of altering the date of or adjourning any trial diet exercisable under the following provisions of the Act of 1995—

section 74(3) (postponement of trial diet in appeals in connection with first diets or preliminary hearings),
section 75 A (adjournment and alteration of diets),
section 76(3) (postponement where not guilty plea accepted),

AMENDMENTS

Rule 13.1 substituted by Act of Adjournal (Criminal Procedure Rules Amendment) (Criminal Procedure (Amendment) (Scotland) Act) 2005 (SSI 2005/44) para.2(14) (subject to para.2(2)-(4)) (effective February 1, 2005).

Rule 13.1 as amended by Act of Adjournal (Criminal Procedure Rules Amendment) (Miscellaneous) 2010 (SSI 2010/184) para.2 (effective June 1, 2010). Only applies to a list of jurors prepared on or after June 1, 2010.

Citation of jurors

13.2.—(1) The citation under section 85(4) of the Act of 1995 of a person summoned to serve as a juror shall be served on that person in Form 13.2-A. **B1-32.1**

(2) The execution of citation under section 85(4) of the Act of 1995 of persons summoned to serve as jurors shall be in Form 13.2-B.

[THE NEXT PARAGRAPH IS B1-33]

GENERAL NOTE

Section 84(1) of the 1995 Act requires sheriffs principal to return such numbers of jurors as they think fit or such number of jurors in cases to be tried in the High Court as the Lord Justice Clerk or a Lord Commissioner of Justiciary directs. The clerk of court shall use only these lists for the trials for which they were required (s. 84(7)). This rule provides that special regard should be had by the clerk of court in determining the number of jurors to be listed to the power of the court to postpone or adjourn trial diets. The accused is entitled to have a copy of the list of jurors supplied to him free of charge on application being made to the appropriate sheriff clerk (see s.85(1)). **B1-33**

Section 84 makes no provision as to the minimum number of potential jurors who should be included in what subs.(8) refers to as the "list of assize". Rule 13.1(a) supplies that want by requiring that there be no fewer than 40 names. The minimum number of potential jurors was previously 30 but was increased to 40 for any list of jurors "prepared on or after" June 1, 2010 (Act of Adjournal (Criminal Procedure Rules Amendment) (Miscellaneous) 2010 (SSI 2010/184) para.2(2)). However, by the time a jury is to be empanelled, there will almost always be a smaller number of available persons to serve on the jury. This can cause problems, both administrative and legal. "The system of jury trial is based on the constitutional principle that a person indicted for trial should be judged by a randomly chosen jury of his peers" (*B. v HM Advocate* 2006 S.L.T. 143, para.21, per Lord Justice Clerk Gill). For that reason, a miscarriage of justice was held to have occurred in *B* when an accused was tried by a jury chosen from a list of 22 names. The High Court stated, however, that it would be wrong to lay down the minimum number from which a jury should be balloted or whether and to what extent a gender imbalance within that number would be acceptable (para.26). In *B* out of a list of 60 names (comprising an equal number of males and females), only 7 men and 15 women constituted the eventual pool of potential jurors. A retrial was authorised.

In order to address the procedural problem which arose in *B v HM Advocate*, supra, the High Court of Justiciary promulgated a new rule which applies where the list of jurors has been prepared on or after June 1, 2010. Rule 14.1 A(1) provides that where there are fewer than 30 names on the list of jurors prepared on or after that date it shall not be competent to ballot the jury. The court must then make such order or orders as it thinks fit in the interests of justice (r.14.1 A(3)).

Chapter 13A

Witnesses

Citation of witnesses for precognition

13A.1 The form of citation of a witness for precognition under section 267A of the Act of 1995 shall be in Form 13A.1. **B1-33.1**

AMENDMENTS

Chapter 13A inserted by Act of Adjournal (Criminal Procedure Rules Amendment No.4) (Criminal Procedure (Amendment) (Scotland) Act 2004) 2004 (SSI 2004/434) para.2 (effective October 4, 2004).

Rule 13A.1 as amended by Act of Adjournal (Criminal Procedure Rules Amendment No.5) (Miscellaneous) 2004 (SSI 2004/481) para.2 (effective November 26, 2004).

Warrants for apprehension

13A.2.—(1) An application made in writing for a warrant for the apprehension of a witness under section 90A or 90D of the Act of 1995 shall be in Form 13A.2-A. **B1-33.2**

(2) On receipt of an application under paragraph (1), the Clerk of Justiciary or sheriff clerk, as the case may be, shall fix a diet for the hearing of the application and intimate the date of that hearing to the parties.

(3) A warrant for the apprehension of a witness under section 90 A of the Act of 1995 shall be in Form 13A.2-B.

AMENDMENTS

Rule 13A.2 inserted by Act of Adjournal (Criminal Procedure Rules Amendment) (Criminal Procedure (Amendment) (Scotland) Act) 2005 (SSI 2005/44) para.2(15) (subject to para.2(2)-(4)) (effective February 1, 2005).

Review of orders

B1-33.3 **13A.3.** An application for review under section 90D of the Act of 1995 of an order under section 90A(1)(a) or (b) of that Act shall be in Form 13A.3.

AMENDMENTS

Rule 13A.3 inserted by Act of Adjournal (Criminal Procedure Rules Amendment) (Criminal Procedure (Amendment) (Scotland) Act 2004) 2005 (SSI 2005/44) para.2(15) (subject to para.2(2)-(4)) (effective February 1, 2005).

Appeals

B1-33.4 **13A.4.** An appeal under section 90E(1) of the Act of 1995 (appeal in respect of an order under section 90B(1) of the Act of 1995) shall be made by lodging a note of appeal in Form 13A.4 with the Clerk of Justiciary.

AMENDMENTS

Rule 13A.4 inserted by Act of Adjournal (Criminal Procedure Rules Amendment) (Criminal Procedure (Amendment) (Scotland) Act) 2005 (SSI 2005/44) para.2(15) (subject to para.2(2)-(4)) (effective February 1, 2005).

GENERAL NOTE

B1-33.5 The common law power of the Crown to secure the attendance at trial of absconding witnesses in solemn proceedings (see Renton & Brown, *Criminal Procedure* (5th edn), para.7-45) was swept away by s.90A(8) which provides: "It shall not be competent, in any proceedings on indictment, for a court to issue a warrant for the apprehension of a witness otherwise than in accordance with this section". Thus a petition to the sheriff for warrant to apprehend the witness and either to detain him in custody until the date of trial (*Stallworth v HM Advocate*, 1978 S.L.T. 93) or unless he can find sufficient caution for his appearance at trial (*Gerrard, Petitioner*, 1984 S.L.T. 108) is no longer competent. The power is now entirely statutory and introduces a greater degree of judicial control over the incarceration of witnesses.

Once a witness has been arrested on a warrant issued under s.90A(1), he must be brought before the court which issued it and, after the witness and both the prosecution and the defence have been afforded an opportunity to make submissions, the witness may be detained by order of the court until the conclusion of the diet at which he is to give evidence (e.g. the trial diet or preliminary hearing) or he may be released on bail or simply liberated (s.90B(1)). The court's power to find the witness in contempt is not affected by this new procedure (s.90B(3)). The court may order the detention of the witness (or grant his release on bail) only if it is satisfied of two matters under s.90B(2). First, the specific order must be necessary with a view to securing that the witness appears at the diet at which he is to give evidence. Secondly, it must be appropriate in all the circumstances that that specific order be made.

A warrant can only be granted under s.90A(1) where either the witness has been duly cited to appear and he "deliberately and obstructively fails to appear at the diet" (s.90A(2)) or the court is satisfied that the witness is being deliberately obstructive *and* is not likely to attend to give evidence at any diet in the proceedings without being compelled to do so (s.90A(3)). A witness who is proved (by production of an execution of service of citation in proper form) to have been duly cited for the purposes of s.90A(2) and fails to appear at the diet is presumed, in the absence of any evidence to the contrary, to have so failed deliberately and obstructively (s.90A(4)).

Rule 13A.1

The citation of a potential witness for precognition by the procurator fiscal must state the place and time of the proposed precognition since s.267A(3)(a) provides that a witness who, having been duly cited, fails without reasonable excuse (after having received at least 48 hours notice) to attend at the time and place mentioned in the citation shall be guilty of an offence (for which the maximum sentence is 21 days' imprisonment). The citation warns the witness of that fact.

Rule 13A.2

The usual situation in which a witness apprehension warrant becomes necessary is at the trial diet. However, it could arise earlier where, for example, the High Court at a preliminary hearing has ordered a further diet under s.72(9) to hear evidence on an objection to the admissibility of evidence. Usually the prosecutor will be the applicant. Usually the application will be made orally at the bar, as is expressly permitted by s.90A(5)(a). However, where the application is made for a witness who has not been cited and the contention is that he has deliberately and obstructively sought to evade citation—as was the position in *Stallworth v HM Advocate*, 1978 S.L.T. 93—it may be preferable to proceed by written application in Form 13A.2-A as that will allow (in para.2 of the application) specification of the circumstances from which the court is to be invited to infer both the witness's intention deliberately and obstructively to evade citation and thus the need to compel his attendance.

The statute does not prescribe the means of proof in cases where no citation has been effected. However, where the application is in writing, s.90A(5)(b) specifically provides that the court may dispose of the application in court or chambers and leaves it to the court to determine whether any inquiry or hearing (if any) is appropriate. The accused has no right to be present in chambers since the application for a warrant under s.90A(1) is not a part of the trial proceedings even if the trial has commenced.

A s.90A(1) warrant has implied in it warrant to officers of law (a term which is defined in s.307(1), but is in practice restricted to police officers, although it may be noted that any person commissioned by the Commissioners of Customs and Excise (now HM Revenue and Customs) may also execute such a warrant) to arrest the witness, to bring him before the court (wherever practicable on the first day the court granting the warrant is sitting after the witness is taken into custody: s.90A(9)), to detain the witness *ad interim* and so far as necessary for the execution of the warrant, to break open shut and lockfast places (s.90A(6)).

Rule 13A.3

A drafting error in this rule has been carried through into para.2 of Form 13A.3. The orders which can be reviewed are those made under s.90B(1)(a) or (b), namely committal of the witness until conclusion of the diet and release of the witness on bail (with such conditions as the court considers necessary to secure the witness's attendance at the diet: s.90B(5)).

Section 90D(1) gives to the witness the right to apply to the court ordering detention to seek recall of the order so that he can be admitted to bail or liberated. The witness must show cause and the court must afford the parties an opportunity to be heard on the review. Section 90D(2)(a) allows the witness to seek review of the bail conditions if he can show cause, and s.90D(2)(b) allows the prosecutor or defence to seek review of the earlier bail order so that the court can be persuaded to recall bail and order detention or impose different bail conditions. It is incompetent for the court to entertain a review at the instance of the Crown or defence unless there is put before the court material information which was not available to the court when the order was originally made (s.90D(3)). The prosecution or defence can obtain issue of a warrant for arrest of the witness who is on bail when it seeks a review but only if the court is satisfied that the interests of justice require the witness's arrest (s.90D(5)(c)).

A review of a first detention order or a first bail order cannot be sought by the witness before the fifth day after the order was made and once a new order has been made, no subsequent review can be sought before the 15th day after that order was made (s.90D(4)).

Rule 13A.4

It is competent for the witness, the Crown and the accused to appeal to the High Court against an order for detention or the witness's liberation or his release on bail or the conditions on which bail is granted, as appropriate (s.90E(1) and (2)). The appeal should be intimated to the other parties and, where appropriate, the witness. The appeal may be disposed of in chambers or court after such inquiry and hearing of the parties as the court considers just. In light of the terms of s.90E(4), a single High Court judge will hear an appeal from an order made in the sheriff court; a quorum of at least two High Court judges should hear an appeal against a High Court order.

[THE NEXT PARAGRAPH IS B1-34]

Chapter 14
Procedure at Trial in Solemn Proceedings

Recording of not guilty plea

14.1. Where the accused pleads not guilty, the clerk of court shall, subject to rule 14.1 A, make an entry in the record of proceedings for the purposes of section 88(1) of the Act of 1995 (recording plea of not guilty and balloting jury) that, in respect that the accused pleaded not guilty, the accused was remitted to an assize and that the jurors were balloted for and duly sworn to try the libel. **B1-34**

AMENDMENTS

Rule 14.1 as amended by Act of Adjournal (Criminal Procedure Rules Amendment) (Miscellaneous) 2010 (SSI 2010/184) para.3 (effective 1 June 2010).

Minimum number of jurors for balloting jury

14.1A.—(1) Notwithstanding section 88(1) of the Act of 1995 (plea of not guilty, balloting and swearing of jury, etc.), where there are fewer than 30 of those named on the list of jurors available for balloting, it shall not be competent to proceed to ballot the jury. **B1-34.0.1**

(2) Where it is not competent to proceed to ballot the jury the court shall make such order or orders as it thinks fit in the interests of justice.

AMENDMENTS

Rule 14.1 A inserted by Act of Adjournal (Criminal Procedure Rules Amendment) (Miscellaneous) 2010 (SSI 2010/184) para.3 (effective 1 June 2010).

Words in r.14.1 substituted by Act of Adjournal (Criminal Procedure Rules 1996 Amendment)

(Miscellaneous) 2019 (SSI 2019/321) para.2(2) (effective 13 November 2019).

Rule 14.1A(1) as amended by Act of Adjournal (Criminal Procedure Rules 1996 Amendment) (Jury Ballot) 2020 (SSI 2020/200) para.2(2) (effective 19 July 2020).

[THE NEXT PARAGRAPH IS B1-34.1]

Balloting of jurors

B1-34.1 **14.2.**—(1) The clerk of court shall cause the name and address of each juror to be written on a separate piece of paper, all the pieces being of the same size, and shall cause the pieces to be folded up, as nearly as may be in the same shape, and to be put into a box or glass and mixed, and the clerk shall draw out the pieces of paper one by one from the box or glass.

(2) After 15 such names have been drawn ("the first list"), the clerk of court must draw a further 5 names ("the reserve list") and where any person on the first list—

(a) does not appear;
(b) is challenged and is set aside; or
(c) before any evidence is led, is excused,

the persons on the reserve list will, in the order in which their names were drawn, replace on the first list each such absent, challenged or excused juror until the number required for the trial is attained.

(3) Paragraph (4) applies where the court considers that a reserve list of 5 jurors may be insufficient to ensure the number required for the trial will be attained.

(4) The court may, of its own accord or on the application of a party, after hearing parties, direct that the reserve list be increased to a maximum of 10 jurors.

Amendments

Rule 14.2 as amended by Act of Adjournal (Criminal Procedure Rules 1996 Amendment) (Jury Ballot) 2020 (SSI 2020/200) para.2(2) (effective 19 July 2010).

Form of oath or affirmation to jurors

B1-34.2 **14.3.**—(1) Where the clerk of court administers the oath to the jury in terms of section 88(6) of the Act of 1995 (administration of oath in common form), he shall do so in accordance with the form in Form 14.3-A.

(2) In the case of any juror who elects to affirm, the clerk of court shall administer the affirmation in accordance with the form in Form 14.3-B.

(3) The oath or the affirmation administered in accordance with paragraph (1) or (2), as the case may be, shall be treated as having been administered for the purposes of section 88(6) of the Act of 1995.

Jurors chosen for one trial may continue to serve

B1-34.3 **14.4.**—(1) Where the conditions in section 88(4) of the Act of 1995 (circumstances in which jurors for one trial may serve on another) are met, and subject to paragraph (2) of this rule, the clerk of court shall at the commencement of the first trial engross the names and addresses of the jurors in the record of proceedings; and in the record of proceedings of the subsequent trial it shall be sufficient to mention—

(a) that the jurors who served on the preceding trial also served on the assize of the accused then under trial; and
(b) that no objection was made to the contrary.

(2) The jurors referred to in paragraph (1) shall be sworn together in the presence of the accused in the subsequent trial.

Form of oath or affirmation to witnesses

B1-34.4 **14.5.**—(1) Where the judge administers the oath to a witness, he shall do so in accordance with the form in Form 14.5-A.

(2) In the case of any witness who elects to affirm, the judge shall administer the affirmation in accordance with the form in Form 14.5-B.

(3) The oath or affirmation administered in accordance with paragraph (1) or (2), as the case may be, shall be treated as having been administered in common form.

Sheriffs notes of evidence

B1-34.5 **14.6.** The sheriff who has presided at a trial on solemn procedure shall duly authenticate and preserve the notes of the evidence taken by him in the trial and, if called upon to do so by the High Court, shall produce them, or a certified copy of them, to the High Court.

Form of record of proceedings

B1-34.6 **14.7.** Where the proceedings at a trial are recorded, the entry in the record of proceedings shall be signed by the clerk of court and shall be in the form in Form 14.7.

Interruption of trial for other proceedings

B1-34.7 **14.8.**—(1) Where a trial is interrupted under section 102 of the Act of 1995 (interruption of trial for other proceedings), a minute of continuation of the diet of the interrupted trial shall be entered in the record of proceedings.

(2) Where a trial is interrupted under section 102 of the Act of 1995, the trial shall be continued to a time later on the same day or to such other time as may be specified in the minute of proceedings.

Interruption of proceedings for the tendering of pleas

14.8A.—(1) Where a case has called the presiding judge may, on a motion made jointly, without adjourning those proceedings interrupt them by calling other proceedings. B1-34.7.1

(2) Such a motion is competent only where in making the motion parties inform the court that—

(a) one or more of the accused in the proceedings is also an accused in other proceedings;

(b) none of the proceedings are going to trial, because (either or both)—

(i) the accused persons are intending to plead guilty as libelled;

(ii) the accused persons are intending to tender pleas which the Crown intends to accept; and

(c) in the interests of justice it is appropriate that the other proceedings be called in order that they be dealt with simultaneously.

(3) Where the judge has interrupted any proceedings under paragraph (1), the proceedings are to be regarded as being before the court simultaneously and pleas shall be recorded in this way.

(4) Where pleas have been recorded in accordance with paragraph (3) the clerk of court may on any subsequent occasion call the proceedings together and they shall be regarded as being before the court simultaneously.

AMENDMENTS

Rule 14.8A inserted by Act of Adjournal (Criminal Procedure Rules Amendment No.4) (Miscellaneous) 2010 (SSI 2010/418) para.4 (effective December 13, 2010).

[THE NEXT PARAGRAPH IS B1-34.8]

Interruption of proceedings for conviction or sentence

14.9.—(1) On conviction of an accused in solemn proceedings, the presiding judge may, without adjourning those proceedings, interrupt them by— B1-34.8

(a) considering a conviction against that accused in other proceedings pending before that court for which he has not been sentenced; or

(b) passing sentence on that accused in respect of the conviction in those other proceedings.

(2) Where the judge has interrupted any proceedings under paragraph (1), he may, in passing sentence on an accused person in respect of a conviction in those proceedings, at the same time pass sentence on that person in respect of any other conviction he has considered.

(3) No interruption of any proceedings under paragraph (1) shall cause the instance to fall in respect of any person accused in those proceedings or shall otherwise affect the validity of those proceedings.

Issue of extract convictions

14.10.—(1) Subject to the following paragraphs, no extract of a conviction shall be issued during the period of four weeks after the day on which the conviction took place. B1-34.9

(2) An extract of a conviction may be issued at any time where it is required as a warrant for the detention of the person convicted under any sentence which shall have been pronounced against him.

(3) In the event of—

(a) an appeal under section 108 (Lord Advocate's appeal against sentence) or section 210F(3) (prosecutor's appeal against refusal to make an order for lifelong restriction),

(b) an intimation of intention to appeal under section 109(1), or

(c) a note of appeal under section 110 in respect of an appeal under section 106(1)(b) (appeal against sentence passed on conviction),

of the Act of 1995 being lodged, no extract of a conviction shall be issued until such appeal, if it is proceeded with, is determined.

(4) Where an accused is convicted on indictment in the sheriff court of any crime or offence and an extract of that conviction is subsequently required in evidence, such extract shall be issued at any time by the clerk of the court having the custody of the record copy of the indictment although the plea of the accused may have been taken and the sentence on him pronounced in another court.

AMENDMENTS

Rule 14.10(3)(a) as amended by Act of Adjournal (Criminal Procedure Rules Amendment No.3) (Risk Assessment Orders and Orders for Lifelong Restriction) 2006 (SSI 2006/302) para.2(2) (effective June 20, 2006).

[THE NEXT PARAGRAPH IS B1-35]

GENERAL NOTE

Sections 88 to 102 of the 1995 Act make detailed provision for the conduct of contested solemn proceedings at the trial stage from the recording of the plea of not guilty, the balloting of the jury, etc., right through to the receiving and recording of the verdict in open court in the presence of the accused. B1-35

It should be noted that the High Court has effectively held that it is incompetent to interfere with the principle of random selection of the jury by "vetting" prospective jurors on the list of assize, in order to determine their individual beliefs and possible prejudices: see *McDonald v HM Advocate*, 1997 S.L.T. 1237. This decision is in line with the English position that the court has no power to ensure that a multiracial jury is empanelled: see *R. v Ford (Royston)* [1989] Q.B. 868.

Rule 14.1

The minutes of proceedings should record the fact that the accused pled not guilty and that the jury were balloted and duly sworn to try the libel under rr.14.2 and 14.3, as these are essential steps in the trial process and accurate information about their having occurred is required in the event of an appeal against conviction. See also Ch.3.

Rule 14.1A

This rule was introduced in order to address the procedural difficulty which arose in *B v HM Advocate*, 2006 S.L.T. 143. It applies only to a list of jurors prepared on or after June 1, 2010 (Act of Adjournal (Criminal Procedure Rules Amendment) (Miscellaneous) 2010 (SSI 2010/184) para.3(3)). In respect of any list of jurors prepared on or after that date, the list must contain "not less than 40 names" (r.13.1(1)(a)).

Rule 14.2

Jurors can now only be challenged for cause (see s.86(2)) although the court is required to excuse a juror before he is sworn if the Crown and the accused agree (see s. 86(1)) and in that event no reason need be given to the court. Any objection for cause must be stated to the court, before the juror is sworn to serve (see s.86(4)) and cannot be founded on any irregularity in the procedures for the preparation of the list of assize unless such irregularity is based on a criminal act by which jurors may be returned to serve in any case contrary to the 1995 Act or the Jurors (Scotland) Act 1825 (see s.84(10)).

Prospective jurors are cited to attend a sitting of the High Court (or the sheriff court) in terms of a warrant issued by the Clerk of Justiciary (or sheriff clerk, as appropriate) in terms of s.66(1) of the 1995 Act. Provision is made in s. 1(2) of the Law Reform (Miscellaneous Provisions) (Scotland) Act 1980 for excusal as of right and, under s. 1(3), for other prospective jurors to be excused in particular circumstances. Furthermore, any juror who cannot escape under these provisions can be excused by the clerk of court if the juror can show to the clerk's satisfaction that "there is good reason why he should be excused from attending in compliance with the citation" (s. 1(5)). These provisions do not undermine the common law principle (expressed by Lord Justice-General Emslie in *M v HM Advocate*, 1974 S.L.T. (Notes) 25) that the jury ultimately balloted must be a random selection of the citizenry. Nor do these provisions provide a relevant ground of challenge under Art.6(1) of the European Convention that the jury is not an independent and impartial tribunal established by law: *Transco Pic v HM Advocate (No.2)*, 2004 S.L.T. 995.

Rule 14.4

Section 88(4) of the 1995 Act permits with the consent of the Crown and the accused, jurors who are chosen for one trial, which has been disposed of, to serve on the jury at other trials without again being selected by ballot. However r. 14.4(2) reaffirms the requirement of s.92(1) that (subject to s.54(4) dealing with the plea of insanity in bar of trial, and where the accused misconducts himself) no part of a trial shall take place outwith the presence of the accused (see *Walker v Emslie* (1899) 3 Adam 102; *Bennett v HM Advocate*, 1980 S.L.T. (Notes) 73. See also notes to Chap. 12 for a qualification to this rule in respect of continuations of the diet).

Rule 14.5

A failure to put the appropriate form of oath or affirmation to the witness would not, it is submitted, invalidate the trial proceedings nor render the witnesses' evidence incompetent: see *McAvoy v HM Advocate*, 1992 S.L.T. 46 (sub nom. *McAvoy and Jackson v HM Advocate*, 1991 S.C.C.R. 123). If the witness is a child or arguably too young to be sworn, but the witness is sworn without the court first ascertaining the witness's age and satisfying itself that the witness is capable of understanding the nature of the oath—in accordance with the procedure desiderated in *Quinn v Lees*, 1994 S.C.C.R. 159—any evidence from the witness should be objected to timeously in order to preserve the accused's right of appeal in accordance with s. 118(8) of the 1995 Act: *Jardine v Howdle*, 1997 S.C.C.R. 294 (applying s. 192(3) in summary proceedings). However, it should be noted that *Jardine* is apparently inconsistent with *Kelly v Docherty*, 1991 S.L.T. 419 and that the court did not appear to consider the additional question of whether the alleged incompetency of the witness rendered the proceedings a fundamental nullity. It seems that no distinction was drawn between the competency of evidence (e.g. hearsay evidence is generally incompetent, but once admitted without objection it becomes competent evidence *in causa*) and the competency of witnesses.

Rule 14.6

No obligation is imposed on High Court judges to authenticate and preserve their notes of the evidence but it is the practice of the High Court for judges to keep detailed notes which can then be furnished to the High Court by way of a report in terms of s. 113 or s.298(1) of the 1995 Act, and accordingly these detailed notes of evidence would be available in the (unlikely) event that the Criminal Appeal Court wished to inspect them.

Rule 14.7

Section 93(1) of the Criminal Procedure (Scotland) Act 1995 provides that the proceedings at the trial of any person who, if convicted, is entitled to appeal under Part VIII of the 1995 Act, shall be recorded by means of shorthand notes or by mechanical means. A breach of that provision, which can perhaps more easily occur now in the High Court because of the use of tape recording equipment, does not alone lead to the conviction being quashed: for a breach of s.93(1) to give rise to a miscarriage of justice the accused must also identify an issue on which it can be said that the trial judge misdirected the jury (*Carroll v HM Advocate*, 1999 S.L.T. 1185; 1999 S.C.C.R. 617).

Section 94 of the 1995 Act makes provision for the making and delivery of transcripts of evidence recorded under s.93(1). The Secretary of State (now Scottish Ministers) and the prosecutor are entitled to request such a transcript which the Clerk of Justiciary must then make available; and the same obligation applies where a request is made by any other person not being a person convicted at the trial although the third party must pay such charges as are fixed by the Treasury as a condition of obtaining the transcript (s.94(2)). Subsection (2A), inserted by s.65 of the Criminal Justice (Scotland) Act 2003, gives a convicted person the right to ask a High Court judge for a transcript where he has been granted leave to appeal and can show cause for his application; but in that case the convicted person must pay such charges as are fixed by the Treasury (just as third parties must do). Where the Crown Agent has received intimation of the High Court's decision on an application for leave to appeal (or a second sift application) under s. 107(10)—whether the decision is to grant leave or to refuse it—the prosecutor is not entitled to a transcript as of right under subs.(2)(a) but must apply in writing to a High Court judge for a transcript and that request may be granted where the prosecutor shows cause for the transcript being made available (s.94(2B)). Cause will exist where the Crown proposes to try a co-accused separately because, for example, the evidence was insufficient in the absence of the first accused as a compellable witness or the co-accused had absconded prior to the first trial, and especially so where an essential witness has died after giving evidence at the first trial. It is necessary to apply to a High Court judge irrespective of whether the trial was in the sheriff court or High Court because it is the High Court which alone regulates appellate procedure.

Section 94(3) repeats the terms of s.275(3) of the Criminal Procedure (Scotland) Act 1975 (as inserted by s.47(1) of, and para.27 of Sch.5 to, the Prisoners and Criminal Proceedings (Scotland) Act 1993) and empowers the Secretary of State (now the Scottish Ministers) to make an order restricting the scope of s.94(2). The power was exercised in 1993 to make the Transcripts of Criminal Proceedings (Scotland) Order 1993 (SI 1993/2226) which, after amendment by the Transcripts of Criminal Proceedings (Scotland) Amendment Order 1995 (SI 1995/1751), provides that no transcript can be supplied unless the Clerk of Justiciary is satisfied that the person requesting the transcript (whether prosecutor, convicted person, any third party named in or immediately affected by an order made by the court in the proceedings, or any person authorised to act on behalf of such persons) intends to use it only for a specified purpose. This applies only to (a) trials where the court has made an order excluding persons from the court room because it is a trial for rape or a like offence (s. 145(3) of the 1975 Act, now s.92(3) of the 1995 Act) or a trial relating to an offence or conduct contrary to decency or morality and a child witness is to give evidence (s. 166(1) of the 1975 Act, now s.50(3) of the 1995 Act) and (b) trials where the court has made an order postponing publication of the proceedings under s.4(2) of the Contempt of Court Act 1981. The specified purposes which alone can be the justification for the supply of a transcript are (1) an appeal to the High Court (which does not include a reference by the Lord Advocate under s.123(1) of the 1995 Act or a reference by the Advocate General of a devolution issue under s.288A(1) of the 1995 Act); (2) a reference of a conviction and/or sentence to the High Court by the Secretary of State for Scotland under s.263(1) of the 1975 Act (which must now mean a reference by the Scottish Criminal Cases Review Commission under s.194B(1) of the 1995 Act, or any application or petition in relation thereto); (3) a petition for the exercise of Her Majesty's Prerogative of Mercy; (4) any proceedings before the European Court of Human Rights; and (5) any proceedings before the Court of Justice of the European Communities.

Rule 14.8

Section 102 of the 1995 Act allows for a jury trial to be interrupted in two distinct situations. First, where the jury is deliberating over its verdict and another trial has been called (it is unnecessary that the first witness has been sworn for this rule to apply), the presiding judge may receive the verdict in the preceding trial and pass sentence, or the presiding judge may give further directions in the preceding trial where the jury has sought a direction (although not where the presiding judge *ex proprio motu* decides to give further directions) or where any request by the jury has been made regarding any matter in the cause. For example the jury may request to examine a production and in such circumstances the procedure laid down in *Hamilton v HM Advocate*, 1980 J.C. 66 should be followed. Secondly, where a trial is "then proceeding", and an accused in a case where the diet has not yet been called intimates a desire to plead guilty or to plead in terms acceptable to the Crown, or where a case is remitted to the High Court for sentence under s. 195, the presiding judge may interrupt the trial. Presumably the trial is "proceeding" immediately on the diet having been called. In either case the interruption is not to be deemed an irregularity, nor can the accused object to the proceedings (s. 102(5)), although subs.(4) requires the trial diet to be called *de novo* after the interruption is concluded in order for the trial competently to be proceeded with anew. The interruption should accordingly be minuted so that there is a record of it and of the commencement of the trial in the event of an appeal against conviction.

Rule 14.9

This rule was first introduced by the Act of Adjournal (Sentencing Powers) 1978 (SI 1978/123) which was intended to assist court administration by curing the technical obstacles to an accused who is awaiting sentence in respect of another conviction being dealt with for both convictions simultaneously (see *Law and Nicol v HM Advocate*, 1973 S.L.T. (Notes) 14). The rule requires that there be a conviction in existence and accordingly does not permit the interruption of the proceedings to receive the plea and then proceed to sentence (*Watters v HM Advocate*, 1992 S.L.T. 149; 1992 S.C.C.R. 104. See also *MacDonald v HM Advocate*, 1994 S.L.T. 44 where a summary complaint in respect of which no conviction had been returned was tendered to but rejected by the sheriff at a deferred sentence diet).

Chapter 15

Appeals from Solemn Proceedings

Register and lists of appeals

B1-36 **15.1.**—(1) The Clerk of Justiciary shall keep a register, in such form as he thinks fit, of all cases in which he receives intimation of intention to appeal or, in the case of an appeal under section 106 (right of appeal), section 108 (Lord Advocate's appeal against sentence) or section 210F(3) (prosecutor's appeal against refusal to make an order for lifelong restriction) of the Act of 1995, a note of appeal under section 110 of that Act.

(2) The register kept under paragraph (1) shall be open for public inspection at such place and at such hours as the Clerk of Justiciary, subject to the approval of the Lord Justice General, considers convenient.

(3) The Clerk of Justiciary shall—

(a) prepare from time to time, a list of appeals to be dealt with by the High Court; and
(b) cause such list to be published in such manner as, subject to the approval of the Lord Justice General, he considers convenient for giving due notice to persons having an interest in the hearing of such appeals by the High Court.

(4) Subject to paragraph (5), the Clerk of Justiciary shall give the respective solicitors representing parties to an appeal so listed at least 14 days notice of the date fixed for the hearing of the appeal.

(5) In an appeal under sections 106(1)(b) to (e), 108(1) or 210F(3) of the Act of 1995, the period of notice mentioned in paragraph (4) shall be 28 days.

AMENDMENTS

Rule 15.1 as amended by Act of Adjournal (Criminal Appeals) 2003 (SSI 2003/387) para.3. Brought into force on September 1, 2003 in accordance with art.1.

Rule 15.1(1) and (5) as amended by Act of Adjournal (Criminal Procedure Rules Amendment No.3) (Risk Assessment Orders and Orders for Lifelong Restriction) 2006 (SSI 2006/302) para.2(3) (effective June 20, 2006).

Rule 15.1(5) as amended by Act of Adjournal (Criminal Procedure Rules Amendment No.2) (Miscellaneous) 2012 (SSI 2012/187) para.2 (effective July 16, 2012, subject to transitional provisions).

Forms of appeal

B1-36.1 **15.2.**—(1) Any intimation under section 109(1) of the Act of 1995 (written intimation of intention to appeal) shall be in Form 15.2-A.

(2) A note under section 110(1) of the Act of 1995 (written note of appeal) shall be in Form 15.2-B.

(3) An application under section 111(2) of the Act of 1995 (application to extend time) shall be made in Form 15.2-C.

(4) An application under section 112(1) of the Act of 1995 (application of appellant for bail) shall be made in Form 15.2-D.

(5) The following documents shall be signed by the appellant or by his counsel or solicitor—

(a) an intimation of intention to appeal under section 109(1) of the Act of 1995 except where the appellant is the Lord Advocate, or;
(b) an application under section 111(2) of the Act of 1995 (application to extend time).

(5A) The note of appeal shall be signed by—

(a) the counsel or solicitor advocate who has drafted it; or
(b) the appellant where the appellant has drafted it and intends to conduct the appeal himself.

(6) An appeal under section 19 of the Prisoners and Criminal Proceedings (Scotland) Act 1993 (appeals in respect of decisions relating to supervised release orders) shall be in Form 15.2-B.

AMENDMENTS

Rule 15.2(5) as amended, and r.15.2(5A) inserted, by Act of Adjournal (Criminal Appeals) 2002 (SSI 2002/387) para.3(2) (effective September 26, 2002).

Appeals against refusal of applications heard by single judge

B1-36.2 **15.3.**—(1) Where an application has been dealt with by a single judge of the High Court by virtue of section 103(5) of the Act of 1995 (powers exercisable by single judge), the Clerk of Justiciary shall notify the decision to the applicant in Form 15.3-A.

(2) In the event of such judge refusing any such application, the Clerk of Justiciary on notifying such refusal to the applicant shall forward to him a form in Form 15.3-B to complete and return forthwith if he desires to have his application determined by the High Court as constituted for the hearing of appeals under Part VIII of the Act of 1995 (appeals from solemn proceedings).

Extension of time by Clerk of Justiciary

15.4. Where, under section 110(2) of the Act of 1995, the Clerk of Justiciary extends the period for lodging a note of appeal, the period of any such extension shall be recorded on the completed form of intimation of intention to appeal. **B1-36.3**

Intimation of appeal against sentence of death

15.5. The Clerk of Justiciary shall intimate an appeal against a conviction in respect of which sentence of death has been pronounced, and the determination in any such appeal, immediately on such intimation or determination, as the case may be, to— **B1-36.4**

(a) the Secretary of State for Scotland; and
(b) the governor of the prison in which the appellant is detained.

Procedural hearing

15.5A—(1) In any appeal the Clerk of Justiciary may fix a procedural hearing for the purposes of determining whether the parties are ready to proceed to a hearing of the appeal. **B1-36.4.1**

(2) The procedural hearing shall be heard by a judge of the High Court and, where the appellant is an individual and is represented, may be held in his absence.

(3) The Clerk of Justiciary shall intimate to the parties in Form 15.5A-A the date of the procedural hearing fixed under paragraph (1), not later than twentyone days before that date.

(4) Not later than seven days before the date of the procedural hearing, the appellant shall complete and lodge a notice in Form 15.5A-B with the Clerk of Justiciary and send a copy to the respondent. The said notice shall be signed by the counsel or solicitor advocate representing the appellant in the appeal, or by the appellant where the appellant intends to conduct the appeal himself.

(5) Where the appellant has lodged a notice in accordance with paragraph (4), the Clerk of Justiciary, having considered the terms of the said notice and any representations made to him by the respondent, may determine that it is unnecessary to proceed with the procedural hearing and, if he so determines, shall intimate this to the parties not less than forty-eight hours before the date of the procedural hearing.

(6) Not later than seven days after the last day of the appeal court sitting during which

(a) the procedural hearing at which it has been determined that the appeal is ready to proceed has been heard; or
(b) the procedural hearing was due to be heard but in respect of which the Clerk of Justiciary has made a determination in terms of paragraph (5),

the Clerk of Justiciary shall fix and intimate to the parties the date when the appeal is to be heard.

(7) [...]

AMENDMENTS

Rule 15.5A inserted by Act of Adjournal (Criminal Appeals) 2002 (SSI 2002/387) para.3(2) (effective September 26, 2002).

Rule 15.5A(7) repealed by Act of Adjournal (Criminal Procedure Rules Amendment No.2) (Presentation of Conviction Appeals in Writing) 2010 (SSI 2010/309) para.2 (effective November 1, 2010).

Rule 15.5A(1) as amended by Act of Adjournal (Criminal Procedure Rules Amendment No.3) (Procedural Hearings in Appeals from Solemn Proceedings) 2012 (SSI 2012/300) para.2 (effective December 10, 2012).

[THE NEXT PARAGRAPH IS B1-36.5]

Abandonment of appeals

15.6. A notice of abandonment under section 116(1) of the Act of 1995 (abandonment of appeal) shall be in Form 15.6. **B1-36.5**

Note of proceedings at trial

15.7. In an appeal under section 106(1) of the Act of 1995 (right of appeal), the High Court may require the judge who presided at the trial to produce any notes taken by him of the proceedings at the trial. **B1-36.6**

Clerk to give notice of date of hearing

15.8.—(1) Where the High Court fixes the date for the hearing of an appeal, or fixes the date for a hearing in chambers of an application under section 111(2) of the Act of 1995 (application to extend time) and makes a direction under section 111(4) of the Act of 1995 (parties to be present), the Clerk of Justiciary shall give notice to the Crown Agent and to the solicitor of the convicted person, or to the convicted person himself if he has no known solicitor; and the appellant or applicant shall, within seven days before the hearing, lodge three copies (typed or printed) of the appeal or application for the use of the court. **B1-36.7**

(2) Where the powers of the court are to be exercised by a single judge under section 103(5) of the Act of 1995 (powers exercisable by single judge), a copy of the application to be determined shall be lodged for the use of the judge.

(3) A notice by the Clerk of Justiciary to the Secretary of State for the purposes of section 117(4) of the Act of 1995 (notice that appellant or applicant be present at a diet) shall be in Form 15.8.

AMENDMENTS

Rule 15.8 as amended by Act of Adjournal (Criminal Procedure Rules 1996 Amendment) (Miscellaneous) 2017 (SSI 2017/144) para.2(5) (effective 29 May 2017).

Continuation of hearings

B1-36.8 **15.9.**—(1) The High Court, or any single judge exercising the powers of the High Court under section 103(5) of the Act of 1995 (powers exercisable by single judge), may continue the hearing of any appeal or application to a date, fixed or not fixed.

(2) Any judge of the High Court, or the person appointed by the court to take additional evidence, may fix any diet or proof necessary for that purpose.

Note to be kept of appeal

B1-36.9 **15.10.**—(1) The Clerk of Justiciary shall, in all cases of appeal from a conviction obtained or sentence pronounced in the High Court, note on the margin of the record of the trial the fact of an appeal having been taken and the result of the appeal.

(2) In the case of an appeal taken against any conviction obtained or sentence pronounced in the sheriff court on indictment, the Clerk of Justiciary shall notify the clerk of that court of the result of the appeal; and it shall be the duty of the clerk of that court to enter on the margin of the record of the trial a note of such result.

Suspension of disqualification from driving pending appeal

B1-36.10 **15.11.**—(1) Where a person who has been disqualified from holding or obtaining a driving licence following a conviction on indictment appeals against that disqualification to the High Court, any application to suspend that disqualification pending the hearing of the appeal shall be made—

(a) if the sentencing court was the sheriff, by application to the sheriff; or
(b) if the sentencing court was the High Court, or if an application to the sheriff under subparagraph (a) has been refused, by petition to the High Court.

(2) An application to the sheriff under paragraph (1)(a) shall be—

(a) in Form 15.11-A, and
(b) lodged with the sheriff clerk with a copy of the note of appeal endorsed with the receipt of the Clerk of Justiciary;

and the sheriff clerk shall record the order made by the sheriff on the application in the minute of proceedings.

(3) A petition to the High Court under paragraph (1)(b) shall be—

(a) in Form 15.11-B; and
(b) lodged with the Clerk of Justiciary.

Provisions supplemental to rule 15.11(3)

B1-36.11 **15.12.**—(1) The petitioner or his solicitor shall, on lodging a petition under rule 15.11(3), send a copy of it to—

(a) the Crown Agent; and
(b) if the sentencing court was the sheriff, the clerk of that court.

(2) The High Court may order such further intimation (including intimation to the Lord Advocate) as it thinks fit, and may dispose of the application in open court or in chambers.

(3) An order made by a single judge under paragraph (2) shall not be subject to review.

(4) On an order being made on a petition under rule 15.11(3), the Clerk of Justiciary shall, if the sentencing court was the sheriff, send a certified copy of the order to the clerk of that court.

(5) Where the order referred to in paragraph (4) suspends a disqualification from driving, the Clerk of Justiciary shall also send a certified copy of the order to the Secretary of State with such further information as the Secretary of State may require.

(6) The Clerk of Justiciary shall, on determination of the appeal against a disqualification from driving—

(a) if the sentencing court was the sheriff, send the clerk of that court a certified copy of the order determining the appeal and the clerk of that court shall, if appropriate, make the appropriate endorsement on the appellant's driving licence and intimate the disqualification to the persons concerned; or
(b) if the appeal against the disqualification is refused, make the appropriate endorsement on the appellant's driving licence and intimate the disqualification to the persons concerned.

(7) Where leave to appeal has been refused under section 107 of the Act of 1995, "determination" in paragraph (6) of this rule means—

(a) the fifteenth day after the date of intimation to the appellant or his solicitor of refusal of leave under subsection (1)(b) of that section, unless the appellant applies to the High Court for leave to appeal; or
(b) the day two days after the date of intimation to the appellant or his solicitor of the refusal of leave by the High Court under subsection (5)(b) of that section.

Suspension of sentence under S.121A of the Act of 1995

B1-36.12 **15.12A.**—(1) Where under section 109(1) of the Act of 1995 a person lodges intimation of intention to appeal, any application for suspension of a relevant sentence under section 121A of that Act shall be made by petition to the High Court in Form 15.12A-A.

(2) Where a convicted person or the prosecutor lodges a note of appeal in respect of an appeal under section 106(1)(b) to (e) or 108 of the Act of 1995, as the case may be, any application for suspension of a relevant sentence under section 121A of that Act shall be made by petition to the High Court in Form 15.12A-B.

(3) A petition to the High Court under paragraph (1) or (2) shall be lodged with the Clerk of Justiciary.

(4) The court shall grant or refuse any application under paragraph (1) or (2) within 7 days of the petition having been lodged as mentioned in paragraph (3).

(5) Where the court grants an application under paragraph (1) or (2) the Clerk of Justiciary shall, if the sentencing court was the sheriff, send a certified copy of the order to the clerk of that court.

(6) In any case where—

(a) intimation of intention to appeal is lodged under section 109(1) of the Act of 1995; and

(b) a relevant sentence is suspended under section 121A of that Act,

but no note of appeal is lodged under section 110 of that Act, the order suspending *ad interim* the relevant sentence shall be recalled with effect from the seventh day after the date on which the Clerk of Justiciary intimates that the appeal is deemed to have been abandoned.

(7) In the application of section 121A of the Act of 1995 (suspension of certain sentences pending appeal) to a case in which leave to appeal has been refused under section 107 of that Act, the word "determined" in subsection (1) of the said section 121A shall be construed as meaning—

(a) the fifteenth day after the date of intimation to the appellant or his solicitor and to the Crown Agent of refusal of leave under subsection (1)(b) of section 107 of that Act, unless the appellant applies to the High Court for leave to appeal; or

(b) the seventh day after the date of intimation to the appellant or his solicitor and to the Crown Agent of the refusal of leave by the High Court under subsection (5)(b) of section 107 of that Act.

AMENDMENTS

Rule 15.12A inserted by Act of Adjournal (Criminal Procedure Rules Amendment No.4) (SI 1997/1834) (effective 1 August 1997).

Suspension of disqualification etc. under section 121 of the Act of 1995

15.13. In the application of section 121 of the Act of 1995 (suspension of disqualification, forfeiture, etc.) to a case in which leave to appeal has been refused under section 107 of the Act of 1995, the word "determined" in subsections (1) and (2) of section 121 of that Act shall be construed as meaning— **B1-36.13**

(a) the fifteenth day after the date of intimation to the appellant or his solicitor of refusal of leave under subsection (1)(b) of section 107 of that Act, unless the appellant applies to the High Court for leave to appeal; or

(b) the day seven days after the date of intimation to the appellant or his solicitor of the refusal of leave by the High Court under subsection (5)(b) of section 107 of that Act.

AMENDMENTS

Rule 15.13 as amended by Act of Adjournal (Criminal Procedure Rules Amendment No.3) 1997 (SI 1997/1788) (effective 11 August 1997).

Remits in applications for leave to appeal

15.14. The judge of the High Court considering an application for leave to appeal under section 107 of the Act of 1995 may, before deciding to grant or refuse leave, remit the case to the judge who presided at the trial for a supplementary report to be produced to him as soon as is reasonably practicable on any matter with respect to the grounds of appeal. **B1-36.14**

AMENDMENTS

Rule 15.14 inserted by Act of Adjournal (Criminal Procedure Rules Amendment) (Miscellaneous) (SI 1996/2747 (S.171)) (effective 9 September 1996).

Amended grounds of appeal

15.15.—(1) On cause shown, the High Court may grant leave to an appellant to amend the grounds of appeal contained in the note of appeal. **B1-36.15**

(2) Where the High Court has granted leave to amend the grounds of appeal under paragraph (1), it may order—

(a) that the Clerk of Justiciary shall send a copy of the amended note of appeal to the judge who presided at the trial; and

(b) that as soon as is reasonably practicable after receiving a copy of the amended note of appeal, the judge who presided at the trial shall provide the Clerk of Justiciary with a written report on the amended grounds of appeal.

(3) Section 113(2) to (4) of the Act of 1995 (judge's report) shall apply to a report on the amended grounds of appeal ordered under paragraph (2) as it applies to a report under subsection (1) of that section.

(4) Where the High Court grants leave to amend under paragraph (1), section 107 of the Act of 1995 shall apply, unless the Court otherwise directs, for the purposes of obtaining leave to appeal for the amended grounds of appeal as it applied for the purposes of the original grounds of appeal and, for the references in subsection (2)(a) and (c) of that section to the note of appeal and the trial judge's report, there shall be substituted references to the amended grounds of appeal contained in the amended note of appeal and the trial judge's report, if any, on the amended grounds of appeal, respectively.

AMENDMENTS

Rule 15.15 inserted by Act of Adjournal (Criminal Appeals) 2002 (SSI 2002/387) art.3(2) (effective 26 September 2002).

Requirement for case and argument

B1-36.15.1 **15.15A.**—(1) Subject to paragraphs (2) and (3), this rule applies to an appeal under section 106(1)(a) or (f) of the Act of 1995.

(2) The court may, of its own motion or on the application of the appellant, order that this rule is not to apply in a particular appeal or to a particular aspect of an appeal.

(3) Where in relation to any ground of appeal an appellant seeks to lead evidence this rule shall apply to that ground of appeal only in relation to the question of whether that evidence should be led; but the court may nevertheless make an order containing provision similar to this rule in relation to the presentation of submissions following the hearing of that evidence.

(4) The appellant must, within 42 days of the granting of leave to appeal in accordance with section 107 of the Act of 1995, lodge a case and argument.

(5) A case and argument must—

(a) set out, for each ground of appeal, a succinct and articulate statement of the facts founded upon and the propositions of law being advanced;
(b) contain an estimate of how long will be required for the hearing of the appeal; and
(c) be signed by counsel or the solicitor advocate instructed to represent the party concerned in the conduct of the appeal, or by the appellant where the appellant intends to conduct the appeal himself.

(6) A case and argument must, when lodged, be accompanied by—

(a) all documents, or a copy thereof, referred to or founded upon in the case and argument and not already lodged in the appeal process; and
(b) all authorities, or a copy thereof, listed in the case and argument and not contained within a publication specified by the Lord Justice General by direction.

(7) The Crown—

(a) must, if the court, considering that the circumstances of the case require it, orders it to do so; and
(b) may, if it considers it appropriate to do so,

lodge a case and argument in response to the appellant's case and argument.

(8) Where the court makes an order under paragraph (7)(a), the Crown must lodge the case and argument within 21 days of the making of that order.

(9) At the same time as a case and argument is lodged, a copy of it and of all the documents accompanying it must be sent to the other party to the appeal.

(10) Where the Deputy Principal Clerk of Justiciary considers a case and argument to be unduly lengthy he shall refer the matter to a judge of the High Court who shall give such directions as he considers appropriate.

(11) Where a case and argument is not lodged timeously, the Deputy Principal Clerk of Justiciary shall refer the matter to the Lord Justice General, whom failing the Lord Justice Clerk, for such action as he considers appropriate.

(12) The court may, on the application of the relevant party and on cause shown, extend the period for lodging a case and argument.

AMENDMENTS

Rule 15.15A inserted by Act of Adjournal (Criminal Procedure Rules Amendment No.2) (Presentation of Conviction Appeals in Writing) 2010 (SSI 2010/309) para.2 (effective November 1, 2010).

Hearing of appeal

B1-36.15.2 **15.15B.**—(1) This Rule applies to the hearing of an appeal in so far as a case and argument has been lodged by the appellant in terms of rule 15.15A(4).

(2) At the hearing of the appeal—

(a) the appellant's case and argument and supporting documents shall constitute the principal submissions of the appellant;
(b) unless it otherwise directs, the court will expect the appellant to rely on the case and argument without reading it over to the court;
(c) the appellant may, subject to the control of the court, make supplementary comment to the case and argument;
(d) the appellant may respond to any case and argument lodged by the Crown; and
(e) the appellant shall answer any points raised by the court.

(3) Where the Crown lodges a case and argument paragraph (2) applies, with the necessary modifications, to the Crown as it applies to the appellant.

(4) The appellant and Crown have a duty to co-operate with each other and the court to ensure the completion of the hearing of the appeal within the time allocated by the court.

(5) The court may, at any point during the hearing, set a timetable for the completion by a party of any submissions permitted in terms of paragraph (2)(b), (c)(d) or (e).

(6) On cause shown, the court may permit the appellant to introduce new information that has come to light in the period since the case and argument was lodged.

(7) Where the court permits the introduction of new information, it may at its discretion permit the lodging of additional documents in support of the new information.

(8) An appellant who wishes to introduce new information and lodge additional documents shall send a copy of the information and documents to the Clerk of Justiciary and to the Crown as soon as the information and documents come into the appellant's possession.

(9) An appellant who has sent new information and documents to the Clerk of Justiciary shall apply at the bar to allow it to be introduced or lodged, as the case may be.

AMENDMENTS

Rule 15.15B inserted by Act of Adjournal (Criminal Procedure Rules Amendment No.2) (Presentation of Conviction Appeals in Writing) 2010 (SSI 2010/309) para.2 (effective November 1, 2010).

[THE NEXT PARAGRAPH IS B1-36.16]

Presentation of solemn sentence appeal in writing

15.16.—(1) This rule applies to an appeal under sections 106(1)(b) to (e), 108(1) or 210F(3) of the Act of 1995 listed in terms of rule 15.1(3) (register and lists of appeals). **B1-36.16**

(2) In an appeal to which paragraph (1) applies, the appellant shall present his case in writing.

(3) The solicitor for the appellant or, if unrepresented, the appellant shall—

(a) not later than 14 days before the date assigned for the appeal court hearing, lodge a case and argument in Form 15.16;

(b) lodge with the case and argument all documents, or a copy thereof, referred to or founded upon in the case and argument and not already lodged; and

(c) at the same time as he lodges the case and argument referred to in subparagraph (a) and the supporting documents referred to in sub-paragraph (b), send a copy to the Crown or, where the Crown is the appellant, to the respondent.

(4) The case and argument referred to in paragraph (3) shall be signed by counsel or the solicitor advocate representing the appellant in the appeal, or by the appellant where the appellant intends to conduct the appeal himself.

(5) At the hearing of the appeal—

(a) the case and argument and supporting documents referred to in paragraph (3) shall constitute the submissions of the appellant;

(b) unless it otherwise directs, the Court will expect the appellant to rely upon the case and argument without reading it over to the Court; and

(c) the appellant may make supplementary comments to the case and argument; and shall answer any points raised by the Court.

(6) On cause shown, the Court may permit the appellant to introduce new information that has come to light in the period since the case and argument was lodged.

(7) Where the Court permits the introduction of new information, it may at its discretion permit the lodging of additional documents in support of the new information.

(8) A party who wishes to introduce new information and lodge additional documents shall send a copy of the information and documents to the Clerk of Justiciary as soon as the information and documents come into the appellant's possession.

(9) A party who has sent new information and documents to the Clerk of Justiciary shall make application at the bar to allow it to be introduced or lodged, as the case may be.

(10) Where the documents referred to in paragraph (3) are not lodged timeously, the Deputy Principal Clerk of Justiciary shall refer the matter to the Lord Justice-General, whom failing the Lord Justice-Clerk, for such action as the Lord Justice-General or Lord Justice-Clerk, as the case may be, considers appropriate.

AMENDMENTS

Rule 15.16 inserted by Act of Adjournal (Criminal Appeals) 2003 (SSI 2003/387) para.3. Brought into force on September 1, 2003 in accordance with art.1.

Rule 15.16(1) as amended by Act of Adjournal (Criminal Procedure Rules Amendment No.3) (Risk Assessment Orders and Orders for Lifelong Restriction) 2006 (SSI 2006/302) para.2(4) (effective June 20, 2006).

Rule 15.16(3) as amended by Act of Adjournal (Criminal Procedure Rules Amendment No.2) (Miscellaneous) 2012 (SSI 2012/187) para.2 (effective July 16, 2012, subject to transitional provisions).

Copying of transcripts to other parties

15.16A.—(1) Where the prosecutor receives a transcript under section 94(2) of the Act of 1995, the prosecutor shall forthwith send a copy to the other parties and to the clerk of court. **B1-36.17**

(2) Where a person receives a transcript under section 94(2A) of the Act of 1995, that person shall forthwith send a copy to the other parties and to the clerk of court.

AMENDMENTS

Rule 15.16A inserted by Act of Adjournal (Criminal Procedure Rules Amendment) (Miscellaneous) 2010 (SSI 2010/184) para.4 (effective June 1, 2010).

Lodging and intimation of transcripts

15.17—(1) This rule applies where a party intends to rely upon a transcript of a record made under section 93(1) of the Act of 1995 (record of trial) in any appeal under section 106 or 108 of that Act. **B1-36.18**

(2) the party shall lodge 4 copies of the transcript or any relevant part thereof with the Clerk of Justiciary in accordance with paragraphs (3) and (4) and shall at the same time send a copy to the other parties.

(3) Where a procedural hearing has been fixed the party shall lodge the copies not later than 7 days before the date of that hearing.

(4) Where no procedural hearing has been fixed the party shall lodge the copies not later than 21 days before the date of the hearing at which he intends to rely upon the transcript.

(5) where a party has not complied with the requirements of paragraphs (3) and (4) he shall not, except by leave of the court on cause shown, be permitted to refer to such transcript in the course of any hearing.

AMENDMENTS

Rule 15.17 inserted by Act of Adjournal (Criminal Procedure Rules Amendment No.5) (Miscellaneous) 2007. Brought into force on December 1, 2007.

Rule 15.17 as amended by Act of Adjournal (Criminal Procedure Rules Amendment) (Miscellaneous) 2010 (SSI 2010/184) para.4 (effective June 1, 2010).

[THE NEXT PARAGRAPH IS B1-37]

GENERAL NOTE

B1-37 The law in relation to an appeal against conviction and/or sentence in solemn proceedings is now radically altered from the state it existed in under the 1975 Act since an appeal on the ground of a miscarriage of justice can only be proceeded with now after the High Court has granted leave to appeal in terms of s.107 of the 1995 Act. Leave to appeal will only be granted in the first instance by a single judge of the High Court or, in the event of his refusing leave, by a quorum of two or three judges (depending on whether the appeal is against sentence alone or conviction (and sentence)), if the accused can satisfy the High Court that he has "arguable grounds of appeal". If the accused satisfies the court that there are arguable grounds then the appeal will be allowed to be proceeded with on these grounds *alone* (although the High Court can permit further grounds to be argued at the appeal hearing).

It is incompetent to apply to judges at a second sift in order to challenge the first sift judge's decision to limit the grounds of appeal on which the first sift judge has granted leave to appeal. The correct procedure, where leave is granted on restricted grounds, is to seek the Appeal Court's leave, under s.107(8) of the 1995 Act, to argue the grounds refused at the sift stage: see *Beggs, Petitioner*, 2005 S.L.T. 165 (para.9). The first sift judge must give reasons for his refusal of leave and these reasons must be "intelligible and deal with the issues of law that are raised in the grounds of appeal" but once that has been done there is no reason in principle for the second sift judges' not being able to express their reasons referentially by adopting those of the first sift judge: see *McSorley, Petitioner*, 2005 S.C.C.R. 508 (para.15). Where leave to appeal against sentence has been refused in respect of all the grounds advanced, it is incompetent to ask the Appeal Court to grant leave on cause shown even though the judges at the second sift have granted leave to appeal against conviction because such an appeal is "a quite different matter" (*McLeod v HM Advocate* [2005] HCJAC 128 (October 12, 2005), para.12).

In light of observations made by the court in *Ryan, Petitioner*, 2002 S.L.T. 275; 2002 S.C.C.R. 295 (para.7), a practice developed in Justiciary Office when leave to appeal had been refused at the first sift of advising solicitors who had intimated an appeal against the refusal of leave that the appeal would be withheld from the second sift for a stated period (in order to allow amplification of the written submissions on the grounds of appeal and quite often also to allow for the obtaining of counsel's opinion). This was nothing more than an informal administrative arrangement which only operated when the solicitor requested that the appeal be withheld from the second sift. If no such request were made and acceded to, the appeal could be considered by the second sift judges forthwith. There is no basis for solicitors believing that an appeal will not be considered at second sift before the 14-day period (under s.107(4)) for marking an appeal to the second sift expires: see *Strang v HM Advocate*, 2005 S.L.T. 1114 (paras 19-20).

It should be noted that where an application for leave to appeal has been refused by a single judge and the accused has failed within 14 days to apply to a quorum of the High Court, the High Court has no power in exercise of its *nobile officium* to waive or extend that time limit on an extra-statutory basis: see *Connolly, Petr*, 1997 S.L.T. 689; 1997 S.C.C.R. 295.

That decision was approved by a Bench of Five Judges in *Ryan, Petitioner*, 2002 S.L.T. 275 where *Connolly* was described as correctly decided although the court expressed concern that s.107(4) was inflexible in its operation because it applied even where an extension of time (which is available for other time limits governing related procedural steps on appeal) would occasion no prejudice to the Crown or any other party. Reconsideration of s.107(4) was therefore urged on the Scottish Parliament so as to avoid a situation where the consequence of failure, even by a day, to comply with the provision "would be out of all proportion to the culpability, if there was any, of a failure to comply with that time limit" (para.25, p.277L).

The remedy in such a situation would therefore appear to rest in the hands of the Scottish Criminal Cases Review Commission which is empowered by s.194B(1) of the 1995 Act to refer a convicted person's whole case to the High Court for determination as if it were an appeal, irrespective of whether an appeal against conviction had previously been heard and determined by the court, on the grounds that the Commission believes that a miscarriage of justice may have occurred *and* that it is in the interests of justice that the case should be referred (s.194C). However, given the limited resources of the Commission and the delay which being required to make application to the Commission would entail, this is at best an uneconomic way of avoiding the consequences of s.107(4) as it is presently framed. The provision has now been amended to give the court a discretion to allow the appeal to proceed.

Crown appeals against sentence

Where the Crown appeals against an unduly lenient sentence it can happen that the accused, though represented by counsel and agents, is absent at the hearing of the appeal when the appeal might be allowed and an increased sentence imposed. The High Court has held that "in principle, proceedings which may have that consequence ought not to take place outwith the presence of the respondent" (*Urquhart v Campbell*, 2006 S.C.C.R. 656, para.[4]). At present the court will therefore continue the appeal for the accused to have the opportunity to attend.

Rule 15.1

The Register of Appeals will be a record of all solemn cases in which an intention to appeal (though the appeal may subsequently be abandoned under s.116 of the 1995 Act) is given to the Justiciary Office in Edinburgh under s. 109, or where a note of appeal against conviction and/or sentence is lodged by an accused after leave has been granted under s. 107, or where the Lord Advocate has lodged a note of appeal against an unduly lenient sentence under s. 108. The Clerk of Justiciary will thereafter prepare a criminal appeal roll detailing the appeals which have been granted leave to proceed and specifying the dates on which they are appointed to be heard. **B1-37.1**

Oddly, r. 15.1 does not make provision for the recording of notes of appeal under r.31.7 against the decision of a solemn court to make a reference to the Court of Justice of the European Communities.

The additional r. 15.1(4) and (5) provides that, except in appeals against sentence and the Lord Advocate's appeals against unduly lenient disposals (under s. 106 and 108 respectively), there should be at least 14 days' notice given to the parties of the date of the proposed appeal hearing. The exception requiring 42 days' notice in sentence appeals is made necessary by the innovation in procedure effected by the Act of Adjournal (Criminal Appeals) 2003 (SSI 2003/387), para.3(b) which provides that these appeals shall be presented in writing.

Rule 15.2

Rule 15.2(1). Written intimation of an intention to appeal against conviction and/or sentence on indictment should be given within two weeks of the final determination of the proceedings (i.e. when sentence is passed in open court: s. 109(4)). **B1-37.2**

Rule 15.2(2). A note of appeal by an accused person against conviction and/or sentence on indictment, should be lodged within six weeks of lodging intimation by way of Form 15.2-A but where the appeal is against sentence only, the note of appeal should be lodged within two weeks of sentence being passed in open court. Where the Lord Advocate appeals against an unduly lenient sentence (or a disposal which is either inappropriate or on unduly lenient terms), there is no requirement to lodge intimation of an intention to appeal as the Lord Advocate does not require leave to appeal. The Lord Advocate has "the right of direct access" to the Appeal Court: see *HM Advocate v McKay*, 1996 S.C.C.R. 410 at 416G-417A). The Lord Advocate's note of appeal must be lodged within four weeks of the passing of the sentence in open court. However, the period of six weeks applying to accused persons may be extended (before it expires) by the Clerk of Justiciary (see s. 110(2)). The Clerk of Justiciary has no such power in relation to an appeal at the instance of the Lord Advocate.

Rule 15.2(3). A single judge of the High Court (see s. 103(5)) may extend (i) the period of two weeks within which intimation of an intention to appeal should be given by the accused, and (ii) the periods of six weeks and two weeks within which the note of appeal should be lodged by the accused (see s.111(2)). This power is additional to the power of the Clerk of Justiciary under s.110(2) since the High Court can grant a retrospective extension of time.

Rule 15.2(4). A single judge of the High Court (see s. 103(5)) may admit a convicted accused to bail pending the determination of his appeal against conviction and/or sentence or pending the Lord Advocate's appeal against an unduly lenient sentence, and an accused who is convicted on indictment should (if he has not yet lodged a note of appeal) apply stating the reasons for granting bail and what his grounds of appeal are (s.112(2)(a)). The scope for the allowance of bail pending an appeal is intended to be "especially limited" in cases where the convicted person has not yet lodged a note of appeal since s.112 of the 1995 Act provides that the High Court shall not admit such a convicted person to bail unless in exceptional circumstances" (see *Ogilvie, Petr*, 1998 S.L.T. 1339; 1998 S.C.C.R. 187). Furthermore, the mere fact that a convicted person has been granted leave to appeal is not in itself sufficient cause why bail should be granted although it is a factor which is relevant to the court's consideration of the merits of the application (*Ogilvie*, supra).

Rule 15.2(5). The Lord Advocate does not require to intimate an intention to appeal under s. 108 (see note to r. 15.2(2)) but Crown Counsel are required to sign the Lord Advocate's note of appeal.

Rule 15.2(5A). Contrary to previous practice, and in order to ensure so far as possible, that frivolous or futile grounds of appeal are not submitted on behalf of persons convicted in solemn proceedings, counsel or the solicitor advocate who drafts the note of appeal must now sign it. He shall then be expected to appear before the Appeal Court to present the appeal (see Practice Note (No.1 of 2002)).

The duties of counsel are made plain in *Smith (C.C.) v HM Advocate*, 2004 S.C.C.R. 521 which, though what was said was said in reference to the drafting of the case and argument (see r.15.16), applies equally to notes of appeal. An allegation of procedural irregularity in solemn proceedings should not be approached as a mere technicality. Proper inquiry must be made as to the factual basis of the allegation before the allegation is drafted or tendered to the court (para. 16).

Rule 15.2(6). An accused in respect of whom a supervised release order has been made (i.e. the accused is a short-term prisoner serving a sentence of not less than 12 months but less than four years), may appeal to the High Court against the decision of the original court which made the order where he is dissatisfied with the court's decision on an application made either by himself or by his local authority supervisor to vary the order. The grounds should be fully set out in Form 15.2-D because the accused will not be allowed to found on any ground not contained in the note of appeal except with leave of the High Court on cause shown (s. 19(2) of the Prisoners and Criminal Proceedings (Scotland) Act 1993).

Rule 15.3

B1-37.3 *Rule 15.3(1).* Section 111(2) provides that the periods of two weeks (in s.109(1)) within which an appellant must lodge with Justiciary Office written intimation of his intention to appeal against conviction or conviction and sentence and of eight weeks (starting when intimation was lodged) within which an appellant must lodge with Justiciary Office a written note of appeal (as set out in s.110(1)(a)) may be extended at any time by the High Court. (The period of eight weeks may be extended by the Clerk of Justiciary *before* it expires: s. 110(2)). Under s. 103(5)(a) a single judge of the High Court may extend these periods as well as allow the appellant to be present at any proceedings in any cases where he is not entitled to be present without leave (s.103(5)(b)) and admit an appellant to bail (s.103(5)(c)).

The purpose of an application for extension under s.111(2) is to secure an indulgence from the court for non-compliance with the time limits. In terms of s. 129(1) non-compliance with these limits "shall not prevent the further prosecution of an appeal if the High Court or a judge thereof considers it just and proper that the non-compliance is waived or, in the manner directed by the High Court or judge, remedied by amendment or otherwise". Thus, for example, an appellant may initially give written intimation of his intention to appeal against conviction but later desire to challenge sentence as well. In such a case the appellant may be allowed to amend his written intimation out of time to include a challenge to sentence.

However, there is no right to a second appeal. It is incompetent to seek extension of time within which to lodge a (further) note of appeal against conviction where the appellant has already had his appeal heard and determined (following which the Clerk of Justiciary will have given notice of final determination to various persons: s. 120(4)). As Lord Osborne said in *Beck v HM Advocate*, 2006 S.L.T. 468 (para.6, p.470I-J): "The premise upon which s.111(2) operates is that there has not been an appeal, but that a convicted person desires that there should be …[Section] 111 (2) was never intended by the legislators to afford to a person who has in fact appealed against conviction and has had that appeal determined upon certain grounds the opportunity again to initiate appeal proceedings, either upon these grounds, or upon some other grounds." (See Peter Ferguson, Q.C., "Late appeals", 2006 S.L.T. (News) 97.)

Rule 15.3(2). In terms of s. 103(6), where a single judge has refused an application referred to in s. 103(5), the appellant is entitled "to have the application determined by the High Court". Such procedure is not an appeal against, or review of, the single judge's decision but a rehearing of the application on its merits. Where the appellant does not desire a rehearing of his application, or fails within five days to return to the Justiciary Office a duly completed Form 15.3-B, the refusal of the application by the single judge becomes final (s. 105(2)).

The High Court as constituted for the hearing of appeals under Pt 8 is a quorum of three judges for appeals against both conviction and sentence (s. 103(2)) but two judges for appeals against sentence alone (s. 102(3)). The single judge may sit as a member of the court and take part in determining the application (s. 105(6)).

B1-37.4 *Rule 15.4* See note to r. 15.2(2).

Rule 15.5 This provision is now redundant. The death sentence for all crimes was finally abolished by s.36 of the Crime and Disorder Act 1998. Section 36(3)—(5) applies also to Scotland (s.121(6)(b)). After the abolition of the death penalty for murder in 1965, the remaining crimes for which the capital sentence was prescribed were certain forms of treason and piracy. On conviction under s1 of the Treason Act 1814 or s.2 of the Piracy Act 1837 the accused is now liable to imprisonment for life.

Rule 15.5A Procedural hearings were introduced into Appeal Court practice in order to reduce the number of appeal continuations which were occasioned by the change of counsel, or motion to amend the note of appeal, or further preparations to be undertaken for the appeal hearing. Not later than seven days before the procedural hearing the appellant's counsel should complete Form 15.5A-B stating whether the appeal will be presented at the proposed appeal sitting dates. If no problem is identified the court can decide that a procedural hearing is unnecessary. If, however, the appeal is not ready to proceed, or if a motion to amend the grounds of appeal is likely to be made (see r.15.15), the court should be advised of this fact. The procedural hearing will enable the court to examine the reasons for the delay or determine whether leave to amend should be granted.

The Appeal Court has recently had occasion to consider the effectiveness of procedural hearings since their introduction in September 2002. The court's observations in this case will be of considerable importance to practitioners. In *Johnston and Woolard v HM Advocate* [2009] HCJAC 38 (April 21, 2009), the court noted (para.23) that procedural hearings had reduced the frequency with which full appeal hearings do not proceed or require to be continued. But these hearings have been attended by the introduction of new problems which are illustrated by *McCarthy v HM Advocate*, 2008 S.L.T. 1038, *S v HM Advocate*, 2008 S.L.T. 1128 and *Johnston and Woolard.* These problems have a number of causes. One of these is the use which has hitherto been made of Form 15.5A-B where appellants' agents have intimated, prior to a procedural hearing, that the appeal is not ready to proceed to a full hearing. In such circumstances the Justiciary Office, after liaising with Crown Office, has removed the case from the roll and the procedural hearing has not proceeded. This practice has resulted in considerable delays spanning years between the lodging of the note of appeal (under s.110(1) of the 1995 Act) and the eventual appeal hearing.

This practice is inconsistent with r.15.5A(6). In *Johnston and Woolard* the court concluded from the terms of the rule that where Form 15.5A-B states that the appeal is not ready to proceed to a full hearing, "the intention of the Act of Adjournal [of 2002] is that the procedural hearing should go ahead, with the court deciding whether the appeal should proceed to a full hearing or whether further time (and, if so, how much time) should be allowed" (para.24).

The court also remarked, for the assistance of appellants' agents, that the court "will not grant continuations as a matter of course whenever the appellant states that the appeal is not ready to proceed and the respondent is content that further time should be allowed." This is because, first, the court has a responsibility to ensure that appeals are heard within a reasonable time, whatever the attitude of the parties to the appeal may be; and, secondly, the court's attention will be focused on the grounds of appeal in the note of appeal: "it will not ordinarily agree to continuations designed to allow additional investigations to be carried out, unless those investigations are related to the grounds of appeal." There has been a tendency on appellants' agents' part to treat the note of appeal as if it were "merely an opening gambit" (para.26). That is neither the nature nor function of the note of appeal.

The court also regretted a change in practice whereby appellants instructed different counsel from those who had conducted the trial (para.27). While that was necessary in some appeals (such as those based on allegations of defective trial representation), this general change in practice led to the unsurprising result that the new counsel preferred to obtain transcripts of the evidence so as to be fully informed of what had occurred at trial, rather than to rely on the original trial counsel's notes. This resulted in delays while transcripts were made available, at considerable public cost.

Rule 15.6 An accused person may abandon his appeal against conviction and/or sentence, or where he has appealed against both conviction and sentence, he may abandon his appeal against conviction and proceed against sentence alone, at any time by lodging a notice with the Clerk of Justiciary. The words "at any time" do not appear in s. 116(1) but this omission has been held to be immaterial: "there is no time-limit on an abandonment" (*Hendry v HM Advocate* [2006] HCJAC 14; 2006 S.C.C.R. 178 (para.7, per Lord Justice Clerk Gill)). The correct principle is not that stated in *Ferguson v HM Advocate*, 1980 J.C. 27, which prevailed for a quarter of a century and required the court's permission to be sought in order to abandon an appeal against sentence once the appeal had been called and was before the court, but that stated in *West v HM Advocate*, 1955 S.L.T. 425. An appeal can be abandoned orally at the bar of the court at any time prior to submissions in support of the appeal being presented to the Appeal Court. Once submissions are begun, the leave of the court is required before abandonment can be effected because the purpose of the court's having a discretion is to allow it to discourage the presentation of speculative appeals by use of the power to increase sentences under s.118(4)(b) (*Hendry* at paras 12-13) and, it may be added, to serve the public interest in doing justice where an inadequate sentence has been passed by the court of first instance. The date of lodging the notice is the time at which the appeal is deemed to have been dismissed by the Appeal Court. **B1-37.5**

Rule 15.7 High Court judges are not statutorily obliged to take or having taken, preserve notes of evidence at the trial. Sheriffs were obliged by s. 146 of the 1975 Act to do so although this provision has not been preserved by the 1995 Act. The sheriff's duty is now imposed by r.14.6. Section 237 of the 1975 Act (as inserted by the Criminal Justice (Scotland) Act 1980) placed a duty on a High Court judge to produce any notes which he had taken at the trial when required to do so by the Appeal Court. The 1995 Act does not not repeat s.237 and this rule fills that gap.

Rule 15.9

Rule 15.9(1). Diets in appeal proceedings are not peremptory and the usual practice is for the hearing to be continued "to a date afterwards to be fixed".

Rule 15.9(2). Section 104(1)(b) of the 1995 Act empowers the Appeal Court to appoint a person other than a High Court judge to hear additional evidence. In *Marshall v MacDougall* 1986 J.C. 77; 1987 S.L.T. 123; 1986 S.C.C.R. 376, under an equivalent power for appeals in summary proceedings under the 1975 Act (s.452(d)), the Appeal Court appointed the sheriff principal rather than a High Court judge to hear additional evidence no doubt because it was a district court prosecution. Section 104(1)(d) of the 1995 Act gives the Appeal Court power to remit to any "fit person" to enquire and report in regard to any matter or circumstance affecting the appeal. This rule does not give such fit person any power to fix a diet of proof but presumably such a power would be regarded as necessarily inherent in a remit in order to allow the person to discharge his duty: cf. *Crossan v HM Advocate*, 1996 S.C.C.R. 279 at 292E and *X, Petr*, 1996 S.C.C.R. 436 at 439D. See also *Robertson v HM Advocate (No.2)*, 1996 S.C.C.R. 243.

B1-37.6 *Rule 15.11* Any disqualification shall not attach for four weeks from the date of the verdict against the accused or, where an intimation of intention to appeal or a note of appeal (by the accused or the Lord Advocate) has been lodged, until the appeal, if it is proceeded with, is determined.

Rule 15.12

Rule 15.12(1). The hearing can take place in open court unlike the sift procedures for appeals under s. 107.

Rule 15.12(2). It is unclear why the Lord Advocate should require intimation when the Crown Agent should already have received a copy of the petition to the High Court.

Rule 15.12(3). Unlike the sift procedures for appeals, there is no appeal to a quorum of judges.

Rule 15.13 The rule takes account of the sift procedures under s. 107 where either a single judge or a quorum of judges has refused leave to appeal. The accused has until the 15th day after intimation that the single judge has refused leave, in order to appeal to a quorum of judges against the refusal of leave to appeal by a single judge. The disqualification attaches seven days after intimation of the refusal of leave by a quorum of judges.

Rule 15.14 Parliament did not give express power to the judge who "sifts" solemn appeals against conviction to obtain a further report but since the 1995 Act envisages that an appeal can be granted leave on grounds which are not contained in the note of appeal (see s. 107(7)), the power to remit to the trial judge is clearly necessary. It will also perhaps be of assistance where the trial judge has developed a practice of not commenting on grounds of appeal, unless questions of fact are raised, in breach of his duty under s.113(1) of the 1995 Act (see, e.g. *McPhelim v HM Advocate*, 1996 S.L.T. 992). It will also be of assistance where the sheriff's report is (at the stage of the "sift") immediately seen to be "conspicuous for its brevity" and lacking in an outline of the relevant matters giving rise to the appeal (as was the case in *McCutcheon v HM Advocate*, 2001 G.W.D. 18-694).

B1-37.7 *Rule 15.15* Section 110(4) of the 1995 Act provides: "Except by leave of the High Court on cause shown, it shall not be competent for an appellant to found any aspect of his appeal on a ground not contained in the note of appeal". In 2002 the Lord Justice-General and the Lord Justice-Clerk issued a consultation paper on appeals procedure and expressed concern that once an appeal had obtained the grant of leave on a specified ground in the note of appeal, there was the risk of abuse because leave could thereafter be sought to introduce a further ground which had not been before the sift judge. Thus, where leave of the High Court—it may be at a procedural hearing or when the appeal is called for a full hearing—is granted for an amendment of the note of appeal, the court *may* direct that the appeal be returned to the sift so that consideration can be given to whether the new ground raises an arguable point (r. 15.15(4)). However, if the worth of an amendment is to be considered by the court, the court may be likely to consider whether the ground is arguable as well as whether there is any good reason for the ground not having been specified in the original note in accordance with the Practice Notice of March 29, 1985 (see C1-02).

In *G v HM Advocate* [2009] HCJAC 52; 2009 S.L.T. 752, after a reference had been made by the Scottish Criminal Cases Review Commission and a note of appeal containing four grounds had been lodged by the appellant, some two years elapsed and 12 procedural hearings were listed in the case. At the last procedural hearing the appellant argued that the appeal was not then ready to proceed because investigations into other possible grounds of appeal had not been completed. Lord Carloway held that Form 15.5A-B asked whether the appeal on the grounds for which leave had been granted was ready to proceed to a full hearing: "If an appellant is ready to proceed with these grounds, or will be given a reasonable amount of time to do so, the appeal should proceed to a determination at a full hearing. If matters were otherwise then the appeal process in some cases would become almost interminable" (para. 17). Approving G the appeal court in *Lowrie v HM Advocate* [2009] HCJAC 71 stated that if the spirit and intention of the procedure are observed, amended grounds of appeal will be unnecessary in all but "the most exceptional of cases" (para.6, per Lord Hardie).

With effect from November 5, 2010, these rules expressly provide that appeals which originate as references by the Scottish Criminal Cases Review Commission under s.194C of the Criminal Procedure (Scotland) Act 1995 are not covered by the High Court's power to allow amendment of the grounds of appeal (see Act of Adjournal (Criminal Procedure Rules Amendment No.3) (Scottish Criminal Cases Review Commission) 2010 (SSI 2010/386) para. 1(1)). This is necessary to reflect the change in procedure introduced by s.83 of the Criminal Justice and Licensing (Scotland) Act 2010 (asp 13) which, however, is not yet in force (see annotations to Ch.19B, at B1-45.4 infra).

B1-37.8 *Rule 15.15A* This new rule applies only to proceedings in appeals in which leave was granted in accordance with s. 107 of the 1995 Act *after* November 1, 2010 (Act of Adjournal (Criminal Procedure Rules Amendment No.2) (Presentation of Conviction Appeals in Writing) 2010 (SSI 2010/309) para.3). It addresses a procedural issue of some importance in solemn conviction appeals. Increasingly appeals against convictions on indictment are brought on the basis of the existence of fresh evidence which either (a) existed at the time of trial but was excusably unknown to the defence at that time (and so was not heard at the trial, as envisaged by s.106(3)(a) of the 1995 Act) or (b) came into existence after the trial proceedings had concluded with a guilty verdict (see *Mackintosh v HM Advocate* [2010] HCJAC 30, para.23; 2010 S.C.L. 863). But this rule is wider than that and applies, as r.15.15A(3) states, where an appellant seeks to lead evidence "in relation to any ground of appeal" and so it will also apply when an appellant founds a ground of appeal on the evidence of alleged juror misconduct during the trial (e.g. *Feely v HM Advocate*, 2000 G.W.D. 12-422).

The rule applies unless the Appeal Court orders that it is not to apply to the appeal or any particular aspect of the appeal (r.15.15A(2)). The appellant may seek to have the rule disapplied. But when the rule is not disapplied, it requires the appellant to lodge with Justiciary Office a written "case and argument" within 42 days of the grant of leave (r.15.15A(4)). At the time of lodging the case and argument, the appellant must also send a copy of it to the other party to the appeal (r.15.15A(9)). If the case and argument is not timeously lodged, the Deputy Principal Clerk of Justiciary must refer the matter to the Lord Justice General whom failing the Lord Justice Clerk (r.15.15A(11)). However, the Appeal Court may extend the time limit for lodging the case and argument if cause for doing so is established to the satisfaction of the court (r.15.15A(12)) and presumably such an application need not be made before the expiry of the 42-day period. An "unduly lengthy" case and argument may be referred to a High Court judge for such directions as he considers appropriate (r.15.15A(10)).

This rule is principally intended to control the conduct of appeals in advance of an appeal hearing at which evidence is proposed to be adduced by or on behalf of the convicted accused. Hence the automatic application of the rule arises only "in relation to the question of whether that evidence should be led"; but the court may in its discretion also apply the requirements of this rule to the presentation of submissions following the hearing of such evidence (r.15.15A(3)). Moreover, the Appeal Court may ordain the Crown as respondent in the appeal to lodge a case and argument in response to the appellant's case and argument, if the court considers "the circumstances of the case require it" (r.15.15A(7)(a)); and the Crown is always entitled to lodge such a response when it considers it appropriate to do so (r.15.15A(7)(b)). When ordained to lodge a case and argument, the Crown must do so within 21 days of the order along with any documents accompanying it (r.15.15A(8)) but that time limit may be extended on cause shown (r.15.15A(12)). The Crown must also send a copy of the case and argument to the appellant at the time of lodging it with Justiciary Office (r.15.15A(9)). The 21-day time limit does not apply to the Crown's case and argument which it elects to lodge but when it does lodge it, a copy should be sent to the appellant.

The case and argument for the appellant must comply with r.15.15A(5). In particular, it should state succinctly and accurately the facts founded on in relation to the relevant ground of appeal and the legal propositions which the appellant desires to advance in respect of that ground (r. 15.15A(5)(a)). Importantly, this statement should be warranted by the signature of counsel (or a solicitor with extended rights of audience) who is going to present the appeal (r.15.15A(5)(b)). Any documents (or copies) referred to in the case and argument should accompany the case and argument when it is lodged with Justiciary Office (unless these documents are already in the appeal process); and, once again importantly, copies of all authorities which are listed in the case and argument should accompany the case and argument if these authorities are not contained in a publication which is to be specified by direction of the Lord Justice General (who has not yet issued such direction).

The purpose of this new rule is plain. It is to control the length of submissions on either the question whether proposed fresh evidence should be heard (such as whether the evidence would be competent or relevant or admissible) or the effect of any such evidence which has been allowed to be adduced. Hence the requirement that the case and argument should record an estimate by counsel of how long will be required for the hearing of the appeal (r.15.15A(5)(2)) and also, significantly, the special provision in r.15.15B(5) for the Appeal Court at any time to prescribe a timetable for completion of any submissions.

Rule 15.15B The use to which the case and argument is intended to be put is demonstrated by the rigour of r.15.15B(2). In most if not all cases the appellant's submissions will be taken as read and it will be superfluous, and indeed time wasting, for counsel to read out the terms of the case and argument and any accompanying documents (r.15.15B(2)(a) and (b)). Supplementary comment will be controlled by the court which shall require an answer to any points which it raises with the appellant or his counsel (r.15.15B(2)(c) and (e)). The greatest scope for oral submissions will arise only in two areas. First, the appellant is entitled to respond to any case and argument lodged by the Crown (r.15.15B(2)(d)); and, secondly, the Appeal Court may, on cause shown, permit the introduction by the appellant of "new information" which has come to light since the case and argument was lodged (r.15.15B(6)) and any additional documents in support of the new information (r.15.15B(7)). But in order to be allowed to found on such new information and documents, the appellant must have given notice of the new information and copied any such additional documents to both the Justiciary Office and the Crown "as soon as" the information and documents came into the appellant's possession (r.15.15B(8)). Application for leave to found on new matter should be made at the bar (r.15.15B(9)) and preferably at the outset of the appeal hearing. **B1-37.9**

Rule 15.16 This innovation in appeals procedure was introduced in September 2003 and is designed to reduce the time the Appeal Court expends on sentence appeals. Sentence appeals under s. 106 and the Lord Advocate's appeals against unduly lenient disposals under s. 108 shall be presented in writing. Thus, under r. 15.1(5), notice of the appeal hearing is 42 days. Not later than 21 days before the hearing the case and argument must be lodged with Justiciary Office. That case and argument will constitute the submissions but "supplementary comments to the case" may be made (r.15.16(5)(c)). In *Houldsworth, Petitioner*, 2006 J.C. 174 (decided on March 14, 2006) a challenge to this new procedure as being incompatible with an accused's art.6 right under the European Convention to a fair and public hearing of his appeal was rejected by the appeal court. The court explained that r.15.16(5)(c) "plainly provides that the appellant may make oral comments on the appeal supplementary to the case and argument required by the earlier parts of the rule. Thus an appellant is not deprived of the right to make oral submissions by the provisions of the rule" (para. 8, per Lord Osborne). **B1-37.10**

The case must be signed by counsel or the solicitor-advocate who is supporting the appeal. This is in line with the change effected in solemn conviction appeals (see Practice Note (No.1 of 2002), C1-24, infra). If new information has come to light since the case and argument were lodged, that will only be admitted if the court is satisfied that cause has been shown for doing so. What amounts to "cause" will likely depend on two factors: (1) why the information was not available when the case and argument were lodged; and (2) whether the new information has a material bearing on the merits of the appeal. If the new information will almost certainly tip the balance in the appellant's favour, the Appeal Court will almost certainly allow it to be received at the hearing, even where there is no proper explanation for its lateness. That new information should be intimated to Justiciary Office immediately.

It should be noted, however, that this rule does not affect the general principle that sentence appeals should be determined on the basis of the information before the sentencing court because it is only on that basis that the actual sentence can be said to be a miscarriage of justice (Nicholson on *Sentencing* (2nd edn), para.8-99), although that principle suffers exceptions (see *McLean v MacDougall*, 1989 S.C.C.R. 625). Similarly, this rule does not affect the power of the Appeal Court under s. 106(3) of the 1995 Act to admit fresh evidence in a sentence appeal when the conditions of that subsection are satisfied (e.g. *Baikie v HM Advocate*, 2000 S.C.C.R. 119). The information referred to in the rule is new only because it is relied upon after the case was lodged.

Rule 15.16A The prosecutor may request the Clerk of Justiciary to provide to him a transcript of any part of the proceedings at the trial recorded under s.93(1) of the 1995 Act. When he receives this transcript he must immediately send a copy to the other parties to the appeal and to the clerk of court (i.e. the Clerk of Justiciary or the sheriff clerk). The same obligation is imposed by r.15.16A(2) on the accused whose request for a transcript to be sent to him is granted by a High Court judge on cause shown after the accused has been granted leave to appeal under s. 107 of the 1995 Act. This is a new obligation and is independent of the duties imposed by r. 15.17 on appellants and respondents who intend to rely on the transcript at the appeal hearing.

Rule 15.17 Section 94 of the 1995 Act makes provision for the making and delivery of transcripts of evidence recorded under s.93(1). Section 94(2A) gives a convicted person the right to request a High Court judge for a transcript of the proceedings in which he was convicted but only if he has been granted leave to appeal and he can show cause for his application. Where the convicted person, or the prosecutor, intends to rely on any part of a transcript in the appeal, he must lodge four copies of the transcript with the Justiciary Office within one or other of two time limits (and intimate to the other parties that the transcript or the relevant part thereof has been so lodged). If a procedural hearing has been fixed by the court under r.15.5A(1), the transcripts must be lodged with the Justiciary Office not later than seven days before the hearing. If no procedural hearing is fixed, the transcripts must be lodged no later than 28 days before the appeal hearing. If this time limit is not adhered to, the court may refuse to allow the offending party to rely on the transcript.

[THE NEXT PARAGRAPH IS B1-38]

PART IV

SUMMARY PROCEEDINGS

Chapter 16

Complaints

Form of complaints and related notices and forms

B1-38 **16.1.**—(1) The form of complaint referred to in section 138(1) of the Act of 1995 shall be in Form 16.1-A.

(2) The form of citation of an accused referred to in section 140(2) and (2A) of the Act of 1995 shall be in Form 16.1-B.

(2A) The notice to be affixed to the door of the dwelling-house or place of business of an accused for the purposes of section 141(2A) of the Act of 1995 (citation of accused by affixing a notice) shall be in Form 16.1-BB

(3) The procurator fiscal shall send to the accused with the citation in Form 16.1-B—

(a) a reply form in Form 16.1-C for completion and return by him stating whether he pleads guilty or not guilty; and

(b) a means form in Form 16.1-D for completion and return by him.

(3A) The form of notice referred to in section 146(3A) of the Act of 1995 shall be in Form 16.1-BA.

(4) The form of notice of previous convictions to be served on an accused under section 166(2) of the Act of 1995 shall be in Form 16.1-E.

AMENDMENTS

Rule 16.1(2) as amended, and r. 16.1(3A) inserted, by Act of Adjournal (Criminal Procedure Rules Amendment No. 3) (Sexual Offences (Procedure and Evidence) (Scotland) Act 2002) 2002 (SSI 2002/454) r.2(8) (effective November 1, 2002).

Rule 16.1(2A) inserted by Act of Adjournal (Criminal Procedure Rules Amendment No.2) (Miscellaneous) 2003 (SSI 2003/468) r.2. Brought into force on October 27, 2003 in accordance with art.1.

Signature of prosecutor

B1-38.1 **16.2.**—(1) The prosecutor shall sign the principal complaint and the citation to the accused.

(2) Any document sent with the citation to the accused including the copy complaint shall, for the purposes of such signature, be treated as part of the citation.

Effect of failure by prosecutor to comply with certain requirements

16.3. The validity of any proceedings against an accused shall not be affected by reason only of the failure of the prosecutor to comply in any respect with a requirement of rule 16.1(3) (reply and means forms). **B1-38.2**

Further procedural forms

16.4.—(1) The form of incidental application referred to in section 134 of the Act of 1995 (incidental applications) shall be in Form 16.4-A. **B1-38.3**

(2) The form of assignation of a diet shall be in Form 16.4-B.

(3) The form of minutes in the record of proceedings in summary proceedings shall be in Form 16.4-C.

Incidental applications out of hours

16.4A—(1) Where the prosecutor makes an incidental application in Form 16.4-A when the office of the prosecutor is closed, the application shall not require to be signed by the prosecutor but shall state the name of the prosecutor. **B1-38.3.1**

(2) The oath of a police officer shall be sufficient to authenticate the application as being an application by the prosecutor named on the application.

AMENDMENT

Rule 16.4A inserted by the Act of Adjournal (Criminal Procedure Rules Amendment No.2) (Miscellaneous) 2005 (SSI 2005/160), r.2 (effective March 31, 2005).

[THE NEXT PARAGRAPH IS B1-38.4]

Form of certain warrants

16.5.—(1) The form of warrant referred to in section 135 of the Act of 1995 (warrants of apprehension and search)— **B1-38.4**

(a) to apprehend an accused shall be in Form 16.5-A;

(b) to search the person, dwelling house and repositories of the accused shall be in Form 16.5-B.

(2) The form of order adjourning a diet and granting warrant to detain an accused shall be in Form 16.5-C.

Citation of witnesses

16.6.—(1) The form of postal citation of a person to appear as a witness at a trial on a summary complaint shall be in Form 16.6-A; and the witness shall complete and return Form 16.6-B to the procurator fiscal, or the accused or his solicitor, as the case may be, in the pre-paid envelope provided within 14 days after the date of citation. **B1-38.5**

(2) The form of personal citation of a witness at a trial on a summary complaint shall be in Form 16.6-C.

(2A) The form of electronic citation of a person to appear as a witness at a trial on summary complaint shall be in Form 16.6-D; and the witness shall complete and return Form 16.6-B to the procurator fiscal, or the accused or his solicitor as the case may be, by electronic mail or by post within 14 days after the date of citation.

(3) In the case of a postal citation in Form 16.6-A by the prosecutor under section 141 of the Act of 1995, the citation may be signed by the prosecutor by use of an official stamp of his signature or by mechanical or electronic means.

AMENDMENT

Rule 16.6 as amended by the Act of Adjournal (Criminal Procedure Rules Amendment No.6) (Criminal Proceedings etc. (Reform) (Scotland) Act 2007) 2007 (SSI 2007/511), r.5 (effective December 10, 2007).

Applications for alteration of diets

16.7.—(1) Where the prosecutor and the accused propose to make a joint application orally to the court under section 137(2) of the Act of 1995 (application for alteration of diet) for postponement of a diet that has been fixed, they may do so only at a diet which has been duly assigned and which has been called. **B1-38.6**

(2) An application by an accused under section 137(5) of the Act of 1995 (application to postpone or accelerate diet) shall be made in Form 16.7.

AMENDMENT

Rule 16.6(3) as inserted by Act of Adjournal (Criminal Procedure Rules Amendment) (Miscellaneous) (SI 1996/2147 (s. 171)) (effective September 9, 1996).

[THE NEXT PARAGRAPH IS B1-39]

GENERAL NOTE

B1-39 Section 307(1) provides that for the purposes of summary proceedings, the word "prosecutor" includes procurator fiscal, and any other person prosecuting in the public interest and complainer and any person duly authorised to represent or act for any public prosecutor. The procurator fiscal is the Lord Advocate's local representative and takes his instructions from the Lord Advocate as the public prosecutor. The procurator fiscal is not the "sheriff's advocate" (see *Green v Smith*, 1988 S.L.T. 175). All prosecutions in the summary courts are by way of complaint. Private prosecutions by individuals who can show title and interest in order to prosecute accused persons for crimes with or without the concurrence of the Lord Advocate, are initiated by way of a Bill for Criminal Letters and these prosecutions are pursued exclusively in the High Court (see *Dunbar v Johnstone* (1904) 4 Adam 505). Section 138(1) of the 1995 Act does, however, recognise that other persons can initiate proceedings by way of a summary complaint (e.g. local education authorities as in *Ross v Simpson*, 1995 S.L.T. 956, and customs officers) and they may be represented by a solicitor. They are not, however, public prosecutors in the true sense of the term but are prosecutors in the public interest under s.307(1).

Note should be made of the fact that it is observed in Renton and Brown, *Criminal Procedure* (5th ed.), para. 13-11 that where the failure of a prosecutor to appear in court had been due to death, disability, or other unavoidable cause, the court has an inherent power to appoint a prosecutor *pro hac vice* to proceed with the prosecution, in order that the ends of justice may not be defeated. (See *Thomson v Scott; Walker v Emslie* (1899) 3 Adam 102; and *Hill v Finlayson* (1883) 5 Couper 284.) It is, however, to be doubted that the court has a power to appoint an ad hoc prosecutor at least in respect of procurators fiscal. Since no part of a criminal trial can take place in the absence of the prosecutor, and most summary prosecutions are instituted by the procurator fiscal as the Lord Advocate's local representative, it would appear that a more appropriate remedy would be adjournment or desertion of the diet *pro loco et tempore* by the court on its own motion. The instance would then be preserved by adjournment or the Crown would be entitled to raise proceedings *de novo* in order to meet the difficulty caused by the unforeseen occurrences of death, illness, or unavoidable absence (cf. *Platt v Lockhart*, 1988 S.L.T. 845 which concerned a sheriff's death during the adjournment of a part-heard trial; and *Annan, Complainer*, 1994 S.L.T. 157).

Rule 16.1

Rule 16.1(1). Form 16.1 - A prescribes the form of summary complaint which should be employed in all prosecutions (see s.138(2)(b) of the 1995 Act). The styles of charge which should be used for common law and statutory offences are set out in Sch.5 to the 1995 Act, which incorporates for the purposes of summary complaints the other styles which are set out for indictment cases in Sch.2 to the 1995 Act. When a charge follows these styles it is most unlikely that the court will hold the charge to be irrelevant or lacking in fair notice (see *Anderson v Allan*, 1985 S.C.C.R. 399; see also *Coventry v Douglas*, 1944 S.C. 13; 1944 S.L.T. 129).

Rule 16.1(2). The citation is to proceed on an inducíae of at least 48 hours unless in the special circumstances of the case the court fixes a shorter inducíae (s. 140(2)). The citation must be signed by the prosecutor in order to be valid (r. 16.2(1)). Failure to state the date of the diet to which the accused is cited renders the citation *funditus* null and void: see *Beattie v McKinnon*, 1977 J.C. 64.

Rule 16.1(3).

Failure to send the pleading and the means forms with the citation to the accused will not invalidate the proceedings (r.16.3).

Rule 16.1(4). Section 311(5) of the 1975 Act required in summary cases that the accused be served with a notice of penalties relevant to any statutory charge in the summary complaint but the 1995 Act (regrettably) makes no such requirement. However, the issue which arose in *Cowan v Guild*, 1991 S.C.C.R. 424, whether the accused was ever served with a notice, can still arise in respect of notices of previous convictions, an issue which is much more likely to surface where personal service has been effected. But if there is "substantial compliance" with a duty under s. 166(2) to serve the notice on the accused with the complaint where he is cited to a diet or if he is in custody, before he is called on to plead, the court is entitled to take into account the previous convictions (cf. *Hutchison v Normand*, 1993 S.C.C.R. 1000 and *Normand v Buchanan*, 1996 S.C.C.R. 355 which were concerned with notices of penalty).

In any event, the court has a very wide power under s. 159(1) of the 1995 Act, unless the court sees just cause to the contrary, to allow amendment of the complaint by deletion, alteration or addition so as inter alia to cure any error or defect in it or to meet any objection to it (such as relevancy or specification). There is only one restriction on the court's power to allow amendment: under s.159(2) the court cannot allow amendment where the effect of the amendment would be to change "the character of the offence charged" (cf. *MacArthur v MacNeill*, 1986 J.C. 182). Where a competent amendment appears to the court to prejudice the accused in any way "in his defence on the merits of the case" the court must grant such remedy to the accused by way of adjournment or otherwise as is just in the opinion of the court. It has been doubted that such other remedy includes refusal of the proposed amendment (*Brooks v HM Advocate* Unreported January 19, 2007; [2007] HCJAC 9 at [12]). If the amendment substitutes a different statutory offence which carries liability to an increased penalty (or a minimum penalty), that does not constitute a prejudice to the defence on the merits of the case (*Brooks* at [12]) nor can it amount to "just cause" under s.159(1) for refusing the amendment (*Brooks* at [13]; cf. *Cook v Jessop*, 1990 J.C. 286).

An essential part of a relevant charge in a summary complaint is specification of the locus of the alleged offence (*Stevenson v McLeavy* (1879) 6 R. (J.) 33). If it is not specified at all then the charge is a fundamental nullity and cannot be amended. The locus of the offence must be adequately specified on the face of the charge itself for two reasons. First, such specification is necessary to demonstrate that the court concerned has jurisdiction to try the case and, secondly, it is necessary so as to give fair notice to the person charged of where the offence is alleged to have been committed (*Caven v Cumming*, 1998 S.L.T. 768 at 770). It has been held not to be fatal to a summary complaint that the town where the offence is said to have taken place is not expressly named provided that the location is sufficiently clear. Moreover, the use of road numbers (which form part of a general system of road numbering that applies throughout the United Kingdom under statutory authority and allows for the specification of a section of road with great precision) is sufficiently specific. The need to use a road map to identify the locus is not fatal to the relevance of the charge (*Strawbridge v Procurator Fiscal, Hamilton* [2014] HCJAC 32 at [4] and [9]).

Rule 16.2

Rule 16.2(1). The prosecutor's signature is essential for the proceedings to be competent (*Lowe v Bee*, 1989 S.C.C.R. 476; see also *Milne v Normand*, 1994 S.L.T. 760; 1993 S.C.C.R. 1058 where, because a two page complaint was signed on the first page but not on the second page, the second page was treated *pro non scripto*).

Rule 16.2(2).

The copy complaint need not be signed by the prosecutor.

Rule 16.4 Incidental applications can be made for a vast range of orders or warrants. One order of importance is where the Crown desires to postpone or accelerate a diet but the accused—or one of them—refuses to agree to a joint application to the court. The Crown may make an incidental application in these circumstances: see s.137(4).

Rule 16.6 The administrative burden imposed by the imperative requirement of r.16.2(1) is eased by allowing for a stamp or other mechanical or electronic means of reproducing the prosecutor's signature so far as the vast majority of citations are concerned.

Rule 16.7 In *White v Ruxton*, 1996 S.L.T. 556; 1996 S.C.C.R. 427, the court held that the authority for the fixing of a diet to hear a joint application to accelerate the diet in order that a later diet could be fixed on account of the absence on holiday of one of the co-accused, was contained in the joint minute signed by both parties under s.314(3) of the 1975 Act. It was, however, observed by the court that the better practice was to include authority in a minute in the record of proceedings.

Chapter 16A

Engagement, Dismissal and Withdrawal of Solicitors in Summary Proceedings

Notification

16A.1.—(1) The notification to the court in writing under section 148C(1) of the Act of 1995 (engagement, dismissal and withdrawal of solicitor representing accused) that a solicitor has been engaged by the accused for the purposes of his defence at trial shall be in Form 16A.1-A. **B1-39.1**

(2) The notification to the court in writing under section 148C(3) of the Act of 1995 that a solicitor has been dismissed by the accused or has withdrawn from acting shall be in Form 16A.1-B.

AMENDMENTS

Chapter 16A inserted by Act of Adjournal (Criminal Procedure Rules Amendment No.6) (Criminal Proceedings etc. (Reform) (Scotland) Act 2007) 2007 (SSI 2007/511) para.6 (effective December 10, 2007).

[THE NEXT PARAGRAPH IS B1-40]

Chapter 17

Summary Pre-Trial Procedure

Applications for extension of period of detention

17.A1. An application made in writing for extension of time under section 147 of the Act of 1995 (prevention of delay in trials) shall be in Form 17.A1 and shall be intimated to the other parties by the applicant. **B1-40**

AMENDMENTS

Rule 17.A1 inserted by Act of Adjournal (Criminal Procedure Rules Amendment) (Criminal Proceedings etc. (Reform) (Scotland) Act 2007) 2008 (SSI 2008/61) para.3 (effective March 10, 2008)

Appeals against extension of period of detention

B1-40.1 **17.1.**—(1) A note of appeal presented to the Sheriff Appeal Court under section 147(3) of the Act of 1995 (appeal against grant or refusal of extension of 40 days detention) shall be made in Form 17.1

(2) Such a note of appeal shall be served by the appellant on—

(a) the respondent; and

(b) the clerk of the court against the decision of which the appeal is taken.

(3) The appellant in such a note of appeal shall lodge with the Clerk of the Sheriff Appeal Court—

(a) the note of appeal; and

(b) the certificate of execution of service in respect of the persons mentioned in paragraph (2).

(4) The clerk of the court against the decision of which the appeal is taken shall, as soon as practicable after being served with the note of appeal, transmit to the Clerk of the Sheriff Appeal Court the original application and all the relative documents; and the Clerk of the Sheriff Appeal Court shall, on receipt of those documents, assign the appeal to the roll and intimate the date of the diet to the appellant and the respondent.

(4A) Where the sheriff's report is not included in the documents mentioned in paragraph (4) the Clerk of the Sheriff Appeal Court shall request the report from the clerk of the court against the decision of which the appeal is taken.

(5) The Clerk of the Sheriff Appeal Court shall intimate the result of the appeal to the court against the decision of which the appeal was taken and to the governor of the institution in which the appellant is detained.

AMENDMENTS

Rule 17.1 as amended by Act of Adjournal (Criminal Procedure Rules Amendment) (Miscellaneous) 2012 (SSI 2012/125) para.4 (effective June 4, 2012).

Rule 17.1 as amended by Act of Adjournal (Criminal Procedure Rules 1996 Amendment) (No. 4) (Sheriff Appeal Court) 2015 (SSI 2015/245) para.4 (effective September 22, 2015 subject to savings provisions in para.6).

Notice of defences

B1-40.2 **17.2.**—(1) Notification to the prosecutor of a defence under section 149B of the Act of 1995 (notice of defences) shall be in Form 17.2.

(2) At the same time as giving notification under paragraph (1) the accused shall serve a copy of the notification on any co-accused.

AMENDMENTS

Rule 17.2 inserted by Act of Adjournal (Criminal Procedure Rules Amendment No.6) (Criminal Proceedings etc. (Reform) (Scotland) Act 2007) 2007 (SSI 2007/511) para.7 (effective December 10, 2007).

[THE NEXT PARAGRAPH IS B1-41]

GENERAL NOTE

B1-41 An accused person is entitled to be liberated forthwith and to be thereafter free from all question or process for an offence charged against him on summary complaint if he has been detained on that charge for a total of more than 40 days after the bringing of the complaint in court unless his trial has been commenced within that period (s.147(1)). However, the sheriff can extend that period for such period as he thinks fit when a delay is caused by illness of the accused or the judge, the absence or illness of any witness or any other sufficient cause not attributable to the prosecutor's fault (s.147(2)). When an extension is granted or refused there is an automatic right of appeal (s.147(3)). The note of appeal should be served on, inter alia, the clerk of the lower court and be lodged with the Clerk of Justiciary. If the note is not lodged with the clerk of the lower court he cannot transmit the documents necessary for the appeal under r.17.1(4) and Justiciary Office cannot assign the appeal to a roll for a hearing. No time-limits are specified and accordingly the onus is on the appellant—who is almost always the accused—to prosecute his appeal expeditiously.

Chapter 17A

Transfer of Summary Proceedings

Transfer of summary proceedings

B1-41.1 **17A.1.**—(1) A written application by the procurator fiscal under—

(a) section 137A(1) or section 137CA(2) of the Act of 1995 (transfer within sheriffdom) shall be in Form 17A.1-A;

(b) section 137B(1) or section 137CB(2) of the Act of 1995 (transfer outwith sheriffdom due to exceptional circumstances) shall be in Form 17A.1-B;

(c) section 137B(1A) or section 137CB(4) of the Act of 1995 (transfer outwith sheriffdom where accused cited to attend diet in other summary proceedings or other summary proceedings commenced) shall be in Form 17A.1-C;

(d) section 137B(1C) or section 137CB(6) of the Act of 1995 (transfer outwith sheriffdom: intention to take summary proceedings where other summary proceedings commenced) shall be in Form 17A.1-D;

(e) section 137B(3) or section 137CB(9) of the Act of 1995 (transfer outwith sheriffdom due to exceptional circumstances: revocation or variation of order) shall be in Form 17A.1-E;

(f) section 137B(4) or section 137CB(10) of the Act of 1995 (transfer outwith sheriffdom where other summary proceedings commenced or intended: revocation or variation of order) shall be in Form 17A.1-F;

(g) section 137C(1) or section 137CC(2) of the Act of 1995 (initiating custody cases outwith sheriffdom: exceptional circumstances) shall be in Form 17A.1-G;

(h) section 137D(1) of the Act of 1995 (transfer of justice of the peace court proceedings where accused person to be sentenced in sheriff court) shall be in Form 17A.1-H.

(2) Where the sheriff principal consents to an application under paragraph (1)(b), (e) or (g), he shall docquet his consent to the application.

(3) Where a sheriff consents to an application under paragraph (1)(c), (d) or (f), he shall docquet his consent to the application.

AMENDMENTS

Chapter 17A inserted by Act of Adjournal (Criminal Procedure Rules Amendment) (Miscellaneous) 2009 (SSI 2009/144) para.3 (effective April 30, 2009).

Rule 17A.1 as amended by Act of Adjournal (Criminal Procedure Rules Amendment No.3) (Miscellaneous) 2011 (SSI 2011/194) para.3 (effective March 28, 2011).

GENERAL NOTE

Section 137A, as amended in 2007, came into force on March 10, 2008 (see SSI 2008/42) and empowers the procurator fiscal to apply to the sheriff for an order transferring summary proceedings to a sheriff court in any other district in the same sheriffdom and for an adjournment of these proceedings to a diet of that other court (s.137A(1)). The order can be made either where the accused has already been cited to attend a diet of the first court or where, he not having been yet cited, summary proceedings have already been commenced against him in the first court (s.137A(2)). **B1-41.2**

Section 137B was also amended and brought into force on the same dates as s.137A. It provides that the procurator fiscal may apply to the sheriff principal of the sheriffdom in which his district lies for an order transferring summary proceedings to a sheriff court in another sheriffdom and for an adjournment of these proceedings to a diet of that other court (s.137B(1)). An application under this power can only be made where, because of "exceptional circumstances which could not reasonably have been foreseen", it is not practicable for the sheriff court *or any other sheriff court in the sheriffdom* to proceed with some or all of the summary cases due to call at a diet. The sheriff principal may make the order if the sheriff principal of the other sheriffdom consents (s.137B(2)). Where the sheriff principal consents, he "shall docquet his consent to the application" (r.17A.1(2)).

Where there are summary proceedings and the accused has already been cited to a diet or where such proceedings have already been commenced but citation has not yet been effected, a similar order may be made to transfer these proceedings to another sheriffdom where there are already extant summary proceedings (s.137B(1A)).

Where the prosecutor intends to take summary proceedings in his sheriff court district, he may also apply to the sheriff for an order for authority for these proceedings to be taken at a sheriff court in another sheriffdom if there are also summary proceedings against the accused in that other court (s.137B(1C)). The sheriff is required to grant the prosecutor's applications under subs.(1A) and (1C) if he considers that (a) it would be expedient for the different cases involved to be dealt with by the same sheriff *and* (b) a sheriff of the other sheriffdom consents (s.137B(2A)). The consenting sheriff must docquet his consent to the application (r.17A.1(3)).

An order made by a sheriff principal on the basis of exceptional circumstances (under s.137B(1)) may be revoked or varied (so as to restrict its effect) by that sheriff principal, on the application of the prosecutor under s.137B(3), with the consent of the other sheriff principal. An order made by the sheriff under s.137B(2A) may be revoked or varied (so as to restrict its effect) on the prosecutor's application under s.137B(4) where the sheriff of the receiving sheriffdom consents. The consents of the sheriff and sheriff principal must be evidenced by a docquet to the prosecutor's applications for revocation or variation (r.17A.1((2) and (3)).

Section 137C makes similar provision for custody cases in summary proceedings as is made for petition cases in s.34A (see Ch.8C). Where the prosecutor believes (a) that because of exceptional circumstances it is likely that there will be an unusually high number of cases of accused persons appearing from custody for the first calling of cases in summary proceedings in the sheriff courts in the sheriffdom and (b) it will not be practicable for those courts to deal with all of these cases, the prosecutor may apply to the sheriff principal of the sheriffdom in which the prosecutor's district lies for an order under subs.(2) (s.137C(1)). That order is authority for summary proceedings against some or all of the accused persons to be taken at a sheriff court in another sheriffdom and maintained there or at any of the sheriff courts in the prosecutor's sheriffdom as may be specified at the first calling of the case appointed for further proceedings (s.137C(2)). The receiving sheriff principal must consent and his consent must be evidenced by a docquet to the application (s.137C(3) and r.17A.1(2)). An order under subs.(2) may be made by reference to a particular period or particular circumstances.

Finally, s.137D(1) confers on the prosecutor in summary proceedings before the sheriff a power to apply to the sheriff for an order for the transfer to that sheriff court of "any case against the accused in respect of which sentencing is pending at any JP court in the sheriffdom" and for that case to call at a diet in that sheriff court. The JP court (which is established by the Scottish Ministers by reference to a particular sheriff court district: Criminal Proceedings etc. (Reform) (Scotland) Act 2007 s.59(3)) need not be situated within the sheriff court district but must be within the sheriffdom within which that sheriff court is situated. The prosecutor can only apply for such an order when the accused in the sheriff court case is "due to be sentenced … for an offence". The sheriff must make the order where he considers that it would be expedient for the different cases to be disposed of at the same court at the same time (s.137D(2)). The consent of the JP court is not required. An order does not increase the sentencing powers of the sheriff in respect of the charges so transferred. These charges remain subject to the sentencing limits set by s.7(6) of the 1995 Act (s.137D(3)).

These statutory provisions are now given effect by the provision, in this new chapter, of the requisite statutory forms. This chapter was brought into force on April 30, 2009 (see Act of Adjournal (Criminal Procedure Rules Amendment) (Miscellaneous) 2009 (SSI 2009/144), para.1(1)). Some of these statutory provisions alter the common law rule which, although over time it has been modified by statute, was explained in *Shields v Donnelly*, 1999 S.C.C.R. 890 at 893B: "the basic position remained that the judge had power to act only within the limits of the area for which he was appointed".

[THE NEXT PARAGRAPH IS B1-42]

Chapter 18

Procedure at Trial in Summary Proceedings

Accused to plead personally and to receive intimation of diets

B1-42 **18.1.**—(1) Subject to paragraph (2), in any summary proceedings where a person accused in those proceedings is present in court, that person shall personally plead to the charge against him whether or not he is represented.

(2) Where the judge is satisfied that the accused is not capable for any reason of pleading personally to the charge against him, it shall be sufficient if the plea is tendered by a solicitor or by counsel on his behalf.

(3) Where an accused is not represented or not personally present and a court continues a diet without taking a plea from the accused, the prosecutor shall intimate the continuation and the date of the adjourned diet to the accused.

(4) Subject to section 150(2) of the Act of 1995 (adjournment to another diet), where an accused is not represented or not personally present, on the fixing of—

(a) a diet of trial,
(b) a diet after conviction, or
(c) any diet after a plea from the accused has been recorded,

the sheriff clerk or clerk of the justice of the peace court shall intimate the diet to the accused.

(5) Where the accused pleads guilty to the charge or to any part of it, and his plea is accepted by the prosecutor, the plea shall be recorded and signed by the judge or clerk of court, and the court shall thereafter dispose of the case at the same or any adjourned diet.

(6) The plea referred to in paragraph (5) and any sentence may be combined, in which case one signature shall be sufficient to authenticate both.

AMENDMENTS

Rule 18.1(4) as amended by Act of Adjournal (Criminal Procedure Rules Amendment) (Criminal Proceedings etc. (Reform) (Scotland) Act 2007) 2008 (SSI 2008/61) para.2 (effective March 10, 2008).

Form of oath or affirmation to witnesses

B1-42.1 **18.2.**—(1) Where the judge administers the oath to a witness in summary proceedings, he shall do so in accordance with the form in Form 14.5-A.

(2) In the case of any witness who elects to affirm, the judge shall administer the affirmation in accordance with the form in Form 14.5-B.

(3) The oath or the affirmation administered in accordance with paragraph (1) or (2), as the case may be, shall be treated as having been administered in common form.

Warrants for apprehension of witnesses

B1-42.2 **18.3.**—(1) An application made in writing for a warrant for the apprehension of a witness under section 156 or 156C of the Act of 1995 (apprehension of witnesses) shall be in Form 18.3-A.

(2) On receipt of an application under paragraph (1), the clerk of court shall fix a diet for the hearing of the application and intimate the date of the hearing to the parties.

(3) A warrant for the apprehension of a witness under section 156(1) of the Act of 1995 shall be in Form 18.3-B.

AMENDMENTS

Rule 18.3 as substituted by Act of Adjournal (Criminal Procedure Rules Amendment) (Criminal Proceedings etc. (Reform) (Scotland) Act 2007) 2008 (SSI 2008/61) para.4 (effective March 10, 2008).

Review by witnesses of orders made under section 156A

B1-42.3 **18.3A.** An application under section 156C(2)(a) of the Act of 1995 (application by party for review of order under section 156A(1)(b)) shall be in Form 18.3A.

AMENDMENTS

Rule 18.3A inserted by Act of Adjournal (Criminal Procedure Rules Amendment) (Criminal Proceedings etc. (Reform) (Scotland) Act 2007) 2008 (SSI 2008/61) para.4 (effective March 10, 2008).

Citation of witnesses under section 156C(5)

18.3B. The citation of a witness under section 156C(5)(b) shall be in Form 18.3B. **B1-42.4**

AMENDMENTS

Rule 18.3B inserted by Act of Adjournal (Criminal Procedure Rules Amendment) (Criminal Proceedings etc. (Reform) (Scotland) Act 2007) 2008 (SSI 2008/61) para.4 (effective March 10, 2008)

Appeals in respect of orders made under section 156A(1)

18.3C. An appeal under section 156D(1) of the 1995 Act (appeals in respect of orders under section 156A(1)) shall be in Form 18.3C. **B1-42.5**

AMENDMENTS

Rule 18.3C inserted by Act of Adjournal (Criminal Procedure Rules Amendment) (Criminal Proceedings etc. (Reform) (Scotland) Act 2007) 2008 (SSI 2008/61) para.4 (effective March 10, 2008).

Record of proceedings to be written or printed

18.4.—(1) The record of proceedings in summary proceedings may be in writing or printed, or may be partly written and partly printed. **B1-42.6**

(2) All forms of minute of proceedings or orders of the court may be on the same sheet of paper as the complaint or on a separate sheet attached to it.

(3) Where the record of proceedings or minute of proceedings or orders of the Court referred to in paragraph (1) or (2) are for whatever reason unavailable to the Court, it shall be competent for the Court to proceed with a copy certified as a true copy by the clerk of court.

AMENDMENTS

Rule 18.4(3) as amended by Act of Adjournal (Criminal Procedure Rules Amendment) (SI 1997/63).

Interruption of proceedings after conviction

18.5.—(1) On conviction of an accused in summary proceedings, the judge may, without adjourning those proceedings, interrupt them by— **B1-42.7**

(a) considering a conviction against that person in other proceedings pending before that court for which he has not been sentenced; or

(b) passing sentence on that person in respect of the conviction in those other proceedings.

(2) When the judge has interrupted any proceedings under paragraph (1), he may, in passing sentence on an accused person in respect of a conviction in those proceedings, at the same time pass sentence on that person in respect of any other conviction he has considered.

(3) No interruption of any proceedings under paragraph (1) shall cause the instance to fall in respect of any person accused in those proceedings or shall otherwise affect the validity of those proceedings.

Detention in precincts of court

18.6. [...] **B1-42.8**

AMENDMENTS

Rule 18.6 repealed by Act of Adjournal (Criminal Procedure Rules Amendment No.4) (Miscellaneous) 2010 (SSI 2010/418) para.7 (effective December 13, 2010; subject to savings in para.7(3)).

[THE NEXT PARAGRAPH IS B1-43]

GENERAL NOTE

By para.2 of the Act of Adjournal (Criminal Procedure Rules Amendment) 1997 (SI 1997/63), it appears that per incuriam the High Court has substituted a new r.18.4(1). It seems that what was intended, but not achieved, was the insertion of a further rule (as r.18.4(3)) allowing for certified copies to be used when the principals are unavailable for whatever reason. **B1-43**

Rule 18.1

The accused, unless he cannot do so because of any infirmity, must tender his plea even when he has legal representation. This is a fundamental requirement and breach of it renders the conviction null and void, although in appropriate circumstances the Appeal Court will authorise a fresh prosecution (see *McGowan v Ritchie*, 1997 S.C.C.R. 322). There is, however, no obligation on the court to enquire if the accused has received the copy complaint or whether he has understood the charge or charges contained in it. If the Crown fails to intimate to the accused the date of the adjourned diet, the court will be entitled, in exercise of its own inherent discretionary power to regulate its own proceedings in the interests of justice, to refuse a further continuation without plea.

Rule 18.2

Form 14.5-A states that the witness is to raise his right hand and repeat the terms of the oath. The rule is directory only: see *McAvoy v HM Advocate*, 1992 S.L.T. 46. If the witness is a child, but is sworn without the court first ascertaining his age and whether or not he understands the nature of the oath—as required by the procedure desiderated in *Quinn v Lees*, 1994 S.C.C.R. 159—the witness's evidence must be objected to timeously in order to avoid losing a right of appeal under s.192(3) of the 1995 Act (*Jardine v Howdle*, 1997 S.C.C.R. 294; but see notes to r.14.5).

Rule 18.3

Form 18.3 requires the place and date of the granting of the warrant and also the signature of the sheriff (or justice of the peace) to be entered. Omission of these essentials will render the warrant bad and liable to suspension in the High Court. Equally, should the warrant be postdated per incuriam to, e.g. a year hence, it will be invalid.

Rule 18.4

The usual practice until the advent of computer technology was for the minutes, unless they became voluminous, to be written down the side of the principal complaint. Now minutes are more likely to be pre-printed and that may give rise to irregularities and inaccuracies in recording. Either party is entitled to insist that any objection taken to the competency or relevancy of the complaint or the proceedings, or to the competency or admissibility of evidence, be entered in the record of the proceedings: see s.157(2).

Rule 18.5

The sheriff may interrupt summary proceedings after he has convicted the accused in order to impose sentence in respect of another conviction irrespective of whether that conviction was in summary proceedings or on indictment so that he can simultaneously determine the appropriate disposal in respect of the original matter before him.

Rule 18.6

The power under s.169 of the 1995 Act is restricted to cases where a custodial sentence (not being a sentence imposed in default of payment of a fine) would be competent and the detention which the court orders does not extend beyond 8 pm. The power should also not be exercised where its exercise would deprive the accused of a reasonable opportunity of getting home in the course of that day.

Chapter 19

Appeals from Summary Proceedings

Appeals relating to preliminary pleas

B1-44 **19.1.**—(1) If—

(a) an accused states an objection to the competency or relevancy of a complaint or the proceedings; and

(b) that objection is repelled,

he may apply for leave to appeal against that decision under section 174(1) of the Act of 1995 (appeals relating to preliminary pleas) only after stating how he pleads to the charge or charges set out in the complaint.

(2) Subject to paragraph (1), the accused shall apply for leave to appeal against any decision to which that paragraph applies; and the court which made the decision shall determine that application immediately following the decision in question.

(3) Where the court grants the application, the clerk of court shall enter in the minute of proceedings—

(a) details of the decision in question; and

(b) the granting of leave to appeal against it.

(4) An appeal to which this rule applies shall be made by note of appeal in Form 19.1-A.

(5) The note of appeal shall be lodged with the clerk of the court which granted leave to appeal not later than seven days after the decision appealed against.

(6) The clerk of court shall, on the lodging of the note of appeal with him—

(a) send a copy to the respondent or his solicitor;

(b) request a report from the presiding judge; and

(c) transmit—

(i) the note of appeal,

(ii) two certified copies of the complaint and the minutes of proceedings, and

(iii) any other relevant documents,

to the Clerk of the Sheriff Appeal Court.

(7) The presiding judge shall, as soon as possible after receiving a request for a report, send his report to the Clerk of the Sheriff Appeal Court who shall send a copy to the appellant and respondent or their solicitors.

(8) The Clerk of the Sheriff Appeal Court shall arrange for the Sheriff Appeal Court to hear the appeal as soon as possible, and shall cause to be copied any documents necessary for the Sheriff Appeal Court.

(9) Where the Sheriff Appeal Court makes any order postponing the trial diet under section 174(2) of the Act of 1995, or makes any such order and gives a direction under that section, the Clerk of the Sheriff Appeal Court shall send a copy of that order and any direction to—

(a) the appropriate clerk of court;
(b) any accused who are not parties to the appeal or to their solicitors; and
(c) the governor of any institution in which any accused is detained.

(10) Any such appeal may be abandoned at any time prior to the hearing of the appeal.

(11) Where an appeal is abandoned, a minute of abandonment in Form 19.1-B shall be lodged with the Clerk of the Sheriff Appeal Court.

(12) On the lodging of a minute of abandonment under paragraph (11), the Clerk of the Sheriff Appeal Court shall inform the appropriate clerk of court and the respondent or his solicitor that the appeal has been abandoned.

AMENDMENTS

Rule 19.1(5) as amended by Act of Adjournal (Criminal Procedure Rules Amendment) (Miscellaneous) 2012 (SSI 2012/125) para.5 (effective June 4, 2012).

Rule 19.1 as amended by Act of Adjournal (Criminal Procedure Rules 1996 Amendment) (No. 4) (Sheriff Appeal Court) 2015 (SSI 2015/245) para.2 (effective September 22, 2015 subject to savings provisions in para.6).

Forms for appeals by stated case

19.2.—(1) An application under section 176(1) of the Act of 1995 (stated case: manner and time of appeal) shall be in Form 19.2-A. **B1-44.1**

(2) A stated case shall be in Form 19.2-B.

(3) The form of minutes of procedure in an appeal by stated case shall be in Form 19.2-C.

Forms for appeals against sentence only

19.3.—(1) A note of appeal under section 186(1) of the Act of 1995 (appeals against sentence only) shall be in Form 19.3-A. **B1-44.2**

(2) The form of minutes of procedure in an appeal under section 186(1) of the Act of 1995 shall be in Form 19.3-B.

Extension of time for appeals

19.4.—(1) An extension of time by the sheriff principal under section 186(5) (extension of time in appeal against sentence only), or section 194(2) (extension of time for stated case), of the Act of 1995 shall be in Form 19.4. **B1-44.3**

(2) Where, by virtue of subsection (8) of section 186 of the Act of 1995 (application of section 181 where appellant in appeal against sentence only fails to comply with a requirement), the court makes an order extending the period within which the note of appeal shall be lodged under subsection (2) of that section, the periods mentioned in subsections (2) and (4) of that section shall run from the date which is two days after the date on which the court makes that order and not from the date of the passing of the sentence.

Abandonment of appeals by stated case

19.5. A minute of abandonment of an appeal under section 184(1) of the Act of 1995 (abandonment of stated case before lodging it with the Clerk of the Sheriff Appeal Court) shall be in Form 19.5. **B1-44.4**

AMENDMENTS

Rule 19.5 as amended by Act of Adjournal (Criminal Procedure Rules 1996 Amendment) (No. 4) (Sheriff Appeal Court) 2015 (SSI 2015/245) para.2 (effective September 22, 2015 subject to savings provisions in para.6).

Abandoning appeals against conviction only

19.6.—(1) This rule applies for the purpose of section 175(8) of the Act of 1995 (abandoning appeal against conviction and proceeding with appeal against sentence alone). **B1-44.5**

(2) An application to abandon an appeal under section 175(8) of the Act of 1995 shall be made by minute in Form 19.6 and intimated by the appellant to the respondent.

(3) Subject to paragraph (4), the minute shall be lodged with the clerk of the court which imposed the sentence being appealed against.

(4) Where, before the lodging of the minute, the stated case has been lodged with the Clerk of Justiciary, the minute shall be lodged with the Clerk of the Sheriff Appeal Court who shall send a copy of the minute to the clerk of the court which imposed the sentence appealed against.

(5) Where, before the lodging of the minute, copies of the stated case and relative proceedings have been lodged with the Clerk of the Sheriff Appeal Court, those copies shall be used for the purposes of the hearing of the appeal against sentence.

(6) On the lodging of the minute, section 186(3) to (9) of the Act of 1995 (provisions relating to appeal against sentence only) shall apply to the stated case as they apply to a note of appeal.

AMENDMENTS

Rule 19.6(4), (5) as amended by Act of Adjournal (Criminal Procedure Rules 1996 Amendment) (No. 4) (Sheriff Appeal Court) 2015 (SSI 2015/245) para.2 (effective September 22, 2015 subject to savings provisions in para.6).

Abandonment of appeals against sentence only

B1-44.6 **19.7.** A minute of abandonment under section 186(9) of the Act of 1995 (abandonment of appeal against sentence only) shall be in Form 19.7.

Intimation of abandonment

B1-44.7 **19.8.** The Clerk of the Sheriff Appeal Court or clerk of court, as the case may be, on the lodging with him of—

(a) a minute abandoning an appeal under section 184(1) of the Act of 1995 (abandonment of appeal by stated case before lodging of case with the Clerk of the Sheriff Appeal Court), or

(b) a minute abandoning an appeal under section 186(9) of the Act of 1995 (abandonment of appeal against sentence only),

shall immediately notify the Crown Agent or the prosecutor, as the case may be, of the lodging of the minute; and the Clerk of the Sheriff Appeal Court shall, where the minute is lodged with him, notify immediately the clerk of the appropriate court.

AMENDMENTS

Rule 19.8 as amended by Act of Adjournal (Criminal Procedure Rules 1996 Amendment) (No. 4) (Sheriff Appeal Court) 2015 (SSI 2015/245) para.2 (effective September 22, 2015 subject to savings provisions in para.6).

Applications for suspension of disqualification from driving in appeals

B1-44.8 **19.9.**—(1) Where a person who has been disqualified from holding or obtaining a driving licence appeals against that disqualification under section 176(1) of the Act of 1995 by stated case, any application to suspend the disqualification shall be made with the application to the court to state a case for the opinion of the Sheriff Appeal Court.

(2) On an application being made under paragraph (1) to suspend a disqualification, the court shall grant or refuse to grant the application within seven days of it being made.

(3) Where the court refuses to grant the application and the appellant applies to the Sheriff Appeal Court to suspend the disqualification, any such application shall be made by note in Form 19.9.

(4) The note shall be lodged by the appellant or his solicitor with the Clerk of the Sheriff Appeal Court.

(5) The appellant or his solicitor shall intimate the lodging of the note to the respondent and the clerk of the court which imposed the disqualification.

(6) The clerk shall, on receiving such intimation, forthwith send to the Clerk of the Sheriff Appeal Court—

(a) a certified copy of the complaint; and

(b) a certified copy of the minute of proceedings.

(7) The Sheriff Appeal Court may order such further intimation (including intimation to the Lord Advocate) as it thinks fit, and may dispose of the application in open court or in chambers after such hearing as it thinks fit.

(8) On the Sheriff Appeal Court making an order on the note, the Clerk of the Sheriff Appeal Court shall send a certified copy of the order to the clerk of the court which imposed the disqualification.

(9) Where the order suspends the disqualification, the Clerk of the Sheriff Appeal Court shall also send a certified copy of the order to the Secretary of State with such further information as the Secretary of State may require.

(10) An order made by a single Appeal Sheriff of the Sheriff Appeal Court under this rule shall not be subject to appeal or review.

AMENDMENTS

Rule 19.9 as amended by Act of Adjournal (Criminal Procedure Rules 1996 Amendment) (No. 4) (Sheriff Appeal Court) 2015 (SSI 2015/245) para.2 (effective September 22, 2015 subject to savings provisions in para.6).

Applications for suspension of disqualification from driving in bills of suspension

B1-44.9 **19.10.**—(1) Where a person who has been disqualified from holding or obtaining a driving licence appeals against that disqualification by bill of suspension, an application to suspend the disqualification shall be made by requesting interim suspension of the disqualification in the prayer of the bill.

(2) Where the courts orders interim suspension, that order shall not have effect until—

(a) the bill has been served on the respondent; and

(b) the principal bill and first deliverance on the bill with an execution, or acceptance, of service—

(i) have been shown to the clerk of the sentencing court and he has endorsed a certificate of exhibition; and

(ii) they have been returned to the Clerk of the Sheriff Appeal Court by the complainer or his solicitor.

(3) On certifying the bill under paragraph (2), the clerk of the court which imposed the disqualification shall send a certified copy of the complaint and the relative minute of proceedings to the Clerk of the Sheriff Appeal Court.

(4) Paragraphs (2), (8), (9) and (10) of rule 19.9 (applications for suspension of disqualification from driving in appeals) apply to this rule as they apply to that rule.

AMENDMENTS

Rule 19.10 as amended by Act of Adjournal (Criminal Procedure Rules 1996 Amendment) (No. 4) (Sheriff Appeal Court) 2015 (SSI 2015/245) para.2 (effective September 22, 2015 subject to savings provisions in para.6).

Suspension of sentence under s.193A of the Act of 1995

19.10A.—(1) Where a convicted person or the prosecutor appeals to the Sheriff Appeal Court under section 175 of the Act of 1995, any application to suspend a relevant sentence shall be made with— **B1-44.10**

(a) the application to the court to state a case for the opinion of the Sheriff Appeal Court; or
(b) the note of appeal, as the case may be.

(2) On an application being made under paragraph (1) to suspend a sentence the court shall grant or refuse to grant the application within seven days of its being made.

(3) In the application of section 193A of the Act of 1995 (suspension of certain sentences pending appeal) to a case in which leave to appeal has been refused under section 180 or 187 of that Act, the word "determined" in subsection (1) of the said section 193A shall be construed as meaning—

(a) the fifteenth day after the date of intimation to the appellant or his solicitor and to the prosecutor of refusal of leave under subsection (1)(b) of section 180 or 187 of that Act, as the case may be, unless the appellant applies to the Sheriff Appeal Court for leave to appeal; or
(b) the seventh day after the date of intimation to the appellant or his solicitor and to the prosecutor of the refusal of leave by the Sheriff Appeal Court under subsection (5)(b) of section 180 or subsection (4)(b) of section 187 of that Act, as the case may be.

AMENDMENTS

Rule 19.10A inserted by Act of Adjournal (Criminal Procedure Rules Amendment No. 4) (SI 1997/1834) effective August 1, 1997).

Rule 19.10A as amended by Act of Adjournal (Criminal Procedure Rules 1996 Amendment) (No. 4) (Sheriff Appeal Court) 2015 (SSI 2015/245) para.2 (effective September 22, 2015 subject to savings provisions in para.6).

Solicitor entering appearance etc.

19.11.—(1) The solicitor for the appellant or the appellant, if unrepresented, must enter appearance— **B1-44.11**

(a) at the same time as lodging a stated case in accordance with section 179(9) of the Act of 1995; or
(b) within 7 days after the Clerk of the Sheriff Appeal Court intimates that leave to appeal has been granted in accordance with section 187(9)(a) of the Act of 1995.

(2) Appearance is entered by lodging Form 19.11-A with the Clerk of the Sheriff Appeal Court

(3) Where an appellant is represented by a solicitor who does not practise in Edinburgh, that solicitor may appoint a solicitor who practises in Edinburgh to carry out the duties of solicitor for the appellant.

(4) If there is a change in representation of an appellant, the new solicitor for the appellant or the appellant, if unrepresented, must lodge Form 19.11—B with the Clerk of the Sheriff Appeal Court within 7 days of that change in representation.

(5) A change in representation occurs where—

(a) an unrepresented appellant instructs a solicitor;
(b) an appellant dismisses the appellant's solicitor and—
  (i) instructs another solicitor; or
  (ii) intends to conduct the appeal in person.

AMENDMENTS

Rule 19.11 substituted by Act of Adjournal (Criminal Procedure Rules 1996 Amendment) (No. 4) (Sheriff Appeal Court) 2015 (SSI 2015/245) para.2 (effective September 22, 2015 subject to savings provisions in para.6).

Rule 19.11 as amended by Act of Adjournal (Criminal Procedure Rules 1996 and Act of Adjournal (Criminal Procedure Rules 1996 Amendment) (No.4) (Sheriff Appeal Court) 2015 Amendment) (Miscellaneous) 2015 (SSI 2015/295) para.6 (effective September 1, 2015).

Duty to print stated case etc.

19.12.—(1) The solicitor for the appellant or, if unrepresented, the appellant shall— **B1-44.12**

(a) print the complaint, minutes of proceedings and stated case or bill of suspension;
(b) not later than twenty-one days before the hearing, return the process to the Clerk of the Sheriff Appeal Court; and
(c) provide—
  (i) the Clerk of the Sheriff Appeal Court with four copies of the print; and
  (ii) the respondent or his solicitor with three copies of the print.

(2) Where the solicitor for the appellant or the appellant, as the case may be, cannot comply with any of the requirements of paragraph (1), he shall, not later than twenty-one days before the hearing, so inform the Clerk of the Sheriff Appeal Court in writing with reasons.

(3) On being so informed, the Clerk of the Sheriff Appeal Court may in his discretion postpone the hearing by dropping the appeal from the Criminal Appeal Roll.

(4) Where the Clerk of the Sheriff Appeal Court does not drop the appeal from the roll under paragraph (3), the court may, at the hearing, allow the appeal to be dropped from the roll or may dismiss the appeal.

AMENDMENTS

Rule 19.12 as amended by Act of Adjournal (Criminal Procedure Rules Amendment No.3) (Extradition etc.) 2004 (SSI 2004/346) para.2 (effective August 18, 2004).

Rule 19.12 as amended by Act of Adjournal (Criminal Procedure Rules 1996 Amendment) (No. 4) (Sheriff Appeal Court) 2015 (SSI 2015/245) para.2 (effective September 22, 2015 subject to savings provisions in para.6).

Duty of solicitor in bill of suspension

B1-44.13 **19.13.** A solicitor who requests a first deliverance in a bill of suspension shall comply with the requirements of rule 19.12(1) and (2) (printing of stated case) whether or not he is the nominated solicitor for the purposes of legal aid.

List of appeals

B1-44.14 **19.14.**—(1) The Clerk of the Sheriff Appeal Court shall, after consultation with the President of the Sheriff Appeal Court, issue a list of appeals with the respective dates of hearing on the Criminal Appeal Roll.

(2) Subject to paragraph (3) the Clerk of the Sheriff Appeal Court shall give the respective solicitors representing parties to an appeal so listed at least 14 days notice of the date fixed for the hearing of the appeal.

(3) In an appeal under section 175(2)(b), (c) or (ca) or by virtue of section 175(4) of the Act of 1995, the period of notice mentioned in paragraph (2) shall be 28 days.

AMENDMENTS

Rule 19.14 as amended by Act of Adjournal (Criminal Appeals) 2003 (SSI 2003/387) para.3. Brought into force on September 1, 2003 in accordance with para.1.

Rule 19.14(3) as amended by Act of Adjournal (Criminal Procedure Rules Amendment No.2) (Miscellaneous) 2012 (SSI 2012/187) para.2 (effective July 16, 2012, subject to transitional provisions).

Rule 19.14(1), (2) as amended by Act of Adjournal (Criminal Procedure Rules 1996 Amendment) (No. 4) (Sheriff Appeal Court) 2015 (SSI 2015/245) para.2 (effective September 22, 2015 subject to savings provisions in para.6).

Diet for interim suspension

B1-44.15 **19.15.** Where a bill of suspension contains a prayer for interim suspension of any order or for interim liberation—

- (a) the Appeal Sheriff before whom the bill is laid for a first deliverance shall assign a diet at which the parties may be heard on the crave for the interim order; and
- (b) the Clerk of the Sheriff Appeal Court shall forthwith give notice of that diet to the parties.

AMENDMENTS

Rule 19.15 as amended by Act of Adjournal (Criminal Procedure Rules 1996 Amendment) (No. 4) (Sheriff Appeal Court) 2015 (SSI 2015/245) para.2 (effective September 22, 2015 subject to savings provisions in para.6).

Intimation of determination of appeal

B1-44.16 **19.16.**—(1) The Clerk of the Sheriff Appeal Court shall send to the clerk of the sentencing court a certified copy of the order made on determination of the appeal from summary proceedings.

(2) Where the appeal against a disqualification from driving is refused or abandoned, the clerk of the sentencing court shall—

- (a) make the appropriate endorsement on the driving licence of the appellant; and
- (b) intimate the disqualification to the appropriate driving licence and police authorities.

(3) In this rule, "appeal" includes any appeal whether by stated case, note of appeal, bill of suspension or advocation.

AMENDMENTS

Rule 19.16(1) as amended by Act of Adjournal (Criminal Procedure Rules 1996 Amendment) (No. 4) (Sheriff Appeal Court) 2015 (SSI 2015/245) para.2 (effective September 22, 2015 subject to savings provisions in para.6).

Suspension of disqualification etc. under section 193 of the Act of 1995

B1-44.17 **19.17.** In the application of section 193 of the Act of 1995 (suspension of disqualification, forfeiture, etc.) to a case in which leave to appeal has been refused under section 180 or 187 of the Act of 1995, the word "determination" in subsection (1) of section 193 of that Act shall be construed as meaning—

(a) the fifteenth day after the date of intimation to the appellant or his solicitor of refusal of leave under subsection (1)(b) of section 180 or 187 of that Act, as the case may be, unless the appellant applies to the Sheriff Appeal Court for leave to appeal; or
(b) the day seven days after the date of intimation to the appellant or his solicitor of the refusal of leave by the Sheriff Appeal Court under subsection (5)(b) of section 180 or subsection (4)(b) of section 187 of that Act, as the case may be.

AMENDMENTS

Rule 19.17 as amended by Act of Adjournal (Criminal Procedure Rules Amendment No. 3) (SI 1997/1788) (effective August 11, 1997).

Rule 19.17 as amended by Act of Adjournal (Criminal Procedure Rules 1996 Amendment) (No. 4) (Sheriff Appeal Court) 2015 (SSI 2015/245) para.2 (effective September 22, 2015 subject to savings provisions in para.6).

Remits in applications for leave to appeal

19.18. The Appeal Sheriff considering an application for leave to appeal under section 180 (leave to appeal against conviction etc.), or section 187 (leave to appeal against sentence), of the Act of 1995 may, before deciding to grant or refuse leave, remit the case to the judge at first instance for a report or a supplementary report to be produced to him as soon as is reasonably practicable on any matter with respect to the grounds of appeal. **B1-44.18**

AMENDMENTS

Rule 19.18 as inserted by Act of Adjournal (Criminal Procedure Rules Amendment) (Miscellaneous) (SI 1996/2147 (S.171)) (effective September 9 1996).

Rule 19.18 as amended by Act of Adjournal (Criminal Procedure Rules 1996 Amendment) (No. 4) (Sheriff Appeal Court) 2015 (SSI 2015/245) para.2 (effective September 22, 2015 subject to savings provisions in para.6).

Presentation of summary conviction appeals in writing

19.18A.—(1) Where the Sheriff Appeal Court considers that the circumstances of the case require it, it may direct that this rule and rule 19.18B apply to an appeal under section 175(2) (a) or (d) of the Act of 1995. **B1-44.18.1**

(2) Where in relation to any ground of appeal an appellant seeks to lead evidence—
(a) this rule applies to that ground of appeal only in relation to the question of whether that evidence should be led;
(b) the court may nevertheless make an order containing provision similar to this rule in relation to the presentation of submissions following the hearing of that evidence.

(3) The appellant must, within 42 days of the granting of leave to appeal in accordance with section 180 of the Act of 1995, lodge a case and argument.

(4) A case and argument must—
(a) set out, for each ground of appeal, a succinct and articulate statement of the facts founded upon and the propositions of law being advanced;
(b) contain an estimate of how long will be required for the hearing of the appeal; and
(c) be signed—
(i) by the solicitor or counsel representing the appellant in the appeal; or
(ii) where the appellant intends to conduct the appeal personally, by the appellant.

(5) A case and argument must, when lodged, be accompanied by—
(a) all documents, or a copy thereof, referred to or founded upon in the case and argument and not already lodged in the appeal process; and
(b) all authorities, or a copy thereof, listed in the case and argument and not contained within a publication specified by the Lord Justice General by direction.

(6) The prosecutor—
(a) may lodge a case and argument in response to the appellant's case and argument if the prosecutor considers it appropriate;
(b) must do so if the court, considering that the circumstances of the case require it, orders the prosecutor to do so.

(7) Where the court makes an order under paragraph (6)(b), the prosecutor must lodge the case and argument within 21 days of the making of that order.

(8) At the same time as a case and argument is lodged, a copy of it and all accompanying documents must be sent to the other party to the appeal

(9) Where the Clerk of the Sheriff Appeal Court considers a case and argument to be unduly lengthy, the matter is to be referred to an Appeal Sheriff who is to give such directions as are considered appropriate.

(10) Where a case and argument is not lodged timeously, the Clerk of the Sheriff Appeal Court is to refer the matter to the President of the Sheriff Appeal Court, whom failing the Vice President of the Sheriff Appeal Court, for such action as is considered appropriate.

(11) The court may, on the application of the relevant party and on cause shown, extend the period for lodging a case and argument.

AMENDMENTS

Rule 19.18A inserted by Act of Adjournal (Criminal Procedure Rules Amendment No.2) (Presentation of Conviction Appeals in Writing) 2010 (SSI 2010/309) para.2 (effective November 1, 2010).

Rule 19.18A substituted by Act of Adjournal (Criminal Procedure Rules 1996 Amendment) (No. 4) (Sheriff Appeal Court) 2015 (SSI 2015/245) para.2 (effective September 22, 2015 subject to savings provisions in para.6).

Hearing of appeal presented in writing

B1-44.18.2 **19.18B.**—(1) This rule applies to the hearing of an appeal where a case and argument has been lodged by the appellant in accordance with rule 19.18A(3).

(2) At the hearing of the appeal—

(a) the appellant's case and argument and supporting documents constitute the principal submissions of the appellant;

(b) unless it otherwise directs, the court will expect the appellant to rely on the case and argument without reading it over to the court;

(c) the appellant may, subject to the control of the court, make supplementary comment to the case and argument;

(d) the appellant may respond to any case and argument lodged by the prosecutor; and

(e) the appellant is to answer any points raised by the court.

(3) Where the prosecutor lodges a case and argument, paragraph (2) applies with the necessary modifications to the prosecutor as it applies to the appellant.

(4) The appellant and the prosecutor have a duty to co-operate with each other and the court to ensure the completion of the hearing within the time allocated by the court.

(5) The court may, at any point during the hearing, set a timetable for the completion by a party of any submissions permitted in terms of paragraph (2)(b), (c), (d) or (e).

(6) On cause shown, the court may permit the appellant to introduce new information that has come to light in the period since the case and argument was lodged.

(7) Where the court permits the introduction of new information, it may at its discretion permit the lodging of additional documents in support of the new information.

(8) An appellant who wishes to introduce new information and lodge additional documents must send a copy of the information and documents to the Clerk of the Sheriff Appeal Court and the prosecutor as soon as the information and documents come into the appellant's possession.

(9) An appellant who has sent new information and documents to the Clerk of the Sheriff Appeal Court must apply at the bar to allow it to be introduced or lodged, as the case may be.

AMENDMENTS

Rule 19.18B inserted by Act of Adjournal (Criminal Procedure Rules 1996 Amendment) (No. 4) (Sheriff Appeal Court) 2015 (SSI 2015/245) para.2 (effective September 22, 2015 subject to savings provisions in para.6).

[THE NEXT PARAGRAPH IS B1-44.19]

Presentation of summary sentence appeal in writing

B1-44.19 **19.19**—(1) This rule applies to an appeal under section 175(2)(b), (c) or (ca) or by virtue of section 175(4) of the Act of 1995 listed in terms of rule 19.14 (list of appeals).

(2) In an appeal to which paragraph (1) applies the appellant shall present his case in writing.

(3) The solicitor for the appellant or, if unrepresented, the appellant shall—

(a) not later than 14 days before the date assigned for the appeal court hearing, lodge a case and argument in Form 19.19;

(b) lodge with the case and argument all documents, or a copy thereof, referred to or founded upon in the case and argument and not already lodged; and

(c) at the same time as he lodges the case and argument referred to in subparagraph (a) and the supporting documents referred to in sub-paragraph (b), send a copy to the Crown or, where the Crown is the appellant, to the respondent.

(4) The case and argument referred to in paragraph (3) shall be signed—

(a) by the solicitor or counsel representing the appellant in the appeal; or

(b) where the appellant intends to conduct the appeal personally, by the appellant.

(5) At the hearing of the appeal—

(a) the case and argument and supporting documents referred to in paragraph (3) shall constitute the submissions of the appellant;

(b) unless it otherwise directs, the Court will expect the appellant to rely upon the case and argument without reading it over to the Court; and

(c) the appellant may make supplementary comments to the case and argument; and shall answer any points raised by the Court.

(6) On cause shown, the Court may permit the appellant to introduce new information that has come to light in the period since the case and argument was lodged.

(7) Where the Court permits the introduction of new information, it may at its discretion permit the lodging of additional documents in support of the new information.

(8) A party who wishes to introduce new information and lodge additional documents shall send a copy of the information and documents to the Clerk of the Sheriff Appeal Court as soon as the information and documents come into the appellant's possession.

(9) A party who has sent new information and documents to the Clerk of the Sheriff Appeal Court shall make application at the bar to allow it to be introduced or lodged, as the case may be.

(10) Where the documents referred to in paragraph (3) are not lodged timeously, the Clerk of the Sheriff Appeal Court shall refer the matter to the President of the Sheriff Appeal Court, whom failing the Vice President of the Sheriff Appeal Court, for such action as the President of the Sheriff Appeal Court or Vice President of the Sheriff Appeal Court, as the case may be, considers appropriate.

AMENDMENTS

Rule 19.19 inserted by Act of Adjournal (Criminal Appeals) 2003 (SSI 2003/387) para.3. Brought into force on September 1, 2003 in accordance with para.1.

Rule 19.19 as amended by Act of Adjournal (Criminal Procedure Rules Amendment No.2) (Miscellaneous) 2003 (SSI 2003/468) para.2. Brought into force on October 27, 2003 in accordance with para.1.

Rule 19.19(3) as amended by Act of Adjournal (Criminal Procedure Rules Amendment No.2) (Miscellaneous) 2012 (SSI 2012/187) para.2 (effective July 16, 2012, subject to transitional provisions).

Rule 19.19 as amended by Act of Adjournal (Criminal Procedure Rules 1996 Amendment) (No. 4) (Sheriff Appeal Court) 2015 (SSI 2015/245) para.2 (effective September 22, 2015 subject to savings provisions in para.6).

[THE NEXT PARAGRAPH IS B1-45]

GENERAL NOTE

In many summary cases the appeal hearing proceeds in the absence of the appellant accused because he is neither in custody nor on bail pending the appeal. Where the accused has been admitted to bail he must attend the hearing (as it is a requirement of bail that he attend all lawful diets) and if he fails to do so the court will decline to entertain the appeal and will usually be persuaded to continue the appeal to a date to be afterwards fixed. However, in exceptional cases the court may be persuaded to hear the appeal in the accused's absence. In Crown appeals against unduly lenient sentences matters are different since the accused is the respondent and he will not be on bail (and it is highly unlikely that he will be in custody). It has been held that in principle the court will not hear an appeal against sentence in the respondent accused's absence but will continue the appeal for the accused to be afforded the opportunity of attending. This is because it is wrong in principle to determine the Crown's appeal when the consequence of that decision could be to increase the sentence imposed on the accused (*Urquhart v Campbell*, 2006 S.C.C.R. 656, para.[4]). **B1-45**

Rule 19.1

An appeal is initiated by lodging a note of appeal with the clerk of the lower court and not with the Justiciary Office. The note must be lodged not later than seven days after the decision of the lower court. If no note of appeal is lodged timeouslythe appeal is never, in fact, insisted in (there is therefore no need for a minute of abandonment in Form 19.1-B to be lodged) and, in the normal course of events, where a trial diet has been fixed already, the case will next call on the day fixed for the trial. Trial diets should, in the normal course, have been fixed because leave can only be applied for after the accused has pled not guilty. However, ifleave to appeal is applied for and granted and per incuriam the accused has not already been asked to state how he intends to plead, the lower court will not have adjourned the diet to a trial diet and (unless a trial diet has previously been fixed when the accused stated his objection at the pleading diet), the instance will fall at midnight: see *Lafferty v Jessop*, 1989 S.L.T. 846; 1989 S.C.C.R. 451. **B1-45.0.1**

The lower court is not entitled to postpone determination of the motion for leave to appeal against its decision but must determine the application "immediately".

Once the appeal calls in the High Court it is necessary to obtain the leave of the High Court to abandon the appeal because the High Court may wish to hear argument on the appeal or (at least) an explanation as to why the appeal was marked in the first place.

Two recent decisions on what does and does not constitute relevancy and/or competency are worthy of notice because of their potentially far reaching implications. First, in *Rosselli v Vannet*, 1997 S.C.C.R. 655 the High Court observed that where in a summary prosecution the Crown's conduct at the intermediate diet was founded on as oppressive, it was open to the accused to raise the issue of oppression at the outset of the trial diet as it was not a matter of competency or relevancy and thus did not require to be stated before the accused was called on to plead (cf. *Normand v Rooney*, 1992 S.C.C.R. 336, to which the court in *Rosselli* made no reference). Secondly, in *McQueen v Hingston*, 1997 S.C.C.R. 765 it was held that where the accused required the Crown to prove by production of a non-statutory document the commencement of a period within which a statutory duty operated, failure to comply with such duty constituting an offence, the accused was bound to state objection to the relevancy and/or competency of the charge. The accused was not entitled to remain silent and submit that the Crown had failed to prove its case (see P.W. Ferguson, "Relevancy and Sufficiency", 1997 S.L.T. (News) 229).

Rule 19.2

Stated case appeals are a creation of statute. They are limited to questions of law which it is for the trial court to formulate with precision. An appellant must set forth "a full statement of all the matters which [he] desires to bring under review" in his application (under s.176(1)) to the lower court for that court to state a case. Where, however, the appellant wishes to amend any matter in his application, or add a new matter on which he seeks review, he is at liberty to do so by intimating that fact during the three- **B1-45.0.2** week period commencing with the issue of the draft stated case (s.179(1)). The case cannot be meaningfully stated unless the grounds of challenge are identified in advance of the issue of the final stated case.

Once the case has been finalised and transmitted to the Clerk of Justiciary in Edinburgh, it is incompetent for an appellant to present argument on matters not previously identified in the application for a stated case (as added to or amended under s.179(1)). However, the High Court has power under s.182(3) to grant leave, on cause being shown to the court's satisfaction, for the appellant to found any aspect of his appeal on a matter not contained in his application under s.176(1). Neither the 1995 Act nor the Criminal Procedure Rules provides a mechanism for seeking leave to amend the grounds of review.

On receipt of the final stated case from the lower court, the High Court must decide whether or not to grant leave to appeal on a consideration of the stated case and other documents specified in s.179(8)(b) (s.180(1) and(2)). Where leave to appeal is refused the appellant may apply to three judges de novo for the grant ofleave to appeal, the so-called second sift (s.180(4)). It is not competent at this stage to seek to amend the stated case (*Gordon v Procurator Fiscal, Aberdeen* [2015] HCJAC 36 at [8]). Unlike solemn appeals where applications for amendment of Notes of Appeal may take place prior to, as well as after, the grant of leave to appeal (and, in particular, leave to amend may be sought at the stage of the second sift), the procedure in summary conviction appeals is quite different. Amendment is "only possible in terms of the statutory scheme. This is that the court may, *at the hearing of the stated case*, remit the case back to the court of first instance to be 'amended and returned' (1995 Act s.182(6)). There is no other method of amending a stated case. It is clear from the statutory provisions that such amendment can only take place at a hearing; that is the point after leave to appeal has been granted on one ground or another." (at [11], emphasis added).

However, in *Gordon* (at [12]) the court noted that there is an additional "safety valve": at the stage of the first or second sift, the court "may specify the arguable grounds of appeal (whether or not they are contained in the stated case) on the basis of which leave to appeal is granted" (1995 Act s.180(7)). Moreover, the court has power under s.182(3) to grant leave, on cause being shown, for the appellant to found any aspect of his appeal on a matter not contained in his initial application for a stated case under s.176(1).

The High Court in *Watt v Ralph* [2007] HCJAC 5; 2007 S.C.C.R. 70 gave the following guidance:

> "[W]here a case has been stated and there subsequently arise matters upon which an appellant wishes to rely, he should promptly make an application to the court under s.182(3) for the relevant leave. That should be done in writing in a document headed 'Application under s.182(3) of the Criminal Procedure (Scotland) Act 1995' and setting out clearly and succinctly the basis upon which the application is made. The document should be lodged in court and intimated to the Crown sufficiently far in advance of the day on which leave is to be sought, so as to allow to the court and to the Crown time to give it mature consideration" (at [9]).

The document should be lodged with the Justiciary Office and intimation should be given to the Crown Office in Edinburgh. This guidance applies also to new grounds of review in respect of sentences which are challenged by way of stated case.

It is competent for an appeal to be taken against the acquittal of the accused even though the Crown seeks to withdraw a concession in law which was the basis of the acquittal in the lower court (see *Brown v Farrel*, 1997 S.C.C.R. 356). There seems no reason in principle forthat rule not to apply equally to a defence appeal. It must, however, be open to serious doubt whether an accused whose conviction proceeded on the basis that it was accepted—as so often happens in the lower court—that the case depended on issues of credibility and reliability, can thereafter appeal on the ground of a legal argument which was not advanced in the lower court either because it was not noticed or it was considered unsound (cf. *McGinty v HM Advocate*, 2000 J.C. 277 where an appellant was refused leave to revert to a ground of appeal which had been expressly abandoned at an earlier hearing).

Rule 19.6

B1-45.0.3 Two different stages can have been reached when the appellant chooses to abandon his appeal. When the stated case has not been transmitted to the Justiciary Office, the appellant should lodge the minute with the clerk of the lower court but, once the stated case has been lodged with the Justiciary Office, the minute should be lodged with the Clerk of Justiciary who will then inform the clerk of the lower court.

Rule 19.9

Where an accused applies for a stated case he should also seek interim suspension of his driving disqualification and, if the court does not suspend the disqualification, the accused can apply to a judge of the High Court who shall normally hear the application in chambers though not necessarily with the attendance of counsel (cf. the situation where a bill of suspension contains a prayer for interim suspension: r.19.15). The judge's decision is final.

Rule 19.10

In bills of suspension the application is made direct to the High Court and no notice is given to the lower court which will therefore be unaware that the conviction and/or disqualification is being appealed. The interim suspension of the disqualification when granted must therefore (for administrative convenience) be postponed until the lower court has been informed that it has been suspended.

Rule 19.11

There is no obligation on agents outside Edinburgh to instruct correspondents in Edinburgh for appeals but they may do so.

Rule 19.12

While rr.19.11 and 19.16 refer to bills of advocation, r.19.12 does not include them although it is conceivable—but hardly likely nowadays—that an accused could bring an advocation during the course of a summary trial.

Rule 19.14

This rule was introduced in September 2003 and does for solemn sentence appeals (including Crown appeals) what is now provided for in summary appeals (see r.15.1(4) and (5), supra). In both such appeals the court must give at least 42 days' notice of the appeal hearing so as to allow the appellant to comply with r.19.19 by lodging a case and argument in Form 19.18. **B1-45.0.4**

Rule 19.17

Section 193(1) of the 1995 Act provides that where a disqualification, forfeiture or disability attaches as a result of conviction, the lower court can, if it thinks fit, suspend the disqualification, etc., pending the determination of any appeal. Where leave to appeal is required under either s.180 or s.187 of the 1995 Act, the single judge's decision to refuse leave will be intimated to the accused and, on the 15th day after the date of intimation, the disqualification, etc., will re-attach. Where, however, the accused applies to a quorum of judges—three judges are appropriate if conviction is being challenged but two judges are appropriate where sentence alone is appealed—the disqualification, etc., will attach seven days after the date of intimation of the refusal of leave to appeal.

Rule 19.18

The High Court when hearing appeals has an inherent power to call for a supplementary report. Presumably on the view that the single judge who "sifts" the appeals has no such inherent power and because (no doubt because it has become apparent in the months since the "sift" procedures have been operating) stated cases may disclose a ground of appeal which is not referred to in the application for a stated case, the single judge is now given a power to remit to the trial judge.

Rule 19.18A

Under procedure governing solemn conviction appeals (in respect of which leave to appeal under s.107 of the 1995 Act has been granted after November 1, 2010),rr.15.15A and 15.15B automatically apply in all cases where an appellant seeks to adduce evidence in support of a ground of appeal. The Appeal Court may, however, disapply the requirements of rr.15.15A and 15.15B. This rule empowers the Appeal Court, in appeals for which leave has been granted after November 1, 2010, to apply the requirements of these solemn appeal rules to summary conviction appeals "if it considers the circumstances of the case require it".

Thus, where the Appeal Court so directs, the appellant is obliged to prepare and lodge "a case and argument" (and any accompanying documents not already in the appeal process but referred to in the case and argument) with Justiciary Office within 42 days of the court so directing. The appellant must also send a copy of the case and argument (and copies of any accompanying documents) to the Crown. The Crown will then be entitled, if its considers it appropriate to do so, to prepare and lodge its response to that case and argument in the form of its own case and argument.

Furthermore, the Appeal Court may ordain the Crown to lodge a case and argument when the court considers that the circumstances of the case require it. When such an order is made, the Crown has 21 days within which to lodge the case and argument. However, as with the 42-day period applying to an appellant, the Appeal Court may, on cause shown, extend the time limit for lodging the case and argument and accompanying documents.

Rule 19.19

This rule is designed to ensure that sentence appeals by accused persons and the Crown do not occupy an undue amount of precious Appeal Court time. Such appeals should be presented in writing although the appellant *may* (at his or the court's discretion?) "make supplementary comments" (r.19.19(5)(c)). Information relied upon at the appeal hearing but not founded on in the case and argument may be admitted. See annotations to r.15.16, supra.

[THE NEXT PARAGRAPH IS B1-45.1]

Chapter 19A

Alteration by Clerk of Justiciary of Place Where Case to be Heard

Power of clerk of Justiciary to alter place where case to be heard

B1-45.1 **19A.1.**—(1) Where the High Court has—

(a) adjourned a case following conviction; or

(b) deferred sentence in a case following conviction,

(c) fixed any diet in respect of any of the following—

(i) [...]

(ii) [...]

(iii) a drug treatment and testing order made under section 234B of the Act of 1995;

(v) a community payback order.

(d) fixed any diet under section 52 or sections 52B to 59 of the Act of 1995,

(e) adjourned a preliminary hearing under section 75A of the Act of 1995,

the Clerk of Justiciary may make an order altering the place where the case is to be heard, not later than two days before the case is to be called.

(2) The Clerk of Justiciary shall intimate an order made under paragraph (1) to—

(a) the parties to the proceedings; and

(b) the governor of any institution in which the accused is detained,

not later than two days before the case is to be called.

AMENDMENTS

Chapter 19A inserted by Act of Adjournal (Criminal Procedure Rules Amendment No.2) (Miscellaneous) 2003 (SSI 2003/468) para.2. Brought into force on 27 October 2003 in accordance with para.1.

Rule 19A.1 and chapter heading as amended by Act of Adjournal (Criminal Procedure Rules Amendment) (Miscellaneous) 2010 (SSI 2010/184) para.5 (effective 1 June 2010).

Rule 19A.1(1)(c) as amended by Act of Adjournal (Criminal Procedure Rules Amendment No.4) (Miscellaneous) 2010 (SSI 2010/418) para.2(4) (effective 1 February 2011; subject to savings in para.2(8)).

Rule 19A.1(1) as amended by Act of Adjournal (Criminal Procedure Rules 1996 and Act of Adjournal (Criminal Procedure Rules 1996 Amendment) (No. 4) (Sheriff Appeal Court) 2015 Amendment) (Miscellaneous) 2015 (SSI 2015/295) para.3 (effective 1 September 2015).

GENERAL NOTE

B1-45.2 When this chapter was introduced in October 2003 it was concerned only to confer a power on the trial court to alter the place where a case was to be heard when the court either had adjourned a case under s.201 of the 1995 Act (to enable inquiries to be made or to determine the most suitable method of dealing with the accused's case) or had deferred sentence under s.202 of the 1995 Act for the accused to be of good behaviour. This amended chapter provides (with effect from June 1, 2010) that the power now applies to a wider range of diets including diets specifically fixed in order to administer various orders which can be made by the court as part of its disposal of the case.

The rule is only necessary for, and therefore only applies to, High Court proceedings. So far as deferred sentences under s.202 are concerned, it is impossible to know where a High Court judge will be in 12 months' time and the same nowadays is true even for four-week adjournments. Thus, to avoid the need of calling the case before the "wrong" judge at the court previously announced (so as to adjourn it to a later date for the original judge to deal with it), Justiciary Office can now alter the place. This must be done not later than two days before the case is to be called; the same period of notice must be given to the accused. Failure to keep to the timetable when making the order could be fatal to the instance if the case then calls where it should not and is therefore not called where it is still bound to call.

Chapter 19B

Scottish Criminal Cases Review Commission

References

B1-45.3 **19B.1.**—(1) This rule applies to a reference by the Scottish Criminal Cases Review Commission to the High Court under section 194B of the Act of 1995.

(2) The Clerk of Justiciary shall—

(a) assign the reference to a procedural hearing fixed for a date not earlier than 21 days after receipt of the reference; and

(b) as soon as possible thereafter, intimate the diet to every party and to the governor of any institution in which any accused is detained.

(2A) Subject to section 194D(4A) of the Act of 1995, within 21 days after the date on which a copy of the Commission's statement is sent under section 194D(4)(b) of the Act of 1995 the appellant shall lodge with the Clerk of Justiciary a note of the grounds of appeal that are to be relied upon at the hearing of the appeal and send a copy to the Crown Agent.

(2B) The High Court may, on cause shown, extend the period of 21 days mentioned in paragraph (2A).

(3) At the procedural hearing the High Court shall consider and make orders in respect of—

(b) any application under section 194D(4B) of the Act of 1995;
(c) any application under section 194D(4D) of the Act of 1995;
(d) the procedure to be followed in the determination of the reference;
(e) any other matter which the Court considers appropriate in respect of the reference.

AMENDMENTS

Rule 19B.1 as amended by Act of Adjournal (Criminal Procedure Rules Amendment No.3) (Extradition etc.) 2004 (SSI 2004/346) para.2 (effective 18 August 2004).

Rule 19B.1 substituted by Act of Adjournal (Criminal Procedure Rules Amendment No.4) (Miscellaneous) 2010 (SSI 2010/418) para.6 (effective 13 December 2010).

Rule 19B.1 as amended by Act of Adjournal (Criminal Procedure Rules Amendment No.2) (Miscellaneous) 2012 (SSI 2012/187) para.3 (effective 16 July 2012, subject to transitional provisions).

Rule 19B.1 as amended by Act of Adjournal (Criminal Procedure Rules 1996 Amendment) (Miscellaneous) 2017 (SSI 2017/144) para.2(6) (effective 29 May 2017).

Applications for requests for assistance

19B.2.—(1) An application under section 194IA of the Act of 1995 shall be in Form 19B.2 and shall be lodged with the Clerk of Justiciary. **B1-45.4**

(2) The High Court shall—

(a) without requiring intimation to any other party, proceed to consider the application;
(b) after considering it shall grant it, with or without any modifications which it deems appropriate, or shall refuse it.

(3) The application shall be registered by the Clerk of Justiciary as if it were an application made under section 7(1) of the Crime (International Co-operation) Act 2003 and rule 36.62 applied.

AMENDMENTS

Chapter 19B inserted by Act of Adjournal (Criminal Procedure Rules Amendment No.2) (Miscellaneous) 2003 (SSI 2003/468) r.2. Brought into force on 27 October 2003 in accordance with r.1.

Rule 19B.2 substituted by Act of Adjournal (Criminal Procedure Rules Amendment No.4) (Miscellaneous) 2010 (SSI 2010/418) para.6 (effective 13 December 2010).

GENERAL NOTE

Solemn cases

Section 194B of the 1995 Act provides, inter alia, that the Scottish Criminal Cases Review Commission may at any time, if it thinks fit (having regard to the grounds in s.194C), refer "the whole case" of a person convicted on indictment to the High Court and "the case shall be heard and determined, subject to any directions the High Court may make, as if it were an appeal under Part VIII" of the 1995 Act (which governs solemn appeals). The practice (whether there was a Secretary of State's reference (*Beattie v HM Advocate*, 1995 S.L.T. 275) or a Commission reference (*Boncza-Tomaszewski v HM Advocate*, 2000 J.C. 586)) has been for the accused to lodge a note of appeal containing all the grounds which he desires to argue: he was entitled to go beyond the specific grounds on which the Commission had stated that it referred the case and he was entitled to seek leave to amend his grounds. This was consistent with the deeming of the reference to be an appeal under the 1995 Act; and the Appeal Court would accordingly put the case out for a procedural hearing to give appropriate directions. **B1-45.5**

However, unlike s.110(1)(a), where the starting point for the eight-week period within which to lodge a note of appeal is prescribed, there was no definite starting point for references. Thus r.19B assimilates references to ordinary appeals by providing for a starting point for the eight-week period: it is either (a) the date of the referral or (b) the date on which an application made under s.194D(4B) of the Criminal Procedure (Scotland) Act 1995 was determined.

Section 83 of the Criminal Justice and Licensing (Scotland) Act 2010 (asp 13), which received the Royal Assent on August 6, 2010 but is not yet in force, introduces a restriction on the scope of an appeal following a reference by the commission. Section 194D(4D) now provides that the grounds of appeal in such a case must relate to one or more of the reasons for making the reference contained in the commission's statement of reasons. However, s.194D(4B) provides that the High Court "may, if it considers it is in the interests of justice to do so, grant leave for the appellant to found the appeal on additional grounds". This innovation in the procedure on references was foreshadowed by the High Court's observations in *Al Megrahi v HM Advocate* [2008] HCJAC 58; 2008 S.L.T. 1008 (para.80). An application for leave to introduce additional grounds of appeal must be made and intimated to the Crown Agent within 21 days after the date on which a copy of the commission's statement of reasons was sent to the appellant (s.194D(4C)) although the High Court may, on cause shown, extend that period (s.194D(4D)). Where the High Court refuses to extend that period, it must give reasons for that refusal to the appellant (s.194D(4E)(b)).

In due course these annotations will take notice of the further restriction on references introduced by s.7(3) of the Criminal Procedure (Legal Assistance, Detention and Appeals) (Scotland) Act 2010 in respect of which, for present purposes, reference should be made to the author's article, " The right to legal advice in detention", 2010 S.L.T. (News) 197 at p.199.

But, as already noted, the reference appellant is also entitled to present in his note of appeal any ground of appeal, even a ground which the Commission considered and rejected as a basis for referring the conviction. This situation has been confirmed by a bench of five judges in *Al Megrahi v HM Advocate* [2008] HCJAC 58; 2008 S.L.T. 1008; 2008 S.C.L. 1346 in which the High Court stated that whether this situation was desirable was a matter for the Scottish Parliament (para.80). That hint has been taken up by the Scottish Parliament in Pt 3 of the Criminal Justice and Licensing Bill presently before Parliament. It should also be noted that the High Court has twice questioned the appropriateness of a reference where the appellant had either not marked an appeal or, having done so, had thereafter abandoned that appeal, prior to applying to the Commission (see *Hunt v Aitken*, 2008 S.C.C.R. 919; *Kelly v HM Advocate* [2010] HCJAC 20; 2010 S.L.T. 967).

Summary cases

Section 194B makes the same provision for summary convictions and sentences. However, while it is provided that the appeal is to be heard and determined as if it were an appeal under Part X of the 1995 Act (which provides the procedure to be followed for the statutory modes of appeal of stated case and note of appeal (where sentence alone is challenged)), it is necessary to avoid the consequences of that provision. Thus, the time limits for stated case procedure do not, because they cannot, apply. A procedural hearing is to be appointed so that the Appeal Court can determine what steps should be taken to advance the appeal and identify the grounds on which it is to be prosecuted. In *Crombie v Clark*, 2001 S.L.T. 635 the Appeal Court ordained the accused to lodge a bill of suspension (para.3) and this seems the likely direction to be given in all cases. The bill will then be the focus of the appeal and the Commission's statement of reasons for referring the case will simply be the background material (as Lord Prosser observed in *Crombie*, para.4).

Chapter 19C

Risk Assessment

Risk assessment orders

B1-45.6 **19C.1.**—(1) A notice of intention to make a motion for a risk assessment order under section 210B(2) of the Act of 1995 [8] shall be in Form 19C.1-A.

(2) A risk assessment order under section 210B(2) of the Act of 1995 shall be in Form 19C.1-B.

(3) An application under section 210B (5) of the Act of 1995 (application for extension of period of adjournment following order) shall be made by letter to the Clerk of Justiciary.

(4) On receipt of a letter under paragraph (3), the Clerk of Justiciary shall—

(a) send a copy of that letter to the prosecutor, the convicted person and the assessor; and

(b) fix a date and time for hearing the application which date and time shall be notified by the Clerk of Justiciary to the prosecutor; the convicted person and the governor of any institution in which the convicted person is detained.

(5) The Clerk of Justiciary shall notify the governor of any institution in which the convicted person is detained of any extension (or further extension) under section 210B(5) of the Act of 1995, of the period mentioned in section 210B(4) of the Act of 1995 (adjournment following risk assessment order).

Reports

B1-45.7 **19C.2.** A report under section 2 10C or 210D of the Act of 1995 shall be in Form 19C.2.

Objections to reports

B1-45.8 **19C.3.**—(1) A convicted person shall intimate any objection under section 210C(7) of Act of 1995 by lodging with the Clerk of Justiciary and serving on the prosecutor a notice of objection in Form 19C.3 within 14 days after receiving a copy of the report.

(2) On receipt of a notice of objection under paragraph (1), the Clerk of Justiciary shall fix a date and time for hearing the objection and shall intimate that date and time to the convicted person, the prosecutor and the governor if any institution in which the convicted person is detained.

(3) The convicted person and the prosecutor shall, not less than 7 days before the hearing mentioned in paragraph (2), lodge and serve on the other party lists of any witnesses and productions on which they propose to rely at the hearing.

AMENDMENTS

Chapter 19C inserted by Act of Adjournal (Criminal Procedure Rules Amendment No.3) (Risk Assessment Orders and Orders for Lifelong Restriction) 2006 (SSI 2006/302) para.2(5) (effective June 20, 2006).

GENERAL NOTE

B1-45.9 Section 1 of the Criminal Justice (Scotland) Act 2003 amends the 1995 Act to insert ss.210B-210G which make provision for risk assessment orders (RAOs) and lifelong restriction orders (LROs). The object of an RAO is to provide the court with sufficient information in the form of a risk assessment report prepared in an accredited manner by a psychologist (to be known as an "assessor": s.210B(5)) accredited by the Risk Management Authority, so as to be able to determine whether a LRO should be made when imposing sentence. The Risk Management Authority was established by s.3 of the 2003 Act (which came into force on June 27, 2003: see Criminal Justice (Scotland) Act 2003 (Commencement No.1) Order 2003 (SSI 2003/288)). The Authority has responsibility for preparing and issuing guidelines as to the assessment and minimisation of risk and for setting and publishing standards according to which measures taken in respect of such assessment and minimisation of risk are to be judged (2003 Act s.5(1)). It is the duty of assessors to have regard to such guidelines and standards (2003 Act s.5(2)). The scheme for accreditation to be administered by the Authority came into force on March 30, 2006 (see Risk Assessment and Minimisation (Accreditation Scheme) (Scotland) Order 2006 (SSI 2006/190)).

A LRO constitutes a sentence of imprisonment or detention for an indeterminate period (s.210F(2)) and may be appealed by note of appeal against sentence. Moreover, if the court refuses to make a LRO, the Crown is entitled to appeal against that refusal on the grounds that on balance of probabilities the risk criteria for making such an order were met (s.210F(3)). Thus, exceptionally in Scottish procedure, the Crown is in effect given a right to appeal on a question of fact. The Crown does not require leave to appeal. If a LRO is made there then arises an obligation on the Scottish Ministers to prepare a risk management plan (2003 Act, s.6(1)). The plan must be completed no later than nine months after sentence was imposed (2003 Act, s.8(1)) and must set out, inter alia, an assessment of the accused's risk to the public, the measures to be taken to minimise that risk and how such measures are to be coordinated (2003 Act, s.6(3)).

Rule 19C.1

The prosecution is not entitled to move for an RAO unless it has given notice of its intention to do so but the court may make an order *ex proprio motu* (s.210B(2)). In any event, the court is bound to make an order if it considers that the risk criteria set out in S.210E *may* be met, unless the court makes an interim hospital order or the accused is already subject to a LRO. An RAO can only be made by the High Court; it cannot be made in respect of a murder conviction; and it is necessary that the conviction before the High Court be for one or all of the following offences: (a) a sexual offence as defined in s.210A(10), (b) a violent offence as so defined, (c) an offence which endangers life (e.g. culpable and reckless conduct); or for (d) an offence the nature of which, or the circumstances of the commission of which, are such that it appears to the court that the accused has a "propensity to commit any such offence as is mentioned" in (a)-(c).

An RAO is an order for the accused to be taken to a place specified in the order so that there can be prepared a risk assessment report on the risk which the accused's being at liberty presents to the safety of the public at large; and the order provides for the accused to be remanded in custody there for so long as is necessary for that purpose (and thereafter detained there or elsewhere until the accused's sentencing diet) (s.210B(3)). On making the RAO the court must adjourn the case for no more than 90 days. However, the court may on one occasion, on cause shown, extend that period by not more than 90 days; and may, exceptionally, further extend the period for as long as the court considers appropriate for completion of the report if the reason for the report not having been completed is attributable to circumstances which were outwith the assessor's control (s.210B(5)). There is no right of appeal against an RAO or the refusal to make one (s.210B(6)).

The High Court made a RAO in *HM Advocate v Henderson*, 2009 S.C.C.R. 30 where it was contended that a LRO was incompetent in any case where the maximum penalty was less than life imprisonment. Lord Uist held that the risk assessment provisions are concerned with the protection of the public at large; they do not amend the maximum punishment laid down for any offence; they permit the court to make a LRO for the purpose of the protection of the public where the risk criteria as defined in s.210E of the 1995 Act are met (para.14). It is therefore competent to make a RAO where the accused has been convicted of a statutory offence the maximum punishment for which is set at a period less than life imprisonment.

Rule 19C.2

The assessor may take into account, for the purposes of assessing the accused's risk, not only the accused's previous convictions but also "any allegation that the [accused] has engaged in criminal behaviour (whether or not that behaviour resulted in prosecution and acquittal)". Where any allegation is taken into account, it must be specified in the risk assessment report, as must any additional evidence which supports the allegation and the assessor must explain the extent to which the allegation and the evidence have influenced him in forming his opinion as to the level of risk which the accused presents (s.210C(2) and (3)). The completed report must be sent by the assessor to the Clerk of Justiciary who must copy it to the Crown and the accused along with any documents available to, and referred to in the report by, the assessor (s.210C(4)). Upon receipt of the report the Clerk of Justiciary must fix a diet for sentence.

Rule 19C.3

An accused is entitled, while detained for the preparation of the risk assessment report, to instruct his own report (s.210C(5)). If he does, that report should be sent to the Clerk of Justiciary who will copy it, and any relevant documents, to the Crown. The accused may then be in a position to challenge the findings and/or opinion contained in the assessor's report. If he wishes to do so he must give notice. If objection is taken by the accused to the assessor's report, evidence may be led before the sentencing judge (s.210C(7)).

Risk criteria

Whether or not objections are intimated and irrespective of whether a proof is held, the task of the sentencing judge is then to determine whether a LRO should be made. He must do so in light of the risk criteria which are that "the nature of, or the circumstances of the commission of, the offence of which the [accused] has been found guilty either in themselves or as part of a pattern of behaviour are such as to demonstrate that there is a likelihood that he, if at liberty, will seriously endanger the lives, or physical or psychological well-being, of members of the public at large" (s.210E). If in light of the RAO, any risk assessment prepared for the accused, any evidence led at a proof on the accused's objections or "any other information before it", the court is satisfied on balance of probabilities that the risk criteria are met, the court must make a LRO (s.210F(1)). Where the court does not make a LRO because it is not satisfied that the risk criteria are met, the court is thereby precluded from imposing an indeterminate sentence (s.210G(1)).

Part IVA

Appeals and Referrals from Sheriff Appeal Court

Chapter 19D

Referral of Point of Law for Opinion of the High Court of Justiciary

Interpretation of this Chapter

B1-45.10 **19D.1.** In this Chapter—

"appeal document" has the meaning given by rule 19E.3(2);

"reference" means a reference made by the Sheriff Appeal Court to the High Court for its opinion on a point of law undersection 175A(1) of the Act of 1995.

Notice of intention to seek reference

B1-45.11 **19D.2.**—(1) Where a party to the appeal proceedings applies to the Sheriff Appeal Court to make a reference, that party must give notice of intention to do so to the Clerk of the Sheriff Appeal Court and to every other party.

(2) A record of that notice is to be entered in the minute of proceedings.

(2) On receiving notice—

(a) the court is to fix a diet at which parties may be heard on the application for a reference;

(b) the Clerk of the Sheriff Appeal Court must give every party to the appeal proceedings notice of the date, time and place of the diet.

Reference proposed by the Sheriff Appeal Court on its own initiative

B1-45.12 **19D.3.**—(1) Where the Sheriff Appeal Court proposes to make a reference on its own initiative, it is to fix a diet at which parties may be heard on the question of whether a reference should be made.

(2) The Clerk of the Sheriff Appeal Court must give every party to the appeal proceedings notice of—

(a) the intention of the court to make a reference; and

(b) the date, time and place of the diet.

(3) A record of that notice is to be entered in the minute of proceedings.

Preparation of a reference

B1-45.13 **19D.4.**—(1) After hearing parties, where the court grants an application for a reference or decides to make a reference on its own initiative, the court is to—

(a) give reasons for that decision and cause those reasons to be recorded in the minute of proceedings;

(b) continue the proceedings from time to time as necessary for the purposes of the reference to the High Court.

(2) The reference is to be drafted—

(a) in Form 19D.4 unless the court directs otherwise;

(b) in accordance with directions given by the court to the parties about the manner in which and by whom the reference is to be drafted and adjusted.

(3) The reference may be further adjusted to take account of any adjustments required by the court.

(4) After approval by the court, the Clerk of the Sheriff Appeal Court must transmit the reference to the Clerk of Justiciary, together with a certified copy of—

(a) the minute of proceedings;

(b) the complaint;

(c) the appeal document.

Procedure before the High Court

B1-45.14 **19D.5.**—(1) On receipt of a reference, the High Court may make such order as it thinks fit in order to determine the reference, and in particular it may—

(a) order that the reference be intimated on any person appearing to the High Court to have an interest, including the Lord Advocate;

(b) order parties to lodge written submissions in such form and on such matters as it considers appropriate;

(c) fix a diet at which parties may be heard on the reference.

(2) The Clerk of Justiciary must send to the Clerk of the Sheriff Appeal Court a certified copy of the opinion of the High Court on the reference, including any direction as to further procedure given in accordance with section 175A(3).

Procedure on receipt of opinion of the High Court

19D.6.—(1) When the Clerk of the Sheriff Appeal Court receives the opinion of the High Court, the clerk must lay the ruling before the Sheriff Appeal Court. **B1-45.15**

(2) The Sheriff Appeal Court is then to give directions as to further procedure.

(3) The Clerk of the Sheriff Appeal Court must give every party to the appeal proceedings—

(a) notice of those directions;

(b) a copy of the opinion of the High Court.

AMENDMENTS

Chapter 19D inserted by Act of Adjournal (Criminal Procedure Rules 1996 Amendment) (No. 4) (Sheriff Appeal Court) 2015 (SSI 2015/245) para.3 (effective September 22, 2015).

[THE NEXT PARAGRAPH IS B1-45.17]

Chapter 19E

Appeals to High Court of Justiciary

Forms for appeals

19E.1.—(1) A note of appeal under section 194ZC(1) of the Act of 1995 (appeals: applications and procedure) is to be in Form 19E.1-A. **B1-45.17**

(2) The form of minutes of procedure in an appeal under section 194ZC(1) is to be in Form 19E.1-B

Lodging of appeal

19E.2.—(1) The note of appeal is to be lodged with the Clerk of the Sheriff Appeal Court within the period specified in section 194ZB(4) of the Act of 1995, unless that period is extended by the High Court in accordance with section 194ZB(5). **B1-45.18**

(2) On receipt of the note of appeal, the Clerk of the Sheriff Appeal Court must—

(a) send a copy of the note to the respondent or the respondent's solicitor;

(b) where the judgment of the Sheriff Appeal Court appealed against is not available, obtain it from the Sheriff Appeal Court.

(3) Within two weeks of receiving the note of appeal, the Clerk of the Sheriff Appeal Court must send—

(a) the note of appeal, together with the documents specified in rule 19E.3(1), to the Clerk of Justiciary;

(b) the judgment of the Sheriff Appeal Court appealed against to the appellant and respondent or their solicitors.

(4) Paragraph (3)(b) does not apply if the judgment was available when the note of appeal was lodged.

(5) The President of the Sheriff Appeal Court may, on cause shown, extend the period of two weeks specified in paragraph (3), and such an extension is to be in Form 19E.2.

Documents to be considered in determining an application for permission

19E.3.—(1) Where an application for permission is being considered and determined under section 194ZD of the Act of 1995, the following documents are specified for the purposes of section 194ZF(1)(c)(ii)— **B1-45.19**

(a) the judgment of the Sheriff Appeal Court appealed against;

(b) the minute of proceedings—

(i) in the Sheriff Appeal Court;

(ii) in the court in which the complaint was brought;

(c) a certified copy of the complaint;

(d) the appeal document;

(e) any other relevant documents sent by the clerk of court to the Clerk of the Sheriff Appeal Court under section 179(8)(b) or section 186(4)(a);

(f) any other documents that the Clerk of the Sheriff Appeal Court considers are relevant.

(2) In paragraph (1), "appeal document" means the document or documents by which the appeal to the Sheriff Appeal Court was instituted, that is in an appeal under the provision mentioned in the first column of the following table, the document or documents mentioned in the second column—

Provision	Appeal document(s)
Section 32(1) or (2)	The notice of appeal and the report mentioned in section 32(3B)(b), unless the sheriff court has determined the appeal without the report in accordance with section 32(3H)(b)
Section 175(2)(a) or (d) or (3)	The stated case
Section 175(2)(b), (c) or (cza) or (4)	The note of appeal and the report mentioned in section 186(3)(b), unless the Sheriff Appeal Court has determined the appeal without the

Provision	Appeal document(s)
	report in accordance with section 186(7)
Section 191	The bill of suspension or bill of advocation

(3) Where an application for permission is being considered and determined under section 194ZE, the following documents are specified for the purposes of section 194ZF(1) (c)(ii)—
(a) the documents specified in paragraph (1);
(b) the reasons in writing given under section 194ZD(3)(a).

Solicitor entering appearance etc.

B1-45.20 **19E.4.**—(1) The solicitor for the appellant or the appellant, if unrepresented, must enter appearance within 7 days after the Clerk of Justiciary intimates that permission has been given in accordance with section 194ZF(2)(a) of the Act of 1995.
(2) Appearance is entered by lodging Form 19E.4-A with the Clerk of Justiciary.
(3) Where an appellant is represented by a solicitor who does not practise in Edinburgh, that solicitor may appoint a solicitor who practises in Edinburgh to carry out the duties of solicitor for the appellant.
(4) If there is a change in representation of an appellant, the new solicitor for the appellant or the appellant, if unrepresented, must lodge Form 19E.4-B with the Clerk of Justiciary within 7 days of that change in representation.
(5) A change in representation occurs where—
(a) an unrepresented appellant instructs a solicitor;
(b) an appellant dismisses the appellant's solicitor and—
(i) instructs another solicitor; or
(ii) intends to conduct the appeal in person.

AMENDMENTS

Rule 19E.4(1) as amended by Act of Adjournal (Criminal Procedure Rules 1996 and Act of Adjournal (Criminal Procedure Rules 1996 Amendment) (No. 4) (Sheriff Appeal Court) 2015 Amendment) (Miscellaneous) 2015 (SSI 2015/295) para.6 (effective September 1, 2015).

List of appeals

19E.5.—(1) The Clerk of Justiciary must, after consultation with the Lord Justice General or the Lord Justice-Clerk, issue a list of appeals under section194ZB of the Act of 1995 with the respective dates of hearing on the Justiciary Roll.
B1-45.21 (2) The Clerk of Justiciary must give the respective solicitors representing parties to an appeal listed in accordance with paragraph (1) at least 14 days' notice of the date fixed for the hearing of the appeal.

Intimation of determination of appeal

B1-45.22 **19E.6.** The Clerk of Justiciary must send the Clerk of the Sheriff Appeal Court a certified copy of the order under section 194ZH of the Act of 1995 disposing of an appeal under section 194ZB.

Abandonment of appeal

B1-45.23 **19E.7.**—(1) A minute of abandonment under section 194ZJ of the Act of 1995 (abandonment of appeal) is to be in Form 19E.7.
(2) When a minute of abandonment is lodged, the Clerk of Justiciary must inform the Clerk of the Sheriff Appeal Court that the appeal has been abandoned.".

AMENDMENTS

Chapter 19E inserted by Act of Adjournal (Criminal Procedure Rules 1996 Amendment) (No. 4) (Sheriff Appeal Court) 2015 (SSI 2015/245) para.3 (effective September 22, 2015).

[THE NEXT PARAGRAPH IS B1-46]

PART V

SENTENCING

Chapter 20

Sentencing

Form of sentence of death

B1-46 **20.1.** […]

AMENDMENTS

Repealed by Act of Adjournal (Criminal Procedure Rules Amendment No. 3) 1999 (SI 1999/1387) para.2(4) (effective May 19, 1999).

Detention in police custody instead of imprisonment

B1-46.1 **20.2.** […]

AMENDMENTS

Rule 20.2 repealed by Act of Adjournal (Criminal Procedure Rules Amendment No.4) (Miscellaneous) 2010 (SSI 2010/418) para.7 (effective December 13, 2010; subject to savings in para.7(3)).

Supervised release orders

20.3.—(1) An order under section 209 of the Act of 1995 (supervised release orders) shall be in Form 20.3-A. **B1-46.2**

(2) The citation of an offender to appear before a court under section 15(5) of the Prisoners and Criminal Proceedings (Scotland) Act 1993 (variation of supervised release order etc.) shall be in Form 20.3-B.

(3) The citation of an offender to appear before a court under section 18(1) of the Prisoners and Criminal Proceedings (Scotland) Act 1993 (breach of supervised release order) shall be in Form 20.3-C.

AMENDMENTS

Rule 20.3 substituted by Act of Adjournal (Criminal Procedure Rules Amendment No.2) (Miscellaneous) 2003 (SSI 2003/468) r.2. Brought into force on October 27, 2003 in accordance with art.1.

Sexual offences to which Part 2 of the Sexual Offences Act 2003 applies

20.3A.—(1) A certificate under section 92(2) of the Sexual Offences Act 2003 (certificate that an accused has been convicted of, found not guilty by reason of insanity of, or found to be under a disability and to have done the act charged against him in respect of, an offence listed in Schedule 3 to that Act) shall be in Form 20.3A-A. **B1-46.3**

(2) Subject to paragraph (3), when a certificate such as is mentioned in paragraph (1) is prepared, the accused shall be given a copy of it by the clerk of the court, together with a notice in Form 20.3A-B.

(3) If the certificate is not prepared immediately after the statement in open court but is to be prepared subsequently, the clerk of the court shall forthwith give the accused the notice required by paragraph (2) and shall in due course send a copy of the certificate to the accused.

(3A) Where sentence has been deferred in respect of an accused who has been given a notice required by paragraph (2), the clerk of the court shall, when sentence is passed, give the accused a notice in Form 20.3A-C.

(4) The clerk of the court shall retain a copy of any notices given to the accused under paragraph (3) or (3A), as the case may be and shall record on those copies the fact that notice has been so given.

(5) The record made under paragraph (4) shall be sufficient evidence of the fact recorded; and a certificate of posting sufficient evidence of the sending of a copy under paragraph (3).

AMENDMENTS

Rule 20.3A inserted by Act of Adjournal (Criminal Procedure Rules Amendment No. 5) (SI 1997/2082) (effective September 1, 1997).

Rule 20.3A substituted by Act of Adjournal (Criminal Procedure Rules Amendment No.2) (Sexual Offences Act 2003) 2004 (SSI 2004/206) r.2 (effective May 1, 2004).

Rule 20.3A(3A) inserted, and r.20.3A(4) as amended, by Act of Adjournal (Criminal Procedure Rules Amendment No. 4) (Miscellaneous) 2006 (SSI 2006/436) r.2 (effective September 1, 2006).

Application of money found on offender towards fine

20.4.—(1) A direction under section 212(1) of the Act of 1995 that money found on an offender should not be applied towards payment of a fine shall be in Form 20.4-A. **B1-46.4**

(2) A notice for the purposes of section 212(7) of the Act of 1995 (notice to governor of prison as warrant to convey offender to court) shall be in Form 20.4-B.

Extension of time for payment of fine

20.5. An order under section 214(7) or 215(3) of the Act of 1995 (order allowing further time for payment of fine) shall be in Form 20.5. **B1-46.5**

Forms for enquiry for non-payment of fine

20.6.—(1) The citation of an offender issued under section 216(3)(a) of the Act of 1995 (citation to appear for enquiry before imprisonment in default of payment of fine) shall be in Form 20.6-A. **B1-46.6**

(2) The execution of a citation referred to in paragraph (1) which is served other than by post shall be in Form 20.6-B.

(3) The—

(a) execution of a citation referred to in paragraph (1) which is served by post,

(b) warrant for apprehension of an offender issued under section 216(3)(b) of the Act of 1995, and

(c) record of proceedings at an enquiry under section 216 of that Act, shall be in Form 20.6-C.

Supervision of payment of fine

20.7. A notice to be sent to an offender under section 217(7) of the Act of 1995 (appointment of different supervising officer to offender allowed time to pay fine) shall be in Form 20.7. **B1-46.7**

Forms of warrant for execution and charge for payment of fine or other financial penalty

20.8.—(1) In every extract of a sentence of a fine or other financial penalty, there shall be included a warrant for execution in the following terms: "and the Lords *[or* sheriff *or* justice(s)] grant(s) warrant for all lawful execution hereon". **B1-46.8**

(2) The charge for payment of a fine or other financial penalty to be used by a sheriff officer under section 90 of the Debtors (Scotland) Act 1987 (provisions relating to charges for payment) shall be in Form 20.8.

Transfer of fines

B1-46.9 **20.9.**—(1) A transfer of fine order under section 222(1), and a notice of it required by section 223(1), of the Act of 1995 shall be in Form 20.9-A.

(2) A transfer of fine order made by virtue of section 222(5) of the Act of 1995, and a notice of it required by section 223(1), shall be in Form 20.9-B.

(3) Where a notice of a transfer of fine order is received by a court in Scotland, the clerk of that court shall serve by post a notice to the offender in Form 20.9-C.

Enforcement orders

B1-46.9.1 **20.9A.** An order under section 226B of the Act of 1995 (enforcement orders) shall be in Form 20.9A and the form of warrant for civil diligence granted under section 226F of that Act (powers of diligence) in respect of the order shall be in the form set out in that Form.

AMENDMENTS

Rule 20.9A inserted by Act of Adjournal (Criminal Procedure Rules Amendment) (Criminal Proceedings etc. (Reform) (Scotland) Act 2007) 2008 (SSI 2008/61) r.5 (effective March 10, 2008).

Application for release of vehicle

B1-46.9.2 **20.9AA.** An application under regulation 19(1)(b) or (c) of the Enforcement of Fines (Seizure and Disposal of Vehicles) (Scotland) Regulations 2008 (release of seized vehicle on application by offender) shall be in Form 20.9AA.

AMENDMENTS

Rule 20.9AA inserted by Act of Adjournal (Criminal Procedure Rules Amendment No. 3) (Seizure and Disposal of Vehicles) 2008 (SSI 2008/275) para.2 (effective August 15, 2008).

Application for an order for sale or disposal of a vehicle

B1-46.9.3 **20.9B.**—(1) An application for an order for sale or disposal of a vehicle under section 226D(6) of the Act of 1995 (seizure of vehicles) shall be in Form 20.9B-A and a copy shall be served on the offender by the fines enforcement officer.

(2) Where an offender objects to an application under paragraph (1) he shall, within 7 days of its receipt, lodge with the clerk of court a response in the form of numbered paragraphs which correspond to the paragraphs of that application.

(3) The court may fix a diet for hearing an application mentioned in paragraph (1) and any response lodged under paragraph (2) in relation to the application.

(4) Where the court fixes a diet under paragraph (3) the clerk of court shall intimate the diet to the offender and the applicant.

(5) An order under section 226D(6) of the Act of 1995 shall be in Form 20.9B-B.

AMENDMENTS

Rule 20.9B inserted by Act of Adjournal (Criminal Procedure Rules Amendment) (Criminal Proceedings etc. (Reform) (Scotland) Act 2007) 2008 (SSI 2008/61) r.5 (effective March 10, 2008).

Application by a third party claiming to own vehicle

B1-46.9.4 **20.9C.**—(1) An application to a sheriff under section 226D(7)(b)(ii) of the Act of 1995 by a third party who claims to own the vehicle shall be in Form 20.9C.

(2) The court may fix a diet for hearing an application mentioned in paragraph (1).

(3) Where the court fixes a diet under paragraph (2) the clerk of court shall intimate—

(a) the application and the diet to—

(i) the offender subject to the enforcement order in terms of which the vehicle seizure order was made;

(ii) any other person from whose possession the vehicle was taken;

(iii) the relevant fines enforcement officer; and

(b) the diet to the applicant.

AMENDMENTS

Rule 20.9C inserted by Act of Adjournal (Criminal Procedure Rules Amendment) (Criminal Proceedings etc. (Reform) (Scotland) Act 2007) 2008 (SSI 2008/61) r.5 (effective March 10, 2008).

Review of actions of fines enforcement officer

B1-46.9.5 **20.9D.**—(1) An application for review under section 226H of the Act of 1995 (review of actions of FEO) shall be in Form 20.9D.

(2) The court may fix a diet for hearing an application mentioned in paragraph (1).

(3) Where the court fixes a diet under paragraph (2) it shall intimate—

(a) the application and the diet to the relevant fines enforcement officer; and

(b) the diet to the applicant.

AMENDMENTS

Rule 20.9D inserted by Act of Adjournal (Criminal Procedure Rules Amendment) (Criminal Proceedings etc. (Reform) (Scotland) Act 2007) 2008 (SSI 2008/61) r.5 (effective March 10, 2008).

[THE NEXT PARAGRAPH IS B1-46.10]

Probation orders

20.10. [...] B1-46.10

AMENDMENTS

Rule 20.10 as amended by Act of Adjournal (Criminal Procedure Rules Amendment No.2) (Miscellaneous) 2003 (SSI 2003/468) r.2. Brought into force on October 27, 2003 in accordance with art.1.

Rule 20.10 repealed by Act of Adjournal (Criminal Procedure Rules Amendment No.4) (Miscellaneous) 2010 (SSI 2010/418) para.2 (effective February 1, 2011; subject to savings in para.2(8)).

Form and notification of non-harassment order

20.10A.—(1) A non-harassment order made under section 234A of the Act of 1995 shall be in Form 20.10A. B1-46.11

(2) A non-harassment order mentioned in paragraph (1) above shall be intimated by the clerk of the court, by which it is made to any person, other than the offender, who is named in the order.

Variation or revocation of non-harassment order

20.10B.—(1) This rule applies to an application under section 234(6) of the Act of 1995 (application for variation or revocation of non-harassment order). B1-46.12

(2) In this rule—

"the offender" means the offender subject to the order to which the application relates; and

"the prosecutor" means the prosecutor at whose instance the order was made.

(3) The application shall—

(a) identify the proceedings in which the order was made;

(b) state the reasons for which the applicant seeks the variation or revocation of the order;

(c) be, as nearly as may be, in Form 20.10B.

(4) The applicant shall serve a copy of the application on—

(a) the clerk of the court which made the order;

(b) any person, other than the offender, who is named in the order; and

(c) where the applicant is—

(i) the offender, the prosecutor; and

(ii) the prosecutor, the offender,

but the application may proceed notwithstanding that, having taken reasonable steps to do so, the applicant has been unable to effect service of it on the offender or any person such as is mentioned in subparagraph (b) above.

(5) Where the offender is the applicant, the prosecutor shall, within fourteen days of the receipt of the copy of the application, notify the clerk of court in writing whether he intends to oppose the application.

(6) Where the prosecutor is the applicant, the offender shall, within fourteen days of receipt of the copy of the application, notify the clerk of court in writing whether he intends to oppose the application.

(7) Where a person notifies the clerk of court under paragraph (5) or (6) above that he does not intend to oppose the application, or fails to make any notification, the court shall proceed to dispose of the application and may do so in the absence of the applicant.

(8) Where a person notifies the clerk of court under paragraph (5) or (6) above that he does intend to oppose the application, the clerk of court shall arrange a hearing before the court at which the prosecutor and the offender may appear or be represented.

(9) The clerk of court shall give notice in writing of the decision of the court on the application to—

(a) the applicant;

(b) any person served with a copy of the application under sub-paragraph (b) or (c) of paragraph (4) above.

Supervised attendance orders

20.11. [...] B1-46.13

AMENDMENTS

Rule 20.11 substituted by Act of Adjournal (Criminal Procedure Rules Amendment No.2) (Miscellaneous) 2003 (SSI 2003/468), r.2. Brought into force on October 27, 2003 in accordance with art.1.

Rule 20.11 repealed by Act of Adjournal (Criminal Procedure Rules Amendment No.4) (Miscellaneous) 2010 (SSI 2010/418) para.2 (effective February 1, 2011; subject to savings in para.2(8)).

Community service orders

20.12. [...] B1-46.14

AMENDMENTS

Rule 20.12 repealed by Act of Adjournal (Criminal Procedure Rules Amendment No.4) (Miscellaneous) 2010 (SSI 2010/418) para.2 (effective February 1, 2011; subject to savings in para.2(8)).

Restriction of liberty orders

B1-46.15 **20.12A.**—(1) A restriction of liberty order made under section 245A(1) of the Act of 1995 shall be in form 20.12A-A.

(2) An application under section 245E(1) (application to review a restriction of liberty order) of that Act shall be in form 20.12A-B.

(3) The citation of an offender under section 245E(3) (citation to appear before a court which proposes to vary or revoke a restriction of liberty order) of that Act shall be in form 20.12A-C.

(4) The citation of an offender under section 245F(1) (citation for failure to comply with requirement of restriction of liberty order) of that Act shall be in form 20.12A-D.

AMENDMENTS

Rule 20.12A inserted by Act of Adjournal (Criminal Procedure Rules Amendment) (Restriction of Liberty Orders) 1998 (SI 1998/1842) (effective August 17, 1998).

Drug treatment and testing orders

B1-46.16 **20.12B.**—(1) A drug treatment and testing order made under section 234B of the Act of 1995 shall be in Form 20.12B-A.

(2) The citation of an offender to appear before a court under section 234E(2) of the Act of 1995 (variation or revocation of drug treatment and testing order) shall be in Form 20.12B-B.

(3) The citation of an offender to appear before a court under section 234G(1) of the Act of 1995 (breach of drug testing and treatment order) shall be in Form 20.12B-C.

AMENDMENT

Rule 20.12B inserted by the Act of Adjournal (Criminal Procedure Rules Amendment No. 4) (Drug Treatment and Testing Orders) 1999 (SSI 1999/191), para.2 (effective December 20, 1999).

Rule 20.12B substituted by Act of Adjournal (Criminal Procedure Rules Amendment No.2) (Miscellaneous) 2003 (SSI 2003/468), r.2. Brought into force on October 27, 2003 in accordance with art.1.

Community reparation orders

B1-46.16.1 **20.12C.** […]

AMENDMENTS

Rule 20.12C inserted by Act of Adjournal (Criminal Procedure Rules Amendment No.2) (Miscellaneous) 2005 (SSI 2005/160) r.2 (effective March 31, 2005).

Rule 20.12C repealed by Act of Adjournal (Criminal Procedure Rules Amendment No.4) (Miscellaneous) 2010 (SSI 2010/418) para.2 (effective February 1, 2011; subject to savings in para.2(8)).

[THE NEXT PARAGRAPH IS B1-46.17]

Terms of compensation orders in record of proceedings

B1-46.17 **20.13.** Entries shall be made in the record of proceedings by the clerk of court on the making of a compensation order, specifying the terms of the order and in particular—

(a) the name of the convicted person required to pay compensation;
(b) the amount of compensation required to be paid by such person;
(c) the name of the person entitled to the compensation payable; and
(d) where there is more than one person entitled to compensation, the amount of compensation each is entitled to and the priority, if any, among those persons for payment.

Legal disability of person entitled to compensation

B1-46.18 **20.14.**—(1) The prosecutor, if he knows that any person entitled to payment of compensation under a compensation order is under any legal disability, shall so inform the court immediately it makes any such order in respect of any such person, and that information shall be entered by the clerk of court in the record of proceedings.

(2) Where payment of any sum is made under a compensation order to the clerk of court in respect of a person known to be under a legal disability, Part IV (except rule 36.17(1) (receipt sufficient discharge)) of Chapter 36 of the Ordinary Cause Rules 1993 in Schedule 1 to the Sheriff Courts (Scotland) Act 1907 (management of damages payable to persons under legal disability) shall apply to the administration of that sum as they apply to the administration of a sum of money paid into court in respect of damages for such a person.

Variation of compensation orders

B1-46.19 **20.15.**—(1) The court may, at any time before a compensation order is fully complied with, and after such further inquiry as the court may order, vary the terms of the order as it thinks fit.

(2) A variation made under paragraph (1) may be made in chambers and in the absence of the parties or any of them.

GENERAL NOTE

B1-46.19.1 Rule 22.15 shall apply in solemn proceedings which commenced after April 1, 2006, and in which there is a vulnerable witness within the meaning of s.271(1)(b) of the Criminal Procedure (Scotland) Act 1995, with proceedings being taken to have commenced when a report of the case has been received by the procurator fiscal (Act of Adjournal (Criminal Procedure Rules Amendment) (Animal Health and

Welfare etc.) 2007 (SSI 2007/238)).

[THE NEXT PARAGRAPH IS B1-46.20]

Discharge or reduction of compensation order

20.16.—(1) An application to discharge a compensation order or to reduce the amount that remains to be paid under section 251(1) of the Act of 1995 (review of compensation order) shall be made in writing to the clerk of the court which made the order. **B1-46.20**

(2) The clerk of court shall, on any such application being made to him, serve a copy of the application on the prosecutor by post.

(3) The court to which the application is made may dispose of the application after such inquiry as it thinks fit.

Use of certified copy documents in certain proceedings

20.17.—(1) Subject to paragraph (2), in proceedings relating to— **B1-46.21**

(a) an order which imposed a fine; or

(f) a community payback order,

in a court other than the court which made the order, the principal indictment, complaint, record or minute of proceedings, or notice of previous convictions need not be before the court.

(2) The court to which paragraph (1) applies shall have before it a copy of the principal of each of such documents certified as a true copy by the clerk of the court which made the order.

AMENDMENTS

Rule 20.17 as amended by Act of Adjournal (Criminal Procedure Rules Amendment No.2) (Miscellaneous) 2005 (SSI 2005/160) para.2 (effective March 31, 2005).

Rule 20.17 as amended by Act of Adjournal (Criminal Procedure Rules Amendment No.4) (Miscellaneous) 2010 (SSI 2010/418) para.2 (effective February 1, 2011; subject to savings in para.2(8)), as amended by SSI 2011/21.

Form of extract of sentence

20.18.—(1) An extract of a custodial sentence following a conviction on indictment, and warrant of detention and return of sentence, required for any purpose in connection with any case shall be in Form 20.18-A. **B1-46.22**

(2) An extract of a sentence of imprisonment, a fine or caution in summary proceedings under the Act of 1995 shall be in the appropriate form in Form 20.18-B.

(3) An extract issued in accordance with paragraph (1) or (2) shall be warrant and authority for execution.

Reduction of disqualification period for drink-drive offenders

20.19.—(1) In this rule— **B1-46.23**

"the Act of 1988" means the Road Traffic Offenders Act 1988;
"course provider" has the meaning assigned in section 34C(3) of the Act of 1988;
"relevant date" means the date specified in an order under section 34A of the Act of 1988;
"supervising court" has the meaning assigned in section 34C(3) of the Act of 1988.

(2) An application to the supervising court for a declaration under section 34B(6) of the Act of 1988 shall be—

(a) in Form 20.19-A;

(b) accompanied by a copy of the written notice required by section 34B(5) of the Act of 1988 intimating the course provider's decision not to give a course completion certificate; and

(c) lodged with the clerk of court within 28 days after the relevant date.

(3) An application to the supervising court for a declaration under section 34B(8) of the Act of 1988 shall be—

(a) in Form 20.19-B; and

(b) lodged with the clerk of court within 28 days after the relevant date.

(4) On the lodging of an application under section 34B(6) or (8) of the Act of 1988—

(a) the sheriff or stipendiary magistrate, as the case may be, shall fix a date for hearing the application; and

(b) the clerk of court shall—

(i) notify the applicant of the date of hearing; and

(ii) serve a copy of the application, with notice of the hearing, on the course provider and the procurator fiscal.

AMENDMENTS

Rule 20.19 as amended by Act of Adjournal (Criminal Procedure Rules Amendment No. 3) (Miscellaneous) 2013 (SSI 2013/198) para.2 (effective 24 June 2013).

Antisocial behaviour orders

20.20. An antisocial behaviour order made under section 234AA of the Act of 1995 shall be in Form 20.20. **B1-46.24**

AMENDMENTS

Rule 20.20 inserted by Act of Adjournal (Criminal Procedure Rules Amendment No.5) (Miscellaneous) 2004 (SSI 2004/481) para.2 (effective 26 November 2004).

Orders for lifelong restriction

B1-46.25 **20.21.** An order for lifelong restriction under section 210F(1) of the Act of 1995 shall be in Form 20.21.

AMENDMENTS

Rule 20.21 inserted by Act of Adjournal (Criminal Procedure Rules Amendment No.3) (Risk Assessment Orders and Orders for Lifelong Restriction) 2006 (SSI 2006/302) para.2(6) (effective 20 June 2006).

Community payback orders

B1-46.26 **20.22**—(1) A community payback order made under section 227A or 227M of the Act of 1995 shall be in Form 20.22-A.

(2) The citation of an offender to appear before a court under section 227X(7)(a) (failure to attend progress review) of the Act of 1995 shall be in Form 20.22-B.

(3) An application under section 227Y(1) (applications to vary, revoke and discharge community payback orders) of the Act of 1995 shall be in Form 20.22-C.

(4) The citation of an offender to appear before a court under section 227ZC(2)(b) (breach of community payback order) of the Act of 1995 shall be in Form 20.22-D.

(5) The citation of an offender to appear before a court under section 227Z(13) (hearing of applications to vary, revoke and discharge community payback orders) shall be in Form 20.22-E.

AMENDMENTS

Rule 20.22 inserted by Act of Adjournal (Criminal Procedure Rules Amendment No.4) (Miscellaneous) 2010 (SSI 2010/418) para.2 (effective 1 February 2011; subject to savings in para.2(8)), as amended by SSI 2011/21.

Supervision default orders

B1-46.27 **20.23**—(1) This rule applies where paragraph 8(2) or (4) of schedule 1 to the Crime (Sentences) Act 1997 (restricted transfers from England and Wales to Scotland) applies to a transfer to Scotland.

(2) A supervision default order made under section 256AC(4)(c) of the 2003 Act (breach of supervision requirements) is to be in Form 20.23-A.

(3) An application under paragraph 10(1) of schedule 19A of the 2003 Act (amendment or revocation of supervision default order) is to be in Form 20.23-B.

(4) The citation of an offender to appear before the sheriff under the following enactments is to be in Form 20.23-C—

- (a) section 256AC(1)(a) of the 2003 Act;
- (b) section 256C(1)(a) of the 2003 Act;
- (c) paragraph 8(1)(a) of schedule 19A of the 2003 Act.

(5) The citation of an offender to appear before the sheriff under paragraph 10(5) of schedule 19A of the 2003 Act (amendment or revocation of supervision default order: hearing) is to be in Form 20.23-D.

(6) In this rule, "the 2003 Act" means the Criminal Justice Act 2003.

AMENDMENTS

Rule 20.23 inserted by Act of Adjournal (Criminal Procedure Rules 1996 Amendment) (No.3) (Supervision Default Orders) 2016 (SSI 2016/300) para.2 (effective 31 October 2016).

Rule 20.23 as amended by Act of Adjournal (Criminal Procedure Rules 1996 Amendment) (Miscellaneous) 2017 (SSI 2017/144) para.2(3) (effective 29 May 2017).

[THE NEXT PARAGRAPH IS B1-47]

GENERAL NOTE

B1-47 Chapter 20 is largely administrative in character in that it provides merely for the appropriate forms which are to be employed by clerks of court at the sentencing stage for different disposals and for consequential matters. Certain provisions should, however, be noted.

Rule 20.2

Section 206(2) provides that where a court of summary jurisdiction has power to impose imprisonment on an offender, it may sentence the offender to be detained in a police cell for a period not exceeding four days as an alternative to imprisonment since s.206(1) provides that no person shall be sentenced to imprisonment by a court of summary jurisdiction for a period of less than five days.

Rule 20.3A

Part I of the Sex Offenders Act 1997 requires persons who are convicted of certain sexual offences to notify their names and addresses to the police. Section 5 provides that where the court before whom an accused is convicted of a sexual offence states and certifies that the offender has been convicted of a sexual offence to which Pt I applies, the certificate granted by the court shall be evidence of that conviction (and therefore of the accused's liability to comply with the notification requirements). The relevant sexual offences are set out in Sch.1 to the 1997 Act (s. 1(9)). It has been held that indecent exposure is a form of shameless indecency (which is listed as a relevant sexual offence in Sch.1) and so is an offence in respect of which the convicting court is entitled to grant a certificate (see *Lees, Petitioner*, 1998 S.C.C.R. 401).

Rule 20.8

Any sentence for any fine pronounced by a sheriff court or a district court may be enforced against the person or effects of any party against whom the sentence was awarded (a) in the district where the sentence or decree was pronounced or (b) in any other district (see s.211(3) of the 1995 Act). The word "or" is conjunctive and the provision does not set out mutually exclusive alternatives. The effect of the warrant which is added to the finding of the court imposing the fine is (under s.221(1)) to authorise the charging of the accused to pay the fine within the period specified in the charge and, in the event of his failure to make such payment within that period, the execution of an earnings arrestment and the poinding of articles belonging to him and, if necessary for the purpose of executing the poinding, the opening of shut and lockfast places. The warrant also has the separate effect of authorising an arrestment other than an arrestment of earnings in the hands of his employer.

Rule 20.10

Section 232(2) of the 1995 Act provides that if it is proved to the satisfaction of the court—for which purpose the evidence of one witness shall be sufficient (s.232(3))—that a probationer has failed to comply with a requirement of his probation order, the court may do one or other of four things: (a) fine the probationer (except where compensation was the requirement which was breached); (b) "sentence the offender for the offence for which the order was made"; (c) vary the requirements of the probation order; or (d) make a community service order in tandem with the probation order. When the court finds that the accused has breached his probation order, the court must proceed to sentence the accused for the original offence in respect of which the probation order had been made and not for the failure to comply with the requirements of the probation order. Thus, the court is obliged by s.210(1) of the 1995 Act to have regard to any period of time spent by the probationer on remand awaiting trial or sentence for the original offence (*Wereszcznski v Procurator Fiscal, Dundee* [2006] HCJAC 58 (Unreported, July 18, 2006), para.11).

Rule 20.10A

Section 234A of the 1995 Act was inserted by s.11 of the Protection from Harassment Act 1997 (c.40) which was brought into force on June 16, 1997. Section 234A(1) provides that where a person is convicted of an offence involving harassment of a person (whether on indictment or on summary complaint), the Crown may apply to the court to make a non-harassment order against the accused. The order shall require him to refrain from such conduct in relation to the victim as may be specified in the order for such period (which includes an indeterminate (i.e. life) period) as may be so specified, at the same time as passing any other sentence. The court can only make such an order if it is satisfied on a balance of probabilities that it is appropriate to do so (s.234A(8)). The order—including any variation or revocation of it (see r. 20.10B)—can be appealed as if it were a sentence.

The 1997 Act also gives civil courts the power to make a non-harassment order when an action of harassment is pursued by the victim (see s.8(5)(b)(ii)). It is essential before a non-harassment order can competently be made that the accused has been convicted of an offence which in itself involves at least two occasions of conduct which amounts to harassment (*McGlennan v McKinnon*, 1998 S.L.T. 494) but presumably the conduct does not require to be the same on each occasion. Section 8 creates an arguably new private law right to be "free from harassment" and provides that a person must not pursue a course of conduct which amounts to harassment of another and (a) is intended to amount to harassment *or* (b) occurs in circumstances where it would appear to a reasonable person that it would amount to harassment (see s.8(1)). Section 8(3) expressly includes speech as prohibited conduct and declares that harassment includes causing the victim alarm and distress. It is essential before a nonharassment order can competently be made that the prohibited conduct be established as having occurred on at least two occasions but presumably the conduct would not require to be the same on each occasion. Threatening words on one occasion and physical gestures on the other will suffice.

It should be noted that s.234A does not specifically require corroboration no doubt on the view that since the conviction will have proceeded on corroborated evidence, that provision would be redundant. However, it is conceivable that the accused could be convicted of breach of the peace involving two occasions, only one of which is corroborated: the uncorroborated incident would not be deleted from the libel as it would be narrative not requiring corroboration (see *Yates v HM Advocate*, 1977 S.L.T. (Notes) 42). It remains to be seen whether that conviction will be sufficient to bring s.234A into operation.

Breach of a non-harassment order is a criminal offence punishable on indictment by up to five years' imprisonment and/or an unlimited fine, or on summary complaint by up to six months' imprisonment and/or a fine not exceeding the statutory maximum (s.234A(4)). The Crown is permitted to appeal the refusal of its application for an order, although no rule prescribes the form which such an appeal should take. It is suggested that it would be perfectly appropriate, therefore, for the Crown to appeal by bill of advocation. However, it seems likely that where a non-harassment order is made on terms which the

Crown consider to be unduly lenient, the Crown cannot appeal against the order under s. 108 because, first, s. 108 has not been amended to include specifically non-harassment orders (no doubt because they are not strictly speaking punishment) and, secondly, s.234A(3) treats variations and revocations as sentences for appeal purposes but excludes the right of the court when varying the order to increase the period for which it is to run.

Rule 20.10B

Section 234A(6) permits the prosecutor or the accused to apply to the court which made the nonharassment order to vary or revoke it though any variation cannot increase the period for which it was originally ordered to run. While an application for variation or revocation must be served on the victim, no provision is made for the victim to be present or represented at the hearing of the application (r.20.10B(8)). His or her only means of representation must therefore be through the prosecutor. The victim is, however, entitled to notice of the court's decision (r.20.10B(9)).

Rule 20.11

Section 235(2) of the 1995 Act provides that a supervised attendance order is an order which requires an offender (1) to attend a place of supervision (determined by the supervising officer appointed by the relevant local authority: s.235(8)) for such period between 10 and 50 hours (where the amount of the fine in question does not exceed level 1 of the standard scale) and (in all other cases) between 10 and 100 hours and (2) to carry out, during that period, such instructions as the supervising officer may give to the offender. Such an order can only competently be made under s.235 where (1) the offender is 16 years old or older; (2) having been convicted of an offence, the offender has had imposed on him a fine which (or any part or instalment of which) he has failed to pay; (3) the court, but for this section, would also have imposed on the offender a period of imprisonment in default of payment (whether immediately or at a future date) under s.219(1) of the 1995 Act; and (4) the court considers the order "more appropriate than the serving of or, as the case may be, the imposition of such a period of imprisonment" (s.235(4)). In short, supervised attendance orders are an alternative to custody for fine defaulters.

Schedule 7 to the 1995 Act makes further provision for supervised attendance orders (s.235(7)). Paragraph 4(2) specifies the course which the court may take in the event of the offender's failure, without reasonable excuse, to comply with any requirements imposed by the order or to notify his supervising officer of a change of address or in the offender's working times. The court may either: (a) revoke the order and imprison the offender for a maximum of (in the sheriff court) 30 days or (in the district court) 20 days; or (b) vary the number of hours specified in the order. An order, unless revoked, shall remain in force until the offender has carried out the instructions given under it for the number of hours specified in it (para. 3 (2)). These two courses are the only options open to the court. It is incompetent for the court to revoke the order and make a community service order (even though the offender consents to such community service order): *Crane, Petitioner* [2006] HCJAC 40 (para. 14).

No right of appeal is conferred on an offender who wishes to challenge the court's order made on a finding of breach of a supervised order. Where the offender wishes to challenge the competency of the court's order, the offender should present a bill of suspension; where the appropriateness of the order is challenged or it is to be argued that the order is excessive, the competent mode of review is a petition to the *nobile officium*: see *Crane* at para.7.

Rule 20.12

Note that a community service order once made by the lower court cannot be competently suspended by the lower court pending determination of an appeal under s. 193 (see *Magee, Petitioner*, 1996 S.L.T. 400).

Rule 20.12A

Sections 234A, 234E and 234F of the 1995 Act were inserted by s.5 of the Crime and Punishment (Scotland) Act 1997 (c.48). Section 245A empowers the court to make a restriction of liberty order in respect of any person aged 16 years or more where he is convicted of an offence (other than murder) if the court is of opinion that the making of such an order is the most appropriate method of disposal. Under s.245A(8) the order may restrict the accused's movements (during a period of up to 12 months (s.245A(3)) to such an extent as the court thinks fit and may include requiring the accused to be in certain places for certain periods in each day or week (for a period or periods not in total exceeding 12 hours per day) or requiring the accused not to be in these specified places for certain periods. Section 245E allows for such an order to be reviewed on the application (to the court which made the order) of either the accused or the person responsible for monitoring compliance with it by means of electronic "tagging". The court can change the order by extending or restricting its requirements, or extending its duration, or can revoke the order (s.245E(2)(a), (b)). Section 245F provides for breach of the requirements of the order being determined by the court which made the order. Where an accused is found to the court's satisfaction, to have failed to comply with any requirement of the order without reasonable excuse, the court can fine the accused without prejudice to the continuation of the order (s.245F(2)(a)). If the accused is fined (the fine being limited to level 3 on the standard scale), the court cannot vary or revoke the order. The fine is deemed to be a summary sentence for the purposes of an appeal to the High Court (s.245F(3)).

Rule 20.15

After the imposition of a compensation order it may come to the court's attention that the person to whom the compensation is payable (which is recorded in the record of proceedings when the compensation order is made: see r.20.13) has died or indeed was dead before the order was made. This rule would allow the court to take that factor into account since s.251(1) does not give the court power on the application of the accused, to discharge or reduce the compensation order. (See *Tudhope v Furphy*, 1982 S.C.C.R. 575.)

Rule 20.18

See s.198(3). In respect of r.20.18(3), see as an illustration, *Thorne v Stott*, 2000 J.C. 13 at 16E.

Rule 20.20

Section 234AA(1) of the 1995 Act provides that where certain conditions are met, the court "may, instead of or in addition to imposing any sentence which it could impose" make an antisocial behaviour order (ASBO). The conditions are: (1) the accused is convicted of an offence; (2) at the time of the offence, he was at least 12 years of age; (3) in committing the offence, he "engaged in antisocial behaviour" (which is defined in s.234AA(3)); and (4) the court is satisfied, on the balance of probabilities, that the making of an ASBO is "necessary for the purpose of protecting other persons from further antisocial behaviour by the offender" (s.234AA(2)).

The accused is held to engage in antisocial behaviour if he *either* acts in a manner that causes or is likely to cause alarm and distress *or* pursues a course of conduct that causes or is likely to cause alarm or distress; and, in either case, the alarm of distress must be to at least one person who is not of the same household as the accused (s.234AA(3)). Conduct includes speech and a course of conduct must involve conduct on at least two occasions (s.234AA(12)). These are essential provisions because they both guide the court as to whether condition (4) above is satisfied (the necessity criterion) and inform the court as to what sort of things should be prohibited. An ASBO is defined in s.234AA(4) as "an order which prohibits, indefinitely or for such period as may be specified in the order, the offender from doing anything described in the order". The prohibitions which may be imposed in an ASBO are those which reflect the necessity criterion in condition (4) above: they must be "necessary for the purpose of protecting other persons from further antisocial behaviour" by the accused (s.234AA(5)).

Before making an ASBO the court must explain to the accused "in ordinary language" the effect of the order and its prohibitions, the consequences for him of breaching the order, the power of the court to revoke or vary the order at the accused's request (under s.234AA(8)) and the accused's right to appeal against the making of the order. The making of an ASBO and any revocation or varying of its terms are deemed to be a sentence for the purposes of s.175(2)(b) of the 1995 Act (s.234AA(10)). However, the failure to explain the order in ordinary language shall not affect the validity of the ASBO (s.234AA(7)).

It is incompetent at one and the same time, in respect of the same charge, to defer sentence and make an ASBO (*Duncan v Spiers* [2008] HCJAC 27 (at [13]).

Rule 20.21

Section 210F(1) (which was brought into force on June 19, 2006) provides that the High Courtmay make an order for lifelong restriction (OLR) in certain circumstances. Before the High Court can make such an order it must have regard to (1) any risk assessment report, (2) any report under s.210D(2) on the assessment of risk to the public at large presented by a convicted person (who is subject to an interim hospital order) being at liberty, (3) any evidence given in respect of an accused's objection to a risk assessment (under s.210C(7)) and (4) any other information before the court. The circumstances under which an OLR can be made are that the High Court is satisfied, on balance of probabilities, that the risk criteria are met in a case where the High Court may make a compulsion order under s.57A but does not make such an order and where these criteria are met in any other case.

An OLR constitutes a sentence ofimprisonment, or detention, for an indeterminate period (s.210F(2)). The accused may, therefore, appeal against such an order (s.106(1)(ba)). The Crown may appeal against any refusal of the court to make an OLR "on the grounds that on balance of probabilities the risk criteria are met" (s.210F(3)).

An OLR can only be made after a risk assessment order has been made. A risk assessment order requires the preparation of a risk assessment report. It is on the basis of such a report that the sentencing judge can determine whether the risk criteria are met; and when the judge is so satisfied, an OLR must be made (*Johnston v HM Advocate*, 2011 S.C.C.R. 470 at [24]). It is incompetent to appeal against the sentencing judge's decision to make a risk assessment order (*Ferguson v HM Advocate* [2014] HCJAC 19 at [86]). There is no requirement for the sentencing judge to order the preparation of a criminal justice social work report although he may do so if he considers it appropriate (at [90])

The risk criteria are set out in s.210E, namely that "the nature of, or the circumstances of the commission of, the offence of which the convicted person has been found guilty either in themselves or as part of a pattern of behaviour are such as to demonstrate that there is a likelihood that he, if at liberty, will seriously endanger the lives, or physical or psychological well-being of members of the public at large". It is for the sentencing judge to determine whether there is such a likelihood; that is a question of fact; and the judge must have regard to the risk assessment report and any other information (s.210F(1)).

In *Ferguson* a bench of three judges has decided that (1) "what the judge must therefore determine before making an OLR is that it is likely (in the sense of more likely than not) that, were the offender to have been sentenced otherwise than by the imposition of an OLR, he would seriously endanger the public once at liberty" (at [95]); and (2) "that assessment is looking forward to the point at which the offender would, but for the OLR, be 'at liberty' … Thus the judge has to contemplate whether there is likely to be serious endangerment at the point in the future when, but for the imposition of an OLR, the offender might be predicted to be at liberty" (at [99]).

When the court is imposing an OLR and there are several offences on the indictment, the court should not impose separate custodial sentences to be served consecutively to the punishment part of the OLR "since the latter [order] ought to have taken full cognisance of the totality of the determinate sentences which would have been imposed on the whole indictment" (*McCluskey v HM Advocate*, 2012 S.C.C.R. 719 at [21]).

Rule 20.22

A community payback order (CPO) is an order imposing one or more of the following nine requirements: (a) an offender supervision requirement; (b) a compensation requirement; (c) an unpaid work or other activity requirement; (d) a programme requirement; (e) a residence requirement; (f) a mental health treatment requirement; (g) a drug treatment requirement; (h) an alcohol treatment requirement; and (i) a conduct requirement (s.227A(2)). It is imposed instead of imposing a sentence of imprisonment (s.227A(1)). A JP court may not make a CPO which imposes requirements (d), (f), (g) or (h) (see s.227A(5)). Imprisonment includes detention (s.227A(9)).

The CPO became available to the court on February 1, 2011 when it replaced such sentences as probation orders, community service orders and supervised attendance orders.

> "[T]he legislative intent in bringing into effect this form of sentencing disposal was to provide for community sentencing options in a package which is tailored for the particular needs and circumstances of the particular offender" (*Kirk v Brown*, 2012 S.C.C.R. 558 at [3]).

It is incompetent to make a CPO which imposes as a conduct requirement that the offender should be of good behaviour or to refrain generally from committing offences (*Kirk v Brown* at [2]).

Rule 20.23

The Offender Rehabilitation Act 2014 (c.11) amended the Criminal Justice Act 2003 (c.44) to introduce a new Sch.19A which deals with supervision default orders (SDO). On release from prison certain categories of offenders in England and Wales may be made subject to supervision requirements specified in a notice given by the Secretary of State. Where this occurs, failure by the offender to comply with these requirements may result in the making of a SDO. Since offenders who are released with supervision requirements may come to live in Scotland, the Secretary of State is empowered to transfer supervision to Scotland in respect of offenders who are either undergoing supervision or about to undergo supervision. Such a transfer is made to "an appropriate person there" (see 2003 Act Sch.19A para.4(1)).

Rule 2.3(1A) provides for the means of citation of an offender in respect of whom it is proposed that a SDO should be made, amended or revoked and that provision is replicated in r.20.23(4) and (5). When application is made to amend or revoke a SDO, the application should be in terms of Form 20.23-B stating the reasons for the application and, where amendment is sought, it should also specify the terms of the proposed amended SDO (and the amended SDO should be set out in a schedule to the application).

PART VI

EVIDENCE

Chapter 21

Uncontroversial Evidence, Hearsay and Prior Statements

Notice of uncontroversial evidence

B1-48 **21.1.**—(1) Where a party to criminal proceedings serves a copy of a statement and document on another party under section 258 of the Act of 1995 (uncontroversial evidence), he shall also serve with that statement and document a statement in Form 21.1-A.

(2) Where a document is annexed to a statement under section 258(2) of the Act of 1995 and is not described in the statement, a docquet in Form 21.1-B shall be endorsed on that document.

Notice of challenge of evidence as uncontroversial

B1-48.1 **21.2.** A notice by a party under section 258(3) of the Act of 1995 (notice challenging fact in statement under section 258(2) of the Act of 1995) shall be in Form 21.2.

Application for direction that challenge be disregarded

B1-48.1.1 **21.2A.** An application under section 258(4A) of the Act of 1995 (application for direction that challenge be disregarded) shall be in Form 21.2A.

AMENDMENTS

Rule 21.2A inserted by Act of Adjournal (Criminal Procedure Rules Amendment) (Criminal Procedure (Amendment) (Scotland) Act) 2005 (SSI 2005/44) para.2(16) (subject to para.2(2)-(4)) (effective 1 February 2005).

[THE NEXT PARAGRAPH IS B1-48.2]

Notice of intention to have hearsay statement admitted

21.3. A notice under section 259(5) of the Act of 1995 (notice of intention to apply to have evidence of hearsay statement admitted) shall be in Form 21.3. **B1-48.2**

Authentication of certain prior statements of witnesses

21.4. A statement in a document which it is sought to be admitted in evidence under section 260(4) of the Act of 1995 (admissibility of certain prior statements of witnesses) shall be authenticated by a certificate in Form 21.4 endorsed on or attached to the first page of the statement or attached to the device on which the statement has been recorded. **B1-48.3**

AMENDMENTS

Rule 21.4 as amended by Act of Adjournal (Criminal Procedure Rules Amendment No.3) (Vulnerable Witnesses (Scotland) Act 2004) 2005 (SSI 2005/188) para.2, subject to the conditions in para.2(2) (effective 1 April 2005).

Form of application to introduce evidence relating to sexual offences

21.5. An application under section 275(1) of the Act of 1995 (exception to restrictions on evidence relating to sexual offences) shall be in Form 21.5. **B1-48.4**

AMENDMENTS

Rule 21.5 inserted by Act of Adjournal (Criminal Procedure Rules Amendment No. 3) (Sexual Offences (Procedure and Evidence) (Scotland) Act 2002) 2002 (SSI 2002/454) para.2(9) (effective 1 November 2002).

Notice of intention to rely on presumption of identification

21.6—(1) A notice under section 281A(2)(a) of the Act of 1995 (notice of intention to rely on presumption of identification prior to trial) shall be in Form 21.6-A **B1-48.5**

(2) A notice under section 281A(2)(b) of the Act of 1995 (notice of intention to challenge facts in report of identification) shall be in Form 21.6-B.

AMENDMENTS

Rule 21.6 inserted by Act of Adjournal (Criminal Procedure Rules Amendment No.3) (Vulnerable Witnesses (Scotland) Act 2004) 2005 (SSI 2005/188) para.2, subject to the conditions in para.2(2) (effective 1 April 2005).

[THE NEXT PARAGRAPH IS B1-49]

GENERAL NOTE

Ch.21 applies to both solemn and summary proceedings. **B1-49**

Rules 21.1 and 21.2

Section 258 of the 1995 Act provides that where either the Crown or the defence considers that any fact is unlikely to be disputed by any other party, he can prepare *and* sign a statement specifying the facts concerned or referring to the facts as set out in the document annexed to the statement, and serve a copy of the statement and the document (where appropriate) on every party not less than 14 days before the trial diet (see subss.(1) and (2)). The facts shall be deemed to have been conclusively proved unless a notice challenging any of the facts is served by any other party not more than seven days after the date of service of the statement and the document (see subs.(3)). It is irrelevant that the evidence is not capable of being led at the trial because the relevant witness or production is not specified in the lists annexed to the indictment.

Rule 21.3

Section 259 of the 1995 Act allows for hearsay evidence to be admitted in evidence in certain circumstances (see subss.(1) and (2)). Notice of intention to apply to the court to have hearsay evidence admitted should be given in writing before the trial diet and should specify the fact(s) and the witnesses and productions to be adduced in connection with such evidence (subs.(5)). Section 262(1) of the 1995 Act adheres to the common law rule and excludes a statement which is a precognition other than a precognition on oath. The most recent and authoritative discussion of the criteria by which the court must determine whether the statement is of the nature of a precognition is provided in *HM Advocate v McSween*, 2007 S.L.T. 645

The statutory regime introduced by s.259 does not provide an optional way of introducing evidence of a person who has died. Where it is desired to lead such evidence the party relying on the evidence should comply with s.259. That section has "abrogated and replaced the common law exceptions [to the rule against hearsay evidence] which fall within its ambit" (*HM Advocate v Malloy and Stewart* [2012] HCJ 124 (opinion of bench of three judges; Unreported September 19, 2011)). In so holding, the court in Malloy and Stewart followed the decision of another bench of three judges in *HM Advocate v Clancy* unreported February 10, 1997 and Lord Matthews's decision in *HM Advocate v Parracho* IN764/08,

Unreported. Section 262(4) only preserves other types of admissible hearsay if they do not fall within the ambit of ss.259 to 261A such as statements forming part of the res gestae and statements made by an accused person (*Malloy and Stewart*, at [22]).

It is important to note that s.259(5A)(a) requires that hearsay evidence which is admissible under that provision cannot be led at trial unless notice of intention to lead the hearsay evidence is given not less than seven days before the preliminary hearing to which the accused is initially cited in the High Court (or such later time, before the trial diet, as the judge may on cause shown allow). It is not compliance with that provision to give notice seven days before a continued preliminary hearing (see *Murphy v HM Advocate*, 2012 S.C.C.R. 542 at [30]).

It has been held that the court will not determine in advance of a trial whether use by the Crown of a statement by a deceased witness (against whom there was possibly some incriminating evidence) would violate the accused's right to a fair trial under art.6(1) of the European Convention on Human Rights and that such a devolution issue had to be determined as and when the Crown sought to make use of the secondary evidence at the trial (*McKenna v HM Advocate*, 2000 J.C. 291).

Rule 21.4

Section 260(1) of the 1995 Act declares that a witness's prior statement shall be admissible if it is contained in a written document and if three conditions which are set out in subs.(2) are met—though precognitions on oath and evidence in earlier criminal or civil proceedings are excepted from these requirements and only require to be authenticated—and if it is sufficiently authenticated (see subs.(4)). The authentication should be by way of a certificate which is endorsed on or attached to the first page of the statement. (Cf. *Jamieson v HM Advocate (No.2)*, 1995 S.L.T. 666 which allowed at common law for a witness to adopt his earlier statement to the police even though he could not recall the details of it so long as he maintained that it was the truth.) Lord Osborne has questioned the precise purpose of ss.260 and 262 in the light of the ruling in *Jamieson (No.2)* (see *Hemming v HM Advocate*, 1997 S.C.C.R. 257 at 267). Section 262(1) provides that "statement" does not include a statement made in a precognition other than a precognition on oath.

Chapter 22

Evidence of Vulnerable Witnesses

Vulnerable witness notice: non-standard special measures

B1-50 **22.1.** Where a vulnerable witness notice under section 271A(2) of the Act of 1995 (vulnerable witness notice)—

(a) specifies a special measure other than a standard special measure; or
(b) seeks an order authorising the giving of evidence by the witness without the benefit of any special measure,

it shall be in Form 22.1 and shall be lodged with the clerk of court.

AMENDMENTS

Chapter 22 substituted by Act of Adjournal (Criminal Procedure Rules Amendment No.3) (Vulnerable Witnesses (Scotland) Act 2004) 2005 (SSI 2005/188) para.2, subject to the conditions in para.2(2) (effective 1 April 2005).

Rule 22.1 substituted by Act of Adjournal (Criminal Procedure Rules 1996 and Act of Adjournal (Criminal Procedure Rules 1996 Amendment) (No. 4) (Sheriff Appeal Court) 2015 Amendment) (Miscellaneous) 2015 (SSI 2015/295) para.4 (effective 1 September 2015).

Vulnerable witness notice: standard special measures

B1-50.0.1 **22.1ZA.** Where a vulnerable witness notice under section 271A(2) of the Act of 1995 (vulnerable witness notice) specifies only a standard special measure, it shall be in Form 22.1ZA and shall be lodged with the clerk of court.

AMENDMENTS

Rule 22.1ZA inserted by Act of Adjournal (Criminal Procedure Rules 1996 and Act of Adjournal (Criminal Procedure Rules 1996 Amendment) (No. 4) (Sheriff Appeal Court) 2015 Amendment) (Miscellaneous) 2015 (SSI 2015/295) para.4 (effective 1 September 2015).

[THE NEXT PARAGRAPH IS B1-50.1]

Vulnerable witness application

B1-50.1 **22.1A.** An application under section 271C(2) of the Act of 1995 (vulnerable witness application) shall be in Form 22.1A and shall be lodged with the clerk of court.

AMENDMENTS

Rule 22.1A inserted by Act of Adjournal (Criminal Procedure Rules Amendment) (Vulnerable Witnesses (Scotland) Act 2004) 2006 (SSI 2006/76) para.2(4) (effective 1 April 2006). See para.2(2) and (3) for transitional provisions.

Procedure on lodging vulnerable witness notice or vulnerable witness application

22.2.—(1) On receipt of a notice under rule 22.1 (vulnerable witness notice: non-standard special measures) or rule 22.1ZA (vulnerable witness notice: standard special measures) or application under rule 22.1A (vulnerable witness application) the clerk of court shall— **B1-50.1.1**

(a) endorse on the notice or application, as the case may be, the time and date on which it was received; and

(b) place the notice or application, as the case may be, before a judge in chambers.

(2) The party that lodges the vulnerable witness notice or vulnerable witness application, as the case may be, shall lodge a certificate of intimation with the clerk of court—

(a) within 7 days after lodging the notice or application, as the case may be; or

(b) at least 2 days before any first diet or preliminary hearing,

whichever is the earlier.

AMENDMENTS

Rule 22.2 substituted by Act of Adjournal (Criminal Procedure Rules Amendment) (Vulnerable Witnesses (Scotland) Act 2004) 2006 (SSI 2006/76) para.2(5) (effective 1 April 2006). See para.2(2) and (3) for transitional provisions.

Rule 22.2 as amended by Act of Adjournal (Criminal Procedure Rules 1996 and Act of Adjournal (Criminal Procedure Rules 1996 Amendment) (No. 4) (Sheriff Appeal Court) 2015 Amendment) (Miscellaneous) 2015 (SSI 2015/295) para.4 (effective 1 September 2015).

Objections to special measures

22.2A.—(1) An objection notice under section 271A(4A) or 271C(4A) of the Act of 1995 (objections to special measures) shall be in Form 22.2A and shall be lodged with the clerk of court. **B1-50.1.2**

(2) On receipt of an objection notice mentioned in paragraph (1)—

(a) the clerk of court shall endorse the time and date on which it is received;

(b) the court shall make an order under section 271A(5A) or 271C(5A) of the Act of 1995; and

(c) the court shall order intimation of the hearing to be made to the parties.

(3) The party that lodges the objection notice shall lodge a certificate of intimation with the clerk of court—

(a) within 7 days after lodging the notice; or

(b) where a diet mentioned in paragraph (4) has been fixed, at least 2 days before that diet,

whichever is earlier.

(4) The diets are—

(a) a first diet;

(b) a preliminary hearing; or

(c) a diet appointed in terms of section 271A(5A)(c) or 271C(5A)(c) of the Act of 1995.

AMENDMENTS

Rule 22.2A inserted by Act of Adjournal (Criminal Procedure Rules 1996 and Act of Adjournal (Criminal Procedure Rules 1996 Amendment) (No. 4) (Sheriff Appeal Court) 2015 Amendment) (Miscellaneous) 2015 (SSI 2015/295) para.4 (effective 1 September 2015).

[THE NEXT PARAGRAPH IS B1-50.2]

Intimation of an order under section 271A

22.3.—(1) An order— **B1-50.2**

(a) under section 271A(5)(a) of the Act of 1995 authorising the use of a special measure;

(b) under section 271A(5)(b) of that Act authorising the giving of evidence without the benefit of any special measures;

(c) appointing a vulnerable witness notice to be disposed of—

(i) under section 271A(5A)(a) of that Act, at a preliminary hearing; or

(ii) under section 271A(5A)(b) of that Act, at a first diet; or

(d) under section 271A(5A)(c) or (7)(b)(ii) of that Act, appointing a diet to be held before the trial diet; or

(e) under section 271A(9) of that Act (order in relation to special measures after hearing),

may be signed by the clerk of court.

(2) An order mentioned in paragraph (1) shall be intimated by the clerk of court to all parties, unless the party was present at the hearing at which the order was made, and in the case of an order under paragraph (1)(c) or (d), to the governor of any institution in which the accused is detained.

AMENDMENTS

Rule 22.3(1)(c) as amended by Act of Adjournal (Criminal Procedure Rules 1996 and Act of Adjournal (Criminal Procedure Rules 1996 Amendment) (No. 4) (Sheriff Appeal Court) 2015 Amendment) (Miscellaneous) 2015 (SSI 2015/295) para.4 (effective 1 September 2015).

Intimation of an order under section 271C

22.3A.—(1) An order— **B1-50.2.1**

(a) under section 271C(5)(a) of the Act of 1995 authorising the use of a special measure;

(b) appointing a vulnerable witness application to be disposed of—

(i) under section 271C(5A)(a) of that Act, at a preliminary hearing; or
(ii) under section 271C(5A)(b) of that Act at a first diet;
(c) under section 271C(5A)(c) of that Act, appointing a diet to be held before the trial diet; or
(d) under section 271C(7) of that Act (order in relation to special measure after hearing),
may be signed by the clerk of court.

(2) An order mentioned in paragraph (1) shall be intimated by the clerk of court to all parties, unless the party was present at the hearing at which the order was made and, in the case of an order under paragraph (1)(b) or (c), to the governor of any institution in which the accused is detained.

AMENDMENT

Rule 22.3A inserted by (effective 1 April 2006). See para.2(2) and (3) for transitional provisions.

[THE NEXT PARAGRAPH IS B1-50.3]

Review of arrangements for vulnerable witnesses

B1-50.3 **22.4.**—(1) An application under section 271D(1)(a) of the Act of 1995 (review of arrangements for vulnerable witnesses) may be made—
(a) orally; or
(b) in writing by minute in Form 22.4.

(2) A minute under paragraph (1)(b) shall be lodged with the clerk of the court.

AMENDMENT

To be read with the transitional provisions contained in the Act of Adjournal (Criminal Procedure Rules Amendment) (Vulnerable Witnesses (Scotland) Act 2004) 2006 (SSI 2006/76), para.2(2) and (3) (effective 1 April 2006).

Rule 22.4(2) as amended by the Act of Adjournal (Criminal Procedure Rules 1996 Amendment) (Miscellaneous) 2020 (SSI 2020/27) r. 2(2)(a) (effective 2 March 2020).

Procedure for review

B1-50.4 **22.5.** On receipt of a minute under rule 22.4(1)(b) (minute for review of arrangements for vulnerable witnesses) or on a review on the court's own motion, the court, after giving the parties an opportunity to be heard by making written submissions within such period as specified by the court, may—
(a) consider and determine the review without a hearing; or
(b) make an order, endorsed on the minute or recorded in the minute of proceedings,
fixing a diet for a hearing of the application and for intimation by the clerk of court of the date of the diet to all parties.

AMENDMENT

To be read with the transitional provisions contained in the Act of Adjournal (Criminal Procedure Rules Amendment) (Vulnerable Witnesses (Scotland) Act 2004) 2006 (SSI 2006/76), para.2(2) and (3) (effective 1 April 2006).

Rule 22.5 as substituted by Act of Adjournal (Criminal Procedure Rules 1996 Amendment) (Miscellaneous) 2020 (SSI 2020/27) para.2 (effective 2 March 2020).

Intimation of the order

B1-50.5 **22.6.** Where an order under section 271D(2) of the Act of 1995 (order after review of arrangements for vulnerable witnesses) is made under rule 22.5 (procedure for review) it shall be intimated by the clerk of court to all parties unless the party was present at a hearing at which the order was made.

AMENDMENT

To be read with the transitional provisions contained in the Act of Adjournal (Criminal Procedure Rules Amendment) (Vulnerable Witnesses (Scotland) Act 2004) 2006 (SSI 2006/76), para.2(2) and (3) (effective 1 April 2006).

Rule 22.6 as amended by Act of Adjournal (Criminal Procedure Rules 1996 Amendment) (Miscellaneous) 2020 (SSI 2020/27) para.2 (effective 2 March 2020).

Notice of prohibition of personal conduct of defence

B1-50.6 **22.7.** In proceedings to which section 288E of the Act of 1995 (prohibition of personal conduct of defence in certain cases involving child witnesses under the age of 12) applies, a notice in Form 22.7 shall be served on the accused by the prosecutor with any vulnerable witness notice, unless a notice in Form 8.2-C has already been served.

AMENDMENTS

Rule 22.7 as amended by Act of Adjournal (Criminal Procedure Rules 1996 and Act of Adjournal (Criminal Procedure Rules 1996 Amendment) (No. 4) (Sheriff Appeal Court) 2015 Amendment) (Miscellaneous) 2015 (SSI 2015/295) para.4 (effective 1 September 2015).

Application for prohibition of personal conduct of defence

B1-50.7 **22.8.**—(1) An application under section 288F(2)(a) of the Act of 1995 (prohibition of personal conduct of defence) shall be made by minute in Form 22.8-A.

(2) The minute shall be lodged with the clerk of court and served on all parties by the minuter.

(3) On receipt of a minute under paragraph (1), or on the court's own motion, the court shall make an order endorsed on the minute or recorded in the minute of proceedings—

(a) fixing a diet for a hearing of the application or to hear parties; and
(b) for service of the minute or order with the date on all parties and to the governor of any institution in which the accused is detained.

(4) Where a party is not represented or personally present at a hearing under paragraph (3) when an order is made under section 288F of the Act of 1995 (order prohibiting personal conduct of defence) the clerk of court shall intimate the order to that party.

(5) On the making of an order under section 288F of the Act of 1995 in the absence of the accused, the prosecutor shall forthwith serve on the accused a notice in Form 22.8-B.

AMENDMENT

To be read with the transitional provisions contained in the Act of Adjournal (Criminal Procedure Rules Amendment) (Vulnerable Witnesses (Scotland) Act 2004) 2006 (SSI 2006/76) para.2(2) and (3) (effective 1 April 2006).

Transfer of cases

22.9.—(1) This rule applies where the sheriff or justice of the peace makes an order under— **B1-50.8**

(a) section 271J(4) of the Act of 1995 (live television link: transfer of proceedings); or
(b) section 271K(3) of the Act of 1995 (screens: transfer of proceedings).

(2) When an order is made, the clerk of court must transmit to the clerk of the court to which the proceedings are transferred—

(a) the record copy of the indictment or complaint;
(b) the minute of proceedings;
(c) any productions;
(d) any relevant documents.

AMENDMENT

To be read with the transitional provisions contained in the Act of Adjournal (Criminal Procedure Rules Amendment) (Vulnerable Witnesses (Scotland) Act 2004) 2006 (SSI 2006/76) para.2(2) and (3) (effective 1 April 2006).

Rule 22.9 substituted by Act of Adjournal (Criminal Procedure Rules 1996 Amendment) (No.6) (Special Measures in the Justice of the Peace Court) 2015 (SSI 2015/443) para.2 (effective 23 December 2015).

Evidence in chief in form of prior statement

22.10. [...] **B1-50.9**

AMENDMENT

Rule 22.10 repealed by Act of Adjournal (Criminal Procedure Rules 1996 Amendment) (Miscellaneous) 2020 (SSI 2020/27) para.2 (effective 2 March 2020).

Appointment of commissioner

22.11.—(1) On making an order under section 271A(5) or (9) of the Act of 1995 (order in relation to special measures) authorising the taking of evidence by a commissioner in accordance with section 271I of that Act, the High Court, the sheriff or the justice of the peace, as the case may be, shall appoint— **B1-50.10**

(a) a commissioner to take the evidence of the vulnerable witness; and
(b) a clerk to assist the commissioner in the carrying out of his duties,

and shall dispense with interrogatories.

(2) On the appointment of a commissioner under paragraph (1), the clerk of court shall send the order to the commissioner or his clerk with such other relative documents as the court may direct.

(3) On sending the order to the commissioner or his clerk under paragraph (2), the clerk of court shall note on the record copy of the indictment or in the minute of proceedings—

(a) the order and the documents sent;
(b) the names of the persons to whom the order and documents were sent;
(c) the date on which the order and documents were sent.

AMENDMENTS

Rule 22.11 inserted by Act of Adjournal (Criminal Procedure Rules Amendment No.6) (Vulnerable Witnesses (Scotland) Act 2004) (Evidence on Commission) 2005 (SSI 2005/574) para.2(3) (effective 30 November 2005).

To be read with the transitional provisions contained in the Act of Adjournal (Criminal Procedure Rules Amendment) (Vulnerable Witnesses (Scotland) Act 2004) 2006 (SSI 2006/76) para.2(2) and (3) (effective 1 April 2006).

Rule 22.11 as amended by Act of Adjournal (Criminal Procedure Rules 1996 Amendment) (No.6) (Special Measures in the Justice of the Peace Court) 2015 (SSI 2015/443) para.2 (effective 23 December 2015).

The commission

B1-50.11 **22.12.**—(1) The commissioner shall, on receiving the order and documents mentioned in rule 22.11(2) (appointment of commissioner), determine the place and date of the diet for the taking the evidence of the witness to whom the order of the court relates, and shall give reasonable notice of those matters to all parties.

(2) The commissioner may vary or revoke his determination or adjourn the taking of the evidence of the witness to such other place, at such other date and time, as he may determine.

(3) If, in the course of the examination of a witness under this rule, any question arises as to the admissibility of any evidence, the commissioner, unless a judge or sheriff of the relevant court, shall not determine any such question but shall allow the evidence subject to all questions of competency and relevancy.

AMENDMENTS

Rule 22.12 inserted by Act of Adjournal (Criminal Procedure Rules Amendment No.6) (Vulnerable Witnesses (Scotland) Act 2004) (Evidence on Commission) 2005 (SSI 2005/574) para.2(3) (effective 30 November 2005).

To be read with the transitional provisions contained in the Act of Adjournal (Criminal Procedure Rules Amendment) (Vulnerable Witnesses (Scotland) Act 2004) 2006 (SSI 2006/76) para.2(2) and (3) (effective 1 April 2006).

Video recording of commission

B1-50.12 **22.13.**—(1) On the carrying out of his commission in accordance with the terms of the order appointing him, or otherwise on concluding his commission, the commissioner or his clerk shall cause the tape or disc of the video recording of the commission to be sealed in an envelope or other similar container, which the commissioner shall sign and date, and on which the following information shall be endorsed—

(a) the name of the accused;
(b) the prosecution and court reference numbers; and
(c) the time of commencement and of termination of the tape or disc;

which sealed envelope shall be returned, with the relative documents, to the clerk of court.

(2) On the video recording and any documents being returned to him, the clerk of court shall—

(a) note—
  (i) the documents returned;
  (ii) by whom the documents were returned; and
  (iii) the date on which the documents were returned;

on the record copy of the indictment or in the minute of proceedings; and

(b) intimate what he has noted to all parties.

(3) The seal on the envelope or container shall be broken only on the authority of the clerk of court.

(4) The clerk of court shall only permit such access to the tape or disc for such period as may be required for the purposes of the authorisation and on expiry of that period, shall again cause the tape or disc of the video recording of the commission to be sealed, which the Clerk of Justiciary or sheriff clerk, as the case may be, shall sign, and on which the following information shall be endorsed—

(a) the name of the accused;
(b) the date of the commission;
(c) the name of the commissioner;
(d) the prosecution and court reference numbers;
(e) the time of commencement and termination of the tape or disc;
(f) the time and date of sealing of the tape or disc.

AMENDMENT

Rule 22.13 inserted by Act of Adjournal (Criminal Procedure Rules Amendment No.6) (Vulnerable Witnesses (Scotland) Act 2004) (Evidence on Commission) 2005 (SSI 2005/574) para.2(3) (effective 30 November 2005).

To be read with the transitional provisions contained in the Act of Adjournal (Criminal Procedure Rules Amendment) (Vulnerable Witnesses (Scotland) Act 2004) 2006 (SSI 2006/76) para.2(2) and (3) (effective 1 April 2006).

Rule 22.13 as amended by Act of Adjournal (Criminal Procedure Rules 1996 Amendment) (No. 6) (Special Measures in the Justice of the Peace Court) 2015 (SSI 2015/443) para.2 (effective 23 December 2015).

Custody of video recording and documents

B1-50.13 **22.14.**—(1) The clerk of court shall keep the tape or disc of the video recording and documents referred to in rule 22.13(1) (video record of evidence on commission) in his custody.

(2) Where the tape or disc of the video recording of the evidence of a witness is in the custody of the clerk of court under this rule and where intimation has been given to that effect under rule 22.13(2)(b) to all the parties, the name and address of the witness and the tape or disc of the video recording of his or her evidence shall be treated as being within the knowledge of those parties; and no party shall be required, notwithstanding any enactment to the contrary, to include the tape or disc of the video recording of that witness's evidence in any list of productions.

AMENDMENTS

Rule 22.14 inserted by Act of Adjournal (Criminal Procedure Rules Amendment No.6) (Vulnerable Witnesses (Scotland) Act 2004) (Evidence on Commission) 2005 (SSI 2005/574) para.2(3) (effective 30 November 2005).

To be read with the transitional provisions contained in Act of Adjournal (Criminal Procedure Rules Amendment) (Vulnerable Witnesses (Scotland) Act 2004) 2006 (SSI 2006/76) para.2(2) and (3) (effective 1 April 2006).

Rule 22.14 as amended by Act of Adjournal (Criminal Procedure Rules 1996 Amendment) (No. 6) (Special Measures in the Justice of the Peace Court) 2015 (SSI 2015/443) para.2 (effective 23 December 2015).

Applications for leave for accused to be present at commission

22.15.—(1) An application in writing under section 271I(3) of the Act of 1995 (application for leave for accused to be present in the room during commission) shall be in Form 22.15. **B1-50.14**

(2) The application shall be lodged with the clerk of court and served on every other party by the applicant.

(3) On receipt of an application under paragraph (2), the clerk of court shall place the application before a judge in chambers.

(4) On considering the application in the absence of parties, or of any person acting on their behalf, the judge shall—

- (a) grant leave as requested; or
- (b) fix a diet for a hearing of the application; and
- (c) make an order for service of the application with the date on all parties and to the governor of any institution in which the accused is detained.

(5) Where an order under section 271I(3) of the Act of 1995 (leave for accused to be present in the room) is granted, it shall be intimated by the clerk of court to all parties unless the party was present at the hearing at which the order was made.

AMENDMENTS

Rule 22.15 inserted by Act of Adjournal (Criminal Procedure Rules Amendment No.6) (Vulnerable Witnesses (Scotland) Act 2004) (Evidence on Commission) 2005 (SSI 2005/574) para.2(3) (effective 30 November 2005).

[THE NEXT PARAGRAPH IS B1-51]

GENERAL NOTE

The expression "vulnerable witness" is defined in s.271 of the 1995 Act as either (1) a witness who is under the age of 16 at the date of the commencement of the proceedings (i.e. when the indictment is served: see s.271(3))—and in such a case he is referred to as a child witness—or (2) a witness in respect of whose evidence there is a significant risk that his evidence will be diminished in quality by reason of either mental disorder within the meaning of s.328 of the Mental Health (Care and Treatment (Scotland) Act 2003 (asp 13) or "fear or distress in connection with giving evidence at the trial". **B1-51**

As a result of the bringing into force of the Act of Adjournal (Criminal Procedure Amendment No.6) (Vulnerable Witnesses (Scotland) Act 2004) (Evidence on Commission) 2005 on November 30, 2005, this chapter is enlarged with rr.22.11-22.15 being inserted to deal with the special measure for taking the evidence of child witnesses on commission. For the assistance of practitioners the High Court has also issued a Practice Note (No.3 of 2005) (effective from November 30, 2005) in which details of what the court will expect the child witness notice (see r.22.1) to contain are identified. The Practice Note should be read in conjunction with this chapter.

Vulnerable witnesses

As para.2 of the Practice Note No.3 of 2005 stated, the 2004 Act only applied to child witnesses in solemn proceedings commenced after 1 April 2005, but it was intended that the 2004 Act would be implemented in due course to apply to vulnerable witnesses in all criminal proceedings. The next stage of the reform programme was reached with the High Court's enactment of the Act of Adjournal (Criminal Procedure Rules Amendment) (Vulnerable Witnesses (Scotland) Act 2004) 2006 (SSI 2006/76) which came into force on 1 April 2006 (para. 1(1)). The Act of Adjournal amends the Criminal Procedure Rules 1996 to apply certain of the rules of Ch.22 to vulnerable witnesses as defined by s.271(1)(b) of the 1995 Act (i.e. witnesses who are not children). The rules which now apply to vulnerable witnesses are: rr.22.4—22.6 and rr.22.8-22.14 (para.2(3)) and (with effect from 26 March 2007) r.22.15 (as a result of further amendment by Act of Adjournal (Criminal Procedure Rules Amendment) (Animal Health and Welfare etc.) 2007 (SSI 2007/238) para.2(2)). Thus, for example, it is now permissible for the evidence of a vulnerable witness who is not a child witness to be taken on commission. This is a significant change in Scottish procedure which has hitherto proceeded on the understandable basis that the jury which is to try the charges should see and hear the witness in court as the witness gives his evidence. The extent to which this new procedure will be utilised must at this stage be unknown, but if it is permitted on a regular basis the disruption and expense which will be occasioned will be considerable. Much may, therefore, turn on the strictness with which the court considers applications for taking evidence on commission.

As in the reform in respect of child witnesses introduced in 2005, the 2006 Act of Adjournal does not apply to summary proceedings. It applies only to solemn proceedings which *commenced* after 1 April 2006 where there is a vulnerable witness. Paragraph 2(2) makes plain that proceedings are commenced for these purposes "when a report of a case has been received by the procurator fiscal". Thus, the new provisions for vulnerable witnesses will apply not only to crimes committed after April 1, 2006 but also to crimes committed before but not reported until after that date.

In order to be applicable to vulnerable witnesses generally, two new rules are inserted into Ch.22. Rule 22.1A provides for the request for a vulnerable witness order to be made by means of a vulnerable witness application in terms of Form 22.1A which is to be lodged with the appropriate clerk; and r.22.3A provides for intimation of an order under S.271C. Rule 22.2 is repealed and re-enacted so as to include reference to vulnerable witness applications.

In *HM Advocate v G*, 2010 S.L.T. 239 the Crown applied to take the evidence of one child complainer by live CCTV link and the evidence of the other complainer on commission. The prosecution case was dependent on the doctrine of mutual corroboration. The defence lodged devolution issue minutes and took a preliminary objection to the admissibility of the evidence of the child complainers on the basis that their evidence was unreliable by reason of the manner in which their evidence had been elicited; the defence proposed that the evidence of psychologists be heard by a judge before trial (but without hearing the evidence of the two complainers) in order to determine the objections. Lord Brodie declined to take that course and deferred consideration of the issues to the trial diet on the view that it would be permissible for the trial judge to hear all the evidence including the defence psychologists' evidence in the presence of the jury and thereafter determine the objection. In the event that the objection succeeded in respect of only one of the complainers, the entire case would fail and require to be withdrawn from the jury.

Summary proceedings

With effect from 1 April 2007, rr.22.1-22.15 are now applied to summary proceedings in the sheriff court where a child witness is to give evidence (see Act of Adjournal (Criminal Procedure Rules Amendment No.2) (Vulnerable Witnesses (Scotland) Act 2004) 2007 (SSI 2007/237) para.2(2)). The proceedings must commence after 1 April 2007 and proceedings are taken to have commenced when a report of the case has been received by the procurator fiscal. In due course vulnerable witnesses within the meaning of s.271(1)(b) (non-child witnesses) will also be brought within the scope of ch.22 for the purposes of summary proceedings.

Rule 22.1

In nearly all cases the application for a vulnerable witness order is made by the Crown. The legislative intent underlying the Vulnerable Witnesses (Scotland) Act 2004 was that such applications should be dealt with speedily by a judge or sheriff in chambers. There is no statutory right on the other party, usually the accused, to a hearing in court. The only ground upon which an accused person is entitled to object to such a special measure is that its use "would give rise to a significant risk of prejudice to the fairness of the hearing or otherwise to the interests of justice" (Criminal Procedure (Scotland) Act 1995 s.271D(4)(b)(i)). That approach has been held to be compliant with the accused's rights under art.6 of the European Convention (see *AMI v Dunn* [2012] HCJAC 108, at [31] and [48], per Lady Paton and Lord Carloway).

Prior to the coming into force of the 2004 Act (on April 1, 2005), the practice was that a party seeking special measures presented an application in court and the other parties had an opportunity to oppose that application. That practice has been altered. Where the party now wishes to oppose the making of the order, he is given information about the grounds upon which the application is based. At that stage the objections should be intimated by letter to the court so that they can be taken into account. That application is then placed before the sheriff or judge in chambers and he may grant the application or order a hearing on it. If the latter occurs the accused can make oral submissions in support of his opposition in order to persuade the court that the order should not be made. But if no letter of opposition has been submitted, the accused is still entitled to make representations by way of a review of the arrangements under s.271D(4). While that provision makes no mention of any party other than the party citing or intending to cite the witness, another party such as the accused is entitled to bring to the court's attention his concerns that the consequences mentioned in s.271D(4)(b)(i) or (ii) will materialise at trial. The court will be obliged to take these concerns into account and, if the court deems it appropriate, should appoint an oral hearing. The hearing might be a preliminary hearing or a first diet or a special diet fixed for review of the special measures under s.271D(1) (*AMI v Dunn*, at [39] and [48]).

Rule 22.4

Section 271D(1)(a) and (b) of the 1995 Act (as amended) envisage only that the party citing or intending to cite the vulnerable witness, or the court on its own motion, may initiate a review of the special measures but in *AMI v Dunn* a majority of the High Court held that another party such as the accused or co-accused could bring to the court's attention concerns about the special measures. If that is done the court is bound to consider them and may appoint a hearing to determine whether the special measures should continue in place.

Chapter 22A

Witness Anonymity Orders

Application for witness anonymity order

22A.1. An application under section 271P of the Act of 1995 for a witness anonymity order shall be in Form 22A.1. **B1-51.1**

Notice of application in summary proceedings

22A.2. Notice for the purpose of section 271Q(2) of the Act of 1995 shall be in Form 22A.2. **B1-51.2**

Discharge and variation of witness anonymity order

22A.3. An application under section 271U(3)(a) of the Act of 1995 to discharge or vary a witness anonymity order shall be made— **B1-51.3**

(a) by motion, at any hearing; or
(b) in Form 22A.3, at any other time.

Appeals

22A.4.—(1) Any appeal mentioned in section 27IV of the Act of 1995 must be taken not later than seven days after the decision. **B1-51.4**

(2) The appeal shall thereafter be treated procedurally, so far as possible—

(a) in solemn proceedings, as if it were an appeal under section 74(1) of the Act of 1995;
(b) in summary proceedings, as if it were an appeal under section 174(1) of the Act of 1995.

AMENDMENTS

Chapter 22A inserted by Act of Adjournal (Criminal Procedure Rules Amendment No.3) (Miscellaneous) 2011 (SSI2011/194) para.4 (effective March 28, 2011).

[THE NEXT PARAGRAPH IS B1-52]

Chapter 23

Letters of Request

Applications for letters of request

23.1.—(1) An application to the court by the prosecutor or the defence under section 272(1)(a) of the Act of 1995 (evidence by letter of request) for the issue of a letter of request shall be made by petition— **B1-52**

(a) where the accused has appeared on petition under Part IV of the Act of 1995 (petition procedure) but an indictment has not been served on him, in Form 23.1-A presented to the High Court; or
(b) where an indictment or a complaint has been served on the accused, in Form 23.1-B presented to the appropriate court.

(2) A petition referred to in paragraph (1) shall—

(a) where it relates to proceedings in the High Court or to proceedings in respect of which the court where the trial is to take place is not yet known, be lodged with the Clerk of Justiciary, or
(b) where it relates to proceedings in the sheriff court, be lodged with the sheriff clerk,

and shall be accompanied by a proposed letter of request in Form 23.1-C.

(3) […]

(4) Such an application made to the High Court may be disposed of by a single judge of that court.

(5) The High Court or the sheriff, as the case may be, shall—

(a) order intimation on the other party or parties to the proceedings;
(b) subject to paragraph (6), allow such time for lodging answers as appears appropriate; and
(c) fix a diet for hearing the petition and answers (if any).

(6) The High Court or the sheriff, as the case may be, may dispense with answers to the petition on cause shown.

AMENDMENTS

Rule 23.1(3) repealed by Act of Adjournal (Criminal Procedure Rules Amendment) (Miscellaneous) 2004 (SSI 2004/195) r.2 (effective April 26, 2004).

Powers of court in applications

23.2.—(1) The High Court or the sheriff, as the case may be, may, after considering the petition for the issue of a letter of request and any answers to it, grant the petition with or without modification or refuse it. **B1-52.1**

(2) On granting the petition, the High Court or the sheriff, as the case may be, shall—

(a) in relation to an application under section 272(1)(a) of the Act of 1995 (evidence by letter of request), allow interrogatories to be adjusted summarily;

(b) pronounce an order approving the terms—
 (i) of the letter of request to be sent;
 (ii) of any interrogatories and cross-interrogatories to be sent; and
(c) if English is not an official language of the body to which the letter of request is addressed, specify a period within which a translation of each of the letter, any interrogatories and cross-interrogatories, and any productions, are to be lodged.

Expenses

B1-52.2 **23.3.**—(1) The solicitor for the petitioner or, if he is unrepresented, the petitioner shall be liable for the expenses of the petition for the issue of a letter of request.

(2) The High Court or the sheriff, as the case may be, may order the solicitor for the petitioner, or the petitioner, to consign into court such sum in respect of those expenses as may be specified, and on or before such date as may be specified, in the order.

(3) In the event of the sum so specified not being consigned into court on or before the date so specified, the petition shall be treated as having been abandoned.

Transmission of letters of request

B1-52.3 **23.4.**—(1) On—

(a) the High Court or the sheriff, as the case may be, pronouncing an order under rule 23.2(2), or
(b) in a case where a translation requires to be lodged, on the lodging of the translation,

the Clerk of Justiciary or the sheriff clerk, as the case may be, shall send the letter of request and any documents to the Secretary of State for Foreign, Commonwealth and Development Affairs for onward transmission to the body to which the letter of request is addressed.

(2) On sending the letter of request and any documents to the Secretary of State, the Clerk of Justiciary or sheriff clerk, as the case may be, shall note, on the petition, record copy of the indictment or in the minute of proceedings—

(a) the documents sent;
(b) to whom the documents were sent; and
(c) the date on which the documents were sent.

(3) On the relative documents being returned to him, the Clerk of Justiciary or sheriff clerk, as the case may be, shall—

(a) note—
 (i) the documents returned,
 (ii) by whom they were returned, and
 (iii) the date on which they were returned,

 on the application, the record copy of the indictment or in the minute of proceedings; and
(b) intimate what he has noted to all parties concerned.

AMENDMENT

Rule23.4(1) as amended by the Transfer of Functions (Secretary of State for Foreign, Commonwealth and Development Affairs) Order 2020 (SI 2020/942) Sch.1(2) para.12 (effective 28 September 2020).

Custody of documents

B1-52.4 **23.5.**—(1) The Clerk of Justiciary or sheriff clerk, as the case may be, shall, subject to paragraph (2), keep the documents referred to in rule 23.4(3) in his custody.

(2) Where the petition for the issue of a letter of request was made to the High Court on the ground that the court in which the trial was to take place was not then known, the prosecutor shall, as soon as that court is known, inform the Clerk of Justiciary of that fact; and if that court is the sheriff court, the Clerk of Justiciary shall, as soon as is practicable, send to the sheriff clerk of that sheriff court the record of the evidence of the witness obtained by a letter of request under section 272(1)(a) of the Act of 1995.

(3) Where the record of the evidence of a witness is in the custody of the Clerk of Justiciary or a sheriff clerk under this rule and where intimation has been given to that effect under rule 23.4(3) to all the parties concerned in the proceedings, the name and address of that witness and the record of his evidence shall be treated as being within the knowledge of those parties; and no party shall be required, notwithstanding any enactment to the contrary—

(a) to include the name of that witness in any list of witnesses; or
(b) to include the record of his evidence in any list of productions.

Prohibition of reference to evidence without leave

B1-52.5 **23.6.**—(1) No reference shall be made either directly or indirectly in any proceedings to the evidence, or any part of the evidence, of a witness whose evidence has been taken by virtue of a letter of request under section 272(1)(a) of the Act of 1995 unless the party seeking to make such reference has made a motion to the court to that effect and that motion has been granted.

(2) The terms of any motion made under paragraph (1) and the grant or refusal of that motion by the court shall be noted by the clerk of court in the record or minute of proceedings.

(3) On any such motion in solemn proceedings being granted—

(a) the judge may direct copies of the evidence, to which he has granted leave for reference to be made, to be provided to the jury by the party making the motion; and

(b) the clerk of court shall read the record of that evidence to the jury and shall then record that he has done so in the record of proceedings.

[THE NEXT PARAGRAPH IS B1-53]

GENERAL NOTE

Section 272 of the 1995 Act allows for the High Court or the sheriff court (but not the district court): (1) to issue a letter of request to a foreign court, i.e. outside the United Kingdom, Channel Islands or Isle of Man, for the taking of evidence from a witness resident there; and (2) to appoint a Commissioner to examine at any place within the United Kingdom, Channel Islands or Isle of Man a witness who cannot attend the trial diet because of illness or infirmity or who is not ordinarily resident here and is unlikely to be present here at the trial diet. No further elaboration is given in the 1995 Act of illness or infirmity but it is submitted that a psychiatric condition which would not render the witness's evidence valueless (e.g. agoraphobia) as well as physical illness is comprehended. A substantial degree of infirmity by reason of old age is sufficient (see *Lang, Petitioner*, 1991 S.L.T. 931). The evidence can be taken with or without interrogatories. **B1-53**

Chapter 23 deals with applications for letters of request to the foreign state to examine witnesses and to receive productions; Ch.24 provides for applications to appoint commissioners to go abroad to examine witnesses and to receive productions.

In either case the court can *only* grant the application if it is satisfied on two matters: (i) that the evidence (which the Crown or defence must narrate as being what the witness is able to give) is "necessary for the proper adjudication of the trial"; and (ii) that there would be no unfairness to the other party in the taking of evidence in that way. The evidence need not be given on oath in order to be competent (s.272(4)). The taking of evidence by way of contemporaneous live television link in the course of the trial proceedings can also be sought by way of application for a letter of request (see s.273 of the 1995 Act).

Rule 23.1

Rule 23.1(1) and (2). The application is by way of petition which must contain averments as to the evidence which the petitioner maintains the witness will be able to give so that the court can be satisfied that the evidence is necessary for the proper adjudication of the trial and that there will be no unfairness (s.272(3)). It can be made in solemn or summary proceedings but must be made before the jury takes the oath or the first witness is sworn in summary proceedings. Except where in applications for the appointment of a commissioner, the court is satisfied by the petitioner that the circumstances justifying the application had not arisen or would not have merited such an application before the jury took the oath or the first witness was sworn (s.272(7)). The use of the word "or" in s.272(7) appears to be disjunctive. There may be cases where evidence which was known before the trial commenced takes on a different complexion once other witnesses have been examined.

Rule 23.1(3). Where in solemn proceedings (but not in summary proceedings) it is sought to take the evidence of a witness by contemporaneous live television link in the course of a trial, the Crown or the accused can apply for the issue of a letter of request which can only be granted if the court is satisfied that the witness's evidence (which should be narrated in the petition) is necessary for the proper adjudication of the trial and the granting of the application is in the interests of justice and, where the applicant is the Crown, there is no unfairness to the accused (s.273(3)).

Rule 23.1(5). The court must order intimation and if the other party does not receive notice the court is not entitled to grant the application. The court could never be satisfied that there would be no unfairness to the accused if he were not heard on the merits of the petition. Accordingly the petitioner should ensure that proof of intimation is available to the court. The hearing should take place in chambers but if a petition is unopposed the hearing can be dispensed with (s.272(2)).

Rule 23.2

The decision of the sheriff or a single judge of the High Court (see r.23.1(4)) is not susceptible of appeal and a petition to the *nobile officium* to review his decision is incompetent (see *Lang, Petitioner*, 1991 S.L.T. 931). However, the issue of fairness can still arise at the trial: see r.23.6 below.

Rule 23.5

Rule 23.5(3). Where the evidence of a witness or productions received at the examination are returned to the appropriate court, they need not be intimated on a list to the other side so long as intimation is given by the clerk of the court that the evidence or productions have been received. Rule 23.4(3) states that the clerk of the court "shall intimate" to the other parties the "documents returned" (though productions are not mentioned) and by whom and when they were returned. However, if the clerk by oversight fails to intimate when or by whom the documents were received by him, it is likely that the court would hold that there had been substantial compliance with the overall purpose of r.23.4(3) when taken together with r.23.5(3). In any event the court must first grant leave in the course of the trial for reference to be made to any part of the evidence or any production (see r.23.6 below).

Rule 23.6

The issue of fairness can be raised at the trial. The court must be requested by way of a motion to allow any part of the evidence or any production to be referred to. If no intimation is given under r.23.4(3) above to the other party then the court could not properly allow reference to be made to the evidence or productions. Equally the circumstances or the form in which the evidence was taken or the absence of cross-examination could arguably be prejudicial to the accused (or the Crown) and that would entitle the presiding judge to refuse to allow reference to the evidence. The judge's decision would however be capable of review on appeal on the ground of a miscarriage of justice in the event of conviction.

Chapter 23A

Television Link Evidence

Application for television link evidence

B1-53.1 **23A.1**—(1) An application to the court by the prosecutor or the defence under section 273(2) or section 273A(2) of the Act of 1995 shall be by petition in Form 23A.1-A and shall be accompanied by a letter of request in Form 23A.1-B.

(2) Such an application made to the Fligh Court may be disposed of by a single judge of that court.

(3) The Fligh Court or the sheriff, as the case may be, shall—

(a) order intimation on the other party or parties to the proceedings;

(b) subject to paragraph (4), allow such time for lodging answers as appears appropriate; and

(c) fix a diet for hearing the petition and answers (if any).

(4) The Fligh Court or the sheriff as the case may be, may dispense with answers to the petition on cause shown.

AMENDMENTS

Chapter 23A heading, r.23A heading and r.23A.1(1) as amended by Act of Adjournal (Criminal Procedure Rules Amendment) (Miscellaneous) 2013 (SSI 2013/72) para.3 (effective April 22, 2013).

Powers of the court in applications

B1-53.2 **23A.2**—(1) The Fligh Court or the sheriff, as the case may be, may, after considering the petition and any answers to it, grant the petition with or without modification or refuse it.

(2) On granting the petition, the Fligh Court or the sheriff, as the case may be, shall—

(a) pronounce an order approving the terms of the letter of request to be sent; and

(b) if English is not an official language of the body to which the letter is addressed, specify a period within which a translation of the letter is to be lodged.

Expenses

B1-53.3 **23A.3**—(1) The solicitor for the petitioner or, if he is unrepresented, the petitioner shall be liable for the expenses of the petition for the issue of a letter of request.

(2) The High Court or the sheriff, as the case may be, may order the solicitor for the petitioner, or the petitioner, to consign into court such sum in respect of those expenses as may be specified, and on or before such date as may be specified, in the order.

(3) In the event of the sum so specified not being consigned into court on or before the date so specified, the petition shall be treated as having been abandoned.

Transmission of letters of request

B1-53.4 **23A.4**—(1) On–

(a) the High Court or the sheriff, as the case may be, pronouncing an order under rule 23 A.2(2), or

(b) in a case where a translation requires to be lodged, on the lodging of the translation,

the Clerk of Justiciary or the sheriff clerk, as the case may be, shall send the letter of request to the Lord Advocate for transmission to the body to which the letter of request is addressed.

(2) The Clerk of Justiciary or sheriff clerk, as the case may be, shall note, on the petition, record copy of the indictment or in the minute of proceedings, the date on which the letter of request was sent to the Lord Advocate for transmission and shall intimate that date to all parties concerned.

Procedural diet

B1-53.5 **23A.5**—(1) On receipt of confirmation that the court, tribunal or other authority to which a letter of request was transmitted will provide assistance in facilitating the giving of evidence through a live television link, the Clerk of Justiciary or sheriff clerk, as the case may be, shall fix a procedural diet in accordance with paragraph (2) and shall intimate that diet to all parties concerned.

(2) The procedural diet shall be fixed for a date which is before the date on which the evidence is to be given by television link.

(3) The accused shall not require to be present at the procedural diet.

(4) At the procedural diet, the judge or sheriff, as the case may be, shall make inquiries as to whether or not arrangements are in place to facilitate the giving of evidence through a live television link.

AMENDMENTS

Chapter 23A inserted by Act of Adjournal (Criminal Procedure Rules Amendment) (Miscellaneous) 2004 (SSI 2004/195) para.2 (effective April 26, 2004).

[THE NEXT PARAGRAPH IS B1-54]

Chapter 24
Evidence On Commission

Applications to take evidence on commission

24.1.—(1) An application to the court by the prosecutor or the defence under section 272(1)(b) of the Act of 1995 for the appointment of a commissioner to examine a witness to whom that section applies, shall be made by petition— **B1-54**

(a) where the accused has appeared on petition under Part IV of the Act of 1995 (petition procedure) but an indictment has not been served on him, in Form 24.1-A presented to the High Court; or

(b) where an indictment or a complaint has been served on the accused, in Form 24.1-B presented to the appropriate court.

(2) A petition referred to in paragraph (1) shall—

(a) where it relates to proceedings in the High Court or to proceedings in respect of which the court where the trial is to take place is not yet known, be lodged with the Clerk of Justiciary; or

(b) where it relates to proceedings in the sheriff court, be lodged with the sheriff clerk.

(3) A petition in relation to section 272(1)(b)(i) of the Act of 1995 (examination of witness ill or infirm) shall be accompanied by an appropriate medical certificate duly certified on soul and conscience by a qualified medical practitioner.

(4) Such an application made to the High Court may be disposed of by a single judge of that court.

(5) The High Court or the sheriff, as the case may be, shall—

(a) order intimation on the other party or parties to the proceedings;

(b) subject to paragraph (6), allow such time for lodging answers as appears appropriate; and

(c) fix a diet for hearing the petition and answers (if any).

(6) The High Court or the sheriff, as the case may be, may dispense with answers to the petition on cause shown.

Appointment of commissioner

24.2.—(1) The High Court or the sheriff, as the case may be, may, after considering the petition for the taking of evidence on commission and any answers to it, grant the petition with or without modifications or refuse it. **B1-54.1**

(2) On making an order granting the petition, the High Court or the sheriff, as the case may be, shall appoint—

(a) a commissioner to examine the witness to whom the order applies, and

(b) a clerk to assist the commissioner in the carrying out of his duties,

and shall dispense with interrogatories.

(3) On the making of an order under paragraph (1), the Clerk of Justiciary or sheriff clerk, as the case may be, shall send the order to the commissioner or his clerk with the other relative documents.

(4) On sending the order to the commissioner or his clerk under paragraph (2), the Clerk of Justiciary or sheriff clerk, as the case may be, shall note on the petition, record copy of the indictment or in the minute of proceedings—

(a) the order and documents sent;

(b) to whom they were sent; and

(c) the date on which they were sent.

Expenses

24.3.—(1) The solicitor for the petitioner or, if he is unrepresented, the petitioner shall be liable for the expenses of the petition for the appointment of a commissioner to take the evidence of a witness on commission. **B1-54.2**

(2) The High Court or the sheriff, as the case may be, may order the solicitor for the petitioner, or the petitioner, to consign into court such sum in respect of those expenses as may be specified, and on or before such date as may be specified, in the order.

(3) In the event of the sum so specified not being consigned into court on or before the date so specified, the petition shall be treated as having been abandoned.

The commission

24.4.—(1) The commissioner shall, on receiving the order and documents mentioned in rule 24.2 (appointment of commissioner), determine the place and the date of the diet for the examination of the witness to whom the order of the court relates, and shall give reasonable notice of those matters to all the parties concerned. **B1-54.3**

(2) The commissioner may vary or revoke his determination or adjourn the examination of any witness to such other place, at such other date and time, as he may determine.

(3) If, in the course of the examination of a witness under this rule, any question arises as to the admissibility of any evidence, the commissioner shall not determine any such question but shall allow the evidence subject to all questions of competency and relevancy.

Commissioner's report

B1-54.4 **24.5.**—(1) On the carrying out of his commission in accordance with the terms of the order appointing him, or otherwise on concluding his commission, the commissioner shall complete a written report of his commission, and he or his clerk shall return the report and relative documents to the Clerk of Justiciary or sheriff clerk, as the case may be.

(2) On the report and any documents being returned to him, the Clerk of Justiciary or sheriff clerk, as the case may be, shall—

(a) note—

(i) the documents returned,

(ii) by whom they were returned, and

(iii) the date on which they were returned, on the application, the record copy of the indictment or in the minute of proceedings; and

(b) intimate what he has noted to all parties concerned.

Custody of documents

B1-54.5 **24.6.**—(1) The Clerk of Justiciary or the sheriff clerk, as the case may be, shall, subject to paragraph (2), keep the documents referred to in rule 24.5(2) in his custody.

(2) In any case where the petition for the taking of evidence on commission was made to the High Court on the ground that the court in which the trial was to take place was not then known, the prosecutor shall, as soon as that court is known, inform the Clerk of Justiciary of that fact; and if that court is the sheriff court, the Clerk of Justiciary shall, as soon as is practicable, send to the sheriff clerk of that sheriff court the record of the evidence of the witness or witnesses.

(3) Where the record of the evidence of a witness is in the custody of the Clerk of Justiciary or a sheriff clerk under this rule and where intimation has been given to that effect under rule 24.5(2) to all the parties concerned in the proceedings, the name and address of that witness and the record of his evidence shall be treated as being within the knowledge of those parties; and no party shall be required, notwithstanding any enactment to the contrary—

(a) to include the name of that witness in any list of witnesses; or

(b) to include the record of his evidence in any list of productions.

Prohibition of reference to evidence without leave

B1-54.6 **24.7.**—(1) No reference shall be made either directly or indirectly in any proceedings to the evidence, or any part of the evidence, of a witness whose evidence has been taken on commission under this Chapter unless the party seeking to make such reference has made a motion to the court to that effect and that motion has been granted.

(2) The terms of any motion made under paragraph (1) and the grant or refusal of that motion by the court shall be noted by the clerk of court in the record or minute of proceedings.

(3) On any such motion in solemn proceedings being granted—

(a) the judge may direct copies of the evidence, to which he has granted leave for reference to be made, to be provided to the jury by the party making the motion; and

(b) the clerk of court shall read the record of that evidence to the jury and shall then record that he has done so in the record of proceedings.

[THE NEXT PARAGRAPH IS B1-55]

GENERAL NOTE

B1-55 Much of what was noted in relation to the procedure for applying for the issue of letters of request is applicable to this chapter and reference should therefore be made to the notes to Ch.23 above.

Additionally, however, it should be noted that the petition seeking the taking of evidence on commission should be supported by a certificate from a qualified medical practitioner that the witness whose evidence is to be taken is ill or infirm in a particular respect. The certificate must be on soul and conscience (r.24.1(3)). The court shall not authorise interrogatories (r.24.2(2)(b)) as the examination is to be left to the discretion of the parties. Any objection to the admissibility cannot be sustained by the commissioner who must allow the question or line of examination under reservation of all questions of relevancy and competency (r.24.4(3)). However it should be noted that objections should nonetheless be timeously taken so that objection can competently be renewed before the trial judge.

As Lord Brodie noted in *HM Advocate v RM* [2009] HCJ 05 (Unreported October 28, 2009), para.8, it is incompetent at common law for evidence to be taken on commission in criminal proceedings and the power of the High Court to authorise such a process is therefore dependent on the precise terms of s.272 of the 1995 Act. Thus his Lordship (under reference to s.272(3)(a) of the 1995 Act requiring that the judge be satisfied that the evidence is "necessary for the proper adjudication of the trial") also held that it was self-evident that a complainer in a fraud charge is "someone who can give necessary evidence in the sense that, prima facie, he is likely to have the most direct experience of what is alleged or at least a material part of it". In *RM* the Crown applied to take evidence on commission from five elderly witnesses who were alleged to be victims of fraud; the witnesses were to be examined and cross-examined in their homes outwith the presence of the accused. Lord Brodie also held (under reference to s.272(3)(b)) that there would be no unfairness to the accused in his being absent, any disadvantage being "more theoretical than real" (para. 10); and that the taking of the complainers' evidence by means of a live CCTV link was not practicable and thus did not provide a reasonable alternative to taking their evidence on commission (para. 11).

Chapter 25

Record of Judicial Examination as Evidence in Solemn Proceedings

Use of transcript of judicial examination

25.1.—(1) The record made under section 37 of the Act of 1995 (judicial examination: record of proceedings) shall be received in evidence in accordance with section 278(1) of that Act by means of the clerk of court, subject to paragraph (2) of this rule, reading the record of those proceedings to the jury. **B1-56**

(2) The clerk of court shall not read to the jury such part of the record as the court refuses to allow to be read to the jury on an application under section 278(2) of the Act of 1995.

(3) The presiding judge may direct that copies of such part of the record as has been read to the jury shall be made available to them together with copies of any written record of a confession allegedly made and received by the accused under section 36(3) of the Act of 1995 (written record of confession allegedly made received from prosecutor or constable).

Chapter 26

Documentary Evidence

Authentication of copies of documents

26.1.—(1) For the purposes of paragraph 1(1) of Schedule 8 to the Act of 1995 (production of copy documents), a copy, or a copy of a material part, of a document shall be authenticated— **B1-57**

(a) by a person who is—

(i) the author of the original of it;

(ii) a person in, or who has been in, possession and control of the original of it or a copy of it; or

(iii) the authorised representative of the person in, or who has been in, possession and control of the original of it or a copy of it; and

(b) by means of a signed certificate, certifying the copy as a true copy, which may be in Form 26.1-A—

(i) endorsed on the copy; or

(ii) attached to the copy.

(2) For the purposes of paragraph 4 of Schedule 8 to Act of 1995 (documents kept by businesses etc.), a document shall be certified by a docquet in Form 26.1-B—

(a) endorsed on the document; or

(b) attached to the document.

(3) For the purposes of paragraph 5(3) of Schedule 8 to the Act of 1995 (statements not contained in business documents), a certificate shall be in Form 26.1-C.

[(4) In this Chapter a reference to a certificate or docquet being endorsed on, or attached to, a copy of a document includes endorsement or attachment by electronic means.]

AMENDMENT

Rule 26.1(4) inserted by the Act of Adjournal (Criminal Procedure Rules 1996 Amendment) (Electronic Authentication of Copy Documents) 2021 (SSI 2021/116) r. 2(2) (effective 22 March 2021).

GENERAL NOTE

Schedule 8 to the 1995 Act makes provision for documentary evidence in all criminal proceedings. Paragraph 1 requires that unless the court otherwise directs, a document which purports to be authenticated in such manner and by such person as may be prescribed, *shall* be deemed to be a true copy and treated as if it were the actual copy whether or not the original is still in existence. It is immaterial whether the copy is a copy of a copy or even more removed from the original. Rule 26.1(1) even allows authentication by a person who at one time had possession of a copy of the original. Note that in *Lord Advocate's Reference No. 1 of 1992*, 1992 S.L.T. 1010 at 1016F the High Court observed that it was open to the court, when considering the exceptions to the hearsay rule which might be permitted, to take account of changing circumstances which might render the continued application of the rule against hearsay unacceptable. **B1-58**

Paragraph 4 is permissive and provides that (unless the court otherwise directs) a document may be taken to be a document kept by a business or by or on behalf of a holder of an office (whether paid or unpaid) if a docquet certifying that that is so is endorsed on or attached to the document. Form 26.1-B is the appropriate docquet style.

Paragraph 5 avoids the necessity of the attendance at court of a witness who is to speak to a negative. A certificate should be produced stating that a document which was created or received in the course of a business or undertaking or in pursuance of functions of an office-holder (whether paid or unpaid) and is or at any time was kept by a business or undertaking or by or on behalf of an office-holder, either does not contain a certain statement or that no such document contains a certain statement.

In *Lord Advocate's Reference No. 1 of 1996*, 1996 S.L.T. 740; 1996 S.C.C.R. 516 it has been held under reference to the statutory predecessor of Sch.8 (namely Sch.3 to the Prisoners and Criminal

Proceedings (Scotland) Act 1993) that there are now two methods by which bank statements and bank documents can be proved in criminal proceedings: either under Sch.8 to the 1995 Act or under the (more strict) Bankers' Books Evidence Act 1879.

Form 26.1-A and Form 26.1-B must either be endorsed on the copy production or business document or be attached to the copy or document. In *HM Advocate v B*, 2012 S.C.C.R. 336 the Appeal Court held that, in either case, the docquet was not part of the text of the production. The docquet is not an integral part of the production itself (at [31]). Accordingly, Lord Malcolm's contrary opinion in *HM Advocate v Qureshi*, 2011 S.C.C.R. 183 was disapproved (at [33]).

Chapter 27

Routine Evidence, Sufficient Evidence and Proof of Previous Convictions

Notices in relation to use of autopsy and forensic science reports

B1-59 **27.1.**—(1) Any notice given by an accused under subsection (1) or (2) of section 281 of the Act of 1995 (routine evidence: autopsy and forensic science reports) shall be in writing and shall be given to the prosecutor.

(2) For the purposes of the application of section 281(1) of the Act of 1995 to any summary proceedings, an autopsy report shall not be treated as having been lodged as a production by the prosecutor unless it has been lodged as a production not later than 14 days before the date of the trial diet.

(3) For the purposes of the application of subsection (2) of section 281 of the Act of 1995 to any summary proceedings, the prosecutor shall intimate his intention in accordance with that subsection by serving a copy of the autopsy or forensic science report lodged by him on the accused or his solicitor with a notice of his intention not later than 14 days before the date of the trial diet.

Form of certificates in relation to certain evidence

B1-59.1 **27.2.** A certificate under any of the following provisions of the Act of 1995 shall be in Form 27.2:—
section 283(1) (certificate as to time and place of video surveillance recordings),
section 284(1) (certificate in relation to fingerprints),
section 285(2) (certificate relating to previous convictions),
section 285(4) (certificate relating to fingerprints),
section 285(5) (certificate relating to fingerprints of previously convicted person).

Form of notice in relation to certain evidential certificates

B1-59.2 **27.3.** A notice under any of the following provisions of the Act of 1995 shall be in Form 27.3:—
section 282(3) (notice not accepting evidence as to controlled drugs or medicinal products),
section 283(2) (notice not accepting evidence as to video surveillance),
section 284(2) (notice not accepting evidence in relation to fingerprints),
section 286(1) (notice denying extract conviction applies to accused).

Notices under section 16A(4) of the Criminal Law (Consolidation) (Scotland) Act 1995

B1-59.3 **27.4.**—(1) A notice under section 16A(4) of the Criminal Law (Consolidation) (Scotland) Act 1995 (notice disputing that condition is satisfied and requiring prosecutor to prove such) shall be in Form 27.4.

(2) A notice by an accused under section 16A(4) of the Criminal Law (Consolidation) (Scotland) Act 1995 (notice disputing condition specified in section 16A(3)) may be served on the prosecutor by any of the methods of service in rule 2.3 (general provisions for service).

(3) At the same time as he serves a notice on the prosecutor under paragraph (2), the accused shall serve a copy of that notice on any co-accused or his solicitor.

(4) An accused shall serve a notice under paragraphs (2) or (3), no later than 21 days before the trial diet.

AMENDMENTS

Rule 27.4 as amended by Act of Adjournal (Criminal Procedure Rules Amendment) 1997 (SI 1997/63).

Subs.(4) as amended by Act of Adjournal (Criminal Procedure Rules Amendment No. 3) (SI 1997/1788) (effective 11 August 1997).

Notice under section 16B(4) of Criminal Law (Consolidation) (Scotland) Act 1995

B1-59.4 **27.5.**—(1) Any notice under section 16B(4) of the Criminal Law (Consolidation) (Scotland) Act 1995 (notice served on prosecutor by person accused of sexual offence disputing whether an act done by him abroad constituted an offence under the law in force in the country or territory in question) shall be in Form 27.5 and may be served on the prosecutor by any of the methods of service mentioned in rule 2.3.

(2) Any such notice shall be served not later than 21 days before the trial diet; and when he serves such a notice the accused shall serve a copy of it on any coaccused or on the solicitor of any co-accused.

AMENDMENTS

Rule 27.5 inserted by Act of Adjournal (Criminal Procedure Rules Amendment No.5) (SI 1997/2082) (effective 1 September 1997).

[THE NEXT PARAGRAPH IS B1-60]

General Note

Chapter 27 mainly provides for the appropriate forms of certificates and notices which require to be given. Rule 27.1 however merits notice. When the prosecutor in solemn or summary proceedings wishes to rely on the presumption in s.281(1) of the 1995 Act that the body examined at a postmortem dissection was the deceased named in the charge, or wishes to rely on only one of two experts who prepared the autopsy report or the forensic science report as being sufficient evidence of the facts and conclusions contained in the report, he should give written notice to the accused. The accused then has to give a counter-notice not less than six days before the trial in order to prevent the prosecutor from relying on the presumption or calling only one expert. In summary proceedings r.27.1(2) and (3) provide that the prosecutor must lodge the autopsy report or give the notice of his intention to rely on only one witness, not later than 14 days before the trial diet. **B1-60**

Rule 27.4 has been rendered necessary by the amendment of the Criminal Law (Consolidation) (Scotland) Act 1995 by s.6 of the Sexual Offences (Conspiracy and Incitement) Act 1996 (c.29) which came into force on 1 October 1996. Section 16A provides that a person shall be guilty of conspiracy or incitement in respect of various sexual offences involving children (i.e. persons under 16 years) where these offences are intended to be committed abroad. Section 16A(4) allows for an essential condition of guilt to be taken as satisfied, unless notice is given by the accused that the condition is disputed (although the court is entitled to permit, if it thinks fit, the accused to require the Crown to prove the condition without prior service of a notice: s.16A(6)). The essential conditions are: either (a) where conspiracy is charged, the criminal purpose would involve at some stage either an act by him or by another party to the conspiracy, or the happening of some event, constituting an offence under the law of the place where the event was intended to take place; or (b) where incitement is libelled, what was in view would involve the commission of an offence under the law of that place. The Act also states that the conduct is an offence under that other country's law, howsoever the foreign law describes it so long as it is punishable under that law. Thus it is for Scots law as the *lex fori* to characterise the purpose of the conspiracy or the object of the incitement as an offence: to regard the foreign law as punishing the conduct the Scots court will ask whether the consequences of the conduct under the foreign law can be regarded as penal in nature.

Chapter 27A

Recovery of Documents

Appeal against decision of sheriff

27A.1.—(1) An appeal under section 301A(5) of the Act of 1995 shall be lodged with the clerk of the appropriate Appeal Court not later than 2 days after the date of the decision of the sheriff and shall be served on the other parties to the application. **B1-60.1**

(2) Where the last day of the period referred to in paragraph (1) falls on a Saturday, Sunday or court holiday, such period shall extend to and include the next day which is not a Saturday, Sunday or court holiday.

(3) An appeal under paragraph (1) shall be in Form 27A. 1.

(4) In this rule, "clerk of the appropriate Appeal Court" means—

(a) in a case where the High Court is the appropriate Appeal Court, the Clerk of Justiciary;

(b) in a case where the Sheriff Appeal Court is the appropriate Appeal Court, the Clerk of the Sheriff Appeal Court.

Amendments

Chapter 27A inserted by Act of Adjournal (Criminal Procedure Rules Amendment No.6) (Criminal Proceedings etc. (Reform) (Scotland) Act 2007) 2007 (SSI 2007/511) r.8 (effective 10 December 2007).

Rule 27A.1 as amended by Act of Adjournal (Criminal Procedure Rules Amendment) (Miscellaneous) 2010 (SSI 2010/184) para.6 (effective 1 June 2010).

Rule 27A.1 as amended by Act of Adjournal (Criminal Procedure Rules 1996 Amendment) (No. 4) (Sheriff Appeal Court) 2015 (SSI 2015/245) para.4 (effective 22 September 2015 subject to savings provisions in para.6).

General Note

Section 301A of the 1995 Act was inserted by s.37 of the Criminal Proceedings etc. (Reform) (Scotland) Act 2007 and brought into force on 10 December 2007. Section 301A(1) provides that it is now competent for the sheriff to make, in connection with any criminal proceedings (whether solemn or summary proceedings before it or before any JP court in the district of that sheriff court:s.301A(2)), either of the orders mentioned in s.301A(3) (viz. an order granting commission and diligence for the recovery of documents or an order on the Crown for the production of documents). However, an application may not be made for either order until an indictment has been served on the accused or the accused has been cited under s.66(4)(b) or the accused has answered the summary complaint (s.301A(4)). **B1-60.2**

This new power was necessary because it was incompetent at common law for the sheriff to grant warrant for commission and diligence (*HM Advocate v Ashrif*, 1988 S.L.T. 567, which Lord Rodger of Earlsferry described in *HM Advocate v Murtagh* [2009] UKPC 36 at para.53 as "the last spurt of a system that was doomed to disappear"). The High Court's jurisdiction in applications for production orders and commission and diligence is now confined to making them in connection with proceedings before that court (s.301A(8)).

The application for either order must be in writing. The unsuccessful party may appeal to the High Court against the decision of the sheriff (s.301A(5)). This is an unqualified right to appeal (*Harvey v HM*

Advocate [2008] HCJAC 46, para.8) so that where, as is often convenient, the application is heard at a first diet in solemn proceedings in the sheriff court, there is no requirement to obtain leave from the sheriff. Form 27A.1 prescribes the form in which the note of appeal should be presented. A copy of the initial application for the order must be attached to the note of appeal. The note of appeal should include a succinct summary of the sheriff's decision (and a copy of it should be attached to the note of appeal). The grounds of challenge to the sheriff's decision should be precisely articulated.

The powers of the High Court on an appeal under s.301A(5) are provided in s.301A(6). The court may uphold, vary or quash the decision of the sheriff. There is a time limit for bringing an appeal: it must be lodged with Justiciary Office not later than two days after the date of the sheriff's decision (r.27A.1(1)). Failure to comply with that requirement will render the appeal incompetent unless the High Court subsequently, on a written application (see r.A4.1(1)), determines that the failure is a procedural irregularity which is due to mistake, oversight or other excusable reason and that it would be in the interests of justice to excuse the failure (see s.300A(4) and (5)(b)).

[THE NEXT PARAGRAPH IS B1-61]

PART VII

MISCELLANEOUS PROCEDURES

Chapter 28

Identification Procedures

Applications for identification parade

B1-61 **28.1.**—(1) An application to the sheriff made by an accused under section 290 of the Act of 1995 (application by accused for identification parade) shall be made—

(a) to the sheriff in whose sheriffdom the proceedings in relation to which the order is sought have been commenced;

(b) by petition—

(i) where the accused has appeared on petition under Part IV of the Act of 1995 (petition procedure) but an indictment has not been served on him, in Form 28.1-A; or

(ii) where an indictment or a complaint has been served on the accused, in Form 28.1-B.

(2) On the petition referred to in paragraph (1) being lodged, the sheriff shall—

(a) order intimation of the petition to be made to the prosecutor;

(b) fix a diet for a hearing of the petition on the earliest practicable date; and

(c) after giving the prosecutor an opportunity to be heard at the hearing and allowing such further procedure as he thinks fit, make an order granting or refusing the petition.

(3) If—

(a) the prosecutor is not present at the hearing of the petition; and

(b) the sheriff makes an order granting the petition,

the sheriff clerk shall issue a certified copy of the order to the petitioner or his solicitor.

(4) The sheriff clerk shall record the order made by the sheriff under paragraph (2)(c) in the minute of proceedings, and shall keep the petition and relative documents in his custody.

Order requiring accused to participate in identification procedure

B1-61.1 **28.2.**—(1) An application made in writing by the prosecutor under section 267B of the Act of 1995 (order requiring accused to participate in identification procedure) shall be in Form 28.2 and shall be served on the other parties.

(2) On an application referred to in paragraph (1) being made, the court may appoint a diet for a hearing of the application.

(3) Where the court appoints a hearing under paragraph (2) it shall order intimation of the diet to the other parties.

AMENDMENTS

Rule 28.2 inserted by Act of Adjournal (Criminal Procedure Rules Amendment No.6) (Criminal Proceedings etc. (Reform) (Scotland) Act 2007) 2007 (SSI 2007/511) r.9 (effective December 10, 2007).

Chapter 28 heading and r.28.2 as amended by Act of Adjournal (Criminal Procedure Rules Amendment) (Miscellaneous) 2009 (SSI 2009/144) r.4 (effective April 30, 2009).

[THE NEXT PARAGRAPH IS B1-62]

GENERAL NOTE

B1-62 When an identification parade involving the accused has not been held by the Crown, the accused is entitled to apply to the sheriff for an order that the prosecutor hold an identification parade in which the accused shall be one of those constituting the parade. The sheriff is only entitled to grant the order when the prosecutor has been requested by the accused to hold such a parade and the prosecutor has either refused to hold the parade or has unreasonably delayed in holding the parade, and the application is considered to be reasonable by the sheriff. Considerations which arose in cases where the Crown applied for a warrant to place accused persons, or suspects (see *Archibald v Lees*, 1995 S.L.T. 231), on an identification parade such as whether there are "special circumstances" justifying the grant of the warrant (see, e.g. *McMurtrie v Annan*, 1995 S.L.T. 642) do not apply when the accused seeks the warrant. Intimation of the petition craving the order on the prosecutor must be given to the prosecutor who is entitled to appear at the hearing of the petition and must be afforded an opportunity to be heard (see s.29(2)). For an example of a successful application, see *Wilson v Tudhope*, 1985 S.C.C.R. 339.

In *Beattie v Hingston*, 1999 S.L.T. 362, the sheriff had refused an accused's application for an identification parade to be held, on the basis that the accused had advanced no reasons for him to assess whether the application was reasonable. On a suspension brought by the accused the High Court remitted the application to be heard *de novo* by a different sheriff in respect that the sheriff had erred in his conclusion. The accused had explained that the parade was sought because (1) identification of the perpetrator was the main issue at the forthcoming trial, and (2) Crown witnesses had variously stated at precognition that they had identified the accused or had not or had been unsure. The High Court, however, expressed no opinion as to the sufficiency of the accused's reasons.

Section 267B(1) provides that the court (which means, in proceedings in the High Court, a single judge of that court and, in any other case, any court with jurisdiction in relation to proceedings: s.267B(10)) may, on an application by the prosecutor in any proceedings, make an order requiring the accused to participate in "an identification parade or other identification procedure". Rule 28.2 (as amended with effect from April 30, 2009) now refers not just to traditional identification parades but also to identification "procedures" because of the increasingly common use made of video identification procedure (VIPER). The prosecutor's application may be made at any time after commencement of the proceedings (s.267B(2)). Thus the sheriff has jurisdiction to determine an application made after appearance of the accused on petition even in cases, such as rape or murder, where the trial will inevitably require to proceed in the High Court.

Section 267B(3)(b) provides that where the accused is not present when the application is made, the court may (if it considers it appropriate) fix a hearing for the purpose of allowing the accused to make representations in relation to the application. Where a hearing is considered necessary, as it should be in almost all cases, the court is directed by r.28.2(3), to order intimation of the diet to the accused who is to participate in the parade or procedure and all co-accused.

Chapter 29

Precognition on Oath of Defence Witnesses

Applications for warrant to cite for precognition

29.1.—(1) An application to the sheriff made by an accused under section 291(1) of the Act of 1995 (warrant to cite any person to appear for precognition on oath) shall be made— **B1-63**

(a) to the sheriff in whose sheriffdom the proceedings, in respect of which the accused seeks the precognition of that person, have been commenced;

(b) by petition—

(i) where the accused has appeared on petition under Part IV of the Act of 1995 (petition procedure) but an indictment has not been served on him, in Form 29.1-A; or

(ii) where an indictment or a complaint has been served on the accused, in Form 29.1-B.

(2) On a petition referred to in paragraph (1) being lodged, the sheriff shall—

(a) order intimation of the application to be made to the procurator fiscal; and

(b) fix a diet for a hearing of the application.

Orders for taking precognition

29.2. Where, after the hearing fixed under rule 29.1(2), the sheriff is satisfied that it is reasonable to require such precognition on oath in the circumstances, he shall— **B1-63.1**

(a) order the precognition to be taken;

(b) fix a diet for it to be taken; and

(c) grant warrant to cite the person from whom it is to be taken.

Citation to attend for precognition

29.3.—(1) Citation of a person to attend the diet fixed for taking his precognition on oath shall be in Form 29.3; and an execution of service shall be produced at the diet fixed under rule 29.1(2). **B1-63.2**

(2) Where a person fails to appear at a diet fixed for taking his precognition and the sheriff issues a warrant for his apprehension under section 291(2) of the Act of 1995, execution of that warrant—

(a) shall be made by an officer of law instructed by the accused or his solicitor; and

(b) may proceed on a copy of the petition and warrant duly certified by the sheriff clerk.

(3) The clerk shall immediately give notice of that person's failure to appear at the diet to the procurator fiscal.

Record of proceedings

29.4.—(1) Where a person appears before the sheriff to have his precognition taken on oath, the proceedings shall be recorded in shorthand by an official shorthand writer instructed by the accused or his solicitor. **B1-63.3**

(2) The shorthand writer shall extend his shorthand notes recording the proceedings, sign the transcript, and lodge it with the sheriff clerk.

(3) On the transcript being lodged, the sheriff clerk shall—

(a) send a copy to the solicitor for the accused or, it he is not represented, to the accused; and

(b) fix a diet for the person whose precognition has been taken on oath to attend before the sheriff to sign the precognition.

Fees of shorth and writer

B1-63.4 **29.5.**—(1) The solicitor for the accused or, if he is not represented, the accused shall be liable for payment of—

(a) the fees of the shorthand writer, and
(b) the reasonable expenses of the person precognosed on oath;

and shall tender any such expenses in advance if required by that person to do so.

(2) Where the accused is not represented, the sheriff may, at the hearing of the application or at any time before the precognition is taken, order the accused to consign into court such sum as he may be required to pay under paragraph (1) in respect of fees and expenses on or before such date as the sheriff may specify in the order.

(3) If the sheriff orders the accused to consign a sum into court under paragraph (2) and that sum is not consigned by the date specified in the order, the petition shall be treated as abandoned.

[THE NEXT PARAGRAPH IS B1-64]

GENERAL NOTE

B1-64 Section 291(1) of the 1995 Act provides that the sheriff may grant warrant to cite any person (other than a co-accused) who is alleged to be a witness in relation to any offence of which the accused has been charged, to appear before him in chambers at such time or place as the sheriff specifies, for precognition on oath by the accused or his solicitor in relation to that offence (cf. *HM Advocate v Campbell*, 1996 S.C.C.R. 419). For an order to be granted the accused must satisfy the sheriff that it is reasonable to require such precognition on oath in the circumstances. For example, the Appeal Court has observed that where a partially dyslexic accused wishes himself to precognosce witnesses who are unwilling, in order to obtain a record of their evidence, his remedy is to apply for an order from the sheriff under s.291(1) which the sheriff should grant if he is satisfied that it is reasonable to require precognition on oath in the particular circumstances: see *Drummond, Petitioner*, 1998 S.L.T. 757 at 758, per Lord Justice General Rodger. As in the case of identification parades in Ch.28, the prosecutor is entitled to receive intimation of the application and is entitled to be heard at the hearing of the application.

Rule 29.1

It is incompetent to apply for an order for citation of a witness to submit to precognition on oath prior to full committal (see *Cirignaco, Petitioner*, 1985 S.C.C.R. 157). If intimation is not made by the accused of the application to the procurator fiscal then the sheriff is entitled—and no doubt would feel bound—to refuse the application.

Rule 29.3

The obligation on the sheriff clerk to give immediate notice of a witness's failure to appear at the diet to the procurator fiscal proceeds on the fact that failure to attend when duly cited and having been given at least 48 hours notice, exposes the witness to the risk of criminal prosecution under s.291(2) of the 1995 Act.

Rule 29.5

It is suggested that the tendering of reasonable witness expenses in advance, when so required, is a condition precedent of the sheriff's allowing the precognition on oath to proceed (irrespective of whether or not the sheriff makes an order in terms of r.29.5(2)). Accordingly, the failure to tender such expenses when they are sought will justify the witness in not attending for precognition and the witness will not incur any criminal liability by not attending.

The Appeal Court has observed that an unrepresented accused has no right to recover the expenses of the shorthand writer and the witnesses from the legal aid fund and accordingly, where such an accused has chosen not to seek legal aid, it has been held that he is not entitled to complain that precognition on oath is financially burdensome and that he should therefore be enabled to compel witnesses to submit to being precognosced by the accused himself in tape-recorded conditions (see *Drummond, Petitioner*, 1998 S.L.T. 759; 1998 S.C.C.R. 42).

Chapter 29A

Service of Bills of Advocation and Suspension and Petitions to the Nobile Officium

Service of bill or petition

B1-64.1 **29A.1.**—(1) Where a first order for service is sought in relation to—

(a) a bill of advocation;
(b) a bill of suspension; or
(c) a petition to the nobile officium,

the complainer or petitioner shall provide two copies of the bill or petition when presenting it to the clerk of the appropriate Appeal Court for registration.

(2) Where a first order for service is granted, the clerk of the appropriate Appeal Court shall provide the complainer or petitioner with a certified copy of—

(a) the bill or petition; and

(b) the interlocutor granting first order for service.

(3) The complainer or petitioner shall serve the certified copy of the bill or petition and interlocutor on the respondent.

(4) Where a bill or petition arises from proceedings in a lower court, the clerk of the appropriate Appeal Court shall intimate a copy to that court.

(5) In this rule, "clerk of the appropriate Appeal Court" means—

(a) in a case where the bill or petition is presented to the High Court, the Clerk of Justiciary;

(b) in a case where the bill is presented to the Sheriff Appeal Court, the Clerk of the Sheriff Appeal Court.

AMENDMENTS

Chapter 29A inserted by Act of Adjournal (Criminal Procedure Rules Amendment) (Miscellaneous) 2009 (SSI 2009/144) para.5 (effective April 30, 2009).

Rule 29A.1 as amended by Act of Adjournal (Criminal Procedure Rules 1996 Amendment) (No. 4) (Sheriff Appeal Court) 2015 (SSI 2015/245) para.4 (effective September 22, 2015 subject to savings provisions in para.6).

GENERAL NOTE

Advocation, suspension and applications to the *nobile officium* of the High Court of Justiciary are common law methods of review. There is little statutory regulation of them. Section 130 of the 1995 Act provides that suspension is incompetent in respect of any "conviction, sentence, judgment or order pronounced in any proceedings on indictment in the sheriff court" (see *George Outram & Co v Lees*, 1992 J.C. 17) although suspension is competent to review a warrant of the sheriff committing an accused for trial on indictment (*Mellors v Normand (No.2)*, 1996 J.C. 148). Suspension is incompetent prior to final judgment in summary proceedings (*Morton v McLeod*, 1982 S.L.T. 187) but incidental warrants may be suspended where they do not form part of the case. **B1-64.2**

Advocation of solemn proceedings is incompetent at the instance of the accused but s.131(1) of the 1995 Act provides that advocation is available to the prosecutor for the review of "a decision of any court of solemn jurisdiction". Hitherto advocation of High Court proceedings was incompetent because of the nature of advocation as a calling up of inferior court proceedings. Under s.191(1) both suspension and advocation are available in summary proceedings where an appeal under s.175 would be incompetent or inappropriate; the accused in such circumstances seeks suspension of the conviction and the prosecutor seeks advocation against the acquittal on the ground of an alleged miscarriage of justice.

In summary proceedings, advocation at the accused's instance is generally not appropriate prior to final determination. Thus bills were competent in *Pollock and Kenmure v Procurator Fiscal, Hamilton* [2009] HCJAC 34 (April 24, 2009) because the impugned decision was that of the sheriff taken in confiscation proceedings which followed conviction on summary complaint. Otherwise, as a matter of expediency, advocation by an accused prior to final determination is excluded unless there are "very special circumstances where grave injustice to an accused would result from an irregularity in preliminary procedure, which injustice could not be reasonably rectified by a bill of suspension brought after the determination of the case" (*Durant v Lockhart*, 1985 S.C.C.R. 72 at 74, per Lord Jauncey). However, in *Lawson v Procurator Fiscal, Falkirk* [2009] HCJAC 56 (June 4, 2009) the High Court reserved its opinion on the continuing soundness of *Durant v Lockhart* (para.15).

When a bill or petition is to be proceeded with, the complainer or petitioner must lodge the writ with Justiciary Office. The writ will then be placed before a single judge of the High Court for the first order for service and any interim orders such as liberation or suspension of a disqualification. Rule 29A.1(1) requires that two copies of the writ be presented to Justiciary Office.

As r.29A.1(2) implies, the single judge may decline to grant a first order. It is not necessary for the judge to remit the case to a quorum of the High Court (see Renton and Brown, *Criminal Procedure* (6th edn), para.33-11). The single judge in *Granger, Petitioner*, 2001 J.C. 183 refused a first order in a petition to the *nobile officium* because it sought an order which was in conflict with s.124(2) of the 1995 Act. The same course could have been followed in *Harris, Petitioner* [2009] HCJAC 85 (September 4, 2009) but was not. Instead a quorum of the High Court concluded after a hearing of the petition and answers in which the Crown challenged the competency of the petition, that the petition was incompetent as it sought a second appeal in respect of a murder conviction which had already been the subject of an unsuccessful appeal. The power of the Appeal Court to consider a second appeal against conviction in solemn proceedings has recently been considered by a bench of five judges in a set of petitions in which the court itself raised the point of competency (see *Beck and Others, Petitioners* [2010] HCJAC 8: it was held to be generally incompetent to petition the *nobile officium* in such circumstances). In *Morton v McLeod*, 1982 S.L.T. 187 Lord Cameron refused a first order in a suspension as incompetent. Where a bill of advocation by an accused is presented prior to final determination, it is submitted that the single judge will be entitled, though not bound, to decline to grant the first order if the test set out in *Durant v Lockhart*, supra is not satisfied on the averments in the bill.

Rule 29A.1(3) requires the complainer or petitioner to serve on the respondent both the certified copy of the writ and the interlocutor granting the first order for service. Section 298A of the 1995 Act addresses the requirements of service by both prosecutor and accused.

Time limits

Section 191A of the 1995 Act introduced a time limit for presentation of bills of suspension and advocation. The party must lodge the bill with Justiciary Office within three weeks of the date of the conviction, acquittal or, as the case maybe, other decision to which the bill relates (s.191A(2)) but the High Court may, on the application of the party, extend the time limit (s.191A(3)). The approach of the High Court to the operation of the power in s.191A(3) has recently been explained in *MacDonald v Procurator Fiscal, Dornoch* [2013] HCJAC 48 (decided on March 13, 2013):

> "The court requires to consider two matters. The first is whether an adequate explanation has been proferred as to why the bill is so late. The second is to determine whether there is any merit in the allegation, such that the bill would be likely to succeed in suspending the conviction" (at [3], per Lord Justice Clerk Carloway).

At the same time as the High Court decided *MacDonald*, it also stated that it did not consider that "ignorance of the law in relation to time limits, professed by agents practising in the very field in which they are applicable, constitutes any form of explanation which can be excused in terms of the statutory provisions" (*Middleton and McAllister v Procurator Fiscal, Livingston* [2013] HCJAC 49, at [3], per Lord Justice Clerk Carloway).

Chapter 29B

Contempt of Court

Application of this Chapter

B1-64.3 **29B.1.**—(1) This Chapter applies where a court considers that a person ("the relevant person") may have committed a contempt of court to which paragraph (2) applies (the "alleged contempt") in, or in connection with, proceedings before that court.

(2) This paragraph applies to an alleged contempt that has been directed at a member of the court personally or any other contempt that it would be inappropriate for that court to deal with.

Withdrawal of jury

B1-64.4 **29B.2.** Where the alleged contempt occurs in proceedings on indictment, the court shall ensure that any step it takes in relation to dealing with the alleged contempt is taken out with the presence of the jury or any persons cited for jury service.

Criminal prosecution

B1-64.5 **29B.3.**—(1) The court shall ascertain from the prosecutor whether he intends to bring criminal proceedings in relation to the alleged contempt.

(2) Where the prosecutor states that he intends to bring criminal proceedings, the court shall take no further action in relation to the alleged contempt.

Procedure where the prosecutor does not intend to bring criminal proceedings

B1-64.6 **29B.4.**—(1) Where the prosecutor has indicated that he does not intend to bring criminal proceedings, the court ("the first court") shall fix a diet for a hearing of the matter ("the contempt hearing") by a differently constituted court ("the other court").

(2) The diet shall be fixed to take place no later than the third court day following the date on which the alleged contempt occurred.

(3) At the same time as fixing the diet for the contempt hearing, the first court shall—

(a) advise the relevant person that legal aid is available for legal advice and assistance;
(b) ascertain the relevant person's current address; and
(c) either—
  (i) ordain the relevant person to appear at the contempt hearing; or
  (ii) exercise its power to remand that person in custody until that hearing.

Statement of facts

B1-64.7 **29B.5.**—(1) The first court shall prepare a statement of the relevant facts ("the statement of facts").

(2) The clerk of court shall make arrangements for the relevant person and the other court to receive a copy of the statement of facts no later than 24 hours before the contempt hearing.

The contempt hearing

B1-64.8 **29B.6.**—(1) At the contempt hearing the other court shall ascertain from the relevant person whether he admits or denies the facts contained in the statement of facts.

(2) Where the relevant person admits the material facts contained in the statement of facts, the other court shall take that statement to be accurate and shall—

(a) hear the relevant person and consider any relevant documents; and
(b) determine whether a contempt of court has been committed by the relevant person.

(3) Where the relevant person denies any of the material facts contained in the statement of facts—

(a) he may give evidence on oath concerning that fact or those facts;
(b) the other court may hear evidence from any persons that it considers relevant ("relevant witnesses") and consider any relevant documents.

(4) Persons identified by the other court as relevant witnesses under paragraph (3) shall be cited to attend that court by the clerk of court.

(5) To the extent that the statement of facts is not denied by the relevant person, the other court shall take it to be accurate.

(6) After having determined under paragraph (3) the accuracy of each of the material facts which is disputed, the other court shall—

(a) hear the relevant person and consider any relevant documents; and

(b) determine whether a contempt of court has been committed by the relevant person.

(7) Where the other court makes a finding of contempt of court, it shall—

(a) give the relevant person the opportunity to apologise; and

(b) after hearing the relevant person, determine the disposal.

Adjournment of the hearing

29B.7.—(1) The other court may adjourn the contempt hearing on its own motion or on the motion of the relevant person. **B1-64.9**

(2) A request by the relevant person for an adjournment of the contempt hearing shall be made orally at the contempt hearing.

(3) A request for an adjournment will be granted on cause shown.

(4) Where the other court adjourns a contempt hearing it shall—

(a) ordain the relevant person to appear at that adjourned hearing; or

(b) exercise its power to remand that person in custody until that hearing.

Remand appeal

29B.8.—(1) The relevant person may appeal to the High Court a decision of the court to exercise its powers to remand him in custody as mentioned in rule 29B.4(3)(c) or rule 29B.7(4) by lodging a written notice of appeal with the Clerk of Justiciary. **B1-64.10**

(2) The appeal shall be treated, so far as possible, as though it were a bail appeal.

Minute of proceedings

29B.9. The clerk of court shall record all proceedings relating to the alleged contempt of court in the court minutes. **B1-64.11**

AMENDMENTS

Chapter 29B inserted by Act of Adjournal (Criminal Procedure Rules Amendment No.2) (Contempt of Court) 2009 (SSI 2009/243) r.2 (effective August 5, 2009).

GENERAL NOTE

This chapter, which came into force on August 5, 2009 (see Act of Adjournal (Criminal Procedure Rules Amendment No.2) (Contempt of Court) 2009 (SSI 2009/243) para.1(1)) is made necessary by the decision of the Grand Chamber of the European Court in *Kyprianou v Cyprus (No.2)* (2007) 44 E.H.R.R. 27 and implements the Lord Justice Clerk's recommendation in *Robertson v HM Advocate*, 2008 J.C. 146 (para.102) that urgent attention be given to the promulgation of an Act of Adjournal to provide appropriate procedures to be followed when the court itself cannot deal with a possible contempt of court. That situation will arise where, as r.29B.1(2) describes it, the alleged contempt "has been directed at a member of the court personally" or where it would be inappropriate for the court to deal with the alleged contempt. **B1-64.12**

Special provision is made in r.29B.2 for such alleged contempt occurring in the course of proceedings on indictment. The court before whom the alleged contempt occurs must ensure that any step it takes in relation to the alleged contempt is taken out with the jury's presence and where the jury has not then been empanelled, out with the presence of any persons cited to attend for jury service. In any case of alleged contempt within the meaning of r.29B.1(2), the court must first ascertain from the Crown whether the Crown intends to bring criminal proceedings in respect of the alleged contempt (r.29B.3(1)) and if the Crown intends to do so, the court should take no further action (r.29B.3(2)). Where the Crown does not intend to bring criminal proceedings, the court must fix a diet for a hearing (called "the contempt hearing") to be held before a differently constituted court. That diet must be fixed so as to take place no later than the third court day following the date on which the alleged contempt occurred (r.29B.4(2)). At the time of fixing the contempt hearing the first court must do three things: advise the alleged contemnor of the availability of legal aid; discover from him his current address; and either ordain him to appear at the contempt hearing or remand him in custody until that hearing (r.29B.4(3)).

The court fixing the contempt hearing must thereafter prepare a "statement of facts" setting out the alleged contempt and the clerk of court must ensure that this statement is supplied to the other court for the contempt hearing, and to the alleged contemnor, no later than 24 hours before the contempt hearing (r.29B.5(2)). The statement of facts must be either admitted or denied (whether in whole or in part) at the contempt hearing. Where the statement of facts is admitted in all material particulars, the court must take the statement of facts as accurate, hear the alleged contemnor, consider any relevant documents and thereafter determine whether a contempt has been committed (r.29B.6(2)).

Where material facts in the statement are denied, the court must determine whether they are accurate or not and in doing so the court may hear evidence from any persons (including the alleged contemnor, whose evidence must be given on oath or affirmation) and consider any relevant documents (r.29B.6(3)). As it will be unknown prior to the contempt hearing whether the statement of facts is admitted or not, it seems inevitable that the contempt hearing may require to be adjourned for the citation of witnesses considered relevant by the court (r.29B.6(4)). Hence the power given by r.29B.7(1) for the court to adjourn the contempt hearing *ex proprio motu* or on the alleged contemnor's motion on cause shown. When the hearing is adjourned, the alleged contemnor must be either ordained to appear at the adjourned diet or remanded in custody until that diet. The alleged contemnor is given the right to appeal against his remand by means of a written notice of appeal which must be lodged with the Justiciary Office (r.29B.8(1)).

After hearing the evidence, considering the relevant documents and affording the alleged contemnor an opportunity to address the court, the court must determine whether a contempt has been committed. Where it does so determine it must make a finding to that effect. When that finding is made the court must give the contemnor the opportunity to apologise and after hearing this, it must determine the appropriate "disposal". The penalty for contempt is not a sentence under the 1995 Act. The contemnor is, however, able to seek review of his finding and disposal by petition to the *nobile officium* of the High Court.

These rules do not mention the Crown at any stage. For example, no requirement is made that the Crown should receive a copy of the statement of facts. The procedure appears to envisage that the alleged contempt is a matter between the court and the alleged contemnor. That may be necessary on one view because the prosecutor may be a witness to the alleged contempt. The requisite standard of proof to be applied when the court determines the facts is proof beyond reasonable doubt since a finding of contempt of court may have penal consequences for the contemnor.

[THE NEXT PARAGRAPH IS B1-65]

Chapter 30

Proceedings for the Execution of Irish Warrants

B1-65 [...]

AMENDMENT

Chapter 30 repealed by the Act of Adjournal (Criminal Procedure Rules Amendment No.3) (Extradition etc.) 2004 (SSI 2004/346), r.2 (effective August 18, 2004).

[THE NEXT PARAGRAPH IS B1-67]

Chapter 31

References to the European Court of Justice

Interpretation of this Chapter

B1-67 **31.1.**—(1) In this Chapter, unless the context otherwise requires—

"the European Court" means the Court of Justice of the European Communities;

"question" means a question or issue in respect of which the European Court has jurisdiction to give a preliminary ruling under the Community Treaties;

"reference" means a request to the European Court for a preliminary ruling on a question.

(2) [...]

AMENDMENT

Rule 31.1(1) as amended, and r.31.1 (2) repealed, by the Act of Adjournal (Criminal Procedure Rules Amendment No. 4) (Miscellaneous) 2006 (SSI 2006/436), r.2 (effective September 1, 2006).

Notice of references in solemn proceedings

B1-67.1 **31.2.**—(1) Where a question is to be raised in any proceedings on indictment (other than proceedings on appeal), notice of intention to do so shall be given to the court before which the preliminary hearing or first diet is to take place, as the case may be, and to the other parties not later than 14 days after service of the indictment.

(2) Where such a notice is given, a record of the notice shall be made on the record copy of the indictment or in the record of proceedings, as the case may be; and the court, in chambers, shall reserve consideration of the question to the preliminary hearing or first diet, as the case may be.

(3) [...]

(4) At the trial diet, the court, after hearing the parties, may determine the question or may decide that a preliminary ruling should be sought.

(5) Where the court determines the question, the accused shall then (if appropriate) be called on to plead to the indictment; and, without prejudice to any other power available to it, the court—

(a) may prorogate the time for lodging any special defence;
(b) may continue the diet to a specified time and place; and
(c) in a case where witnesses and jurors have not been cited to attend at the trial diet, shall continue the diet and order the citation of witnesses and jurors to attend the continued diet.

(6) No period during which the diet is continued under paragraph (5) shall—

(a) subject to paragraph (7), be longer than 21 days; or
(b) be taken into account for the purposes of determining whether any time limit has expired.

(7) The court may, on the application of the prosecutor or defence, extend any period during which the diet is continued for such longer period than 21 days as it thinks fit on special cause shown.

AMENDMENTS

Rule 31.2(1) and (2) as amended, and r.31.2(3) repealed, by Act of Adjournal (Criminal Procedure Rules Amendment No. 4) (Miscellaneous) 2006 (SSI 2006/436) para.2 (effective September 1, 2006).

Notice of references in summary proceedings

31.3.—(1) Where a question is to be raised in any summary proceedings (other than proceedings on appeal), notice of intention to do so shall be given before the accused is called on to plead to the complaint. **B1-67.2**

(2) Where such notice is given, a record of the notice shall be entered in the minute of proceedings and the court shall not then call on the accused to plead to the complaint.

(3) The court may hear parties on the question forthwith or may adjourn the case to a specified date for such hearing.

(4) After hearing parties, the court may determine the question or may decide that a preliminary ruling should be sought.

(5) Where the court determines the question, the accused shall then (where appropriate) be called on to plead to the complaint.

References in proceedings in the Sheriff Appeal Court

31.3A.—(1) Where a question is to be raised in the Sheriff Appeal Court in any proceedings, notice of intention to do so shall be given by the party raising the question **B1-67.2.1**

(2) Where such notice is given, a record of the notice shall be entered in the minute of proceedings.

(3) The court may hear parties on the question forthwith or may adjourn the case to a specified date for such hearing.

(4) After hearing parties, the court may determine the question or may decide that a preliminary ruling should be sought.

(5) Where the court determines the question, it shall then make such order in respect of further procedure as it thinks fit.

AMENDMENTS

Rule 31.3A inserted by Act of Adjournal (Criminal Procedure Rules 1996 Amendment) (No. 4) (Sheriff Appeal Court) 2015 (SSI 2015/245) para.4 (effective September 22, 2015).

[THE NEXT PARAGRAPH IS B1-67.3]

Proceedings on appeal etc. to the High Court

31.4.—(1) Where a question is raised in the High Court in any proceedings on appeal or on a petition for the exercise of the *nobile officium*, the court shall proceed to make a reference. **B1-67.3**

(2) In paragraph (1), the reference to proceedings on appeal is a reference to proceedings on appeal under the Act of 1995 or on appeal by bill of suspension, bill of advocation or otherwise.

AMENDMENTS

Rule 31.4 as amended by Act of Adjournal (Criminal Procedure Rules 1996 Amendment) (No. 4) (Sheriff Appeal Court) 2015 (SSI 2015/245) para.4 (effective September 22, 2015).

Preparation of case for reference

31.5.—(1) Where the court decides that a preliminary ruling should be sought, the court shall— **B1-67.4**

(a) give its reasons and cause those reasons to be recorded in the record or minute of proceedings, as the case may be; and
(b) continue the proceedings from time to time as necessary for the purposes of the reference.

(2) The reference—

(a) except in so far as the court may otherwise direct, shall be drafted in Form 31.5 and the court may give directions to the parties as to the manner in which and by whom the case is to be drafted and adjusted;
(b) shall thereafter if necessary, be further adjusted to take account of any adjustments required by the court; and
(c) after approval and the making of an appropriate order by the court, shall (after the expiry of the period for appeal) be transmitted by the clerk of court to the Registrar of the European Court with a certified copy of the record or minute of proceedings, as the case may be, and, where applicable, a certified copy of the relevant indictment or complaint.

(3) In preparing a reference, the parties shall have regard to guidance issued by the European Court.

AMENDMENT

Rule 31.5(3) substituted by the Act of Adjournal (Criminal Procedure Rules Amendment No. 4) (Miscellaneous) 2006 (SSI 2006/436), r.2 (effective September 1, 2006).

Procedure on receipt of preliminary ruling

31.6.—(1) Where a preliminary ruling has been given by the European Court on a question referred to it and the ruling has been received by the clerk of the court which made the reference, the ruling shall be laid by the clerk before the court. **B1-67.5**

(2) On the ruling being laid before the court, the court shall then give directions as to further procedure, which directions shall be intimated by the clerk, with a copy of the ruling, to each of the parties to the proceedings.

Appeals against references

B1-67.6 **31.7.**—(1) Subject to paragraph (2), where an order making a reference is made, any party to the proceedings who is aggrieved by the order may, within 14 days after the date of the order, appeal against the order to the High Court sitting as a court of appeal.

(2) Paragraph (1) shall not apply to such an order made in proceedings in the High Court sitting as a court of appeal or in proceedings on petition to that court for the exercise of its *nobile officium*.

(3) Any appeal under this rule shall be taken by lodging with the clerk of the court which made the order a note of appeal in Form 31.7 and signed by the appellant or his solicitor; and a copy of the note shall be served by the appellant on every other party to the proceedings.

(4) The clerk of court shall record the lodging of the note in the record or minute of proceedings, as the case may be, and shall forthwith transmit the note to the Clerk of Justiciary with the record or minute of proceedings and a certified copy of the relevant indictment or complaint.

(5) In disposing of an appeal under this rule, the High Court (sitting as a court of appeal) may—

(a) sustain or dismiss the appeal, and in either case remit the proceedings to the court of first instance with instructions to proceed as accords; and

(b) give such directions for other procedure as it thinks fit.

(6) Unless the court making the order otherwise directs, a reference shall not be transmitted to the Registrar of the European Court before the time allowed by this rule for appealing against the order has expired or before the appeal has been disposed of or abandoned.

AMENDMENTS

Rules 31.1 and 31.7 as amended by the Act of Adjournal (Criminal Procedure Rules Amendment No. 2) 1999 (SI 1999/1282), para.2(2) (effective May 1, 1999).

Rule 31.5(2) as amended by the Act of Adjournal (Criminal Procedure Rules Amendment No. 2) 1999 (SI 1999/1282), para.2(3)(a) (effective May 1, 1999). Rule 31.5(3) inserted by the Act of Adjournal (Criminal Procedure Rules Amendment No. 2) 1999 (SI 1999/1282), para.2(3)(b) (effective May 1, 1999).

Para.B1-67 as amended by Act of Adjournal (Criminal Procedure Rules Amendment) (Miscellaneous) (SI 1996/2147 (s.171)) (effective September 9, 1996).

[THE NEXT PARAGRAPH IS B1-68]

GENERAL NOTE

B1-68 Rules 63 to 67 and 112 to 118 of the 1988 Rules provided separately for solemn and summary proceedings in which references were made to the Court of Justice of the European Communities for a preliminary ruling on a question or issue of European law concerning the interpretation or validity of the Treaty provisions or an act of the Community institutions. The 1996 Rules bring these rules together under one chapter. A reference is a request for a preliminary ruling on a European legal question which *must* be made by the High Court when it sits as a Court of Appeal because there is no right of appeal from that court. Lower courts are not however compelled to make a reference but may do so (except in the case of a question or an issue arising under the European Coal and Steel Community Treaty (see Art. 41)) if they consider it appropriate.

A lower court is entitled to seek a preliminary ruling from the European Court of Justice if the lower court considers that a decision on the question raised before it is necessary to enable the court to give judgment (*Wither v Cowie*, 1991 S.L.T. 401 at 405F). National Courts have the widest discretion in seeking such a ruling (see *Rheinmuhlen-Dusseldorf v Einfuhr-Und Vorratsstelle fur Getreide undFuttermittel* (166/73) [1974] E.C.R. 33), although in *Wither v Cowie*, supra, Lord Justice-Clerk Ross referred only to the lower court's having "a wide discretion".

Where a sheriff, or justice of the peace or High Court judge sitting at first instance decides to make a reference to the European Court of Justice either at the suggestion of one of the parties or *ex proprio motu*—as the sheriff did in *Wither v Cowie*, supra—his decision can be appealed to the High Court of Justiciary sitting as a Court of Appeal. In such cases however the Appeal Court will not lightly interfere with the decision of the lower court to seek a preliminary ruling. In *Wither v Cowie*, supra, it was said that the Appeal Court "would not be justified in interfering with that exercise of the sheriffs discretion unless it felt that the sheriffs decision was plainly wrong" (1991 S.L.T. 401 at 406A) and Stephenson L.J.'s dictum in *Bulmer (H.P.) Ltd v J Bollinger S.A.* [1974] Ch. 401 was approved to the effect that the Appeal Court will only interfere when the lower court's decision "exceeds the generous ambit within which reasonable disagreement is possible and is, in fact, plainly wrong".

It has been argued that the provision of a right to appeal against the decision to make a reference is a fetter on the wide powers conferred on the national court by Art. 177 of the Treaty of Rome. However, the Court of Justice has not regarded the application of national appeal procedures to decisions to refer as being incompatible with Art. 177 (see *Kledingverkoopbedrijf de Geus en Uitdenbogerd v Bosch* (13/61) [1962] E.C.R. 45 at 50; see also Anderson, *References to the European Court* (1995), paras 7-083 to 7-088).

It might also be questioned whether the fact that the power to make a reference is only available prior to the accused being called on to plead is itself an unlawful restriction on the powers conferred on the national courts by Art. 177. However, the Court of Justice has held that national procedural rules which impinge on the power to refer a question for a preliminary ruling are not incompatible with Art. 177 unless they either are less favourable than the rules governing domestic actions or render the rights conferred by Community law virtually impossible or extremely difficult to invoke (*Rheinmuhlen-Dusseldorf* supra; *S.C.S. Peterbroeck van Campenhout & Cie. v Belgium* (C-312/93) [1996] All E.R. (E.C.) 242 at 257 (para. 12)).

Most European questions will involve a point of relevancy or competency and should be raised before the accused is called on to plead. For those cases which require the facts to be established before the question can be said to be raised, the accused or the Crown (at least in summary cases) can obtain his remedy on appeal when, if the High Court considers that a European question is raised, the court must make a reference (cf the position envisaged in *Wither v Cowie*, 1991 S.L.T. 401 and the notes to rr.31.2 and 31.3).

For examples of decisions of the European Court of Justice on references for preliminary rulings, see *Walkingshaw v Marshall*, 1991 S.C.C.R. 397; *Wither v Cowie*, 1994 S.L.T. 363; and *Mehlich v Mackenzie; Gewiese v Mackenzie*, 1984 S.L.T. 449; 1984 S.C.C.R. 130.

Rule 31.1

The reference procedure most frequently invoked is that provided for in Art.234 of the EC Treaty (formerly Art. 177 EEC) (see *Law of the European Union*, Vol.1, para.[308]). Prior to amendment of this chapter with effect from September 1, 2006, the preliminary ruling which a domestic court could seek was on a question or issue under Art.234, Art. 150 of the Euratom Treaty or Art.41 of the ECSC Treaty. The change in definition of "question" in r.31.1(1) reflects the now enlarged jurisdictional competence of the Court of Justice. For example, the Treaty of Amsterdam introduced a new provision, Art.68, into the EC Treaty. That provision modifies the application of Art.234 EC (and in particular, by Art.68(2), provides that the Court of Justice does not have jurisdiction to rule on measures taken pursuant to Art.62(1) EC in relation to the maintenance of law and order and the safeguarding of internal security). Moreover, while the UK has not yet made a declaration of acceptance, Art.35 of the Treaty on European Union gives jurisdiction to the Court of Justice to provide preliminary rulings on inter alia the validity and interpretation of framework decisions and decisions under Title VI in respect of police and judicial cooperation in criminal matters.

Rule 31.2

While it is possible for the court ex proprio motu to seek a preliminary ruling on a question or issue under the Community Treaties (see *Rheinmuhlen-Dusseldorf,*' at 38 (para.3)), it will normally be the parties who wish a reference to be made. To take account of the introduction of preliminary hearings in the High Court and to acknowledge belatedly the creation of mandatory first diets in the sheriff court, the notice which formerly had to be given by a party seeking a reference 14 days before the trial diet is now amended (as from September 1, 2006) to be 14 days before the preliminary hearing or first diet.

Rule 31.3

Notice of an intention to raise a question in summary proceedings need only be given at the pleading diet and can be determined there and then or at an adjourned diet. The court can also, as in solemn cases, decide to reserve the question if it is the course least likely to lead to long delay. In that case the court allows in effect a proof before answer, which was the course which the Appeal Court in *Wither v Cowie*, 1991 S.L.T. 401 appeared to approve.

Rule 31.4

The Appeal Court has no discretion and must seek a preliminary ruling. There is no appeal against the Appeal Court's decision to make a reference to the European Court of Justice: see r.31.7(2). Indeed where an appeal against the lower court's decision to seek a preliminary ruling is taken under r.31.7, it is arguable that since there is no appeal beyond the Appeal Court, the reference should be made in all cases. (Cf. McCluskey, *Criminal Appeals*, para.5.17.)

Rule 31.5

The parties should prepare the draft reference which it is proposed that the court should make to the Court of Justice and, where the referring court so directs (because, for example, the parties cannot agree on the final terms of the reference), they should make further adjustments to the proposed reference before the court will sanction its terms.

The reference is made because the court considers that a preliminary ruling is necessary and accordingly the court has the duty to control the terms of the reference which must contain, inter alia, (1) a statement of the facts which are essential to a full understanding of the legal significance of the proceedings which give rise to the question and (2) an exposition of the national law in which the question arises. Such details will usually appear in the opinion of the court on an appeal but that will not suffice because, while the opinion will accompany the reference, it may not be translated into the other official languages of the Community. In the case of references from inferior courts there will not usually be a written decision or note from the sheriff or justice.

The reference after having been approved by the lower court, cannot be transmitted to the European Court of Justice until after the expiry of the 14 day time-limit for appeal under r.31.7(1) (see r.31.7(6)).

However it should be noted that the High Court can in exercise of its *nobile officium* relieve a party from the consequences of a failure to comply with that time-limit: see *HM Advocate, Petitioner*, 1990 S.L.T. 798; 1990 S.C.C.R. 195.

The Notes for Completion of Form 31.5 have been issued by the Court of Justice but have no binding or interpretative effect. They draw to practitioners' attention the fact that proceedings for a preliminary ruling under Art.234 are free of charge before the Court of Justice which will not award expenses to any party.

Rule 31.7

An appeal against the order making a reference is competent at the instance of any party to the proceedings who is aggrieved by the order. A co-accused who is not involved in any charge raising a question on which a preliminary ruling is sought, could therefore be prejudiced by the delay which will be occasioned by a reference and might be well advised to appeal against the order. If his appeal fails—as it is likely to do—he can then seek a separation of trials: see McCluskey, *Criminal Appeals*, para.5.16.

Chapter 32

Annoying Creature

Interpretation of this Chapter

B1-69 **32.1.** In this Chapter, "the Act of 1982" means the Civic Government (Scotland) Act 1982.

Form of application to district court and service

B1-69.1 **32.2.**—(1) An application to a justice of the peace court under section 49(3) of the Act of 1982 (annoying creatures) shall be made in Form 32.2.

(2) On the lodging of any such application, the district court shall make an order for service of a copy of the application on any person mentioned in the application as having the creature so mentioned in his charge or keeping the creature, and fixing a date and time for the hearing of the application.

(3) A copy of the application and of the order made under paragraph (2) shall be served on any such person by recorded delivery at the normal place of residence or place of business of that person, and such service shall be treated as sufficient notice to that person of the terms of the application and the order for the purposes of paragraph (4).

(4) If any person upon whom service has been made in accordance with paragraph (3) fails to appear or be represented at the time and date of the hearing specified in the order without reasonable excuse, the court may proceed to hear and decide the application in his absence.

(5) Where the court makes an order in respect of any person under section 49(2) of the Act of 1982, the clerk of court shall, within seven days after the date on which the order was made, serve on that person, by recorded delivery at the normal place of residence or place of business of that person, a copy of the order and a notice setting out the terms of section 49(4) of the Act of 1982.

AMENDMENTS

Rule 32.2(1) as amended by Act of Adjournal (Criminal Procedure Rules Amendment) (Criminal Proceedings etc. (Reform) (Scotland) Act 2007) 2008 (SSI 2008/61) r.2 (effective March 10, 2008).

[THE NEXT PARAGRAPH IS B1-70]

Chapter 33

Legal Aid

Interpretation of this Chapter

B1-70 **33.1.** In this Chapter, unless the context otherwise requires—

"the Act of 1986" means the Legal Aid (Scotland) Act 1986;

"assisted person" means a person who is in receipt of criminal legal aid in the proceedings in question;

"the Regulations" means the Criminal Legal Aid (Scotland) Regulations 1996.

AMENDMENTS

Rule 33.1 as amended by Act of Adjournal (Criminal Procedure Rules Amendment No.4) (Miscellaneous) 2010 (SSI 2010/418) para.8 (effective December 13, 2010).

Legal aid in High Court

B1-70.1 **33.2.** [...]

AMENDMENTS

Rule 33.2 repealed by Act of Adjournal (Criminal Procedure Rules Amendment No.4) (Miscellaneous) 2010 (SSI 2010/418) para.8 (effective December 13, 2010).

Discontinuance of entitlement to legal aid

B1-70.2 **33.3.**—(1) Subject to paragraph (1A) below, where the court before which there are proceedings in which an assisted person is an accused or appellant is satisfied, after hearing that person—

(a) that he—
(i) has without reasonable cause failed to comply with a proper request made to him by the solicitor acting for him to supply any information relevant to the proceedings,
(ii) has delayed unreasonably in complying with any such request,
(iii) has without reasonable cause failed to attend at a diet of the court at which he has been required to attend or at a meeting with the counsel or solicitor acting for him under the Act of 1986 at which he has reasonably and properly been required to attend,
(iv) has conducted himself in connection with the proceedings in such a way as to make it appear to the court unreasonable that he should continue to receive criminal legal aid,
(v) has wilfully or deliberately given false information for the purpose of misleading the court in considering his financial circumstances under section 23(1) of the Act of 1986, or
(vi) has without reasonable cause failed to comply with a requirement of the Regulations, or
(b) that it is otherwise unreasonable for the solicitor to continue to act on behalf of the assisted person in the proceedings,

the court may direct that the assisted person shall cease to be entitled to criminal legal aid in connection with those proceedings.

(1A) Where the solicitor acting for the assisted person was appointed by the court under section 288D of the Act of 1995 (appointment of solicitors by court in proceedings in respect of sexual offence), paragraph (1) shall not apply.

(2) Where a direction is made under paragraph (1) of this rule in the course of proceedings to which section 22 of the Act of 1986 (automatic availability of criminal legal aid) applies, the accused shall not be entitled to criminal legal aid in relation to any later stages of the same proceedings before the court of first instance.

(3) Where a court issues a direction under paragraph (1), the clerk of court shall send notice of it to the Scottish Legal Aid Board.

(4) Where a court of first instance has made a direction under paragraph (1)(a), it shall instruct the clerk of court to report the terms of the finding made by the court to the Scottish Legal Aid Board for its consideration in any application for criminal legal aid in an appeal in connection with the proceedings in that court.

AMENDMENTS

Rule 33.3(1) as amended, and (1A) inserted, by Act of Adjournal (Criminal Procedure Rules Amendment No.3) (Sexual Offences (Procedure and Evidence) (Scotland) Act 2002) 2002 (SSI 2002/454) r.2(10) (effective November 1, 2002).

Statements on oath

33.4. In considering any matter in regard to the entitlement of a person to criminal legal aid, the court may require that person to make a statement on oath for the purpose of ascertaining or verifying any fact material to his entitlement to criminal legal aid. **B1-70.3**

Intimation of determination of High Court

33.5. The Clerk of Justiciary shall intimate to the Scottish Legal Aid Board any decision of the High Court made under section 25(2A) of the Act of 1986 (determination by High Court that applicant should receive legal aid). **B1-70.4**

Intimation of appointment of solicitor by court in certain proceedings

33.6. The clerk of court shall intimate to the Scottish Legal Aid Board any decision of the court to appoint a solicitor under section 288D(2) of the Act of 1995 (appointment of solicitors by court in certain proceedings). **B1-70.5**

AMENDMENTS

Rule 33.6 inserted by Act of Adjournal (Criminal Procedure Rules Amendment No.3) (Sexual Offences (Procedure and Evidence) (Scotland) Act 2002) 2002 (SSI 2002/454) r.2(11) (effective 1 November 2002).

In the heading of r 33.6 words substituted by Act of Adjournal (Criminal Procedure Rules 1996 Amendment) (Miscellaneous) 2019 (SSI 2019/321) para. 2(3)(a) (effective 13 November 2019).

Words in r.33.6 substituted by Act of Adjournal (Criminal Procedure Rules 1996 Amendment) (Miscellaneous) 2019 (SSI 2019/321) para.2(3)(b) (effective 13 November 2019).

[THE NEXT PARAGRAPH IS B1-71]

GENERAL NOTE

Rule 33.3

Rule 33.3(1). It is incompetent for the court to make a direction that the assisted person shall cease to be entitled to criminal legal aid in connection with the proceedings unless the assisted person has been afforded an opportunity to be heard on that question: see *Lamont, Petitioner*, 1995 S.L.T. 566. It is **B1-71** competent for an assisted person who has had his entitlement to criminal legal aid terminated by the court without being heard, to petition the *nobile officium* of the High Court of Justiciary to quash that direction: see *Lamont, Petitioner*, above, following *Hartley, Petitioner* (1968) 32 J.C.L. 191. Equally, it is incompetent for the court to refuse to hear an accused's legal representative and to insist in hearing the accused himself prior to revoking his legal aid certificate: such a decision to revoke legal aid can be reversed by the High Court in exercise of its *nobile officium* (see *Ness, Petitioner*, 1999 S.L.T. 214; 1998 S.C.C.R. 589).

In *Russell v Wilson*, 1994 S.C.C.R. 13 the sheriff, after the accused had pled guilty during a summary trial, adjourned the diet and remanded the accused in custody in order for investigations to be carried out into whether, as the sheriff strongly suspected, the accused had committed an offence under the Legal Aid (Scotland) Act 1986 in connection with his application for legal aid. The High Court suspended both the conviction and subsequent sentence on the ground that the adjournment was an extraneous and collateral matter with no legitimate bearing on any decision which the sheriff might have required to take and that the proceedings had accordingly come to an end at midnight on the day of the purported adjournment. The High Court also observed that it was unreasonable for the sheriff to remand the accused in custody simply on the basis of a suspicion.

Rule 33.3(2). Once the Court has made a direction that the assisted person should cease to be entitled to criminal legal aid, it is incompetent to petition the *nobile officium* to obtain an order restoring legal aid in relation to any later stages of the same proceedings before the court of first instance: see *McGettigan, Petitioner*, 1996 S.L.T. 76. However, where what is challenged before the High Court is the propriety of the order of the lower court revoking the legal aid certificate (which was not in issue in *McGettigan*), a petition to the *nobile officium* is competent (see *Anderson, Petr*, 1998 S.L.T. 101). Thus in *Reid, Petitioner*, 1998 S.C.C.R. 430 the High Court restored an accused's legal aid certificate because the sheriff at the trial diet had revoked the accused's certificate and backdated the revocation to the intermediate diet. While the High Court understood the sheriff's reasons for backdating the order revoking the certificate, backdating was not competent.

The principles on which the revocation of a legal aid certificate will be reviewed in a petition to the *nobile officium* are, with one possible exception, likely to be the same as for judicial review of administrative decisions (see *Council of Civil Service Unions v Minister for the Civil Service* [1985] A.C. 374). Thus taking into account an irrelevant consideration vitiates the decision to revoke a certificate (*Anderson*) and leaving out of account a relevant factor which favours not revoking a certificate would presumably also found a petition to the *nobile officium* (see Lord President Emslie's opinion in *Wordie Property Co. Ltd v Secretary of State for Scotland*, 1984 S.L.T. 345). Furthermore, r. 33.3(1) expressly requires that the accused be heard before the order to revoke the certificate is made and accordingly a breach of that requirement would also open up the order to review in the High Court (see, e.g. *Brannigan, Petitioner*, 1999 S.L.T. 679; 1999 S.C.C.R. 274 where the sheriff granted warrant for the accused's arrest on the third occasion when she failed to appear for sentence and simultaneously directed that her legal aid certificate be withdrawn). However, it is doubtful whether the High Court would permit review on the grounds of *Wednesbury* unreasonableness (see *Associated Provincial Picture Houses v Wednesbury Corporation* [1948] 1 K.B. 223) since to do so would effectively subvert entirely the otherwise final nature of the decision which the rule has by implication entrusted exclusively to the lower court.

While the above propositions are not explicitly warranted by judicial authority, they do receive considerable support from two recent decisions of the Appeal Court. In *Ness*, above, the High Court observed that cases involving the revocation of legal aid certificates raised "very real questions" about the factors which should be taken into account when a court decides to deprive an accused person of legal representation on charges which can result in his imprisonment. The reference to imprisonment is no doubt an oblique allusion to the decisions of the European Court of Human Rights in *Boner v United Kingdom*; Maxwell v United Kingdom, 1995 S.C.C.R. 1 and *Granger v United Kingdom, Series A, No.174* (1990) 12 E.H.R.R. 469 and perhaps indicates that the scope for review might be broader since the European Court of Human Rights is likely to require that the sanction of the withdrawal of legal aid be a proportionate response to the accused's failures. The European Court's insistence on proportionality will, however, require a consideration of the likely length of the period of imprisonment and so it may be that at least for the usual type of summary trial where the maximum sentence is 3 or 6 months' imprisonment, the revocation of legal aid will be less open to being characterised as disproportionate.

The more significant decision is, however, *Shaw, Petr*, 1999 S.L.T. 215; 1998 S.C.C.R. 672 in which the Appeal Court stated that an accused's interest in having a fair trial was not merely a private interest but was an interest shared by the whole of society and that the availability of legal aid was of fundamental importance in helping the criminal justice system achieve its objective of securing a fair trial. The Appeal Court accordingly requires the court contemplating making an order revoking legal aid to bear these factors in mind and to make the order only where satisfied that by reason of some conduct on the accused's part falling within r.33.3(1), it would be unreasonable for the accused's solicitor to continue to act for the accused. The court should also be satisfied that such an order would be a reasonable or proportional response to the accused's conduct when measured against the potential effect of revocation on the accused's right to a fair trial. It was also observed that the power to revoke a legal aid certificate was not conferred on the court for use as a punishment of the accused.

Chapter 34

Extradition

Interpretation of this Chapter

34.1. In this Chapter— **B1-72**

"the Act of 2003" means the Extradition Act 2003;
"arrested person" means a person who has been arrested under the Act of 2003; and
"required period" shall be construed in accordance with section 74(11) of the Act of 2003.

Provisional arrest

34.1A.—(1) Notice of an application under section 6(3A) of the Act of 2003 must be given to the arrested person by giving him or her, or his or her solicitor, a letter to that effect. **B1-72.0.1**

(2) Such notice must be given before the hearing at which the application is to be made.

AMENDMENTS

Rule 34.1A inserted by Act of Adjournal (Criminal Procedure Rules Amendment No.3) (Miscellaneous) 2011 (SSI 2011/194) para.5 (effective March 28, 2011).

[THE NEXT PARAGRAPH IS B1-72.1]

Arrest under provisional warrant

34.2.—(1) This rule applies where an arrested person is brought before the sheriff at Lothian and Borders under section 74(3) (person arrested under provisional warrant) of the Act of 2003. **B1-72.1**

(2) The sheriff—

(a) may fix a date for a review hearing to take place before the expiry of the required period; and
(b) shall fix a date for a review hearing to take place as soon as practicable after the expiry of the required period.

(3) At a review hearing under paragraph (2), the sheriff shall ascertain, so far as reasonably practicable, the state of preparation of the parties and may fix a further hearing to take place before the extradition hearing; and this paragraph may apply more than once.

Procedural hearing

34.2A.—(1) This rule applies where the sheriff of Lothian and Borders has fixed a date on which an extradition hearing is to begin in terms of section 8(1), section 75(1) or section 76(2) of the Act of 2003. **B1-72.1.1**

(2) The sheriff may fix a procedural hearing for the purposes of determining whether parties are ready to proceed to the extradition hearing.

(3) Where the extradition hearing is subsequently fixed for a later date the sheriff may discharge the procedural hearing and fix a new procedural hearing for a later date or, if the later date for the extradition hearing is fixed at or following the procedural hearing, fix a further procedural hearing.

(4) Where the extradition hearing has been adjourned the sheriff may fix a further procedural hearing.

(5) On fixing a procedural hearing under paragraph (2) the sheriff shall—

(a) grant warrant for the citation of witnesses and the lodging of productions by the parties;
(b) specify the last date for lodging witness lists and productions;
(c) specify the last date for the relevant person to lodge a case and argument.

(6) A case and argument must be lodged by the relevant person and—

(a) set out, for each ground of opposition to the extradition, a succinct and articulate statement of the facts founded upon and the propositions of law being advanced;
(b) be accompanied by all authorities, or a copy thereof, listed in the case and argument;
(c) be signed by counsel or the solicitor instructed to represent the relevant person at the extradition hearing, or by the relevant person where he or she intends to conduct the extradition hearing himself or herself.

(7) The Lord Advocate—

(a) must, if the sheriff, considering that the circumstances of the case require it, orders him to do so;
(b) may, if he considers it appropriate to do so,

lodge a case and argument in response to the relevant person's case and argument.

(8) At the same time as lodging a case and argument, witness lists and productions, the party lodging them shall intimate copies to the other party.

(9) In this rule, "relevant person" means the person to whom the extradition proceedings relate.

(10) Paragraphs (3) and (4) may apply more than once.

(11) The sheriff may vary or dispense with any of the requirements mentioned in or made under this rule.

AMENDMENTS

Rule 34.2A inserted by Act of Adjournal (Criminal Procedure Rules Amendment) (Miscellaneous) 2012 (SSI 2012/125) para.6 (effective 4 June 2012).

[THE NEXT PARAGRAPH IS B1-72.2]

Application for leave to appeal

B1-72.2 **34.3.**—(1) An application for leave to appeal under—

(a) section 26 of the Act of 2003 (appeal against extradition order) is made in Form 34.3-A;

(b) section 28 of the Act of 2003 (appeal against discharge at extradition hearing) is made in Form 34.3-B;

(c) section 103 (appeal where case sent to Scottish Ministers) or 108 (appeal against extradition order) of the Act of 2003 is made in Form 34.3-C;

(d) section 105 (appeal against discharge at extradition hearing) or section 110 (appeal against discharge by Scottish Ministers) of the Act of 2003 is made in Form 34.3- D.

(2) Notice of an application for leave to appeal mentioned in paragraph (1) must be given by serving a copy of the application—

(a) in the case of an appeal under section 26, 103 or 108 of the Act of 2003, on the Crown Agent; and

(b) in the case of an appeal under section 28, 105 or 110 of the Act of 2003, on the arrested person.

(3) An application for leave to appeal under paragraph (1)—

(a) must be accompanied by an execution of service; and

(b) is made when it is lodged with the Clerk of Justiciary.

AMENDMENTS

Rule 34.3 substituted by Act of Adjournal (Criminal Procedure Rules 1996 Amendment) (Miscellaneous) 2016 (SSI 2016/103) para.2 (effective 1 March 2016, subject to para.5).

Hearing of appeals

B1-72.2.1 **34.3A.**—(1) When an application for leave to appeal is made under—

(a) section 26 (appeal against extradition order);

(b) section 28 (appeal against discharge at extradition hearing);

(c) section 103 (appeal where case sent to Scottish Ministers); or

(d) section 105 (appeal against discharge at extradition hearing),

of the Act of 2003, the Clerk of Justiciary must intimate the application to the sheriff clerk.

(2) On intimation, the sheriff clerk must request a report from the presiding sheriff.

(3) The sheriff is to comply with that request within 14 days of receiving it.

(4) On receipt of the report from the sheriff the sheriff clerk must transmit that report together with two certified copies of the minutes of proceedings and any other relevant documents to the Clerk of Justiciary.

(5) When an application for leave to appeal is made under—

(a) section 108 (appeal against extradition order); or

(b) section 110 (appeal against discharge by Scottish Ministers),

of the Act of 2003, the Clerk of Justiciary must request a report from the Scottish Ministers.

(6) The Scottish Ministers are to comply with that request within 14 days of receiving it.

(7) Upon receipt of the report from the sheriff or the Scottish Ministers, the Clerk of Justiciary must—

(a) send a copy to the arrested person and the Crown Agent; and

(b) fix a diet for the hearing of the application for leave to appeal.

(8) At that diet the court may—

(a) refuse leave to appeal;

(b) grant leave to appeal and determine the appeal; or

(c) grant leave to appeal and order that a further diet be fixed for hearing the appeal.

(9) When leave to appeal is granted under paragraph (8)(c) the Clerk of Justiciary must fix a further diet for hearing the appeal.

AMENDMENTS

Rule 34.3A inserted by Act of Adjournal (Criminal Procedure Rules 1996 Amendment) (Miscellaneous) 2016 (SSI 2016/103) para.2 (effective 1 March 2016, subject to para.5).

[THE NEXT PARAGRAPH IS B1-72.3]

Time limits

B1-72.3 **34.4.**—(1) The High Court is to begin to hear an appeal under section 26 or 28 of the Act of 2003 within 40 days after the date on which the arrested person was arrested.

(2) The High Court is to begin to hear an appeal under section 103, 105, 108 or 110 of the Act of 2003 within 76 days after the date on which the note of appeal is lodged.

AMENDMENTS

Rule 34.4 substituted by Act of Adjournal (Criminal Procedure Rules 1996 Amendment) (Miscellaneous) 2016 (SSI 2016/103) para.2 (effective 1 March 2016, subject to para.5).

Applications for extension of time

34.5—(1) Subject to paragraph (2), an application seeking an extension of the relevant period under section 31(4) (extension of time limit for start of hearing) or section 113(4) (extension of time limit for start of hearing) of the Act of 2003 shall be lodged with the Clerk of Justiciary in Form 34.5, and the applicant shall serve a copy of the application on the other party in the appeal. **B1-72.4**

(2) At the diet fixed for the hearing of the appeal or an application mentioned in paragraph (1), the court may dispense with the requirements of paragraph (1).

Consent to extradition

34.6. Notice of consent to extradition shall be given— **B1-72.5**

(a) in the case of extradition to a category 1 territory, in Form 34.6-A; and

(b) in the case of extradition to a category 2 territory, in Form 34.6-B.

Post-extradition matters

34.7.—(1) A notice under section 54(4) (notice of request for consent to another offence being dealt with) of the Act of 2003 shall be in Form 34.7-A. **B1-72.6**

(2) A notice under section 56(4) (notice of request for consent extradition to another category 1 territory) of the Act of 2003 shall be in Form 34.7-B.

Part 3 warrants

34.8. Subject to section 142 of the Act of 2003, a Part 3 warrant issued by a sheriff shall be in the form set out in the Annex to Council Framework Decision 2002/584/JHA of 13 June 2002 on the European arrest warrant and the surrender procedures between Member States, with such variation as circumstances may require. **B1-72.7**

AMENDMENTS

Chapter 34 substituted by Act of Adjournal (Criminal Procedure Rules Amendment No.3) (Extradition etc.) 2004 (SSI 2004/346) r.2 (effective 18 August 2004).

[THE NEXT PARAGRAPH IS B1-73]

GENERAL NOTE

Part 2 of the Extradition Act 2003 (which comprises ss.69-141) makes provision for extradition to what are termed "category 2" territories. These territories are states which, although they have an extradition treaty with the United Kingdom, are not party to the EU Council Framework Decision of June 13, 2002 on the European Arrest Warrant (see O.J. 2002 L 190). However, it is not a prerequisite for designation as a category 1 territory that the Framework Decision should apply to that state. The power to designate category 1 territories is not limited to member states of the European Union. The only restriction on designation is in s.1(3) of the 2003 Act, namely that a territory may not be designated for the purposes of Part I if a person found guilty in that territory of a criminal offence may be sentenced to death for the offence under the general criminal law of the territory (*Dabas v High Court of Justice in Madrid, Spain* [2007] 2 W.L.R. 254 at 263 ([24]), per Lord Hope of Craighead). **B1-73**

It is worth noticing that the High Court in an appeal concerning an extradition request from the USA, stated:

> "There is a strong public interest in the United Kingdom meeting its treaty obligations. There is also a strong public interest in the effective prosecution of trans-national crimes … It is important to the rule of law and to international comity that a person who is the subject of a proper request should be extradited to stand trial … There is also a strong public interest in honouring extradition treaties made with other states … It would only be in exceptional circumstances that the courts would be justified in not ordering extradition where that would otherwise be lawful." (*Calder v HM Advocate*; *Calder v The Scottish Ministers* [2006] HCJAC 71; 2006 S.C.C.R. 609 at [17]).

Provisional warrants

Section 73 of the 2003 Act provides, so far as concerns Scotland (see s.73(10)), that the sheriff may issue a warrant for the arrest of a person who is either accused in a category 2 territory of the commission of an offence or alleged to be unlawfully at large after conviction of an offence by a court in a territory 2 country where the sheriff is satisfied on an application by the procurator fiscal that that person (a) is or is believed to be in the United Kingdom, or (b) is or is believed to be "on his way" to the United Kingdom (s.73(1) and (2)). Such a warrant is known as a "provisional warrant" (ss.73(3) and 216(12)) and may be issued if the sheriff has reasonable grounds for believing that (a) the offence of which the person is accused or has been convicted is an extradition offence, and (b) there is written evidence that would either justify the issue of a warrant for the person's arrest for the offence if committed in the sheriff's jurisdiction or justify his arrest for being unlawfully at large within the sheriff's jurisdiction (s.73(3) and (4)). (Where the category 2 territory has been designated for the purposes of s.73, information and not evidence will suffice: s.73(5)).

Rule 34.2

Where a person is arrested under a provisional warrant, he must be given a copy of the warrant as soon as practicable after his arrest (s.74(2)) and if that direction is not complied with and the arrested person applies to the sheriff to be discharged, the sheriff *may* order his discharge (s.74(5)). Further, the arrested person must be brought before the sheriff as soon as practicable after his arrest (s.74(3)) and if that is not done and the person applies to the sheriff to be discharged, the sheriff *must* order his discharge (s.74(6)). This latter requirement does not apply where either the person is granted bail following his arrest or the Scottish Ministers, having received a valid request for his extradition, decide under s.126 because of competing extradition requests, that the particular request is not to be proceeded with (s.74(4)).

Prior to the extradition hearing held under s.76, there must be at least one review hearing at which the sheriff must ascertain the state of preparation of the parties for the extradition hearing. The first review hearing should be fixed when the arrested person is first brought before the court. At that time the sheriff must also (i) inform the person that he is accused of the commission of an offence in the category 2 territory or that he is alleged to be unlawfully at large following conviction there; (ii) give the person the required information (defined in s.74(8)) about his option of consenting to extradition, whereby the procedure is expedited; and (iii) remand the person in custody or on bail (s.74(7)).

The "required period" referred to in r.34.2(2) is either (a) 45 days starting with the day on which the person was arrested, or (b) if the category 2 territory has been designated for the purposes of this provision, any longer period permitted by the designation order (s.74(10)).

Chapter 34A

Interpretation and Translation in European Arrest Warrant Proceedings

Interpretation and application

B1-73.1 **34A.1.**—(1) In this Chapter—

"the Act of 2003" means the Extradition Act 2003;

"the Directive" means Directive 2010/64/EU of the European Parliament and of the Council on the right to interpretation and translation in criminal proceedings;

"interpretation assistance" means—

- (a) in relation to a person who does not speak or understand English, an oral translation of—
  - (i) the proceedings into the person's native language or any other language which the person speaks or understands; and
  - (ii) any communication by the person into English; or
- (b) in relation to a person who has a hearing or speech impediment, such appropriate assistance as the person requires to be able to understand the proceedings and communicate effectively;

"Part 1 proceedings" means court proceedings relating to the execution of a Part 1 warrant;

"Part 1 warrant" is to be construed in accordance with section 2(2) of the Act of 2003.

(2) This Chapter applies to Part 1 proceedings.

Right to interpretation assistance

B1-73.2 **34A.2.**—(1) The court must take all reasonable steps to determine whether the person who is subject to the Part 1 proceedings requires interpretation assistance because the person—

- (a) does not speak English;
- (b) does not understand English;
- (c) has a hearing impediment; or
- (d) has a speech impediment.

(2) Where the court determines that the person requires interpretation assistance, it must ensure that arrangements are made for the person to be provided with that assistance—

- (a) at every diet in the Part 1 proceedings at which the person is due to appear;
- (b) for the purpose of safeguarding the fairness of proceedings in accordance with the Directive.

(3) The court must ensure that interpretation assistance provided under this paragraph is of a quality sufficient to safeguard the fairness of proceedings.

Right to translation of Part 1 warrant

B1-73.3 **34A.3.**—(1) The court must take all reasonable steps to determine whether the person who is subject to the Part 1 proceedings understands the language in which the Part 1 warrant is drawn up or into which it has been translated.

(2) Where the court determines that the person does not understand the language in which the Part 1 warrant is drawn up or into which it has been translated, it must ensure that arrangements have been or are made to provide the person with a written translation of that document.

(3) Despite paragraph (2), the person may be provided with an oral translation or oral summary of the Part 1 warrant, instead of a written translation, unless this would prejudice the fairness of proceedings.

(4) A person entitled under this rule to be provided with a translation of a Part 1 warrant may waive that right.

(5) A waiver under paragraph (4) must be—
(a) voluntary and unequivocal; and
(b) informed by legal advice, unless the person otherwise fully understands the consequences of waiving the right.

(6) The court must ensure that any translation provided under this paragraph is of a quality sufficient to safeguard the fairness of proceedings.

Application for review of a determination about rights to interpretation or translation

34A.4.—(1) Paragraph (2) applies where a court has determined— **B1-73.4**
(a) under rule 34A.2 that a person does not require any interpretation assistance; or
(b) under rule 34A.3 that a person does not require a translation of a Part 1 warrant.

(2) The person may, on one occasion only, apply to the court which made the determination for a review of its determination.

(3) If, on reviewing its determination, the court determines that the person requires interpretation assistance or a translation of the Part 1 warrant, it must give such direction as it considers necessary to safeguard the fairness of the proceedings.

(4) Nothing in this rule affects any right of appeal in relation to the determination being reviewed.

Application for a direction relating to interpretation or translation

34A.5.—(1) A person entitled under this Chapter to be provided with interpretation assistance, or a translation of a Part 1 warrant, may apply to the court to give a direction if, as the case may be— **B1-73.5**
(a) the person is not provided with interpretation assistance;
(b) the person considers that the interpretation assistance is of insufficient quality to safeguard the fairness of the proceedings;
(c) the person is not provided with a written translation, an oral translation or an oral summary of a Part 1 warrant; or
(d) the person considers that any written translation, oral translation or oral summary provided is of insufficient quality to safeguard the fairness of the proceedings.

(2) On determining an application under paragraph (1), the court must give such direction as it considers necessary to safeguard the fairness of the proceedings.

Applications under rule 34A.4 and 34A.5

34A.6.—(1) An application under rule 34A.4(2) or 34A.5(1)— **B1-73.6**
(a) is to be made orally; and
(b) must be made as soon as reasonably practicable.

(2) Before determining an application made under rule 34A.4(2) or 34A.5(1), the court must give the prosecutor an opportunity to make representations.

Information to be recorded by the clerk of court

34A.7. The clerk of court must make a record of any of the following which apply— **B1-73.7**
(a) the fact that interpretation assistance is provided under this Chapter;
(b) the fact that an oral translation or oral summary of the Part 1 warrant is provided;
(c) the fact that a waiver is given to the court under rule 34A.3(4).

Provision of interpretation assistance and translation free of charge

34A.8. Any interpretation assistance, translation or oral summary provided to a person under this Chapter must be provided free of charge. **B1-73.8**

GENERAL NOTE

The purpose of this chapter, which came into force on October 10, 2014 (see para.1(2) of Act of Adjournal (Amendment of the Criminal Procedure (Scotland) Act 1995 and the Criminal Procedure Rules 1996) (Miscellaneous) 2014 (SSI 2014/242)) is to implement the European Union Directive of the Council and Parliament of October 26, 2010 (2010/64/EU) (OJ L. 280). The preamble to the Directive states that "the principle of mutual recognition of judgments and other decisions of judicial authorities should become the cornerstone of judicial cooperation in civil and criminal matters within the Union because enhanced mutual recognition and the necessary approximation of legislation would facilitate cooperation between competent authorities and the judicial protection of individual rights" (Preamble (1)). However, enhanced cooperation between Member States of the EU presupposes that Member States have trust in each other's criminal justice systems (Preamble (3)). **B1-73.9**

The Directive notes that both art.6 of the European Convention and art.47 of the European Charter of Fundamental Rights guarantee a fair trial (and art.48(2) of the Charter guarantees the right of defence) but states that the "Directive respects those rights and should be implemented accordingly" (Preamble (5)). This is necessary because, although all Member States of the EU are parties to the European Convention, the Directive records "experience has shown that that alone does not always provide a sufficient degree of trust in the criminal justice systems of other member states" (Preamble (6)): cf. *Kapri v Lord Advocate*, 2013 S.C.C.R. 430 at [28].

The Directive is concerned with laying down rules regarding "the right to interpretation and translation in criminal proceedings and proceedings for the execution of a European Arrest Warrant" (art.1(1)). The Directive thereafter makes specific provision for the right to interpretation in art.2 and the right to translation of essential documents in art.3 and in each case extends these rights to proceedings for the execution of European Arrest Warrants (see art.2(7) and art.3(6)). In each case the quality of the interpretation or translation (as the case may be) must be "of a quality sufficient to safeguard the fairness of the proceedings, in particular by ensuring that suspected or accused persons have knowledge of the case against them and are able to exercise their right of defence" (art.2(8)).

Rule 34A.1

As the Directive requires, the right to interpretation assistance is afforded to persons who do not speak or read English and also to persons who suffer hearing or speech impediments. Scots criminal procedure already has well established principles concerning an accused's right to an interpreter for any essential part of criminal proceedings and accordingly Chapter 34A is restricted to proceedings for execution of a European Arrest Warrant ("EAW") (r.34A.1(2)).

Rule 34A.2

The right provided for here is strictly speaking unnecessary since Scots procedure would always provide interpreters to persons who are the subject of proceedings relating to execution of a EAW. This rule merely puts the matter beyond doubt.

Rule 34A.3

This right relates to the EAW. A person subject to a EAW should know what he is accused of when he is made the subject of a Member State's application for his return to that state. Without such knowledge the accused may not be able to participate fully in the first issue the sheriff must determine, namely whether the offence for which the EAW has been issued is an extradition offence.

It may be that an accused will not need a written translation of the EAW and that an oral description of the terms of the warrant will suffice. Moreover, an accused may waive the right to translation of the EAW (r.34A.3(4)) but where waiver is to be effectual, it must be voluntary, unequivocal and informed by legal advice unless the accused otherwise fully understands the consequences of waiving his right (r.34A.3(5)). These requirements for effective waiver reflect the European Court's case law: see *Millar v Dickson*, 2002 S.C. (P.C.) 30.

[THE NEXT PARAGRAPH IS B1-74]

Chapter 35

Computer Misuse Act 1990

Notices in relation to relevance of external law

B1-74 **35.1.** A notice under section 8(5) of the Computer Misuse Act 1990 (notice by defence that conditions not satisfied) shall be served on the prosecutor not later than 14 days before the trial diet.

Chapter 36

Crime (International Co-operation) Act 2003

Interpretation of this Chapter

B1-75 **36.1.** In this Chapter—

"Act of 2003" means the Crime (International Co-operation) Act 2003; and

"external court" means the court mentioned in section 30(1) or, as the case may be, section 31(1) of the Act of 2003; and.

"nominated court" means a court nominated under section 15(3), section 30(3) or section 31(4) of the Act of 2003.

Effecting citation or service of documents outside the United Kingdom

B1-75.1 **36.2.**—(1) A notice under section 5(5)(b) of the Act of 2003 (notice to accompany citation being effected outside the United Kingdom) shall be in Form 36.2 and shall give the information specified in that form.

(2) Where citation is being effected outside the United Kingdom under section 5 or 6 of the Act of 2003, in the form of citation for—

"IF YOU DO NOT ATTEND COURT WITHOUT A LAWFUL EXCUSE THE COURT MAY ORDER THAT YOU BE APPREHENDED AND PUNISHED."

or

"IF YOU FAIL TO ATTEND WITHOUT A LAWFUL EXCUSE THE COURT MAY ISSUE A WARRANT FOR YOUR ARREST."

or

"A warrant may be issued for your arrest",

there shall be substituted the following—

"As this citation is being effected outside the United Kingdom, no obligation under the law of Scotland to comply with the citation is imposed by virtue of its being so effected. Accordingly, failure to comply with the citation does not constitute contempt of court and is not a ground for issuing a warrant to secure your attendance or for imposing a penalty. But this citation may subsequently be effected against you in the United Kingdom, in which case, if you fail to attend without a lawful excuse, the court may issue a warrant for your arrest."

(3) Where a document is to be served on a person outside the United Kingdom under section 6 of the Act of 2003 (effecting citation etc. otherwise than by post), it shall be sent by the Clerk of Justiciary, sheriff clerk or clerk of the justice of the peace court, as the case may be, to the Lord Advocate.

AMENDMENT

Rule 36.2(3) as amended by the Act of Adjournal (Criminal Procedure Rules Amendment) (Criminal Proceedings etc. (Reform) (Scotland) Act 2007) 2008 (SSI 2008/61), r.2 (effective March 10, 2008).

Proof of citation or service outside the United Kingdom

36.3. The service on any person of a citation or document under section 6 of the Act of 2003 (effecting citation etc. otherwise than by post) may be proved in any legal proceedings by a certificate given by or on behalf of the Lord Advocate. **B1-75.2**

Applications for requests for assistance

36.4. An application under section 7(1) of the Act of 2003 (application for request for assistance) shall— **B1-75.3**

(a) be in Form 36.4-A;
(b) be lodged with the Clerk of Justiciary or sheriff clerk, as the case may be; and
(c) state the particulars of the offence which it is alleged has been committed or the grounds on which it is suspected that an offence has been committed;
(d) state whether proceedings in respect of the offence have been instituted or the offence is being investigated; and
(e) include particulars of the assistance requested and a draft request in Form 36.4-B.

Hearing of applications for requests for assistance

36.5.—(1) Where the prosecutor presents an application under section 7(1) of the Act of 2003 (application for request for assistance) before either the first appearance of the accused on petition or the service of a summary complaint, the High Court or the sheriff, as the case may be, shall, without requiring intimation to any other party, proceed to consider the application. **B1-75.4**

(2) Where any party presents such an application following the first appearance of the accused on petition or the service of a summary complaint, the High Court or sheriff, as the case may be, may—

(a) before the lodging of an indictment, dispense on cause shown with intimation to any other party and proceed to consider the application; or
(b) fix a diet for hearing the application and order intimation of the diet and application to any other party.

(3) The High Court or sheriff, as the case may be, after considering such application—

(a) may allow summary adjustment of the statement of assistance required in the draft request;
(b) shall grant the application, with or without any modifications which it or he deems appropriate, or shall refuse it.

(4) On granting such application the High Court or sheriff, as the case may be, shall—

(a) approve and sign the draft request;
(b) if English is not an official language of the court or authority to which the request is addressed, specify a period within which a translation of the request and of any production is to be lodged.

Register of applications for requests for assistance

36.6.—(1) A register shall be kept by the Clerk of Justiciary and by the sheriff clerk of applications under section 7(1) of the Act of 2003 (application for request for assistance). **B1-75.5**

(2) Save as authorised by the court, the register mentioned in paragraph (1) shall not be open to inspection by any person.

Notification of requests for assistance

36.7. Where a court sends a request for assistance under section 8 of the Act of 2003 other than on an application by or on behalf of the Lord Advocate, the Clerk of Justiciary or sheriff clerk, as the case may be, shall forthwith notify the Lord Advocate of this and send with the notification a copy of the letter of request. **B1-75.6**

Citation for proceedings before a nominated court

36.8.—(1) The warrant to cite a person to proceedings before a nominated court shall be in Form 36.8-A. **B1-75.7**

(2) The form of postal citation of a person to proceedings before a nominated court shall be in Form 36.8-B; and the person shall complete and return Form 36.8-C to the procurator fiscal.

(3) The form of personal citation of a person to proceedings before a nominated court shall be in Form 36.8-D.

Proceedings before a nominated court

B1-75.8 **36.9.**—(1) In proceedings before a nominated court—

(a) the procurator fiscal or Crown counsel shall participate in any hearing;
(b) the prosecutor of the requesting country mentioned in the request under section 13(1) of the Act of 2003 (request for assistance from overseas authorities) may participate in any hearing;
(c) where the request under section 13(1) of the Act of 2003 originates from current criminal proceedings any party to or persons with an interest in those proceedings may attend and, with the leave of the court, participate in any hearing;
(d) a judge or investigating magistrate in the current criminal proceedings may participate in any hearing;
(e) a lawyer or person with a right of audience from the requesting country who represents any party to the current criminal proceedings may participate in any hearing;
(f) a solicitor or counsel instructed by any party may participate in any hearing;
(g) any other person may, with the leave of the court, participate in any hearing;
(h) a shorthand writer may be present to record the proceedings; and
(i) the proceedings shall be in private.

(2) Where any person applies for leave to participate in any hearing the court shall, in determining such application, consider any relevant representations made by the court or authority making the request under section 13(1).

Time period for consideration of overseas freezing order

B1-75.8.1 **36.9A.**—(1) This rule applies where the Lord Advocate has nominated a sheriff to give effect to an overseas freezing order under section 21(2) of the Act of 2003 (considering the overseas freezing order).

(2) Subject to paragraph (3), the sheriff shall consider the order no later than the day after receipt of the order.

(3) The sheriff may, exceptionally, consider the order later than the period prescribed in paragraph (2) but shall do so no later than 5 days after receipt of the order.

(4) Where the day mentioned in paragraph (2) or the last day of the period mentioned in paragraph (3) falls on a Saturday, Sunday or court holiday, such period shall extend to and include the next day which is not a Saturday, Sunday or court holiday.

(5) In calculating the period mentioned in paragraph (3), any Saturday, Sunday or court holiday that falls within that period shall be disregarded.

AMENDMENTS

Rule 36.9A inserted by Act of Adjournal (Criminal Procedure Rules Amendment No.5) (Miscellaneous) 2009 (SSI 2009/345) para.2 (effective October 27, 2009).

Form of warrant for seizure and retention of evidence

B1-75.8.2 **36.9B.** A warrant under section 22(1) of the Act of 2003 (giving effect to the overseas freezing order) shall be in Form 36.9B.

AMENDMENTS

Rule 36.9B inserted by Act of Adjournal (Criminal Procedure Rules Amendment No.5) (Miscellaneous) 2009 (SSI 2009/345) para.2 (effective October 27, 2009).

Application for release of evidence

B1-75.8.3 **36.9C.** An application under section 25(1) of the Act of 2003 (release of evidence held under overseas freezing order) shall be in Form 36.9C.

AMENDMENTS

Rule 36.9C inserted by Act of Adjournal (Criminal Procedure Rules Amendment No. 5) (Miscellaneous) 2009 (SSI 2009/345) para.2 (effective October 27, 2009).

[THE NEXT PARAGRAPH IS B1-75.9]

Provision of interpreters

B1-75.9 **36.10.**—(1) This rule applies where a court has been nominated under section 30(3) (nomination to facilitate the giving of evidence by live television link) or section 31(4) (nomination to facilitate the giving of evidence by telephone) of the Act of 2003.

(2) Where it appears to the Clerk of Justiciary or sheriff clerk, as the case may be, that the witness is likely to give evidence in a language other than English, he shall make arrangements for an interpreter to be present at the proceedings to translate what is said into English.

(3) Where it appears to the Clerk of Justiciary or sheriff clerk, as the case may be, that the witness is likely to give evidence in a language other than that in which the proceedings of the external court will be conducted, he shall make arrangements for an interpreter to translate what is said into the language in which the proceedings of the external court will be conducted.

(4) Where the evidence in proceedings before a nominated court is either given in a language other than English or is not translated into English by an interpreter, the High Court or, as the case may be, the sheriff, shall continue the proceedings until such time as a translator can be present to provide a translation into English.

Court record of proceedings before a nominated court

36.11.—(1) Where a court receives evidence in proceedings by virtue of a nomination under section 15(3) (nomination to receive evidence), section 30(3) (nomination to facilitate the giving of evidence by live television link), or section 31(4) (nomination to facilitate the giving of evidence by telephone) of the Act of 2003, the Clerk of Justiciary or sheriff clerk, as the case may be, shall record in the minute of proceedings— **B1-75.10**

(a) particulars of the proceedings; and
(b) without prejudice to the generality of (a) above—
  (i) which persons were present;
  (ii) which of those persons was represented and by whom; and
  (iii) whether any of those persons was denied the opportunity of cross-examining a witness as to any part of his testimony.

(2) Save as authorised by the Lord Advocate or, with the leave of the court, the minute of proceedings mentioned in paragraph (1) above shall not be open to inspection by any person.

(3) The Clerk of Justiciary or sheriff clerk, as the case may be, shall send to the Lord Advocate and to the external authority a certified copy of the minute of proceedings.

(4) Where the court has been nominated under section 15(3) of the Act of 2003 the Clerk of Justiciary or sheriff clerk, as the case may be, shall comply with paragraph 6 of Schedule 1 to the Act of 2003 with regard to the forwarding of evidence received by the court.

AMENDMENTS

Chapter 36 substituted by Act of Adjournal (Criminal Procedure Rules Amendment) (Miscellaneous) 2004 (SSI 2004/195) para.2 (effective April 26, 2004).

[THE NEXT PARAGRAPH IS B1-76]

GENERAL NOTE

Part 1 of the Crime (International Co-operation) Act 2003 deals with mutual assistance to be given by UK courts in respect of criminal proceedings and investigations. Sections 7-12 of Ch.2 of Pt 1 provide for assistance in obtaining evidence from abroad. If it appears to any judge of the High Court of Justiciary or any sheriff, on an application made by: (a) a prosecuting authority in England and Wales or Northern Ireland; (b) the Lord Advocate or a procurator fiscal; or (c) where proceedings have been instituted, the person charged in those proceedings (s.7(3)), that an offence has been committed (or that there are reasonable grounds for suspecting that that is so) *and* that proceedings in respect of that offence have been instituted (or that the offence is being investigated), the judge or sheriff may request assistance "in obtaining outside the United Kingdom any evidence specified in the request for use in the proceedings or investigation" (s.7(1) and (2)). **B1-76**

Section 13 makes provision for the reverse of s.7, namely assistance to overseas authorities in obtaining evidence within the United Kingdom. Where a request for assistance in obtaining evidence in Scotland is received by the Lord Advocate (who is the "territorial authority" in Scotland: s.28(9)) he may, if conditions specified in s. 14 are met, arrange for the evidence to be obtained under s. 15; or he may direct that a search warrant be applied for under or by virtue of s. 18 (s. 13(1)). Such a request for assistance may be made *only* by a court exercising criminal jurisdiction, or a prosecuting authority, in a foreign country; or any other foreign authority which appears to the Lord Advocate to have "the function of making such requests for assistance"; or the International Criminal Police Organisation; or any other body or person competent to make such a request under any provisions adopted under the Treaty on European Union (s. 13(2) and (3)).

Nominated court

Under s. 15(3) the Lord Advocate, upon receipt of such a request, may by a notice nominate a sheriff court to receive any evidence which relates to that request and appears to that court to be appropriate for the purpose of giving effect to the request. However, where it appears to the Lord Advocate that the request relates to an offence involving serious or complex fraud, he may give a direction under s.27 of the Criminal Law (Consolidation) (Scotland) Act 1995 (s. 15(4)). Section 27 provides that the Lord Advocate may give a direction (which must be personally signed by the Lord Advocate: s.27(4)) when, for the purpose of investigating the affairs or any aspect of the affairs of any person (in the course of investigating a suspected offence which may involve serious or complex fraud), he is satisfied that there is good reason to do so (s.27(1) and (2)). The direction may also be made at the request of the Attorney-General of the Isle of Man, Jersey or Guernsey acting under legislation corresponding to Part IV of the 1995 Act (s.27(2)). The direction nominates a person who is then entitled to exercise the powers and functions conferred by Part IV (s.27(3)).

The sheriff's jurisdiction is to determine whether the evidence which he is asked to receive is evidence falling within the description in s. 15(3). The High Court has stated: "The sheriff has no broader discretion to exercise than that ... His sole concern is whether the evidence which he is asked to receive is within the proper scope of the request ... the sheriff is concerned only with a process of evidence gathering. It is no part of his function to consider what may be made of the evidence by the requesting State. Nor is it part of his function to consider whether the evidence may lead the requesting State to request the extradition of the suspect. These are matters for the requesting State ... Equally, it is no part of the sheriff's function to consider whether sending the evidence to the requesting State will affect the ability of the Scottish prosecuting authorities to prosecute the suspect in Scotland. That is a matter for the Lord Advocate in deciding whether in principle to give effect to the request by nominating a court to receive the evidence." (*Calder v Frame* [2006] HCJAC 62; 2006 S.L.T. 862; 2006 S.C.C.R. 487, para.[31]).

Evidence by television link or telephone for use in overseas proceedings

The last two rules in this chapter are required to give effect to two provisions of Ch.3 of Part 1 of the 2003 Act, namely the hearing of evidence through television links and by telephone. Under s.30(3), unless the Lord Advocate considers it inappropriate to do so, where he receives a request from an external authority (which is defined in s.30(2)) for "a person in the United Kingdom to give evidence through a live television link in criminal proceedings before a court in a country outside the United Kingdom", he *must* by written notice nominate a court in Scotland where that can be done. The nominated court must be either the High Court or the sheriff court. The notice need not be personally authorised by the Lord Advocate (see *HM Advocate v Copeland*, 1988 S.L.T. 249 and note to r.36.8 infra). Foreign proceedings include any proceedings on an appeal "before a court against a decision in administrative proceedings" (s.30(1)) and will by parity of reasoning also include evidence in the course of criminal appeals.

Section 31 replicates s.30 in respect of requests from an external authority to take evidence by telephone. The Lord Advocate must nominate a court unless he considers it inappropriate for the request to be acceded to. The request under s.31, unlike a request under s.30, must specify the external court, the name and address of the witness and state whether the witness is willing to give evidence by telephone in the proceedings before the external court (s.31(3)).

Rule 36.4

Applications under s.7 are for the issue of a request to a foreign state for assistance in obtaining evidence abroad. Such requests can be made either because proceedings have been raised or because a suspected offence is under investigation. Hence the requirement in r.36.4(d). The offences must have been committed in Scotland. Applications can be made to either the High Court or the sheriff court and are made by the Lord Advocate or the appropriate procurator fiscal.

Rule 36.5

For the purposes of intimation of an application for the issue of a request for foreign assistance, a distinction is drawn on the basis of the stage of the proceedings. Where neither petition nor summary complaint has been served, the court need not require intimation be given to the suspect. However, once the initiating document has been served the party making the application may seek dispensation from intimation to the suspect if he can show cause. Rule 36.5(2)(a) refers only to the period prior to the lodging of an indictment but that is inconsistent with the preceding reference to service of a summary complaint. Does it not make sense for the court also to be able to dispense with intimation on cause shown after service of a complaint?

Rule 36.8

The Lord Advocate may nominate an appropriate court to receive the evidence which the foreign authority seeks to obtain in Scotland. Such nomination must be given in writing (s. 15(3)) but, unlike the direction under s.27 of the Criminal Law (Consolidation) (Scotland) Act 1995 (see above), does not require to be personally signed by the Lord Advocate (see *HM Advocate v Copeland*, 1988 S.L.T. 249; *Somerville v The Scottish Ministers*, [2006] CSIH 52; 2007 S.L.T. 96, para.[101]; and *Carltona Limited v Commissioners of Works* [1943] 2 All E.R. 560).

Rule 36.9

It is competent for the sheriff, at the hearing when he is to take his decision on the evidence which he is to receive, to proceed without intimation of the hearing having been given to the suspect. Rule 36.9 contains no requirement to notify (or even to consider notifying) the suspect of the hearing and the absence of any such requirement cannot amount to an absence of sufficient procedural safeguards such as to render the sheriff's decision unlawful under Art.8(1) of, and Art.1 of the First Protocol to, the European Convention on Human Rights (*Calder v Frame*, 2006 S.L.T. 862 at para.[33]).

Rule 36.10

Most external courts will not conduct their proceedings in English and it is also to be readily anticipated that witnesses will not speak English and may indeed speak neither English nor the language of the external court. Since the giving of the witness's evidence by either television link or telephone must be controlled by the judge of the nominated court (especially since any contempt by the witness in the presence of the nominated court is a contempt of that court: ss.30(4) and 31 (5)), the nominated court must have available an interpreter to translate the witness's evidence into English for the benefit of the nominated court. Hence the direction in r.36.10(4). However, whatever the language in which the witness depones, it must be translated into the language of the external court if that witness's language is foreign to the external court. Wilfully false testimony before the nominated court is deemed perjury and liable to prosecution in Scotland (see ss.30(5) and 31(6)) even though the proceedings are foreign in nature and evidence given in pursuance of ss.30 and 31 is not to be treated for any purpose as evidence given in proceedings in Scotland (see ss.30(7) and 31(8)).

Rule 36.11

The proceedings before the nominated court are necessarily adjectival to the proceedings before the external criminal court. Accordingly, they are not a public matter as proceedings must be when the nominated court is exercising its domestic powers, although they may form part of public proceedings in the external court. Hence, the nominated court's proceedings are not held in public, the persons present and any legal representatives are to be named in the minute of proceedings (r.36.11(1)(b)) and the minute of proceedings are confidential and not to be inspected by anyone except where inspection is authorised by the Lord Advocate or the nominated court (r.36.11(2)). The direction to the appropriate clerk to transmit a certified copy of the minute of proceedings to the Lord Advocate and the external authority which requested the witness's testimony (r.36.11(3)) is not of such a nature that a failure to comply with it would open the proceedings to challenge in the domestic courts. Parliament could not be taken to have intended such failure to invalidate the proceedings (see *R. v Soneji* [2006] 1 A.C. 340 and *R. v Ashton* [2007] 1 W.L.R. 181).

Chapter 37

Proceedings under the Proceeds of Crime (Scotland) Act 1995

Orders to make material available

37.1.—(1) An application by the procurator fiscal to the sheriff for an order under section 18(2) of the Proceeds of Crime (Scotland) Act 1995 (order to make material available in investigation into whether a person has benefited from commission of an offence shall be made by petition; and section 134 (incidental applications) of the Act of 1995 shall apply to any such application as it applies to an application referred to in that section. **B1-77**

(2) The sheriff may make the order sought in the petition under paragraph (1) before intimation of the petition to the person who appears to him to be in possession of the material to which the application relates.

(3) An application by the procurator fiscal for an order under section 18(5) of the Proceeds of Crime (Scotland) Act 1995 (order to allow constable to enter premises to obtain access to material) may be made in the petition applying for an order under section 18(2); and paragraph (2) of this rule shall apply to an order in respect of a person who appears to the sheriff to be entitled to grant entry to the premises in question as it applies to an order in respect of the person mentioned in that paragraph.

Discharge and variation of orders

37.2.—(1) A person, in respect of whom an order has been made under section 18(2) or (5) of the Proceeds of Crime (Scotland) Act 1995 (which relate to orders to make material available in investigating whether a person has benefited from commission of a offence), may apply to the sheriff for discharge or variation of the order in question. **B1-77.1**

(2) The sheriff may, after hearing the parties, grant or refuse to grant the discharge or variation sought.

Warrants to search premises

37.3. An application by the procurator fiscal to the sheriff under section 19(1) of the Proceeds of Crime (Scotland) Act 1995 (authority for search) shall be made by petition; and section 134 (incidental applications) of the Act of 1995 shall apply to any such application for a warrant as it applies to an application for a warrant referred to in that section. **B1-77.2**

Orders under sections 25 and 26

37.4. An application under section 25 (recall etc. of suspended forfeiture order) or 26 (return of property wrongly confiscated etc.) of the Proceeds of Crime (Scotland) Act 1995 by a person other than the accused to the court shall be made by petition in Form 37.4. **B1-77.3**

Appeals under section 27

37.5. An appeal under section 27 of the Proceeds of Crime (Scotland) Act 1995 (appeal against grant or refusal of application under section 25(1)26(1)) shall be in Form 37.5. **B1-77.4**

Amendments

Rules 37.1(1), 37.2(1) as amended by Act of Adjournal (Criminal Procedure Rules Amendment) (Miscellaneous) (SI 1996/2147 (S.171)) (effective 9 September 1996).

Rules 37.4 and 37.5 inserted by Act of Adjournal (Criminal Procedure Rules Amendment No.7) (SI 1997/2653) (effective 21 November 1997).

[THE NEXT PARAGRAPH IS B1-78]

General Note

Section 18(1) of the Proceeds of Crime (Scotland) Act 1995 provides that the procurator fiscal may, for the purpose of an investigation into whether a person has benefited from the commisison of an offence described in s.1(2) of that Act and as to the amount of that benefit, apply to the sheriff for an order: **B1-78**

(a) to produce material to a constable for the constable to take away; or (b) to give a constable access to it within such period as the sheriff specifies in the order (s.18(2)). Section 18(5) of the 1990 Act provides that where the sheriff makes an order requiring access to be given to a constable he may also, on the application of the procurator fiscal, order any person who appears to him to be entitled to grant entry to the premises to allow a constable to enter the premises to obtain access to the material.

Section 19(1) of the 1995 Act provides that the procurator fiscal may, for the purpose of an investigation as aforesaid and as to the amount of that benefit, apply to the sheriff for a warrant authorising a constable to enter and search specified premises (see s.19(2)).

Section 18(1) and s.19(1) (see r.37.3) do not apply to offences of drug trafficking as that phrase is defined in s.49(2) and (3) of the Proceeds of Crime (Scotland) Act 1995 (see s.18(11))—which are provided for by equivalent legislation in s.31 of the Criminal Law (Consolidation) (Scotland) Act 1995—or into an offence under Pt III of the Prevention of Terrorism (Temporary Provisions) Act 1989 which deals with financial assistance from terrorism (see s.1(2) of the Proceeds of Crime (Scotland) Act 1995), but otherwise they have application in respect of any offence which has been prosecuted on indictment or on summary complaint, if the offence is punishable by a fine of an amount greater than the amount corresponding to level 5 on the standard scale or by imprisonment for a period longer than three months or by both such fine and imprisonment.

Rules 37.1 and 37.3 apply the provisions of s.134 of the 1995 Act to such warrants which should in each case be applied for to the sheriff by way of petition. In view of the need to avoid giving warning to persons who are suspected of benefiting from drug trafficking the sheriff is entitled to grant the warrant before intimation has been given to the "suspects" of the procurator fiscal's application.

Chapter 37AA

Proceedings under the Proceeds of Crime Act 2002

Interpretation of this Chapter

B1-78.0.1 **37AA.1** In this Chapter—

"the Act of 2002" means the Proceeds of Crime Act 2002;

"the 2014 Regulations" means the Criminal Justice and Data Protection (Protocol No. 36) Regulations 2014;

"appropriate person" has the meaning given by section 412 (interpretation) of the Act of 2002;

"compliance order" has the meaning given by section 97B(2) of the Act of 2002;

"interested person" and "senior officer" have the meanings given by section 336D (sections 336A to 336C: interpretation) of the Act of 2002;

"relevant person" has the meaning given by section 339ZH(12) (further information orders) of the Act of 2002.

AMENDMENTS

Rule 37AA.1 substituted by Act of Adjournal (Criminal Procedure Rules 1996 Amendment) (Miscellaneous) 2016 (SSI 2016/103) para.3 (effective 1 March 2016).

Rule 37AA.1 as amended by Act of Adjournal (Criminal Procedure Rules 1996 Amendment) (No. 5) (Proceeds of Crime etc.) 2017 (SSI 2017/429) para.2(2) (effective 21 December 2017).

Confiscation

Confiscation orders

B1-78.0.2 **37AA.2**—(1) A request by the prosecutor under subsection (3) of section 92 of the Act of 2002 (making of order) may be made orally at the bar.

(2) A person who wishes to make representations to the court under subsection (8) of section 92 of the Act of 2002 shall do so—

(a) in writing to the Clerk of Court, unless the court otherwise directs; and
(b) by such date as the court directs.

(2A) In the High Court, where written representations are made under paragraph (2) after the second procedural hearing fixed under rule 37AA.5B(4)(i) has taken place—

(a) a hearing shall be fixed for a date no later than 4 weeks after the date of lodging of the written representations; and
(b) the Clerk of Justiciary shall intimate the date of that hearing and a copy of the written representations to the parties.

(3) An application under—

(a) subsection (2) of section 111 (conviction or other disposal of accused); or
(b) subsection (2) of section 112 (accused neither convicted nor acquitted),

of the Act of 2002 may be made—

(i) orally at the bar; or
(ii) by minute.

(4) An application by the prosecutor under subsection (6)(a) of section 131ZA of the Act of 2002 (seized money) may be made orally at the bar or by minute.

AMENDMENTS

Rule 37AA.2 as amended by Act of Adjournal (Criminal Procedure Rules Amendment No.3) (Confiscation Proceedings) 2009 (SSI 2009/244) para.2 (effective 5 August 2009, subject to transitional provisions in para.1(4)).

Subs.(4) inserted by Act of Adjournal (Criminal Procedure Rules 1996 Amendment) (Miscellaneous) 2018 (SSI 2018/12) para.2(2) (effective 31 January 2018).

Confiscation orders: certification

37AA.2A.—(1) A request by the prosecutor for a certificate under paragraph 7(1) of Schedule 1 to the 2014 Regulations must— **B1-78.0.2.1**

(a) be made by minute prior to the making of a domestic confiscation order;

(b) set out why the prosecutor considers that the property to which the application relates—

(i) was used or was intended to be used for the purposes of an offence; or

(ii) is the proceeds of an offence;

(c) contain the specified information.

(2) Where the court issues a certificate, it must—

(a) do so in the form annexed to Council Framework Decision 2006/783/JHA of 6th October 2006 on the application of the principle of mutual recognition to confiscation orders;

(b) provide in the domestic confiscation order for notice to be given in accordance with paragraph 7(4) of Schedule 1 to the 2014 Regulations.

(3) In this rule, "domestic confiscation order" and "specified information" have the meanings given by paragraph 1 of Schedule 1 to the 2014 Regulations.

AMENDMENTS

Rule 37AA.2A inserted by Act of Adjournal (Criminal Procedure Rules 1996 Amendment) (Miscellaneous) 2016 (SSI 2016/103) para.3 (effective 1 March 2016).

Compliance orders

37AA.2B.—(1) An application by the prosecutor for a compliance order is to be made in Form 37AA.2B-A. **B1-78.0.2.2**

(2) When an application is lodged, the court must—

(a) order intimation of the application to the accused;

(b) appoint a hearing on the application.

(3) A compliance order is to be in Form 37AA.2B-B.

AMENDMENTS

Rule 37AA.2B inserted by Act of Adjournal (Criminal Procedure Rules 1996 Amendment) (Miscellaneous) 2016 (SSI 2016/103) para.3 (effective 1 March 2016, subject to para.5).

Compliance orders: discharge and variation

37AA.2C.—(1) An application to discharge or vary a compliance order is to be made in Form 37AA.2C-A. **B1-78.0.2.3**

(2) When an application is lodged, the court must—

(a) order intimation of the application to—

(i) the prosecutor, where the application is made by the accused;

(ii) the accused, where the application is made by the prosecutor;

(b) appoint a hearing on the application.

(3) Where the court discharges or varies a compliance order, it is to do so in Form 37AA.2C-B.

(4) An appeal under section 97D of the Act of 2002 is to be made by lodging a note of appeal in Form 37AA.2C-C.

(5) When an appeal is lodged, the court must—

(a) order intimation of the application to—

(i) the prosecutor, where the accused is the appellant;

(ii) the accused, where the prosecutor is the appellant;

(b) appoint a hearing on the appeal.

AMENDMENTS

Rule 37AA.2C inserted by Act of Adjournal (Criminal Procedure Rules 1996 Amendment) (Miscellaneous) 2016 (SSI 2016/103) para.3 (effective 1 March 2016, subject to para.5).

Compliance orders: breach

37AA.2D.—(1) Where the prosecutor considers that an accused who is subject to a compliance order has failed to comply with it, the prosecutor must notify the court. **B1-78.0.2.4**

(2) That notification is to be given in Form 37AA.2D-A.

(3) A citation under section 97C(2)(b) of the Act of 2002 is to be in Form 37AA.2D-B.

(4) Where the court revokes or varies a compliance order under section 97C(6) or (7), it is to do so in Form 37AA.2D-C.

AMENDMENTS

Rule 37AA.2D inserted by Act of Adjournal (Criminal Procedure Rules 1996 Amendment) (Miscellaneous) 2016 (SSI 2016/103) para.3 (effective 1 March 2016, subject to para.5).

[THE NEXT PARAGRAPH IS B1-78.0.3]

Disposal of family home

B1-78.0.3 **37AA.3** An application by an administrator under subsection (2) of section 98 of the Act of 2002 (disposal of family home) to dispose of a right or interest in a person's family home shall be—

(a) by petition; and
(b) served on—
  (i) the person in respect of whose right or interest the application is made; and
  (ii) any other person likely to be affected by the application.

Application for postponement

B1-78.0.4 **37AA.4** An application by the accused or the prosecutor for postponement or extension under subsection (7) of section 99 of the Act of 2002 (postponement)—

(a) may be made either—
  (i) orally at the bar; or
  (ii) in writing by minute; and
(b) may be determined by the court without a hearing.

Statement of information

B1-78.0.5 **37AA.5**—(1) This rule applies where the court ordains the prosecutor to give a statement of information or further statement of information, as the case may be, under any of the following provisions of the Act of 2002—

(a) subsection (1) of section 101 (statement of information);
(b) subsection (5) of that section; or
(c) paragraph (b) of subsection (2) of section 110 (information).

(2) The prosecutor shall give a statement referred to in the foregoing paragraph within such period as the court determines.

(3) At the same time as giving a statement under paragraph (2) the prosecutor shall—

(a) serve a copy on the accused; and
(b) make arrangements, where applicable, for the accused to view, and copy if required, any documents that the prosecutor intends to rely upon.

(4) An accused who gives an indication under subsection (1) of section 102 of the Act of 2002 (accused's response to statement of information) (called the "response") shall do so in writing to the Clerk of Court.

(5) At the same time as giving a response under paragraph (4), the accused shall serve a copy on the prosecutor.

AMENDMENTS

Rule 37AA.5 as amended by Act of Adjournal (Criminal Procedure Rules Amendment No.3) (Confiscation Proceedings) 2009 (SSI 2009/244) para.2 (effective 5 August 2009, subject to transitional provisions in para.1(4)).

Initial period of adjustment

B1-78.0.6 **37AA.5A.** In the High Court, parties may adjust their respective statements during the 6 week period following the expiry of the period ordered by the court under section 102(1) of the Act of 2002 for the lodging of the response.

AMENDMENTS

Rule 37AA.5A inserted by Act of Adjournal (Criminal Procedure Rules Amendment No.3) (Confiscation Proceedings) 2009 (SSI 2009/244) para.2 (effective 5 August 2009, subject to transitional provisions in para.1(4)).

First procedural hearing

B1-78.0.7 **37AA.5B.**—(1) Where the High Court is proceeding under section 92 of the Act of 2002, a procedural hearing called "the first procedural hearing" shall take place on the first Monday after the period for adjustment mentioned in rule 37AA.5A has expired.

(2) At the first procedural hearing the High Court shall ascertain the state of readiness of the parties to conduct a hearing to dispose of the matter.

(3) The High Court may—

(a) set a date for the lodging of any forensic report by the accused;
(b) make an order for exchange of documents between parties;
(c) make an order for the production of documents;
(d) provide for further adjustment of the respective statements of the parties;
(e) make any further order it considers necessary.

(4) The High Court shall either—

(a) order that there shall be a further procedural hearing (called "the second procedural hearing") and fix a date for that hearing; or
(b) order a hearing to dispose of the matter (called "the determination hearing") and the Clerk of Justiciary shall fix a date for that hearing.

(5) Where the High Court orders a determination hearing, it shall ascertain from the parties their estimates of the likely length of that hearing.

AMENDMENTS

Rule 37AA.5B inserted by Act of Adjournal (Criminal Procedure Rules Amendment No.3) (Confiscation Proceedings) 2009 (SSI 2009/244) para.2 (effective 5 August 2009, subject to transitional provisions in para.1(4))

Second procedural hearing

37AA.5C.—(1) At the second procedural hearing, the High Court shall— **B1-78.0.8**

(a) ascertain the state of readiness of the parties to conduct a determination hearing;
(b) make such further orders as the High Court thinks fit for the purpose of reaching a position where the parties are so ready; and
(c) either—
  (i) continue the hearing for a period of not longer than 4 weeks; or
  (ii) order a determination hearing and the Clerk of Justiciary shall fix a date for that hearing.

(2) Where the High Court orders a determination hearing, it shall ascertain from the parties their estimates of the likely length of that hearing.

AMENDMENTS

Rule 37AA.5C inserted by Act of Adjournal (Criminal Procedure Rules Amendment No.3) (Confiscation Proceedings) 2009 (SSI 2009/244) para.2 (effective 5 August 2009, subject to transitional provisions in para.1(4)).

Preparation for determination hearing

37AA.5D.—(1) Where the High Court fixes a determination hearing it shall— **B1-78.0.9**

(a) direct the Clerk of Justiciary to issue a timetable specifying—
  (i) that a pre-determination hearing meeting is to take place at least 8 weeks before the determination hearing;
  (ii) the date for lodging of the minute in Form 37AA.5D-A of the above meeting, to be at least 5 weeks before the determination hearing;
  (iii) the last date for lodging productions, to be at least 4 weeks before the determination hearing;
  (iv) the last date for lodging witness lists, to be at least 4 weeks before the determination hearing.
(b) make such further orders regarding preparation as it sees fit.

(2) The timetable issued under paragraph (1)(a) shall be in Form 37AA.5D-B and shall be treated for all purposes as an interlocutor of the High Court signed by a judge of that court.

(3) A party shall not be permitted to refer to any document that has not been lodged by the date required under paragraph (1)(a)(iii) except by leave of the High Court on cause shown.

(4) At the same time as lodging productions and witness lists, copies shall be intimated to the other parties.

AMENDMENTS

Rule 37AA.5D inserted by Act of Adjournal (Criminal Procedure Rules Amendment No.3) (Confiscation Proceedings) 2009 (SSI 2009/244) para.2 (effective 5 August 2009, subject to transitional provisions in para.1(4)).

Hearing to check preparation

37AA.5E.—(1) A hearing shall take place on the last Monday which is at least 4 weeks before the determination hearing. **B1-78.0.10**

(2) At the hearing the High Court shall—

(a) consider the minute in Form 37AA.5D-A;
(b) ascertain the state of readiness of the parties to conduct the determination hearing; and
(c) make such further orders as the High Court thinks fit for the purpose of ensuring that the parties are so ready.

AMENDMENTS

Rule 37AA.5E inserted by Act of Adjournal (Criminal Procedure Rules Amendment No.3) (Confiscation Proceedings) 2009 (SSI 2009/244) para.2 (effective 5 August 2009, subject to transitional provisions in para.1(4)).

General provision on adjustment

37AA.5F.—(1) In the High Court, any adjustments to the statement of information or response must be intimated as soon as practicable to the other party. **B1-78.0.11**

(2) The statement of information and response, as adjusted, shall be lodged by the respective parties on the day after the adjustment period ends and at the same time a copy fully adjusted to date shall be intimated to the other party.

AMENDMENTS

Rule 37AA.5F inserted by Act of Adjournal (Criminal Procedure Rules Amendment No.3) (Confiscation Proceedings) 2009 (SSI 2009/244) para.2 (effective 5 August 2009, subject to transitional provisions in para.1(4)).

Public holidays

B1-78.0.12 **37AA.5G.** Where any hearing on a Monday set by virtue of rule 37AA.5B or 37AA.5E would otherwise fall on a public holiday, it shall take place on the next Monday following which is not a public holiday.

AMENDMENTS

Rule 37AA.5G inserted by Act of Adjournal (Criminal Procedure Rules Amendment No.3) (Confiscation Proceedings) 2009 (SSI 2009/244) para.2 (effective 5 August 2009, subject to transitional provisions in para.1(4)).

Reconsideration of case, benefit or available amount

B1-78.0.13 **37AA.6—** (1) This rule applies to an application by the prosecutor under any of the following provisions of the Act of 2002—

(a) to consider new evidence under—
  (i) paragraph (c) of subsection (1) of section 104 (no order made: reconsideration of case);
  (ii) paragraph (b) of subsection (3) of section 105 (no order made: reconsideration of benefit); or
  (ii) paragraph (d) of subsection (1) of section 106 (order made: reconsideration of benefit); and
(b) to make a new calculation of the available amount under paragraph (c) of subsection (1) of section 107 (order made: reconsideration of available amount).

(2) An application mentioned in the foregoing paragraph—
(a) shall be made by minute; and
(b) shall be served by the prosecutor on the accused and any other person likely to be affected by it.

Variation or discharge of confiscation order

B1-78.0.14 **37AA.7—**(1) Any of the following applications made under any of the following provisions of the Act of 2002 shall be by minute—

(a) by the accused or the prosecutor under paragraph (b) of subsection (1) of section 108 (inadequacy of available amount: variation of order);
(b) by the prosecutor under paragraph (b) of subsection (1) of section 109 (inadequacy of available amount: discharge of order);
(c) by the accused under paragraph (e) of subsection (1) of section 113 (variation of order); or
(d) by the accused under—
  (i) paragraph (c) of subsection (1); or
  (ii) paragraph (d) of subsection (3),
of section 114 (discharge of order).

(2) A party who makes an application mentioned in the foregoing paragraph shall serve a copy on every person likely to be affected by it.

Time for payment

B1-78.0.15 **37AA.8—**(1) An application by the accused under subsection (4) of section 116 of the Act of 2002 (time for payment) may be made—

(a) by minute; or
(b) orally at the bar.

(2) Where an accused makes an application by minute, he shall serve a copy on the prosecutor.

Hearings

B1-78.0.16 **37AA.9** Any request or application mentioned in the following rules shall be determined at a hearing, unless the court otherwise directs:

(a) 37AA.2 (confiscation orders);
(aa) 37AA.2A (confiscation orders: certification);
(ab) 37AA.2B (compliance orders);
(ac) 37AA.2C(1) (compliance orders: discharge and variation applications);
(ad) 37AA.2C(4) (compliance orders: discharge and variation appeals);
(b) 37AA.3 (disposal of family home);
(c) 37AA.6 (reconsideration of case, benefit or available amount);
(d) 37AA.7 (variation or discharge of confiscation order),
(e) 37AA.8 (time for payment);
(f) 37AA.10 (application, discharge and variation).

AMENDMENTS

Rule 37AA.9 as amended by Act of Adjournal (Criminal Procedure Rules Amendment No.2) (Miscellaneous) 2003 (SSI 2003/468) para.2. Brought into force on 27 October 2003 in accordance with para.1.

Rule 37AA.9 as amended by Act of Adjournal (Criminal Procedure Rules 1996 Amendment) (Miscellaneous) 2016 (SSI 2016/103) para.3 (effective 1 March 2016, subject to para.5).

Investigations

Application, discharge and variation

37AA.10—(1) The following applications shall be by petition— **B1-78.0.17**

(a) by the appropriate person to the Sheriff under any of the following provisions of the Act of 2002—

(i) subsection (1) of section 380 (production orders);

(ii) subsection (1) of section 387 (search warrants);

(iii) subsection (1) of section 397 (customer information orders);

(iv) subsection (1) of section 404 (account monitoring orders),

in relation to a confiscation investigation or money laundering investigation; and

(b) by the Lord Advocate, to the High Court of Justiciary under subsection (1) of section 391 of that Act (disclosure orders) for a disclosure order in relation to a confiscation investigation or a money laundering investigation.

(2) An application under subsection (2) of section 382 of the Act of 2002 (order to grant entry)—

(a) may be included in a petition in respect of an application under paragraph (1)(a)(i) of this rule; or

(b) if made after the lodging of the petition, shall be by minute,

and paragraph (3) of this rule shall apply to such an application.

(3) An application under any of the following provisions of the Act of 2002 shall be by minute and shall be intimated to any person affected by it—

(a) subsection (4) of section 386 (production orders: supplementary) to discharge or vary a production order or an order to grant entry;

(b) subsection (4) of section 396 (disclosure orders: supplementary) to discharge or vary a disclosure order;

(c) subsection (4) of section 403 (customer information orders: supplementary) to discharge or vary a customer information order;

(d) subsection (4) of section 408 (account monitoring orders: supplementary) to discharge or vary an account monitoring order.

AMENDMENTS

Rule 37AA.10(1) as amended by Act of Adjournal (Criminal Procedure Rules 1996 Amendment) (Miscellaneous) 2018 (SSI 2018/12) para.2(2) (effective 31 January 2018).

Appeal to the Sheriff Appeal Court

37AA.11.—(1) An appeal to the Sheriff Appeal Court under section 336B(8) (proceedings under section 336A: supplementary) of the Act of 2002 is to be made by lodging a note of appeal in Form 37AA.11-A. **B1-78.0.18**

(2) When an appeal is lodged, the court must—

(a) order intimation of the appeal to—

(i) the senior officer and any interested person other than the appellant, where an interested person is the appellant; or

(ii) any interested person, where the senior officer is the appellant; and

(b) appoint a hearing on the appeal.

(3) An appeal to the Sheriff Appeal Court under section 339ZJ(1) (appeals) of the Act of 2002(e) is to be made by lodging a note of appeal in Form 37AA.11-B.

(4) When an appeal is lodged the court must—

(a) order intimation of the appeal to—

(i) the procurator fiscal and any other person who was a party to the proceedings on the application, where a respondent to the proceedings on the application is the appellant; or

(ii) any respondent to the proceedings on the application, where the procurator fiscal is the appellant; and

(b) appoint a hearing on the appeal.

AMENDMENTS

Chapter 37AA inserted by Act of Adjournal (Criminal Procedure Rules Amendment) (Proceeds of Crime Act 2002) 2003 (SSI 2003/120) para.2. Brought into force on 24 February 2003 (for proceedings under Ch.3 of Pt 8 of the Proceeds of Crime Act 2002) and on 24 March 2003 (for proceedings under Pt 3 of that Act).

Rule 37AA.11 inserted by Act of Adjournal (Criminal Procedure Rules 1996 Amendment) (No. 5) (Proceeds of Crime etc.) 2017 (SSI 2017/429) para.2(2) (effective 21 December 2017).

GENERAL NOTE

B1-78.0.19 Section 92 of the Proceeds of Crime Act 2002 requires the High Court or the sheriff court (s.92(13)) to consider whether or not to make a confiscation order ("CO") when three conditions are satisfied. These conditions are: (1) that the accused has been convicted of an offence or offences (s.92(2)); (2) that the prosecutor has asked the court to proceed under s.92 (s.92(3)); and (3) that the court decides to order some disposal in respect of the accused (s.92(4)). Where the court acts under s.92, the court must proceed in a specified way. The court must: (a) decide whether the accused has a criminal lifestyle as defined in s.142; (b) where the court so decides, it must then decide whether the accused has benefited from his general criminal conduct as defined in s.143(2); and (c) if the court decides that the accused does not have a criminal lifestyle, it must decide whether he has benefited from "his particular criminal conduct" as defined in s.143(3) (s.92(5)). If the court decides that the accused has benefited from the criminal conduct, it must then proceed to decide the recoverable amount (which under s.93(1) is an amount equal to the accused's benefit from the criminal conduct) and then make a CO which requires the accused to pay that amount (s.92(6)). Before making a CO the court must take into account any representations made to it by "any person" who the court thinks is "likely to be affected by the order" (s.92(8)). The procedure envisages that either agreement will be reached between the Crown and the accused as to the amount which is due under a CO or a hearing will require to be held in order for evidence to be led and for the court to determine the amount if any due under the CO. The standard of proof which must be met when the court is determining issues such as whether the accused has a criminal lifestyle, whether he has benefited from either general criminal conduct or the accused's particular criminal conduct and how much is recoverable, is the balance of probabilities (s.92(9)). A CO is deemed to be a sentence for the purposes of any appeal or review (s.92(11)).

Chapter 37AA in its present state following amendment with effect from 5 August 2009 (see Act of Adjournal (Criminal Procedure Rules Amendment No.3) (Confiscation Proceedings) 2009 (SSI 2009/244) para.1(1)) provides a procedure which the High Court must follow in respect of confiscation proceedings in which the prosecutor gives to the High Court his statement of information under s.101(1) or s.110(2)(b) on or after 5 August 2009. In High Court cases where the statement of information was given before that date, the procedure set out under Ch.37AA prior to amendment is to be followed (para.1(4)). The newprocedure allows forgreaterjudicial control to be exercised in confiscation proceedings.

The initiating document is the prosecutor's statement of information (which is defined in s.101). At the same time as he gives this statement of information to the High Court the prosecutor must also serve a copy of it on the accused and he must also make arrangements, where applicable, for the accused to view and, if need be, copy any documents on which the prosecutor intends to rely (r.37AA.5(3)(b)). Within such time as the High Court directs, the accused must then supply his "response" to the prosecutor's statement of information (r.37AA.2(2)). Moreover, other persons who appear to the court likely to be affected by the making of a CO are entitled to submit written representations since the court is obliged to take into account any such written representations before proceeding to make a CO (s.92(8)).

After the period for submitting the response has expired, there is then an adjustment period of six weeks commencing on the date previously fixed by the High Court for lodging the response (r.37AA.5A). The High Court must then fix a procedural hearing to take place on the first Monday after the adjustment period has ended (r.37AA.5B(1)). At that procedural hearing the High Court must ascertain the parties' state of readiness to conduct a hearing to dispose of the prosecutor's application for a CO (called "the determination hearing"); and the High Court may set a date for lodging of any forensic report commissioned by the accused, order the exchange of documents between the parties, order the production of any documents and allow further adjustment of the statement of information and response. Finally, at that procedural hearing the High Court must thereafter either order a second procedural hearing or fix the determination hearing (r.37AA.5B(4)).

If a second procedural hearing is ordered, the High Court must once again at that second hearing, ascertain the parties' state of readiness for the determination hearing and either continue the second procedural hearing for a period not exceeding four weeks or fix the determination hearing (r.37AA.5C(1)). When the determination hearing is ordered, the High Court must issue a timetable (in Form 37AA.5D-B). The timetable must specify: (1) that a pre-determination hearing meeting is to take place on a date at least eight weeks before the date of the determination hearing; (2) the date for lodging the minute of that meeting (Form 37AA.5D-A), which date is to be at least five weeks before the determination hearing; and (3) the last dates (which must be at least four weeks before the determination hearing) for lodging productions and lists of witnesses (r.37AA.5D).

The final hearing which the new provisions envisage before the holding of the determination hearing is a hearing which is to be held on the last Monday which is at least four weeks before the determination hearing. At that final preliminary hearing the High Court must ascertain the parties' state of readiness for the determination hearing (r.37AA.5E(1)).

[THE NEXT PARAGRAPH IS B1-78.1]

Chapter 37A

Proceedings under Section 7 of the Knives Act 1997

Proceedings under Section 7 of the Knives Act 1997

37A. An application to the sheriff under section 7(3) of the Knives Act 1997 (recovery order for delivery of property to applicant if it appears to court that he owns it) shall be made by petition in Form 37A. **B1-78.1**

AMENDMENTS

Rule 37A inserted by Act of Adjournal (Criminal Procedure Rules Amendment No.6) (SI 1997/2081) (effective 1 September 1997).

Chapter 38

Transfer of Rights of Appeal of Deceased Persons

Applications for transfer under section 303A of the Act of 1995

38. Any application to the appropriate Appeal Court under section 303A of the Act of 1995 for an order authorising a person (the "applicant") as executor, or as the case may be by reason of his having a legitimate interest, to institute or continue any appeal which could have been or has been instituted by a deceased person shall be made in Form 38 and shall be accompanied by a copy of the confirmation of the applicant as executor or evidence of his legitimate interest, as the case may be. **B1-78.2**

AMENDMENTS

Rule 38 inserted by Act of Adjournal (Criminal Procedure Rules Amendment No.4) (SI 1997/1834) (effective August 1, 1997).

Rule 38 as amended by Act of Adjournal (Criminal Procedure Rules 1996 Amendment) (No. 4) (Sheriff Appeal Court) 2015 (SSI 2015/245) para.4 (effective September 22, 2015 subject to savings provisions in para.6).

GENERAL NOTE

Section 20 of the Crime and Punishment (Scotland) Act 1997 (c.48) amended the 1995 Act by inserting a new provision (s.303A) in implementation of recommendation 16 of the *Sutherland Committee's Report on Appeals Criteria and Miscarriages of Justice* (Cmnd 3245 (1996), para.5.61) which itself was strongly influenced by the introduction in England in the Criminal Appeal Act 1995 of a similar right of appeal where the convicted person had died. **B1-78.3**

The convicted person's executor or anyone having a legitimate interest in the outcome of the appeal can not only continue with an appeal already commenced by the deceased before his death but also commence such an appeal (s.303A(1) and (4)). The deceased's representative requires the High Court's authority which must be sought within three months of the deceased's death or, where cause is shown, at such later time as the court allows (s.303A(2)). The transferred right relates not only to all statutory appeals relating to conviction and sentence but also to bills of suspension, bills of advocation and petititons to the *nobile officium* for review of "any conviction, penalty or other order made in respect of the deceased" (s.303A(6)).

In such appeals the deceased's representative or other person having a legitimate interest must stand in the deceased's shoes and accordingly where time has begun to run against the deceased, his representative only has the benefit of that portion of the time limit which remains unexpired at the date of the deceased's death (s.303A(5)).

The Sutherland Committee recommended a right of appeal should exist in someone other than the convicted person when the convicted person died if there was "good reason for pursuing such an appeal, for example a personal or business partner, close relation or executor" (para.5.61). It has been held that the term "legitimate interest" in s.303A(4)(b) does not include deceased victims or their representatives. In *Scottish Criminal Cases Review Commission v Swire and Mosey* [2015] HCJAC 76 (decided on 3 July 2015) the Lord Justice Clerk (Carloway) stated:

> "What the statute is intended to provide is an avenue whereby an executor, as of right, and others in a similar relationship with the deceased, can continue or institute appeal proceedings in his stead. It is not designed to give relatives of victims a right to pursue an appeal for their own, or the public interest in securing that miscarriages ofjustice should not occur." (at [23]).

Following the recommendation of the Sutherland Committee's Report (supra, para.5.50), the Scottish Criminal Cases Review Commission was created by s.25 of the Crime and Punishment (Scotland) Act 1997 (inserting Part XA into the Criminal Procedure (Scotland) Act 1995) and became operational on April 1, 1999. The transferred right shall apply also to appeals resulting from references by the Commission, but in such cases the executor or other interested person will require to apply to the court for an order under s.303A(1) within one month of the date of the deceased's death (s.303A(3)). In *Coughbrough's*

Executrix v HM Advocate [2010] HCJAC 32 (decided on April 1, 2010), the convicted person secured a reference to the High Court of his conviction but, after certain grounds of appeal had been heard and finally determined, he died. His sister was appointed executor and was permitted by the High Court to proceed with the two remaining grounds of appeal, neither of which had been the basis of the Scottish Criminal Cases Review Commission's reference (para.3). The mother of a man convicted of lewd, indecent and libidinous practices was authorised to continue with her son's appeal against conviction when he died after having marked an appeal and obtained interim liberation. The appeal was successful: see *Cowan (Deceased) v HM Advocate*, May 3, 2001, Appeal Court (unreported).

In *R. v Whelan* [1997] Crim.L.R. 659, the Court of Appeal (Criminal Division) in England allowed a widow to continue with her deceased's husband's appeal against conviction for sexual offences because the couple had been close and she was doing what her husband had wished to be done to clear his name. In *R. v Bentley* [1998] T.L.R. 492 the Court of Appeal quashed a conviction for murder (in respect of which the accused had been hanged) on an appeal brought by the accused's niece following a reference to the Court of Appeal by the English Criminal Cases Review Commission. In *R. v Hanratty* (October 17, 2000) *The Times,* October 26, 2000, the Court of Appeal gave directions for the exhumation of the remains of a convicted murderer so that DNA samples could be obtained in order to assist in the determination of the murderer's appeal which was brought by the murderer's brother after a reference to the Court of Appeal by the Criminal Cases Review Commission.

Chapter 39

Proceedings under Criminal Law (Consolidation) (Scotland) Act 1995

Orders to make material available

B1-78.4 **39.1.**—(1) An application by the procurator fiscal to the sheriff for an order under section 31(2) of the Criminal Law (Consolidation) (Scotland) Act 1995 (order to make material available in investigation into drug trafficking) shall be made by petition; and section 134 of the Act of 1995 (incidental applications) shall apply to an application under section 31(2) as it applies to an application under section 31(2) as it applies to an application to which section 134 applies.

(2) The sheriff may make the order sought in the petition under paragraph (1) before intimation of the petition to the person who appears to him to be in possession of the material to which the application relates.

(3) An application by the procurator fiscal for an order under section 31(5) of the Criminal Law (Consolidation) (Scotland) Act 1995 (order allowing constable or person commissioned by Customs and Excise access to premises to obtain material) may be made in the petition applying for an order under section 31(2) of that Act; and paragraph (2) shall apply to an order in respect of a person who appears to the sheriff to be entitled to grant entry to the premises in question as it applies to an order in respect of the person mentioned in that paragraph.

Discharge and variation of orders

B1-78.5 **39.2.**—(1) A person in respect of whom an order has been made under section 31(2) or (5) of the Criminal Law (Consolidation) (Scotland) Act 1995 may apply to the sheriff for discharge or variation of the order in question.

(2) The sheriff may, after hearing the parties, grant or refuse to grant the discharge or variation sought.

Warrants to search premises

B1-78.6 **39.3.** An application by the procurator fiscal to the sheriff under section 32(1) of the Criminal Law (Consolidation) (Scotland) Act 1995 (authority for search) shall be made by petition; and section 134 of the Act of 1995 (incidental applications) shall apply to an application under section 32(1) as it applies to an application to which section 134 applies.

AMENDMENTS

Chapter 39 inserted by Act of Adjournal (Criminal Procedure Rules Amendment No.7) (SI 1997/2653) (effective November 21, 1997) as Chapter 38.

GENERAL NOTE

B1-78.6.1 This rule has been superseded by legislation. Sections 31 and 32 of the Criminal Law (Consolidation) (Scotland) Act 1995 were repealed by Sch.12 to the Proceeds of Crime Act 2002 from and after February 24, 2003.

[THE NEXT PARAGRAPH IS B1-78.7]

Chapter 40

Compatibility Issues and Devolution Issues

Interpretation

B1-78.7 **40.1.** In this Chapter—

"Advocate General" means the Advocate General for Scotland;

"compatibility issue" means a compatibility issue within the meaning of section 288ZA(2) of the Act of 1995;

"devolution issue" means a devolution issue within the meaning of paragraph 1 of Schedule 6 to the Scotland Act 1998;
"Schedule 6" means Schedule 6 to the Scotland Act 1998;
"the 2010 Act" means the Criminal Justice and Licensing (Scotland) Act 2010.

Raising compatibility issues and devolution issues: solemn proceedings

40.2.—(1) This rule applies to solemn proceedings. **B1-78.8**

(2) In proceedings at first instance, where a party proposes to raise a compatibility issue or devolution issue he shall give written notice of his intention to do so by minute in Form 40.2.

(3) The minute must be lodged with the clerk of court and served on the other parties no later than 14 clear days before the preliminary hearing or, as the case may be, first diet.

(4) In proceedings on appeal (where the issue is being raised for the first time), where a party proposes to raise a compatibility issue or devolution issue he shall, subject to section 107 of the Act of 1995, do so in the note of appeal.

Raising compatibility issues and devolution issues: summary proceedings

40.3.—(1) This rule applies to summary proceedings. **B1-78.9**

(2) In proceedings at first instance, where a party proposes to raise a compatibility issue or devolution issue he shall give written notice of his intention to do so by minute in Form 40.3.

(3) The minute must be lodged with the clerk of court and served on the other parties—

(a) where an intermediate diet is to be held, before the first such diet; or

(b) where such a diet is not to be held, no later than 14 clear days before the trial diet.

(4) In proceedings on appeal (where the issue is being raised for the first time), where a party proposes to raise a compatibility issue he shall, subject to section 176of the Act of 1995, do so in the application for a stated case.

Raising compatibility issues and devolution issues: other proceedings

40.4.—(1) This rule applies to criminal proceedings which are not proceedings on indictment or summary proceedings, including bills of advocation and bills of suspension. **B1-78.10**

(2) Where a party to proceedings proposes to raise a compatibility issue or devolution issue he shall raise such an issue as a point of law in the pleadings.

Specification of compatibility issue or devolution issue

40.5. Where a compatibility issue or devolution issue is raised in accordance with rule 40.2, rule 40.3 or rule 40.4 the facts and circumstances and contentions of law on the basis of which it is alleged that a compatibility issue or devolution issue arises in the proceedings shall be specified in sufficient detail to enable the court to determine whether such an issue arises. **B1-78.11**

Time for raising compatibility issue or devolution issue

40.6.—(1) No party to criminal proceedings shall raise a compatibility issue or devolution issue in those proceedings except as in accordance with rule 40.2, 40.3 or 40.4, unless the court, on cause shown, otherwise directs. **B1-78.12**

(2) Where the court determines that a devolution issue may be raised as mentioned in paragraph (1), it shall order that intimation of the devolution issue is given in writing to the Advocate General.

Intimation of compatibility issues and devolution issues to the Advocate General

40.7.—(1) Where a party raises a devolution issue in accordance with rule 40.2, rule 40.3 or rule 40.4 a copy of the document in which it is raised shall be served on the Advocate General. **B1-78.13**

(2) A copy document served on the Advocate General under paragraph (1) shall be treated as intimation of the devolution issue arising in the proceedings as mentioned in paragraph 5 of Schedule 6.

Participation of Advocate General in proceedings

40.8. Where the Advocate General intends to take part in the proceedings as mentioned in paragraph 6 of Schedule 6 or, as the case may be, section 288ZA(1) of the Act of 1995, he shall give written notice of his intention to do so to the clerk of court and the other parties. **B1-78.14**

Appeals to the Supreme Court

40.9.—(1) An application to the High Court under section 288AA(5) of the Act of 1995 (appeals to the Supreme Court: compatibility issues) or paragraph 13 of Schedule 6 (appeals to the Supreme Court: devolution issues) shall be in Form 40.9. **B1-78.15**

(2) Where the Advocate General is not already a party to the proceeding, the applicant shall, at the same time as lodging the application, intimate a copy to the Advocate General.

Reference of compatibility issues and devolution issues to the High Court

40.10.—(1) This rule applies where a court, other than a court consisting of two or more judges of the High Court of Justiciary decides or, as the case may be, is required to refer— **B1-78.16**

(a) a compatibility issue to the High Court of Justiciary under section 288ZB(1) or (2) of the Act of 1995;

(b) a devolution issue to the High Court of Justiciary under paragraph 9 of Schedule 6.

(2) The court shall—

(a) pronounce an order giving directions to the parties about the manner and time in which the reference is to be drafted;

(b) give its reasons for making the reference and cause those reasons to be recorded in the record or minutes of proceedings, as the case may be;
(c) give written notice of the reference to the Advocate General where the reference relates to a devolution issue and the Advocate General is not already a party to the proceedings;
(d) continue the proceedings from time to time as necessary for the purposes of the reference.

(3) The reference shall—

(a) be adjusted at the sight of the court in such manner as the court may direct;
(b) after approval and the making of an appropriate order by the court (after the expiry of any period for appeal) be transmitted by the clerk of court to the Clerk of Justiciary with a certified copy of the record or minutes of proceedings, as the case may be, and, where applicable a certified copy of the relevant indictment or complaint.

Reference of compatibility issues and devolution issues to the Supreme Court

B1-78.17 **40.11.**—(1) This rule applies where a court consisting of two or more judges of the High Court of Justiciary decides or, as the case may be, is required to refer—

(a) a compatibility issue to the Supreme Court under section 288ZB(3), (4) or (5) of the Act of 1995;
(b) a devolution issue to the Supreme Court under paragraph 11 or 33 of Schedule 6.

(2) The court shall—

(a) pronounce an order giving directions about the manner and time in which the reference is to be drafted (including such matters as may be required by Supreme Court Practice Direction 10);
(b) give its reasons for making the reference and cause those reasons to be recorded in the record or minutes of proceedings, as the case may be;
(c) give written notice of the reference to the Advocate General where the Advocate General is not already a party to the proceedings;
(d) continue the proceedings from time to time as necessary for the purposes of the reference.

(3) The reference shall—

(a) be adjusted at the sight of the court in such manner as the court may direct;
(b) after approval and the making of an appropriate order by the court, shall be transmitted by the clerk of court to the Registrar of the Supreme Court with a certified copy of the record or minutes of proceedings, as the case may be, and, where applicable, a certified copy of the relevant indictment or complaint.

Orders pending determination of compatibility issues or devolution issues

B1-78.18 **40.12.**—(1) Where a court makes a reference mentioned in rule 40.10 or rule 40.11 it may make such orders as it considers just and equitable in the circumstances pending the determination of the compatibility issue or devolution issue.

(1A) Where an appeal under paragraph 13(a) of Schedule 6 is taken, the High Court of Justiciary may make such orders as it considers just and equitable in the circumstances pending the determination of that appeal.

(1B) Without prejudice to the generality of paragraphs (1) and (1A), orders made under those paragraphs may include—

(a) an order postponing any diet, including a trial diet, fixed in the case;
(b) such orders as the court considers appropriate in relation to bail;
(c) subject to paragraph (2), an order extending the period within which any step requires to be taken or event to have occurred.

(2) An order extending a period which may be extended under section 65 or section 147 of the Act of 1995 may be made only by a court which has power to do so under that section, and for the purposes of that section, the fact that a devolution issue has been raised by the prosecutor shall not, without more, be treated as fault on the part of the prosecutor.

AMENDMENTS

Rule 40.12 as amended by Act of Adjournal (Criminal Procedure Rules Amendment No.3) (Miscellaneous) 2013 (SSI 2013/198) para.3 (effective June 24, 2013).

Procedure on receipt of determination of compatibility issue or devolution issue

B1-78.18.1 **40.13.**—(1) This rule applies where—

(a) the High Court has determined a reference mentioned in rule 40.10;
(b) the Supreme Court has determined a reference mentioned in rule 40.11.

(2) The determination shall be laid before the court that made the reference.

(3) The court shall then give directions as to further procedure which shall be intimated by the clerk of court with a copy of the determination to each of the parties to the proceedings.

AMENDMENTS

Rule 40.13(1)(b) as amended by Act of Adjournal (Criminal Procedure Rules Amendment No.3) (Miscellaneous) 2013 (SSI 2013/198) para.3 (effective June 24, 2013).

Procedure following determination of an appeal by the Supreme Court

B1-78.18.2 **40.14.**—(1) This rule applies where the Supreme Court has—

(a) determined a compatibility issue on appeal and remitted the proceedings to the High Court in accordance with section 288AA(3) of the Act of 1995;

(b) determined a devolution issue on appeal under paragraph 13(a) of Schedule 6.

(2) The High Court of Justiciary shall then give direction as to further procedure which shall be intimated by the Clerk of Justiciary to each of the parties to the proceedings.

Orders mitigating the effect of certain decisions

40.15. Where the court is considering making an order under section 102 of the Scotland Act 1998 (power of court to vary or suspend the effect of certain decisions) the court shall order intimation of the fact to be made by the clerk of court, in writing, to every person to whom intimation is required to be given by that section. **B1-78.18.3**

AMENDMENTS

Chapter 40 as substituted by Act of Adjournal (Criminal Procedure Rules Amendment) (Miscellaneous) 2013 (SSI 2013/72) para.4 (effective 22 April 2013, subject to transitional provisions).

[THE NEXT PARAGRAPH IS B1-78.19]

GENERAL NOTE

In the aftermath of the Supreme Court's constitutionally contentious decision in *Fraser v HM Advocate*, 2011 S.L.T. 515 there was urgent consideration given in Scotland to the relationship between the High Court and the Supreme Court in respect of the jurisdiction of the latter court in devolution issue appeals. A Review Group under the chairmanship of Lord McCluskey was appointed and issued a First Report and its Final Report in quick succession (see *Examination of the Relationship between the High Court of Justiciary and the Supreme Court in Criminal Cases* (2011)). In summary the Review Group concluded (1) that there should remain an appellate jurisdiction in the Supreme Court to determine human rights questions arising in Scottish criminal proceedings; (2) that the Lord Advocate in his role as public prosecutor should be removed from s.57 of the Scotland Act 1998; and (3) that the "true distinction" which should be reflected in statute is "the distinction between Convention rights and real *vires* devolution issues, i.e. disputes as to whether legislative or executive acts are ultra vires because they are outwith the competence of the Scottish Parliament or Executive" (Final Report, para.28). **B1-78.19**

Part 4 of the Scotland Act 2012 (c.11) contains important changes to the procedure regulating devolution issues that are raised in criminal proceedings in order to reflect the recommendations of the Review Group. These changes are set out in ss.34-38 of the 2012 Act. These provisions came into force on 22 April 2013 (see Scotland Act 2012 (Commencement No.3) Order 2013 (SI 2013/6) art.2). In order to take account of these provisions the original Ch.40 required to be replaced with a new provision which was introduced by para.4 of the Act of Adjournal (Criminal Procedure Rules Amendment) (Miscellaneous) 2013 (SSI 2013/72).

The thrust of ss.34-38 of the 2012 Act is that there are now two types of issues which can arise: devolution issues and compatibility issues. From 22 April 2013 any new issues arising in Scottish criminal proceedings in respect of the Convention rights or European Union law will cease to be devolution issues and must thereafter be raised as compatibility issues. This change in procedure is important as the vast bulk of what were devolution issues in criminal proceedings were in respect of the fair trial right under art.6 of the European Convention: the accused must now raise this matter as a compatibility issue.

Compatibility issues

A compatibility issue is defined in s.288ZA(2) of the Criminal Procedure (Scotland) Act 1995 (as inserted by s.34(3) of the 2012 Act) as "a question arising in criminal proceedings, as to—(a) whether a public authority has acted (or proposes to act)—(i) in a way which is made unlawful by s.6(1) of the Human Rights Act 1998, or (ii) in a way which is incompatible with EU law, or (b) whether an Act of the Scottish Parliament or any provision of an Act of the Scottish Parliament is incompatible with any ofthe Convention rights or with EU law". The expression "public authority" in s.288ZA(2)(a) has the same meaning as in s.6 of the Human Rights Act 1998; EU law has the same meaning as in s.126(9) ofthe Scotland Act 1998; and references to acting include failing to act (s.288ZA(3)). **B1-78.19.1**

The Supreme Court has confirmed that its jurisdiction in compatability issues is "limited" (*Macklin v HM Advocate* [2015] UKSC 77 at [11]) and that it extends only to determining whether the High Court has applied the correct test in a compatability issue and does not include determining whether the High Court's decision is correct: *Macklin*, at [20] (Lord Reed) and at [38] (Lord Gill).

For the purposes of determining any compatibility issue an appeal lies, as it continues to do with "real" devolution issues, to the Supreme Court against a determination in criminal proceedings by a court of two or more judges of the High Court of Justiciary (s.288AA(1)). However, appeal can only be taken with the permission of the High Court or (failing the grant of leave) the permission of the Supreme Court. However, despite a recommendation by the Review Group in favour of the introduction of a requirement of certification of a point of law of general public importance before an appeal can be taken to the Supreme Court (Final Report, paras 42-43), there is no such requirement.

In relation to the practice of the Inner House on whether or not to grant leave to appeal, it has recently been stated in *Massie v McCaig* [2013] CSIH 37 that

> "appeals to the United Kingdom Supreme Court are not normally appropriate unless they raise an issue of law of general or public importance (*G Hamilton (Tullochgribban Mains) v Highland Council*, 2012 S.L.T. 1148, Lord Walker at para.29)." (at[7], per Lord Justice Clerk Carloway).

It is likely that such an approach will be taken in applications for leave to appeal in the High Court.

Consistent with the introduction of compatibility issues, para.1 of Sch.6 to the Scotland Act 1998 has been amended by the addition of the qualification that "a question arising in criminal proceedings … that would, apart from this paragraph, be a devolution issue is not a devolution issue if (however formulated) it relates to the compatibility with any of the Convention rights or with EU law" of (a) an or any provision of an Act of the Scottish Parliament, (b) a function, (c) the purported or proposed exercise of a function and (d) a failure to act (2012 Act s.36(4)). So a complaint that the prosecutor's acts are in breach of art.6 of the European Convention must now be raised as a compatibility issue.

Rule 40.2

As with the previous Ch.40, separate provision is made for the raising of compatibility issues and devolution issues in solemn and summary proceedings. Subject to the power of the court in r.40.6 to direct otherwise, such issues must in solemn proceedings be intimated in writing by minute (the style of which is Form 40.2) lodged with the clerk of the court and served on the other parties to the proceedings no later than 14 clear days before the preliminary hearing in the High Court or the first diet in the sheriff court. However, where the issue is raised for the first time on appeal, that must be done in the note of appeal (r.40.2(4)).

Rule 40.3

In summary proceedings, notice of a compatibility issue or a devolution issue must be given in Form 40.3 lodged with the court and served on the other parties either before the first intermediate diet or no later than 14 clear days before the trial diet. Any such issue which is raised for the first time on appeal must be specified in the application for a stated case (r.40.3(4)).

Rule 40.4

In the case of bills of suspension and advocation, and presumably also petitions to the *nobile officium*, compatibility issues and devolution issues must be raised as a point of law in the pleadings. Bills of advocation and suspension are now subject to a time limit of three weeks for presentation to the High Court (s.191A(2)) but the High Court may extend that time limit (s.191A(3); see *MacDonald vProcurator Fiscal, Dornoch* [2013] HCJAC 48 and *Middleton and McAllister v Procurator Fiscal, Livingston* [2013] HCJAC 49).

Rule 40.5

B1-78.19.2 As with the old provisions of Ch.40 which dealt only with devolution issues (see r.40.6), there is a requirement that the issue—whether a compatibility issue or a devolution issue—should be stated in sufficient detail so as to allow the court to determine that such an issue is in law raised. Sch.6 para.2 to the Scotland Act 1998 provides that a devolution issue shall not be taken to arise "merely because of any contention of a party to the proceedings which appears to the court … to be frivolous or vexatious". It has been stated by the Appeal Court that

> "it is not sufficient for a party simply to aver that a devolution issue has arisen. The court must consider whether, in light of the particular circumstances of each individual case, it has been demonstrated that a devolution issue does relevantly arise." (BBC, Petrs (No.2), 2000 J.C. 521 at 532G, per Lord Kirkwood).

See also Lord Hope of Craighead's discussion of what constitutes a relevant devolution issue minute in *Montgomery v HM Advocate*, 2001 S.L.T. 37. This approach will likely also be adopted for compatibility issues.

Rule 40.6

Where the court is satisfied on cause shown it may direct that the time limits already noticed need not be complied with. It was held that the mere fact that there had been some failure by the accused or his representatives to raise a devolution issue timeously did not necessarily mean that cause had not been shown for allowing an issue to be raised late and that part of the cause for allowing a late issue to be raised might be the prima facie significance of the issue, particularly for the proceedings as a whole (*HM Advocate v Montgomery*, 2000 J.C. 111 at 121C, per Lord Justice General Rodger). It was also observed that it is not particularly helpful for the court simply to ask itself whether it is in the interests of justice to depart from the timetable requirements.

Rule 40.7

Despite the terms of the heading of this rule, it only applies to devolution issues (as does r.40.6(2)). Sch.6 para.5 to the Scotland Act 1998 requires intimation of any devolution issue which arises in any proceedings before a court or tribunal to be given to the Advocate General and the Lord Advocate (unless the person to whom the intimation would be given is a party to the proceedings). The Lord Advocate is not a party to summary criminal proceedings.

Rule 40.8

B1-78.19.3 Section 288ZA(1) of the 1995 Act (as inserted by the 2012 Act) provides that the Advocate General may take part as a party in criminal proceedings so far as they relate to a compatibility issue; and in the event that upon learning of the compatibility issue, the Advocate General decides to join the proceedings, he must give written notice of that decision to the court and all other parties. The same duty is imposed in respect of devolution issues where the Advocate General intends to intervene.

Rule 40.9

Section 288AA(5) of the 1995 Act (as inserted by the 2012 Act) provides that, as with devolution issues under the 1998 Act, an appeal against a determination of two or more judges of the High Court of a compatibility issue lies to the Supreme Court only with the leave of the High Court or (failing that grant of leave) with the permission of the Supreme Court. Notice of the application must be given to the Advocate General if he is not already a party (as in most cases he will not be).

Section 37 of the 2012 Act introduced for devolution issues an important change which will assist the efficient administration of justice. Time limits are now prescribed for applications for leave to appeal in respect of both compatibility issues and devolution issues (see respectively, s.288AA(7) and (8) of the 1995 Act and paras 13A and 13B of Sch.6 to the 1998 Act). An application to the High Court must be made within 28 days of the date of the determination against which the appeal is sought to be taken or within such longer period as the High Court considers "equitable having regard to all the circumstances"; and application to the Supreme Court must be made within 28 days of the date on which the High Court refused that permission to appeal or such longer period as the Supreme Court considers equitable in light of all the circumstances. It is likely that leave to appeal will not be granted unless the proposed appeal raises "an issue of law of general or public importance" (see *Massie v McCaig* [2013] CSIH 37 at [7]).

Rule 40.10

Where a compatibility issue arises in any court of first instance (other than the High Court when constituted by two or more judges), that court may refer the compatibility issue to the High Court for determination instead of determining the issue itself (s.288ZB(1)). The same is true for devolution issues arising in proceedings before any such first instance court (1998 Act Sch.6 para.9). Where the Lord Advocate or Advocate General is a party to criminal proceedings before a court other than a court consisting of two or more judges of the High Court, he may *require* the court to refer the compatibility issue to the High Court for determination (s.288ZB(2)). Where the Advocate General is not already a party to the criminal proceedings, the court must give written notice to him when the issue is a devolution issue (r.40.10(2)(c)).

Rule 40.11

Where a compatibility issue has been referred to the High Court because either the Lord Advocate or Advocate General required that a reference be made, the High Court may, instead of determining the issue itself, refer the issue to the Supreme Court (s.288ZB(3)). When a compatibility issue arises in proceedings before a court comprising two or more High Court judges, that court may refer the issue to the Supreme Court rather than determine the issue itself (s.288ZB(4)). The Lord Advocate and Advocate General (if he is already a party to the proceedings) may also require the High Court to refer a compatibility issue to the Supreme Court (s.288ZB(5)). The Lord Advocate and the Advocate General are entitled to require the High Court to refer a devolution issue to the Supreme Court when the Law Officer is a party to the proceedings (1998 Act Sch.6 para.33). A court comprising two or more High Court judges may refer a devolution issue to the Supreme Court other than a devolution issue which has been referred to it by an inferior court (Sch.6 para.11). Where the Advocate General is not already a party to the proceedings, the court must give written notice of the reference to the Advocate General (r.40.11(2)(c)). **B1-78.19.4**

Rule 40.13

Section 288ZB(7) of the 1995 Act provides: "When it has determined a compatibility issue on a reference ... the Supreme Court must remit the proceedings to the High Court." It is of importance to note what r.40.13(2) and (3) seek to achieve. The objective is to ensure that the Supreme Court's determination of a compatibility issue referred to it by the High Court is then laid before the High Court, and the High Court thereafter gives effect to the determination as it considers appropriate. That was what the Review Group considered to be necessary so as to preserve the constitutional relationship between the High Court and the Supreme Court in criminal proceedings (see Final Report, para.10).

Rule 40.14

Likewise s.288AA(3) provides that on determining an appeal on a compatibility issue, the Supreme Court must remit the case to the High Court. It is thereafter for the High Court to give directions as to further procedure.

[THE NEXT PARAGRAPH IS B1-78.20]

Chapter 41

Human Rights Act 1998

Application and interpretation

B1-78.20 **41.1.**—(1) This Chapter deals with various matters relating to the Human Rights Act 1998.

(2) In this Chapter—

"the 1998 Act" means the Human Rights Act 1998;

"declaration of incompatibility" has the meaning given by section 4 of the 1998 Act.

Evidence of judgments etc

B1-78.21 **41.2.**—(1) Evidence of any judgment, decision, declaration or opinion of which account has to be taken by the court under section 2 of the 1998 Act shall be given by reference to any authoritative and complete report of the said judgment, decision, declaration or opinion and may be given in any manner.

(2) Evidence given in accordance with paragraph (1) shall be sufficient evidence of that judgment, decision, declaration or opinion.

Declaration of incompatibility

B1-78.22 **41.3.**—(1) Where in any proceedings a party seeks a declaration of incompatibility or the court is considering whether to make such a declaration at its own instance—

(a) notice in Form 41.3-A shall be given as soon as reasonably practicable to such person as the Lord Justice General may from time to time direct—

(i) by the party seeking the declaration; or

(ii) by the clerk of court,

as the case may be, provided that there shall be no requirement to give such notice to a party or to the representative of a party; and

(b) where notice is given by the party seeking the declaration the party shall lodge a certificate of notification in process.

(2) Where any—

(a) Minister of the Crown (or person nominated by him);

(b) member of the Scottish Executive;

(c) Northern Ireland Minister;

(d) Northern Ireland department,

wishes to be joined as a party to proceedings in relation to which the Crown is entitled to receive notice under section 5 of the 1998 Act he or, as the case may be, it shall serve notice in Form 41.3-B to that effect on the Deputy Principal Clerk of Justiciary and shall serve a copy of the notice on all other parties to the proceedings.

AMENDMENTS

Rule 41.3(1) substituted by Act of Adjournal (Criminal Procedure Rules Amendment No.4) (Miscellaneous) 2006 (SSI 2006/436) r.2 (effective September 1, 2006)

B1-78.23 **41.4.** Within 14 days after the date of service of the notice under rule 41.3(2), the person serving the notice shall lodge a minute in the proceedings in Form 41.4 and shall serve a copy of that minute on all other parties to the proceedings.

B1-78.24 **41.5.** The court may fix a diet for a hearing on the question of incompatibility as a separate hearing from any other hearing in the proceedings and may sist the proceedings if it considers it necessary to do so while the question of incompatibility is being determined.

AMENDMENTS

Chapter 41 inserted by Act of Adjournal (Criminal Procedure Rules Amendment No.2) (Human Rights Act 1998) 2000 (SSI 2000/315) (effective October 2, 2000).

GENERAL NOTE

B1-78.25 The Human Rights Act 1998 was brought into force on October 2, 2000. Subject to what is said below, the effect of the coming into force of that statute might have been though to be to eliminate any need to raise a devolution issue when an accused wishes to challenge the Crown's conduct in a prosecution since (in terms of s.6(3)(a)) all courts are public authorities for the purposes of the Human Rights Act 1998 (with the exception of claims for damages for judicial acts done in good faith, in respect of which damages may not be awarded otherwise than to compensate a person to the extent required by art.5(5) of the European Convention on Human Rights: see s.9(3)) and are therefore bound to refrain from acting in a manner incompatible with the European Convention. The availability of the regime created by the Human Rights Act 1998 might therefore have been thought to rob of significance—except perhaps in the context of rights of appeal (see *Montgomery v HM Advocate*, 2001 S.L.T. 37 at 40K, per Lord Nicholls of Birkenhead)—any dispute over the scope of the devolution issues specified in Sch.6 to the Scotland Act 1998.

The purpose of this new chapter is necessarily very limited. This is because the duty of the court in its handling of all criminal business will be to ensure that it acts in a manner compatible with all of the Convention rights enumerated in s.1 of, and Sch.1 to, the Human Rights Act 1998. Accordingly, a human rights issue will be capable of arising at any stage in criminal proceedings prior to final determination in the Appeal Court and will not be dependent on demonstrating that the Lord Advocate or a procurator fiscal is acting incompatibly with a Convention right. Thus, no procedural rules for the raising of a human rights issue have been made in contradistinction to the provision made in Ch.40 of the Criminal Procedure Rules for the raising of devolution issues. Yet it may remain to be seen whether the use of the concept of waiver, which has been approved in devolution issues cases (see *Millar v Dickson*, 2000 J.C. 648 and *Clancy v Caird*, 2000 S.C. 441) will not also be considered appropriate to bar an accused from raising a challenge to certain procedural matters when he could have done so at an earlier stage in the proceedings.

Moreover, the related plea of acquiescence has also been approved by the High Court for use by the Crown in devolution issues cases (see *Lochridge v Miller*, 2002 S.L.T. 906; 2002 S.C.C.R. 628) and the Privy Council (see *Robertson v Frame*, 2006 S.L.T. 478; 2006 S.C.C.R. 151). Thus, once the trial proceedings are at an end without any complaint of a Convention breach having been stated, it will be necessary for any such complaint to be raised on appeal in a devolution issue minute without significant delay. If the point is not raised quickly the inference may be drawn that the accused has acquiesced in the breach and thereby lost his right to redress by suspension or advocation (or, indeed, any other remedy: see *Dickson v HM Advocate* [2006] HCJAC 74; 2006 S.L.T. 1027, para.43.). However, especially where the Convention breach is said to have occurred prior to the commencement of the Scotland Act 1998 (where the retrospective application of Convention rights under the Human Rights Act 1998 will then be in issue (cf. *Dickson*, supra)), the plea will fail where "the circumstances do not disclose that the appellants during the relevant period had the requisite knowledge of the availability of the grounds of challenge to the validity of the ... decisions which they [later] maintain to enable it to be inferred that they made an informed decision not to take the point" (*Dickson*, para.40).

Subject to the qualification which was expressed in *Mills v HM Advocate (No.2)*, 2001 S.L.T. 1359 (see B1-78.19 above), the Human Rights Act does not provide for a special procedure for raising human rights challenges but there is need for notice to be given by the *court* when it is considering whether or not to exercise its powers under s.4(2) or (4). These provisions provide respectively for the power of the court (which for these purposes is restricted to the High Court of Justiciary sitting otherwise than as a trial court, the Courts-Martial Appeal Court and the Judicial Committee of the Privy Council: s.4(5)) to make a "declaration of incompatibility" where the court determines that a provision of primary legislation or a provision of subordinate legislation made in the exercise of a power conferred by primary legislation is incompatible with a Convention right. In such cases it may be necessary for a government department (other than the Lord Advocate) to be afforded the opportunity of making submissions on the proposal to make a declaration of incompatibility.

The Appeal Court's powers of interpretation of potentially incompatible legislation are specified in s.3. So far as it is possible to do so, primary legislation and subordinate legislation (whenever enacted) must be read and given effect in a way which is compatible with the Convention rights (s.3(1)). Thus, when dealing with s. 172 of the Road Traffic Act 1988, the Appeal Court in determining a devolution issue minute and having found that s. 172 was incompatible with an accused's right to silence and privilege against self-incrimination, considered that it was obliged thereafter to consider whether that provision could be "read down" so as to be compatible with art.6(1) (see *Brown v Stott*, 2000 J.C. 328 at 354E-355C, per Lord Justice General Rodger). The duty to "read down" legislation does not, however, affect the validity, continuing operation or enforcement of any incompatible primary legislation or of any incompatible subordinate legislation which (disregarding any possibility of revocation) is prevented by primary legislation from being cured of its incompatibility (s.3(2)(b) and (c)). A declaration of incompatibility is declared by s.6(6) not to affect the validity, continuing operation or enforcement of the legislative provision in respect of which it is made and is also declared not to be binding on the parties to the proceedings in which it is made.

The approach to be adopted to whether a declaration of incompatibility should be made, or whether the statutory provision in question can be "read down" so as to be compatible with a Convention right has been considered in several cases. See *R. v Lambert* [2001] 3 W.L.R. 206 and *R. v A (No.2)* [2001] 2 W.L.R. 1546, both decided in the House of Lords; and *Wilson v First County Trust Ltd (No.2)* [2001] 3 W.L.R. 42 decided in the Court of Appeal (Civil Division). The interpretative obligation imposed on the courts by s.3, which has unsurprisingly been described as "the Humpty Dumpty rule of construction" (see Sir John Smith, Q.C. at [2001] Crim.L.R. 843) at best requires a strained construction and at worst frees the court to construe legislative provisions in terms in which Parliament on no reasonable view could ever have intended them to be understood. That course was followed in *McLean (Duncan) v HM Advocate* [2009] HCJAC 97 (Unreported October 22, 2009). A bench of seven judges of the High Court of Justiciary declined to apply in Scots practice the decision of the Grand Chamber of the European Court in *Salduz v Turkey* [2008] ECHR 1542 (see paras 26 and 29-31).

The leading decision on the scope of the interpretative obligation in s.3 is *Ghaidan v Godin-Mendoza* [2004] 3 W.L.R. 113 in which the House of Lords recognised that s.3 was not confined to resolving ambiguities but was of an "unusual and far-reaching character" (para.30). There were bound to be cases in which "reading down" could not be possible (Lord Nicholls, para. 27) and these would arise where the Convention-compliant interpretation would go against the grain of the legislation (Lord Rodger, para. 121). What is essential is that any modified meaning given under s.3 had to remain consistent with the fundamental features of the legislative scheme. If the modified meaning failed that test then the superior courts would be crossing the constitutional line between interpretation and statutory amendment. Certain

Convention-compatible interpretations of legislation would not be possible because such alterations would involve consideration of issues which could only properly be decided upon by Parliament.

Rule 41.2

B1-78.25.1 Section 2(1) of the Human Rights Act 1998 provides that a court determining a question which has arisen in connection with a Convention right must take into account any judgment, decision, declaration or advisory opinion of the European Court and various opinions or decisions of the European Commission—which ceased to function from and after November 1, 1998 by virtue of the merger of the Commission and Court in accordance with the Eleventh Protocol—and the Committee of Ministers. Section 2(2) provides that evidence of any such judgment, etc. is to be given in proceedings in such manner as may be provided by rules of court (s.2(3)). This rule implements that provision. It may seem odd that such provision should be seen as necessary but the necessity for rules about the form and manner of evidencing the judgments, etc. of the European Court and the other bodies follows from the fact that foreign (including international) court judgments are not self-proving and require to be proved. Equally, since the authenticity of foreign public registers may be called into question, the Parliamentary practice is to provide for a means of proving judgments entered in foreign court registers (see, e.g. Evidence (Foreign, Dominion, etc., Documents) Act 1933. s.1).

Rule 41.2(1) requires that to be admissible, the evidence of the judgment, etc. must be by reference to any "authoritative and complete" report. The same expression is used in the *Practice Direction* [2000] 4 All E.R. 288 issued by the President of the Family Division of the High Court in England in July, 2000. A précis of the decision in a legal publication will not suffice. The standard law reports cited as E.H.H.R. will be the norm for most practitioners although the official series of law reports will be preferable. The official series of reports of the European Court decisions, up to 1996, was called "Series A (Judgments and Decisions)". After 1996 the official series became "Reports of Judgments and Decisions". More recent reports of the European Court are referred to by the application number: transcripts of these reports are available from the European Court's website (*www.echr.coe.int*). The official series of reports of European Commission decisions is called "Decisions and Reports" (cited as "DR") and is published by the Council of Europe.

The doctrine of stare decisis and Strasbourg jurisprudence

What is the position where there is domestic judicial precedent of a superior court binding on an inferior court but that domestic authority is inconsistent with a European Court decision? Should the lower domestic courts disregard the binding domestic authority or the European decision? This difficulty arises from s.2 of the Human Rights Act 1998 which imposes what Lord Bingham of Cornhill has termed "the mandatory duty imposed on domestic courts …to take into account any judgment of the Strasbourg court and any opinion of the commission" (*Kay v Lambeth LBC* [2006] 2 W.L.R. 570 (para.28, p.583H). The House of Lords in *Kay* has provided the answer for England and Wales. The Court of Appeal in *Leeds City Council v Price* [2005] 1 W.L.R. 1825 had followed a House of Lords' decision but granted leave to appeal because of the obvious inconsistency of domestic and European decisions. That course was approved in *Kay*. Lord Bingham, with the express concurrence of the other six Law Lords (see paras 50, 62, 121, 177, 178 and 213), made the following points: first, adherence to precedent is a cornerstone of the English legal system (para.42); secondly, the need for certainty and the avoidance of conflicting decisions of lower courts on whether there is a "clear inconsistency" between the European and domestic authorities before disregarding domestic decisions are best achieved by adhering to domestic rules of precedent (para.43); thirdly, thus domestic courts should review Convention arguments and if they consider domestic precedents to be—or possibly to be—inconsistent with Strasbourg authority, they *may* express their views and give leave to appeal (para.43); and, fourthly, there is one "partial exception" to this approach: in an exceptional case, where the facts are of such an extreme character as existed in *D v East Berkshire Community NHS Trust* [2004] Q.B. 558, the lower court can depart from the superior court's decision and follow the Strasbourg authority (para.45).

The same approach would seem eminently sensible for Scotland. Where a sheriff or Lord Commissioner of Justiciary is confronted by a binding decision of a quorum of the High Court and it is arguably, or even clearly, incompatible with Strasbourg jurisprudence, the domestic court should follow the Scottish decision. If an appeal is taken the High Court can determine the present state of the law. Alternatively, as human rights issues are properly raised by way of devolution minutes, to which Ch.40 applies, the lower court may decide to refer the issue to the Appeal Court if that option remains open. For example, in *McLean v HM Advocate* [2009] HCJAC 97; 2010 S.L.T. 73; 2010 S.C.L. 166 the sheriff referred a preliminary issue to the Appeal Court (which convened a bench of five judges) so that the inconsistency of a recent decision of the Grand Chamber of the European Court (*Salduz v Turkey* (2008) 49 EHRR 19) with two binding Scottish decisions (*Paton v Ritchie*, 2000 S.L.T. 239; 2000 S.C.C.R. 151 and *Dickson v HM Advocate*, 2001 S.L.T. 674; 2001 S.C.C.R. 297) could be resolved (see P.W. Ferguson, "The status of Salduz v Turkey in Scotland" 2010 S.C.L. 215).

Rule 41.3(1)

B1-78.25.2 Until amendment with effect from September 1, 2006 this rule required the court to give notice to persons specified by the Lord Justice General whenever the court was considering whether to make a declaration of incompatibility. Now the rule recognises that a party may seek the making of such a declaration and so requires that party to give notice to relevant persons. However, as the notice procedure is designed to alert vested governmental interests (such as the Advocate General for Scotland), there is no obligation on the court to give notice to the parties to the proceedings (or for the party seeking the declaration to give notice to other parties to the proceedings).

Rule 41.3(2)

Section 5(1) provides that where the Appeal Court is considering whether to make a declaration of incompatibility, the Crown is entitled to notice of that fact in accordance with rules of court. Section 5(2) provides that in any case to which subs.(1) applies, the persons or departments identified are entitled to be joined as a party to the proceedings if they give notice in accordance with the rules of court. Where the Ministers or departments wish to be joined as parties to the proceedings, it will be necessary for them to serve notice on the court and all other parties.

Paragraphs (a) and (b) draw the distinction, which is in terms of constitutional law correct, between members of the Scottish Executive (including the so-called Scottish "Cabinet") and Ministers of the Crown. Scottish Executive ministers are not Ministers of the Crown. The statutory functions of the Scottish Ministers are exercisable on behalf of Her Majesty (Scotland Act 1998, s.52(2)) but, as was recently observed, that does not mean that they are the Crown (see Lord Boyd of Duncansby Q.C., "Ministers and the Law", 2006 J.R. 179 at p. 183).

According to the strict terms of s.5(1) the entitlement to notice arises only once the court is considering whether to make a declaration of incompatibility and thus the court has by that stage already in effect decided that the statutory provision cannot be "read down" so as to be compatible with the Convention rights scheduled to the 1998 Act. This procedural difficulty (which appears to have first surfaced in the course of a hearing of a purely private law civil appeal in the Court of Appeal (Civil Division) in *Wilson v First County Trust Ltd* [2001] 2 W.L.R. 302) has been addressed both by a committee of the House of Lords in a criminal appeal in *R v A (Joinder of appropriate minister)* [2001] 1 W.L.R. 789 and by the First Division in *Gunn v Newman*, 2001 S.L.T. 776 in a reclaiming motion arising out of a purely private law issue concerning the availability of civil jury trial and ss.9 and 11 of the Court of Session Act 1988.

In *Gunn*, following *R v A*, the First Division held that notice of the proposal to consider whether or not a statutory provision was incompatible, or could be "read down" and so avoid the necessity of making a declaration of incompatibility, should be given in advance of the hearing of the reclaiming motion so as to avoid the risk that the hearing would commence and then require to be adjourned so as to allow notice to be given to the appropriate ministers (as occurred in *Wilson v First County Trust Ltd*). Lord President Rodger stated: "[The purpose of intervention under s.5(2)] is not confined simply to arguing as to whether a court, which had in effect decided that a provision was incompatible with the Convention, should make a declaration in terms of s.4(1). That would be, at best, a most limited and unconstructive role. Rather, the minister has an opportunity to address the court on the objects and purposes of the legislation in question and on any other matters which may be relevant." (para.[9]). Thus notice was given under s.5(1) to the Lord Advocate as representing the Scottish Ministers who have the policy responsibility for Scots private law and to the Advocate-General as representing the UK Government who have responsibility for international relations including compliance with the European Convention.

Rule 41.4

No time limit is set for compliance with the requirement of notice under r.41.3(2) but once notice has been given, a 14 day time limit is imposed for lodging a minute with the court and serving a copy of the minute on all other parties to the proceedings. It may be that failure to comply with that time limit will be fatal to the intervener's right to be heard.

Rule 41.5

This rule gives the court power to sist an appeal (including petition to the *nobile officium* or bill) or reference from an inferior court in which a declaration of incompatibility is being considered and also enables the court to hold a diet for a hearing on that issue as a separate hearing from any other hearing in the proceedings. It is an unusual provision and may be explained by the fact that the declaration of incompatibility will not affect the validity of the statutory provision or be binding on the parties to the proceedings (see s.4(6)) and so can conveniently be determined apart from the proceedings which have given rise to the declaration. However, the court's recently adopted approach to the timing of the notice to be given when the court is considering making a declaration (referred to above) suggests that hearings will not be held separately from the review proceedings and that a sist will be the only likely power exercised by the Appeal Court (and only when it appears necessary).

[THE NEXT PARAGRAPH IS B1-78.26]

Chapter 42

Convention Rights (Compliance) (Scotland) Act 2001

Application and interpretation

42.1.—(1) This Chapter applies to punishment part hearings. B1-78.26

(2) In this Chapter—

"the 2001 Act" means the Convention Rights (Compliance) (Scotland) Act 2001;

"punishment part hearing" means a hearing in terms of paragraph 12 of Part 1 or paragraph 59 of Part 4 of the Schedule to the 2001 Act;

"life prisoners" has the meaning given in paragraph 2 of Part 1 of the Schedule to the 2001 Act;

"procedural hearing" means a hearing, held in terms of rule 42.4, for the purpose of determining any matter raised in terms of rule 42.3.

Intimation

B1-78.27 **42.2.**—(1) The Deputy Principal Clerk of Justiciary shall intimate the date, time and place of a punishment part hearing in Form 42.2.

Disputed or additional documents

B1-78.28 **42.3.**—(1) If a life prisoner who has received intimation of a punishment part hearing in terms of rule 42.2(1) wishes to—

(a) dispute the terms of any document, or a part of any document, sent to him by the Scottish Ministers in terms of paragraph 9 of Part 1 or paragraph 56 of Part 4 of the Schedule to the 2001 Act; or

(b) lodge any other document,

he shall, not later than 21 days before the date of the punishment part hearing, give written intimation to the Deputy Principle Clerk of Justiciary.

(2) A life prisoner who gives intimation in terms of paragraph (1) of this rule shall, at the same time, specify the grounds upon which he seeks to—

(a) dispute the document or part of the document; or

(b) lodge any other document,

and shall lodge any document referred to in, or to which he intends to refer, in support of such grounds.

(3) None of the matters mentioned in paragraph (1) of this rule may be raised after the time specified in that paragraph.

Procedural hearing

B1-78.29 **42.4.** Where a life prisoner gives intimation in terms of paragraph (1) of rule 42.3, there shall, 14 days before the date of the punishment part hearing, be a procedural hearing.

AMENDMENT

Chapter 42 inserted by Act of Adjournal (Criminal Procedural Rules Amendment) (Convention Rights (Compliance) (Scotland) Act 2001) 2001 (SSI 2001/479 (effective December 21, 2001).

Rules 42.1, 42.3 and 42.4 as amended by Act of Adjournal (Criminal Procedure Rules Amendment) (Convention Rights (Compliance) (Scotland) Act 2001) 2002 (SSI 2002/137) r.2 (effective March 4, 2002).

GENERAL NOTE

B1-78.29.1 The Convention Rights (Compliance) (Scotland) Act 2001 was passed to deal with, inter alia, the arguable incompatibility of the indeterminate life sentence for murder with the accused's rights under the European Convention to a review of the lawfulness of his detention after the punitive part of his sentence had elapsed. Judgments of the European Court had already considered the issue in respect of an accused convicted of murder when under-age and persons sentenced to a discretionary life term. In due course the European Court decided *Stafford v United Kingdom* [2002] 35 E.H.R.R. 1121 on May 25, 2002.

Consequently, s.2 of the 2001 Act, which came into force before the decision in *Stafford*, repealed s.205(4) of the 1995 Act (which permitted the trial judge to make a minimum recommendation) and amended the Prisoners and Criminal Proceedings (Scotland) Act 1993 so that in terms of s.2(2) the trial judge should make an order known as the "punishment part" which is the part of the life sentence for murder appropriate "to satisfy the requirements of retribution and deterrence (ignoring the period of confinement, if any, which may be necessary for the protection of the public)". Since there were existing life sentence prisoners convicted of murder before the coming into force of the 2001 Act, Part I of the Schedule to the 2001 Act made provision for persons who had been sentenced (before October 8, 2001) for murder committed when they were aged 18 or over.

In terms of para. 12 of the Schedule, there must be a hearing at which the High Court shall make an order which is to be what the court considers would have been ordered as a punishment part had the relevant provisions been in force when the accused was sentenced for murder (para. 13). For the purposes of the hearing the court will have available to it various documentary productions including the post-mortem report, the accused's previous convictions and the trial judge's report to the Parole Board (regarding the circumstances of the offence). These documents are to be sent to the accused before the hearing. Where the accused disputes the terms of any of these documents, or wishes to rely on another document, he must give notice of that fact to the court. At the same time he must state why he takes issue with the document or wishes to found on another document (which he must lodge with Justiciary Office). If he fails in any of these respects, within the timescale, he is precluded from raising his dispute or relying on the document at the punishment part hearing.

In *Flynn v HM Advocate*, 2004 S.C.C.R. 281 the Privy Council disapproved the High Court's decisions in *Stewart v HM Advocate*, 2002 S.L.T. 1307 and *McCreaddie v HM Advocate*, 2002 S.L.T. 1311 (which held as irrelevant to fixing the punishment part the views of the Preliminary Review Committee (PRC) of the Parole Board as to the appropriate review date for considering the accused's release) and decided that such views were relevant although not determinative. A bench of five judges subsequently overruled *Stewart* and *McCreaddie* in light of the Privy Council's judgments (see *Flynn v HM Advocate*,

2004 S.L.T. 1195 (para.15)) and held that (1) the PRC'S proposed review date was a relevant but not decisive factor in fixing the punishment part; (2) the weight to be given to it depended on the accused's prospects of release at that review date (para. 19); and (3) in fixing the punishment part, the court had to start by considering what punishment part would have been set if it had been set at the date of the sentence (thus disregarding all subsequent events) and then look at subsequent events having a possible bearing on the accused's possible release and decide what weight, if any, should be given to them by way of adjustment of the punishment part (para.22).

It should also be noted that the Appeal Court has held that the *Practice Statement (Crime: Life Sentences)* [2002] 1 W.L.R. 1789 (which has been consolidated into the *Practice Direction (Criminal Proceedings: Consolidation)* [2002] 1 W.L.R. 2870 (paras 49.2-49.28)) setting out the normal "starting point" of 12 years and a "higher starting point" of 15-16 years for adult offenders, are guidelines which do not apply in Scotland although they may be useful for drawing attention to matters which may be relevant in the particular case (*Flynn v HM Advocate*, 2003 S.L.T. 954 (para.87); *Brown v HM Advocate*, HCJ, November 20, 2002 (unreported), para.7). In particular, it seems appropriate for the mitigating factors mentioned in paras 49.11, 49.17 and 49.18 and the aggravating factors set out in paras 49.13, 49.15, 49.16 and 49.20 to be taken into account, although the normal, higher and very serious offence tariffs are irrelevant in Scotland. (The relevant English guidance has been amended and is now to be found in *Practice Direction (Crime: Mandatory Life Sentences) (No.2)* [2004] 1 W.L.R. 2551.)

Authoritative guidance has been provided by a bench of five judges of the High Court of Justiciary under s. 118(7) of the Criminal Procedure (Scotland) Act 1995 as to the appropriate levels of punishment parts which should be fixed for life sentences for murder: see *HM Advocate v Boyle, Maddock and Kelly* [2009] HCJAC 89 (November 29, 2009), especially paras 13, 14 and 16).

[THE NEXT PARAGRAPH IS B1-78.30]

Chapter 43

Terrorism Act 2000 and Anti-Terrorism, Crime and Security Act 2001

Interpretation

43.1.—(1) In this Chapter— **B1-78.30**

"the Act of 2000" means the Terrorism Act 2000;

"the Act of 2001" means the Anti-Terrorism, Crime and Security Act 2001; and

"law enforcement officer" has the meaning given by section 22B(14) (further information orders) of the Act of 2000.

AMENDMENTS

Rule 43.1 as amended by Act of Adjournal (Criminal Procedure Rules 1996 Amendment) (No. 5) (Proceeds of Crime etc.) 2017 (SSI 2017/429) para.2(3) (effective 21 December 2017).

Applications under the Act of 2000 or 2001

43.2.—(1) An application under any of the following provisions shall be made by petition— **B1-78.31**

(za) section 22B(1) (further information order) of the Act of 2000;

(a) paragraph 22(1) (production of material for the purposes of a terrorist investigation) of Schedule 5 to the Act of 2000;

(b) paragraph 30(1) (explanation of material seized or produced shall for the purposes of a terrorist investigation) of Schedule 5 to the Act of 2000;

(ba) paragraph 19(1) (disclosure orders) of Schedule 5A to the Act of 2000;

(bb) paragraph 24(3) (variation or discharge of a disclosure order) of Schedule 5A to the Act of 2000;

(c) paragraph 2(b) (procedure for order requiring financial information) of Schedule 6 to the Act of 2000;

(d) paragraph 2(1) (account monitoring order) of Schedule 6A to the Act of 2000;

(e) paragraph 4(1) (discharge or variation of account monitoring order) of Schedule 6A to the Act of 2000.

(2) The sheriff may make the order sought in an application under paragraph 22(1) of Schedule 5 to the Act of 2000 before intimation of the application to the person who appears to him to be in possession of the material to which the application relates.

(3) The sheriff may make the order sought in an application under:—

(a) paragraph 2(b) of Schedule 6 to the Act of 2000;

(b) paragraph 2(1) of Schedule 6A to the Act of 2000; or

(c) paragraph 4(1)(a) of Schedule 6A to the Act of 2000,

before intimation of the application to the person who appears to him to be in possession of the information to which the application relates and the person who is the subject of that information.

(4) Notice under paragraph 5(3) of Schedule 1 to the Act of 2001 (release of cash where retention no longer justified) shall be given in writing.

AMENDMENTS

Rule 43.2 as amended by Act of Adjournal (Criminal Procedure Rules Amendment No.2) (Anti-Terrorism, Crime and Security Act 2001) 2002 (SSI 2002/136) para.2 (effective 4 March 2002).

Rule 43.2 as amended by Act of Adjournal (Criminal Procedure Rules 1996 Amendment) (No. 5) (Proceeds of Crime etc.) 2017 (SSI 2017/429) para.2(3) (effective 21 December 2017).

Rule 43.2(1) as amended by Act of Adjournal (Criminal Procedure Rules 1996 Amendment) (Miscellaneous) 2018 (SSI 2018/12) para.2(3) (effective 31 January 2018).

Appeal to the Sheriff Appeal Court

B1-78.31.1 **43.3.**—(1) An appeal to the Sheriff Appeal Court under section 22D(1) (appeals) of the Act of 2000 is to be made by lodging a note of appeal in Form 43.3.

(2) When an appeal is lodged, the court must—

(a) order intimation of the appeal to—

(i) the law enforcement officer and any other person who was a party to the proceedings on the application, where a respondent to the proceedings on the application is the appellant; or

(ii) any respondent to the proceedings on the application, where the law enforcement officer is the appellant; and

(b) appoint a hearing on the appeal.

Amendments

Rule 43.3 inserted by Act of Adjournal (Criminal Procedure Rules 1996 Amendment) (No. 5) (Proceeds of Crime etc.) 2017 (SSI 2017/429) para.2(3) (effective 21 December 2017).

General Note

B1-78.31.2 Chapter 43 inserted by Act of Adjournal (Criminal Procedural Rules Amendment No.2) (Terrorism Act 2000 and Anti-Terrorism, Crime and Security Act 2001) 2001 (SSI 2001/486) (effective 22 December 2001).

[THE NEXT PARAGRAPH IS B1-78.32]

Chapter 44

International Criminal Court Act 2001

Interpretation of this Chapter

B1-78.32 **44.1.** In this Chapter, "the Act of 2001" means the International Criminal Court Act 2001.

Consent to surrender

B1-78.33 **44.2.** Consent to surrender given under section 7 of the Act of 2001 (consent to surrender) shall be in writing in Form 44.2.

Waiver of right to review

B1-78.34 **44.3.** Waiver given under section 13 of the Act of 2001 (waiver of the right to review) shall be in writing in Form 44.3.

Amendment

Chapter 44 inserted by Act of Adjournal (Criminal Procedure Rules Amendment No.2) (Miscellaneous) 2003 (SSI 2003/468) para.2. Brought into force on 27 October 2003 in accordance with para.1.

General Note

B1-78.35 Part 2 of the International Criminal Court Act 2001 (c.17) provides for the arrest and delivery of persons who either are the subject of investigation for an "ICC crime" (i.e. genocide, war crimes and crimes against humanity (s.1)) or have been convicted (with or without sentence having been imposed) of such a crime by the International Criminal Court. The Act is intended to provide an expeditious procedure which takes two forms.

Under s.2 the United Kingdom Government receives a request for the arrest and surrender of such persons and, after its transmission to the Scottish Ministers, if the request is accompanied by a warrant, the warrant must be endorsed for execution by the sheriff at Edinburgh (only Lothian and Borders has jurisdiction: s.26(c)) if the sheriff "is satisfied that the warrant appears to have been issued by the ICC" (s.2(3)). Where there is no arrest warrant, the sheriff must issue a warrant. Both warrants are termed " section 2 warrants" (s.2(5)).

In cases of urgency, the ICC may request the United Kingdom Government to secure the issue of an arrest warrant. There will not be time available for the ICC to supply the Government with the necessary documentation supporting a section 2 warrant request. Thus the Government may transmit the request to the Scottish Ministers "who shall instruct the procurator fiscal to apply for a w arrant" to arrest the named individual. On that application being made, the sheriff " shall issue a warrant" (s.3(3)). Such warrants are termed "provisional warrants" (s.3(5)). Persons arrested on provisional warrants must be brought before the sheriff as soon as is practicable (s.4(1)) and must be remanded in custody pending the production of a section 2 warrant (s.4(3)). Where no section 2 warrant is produced the arrested person must be discharged but may subsequently be arrested under a section 2 warrant (s.4(7)).

Rule 44.2

Persons arrested under a section 2 warrant must be brought before the sheriff as soon as is practicable (s.5(1)) so that a delivery order can be made whereby they are delivered up to the ICC or, if they have been convicted, to the state which is to enforce the ICC's sentence. A person so arrested can consent to the delivery order (s.7) but such consent must be in a written form prescribed by Act of Adjournal and be signed in the presence of a sheriff (s.7(3)).

Rule 44.3

The Government may not instruct the execution of the delivery order under s.5 until "the end of the period of 15 days beginning with the date on which the order is made" (s.12(1)). This is to allow for review of the delivery order to be sought by bill of suspension (s.12(5)). However, the subject of the delivery order is entitled to waive his right to review of the delivery order under s.13. The waiver must be in writing in the prescribed form and signed in the presence of a sheriff (s.3(3)).

Chapter 45

Fur Farming (Prohibition) (Scotland) Act 2002

Interpretation of this Chapter

45.1. In this Chapter, "the Act of 2002" means the Fur Farming (Prohibition) (Scotland) Act 2002. **B1-78.36**

Representations in forfeiture orders

45.2.—(1) This rule applies where the Court is deciding whether to make a forfeiture order in terms of section 2 of the Act of 2002 (forfeiture orders). **B1-78.37**

(2) A person who wishes to make representations to the court under subsection (7) of section 2 of the Act of 2002 shall do so—

(a) in writing to the Clerk of Court, unless the court otherwise directs; and
(b) by such date as the court directs.

AMENDMENTS

Chapter 45 inserted by Act of Adjournal (Criminal Procedure Rules Amendment No.2) (Miscellaneous) 2003 (SSI 2003/468) r.2. Brought into force on 27 October 2003 in accordance with r.1.

GENERAL NOTE

Section 1(1) of the Fur Farming (Prohibition) (Scotland) Act 2002 makes it an offence for anyone to keep animals solely or principally for slaughter (whether by that person or another) for the value of the animals' fur or to breed progeny for such slaughter. This offence includes keeping or breeding animals for sale for subsequent slaughter (s. 1(3)). It is also an offence for anyone to cause or permit an offence under s. 1(1). The maximum penalty is a fine of £20,000. The offence is triable only summarily (s. 1(6)). **B1-78.37.1**

In terms of s.2(1) a court in dealing with a person convicted of an offence under s. 1(1) may make a forfeiture order (FO) in respect of any animals of any type to which the offence related if these animals are kept by the accused when the order is made or came into his keeping during the period (as defined in s.2(3)) beginning with the making of the FO and ending with the destruction or other disposal of the animals in pursuance of the order. A FO may also be made on conviction of an accused for causing or permitting the offence (s.2(2)). A FO is "an order for the forfeiture and destruction or other disposal of the animals to which the order applies (including any subsequent progeny of those animals)" (s.2(4)). It operates so as to deprive "any person of that person's rights in the animals" (s.2(5)). However, in deciding whether to make a FO the court must take into account any representations made to it by "any person who has an interest in any animals to which the order may apply" (s.2(7)). Persons with an interest in the animals are given a right to appeal to the High Court within seven days beginning with the date of the order (s.2(8)).

Thus it is imperative that any person with an interest in the animals should have notice of the proposed making of a FO so that he can make representations to the sheriff. Such persons are not given a right to appear although r.45.2(2) does not preclude the sheriff's allowing personal appearance or legal representation. Since legal representation or at least legal advice may be necessary (as there may be delicate legal rights in issue) the sheriff should allow a reasonable period within which any representations should be submitted or advice taken by persons whose rights or interests may be affected.

[THE NEXT PARAGRAPH IS B1-78.38]

Chapter 46

Parental Directions under the Sexual Offences Act 2003

Young offenders: parental directions

46.1. Where a court makes a direction under section 89(1) of the Sexual Offences Act 2003 (young offenders: parental directions) in respect of an individual having parental responsibilities in relation to a young offender, the clerk of the court shall— **B1-78.38**

(a) intimate the making of the direction; and

(b) deliver or send by post a copy of the notice in Form 20.3A-B (notice of requirement to notify police under Part 2 of the Sexual Offences Act 2003),

to that individual and to the chief constable of the police force within the area of which the young offender resides.

Applications to vary, renew or discharge parental directions

B1-78.39 **46.2.** An application under section 90(1) of the Sexual Offences Act 2003 (parental directions: variations, renewals and discharges) shall be made by petition in Form 46.2.

AMENDMENTS

Chapter 46 inserted by Act of Adjournal (Criminal Procedure Rules Amendment No.2) (Sexual Offences Act 2003) 2004 (SSI 2004/206) r.2 (effective 1 May 2004).

GENERAL NOTE

B1-78.39.1 Under s.89(2) of the Sexual Offences Act 2003, a young offender, in respect of whom a parental direction can be made, must be under 16 years of age (though in England he must be under 18 years). Where such a young offender is before the court in respect of a sexual offence the court may direct that the obligations in ss.83-86 (such as notification requirements) for sexual offenders should apply to the parent so that, for example, the parent must attend at the police station with the young offender when notifications obligations are complied with. The chief constable of the police force for the area within which the young offender resides has an interest to be informed of the direction as he is entitled to apply for variation, renewal or discharge of the parental directions (s.90(2)). Under s.90(4) the court, in adjudicating on a petition under r.46.2, must hear the party making the application and any other persons specified in s.90(2), if they wish to be heard, before making any order varying, renewing or discharging the direction as the court considers appropriate.

[THE NEXT PARAGRAPH IS B1-78.40]

Chapter 47

Protection of Children (Scotland) Act 2003

B1-78.40 **47.1.** […]

AMENDMENTS

Chapter 47 inserted by Act of Adjournal (Criminal Procedure Rules Amendment No.5) (Miscellaneous) 2004 (SSI 2004/481) r.2 (effective 26 November 2004).

Chapter 47 substituted with Chapter 47A by Act of Adjournal (Criminal Procedure Rules Amendment No. 2) (Protection of Vulnerable Groups (Scotland) Act 2007) 2010 (SSI 2011/167) para.2 (effective 28 February 2011), subject to savings provisions in para.2(4).

Chapter 47A

Protection of Vulnerable Groups (Scotland) Act 2007

References under the Protection of Vulnerable Groups (Scotland) Act 2007

B1-78.40.1 **47A.1** Where a court is giving the Scottish Ministers information under section 7 of the Protection of Vulnerable Groups (Scotland) Act 2007 it shall do so by—

(a) posting a notice of reference in Form 47A.1; or
(b) transmitting a copy of that notice, by facsimile or other electronic means.

AMENDMENTS

Chapter 47A substituted for Chapter 47 by Act of Adjournal (Criminal Procedure Rules Amendment No. 2) (Protection of Vulnerable Groups (Scotland) Act 2007) 2010 (SSI 2011/167) para.2 (effective 28 February 2011), subject to savings provisions in para .2(4).

[THE NEXT PARAGRAPH IS B1-78.41]

Chapter 48

Protection of Children and Prevention of Sexual Offences (Scotland) Act 2005

Interpretation

B1-78.41 **48.1.** In this Chapter "sexual offences prevention order" means a sexual offences prevention order made where subsection (2) or (3) of section 104 of the Sexual Offences Act 2003 applies.

Sexual offences prevention orders

B1-78.42 **48.2.** A sexual offences prevention order shall be in Form 48.2.

Variation, renewal or discharge of sexual offences prevention orders

B1-78.43 **48.3.** An application for the variation, renewal or discharge of a sexual offences prevention order shall be made by petition in Form 48.3.

AMENDMENTS

Chapter 48 inserted by Act of Adjournal (Criminal Procedure Rules Amendment No. 5) (Sexual Offences Prevention Orders) 2005 (SSI 2005/472) para.2(2) (effective 7 October 2005).

GENERAL NOTE

Sections 104–113 of the Sexual Offences Act 2003 (c.42) introduced the sexual offences prevention order (SOPO). The 2003 Act is principally concerned with English criminal law, and when it was passed it did not confer on Scottish courts the power given to English courts to make a SOPO. The Protection of Children and Prevention of Sexual Offences (Scotland) Act 2005 (asp 9) gives Scottish courts that power. In terms s.107(1) of the 2003 Act a SOPO prohibits the accused from doing anything described in the order and has effect for a fixed period (which must be not less than five years) specified in the order "or until further order". Where an accused is convicted of an offence listed in paras 36-60 of Sch.3 to the 2003 Act the court may make a SOPO if it is satisfied that "it is necessary to make such an order, for the purpose of protecting the public or any particular members of the public from serious sexual harm from the [accused]" (s.104(1)). The phrase "protecting the public ..." is defined in s.106(3) as meaning protecting the public in the UK or any particular members of that public from serious physical or psychological harm caused by the accused committing one or more of the scheduled offences. **B1-78.43.1**

Schedule 3 is out of date and was not amended by the Scottish Parliament in the 2005 Act to take account of changes in the common law. Thus, para.37 refers to clandestine injury to women although that crime is now comprehended in rape (para.36). Paragraph 42 also specifies "shameless indecency, if a person (other than the offender) involved in the offence was under 18". Shameless indecency is not a crime (see *Webster v Dominick*, 2003 S.L.T. 975 and *Clark v HM Advocate*, 2008 S.L.T. 787; 2008 S.C.C.R. 648; 2008 S.C.L. 923). Paragraph 60 is also important. It lists "an offence in Scotland other than [paras 36-59] if the court, in imposing sentence or otherwise disposing of the case, determines for the purposes of this paragraph that there was a significant sexual aspect to the offender's behaviour in committing the offence". A SOPO can be made in respect of behaviour occurring before the commencement of the 2003 Act (s.106(4)).

Rule 48.2

The court may only include in a SOPO prohibitions which are necessary for the purpose of protecting the public or any particular members of the public from serious sexual harm from the accused (s.107(2)). The scope of the phrase "serious sexual harm" has been described by the Court of Appeal in Northern Ireland as relatively wide (*R. v Shannon* [2008] NICA 38 (para.18)). In that decision Campbell, L.J. said: "The test to be applied ... involves an assessment of the level of risk of recurrence, first, and of the level of risk of harm if recurrence there be, second. The second exercise involves assessing how much harm is likely to be done and whether it can properly be called serious or not, and if it were the case that only a small number of people would be likely to suffer such harm that would be a relevant factor in assessing the risk" (para.19; see also *R. (Commissioner of Police for the Metropolis) v Croydon Crown Court* [2007] EWHC 1792). Any prohibition must not be disproportionate to the risk of serious sexual harm. Proportionality is a question of law for the Appeal Court to determine; it is not a question of discretion subject to review only on grounds of *Wednesbury* unreasonableness. Appeal against the making of a SOPO is by note of appeal. It is appealable as if it were an order referred to in s.106(1)(d) of the 1995 Act for solemn proceedings or, in summary proceedings, an order referred to in s.175(2)(c) (2003 Act s.111(c) as amended by 2005 Act s.17(2)). The Appeal Court may suspend a SOPO pending the disposal of the appeal (2003 Act s.111(d)).

Rule 48.3

The only persons who may apply for variation, discharge or renewal are the accused and the prosecutor (2003 Act s.112(1)(g) as inserted by 2005 Act s.17(4)(f)). The appropriate court to apply to under this rule is either the High Court where the SOPO was made in that court or, where it was made in the sheriff court, the sheriff court for the area in which the accused is resident at the time of application and, in any other case, the sheriff court which originally made the order (2003 Act s.112(1A) as inserted by 2005 Act s.17(5)). The court must hear the applicant (and any other person if he wishes to be heard) before it determines whether to grant the application (s.108(4)).

A SOPO may be renewed or varied so as to impose additional prohibitions on the accused "only if it is necessary to do so for the purpose of protecting the public or any particular member of the public from serious sexual harm from the [accused] (and any renewed or varied order may contain only such prohibitions as are necessary for this purpose)" (2003 Act s.108(5)). The accused is entitled to be given by the clerk of court, or sent to him by the clerk by registered post or recorded delivery service, a copy of the order and its renewal, variation or discharge (2003 Act s.112(3)). There is no provision for an appeal against the court's decision to refuse a petition under r.48.3.

[THE NEXT PARAGRAPH IS B1-78.44]

Chapter 49

Financial Reporting Orders

49.1.–49.3. [...] **B1-78.44**

AMENDMENTS

Chapter 49 inserted by Act of Adjournal (Criminal Procedure Rules Amendment No.2) (Financial Reporting Orders) 2006 (SSI 2006/205) para.2(2) (effective 1 May 2006).

Chapter 49 is revoked by Act of Adjournal (Criminal Procedure Rules 1996 Amendment) (No.2) (Serious Crime Prevention Orders) 2016 (SSI 2016/137) para.2 and Sch (effective 17 March 2016), subject to savings in para.3.

[THE NEXT PARAGRAPH IS B1-78.47]

GENERAL NOTE

B1-78.47 Section 77 of the Serious Organised Crime Act 2005 (c.15) applies to Scotland (s.179(4)) and, taking account of Scottish procedure, makes separate provision for the making of financial reporting orders (FROs) along the lines provided in s.76 for FROs in England and Wales. Section 77(1) provides that a court sentencing or otherwise dealing with a person convicted of specific offences may also make an FRO in respect of him. However, an FRO may only be made where the court "is satisfied that the risk of the person's committing another [relevant offence] is sufficiently high to justify the making of a FRO" (s.77(2)). The relevant offences for subs.(1) and (2) are: common law fraud and any of the "lifestyle offences" specified in Sch.4 to the Proceeds of Crime Act 2002 (s.77(3)).

The effect of an FRO is set out in s.79. The person subject to it must make a report in respect of the period specified in the order starting with the date when the order comes into force (which is the date when it is made: s.77(5)) and for subsequent periods of specified lengths (s.79(2)); set out in the report in the manner specified in the order "such particulars of his financial affairs relating to the period in question as may be specified" (s.79(3)); he must include any specified documents with the report (s.79(4)); make each report within the specified number of days after the end of the specified period (s.79(5)); and make the report to the person specified in the FRO (s.79(6)). An FRO must, therefore, be highly detailed as to what is required (s.79(8)). The Scottish Ministers must make an order specifying the persons who are qualified to act as the persons to whom the report must be made (s.79(9)). This has been done. The list of persons from whom the court may select a specified person is specified as being either a chief constable of a Scottish police force or the Director of the Scottish Drug Enforcement Agency (see art.2 of the Serious Organised Crime and Police Act 2005 (Specified Persons for Financial Reporting Orders) (Scotland) Order 2006 (SSI 2006/170) which came into force on May 1, 2006 (para.1(1)).

An FRO may be made in the sheriff court or High Court. However, where it is made in the sheriff court, the duration of the order must not exceed five years (s.77(6)). If the order is made by the High Court, the order must be for a period not exceeding 20 years if the person is sentenced to life imprisonment (s.77(7)(a)) and otherwise must not exceed 15 years (s.77(7)(b)). Provision may in due course be made, by Act of Adjournal, for the maximum length of reporting periods to be specified in the orders (s.79(7)).

In terms of s.79(10) it is an offence for a person subject to an FRO, without reasonable excuse, to include false or misleading information in a report, or otherwise fail to comply with any requirement of s.79. The offence is prosecutable only on summary complaint but carries a maximum sentence of 12 months' imprisonment and a fine not exceeding level 5 on the standard scale.

Rule 49.1

An order can only be made in the sheriff court or the High Court and cannot be made unless (i) the person to be subject to it has been convicted of either fraud at common law or a lifestyle offence under Sch.4 to the Proceeds of Crime Act 2002; and (ii) the court is satisfied that there is a sufficiently high risk of his committing another offence (whether fraud or lifestyle offence) to justify making the order (s.77(1) and (2)). Convictions for theft, embezzlement, uttering and practical cheating are not qualifying offences.

Rule 49.3

Section 80 provides for variation and recall of an FRO. Application for recall or variation of an FRO may be made by either the person subject to it or the specified person to whom the reports during the reporting periods are to be made (s.80(1)). The application must be made by petition (r.49.3(1)) which must be presented to the court which made the order (s.80(2)).

Chapter 50

Football Banning Orders

Interpretation

B1-78.48 **50.1.** In this Chapter—

"the 2006 Act" means the Police, Public Order and Criminal Justice Act 2006;
"football banning order" means an order made under section 51(2) of the 2006 Act;
"football banning orders authority" has the meaning given in section 69 of the 2006 Act.

Football banning orders

B1-78.49 **50.2.** A football banning order shall be in Form 50.2.

Variation or termination of football banning orders

50.3.—(1) An application for the variation or termination of a football banning order shall be made by petition in Form 50.3. **B1-78.50**

(2) On a petition referred to in paragraph (1) being lodged, the court shall—

(a) order intimation of the application to—

(i) in the case of an application by the person subject to the order, the football banning orders authority; or

(ii) in any other case, to the person subject to the order;

(b) appoint a hearing on the application; and

(c) order intimation of the hearing to the persons referred to in sub-paragraph (a) and to the governor of any institution in which the person in respect of whom the football banning order was made is detained.

AMENDMENTS

Chapter 50 inserted by Act of Adjournal (Criminal Procedure Rules Amendment No. 4) (Miscellaneous) 2006 (SSI 2006/436) r.2 (effective September 1, 2006).

GENERAL NOTE

Football banning orders

A football banning order (FBO) under s.51(2) of the Police, Public Order and Criminal Justice Act 2006 (asp 10) can be made instead of, or in addition to, any sentence which the court passes on an accused for an offence which must involve the accused "engagingin violence or disorder" and relate to a football match (s.51(4)). The accused must also have been 16 or over at the time he committed the offence (s.51(1)). Further, an FBO can only be made where there are reasonable grounds to believe that making it would "help to prevent violence or disorder at or in connection with any football matches" (s.51(3)(b)). The index offence relates to a football match if it is committed (a) at a football match or while the accused is entering or leaving (or trying to enter or leave) the ground; or (b) on a journey to or from a football match; or (c) "otherwise, where it appears to the court from all the circumstances that the offence is motivated (wholly or partly) by a football match" (s.51(6)). Posting an offensive message on Twitter is not an offence related to a football match played or intended to be played and nor is it an offence motivated wholly or partly by a football match played or intended to be played: see *MacDonald v Dunn*, 2013 S.C.C.R. 11 at [12]. A person may be regarded as having been on a journey to or from a football match whether or not he attended, or intended to attend, the match and "journey" includes breaks (including overnight breaks) (s.51(8)). References to a "football match" include any place, other than domestic premises, at which a football match is being televised (s.51(7)). **B1-78.51**

Declarations Section 51(5) provides that where the court does not make a FBO but the court is satisfied that the offence of which the accused was convicted involved the accused engaging in violence or disorder and related to a football match, the court *may* declare that that be the case. This provision is permissive; the court is not required to make this declaration but may consider it appropriate to make the declaration where reasonable grounds do not exist for believing that the making of a FBO would help to prevent violence or disorder at another match.

Violence or disorder The requirement that the accused's offence involved him in engaging in violence or disorder is a disjunctive condition. Either violence or disorder will suffice. Violence is defined as "violence against persons or intentional damage to property and includes (a) threatening violence and (b) doing anything which endangers the life of a person" (s.56(2)). Assault, breach of the peace by shouting menaces or even gesticulating in a manner to threaten violence (cf. *Dyer v Hutchison, Bell and Johnstone*, 2006 S.C.C.R. 377) are covered by this definition but apparently reckless vandalism is for some reason excluded.

Disorder is given an enormously detailed treatment but not an exhaustive definition. Section 56(3) provides that disorder includes (a) stirring up hatred against a group of persons based on their membership (or presumed membership, i.e. presumed by the accused) of a group defined by reference to characteristics specified in s.56(5). These are: colour, race, nationality (including citizenship), ethnic or national origins, membership of a religious group (within the meaning of s.74(7) of the Criminal Justice (Scotland) Act 2003 (asp 7)) or of a social or cultural group with a perceived religious affiliation, sexual orientation, transgender identity (which is defined in subs.(6)) and disability (which means physical or mental impairment of any kind). Transgender identity means any of the following: transvestism, transsexualism, intersexuality or having by virtue of the Gender Recognition Act 2004 (c.7) changed gender by gender reassignment surgery. Presumably sexual orientation, which is not further defined, means male homosexuality, lesbianism and bisexuality.

Appeals For the purposes of the appeal provisions under the 1995 Act, a FBO and a declaration under s.51(5) as well as an order varying a FBO under s.57 and an order terminating a FBO under s.58 are sentences (s.60(1)). Where the High Court quashes a FBO on appeal, that court may make a declaration under s.51(5) unless one of the grounds for quashing the order is that the lower court erred in holding that the index offence was one to which s.51(4) applied (i.e. the offence related to a football match and involved violence or disorder in which the accused engaged) (s.60(3)).

Offences Failure to comply with any condition imposed in a FBO is an offence (s.68(1)) which is triable only on summary complaint. The offence-creating provision makes no reference to any necessary mental element in the offence but it is provided that it is a defence for the accused to prove that he had a reasonable excuse for failing to comply with the requirement (s.68(2)). It is therefore a strict liability offence but subject to a defence which the accused must establish on balance of probabilities. The maximum penalties are six months' imprisonment or a fine not exceeding level 5, or both (s.68(3)).

Rule 50.2

Form 50.3 reflects the requirements in s.53 as to the content of a FBO. A FBO prohibits the accused from entering any premises for the purposes of attending any *regulated* football matches in the UK and requires him to report to a police station in connection with football matches outside the UK (s.53(1)). The order must require the accused (a) to report initially at a police station in Scotland specified in the FBO within five days beginning with the day on which the FBO was made and (b) where a relevant event as specified in Sch.5 to the 2006 Act occurs, to notify the football banning orders authority (i.e. the chief constable of Strathclyde Police: s.69(1)) of the prescribed information as defined in that schedule in relation to that event within seven days beginning with the day on which the event occurs (s.53(2)). All FBOs must require the accused to surrender his passport in connection with regulated football matches outside the UK unless it appears to the court that there are "exceptional circumstances" (s.53(3)). Additional requirements may be imposed in a FBO where the court "considers it would help to prevent violence or disorder at or in connection with any football match" (s.53(4)). Such additional requirements can include prohibiting the accused from entering any premises (including premises to be entered for the purposes of attending non-regulated football matches) (s.53(5)).

A copy of the FBO must be served on the accused and copies must also be sent as soon as reasonably practicable to both the chief constable of Strathclyde Police as the FBO authority and the named police station to which the accused must initially report and also, where the accused is in custody, to the relevant custodian (s.59(1)).

Duration A FBO must specify the period for which it is to have effect and that period must not exceed (a) 10 years where the order is made in tandem with a custodial sentence (whether detention or imprisonment: s.54(3)) or (b) 5 years where either no sentence is imposed or the sentence is noncustodial (s.53(6)-(7)). The period runs from the day on which the FBO is made (s.54(2)).

Regulated football matches This concept is central to FBOs and is defined in s.55. For football matches anywhere within the UK, regulated football matches involve at least one national or territorial team, or SPL club team or member of the Scottish Football League or other team which is a full or associate member of the Football League, the FA Premier League, Football Conference or League of Wales. Regulated matches outside the UK involve a national team appointed to represent Scotland, England or Wales by their respective football associations or a team representing a club.

Rule 50.3

A FBO may be varied by the court which made it where application for variation is made by (a) the accused, (b) the chief constable of the area where the accused resides or (c) the chief constable of an area either in which the police believe the accused already is present or to which the police believe the accused intends to come (s.57(1)). Variation is effected by omitting or imposing the requirement anent passport surrender (but the court can only omit that requirement where there are exceptional circumstances: s.57(2)); and by imposing, replacing or omitting any additional requirements.

Termination of a FBO may be ordered by the court which made the order (s.58(5)) where the accused applies to that court for that purpose but the accused may not seek termination unless the order has had effect for at least two-thirds of the period specified in the order (s.58(2)). In considering whether to order termination, the court is directed to have regard to (a) the accused's character; (b) his conduct since the order was made; (c) the nature of the offence which led to the making of the order; and (d) any other circumstances which the court thinks are relevant (s.58(3)). Where termination is refused, the accused may not re-apply for termination of that same order during a further period of six months beginning with the date of refusal (s.58(4)).

The same requirements for service of copies of orders varying or terminating a FBO apply as are applicable in respect of the original order (see r.50.2).

Chapter 51

Animal Health and Welfare

Interpretation

B1-78.52 **51.1** In this Chapter-

"the 1981 Act" means the Animal Health Act 1981;
"the 2006 Act" means the Animal Health and Welfare (Scotland) Act 2006;

"deprivation order" means an order made under section 28E of the 1981 Act, section 39 of the 2006 Act, or section 47 of the Animal Welfare Act 2006

"disqualification order" means an order made under section 28F of the 1981 Act, section 40 of the 2006 Act or regulation 21(2) of the Licensing of Animal Dealers (Young Cats and Young Dogs) (Scotland) Regulations 2009.

AMENDMENTS

Rule 51.1 as amended by Act of Adjournal (Criminal Procedure Rules Amendment) (Miscellaneous) 2009 (SSI 2009/144) r.6 (effective April 30, 2009).

Deprivation Orders

51.2 A deprivation order shall be in Form 51.2. **B1-78.53**

Representations

51.3—(1) Where the court is considering making a deprivation order and it is practicable to do so— **B1-78.54**

(a) the court shall appoint a diet for parties to be heard; and
(b) the clerk of court shall intimate the diet to the owner of any animal to which the order would apply.

(2) A person who has received intimation under paragraph (1)(b) and wishes to make representations to the court under section 28E(9) of the 1981 Act, section 39(9) of the 2006 Act or section 47(9) of the Animal Welfare Act 2006 shall do so—

(a) in writing to the clerk of court, unless the court otherwise directs; and
(b) by such date as the court directs.

Forms of appeal by person with interest in animal

51.4 An application under section 28E(11) of the 1981 Act, section 43(2) of the 2006 Act or section 49(2) of the Animal Welfare Act 2006 (appeal) shall be in Form 51.4. **B1-78.55**

Disqualification Orders

51.5 A disqualification order shall be in Form 51.5. **B1-78.56**

Termination or variation of disqualification orders

51.6 An application for the termination or variation of a disqualification order shall be made by petition in Form 51.6. **B1-78.57**

GENERAL NOTE

The Animal Health and Welfare (Scotland) Act 2006 (asp 11) amends the Animal Health Act 1981 (c.22) and makes provision for various offences in relation to protected animals. These offences are termed "relevant offences" for the purposes of ss.39 and 40 of the 2006 Act (see s.39(10) and s.40(13)) and are: (i) causing unnecessary suffering to an animal (s.19); (ii) mutilation (by carrying out a prohibited act) (s.20); (iii) performing an operation without due care and humanity (s.21); (iv) administration of poison, etc (s.22); (v) organising and other activities in connection with animals fights (s.23); (vi) failing to take reasonable steps to ensure the needs of an animal are met to the extent required by good practice (s.24(1)); (vii) failing, without reasonable excuse, to comply with a care notice (s.25(7)); (viii) abandonment of an animal in circumstances likely to cause it unnecessary suffering (s.29); and (ix) breaching a disqualification order (s.40(11)). **B1-78.58**

The 2006 Act also makes provision for two orders which the court may make in the exercise of its discretion on the conviction of any person (including bodies corporate, unincorporated associations and Scottish partnerships: (s.45) of any of these nine relevant offences. The orders are deprivations orders and disqualification orders.

Deprivation orders Where a person is convicted of a relevant offence (as defined in s.39(10)) the convicting court may make an order to be known as a "deprivation order" in addition to, or instead of, any other order or penalty which may be imposed in relation to a relevant offence (s.39(1) and (5)). A deprivation order is an order depriving a person of possession or ownership (or both) of an animal for the purpose of its destruction or sale or any other disposal. Such an order may include (1) a provision appointing a person who is to secure that the order is carried out and requiring any possessor of the animal in question to give it up to such appointed person; (2) a provision authorising an appointed person and any other person acting on the appointed person's behalf to enter (for the purposes of securing that the deprivation order is carried out) any premises where an animal to which the order applies is kept; and (3) any other provision "as the court considers appropriate in connection with the order" (s.39(6)).

It is further provided that, so far as (3) above is concerned, that power includes in particular the power to require reimbursement of any expenses reasonably incurred in carrying out the deprivation order and the power to give directions as to the retention of any proceeds arising from the disposal of the animal (s.39(7)). This power is necessary to cater for the accused who is unwilling to shoulder the costs of keeping his animals after his conviction (cf. *Debidin v Chief Constable, Northern Constabulary*, 2002 S.L.T. (Sh. Ct.) 125 where the chief constable was left to bear the costs of kennelling 35 dogs under s.68 of the Civic Government (Scotland) Act 1982.

In respect of all but one of the relevant offences the court may not order destruction of the animal unless the court is satisfied, on evidence provided (orally or in writing) by a veterinary surgeon, that destruction would be "in the interests of the animal". The one exception is the offence under s.23 (animal fighting) (s.39(8)).

Disqualification orders Under s.40(1) of the 2006 Act, where a person is convicted of a relevant offence the court may make an order to be known as a "disqualification order" by which the court imposes on the convicted person one or more of the disqualifications listed in s.40(2). These disqualifications are from (1) owning or keeping animals (or both); (2) dealing in animals; (3) transporting animals; (4) working with or using animals; (5) riding or driving animals; (6) providing any service including care to animals such that the provision of the service requires taking possession of the animals; (7) taking possession of animals for any activity mentioned in (1)–(6); and (8) taking charge of animals for any, or any other, purpose.

The scope of the disqualification is wide and includes "disqualification from any participation in the activity" identified in the order (s.40(3)). The disqualification order can be made either in addition to, or instead of, any other order or penalty (s.40(6)); and it can be general or restricted to particular kinds of animals (s.40(7)). Where there is a restriction of that sort, the restriction may be expressed so as to allow the convicted person to own or possess a maximum number of the animals before the disqualification applies (s.40(8)). A disqualification order must prescribe its duration and may specify the period during which an application cannot be made under s.42(2) to terminate or vary the order (s.40(9)).

The court in making the order is empowered to suspend its operation (a) for such period as the court considers necessary for enabling arrangements to be made for the keep of the animals and (b) pending an appeal against the making of the order (s.40(10)).

Appeals Where a deprivation order or a disqualification order is made against a person convicted of a relevant offence, the order is to be treated as a sentence for the purposes of any appeal under the Criminal Procedure (Scotland) Act 1995 (s.43(1)). Special provision required to be made for persons who have an interest in any animal where that person's interests are affected by the making of a deprivation order. In such cases the third party is given the same rights of appeal as the convicted person (s.43(2)).

Rule 51.3

Before the court can make a deprivation order, the court must give the owner of the animal in question an opportunity to make representations unless it is not practicable for the court to do so (s.39(9)). It is suggested that where there is a failure to obtemper this precondition the deprivation order is null and void but only to the extent that any such representations would have materially affected the court's decision to make an order (cf. *Seal v Chief Constable of South Wales Police* [2007] 1 W.L.R. 1910).

Rule 51.4

Section 43(2) gives any person who has an interest in the animal in respect of which a deprivation order is made the same right of appeal as the convicted person. The third party may appeal to the High Court of Justiciary against the order "by the same procedure as applies [for convicted persons] in relation to a deprivation order". Thus, where a third party has not been given an opportunity to make representations before the deprivation order is made, he may appeal against the order. To make the right to make representations effectual it should not be material, for the purposes of exercising this right of appeal where the third party was not notified of the proposed order (see r.51.3(1)), whether it was practicable at the time to give him notice.

The operation of a deprivation order is suspended until (a) any period for an appeal has expired; (b) the period for an appeal against conviction on which the order depends has expired; and (c) any appeal against the deprivation order (or the conviction) has been withdrawn or finally determined (s.43(4)). However, where an appeal is taken thereby suspending the operation of the order, the court which made the order may make an order to be known as an "interim order" containing such provision as the court considers appropriate in relation to the keeping of the animal for so long as the principal order remains suspended (s.43(5)). Where the order is suspended any person who sells or otherwise parts with an animal to which the order applies commits an offence (s.43(8)). The maximum penalty for this offence, which is a summary offence, is six months' imprisonment or a fine not exceeding level 5 on the standard scale, or both (s.46(2)).

Rule 51.6

A disqualification order may be terminated or varied under s.42(1). However, the court in making the order may provide that any application to vary or terminate it cannot be made before the expiry of a certain period (s.40(9)).

Chapter 52

Investigation of Revenue and Customs Offences

Interpretation

B1-78.59 **52.1** In this Chapter-

"the 1995 Act" means the Criminal Law (Consolidation) (Scotland) Act 1995;

"authorised officer" shall have the same meaning as in s.26B(1) of the 1995 Act;

Production Orders

B1-78.60 **52.2**—(1) An application by an authorised officer for a production order under s.23B(1) of the 1995 Act shall be by petition in Form 52.2.

(2) A production order shall specify the period within which—

(a) the haver must fulfil the requirements of the production order; and

(b) the production order must be served on the haver by the authorised officer.

Revenue and Customs warrants

52.3 An application by an authorised officer for a Revenue and Customs warrant under s.23E(1) of the 1995 Act shall be by petition in Form 52.3 **B1-78.61**

Applications for variation, discharge or failure to comply with sections 23F or 23G

52.4—(1) An application under s.23C(2) of the 1995 Act for an order to vary or discharge a production order shall be by minute in Form 52.4-A. **B1-78.62**

(2) An application under s.23H(2) of the 1995 Act for an order that there has been a failure to comply with requirements of ss.23F or 23G shall be by minute in Form 52.4-B.

(3) A minute under para.(1) or (2) shall be lodged with the clerk of court.

(4) On receipt of a minute under para.(1) or (2) the court shall make an order endorsed on the minute—

(a) fixing a diet for the hearing of the minute; and

(b) for service of the minute with the date of the diet on all relevant persons.

(5) For the purpose of para.(4)(b), the relevant persons are—

(a) in the case of an application under para.(1), every person who is entitled, by virtue of that section, to apply for variation or discharge of the order;

(b) in the case of an application under para. (2)—

(i) the officer in respect of whose alleged failure the order is sought; and

(ii) every other person who is entitled by virtue of s.23H(3) to apply for an order under s.23H(4) in respect of the alleged failure in question.

(6) Where an order mentioned in para.(1) or (2) is made at a hearing fixed under para.(4) it shall be intimated by the clerk of court to all parties unless the party was present at the hearind at which the order was made.

AMENDMENTS

Chapter 52 inserted by Act of Adjournal (Criminal Procedure Rules Amendment No.5) (Miscellaneous) 2007 (SSI 2007/495) (effective 1 December 2007).

GENERAL NOTE

Section 85 of, and Sch.23 to, the Finance Act 2007 amended Part III of the Criminal Law (Consolidation) (Scotland) Act 1995 to update and expand on the powers of HM Revenue and Customs (HMRC) which, in terms of s.5 of the Commissioners for Revenue and Customs Act 2005, assumed responsibility for the matters for which the Inland Revenue and Customs and Excise had previously been responsible. Both production orders and Revenue and Customs warrants can only be granted by sheriffs (and no other judges) and can only be applied for by authorised officers of HMRC. An authorised officer is "an officer acting with the authority (which may be general or specific) of" HMRC and only officers of HMRC may be so authorised (s.26B(1)). In any criminal proceedings a certificate from HMRC that its officers had authority to exercise a power or function conferred by a provision of Part III of the 1995 Act is to be conclusive proof of that fact (s.26B(2)). The foundation for the grant of both production orders and Revenue and Customs warrants is reasonable grounds to suspect that a Revenue and Customs offence "has been or is being committed" (s.23B(2) for orders and s.23F(2) for warrants). **B1-78.63**

A Revenue and Customs offence is "an offence which relates to a matter in relation to which HMRC have functions" other than certain specified matters (s.23A(2)). These excepted matters are (1) disabled person's tax credit, working families tax credit, child benefit, guardian's allowance, the issue of bank notes, N.I. contributions, oil and gas royalties, payment of or in lieu of rates, rating lists, statutory adoption pay, statutory maternity or paternity pay and statutory sick pay, student loans and valuation lists in relation to council tax; and (2) "any matter relating to the movement of goods which is subject to any prohibition or restriction for the time being in force under or by virtue of any enactment" (s.23A(3)).

Production orders

Production orders relate only to documents. A production order is an order requiring the haver, before the expiry of the period specified in the order, either (a) to deliver a specified document to an officer of HMRC or (b) to give an officer of HMRC access to the document and permit the officer to make copies of it or remove it (s.23B(3)). Production orders are to be granted only when the sheriff is satisfied on information on oath given by an authorised officer that (1) there are reasonable grounds to suspect that a Revenue and Customs offence has been or is being committed and (2) a person (known as the haver) specified by the authorised officer has possession or control of a document which may be required as evidence for the purposes of any proceedings in respect of such offence (s.23B(2)). The period within which the haver must comply with the requirements is either 10 working days beginning with the day on which the order is made or such other period as the sheriff considers appropriate (s.23B(4)). Production orders may be made by the sheriff in respect of parts of Scotland lying outwith his jurisdiction and in such cases the order shall have effect throughout Scotland without the necessity of being backed or endorsed by another sheriff (s.23B(5)). "Working days" excludes the weekend and any public holiday in the area in which the production order is to have effect (s.23B(8)).

Subject to the claim of legal privilege (see below), the order has effect "in spite of any restriction on disclosure of information (however imposed)" (s.23B(6)). So the haver cannot refuse to obtemper the order on the ground of contractual duty of confidence, or apprehended liability in delict for breach of confidence, or any statutory obligation to preserve confidentiality. Failure by any person to comply with a production order may be dealt with as a contempt of court (s.23B(7)). Furthermore, a person who falsifies, or conceals, or destroys or otherwise disposes of a document, which a person is required to deliver to an officer or to give an officer access to, commits an offence under s.23D(1). The falsification, concealment or destruction or disposal must be intentional. Recklessness will not suffice. It is also an offence to cause or permit any of those acts to be done. The maximum penalty on summary conviction is 12 months' imprisonment or a fine not exceeding the statutory maximum, or both; and on indictment it is two years' imprisonment or an unlimited fine, or both (s.23D(5)).

Revenue and Customs warrants

Revenue and Customs warrants relate to documents and other things. They are warrants authorising an officer of HMRC to enter, if needs be by force, the premises named in the information on oath and to search those premises before the expiry of the period of one month beginning with the day on which the warrant is granted (s.23E(3)). The sheriff may impose such conditions as he considers appropriate when granting the warrant (s.23E(4)). Thus the warrant may provide that it is not to be executed during certain hours of any day. The warrant can only be granted when the sheriff is satisfied on information on oath given by an authorised officer that there are the same reasonable grounds as are necessary for production orders and that evidence of that offence is to be found in or on the named premises (s.23E(1)). "Premises" include any place and, in particular, any vehicle, vessel, aircraft or hovercraft; any offshore installation within the meaning of s. 12(1) of the Mineral Workings (Offshore Installations) Act 1971; and any tent or other movable structure (s.23E(9)). As with production orders, warrants may be granted for premises outwith the sheriff's jurisdiction so long as they are in Scotland (s.23E(8)).

An officer to whom the warrant is granted may, subject to any condition imposed by the sheriff under s.23E(4), take with him when executing the warrant any person (including persons who are not officers of HMRC) as appear to him to be necessary (s.23E(5)(a)). Thus, no question such as arose in *Lord Advocate's Reference (No.1 of 2002)*, 2002 S.C.C.R. 743 should arise. The officer empowered by the warrant need not be the authorised officer whose information is the basis for the grant of the warrant. In the course of executing the warrant and subject to the power to make copies of documents or other things (under s.23E(6)), the officer to whom the warrant is granted may seize and remove any document or other thing found there when the officer has reasonable cause to believe that it may be required as evidence for the purposes of proceedings in respect of the offence (s.23E(5)(b)). Further, at that time he may search, or cause to be searched, any person found on or in the named premises if that officer has reason to believe that that person may be in possession of any such document or thing; and he may seize and remove any item recovered (s.23E(5)(c)).

Legal privilege

Neither a production order nor a warrant authorises the seizure, removal or copying of any documents or other things subject to legal privilege (s.23J(1)). However, that otherwise absolute prohibition does not apply where the document or thing is "held for the purposes of furthering a criminal purpose" (s.23J(2)). Whether the holding of the document or thing is innocent or not, legal privilege will not attach (cf. *Kelly v Vannet*, 1999 S.C.C.R. 169, approving Dickson, *Evidence* (3rd edn), para.1678; *B v Auckland District Law Society* [2003] 3 W.L.R. 859 at [44]) where the document furthers a criminal purpose. The term "privilege" means communications between a professional legal adviser and the adviser's client *or* communications made in connection with, or in contemplation of, legal proceedings and for the purposes of those proceedings, which would, in legal proceedings, be protected from disclosure by virtue of any rule of law relating to confidentiality of communications (s.23J(3)). Thus "privilege" under the 1995 Act covers both aspects of what the common law now terms legal professional privilege: legal advice privilege where there are "communications between lawyers and their clients whereby legal advice is sought or given" (*Three Rivers District Council v Governor and Company of the Bank of England* [2004] 3 W.L.R. 1274 at [10]); and litigation privilege which covers all documents brought into existence for the purposes of litigation, whether or not legal proceedings have begun (*R. (Morgan Grenfell Ltd) v Special Commissioner of Income Tax* [2002] 2 W.L.R. 1299 at [22]).

Consequential obligations of HMRC officers

Section 23F(2) of the 1995 Act provides that where a document or thing, as the case may be, is removed under a production order or Revenue and Customs warrant, the officer who removes it shall, if requested to do so by: (a) the haver; (b) the occupier of the premises searched; or (c) the person having possession of the document or other thing before it was removed (s.23F(3)), provide to that person a record of what that officer removed. This record must be provided within a reasonable time of the request for it (s.23F(4)).

Similarly, under s.23G(4) it is provided that where the officer in overall charge of the investigation to which the order or warrant relates is requested to do so, he must allow supervised access to the document or thing or for a copy or photograph of the item to be taken.

Under s.23H(2), where there is a claimed failure on the part of the relevant officer under s.23F or s.23G, the person whose request has not been complied with may apply to the sheriff for an order under s.23H(4). If the sheriff is satisfied that there has been such failure, he may order the relevant officer "to comply with the requirements within such time and in such manner as the sheriff specifies in the order" (s.23H(4)). Presumably a failure to comply with that order would constitute a contempt of court if done intentionally.

Chapter 53

Review of Fixed Penalty or Compensation Conditional Offers by Procurator Fiscal

Review by court of fixed penalty or compensation conditional offers by procurator fiscal

53.1.—(1) An application for review under section 302C(6) of the Act of 1995 (recall of fixed penalty or compensation offer) shall be in Form 53.1. **B1-78.64**

(2) The court may fix a diet for hearing an application mentioned in paragraph (1).

(3) Where the court fixes a diet under paragraph (2) it shall—

(a) send a copy of the application to the prosecutor; and

(b) intimate the diet to the parties.

AMENDMENTS

Chapter 53 inserted by Act of Adjournal (Criminal Procedure Rules Amendment) (Criminal Proceedings etc. (Reform) (Scotland) Act 2007) 2008 (SSI 2008/61) para.6 (effective 10 March 2008).

GENERAL NOTE

Section 302C was inserted in the 1995 Act at the same time as s.302 was amended and s.302A was inserted in the 1995 Act by s.50 of the Criminal Proceedings etc. (Reform) (Scotland) Act 2007 (which came into force on March 10, 2008). A new and enlarged system for conditional offers by the procurator fiscal of fixed penalties to alleged offenders was introduced by the amendments to s.302 while s.302A introduced a new scheme for an offer by the procurator fiscal of the option to pay compensation in respect of an alleged offence. In either case where the alleged offender does not give notice to the clerk of court that he refuses the conditional offer of a fixed penalty (under s.302(2)(ca)(i)) or that he refuses the compensation offer (s.302A(2)(d)(i)), the alleged offender is deemed to have accepted the offer (s.302(4B) and s.302A(6) respectively). When there is a deemed acceptance of the fixed penalty conditional offer or the compensation offer, and the offer is not recalled, no proceedings "shall be brought against the alleged offender for the offence" (s.302(4C)(b) and s.302A(7)(b) respectively). **B1-78.65**

Section 302C(1) provides that where an alleged offender has been deemed to have accepted either offer, he may request that the offer be recalled. The effect of recall is that the alleged offender's discharged liability to conviction (which is the consequence of acceptance of the offer) is revoked. The alleged offender can then proceed to trial. An alleged offender's request for recall under s.302C(1) is valid only if (a) he claims that he (i) did not receive the offer concerned; and (ii) would (if he had received it) have refused the offer; or (b) he claims that (i) although he received the offer, it was not "practicable by reason of exceptional circumstances" for him to give notice of refusal of the offer; and (ii) he would (but for these exceptional circumstances) have refused the offer (s.302C(2)). The request for recall requires to be made to the clerk of court no later than seven days after the expiry of the period specified in the original offer (viz, 28 days or such longer period as may be specified in the offer) or, where a notice of intention to take enforcement action under s.303(1A)(a) has been sent to the alleged offender, no later than seven days after that notice is sent (s.302C(3)). However, the clerk may, on cause shown, consider a request for recall although late (s.302C(4)).

Following receipt of the request for recall, the clerk of court may either uphold the offer or recall it (s.302C(5)). The alleged offender may then seek review of the clerk of court's decision by application to the court within seven days of that decision (s.302C(6)). Rule 53.1 provides for the appropriate form for seeking review of the clerk of court's decision. In a review the court may confirm or quash the decision of the clerk of court and, in either event, give such direction to the clerk of court as it considers appropriate (s.302C(7)). The decision of the court is declared to be final (s.302C(8)). There is, therefore, no right of appeal to the High Court whether by suspension or petition to the *nobile officium*.

Section 302C(9) provides that the clerk of court must without delay notify the procurator fiscal of a request for recall, of an application for review of the refusal to recall and of any decision on either of these matters. Accordingly, where the court on an application for review considers that it should fix a hearing, r.53.1(3)(a) provides that the court shall send a copy of the application to the procurator fiscal.

Chapter 54

Mutual Recognition of Criminal Financial Penalties

Form of certificate

54.1. A certificate issued under section 223A(1) of the Act of 1995 (recognition of financial penalties: requests to other member States) shall be in Form 54.1. **B1-78.66**

AMENDMENTS

Chapter 54 inserted by Act of Adjournal (Criminal Procedure Rules Amendment No. 5) (Miscellaneous) 2009 (SSI 2009/345) para.4 (effective 27 October 2009).

GENERAL NOTE

B1-78.67 Section 223A(1) of the 1995 Act was inserted by art.3 of the Mutual Recognition of CriminalFinancial Penalties in the European Union (Scotland) Order 2009 (SSI 2009/342) and came into force on October 12, 2009. That subsection provides machinery by which a Scottish fine or other order can be enforced in other member States of the European Union: the designated officer of the competent authority for Scotland may issue a certificate, in a form prescribed by Act of Adjournal, so as to request enforcement under the Council Framework Decision 2005/214/JHA of February 24, 2005 on the application of the principle of mutual recognition to financial penalties, where (a) a person is required to pay a financial penalty (as defined in s.223A(5) including fines, compensation orders and the like); (b) the financial penalty is not paid in full within the time allowed for payment; (c) there is no appeal outstanding in relation to the penalty ("appeal outstanding" being defined in s.223A(2)); and (d) it appears to the designated officer of the competent authority for Scotland that the person is "normally resident, or has property or income, in a member State other than the United Kingdom". (The "designated officer" of the competent authority for Scotland is defined in s.223T(3) and (4).)

The certificate which is provided for in s.223A(1) must be the certificate as is provided for by art.4 of the Council Framework Decision (s.223T(1)). Form 54.1 is the Scottish version of what art.4 requires.

Chapter 55

Recovery Orders under section 27K(3) of the Civic Government (Scotland) Act 1982

B1-78.68 **55.1.** An application under section 27K(3) of the Civic Government (Scotland) Act 1982 (application for recovery order) shall be made by petition in Form 55.

AMENDMENTS

Chapter 55 inserted by Act of Adjournal (Criminal Procedure Rules Amendment) (Miscellaneous) 2010 (SSI 2010/184) para.7 (effective 1 June 2010).

GENERAL NOTE

B1-78.69 A court may now make a forfeiture order ("FO") under s.27J(2) of the Civic Government (Scotland) Act 1982 where a person is convicted of certain offences under s.7 of the 1982 Act. Sections 27J and 27K were inserted into the 1982 Act as part of a scheme aimed at licensing and regulating knife dealers by Part 3of the Custodial Sentences and Weapons (Scotland) Act 2007 (asp 17). Section 27K(1) provides that the effect of a FO is "to deprive the offender of any rights he has in the property to which it relates". The property to which a FO relates must be taken into the possession of the police (s.27K(2)). However, s.27K(3) makes provision for an innocent third party who has title in the property which is the subject of the FO to obtain delivery of the property.

That subsection provides that the court by which the offender is convicted may, on the application of a person who (a) claims property to which a FO relates but (b) is not the offender from whom it was forfeited, make an order (a "recovery order") for "delivery of the property to the applicant if it appears to the court that he owns it". The third party's application for a recovery order must be in such manner as may be prescribed by Act of Adjournal and must be made before the end of the period of six months beginning with the date on which the FO was made (s.27K(4)).

In terms of s.27K(5) a recovery order can *only* be made if the applicant satisfies the court that (a) he had not consented to the offender's having possession of the property or (b) he did not know, and had no reason to suspect, that the offence was likely to be committed. Thus, the innocent third party bears the burden of establishing grounds for the making of a recovery order; and his negligence (in failing to suspect, when reasonable people would suspect, that the offence was likely to be committed by the offender who has his property with his consent) is a bar to recovery of his property.

Chapter 56

Reporting Restrictions

Interpretation and application of this Chapter

B1-78.70 **56.1.**—(1) This Chapter applies to orders which restrict the reporting of proceedings.

(2) In this Chapter, "interested person" means a person—

(a) who has asked to see any order made by the court which restricts the reporting of proceedings, including an interim order; and

(b) whose name is included on a list kept by the Lord Justice General for the purposes of this Chapter.

Interim orders

B1-78.71 **56.2.**—(1) Where the court is considering making an order, it must first make an interim order.

(2) The clerk of court shall immediately send a copy of the interim order to any interested person.

(3) The court shall specify in the interim order why it is considering making an order.

AMENDMENT

Rule 56.2 as amended by Act of Adjournal (Criminal Procedure Rules 1996 Amendment) (Miscellaneous) 2020 (SSI 2020/27) para.2 (effective 2 March 2020).

Representations

56.3.—(1) [...] B1-78.72

(2) An interested person who would be directly affected by the making of an order shall have an opportunity to make representations to the court before an order is made.

(3) Representations shall—

(a) be made in Form 56.3;

(b) where an urgent hearing is sought, include reasons explaining why an urgent hearing is necessary;

(c) be lodged no later than 2 days after the interim order is sent to interested persons in accordance with rule 56.2(2).

(4) Where the period for lodging representations expires on a Saturday, Sunday or public or court holiday, it shall be deemed to expire on the next day on which—

(a) the Justiciary Office is open, where the interim order was made by the High Court; or

(aa) the office of the Sheriff Appeal Clerk is open for criminal court business, where the interim order was made by the Sheriff Appeal Court;

(b) the sheriff clerk's office is open for criminal court business, where the interim order was made by the sheriff or the JP court.

(5) On representations being made—

(a) the court shall appoint a date and time for a hearing—

(i) on the first suitable court day thereafter; or

(ii) when the court is satisfied that an urgent hearing is necessary, at such earlier date and time as the court may determine;

(b) the clerk of court shall—

(i) notify the date and time of the hearing to the parties to the proceedings and the person who has made representations;

(ii) send a copy of the representations to the parties to the proceedings.

(6) Where no interested party makes representations in accordance with rule 56.3(2), the clerk of court shall put the interim order before the court in chambers in order that the court may resume consideration as to whether to make an order.

(7) Where the court, having resumed consideration under rule 56.3(6), makes no order, it shall recall the interim order.

(8) Where the court recalls an interim order, the clerk of court shall immediately notify any interested person.

AMENDMENTS

Rule 56.3(4) as amended by Act of Adjournal (Criminal Procedure Rules 1996 Amendment) (No.4) (Sheriff Appeal Court) 2015 (SSI 2015/245) para.4 (effective 22 September 2015).

Rule 56.3(1) repealed by Act of Adjournal (Criminal Procedure Rules 1996 Amendment) (Miscellaneous) 2020 (SSI 2020/27) para.2 (effective 2 March 2020).

Notification of reporting restrictions

56.4. Where the court makes an order, the clerk of court shall immediately— B1-78.72.1

(a) send a copy of the order to any interested person;

(b) arrange for the publication of the making of the order on the Scottish Courts and Tribunals Service website.

AMENDMENTS

Rule 56.4(b) as amended by Act of Adjournal (Criminal Procedure Rules 1996 Amendment) (No.4) (Sheriff Appeal Court) 2015 (SSI 2015/245) para.4 (effective 22 September 2015).

Applications for variation or revocation

56.5.—(1) A person aggrieved by an order may apply to the court for its variation or revocation. B1-78.72.2

(2) An application shall be in Form 56.5.

(3) On an application being made—

(a) the court shall appoint the application for a hearing;

(b) the clerk of court shall—

(i) notify the date and time of the hearing to the parties to the proceedings and the applicant;

(ii) send a copy of the application to the parties to the proceedings.

(4) The hearing shall, so far as reasonably practicable, be before the judge or judges who made the order.

AMENDMENTS

Chapter 56 inserted by Act of Adjournal (Criminal Procedure Rules Amendment No.3) (Miscellaneous) 2011 (SSI 2011/194) para.6 (effective 28 March 2011).

Chapter 56 substituted by Act of Adjournal (Criminal Procedure Rules Amendment) (Reporting Restrictions) 2015 (SSI 2015/84) para.2 (effective 1 April 2015).

[THE NEXT PARAGRAPH IS B1-78.73]

GENERAL NOTE

B1-78.73 This chapter was substituted by Act of Adjournal (Criminal Procedure Rules Amendment) (Reporting Restrictions) 2015 (SSI 2015/84) for the previous chapter which had been in force since 28 March 28, 2011. The new chapter came into force on 1 April 2015 and widens the scope of the rules. The previous chapter was confined to reporting restrictions imposed by the court under s.4(2) of the Contempt of Court Act 1981. The motivation for the old Ch.56 was criticism by the European Court of Human Rights of the Scottish practice in relation to the making of s.4(2) orders (see *Mackay and BBC Scotland v United Kingdom* [2010] ECHR 1968 (7 December 2010); (2010) 53 E.H.H.R. 19 at [32]).

However, it is now clear since the Supreme Court's decision in *A v British Broadcasting Corp* [2014] UKSC 25; 2014 S.L.T. 613, that while the principle of open justice is inextricably linked to the freedom of the media to report on court proceedings, the court's power to restrict such reports is not limited to those cases covered by statute: the basis of the court's power to make such exceptions is its inherent power to control its own procedure in the interests of justice (at [33] per Lord Reed affirming Lord President Gill's dictum at 2013 S.C. 533 at 542). Hence, this new chapter applies generally to "orders which restrict the reporting of proceedings" (r.56.1(1)).

What these orders consist of is made plain by Practice Note No.1 of 2015 which also came into force on 1 April 2015. In para.3 the court states that what it terms "a reporting restriction" may be made where the court makes an order (a) under statute, (b) at common law or (c) to ensure that the court does not act in a way which is incompatible with the European Convention on Human Rights.

Interim reporting restriction orders

This new chapter introduces the interim order which the court may make where it is considering making a reporting restriction. Part of the European Court's concern in its 2010 decision was the inability of the media to challenge a s.4(2) order before it was made. The old Ch.56 gave the media a limited right to make representations against an order within 48 hours of such an order being mooted. The new Ch.56 provides that "interested persons",whose names appear at their initial request on a list kept by the Lord Justice General (r.56.1(2)), should receive intimation from the court of a proposed reporting restriction including an interim order in the form of a copy of the order (r.56.2(2)). This proposed order should specify why the court is considering making an interim order (r.56.2(3)). The interested person then has two days within which to lodge with the court its representations against the making of the interim order in the style of Form 56.3 (r.56.3(c)). A hearing then must be ordered for the next suitable court date or, if the court is satisfied that an urgent hearing is appropriate, at an earlier time (r.56.3(5)(a)(ii)). However, the court will not order an urgent hearing unless the interested person specifies in its Form 56.3 why such a hearing is necessary (r.56.3(2)(b)).

Once the court has determined that an interim order is necessary, it should immediately send a copy of the order to all interested persons *and* publicise the order on its official website (r.56.4).

Criteria for making a reporting restriction

A reporting restriction should not be made in terms which are more than are strictly necessary, otherwise the legitimate interests of the media and the public, whose right to open justice is served by the media, will be unjustifiably interfered with. In *A v British Broadcasting Corporation* Lord Reed stated (2014 S.L.T. 613 at 621 and [41]):

> "Whether a departure from the principle of open justice was justified in any particular case would depend on the facts of that case. As Lord Toulson observed in *Kennedy v Charity Commission* [2014] 2 W.L.R. p.856, para.113, the court has to carry out a balancing exercise which will be fact specific. Central to the court's evaluation will be the purpose of the open justice principle, the potential value of the information in question in advancing that purpose and, conversely, any risk of harm which its disclosure may cause to the maintenance of an effective judicial process or to the legitimate interests of others."

Variation and revocation

Once a reporting restriction has been made any person aggrieved by the order may apply to the court for its variation or revocation (r.56.5(1)). Persons may be aggrieved by the making of the order without being interested persons as defined in r.56.1(2). Any such application should be made in Form 56.5.

Chapter 57

Regulation of Investigatory Powers Act 2000

Interpretation

B1-78.74 **57.1.** In this Chapter "the 2000 Act" means the Regulation of Investigatory Powers Act 2000.

Disclosed information: hearing

B1-78.75 **57.2.—**(1) This rule applies where a prosecutor of a case has had disclosed to him or her information under section 18(7)(a) of the 2000 Act and considers it appropriate to invite the judge to order disclosure in terms of section 18(7)(b) of the 2000 Act.

(2) The prosecutor may request a hearing before the judge.

(3) A request for a hearing under paragraph (2)—
- (a) may be made at any time, either verbally or in writing;
- (b) shall be to either the Clerk of Justiciary or the clerk of court, whoever being more appropriate in the circumstances.

(4) The hearing shall be—
- (a) in court;
- (b) in private.

(5) In paragraph (4), "private" means outwith the presence of any person (including, in a trial, the accused, his representatives and the jury) except the judge, the prosecutor and any other person whose presence the judge considers necessary for the proper determination of the matter.

(6) The hearing shall be recorded by mechanical means as if it were a trial in solemn proceedings.

(7) Paragraph (8) applies where the prosecutor indicates that information disclosed during the hearing has a particular status under any scheme operated by the United Kingdom Government for the protection of sensitive information.

(8) The record of the hearing and any retained documents shall be stored by the court in accordance with the security measures which the scheme stipulates for information of that status.

AMENDMENTS

Chapter 57 inserted by Act of Adjournal (Criminal Procedure Rules Amendment No.3) (Miscellaneous) 2011 (SSI 2011/194) para.6 (effective March 28, 2011).

Chapter 58

Control of Dogs (Scotland) Act 2010

Interpretation

58.1. In this Chapter "the 2010 Act" means the Control of Dogs (Scotland) Act 2010. **B1-78.76**

Application for discharge of disqualification

58.2.—(1) Paragraph (2) applies where a person has been disqualified by virtue of section 5(2)(a) of the 2010 Act. **B1-78.77**

(2) An application for the discharge of the disqualification under section 11(3) of the 2010 Act shall be made by petition in Form 58.2.

Appeal to the High Court

58.3. An appeal to the High Court under section 11(4) of the 2010 Act shall be made by lodging a note of appeal in Form 58.3. **B1-78.78**

AMENDMENTS

Rule 58.3 as amended by Act of Adjournal (Criminal Procedure Rules 1996 Amendment) (No. 4) (Sheriff Appeal Court) 2015 (SSI 2015/245) para.4 (effective September 22, 2015 subject to savings provisions in para.6).

Hearing and intimation

58.4. On an application or appeal being lodged the court shall— **B1-78.79**
- (a) appoint a hearing on the application or appeal;
- (b) make an order for service of the application, or appeal, with the date and time of the hearing on all parties.

AMENDMENTS

Chapter 58 inserted by Act of Adjournal (Criminal Procedure Rules Amendment No.3) (Miscellaneous) 2011 (SSI 2011/194) para.6 (effective March 28, 2011).

Chapter 59

Double Jeopardy (Scotland) Act 2011

Interpretation

59.1. In this Chapter, "the 2011 Act" means the Double Jeopardy (Scotland) Act 2011. **B1-78.80**

Exceptions to the rule against Double Jeopardy: applications by the Lord Advocate

59.2.—(1) An application by the Lord Advocate to set aside a person's acquittal and grant authority to bring a new prosecution— **B1-78.81**
- (a) under section 2(2) of the 2011 Act (tainted acquittals);
- (b) under section 3(3)(b) of the 2011 Act (admission made or becoming known after acquittal);
- (c) under section 4(3)(b) of the 2011 Act (new evidence),

shall be in Form 59.2.

(2) On making an application the Lord Advocate shall send a copy of the application to the acquitted person.

Other subsequent prosecutions: applications by the prosecutor

59.3.—(1) An application by the prosecutor— **B1-78.82**

(a) under section 11(3) of the 2011 Act (eventual death of injured person) shall be in Form 59.3-A;
(b) under section 12(3) of the 2011 Act (nullity of proceedings on previous indictment or complaint) shall be in Form 59.3-B.

(2) On making an application the prosecutor shall send a copy of the application to the person to whom the application relates.

Hearing and determination of applications

B1-78.83 **59.4.**—(1) This rule applies to the hearing and determination of an application mentioned in this Chapter.

(2) On an application being lodged the Clerk of Justiciary shall—
(a) appoint a hearing on the application;
(b) intimate the date and time of the hearing to the parties;
(c) grant warrant for the citation of witnesses and the lodging of productions by the parties;
(d) specify the last date for lodging witness lists and productions.

(3) At the same time as lodging witness lists and productions, the party lodging them shall intimate copies to the other party.

(4) Where a production cannot reasonably be copied the list of productions shall be intimated.

(5) Parties shall be entitled to see the productions according to the existing law and practice of the High Court.

(6) Section 90A of the Act of 1995 (obstructive witnesses) applies, with the necessary modifications.

(7) A party shall not be permitted to—
(a) examine any witness not listed as a witness;
(b) put in evidence any production not lodged,

in accordance with paragraph 2(d) except by leave of the High Court on cause shown.

(8) Without prejudice to any existing power of the High Court, it may—
(a) order the production of any document or thing concerned with the application;
(b) hear any evidence relevant to the application;
(c) remit to any fit person to enquire and report on any matter affecting the application;
(d) appoint a person with expert knowledge to act as assessor to the High Court where it appears to the court that such expert knowledge is required.

(9) Where the High Court hears any evidence it shall do so in accordance with the existing law and practice as to the taking of evidence in criminal trials in Scotland.

Appeal to the High Court

B1-78.84 **59.5**—(1) An appeal to the High Court under section 11(6) of the 2011 Act shall be made by lodging a note of appeal in Form 59.5.

(2) The note of appeal shall be lodged with the Clerk of Justiciary not later than 7 days after the making of the decision in question.

(3) At the same time as lodging a note of appeal the appellant shall send a copy of the note of appeal to the other party.

(4) On an appeal being lodged the Clerk of Justiciary shall—
(a) appoint a hearing on the appeal;
(b) intimate the time and date of the hearing to the parties.

AMENDMENTS

Chapter 59 inserted by Act of Adjournal (Criminal Procedure Rules Amendment No.7) (Double Jeopardy (Scotland) Act 2011) 2011 (SSI 2011/387) para.3 (effective 28 November 2011).

GENERAL NOTE

B1-78.85 The Double Jeopardy (Scotland) Act 2011 (asp 16) was fully brought into force on 28 November 2011. The 2011 Act was passed by the Scottish Parliament to give effect in large measure to the recommendations of the Scottish Law Commission in its *Report on Double Jeopardy* (Scot. Law Com. No.218) which was published in December 2009. The commission earlier that year had consulted on a reference from the Scottish Executive (see Discussion Paper on Double Jeopardy (DP No.141) January 2009). The reference was made following the failure of the "World's End" prosecution.

The commission proposed that there should continue to be a general rule against double jeopardy but that it should be reformed and restated in statute (Report, paras 2.3 and 2.7). However, exceptions were recommended. First, it should be possible to retry an acquitted person where that person's acquittal is tainted by an offence against the administration of justice in relation to the original trial (para.3.8). The commission also proposed that an application to have the acquittal set aside as tainted should be made to a quorum of three judges of the High Court (para.3.51). Secondly, the commission proposed that there should be power to retry an acquitted person who had after trial confessed to having committed the offence of which he had been acquitted (para.4.7). This power should be exercisable only with the authority of the High Court. Thirdly, there should be an exception to the rule against double jeopardy in respect of the crimes of murder and rape: where new evidence which was not, and could not with the exercise of reasonable diligence have been, available at the original trial comes to light after the acquittal, the Lord Advocate should have power to apply to the High Court to allow a retrial (paras 5.6 and 5.15).

General rule against double jeopardy

Section 1(1) provides that it is not competent to charge a person who, whether on indictment or summary complaint, has been convicted or acquitted of an offence with (a) the original offence, (b) any other offence of which it would have been competent to convict the person on the original indictment or complaint, or (c) an offence which (i) arises out of the same, or largely the same, acts or omissions as gave rise to the original indictment or complaint, and (ii) is an aggravated way of committing the original offence. This general rule is subject to limited exceptions which are tainted acquittals (s.2), post-acquittal confessions by the accused (s.3) and new evidence of guilt (s.4).

Tainted acquittals

It should be noted that an acquittal is not to be set aside as tainted if, in the course of the original trial, the interference with the course of justice with the juror (but not the trial judge) became known to the trial judge and he allowed the trial to proceed to its conclusion (s.2(5)). Furthermore, for the acquittal to be tainted there must have been an offence of perverting or attempting to pervert the course of justice (by whatever means and however the offence is described). That includes subornation of perjury and bribery but does not include perjury or an offence under s.44(1) of the Criminal Law (Consolidation) (Scotland) Act 1995 (s.2(8)).

New evidence

It is specifically provided that evidence is not new for the purposes of this exception when it was inadmissible at the original trial but has become admissible after the acquittal (s.4(4)). Only one application may be made by the Lord Advocate to retry an accused on the basis of new evidence (s.4(5)). The High Court may set aside the acquittal on the basis of the existence of the new evidence only if it is satisfied of the following matters (see s.4(7)). First, the case against the accused is "strengthened substantially by the new evidence". Secondly, the new evidence was not available, and could not with the exercise of reasonable diligence have been made available, at the trial. Thirdly, on the new evidence and the evidence led at the trial, it is "highly likely that a reasonable jury properly instructed" would have convicted the accused of the original offence or an offence within the terms of the original libel. Fourthly, it must be in the interests of justice to grant authority for the retrial of the accused. These conditions must all be satisfied.

Rule 59.2

The Lord Advocate's applications under ss.2–4 to set aside an acquittal in order to retry an accused must be made in Form 59.2 and that application must be intimated to the accused (see 2011 Act s.5(1)). The accused is entitled to appear or to be represented at "any hearing of the application" (s.5(2)).

Rule 59.3

The Scottish Law Commission also recommended reform of the old rule that where a person had been tried for assault and the victim later died as a result of the assault, it was competent to try the accused for murder or culpable homicide whether or not the original trial had ended in acquittal. That should continue to be so for convicted persons but should cease to be so for persons who had been acquitted at the original trial (*Report*, para.2.48). The commission also proposed that that should also be true for a later charge of culpable homicide or for a statutory offence of causing death where the accused had previously been convicted of an offence relating to the act or omission which is alleged to have led to the victim's death (para.2.53). Where the Lord Advocate desires to prosecute the accused for a crime of homicide he must obtain the authority of the High Court but that authority will only be granted if the High Court is satisfied that it is in the interests of justice to permitthat new prosecution (s.11(3)). An application to bring such a new prosecution must be made in Form 59.3-A and must be intimated to the accused.

The prosecutor is also entitled to seek authority to bring a new prosecution where the earlier trial was a nullity. When it is desired to bring a new prosecution, the Lord Advocate must apply to the High Court in Form 59.3-B.

Rule 59.4

Section 5(3) of the 2011 Act provides that for the purposes of hearing and determining the Lord Advocate's applications under ss.2–4 in respect of tainted acquittals, post-acquittal confessions and new evidence, the High Court must have a quorum of three judges whose decision may be by majority voting (s.11(3)). However, that requirement is subject to "any power of those sitting to remit the application to a differently constituted sitting of the court (as for example to the whole court sitting together)" (s.11(6)). The decision on the application is final and not subject to appeal (s.11(5)).

It is envisaged that, in the course of hearing the applications, it will be necessary to lead evidence. The parties will not be permitted to call any witness or rely on any production which has not been intimated to the court in accordance with the Clerk of Justiciary's direction unless the High Court grants leave on cause shown.

When a retrial takes place under s.11 and the accused is convicted, if he had previously been convicted of the non-fatal offence, he may, immediately on being convicted, move the trial judge to quash the original conviction (s.11(5)). The trial judge can only do so after hearing parties if he is satisfied that it is appropriate to do so. The grant or refusal of the motion may be the subject of appeal to the High Court (s.11(6)).

Chapter 60

Regulatory Reform (Scotland) Act 2014

Interpretation

B1-78.86 **60.1.** In this Chapter—

"the Act of 2014" means the Regulatory Reform (Scotland) Act 2014.

"the Act of 2016" means the Health (Tobacco, Nicotine etc. and Care) (Scotland) Act 2016.

"publicity order" means an order made under section 36(2) of the Act of 2014 or an order made under section 30(4) of the Act of 2016..

"remedial order" means an order made under section 30(3) of the Act of 2016.

"remediation order" means an order made under section 41(2) of the Act of 2014.

"SEPA" means the Scottish Environment Protection Agency.

AMENDMENTS

Definition of "the Act of 2016" was inserted by the Act of Adjournal (Criminal Procedure Rules 1996 Amendment) (No.4) (Publicity, Remedial and Remediation Orders) 2017 (SSI 2017/298) r. 2(2)(b)(i) (effective 1 October 2017).

Definition of "publicity order" was as amended by the Act of Adjournal (Criminal Procedure Rules 1996 Amendment) (No.4) (Publicity, Remedial and Remediation Orders) 2017 (SSI 2017/298) r.2(2)(b)(ii) (effective 1 October 2017).

Definition of "remedial order" was inserted by the Act of Adjournal (Criminal Procedure Rules 1996 Amendment) (No.4) (Publicity, Remedial and Remediation Orders) 2017 (SSI 2017/298) r. 2(2)(b)(iii) (effective 1 October 2017).

Publicity orders

B1-78.87 **60.2.** A publicity order shall be in Form 60.2.

Remedial and Remediation Orders

B1-78.88 **60.3.** A remedial order or remediation order shall be in Form 60.3.

AMENDMENTS

Rule 60.3 as amended by the Act of Adjournal (Criminal Procedure Rules 1996 Amendment) (No.4) (Publicity, Remedial and Remediation Orders) 2017 (SSI 2017/298) r. 2(2)(c) (effective 1 October 2017).

Variation of orders

B1-78.89 **60.4.—**(1) An application for the variation of—

(a) a publicity order under section 30(8) of the Act of 2016;
(b) a remedial order; or
(c) a remediation order;

shall be made by petition in Form 60.4.

(2) On a petition referred to in paragraph (1) being lodged, the court shall—

(a) order intimation of the application to be made to the prosecutor and, in the case of an application under section 41(5) of the Act of 2014, to SEPA;
(b) appoint a hearing on the application; and
(c) order intimation of the hearing to the persons referred to in subparagraph (a), the petitioner or the petitioner's agent, and to the governor of any institution in which the petitioner is detained.

AMENDMENTS

Rule 60.4 as amended by the Act of Adjournal (Criminal Procedure Rules 1996 Amendment) (No.4) (Publicity, Remedial and Remediation Orders) 2017 (SSI 2017/298) r. 2(2) (effective 1 October 2017).

GENERAL NOTE

B1-78.90 The Regulatory Reform (Scotland) Act 2014 (asp 3) received Royal Assent on 19 February 2014. Its preamble states that the purpose of the 2014 Act is, inter alia, "to enable provision to be made, and to make provision, as respects regulatory activities, and offences, relating to the environment". The entirety of the Act (apart from s.57) was brought into force on 30 June 2014. Chapter 60 was inserted by para.2(2) of the Act of Adjournal (Criminal Procedure Rules Amendment) (Regulatory Reform (Scotland) Act 2014) 2014 (SSI 2014/162) and likewise came into force on 30 June 2014 (para.1(1)). Chapter 60 provides rules in relation to two new orders which can be made, following conviction, for certain environmental offences, namely publicity orders and remediation orders.

Publicity orders

A publicity order ("PO") is an order made following conviction of a person for a relevant environmental offence (2014 Act s.36(1)). A relevant offence means an offence specified in an order made by the Scottish Ministers (2014 Act s.53). No such order has yet been made. The court may make a PO instead of, or in addition to, making any other sentencing disposal and as such it counts as a sentence for the purposes of appeal (s.36(3)). A PO requires the convicted person to publicise in a specified manner three facts: (a) the fact that the person has been convicted of the relevant offence; (b) specified particulars of the offence; and (c) specified particulars of any other sentence passed by the court in respect of the offence (s.36(2)). Furthermore, a PO must also specify *in gremio* (s.36(7)) the period within which the requirement to publicise must be complied with (s.36(6)(a)) and may require the convicted person to supply the Scottish Environment Protection Agency (SEPA), within a specified period, evidence that that requirement to publicise has been complied with (s.36(6)(b)). Such an order may be made either by the court at its own instance or on the application of the prosecution. In deciding on the particular terms of the PO the court must have regard to any representations made by the prosecution and the defence (s.36(5)). A person who fails to comply with the terms of a PO commits an offence (s.36(8)) and is liable on summary conviction to a fine not exceeding £40,000 and on indictment to an unlimited fine (s.36(9)). It is likely that the offence under s.36(8) is one of strict liability especially in view of the penalty provided in s.36(9), the wording of the offence-creating provision, which does not provide for a defence of reasonable practicability or excuse for noncompliance, and the overall regulatory purpose of the offence (viz to ensure compliance with the sentence of the court). A person will be guilty of the offence where he fails to publicise the three particulars stipulated in s.36(2); where he fails to do so within the period specified in the PO; and (as appropriate) where he fails to supply evidence of publicising the particulars within the period within which he must do so as specified in the PO.

It is plain from the regulatory nature of the 2014 Act and the terms of s.37 that the relevant offences which are to be specified by the Scottish Ministers under s.53 are capable of commission by legal persons as well as natural persons. Furthermore, s.37(1) and (2) provide that where an offence of failure to comply with a PO is committed under s.36(8) by a company, limited liability partnership, partnership or another body or association *and* the commission of that offence of failure to comply with a PO involves "the connivance or consent, or is attributable to the neglect, of a responsible official [as defined in s.37(3)] of the relevant organisation ... [that] official (as well as the relevant organisation) commits the offence". Section 37(3) provides that for companies, the responsible official is a director, secretary, manager or similar officer; for LLPs and ordinary partnerships, it is a partner; and for other bodies and associations it is a person "concerned in the management or control of [the association's] affairs". In each case, a person who purports to act in such a capacity is also liable to conviction.

Remediation orders

Where a person is convicted of an offence under s.40(1) of the 2014 Act (an offence of causing, permitting or failing to prevent significant environmental harm, or acts likely to cause such harm) and it appears to the court that it is within the person's power to remedy or mitigate the significant environmental harm, the court may make a remediation order (RO) (s.41(1)). Such an order may be made in addition to, or instead of, any other sentence (and can be challenged in an appeal against sentence (s.41(3)); and it requires the person to "take such steps as may be specified in the order to remedy or mitigate the harm" (s.41(2)). The RO must specify the period within which the specified steps must be taken (the "compliance period") (s.41(4)) but such compliance period may be extended on more than one occasion on the application of the convicted person; and the specified steps to remedy or mitigate the harm may also be varied by the court at that person's request (s.41(5)). However, where application is made to the court for extension or variation of the RO, it must be made before the expiry of the compliance period (s.41(6)). An application for variation must be made by petition in the style of Form 60.4 (r.60.4). A person who fails to comply with a RO commits an offence (s.41(7)) which is punishable on summary conviction by a fine not exceeding £40,000 or up to 12 months' imprisonment (or both) and, on conviction on indictment, to an unlimited fine or up to five years' imprisonment (or both) (s.41(8)).

Where a convicted person desires a variation of the steps he is required to take to remedy or mitigate the environmental harm, the court must order intimation of the petition to SEPA; and, thereafter, on fixing a hearing on the petition, the court must give notice of the date to the parties and SEPA (r.60.4(2)).

An offence of failing to comply with a RO can also be committed by responsible officers of companies, LLPs, partnerships and other bodies and associations where there has been connivance, consent or neglect on the part of the responsible officer (s.42(1)). Section 42 makes similar provision to s.37 in respect of who counts as a responsible officer.

Chapter 61

European Protection Orders

Interpretation

61.1. In this Chapter words and expressions have the same meaning as that given by section 254A or section 254B(7) of the Act of 1995. **B1-78.91**

Information about European Protection Orders

61.2.—(1) Where a court makes a protection measure, it must— **B1-78.92**

(a) where the protection measure is made before conviction, direct the prosecutor to inform the protected person under paragraph (2); or

(b) otherwise, direct the clerk of court to inform the protected person under paragraph (2).

(2) A person is informed under this paragraph if—

(a) informed of the possibility of applying for a European Protection Order if that person decides to reside or stay in another Member State of the European Union and of the basic conditions for making such a request; and

(b) advised that an application for a European Protection Order should be made before leaving the United Kingdom.

Application for a European Protection Order

B1-78.93 **61.3.**—(1) An application is to be made by minute in Form 61.3.

(2) An application which relates to a protection measure issued by a court in Scotland must be made to the court which issued that protection measure.

(3) The court must send to the competent authority of the issuing state an application which relates to a protection measure issued in the issuing state.

(4) An application may be granted by the court in chambers.

Issuing of a European Protection Order

B1-78.94 **61.4.**—(1) A European Protection Order is to be issued in Form 61.4-A.

(2) Where the court refuses an application, it must send that decision to the protected person in Form 61.4-B.

(3) The court must arrange for the translation of a European Protection Order into the official language (or into one of the official languages) of the executing state.

Recognition of a European Protection Order

B1-78.95 **61.5.**—(1) Where the sheriff has to inform the competent authority of the issuing state of refusal and the grounds of refusal under section 254C(5) of the Act of 1995, it must be done in Form 61.5-A.

(2) Where the sheriff has to inform the protected person of refusal and the grounds of refusal under section 254C(5) of the Act of 1995, it must be done in Form 61.5-B.

Implementation of a recognised European Protection Order

B1-78.96 **61.6.**—(1) A non-harassment order made under section 245D of the Act of 1995 is to be made in Form 61.6-A.

(2) An order may be granted by the sheriff in chambers.

(3) Where the sheriff has to provide information under section 254D(6) of the Act of 1995, it must be done in Form 61.6-B.

(4) Where the court must notify the competent authority of the issuing state of a conviction under section 254D(8) of the Act of 1995, it must send that notification in Form 61.6-C.

(5) The court must arrange for the translation of a notification under paragraph (4) into the official language (or into one of the official languages) of the issuing state.

Modification and revocation of a non-harassment order

B1-78.97 **61.7.**—(1) An application by an offender to modify or revoke a non-harassment order under section 254E (3) or (5) of the Act of 1995 is to be made in Form 61.7-A.

(2) Where the sheriff has to provide information under section 254E(6) of the Act of 1995, it must be done in Form 61.7-B.

Translation free of charge

B1-78.98 **61.8.** Translation required under this Chapter must be provided free of charge.

Where competent authority not known

B1-78.99 **61.9.**—(1) This rule applies where the court has to send information to the competent authority of an issuing state under rule 61.3(3), 61.5(1), 61.6(3) or (4) or 61.7(2), but that competent authority is not known to the court.

(2) The court must make all relevant inquiries to identify the competent authority, including via the contact points of the European Judicial Network referred to in the Council Decision 2008/976/JHA of 16 December 2008 on the European Judicial Network(a), the National Member of Eurojust or the National System for the coordination of Eurojust of the United Kingdom.

AMENDMENTS

Chapter 61 inserted by Act of Adjournal (Criminal Procedure Rules Amendment No.2) (European Protection Orders) 2015 (SSI 2015/121) para.2 (effective April 1, 2015).

Rule 61.9(1) as amended by Act of Adjournal (Criminal Procedure Rules 1996 Amendment) (No.3) (Miscellaneous) 2015 (SSI 2015/201) para.2 (effective June 8, 2015).

GENERAL NOTE

B1-78.100 Directive 2011/99/EU of the European Parliament and of the European Council dated 13 December 2011 (and published on 21 December 2011: see OJ L338/2) makes provision for protection measures adopted by a court or equivalent judicial authority in one member state of the European Union to be made effective in another member state to which the person intended to be protected by the measures (known as the "protected person") moves or has moved. (The Directive also allows for that category to include relatives of such victims (Directive, Preamble (12)) but the Scottish Parliament has chosen not to include relatives as protected persons.) Preamble (6) to the Directive presents the Directive as being necessary "in a common area of justice without internal borders" so as to ensure the legitimate exercise by EU citizens of their right to move and reside freely within the territory of the EU. Preamble (9) provides that the Directive applies to protection measures which arise specifically to protect a person (A) against another person's (B) criminal act which may, in any way, endanger A's life or physical, psychological and sexual integrity (e.g. by preventing any form of harassment), as well as A's dignity or personal liberty (e.g. by preventing abductions, stalking and other forms of indirect co-ercion), and which aim to prevent new criminal acts or to reduce the consequences of previous criminal acts. The Directive applies to measures adopted in criminal matters (Preamble (10)) but not to measures which primarily serve the aim of the social rehabilitation of an offender (Preamble (9)) or to measures "adopted with a view to witness protection" (Preamble (11)). The UK was at liberty to refrain from participating in this Directive but notified its desire to apply it. The Republic of Ireland and Denmark on the other hand elected not to be bound by the Directive (Preambles (41) and (42)).

In implementation of the Directive the Scottish Ministers amended the 1995 Act by statutory instrument authorised by s.2(2) of the European Communities Act 1972 (c.68). The European Protection Order (Scotland) Regulations 2015 (SSI 2015/107) came into force on 11 March 2015. The 2015 Regulations insert new provisions (ss.254A to 254E) into the 1995 Act to provide for the making by Scottish courts (High Court, sheriff court and JP court) of European Protection Orders (EPOs) and for the recognition and implementation in the sheriff court of EPOs made in other member states of the EU. To give administrative effect to ss.254A to 254E, Ch.61 was therefore necessary.

The terminology of this new rule is taken from the statute (r.61.1) which is, in turn, very largely but not wholly translated from the Directive. Chapter 61 is virtually unintelligible without noting the definition of various expressions provided in s.254A. A "competent authority" is the judicial or equivalent authority in a EU member state having the power to issue and recognise an EPO. A "protected person" is "the individual who is the object of the protection given by the measure or order" and an "offender" is the individual whose conduct is the subject of the protection measure or order. The "issuing state" means the EU member state (other than the UK) whose competent authority has issued the EPO and (in terms of s.254B(7)) the "executing state" is a EU member state (other than the UK) in which the protected person resides, stays or intends to reside or stay.

A "protection measure" is defined as "a decision taken in criminal matters which is intended to protect a protected person from the criminal conduct of the offender by imposing one or more of the following prohibitions or restrictions—(a) prohibiting the offender from entering certain localities, places or defined areas where the protected person resides or visits; (b) prohibiting the offender from contacting, or regulating the offender's contact with, the protected person in any form (for example, by telephone, electronic or ordinary mail or fax); or (c) prohibiting the offender from coming closer than a prescribed distance to the protected person or regulating the approach of the offender to the protected person within such a distance" (see also art.5 of the Directive). An EPO means "a decision (a) taken in relation to a protection measure by a competent authority in a member state of the EU; and (b) on the basis of which the competent authority of another member state of the EU may take any appropriate measure or measures under its own national law with a view to continuing the protection of the protected person" (see art.2(1) of the Directive).

Rule 61.2

It is plain from the definition of protection measures that the grant of bail with an additional condition that the accused should not approach the complainer or enter the locality of her home or employment is such a measure. Where, however, the bail condition also refers to approaching other witnesses, that condition is not a protection measure. When bail before trial contains such a special condition in relation to the complainer, the prosecutor *must* be directed by the court (1) to inform the complainer of the possibility of applying for (and the basic conditions for requesting the making of) an EPO and (2) to advise the complainer to apply for an EPO before leaving the UK (r.61.2(1)(a)). Where bail is granted pending sentence or interim liberation granted on appeal, the court must take these steps.

Rule 61.3

Article 6(4) of the Directive provides that, before issuing an EPO, the offender must be given the right to be heard and the right to challenge the protection measure but only if these rights have not been afforded him in the procedure leading to the adoption of the protection measure. As bail is always granted in the presence of the accused, this provision is complied with and, accordingly the court may grant an EPO in chambers (r.61.3(4)).

Rule 61.4

A court may issue an EPO if it is satisfied that, first, a protection measure which has been taken in Scotland is in force and, secondly, the protected person either resides or stays in the executing state (i.e. another EU member state apart from Denmark and the Republic of Ireland) or has decided to reside or stay there (s.254B(2)). In deciding whether to issue an EPO the court is directed that it must take into account two matters: first, the period or periods during which the protected person intends to reside or stay in the executing state; and, secondly, the seriousness of the need for protection of the protected person (s.254B(3)).

The Directive provides that any request for the issue of an EPO should be treated with "appropriate speed" when regard is had to the specific circumstances of the case, including the urgency of the matter, the date foreseen for the arrival of the protected person on the territory of the executing state and, where possible, the degree of risk for the protected person (Preamble (13)). That exhortation does not appear in the Scottish enactment, or the rules, but it can be expected to be followed in practice. Where the court refuses the protected person's request for an EPO, the court must inform the protected person of that decision (s.254B(4); r.61.4(2)). Where the EPO is issued, the court must, as soon as reasonably practicable, transmit a translation of the EPO to the competent authority of the executing state (s.254B(5)).

Rule 61.5

Section 254C of the 1995 Act provides for the recognition by the sheriff of an EPO issued in another member state of the EU apart from Denmark and the Republic of Ireland. The grounds for refusing recognition of an EPO are: (1) the EPO is incomplete (a decision which can only be taken after the sheriff has sought unsuccessfully to obtain the necessary further information from the issuing member state: s.254C(4)); (2) the EPO does not relate to a protection measure; (3) the prohibitions or restrictions in the EPO have been adopted in relation to conduct that does not constitute a criminal offence under the law of Scotland; (4) the protection created by the prohibitions or restrictions contained in the EPO derives from the execution of a penalty or measure that is covered by an amnesty under the law of Scotland; (5) there is an immunity conferred on the offender in Scotland making it impossible to adopt a protection measure following recognition of the EPO; (6) criminal proceedings against the offender for the conduct in relation to which the prohibitions or restrictions contained in the EPO have been adopted, would be prohibited in Scotland under any enactment had the conduct occurred in Scotland; (7) recognition of the EPO would be inconsistent with the rule against double jeopardy provided for in s.1(1) of the Double Jeopardy (Scotland) Act 2011 (asp 16); (8) the offender, by reason of his age, could not have been held criminally responsible for the conduct in relation to which the prohibitions or restrictions contained in the EPO have been adopted had the conduct occurred in Scotland; and (9) the prohibitions or restrictions contained in the EPO relate to a criminal offence which, under Scots law, is regarded as having been committed (either wholly or for a major or essential part) within Scotland.

Rule 61.6

Section 254D(1) provides that where the sheriff recognises the EPO he must make a non-harassment order in respect of the offender. The non-harassment order shall require the offender to refrain from such conduct in relation to the protected person as may be specified in the order for such period (which includes an indeterminate period) as may be so specified. A non-harassment order may impose on the offender *only* such requirements as to his conduct as may constitute a protection measure and these requirements must correspond, to the highest degree possible, to the prohibitions or restrictions contained in the EPO (s.254D(4)). In terms of s.254D(6), where the sheriff makes a non-harassment order, he must provide certain information to the offender, the competent authority of the member state issuing the EPO and to the protected person. The information to be communicated to these persons and authorities must comprise the following: (1) that the non-harassment order has been made; (2) that breach of the non-harassment order is a criminal offence; (3) what punishments are competent for such a breach; and (4) information about the powers of arrest given to police constables in respect of the non-harassment order (s.254D(7)). When an offender is convicted of breaching a non-harassment order, the court convicting the offender must inform the issuing state of that fact (s.254D(8)).

Chapter 62

Request for Final Decision and Reasons

Application and interpretation of this Chapter

B1-78.101 **62.1.**—(1) This Chapter applies where a request for qualifying information which falls within section 6(7)(j) of the Victims and Witnesses (Scotland) Act 2014 is made to the Scottish Courts and Tribunals Service.

(2) In this Chapter "qualifying information" has the meaning given by section 6(6) of the Victims and Witnesses (Scotland) Act 2014.

Form in which information to be provided

B1-78.102 **62.2.**—(1) The clerk of the relevant court is to complete Part 1 of Form 62.2.

(2) Where the information requested includes a request for any reasons for a final decision, the presiding judge is to complete Part 2 of Form 62.2.

(3) When Form 62.2 is completed, the clerk is to give it to the Scottish Courts and Tribunals Service.

AMENDMENTS

Chapter 62 inserted by Act of Adjournal (Criminal Procedure Rules 1996 Amendment) (No.5) (Request for Final Decision and Reasons) 2015 (SSI 2015/375) para.2 (effective 2 December 2015).

Chapter 63

Serious Crime Prevention Orders

Interpretation of this Chapter

B1-78.103 **63.1.**—(1) In this Chapter—

"the 2007 Act" means the Serious Crime Act 2007;

"person who is the subject of a serious crime prevention order" is to be construed in accordance with section 1(6) of the 2007 Act;

"serious crime prevention order" has the meaning given by section 1(5) of the 2007 Act;

"subject" means the person who is the subject of a serious crime prevention order.

Serious crime prevention orders

63.2.—(1) An application by the Ford Advocate under section 22A of the 2007 Act (orders by High Court of Justiciary and sheriff on conviction)(a) is to be in Form 63.2–A. **B1-78.104**

(2) When an application is lodged, the court must—

(a) order intimation of the application to the person who is the proposed subject;

(b) appoint a hearing on the application.

(3) A serious crime prevention order made under section 22A of the 2007 Act is to be in Form 63.2.

Variation or replacement of serious crime prevention orders

63.3.—(1) An application by the Lord Advocate under section 22B of the 2007 Act (powers of High Court and sheriff to vary orders on conviction)(b) is to be made in Form 63.3–A. **B1-78.105**

(2) An application by the Lord Advocate under section 22C of the 2007 Act (powers of High Court and sheriff to vary or replace orders on breach)(c) is to be made in Form 63.3-B.

(3) When an application under section 22B or 22C is lodged, the court must—

(a) order intimation of the application to the subject;

(b) appoint a hearing on the application.

(4) Where the court grants an application under section 22B or 22C and varies a serious crime prevention order, the varied order is to be in Form 63.3-C.

(5) Where the court grants an application under section 22C and replaces a serious crime prevention order, the new order is to be in Form 63.3-D.

Extension of serious crime prevention orders

63.4.—(1) An application by the Lord Advocate under section 22E of the 2007 Act (extension of orders pending outcome of criminal proceedings)(d) is to be in Form 63.4–A. **B1-78.106**

(2) When an application is lodged, the court must—

(a) order intimation of the application to the subject;

(b) appoint a hearing on the application.

(3) Where the court grants an application under section 22E and varies a serious crime prevention order, the varied order is to be in Form 63.4–B.

Notification of making or variation of order

63.5.—(1) This rule applies where a serious crime prevention order is— **B1-78.107**

(a) made under section 22A of the 2007 Act;

(b) varied under section 22B, 22C or 22E of the 2007 Act; or

(c) replaced under section 22C of the 2007 Act.

(2) Where the subject is present or represented at the hearing where the order is made, varied or replaced, the clerk of court must give a copy of the order or the variation to—

(a) the subject;

(b) any other person specified in the order or the variation.

(3) Where the subject is not present or represented at the hearing where the order is made, varied or replaced, the Lord Advocate must give notice of the making, variation or replacement of the order on—

(a) the subject;

(b) any other person specified in the order or the variation.

(4) Notice is to be given by serving a copy of the order, the variation or the replacement order in accordance with section 10(2) of the 2007 Act.

AMENDMENTS

Chapter 63 inserted by Act of Adjournal (Criminal Procedure Rules 1996 Amendment) (No.2) (Serious Crime Prevention Orders) 2016 (SSI 2016/137) para.2 and Sch (effective 17 March 2016), subject to savings in para.3.

Chapter 64

Trafficking and Exploitation Prevention Orders

Interpretation

64.1. In this Chapter— **B1-78.108**

"the 2015 Act" means the Human Trafficking and Exploitation (Scotland) Act 2015;
"prosecutor" has the meaning given in section 22 of the 2015 Act;
"trafficking and exploitation prevention order" means an order made under section 17 of the 2015 Act.

Trafficking and exploitation prevention order

64.2. A trafficking and exploitation prevention order is to be in Form 64.2. **B1-78.109**

Variation, renewal or discharge of trafficking and exploitation prevention order

64.3.—(1) An application under section 22 of the 2015 Act for the variation, renewal or discharge of a trafficking and exploitation prevention order is to be made in Form 64.3. **B1-78.110**

(2) When an application under paragraph (1) is lodged, the court must—

(a) order intimation of the application—

(i) in the case of an application by the person subject to the order, to the prosecutor and chief constable; or
(ii) in the case of an application by the prosecutor, to the person subject to the order and to the chief constable;
(b) appoint a hearing on the application; and
(c) order intimation of the hearing to the persons referred to in sub-paragraph (a).

Representations by a third party claiming an interest in a vehicle, ship or aircraft

B1-78.111 **64.4.**—(1) An application to make representations to the court under section 14(5) of the 2015 Act by a person who claims an interest in a vehicle, ship or aircraft shall be in Form 64.4.

(2) The court may fix a diet for considering representations mentioned in paragraph (1).

(3) Where the court fixes a diet under paragraph (2) the clerk of court shall intimate—
(a) the representations and the diet to—
(i) the person convicted on indictment of the offence of human trafficking;
(ii) any other person from whose possession the vehicle, ship or aircraft was taken; and
(b) the diet to the person claiming an interest.

AMENDMENTS

Chapter 64 inserted by Act of Adjournal (Criminal Procedure Rules 1996 Amendment) (No.2) (Human Trafficking and Exploitation) 2017 (SSI 2017/145) para.2 (effective 30 June 2017).

GENERAL NOTE

B1-78.112 The Human Trafficking and Exploitation (Scotland) Act 2015 (asp 12) was passed by the Scottish Parliament on 1 October 2015. It introduced an offence to be known as "human trafficking" (s.1(5)) in s.1. A person commits that offence if, with a view to another person being exploited, the accused (a) recruits another person, (b) transports or transfers another, (c) harbours or receives another, (d) exchanges control or transfers control over another, or (e) arranges or facilitates any of the foregoing acts (s.1(1) and (2)). Where an adult is in Scotland convicted of human trafficking or of any one of a further 11 separate statutory offences set out in s.16 (referred to as "relevant trafficking or exploitation offences"), the court may make a trafficking and exploitation order (TEO) in addition to or instead of any other disposal (s.17). This power is also available where an adult offender is acquitted of such relevant offence by reason of mental disorder and where an adult offender is found to be unfit to stand trial and the trial court determines that the adult offender had committed the relevant acts (s.17(1) (b) and (c)). The court (which can be either the High Court or the sheriff court: s.17(5)) may make a TEO at its own instance or on the Crown's motion (s.17(3)).

A TEO may only be made when the court is satisfied of two matters: first, that there is "a risk that the adult … may commit a relevant trafficking or exploitation offence"; and, secondly, that each prohibition or requirement in the TEO is "necessary for the purpose of protecting persons generally, or particular persons, from the physical or psychological harm which would be likely to occur if the adult committed such an offence" (s.17(4)).

The TEO may contain prohibitions or requirements (or both) in relation to the adult (s.20(1)) but both of these matters (and the order itself) must have effect for at least five years and the precise period(s) must be specified in the TEO (s.20(2)) with the exception of a prohibition on foreign travel or an order containing such a prohibition (s.20(3)). The court may include in a TEO provisions prohibiting the adult from "doing things", or may require that he do things, in any part of Scotland and anywhere outwith Scotland, and the court may specify different periods for different prohibitions or requirements (s.20(4)). However, where the adult is already subject to a TEO at the time a new one is made, the earlier one must cease to have effect (s.20(5)).

Under s.22 of the 2015 Act it is provided that a TEO (or a TEO which has already been varied or renewed) may be the subject of an application for varying or renewal (s.22(1)). On an application made to it in Form 64.3, the court may vary, renew or discharge any prohibition or requirement, as well as add a new prohibition or requirement. Furthermore, the court may renew the order or discharge it (s.22(2)). However, before determining the application, the court must give an opportunity to make representations to the adult, the prosecutor and the chief constable.

Chapter 65

Psychoactive Substances Act 2016

Interpretation of this Chapter

B1-78.113 **65.1.**—(1) In this Chapter—

"the 2016 Act" means the Psychoactive Substances Act 2016;
"forfeiture order" has the meaning given by section 54(5) of the 2016 Act;
"premises order" has the meaning given by section 20(2) of the 2016 Act;
"prohibition order" has the meaning given by section 17(1) of the 2016 Act;
"subject" means the person against whom the prohibition order or the premises order has been made.

Prohibition orders

B1-78.114 **65.2.** A prohibition order made under section 19 of the 2016 Act (prohibition orders following conviction) is to be in Form 65.2.

Variation or discharge of orders

65.3—(1) An application under section 28 of the 2016 Act (variation and discharge on application) for the variation or discharge of a prohibition order which was made under section 19 of the 2016 Act is to be made in Form 65.3-A. **B1-78.115**

(2) When an application is lodged, the court must—

(a) order intimation of the application to the subject, where the application is made by a person other than the subject;

(b) order intimation of the application to the Lord Advocate or procurator fiscal, where the application is made by a person other than the Lord Advocate or procurator fiscal;

(c) order intimation of the application to any other person who the court considers may have an interest in the prohibition order; and

(d) appoint a hearing on the application.

(3) Where the court varies or discharges a prohibition order under section 28 or section 29 of the 2016 Act, it is to do so in Form 65.3-B.

(4) Where the court varies a premises order under section 29 of the 2016 Act (variation following conviction), it is to do so in Form 65.3-C.

Notification of making, variation or discharge of orders

65.4—(1) This rule applies where— **B1-78.116**

(a) a prohibition order is made under section 19 of the 2016 Act;

(b) a prohibition order is discharged under section 28 of the 2016 Act;

(c) a prohibition order is varied under section 28 or section 29 of the 2016 Act; or

(d) a premises order is varied under section 29 of the 2016 Act.

(2) The clerk of court must give a copy of the order, variation or discharge to—

(a) the subject;

(b) any other person specified in the order, variation or discharge; and

(c) the court that made the prohibition order or premises order, where that order was made by a court other than the court varying or discharging it.

(3) The clerk of court may give a copy of the order by—

(a) delivering it in person; or

(b) sending it by recorded delivery.

Forfeiture orders

65.5. A forfeiture order is to be in Form 65.5. **B1-78.117**

Forfeiture orders: representations

65.6—(1) This rule applies where the court is considering making a forfeiture order in relation to an item that was used in the commission of an offence. **B1-78.118**

(2) In this rule, "convicted person" means a person who has been convicted of an offence to which section 54 of the 2016 Act applies.

(3) The court must appoint a hearing at which a forfeiture order may be made.

(4) The clerk of court must intimate the date and time of that hearing to—

(a) the convicted person;

(b) the owner of the item (where known); and

(c) any other person who the court considers may have an interest in the item.

(5) The court must give the convicted person and any person who claims to be the owner of, or has an interest in, the item an opportunity to make representations before a forfeiture order is made.

(6) Those representations must—

(a) be made in Form 65.6; and

(b) be sent to the court by such date as the court directs.

AMENDMENTS

Chapter 65 inserted by Act of Adjournal (Criminal Procedure Rules 1996 Amendment) (No. 3) (Miscellaneous) 2017 (SSI 2017/251) para.2 (effective 21 August 2017).

[THE NEXT PARAGRAPH IS B1-78.120]

Chapter 66

Review of Liberation Conditions and Authorisation for Questioning

Interpretation of this Chapter

66.1. In this Chapter— **B1-78.120**

"the 2016 Act" means the Criminal Justice (Scotland) Act 2016(d);

"intimate" includes intimation by electronic means (and "intimation" is construed accordingly).

Review of investigative liberation conditions

66.2.—(1) An application under section 19(1) of the 2016 Act (review of conditions) is to be made in Form 66.2–A. **B1-78.121**

(2) On receipt of an application under paragraph (1) the court must—

(a) appoint a hearing on the application to take place in private within 7 days of the date of receipt of the application;
(b) intimate the application and the date of the hearing to the procurator fiscal; and
(c) intimate the date of the hearing to the applicant.

(3) The applicant must be personally present at the hearing.

(4) An order to remove a condition or to impose an alternative condition is to be made in Form 66.2–B.

Review of undertaking conditions

B1-78.122 **66.3.**—(1) An application under section 30(1) of the 2016 Act (review of undertaking) is to be made in Form 66.3–A.

(2) On receipt of an application under paragraph (1) the court must—

(a) appoint a hearing on the application to take place in private within 7 days of the date of receipt of the application;
(b) intimate the application and the date of the hearing to the procurator fiscal; and
(c) intimate the date of the hearing to the applicant.

(3) The applicant must be personally present at the hearing.

(4) An order to remove a condition or to impose an alternative condition is to be made in Form 66.3–B.

Authorisation for questioning

B1-78.123 **66.4.**—(1) When made in writing, an application under section 36(1) of the 2016 Act (authorisation: further provision) is to be made in Form 66.4–A.

(2) Before granting an application under section 36(1) of the 2016 Act (whether made in writing or not) the court must appoint a hearing to take place in private.

(3) Where section 35(5) of the 2016 Act (authorisation for questioning) applies the court must—

(a) order intimation of the application to the person to be questioned; and
(b) give the person to be questioned an opportunity to make representations at the hearing fixed under Rule 66.4(2).

(4) Where the court grants an application for authorisation for questioning under section 35 of the 2016 Act (whether made orally or in writing) the authorisation is to be in Form 66.4–B.

AMENDMENTS

Chapter 66 inserted by Act of Adjournal (Criminal Procedure Rules 1996 Amendment) (Miscellaneous) 2018 (SSI 2018/12) para.2(4) (effective 25 January 2018).

[THE NEXT PARAGRAPH IS B1-78.125]

Chapter 67

European Investigation Orders

Interpretation of this Chapter

B1-78.125 **67.1.** In this Chapter—

"the 2017 Regulations" means the Criminal Justice (European Investigation Order) Regulations 2017(a);

"account monitoring order" has the meaning given by regulation 45(3) of the 2017 Regulations;

"customer information order" has the meaning given by regulation 44(3) of the 2017 Regulations;

"European investigation order" has—

(a) in rules 67.2 and 67.3, the meaning given by regulation 5; and
(b) in rule 67.6, the meaning given by regulation 25,

of the 2017 Regulations;

"issuing State" has the meaning given by regulation 25 of the 2017 Regulations;

"nominated court" means a court nominated under regulation 35, 36, 37, 38 or 43 of the 2017 Regulations.

Application for a European investigation order

B1-78.126 **67.2.**—(1) An application under regulation 6(3)(b) or (c) (power of a judicial authority to make a European investigation order) of the 2017 Regulations for a European investigation order is to be made in Form 67.2.

(2) Where any party presents an application under paragraph (1) after proceedings have been instituted the High Court or sheriff, as the case may be, may—

(a) dispense, on cause shown, with intimation to any other party and proceed to consider the application;
(b) fix a date for hearing the application and order intimation of the diet and application to any other party; or
(c) fix a date for hearing the application, order intimation of the diet to any other party and, on special cause shown, dispense meantime with intimation of the schedule of the application.

Variation or revocation of a European investigation order

67.3.—(1) An application to vary or revoke a European investigation order under regulation 10 (variation or revocation of a European investigation order) of the 2017 Regulations is to be made in Form 67.3. **B1-78.127**

(2) When an application under paragraph (1) is lodged, the court may either—

(a) dispense, on cause shown, with intimation to any other party and proceed to consider the application; or

(b) order intimation of the application to—

(i) the Lord Advocate or the procurator fiscal, as the case may be, and the person affected by the order, where the person who applied for the order is seeking to vary or revoke the order;

(ii) the person who applied for the order and the person affected by the order, where the Lord Advocate or the procurator fiscal, as the case may be, is seeking to vary or revoke the order; or

(iii) the person who applied for the order and the Lord Advocate or the procurator fiscal, as the case may be, where the person affected by the order is seeking to vary or revoke the order.

(3) Where the court orders intimation of the application under paragraph (2)(b) it must appoint a hearing on the application.

Citation for proceedings before a nominated court

67.4.—(1) A warrant to cite a person to proceedings before a nominated court is to be made in Form 67.4-A. **B1-78.128**

(2) The form of postal citation of a person to proceedings before a nominated court is to be made in Form 67.4-B, and the person must complete and return Form 67.4-C to the procurator fiscal.

(3) The form of personal citation of a person to proceedings before a nominated court is to be made in Form 67.4-D.

Proceedings before a nominated court

67.5. In proceedings before a nominated court— **B1-78.129**

(a) the procurator fiscal or Crown counsel must participate in any hearing;

(b) a solicitor or counsel instructed by any party may participate in any hearing;

(c) any other person may, with the leave of the court, participate in any hearing;

(d) a shorthand writer may be present to record the proceedings; and

(e) the proceedings must be in private.

Time periods

67.6.—(1) This rule applies where a court is giving effect to a European investigation order— **B1-78.130**

(a) by issuing a warrant under regulation 39(1) (search warrants and production orders: giving effect to the European investigation order);

(b) by making a customer information order under regulation 44 (court's power to make a customer information order); or

(c) by making an account monitoring order under regulation 45 (court's power to make an account monitoring order),

of the 2017 Regulations.

(2) Subject to paragraph (3), the sheriff must give effect to the European investigation order no later than the day after receipt of a nomination notice made under either—

(a) regulation 38(2) (search warrants and production orders: nominating a court); or

(b) regulation 43(2) (nominating a court to make a customer information order or an account monitoring order),

of the 2017 Regulations.

(3) The sheriff may, exceptionally, give effect to the European investigation order later than the period prescribed in paragraph (2) but must do so no later than 5 days after receipt of the nomination notice.

(4) Where the day mentioned in paragraph (2) or the last day of the period mentioned in paragraph (3) falls on a Saturday, Sunday or court holiday, such day or period is to extend to and include the next day which is not a Saturday, Sunday or court holiday.

(5) In calculating the period mentioned in paragraph (3), any Saturday, Sunday or court holiday that falls within that period is to be disregarded.

Form of warrant giving effect to European investigation order

67.7. A warrant issued under regulation 39(1) (search warrants and production orders: giving effect to the European investigation order) of the 2017 Regulations is to be made in Form 67.7. **B1-78.131**

Application to revoke or vary a search warrant or to authorise the release of evidence

67.8.—(1) An application made under regulation 41(1) (power to revoke or vary a search warrant or production order or to authorise the release of evidence seized or produced) of the 2017 Regulations is to be made in Form 67.8. **B1-78.132**

(2) When an application made under paragraph (1) is lodged, the court may either—

(a) dispense, on cause shown, with intimation to any other party and proceed to consider the application; or

(b) order intimation of the application to—
(i) the procurator fiscal, where the person affected by the order is seeking the release of evidence or to revoke or vary the search warrant; or
(ii) the person affected by the order where the procurator fiscal is seeking the release of evidence or to revoke or vary the search warrant.

(3) Where the court orders intimation of the application under paragraph (2)(b) it must appoint a hearing on the application.

Application to vary or revoke a customer information order or an account monitoring order

B1-78.133 **67.9.**—(1) An application under regulation 48(1) (power to vary or revoke customer information and account monitoring orders) of the 2017 Regulations is to be made in Form 67.9.

(2) When an application made under paragraph (1) is lodged, the court may either—
(a) dispense, on cause shown, with intimation to any other party and proceed to consider the application; or
(b) order intimation of the application to either—
(i) the procurator fiscal where the person affected by the order is seeking to vary or revoke the order; or
(ii) the person affected by the order where the procurator fiscal is seeking to vary or revoke the order.

(3) Where the court orders intimation of the application under paragraph (2)(b) it must appoint a hearing on the application.

Provision of interpreters

B1-78.134 **67.10.**—(1) This rule applies where a court has been nominated under either—
(a) regulation 35(2) (nominating a court to hear evidence from a person);
(b) regulation 36(2) (hearing a person through videoconference or other audio visual transmission); or
(c) regulation 37(2) (hearing a person by telephone conference),
of the 2017 Regulations.

(2) Where it appears to the sheriff clerk that the witness is likely to give evidence in a language other than English, arrangements must be made for a translator to be present at the proceedings to translate what is said into English.

(3) Where it appears to the sheriff clerk that the witness is likely to give evidence in a language other than that in which the proceedings in the issuing State will be conducted, arrangements must be made for a translator to translate what is said into the language in which the proceedings of the issuing State will be conducted.

(4) Where the evidence in proceedings before a nominated court is given in a language other than English, the sheriff must continue proceedings until such time as an interpreter can be present to provide a translation into English.

Court record of proceedings before a nominated court

B1-78.135 **67.11.**—(1) This rule applies where a court has received evidence in proceedings by virtue of a nomination under—
(a) regulation 35(2) (nominating a court to receive evidence from a person);
(b) regulation 36(2) (hearing a person through videoconference or other audio visual transmission); or
(c) regulation 37(2) (hearing a person by telephone conference),
of the 2017 Regulations.

(2) The sheriff clerk must record in the minute of proceedings—
(a) particulars of the proceedings; and
(b) without prejudice to the generality of sub-paragraph (a) above—
(i) which persons were present;
(ii) which of those persons were represented and by whom; and
(iii) whether any of those persons were denied the opportunity of cross-examining a witness as to any part of his or her testimony.

(3) Save as authorised by the Lord Advocate or with the leave of the court, the minute of proceedings mentioned in paragraph (1) above is not open to inspection by any person.

(4) The sheriff clerk must send to the issuing authority a certified copy of the minute of Proceedings.

AMENDMENTS

Chapter 67 inserted by Act of Adjournal (Criminal Procedure Rules 1996 Amendment) (European Investigation Orders) 2018 (SSI 2018/150) para.2 (effective 31 May 2018).

Chapter 68

Approval of Sentencing Guidelines

Interpretation of this Chapter

B1-78.136 **68.1.** In this Chapter "the Council" means the Scottish Sentencing Council within the meaning of section 1 of the Criminal Justice and Licensing (Scotland) Act 2010.

Application for approval of sentencing guidelines

68.2.—(1) An application by the Council for approval by the High Court of sentencing guidelines is to be made in Form 68.2. **B1-78.136.1**

(2) On receipt of an application made under paragraph (1), the High Court must appoint a diet for the consideration of the application to take place as soon as practicable.

Consideration and determination of an application

68.3.—(1) On receipt of an application made under rule 68.2(1), the High Court may request such further information from the Council as it considers necessary. **B1-78.136.2**

(2) If the High Court is considering either—

(a) approving the proposed guidelines, in part or with modifications; or
(b) rejecting the proposed guidelines, in whole or in part,

it must intimate to the Council that it is considering such a course of action.

(3) The Council may submit to the High Court a written response to the intimation made under paragraph (2) within a period of 8 weeks from the date of receipt of the intimation.

(4) Approval or rejection of the proposed guidelines by the High Court must take place in open court.

(5) The court must be chaired by the Lord Justice General, whom failing the senior judge of the High Court.

(6) The court cannot include a judge who is a member of the Council.

AMENDMENTS

Chapter 68 inserted by Act of Adjournal (Criminal Procedure Rules 1996 Amendment) (Approval of Sentencing Guidelines) 2018 (SSI 2018/ No.229) para.2 (effective 4 September 2018).

[THE NEXT PARAGRAPH IS B1-78.137]

Chapter 69

Labour Market Enforcement Orders

Interpretation of this Chapter

69.1. In this Chapter — **B1-78.137**

"the 2016 Act" means the Immigration Act 2016;
"enforcing authority" has the meaning given by section 14 of the 2016 Act;
"labour market enforcement order" has the meaning given by section 18 of the 2016 Act;
"trigger offence" has the meaning given by section 14 of the 2016 Act.

Variation and discharge of a labour market enforcement order

69.2.—(1) An application under section 23 of the 2016 Act for variation or discharge of a labour market enforcement order made under section 20 of that Act is to be made in Form 69.2. **B1-78.137.1**

(2) When an application under section 23 of the 2016 Act is lodged, the court must—

(a) appoint a hearing on the application; and
(b) order intimation of the application—
  (i) where the application is made by the respondent to the original order made under section 20 of the 2016 Act, on the enforcing authority whose officer conducted the investigation which resulted in the prosecution of the respondent for the trigger offence; or
  (ii) where the application is made by the enforcing authority whose officer conducted the investigation which resulted in the prosecution of the respondent for the trigger offence, on the respondent to the original order made under section 20 of the 2016 Act.

(3) Where an application referred to in paragraph (1) is made in respect of a labour market enforcement order which was made by the High Court of Justiciary and which has not subsequently been varied in the sheriff court—

(a) the sheriff clerk with whom the application is lodged is to notify the Clerk of Justiciary; and
(b) the Clerk of Justiciary is,
  (i) not later than 4 days after receipt of such notification, to send a certified copy of the indictment and of the labour market enforcement order to the sheriff clerk of the court in which the application is made; and
  (ii) not later than 21 days after receipt of such notification, to obtain a report from the judge who made the labour market enforcement order in respect of which variation or discharge is sought and send that report to the sheriff clerk of the court in which the application is made.

(4) Where the judge's report as mentioned in paragraph (3)(b)(ii) above is not furnished within the period specified in that provision, the sheriff may hear and determine the application without the report.

Appeals

69.3.—(1) An appeal to the Sheriff Appeal Court under section 24(1)(b) of the 2016 Act against the making of, or refusal to make, an order under section 23 varying or discharging a labour market enforcement order made under section 20 is to be made by note of appeal in Form 69.3. **B1-78.137.2**

(2) The note of appeal is to be lodged no later than 7 days after the decision appealed against with the clerk of the court from which the appeal is to be taken.

(3) On receipt of the note of appeal the clerk of court must send a copy of the note to the respondent in the appeal or to the respondent's solicitor, and obtain a report from the sheriff who made the decision appealed against.

(4) Subject to paragraph (5), the clerk of court must no later than 14 days after the decision against which the appeal is taken—

(a) send to the Clerk of the Sheriff Appeal Court the note of appeal, together with the report mentioned in paragraph (3) above, the minute of proceedings and any other relevant documents; and

(b) send copies of that report to the appellant and respondent in the appeal or to their solicitors.

(5) The sheriff principal of the sheriffdom in which the judgment was pronounced may, on cause shown, extend the period of 14 days specified in paragraph (4) above for such period as the sheriff principal considers reasonable.

(6) Where the sheriff's report as mentioned in paragraph (3) above is not furnished within the period mentioned in paragraph (4) above, or such period as extended under paragraph (5) above, the Sheriff Appeal Court may extend such period, or, if it thinks fit, hear and determine the appeal without the report.

(7) For the purposes of hearing and determining any appeal under this rule three of the Appeal Sheriffs is a quorum of the Sheriff Appeal Court, and the determination of any question under this rule by the court is to be according to the votes of the majority of the members of the court sitting, including the presiding Appeal Sheriff, and each Appeal Sheriff so sitting is entitled to pronounce a separate opinion.

(8) Rule 19.14 (list of appeals) and rule 19.16 (intimation of determination of appeal) of Chapter 19 (Appeals from Summary Proceedings) apply to any appeal made under this Chapter.

AMENDMENT

Chapter 69 inserted by Act of Adjournal (Criminal Procedure Rules 1996 Amendment) (Labour Market Enforcement Orders) 2019 (SSI 2019/ No.139) para.2 (effective 18 May 2019).

[THE NEXT PARAGRAPH IS B1-500]

SCHEDULE 3

ACTS OF ADJOURNAL REVOKED

Paragraph 3

B1-500

Statutory Instrument Year and Number	*Title of* Act of Adjournal	*Extent of Revocation*
1988/110	Act of Adjournal (Consolidation) 1988	The whole Act of Adjournal
1989/48	Act of Adjournal (Consolidation Amendment) (Reference to European Court) 1989	The whole Act of Adjournal
1989/1020	Act of Adjournal (Consolidation Amendment No.2) (Forms of Warrant for Execution and Charge for Payment of Fine or Other Financial Penalty) 1989	The whole Act of Adjournal
1990/718	Act of Adjournal (Consolidation Amendment No.2) (Drug Trafficking) 1990	The whole Act of Adjournal
1990/2106	Act of Adjournal (Consolidation Amendment No.2) (Miscellaneous) 1990	The whole Act of Adjournal
1991/19	Act of Adjournal (Consolidation Amendment) (Extradition Rules and Backing of Irish Warrants) 1991	The whole Act of Adjournal
1991/847	Act of Adjournal (Consolidation Amendment No.1) 1991	The whole Act of Adjournal
1991/1916	Act of Adjournal (Consolidation Amendment No.2) (Evidence of Children) 1991	The whole Act of Adjournal
1991/2676	Act of Adjournal (Consolidation Amendment No.3) 1991	The whole Act of Adjournal
1991/2677	Act of Adjournal (Consolidation Amendment No.4) (Supervised Attendance Orders) 1991	The whole Act of Adjournal
1992/1489	Act of Adjournal (Consolidation Amendment) (Criminal Justice International Co-operation Act 1990) 1992	The whole Act of Adjournal

Schedule 3 Acts of Adjournal Revoked

Statutory Instrument Year and Number	*Title of* Act of Adjournal	*Extent of Revocation*
1993/1955	Act of Adjournal (Consolidation Amendment) (Courses for Drink-drive Offenders) 1993	The whole Act of Adjournal
1993/2391	Act of Adjournal (Consolidation Amendment No.2) (Miscellaneous) 1993	The whole Act of Adjournal
1994/1769	Act of Adjournal (Consolidation Amendment) (Miscellaneous) 1994	The whole Act of Adjournal
1995/1875	Act of Adjournal (Consolidation Amendment) (Supervised Release Orders) 1995	The whole Act of Adjournal